THE WESLEYAN BIBLE COMMENTARY

Genesis - Exodus - Leviticus - Numbers - Deuteronomy
Joshua - Judges - Ruth - I & II Samuel - I & II Kings
I & II Chronicles - Ezra - Nehemiah - Esther

The Wesleyan Bible Commentary

Editorial Board

The Six Volumes

I. PART I. GENESIS – DEUTERONOMY

I. PART II. JOSHUA – ESTHER

II. JOB – SONG OF SOLOMON

III. ISAIAH – MALACHI

IV. MATTHEW – ACTS

V. ROMANS – PHILEMON

VI. HEBREWS – REVELATION

The Wesleyan Bible Commentary

Volume One

Part I

GENESIS AND EXODUS

LEE HAINES

Formerly Office Editor
Wesleyan Methodist Sunday School Literature

LEVITICUS

ARMOR D. PEISKER

Editor, The Pilgrim Holiness Advocate

NUMBERS AND DEUTERONOMY

HOWARD A. HANKE

Professor of Bible
Asbury College

Volume One

Part II

JOSHUA – ESTHER

CHARLES R. WILSON

Head of Religion Department
Taylor University

HENDRICKSON PUBLISHERS
PEABODY, MASSACHUSETTS 01961-3473

The Wesleyan Bible Commentary
General Introduction

The Wesleyan Bible Commentary is a six-volume set covering the entire Bible. It consists of three volumes on the New Testament and
three volumes on the Old Testament, with Vol. I divided into two
books, Vol. I—Part I, and Vol. I—Part II. In consideration of the important contemporary revival of interest in and emphasis upon John
Wesley, the renowned English preacher and scholar of the eighteenth
century, and the Father of Methodism in all of its multifold branches,
a group of scholars in the Wesleyan tradition responded to what
they believed to be the movings of God's Spirit in the religious
climate of today to produce a set of commentaries within the
Wesleyan theological frame of reference. The design of the WBC
is evangelical, expositional, practical, homiletical, and devotional. It
is cast in the framework of contemporary evangelical Wesleyan Bible
scholarship. Herein lies the justification for the title of the work:
Wesleyan Bible Commentary.

The staff of contributors to the WBC includes more than twenty
Bible scholars from throughout the nation. They have been selected
from nine different denominations, which include the Church of
God (with headquarters in Anderson, Indiana), Church of the
Nazarene, Evangelical United Brethren, Free Methodist, Friends,
Methodists, Missionary Church Association, Pilgrim Holiness, and
Wesleyan Methodist. The commentary is interdenominational in
representation, nonsectarian, and non-polemical.

The aim of the WBC is to maintain both the spiritual insight
and sound biblical scholarship of John Wesley and Adam Clarke,
but to express these characteristics in the context of contemporary
thought and life. While the WBC contributors aim to maintain the
faith of the Fathers of Methodism, they have not neglected the use
of the latest and best information and tools available to present-day
Bible scholarship. Again, while the WBC is evangelical in the sense
of expounding God's provisions for man's personal regeneration and
sanctification, it does not overlook the social implications and provisions of the gospel of Jesus Christ.

The WBC aims at a high level of sound biblical scholarship,
with a purpose that is practical rather than technical. It is produced with a view to the needs of the average Christian minister,
Sunday school officer and teacher, Bible class leader, college Bible
teacher and student, and all other alert students of the Bible
who seek help in understanding the spiritual message of the Word
of God as recorded in the Bible.

While the Editorial Board assumes responsibility for the general
purpose and production of the WBC, the views expressed in the
commentary are those of the individual contributors. The Editorial
Board has aimed at a reasonable degree of uniformity in the format
and general design of the commentary, but its purpose and desire

have been that each contributor should realize the freedom necessary to discover the truth for himself and express his own personal insights into the unsearchable riches of God's Word. Although both the Editorial Board and the contributors represent the evangelical Wesleyan position, they lay no claim to a monopoly upon the truth of God as revealed in the Bible. They have aimed to make use of the best insights into God's revealed truth that are available in the scholarship of all communions of the Christian faith. The American Standard Version is the basic Bible text used by the contributors, and it is the text printed in the commentary. Free and large use, however, has been made of many other versions of the Bible, as also occasional individual translations by the respective contributors.

General guidance in the development and execution of the WBC has been afforded the Editorial Board by the wise counsel of a carefully selected Advisory Board consisting of eminent leaders in the field of evangelical Christianity today. This Board includes Drs. Paul S. Rees, Vice President of World Vision; Leslie R. Marston, Bishop of the Free Methodist Church; Hugh H. Benner, General Superintendent of the Church of the Nazarene; Roy S. Nicholson, formerly General President of the Wesleyan Methodist Church of America; Paul F. Elliott, President of Owosso College; Everett L. Cattell, President of Malone College; George E. Failing, Editor of the *Wesleyan Methodist;* and Paul P. Petticord, President of Western Theological Seminary.

It is the earnest desire and sincere prayer of those responsible for the production of this commentary that it will make a significant and lasting contribution to the contemporary revival of interest in vital Christian faith and practice throughout the world.

THE EDITORIAL BOARD

CHAS. W. CARTER
    Chairman and General Editor
RALPH EARLE
    New Testament Editor
W. RALPH THOMPSON
    Old Testament Editor
LEE HAINES
    Associate Editor

Volume One

Part I

GENESIS AND EXODUS

LEE HAINES

Formerly Office Editor
Wesleyan Methodist Sunday School Literature

LEVITICUS

ARMOR D. PEISKER

Editor, The Pilgrim Holiness Advocate

NUMBERS AND DEUTERONOMY

HOWARD A. HANKE

Professor of Bible
Asbury College

Contents

General Introduction to the Pentateuch

by
George H. Livingston

Since the first five books of the Old Testament, commonly known as the Pentateuch, have traditionally been understood to have come from Moses, it is best to consider the problem of the authorship and dating of these books together. Though the text of Genesis never mentions the name of Moses, it has been customary for editions of the Bible to designate this book, in the heading, as "The First Book of Moses." Moses is a central figure in the other four books, which constantly present God as speaking directly to Moses, or Moses proclaiming the message of God to Israel.

A large number of the books of both the Old Testament and the New Testament refer to the first five books as the "law of Moses," or some similar phrase. The common Hebrew name for these books is *Torah,* which includes in its meaning more than just the concept of law. It also means "instruction."

With only widely scattered exceptions, scholars in both the Jewish and the Christian traditions upheld the Mosaic origin of these five books until a ground swell of opposition developed during the nineteenth century. Modern rejection of Moses' relationship with the Pentateuch is generally understood to have its roots in the work of Jean Astruc, a French physician, whose work on Genesis appeared in 1753. Astruc did not deny Moses' relationship to Genesis but felt that he had succeeded in his effort to show that Moses used ancient sources. One of these sources, he claimed, used the Hebrew name for God, Elohim, predominantly and the other source used the other common Hebrew name for God, Jahweh or Jehovah, heavily. Besides these were lesser sources. Astruc's views did not meet with immediate acceptance, so the matter rested for three decades.

It was a professor in the German University of Jena, Johann Eichhorn, who revived this view and suggested that the source which used Elohim be designated as the E document and that the source containing Jehovah be known as the J document. Eichhorn carried his source analysis into Exodus, with an accompanying denial that Moses had anything to do with either book. Other German scholars soon carried this twofold division of J and E throughout the first five books and into the book of Joshua, also denying Mosaic authorship.

In 1792 a Catholic priest named Alexander Geddes proposed a more radical approach. He suggested that instead of two major "documents" there were in fact a mass of fragments of varied age which someone compiled as the Pentateuch during the reign of Solomon. An impressive number of German scholars rallied to this view, but by the turn of the nineteenth century a reaction set in. The unity of the five books of the Pentateuch in their present form had to be taken seriously.

No believer in the role of Moses in the production of the Pentateuch, Heinrich Ewald published a work on Genesis which effectively supported the literary unity of the Pentateuch. As a result, early in the nineteenth century some German scholars proposed a basic E document as the core of the Pentateuch, supplemented from time to time by lesser bits of literature. It was claimed that this E document was produced soon after the division of the kingdom under Jeroboam I. During the second quarter of the nineteenth century some German scholars began to promote the idea that the main body of Deuteronomy was a product of the seventh century B.C., made public by Josiah in 621 B.C.

The surge of literary analysis based upon variety of divine names, differences of vocabulary and style, alleged disagreements in narrative and law, and divergences of theological, ecclesiastical and political views, was too powerful. Heinrich Ewald, himself a champion of the concept of unity, eventually yielded and proposed a theory that there were five basic narrators of the early kingdom period whose works were fused or crystallized together sometime in the sixth century B.C.

A German by the name of Hermann Hupfeld made a strong effort to conserve some unity in the Pentateuch by declaring that the core document of the Pentateuch was not the E document but rather the J document. He revived an earlier view that the E document was not really one but two distinct productions. He also insisted that the main body of Deuteronomy was a separate D document. Above all, the J document towered as the most important.

By the third quarter of the nineteenth century, a basic dilemma was becoming apparent to the scholars who denied Moses' role in the Pentateuch and accepted source analysis as a valid methodology. If source analysis was carried to its logical conclusion, the Pentateuch disintegrated into a mass of fragments. If the apparent unity of the books was maintained, there seemed to be little room for development and growth in the history of Israel's literature.

In the preceding quarter of the nineteenth century a few scholars, notably C. P. W. Gramberg, Wilhelm Vatke, and J. F. L. George, suggested that they saw in the currently popular philosophical system of G. W. F. Hegel a concept of unity which would be helpful in solving the problem of how the Pentateuch was produced and when it was produced. For several decades this idea gained little headway until the combined work of K. H. Graf, A. Kuenen and J. Wellhausen brought forth what has become known as the J E D P theory, between 1865 and 1880.

Recognizing four basic documents, this theory proposes that since the J document is to be connected with the divine name Jehovah and the kingdom of Judah and since it is the most theologically naive in its portrayal of God in relation to man, it should be understood to be the earliest of the four documents. A date soon after the division of the kingdom under Rehoboam has been favored.

In contrast, the newly formed kingdom of northern Israel led by the tribe of Ephraim seemed a natural place for the E document to be formed as a history to weaken Judah's claim to possess the right to rule over all Israel through the House of David. The E document is supposed to be marked by a more sophisticated concept of God. Hence Hegel's theory of thesis (J) and antithesis (E) seemed to provide a rational explanation for the relationship of these two documents. E is usually dated as much as a century later than J. After the destruction of northern Israel in 722 B.C., concerned individuals in Judah, often designated as redactors, or editors, are understood to have fused these histories together as the JE document. This fits in well with Hegel's concept of synthesis.

The keystone of the J E D P theory is the so-called D document which is the core of the book of Deuteronomy. Accepting as valid the theory that this document was written early in the seventh century B.C. and "discovered" in 621 B.C., the proponents of the J E D P theory are convinced that this date is a solid anchorage for their reconstruction of how and when the Pentateuch was compiled.

The argument goes that since D presupposes the contents of JE and is itself a synthesis of prophetic and priestly viewpoints, it serves as a significant new antithesis to the prevalent Hebrew theology of the late kingdom period. It is alleged that D is unaware of much of the content of other material called the P document, so called because it is regarded as the work of a group of priests. Hence the P document is declared to be later than the D document by at least two centuries, and served as an antithesis to the growing body of Deuteronomic histories now found in the books from Joshua through II Kings. The P document is said to understand God to be an extremely transcendent being, and its literary style is very formal and repetitious. The fusion of all these documents is said to have taken place late in the fifth century B.C., with P providing the basic framework for the first four books of the Pentateuch and Joshua.

In the last quarter of the nineteenth century the J E D P theory became the predominant view among Protestant Old Testament scholars in Germany and quickly spread to Great Britain and the United States where in the first half of the twentieth century it has enjoyed overwhelming support from Old Testament scholars of the liberal wing of Protestantism. It also claims followers among Jewish scholars and to a limited extent it has adherents among Catholic scholars.[1]

In spite of its compact rationale, time has shown that the J E D P theory possesses several inherent weaknesses. In the first place, there has never appeared in any ancient literature, in ancient manuscripts of the Old Testament, and certainly not in the present Old Testament, any specific reference to a J, an E, a D or a P document. So far these are merely symbols for masses of scattered bits of Scripture said to possess, in total, characteristics of these documents. Second, the Hegelian theory of dialectical evolution which was appropriated as the unifying cord of the J E D P theory has fallen into disrepute and presently few Old Testament scholars will pay allegiance to it. Without the cohesiveness of the Hegelian dialectic the theory has inevitably fallen apart. Third, the J E D P theory has been overly dependent upon unknown redactors to whom has been credited all portions of Scripture which have refused to fall into place in either of the documents. To resort to a redactor has been an easy way out of difficult analytical problems.

In a footnote C. G. Howie has made a remark about redaction in the book of Ezekiel which also holds true of literary analysis of the Pentateuch. He said:

> When an author seeks in one or more redactors the answer to minor literary difficulties, he makes it likely that eventually his reconstruction will become almost completely subjective. The dangers of this method can hardly be overemphasized.[2]

Fourth, though the theory appeared to be neat and clear-cut, much detail remained obscure, which gave rise to suspicions that the structure of the documents may have been actually forced upon them by their modern architects rather than being a reality of the history of the literature. Hence, search for ancient materials in the documents was made by some of its adherents, resulting in what is known as form and tradition criticism. Hermann Gunkel, whose work on Genesis has recently been translated into English, pioneered this method of approach. He had no intention of disproving the J E D P theory, yet his views have radically modified it.[3]

Fifth, archaeologists have brought forth a mass of literary and cultural information which has greatly illuminated the biblical text, showing that ancient culture in the Near East was in line with the testimony of Scripture, but not in line with the reconstructions of the J E D P theory.

Although W. F. Albright allows for much more editing than do conservative Old Testament scholars, he has declared: "It is, accordingly, sheer hypercriticism to deny the substantially Mosaic character of the Pentateuchal tradition."[4]

Finally, theories which deny a relationship between Moses and the Pentateuch disregard a mass of evidence in the Scripture itself, which remains the only significant witness to Hebrew life and faith in Old Testament times. Extant texts cannot be so easily ignored.

Few conservative scholars hold that Moses wrote with his own hand the bulk

[1] The leading advocates of the J E D P theory among English-speaking people have been W. O. E. Oesterly and T. H. Robinson, *An Introduction to the Books of the Old Testament* (New York: Meridian Books, Inc., 1958), and H. H. Rowley, *The Growth of the Old Testament* (London: Hutchinsons, 1950), in England; and J. A. Bewer, *The Literature of the Old Testament* (New York: Columbia University Press, 1962), and R. H. Pfeiffer, *Introduction to the Old Testament* (New York: Harper and Bros., 1941), in the United States.

[2] C. G. Howie, *The Date and Composition of Ezekiel* (Philadelphia: Society of Biblical Literature, 1950), p. 107.

[3] H. Gunkel, *Legends of Genesis* (New York: Schocken Books, 1964).

[4] W. F. Albright, *The Archaeology of Palestine* (Baltimore: Penguin Books, 1954), p. 225.

of the five books of the Pentateuch, nor is there an insistence that no sources, oral or written, were used in producing these books. Most conservative scholars do insist that, with limited later additions, the Pentateuch was produced under the supervision of Moses and that some of it was actually written by him. Above all, there was the guiding and inspiring presence of the Holy Spirit.

Later additions to the Pentateuch no doubt occurred, as suggested by such passages as Genesis 12:6b; 13:7b, 18; 14:14; 22:14; 23:19b; 36:31; 49:5-7; Exodus 6:26, 27; 16:33-35, 36; Numbers 4:3; 12:3; 13:16; 21:14; 24:7; Deuteronomy 2:4-7, 26-30; 3:14-17; 10:6, 7; 32:7-12; 32:13-30 and chapter 34. But the final test of any passage being an addition must be manuscript evidence, and at the present time this is limited in scope.

Besides the clear testimony of Scripture to the Mosaic character of the Pentateuch, there has been a growing body of evidence which not only supports the possibility of the Pentateuch coming from Moses but also makes it highly probable. Information from ancient ruins of long forgotten cities shows that the book of Genesis is deeply rooted in the Mesopotamian culture of the third millennium and the early half of the second millennium B.C. Without a doubt there came to Moses a wealth of materials bearing knowledge of God's dealings with ancient man, and particularly the patriarchs.

Research has revealed that not only the cuneiform script of Mesopotamia and the hieroglyphics of the Nile valley were ancient and widespread in Moses' time, but the alphabetic writing had long since been developed into an effective medium of communication. There was nothing which need prevent Moses or some of his scribes from recording whatever God commanded them to write. With the script, a wide range of materials upon which to write was available, among which were parchment and papyrus.

It is now common knowledge that a variety of literary forms and motifs of narrative and poem construction were available in Moses' day. Poems found at Ras Shamra have specifically demonstated that Moses' song (Exod. 15:1-18) and Miriam's song (Exod. 15:21) were not post-exilic, but rather as ancient as Moses and Miriam themselves.

Of prime importance has been the wealth of light which ancient covenant forms, found on cuneiform tablets, have thrown on the ancient rootage of the covenants of Abraham, Isaac, Jacob and that of the nation at Sinai. This, too, has aided greatly in understanding the structure of the book of Deuteronomy as not a forgery of the seventh century B.C. but an authentic covenant renewal by the children of Israel in Moses' time.[5]

Since law is so prominent in several of the books of the Pentateuch, it is helpful to have a growing body of law codes from Mesopotamia to Asia Minor show that the laws of the Pentateuch are congenial to the legal environment of the second quarter of the second millennium, though at the same time such laws as the Ten Commandments are both old and uniquely superior to any pagan codes.

These evidences do not conclusively prove Mosaic authorship of the Pentateuch, but they do make it far from incredible. Nor do these evidences yet indicate how the contents of Genesis came into Moses' hands. The extent of valid additions to the literary work of the Mosaic period is still unclear.

Definitely, there is a trend away from the late dates of the J E D P theory to much earlier dates, resulting in a variety of opinions and theories. At present, discussion of the date and composition of any of the books of the Pentateuch is in a state of flux such as has not been known for over a century. Conservative Old Testament scholars thus have an obligation and an opportunity to contribute to the resolution of weighty problems in a most difficult area of research and evaluation.

For helpful discussions on the problem of Mosaic authorship, besides the books mentioned in the footnotes, the reader is invited to consider the following:

Aalders, T. C. *A Short Introduction to the Pentateuch.* London: Tyndale Press, 1949.

[5] M. G. Kline, *Treaty of the Great King* (Grand Rapids: Wm. B. Eerdmans Publishing Co., 1963). For a more extensive treatment see D. J. McCarthy, *Treaty and Covenant* (Rome: Analecta Biblia, 1963).

Allis, O. T. *The Five Books of Moses.* Philadelphia: The Presbyterian and Reformed Publishing Co., 1943.

Anderson, Bernhard W. *Understanding the Old Testament.* Englewood Cliffs, N. J., 1957.

Archer, G. L. *A Survey of Old Testament Introduction.* Chicago: Moody Press, 1964.

Cassuto, U. *The Documentary Hypothesis.* Jerusalem: Magness Press, 1961.

Driver, S. R. *An Introduction to the Literature of the Old Testament.* New York: Charles Scribner's Sons, 1922.

Eissfeldt, O. *The Old Testament: An Introduction.* New York: Harper and Row, 1965.

Green, W. H. *The Higher Criticism of the Pentateuch.* New York: Charles Scribner's Sons, 1896.

Harrelson, W. *Interpreting the Old Testament.* New York: Holt, Rinehart and Winston, Inc., 1964.

Kyle, M. G. *The Problem of the Pentateuch.* Oberlin: Bibliotheca Sacra Co., 1920.

Lewy, I. *The Growth of the Pentateuch.* New York: Bookman Associates, 1955.

Pfeiffer, Robert H. *Introduction to the Old Testament.* New York: Harper and Row, 1941.

Simpson, C. A. *The Early Traditions of Israel.* Oxford: B. Blackwell, 1948.

Unger, M. F. *Introductory Guide to the Old Testament.* Grand Rapids: Zondervan Publishing House, 1951.

Winnett, F. V. *The Mosaic Tradition.* Toronto: University of Toronto Press, 1949.

Young, Edward J. *An Introduction to the Old Testament.* Grand Rapids: Wm. B. Eerdmans Publishing Co., 1960.

The Book of Genesis

by Lee Haines

Editor's Preface to Genesis and Exodus

The author of the commentaries on Genesis and Exodus is the Reverend Lee Haines, presently pastor of the Eastlawn Wesleyan Methodist Church in Indianapolis, Indiana.

Mr. Haines graduated from Marion College in 1950 with the Bachelor of Religion degree, *summa cum laude*. In 1959 he was awarded the B.D. degree, *cum laude*, by Christian Theological Seminary. He is presently a candidate for the M.A. degree at Butler University.

Mr. Haines holds membership in Theta Phi, international honor society, Eta Beta Rho, national Hebrew honor society, the Evangelical Theological Society, and the Wesleyan Theological Society.

The Rev. Mr. Haines is an ordained minister in the Indiana Conference of the Wesleyan Methodist Church of America. His pastoral service in that conference extends over a period of sixteen years. He served as an instructor in Greek and religion at Marion College for one year. For two and a half years he was office editor of the adult curriculum, Department of Sunday Schools, the Wesleyan Methodist Church of America. He has been a leader in Sunday school convention work both on the state and national level. He has carried heavy official responsibilities in his conference, and is presently a member of the executive committee of the Board of Trustees of Marion College, the Committee on Itineracy and Orders of the Indiana Conference, and is a second consecutive time delegate to the General Conference of his denomination.

Mr. Haines has been a regular writer for the Wesleyan Methodist Sunday school literature for the past six years. He has written for *The Evangelical Sunday School Lesson Commentary* (Higley Press); he was editor of the first unit of the interdenominational work, "Aldersgate Doctrinal Studies," and wrote a substantial portion of that publication; and he is author of *The Story of Indiana Wesleyan Youth* (Indiana Wesleyan Youth, 1955).

Though one of the younger writers for the *Wesleyan Bible Commentary*, Mr. Haines brings to his expositions on Genesis and Exodus a sound theological training and a rich background of ministerial service and Christian writing. He has excellently and admirably elucidated the great central truths of these first two great books of the Hebrew-Christian Bible which are so basic and fundamental to a correct understanding of the rationale of the entire plan of human redemption as revealed in the Bible. It is a pleasure to commend these expositions to the readers of this volume.

CHAS. W. CARTER
General Editor
Wesleyan Bible Commentary

Outline

Introduction

I. NAME

The first book of the Bible commonly bears a name which is never applied to it in the Scriptures themselves — *Genesis.* This is a Greek word meaning variously: birth, existence, origin, genealogy, source, generation. It was used in the ancient Greek translation of the Old Testament called the Septuagint to translate one of the key Hebrew words of the book, *toledoth,* or "generations" as it commonly appears in our English versions (2:4; 5:1; 6:9; 10:1; 11:10, 27; 25:12, 19; 36:1, 9; 37:1).[1] Because of the importance of the word to the structure of Genesis, the translators of the Septuagint applied the word to the book as a title. From this it was adopted as a title by Jerome in his standard Latin translation, the Vulgate, and from there by practically every modern translation. The ancient Hebrews simply called it by its first word, *bereshith,* meaning, "In the beginning." Martin Luther, in his German translation, entitled it, "The First Book of Moses." This has been combined with the ancient Greek title in the major English translations as, "The First Book of Moses, (Commonly) Called Genesis."

II. STRUCTURE

The book of Genesis has one of the most clearly discernible literary structures of any of the biblical books. Ten times the author introduces a new section with the phrase, *eleh toledoth,* commonly translated, "These are the generations." The phrase always refers to what follows,[2] and is to be understood in the sense, "This is the account of this man and his descendants."[3] In every instance but one the primary emphasis is on the descendants rather than upon the man. The author's outline of the book would accordingly look something like this.

Introduction: the Creation (1:1—2:3)
The offspring of heaven and earth — Adam (2:4—4:26)
The offspring of Adam — Ten Generations (5:1—6:8)
The story of Noah and his offspring — the Flood (6:9—9:29)
The offspring of Shem, Ham, Japheth — the Nations (10:1—11:9)
The offspring of Shem — Another Ten Generations (11:10-26)
The offspring of Terah — Abram or Abraham (11:27—25:11)
The offspring of Ishmael — the Ishmaelites (25:12-18)
The offspring of Isaac — Esau and Jacob (25:19—35:29)
The offspring of Esau — the Edomites (36:1-43)
The offspring of Jacob or Israel — Joseph and his brethren (37:1—50:26)

Expositors of Genesis do not always follow the author's outline in explaining the message and meaning of the book. A quick comparison of this list of eleven sections with the fully developed outline which precedes this "Introduction" will show that the present writer has not. There are sound reasons for this. While the author used the *toledoth* as a mechanical structure around which to build his stories, he also followed a theological progression which helped to fulfill his purpose in writing. This also is discernible, although not so obvious. According to this approach, the turning point of the book is at 12:1, which is part way through the sixth *toledoth.* Here, at the call of Abram, there is an arresting turn from universal history to selective history, from the story of the human race to the story of the chosen family. All that has gone before has simply unfolded the reasons why the chosen man and his family were necessary. The change in setting and mood are dramatically evident. The best way to demonstrate this all-important change, and to

---

[1] Edward J. Young, *An Introduction to the Old Testament,* p. 49.   [2] *Ibid.,* p. 50.
[3] Francis Brown, S. R. Driver, and Charles A. Briggs, eds., *A Hebrew and English Lexicon of the Old Testament,* p. 410.

unfold the progression leading up to it and the significant developments following it, is to divide the book into two major portions at this point. Then subdivisions can be marked off around major events or persons, much as J. Sidlow Baxter has distinguished in the first division four outstanding events: creation, fall, flood, Babel; and in the second, four outstanding persons: Abraham, Isaac, Jacob, Joseph.[4] The major *toledoth* sections often provide proper subdivisions in this scheme, while those which are extremely short and significant only in showing what happened to some side branch of the human race or chosen family are incorporated in the larger and more significant subdivisions. Thus, instead of the mechanical *toledoth* outline, which may have had a unique value to the author (see "Authorship") but which has definite shortcomings for the reader, we have a more practical topical and theological outline, at once more true to the author's overriding purpose and more effective for the modern mind.

III. AUTHORSHIP

From as far back as human memory is able to reach, Genesis has been considered as part of a larger unit involving the first five books of the Bible. The ancient Hebrews called the five books the *Torah,* a word which can mean both "law" and "instruction," and referred to them as "the five fifths of the Torah." Origen, a Christian scholar of the early third century A.D., called them a *pentateuch,* a Greek word meaning "a five-volumed book."[5] This term has become the common name for the five books. The man traditionally recognized both by the Jews and by Christians as the author of the Pentateuch is Moses. The reasons for this are many.

For one thing, Moses is the central character of the five books. Genesis covers the history of the human race and of the chosen family prior to Moses. Exodus records his birth and call, and the beginning of his forty years of leadership of the nation. Leviticus incorporates much

of the law which Jehovah revealed through Moses. Numbers records the closing years of his leadership. Deuteronomy consists almost entirely of his farewell addresses to his people.

Furthermore, Moses had the training necessary for the research, organization, and actual composition of such documents, since he was raised as the son of the daughter of the Pharaoh of a highly civilized Egypt. And the Scriptures make it clear that he did write, the Pentateuch itself mentioning this in conjunction with some of its portions (Exod. 17:14; 24:4-8; 34:27; Num. 33:1-2; Deut. 31:9, 22, 24). A specific document is referred to on occasion, with reference being made to "the book" (Exod. 17:14, see ASV margin), "the book of the covenant" (Exod. 24:7), and "this book of the law" which Moses gave to the Levites to be placed inside the ark in the tabernacle's Holy of Holies (Deut. 31:24-26).

The book which Moses had written played a large part in the guidance of Joshua, the man who followed him. There are many references in the book of Joshua to him doing "as the Lord commanded Moses" or "the word of the Lord by the hand of Moses," and some to the book itself (1:7-8; 8:31; 23:6). And the book continued to play a large part in the history of the nation throughout the Old Testament, with many references to "the law of Moses" and a few to "the book" (II Kings 14:6; 22:8; Ezra 6: 18; Neh. 13:1). The New Testament also refers to the writings of Moses, both in individual citations of stories or commandments and also in more general terms. These references include several from the lips of Jesus, others from the apostles, and some from the writers. By the time of the New Testament, the Old Testament was divided by the Jews into the Law, the Prophets, and the Writings (the latter division was sometimes called the Psalms because Psalms was the first book in the collection). On the two occasions in which the New Testament uses this classification, it substitutes the term "law of Moses," or simply "Moses"

[4] J. Sidlow Baxter, *Explore the Book,* I, 27-29.
[5] Young, *op. cit.,* p. 44.

for the law or the Pentateuch (Luke 24:27, 44).[6]

The tradition of the Mosaic authorship was thus universal down to the close of the biblical canon, and continued so for several centuries thereafter. The first questions were raised during the Middle Ages by certain Jewish scholars, but these dealt only with scattered verses or passages, not with the entire work. After the Reformation, the different suggestions about authorship began to multiply. Some suggested that Moses wrote certain originals which were later enlarged and edited to produce our present Pentateuch. Others suggested that Moses supervised the writing. Many mentioned Ezra as either the author, the reviser, or the editor.[7] Then a whole new school of thought developed on the basis of the observations of Jean Astruc in the eighteenth century, and their elaboration by subsequent scholars including Karl H. Graf and Julius Wellhausen in the nineteenth century. This school claimed to find embedded within the Pentateuch older documents on which the final product was based, documents which had not been rewritten into a single work but rather loosely interwoven. The supporters of the theory claimed to find all kinds of duplications and contradictions within the sacred writings which could only be explained on the basis of multiple and contradicting traditions. The sources were eventually classified as documents J, E, D, and P (see General Introduction to the Pentateuch at the front of this volume). And instead of being pre-Mosaic documents used by him as sources for Genesis, the claim was made that the earliest of the four documents could not have been composed before the time of David, and that the Pentateuch in its final form could not have been put together until after the exile in the early fourth century B.C. Thus Moses, if such a person ever existed, could have had noth-

ing at all to do with the composition of the Pentateuch.

The weaknesses of the Graf-Wellhausen theory, and of its successors which are still taught in the majority of theological seminaries today, are many and can be discussed only sketchily here. The whole movement is based upon skepticism of the miraculous and supernatural, and a blinding devotion to the theory of evolution as the force which has produced modern man, spiritually as well as physically. The critical position has been made attractive by its claim to be a new knowledge, a break-through accomplished by the tools of modern science. It is true that the countless varieties of Scripture dissection, the countless volumes in which the division of the Pentateuch into infinitesimal parts has been carried out, the mumble-jumble of new words and terms and symbolic initials have so befogged the issue that the average man surrenders the whole matter to the scholars and usually submits meekly to their findings! But a careful examination of the evidence reveals that these so-called scholars have often been anything but scientific and critical in their approach. They have divided up the Scriptures arbitrarily, observing certain types of writing and characteristics of writing, manufacturing authors or schools of authors to fit these types, and assigning all the parts to the respective writers. Thus they have argued in a circle, using the theory they are attempting to support to support the arguments which are supposed to support it! And this self-supporting toothpick house becomes ever larger and more elaborate until self-destruction is assured. The critics do not agree with each other on the parts into which the Scriptures are to be dissected, the documents to which they are to be assigned, the type of men who have produced them, or the dates at which they were written. In fact, many a critic does not agree with himself from one time of writing until the next! Thus

---

[6] Sandmel further notes that "when Jews speak of *Bible* they mean what Christians mean by Old Testament; the term that Jews customarily use is *Tanak* (tah-náhk) . . . . The term is formed from the first letters of the names of the three divisions [of the O. T.]. Torah ('Revelation' [technically, the Pentateuch or first five books of the O. T.]), Neviim [or Nebhi'im] ('Prophets' ['Former Prophets'— Josh., Judg., Sam., Kings; and 'Latter Prophets' — Isa., Jer., Ezek. and the Twelve (Minor Prophets)], and Kesuvim ('Writings' [Pss., Prov., Job, Lam., S. S., Eccle., Esther, Dan., Chron., Ezra, Neh.]). Jews actually pronounce the word Tana*ch*, ending with the German *ch*, not *k*." Samuel Sandmel, *The Hebrew Scriptures*, p. 3.

[7] One of the best reviews of this earlier development of criticism is found in John Peter Lange, *Commentary on the Holy Scriptures*, trans. by Philip Schaff, I, 94ff.

the contradictions of the critical school often far exceed the contradictions they claim to find in the Pentateuch.

On the whole, the results of this type of study have been destructive. The inspired Word of God has been reduced for countless ministers and congregations from the level of an authoritative revelation to a fallible record of the religious evolution of finite men groping after eternal truth. Scores of able exegetes have wasted their time and energies, and cluttered up their writings with meaningless analyses of the chapters and verses into their various sources, losing precious opportunities to unlock the true significance of the sacred Word.

Probably the only good things to come out of the critical approach have been the renewed study of the Scriptures by those most fully committed to them, and the necessity of taking a new look at old traditions. While the so-called documentary hypothesis is probably the worst possible explanation for the Pentateuch, it has raised certain valid questions about Mosaic authorship. For example, there are passages in the Pentateuch which sound as though they were written at a later period than Moses, including the identification of ancient sites by their later names or terms best understood after Israel returned to Canaan (Gen. 14:2, 3, 7, 8, 14; 23:2; 28:19; 31:21ff.; 35:6, 19, 27; 37:25; 48:7; 50:10), the explanation of conditions which still obtained in Moses' time but which would have needed such explanation at a later period (12:6b; 13:7b), and the reference to conditions which did not prevail until after Moses' time (36:31ff.). There are what may be parenthetical statements characterized by the reference "unto this day" which take on added significance if they are post-Mosaic (19:37, 38; 22:14; 31:32; 35:20). There are evaluations of Moses which would be out of character for the world's meekest man to write about himself (Num. 12:3). And Deuteronomy 34, which records Moses' own death and burial, and the statement that after him there had not arisen "since" a prophet like him, could certainly not be credited to Moses. Fur-

thermore, while the Pentateuch specifically says that Moses wrote certain of its sections, it nowhere says that he wrote all of it. And when we begin to examine the word *torah* or "law," which was universally ascribed to Moses, it is found that from the first it had various meanings, including one sufficiently limited so that Joshua was able to copy it in its entirety upon the stones of his altar in Mt. Ebal, *while the assembled nation watched him* (Josh. 8:30-32). It is true that Christ and the inspired apostles cited many passages in Exodus, Leviticus, Numbers, and Deuteronomy as the product of Moses. It is also true that on occasion New Testament writers used Moses' name in connection with the entire Pentateuch. The former, however, could be admitted without proving his authorship of all five books as they now stand. And the latter could be the result of using his name in a broad sense, including those portions he did write as well as those he did not, in much the same fashion that Psalms was used as the title for the entire third division of the Hebrew Old Testament, although it included twelve other books, most of which were not poetic in form at all. We have a parallel situation today in referring to the two books of Samuel, since Samuel died before the conclusion of the first of the two books and could not possibly have written the rest. The present writer finds it highly significant that he is not able to find anywhere in the Bible a quotation or citation of Genesis which specifically ascribes any portion of it to Moses, though there may be a suggestion of Genesis in Luke 24:27.

Such observations as these have led present-day evangelical scholars to conclude that there are three factors involved in the authorship of Genesis: pre-Mosaic sources, Mosaic originals, and post-Mosaic additions and editing.[8] The range of possible variations in the relative importance of these factors is great. Some will say that Moses used the earlier sources to produce Genesis and the rest of the Pentateuch almost as we have it today, with only minor additions such as the account of his death.[9] Others would concede to Moses a much smaller

[8] G. C. Aalders, "The Historical Literature of the Old Testament," in *The New Bible Commentary,* ed. by Francis Davidson, p. 34. [9] H. C. Leupold, *Exposition of Genesis,* pp. 5-9.

part in the production, writing large sections of the Pentateuch, but yielding its final composition to an anonymous writer of the early monarchy who may have directly used some pre-Mosaic materials not included by Moses himself.[10] Probably most would agree with the judgment that Moses was "the responsible author of the book," while the final editing may have come as late as the time of Ezra.[11] Such admission of the probability of post-Mosaic additions and editing in no way detracts from the status of Genesis as a divinely inspired record. It simply assumes that the later writers and editors were also fully inspired by the Holy Spirit.

That Moses wrote at least sections of the Pentateuch is clear from the direct testimony of the Scriptures as cited above. That he wrote portions, if not the bulk, of Genesis seems likely, for he is the person best fitted to have done so, both as to the critical period in which he lived and served and as to his training and abilities. That some later editing was also done has already been supported by examples. But it is also possible to support the claim for pre-Mosaic sources for Genesis. Moses could have known the history recorded in Genesis only in one of three ways: divine revelation, oral tradition, or written records. Divine revelation is the only means by which Genesis 1 and 2 could have been produced. Oral tradition may be reflected in the snatches of poetry preserved in the book, since the rhythmic lines of a poem are more easily remembered than prose (4:23-24; 9:25-27; 25:23; 27:27-29, 39-40; 49:2-27). The English divine and scholar, George Matheson, records of the first of these that "there arose in that age a great poet, a poet the rhythm of whose words has not been drowned by the noise of the deluge. A fragment of his verse has come *over* the flood, and is known to us as '*The Song of the Sword.*'"[12] One type of record which involved both an element of oral tradition and an element of writing was that of the erection of altars and

monuments and the digging of wells, to which meaningful names and/or proverbs were applied (16:13-14; 21:27-31; 22:14; 26:18-33; 28:16-22; 31:45-52; 33:20; 35:7, 8, 14-15, 20). Actual written records are indicated by the word "book" in Genesis 5:1 (cf. Num. 21:14). It is almost certain that the genealogical lists would have been among the first things written down. To the present writer it seems extremely likely that all ten of the *toledoth* were originally written genealogies which the author of Genesis used as a framework around which to arrange his other material. For some there was little or no material pertinent to the author's purpose, so they remained genealogies. For others there was a large quantity of important material so the genealogy was expanded into an effective narrative. Much of this material must also have been written down at an early date, most of it at or close to the time when it took place. It is now known that writing dates from very ancient times. And the historical accuracy of Genesis, once challenged by the critics, has now been amply vindicated. The conditions of ancient Mesopotamia in the time of the patriarchs, the conditions of ancient Canaan while they sojourned there, and the conditions of ancient Egypt when Joseph and his brethren were there are all depicted so accurately that they could only have been recorded by men who were there at the particular times designated. Furthermore, there are repeated instances of precise and detailed dating of events by years and even days which would strongly suggest written records or journals. And even in as early a story as that of the flood there is such rich visual imagery as could come only from an eyewitness.[13]

The present writer would conclude that the truth about the authorship of Genesis lies somewhere between the opinions of Aalders and Yates as cited above: large portions written by Moses using pre-existing sources, substantial editing

---

[10] Aalders, *loc. cit.*

[11] Kyle M. Yates, Sr., "Genesis," in *The Wycliffe Bible Commentary*, ed. by Charles F. Pfeiffer and Everett F. Harrison, pp. 1-2.

[12] George Matheson, *The Representative Men of the Bible*, "*Adam to Job*" (New York: George H. Doran Company, n.d.), pp. 96, 97.   [13] Lange, *op. cit.*, I, 316.

by a later editor or editors with the slight possibility that they also used some pre-Mosaic sources either not available or not used by Moses himself. In order to avoid confusion, we shall not use any proper name in references to the author throughout the commentary but simply refer to him as "the author."

IV. DATE

The date of the writing of Genesis of course depends upon one's view of its authorship. The date of the pre-Mosaic sources and that of the writings of Moses himself depend in turn upon the dating of the events in Genesis, especially those of the patriarchal age. There are two ways in which the dating of the patriarchs can be made: the biblical chronology itself, and the contacts between the patriarchs and the cultures of their day which have left dated records.

All through Genesis there are recorded various references to the passage of time, particularly the ages of the principal characters, both at the time of the birth of their sons and at the time of their own death. These, coupled with other key verses (such as Gen. 15:13; Exod. 12:40-41; Acts 7:6) and the later chronology of the nation of Israel which is more easily coordinated with world history, make it possible to arrive at an approximate dating. The accuracy of such dating is tempered by the recognition that it is virtually impossible to translate ancient methods of dating into the precise terms of modern times. For instance, the ancient Hebrews used lunar months of about 28 days which necessitated the frequent insertion of an entire thirteenth month in the calendar to bring it back into harmony with the solar year. Thus some years were noticeably longer than others. Furthermore, in counting the years of the various kings' reigns, partial years were frequently counted as whole years; the year in which one king died and his son succeeded him were often counted in both reigns; there were times when a father and son ruled jointly and yet the overlapping years were counted in both reigns; and there were times when there was not an immediate suc-

cession to the throne and no record is made of the years thus spent in political chaos. To complicate the whole picture, ancient Hebrew numbers were represented by the letters of the alphabet. There are several pairs of letters which differ only in a very slight detail. Thus the point at which a copyist's error would be most likely to occur would be in connection with numbers. And some scholars suspect that many of the Old Testament numbers have been deliberately enlarged or exaggerated by a well-meaning but unwise scribe. Thus a great deal of caution must be exercised when attempting to arrive at a biblical chronology, always seeking some checkpoint from secular chronology or archaeology. Secular chronology is subject to the same problems as is the biblical, but if the two agree and there is some way to pinpoint the agreement through the findings of archaeology, we can feel that we have a relatively accurate date.

When all the pertinent scriptural passages are examined, we arrive at the date of 2161 B.C. for the birth of Abraham, 2086 B.C. for his entrance into Canaan, and 1871 B.C. for the migration of Jacob and his family into Egypt.[14] There are three points at which the patriarchs came into contact with secular cultures in such a way as to make checkpoints possible: the invasion of Trans-Jordan and the region around Sodom by the four Mesopotamian kings in Genesis 14, the destruction of Sodom and its neighbors in Genesis 19, and the service of Joseph as prime minister of Egypt. The destruction of Sodom provides the key event, for archaeology has shown that there was a flourishing civilization in the area south of the Dead Sea in the late third millennium B.C., which came to an abrupt end sometime in the twentieth or twenty-first century — about 2000 B.C. This supports the biblical chronology. The other two checkpoints cannot be made to yield such dramatic evidence, but there is much about them which supports this general period and nothing which contradicts it. William F. Albright, the renowned American archaeologist, points out: (1) that most of the towns mentioned in conjunction with the patriarchs

[14] Merrill F. Unger, *Archaeology and the Old Testament*, pp. 105-07.

have been proven by archaeology to have been occupied in the period around 2000 B.C.; (2) that archaeology has confirmed that there were conquerors like those described in Genesis 14 who flourished at that same date; (3) that some of the words and data in Genesis 14 mystified the scholars until archaeology confirmed them as historically correct for the early second millennium B.C.; (4) that the route taken by the Mesopotamian conquerors in Genesis 14 through Trans-Jordan was densely populated around 2000 B.C. but desolate before 1800 B.C.; and (5) that a possible explanation for the silence of Egyptian records about Joseph may be found in the fact that the period in which he died was one of decadence and anarchy from which few inscriptions have survived.[15] This scheme receives additional support from the fact that it would place Israel in Egypt before, during, and after the period in which Egypt was ruled by the foreign "shepherd kings" or Hyksos. They were Semites like the Israelites, and when the Egyptians managed to throw off their yoke, it would be natural for the new Egyptian rulers to treat all foreigners harshly, just as the new king "who knew not Joseph" did to Israel (Exod. 1:8ff.).[16]

Some critical scholars prefer to place these events 150 to 200 years later than the biblical chronology would indicate, either because they think it more likely that Joseph became prime minister under the Semitic Hyksos,[17] or because of their particular interpretation of Exodus 1:11 and their persuasion that a later date is necessary for the conquest of Canaan.[18] But such reasoning seems quite weak when compared with the strong support cited for the earlier date above.

As will be shown in the comments under the various passages, it is exceedingly difficult to do any dating prior to the time of Abraham. There is strong evidence that the genealogy tracing the descent from Shem to Abraham is schematic rather than exhaustive, making any dating of the flood most precarious. And since similar evidence exists for the gene-

alogies prior to the flood, it is absolutely impossible to date the creation and the fall. So for the earliest sources of Genesis, both oral tradition and written record, no dates can be determined. It is probable that at least from the time of Noah or his sons some written records did exist. It is likely that Abraham, Isaac, and Jacob had among their many slaves those skilled in the art of writing, and earlier records and traditions may have been collected and the marvelous records of God's calls and promises may have been added to them. The further writings of Moses would have taken place during the forty years of wilderness wanderings, 1441-01 B.C. The subsequent additions and editings must then have been almost entirely completed by the third century B.C., since the Greek Septuagint translation was completed then, and it has only minor differences from the accepted Hebrew manuscripts. Some critical scholars would push the final revisions practically that late. But conservative evangelical scholars would prefer to think of Ezra as the last of the revisers, with a strong possibility that some additions were made by Joshua, since he did do some writing in the book of the law (Josh. 24:22), and that most of the work was completed in the early years of the monarchy.

V. SCOPE AND SIGNIFICANCE

Genesis is one of the greater books of the Bible. For vastness of historical scope it cannot be equaled. If even the most conservative chronology, that of Ussher, should be used, from the 4004 B.C. date he ascribed to creation to the year 1800 B.C. when Joseph died, the sweep of Genesis records over half the period covered by both the Old and New Testaments. And when we consider the probability that the date of creation was much earlier than Ussher realized, we see that over half of the entire period of human history is covered in this book, perhaps far more than half.

But the greatness of Genesis does not depend upon the expanses of time which

[15] William F. Albright, "Recent Discoveries in Bible Lands," in Robert Young, *Analytical Concordance to the Bible*, pp. 26-27.

[16] Unger, *op. cit.*, p. 107. See also his article, "The Date of Exodus," in *Unger's Bible Dictionary*, pp. 331-34.

[17] E. A. Speiser, *Genesis*, "The Anchor Bible," p. 316.

[18] J. Coert Rylaarsdam, "Exodus" (Introduction), *The Interpreter's Bible*, I, 836.

it covers. It is rather the result of its theme, its purpose, and its significant relationship to all the rest of the divine revelation, and indeed to all of philosophy and religion.

The theme of Genesis is *God and man*. It tells how God, the Almighty One, desired a creature with whom He could have fellowship. Consequently, He created an entire universe in a state of perfect beauty, filled at least one of the planets with a rich diversity of plant and animal life, and placed in the midst of this natural paradise one made in His own image, perfect in body, mind, and spirit, at once the object of divine love and providential care, the crown of creation, the servant and companion of God, the lord of the earth (Gen. 1:24-31; cf. Ps. 8; Heb. 2:5-8). It also tells how this man despised his Maker and his privileges and, seeking by his own means a deceptive exaltation of himself at the expense of the divine glory, plunged himself and all his progeny into a horrible abyss of sin and rebellion which could only end in his complete and final destruction. But it also tells of the marvelous grace of God which would not give up the object of His affection, the man whom He had so perfectly designed. It reveals that from the moment of man's sin God promised his redemption. And it tells us that, while sin follows a course of becoming increasingly sinful, the grace of God follows a course of becoming increasingly gracious, that even when sin demands justice the glorious radiance of mercy will be seen in the clouds of divine wrath. It makes clear that God's power is sufficient to cause all things to work to His glory and to the good of the object of His love.

The purpose of Genesis is *to unfold the beginnings of redemption*. The author puts man in his proper perspective, describing his origin and destiny, recognizing his wilfulness and its consequences. And against the background of man's desperate need he reveals how God will meet that need — eventually by the promised Seed of the woman, the Christ of the New Testament, but first progressively narrowing down the group through whom He must come. In each generation He finds a man, a family, a tribe, a nation — a remnant through whom He can work out His plan, a servant whom He can use in revealing His nature and purpose to the entire race.

The relationship of Genesis to the whole of religion is one of primary importance: *it is in all things the beginning*. For all the questions which have tortured the mind and soul of man about himself and his place under the sun, it contains the beginnings of a most profound and satisfying answer. For all the rest of divine revelation it is the foundation, introducing all the important themes of Scripture, all the doctrines of the Christian faith, giving to the other books perspective and meaning. In Genesis all the rest is found in embryo. Without Genesis all the rest would be a haunting riddle. Genesis is indeed one of God's most precious gifts, one that is not quickly exhausted and with which we can profitably tarry, seeking to plumb ever more deeply its treasures of promise and assurance.

(For additional introductory material see General Introduction to the Pentateuch at the front of this volume.)

Commentary on Genesis

I. THE STORY OF MAN (Gen. 1:1—11:32)

A. THE CREATION (1:1—2:25)

1. The Origin of the Universe (1:1)

1 In the beginning God created the heavens and the earth.

This is the most sublime and satisfying statement ever made concerning the origin of the universe. It is not a statement which can be proven or disproven by the empirical sciences. Rather, it is a statement of divine revelation and of human faith. It contains the testimony of God, the only One who witnessed the beginning in its entirety, to man, whose searching mind and heart reach deep into the eternal past for a secret he cannot personally uncover. It is a statement which transforms all things, for if it were not true, the universe and all it contains would be an enigma of despair; but since it is true, the universe, history, and man himself are possessed of design and purpose.

In the beginning provides the only dating of the creation given by the scriptural record. In many copies of the English Bible still printed today, one will find the date of 4004 B.C. in the margin. This was the date arrived at by Archbishop Ussher in the seventeenth century by adding together the ages of the patriarchs, the years of the reigns of the kings of Israel, and other scattered bits of chronological information found in the Scriptures. But others took the same figures and arrived at different conclusions. Bible scholars discovered that some of the genealogical lists skipped over entire generations[1] and were faced with the possibility that such gaps might also exist in instances where there were no parallels for cross-checking. Furthermore, there have been discovered instances in which the reigns of kings overlapped or periods of political confusion separated them. As science began to study the geological age of the earth and to discover the vast distances which separated the stars from the earth and which require millions of years for their light to span, a much earlier date for the creation was required. No one today, Bible scholar or scientist, knows with any degree of authority when creation occurred. But this verse tells us that whenever it was, however remote or recent, God was there and He was acting, bringing to pass that which His sovereign will proposed.

Created is from the Hebrew *bara*. This verb is one of three used to describe God's creative work in Genesis 1 and 2. It appears in three connections: the creation of the universe (1:1), the initial creation of animal life (1:21), and the creation of man (1:27). Its meaning is summarized in an excellent fashion by Skinner.

(a) The most important fact is that it is used exclusively of *divine* activity — a restriction to which perhaps no parallel can be found in other languages. . . . (b) The idea of *novelty* . . . or *extraordinariness* . . . of result is frequently implied. . . . (c) It is probable also that it contains the idea of *effortless* production (such as befits the Almighty) by word or volition.[2]

Skinner goes on to observe that the concept of creation *ex nihilo* (out of nothing) is not necessarily included in the word. This is true. But if the author wanted to express that concept, this is the word he would use. The meaning of *bara* here in that respect must be determined by the context. This resolves itself largely into the question, What is the relationship of verse 1 to verses 2 and 3?

Many liberal scholars insist that verse

---

[1] Compare Matthew 1:8 with I Chronicles 3:11-12.
[2] John Skinner, *A Critical and Exegetical Commentary on Genesis*, pp. 14-15.

1 is a dependent clause and that it must be translated with the following verse in some such fashion as this: "When God began to create the heavens and the earth, the earth was a desolate waste, with darkness covering the abyss and a tempestuous wind raging over the surface of the waters."[3] This would mean that when God began His creative activity the universe already existed in a chaotic state and that He merely reshaped some pre-existing material. This would bog down the biblical account in all the philosophical impossibilities of an eternal dualism of God and matter. It is based on technical points of Hebrew grammar which range far beyond the scope of this commentary. Suffice it to say that most conservative scholars reject this translation and find grammatical justification for translating verse 1 as an independent sentence, as it is in every major version.[4] But not only must verse 1 be treated independently because of grammatical possibility and philosophical necessity, but also because of the plan followed by the author of Genesis throughout the book. Repeatedly he depicts a large scene, a fast-moving series of events, a large group of people or an older generation, and then narrows his focus to a smaller scene and enlarges the details as he carries on his narrative. This he does repeatedly in the creation account. So in verse 1 he sets the largest possible stage — the beginning of all things. Then in verse 2 he narrows his focus to the earth and its detailed formation. When verse 1 is seen in this light, there is no mention of a pre-existing material for God to reshape. Rather, in the beginning there was nothing but God and His creative power. Creation *ex nihilo* is again a matter which cannot be proven nor disproven by empirical science, but it is a truth which appeals to human reason, which has every possible support in this verse, and which the Christian believer feels is demanded by His exalted concept of God (cf. John 1:3; Heb. 11:3).

The opening words of this verse at one and the same time refute many philosophical and theological errors and support some significant Christian doctrines. *Polytheism* is precluded, for it is **God** not "gods" who **created**. So are *atheism,* for God exists here in His own right and all other existence is contingent upon Him; *agnosticism,* for in this God of beginnings is found the final and inescapable resting place of the mind's quest for reality; *essential dualism,* for it is not God and matter who created, but only God; *pantheism,* for God **created**, making nature His handiwork, but not of His essence; *the eternal existence of matter,* for there was a beginning when God **created**. On the other hand, we find evidence of the unity of God, the priority of God (God first and then all created things), the self-existence of God, the divine energy, and the divine intelligent purpose. All of this is summed up in the sublime words, **In the beginning God created the heavens and the earth.**

Since verse 1 is the one part of Genesis 1 that is most largely beyond challenge by the empirical sciences, it is perhaps well at this point to confront an unfortunate problem which must be encountered in any intelligent discussion of Genesis. This is the problem of the recurring conflict of science and religion.

There have always been men who refused to admit God's right to rule the universe and them. They have been quick to attack His authority, His Word, and His people whenever opportunity presented itself. When modern science first stretched its infant limbs and began to explore the secrets of the material universe, such men were quick to seize upon the first suggestions which seemed to differ from the dictums of theology. In response, theologians who had long reigned supreme over the world of knowledge sprang to the defense, not only of the Bible, but also of many of their ill-informed interpretations of it. They often did not distinguish between honest inquiry, the scientific method, factual data, preliminary conclusions, and those who were misusing these. There were tragic consequences. On the one hand, science became increasingly non-religious in its orientation. On the other, the church was rent asunder between a

[3] Theophile J. Meek in *The Bible, an American Translation.*
[4] For a detailed and scholarly answer to the liberal position, see Edward J. Young, *Studies in Genesis One,* pp. 1-14.

liberalism which too often lost its religious certainty in its supposed scientific respectability and a conservatism which too frequently turned its back on anything which would make it rethink its position and seek a larger truth than that of which it had hitherto been aware.

All of this was unnecessary. Both scientists and theologians should have had greater humility. Science was, and still is — in spite of its astonishing accomplishments — in its infancy. It proceeds on the basis of hypotheses which it proposes as attempts to explain the data it accumulates. Even when these hypotheses stand up under continued testing and study, they are frequently discarded for fresh ones at a later date. The biblical records *per se* have stood unchanged for millenniums. But the claims of science can change overnight. One Bible believer was asked how he reconciled Genesis with the latest conclusion of modern science. He naively replied, "I haven't read this morning's newspaper. What are the latest conclusions of modern science?" Just so the very hypotheses of science which many felt earlier had undermined the biblical record are now being re-examined and in many cases discarded.

On the other hand, students of the Bible should not be presumptuous in assuming they have the last word on the biblical record. Men must have puzzled over Isaiah 53 for centuries between the time Isaiah wrote it and Christ fulfilled it. It had a partial meaning during those years but its full meaning was not yet clear. It is quite possible that God so inspired His servant in the writing of Genesis 1 and 2 that while its witness to the divine creativity has been clear through all the centuries, the grandeur and scope of that creativity will only unfold in their fullness through the amplifying testimony of modern science.

It is cause for thanksgiving that a climate more favorable to the cooperation of biblical studies and of science is developing. The discoveries of the twentieth century have shaken the earlier presuppositions of the scientists and have caused many of them to accept some kind of belief in God. For example,

nineteenth-century science denied the possibility that either matter or energy could be created or destroyed: they were eternal. But the pioneering studies of Albert Einstein and the subsequent splitting of the atom have proven that matter can be turned into energy and energy into matter. This has led in very recent times to the "big bang" theory of the origin of the universe — a theory which suggests that the entire universe originated in an instant when a tremendous amount of energy was converted into matter. The compatibility of this theory with the mighty, creative commands of God in Genesis 1 is immediately apparent. Again, there is a growing community of Bible-believing scientists who are committed to the best in both science and religion. And there is a new generation of Bible students, fully as committed to the inspired and inerrant Word as were their forefathers, but who have grown up in a world in which they have learned to respect science for its genuine contributions to man's knowledge and welfare, and to use its tools in their own search for truth.

The man of faith today reads God's Word and is enraptured at the sublime truths there revealed concerning creation. He thrills at every new discovery science makes, for in the increasing vastness and complexity of the apprehended universe he sees a further testimony to the greatness of the God he serves. His is the spirit of the old minister in a New England mill town who once each year preached a sermon on the latest discoveries of astronomy. When his assistant wanted to know what possible use such a sermon could have in such a place, the older man answered, "My dear boy, of course it is of no use at all, but it greatly enlarges my idea of God."[5] He does not fear man's search for truth as long as it is honestly conducted. For he knows that the closer science comes to absolute truth, the more it will confirm and amplify the biblical record. He is convinced that someday the Word-book and the world-book, both of which God has authored, will be so read as to be in perfect harmony.

5 Willard L. Sperry, *"Yes, But—"* (New York: Harper, 1931), p. 127, quoted by Walter Russell Bowie in *The Interpreter's Bible*, Vol. I, pp. 476-77.

2. The Origin of the Earth (1:2—2:3)

a. The First Day — Light (1:2-5)

2 And the earth was waste and void; and darkness was upon the face of the deep: and the Spirit of God moved upon the face of the waters. 3 And God said, Let there be light: and there was light. 4 And God saw the light that it was good: and God divided the light from the darkness. 5 And God called the light Day, and the darkness he called Night. And there was evening and there was morning, one day.

Verse 2 marks a new beginning point in the account of creation, a refocusing of attention, a reduction of the field to be covered from "the heavens and the earth" to **the earth**, which word appears first in the Hebrew for the sake of emphasis.[6] The earth, however, is not taken up at the point it was left in verse 1, but rather at a point subsequent to or consequent upon its initial creation in which it was in an uninhabitable state.

Three things are said of the earth: it **was waste and void: and darkness was upon the face of the deep.** The first two terms are normally used together in the Old Testament and can be translated as a single term, such as "formless waste."[7] Many scholars have felt that the earth could not have left the hands of God in such a near-chaotic state. They have proposed therefore the "gap" theory which suggests that thousands or even millions of years may have intervened between the creation of an apparently complete and perfect universe in verse 1 and the re-creation of the earth described in verses 2-31. Into this gap these scholars would put the fall of the angels (II Pet. 2:4; Jude 6), and the fall of Satan (Isa. 14: 12-15; Ezek. 28:11-19. Of course, neither of these O.T. references, when read in context, can refer to Satan.) Their fall somehow involved the earth and the resulting judgment left this planet an uninhabited waste. This gap also makes room for the geologic ages and for the fossils of extinct, prehistoric beasts.[8] This theory is supported, they believe, by the appearance of one of the words of Genesis 1:2 in Isaiah 45:18 where the prophet says God did not create the world "a waste."

This theory is one of the possible ways of reconciling a very old universe, as described by science, with an apparently more recent creation of the present earth in Genesis. But it is almost entirely based on supposition. The faint echoes of the fall of Satan and the angels which are found in the Bible speak with a much louder voice than their context justifies, largely due to the writings of John Milton in *Paradise Lost*. We just do not have enough data available to substantiate such a theory. And Isaiah 45:18 explains itself, for it goes on to say that God did not create the world a waste, but rather "formed it to be inhabited." This would not exclude His having created the earth in an initial, imperfect state as a first stage toward the finished earth of Genesis 1:31. God first made the dust and then the man. The natural sense of Genesis 1:2 is that He initially created the raw materials of the earth and then gradually perfected it. That future perfection was already promised in that the **Spirit of God moved** or "hovered" or "brooded" like a great mother-bird **upon the face of the waters.**[9]

The great creative work of the first day was the creation of light and its separation from darkness. The divine creation was majestically effortless. The original makes this even more vivid than do the translations: "God said, 'Light be.' And light was." For the Hebrew mind, God's speaking and God's doing were one and the same. He did not first command that light should be made and afterwards do it. His Word was itself creative, and the saying was itself the making. And God approved His work, for He **saw the light, that it was good.** This judgment is repeated in verses 10, 12, 18, 21, 25, and 31. It is one of the chief characteristics of the biblical account. For His created handiwork to be **good** meant that it was exactly that which He had designed it to be.

[6] Young, *op cit.*, pp. 30-31.   [7] E. A. Speiser in *The Anchor Bible*, Vol. 1, p. 3.
[8] Robert Jamieson, A. R. Fausset, and David Brown, *A Commentary Critical and Explanatory on the Whole Bible*, p. 17; J. Sidlow Baxter, *Explore the Book*, Vol. 1, pp. 34-35; 45-50; and Joseph P. Free, *Archaeology and Bible History*, pp. 19-20.
[9] Fully as many if not more present-day conservative scholars reject the gap theory as accept it. See Thomas Whitelaw in *The Pulpit Commentary*, Vol. I, p. 4; E. F. Kevan in *The New Bible Commentary*, p. 77; and Kyle M. Yates, Sr. in *The Wycliffe Bible Commentary*, p. 3.

And there was evening and there was morning, one day. Thus is introduced the framework on which the writer of Genesis tells his story — a week of six creative days and one of Sabbath rest. What were these days? Were they the same solar days by which we now measure our time — twenty-four hours long? Could they have been, since the sun is not described as controlling earth's days until the fourth creative day? Or were they rather periods of indeterminate length, perhaps long enough to provide for the geologic ages? These questions are not recent ones, for they were asked in one form or another even before the Bible was completed. Jewish writers as early as Josephus and Philo are said to have discussed this matter. Origen seems to have suggested the possibility that each day was a thousand years in length, apparently on the basis of II Peter 3:8[10] And Augustine stated in classic language the puzzle all biblical interpreters face in these days when he said, "What kind of days these were it is extremely difficult, or perhaps impossible for us to conceive, and how much more to say!"[11]

There is no dogmatic answer to these questions. The Hebrew word for **day** is *yom*. It can mean the daylight hours as opposed to the night (Gen. 7:4), the twenty-four-hour day as a unit of time (Gen. 7:17), or an indeterminate period such as the day or time of harvest (Prov. 25:13), or the judgment period as the day of the Lord (Amos 5:18).[12] (We use the English word in the same three senses; for example, "There were no airplanes in George Washington's day.") The possibility that the six days of Genesis 1 were periods of indeterminate length is strengthened by the fact that *yom* is apparently used in this more general sense in Genesis 2:4 to describe the entire creative period — "the day that Jehovah God made earth and heaven." And when one compares the latter half of the sixth day, when man was created, with the scenes in Genesis 2, he finds it difficult to see how man could have been created in the latter part of a twenty-four-hour day, been introduced to all the animals, have named them, been caused to fall into a deep sleep, had a rib removed, and awakened to find the new companion God had made for him all before sunset without a haste that seems completely foreign to the language of both chapters. When one adds the testimony of the natural sciences that evidence points to the existence of the plants of the third day long ages before the man of the sixth day, and also of other such problems for the theory of the twenty-four-hour day, there is added the attraction of a possible harmonization of science with Scripture. One scientist finds the longer day quite attractive, suggesting that we speak of six "spans" which need not necessarily be exclusive and purely consecutive. He summarizes the six spans in geological terms and describes the first day as the period in which the world was enveloped in a heavy carbon dioxide shroud much like the one which surrounds the planet Venus today — translucent and thus permitting a distinction between night and day but shutting out a clear view of all other heavenly bodies.[13] The **evening** and the **morning** would still be pertinent as indications of a beginning and an ending to the period — an orderly sequence.

On the other hand, the opponents of the six-period theory point out that the natural interpretation of Genesis 1 would be that of twenty-four-hour days. They insist that God's power is sufficient to do in one day what would apparently take millenniums (there is no argument on this score). There are scientific problems either way; e.g., how could clover have reproduced itself for centuries (or at all) without bees to pollinate it? And they appeal to the seventh day which God honored, on which He rested, and which became the basis of His commandment for men to rest once each week (Exod. 20:11). Many of those who accept the "gap" theory discussed earlier reject the "period" theory, and vice versa. The evidence

---

[10] See the "Fragments" of Methodius in *The Ante-Nicene Fathers*, Alexander Roberts and James Donaldson, eds., Vol. VI, p. 381.

[11] "The City of God," in *The Nicene and Post-Nicene Fathers*, Philip Schaff, ed., First Series, Vol. II, p. 208.

[12] See Francis Brown, S. R. Driver, and Charles A. Briggs, *A Hebrew and English Lexicon of the Old Testament*, pp. 398ff.

[13] William F. Tanner, "Geology and the Days of Genesis," in *The Journal of the American Scientific Affiliation*, Vol. 16, No. 3, September 1964, pp. 82-85.

is simply not sufficient at this point to determine the truth or to decide if these two attempts at harmonization need to exclude each other. There is room instead for absolute belief in the divine creation and in God's purpose to reveal these matters more fully in His own time, and room for tolerance and charity in differences of opinion such as these.

b. The Second Day — Atmosphere (1:6-8)

6 And God said, Let there be a firmament in the midst of the waters, and let it divide the waters from the waters. 7 And God made the firmament, and divided the waters which were under the firmament from the waters which were above the firmament: and it was so. 8 And God called the firmament Heaven. And there was evening and there was morning, a second day.

As Adam Clarke points out, **firmament** is a most unfortunate mistranslation.[14] Firmament means "something firm" and seems to imply a sky something like a solid vault in which the sun, moon, and stars are fixed like light bulbs. The error had its beginning in the translation of the Hebrew Old Testament into Greek which was made in the third century B.C. and which we call the Septuagint. The ancient Greeks conceived of the sky as a solid crystalline sphere. It was their false science which determined the Greek word used in this verse. The error was copied by Jerome in the Latin Vulgate and in turn by the translators of the King James Version. Modern science has ridiculed what it thought to be a biblical error when it was actually a scientific error of another era![15] The true meaning of the Hebrew original here is that of something "stretched out" or "extended" like a tent, and the better translation is "expanse." As such it exactly fits the earth's atmosphere, which is here intended.

This expanse was to separate the earth's waters into those above it and those beneath it. The natural explanation for this seems to be the waters contained in evaporated form in the clouds as separated from the waters which re-

mained in liquid form on the surface of the earth. Some believe, however, that an unusual and entirely different kind of atmospheric reservoir is here intended, containing a far greater amount of water than would normally be found in the clouds, which ceased to exist after it was emptied on the earth at the time of Noah.[16]

And God called the firmament Heaven. Heaven here, as "heavens" in verse 1, is literally "the heights." There it apparently refers to all of the universe which lies beyond our earth. Here it refers to the atmosphere which surrounds the earth. Later, in verse 17, it refers to outer space where are to be found the sun, moon, and stars. In Genesis 7:11 it is again the nearer expanse from which the clouds pour rain upon the earth. In Genesis 7:23 it is the region immediately above the earth in which the birds fly. And in Psalm 11:4 it refers to the abode of God.

c. The Third Day — Land, Seas, Plants (1:9-13)

9 And God said, Let the waters under the heavens be gathered together unto one place, and let the dry land appear: and it was so. 10 And God called the dry land Earth; and the gathering together of the waters called he Seas: and God saw that it was good. 11 And God said, Let the earth put forth grass, herbs yielding seed, and fruit-trees bearing fruit after their kind, wherein is the seed thereof, upon the earth: and it was so. 12 And the earth brought forth grass, herbs yielding seed after their kind, and trees bearing fruit, wherein is the seed thereof, after their kind: and God saw that it was good. 13 And there was evening and there was morning, a third day.

The third creative day was marked by two distinct events: the separating of land from the waters, and the introduction of organic life in the form of plants.

The picture described in verse 2 and here is of the planet entirely covered with water. Now parts of the planet sink to provide beds for the oceans and other sections push their way up through the waters to form the backbone of the continents. Whitcomb and Morris sug-

---

[14] *A Commentary and Critical Notes,* I, 33. [15] Free, *op. cit.,* pp. 23-24.
[16] John C. Whitcomb, Jr., and Henry M. Morris, *The Genesis Flood,* pp. 215, 229, 240-41, 255ff.

gest that this took place by "isostasy," meaning "equal weights," a principle quite basic in geology and geophysics. It would involve the differential sorting of the surface materials in accordance with their weights — materials of greater density drawing together and sinking, thus squeezing outward and upward the lighter elements. When the whole was completed, the heavy materials with their superimposed weights of water would be in balance with the greater thicknesses of lighter materials elsewhere. These writers point appropriately to Isaiah 40:12, "Who hath measured the waters in the hollow of his hand, and meted out heaven with the span, and comprehended the dust of the earth in a measure, and weighed the mountains in scales, and the hills in a balance?"[17]

Once the land had been brought to the surface, something near the conditions with which we are familiar was in existence. Now life could be sustained. Science agrees with the Scriptures that plant life was the first form of life on the earth. The Genesis record tells us that God called the plants forth from the earth, apparently using the earth in some way in creating them or at least bringing them to maturity. It mentions three classes: the grasses, the seed-bearing herbs, and the fruit-bearing trees. All reproduced after their kind. This phrase which appears in verses 11, 12, 21, 24, and 25 militates against the theory of evolution as explaining the origin of all forms of life from one original form. This phrase would seem to allow for variation only within certain undefined categories.[18] Some have attempted to limit this variation to the category scientists call "species," but that term seems to have been used so freely as to be applied to variations of a single kind of animal. There is no word in the scientific vocabulary which exactly parallels the kind of Genesis 1.

d. The Fourth Day — Sun, Moon, Stars (1:14-19)

14 And God said, Let there be lights in the firmament of heaven to divide the day from the night; and let them be for signs, and for seasons, and for days and years: 15 and let them be for lights in the firmament of heaven to give light upon the earth: and it was so. 16 And God made the two great lights; the greater light to rule the day, and the lesser light to rule the night: *he made* the stars also. 17 And God set them in the firmament of heaven to give light upon the earth, 18 and to rule over the day and over the night, and to divide the light from the darkness; and God saw that it was good. 19 And there was evening and there was morning, a fourth day.

How could there have been light before the creation of the sun? And how could the plants of the third day live, grow, and produce without the energy of the sun's rays? Many attempts have been made to unravel this problem, a knotty one in any effort to harmonize science and Scripture. Some think that enough light was available from other sources to make the first three days possible without the sun — if by no other means than God's omnipotence. Some think that the creation of the sun, moon, and stars paralleled that of the earth, being begun in an imperfect form at the beginning and brought to perfection one day after the land emerged from the primeval oceans.[19] Some think that the sun, moon, and stars had already been created, but that they were shrouded from view by the earth's atmosphere which was yet in a state different from that of today. They point out that the Bible does not say that God created them on the fourth day, but that He made them or "fashioned" them and set, or more literally "gave" or "appointed," them in the expanse of heaven to give light to the earth. Thus they did not assume their present function in relationship to the earth until the fourth day.[20] Tanner explains the appearance of the sun, moon, and stars on the fourth day in geological terms as the replacement of the gradually thinning carbon dioxide atmosphere with the present one with its high concentration of oxygen which is transparent rather than merely translucent.[21]

The fourth through the sixth days show a remarkable parallel, although also an

[17] *Ibid.*, p. 230.   [18] See Kevan, *op. cit.*, p. 78.
[19] Young, *op. cit.*, pp. 93-97.   [20] Free, *op. cit.*, pp. 24-25.   [21] *Op. cit.*, p. 84.

advancement over the first through the third.

1. Light   4. Light-bearers

2. Atmosphere   5. Fowl
   Waters separated   Fish

3. Dry land   6. Land animals
   Plants   Man — to whom,
                           as to the
                           animals, the
                           plants were giv-
                           en as food

It is almost as if there were two triads within the six days, with the second triad completing and perfecting the creative work of the first.

e. The Fifth Day — Fish and Fowl (1:20-23)

20 And God said, Let the waters swarm with swarms of living creatures, and let birds fly above the earth in the open firmament of heaven. 21 And God created the great sea-monsters, and every living creature that moveth, wherewith the waters swarmed, after their kind, and every winged bird after its kind: and God saw that it was good. 22 And God blessed them, saying, Be fruitful, and multiply, and fill the waters in the seas, and let birds multiply on the earth. 23 And there was evening and there was morning, a fifth day.

The fifth day saw the introduction of an entirely new form of life — that of the animal world. Science agrees with the Scriptures that fish and fowl followed the plants in their appearance on the earth, preceding the land animals. But many scientists have attempted to explain the origin of animal life as a development from plant life or as developing in some parallel fashion from a type of life neither exclusively plant nor animal. That God may have used some kind of process in the creation of animal life is evident from His call here for **the waters** to swarm with living creatures and in verse 24 for "the earth" to bring forth or "lead out" the land animals. He used the waters and the soil

as some type of intermediate instruments. But it is highly significant that the exclusively divine word for create, bara, again makes its appearance in the creation of the animal world (v. 21). God leaves no doubt as to who was the Creator. The animal world, whatever process may have been involved, did not come into existence through some mechanical principle at work in lower forms of life. It came into existence because it was called into existence by God Himself. The theory of evolution almost always questions this to some extent. Theistic evolution (an exceedingly ambiguous term), which claims that God simply used evolution as His method of creation, is very closely related to deism and the concept of God's relation to the universe as that of a watchmaker who wound the watch and let it run by itself without further intervention from him. God can only be involved indirectly, through the natural laws with which His activity must henceforth be identified.[22] Such a distant creativity is not that of Genesis 1. But the theory of evolution in its classic form is no longer the "bugaboo" of biblical scholars that it once was. It is being challenged by its own proponents. G. A. Kerkut, a leading British comparative physiologist, who has no theological axe to grind, in his book, Implications of Evolution, declares:

I think that the attempt to explain all living forms in terms of an evolution from a unique source, though a brave and valid attempt, is one that is premature and not satisfactorily supported by present-day evidence. It may in fact be shown ultimately to be the correct explanation, but the supporting evidence remains to be discovered.

He lists seven basic assumptions which are seldom regarded as such in discussions of evolution, all of which by their nature are not capable of experimental verification. And he declares that the evidence for the evolution of all forms from one is not sufficiently strong to allow anything more than its use as a working hypothesis.[23]

[22] John W. Klotz, "Theistic Evolution: Some Theological Implications," in The Journal of the American Scientific Affiliation, Vol. 15, No. 3, September 1963, p. 85.
[23] Kerkut's book is reviewed by Wilbur Bullock in The Journal of the American Scientific Affiliation, Vol. 16, No. 4, December 1964, pp. 125-26.

f. The Sixth Day — Animals and Man (1:24-31)

24 And God said, Let the earth bring forth living creatures after their kind, cattle, and creeping things, and beasts of the earth after their kind: and it was so. 25 And God made the beasts of the earth after their kind, and the cattle after their kind, and everything that creepeth upon the ground after its kind: and God saw that it was good. 26 And God said, Let us make man in our image, after our likeness: and let them have dominion over the fish of the sea, and over the birds of the heavens, and over the cattle, and over all the earth, and over every creeping thing that creepeth upon the earth. 27 And God created man in his own image, in the image of God created he him; male and female created he them. 28 And God blessed them: and God said unto them, Be fruitful, and multiply, and replenish the earth, and subdue it; and have dominion over the fish of the sea, and over the birds of the heavens, and over every living thing that moveth upon the earth. 29 And God said, Behold, I have given you every herb yielding seed, which is upon the face of all the earth, and every tree, in which is the fruit of a tree yielding seed; to you it shall be for food: 30 and to every beast of the earth, and to every bird of the heavens, and to everything that creepeth upon the earth, wherein there is life, *I have given* every green herb for food: and it was so. 31 And God saw everything that he had made, and, behold, it was very good. And there was evening and there was morning, the sixth day.

The sixth day began with the completion of the creation of the animal world. It is probable that the land animals shared in some fashion the commission to multiply and fill the entire earth, water and land, which had been given to the fish and fowl in verse 22.

But the climax of God's creative work, the focal point of His grand design, made its appearance toward the close of this sixth and last creative day. It was then that He made man. The creation of man is set apart from all other creative acts in several ways. For one, it was so important, so vital, to the accomplishment of the divine purpose that it was preceded by a divine consultation. There

are many hints at the doctrine of the Trinity in Genesis 1 which cannot be overlooked by the Christian believer — *Elohim* the plural Hebrew word for God, the brooding presence of the Spirit of God on the primeval chaos, the mighty utterances of God which John 1 tells us was the pre-existent Word — the Christ — acting as the agent of creation (cf. Heb. 11:3), and here the divine decision, **Let us make man in our image, after our likeness.** This agreement could not have been made with the angels but only between the Father, the Son, and the Holy Spirit. How beautifully God anticipates the fuller revelation of the New Testament in the opening verses of the Old, always giving to man all the truth he can receive in the way he can best receive it!

A second distinctive element in the story of man's creation is that of his being made in the **image** and **likeness** of God. There is not the least suggestion that this likeness is a physical one. The only hint which is given in the text is that man is to exercise dominion over his appointed domain as God does over the entire universe. The likeness is thus one of nature and involves man's spirituality, intelligence, sensibilities or emotional nature and will, with the consciousness of moral responsibility. Bowie suggests that it includes man's power of thought, his power of communication, and his power of self-transcendence.[24] It is significant in this connection that the word *bara* reappears at this point to designate man as the direct handiwork of God. And apparently for emphasis it is repeated three times in verse 27 to underscore God's involvement.

A third distinctive element is that of the mention of sex — **male and female created he them.** The division of sex had already appeared in lower forms of life but it had not been mentioned there. Man is the only creature of whom God makes requirements in the area of sex, and his responsibility to God for his conduct in this important area of his life is here clearly implied. Combined with the description of man's relationship to woman given in Genesis 2:21-25, it gives strong and needed support to the concept of marriage and the family as a divinely

[24] *Op. cit.*, p. 485.

established institution with which man's righteousness and happiness are closely involved.

The fourth distinctive element in man's creation is the particular commission given to him in relation to his world. God had commissioned the animals to multiply and fill the earth. Now He commissioned men to **multiply**, to **replenish** or better "fill" the earth, to **subdue** it, and to **have dominion over** all the other living creatures which inhabited it. In addition He gave to man and the animals all of the plant world for food. Science confirms the Scripture by teaching us that man and the animals are entirely dependent, directly or indirectly, upon the plant kingdom for sustenance.

Finally, God once more looked over His handiwork. Six times before He had seen that it was good. Now His judgment was that **it was very good.** What a testimony to the perfection of His labors! Everything was exactly as He had designed it to be. And what a testimony to the original condition of man as that of holiness and righteousness! He, too, was very good — just as God had intended him to be.

g. The Seventh Day — The Sabbath Rest (2:1-3)

1 And the heavens and the earth were finished, and all the host of them. 2 And on the seventh day God finished his work which he had made; and he rested on the seventh day from all his work which he had made. 3 And God blessed the seventh day, and hallowed it; because that in it he rested from all his work which God had created and made.

The significance of these verses is evident in their verbs: **finished, rested, blessed, hallowed.** The grand design of **the heavens and the earth** was brought to perfect completion. **The host,** or more literally "the army," of the heavens and the earth was in its place. The picture is a beautiful one, with the stars marching across the heavens in their appointed courses like soldiers on the parade ground and the countless creatures of earth busily carrying out every wish of their divine

Commander. God's creation was marked by its order and abundance.

The seventh day brought a cessation of God's original creative activity. Whether the day of rest is to be thought of as a continuing period into the present, as far as the type of creativity exercised during the six days is concerned, or whether God renewed His creativity in some sense after a day or period of rest, is not made clear. "Finished" (2:1, 2) at least indicates that the original, basic work was done. But He used His own experience and example as the basis for establishing a pattern of six days of work followed by one of rest for man. A special reverence for the seventh day seems to have existed from the beginning of the human race, and has been observed by scholars and travelers among the ancient Persians, Indians, Teutons, Greeks, Phoenicians, Assyrians, Babylonians, Egyptians, and the primitive tribes of Africa and the Americas. All of this witnesses to the truth of the biblical record and its account of the original institution of the Sabbath. Men have wandered far from God in many ways and have corrupted His commandments, but here is one commandment which still casts feeble rays of light in the darkest places.[25] The Babylonian reverence for the seventh day reminds us that the Babylonians also had a creation account, written on seven tablets, discovered at the site of Nineveh in the nineteenth century. The account has many parallels to the biblical one but is revolting to a modern reader because of its gross polytheism. While it has a certain value in confirming the truth of the biblical account, its value is partially seen in the contrasts between the accounts. One can only see in it how far astray man can wander from God-revealed truth when he rejects God's direction of his life.[26]

Hallowed, it is interesting to note, is the first appearance of one of the biblical words for "sanctified" (cf. KJV) or any of its kindred words, "holy," "holiness," etc. Here it applies to His setting apart of the Sabbath peculiarly unto Himself, for the resting of man's body and the

25 Whitelaw, *op. cit.*, p. 36.
26 Merrill F. Unger, *Archaeology and the Old Testament*, pp. 26-38.

deepening of his spirit's fellowship with the God who made him.

3. The Origin of Man (2:4-25)

a. Man's Creator (2:4-6)

4 These are the generations of the heavens and of the earth when they were created, in the day that Jehovah God made earth and heaven. 5 And no plant of the field was yet in the earth, and no herb of the field had yet sprung up; for Jehovah God had not caused it to rain upon the earth: and there was not a man to till the ground; 6 but there went up a mist from the earth, and watered the whole face of the ground.

Just as the writer of Genesis narrowed his focus between Genesis 1:1 and 1:2 from the entire universe to the earth, and accordingly enlarged the details of his picture, just so he now narrows his focus from the creation of the entire earth to the creation of man. Some of the other facets of creation are touched upon, but only those which touch man directly, and they are viewed from man's point of view.

These are the generations of is one of the characteristic phrases of Genesis. It occurs also in 5:1; 6:9; 10:1; 11:10, 27; 25:12, 19; 36:1; 37:2. Each time it is introduced it narrows the focus of the narrative, turning the attention to the result of something previously mentioned (as here), or to the descendants of an individual mentioned in the foregoing section (as in the other instances). So here, while it leads first to another point of view of the creation, it leads also to an account of what followed as a result of the creation. Many scholars use this phrase as a means of outlining the book of Genesis. It probably played a large part in the framework of the author's thinking. One wonders if the ten occurrences of this phrase may not reflect early written records and oral tradition that had come down from the earliest times and around which the author organized all other material. This possibility seems more plausible than dissecting this book in a frantic attempt to find the author's sources. That there are some differences

in style between Genesis 1 and 2 is almost instantly apparent. Long before modern liberalism raised the question, Josephus remarked that "Moses, after the seventh day was over, begins to talk philosophically." What he meant may be best explained from his preface in which he said that Moses spoke some things plainly but others enigmatically and allegorically.[27] Liberal scholars insist that Genesis 2 is another independent account of creation which hopelessly contradicts Genesis 1. Such is not necessary at all. Genesis 1 described creation from God's point of view in a way that man could understand. Genesis 2 gives a series of pictures of the creation events from Adam's point of view. It uses graphic, pictorial language, and may smack of the allegory or parable as it touches upon some of the deepest mysteries of human nature and history. It may very well have been handed down in germ form from Adam himself. It is not intended to be chronological in its treatment, but topical.

Verses 4b-6 are very difficult to relate to the rest of the passage, especially as translated in the standard versions. They appear to say that God created man before the plants, a statement which would be hopelessly in conflict with Genesis 1.[28] The Berkeley Version is faithful to the original yet helps us relate the passage to its context.

These are the generations of the heavens and the earth in their creation. When the Lord God made earth and heaven, there was as yet not a shrub on the earth, nor any plant sprouting in the field; for the Lord God had not made it to rain on the earth, and there was no man to cultivate the soil; but a vapor used to rise from the earth to moisten all the surface of the ground.

Thus we have a simple statement that God carried on His work in stages, that there was a time when the earth existed before there were plants or man or rain. The emphasis of the passage is on **the Lord God** as the Creator. He it was who made **earth and heaven,** and without His creative power there could be neither **plant, man** or **rain.** The stage is being

---

[27] *The Antiquities of the Jews,* Preface, 4; Book I, Chap. 1, para. 2.
[28] The King James Version is an exception, but it does not seem to do justice to the Hebrew, and its meaning remains obscure.

set for the creation of man by the only possible Creator.

For the account of man's creation, a new form of the divine name is introduced — **Jehovah God**. This combines the plural *elohim* of Genesis 1, the more general name for God, with its concept of majesty and power (Creator, Ruler, Lord), with *yahweh*, the name which specifies Israel's covenant-making and covenant-keeping God. "God's personal existence, the continuity of His dealings with man, the unchangeableness of His promises, and the whole revelation of His redeeming mercy, gather round the name *Jehovah*."[29] How appropriate this double form in connection with the intimate account which follows of God's culmination of His creative plan in the formation of man!

An interesting misinterpretation of Scripture comes to light in this section. The statement, **Jehovah God had not caused it to rain upon the earth,** has been taken by many to apply to the entire period from creation to the flood. But Genesis 2 specifically says that the reason there were no plants in the primitive earth at this early stage was that there had been no rain. The plain implication is that it did rain before the plants were created and that it continued to do so afterwards.

b. Man's Constituency (2:7)

7 And Jehovah God formed man of the dust of the ground, and breathed into his nostrils the breath of life; and man became a living soul.

The dual nature of man as both a part of earth and a part of heaven is implicit in the statement rather than explicit. Just as the earth had been in some sense the "mother" of the plant and animal kingdoms, so God took of the soil the physical materials for His man. The kinship is apparent even in the Hebrew words, for **ground** is *adamah* and **man** is *adam*. But **the breath of life** and **a living soul** do not speak expressly of a spiritual nature. They are rather, in the original, terms which refer to the physical life which man shares with the animals. **A living soul** is in fact exactly the same word as

that translated "living creatures" in Genesis 1:20, 21, and 24. But the distinctive elements of the creation of man given in Genesis 1 are amplified here. For God is pictured as shaping man personally and carefully, as a potter the vessel of clay. He personally breathes into him the breath of life, taking a far more intense interest in man than any of the creatures which preceded him. Such a direct and intense involvement of the divine in the creation of man evidences a more lofty destiny, a similarity of nature, a kinship of the spirit as genuine as the kinship with the earth.

This verse explains at once the frailty of man and the infinite potential of man. In him is both time and eternity. In him the world and heaven meet. He is at once a part of the lowest order of God's creation and also the image of God Himself. Man is only truly man as he makes the best possible use of both parts of his nature, disciplining the earthly, enjoying its pleasures only within the divinely appointed bounds, making it the tool of the heavenly, and so committing himself to the pursuit of heaven and the service of its King as to fulfill the divine purpose in an exquisite and eternal fellowship.

c. Man's Circumstances (2:8-17)

8 And Jehovah God planted a garden eastward, in Eden; and there he put the man whom he had formed. 9 And out of the ground made Jehovah God to grow every tree that is pleasant to the sight, and good for food; the tree of life also in the midst of the garden, and the tree of the knowledge of good and evil. 10 And a river went out of Eden to water the garden; and from thence it was parted, and became four heads. 11 The name of the first is Pishon: that is it which compasseth the whole land of Havilah, where there is gold; 12 and the gold of that land is good: there is bdellium and the onyx stone. 13 And the name of the second river is Gihon: the same is it that compasseth the whole land of Cush. 14 And the name of the third river is Hiddekel: that is it which goeth in front of Assyria. And the fourth river is the Euphrates. 15 And Jehovah God took the man, and put him into the garden of Eden to dress it and to keep it. 16 And Jehovah God commanded the

29 Robert Baker Girdlestone, *Synonyms of the Old Testament,* pp. 18-44; the quote is from p. 38.

man, saying, Of every tree of the garden thou mayest freely eat: 17 but of the tree of the knowledge of good and evil, thou shalt not eat of it: for in the day that thou eatest thereof thou shalt surely die.

Genesis 2 does not say that God prepared the garden after He had made the man. Chronology is not involved. Having more fully revealed the character of the Creator, and having more intimately depicted the creation of man and the constituency of his nature, the writer now describes the original environment of man. It is an idyllic scene indeed, an oriental garden containing **every tree that is pleasant to the sight and good for food.** Adam was surrounded with all the beauty and bounty which a God of infinite power and love could provide. But for all of His careful provision, He did not over-indulge His child and impose upon him a boredom which would have destroyed his happiness. He **took the man, and put him into the garden of Eden to dress it and to keep it.** While labor became extremely hard and grueling after the fall, it was not in itself outside the divine plan for man. It was rather part of his original destiny and will probably be involved in some form in his eternal destiny.

Special attention is given to the two trees in **the midst of the garden: the tree of life** and **the tree of the knowledge of good and evil.** The first was readily available to Adam as long as he continued in his original state of righteousness, but he was immediately denied access to it when he fell into sin (3:22-24). It teaches that eternal life is not inherent to man but available to him only through the grace and power of God. He was dependent upon constant access to its fruit and was doomed to death when separated from it. Access to the tree will be renewed in heaven (Rev. 22:2). The second tree was a means of making man morally accountable. It was to be seen yet avoided, present but not to be partaken of. It and the tree of life were mutually exclusive. One could not partake of the fruit of both. The enjoyment of the tree of knowledge could only lead to the loss of the tree of life and the certain death which would follow.

The data given in these verses concerning the location of **the garden of Eden** has led to a multitude of interpretations, some almost too wild to imagine. Two of the rivers, the **Hiddekel** or Tigris and the **Euphrates,** are quite plainly the two great streams of Mesopotamia. The garden then must be located at some point where these two streams come close together. The two other rivers are not identified but are believed by one scholar to have been small streams whose names have been Hebraized into something like "the Gusher" and "the Bubbler." He translates verse 10, "A river rises in Eden to water the garden; outside, it forms four separate branch streams." He pictures the garden as being close to the Persian Gulf in the area where the two large rivers and other streams converge together — making one river inside the garden but four branch streams before entering the garden.[30] Support for this view is also found in the Babylonian tablets which say that Eridu, a town in this vicinity, "was reputed to have in its neighborhood a garden, a 'holy place' in which there grew a sacred palm tree."[31] Archaeology testifies that the Mesopotamian valley has no rival as the most ancient site of civilization.

d. Man's Companion (2:18-25)

18 And Jehovah God said, It is not good that the man should be alone; I will make him a help meet for him. 19 And out of the ground Jehovah God formed every beast of the field, and every bird of the heavens; and brought them unto the man to see what he would call them: and whatsoever the man called every living creature, that was the name thereof. 20 And the man gave names to all cattle, and to the birds of the heavens, and to every beast of the field; but for man there was not found a help meet for him. 21 And Jehovah God caused a deep sleep to fall upon the man, and he slept; and he took one of his ribs, and closed up the flesh instead thereof: 22 and the rib, which Jehovah God had taken from the man, made he a woman, and brought her unto the man. 23 And the man said, This is now bone of my bones, and flesh of my flesh; she shall be called Woman, because she was taken out of Man. 24 Therefore shall

---

[30] Speiser, *op. cit.*, pp. 14-20.   [31] Free, *op. cit.*, p. 31.

a man leave his father and his mother, and shall cleave unto his wife: and they shall be one flesh. 25 And they were both naked, the man and his wife, and were not ashamed.

For the first time, God surveyed what He had done and said, **It is not good** — that is, **that the man should be alone.** Because of this, He determined to make **a help** or helper **meet** or suitable **for him.** The original is literally, "a helper corresponding to him."

The following verses are not intended to mean that God, according to this supposed second and contradicting account of creation, created the animals after man. Chronology is not in the picture. But in connection with the search for a companion for man, God's creation of the beasts and birds is mentioned as a matter of course and the similarity of their origin in the dust of the ground is emphasized. Now He brought them to man, who became sufficiently acquainted with them to name each one. But in spite of a partially similar origin and close acquaintanceship no proper companion was found.

Then follows one of the most beautiful and profound passages in the Bible. God decided to create a special companion for man, one designed especially for him and formed out of a part of his body. Thus man's mate did not originate simultaneously with him as apparently did the female of all other species, but afterwards, with her very body dependent upon him for its existence, yet so designed as to supply that in which he was lacking. Adam recognized her as bone of his bones and flesh of his flesh, and gave to her the name of **Woman** (Hebrew *ishshah*) **because she was taken out of Man** (Hebrew *ish*). The Scriptures do not make clear whether Adam, or the writer of Genesis, or God Himself spoke the words of verse 24. But their later use by Christ (Matt. 19:5) only enhances their authority and makes clear that the relationship of husband and wife is the strongest, the most indissoluble of all human relationships — stronger even than that of parent and child. In the mysteries of divine providence, they are one biologically and to some degree

spiritually. The story of creation ends with them sharing a beautiful and ideal life — **naked, not ashamed,** holy, innocent, the perfect creatures of a perfect God, surrounded by every evidence of His love and care.

B. THE FALL (3:1—4:26)

1. The Introduction of Sin (3:1-6)

1 Now the serpent was more subtle than any beast of the field which Jehovah God had made. And he said unto the woman, Yea, hath God said, Ye shall not eat of any tree of the garden? 2 And the woman said unto the serpent, Of the fruit of the trees of the garden we may eat: 3 but of the fruit of the tree which is in the midst of the garden, God hath said, Ye shall not eat of it, neither shall ye touch it, lest ye die. 4 And the serpent said unto the woman, Ye shall not surely die: 5 for God doth know that in the day ye eat thereof, then your eyes shall be opened, and ye shall be as God, knowing good and evil. 6 And when the woman saw that the tree was good for food, and that it was a delight to the eyes, and that the tree was to be desired to make one wise, she took of the fruit thereof, and did eat; and she gave also unto her husband with her, and he did eat.

Many different interpretations have been made of this chapter. Some liberal scholars say that it is a collection of myths, or a revision of them, originally handed down from generation to generation of primitive peoples. Some commentators would make of it an allegory, something like the parables of Jesus, in which a fictional narrative is used to portray spiritual and eternal truths. Some would stress that they accept it as literal history but they would nevertheless see in the serpent more than a serpent and in the fruit more than mere fruit. The vast majority of ancient Jewish commentators, the church fathers, and evangelical students of the Word in modern times would agree with H. Orton Wiley's interpretation of it "as an inspired record of historical facts, bound up with a deep and rich symbolism."[32] This interpretation is that which is assumed by the divinely inspired Scriptures (see Job 31:

---

[32] H. Orton Wiley, *Christian Theology*, Vol. II, p. 52.

33; Hos. 6:7; Rom. 5:12-21; I Cor. 15: 22; II Cor. 11:3; I Tim. 2:13-14).

The serpent is pictured as the instrument of the temptation. He is described as more subtle than any beast of the field, as having the power of speech, and there is a possible implication later that he was not crawling upon his belly prior to the fall but perhaps standing erect or at least walking upon legs (3:14). Nothing is said in Genesis about some celestial or demonic being approaching Eve. But the New Testament makes it clear that Satan was the real tempter (John 8:44; II Cor. 11:3; Rev. 12:9, 14-15; 20:2). Just as on other occasions he disguised himself as an angel of light, so here he adopts a form to which the woman was apparently accustomed and of which she shows no fear nor amazement.

The origin of Satan is not explicitly described in the Scriptures. Traditionally, Christians have believed that he was once an archangel of the highest rank. He is supposed to have coveted after the supreme position of God Himself. His envy and pride spurred him to enlist as many as one-third of the angels in a revolt against the King of heaven. He was defeated and cast out, and now he makes the earth the scene of his activity in a further attempt to incite revolt against God. While God will permit his activity to continue for a time, hell itself has been prepared for him and his angels. While the fall of the angels is clearly stated (Jude 6) and also their eventual fate (Matt. 25:41), the rest of the traditional explanation rests upon the tenuous foundation of a highly symbolic passage (Rev. 12:3-4, 7-9) and the reading in of a deeper meaning into two poetic denunciations of the kings of Babylon and Tyre (Isa. 14:12-14; Ezek. 28:12-17). One almost suspects that the theory owes as much to the details added by John Milton in *Paradise Lost* as to what the Bible actually says. In the main, however, the theory seems to be the best that can be offered on the meager basis available for interpretation. It is in accord with what we know about the nature of God, the nature of evil, and the activities of Satan.

The tempter's words show a three-step progression. (1) His first recorded speech seems to express incredulity: Has God really forbidden you to eat of one of the trees? The injection of the idea of surprise or wonder and doubt at one of God's commands into the mind of Eve was Satan's attempt to establish a beachhead from which he could complete his work of destruction. (2) He followed this with a flat denial of the divine warning, Ye shall not surely die. While Eve's response to the serpent gave little indication of her taking the bait, he followed up his first subtle suggestion with a bold attack which left her little question as to his opinion of God. (3) Then to the insidiousness of doubt and the sacrilege of attempting to rob God of His truthfulness, he added the blasphemy of suggesting that God's command was due to ulterior and selfish motives, for God doth know that in the day ye eat thereof, then your eyes shall be opened, and ye shall be as God, knowing good and evil.

Even for Eve in her state of innocence, the tempter's true character and purpose should have been immediately clear. She and Adam had experienced enough of the goodness of God to give the lie to all Satan said. Her initial response to the tempter held promise of good. He had asked her about the commandment in a negative fashion, hath God said, Ye shall not? She answered him in the same manner in which God had given the commandment, first referring positively to their free access to all the other trees, thus giving the prohibition its proper perspective as anything else but harsh or cruel. The commandment had evidently been given to Adam alone, since it was before Eve's creation, and even the form of the verb is singular (2: 16-17). But Eve knew about it and recognized it as binding upon her as well, and she faithfully responded to Satan with almost the exact words the Lord had used.

Eve's error is not apparent in her initial response but in her continuing to listen to the tempter and to follow his words to the point of looking at the forbidden fruit in the light of what he said. Three reasons are given for her final surrender: the tree was (1) good for food, (2) a delight to the eyes, and (3) desired to make one wise. It has been frequently pointed out that these three desires, all natural and legitimate as long as limited to the sphere for which God has designed them, now passed over into that which a later writer called "the lust of the flesh, and the lust of the eyes, and the pride of life" (I John 2:16). 33 She had listened to Satan too long, so long that her desires were aroused and she yielded, for **she took of the fruit thereof, and did eat; and she gave also unto her husband.** Satan had won a double victory: Eve had yielded to his temptation, and Eve in turn had become the instrument of temptation for Adam.

The Scriptures make it very plain that Eve was the one who was deceived by Satan (I Tim. 2:14). The actual partaking of the fruit, however, must have been nearly simultaneous. Such is indicated by the close connection of **did eat** and **gave,** the words **with her,** and the fact that the awareness of guilt was experienced together (v. 7). And whatever Eve's choice may have been, it was to Adam that God had directly given the commandment and it was on Adam's choice that the destiny of all mankind rested (Rom. 5:12), and it was Adam who must accept the final responsibility for his own fall and that of the entire human race.

Many attempts have been made to explain the tree of the knowledge of good and evil and to identify its fruit. For some unexplained reason popular tradition points to the apple. And many have been convinced that the tree and its fruit could only be a symbol of some act which involved moral choice somehow involved in the sexual relationship of man and woman. But the Bible nowhere pictures sex within the marriage relationship as intrinsically evil. God had in fact created the first human pair male and female and commanded them to multiply and fill the earth (1:27-28), and had caused them to cleave together as one flesh (2:24). That this tree and its fruit were unique, that they existed only in Eden, and that their mystical properties exceeded in importance their physical properties seems very clear indeed. The tree stood as a constant reminder of God's sovereignty and of His desire for man's loving obedience. God had designed man for fellowship with

Himself, but that fellowship could not be realized in the fullness and richness God purposed if man did not enter into it freely and lovingly, not by the necessity of his origin but by his own choice. This required a test of some type, and this the tree provided. It was a gift of God's grace, intended for man's improvement, but turned by Satan's wiles and man's rebellion into the means of man's destruction.

Some interesting bits of evidence supporting the biblical account of the fall have been turned up by archaeologists. In the so-called Gilgamesh epic, an ancient Babylonian tale, the hero after a long and difficult quest obtains the plant of life only to have it stolen by a serpent.34 And in the vicinity of Nineveh two seals have been found, dating from 3000 B.C. and earlier, the one depicting a man, a woman, and a serpent, the other a tree in the center, a man on the right, a woman on the left plucking fruit, and a serpent standing erect behind her.35 However the heathen nations may have twisted the details, it is evident that much of the truth about the origin of man and of sin remained widespread knowledge in ancient times.

2. The Consequences of Sin (3:7—4:26)

a. The Spiritual Consequences (3:7-8)

7 And the eyes of them both were opened, and they knew that they were naked; and they sewed fig-leaves together, and made themselves aprons. 8 And they heard the voice of Jehovah God walking in the garden in the cool of the day: and the man and his wife hid themselves from the presence of Jehovah God amongst the trees of the garden.

Two inner consequences of the fall are immediately apparent. Adam and Eve felt *shame* and *fear.* The first was apparent in their sudden consciousness of their nakedness and their attempt to cover themselves with **aprons** of **fig-leaves.** The second was apparent in their attempt to further cover themselves by hiding amongst the trees when God came for His daily period of fellowship with them.

---

33 Compare also the threefold temptation of Jesus in Luke 4:1-13.
34 Jack Finegan, *Light from the Ancient Past,* p. 28.   35 Free, *op. cit.,* p. 34.

H. Orton Wiley summarizes these consequences in theological terms when he says, "Externally, it was an alienation from God and an enslavement to Satan; internally, it was the loss of divine grace by which man became subject to physical and moral corruption."[36] The shame they felt was due to their loss of grace, the fear to their alienation from God.

The serpent had promised Eve that the fruit of the tree would open their eyes and make them like God, knowing good and evil. The promise was fulfilled to the extent that their eyes were opened, but the new knowledge was not that which exalted but that which abased. They had known all along that there was a difference between right and wrong, but the distinction had been limited to the use or non-use of the tree. Now they had gone beyond distinguishing between right and wrong to knowing evil experientially. And all that that knowledge added was the burden of guilt. Their shame had nothing to do with sex. Rather, the nakedness which caused their frantic invention of clothing was their sudden awareness that they had lost the divine glory which had previously enshrouded them. The image of God in the sense of a conscious, rational personality was retained, but the glory of divine holiness, the full moral likeness to God, was gone. Adam and Eve stood exposed to all around them — plant world, animal world, spiritual world — as they never had been before. And when the sound of Jehovah's voice calling them to what had been their daily and beloved visit echoed among the trees, they discovered that they had not only forfeited their high position in the created world but they had forfeited their right to intimate fellowship with the God who had designed them for that purpose. By reaching for what they felt was a higher level of life they had lost the highest and plunged to the lowest.

b. The Physical Consequences (3:9-21)

9 And Jehovah God called unto the man, and said unto him, Where art thou? 10 And he said, I heard thy voice in the garden, and I was afraid, because I was naked; and I hid myself. 11 And he said, Who told thee that thou wast naked? Hast thou eaten of the tree, whereof I commanded thee that thou shouldest not eat? 12 And the man said, The woman whom thou gavest to be with me, she gave me of the tree, and I did eat. 13 And Jehovah God said unto the woman, What is this thou hast done? And the woman said, The serpent beguiled me, and I did eat. 14 And Jehovah God said unto the serpent, Because thou hast done this, cursed art thou above all cattle, and above every beast of the field; upon thy belly shalt thou go, and dust shalt thou eat all the days of thy life: 15 and I will put enmity between thee and the woman, and between thy seed and her seed: he shall bruise thy head, and thou shalt bruise his heel. 16 Unto the woman he said, I will greatly multiply thy pain and thy conception; in pain thou shalt bring forth children; and thy desire shall be to thy husband, and he shall rule over thee. 17 And unto Adam he said, Because thou hast hearkened unto the voice of thy wife, and hast eaten of the tree, of which I commanded thee, saying, Thou shalt not eat of it: cursed is the ground for thy sake; in toil shalt thou eat of it all the days of thy life; 18 thorns also and thistles shall it bring forth to thee; and thou shalt eat the herbs of the field; 19 in the sweat of thy face shalt thou eat bread, till thou return unto the ground; for out of it wast thou taken: for dust thou art, and unto dust shalt thou return. 20 And the man called his wife's name Eve; because she was the mother of all living. 21 And Jehovah God made for Adam and for his wife coats of skins, and clothed them.

Verses 9-13 outline the series of questions by which God sought the truth about the fall. Adam refused to face his personal responsibility and blamed his sin on **the woman whom thou gavest to be with me,** thus implying that God Himself was partially to blame. Eve refused to face her personal responsibility and pointed the finger of accusation at the serpent. Thus we have the first recorded instance of the familiar device known as psychological projectionism. Both, however, were forced to admit, **I did eat.** Whatever the part played by others, the fact of sin could not be dodged.

---

[36] *Op. cit.,* Vol. II, p. 64.

No mention is made of the serpent's attempt to avoid responsibility. In any event, God began His pronouncement of judgment with the serpent. The judgment upon the serpent, the woman, the man, and even the earth itself consisted largely of physical or external changes — not necessarily the introduction of new factors but the modification or exaggeration of those already existing. The serpent was to crawl in the dust and to be faced with continuous enmity on the part of man. It is doubtful from the principles manifested in the other judgments that this was a total change of bodily structure and way of life for the serpent, but rather an intensification of his generally abject posture and of man's attempt to control or slay him. The woman had been appointed as man's helper and the bearer of children, but she was demoted to the extent that her husband was her master, and the highest fulfillment of her destiny was involved in pain and risk. The man had always been expected to work, but now his labor was to be intensified. He was no longer to be readily and easily the master of his world but was to be forced to toil for the very necessities of life, struggling against the thorns and the thistles the earth would produce, facing only the prospect of returning to the ground from which he had originally been taken.

But in the very moment of judgment, the sovereignty and the grace of God were clearly revealed. God had indeed designed man for fellowship with Himself and even rebellion and sin were not going to thwart the grand design. God had loved man from the beginning and His love did not desert Adam now. Even when speaking to the serpent, God declared, **I will put enmity between thee and the woman, and between thy seed and her seed: he shall bruise thy head, and thou shalt bruise his heel.** While the reference to the woman's **seed** bruising the serpent's **head** refers in part to the enmity of man for the serpent, it must also mean that God has provided for the final triumph of man over the tempter. When this verse is viewed in the light of the Christian gospel, it is impossible not to see a veiled reference to Christ, the God-man who was indeed the seed of the woman, and by whose death and resurrection and intercession man is redeemed and Satan defeated. This impression is heightened when one observes that **seed** is singular and the personal pronoun referring to it is **he.** And one certainly sees no conflict between the prediction that this victory comes through the seed of the woman (rather than the seed of the man and the woman) and the fact that Christ was conceived of the virgin Mary without the concurrence of a man.

God's grace was further revealed when He replaced the inadequate fig-leaf aprons Adam and Eve had made for themselves with coats of skin. It is possible that God thus introduced the blood sacrifice as man's only hope of access to God. It is certain that blood was shed in this gracious act to meet man's need. And the lesson is clearly revealed that man's attempts to cover his shame are never adequate. The only covering for shame and guilt, the only hope for forgiveness and restoration must come through God and the remedy which He devises and provides. Thus, in man's darkest hour, when sin had marred the divine image in him, when judgment had been pronounced upon him, when his whole world was changing, even then God's grace and mercy were revealed as in veiled promise and symbolic act He foretold the coming Savior and His redemptive work.

c. The Dispensational Consequences (3:22-24)

22 And Jehovah God said, Behold, the man is become as one of us, to know good and evil; and now, lest he put forth his hand, and take also of the tree of life, and eat, and live for ever — 23 therefore Jehovah God sent him forth from the garden of Eden, to till the ground from whence he was taken. 24 So he drove out the man; and he placed at the east of the garden of Eden the Cherubim, and the flame of a sword which turned every way, to keep the way of the tree of life.

The final act of God in judgment upon Adam involved a divine conference, apparently within the Trinity, of the same type as that which resulted in his creation: **Behold, the man is become as one of us** (cf. 1:26). God faced the possibility that now since man had sinned, if man retained constant access to the tree of life, he could perpetuate his independent, rebellious, and sinful state forever. So God thrust Adam and Eve out of the garden, thus fulfilling the warning that if they partook of the fruit of the tree they would die. For now they were cut off from the source of life and the mortality inherent in their bodies of dust began to assert itself. Thus the means of God's dispensing life to man was changed as a consequence of the fall. Before it he had free and ready access to the source of life. Now it could only be had if God provided some new means — which He had indeed promised to do, but which would be so hedged about by conditions as to fulfill God's original purpose of loving, willing fellowship.

d. The Racial Consequences (4:1-26)

(1) Cain's Sin (4:1-8)

1 And the man knew Eve his wife; and she conceived, and bare Cain, and said, I have gotten a man with *the help of* Jehovah. 2 And again she bare his brother Abel. And Abel was a keeper of sheep, but Cain was a tiller of the ground. 3 And in process of time it came to pass, that Cain brought of the fruit of the ground an offering unto Jehovah. 4 And Abel, he also brought of the firstlings of his flock and of the fat thereof. And Jehovah had respect unto Abel and to his offering: 5 but unto Cain and to his offering he had not respect. And Cain was very wroth, and his countenance fell. 6 And Jehovah said unto Cain, Why art thou wroth? and why is thy countenance fallen? 7 If thou doest well, shall it not be lifted up? and if thou doest not well, sin coucheth at the door; and unto thee shall be its desire; but do thou rule over it. 8 And Cain told Abel his brother. And it came to pass, when they were in the field, that Cain rose up against Abel his brother and slew him.

The account of the fall as such is limited to Genesis 3. But the consequences of the fall were not limited to the characters mentioned in that chapter. The sin of disobedience in Eden was not to be an isolated act. Evidence would soon accrue that man's very nature was now bent toward evil, and he would go on from rebellion to murder, and from murder to such self-indulgence and wickedness as to move God to wipe out all the race except one family and begin anew. This evidence is sufficient in chapter 4 to round out the picture by showing the racial consequences of sin. In chapter 3, man sinned against God. Now he sins against his fellow man, thus completing his violation of the two most fundamental laws of his nature.

The first significant event after the first human couple was exiled from Eden was the birth of their two sons. The first was named **Cain,** which Eve explained with her exclamation, **I have gotten a man with the help of Jehovah.** ("Get" in Hebrew is *qanah* and "Cain" is *qayin*.) Eve looked upon her first-born son as a gift from God. Certainly the wonder of childbirth, especially since Cain was the first ever born, and the joy of any mother over her baby would prompt such an expression of praise and gratitude. She may also have seen in him further evidence that God had not abandoned them, but that His somewhat veiled promises concerning the future were going to be worked out. Cain's birth was followed by that of Abel. The fact that no separate conception is mentioned as is usually done in the Scriptures, and the peculiar construction of the Hebrew which says literally, "and she added to bare," has led many scholars to believe that Abel was Cain's twin. In any event, the two brothers were bound by the closest of ties — the same father and mother, the same home, the same spiritual heritage.

No mention is made of the childhood of the two sons. Rather the story moves immediately to their manhood when each had taken up his livelihood. Cain followed in the footsteps of his father and tilled the soil; Abel became a shepherd. Then in **process of time** the two brothers came to worship by the means of sacrifice. This is literally "in end of days," and may mean on the Sabbath Day or at the end of the growing season in a thanksgiving-type religious festival. **Cain brought of the fruit of the ground an offering unto Jehovah. Offering** is literally "gift" and can refer to anything given to God, whether grain or animals. However, it is frequently used particularly of the grain offerings, such as the one described in Leviticus 2:1ff. Such offerings were not contrary to the God-ordained sacrificial system of the

Old Testament, but were rather an integral part of that system. **And Abel, he also brought of the firstlings of his flock and of the fat thereof.** Abel offered of the first-born lambs and either the fattest ones of the flock or the fatty portions of those which he offered. This was in full accord with the later provisions of the Mosaic law (Exod. 13:1-2, 11-16; Lev. 3:16-17).

Now comes the turning point of the story. For **Jehovah had respect unto Abel and to his offering: but unto Cain and to his offering he had not respect. Had respect** is literally "gazed at" or "regarded with favor." How Jehovah expressed His approval is not made clear. Some have supposed that the offering was consumed by fire from heaven much as some later sacrifices, especially since Hebrews 11:4 can be translated, "God bearing witness upon his gifts." Neither is the reason for the Lord's acceptance of Abel and rejection of Cain made crystal clear. It could not have been in the physical nature of the sacrifices, for each brought the fruit of his labors. Abel did offer a blood sacrifice, but Cain's line of work could not have provided such, and both sacrifices, as pointed out above, were later sanctioned in the Mosaic code. There is a slight hint at a difference in spirit, for no qualifying words are used concerning Cain's sacrifice while Abel offered the first-born and the fat. It is possible that Cain merely followed the form of worship without the attitude of heart necessary to worship while Abel sought to give God the best he had as an expression of his reverence and devotion. Hebrews 11:4 makes it clear that the difference was one of heart and attitude, for it says, "By faith Abel offered unto God a more excellent sacrifice than Cain," and in Hebrews 11:6 the writer declares, "Without faith it is impossible to be well-pleasing unto him; for he that cometh to God must believe that he is, and that he is a rewarder of them that seek after him." Cain somehow lacked this faith, and his subsequent acts show him to have been of a

spirit completely foreign to the nature of God.

Cain was very wroth, and his countenance fell. Cain was aware by some means that Abel was accepted and he rejected. His reaction was a negative one. But just as the Lord had not abandoned Adam and Eve after their sin in the garden, so He refused to abandon Cain. He would not look upon Cain's sacrifice, but He did not lose sight of Cain. In verse 7 God seeks to warn Cain against the hazards of the sin-force which lurks in his heart and to point the way to victory over it. The verse is a difficult one to translate and the ASV as given above does about the best that can be done. There was no reason for Cain's countenance to be fallen. If he did well, his countenance would be lifted up. If he did not well, it was because sin made its lair like a wild beast at the door of his heart, setting its desire upon Cain to consume him. But the divine exhortation was that Cain should rule over it, something which he could do if he sought divine help.[37] But Cain did not heed God's warning. He went out and **told Abel** (either the Scripture implies that he told Abel what God had said to him or the content of the conversation is not given). And then when they were in the field, he slew Abel in the heat of anger under the control of the wild beast of sin against which he had been warned.

(2) Cain's Punishment (4:9-15)

9 And Jehovah said unto Cain, Where is Abel thy brother? And he said, I know not: am I my brother's keeper? 10 And he said, What hast thou done? the voice of thy brother's blood crieth unto me from the ground. 11 And now cursed art thou from the ground, which hath opened its mouth to receive thy brother's blood from thy hand; 12 when thou tillest the ground, it shall not henceforth yield unto thee its strength; a fugitive and a wanderer shalt thou be in the earth. 13 And Cain said unto Jehovah, My punishment is greater than I can bear. 14 Behold, thou hast driven me out this day from the face of the ground;

[37] E. A. Speiser makes an intriguing suggestion as to the translation of Genesis 4:7. He suggests that the word translated "coucheth" is actually an early Akkadian loan-word meaning "demon." Demons were often thought of as lurking at the entrance of a building, either to help or hurt the inhabitants, depending on the nature of the demon. He would read the verse, "Surely, if you act right, it should mean exaltation. But if you do not, sin is the demon at the door, whose urge is toward you; yet you can be his master." *Op. cit.*, pp. 29, 32-33.

and from thy face shall I be hid; and I shall be a fugitive and a wanderer in the earth; and it will come to pass, that whosoever findeth me will slay me. 15 And Jehovah said unto him, Therefore whosoever slayeth Cain, vengeance shall be taken on him sevenfold. And Jehovah appointed a sign for Cain, lest any finding him should smite him.

How soon after Cain's awful deed this scene occurred is not stated. Some have conjectured that it took place the next time Cain went to worship. But again the Lord pursued the sinner. Just as He had relentlessly questioned His way to the truth in the garden, He now began the questioning of Cain: **Where is Abel thy brother?** The quick, downward progression of sin is revealed in Cain's answer, **I know not: am I my brother's keeper?** Neither Adam nor Eve had dared to deny their sin completely. But now Cain follows murder with lying and adds to both a blasphemous insolence to God Himself. But Cain's attempt to dodge God's question with another question failed. For as always God asked the last question — a question to which Cain had no satisfactory answer: **What hast thou done?** The voice of Abel's blood had spoken to God from the ground. No sin can ever be kept hidden or quiet. Even if man knows nothing of it, God can still see things invisible to human eyes and hear sounds inaudible to human ears. It is significant that each time God spoke to Cain about Abel He used the words **thy brother** or **thy brother's** — three times in three verses (vv. 9, 10, 11). Thus God refuted the implication of Cain's question. He is responsible for his brother, not only to avoid intentional injury or violence against him, but to assume responsibility for his total well-being. God makes it clear that man's conduct toward his brother is to be judged on the basis of practical love.

Once the question was at an end, judgment was again pronounced. And like the previous time in Eden, it was again tempered with mercy. God declared that the ground would henceforth not yield its strength at all to Cain, but he would become **a fugitive and a wanderer.** Cain began to whimper and complain, **My punishment is greater than I can bear.**

The tragedy is that Cain did not break down under his guilt, but rather broke down under his punishment.[38] The grace of God was sufficient to have forgiven and redeemed Cain, had he been willing to appropriate it, but all he sought was some alleviation of his punishment: how typical this is of the convinced but rebellious sinful man. The Lord in His mercy put some kind of sign on Cain and declared that whoever took his life would be repaid sevenfold.

(3) Cain's Descendants (4:16-24)

16 And Cain went out from the presence of Jehovah, and dwelt in the land of Nod, on the east of Eden. 17 And Cain knew his wife; and she conceived, and bare Enoch: and he builded a city, and called the name of the city, after the name of his son, Enoch. 18 And unto Enoch was born Irad: and Irad begat Mehujael; and Mehujael begat Methushael; and Methushael begat Lamech. 19 And Lamech took unto him two wives: the name of the one was Adah, and the name of the other Zillah. 20 And Adah bare Jabal: he was the father of such as dwell in tents and *have* cattle. 21 And his brother's name was Jubal: he was the father of all such as handle the harp and pipe. 22 And Zillah, she also bare Tubal-cain, the forger of every cutting instrument of brass and iron: and the sister of Tubal-cain was Naamah. 23 And Lamech said unto his wives:

Adah and Zillah, hear my voice;
Ye wives of Lamech, hearken unto my speech:
For I have slain a man for wounding me,
And a young man for bruising me:
24 If Cain shall be avenged sevenfold, Truly Lamech seventy and sevenfold.

Many significant things can be discovered in what seems to be a dry list of names, and such is true of the list of Cain's descendants. **Cain went out from the presence of Jehovah, and dwelt in the land of Nod,** or "the land of wandering." God had sentenced him to wandering, and although his wandering seems to have been limited to a vague area **east of Eden,** he did indeed become a wanderer. He apparently married one of his sisters, not an uncommon practice among the ancients, and some modern royal

---

[38] Albert van der Ziel, *Genesis and Scientific Inquiry*, p. 89.

families (Adam's daughters are mentioned in 5:4), and when his son was born he was in the process of building a city which he named Enoch, after his son. This city did not frustrate the divine sentence to wandering, however, for the Hebrew seems to imply that he was in the process of building and never finished it.[39] As one reads on in the verses he discovers that Cain and his descendants were responsible not only for the first murder and the first city, but also the origin of polygamy (v. 19), the beginning of the nomadic way of life (v. 20), the invention of string and wind instruments of music (v. 21), the use of metal in the manufacture of tools (v. 22), and apparently the first poem (vv. 23-24). The line of Cain is definitely set by the writer of Genesis in contrast with the line of Seth: the former, though having many gifted members, devoted those gifts to evil; the latter turned their powers to doing good. It is easy to see how Cain and his descendants would be responsible for murder and polygamy. But why was the rebellious line the one which made the great advances culturally? It is possible that Cain and his descendants were so committed to finding happiness and comfort in the things of earth and time that they were driven in desperation to improving their lot.[40] However, the writer's silence concerning the descendants and temporal attainments of Seth may be due to his desire to emphasize their moral and spiritual qualities.

This section closes out with Lamech, the first polygamist, boasting to his two wives of a murder which he had committed at only slight provocation. And he declares in what has been called his "Sword Song" that if his ancestor **Cain** was **avenged sevenfold,** he would be avenged **seventy and sevenfold.** It is apparent that sin has continued to grow exceedingly sinful, that man has reached a new low in brutality and beastliness. The sin of Adam alienated him from God, enslaved him to Satan, deprived him of the divine glory with which his creation in the image of God had originally clothed him, condemned him to hard labor in the earning of his bread,

and separated him from the free and ready access he had had to the tree of life. But it had done even more, for it had left its stamp upon all his descendants, bequeathing to them a blindness of the heart — a lack of spiritual discernment, an evil concupiscence or unregulated carnal craving, and moral inability — a weakness in the presence of sin.[41] This was patently apparent in the line of Cain. And time would soon reveal its truth in the case of the supposedly godly line of Seth. As long as human history continued, men would suffer because of the sin of Adam.

(4) Seth's Appointment (4:25-26)

25 And Adam knew his wife again; and she bare a son, and called his name Seth: For, *said she,* God hath appointed me another seed instead of Abel; for Cain slew him. 26 And to Seth, to him also there was born a son; and he called his name Enosh. Then began men to call upon the name of Jehovah.

God's Word always seems to relieve the darkest moments with a quick ray of divine mercy. And the sordid story of Cain is relieved by the record of the birth of a new son to Adam and Eve. Eve named him **Seth** (Hebrew *sheth*) because, said she, **God hath appointed** (Hebrew *sheth*) **me another seed instead of Abel.** (The biblical explanation of names seems not always to be based upon the etymology of the name but upon its similarity in sound to a particular word. It is thus a kind of pun or play on words.) The divine appointment promised better things. And the impression was heightened when later Seth had a son named **Enosh,** for then men began **to call upon the name of Jehovah.** The force of the original is that of "invoke" or "call upon in prayer." Thus while the line of Cain was first in many things, the line of Seth was first in public worship. The name of Jehovah had been known by man from the beginning (4:1), and Cain and Abel had in some manner worshiped Him (4:3-4). But the use of the name **Jehovah** in prayer and apparently public forms and rituals which accompanied it were now introduced.

[39] H. C. Leupold, *Exposition of Genesis,* p. 216.
[40] *Ibid.,* pp. 214-15.   [41] Wiley, *op. cit.,* Vol. II, p. 65.

C. THE TEN PATRIARCHS (5:1-32)

1 This is the book of the generations of Adam. In the day that God created man, in the likeness of God made he him; 2 male and female created he them, and blessed them, and called their name Adam, in the day when they were created. 3 And Adam lived a hundred and thirty years, and begat *a son* in his own likeness, after his image; and called his name Seth: 4 and the days of Adam after he begat Seth were eight hundred years: and he begat sons and daughters. 5 And all the days that Adam lived were nine hundred and thirty years: and he died.

6 And Seth lived a hundred and five years, and begat Enosh: 7 and Seth lived after he begat Enosh eight hundred and seven years, and begat sons and daughters: 8 and all the days of Seth were nine hundred and twelve years: and he died.

9 And Enosh lived ninety years, and begat Kenan: 10 and Enosh lived after he begat Kenan eight hundred and fifteen years, and begat sons and daughters: 11 and all the days of Enosh were nine hundred and five years: and he died.

12 And Kenan lived seventy years, and begat Mahalalel: 13 and Kenan lived after he begat Mahalalel eight hundred and forty years, and begat sons and daughters: 14 and all the days of Kenan were nine hundred and ten years: and he died.

15 And Mahalalel lived sixty and five years, and begat Jared: 16 and Mahalalel lived after he begat Jared eight hundred and thirty years, and begat sons and daughters: 17 and all the days of Mahalalel were eight hundred ninety and five years: and he died.

18 And Jared lived a hundred sixty and two years, and begat Enoch: 19 and Jared lived after he begat Enoch eight hundred years, and begat sons and daughters: 20 and all the days of Jared were nine hundred sixty and two years: and he died.

21 And Enoch lived sixty and five years, and begat Methuselah: 22 and Enoch walked with God after he begat Methuselah three hundred years, and begat sons and daughters: 23 and all the days of Enoch were three hundred sixty and five years: 24 and Enoch walked with God: and he was not; for God took him.

25 And Methuselah lived a hundred eighty and seven years, and begat Lamech: 26 and Methuselah lived after he begat Lamech seven hundred eighty and two years, and begat sons and daughters: 27 and all the days of Methuselah were nine hundred sixty and nine years: and he died.

28 And Lamech lived a hundred eighty and two years, and begat a son: 29 and he called his name Noah, saying, This same shall comfort us in our work and in the toil of our hands, *which cometh* because of the ground which Jehovah hath cursed. 30 And Lamech lived after he begat Noah five hundred ninety and five years, and begat sons and daughters: 31 And all the days of Lamech were seven hundred seventy and seven years: and he died.

32 And Noah was five hundred years old: and Noah begat Shem, Ham and Japheth.

This is the book of the generations of Adam. This is the second time in Genesis that the characteristic phrase is used to introduce a new section, and the only time the term **book** is used in conjunction with it. The author of Genesis has completed the section on the offspring of the heavens and earth begun in 2:4 and now turns his attention to the main line of descent from Adam. In so doing, he remarks again that God created man in His own likeness, and adds that Seth was begotten in Adam's likeness. There is here a possible twofold implication: (1) Adam passed on the image of God, defaced as it was by sin, and (2) Adam passed on his own nature, now sinful because of the fall.

The genealogy found in this chapter is most interesting. It refers to ten patriarchs: Adam, Seth, Enosh, Kenan, Mahalalel, Jared, Enoch, Methuselah, Lamech, and Noah. These men begat their sons at ages ranging from sixty-five years to five hundred years, and lived for periods ranging from 365 to 969 years. There is some evidence that this is a "schematic" genealogy rather than a complete or exhaustive one. In other words, it may be a list of the most important men in the family line at this time but may not include a representative of each generation. Such a genealogy is included in Holy Writ in Matthew 1, for there the author is carrying out a "scheme" of three periods of fourteen generations each, and in the second period, in order to get the fourteen names, he omits three generations (the kings Ahaziah, Joash, and Amaziah, I Chron. 3:11-12). The very fact that *ten* names are here given from Adam to Noah, and in Genesis 11:

10-26 ten are given from Noah to Terah would suggest the possibility that these, too, are schematic. And when we add for further comparison the genealogy of Adam through Cain in 4:16-22 with its seven generations from Adam to Lamech, and note that all three of these genealogies end with a patriarch who had three sons, the evidence is a bit stronger.

The extreme ages of these men have caused problems for many. It needs to be pointed out that Hebrew numbers in ancient times were represented by Hebrew letters, several of which are easily confused with one another, thus making numbers the most likely center of error in copying. It needs also to be pointed out that the most ancient versions of the Old Testament with which we can compare our Hebrew text, the Greek Septuagint dating from the third century B.C. and the Samaritan Pentateuch dating from perhaps the fifth century B.C., each has a different set of numbers. One possibility is suggested by the ancient "Sumerian King List," an interesting archaeological find which in its various editions lists eight or ten kings as dominant in lower Mesopotamia prior to the flood. It gives tremendously long periods for the reigns of its kings — up to 64,800 years. But in the post-flood period, when its lengths for reigns are more normal, a separate tablet reveals that the King List has omitted a name while adding the years to the reign of his predecessor.[42] Thus the extremely long periods may in some manner preserve the total years of the generations represented by the patriarch whose name is preserved. On the other hand, it must also be pointed out that we know little about our race prior to the flood and there is scriptural evidence that early man lived longer and that God purposefully shortened his life span (Gen. 6:3; Ps. 90:10).

It is refreshing in the midst of a rather monotonous summary of men's lives in terms of their births, begettings, and ages to find the account of one man whose life was remarkably different. **Enoch walked with God,** a tremendously high evaluation of a spiritual life which was shared by none other except Noah (6:9). With Enoch this fellowship possibly rescued him from death, for God took him to heaven that their walk might continue uninterrupted (cf. comment on Heb. 11:5 in WBC, Vol. VI). Here again is the gleam of divine grace amidst darkness. The clouds of destruction were gathering for the antediluvian world. But in the midst of universal depravity it was still possible for a man to know God and to commune with Him. The mere mention of Enoch has been sufficient encouragement for countless saints in dark days since.

D. THE FLOOD (6:1—9:29)

1. The Nature of the Flood (6:1—7:24)

a. Judgment Determined — Mercy Demanded (6:1-8)

1 And it came to pass, when men began to multiply on the face of the ground, and daughters were born unto them, 2 that the sons of God saw the daughters of men that they were fair; and they took them wives of all that they chose. 3 And Jehovah said, My Spirit shall not strive with man for ever, for that he also is flesh: yet shall his days be a hundred and twenty years. 4 The Nephilim were in the earth in those days, and also after that, when the sons of God came in unto the daughters of men, and they bare children to them: the same were the mighty men that were of old, the men of renown.

5 And Jehovah saw that the wickedness of man was great in the earth, and that every imagination of the thoughts of his heart was only evil continually. 6 And it repented Jehovah that he had made man on the earth, and it grieved him at his heart. 7 And Jehovah said, I will destroy man whom I have created from the face of the ground; both man, and beast, and creeping things, and birds of the heavens; for it repenteth me that I have made them. 8 But Noah found favor in the eyes of Jehovah.

Two types of persons are mentioned in verses 1 and 2: **the sons of God** and **the daughters of men.** These two intermarried, apparently thus displeasing Jehovah (v. 3), and also apparently producing among their offspring some men who were veritable giants (v. 4). The pas-

---

[42] Finegan, *op. cit.*, pp. 24-25, 33.

sage also seems to imply that there were other giants who were not the offspring of the two groups (v. 4). Two major interpretations have dominated scholarly thinking on these verses: (1) that **the sons of God** are fallen angels who lust after and marry **the daughters of men,** producing through their intercourse a race of monstrous men, (2) that **the sons of God** are the Sethites who now forgot their spiritual heritage and inclinations and chose themselves wives of **the daughters of men,** including those of the Cainites, choosing freely whomever they desired on the basis of physical attraction alone. The first interpretation is thought by some to be supported by the fact that **the sons of God** is a technical term used in the Old Testament to refer to heavenly beings (Job 1:6; 2:1; 38:7), though the reference in Job may not be so .considered. New Testament references to fallen angels seem friendly to this interpretation (II Pet. 2:4; Jude 6-7). But there are many difficulties. For one thing, such a story smacks of the myths of paganism. It seems also to contradict Jesus' plain statement that angels do not marry (Matt. 22:30). Moreover, angels are spirits and have no physical bodies (Heb. 1:14). And in verse 3, Jehovah pronounces judgment upon men, not upon angels. The second view is the one which is rationally most appealing. It finds support in Seth being referred to as a son appointed by God (4:25), in the introduction at the birth of his son of the name Jehovah in public worship (4: 26), and in the entire Sethite line which produced such godly men as Enoch and Noah. While the exact words **the sons of God** are not elsewhere applied in the Old Testament to the righteous, they are in the New, and the thought is often expressed in the Old (Deut. 14:1; Ps. 73: 15; Prov. 14:26; Hos. 1:10). The problem of the indiscriminate marriage of those devoted to God with those who have no loyalties to Him often brought calamity (Num. 35; Judg. 3). The main difficulty with this interpretation is the reference to the **Nephilim** or giants which were produced by this intermarriage. But a Lutheran scholar (among others) makes a strong case for rejecting "giants"

as the meaning of Nephilim. He traces the word to a Hebrew root which would make it mean "attackers," and blames the Greek Septuagint for misdirecting thought to the giants. Thus these men, who also existed prior to the intermarriage of the Sethites with the Cainites, were the violent robbers and marauders whose infamy spread throughout the ancient world.[43]

The long history of sin in the line of Cain, the breakdown of the line of Seth due to their indiscriminate marriages, and the dedication of man from both lines, as also from the intermingled line, to lives of brutality and violence moved toward a climax. God had pronounced judgment on Adam and Eve for their disobedience, and upon Cain for his murderous act. Now He pronounced judgment upon the entire race, announcing in verse 3 that either man's life span was to be reduced to 120 years or that a period of 120 years would be granted as the extent of his further probation before universal destruction (the context seems to favor the latter interpretation). The depravity of man was now so evident that it could be said, **Every imagination of the thoughts of his heart was only evil continually.** God actually repented that He had made man and He announced His intention to destroy man, beast, creeping things, and the birds of heaven. But once again there is the gleaming ray of mercy. For **Noah** — only Noah, only one man — **found favor in the eyes of Jehovah.** And the nature of God which determined universal judgment for man's sin also demanded mercy for Noah.

b. Judgment Predicted — Mercy Planned (6:9-22)

9 These are the generations of Noah. Noah was a righteous man, *and* perfect in his generations: Noah walked with God. 10 And Noah begat three sons, Shem, Ham, and Japheth. 11 And the earth was corrupt before God, and the earth was filled with violence. 12 And God saw the earth, and, behold, it was corrupt; for all flesh had corrupted their way upon the earth.

13 And God said unto Noah, The end

---

[43] Leupold, *op. cit.*, pp. 258-60. The best analyses of this entire problem in interpretation are to be found in his book, pp. 249-60, and in Whitelaw in *The Pulpit Commentary*, I, 101-03.

of all flesh is come before me; for the earth is filled with violence through them; and, behold, I will destroy them with the earth. 14 Make thee an ark of gopher wood; rooms shalt thou make in the ark, and shalt pitch it within and without with pitch. 15 And this is how thou shalt make · it: the length of the ark three hundred cubits, the breadth of it fifty cubits, and the height of it thirty cubits. 16 A light shalt thou make to the ark, and to a cubit shalt thou finish it upward; and the door of the ark shalt thou set in the side thereof; with lower, second, and third stories shalt thou make it. 17 And I, behold, I do bring the flood of waters upon the earth, to destroy all flesh, wherein is the breath of life, from under heaven; everything that is in the earth shall die. 18 But I will establish my covenant with thee; and thou shalt come into the ark, thou and thy sons, and thy wife, and thy sons' wives with thee. 19 And of every living thing of all flesh, two of every sort shalt thou bring into the ark, to keep them alive with thee; they shall be male and female. 20 Of the birds after their kind, and the cattle after their kind, of every creeping thing of the ground after its kind, two of every sort shall come unto thee, to keep them alive. 21 And take thou unto thee of all food that is eaten, and gather it to thee; and it shall be for food for thee, and for them. 22 Thus did Noah; according to all that God commanded him, so did he.

These are the generations of Noah. Thus our author uses again his characteristic title of a new section. The genealogy of the descent of the heavens and the earth and that of Adam have been completed. Now a new series is to be considered. Just as in 2:4 the reference to "generations" led to a brief summary of the account of creation previously given, and just as in 5:1 it led to a brief summary of Adam's origin as previously given, just so it now leads to a brief summary of facts about Noah which have already been stated — his righteousness, his progeny, and his surroundings.

Then God speaks to Noah, announcing His purpose and its justification (v. 13), and the means by which His purpose will be carried out — a tremendous, destructive flood (v. 17). But most of His message is given to outlining the means whereby Noah can escape this destruction. He is to build an ark or boat of gopher wood, 450 feet long, 75 feet wide, and 45 feet high. It is to have three stories, divided into rooms, and a door and a window. Into it are to come Noah, his wife, his three sons and their three wives, and they are to bring a pair of every living creature — birds, cattle, creeping things — into the ark, and also all the various kinds of food which will be needed by the men and the animals. The beauty of Noah's faith and obedience are given in the simple statement, **Thus did Noah; according to all that God commanded him, so did he.** To build such a vessel would have been a tremendous undertaking for a man already extremely old. And to build it on dry land would certainly have brought the ridicule of all his neighbors and associates. But there is no evidence of debate or hesitation, only belief and obedience.

c. Judgment Executed — Mercy Exemplified (7:1-24)

1 And Jehovah said unto Noah, Come thou and all thy house into the ark; for thee have I seen righteous before me in this generation. 2 Of every clean beast thou shalt take to thee seven and seven, the male and his female; and of the beasts that are not clean two, the male and his female: 3 of the birds also of the heavens, seven and seven, male and female, to keep seed alive upon the face of all the earth. 4 For yet seven days, and I will cause it to rain upon the earth forty days and forty nights; and every living thing that I have made will I destroy from off the face of the ground. 5 And Noah did according unto all that Jehovah commanded him.

6 And Noah was six hundred years old when the flood of waters was upon the earth. 7 And Noah went in, and his sons, and his wife, and his sons' wives with him, into the ark, because of the waters of the flood. 8 Of clean beasts, and of beasts that are not clean, and of birds, and of everything that creepeth upon the ground, 9 there went in two and two unto Noah into the ark, male and female, as God commanded Noah. 10 And it came to pass after the seven days, that the waters of the flood were upon the earth. 11 In the six hundredth year of Noah's life, in the second month, on the seventeenth day of the month, on the same day were all the fountains of the great deep broken up, and the windows of heaven were

opened. 12 And the rain was upon the earth forty days and forty nights.

13 In the selfsame day entered Noah, and Shem, and Ham, and Japheth, the sons of Noah, and Noah's wife, and the three wives of his sons with them, into the ark; 14 they, and every beast after its kind, and all the cattle after their kind, and every creeping thing that creepeth upon the earth after its kind, and every bird after its kind, every bird of every sort. 15 And they went in unto Noah into the ark, two and two of all flesh wherein is the breath of life. 16 And they that went in, went in male and female of all flesh, as God commanded him: and Jehovah shut him in. 17 And the flood was forty days upon the earth; and the waters increased, and bare up the ark, and it was lifted up above the earth. 18 And the waters prevailed, and increased greatly upon the earth; and the ark went upon the face of the waters. 19 And the waters prevailed exceedingly upon the earth; and all the high mountains that were under the whole heaven were covered. 20 Fifteen cubits upward did the waters prevail; and the mountains were covered. 21 And all flesh died that moved upon the earth, both birds, and cattle, and beasts, and every creeping thing that creepeth upon the earth, and every man: 22 all in whose nostrils was the breath of the spirit of life, of all that was on the dry land, died. 23 And every living thing was destroyed that was upon the face of the ground, both man, and cattle, and creeping things, and birds of the heavens; and they were destroyed from the earth: and Noah only was left, and they that were with him in the ark. 24 And the waters prevailed upon the earth a hundred and fifty days.

In verses 1-5 the Lord gives Noah fuller instructions and more complete details about the impending flood. This warning came seven days before the beginning of the flood and enlarged the previous commandment by asking for seven pairs of each of the clean beasts and birds and only one pair of each of the unclean beasts. Again, **Noah did according unto all that Jehovah commanded him.**

In verses 6-12 an account is given of Noah's entry into the ark, with his family and the animals. Here also is a beginning of the account of the flood itself. In verses 13 to 24 is found the full account of the flood up to the time the waters began receding. For the sake of em-

phasis, it begins with a restatement of the entry.

Putting these overlapping sections together certain facts appear evident. The flood began in the six-hundredth year of Noah's life, on the seventeenth day of the second month. The waters of the flood had two sources: **the fountains of the great deep** and **the windows of heaven.** The rain fell for forty days and nights. The waters rose until **the high mountains that were under the whole heaven were covered,** apparently to a depth of fifteen cubits or twenty-two and one-half feet, half the height of the ark. **Every living thing** which normally found its existence on the land died. Only Noah and his companions survived. The waters apparently continued at their maximum height for another 110 days in addition to the forty days in which they were rising.

That in the dim past of human history there was a flood which profoundly affected the entire human race is virtually beyond debate. Stories of a flood which parallel the Noahic story in many precise details are found in virtually every part of the earth, from the Babylonian account in the Gilgamesh epic to the legends of some of the tribes of the Western hemisphere. Three possible interpretations present themselves: (1) that this was an extra large, extra destructive flood experienced on an entirely natural basis in some river valley, and used by the Lord as an instrument of judgment on mankind, (2) that this was a unique flood which inundated the entire Near East, covering all the inhabited earth, and destroying all mankind and those animals which lived in the area inhabited by man, or (3) that this was a flood which covered the entire globe, blotting out all life which was dependent upon land as its natural habitat, and bringing drastic geological upheavals and changes in its train.

The first interpretation is that which liberal scholars by and large would support, and they would not necessarily think that all the legends about the flood stemmed from the same flood or that only one family actually survived. However, the language of Scripture plainly rules out a river-valley flood. The scope is too large, the preparations too elaborate, the ark too massive, the dimensions of the flood too extensive, the period of more than a year described in the rising and falling of the waters entirely too long for any such "normal" flood.

The second interpretation has found rather widespread support among evangelical scholars. They have found no scriptural necessity for the flood being geographically universal, but rather anthropologically — universal only where man was dwelling. They point out that the universal terms used in relation to the flood are used in other Scriptures in a relative sense. And they believe that the difficulties of a geographically universal flood are so extreme that since they are not necessary they are also improbable. These include the difficulty of Noah's gathering of animals such as those which are found only in Australia, the inability of any structure like the ark holding the prescribed number of animals if all the species of the entire globe must be considered, the task of caring for the feeding and cleaning of that many animals, the tremendous amount of water required to cover the earth to a sufficient depth to submerge the mountains, and the disposition of the water after the flood.[44] But this view does not avoid all difficulties; it simply decreases their number. To imagine a flood too big for a river valley, blotting out the entire human race which had had several centuries to multiply and spread out from the Mesopotamian valley, would involve a tremendous miracle by itself. Since water always seeks its own level, the only way a large area of the earth's surface could become exclusively flooded would be for it to be temporarily depressed until the oceans themselves would help to flood it. This Whitelaw proposes — a depression of the land mass between the Indian Ocean and the Mediterranean Sea.[45]

The third interpretation is the traditional one and it still finds strong support among evangelical scholars. One of the most exhaustive studies of the entire problem has been made in recent years by John C. Whitcomb, Jr., an Old Testament scholar, and Henry M. Morris, a university professor of civil engineering.

This study has resulted in a controversial work called *The Genesis Flood*. It stands solidly for a geographically universal flood, listing seven reasons the scriptural records demand such an interpretation and then attempting to answer all arguments advanced against such an interpretation. In the process, it is pointed out that the topography of the earth may have been considerably different prior to the flood. The mountains may have been much lower and the continents connected so that unusual varieties of animals could have followed God-implanted instincts in their migrations to the ark. There is also the possibility that there was a great store of water in the outer atmosphere and another beneath the earth's crust, that the breaking up of the fountains of the deep involved violent shifts in the earth's crust, submerging entire continents, raising the floors of the oceans, and returning the earth for a time to a state somewhat comparable to that of Genesis 1:2 when the entire earth was covered by primeval oceans. Such a tremendous flood, the authors believe, would account for many of the phenomena studied by geologists, accomplishing in one short year through the sheer size and power of the flood what by the processes now discernible in nature would have taken millions of years to do — thus solving part of the problem of harmonizing the apparent Genesis chronology with the theories of modern science.

It is unwise to be dogmatic in interpreting such a controversial passage as this. The present writer finds himself attracted to both the second and third interpretations of the flood. There is perhaps something of a preference for the third because its case has been stated far more completely and ably by a host of writers than has that of the second, but certain difficulties still remain. In any event there was a flood, one of dimensions sufficient to accomplish the divine purpose, one which could only have been brought about by divine power, one in which the grace of God was as fully revealed as His judgment. For the God who had granted His favor to Noah,

---

[44] Kevan, *op. cit.*, p. 84, and Whitelaw, *op. cit.*, pp. 118-121, are proponents of this interpretation.
[45] *Ibid.*, p. 121. There is some geological evidence that much of the Mesopotamian coastland area was once submerged by waters from the Persian Gulf; see Speiser, *op. cit.*, pp. 55-56.

and who had planned with Noah for his deliverance, now demonstrated His mercy by shutting him in the ark and watching over him through all the turbulence of the flood. The miracle of Noah's escape was fully as great as that of the flood itself. And whatever the truth about the details of the flood, the story of Noah's deliverance conveys to us the most essential truth of all — the constant care of God for His own.

2. The Receding of the Flood (8:1-19)

1 And God remembered Noah, and all the beasts, and all the cattle that were with him in the ark: and God made a wind to pass over the earth, and the waters assuaged; 2 the fountains also of the deep and the windows of heaven were stopped, and the rain from heaven was restrained; 3 and the waters returned from off the earth continually: and after the end of a hundred and fifty days the waters decreased. 4 And the ark rested in the seventh month, on the seventeenth day of the month, upon the mountains of Ararat. 5 And the waters decreased continually until the tenth month: in the tenth month, on the first day of the month, were the tops of the mountains seen.

6 And it came to pass at the end of forty days, that Noah opened the window of the ark which he had made: 7 and he sent forth a raven, and it went forth to and fro, until the waters were dried up from off the earth. 8 And he sent forth a dove from him, to see if the waters were abated from off the face of the ground; 9 but the dove found no rest for the sole of her foot, and she returned unto him to the ark; for the waters were on the face of the whole earth; and he put forth his hand, and took her, and brought her in unto him into the ark. 10 And he stayed yet other seven days; and again he sent forth the dove out of the ark; 11 and the dove came in to him at eventide; and, lo, in her mouth an olive-leaf plucked off: so Noah knew that the waters were abated from off the earth. 12 And he stayed yet other seven days, and sent forth the dove; and she returned not again unto him any more.

13 And it came to pass in the six hundred and first year, in the first month, the first day of the month, the waters were dried up from off the earth: and

Noah removed the covering of the ark, and looked, and, behold, the face of the ground was dried. 14 And in the second month, on the seven and twentieth day of the month, was the earth dry. 15 And God spake unto Noah, saying, 16 Go forth from the ark, thou, and thy wife, and thy sons, and thy sons' wives with thee. 17 Bring forth with thee every living thing that is with thee of all flesh, both birds, and cattle, and every creeping thing that creepeth upon the earth; that they may breed abundantly in the earth, and be fruitful, and multiply upon the earth. 18 And Noah went forth, and his sons, and his wife, and his sons' wives with him: 19 every beast, every creeping thing, and every bird, whatsoever moveth upon the earth, after their families, went forth out of the ark.

The timetable of the flood, both as to its rise and its fall, is fairly easily determined from the scriptural record. Chapter 7 told of forty days of rainfall and a total of 150 days that the waters prevailed. Now we are told that at the end of the 150 days **the waters decreased** (v. 3), and on the same day, the seventeenth day of the seventh month, the ark came to rest upon the mountains of Ararat. (The months of the Jewish calendar were lunar months, consisting of either twenty-nine or thirty days each. In order to adjust the lunar months to the solar year, many years had to have an additional month.[46]) In seventy-four more days the tops of the mountains were clearly seen (v. 5). After forty more days, or 264 days from the beginning of the flood, Noah sent forth a raven from the ark. The raven found plenty of floating carrion to light upon and feed upon. Noah also sent out a dove which returned to the ark because it could not find a place to land. Seven days later he sent it out again and it returned in the evening with an olive leaf in its mouth. After seven more days he sent the dove out the third time and it did not return. Thirty-six days later, on the first day of the first month of Noah's 601st year, he removed the covering from the ark and saw that **the face of the ground was dried.** Apparently this meant only the surface was dry, for Noah waited fifty-six more days until the second month, the twenty-seventh day, and then **was the earth dry.**

46 "Time, Divisions of," in *Unger's Bible Dictionary*, pp. 1097-98.

A period of 370 days had passed from the entrance into the ark to the exit from it. However, the 370 figure is based on a straight thirty-day month. Since some lunar months had only twenty-nine days, the actual length of time was very near our 365-day solar year.[47]

The mercy of God is again clearly revealed in the receding of the flood and the exit from the ark. The writer introduces the recession with the words, **And God remembered Noah.** In the great violence of His wrath He still remembered the one righteous man. It was God who actively initiated the recession, just as He had actively initiated the flood itself. And while Noah carried on his observation of the drying earth without any recorded instructions from the Lord, God was the One who finally spoke the command to come forth from the ark. Noah's patience and obedience are again manifest. God had told him when to enter the ark. Now Noah refused to let the tensions of a year's confinement in the ark force him into a presumptuous disembarking. He waited for God's command to leave.

One of the great problems with the theory of a geographically universal flood is the question, Where did the waters go? Several factors are mentioned here which contributed to the recession of the waters: a wind caused by God to pass over the earth, the stopping of the fountains of the deep, the stopping of the windows of heaven and the restraining of the rain from heaven, and the returning of the waters from off the earth. There is apparently indicated not only the evaporation of the waters but also their return either to the ocean basins or to great storage chambers beneath the surface of the earth. It is possible that the great shifts in the earth's crust, supposed by some to have helped cause the flood, now continued to assist in its recession, rearing mountains and plateaus higher than they had ever been, and creating even deeper ocean basins for the storage of the waters. In any event, the timetable reveals a much slower and more gradual recession of the waters in comparison to their rapid rise in the terrible coming of the flood.

The mountains of Ararat, or Urartu,

the landing place of the ark, refers to a range of mountains in Armenia, some six hundred miles north and slightly west of the probable site of Eden. They are the highest mountains in the Near East. The highest peak is approximately three miles high. Local tradition insists that the ark is still preserved in the eternal snows on its southern slopes. It is the most inaccessible of all the peaks, however, making it at once unlikely that the ark landed there, since descent would have been difficult for many of the animals, and also impossible thus far to confirm the traditions.

3. The Aftermath of the Flood (8:20—9:29)

a. The Consistency of the Seasons Promised (8:20-22)

20 And Noah builded an altar unto Jehovah, and took of every clean beast, and of every clean bird, and offered burnt-offerings on the altar. 21 And Jehovah smelled the sweet savor; and Jehovah said in his heart, I will not again curse the ground any more for man's sake, for that the imagination of man's heart is evil from his youth; neither will I again smite any more everything living, as I have done. 22 While the earth remaineth, seedtime and harvest, and cold and heat, and summer and winter, and day and night shall not cease.

Noah's first act after leaving the ark was to build an altar, the first one mentioned in the Scriptures, although not necessarily the first one built, and offered of each kind of clean beast and clean bird **burnt-offerings** unto the Lord. Seven pairs of the clean beasts and birds had been taken into the ark; now apparently one pair of each was used as sacrifices. The sudden introduction of the idea of clean and unclean animals in 7:2 and here is without any explanation. There is the implication that the classification embodied in Moses' law had been recognized from antediluvian times.

Noah's offering was at once an expression of thanksgiving for deliverance and an attempt to propitiate the God whose just anger had destroyed the earth. The sacrifice was successful and Jehovah re-

---

[47] Compare Kevan, *op. cit.*, pp. 84-85.

sponded with a promise that He would not again **curse the earth** nor **smite . . . everything living,** as He had done, on account of man. His reason is **that the imagination of man's heart is evil from his youth.** It is interesting to note that this same lifelong depravity led God to determine upon judgment in 6:6-7; now it leads to the suspension of judgment. The enigma of man's natural depravity is thus clearly revealed. It is just cause for the anger of God — thus the flood. But it is at the same time something for which the individual is not initially responsible — hence God's promise after the flood.

God now promised that as long as the earth remains, **seedtime and harvest, and cold and heat, and summer and winter, and day and night shall not cease.** The regular cycles of nature were not again to be disturbed. But these verses do not teach a clocklike universe operated by unchangeable laws. This regularity is rather explained as the sovereign decision of an omnipotent God who is actively interested in His world and who actively participates in its operation and management.

b. The Commission of Man Restated (9:1-7)

1 And God blessed Noah and his sons, and said unto them, Be fruitful, and multiply, and replenish the earth. 2 And the fear of you and the dread of you shall be upon every beast of the earth, and upon every bird of the heavens; with all wherewith the ground teemeth, and all the fishes of the sea, into your hand are they delivered. 3 Every moving thing that liveth shall be food for you; as the green herb have I given you all. 4 But flesh with the life thereof, *which is* the blood thereof, shall ye not eat. 5 And surely your blood, *the blood* of your lives, will I require; at the hand of every beast will I require it: and at the hand of man, even at the hand of every man's brother, will I require the life of man. 6 Whoso sheddeth man's blood, by man shall his blood be shed: for in the image of God made he man. 7 And you, be ye fruitful, and multiply; bring forth abundantly in the earth, and multiply therein.

Noah's exit from the ark brought a new beginning to human history. It called for a restatement of the commission God had originally given to Adam and Eve in 1:28. But there are some modifications in this commission — man's relationship to God had changed and as a result his relationship to his world had changed. Formerly he was not only commissioned to populate the earth but to subdue it and to have dominion over all living creatures. Now he is to populate but no mention is made of subduing or having dominion. Rather, he is reduced to a superiority which is dependent upon the **fear** and **dread** (or better "terror," for it is a strong word) of man which God has put in the beasts and the birds. Only the creeping things and the fish are completely delivered into his hand. Just as the human image of God was marred by Adam's fall, just so the human sovereignty was marred. This sovereignty can only be restored in Christ (see Heb. 2:5-9).

God had appended to His first commission a granting of all the plant world as food for man and the animals (1:29-30). Now He added to His recommission a granting of the animal world as well as the plant world to man for food. The only qualification here stated was that the blood should not be eaten with the flesh, for it represented life itself.

There is no record of earlier commandments from the Lord, except that which pertained to the tree of knowledge. But now God recognizes that man must learn to govern himself and He issues the command that human life is to be sacred, since man is made in the image of God. Whoever slays man is striking indirectly at God Himself, and whether man or beast his blood must in turn be shed by man. God will require man's life at **the hand of every man's brother,** thus implying that to protect a murderer is to share a murderer's punishment. It is difficult for one who takes the plenary dynamic inspiration of the Old Testament seriously to reconcile this plain statement with modern attempts to abolish the death penalty.

c. The Covenant of the Rainbow Established (9:8-17)

8 And God spake unto Noah, and to his sons with him, saying, 9 And I, behold, I establish my covenant with you,

and with your seed after you; 10 and with every living creature that is with you, the birds, the cattle, and every beast of the earth with you; of all that go out of the ark, even every beast of the earth. 11 And I will establish my covenant with you; neither shall all flesh be cut off any more by the waters of the flood; neither shall there any more be a flood to destroy the earth. 12 And God said, This is the token of the covenant which I make between me and you and every living creature that is with you, for perpetual generations: 13 I do set my bow in the cloud, and it shall be for a token of a covenant between me and the earth. 14 And it shall come to pass, when I bring a cloud over the earth, that the bow shall be seen in the cloud, 15 and I will remember my covenant which is between me and you and every living creature of all flesh; and the waters shall no more become a flood to destroy all flesh. 16 And the bow shall be in the cloud; and I will look upon it, that I may remember the everlasting covenant between God and every living creature of all flesh that is upon the earth. 17 And God said unto Noah, This is the token of the covenant which I have established between me and all flesh that is upon the earth.

The first covenant mentioned in the Scriptures was that established between God and Noah and his descendants. It was promised before the flood (6:18) and was now initiated after the flood, apparently while Noah was still before the altar. The Hebrew *berith* has been a problem for translators, for while "covenant" translates it well enough as an agreement between man and man, there is no word which adequately carries the full meaning of the agreement between God and man in which God graciously grants all the benefits and in turn spells out the conditions by which man will receive them. The God-to-man **covenant** usually involved a blood sacrifice, fulfilled here by Noah's offering. The word **covenant** becomes a familiar one in the history of God's dealings with His people, and its final fulfillment is seen in the new covenant, or new testament, sealed by the blood of Christ (Heb. 9:15-22).

In this particular covenant, God promised that never again would the earth and all flesh be destroyed by a flood. The only demands He made upon man were those mentioned in the preceding paragraph — abstention from eating blood and respect for the life of man. He graciously granted a sign to remind man of God's promise — His **bow in the cloud.** It takes only a little sympathetic imagination to recover something of the terrible dread which would naturally have seized the hearts of men after the flood whenever the sky clouded over and rain began to fall. But God said that in the very threatening clouds themselves His bow, the rainbow, would remind Him of His promise and secure the safety of all the earth. It is impossible to ascertain from this passage whether the rainbow had existed prior to the flood or was just now introduced. The original can be taken as meaning that God now appointed the rainbow as His sign of this covenant. But there is nothing to exclude the more dramatic possibility that the rainbow was now seen for the first time, though it would seem reasonable that as a natural phenomenon it had existed from the first appearance of the cosmic lights.

d. The Curse of the Vine Demonstrated (9:18-29)

18 And the sons of Noah, that went forth from the ark, were Shem, and Ham, and Japheth: and Ham is the father of Canaan. 19 These three were the sons of Noah: and of these was the whole earth overspread.

20 And Noah began to be a husbandman, and planted a vineyard: 21 and he drank of the wine, and was drunken; and he was uncovered within his tent. 22 And Ham, the father of Canaan, saw the nakedness of his father, and told his two brethren without. 23 And Shem and Japheth took a garment and laid it upon both their shoulders, and went backward, and covered the nakedness of their father; and their faces were backward, and they saw not their father's nakedness. 24 And Noah awoke from his wine, and knew what his youngest son had done unto him. 25 And he said,

Cursed be Canaan;
A servant of servants shall he be unto his brethren.

26 And he said,
Blessed be Jehovah, the God of Shem;
And let Canaan be his servant.

27 God enlarge Japheth,

And let him dwell in the tents of
Shem;
And let Canaan be his servant.
28 And Noah lived after the flood three
hundred and fifty years. 29 And all the
days of Noah were nine hundred and fifty
years: and he died.

The last scene in which the Bible pictures Noah is a tragic one. Apparently
Noah had had some other occupation
prior to the flood, but now the necessity
of beginning life anew forced him to get
his food directly from the soil, and he
began to be a husbandman. In the
process, he planted a vineyard, and later,
he became drunken with the wine which
he produced from it. In his drunken
state he immodestly exposed himself.
Ham, his son, saw him thus exposed and
reported the incident to his brothers.
They, with greater respect for their father's dignity, took a garment, walked back-
wards into the tent, and covered him
without gazing upon him. When Noah
awakened, he cursed Ham's son, Canaan,
and blessed Shem and Japheth. Why
he cursed Canaan instead of Ham is not
clear. One suggestion is that Ham had
a natural tendency to the unclean, a
tendency which led him to enjoy thus
gazing upon his father and to delight in
telling his brothers about what he saw
— a tendency which Noah had already
observed in an enlarged sense in Ham's
son, Canaan, in whose descendants the
tendency led to their extreme depravity,
their enslavement to immorality, and
their eventual destruction (Gen. 18:20-
21; 19:1-28; Deut. 9:4-5). Noah's words
were then not merely an outburst of resentment, but a prophetic pronouncement concerning the future of his descendants, similar to those of Isaac (Gen.
27:27-29, 39-40) and Jacob (49:1-28).[48]

Concerning the other sons of Ham, and
Ham himself, Noah said nothing, either
of curse or blessing. Concerning Canaan, he declared, **A servant of servants
shall he be unto his brethren.** Only in
connection with Shem did he use the
name **Jehovah,** in fact, calling Him **the
God of Shem,** and outside of Canaan's
service to Shem he let Shem's blessing
consist in the worship of Jehovah — especially significant since the promised

line of descent went through Shem to
Abraham. For Japheth he called for
Elohim to enlarge him and predicted that
he would **dwell in the tents of Shem,**
and be served by Canaan. In the nineteenth century much was made of the
so-called curse of Ham, it being used as a
scriptural justification for the enslaving
of Africans! This of course overlooked
the fact that it was Canaan, not Ham,
who was cursed, and not by the wildest
of interpretations can the Africans be said
to be descendants of Canaan. Further,
anthropologically considered, Negroids
are not Hamitic. There is a remarkable
prophetic element in this ancient poem,
however, for Shem's glory was his spiritual tendency, Japheth through his Euro-
pean descendants established the world's
most "enlarged" empires, and Canaan
was enslaved by sin to his own destruction.

Thus even the flood did not rid men of
sinful inclinations. Noah, the righteous
one, fell into sin in what should have
been a day of unparalleled opportunity
to serve God. And among his immediate
descendants there appeared a weakness
toward fleshly lusts that would eventually
write an indelible record of unnatural
wickedness. God had much yet to do before He could meet man's tremendous
needs. While punishment through judgment is sometimes necessary, whether by
God or man, as a deterrent to evil, mercy,
which is a higher court of appeal than
justice, is required to save man from evil
and its consequences (cf. Ps. 51:1, 2).

E. THE NATIONS (10:1—11:32)

1. The Familial Divisions (10:1-32)

1 Now these are the generations of the
sons of Noah, *namely,* of Shem, Ham, and
Japheth: and unto them were sons born
after the flood.
2 The sons of Japheth: Gomer, and
Magog, and Madai, and Javan, and Tubal, and Meshech, and Tiras. 3 And the
sons of Gomer: Ashkenaz, and Riphath,
and Togarmah. 4 And the sons of Javan:
Elishah, and Tarshish, Kittim, and Dodanim 5 Of these were the isles of the
nations divided in their lands, every one
after his tongue, after their families, in
their nations.

---

[48] Leupold, *op. cit.,* pp. 343-53.

6 And the sons of Ham: Cush, and Mizraim, and Put, and Canaan. 7 And the sons of Cush: Seba, and Havilah, and Sabtah, and Raamah, and Sabteca; and the sons of Raamah: Sheba, and Dedan. 8 And Cush begat Nimrod: he began to be a mighty one in the earth. 9 He was a mighty hunter before Jehovah: wherefore it is said, Like Nimrod a mighty hunter before Jehovah. 10 And the beginning of his kingdom was Babel, and Erech, and Accad, and Calneh, in the land of Shinar. 11 Out of that land he went forth into Assyria, and builded Nineveh, and Rehoboth-Ir, and Calah, 12 and Resen between Nineveh and Calah (the same is the great city). 13 And Mizraim begat Ludim, and Anamim, and Lehabim, and Naphtuhim, 14 and Pathrusim, and Casluhim (whence went forth the Philistines), and Caphtorim.

15 And Canaan begat Sidon his firstborn, and Heth, 16 and the Jebusite, and the Amorite, and the Girgashite, 17 and the Hivite, and the Arkite, and the Sinite, 18 and the Arvadite, and the Zemarite, and the Hamathite: and afterward were the families of the Canaanite spread abroad. 19 And the border of the Canaanite was from Sidon, as thou goest toward Gerar, unto Gaza; as thou goest toward Sodom and Gomorrah and Admah and Zeboiim, unto Lasha. 20 These are the sons of Ham, after their families, after their tongues, in their lands, in their nations.

21 And unto Shem, the father of all the children of Eber, the elder brother of Japheth, to him also were children born. 22 The sons of Shem: Elam, and Asshur, and Arpachshad, and Lud, and Aram. 23 And the sons of Aram: Uz, and Hul, and Gether, and Mash. 24 And Arpachshad begat Shelah, and Shelah begat Eber. 25 And unto Eber were born two sons: the name of the one was Peleg; for in his days was the earth divided; and his brother's name was Joktan. 26 And Joktan begat Almodad, and Sheleph, and Hazarmaveth, and Jerah, 27 and Hadoram, and Uzal, and Diklah, 28 and Obal, and Abimael, and Sheba, 29 and Ophir, and Havilah, and Jobab: all these were the sons of Joktan. 30 And their dwelling was from Mesha, as thou goest toward Sephar, the mountain of the east. 31 These are the sons of Shem, after their families, after their tongues, in their lands, after their nations.

32 These are the families of the sons of Noah, after their generations, in their nations: and of these were the nations divided in the earth after the flood.

In 10:1 we find the fourth use of the familiar words, these are the generations. This time interest is shifted from Noah to his three sons.

Sometimes Genesis 10 has been broadly interpreted as saying that the sons of Japheth populated Europe, the sons of Ham Africa, and the sons of Shem Asia. And some scholars have drawn up elaborate maps to show the location of each tribe as if it were a well-established fact. But such approaches are overdone. For example, anthropologists do not classify the Negroids, who make up the bulk of the African population, as Hamitic. The so-called "Table of the Nations" provides us with invaluable information, and it teaches some solid spiritual lessons. But there are many names in it which have no meaning today with the knowledge available to us. There are some about which we can make an educated guess, and only a few that other biblical passages or other sources enable us to identify beyond question. What it does tell us is that there were no hard-and-fast lines drawn between the descendants of Noah's three sons.

It is interesting that the three sons are treated in reverse order to that of their usual listing. Japheth was apparently the middle son (9:24; 10:21). He is listed as having seven sons. Concerning Gomer and his three sons, and Magog, little is really known except that they probably settled in the vague region north of Mesopotamia (Ashkenaz may be identified with the Scythians). Madai was probably the father of the Medes. Javan can be most definitely identified as Greece, particularly Ionia, and his sons represent the various Greek colonies on the islands and coastal lands of the Mediterranean; Elishah as Cyprus, Tarshish perhaps as Spain, Kittim as the islands and coasts of the eastern Mediterranean, the Dodanim as the Dardani who lived in Illyricum and Troy. Tubal and Meshech apparently settled in eastern Asia Minor, not far from the Black Sea. From Tiras may have come the Thracians or other of the Aegean coastland peoples.

Ham was apparently the youngest of the sons of Noah (9:24). He had four sons. Cush was probably the father of the Mesopotamian Kassites. The first five sons credited to him apparently settled in the Mesopotamian and Arabian areas. The sixth, **Nimrod,** is singled out for special attention, as **a mighty one in the earth,** and **a mighty hunter.** He is the first man mentioned in the Scriptures as having had a kingdom, and it was indeed a mighty one, for in the land of Shinar it included Babylon and three other leading cities, and in Assyria it included Nineveh and three other cities. The name of Ham's second son, **Mizraim,** is a dual form which is the standard Hebrew name for Egypt — perhaps referring to the upper and lower Egypts of ancient times. His sons are all listed by names that end in -*im,* the Hebrew plural, thus referring to peoples rather than individuals. These are apparently tribes which settled in or near Egypt, with the **Lehabim** as the inhabitants of Lybia, and the **Caphtorim** as the inhabitants of Crete. Apparently a copyist has at some time misplaced the reference to the **Philistines,** for comparison with other Scriptures shows they were descended from the **Caphtorim,** not the **Casluhim** (Jer. 47:4; Amos 9:7). Ham's third son, **Put,** probably settled in Africa, perhaps south of Egypt in the vicinity of Somaliland where they with the Ethiopians are presently classified as Hamitic, though not Negroid. The fourth son, **Canaan,** had a numerous progeny which is listed mostly by tribal names. **Sidon** probably founded the city of that name. **Heth** fathered the Hittites. They, plus the **Jebusite** of Jerusalem, the **Amorite,** the **Girgashite,** and the **Hivite** were among the seven nations to be displaced by Israel from Canaan (Deut. 7:1); but the Hittites and Amorites were found far beyond Palestine, with the former centering in Asia Minor and the latter reaching into Mesopotamia. The **Arkite** and the **Sinite** apparently settled in Lebanon, the **Arvadite** on Arvad, an island off Phoenicia, and the **Hamathite** of course in Hamath, the capital of upper Syria. The **Zemarite** may be reflected in Joshua 18:22.

Shem was probably the eldest of Noah's sons, certainly older than Japheth (v. 21). He is best known as the ancestor of **Eber,** the founder of the Hebrews. He had five sons. **Elam** was the name of a country east of Babylonia. The descendants of **Asshur** apparently peopled Assyria. The line of **Arpachshad** is of little note as to the establishing of nations down to the sons of Eber, Arpachshad's grandson. One of his sons, **Peleg,** was distinguished because in his day the earth was divided (perhaps a reference to the confusion of tongues at Babel, 11:9), and the other, **Joktan,** fathered thirteen sons who settled in Arabia, largely in the Yemen area to the south, including three whose names were perpetuated in nations familiar in the Old Testament: **Sheba, Ophir,** and **Havilah.** The descendants of Shem's fourth son, **Lud,** are not readily indentifiable. But the fifth, **Aram,** was the father of the vast Aramaean peoples of Syria and Mesopotamia.[49]

Some things are immediately apparent from this list. Probably not all of Noah's grandsons and great-grandsons each produced his tribe or nation — some were simply absorbed into the tribes others established. Sometimes tribes from two or more ancestral lines settled in the same area; no doubt they intermarried, thus providing the basis for the similarities in names which one can discover in the three family lines. Some names are not of individual sons but of nations or tribes, and some of these may not reflect the names of their fathers but of the regions where the tribes settled. Some of the names probably refer to temporary tribes. Practically none of these names is in use today. Thus it is impossible to trace the descent of all modern peoples from these early tribes with the knowledge presently available to us.

But there are lasting truths even in these dusty lists. Noah's sons set out to obey God's command and repopulated the earth. This is always the wise and proper course, whatever the command. And while man obeyed, God was exercising His divine sovereignty to select the right family line, the right men through whom to fulfill His promises and His purposes. In recording the peopling of the earth by the three brothers, God not only has recorded their obedience and His sovereignty, but He has also plainly

---

[49] Much of the information found here was gleaned from the many articles under the individual names in *Unger's Bible Dictionary.* Where uncertainty is reflected, other writers may vary in their identification.

declared the unity of the human race — a brotherhood of man, not of the spirit but of the flesh. We all are blood-brothers. No individual or tribe or nation has a right to consider itself naturally superior to another. No one has a right to enslave or degrade another. There is only one race — the human race (*homo sapiens*), and differences in color and other physical characteristics are simply varieties which have developed within the family on the basis of the laws of heredity, the "natural selection" of the climates where men have settled, and perhaps other unknown factors. In all this there is implied clearly the concern of God for all nations. While He was choosing one to be His representative among the others, He was also planning for the redemption of the whole earth.

2. The Language Division (11:1-9)

1 And the whole earth was of one language, and of one speech. 2 And it came to pass, as they journeyed east, that they found a plain in the land of Shinar; and they dwelt there. 3 And they said one to another, Come, let us make brick, and burn them thoroughly. And they had brick for stone, and slime had they for mortar. 4 And they said, Come, let us build us a city, and a tower, whose top *may reach* unto heaven, and let us make us a name; lest we be scattered abroad upon the face of the whole earth. 5 And Jehovah came down to see the city and the tower, which the children of men builded. 6 And Jehovah said, Behold, they are one people, and they have all one language; and this is what they begin to do: and now nothing will be withholden from them, which they purpose to do. 7 Come, let us go down, and there confound their language, that they may not understand one another's speech. 8 So Jehovah scattered them abroad from thence upon the face of all the earth: and they left off building the city. 9 Therefore was the name of it called Babel; because Jehovah did there confound the language of all the earth: and from thence did Jehovah scatter them abroad upon the face of all the earth.

The picture contained in these verses is that of a large company of people, consisting of nearly all the descendants of Noah, migrating slowly southeastward from the mountains of Ararat back to the plains of Mesopotamia. They had

one language and one speech, or more literally, "one lip" and "one word" — one way of forming the sounds and one vocabulary. When they came to the land of Shinar, the broad fertile plain between the Tigris and the Euphrates where Babylon later stood, they stopped migrating and planned to set up permanent residence. They counseled together to make kiln-burnt brick and put it together with slime or "bitumen" and build a city, and a tower. There were eventually many great, walled cities in Mesopotamia in antiquity, of course, and one of the chief characteristics of most of them was a tower known as a *ziggurat,* usually crowned by a temple dedicated to the city deity. It was apparently the first *ziggurat* which was planned at this time, probably on the site of the city of Babylon itself. It is worthy of special note that at this early period the genius of these people manifested itself in their invention of kiln-burnt brick which became one of man's best building materials, and continues so to the present.

Although there was doubtless a religious significance to the tower, it probably did not represent a developed state of idolatry. It appears certain that it represented a humanistic venture from which God was excluded. The later development of idolatry here seems to indicate that this tower signifies early man's attempt at self-salvation — another way to heaven. God had commanded Noah and his sons to populate the earth, a command which necessitated their scattering abroad. Now they announced their purpose to stay together and to build a city and tower for themselves, with the tower reaching unto heaven itself, that they might make a name for themselves — a name which would hold them together. The five occurrences of the first person pronoun in their recorded speech hints at thoughts of self-sufficiency and self-exaltation. Here is the first recorded evidence of man's disposition to thwart God's purpose by an attempted inbred self-sufficient exclusiveness. This was repeated by the Hebrews whom God placed at the crossroads of the ancient world that they might become the disseminators of God's revealed truth concerning the coming Messiah to the nations of the ancient world. At Jerusalem they built themselves a city and a temple around which they centered their interest and their lives to the exclusion of the pagan world and often made of the temple and even the city itself an object of worship — an idol, instead of worshiping the God of the temple. Thus God allowed their forceful dispersion among the nations in order to fulfill His purpose to get His message to those nations. Again and again the Christian Church has repeated this error and thus failed God's purpose of world evangelism through her.

In recognition of their activities Jehovah came down to evaluate the situation Himself. The usual divine council was held. The expressed decision was that as long as man was one and his language one he would be able to carry out any project he set for himself and that therefore his language must be confounded. The divine decision was carried out. The means or the time involved are not stated. Some have supposed a miracle involving the hearing of the words, others have understood it as something involving the formation of the words, and still others see something involving the thoughts behind the words. It is possible that the change was simply an acceleration of the natural differences which constantly arise in human speech. But it must have taken place quickly enough to frustrate their purpose, for **they left off building the city.** The name of the city was then called **Babel** from *balbel,* a form of the word *balal,* "to confuse." The Hebrew play on words can be carried over into English thus: "Called Babel because there the Lord made a babble."[50]

In our century, there is a new effort to re-establish the unity of the human race. Many good things have come from this effort and no doubt many more good things will come. But there is a lesson in Babel that as long as man attempts to unite apart from God, God cannot but frown upon his attempts. In fact, man's attempts to unite himself without reference to God and His appointed mediator, Jesus Christ, are more likely to end in his greater disunity.[51]

3. The Redemptive Division (11:10-32)

10 These are the generations of Shem. Shem was a hundred years old, and begat Arpachshad two years after the flood: 11 and Shem lived after he begat Arpachshad five hundred years, and begat sons and daughters.

12 And Arpachshad lived five and thirty years, and begat Shelah: 13 and Arpachshad lived after he begat Shelah four hundred and three years, and begat sons and daughters.

14 And Shelah lived thirty years, and begat Eber: 15 and Shelah lived after he begat Eber four hundred and three years, and begat sons and daughters.

16 And Eber lived four and thirty years, and begat Peleg: 17 and Eber lived after he begat Peleg four hundred and thirty years, and begat sons and daughters.

18 And Peleg lived thirty years, and begat Reu: 19 and Peleg lived after he begat Reu two hundred and nine years, and begat sons and daughters.

20 And Reu lived two and thirty years, and begat Serug: 21 and Reu lived after he begat Serug two hundred and seven years, and begat sons and daughters.

22 And Serug lived thirty years, and begat Nahor: 23 and Serug lived after he begat Nahor two hundred years, and begat sons and daughters.

24 And Nahor lived nine and twenty years, and begat Terah: 25 and Nahor lived after he begat Terah a hundred and nineteen years, and begat sons and daughters.

26 And Terah lived seventy years, and begat Abram, Nahor, and Haran.

27 Now these are the generations of Terah. Terah begat Abram, Nahor, and Haran; and Haran begat Lot. 28 And Haran died before his father Terah in the land of his nativity, in Ur of the Chaldees. 29 And Abram and Nahor took them wives: the name of Abram's wife was Sarai; and the name of Nahor's wife, Milcah, the daughter of Haran, the father of Milcah, and the father of Iscah. 30 And Sarai was barren; she had no child. 31 And Terah took Abram his son, and Lot the son of Haran, his son's son, and Sarai his daughter-in-law, his son Abram's wife; and they went forth with them from Ur of the Chaldees, to go into the land of Canaan; and they came unto

---

50 *The Bible, an American Translation.*
51 Kevan remarks that it is highly significant that throughout the Scriptures, all the way to the Revelation, Babel or Babylon stands for the idea of materialistic and humanistic federation in opposition to God (*op. cit.,* p. 87).

Haran, and dwelt there. 32 And the days of Terah were two hundred and five years: and Terah died in Haran.

We again find the key words, **These are the generations,** terminating the account which began in 10:1 of the generations of the sons of Noah, and now concentrating on the generations of one of those sons, Shem. It was pointed out in the comments on chapter 5 that this is probably a schematic genealogy. If Noah is added to the beginning of this genealogy, we again have ten patriarchs as we had in chapter 5. The nine added here are Shem, Arpachshad, Shelah, Eber, Peleg, Reu, Serug, Nahor, and Terah. To support the idea of the schematic genealogy, there is evidence that at least one generation has been omitted (Luke 3:36 — Cainan is not mentioned in Genesis). And again, like the genealogies of chapters 4 and 5, this one ends with a patriarch who had three sons.

In 11:27, the key words, **these are the generations,** again appear, narrowing the field of interest from the generations of Shem to the generations of Terah, one of Shem's distant descendants. The remaining verses give a brief history of the family of Terah: the names of his three sons, Abram, Nahor, and Haran, the premature death of Haran in the family home at Ur of the Chaldees, the marriage of the other two sons, the barrenness of Abram's wife, Sarai, the pilgrimage of the entire family, including Haran's son Lot, to the northern city of Haran, and the death of Terah. Of greatest significance is the revelation of Abram's background. **Ur of the Chaldees** was southeast of Babylon, and was probably then at the head of the Persian Gulf. It was one of the most magnificent cities of its day with a splendid *ziggurat* and temple to the moon god, a highly developed school system where reading, writing, and arithmetic were studied, a commerce that drew ships and caravans from all over the known world, and a standard of living that put the middle-class family in a house of from ten to twenty rooms amid conditions not altogether foreign to twentieth-century luxury.[52] Thus Abraham's later life as

a nomadic pilgrim was not the one to which he was accustomed, but which could only have been adopted from extremely strong motivation. **Haran,** the second city mentioned in the family history, like Ur, was a city devoted to the worship of the moon god, but was located some six hundred miles northwest of Ur, far up in the headwaters of the Euphrates in the region called Padan-Aram or "land of Aram." The region about Haran abounds in place names which reflect the ancestors and kindred of Abraham.

The families of Noah's sons had gradually broken up the human race into nations. And God's judgment at Babel had introduced the division of language. But it was again God's sovereign and gracious purpose to narrow down His selection for service from generation to family to man until out of the chosen line of Shem He called the chosen man Abram. With this selection, the first major division of Genesis closes. The story of man as given in Genesis 1-11 is largely one of reoccurring sin and failure on man's part, of tragic loss and declension. But now attention is turned to the story of the chosen family through whom God planned to bring hope and eventual restoration to all mankind.

II. THE STORY OF THE CHOSEN PEOPLE (Gen. 12:1—50:26)

A. THE STORY OF ABRAHAM (12:1—23:20)

1. Abram's Call (12:1-20)

a. The First and Second Promises — Blessing and Land (12:1-9)

1 Now Jehovah said unto Abram, Get thee out of thy country, and from thy kindred, and from thy father's house, unto the land that I will show thee: 2 and I will make of thee a great nation, and I will bless thee, and make thy name great; and be thou a blessing: 3 and I will bless them that bless thee, and him that curseth thee will I curse: and in thee shall all the families of the earth be blessed. 4 So Abram went, as Jehovah had spoken unto him; and Lot went with him: and Abram was seventy and five years old when he departed out of Haran. 5 And Abram took Sarai his wife, and

---

[52] Unger, *Archaeology and the Old Testament,* pp. 105-12, and Free, *op. cit.,* pp. 49-50.

Lot his brother's son, and all their substance that they had gathered, and the souls that they had gotten in Haran; and they went forth to go into the land of Canaan; and into the land of Canaan they came. 6 And Abram passed through the land unto the place of Shechem, unto the oak of Moreh. And the Canaanite was then in the land. 7 And Jehovah appeared unto Abram, and said, Unto thy seed will I give this land: and there builded he an altar unto Jehovah, who appeared unto him. 8 And he removed from thence unto the mountain on the east of Beth-el, and pitched his tent, having Beth-el on the west, and Ai on the east: and there he builded an altar unto Jehovah, and called upon the name of Jehovah. 9 And Abram journeyed, going on still toward the South.

Chapter 11 has already introduced us to Abram, his father and brothers, his wife Sarai, his nephew Lot, his birthplace at Ur of the Chaldees, and his later home at Haran. Chapter 11 also hints that the call of Abram by the Lord began at Ur, for it says that when the family left there, "they went forth . . . to go into the land of Canaan." This hint is confirmed in Acts 7:2-8, where Stephen declares that the words of Genesis 12:1 were spoken in Ur, and that Abram completed his obedience to them after Terah's death.

The methods by which God called Abram are not specified. His father, and apparently all of the family, were idolaters (Josh. 24:2). Both Ur and Haran were strong centers of moon-worship. Perhaps through the death of Abram's brother (11:28), the family was made aware of the spiritual poverty of the materially rich culture around them, and Abram specifically heard the call of God to a pilgrimage of faith, a spiritual adventure of the highest order.

God's call began with a command for a threefold separation from all Abram had known and loved: (1) **out of thy country**, (2) **from thy kindred**, (3) **from thy father's house**. The old relationships and attachments were too strong, too sensibly real for Abram to retain them and at the same time develop the capacity to receive God's message. It was only as God drew him apart for Himself, made him dependent upon Him alone for fellowship, guidance, comfort, and

strength, that He would be able to make of him the man He needed.

Abram was not only asked to abandon the familiar and dependable life he had known, but also to pursue a strange and unseen goal: **unto the land that I will show thee**. This was similar to buying a traveling ticket without knowing the destination! He indeed "went out, not knowing whither he went" (Heb. 11: 8). This called for faith that would do justice to the most mature saint of the Christian era.

But for all that God demanded of Abram, He devoted most of His words to promises as to what He would do for Abram. The promise is sevenfold: (1) **I will make of thee a great nation**. This promise was often repeated to Abram. It takes on special significance since the author of Genesis has already emphasized the fact that his wife was childless (11: 30). (2) **I will bless thee**. This was not simply to be an isolated wishing of good upon Abram, but the constant, lifelong conferring of good upon him, the prospering of all he did in obedience to God. (3) **And make thy name great**. In 11:4, the men who were proposing to build the tower of Babel had expressed their intention as that of making themselves a name. Again God demonstrates that such cannot be achieved through human ability nor power, but only as the Lord chooses and assigns. This prophecy has been gloriously fulfilled, since three of earth's largest religious followings (Jews, Christians, Moslems) all look to Abram as one of their greatest men. (4) **And be thou a blessing**. This clause appears in an altogether different form, not simply predicting that such shall be the case, but commanding Abram to make it so. He is not only to be blessed and to be the means of blessing, but he is actively to seek to be a blessing. (5) **I will bless them that bless thee**. God identifies Himself in a unique manner with Abram, to the extent that God's blessings upon others will depend upon their attitude toward Abram. (6) **And him that curseth thee will I curse**. The degree of identification is intensified, for the one who opposes himself to Abram will find God opposed to him. But God's words indicate that many (**them**) will seek to bless Abram, while only a few (him) will dare to curse him. (7) **And in thee shall all the families of the earth be blessed.** This is the key clause of the entire call and promise. It reveals God's true purpose for Abram and sharpens the first faint promise of the Messiah made to Adam and Eve in the garden. It helps us to relate God's words and acts involved in this call and its consequences to all that God had said and done previously.

In Genesis 1-11, it is plain that we are reading universal history. There is a certain narrowing of interest, a certain marking of persons divinely selected for particular responsibilities. But the stage for the drama is always the entire world of man. But from what we have already read in chapter 12, and what we will continue to read throughout the Old Testament and part of the New, it would appear that the larger stage is abandoned and that God will now concentrate His attention on a small and oft-despised portion of the human race.

Closer examination, however, reveals that there is no change in the divine purpose in Genesis 12. God made man as the crowning work of His creative activity and for fellowship with Himself. In chapters 1-11, man rebelled at every turn against God's purpose, until he forfeited his right to fellowship with God and his ability to unite with his fellows in any common enterprise. The most recent judgment of God upon man's misdirected ambitions (the confusion of tongues at Babel) rendered unpromising and impractical any further attempt to deal with him as a whole. So God took an important new step in fulfilling His purpose, a step which is basic to an understanding of all the Old Testament and, in fact, to an understanding of the Bible as a whole. He chose a man, and through him a people, to whom He planned to reveal Himself, among whom He planned to do mighty deeds, and through whom He intended to win the whole race to Himself once again. The election of this man and this people did not mean that all of God's redemptive activity was henceforth to be limited to them, nor that His mercies and blessings were to be restricted to them alone.

God had not abandoned mankind as a whole. He still desired fellowship with the whole human family. He still intended to redeem all mankind. But He was introducing a new stage in that redemption. Blauw states:

> The call of Abraham, and the history of Israel which begins at that point, is the beginning of the restoration of the lost unity of mankind and of the broken fellowship with God. . . . it becomes clear *that the whole history of Israel is nothing but the continuation of God's dealings with the nations, and that therefore the history of Israel is only to be understood from the unsolved problem of the relation of God to the nations.*[53]

Thus Abram's election is seen to be not one of privilege, but one of responsibility. Such has been true of his natural descendants, the people of Israel, and his spiritual descendants, the Church of Jesus Christ.

Abram obeyed God's command. He took with him Sarai, Lot his nephew (the dead brother Haran's son), and all those who had been added to their household in Haran (apparently servants). The first stopping point was Shechem at the **oak of Moreh,** or as it is better translated, the "terebinth (a large evergreen tree of Palestine) of the teacher" or "wise man." Among the pagan peoples which inhabited the land before the coming of Israel centuries later, the terebinth tree was often looked upon as sacred. It seems at this place to have been associated with some person who sought to give guidance to those who came to him. This particular tree must have been a remarkable one, for it (or its successors) appears again many years later (Gen. 35:4; Josh. 24:26; Judg. 9:6). The land was already inhabited by the Canaanites, but the Lord gave to Abram a second promise, identifying this land as the goal of his pilgrimage, and promising it to his descendants. Abram responded by building an altar, a practice which he repeated at almost every stopping place. He then continued his journey southward, going by stages toward the **South,** or the "Negeb" as the southern part of the country is called.

---

[53] Johannes Blauw, *The Missionary Nature of the Church,* p. 19.

b. The First Presumption — Egypt (12:10-20)

10 And there was a famine in the land: and Abram went down into Egypt to sojourn there; for the famine was sore in the land. 11 And it came to pass, when he was come near to enter into Egypt, that he said unto Sarai his wife, Behold now, I know that thou art a fair woman to look upon: 12 and it will come to pass, when the Egyptians shall see thee, that they will say, This is his wife: and they will kill me, but they will save thee alive. 13 Say, I pray thee, thou art my sister; that it may be well with me for thy sake, and that my soul may live because of thee. 14 And it came to pass, that, when Abram was come into Egypt the Egyptians beheld the woman that she was very fair. 15 And the princes of Pharaoh saw her, and praised her to Pharaoh: and the woman was taken into Pharaoh's house. 16 And he dealt well with Abram for her sake: and he had sheep, and oxen, and he-asses, and menservants, and maid-servants, and she-asses, and camels. 17 And Jehovah plagued Pharaoh and his house with great plagues because of Sarai, Abram's wife. 18 And Pharaoh called Abram, and said, What is this that thou hast done unto me? why didst thou not tell me that she was thy wife? 19 why saidst thou, She is my sister, so that I took her to be my wife? now therefore behold thy wife, take her, and go thy way. 20 And Pharaoh gave men charge concerning him: and they brought him on the way, and his wife, and all that he had.

Abram's act of faith in accepting the divine call promised much for God's new method of dealing with man. But the scrupulously honest biblical writer follows this bright picture of Abram with one which shows him to be plagued by the same tendency to evil as his forebears. A famine developed, and Abram went down to Egypt where the waters of the Nile, dispersed through irrigation canals, consistently protected that land from food shortages (cf. 26:1-2; 41:54). But upon entering this land, far more alien to Abram in its people, laws, and customs than Canaan had been, he became fearful lest the powerful Egyptians should kill him in order to seize his beautiful wife. His fears had good

grounds, for an ancient papyrus document reveals that one of the Pharaohs did bring a beautiful woman to his court and murdered her husband.[54] But instead of seeking the Lord's guidance or simply trusting Him for protection, Abram devised his own means of meeting this emergency. He proposed that Sarai pass herself off as his sister (she was his half-sister, Gen. 20:12). The shocking but plain implication is that Abram was willing to risk his wife's honor to save his own life. The whole thing could have ended in catastrophe. For Pharaoh took Sarai into his harem and gave rich gifts to Abram, her supposed brother. But before irreparable damage was done, God intervened. He plagued Pharaoh's house in some manner not specified, and somehow brought Pharaoh to understand his own danger and the deception of Abram. Pharaoh, the proud monarch of a line notably opposed to God, called before him Abram, the supposed representative of God, and gave him a stern rebuke for his cowardice and sin. He was permitted to keep his increased wealth, but he was immediately banished from the land. Abram in his presumption had threatened God's entire redemptive process, but God had overruled his transgression and kept alive His own purpose. Von Rad remarks:

> One must remember that the jeopardizing of the ancestress called into question everything that Yahweh [Jehovah] had promised to do for Abraham. But Yahweh does not allow his work to miscarry right at the start; he rescues it and preserves it beyond all human failure.[55]

2. Abram's Nephew (13:1—14:24)

a. Lot's Portion (13:1-13)

1 And Abram went up out of Egypt, he, and his wife, and all that he had, and Lot with him, into the South. 2 And Abram was very rich in cattle, in silver, and in gold. 3 And he went on his journeys from the South even to Beth-el, unto the place where his tent had been at the beginning, between Beth-el and Ai, 4 unto the place of the altar, which he had made there at the first: and there Abram called on the name of Jehovah. 5 And Lot also, who went with

---

54 Free, *op. cit.*, p. 55.
55 Gerhard von Rad, *Genesis, a Commentary*, trans. by John H. Marks, p. 164.

Abram, had flocks, and herds, and tents.
6 And the land was not able to bear
them, that they might dwell together: for
their substance was great, so that they
could not dwell together. 7 And there
was a strife between the herdsmen of
Abram's cattle and the herdsmen of Lot's
cattle: and the Canaanite and the Perizzite dwelt then in the land. 28 And
Abram said unto Lot, Let there be no
strife, I pray thee, between me and thee,
and between my herdsmen and thy herdsmen; for we are brethren. 9 Is not the
whole land before thee? separate thyself,
I pray thee, from me: if *thou wilt take*
the left hand, then I will go to the right;
or if *thou take* the right hand, then I will
go to the left. 10 And Lot lifted up his
eyes, and beheld all the Plain of the Jordan, that it was well watered everywhere,
before Jehovah destroyed Sodom and
Gomorrah, like the garden of Jehovah,
like the land of Egypt, as thou goest unto
Zoar. 11 So Lot chose him all the Plain of
the Jordan; and Lot journeyed east: and
they separated themselves the one from
the other. 12 Abram dwelt in the land of
Canaan, and Lot dwelt in the cities of
the Plain, and moved his tent as far as
Sodom. 13 Now the men of Sodom were
wicked and sinners against Jehovah exceedingly.

When Abram and his company returned from Egypt to Canaan, they proceeded by stages again up through the
Negeb and on to the second spot mentioned in their initial visit to the land,
a spot between Bethel and Ai where
Abram had built an altar. Here Abram
worshiped again. But a new problem
faced him and Lot. Both of them had
become extremely wealthy, and their
multiplying flocks and herds could not
be pastured together, for **the land was
not able to bear them.** The shortage
of pastures led to conflicts between their
herdsmen. This Abram could not bear.
So, painful though it was, he proposed
that they separate, and he magnanimously
left it to the younger man to take the
first choice. Lot looked at **the Plain of
the Jordan,** the southern end of the Jordan valley and particularly the area
about the southern end of the Dead Sea,
which, as is confirmed by archaeological
evidence, was then at its peak of cultivation and prosperity. It was the richest,
most fertile portion of Palestine at the
time, **well watered everywhere,** equal

even **to the land of Egypt.** This was the
area Lot chose. He journeyed east, leaving Abram behind in the upland region.

This meant for Lot a complete change
in his way of life. He no longer lived as
a nomad, moving from tenting place to
tenting place. Rather, he dwelt in the
cities of the plain, going back to the form
of life they had known at Ur and Haran.
The hills were the proper place for pasture, so Lot must also have changed his
livelihood. But most serious of all, he
again exposed himself to the environment from which Abram had been called.
For the people with whom he associated
himself **were wicked and sinners against
Jehovah exceedingly.**

b. The Third Promise — Seed as the Sand (13:14-18)

14 And Jehovah said unto Abram, after
that Lot was separated from him, Lift
up now thine eyes, and look from the
place where thou art, northward and
southward and eastward and westward:
15 for all the land which thou seest, to
thee will I give it, and to thy seed for
ever. 16 And I will make thy seed as the
dust of the earth: so that if a man can
number the dust of the earth, then may
thy seed also be numbered. 17 Arise,
walk through the land in the length of it
and in the breadth of it; for unto thee
will I give it. 18 And Abram moved his
tent, and came and dwelt by the oaks of
Mamre, which are in Hebron, and built
there an altar unto Jehovah.

No doubt, Lot's choice of the already
rich plain, and his association with men
known for their wickedness, must have
troubled Abram. He may even have
longed for a moment to have returned
to the easier life of the city to which
he had formerly been accustomed. The
Lord sensed his need, whatever it was,
and came to renew His promise. He told
him to look in all directions, for all that
he saw the Lord would give to him. He
promised that his **seed** would be **as the
dust of the earth** (cf. 22:17). He instructed him to arise and **walk through
the land in the length of it and in the
breadth of it; for unto thee will I give
it.** So Abram left Bethel, where the
division of the land had evidently taken
place, and journeyed southwest to the
vicinity of Hebron, pitching his tent in

a grove known as "the terebinths" of Mamre. Here again he built an altar to the Lord.

In the early development of the critical study of the Scriptures, many scholars questioned the historical validity of the stories of the patriarchs. They were assigned to the level of legends, and some took the extreme position that Abraham, Isaac, and Jacob themselves never existed except as characters in popular stories which developed over centuries. But the painstaking work of the archaeologists has slowly but surely accumulated substantial evidence that Genesis records quite accurately the conditions of life at the time the patriarchs lived. The accuracy is so remarkable that one is driven to the conclusion that here are historical accounts of actual happenings, accounts which must have been preserved in some form from the very time the events occurred. This is seen in the account of Abram's camping in the hill country of Palestine. There is nothing in the later history of the land or in modern life there which quite parallels this semi-nomadic condition operating as it did around certain rather permanent bases, and yet including in its itinerary everything from Mesopotamia to Egypt, and particularly all of central and southern Palestine. But archaeology has provided the explanation. In this period the hill country was sparsely populated, the bulk of the population living on the coastal plains and in the valley of Esdraelon and the Jordan valley. Only a few fortified towns existed in the mountains. On the slopes in between there was plenty of room for semi-nomadic groups, which have indeed left many traces of their existence in cemeteries far removed from the towns.[56] It was to this sparsely populated region that Abram was committed by Lot's choice. It was the best possible place for his immense flocks and herds. And when the cities of the plain had long since been consumed by the fiery wrath of God, the hills would provide a home for the people of God. It was there that their greatest men would live and labor, and their best years would be spent.

c. Lot's Plight (14:1-12)

1 And it came to pass in the days of Amraphel king of Shinar, Arioch king of Ellasar, Chedorlaomer king of Elam, and Tidal king of Goiim, 2 that they made war with Bera king of Sodom, and with Birsha king of Gomorrah, Shinab king of Admah, and Shemeber king of Zeboiim, and the king of Bela (the same is Zoar). 3 All these joined together in the vale of Siddim (the same is the Salt Sea). 4 Twelve years they served Chedorlaomer, and in the thirteenth year they rebelled. 5 And in the fourteenth year came Chedorlaomer, and the kings that were with him, and smote the Rephaim in Ashterothkarnaim, and the Zuzim in Ham, and the Emim in Shavehkiriathaim, 6 and the Horites in their mount Seir, unto El-paran, which is by the wilderness. 7 And they returned, and came to En-mishpat (the same is Kadesh), and smote all the country of the Amalekites, and also the Amorites, that dwelt in Hazontamar. 8 And there went out the king of Sodom, and the king of Gomorrah, and the king of Admah, and the king of Zeboiim, and the king of Bela (the same is Zoar); and they set the battle in array against them in the vale of Siddim; 9 against Chedorlaomer king of Elam, and Tidal king of Goiim, and Amraphel king of Shinar, and Arioch king of Ellasar; four kings against the five. 10 Now the vale of Siddim was full of slime pits; and the kings of Sodom and Gomorrah fled, and they fell there, and they that remained fled to the mountain. 11 And they took all the goods of Sodom and Gomorrah, and all their victuals, and went their way. 12 And they took Lot, Abram's brother's son, who dwelt in Sodom, and his goods, and departed.

Sometime after Lot moved to Sodom, four kings from Mesopotamia led a military invasion of the area east of the Jordan, swinging in a large circle into southern Canaan, and climaxing the whole with the capture and spoiling of the cities of the plain. The five cities of the plain, as indicated earlier, were probably located at the southern end of the Dead Sea, which has been slowly rising for centuries and has since covered their sites. Several fresh-water streams

---

[56] William Foxwell Albright, *The Archaeology of Palestine and the Bible*, pp. 129-33. Dr. Albright, long considered one of the most eminent authorities in the field of archaeology, and himself devoted to the critical method of Bible study, devotes much space in this book to pointing out how archaeology has upset the earlier theories of the critics, including some of his own. His own conclusions have become increasingly conservative.

empty into the Dead Sea from the south, making possible the extensive irrigation and cultivation indicated in the story of Lot's choice. These cities had apparently been subjugated in an earlier invasion by Chedorlaomer, king of Elam, and after serving him for twelve years, rebelled. Chedorlaomer and his allies set out to punish the rebels and broadened the campaign into one of violence and plunder along their entire route. When the pitched battle was fought on the shores of the Dead Sea, the invaders triumphed, the kings of Sodom and Gomorrah fell into the **slime** or asphalt **pits** which abound in the area, and the remnant of their army fled to the mountains. The cities were sacked and Lot and all he had were also taken.

This chapter is an important one, for it gives one of the few detailed points of contact between Abram and the political world of his day. Critics at an early date assigned the whole story to the realm of legend. They pointed to the apparently poetic character of the story, the unknown kings, the impossible line of march. But again archaeology proved them wrong. The names of the kings were found to be similar to those recorded on ancient monuments and in ancient manuscripts. Practically all of the countries mentioned are identifiable. Dr. Albright confesses that he himself had considered the "extraordinary line of march as being the best proof of the essentially legendary character of the narrative."[57] But in 1929 he discovered a line of mounds, covering the remains of ancient cities and towns, following the course mentioned in Genesis 14. As he dug up some of the very sites mentioned, he found proof again of the historical accuracy of Genesis. This route was later called, "The King's Highway," or "The Way of the King." It apparently was never used as an invasion route in the later history of Israel. But the archaeological discovery of ancient mines far to the south of the cities of the plain helps to explain its use at this time, and also the far-ranging excursion to the south and west of Sodom before the actual attack.[58] Many attempts have been made to identify the Mesopotamian kings listed here (including one attempt to identify Amraphel with the famous Hammurabi of Babylon), thus providing a basis for accurately dating the time of Abraham. All attempts thus far have failed, but each new discovery has helped to make more probable the traditional date of about 2000 B.C.[59]

d. Abram's Princeliness (14:13-24)

13 And there came one that had escaped, and told Abram the Hebrew: now he dwelt by the oaks of Mamre, the Amorite, brother of Eshcol, and brother of Aner; and these were confederate with Abram. 14 And when Abram heard that his brother was taken captive, he led forth his trained men, born in his house, three hundred and eighteen, and pursued as far as Dan. 15 And he divided himself against them by night, he and his servants, and smote them, and pursued them unto Hobah, which is on the left hand of Damascus. 16 And he brought back all the goods, and also brought back his brother Lot, and his goods, and the women also, and the people.

17 And the king of Sodom went out to meet him, after his return from the slaughter of Chedorlaomer and the kings that were with him, at the vale of Shaveh (the same is the King's Vale). 18 And Melchizedek king of Salem brought forth bread and wine: and he was priest of God Most High. 19 And he blessed him, and said, Blessed be Abram of God Most High, possessor of heaven and earth: 20 and blessed be God Most High, who hath delivered thine enemies into thy hand. And he gave him a tenth of all. 21 And the king of Sodom said unto Abram, Give me the persons, and take the goods to thyself. 22 And Abram said to the king of Sodom, I have lifted up my hand unto Jehovah, God Most High, possessor of heaven and earth, 23 that I will not take a thread nor a shoe-latchet nor aught that is thine, lest thou shouldest say, I have made Abram rich: 24 save only that which the young men have eaten, and the portion of the men that went with me, Aner, Eshcol, and Mamre; let them take their portion.

The greatness of Abram was never more clearly manifested than when a refugee from the battle arrived and told him of Lot's plight. Abram was still dwelling by the **oaks of Mamre,** or better, "the terebinth grove of Mamre," and had

[57] *Ibid.*, p. 142.   [58] *Ibid.*, pp. 142-43.   [59] Unger, *op. cit.*, p. 118.

established what was apparently a mutual protection confederacy with Mamre and his two brothers, Eshcol and Aner. Abram mustered 318 slaves who had been born in his house, combined them with the forces of his confederates, pursued the invaders to the northern extremities of Canaan, surprised them in a night attack, and recovered their captives and loot. The invading army was probably not exceptionally large as were many of the armies at a somewhat later period in biblical history. They were a fast-moving band of marauders, readily scattered by a surprise attack of the size Abram and the others staged.

Abram was given a royal welcome on his triumphal return. The new king of Sodom traveled northward to **the vale of Shaveh,** later called **the King's Vale.** This was the valley of the Kidron, just north of Jerusalem. And Melchizedek, the king of Salem, the old name for Jerusalem, came out to meet him with bread and wine. This Melchizedek was also the priest of *El Elyon,* the name of a Canaanite deity which meant **God Most High.** Apparently, from the approving manner in which this mysterious king-priest is mentioned here, the way in which Abram himself used his name for God (v. 22), and from the place given him in biblical typology (cf. Ps. 110:4; Heb. 5-7), he had somehow risen above the pagan worship of his environment and was serving the true God by this significant name. (This **God Most High** is likely identifiable with the High-God concept found in most if not all pagan religions; see additional note VI, The High-God Theory, WBC, IV, 733-735.) He proceeded to bless Abram in that name of God which he commonly used. And Abram **gave him a tenth of all.** The source of this tithe was evidently not the goods belonging to the cities of the plain (vv. 22-24), but either other spoils which Abram had captured from the invaders or his own abundant riches.

After Abram's interview with Melchizedek, the new king of Sodom offered to give him all the goods he had recovered, asking only for the people. But Abram announced that he would not accept even the smallest item lest the king of Sodom, the representative of all that stood for sin and wickedness, should say

he had made him rich. Abram had revealed the princeliness of his spirit in aiding Lot who had so readily abandoned him and his way of life for the fleeting riches of the plain, and he demonstrated it even further in his unrelenting refusal to be contaminated by Sodom in any way.

3. Abraham's Covenant (15:1—17:27)

a. The Fourth Promise — Seed as the Stars (15:1-21)

1 After these things the word of Jehovah came unto Abram in a vision, saying, Fear not, Abram: I am thy shield, *and* thy exceeding great reward. 2 And Abram said, O Lord Jehovah, what wilt thou give me, seeing I go childless, and he that shall be possessor of my house is Eliezer of Damascus? 3 And Abram said, Behold, to me thou hast given no seed: and, lo, one born in my house is mine heir. 4 And, behold, the word of Jehovah came unto him, saying, This man shall not be thine heir; but he that shall come forth out of thine own bowels shall be thine heir. 5 And he brought him forth abroad, and said, Look now toward heaven, and number the stars, if thou be able to number them: and he said unto him, So shall thy seed be. 6 And he believed in Jehovah; and he reckoned it to him for righteousness. 7 And he said unto him, I am Jehovah that brought thee out of Ur of the Chaldees, to give thee this land to inherit it. 8 And he said, O Lord Jehovah, whereby shall I know that I shall inherit it? 9 And he said unto him, Take me a heifer three years old, and a she-goat three years old, and a ram three years old, and a turtle-dove, and a young pigeon. 10 And he took him all these, and divided them in the midst, and laid each half over against the other: but the birds divided he not. 11 And the birds of prey came down upon the carcasses, and Abram drove them away.

12 And when the sun was going down, a deep sleep fell upon Abram; and, lo, a horror of great darkness fell upon him. 13 And he said unto Abram, Know of a surety that thy seed shall be sojourners in a land that is not theirs, and shall serve them; and they shall afflict them four hundred years; 14 and also that nation, whom they shall serve, will I judge: and afterward shall they come out with great substance. 15 But thou shalt go to thy fathers in peace; thou shalt be

buried in a good old age. 16 And in the fourth generation they shall come hither again: for the iniquity of the Amorite is not yet full. 17 And it came to pass, that, when the sun went down, and it was dark, behold, a smoking furnace, and a flaming torch that passed between these pieces. 18 In that day Jehovah made a covenant with Abram, saying, Unto thy seed have I given this land, from the river of Egypt unto the great river, the river Euphrates: 19 the Kenite, and the Kenizzite, and the Kadmonite, 20 and the Hittite, and the Perizzite, and the Rephaim, 21 and the Amorite, and the Canaanite, and the Girgashite, and the Jebusite.

After Abram's rescue of Lot, Jehovah appeared to him and renewed the promise **in a vision.** This is the only time these words are used to indicate the means by which the Lord communicated with Abram, and the first time this particular means is mentioned in the Bible.

Apparently the passage of time was having its effect on Abram, for the Lord had little more than greeted him than he began to complain about his childlessness and the necessity of leaving all his possessions to one **Eliezer of Damascus,** a slave born in his house. It might seem strange that a slave would be his owner's heir. But, according to Unger, clay tablets excavated at Nuzu, southeast of Nineveh, reveal that it was customary in that day for a childless couple to adopt a freeborn person or a slave to care for them in old age, bury them and carry out all necessary funeral customs, and inherit their property. But if afterwards the adopter would beget a son of his own, the adopted son must yield to him the place of the chief heir.[60]

The Lord reassured Abram that he would have descendants of his own. He had earlier declared they would be in number like the sand of the seashore; now He took Abram out and pointed him to the heavens and declared they would be in number like the stars of the heaven. Some have thought that the former referred to his physical posterity and the latter to his spiritual posterity.

Then occurs one of the key statements of the Bible: **And he believed in Jehovah; and he reckoned it to him for righteousness.** It has been pointed out that this marks the first occurrence of three of the great doctrinal words of the Bible: **believed, reckoned** or **imputed,** and **righteousness.**[61] This verse is quoted in the New Testament and used there as the cornerstone of the great doctrine of justification by faith (Rom. 4:3; Gal. 3:6). Its appearance in Genesis reveals that the divinely appointed basis for the salvation of the individual has always been the same. It also reveals the divine inspiration of the Scriptures, their basic unity that transcends the limitations of the period and understanding of the human writer.

Still Abram asked for some means whereby he might know that he would inherit the land. The Lord answered with instructions to prepare a sacrifice. Abram took the proper animals and divided them in half, laying **each half over against the other: but the birds divided he not.** The halving of the sacrificed animals was in full accord with the customs of making a covenant. In establishing an agreement between two parties, a ritual which apparently reflected some concern for sympathetic magic was commonly followed. An animal was slain and the parties passed between the parts, thus wishing death and partition upon themselves if they did not keep the covenant. The Hebrew word translated **made** in verse 18 is literally "cut," the practice being so general that "to cut a covenant" meant "to make a covenant."[62] Abram then watched over the prepared carcasses, driving away the birds of prey.

Apparently this encounter with Jehovah had passed over into its second day, for the Lord had pointed out the stars to Abram in verse 5, while in verse 12 it is again growing dark. Sleep came to Abram. And then God appeared, His presence symbolized by the **smoking furnace** and **flaming torch** which passed between the pieces. He promised to Abram the land from **the river of Egypt** (not the Nile but a wadi or brook southwest of Canaan) to **the river Euphrates** (not in southern Mesopotamia but at its headwaters in the vicinity of Hamath). These were the boundaries approximated under David and Solomon. He lists ten nations which would be displaced, in-

⁶⁰ *Ibid.,* pp. 121-22.   ⁶¹ Free, *op. cit.,* p. 58.   ⁶² Speiser, *op. cit.,* pp. 112-14.

cluding six of the traditional seven (cf. Deut. 7:1). He also informed Abram that the chosen people would spend four hundred years in a country not their own (apparently a round number for the 430 years mentioned in Exodus 12:40), but that Abram would die a peaceful death in his old age. He also added that **in the fourth generation** they would return to Canaan when the iniquity of the Amorite was full. **The fourth generation** is preferably translated "the fourth time span," since it only secondarily refers to generation in the modern sense.[63] Moses did represent the fourth generation from Jacob in the genealogies, but the number of years involved would imply that these genealogies are probably schematic as was suggested of earlier ones (cf. comments on chapter 5).

The Lord had indeed honored Abram, first, by speaking to him once again; second, by renewing the promise and reckoning his faith as righteousness; and third, by granting his request for additional evidence in this remarkable vision and covenant. God had bound Himself in every possible way to keep His word to Abram.

b. The Second Presumption — Ishmael (16:1-16)

1 Now Sarai, Abram's wife, bare him no children: and she had a handmaid, an Egyptian, whose name was Hagar. 2 And Sarai said unto Abram, Behold now, Jehovah hath restrained me from bearing; go in, I pray thee, unto my handmaid: it may be that I shall obtain children by her. And Abram hearkened to the voice of Sarai. 3 And Sarai, Abram's wife, took Hagar the Egyptian, her handmaid, after Abram had dwelt ten years in the land of Canaan, and gave her to Abram her husband to be his wife. 4 And he went in unto Hagar, and she conceived: and when she saw that she had conceived, her mistress was despised in her eyes. 5 And Sarai said unto Abram, My wrong be upon thee: I gave my handmaid into thy bosom; and when she saw that she had conceived, I was despised in her eyes: Jehovah judge between me and thee. 6 But Abram said unto Sarai, Behold, thy maid is in thy hand; do to her that which is good in thine eyes. And Sarai dealt hardly with her,

and she fled from her face.

7 And the angel of Jehovah found her by a fountain of water in the wilderness, by the fountain in the way to Shur. 8 And he said, Hagar, Sarai's handmaid, whence camest thou? and whither goest thou? And she said, I am fleeing from the face of my mistress Sarai. 9 And the angel of Jehovah said unto her, Return to thy mistress, and submit thyself under her hands. 10 And the angel of Jehovah said unto her, I will greatly multiply thy seed, that it shall not be numbered for multitude. 11 And the angel of Jehovah said unto her, Behold, thou art with child, and shalt bear a son; and thou shall call his name Ishmael, because Jehovah hath heard thy affliction. 12 And he shall be *as* a wild ass among men; his hand *shall be* against every man, and every man's hand against him; and he shall dwell over against all his brethren. 13 And she called the name of Jehovah that spake unto her, Thou art a God that seeth: for she said, Have I even here looked after him that seeth me? 14 Wherefore the well was called Beer-lahai-roi; behold, it is between Kadesh and Bered.

15 And Hagar bare Abram a son: and Abram called the name of his son, whom Hagar bare, Ishmael. 16 And Abram was fourscore and six years old, when Hagar bare Ishmael to Abram.

Just as the high point of Abram's call and response had been followed by the low point of his presumptive flight to Egypt and dishonorable conduct while there, just so the high point of the vision of the covenant was followed by another low point of presumption. It was customary among the people of Mesopotamia for a barren wife to supply her husband with a slave girl as a concubine. If the slave girl conceived, she was delivered of the child on the knees of her mistress and the child was looked upon as belonging to the mistress and as the heir of the father (cf. 30:3-13). So after they had dwelt in Canaan ten years and Sarai had not yet borne children, she suggested to Abram that he take her Egyptian handmaid, Hagar, as a secondary wife so that Sarai could have children by her. Abram agreed. But when Hagar conceived, she despised her mistress. Sarai complained to Abram, was told that Hagar was hers to dispose of as

[63] *Ibid.*, p. 113.

she pleased, and dealt with her so severely that she ran away into the desert. There the angel of the Lord found her at an oasis, promised her a son to be known as Ishmael ("God hears"), foretold his rough life in the desert, and instructed her to return and submit herself to Sarai. She was so impressed by the experience that she called Jehovah *El roi*, "God of seeing," which led to the naming of the well **Beer-lahai-roi**, "The well of the living one who sees me." She returned to Sarai and bore Ishmael when Abram was eighty-six years of age.

It is possible that Abram and Sarai acquired this Egyptian handmaid along with the other gifts by Pharaoh when he took Sarai into his harem (12:16). If so, the one presumption paved the way for the other. In any event, Sarai's self-designed method of fulfilling their natural desires for children and God's promise of a multitude of descendants led only to trouble. She reaped the harvest first in Hagar's attitude and later in Ishmael's mockery of Isaac (21:9). The bitter fruit continued long after Sarai's death when the Ishmaelites warred against the chosen people. The lesson is clear that it is never wise to try to speed up the processes of divine providence. God's timetable is perfect. For us to tamper with it will only lead to tragedy.

c. The Fifth Promise — Name and Circumcision (17:1-27)

1 And when Abram was ninety years old and nine, Jehovah appeared to Abram, and said unto him, I am God Almighty; walk before me, and be thou perfect. 2 And I will make my covenant between me and thee, and will multiply thee exceedingly. 3 And Abram fell on his face: and God talked with him, saying, 4 As for me, behold, my covenant is with thee, and thou shalt be the father of a multitude of nations. 5 Neither shall thy name any more be called Abram, but thy name shall be Abraham; for the father of a multitude of nations have I made thee. 6 And I will make thee exceeding fruitful, and I will make nations of thee, and kings shall come out of thee. 7 And I will establish my covenant between me and thee and thy seed after thee throughout their generations for an everlasting covenant, to be a God unto thee and to thy seed after thee. 8 And I will give unto thee, and to thy seed after thee, the land of thy sojournings, all the land of Canaan, for an everlasting possession; and I will be their God.

9 And God said unto Abraham, And as for thee, thou shalt keep my covenant, thou and thy seed after thee throughout their generations. 10 This is my covenant, which ye shall keep, between me and you and thy seed after thee: every male among you shall be circumcised. 11 And ye shall be circumcised in the flesh of your foreskin; and it shall be a token of a covenant betwixt me and you. 12 And he that is eight days old shall be circumcised among you, every male throughout your generations, he that is born in the house, or bought with money of any foreigner that is not of thy seed. 13 He that is born in thy house, and he that is bought with thy money, must needs be circumcised: and my covenant shall be in your flesh for an everlasting covenant. 14 And the uncircumcised male who is not circumcised in the flesh of his foreskin, that soul shall be cut off from his people; he hath broken my covenant.

15 And God said unto Abraham, As for Sarai thy wife, thou shalt not call her name Sarai, but Sarah shall her name be. 16 And I will bless her, and moreover I will give thee a son of her: yea, I will bless her, and she shall be *a mother of* nations; kings of peoples shall be of her. 17 Then Abraham fell upon his face, and laughed, and said in his heart, Shall a child be born unto him that is a hundred years old? and shall Sarah, that is ninety years old, bear? 18 And Abraham said unto God, Oh that Ishmael might live before thee! 19 And God said, Nay, but Sarah thy wife shall bare thee a son; and thou shalt call his name Isaac: and I will establish my covenant with him for an everlasting covenant for his seed after him. 20 And as for Ishmael, I have heard thee: behold, I have blessed him, and will make him fruitful, and will multiply him exceedingly; twelve princes shall he beget, and I will make him a great nation. 21 But my covenant will I establish with Isaac, whom Sarah shall bear unto thee at this set time in the next year.

22 And he left off talking with him, and God went up from Abraham. 23 And Abraham took Ishmael his son, and all that were born in his house, and all that were bought with his money, every male among the men of Abraham's house, and circumcised the flesh of their foreskin in the selfsame day, as God had said unto him. 24 And Abraham was ninety years old and nine, when he was circum-

cised in the flesh of his foreskin. 25 And Ishmael his son was thirteen years old, when he was circumcised in the flesh of his foreskin. 26 In the selfsame day was Abraham circumcised, and Ishmael his son. 27 And all the men of his house, those born in the house, and those bought with money of a foreigner, were circumcised with him.

One of the longest periods of divine silence Abram had ever experienced followed the birth of Ishmael. The next divine visitation did not occur until after thirteen years when Abram was ninety-nine. John Calvin has well suggested that God's long silence may have been in disapproval of Abram and Sarai's attempt to provide for themselves the promised son.

The Lord introduces Himself by a new name in appearing to Abram this time, El Shaddai, **God Almighty.** Thus three of the most prominent Old Testament names for God appear in this chapter: El Shaddai, **Jehovah** or Yahweh (the particularly Hebrew name for God), and Elohim (translated God in our versions, a plural form). While not everything is known concerning the origin and full significance of these names, each helps us better to understand the character of God. One scholar notes:

> Elohim sets forth God's creative and sustaining Power, Shaddai His Bounty, and . . . Jehovah sets forth His essential and unswerving principles of mercy and judgment, and presents Him as a Father, a Friend, and a Moral Governor.[64]

The significance of the use of El Shaddai, the term which speaks of God as a bountiful Giver, is immediately apparent. For the Lord has reappeared to renew His promises and covenant, to amplify the nature of the promises, and to clarify the conditions expected of Abram and his descendants. In renewing the promise, He repeats certain factors which He had announced earlier, namely, the everlasting nature of the promise, and the possession of the land of Canaan. But He adds that Abram will become **the father of a multitude of nations,** and kings shall come out of him. It is clear from the biblical record that not only Israel, but also the Ishmaelites and

Edomites as well as perhaps other desert tribes, were descended from Abraham. Israel and Edom both had kings, and the former included some of the most illustrious in human history: David, Solomon, Hezekiah, Josiah, and the greatest of all, Jesus Christ. These promises were abundantly fulfilled by the God of bountiful giving.

God also announced a change of names for Abram and Sarai. **Abram** ("exalted father") was to become **Abraham,** a name whose etymology cannot now be traced with certainty, but which the author explains as somehow indicating "father of a multitude." **Sarai** was to become **Sarah,** not involving a change in the meaning, since both meant "princess," but a change of an older, specialized feminine ending to the more common feminine ending.[65] It was, in a sense, a freshening of the name. Such changes were thought of as symbolizing a change in a person's status, much as kings, both ancient and modern, commonly assume a new name when ascending the throne. For Abraham, the change in status was that of an end to his early period of probation and waiting, and the entering in upon the period of fulfillment of the divine promises. For Sarah, this is the first specific announcement that she will be the mother of the promised seed.

The Lord also announced the name of the promised son: it was to be **Isaac,** a name derived from the Hebrew word meaning "to laugh." It was apparently here an implied rebuke to Abraham. For all his faith, when the Lord assured him Sarah would bear this son, Abraham laughed secretly, wondering how a man one hundred years old and a woman ninety years old could have a child. He asked instead that Ishmael might live before the Lord. The Lord refused to accept Ishmael as the promised seed, but promised that he would become a great nation.

The Lord also clarified the conditions demanded of Abraham in the covenant. The only conditions indicated prior to this were the implied conditions of faith and obedience, both of which Abraham had met. But now the Lord becomes more specific about Abraham's conduct and character. As to his conduct, he is told, **Walk before me.** Enoch and Noah

[64] Girdlestone, *op. cit.,* p. 40.   [65] Speiser, *op. cit.,* p. 75.

had walked "with" God (5:22-24; 6:9), but Abraham is to walk **before Him** — living his life as being constantly under the scrutiny and judgment of the Lord. As to his character, he is told, **And be thou perfect. Perfect** is literally "whole" or "complete." It is "completeness of being in respect of purity."[66] And in addition to these internal and spiritual conditions, God adds an external sign of the covenant, the rite of circumcision. This surgical procedure was virtually unknown in Mesopotamia, but was widely practiced among the people of Egypt and by some of the nomads.[67] But its introduction among the Hebrews carried from the beginning a spiritual significance. It marked those chosen of God. Paul later pointed out that the true mark was not the external one in the flesh, but the internal one in the heart (Rom. 2:29; Col. 2:11).

When God left off talking with Abraham, Abraham immediately obeyed this new instruction from the Lord, circumcising every male in his household, himself, Ishmael, every slave born in the home, and everyone purchased from a foreigner. His obedience was complete.

4. Abraham's Intercession (18:1—19:38)

a. The Sixth Promise — a Son (18:1-15)

1 And Jehovah appeared unto him by the oaks of Mamre, as he sat in the tent door in the heat of the day; 2 and he lifted up his eyes and looked, and, lo, three men stood over against him: and when he saw them, he ran to meet them from the tent door, and bowed himself to the earth, 3 and said, My lord, if now I have found favor in thy sight, pass not away, I pray thee, from thy servant: 4 let now a little water be fetched, and wash your feet, and rest yourselves under the tree: 5 and I will fetch a morsel of bread, and strengthen ye your heart; after that ye shall pass on: forasmuch as ye are come to your servant. And they said, So do, as thou hast said. 6 And Abraham hastened into the tent unto Sarah, and said, Make ready quickly three measures of fine meal, knead it, and make cakes. 7 And Abraham ran unto the herd, and fetched a calf tender and good, and gave it unto the servant; and

he hasted to dress it. 8 And he took butter, and milk, and the calf which he had dressed, and set it before them; and he stood by them under the tree, and they did eat.

9 And they said unto him, Where is Sarah thy wife? And he said, Behold, in the tent. 10 And he said, I will certainly return unto thee when the season cometh round; and, lo, Sarah thy wife shall have a son. And Sarah heard in the tent door, which was behind him. 11 Now Abraham and Sarah were old, *and* well stricken in age; it had ceased to be with Sarah after the manner of women. 12 And Sarah laughed within herself, saying, After I am waxed old shall I have pleasure, my lord being old also? 13 And Jehovah said unto Abraham, Wherefore did Sarah laugh, saying, Shall I of a surety bear a child, who am old? 14 Is anything too hard for Jehovah? At the set time I will return unto thee, when the season cometh round, and Sarah shall have a son. 15 Then Sarah denied, saying, I laughed not; for she was afraid. And he said, Nay; but thou didst laugh.

God has infinite ways of revealing Himself to men. He had earlier simply spoken to Abraham and also revealed Himself in a vision. Now He comes with two angels, the three in human form. The picture is a sharply detailed one of the semi-nomadic life Abraham lived. He is sitting at the entrance to his tent in the terebinth grove of Mamre in the hottest part of the day, the time during which all inhabitants of tropical or semi-tropical countries must hide from the sun and rest. Suddenly he looks up to see what he takes to be three men. They are standing, waiting for an invitation to come closer. With elaborate oriental hospitality, he rushes to greet them, bows before them, and addresses words of welcome to the one who is obviously the leader. He asks them to recline under the tree which customarily shaded the tent, and rushes away to prepare **a morsel of bread,** which turns out to be a full-fledged feast! The heavenly beings, still appearing as men to him, proceed to eat — apparently demonstrating the ability to eat but not the necessity of eating, which the resurrected Christ later also manifested (Luke 24:41-43).

The meal was eaten outside. Sarah,

---

[66] Whitelaw, *op. cit.*, Vol. I, p. 232.   [67] Speiser, *op. cit.*, pp. 126-27.

as was proper in the Orient, remained inside the tent, out of sight, but out of natural curiosity, close to the door where she could listen. It was not proper for anyone except close friends to inquire after one's wife, but suddenly, with a note of authority, the visitors asked Abraham, **Where is Sarah thy wife?** This was apparently the first subtle hint of the leading visitor's identity. Informed by Abraham of her whereabouts, He replied that He would **return when the season cometh round** and Sarah would have a son. Certainly Abraham's startled thoughts must have immediately recalled that only Jehovah had talked to him about this before. But in the tent Sarah was remembering her age, the fact that she had already long ago passed through menopause, and she laughed at such a suggestion — laughing apparently at the suggestion of three utter strangers that such could be possible. But now Jehovah fully revealed His identity, for He questioned Abraham about Sarah's secret laughter, her doubts, something He could only have known about through His omniscience. And when the startled Sarah attempted to cover up her unwitting irreverence with a lie, He emphatically refuted her claim.

In this beautiful visit to Abraham's tent, God had indeed renewed His promise to Abraham. The visit must have come shortly after the institution of the rite of circumcision, for at that time, too, God had told Abraham that Isaac's birth would occur the next year. His term here, **when the season cometh round,** can be taken in several ways: next year, next spring, or at the end of the normal period of pregnancy. In any event, the immediate fulfillment of the promise was assured and Sarah herself was involved in the revelation so that spiritually she could also be prepared.

b. The Judgment of Sodom (18:16-21)

16 And the men rose up from thence, and looked toward Sodom: and Abraham went with them to bring them on the way. 17 And Jehovah said, Shall I hide from Abraham that which I do; 18 seeing that Abraham shall surely become a great and mighty nation, and all the nations of the earth shall be blessed in him? 19 For I have known him, to the end that he may command his children and his household after him, that they may keep the way of Jehovah, to do righteousness and justice; to the end that Jehovah may bring upon Abraham that which he hath spoken of him. 20 And Jehovah said, Because the cry of Sodom and Gomorrah is great, and because their sin is very grievous; 21 I will go down now, and see whether they have done altogether according to the cry of it, which is come unto me; and if not, I will know.

After Jehovah had fulfilled His purpose in visiting Abraham's tent, He and His companions arose and turned their faces toward Sodom. Abraham walked a little way with them, as if to point out the road they sought. The very picturesque, anthropomorphic way of describing God's actions is continued, with the writer suggesting that Jehovah had not yet made up His mind whether to tell Abraham what He planned to do. But finally, on the basis of Abraham's known character and future destiny, Jehovah told Abraham the second reason for His appearance in this guise. The sinfulness of Sodom and Gomorrah had become so great that judgment could no longer tarry. He had come for a personal observation. He did not say what would happen if He found the report to be true. He did not need to. Abraham was well aware what would happen to the wicked cities in the presence of the holy God he served.

c. The Prayer for Sodom (18:22-33)

22 And the men turned from thence, and went toward Sodom: but Abraham stood yet before Jehovah. 23 And Abraham drew near, and said, Wilt thou consume the righteous with the wicked? 24 Peradventure there are fifty righteous within the city: wilt thou consume and not spare the place for the fifty righteous that are therein? 25 That be far from thee to do after this manner, to slay the righteous with the wicked, that so the righteous should be as the wicked; that be far from thee: shall not the Judge of all the earth do right? 26 And Jehovah said, If I find in Sodom fifty righteous within the city, then I will spare all the place for their sake. 27 And Abraham answered and said, Behold now, I have taken upon me to speak unto the Lord,

who am but dust and ashes: 28 peradventure there shall lack five of the fifty righteous: wilt thou destroy all the city for lack of five? And he said, I will not destroy it, if I find there forty and five. 29 And he spake unto him yet again, and said, Peradventure there shall be forty found there. And he said, I will not do it for the forty's sake. 30 And he said, Oh let not the Lord be angry, and I will speak: peradventure there shall thirty be found there. And he said, I will not do it, if I find thirty there. 31 And he said, Behold now, I have taken upon me to speak unto the Lord: peradventure there shall be twenty found there. And he said, I will not destroy it for the twenty's sake. 32 And he said, Oh let not the Lord be angry, and I will speak yet but this once: peradventure ten shall be found there. And he said, I will not destroy it for the ten's sake. 33 And Jehovah went his way, as soon as he had left off communing with Abraham: and Abraham returned unto his place.

The two companions of Jehovah apparently moved on, but Abraham tarried as if to hold his Divine Guest a little longer. Then he began to pray one of the most remarkable prayers of intercession ever recorded. He spoke to God almost as one man might speak to another, pointing out the injustice of slaying the righteous with the wicked, calling for **the Judge of all the earth** to do right, admitting his own lack of status in making his requests, praying for forbearance that he might speak just a little longer. He secured Jehovah's promise that He would not destroy Sodom if fifty righteous were to be found there. He pressed his claim, lowering the number to forty-five, then forty, thirty, twenty, and finally ten. Some have wondered if Sodom might not have been saved if only Abraham had continued his prayer until only one righteous man would have saved it! One cannot but marvel at the spiritual insights of this man so recently called out of idolatry, at his understanding of Jehovah's relation to all the earth, at his faith, at his compassion. There is a lesson here in the need for and the effectiveness of true intercession which needs to be learned and applied in our day. And there is here a demonstration both of the gracious hospitality and the neighborly concern of a great man of God which would do justice to the twentieth-century Christian. Abraham did not hide in the comfort of his own wealth and security. He insisted on being involved in the needs of the world about him.

d. The Sinfulness of Sodom (19:1-11)

1 And the two angels came to Sodom at even; and Lot sat in the gate of Sodom: and Lot saw them, and rose up to meet them; and he bowed himself with his face to the earth; 2 and he said, Behold now, my lords, turn aside, I pray you, into your servant's house, and tarry all night, and wash your feet, and ye shall rise up early, and go on your way. And they said, Nay; but we will abide in the street all night. 3 And he urged them greatly; and they turned in unto him, and entered into his house; and he made them a feast, and did bake unleavened bread, and they did eat. 4 But before they lay down, the men of the city, *even* the men of Sodom, compassed the house round, both young and old, all the people from every quarter; 5 and they called unto Lot, and said unto him, Where are the men that came in to thee this night? bring them out unto us, that we may know them. 6 And Lot went out unto them to the door, and shut the door after him. 7 And he said, I pray you, my brethren, do not so wickedly. 8 Behold now, I have two daughters that have not known man; let me, I pray you, bring them out unto you, and do ye to them as is good in your eyes: only unto these men do nothing, forasmuch as they are come under the shadow of my roof. 9 And they said, Stand back. And they said, This one fellow came in to sojourn, and he will needs be a judge; now will we deal worse with thee, than with them. And they pressed sore upon the man, even Lot, and drew near to break the door. 10 But the men put forth their hand, and brought Lot into the house to them, and shut to the door. 11 And they smote the men that were at the door of the house with blindness, both small and great, so that they wearied themselves to find the door.

The two angels who had accompanied Jehovah, still bearing the appearance of men, apparently entered Sodom the same evening. Lot was sitting in the gate, the center of city life and the seat of its council and court. It is possible that Lot had become one of the city elders or judges. If so, he would have been in an excellent position to have "vexed his righteous soul from day to day with their lawless deeds" (II Pet. 2:8). In any event, he saw the strangers enter the city, and immediately demonstrated the same gracious hospitality which had characterized Abraham, bowing before them and inviting them to his house. They deferred, expressing their intention to abide in the street. But he insisted and again a feast was spread before them. Before the time for retirement, a clamor was heard without. A crowd of men, young and old, from every quarter of the city, had gathered. They demanded that Lot bring out his guests in order that they might **know them**, the common Hebrew term for sexual intimacy, which reveals the awful truth about the sinfulness of Sodom (see Ezek. 16:50). It had fallen into mass perversion, had so given itself to homosexuality that its very name is used in English today to describe this unnatural relationship — sodomy. Lot went out and shut the door behind him. He had a solemn responsibility to protect his guests — such was involved in oriental hospitality. In order to protect them, he offered his two virgin daughters to the mob. But they had no desire for his alternative, denounced his "holier-than-thou" attitude, and threatened him personally. As they pressed upon him, the angels intervened, pulling Lot inside, shutting the door, and smiting the mob with blindness so that they could not find the door. All the rumors concerning Sodom had been confirmed. Its debauchery demanded judgment.

e. The Escape from Sodom (19:12-22)

12 And the men said unto Lot, Hast thou here any besides? son-in-law, and thy sons, and thy daughters, and whomsoever thou hast in the city, bring them out of the place: 13 for we will destroy this place, because the cry of them is waxed great before Jehovah; and Jehovah hath sent us to destroy it. 14 And Lot went out, and spake unto his sons-in-law, who married his daughters, and said, Up, get you out of this place; for Jehovah will destroy the city. But he seemed unto his sons-in-law as one that mocked. 15 And when the morning arose, then the angels hastened Lot, saying, Arise, take thy wife, and thy two daughters that are here, lest thou be consumed in the iniquity of the city. 16 But he lingered; and the men laid hold upon his hand, and upon the hand of his wife, and upon the hand of his two daughters, Jehovah being merciful unto him: and they brought him forth, and set him without the city. 17 And it came to pass, when they had brought them forth abroad, that he said, Escape for thy life; look not behind thee, neither stay thou in all the Plain; escape to the mountain, lest thou be consumed. 18 And Lot said unto them, Oh, not so, my lord: 19 behold now, thy servant hath found favor in thy sight, and thou hast magnified thy lovingkindness, which thou hast showed unto me in saving my life; and I cannot escape to the mountain, lest evil overtake me, and I die: 20 behold now, this city is near to flee unto, and it is a little one. Oh let me escape thither (is it not a little one?), and my soul shall live. 21 And he said unto him, See, I have accepted thee concerning this thing also, that I will not overthrow the city of which thou hast spoken. 22 Haste thee, escape thither; for I cannot do anything till thou be come thither. Therefore the name of the city was called Zoar.

The angels had revealed their true identity by the miracle. Now they revealed the nature of their errand to Lot. They warned him to gather together all who pertained to him and to flee the city. But Lot's efforts were unavailing. His **sons-in-law** (the Hebrew can mean either those already married to older daughters not mentioned in the text, or those already pledged to marry the two daughters still at home) considered him as one beside himself. And as dawn was breaking, the angels practically dragged Lot, his wife, and his two daughters out and thrust them from the city. They warned them to flee for their lives, not to tarry until they arrived in the mountains, and not to look behind them. Lot's chronic weakness manifested itself again as he begged for Zoar, apparently the smallest and the southernmost of the five cities, to be spared. The request was granted and haste was again urged. The effectiveness of Abraham's prayer and the constant concern of God for the righteous are revealed in the angel's confession, **I cannot do anything till thou be come thither.**

The error of Lot's choice of the wealth of the plains was now clearly revealed. All he had invested in Sodom, all he now possessed, was left behind. He is indeed an example of one who is himself saved, but whose works are burned (I Cor. 3:11-15).

f. The Destruction of Sodom (19:23-29)

23 The sun was risen upon the earth when Lot came unto Zoar. 24 Then Jehovah rained upon Sodom and upon Gomorrah brimstone and fire from Jehovah out of heaven; 25 and he overthrew those cities, and all the Plain, and all the inhabitants of the cities, and that which grew upon the ground. 26 But his wife looked back from behind him, and she became a pillar of salt. 27 And Abraham gat up early in the morning to the place where he had stood before Jehovah: 28 and he looked toward Sodom and Gomorrah, and toward all the land of the Plain, and beheld, and, lo, the smoke of the land went up as the smoke of a furnace.

29 And it came to pass, when God destroyed the cities of the Plain, that God remembered Abraham, and sent Lot out of the midst of the overthrow, when he overthrew the cities in which Lot dwelt.

When Lot arrived at Zoar, doomsday dawned for the other cities of the plain. The tremendous catastrophe so attracted the curiosity of his wife that she disobeyed the angelic command, looked back, and was turned into a pillar of salt. Far off near Hebron, Abraham rose early in the morning and walked out to where he had interceded with Jehovah for Sodom. Even from a distance of forty miles or more, he could see **the smoke of the land** rising as **the smoke of a furnace.**

Archaeological evidence confirms the fact that the flourishing civilization of the plain came to an abrupt end at the approximate time of Abraham. The region was full of bitumen or asphalt pits and petroleum deposits are still to be found there. The entire region is on the so-called "fault line" which formed the Jordan valley, the Dead Sea, and the Arabah to the south. It has been the scene of countless earthquakes. It is possible that God simply set off the natural powderkeg, using an earthquake to mingle the salt and free sulphur of the area, resulting in a tremendous explosion, showering fire and brimstone all over the plain, setting fire to the asphalt and petroleum, and consuming the cities, their inhabitants, and the rich farmlands about them.[68] Access to the ruins of the cities has been denied archaeologists by the rising waters of the Dead Sea, which have slowly covered their site in its shallow southern basin. There is some evidence that the ruins were still visible in classical and New Testament times, and that the biblical Zoar still survived at that later period, although it, too, has now gone beneath the waters.[69]

The severe judgment on the cities of the plain for their perversion, and the extreme aversion to this sin shown by the Lord throughout the Old Testament laws (Lev. 18:22; 20:13; Deut. 23:17) is worthy of note. In our contemporary culture, efforts are being made to accept the homosexual person as naturally different from others, to recognize his "right" to mutually voluntary relations with other adults, and to alleviate the laws and penalties formerly enacted by society against him. When we read what the Bible has to say about God's attitude toward this practice, we cannot but wonder if this move to neutralize the traditional sinfulness of sodomy is not in itself part of the moral breakdown which is so general now, and which must have preceded Sodom's plunge into mass perversion. Certainly no sincere Christian could advocate the execution of every homosexual on the basis of the Old Testament law. And where there is need for medical help in dealing with a physiological problem, it certainly should be available with as little embarrassment as possible. But to nullify the sinfulness of sin is to foster it. And to foster this sin is to invite the fate of Sodom itself.

g. The Aftermath of Sodom (19:30-38)

30 And Lot went up out of Zoar, and dwelt in the mountain, and his two daughters with him; for he feared to

[68] Unger, op. cit., p. 115.

[69] Ibid. See also Josephus, Wars of the Jews, Book IV, Chap. VIII, para. 4.

dwell in Zoar: and he dwelt in a cave, he and his two daughters. 31 And the first-born said unto the younger, Our father is old, and there is not a man in the earth to come in unto us after the manner of all the earth: 32 come, let us make our father drink wine, and we will lie with him, that we may preserve seed of our father. 33 And they made their father drink wine that night: and the first-born went in, and lay with her father; and he knew not when she lay down, nor when she arose. 34 And it came to pass on the morrow, that the first-born said unto the younger, Behold, I lay yesternight with my father: let us make him drink wine this night also; and go thou in, and lie with him, that we may preserve seed of our father. 35 And they made their father drink wine that night also: and the younger arose, and lay with him; and he knew not when she lay down, nor when she arose. 36 Thus were both the daughters of Lot with child by their father. 37 And the first-born bare a son, and called his name Moab: the same is the father of the Moabites unto this day. 38 And the younger, she also bare a son, and called his name Ben-ammi: the same is the father of the children of Ammon unto this day.

The story of Lot is one of the great tragedies of the Bible. It is possible that, in spite of all the failures, all the compromises, all the sordid involvements of this man, he was somehow saved (cf. II Pet. 2:6-9). But he failed at every point to realize the promise which his relationship to God and God's man held for him. And the final chapter in the biblical record of his life is one of the saddest of all.

While Lot had sought for Jehovah to spare Zoar, he was not content to stay there. The awful desolation of the plain was too vivid a reminder of the past and he moved on to the mountains. He was afraid Zoar might yet be destroyed. In the mountains he lived in a cave with his two daughters. And there the moral infection of Sodom brought forth its final evil fruit. For the daughters, cut off from association with other people and from the hope of natural marriage, plotted together to bring about the drunkenness of their father, tricked him into incestuous relations with them, and bore him two sons, one the father of the Moabites,

the other the father of the Ammonites. The daughters had learned nothing from the holocaust but continued to decide questions of conduct on the basis of their own personal desires and the convenience of the moment. Lot's final degradation cost the chosen people much suffering, for the Moabites and Ammonites were their bitterly hostile neighbors centuries later.

5. Abraham's Fulfillment (20:1—23:18)

a. The Third Presumption — Encounter with Abimelech (20:1-18)

1 And Abraham journeyed from thence toward the land of the South, and dwelt between Kadesh and Shur; and he sojourned in Gerar. 2 And Abraham said of Sarah his wife, She is my sister: and Abimelech king of Gerar sent, and took Sarah. 3 But God came to Abimelech in a dream of the night, and said to him, Behold, thou art but a dead man, because of the woman whom thou hast taken; for she is a man's wife. 4 Now Abimelech had not come near her: and he said, Lord, wilt thou slay even a righteous nation? 5 Said he not himself unto me, She is my sister? and she, even she herself said, He is my brother: in the integrity of my heart and the innocency of my hands have I done this. 6 And God said unto him in the dream, Yea, I know that in the integrity of thy heart thou hast done this, and I also withheld thee from sinning against me: therefore suffered I thee not to touch her. 7 Now therefore restore the man's wife; for he is a prophet, and he shall pray for thee, and thou shalt live: and if thou restore her not, know thou that thou shalt surely die, thou, and all that are thine.

8 And Abimelech rose early in the morning, and called all his servants, and told all these things in their ears: and the men were sore afraid. 9 Then Abimelech called Abraham, and said unto him, What hast thou done unto us? and wherein have I sinned against thee, that thou hast brought on me and on my kingdom a great sin? thou hast done deeds unto me that ought not to be done. 10 And Abimelech said unto Abraham, What sawest thou, that thou hast done this thing? 11 And Abraham said, Because I thought, Surely the fear of God is not in this place; and they will slay me for my wife's sake. 12 And moreover she is indeed my sister, the daughter of

my father, but not the daughter of my mother; and she became my wife: 13 and it came to pass, when God caused me to wander from my father's house, that I said unto her, This is thy kindness which thou shalt show unto me: at every place whither we shall come, say of me, He is my brother. 14 And Abimelech took sheep and oxen, and men-servants and women-servants, and gave them unto Abraham, and restored him Sarah his wife. 15 And Abimelech said, Behold, my land is before thee: dwell where it pleaseth thee. 16 And unto Sarah he said, Behold, I have given thy brother a thousand pieces of silver: behold, it is for thee a covering of the eyes to all that are with thee; and in respect of all thou art righted. 17 And Abraham prayed unto God: and God healed Abimelech, and his wife, and his maid-servants; and they bare children. 18 For Jehovah had fast closed up all the wombs of the house of Abimelech, because of Sarah, Abraham's wife.

Twice before, when Abraham reached a pinnacle of spiritual life, he followed with an act unworthy of his high calling (cf. comments on 12:10-20; 16:1-16). Now, just when he seemed ready to graduate from his probationary period, just when God had dated the fulfillment of His promise, Abraham stooped again.

He left the grove of Mamre near Hebron and migrated toward **the South** or the Negeb. There he camped for a while in the area between **Kadesh** (probably Kadesh-barnea) and **Shur** (the word probably means "wall" and may have referred to a line of fortresses maintained by Egypt at the isthmus of Suez, protecting its border from invasion[70]). Then he moved on to **Gerar**, to the northwest, about ten miles south of Gaza, in the southern part of the territory of the Philistines. Again Abraham called Sarah his sister, and Abimelech, the local monarch, took her into his harem. But Abimelech seems to have stood out among the inhabitants of the land for his spirituality and piety, for God spoke to him in a dream, revealing what had actually happened and threatening him with judgment if Sarah were not returned to her husband. Abimelech protested his innocence in motive and act — **in the integrity of my heart and the innocency**

of my hands have I done this, recounting how both Abraham and Sarah had deceived him. God granted the innocence of his motive, and said Abraham was a prophet and would pray for him that judgment would not fall. Abimelech's obedience was prompt. He arose early in the morning, related the news to his servants, and summoned Abraham before him. Again, the man of lesser spiritual privilege rebuked the man chosen of God, and asked for an explanation. Abraham explained himself as he had not done to Pharaoh, saying (1) he thought there was no fear of God in this place and thus no respect for man's rights, (2) she really was his half-sister, and (3) they had made a mutual agreement at the beginning of their pilgrimage that such would be their habitual custom in going into strange places. Abimelech bestowed rich gifts upon Abraham, amounting to a sufficient sum to veil Sarah's eyes from those of her own household — apparently restoring her dignity in relation to her servants who might otherwise have despised her.[71] Then Abraham prayed and Abimelech and all his household were healed of a mysterious affliction which had stopped their reproductive functions. God had once again protected His redemptive program from Abraham's presumption.

One might wonder how Abraham could make the same mistake twice. In fact, critics have long since declared that the two accounts in 12:10-20 and 20:1-18 as well as the similar one about Isaac in 26:6-11 are simply three versions of the same incident, the differences having developed through centuries of oral tradition. But men do make the same mistake twice. Furthermore, Abraham indicates here that this was an habitual practice with him and Sarah, making its repetition extremely likely. And the differences of this account are marked — different reasons for entering the strange area, different countries and different kings, different ways in which the kings discovered the truth, different spiritual levels as far as the kings were concerned, different responses on the part of Abraham when rebuked. And it is very significant that nothing is said in this later incident about Sarah's beauty. She was

70 Leupold, op. cit., p. 500.   71 Ibid., pp. 591-92.

now far along in years. Abimelech's desire for her was not one of physical attraction, but to ally himself by marriage with a powerful nomad who was visiting his area.[72] Abraham's fear must have been more a matter of habit than anything else. The alarming thing is that he could be so thoughtless just at the time God was fulfilling His promise. Only divine providence prevented catastrophe.

b. The Birth of Isaac (21:1-7)

1 And Jehovah visited Sarah as he had said, and Jehovah did unto Sarah as he had spoken. 2 And Sarah conceived, and bare Abraham a son in his old age, at the set time of which God had spoken to him. 3 And Abraham called the name of his son that was born unto him, whom Sarah bare to him, Isaac. 4 And Abraham circumcised his son Isaac when he was eight days old, as God had commanded him. 5 And Abraham was a hundred years old, when his son Isaac was born unto him. 6 And Sarah said, God hath made me to laugh; every one that heareth will laugh with me. 7 And she said, Who would have said unto Abraham, that Sarah should give children suck? for I have borne him a son in his old age.

The long-desired day arrived. At the very time God had appointed, Sarah gave birth to the promised son. Abraham called him **Isaac,** as God had instructed (17:19), and circumcised him on the eighth day in keeping with the conditions of the covenant. Abraham was now one hundred years old and Sarah ninety — truly this was a miracle child. Isaac's name, "Laughter," was a reminder to both Abraham and Sarah that in unbelief they had laughed at the promises of God (17:17; 18:12). For not even the physically impossible had proved too hard for God. And the grateful Sarah saw in it also a more pleasant thought — that God had now caused her to laugh for joy, and would cause all who heard to rejoice with her.

Isaac was living proof to Abraham of a lesson he had been slow to learn. God did plan to redeem mankind through Abraham and his seed, but this redemption would never be the result of mere natural processes, nor of human in-

genuity or effort. It could only result through the sovereign grace of God at work in and through Abraham. The man of God must be yielded, never presumptive on the one hand nor stubborn on the other, ready to do God's bidding without hesitation and ready to wait God's time without complaining. Obedient faith involved much more than mental assent and occasional altar-building. It involved constant dependence upon God with all the denial of self that implies.

c. The Destiny of Ishmael (21:8-21)

8 And the child grew, and was weaned: and Abraham made a great feast on the day that Isaac was weaned. 9 And Sarah saw the son of Hagar the Egyptian, whom she had borne unto Abraham, mocking. 10 Wherefore she said unto Abraham, Cast out this handmaid and her son: for the son of this handmaid shall not be heir with my son, even with Isaac. 11 And the thing was very grievous in Abraham's sight on account of his son. 12 And God said unto Abraham, Let it not be grievous in thy sight because of the lad, and because of thy handmaid; in all that Sarah saith unto thee, hearken unto her voice; for in Isaac shall thy seed be called. 13 And also of the son of the handmaid will I make a nation, because he is thy seed. 14 And Abraham rose up early in the morning, and took bread and a bottle of water, and gave it unto Hagar, putting it on her shoulder, and *gave her* the child, and sent her away: and she departed, and wandered in the wilderness of Beersheba. 15 And the water in the bottle was spent, and she cast the child under one of the shrubs. 16 And she went, and sat her down over against him a good way off, as it were a bowshot: for she said, Let me not look upon the death of the child. And she sat over against him, and lifted up her voice, and wept. 17 And God heard the voice of the lad; and the angel of God called to Hagar out of heaven, and said unto her, What aileth thee, Hagar? fear not; for God hath heard the voice of the lad where he is. 18 Arise, lift up the lad, and hold him in thy hand; for I will make him a great nation. 19 And God opened her eyes, and she saw a well of water; and she went, and filled the bottle with water, and gave the lad drink. 20 And God was with the lad, and he grew; and he dwelt in the wilderness,

[72] *Ibid.,* pp. 582-83.

and became, as he grew up, an archer. 21 And he dwelt in the wilderness of Paran: and his mother took him a wife out of the land of Egypt.

As Isaac grew, the time for weaning came, and Abraham celebrated this day with a great feast. But the day was spoiled for Sarah when she saw Ishmael, now about fourteen years old, mocking. She went to Abraham and demanded that Hagar and Ishmael be expelled from the household. This Abraham was reluctant to do, and well he might have been. For the same law which provided for a barren wife to have children through her slave girl also prohibited the setting aside of such children if the wife herself later became a mother.[73] But the Lord encouraged Abraham to grant Sarah's request, for Isaac was the divinely appointed heir. He promised to make also of Ishmael a nation.

So Abraham supplied Hagar and Ishmael with provisions and sent them away into the desert. When the water was spent, Hagar despaired of life itself. But an angel spoke to her, reassured her of God's interest and care, showed her a well, and promised to make of Ishmael a great nation. So Ishmael's life was preserved. He grew, became an archer, settled in **the wilderness of Paran,** a region in the east-central part of the Sinai peninsula, and married a girl from Egypt.

d. The Covenant with Abimelech (21:22-34)

22 And it came to pass at that time, that Abimelech and Phicol the captain of his host spake unto Abraham, saying, God is with thee in all that thou doest: 23 now therefore swear unto me here by God that thou wilt not deal falsely with me, nor with my son, nor with my son's son: but according to the kindness that I have done unto thee, thou shalt do unto me, and to the land wherein thou hast sojourned. 24 And Abraham said, I will swear. 25 And Abraham reproved Abimelech because of the well of water, which Abimelech's servants had violently taken away. 26 And Abimelech said, I know not who hath done this thing: neither didst thou tell me, neither yet heard I of it, but to-day. 27 And Abra-

ham took sheep and oxen, and gave them unto Abimelech; and they two made a covenant. 28 And Abraham set seven ewe lambs of the flock by themselves. 29 And Abimelech said unto Abraham, What mean these seven ewe lambs which thou hast set by themselves? 30 And he said, These seven ewe lambs shalt thou take of my hand, that it may be a witness unto me, that I have digged this well. 31 Wherefore he called that place Beer-sheba; because there they sware both of them. 32 So they made a covenant at Beer-sheba: and Abimelech rose up, and Phicol the captain of his host, and they returned into the land of the Philistines. 33 And *Abraham* planted a tamarisk tree in Beer-sheba, and called there on the name of Jehovah, the Everlasting God. 34 And Abraham sojourned in the land of the Philistines many days.

Abimelech had earlier given Abraham the free run of his country. Apparently, after a time at least, Abraham had migrated inland to the spot later called Beersheba, which was farther east than Philistine territory normally extended. But Abraham's vast herds no doubt ranged far and wide, some of them being pastured close to Gerar. Abimelech observed the increasing wealth and strength of Abraham and felt that it would be a wise political measure to formalize the good relations they had thus far maintained. He came with **Phicol,** the head of his army, and proposed to Abraham such a non-aggression pact, which would be binding upon them and their descendants forever. Abraham agreed that such would be wise. But he called to Abimelech's attention a matter which needed adjustment first. The well which Abraham had dug at Beersheba had been forcibly seized by Abimelech's people and Abraham felt that it must be restored. Abimelech protested his complete innocence, and the implication is that he agreed to the restoration. Then Abraham gave to Abimelech, the militarily stronger party to the pact, sheep and oxen as a sign of confirmation of their agreement. But he also set aside seven ewe lambs by themselves which he gave to Abimelech with the explanation that this gift signified their agreement that Abraham had dug the well and that all rights pertaining to

---

[73] Unger, *op. cit.,* pp. 122-23.

it were his. So the place was named **Beer-sheba,** the first part of the word meaning "well" and the last part meaning either "seven" or "oath." Thus the name of the well commemorated both the oath taken between the two men and the seven lambs which especially signified the ownership of the well itself.

When Abimelech and Phicol returned to their capital, Abraham planted a **tamarisk tree** in Beersheba. The tamarisk is something like the cypress and its wood is especially firm and durable. This lasting quality takes on additional significance when we read that now Abraham called Jehovah by a new name, *El olam,* **the Everlasting God.** The perpetual covenant which he had made with Abimelech no doubt reminded him of the perpetual covenant he had with Jehovah and the constant faithfulness Jehovah had manifested toward him across the years.

e. The Testing of Abraham (22:1-14)

1 And it came to pass after these things, that God did prove Abraham, and said unto him, Abraham; and he said, Here am I. 2 And he said, Take now thy son, thine only son, whom thou lovest, even Isaac, and get thee into the land of Moriah; and offer him there for a burnt-offering upon one of the mountains which I will tell thee of. 3 And Abraham rose early in the morning, and saddled his ass, and took two of his younger men with him, and Isaac his son; and he clave the wood for the burnt-offering, and rose up, and went unto the place of which God had told him. 4 On the third day Abraham lifted up his eyes, and saw the place afar off. 5 And Abraham said unto his young men, Abide ye here with the ass, and I and the lad will go yonder; and we will worship, and come again to you. 6 And Abraham took the wood of the burnt-offering, and laid it upon Isaac his son; and he took in his hand the fire and the knife; and they went both of them together. 7 And Isaac spake unto Abraham his father, and said, My father: and he said, Here am I, my son. And he said, Behold, the fire and the wood: but where is the lamb for a burnt-offering? 8 And Abraham said, God will provide himself the lamb for a burnt-offering, my son: so they went both of them together.

9 And they came to the place which God had told him of; and Abraham built the altar there, and laid the wood in order, and bound Isaac his son, and laid him on the altar, upon the wood. 10 And Abraham stretched forth his hand, and took the knife to slay his son. 11 And the angel of Jehovah called unto him out of heaven, and said, Abraham, Abraham: and he said, Here am I. 12 And he said, Lay not thy hand upon the lad, neither do thou anything unto him; for now I know that thou fearest God, seeing thou hast not withheld thy son, thine only son, from me. 13 And Abraham lifted up his eyes, and looked, and, behold, behind *him* a ram caught in the thicket by his horns: and Abraham went and took the ram, and offered him up for a burnt-offering in the stead of his son. 14 And Abraham called the name of that place Jehovah-jireh: as it is said to this day, In the mount of Jehovah it shall be provided.

After these things — after all that God had done to develop in Abraham the highest possible level of faith and spiritual achievement — **God did prove Abraham,** giving him his final examination in the school of faith. And it was a severe one. After securing Abraham's attention, the original word order has Jehovah saying, "Take, I pray, your son, the only one, whom you love, even Isaac." Each short phrase made the dread command even more specific, so there could be no mistake. How instantly and completely Abraham's entire emotional and spiritual being was involved! And then the Lord said to go into **the land of Moriah,** and offer him there as a **burnt-offering,** with the original being a technical term describing the kind of sacrifice which is wholly consumed on the altar. Abraham must have been utterly shaken by such a command, for it not only demanded that from which any man would recoil, but it threatened the loss of all that to which Abraham had dedicated his life — the promises of God. But there is absolutely nothing in his conduct which reveals disturbance. He does not argue with God or question Him. The next morning he arises, saddles his ass, takes along two servants and Isaac, splits the wood for the sacrifice, and departs. The short rhythmic clauses of the biblical account picture the prompt, methodical way he went about obeying

God — almost like a soldier marching off to do his duty!

On the third day, some forty miles or more from his starting point, Abraham understands by some means that the mountain before him is the one God had promised to point out. **The land of Moriah** cannot be located with certainty. Solomon built his temple upon Mount Moriah in Jerusalem (II Chron. 3:1), and some have thought that the temple sacrifices were offered on the same spot as Isaac. Adam Clarke suggests that all the mountains of Jerusalem made up the land of Moriah, and that Calvary was the particular one used for the altar upon which Isaac was offered.[74] While the symbolic truth of the story is rich and significant, these identifications of place cannot be pressed too far. Jerusalem was already a city in Abraham's day, and the scene described fits much more readily with an uninhabited region.

At the foot of the mountain Abraham leaves his servants. His prompt, unquestioning obedience had already indicated that his faith was greater than the test. Now a second indication of the sufficiency of his faith appears as he tells the servants, **I and the lad will go yonder; and we will worship, and come again to you** — all three of the verbs being first person plural forms — we will go, we will worship, we will come again! Little wonder that such faith prompted the writer of the Epistle to the Hebrews to say that Abraham obeyed, "accounting that God is able to raise up, even from the dead" (Heb. 11:17-19). Abraham laid the wood on Isaac (apparently now in his teens and better able to carry this burden than his aged father) and took the fire, carried in some kind of brazier, and a knife, and began the ascent. Isaac wondered if his aged father had forgotten the most important detail, but his query brought forth a third indication of Abraham's great faith, **God will provide himself the lamb, my son.**

When they came to the place God had indicated, Abraham built an altar, laid in order the wood, bound Isaac, and placed him on the wood. It seems impossible that even Abraham's faith could have gone through all this without emotion. But his methodical preparation indicates sublime composure. And the whole story says much for Isaac too. For the boy could not have been bound without his consent, but he seems to have had complete trust in his father. Then Abraham took the knife and reached out to slay Isaac. Not one hesitation is recorded, not one prayer for new guidance or instruction. To all intents and purposes, Abraham had already offered his son on the altar of sacrifice to the God who had given him.

But then came a providential interruption. **The angel of Jehovah** called Abraham's name twice as if anxious to interrupt him before he went too far. Abraham's reply was as calm as he had been throughout, as if he were not at all surprised that God had intervened but had been expecting it all the time! Now he was commanded to refrain from the offering up of Isaac. God was satisfied with Abraham's demonstration of faith and obedience. He asked no more. Speaking in human terms, now He knew that Abraham served Him with all his heart.

Turning about, Abraham found **a ram caught in the thicket by his horns.** Quickly he took it and offered it in place of Isaac. He had every reason for worship at this juncture, and he was quick to use the substitute which divine mercy had provided. Abraham named this place **Jehovah-jireh,** meaning "Jehovah will see" or "Jehovah will provide." The verb is the same as that used in verse 8 when Abraham said, "God will provide himself a lamb." Out of this experience a proverb developed, **In the mount of Jehovah it shall be provided.** The exact meaning of the proverb is not clear. One possibility is that it is a reminder that whenever the Lord calls us to a difficult task (an appointment which took Abraham to this mountain), He will provide all we need for the occasion.

The purpose of the trial is immediately apparent. It would have been easy for Abraham to have loved Isaac, the miracle son of his old age, to such an extent as to permit affection for him to have replaced loyalty to Jehovah as the primary principle of his life. Now the Lord is pleased to examine Abraham to the fullest extent possible, to demand a

[74] Op. cit., I, 139.

sacrifice of Isaac. It is true that human sacrifice was contrary to the will of God. But the heathen religions around Abraham practiced it, giving their best to their false gods, offering the bodies of their children upon the altar. God had not yet forbidden such by His express command as He did later with Moses (Lev. 18:21). And there was no other way to test Abraham's willingness to sacrifice Isaac in his primary obedience to God than to let him proceed on the basis of a physical sacrifice — and then stop him in the nick of time.

The story in itself is one of the most beautiful in all of literature. But the Christian cannot help but see in it shadows of the great truths of the gospel. In Abraham's unhesitating denial of his own emotions and feelings, we see a picture of God's unswerving intention to redeem man, for He "spared not his own Son, but delivered him up for us all" (Rom. 8:32). In Isaac's meek submission to his father's will, we see pictured the submission of Christ to the cross, His willingness to drink the cup His Father's plan required. In Abraham's words, "God will provide himself the lamb," we see foreshadowed the providing of Christ as the eternal sacrifice. In the substitutionary ram caught in the thicket, we see foreshadowed not only the entire sacrificial system of the Old Testament but also the divine Substitute who suffered in our stead. One cannot read this passage in the light of the New Testament without being convinced afresh of the God-inspired unity of the Scriptures, the harmonious unfolding of God's self-revelation.

f. The Seventh Promise — Victory (22:15-19)

15 And the angel of Jehovah called unto Abraham a second time out of heaven, 16 and said, By myself have I sworn, saith Jehovah, because thou hast done this thing, and hast not withheld thy son, thine only son, 17 that in blessing I will bless thee, and in multiplying I will multiply thy seed as the stars of the heavens, and as the sand which is upon the seashore; and thy seed shall possess the gate of his enemies; 18 and in thy seed shall all the nations of the earth be blessed; because thou hast obeyed

my voice. 19 So Abraham returned unto his young men, and they rose up and went together to Beer-sheba; and Abraham dwelt at Beer-sheba.

Again the angel of Jehovah called Abraham, and communicated to him God's seventh promise, one based on Abraham's proven faith and obedience in the experience which had just transpired. In this promise there is a summing up of many of the provisions included in the first six. There is only one addition: **thy seed shall possess the gate of his enemies.** To all the promises of multiplied descendants, great nations and mighty kings, and a blessing for all the nations, was added this one of victory and triumph over enemies. While this promise has been fulfilled literally in a physical way many times and perhaps will yet again be so fulfilled for Israel, its ultimate fulfillment must be in a spiritual sense since even the gates of Hades cannot prevail against Abraham's spiritual descendants, the Church of Jesus Christ (Matt. 16:18).

g. The News from Nahor (22:20-24)

20 And it came to pass after these things, that it was told Abraham, saying, Behold, Milcah, she also hath borne children unto thy brother Nahor: 21 Uz his first-born, and Buz his brother, and Kemuel the father of Aram, 22 and Chesed, and Hazo, and Pildash, and Jidlaph, and Bethuel. 23 And Bethuel begat Rebekah: these eight did Milcah bear to Nahor, Abraham's brother. 24 And his concubine, whose name was Reumah, she also bare Tebah, and Gaham, and Tahash, and Maacah.

Now late in Abraham's life, probably at least forty years after his departure from Haran, he receives news of his brother Nahor whom he had left behind. The news probably traveled with one of the merchants' caravans which even then plied busily back and forth from one part of the fertile crescent to the other. Even as Abraham had been blessed with a son, so God had blessed Nahor with children. His wife Milcah had borne him eight sons and his concubine Reumah had borne him four, making twelve altogether, just as in the case of Ishmael (25:13-15) and Jacob. These twelve apparently fathered Aramaean tribes, with Chesed the possible ancestor of the Chaldeans, and others settling to the south of Canaan.[75]

h. The Death of Sarah (23:1-20)

1 And the life of Sarah was a hundred and seven and twenty years: these were the years of the life of Sarah. 2 And Sarah died in Kiriath-arba (the same is Hebron), in the land of Canaan: and Abraham came to mourn for Sarah, and to weep for her. 3 And Abraham rose up from before his dead, and spake unto the children of Heth, saying, 4 I am a stranger and a sojourner with you: give me a possession of a burying-place with you, that I may bury my dead out of my sight. 5 And the children of Heth answered Abraham, saying unto him, 6 Hear us, my lord; thou art a prince of God among us: in the choice of our sepulchres bury thy dead; none of us shall withhold from thee his sepulchre, but that thou mayest bury thy dead. 7 And Abraham rose up, and bowed himself to the people of the land, even to the children of Heth. 8 And he communed with them, saying, If it be your mind that I should bury my dead out of my sight, hear me, and entreat for me to Ephron the son of Zohar, 9 that he may give me the cave of Machpelah, which he hath, which is in the end of his field; for the full price let him give it to me in the midst of you for a possession of a burying-place. 10 Now Ephron was sitting in the midst of the children of Heth: and Ephron the Hittite answered Abraham in the audience of the children of Heth, even of all that went in at the gate of his city, saying, 11 Nay, my lord, hear me: the field give I thee, and the cave that is therein, I give it thee; in the presence of the children of my people give I it thee: bury thy dead. 12 And Abraham bowed himself down before the people of the land. 13 And he spake unto Ephron in the audience of the people of the land, saying, But if thou wilt, I pray thee, hear me: I will give the price of the field; take it of me, and I will bury my dead there. 14 And Ephron answered Abraham, saying unto him, 15 My lord, hearken unto me: a piece of land worth four hundred shekels of silver, what is that betwixt me and thee? bury therefore thy dead. 16 And Abraham hearkened unto Ephron; and Abraham

weighed to Ephron the silver which he had named in the audience of the children of Heth, four hundred shekels of silver, current *money* with the merchant.

17 So the field of Ephron, which was in Machpelah, which was before Mamre, the field, and the cave which was therein, and all the trees that were in the field, that were in all the border thereof round about, were made sure 18 unto Abraham for a possession in the presence of the children of Heth, before all that went in at the gate of his city. 19 And after this, Abraham buried Sarah his wife in the cave of the field of Machpelah before Mamre (the same is Hebron), in the land of Canaan. 20 And the field, and the cave that is therein, were made sure unto Abraham for a possession of a burying-place by the children of Heth.

Sarah lived to be 127 years old. She died in **Kiriath-arba,** which is the old name for **Hebron.** Apparently Abraham had moved back to Hebron from Beersheba. After an initial period of mourning, Abraham went out to buy a burial site from the native inhabitants of the land. The account is a classic portrayal of oriental business transactions, with its exaggerated courtesy, its insistence that the money is insignificant, its final agreement for purchase at what must have been an exorbitant price, freely paid by Abraham since he was in no position to bargain.[76] The burial site was a cave, in a field formerly belonging to **Ephron,** one of the Hittites who inhabited the vicinity. The locale of the field was called **Machpelah,** and it was apparently opposite the gate of **Mamre,** which appears here as still another name for Hebron. The field, the cave, and all the trees included in the field became Abraham's possession, with a firm title to the land secured before the city council of Hebron. Here Sarah was buried, and here later were buried Abraham (25:9-10), and also Isaac and Rebekah, and Leah and Jacob (49:31; 50:13).

B. THE STORY OF ISAAC (24:1—27:46)

1. Isaac's Wife (24:1-67)

1 And Abraham was old, *and* well stricken in age: and Jehovah had blessed

---

[75] Speiser, *op. cit.,* p. 167.
[76] *Ibid.,* p. 171. Speiser's translation brings out even more clearly the undertones of the oriental business transaction.

Abraham in all things. 2 And Abraham said unto his servant, the elder of his house, that ruled over all that he had, Put, I pray thee, thy hand under my thigh: 3 and I will make thee swear by Jehovah, the God of heaven and the God of the earth, that thou wilt not take a wife for my son of the daughters of the Canaanites, among whom I dwell: 4 but thou shalt go unto my country, and to my kindred, and take a wife for my son Isaac. 5 And the servant said unto him, Peradventure the woman will not be willing to follow me unto this land: must I needs bring thy son again unto the land from whence thou camest? 6 And Abraham said unto him, Beware thou that thou bring not my son thither again. 7 Jehovah, the God of heaven, who took me from my father's house, and from the land of my nativity, and who spake unto me, and who sware unto me, saying, Unto thy seed will I give this land; he will send his angel before thee, and thou shalt take a wife for my son from thence. 8 And if the woman be not willing to follow thee, then thou shalt be clear from this my oath; only thou shalt not bring my son thither again. 9 And the servant put his hand under the thigh of Abraham his master, and sware to him concerning this matter.

10 And the servant took ten camels, of the camels of his master, and departed, having all goodly things of his master's in his hand: and he arose, and went to Mesopotamia, unto the city of Nahor. 11 And he made the camels to kneel down without the city by the well of water at the time of evening, the time that women go out to draw water. 12 And he said, O Jehovah, the God of my master Abraham, send me, I pray thee, good speed this day, and show kindness unto my master Abraham. 13 Behold, I am standing by the fountain of water; and the daughters of the men of the city are coming out to draw water: 14 and let it come to pass, that the damsel to whom I shall say, Let down thy pitcher, I pray thee, that I may drink; and she shall say, Drink, and I will give thy camels drink also: let the same be she that thou hast appointed for thy servant Isaac; and thereby shall I know that thou hast showed kindness unto my master. 15 And it came to pass before he had done speaking, that, behold, Rebekah came out, who was born to Bethuel the son of Milcah, the wife of Nahor, Abraham's brother, with her pitcher upon her shoulder. 16 And the damsel was very fair to look upon, a virgin, neither had any man known

her: and she went down to the fountain, and filled her pitcher, and came up. 17 And the servant ran to meet her, and said, Give me to drink, I pray thee, a little water from thy pitcher. 18 And she said, Drink, my lord: and she hasted, and let down her pitcher upon her hand, and gave him drink. 19 And when she had done giving him drink, she said, I will draw for thy camels also, until they have done drinking. 20 And she hasted, and emptied her pitcher into the trough, and ran again unto the well to draw, and drew for all his camels. 21 And the man looked stedfastly on her, holding his peace, to know whether Jehovah had made his journey prosperous or not. 22 And it came to pass, as the camels had done drinking, that the man took a golden ring of half a shekel weight, and two bracelets for her hands of ten shekels weight of gold, 23 and said, Whose daughter art thou? tell me, I pray thee. Is there room in thy father's house for us to lodge in? 24 And she said unto him, I am the daughter of Bethuel the son of Milcah, whom she bare unto Nahor. 25 She said moreover unto him, We have both straw and provender enough, and room to lodge in. 26 And the man bowed his head, and worshipped Jehovah. 27 And he said, Blessed be Jehovah, the God of my master Abraham, who hath not forsaken his lovingkindness and his truth toward my master: as for me, Jehovah hath led me in the way to the house of my master's brethren.

28 And the damsel ran, and told her mother's house according to these words. 29 And Rebekah had a brother, and his name was Laban: and Laban ran out unto the man, unto the fountain. 30 And it came to pass, when he saw the ring, and the bracelets upon his sister's hands, and when he heard the words of Rebekah his sister, saying, Thus spake the man unto me; that he came unto the man; and, behold, he was standing by the camels at the fountain. 31 And he said, Come in, thou blessed of Jehovah; wherefore standest thou without? for I have prepared the house, and room for the camels. 32 And the man came into the house, and he ungirded the camels; and he gave straw and provender for the camels, and water to wash his feet and the feet of the men that were with him. 33 And there was set food before him to eat: but he said, I will not eat, until I have told mine errand. And he said, Speak on. 34 And he said, I am Abraham's servant. 35 And Jehovah hath blessed my master greatly; and he is become great: and he hath

given him flocks and herds and silver and gold, and men-servants and maid-servants, and camels and asses. 36 And Sarah my master's wife bare a son to my master when she was old: and unto him hath he given all that he hath. 37 And my master made me swear, saying, Thou shalt not take a wife for my son of the daughters of the Canaanites, in whose land I dwell: 38 but thou shalt go unto my father's house, and to my kindred, and take a wife for my son. 39 And I said unto my master, Peradventure the woman will not follow me. 40 And he said unto me, Jehovah, before whom I walk, will send his angel with thee, and prosper thy way; and thou shalt take a wife for my son of my kindred, and of my father's house: 41 then shalt thou be clear from my oath, when thou comest to my kindred; and if they give her not to thee, thou shalt be clear from my oath. 42 And I came this day unto the fountain, and said, O Jehovah, the God of my master Abraham, if now thou do prosper my way which I go: 43 behold, I am standing by the fountain of water; and let it come to pass, that the maiden that cometh forth to draw, to whom I shall say, Give me, I pray thee, a little water from thy pitcher to drink; 44 and she shall say to me, Both drink thou, and I will also draw for thy camels: let the same be the woman whom Jehovah hath appointed for my master's son. 45 And before I had done speaking in my heart, behold, Rebekah came forth with her pitcher on her shoulder; and she went down unto the fountain, and drew: and I said unto her, Let me drink, I pray thee. 46 And she made haste, and let down her pitcher from her shoulder, and said, Drink, and I will give thy camels drink also: so I drank, and she made the camels drink also. 47 And I asked her, and said, Whose daughter art thou? And she said, The daughter of Bethuel, Nahor's son, whom Milcah bare unto him: and I put the ring upon her nose, and the bracelets upon her hands. 48 And I bowed my head, and worshipped Jehovah, and blessed Jehovah, the God of my master Abraham, who had led me in the right way to take my master's brother's daughter for his son. 49 And now if ye will deal kindly and truly with my master, tell me: and if not, tell me; that I may turn to the right hand, or to the left.

50 Then Laban and Bethuel answered and said, The thing proceedeth from Jehovah: we cannot speak unto thee bad or good. 51 Behold, Rebekah is before thee, take her, and go, and let her be thy master's son's wife, as Jehovah hath spoken. 52 And it came to pass, that, when Abraham's servant heard their words, he bowed himself down to the earth unto Jehovah. 53 And the servant brought forth jewels of silver, and jewels of gold, and raiment, and gave them to Rebekah: he gave also to her brother and to her mother precious things. 54 And they did eat and drink, he and the men that were with him, and tarried all night; and they rose up in the morning, and he said, Send me away unto my master. 55 And her brother and her mother said, Let the damsel abide with us *a few* days, at the least ten; after that she shall go. 56 And he said unto them, Hinder me not, seeing Jehovah hath prospered my way; send me away that I may go to my master. 57 And they said, We will call the damsel, and inquire at her mouth. 58 And they called Rebekah, and said unto her, Wilt thou go with this man? And she said, I will go. 59 And they sent away Rebekah their sister, and her nurse, and Abraham's servant, and his men. 60 And they blessed Rebekah, and said unto her, Our sister, be thou *the mother* of thousands of ten thousands, and let thy seed possess the gate of those that hate them.

61 And Rebekah arose, and her damsels, and they rode upon the camels, and followed the man: and the servant took Rebekah, and went his way. 62 And Isaac came from the way of Beer-lahai-roi; for he dwelt in the land of the South. 63 And Isaac went out to meditate in the field at the eventide: and he lifted up his eyes, and saw, and, behold, there were camels coming. 64 And Rebekah lifted up her eyes, and when she saw Isaac, she alighted from the camel. 65 And she said unto the servant, What man is this that walketh in the field to meet us? And the servant said, It is my master: and she took her veil, and covered herself. 66 And the servant told Isaac all the things that he had done. 67 And Isaac brought her into his mother Sarah's tent, and took Rebekah, and she became his wife; and he loved her: and Isaac was comforted after his mother's death.

While Isaac is regularly listed with Abraham and Jacob as one of the three patriarchs from which God's chosen people took their start, in Genesis he is mostly just a connecting link between the two more prominent men. The book does not even need to be divided so as to have a section given to the story of Isaac; for the securing of Isaac's wife in chapter 24 was initiated by Abraham. The first part of chapter 25 deals with Abraham's closing days and other sons, and the last part of 25 and all of 27 actually deal more with Jacob and Esau than with Isaac. This leaves only chapter 26 which concentrates on Isaac. He seems to have been a neutral type of personality — there was little which made him stand out as an individual. But there is value in studying the religious life of such a man, for he is so much like the average person. The average person may read about Abraham and Jacob and be awed by the grandeur of their religious experiences, but feel that this is beyond him. But when one reads concerning Isaac, his quiet ways, his unheralded tragedies, his faithfulness, and God's concern for him and use of him, one becomes convinced that there is a place in God's plan even for connecting links!

As Abraham neared the end of life, he called in his most trusted servant, the head over all his household. (This may have been the very Eliezer to whom Abraham had earlier expected to leave his wealth, 15:2, but his name is not mentioned and it may have been Eliezer's successor.) He caused this man to put his hand under Abraham's thigh, a very solemn kind of oath the significance of which is now largely lost. It appears in the Bible only here and in 47:29-31 when Jacob was nearing death. The servant implied in verse 41, when relating his vow to Rebekah's family, that a curse rested upon him if he did not carry out his promise. In any event, the solemn promise was that he would not take a wife for Isaac from among the Canaanites, nor would he take Isaac back to the family home, but that he would go and bring a wife from the homeland to Isaac. Abraham assured him that God would prosper his efforts.

So the servant took ten camels and such provisions and gifts as he needed, and departed on a journey which would have taken at least a month. He came to **Mesopotamia,** or as the Hebrew actually expresses it, "the Aram of the two rivers," to **the city of Nahor,** which was either Nahor's home or the city bearing Nahor's name. He came to the well outside the city in the evening, and caused the camels to kneel at just about the time the women of the city were coming out for water. He prayed and asked Jehovah for a supernatural sign designating the girl God had chosen for Isaac. He had barely quit praying when Rebekah, granddaughter of Nahor, Abraham's brother, came and fulfilled the sign he had appointed to the very letter. The servant immediately produced gifts for her, inquired as to her identity, and then revealed the name of his master, thanking the Lord for His guidance and assistance. Rebekah ran to her mother's house (apparently her father, Bethuel, had died) with the news. When her brother Laban saw the jewelry she had received, he, too, became interested and invited Abraham's servant to the house. There the servant related his errand and the way in which God had singled out Rebekah as the designated object of his mission. A most suggestive expression occurs in the KJV rendering at this point: "I being in the way, the Lord led me." There is always assurance of divine guidance when there is obedience to the divine will.

According to the laws of the land, when a father died, the eldest son would become the leading negotiator in the marriage arrangements for the daughters. Accordingly, Laban is pictured as assuming authority in this transaction. A **Bethuel** is mentioned in verse 50, but it cannot be the father or his name would have been first; he may have been a younger brother. When the brother acted in the place of the father, the marriage contract came under the heading of a "sistership document." This ordinarily involved the following specifications: (1) the principals in the case, (2) nature of the transaction, (3) details of payments, (4) the girl's declaration of concurrence, (5) penalty clause. A close study of verses 50-60 reveals that here is virtually a restatement in literary form of such a document, omitting only the penalty clause.[77]

The transaction was satisfactorily completed. Rebekah and her slave girls accompanied the servant back to Canaan,

77 *Ibid.*, pp. 184-85.

where she met Isaac near Hagar's memorable spot, **Beer-lahai-roi.** Isaac took her as his wife and was comforted over his mother's death. Once again divine providence had fulfilled the divine purpose in selecting the proper ancestress of the chosen people.

2. Isaac's Brothers (25:1-18)

a. Keturah's Sons (25:1-6)

1 And Abraham took another wife, and her name was Keturah. 2 And she bare him Zimran, and Jokshan, and Medan, and Midian, and Ishbak, and Shuah. 3 And Jokshan begat Sheba, and Dedan. And the sons of Dedan were Asshurim, and Letushim, and Leummim. 4 And the sons of Midian: Ephah, and Epher, and Hanoch, and Abida, and Eldaah. All these were the children of Keturah. 5 And Abraham gave all that he had unto Isaac. 6 But unto the sons of the concubines, that Abraham had, Abraham gave gifts; and he sent them away from Isaac his son, while he yet lived, eastward, unto the east country.

We have here the record of another marriage by Abraham to **Keturah.** In verse 6, she and Hagar are referred to as **concubines.** She was therefore a secondary wife, and as such, may have been taken by Abraham prior to Sarah's death. It is evident that this chapter does not deal with events in chronological order, for Abraham's death appears before the birth of Esau and Jacob. Since he was a hundred years old at the time of Isaac's birth, 175 at the time of his own death, and Isaac was sixty when the twins were born, Abraham lived for fifteen years after the birth of his grandsons. Abraham had himself realized the human impossibility of his becoming a father at the age of one hundred years (17:17). Since Sarah did not die until he was 137, if he waited until after that to marry Keturah, he would have been nearly 150 before her sixth and last son was born. It is possible, as some have suggested, that the rejuvenation of Abraham's body which made possible the birth of Isaac was miraculously continued to enable him to father the multitude of nations God had promised him.[78] But this seems

to be straining after support for an interpretation which is not necessary.

The genealogy of Keturah's sons lists six of them, and traces some of them to the second and third generation. They can be rather loosely identified as the ancestors of Arabian tribes living south and southeast of Canaan.[79] The most familiar names are those of Midian (the Midianites are frequently mentioned as neighbors of Israel) and Sheba and Dedan. The latter two names are also mentioned in 10:7 as descendants of Ham. It is possible that the descendants of the two lines intermingled in the countries mentioned.

Abraham fully recognized the priority of Isaac's claim as the promised son and gave to him his vast wealth. The other sons, apparently including Ishmael as well as the sons of Keturah, received gifts and were sent away from Isaac while Abraham still lived. He attempted to make the wisest possible arrangement to secure peace and prosperity for the one through whom God would continue to work.

b. Abraham's Death (25:7-11)

7 And these are the days of the years of Abraham's life which he lived, a hundred threescore and fifteen years. 8 And Abraham gave up the ghost, and died in a good old age, an old man, and full *of years,* and was gathered to his people. 9 And Isaac and Ishmael his sons buried him in the cave of Machpelah, in the field of Ephron the son of Zohar the Hittite, which is before Mamre; 10 the field which Abraham purchased of the children of Heth: there was Abraham buried, and Sarah his wife. 11 And it came to pass after the death of Abraham that God blessed Isaac his son: and Isaac dwelt by Beer-lahai-roi.

The story of Abraham's life has been told in full. There is little to add in connection with the notice of his death except his age at passing, the joining of hands by Isaac and Ishmael in caring for his remains, and his burial in the cave which he himself had purchased. Now the divine blessing which had always attended Abraham passed to his

[78] R. Payne Smith, "Genesis," *Ellicott's Commentary on the Whole Bible,* ed. by Charles John Ellicott, I, 95-96.
[79] S. R. Driver, *The Book of Genesis,* "Westminster Commentaries," ed. by Walter Lock, pp. 239-40.

son Isaac, who continued to dwell by Beer-lahai-roi where Rebekah had found him.

c. Ishmael's Sons (25:12-18)

12 Now these are the generations of Ishmael, Abraham's son, whom Hagar the Egyptian, Sarah's handmaid, bare unto Abraham: 13 and these are the names of the sons of Ishmael, by their names, according to their generations: the first-born of Ishmael, Nebaioth; and Kedar, and Adbeel, and Mibsam, 14 and Mishma, and Dumah, and Massa, 15 Hadad, and Tema, Jetur, Naphish, and Kedemah: 16 these are the sons of Ishmael, and these are their names, by their villages, and by their encampments; twelve princes according to their nations. 17 And these are the years of the life of Ishmael, a hundred and thirty and seven years: and he gave up the ghost and died, and was gathered unto his people. 18 And they dwelt from Havilah unto Shur that is before Egypt, as thou goest toward Assyria: he abode over against all his brethren.

It has been evidenced repeatedly throughout Genesis that the author habitually completes whatever is important enough to be said about the individuals or families which represent side lines from the main line of interest, before he continues with the main story. So here he lists the twelve sons of Ishmael (same number as the sons of Nahor, 23:20-24, and of Jacob), and suggests that the names were also applied to the villages and encampments which they established. Some of the names are recognizable as those of clans or tribes living in the Arabian desert. Their dwelling places are given as **from Havilah unto Shur that is before Egypt, as thou goest toward Assyria,** describing the desert areas east of Egypt.

3. Isaac's Sons (25:19-34)

a. Their Birth (25:19-26)

19 And these are the generations of Isaac, Abraham's son: Abraham begat Isaac: 20 and Isaac was forty years old when he took Rebekah, the daughter of Bethuel the Syrian of Paddan-aram, the sister of Laban the Syrian, to be his wife. 21 And Isaac entreated Jehovah for his wife, because she was barren: and Jehovah was entreated of him, and Rebekah

his wife conceived. 22 And the children struggled together within her; and she said, If it be so, wherefore do I live? And she went to inquire of Jehovah. 23 And Jehovah said unto her,

Two nations are in thy womb,
And two peoples shall be separated from thy bowels:
And the one people shall be stronger than the other people;
And the elder shall serve the younger.

24 And when her days to be delivered were fulfilled, behold, there were twins in her womb. 25 And the first came forth red, all over like a hairy garment; and they called his name Esau. 26 And after that came forth his brother, and his hand had hold on Esau's heel; and his name was called Jacob: and Isaac was threescore years old when she bare them.

Again we encounter the familiar words, **these are the generations.** The story of the offspring of Terah, begun in 11:27, has been completed. Now the emphasis shifts to the descendants of Isaac. Again we have a brief summary of what has already transpired — Isaac's birth and marriage.

History repeated itself somewhat in the case of Isaac and Rebekah, for they, too, went childless for twenty years. Isaac prayed, the Lord heard, and Rebekah conceived. Unbeknown to her, she conceived twins. She sensed something unusual in the lively movements she felt within her, so she sought an explanation from the Lord. How she sought divine enlightenment is not indicated. It may have been in prayer, by sacrifice, or from some holy man known for his ability to converse with God, and who was respected by Isaac and Rebekah. In any event, the answer was given in poetic form, revealing that two nations were in her womb in the form of the twins, nations that would be unalterably opposed to each other from birth. The divine oracle also announced that one would be stronger than the other, and the elder would serve the younger. This is the first of four places in which Jehovah definitely revealed His choice of Jacob as the heir of Abraham's call and blessing — here in the birth oracle, and later in the bartering for the birthright, in the matter of the blessing, and in the dream at Bethel.

In due time, the twins were born. The

oldest was **red** (Hebrew *admoni,* a word-play on Esau's other name, Edom — see v. 30), having the appearance of a garment of hair (Hebrew *seyar,* apparently a word-play on Seir, the land in which Esau eventually settled). Because of his hairy appearance, he was named **Esau.** While the connection of Esau with **hairy** cannot be established with our present knowledge of Hebrew, a study of the closely related Arabic makes it likely.[80] The younger brother was born very closely behind his brother Esau, with his hand grasping Esau's heel. So he was named **Jacob,** or Hebrew *ya'aqob* from the root *'aqob,* which means "heel." The verbal form of the word means "follow at the heel," "assail insidiously," "circumvent," or "overreach."

b. The Birthright (25:27-34)

27 And the boys grew: and Esau was a skilful hunter, a man of the field; and Jacob was a quiet man, dwelling in tents. 28 Now Isaac loved Esau, because he did eat of his venison: and Rebekah loved Jacob. 29 And Jacob boiled pottage: and Esau came in from the field, and he was faint: 30 and Esau said to Jacob, Feed me, I pray thee, with that same red *pottage;* for I am faint: therefore was his name called Edom. 31 And Jacob said, Sell me first thy birthright. 32 And Esau said, Behold, I am about to die: and what profit shall the birthright do to me? 33 And Jacob said, Swear to me first; and he swear unto him: and he sold his birthright unto Jacob. 34 And Jacob gave Esau bread and pottage of lentils; and he did eat and drink, and rose up, and went his way: so Esau despised his birthright.

The twins grew up to be as different as the divine oracle had indicated. Esau became the restless hunter, roaming the countryside. Jacob became the typical semi-nomad, content to dwell in a tent and tend his flocks and herds. For some reason or other, the passive Isaac was attracted to the active Esau, and the more impulsive Rebekah was attracted by the nomadic Jacob, who nevertheless reflected many of his mother's traits. This parental favoritism was to play a large part in the troubles which developed between the two sons (chap. 27).

One day Jacob was cooking lentils when Esau came in from hunting, weak with weariness and hunger. He exclaimed, "Let me have a swallow of that red stuff there; for I am famishing."[81] This is again a play upon his nickname **Edom** or "Red." But Jacob was not so free with his lentils. He was an ambitious young man. He may have been told by his doting mother of the revelation made to her before the birth of the twins. And it is possible that Esau and he had discussed the birthright before and Esau had taken only a slight interest in it.[82] In any event, the oriental trader was manifest in the proposition he made to Esau: **Sell me first** (or "today") **thy birthright.** Jacob no doubt knew his brother's weaknesses, his unworthiness to carry on the family's spiritual heritage, and he was ready to take advantage of them — although he may have thought it was for a worthy cause! Esau demonstrated his true character with his answer, **Behold, I am about to die: and what profit shall the birthright do to me?** It is questionable whether such a strong, robust, out-of-doors man as Esau really thought he was going to die because of his intense hunger. It seems rather that he was half joking at this point, but in any event his present, physical needs were more important to him than anything of spiritual significance. Jacob insisted upon a serious, oath-bound agreement **first** or "today." With this Esau complied and the trade was consummated.

The **birthright** gave to the eldest son a double portion of his father's goods and also made him head of the family upon his father's death, making him ruler over his brothers and provider for his mother and unmarried sisters if there were any. But according to the laws and customs by which the patriarchs lived, as is evidenced through the discoveries of archaeology, the eldest son could sell his birthright to a younger brother or even to an adopted brother. One such instance is recorded in which a youth traded his away for three sheep.[83] It was this provision which Jacob and Esau followed. Blame rests on both the brothers for this act. Jacob had already been

[80] Leupold, *op. cit.,* p. 707.   [81] *The Bible, an American Translation.*
[82] Leupold, *op. cit.,* pp. 711-13.   [83] Unger, *op. cit.,* p. 123.

chosen by God for the most important heritage, the family calling, and God did not need his help in bringing it about. Isaac could have transferred it to him as we shall see in chapter 27. So Jacob was guilty of presumption as well as sharp bargaining. Esau was guilty of disrespect for the family name, the rich heritage in which he shared. He was fleshly-minded, a materialist in the extreme.

4. Isaac's Neighbors (26:1-35)

a. The First Promise — This Land (26:1-5)

1 And there was a famine in the land, besides the first famine that was in the days of Abraham. And Isaac went unto Abimelech king of the Philistines, unto Gerar. 2 And Jehovah appeared unto him, and said, Go not down into Egypt; dwell in the land which I shall tell thee of: 3 sojourn in this land, and I will be with thee, and will bless thee; for unto thee, and unto thy seed, I will give all these lands, and I will establish the oath which I sware unto Abraham thy father; 4 and I will multiply thy seed as the stars of heaven, and will give unto thy seed all these lands; and in thy seed shall all the nations of the earth be blessed; 5 because that Abraham obeyed my voice, and kept my charge, my commandments, my statutes, and my laws.

Famines were frequent in Canaan and neighboring lands, and the second one mentioned in Genesis came during Isaac's life. Isaac moved closer to the coastal plain, a fertile area occupied by **the Philistines**. Archaeology has not found any trace of this people, who migrated from Crete, along this coast prior to the twelfth century B. C., hundreds of years after the time of Abraham. It is possible, however, that there was an earlier wave of migrants, evidence of which has not yet been discovered. Or it may be that the term Philistine is used in a more geographic sense as referring to the country where they later lived.

As if to anticipate Isaac's partial repetition of his father's earlier errors, the Lord appeared to warn him against moving to Egypt. This was the Lord's first appearance to Isaac which is recorded. In it He commanded Isaac to dwell in

Canaan, and passed on to him the blessings earlier pronounced on Abraham, including the redemptive promise: **in thy seed shall all the nations of the earth be blessed.** The promise was significantly dependent upon the land, something Abraham had also stressed in forbidding his servant to take Isaac back to Paddanaram again (24:6-7). It is possible that this encounter with the Lord and the related events took place shortly after Abraham's death, since in connection with the account of his death mention is made of the subsequent blessing of Isaac (25:11).

b. Encounter with Abimelech (26:6-11)

6 And Isaac dwelt in Gerar: 7 and the men of the place asked him of his wife; and he said, She is my sister: for he feared to say, My wife; lest, *said he,* the men of the place should kill me for Rebekah; because she was fair to look upon. 8 And it came to pass, when he had been there a long time, that Abimelech king of the Philistines looked out at a window, and saw, and, behold, Isaac was sporting with Rebekah his wife. 9 And Abimelech called Isaac, and said, Behold, of a surety she is thy wife: and how saidst thou, She is my sister? And Isaac said unto him, Because I said, Lest I die because of her. 10 And Abimelech said, What is this thou hast done unto us? one of the people might easily have lain with thy wife, and thou wouldest have brought guiltiness upon us. 11 And Abimelech charged all the people saying, He that toucheth this man or his wife shall surely be put to death.

As pointed out in the comments on chapter 20, critics have insisted that the three similar accounts of 12:10-20; 20:1-18; and the present paragraph are simply conflicting accounts of the same event. This of course can only be accepted if one is ready to think of the Bible as almost entirely a human work, inspired only in the sense that other great literary works are inspired. But such a supposition is self-defeating, for it is extremely doubtful that any writer or group of writers would preserve three different stories or versions all of which placed their revered ancestors in a bad light. It is true that the setting is the same in the second two stories, the king's name is the same; the cause for the patriarch's move is the same in the first and third as is the cause of his fear. But as already indicated, famines were frequent and migrations to escape them were also (cf. Gen. 45:9-11; Ruth 1:1; II Kings 8:1-2). It is quite possible that Rebekah was just as beautiful as Sarah (cf. 24:16), and she was Isaac's cousin, a relationship to which the term "sister" was (and still is among primitive people) sometimes loosely applied. From what we know of names in biblical times, there is nothing unusual in two kings of the same city having the same name. And it is altogether possible that **Abimelech** was a standing designation for Philistine kings as Pharaoh was for the Egyptian monarchs. (Cf. the superscription of Psalm 34 with II Sam. 21:10-15.[84]) Furthermore, the biblical writer emphasizes that this is a different famine than the one which sent Abraham to Egypt (v. 1). And in this third incident, Rebekah was not taken into the king's harem. The truth was discovered accidentally by Abimelech when he saw Isaac caressing Rebekah in a manner not usually practiced with sisters! Abimelech questioned Isaac about his deceit, pointing out the danger of his act, and commanded his people not to harm this man or his wife.

It is impossible to determine if this scene transpired after the birth of the twins recorded in the preceding chapter. If the visit to Gerar was earlier, once again God protected the promised line. If it came later, He still protected His chosen man from embarrassment and disgrace.

c. Envy of the Philistines (26:12-22)

12 And Isaac sowed in that land, and found in the same year a hundredfold: and Jehovah blessed him. 13 And the man waxed great, and grew more and more until he became very great: 14 and he had possessions of flocks, and possessions of herds, and a great household: and the Philistines envied him. 15 Now all the wells which his father's servants had digged in the days of Abraham his father, the Philistines had stopped, and filled with earth. 16 And Abimelech said unto Isaac, Go from us; for thou art much mightier than we. 17 And

Isaac departed thence, and encamped in the valley of Gerar, and dwelt there.

18 And Isaac digged again the wells of water, which they had digged in the days of Abraham his father; for the Philistines had stopped them after the death of Abraham: and he called their names after the names by which his father had called them. 19 And Isaac's servants digged in the valley, and found there a well of springing water. 20 And the herdsmen of Gerar strove with Isaac's herdsmen, saying, The water is ours: and he called the name of the well Esek, because they contended with him. 21 And they digged another well, and they strove for that also: and he called the name of it Sitnah. 22 And he removed from thence, and digged another well; and for that they strove not: and he called the name of it Rehoboth; and he said, For now Jehovah hath made room for us, and we shall be fruitful in the land.

Abraham's relations with the Philistines had been cordial, with the exception of controversy over the well at Beersheba, far removed from Gerar. He and the Abimelech of his day had even concluded a non-aggression pact which was supposed to be binding on their descendants (21:22-34). But Isaac's experiences were not so pleasant. His first year in the area of Gerar he reaped a hundredfold what he had planted. His flocks, herds, and servants grew so rapidly and to such vast proportions that the Philistines were filled with envy. As a result, they spitefully filled up the wells which dated back to Abraham's sojourn in the land, one of the meanest possible acts in a semi-desert land. Then Abimelech came and asked Isaac to leave, since he was becoming too strong for the Philistines — implying that he, Isaac, was the troublemaker. Isaac seems to have been a pacifist. He moved away from Gerar itself, although he stayed in **the valley of Gerar**. He began to reopen the wells of Abraham in this distant area, but still did not find peace. The first well was named **Esek** or "Contention," and the second **Sitnah** or "Enmity," because of the continued effort of the Philistines to deprive him of that which belonged to him. So he moved again, opened a third well, and when no strife resulted, called it **Rehoboth,** "Broad Places" or "Room."

d. The Second Promise — Fear Not (26:23-25)

23 And he went up from thence to Beer-sheba. 24 And Jehovah appeared unto him the same night, and said, I am the God of Abraham thy father: fear not, for I am with thee, and will bless thee, and multiply thy seed for my servant Abraham's sake. 25 And he builded an altar there, and called upon the name of Jehovah, and pitched his tent there: and there Isaac's servants digged a well.

For some reason, Isaac moved again, going up to **Beer-sheba,** the inland oasis where Abraham had agreed to a covenant with the Philistines. Here the Lord appeared to him again, reassuring him that he need not fear, and renewing His promise. Here Isaac built an altar and dug a well. (This may or may not have been a redigging of the well dug there by Abraham. Beersheba may be translated as "The Well of the Seven," or as "The Seven Wells." Several wells have been found in the area.) The dual practice of Abraham and Isaac, building altars and digging wells, has a symbolic application worthy of any life — worshiping God and providing refreshing resources for others as well as self.

e. End of Hostilities (26:26-33)

26 Then Abimelech went to him from Gerar, and Ahuzzath his friend, and Phicol the captain of his host. 27 And Isaac said unto them, Wherefore are ye come unto me, seeing ye hate me, and have sent me away from you? 28 And they said, We saw plainly that Jehovah was with thee: and we said, Let there now be an oath betwixt us, even betwixt us and thee, and let us make a covenant with thee, 29 that thou wilt do us no hurt, as we have not touched thee, and as we have done unto thee nothing but good, and have sent thee away in peace: thou art now the blessed of Jehovah. 30 And he made them a feast, and they did eat and drink. 31 And they rose up betimes in the morning, and sware one to another: and Isaac sent them away, and they departed from him in peace. 32 And it came to pass the same day, that Isaac's servants came, and told him concerning the well which they had

digged, and said unto him, We have found water. 33 And he called it Shibah: therefore the name of the city is Beer-sheba unto this day.

Now came **Abimelech** with a friend, **Ahuzzath,** and his army commander, **Phicol** (the name is the same as the one in Abraham's day). Isaac wondered at their appearance after his recent, curt dismissal. But Abimelech declared that they were convinced that Jehovah was with him, and they preferred to be on friendly terms — perhaps thinking that some of the blessings might magically come their way! They ate together, a common way of expressing agreement, and swore not to hurt each other. Apparently, just after the Philistines departed, Isaac's servants came to tell him that the well which they had been digging was now complete. He named it **Shibah** which, like the term used by his father, could mean either "Seven" or "Oath." Thus Beersheba had a double reason for its name.

f. Esau's Wives (26:34-35)

34 And when Esau was forty years old he took to wife Judith the daughter of Beeri the Hittite, and Basemath the daughter of Elon the Hittite: 35 and they were a grief of mind unto Isaac and to Rebekah.

Esau had now reached maturity. But in marrying, he did not return to the homeland to find a wife and preserve the purity of the family line. Instead he married two Hittite girls, probably from the vicinity of Hebron. This brought grief to his parents and later played a key part in shaping the destiny of his brother Jacob.

5. Isaac's Prophecies (27:1-46)

a. The Blessing of Jacob (27:1-29)

1 And it came to pass, that when Isaac was old, and his eyes were dim, so that he could not see, he called Esau his elder son, and said unto him, My son: and he said unto him, Here am I. 2 And he said, Behold now, I am old, I know not the day of my death. 3 Now therefore take, I pray thee, thy weapons, thy quiver and thy bow, and go out to the field, and take me venison; 4 and make me savory food, such as I love, and

bring it to me, that I may eat; that my soul may bless thee before I die.

5 And Rebekah heard when Isaac spake to Esau his son. And Esau went to the field to hunt for venison, and to bring it. 6 And Rebekah spake unto Jacob her son, saying, Behold, I heard thy father speak unto Esau thy brother, saying, 7 Bring me venison, and make me savory food, that I may eat, and bless thee before Jehovah before my death. 8 Now therefore, my son, obey my voice according to that which I command thee. 9 Go now to the flock, and fetch me from thence two good kids of the goats; and I will make them savory food for thy father, such as he loveth: 10 and thou shalt bring it to thy father, that he may eat, so that he may bless thee before his death. 11 And Jacob said to Rebekah his mother, Behold, Esau my brother is a hairy man, and I am a smooth man. 12 My father peradventure will feel me, and I shall seem to him as a deceiver; and I shall bring a curse upon me, and not a blessing. 13 And his mother said unto him, Upon me be thy curse, my son; only obey my voice, and go fetch me them. 14 And he went, and fetched, and brought them to his mother: and his mother made savory food, such as his father loved. 15 And Rebekah took the goodly garments of Esau her elder son, which were with her in the house, and put them upon Jacob her younger son; 16 and she put the skins of the kids of the goats upon his hands, and upon the smooth of his neck: 17 and she gave the savory food and the bread, which she had prepared, into the hand of her son Jacob.

18 And he came unto his father, and said, My father: and he said, Here am I; who art thou, my son? 19 And Jacob said unto his father, I am Esau thy first-born; I have done according as thou badest me: arise, I pray thee, sit and eat of my venison, that thy soul may bless me. 20 And Isaac said unto his son, How is it that thou hast found it so quickly, my son? And he said, Because Jehovah thy God sent me good speed. 21 And Isaac said unto Jacob, Come near, I pray thee, that I may feel thee, my son, whether thou be my very son Esau or not. 22 And Jacob went near unto Isaac his father; and he felt him, and said, The voice is Jacob's voice, but the hands are the hands of Esau. 23 And he discerned him not, because his hands were hairy, as his brother Esau's hands: so he blessed him. 24 And he said, Art thou my very son Esau? And he said,

I am. 25 And he said, Bring it near to me, and I will eat of my son's venison, that my soul may bless thee. And he brought it near to him, and he did eat: and he brought him wine, and he drank. 26 And his father Isaac said unto him, Come near now, and kiss me, my son. 27 And he came near, and kissed him: and he smelled the smell of his raiment, and blessed him, and said,

See, the smell of my son
Is as the smell of a field which Jehovah hath blessed:
28 And God give thee of the dew of heaven,
And of the fatness of the earth,
And plenty of grain and new wine:
29 Let peoples serve thee,
And nations bow down to thee:
Be lord over thy brethren,
And let thy mother's sons bow down to thee:
Cursed be every one that curseth thee,
And blessed be every one that blesseth thee.

This chapter brings us to a third and quite decisive incident in which Jacob is marked as the one through whom the promises of God would be worked out. In an earlier encounter, Jacob purchased from Esau the *birthright*. In this event, the matter at stake is the paternal *blessing*. There was some overlapping of the two, and yet some differences. It has already been indicated that the birthright customarily belonged to the oldest son, giving to him a double portion in inheriting his father's goods, and making him also the head of the family. It was also pointed out that the birthright could be sold by one son to another. However, it was also possible for the father to designate which son should receive the birthright, transferring it from the eldest to one of the younger ones.[85] This was frequently done by the father in an oral blessing, which sometimes occurred on his deathbed, but which always had full legal validity just as a written will in our own day.[86] The paternal blessing in biblical times had also a prophetic function, predicting the futures of the children. The present writer has not been able to discover anything written upon the ancient laws which governed the patriarchs which would indicate which took precedence: the barter

[85] Speiser, *op. cit.*, pp. 194-95.　　[86] Free, *op. cit.*, p. 70.

agreement between the brothers, or the oral blessing of the father. It is not stated that Rebekah related to Isaac what God had told her before the birth of the twins. If she had done so, Isaac did not take it as binding upon himself. And it is doubtful whether either of the sons, each for his own reason, had told Isaac about their transaction. It is possible that he still could have overruled their agreement. It is certain that he could not have blessed Esau in the terms with which he unintentionally blessed Jacob without contradicting the earlier transaction. In any event, when Isaac announced that the time had come for the oral blessing, Esau saw in it an opportunity to undo what he had earlier done and which he evidently now regretted, and Rebekah saw in it an opportunity to obtain for Jacob once for all that which God had promised for him and which she probably knew he had purchased. Thus both brothers were involved in trickery on this occasion, each with motives and methods which were completely out of place in relation to the holy promise of God.

The scene is set when Isaac was old, his eyes dim, and the thought of approaching death kept nagging him. From a comparison of various passages (47:9; 45:6; 41:46, 53-54; 31:41; 30:25; 25:26), Isaac must have been approximately 137 years old at this time. Ishmael had already been dead fourteen years, having died at 137. This probably intensified Isaac's concern about the approaching end. He wanted to confirm his eldest and favorite son's birthright. So he instructed Esau to go out and get some game and prepare a tasty meal as the proper setting for the blessing. Rebekah overheard the conversation and proposed to Jacob that he slay two young goats and she would attempt to prepare them in such a way that Isaac would take them for venison. Jacob demurred, pointing out that Esau was hairy and he was smooth. He feared lest instead of a blessing he receive a curse. But Rebekah was up to this too, dressing him in Esau's clothes and covering his hands and forearms with hairy goatskins. When Jacob entered his father's quarters, Isaac questioned him on four counts: who he was, how he got the meat so quickly, why his voice sounded like Ja-

cob's instead of Esau's, and then a final, pointed question, if he were really Esau. Jacob replied with repeated deceptions: claiming to be Esau, claiming to have obeyed his father's instructions to bring game, blasphemously crediting Jehovah with his quick success, using the goatskins to satisfy his father's searching fingers, and insisting on the closest questioning that he was indeed his very son Esau. Isaac was finally satisfied and ate the meat. Then he blessed Jacob, giving him abundance of material things, dominion over other peoples and nations, the headship over the family, and passed on part of the covenant promise — that the one who blessed him would be blessed and the one who cursed him would be cursed.

b. The Blessing of Esau (27:30-40)

30 And it came to pass, as soon as Isaac had made an end of blessing Jacob, and Jacob was yet scarce gone out from the presence of Isaac his father, that Esau his brother came in from his hunting. 31 And he also made savory food, and brought it unto his father; and he said unto his father, Let my father arise, and eat of his son's venison, that thy soul may bless me. 32 And Isaac his father said unto him, Who art thou? And he said, I am thy son, thy first-born, Esau. 33 And Isaac trembled very exceedingly, and said, Who then is he that hath taken venison, and brought it me, and I have eaten of all before thou camest, and have blessed him? yea, *and* he shall be blessed. 34 When Esau heard the words of his father, he cried with an exceeding great and bitter cry, and said unto his father, Bless me, even me also, O my father. 35 And he said, Thy brother came with guile, and hath taken away thy blessing. 36 And he said, Is not he rightly named Jacob? for he hath supplanted me these two times: he took away my birthright; and, behold, now he hath taken away my blessing. And he said, Hast thou not reserved a blessing for me? 37 And Isaac answered and said unto Esau, Behold, I have made him thy lord, and all his brethren have I given to him for servants; and with grain and new wine have I sustained him: and what then shall I do for thee, my son? 38 And Esau said unto his father, Hast thou but one blessing, my father? bless me, even me also,

O my father. And Esau lifted up his voice, and wept. 39 And Isaac his father answered and said unto him,

Behold, of the fatness of the earth shall be thy dwelling,
And of the dew of heaven from above;
40 And by thy sword shalt thou live, and thou shalt serve thy brother;
And it shall come to pass, when thou shalt break loose,
That thou shalt shake his yoke from off thy neck.

Jacob barely escaped from his father's presence before Esau returned from the chase. Esau hastened his preparation of the game and took it to his father. Isaac again questioned concerning the visitor's identity. And when the familiar voice of Esau revealed to Isaac that it was indeed his eldest son, Isaac trembled exceedingly and asked who his earlier visitor had been, whom he had blessed, and concerning whom he now declared, **yea, and he shall be blessed.** Isaac had apparently been meditating upon the events which had just transpired and perhaps had felt a sense of divine approval even before he knew really what had happened. Or perhaps in the flash of understanding what had happened, he also was intuitively assured that God had overruled his own intention and accomplished that which He had purposed all along. Esau was overwhelmed with disappointment, but he found no way of changing what he had earlier done nor of persuading his father to change his blessing "though he sought it diligently with tears" (Heb. 12:17). It is worthy of note that it seems Esau was more concerned about his father's blessing than he was with the birthright. The blessing, however, was contingent upon the birthright and the latter was necessary to the former. Likewise, many since Esau have vainly sought God's blessings in the absence of a spiritual birthright. He asked if something had not been reserved which could be given to him. Isaac replied that he had given everything to Jacob. But as Esau wept, Isaac sought to console him with what was scarcely a blessing yet not a curse: giving him of the riches of the earth, a life lived by the sword, and the promise of temporary respite from the control of his brother (cf. II Kings 8:20-22).

c. The Burden of Rebekah (27:41-46)

41 And Esau hated Jacob because of the blessing wherewith his father blessed him: and Esau said in his heart, The days of mourning for my father are at hand; then will I slay my brother Jacob. 42 And the words of Esau her elder son were told to Rebekah; and she sent and called Jacob her younger son, and said unto him, Behold, thy brother Esau, as touching thee, doth comfort himself, *purposing* to kill thee. 43 Now therefore, my son, obey my voice; and arise, flee thou to Laban my brother to Haran; 44 and tarry with him a few days, until thy brother's fury turn away; 45 until thy brother's anger turn away from thee, and he forget that which thou hast done to him: then I will send, and fetch thee from thence: why should I be bereaved of you both in one day?

46 And Rebekah said to Isaac, I am weary of my life because of the daughters of Heth: if Jacob take a wife of the daughters of Heth, such as these, of the daughters of the land, what good shall my life do me?

Even in his father's presence, Esau had charged that his brother was rightly named, for twice he had "supplanted" him, taking both his birthright and his blessing. Esau of course failed to confess his own indifference to the birthright which made Jacob's success possible, and his own deceit in attempting to circumvent that earlier arrangement through the blessing. But in private his wrath knew no bounds. His true character was now revealed. He would kill Jacob just as soon as Isaac died. The news of his intention somehow reached Rebekah, who shared it now with Jacob. Quickly she decided what must be done. She complained to Isaac about Esau's Hittite wives, a sore point with Isaac also, and said that if Jacob should take such a wife her own life would not be worth living. Rebekah's resourcefulness is amazing. She certainly knew how to manage her husband without his knowing that he was being managed!

C. THE STORY OF JACOB (28:1–36:43)

1. Jacob's Flight (28:1–29:14)

a. A High Mission (28:1-9)

1 And Isaac called Jacob, and blessed him, and charged him, and said unto him, Thou shalt not take a wife of the daughters of Canaan. 2 Arise, go to Paddan-aram, to the house of Bethuel thy mother's father; and take thee a wife from thence of the daughters of Laban thy mother's brother. 3 And God Almighty bless thee, and make thee fruitful, and multiply thee, that thou mayest be a company of peoples; 4 and give thee the blessing of Abraham, to thee, and to thy seed with thee; that thou mayest inherit the land of thy sojournings, which God gave unto Abraham. 5 And Isaac sent away Jacob: and he went to Paddan-aram unto Laban, son of Bethuel the Syrian, the brother of Rebekah, Jacob's and Esau's mother.

6 Now Esau saw that Isaac had blessed Jacob and sent him away to Paddan-aram, to take him a wife from thence; and that as he blessed him he gave him a charge, saying, Thou shalt not take a wife of the daughters of Canaan; 7 and that Jacob obeyed his father and his mother, and was gone to Paddan-aram: 8 and Esau saw that the daughters of Canaan pleased not Isaac his father; 9 and Esau went unto Ishmael, and took, besides the wives that he had, Mahalath the daughter of Ishmael Abraham's son, the sister of Nebaioth, to be his wife.

Apparently Rebekah did not have to make any concrete suggestions to Isaac. She had already told Jacob what he needed to do (27:43-45), arranging to bring him back when it was safe. But she knew the working of her husband's mind as well. For just at the mention of Jacob's need of a wife, Isaac called him in and made the same suggestion that Rebekah had made, but for a different reason. He suggested that Jacob return to the home country to take a wife of their own family. And he blessed Jacob again, fully committing to him this time the family heritage, **the blessing of Abraham,** including the right to inherit Canaan. No doubt Rebekah had shared with Isaac now what God had told her before the birth of the two boys. The whole story was probably known now about the trading of the birthright. Esau

had already married outside the family, and Isaac was now convinced that Jacob was God's chosen representative. So Jacob was sent to the home of Laban, Rebekah's brother.

A brief note appears at this point in the narrative to the effect that when Esau learned of Jacob's journey and mission, he sought to compensate for his earlier error by marrying a daughter of Ishmael. It of course got him nowhere in repairing the past. And what a poor foundation for a marriage — the frustrated hatred of the husband towards his brother!

b. A Heavenly Vision — First Promise (28:10-22)

10 And Jacob went out from Beersheba, and went toward Haran. 11 And he lighted upon a certain place, and tarried there all night, because the sun was set; and he took one of the stones of the place, and put it under his head, and lay down in that place to sleep. 12 And he dreamed; and, behold, a ladder set up on the earth, and the top of it reached to heaven; and, behold, the angels of God ascending and descending on it. 13 And, behold, Jehovah stood above it, and said, I am Jehovah, the God of Abraham thy father, and the God of Isaac: the land whereon thou liest, to thee will I give it, and to thy seed; 14 and thy seed shall be as the dust of the earth, and thou shalt spread abroad to the west, and to the east, and to the north, and to the south: and in thee and in thy seed shall all the families of the earth be blessed. 15 And, behold, I am with thee, and will keep thee whithersoever thou goest, and will bring thee again into this land; for I will not leave thee, until I have done that which I have spoken to thee of. 16 And Jacob awakened out of his sleep, and he said, Surely Jehovah is in this place; and I knew it not. 17 And he was afraid, and said, How dreadful is this place! this is none other than the house of God, and this is the gate of heaven.

18 And Jacob rose up early in the morning, and took the stone that he had put under his head, and set it up for a pillar, and poured oil upon the top of it. 19 And he called the name of that place Beth-el: but the name of the city was Luz at the first. 20 And Jacob vowed a vow, saying, If God will be with me, and will keep me in this way that I go, and will give me bread to eat, and

raiment to put on, 21 so that I come again to my father's house in peace, and Jehovah will be my God, 22 then this stone, which I have set up for a pillar, shall be God's house: and of all that thou shalt give me I will surely give the tenth unto thee.

From Beersheba to Luz was approximately a three-day's journey. Apparently Rebekah managed the actual departure of Jacob, for it seems to have been done in haste. Otherwise it would have been strange for the chosen son of a wealthy family to have embarked on such a journey with no accompanying servants. The picture is one of complete aloneness. No doubt Jacob had ample opportunity to think during those three days. He found himself hated by his brother and exiled from his parents and all that was familiar to him. He was faced with all the dangers and uncertainties of a long journey in a lawless age among people who were more likely to be hostile than friendly. No doubt he began to wonder about the "success" of his scheming and the "wisdom" of his unbridled ambition. He probably shared more seriously Esau's earlier question about the present value of the birthright and the blessing. It seems certain that by the time Jacob reached Luz he was completely disillusioned with himself and his future. He was indeed at the end of himself.

On the evening described in the Scriptures, Jacob reached the vicinity of the ancient city of Luz. It is impossible to say whether the city had actually been established as yet. But if so, either Jacob did not quite reach it before the gates closed or he chose to take his chances in the open rather than among strangers. The area was extremely rocky and, strange as it seems in a day of foam-rubber pillows, Jacob simply followed a common custom of travelers in his day by propping his head on a stone.

It is not surprising that Jacob dreamed that night. No doubt his conscience was aroused. No doubt he was frightened by the uncertainties which faced him. The area in which he slept was surrounded by piles of ledgelike rocks which some have thought suggested to the physical eye the form of giant stairways going up into the sky.[87] To what extent God used such natural means to reveal himself to Jacob we cannot be sure. But it is quite evident that this dream was far more than just another dream.

In his dream, Jacob saw a ladder reaching from earth to heaven, with the angels of God ascending and descending on it. Above it stood Jehovah, who identified himself as the God of Abraham and Isaac. The Lord spoke to Jacob, imparting to him the full promise earlier given to the other two patriarchs, thus confirming Isaac's blessings of Jacob. When Jacob awoke, he was first surprised, then frightened. His surprise was due to his personal ignorance of Jehovah. No doubt he had heard from Isaac the story of the earlier revelations. But Jacob's life up to this point demonstrated no personal acquaintance with the God of purity who commanded Abraham to walk before Him and be perfect. Besides, the heathen nations around Jacob thought of their gods as local deities, exercising their authority only over a city or village or small country. It is quite possible that Jacob thought in the same terms about Isaac's God. He thought Jehovah had been left at Beersheba. His dream convinced him otherwise. Jacob's fear was the natural fear that a sinful man always feels in the presence of a holy God.

Jacob declared this place to be the house (Beth) of God (el). This name later replaced that of Luz. He also took his stone pillow, set it up as a pillar, and poured oil upon it. Such a setting up of stones to mark a place of worship, and the pouring of oil upon them as an act of worship is a custom known to have been used by many ancient peoples. Jacob may well have seen his heathen neighbors engaging in such practices, or even bowing down to such stones as rude idols. But this was no idol worship. for him. There was something so sacred about this spot that he must commemorate what had taken place.

Jacob was overwhelmed at the historic blessing and personal assurance God had given him. He had been promised multiplied descendants — a promise given to Abraham when he was childless and now given to Jacob when he was not even married, and when his present circum-

[87] Cuthbert A. Simpson, The Interpreter's Bible, I, 689.

stances threatened an end to his future. He had also been promised he would be a means of blessing for all nations. All he had schemed to get, God now tells him is to be his by divine appointment. But with it would come a tremendous responsibility. For he was not to receive this fabulous spiritual heritage simply for self-satisfaction, but for the service of mankind. And God told him that He would be his constant companion from this moment on, never leaving him until He had accomplished that which He had promised. Jacob had been aware of his wrongdoing; now he found his life in the hands of a holy God who designed to make of him a servant suitable for His service. He had been conscious of his loneliness; now he was assured of a divine Guide who would see him safely through his journey and return him to the promised land.

When God had made His covenant with Abraham and Isaac, He had stipulated the conditions. As far as the Scriptures reveal, they said nothing. But different personalities call for different types of religious experiences. Jacob had not been a religious man, but rather a deep-dyed sinner. He felt that he must express himself, that God's promises must call from him some response. He began by repeating some of the provisions of the divine promise, but in a much smaller degree than God had given them. He has been accused of trying to bargain with God here as he had been accustomed to doing with others. But he is rather saying that the Lord need not do nearly all He has promised, but that if He will provide companionship, a safe journey, food and raiment (the bare necessities of life), and a safe return to Canaan, then he would indeed serve the Lord, and Bethel would be his place of worship, and he would give the tenth of all God gave him back to Him again. While Jacob had always been first in trying to get material possessions, when God spoke to him he was among the first to use what he owned in the worship of God. His vow, along with Abraham's tithe to Melchizedek (14:20), serves to indicate that the principle of the tithe as a part of man's duty in the service of God is as old as man's worship of God. And while one hesitates to press New

Testament terminology on Old Testament experiences, it would indicate that Jacob had indeed been born anew in this encounter with God.

c. A Hearty Reception (29:1-14)

1 Then Jacob went on his journey, and came to the land of the children of the east. 2 And he looked, and, behold, a well in the field, and, lo, three flocks of sheep lying there by it; for out of that well they watered the flocks: and the stone upon the well's mouth was great. 3 And thither were all the flocks gathered: and they rolled the stone from the well's mouth, and watered the sheep, and put the stone again upon the well's mouth in its place. 4 And Jacob said unto them, My brethren, whence are ye? And they said, Of Haran are we. 5 And he said unto them, Know ye Laban the son of Nahor? And they said, We know him. 6 And he said unto them, Is it well with him? And they said, It is well: and, behold, Rachel his daughter cometh with the sheep. 7 And he said, Lo, it is yet high day, neither is it time that the cattle should be gathered together; water ye the sheep, and go and feed them. 8 And they said, We cannot, until all the flocks be gathered together, and they roll the stone from the well's mouth; then we water the sheep. 9 While he was yet speaking with them, Rachel came with her father's sheep; for she kept them. 10 And it came to pass, when Jacob saw Rachel the daughter of Laban his mother's brother, and the sheep of Laban his mother's brother, that Jacob went near, and rolled the stone from the well's mouth, and watered the flock of Laban his mother's brother. 11 And Jacob kissed Rachel, and lifted up his voice, and wept. 12 And Jacob told Rachel that he was her father's brother, and that he was Rebekah's son: and she ran and told her father.

13 And it came to pass, when Laban heard the tidings of Jacob his sister's son, that he ran to meet him, and embraced him, and kissed him, and brought him to his house. And he told Laban all these things. 14 And Laban said to him, Surely thou art my bone and my flesh. And he abode with him the space of a month.

Jacob's journey was apparently uneventful after his experience at Bethel. Arriving in the vicinity of his destination, he found a well in the open countryside, with three flocks of sheep lying nearby. The well was covered, as was customary, by a huge rock. The rock was placed upon the well only partially to keep dirt out of the water; it was placed there primarily to discourage any individual from stealing the precious water without the knowledge of the group which shared in its use. It apparently was large enough to require two or more ordinary individuals to move it, and the Scripture implies that by common agreement the shepherds daily waited until all had gathered before proceeding with the watering. Jacob, himself an experienced and effective shepherd, could not understand the waste of time away from the pastures while the shepherds waited for one another.

Jacob inquired of the shepherds with the three flocks where they lived. On learning they were from Haran, he inquired further concerning their acquaintance with his uncle, Laban, and concerning his welfare. To his delight, they assured him that Laban was well and that his daughter was approaching with her sheep. When Rachel arrived, Jacob, who was apparently an unusually strong person, and for whom the joy and excitement of the moment no doubt gave added energy, disregarded the local custom and rolled away the stone from the well. He watered Laban's sheep, and kissed Rachel. While it was rather unusual, according to the custom of the country, for cousins to express affection in public in this manner, especially when Rachel did not yet know who Jacob was, women of the Orient were not yet under the severe restrictions of a later day. And Jacob was apparently overcome by the joy and relief at having safely completed his journey. Some have also suggested that he experienced love at first sight when he met Rachel![88]

After kissing Rachel, Jacob wept. This was probably also an expression of joy and relief, perhaps also a release of the pent-up feelings of remorse and loneliness over the real cause of his flight. While such a demonstration of emotion among Western peoples might be less likely, the Orientals of Jacob's day were not restricted by any artificial standards. No doubt Rachel was startled; but he told her who he was, and she ran to tell

her father. Laban also hurried to welcome him. When Jacob had told enough about his home and family, and his journey, no doubt having to tell at least part of the real reason for his unattended flight, Laban was convinced of the truth of their relationship. Jacob then tarried for a month as a guest in Laban's home.

2. Jacob's Family (29:15—32:2)

a. A Deceitful Foundation (29:15-30)

15 And Laban said unto Jacob, Because thou art my brother, shouldest thou therefore serve me for nought? tell me, what shall thy wages be? 16 And Laban had two daughters: the name of the elder was Leah, and the name of the younger was Rachel. 17 And Leah's eyes were tender; but Rachel was beautiful and well-favored. 18 And Jacob loved Rachel; and he said, I will serve thee seven years for Rachel thy younger daughter. 19 And Laban said, It is better that I give her to thee, than that I should give her to another man: abide with me. 20 And Jacob served seven years for Rachel; and they seemed unto him but a few days, for the love he had to her.

21 And Jacob said unto Laban, Give me my wife, for my days are fulfilled, that I may go in unto her. 22 And Laban gathered together all the men of the place, and made a feast. 23 And it came to pass in the evening, that he took Leah his daughter, and brought her to him; and he went in unto her. 24 And Laban gave Zilpah his handmaid unto his daughter Leah for a handmaid. 25 And it came to pass in the morning that, behold, it was Leah: and he said to Laban, What is this thou hast done unto me? did not I serve with thee for Rachel? wherefore then hast thou beguiled me? 26 And Laban said, It is not so done in our place, to give the younger before the first-born. 27 Fulfil the week of this one, and we will give thee the other also for the service which thou shalt serve with me yet seven other years. 28 And Jacob did so, and fulfilled her week: and he gave him Rachel his daughter to wife. 29 And Laban gave to Rachel his daughter Bilhah his handmaid to be her handmaid. 30 And he went in also unto Rachel, and he loved also Rachel more than Leah, and served with him yet seven other years.

[88] Leupold, op. cit., pp. 788-89.

As was noted in connection with Abraham's servant's visit to this area to secure a wife for Isaac, Laban was a greedy man (24:29-31). So after Jacob had tarried in his home for a month, Laban decided it was time to put his visitor to work. It is probable that the industrious Jacob had already voluntarily done some labor, and perhaps had revealed by his words and actions his wisdom and skill in the care of animals. So now Laban suggested, **Because thou art my brother, shouldest thou therefore serve me for nought? tell me, what shall thy wages be?** Jacob had come here ostensibly to get a wife. And he apparently did feel an interest in Rachel from the start. She **was beautiful and well-favored,** or to put it in our present-day terms, "she was beautiful both in face and form." Her eldest sister Leah had **tender** eyes, an expression which some have taken to mean that her eyes distracted from whatever other beauty she might have had, and yet others have taken it to mean that her eyes were the only attractive thing about her. But Jacob was in an awkward position. A dowry was expected for the bride. And Jacob had come away from home without wealth sufficient for such a gift. So he proposed to work out the dowry. To have met the formal requirements of the situation, a year's labor would have been sufficient.[89] But it is probable that Laban had already observed Jacob's affection for Rachel, had surmised the basic nature of Jacob's proposal, and felt that if he let Jacob set the terms they might be very generous indeed. And they were, for Jacob proposed to work seven years for Rachel. Laban immediately accepted, this being far more than he could have expected.

A beautiful picture of the strength of human love is given when the author tells us that the seven years seemed like only a few days to Jacob because of the love he had for Rachel. At the end of the seven years, Laban apparently took no initiative in fulfilling his part of the contract. So Jacob demanded payment. Laban threw the customary bridal feast, inviting all of his neighbors. The bride was veiled from the beginning of the feast until after the consummation of the marriage. Laban took advantage of this

to trick Jacob in one of the basest ways possible. He put Leah under the veil instead of Rachel! By some means or other, apparently with Leah's full cognizance and cooperation, the deception was successful and Jacob did not discover the truth until the morning after his first night with his bride. Truly Jacob was finding out what it was like to be "supplanted," and he must have been reminded of his earlier deception of Isaac and Esau. But he was justly angry. He had served Laban faithfully, and he demanded to know why he had been so treated. Laban rather weakly explained that it was the custom to marry off the elder daughter first in that place. If such had been the case, Jacob would have heard of it before this. The real explanation was that Laban was afraid no one would ever ask for Leah, so he palmed her off on Jacob. But now Laban proposed a remedy for the situation. If Jacob would only finish out the bridal week with Leah (a seven-day period in which the newlyweds ruled as king and queen over the festivities[90]), he would give him Rachel and trust him for another seven years' labor as payment! Jacob was in an awkward position. He would become the laughingstock of the community if his situation became public knowledge, and no doubt he would be forced to return home with nothing to show for his seven years of labor if he refused. So he accepted the exorbitant terms Laban proposed, and at the end of seven days the second marriage was consummated.

In connection with the marriages, the author adds brief notices that Laban gave Leah a slave-girl by the name of Zilpah and Rachel one by the name of Bilhah. Such was the custom among families on Laban's social level. The girl was given not only to serve her mistress but to become her substitute in the bearing of children if she proved to be barren (as Hagar had been for Sarah, and these girls later became for Rachel and Leah). Among the archaeological discoveries in Mesopotamia has been found an ancient marriage contract which gave notice of the accompanying slave-girl in words almost exactly paralleling these verses in Genesis.[91]

[89] Ibid., p. 792.   [90] Ibid., p. 798.   [91] Speiser, op. cit., pp. 226-27.

b. An Abnormal Situation (29:31—30:24)

31 And Jehovah saw that Leah was hated, and he opened her womb: but Rachel was barren. 32 And Leah conceived, and bare a son, and she called his name Reuben: for she said, Because Jehovah hath looked upon my affliction; for now my husband will love me. 33 And she conceived again, and bare a son: and said, Because Jehovah hath heard that I am hated, he hath therefore given me this *son* also: and she called his name Simeon. 34 And she conceived again, and bare a son; and said, Now this time will my husband be joined unto me, because I have borne him three sons: therefore was his name called Levi. 35 And she conceived again, and bare a son: and she said, This time will I praise Jehovah: therefore she called his name Judah; and she left off bearing.

1 And when Rachel saw that she bare Jacob no children, Rachel envied her sister; and she said unto Jacob, Give me children, or else I die. 2 And Jacob's anger was kindled against Rachel: and he said, Am I in God's stead, who hath withheld from thee the fruit of the womb? 3 And she said, Behold, my maid Bilhah, go in unto her; that she may bear upon my knees, and I also may obtain children by her. 4 And she gave him Bilhah her handmaid to wife: and Jacob went in unto her. 5 And Bilhah conceived, and bare Jacob a son. 6 And Rachel said, God hath judged me, and hath also heard my voice, and hath given me a son: therefore called she his name Dan. 7 And Bilhah Rachel's handmaid conceived again, and bare Jacob a second son. 8 And Rachel said, With mighty wrestlings have I wrestled with my sister, and have prevailed: and she called his name Naphtali.

9 When Leah saw that she had left off bearing, she took Zilpah her handmaid, and gave her to Jacob to wife. 10 And Zilpah Leah's handmaid bare Jacob a son. 11 And Leah said, Fortunate! and she called his name Gad. 12 And Zilpah Leah's handmaid bare Jacob a second son. 13 And Leah said, Happy am I! for the daughters will call me happy: and she called his name Asher.

14 And Reuben went in the days of wheat harvest, and found mandrakes in the field, and brought them unto his mother Leah. Then Rachel said to Leah, Give me, I pray thee, of thy son's mandrakes. 15 And she said unto her, Is it a small matter that thou hast taken away my husband? and wouldest thou take away my son's mandrakes also? And Rachel said, Therefore shall he lie with thee to-night for thy son's mandrakes. 16 And Jacob came from the field in the evening, and Leah went out to meet him, and said, Thou must come in unto me; for I have surely hired thee with my son's mandrakes. And he lay with her that night. 17 And God hearkened unto Leah, and she conceived, and bare Jacob a fifth son. 18 And Leah said, God hath given me my hire, because I gave my handmaid to my husband: and she called his name Issachar. 19 And Leah conceived again, and bare a sixth son to Jacob. 20 And Leah said, God hath endowed me with a good dowry; now will my husband dwell with me, because I have borne him six sons: and she called his name Zebulun. 21 And afterwards she bare a daughter, and called her name Dinah. 22 And God remembered Rachel, and God hearkened to her, and opened her womb. 23 And she conceived, and bare a son: and said, God hath taken away my reproach: 24 and she called his name Joseph, saying, Jehovah add to me another son.

Laban's treachery had saddled Jacob with a situation he had not wanted, and which created almost endless problems for him. While multiple wives were accepted in his day, God had not so planned the human family from the beginning, and the transgression of the divine will in this area can do nothing but cause strife and dissension, destroying family unity and discipline among the children.

Jacob naturally loved Rachel more than Leah. He had been attracted to her from the first. It was for her he had labored. Leah was not only not as attractive, she had joined her father in deceiving him. But Jacob permitted his preference to be shown to an unwise degree. As a result, the Lord took pity on the hurt and lonely Leah and gave her a son. From this point on, the bearing of children became a contest between the two wives and their eventually involved slave-girls.

First, Leah gave birth to four sons, one after the other. The first was named **Reuben,** meaning, "See, a son!" probably from Leah's first joyous exclamation after his birth. There is also a play on words in the expression "he looked" and "he will love me" in her hopeful declaration, **Because Jehovah hath looked upon my affliction; for now my husband will love** me. The second son she named **Simeon,** "Hearing," because Jehovah had **heard** of her plight. The third son she called **Levi,** "Attachment," since on learning she had conceived again, she had expressed hope that now her husband would be **joined** or attached to her because of the three sons she had borne him — the highest service a wife could give her husband in that day was the bearing of sons. The fourth son she called **Judah,** "Praised," for she reacted to his birth with a declaration that she would **praise** Jehovah.

Meanwhile, Rachel saw to her dismay that she was barren. Foolishly, she demanded children of Jacob. He angrily reminded her that he was not God. So she gave him her slave-girl, Bilhah. To Bilhah were born two sons: **Dan,** "Vindication," for Rachel felt that God had **judged** her and now, vindicated, she had been given a son through Bilhah; and **Naphtali,** "Wrestling," for "with wrestlings of God" (rather than merely **mighty wrestlings**) or by means of prayer she had wrestled with her sister and now had prevailed. It is doubtful whether Bilhah's two sons were born after Leah's fourth, for eleven of Jacob's sons were born in the second period of seven years he served for Rachel. If each group had to wait on the other to be completed, there would not have been time for all eleven. It is probable that Rachel gave Bilhah to Jacob after the birth of Leah's first or second son.

Meanwhile, Leah had ceased to bear. So she took her cue from Rachel and gave Zilpah to Jacob. Two sons were then born: **Gad,** "Fortune," for at his birth Leah exclaimed, **Fortunate!** or "Fortune is come!"; and **Asher,** "Happy," for Leah had said, **Happy am I! for the daughters** (or "the girls"[92]) **will call me happy.**

By this time Reuben was about four years old, and he toddled after the reapers into the wheat fields. There his eye was attracted to the yellow berries of the mandrake, about the size of a nutmeg. The Hebrew word for them meant "love-apple," and they were widely considered as a stimulant of sexual desire and acttivity as well as a promoter of fertility.[93] Reuben innocently carried some home to his mother, Leah. Rachel saw them and

asked for some. Leah's pent-up anger exploded, charging Rachel first with stealing her husband, and second, with taking her mandrakes. Then the evil consequences of polygamy were fully revealed as the two wives bargained with each other who would get the husband for the night! Rachel got some mandrakes and Leah greeted Jacob that night with the sarcastic statement that she had **hired** him for the night. She conceived and bore a fifth son, calling him **Issachar,** "There is hire" or "reward," playing both on the fact that Leah claimed God had given her her **hire** or reward for giving Zilpah to Jacob, and also on the earlier hiring of her husband. Then came her sixth son, named **Zebulun,** meaning both "Dowry" and "Dwelling," believing now that God had given her a good **dowry** and that her husband would **dwell** with her. Later, but not much later, she gave birth to a daughter, **Dinah.** Her name is mentioned because of her involvement in one of the family's later adventures (chap. 34), but Jacob had other daughters whose births and names are not mentioned (37:35; 46:7, 15b).

Finally, the Lord answered Rachel's prayers, and she bore Jacob's eleventh son. She named him **Joseph,** "May he add," asking that Jehovah might **add** yet another son.

c. An Unreliable Compensation (30: 25-43)

25 And it came to pass, when Rachel had borne Joseph, that Jacob said unto Laban, Send me away, that I may go unto mine own place, and to my country. 26 Give me my wives and my children for whom I have served thee, and let me go: for thou knowest my service wherewith I have served thee. 27 And Laban said unto him, If now I have found favor in thine eyes, *tarry: for* I have divined that Jehovah hath blessed me for thy sake. 28 And he said, Appoint me thy wages, and I will give it. 29 And he said unto him, Thou knowest how I have served thee, and how thy cattle have fared with me. 30 For it was little which thou hadst before I came, and it hath increased unto a multitude; and Jehovah hath blessed thee whithersoever I turned: and now when shall I provide for mine own house also? 31 And he said, What

[92] *Ibid.,* p. 231.   [93] Leupold, *op. cit.,* pp. 811-12.

shall I give thee? And Jacob said, Thou shalt not give me aught: if thou wilt do this thing for me, I will again feed thy flock and keep it. 32 I will pass through all thy flock to-day, removing from thence every speckled and spotted one, and every black one among the sheep, and the spotted and speckled among the goats: and of such shall be my hire. 33 So shall my righteousness answer for me hereafter, when thou shalt come concerning my hire that is before thee: every one that is not speckled and spotted among the goats, and black among the sheep, that, if found with me, shall be counted stolen. 34 And Laban said, Behold, I would it might be according to thy word. 35 And he removed that day the he-goats that were ringstreaked and spotted, and all the she-goats that were speckled and spotted, every one that had white in it, and all the black ones among the sheep, and gave them into the hand of his sons; 36 and he set three days' journey betwixt himself and Jacob: and Jacob fed the rest of Laban's flocks.

37 And Jacob took him rods of fresh poplar, and of the almond and of the plane-tree; and peeled white streaks in them; and made the white appear which was in the rods. 38 And he set the rods which he had peeled over against the flocks in the gutters in the watering-troughs where the flocks came to drink; and they conceived when they came to drink. 39 And the flocks conceived before the rods, and the flocks brought forth ringstreaked, speckled, and spotted. 40 And Jacob separated the lambs, and set the faces of the flocks toward the ring-streaked and all the black in the flock of Laban: and he put his own droves apart, and put them not unto Laban's flock. 41 And it came to pass, whensoever the stronger of the flock did conceive, that Jacob laid the rods before the eyes of the flock in the gutters, that they might conceive among the rods; 42 but when the flock were feeble, he put them not in: so the feebler were Laban's, and the stronger Jacob's. 43 And the man increased exceedingly, and had large flocks, and maidservants and men-servants, and camels and asses.

The second period of seven years of service ended just after Joseph's birth. Jacob had acquired the wife he had come to seek and more — another wife, two concubines, eleven sons. So he asked permission from Laban to return home. He was somewhat in the position of a hired servant, with his family not entirely belonging to him until he had completed his fourteen years of labor. What he wanted now was recognition that full payment had been made. Furthermore, Laban had a certain degree of authority over him as the head of the local family. He wished now to escape all this and Laban's double-dealing and get back home.

But Laban had observed the profit Jacob's hard work had brought him, and claimed that by some superstitious means he had **divined** that Jehovah had blessed him for Jacob's sake. So he asked Jacob to stay, and offered to let him set his own wages. Jacob had built a large family, but he had no personal wealth. So he proposed now to build himself flocks and herds. In the Orient, sheep are normally white and goats black or brown-black. What Jacob suggested was that all abnormally colored sheep and goats would become his. If any normally colored ones were found among Jacob's flocks and herds, it could be counted by Laban as stolen and he could demand restitution. Laban gleefully thought Jacob was indeed a foolish bargainer and he jumped at the chance. It is not clear whether Jacob intended that the spotted, speckled, and black sheep, and the spotted and speckled goats which were already in Laban's herd should immediately become his, or whether he was asking only for such animals which should be born in the future. He did say that he wanted no gifts. Yet he did propose to divide the animals that day — either to take his initial wages or to make Laban's advantage even stronger by removing the animals most likely to reproduce the coloring Jacob was to receive. In any event, Laban did the dividing, turned the abnormally colored animals over to his sons, and removed them three-days' journey from Jacob. Laban could not be trusted and he did not trust Jacob even yet.

But Jacob had plans of his own. He prepared rods which were striped and spotted and placed them where the animals could see them during breeding season. He learned to differentiate between the stronger strains of stock and attempted to determine their coloring to suit his advantage and left the weaker strains for Laban. Jacob was attempting to win the day by prenatal marking, something in which the people of his day believed strongly although its possibility is emphatically denied by scientists today. But in any event, the Lord blessed Jacob's efforts and his stock increased tremendously and he began to build a strong staff of servants of his own. Laban apparently tried to outfox him repeatedly (31:41), but the Lord prospered Jacob in spite of Laban. There is a moral problem here. However just Jacob may have felt his cause to be, and however futile his methods might have been without divine aid, his motives and intentions were wrong. The only way we can explain the Lord's blessing is to remember the common state of moral ignorance in that day, and to understand that the Lord blessed in accordance with His eternal purpose through Jacob, and in condemnation of Laban's more dishonest and provocative behavior.

d. A Painful Separation (31:1–32:2)

1 And he heard the words of Laban's sons, saying, Jacob hath taken away all that was our father's; and of that which was our father's hath he gotten all this glory. 2 And Jacob beheld the countenance of Laban, and, behold, it was not toward him as beforetime. 3 And Jehovah said unto Jacob, Return unto the land of thy fathers, and to thy kindred; and I will be with thee. 4 And Jacob sent and called Rachel and Leah to the field unto his flock, 5 and said unto them, I see your father's countenance, that it is not toward me as beforetime; but the God of my father hath been with me. 6 And ye know that with all my power I have served your father. 7 And your father hath deceived me, and changed my wages ten times; but God suffered him not to hurt me. 8 If he said thus, The speckled shall be thy wages; then all the flock bare speckled: and if he said thus, The ringstreaked shall be thy wages; then bare all the flock ringstreaked. 9 Thus God hath taken away the cattle of your father, and given them to me. 10 And it came to pass at the time that the flock conceive, that I lifted up mine eyes, and saw in a dream, and, behold, the he-goats which leaped upon the flock were ringstreaked, speckled, and grizzled. 11 And the angel of God said unto me in the dream, Jacob: and I said, Here am I. 12 And he said, Lift up now thine eyes, and see: all the he-goats which leap upon the flock are ringstreaked, speckled, and griz-

zled: for I have seen all that Laban doeth unto thee. 13 I am the God of Beth-el, where thou anointedst a pillar, where thou vowedst a vow unto me: now arise, get thee out from this land, and return unto the land of thy nativity. 14 And Rachel and Leah answered and said unto him, Is there yet any portion or inheritance for us in our father's house? 15 Are we not accounted by him as foreigners? for he hath sold us, and hath also quite devoured our money. 16 For all the riches which God hath taken away from our father, that is ours and our children's: now then, whatsoever God hath said unto thee, do.

17 Then Jacob rose up, and set his sons and his wives upon the camels; 18 and he carried away all his cattle, and all his substance which he had gathered, the cattle of his getting, which he had gathered in Paddan-aram, to go to Isaac his father unto the land of Canaan. 19 Now Laban was gone to shear his sheep: and Rachel stole the teraphim that were her father's. 20 And Jacob stole away unawares to Laban the Syrian, in that he told him not that he fled. 21 So he fled with all that he had; and he rose up, and passed over the River, and set his face toward the mountain of Gilead.

22 And it was told Laban on the third day that Jacob was fled. 23 And he took his brethren with him, and pursued after him seven days' journey; and he overtook him in the mountain of Gilead. 24 And God came to Laban the Syrian in a dream of the night, and said unto him, Take heed to thyself that thou speak not to Jacob either good or bad. 25 And Laban came up with Jacob. Now Jacob had pitched his tent in the mountain: and Laban with his brethren encamped in the mountain of Gilead. 26 And Laban said to Jacob, What hast thou done, that thou hast stolen away unawares to me, and carried away my daughters as captives of the sword? 27 Wherefore didst thou flee secretly, and steal away from me, and didst not tell me, that I might have sent thee away with mirth and with songs, with tabret and with harp; 28 and didst not suffer me to kiss my sons and my daughters? now hast thou done foolishly. 29 It is in the power of my hand to do you hurt: but the God of your father spake unto me yesternight, saying, Take heed to thyself that thou speak not to Jacob either good or bad. 30 And now, *though* thou wouldest needs be gone, because thou sore longedst after thy father's house, *yet* wherefore hast thou stolen my gods? 31 And Jacob answered and said to Laban, Because I was afraid: for

I said, Lest thou shouldest take thy daughters from me by force. 32 With whomsoever thou findest thy gods, he shall not live: before our brethren discern thou what is thine with me, and take it to thee. For Jacob knew not that Rachel had stolen them.

33 And Laban went into Jacob's tent, and into Leah's tent, and into the tent of the two maid-servants; but he found them not. And he went out of Leah's tent, and entered into Rachel's tent. 34 Now Rachel had taken the teraphim, and put them in the camel's saddle, and sat upon them. And Laban felt about all the tent, but found them not. 35 And she said to her father, Let not my lord be angry that I cannot rise up before thee; for the manner of women is upon me. And he searched, but found not the teraphim.

36 And Jacob was wroth, and chode with Laban: and Jacob answered and said to Laban, What is my trespass? what is my sin, that thou hast hotly pursued after me? 37 Whereas thou hast felt about all my stuff, what hast thou found of all thy household stuff? Set it here before my brethren and thy brethren, that they may judge betwixt us two. 38 These twenty years have I been with thee; thy ewes and thy she-goats have not cast their young, and the rams of thy flocks have I not eaten. 39 That which was torn of beasts I brought not unto thee! I bare the loss of it; of my hand didst thou require it, whether stolen by day or stolen by night. 40 Thus I was; in the day the drought consumed me, and the frost by night; and my sleep fled from mine eyes. 41 These twenty years have I been in thy house; I served thee fourteen years for thy two daughters, and six years for thy flock: and thou hast changed my wages ten times. 42 Except the God of my father, the God of Abraham, and the Fear of Isaac, had been with me, surely now hadst thou sent me away empty. God hath seen mine affliction and the labor of my hands, and rebuked thee yesternight.

43 And Laban answered and said unto Jacob, The daughters are my daughters, and the children are my children, and the flocks are my flocks, and all that thou seest is mine: and what can I do this day unto these my daughters, or unto their children whom they have borne? 44 And now come, let us make a covenant, I and thou; and let it be for a witness between me and thee. 45 And Jacob took a stone, and set it up for a pillar. 46 And Jacob said unto his brethren, Gather stones; and they took stones, and made a heap: and they did eat there by the heap. 47 And Laban called it Jegar-saha-dutha: but Jacob called it Galeed. 48 And Laban said, This heap is witness between me and thee this day. Therefore was the name of it called Galeed: 49 and Mizpah, for he said, Jehovah watch between me and thee, when we are absent one from another. 50 If thou shalt take wives besides my daughters, no man is with us; see, God is witness betwixt me and thee. 51 And Laban said to Jacob, Behold this heap, and behold the pillar, which I have set betwixt me and thee. 52 This heap be witness, and the pillar be witness, that I will not pass over this heap to thee, and that thou shalt not pass over this heap and this pillar unto me, for harm. 53 The God of Abraham, and the God of Nahor, the God of their father, judge betwixt us. And Jacob sware by the Fear of his father Isaac. 54 And Jacob offered a sacrifice in the mountain, and called his brethren to eat bread: and they did eat bread, and tarried all night in the mountain. 55 And early in the morning Laban rose up, and kissed his sons and his daughters, and blessed them: and Laban departed and returned unto his place. 1 And Jacob went on his way, and the angels of God met him. 2 And Jacob said when he saw them, This is God's host: and he called the name of that place Mahanaim.

As the years went by, Jacob became aware of increasing hostility on the part of Laban and his sons toward him. Then the Lord spoke to him, commanding him to return to Canaan. So Jacob called Rachel and Leah to the field where he was watching the flock. He told them what he had sensed and reminded them of his faithful service to their father, of Laban's treachery, and of God's overruling providence. And he told how the Lord had appeared to him at breeding time, revealing that He had been the cause of his prospering in the multiplying of the abnormally colored animals, and commanding him to return home. Rachel and Leah were quick to support such a move. They declared that Laban had treated them more like outsiders than daughters. For they had been practically sold like slaves through his deception of Jacob. And Jacob's labor for their dowry, instead of resulting in its having been given at least in part to them, as was the custom, the father had himself greedily appropriated. So they reasoned that all the wealth God had transferred from Laban to Jacob should be considered as rightfully belonging to them and their children anyway.

So Jacob stole away secretly from Laban while Laban was shearing his sheep. It was not until the third day that Laban was told. It took seven days for him to overtake Jacob. Just before he caught up, God appeared to Laban in a dream and warned him not to speak to Jacob **either good or bad.** The next day Laban asked Jacob for an explanation as to his secret exit. He claimed the power to do him injury, but confessed that God had ordered otherwise. And finally he accused him of taking his **gods,** his household **teraphim** or images, which Rachel had slipped away without Jacob's knowledge. Jacob answered that he had left secretly lest Laban take away his wives by force. And he declared that whoever had taken the images would die. He asked Laban to search everything in front of the relatives he had brought along. Laban did search, going from tent to tent. Rachel had placed them in **the camel's saddle,** a large saddle with compartments attached, which evidently made a comfortable stool even when off the camel. She sat on them and, when her father entered her tent, excused herself from rising on the basis that **the manner of women is upon me.** This has usually been interpreted as a claim that she was menstruating. So Laban's search was in vain.

For a long time the reason for Rachel's theft and Laban's great concern over the images was unknown. Now it is known that according to the laws of the land, a son-in-law possessing the family images could go to court and lay a strong claim to all the family's wealth. Rachel had taken the law into her own hands in an effort to claim for Jacob what she felt he had been cheated of by Laban. Laban was afraid of what Jacob could do with the images and he felt that he must regain them.[94]

Now it was Jacob's time to speak. And he was very angry. He asked Laban the reason for this pursuit, this "feeling about" all his property. He rehearsed the twenty years' working arrangements, telling of repeated changes of wages, and reminding Laban of his (Jacob's) faithfulness. He had stood all of Laban's losses, something which could not legally have been required.[95] Laban attempted to bluster, but proposed a covenant between them, apparently fearing lest an angry Jacob organize a band and return to punish him. So Jacob set up a pillar and asked the relatives accompanying Laban to build a heap of stones also, the pillar and the heap serving as a dual testimony to the non-aggression pact between the two. Laban gave this spot an Aramaic name, reflecting his native tongue, and Jacob gave it a Hebrew name, reflecting his. Both names mean, "The heap of witness." The place was also called **Mizpah,** "The watchtower," a common place name in Bible lands. This was due to Laban's last effort to slander Jacob's name, suggesting that Jehovah was thus called upon to watch between them, lest Jacob mistreat Laban's daughters or take other wives besides them. Each swore not to pass over this boundary to hurt the other, Jacob offered a sacrifice, they ate bread together (a common way of sealing an agreement) and the next morning Laban went on his way.

As Jacob departed this scene, he met some angels in whom he apparently recognized the protective hand of God. Because of this he called the place **Mahanaim,** "Two hosts," the one apparently being Laban's which had threatened him, and the other being the Lord's which had protected him.

3. Jacob's Fears (32:3—33:17)

a. A Threatened Retaliation (32:3-21)

3 And Jacob sent messengers before him to Esau his brother unto the land of Seir, the field of Edom. 4 And he commanded them, saying, Thus shall ye say unto my lord Esau: Thus saith thy servant Jacob, I have sojourned with Laban, and stayed until now: 5 and I have oxen, and asses, *and* flocks, and men-servants, and maid-servants: and I have sent to tell my lord, that I may find favor in thy sight. 6 And the messengers returned to Jacob, saying, We came to thy brother

---

94 Albright, *op. cit.,* pp. 138-39; and Unger, *op. cit.,* pp. 123-24.
95 Speiser, *op. cit.,* p. 247.

Esau, and moreover he cometh to meet thee, and four hundred men with him. 7 Then Jacob was greatly afraid and was distressed: and he divided the people that were with him, and the flocks, and the herds, and the camels, into two companies; 8 and he said, If Esau come to the one company, and smite it, then the company which is left shall escape. 9 And Jacob said, O God of my father Abraham, and God of my father Isaac, O Jehovah, who saidst unto me, Return unto thy country, and to thy kindred, and I will do thee good: 10 I am not worthy of the least of all the lovingkindness, and of all the truth, which thou hast showed unto thy servant; for with my staff I passed over this Jordan; and now I am become two companies. 11 Deliver me, I pray thee, from the hand of my brother, from the hand of Esau: for I fear him, lest he come and smite me, the mother with the children. 12 And thou saidst, I will surely do thee good, and make thy seed as the sand of the sea, which cannot be numbered for multitude.

13 And he lodged there that night, and took of that which he had with him a present for Esau his brother: 14 two hundred she-goats and twenty he-goats, two hundred ewes and twenty rams, 15 thirty milch camels and their colts, forty cows and ten bulls, twenty she-asses and ten foals. 16 And he delivered them into the hand of his servants, every drove by itself, and said unto his servants, Pass over before me, and put a space betwixt drove and drove. 17 And he commanded the foremost, saying, When Esau my brother meeteth thee, and asketh thee, saying, Whose art thou? and whither goest thou? and whose are these before thee? 18 then thou shalt say, *They are* thy servant Jacob's; it is a present sent unto my lord Esau: and, behold, he also is behind us. 19 And he commanded also the second, and the third, and all that followed the droves, saying, On this manner shall ye speak unto Esau, when ye find him; 20 and ye shall say, Moreover, behold, thy servant Jacob is behind us. For he said, I will appease him with the present that goeth before me, and afterward I will see his face; peradventure he will accept me. 21 So the present passed over before him: and he himself lodged that night in the company.

Jacob's return to Canaan was hedged about with difficulties. One of the most serious problems which he encountered was the pursuit by Laban, with the prob-able intention of keeping him in Paddan-aram. That had now been disposed of. But Jacob must also deal with his long-estranged brother Esau, who not only might want to prevent his return, but also to avenge himself by carrying out his old vow to kill Jacob.

It is noteworthy that Jacob did not try to slip into Canaan without Esau knowing it. He had secretly fled from Laban and earlier had fled in haste lest this same Esau pursue and kill him. But apparently Jacob was learning that deceit and unprincipled cleverness were not the best ways to happiness and success. Now he sent messengers to Esau, announcing his return. Esau was living in **Seir,** the land later known after his nickname as **Edom** ("Red"). How Jacob knew where to send the messengers is not revealed. Perhaps Esau had already taken the initial steps toward making Seir his home even before Jacob left twenty years before. Or, more likely, Jacob had learned of his brother's present residence from some of the caravans encountered on his journey.

The Jacob who was returning to Canaan was not the same Jacob who had left Beersheba twenty years before. From the moment he had met God at Bethel, he had been different. Previously there was no record that he had any kind of religious life. He depended entirely upon his own wits and his mother's counsel. He was intensely selfish. He gave no evidence of being conscience-stricken over his ill treatment of his twin brother. But after Bethel, the name of God was often upon Jacob's lips. He frequented the place of prayer and angels came repeatedly to reassure or direct him. He now gave God the credit for his success, and obeyed God's command to return to his homeland. His love was now turned outward, especially to Rachel, but also to all the members of his family. He still tried to take advantage of Laban, but only in retaliation in an age when the law was "an eye for an eye," and under circumstances in which God evidently approved, for only He could have given success to Jacob's efforts. Now, the changed Jacob becomes more evident in his message to his estranged brother. He calls Esau **my lord** and himself **thy servant Jacob.** He tells him that he has sojourned or "resided temporarily" with Laban, and has stayed or "tarried" or "delayed" until now. He also lists the various categories of his possessions: oxen, asses, flocks, men-servants, maid-servants. And he closes by explaining his communication as intended to find favor with Esau. He is in effect renouncing claim to all the natural and material advantages which would have been his by virtue of the birthright and the blessing. He assumes no superiority over Esau, but rather the position of humble submission. He explains his departure from and return to a land over which Esau for the time being has a certain degree of control. He lists his possessions so Esau will know that he needs neither his father's riches nor his brother's charity.

But when Jacob's messengers returned, they brought alarming news. They had found Esau, and he was coming to meet Jacob with four hundred men. Apparently Esau had said nothing in reply to the messengers which indicated either his acceptance or rejection of Jacob's humble request for favor. And this silence distressed Jacob exceedingly. He divided his people and livestock into two companies, with the hope that if Esau attacked the one, the other would have a chance to escape. This seems to have been a standard procedure for threatened caravans from the earliest times.[96] It is not clear whether he so divided his wives and children. Rather it would seem that Jacob and his family either stayed with one of the groups or lagged somewhat behind and apart from both of them. Then Jacob went to prayer. He addressed the *Elohim* of Abraham and Isaac who was also the *Jehovah* who had given him a promise at Bethel those twenty years ago. He declared that he was not worthy of the least of the divine blessings, and contrasted his crossing over Jordan in that earlier day carrying only his staff, with his return accompanied by enough servants and stock to make two companies. Then he asked for deliverance from Esau, for he feared that he would be stricken completely — himself and all that pertained to him, me, the mother with the children. And the reference to the children led him to still a further reminder of the divine promise, for Je-

hovah had told him that He would make his descendants as innumerable as the sand of the sea. The order of the prayer is an instructive one, a pattern for any age: address, promise-reference, humility, thanksgiving, petition, intercession, promise-reference. It was a remarkable prayer by a changed Jacob face-to-face with a situation far beyond his ability to handle.

Jacob had acted quickly and decisively, and then prayed. Now he follows the prayer with further action. Sometimes activity must precede prayer; often it follows prayer. Prayer frequently leads to immediate insights which help to solve our difficulties. Perhaps it was so with Jacob. In any event, he camped at the spot where his messengers had found him. And even as night was settling, he sorted out a present for Esau, consisting of two hundred twenty goats, two hundred twenty sheep, thirty milk camels with their colts, fifty cattle, and thirty asses — a total of five hundred fifty animals, a splendid gift indeed, and a significant hint at the wealth of Jacob. He organized them in five droves, each kind of animal by itself, and sent them ahead of him, each drove being driven by his servants. A space was left between drove and drove. And the servants were instructed that when Esau met them and inquired who they were, where they were going, and whose were the droves, they were to reply that these were the property of his servant Jacob, sent as a present to his lord Esau, and that Jacob was following them. All of this was done in the hope of changing Esau's attitude from one of anger to one of welcome. An interesting play on the word "face" appears in verses 20-21, which is quite significant in the light of Jacob's later experience at Peniel ("the face of God," 32:22-32), and his words upon meeting Esau (33:10). The Hebrew literally says, "For he said, I will cover his *face* with the present which goes before my *face,* and afterwards I will see his *face;* perhaps he will lift up my *face.* And the present passed over before his *face.*"

b. A Glorious Renunciation — Second Promise (32:22-32)

22 And he rose up that night, and took

96 Leupold, *op. cit.,* p. 865.

his two wives, and his two handmaids, and his eleven children, and passed over the ford of the Jabbok. 23 And he took them, and sent them over the stream, and sent over that which he had. 24 And Jacob was left alone; and there wrestled a man with him until the breaking of the day. 25 And when he saw that he prevailed not against him, he touched the hollow of his thigh; and the hollow of Jacob's thigh was strained, as he wrestled with him. 26 And he said, Let me go, for the day breaketh. And he said, I will not let thee go, except thou bless me. 27 And he said unto him, What is thy name? And he said, Jacob. 28 And he said, Thy name shall be called no more Jacob, but Israel: for thou hast striven with God and with men, and hast prevailed. 29 And Jacob asked him, and said, Tell me, I pray thee, thy name. And he said, Wherefore is it that thou dost ask after my name? And he blessed him there. 30 And Jacob called the name of the place Peniel: for, *said he*, I have seen God face to face, and my life is preserved. 31 And the sun rose upon him as he passed over Penuel, and he limped upon his thigh. 32 Therefore the children of Israel eat not the sinew of the hip which is upon the hollow of the thigh, unto this day: because he touched the hollow of Jacob's thigh in the sinew of the hip.

After Jacob had sent the droves away into the gathering darkness, he apparently attempted to settle down for a night's rest. But he could not sleep. This was probably more than a matter of fear of Esau, for the Spirit of God must already have been preparing him for the profound spiritual experience which was soon to occur. He arose in the night and took his wives and children across the **Jabbok,** a brook which empties into the Jordan from the east, about fifteen miles north of the Dead Sea. Whether Jacob himself actually crossed the brook cannot be determined, but it is apparent that while he supervised the crossing by his family, he himself returned to the north bank to spend the remainder of the night in solitary prayer and meditation.

By sending all of his earthly possessions and all of his loved ones from him, Jacob had in effect abandoned all that he had to God's care. Step by step the

Lord had led him in the direction of complete self-surrender. Now the final step was to be taken. Suddenly, out of the darkness, **a man** grappled with Jacob and wrestled **with him until the breaking of the day.** Jacob later called his antagonist an angel (48:16), as did the inspired prophet Hosea (Hos. 12:4). However, the term *angel* (which means "messenger" both in the Old Testament Hebrew and the New Testament Greek) is apparently used in the Old Testament both of spiritual beings which serve as God's messengers and also of the guise in which God Himself sometimes appears. This is especially true of "the Angel of the Covenant,"[97] who is called "the angel of Jehovah" or "the angel of Elohim" in the Scriptures, who is frequently identified with Jehovah, so that the terms are used interchangeably (cf. Gen. 16:7-13; 28:13 with 31:11, 13; Exod. 3:2, 4, 6, 7; Judg. 6:11, 12, 14, 16, 20, 21), and who many scholars believe to have been the preincarnate Christ.[98] It appears certain that God Himself was Jacob's antagonist as is evidenced by (1) the power of His touch upon Jacob's thigh, (2) Jacob's insistence that He bless him, (3) the new name He gave to Jacob, (4) the refusal to reveal His own name, (5) the blessing which He gave Jacob, and (6) the name by which Jacob commemorated the spot. God had assumed the form of a man when He wanted to speak to Abraham (chap. 18). On that occasion Abraham interceded for Sodom, and his prayer was in the form of a conversation. Now God comes to complete the transformation of Jacob into a man He can use, and the encounter takes the form of an intense struggle.

As dawn approached, Jacob's antagonist **saw that he prevailed not against** this man, whose unusual strength has already been noted (see exposition of 29:10). So he **touched the hollow** or "socket" where Jacob's thigh bone connected with the pelvis, throwing it out of the socket. Jacob had no doubt been astonished that his solitary meditation had been so rudely interrupted. He had wondered from the first concerning the identity of his adversary, probably sensing something unusual about Him. But the

97 Robert S. Candlish, *Commentary on Genesis*, "Classic Commentary Library," II, 74.
98 Girdlestone, *op. cit.*, pp. 41-42.

moment that the mere touch of His hand crippled Jacob, he immediately knew who it was whom he held in his grasp. The strong-willed, strong-armed Jacob was changed in an instant from a wrestler who could not be thrown into one who could not stand unaided. He quit fighting and began clinging. God asked to be released, for day was breaking. Perhaps He did not want Jacob to see His face clearly in the light. Perhaps He was reminding him that it was time to go on and face Esau. But more probably, He was testing Jacob to see if he would benefit by the night's experience, and hold on until he had received from the Lord all that He had planned for him. Jacob's rebellious spirit was broken; but he yet needed a deeper consciousness of God's blessing and empowering grace. He met the test, for he declared, **I will not let thee go, except thou bless me.** Here was a holy boldness, a holy determination. Here was Jacob at his best. Formerly he had deceived his father to get his human blessing. But he had long since been convinced of the inadequacy of that blessing obtained by those means. Now he wanted a blessing from God and he refused to go until it was given.

God's answer to Jacob's insistence on a blessing was to ask, **What is thy name? And he said, Jacob.** Such an exchange would mean little today. But Hebrew names had definite meanings. Jacob's name came from a root which as a noun meant "heel," and as a verb meant "overreach," "assail insidiously," or "circumvent." He had been marked since birth as the heel-grasper, the supplanter. For him to say his name was at the same time to confess his nature. This God required him to do, painful as it was. But a change was taking place in Jacob's nature, in his spiritual status. And as a sign of this change, God gave him a new name, **Israel** ("wrestler with God"[99]): **for thou hast striven with God and with men, and hast prevailed.**

Jacob now asked to know the name of his antagonist. He certainly had recognized Him. But as God had asked for his name, already knowing it, so now he asks for a further self-revelation on the

part of God. His was a natural desire to receive from the Lord all he could while this wonderful encounter was still a present fact. But the Lord evidently deemed any further revelation unnecessary and unwise at this time. So He side-stepped the question and honored Jacob's previous insistence on a blessing. Its nature is not here disclosed. But it no doubt restated and clarified the promises God had already given Jacob, perhaps stamping the divine approval on the blessing Isaac had given long before. How much happier was this latter experience than the sorry situation when he deceived his father! How much better it would have been if Jacob had been intent on this blessing all along.

Jacob also did some naming on this occasion. He named the site of his climactic experience **Peniel** or **Penuel**, different forms of the same Hebrew word, meaning "the face of God." Faces had been much on Jacob's mind during his return homeward (cf. comments on verses 20-21). No doubt the voice of conscience had been holding before Jacob the angry face of his wronged brother, especially in the darkness after his family had been sent away. But instead of Esau, he had first encountered God **face to face,** and once having settled matters with Him, he was ready for his encounter with Esau. Jacob especially noted one result of his meeting with God: **my life is preserved.** This may reflect the typical Old Testament fear of seeing God and the corresponding thanksgiving when such occurs without death ensuing (cf. Exod. 33:20; Judg. 6:22-24; 13:22-23). But it can just as well be translated, "my soul is delivered," or as Luther renders it, "my soul is healed, saved."[100] The verb is used in the Psalms to speak of deliverance from guilt and sin. This second meaning may well have been included in Jacob's expression since he later refers to his antagonist on this occasion as "the angel who hath redeemed me from all evil" (48:16).

As the sun arose, Jacob went limping on his way to rejoin his family, a changed man physically and spiritually. As a memorial to his experience and the crippling

[99] *The Bible, an American Translation.*
[100] Quoted by John Peter Lange, *Commentary on the Holy Scriptures,* trans. from the German by Philip Schaff, I, 550.

touch of God, his descendants refuse to eat the sinew of the hip, the powerful sciatic muscle which passes along the thigh. The custom is not mentioned elsewhere in the Old Testament, but is encouraged by the Mishna, the topical arrangement of the Jewish oral law which was written in the second century A.D.[101]

c. A Joyful Reconciliation (33:1-17)

1 And Jacob lifted up his eyes, and looked, and, behold, Esau was coming, and with him four hundred men. And he divided the children unto Leah, and unto Rachel, and unto the two handmaids. 2 And he put the handmaids and their children foremost, and Leah and her children after, and Rachel and Joseph hindermost. 3 And he himself passed over before them, and bowed himself to the ground seven times, until he came near to his brother. 4 And Esau ran to meet him, and embraced him, and fell on his neck, and kissed him: and they wept. 5 And he lifted up his eyes, and saw the women and the children; and said, Who are these with thee? And he said, The children whom God hath graciously given thy servant. 6 Then the handmaids came near, they and their children, and they bowed themselves. 7 And Leah also and her children came near, and bowed themselves: and after came Joseph near and Rachel, and they bowed themselves. 8 And he said, What meanest thou by all this company which I met? And he said, To find favor in the sight of my lord. 9 And Esau said, I have enough, my brother; let that which thou hast be thine. 10 And Jacob said, Nay, I pray thee, if now I have found favor in thy sight, then receive my present at my hand; forasmuch as I have seen thy face, as one seeth the face of God, and thou wast pleased with me. 11 Take, I pray thee, my gift that is brought to thee, because God hath dealt graciously with me, and because I have enough. And he urged him, and he took it. 12 And he said, Let us take our journey, and let us go, and I will go before thee. 13 And he said unto him, My lord knoweth that the children are tender, and that the flocks and herds with me have their young: and if they overdrive them one day, all the flocks will die. 14 Let my lord, I pray thee, pass over before his servant: and I will lead on gently, according to the pace of the cattle that are before me and according to the pace of the children, until I come unto my lord unto Seir. 15 And Esau said, Let me now leave with thee some of the folk that are with me. And he said, What needeth it? let me find favor in the sight of my lord. 16 So Esau returned that day on his way unto Seir. 17 And Jacob journeyed to Succoth, and built him a house, and made booths for his cattle: therefore the name of the place is called Succoth.

As Jacob rejoined his family, he could see in the distance the cloud of dust which marked the approach of Esau and his four hundred men. So he divided his family into four groups, putting the slave-girls and their children first, then Leah and her children, and Rachel and Joseph in the rear. He preceded them, bowing his head almost to the ground seven times, a sign of respect which according to ancient documents found by archaeologists was customarily given in homage to kings.[102] Just what Esau's original intentions were when he came to meet Jacob cannot be known with certainty. Perhaps he did not even know himself what he was going to do. Neither can we know just what persuaded him to accept Jacob's offer of good will. God had warned Laban in a dream not to harm Jacob (31:24). Perhaps He also spoke to Esau. Or perhaps the total effect of all Jacob had done to placate him — the humble request through the messengers for permission to return to Canaan (32:4-5), the costly gift which Esau met before he encountered Jacob (32:13-21), the deep respect shown in Jacob's bowing before him — had convinced Esau that Jacob was indeed a changed man who was sorry for his previous misbehavior, or perhaps it was the result of direct divine intervention in answer to Jacob's prevailing prayer. He probably felt that he need no longer fear his brother, for his character and methods were now altogether different. In any event, Esau ran to meet him, embraced him as a brother, kissed him, and wept with him in a glad reunion made even more emotional by the bitter memories of the past.

After the greeting of the two brothers, Esau inquired concerning the company of women and children standing somewhat uncertainly at one side. As Jacob introduced them, they, too, came for-

101 Driver, *op. cit.*, p. 296.   102 Leupold, *op. cit.*, p. 886.

ward and bowed in respect to Esau. Then he inquired concerning the droves of animals he had met on the way. Jacob frankly told him they were intended, **To find favor in the sight of my lord.** All through their conversation, Jacob continued to address Esau as **my lord,** and to refer to himself as **thy servant,** maintaining the spirit of respect for his elder brother. But Esau was reluctant to accept Jacob's gifts, saying, **I have enough,** or more literally, "I have much." But Jacob insisted, asking that the gift be accepted as evidence that he had found favor in Esau's sight — somewhat in the manner used to confirm the covenant between Abraham and Abimelech at Beersheba years before (21:27-31). He was intent on carrying to completion what amounted to apology and restitution for the wrongs he had committed against Esau many years earlier. His insistence on respect for his brother was a renunciation of the favored position he had acquired through the deceitfully obtained birthright and blessing. The gift was in atonement — a kind of punitive compensation for the hurt and injury which Esau had suffered. If Esau accepted it, according to oriental custom, it would indicate that he forgave Jacob and that good relations were restored. Jacob declared that this would make complete his joy over their meeting, for then his glimpse of Esau's face would be like a glimpse of the face of God, who only manifests Himself to those with whom He is pleased.[103] No doubt there was an allusion in Jacob's mind to the experience at Peniel. He had seen God's face and received a blessing. Now he saw Esau's face and was also seeking a conclusive sign of his favor. He clinched his argument for Esau's acceptance of the gift by saying **I have enough,** but literally his statement differed from Esau's, for he said, "I have all" or "everything." He may have meant he had everything he needed. He may have actually had greater acquired wealth than did Esau at this time and intended to contrast their positions in his words. Some scholars feel that he was thinking primarily of his spiritual wealth, of the divine

prospering of which he was now assured, and felt that as long as he had the Lord he needed nothing else.[104] To have these two brothers each claiming that they had enough was indeed a change! But Esau, seeing what the gift really meant, yielded to his brother's urging and accepted it.

Esau then proposed closer ties between the brothers. He first suggested that they proceed together, with Esau and his men serving as an armed guard for Jacob and his caravan. But Jacob pointed out how difficult this would be, for he must move slowly with his stock. Then Esau offered to leave a small group of men with him. But Jacob replied, **What needeth it?** and hinted that such an act might indicate less than Esau's full acceptance of Jacob. Jacob no doubt wanted to retain independence of movement. And he probably also realized that the great differences in disposition and temperament between him and Esau might well lead to further difficulties if they associated closely over an extended period of time. So he tactfully but firmly avoided such association.[105]

So Esau returned to Seir, with a promise of a visit from Jacob. Such a visit is not recorded in the Scriptures, but certainly not all of Jacob's actions are so recorded. Jacob went on to **Succoth,** a site near the Jabbok, apparently west of Peniel, closer to the Jordan. Here he did something most unusual, building himself **a house,** rather than dwelling in a tent, and constructing **booths** (Heb. *succoth*) or "sheds"[106] for his cattle. He apparently stayed here for several years, for Reuben could not have been much over twelve years of age at the time of his return, and Joseph and Dinah would have been about six years old. Dinah's part in the succeeding narrative would have required at the very least another six or seven years.

4. Jacob's Fortune (33:18—35:29)

a. A Period of Violence (33:18—34:31)

18 And Jacob came in peace to the city of Shechem, which is in the land of Canaan, when he came from Paddan-aram;

[103] A. Dillmann, *Genesis, Critically and Exegetically Expounded*, trans. from the German by William B. Stevenson, II, 284.   [104] Leupold, *op. cit.*, p. 890.
[105] Candlish, *op. cit.*, II, 90-91.   [106] *The Bible, an American Translation*.

and encamped before the city. 19 And he bought the parcel of ground, where he had spread his tent, at the hand of the children of Hamor, Shechem's father, for a hundred pieces of money. 20 And he erected there an altar, and called it El-Elohe-Israel.

1 And Dinah the daughter of Leah, whom she bare unto Jacob, went out to see the daughters of the land. 2 And Shechem the son of Hamor the Hivite, the prince of the land, saw her; and he took her, and lay with her, and humbled her. 3 And his soul clave unto Dinah the daughter of Jacob, and he loved the damsel, and spake kindly unto the damsel. 4 And Shechem spake unto his father Hamor, saying, Get me this damsel to wife. 5 Now Jacob heard that he had defiled Dinah his daughter; and his sons were with his cattle in the field: and Jacob held his peace until they came. 6 And Hamor the father of Shechem went out unto Jacob to commune with him. 7 And the sons of Jacob came in from the field when they heard it: and the men were grieved, and they were very wroth, because he had wrought folly in Israel in lying with Jacob's daughter; which thing ought not to be done. 8 And Hamor communed with them, saying, The soul of my son Shechem longeth for your daughter: I pray you, give her unto him to wife. 9 And make ye marriages with us; give your daughters unto us, and take our daughters unto you. 10 And ye shall dwell with us: and the land shall be before you; dwell and trade ye therein, and get you possessions therein. 11 And Shechem said unto her father and unto her brethren, Let me find favor in your eyes, and what ye shall say unto me I will give. 12 Ask me never so much dowry and gift, and I will give according as ye shall say unto me: but give me the damsel to wife. 13 And the sons of Jacob answered Shechem and Hamor his father with guile, and spake, because he had defiled Dinah their sister, 14 and said unto them, We cannot do this thing, to give our sister to one that is uncircumcised; for that were a reproach unto us. 15 Only on this condition will we consent unto you: if ye will be as we are, that every male of you be circumcised; 16 then will we give our daughters unto you, and we will take your daughters to us, and we will dwell with you, and we will become one people. 17 But if ye will not hearken unto us, to be circumcised; then will we take our daughter, and we will be gone. 18 And their words pleased Hamor, and Shechem Hamor's son. 19 And the young man deferred not to do the thing, be-cause he had delight in Jacob's daughter: and he was honored above all the house of his father. 20 And Hamor and Shechem his son came unto the gate of their city, and communed with the men of their city, saying, 21 These men are peaceable with us; therefore let them dwell in the land, and trade therein; for, behold, the land is large enough for them; let us take their daughters to us for wives, and let us give them our daughters. 22 Only on this condition will the men consent unto us to dwell with us, to become one people, if every male among us be circumcised, as they are circumcised. 23 Shall not their cattle and their substance and all their beasts be ours? only let us consent unto them, and they will dwell with us. 24 And unto Hamor and unto Shechem his son hearkened all that went out of the gate of his city; and every male was circumcised, all that went out of the gate of his city. 25 And it came to pass on the third day, when they were sore, that two of the sons of Jacob, Simeon and Levi, Dinah's brethren, took each man his sword, and came upon the city unawares, and slew all the males. 26 And they slew Hamor and Shechem his son with the edge of the sword, and took Dinah out of Shechem's house, and went forth. 27 The sons of Jacob came upon the slain, and plundered the city, because they had defiled their sister. 28 They took their flocks and their herds and their asses, and that which was in the city, and that which was in the field; 29 and all their wealth, and all their little ones and their wives, took they captive and made a prey, even all that was in the house. 30 And Jacob said to Simeon and Levi, Ye have troubled me, to make me odious to the inhabitants of the land, among the Canaanites and the Perizzites: and, I being few in number, they will gather themselves together against me and smite me; and I shall be destroyed, I and my house. 31 And they said, Should he deal with our sister as with a harlot?

After a lengthy stay at Succoth, Jacob crossed the Jordan into Canaan proper — hence the clause, **when he came from Paddan-aram.** This was the first time he had set foot in the promised land itself since he had left it nearly thirty years before. He pitched his tent outside but near the city of Shechem, about twenty miles west of Succoth, almost in the center of Canaan. The city was located under the summit of Mt. Gerizim, part of what was later called the Ephraimite range of mountains. Here he bought a parcel of ground on which to pitch his tent. (This later became part of the tribal inheritance of Ephraim, and here Joseph was buried.) Here Jacob erected the first altar which he is recorded as having built, and called it **El-Elohe-Israel,** "God, the God of Israel."

While Jacob and his family were camped near Shechem, his daughter by Leah, Dinah, **went out to see the daughters of the land.** Whether this was a sudden impulse on her part, the result of curiosity and perhaps girlish loneliness, is not revealed. Perhaps she had made some friends and slipped away to visit them. Almost certainly she went without her family's knowledge, for unattended girls were considered legitimate prey by Canaanite and Egyptian men. (Even the later Mosaic law did not provide for the punishment of a rape of this kind by death as it did acts of fornication and adultery, but only the payment of a dowry and the requirement of marriage if the father consented. Cf. Exod. 22:16-17; Deut. 22:28-29.) The result of her excursion was tragic. For **Shechem the son of Hamor,** and thus the son of the city's leading citizen, seized her and ravished her. Furthermore, he fell in love with her, kept her in his house, speaking kindly to her as he no doubt told her of his plans to make the union a permanent one in marriage. According to the custom of the day, parents arranged marriages, so Shechem went to Hamor with the demand that he secure Dinah as his wife.

The news of Dinah's misadventure reached Jacob before Hamor did. The peculiar emphasis laid upon Jacob's sons, both in the story as a whole and in the word order of the Hebrew, would indicate that Jacob depended upon them to carry a heavy share of responsibility in dealing with the situation. This may have been because it was the custom for grown sons to share in the protection of unmarried daughters, or it may have been due to necessity imposed by Jacob's advancing age. The sons were out with the stock when Jacob heard of the incident, but word had reached them and they had returned home by the time Hamor arrived, or shortly after. Hamor and

Shechem revealed the low moral level of the age and country, since they felt no need of an apology for what had happened. Hamor proposed the marriage of Shechem and Dinah, and enlarged this with a proposal for the intermarriage of Jacob's entire family with the Shechemites. He pointed out the advantages which this would bring Israel — greater freedom in moving about the land, and valuable, permanent possessions. Shechem added his voice to his father's, promising to pay whatever marriage price and bridal gift Jacob and his sons might impose.

Jacob's sons had apparently inherited their father's tendency to deceitful dealing. They were justly angry, but their tactics in punishing Dinah's attacker and his people were dishonorable to say the least. They insisted that they could not marry their sister to an uncircumcised man, but if Shechem and all his people would be circumcised, then they would be content to become one people. Circumcision, as was noted in connection with chapter 17, was a common practice among the people of Canaan. So Hamor and Shechem were not at all repelled by the demand. They returned to their city council in its regular meeting place, the city gate, and relayed the proposal to the men of the city, stressing now the other side of what they had advertised to Jacob and his sons — that the Shechemites would thus possess Israel's riches. The men of the city agreed and the mass circumcision of **all that went out of the gate of the city** (a technical term referring to those capable of military service[107]) was carried out.

All through this narrative, the members of Jacob's family which play the leading role keep shifting. Hamor came to see Jacob (v. 6). He and Shechem spoke both to Jacob and to his sons (v. 11). But when the circumcision proposal was made to Hamor and Shechem, only Jacob's sons are in the picture (v. 13). Either Jacob had grown too weak to continue negotiations, due to his age and his anxiety over Dinah, and had retired, or else the family's answer was postponed for a time of counsel and Jacob's sons later made the proposal without their father's knowledge. If the latter is true, then it

---

[107] Speiser, *op. cit.,* p. 265.

is almost certain that it was only Simeon and Levi, two of Dinah's full brothers, who made the proposal. For whoever persuaded Hamor and Shechem to circumcise the entire male population of the city must have had in mind exactly that which Simeon and Levi subsequently did, and for which Jacob blamed them entirely (v. 30; 49:5-7). **On the third day,** the time when soreness from any surgical operation is usually at its worst, these two brothers walked boldly into Shechem and massacred all the men. Ancient cities were sometimes quite small, both in area and population. And with the advantage of surprise and the indisposition of the men of the city, it would have been by no means impossible for the two men to have moved quickly from house to house on their murderous mission. They may also have taken along some of their father's slaves.[108] They took Dinah from Shechem's house and departed. Later they apparently returned with their other brothers to plunder the city, seizing all the stock and other portable wealth, and enslaving the women and children. Jacob rebuked them for their acts, pointing out the danger which would arise from the other Canaanites when they heard of the violence of these outsiders. The brothers insisted that Shechem must not be allowed to treat their sister as **a harlot.** Jacob did not rebuke them in terms as strong as those used later on his deathbed (49:5-7), and strangely enough nothing is said of his making them release their captives and restore their goods. Apparently his own distress over Shechem's act made it difficult for him to know where just revenge ended and cruelty began. Again Jacob and his sons reflect the ethical limitations of their age.

b. A Period of Renewal — Third Promise (35:1-15)

1 And God said unto Jacob, Arise, go up to Beth-el, and dwell there: and make there an altar unto God, who appeared unto thee when thou fleddest from the face of Esau thy brother. 2 Then Jacob said unto his household, and to all that were with him, Put away the foreign gods that are among you, and purify yourselves, and change your garments: 3 and let us arise, and go up to Beth-el; and I will make there an altar unto God, who answered me in the day of my distress, and was with me in the way which I went. 4 And they gave unto Jacob all the foreign gods which were in their hand, and the rings which were in their ears; and Jacob hid them under the oak which was by Shechem. 5 And they journeyed: and a terror of God was upon the cities that were round about them, and they did not pursue after the sons of Jacob. 6 So Jacob came to Luz, which is in the land of Canaan (the same is Beth-el), he and all the people that were with him. 7 And he built there an altar, and called the place El-beth-el; because there God was revealed unto him, when he fled from the face of his brother. 8 And Deborah Rebekah's nurse died, and she was buried below Beth-el under the oak: and the name of it was called Allon-bacuth.

9 And God appeared unto Jacob again, when he came from Paddan-aram, and blessed him. 10 And God said unto him, Thy name is Jacob: thy name shall not be called any more Jacob, but Israel shall be thy name: and he called his name Israel. 11 And God said unto him, I am God Almighty: be fruitful and multiply; a nation and a company of nations shall be of thee, and kings shall come out of thy loins: 12 and the land which I gave unto Abraham and Isaac, to thee I will give it, and to thy seed after thee will I give the land. 13 And God went up from him in the place where he spake with him. 14 And Jacob set up a pillar in the place where he spake with him, a pillar of stone: and he poured out a drink-offering thereon, and poured oil thereon. 15 And Jacob called the name of the place where God spake with him, Beth-el.

No direct contact with Jehovah is recorded in Jacob's life from Peniel until after the shameful affair at Shechem. Then God reminded Jacob of his promise to return to Bethel and build an altar unto the Lord who had appeared to him there (cf. 28:22). Jacob, like many others, probably had been postponing the keeping of his vow and may have been in danger of forgetting it altogether. Perhaps his troubles at Shechem could have been avoided if he had more promptly moved on to Bethel. In any event, the Shechem episode made him ready to move and he promptly obeyed. But before departing, he called for a general, spiritual

---

[108] Leupold, *op. cit.,* p. 908.

housecleaning. He commanded that all **foreign gods** be discarded. These would have included Laban's images which Rachel had stolen (31:19, 30-35), and which Jacob had probably long since discovered, images which Jacob's slaves had secretly kept and worshiped, and probably some images picked up with the loot from Shechem. He also called for them to purify themselves, perhaps by means of some ceremonial washing, and to change their clothes, as was customary when going to worship (cf. Exod. 19:10, 14). So the heathen gods, and also the earrings which served an idolatrous function, often being covered with allegorical figures and mysterious sentences and serving as charms, [109] were collected and buried beneath **the oak** or terebinth tree near Shechem — apparently the same one visited by Abraham long before (12:6). Then they took their journey to Bethel, which lay some twenty miles south of Shechem. **A terror of God** rested upon the Canaanite towns around, and Jacob's fears were not realized concerning his neighbors' revenge for the massacre and looting of Shechem (34:30). Divine protection had been granted once more. At Bethel, Jacob built an altar, calling it **El-beth-el,** "The God of Bethel."

Verse 8 appears almost to be out of context in this chapter, with its abrupt notice of the death of **Deborah Rebekah's nurse,** apparently the same one who had accompanied Jacob's mother on her journey to Canaan to marry Isaac (24:59). How she came to be with Jacob, as is here implied, is not explained. She would have been extremely old by this time. Either she had joined Jacob after Rebekah's death upon his return to Canaan, and her death occurred just after he built the altar at Bethel, or she had died at an earlier time and her death is recorded here simply because of the proximity of her burial place to Bethel. In any event, it is highly instructive that God's revealed Word can take note of the death of a faithful servant, and memorialize her burial place as **Allon-bacuth,** "the oak" or "terebinth of weeping."[110]

While Jacob was still at Bethel (this being in one sense still part of his journey home — **when he came from Paddan-aram**), the Lord appeared to him again

with a renewal of the promise originally given at Bethel long before. It included a repetition of the promise concerning possession of the land, and the addition of promises that out of Jacob would come **a nation and a company of nations,** and also **kings.** It also involved a repetition of the changing of his name from Jacob to Israel. When the Lord departed, Jacob repeated his acts of long ago, setting up a pillar and anointing it with wine and oil. Again he declared that this was **Beth-el,** "the house of God." It was not surprising that Jacob's return visit to this place of sacred memory would bring a renewal of divine promise and human worship.

c. A Period of Lamentation (35:16-29)

16 And they journeyed from Beth-el; and there was still some distance to come to Ephrath: and Rachel travailed, and she had hard labor. 17 And it came to pass, when she was in hard labor, that the midwife said unto her, Fear not; for now thou shalt have another son. 18 And it came to pass, as her soul was departing (for she died), that she called his name Ben-oni: but his father called him Benjamin. 19 And Rachel died, and was buried in the way to Ephrath (the same is Beth-lehem). 20 And Jacob set up a pillar upon her grave: the same is the Pillar of Rachel's grave unto this day. 21 And Israel journeyed, and spread his tent beyond the tower of Eder. 22 And it came to pass, while Israel dwelt in that land, that Reuben went and lay with Bilhah his father's concubine: and Israel heard of it.

Now the sons of Jacob were twelve: 23 the sons of Leah: Reuben, Jacob's firstborn, and Simeon, and Levi, and Judah, and Issachar, and Zebulun; 24 the sons of Rachel: Joseph and Benjamin; 25 and the sons of Bilhah, Rachel's handmaid: Dan and Naphtali; 26 and the sons of Zilpah, Leah's handmaid: Gad and Asher: these are the sons of Jacob, that were born to him in Paddan-aram. 27 And Jacob came unto Isaac his father to Mamre, to Kiriath-arba (the same is Hebron), where Abraham and Isaac sojourned.

28 And the days of Isaac were a hundred and fourscore years. 29 And Isaac gave up the ghost, and died, and was

---

109 Whitelaw, *op. cit.*, I, 411.   110 Leupold, *op. cit.*, pp. 919-20.

gathered unto his people, old and full of days: and Esau and Jacob his sons buried him.

Jacob did not tarry long at Bethel. He moved on with his family toward **Eph-rath,** the old name for **Beth-lehem.** Before they arrived, Rachel began to travail in birth. She died in giving birth to her second son for which she had hoped ever since the birth of Joseph, some thirteen years or more earlier (30:24). With her dying breath she called him **Ben-oni,** "the son of my sorrow," but Jacob renamed him **Benjamin,** "the son of the right hand." Rachel was buried outside Bethlehem, and Jacob marked her grave with a memorial pillar, still known as the Pillar of Rachel's Grave at the time Genesis was written. A chapel marks the traditional spot yet today, one mile north of Bethlehem.

Jacob camped not far from the site of Rachel's death, **beyond the tower of Eder,** or "the tower of the flock," a shepherd's watchtower located between Bethlehem and Jerusalem. Such towers persisted in this area for centuries, probably built on the same vantage-point. One was later mentioned by the prophet Micah (Mic. 4:8), and still later Jewish tradition held that the Messiah was first to be revealed at the tower of the flock near Bethlehem, where in Jesus' day the shepherds watched over flocks destined for the temple sacrifices in Jerusalem.[111] It was here that another sad event occurred in Jacob's long and troubled life. Reuben, his firstborn son, committed fornication with his father's concubine Bilhah, Rachel's slave-girl. Jacob, or Israel, heard of it, but is not recorded to have done anything about it at the time. Later, he deprived Reuben of the birthright because of this act, giving it to Joseph (49:3-4; I Chron. 5:1).

In verses 22b-26 the author of Genesis summarizes the twelve sons of Jacob, listing them not in the order of their birth, but grouping them under their respective mothers in the order in which the four women became Jacob's wives and concubines. He lists them as **the sons of Jacob, that were born to him in Paddan-aram,** which could only be true as a generalization since Benjamin was not born until they were back in Canaan. It is natural

that this summary should appear at this point, for immediately afterward appears the record of Jacob's return home to his father Isaac. He found him at **Mamre** or **Hebron,** which had been one of Abraham's favorite tenting places, and where the family burial grounds were located. It was here that Isaac died, being 180 years old, and Esau and Jacob joined together in burying him. Isaac's death is not listed here in chronological order, for he could not have been 180 until after Joseph was sold into slavery (cf. 47:9; 45:6; 41:46, 53-54; 37:2; 31:41; 30:25ff.; 25:26). The writer is bringing to conclusion the story of Isaac's sons and before moving on to the sons of Esau and the sons of Jacob he records the last event which was primarily related to the older generations.

5. Esau's Family (36:1-43)

1 Now these are the generations of Esau (the same is Edom). 2 Esau took his wives of the daughters of Canaan: Adah the daughter of Elon the Hittite, and Oholibamah the daughter of Anah, the daughter of Zibeon the Hivite, 3 and Basemath Ishmael's daughter, sister of Nebaioth. 4 And Adah bare to Esau Eliphaz; and Basemath bare Reuel; 5 and Oholibamah bare Jeush, and Jalam, and Korah: these are the sons of Esau, that were born unto him in the land of Canaan. 6 And Esau took his wives, and his sons, and his daughters, and all the souls of his house, and his cattle, and all his beasts, and all his possessions, which he had gathered in the land of Canaan; and went into a land away from his brother Jacob. 7 For their substance was too great for them to dwell together; and the land of their sojournings could not bear them because of their cattle. 8 And Esau dwelt in mount Seir: Esau is Edom.

9 And these are the generations of Esau the father of the Edomites in mount Seir: 10 these are the names of Esau's sons: Eliphaz the son of Adah the wife of Esau, Reuel the son of Basemath the wife of Esau. 11 And the sons of Eliphaz were Teman, Omar, Zepho, and Gatam, and Kenaz. 12 And Timna was concubine to Eliphaz Esau's son; and she bare to Eliphaz Amalek: these are the sons of Adah, Esau's wife. 13 And these are the sons of Reuel: Nahath, and Zerah, Shammah, and Mizzah: these were the sons of Basemath, Esau's wife. 14 And these were

[111] Alfred Edersheim, *The Life and Times of Jesus the Messiah,* I, 186-87.

the sons of Oholibamah the daughter of
Anah, the daughter of Zibeon, Esau's wife:
and she bare to Esau Jeush, and Jalam,
and Korah.

15 These are the chiefs of the sons of
Esau: the sons of Eliphaz the first-born
of Esau: chief Teman, chief Omar, chief
Zepho, chief Kenaz, 16 chief Korah, chief
Gatam, chief Amalek: these are the chiefs
that came of Eliphaz in the land of Edom;
these are the sons of Adah. 17 And these
are the sons of Reuel, Esau's son: chief
Nahath, chief Zerah, chief Shammah, chief
Mizzah: these are the chiefs that came
of Reuel in the land of Edom; these are
the sons of Basemath, Esau's wife. 18 And
these are the sons of Oholibamah, Esau's
wife: chief Jeush, chief Jalam, chief
Korah: these are the chiefs that came of
Oholibamah the daughter of Anah, Esau's
wife. 19 These are the sons of Esau, and
these are their chiefs: the same is Edom.

20 These are the sons of Seir the Horite,
the inhabitants of the land: Lotan and
Shobal and Zibeon and Anah, 21 and
Dishon and Ezer and Dishan: these are
the chiefs that came of the Horites, the
children of Seir in the land of Edom.
22 And the children of Lotan were Hori
and Heman; and Lotan's sister was Timna. 23 And these are the children of
Shobal: Alvan and Manahath and Ebal,
Shepho and Onam. 24 And these are the
children of Zibeon; Aiah and Anah; this
is Anah who found the hot springs in the
wilderness, as he fed the asses of Zibeon
his father. 25 And these are the children
of Anah: Dishon and Oholibamah the
daughter of Anah. 26 And these are the
children of Dishon: Hemdan and Eshban
and Ithran and Cheran. 27 These are the
children of Ezer: Bilhan and Zaavan and
Akan. 28 These are the children of Dishan: Uz and Aran. 29 These are the chiefs
that came of the Horites: chief Lotan,
chief Shobal, chief Zibeon, chief Anah,
30 chief Dishon, chief Ezer, chief Dishan:
these are the chiefs that came of the
Horites, according to their chiefs in the
land of Seir.

31 And these are the kings that reigned
in the land of Edom, before there reigned
any king over the children of Israel. 32
And Bela the son of Beor reigned in
Edom: and the name of his city was
Dinhabah. 33 And Bela died, and Jobab
the son of Zerah of Bozrah reigned in his
stead. 34 And Jobab died, and Husham
of the land of the Temanites reigned in
his stead. 35 And Husham died, and Ha-

dad the son of Bedad, who smote Midian
in the field of Moab, reigned in his stead:
and the name of his city was Avith. 36
And Hadad died, and Samlah of Masrekah reigned in his stead. 37 And Samlah
died, and Shaul of Rehoboth by the River
reigned in his stead. 38 And Shaul died,
and Baal-hanan the son of Achbor reigned
in his stead. 39 And Baal-hanan the son
of Achbor died, and Hadar reigned in his
stead: and the name of his city was Pau;
and his wife's name was Mehetabel, the
daughter of Matred, the daughter of
Me-zahab.

40 And these are the names of the
chiefs that came of Esau, according to
their families, after their places, by their
names: chief Timna, chief Alvah, chief
Jetheth, 41 chief Oholibamah, chief Elah,
chief Pinon, 42 chief Kenaz, chief Teman,
chief Mibzar, 43 chief Magdiel, chief Iram:
these are the chiefs of Edom, according to
their habitations in the land of their possession. This is Esau, the father of the
Edomites.

Again we find the familiar words, **these
are the generations.** The author has completed his narrative about the sons of
Isaac, and now moves on to the sons or
descendants of Isaac's sons, beginning
first with **Esau.** The chapter divides into
six parts: (1) the sons of Esau born in
Canaan, verses 1-8, (2) the grandsons of
Esau born after his move to Seir, verses
9-14, (3) the tribal chiefs of the nation
of Edom, verses 15-19, (4) the genealogy and chiefs of the Horites of Mt. Seir,
the survivors of whom became amalgamated with Esau's offspring in the nation
of Edom, verses 20-30, (5) a list of early
kings of Edom who reigned there before
the establishment of the kingdom in Israel, verses 31-39, and (6) a geographical list of the clans or tribes of Edom,
verses 40-43.

In verses 1-8, Esau's three wives are
listed by somewhat different names than
previously (cf. 26:34; 28:9). Apparently
Adah the daughter of Elon the Hittite
is the same as "Basemath the daughter of
Elon the Hittite." **Oholibamah the daughter of Anah, the daughter of Zibeon
the Hivite** appears to be the same person as "Judith the daughter of Beeri
the Hittite." (*Beeri* means "spring man"
and **Anah** was the discoverer of springs,

36:24.[112] Anah was not a woman but a man, the second word **daughter** being used in the sense of "granddaughter," which was quite legitimate in the Hebrew.) **Basemath** must be the same person as "Mahalath," since both are designated as daughter of Ishmael, and sister of Nebaioth, Ishmael's first-born son. After the birth of his five sons, Esau took his family and all of his possessions and left Canaan for Mt. Seir, since there was not enough pasture for him and Jacob both (cf. Abram and Lot, 13:5ff.). This was apparently Esau's final move to Seir which probably occurred after Jacob's return and perhaps even after Isaac's death. It marked his final recognition that the birthright belonged to Jacob. Seir's general location was south of the Dead Sea, centering in a range of mountains running along the east side of the Arabah to the Elanitic Gulf.

Verses 9-14 begin with a repetition of the familiar words, **these are the generations of Esau.** But here is introduced not a new person or line, but the shift is from the offspring of Esau, as they were when he lived in Canaan, to them as they were later in Seir. The only addition is to list the ten grandsons born to two of Esau's sons — the two born to two of his wives, Adah and Basemath. Then in verses 15-19, fourteen chiefs of the clans or tribes (more literally "chiliarchs" or "rulers of a thousand") of Edom are listed, including the ten grandsons, the three sons of Esau's other wife, Oholibamah, and an additional **Korah,** listed among the descendants of Eliphaz, Esau's first-born son, but bearing a name identical to that of Oholibamah's youngest son. It is possible that this was a great-grandson of Esau who rose to such prominence as to be included among the chiefs.

Verses 20-30 give a brief summary of the descendants of **Seir the Horite,** the people who preceded Esau in the land, whom he partially conquered and destroyed (Deut. 2:12, 22), and with whom he partially amalgamated through intermarriage. Seir's six sons are listed together with their sons. In only one case, that of Anah, are the children of a grandson given. This is evidently to trace the lineage of Oholibamah, Esau's wife. So in Esau's marriage the two lines joined. There is also mention of a daughter of Seir by the name of Timna, the same as the concubine of Esau's first-born son, Eliphaz (vv. 10-12). This Timna would have been a great-aunt to Oholibamah, Esau's wife, and only if she had been the child of Seir's extremely old age could she have been the same person as Eliphaz's concubine. Mention is made in connection with Anah of his discovery of **hot springs,** a phenomenon still to be observed in the area south of the Dead Sea.[113] Only the six sons of Seir are listed as having obtained the rank of chiefs among the Horites.

Verses 31-39 list some of the early kings of Edom. They are said to have reigned **before there reigned any king over the children of Israel.** This clause has been used by many critical scholars as an unassailable proof that the book of Genesis could not have been written for hundreds of years after the time of Moses. It is possible, however, that these kings had already reigned by the time of Moses and he simply spoke prophetically concerning the kings of Israel. Or, although the book must have been written in essentially the same form as it appears today about the time of Moses and probably by that great leader himself, there is evidence that a later hand added such

---

[112] Leupold, *op. cit.*, p. 934. The father of this wife appears variously as a Hittite (26:34), a Hivite (36:2), and a Horite (36:20, 24). The Hittites were one of the great powers of the ancient world, long forgotten, but recently rediscovered by archaeologists; the center of their power was in Asia Minor, but they also spread throughout Mesopotamia and Syria-Palestine. The Hivites were one of the seven nations of Canaan, with their center of power in the northern part of the land, but also to be found throughout the country. The Horites are now known in secular history as the Hurrians, another people recently brought to light by archaeologists, who came from the region just south of the Caucasus, and who moved in great numbers into Mesopotamia, indelibly stamping upon all the ancient peoples their cultural ideas and laws — it was their laws which governed the lands from which Abraham came and which explain many of the otherwise mysterious actions recorded in the patriarchal stories. How could this man have been from all three nationalities? The terms *Hittite* and *Hivite* both seem to have achieved a broader meaning and been applied to other peoples in Canaan much the same as Amorite and Canaanite. There is some possibility that the Hivites were an ethnic division of the Hurrians. And the term *Horite* also means "cave-dweller," and may in the Scriptures refer at times to literal cave-dwellers rather than the Hurrians. So it is possible that Anah or Beeri was technically any one of the three nationalities and yet the other two terms could have been quite correctly applied to him in the proper setting.

[113] *Ibid.*, p. 943.

passages as this one and the parenthetical identification of ancient sites by their later names — those current in the time of the later scribe (cf. 35:19, 27 and see "Authorship" under "Introduction"). The chapter closes out with another list of the chiefs of Edom, only two of which have the same names as those in verses 15-19. The former, however, represented the ancestral founders of the clans; the latter refer to those who ruled the clans according to their geographical distribution — according to their families, after their places, by their names. Dillmann calls the former list "historico-genealogical" and the latter "geographic-statistical."[114] Of all the names listed in the chapter, only a few seem to be echoed in the names of known tribes of the desert dwellers. The exception is Amalek, the son borne by Timna the concubine to Eliphaz, Esau's first-born. The Amalekites lived apart from Edom, inhabiting the area farther to the west. It is possible that since Amalek was a concubine's son, the other sons forced him and therefore his descendants into a separate existence.[115]

D. THE STORY OF JOSEPH AND HIS BRETHREN (37:1—50:26)

1. Joseph's Tribulation (37:1-36)

a. Course: Favored (37:1-11)

1 And Jacob dwelt in the land of his father's sojournings, in the land of Canaan. 2 These are the generations of Jacob. Joseph, being seventeen years old, was feeding the flock with his brethren; and he was a lad with the sons of Bilhah, and with the sons of Zilpah, his father's wives: and Joseph brought the evil report of them unto their father. 3 Now Israel loved Joseph more than all his children, because he was the son of his old age: and he made him a coat of many colors. 4 And his brethren saw that their father loved him more than all his brethren; and they hated him, and could not speak peaceably unto him.

5 And Joseph dreamed a dream, and he told it to his brethren: and they hated him yet the more. 6 And he said unto them, Hear, I pray you, this dream which I have dreamed: 7 for, behold, we were binding sheaves in the field, and, lo, my sheaf arose, and also stood upright; and, behold, your sheaves came round about, and made obeisance to my sheaf. 8 And his brethren said to him, Shalt thou indeed reign over us? or shalt thou indeed have dominion over us? And they hated him yet the more for his dreams, and for his words. 9 And he dreamed yet another dream, and told it to his brethren, and said, Behold, I have dreamed yet a dream; and, behold, the sun and the moon and eleven stars made obeisance to me. 10 And he told it to his father, and to his brethren; and his father rebuked him, and said unto him, What is this dream that thou hast dreamed? Shall I and thy mother and thy brethren indeed come to bow down ourselves to thee to the earth? 11 And his brethren envied him; but his father kept the saying in mind.

Verse 1 is transitional. In contrast with Esau's permanent dwelling in Seir, Jacob continues in Canaan, the land of the patriarchs. Then in verse 2 we find the familiar words introducing a new section: These are the generations of Jacob. The author has once more disposed of a sideline (cf. 25:12-19) and is returning to the main line in the story of Jacob's offspring. Up to this point, the course of Genesis has followed the Messianic line. Now there is a deviation of sorts. For instead of Judah being the leading character in the remaining chapters, he takes second place far behind Joseph. There are several reasons for this. From this time on the entire people of Israel were closely involved in God's revelation of Himself. Furthermore, Joseph, not Judah, was the key person in God's unfolding plan at this particular moment. It was he who was to save the chosen family from starvation, and in the process he was to provide a beautiful picture of the Christ who was yet to come.

In verses 2-11, Joseph is introduced as a young man of seventeen, and the reasons are given for his early prominence and particularly for the animosity of his brethren toward him. Of these there are three. (1) While serving as a lad, or something of an apprentice shepherd, with the four sons of the two slave-girls (Dan, Naphtali, Gad, Asher), he observed in their conduct certain

[114] Dillmann, op. cit., II, 328.
[115] Leupold, op. cit., p. 939. For a parallel, see Judges 11:1ff.

things which were not proper and reported the same to their father. These four brothers would naturally have considered him a tattler. (2) Jacob or **Israel loved Joseph more than all his children.** The reason given is that **he was the son of his old age.** This can only be interpreted in a relative sense. The eleven older sons of Jacob, from Reuben to Joseph, had all been born in a period of slightly over six years. Thus several of the brothers could not have been more than two or three years older than Joseph, one or two only a year or less. Benjamin, who was about thirteen years younger than Joseph, would really have been the son of Jacob's old age. Jacob, however, was already an old man when he went to Laban's house seeking a wife. He worked seven years for Rachel only to get Leah instead. And when he did subsequently marry Rachel, it was six years before a son was born to them — Joseph. Thus Joseph was in a sense the son he had wanted from the beginning and it was only after a long period of repeated frustrations that he was obtained. Thus he was the one waited for and in that sense a son of Jacob's old age. Furthermore, he was the first-born son of Jacob's favorite wife who had later died prematurely. And he seems to have been by far the most spiritually responsive of all the brothers. Because of this Jacob preferred him and showed this preference by making him a very special garment (the Hebrew carries the idea of "continuing to make," thus furnishing replacements as needed). The exact meaning of the Hebrew word translated a **coat of many colors** is uncertain. Some translate it "a long garment with long sleeves." One scholar finds in ancient clay tablets a clue which suggests that it was something of a ceremonial robe with costly ornaments of gold sewed onto it.[116] In any event, it was the distinctive garment of royalty (cf. II Sam. 13:18-19). Jacob should have learned from his own childhood that open parental preference could only lead to bitter strife among the children. But the error was repeated and all ten of Joseph's brothers **hated him, and could not speak peaceably unto him.** (3) Then Joseph had two dreams. The first revealed a harvest field, with his brothers'

sheaves bowing humbly before his sheaf. The second was staged in the heavens with the sun and moon and eleven stars bowing before him. Nothing is said that these dreams were divinely inspired. The Lord must have had a hand in them to the extent that they were later remarkably fulfilled. But it is quite likely that Joseph's personal ambitions played a part in their formation too.[117] But such is doubtless true of most if not all of life's really worthy dreams (cf. Rom. 8:28). Joseph seems to have told the first dream only to his brothers. The second he related to his father and his brothers. Both angered his brothers, brought their mockery, and increased their hatred. The second brought the rebuke of Jacob but also left an indelible impression on his mind.

b. Crisis: Hatred (37:12-24)

12 And his brethren went to feed their father's flock in Shechem. 13 And Israel said unto Joseph, Are not thy brethren feeding the flock in Shechem? come, and I will send thee unto them. And he said to him, Here am I. 14 And he said to him, Go now, see whether it is well with thy brethren, and well with the flock; and bring me word again. So he sent him out of the vale of Hebron, and he came to Shechem. 15 And a certain man found him, and, behold, he was wandering in the field: and the man asked him, saying, What seekest thou? 16 And he said, I am seeking my brethren: tell me, I pray thee, where they are feeding *the flock.* 17 And the man said, They are departed hence; for I heard them say, Let us go to Dothan. And Joseph went after his brethren, and found them in Dothan.

18 And they saw him afar off, and before he came near unto them, they conspired against him to slay him. 19 And they said one to another, Behold, this dreamer cometh. 20 Come now therefore, and let us slay him, and cast him into one of the pits, and we will say, An evil beast hath devoured him: and we shall see what will become of his dreams. 21 And Reuben heard it, and delivered him out of their hand, and said, Let us not take his life. 22 And Reuben said unto them, Shed no blood; cast him into this pit that is in the wilderness, but lay no hand upon him: that he might deliver him out of their hand, to restore him to his father. 23 And it came to pass, when

---

[116] Speiser, *op. cit.,* pp. 289-90.   [117] Leupold, *op. cit.,* pp. 956-57.

Joseph was come unto his brethren, that they stripped Joseph of his coat, the coat of many colors that was on him; 24 and they took him, and cast him into the pit: and the pit was empty, there was no water in it.

Up to this point, everything about Joseph marked him for an upward climb to success. But in keeping with a pattern which reflected itself repeatedly in his life, this upward climb now faced a rude interruption.

Apparently the ten older brothers had all gone together to watch after the flocks. Perhaps because of a temporary drought near Hebron, they had ranged far to the north. When they had been gone for some time, Jacob sent Joseph to see if all was well and bring word again. He left Hebron where Jacob now made his home, and went some fifty to sixty miles north to the vicinity of Shechem. Here he was told they had gone on to the neighborhood of Dothan, on the edge of the Plain of Esdraelon or Jezreel, some ten to fifteen miles farther. Here they were in the most productive area of Canaan, and incidentally on the route by which caravans traveled from Gilead and the east to Egypt.

Joseph was wearing the special garment made for him by his father. The brothers recognized the hated garment from afar, and for some of them, their emotions reached the boiling point. They began to plan his murder — not a killing on the spur of the moment under provocation, but a premeditated and cold-blooded murder of their own brother. They planned to kill him, throw his body into one of the pits or empty cisterns which abounded in the area, and report to his father that he had been killed by a wild beast. Then, they exulted in wicked glee, **we shall see what will become of his dreams.** However, while hatred for Joseph seems to have been general among the brothers, there were those whose emotions did not overcome their reason or entirely becloud their sense of right. Reuben, Jacob's first-born, tried by strategy to rescue Joseph. He suggested that they not kill him but imprison him in one of the cisterns where he would die eventually of thirst and starvation. He planned to come back later alone and rescue his younger brother,

but did not feel at the time that he could oppose his brothers directly. So they seized Joseph, stripped him of the despised coat, and threw him into an empty cistern. There were many of these in Canaan, dug out to conserve whatever rain might fall in that semi-desert land. Some of them were extremely narrow at the top, and were covered with a heavy stone. They were frequently used as prisons (cf. Jer. 38:6; Zech. 9:11).

c. Consequence: Slavery (37:25-36)

25 And they sat down to eat bread: and they lifted up their eyes and looked, and, behold, a caravan of Ishmaelites was coming from Gilead, with their camels bearing spicery and balm and myrrh, going to carry it down to Egypt. 26 And Judah said unto his brethren, What profit is it if we slay our brother and conceal his blood? 27 Come, and let us sell him to the Ishmaelites, and let not our hand be upon him; for he is our brother, our flesh. And his brethren hearkened unto him. 28 And there passed by Midianites, merchantmen; and they drew and lifted up Joseph out of the pit, and sold Joseph to the Ishmaelites for twenty pieces of silver. And they brought Joseph into Egypt.

29 And Reuben returned unto the pit; and, behold, Joseph was not in the pit; and he rent his clothes. 30 And he returned unto his brethren, and said, The child is not; and I, whither shall I go? 31 And they took Joseph's coat, and killed a he-goat, and dipped the coat in the blood; 32 and they sent the coat of many colors, and they brought it to their father, and said, This have we found: know now whether it is thy son's coat or not. 33 And he knew it, and said, It is my son's coat; an evil beast hath devoured him; Joseph is without doubt torn in pieces. 34 And Jacob rent his garments, and put sackcloth upon his loins, and mourned for his son many days. 35 And all his sons and all his daughters rose up to comfort him; but he refused to be comforted; and he said, For I will go down to Sheol to my son mourning. And his father wept for him. 36 And the Midianites sold him into Egypt unto Potiphar, an officer of Pharaoh's, the captain of the guard.

Reuben left. The other brothers sat down to eat. Their extreme callousness is thus revealed, for Joseph was confined without water or food, and they were probably within earshot of his cries for mercy (cf. 42:21). While they were eating, a caravan appeared on the road leading across the plain to the seacoast, whence it turned southward through the Philistine country to Egypt. This caravan was **bearing spicery** (gum tragacanth) **and balm** (mastic or balsam) **and myrrh** (ladanum), all products highly valued in Egypt both for medicinal use and for use in embalming the bodies of the dead. Judah, like Reuben, had apparently been looking for some way to save Joseph. He was not aware of Reuben's plan, so he suggested one of his own — that they sell Joseph to the caravan. This way they would be rid of him, yet not guilty of Cain's sin. To this the other brothers readily agreed. So they drew Joseph out of the cistern, and sold him to the caravan traders for **twenty pieces of silver,** the standard price for a boy between five and twenty years of age (Lev. 27:5), being somewhat less than the price of an adult slave which was thirty pieces (Exod. 21:32; cf. Matt. 26:14-16).

Many readers of this chapter have been confused by the various terms used of the people in the caravan: **Ishmaelites** (vv. 25, 27, 28), and **Midianites** (vv. 28, 36 — the Hebrew for the latter verse gives it *Medanites*). This has led some critical scholars to declare that the story is the mingling of two conflicting accounts. The Ishmaelites, Midianites, and Medanites, however, were all descendants of Abraham (25:1-2, 12). They all were desert-dwellers and seem to have intermarried with each other and with other nomadic groups until they blended together in the modern Arabs. Because of this the names could almost be used interchangeably. The term **Ishmaelites** seems also to have been used of caravan traders in general, irrespective of their national origin, and a group of Midianite merchants may have made up one part of the large "Ishmaelite" caravan.[118] If the word **Ishmaelites** is in each instance translated "traders" or "caravan traders," the difficulty disappears.

When Reuben returned and found Joseph gone, he rent his clothes and said in desperation to his brothers, **Whither shall I go?** — What shall I do now? They replied by carrying out their earlier plan for a false report to their father, killing **a he-goat,** and dipping Joseph's famous coat in its blood. Rather than taking it, they sent it to Jacob saying that they had found it — he would know whether it was Joseph's or not! Jacob was wild with grief, so much that even Joseph's hypocritical brothers tried to comfort him, but he refused their comfort. He expected to go down to **Sheol** or "the grave" to Joseph, mourning.[119]

Meanwhile, the Midianite merchants in the caravan of traders had gone on to Egypt. There they sold Joseph to Potiphar, one of Pharaoh's officials, and in fact, **captain of the guard** — perhaps the king's bodyguard.

2. Judah's Indiscretion (38:1-30)

1 And it came to pass at that time, that Judah went down from his brethren, and turned in to a certain Adullamite, whose name was Hirah. 2 And Judah saw there a daughter of a certain Canaanite whose name was Shua; and he took her, and went in unto her. 3 And she conceived and bare a son; and he called his name Er. 4 And she conceived again, and bare a son; and she called his name Onan. 5 And she yet again bare a son, and called his name Shelah: and he was at Chezib, when she bare him. 6 And Judah took a wife for Er his first-born, and her name was Tamar. 7 And Er, Judah's firstborn, was wicked in the sight of Jehovah; and Jehovah slew him. 8 And Judah said unto Onan, Go in unto thy brother's wife, and perform the duty of a husband's brother unto her, and raise up seed to thy brother. 9 And Onan knew that the seed would not be his; and it came to pass, when he went in unto his brother's wife, that he spilled it on the ground, lest he should give seed to his brother. 10 And the thing which he did was evil in the sight of Jehovah: and he slew him also. 11 Then said Judah to Tamar his daughter-in-law, Remain a widow in thy father's house, till Shelah my son be grown up; for he said, Lest he also die, like his brethren. And Tamar went and dwelt in her father's house.

12 And in process of time Shua's daughter, the wife of Judah, died; and

---

[118] *Ibid.*, pp. 968-971. In Judges 8:24 the Midianites whom Gideon overcame are also called Ishmaelites. Compare also W. Haskell, "Ishmaelite," in *Unger's Bible Dictionary*, p. 540.

[119] **Sheol**, while generally referring to a condition of shadowy darkness, is usually used in the Old Testament in reference merely to the grave, and not to a place of punishment after death. This latter truth was only gradually revealed and that in its fullness only in the New Testament.

Judah was comforted, and went up unto his sheep-shearers to Timnah, he and his friend Hirah the Adullamite. 13 And it was told Tamar, saying, Behold, thy father-in-law goeth up to Timnah to shear his sheep. 14 And she put off from her the garments of her widowhood, and covered herself with her veil, and wrapped herself, and sat in the gate of Enaim, which is by the way to Timnah; for she saw that Shelah was grown up, and she was not given unto him to wife. 15 When Judah saw her, he thought her to be a harlot; for she had covered her face. 16 And he turned unto her by the way, and said, Come, I pray thee, let me come in unto thee: for he knew not that she was his daughter-in-law. And she said, What wilt thou give me, that thou mayest come in unto me? 17 And he said, I will send thee a kid of the goats from the flock. And she said, Wilt thou give me a pledge till thou send it? 18 And he said, What pledge shall I give thee? And she said, Thy signet and thy cord, and thy staff that is in thy hand. And he gave them to her, and came in unto her, and she conceived by him. 19 And she arose, and went away, and put off her veil from her, and put on the garments of her widowhood. 20 And Judah sent the kid of the goats by the hand of his friend the Adullamite, to receive the pledge from the woman's hand: but he found her not. 21 Then he asked the men of her place, saying, Where is the prostitute, that was at Enaim by the wayside? And they said, There hath been no prostitute here. 22 And he returned to Judah, and said, I have not found her; and also the men of the place said, There hath been no prostitute here. 23 And Judah said, Let her take it to her, lest we be put to shame: behold, I sent this kid, and thou hast not found her.

24 And it came to pass about three months after, that it was told Judah, saying, Tamar thy daughter-in-law hath played the harlot; and moreover, behold, she is with child by whoredom. And Judah said, Bring her forth, and let her be burnt. 25 When she was brought forth, she sent to her father-in-law, saying, By the man, whose these are, am I with child: and she said, Discern, I pray thee, whose are these, the signet, and the cords, and the staff. 26 And Judah acknowledged them, and said, She is more righteous than I, forasmuch as I gave her not to Shelah my son. And he knew her again no more. 27 And it came to pass in the time of her travail, that, behold, twins were in her womb. 28 And it came to pass, when she travailed, that one put

out a hand: and the midwife took and bound upon his hand a scarlet thread, saying, This came out first. 29 And it came to pass, as he drew back his hand, that, behold, his brother came out: and she said, Wherefore hast thou made a breach for thyself? therefore his name was called Perez. 30 And afterward came out his brother, that had the scarlet thread upon his hand: and his name was called Zerah.

Chapter 38 seems at first glance to be an inexcusable interruption of the fascinating story of Joseph. However, it is in accord with the general theme of the last fourteen chapters of Genesis — the story of Jacob's offspring. And it serves the purpose of an interlude between Acts I and II of the drama of Joseph, helping to mark the passage of time and the shift in background. Its position in the book also contrasts the low morals of Judah and his sons with the purity of Joseph (cf. Gen. 38 with 39:6b-18). It does focus attention on the Messianic line again, but not in a very complimentary way. Rather, as in other similar stories about biblical characters, it frankly tells even the worst side of the men who were the best God could find to serve as the instruments of His divine purpose and will.

The chapter begins with an expression which is intended in a general way to date the story: **And it came to pass at that time.** This would seem to mark the beginning of the following series of events as occurring at the time of Joseph's enslavement or immediately· afterward. However, the total number of years Joseph spent in Egypt before the rest of the family left Canaan to join him was only twenty-two (cf. 37:2; 41:46, 53; 45: 7ff.). This would not be sufficient to allow comfortably for all the events of the chapter to occur. So it is likely that Judah's friendship with the Canaanites began at an earlier time, perhaps when Jacob first tented at Shechem or soon after he returned to his father at Hebron. But most of the events of this chapter occurred while Joseph was in Egypt. Since they affected the founder of the leading tribe of the chosen people, the man through whom God's most important promises were to be fulfilled, they were the most noteworthy items of the family history during Joseph's absence.

The whole story, with all of its shameful development, began when Judah partially broke away from the family and formed a friendship and business relation with **Hirah**, a Canaanite from the city of Adullam, located at the edge of the *Shephelah* or foothills southwest of Jerusalem. The Lord had always sought to prevent entangling alliances such as this and later forbade them in the law of Moses. The dangers are evident in the case of Judah. While visiting Hirah, Judah saw the daughter of **Shua**, another Canaanite, and married ˋher. She bore him three sons: **Er, Onan,** and **Shelah.** When Er reached maturity his father took for him a wife named **Tamar.** Jacob, in spite of prevailing custom (cf. 24:1ff.; 28:1-5), had almost certainly had no say in the choice of a wife for Judah. But it is possible that Er was still quite young since marriages were common in the teens, and his father would have been that much more likely to have dominated his choice. His bride also was apparently a Canaanite. But Er proved to be displeasing to the Lord. He was wicked and he was slain — the wages of sin have always been death, from the garden of Eden to the present. So Judah gave his widow to Onan, asking him to raise up children who would bear his brother's name and keep alive his memory. This was in full accord with the so-called law of the levirate marriage, later set forth in the Mosaic law (Deut. 25: 5-10), but also generally practiced among ancient, as also many contemporary primitive, peoples.[120] But Onan had no interest in his brother's name and consistently prevented a natural conclusion to their intercourse in order to avoid fathering children for Er. This, too, was evil in the Lord's sight and Onan also died. Judah then advised Tamar to return to her father's house until his third son, Shelah, was grown. But secretly he had decided that Tamar must be the cause of his sons' deaths and he determined to save Shelah from a similar fate.

Some time passed. Shelah reached the same age at which his brothers had married. Then his mother died. Judah ended his period of mourning and went with his friend Hirah to shear the sheep. Tamar knew that Shelah was grown and that Judah was trying to avoid his responsibilities toward her. She knew, too, that he was now a widower and that he had gone to the sheep-shearing where there was usually much feasting and drinking.[121] She took off her widow's garments, wrapped around herself "the veil" as the Hebrew literally reads, apparently designating that particular veil which was customarily worn by prostitutes of that area, slipped away from her father's home, and sat down by the road which led to Timnah, the site of the shearing. Judah came by, took her to be the prostitute she appeared to be, and proposed to employ her services. The writer indicates that Judah would certainly not have done so if he had known she was his daughter-in-law. Thus Judah was not intentionally guilty of incest. But his moral character is depicted as very low. While Tamar knew that his resistance to this temptation would be particularly low at this time, it is also possible that she had heard previous reports of such escapades on his part.[122] The price agreed upon was **a kid of the goats.** But since Judah would have to send the kid later, Tamar asked for something to be deposited as a pledge of payment. She asked for his **signet** and **cord** and his **staff.** The signet and cord were almost certainly the cylindrical seal which was suspended by a cord from the owner's sash or other garment. Such seals marked persons of importance in Mesopotamia and their use spread throughout the Near East.[123] The staff was probably the one he used in shepherding, and which would have been easily identifiable as his. Thus in both cases Tamar asked not only for things of value but those about which there could be no error in identification. All that she asked he gave to her. The shameful bargain was then carried to completion.

After Judah left, Tamar slipped away, discarded her disguise, and attired herself once again as a widow. Judah sent the payment of the kid by the hand of his friend Hirah. The low moral state of Canaan is evidenced by the fact that Hirah apparently felt honored so to

[120] Skinner, *op. cit.*, p. 452.   [121] Leupold, *op. cit.*, p. 982.   [122] *Ibid.*, p. 983.
[123] Speiser, *op. cit.*, p. 298.

serve his friend. But when Hirah came to the place where the "prostitute" was supposed to be plying her trade, he found her not. So he inquired concerning her whereabouts. But he attempted to raise the moral tone of the whole incident by asking instead concerning the "sacred prostitute," a woman dedicated to prostitution as an act of worship of the heathen gods of the land. These gods were especially thought of in terms of fertility and productivity, both in crops and animals and in children. And it was thought their favor and active blessing could be incited by human intercourse. Accordingly, a woman who dedicated herself to use in connection with the shrines held a much higher place socially than a prostitute who merely sought personal gain. But Hirah was told there had been no sacred prostitute there. He reported the failure of his mission to Judah, who wished to avoid any notoriety which might arise from further inquiry and who decided to let the unknown woman keep his pledge. How low man can sink when he ignores God! And how easily man can excuse his conduct while hiding from its consequences!

Three months later, Judah heard the news that Tamar was pregnant. Everyone knew that it must be illegitimately. So Judah condemned her to be burned. But on the way to the place of execution, she sent his seal and cord and staff that Judah might identify the man who shared her guilt. Judah immediately confessed them as his own and declared that her righteousness exceeded his own. Since the conduct of both Judah and Tamar must stand condemned in the light of God's revealed will, it would be better to say that his guilt was greater than hers! He had not only committed fornication, but he had also deprived her of the husband who was rightfully hers. Judah knew her no more as a wife and apparently and justifiably never permitted her marriage to Shelah. When the time came for her to be delivered, she gave birth to twins, Perez and Zerah. Perez became the ancestor of Christ. Thus Tamar became the first of four women in the ancestral line of Christ whom men would have excluded because of race or character or both (cf. Matt. 1:3, 5, 6).

3. Joseph's Vindication (39:1—41:57)

a. The Test in Potiphar's House (39: 1-20)

(1) Course: Prosperity (39:1-6)

1 And Joseph was brought down to Egypt; and Potiphar, an officer of Pharaoh's, the captain of the guard, an Egyptian, bought him of the hand of the Ishmaelites, that had brought him down thither. 2 And Jehovah was with Joseph, and he was a prosperous man; and he was in the house of his master the Egyptian. 3 And his master saw that Jehovah was with him, and that Jehovah made all that he did to prosper in his hand. 4 And Joseph found favor in his sight, and he ministered unto him: and he made him overseer over his house, and all that he had he put into his hand. 5 And it came to pass from the time that he made him overseer in his house, and over all that he had, that Jehovah blessed the Egyptian's house for Joseph's sake; and the blessing of Jehovah was upon all that he had, in the house and in the field. 6 And he left all that he had in Joseph's hand; and he knew not aught *that was* with him, save the bread which he did eat. And Joseph was comely, and well-favored.

Now the story returns to Joseph. He is now a slave in the household of Potiphar, the captain of Pharaoh's guard. From the moment of his arrival, the blessing of the Lord was evident upon him. Potiphar recognized this and began to trust him with ever-increasing responsibilities. Finally he made him the overseer of his house, and as the blessings continued, falling not only upon Joseph but also upon Potiphar, he completely turned over the care of all his possessions, **in the house and in the field,** no longer taking account of his riches except for that which he enjoyed at the table each day. The pattern which was noted in chapter 37 again begins to develop. Joseph was again climbing surely toward success. But the crisis is at hand, and its nature is hinted in the author's reference to Joseph's handsomeness, both in features and form — in the exact words applied earlier to Rachel, Joseph's mother (29:17).

(2) Crisis: Temptation (39:7-12)

7 And it came to pass after these things, that his master's wife cast her eyes upon

Joseph; and she said, Lie with me. 8 But he refused, and said unto his master's wife, Behold, my master knoweth not what is with me in the house, and he hath put all that he hath into my hand: 9 he is not greater in this house than I; neither hath he kept back anything from me but thee, because thou art his wife: how then can I do this great wickedness, and sin against God? 10 And it came to pass, as she spake to Joseph day by day, that he hearkened not unto her, to lie by her, *or* to be with her. 11 And it came to pass about this time, that he went into the house to do his work; and there was none of the men of the house there within. 12 And she caught him by his garment, saying, Lie with me: and he left his garment in her hand, and fled, and got him out.

Archaeology has confirmed the fact that Syrian slaves were highly prized in Egypt and that slaves were frequently appointed as superintendents of the houses of the more important Egyptians. It has also revealed why Joseph and Potiphar's wife were thrown into close and frequent contact with each other. Many of the houses had the storerooms at the back, where they could only be reached by going through the main part of the house.[124] Thus Joseph would constantly be going past the inner compartments where his mistress leisurely whiled away her time. She soon noticed this handsome and talented slave, and in her boredom she boldly and unashamedly invited him to commit adultery with her. Formerly Joseph's own talkativeness and perhaps a kind of virtuous pride had provided the crisis which abruptly ended his upward climb. But now it was a temptation to evil which he steadfastly refused. He pointed out to his mistress three reasons for his refusal: (1) his master's great trust in him which he could not betray, (2) the fact that she was his master's wife whom he could not legally touch, and (3) his own conviction, which she probably could not understand, that such would be **great wickedness** and a sin **against God**. She repeated her invitation frequently. But not only did Joseph consistently refuse; he did all he could to avoid her presence. But finally one day he entered the house when all the other servants were out. Potiphar's wife went

beyond any previous attempt and this time actually laid hold of Joseph's garment. He left the garment in her hand and fled. There are some temptations against which argument is not in order, but rather flight is called for. This was one as far as Joseph was concerned.

(3) Consequence: Prison (39:13-20)

13 And it came to pass, when she saw that he had left his garment in her hand, and was fled forth, 14 that she called unto the men of her house, and spake unto them, saying, See, he hath brought in a Hebrew unto us to mock us: he came in unto me to lie with me, and I cried with a loud voice: 15 and it came to pass, when he heard that I lifted up my voice and cried, that he left his garment by me, and fled, and got him out. 16 And she laid up his garment by her, until his master came home. 17 And she spake unto him according to these words, saying, The Hebrew servant, whom thou hast brought unto us, came in unto me to mock me: 18 and it came to pass, as I lifted up my voice and cried, that he left his garment by me, and fled out.

19 And it came to pass, when his master heard the words of his wife, which she spake unto him, saying, After this manner did thy servant to me; that his wrath was kindled. 20 And Joseph's master took him, and put him into the prison, the place where the king's prisoners were bound: and he was there in the prison.

Once before Joseph had been rising to a position of prominence only to be thrown into slavery. Now he has risen out of slavery to another position of prominence only to be thrown into prison. When Potiphar's wife saw that Joseph had run out leaving her with his coat, she knew that she must cover up her indiscretion. So she sounded the alarm, called in other servants and told them that her husband had brought in a Hebrew to the household with the net result that all the women were in danger of being mocked, or better "toyed with" or "violated." She accused Joseph of attempting to rape her, and declared that it was as a result of her cries that he had fled leaving his coat behind. She put the garment in a safe place until Potiphar came home and then repeated her charge. Potiphar was very angry, putting Joseph into a prison

---

[124] Free, *op. cit.*, pp. 74-75.

where the king's prisoners were ordinarily kept. Leupold thinks that there is a hint that Potiphar halfway suspected the truth, in the fact that Joseph is not mentioned as the object of his wrath and in the comparatively light punishment which he meted out — prison instead of death.[125] (See also comments on 39:21—40:4.)

b. The Test in Prison (39:21—40:23)

(1) Course: Trusted (39:21—40:4)

21 But Jehovah was with Joseph, and showed kindness unto him, and gave him favor in the sight of the keeper of the prison. 22 And the keeper of the prison committed to Joseph's hand all the prisoners that were in the prison; and whatsoever they did there, he was the doer of it. 23 The keeper of the prison looked not to anything that was under his hand, because Jehovah was with him; and that which he did, Jehovah made it to prosper. 1 And it came to pass after these things, that the butler of the king of Egypt and his baker offended their lord the king of Egypt. 2 And Pharaoh was wroth against his two officers, against the chief of the butlers, and against the chief of the bakers. 3 And he put them in ward in the house of the captain of the guard, into the prison, the place where Joseph was bound. 4 And the captain of the guard charged Joseph with them, and he ministered unto them: and they continued a season in ward.

Again Joseph had been plunged into the depths. But again **Jehovah was with him.** And this time it was the warden who looked kindly upon him. He turned over all the prisoners into Joseph's care, and just as Potiphar had not kept account of his wealth, so the warden no longer worried about anything that was under Joseph's supervision. As always, the Lord made Joseph prosper. And after he had been in the prison for some time, the chief butler or cup-bearer and the chief baker of Pharaoh were confined in the same prison for some unidentified crime against their master. In 40:3 the prison is described as being **in the house of the captain of the guard,** which would have been Potiphar's house. This explains how easy it was for Potiphar to confine Joseph there, since the king's prison was close

by or connected with his home. It also helps to explain the manner in which Joseph won the confidence of the warden. Either Potiphar was himself the warden, or one of his servants who would have already known and respected Joseph before his imprisonment. The loose character of Potiphar's wife was probably general knowledge within the household, and thus the warden would almost certainly have believed Joseph to be innocent. The cup-bearer and baker of the king were important officials in ancient courts, far beyond what their titles would indicate to a modern reader. Therefore, as prisoners they were accorded special treatment. And Potiphar himself charged Joseph with their care, giving them the best care possible, and bringing Joseph within one step, although at the time a distant step, of Pharaoh's court.

(2) Crisis: Dreams (40:5-19)

5 And they dreamed a dream both of them, each man his dream, in one night, each man according to the interpretation of his dream, the butler and the baker of the king of Egypt, who were bound in the prison. 6 And Joseph came in unto them in the morning, and saw them, and, behold, they were sad. 7 And he asked Pharaoh's officers that were with him in ward in his master's house, saying, Wherefore look ye so sad to-day? 8 And they said unto him, We have dreamed a dream, and there is none that can interpret it. And Joseph said unto them, Do not interpretations belong to God? tell it me, I pray you.

9 And the chief butler told his dream to Joseph, and said to him, In my dream, behold, a vine was before me; 10 and in the vine were three branches: and it was as though it budded, *and* its blossoms shot forth; *and* the clusters thereof brought forth ripe grapes: 11 and Pharaoh's cup was in my hand; and I took the grapes, and pressed them into Pharaoh's cup, and I gave the cup into Pharaoh's hand. 12 And Joseph said unto him, This is the interpretation of it: the three branches are three days; 12 within yet three days shall Pharaoh lift up thy head, and restore thee unto thine office: and thou shalt give Pharaoh's cup into his hand, after the former manner when thou wast his butler. 14 But have me in thy remembrance when it shall be well with thee, and show kindness, I

---

[125] Leupold, *op. cit.,* p. 1001.

pray thee, unto me, and make mention of me unto Pharaoh, and bring me out of this house: 15 for indeed I was stolen away out of the land of the Hebrews: and here also have I done nothing that they should put me into the dungeon.

16 When the chief baker saw that the interpretation was good, he said unto Joseph, I also was in my dream, and, behold, three baskets of white bread were on my head: 17 and in the uppermost basket there was of all manner of baked food for Pharaoh; and the birds did eat them out of the basket upon my head. 18 And Joseph answered and said, This is the interpretation thereof: the three baskets are three days; 19 within yet three days shall Pharaoh lift up thy head from off thee, and shall hang thee on a tree; and the birds shall eat thy flesh from off thee.

Joseph was once more on the ascent, and once more a crisis arose. This time it was of a different nature. While it could have brought him the disfavor of his fellow-prisoners if he had misled them, it held no real danger for him as had the hatred of his brothers and the passion of Potiphar's wife. But it did hold out promise of escape and deliverance.

The cup-bearer and the baker were observably sad one morning. Joseph, fully conscious of his heavy responsibility for their welfare, inquired as to the cause of their sadness. They told him that each had had a dream and there was no interpreter available to explain the dreams. Dreams were taken very seriously in ancient times, and interpreters were common at the royal courts, and would have been available to these men if they had not been in prison. But Joseph reminded them that **interpretations belong to God** and asked them to tell him their dreams. The cup-bearer told of a vine with three branches which budded, blossomed, and produced mature fruit while he watched. In the dream he held Pharaoh's cup in his hand, squeezed the juice of the grapes into the cup, and served the wine to his master. Joseph told him that the three branches were three days and that in that length of time Pharaoh would restore him to his office. And he added a request that he might be remembered by the cup-bearer when so restored, to mention him to Pharaoh and to seek his

release. Joseph supported his petition with a declaration of innocence both as to his original enslavement and his current imprisonment. The baker had no doubt been listening with keen interest. And when he heard the good news announced to the cup-bearer, and observed the similarity of their dreams, he was quick to tell Joseph his dream also. He had seen three baskets of white bread on his head, and in the top basket all kinds of baked goods for Pharaoh which the birds were eating. This was a normal picture in Egyptian life, for the monuments picture bakers carrying their goods in just this manner.[126] But Joseph's interpretation was now altogether different. The three baskets were three days. And in three days Pharaoh would **lift up** his **head** also, but not in promotion, but rather to remove it from his shoulders! Instead of eating baked goods, the birds would be eating the baker's flesh.

(3) Consequence: Forgotten (40:20-23)

20 And it came to pass the third day, which was Pharaoh's birthday, that he made a feast unto all his servants: and he lifted up the head of the chief butler and the head of the chief baker among his servants. 21 And he restored the chief butler unto his butlership again; and he gave the cup into Pharaoh's hand: 22 but he hanged the chief baker: as Joseph had interpreted to them. 23 Yet did not the chief butler remember Joseph, but forgat him.

At the end of three days, Pharaoh's birthday was celebrated. At such a time it was customary to hold banquets and grant amnesty to political prisoners.[127] And all that Joseph had foretold came to pass. Pharaoh did lift up the heads of the cup-bearer and the baker, restoring the one to his exalted office and decapitating and subsequently hanging the other.

But the sad end of this period of testing for Joseph is found in the words, **Yet did not the chief butler remember Joseph, but forgat him.** How Joseph must have waited in eager hope during those first few days after the cup-bearer had returned to the royal palace! How

---

[126] Free, op. cit., p. 76.   [127] Leupold, op. cit., pp. 1016-17.

depressing must have been the reluctant recognition that he was forgotten and his one human ray of light was extinguished! Repeatedly tragedy had seemed to dog his footsteps. Possessed of bright dreams about his future and of the intellectual, personal, and spiritual capabilities needed to fulfill them, he was nevertheless crushed every time it seemed that he was rising. A lesser man would have sunk into bitterness and despair, resigned to a life of uselessness and meaninglessness. But Joseph was pure gold, and gold is only refined when placed in the f're. He never gave in to despair, but maintained the same confidence in God and in his own destiny which he had had all along.

c. The Test in Pharaoh's Court (41: 1-57)

(1) Course: Opportunity (41:1-24)

1 And it came to pass at the end of two full years, that Pharaoh dreamed: and, behold, he stood by the river. 2 And, behold, there came up out of the river seven kine, well-favored and fatfleshed; and they fed in the reed-grass. 3 And, behold, seven other kine came up after them out of the river, ill-favored and lean-fleshed, and stood by the other kine upon the brink of the river. 4 And the ill-favored and lean-fleshed kine did eat up the seven well-favored and fat kine. So Pharaoh awoke. 5 And he slept and dreamed a second time: and, behold, seven ears of grain came up upon one stalk, rank and good. 6 And, behold, seven ears, thin and blasted with the east wind, sprung up after them. 7 And the thin ears swallowed up the seven rank and full ears. And Pharaoh awoke, and, behold, it was a dream. 8 And it came to pass in the morning that his spirit was troubled; and he sent and called for all the magicians of Egypt, and all the wise men thereof: and Pharaoh told them his dream; but there was none that could interpret them unto Pharaoh.

9 Then spake the chief butler unto Pharaoh, saying, I do remember my faults this day: 10 Pharaoh was wroth with his servants, and put me in ward in the house of the captain of the guard, me and the chief baker: 11 and we dreamed a dream in one night, I and he; we dreamed each man according to the interpretation of his dream. 12 And there was with us there a young man, a Hebrew, servant to the captain of the guard; and we told him, and he interpreted to us our dreams; to each man according to his dream he did interpret. 13 And it came to pass, as he interpreted to us, so it was; me he restored unto mine office, and him he hanged.

14 Then Pharaoh sent and called Joseph, and they brought him hastily out of the dungeon: and he shaved himself, and changed his raiment, and came in unto Pharaoh. 15 And Pharaoh said unto Joseph, I have dreamed a dream, and there is none that can interpret it: and I have heard say of thee, that when thou hearest a dream thou canst interpret it. 16 And Joseph answered Pharaoh, saying, It is not in me: God will give Pharaoh an answer of peace. 17 And Pharaoh spake unto Joseph, In my dream, behold, I stood upon the brink of the river: 18 and, behold, there came up out of the river seven kine, fat-fleshed and well-favored; and they fed in the reed-grass: 19 and, behold, seven other kine came up after them, poor and very ill-favored and leanfleshed, such as I never saw in all the land of Egypt for badness: 20 and the lean and ill-favored kine did eat up the first seven fat kine: 21 and when they had eaten them up, it could not be known that they had eaten them; but they were still ill-favored, as at the beginning. So I awoke. 22 And I saw in my dream, and, behold, seven ears came up upon one stalk, full and good: 23 and, behold, seven ears, withered, thin, *and* blasted with the east wind, sprung up after them: 24 and the thin ears swallowed up the seven good ears: and I told it unto the magicians; but there was none that could declare it to me.

Two years passed after the departure of the cup-bearer from the prison. One night Pharaoh had a dream — in fact, a double dream. In the first he was standing by the Nile. Up out of the river came seven perfect cows, to feed upon **the reed-grass.** They were followed out of the river by seven miserable specimens, whom Pharaoh later described as worse than any he had ever seen in Egypt, and who proceeded to devour the others, appearing none the better for it. This unnatural act startled Pharaoh awake. But he slept again. Now he saw seven outstanding ears of grain on a single stalk (not unusual in Egypt), followed by seven poor ears, apparently on seven stalks. Again the thin devoured the fat. Pharaoh was again startled awake. The dreams had made quite an impression on him and he demanded of **the magicians** ("sacred scribes" — those accustomed to inscribing and deciphering hieroglyphics) and **the wise men** an interpretation of the dreams. As dreams go, these dreams should have been readily interpreted by men so accustomed to such practices and to such symbols. But apparently the Lord blinded their eyes to the transparent truth and they failed to enlighten their master.

This incident reminded the cup-bearer of his earlier experience. And reluctantly referring to his earlier imprisonment, he related his encounter with Joseph and the accuracy of his interpretations. Immediately Pharaoh sent for Joseph. He was brought out of his prison, he shaved (probably the head as well as the face as was the Egyptian custom), changed his clothes as was proper in approaching Pharaoh, and was ushered into the royal presence. Pharaoh told Joseph why he had been called, but Joseph refused to acknowledge any inherent ability to interpret dreams. Instead he declared, consistent with his unquenchable faith, **God will give Pharaoh an answer of peace.** Thus encouraged, Pharaoh related to Joseph his dreams.

(2) Crisis: Interpretation (41:25-36)

25 And Joseph said unto Pharaoh, The dream of Pharaoh is one: what God is about to do he hath declared unto Pharaoh. 26 The seven good kine are seven years; and the seven good ears are seven years: the dream is one. 27 And the seven lean and ill-favored kine that came up after them are seven years, and also the seven empty ears blasted with the east wind; they shall be seven years of famine. 28 That is the thing which I spake unto Pharaoh: what God is about to do he hath showed unto Pharaoh. 29 Behold, there come seven years of great plenty throughout all the land of Egypt: 30 and there shall arise after them seven years of famine; and all the plenty shall be forgotten in the land of Egypt; and the famine shall consume the land; 31 and the plenty shall not be known in the land by reason of that famine which followeth; for it shall be very grievous. 32 And for that the dream was doubled unto Pharaoh, it is because the thing is established by God, and God will shortly bring it to pass. 33 Now therefore let Pharaoh look out a man discreet and wise, and set him over the land of Egypt. 34 Let Pharaoh do *this*, and let him appoint overseers over the land, and take up the fifth part of the land of Egypt in the seven plenteous years. 35 And let them gather all the food of these good years that come, and lay up grain under the hand of Pharaoh for food in the cities, and let them keep it. 36 And the food shall be for a store to the land against the seven years of famine, which shall be in the land of Egypt; that the land perish not through the famine.

Again Joseph was on the ascent. And again he faced a crisis. If he failed to give an interpretation, or to give the correct one, he might well lose his life this time. But the Lord did not fail him. He declared that the message of the two dreams was one, doubled to impress upon Pharaoh the certainty and proximity of the events they foretold. Seven years of great plenty were to come upon Egypt, to be followed by seven years of extreme famine which would cause the years of plenty to be forgotten. And Joseph moved beyond interpretation to advise Pharaoh on the proper course of action. He recommended that **a man discreet and wise** be selected and placed in charge of all of Egypt, with other qualified overseers under him, to collect one-fifth of all that was produced in the seven years of plenty, storing it up for use during the famine.

(3) Consequence: Promotion (41:37-57)

37 And the thing was good in the eyes of Pharaoh, and in the eyes of all his servants. 38 And Pharaoh said unto his servants, Can we find such a one as this, a man in whom the spirit of God is? 39 And Pharaoh said unto Joseph, Forasmuch as God hath showed thee all this, there is none so discreet and wise as thou: 40 thou shalt be over my house, and according unto thy word shall all my people be ruled: only in the throne will I be greater than thou. 41 And Pharaoh said unto Joseph, See, I have set thee over all the land of Egypt. 42 And Pharaoh took off his signet ring from his hand, and put it upon Joseph's hand, and arrayed him in vestures of fine linen, and put a gold chain about his neck; 43 and he made him to ride in the second chariot which he had; and they cried before him, Bow the knee: and he set him over all

the land of Egypt. 44 And Pharaoh said unto Joseph, I am Pharaoh, and without thee shall no man lift up his hand or his foot in all the land of Egypt. 45 And Pharaoh called Joseph's name Zaphenath-paneah; and he gave him to wife Asenath, the daughter of Poti-phera priest of On. And Joseph went out over the land of Egypt.

46 And Joseph was thirty years old when he stood before Pharaoh king of Egypt. And Joseph went out from the presence of Pharaoh, and went throughout all the land of Egypt. 47 And in the seven plenteous years the earth brought forth by handfuls. 48 And he gathered up all the food of the seven years which were in the land of Egypt, and laid up the food in the cities: the food of the field, which was round about every city, laid he up in the same. 49 And Joseph laid up grain as the sand of the sea, very much, until he left off numbering; for it was without number. 50 And unto Joseph were born two sons before the year of famine came, whom Asenath, the daughter of Poti-phera priest of On, bare unto him. 51 And Joseph called the name of the first-born Manasseh: For, said he, God hath made me forget all my toil, and all my father's house. 52 And the name of the second called he Ephraim: For God hath made me fruitful in the land of my affliction. 53 And the seven years of plenty, that was in the land of Egypt, came to an end. 54 And the seven years of famine began to come, according as Joseph had said: and there was famine in all lands; but in all the land of Egypt there was bread. 55 And when all the land of Egypt was famished, the people cried to Pharaoh for bread: and Pharaoh said unto all the Egyptians, Go unto Joseph; what he saith to you, do. 56 And the famine was over all the face of the earth: and Joseph opened all the storehouses, and sold unto the Egyptians; and the famine was sore in the land of Egypt. 57 And all countries came into Egypt to Joseph to buy grain, because the famine was sore in all the earth.

Now came the turning point in Joseph's life, the one time when his upward course did not end in tragedy. Whether Joseph himself had his own promotion in mind when he added his recommendations to the interpretation of the dreams cannot be known with certainty. It is possible that Joseph saw this outcome as clearly as the meaning of the dreams.

But in any event Pharaoh was so overwhelmed by the marked superiority of this young man to all his wise men, the evident dwelling within him of the spirit of God, that he immediately assigned to Joseph the task of preparing Egypt for the famine. Actually he went far beyond Joseph's recommendation, for he made him the ruler of the land in all matters, lacking only the throne as far as equality to Pharaoh himself was concerned. He gave him his signet ring (the royal seal, both the symbol and instrument of royal authority), clothed him in fine linen, circled his neck with a gold chain (an Egyptian decoration conferred for outstanding service to the crown[128]), provided him with the second ranking "limousine" or chariot, and sent him out to be introduced to the people as their new ruler. His power was to be so complete that no one could move in Egypt contrary to his wishes. He was in effect the prime minister of the empire. Then he gave him the necessary social rank, giving him an Egyptian name and marrying to him Asenath, the daughter of Poti-phera priest of On or Heliopolis, a city seven miles northeast of modern Cairo.

Joseph was now thirty years old, having spent thirteen years in slavery and prison. The shock of such an abrupt change from the most unhappy level of existence to the most exalted would have turned the head of nearly any man this young. But God's refining work had been well done. Joseph went out to assume his responsibilities in the same faith and poise that had carried him through the darkest moments of his life. During the seven years of plenty, he stored up grain until the primitive arithmetic of the day was no longer able to total it. And when the years of plenty were over, he wisely waited until the famine had really begun to pinch before he opened the storehouses and began to ration out the precious food. Soon even the neighboring countries were coming to Egypt to obtain food from Joseph, for the famine extended over all that portion of the earth.

Meanwhile Joseph had himself been blessed again. For Asenath had borne him two sons: Manasseh, "Making to forget," and Ephraim, "Double fruit" or

---

[128] Simpson, op. cit., I, 779.

"Fruitful." He had not forgotten his father's house to the degree of not remembering God's covenant with it, nor of being disinterested in its welfare. But his new joy had blotted out all the horror of the past, both as related to his life of slavery and the hateful conduct of his brothers. God had indeed made him fruitful in the very land where he had been most afflicted.

Many attempts have been made to identify the Pharaoh under whom Joseph served. The only result has been a multiplication of possibilities. One strong possibility is that it was one of the so-called *Hyksos,* the Semitic foreigners who ruled Egypt during the fifteenth and sixteenth dynasties, about 1720–1550 B.C. They were also called the "shepherd kings," and they would have had special affinity for other Semites such as Joseph.[129] However, the historical data in the biblical story is insufficient to permit a definite identification. Famines in Egypt are a matter of monumental record in this period, and one of this duration has been observed in more recent times.[130] The most significant thing about the biblical record is its detailed accuracy about Egyptian life and customs. Some critical scholars used to pronounce the story of Joseph's rise to the premiership as an impossibility. The Egyptians with their hostility toward aliens would never permit a Hebrew slave to hold such a position. However, archaeology has now uncovered evidence of many Canaanite immigrants who achieved prominence in Egyptian history, including some who may have first been slaves. Some assumed Egyptian names as did Joseph, and one was in charge of a grain-growing district. Furthermore, there is record of one prime minister in the seventeenth century B.C., who bore the good Hebrew name of Hur.[131] As knowledge of ancient Egyptian life has grown, the faithfulness of the Genesis record to historical fact has been revealed to such an extent that even those who would most emphatically deny Moses any connection with its writing admit that the later writers of the record must have visited Egypt![132] Speiser is constrained to say:

> On the other hand, the incidental detail is authentically Egyptian. Pharaoh elevates Joseph to the typically Egyptian post of Vizier (43). This is corroborated by the transfer to Joseph of the royal seal (42), inasmuch as the Vizier was known as the "Sealbearer of the King of Lower Egypt" as far back as the third millennium. . . . The gift of the gold chain is another authentic touch. The three names in vs. 45 are Egyptian in type and components; so, too, in all probability, is the escorts' cry "Abrek" (43 . . .).

While the story is the main thing, the setting is thus demonstrably factual. And although the theme and the setting together cannot as yet be fitted into an established historical niche, the details are not out of keeping with that phase of Egyptian history which can be independently synchronized with the patriarchal period.[133]

4. Israel's Reunion (42:1—47:12)

a. The First Journey to Egypt (42:1-38)

(1) The Brethren's Accusation (42:1-17)

1 Now Jacob saw that there was grain in Egypt, and Jacob said unto his sons, Why do ye look one upon another? 2 And he said, Behold, I have heard that there is grain in Egypt: get you down thither, and buy for us from thence; that we may live, and not die. 3 And Joseph's ten brethren went down to buy grain from Egypt. 4 But Benjamin, Joseph's brother, Jacob sent not with his brethren; for he said, Lest peradventure harm befall him. 5 And the sons of Israel came to buy among those that came: for the famine was in the land of Canaan. 6 And Joseph was the governor over the land; he it was that sold to all the people of the land. And Joseph's brethren came, and bowed down themselves to him with their faces to the earth. 7 And Joseph saw his brethren, and he knew them, but made himself strange unto them, and spake roughly with them; and he said

129 Speiser, *op. cit.,* p. 316.
130 Whitelaw, *op. cit.,* I, 470.
131 Free, *op. cit.,* pp. 76-77. The record of Hur he finds in W. F. Albright's article, "The Old Testament and Archaeology," in *Old Testament Commentary,* edited by Herbert C. Alleman and Elmer E. Flack, (Philadelphia: Muhlenberg, 1948), p. 141.
132 Simpson, *op. cit.,* I, 778-79.
133 Speiser, *op. cit.,* pp. 316-17.

unto them, Whence come ye? And they said, From the land of Canaan to buy food. 8 And Joseph knew his brethren, but they knew not him. 9 And Joseph remembered the dreams which he dreamed of them, and said unto them, Ye are spies; to see the nakedness of the land ye are come. 10 And they said unto him, Nay, my lord, but to buy food are thy servants come. 11 We are all one man's sons; we are true men, thy servants are no spies. 12 And he said unto them, Nay, but to see the nakedness of the land ye are come. 13 And they said, We thy servants are twelve brethren, the sons of one man in the land of Canaan; and behold, the youngest is this day with our father, and one is not. 14 And Joseph said unto them, That is it that I spake unto you, saying, Ye are spies: 15 hereby ye shall be proved: by the life of Pharaoh ye shall not go forth hence, except your youngest brother come hither. 16 Send one of you, and let him fetch your brother, and ye shall be bound, that your words may be proved, whether there be truth in you: or else by the life of Pharaoh surely ye are spies. 17 And he put them all together into ward three days.

Now the story reverts to that family Joseph had been forced to leave so long before. And the famine which engaged Joseph's labors in Egypt was also causing difficulty in Canaan where Jacob and his other sons were still living. Jacob soon learned from passing caravans, or from neighbors who had gone to Egypt to satisfy their own needs, that there was grain in Egypt. While his sons looked uncertainly at each other, not knowing what to do, his still agile mind demanded immediate action in the only way which would alleviate their difficulty. Thus "the energy and resourcefulness of the father is set in striking contrast to the perplexity of the sons."[134] Ten of the brothers were dispatched to Egypt, but Benjamin was kept at home, for Jacob feared lest some disaster would befall him as it had Joseph, and he would be deprived of both sons of his favorite wife.

In Egypt, Joseph was busy supervising the distribution of the grain. It seems probable that he took a large, personal part in dealing with visitors from foreign countries. In any event, he was on hand when his brethren arrived. From the deference shown him by his subordinates, and from his dress and manner, the brethren recognized him as a person of elevated position and bowed humbly before him. Joseph had been only seventeen when they sold him into slavery. Now he was about thirty-eight, shaven and attired like an Egyptian, using a foreign language, and appearing under circumstances where they would never have expected their brother. But on the other hand, while Joseph's brothers had been only slightly older than he, their language and clothes were still the same, and since there were ten of them, at least some of them would have changed little in appearance. So he recognized them immediately. He spoke roughly, as is sometimes customary with government officials dealing with aliens, and demanded to know whence they came. They told him they were from Canaan. Remembering his dreams and observing his brethren's present humility, Joseph determined upon a course of action calculated to test them and discover their present character. He charged them with being spies, come to spy out the weaknesses of the land. Such a charge had a ring of reality to it, for the Egyptians were especially sensitive about the possibility of invasion across their unprotected borders with Canaan. This they quickly denied, claiming that they were brothers, all the sons of one man. Spies would not likely be all brothers, for no father would risk his entire progeny on such a venture. When Joseph maintained his charge, the brothers enlarged their account of their family, telling Joseph that there were twelve brothers altogether, the youngest at home and one who was no longer alive. Joseph may have been alarmed at the absence of Benjamin, fearing lest the brothers had also done away with him. Now he determined to have proof, declaring his intention to imprison the brothers, permitting one to return home to fetch the younger brother. If the younger brother was not brought, they would not be released. And to enforce his charge and demand, he shut all of them up for three days.

(2) The Brethren's Admission (42: 18-25)

18 And Joseph said unto them the third day, This do, and live; for I fear God: 19 if ye be true men, let one of your brethren be bound in your prison-house; but go ye, carry grain for the famine of your houses: 20 and bring your youngest brother unto me; so shall your words be verified, and ye shall not die. And they did so. 21 And they said one to another, we are verily guilty concerning our brother, in that we saw the distress of his soul, when he besought us, and we would not hear; therefore is this distress come upon us. 22 And Reuben answered them, saying, Spake I not unto you, saying, Do not sin against the child; and ye would not hear? therefore also, behold, his blood is required. 23 And they knew not that Joseph understood them; for there was an interpreter between them. 24 And he turned himself about from them, and wept; and he returned to them, and spake to them, and took Simeon from among them, and bound him before their eyes. 25 Then Joseph commanded to fill their vessels with grain, and to restore every man's money into his sack, and to give them provision for the way: and thus was it done unto them.

After the three days, Joseph called them out of prison, appearing to relent a little. He proposed to keep one of them as a hostage, sending the others back with the necessary grain and promising them their lives if they returned with their younger brother.

Joseph's action was not dictated by a spirit of revenge. He does not seem to have been capable of such. Rather, before he revealed himself to them, he wanted to know whether they were still the same evil men they had once been. And he was "well aware that in the analysis of character the most potent elements are only brought into clear view when the test of severe trouble is applied."[135] The approach he used fit perfectly the men and their past. He lodged a false accusation against them, unjustly imprisoned them, and left them completely uncertain of their future. It was so nearly the same as their hateful act against Joseph some twenty years or more before that their consciences were immediately quick-

ened. When they were brought out to hear his final decision about the hostage, they confessed to one another that this had come upon them because of their merciless conduct toward their brother. And Reuben reminded the others how he had opposed them, however making his opposition stronger than it originally was, and partially admitting his own guilt by saying, **his blood is required.** The brothers had no idea that Joseph understood, for he completed his disguise by speaking to them through an interpreter. When he heard their confession, he had to leave and weep, returning when he had regained his composure. Then he had Simeon bound before the eyes of the others, and gave the necessary instructions to his servants to supply the needs of the brothers and sent them on their way. It is possible that Simeon was selected as the hostage because he was the second oldest, Reuben having somewhat extricated himself from responsibility for the brothers' wickedness. It is also possible that Simeon, whose evil temper and cruelty had been so evident at Shechem (34:25-31), played a leading part in the violence against Joseph. Joseph may have felt that he especially needed some testing and mellowing!

(3) The Brethren's Apprehension (42:26-38)

26 And they laded their asses with their grain, and departed thence. 27 And as one of them opened his sack to give his ass provender in the lodging-place, he espied his money; and, behold, it was in the mouth of his sack. 28 And he said unto his brethren, My money is restored; and, lo, it is even in my sack: and their heart failed them, and they turned trembling one to another, saying, What is this that God hath done unto us? 29 And they came unto Jacob their father unto the land of Canaan, and told him all that had befallen them, saying, 30 The man, the lord of the land, spake roughly with us, and took us for spies of the country. 31 And we said unto him, We are true men; we are no spies: 32 we are twelve brethren, sons of our father; one is not, and the youngest is this day with our father in the land of Canaan. 33 And the man, the lord of the land, said unto us, Hereby shall I know that

135 Marcus Dods, *The Book of Genesis*, "The Expositor's Bible," ed. W. Robertson Nicoll, p. 384.

ye are true men: leave one of your brethren with me, and take *grain for* the famine of your houses, and go your way; 34 and bring your youngest brother unto me: then shall I know that ye are no spies, but that ye are true men: so will I deliver you your brother, and ye shall traffic in the land.

35 And it came to pass as they emptied their sacks, that, behold, every man's bundle of money was in his sack: and when they and their father saw their bundles of money, they were afraid. 36 And Jacob their father said unto them, Me have ye bereaved of my children: Joseph is not, and Simeon is not, and ye will take Benjamin away: all these things are against me. 37 And Reuben spake unto his father, saying, Slay my two sons, if I bring him not to thee: deliver him into my hand, and I will bring him to thee again. 38 And he said, My son shall not go down with you; for his brother is dead, and he only is left: if harm befall him by the way in which ye go, then will ye bring down my gray hairs with sorrow to Sheol.

On the way home, although they had provision for the way in addition to the grain they were taking back home (v. 25), one of them apparently ran low on food for his beast. So when stopping in the empty shelter called a caravansary, e-rected for travelers such as these, he opened his bag of grain only to discover that his money had been returned and was just inside the bag.[136] The brothers were immediately filled with fear, wondering to what extent God was going to carry their punishment. They knew now that they might face new charges of theft when they returned to Egypt.

Arriving back home, they made a full report on their adventures to their father. As they emptied their sacks, they discovered that all of them had had their money returned. Jacob also became a-fraid. And he charged them with be-reaving him of his children: **Joseph is not, and Simeon is not, and ye will take Benjamin away.** While the charge was prob-ably an unreasoned one as far as Jacob was concerned, based only on the present loss of Simeon and threat to Benjamin, it no doubt startled the brothers whose consciences had been so recently and keenly sensitized. Reuben blurted out a wild offer that if Benjamin were en-trusted to his care, he would bring him back or Jacob could slay two of Reuben's sons. What consolation — avenging the loss of a son on two grandsons! But Ja-cob was adamant; he would not permit Benjamin to go.

b. The Second Journey to Egypt (43: 1—45:28)

(1) Jacob's Resignation (43:1-15)

1 And the famine was sore in the land. 2 And it came to pass, when they had eaten up the grain which they had brought out of Egypt, their father said unto them, Go again, buy us a little food. 3 And Judah spake unto him, say-ing, The man did solemnly protest un-to us, saying, Ye shall not see my face, ex-cept your brother be with you. 4 If thou wilt send our brother with us, we will go down and buy thee food: 5 but if thou wilt not send him, we will not go down; for the man said unto us, Ye shall not see my face, except your brother be with you. 6 And Israel said, Wherefore dealt ye so ill with me, as to tell the man whether ye had yet a brother? 7 And they said, The man asked straitly con-cerning our kindred, saying, Is your fa-ther yet alive? have ye *another* brother? and we told him according to the tenor of these words: could we in any wise know that he would say, Bring your brother down? 8 And Judah said unto Israel his father, Send the lad with me, and we will arise and go; that we may live, and not die, both we, and thou, and also our little ones. 9 I will be surety for him; of my hand shalt thou require him: if I bring him not unto thee, and set him before thee, then let me bear the blame for ever: 10 for except we had lingered, surely we had now returned a second time. 11 And their father Israel said unto them, If it be so now, do this: take of the choice fruits of the land in your vessels, and carry down the man a present, a little balm, and a little honey, spicery and myrrh, nuts, and almonds; 12 and take double money in your hand; and the money that was returned in the mouth of your sacks carry again in your hand; peradventure it was an oversight: 13 take also your brother, and arise, go again unto the man: 14 and God Al-mighty give you mercy before the man, that he may release unto you your other brother and Benjamin. And if I be be-reaved of my children, I am bereaved.

---

[136] Leupold, *op. cit.,* p. 1055.

15 And the men took that present, and they took double money in their hand, and Benjamin; and rose up, and went down to Egypt, and stood before Joseph.

Physical hunger is a powerful argument in any dispute. And in spite of Jacob's insistence that Benjamin could not go to Egypt, the supply of grain was soon exhausted. When Jacob told them to go to Egypt again, the brothers reminded him that it would do no good unless Benjamin went too. And now Judah, who like Reuben had tried to mitigate Joseph's fate, revealed once more his nobler side, explaining patiently to his aged father the nature of the trap into which they had fallen, and offering to accept personal responsibility for Benjamin's welfare, bearing the blame in perpetuity if he did not bring him back. So Jacob agreed, commanding them to take a gift of the fruits of the land, and double money plus the money they had found in their bags. He permitted Benjamin to go, praying for God's help in tendering this cruel Egyptian, and accepting the fact that if he must be bereaved he would have to bear his sorrow.

(2) The Brethren's Reception (43: 16-34)

16 And when Joseph saw Benjamin with them, he said to the steward of his house, Bring the men into the house, and slay, and make ready; for the men shall dine with me at noon. 17 And the man did as Joseph bade; and the man brought the men to Joseph's house. 18 And the men were afraid, because they were brought to Joseph's house; and they said, Because of the money that was returned in our sacks at the first time are we brought in; that he may seek occasion against us, and fall upon us, and take us for bondmen, and our asses. 19 And they came near to the steward of Joseph's house, and they spake unto him at the door of the house, 20 and said, Oh, my lord, we came indeed down at the first time to buy food: 21 and it came to pass, when we came to the lodging-place, that we opened our sacks, and, behold, every man's money was in the mouth of his sack, our money in full weight: and we have brought it again in our hand. 22 And other money have we brought down in our hand to buy food: we know not

who put our money in our sacks. 23 And he said, Peace be to you, fear not: your God, and the God of your father, hath given you treasure in your sacks: I had your money. And he brought Simeon out unto them. 24 And the man brought the men into Joseph's house, and gave them water, and they washed their feet; and he gave their asses provender. 25 And they made ready the present against Joseph's coming at noon: for they heard that they should eat bread there.

26 And when Joseph came home, they brought him the present which was in their hand into the house, and bowed down themselves to him to the earth. 27 And he asked them of their welfare, and said, Is your father well, the old man of whom ye spake? Is he yet alive? 28 And they said, Thy servant our father is well, he is yet alive. And they bowed the head, and made obeisance. 29 And he lifted up his eyes, and saw Benjamin his brother, his mother's son, and said, Is this your youngest brother, of whom ye spake unto me? And he said, God be gracious unto thee, my son. 30 And Joseph made haste; for his heart yearned over his brother: and he sought where to weep; and he entered into his chamber, and wept there. 31 And he washed his face, and came out; and he refrained himself, and said, Set on bread. 32 And they set on for him by himself, and for them by themselves, and for the Egyptians, that did eat with him, by themselves: because the Egyptians might not eat bread with the Hebrews; for that is an abomination unto the Egyptians. 33 And they sat before him, the first-born according to his birthright, and the youngest according to his youth: and the men marvelled one with another. 34 And he took and sent messes unto them from before him: but Benjamin's mess was five times so much as any of theirs. And they drank, and were merry with him.

When Joseph saw the brothers with Benjamin, he instructed the man in charge of his house to prepare a meal for them. There were sacred animals in Egypt which were not eaten, but the monuments show that there were large portions of meat consumed, especially when foreigners were being entertained.[137] But when the brothers heard that they were summoned to Joseph's house, they were frightened even more, and feared that it might be due to their money which had somehow been restored to

---

[137] Whitelaw, *op. cit.*, I, 484.

them after the first journey. The common punishment for theft was enslavement and confiscation of property, which they now feared. So they stopped at the door of Joseph's house to explain to his servant about their money and the fact that they had brought it again. The servant calmed their fears and declared that the God of their family had given them treasure, for he had had their money. Now Simeon was reunited with them, they were received hospitably as guests, water was provided for the washing of their feet, and their animals were fed. They then prepared their gift for Joseph's arrival, for they had learned they were to eat with him. No doubt Joseph's sudden and extraordinary kindness perplexed his brothers as much as his earlier harshness!

When Joseph arrived, they presented their gift, and bowed down to the ground according to oriental custom, once again fulfilling Joseph's dreams. He inquired of their welfare, their father's health, and the identity of the younger brother they had brought with them. Benjamin was only an infant when Joseph had been sold, and now was in his early twenties. When Joseph had spoken a blessing to his younger full brother, he could no longer restrain himself. He left to weep, washed his face, and returned to the dining room. The meal was a segregated one, with Joseph at his own table, the Egyptians of his household at theirs, and the brothers at still another. The explanation given is that the Egyptians refused to eat with Hebrews, as indeed they did with all foreigners. While it is possible that this exclusion applied even to the "naturalized Egyptian" and prime minister Joseph, it is more probable that his high position and his relationship to the priestly caste necessitated his separateness from the more common Egyptians.[138] But the most amazing thing about the meal to the brothers was the fact that they found themselves seated in the order of their ages. Their food was sent in portions from Joseph's table, a high honor indeed. But Joseph sent five times as many portions for Benjamin as the others. It was customary among the ancients to give the honored guest the larg-est and finest pieces. Among the Spartans the king received a double portion, among the Cretans the *archon* four times as much as others. The number five was particularly Egyptian.[139] It is possible that Joseph manifested such extreme favoritism toward Benjamin to test whether the older brothers were still capable of the bitter jealousy they had felt towards him. If so, they passed the test with flying colors, continuing in jovial spirits even after drinking largely (the literal meaning of the Hebrew for **were merry**) with Joseph.[140]

(3) The Brethren's Retribution (44:1-13)

1 And he commanded the steward of his house, saying, Fill the men's sacks with food, as much as they can carry, and put every man's money in his sack's mouth. 2 And put my cup, the silver cup, in the sack's mouth of the youngest, and his grain money. And he did according to the word that Joseph had spoken. 3 As soon as the morning was light, the men were sent away, they and their asses. 4 *And* when they were gone out of the city, and were not yet far off, Joseph said unto his steward, Up, follow after the men; and when thou dost overtake them, say unto them, Wherefore have ye rewarded evil for good? 5 Is not this that in which my lord drinketh, and whereby he indeed divineth? ye have done evil in so doing. 6 And he overtook them, and he spake unto them these words. 7 And they said unto him, Wherefore speaketh my lord such words as these? Far be it from thy servants that they should do such a thing. 8 Behold, the money, which we found in our sacks' mouths, we brought again unto thee out of the land of Canaan: how then should we steal out of thy lord's house silver or gold? 9 With whosoever of thy servants it be found, let him die, and we also will be my lord's bondmen. 10 And he said, Now also let it be according unto your words: he with whom it is found shall be my bondman; and ye shall be blameless. 11 Then they hasted, and took down every man his sack to the ground, and opened every man his sack. 12 And he searched, *and* began at the eldest, and left off at the youngest: and the cup was found in Benjamin's sack. 13 Then they rent their clothes, and laded every man his ass, and returned to the city.

[138] Leupold, *op. cit.*, p. 1075.   [139] Quoted from Knobel by Dillmann, *op. cit.*, II, 396-97.
[140] Leupold, *op. cit.*, p. 1076.

After the meal, Joseph commanded his servant to give the brethren all the grain they could carry, to return their money once again, and also to include his **silver cup** inside the mouth of Benjamin's sack. His instructions were carried out, and by the end of the day all was in readiness for their return homeward. As soon as it was light the next morning, they were sent away. Shortly afterward, Joseph sent his servant after them, to accuse them of the theft of his cup. It is spoken of as a divining cup. Such were commonly used in the Near East as a means of seeking guidance from a deity, oil or water being poured into the bowl or cup and omens being found on the basis of the appearance of the liquids.[141] While this would appear to us to be gross superstition, somewhat on the level of reading tea leaves, this passage definitely indicates that Joseph used the cup in this way to secure Jehovah's leadership. Other similar methods later received a measure of divine approval in the Mosaic law (cf. Exod. 28:30; Num. 27:21; I Sam. 28:6; Num. 5:11-31; and Acts 1:26).

When the servant carried out his instructions, the brethren stoutly denied the theft. They reminded him of their return of the money they had found in their sacks on the previous trip. And they declared that if they had the cup, the one who had stolen it could be executed and the rest bound as slaves. The servant responded that such extreme punishment would not be necessary, but that the thief himself would be enslaved — the customary punishment for such an act. So the search began, moving from the oldest to the youngest, and to the dismay of all of them, the cup was found in Benjamin's sack. The brothers were so overwhelmed, sensing anew their previous guilt and the doom which threatened, that they rent their clothes, the customary sign of extreme distress.

(4) Judah's Response (44:14-34)

14 And Judah and his brethren came to Joseph's house; and he was yet there: and they fell before him on the ground. 15 And Joseph said unto them, What deed is this that ye have done? know ye

141 Speiser, op. cit., p. 333.

not that such a man as I can indeed divine? 16 And Judah said, What shall we say unto my lord? what shall we speak? or how shall we clear ourselves? God hath found out the iniquity of thy servants: behold, we are my lord's bondmen, both we, and he also in whose hand the cup is found. 17 And he said, Far be it from me that I should do so: the man in whose hand the cup is found, he shall be my bondman; but as for you, get you up in peace unto your father.

18 Then Judah came near unto him, and said, Oh, my lord, let thy servant, I pray thee, speak a word in my lord's ears, and let not thine anger burn against thy servant; for thou art even as Pharaoh. 19 My lord asked his servants, saying, Have ye a father, or a brother? 20 And we said unto my lord, We have a father, an old man, and a child of his old age, a little one; and his brother is dead, and he alone is left of his mother; and his father loveth him. 21 And thou saidst unto thy servants, Bring him down unto me, that I may set mine eyes upon him. 22 And we said unto my lord, The lad cannot leave his father: for if he should leave his father, his father would die. 23 And thou saidst unto thy servants, Except your youngest brother come down with you, ye shall see my face no more. 24 And it came to pass when we came up unto thy servant my father, we told him the words of my lord. 25 And our father said, Go again, buy us a little food. 26 And we said, We cannot go down: if our youngest brother be with us, then will we go down; for we may not see the man's face, except our youngest brother be with us. 27 And thy servant my father said unto us, Ye know that my wife bare me two sons: 28 and the one went out from me, and I said, Surely he is torn in pieces; and I have not seen him since: 29 and if ye take this one also from me, and harm befall him, ye will bring down my gray hairs with sorrow to Sheol. 30 Now therefore when I come to thy servant my father, and the lad is not with us; seeing that his life is bound up in the lad's life; 31 it will come to pass, when he seeth that the lad is not *with us,* that he will die: and thy servants will bring down the gray hairs of thy servant our father with sorrow to Sheol. 32 For thy servant became surety for the lad unto my father, saying, If I bring him not unto thee, then shall I bear the blame to my father for ever. 33 Now therefore, let thy servant, I pray

thee, abide instead of the lad a bondman
to my lord; and let the lad go up with
his brethren. 34 For how shall I go up to
my father, if the lad be not with me?
lest I see the evil that shall come on my
father.

Judah assumed the leadership from the
moment the cup was discovered. He led
the brothers back to Joseph's house. Here
Joseph was waiting. He was intent on
one final test of his brethren. He had
attempted to reproduce as nearly as possible the circumstances leading to their
sin against him twenty-two years before.
He knew that Benjamin must have largely taken his own place as his father's
favorite since his disappearance. He knew
that many of the same reasons for jealousy on the part of the older brothers
were present in Benjamin's case as had
been true in his own. He had perhaps
attempted to incite that jealousy just the
day before with the .extra large portions
for Benjamin at the feast. Now he was
giving the brothers a golden chance to
reveal their true character, their true
feelings toward Benjamin. They could
escape from the wiles of this Egyptian
dictator and at the same time be rid of
Benjamin once and for all — all this
without any personal sin or blame.

But the change which the years and
recent events had wrought in the brothers
now became evident. Instead of abandoning Benjamin to his fate, they returned with him to plead his cause. They
fell before Joseph, who chided them with
the folly of their "crime." Judah replied,
despairing of clearing himself and his
brothers, for God had **found out the iniquity** of the brothers — not meaning, of
course, the present theft, but the former
sin against Joseph. This could no longer
be hidden. All would now be enslaved
by the Egyptian. But Joseph said only
the thief would thus be punished; the
others could leave in peace. Judah could
not accept this, but spoke again, uttering
one of the most eloquent pleas to be
found anywhere in literature. He reminded this Egyptian lord of the history
of their encounters, the words which had
passed between them, and the demand
that Benjamin be brought down. In the
process, Judah either brought out details
not previously mentioned in the record,
or he so reconstructed their conversations

as to lay great stress on the tender e-
motions involved in their aged father's
love for Benjamin. He then related how
reluctant Jacob had been to let him come.
He told how he himself had taken a
solemn pledge to be responsible for young
Benjamin's safety. And he climaxed this
moving speech with an offer to stay in
Benjamin's place, to become a slave so
the young man could be returned safely
to his father. While Judah had helped
to save Joseph's life years before, he had
done so by taking the course of least resistance, a course which accomplished in
essence the evil the brothers had designed. But now he is ready to be a substitute for his brother. Judah as well as
the other brothers had changed indeed!

(5) Joseph's Revelation (45:1-15)

1 Then Joseph could not refrain himself before all them that stood by him;
and he cried, Cause every man to go out
from me. And there stood no man with
him, while Joseph made himself known
unto his brethren. 2 And he wept aloud:
and the Egyptians heard, and the house
of Pharaoh heard. 3 And Joseph said
unto his brethren, I am Joseph; doth
my father yet live? And his brethren
could not answer him; for they were
troubled at his presence. 4 And Joseph
said unto his brethren, Come near to
me, I pray you. And they came near.
And he said, I am Joseph your brother,
whom ye sold into Egypt. 5 And now be
not grieved, nor angry with yourselves,
that ye sold me hither: for God did send
me before you to preserve life. 6 For
these two years hath the famine been
in the land: and there are. yet five years,
in which there shall be neither plowing
nor harvest. 7 And God sent me before
you to preserve you a remnant in the
earth, and to save you alive by a great
deliverance. 8 So now it was not you
that sent me hither, but God: and he hath
made me a father to Pharaoh, and lord
of all his house, and ruler over all the
land of Egypt. 9 Haste ye, and go up to
my father, and say unto him, Thus saith
thy son Joseph, God hath made me lord
of all Egypt: come down unto me, tarry
not; 10 and thou shalt dwell in the
land of Goshen, and thou shalt be near
unto me, thou, and thy children, and
thy children's children, and thy flocks,
and thy herds, and all that thou hast:
11 and there will I nourish thee; for there
are yet five years of famine; lest thou

come to poverty, thou, and thy household, and all that thou hast. 12 And, behold, your eyes see, and the eyes of my brother Benjamin, that it is my mouth that speaketh unto you. 13 And ye shall tell my father of all my glory in Egypt, and of all that ye have seen: and ye shall haste and bring down my father hither. 14 And he fell upon his brother Benjamin's neck, and wept; and Benjamin wept upon his neck. 15 And he kissed all his brethren, and wept upon them: and after that his brethren talked with him.

Judah's nobility broke completely Joseph's self-control. He ordered all his Egyptian servants out. Once he was alone, he revealed his true identity to his brothers, his words being at first mixed with such great sobs that the servants heard him outside and the report reached even the house of Pharaoh. Again he asked about his father's health, but his brothers were so astonished and frightened that they had become speechless. They had never had the least suspicion as to who he really was. But now that they knew, the different actions he had taken to test them may well have made them uneasy about his further plans. Joseph now calms himself a bit and calls them nearer to him. He repeats his name, confirming it by a reminder of their sin: **I am Joseph . . . whom ye sold.** And he tries to calm their troubled spirits by telling them not to be grieved or angry with themselves any longer. For while they had **sold** him, it was God who **did send** him to Egypt. Joseph does not thus make God responsible for the sin of his brethren, nor lightly excuse their conduct. But he does express his forgiveness of them, and he gives voice to that tremendous faith which had sustained him through the years. He had gradually become able to see the glorious truth behind the dark clouds of his life. God overrules things in the lives of those who serve Him for His own honor and for their good (cf. Rom. 8:28). Joseph sought now to share this comforting truth with his brethren, pointing out three reasons for his presence in Egypt: (1) **to preserve life** — the life of the Egyp-

tians and of other neighboring nations, a preservation which must be carried on for five more years; (2) to **preserve God's people — to preserve you a posterity in the earth, and to save your lives by a great deliverance;** (3) to provide leadership, for God had made him **a father to Pharaoh, and lord of all his house, and ruler over all the land of Egypt.**[142]

Now Joseph shared his plans for the future with his brothers. He wanted them to go at once, report to Jacob that he was alive and that he ruled Egypt, and bring back the entire family, including their own wives and children, so Joseph could take care of them through the remaining years of famine, lest they lose all the family wealth and come to poverty. He called on them and Benjamin to witness to their father concerning the truth of the report. His lifelong tendency to leadership and the rather lengthy experience he had now had as master of Egypt flashed forth in a strong imperative, **and ye shall haste and bring down my father hither.** Then he and Benjamin fell into each other's arms, weeping. He kissed all his brethren and wept upon their shoulders as well. By this time they were sufficiently recovered from their shock, and sufficiently convinced of Joseph's kind intentions, that they could converse with him. This very one they had hated so bitterly, and whom they had treated so harshly when he was little more than a child, was now proposing to provide for their needs and those of their children. They had no choice but to accept his aid and to hope that his attitude would continue to be favorable toward them.

(6) The Brethren's Report (45:16-28)

16 And the report thereof was heard in Pharaoh's house, saying, Joseph's brethren are come: and it pleased Pharaoh well, and his servants. 17 And Pharaoh said unto Joseph, Say unto thy brethren, This do ye: lade your beasts, and go, get you unto the land of Canaan; 18 and take your father and your households, and come unto me: and I will give you the good of the land of Egypt, and ye

[142] Joseph is here using regular official Egyptian titles in describing his office, thus evidencing once again the remarkable historical accuracy of Genesis. As father to Pharaoh, he was his adviser; as lord of his house, he managed all the affairs of the court; and as ruler over the land, he was supreme in the administration of the entire nation. See Free, *op. cit.*, p. 78.

shall eat the fat of the land. 19 Now thou art commanded, this do ye: take you wagons out of the land of Egypt for your little ones, and for your wives, and bring your father, and come. 20 Also regard not your stuff; for the good of all the land of Egypt is yours.

21 And the sons of Israel did so: and Joseph gave them wagons, according to the commandment of Pharaoh, and gave them provision for the way. 22 To all of them he gave each man changes of raiment; but to Benjamin he gave three hundred pieces of silver, and five changes of raiment. 23 And to his father he sent after this manner: ten asses laden with the good things of Egypt, and ten she-asses laden with grain and bread and provision for his father by the way. 24 So he sent his brethren away, and they departed: and he said unto them, See that ye fall not out by the way. 25 And they went up out of Egypt, and came into the land of Canaan unto Jacob their father. 26 And they told him, saying, Joseph is yet alive, and he is ruler over all the land of Egypt. And his heart fainted, for he believed them not. 27 And they told him all the words of Joseph, which he had said unto them: and when he saw the wagons which Joseph had sent to carry him, the spirit of Jacob their father revived: 28 and Israel said, It is enough; Joseph my son is yet alive: I will go and see him before I die.

Before Joseph's brothers could start on their return journey, a message came from Pharaoh himself. The good news of the family reunion had reached his ears and he was very pleased. He instructed Joseph to give his brothers ample provisions and wagons for transporting their families and goods back to Egypt. He promised them that they would **eat the fat of the land.** They were not to worry about their **stuff,** their less significant possessions, for the good of Egypt would be theirs. Joseph not only supplied the wagons, but he also gave to each of them a change of clothes, to Benjamin 300 pieces of silver and five changes of clothes, and to his father **ten asses laden with the good things of Egypt** and ten she-asses carrying grain, bread, and other provisions for his father on the way.

So the brothers departed. They came to Jacob and reported that Joseph was alive and that he was the mysterious, "harsh" ruler of Egypt. Jacob could not

believe the report until he heard all the words that Joseph had spoken (which necessitated a full confession on the part of the brothers as to how Joseph came to be in Egypt), and saw the gifts he had sent. Then his spirit revived, he felt that this was all he could possibly have asked, and he declared his intention to go to see Joseph.

c. The Third Journey into Egypt (46:1—47:12)

(1) Jacob's Fourth Promise (46:1-7)

1 And Israel took his journey with all that he had, and came to Beer-sheba, and offered sacrifices unto the God of his father Isaac. 2 And God spake unto Israel in the visions of the night, and said, Jacob, Jacob. And he said, Here am I. 3 And he said, I am God, the God of thy father: fear not to go down into Egypt; for I will there make of thee a great nation: 4 I will go down with thee into Egypt; and I will also surely bring thee up again: and Joseph shall put his hand upon thine eyes. 5 And Jacob rose up from Beer-sheba: and the sons of Israel carried Jacob their father, and their little ones, and their wives, in the wagons which Pharaoh had sent to carry him. 6 And they took their cattle, and their goods, which they had gotten in the land of Canaan, and came into Egypt, Jacob, and all his seed with him: 7 his sons, and his sons' sons with him, his daughters, and his sons' daughters, and all his seed brought he with him into Egypt.

Jacob (or Israel) and all his family and possessions departed from their home, which was probably still near Hebron, and traveled to the southern extremity of Canaan, to Beersheba. Here he offered sacrifices to his father's God. And in the night another vision occurred. Ever since Abraham's disgraceful exit from Egypt on his visit there during a famine (12:10-20), the chosen family had been forbidden by the Lord to go to Egypt (26:1-6). Now the Lord told Jacob not to fear to make this journey, for in Egypt He would make of Israel a great nation. He would go down with him into Egypt, and He would bring him out again — not as a living person indeed, as time would tell, but as a nation. And he promised Jacob that Joseph would put his hand upon his father's eyes, an expression taken by many scholars to mean the closing of his eyes after death. So Jacob's last reservations were removed and he and his family moved on to Egypt, with their cattle and goods.

The Lord had predicted the sojourn of Israel in Egypt to Abraham, many years before (15:13-14). It is plain from the viewpoint of biblical history that His providential hand was as active in their removal to Egypt and the subsequent testing and training experiences which they encountered there as it had been in all the protection and development of Joseph. Why did God lead Israel into Egypt? The immediate reason was, of course, to preserve them alive through the food to be found there. But the more long-range reasons involved their development into a nation, fitted for dependence upon His grace and power and for obedience to his commission. Judah had already married a Canaanite woman as had Simeon (v. 10). On the basis of the mention of these two as if they were unique situations, most of the brothers must have married wives imported from the homeland or from related tribes. Yet their sons were in danger of being absorbed by the Canaanites, a very wicked people with a way of life not conducive to the mission of the chosen people. In Egypt, such intermarriage and amalgamation would be discouraged by the very exclusiveness of the Egyptians themselves. The religious barriers would be more easily maintained. And yet Israel would be exposed to one of the highest cultures known in the ancient world. The promises of their own eventual inheritance of Canaan would help to keep their eyes on the divine plan, and the persecutions of Egypt would keep alive their hope for its soon realization.[143] God called Israel into Egypt to shape them for their task. He called them out later when Egypt's work was done and when it was time to begin their mission more fully.

(2) Jacob's Progeny (46:8-27)

8 And these are the names of the children of Israel, who came into Egypt, Jacob and his sons: Reuben, Jacob's first-born. 9 And the sons of Reuben: Hanoch, and Pallu, and Hezron, and Carmi. 10 And the sons of Simeon: Jemuel, and Jamin, and Ohad, and Jachin, and Zohar, and Shaul the son of a Canaanitish woman. 11 And the sons of Levi: Gershon, Kohath, and Merari. 12 And the sons of Judah: Er, and Onan, and Shelah, and Perez, and Zerah; but Er and Onan died in the land of Canaan. And the sons of Perez were Hezron and Hamul. 13 And the sons of Issachar: Tola, and Puvah, and Iob, and Shimron. 14 And the sons of Zebulun: Sered, and Elon, and Jahleel. 15 These are the sons of Leah, whom she bare unto Jacob in Paddan-aram, with his daughter Dinah: all the souls of his sons and his daughters were thirty and three. 16 And the sons of Gad: Ziphion, and Haggi, Shuni, and Ezbon, Eri, and Arodi, and Areli. 17 And the sons of Asher: Imnah, and Ishvah, and Ishvi, and Beriah, and Serah their sister; and the sons of Beriah: Heber, and Malchiel. 18 These are the sons of Zilpah, whom Laban gave to Leah his daughter; and these she bare unto Jacob, even sixteen souls. 19 The sons of Rachel Jacob's wife: Joseph and Benjamin. 20 And unto Joseph in the land of Egypt were born Manasseh and Ephraim, whom Asenath, the daughter of Poti-phera priest of On, bare unto him. 21 And the sons of Benjamin: Bela, and Becher, and Ashbel, Gera, and Naaman, Ehi, and Rosh, Muppim, and Huppim, and Ard. 22 These are the sons of Rachel, who were born to Jacob: all the souls were fourteen. 23 And the sons of Dan: Hushim. 24 And the sons of Naphtali: Jahzeel, and Guni, and Jezer, and Shillem. 25 These are the sons of Bilhah, whom Laban gave unto Rachel his daughter, and these she bare unto Jacob: all the souls were seven. 26 All the souls that came with Jacob into Egypt, that came out of his loins, besides Jacob's sons' wives, all the souls were threescore and six; 27 and the sons of Joseph, who were born to him in Egypt, were two souls: all the souls of the house of Jacob, that came into Egypt, were threescore and ten.

Just as the author of Genesis had felt that it was appropriate to list the sons of Jacob just before he returned to Isaac at Hebron (35:22b-27), so now he lists Jacob's descendants just before he enters Egypt on his journey from Hebron. In both lists, the descendants are grouped according to their four mothers. In the previous list, the groups were given in the order that Jacob married the four women; here in the order of the marriage of Leah and Rachel only, with the concubines following in each instance immediately after their respective mistresses.

This list presents several difficulties. It purports to be a list of those who entered Egypt with Jacob. But this can only be understood in some general fashion. For Joseph and his two sons are included, and they were already in Egypt. Judah's eldest two sons, Er and Onan, are included, and they had already died. Furthermore, there are included two sons of Perez, one of the twins born to Judah by his daughter-in-law. As we saw in chapter 38, the twins would have been only infants or small boys at the most when the family joined Joseph in Egypt. So the sons of Perez could not have been born for several years after the family migration. And ten sons are listed for Benjamin, who is constantly referred to as being only a youth, and who as we have seen could not have been over twenty-two or twenty-three years of age. A comparison with Numbers 26 finds Benjamin having only five sons, with two of those listed in Genesis 46 given as grandsons. (There are also differences in names in Numbers 26 and other parallel listings, but some of these are merely the result of variations in the forms of names or the use by some men of a second name.) And finally, verse 26 says that there were sixty-six persons in the migration, verse 27 says seventy, and Stephen in Acts 7:14 says there were seventy-five!

The resolution of all these difficulties would require far more space than is available in this treatment of the passage. But some general observations will lay the groundwork for such resolution. This must again be a schematic genealogy such as is also probable in chapters 5 and 10, and is certain in Matthew 1. The author is not listing just those who accompanied Jacob, but those who had previously belonged to the family, those who presently belonged to it, even though not physically with the majority, and those who potentially were part of the family, and who would father some of the major clans which would constitute the nation

at the time of the Exodus. This would also help to explain the presence of some of Benjamin's grandsons among his sons — they became equal in importance through fathering clans. The variation in the total depended upon the inclusion or exclusion of Jacob, Dinah, and Joseph and his two sons, as well as that of Er and Onan. Stephen's reference was dependent upon the Septuagint, the ancient Greek version of the Old Testament, which adds to our list five of Joseph's grandsons.[144] Some of the confusion in attempting to harmonize this list with later ones can perhaps be avoided by remembering that no mention is made in this list of the servants of the family, who must have exceeded the family itself in number. Many of these were also Semites, some descended from Abraham's slaves or Isaac's, others acquired by Jacob while in Paddan-aram (30:43). No doubt most of these and their descendants remained with the family of Israel throughout its sojourn in Egypt, with some change in relationship, especially when the Israelites themselves became slaves, and helped to constitute the "mixed multitude" which went out of Egypt with them many years later (Exod. 12:38). Some of these may have been adopted as children and still others may have simply become known as part of their master's clan. Thus an absolute tracing out of every man's ancestry would become an impossibility and would introduce countless variations into the genealogical lists, depending upon their purpose and the period of which they spoke.

(3) Joseph's Plan (46:28-34)

28 And he sent Judah before him unto Joseph, to show the way before him unto Goshen; and they came into the land of Goshen. 29 And Joseph made ready his chariot, and went up to meet Israel his father, to Goshen; and he presented himself unto him, and fell on his neck, and wept on his neck a good while. 30 And Israel said unto Joseph, Now let me die, since I have seen thy face, that thou art yet alive. 31 And Joseph said unto his brethren, and unto his father's house, I will go up, and tell Pharaoh, and will say unto him, My brethren, and my father's house, who were in the land of

---

[144] Whitelaw, op. cit., I, 503.

Canaan, are come unto me; 32 and the men are shepherds, for they have been keepers of cattle; and they have brought their flocks, and their herds, and all that they have. 33 And it shall come to pass, when Pharaoh shall call you, and shall say, what is your occupation? 34 that ye shall say, Thy servants have been keepers of cattle from our youth even until now, both we and our fathers: that ye may dwell in the land of Goshen; for every shepherd is an abomination unto the Egyptians.

Judah's strong and noble leadership in pleading for Benjamin had brought him permanently to the fore among his brethren. As a result, his father used him as a messenger to go ahead to Joseph to seek guidance as to their lodging-place. Joseph got in his chariot, probably the same one with which Pharaoh had honored him (41:43), and went to meet his father. Their meeting was understandably an emotional one, and when Jacob was again able to speak he declared that now he could die in contentment, knowing that his son was truly alive.

Now Joseph revealed his strategy for securing a proper home for his family. He was going up to report to Pharaoh on their arrival. He would also tell him that they were shepherds and that they had brought their flocks and herds with them. Afterward, when they were called into Pharaoh's presence and he inquired after their occupation, they, too, were to stress that they were **keepers of cattle**, and their ancestors had been the same before them. This was to pave the way for their settlement in Goshen, in the eastern part of the rich Nile delta. This would be advantageous because of the rich pastures available for their animals, because it would help to keep them isolated from the Egyptians, and because it was so close to Canaan and thus made the eventual return easier.[145] Furthermore, an ancient Egyptian inscription reveals that from time immemorial it had been customary for frontier officials to allow people from Palestine to enter this area during periods of famine. A long occupation of the area by a Semitic group like Israel is indicated by the many

Canaanite place names found there later. And it was here that the capital of the Semitic Hyksos or foreign "shepherd" kings was located when they ruled Egypt, probably during the period of Israel's sojourn there.[146] All of this fit in with the basis of Joseph's approach — **every shepherd is an abomination unto the Egyptians.** The Egyptian monuments reveal the truth of this statement, for even native shepherds are pictured as the most degraded of men. This antipathy may have been based on the fact that the Egyptians were settled agriculturalists and naturally suspicious of roving tenders of livestock, on a long history of attacks from the nomadic shepherds of the desert, and on the violation of Egyptian taboos against certain kinds of meat which were commonly committed by shepherds.[147]

(4) Pharaoh's Present (47:1-12)

1 Then Joseph went in and told Pharaoh, and said, My father and my brethren, and their flocks, and their herds, and all that they have, are come out of the land of Canaan; and, behold, they are in the land of Goshen. 2 And from among his brethren he took five men, and presented them unto Pharaoh. 3 And Pharaoh said unto his brethren, What is your occupation? And they said unto Pharaoh, Thy servants are shepherds, both we, and our fathers. 4 And they said unto Pharaoh, To sojourn in the land are we come; for there is no pasture for thy servants' flocks; for the famine is sore in the land of Canaan: now therefore, we pray thee, let thy servants dwell in the land of Goshen. 5 And Pharaoh spake unto Joseph, saying, Thy father and thy brethren are come unto thee: 6 the land of Egypt is before thee; in the best of the land make thy father and thy brethren to dwell; in the land of Goshen let them dwell: and if thou knowest any able men among them, then make them rulers over my cattle. 7 And Joseph brought in Jacob his father, and set him before Pharaoh: and Jacob blessed Pharaoh. 8 And Pharaoh said unto Jacob, How many are the days of the years of thy life? 9 And Jacob said unto Pharaoh, The days of the years of my pilgrimage are a hundred and thirty years: few and evil have been the days of the years of my life, and they have not attained unto the days of the years of the life of

145 *Ibid.*, I, 504.   146 Unger, *Archaeology and the Old Testament*, pp. 134-35.
147 Whitelaw, *op. cit.*, I, 504-05.

my fathers in the days of their pilgrimage. 10 And Jacob blessed Pharaoh, and went out from the presence of Pharaoh. 11 And Joseph placed his father and his brethren, and gave them a possession in the land of Egypt, in the best of the land, in the land of Rameses, as Pharaoh had commanded. 12 And Joseph nourished his father, and his brethren, and all his father's household, with bread, according to their families.

Joseph carried out his plan and it proved to be quite successful. He reported to Pharaoh the arrival of his family and that they were presently in Goshen, which would have been a logical place for them to await further orders because of its proximity to Canaan. He brought five of his brothers before Pharaoh. The king inquired concerning their occupation, and was answered as Joseph had instructed them. They told him whence they had come and why, and requested permission to stay in Goshen. Pharaoh had earlier given an indirect invitation to Joseph's family when he had instructed Joseph to send for them (45:16-20). Now he confirmed that invitation to Joseph in the presence of his brethren, specifying Goshen as the approved site of their home. And he added that if there were able men among them, they should be placed over his cattle as well.

Then Joseph brought his father before Pharaoh. It would appear that Jacob sat in the presence of Pharaoh and pronounced a blessing upon him. And in Jacob's conversation with Pharaoh, the patriarch does not call himself "thy servant," as had his sons (vv. 3-4). This probably reflects the high standing of Jacob as a nomadic chief or sheik, and the great reverence all ancient peoples had for advanced age. Thus he met Pharaoh, in some sense at least, as an equal, and assumed the position of superiority because of seniority in blessing him.

5. Joseph's Administration (47:13-26)

13 And there was no bread in all the land; for the famine was very sore, so that the land of Egypt and the land of Canaan fainted by reason of the famine. 14 And Joseph gathered up all the money that was found in the land of Egypt, and in the land of Canaan, for the grain which they bought: and Joseph brought the money into Pharaoh's house. 15 And when the money was all spent in the land of Egypt, and in the land of Canaan, all the Egyptians came unto Joseph, and said, Give us bread: for why should we die in thy presence? for *our* money faileth. 16 And Joseph said, Give your cattle; and I will give you for your cattle, if money fail. 17 And they brought their cattle unto Joseph; and Joseph gave them bread in exchange for the horses, and for the flocks, and for the herds, and for the asses: and he fed them with bread in exchange for all their cattle for that year. 18 And when that year was ended, they came unto him the second year, and said unto him, We will not hide from my lord, how that our money is all spent; and the herds of cattle are my lord's; there is nought left in the sight of my lord, but our bodies, and our lands: 19 wherefore should we die before thine eyes, both we and our land? buy us and our land for bread, and we and our land will be servants unto Pharaoh: and give us seed, that we may live, and not die, and that the land be not desolate.

20 So Joseph bought all the land of Egypt for Pharaoh; for the Egyptians sold every man his field, because the famine was sore upon them: and the land became Pharaoh's. 21 And as for the people, he removed them to the cities from one end of the border of Egypt even to the other end thereof. 22 Only the land of the priests bought he not: for the priests had a portion from Pharaoh, and did eat their portion which Pharaoh gave them; wherefore they sold not their land. 23 Then Joseph said unto the people, Behold, I have bought you this day and your land for Pharaoh: lo, here is seed for you, and ye shall sow the land. 24 And it shall come to pass at the ingatherings, that ye shall give a fifth unto Pharaoh, and four parts shall be your own, for the seed of the field, and for your food, and for them of your households, and for food for your little ones. 25 And they said, Thou hast saved our lives: let us find favor in the sight of my lord, and we will be Pharaoh's servants. 26 And Joseph made it a statute concerning the land of Egypt unto this day, that Pharaoh should have the fifth; only the land of the priests alone became not Pharaoh's.

Now the author turns attention to the manner in which Joseph carried on his government of the land during the famine. First he sold the grain until he had collected all the money in the land. Then when the people asked for food, he proposed to exchange the stored-up grain for their cattle. The next year they returned, admitting that money and livestock were both gone, but proposing to sell their land and themselves unto Pharaoh in exchange for food. So Joseph bought all the land except that which belonged to the priests, and laid a permanent rent or tax upon the entire population of one-fifth of the harvests. The people he gathered together in and around the cities so as better to distribute food to them and to organize them for labors in service to Pharaoh. The ownership of all the land by Pharaoh and the priests and the heavy taxation placed upon it are all amply supported by archaeological evidence.[148] While such procedures on the part of Joseph appear somewhat harsh to an age conditioned by socialism, they were far from harsh for the age in which Joseph lived, especially under the extreme emergency which existed.

6. Jacob's Consummation (47:27 — 50:14)

a. Burial Plans (47:27-31)

27 And Israel dwelt in the land of Egypt, in the land of Goshen; and they gat them possessions therein, and were fruitful, and multiplied exceedingly. 28 And Jacob lived in the land of Egypt seventeen years: so the days of Jacob, the years of his life, were a hundred forty and seven years. 29 And the time drew near that Israel must die: and he called his son Joseph, and said unto him, If now I have found favor in thy sight, put, I pray thee, thy hand under my thigh, and deal kindly and truly with me: bury me not, I pray thee, in Egypt; 30 but when I sleep with my fathers, thou shalt carry me out of Egypt, and bury me in their burying-place. And he said, I will do as thou hast said. 31 And he said, Swear unto me: and he sware unto him. And Israel bowed himself upon the bed's head.

The family of Israel had been placed by Joseph in Goshen, in fulfillment of his own plans and Pharaoh's command. They prospered there. In five years the famine ended and the rich delta area yielded abundant harvests so that their wealth multiplied. The family itself was increasing rapidly. For seventeen years, Jacob lived on in Egypt, the happiest, most peaceful years of his life. But as the end drew near, he called Joseph to his bedside, and made him swear that he would not bury his body in Egypt, but would take it back to the family burying-place near Hebron. The form of the oath was the same as that demanded by Abraham when sending his servant to seek a wife for Isaac, the hand of the one making the promise under the thigh of the other (see comments on 24:1-9). When Joseph had made the solemn promise, Jacob bowed his head in a gesture of appreciation, or in a prayer of thanksgiving.

b. Blessing of Joseph's Sons (48:1-22)

1 And it came to pass after these things, that one said to Joseph, Behold, thy father is sick: and he took with him his two sons, Manasseh and Ephraim. 2 And one told Jacob, and said, Behold, thy son Joseph cometh unto thee: and Israel strengthened himself, and sat upon the bed. 3 And Jacob said unto Joseph, God Almighty appeared unto me at Luz in the land of Canaan, and blessed me, 4 and said unto me, Behold, I will make thee fruitful, and multiply thee, and I will make of thee a company of peoples, and will give this land to thy seed after thee for an everlasting possession. 5 And now thy two sons, who were born unto thee in the land of Egypt before I came unto thee into Egypt, are mine; Ephraim and Manasseh, even as Reuben and Simeon, shall be mine. 6 And thy issue, that thou begettest after them, shall be thine; they shall be called after the name of their brethren in their inheritance. 7 And as for me, when I came from Paddan, Rachel died by me in the land of Canaan in the way, when there was still some distance to come unto Ephrath: and I buried her there in the way to Ephrath (the same is Beth-lehem).

8 And Israel beheld Joseph's sons, and said, Who are these? 9 And Joseph said unto his father, They are my sons, whom God hath given me here. And he said, Bring them, I pray thee, unto me, and I will bless them. 10 Now the eyes of Israel were dim for age, so that he could not see. And he brought them near unto him; and he kissed them, and embraced them. 11

And Israel said unto Joseph, I had not thought to see thy face: and, lo, God hath let me see thy seed also. 12 And Joseph brought them out from between his knees; and he bowed himself with his face to the earth. 13 And Joseph took them both, Ephraim in his right hand toward Israel's left hand, and Manasseh in his left hand toward Israel's right hand, and brought them near unto him. 14 And Israel stretched out his right hand, and laid it upon Ephraim's head, who was the younger, and his left hand upon Manasseh's head, guiding his hands wittingly; for Manasseh was the first-born. 15 And he blessed Joseph, and said, The God before whom my fathers Abraham and Isaac did walk, the God who hath fed me all my life long unto this day, 16 the angel who hath redeemed me from all evil, bless the lads; and let my name be named on them, and the name of my fathers Abraham and Isaac; and let them grow into a multitude in the midst of the earth. 17 And when Joseph saw that his father laid his right hand upon the head of Ephraim, it displeased him: and he held up his father's hand to remove it from Ephraim's head unto Manasseh's head. 18 And Joseph said unto his father, Not so, my father; for this is the first-born; put thy right hand upon his head. 19 And his father refused, and said, I know *it,* my son, I know *it;* he also shall become a people, and he also shall be great: howbeit his younger brother shall be greater than he, and his seed shall become a multitude of nations. 20 And he blessed them that day, saying, In thee will Israel bless, saying, God make thee as Ephraim and as Manasseh: and he set Ephraim before Manasseh. 21 And Israel said unto Joseph, behold, I die: but God will be with you, and bring you again unto the land of your fathers. 22 Moreover I have given to thee one portion above thy brethren, which I took out of the hand of the Amorite with my sword and with my bow.

Not long after Joseph was called to his father's bedside, he was told that his condition had grown worse. So he went again, this time taking his two sons, Manasseh and Ephraim. When Jacob heard of it, he sat up in the bed and gathered his strength for something he must have been thinking about for some time. When Joseph came in, Jacob proceeded to tell him that he was adopting Manasseh and Ephraim as his own. This was

done for three reasons, two stated, the other implied. (1) God had promised him at Luz or Bethel that he would make him a company of peoples. The adoption of two more sons would further that development. (2) They were to be his as much as Reuben and Simeon, his oldest sons by Leah, were his. Reuben had forfeited his birthright by his transgression with Bilhah (35:22; 49:3-4; I Chron. 5: 1-2), and Simeon lost any right to succeed him through his uncontrolled anger at Shechem (34:30-31; 49:5-7). The birthright was to go to Joseph instead (v. 22; I Chron. 5:1-2), and the double portion would be at least in part realized through his two sons' sharing equally with Jacob's own. (3) Rachel, Jacob's chosen and beloved wife, had died having given birth to only two sons. By adopting Manasseh and Ephraim, Jacob would be making up for some of the other sons he had hoped for through Rachel, but never received. Jacob's vision had grown dim, like that of Isaac before him, He had only dimly observed that Joseph was not alone, perhaps being so intent upon making his announcement that he had not even noticed Joseph's sons until after he had spoken. Then he asked, **Who are these?** The boys were now in their twenties and may not have visited with their grandfather frequently. But in any event, Joseph identified them. Jacob asked that they be brought near and he kissed them and embraced them, remembering how once he had no hope of seeing Joseph and now God had permitted him to see Joseph's sons. Apparently Jacob took the boys, young men though they were, on or between his knees as was the customary way of formalizing adoption.[149] Now Joseph positioned them before their grandfather, with Manasseh the eldest facing Jacob's right hand and Ephraim his left, and probably all three of them knelt beside Jacob's bed. But Jacob crossed his hands intentionally, placing his right hand on the younger Ephraim's head and his left on Manasseh. He proceeded to bless them, asking that they might be called by the name of Abraham, Isaac, and Jacob, and that they might grow into a multitude. In his threefold reference to God at the beginning of the

149 Speiser, *op. cit.,* p. 357.

blessing, the second part of it is better translated, "the God who has shepherded me all my life long unto this day," thus giving the testimony of the expert shepherd that God was indeed his shepherd — the first use of this precious symbol recorded in the Bible. Meanwhile Joseph was displeased and attempted to move Jacob's hands. But Jacob insisted that he knew what he was doing, that Manasseh would become a great people but Ephraim a greater. No doubt his own mind went back to the time Isaac had blessed him instead of the elder Esau, although it was not simply a sentimental memory but the Spirit of God which directed his present choice. He declared that Ephraim and Manasseh would be so blessed that their prosperity would become proverbial in the wishing of a blessing upon others. And he assured Joseph that some day God would restore him to the land of his fathers. And he told Joseph that he was indeed to receive a portion above his brothers, the mark of the birthright, and that it was to be that which he had **taken out of the hand of the Amorite with my sword and with my bow.** The word for **portion** is virtually the same as the name of the city Shechem, which Simeon and Levi and the other sons had so violently taken. While Jacob had rebuked them for the way they had done it, it is possible that he felt his own subsequent action had earned him the permanent possession of the city. In any event, it was the territory around Shechem which was traditionally looked upon as his gift to Joseph (Josh. 24:32; John 4:5-6).

c. Blessing of the Twelve Sons (49:1-28)

1 And Jacob called unto his sons, and said: Gather yourselves together, that I may tell you that which shall befall you in the latter days.
2 Assemble yourselves, and hear, ye sons of Jacob;
And hearken unto Israel your father.
3 Reuben, thou art my first-born, my might, and the beginning of my strength;
The pre-eminence of dignity, and the pre-eminence of power.
4 Boiling over as water, thou shalt not have the pre-eminence;
Because thou wentest up to thy father's bed;
Then defiledst thou it: he went up to my couch.
5 Simeon and Levi are brethren;
Weapons of violence are their swords.
6 O my soul, come not thou into their council;
Unto their assembly, my glory, be not thou united;
For in their anger they slew a man,
And in their self-will they hocked an ox.
7 Cursed be their anger, for it was fierce;
And their wrath, for it was cruel:
I will divide them in Jacob,
And scatter them in Israel.
8 Judah, thee shall thy brethren praise:
Thy hand shall be on the neck of thine enemies;
Thy father's sons shall bow down before thee.
9 Judah is a lion's whelp;
From the prey, my son, thou art gone up:
He stooped down, he couched as a lion,
And as a lioness; who shall rouse him up?
10 The sceptre shall not depart from Judah,
Nor the ruler's staff from between his feet,
Until Shiloh come;
And unto him shall the obedience of the peoples be.
11 Binding his foal unto the vine,
And his ass's colt unto the choice vine;
He hath washed his garments in wine,
And his vesture in the blood of grapes:
12 His eyes shall be red with wine,
And his teeth white with milk.
13 Zebulun shall dwell at the haven of the sea;
And he shall be for a haven of ships;
And his border shall be upon Sidon.
14 Issachar is a strong ass,
Couching down between the sheepfolds:
15 And he saw a resting-place that it was good,
And the land that it was pleasant;
And he bowed his shoulder to bear,
And became a servant under taskwork.
16 Dan shall judge his people,
As one of the tribes of Israel.
17 Dan shall be a serpent in the way,
An adder in the path,
That biteth the horse's heels,
So that his rider falleth backward.

18 I have waited for thy salvation, O
Jehovah.
19 Gad, a troop shall press upon him;
But he shall press upon their heel.
20 Out of Asher his bread shall be fat,
And he shall yield royal dainties.
21 Naphtali is a hind let loose:
He giveth goodly words.
22 Joseph is a fruitful bough,
A fruitful bough by a fountain;
His branches run over the wall.
23 The archers have sorely grieved him,
And shot at him, and persecuted him:
24 But his bow abode in strength,
And the arms of his hands were made
strong,
By the hands of the Mighty One of
Jacob
(From thence is the shepherd, the
stone of Israel),
25 Even by the God of thy father, who
shall help thee,
And by the Almighty, who shall bless
thee,
With blessings of heaven above,
Blessings of the deep that coucheth
beneath,
Blessings of the breasts, and of the
womb.
26 The blessings of thy father
Have prevailed above the blessings
of my progenitors
Unto the utmost bound of the everlasting hills:
They shall be on the head of Joseph,
And on the crown of the head of
him that was separate from his
brethren.
27 Benjamin is a wolf that raveneth:
In the morning he shall devour the
prey,
And at even he shall divide the spoil.
28 All these are the twelve tribes of
Israel: and this is it that their father spake
unto them and blessed them; every one
according to his blessing he blessed them.

Finally the time came when Jacob
called together his twelve sons to pronounce his final blessing upon them. No
doubt his thoughts went back to the
blessing Isaac had pronounced upon him,
and no doubt he intended his blessing
also as a legal will and testament (see
comments on chapter 27). His invitation
to this special occasion indicated that he
was going to tell them something of the
secrets of the future — something often
done in such blessings. This one compares most readily with the similar one

of Moses concerning the twelve tribes
(Deut. 33).

Jacob's order is different than in any
other listing of the twelve sons. Leah's
six are mentioned first, with Zebulun the
sixth preceding Issachar the fifth. Then
follow the slave-girls' four, but with Zilpah's two sandwiched between Bilhah's
two. Finally come Rachel's two.

Concerning **Reuben**, Jacob mentions
his joy over his first-born. But he also
speaks of his sin of incest and denies
him the pre-eminence among his brethren
because of it. **Simeon** and **Levi** are described in terms of their violent anger
at Shechem and it is predicted that they
will be divided and scattered. This was
remarkably fulfilled, for Simeon received
his inheritance within that of Judah, and
Levi received no single inheritance but
only cities and fields scattered throughout the entire nation. **Judah** is mentioned as the one who would be praised
by his brethren, who would pursue his
enemies, be served by his brethren, who
would be the ruler until he gave way to
a greater one, and who would make his
home in a land rich with the fruit of the
vine. The latter was clearly fulfilled in
southern Canaan. The word **Shiloh,** referring to the great ruler to come, may
mean "Rest-giver," and is best understood as containing a Messianic promise.[150] Judah shares with Joseph the
most prominent place among the brethren in Jacob's blessing. And he shares
with Joseph in assuming Reuben's natural office as the first-born, Joseph getting
the double portion and Judah the position of leadership (I Chron. 5:1-2).
The highest of the promises made to the
chosen people are to be fulfilled in Judah and in the Messiah who will be his
descendant. **Zebulun** was to dwell at or
near the seacoast, and be a haven for
ships. No claim is made that Jacob's
words were divinely inspired, at least in
their entirety. Here he seems to have
slightly missed the mark. Zebulun was
located about halfway between the Mediterranean and Galilean Seas, but did not
touch either one. However, it was a land
of commerce, with its trade routes feeding
the seaports, and with its boundaries
touching Phoenicia near Sidon, and prospering because of the ships which con-

150 Leupold, *op. cit.*, pp. 1178-83.

stantly moved in and out of that place. **Issachar** is noted for his strength, and is apparently chided for a tendency to settle for the least possible expenditure of his energy. **Dan** is singled out for his judging ability, perhaps predicting the services of such men as Samson and also the renowned shrine located at the northern city of Dan where many would come to be judged. There is also reference to his tendency to treacherous attack, such as that which seized the peaceful city of Laish and turned it into Dan (Judg. 18: 27-31). Jacob at this point interrupted his discourse to cry, **I have waited for thy salvation, O Jehovah.** This may have been a reference to Dan's trust in his cleverness, something which Jacob had long since learned was not adequate. **Gad,** whose descendants were to settle in an exposed position east of the Jordan, would be subjected to many attacks, but would be enabled to retaliate against his enemies. **Asher,** who was to dwell between Zebulun and the seacoast and even closer to Phoenicia, would indeed have abundant bread and be filled with dainties fit for kings. **Naphtali** was to be noted for his swiftness and eloquence. **Joseph** was to be a fruitful branch, one fed by the waters of a fountain. He would be shot at by his enemies, but his bow would retain its strength and his arms their agility because of **the hands of the Mighty One of Jacob,** who was indeed **the shepherd** and **the stone** or rock of **Israel.** All the blessings that Jacob could heap upon Joseph he did — from above, from beneath, pertaining to reproduction and care of children — all the multiplied blessings of Jacob would be passed on to Joseph, who stood distinct among his brethren. **Benjamin** was characterized as a wolf that seized that which he needed.

The blessing of Jacob was itself a beautiful poem. The author follows it with an explanation that it refers to the twelve tribes of Israel. It, of course, did apply more to the tribes than to the individual sons, except as the tribes in many cases inherited the weaknesses or strengths of their respective fathers.

d. Burial in Canaan (49:29 — 50:14)

29 And he charged them, and said unto them, I am to be gathered unto my peo-

ple: bury me with my fathers in the cave that is in the field of Ephron the Hittite, 30 in the cave that is in the field of Machpelah, which is before Mamre, in the land of Canaan, which Abraham bought with the field from Ephron the Hittite for a possession of a burying-place. 31 There they buried Abraham and Sarah his wife; there they buried Isaac and Rebekah his wife; and there I buried Leah — 32 the field and the cave that is therein, which was purchased from the children of Heth. 33 And when Jacob made an end of charging his sons, he gathered up his feet into the bed, and yielded up the ghost, and was gathered unto his people. 1 And Joseph fell upon his father's face, and wept upon him, and kissed him. 2 And Joseph commanded his servants the physicians to embalm his father: and the physicians embalmed Israel. 3 And forty days were fulfilled for him; for so are fulfilled the days of embalming: and the Egyptians wept for him threescore and ten days.

4 And when the days of weeping for him were past, Joseph spake unto the house of Pharaoh, saying, If now I have found favor in your eyes, speak, I pray you, in the ears of Pharaoh, saying, 5 My father made me swear, saying, Lo, I die: in my grave which I have digged for me in the land of Canaan, there shalt thou bury me. Now therefore let me go up, I pray thee, and bury my father, and I will come again. 6 And Pharaoh said, Go up, and bury thy father, according as he made thee swear. 7 And Joseph went up to bury his father; and with him went up all the servants of Pharaoh, the elders of his house, and all the elders of the land of Egypt, 8 and all the house of Joseph, and his brethren, and his father's house: only their little ones, and their flocks, and their herds, they left in the land of Goshen. 9 And there went up with him both chariots and horsemen: and it was a very great company. 10 And they came to the threshing-floor of Atad, which is beyond the Jordan, and there they lamented with a very great and sore lamentation: and he made a mourning for his father seven days. 11 And when the inhabitants of the land, the Canaanites, saw the mourning in the floor of Atad, they said, This is a grievous mourning to the Egyptians: wherefore the name of it was called Abel-mizraim, which is beyond the Jordan. 12 And his sons did unto him according as he commanded them: 13 for his sons carried him into the land of Canaan, and buried him in the cave of the field of Machpelah, which Abraham bought with the field, for a

possession of a burying-place, of Ephron the Hittite, before Mamre. 14 And Joseph returned into Egypt, he, and his brethren, and all that went up with him to bury his father, after he had buried his father.

When Jacob completed the blessing of his sons, he then gave to them the same charge he had earlier given to Joseph (47:29-31) — that he was not to be buried in Egypt but returned to the family burying-place outside Hebron. Then he pulled his feet back on the bed, and died. Such scenes, with death coming almost immediately after a full and official farewell, are not unknown in modern times.

Joseph wept over his dead father and kissed him. Then he commanded the Egyptian physicians who were assigned to his service to embalm his father. The embalming process was an elaborate one. Ancient secular historians assign various lengths of thirty or seventy days for its completion. In Jacob's case it was forty. The brain as well as the heart, liver, lungs, stomach, and intestines were removed from the body cavities. These organs were placed separately in jars. The body was treated for an extended period with either saltpeter or natron, then the cranial and abdominal cavities were filled with spices, and the body was wrapped in many yards of fine linen. The dry climate of Egypt helped to complete the process of preservation so effectively that mummies prepared in this fashion are in excellent condition yet today, thousands of years after burial.[151]

The period of mourning for Jacob lasted for a total of seventy days, only two short of that commonly observed for Pharaohs.[152] This plus the fact that the Egyptians themselves joined in the mourning is an indication of the high esteem in which Jacob was held in that nation.

At the close of the period of mourning, Joseph asked members of Pharaoh's court to act as intercessors for him with the king. He communicated to Pharaoh his vow to Jacob that he would bury his body in Canaan. Now he wanted royal permission to go to Hebron to fulfill his father's wish. Joseph did not attempt to presume upon his high position and disregard Pharaoh's authority over him. If he had gone without asking permission, Pharaoh might well have feared that Joseph was abandoning his adopted country for his earlier home. Joseph showed wisdom in using go-betweens at this time and under these circumstances, and permission was granted. It was a tremendous funeral procession which wound its way across the desert. With Joseph the prime minister went **all the servants of Pharaoh, the elders of his house, and all the elders of the land of Egypt** (courtiers, leading aids, national officials), plus Joseph's entire household, his brothers, and all his father's household, including no doubt many of the faithful and beloved servants who had ministered to him for so long. Only the small children and livestock were left in Goshen. And they were also provided a military escort of chariots and horsemen.

It is impossible to determine the route of the funeral procession on its way to Hebron. The one stopping-place mentioned is that of Goren-ha-Atad, **the threshing-floor of Atad,** or "The threshing place of brambles." It is described as being **beyond the Jordan.** This is the normal Israelite designation of the area east of the Jordan. If so, it would mean that the procession took the longer, more peaceful route to Canaan later followed by the nation on its journey to the promised land, across the Sinai Peninsula, around the lower end of the Dead Sea, and back up to cross the Jordan north of the Sea. In this event, the Egyptians must have halted there and conducted an additional mourning for Jacob, apparently for seven days. Joseph and his brethren went on across the Jordan to Hebron to complete the actual burial. On the other hand, many scholars have felt that Moses wrote this part of Genesis while he and the children of Israel were encamped on the east side of the Jordan, shortly before his death. In that event, Goren-ha-Atad would be a place on the west side, near Hebron, where the Egyptians camped during their period of mourning.

[151] Free, *op. cit.*, pp. 80-81; and Leupold, *op. cit.*, pp. 1205-06.
[152] Speiser, *op. cit.*, p. 376.

7. Joseph's Vision (50:15-26)

a. Forgiveness for Today (50:15-21)

15 And when Joseph's brethren saw that their father was dead, they said, It may be that Joseph will hate us, and will fully requite us all the evil which we did unto him. 16 And they sent a message unto Joseph, saying, Thy father did command before he died, saying, 17 So shall ye say unto Joseph, Forgive, I pray thee now, the transgression of thy brethren, and their sin, for that they did unto thee evil. And now, we pray thee, forgive the transgression of the servants of the God of thy father. And Joseph wept when they spake unto him. 18 And his brethren also went and fell down before his face; and they said, Behold, we are thy servants. 19 And Joseph said unto them, Fear not: for am I in the place of God? 20 And as for you, ye meant evil against me; but God meant it for good, to bring to pass, as it is this day, to save much people alive. 21 Now therefore fear ye not: I will nourish you, and your little ones. And he comforted them, and spake kindly unto them.

After Jacob's death, Joseph's ten older brothers became fearful lest Joseph had only been feigning forgiveness in order to avoid causing his father further suffering. Now they were completely at his mercy. It is worthy of note that prior to this time we have no record of their expressed repentance and confession, and an actual request for forgiveness. They had expressed regret for their sin while talking together in the presence of the man they thought could not understand them (42:21-23). And Joseph had allayed their fears by his assurance of forgiveness when he made himself known to them. But sin is never adequately dealt with until repentance and confession are personal and thorough. So they sent a messenger (perhaps Benjamin?[153]) with a twofold message: their father's instruction to them to seek forgiveness with its implied request from Jacob that Joseph grant such forgiveness, and their own personal request for forgiveness. The Scriptures do not say whether Jacob had actually made such a command or not. But deception at this stage would be entirely out of keeping with the transformation of their character which now

seemed almost complete. The failure of the author of Genesis to call their act a deception would indicate that their claim was true. And as Whitelaw says, "Nothing is more inherently probable than that the good man on his deathbed did request his sons to beg their brother's pardon."[154] In their own request, for the first time they laid claim to a relationship to God, **the servants of the God of thy father.** They wanted, too, to be known, as their father and Joseph had, as worshipers of the true God. Such would indicate that they were at least ready to come to grips with their own spiritual need. The reminder of the past which Joseph had so readily forgotten stirred his emotions once more. He wept, perhaps over all the pain those past experiences had caused, perhaps in sympathy for his guilt-oppressed brothers, perhaps in disappointment that they would still question his forgiveness. While he was still weeping, the brothers followed hard on the heels of their messenger. They could not rest content until their repentance was made definite and personal, face to face with the man they had injured. And they threw themselves down before him, offering themselves as his slaves. The very thing which had so long ago antagonized them — bowing down to Joseph as pictured in his dreams — they were now quite ready to do.

Joseph was quick to reassure his brethren. He told them not to fear, for he did not feel himself to be in the place of God. While he had the physical power to punish them, he felt he had no moral right to do so. This was God's prerogative, not his. There is the implication here that the whole realm of man's responsibility for his acts, of punishments and rewards, and even of forgiveness, belongs entirely to the Lord and not to man. Forgiveness was the only proper thing for Joseph. Vengeance belonged unto the Lord (Deut. 32:35; Rom. 12:19) and Joseph did not intend to tamper with it. He reminded the brethren again of his insight into the providences of God. They had **meant,** or "intended," evil against him, but God had **meant,** or "intended," **it for good** for the benefit

---

[153] Leupold, *op. cit.,* p. 1214.   [154] Whitelaw, *op. cit.,* I, 539.

of many people. Whenever man intends one thing and God intends another, it is God's intentions which are accomplished! Joseph promised once again that he would care for them and their families. The famine was long since over, but Joseph would continue to patronize them, to protect their rights to secure a living, to provide for them whenever they could not provide for themselves.

Joseph's sweet, forgiving spirit calls to mind the parallels between his life and character and that of Jesus Christ which have so often been observed. The New Testament in no place describes Joseph as a type of Christ. But the points of agreement are so striking as to demonstrate anew the marvelous providences of God. Lange has summarized some of these similarities.

> Joseph's history is considered . . . as a type of the fundamental law of God in guiding the elect from suffering to joy, from humiliation to exaltation . . . Hence the appearance, in our history, of individual types representing the New-Testament history of Jesus, such as the jealousy and hatred of Joseph's brethren, the fact of his being sold, the fulfilment of Joseph's prophetic dreams in the very efforts intended to prevent his exaltation, the turning of his brothers' wicked plot to the salvation of many, even of themselves, and of the house of Jacob, the spiritual sentence pronounced on the treachery of the brethren, the victory of pardoning love, Judah's suretyship for Benjamin, his emulating Joseph in a spirit of redeeming resignation, Jacob's joyful reviving on hearing of the life and glory of his favorite son, whom he had believed to be dead.[155]

Pascal has also listed some of the likenesses.

> Jesus Christ is prefigured by Joseph: the beloved of his father, sent by the father to his brethren, the innocent one sold by his brethren for twenty pieces of silver and so made their lord, their savior and the savior of strangers and the savior of the world; all of which would not have happened if they had not had the purpose to destroy him, if they had not sold and rejected him. In prison Joseph the innocent one between two malefactors —

Jesus on the cross between two evildoers: Joseph predicts good fortune to the one and death to the other, though both appear alike — Jesus saves the one and leaves the other in his just condemnation, though both stood charged with the same crime. Joseph begs of the one who is to be delivered to remember him when he is restored to honor, and he whom Jesus saves asks to be remembered when He comes in His kingdom.[156]

b. Faith for Tomorrow (50:22-26)

22 And Joseph dwelt in Egypt, he, and his father's house: and Joseph lived a hundred and ten years. 23 And Joseph saw Ephraim's children of the third generation: the children also of Machir the son of Manasseh were born upon Joseph's knees. 24 And Joseph said unto his brethren, I die; but God will surely visit you, and bring you up out of this land unto the land which he sware to Abraham, to Isaac, and to Jacob. 25 And Joseph took an oath of the children of Israel, saying, God will surely visit you, and ye shall carry up my bones from hence. 26 So Joseph died, being a hundred and ten years old: and they embalmed him, and he was put in a coffin in Egypt.

Joseph had been thirty-nine years old when his father moved to Egypt, or ninety-one years younger than his father. When his father died at the age of 147, Joseph would have been fifty-six. So he lived fifty-four years, or nearly half of his entire life, after Israel's death. Old age was looked upon in Old Testament times as a special blessing from God, the reward of the righteous man. While the biblical genealogies indicate that the length of man's life was gradually shortening during this period, and Joseph's life was shorter than that of Abraham, Isaac, or Jacob, yet he lived to a good old age with all the evidences of divine favor surrounding him. In fact, his 110 years was the span considered by the Egyptians to be the ideal lifetime for a man.[157] As he drew near the end of his life, he was able to look forward with faith as far as the future of his people was concerned, because of the faithfulness of God to him throughout his life. And that faithfulness did not end with

[155] Lange, op. cit., I, 581.
[156] From Pensees, quoted by Delitzsch and in turn by Leupold, op. cit., p. 951.
[157] Speiser, op. cit., p. 376.

the providences of his earlier years, but attended him to the very end. He saw **Ephraim's children of the third generation,** and the children of Machir, Manasseh's son, were set upon his knees for his official recognition of them as part of the family. **The third generation** has been variously interpreted as referring to Ephraim's grandchildren or his great-grandchildren, depending upon whether the first generation counted would be Ephraim or his children. The former is favored by the fact that Manasseh's grandchildren are specifically mentioned, but the latter is favored by Joseph's very long life.

As Joseph's end approached, he called in his brethren. His address to **his brethren** need not imply that all of Joseph's eleven brothers outlived him. The term is frequently used in the Scriptures in the sense of "kindred." But even though Joseph was next to the youngest, some of his brothers may have survived him. Levi certainly did (Exod. 6:16). When all his kindred were assembled, Joseph reminded them that their presence in Egypt was not to be permanent. God would some day visit them and take them back to the promised land. And he, like his father before him, wanted to be buried in Canaan rather than in Egypt. His ninety-three years in Egypt and his long service to its government had not dimmed his memory of the covenant. He did not insist on an immediate removal of his body to Canaan, but he did ask that his **bones** might be carried there when the time came for the family to return. He wanted to retain his identity with the chosen family, and his request was at the same time an expression of his undying faith. Joseph was embalmed and placed in a coffin in Egypt. Later, Moses helped to fulfill the promise made to Joseph (Exod. 13:19). Joshua completed its provisions by burying the body in Shechem (Josh. 24:32). Of all the acts of faith which marked the life of Joseph, this one was singled out by the writer to the Hebrews as making him worthy of entry in faith's "hall of fame" (Heb. 11:22).

As one reads the closing chapters and verses of Genesis, he can not escape the conviction that an era is drawing to a close. But as he views the closing scene and catches the echo of Joseph's faith, he is also convinced that the story of redemption is yet unfinished. The outlook of Genesis 50 is not backward at the monuments of faith behind it, but forward to the accomplishment of all faith has dared to claim.

Bibliography

I. COMMENTARIES

Aalders, G. C. "The Historical Literature of the Old Testament," *The New Bible Commentary.* Ed. Francis Davidson. Grand Rapids: Eerdmans, 1963.

Baxter, J. Sidlow. *Explore the Book.* Vol. 1. Grand Rapids: Zondervan, 1960.

Bowie, Walter Russell. "The Book of Genesis" (Exposition), *The Interpreter's Bible.* Ed. George Arthur Buttrick. Vol I. New York-Nashville: Abingdon, 1952.

Candlish, Robert S. *Commentary on Genesis,* "Classic Commentary Library." 2 vols. Grand Rapids: Zondervan, rep., n.d.

Clarke, Adam. *The Holy Bible with a Commentary and Critical Notes,* Vol. I. New York-Nashville: Abingdon-Cokesbury, rep., n.d.

Dillmann, A. *Genesis, Critically and Exegetically Expounded.* 2 vols. Trans. William B. Stevenson. Edinburgh: T. and T. Clark, 1897.

Dods, Marcus. *The Book of Genesis,* "The Expositor's Bible." Ed. W. Robertson Nicoll. New York: Hodder and Stoughton, n.d.

Driver, S. R. *The Book of Genesis,* "Westminster Commentaries." Ed. Walter Lock. London: Methuen, 1905.

Griffith-Jones, E., and A. C. Welch. *Genesis,* "The Study Bible." Ed. John Stirling. Garden City, N. Y.: Doubleday, Doran, n.d.

Henry, Matthew and Thomas Scott. *Commentary on the Holy Bible.* Vol. I. Grand Rapids: Baker, rep. 1960.

Jamieson, Robert, A. R. Fausset, and David Brown. *Commentary Critical and Explanatory on the Whole Bible.* Grand Rapids: Zondervan, rep., n.d.

Kevan, Ernest F. "Genesis," *The New Bible Commentary.* Ed. Francis Davidson. Grand Rapids: Eerdmans, 1963.

Lange, John Peter. *Commentary on the Holy Scriptures.* Vol. I. Trans. Philip Schaff. Grand Rapids: Zondervan, rep., n.d.

Leupold, H. C. *Exposition of Genesis.* Columbus, Ohio: Wartburg, 1942.

Rad, Gerhard von. *Genesis, a Commentary.* Trans. John H. Marks. Philadelphia: Westminister, 1961.

Rylaarsdam, J. Coert. "Exodus" (Introduction), *The Interpreter's Bible.* Ed. George Arthur Buttrick. Vol. I. New York-Nashville: Abingdon, 1952.

Simpson, Cuthbert A. "The Book of Genesis" (Introduction and Exegesis), *The Interpreter's Bible.* Ed. George Arthur Buttrick. Vol. I. New York-Nashville: Abingdon, 1952.

Skinner, John. *A Critical and Exegetical Commentary on Genesis,* "The International Critical Commentary." Eds. Samuel Rolles Driver, Alfred Plummer, and Charles Augustus Briggs. New York: Scribner, 1910.

Smith, R. Payne. "Genesis," *Commentary on the Whole Bible.* Ed. Charles John Ellicott. Vol I. Grand Rapids: Zondervan, rep., n.d.

Speiser, E. A. "Genesis," *The Anchor Bible.* Eds. William Foxwell Albright and David Noel Freedman. Vol. I. Garden City, N.Y.: Doubleday, 1964.

Whitelaw, Thomas. "Genesis," *The Pulpit Commentary.* Eds. H. D. M. Spence and Joseph S. Exell. Vol. I. Grand Rapids: Eerdmans, rep. 1958.

Yates, Kyle M., Sr. "Genesis," *The Wycliffe Bible Commentary.* Eds. Charles F. Pfeiffer and Everett F. Harrison. Chicago: Moody, 1963.

II. OTHER REFERENCE WORKS

Albright, William Foxwell. *The Archaeology of Palestine and the Bible.* New York: Revell, 1932-33.

————. "Recent Discoveries in Bible Lands," in Robert Young, *Analytical Concordance to the Bible.* New York: Funk and Wagnalls, 1936.

————. "The Rediscovery of the Biblical World," in *The Westminster Historical Atlas to the Bible.* Eds. George Ernest Wright and Floyd Vivian Filson. Philadelphia: Westminster, 1946.

Allis, Oswald T. *God Spake by Moses.* Nutley, N. J.: Presbyterian and Reformed, 1958.

Blaikie, William G., rev. by Charles D. Matthews. *A Manual of Bible History.* New York: Ronald Press, 1940.

Blauw, Johannes. *The Missionary Nature of the Church.* New York: McGraw-Hill, 1962.

Brown, Francis, S. R. Driver, and Charles A. Briggs, eds. *A Hebrew and English Lexicon of the Old Testament.* Oxford: Clarendon, rep. 1959.

Bullock, Wilbur. "Book Review of G. A. Kerkut's *Implications of Evolution,*" in *Journal of the American Scientific Affiliation,* Vol. 16, No. 4, December 1964, pp. 125-26.

Edersheim, Alfred. *The Life and Times of Jesus the Messiah.* 2 vols. New York: Longmans, Green, 1899.

Finegan, Jack. *Light from the Ancient Past.* Princeton, N. J.: Princeton, 1959.

Free, Joseph P. *Archaeology and Bible History.* Rev. ed. Wheaton, Ill.: Scripture Press, 1962.

Girdlestone, Robert Baker. *Synonyms of the Old Testament.* Grand Rapids: Eerdmans, rep. 1948.

Green, William Henry. *The Unity of the Book of Genesis.* New York: Scribner, 1910.

Hurlbut, Jesse Lyman. *A Bible Atlas.* New York: Rand McNally, 1943.

Jackson, Samuel Macauley, ed. *The New Schaff-Herzog Encyclopedia of Religious Knowledge.* Grand Rapids: Baker, rep. 1951.

Josephus, Flavius. *Complete Works.* Trans. William Whiston. Grand Rapids: Kregel, 1964.

Klotz, John W. "Theistic Evolution: Some Theological Implications," in *Journal of the American Scientific Affiliation,* Vol. 15, No. 3, September 1963, pp. 82-86.

Loetscher, Lefferts A., ed. *Twentieth Century Encyclopedia of Religious Knowledge.* Grand Rapids: Baker, 1955.

Nelson, Byron C. *After Its Kind.* Minneapolis: Augsburg, 1958.

Purkiser, W. T., ed. *Exploring the Old Testament.* Kansas City, Mo.: Beacon Hill, 1964.

Roberts, Alexander, and James Donaldson, eds. *The Ante-Nicene Fathers.* 10 vols. Grand Rapids: Eerdmans, rep. 1956.

Sandmel, Samuel. *The Hebrew Scriptures.* New York: Alfred A. Knopf, 1963.

Schaff, Philip, ed. *A Select Library of the Nicene and Post-Nicene Fathers of the Christian Church, Series I.* 14 vols. Grand Rapids: Eerdmans, rep. 1956.

Schaff, Philip, and Henry Wace, eds. *A Select Library of Nicene and Post-Nicene Fathers of the Christian Church, Series II.* 14 vols. Grand Rapids: Eerdmans, rep. 1952.

Tanner, William F. "Geology and the Days of Genesis," in *Journal of the American Scientific Affiliation,* Vol. 16, No. 3, September 1964, pp. 82-85.

Unger, Merrill F. *Archaeology and the Old Testament.* Grand Rapids: Zondervan, 1954.

————, ed. *Unger's Bible Dictionary.* Chicago: Moody Press, 1957.

Whitcomb, John C., Jr., and Henry M. Morris. *The Genesis Flood.* Philadelphia: Presbyterian and Reformed, 1963.

Wiley, H. Orton. *Christian Theology.* 3 vols. Kansas City: Beacon Hill, 1940.

Wright, George Ernest, and Floyd Vivian Filson, eds. *The Westminster Historical Atlas to the Bible.* Philadelphia: Westminster, 1946.

Young, Edward J. *An Introduction to the Old Testament.* Rev. ed. Grand Rapids: Eerdmans, 1960.

————. *Studies in Genesis One,* "International Library of Philosophy and Theology: Biblical and Theological Studies." Ed. J. Marcellus Kik. Grand Rapids: Baker, n.d.

Young, Robert. *Analytical Concordance to the Bible.* New York: Funk and Wagnalls, rep. 1936.

Ziel, Aldert van der. *Genesis and Scientific Inquiry.* Minneapolis: T. S. Denison, 1965.

————. *The Natural Sciences and the Christian Message,* "The Lutheran Studies Series," Vol. I. Minneapolis: T. S. Denison, 1960.

III. Bible Versions

American Standard Version of The Holy Bible. New York: Thomas Nelson, 1901.

King James Version of The Holy Bible. 1611 (1st ed.).

Leupold, H. C. Translation incorporated in *Exposition of Genesis.* Columbus, Ohio: Wartburg, 1942.

Meek, Theophile J. "Genesis," in *The Bible, an American Translation*, Old Testament ed. by J. M. Powis Smith, New Testament trans. by Edgar J. Goodspeed. Chicago: University of Chicago, 1939.

The Revised Standard Version of the Holy Bible. New York: Thomas Nelson, 1952.

Speiser, E. A. Translation incorporated in "Genesis," *The Anchor Bible*, Eds. William Foxwell Albright and David Noel Freedman. Vol. I. Garden City, N. Y.: Doubleday, 1964.

Verkuyl, Gerrit, ed. *The Holy Bible: The Berkeley Version in Modern English*. Grand Rapids: Zondervan, 1959.

The Book of Exodus

by Lee Haines

Outline

Introduction

I. NAME AND CONTENTS

The five books of the Pentateuch were commonly titled by the Jews on the basis of their initial words. The second book was thus called *we'elleh shemoth* ("Now these are the names"), or in a shortened form, *shemoth* ("names"). But such a title in no way describes the book or its contents. When the Jews in Egypt translated the Old Testament into Greek in the third century B.C. (the Septuagint translation), they titled it with the Greek word *Exodos* (the marching out *en masse* of a large group of people), which they used in translating 19:1. The word fit well the theme of the first part of the book, and it was transliterated into Latin as *Exodus* when the Bible was later translated into Latin.[1] The name has been carried over into practically every modern language. When Martin Luther translated the Bible into German, he called this book, "The Second Book of Moses." The popular Greek name has been combined with this title in the standard English translations as, "The Second Book of Moses (Commonly) Called Exodus."

But the title does not fit this book as well as Genesis fits the first book. Exodus is indeed the theme of the early part of the book, but not from 15:22 on. The book revolves around two great historical events: the exodus from Egypt, and the giving of the law at Mt. Sinai. There are three chief characters in the book: God, Moses, and Israel. In the first part of the book, as it revolves about God, the stress is on the revelation of the divine nature — the power of God, and in the second part it is on the revelation of the divine will — the purpose of God for His holiness to be reflected in His people.[2] From the viewpoint of Moses, the first part of the book tells of his use by the Lord as a reluctant instrument in freeing His people, but in the second part, he is not only the instrument by which the law is revealed and the covenant established, but also the intercessor and mediator through whom God's plan is preserved from a most serious interruption, and through whom God's people secure an extended probation. From the viewpoint of Irael, the first part of the book is a marvelous *deliverance* of the chosen people from slavery in Egypt, a deliverance brought about first by Jehovah's victory over Egypt in the ten plagues, and finally culminated by His slaughter of the Egyptian armies at the Red Sea. The last part deals with the *discipline* or training of Israel, shaping it by the experience of a series of difficulties, by the revelation of God's law and the provisional plan of salvation, by judgment pronounced and executed upon disobedience, and by service in building the divinely appointed place of worship. The discipline was fully as marvelous as the deliverance, a disorganized mob of slaves becoming a nation in a one-year period. Since the lasting, significant result of the historical events described in the Bible's second book was the emergence of a new nation devoted to God's service, the present commentary outlines the book from Israel's point of view. And on the basis of this approach, a fitting title for the book would be "The Birth of a Nation."

II. AUTHORSHIP

The authorship of Exodus is a matter which also involves the authorship of four other books — Genesis, Leviticus, Numbers, and Deuteronomy. It is evident that Exodus continues the story of Genesis, as when the closing portions of Genesis are either assumed or used in Exodus 1:1-8, and when the covenant with Abraham, Isaac, and Jacob is referred to (2:24) without any further explanation. It is also evident that Leviti-

---

[1] Edward J. Young, *An Introduction to the Old Testament*, p. 65.
[2] J. Coert Rylaarsdam, "Exodus" (Introduction and Exegesis), in *The Interpreter's Bible*, I, 834.

cus and Numbers continue the story, for the priesthood set up in Exodus is ordained in Leviticus, and the encampment at Sinai begun in Exodus continues through Leviticus into Numbers. And Deuteronomy presents itself as a resumé of the events recorded in the three preceding books.

Traditionally, Moses has been thought of as the author of the five books. The books revolve around him in such a way that on the surface he is the only logical candidate. But over the past two centuries there has arisen an increasing chorus of questions and denials. Critical scholarship has proposed an altogether different solution to the problem of authorship, that of four different literary documents, based on an oral tradition, which over the centuries were first composed and *then* fused together by a succession of editors. Perhaps the majority of scholars have been won to this radical and questionable position. But others, driven to more careful and diligent study, are convinced still that Moses wrote or supervised the writing of at least a core of the Pentateuch, using older documents in Genesis, and in turn having his work revised, enlarged, and explained by subsequent editors down to the time of Ezra.

The present writer has rather fully developed his own support of this latter position in the Introduction to Genesis, section on "Authorship." For the basic arguments, the reader is referred to that section. (See also the General Introduction to the Pentateuch at the front of this volume.) But there are also some points which need to be re-emphasized because of their particular pertinence in the case of Exodus, and some points which Exodus itself contributes which are additional to those pertinent to Genesis.

There are several specific references to Moses writing in Exodus, the first being Jehovah's instructions for him to record "in *the book*" (literal translation of 17:14) His declaration of war on Amalek. Others are to "the book of the covenant" in which he wrote the Ten Commandments and the other laws given as a basis of a Jehovah-Israel covenant (24: 4-8), and to Jehovah's instructions that he write down the restatement of the covenant provisions needing emphasis be-

cause of Israel's lapse into idolatry (34: 27). There are also several references to Jehovah Himself writing the Ten Commandments on the two sets of two stone tablets (24:12; 31:18; 32:15-16; 34:1, 28).

There are strong evidences that much of Exodus was recorded in just the kind of book apparently indicated by Jehovah in 17:14, a diary or journal of the events leading up to the Exodus and of those culminating in the establishment of the covenant at Mt. Sinai. One of these is the constant dating of various events, by year, month, and day (cf. 12:1ff.; 16:1; 19:1; 40:1, 17). Another is the intense sensory descriptions which almost necessitate that the account be written by an eyewitness. We cannot be exhaustive here, but notice the fine details of things seen (3:2; 4:3, 6-7; 13:21-22; 16:14; 19:18a; 34:29ff.), of things heard (9:23, 28; 19: 16, 19; 20:18-19), of things felt (10:21; 19:18b), of things tasted (15:23; 16:31), and of things smelled (8:14; 16:20). Related to this is the precise accuracy with which life both in Egypt and in the desert is pictured, both as to customs and geographical locations, including the topography of Sinai.[3] Still another evidence is the many direct quotations of words spoken by Jehovah, including some lengthy ones which could only be authoritative if recorded by the person who heard them, at the time of or immediately after hearing them. Most of these purport to have been heard by Moses only. They involve 580 of the book's 1213 verses — almost one-half.

Critical scholars have been quick to point out that the book has some abrupt breaks, blocks of material which appear to be out of chronological order, in some places interrupting an account which is later resumed. No one can deny that these exist. But many of them could easily have been added by Moses or those writing under his supervision. In fact, the book bears the appearance of having been written in short sections, in odd moments of time, with the author coming back later to revise his rough draft, adding statements which anticipate events related to the topic at hand but which happened actually some time

---

[3] George Rawlinson, *The Pulpit Commentary: Exodus*, I, xii-xiv.

later. Some of these are: the abrupt insertion of a genealogy of the tribes descended from the three oldest sons of Leah, aimed at tracing the origin of Moses and Aaron, and ending with a threefold designation of "these are that," "these are they," and "these are that Moses and Aaron" who led Israel out (6:14-27) ; the lengthy instructions concerning the Feast of the Passover and of Unleavened Bread as it was to be observed in Canaan recorded in the midst of Israel's hurried exit from Egypt (12: 43—13:16) ; the last six verses of Moses' song by the Red Sea which seem to refer to the conquest of Canaan and the building of Solomon's temple as past events (15:13-18) ; the record of the preserving of a memorial pot of manna in the ark at a time previous to the construction of the ark, and a reference to the forty years in the wilderness and of the arrival at the borders of Canaan at a time almost at the beginning of the forty years (16: 32-35) ; a record of Moses' following Jethro's advice in sharing his judicial responsibilities with subordinates some months before he actually did (cf. 18:24-26 with Num. 11:11-30; Deut. 1:6-18) ; the explanatory portions of the Ten Commandments (see comments on 20:1-17) ; the closing paragraphs of instructions about the tabernacle and its furnishings and use, in a surprising sequence and most with a separate, introductory, "And Jehovah spake unto Moses, saying," rather than the extended quotation as previously (30:1—31:17) ; and references to "all their journeys" when Israel had as yet only journeyed from Egypt to Sinai (40:36-38). The present writer's position would allow some of these to have been added by later revisers or editors of the Pentateuch, and would especially suggest that this is true of the 6:14-27 and 15:13-18 passages and perhaps of 16:32-35. There are three explanatory notes similar to those made in Genesis to explain ancient concepts or words to later readers, almost certainly the work of the editor (4:26b; 16:36; 30:13). But one is surprised that there are not more. The author seems under no compulsion thus to update the record, but expects his readers to understand fully the setting and color of his narrative.

III. DATE

The problem of dating the book of Exodus is actually one of dating the historical event of the Exodus. Even many critical scholars are now ready to admit that Moses did exist, that he led Israel out of Egypt, that he helped to establish the tribes as a people, and that he wrote at least a primitive core of what is now recorded as his law. The evangelical scholar, while allowing for some additions to Exodus after Moses, will find an even larger portion of the work due to his labors. So the beginnings at least of the book date from the period of the event or very shortly thereafter.

But the dating of the Exodus as an event is not easy. While the general background of Egyptian history during the middle of the second millennium B.C. is just what the Scriptures picture them as being, even to the presence of alien nomads there and their enslavement by the Egyptians, there is no record on Egypt's monuments or in its literature of the Exodus. There is good reason for this. The Egyptians, like other ancient empires, never recorded their defeats or disasters. They boasted only of their victories and prosperity. So this leaves the dating of the event largely to the biblical data. But as we saw in the Introduction to Genesis, under "Date," it is exceedingly difficult to translate ancient dates into ones understandable from the modern point of view. Some type of corroboration from secular history or archaeology is extremely helpful for arriving at a precise date. Such corroboration was found in the case of Genesis, where we felt fairly certain about the entrance of Jacob and his family into Egypt in about 1871 B.C. In Exodus 12:40-41, we are told that Israel was in Egypt 430 years. So it would seem to be a simple matter to make the proper subtraction and arrive at the date of 1441 B.C. for the Exodus. This date is also supported by I Kings 6:1, which states that Solomon began to build his temple in the four-hundred-eightieth year after the Exodus, which was also the fourth year of his reign. Solomon's reign is more readily dated from secular history and archaeology, and it is generally agreed that the fourth year of his reign would fall in the decade between 967 and 958 B.C.[4] Testing our proposed date for the Exodus, we subtract 480 from 1441 and arrive at 961 B.C., well within the probable period of the fourth year of Solomon's reign.

But the matter is not so easily settled. There are other pertinent scriptural data. In Genesis 15:13, the Lord had forewarned Abraham that the chosen people would be *afflicted* by an alien nation for 400 years, a statement which could be interpreted as predicting a longer sojourn than 430 years (since Joseph lived seventy-one years after Israel entered Egypt, and the persecution did not begin until sometime after his death) or as a reference to the 430 years in round numbers. (Acts 7:6 also refers to this prediction.) But in Genesis 15:16, the Lord said they would return to Canaan "in the fourth generation," a phrase which might imply a much shorter period than 430 years, unless "generation" be translated "time span" (see comments on Genesis 15:1-21). And in Galatians 3:17, Paul refers to 430 years as running from the covenant to the law. If by this he means the entire period from Abraham to Sinai, 215 years of that period would be absorbed by the three patriarchs themselves in Canaan, leaving only 215 years for Israel to have been in Egypt. (But Paul may have been thinking of the "covenant" as including all three patriarchs, and the period being the time between Jacob and Sinai.) Finally, in Exodus 1:11, reference is made to Israel's employment by Pharaoh in the building of the city of Raamses. This city was known by this name only from c. 1300-1100 B.C.[5] And Rameses II, Pharaoh from c. 1290-1224 B.C., claims to have built it. If the Israelites built it under Rameses II, they could not have left Egypt until 150 years or more after 1441 B.C.

Thus the dating of the Exodus has been thrown into a welter of confusion. Even if the date suggested by the present writer under Genesis is accepted for the date of Abraham and the migration of Jacob, it is possible to claim a period of sojourn longer than 430 years and arrive at a date later than 1441 B.C. Some scholars are not ready to accept the dates for Abraham and Jacob, and finding in the rule over Egypt by the foreign, Semitic kings, the Hyksos (c. 1720-1550 B.C.), the most logical time for their relatives, Israel, to enter Egypt, they are able to use the figure of 430 years sojourn and still come out with a date for the Exodus which coincides with the reign of Rameses II. Others would say that Israel must have been expelled from Egypt when the Hyksos were, thus placing the Exodus 100 years before the 1441 B.C. date. And of those who support a later date, some would find room for the Exodus in the reign of Rameses II, others would say he was the oppressor and his son, Merenptah, was the Pharaoh of the Exodus itself. The date has thus been placed by scholars all the way from the sixteenth to the late thirteenth century B.C. — sometime between 1550 and 1225. In fact, the evidence has confused some to the point that they have been ready to propose two different exoduses, and also to suggest that some of the tribes may never have been in Egypt![6] In general, however, scholars have settled on one of two dates: either a date near 1441 B.C., or a date somewhere between 1290 and 1225 B.C. While most of the supporters of the early date are evangelicals, both evangelicals and liberals are found among the supporters of the later date. It is not a matter of doctrine, but a matter of interpreting the data. We will now attempt to summarize the main evidence for the two dates largely as it is given by Unger.[7]

Those who support the late date appeal basically to four facts: (1) The likelihood that Israel entered Egypt under the Hyksos. (2) The statement in Exodus 1:11 that Israelite slaves built Raamses. (3) Archaeological evidence which shows no settled population in the region of Trans-Jordan and the Arabah in the centuries preceding 1300 B.C., and thus no Edomite, Moabite, and Ammonite nations to resist Israel's advance in the period between 1441 and 1401. The situation described in Numbers 20:14-17 seems to them impossible prior to 1300.[8]

[4] Merrill F. Unger, *Archaeology and the Old Testament*, p. 141.
[5] *Ibid.*, p. 149.
[6] William G. Blaikie, rev. by Charles D. Matthews, *A Manual of Bible History*, pp. 76-78.
[7] Unger, *op. cit.*, Chapter XII, "The Date of the Exodus," pp. 140-52.
[8] See Blaikie and Matthews, *op. cit.*, pp. 77-78.

(4) The first mention of Israel in Egyptian records on an inscription dating from the reign of Merenptah, son of Rameses II, who began to rule c. 1223 B.C. The inscription records his crushing of a revolt in Palestine, and gloats over the unhappy victims, including "the people of Israel" who "is desolate, it has no offspring."[9] The assumption is that Israel had only recently arrived. The supporters of the late date attempt to refute the claim by their opponents that the biblical Hebrews are the same as the Habiru invaders of Canaan mentioned in letters found at El-Amarna, and dating from the period just after 1400 B.C., by pointing out that they were written by the alarmed governor of Jerusalem while Israel did not capture Jerusalem during the conquest (see below). And they disagree with their interpretation of the archaeological evidence on the date of Jericho's destruction.

Those who support the early date appeal basically to three sets of facts: (1) The chronological data supplied by Exodus 12:40-41 and I Kings 6:1 as discussed above. (2) The ease with which the Exodus fits into Egyptian history at this point, with the expulsion of the Hyksos just about one century earlier. The newly liberated Egyptians would have been prone to harass the Hebrew relatives of the Hyksos, and their ruler the most likely person to be the king "who knew not Joseph." Thutmose I, who began to rule about twenty-five years after the expulsion of the Hyksos, would according to this chronology have been reigning when Moses was born. He had a strong-willed daughter who later was known as Queen Hatshepsut, and who fits the description of one who would dare to thwart her father's decree by saving a Hebrew baby from the Nile. She later served as regent over Egypt, for some time preventing her stepson and Thutmose I's grandson, Thutmose III, from taking over the government. This restive and jealous king, destined to become one of the greatest Pharaohs, a conqueror and empire builder, would have been raised in the palace with Moses. He would have recently come to the throne when Moses killed an Egyptian, and his resentment of Hatshepsut would fit in admirably with the zeal with which he sought to kill Moses, who fled to Midian instead. He would have died just shortly before Moses returned to lead the Exodus. His son, Amenhotep II, was busily occupied for some time after his father's death in crushing the revolt of outlying provinces in Syria and Palestine — an excellent time for Israel to escape, and an excellent reason why the Lord led them into the desert instead of along by the Mediterranean Sea (13:17). Amenhotep's son, Thutmose IV, who succeeded him to the throne, was not his first-born, who would have died on the night of the first Passover. (3) Archaeological evidence that Israel arrived in Canaan at about 1400 B.C. The destruction of the city of Jericho, whose walls have been found flattened just as described in Joshua 6, has been dated by one leading archaeologist as 1400 B.C. Furthermore, under the Egyptian Pharaoh Akhnaton (1387-1366 B.C.), the governor of Jerusalem wrote numerous letters which have now been recovered asking for aid against the invading Habiru, who were taking possession of Canaan. Even though Jerusalem itself was not captured by Israel, the governor would naturally have been alarmed by reports of their widespread victories. The supporters of the early date attempt to refute their opponents by pointing out Rameses II's tendency to claim credit for achievements of others, and the strong probability that the city which he later named after himself was rebuilt much earlier and merely remodeled by him. They also point out that the descriptions of Edom, Moab, and Ammon given in Numbers do not require a settled, urbanized population, but would fit with a semi-nomadic state like that of Israel which would leave archaeology little evidence of its presence. And they see in Merenptah's inscription only evidence that Israel was an established nation by the late thirteenth century, a fact which fits better with their arrival 150 years before than with a supposed arrival just before Merenptah's victory.

The present writer (as might be guessed from the bulk of the evidence!) supports the early date for Exodus. It is assumed throughout the exposition of the book. But he does so fully conscious

9 Unger, op. cit., p. 184.

that those who differ have sound reasons for doing so. Perhaps future discoveries will solve this chronological riddle.

IV. SIGNIFICANCE

The book of Exodus is almost as significant in its own way as the book of Genesis is in its unique service as the foundation of all understanding of man's relationship to God. Between "Paradise Lost" and "Paradise Regained," between the beginning of this age at man's creation and its consummation at the great judgment, four events tower like great mountain peaks far above all their neighbors: Jehovah's covenant with Abraham, His creation of a community of faith at Sinai, the death and resurrection of Jesus Christ, and the effusion of the Holy Spirit on the Day of Pentecost. The first is recorded in Genesis, which deals with all beginnings. The third is recorded in the gospels and expounded in the epistles. The last is recorded in Acts 2 and became the instrument of the Christian movement for all time. The second is recorded in Exodus, is expounded throughout the Old Testament, and reaches its fulfillment in the body of Christ known as the Church in the New Testament. The Day of Pentecost itself is thought by many scholars to be the commemoration of the giving of the law on Sinai.

The entire national and religious history and life of the Jew, even today, revolve around the dual deliverance from Egypt and discipline at Sinai. The Lord Himself becomes identified by His role in the deliverance, for He consistently thereafter calls Himself, "Jehovah thy God, who brought thee out of the land of Egypt." And only those laws which can be traced to Sinai, as mediated through Moses, have won for themselves a permanent place among Jehovah's people. Kings and rulers have come and gone since, but it is Sinai that has stamped upon these people an indelible national character. This is evident even in the book of Exodus itself. Constantly instruction is given as to how the various observances are to be used in perpetuating the knowledge of divine deliverance,

being introduced by the formula, "When thy son asketh thee in time to come, saying, What is this?" and completed in "Thou shalt say unto him . . . Jehovah brought us out." And many times perpetual observance is called for in such words as "ye shall keep it . . . for ever" or "it shall be a statute for ever throughout their generations."

All religious and spiritual truth, both for Judaism and Christianity, can only be understood in the light of Exodus.[10] Even Genesis and the Abrahamic covenant have to be understood in terms of Sinai, for the first book was written after the great events of the second. All that God had done before was interpreted by His nature and will as revealed in the creation of Israel. The great prophets can only be understood in relation to Exodus, for it was to the great spiritual insights first glimpsed at Sinai that they constantly turned in order to restore the nation. And the prophet of Galilee was no exception. He came not to destroy the product of Sinai, but to fulfill it — carry it to its ultimate and highest demonstration and application. The spiritual perfection which He saw in His Father and which He demanded in His disciples was that same holiness which Israel first began to understand at Sinai. The offering of Himself as the unblemished Lamb for the redemption of all mankind brought to complete realization the redemption first glimpsed at the institution of the Passover. His institution of a new supper of bread and wine to commemorate His sacrifice unfolded the fuller meaning of that Passover meal so insistently commanded in Exodus. His entrance into heaven to intercede in our behalf made clear the mystic meaning of the priest's annual entrance into the inner compartment of the tabernacle described in Exodus, the Holy of Holies — a place once prohibited to men because of their sinfulness and God's holiness, but now freely open to those who come through the veil of His flesh. His commission to His disciples to go into all the world and preach the gospel to every creature is simply the logical fulfillment of the divine purpose for the community of faith expressed at Sinai — to be "a

---

[10] Samuel Sandmel, *The Hebrew Scriptures: an Introduction to Their Literature and Religious Ideas*, p. 387.

kingdom of priests, and a holy nation," the ambassadors of God to a world in darkness.

The Christian will find much in Exodus, if he only reads with a searching mind and a prayerful heart. He will see in Egyptian bondage a picture of his own bondage in sin, in the passage through the Red Sea a picture of his own conversion as symbolized in baptism, in Moses the leader of Israel along unknown but purposeful paths a picture of the Christ who today leads the spiritual pilgrim along "the Way," in the tests which faced Israel a picture of his own tests and the lessons which they teach, in God's provision for Israel of super-natural food and drink a promise that his own need for spiritual sustenance will always be graciously provided (cf. I Cor. 10:1-4).[11] At Sinai, he will see that salvation comes only by a divinely appointed way — through grace. He will find guidelines for his moral conduct as pertinent to the twentieth century A.D. as to the fifteenth B.C. He will find assurance in divine compassion, inspiration in divine demands, and security in the persistent unfolding of the divine plan.

(For additional introductory information on Exodus see General Introduction to the Pentateuch at the front of this volume.)

---

[11] Jack Finegan, *Let My People Go*, pp. 99-100.

Commentary on Exodus

I. THE DELIVERANCE OF ISRAEL (Exod. 1:1-15:21)

A. THE NEED FOR DELIVERANCE (1:1-22)

1. The Resumé of the Past (1:1-7)

1 Now these are the names of the sons of Israel, who came into Egypt (every man and his household came with Jacob) : 2 Reuben, Simeon, Levi, and Judah, 3 Issachar, Zebulun, and Benjamin, 4 Dan and Naphtali, Gad and Asher. 5 And all the souls that came out of the loins of Jacob were seventy souls: and Joseph was in Egypt already. 6 And Joseph died, and all his brethren, and all that generation. 7 And the children of Israel were fruitful, and increased abundantly, and multiplied, and waxed exceeding mighty; and the land was filled with them.

The first seven verses of Exodus are intended to relate the book to Genesis, summarizing both the closing events of that book and the most significant changes of the centuries which intervened between the death of Joseph and the birth of Moses. The **now** with which it begins is the common Hebrew conjunction most frequently translated "and," indicating that this is a continuation of the previous account. It lists again the names of the sons of Jacob who went down into Egypt, grouping them according to their four mothers with the groups in the order that Jacob married the two wives and the two concubines, and listing those within each group in the order of their birth (cf. the order in Gen. 35:22b-26). Joseph is omitted from the list, because he **was in Egypt already.** The number of Jacob's immediate descendants is again given as seventy (cf. Gen. 46:26-27 and comments there), but since this number refers almost entirely to the males, a much larger number is hinted at in that each man took also his **household,** including wives, daughters, and servants.

The change in setting from the closing verses of Genesis is marked in two ways: the death not only of Joseph (Gen. 50: 26), but also of the rest of his brothers, their wives and sisters, and the servants — **all that generation;** and the subsequent development of the clan into a great nation. This "population explosion" is indicated by a five-step progression: they (1) **were fruitful,** and (2) **increased abundantly,** and (3) **multiplied,** and (4) **waxed exceeding mighty;** and (5) **the land was filled with them.** Such a heaping up of expressions indicates that the gain was more than a merely natural one. It was the result of direct divine blessing. This conviction of divine providence in the life of the chosen family was evident throughout Genesis, and particularly in the experiences of Joseph. It appears again in these opening verses of Exodus, and remains a dominant theme throughout the book.

2. The Reproach of Slavery (1:8-14)

8 Now there arose a new king over Egypt, who knew not Joseph. 9 And he said unto his people, Behold, the people of the children of Israel are more and mightier than we: 10 come, let us deal wisely with them, lest they multiply, and it come to pass, that, when there falleth out any war, they also join themselves unto our enemies, and fight against us, and get them up out of the land. 11 Therefore they did set over them taskmasters to afflict them with their burdens. And they built for Pharaoh storecities, Pithom and Raamses. 12 But the more they afflicted them, the more they multiplied and the more they spread abroad. And they were grieved because of the children of Israel. 13 And the Egyptians made the children of Israel to serve with rigor: 14 and they made their lives bitter with hard service, in mortar and in brick, and in all manner of service in the field, all their service, wherein they made them serve with rigor.

While conditions were changing within Israel, they were also changing in their temporary home, the land of Egypt. A new king ascended the throne, one **who knew not Joseph.** The peculiar way in which this is emphasized indicates more than simply a new heir to the throne who because of the passage of time was not personally acquainted with Joseph. It rather marks the beginning of a new era, when Joseph's influence and precedent were forgotten or ignored, when the Pharaoh felt no responsibility or desire to grant special favors to Israel. It probably marked the beginning of an entire new dynasty of kings, the eighteenth, which took over the rule of Egypt after the expulsion of the Hyksos, the foreign shepherd kings who like the Israelites were Semitic in origin. While the Hyksos gained control of Egypt after Joseph's day, it is likely that his rule was still remembered, and the kinship of him and his people to the Hyksos would have won for Israel continued kindnesses. But when native Egyptian rule was re-established, patriotic emotions would easily have cast suspicion upon the other foreigners living in Goshen.[1] (For a fuller discussion of the dating of events in Exodus, see "Date" under "Introduction.")

The new king of Egypt committed himself to the oppression of Israel. He explained this to the Egyptians on the basis of their numerical strength, exaggerating their number by saying that the Israelites were **more and mightier** than the Egyptians, a term better translated "too many and too mighty for us" (ASV margin). He pointed out the danger, in the case of war and invasion from the east, of Israel's rising to join Egypt's enemies and using the opportunity to leave the country. Israel's residence in Goshen, in the eastern part of the Nile delta, near the desert routes from Palestine and Syria, did make such an action possible. And, in spite of the Egyptian king's hatred for Israel, he did not want them to leave. They represented too much potential wealth for him and his nation.

The first countermeasure the king proposed was that of conscripting the Israel-ites for "forced labor-gangs." It was a common practice in ancient times thus to enslave subject peoples.[2] Solomon did it in building the temple and his other public works (I Kings 5:13-16; 9:15-22). And archaeological records indicate that the ancient Egyptians were notorious for this practice. From the fifteenth century on, the ancient Egyptian inscriptions mention a people called the *'Apiru,* a foreign term equivalent to the Habiru mentioned in Mesopotamia and Syria. The word apparently means "those who cross over" or "immigrants." It is thought by many scholars that this word is the equivalent of the biblical "Hebrews," applied in Genesis to Abraham and to Joseph and his brethren (14:13; 39:14, 17; 40:15; 41:12; 43:32), and frequently in the early chapters of Exodus to the Israelites while they were still in Egypt. It is sometimes thought that "Hebrew" is an ethnic name derived from Eber, the ancestor of Abraham. But it now seems more likely that the term was a general one applied to migrant peoples, of which the biblical Hebrews would have been a part. And these 'Apiru are mentioned in the Egyptian records as being forced to work on the royal building projects.[3]

This type of labor was well calculated to hinder the growth and aspirations of the people, for under the Egyptian **taskmasters** they were set to building cities, working with mortar and brick, and also **in the field,** no doubt involving the digging and maintaining of irrigating canals, planting and cultivating the crops, etc. The **rigor** of such conscripted labor is evidenced in the record of Herodotus, the ancient Greek historian, who relates that Pharaoh Necho lost 120,000 men in digging a canal from the Red Sea to the Nile,[4] and in the experience of a more modern ruler, Mehemet Ali, who lost 20,000 out of a total of 120,000 laborers in digging the Alexandrian Canal in the middle of the nineteenth century A.D.[5]

Two cities are specifically mentioned as centers of Israelite labor, **Pithom** and **Raamses.** This has caused verse 11 to

---

[1] Merrill F. Unger, *Archaeology and the Old Testament,* pp. 143-44.
[2] S. R. Driver, *The Book of Exodus,* in "The Cambridge Bible for Schools and Colleges," Old Testament and Apocrypha, ed. by A. F. Kirkpatrick, p. 3.
[3] Jack Finegan, *Let My People Go,* pp. 20-21.
[4] J. Clement Connell, "Exodus," *The New Bible Commentary,* ed. by Francis Davidson, p. 108.
[5] George Rawlinson, *The Pulpit Commentary: Exodus,* ed. by H. D. M. Spence and Joseph S. Exell, I, 11.

become the center of the storm of controversy over the date of the Exodus of Israel from Egypt. The most natural reading of the data given in the Scriptures would indicate a date of approximately 1441 B.C. But the Pharaohs whose names were given to the city of Raamses (Rameses I, 1319-18, and Rameses II, 1301-1234) did not rule until much later. It is also recorded that Rameses II built the city which bore his name, and he speaks of using the 'Apiru in building it.[6] This has led practically all liberal scholars and a few conservative ones to settle on a date sometime in the thirteenth century B.C. for the Exodus. But this evidence is also subject to a different interpretation. Rameses II was notorious for claiming the credit for the achievements of his predecessors and it is likely that he merely rebuilt or enlarged the city which bore his name. The city was best known to the Israelites under the name Zoan. It had apparently been built by the time of Abraham, thus being only seven years younger than Hebron (Num. 13:22). It was known by the name of Avaris when it was the capital of the Hyksos rulers, and it was destroyed when they made their last stand there. So the Israelites could have been employed in construction work on the city at any time subsequent to the Hyksos. As we have seen, the 'Apiru included other foreigners, and those mentioned by Rameses II need not be Israelites. It is true that the city was known by the name Rameses only from 1300-1100 B.C., but the occurrence of the name in the Pentateuch (Gen. 47:11; Exod. 1:11; 12:37; Num. 33:3, 5) may be due to the modernization of an ancient place name by a scribe from that period just as Laish is called Dan in Genesis 14:14, although it did not receive that name until centuries after the time of Moses (Judg. 18:27-31).[7] (For a fuller discussion of the dating of the events of this book, see "Date" under "Introduction.") Practically all scholars, whatever their opinions about the date of the Exodus, do agree on the location of the two ancient cities mentioned here. Pithom is located at the modern Tell er-Retabeh, in the Wadi Tumilat, a valley which connects the Nile and Lake Tim-

sah, near the eastern borders of Egypt. Raamses, as already indicated, is the same as Zoan or Avaris, also designated later in Greek as Tanis. It also was located in the eastern delta, about thirty miles north and a little west of Pithom, on the ancient Tanitic branch of the Nile.[8] The cities were built as store-cities, depots for war materials backing up the front line of defense along the eastern borders of the nation.

The significant result of Pharaoh's plan to hamper Israel's growth was its complete failure. **The more they afflicted them, the more they multiplied and the more they spread abroad.** This was further evidence of divine intervention and providence, and it caused even the Egyptians to be **grieved because of** the Israelites, or as it is better translated, "felt a dread of," or "became apprehensive about." They recognized the unusual character of Israel's prosperity.

3. The Risk of Extinction (1:15-22)

15 And the king of Egypt spake to the Hebrew midwives, of whom the name of the one was Shiphrah, and the name of the other Puah: 16 and he said, When ye do the office of a midwife to the Hebrew women, and see them upon the birth-stool; if it be a son, then ye shall kill him; but if it be a daughter, then she shall live. 17 But the midwives feared God, and did not as the king of Egypt commanded them, but saved the men-children alive. 18 And the king of Egypt called for the midwives, and said unto them, Why have ye done this thing, and have saved the men-children alive? 19 And the midwives said unto Pharaoh, Because the Hebrew women are not as the Egyptian women; for they are lively, and are delivered ere the midwife come unto them. 20 And God dealt well with the midwives: and the people multiplied, and waxed very mighty. 21 And it came to pass, because the midwives feared God, that he made them households. 22 And Pharaoh charged all his people, saying, Every son that is born ye shall cast into the river, and every daughter ye shall save alive.

When Pharaoh observed that his efforts to stop Israel's rapid growth had failed, he took a new approach. He called to

---

[6] Finegan, *op. cit.*, pp. 18, 21.   [7] Unger, *op. cit.*, pp. 149-50.
[8] For a very full support of these locations, and their description, see Finegan, *op. cit.*, pp. 3-15, 29-38.

his aid the midwives who helped to deliver Israel's babies. Only two are mentioned, a fact which is frequently cited as evidence that the biblical figures indicating the number of Israelites at the time of the Exodus as more than two million are in error. While this may be a valid observation, it must be remembered that this first command was issued at least eighty years before the Exodus, perhaps more, when the number of Israelites could easily have been much smaller than at the time of the Exodus. It is also possible that only the leading families were served by the midwives, or that these two are the only ones of a larger group whose names have been preserved, or that they were supervisors of the rest.[9] He told them that when the Hebrew women were **upon the birth-stool** (the original is plural and refers to "two stones, bricks, or low stools upon which it was the custom for the women to kneel or sit during delivery"[10]), they were to kill every boy-baby, but save alive every girl. This would eventually annihilate the nation, for the girls could be absorbed by marriage into the Egyptians. It is not clear whether these midwives were Egyptian or Hebrew. **The Hebrew midwives** may mean "the Egyptian midwives serving the Hebrew women." The fact that God's blessings were added to the midwives would hint that they were not Israelites since they had not had His blessings until now. Their names are Hebrew, meaning "Beauty," and "Splendor,"[11] although these may have been merely translations of their Egyptian names. But whether Egyptian or Hebrew, they refused to obey Pharaoh's commands, for they **feared God.** When called to account for the survival of the boys, they replied that the Israelite women were not as dependent as the Egyptian women upon the midwives and were usually delivered of their children before they arrived. This may have been a partial truth,[12] as it succeeded in allaying the suspicions of Pharaoh. Their heroic devotion to their ethical duty also led to their being blessed by the Lord so that they too had large families, the greatest blessing any woman could have in that day.

But Pharaoh insisted on doing away with the people of Israel. So he now issued a proclamation calling on all Egyptians to join him in killing all the infant boys of Israel and saving the girls alive for future slavery. The case of Moses indicates that this proclamation was carried out to some extent, but such a practice was probably never fully operative nor of long duration. It, too, was doomed to failure.

B. THE AGENT OF DELIVERANCE (2:1—4:31)

1. The Birth of Moses (2:1-10)

1 And there went a man of the house of Levi, and took to wife a daughter of Levi. 2 And the woman conceived, and bare a son: and when she saw him that he was a goodly child, she hid him three months. 3 And when she could no longer hide him, she took for him an ark of bulrushes, and daubed it with slime and with pitch; and she put the child therein, and laid it in the flags by the river's brink. 4 And his sister stood afar off, to know what would be done to him. 5 And the daughter of Pharaoh came down to bathe at the river; and her maidens walked along by the riverside; and she saw the ark among the flags, and sent her handmaid to fetch it. 6 And she opened it, and saw the child: and, behold, the babe wept. And she had compassion on him, and said, This is one of the Hebrews' children. 7 Then said his sister to Pharaoh's daughter, Shall I go and call thee a nurse of the Hebrew women, that she may nurse the child for thee? 8 And Pharaoh's daughter said to her, Go. And the maiden went and called the child's mother. 9 And Pharaoh's daughter said unto her, Take this child away, and nurse it for me, and I will give thee thy wages. And the woman took the child, and nursed it. 10 And the child grew, and she brought him unto Pharaoh's daughter, and he became her son. And she called his name Moses, and said, Because I drew him out of the water.

It was with this background of oppression and the attempted annihilation of infant boys that the main character of

---

[9] Solomon Goldman, *From Slavery to Freedom*, pp. 85-86.
[10] Philip C. Johnson, "Exodus," *The Wycliffe Bible Commentary*, ed. by Charles F. Pfeiffer and Everett F. Harrison, p. 53.
[11] Martin Noth, *Exodus*, trans. by J. S. Bowden, p. 23.
[12] C. F. Keil and F. Delitzsch, *Biblical Commentary on the Old Testament*, "The Pentateuch," I, 425.

Exodus entered upon the scene. A Levite man married a Levite woman. Their names are revealed later to be Amram and Jochebed (6:20). Three of their children are mentioned in the Scriptures, both Miriam and Aaron being older than Moses. Since no mention is made of difficulties at the time of Aaron's birth, it seems probable that Pharaoh's decree concerning Hebrew boys was issued between the births of the two brothers.[13]

When the third child was born, Jochebed saw that **he was a goodly** (beautiful, handsome) **child.** To the natural affection she would have felt for the infant was added the undeniable fact that he was well-formed, healthy, holding great promise for the future. He was a child for whom one could well afford to take a risk. The author of Hebrews declares that the promising appearance of the child became the basis for his parents' faith in preserving him (Heb. 11:23). As a result, his mother hid him for **three months.** But then the increasing vigor of his crying made it increasingly doubtful that her efforts would much longer succeed. So she made a little box out of the papyrus plants which grew in profusion along the banks of the Nile,[14] coated it with **slime** (the bitumen or asphalt from the Dead Sea area) and **pitch,** placed her boy in it, and set him afloat among the reeds along the river bank. Miriam was placed close by to watch what would happen. Soon Pharaoh's daughter came down to bathe in the river, and spying the little box she sent one of her maidservants **to fetch it.** When she opened the box, the baby was crying and her heart was touched. She immediately recognized it as one of the Hebrew babies. Miriam then ran forward and volunteered to find a Hebrew nurse to nurse the baby. Pharaoh's daughter agreed, and Jochebed was hired to care for her own baby. As the child grew older, Jochebed took him to Pharaoh's daughter and he was apparently formally adopted as her son. Pharaoh's daughter named him **Moses,**

saying, **Because I drew him out of the water** (cf. Heb. 11:24-26; the name Moses has a relationship in sound both to an Egyptian word, *mesu,* a noun meaning "child" or "son" from a verb meaning "to produce" or "to draw forth," and to a Hebrew word, *mashah,* meaning "to draw out"[15]).

If the earlier date for the Exodus is correct, as the present writer holds, Moses was born in the reign of Thutmose I (1525-08 B.C.). This Pharaoh had an outstanding daughter, Hatshepsut, who later virtually ruled Egypt as queen-regent in the early years of her stepson and son-in-law, Thutmose III. It is quite possible that she was the one who adopted Moses. Egyptian law prevented her from becoming queen in fact.[16] It is probable that Jochebed had observed the princess coming regularly to the Nile to bathe, and placed Moses where he was most likely to be found by her, depending upon his natural beauty and divine providence to win the royal favor. It is also probable that Pharaoh's daughter was not fooled at all by what happened, but easily guessed from Miriam's quick appearance and quick finding of a nurse capable of breast-feeding the baby that these were his real mother and sister. She was probably not in sympathy with her father's cruelty. But in any event, the providences of God again overruled the very wrath of man, using Pharaoh's oppression to secure for Moses a place in the royal court itself, where he received invaluable preparation for his later mission, being "instructed in all the wisdom of the Egyptians" (Acts 7:22). No better secular education could have been found in Moses' age.

There are many parallels to the story of Moses' being found by the princess in the river in the stories of other ancient heroes—Romulus and Remus the founders of Rome, Bacchus and Perseus of Greek mythology, and Sargon I of Akkad in Mesopotamia.[17] This has led some critical scholars to assume that the story

---

[13] Some scholars insist that the wording of Exodus 2:1-2 indicates that Moses was the first-born son of the marriage, and theorize that Miriam and Aaron were the children of a former marriage of Amram. See A. H. McNeile, *The Book of Exodus,* "The Westminster Commentaries," ed. by Walter Lock, p. 6. But while the wording is open to such an interpretation, it does not require it, and Exodus 6:20 seems to settle the question.

[14] The pith of the papyrus plant was used to produce writing materials, hence our English word "paper." The stems were used to form light boats. For an interesting description of the plant and how it was used, see Driver, *op. cit.,* pp. 8-9.

[15] Connell, *op. cit.,* pp. 108-09.   [16] Unger, *op. cit.,* pp. 144-45.   [17] *Ibid.,* p. 135.

of Moses' birth is fiction rather than fact, claiming that there was a standard literary form for relating the birth of a deliverer, and a natural desire to connect the deliverer with the proper persons and activities.[18] But the mere appearance of similar stories does not automatically mean that all of them are fictional. Where there are counterfeits there is always somewhere a genuine. The naturalness of the setting of Moses' story and its consequences, the inclusion of it in the divinely inspired record, the stamp of approval put upon it by similarly inspired New Testament writers all insist that the story of Moses is a fact as well as a fascinating story.

2. The Exile of Moses (2:11-22)

11 And it came to pass in those days, when Moses was grown up, that he went out unto his brethren, and looked on their burdens: and he saw an Egyptian smiting a Hebrew, one of his brethren. 12 And he looked this way and that way, and when he saw that there was no man, he smote the Egyptian, and hid him in the sand. 13 And he went out the second day, and, behold, two men of the Hebrews were striving together: and he said to him that did the wrong, Wherefore smitest thou thy fellow? 14 And he said, Who made thee a prince and a judge over us? thinkest thou to kill me, as thou killedst the Egyptian? And Moses feared, and said, Surely the thing is known. 15 Now when Pharaoh heard this thing, he sought to slay Moses. But Moses fled from the face of Pharaoh, and dwelt in the land of Midian; and he sat down by a well.
16 Now the priest of Midian had seven daughters: and they came and drew water, and filled the troughs to water their father's flock. 17 And the shepherds came and drove them away; but Moses stood up and helped them, and watered their flock. 18 And when they came to Reuel their father, he said, How is it that ye are come so soon to-day? 19 And they said, An Egyptian delivered us out of the hand of the shepherds, and moreover he drew water for us, and watered the flock. 20 And he said unto his daughters, And where is he? why is it that ye have left the man? call him, that he may eat bread. 21 And Moses

was content to dwell with the man: and he gave Moses Zipporah his daughter. 22 And she bare a son, and he called his name Gershom; for he said, I have been a sojourner in a foreign land.

Apparently Jochebed had opportunity, either before she first turned Moses over to Pharaoh's daughter or subsequently in contacts not mentioned in the Scriptures, to instruct him concerning his true identity. When he was grown (Stephen says he was nearly forty years old, Acts 7:23), he went out to see for himself how his people were being oppressed. One of the first things he saw was an Egyptian, probably one of the "taskmasters" of 1:11, striking a Hebrew. Looking around, and thinking no one was watching, he killed the Egyptian and buried him in the sand. Such an act was inexcusable, either from divine or human law. And such impulsive violence revealed that whatever natural abilities and secular training Moses may have had, he was not ready to lead his people. The next day, he discovered two Hebrew men struggling with each other, and when he attempted to correct the offender, was immediately rejected as a prince and a judge over the Israelites, with a reference to his crime of the day before. Moses was alarmed to discover that his secret was known. The news spread to Pharaoh who ordered his capture and execution. But Moses fled eastward into a part of the desert occupied by some nomadic Midianites. It might be expected that his connections with Egypt's royal family would have helped to hush the whole matter up. But if Hatshepsut really was his adopted mother (see comments on 2:1-10), she died during the 1480's B.C., shortly before Moses would have been forty years old. She had dominated the early years of the reign of her stepson and son-in-law, Thutmose III, a domination which he resented intensely. Upon her death, he sought to obliterate her monuments, and it is easy to imagine that he would eagerly have sought the death of the Hebrew boy she had favored and brought into the palace with him.[19]

Arriving in Midian, Moses sat down by a well. The Midianites were related to

[18] J. Coert Rylaarsdam, "Exodus" (Introduction and Exegesis), in *The Interpreter's Bible*, ed. by George Arthur Buttrick, I, 857-60.
[19] Unger, *op. cit.*, pp. 144-45.

Israel, being descended from Abraham (Gen. 25:1-6). Their home was usually in Arabia, on beyond the Sinai Peninsula, across the eastern arm of the Red Sea. But they were nomads, and frequently wandered into Sinai and the borders of Canaan. The group that Moses encountered included a priest, known variously as Reuel or Jethro (2:18; 3:1). The Midianites were not as a group worshipers of Jehovah. But it is possible that some dim light about the true God had filtered down to Reuel from Abraham, and that even if he used a different name for God, like Melchizedek he could be recognized as a true worshiper of the true God (Gen. 14:18-19). It is probable that Moses helped later to draw him away from idolatry to the worship of Jehovah. In any event, he was later respected as a true priest by the Israelites (Exod. 18: 8-12). This man's sheep were cared for by his seven daughters — girls were frequently employed as shepherds in the ancient world (cf. Gen. 29:6-12). But when they came to draw water from the well and put it in the troughs to water their flock, the stronger male shepherds drove them off, bullying their own way in first. The stranger from Egypt, so intent upon justice for all men, again intervened in the quarrel of others, and made it possible for the girls to take their turn. As a result, they made it back home much earlier than usual. Their father inquired why, and when told, was disappointed and reproachful over their failure to invite such a helpful stranger home for supper. The oversight was quickly remedied and Moses came not only for supper, but remained to marry **Zipporah,** one of the seven sisters, and to take up his dwelling with Reuel. In time, a son was born, and Moses named him **Gershom,** best explained from the Hebrew words *ger* ("foreigner") *sham* ("there").[20] Later another son was born (4:20; 18:2-4).

3. The Prayer of Israel (2:23-25)

23 And it came to pass in the course of those many days, that the king of Egypt died: and the children of Israel sighed by reason of the bondage, and they cried, and their cry came up unto God by reason

of the bondage. 24 And God heard their groaning, and God remembered his covenant with Abraham, with Isaac, and with Jacob. 25 And God saw the children of Israel, and God took knowledge *of them.*

If the chronology we have been following is correct, Thutmose III, stepson and son-in-law of Queen Hatshepsut, the Pharaoh from whom his foster-brother Moses had fled into exile, would have ended his outstanding reign by death at about 1450 B.C. or shortly thereafter.[21] This would have been shortly before Moses reached the age of eighty (7:7), and would have removed the most serious hindrance to his return to Egypt (4:19). But the death of Thutmose III did not bring respite to the oppressed people of Israel. He was succeeded by his son, Amenhotep II, a somewhat weaker monarch against whom the outlying tribes in Syria and Palestine rebelled.[22] But he had the same stubbornness characteristic of all the rulers who had oppressed Israel. The people of Israel sank even lower in their despair. The Lord **heard their groaning,** remembered the covenant He had established with their ancestors, and moved to bring to a climax the deliverance He had been preparing all through the years.

4. The Call of Moses (3:1—4:17)

a. The Nature of the Call (3:1-12)

1 Now Moses was keeping the flock of Jethro his father-in-law, the priest of Midian; and he led the flock to the back of the wilderness, and came to the mountain of God, unto Horeb. 2 And the angel of Jehovah appeared unto him in a flame of fire out of the midst of a bush: and he looked, and, behold, the bush burned with fire, and the bush was not consumed. 3 And Moses said, I will turn aside now, and see this great sight, why the bush is not burnt. 4 And when Jehovah saw that he turned aside to see, God called unto him out of the midst of the bush, and said, Moses, Moses. And he said, Here am I. 5 And he said, Draw not nigh hither: put off thy shoes from off thy feet, for the place whereon thou standest is holy ground. 6 Moreover he said, I am the God of thy father, the God of Abraham, the God of Isaac, and the God of Jacob. And Moses hid his face; for he was afraid to look upon

---

[20] Goldman, *op. cit.,* p. 130.   [21] Cf. Unger, *op. cit.,* p. 142, and Finegan, *op. cit.,* p. 18.

[22] Unger, *op. cit.,* pp. 142-43.

God. 7 And Jehovah said, I have surely seen the affliction of my people that are in Egypt, and have heard their cry by reason of their taskmasters; for I know their sorrows; 8 and I am come down to deliver them out of the hand of the Egyptians, and to bring them up out of that land unto a good land and a large, unto a land flowing with milk and honey; unto the place of the Canaanite, and the Hittite, and the Amorite, and the Perizzite, and the Hivite, and the Jebusite. 9 And now, behold, the cry of the children of Israel is come unto me: moreover I have seen the oppression wherewith the Egyptians oppress them. 10 Come now therefore, and I will send thee unto Pharaoh, that thou mayest bring forth my people the children of Israel out of Egypt. 11 And Moses said unto God, Who am I, that I should go unto Pharaoh, and that I should bring forth the children of Israel out of Egypt? 12 And he said, Certainly I will be with thee; and this shall be the token unto thee, that I have sent thee: when thou hast brought forth the people out of Egypt, ye shall serve God upon this mountain.

Years passed, and the once headstrong prince of Egypt had become a patient shepherd in the desert. How difficult those first few months and years must have been for this man filled with a sense of mission, with ambition, with dynamic energy! How long it takes sometimes for God to prepare His instruments! For forty years God had trained Moses in the best schools of the age. And Moses would have been at a complete loss in dealing with Pharaoh and in organizing his motley company of slaves without that earlier courtly education. Now for forty years God had to teach Moses humility, dependence, patience. And Moses would have been swallowed up with all of Israel in the desert if he had not first returned to the simple life of Abraham, Isaac, and Jacob, meditating on eternal truths under the starry heavens and among the awe-inspiring mountains and the desert's shifting sands, and learning firsthand the fundamental laws of survival. How profitable it is to abide God's timetable, to submit to God's pruning and molding!

While tending Jethro or Reuel's flock,

Moses directed it **to the back of the wilderness.** This seems to be a technical term meaning the western part or western side of the desert.[23] Either Jethro's permanent home was like that of the major part of his people, in Arabia east of the eastern arm of the Red Sea, and Moses had brought the flock around that arm into the Sinai Peninsula, or the Midianite clan of which Jethro was a part had been camping on the eastern side of the Sinai Peninsula and Moses now led the flock toward the western side. In any event, he came **to the mountain of God, unto Horeb. The mountain of God** apparently refers to Sinai, either due to the sacred character it had assumed by the time this story was recorded, or as some scholars believe, due to its habitual use as a place of worship by the nomadic tribes in the area. While Horeb appears to be used interchangeably with Sinai in the accounts of Israel's wanderings, the evidence is strong that it refers to the larger vicinity in which the single Mt. Sinai is located. Mt. Sinai itself is traditionally identified with the present *Jebel Musa* (Arabic for "Mountain of Moses"), one of the most outstanding peaks in the range near the southern end of the Peninsula.[24]

Here **the angel of Jehovah** appeared to him through the instrumentality of a thornbush all aglow with fire but unconsumed. **The angel of Jehovah** "is a temporary, but full, *self-manifestation of Jehovah,* a manifestation usually, at any rate, in human form, possessing no distinct and permanent personality, as such, but speaking and spoken of, sometimes as Jehovah Himself . . . , and sometimes as distinct from Him."[25] As in all cases where the Bible pictures something unusual or bordering on the miraculous, certain naturalistic, critical scholars have come up with suggestions as to a natural explanation for the bush that burned but was not consumed. But no natural phenomenon can be described which would have been normal in that region without Moses almost certainly having been familiar with it. This was something which he had not seen before, which God

[23] See Theophile J. Meek's translation in *The Bible, an American Translation,* Old Testament ed. by J. M. Powis Smith, p. 52.

[24] Driver, *op. cit.,* pp. 18-19; and Goldman, *op. cit.,* pp. 155-67.

[25] Driver, *op. cit.,* p. 19. See also the present writer's comments on Genesis 32:22-32.

used to arouse his curiosity and to prompt his investigation. There is no reasonable explanation for it except that God chose, according to His sovereign pleasure and His divine wisdom, to clothe Himself in the fire He so frequently used as a symbol of His presence (cf. Heb. 12:29).

The Lord's first words to Moses mentioned his name, cautioned him against closer approach to the divine presence, and commanded the removal of his sandals from his feet, a widespread custom in the Orient when approaching a sacred spot or entering a house of worship.[26] Then came the identification of the voice, the God of the patriarchs, resulting in Moses' fearful hiding of his face. Jehovah then moved to the reason for His appearance. He had **seen** the Israelites' affliction and had **heard** their cry. So He had stepped down to earth personally to rescue them from the Egyptians and to take them to the land of **milk and honey.** He wished to send Moses to Pharaoh, using him as the human instrument of deliverance. Immediately there arose a cry of protest from Moses, **Who am I,** either to go to Pharaoh or to bring out Israel? The impulsive, self-confident prince had changed indeed. He no longer thought of his natural talents nor his excellent training. He thought instead of the utter failure of his previous attempt to help his people, of the hostility of Pharaoh and the rejection of his leadership by his own brethren. But the Lord quickly reassured him that the important thing was not his own identity or importance but the fact of the divine presence accompanying him. And He promised, as a sign that He had sent Moses, that Moses and his people would worship Him upon this very same mountain.

b. The Authority of the Call (3:13-22)

13 And Moses said unto God, Behold, when I come unto the children of Israel, and shall say unto them, The God of your fathers hath sent me unto you; and they shall say to me, What is his name? what shall I say unto them? 14 And God said unto Moses, I AM THAT I AM: and he said, Thus shalt thou say unto the children of Israel, I AM hath sent me

unto you. 15 And God said moreover unto Moses, Thus shalt thou say unto the children of Israel, Jehovah, the God of your fathers, the God of Abraham, the God of Isaac, and the God of Jacob, hath sent me unto you: this is my name for ever, and this is my memorial unto all generations. 16 Go, and gather the elders of Israel together, and say unto them, Jehovah, the God of your fathers, the God of Abraham, of Isaac, and of Jacob, hath appeared unto me, saying, I have surely visited you, and *seen* that which is done to you in Egypt: 17 and I have said, I will bring you out of the affliction of Egypt unto the land of the Canaanite, and the Hittite, and the Amorite, and the Perizzite, and the Hivite, and the Jebusite, unto a land flowing with milk and honey. 18 And they shall hearken to thy voice: and thou shalt come, thou and the elders of Israel, unto the king of Egypt, and ye shall say unto him, Jehovah, the God of the Hebrews, hath met with us: and now let us go, we pray thee, three days' journey into the wilderness, that we may sacrifice to Jehovah our God. 19 And I know that the king of Egypt will not give you leave to go, no, not by a mighty hand. 20 And I will put forth my hand, and smite Egypt with all my wonders which I will do in the midst thereof: and after that he will let you go. 21 And I will give this people favor in the sight of the Egyptians: and it shall come to pass, that, when ye go, ye shall not go empty: 22 but every woman shall ask of her neighbor, and of her that sojourneth in her house, jewels of silver, and jewels of gold, and raiment: and ye shall put them upon your sons, and upon your daughters; and ye shall despoil the Egyptians.

Moses immediately saw another problem. When he arrived again among his people and told them his mission, they would demand to know the name of the God who had sent him. Names were extremely important among the ancient Hebrews, for they revealed character even more than simply providing a tag for identification. Many times in the days of the patriarchs an outstanding religious experience centering around a vision of God or the building of an altar brought the revelation or adoption of a new name for God, either in a larger understanding of His nature or in a sense reminiscent

[26] McNeile, *op. cit.*, p. 17.

of that particular incident and place.[27] So when Moses came with his story of a marvelous vision from God, one of the most natural questions that could be asked to test the genuineness of his account would be, What was the name? And the Lord quickly supplied that answer: My name is *Ehyeh-asher-ehyeh;* tell them *Ehyeh* has sent you. The long phrase is traditionally translated **I AM THAT I AM,** although three other possibilities are given in the ASV margin and one scholar occupies nearly two large pages to list the several possibilities which have been suggested.[28] *Ehyeh* is from the same root as Jehovah or Yahweh. The root has many possible meanings and this particular form makes it indefinite as to whether the verb is past, present, or future. This is most fitting. For it reveals God as the self-sufficient One, as the unlimited One, as the eternal One, as the God of the "eternal Now." It speaks of His self-existence, His mystery, His unapproachableness, His majesty, His omnipotence, His omniscience, His goodness and His grace all at once. Then He advised Moses to add the more familiar name of Jehovah, the God of the patriarchs, the name which was His forever, His peculiar **memorial unto all generations.** He gave to Moses in detail the words he was to speak to Israel, relaying to them the same message of comfort and promise He had just given to Moses (3:7-10). And He promised Moses that the elders of Israel would listen to him and would go with him to make their request of Pharaoh. This request was to be for permission to go **three days' journey into the wilderness** for sacrifices to Jehovah. Since Israel would be sacrificing animals sacred to the Egyptians, they could do so only at a distance. And while the Lord had no intention to halt His deliverance at such a remote point from Canaan, it is doubtful that He meant it for the deception of Pharaoh. Rather, this was to be the beginning of negotiations, the first step in a final exodus from the land. But Jehovah warned Moses that Pharaoh would not be so easily persuaded as Israel. Even after he was stricken by the **mighty hand** of God, he would still stubbornly refuse to yield, until God had completed all His **wonders.** Then he would let them go, and the Egyptians would enrich the Israelites with their jewels, a sign of Israel's final triumph over their masters, a sort of long-delayed payment for their services while in Egypt.

c. The Evidence of the Call (4:1-9)

1 And Moses answered and said, But, behold, they will not believe me, nor hearken unto my voice; for they will say, Jehovah hath not appeared unto thee. 2 And Jehovah said unto him, What is that in thy hand? And he said, A rod. 3 And he said, Cast it on the ground. And he cast it on the ground, and it became a serpent; and Moses fled from before it. 4 And Jehovah said unto Moses, Put forth thy hand, and take it by the tail (and he put forth his hand, and laid hold of it, and it became a rod in his hand); 5 that they may believe that Jehovah, the God of their fathers, the God of Abraham, the God of Isaac, and the God of Jacob, hath appeared unto thee. 6 And Jehovah said furthermore unto him, Put now thy hand into thy bosom. And he put his hand into his bosom: and when he took it out, behold, his hand was leprous, as *white as* snow. 7 And he said, Put thy hand into thy bosom again. (And he put his hand into his bosom again; and when he took it out of his bosom, behold, it was turned again as his *other* flesh.) 8 And it shall come to pass, if they will not believe thee, neither hearken to the voice of the first sign, that they will believe the voice of the latter sign. 9 And it shall come to pass, if they will not believe even these two signs, neither hearken unto thy voice, that thou shalt take of the water of the river, and pour it upon the dry land: and the water which thou takest out of the river shall become blood upon the dry land.

---

[27] Thus for Abraham when meeting Melchizedek there had come the new insight of *El Elyon* (God Most High), Gen. 14:18-22; at the institution of circumcision the divine use of *El Shaddai* (God Almighty), Gen. 17:1; and after the planting of the tamarisk tree in Beersheba, in the identification of Jehovah with *El Olam* (God of Eternity), Gen. 21:33; for the pregnant and abused Hagar fleeing from her mistress and instructed by the angel, the new insight of the name *El Rôi* (God of seeing), Gen. 16:13; for Jacob at the building of an altar at Shechem the identifying name *El-Elohe-Israel* (God, the God of Israel), Gen. 33:20; and another at Bethel with the identifying name *El-beth-el* (The God of the House of God), Gen. 35:7.
[28] Goldman, *op. cit.,* pp. 142-44.

Moses did not soon run out of excuses for not accepting the divine commission. Even if the Lord went with him, and even with a new name of God to announce, the people still might not believe that the Lord had appeared *to him*. He needed some evidence that he personally had received a commission from the Lord. So the Lord gave him three signs: the first using the simple shepherd's rod which he carried, it becoming first a serpent and then being changed again into a rod; the second using only his hand and his garment, covering his skin first with leprosy and then immediately healing him of the dread, and at that time incurable, disease; and the third, as a final emergency measure, pouring water from the Nile upon the ground and turning it into blood. Moses was going to be dealing with a people steeped in superstition, a people surrounded by a heathen nation which practiced magic in all of its forms. The Lord adapted the evidence which He granted to the state of the people, to that which they would most readily understand and accept.

d. The Sharing of the Call (4:10-17)

10 And Moses said unto Jehovah, Oh, Lord, I am not eloquent, neither heretofore, nor since thou hast spoken unto thy servant; for I am slow of speech, and of a slow tongue. 11 And Jehovah said unto him, Who hath made man's mouth? or who maketh a *man* dumb, or deaf, or seeing, or blind? Is it not I, Jehovah? 12 Now therefore go, and I will be with thy mouth, and teach thee what thou shalt speak. 13 And he said, Oh, Lord, send, I pray thee, by the hand of him whom thou wilt send. 14 And the anger of Jehovah was kindled against Moses, and he said, Is there not Aaron thy brother the Levite? I know that he can speak well. And also, behold, he cometh forth to meet thee: and when he seeth thee, he will be glad in his heart. 15 And thou shalt speak unto him, and put the words in his mouth: and I will be with thy mouth, and with his mouth, and will teach you what ye shall do. 16 And he shall be thy spokesman unto the people; and it shall come to pass, that he shall be to thee a mouth, and thou shalt be to him as God. 17 And thou shalt take in thy hand this rod, wherewith thou shalt do the signs.

But Moses had one last excuse to offer. He was not an outstanding public speaker. He had never been before, and even this appearance of the Lord and the miraculous power here displayed had not changed the situation. Moses had no doubt studied public speaking in the schools of Egypt and could well remember that it was his weakest point. No doubt he had been struggling with words in trying to express to the Lord his reluctance to accept this task. But the Lord reminded him that it was He who had made man's mouth, who in fact made man with either gifted or handicapped faculties. He would not only be with Moses, but also with his mouth, and would teach him what he should speak. But still Moses hesitated. He said, **Oh, Lord, send, I pray thee, by the hand of him whom thou wilt send.** This was a grudging acceptance of the divine commission, given as Driver describes it, "unwillingly and ambiguously."[29] The immediate result was the anger of the Lord. God is very patient with His servants' honest questions, with their genuine concern over their limitations, but He has no patience with a stubborn reluctance to do His will. It was a virtue for Moses to be humble; it was a vice for him to continue to question the wisdom of God when all of his questions had been answered. It cost him the honor which would have been solely his both in his lifetime and afterwards, for Jehovah now decided he must share the mission with someone else. He reminded him of Aaron, his brother. Aaron was well known as a gifted speaker, and he was even now on his way to meet Moses. Aaron was to be Moses' "mouth" and Moses was to be Aaron's "God" as far as the presentation of the message to Israel was concerned. These terms were exactly those used in Egypt of Pharaoh and his chief deputy — the god and his mouth or "chief mouth." Thus Aaron was to become Moses' mouthpiece and chief helper.[30] Aaron is specified as **the Levite,** a term ordinarily thought to refer to members of the tribe of Levi. But Moses was also of the tribe of Levi, and the use of the distinguishing term here could have meaning only if it referred to some-

29 Driver, *op. cit.*, p. 28.   30 Professor Yahuda, cited by Goldman, *op. cit.*, p. 215.

thing else. This, plus other passages, has led scholars to believe that the term also referred to a function as a religious instructor or priest, regardless of a man's tribal ancestry (cf. Judg. 17:7 where a Levite is descended from Judah). It is quite likely that Israel had some type of spiritual leaders while in slavery, although their activities would have been necessarily limited. Aaron was apparently one of these, and is so designated by the term "Levite" in this setting.[31] Thus equipped, with Aaron as his speaker, and his own shepherd's rod as the visible instrument of divine power for use both in the sign of the serpent (4:2-5) and in the wonders to be wrought upon Egypt (3:30), Moses went forth from the presence of God to carry out the task assigned to him.

5. The Return of Moses (4:18-31)

a. A Wretched Farewell (4:18-26)

18 And Moses went and returned to Jethro his father-in-law, and said unto him, Let me go, I pray thee, and return unto my brethren that are in Egypt, and see whether they be yet alive. And Jethro said to Moses, Go in peace. 19 And Jehovah said unto Moses in Midian, Go, return into Egypt; for all the men are dead that sought thy life. 20 And Moses took his wife and his sons, and set them upon an ass, and he returned to the land of Egypt: and Moses took the rod of God in his hand. 21 And Jehovah said unto Moses, When thou goest back into Egypt, see that thou do before Pharaoh all the wonders which I have put in thy hand: but I will harden his heart, and he will not let the people go. 22 And thou shalt say unto Pharaoh, Thus saith Jehovah, Israel is my son, my first-born: 23 and I have said unto thee, Let my son go, that he may serve me; and thou hast refused to let him go: behold, I will slay thy son, thy first-born. 24 And it came to pass on the way at the lodging-place, that Jehovah met him, and sought to kill him. 25 Then Zipporah took a flint, and cut off the foreskin of her son, and cast it at his feet; and she said, Surely a bridegroom of blood art thou to me. 26 So he let him alone. Then she said, A bridegroom of blood *art thou*, because of the circumcision.

The stages of Moses' farewell to his home in Midian are given in a rather sketchy fashion, which makes positive interpretation difficult. Five different scenes or events are included: (1) the obtaining from Jethro of permission to leave (4:18), (2) a further communication from Jehovah assuring Moses that those in Egypt who had sought to kill him were now dead (4:19), (3) the departure of Moses and his family for Egypt (4:20), (4) a still further communication from Jehovah advising Moses of Pharaoh's stubbornness (4:21-23), and (5) an amazing and perplexing experience in which Moses' life was only saved by the circumcision of one of his sons (4:24-26). Some parts, especially the last, are so brief and omit so many pertinent details that it becomes extremely difficult to reconstruct exactly what happened. It is also difficult to be certain whether the events are given in strict chronological order, or whether this is just a collection of isolated items connected with his leave-taking.

Moses' seeking of permission from Jethro to return to his home is reminiscent of Jacob's similar request to Laban at the end of his first fourteen years of service (Gen. 30:25ff.). The reason was the same. Moses, by marrying Jethro's daughter, had become a part of the clan which Jethro led, and as shown in his tending of Jethro's flock, owed him his loyal service and obedience. While the Lord had called Moses, this did not release him from fulfilling insofar as possible those duties dictated by human custom and courtesy.

The fact that the Lord spoke to Moses again before his departure from Midian may indicate that Moses was still hesitating. Perhaps he thought up an additional excuse after leaving the burning bush — I am a wanted man; to return to Egypt will simply mean my death. But the Lord reassured him that those who would have punished him were now themselves dead. This further communication also indicates that the Lord kept in frequent and continuous contact with his servant, giving him additional encouragement and instruction as they were needed and as he had the capacity to receive them.

---

[31] Driver, *op. cit.*, p. 29.

There are many difficulties involved in the pictures of Moses' family contained in this chapter. According to the data given in other Scriptures, Moses spent about forty years in Midian (Acts 7:23; Exod. 7:7). He apparently married Jethro's daughter, Zipporah, soon after his arrival in Midian, and there is no mention of a long delay before the birth of his eldest son, Gershom (2:21-22). His younger son is not mentioned at all until the present passage by the reference to sons, and is not distinguished by name until 18:4. If Gershom was born even in the first ten years of Moses' exile, he would long since have been a grown man. But now, at the end of Moses' exile, Moses places his wife and both sons on one beast of burden — as if they were very little boys. Two possibilities present themselves for reconciling these apparently contradictory factors. One suggested by Jack Finegan is that the number forty is used so frequently both in the Bible and in rabbinic literature as to suggest that it is used in many instances not as an exact figure but as a round number meaning "many." In fitting Moses' life into the later chronology suggested for the Exodus, and particularly in conjunction with the reign of Rameses II, Finegan reduces Moses' three periods of forty years each to a total of ninety.[32] This would, of course, give a great deal of flexibility to the chronology of Moses' life. It has favorable support in the fact that the impatience manifested in Moses' murder of the Egyptian (2:11-12) is more typical of a man twenty years old than of a man forty, and is evidence that his desire to help his people could not easily have been restrained that long. It would also make possible a much shorter period of exile and the youth of his sons at the time of his departure. But it requires a great deal of freedom in interpreting the Scriptures, and runs afoul of the chronology which we have been following for the earlier date of the Exodus. The other possibility is that Zipporah was one of the youngest daughters of Jethro, that she was not given to Moses until many years after he arrived in Midian, and

that like Sarah, Rebekah, and Rachel, she experienced a long period of barrenness before the birth of her two sons. In any event, Moses mounted them on the ass, took his rod which had now become the rod of God by divine appointment, and departed for Egypt.

Again the Lord spoke to Moses, reemphasizing the need for his showing to Pharaoh all the wonders which Jehovah had put in Moses' hand. It is possible that this included the three signs appointed for Israel (4:1-9), one of which he is recorded as having demonstrated before Pharaoh (7:8-13), but may also have included the plagues which God had mentioned by implication (3:20), and perhaps in unrecorded communications somewhat more explicitly. And the Lord repeated His warning that in spite of the divine power Moses might demonstrate before Pharaoh, that haughty ruler would not let the people go (cf. 3:19). In fact, He said, I will harden his heart.

This prediction by Jehovah introduces a very important line of truth which is central to the whole account of the Exodus. There are frequent references to Pharaoh's hardening of his own heart and frequent references to Jehovah's hardening of Pharaoh's heart. So the old problem of the sovereignty of God versus the freedom of man is raised. And a reference by Paul to Pharaoh's experience when illustrating the divine sovereignty in the selection and use of men (Rom. 9:17-18) has unfortunately led to the misinterpretation by many of the entire matter.[33] Pharaoh's hardening has been claimed as evidence of the unconditional election and predestination by God of some to be saved and of others to be eternally lost. And if the present verse is taken out of context, it might appear to be so. But there is much more to be considered. In the whole account of Moses' dealings with Pharaoh, there are nineteen references to the hardening of his heart, in ten of which Jehovah is the source of the hardening and in nine Pharaoh is his own cause of hardening. Three Hebrew roots are used to express this hardening of Pharaoh's heart. Chazaq

---

[32] Finegan, op. cit., pp. 44-45.

[33] For outstanding treatments of the entire passage in Romans (chaps. 9-11), see W. T. Dayton's comments in this commentary, Vol. V, pp. 60-74; and A. Berkeley Mickelsen, "Romans," in The Wycliffe Bible Commentary, ed. by Charles F. Pfeiffer and Everett F. Harrison, pp. 1209-19.

is used twelve times. It basically means "to grow firm, strong," and in this context, "to grow stout, rigid, hard." It refers to a process of becoming fixed in a state of disobedience. *Kabed* is used six times. It basically means "to be heavy, weighty," and in this context, "to be insensible, unresponsive." It refers to a state in which there is an obstinate resistance to change. *Qashah* is used only once. It basically means "to be hard, severe, fierce." It is the common word in the Old Testament used in the phrase "stiffened the neck." The picture is of an animal who refuses to obey the instructions of his master, stiffens his neck against being turned in the direction of the master's choice, perversely insists on his own way. Using the key words, "grow hard," "be obstinate," and "be perverse" to indicate the three different roots, the nineteen references can be analyzed as follows:

4:21 — when Moses was on the way to Egypt, God foretold that He would make Pharaoh's heart *hard.*

7:3 — after Moses reached Egypt, God foretold that He would make Pharaoh's heart *perverse.*

7:13 — after the sign of the rods, Pharaoh's heart *grew hard.*

7:14 — at the same time, the Lord describes Pharaoh's heart as *obstinate.*

7:22 — after the plague of the water turned to blood, Pharaoh's heart *grew hard.*

8:15 — after the plague of the frogs, Pharaoh made his heart *obstinate.*

8:19 — after the plague of the lice, Pharaoh's heart *grew hard.*

8:32 — after the plague of the flies, Pharaoh made his heart *obstinate.*

9:7 — after the plague of the disease of the livestock, Pharaoh's heart was *obstinate.*

9:12 — after the plague of boils, Jehovah made Pharaoh's heart *hard.*

9:34 — after the plague of hail, Pharaoh made his heart *obstinate.*

9:35 — and at the same time, Pharaoh's heart grew *hard.*

10:1 — before the plague of locusts, the Lord declared, "I have made *obstinate* the heart of Pharaoh."

10:20 — after the plague of locusts, Jehovah made the heart of Pharaoh *hard.*

10:27 — after the plague of darkness, the Lord made the heart of Pharaoh *hard.*

11:10 — by way of summary, before the slaying of the first-born, it is said that the Lord made Pharaoh's heart *hard.*

14:4 — the Lord foretold Pharaoh's pursuit of Israel, declaring, I will make Pharaoh's heart *hard.*

14:8 — in connection with the pursuit, the Lord made Pharaoh's heart *hard.*

14:17 — the Lord foretells the pursuit of Israel by the Egyptians into the Red Sea itself, declaring, "I will make the hearts of the Egyptians *hard.*"

Several interesting facts emerge from this analysis. The Lord, in His omniscience, foretold His hardening of Pharaoh's heart. But the hardening process itself was initiated by Pharaoh. Six times, following the swallowing up of his magicians' rods by the rod of God, and following each of the first five plagues, it is declared that his heart grew hard, that he made it obstinate, or that it was obstinate. Only after this, only after Pharaoh's magicians had been forced to admit that the wonders Moses and Aaron were performing were no mere magical tricks but the handiwork of God, only after the Lord had further evidenced His power by limiting the plagues to those territories outside of Goshen, thus protecting Israel from harm, only after Pharaoh had twice broken his promise to let the people go — only after all of this is it finally said that the Lord made Pharaoh's heart hard. Thus it is made clear that God hardens no man capriciously. He gives every man ample opportunity for obedience and repentance. Even after the Lord joined in the hardening of Pharaoh's heart, Pharaoh himself had further opportunity to contribute to the process. So it is understood that he could even then have turned back in repentance. But after the double reference to his stubbornness following the seventh plague (9:34-35), the Scriptures speak only of the Lord as carrying on the process of hardening. Whenever man insists on his own way, God grants him that freedom. The frightening thing is that while man initiates the hardening process, he does not control the speed with which, nor the extent to which, it will carry out its deadly work. Just as God gave up the heathen to their lusts, their passions, and a reprobate mind — the very things they insisted on having (Rom. 1:24, 26, 28) — so He gave up Pharaoh to the stubborn heart he insisted on developing. He committed him irrevocably to the fate he had chosen. Pharaoh had been honored by the Lord in bringing him to the throne of Egypt at this juncture, when he could have rendered invaluable service to the cause of human redemption (Rom. 9:17). But his stubborn disobedience meant that the Lord could use him only as a tragic example of the impotence of the proudest sinner before the wrath of an offended and angry God.[34]

One might wonder why the Lord told Moses so far in advance about His part in the hardening of Pharaoh without balancing this with a revelation about Pharaoh's part in it. Keil and Delitzsch have aptly answered this question. Moses would learn soon enough about Pharaoh's personal stubbornness. But he needed to know beforehand that this came as no surprise to Jehovah, and would in fact be used to advance His design for Israel. Thus he was encouraged in advance for the repeated disappointments he would have to endure in his dealings with Pharaoh.[35]

It was in connection with this advance encouragement that the Lord also revealed another facet of His relationship to Israel. Israel was His son, and his son in a peculiar way — the first-born. This was a reference to His choice of Israel to be separate unto Him, to be His helpers in the cause of redemption. And it was the basis for His most solemn warning to Pharaoh: Because you will not let my first-born son go free, I will slay your first-born son. This warning Moses was to carry.

The last incident in Moses' farewell is that which made it a "wretched" one, and is one of the most baffling incidents in all the Scriptures. The critics, in their analysis of the Pentateuch into different documents and these in turn into their ancient sources, are quick to classify this as one of the oldest and most primitive bits of folklore to be found in the Old Testament.[36] But by carefully filling in the background, one is able to arrive at at least a partial interpretation which is by and large faithful to the details of the

story as given and also to the Scriptures as a whole. Moses' marriage to the Midianite Zipporah had brought together two individuals with quite different cultural backgrounds. In the matter of circumcision, for example, the custom of Moses' people was to circumcise the boys as infants, when they were eight days old. Failure to be circumcised made a person subject to the death-penalty, and it seems probable that this penalty was also exacted of a father who failed to circumcise his sons (Gen. 17:9-14). Zipporah's people were also accustomed to circumcising, but it was done to a young man as a part of his preparation for marriage. Because of this, the circumcision of a baby seemed to her barbaric and cruel. When Gershom was born, Moses apparently carried out Israel's custom either over his wife's objections or before he became aware of them. But when Eliezer was born, Moses did not override her opposition, and they were headed for Egypt with the younger son yet uncircumcised. The Lord had been speaking to Moses about His demand for Pharaoh's obedience, and the cost of disobedience. He must now secure the explicit obedience of the appointed leader of His people. When the family camped at an oasis for the night, the Lord suddenly attacked Moses in such a way as to threaten his life. This may have been by means of an acute illness; it may have been in some bodily form such as that experienced by Jacob when he wrestled with the Lord (Gen. 32:24ff.). However it was, Zipporah got the message. She took a flint knife, the tool used for centuries by ancient Israel for circumcising (see Josh. 5: 2ff.), cut off her younger son's foreskin and as the original has it, "made it touch his feet." Whose feet and why? The feet of an incarnate Jehovah to prove her obedience? The feet of the sick Moses in an expression of disgust and bitterness, or of hope that this would bring his healing? The feet of her little son in some primitive ceremony long since forgotten and abandoned? This it

---

[34] For the meaning of the Hebrews words discussed above, see Francis Brown, S. R. Driver, and Charles A. Briggs, eds., *A Hebrew and English Lexicon of the Old Testament*, pp. 304-05, 457-58, 904; also, Robert Baker Girdlestone, *Synonyms of the Old Testament*, pp. 66-67. For outstanding discussions of the entire problem in this context, see Keil and Delitzsch, *op. cit.*, I, 453-57; and Mickelsen, *op. cit.*, pp. 1211-12.

[35] Keil and Delitzsch, *op. cit.*, I, 457.

[36] For a typical critical reconstruction of the story, see Rylaarsdam, *op. cit.*, I, 882.

is impossible to say. So is it impossible to determine the person addressed or the meaning of her cry, **a bridegroom of blood art thou to me.** Was this the common term describing a young Midianite man circumcised just prior to his marriage? If so, was she using it in bitter mockery of Moses, who had never been such a bridegroom of blood for her but had required the shedding of her son's blood? Or was it a phrase that she coined on the spot in recognition that Moses had been given back to her from the brink of the grave, a new bridegroom as it were, purchased by the blood of her son? Whatever the nature of these details, it seems evident that Moses decided to send Zipporah and the children back to Jethro (18:2ff.). Such a separation at this point would seem to support the theory that Zipporah's attitude was anything else but that of loyalty to her husband's religion and respect for his convictions. Whatever the details which we cannot now recover, we are reminded again that God adapts His methods to the state of the people with whom He must deal. This is just one more evidence of His grace and mercy.[37]

b. A Warm Welcome (4:27-31)

27 And Jehovah said to Aaron, Go into the wilderness to meet Moses. And he went, and met him in the mountain of God, and kissed him. 28 And Moses told Aaron all the words of Jehovah wherewith he had sent him, and all the signs wherewith he had charged him. 29 And Moses and Aaron went and gathered together all the elders of the children of Israel: 30 and Aaron spake all the words which Jehovah had spoken unto Moses, and did the signs in the sight of the people. 31 And the people believed: and when they heard that Jehovah had visited the children of Israel, and that he had seen their affliction, then they bowed their heads and worshipped.

While the Lord was guiding Moses, He was also guiding Aaron. At His command, Aaron went into the desert to meet Moses. The meeting, quite appropriately, took place on Mt. Sinai, **the mountain of God.** There was the usual greeting of the kiss, and the sharing

with Aaron by Moses of **all the words** and **all the signs** with which God had commissioned him. Together they went on to Egypt. There, when they had gathered together **the elders** of Israel (these were generally older men, but the term applied to the heads of the various tribes and clans — the leaders or chiefs), Aaron spoke to them all the words of the Lord, and demonstrated before them the signs the Lord had given Moses as evidence of his call (4:1-9). And just as the Lord had promised (3: 18) the people believed them and bowed their heads in reverent thanksgiving for the Lord's remembrance and intervention in their behalf.

C. THE PROCESS OF DELIVERANCE (5:1—15:21)

1. The First Audience with Pharaoh (5:1—6:13)

a. The Royal Contempt (5:1-18)

1 And afterward Moses and Aaron came, and said unto Pharaoh, Thus saith Jehovah, the God of Israel, Let my people go, that they may hold a feast unto me in the wilderness. 2 And Pharaoh said, Who is Jehovah, that I should hearken unto his voice to let Israel go? I know not Jehovah, and moreover I will not let Israel go. 3 And they said, The God of the Hebrews hath met with us; let us go, we pray thee, three days' journey into the wilderness, and sacrifice unto Jehovah our God, lest he fall upon us with pestilence, or with the sword. 4 And the king of Egypt said unto them, Wherefore do ye, Moses and Aaron, loose the people from their works? get you unto your burdens. 5 And Pharaoh said, Behold, the people of the land are now many, and ye make them rest from their burdens. 6 And the same day Pharaoh commanded the taskmasters of the people, and their officers, saying, 7 Ye shall no more give the people straw to make brick, as heretofore: let them go and gather straw for themselves. 8 And the number of the bricks, which they did make heretofore, ye shall lay upon them; ye shall not diminish aught thereof: for they are idle; therefore they cry, saying, Let us go and sacrifice to our God. 9 Let heavier work be laid upon the men, that they

---

[37] See Keil and Delitzsch, *op. cit.,* I, 459-61; Rawlinson, *op. cit.,* I, 109-10; Johnson, *op. cit.,* p. 56; Connell, *op. cit.,* pp. 110-11.

may labor therein; and let them not regard lying words.

10 And the taskmasters of the people went out, and their officers, and they spake to the people, saying, Thus saith Pharaoh, I will not give you straw. 11 Go yourselves, get you straw where ye can find it; for nought of your work shall be diminished. 12 So the people were scattered abroad throughout all the land of Egypt to gather stubble for straw. 13 And the taskmasters were urgent, saying, Fulfil your works, *your* daily tasks, as when there was straw. 14 And the officers of the children of Israel, whom Pharaoh's taskmasters had set over them, were beaten, and demanded, Wherefore have ye not fulfilled your task both yesterday and to-day, in making brick as heretofore?

15 Then the officers of the children of Israel came and cried unto Pharaoh, saying, Wherefore dealest thou thus with thy servants? 16 There is no straw given unto thy servants, and they say to us, Make brick: and, behold, thy servants are beaten; but the fault is in thine own people. 17 But he said, Ye are idle, ye are idle: therefore ye say, Let us go and sacrifice to Jehovah. 18 Go therefore now, and work; for there shall no straw be given you, yet shall ye deliver the number of bricks.

Moses and Aaron apparently moved with dispatch. After their meeting with the elders, they sought and obtained an audience with Pharaoh. This Pharaoh was of course a different man than the one from whom Moses had fled. **Pharaoh** was merely his title. It is the English form of an Egyptian word, *per-o,* which originally meant "the Great House" and was applied to the palace of the king in much the same way that Americans call their President's residence "the White House." The Egyptian monarch's full title was a lengthy one indeed. So it became convenient and customary to call him "the Great House," much as we today refer to the President and his staff as "the White House says," or "the White House has decided to," etc.[38] This particular Pharaoh was either Amenhotep II of the eighteenth dynasty, or Rameses II of the nineteenth dynasty, depending upon how one dates the Exodus. If it was Amenhotep, he was the son of the great conqueror and builder, Thutmose III.

He was born at Memphis, a point not too distant from Goshen, and it is probable that, due to the revolt of the tribes of Palestine and Syria against his rule, he was at this time maintaining at least a temporary capital at the ancient city of Zoan-Avaris (later called Raamses) which his father had probably begun rebuilding with conscripted Hebrew labor, and which was in the vicinity of Goshen and near the border with the outlying dependencies.[39] If the Pharaoh Moses faced was Rameses II, he was one of the strongest monarchs Egypt ever had, ruling for fifty or sixty years, conquering the surrounding nations, building cities, temples, and monuments all over Egypt. His capital was at the city whose rebuilding he completed and which he named Raamses after himself and Rameses I.[40] The present writer prefers to consider Amenhotep II as the Pharaoh of the Exodus. (See "Date" under "Introduction.")

Moses and Aaron made their first request one of permission to take the people into the desert for a feast in honor of Jehovah. Their request was given in the form of a command from Jehovah. But Pharaoh insisted that he knew no Jehovah and declared he would not let Israel go. Moses and Aaron had identified Jehovah as **the God of Israel,** and now again as **the God of the Hebrews,** asking respectfully that they be permitted a **three days' journey into the desert** (see 3:18), lest He fall upon them in pestilence or with the sword. But Pharaoh refused to discuss the issue further, charging Moses and Aaron with releasing the people from their duties, and ordering them and the elders who may have accompanied them (3:18) to get back to their own burdens.

When Moses and Aaron had left, Pharaoh showed his contempt for Israel and its God by ordering an intensification of the bondage imposed upon the nation. The Egyptians made bricks by breaking up the Nile mud with mattocks, moistening it with water, mixing it with sand and sometimes with chopped straw, and afterwards forming it in molds and baking it in the sun. The tomb of Rekhmire, the prime minister of Thutmose III, the Pharaoh from whom Moses had fled

---

[38] Finegan, *op. cit.,* pp. 24-25.   [39] Unger, *op. cit.,* pp. 143, 150.   [40] Finegan, *op. cit.,* pp. 23-39.

into exile and the father of the one with whom he was now dealing, still bears a picture of Semitic foreigners like the Israelites making and laying bricks.[41] Now Pharaoh proposed that the Egyptian **taskmasters** and their assistants quit furnishing straw to the Israelites. Modern experiments have demonstrated that the addition of organic matter to the Nile mud makes it easier to work. Thus while not all Egyptian bricks contain straw, they can be made easier and faster with it.[42] Now the Israelites must find their own straw but still meet the same daily quotas. Heavier work would eliminate dreams about getting away for a religious holiday!

So the cruel order was carried into effect. And when the quotas were not met, the Israelite officers who served under the Egyptian taskmasters and their deputies were called on the green carpet, questioned severely, and beaten. They in turn went to Pharaoh, charging their superiors with injustice. But they found no comfort there, but a charge of idleness because of their desire to go and worship Jehovah.

b. The Human Complaint (5:19-23)

19 And the officers of the children of Israel did see that they were in evil case, when it was said, Ye shall not diminish aught from your bricks, *your* daily tasks. 20 And they met Moses and Aaron, who stood in the way, as they came forth from Pharaoh: 21 and they said unto them, Jehovah look upon you, and judge; because ye have made our savor to be abhorred in the eyes of Pharaoh, and in the eyes of his servants, to put a sword in their hand to slay us. 22 And Moses returned unto Jehovah, and said, Lord, wherefore hast thou dealt ill with this people? why is it that thou hast sent me? 23 For since I came to Pharaoh to speak in thy name, he hath dealt ill with this people; neither hast thou delivered thy people at all.

As the Israelite officers came out of Pharaoh's presence, they met Moses and Aaron. Apparently the two brothers had been on their way to talk to Pharaoh again. But when the physically and emotionally beaten men met them, they bitterly called upon Jehovah to judge

Moses and Aaron because they had put a sword in the hand of the Egyptians to slay them. These **officers** were not the same as the "elders" with whom Moses had been dealing. The elders were the leaders chosen or recognized by the Israelites themselves who had jurisdiction over purely internal matters. The officers were those chosen by the Egyptians to be the lowest ranked supervisors of the slave-labor rendered by the Israelites. Only rarely would they have been the same individuals. It is impossible to say how extensively the news of Moses' mission had penetrated among the people at this stage, nor to what degree his support went beyond the elders. But for the moment, the officers deeply regretted his coming. Quite naturally, Moses was deeply hurt, both for his people and over the unjust charge made against him. So he carried the complaint in turn to Jehovah, asking why he had been sent when it only led to greater difficulty rather than to deliverance.

c. The Divine Charge (6:1-13)

1 And Jehovah said unto Moses, Now shalt thou see what I will do to Pharaoh: for by a strong hand shall he let them go, and by a strong hand shall he drive them out of his land.
2 And God spake unto Moses, and said unto him, I am Jehovah: 3 and I appeared unto Abraham, unto Isaac, and unto Jacob, as God Almighty: but by my name Jehovah I was not known to them. 4 And I have also established my covenant with them, to give them the land of Canaan, the land of their sojournings, wherein they sojourned. 5 And moreover I have heard the groaning of the children of Israel, whom the Egyptians keep in bondage; and I have remembered my covenant. 6 Wherefore say unto the children of Israel, I am Jehovah, and I will bring you out from under the burdens of the Egyptians, and I will rid you out of their bondage, and I will redeem you with an outstretched arm, and with great judgments: 7 and I will take you to me for a people, and I will be to you a God; and ye shall know that I am Jehovah your God, who bringeth you out from under the burdens of the Egyptians. 8 And I will bring you in unto the land which I sware to give to Abraham, to Isaac, and to Jacob;

---

[41] Unger, *op. cit.*, p. 143.   [42] Joseph P. Free, *Archaeology and Bible History*, pp. 91-92.

and I will give it you for a heritage: I am Jehovah. 9 And Moses spake so unto the children of Israel: but they hearkened not unto Moses for anguish of spirit, and for cruel bondage.

10 And Jehovah spake unto Moses, saying, 11 Go in, speak unto Pharaoh king of Egypt, that he let the children of Israel go out of his land. 12 And Moses spake before Jehovah, saying, Behold, the children of Israel have not hearkened unto me; how then shall Pharaoh hear me, who am of uncircumcised lips? 13 And Jehovah spake unto Moses and unto Aaron, and gave them a charge unto the children of Israel, and unto Pharaoh king of Egypt, to bring the children of Israel out of the land of Egypt.

The Lord had already warned Moses how things would go. But in divine patience He reassured him once more that if he would patiently trust and obey, he would yet see how Jehovah would use Pharaoh to accomplish His purpose. He reminded Moses that He was Jehovah, and for the first time that it is recorded, referred Moses to the covenant He had established with the patriarchs. And He gave to him in greater fullness the message which He had spoken personally to Moses (3:7-9) and had instructed him to proclaim to Israel (3:15-17). It is possible that Moses had not made a general proclamation of this comforting announcement prior to this. But now he did, yet the people were in such bitter bondage that they refused to find comfort in his words. Again the Lord spoke to Moses that he bear the divine message to Pharaoh. But Moses remarked that if Israel would not hear him, what hope could he have of impressing Pharaoh? But the Lord pressed His command upon Moses and Aaron, giving them a charge in relationship to Israel and Pharaoh that they bring Israel out. Their assignment was one of the most solemn responsibilities possible.

In the process of the Lord's communication with Moses, He said that He was Jehovah, that He had appeared to the three patriarchs as El Shaddai (God Almighty, see Gen. 17:1; 28:3; 35:11; 43:14; 48:3; 49:25), but He had not been known by them, or as it is better translated, had not made Himself known to them, by His name Yahweh or Jehovah. This raises a perplexing problem. For the name Jehovah appears about sixty-one times in Genesis. These include not simply references to Him by that name in the narrative, but specific statements that the name was u ed in worship as far back as the time of Seth (Gen. 4:26), that Abraham worshiped him by this name (Gen. 12:8; 13:4; 21:33), that Isaac worshiped him by this name (Gen. 26: 22, 25), that He called Himself Jehovah when conversing with Abraham (18:14) and when first revealing Himself to Jacob at Bethel (28:13), that the name was used in extremely ancient proverbs (10:9; 22:14), that Abraham used this name in naming the place where he bound Isaac (22:14), and numerous instances in which an angel called Him Jehovah or the patriarchs or members of their families referred to Him under that name.

There are three possible explanations for this apparent contradiction. Critical scholars have seized upon this verse as the key to the so-called "documentary hypothesis," the division of the Pentateuch and the book of Joshua into various independent and contradictory documents that were eventually woven rather loosely together by editors who feared to tamper to any great extent with the already sacred documents, and who accordingly did not eliminate the contradictions. According to this theory, the instances in which Jehovah is used prior to Exodus are almost entirely from the document called J for Jehovistic, for this is considered one of its major characteristics. Another major document is supposed to be E which commonly uses Elohim or "God" as the name for the deity. The passage in Exodus 3:13-15 is supposed to be E's first independent use of the name Jehovah and to contain the implication that it had not been previously known. The present passage is supposed to be from still a third document known as P because of its priestly interests and emphasis. In this setting it makes the positive statement that the name Jehovah was not known nor used among the chosen people until after the Lord appeared to Moses.[43] (For discussion of the inherent weaknesses of this

[43] See Driver, *op. cit.*, pp. 23-24; Rylaarsdam, *op. cit.*, I, 889.

theory and the reasons for the present writer's rejection of it, see the General Introduction to the Pentateuch at the front of this volume and also "Authorship" under "Introduction" to Exodus.)

A second possibility is that Jehovah or Yahweh was not known as the name of God prior to the time of Moses, and that its earlier occurrences in Genesis are simply the result of the author's knowledge of God by that name. But this would necessitate a great deal of freedom in recording speeches both of Jehovah and of the patriarchs. It trips up over specific declarations that men called upon the name of Jehovah, the proverbs using it, and Abraham's place name which included it. And it involves the author of the Pentateuch in such a flagrant self-contradiction, using the name in the early narratives and then recording its later introduction and the denial that it had been previously known, as to make it virtually impossible to conceive that an intelligent writer could have followed such a course. The present writer does not feel, of course, that historical accuracy depends upon every speech recorded in Genesis reproducing the original statements word for word. A comparison of the four gospels in the New Testament in relation to the words of Jesus and His contemporaries makes it abundantly clear that such exactness is not a necessary characteristic of inspired writing. But it is asking too much to propose that Moses or whoever wrote Genesis incorporated all that is there said about the name of Jehovah from his own later knowledge of that name.

The third explanation is the one almost universally adopted among evangelical scholars. As was noted in conjunction with the change in name from Jacob to Israel (Gen. 32:27-28), and in conjunction with the scene at the burning bush (Exod. 3:13ff.), names were more than identification tags for the Hebrews. They revealed character as well as identity. The name Jehovah is closely related to that other name which was revealed for the first time to Moses at the burning bush — *Eyeh,* traditionally translated, "I am." Jehovah is the third personal

form rather than the first, meaning "He is" or "He will be," and as a name, "the one who is," "the absolute and unchangeable one," "the one ever coming into manifestation," or even, "he who brings to pass" or "the performer of his promises."[44] Now, while the name itself was much older than Abraham, and was known and used by him as the identifying name of his God, God never called attention to the meaning of the name when revealing Himself to the three patriarchs, nor explained it. He did reveal the name El Shaddai or God Almighty to Abraham, and followed it with promises that would necessitate the power of God for fulfillment. But it was impossible for the patriarchs to know the full meaning of Jehovah, for it stressed His eternity, His performance of His promises. It gathered round itself the concepts of "God's personal existence, the continuity of His dealings with man, the unchangeableness of His promises, and the whole revelation of His redeeming mercy."[45] As such, Jehovah could only make the character behind the name known to the descendants of the patriarchs — to the children of Israel at the time of the Exodus. Connell has called attention to the fact that men as late as the time of Jeremiah and Ezekiel, who most assuredly knew the name Jehovah, still needed *to know the name* in the truer sense of a personal knowledge of the character behind it.[46]

To know God by the name Jehovah was to know Him as the covenant-keeping God. And it was in that way that this further, richer revelation of the Lord to Moses made Him known. The Lord now mentions the covenant which He had made with the patriarchs for the first time (6:4). He defines it as the promise of a home in Canaan. He has heard Israel's groans and remembered His covenant — this is true to the character of Jehovah. So now He will bring them out, **redeem** them with a stretched-out arm — the first time that the concept of redemption is introduced in the Scriptures and again that which is true to the character of Jehovah. And He assures them that He has in mind the closest of

[44] Brown, Driver, and Briggs, *op. cit.,* p. 218.
[45] Girdlestone, *op. cit.,* p. 38. His entire chapter on "The Names of God" (pp. 18-44), including the section on "Jehovah" (pp. 35-40), is extremely helpful.
[46] Connell, *op. cit.,* p. 111; cf. Jer. 16:21; Ezek. 11:12.

relationships. They will be His people and He will be their God — this close, personal tie again true to the character of Jehovah. And all this proves that He is indeed Jehovah, their God. He promises to fulfill His oath to the patriarchs and to bring them in. And He concludes His entire address to Moses and the smaller address to the people contained therein with the same words with which He *commenced them, **I am Jehovah.** What a rich unfolding of the character of God! How meaningful even today for those He seeks to redeem from sin as He once redeemed Israel from Egypt's bondage!

2. The Ancestry of Moses and Aaron (6:14-27)

14 These are the heads of their fathers' houses. The sons of Reuben the firstborn of Israel: Hanoch, and Pallu, Hezron, and Carmi; these are the families of Reuben. 15 And the sons of Simeon: Jemuel, and Jamin, and Ohad, and Jachin, and Zohar, and Shaul the son of a Canaanitish woman; these are the families of Simeon. 16 And these are the names of the sons of Levi according to their generations: Gershon, and Kohath, and Merari; and the years of the life of Levi were a hundred thirty and seven years. 17 The sons of Gershon: Libni and Shimei, according to their families. 18 And the sons of Kohath: Amram, and Izhar, and Hebron, and Uzziel; and the years of the life of Kohath were a hundred thirty and three years. 19 And the sons of Merari: Mahli and Mushi. These are the families of the Levites according to their generations. 20 And Amram took him Jochebed his father's sister to wife; and she bare him Aaron and Moses: and the years of the life of Amram were a hundred and thirty and seven years. 21 And the sons of Izhar: Korah, and Nepheg, and Zichri. 22 And the sons of Uzziel: Mishael, and Elzaphan, and Sithri. 23 And Aaron took him Elisheba, the daughter of Amminadab, the sister of Nahshon, to wife; and she bare him Nadab and Abihu, Eleazar and Ithamar. 24 And the sons of Korah: Assir, and Elkanah, and Abiasaph; these are the families of the Korahites. 25 And Eleazar Aaron's son took him one of the daughters of Putiel to wife; and she bare him Phinehas. These are the heads of the fathers' *houses* of the Levites according to their families. 26 These are that Aaron and Moses, to whom Jehovah said, Bring out the children of Israel from the land of Egypt according to their hosts. 27 These are they that spake to Pharaoh king of Egypt, to bring out the children of Israel from Egypt: these are that Moses and Aaron.

At this point, the writer of Exodus seeks to identify Moses and Aaron more fully. To do this, he begins to repeat almost word for word the genealogical list of the sons of Israel found in Genesis 46:8ff. But after thus giving Levi the proper setting as the third of Leah's sons, he breaks off to amplify the genealogy of Levi. He lists Levi's three sons, and in turn the two sons of Gershon, the four sons of Kohath, and the two sons of Merari. The genealogy apparently pictures Moses and Aaron as representing the fourth generation from Jacob himself. Such might seem related to the prediction made by the Lord to Abraham that his descendants would be brought out of the land of oppression in the fourth generation (Gen. 15:16). But as was remarked in commenting on that passage, "generation" there probably refers to "time span" rather than generation in the modern sense. For the Lord also told Abraham that the oppression would last 400 years (Gen. 15:13), and the writer of Exodus gives the total sojourn in Egypt as 430 years (12:40-41). The ages of Levi, Kohath, and Amram are all given in this genealogy, and that of Aaron and Moses in 7:7 immediately afterward. If Levi had begotten his second of three sons, Kohath, at the age of 100, and Kohath had in turn begotten Amram and Amram Aaron at the same age, there would still be nearly a century left over that could not be accounted for in their lifetimes. Thus this, too, is a schematic, contracted or "accordionized" genealogy.

A few interesting highlights stand out as the descent of three of the four sons of Kohath is traced schematically to the generation after Moses and Aaron. Moses' mother is revealed to have been his father's aunt, a marriage later forbidden (Lev. 18:12) but apparently acceptable at this time. Korah, who later caused Moses trouble (Num. 16:1ff.), is described as Moses' cousin. Aaron's wife is revealed to have been a sister of Nahshon, the son of Amminadab, who was the ruler of the tribe of Judah (Num.

1:7). Aaron's descent is traced farther than any of the others, to Phinehas his grandson, because of the importance of the priestly line. The writer lays great stress on the fact that this is that particular Aaron and Moses whom God called to bring His people out (vv. 26-27).

3. The Second Audience with Pharaoh (6:28—7:13)

a. A Mandate and Its Acceptance (6:28—7:7)

28 And it came to pass on the day when Jehovah spake unto Moses in the land of Egypt, 29 that Jehovah spake unto Moses, saying, I am Jehovah: speak thou unto Pharaoh king of Egypt all that I speak unto thee. 30 And Moses said before Jehovah, Behold, I am of uncircumcised lips, and how shall Pharaoh hearken unto me? 1 And Jehovah said unto Moses, See, I have made thee as God to Pharaoh; and Aaron thy brother shall be thy prophet. 2 Thou shalt speak all that I command thee; and Aaron thy brother shall speak unto Pharaoh, that he let the children of Israel go out of his land. 3 And I will harden Pharaoh's heart, and multiply my signs and my wonders in the land of Egypt. 4 But Pharaoh will not hearken unto you, and I will lay my hand upon Egypt, and bring forth my hosts, my people the children of Israel, out of the land of Egypt by great judgments. 5 And the Egyptians shall know that I am Jehovah, when I stretch forth my hand upon Egypt, and bring out the children of Israel from among them. 6 And Moses and Aaron did so; as Jehovah commanded them, so did they. 7 And Moses was fourscore years old, and Aaron fourscore and three years old, when they spake unto Pharaoh.

It is evident that Moses faced a crisis after his first audience with Pharaoh. The contempt of the king, the bitterness of the mistreated Hebrew officers, and the anguished refusal of Israel to listen to him any further had brought him to the brink of defeat. **The day when Jehovah spake unto Moses in the land of Egypt** is not a reference to a conflicting account of the call of Moses as the critics would affirm — as if he here received his call rather than earlier at Sinai. It is instead the day on which Jehovah finally overcame all of Moses' reservations and doubts

and got him well started on the road to final victory over Pharaoh. Moses had started the exchange by a prayer of complaint (5:22-23). The Lord had answered it with a fuller revelation of His character (6:1-8). Moses had carried His message to Israel, only to return more depressed than ever (6:9-12). The Lord had responded with a renewed command to carry out the mission (6:13), a command mentioned only in general terms until after the sideline of the genealogy was taken care of (6:14-27), and now given in detail. As the writer reintroduces this scene, he repeats almost verbatim the conversation of 6:10-13, except that he expands the charge to its original fullness. Moses is still worried about his inadequacy as a messenger, referring to himself as one with **uncircumcised lips,** as if his lips were covered with something like a foreskin, so that they opened and closed with difficulty.[47] But the Lord reassures him that he has no need to feel inferior to Pharaoh. His supernaturally provided power has made him like a god to Pharaoh, and Aaron is his prophet. They are to speak the words the Lord will give them. Pharaoh's heart will be hardened (see comments on 4:21), but this will only lead to a multiplication of Jehovah's signs and wonders. When His judgments of Egypt are complete, all the Egyptians will know, as will Israel, that He is Jehovah — that He keeps His promises. At last Moses is convinced. He and Aaron go out to do the bidding of the Lord. There was never again a serious question as to whether Moses would fulfill his mission. The divine patience is beyond our comprehension, but it was only patience like this that could have succeeded with Moses. How often such patience must be practiced with us! No doubt its accomplishments in our lives are more than we know.

b. A Miracle and Its Counterfeit (7:8-13)

8 And Jehovah spake unto Moses and unto Aaron, saying, 9 When Pharaoh shall speak unto you, saying, Show a wonder for you; then thou shalt say unto Aaron, Take thy rod, and cast it down before Pharaoh, that it become a serpent. 10 And Moses and Aaron went in unto

---

[47] Johnson, *op. cit.,* p. 57.

Pharaoh, and they did so, as Jehovah had commanded: and Aaron cast down his rod before Pharaoh and before his servants, and it became a serpent. 11 Then Pharaoh also called for the wise men and the sorcerers: and they also, the magicians of Egypt, did in like manner with their enchantments. 12 For they cast down every man his rod, and they became serpents: but Aaron's rod swallowed up their rods. 13 And Pharaoh's heart was hardened, and he hearkened not unto them; as Jehovah had spoken.

On the occasion of the first audience with Pharaoh, there had only been an exchange of words. The Lord foresaw that on the occasion of the second, Pharaoh would ask for the credentials of the two brothers. Such credentials would be understood only in terms of the supernatural, comparable to the magic so highly valued in Egypt. So He instructed Moses and Aaron to use the rod-serpent sign. This they did. But the wonders did not end there. Pharaoh, only slightly impressed, called his own magicians. Their leaders were traditionally known as Jannes and Jambres (II Tim. 3:8). They also cast down their "rods" and they became serpents. This trick is still standard equipment for modern Egyptian magicians on the streets of Cairo, and its secret is well known. The Egyptian cobra can be paralyzed by applying pressure to a nerve in its neck. When thus rendered motionless, it appears at a distance to be a cane or rod. But when it is thrown to the ground, the jar recovers it, and it slithers away.[48] But the Lord proved that Moses' sign was not the result of any such trick, for the serpent into which his rod had turned swallowed up the "rods" of the magicians!

From this first clash of supernatural power, Jehovah's program to free Israel from Egypt was in terms of a test of strength or conflict between the true God of Israel and the false gods of Egypt. He Himself described it in these terms (12: 12). And many of the objects which became a curse to the land or were themselves cursed through the plagues were sacred objects of worship for the Egyptians. Pharaoh himself was considered a god, and the serpent was one of the most common symbols of the divine.[49] Jehovah had decidedly won the first skirmish prior to the actual conflict of the plagues, but Pharaoh was not convinced. His heart was "growing hard" (see comments on 4:21).

4. The Account of the Ten Plagues (7:14—12:36)

a. First Plague — Water Turned to Blood (7:14-25)

14 And Jehovah said unto Moses, Pharaoh's heart is stubborn, he refuseth to let the people go. 15 Get thee unto Pharaoh in the morning; lo, he goeth out unto the water; and thou shalt stand by the river's brink to meet him; and the rod which was turned to a serpent shalt thou take in thy hand. 16 And thou shalt say unto him, Jehovah, the God of the Hebrews, hath sent me unto thee, saying, Let my people go, that they may serve me in the wilderness: and, behold, hitherto thou hast not hearkened. 17 Thus saith Jehovah, In this thou shalt know that I am Jehovah: behold, I will smite with the rod that is in my hand upon the waters which are in the river, and they shall be turned to blood. 18 And the fish that are in the river shall die, and the river shall become foul; and the Egyptians shall loathe to drink water from the river. 19 And Jehovah said unto Moses, Say unto Aaron, Take thy rod, and stretch out thy hand over the waters of Egypt, over their rivers, over their streams, and over their pools, and over all their ponds of water, that they may become blood; and there shall be blood throughout all the land of Egypt, both in vessels of wood and in vessels of stone.

20 And Moses and Aaron did so, as Jehovah commanded; and he lifted up the rod, and smote the waters that were in the river, in the sight of Pharaoh, and in the sight of his servants; and all the waters that were in the river were turned to blood. 21 And the fish that were in the river died; and the river became foul, and the Egyptians could not drink water from the river: and the blood was throughout all the land of Egypt. 22 And the magicians of Egypt did in like manner with their enchantments: and Pharaoh's heart was hardened, and he hearkened not unto them; as Jehovah had spoken. 23 And Pharaoh turned and went into his house, neither did he lay even this to heart. 24 And all the Egyptians digged round about the river for water to drink; for they could not drink

[48] Finegan, *op. cit.*, p. 48.   [49] Charles F. Pfeiffer, *Egypt and the Exodus*, pp. 21-22.

of the water of the river. 25 And seven days were fulfilled, after that Jehovah had smitten the river.

The plagues which now befell Egypt are described by various terms: *wonders* (3:20; 4:21; 7:3), *signs* (7:3), *judgments* (6:6; 7:4), and three Hebrew words translated as *plague* or *plagues,* all three carrying the picture of a stroke or blow which would wound or kill (9:14; 11:1; 12:13). They were to prove the identity of the God of Israel as Jehovah. The first nine can be divided into three groups of three each, with the first two in each triad being announced beforehand to Pharaoh, but the third in each case (the third, sixth, and ninth) striking without warning. The first triad affected both Israel and the Egyptians, the last two only the Egyptians. There was a steady progression from annoying to serious to destructive to deadly.[50] The first nine were made up of calamities natural to Egypt. The tenth has no explanation short of a direct divine intervention in the lives of men, and the first nine are also miraculous because of their intensification of natural calamities, their prediction by the Lord's messenger, their discrimination which freed Goshen from the later plagues, their orderliness in following one heavy blow with another yet heavier, and their moral purpose in discrediting Egypt's gods, forcing Pharaoh to acknowledge Jehovah as God, and revealing Him as Savior to Israel.[51]

In the first plague, Moses met Pharaoh in the morning as he went out to the Nile. He was to carry the rod and to announce to Pharaoh that because he had stubbornly refused to obey, he would now be made to know that the God who sent him was Jehovah. He would turn all the river into blood, killing the fish, and making it impossible to drink the water. Not only the Nile, but all its branches, its **streams** (better translated "irrigation canals"), its **pools** and **ponds,** and even water collected in vessels would be affected. And Moses carried out Jehovah's instructions fully. The Nile, the one geographic feature which made the Egyptian civilization possible in the midst of an otherwise desert waste, the divine

river which the Egyptians worshiped through the god Hapi, had now become a curse instead of a blessing to its people. Once each year, two of the three streams which make up the lower Nile pour a much greater volume of water down from the melting snows and the summer rains, usually causing the river to reach flood stage in September. The highlands where these two streams rise and make their descent are made up of red earth. The flooding streams wash away this red soil and take on its color. The more severe the flood, the redder the water. Extreme inundations also bring down minute organisms which infect the fish, cause the water to stink, and make it unfit to drink. The Lord apparently caused such a tremendous flood this year as to result in the intensification of these conditions far beyond anything in the memory of the inhabitants. The flood was so great as even to break into and contaminate the wells. As a result, the water thereafter collected in **vessels of wood and in vessels of stone** was all contaminated (7:19). Only one resort was left, that of digging beside the river and thus filtering the water through the soil (7:24). The fact that no definite termination is indicated for this first plague would support the fact that it was an extreme instance of the annual flood.[52]

b. Second Plague — Frogs (8:1-15)

1 And Jehovah spake unto Moses, Go in unto Pharaoh, and say unto him, Thus saith Jehovah, Let my people go, that they may serve me. 2 And if thou refuse to let them go, behold, I will smite all thy borders with frogs: 3 and the river shall swarm with frogs, which shall go up and come into thy house, and into thy bedchamber, and upon thy bed, and into the house of thy servants, and upon thy people, and into thine ovens, and into thy kneading-troughs: 4 and the frogs shall come up both upon thee, and upon thy people, and upon all thy servants. 5 And Jehovah said unto Moses, Say unto Aaron, Stretch forth thy hand with thy rod over the rivers, over the streams, and over the pools, and cause frogs to come up upon the land of Egypt. 6 And Aaron stretched out his hand over the waters of Egypt; and the frogs came up, and covered the land of Egypt. 7

[50] See Johnson, *op. cit.,* p. 57; and Keil and Delitzsch, *op. cit.,* I, 472-75.
[51] Free, *op. cit.,* p. 95.   [52] Finegan, *op. cit.,* pp. 48-51.

And the magicians did in like manner with their enchantments, and brought up frogs upon the land of Egypt.

8 Then Pharaoh called for Moses and Aaron, and said, Entreat Jehovah, that he take away the frogs from me, and from my people; and I will let the people go, that they may sacrifice unto Jehovah. 9 And Moses said unto Pharaoh, Have thou this glory over me: against what time shall I entreat for thee, and for thy servants, and for thy people, that the frogs be destroyed from thee and thy houses, and remain in the river only? 10 And he said, Against to-morrow. And he said, Be it according to thy word; that thou mayest know that there is none like unto Jehovah our God. 11 And the frogs shall depart from thee, and from thy houses, and from thy servants, and from thy people; they shall remain in the river only. 12 And Moses and Aaron went out from Pharaoh: and Moses cried unto Jehovah concerning the frogs which he had brought upon Pharaoh. 13 And Jehovah did according to the word of Moses; and the frogs died out of the houses, out of the courts, and out of the fields. 14 And they gathered them together in heaps; and the land stank. 15 But when Pharaoh saw that there was respite, he hardened his heart, and hearkened not unto them; as Jehovah had spoken.

When Pharaoh's heart remained unchanged, the Lord sent Moses with another warning: Either let my people go or I will plague the land with frogs — they will invade your houses, your bedrooms, your beds, your ovens, your very kneading-troughs. And so the rod was stretched out again and the frogs came in from the waters in numbers beyond reckoning.

Frogs are common in Egypt. And each year, after the flooding Nile subsides in October, the frogs come out on the banks of the river. But 7:25 says that this plague followed only seven days after the waters had turned to blood, so it was still late in August or early in September. The dying fish had polluted the home of the frogs and they stampeded out of the waters long before their normal migration, and went everywhere seeking pure water and shelter from the sun. Pharaoh was so disturbed at this nuisance that he told Moses to ask Jehovah to take away the frogs and he would let Israel go to offer sacrifice. The frog was sacred to the Egyptians and thus could not be killed by them. Moses perceived Pharaoh's insincerity, but seized upon this as a further opportunity to glorify Jehovah. He asked Pharaoh to set the time for the frogs to die, and he chose the next day. The Lord had, no doubt, due to His foreknowledge, already prepared for the frogs' destruction by permitting them to be infected by bacteria from the decaying fish. So they died. And they were stacked in stinking heaps all over Egypt.[53]

Jehovah had won the second round of the conflict. The frogs who were associated with the gods of fruitfulness were instead made objects of loathing.[54] And Pharaoh who had contemptuously asked, "Who is Jehovah?" (5:2) had now asked that Moses might pray to Jehovah in his behalf. But he made his heart obstinate and failed to keep his promise.

c. Third Plague — Lice or Mosquitoes (8:16-19)

16 And Jehovah said unto Moses, Say unto Aaron, Stretch out thy rod, and smite the dust of the earth, that it may become lice throughout all the land of Egypt. 17 And they did so; and Aaron stretched out his hand with his rod, and smote the dust of the earth, and there were lice upon man and upon beast; all the dust of the earth became lice throughout all the land of Egypt. 18 And the magicians did so with their enchantments to bring forth lice, but they could not: and there were lice upon man, and upon beast. 19 Then the magicians said unto Pharaoh, This is the finger of God: and Pharaoh's heart was hardened, and he hearkened not unto them; as Jehovah had spoken.

The third plague was not announced in advance to Pharaoh. The rod was used to strike the dust of the land and thus bring tremendous clouds of small insects upon the land. The Hebrew word has been variously translated "lice," "sand flies," "fleas," and "mosquitoes." Many modern scholars are settling on the latter translation. They are what one would expect under the circumstances. They are always numerous in October and November in Egypt, due to the natural

---

[53] Ibid., pp. 51-52.   [54] Pfeiffer, op. cit., p. 49.

breeding places left by the river as it recedes from flood stage. At that time, with one of the worst floods ever, they would have been unusually numerous. No end to this plague is indicated, so it probably continued for some time, helping to confirm the identification of the insects as mosquitoes the Lord brought on in unusual numbers through the natural results of the first plague.[55]

This time the Lord won a notable victory. Pharaoh's magicians had matched Moses on a smaller scale by turning water into blood and producing frogs. But they could not produce the mosquitoes. And they reported to their master, **This is the finger of God.** Also the river-god had once again been humiliated. But Pharaoh's heart grew harder still.

d. Fourth Plague — Flies (8:20-32)

20 And Jehovah said unto Moses, Rise up early in the morning, and stand before Pharaoh; lo, he cometh forth to the water; and say unto him, Thus saith Jehovah, Let my people go, that they may serve me. 21 Else, if thou wilt not let my people go, behold, I will send swarms of flies upon thee, and upon thy servants, and upon thy people, and into thy houses: and the houses of the Egyptians shall be full of swarms of flies, and also the ground whereon they are. 22 And I will set apart in that day the land of Goshen, in which my people dwell, that no swarms of flies shall be there; to the end thou mayest know that I am Jehovah in the midst of the earth. 23 And I will put a division between my people and thy people: by to-morrow shall this sign be. 24 And Jehovah did so; and there came grievous swarms of flies into the house of Pharaoh, and into his servants' houses: and in all the land of Egypt the land was corrupted by reason of the swarms of flies.

25 And Pharaoh called for Moses and for Aaron, and said, Go ye, sacrifice to your God in the land. And Moses said, It is not meet so to do; for we shall sacrifice the abomination of the Egyptians to Jehovah our God: lo, shall we sacrifice the abomination of the Egyptians before their eyes, and will they not stone us? 27 We will go three days' journey into the wilderness, and sacrifice to Jehovah our God, as he shall command us. 28 And Pharaoh said, I will let you go, that ye may sacrifice to Jehovah your God in the wilderness; only ye shall not go very far away: entreat for me. 29 And Moses said, Behold, I go out from thee, and I will entreat Jehovah that the swarms of flies may depart from Pharaoh, from his servants, and from his people to-morrow: only let not Pharaoh deal deceitfully any more in not letting the people go to sacrifice to Jehovah. 30 And Moses went out from Pharaoh, and entreated Jehovah. 31 And Jehovah did according to the word of Moses; and he removed the swarms of flies from Pharaoh, from his servants, and from his people; there remained not one. 32 And Pharaoh hardened his heart this time also, and he did not let the people go.

Just as Moses began the first triad of plagues by meeting Pharaoh in the morning on the bank of the Nile, so he began the second triad. He warned Pharaoh that if he did not let Israel go, the Lord would send swarms of flies upon the land. He also announced a new purpose for these signs. The first triad had been intended to prove that He was Jehovah (7:17). The second was aimed at convincing Pharaoh that He was **Jehovah in the midst of the earth,** not only a god of the Hebrews after the fashion of one of the gods of Egypt, but the supreme and only deity, who ruled over Egypt as well as Israel. To this end, beginning with this plague He would divide between Egypt and Israel and permit the flies only in Egypt.

The flies which now plagued Egypt are simply called a "swarm" or a "mixture" in the Hebrew. It is possible that more than one kind of insect was included. Since this plague came in the winter and the flies did not invade Goshen in the cooler northern part of the land, Finegan suggests the fly called *stomoxys calcitrans*, which could have bred prolifically along the receding Nile among the decaying fish and frogs, but would have been restricted to the warmer climate of the central and southern parts of Egypt. This insect could also have played a part in the sixth plague.[56] Others suggest a species of beetle known as the scarab, an emblem of Egypt's sun-god, and so like the frog beyond the reach of the injured Egyptians. The writer indicates that this plague **corrupted** or still better "de-

[55] Finegan, *op. cit.*, p. 52. [56] *Ibid.*, pp. 52-53. Pfeiffer concurs, *op. cit.*, p. 48.

stroyed" the land, hinting at injury to the crops as well as to men.[57]

Now Pharaoh called Moses and suggested a compromise: Sacrifice in Egypt rather than out in the desert. But Moses pointed out the impossibility of this, since the Israelites would be sacrificing animals sacred to the Egyptians. Such would only lead to mob attack. He insisted on **three days' journey** away from Egypt. Pharaoh appeared to relent a little, promising permission but asking that they not go far. As Connell aptly puts it, "His sin was within as easy range of recall as he desired the Israelites to be."[58] Moses agreed to pray for the removal of the flies, but warned Pharaoh against further trifling with Jehovah. The flies were removed on the morrow as quickly as they had appeared. Not one remained. But all these miraculous displays of power did not change Pharaoh. He continued to make his heart obstinate.

e. Fifth Plague — Disease of Livestock (9:1-7)

1 Then Jehovah said unto Moses, Go in unto Pharaoh, and tell him, Thus saith Jehovah, the God of the Hebrews, Let my people go, that they may serve me. 2 For if thou refuse to let them go, and wilt hold them still, 3 behold, the hand of Jehovah is upon thy cattle which are in the field, upon the horses, upon the asses, upon the camels, upon the herds, and upon the flocks: *there shall be* a very grievous murrain. 4 And Jehovah shall make a distinction between the cattle of Israel and the cattle of Egypt; and there shall nothing die of all that belongeth to the children of Israel. 5 And Jehovah appointed a set time, saying, To-morrow Jehovah shall do this thing in the land. 6 And Jehovah did that thing on the morrow; and all the cattle of Egypt died; but of the cattle of the children of Israel died not one. 7 And Pharaoh sent, and, behold, there was not so much as one of the cattle of the Israelites dead. But the heart of Pharaoh was stubborn, and he did not let the people go.

Again the Lord warned Pharaoh through Moses that if he did not let the people go, He would send a plague or pestilence on all of his livestock that were out in the fields or in the open. A "murrain" is simply an English word meaning a deadly plague or pestilence, especially one which affects domestic animals or plants. Finegan believes that this plague occurred in December-January, after some of the cattle had been turned out into the pastures from which the flood-waters had receded. Here where the frogs had been piled up, they contracted the same dread anthrax disease which had killed the frogs.[59] Again the Lord won a clear-cut victory over the false gods of Egypt. The goddess Hathor was symbolized by a bull, and the Apis-bull had been venerated for centuries in Egypt.[60] In fact, all bulls were sacred. Now Jehovah showed the folly of such superstition. Again He divided between Egypt and Israel, not one animal dying in Goshen. This time Pharaoh's interest was sufficiently aroused to check on the factualness of this division, but still his heart was obstinate and he refused to obey Jehovah's command.

f. Sixth Plague — Boils (9:8-12)

8 And Jehovah said unto Moses and unto Aaron, Take to you handfuls of ashes of the furnace, and let Moses sprinkle it toward heaven in the sight of Pharaoh. 9 And it shall become small dust over all the land of Egypt, and shall be a boil breaking forth with blains upon man and upon beast, throughout all the land of Egypt. 10 And they took ashes of the furnace, and stood before · Pharaoh; and Moses sprinkled it up toward heaven; and it became a boil breaking forth with blains upon man and upon beast. 11 And the magicians could not stand before Moses because of the boils; for the boils were upon the magicians, and upon all the Egyptians. 12 And Jehovah hardened the heart of Pharaoh, and he hearkened not unto them; as Jehovah had spoken unto Moses.

In the first three plagues, Moses and Aaron had used the rod of God. No mention of it is made in the fourth and fifth. In the sixth, a different visible instrument is used. Moses was to "take two handfuls of soot from a kiln" and "toss it up to the sky,"[61] and there would break forth an epidemic of boils or sores break-

---

[57] Connell, *op. cit.*, pp. 112-13.   [58] *Ibid.*, p. 113.   [59] Finegan, *op. cit.*, p. 53.
[60] Pfeiffer, *op. cit.*, p. 48.   [61] Meek, *The Bible, an American Translation*, p. 58.

ing into pustules **upon man and upon beast.** It is possible that this was an extension of the epidemic of anthrax which had stricken the livestock in the fifth plague. No sudden end is mentioned to that plague. Now it reaches the stock in the stalls and folds, and from them to the people of the land. This disease is characterized by ulcerations of the skin and the forming of pustules. It chiefly affects the legs and feet, being commonly called "blackleg." The magicians were unable even to stand before Moses because of it. It is spread chiefly by the *stomoxys calcitrans,* one of the insects mentioned in connection with the fourth plague.[62]

Now, after Pharaoh's stubbornness had been fully demonstrated, after he had twice broken his promise to let Israel go, the Lord gave him over to the willful sin he had chosen (see comments on 4:21).

g. Seventh Plague — Hail (9:13-35)

13 And Jehovah said unto Moses, Rise up early in the morning, and stand before Pharaoh, and say unto him, Thus saith Jehovah, the God of the Hebrews, Let my people go, that they may serve me. 14 For I will this time send all my plagues upon thy heart, and upon thy servants, and upon thy people; that thou mayest know that there is none like me in all the earth. 15 For now I had put forth my hand, and smitten thee and thy people with pestilence, and thou hadst been cut off from the earth: 16 but in very deed for this cause have I made thee to stand, to show thee my power, and that my name may be declared throughout all the earth. 17 As yet exaltest thou thyself against my people, that thou wilt not let them go? 18 Behold, to-morrow about this time I will cause it to rain a very grievous hail, such as hath not been in Egypt since the day it was founded even until now. 19 Now therefore send, hasten in thy cattle and all that thou hast in the field; *for* every man and beast that shall be found in the field, and shall not be brought home, the hail shall come down upon them, and they shall die. 20 He that feared the word of Jehovah among the servants of Pharaoh made his servants and his cattle flee into the houses: 21 and he that regarded not the word of

Jehovah left his servants and his cattle in the field.
22 And Jehovah said unto Moses, Stretch forth thy hand toward heaven, that there may be hail in all the land of Egypt, upon man, and upon beast, and upon every herb of the field, throughout the land of Egypt. 23 And Moses stretched forth his rod toward heaven: and Jehovah sent thunder and hail, and fire ran down unto the earth; and Jehovah rained hail upon the land of Egypt. 24 So there was hail, and fire mingled with the hail, very grievous, such as had not been in all the land of Egypt since it became a nation. 25 And the hail smote throughout all the land of Egypt all that was in the field, both man and beast; and the hail smote every herb of the field, and brake every tree of the field. 26 Only in the land of Goshen, where the children of Israel were, was there no hail.
27 And Pharaoh sent, and called for Moses and Aaron, and said unto them, I have sinned this time: Jehovah is righteous, and I and my people are wicked. 28 Entreat Jehovah; for there hath been enough of *these* mighty thunderings and hail; and I will let you go, and ye shall stay no longer. 29 And Moses said unto him, As soon as I am gone out of the city, I will spread abroad my hands unto Jehovah; the thundering shall cease, neither shall there be any more hail; that thou mayest know that the earth is Jehovah's. 30 But as for thee and thy servants, I know that ye will not yet fear Jehovah God. 31 And the flax and the barley were smitten: for the barley was in the ear, and the flax was in bloom. 32 But the wheat and the spelt were not smitten: for they were not grown up. 33 And Moses went out of the city from Pharaoh, and spread abroad his hands unto Jehovah: and the thunders and hail ceased, and the rain was not poured upon the earth. 34 And when Pharaoh saw that the rain and the hail and the thunders were ceased, he sinned yet more, and hardened his heart, he and his servants. 35 And the heart of Pharaoh was hardened, and he did not let the children of Israel go; as Jehovah had spoken by Moses.

At the beginning of the third triad of the plagues, the Lord sent Moses into Pharaoh's presence early in the morning, just as had been true in connection with the first and fourth plagues. There was a warning that the plagues would now

---

[62] Finegan, *op. cit.,* p. 54.

intensify for a new purpose — that Pharaoh might know that there was none like Jehovah in all the earth (cf. 7:17; 8:22). The Lord reminded Pharaoh that He could easily have annihilated the Egyptians by now, but that He had preserved them so as better to demonstrate His power on them — so that all the world would know. Then came the announcement of the seventh plague, the most deadly hailstorm ever to strike Egypt, and the warning that men and cattle be brought in out of the fields lest they die. It is interesting to note that while Pharaoh stubbornly refused to be convinced, some of his people were ready to listen.

When Pharaoh sought deliverance from the second plague, he had appointed "tomorrow" as the time for the removal of the frogs. From then on, in every plague that was announced in advance to Pharaoh (the fourth, fifth, seventh, and eighth), the appointed time was to-morrow. And so on the next day, under Moses' uplifted rod, the tremendous hailstorm came. In upper Egypt, that part south of Goshen (where Israel dwelt and where no hail fell), hailstorms can occur at any time of the year. In Goshen they occur only in the summer. This hailstorm is dated by the fact that flax was in bloom and barley in the ear, but the wheat and spelt were not yet matured. The flax is usually in bloom there in late January and the barley harvested in February, while wheat and spelt are not harvested until late March. So the hailstorm struck near the end of January or the beginning of February.[63] It was accompanied by lightning (v. 24) and thunder (vv. 28, 29, 33, 34). And its destruction was phenomenal, killing man and beast, shredding the vegetation, breaking the trees, destroying the flax and barley crops.

Again Pharaoh called Moses and begged for respite, promising for the third time to let the people go. Moses said that he would go ask the Lord to stop the hail, but he knew that Pharaoh and his servants did **not yet fear Jehovah God.** And when the storm abated, Pharaoh sinned even more, making his heart obstinate and permitting it to grow hard. Up to this point, Pharaoh had taken the initia-

tive in the hardening process which wrought his final destruction. Only once (9:12) is it said prior to this that the Lord hardened his heart. But once this double reference to his own hardening is given, his destiny is apparently sealed. From this time on the hardening is ascribed entirely to the Lord (see comments on 4:21).

h. Eighth Plague — Locusts (10:1-20)

1 And Jehovah said unto Moses, Go in unto Pharaoh: for I have hardened his heart, and the heart of his servants, that I may show these my signs in the midst of them, 2 and that thou mayest tell in the ears of thy son, and of thy son's son, what things I have wrought upon Egypt, and my signs which I have done among them; that ye may know that I am Jehovah. 3 And Moses and Aaron went in unto Pharaoh, and said unto him, Thus saith Jehovah, the God of the Hebrews, How long wilt thou refuse to humble thyself before me? let my people go, that they may serve me. 4 Else, if thou refuse to let my people go, behold, to-morrow will I bring locusts into thy border: 5 and they shall cover the face of the earth, so that one shall not be able to see the earth: and they shall eat the residue of that which is escaped, which remaineth unto you from the hail, and shall eat every tree which groweth for you out of the field: 6 and thy houses shall be filled, and the houses of all thy servants, and the houses of all the Egyptians; as neither thy fathers nor thy fathers' fathers have seen, since the day that they were upon the earth unto this day. And he turned, and went out from Pharaoh. 7 And Pharaoh's servants said unto him, How long shall this man be a snare unto us? let the men go, that they may serve Jehovah their God: knowest thou not yet that Egypt is destroyed? 8 And Moses and Aaron were brought again unto Pharaoh: and he said unto them, Go, serve Jehovah your God; but who are they that shall go? 9 And Moses said, We will go with our young and with our old; with our sons and with our daughters, with our flocks and with our herds will we go; for we must hold a feast unto Jehovah. 10 And he said unto them, So be Jehovah with you, as I will let you go, and your little ones: look to it; for evil is before you. 11 Not so: go now ye that are men, and serve Jehovah; for that is what ye de-

63 *Ibid.*, p. 54.

sire. And they were driven out from Pharaoh's presence.

12 And Jehovah said unto Moses, Stretch out thy hand over the land of Egypt for the locusts, that they may come up upon the land of Egypt, and eat every herb of the land, even all that the hail hath left. 13 And Moses stretched forth his rod over the land of Egypt, and Jehovah brought an east wind upon the land all that day, and all the night; and when it was morning, the east wind brought the locusts. 14 And the locusts went up over all the land of Egypt, and rested in all the borders of Egypt; very grievous were they; before them there were no such locusts as they, neither after them shall be such. 15 For they covered the face of the whole earth, so that the land was darkened; and they did eat every herb of the land, and all the fruit of the trees which the hail had left: and there remained not any green thing, either tree or herb of the field, through all the land of Egypt. 16 Then Pharaoh called for Moses and Aaron in haste; and he said, I have sinned against Jehovah your God, and against you. 17 Now therefore forgive, I pray thee, my sin only this once, and entreat Jehovah your God, that he may take away from me this death only. 18 And he went out from Pharaoh, and entreated Jehovah. 19 And Jehovah turned an exceeding strong west wind, which took up the locusts, and drove them into the Red Sea; there remained not one locust in all the border of Egypt. 20 But Jehovah hardened Pharaoh's heart, and he did not let the children of Israel go.

After the double reference to Pharaoh's hardening of his own heart, the Lord told Moses that He had made his heart *obstinate,* the only time the Lord's work is described by this particular Hebrew word (see comments on 4:21). He was now prolonging the conflict in order to provide Israel, both as to the present generation and as to future generations, with an indelible lesson about His reality and power. He sent Moses to Pharaoh with still another warning, that if he did not let Israel go, locusts would invade the land and devour what little remained. After he left, Pharaoh's courtiers spoke rather plainly to their master, suggesting that they let **the men** of Israel go to worship Jehovah, asking him if he did not yet realize that Egypt was on the brink

of complete collapse. So Moses and Aaron were called back. Pharaoh inquired who was to go to this religious feast. Moses replied that young and old, male and female, men and beasts. Pharaoh was incensed and cried out that such a plan could only be part of an evil design. They were to take the men and go to worship, for he felt this was all that was needed to fulfill their original request. And in his anger he had them driven from the throneroom.

Moses apparently stretched out his rod that same day, and during the following night the locusts came. In autumn the locusts migrate from the Sudan south of Egypt to the coastal regions halfway down the Red Sea, east and a bit south of Egypt. Here they lay their eggs. During the winter the new generation hatches. In February-March they migrate either to Palestine or Egypt, depending upon which way the wind blows. In response to Moses' upraised rod, God caused an east wind to blow all day and all night, bringing the locusts in in unprecedented numbers. Tremendous plagues of them have been known even in modern times, their flights literally blacking out the sun. On this occasion they darkened the land, devouring everything that was left from the hail, thus destroying not only the leaves of the trees and mopping up whatever flax and barley might be left, but also destroying the wheat and smelt which had escaped serious hail damage before. Again Pharaoh called for Moses and entreated him to pray for him. Again Moses prayed, and the Lord sent a strong west wind, driving the locusts out of Egypt and apparently dumping them in the Red Sea itself.[64]

i. Ninth Plague — Darkness (10:21-29)

21 And Jehovah said unto Moses, Stretch out thy hand toward heaven, that there may be darkness over the land of Egypt, even darkness which may be felt. 22 And Moses stretched forth his hand toward heaven; and there was a thick darkness in all the land of Egypt three days; 23 they saw not one another, neither rose any one from his place for three days: but all the children of Israel had light in their dwellings. 24 And Pharaoh

[64] *Ibid.,* pp. 54-55.

called unto Moses, and said, Go ye, serve Jehovah; only let your flocks and your herds be stayed: let your little ones also go with you. 25 And Moses said, Thou must also give into our hand sacrifices and burnt-offerings, that we may sacrifice unto Jehovah our God. 26 Our cattle also shall go with us; there shall not a hoof be left behind; for thereof must we take to serve Jehovah our God; and we know not with what we must serve Jehovah, until we come thither. 27 But Jehovah hardened Pharaoh's heart, and he would not let them go. 28 And Pharaoh said unto him, Get thee from me, take heed to thyself, see my face no more; for in the day thou seest my face thou shalt die. 29 And Moses said, Thou hast spoken well; I will see thy face again no more.

The third plague in each triad came without advance warning. And the ninth was no exception. The Lord told Moses to stretch out his hand toward heaven and a darkness would come upon Egypt so thick that men would have to grope about, trying to feel their way. Most scholars believe this was the result of the *khamsin,* a hot southerly wind that comes in off the Sahara, carrying some of the desert sand. It usually blows for two or three days, and strikes any time from March to May. The tremendous flood of the preceding summer had left a heavy deposit of red soil all over Egypt. It was now as dry as powder. The hail and the locusts had destroyed the vegetation, and there was nothing to hold the soil and sand in place. So to the sand of the Sahara was added the dust of Egypt until the air was full of the little particles. The very sun was blotted out, and no Egyptian left his house for three days. Jehovah had defeated the very sun-god, Re, one of the greatest of the Egyptian deities. But the wind did not reach into the more protected areas of Goshen where the Israelites dwelt, so they had light.[65] Again Pharaoh proposed a compromise: all the people could go, but the stock must remain. This would be a kind of guarantee they would come back. When Moses insisted all must go, Pharaoh angrily banished him from his presence on pain of death.

65 *Ibid.,* p. 55; and Pfeiffer, *op. cit.,* pp. 48-49.

j. Tenth Plague — Slaying of the First-born (11:1—12:36)

(1) The Announcement to Pharaoh (11:1-10)

1 And Jehovah said unto Moses, Yet one plague more will I bring upon Pharaoh, and upon Egypt; afterwards he will let you go hence: when he shall let you go, he shall surely thrust you out hence altogether. 2 Speak now in the ears of the people, and let them ask every man of his neighbor, and every woman of her neighbor, jewels of silver, and jewels of gold. 3 And Jehovah gave the people favor in the sight of the Egyptians. Moreover the man Moses was very great in the land of Egypt, in the sight of Pharaoh's servants, and in the sight of the people.

4 And Moses said, Thus saith Jehovah, About midnight will I go out into the midst of Egypt: 5 and all the first-born in the land of Egypt shall die, from the first-born of Pharaoh that sitteth upon his throne, even unto the first-born of the maid-servant that is behind the mill; and all the first-born of cattle. 6 And there shall be a great cry throughout all the land of Egypt, such as there hath not been, nor shall be any more. 7 But against any of the children of Israel shall not a dog move his tongue, against man or beast: that ye may know how that Jehovah doth make a distinction between the Egyptians and Israel. 8 And all these thy servants shall come down unto me, and bow down themselves unto me, saying, Get thee out, and all the people that follow thee: and after that I will go out. And he went out from Pharaoh in hot anger.

9 And Jehovah said unto Moses, Pharaoh will not hearken unto you; that my wonders may be multiplied in the land of Egypt. 10 And Moses and Aaron did all these wonders before Pharaoh: and Jehovah hardened Pharaoh's heart, and he did not let the children of Israel go out of his land.

In the encounter between Moses and Pharaoh after the ninth plague, the king told Moses to get out and not to come back to speak to him again or he would die. To this cessation of face-to-face contact Moses agreed. But before he departed from Pharaoh's presence, he had one last message to deliver. The Lord had been revealing the various parts of the message for quite some time (cf. vv. 1-2 with

3:21-22; 4:22-23; 6:1). Now He had either revealed to Moses just prior to his coming to the palace that this was the time for the message to be delivered, or in a flash of inspiration Moses realized that the key moment in the conflict had arrived. He had a twofold message for Pharaoh: the threat of one final plague, and the prophecy that after this he would no longer hold Israel but compel them to go. And he also had a message for the people: that they were to ask from the Egyptians their jewels and ornaments — final preparation for quitting the land. This was made possible through the increasing respect of the Egyptians for Israel in general and for Moses in particular.

So before leaving Moses announced to Pharaoh that at **midnight** (either of that same day or of an indefinite day in the near future) Jehovah Himself would go through Egypt to slay the first-born son of every family, from the palace of Pharaoh to the hovel of the most menial slave who ground the grain in the crude millstones. There would be oriental wailing and mourning such as had never been heard in Egypt before. But not even a dog would threaten Israel — using a proverbial expression.[66] Then all the courtiers of Pharaoh, who were even then listening to Moses' announcement, would descend from their plush palaces to find Moses, and bowing in obeisance before him plead with him to depart from Egypt. Then Moses declared he would go. And he marched out of Pharaoh's presence **in hot anger.** The personal crisis between Pharaoh and Moses had been building up for some time. Moses had made increasing demands that the haughty monarch, who considered himself a god and was so considered by his people, humble himself before Jehovah whom Moses represented. To this kind of speech Pharaoh was not accustomed. After the seventh plague, he had had Moses and Aaron driven from his presence. Now he had ordered them to leave and see him no more on pain of death. But it was Moses who spoke the last hot word and marched out of Pharaoh's presence unimpressed by the royal threats. The man who had told God he could not speak had come a long way in the year since he first spoke to Pharaoh!

(2) The Announcement to Israel (12:1-28)

1 And Jehovah spake unto Moses and Aaron in the land of Egypt, saying, 2 This month shall be unto you the beginning of months; it shall be the first month of the year to you. 3 Speak ye unto all the congregation of Israel, saying, In the tenth *day* of this month they shall take to them every man a lamb, according to their fathers' houses, a lamb for a household: 4 and if the household be too little for a lamb, then shall he and his neighbor next unto his house take one according to the number of the souls; according to every man's eating ye shall make your count for the lamb. 5 Your lamb shall be without blemish, a male a year old: ye shall take it from the sheep, or from the goats: 6 and ye shall keep it until the fourteenth day of the same month; and the whole assembly of the congregation of Israel shall kill it at even. 7 And they shall take of the blood, and put it on the two side-posts and on the lintel, upon the houses wherein they shall eat it. 8 And they shall eat the flesh in that night, roast with fire, and unleavened bread; with bitter herbs they shall eat it. 9 Eat not of it raw, nor boiled at all with water, but roast with fire; its head with its legs and with the inwards thereof. 10 And ye shall let nothing of it remain until the morning; but that which remaineth of it until the morning ye shall burn with fire. 11 And thus shall ye eat it: with your loins girded, your shoes on your feet, and your staff in your hand; and ye shall eat it in haste: it is Jehovah's passover. 12 For I will go through the land of Egypt in that night, and will smite all the first-born in the land of Egypt, both man and beast; and against all the gods of Egypt I will execute judgments: I am Jehovah. 13 And the blood shall be to you for a token upon the houses where ye are: and when I see the blood, I will pass over you, and there shall no plague be upon you to destroy you, when I smite the land of Egypt. 14 And this day shall be unto you for a memorial, and ye shall keep it a feast to Jehovah: throughout your generations ye shall keep it a feast by an ordinance for ever.

15 Seven days shall ye eat unleavened bread; even the first day ye shall put away leaven out of your houses: for whosoever eateth leavened bread from the first day until the seventh day, that soul shall be cut off from Israel. 16 And in the first day there shall be to you a holy

---

[66] Connell, *op. cit.*, p. 114.

convocation, and in the seventh day a holy convocation; no manner of work shall be done in them, save that which every man must eat, that only may be done by you. 17 And ye shall observe the *feast of* unleavened bread: for in this self-same day have I brought your hosts out of the land of Egypt: therefore shall ye observe this day throughout your generations by an ordinance for ever. 18 In the first *month*, on the fourteenth day of the month at even, ye shall eat unleavened bread, until the one and twentieth day of the month at even. 19 Seven days shall there be no leaven found in your houses: for whosoever eateth that which is leavened, that soul shall be cut off from the congregation of Israel, whether he be a sojourner, or one that is born in the land. 20 Ye shall eat nothing leavened; in all your habitations shall ye eat unleavened bread.

21 Then Moses called for all the elders of Israel, and said unto them, Draw out, and take you lambs according to your families, and kill the passover. 22 And ye shall take a bunch of hyssop, and dip it in the blood that is in the basin, and strike the lintel and the two side-posts with the blood that is in the basin; and none of you shall go out of the door of his house until the morning. 23 For Jehovah will pass through to smite the Egyptians; and when he seeth the blood upon the lintel, and on the two side-posts, Jehovah will pass over the door, and will not suffer the destroyer to come in unto your houses to smite you. 24 And ye shall observe this thing for an ordinance to thee and to thy sons for ever. 25 And it shall come to pass, when ye are come to the land which Jehovah will give you, according as he hath promised, that ye shall keep this service. 26 And it shall come to pass, when your children shall say unto you, What mean ye by this service? 27 that ye shall say, It is the sacrifice of Jehovah's passover, who passed over the houses of the children of Israel in Egypt, when he smote the Egyptians, and delivered our houses. And the people bowed the head and worshipped. 28 And the children of Israel went and did so; as Jehovah had commanded Moses and Aaron, so did they.

The announcement to Israel of the final plague is recorded as a longer set of instructions for escaping it, as given by the Lord to Moses, and a shorter set, as given by Moses to the elders of Israel. Involved in these instructions, of course,

was the establishment of one of the great national feasts of Israel, the Passover. The longer set of instructions need not be thought of as having been received by Moses between the time of his visit to Pharaoh which ended in 11:8 and his meeting with the elders in 12:21. Rather, this partakes of the nature of a summary of divine instructions which had been received over a number of days. It must have begun during the first nine days of the month, since the Lord refers to **this month,** and gives instructions concerning the tenth day, the fourteenth, and the fifteenth through the twenty-first. Many scholars believe that Moses' promise that the first-born would be slain at midnight (11:4) did not refer to the night following the day on which he spoke, but an indefinite midnight in the future. While this is possible, it is also possible that the announcement was made on the fourteenth day while Israel already had the lambs penned up since the tenth day, ready for Moses' final instruction (12:3). This possibility is strengthened by the fact that when Moses addressed the elders of Israel just before the Passover, he made no reference to a preliminary penning up of the lambs, as if that had already been taken care of, and he referred to the lamb itself in words which indicated they were already familiar with its significance — **kill the passover** (12:21). The greater length of the Lord's instructions to Moses as compared with his address to the elders may also be explained in the possibility that they include some items, especially in verses 15-20, which Moses was instructed about at a later time. When Exodus was written, this was a logical place to include them.

The instructions involved the establishment of a religious calendar for Israel. Their previous calendar, which continued as their civil calendar, began in the fall, in the month of *Tisri,* corresponding roughly with the last half of September and the first half of October (see 34:22). But now the Lord tells them that the month **Abib,** later called *Nisan,* corresponding to the last half of March and the first half of April, is to mark **the beginning of months.**[67] Practically all ancient peoples observed a spring festi-

---

[67] Merrill F. Unger, ed., "Calendar, Jewish," *Unger's Bible Dictionary,* pp. 163-66.

val of a religious nature. Visitors have also observed among the nomads of the Near East many of the features of the Passover itself: an annual dedication of the first-born of the flocks, the use of these the following spring for a festival meal, the eating with them of unleavened bread, and the marking of the tent with blood for protection and blessing. The Passover itself partook of the spirit of a spring festival, for during the total period of eight days a sheaf of barley, the first-fruits of the year's harvest, was to be waved before the Lord (Lev. 23:4-14). This, along with the implied familiarity of the elders with the slaying of the lambs (Exod. 12:21), has led many scholars to believe that from time immemorial Israel had observed a springtime religious festival with many of the ingredients of the Passover. It may even have been called a "passover" although if so the reason is not now known.[68] But however familiar Israel may have been with a springtime religious festival, and with some of the ingredients of the Passover, it is clear that this was the initiation of a new observance as far as its meaning and significance were concerned. This was the birth of a nation, a birth brought about by the gracious power of Jehovah, a birth which Israelites would never forget, and a birth which carried within its symbolism the seeds of an even higher revelation of the character and goodness of God.

The instructions required the taking of a perfect, year-old male lamb or kid for each household. If the family was too small, it was to join with a neighboring family. Eventually the minimum was fixed at ten persons to the lamb.[69] It was to be killed on the fourteenth day at even, or as the Hebrew says it, "between the two evenings." This was variously interpreted as being between the first noticeable lengthening of the shadows in the afternoon and sunset, or between sunset and total darkness. It was later done between 3 p.m. and 5 p.m.[70] The blood of the sacrifice was to be put above and on both sides of the door of each Israelite home, being applied by a bunch of hyssop, a vine-like plant which

grew in the clefts of walls (I Kings 4:33). The animal was to be roasted whole, and eaten with **unleavened bread** and **bitter herbs.** Unleavened bread was quite common among the nomads, although probably not so common among the Egyptians. The bitter herbs included lettuce, peppermint, snakeroot, and dandelion.[71] Leaven in the Scriptures generally symbolizes impurity or corruption, and seems to have had this meaning for other ancient peoples besides the Jews.[72] Its use was quite logically prohibited in connection with the worship of Jehovah. The bitter herbs were to remind Israel of the bitterness of their slavery in Egypt. The meal was to be eaten as if they were outside on the march, their sandals on, their belts tightened, their staffs in their hands. None of the sacrificial lamb was to be left until morning, and if some remnants were left they were to be burned.

The Lord's words to Moses also included instructions concerning the religious Feast of Unleavened Bread (vv. 15-20). The Passover proper was observed for only one day. But the week which immediately followed it was to continue the abstinence from leaven. The first instance of this abstinence is recorded at the time of the Exodus, and is there explained on the basis of the haste with which Israel departed from Egypt (vv. 34, 39). Moses did not relay instructions concerning the memorializing of this event until after their flight (13:3-10), and this strengthens the possibility that the lengthy instructions from the Lord to him were given before, during, and after the Exodus itself rather than at one time. There are several references to the conjoined Feasts of Passover and Unleavened Bread throughout the Pentateuch, but those which significantly enlarged upon these early instructions are those which command the consecration of the first-born (Exod. 13:11-16), command the offering of the first-fruits during the Feast of Unleavened Bread (Lev. 23:4-14), provide for a second Passover for those ceremonially unfit for the regular one (Num. 9: 1-14), command the offering of special daily sacrifices during the Feast of Unleavened Bread (Num. 28:16-25), and

---

[68] Finegan, *op. cit.*, pp. 67-69; see also Rawlinson, *op. cit.*, I, 257.
[69] Flavius Josephus, *Wars of the Jews*, Book VI, Chap. IX, para. 3.
[70] *Ibid.* See also Connell, *op. cit.*, p. 114.   [71] Rylaarsdam, *op. cit.*, I, 920.
[72] Rawlinson, *op. cit.*, I, 261.

shift the festival from the home to the city where the central sanctuary would be located in Canaan (Deut. 16:1-8).

The reason for the initial slaying of the lambs, and the meaning of the feast which commemorated it were to be found in the tenth plague. Egypt's first-born men and beasts were to be slain that night. Since this included the house of Pharaoh, who was considered a god, and since many of the false gods of Egypt were symbolized by various animals, God would now strike the most meaningful blow of His conflict with these false deities, executing judgments against **all the gods of Egypt.** Only those houses which had the sign of blood upon them would be "passed over." Thus the feast would serve as a living memorial throughout all coming generations to the miraculous deliverance of the nation by Jehovah — both as to the slaying of the Egyptians and the sparing of Israel. Moses made the memorial even more meaningful when for the first time he instructed the people how to use the questions of their children to give them religious instruction (vv. 26-27).

A Christian cannot fail to see in the Passover and the Feast of Unleavened Bread something more than a memorial to Israel's deliverance from Egypt. The New Testament suggests a deeper significance. We are told that the Jewish feast days were "a shadow of the things to come" (Col. 2:17; Heb. 10:1), the old order of worship was "a copy and shadow of the heavenly things" (Heb. 8:5; 9:23), "a figure for the time present" (Heb. 9:9). The prophet Isaiah anticipated the revelation of the Messiah as a lamb (Isa. 53:7; Acts 8:32-35). John the Baptist announced Him to the multitudes as "the Lamb of God, that taketh away the sin of the world" (John 1:29, 36). The Apostle Peter spoke of Him in the exact words describing the Passover lamb, "as of a lamb without blemish and without spot" (I Pet. 1:19). John the Revelator used "the Lamb" as the title of the Messiah twenty-eight times, and referred to Him as "the Lamb slain from the foundation of the world" (Rev. 13:8, KJV, Weymouth, Phillips, Berkeley). Paul went even farther in his identification, declaring, "our passover also hath been sacrificed, even Christ" (I Cor. 5:7). The unblemished lamb whose blood caused Jehovah to pass over the dwellings of Israel speaks eloquently of the Lamb whose blood could deliver a man forever from the punishment due for his sins. It was at the same hour that the Passover lamb was slain (the ninth to the eleventh, 3 p.m. to 5 p.m.) that Christ died on the cross (the ninth hour, or 3 p.m., Matt. 27:46-50), although it was on the first day of the Feast of Unleavened Bread rather than on the Passover proper. Even the accompanying features of the feast held a deeper meaning, the prohibited leaven symbolizing moral and spiritual impurity which for the Christian was permanently forbidden in his perpetual observance of the true Passover (I Cor. 5:6-8), and the bitter herbs speaking of the repentant spirit, the memory of the worshiper's own unfitness for communion with God which must always accompany him to the place of worship.[73] The Passover Supper itself is perpetuated in the Lord's Supper, established at the Passover He kept with His disciples on the night before the crucifixion. The partaking of the flesh of the Lamb is now in symbol, the unleavened bread representing His broken body and the wine the shed blood which was earlier forbidden to Israel. When one perceives the deeper meaning of the Passover, a meaning which the Israelites could not even faintly have foreseen at this time, he is reminded again of the profundity of the divine plan for human redemption, of the beautiful manner in which it unfolds from the beginning, of the wonderful unity of revelation.

(3) The Act of Jehovah (12:29-36)

29 And it came to pass at midnight, that Jehovah smote all the first-born in the land of Egypt, from the first-born of Pharaoh that sat on his throne unto the first-born of the captive that was in the dungeon; and all the first-born of cattle. 30 And Pharaoh rose up in the night, he, and all his servants, and all the Egyptians; and there was a great cry in Egypt; for there was not a house where there was not one dead. 31 And he called for Moses and Aaron by night, and said, Rise up, get you forth from among my people, both ye and the children of Israel;

---

[73] Connell, *op. cit.*, p. 114.

and go, serve Jehovah, as ye have said. 32 Take both your flocks and your herds, as ye have said, and be gone; and bless me also. 33 And the Egyptians were urgent upon the people, to send them out of the land in haste; for they said, We are all dead men. 34 And the people took their dough before it was leavened, their kneading-troughs being bound up in their clothes upon their shoulders. 35 And the children of Israel did according to the word of Moses; and they asked of the Egyptians jewels of silver, and jewels of gold, and raiment: 36 and Jehovah gave the people favor in the sight of the Egyptians, so that they let them have what they asked. And they despoiled the Egyptians.

The tenth plague was markedly different from the other nine. The nine had been basically natural calamities, natural calamities which God turned into miracles by His prediction and exact timing, the inexorable sequence in which one calamity followed another to a degree without parallel, and the extreme intensity with which they struck. That they were the work of God, any unrebellious heart could easily see. But Pharaoh refused to see. So the final stroke must be one which could not possibly be explained on any other basis than that it was the work of Jehovah. So in connection with this plague there is virtually no reference to any natural phenomenon. Jehovah declared that He Himself would pass through Egypt, smiting and executing judgments (11:4; 12:12). While it is common in our references to this plague to speak of the "death-angel" passing over Egypt slaying the first-born, the Bible nowhere refers this act to an angel. Always Jehovah is the immediate agent of this destruction. The only references which remotely suggest a natural or intermediate instrument are those to a "destroyer" (12:23), and to a "plague" (12:13) using a Hebrew word which elsewhere refers to a pestilence of epidemic proportions (30:12; Num. 8:19; 16:46-47; Josh. 22:17). But when it is said that Jehovah will not permit the destroyer to enter homes marked with blood, it is also said that Jehovah Himself will pass over that home rather than smiting the first-born there, indicating that Jehovah and the destroyer were one and the same. And it is quite evident that this

was not an epidemic such as has ever been known to man, for it struck only the first-born son of each home, and then only in homes not marked by blood.

When the Lord struck the first-born, Pharaoh's reaction was immediate. He and all his courtiers and all of the Egyptians arose in the night and began their mourning. He personally commanded Moses and Aaron to get Israel out of the land immediately, taking with them their flocks and herds, and amazingly added a request for a blessing — a strange comedown for a human god! The Egyptians in general joined in urging them to hurry out of the land, for they feared that death would extend beyond the firstborn to include the entire nation if obedience was not immediate. And when Israel, at the command of Jehovah (3:22; 11:2), asked that the Egyptians give them of their expensive clothing and jewelry, the Egyptians were quick to do so, letting them have whatever they asked.

5. The Abandonment of Egypt (12: 37—13:22)

a. The Conditions of the March (12: 37-42)

37 And the children of Israel journeyed from Rameses to Succoth, about six hundred thousand on foot that were men, besides children. 38 And a mixed multitude went up also with them; and flocks, and herds, even very much cattle. 39 And they baked unleavened cakes of the dough which they brought forth out of Egypt; for it was not leavened, because they were thrust out of Egypt, and could not tarry, neither had they prepared for themselves any victuals. 40 Now the time that the children of Israel dwelt in Egypt was four hundred and thirty years. 41 And it came to pass at the end of four hundred and thirty years, even the selfsame day it came to pass, that all the hosts of Jehovah went out from the land of Egypt. 42 It is a night to be much observed unto Jehovah for bringing them out from the land of Egypt: this is that night of Jehovah, to be much observed of all the children of Israel throughout their generations.

Israel was accompanied by a **mixed multitude** when they went up out of Egypt, taking with them large flocks and herds of various animals. The **mixed** multitude probably included descendants of non-Israelite slaves which had accompanied Jacob and his sons into Egypt, other Semitic tribes which were sojourning in Egypt, and others who for various reasons wanted to leave Egypt. The confusion of a large group of people, having spent years in slavery, being joined by others of diverse backgrounds, routed out in the darkness of the night, and started on a journey into unfamiliar areas, must have been great indeed. They left Goshen or the land of Rameses for **Succoth,** either the area at the east end of the Wadi Tumilat, the valley running from the Nile to Lake Timsah, or specifically a city located at the present Tell-el-Maskhutah, ten miles east of Pithom, in that area.[74]

Note is taken by the writer of Exodus that Israel left after being in Egypt 430 years. In Genesis 15:13 Jehovah had foretold to Abraham that his descendants would be afflicted in a strange land for 400 years, Also in Acts 7:8 Stephen uses the round number of 400 years in referring to this announcement to Abraham. But Paul, in Galatians 3:17, speaks of 430 years as reaching from the covenant with Abraham to the giving of the law at Sinai. And the Septuagint, the most ancient translation of the Old Testament into Greek, dating from the third century B.C., makes this present passage read, "in the land of Egypt, and in the land of Canaan, was 430 years."[75] This would diminish the 430 years in Egypt to 215, since 215 years were spent by the three patriarchs in Canaan from the entry of Abraham into Canaan to the entry of Jacob into Egypt. However, the Septuagint reading does not make sense, since the children of Israel had not spent 215 years in Canaan but only the patriarchs had done so. And Paul could well have been thinking of the renewal of the covenant with Jacob rather than simply its original establishment with Abraham, at least when referring to the time-gap between it and the law. The figure of 430 years becomes an all-important figure in determining the period in which the patriarchs lived.

One serious problem arises in connection with the Exodus, for the writer says

that **about six hundred thousand . . . men, besides children** (and women) and **a mixed multitude** of indefinite number went out of Egypt. This would mean an absolute minimum of two million people and more likely as many as three or four million. This number is exceedingly difficult to accept, not simply from the basis of human reason but also from the plain statement of other Scriptures. The total population of Egypt was only about seven million as late as the time of Christ and it is quite likely that it was no larger if as large at the time of the Exodus. This would mean that Israel would have been as large as the balance of the population of Egypt, and could hardly have been held in bondage so long as they were. Furthermore, the land of Goshen was only a small part of Egypt, the Wadi Tumilat in modern times supporting only from four thousand nomads to twelve thousand farmers. The oases of the Sinai Peninsula can take care of only about five thousand nomads.[76] And while God miraculously provided food for Israel in their journeys through the Peninsula, it is only recorded three times that He miraculously gave them water, and it is never recorded that He miraculously provided pasture for their herds and flocks which are pictured in verse 38 as being quite numerous in proportion to the number of Israelites. Furthermore, Israel is consistently spoken of as being small in number in comparison with other nations. In Deuteronomy 7:7, Israel is assured that the Lord did not choose them because they were more in number than other peoples, "for ye were the fewest of all peoples," which made even more evident the mighty hand of the Lord in bringing them out of Egypt. In Deuteronomy 4:38 it is said that the Lord chose Israel to displace nations "greater and mightier" than themselves; but the nations Israel displaced in Canaan could not possibly have been more numerous than a people numbering into the millions. And in Exodus 23:29-30, the Lord plainly states that it would be unwise for Him to drive out all the Canaanites in one year, since the Israelites were so few in number that the land would become desolate and the wild

---

[74] Rylaarsdam, *op. cit.*, I, 925; and Johnson, *op. cit.*, p. 62.   [75] Driver, *op. cit.*, pp. 101-02.
[76] Finegan, *op. cit.*, pp. 90-91.

beasts would multiply against them. Instead, He would drive them out gradually so the number of Israelites could increase sufficiently to populate the land. Yet a population of from two to five million would have adequately filled the land of Canaan, which is no larger in area than the state of Vermont — which even today has only a fraction of such a population. As we read the description of Israel's march, it is the fairly rapid march of a compact body, not the slow meanderings of millions of people over a vast area. And neither was the camp spread all over the Sinai Peninsula, but was organized in a relatively small area around the tabernacle (Num. 2:1-34).

The question is not simply one of belief in miracles. Of course the omnipotent God can do anything He chooses to do. The question is not whether He could but whether He did.[77] The plain testimony of Scripture in the present writer's opinion is that He did not. How then do we explain these numbers? The critical scholar simply says, "The figures do not come to us from eye-witnesses; and tradition, in the course of years, greatly exaggerated the numbers."[78] The evangelical scholar cannot accept the record of the Exodus itself as anything else but that of an eyewitness. On the other hand, he observes that, as has been mentioned before, Hebrew numbers were originally symbolized by the letters of the alphabet. The extremely close similarity of some letters would make numbers the most likely point for copying errors to occur. An explanation first suggested by W. M. Flinders Petrie is that the Hebrew word 'elef need not here be translated as **thousand**. It does have this meaning in certain contexts, but in others it refers to a unit of fighting men. Eventually these units were standardized as 1,000 each. But they apparently could be much smaller family groups in earlier times, as is indicated by Gideon's words, "How can I save Israel, seeing that my clan ('elef) is the weakest in Manasseh?" (Judg. 6:15).[79] If this translation be applied here in Exodus, we have record of about 600 clans or military units going out of Egypt, bringing the number down from millions to per-

haps thirty thousand or so — a number which would still require a miracle for sustenance in the Sinai Peninsula, but which fits the language of Scripture much better. Finegan makes a similar translation in the two censuses in Numbers, taking the number of "thousands" for each tribe as the number of 'elefs and the hundreds and tens as the actual number of fighting men in each case. He arrives at 598 'elefs and 5,550 fighting men in Numbers 1, and 596 'elefs and 5,750 fighting men in Numbers 26.[80] This is extremely interesting and may well be the proper interpretation. It still leaves some problems such as the totals in the two censuses which seem to indicate that the 'elefs must be thousands in the numerical sense. Yet it is possible that after a few errors had been made by copyists, a well-meaning scribe, misreading 'elef here in Exodus, sought to harmonize the numbers again as he thought they ought to be, revising the few numbers necessary to make the lists agree with his misreading. Thus, while the original meaning is still preserved, it is somewhat veiled. That the numbers cannot be reconciled in their present state is dramatically evidenced by comparing the references to 600,000 men twenty years of age or older with the statement in Numbers 3:43 that all the first-born sons of Israel from *a month old* and older numbered only 22,273. Even disregarding the group under twenty, each first-born son would have had to have twenty-six younger brothers — besides sisters. If there were as many males under twenty as over, this would demand an average family of 100 children or more throughout the entire nation! Such problems as these need not disturb the faith of God's child in the inspired authority of the Word. Future discoveries of older copies of the Old Testament may well clear up all of these difficulties. Thank the Lord our salvation doesn't depend upon Old Testament numbers!

b. The Commemoration of the Passover (12:43—13:16)

43 And Jehovah said unto Moses and Aaron, This is the ordinance of the passover: there shall no foreigner eat thereof;

44 but every man's servant that is bought for money, when thou hast circumcised him, then shall he eat thereof. 45 A sojourner and a hired servant shall not eat thereof. 46 In one house shall it be eaten; thou shalt not carry forth aught of the flesh abroad out of the house; neither shall ye break a bone thereof. 47 All the congregation of Israel shall keep it. 48 And when a stranger shall sojourn with thee, and will keep the passover to Jehovah, let all his males be circumcised, and then let him come near and keep it; and he shall be as one that is born in the land: but no uncircumcised person shall eat thereof. 49 One law shall be to him that is home-born, and unto the stranger that sojourneth among you. 50 Thus did all the children of Israel; as Jehovah commanded Moses and Aaron, so did they. 51 And it came to pass the selfsame day, that Jehovah did bring the children of Israel out of the land of Egypt by their hosts.

1 And Jehovah spake unto Moses, saying, 2 Sanctify unto me all the first-born, whatsoever openeth the womb among the children of Israel, both of man and of beast: it is mine.

3 And Moses said unto the people, Remember this day, in which ye came out from Egypt, out of the house of bondage; for by strength of hand Jehovah brought you out from this place: there shall no leavened bread be eaten. 4 This day ye go forth in the month Abib. 5 And it shall be, when Jehovah shall bring thee into the land of the Canaanite, and the Hittite, and the Amorite, and the Hivite, and the Jebusite, which he sware unto thy fathers to give thee, a land flowing with milk and honey, that thou shalt keep this service in this month. 6 Seven days thou shalt eat unleavened bread, and in the seventh day shall be a feast to Jehovah. 7 Unleavened bread shall be eaten throughout the seven days; and there shall no leavened bread be seen with thee, neither shall there be leaven seen with thee, in all thy borders. 8 And thou shalt tell thy son in that day, saying, It is because of that which Jehovah did for me when I came forth out of Egypt. 9 And it shall be for a sign unto thee upon thy hand, and for a memorial between thine eyes, that the law of Jehovah may be in thy mouth: for with a strong hand hath Jehovah brought thee out of Egypt. 10 Thou shalt therefore keep this ordinance in its season from year to year.

11 And it shall be, when Jehovah shall bring thee into the land of the Canaanite as he sware unto thee and to thy fathers, and shall give it thee, 12 that thou shalt set apart unto Jehovah all that openeth the womb, and every firstling which thou hast that cometh of a beast; the males shall be Jehovah's. 13 And every firstling of an ass thou shalt redeem with a lamb; and if thou wilt not redeem it, then thou shalt break its neck: and all the first-born of man among thy sons shalt thou redeem. 14 And it shall be, when thy son asketh thee in time to come, saying, What is this? that thou shalt say unto him, By strength of hand Jehovah brought us out from Egypt, from the house of bondage: 15 and it came to pass, when Pharaoh would hardly let us go, that Jehovah slew all the first-born in the land of Egypt, both the first-born of man, and the first-born of beast: therefore I sacrifice to Jehovah all that openeth the womb, being males; but all the first-born of my sons I redeem. 16 And it shall be for a sign upon thy hand, and for frontlets between thine eyes: for by strength of hand Jehovah brought us forth out of Egypt.

Now there are added instructions given concerning the Passover. The people are apparently informed for the first time of the yearly observance of the Feast of Unleavened Bread commemorating the Exodus. The Lord instructs Moses, and he in turn the people, about the dedication of all the first-born to Jehovah. The instructions concerning the Passover included directions prohibiting its observance by foreigners. Only circumcised Israelites, their circumcised slaves, and those foreigners who were willing to become Israelites by means of circumcision, could partake. This is the original provision for the admission of Gentile proselytes to the covenant family. It indicates that from the beginning God's plan of redemption included others besides Israelites. The instructions concerning the Feast of Unleavened Bread were largely a repetition of the instructions earlier given to Moses (12:15-20). This, too, was to be used as a means of religious instruction for the children (cf. v. 8 with 12:26-27). The consecration of the first-born is based on the slaying of the first-born of Egypt and the simultaneous sparing of the first-born of Israel. All the first-born had been consecrated to God, the Egyptians by death, the Israelites in life. So every first-born male animal was to be offered to the Lord as a sacrifice, the meat of these animals providing much of the sustenance for the priests and Levites (Num. 18:17-20). In the case of an unclean animal, such as an ass, not acceptable as sacrifice, a lamb was to be substituted. If the owner was not willing to give a lamb, he must kill the colt. Since commercially an ass was much more valuable than a lamb, this almost assured compliance.[81] In the case of humans, the first-born must not be offered as a burnt-sacrifice as did the heathen. It is interesting, however, that the Hebrew word translated **set apart** (literally, "cause to pass over") is the very word used elsewhere to describe heathen sacrifice of children (II Kings 16:3; Ezek. 20:31). It is probably intended as a subtle contrast of Jehovah's way with that of paganism.[82] Human first-born were to be redeemed or ransomed. The fact that by rights they belonged to God was to be recognized by the payment of a set price. The first-born of both men and beasts who had come out of Egypt were ransomed *en masse* by the consecration of the Levites and their cattle to the service of Jehovah (Num. 3:40-51). The excess in number of first-born over Levites, and all subsequent first-born were redeemed by the payment of five shekels or about three dollars (Num. 3:47; 18:16).[83] The first-born of animals were to be sacrificed or redeemed when eight days old (Exod. 22:30), and the first-born of men to be redeemed when one month old (Num. 18:16). This observance would be to Israel a sign upon their hands and frontlets between their eyes, reminders of spiritual truth which would always be before their eyes. From this phrasing the rabbis later developed the phylacteries worn by Jewish males — passages of Scripture in little leather boxes worn on their wrists and foreheads.

c. The Certainty of Divine Leadership (13:17-22)

17 And it came to pass, when Pharaoh had let the people go, that God led them not by the way of the land of the Philistines, although that was near; for God said, Lest peradventure the people repent when they see war, and they return to Egypt: 18 but God led the people about, by the way of the wilderness by the Red Sea: and the children of Israel went up armed out of the land of Egypt. 19 And Moses took the bones of Joseph with him: for he had straitly sworn the children of Israel, saying, God will surely visit you; and ye shall carry up my bones away hence with you. 20 And they took their journey from Succoth, and encamped in Etham, in the edge of the wilderness. 21 And Jehovah went before them by day in a pillar of cloud, to lead them the way, and by night in a pillar of fire, to give them light; that they might go by day and by night: 22 the pillar of cloud by day, and the pillar of fire by night, departed not from before the people.

There were two routes by which God could lead Israel to Palestine. One was a coastal route running from the city of Raamses northeast to the edge of the Mediterranean and thence up to Gaza. It was the **near** or short route, but the Lord did not lead them that way because it was the military route used by the armies of Egypt and invading armies as well. No doubt it was well patrolled by the Egyptians and the people could easily have become fearful and turned back. The second route was one across the desert, longer, but more peaceful. It went toward the Red Sea rather than the Mediterranean. The first stopping point, at the edge of **the wilderness** or desert, was **Etham,** apparently the Hebrew form of the Egyptian *hetem* or "fort," referring to the fortress which commanded the eastern entrance to the Wadi Tumilat, standing between Crocodile Lake and Bitter Lake.[84] It was in this direction that Jehovah led His people, clothing Himself in a pillar of cloud by day and a pillar of fire by night, giving them visible guidance by day and light by night. This visible representation of the Lord's presence continued with them until they reached Canaan forty years later. Its usual resting-place when Israel was camped was over the place of worship (33:9-10; 40:34-38).

A note is added at this point to the effect that the children of Israel fulfilled the vows of their fathers to Joseph by carrying his mummy with them on their journey. His faith was fully vindicated (Gen. 50:24-26).

---

[81] Connell, *op. cit.*, pp. 115-16.   [82] Johnson, *op. cit.*, p. 63.   [83] Rylaarsdam, *op. cit.*, I, 927.
[84] Finegan, *op. cit.*, pp. 78-85.

6. The Avenging of God's People (14: 1—15:21)

a. The Reaction of Pharaoh (14:1-9)

1 And Jehovah spake unto Moses, saying, 2 Speak unto the children of Israel, that they turn back and encamp before Pi-hahiroth, between Migdol and the sea, before Baal-zephon: over against it shall ye encamp by the sea. 3 And Pharaoh will say of the children of Israel, They are entangled in the land, the wilderness hath shut them in. 4 And I will harden Pharaoh's heart, and he shall follow after them; and I will get me honor upon Pharaoh, and upon all his host; and the Egyptians shall know that I am Jehovah. And they did so. 5 And it was told the king of Egypt that the people were fled: and the heart of Pharaoh and of his servants was changed towards the people, and they said, What is this we have done, that we have let Israel go from serving us? 6 And he made ready his chariot, and took his people with him: 7 and he took six hundred chosen chariots, and all the chariots of Egypt, and captains over all of them. 8 And Jehovah hardened the heart of Pharaoh king of Egypt, and he pursued after the children of Israel: for the children of Israel went out with a high hand. 9 And the Egyptians pursued after them, all the horses *and* chariots of Pharaoh, and his horsemen, and his army, and overtook them encamping by the sea, beside Pi-hahiroth, before Baal-zephon.

Having arrived before the Egyptian fortress at Etham, the Lord turned the people back to the southwest. The commander of the fortress probably had no intention to let Israel pass. The Lord knew well what Pharaoh's second thoughts would be, so still seeking a peaceful exit, He led Israel back around the bulge of the large Bitter Lake. Here they encountered a mountain range, Jebel Jenefeh, running in from the west, which forced them to move southeastward between the mountains and the Bitter Lakes. There is evidence that in these times the Gulf of Suez, the western arm of the Red Sea, reached all the way to the Bitter Lakes, being connected by shallow channels that in at least one spot could be crossed under extremely favorable conditions. Between the mountains to the west and the sea is a small plain about five miles across. On the mountain, overlooking the sea, even today can be found the ruins of a watchtower or **Migdol,** as such a structure is known in Hebrew, dating from the time of the Exodus. Here is a spot that fits perfectly the biblical description, **encamp . . . between Migdol and the sea.**[85]

Not all biblical scholars agree that this was the route taken by Israel. The Hebrew words used wherever "Red Sea" appears in English, literally mean "Sea of Reeds." It is thought by many that this term referred to a marshy area in the lake region north of the Gulf of Suez, and that it was this marsh rather than our present Red Sea which Israel crossed. Both critical and evangelical scholars are represented among those who take this position.[86] But as Finegan keenly observes, the name "Sea of Reeds" was applied by ancient Israel to our present Red Sea, including the eastern arm or the Gulf of Aqabah (I Kings 9:26). And the picture he draws of the route is so closely fitted to the language of the Scriptures as to convince the present writer that it was the extension of the Gulf of Suez up into the Bitter Lakes which Israel crossed rather than the marshy area to the north of the lakes.[87]

The Lord knew that reports would reach Pharaoh of the movements of Israel. He knew the covetous, proud heart of that monarch. He knew that Pharaoh was not yet finally and completely defeated. He decided that Pharaoh's punishment was not yet complete. So He baited a trap for the Egyptians by apparently leading Israel into a corner from which they could not escape. Pharaoh arose to the occasion, and with the chariots and soldiers of whom he was so proud, he moved out to attack Israel.

b. The Perception of Faith (14:10-14)

10 And when Pharaoh drew nigh, the children of Israel lifted up their eyes, and, behold, the Egyptians were marching after them; and they were sore afraid: and the children of Israel cried out unto Jehovah. 11 And they said unto Moses, Because there were no graves in Egypt, hast thou taken us away to die in the

---

[85] *Ibid.,* pp. 85-87.

[86] See Johnson, *op. cit.,* p. 64; Pfeiffer, *op. cit.,* p. 54; Rylaarsdam, *op. cit.,* I, 930-31.

[87] Finegan, *op. cit.,* p. 87.

wilderness? wherefore hast thou dealt thus with us, to bring us forth out of Egypt? 12 Is not this the word that we spake unto thee in Egypt, saying, Let us alone, that we may serve the Egyptians? For it were better for us to serve the Egyptians, than that we should die in the wilderness. 13 And Moses said unto the people, Fear ye not, stand still, and see the salvation of Jehovah, which he will work for you to-day: for the Egyptians whom ye have seen to-day, ye shall see them again no more for ever. 14 Jehovah will fight for you, and ye shall hold your peace.

The armies of Egypt had no sooner come into view in the distance than Israel was terrified. Their weakness in the face of any kind of opposition or problem had been in evidence from the time of Moses' first interview with Pharaoh (chap. 5), and was to plague Moses throughout the wilderness journeyings. They cried that there were sufficient graves in Egypt for them without dragging them into the desert to die, and reminded Moses that they had preferred to remain in Egypt rather than follow him anyway! But Moses had learned much in the year he had spent on his mission. He told them not to fear. By faith he had already perceived that Jehovah was a master strategist and that He was about to win the biggest victory of His war with Egypt and its gods.

c. The Intervention of Jehovah (14:15-31)

15 And Jehovah said unto Moses, Wherefore criest thou unto me? speak unto the children of Israel, that they go forward. 16 And lift thou up thy rod, and stretch out thy hand over the sea, and divide it: and the children of Israel shall go into the midst of the sea on dry ground. 17 And I, behold, I will harden the hearts of the Egyptians, and they shall go in after them: and I will get me honor upon Pharaoh, and upon all his host, upon his chariots, and upon his horsemen. 18 And the Egyptians shall know that I am Jehovah, when I have gotten me honor upon Pharaoh, upon his chariots, and upon his horsemen. 19 And the angel of God, who went before the camp of Israel, removed and went behind them; and the pillar of cloud removed from before them, and stood behind them: 20 and it came between the camp of Egypt and the camp of Israel;

and there was the cloud and the darkness, yet gave it light by night: and the one came not near the other all the night.

21 And Moses stretched out his hand over the sea; and Jehovah caused the sea to go *back* by a strong east wind all the night, and made the sea dry land, and the waters were divided. 22 And the children of Israel went into the midst of the sea upon the dry ground: and the waters were a wall unto them on their right hand, and on their left. 23 And the Egyptians pursued, and went in after them into the midst of the sea, all Pharaoh's horses, his chariots, and his horsemen. 24 And it came to pass in the morning watch, that Jehovah looked forth upon the host of the Egyptians through the pillar of fire and of cloud, and discomfited the host of the Egyptians. 25 And he took off their chariot wheels, and they drove them heavily; so that the Egyptians said, Let us flee from the face of Israel; for Jehovah fighteth for them against the Egyptians.

26 And Jehovah said unto Moses, Stretch out thy hand over the sea, that the waters may come again upon the Egyptians, upon their chariots, and upon their horsemen. 27 And Moses stretched forth his hand over the sea, and the sea returned to its strength when the morning appeared; and the Egyptians fled against it; and Jehovah overthrew the Egyptians in the midst of the sea. 28 And the waters returned, and covered the chariots, and the horsemen, even all the host of Pharaoh that went in after them into the sea; there remained not so much as one of them. 29 But the children of Israel walked upon dry land in the midst of the sea; and the waters were a wall unto them on their right hand, and on their left. 30 Thus Jehovah saved Israel that day out of the hand of the Egyptians; and Israel saw the Egyptians dead upon the sea-shore. 31 And Israel saw the great work which Jehovah did upon the Egyptians, and the people feared Jehovah: and they believed in Jehovah, and in his servant Moses.

The Lord instructed Moses how Israel was to escape, and called for the use of the sacred rod in making it possible. The cloudy pillar moved between Israel and the Egyptian army, blinding the Egyptians, stopping their progress for the night, and on the other hand, giving light to the Israelite camp. When Moses stretched out his hand, the Lord caused **a strong east wind** to blow all night long, literally blowing the waters of the Red

Sea's western arm off the area before Israel. Strong winds have been observed to do this in the same general region in modern times, and of course move vast quantities of water on lakes and oceans around the world. But the miracle was unquestionably there — in the prediction, in the timing, in the way the Lord used His power over nature to save His people and punish His enemies. Very early in the morning, the waters had been literally piled back and the Israelites saw a firm path awaiting them across what had shortly before been an impassible barrier. They were quick to take advantage of it. But as they passed through, the cloud lifted from between them and the Egyptians. The armed might of Egypt was not so easily to be escaped, and they dashed wildly after Israel. But the ground which had been firm enough for people and animals quickly became soft and mushy under the wheels of the chariots. The cloud apparently settled down in a very discomfiting manner again. And at the command of the Lord, Moses stretched out his hand once more, the wind died down, and the waters, no longer restrained, rushed back together with a force and velocity that buried forever the army that had dominated all that part of the world. Not one survived. As dawn broke and the dead bodies were washed up on the shore by the still-churning waters, Israel had its final reason for fearing Jehovah, for believing Him and His servant Moses.

d. The Celebration of Victory (15:1-21)

1 Then sang Moses and the children of Israel this song unto Jehovah, and spake, saying,
   I will sing unto Jehovah, for he hath triumphed gloriously:
   The horse and his rider hath he thrown into the sea.
2 Jehovah is my strength and song,
   And he is become my salvation:
   This is my God, and I will praise him;
   My father's God, and I will exalt him.
3 Jehovah is a man of war:
   Jehovah is his name.
4 Pharaoh's chariots and his host hath he cast into the sea;
   And his chosen captains are sunk in the Red Sea.

5 The deeps cover them:
   They went down into the depths like a stone.
6 Thy right hand, O Jehovah, is glorious in power.
   Thy right hand, O Jehovah, dasheth in pieces the enemy.
7 And in the greatness of thine excellency thou overthrowest them that rise up against thee:
   Thou sendest forth thy wrath, it consumeth them as stubble.
8 And with the blast of thy nostrils the waters were piled up,
   The floods stood upright as a heap;
   The deeps were congealed in the heart of the sea.
9 The enemy said,
   I will pursue, I will overtake, I will divide the spoil;
   My desire shall be satisfied upon them;
   I will draw my sword, my hand shall destroy them.
10 Thou didst blow with thy wind, the sea covered them:
   They sank as lead in the mighty waters.
11 Who is like unto thee, O Jehovah, among the gods?
   Who is like thee, glorious in holiness, Fearful in praises, doing wonders?
12 Thou stretchedst out thy right hand, The earth swallowed them.
13 Thou in thy lovingkindness hast led the people that thou hast redeemed:
   Thou hast guided them in thy strength to thy holy habitation.
14 The peoples have heard, they tremble:
   Pangs have taken hold on the inhabitants of Philistia.
15 Then were the chiefs of Edom dismayed;
   The mighty men of Moab, trembling taketh hold upon them:
   All the inhabitants of Canaan are melted away.
16 Terror and dread falleth upon them;
   By the greatness of thine arm they are as still as a stone;
   Till thy people pass over, O Jehovah,
   Till the people pass over that thou hast purchased.
17 Thou wilt bring them in, and plant them in the mountain of thine inheritance,
   The place, O Jehovah, which thou hast made for thee to dwell in,
   The sanctuary, O Lord, which thy hands have established.
18 Jehovah shall reign for ever and ever.
19 For the horses of Pharaoh went in with his chariots and with his horsemen into the sea, and Jehovah brought back

the waters of the sea upon them; but the children of Israel walked on dry land in the midst of the sea. 20 And Miriam the prophetess, the sister of Aaron, took a timbrel in her hand; and all the women went out after her with timbrels and with dances. 21 And Miriam answered them,

Sing ye to Jehovah, for he hath triumphed gloriously;
The horse and his rider hath he thrown into the sea.

Such a marvelous and glorious deliverance naturally called for a fitting celebration. Two songs are recorded as part of that celebration, the first known as the song of Moses, verses 1-18, and the second known as the song of Miriam, verse 21. The latter, while poetic in nature, is the short kind of verse which would spring quickly and easily out of such a situation. It is the kind of spontaneous chant which would be easily inspired by the occasion and which would lend itself to the sacred dance of the Israelite women, led by Miriam and her **timbrel,** either a tambourine or a small drum. The former song begins with the words of the briefer one. It is as beautiful a specimen of Hebrew poetry as will be found anywhere in the Bible. The imagery is outstanding; the highly anthropomorphic references to Jehovah's work of deliverance beautifully express the thankful praise of His people. It is possible that a man of genius such as Moses, inspired of the Lord, could compose such a work in a relatively short length of time, taking his cue from the song of Miriam, which was probably sung immediately. However, the second part of the song, verses 13-18, refers not to the deliverance at the Red Sea, but to subsequent deliverance in the wilderness journeys, to the fear of Israel felt by the nations in and around Canaan, of Israel's triumphal entry into Canaan, and finally of the establishment of the sanctuary on a mountain, apparently the temple in Jerusalem. This has caused some critical scholars to say that it could not have been composed before the time of Solomon, perhaps later.[88] Most evangelical scholars take the view that the second part is prophetic, Moses in his prophetic office adding to the present triumphs of Jehovah His prospective triumphs. Raw-linson understands it thus. He points out that the first part, verses 2-12, divides naturally into three parts, each beginning with an address to Jehovah and closing with a reference to the fate of the Egyptians. In verses 2-5, it runs from **Jehovah is my strength** to **They went down into the depths like a stone;** in 6-10, from **Thy right hand, O Jehovah** to **They sank as lead in the mighty waters;** in 11-12, from **Who is like unto thee, O Jehovah** to **The earth swallowed them.** He suggests that Moses and the men may have sung these various sections with Miriam and the women following in each case with their refrain, and then again at the end of the entire song.[89] While such prophetic revelation of God's future deliverances would certainly be no more difficult than many others recorded in the Old Testament, it should be observed that both sections of the song are written mostly as history. While the past tense is used in prophecy, it seems strange that no distinction is made. Perhaps the first half of the poem may have been composed immediately by Moses, the latter half by him at a date nearer Israel's entry into Canaan. Or the first half by him may have been added to in the days of the kings and the longer poem substituted here by a later editor or copyist.

II. THE DISCIPLINE OF ISRAEL (Exod. 15:22—40:38)

A. TRAINING THROUGH EXPERIENCE (15:22—18:27)

1. First Encounter with Thirst (15:22-27)

22 And Moses led Israel onward from the Red Sea, and they went out into the wilderness of Shur: and they went three days in the wilderness, and found no water. 23 And when they came to Marah, they could not drink of the waters of Marah, for they were bitter: therefore the name of it was called Marah. 24 And the people murmured against Moses, saying, What shall we drink? 25 And he cried unto Jehovah; and Jehovah showed him a tree, and he cast it into the waters, and the waters were made sweet. There he made for them a statute and an ordinance, and there he proved them; 26 and he said, If thou wilt diligently hearken to the voice of Jehovah thy God, and wilt do

that which is right in his eyes, and wilt give ear to his commandments, and keep all his statutes, I will put none of the diseases upon thee, which I have put upon the Egyptians: for I am Jehovah that healeth thee.

27 And they came to Elim, where were twelve springs of water, and threescore and ten palm-trees: and they encamped there by the waters.

The deliverance from Egypt was now complete. The mighty deeds of Jehovah had built up to a crescendo. Egypt was crippled economically and militarily. Israel was free. Now, just as so often happens, Israel turned from the mountain peak of a tremendous experience with God to the valley of difficulty and defeat. Immediately after crossing the shallow extension of the Gulf of Suez in the area of the present Bitter Lakes, they journeyed into **the wilderness of Shur. Shur** means "wall," and refers to the barrier ancient Egypt erected across its northeastern frontiers, similar to the ancient wall of China. The desert which bordered this wall on the east side became known as "the Desert of the Wall."[90] Here they encountered a quite natural problem — they could find **no water** in the desert. After three days' journey they came to **the waters of Marah,** a site identified convincingly by Finegan with a spring, Ain Hawarah, close by the Wadi 'Amarah, which apparently preserves the name Marah.[91] The waters, however, were bitter. And the people who so recently had praised Jehovah now were quick to murmur. The Lord directed Moses to correct the problem by casting a tree into the waters. Then He used the occasion to establish an agreement with Israel that if they would obey Him, He would never visit upon them **the diseases** of the Egyptians — probably not a reference to the plagues but to diseases which were peculiarly active among the inhabitants of Egypt. His healing of the waters had already identified Him as **Jehovah that healeth thee,** and He was promising to do so in a fuller and larger sense.

The next move was to **Elim,** a place of twelve springs and seventy palms. Finegan identifies this with the "pleasant oasis and very good water supply" at the Wadi

Gharandel, about one day's march from his location of the waters of Marah.[92] There was respite now from thirst.

2. Encounter with Hunger (16:1-36)

1 And they took their journey from Elim, and all the congregation of the children of Israel came unto the wilderness of Sin, which is between Elim and Sinai, on the fifteenth day of the second month after their departing out of the land of Egypt. 2 And the whole congregation of the children of Israel murmured against Moses and against Aaron in the wilderness: 3 and the children of Israel said unto them, Would that we had died by the hand of Jehovah in the land of Egypt, when we sat by the flesh-pots, when we did eat bread to the full; for ye have brought us forth into this wilderness, to kill this whole assembly with hunger.

4 Then said Jehovah unto Moses, Behold, I will rain bread from heaven for you; and the people shall go out and gather a day's portion every day, that I may prove them, whether they will walk in my law, or not. 5 And it shall come to pass on the sixth day, that they shall prepare that which they bring in, and it shall be twice as much as they gather daily. 6 And Moses and Aaron said unto all the children of Israel, At even, then ye shall know that Jehovah hath brought you out from the land of Egypt; 7 and in the morning, then ye shall see the glory of Jehovah; for that he heareth your murmurings against Jehovah: and what are we, that ye murmur against us? 8 And Moses said, *This shall be,* when Jehovah shall give you in the evening flesh to eat, and in the morning bread to the full; for that Jehovah heareth your murmurings which ye murmur against him: and what are we? your murmurings are not against us, but against Jehovah. 9 And Moses said unto Aaron, Say unto all the congregation of the children of Israel, Come near before Jehovah; for he hath heard your murmurings. 10 And it came to pass, as Aaron spake unto the whole congregation of the children of Israel, that they looked toward the wilderness, and, behold, the glory of Jehovah appeared in the cloud. 11 And Jehovah spake unto Moses, saying, 12 I have heard the murmurings of the children of Israel: speak unto them, saying, At even ye shall eat flesh, and in the morning ye shall be

[90] Unger, ed., "Shur," in *Unger's Bible Dictionary*, p. 1022.   [91] Finegan, *op. cit.*, p. 95.
[92] *Ibid.*

filled with bread; and ye shall know that I am Jehovah your God.

13 And it came to pass at even, that the quails came up, and covered the camp: and in the morning the dew lay round about the camp. 14 And when the dew that lay was gone up, behold, upon the face of the wilderness a small round thing, small as the hoar-frost on the ground. 15 And when the children of Israel saw it, they said one to another, What is it? for they knew not what it was. And Moses said unto them, It is the bread which Jehovah hath given you to eat. 16 This is the thing which Jehovah hath commanded. Gather ye of it every man according to his eating; an omer a head, according to the number of your persons, shall ye take it, every man for them that are in his tent. 17 And the children of Israel did so, and gathered some more, some less. 18 And when they measured it with an omer, he that gathered much had nothing over, and he that gathered little had no lack; they gathered every man according to his eating. 19 And Moses said unto them, Let no man leave of it till the morning. 20 Notwithstanding they hearkened not unto Moses; but some of them left of it until the morning, and it bred worms, and became foul: and Moses was wroth with them.

21 And they gathered it morning by morning, every man according to his eating: and when the sun waxed hot, it melted. 22 And it came to pass, that on the sixth day they gathered twice as much bread, two omers for each one: and all the rulers of the congregation came and told Moses. 23 And he said unto them, This is that which Jehovah hath spoken, To-morrow is a solemn rest, a holy sabbath unto Jehovah: bake that which ye will bake, and boil that which ye will boil; and all that remaineth over lay up for you to be kept until the morning. 24 And they laid it up till the morning, as Moses bade: and it did not become foul, neither was there any worm therein. 25 And Moses said, Eat that to-day; for to-day is a sabbath unto Jehovah: to-day ye shall not find it in the field. 26 Six days ye shall gather it; but on the seventh day is the sabbath, in it there shall be none. 27 And it came to pass on the seventh day, that there went out some of the people to gather, and they found none. 28 And Jehovah said unto Moses, How long refuse ye to keep my laws? 29 See, for that Jehovah hath given you the sabbath, therefore he giveth you on

the sixth day the bread of two days; abide ye every man in his place, let no man go out of his place on the seventh day. 30 So the people rested on the seventh day.

31 And the house of Israel called the name thereof Manna: and it was like coriander seed, white; and the taste of it was like wafers *made* with honey. 32 And Moses said, This is the thing which Jehovah hath commanded, Let an omerful of it be kept throughout your generations, that they may see the bread wherewith I fed you in the wilderness, when I brought you forth from the land of Egypt. 33 And Moses said unto Aaron, Take a pot, and put an omerful of manna therein, and lay it up before Jehovah, to be kept throughout your generations. 34 As Jehovah commanded Moses, so Aaron laid it up before the Testimony, to be kept. 35 And the children of Israel did eat the manna forty years, until they came to a land inhabited; they did eat the manna, until they came unto the borders of the land of Canaan. 36 Now an omer is the tenth part of an ephah.

After leaving **Elim,** Israel journeyed into **the wilderness of Sin.** In Numbers, where Moses wrote down a complete list of their stopping-places (Num. 33:1ff.), it is recorded that they went from Elim to the Red Sea and then to the wilderness of Sin. The spot at which they touched the Red Sea was south of their crossing, probably at or near Merkhah, where the Egyptians had a port as early as the fifteenth century B.C. — the probable century of the Exodus (see "Date" under "Introduction").[93] From here they turned inland, proceeding up one of the wadies or dry creek-beds to a large plain, Debbet er-Ramlah, which is frequently identified with the wilderness of Sin.[94] They arrived here exactly one month or exactly two months after leaving Egypt, depending upon how one understands **the second month after** — as referring to the second month of the new religious calendar or referring to the second month after their departure, which would be the third month on the calendar.

Here they encountered another quite normal problem for the desert — they began to run short of food. Despite the advance warning they had had of their departure, they had still been hurried out

[93] Pfeiffer, *op. cit.,* p. 54.   [94] *Ibid.;* and Finegan, *op. cit.,* p. 96.

of Egypt so fast that they had no time to prepare food for the journey (12:39). No doubt most of the families had some small stock of food. And milk was to be had from the flocks and the herds, and also some meat. But Israel had long since ceased to depend entirely or almost entirely upon their stock for their food supply. They had become partially adapted to agricultural ways even in the days of Isaac (Gen. 26:12) and Jacob (Gen. 30:14-16), were seriously handicapped when famine deprived them of their personal supply of grain in the days of Joseph (Gen. 42:1-2), and during their 430-year sojourn in Egypt had become quite dependent upon the produce of the ground (Num. 11:5). And if they had now started living entirely off their flocks and herds, these would soon have been depleted in spite of their numbers. So for the third time since they had left Egypt they began to murmur and complain, taking out their feelings on Moses and Aaron, their leaders and God's representatives. They were quick to forget their earlier cries for freedom and to exaggerate the physical comforts of Egypt.

The Lord's response to the people's murmuring continued to be a patient, mild one. Verses 4-12 record His instructions to Moses, and Moses and Aaron's transmission of them to Israel. Apparently some ancient scribe misplaced verses 9-12, the Lord's command to tell the people about His gift of flesh in the evening and of bread in the morning, otherwise Moses would have already told Israel this in verses 6-8 before the Lord told him. Driver would move verses 9-12 in front of verses 6-8,[95] but the present writer would place them before verse 4. This would afford a natural sequence for the entire passage. According to this arrangement of the verses, Moses first called Israel **before Jehovah** because of their murmurings (v. 9). This meeting may have been held before a primitive "tent of meeting," which seems to have been the center of worship prior to the construction of the tabernacle (33:7-11). It was held apparently at the edge of the encampment, where, as they watched, the Lord in some fashion manifested His glory in the cloud by which He had been guiding them (v. 10). Then the Lord

spoke to Moses, announcing that "between the evenings" they would eat flesh, and in the morning they would be filled with bread. This would be done for the same purpose that the plagues had been visited upon Egypt — **and ye shall know that I am Jehovah your God** (vv. 11-12). In addition, the Lord instructed Moses concerning the daily portion of manna which was to be collected and the double portion for weekends — instructions not pertinent yet for the public but to be used when the need arose (vv. 4-5). Then Moses and Aaron spoke to Israel, announcing that **at even** they would know Jehovah had brought them out of Egypt, for they would eat flesh, and **in the morning** they would see the glory of the Lord in an even more tangible way, for they would be eating bread to the full (vv. 6-8). Moses also rebuked their murmurings, explaining why the Lord must prove that He brought Israel out of Egypt. Israel had, in their murmurings, just blamed Moses and Aaron for bringing them out (v. 3). But neither their deliverance nor their problems could be blamed on human leaders. Complainings about divine leadership can never be leveled at God's appointed and directed leaders without really being aimed at God Himself.

True to God's promise, at even **quails came up, and covered the camp.** Quails migrate southward across the Mediterranean in September and October each year to winter in Arabia or Africa, and fly northward again in the spring. Since Israel arrived in the wilderness of Sin on about May 1 or June 1, the spring migrations could still have been crossing Sinai. When wearied by extended flight, the quail fly quite low or land and are easily caught.[96] Through His divine power, the Lord brought a large flock directly to Israel's camp. Since the quail were to provide only a "one-time special" addition to Israel's menu, not nearly as much is said concerning them as is said of the manna, which was to be a continuous addition to their diet.

The next morning, when the dew evaporated, a **small round** ("fine, flake-like," RSV) object lay upon the ground all around the camp, like frost crystals. It was discovered that it melted when the hot sun shone on it, that it became

[95] Driver, op. cit., p. 146.   [96] McNeile, op. cit., p. 97; Pfeiffer, op. cit., p. 55.

wormy and evil-smelling if kept too long, and that it could be baked or boiled. It was white like a coriander seed — a small, round seed of whitish or yellowish gray,[97] and tasted like wafers made with honey. An omer (variously defined by authorities as from three to six pints, by a plurality as four pints or two quarts) of it provided the average daily supplement needed in Israel's diet. In Numbers 11: 7-9, it is described as appearing like bdellium, a fragrant gum obtained from a tree in Arabia and other eastern countries, and yellowish gray in color. It is also said that the people "ground it in mills" and "beat it in mortars," "boiled it in pots, and made cakes of it." There it is described as having the taste of cakes baked with fresh oil. When the people saw it, they exclaimed, Man hu? or What is it? Moses explained that it was the bread Jehovah had promised to give them. He instructed them how much to gather. And when his instructions were followed, the man with a large family who had gathered much and the man with a small family who had gathered less, both discovered that it averaged out exactly right when divided up within their families. Moses instructed them not to try to save any of it. But as always, there were some people who could only learn from experience. They tried with unpleasant results, including the anger of Moses. On the sixth day they collected twice as much, so they would not have to gather on the Sabbath. And those who again contrary to Moses' instructions went out to seek it on the Sabbath found none.

Attempts have been made to find a natural explanation for the manna. Various insects sustain life by sucking the sap of plants and then produce sweet secretions. In Sinai, two kinds of scale-insects do this in relation to the tamarisk trees. The secretion forms large, transparent drops which dry and fall to the ground. During the night, when the ants cannot carry these off, they accumulate. They are composed of a rare sugar and are delightful as a candy. These secretions appear in the late spring and early summer at about the time Israel arrived in the wilderness of Sin.[98] Many scholars have sought to identify manna with these sweet secretions. There are many points of similarity, but there are also differences, chief of which are the ways in which the manna was used and the constant references by the Scriptures to it as a substitute for bread or grain.[99] The amount of manna needed would have far exceeded the capacity of the insects of Sinai! And its miraculous doubling on Friday and absence on Saturday, and its continuation not just for a few weeks in this area but for forty years throughout the entire peninsula remove it from the realm of the natural. The best that this present-day "parallel" can offer is a hint at how God may have modified and augmented a natural process in this miracle.

The Lord instructed Moses to preserve an omer, the standard daily individual portion, of the manna as a testimony to future generations of His providential care for His people. This was done, and Aaron laid it up before the Testimony, a reference to the tables of stone on which were written the Ten Commandments (34:28-29), and which were kept in the ark in the innermost sanctuary of the tabernacle (25:16). Since the instructions for constructing the tabernacle had not yet been given at the time manna was first given, this is probably a reference to action taken much later, after the tabernacle was erected and perhaps toward the end of the wilderness wanderings.

In Deuteronomy 8:3, 16-17, it is made clear that the gift of manna was intended to meet not only a physical need but also a spiritual. It was given to humble Israel, make it conscious of its daily dependence upon God's provision. And it pointed beyond itself to the truth "that man doth not live by bread only, but by everything that proceedeth out of the mouth of Jehovah doth man live." Even here in Exodus 16:4 the Lord indicated that it was given as a test of Israel's obedience (the second one since leaving Egypt, cf. 15:25), of their willingness to accept "trustfully and contentedly . . . this state of continued dependence."[100] His words instructing them to "gather

---

[97] Rawlinson, op. cit., II, 58.   [98] Finegan, op. cit., p. 99.
[99] For a complete summary of similarities and differences, see Driver, op. cit., pp. 153-54.
[100] Driver, op. cit., p. 154.

a day's portion every day" find an echo in the words of the Lord's Prayer, "Give us this day our daily bread" (Matt. 6:11). In I Corinthians 10:3, Paul called manna "spiritual food." In John 6:30ff., following the feeding of the five thousand, Jesus used the manna as a type of Himself, saying that He alone was "the bread of life," "the true bread out of heaven." Truly all that could be said in relationship to daily dependence upon God for manna or for food in general can be underscored in relationship to daily dependence upon God for the spiritual bread available through Christ.

An interesting sidelight appears in conjunction with the story of the manna. It is a reference to the Sabbath Day before the giving of the Ten Commandments (20:8-11). It is apparent that its observance did not begin at Sinai, but was probably as old as creation itself (Gen. 2:2-3). The week was known as early as the time of Jacob and Laban (Gen. 29:27-28). A similar pattern was followed in Babylonia earlier than the Exodus, with the seventh, fourteenth, twenty-first, and twenty-eighth days of each lunar month observed as sabbaths.[101] But while these called for physical rest, they were thought of as days of evil.[102] The Lord was now preparing His people for a higher and holier keeping of His day.

3. Second Encounter with Thirst (17:1-7)

1 And all the congregation of the children of Israel journeyed from the wilderness of Sin, by their journeys, according to the commandment of Jehovah, and encamped in Rephidim: and there was no water for the people to drink. 2 Wherefore the people strove with Moses, and said, Give us water that we may drink. And Moses said unto them, Why strive ye with me? wherefore do ye tempt Jehovah? 3 And the people thirsted there for water; and the people murmured against Moses, and said, Wherefore hast thou brought us up out of Egypt, to kill us and our children and our cattle with thirst? 4 And Moses cried unto Jehovah, saying, What shall I do unto this people? they are almost ready to stone me. 5 And Jehovah said unto Moses, Pass on be-

fore the people, and take with thee of the elders of Israel; and thy rod, wherewith thou smotest the river, take in thy hand, and go. 6 Behold, I will stand before thee there upon the rock in Horeb; and thou shalt smite the rock, and there shall come water out of it, that the people may drink. And Moses did so in the sight of the elders of Israel. 7 And he called the name of the place Massah, and Meribah, because of the striving of the children of Israel, and because they tempted Jehovah, saying, Is Jehovah among us, or not?

From the wilderness of Sin, Israel journeyed on by "stages," as the margin gives it. In Numbers 33:13-14, two intermediate stopping-points are mentioned before their arrival at **Rephidim**. The first was Dophkah, a name which may be derived from *mafqat,* the Egyptian word for turquoise. The Egyptians had copper and turquoise mines in the area identified by Finegan as the wilderness of Sin, although the mines may have been idle during this period. The second stop was at Alush, probably to be identified with Wadi el-'Eshsh, southeastward of the wilderness of Sin. Rephidim, the third stop, and the site of the next incident, may have been in Wadi Refajid at the foot of Jebel Refajid.[103]

In Rephidim, Israel encountered an old problem. There was no water to drink. At Marah, there had been bitter water which Jehovah had healed, but here there was none. So they demanded water of Moses. It is evident that their murmuring is growing more severe and Moses' patience shorter with each incident. But Jehovah is still quite patient. He told Moses to go to **the rock in Horeb,** where Jehovah would be standing, and to strike the rock and water would come out of it. (For the relationship of Horeb and Sinai, see comments on 3:1-12.) Moses did accordingly. Major C. S. Jarvis tells of a camel corps digging for water in this general area, and of how a hammer accidentally hit a rock and water came out of the rock. The explanation given is that underneath the polished, hard surface of limestone, there is soft, porous rock.[104] That water does gather in this porous rock seems certain, but only the

---

[101] Rawlinson, "Exodus," in *Ellicott's Commentary on the Whole Bible,* ed. by Charles John Ellicott, I, 247.   [102] Rylaarsdam, *op. cit.,* I, 954.   [103] Finegan, *op. cit.,* p. 96. [104] Pfeiffer, *op. cit.,* pp. 55-56.

Lord could have directed Moses to a deposit large enough to meet the needs of the children of Israel.

Moses commemorated this incident by naming the place **Massah** ("testing") and **Meribah** ("fault-finding").[105] The New Testament also draws from it a spiritual lesson, Paul declaring that they drank of "a spiritual rock" which was Christ. He refers to this rock as having followed them, thought by some to be evidence of his acceptance of a rabbinic tradition that the rock thenceforth followed Israel, providing their constant supply of water.[106] But since Moses had on still another occasion to strike water from a rock (Num. 20:2ff.), Paul may simply have been expressing his faith that Christ was always on hand to supply what was needed.

4. Encounter with Hostility (17:8-16)

8 Then came Amalek, and fought with Israel in Rephidim. 9 And Moses said unto Joshua, Choose us out men, and go out, fight with Amalek: to-morrow I will stand on the top of the hill with the rod of God in my hand. 10 So Joshua did as Moses had said to him, and fought with Amalek: and Moses, Aaron, and Hur went up to the top of the hill. 11 And it came to pass, when Moses held up his hand, that Israel prevailed; and when he let down his hand, Amalek prevailed. 12 But Moses' hands were heavy; and they took a stone, and put it under him, and he sat thereon; and Aaron and Hur stayed up his hands, the one on the one side, and the other on the other side; and his hands were steady until the going down of the sun. 13 And Joshua discomfited Amalek and his people with the edge of the sword. 14 And Jehovah said unto Moses, Write this for a memorial in a book, and rehearse it in the ears of Joshua: that I will utterly blot out the remembrance of Amalek from under heaven. 15 And Moses built an altar, and called the name of it Jehovah-nissi; 16 and he said, Jehovah hath sworn: Jehovah will have war with Amalek from generation to generation.

Perhaps as a judgment upon Israel for its murmurings,[107] the Lord permitted them to taste war for the first time. The Amalekites, descendants of Esau (Gen. 36:12), were nomads who lived in the desert southwest of Canaan. They had apparently wandered farther south than usual, and attacked the Israelite encampment. Joshua is introduced for the first time as an assistant to Moses, this time as the commander of the armed forces. He led the men into battle while Moses, sustained by Aaron and Hur (a Judahite, grandfather of Bezalel, craftsman of the tabernacle, 31:2), went up to the top of the hill to intercede with God in their behalf. Two pictures seem to blend here, the one being an adaptation by the Lord to the common belief of the day in defeating the enemy by oath and imprecation (such as that sought by Balak from Balaam, Num. 22:5-6),[108] and the other being a telling demonstration of the effectiveness of intercessory prayer. As long as Moses held up his hands, the one holding the rod of God, both in a curse upon Amalek and a prayer to Jehovah, Israel prevailed. But when he tired and ceased, Amalek prevailed. Finally Aaron and Hur seated Moses upon a rock and helped him hold aloft his hands until victory was final.

The result of Amalek's unprovoked attack upon Israel was a perpetual declaration of war by Jehovah upon Amalek. This He commanded Moses to write as **a memorial in a book,** or as the Hebrew gives it, "the book." This plainly implies that Moses was already writing a record of the experiences of God's people. It was also to be rehearsed in the ears of Joshua, whom the Lord was already grooming as Moses' successor. Moses built an altar to commemorate the event, calling it **Jehovah-nissi,** "The Lord is my banner." God's war with Amalek was almost completed by Saul (I Sam. 15), prosecuted by David (I Sam. 27:8-9; 30:1ff.), and apparently completed in the days of Hezekiah (I Chron. 4:39-43).

5. Encounter with Organizational Problems (18:1-27)

1 Now Jethro, the priest of Midian, Moses' father-in-law, heard of all that God had done for Moses, and for Israel his people, how that Jehovah had brought Israel out of Egypt. 2 And Jethro, Moses' father-in-law, took Zipporah, Moses' wife, after he had sent her away, 3 and her two

---

[105] Meek, *The Bible, an American Translation,* p. 67.   [106] Rylaarsdam, *op. cit.,* I, 959.
[107] Connell, *op. cit.,* p. 118.   [108] Rylaarsdam, *op. cit.,* I, 960.

sons; of whom the name of the one was Gershom; for he said, I have been a sojourner in a foreign land: 4 and the name of the other was Eliezer; for *he said,* The God of my father was my help, and delivered me from the sword of Pharaoh. 5 And Jethro, Moses' father-in-law, came with his sons and his wife unto Moses into the wilderness where he was encamped, at the mount of God: 6 and he said unto Moses, I, thy father-in-law Jethro, am come unto thee, and thy wife, and her two sons with her. 7 And Moses went out to meet his father-in-law, and did obeisance, and kissed him; and they asked each other of their welfare; and they came into the tent. 8 And Moses told his father-in-law all that Jehovah had done unto Pharaoh and to the Egyptians for Israel's sake, all the travail that had come upon them by the way, and how Jehovah delivered them. 9 And Jethro rejoiced for all the goodness which Jehovah had done to Israel, in that he had delivered them out of the hand of the Egyptians. 10 And Jethro said, Blessed be Jehovah, who hath delivered you out of the hand of the Egyptians, and out of the hand of Pharaoh; who hath delivered the people from under the hand of the Egyptians. 11 Now I know that Jehovah is greater than all gods; yea, in the thing wherein they dealt proudly against them. 12 And Jethro, Moses' father-in-law, took a burnt-offering and sacrifices for God: and Aaron came, and all the elders of Israel, to eat bread with Moses' father-in-law before God.

13 And it came to pass on the morrow, that Moses sat to judge the people: and the people stood about Moses from the morning unto the evening. 14 And when Moses' father-in-law saw all that he did to the people, he said, What is this thing that thou doest to the people? why sittest thou thyself alone, and all the people stand about thee from morning unto even? 15 And Moses said unto his father-in-law, Because the people come unto me to inquire of God: 16 when they have a matter, they come unto me; and I judge between a man and his neighbor, and I make them know the statutes of God, and his laws. 17 And Moses' father-in-law said unto him, The thing that thou doest is not good. 18 Thou wilt surely wear away, both thou, and this people that is with thee: for the thing is too heavy for thee; thou art not able to perform it thyself alone. 19 Hearken now unto my voice, I will give thee counsel, and God be with thee: be thou for the people to Godward, and bring thou the

causes unto God: 20 and thou shalt teach them the statutes and the laws, and shalt show them the way wherein they must walk, and the work that they must do. 21 Moreover thou shalt provide out of all the people able men, such as fear God, men of truth, hating unjust gain; and place such over them, to be rulers of thousands, rulers of hundreds, rulers of fifties, and rulers of tens: 22 and let them judge the people at all seasons: and it shall be, that every great matter they shall bring unto thee, but every small matter they shall judge themselves: so shall it be easier for thyself, and they shall bear *the burden* with thee. 23 If thou shalt do this thing, and God command thee so, then thou shalt be able to endure, and all this people also shall go to their place in peace. 24 So Moses hearkened to the voice of his father-in-law, and did all that he had said. 25 And Moses chose able men out of all Israel, and made them heads over the people, rulers of thousands, rulers of hundreds, rulers of fifties, and rulers of tens. 26 And they judged the people at all seasons: the hard causes they brought unto Moses, but every small matter they judged themselves. 27 And Moses let his father-in-law depart; and he went his way into his own land.

The last notice given of Moses' own wife and children was in 4:20, 24-26, where Zipporah was forced to circumcise one of her sons. We are now informed that Moses had subsequently sent them back to her paternal home. As Israel is approaching Sinai, Jethro, the father-in-law of Moses, comes to meet him, bringing them back to him, now that he has led the people safely out of Egypt. Jethro, also known as Reuel (2:18), was a priest of Midian. After a typically elaborate oriental greeting, Moses took him to his tent and related to him all that Jehovah had done for Israel. Jethro rejoiced at the account, blessed Jehovah, and declared that now he knew **that Jehovah is greater than all gods.** Then he presided over a sacrificial feast, attended by Moses, who was already with him, and by Aaron and the elders of Israel, who now joined them. This type of religious meal commonly occurred on a "high place."

A rectangular area on top of a natural rock was smoothed off. At one end a somewhat higher rock surface sometimes projected slightly into the rectangle: it represented the seat of the deity before whom the brotherhood gathered. Those who shared in the feast reclined along the sides and at the lower end of the rectangle. An altar on which certain parts of victims were burned, and at which libations were poured out, stood to one side of the rectangular place . . . A striking picture of such a meal is given in the account of the choice of Saul as king (cf. I Sam. 9:11-14).[109]

The animal was slain at the altar and only portions of it offered there for sacrifice. The remainder was consumed by the worshipers.

The appearance of Jethro at this juncture, just prior to the giving of the law, and in this manner, leading the leaders of Israel in worship, has led some critical scholars to propose the theory that it was from the Kenite clan of the Midianites that Israel adopted Jehovah as their God, and also received many other elements of their worship. But it is quite evident that it was Jethro who was changed, rather than Moses and Israel. He may, like Melchizedek, have been a priest of the true God under a different name (cf. Gen. 14:18-19); or, as also a descendant of Abraham (Gen. 25:1-6), some dim light about the true God may have reached down through the generations to him. Probably Moses had exerted some influence on him while in exile. It is significant that Moses told him nothing about Jehovah's appearance to him nor the mission on which he was sent when he asked permission to return to Egypt (Exod. 4:18). But now, having heard Moses' report of Jehovah's mighty deeds, he is convinced that He is not merely one god among others, but that He is greater than all others. And as evidence of his conversion to the worship of Jehovah, he officiates at the offering of a sacrifice at Moses' newly constructed altar, Jehovah-nissi (17:15).[110]

Jethro tarried with Moses for at least another day. And as he did so, he observed Moses, like a typical nomad "sheik," sitting as a judge over the people. Upon inquiry, Moses explained that he was serving both as the one who pro-

claimed the basis upon which judgments were rendered (inquiring of the Lord), and also as the one who decided their application in individual cases (making **them know the statutes of God, and his laws**). Jethro was quick to point out that this was a foolish course. There were far too many people for Moses to try to play "sheik" to all of them. He would exhaust himself, and the nation's morale would be destroyed because of long delays in the judicial procedure. He recommended that Moses specialize in determining the basis for judgments or inquiring of the Lord, in teaching the people God's laws, and in serving as a kind of supreme court to which hard cases could be brought. But he was to call into his service lower levels of judges, those serving ten families, those fifty, one hundred, and one thousand. They must be capable (**able men**), devout (**such as fear God**), devoted to justice (**men of truth**), and not responsive to bribes (**hating unjust gain**). Jethro implies that Moses is to submit this plan to God for His approval (v. 23). The record here is that Moses adopted his plan. In Deuteronomy 1:6ff., it is indicated that he did not implement the plan immediately, but rather after the law was given at Sinai and they were ready to depart for Canaan. In Numbers 10:33 —11:30, an account is given of their departure from Sinai, and of a murmuring after meat which soon followed. At that time Moses' patience was exhausted, and he asked the Lord to give him helpers. Seventy of the elders of Israel were set apart and the Spirit of God descended upon them, causing them to prophesy. It is quite possible that this marks the time when Moses implemented Jethro's plan in the way the Lord wanted it implemented. The seventy elders would compose the group or groups immediately under Moses. Lower levels of judges may not have been set aside in such a definite manner. It is also possible that the Numbers account records a second division of responsibility, the first marking Moses' sharing of the judicial function, the second his sharing of the oracular or prophetic function. In any event, the

---

[109] *Ibid.*, I, 966.
[110] The Kenite hypothesis has never received full acceptance even among critical scholars. For a summary of its strengths and weaknesses by a critical scholar who certainly does not fully accept it, see Rylaarsdam, *op. cit.*, I, 839-40.

Numbers account goes beyond anything Jethro proposed or foresaw.

Jethro did not stay with Moses, but departed for his homeland. Later, his son Hobab paid Moses a visit, and was urged to cast in his lot with Israel (Num. 10:29-32). While it is not clear whether he did, some of Jethro's descendants did dwell in Canaan among the Israelites (Judg. 1:16).

B. TRAINING THROUGH REVELATION — THE BOOK OF THE COVENANT (19:1–24:11)

1. The Preparation for the Covenant (19:1-25)

a. Introduction of the Covenant (19: 1-8)

1 In the third month after the children of Israel were gone forth out of the land of Egypt, the same day came they into the wilderness of Sinai. 2 And when they were departed from Rephidim, and were come to the wilderness of Sinai, they encamped in the wilderness; and there Israel encamped before the mount. 3 And Moses went up unto God, and Jehovah called unto him out of the mountain, saying, Thus shalt thou say to the house of Jacob, and tell the children of Israel: 4 Ye have seen what I did unto the Egyptians, and how I bare you on eagles' wings, and brought you unto myself. 5 Now therefore, if ye will obey my voice indeed, and keep my covenant, then ye shall be mine own possession from among all peoples: for all the earth is mine: 6 and ye shall be unto me a kingdom of priests, and a holy nation. These are the words which thou shalt speak unto the children of Israel. 7 And Moses came and called for the elders of the people, and set before them all these words which Jehovah commanded him. 8 And all the people answered together, and said, All that Jehovah hath spoken we will do. And Moses reported the words of the people unto Jehovah.

The children of Israel had only one stage of their journey to go when they left Rephidim. They arrived at Sinai **in the third month** after their departure from Egypt. As noted in connection with

16:1, this could be interpreted either as the third month of the year which started just before the Exodus, or the third month **after** the first month. However, the word **month** can also be translated "new moon," and the following words, **the same day,** have led some scholars to translate it, "On the third new moon" (RSV). This would then be the first day of either the third or the fourth month of the religious year. Later Jewish tradition declared that the Feast of Pentecost, celebrated on the sixth day of the third month, commemorated the giving of the Ten Commandments.[111] This would, of course, support their arrival on the new moon of the third month.

Their destination had been reached. But there has not been unanimity of opinion about its location. The identification of the various camping-sites followed by the present writer leads us to the southern part of the Sinai Peninsula, where tradition has always located the mountain of divine revelation. Since the fourth century A.D., a particular mountain, Jebel Musa (Mountain of Moses), has been identified as the one on which the law was given. It stands on the southeast of a wide valley called er-Raha, two miles long and one-third to two-thirds of a mile wide, which would have provided an ideal camping-site. On the northwest is another mountain, Ras es-Safsaf, even closer to the plain, and on the southwest, a higher mountain, Jebel Katarin. All three of the mountains, as well as others in the general area, have been suggested as Mt. Sinai.[112] Most conservative and some critical scholars have accepted this area as the correct one. But two other schools of thought have developed, one suggesting that Mt. Sinai was in Midian proper, clear over on the east side of the Gulf of Aqabah, where there are volcanic mountains which could give a natural setting for the quaking, flaming, smoking summit seen by Israel, and the other, with somewhat more of a biblical foundation, proposing a site near the head of the Gulf of Aqabah.[113] The traditional appears to be the most likely. In any event, here they were and here they were to stay for nearly a year,

---

[111] Johnson, *op. cit.,* p. 67; Unger, ed., "Festivals," in *Unger's Bible Dictionary,* p. 356.
[112] Pfeiffer, *op. cit.,* pp. 56-7.
[113] For a comprehensive summary of the strengths and weaknesses of all three theories, see Rylaarsdam, *op. cit.,* I, 836-37.

while the events recorded in the rest of Exodus, all of Leviticus, and the early chapters of Numbers transpired (Num. 10:11ff.).

Moses had no doubt looked forward eagerly to returning with Israel to the mountain where God had appeared to him in the burning bush. And he did not tarry long before climbing up into the mountain. He was not disappointed, for **Jehovah called unto him,** commanding him to call the attention of Israel to what He had done: (1) His judgments upon the Egyptians, (2) His sure and loving care for Israel, bearing them on **eagles' wings** (the Hebrew refers to the griffon-vulture, a large and majestic bird abundant in Palestine[114]), and (3) His bringing of Israel unto Himself. Now He proposed a **covenant** between Himself and Israel. *Berith,* the Hebrew word for **covenant,** is one of the great words of the Bible. There were two kinds of compacts or agreements covered by the word, that which was established between equals, and that which was established between a superior and an inferior — a king and his subjects, or a master and his servant.[115] The covenant Jehovah proposed was, of course, of the latter type. It was typical of such a covenant that the stronger party made a promise or gift, which was the heart of the agreement, but which was conditioned upon obligations to be fulfilled by the weaker parties. The Lord proposed here to make Israel His **own possession.** This did not involve the exclusion of other peoples, for all the earth is Jehovah's. But it did involve their separation **from among all peoples** in order that they might serve the Lord as **a kingdom of priests** and as **a holy nation** — an entire people consecrated to the service of God, to serving as mediators between Jehovah and all other nations. What Jehovah was proposing was the granting of the highest and most blessed of privileges which was at the same time the most solemn of responsibilities, the whole to be evidenced in the observance of the covenant or law which He was about to reveal. The missionary implications of the divine plan must not be overlooked. The salvation of the whole human race has always been God's ultimate objective, and to this end and purpose He called first the Jewish Church and later the Christian Church.[116]

It is interesting to observe the importance of **the words** which Jehovah spoke to Moses. Before Moses returned to Israel, He stressed that **These are the words which thou shalt speak.** When Moses reached the people, he **set before them all these words,** just as a man would arrange objects on a table before the eyes of his audience (cf. KJV). When the people added their preliminary consent to the establishment of a covenant, Moses **reported,** or as the Hebrew says, "caused to return," or "brought back," their words to Jehovah, just like a man would carry a precious burden. For the Hebrews, a word is a very concrete thing. It does not vanish on the sound waves, but it is permanent and powerful. This underscores the importance of Jehovah's words, the care with which they were preserved, and the reliability of our Scriptures which have come down to us.

b. Readiness for the Covenant (19:9-15)

9 And Jehovah said unto Moses, Lo, I come unto thee in a thick cloud, that the people may hear when I speak with thee, and may also believe thee for ever. And Moses told the words of the people unto Jehovah. 10 And Jehovah said unto Moses, Go unto the people, and sanctify them to-day and to-morrow, and let them wash their garments, 11 and be ready against the third day; for the third day Jehovah will come down in the sight of all the people upon mount Sinai. 12 And thou shalt set bounds unto the people round about, saying, Take heed to yourselves, that ye go not up into the mount, or touch the border of it: whosoever toucheth the mount shall be surely put to death: 13 no hand shall touch him, but he shall surely be stoned, or shot through; whether it be beast or man, he shall not live: when the trumpet soundeth long, they shall come up to the mount. 14 And Moses went down from the mount unto the people, and sanctified the people; and they washed their garments. 15 And he said unto the people, Be ready against the third day: come not near a woman.

---

[114] Driver, *op. cit.,* p. 170.   [115] Rylaarsdam, *op. cit.,* I, 841.
[116] This position has been fully developed in the work of the Dutch scholar, Johannes Blauw, *The Missionary Nature of the Church.*

After the Lord and the people had both expressed their willingness to enter into a covenant relationship, the Lord instructed Moses to prepare the people for a meeting of the parties of the covenant. He was going to appear before Israel in a thick cloud in order that the people might hear Him speaking to Moses and might gain permanent confidence in Moses as Jehovah's spokesman. But before the encounter could take place, the people must be adequately prepared. According to the instructions given by the Lord to Moses and their application by Moses to the people, this preparation consisted of four steps: (1) a sanctifying of themselves — apparently a ceremonial washing of their own bodies, (2) a washing also of their clothes, (3) abstention for three days from sexual relations (this appears to have been standard procedure in the Old Testament as preparation for close contact with Jehovah or His sacred things, I Sam. 21:4-6, and may also have been observed in New Testament times, at least by Jewish Christians, I Cor. 7:5), and (4) the placing of **bounds** or a fence around the mountain that no one might touch it. If the latter regulation was violated, the offending party was to **be stoned, or shot through** on the spot. No one was to go after him to bring him back, nor to touch him.

It is by means of these preparations that we are introduced for the first time in the Bible to the primitive meaning of *holiness.* The Hebrew *qadash* is the root of the noun meaning "holiness," the adjective "holy," and the verb "sanctify" or "make holy." Prior to the experience of Moses at the burning bush (3:5), there is only one use of any of these words in the Bible, that of "sanctified" (KJV), or "hallowed," in conjunction with God's original establishment of the Sabbath (Gen. 2:3). Prior to Exodus 19, there are only five other uses of "holy" (*holy ground,* 3:5; *holy convocation* used twice with reference to the opening and closing days of the Feast of Unleavened Bread, 12:16; *holy habitation* used in the song of Moses either of Canaan or the Jerusalem temple, 15:13; and *holy sabbath* in the instructions about collecting manna,

16:23), and one other use of "sanctify" (in relation to the first-born, 13:2). But now in this one chapter we find "holy" once and "sanctify" four times. And the setting is such as to make clear what the basic concept is.

The first reference is to a holy nation. This is at the end of a whole series of phrases in which God is proposing to separate Israel from all other nations to a peculiar relationship to Himself. The other references to **sanctify** all have to do with their preparing themselves or their environment for this separateness — in effect, setting themselves apart unto God, separating themselves from all things common or unhallowed. In the case of the sanctifying of the mountain (cf. vv. 12, 23), the sanctifying is closely involved with fencing it off and forbidding anyone to touch it. The basic meaning of the Hebrew root is "separateness," and this is apparent in its use here.[117] Later God Himself is spoken of as holy, and His holiness is made the basis for requiring other persons and things related to Him to be holy (Lev. 11:44-45; 19:2). As one reads the Old Testament, it becomes clear, as H. Orton Wiley has pointed out, that holiness is of the essence of the divine nature.

> It is characteristic of personality to mark itself off as separate and distinct from all other existences, personal or otherwise, in what is commonly known as self-grasp or self-affirmation. . . . If, then, we view the ethical nature of God from this standpoint of self-grasp or self-affirmation, we have the concept of divine holiness.[118]

James F. Gregory carries the explanation even farther.

> This separateness of God is more than simply the distinctiveness of His personality: it is a distant separation. He and all who in any way understand Him know that there is a dividing line between Him and all other things and persons lumped together. It is even more than a line; it is a gulf, and a great one. There is a difference as to nature — God is the uncreated one, all else is created; God is the unlimited one, all else is timebound. Thus the scriptures declare Him to be the incomparable one (Isa. 40:25), the unapproachable one (I Sam. 6:20), the one in utter contrast to man

---

[117] Girdlestone, *op. cit.,* pp. 175ff.   [118] H. Orton Wiley, *Christian Theology,* I, 366-67.

(Hos. 11:9), the exalted and sublime one (Isa. 57:15).[119]

It is evident that this holiness of God can be communicated to other persons and to things. God is separated from all else. But He can call His creatures across the gulf to be closer to Him or even with Him, separating them from common or profane activities and reserving them entirely for Himself. He can thus sanctify the Sabbath, the ground on which is a bush burning with His holy fire, even the nation He chooses for a universal mission. In fact, direct contact between this holy God and any person or thing always changes the creature — hallowing for God's service that which can be fitted for His use, destroying that which can not or will not be thus fitted. It is also evident that there are degrees of this sanctification or being set apart to God, for Moses and Aaron may ascend the mountain to God's very presence, the priests may approach the altar but not climb the mountain, and the people while sanctified cannot even touch the mountain but only see the cloud and hear the voice. Holiness, whatever its degree, is initially a matter of relationship or position.

As the children of Israel came to understand this separate holiness of God, they quickly recognized that an important part of this separateness was His utter contradiction of everything wicked, sinful, or immoral (Josh. 24:19). Sin was rebellion against His will and contrary to His very character, and naturally He was, if anything, more distinctly separate from it than anything else. So if a person was to be separated unto God, to be sanctified, he must not only be ceremonially cleansed from his unhallowed state, but also morally and spiritually cleansed from his sinful state. This conception of holiness and sanctification looms especially large in the New Testament, and becomes the basis for the doctrine of entire sanctification preached by John Wesley and his followers. Even here, the concept of separateness is basic and must always loom large in the experience and practice of holiness. Insofar as man separates, it is consecration, and insofar as God completes the separation, it is sanctification — separation from sin, from self, from the world, from everything unlike God, to righteousness, to God's service, to heaven, to the very nature of God Himself.

c. Setting of the Covenant (19:16-25)

16 And it came to pass on the third day, when it was morning, that there were thunders and lightnings, and a thick cloud upon the mount, and the voice of a trumpet exceeding loud; and all the people that were in the camp trembled. 17 And Moses brought forth the people out of the camp to meet God; and they stood at the nether part of the mount. 18 And mount Sinai, the whole of it, smoked, because Jehovah descended upon it in fire; and the smoke thereof ascended as the smoke of a furnace, and the whole mount quaked greatly. 19 And when the voice of the trumpet waxed louder and louder, Moses spake, and God answered him by a voice. 20 And Jehovah came down upon mount Sinai, to the top of the mount; and Jehovah called Moses to the top of the mount: and Moses went up. 21 And Jehovah said unto Moses, Go down, charge the people, lest they break through unto Jehovah to gaze, and many of them perish. 22 And let the priests also, that come near to Jehovah, sanctify themselves, lest Jehovah break forth upon them. 23 And Moses said unto Jehovah, The people cannot come up to mount Sinai: for thou didst charge us, saying, Set bounds upon the mount, and sanctify it. 24 And Jehovah said unto him, Go, get thee down; and thou shalt come up, thou, and Aaron with thee: but let not the priests and the people break through to come up unto Jehovah, lest he break forth upon them. 25 So Moses went down unto the people, and told them.

When the period of preparation was complete, the camp of Israel awoke to some awe-inspiring sights and sounds. **Thunders and lightnings, and a thick cloud** crowned the mountain, and there was the exceedingly loud blast of a **trumpet,** the appointed signal to gather, but apparently not blown by human lips. Now **fire** and **smoke** appeared upon the mountain, and it **quaked greatly.** Some have attempted to explain these phenomena in terms of thunderstorm activity or earthquake and volcano. While God could have used such natural forces to reveal His presence, the record seems to

---

[119] James F. Gregory, "The Holiness of God," in *Entire Sanctification: Studies in Christian Holiness,* "Aldersgate Doctrinal Studies," ed. by Paul L. Kindschi, Lee Haines, *et al.,* pp. 13-14.

indicate something more unusual than this. The people were impressed, to the point of trembling, that God was truly meeting with them.

As the trumpet sounded louder and louder, Moses called out to the Lord, and Jehovah called him to the top of the mountain. But despite the elaborate preparations to observe the sanctity of the mountain, the Lord was not yet satisfied. He insisted that Moses go back to the people and stress the importance of staying in their appointed places. The person who violated Jehovah's command and invaded the holy precincts — upon him Jehovah would **break forth**. If the violator escaped the hand of human punishment (vv. 12-13), he would not escape the hand of divine judgment.

2. The Establishment of the Covenant (20:1—24:11)

a. The Principles of the Covenant — The Ten Commandments (20: 1-17)

1 And God spake all these words, saying,

2 I am Jehovah thy God, who brought thee out of the land of Egypt, out of the house of bondage.

3 Thou shalt have no other gods before me.

4 Thou shalt not make unto thee a graven image, nor any likeness *of any thing* that is in heaven above, or that is in the earth beneath, or that is in the water under the earth: 5 thou shalt not bow down thyself unto them, nor serve them; for I Jehovah thy God am a jealous God, visiting the iniquity of the fathers upon the children, upon the third and upon the fourth generation of them that hate me, 6 and showing lovingkindness unto thousands of them that love me and keep my commandments.

7 Thou shalt not take the name of Jehovah thy God in vain; for Jehovah will not hold him guiltless that taketh his name in vain.

8 Remember the sabbath day, to keep it holy. 9 Six days shalt thou labor, and do all thy work; 10 but the seventh day is a sabbath unto Jehovah thy God: *in it* thou shalt not do any work, thou, nor thy son, nor thy daughter, thy man-servant, nor thy maid-servant, nor thy cattle, nor thy stranger that is within thy gates: 11 for in six days Jehovah made heaven and earth, the sea, and all that in them is, and rested the seventh

day: wherefore Jehovah blessed the sabbath day, and hallowed it.

12 Honor thy father and thy mother, that thy days may be long in the land which Jehovah thy God giveth thee.

13 Thou shalt not kill.

14 Thou shalt not commit adultery.

15 Thou shalt not steal.

16 Thou shalt not bear false witness against thy neighbor.

17 Thou shalt not covet thy neighbor's house, thou shalt not covet thy neighbor's wife, nor his man-servant, nor his maid-servant, nor his ox, nor his ass, nor anything that is thy neighbor's.

The moment had arrived for which all preceding events had prepared Israel. God was now to reveal His law, by which they were to relate themselves to Him and by which they were to order their lives. The first part occupies most of chapters 20-23, and is called "the book of the covenant" (24:7) since it sets forth the basis of the agreement between Jehovah and Israel. Many scholars mark 20:22 as the beginning of the Book of the Covenant, thus omitting the Ten Commandments. However 20:1 begins the recounting of the Ten Commandments by reference to **these words** and 21:1 begins the central portion of the remainder by reference to "these . . . ordinances." In 34:28b, "the words of the covenant" are identified as "the ten commandments," or as the Hebrew literally says, "the ten words." In 24:3 it is said that Moses told the people "all the words" and "all the ordinances," and in 24:4 that he wrote "all the words" in what must have been called immediately after the Book of the Covenant. Thus it is apparent that the Ten Commandments were in the Book of the Covenant, and it is probable that the ordinances were also included.

In the early days of biblical criticism, it was commonly taught that Moses, even if such a person really existed, could not have written the law. For one thing, it was thought that writing was not yet known among the Hebrews, and for another, that ancient legal codes of this complexity were unknown at this date. But these contentions have had to be abandoned. Writing is now known to date from at least 2000 years before the time of Moses, both in Mesopotamia and in Egypt, the two great civilizations which provide most of the background for the early history of the chosen people. And ancient legal codes centuries older than Moses have been discovered. These include one from Abraham's native city of Ur, dating from about his period, 2050 B.C.; one from Eshnunna, a century and a half later; a Sumerian Code of about the same time; and the most famous of them all, that of Hammurabi of Babylon, who reigned approximately 1728-1686 B.C. There is even a similarity in the form of the laws in these codes and some of those in the Old Testament, especially those in Exodus 21:1 − 22:17.[120] But the differences are as marked as the similarities, precluding any mere borrowing from the older ones. As a result of these discoveries, and of additional study of the Old Testament itself, many critical scholars now admit the probability that Moses was the human instrument by which the covenant was established and that he or his scribes wrote down at least a part of what we now have as the law. By some this probability is extended to include at least the core of the Ten Commandments.[121] Thus again critical scholarship is being forced back ever closer to the evangelical position on the origin and authority of the Mosaic law.

In giving the law, the Lord began with a listing of principles, which are entirely different from anything else found in the other ancient legal codes. These principles have had an immeasurable effect on the history of mankind, not only among the descendants of Jacob but also among all Christian groups and even beyond. These principles we call the Ten Commandments (see 34:28b). They are given again, with only slight variation

in explanation and application, when Moses gives his farewell instructions at the borders of Canaan (Deut. 5:7-21). Some scholars claim to find another set of ten commandments or decalogue in Exodus 34:12-26. Because of its different composition and emphasis, it is frequently called "the ritual decalogue." (But see comments on that passage.) The Ten Commandments are not laws in the sense that a human court can enforce them. They are divine laws which can only be implemented by additional legislation such as that which follows them in the Book of the Covenant. They were set apart from all the rest of the law not only by their nature, but also by the manner in which they were given. For all the rest of the law, Moses was the go-between, the one to whom God spoke and the one who relayed the divine communication to the people. But for the Ten Commandments, God spoke directly to the people out of the fire which burned upon the mountain without consuming it, much as the burning bush which first drew Moses to the divine presence. (See 19:9; 20:1, 18-22; Deut. 4:36; 5:4, 22-31.)

Surprisingly enough, there has not been unanimity in identifying the individual commandments of the Ten. Modern Jewish expositors find the first one in what Christian scholars see as an introductory statement, and combine what Orthodox and non-Lutheran Protestant Christians call the first and second as their second. Catholics and Lutherans also make this combination, calling it the first commandment, and dividing the prohibition of coveting into two commandments. The various lists compare as follows.

	Jews	Cath.-Luth.	Orth. and non-Lutheran Prot.
1st	20:2	20:3-6	20:3
2nd	20:3-6	20:7	20:4-6
3rd	20:7	20:8-11	20:7
4th	20:8-11	20:12	20:8-11
5th	20:12	20:13	20:12
6th	20:13	20:14	20:13
7th	20:14	20:15	20:14
8th	20:15	20:16	20:15
9th	20:16	20:17b (Deut. 5:21a)	20:16
10th	20:17	20:17ac (Deut. 5:21b)	20:17

[120] Finegan, *op. cit.*, pp. 118-20.   [121] Rylaarsdam, *op. cit.*, I, 842.

The Orthodox and non-Lutheran Protestant classification follows the earliest one known, dating from at least as far back as Josephus.[122]

The Ten Commandments individually reveal a fascinating variety of form and subject matter. Three of them consist of two words each in the Hebrew, the first word in each case being the negative **not** or "no." They graphically declare: No murder! No adultery! No stealing! Two other commandments (the first and the ninth) consist of only one brief sentence each. The other five begin as briefly but are completed by specific applications, explanations, or promises. This has led to the supposition that all ten were originally given in the shorter form, and that everything additional is Moses' inspired commentary on the five he felt needed elucidation.[123] This finds support in their being called "the ten words" (original of 34:28b), and in the fact that when Moses repeated the commandments some thirty-eight years or so later, in a somewhat different context and when the nation was facing different challenges, the additional material is somewhat different (Deut. 5:7-21). Eight of the commandments are prohibitions, only two are positive. These are the fourth and the fifth, the one ending the list of man's duties toward God, the other beginning the list of man's duties toward his fellows.

The Ten Commandments are commonly divided into the two groups, the first through the fourth providing a vertical standard or our duties toward God, the fifth through the tenth providing a horizontal standard, or our duties toward man. Jesus summarized the first four in what He called "the great and first commandment," and the last six in "a second like unto it." Upon the love of God and the love of neighbor He hung "the whole law" and "the prophets" (Matt. 22:34-40). The duties to men have been subdivided by some into commandments directed against mean deeds (the sixth through the eighth), that against mean words (the ninth), and that against mean thoughts (the tenth).[124] Another division, suggested by Martin Buber, sees the first part as dealing with the God of the spiritual community (the first through the third commandments, prohibiting idol-worship, image-worship, and magic-worship), the second part as dealing with time or "the one-after-the-other" of the community (the fourth and fifth commandments), and the third part as dealing with space or "the with-one-another" of the community (the sixth through the tenth commandments).[125]

In spite of the traditionally high regard given to the Ten Commandments by men of every age, culture, and creed, there are still some who would say that they are antiquated and are no longer pertinent either to Christianity or to the twentieth century. This attitude is pointedly illustrated by a story told by Clovis G. Chappell.

> There is the story of a certain master and slave who years ago went deep-sea fishing. When they were making their way back to shore late in the night, the master became sleepy and turned the helm over to his faithful servant, Mose. Before doing this, however, he pointed out the north star to Mose and urged him to keep his eye on it. But the master had not been asleep very long before Mose snatched forty winks himself. When he awakened he was in utter confusion. He called his master frantically. "Wake up!" he said, "and show me another star. I've done run clean past that one!"[126]

But the Ten Commandments are one constellation past which we will never sail! Their eternal significance and pertinence are self-evident. And if there were ever any doubt, Jesus and his followers who have provided us with the New Testament have silenced it for ever. Each of the Ten Commandments is reaffirmed in the New Testament, as we shall see in treating them individually. In fact, Jesus declared in the Sermon on the Mount that He "came not to destroy" the law, "but to fulfil" it (Matt. 5:17). And that very Sermon on the Mount, which holds much the same place in the new covenant as the Ten Commandments held in the old, makes wide use of the Ten Commandments, making their appli-

---

[122] Johnson, *op. cit.*, p. 69.   [123] Connell, *op. cit.*, p. 120.

[124] J. Edgar Park, "Exodus" (Exposition), in *The Interpreter's Bible*, ed. by George Arthur Buttrick, I, 980.   [125] Martin Buber, *Moses*, pp. 131-34.   [126] Clovis G. Chappell, *Ten Rules for Living*, p. 12.

cation even clearer and stricter in reference to the Kingdom of God.[127]

Thou shalt have no other gods before me. The word **before** does not here carry the idea of order of preference, for this is not a commandment to give Jehovah first place among many gods. **Before me** is literally "before my face," and carries the idea of "in addition to me," or as the margin gives it, "besides me." Jehovah who brought them out of Egypt was to be worshiped exclusively. Some have questioned whether this actually teaches monotheism (the belief in only one God) or instead teaches only monolatry (the worship of only one God even though others may be recognized as existing). Monotheism was virtually unknown in the ancient world, and was in fact at complete variance with all prevailing religious systems. The only moves in this direction among the ancient Egyptians had quickly died. Moses could have believed it and taught it only by setting himself against the beliefs of all the rest of mankind.[128] But it was the natural conclusion of the religious experiences of the patriarchs and Moses' own experiences. He had taught in Egypt that Jehovah was superior to all other gods, saying "there is none like unto Jehovah" (8:10; 9:14). And before the wilderness wanderings were ended, he would declare that He was the only God, saying "there is none else beside him" (Deut. 4:35, 39). Certainly the First Commandment is also a declaration of the unity of God, the strongest and clearest up to this time. That it finds reaffirmation in the New Testament needs not to be proven. In Mark's account of Jesus' pronouncement concerning the greatest commandment, the unity of God and the priority He holds to our reverence and worship are clearly stated (Mark 12:29-30).

Thou shalt not make unto thee a graven image. The prohibition of idols was to include any representation of things **in heaven, in the earth,** or **under the earth.** How soon idols came into use after the fall of Adam or again after the flood is not known. But they are accurately depicted by St. Paul as the result of man's ignorance of and substitution for the true God (Rom. 1:23). They assumed many forms — animal, human, monstrous. In Egypt, from which Israel had so recently departed, all the gods were so represented, as they were also in Mesopotamia and in Canaan. Their worship involved some of the most immoral and loathsome activities ever devised by man. Idolatry had a natural tendency in such a direction and such degradation was also a divine punishment for idolatry (Rom. 1:24ff.). That which was specifically forbidden in the Second Commandment was the use of **graven** or sculptured images. But the word used here also came to refer to all idols. Molten images are also specifically forbidden in verse 23 and in 34:17. There is some evidence that Israel was slow to abide by this rule, for they certainly used images in the worship of Baal and other heathen gods clear down to the time of the exile, and they possibly also used images as an aid in the worship of Jehovah.[129] But it is also important to note that this is not a prohibition of art in general. While there appears to be no reference in the Scriptures to painting, and while the ancient Jews were very cautious about any kind of reproduction, sculpture in its various types was used by divine command both in the tabernacle and the temple (25:18-20; I Kings 6:18, 23-29, 32-35; 7:13-39). What were forbidden were images which men would **bow down** to or **serve** — "religious images, or *worship-related* images."[130] This commandment has especially seemed outdated to many. It was still quite pertinent in New Testament times (see I Cor. 10:14, 20; I John 5:21; Rev. 21:8). And it certainly applies to many modern mission fields, and to those segments of Christianity so infested by paganism that images are used as an aid in worship. Elton Trueblood well remarks that there are more references to this commandment in the Bible than to any of the others, which should be an indication of its great and lasting importance. He points out that it was emphasized to counteract the danger of easy tolerance which constantly tended to produce a syn-

---

[127] For a fascinating analysis of the relationship of the Ten Commandments to the Sermon on the Mount in chart form, see Park, *op. cit.*, I, 989.

[128] For an outstanding treatment of "Moses and Monotheism," see Finegan, *op. cit.*, pp. 101-16.

[129] For a full summary of the evidence, see Rylaarsdam, *op. cit.*, I, 981-82.

[130] James Burton Coffman, *The Ten Commandments, Yesterday and Today*, p. 31.

cretistic worship, incorporating pagan ideas and rituals in the worship of Jehovah.[131] This is certainly a live danger in the present age when some say we are living in a "post-Christian" age, and call for a synthesis of Christian thought with the best to be found in other world religions. It is well also to remember that secularism and materialism can also provide us ready-made idols, for covetousness itself is idolatry (Col. 3:5). The Second Commandment has a timeless message in its insistence on the invisibility, the immateriality, and the spirituality of God.[132]

Thou shalt not take the name of Jehovah thy God in vain. Take is literally "lift" or "carry," and is here used in the sense of "utter." Vain is literally "emptiness," "nothingness," or "unreality." Thus the Third Commandment prohibits the use of the name of Jehovah in any way that falls short of His own reality and truthfulness. It is probable that initially this was aimed at the use of the divine name in false testimony, and also at the use of His name in such an appeal to unreality as the practice of magic. As we have already noted in connection with Genesis 32:22-32, names were far more significant in Old Testament times than they are in our age. The name of Jehovah in a very concrete fashion conveyed something of the character of God. The name was highly revered by the ancient Jews,[133] even to the point that they came not to pronounce it even in the reading of the Scriptures in public worship. They substituted the word *Adonai*, which means "lord" or "master," and may be applied to men as well as God. Thus anything which did not manifest reverence for the name was a violation of the law of God. In addition to perjury and incantation, this would include common profanity, the frivolous use of the name, hypocrisy (the taking of the name upon oneself to designate a relationship which is not real), and the presumptuous use of the name (the claim to do things in the name of God without His authority and blessing).[134] In the New Testament, Jesus not only reaffirmed this commandment in His

model prayer, "Hallowed be thy name" (Matt. 6:9), but He intensified it to the point of prohibiting all oaths, not only those using the name of God, but those referring to heaven (His throne) or to earth (His footstool), or even those referring to one of His creatures (Matt. 5: 33-37). In fact, He extended the demands of holiness to man's total speech, insisting that words reveal the true character of the heart to the point that "by thy words thou shalt be justified, and by thy words thou shalt be condemned" (Matt. 12:34b-37).

Remember the sabbath day, to keep it holy. The principle of six units of labor and one of rest had been followed by Jehovah Himself in the creation of the universe (Gen. 2:2-3). The week itself as a unit of time had been known at least as early as the days of Jacob and Laban (Gen. 29:27-28; see also comments on Exod. 16:1-36). But the first commandment to observe the day had been given to Israel just a short time prior to their arrival at Sinai (Exod. 16:22-30). The principle was later extended to sabbatical years as well (23:10-11; Lev. 25: 1-7). Its commandment here in Exodus is based on the divine pattern. In 23:12 and in Deuteronomy 5:14 a humanitarian purpose is indicated — that of kindness to slaves and servants. And in Deuteronomy 5:15 it is implied that it is to be a weekly commemoration of the deliverance from Egypt — a kind of little Passover. It was a peculiar and permanent sign of God's covenant with Israel (Exod. 31:12-17). While faithful observance of the Sabbath was slow in coming (see Neh. 13:15-22), by the time of Christ it was kept with a vengeance. The rabbis had in fact so multiplied their interpretations of the Sabbath law as to make the day a burden and a subject of ridicule. Jesus was forced to rescue the day from a false and excessive observance, declaring that "the sabbath was made for man, and not man for the sabbath," and that "the Son of man is lord even of the sabbath" (Mark 2:27). The Old Testament made it clear that proper observance of the Sabbath involved rest from all ordinary labor not essential to life. By His ex-

---

[131] Elton Trueblood, *Foundations for Reconstruction*, pp. 12ff.   [132] Finegan, *op. cit.*, p. 126.
[133] For references evidencing this high regard in both Testaments, see Coffman, *op. cit.*, pp. 39-40.
[134] *Ibid.*, pp. 42-45.

ample, Jesus approved a second principle of observance, that of attendance at public worship (Luke 4:16). And by His action, He approved still a third principle of observance, that of doing good to men (Mark 3:1-5). The Fourth Commandment is one that the New Testament does not reaffirm in the letter, although it adopts it and redirects it in principle. Christ contributed nothing in the way of a reaffirmation of the commandment, although He did rebuke its misuse and introduce new light on its true meaning and purpose as indicated above. Not one commendatory word was ever spoken of the Sabbath by His followers, the word being mentioned only in Acts as a time of opportunity for missionaries to preach to the Jews, and only twice elsewhere, once in connection with things peculiarily Jewish (Col. 2:16), and once in a strictly historical reference to the divine rest after creation (Heb. 4:4). Instead, a new day came into prominence among the Christians. The first day of the week was the day on which Christ had arisen from the dead (Matt 28:1; Mark 16:2; Luke 24:1; John 20:1, 19). Pentecost was also most likely on the first day of the week (see Lev. 23:11, 15-16). Very early the Christians began to meet regularly on the first day of the week (Acts 20:7), and were exhorted to contribute regularly to the Jerusalem offering on that day (I Cor. 16:2). The seventh day had been God's perpetual sign of covenant with the Jews, a weekly Passover. Under the guidance of the Holy Spirit, the early Christians received the first day as God's perpetual sign for them, a weekly Easter. It received a new name — no longer the Sabbath or seventh day or day of rest, but the Lord's Day (Rev. 1: 10). It was peculiarly fitting that He who declared Himself to be the Lord of the Sabbath, by sovereign choice had replaced the Sabbath with a day even more fittingly His. The principles of rest, worship, and helpfulness still apply to this day, although it is difficult on the basis of the New Testament to be legalistic about the rest factor. For Christians, this must find its basis in the demand of the body and mind for such relief. It is especially fitting in an age of abundant leisure to stress another part of the Fourth

Commandment, **Six days shalt thou labor.** Paul reaffirmed this by saying, "If any will not work, neither let him eat" (II Thess. 3:10). Labor was part of God's original plan for man, even before the fall (Gen. 2:5, 15), and it is only the man who has labored as best he can who is truly prepared to worship the Lord on His day.

Honor thy father and thy mother. The list of man's duties to his fellow men begins with his duties at home in regards to his parents. This was regarded as one of the most sacred obligations by the Israelites. In some ancient societies, the helpless aged were thrust out of the dwellings of their children to be eaten by beasts or die of exposure.[135] But respect for parents and for old age seems to have been traditional among the peoples from which Israel sprang. And this respect now received the support of divine command. In subsequent legislation this commandment was applied in the strictest manner. A curse was pronounced upon him that "set light by" (more literally "dishonored," "despised," or "esteemed lightly") his parents (Deut. 27:16). He that cursed his father or his mother was to be put to death (Exod. 21:17; Lev. 20:9; Prov. 20: 20). Even a son who willfully and stubbornly disobeyed his parents was to be brought before the elders of his city and stoned to death (Deut. 21:18-21). Much of the book of Proverbs is an inspired commentary on this commandment. In the New Testament, Jesus approved this commandment by His own subjection to His earthly parents (Luke 2:51). On one occasion, He reaffirmed this commandment and rebuked the scribes and Pharisees for circumventing it with their traditions (Mark 7:1-13). Paul rephrased it as a Christian commandment, and called attention to it as the first commandment with promise (Eph. 6:1-4; Col. 3:20-21). The restoration of parental authority is a much needed corrective for the rampant increase of juvenile delinquency in the twentieth century. The revival of filial respect for aged parents would do much to solve the financial and emotional needs of the ever-increasing older generation.

Thou shalt not kill. The verb **kill** used here is the technical Hebrew word

---

135 Rylaarsdam, op. cit., I, 985.

for "murder" or "slaying with premeditation." It voices a law which is intuitive to human nature. Cain had been the first one to violate it and bring forth the rebuke of God (Gen. 4:10-12). After the flood, God spoke very pointedly against murder, telling Noah, "Whoso sheddeth man's blood, by man shall his blood be shed." And He also revealed the real crime of murder as a blow against God Himself, "for in the image of God made he man" (Gen. 9:5-6). There is no prohibition of capital punishment or of war explicit in the Sixth Commandment or in the Old Testament as a whole. In fact, capital punishment was decreed by God for murder from the time of the flood, as indicated above, and for a variety of offenses under the Mosaic law (Exod. 21:12-17, 29; 22:18; 31:14; Lev. 20:1-21, 27; 21:9; 24:16; Deut. 13:5; 17:2-7; 18:20; 22:13-27; 24:7). And God frequently commanded His people to go to war, even wars designed to exterminate entire nations (Deut. 7:1-5; I Sam. 15:1-3). In the New Testament, Jesus quoted this commandment in His answer to the rich, young ruler (Luke 18: 20). But in the Sermon on the Mount, He reached behind the commandment to the principle involved — the sacredness not only of human life but also of human personality. And He outlawed not only murder but also strife, hatred, spite, and even mockery (Matt. 5:21-26). He seems to have forbidden resistance or self-defense, at least on an individual basis (Matt. 5:25, 38-42). He called for active love for enemies, even those who actually mistreat us (Matt. 5:43ff.). It is clear that for the Christian there can never be anything but love and helpfulness on the part of one individual for another. Many earnest Christians feel that this principle must be carried over to the state — thus prohibiting both capital punishment and war. That complete escape from the necessity of taking another human life in any manner is ideal cannot be denied. But the fact that the New Testament does not explicitly instruct soldiers to give up their career (Luke 3:14; Acts 10; Phil. 1:13), but does command obedience to those having civil authority, who do not bear "the sword in vain" but are God's ministers as avengers "for wrath to him that doeth

evil" (Rom. 13:1-7) and are "sent by him for vengeance on evil doers" (I Pet. 2: 13-17), leaves room for other earnest Christians to maintain the state has a duty to defend its citizens and to execute its most serious offenders (see also I Tim. 2:1-2; Tit. 3:1-2). It is entirely possible that love's objectives are sometimes best accomplished by what would otherwise seem to be violent methods.

Thou shalt not commit adultery. The verb used here refers to a violation of the marriage vows, not to fornication in general. All types of sexual offenses were dealt with severely under the Mosaic code, however, as is indicated in many of the references given in the paragraph above concerning capital punishment. The home is the oldest institution known to man, having been founded by the Lord Himself immediately upon the creation of Adam's helpmeet. The inspired writer marked that occasion with a comment beautiful in its simplicity and yet profound in its implications: "Therefore shall a man leave his father and his mother, and shall cleave unto his wife: and they shall be one flesh" (Gen. 2:24). From the beginning, God's design for marriage was that it should be the permanent, loving, God-serving union of one man and one woman. He made of the marriage union one of His favorite symbols of His relationship to His people (Jer. 3:14; Hos. 2:19-20; Eph. 5:22-33). His will is violated whenever the marriage union is jeopardized. His precious gifts of marital love and happiness are defiled whenever the partner to a marriage defiles himself by unfaithfulness. In the New Testament Jesus redefined adultery, condemning not only the overt act but also the inner desire which prompted the act (Matt. 5:27-32). Paul pressed the positive side of the matter with a call for love within the home which would reflect the strength and purity of Christ's love for the Church (Eph. 5:22-33). In the day of "the new morality," of an increasing preoccupation with sex for its own sake without any legal or moral basis, there is need for a new emphasis on the Seventh Commandment and its New Testament applications.

Thou shalt not steal. Not only is man's life sacred and his home sacred, but also his right to his property is sacred. The

Old Testament recognized that there were many ways in which this commandment could be violated and demanded multiple restitution, even if the offender had to be sold as a slave to pay it (Exod. 22:1-15; Lev. 6:1-7). In the New Testament, Jesus quoted this commandment to the rich, young ruler as one of the principles involved in securing eternal life (Luke 18:20). And Paul listed thieves among those who would not inherit the Kingdom of God (I Cor. 6:10). The principle involved here is not a simple one. Stealing can involve theft (the covert taking of another's goods), burglary (unlawful entry of a building to steal), robbery (stealing by force or threat), fraud, cheating, swindling, embezzlement, violations of trust, excessive charges, nonpayment of debts, underpayment of employees, the failure to give an employer the labor for which he pays, and gambling in all of its many forms. Padded expense accounts, falsified tax returns, rigged contests, bribery of officials, cheating as an easy road to academic recognition — all these are contemporary violations of the Eighth Commandment which cry for its reaffirmation and observance. The principle of private property which it recognizes is also a strong answer to Communism and its teaching that all property belongs to the state. For the state to confiscate that which belongs to the private citizen is robbery of the most blatant fashion.[136] The proper safeguards on the ownership of private property lie not in its confiscation by the state but in recognition of Christ's principle that all men are simply stewards of what God has entrusted to their care (Matt. 5:42), and in acceptance of His reminder that earthly riches are only temporary, not worthy of our devotion (Matt. 6:19-34).

Thou shalt not bear false witness against thy neighbor. Now the sacredness of truth is declared. This is not a direct prohibition of lying in general, but deals with a specific type of lying — perjury in reference to a fellow Israelite. Perjury was a crime which under Hammurabi's law brought upon the offender the same penalty which his testimony would have brought upon the accused.[137] The same was also true under the Mosaic code (Deut. 19:15-19). But this narrow application of the Ninth Commandment does not mean that this is the only kind of untruthfulness to which God is opposed. It is simply the beginning of instruction which starts with a concrete case. Later the law declared, "neither . . . lie one to another" (Lev. 19:11). As was noted in connection with 19:1-8, a word was very important in the minds of the Israelites. It was also very important to God. By a word He had created the universe. His Son was to be known as "The Word." Thus a word should always be used in truth. To lie is to destroy all basis for communication, to make a mockery of human relations, to reduce all dealings to the jungle level. A false witness can destroy the reputation, the happiness, the freedom, the life of another. Perjury is simply lying at its worst. Jesus also quoted the Ninth Commandment in His answer to the rich, young ruler's quest for eternal life (Luke 18:20). And John the Revelator saw that all liars were to be cast into the lake of fire forever (Rev. 21:8). In a day of propaganda, of "managed news," of clever double-talk and fine print, of the "white lie" and the constant deceit of polite society, there is need for reaffirmation and emphasis of the Ninth Commandment.

Thou shalt not covet. The Tenth Commandment stands in marked contrast to all the others. While the first nine deal almost entirely with outward behavior, only the tenth deals entirely with inner attitudes. While men may pass laws which would enforce outward conformity with the first nine, only God and conscience can police the sphere of the tenth and apprehend the criminal. Here is an Old Testament anticipation of a basic New Testament principle — that sin really lies in the heart and not in the hands, in a man's attitudes before his actions, in his desires before his deeds, in his motives before his manners. The violation of the Tenth Commandment can lead to the violation of the other nine: to covet

---

[136] For an outstanding discussion of all aspects of the Eighth Commandment, including its contradiction of Communism, and its implications for the state, see Coffman, *op. cit.*, pp. 93-103.

[137] Hammurabi's Code, paragraphs 1-4, in *Documents from Old Testament Times*, ed. by Winton Thomas, p. 29.

first place is to deify self and set God aside, to covet physical assurances in worship can lead to idolatry, to covet the recognition of others, whatever the cost, can lead to taking God's name in vain, to covet time to advance our own selfish plans can lead to violation of the Sabbath, to covet our parents' freedom can lead to a rejection of their authority, to covet our neighbor's position in society can lead to murder, to covet his wife can lead to adultery, to covet his property can lead to stealing, to covet his good name can lead to our false witness. Jesus also concentrated on the inward nature of sin. His reinterpretation of the commandments in the Sermon on the Mount is definitely a part of this emphasis (see especially Matt. 7:15-23). And He had much to say about coveting in general, warning the man who asked Him to arbitrate his inheritance: "Take heed, and keep yourselves from all covetousness: for a man's life consisteth not in the abundance of the things which he possesseth" (Luke 12:15). He followed His answer with the parable of the rich fool and a call to put the Kingdom of God first, trusting the heavenly Father to take care of material needs (Luke 12:13-34). Paul confessed that it was at this point that the law had condemned him (Rom. 7:7ff.). He admonished his readers not even to name covetousness in their conversations with one another (Eph. 5:3), identified it with idolatry, and called for its mortification (Col. 3:5). The call of the New Testament is for contentment in material things (Phil. 4:11; Heb. 13: 5), and for sanctified covetousness only in spiritual things (I Cor. 11:31; 14:39, KJV). In the twentieth century, with its unprecedented material abundance, there is need to heed the scriptural warnings against covetousness. The line between necessity and luxury, between legitimate enjoyment and wastefulness has become hazy for many people. Only a proper devotion to God and His Kingdom will help make it clear again.

b. The Fear of the People (20:18-21)

18 And all the people perceived the thunderings, and the lightnings, and the voice of the trumpet, and the mountain smoking: and when the people saw it, they trembled, and stood afar off. 19 And they said unto Moses, Speak thou with us, and we will hear; but let not God speak with us, lest we die. 20 And Moses said unto the people, Fear not: for God is come to prove you, and that his fear may be before you, that ye sin not. 21 And the people stood afar off, and Moses drew near unto the thick darkness where God was.

The actual vocalization of the Ten Commandments could not have taken long. But by the time those very few minutes were over, the people had had all they wanted of **the thunderings, and the lightnings, and the voice of the trumpet, and the mountain smoking,** and direct reception of the divine revelation. They were frightened and retreated. Apparently Moses had remained with them at the foot of the mountain after God sent him down (19:21-25). And they took advantage of the completion of the Ten Commandments, when the divine voice apparently paused, to ask Moses to serve as their intermediary lest God's voice bring death upon them. Moses comforted them, explaining that God had once again sought **to prove** them (15:25; 16:4), testing the sincerity of their covenant pledge, and to impress indelibly upon their hearts the desirability of obedience and the danger of sin. But their request was granted, for they remained at a distance, **and Moses drew near unto the thick darkness,** which apparently mixed with the flames on the mountain, and in which God's presence was hidden (cf. Deut. 5:23-31).

c. The Rules of the Covenant (20: 22—23:19)

(1) Special Rules About Worship (20:22-26)

22 And Jehovah said unto Moses, Thus thou shalt say unto the children of Israel, Ye yourselves have seen that I have talked with you from heaven. 23 Ye shall not make *other gods* with me; gods of silver, or gods of gold, ye shall not make unto you. 24 An altar of earth thou shalt make unto me, and shalt sacrifice thereon thy burnt-offerings, and thy peace-offerings, thy sheep, and thine oxen: in every place where I record my name I will come unto thee and I will bless thee. 25 And if thou make me an altar of stone, thou shalt not build it of hewn stones; for if thou lift up thy

tool upon it, thou hast polluted it. 26 Neither shalt thou go up steps unto mine altar, that thy nakedness be not uncovered thereon.

Jehovah's first words to Moses had to do with applying in a practical way what Israel had learned about Him through listening to Him directly. Four rules are to be followed in divine worship: (1) idols are not to be used (molten ones are now prohibited as graven ones had been in the Second Commandment), (2) altars are to be quite simple, made only of earth, and erected in places approved by the Lord Himself, (3) if altars are made of stone, they are to be natural, uncut stones, maintaining the principle of simplicity, and (4) altars are not to be highly elevated to the point that they must be reached by steps, lest the modesty of the worshipers be violated due to their flowing garments. The apparent provision here for a multiplicity of altars, the difference between these simple altars and the ones in the tabernacle and the temple, and the apparent provision for private individuals to offer sacrifices since provision was made for the maintenance of the priests' modesty at the more elaborate altars (28:42-43), has caused critical scholars to claim a basic contradiction. They declare that there was an earlier period when private altars were accepted and private sacrifices could be offered, but that the construction of Solomon's temple and the rise of a vested, priestly class led to a gradual change to worship at only one place. They teach that the Pentateuch, written not by Moses, but rather by different individuals at different periods of Jewish history, has woven various threads of this essentially evolutionary development into what claims to be a coherent historical account, thus giving the reader a hopeless series of contradictions. But such is not the case. Here in Exodus we have provision made for the simple, local, private altars which had been erected by the patriarchs from time immemorial at places made memorable by the appearance of Jehovah. Countless altars of this type were erected all through the period of the conquest, the judges, the early kings, and even under some of the prophets (Josh. 9:30-31; 22:10-29; Judg. 6:24ff.; 13:19-20; 21:4; I Sam. 7:17; 14:35; II Sam. 24:18-25;

I Kings 18:30ff.; 19:10, 14). For the time that the nation lived closely together in the wilderness, such would not be necessary, and the tabernacle was provided instead. In Deuteronomy 12, where Moses gives instructions about the eventual centralization of worship in Canaan itself, there are nevertheless implications that there will be quite a period intervening before that day is fully realized. And there is still provision for the eating of meat in their private homes — in terms that may have allowed sacrificial feasts to continue in a modified form with the father being in a sense his own priest. It was for the transitional period from the wilderness to the temple that Jehovah wisely provided for the altars of earth and uncut stone. All heathen altars were to be torn down. And new ones for Jehovah were not to be put up promiscuously, but only in places of His appointment. It is significant that after Deuteronomy has so much to say about the centralization of worship around one central altar, one of the final instructions it records Moses as having given Joshua is to build an altar in Mt. Ebal, where the words of the law can be recorded (Deut. 27:5-7). The central place of worship in Canaan was first at Shiloh and later at Jerusalem. When the eventual centralization of worship for which Jehovah had planned and instructed took place, the prophets, priests, and people alike saw with increasing clarity the danger of private altars and private sacrifices and they were eventually abandoned.

(2) Judgment Rules About People and Possessions (21:1—22:17)

(a) Relating to Persons (21:1-32)

1 Now these are the ordinances which thou shalt set before them.
2 If thou buy a Hebrew servant, six years he shall serve: and in the seventh he shall go out free for nothing. 3 If he come in by himself, he shall go out by himself: if he be married, then his wife shall go out with him. 4 If his master give him a wife, and she bear him sons or daughters; the wife and her children shall be her master's, and he shall go out by himself. 5 But if the servant shall plainly say, I love my master, my wife, and my children; I will not go out free: 6 then his master shall bring him unto God, and shall bring him to the door, or unto the

door-post; and his master shall bore his ear through with an awl; and he shall serve him for ever.

7 And if a man sell his daughter to be a maid-servant, she shall not go out as the men-servants do. 8 If she please not her master, who hath espoused her to himself, then shall he let her be redeemed: to sell her unto a foreign people he shall have no power, seeing he hath dealt deceitfully with her. 9 And if he espouse her unto his son, he shall deal with her after the manner of daughters. 10 If he take him another *wife;* her food, her raiment, and her duty of marriage, shall he not diminish. 11 And if he do not these three things unto her, then shall she go out for nothing, without money.

12 He that smiteth a man, so that he dieth, shall surely be put to death. 13 And if a man lie not in wait, but God deliver *him* into his hand; then I will appoint thee a place whither he shall flee. 14 And if a man come presumptuously upon his neighbor, to slay him with guile; thou shalt take him from mine altar, that he may die.

15 And he that smiteth his father, or his mother, shall be surely put to death.

16 And he that stealeth a man, and selleth him, or if he be found in his hand, he shall surely be put to death.

17 And he that curseth his father or his mother, shall surely be put to death.

18 And if men contend, and one smite the other with a stone, or with his fist, and he die not, but keep his bed; 19 if he rise again, and walk abroad upon his staff, then shall he that smote him be quit: only he shall pay for the loss of his time, and shall cause him to be thoroughly healed.

20 And if a man smite his servant, or his maid, with a rod, and he die under his hand; he shall surely be punished. 21 Notwithstanding, if he continue a day or two, he shall not be punished: for he is his money.

22 And if men strive together, and hurt a woman with child, so that her fruit depart, and yet no harm follow; he shall be surely fined, according as the woman's husband shall lay upon him; and he shall pay as the judges determine. 23 But if any harm follow, then thou shalt give life for life, 24 eye for eye, tooth for tooth, hand for hand, foot for foot, 25 burning for burning, wound for wound, stripe for stripe.

26 And if a man smite the eye of his servant, or the eye of his maid, and destroy it; he shall let him go free for his eye's sake. 27 And if he smite out his man-servant's tooth, or his maid-servant's tooth; he shall let him go free for his tooth's sake.

28 And if an ox gore a man or a woman to death, the ox shall be surely stoned, and its flesh shall not be eaten; but the owner of the ox shall be quit. 29 But if the ox was wont to gore in time past, and it hath been testified to its owner, and he hath not kept it in, but it hath killed a man or a woman; the ox shall be stoned, and its owner also shall be put to death. 30 If there be laid on him a ransom, then he shall give for the redemption of his life whatever is laid upon him. 31 Whether it have gored a son or have gored a daughter, according to this judgment shall it be done unto him. 32 If the ox gore a man-servant or a maid-servant, there shall be given unto their master thirty shekels of silver, and the ox shall be stoned.

The next series of commandments or laws given by Jehovah to Moses are called **ordinances,** or better, "judgments." Two types of law have been identified in the Pentateuch: the casuistic and the apodictic.[138] The apodictic law is the type found in the Ten Commandments, short, positive. declaratory sentences, and is found only among the Hebrews. The casuistic is case-law, decisions made by a judge or judges in particular cases which serve as precedents for other decisions. This kind of law is characterized by a protasis stating that *if* or *when* a certain action is taken *and* a certain result follows, and an apodosis concluding *then* a certain disposition must be made. This is the form followed in the ancient Code of Hammurabi and other ancient legal codes and it is the form followed here in the **ordinances.** There are points of great similarity between the **ordinances** and the ancient legal codes, in some instances to the point of exact similarity. This does not indicate that Moses copied the older codes. It does indicate that the Lord drew on a general legal background already familiar to Israel in regulating their social order. It is probable that some of these rules had already been revealed by the Lord to Moses in the months spent traveling from Egypt, for he had constantly been taking cases to the Lord for

138 Noth, *op. cit.,* pp. 174-75; Finegan, *op. cit.,* pp. 123-24.

decision (18:14-16, 19). Now the Lord incorporates what Moses has already learned from Him with additional rules in the Book of the Covenant. It was probably by this same means that the law was expanded and modified throughout the rest of the Pentateuch. Critical scholars see in additional provisions in Leviticus and Deuteronomy later stages of evolutionary development. But no doubt as Israel continued in the wilderness, new cases arose not provided for by the set of rules in the Book of the Covenant. And as Moses learned from the Lord how to deal with them, the additional and more complex provisions were recorded.

McNeile has remarked that these judgment rules are in sets of five, or pentads. Five of these appear in this section: a pentad on male slaves (vv. 2-6), a pentad on female slaves (vv. 7-11), a pentad on acts of violence (vv. 12-17), a pentad on injuries inflicted by men (vv. 18-27), and a pentad on injuries inflicted by animals (vv. 28-32) .[139]

In the first pentad (vv. 2-6), the word **servant** is more accurately translated "slave." But this is a particular kind of slave, for it deals only with Hebrews who could only be enslaved for a six-year period. Such slavery could originate through the man selling himself because of financial need (Lev. 25:39), or through his being sold to pay a debt (II Kings 4:1) or to make restitution for theft (Exod. 22:3), or through his being sold as a child by his parents because of their financial need (Exod. 21:7; Neh. 5:5). The five rules are each introduced by **if,** and provide (1) for the release of the slave free of cost at the end of six years, (2) for his release singly if he was single at the beginning of his service, (3) for the release with him of his family if he had a family at the beginning, (4) for the retention by the master of wife and children acquired through the master during his enslavement (apparently this wife would have been a foreigner who could be enslaved permanently, Lev. 25:44-46), and (5) for his voluntary enslavement on a lifelong basis in order to stay with his wife and children. This involved a ceremony in which he was first brought before **God.** The word *elohim* here has three possible translations: God, gods, judges. It is probable that he was literally taken before the judges of his town, either at a local sanctuary in the early days of the nation, or when possible to the temple later, where the judges were thought to act under God's direction and for Him. Then he was returned home and an awl driven through his ear, the organ of hearing and thus the key to obedience,[140] into the doorpost of the master's house as a sign that to this household he now belonged for the rest of his life. Later, provisions were made for extending these rules to female slaves who were not chosen as concubines, and for giving the slave who had completed his term of service a "grubstake" on which to begin life anew (Deut. 15:12-18). Care was taken too to provide for the redemption of a Hebrew who had to sell himself into slavery to a rich Gentile living in Israel, and to provide for a general time of release in the year of jubilee which occurred every fifty years. The Lord also made it clear that the differences between foreign slaves and Hebrew slaves were based on His own priority to Israel's services. He had redeemed them from Egypt and they were His servants and should not readily become permanently the property of another (Lev. 25:35-55).

In the section on female slaves (vv. 7-11), the five rules provide (1) that the female slave will not be released at the end of six years — the word used here for **maid-servant** frequently means "concubine" and that relationship could not properly be terminated so mechanically, (2) that if her master changes his mind after buying her, he cannot sell her to a foreigner, but must **let her be redeemed** — be bought back by her family or by some other Israelite, (3) that if from the first he has planned to give her to his son or after buying her decides that this would be the best arrangement, she must marry his son not as a concubine but as a wife—becoming her master's daughter,[141] (4) that if he take another marriage partner (**wife** is not in the original, so either wife or concubine), he must continue to furnish the former one food and raiment, and to maintain the marriage relationship,

[139] McNeile, *op. cit.*, pp. 126ff.   [140] Johnson, *op. cit.*, p. 70.   [141] Rylaarsdam, *op. cit.*, I, 996.

and (5) that if he fails at any of the three points (either the three just mentioned or the three basic provisions — rules 2, 3, and 4 — for his conduct toward her) she shall be set free without any obligation.

The next five rules (vv. 12-17) deal with acts of violence normally punishable by death, beginning with (1) the general statement that he who kills another man shall himself be killed, but also providing (2) that if the killing is accidental, the slayer may flee to an appointed haven — the six cities of refuge later provided (Num. 35:10-34; Deut. 4:41-43; 19:1-13; Josh. 20:1-9 — this was necessary because executions were not carried out by police forces, but according to primitive custom by the victim's next of kin, "the avenger of blood"), and (3) that if in the subsequent trial at the city of refuge it be proven that the slayer acted intentionally, he must be executed even if he has seized hold of Jehovah's altar itself as a sanctuary — another indication that there was an extended period when multiple places of worship were permitted by the Lord, since neither Shiloh nor Jerusalem was among the cities of refuge and thus the central place of worship was never located at a city of refuge. The same provision for capital punishment prevailed (4) in the case of one who struck a parent (v. 17 carries this on to one who curses a parent; in the Septuagint, the oldest translation of the Old Testament into Greek, this statement immediately follows v. 15 — it must be counted with it to preserve the pentad arrangement and may have been added by Moses later in the wilderness wanderings through further divine revelation), and (5) in the case of a man-stealer or kidnapper.

The next section (vv. 18-27) deals with injuries inflicted by men on one another. The five rules provide (1) that if in a struggle one man is injured but survives to walk again, the other will not be tried before the courts to determine his guilt but will have to pay for the loss of his time and for his medical expenses, (2) that if a man strikes his slave so that he dies on the spot **he shall surely be punished** for murder, but if the slave lives for a time it indicates that he did not intend to kill him and the loss of

the slave's services will be his punishment, (3) that if in a struggle between two men, one of them injure a pregnant woman so that she miscarries but she herself recovers, her husband shall set the fine the man shall pay, subject to its review by the judges, (4) but that if she suffers permanent injury or death, the basic law since called *lex talionis* shall apply — **life for life, eye for eye,** etc., and (5) that if a master strike a slave so that an eye or tooth be lost, the slave shall be set free without charge because of the injury — the master being punished by the loss of his services. While the Mosaic code permits slavery, its advancement over all other ancient law codes is shown in its consideration of the slave as one who still has rights — not as great as those of a free citizen, but yet such as put him far above the slaves of ancient Rome who could be killed upon the mere whim of the master.

The next section (vv. 28-32) deals with injuries inflicted by animals. The five rules provide (1) that if an ox kill a human being, the ox will be stoned but its flesh not eaten, and the owner of the ox shall have no further responsibility, but (2) if the ox has been violent before, and the owner has not kept it shut up, then he becomes fully responsible, and both the ox and the owner are to be executed, unless (3) the next of kin of the victim choose instead to levy a fine, the payment of which will ransom the ox's owner. These provisions are to prevail also (4) in the event that the victim is a minor, but (5) if he is a slave, then the slave's master will be paid the full price of a slave, **thirty shekels of silver** (about $22.50), and only the ox will be executed.

(b) Relating to Property (21:33 —22:17)

33 And if a man shall open a pit, or if a man shall dig a pit and not cover it, and an ox or an ass fall therein, 34 the owner of the pit shall make it good; he shall give money unto the owner thereof, and the dead *beast* shall be his.

35 And if one man's ox hurt another's, so that it dieth, then they shall sell the live ox, and divide the price of it; and the dead also they shall divide. 36 Or if it be known that the ox was wont to gore in time past, and its owner hath not

kept it in; he shall surely pay ox for ox, and the dead *beast* shall be his own.

1 If a man shall steal an ox, or a sheep, and kill it, or sell it; he shall pay five oxen for an ox, and four sheep for a sheep. 2 If the thief be found breaking in, and be smitten so that he dieth, there shall be no bloodguiltiness for him. 3 If the sun be risen upon him, there shall be bloodguiltiness for him; he shall make restitution: if he have nothing, then he shall be sold for his theft. 4 If the theft be found in his hand alive, whether it be an ox, or ass, or sheep; he shall pay double.

5 If a man shall cause a field or vineyard to be eaten, and shall let his beast loose, and it feed in another man's field; of the best of his own field, and of the best of his own vineyard, shall he make restitution.

6 If fire break out, and catch in thorns, so that the shocks of grain, or the standing grain, or the field are consumed; he that kindled the fire shall surely make restitution.

7 If a man shall deliver unto his neighbor money or stuff to keep, and it be stolen out of the man's house; if the thief be found, he shall pay double. 8 If the thief be not found, then the master of the house shall come near unto God, *to see* whether he have not put his hand unto his neighbor's goods. 9 For every matter of trespass, whether it be for ox, for ass, for sheep, for raiment, ~or~ for any manner of lost thing, whereof one saith, This is it, the cause of both parties shall come before God; he whom God shall condemn shall pay double unto his neighbor.

10 If a man deliver unto his neighbor an ass, or an ox, or a sheep, or any beast, to keep; and it die, or be hurt, or driven away, no man seeing it: 11 the oath of Jehovah shall be between them both, whether he hath not put his hand unto his neighbor's goods; and the owner thereof shall accept it, and he shall not make restitution. 12 But if it be stolen from him, he shall make restitution unto the owner thereof. 13 If it be torn in pieces, let him bring it for witness; he shall not make good that which was torn.

14 And if a man borrow aught of his neighbor, and it be hurt, or die, the owner thereof not being with it, he shall surely make restitution. 15 If the owner thereof be with it, he shall not make it good: if it be a hired thing, it came for its hire.

16 And if a man entice a virgin that is not betrothed, and lie with her, he shall surely pay a dowry for her to be his wife. 17 If her father utterly refuse to give her unto him, he shall pay money according to the dowry of virgins.

The first pentad or set of five rules (21:33—22:4) deals with the loss of animals by neglect or theft. They provide (1) that if a man uncovers **a pit** or cistern, or digs one and leaves it uncovered, and another man's animal falls in, the careless one shall pay the owner the price of the animal and the carcass shall be his — the value being only in the hide since the meat could not be eaten (Lev. 22:8), (2) that if one man's animal kills another's, they shall sell the live animal and divide the price, and also share the carcass, but (3) if the animal has been vicious before and its owner warned, but he has not kept it penned up, he shall replace the dead animal and keep the carcass. If on the other hand, (4) a man steal an ox or sheep and kill it or sell it, he must repay the owner **five oxen for an ox, and four sheep for a sheep,** or if he cannot make such restitution, he himself will be sold into slavery and the money used as restitution, but (5) if the animal is found alive in his possession, he will only have to pay back double. Verses 2-3a are parenthetical, applying the earlier rules on manslaughter to the thief caught in the act (cf. 21:12-14). If the thief is struck and killed in the dark, the owner will not be held responsible. But if he kills the thief in the daylight, this is not necessary and makes him guilty of murder.

The next section (22:5-6) breaks with the pentad arrangement, listing only two rules on the intentional or careless destruction of another man's crops. (1) If he deliberately turns his beasts loose in another man's vineyard or field, he shall make restitution from the best of his own produce, but (2) if he is burning off his own land and the fire accidentally spreads to his neighbor's grain, he shall only make restitution for the actual loss. **Beast, eaten, feed, kindled,** and **fire** are all from the same Hebrew root. Because of this McNeile would translate verse 5 to make it describe an intentional burning of the neighbor's field.[142]

---

[142] McNeile, *op. cit.*, p. 132.

The next five rules (22:7-13) have to do with trusts. (1) If a man entrusts his money or goods to his neighbor and they are stolen, the thief shall if caught pay double, but (2) if no thief is found, then the one trusted shall be brought before **God** (or "the judges," see comments on 21:2-6), and if held guilty shall pay double just like the thief. (3) If the trust be in the form of livestock, and the animal die, or is hurt, or wanders away, the one entrusted can take an oath before Jehovah that he is not responsible and he will be cleared — it would then be up to the Lord to punish him if guilty, but (4) if it is stolen from him, he shall make restitution for it, or (5) if torn in pieces by some wild beast, the carcass will clear him.

The last pentad (22:14-17) applies to loans, although the latter portion can be thought of as a loan only in the terms of the primitive society addressed through the Mosaic code. (1) If a man borrows an animal from his neighbor and it is hurt or dies when the owner is not present, he must pay for the loss, but (2) if the owner is present, no restitution is necessary, and (3) if the beast was hired, there is no further obligation, for the hiring involved a risk. The rest of this pentad refers to the seduction of (and probably also the rape of, see Deut. 22:28-29) an unbetrothed virgin. When girls were betrothed by their parents to their prospective husbands, the grooms paid a dowry or marriage-price, much as they would have done in buying a slave. So each girl represented potential wealth to her father. If a man seized such a girl by persuasion or force, he must (4) repay this "loan" by paying the proper dowry (set at fifty shekels of silver or approximately $37:50, Deut. 22:29) to her father, and then he could keep her as his wife, but (5) if the father did not approve of him as a son-in-law, he would have to return the girl and still pay the dowry. This rule did not of course apply if the girl had already been betrothed to another, for then if she had consented, she and her illicit lover would both have been executed, or in case of rape, he alone would have paid the extreme penalty (Deut. 22:23-27).

(3) Miscellaneous Rules About Social Order and Worship (22:18—23:19)

18 Thou shalt not suffer a sorceress to live.

19 Whosoever lieth with a beast shall surely be put to death.

20 He that sacrificeth unto any god, save unto Jehovah only, shall be utterly destroyed. 21 And a sojourner shalt thou not wrong, neither shalt thou oppress him: for ye were sojourners in the land of Egypt. 22 Ye shall not afflict any widow, or fatherless child. 23 If thou afflict them at all, and they cry at all unto me, I will surely hear their cry; 24 and my wrath shall wax hot, and I will kill you with the sword; and your wives shall be widows, and your children fatherless.

25 If thou lend money to any of my people with thee that is poor, thou shalt not be to him as a creditor; neither shall ye lay upon him interest. 26 If thou at all take thy neighbor's garment to pledge, thou shalt restore it unto him before the sun goeth down: 27 for that is his only covering, it is his garment for his skin: wherein shall he sleep? and it shall come to pass, when he crieth unto me, that I will hear; for I am gracious.

28 Thou shalt not revile God, nor curse a ruler of thy people. 29 Thou shalt not delay to offer of thy harvest, and of the outflow of thy presses. The first-born of thy sons shalt thou give unto me. 30 Likewise shalt thou do with thine oxen, *and* with thy sheep: seven days it shall be with its dam; on the eighth day thou shalt give it me. 31 And ye shall be holy men unto me: therefore ye shall not eat any flesh that is torn of beasts in the field; ye shall cast it to the dogs.

1 Thou shalt not take up a false report: put not thy hand with the wicked to be an unrighteous witness. 2 Thou shalt not follow a multitude to do evil; neither shalt thou speak in a cause to turn aside after a multitude to wrest *justice*: 3 neither shalt thou favor a poor man in his cause.

4 If thou meet thine enemy's ox or his ass going astray, thou shalt surely bring it back to him again. 5 If thou see the ass of him that hateth thee lying under his burden, thou shalt forbear to leave him, thou shalt surely release *it* with him.

6 Thou shalt not wrest the justice *due* to thy poor in his cause. 7 Keep thee far from a false matter; and the innocent and righteous slay thou not: for I will

not justify the wicked. 8 And thou shalt take no bribe: for a bribe blindeth them that have sight, and perverteth the words of the righteous. 9 And a sojourner shalt thou not oppress: for ye know the heart of a sojourner, seeing ye were sojourners in the land of Egypt.

10 And six years thou shalt sow thy land, and shalt gather in the increase thereof: 11 but the seventh year thou shalt let it rest and lie fallow, that the poor of thy people may eat: and what they leave the beast of the field shall eat. In like manner thou shalt deal with thy vineyard, *and* with thy oliveyard. 12 Six days thou shalt do thy work, and on the seventh day thou shalt rest; that thine ox and thine ass may have rest, and the son of thy handmaid, and the sojourner, may be refreshed. 13 And in all things that I have said unto you take ye heed: and make no mention of the name of other gods, neither let it be heard out of thy mouth.

14 Three times thou shalt keep a feast unto me in the year. 15 The feast of unleavened bread shalt thou keep: seven days thou shalt eat unleavened bread, as I commanded thee, at the time appointed in the month Abib (for in it thou camest out from Egypt); and none shall appear before me empty: 16 and the feast of harvest, the first-fruits of thy labors, which thou sowest in the field: and the feast of ingathering, at the end of the year, when thou gatherest in thy labors out of the field. 17 Three times in the year all thy males shall appear before the Lord Jehovah.

18 Thou shalt not offer the blood of my sacrifice with leavened bread; neither shall the fat of my feast remain all night until morning. 19 The first of the first-fruits of thy ground thou shalt bring into the house of Jehovah thy God. Thou shalt not boil a kid in its mother's milk.

The balance of the Book of the Covenant does not consist of formal statements of hypothetical situations which shall be dealt with according to a prescribed precedent. Neither do the statements divide into such nicely organized topical groups as in the preceding section. Rather only a few are hypothetical in structure, and all deal with principles, much like the Ten Commandments do. Three general subjects are dealt with, being intertwined or woven together rather than sharply separated. These are

social order, social justice, and the worship of Jehovah.

In 22:18-20, three capital crimes are listed: sorcery, bestiality, and idolatry. All forms of divination and witchcraft were common in biblical times. Bestiality seems to have been a vice characteristic of the nations of Canaan (Lev. 18:23-24). While idolatry was condemned in the Ten Commandments, this is the first time the sentence of death is passed upon it.

In 22:21-27 the matter of social justice is dealt with. The people are commanded to avoid mistreatment of the sojourner, probably either a foreigner or a Hebrew residing elsewhere than his family home, since the entire nation had once been sojourners. Neither are orphans and widows to be afflicted. The Lord Himself will be the judge and executioner in such cases. And the poor of the nation are not to be taken advantage of, nor interest charged on loans to them. If a poor man gave his garment as a pledge for a loan, it must be returned to him before sundown. The outer garment worn by the Jews at this time was a large, rectangular piece of cloth. It was used as a blanket at night. It would probably have been the only property a poor man could give as security, but he would need it at night or he would suffer from the cold.[143] The Lord would certainly hear his complaints. The prohibition here against charging interest applies not just to excessive interest but to interest of any kind. This deals with a man in need, a man who is a part of the religious community. It does not apply to modern methods of doing business in which loans are sought to increase the capital of an individual or business — such were then unknown.

In 22:28-31, the rules apply particularly to the religious sphere. There is to be no reviling of God (perhaps "the judges" — see comments on 21:2-6) or His appointed representatives. There must be promptness in the offering of sacrifices, both in relationship to produce (cf. 23: 14-17), first-born sons, and first-born animals. And the prohibition of eating blood must be carried to the extent that no animal found torn by wild beasts is to be

---

[143] Driver, *op. cit.*, p. 233.

eaten as food, but is to be thrown to the dogs.

In 23:1-3 three basic principles of justice are announced: there is to be no conspiracy to give false witness, there is to be no mob action calculated to pervert justice, and there is to be no support of a poor man's cause simply because of his poverty and without regard to the justice of his case.

In 23:4-5, a New Testament principle of kindness to one's enemy is clearly anticipated. If a man finds his enemy's livestock wandering off, he is to return it to him. If he finds his enemy's beast of burden fallen under his load, he is not to leave his enemy to struggle with it alone, but he is to "help with him" — as the original probably should be rendered.[144]

In 23:6-12, we return again to the subject of the treatment of the poor and the sojourner (cf. 22:21-27). Just as the poor is not to receive preferential treatment before the courts (see 23:3), so he is not to be slighted either. The innocent and righteous, however poor and helpless they may be, have the special protection of Jehovah. The rich man is not to win the day over them through a bribe, for bribes blind men with good eyes and twist legal cases out of all true perspective. The sojourner, too, is to receive justice before the courts, just as Israel would have wished to receive in Egypt — a plain application of the Golden Rule of doing to others what we would like done to us, long before the Golden Rule was given (Matt. 7:12). In fact, in order to provide for the poor and the slave and the sojourner, not only is there to be a principle of six days of labor and the Sabbath of rest, but after the land is worked for six years, it is to be let lie fallow for the seventh year. That which does grow on it will be for the poor, and what they do not eat will be for the wild beasts.

In 23:13-19, the subject is again that of religious duties and observances. First is an admonition not even to mention the names of other gods besides Jehovah. Then is outlined for the first time the list of three great feasts to be observed by the Jewish nation, at which times all the males are to appear before Jehovah

at the place of worship. The first is **the feast of unleavened bread,** which would include the Passover, and during which the first-ripe sheaf of barley was offered. The second is **the feast of harvest,** elsewhere called "the feast of weeks" (34:22), known to us as Pentecost, and occurring at the conclusion of wheat-harvest. The third is **the feast of in-gathering,** elsewhere called "the feast of tabernacles" or "booths" (Lev. 23:39-43; II Chron. 8:13), and occurring "at the final harvest of the fruits — mainly grapes and olives."[145] The last few rules remind them that no leavened bread is to be used in sacrifice, nor the fat which was to be burned on the altar left unconsumed. The first-fruits were faithfully to be offered at **the house of Jehovah.** And finally, a kid was not to be boiled in its mother's milk. This is a most obscure reference to us. But in some heathen sacrificial feasts this was done. Apparently it was so characteristic of some particular heathen act of worship that Jehovah did not want His people to be identified with it.[146]

d. The Advantages of the Covenant (23:20-33)

20 Behold, I send an angel before thee, to keep thee by the way, and to bring thee into the place which I have prepared. 21 Take ye heed before him, and hearken unto his voice; provoke him not; for he will not pardon your transgression: for my name is in him. 22 But if thou shalt indeed hearken unto his voice, and do all that I speak; then I will be an enemy unto thine enemies, and an adversary unto thine adversaries. 23 For mine angel shall go before thee, and bring thee in unto the Amorite, and the Hittite, and the Perizzite, and the Canaanite, the Hivite, and the Jebusite: and I will cut them off. 24 Thou shalt not bow down to their gods, nor serve them, nor do after their works; but thou shalt utterly overthrow them, and break in pieces their pillars. 25 And ye shall serve Jehovah your God, and he will bless thy bread, and thy water; and I will take sickness away from the midst of thee. 26 There shall none cast her young, nor be barren, in thy land: the number of thy days I will fulfil. 27 I will send my terror before thee, and will discomfit all the people to whom thou shalt come, and I

---

[144] *Ibid.,* pp. 237-38.   [145] McNeile, *op. cit.,* p. 141.   [146] Rylaarsdam, *op. cit.,* I, 1013-14.

will make all thine enemies turn their backs unto thee. 28 And I will send the hornet before thee, which shall drive out the Hivite, the Canaanite, and the Hittite, from before thee. 29 I will not drive them out from before thee in one year, lest the land become desolate, and the beasts of the field multiply against thee. 30 By little and little I will drive them out from before thee, until thou be increased, and inherit the land. 31 And I will set thy border from the Red Sea even unto the sea of the Philistines, and from the wilderness unto the River: for I will deliver the inhabitants of the land into your hand; and thou shalt drive them out before thee. 32 Thou shalt make no covenant with them, nor with their gods. 33 They shall not dwell in thy land, lest they make thee sin against me; for if thou serve their gods, it will surely be a snare unto thee.

The remainder of the Book of the Covenant does not consist of rules, but of concluding remarks with something of a restatement of conditions and of the resulting promises or blessings which God will bestow upon Israel. He promises to send before them **an angel** (v. 20), in whom shall be the very name of Jehovah (v. 21), and whose voice is the equivalent of Jehovah's voice (v. 22). This angel was not merely a heavenly creature, but must indeed have been that particular "angel of Jehovah" who many scholars believe to have been the preincarnate Christ (see comments on Gen. 32:22-32). This angel would not tolerate sin, but if Israel obeyed Jehovah's will, Jehovah would become an enemy to their enemies. The angel would lead them to Canaan and Jehovah would cut off the nations already there. Israel was not to worship their gods nor follow their customs, but rather destroy them and their sacred **pillars.** As they worshiped Him, He would bless their bread and water, delivering them from disease, causing their livestock to multiply, and giving them long life. Terror would precede them into Canaan, causing the other nations to flee before them. Even insects (**hornet** is a collective noun and may involve several types of insects[147]) would aid them as they had aided in delivering them from bondage in Egypt. However, the other nations would not be driven out

immediately, but gradually, lest Israel be unable to possess the land adequately and their problems be multiplied. The border would run from the Red Sea (apparently here referring to the eastern branch, the Gulf of Aqabah) to the Mediterranean, and from the wilderness to the Euphrates far to the north. The closest approach to this was made in the days of David and Solomon. But this only could be accomplished by maintaining the strictest of separation from these other peoples, not permitting them to remain in Canaan, not making any covenant with them, above everything not becoming involved with their gods.

e. The Ratification of the Covenant (24:1-11)

1 And he said unto Moses, Come up unto Jehovah, thou, and Aaron, Nadab, and Abihu, and seventy of the elders of Israel; worship ye afar off: 2 and Moses alone shall come near unto Jehovah; but they shall not come near; neither shall the people go up with him. 3 And Moses came and told all the people all the words of Jehovah, and all the ordinances: and all the people answered with one voice, and said, All the words which Jehovah hath spoken will we do. 4 And Moses wrote all the words of Jehovah, and rose up early in the morning, and builded an altar under the mount, and twelve pillars, according to the twelve tribes of Israel. 5 And he sent young men of the children of Israel, who offered burnt-offerings, and sacrificed peace-offerings of oxen unto Jehovah. 6 And Moses took half of the blood, and put it in basins; and half of the blood he sprinkled on the altar. 7 And he took the book of the covenant, and read in the audience of the people: and they said, All that Jehovah hath spoken will we do, and be obedient. 8 And Moses took the blood, and sprinkled it on the people, and said, Behold the blood of the covenant, which Jehovah hath made with you concerning all these words.

9 Then went up Moses, and Aaron, Nadab, and Abihu, and seventy of the elders of Israel: 10 and they saw the God of Israel; and there was under his feet as it were a paved work of sapphire stone, and as it were the very heaven for clearness. 11 And upon the nobles of the children of Israel he laid not his hand: and they beheld God, and did eat and drink.

---

[147] *Ibid.,* I, 1015.

When the Lord had completed giving these instructions to Moses, He called for Moses and Aaron, Aaron's two older sons, Nadab and Abihu, and seventy of the elders of Israel to ascend the mountain. Even though this marked an advance for all besides Aaron (19:24), they still were to ascend only part way with Moses alone coming actually near Jehovah. The people were to remain at the foot of the mountain.

In preparation for this formal ratification of the covenant by the representatives of the people, Moses first rehearsed **all the words** and **all the ordinances** in the hearing of the people as a whole. The entire nation had given their consent to the covenant in principle before the divine revelation of its details (19:8). Now they again gave their consent when the various commandments, rules, and instructions were spelled out for them. Then he wrote **all the words of Jehovah** in the Book of the Covenant. And he rose early the next day and built an altar **under the mount** and with it **twelve pillars** (*matzebah* — the same Hebrew word as that designating the heathen pillars which were to be destroyed, 23:24, but here referring to memorial pillars representing the tribes rather than sacred pillars representing deities). Here **young men of the children of Israel** (the Levitic priesthood had not yet been established, so Moses simply appointed those he felt suitable for the task) offered **burnt-offerings** and **peace-offerings.** Moses sprinkled half of the blood on the altar, but reserved the other half in basins. Then he read again before all the people **the book of the covenant,** and again they consented thereto. Then he used the rest of the blood to sprinkle the people. The slaying of an animal was the normal symbol for establishing a covenant, both parties being identified in the life thus taken (cf. comments on Gen. 15:1-21).

Then the sacrificial meal which normally accompanied sacrifice and especially a covenant (cf. 18:12) followed. God had provided for this in verses 1-2. It was shared by the seventy-four men there mentioned, and it was honored by a revelation of the presence of God which did not cause the death of the men. Even Moses was not permitted to see God's face (33:20), so this must only have been a remarkable manifestation of His glory, similar to that on the Mount of Transfiguration (Matt. 17:1ff.). Rylaarsdam suggests that, "They looked up at the sky, *a pavement of sapphire stone,* on which the feet of God were supposed to rest. God was thought of as throned above the waters that were over the canopy of heaven (Ps. 29:10). The Presence is so real that it is as if 'the heavens were opened' (Ezek. 1:1)."[148]

C. TRAINING THROUGH REVELATION — THE PLAN OF WORSHIP (24:12—31:18)

1. The Setting for the Revelation (24:12-18)

12 And Jehovah said unto Moses, Come up to me into the mount, and be there: and I will give thee the tables of stone, and the law and the commandment, which I have written, that thou mayest teach them. 13 And Moses rose up, and Joshua his minister: and Moses went up into the mount of God. 14 And he said unto the elders, Tarry ye here for us, until we come again unto you: and, behold, Aaron and Hur are with you; whosoever hath a cause, let him come near unto them. 15 And Moses went up into the mount, and the cloud covered the mount. 16 And the glory of Jehovah abode upon mount Sinai, and the cloud covered it six days: and the seventh day he called unto Moses out of the midst of the cloud. 17 And the appearance of the glory of Jehovah was like devouring fire on the top of the mount in the eyes of the children of Israel. 18 And Moses entered into the midst of the cloud, and went up into the mount: and Moses was in the mount forty days and forty nights.

There had been two periods of contact between Jehovah and Moses since Israel arrived at Mt. Sinai. The first involved preliminary consent to the establishment of the covenant and the giving of instructions for preparing the people for its actual pronouncement (19:3-15). The second involved the actual giving and formal enactment of the covenant (19:16—24:11). Now there was to be a third. The Lord's invitation to Moses was to come up **into the mount** to receive from His hand two **tables of stone,** bearing the law (Hebrew *Torah,* which essentially means "direction" or "instruction" and is the usual Jewish term for the Mosaic law and especially the Pentateuch) **and the commandment,** which Jehovah Himself had written to give Moses a permanent and tangible basis for teaching the people. Since the only material said to have been written by the Lord was that on the two tablets of stone, and they contained only the Ten Commandments (34:28; Deut. 4:13; 10:4), **the law** and **the commandment** must be synonymous terms describing "the ten words" themselves.[149] But the mere handing over of the stone tablets, containing as they did laws already given, would not take long. So Jehovah's invitation for Moses to come up **and be there** or "continue there" was a hint of an extended period of contact and of additional revelation to be given. Apparently Moses, Aaron and his sons, and the seventy elders had returned to the foot of the mount after the sacrificial meal. Now, at the call of Jehovah, Moses instructed the elders as the representatives of the people to tarry in their present encampment until his return, and appointed Aaron and Hur as final authorities until his return. Then he took Joshua, now called for the first time **his minister** or "servant" (RSV) or "attendant,"[150] and together they ascended the mountain. Joshua is not mentioned again until 32:17 when Moses was on his way back down the mountain. So apparently he stopped off at some intermediary point, perhaps the same spot at which Moses waited for six days before being called into the cloud which covered God's presence (24:15-18). The preparation for the next step in divine revelation was calculated to impress all who saw with the seriousness and importance of what Jehovah had to say. The cloud containing the divine glory covered the mountain, and for six days all Moses could do was wait. Only on the seventh day was he invited closer to hear God's words. The total time he was to tarry on the mount was **forty days and forty nights.**

2. The Construction of the Tabernacle (25:1—27:19)

a. The Financing of the Tabernacle (25:1-9)

1 And Jehovah spake unto Moses, saying, 2 Speak unto the children of Israel, that they take for me an offering: of every man whose heart maketh him willing ye shall take my offering. 3 And this is the offering which ye shall take of them: gold, and silver, and brass, 4 and blue, and purple, and scarlet, and fine linen, and goats' *hair,* 5 and rams' skins dyed red, and sealskins, and acacia wood, 6 oil for the light, spices for the anointing oil, and for the sweet incense, 7 onyx stones, and stones to be set, for the ephod, and for the breastplate. 8 And let them make me a sanctuary, that I may dwell among them. 9 According to all that I show thee, the pattern of the tabernacle, and the pattern of all the furniture thereof, even so shall ye make it.

The Lord had first given Moses in the Ten Commandments instructions for ordering the moral life of His people, then in the balance of the Book of the Covenant instructions for ordering the social life of His people, and now He begins to unfold in detail those instructions governing the religious life of His people.[151] This was partially due to the need to give His people a visible expression of His relationship to them, and also to the need for their larger understanding of His character, and of the grand means of salvation He had provided for them and for all the world, which would now begin to be revealed in a manner best calculated to catch their interest and instruct their minds and hearts.

The Lord began His instructions to Moses concerning the plan of worship for Israel with a command to take an offering. It was to be general but voluntary — **of every man whose heart maketh him willing ye shall take my offering.** The offering was not to consist basically of money, but of materials. Some of these would have been normally found in their homes: **goats' hair, rams' skins** (given a reddish hue by the tanning process),

[149] Scholars differ widely in their interpretation of the relationship of these words to the tables of stone. But this view best accords with Scripture itself and is supported by the best authorities on the meaning of Hebrew words. See Brown, Driver, and Briggs, *op. cit.,* pp. 435-36, 846; and also Rawlinson, *The Pulpit Commentary: Exodus,* II, 236.   [150] Meek, *The Bible, an American Translation,* p. 73.

[151] J. Sidlow Baxter, *Explore the Book,* I, 84.

sealskins (variously translated as "porpoise-skins," ASV margin; "badgers' skins," KJV; "goatskins," RSV; referring to some type of leather, perhaps from some marine animal[152]), and the olive oil used in lamps. One article, the acacia wood, would have been found in the desert itself. But the other articles would be available only through the spoiling of the Egyptians (12:35-36): gold, silver, brass, blue and purple and scarlet cloth, fine linen, rare spices, onyx stones, and other precious stones. These were to be u ed to make Jehovah a sanctuary ("sacred place" or "holy place") or tabernacle (here literally "dwelling" or "habitation"), that He might dwell among them. Our popular name for this structure, "tabernacle," is simply an Anglicizing of the Latin tabernaculum, used by Jerome in his Vulgate translation. In addition to "sanctuary" and "dwelling," the Bible calls it "the Tent" (33:8, usually translated "tabernacle" in KJV), "the tent of the testimony" or witness (Num. 17:4, 7 — because it housed the ark which contained the tablets of stone which the Lord frequently called "the testimony"), "the dwelling of the testimony" (Exod. 38:21 — literal translation), and "the dwelling of Jehovah" (Num. 16:9 — literal translation).[153] Not only was Moses to be given detailed instructions concerning the various parts and furnishings of the building, including their dimensions, materials, and relationships, but he was also to be shown a pattern of the dwelling and of its furniture. The Hebrew word here "denotes not a ground plan or picture, but a solid structure — a heavenly model of the completely erected building."[154] (Cf. Acts 7:44.) It is no doubt this which enabled Moses to superintend the actual construction of the tent, and our lack of such a model which makes it impossible for us to picture some of the details.[155]

There is no direct and specific reference in the description of the tabernacle to a deeper meaning and purpose of the structure, its contents, and its forms of worship. But one does not think it through carefully without seeing that it depicts beautifully and helpfully some rich spiritual truths. For the Israelites it was a dramatic representation of God's holiness which separated Him from all else, and of sinful man who could approach Him only by His graciously appointed means. And the Jews themselves saw even more detailed typologies or allegories.[156] But it remained for early Christian writers to reveal and apply the deepest meaning of the tabernacle. The writer to the Hebrews thought of the earthly tabernacle as "a copy and shadow" of a heavenly tabernacle, making pointed reference to the pattern or model shown Moses in the mount, serving as "a figure" for the present age (Heb. 8:5; 9:9). This heavenly structure is "the true tabernacle, which the Lord pitched, not man" (Heb. 8:2), a "greater and more perfect tabernacle, not made with hands" (Heb. 9:11). While this is pictured at times as if it were within heaven, it seems also to be identified with heaven itself, for when Jesus entered the compartment within the veil (Heb. 6:19-20), the "Holy of holies" or "the holy place" as it is frequently called in Hebrews (Heb. 9:3, 12), it was "not into a holy place made with hands, like in pattern to the true" but rather "into heaven itself" (Heb. 9:24). The writer indicates that there are detailed meanings of every separate part and furnishing of the structure, for after listing them he regrets, "of which things we cannot now speak severally" (Heb. 9:5). John the Revelator also saw heaven in terms of the tabernacle. God's tabernacle is in heaven, just as is His name (Rev. 13:6). He shares it with those who victoriously endure the great tribulation (Rev. 7:15). It is revealed as the prototype of the tabernacle of the wilderness when it is called "the tabernacle of the testimony in heaven" (Rev. 15:5). It seems to be coextensive with heaven itself, for it contains a kind of inner sanctum or Holy of Holies, usually designated "temple" in the standard English versions. However, it cannot be "temple" in the sense of Solomon's or Herod's, for it is called "the temple of the tabernacle" (Rev. 15:5). The Greek word in the classics was used of the sanctuary or cell of a temple, where the actual image of

---

[152] Johnson, op. cit., pp. 74-5.   [153] Driver, op. cit., p. 257.   [154] McNeile, op. cit., p. 158.
[155] Johnson, op. cit., p. 75.
[156] For example, Josephus' likening of the structure to the universe, with the Holy Place as the earth and sea and the Holy of Holies as heaven, Antiquities of the Jews, Book III, Chapter VI, paragraph 4.

the god was placed, and was distinguished from the temple as a whole.[157] The ASV translates it in the margin as "sanctuary." This Holy of Holies contains not merely a symbol of God's throne like the mercy seat between the cherubim, but the actual throne (Rev. 16:17). From it angels go forth to carry out the divine commands (Rev. 14:15, 17; 15:6), and into it are admitted those who victoriously endure the great tribulation (Rev. 7:15). It apparently was customarily closed off from the rest of heaven, for twice it is said to have been opened (Rev. 11:19; 15:5), and once was so filled with the smoke of God's glory and power that no one could enter it (Rev. 15:8). In it was to be seen the archetype of the ark of the covenant (Rev. 11:19). Apparently either just outside the entrance to this inner sanctuary or actually inside, in front of the divine throne, was a horned, golden altar, beneath which were the souls of the martyrs, and from which incense mingled with the prayers of the saints ascended before God (Rev. 6:9; 8:3-5; 9:13). But while heaven in the present age is thus structured, the new Jerusalem which descends out of heaven to provide the eternal home of the redeemed shall not be so. It shall indeed bring the tabernacle of God directly to men (Rev. 21:3), but no one will find an inner sanctuary there, for the Lord and the Lamb will be its temple or sanctuary, affording all the saints immediate and ready access to the divine presence (Rev. 21:22).

On the one hand, it lies far beyond the limits of the present commentary to expect an exhaustive treatment of the types suggested by the tabernacle and its furnishings and rituals, or of the multitude of applications which have been given them across the centuries. On the other hand, we dare not avoid entirely those which are most apparent or are actually suggested by the Scriptures. Most of these will be mentioned in reference to the separate parts or pieces. However, some of its lessons are best summarized in relationship to the whole as Driver has done.

By one of its principal names, the . . . 'Dwelling' . . . the Tabernacle expresses in a sensible form the truth of God's presence in the midst of His people; by another of its principal names, the 'Tent of Meeting' . . . , it gives expression to the truth that God is not only present with His people, but that He reveals Himself to them; by its third name, the 'Tent (or Dwelling) of the Witness or Testimony,' it reminded the Israelite that in the Decalogue, inscribed on the Tables in the Ark, it contained an ever-present witness to the claims of God and the duty of man . . . . the gold, and costly, beautifully worked fabrics, which decorated, especially, the Holy of holies, and were also conspicuous in the gorgeous vestments of the high priest, give expression to the thought that the Dwelling, and the most responsible ministers of God, should be decked, or apparelled, with becoming splendour and dignity . . . the ascending degrees of sanctity, attaching to the court, the Holy place, and the Holy of holies, marked both by the materials of which they were constructed, and by the fact that while the people generally might enter the court, only the priests could enter the Holy place, and only the high priest, and he only once a year, and that 'not without blood,' the Holy of holies, safeguarded, in an impressive and significant manner, the holiness of God; and shewed that, though the way to Him was open, it was open only under restrictions . . . , and especially that the Presence of God Himself could be approached only by those who were, in a special sense, 'holy' . . . , and who carried with them the blood of atonement.[158]

b. The Furniture of the Tabernacle (25:10-40)

(1) The Ark (25:10-22)

10 And they shall make an ark of acacia wood: two cubits and a half shall be the length thereof, and a cubit and a half the breadth thereof, and a cubit and a half the height thereof. 11 And thou shalt overlay it with pure gold, within and without shalt thou overlay it, and shalt make upon it a crown of gold round about. 12 And thou shalt cast four rings of gold for it, and put them in the four feet thereof; and two rings shall be on the one side of it, and two rings on the other side of it. 13 And thou shalt make staves of acacia wood, and overlay them with gold. 14 And thou shalt put the staves into the rings on the

[157] Joseph Henry Thayer, *Greek-English Lexicon of the New Testament*, pp. 299, 422.
[158] Driver, *op. cit.*, pp. 260-61.

sides of the ark, wherewith to bear the ark. 15 The staves shall be in the rings of the ark: they shall not be taken from it. 16 And thou shalt put into the ark the testimony which I shall give thee. 17 And thou shalt make a mercy-seat of pure gold: two cubits and a half *shall be* the length thereof, and a cubit and a half the breadth thereof. 18 And thou shalt make two cherubim of gold; of beaten work shalt thou make them, at the two ends of the mercy-seat. 19 And make one cherub at the one end, and one cherub at the other end: of one piece with the mercy-seat shall ye make the cherubim on the two ends thereof. 20 And the cherubim shall spread out their wings on high, covering the mercy-seat with their wings, with their faces one to another; toward the mercy-seat shall the faces of the cherubim be. 21 And thou shalt put the mercy-seat above upon the ark; and in the ark thou shalt put the testimony that I shall give thee. 22 And there I will meet with thee, and I will commune with thee from above the mercy-seat, from between the two cherubim which are upon the ark of the testimony, of all things which I will give thee in commandment unto the children of Israel.

The description of the house of worship begins, not with the shell itself nor its surroundings, but rather with its furnishings, and particularly with the most sacred and most important item. Then the instructions proceed outward to the progressively less sacred. When the furnishings are completed, the actual structure is described, but again it is the Holy of Holies which is first completely enclosed and then the Holy Place and finally the court. The only break with this pattern occurs in chapter 30 where two items of furniture are treated after the structure is completely described, in conjunction with some miscellaneous items to be used regularly in the tabernacle.

The first item is the **ark,** which with the objects it held and supported was the only furnishing in the Holy of Holies. The ark was a chest made of **acacia wood,** a hard and durable wood native to the desert. It was forty-five inches long and twenty-seven inches wide by twenty-seven inches high. It was plated **with pure gold,** both inside and outside. It also

had **a crown** or rim of gold which ran all the way around it, probably at the upper edge. Since the tabernacle was essentially a portable temple, and both it and all of its furnishings must be capable of being easily transported, **four rings of gold** were to be cast for the ark and attached to the lower corners. Then poles, also made of acacia wood and plated with gold, were to be slipped into the rings. Inside the ark was to be placed **the testimony,** the two tables of stone bearing the Ten Commandments (cf. Heb. 9:4). The ark was to be covered with a lid which was a slab of pure gold and which bore the name of **mercy-seat** or "propitiatory." (The Hebrew word is from a root which basically means "to cover," and particularly "to cover sin"; the word *ransom* comes from the same root.) Rising from each end of the golden slab and forming one piece with it was to be a **cherub,** of hammered gold. The **cherubim** (-*im* marks the Hebrew plural here) were to face each other and to spread their wings out in such a way as to shadow the mercy-seat. The cherubim are first mentioned in Genesis 3:24 when they were placed as guards at the gate of Eden. They were not the chubby little baby angels now so designated. Ezekiel described them as having four faces (of a man, a lion, an ox, and an eagle), four wings (two of which covered their bodies), "straight feet" with soles like those of a calf's foot, and apparently four hands like the hands of a man. They "sparkled like burnished brass." (See Ezek. 1:4ff.; 10:1-20.) In heathen sculpture, they were symbolic winged creatures, with a lion's body, a human face, and conspicuous wings. They and other such hybrid animals are very frequently pictured as supporting in pairs the throne of a king or god.[159] In the Scriptures, the cherubim apparently constitute one order of angelic beings. On one occasion, Jehovah is said to have ridden upon a cherub (II Sam. 22:11; Ps. 18:10). Above the mercy-seat and between the cherubim was to be the dwelling-place of Jehovah, the supreme meeting-place between Him and man, the focus of the divine-human communication. It was here that only the high priest could approach, and he only once

---

[159] Unger, ed., "Cherub," in *Unger's Bible Dictionary,* pp. 191-92.

a year and with the proper preliminary sacrifices. And he was to do so only after having filled the Holy of Holies with the smoke of burning incense so he could not see the divine glory. And he was to sprinkle upon the mercy-seat and before it the blood of the sin-offering. (See Lev. 16:1-34.)

Thus the very heart of Israel's worship was to be found in the permanent record of God's will for His people's moral life (the ark with the tablets it contained), and in an invisible throne for an invisible God that rested over the mercy-seat — the meeting-place of man's obedience and faith with God's grace and forgiveness.

(2) The Table of Showbread (25: 23-30)

23 And thou shalt make a table of acacia wood: two cubits *shall be* the length thereof, and a cubit the breadth thereof, and a cubit and a half the height thereof. 24 And thou shalt overlay it with pure gold, and make thereto a crown of gold round about. 25 And thou shalt make unto it a border of a handbreadth round about; and thou shalt make a golden crown to the border thereof round about. 26 And thou shalt make for it four rings of gold, and put the rings in the four corners that are on the four feet thereof. 27 Close by the border shall the rings be, for places for the staves to bear the table. 28 And thou shalt make the staves of acacia wood, and overlay them with gold, that the table may be borne with them. 29 And thou shalt make the dishes thereof, and the spoons thereof, and the flagons thereof, and the bowls thereof, wherewith to pour out: of pure gold shalt thou make them. 30 And thou shalt set upon the table showbread before me alway.

The ark as well as the other items of furniture in the tabernacle and the later temple were apparently destroyed or hopelessly lost at the time of the destruction of Jerusalem by the Babylonians. The temple built after the return from exile and the temple of Jesus' day did not contain an ark. But they did contain a later edition of the second piece of furniture described, the **table** of **showbread** or "Presence-bread." This piece was apparently taken to Rome when Jerusalem

was destroyed in A.D. 70, and its likeness was carved there on the Arch of Titus, where it can still be seen.

The table sat on the north side of the outer compartment of the tabernacle (40: 22). It also was of acacia wood and plated with gold, thirty-six inches long, twenty-seven inches high, and eighteen inches wide. Around the edge of the tabletop, probably projecting slightly above, was a golden crown like that on the ark. Halfway down the legs (so it is in the likeness on the Arch of Titus[160]) was a border the width of a man's hand, joining the legs together, and bearing upon it a golden crown matching the one above. On the four legs were four golden rings, close to the border, into which were slipped four gold-plated poles for carrying it. The table was to be the depository of the twelve loaves of showbread which were to be laid out before the Lord each Sabbath (Lev. 24:5-9). To aid the fulfillment of its function, there were also to be made **dishes** or platters on which the bread could be carried, **spoons** or rather cups in which the frankincense could be placed upon the loaves, and **flagons** and **bowls** or chalices apparently for the drink-offerings which are mentioned in connection with certain sacrifices but never specifically related to this table (29:40).

Other ancient peoples had tables on which they laid out food for their gods to satisfy the divine appetites. Since the priests were instructed to eat the showbread (Lev. 24:5-9), it could not have had that precise meaning for Israel at any time. Rather, it was a recognition that all of Israel's material possessions really belonged to God, and symbolized their dedication to Him. It was also a recognition of their dependence upon God, of that expressed in the Lord's Prayer in the words, "Give us this day our daily bread." No doubt the Lord also sought through it to remind Israel "that man does not live by bread only, but by everything that proceedeth out of the mouth of Jehovah" (Deut. 8:30), and perhaps to foreshadow the coming of Him who is indeed the Bread of Life (John 6:35).

---

[160] Johnson, *op. cit.*, p. 75.

(3) The Candlestick (25:31-40)

31 And thou shalt make a candlestick of pure gold: of beaten work shall the candlestick be made, even its base, and its shaft; its cups, its knops, and its flowers, shall be of one piece with it: 32 and there shall be six branches going out of the sides thereof; three branches of the candlestick out of the one side thereof, and three branches of the candlestick out of the other side thereof: 33 three cups made like almond-blossoms in one branch, a knop and a flower; and three cups made like almond-blossoms in the other branch, a knop and a flower: so for the six branches going out of the candlestick: 34 and in the candlestick four cups made like almond-blossoms, the knops thereof, and the flowers thereof; 35 and a knop under two branches of one piece with it, and a knop under two branches of one piece with it, and a knop under two branches of one piece with it, for the six branches going out of the candlestick. 36 Their knops and their branches shall be of one piece with it; the whole of it one beaten work of pure gold. 37 And thou shalt make the lamps thereof, seven: and they shall light the lamps thereof, to give light over against it. 38 And the snuffers thereof, and the snuff-dishes thereof, shall be of pure gold. 39 Of a talent of pure gold shall it be made, with all these vessels. 40 And see that thou make them after their pattern, which hath been showed thee in the mount.

The **candlestick** ought better to be called the "lampstand," as this is what the Hebrew word means, and it bore, not a single candle, but rather lamps. Since there were no windows in the tabernacle, the lampstand was the only means of light in the house of worship. It stood on the south side of the outer compartment, opposite the table (40:24). It consisted of a **base** (perhaps of a tripod nature), a central **shaft**, and six **branches**, three on each side of the shaft. Like the cherubim, it was to be hammered gold, all of one piece, weighing **one talent** or about ninety-four pounds. It had something of the appearance of an almond tree,[161] having **four cups shaped like almond-blossoms** each with **a knop** (an archaic word meaning "knob" or here "bud") and **a flower**, or more technically, the calyx and carolla (the outer leaves and inner petals) of the almond-flower. Apparently there was also the knop or outer part of the flower only at each spot on the shaft where two opposing branches separated. And each branch also had three cups shaped like almond-blossoms with the entire flower represented.[162] On top of the six branches and the shaft, thus making seven in all, were to be placed the lamps. They were shaped like saucers with the rim pinched together at one spot, and the wick protruded from the pinched part. The lamps were to be lighted or rather "set up" in their places. Also out of the talent of gold were to be made **snuffers** (but the Hebrew word here means "tweezers" or literally "the takers" — for drawing up the wick) and **snuffdishes** (literally "fire-holders" or holders for the hot tweezers).

The lampstand and its continually burning lamps symbolized that Israel's spiritual light could come only from Jehovah. It also symbolized Israel's relationship to the nations — a God-provided light in the midst of darkness. It spoke also of the coming Light of the world (John 8:12) and of the spiritual successors of Israel, who were also to be the light of the world — lamps that must be put on the stand so that all could see (Matt. 5:14-16).

In connection with the symmetry of the lampstand as well as of the other pieces of furniture, and the occurrence of the number seven in the lamps, it might be well to consider an observation by Driver.

> In their dimensions, both the 'Tabernacle' and the court display great symmetry. The ruling numbers are 3, 4, 7, 10, their parts (1½, 2, 2½, 5), and their multiples (6, 9, 12, 20, 28, 30, 42, 48, 50, 60, 100). If, without indulging in fantastic extravagances, we may discern a symbolism in numbers, we may perhaps see in *three* a symbol of the divine, in *four* — suggesting the four quarters of the earth — the totality of what is human, in *seven* and *twelve* numbers which, deriving their original significance from astronomy, came to be regarded as symbols of completeness, and in *ten* and its

---

[161] *Ibid.*, p. 76.

[162] A clear description of the lampstand is given by Driver, and he incorporates a very enlightening drawing by Professor A. R. S. Kennedy, from Hastings' *Dictionary of the Bible.* See Driver, *op. cit.*, pp. 275-78.

multiples numbers specially suggestive of symmetry and perfection.[163]

c. The Formation of the Tabernacle (26:1-37)

(1) The Inner Curtains (26:1-6)

1 Moreover thou shalt make the tabernacle with ten curtains; of fine twined linen, and blue, and purple, and scarlet, with cherubim the work of the skilful workman shalt thou make them. 2 The length of each curtain shall be eight and twenty cubits, and the breadth of each curtain four cubits: all the curtains shall have one measure. 3 Five curtains shall be coupled together one to another; and *the other* five curtains shall be coupled one to another. 4 And thou shalt make loops of blue upon the edge of the one curtain from the selvedge in the coupling; and likewise shalt thou make in the edge of the curtain that is outmost in the second coupling. 5 Fifty loops shalt thou make in the one curtain, and fifty loops shalt thou make in the edge of the curtain that is in the second coupling; the loops shall be opposite one to another. 6 And thou shalt make fifty clasps of gold, and couple the curtains one to another with the clasps: and the tabernacle shall be one *whole*.

The term **tabernacle** or "dwelling," while perhaps at times applied to the entire structure, was particularly applied to the beautiful widths of cloth which enclosed the two compartments. **Ten curtains** or widths were to be made, of the **fine twined linen** for which Egypt was known, and of materials dyed **blue** (more exactly a violet or blue-violet, a dye obtained from a shellfish which adheres to rocks in the Mediterranean), **purple** (more exactly a red-violet, a dye extracted from a small gland in the throat of two other kinds of shellfish found on the coasts of Phoenicia, and used in the clothes of kings and wealthy men), and **scarlet** (literally "worm of brilliance," the dye being obtained from the dried bodies of female cochineal insects, scale insects which resemble berries and attach themselves to the leaves and twigs of a Syrian tree). The first two colors were especially prized among the ancients because of their brilliance and costliness.[164] On the curtains or strips of cloth, were

to be pictured cherubim, like those on the mercy-seat. This was either done by embroidering the figures on the material or by so weaving the blue, purple, and red yarns, the linen, and perhaps fine gold wires as to produce them. Driver translates **the skilful workman** as "the skilful designer" or "pattern-maker" which would support the weaving theory.[165] Each strip of cloth was to be forty-two feet long by six feet wide. They were to be fastened together, perhaps sewn together, in sets of five. **Loops of blue** or blue-violet were to be made **upon the edge of the one curtain from the selvedge in the coupling** — or as it is much more clearly translated, "on the edge of the outermost curtain in the one set you are to make loops of violet" and likewise "the same on the edge of the outermost curtain in the other set."[166] There were to be fifty loops on each of the curtains involved, and they were to be fastened together with **fifty clasps of gold,** making one large covering, forty-two by sixty feet in size. Their being in two parts would make them easier to transport from place to place, but their efficient combination in one piece was essential for their purpose in the building. The way in which they were hung will be discussed in the comments on 26:15-30.

(2) The Outer Covers (26:7-14)

7 And thou shalt make curtains of goats' *hair* for a tent over the tabernacle: eleven curtains shalt thou make them. 8 The length of each curtain shall be thirty cubits, and the breadth of each curtain four cubits: the eleven curtains shall have one measure. 9 And thou shalt couple five curtains by themselves, and six curtains by themselves, and shalt double over the sixth curtain in the forefront of the tent. 10 And thou shalt make fifty loops on the edge of the one curtain that is outmost in the coupling, and fifty loops upon the edge of the curtain which is *outmost in* the second coupling. 11 And thou shalt make fifty clasps of brass, and put the clasps into the loops, and couple the tent together, that it may be one. 12 And the overhanging part that remaineth of the curtains of the tent, the half curtain that remaineth, shall hang over the back of the tabernacle. 13 And

---

[163] *Ibid.,* pp. 259-60.   [164] *Ibid.,* pp. 264-65.   [165] *Ibid.,* pp. 280-81.
[166] Meek, *The Bible, an American Translation,* p. 74.

the cubit on the one side, and the cubit on the other side, of that which remaineth in the length of the curtains of the tent, shall hang over the sides of the tabernacle on this side and on that side, to cover it. 14 And thou shalt make a covering for the tent of rams' skins dyed red, and a covering of sealskins above.

While the covering described in verses 1-6 would be beautiful, it would do little to protect the interior of the sanctuary from the weather. So a tent was to be placed over the **tabernacle** or "dwelling." It was to be made of cloth woven from **goats' hair,** the common material for Bedouin tents in that part of the world yet today. There were to be eleven curtains or strips in this outer covering, each forty-five feet long (three feet longer than the interior ones) and six feet wide. They were to be fastened in one set of five and one of six, and then the sets coupled together in the same fashion as the inner covering, only using **brass** or, more accurately, "bronze" or "copper"[167] clasps instead of gold ones. The entire goats' hair covering would be forty-five by sixty-six feet in size. Then over this there were apparently still two other coverings of even stronger and more durable materials, the inner one of **rams' skins** turned **red** by the tanning process, and the outer one of a type of skins not now precisely identifiable (see comments on 25:1-9). The use of skins to protect tents was also known to the Romans.[168] The manner in which the goats' hair covering was hung in place will be discussed in the next section.

(3) The Boards and Bars (26:15-30)

15 And thou shalt make the boards for the tabernacle of acacia wood, standing up. 16 Ten cubits shall be the length of a board, and a cubit and a half the breadth of each board. 17 Two tenons shall there be in each board, joined one to another: thus shalt thou make for all the boards of the tabernacle. 18 And thou shalt make the boards for the tabernacle, twenty boards for the south side southward. 19 And thou shalt make forty sockets of silver under the twenty boards; two sockets under one board for its two tenons, and two sockets under another

board for its two tenons: 20 and for the second side of the tabernacle, on the north side, twenty boards, 21 and their forty sockets of silver; two sockets under one board, and two sockets under another board. 22 And for the hinder part of the tabernacle westward thou shalt make six boards. 23 And two boards shalt thou make for the corners of the tabernacle in the hinder part. 24 And they shall be double beneath, and in like manner they shall be entire unto the top thereof unto one ring: thus shall it be for them both; they shall be for the two corners. 25 And there shall be eight boards, and their sockets of silver, sixteen sockets; two sockets under one board, and two sockets under another board.

26 And thou shalt make bars of acacia wood; five for the boards of the one side of the tabernacle, 27 and five bars for the boards of the other side of the tabernacle, and five bars for the boards of the side of the tabernacle, for the hinder part westward. 28 And the middle bar in the midst of the boards shall pass through from end to end. 29 And thou shalt overlay the boards with gold, and make their rings of gold for places for the bars: and thou shalt overlay the bars with gold. 30 And thou shalt rear up the tabernacle according to the fashion thereof which hath been showed thee in the mount.

The exact form of the tabernacle cannot be determined with finality from the description given in Exodus. The vision of a model which Moses beheld no doubt clarified all the points which now confuse the modern reader. But because of the incompleteness of the description as we have it, endless controversy has developed. Critical scholars are prone to say that the tabernacle as here described never existed in concrete form. Rather it was an ideal tabernacle which later writers wrote into the history of Israel in the wilderness, transforming the simple "tent of meeting" mentioned in 33:7ff. into a portable replica of Solomon's temple.[169] Because of this, they do not believe it essential to understand the tabernacle as a structure which would be practical for a sojourn in the wilderness, and they interpret details in the light of the similarity of the tabernacle to the temple. On the other hand, evangelical

---

[167] Unger, ed., "Mineral Kingdom: Brass," in *Unger's Bible Dictionary*, pp. 733-34.
[168] Driver, *op. cit.*, p. 285.
[169] See Rylaarsdam, *op. cit.*, I, 1027, and also 844-46, 1020ff.; and Driver, *op. cit.*, pp. 257ff., 426ff.

scholars believe that the tabernacle did exist, was used in the wilderness, and that the temple was in turn modeled after the tabernacle. Thus they are committed to understanding the tabernacle as a structure which was practical for life in the desert, and which would be expected to manifest traits characteristic of the dwellings found in the desert.

Basically there are two interpretations of the form of the tabernacle. The one followed by most critical scholars and some evangelicals is that proposed by Professor A. R. S. Kennedy in Hastings' *Dictionary of the Bible*. It looks upon the tabernacle as a flat-topped, essentially box-like structure.[170] In this view, **the boards of . . . acacia wood standing up** are rather "frames," composed of two upright members or **tenons, joined one to another** by means of crossrails or crossbars (as the Hebrew word implies) somewhat like a ladder. These frames were fifteen feet high, and twenty-seven inches wide — wider than one would expect a plank of acacia wood to be, but reasonable for a frame. Kennedy suggests that they were about nine inches thick. The lower part of each tenon or upright fitted into a socket or base of silver (thus two **sockets** to each frame) with each base weighing one talent or about ninety-four pounds (38:27). Twenty of these frames composed each of the long sides of the structure, and six the back end, making it thirty cubits or forty-five feet long, by ten cubits (the nine cubits of the six frames plus the two half-cubits thickness of the side frames) or fifteen feet wide, and fifteen feet high. (This compared with ninety by thirty by forty-five for Solomon's temple, I Kings 6:2ff.) Two extra frames were made to add support to the rear corners, perhaps set out from the others and sloping upward to fit under and support the upper bar which held the frames together. Five bars were to be made for each side and the end, running through rings in the frames, securing them in place. Only the middle bar (v. 28) ran all the way through, with the others probably serving in pairs, each running only half the length of its wall. Both frames and bars

were to be plated with gold. Over the assembled framework the beautifully figured inner cover would have been laid, being visible through the open frames. Its forty-two-foot width would have covered the top and reached down the sides to within one cubit or eighteen inches of the ground, while its sixty-foot length would have covered the top from front to back and reached down the back side to the ground. Over it would have been laid in turn the goats' hair covering, its forty-five-foot width covering the top and both sides all the way to the ground, being one cubit or eighteen inches longer than the inner cover (tabernacle or "dwelling") on each side (v. 13), and its sixty-six-foot length providing a doubled-over valance to help protect the entrance plus covering the length of the top and the end and leaving a half-curtain extra at the back. Over this would have been put the coverings of rams' skins and sealskins. And each successive layer would have been drawn tight and secured to the ground by cords and stakes or "pins" (35:18).

The other view of the tabernacle is that it had a ridgepole running lengthwise at the top, and thus slanting sides as we would normally expect in a tent. This view has many varieties as to some of the details, and can borrow certain parts of the other view. Our description here will take those options which are most different from the other view. The framework then becomes solid boards or planks instead of frames, with projecting tenons fastening into the sockets of the silver bases, and the whole joined together by the poles. The center pillar of the front screen (v. 37) would have served as a front support for the ridgepole, while the back support is not described in the Scriptures (nor is the ridgepole mentioned). The ridgepole was at such a height (about fifteen cubits or twenty-two-and-one-half feet) that when the "dwelling" or beautiful inner covering was thrown over it and drawn tight to the ground, the roof would have had a right angle. Thus approximately half of the covering would be used up as a roof, the other half extending about half-

[170] Drawings of Professor Kennedy's conception are reproduced in McNeile, *op. cit.*, following p. lxxiv, and in Driver, *op. cit.*, p. 283. His view is adopted by and large by such critical scholars as McNeile, Driver, Noth, and Rylaarsdam, and by such an evangelical scholar as Johnson.

way to the ground on each side as large eaves extending beyond the solid board sides. Since the length of the inner covering was sixty feet and of the framework only forty-five, the covering would have extended beyond both ends of the wooden framework about seven-and-one-half feet. This would require additional poles to stretch it upon. On this basis, one standing inside the structure would have seen gold-plated boards down the sides and the beautiful fabric with its figures or cherubim only above. The rest of the inner fabric and the outside of the gold-plated boards would have been visible from the outside due to the overhang. The goats' hair covering or tent would then have been put over the tapestry, with it extending some eighteen inches farther on each overhanging eave, with one-half of the extra width of cloth doubled over at the front to protect the edge of the tapestry from the weather, and the other half hanging down in the back for the same purpose. The two corner boards would have doubled as supports and as closing up the one-cubit shortage of material left by the six end boards. The rams' skins and sealskins would each in turn have been laid over the tent and drawn tight as it was by cords and stakes.[171]

(4) The Veil (26:31-35)

31 And thou shalt make a veil of blue, and purple, and scarlet, and fine twined linen: with cherubim the work of the skilful workman shall it be made: 32 and thou shalt hang it upon four pillars of acacia overlaid with gold; their hooks *shall be* of gold, upon four sockets of silver. 33 And thou shalt hang up the veil under the clasps, and shalt bring in thither within the veil the ark of the testimony: and the veil shall separate unto you between the holy place and the most holy. 34 And thou shalt put the mercy-seat upon the ark of the testimony in the most holy place. 35 And thou shalt set the table without the veil, and the candlestick over against the table on the side of the tabernacle toward the south: and thou shalt put the table on the north side.

The structure was to be divided internally into two compartments by a veil made of the same beautiful material and design as the "dwelling" or inner cover. It was to be hung upon four pillars of acacia wood plated with gold, hooked to them with gold hooks, and the pillars resting in sockets identical to those holding the boards at the sides (38:27). The veil was to be located beneath the juncture of the "dwelling" or inner cover, where the clasps held the two sets of curtains together. The compartment at the west end, farthest from the door and thus hidden by the veil, was to be known as **the most holy** place, and the compartment at the east end next to the door as **the holy place.** The ark and mercy-seat were to go in the inner one, the table and the candlestick in the outer one.

Both views of the form of the tabernacle hold that the four pillars were each of the same height. Professor Kennedy's view would picture the veil as reaching to the flat roof, and enclosing a perfect cube, fifteen feet long, wide, and high — each dimension being just one-half of the corresponding one in Solomon's temple (I Kings 6:20). The more traditional view would picture a triangular opening above the veil because of the pitch of the roof. If the inner covering or "dwelling" extended an equal distance in front of and behind the wooden framework, the veil would have to be located in the middle, dividing the structure in two equal parts, and destroying the comparison with the temple. But many who hold the tent-view here adopt the arrangement of Professor Kennedy, moving all the overhang to the rear and maintaining the Holy of Holies as a cube — except for the open triangular space above it.

The inner compartment of the tabernacle was entered only once a year by the high priest, on the Day of Atonement. But the writer to the Hebrews tells us that this was because the way into the Holy of Holies, the means of ready access to the immediate presence of God, had not yet been made apparent (Heb. 9:8). But at Calvary, Christ tore away the old veil, entered it once and for all (Heb. 6:19-20; 9:12), and substituted a new veil, His own flesh (Heb.

---

171 For a pictorial representation of this view, see William Smith, ed., "Temple," in *Smith's Bible Dictionary*, pp. 303-04. This view in some form or other is supported by Rawlinson, Unger, Connell, and also by G. A. Chadwick, *The Book of Exodus*, in "The Expositor's Bible," ed. by W. Robertson Nicoll.

10:20), so that we can now, all of us, enter confidently into heaven, the true Holy of Holies (Heb. 9:24; 10:19), and have access to the immediate presence of God, through Jesus Christ.

(5) The Screen (26:36-37)

36 And thou shalt make a screen for the door of the Tent, of blue, and purple, and scarlet, and fine twined linen, the work of the embroiderer. 37 And thou shalt make for the screen five pillars of acacia, and overlay them with gold: their hooks shall be of gold: and thou shalt cast five sockets of brass for them.

At the entrance of the structure, a screen was to be made to cover the door, of the same type of material as the inner cover and the veil, but with less elaborate figuration, being the work of the embroiderer rather than of the weaver. It was to be hung upon five pillars, rather than four, also made of acacia and plated with gold, the screen attached to it by gold hooks and the pillars resting in brass bases rather than silver. According to the flat-roof view of the tabernacle, all five of these pillars were of the same height. According to the sloping-roof view, the center one was twenty-two-and-one-half feet high and supported the ridgepole, the next one on each side would have been fifteen feet high, as were the gold-plated boards at the side, and the outside one on each side would have been seven-and-one-half feet high, standing approximately at the lower edge of the inner covering or "dwelling."

d. The Fencing of the Tabernacle (27:1-19)

(1) The Altar of Burnt-Offering (27:1-8)

1 And thou shalt make the altar of acacia wood, five cubits long, and five cubits broad; the altar shall be four-square: and the height thereof shall be three cubits. 2 And thou shalt make the horns of it upon the four corners thereof; the horns thereof shall be of one piece with it: and thou shalt overlay it with brass. 3 And thou shalt make its pots to take away its ashes, and its shovels, and its basins, and its flesh-hooks, and its firepans: all the vessels thereof thou shalt make of brass. 4 And thou shalt make

for it a grating of network of brass; and upon the net shalt thou make four brazen rings in the four corners thereof. 5 And thou shalt put it under the ledge round the altar beneath, that the net may reach halfway up the altar. 6 And thou shalt make staves for the altar, staves of acacia wood, and overlay them with brass. 7 And the staves thereof shall be put into the rings, and the staves shall be upon the two sides of the altar, in bearing it. 8 Hollow with planks shalt thou make it: as it hath been showed thee in the mount, so shall they make it.

Having completed the description of the sanctuary proper, we are now conveyed to the courtyard which surrounded it. Here the object closest to the tabernacle was a large altar, seven-and-one-half feet square and four-and-one-half feet high, built of acacia wood and plated with brass or, more exactly, bronze or copper. Of one piece with the bronze of the altar were the four horns which projected above its corners. Around the altar was built a grating of network of bronze, reaching halfway up the side of the altar, and serving as the support of the ledge which ran around the altar and on which the priests had to stand when carrying out their service on the altar itself. It was hollow, made of planks, and may have had neither top nor bottom. If so, it may have been set down at each camping spot over a natural rock altar or filled with earth somewhat in keeping with 20:24-25. It, too, was to have rings and poles, the material used for the rings and for plating the acacia poles in this case being bronze. It was to have a complete set of pots for carrying away the ashes (literally "fat," referring to the melted fat which ran down among the ashes), shovels for scooping up the ashes, basins or "tossing vessels" for throwing the blood in a quantity against the sides of the altar, flesh-hooks for moving the sacrifice about, and fire-pans for laying the hot instruments in.[172] All of these were to be of brass.

This altar was called "the altar of burnt-offering" (30:28) to distinguish it from the altar of incense inside the sanctuary. It taught Israel and symbolizes to Christians today the truth that man's sin is destructive and God's forgiveness costly. It insists that without the shedding

---

[172] Driver, op. cit., pp. 291-93.

of blood there can be no remission of sin (Heb. 9:22). And the offering there of the daily morning and evening sacrifices spoke clearly of the need for constant dependence upon God's grace and His appointed means for our approach, and for our constant devotion to and worship of Him.

(2) The Curtains of the Court (27: 9-19)

9 And thou shalt make the court of the tabernacle: for the south side southward there shall be hangings for the court of fine twined linen a hundred cubits long for one side: 10 and the pillars thereof shall be twenty, and their sockets twenty, of brass; the hooks of the pillars and their fillets *shall be* of silver. 11 And likewise for the north side in length there shall be hangings a hundred cubits long, and the pillars thereof twenty, and their sockets twenty, of brass; the hooks of the pillars, and their fillets, of silver. 12 And for the breadth of the court on the west side shall be hangings of fifty cubits; their pillars ten, and their sockets ten. 13 And the breadth of the court on the east side eastward shall be fifty cubits. 14 The hangings for the one side *of the gate* shall be fifteen cubits; their pillars three, and their sockets three. 15 And for the other side shall be hangings of fifteen cubits; their pillars three, and their sockets three. 16 And for the gate of the court shall be a screen of twenty cubits, of blue, and purple, and scarlet, and fine twined linen, the work of the embroiderer; their pillars four, and their sockets four. 17 All the pillars of the court round about shall be filleted with silver; their hooks of silver, and their sockets of brass. 18 The length of the court shall be a hundred cubits, and the breadth fifty every where, and the height five cubits, of fine twined linen, and their sockets of brass. 19 All the instruments of the tabernacle in all the service thereof, and all the pins thereof, and all the pins of the court, shall be of brass.

The courtyard of the tabernacle was also to be enclosed. It was to be one-hundred-fifty feet long by seventy-five feet wide. On the north and south sides would be twenty **pillars** standing in **sockets** or bases of brass or bronze, having silver **hooks** to which the seven-and-one-half-feet-high strip of cloth was to be con-

nected by silver **fillets** or "binding-rings" or "binding-threads." The west side and east side would have only ten pillars apiece. The hangings themselves were apparently of white **linen.** On the east side, the hangings extended only twenty-two-and-one-half feet in from each corner, leaving a thirty foot opening in the center. Apparently just inside this were to be set up the four middle pillars and a thirty foot hanging embroidered of the same rich materials and designs as the screen at the entrance to the tabernacle itself. This would leave an opening at each end for entrance, but would protect the privacy of the tabernacle and its courtyard from the curious gaze of those outside. The various pillars and hangings of the entire courtyard would be secured in place by cords and pins, all made of brass.

3. The Ministers of the Tabernacle (27:20—29:46)

a. The Commission of the Priests— A Perpetual Light (27:20-21)

20 And thou shalt command the children of Israel, that they bring unto thee pure olive oil beaten for the light, to cause a lamp to burn continually. 21 In the tent of meeting, without the veil which is before the testimony, Aaron and his sons shall keep it in order from evening to morning before Jehovah: it shall be a statute for ever throughout their generations on the behalf of the children of Israel.

This paragraph seems awkward at this point, being related not to what immediately precedes, but to the outer compartment of the sanctuary which had been considered much earlier. Some have supposed it to be out of place, or introduced by a later editor from Leviticus 24:1-4. However, it is possible that it is the divinely inspired introduction to the Aaronic priesthood, prefacing the instructions concerning their garments and consecration with an announcement concerning one of their most symbolic and important duties.

Pure, beaten **olive oil,** considered the best of all for lighting,[173] was to be furnished by the people so that the priests, Aaron and his sons, could keep one of

---

[173] *Ibid.,* p. 296.

the seven lamps burning continuously throughout each night. It is possible that some daylight came through or around the screen to the door of the tabernacle, or perhaps it was thrown open part of the time, and thus the lamps would not be needed in the daytime. It is more probable that all the lamps were lighted during the day, before the night lamp burned out.

b. The Clothing of the Priests (28: 1-43)

(1) Its Nature and Purpose (28:1-5)

1 And bring thou near unto thee Aaron thy brother, and his sons with him, from among the children of Israel, that he may minister unto me in the priest's office, even Aaron, Nadab and Abihu, Eleazar and Ithamar, Aaron's sons. 2 And thou shalt make holy garments for Aaron thy brother, for glory and for beauty. 3 And thou shalt speak unto all that are wise-hearted, whom I have filled with the spirit of wisdom, that they make Aaron's garments to sanctify him, that he may minister unto me in the priest's office. 4 And these are the garments which they shall make: a breastplate, and an ephod, and a robe, and a coat of checker work, a mitre, and a girdle: and they shall make holy garments for Aaron thy brother, and his sons, that he may minister unto me in the priest's office. 5 And they shall take the gold, and the blue, and the purple, and the scarlet, and the fine linen.

These verses contain the first specific announcement that Aaron and his sons were to exercise perpetually the office of the priesthood. Aaron had had an important office as Moses' spokesman since his younger brother returned from the desert to lead Israel out of Egypt. And his two older sons had been privileged to join in the sacrificial feast which formalized the covenant (24:1, 9). But now Aaron and all four of his sons are set aside for their sacred task. For this task, they would need special garments, **holy** (reflecting the separateness of God), **for glory and for beauty** — exalting the office in the eyes of the people and in keeping with the beauty God had made in the universe and designed in the place of worship. The garments are in themselves

to sanctify Aaron, or set him apart for his ministry, in the manner indicated. The sacred garments were to include a **breastplate, an ephod, a robe, a coat of checker work, a mitre, and a girdle**—or, in terms much more intelligible to our day, "a pouch, an apron, a robe, a tunic in checkered work, a turban, and a sash."[174] They, too, would require **gold, blue, purple, scarlet,** and **linen.**

(2) Its Design for the High Priest (28:6-39)

(a) The Ephod and the Onyx Stones (28:6-14)

6 And they shall make the ephod of gold, of blue, and purple, scarlet, and fine twined linen, the work of the skilful workman. 7 It shall have two shoulder-pieces joined to the two ends thereof, that it may be joined together. 8 And the skilfully woven band, which is upon it, wherewith to gird it on, shall be like the work thereof *and* of the same piece; of gold, of blue, and purple, and scarlet, and fine twined linen. 9 And thou shalt take two onyx stones, and grave on them the names of the children of Israel: 10 six of their names on the one stone, and the names of the six that remain on the other stone, according to their birth. 11 With the work of an engraver in stone, like the engravings of a signet, shalt thou engrave the two stones, according to the names of the children of Israel: thou shalt make them to be inclosed in settings of gold. 12 And thou shalt put the two stones upon the shoulder-pieces of the ephod, to be stones of memorial for the children of Israel: and Aaron shall bear their names before Jehovah upon his two shoulders for a memorial. 13 And thou shalt make settings of gold, 14 and two chains of pure gold; like cords shalt thou make them, of wreathen work: and thou shalt put the wreathen chains on the settings.

The **ephod** was made something like an apron suspended from the shoulders, but probably reached no lower than the waist. It had a **band,** apparently at the bottom, by which it was tied around the body, and **shoulder-pieces** by which it was suspended from the shoulders. It was woven by the same type of workman as the inner covering or "dwelling" of the house of worship — the skillful pattern

---

[174] Meek, *The Bible, an American Translation,* p. 76.

weaver. On the two shoulder-pieces were to be placed **two onyx stones,** either the onyx, which is a stratified stone, consisting of layers of white and other colors, or a beryl, a clear blue, green, or pale yellow stone.[175] The stones were to be set in gold, and each was to have engraved upon it the names of six of the twelve tribes of Israel. Thus Aaron was to bear the names of Israel upon his shoulders for a **memorial,** signifying both those for whom he interceded and those he represented and in whose interests he dared approach the Lord, whenever he carried out his official duties. Suspended from the settings of the stones were to be **two chains of pure gold,** made **like cords** apparently by twisting together some of the fine golden wires also used in weaving the ephod itself.

(b) The Breastplate (28:15-30)

15 And thou shalt make a breastplate of judgment, the work of the skilful workman; like the work of the ephod thou shalt make it; of gold, of blue, and purple, and scarlet, and fine twined linen, shalt thou make it. 16 Foursquare it shall be *and* double; a span shall be the length thereof, and a span the breadth thereof. 17 And thou shalt set in it settings of stones, four rows of stones: a row of sardius, topaz, and carbuncle shall be the first row; 18 and the second row an emerald, a sapphire, and a diamond; 19 and the third row a jacinth, an agate, and an amethyst; 20 and the fourth row a beryl, and an onyx, and a jasper: they shall be inclosed in gold in their settings. 21 And the stones shall be according to the names of the children of Israel, twelve, according to their names; like the engravings of a signet, every one according to his name, they shall be for the twelve tribes. 22 And thou shalt make upon the breastplate chains like cords, of wreathen work of pure gold. 23 And thou shalt make upon the breastplate two rings of gold, and shalt put the two rings on the two ends of the breastplate. 24 And thou shalt put the two wreathen chains of gold in the two rings at the ends of the breastplate. 25 And the *other* two ends of the two wreathen chains thou shalt put on the two settings, and put them on the shoulder-pieces of the ephod in the forepart thereof. 26 And thou shalt make two rings of gold, and thou shalt put them upon the two ends

of the breastplate, upon the edge thereof, which is toward the side of the ephod inward. 27 And thou shalt make two rings of gold, and shalt put them on the two shoulder-pieces of the ephod underneath, in the forepart thereof, close by the coupling thereof, above the skilfully woven band of the ephod. 28 And they shall bind the breastplate by the rings thereof unto the rings of the ephod with a lace of blue, that it may be upon the skilfully woven band of the ephod, and that the breastplate be not loosed from the ephod. 29 And Aaron shall bear the names of the children of Israel in the breastplate of judgment upon his heart, when he goeth in unto the holy place, for a memorial before Jehovah continually. 30 And thou shalt put in the breastplate of judgment the Urim and the Thummim; and they shall be upon Aaron's heart, when he goeth in before Jehovah: and Aaron shall bear the judgment of the children of Israel upon his heart before Jehovah continually.

The Hebrew word translated **breastplate** cannot be precisely defined since it is never used in any other connection except this portion of the high priest's attire. But since it was doubled (v. 16) and served to hold things (v. 30), it is evident that it was some kind of pouch or pocket. It was made of the same material as the ephod, and by the same type of craftsman as the ephod and the inner curtains of the sanctuary. It was about nine inches square. At the top, where the two ends doubled back together, a golden ring was placed at each corner, and the twisted gold chains attached to the shoulder-piece settings were also attached to the breastplate. At the lower corners of the pouch, on the inside, two other gold rings were attached, and a blue or blue-violet **lace** ran from these rings to two others attached to the ephod, probably behind the priest, on the lower part of the shoulder-pieces, just above the band, close to where it itself was tied — **close by the coupling thereof.** On the front of the pouch were to be set twelve precious stones, each engraved with the name of one of the tribes of Israel. It is very difficult to identify precious stones with precision when translating from an ancient language to a modern. Driver identifies the first row

---

[175] Driver, *op. cit.*, p. 305.

as the carnelian or red jasper, chrysolite, and rock-crystal; the second row as red garnet, lapis lazuli, and sardonyx; the third row as cairngorm, agate, and amethyst; and the fourth row as yellow jasper, onyx or beryl, and green jasper.[176] Thus Aaron was to **bear the names of the children of Israel . . . upon his heart . . . for a memorial before Jehovah continually.**

In addition to the stones in gold settings on the outside of the pouch, it is to contain objects called **the Urim and the Thummim,** objects which have a peculiar relationship to **the judgment of the children of Israel,** and in fact cause the pouch to be called **the breastplate of judgment.** They are nowhere explained in the Bible, nor is any ancient writer able to explain them convincingly. Their names mean either "Light and Perfection" or "Lights and Perfections." They were used in some fashion to determine the Lord's will in questions brought to the priests (see Lev. 8:8; Deut. 33:8; Ezra 2:63; Neh. 7:65). Josephus identified them with the two precious stones on the shoulders of the high priest, which when clear indicated approval and when cloudy disapproval. Another suggestion identifies them with the twelve tribal gems which in some manner helped the high priest to pass into a true prophetic state. Still another suggests that they were three stones, one of which signified Yes, another No, and the third neutrality, and that they were used as sacred lots to determine the divine will.[177]

(c) The Robe of the Ephod (28:31-35)

31 And thou shalt make the robe of the ephod all of blue. 32 And it shall have a hole for the head in the midst thereof: it shall have a binding of woven work round about the hole of it, as it were the hole of a coat of mail, that it be not rent. 33 And upon the skirts of it thou shalt make pomegranates of blue, and of purple, and of scarlet, round about the skirts thereof; and bells of gold between them round about: 34 a golden bell and a pomegranate, a golden bell and a pomegranate, upon the skirts of the robe round about. 35 And it shall be

upon Aaron to minister: and the sound thereof shall be heard when he goeth in unto the holy place before Jehovah, and when he cometh out, that he die not.

The next piece of attire was apparently woven in one piece like Christ's seamless robe (John 19:23-24), with a reinforced hole through which the head was slipped, and probably also armholes. It was to be entirely of blue or blue-violet material, a royal garment indeed. On the hem were to be attached tassels in the shape of pomegranates, in all the different colors — blue-violet, red-violet, and scarlet. And alternating with them were to be little golden bells. These would tinkle as he moved in and out of **the holy place,** apparently here referring to the Holy of Holies since it was the only place he alone could go, and serve to protect him from death. They were a kind of audible credential, which marked him as the person authorized to approach Jehovah.

(d) The Crown (28:36-39)

36 And thou shalt make a plate of pure gold, and grave upon it, like the engravings of a signet, HOLY TO JEHOVAH. 37 And thou shalt put it on a lace of blue, and it shall be upon the mitre; upon the forefront of the mitre it shall be. 38 And it shall be upon Aaron's forehead, and Aaron shall bear the iniquity of the holy things, which the children of Israel shall hallow in all their holy gifts; and it shall be always upon his forehead, that they may be accepted before Jehovah. 39 And thou shalt weave the coat in checker work of fine linen, and thou shalt make a mitre of fine linen, and thou shalt make a girdle, the work of the embroiderer.

Only the final touches remain for Aaron's attire. Chief among these was to be a golden **plate,** engraved with the words **HOLY TO JEHOVAH** which was to be attached by a lace of blue to the linen **mitre** or turban, and thus worn on or just above his forehead. It was to signify Aaron's responsibility for the holy things dedicated by Israel to the Lord, and was to secure their acceptance by the Lord. Much is suggested here of the office and work of Christ in whom men and their gifts are consecrated to God,

---

[176] See his descriptions, *ibid.,* pp. 302-05.
[177] Unger, ed., "Urim and Thummim," in *Unger's Bible Dictionary,* pp. 1128-29.

and much is also implied of the solemn responsibilities of those who stand to minister between God and men.

One final word is given in verse 29 that the high priest's **coat** (apparently a long tunic reaching down to the feet, fiting closely, and having tight sleeves[178]), and the **mitre** or turban were to be woven of fine linen. The tunic was to be so woven that it bore a checkered effect. The girdle or sash was to be **the work of the embroiderer,** and was to be not only of white linen but also of the blue-violet, red-violet, and scarlet cloth (39:29). The tunic was to be worn under the robe of the ephod. From its beauty, one would expect the sash to have been worn over the robe, but it may have been within it, over the tunic.

(3) Its Design for the Other Priests (28:40-43)

40 And for Aaron's sons thou shalt make coats, and thou shalt make for them girdles, and head-tires shalt thou make for them, for glory and for beauty. 41 And thou shalt put them upon Aaron thy brother, and upon his sons with him, and shalt anoint them, and consecrate them, and sanctify them, that they may minister unto me in the priest's office. 42 And thou shalt make them linen breeches to cover the flesh of their nakedness; from the loins even unto the thighs they shall reach: 43 And they shall be upon Aaron, and upon his sons, when they go in unto the tent of meeting, or when they come near unto the altar to minister in the holy place; that they bear not iniquity, and die: it shall be a statute for ever unto him and unto his seed after him.

For Aaron's sons, there were also to be prepared tunics, sashes, and headbands. No details concerning them are given except that they also were **for glory and for beauty.** The tunics and headbands, following the parallel of the high priest's, would have been white, and the sashes multicolored. For Aaron and the others, breeches of linen were to be made reaching from the waist to the thighs, keeping them modestly covered when they climbed up on the ledge that ran about the altar of burnt-offering. These garments were to be upon Aaron and his sons when they were anointed and installed in office. And they were to wear them always when

carrying out their priestly tasks, lest they die. Their approaching to the Lord was never to be done lightly nor flippantly, but with careful regard for His expressed will in the matter. Thus proper reverence for God and His holiness were to be instilled in both the priesthood and the people.

c. The Consecration of the Priests and the Tabernacle (29:1-46)

(1) The Dedication of the Priests (29:1-35)

1 And this is the thing that thou shalt do unto them to hallow them, to minister unto me in the priest's office: take one young bullock and two rams without blemish, 2 and unleavened bread, and cakes unleavened mingled with oil, and wafers unleavened anointed with oil: of fine wheaten flour shalt thou make them. 3 And thou shalt put them into one basket, and bring them in the basket, with the bullock and the two rams. 4 And Aaron and his sons thou shalt bring unto the door of the tent of meeting, and shalt wash them with water. 5 And thou shalt take the garments, and put upon Aaron the coat, and the robe of the ephod, and the ephod, and the breastplate, and gird him with the skilfully woven band of the ephod; 6 and thou shalt set the mitre upon his head, and put the holy crown upon the mitre. 7 Then shalt thou take the anointing oil, and pour it upon his head, and anoint him. 8 And thou shalt bring his sons, and put coats upon them. 9 And thou shalt gird them with girdles, Aaron and his sons, and bind head-tires on them: and they shall have the priesthood by a perpetual statute: and thou shalt consecrate Aaron and his sons.

10 And thou shalt bring the bullock before the tent of meeting: and Aaron and his sons shall lay their hands upon the head of the bullock. 11 And thou shalt kill the bullock before Jehovah, at the door of the tent of meeting. 12 And thou shalt take of the blood of the bullock, and put it upon the horns of the altar with thy finger; and thou shalt pour out all the blood at the base of the altar. 13 And thou shalt take all the fat that covereth the inwards, and the caul upon the liver, and the two kidneys, and the fat that is upon them, and burn them upon the altar. 14 But the flesh of the bullock, and its skin, and its dung, shalt thou burn with fire without the camp: it is a sin-offering.

[178] Driver, *op. cit.,* p. 309. His authority is Josephus.

15 Thou shalt also take the one ram; and Aaron and his sons shall lay their hands upon the head of the ram. 16 And thou shalt slay the ram, and thou shalt take its blood, and sprinkle it round about upon the altar. 17 And thou shalt cut the ram into its pieces, and wash its inwards, and its legs, and put them with its pieces, and with its head. 18 And thou shalt burn the whole ram upon the altar: it is a burnt-offering unto Jehovah; it is a sweet savor, an offering made by fire unto Jehovah.

19 And thou shalt take the other ram; and Aaron and his sons shall lay their hands upon the head of the ram. 20 Then shalt thou kill the ram, and take of its blood, and put it upon the tip of the right ear of Aaron, and upon the tip of the right ear of his sons, and upon the thumb of their right hand, and upon the great toe of their right foot, and sprinkle the blood upon the altar round about. 21 And thou shalt take of the blood that is upon the altar, and of the anointing oil, and sprinkle it upon Aaron, and upon his garments, and upon his sons, and upon the garments of his sons with him: and he shall be hallowed, and his garments, and his sons, and his sons' garments with him. 22 Also thou shalt take of the ram the fat, and the fat tail, and the fat that covereth the inwards, and the caul of the liver, and the two kidneys, and and the fat that is upon them, and the right thigh (for it is a ram of consecration), 23 and one loaf of bread, and one cake of oiled bread, and one wafer, out of the basket of unleavened bread that is before Jehovah: 24 and thou shalt put the whole upon the hands of Aaron, and upon the hands of his sons, and shalt wave them for a wave-offering before Jehovah. 25 And thou shalt take them from their hands, and burn them on the altar upon the burnt-offering, for a sweet savor before Jehovah: it is an offering made by fire unto Jehovah.

26 And thou shalt take the breast of Aaron's ram of consecration, and wave it for a wave-offering before Jehovah: and it shall be thy portion. 27 And thou shalt sanctify the breast of the wave-offering, and the thigh of the heave-offering, which is waved, and which is heaved up, of the ram of consecration, even of that which is for Aaron, and of that which is for his sons: 28 and it shall be for Aaron and his sons as *their* portion for ever from the children of Israel; for it is a heave-offering: and it shall be a heave-offering from the children of Israel of the sacrifices of their peace-offerings, even their heave-offering unto Jehovah.

29 And the holy garments of Aaron shall be for his sons after him, to be anointed in them, and to be consecrated in them. 30 Seven days shall the son that is priest in his stead put them on, when he cometh into the tent of meeting to minister in the holy place.

31 And thou shalt take the ram of consecration, and boil its flesh in a holy place. 32 And Aaron and his sons shall eat the flesh of the ram, and the bread that is in the basket, at the door of the tent of meeting. 33 And they shall eat those things wherewith atonement was made, to consecrate *and* to sanctify them: but a stranger shall not eat thereof, because they are holy. 34 And if aught of the flesh of the consecration, or of the bread, remain unto the morning, then thou shalt burn the remainder with fire: it shall not be eaten, because it is holy.

35 And thus shalt thou do unto Aaron, and to his sons, according to all that I have commanded thee: seven days shalt thou consecrate them.

Verses 1-3 list the things which are to be prepared for sacrifice: **one young bullock, two** unblemished **rams,** and three kinds of bread: simple **unleavened bread** like that used in the Passover meal, unleavened cakes **mingled with oil** (termed by Driver "perforated cakes"[179]), **and unleavened wafers anointed** or "smeared" **with oil** — very thin oiled cakes.

Then follow the actual instructions for dedicating the priests. The carrying out of the instructions is recorded in Leviticus 8. The ceremony involved four steps: washing, dressing, anointing, and consecrating or installing.

The first three steps are given only a brief description (vv. 4-9). The washing was not that symbolic washing of the hands and feet which the priest later was to perform for himself every time he approached to minister at the altar or in the tent (30:19-21), but a washing of **them,** their entire bodies, by Moses. The dressing was an arraying of Aaron with the beautiful garments of the high priest, and in the same sequence, of his sons with their simpler clothes. The anointing of Aaron was to be accomplished by the pouring of **anointing oil** upon his head. The sons were also anointed (28:41; 30: 30; 40:15), but no specific instructions are given concerning their anointing. The actual anointing service included much not mentioned here (Lev. 8:10-13). Tradition tells us that the subordinate priests were anointed, not by oil being poured on them, but by having it smeared on their foreheads (the Hebrew word **anoint** also means "smear").[180] The binding upon the sons of the **head-tires** or headbands is the climactic act both here and in the actual anointing ceremony, so it is probable that the smearing was done in conjunction with that.

Anointing was also used in setting apart kings (I Sam. 10:1) and prophets (I Kings 19:16). The use of oil upon the person medicinally and even religiously was quite common in ancient times, and the pouring of it out as an act of dedication and worship was also known (see comments on Gen. 28: 10-22). Among the Israelites, its use in setting aside a person as priest or king or prophet was closely connected with his being endued by the Holy Spirit for his task (see I Sam. 10:1, 6, 9-11; 16:13; Isa. 61:1). It is apparently this which has caused many interpreters of the Bible to say that oil is a type of the Holy Spirit. For the priests, the anointing was a fitting climax to their personal preparation for the formal act of installation. They were being sanctified or set apart unto the Lord, and there had first been the negative step of washing and now the positive steps of dressing and anointing. Johnson well remarks, "Certainly this is a very clear indication of their being cleansed spiritually, clothed with God's righteousness, and empowered by the Holy Spirit."[181]

Only after these three steps were completed were the priests ready for what the KJV and ASV call **consecration,** but the RSV and the Berkeley Version call "ordination," and Meek translates "installation."[182] The idea expressed in the Hebrew is not exactly that of our modern theological concept of consecration. Both in the Hebrew of the Old Testament and the Greek of the New, the part which man plays in setting himself apart for the service of God, and the part which God plays in accomplishing that separation by making him holy, are both expressed by the same words. The context helps to make the distinction. In English, we use two different words to assure the distinction: consecration for man's part and sanctification for God's part. But the word used in this chapter and in most of the places in the Old Testament where the older versions have "consecration," or one of its cognates, has nothing to do with this distinction. It literally means "the filling of the hands," and in the verb form, "to fill the hands." Adam Clarke lists two reasons for the use of this expression in this connection.

> When a person was dedicated or consecrated to God, his hands were filled with some particular offering proper for the occasion, which he presented to God. Hence the word *consecration* signifies the *filling up* or *filling the hands,* some part of the sacrifice being put into the hands of such persons, denoting thereby that they had now a right to offer sacrifices and oblations to God. It seems in reference to this ancient mode of consecration, that in the Church of England, when a person is ordained priest, a Bible is put into his hands with these words, "Take thou authority to preach the word of God," &c. The *filling the hands* refers also to the *presents* which, in the eastern countries, every inferior was obliged to bring when brought into the presence of a superior. Thus the sacrifice was considered, not only as an atonement for sin, but also as a means of approach and as a *present* to Jehovah.[183]

In every instance but one where this word in any of its forms is used in the Old Testament, it refers indisputably to the ordination or installation of the priests.[184] In this first occurrence of such ordination, it is revealed that just as the priests' personal preparation involved a negative and positive aspect, just so the formal rite of ordination would have negative and positive aspects. The bullock and one of the rams which had been brought for sacrifice would be offered first as a sin-offering and a whole burnt-offering. Part of the remaining ram and part of the three

[180] Unger, ed., "Priesthood, Hebrew," in *Unger's Bible Dictionary,* p. 883.   [181] Johnson, *op. cit.,* p. 80.
[182] *The Bible, an American Translation,* pp. 77-78.
[183] Adam Clarke, *The Holy Bible with a Commentary and Critical Notes,* I, 452-53.
[184] The one exception is Ezek. 43:26, but cf. KJV.

kinds of bread would also be offered on the altar. But at that point the negative aspect would end. The positive aspect would be found in the filling of the hands of the priests with portions to wave before the Lord, symbolizing their fitness now to offer sacrifices before the Lord.

Before Aaron and his sons could be accepted to serve in behalf of Israel, they must offer a sin-offering to provide for their own atonement. The **bullock** was to serve this purpose (vv. 10-14) .[185] Aaron and his sons would identify themselves with their offering by laying **their hands upon** its head in front of **the tent of meeting.** Moses was to kill the bullock **at the door,** daub some of the blood upon the four **horns of the altar** with his **finger,** and pour out the rest of the blood **at the base of the altar.** Then he was to take the **fat** that covered the various internal organs, the **caul upon the liver** (the lobe or appendage of the liver, a fatty mass at the opening of the liver extending to the kidneys[186]), and the **kidneys** and the **fat** on them, and burn them upon the altar. Ordinarily, the priest ate the remaining flesh of the sin-offering. But this was not so when it was a sin-offering for the priests or for the entire nation of which they were a part. So the remaining flesh, the hide, and the excrement must be taken outside the camp and burned.

Next, one of the rams was to be offered as a burnt-offering (vv. 15-18). Sin-offerings were offered on the annual Day of Atonement, or when the nation or any individual was guilty of sin. But burnt-offerings were proper at any time as an act of sheer adoration or worship of Jehovah. Again Aaron and his sons were to identify themselves with the sac-rifice, and Moses was to slay it. This time the blood was to be sprinkled **round about upon the altar** (or to translate more correctly, "thrown" or "splashed" against the sides of the altar, using the basins mentioned in 27:3[187]). The an-imal was then cut in pieces, the inner

parts and legs washed, and the whole burnt upon the altar. No part of a burnt-offering was ever to be eaten.

Finally, the remaining ram and the bread were to be used in what was actu-ally a modification of a peace-offering (vv. 19-34). The peace-offering was or-dinarily made as an expression of thanks-giving or as a vow or freewill-offering. While the sin-offering was the sacrifice of contrition, and the burnt-offering of ad-oration, the peace-offering was the sac-rifice of fellowship.[188] Only a representa-tive portion of it was actually burned up-on the altar, the breast and one thigh was given to the officiating priest, and the per-son or persons offering the sacrifice were to eat the rest in the courtyard of the tabernacle. It was a sacred sacrificial meal.

Again Aaron and his sons were to i-dentify themselves with the sacrifice, and Moses was to slay the animal. He was to take of its blood and put it upon the right ear, the right thumb, and the right big toe of Aaron and each of his sons. Thus there was to be "the consecration of their attention to God's word, of the service of their hands and of their walk in the way of holiness."[189] The rest of the blood was to be splashed against the side of the altar. Then of this blood which had touched the altar Moses was to take, and also of the anointing oil, and sprinkle Aaron and his sons and their garments, setting them apart for the Lord. Then the same pieces which in the bullock's case had been burned were to be taken, along with the ram's fatty tail, the right thigh, and one piece of each kind of bread. They were first to be placed in the hands of Aaron and his sons and offered as a wave-offering — thus filling their hands for the first time. The wave-offering seems to have been accomplished by extending the pieces first toward the altar and then with-drawing them. Usually only those pieces which would be given to the priest would be waved, and the waving must have symbolized their being given to the Lord

[185] Full instructions concerning the various kinds of sacrifices are found in Lev. 1-7. See the com-ments there for greater detail in analyzing the various steps and the symbolism involved. For the sin-offering see Lev. 4:1-35; 6:24-29; the burnt-offering, Lev. 1:1-17; the peace-offering (which was adapted as Aaron's ordination offering), Lev. 3:1-17; 7:11-36; and the meal-offering (which has something of a relationship to the bread offered in the peace-offering), Lev. 2:1-16; 6:14-23.

[186] Brown, Driver, and Briggs, op. cit., p. 452.   [187] Driver, op. cit., pp. 318-19.
[188] Rylaarsdam, op. cit., I, 1048.   [189] Connell, op. cit., p. 128.

who then gave them back. But here these waved objects were later burned, so the symbolism must have involved the induction of Aaron and his sons "into their office of presenting sacrifices upon the altar."[190] After they were waved, they were burned on the altar. Then the breast, which in an ordinary peace-offering would have gone to the officiating priest along with the right thigh just burned on the altar, was to be waved by Moses and given to him as the officiating priest in this instance.

Verses 27-28 contain a parenthetical instruction perpetuating the practice of giving these two pieces to the officiating priests. (The term **heave-offering** does not designate a different kind of offering from the wave-offering, but is rather an unfortunate mistranslation. It means "contribution" or "offering" with the literal meaning of something "lifted off" or "separated." Cf. RSV, Berkeley, and *The Bible, an American Translation*.) Verses 29-30 also contain a parenthetical instruction that the high priest's garments now being used by Aaron, were to be passed on to his descendants, with the same seven-day ordination ceremony being observed for each succeeding high priest.

Then instructions concerning the ordination-offering are resumed. Moses is to boil the remaining portions of the ram in the tabernacle courtyard, and Aaron and his sons are to eat it and the rest of the bread at the entrance to the tent. No one but a priest could eat of them. And if any of the meat or bread remained until the next morning, it was to be burned. The hand-filling or ordination ceremony was to be continued for seven days. This would not have involved a sevenfold repetition of the washing, dressing, and anointing of the priests. But it apparently did involve the sevenfold repetition of the sacrifices.

(2) The Dedication of the Altar and the Tent (29:36-46)

36 And every day shalt thou offer the bullock of sin-offering for atonement: and thou shalt cleanse the altar, when thou makest atonement for it; and thou shalt anoint it, to sanctify it. 37 Seven days thou shalt make atonement for the altar,

and sanctify it: and the altar shall be most holy; whatsoever toucheth the altar shall be holy.

38 Now this is that which thou shalt offer upon the altar: two lambs a year old day by day continually. 39 The one lamb thou shalt offer in the morning; and the other lamb thou shalt offer at even: 40 and with the one lamb a tenth part *of an ephah* of fine flour mingled with the fourth part of a hin of beaten oil; and the fourth part of a hin of wine for a drink-offering. 41 And the other lamb thou shalt offer at even, and shalt do thereto according to the meal-offering of the morning, and according to the drink-offering thereof, for a sweet savor, an offering made by fire unto Jehovah. 42 It shall be a continual burnt-offering throughout your generations at the door of the tent of meeting before Jehovah, where I will meet with you, to speak there unto thee. 43 And there I will meet with the children of Israel; and *the Tent* shall be sanctified by my glory. 44 And I will sanctify the tent of meeting, and the altar: Aaron also and his sons will I sanctify, to minister to me in the priest's office. 45 And I will dwell among the children of Israel, and will be their God. 46 And they shall know that I am Jehovah their God, that brought them forth out of the land of Egypt, that I might dwell among them: I am Jehovah their God.

Each day during the seven days of the ordination service, there was also to be offered a **bullock** as a **sin-offering for atonement** in purging the altar itself. The word **cleanse** is translated by Driver with a word coined for the occasion — "un-sin." The Hebrews understood sin in a very broad sense, regarding it as capable of infecting even a material object. Since the altar was the work of human hands, it was infected by a natural uncleanness, and must be "un-sinned" or "de-sinned" before it could be used for sacred purposes.[191] The altar was also to be anointed. Thus set apart, it would truly be holy, and everything and everyone (see ASV margin) would be holy — belonging to the Lord, to be used as He saw fit. If this was an unauthorized person, he would probably die. If it was an authorized person, he would be used in divine service.

Also beginning with the week of ordination, there were to be instituted the per-

190 Driver, *op. cit.*, p. 321.   191 *Ibid.*, p. 324.

petual morning and evening sacrifices. Each sacrifice was to consist of a lamb plus about three quarts of the best flour, a little over one quart of the best olive oil, and a little over one quart of wine. These were to be offered by fire. Thus the dedication of the altar now initiated would be continued **throughout** all **generations.**

The closing verses of the chapter reveal that the twofold aspect of sanctification discussed in the opening comments on verses 10-14 applied also in the case of the tent, the altar, and the priests. All that has been described in this chapter was man's preparation or consecration. But once it was carried out, and as long as it was perpetuated, the Lord would make the consecration complete by sanctifying the tent, the altar, and the priests. As long as Israel offered the sacrifices, the Lord would dwell among them and be their God, and they would know that He was their God who had brought them out of Egypt.

4. The Completion and Use of the Tabernacle (30:1—31:17)

a. The Altar of Incense (30:1-10)

1 And thou shalt make an altar to burn incense upon: of acacia wood shalt thou make it. 2 A cubit shall be the length thereof, and a cubit the breadth thereof; foursquare shall it be; and two cubits shall be the height thereof: the horns thereof shall be of one piece with it. 3 And thou shalt overlay it with pure gold, the top thereof, and the sides thereof round about, and the horns thereof; and thou shalt make unto it a crown of gold round about. 4 And two golden rings shalt thou make for it under the crown thereof; upon the two ribs thereof, upon the two sides of it shalt thou make them; and they shall be for places for staves wherewith to bear it. 5 And thou shalt make the staves of acacia wood, and overlay them with gold. 6 And thou shalt put it before the veil that is by the ark of the testimony, before the mercy-seat that is over the testimony, where I will meet with thee. 7 And Aaron shall burn thereon incense of sweet spices: every morning when he dresseth the lamps, he shall burn it. 8 And when Aaron lighteth the lamps at even, he shall burn it, a perpetual incense before Jehovah through-

out your generations. 9 Ye shall offer no strange incense thereon, nor burnt-offering, nor meal-offering; and ye shall pour no drink-offering thereon. 10 And Aaron shall make atonement upon the horns of it once in the year; with the blood of the sin-offering of atonement once in the year shall he make atonement for it throughout your generations: it is most holy unto Jehovah.

Chapter 30 contains instructions about five more things connected with the place of worship. The collection of especially some of them here, after the main body of instructions, as if they represented miscellaneous afterthoughts, is a bit puzzling. One would expect the section on the altar of incense to have appeared in chapter 25 immediately after the description of the ark and the mercy-seat, following the principle of moving from the most sacred on out to the courtyard and the least sacred.[192] One would also expect the laver to have been described in conjunction with the altar of burnt-offering and the courtyard enclosure in chapter 27. Critical scholars insist that the things contained in this chapter were late additions to Israel's worship. But such is not a necessary conclusion. The record of the actual construction and the record of the assembly of the tabernacle and its furnishings both mention the incense altar and the laver in their proper places (37:25-28; 38:8; 40:26-27, 30 — the altar of incense is always mentioned after the table and the candlestick). Rather, it seems that the Lord first gave Moses instructions concerning the parts which were most essential to worship, then filled out some details which Moses probably had glimpsed in the model. The altar of incense and laver were not used in conjunction with the service of ordination of the priests and dedication of the tabernacle except as they themselves were included in that which was thus sanctified. And incense was apparently not always offered on the altar designed for that purpose, but was burned directly upon the censer, or long-handled panlike instrument with which burning coals were taken from the altar of burnt-offering (Lev. 10:1; 16:12; Num. 16:6ff.). Thus, while the laver and the

[192] In the very ancient Samaritan Pentateuch, verses 1-10 do appear immediately after 26:32, where Adam Clarke believed they originally were. See Clarke, *op. cit.*, I, 439, 457.

incense altar had a divinely appointed place in Israel's worship and each symbolized a deep spiritual truth, in the plan of God they held what must be regarded as a secondary place and are accordingly included in this summary.

The **altar** of **incense** was also to be of acacia wood, eighteen inches square by thirty-six inches high, with its four horns formed in one piece with it. It was to be plated with pure gold, including its top, sides, and horns, and a rim or molding running around it. Two rings would be sufficient for carrying it, and would be located under the molding, apparently upon two vertical studs which made up part of the interior framework. The poles were also to be made of acacia wood and overlaid with gold. It was to be placed **before the veil,** in front of the ark and the mercy-seat, in the outer compartment between the table and the lampstand. Sweet spices were to be burned on it in the morning when the lamps were trimmed, and at night when they were lit. But no strange incense nor any type of offering was to be offered there, except that on the annual Day of Atonement the high priest would daub blood from the sin-offering upon its horns.

The secondary role of the altar of incense in relationship to the altar of burnt-offering is perhaps best understood in terms of their symbolism. The altar of burnt-offering was used for those sacrifices which spoke of the coming sacrifice of the divine-human Savior for the sins of the world. The altar of incense was used for those sacrifices which spoke of human aspiration and prayer (Ps. 141:2; Rev. 5:8; 8:3-4).

b. The Atonement Money (30:11-16)

11 And Jehovah spake unto Moses, saying, 12 When thou takest the sum of the children of Israel, according to those that are numbered of them, then shall they give every man a ransom for his soul unto Jehovah, when thou numberest them; that there be no plague among them, when thou numberest them. 13 This they shall give, every one that passeth over unto them that are numbered: half a shekel after the shekel of the sanctuary (the shekel is twenty gerahs), half a shekel for an offering to Jehovah. 14 Every one that passeth over unto them that are

numbered, from twenty years old and upward, shall give the offering of Jehovah. 15 The rich shall not give more, and the poor shall not give less, than the half shekel, when they give the offering of Jehovah, to make atonement for your souls. 16 And thou shalt take the atonement money from the children of Israel, and shalt appoint it for the service of the tent of meeting; that it may be a memorial for the children of Israel before Jehovah, to make atonement for your souls.

The second additional bit of instruction had to do with **the atonement money,** which was to be paid whenever a census of the nation was made. Each man of military age (cf. 38:26; Num. 1:2; 26:2) was to pay half of a sanctuary shekel as an offering to Jehovah for the maintenance and use of the tent. Such a census was largely a military act and would likely occur in connection with the mustering of the men for a major conflict. It could easily lead to human pride and self-confidence which would bring the judgment of God in a **plague,** for their confidence and strength were to be in Him alone. So a special offering must be provided for their atonement. Apparently David both yielded to the pride and forgot the atonement-offering (II Sam. 24:1ff.; I Chron. 21:1ff.). **The shekel of the sanctuary** is thought to have been a Phoenician shekel, which was larger than the more common Babylonian shekel — a fact which is indicated by the parenthetical statement, **the shekel is twenty gerahs,** gerah being a Babylonian weight. Later Jewish custom changed this from a census-offering to an annual temple-tax, amounting in Nehemiah's day to one-third of what was probably the smaller Babylonian shekel (Neh. 10: 32), and in Jesus' day to the full half-shekel of the census-offering (Matt. 17: 24-27).[193]

c. The Brazen Laver (30:17-21)

17 And Jehovah spake unto Moses, saying, 18 Thou shalt also make a laver of brass, and the base thereof of brass, whereat to wash. And thou shalt put it between the tent of meeting and the altar, and thou shalt put water therein. 19 And Aaron and his sons shall wash their hands and their feet thereat: 20 when they go into the tent of meeting, they shall wash

193 Rylaarsdam, op. cit., I, 1054-56.

with water, that they die not; or when they come near to the altar to minister, to burn an offering made by fire unto Jehovah. 21 So they shall wash their hands and their feet, that they die not: and it shall be a statute for ever to them, even to him and to his seed throughout their generations.

The third bit of instruction involved a laver, a brazen or bronze basin of some type which was to be placed between the altar of burnt-offering and the entrance to the tent, and to be used for the washing of the hands and feet of the priests before they approached the altar of burnt-offering or entered the tent to carry out their priestly functions. Virtually no information is given concerning its form. It was made out of the bronze mirrors of a group of women who apparently helped in the cleaning of the tabernacle precincts (38:8). Unger suggests that it had an upper and lower level, and some provision for storage, flow, and drainage, and may have also been used in the washing of sacrifices (cf. 29:17).[194]

It no doubt was a memorial to the offering of the women. It also served as a daily reminder of that complete washing required in the ordination of the priests, and in turn of the need for spiritual purity in the service of Jehovah.

d. The Holy Anointing Oil (30:22-33)

22 Moreover Jehovah spake unto Moses, saying, 23 Take thou also unto thee the chief spices: of flowing myrrh five hundred *shekels*, and of sweet cinnamon half so much, even two hundred and fifty, and of sweet calamus two hundred and fifty, 24 and of cassia five hundred, after the shekel of the sanctuary, and of olive oil a hin; 25 and thou shalt make it a holy anointing oil, a perfume compounded after the art of the perfumer: it shall be a holy anointing oil. 26 And thou shalt anoint therewith the tent of meeting, and the ark of the testimony, 27 and the table and all the vessels thereof, and the candlestick and the vessels thereof, and the altar of incense, 28 and the altar of burnt-offering with all the vessels thereof, and the laver and the base thereof. 29 And thou shalt sanctify them, that they may be most holy: whatsoever toucheth

them shall be holy. 30 And thou shalt anoint Aaron and his sons, and sanctify them, that they may minister unto me in the priest's office. 31 And thou shalt speak unto the children of Israel, saying, This shall be a holy anointing oil unto me throughout your generations. 32 Upon the flesh of man shall it not be poured, neither shall ye make any like it, according to the composition thereof: it is holy, *and* it shall be holy unto you. 33 Whosoever compoundeth any like it, or whosoever putteth any of it upon a stranger, he shall be cut off from his people.

The use and symbolism of this oil have already been indicated in connection with the comments on 29:1-35. It is quite reasonable that the recipe for its composition would not interrupt the instructions for the ordination service, but be saved for a "footnote" or "appendix" as it is here. It was to consist of **the chief spices,** the very best: 500 shekels of liquid **myrrh,** 250 of **sweet cinnamon** (probably moved by various caravans from the Far East), 250 of **sweet calamus** (a sweet-smelling cane from India), 500 of **cassia** (obtained from the cinnamon bark, also from the Far East), and one-and-one-half gallons of olive oil. The heavier **shekel of the sanctuary** is again the standard of weight, weighing roughly one ounce. This, with the oil, would mean that the recipe would make up about 100 pounds.[195] It was to be put together according to **the art of the perfumer.**

Some additional items are listed for anointing, including the tent and all of its furnishings. When so anointed, they, like the altar of burnt-offering (29:37), would be holy and would devote to the Lord whatsoever or whosoever touched them. It was also to be used in perpetuity in the anointing of Aaron and his descendants for the priesthood. No one was to attempt to duplicate it for secular purposes or to apply it to anyone not a priest. Transgression of the prohibition would bring death.

e. The Holy Incense (30:34-38)

34 And Jehovah said unto Moses, Take unto thee sweet spices, stacte, and onycha, and galbanum; sweet spices with pure

194 Unger, ed., "Tabernacle of Israel," in *Unger's Bible Dictionary*, p. 1063.
195 Rylaarsdam, *op. cit.*, I, 1057.

frankincense: of each shall there be a like weight; 35 and thou shalt make of it incense, a perfume after the art of the perfumer, seasoned with salt, pure *and* holy: 36 and thou shalt beat some of it very small, and put of it before the testimony in the tent of meeting, where I will meet with thee: it shall be unto you most holy. 37 And the incense which thou shalt make, according to the composition thereof ye shall not make for yourselves: it shall be unto thee holy for Jehovah. 38 Whosoever shall make like unto that, to smell thereof, he shall be cut off from his people.

The regular use and symbolism of the incense are described in the comments on 30:1-10. Now appears the recipe for its composition. It was to consist of equal parts of four **sweet spices: stacte** (a type of myrrh oil), **onycha** (refers to the "mouth" or flap of a mollusk found in the Red Sea), **galbanum** (a resin now found chiefly in Iran), and **frankincense** (a prized perfume made from a gum resin, whitish in color, found in Somaliland and South Arabia).[196] It was to be **seasoned with salt** and beaten very fine. Like the anointing oil, its duplication for secular use was prohibited under pain of death.

f. The Builders (31:1-11)

1 And Jehovah spake unto Moses, saying, 2 See, I have called by name Bezalel the son of Uri, the son of Hur, of the tribe of Judah: 3 and I have filled him with the Spirit of God, in wisdom, and in understanding, and in knowledge, and in all manner of workmanship, 4 to devise skilful works, to work in gold, and in silver, and in brass, 5 and in cutting of stones for setting, and in carving of wood, to work in all manner of workmanship. 6 And I, behold, I have appointed with him Oholiab, the son of Ahisamach, of the tribe of Dan; and in the hearts of all that are wise-hearted I have put wisdom, that they may make all that I have commanded thee: 7 the tent of meeting, and the ark of the testimony, and the mercy-seat that is thereupon, and all the furniture of the Tent, 8 and the table and its vessels, and the pure candlestick with all its vessels, and the altar of incense, 9 and the altar of burnt-offering with all its vessels, and the laver and its base, 10 and the finely wrought garments, and the holy garments for Aaron the priest, and the garments of his sons, to minister in the priest's office, 11 and the anointing oil, and the incense of sweet spices for the holy place: according to all that I have commanded thee shall they do.

The Lord now called by name the two men He wanted to supervise the construction of the tabernacle and its furnishings. The calling of men by name was reserved for positions of great responsibility. The two selected were **Bezalel,** grandson of Hur, of the tribe of Judah, and **Oholiab,** of the tribe of Dan. Others were to be chosen by Moses to assist them (v. 6b).

Critical scholars have questioned whether there could have been found among a group of slaves so recently freed craftsmen sufficiently skilled and experienced to have produced such a beautiful and elaborate structure with its furnishings. However, the nation as a whole had been engaged in construction in Egypt. And it is hard to imagine that among Israel's thousands there had not been found individuals with outstanding natural abilities who were accordingly recognized and trained by the Egyptians in other things besides brick-making and laying. Oholiab apparently had already distinguished himself as a craftsman with fabrics (38:23), and the ones to be appointed by Moses were already worthy of the term **wise-hearted.** And, in addition to whatever outstanding natural abilities the builders might have, the Lord was filling Bezalel with His own Spirit, **in wisdom, and in understanding, and in knowledge, and in all manner of workmanship.** Rawlinson identifies these as (1) inventive or creative ability, (2) the ability to follow directions, (3) the know-how of experience and study, and (4) manual dexterity.[197] Oholiab and all those already fitted for such work would also have a special divine gift of wisdom, heightening their natural abilities. Thus fitted, they would be well able to **devise** those matters left to their own originality and to execute faithfully the instructions given by Moses.

---

[196] *Ibid.,* I, 1059. [197] Rawlinson, *The Pulpit Commentary: Exodus,* II, 314.

g. The Sabbath (31:12-17)

12 And Jehovah spake unto Moses, saying, 13 Speak thou also unto the children of Israel, saying, Verily ye shall keep my sabbaths: for it is a sign between me and you throughout your generations; that ye may know that I am Jehovah who sanctifieth you. 14 Ye shall keep the sabbath therefore; for it is holy unto you: every one that profaneth it shall surely be put to death; for whosoever doeth any work therein, that soul shall be cut off from among his people. 15 Six days shall work be done; but on the seventh day is a sabbath of solemn rest, holy to Jehovah; whosoever doeth any work on the sabbath day, he shall surely be put to death. 16 Wherefore the children of Israel shall keep the sabbath, to observe the sabbath throughout their generations, for a perpetual covenant. 17 It is a sign between me and the children of Israel for ever: for in six days Jehovah made heaven and earth, and on the seventh day he rested, and was refreshed.

It might seem strange that the Lord would insert a section on keeping the Sabbath at this point. The point had already been covered in the Ten Commandments (20:8-11) and in a later portion of the Book of the Covenant (23:12). But it is brought up again, and two additional things are remarked: one, that the keeping of the Sabbath is here to be a perpetual sign between the Lord and Israel, and the other that he who violates the Sabbath is to be executed. Apparently the Lord wanted to reinforce the law of the Sabbath rest particularly at this time since the urgency of what was in truth sacred work might lead Israel to extend its building of the tabernacle through the Sabbath Day. But not even in such a worthy purpose was the perpetual sign to be broken.

5. The Tables of Testimony (31:18)

18 And he gave unto Moses, when he had made an end of communing with him upon mount Sinai, the two tables of the testimony, tables of stone, written with the finger of God.

Now the long forty days of revelation concerning the place and manner of worship are at an end. Moses had been invited to the mount this time for only one explicit purpose — to receive the divinely inscribed tablets of stone bearing the Ten Commandments (24:12). The Lord first gave him instructions on how and where the tablets were to be preserved, which involved particularly the ark and the mercy-seat but also the entire tabernacle with its court and furnishings. Now the instructions were ended, and He gave the tablets to Moses, **written with the finger of God.**

D. TRAINING THROUGH CORRECTION — THE COVENANT BROKEN AND RESTORED (32:1—34:35)

1. The Reoccurrence of the Problem of Sin (32:1—33:23)

a. Human Sin and Intercession (32:1-14)

1 And when the people saw that Moses delayed to come down from the mount, the people gathered themselves together unto Aaron, and said unto him, Up, make us gods, which shall go before us; for as for this Moses, the man that brought us up out of the land of Egypt, we know not what is become of him. 2 And Aaron said unto them, Break off the golden rings, which are in the ears of your wives, of your sons, and of your daughters, and bring them unto me. 3 And all the people brake off the golden rings which were in their ears, and brought them unto Aaron. 4 And he received it at their hand, and fashioned it with a graving tool, and made it a molten calf: and they said, These are thy gods, O Israel, which brought thee up out of the land of Egypt. 5 And when Aaron saw *this,* he built an altar before it; and Aaron made proclamation, and said, To-morrow shall be a feast to Jehovah. 6 And they rose up early on the morrow, and offered burnt-offerings, and brought peace-offerings; and the people sat down to eat and to drink, and rose up to play.

7 And Jehovah spake unto Moses, Go, get thee down; for thy people, that thou broughtest up out of the land of Egypt, have corrupted themselves: 8 they have turned aside quickly out of the way which I commanded them: they have made them a molten calf, and have worshipped it, and have sacrificed unto it, and said, These are thy gods, O Israel, which brought thee up out of the land of Egypt. 9 And Jehovah said unto Moses, I have seen this people, and, behold, it is a stiffnecked people: 10 now therefore let

me alone, that my wrath may wax hot against them, and that I may consume them: and I will make of thee a great nation. 11 And Moses besought Jehovah his God, and said, Jehovah, why doth thy wrath wax hot against thy people, that thou hast brought forth out of the land of Egypt with great power and with a mighty hand? 12 Wherefore should the Egyptians speak, saying, For evil did he bring them forth, to slay them in the mountains, and to consume them from the face of the earth? Turn from thy fierce wrath, and repent of this evil against thy people. 13 Remember Abraham, Isaac, and Israel, thy servants, to whom thou swarest by thine own self, and saidst unto them, I will multiply your seed as the stars of heaven, and all this land that I have spoken of will I give unto your seed, and they shall inherit it for ever. 14 And Jehovah repented of the evil which he said he would do unto his people.

When God first made man in His own image, He designed him as a companion for Himself, the object of divine love and fellowship. But inherent in the freedom of choice given to man with the divine image was the risk of his rejection of God. And that risk became a reality with the fall of Adam and Eve in the Garden of Eden (Gen. 3). From the moment of that fall, all of God's dealings with men built toward the time when He could establish His covenant of grace with a people of His own choosing, who would live in obedience to His will. That moment in history had arrived. God had hewn out the nation of Israel, and Israel had pledged to live in obedience to the conditions of God's proposed covenant. But Israel still had the power of choice, and a fall occurred once again, not the fall of the father of all mankind but the fall of the chosen people God had called forth. A crisis was once more present. What could now be done to remedy the problem of sin and its effects?

The opening verses of chapter 32 take us down from the mountain where Moses has been receiving instructions from Jehovah, to the plain below where the people have been waiting. Nearly six weeks passed while Moses was up in the mountain. Israel had been a slave nation, living under human domination, and they were quite dependent upon a leader they could see and from whom

they could seek counsel. Finally they decided that something mysterious must have happened to him, and they cast about for some concrete type of leadership. Contrary to what is commonly assumed, they had a long background of idolatry. The patriarchs had worshiped idols in Mesopotamia and Israel had worshiped idols in Egypt (Lev. 17:7; Josh. 24:14; Ezek. 20:8). They did not at the moment have even the elaborate tabernacle and its furnishings, or Moses the representative of God. So they cried out to Aaron, **Make us gods**, or perhaps better, "a god." Aaron may have thought they would be easily dissuaded, for he told them they must give their golden earrings in order to have an idol. But if so, he had not correctly gauged the intensity of their desire. They quickly responded. And the surprisingly weak Aaron gave in to their demand. The **calf** which he fashioned would have been a familiar sight to all those coming out of Egypt, for bulls were sacred there, and one of Egypt's deities was symbolized by the bull. The image was probably not a solid gold one, but a wooden one over which Aaron poured the **molten** gold. He then used a **graving tool** to put the finishing touches on the image. Then the people proclaimed to one another that this was the god which had brought them out of Egypt. Aaron apparently still wanted to stay as close to the right as he could, so he built an altar before the image and announced that the next day there would be a feast there in honor of Jehovah. Thus the calf was intended, at least by the reluctant Aaron, as a representation of the Lord Himself. On the next day, the people came to eat and drink, probably referring to a sacrificial meal in the presence of the image, and then **rose up to play,** a term which hints at some of the wanton, abandoned, immoral dancing and debauchery connected with the fertility rites of the ancient heathen nations.

It was at this point the Lord concluded His instructions to Moses. He commanded Moses to go down, saying that Moses' people whom Moses had brought out of Egypt had **corrupted themselves.** He informed Moses what had happened, reminding him of the provisions of the covenant which they had thus broken. He remarked that they were a stiffnecked people, an expression used many times in the Old Testament of Israel, and picturing an animal hardening the muscles of his neck against turning in the direction his master wants him to go. He asked that Moses leave Him alone that He might annihilate Israel. And He proposed to replace Israel in His plans with a new nation to be descended from Moses himself.

In all preceding instances in which the rebellious nature of Israel had been manifest, it had been Moses who had been impatient with them. Now in the face of their worst crime by far, the Lord offers to relieve Moses of his frustrating burden and to elevate him even higher in the divine purpose. It is a stern test of Moses' character, but he comes through with flying colors. He refused to accept the Lord's rejection implied in making Israel Moses' people. In his answer he calls them **thy people,** and in his impassioned intercession, the first of three such intercessions in chapters 32 and 33, bases his plea on three points: (1) the destruction of Israel would cancel out the mighty work of deliverance thus far achieved, (2) the Egyptians would charge Jehovah with unworthy motives in delivering them in the first place, and (3) the covenant with the three patriarchs would be broken — which covenant the Lord had sworn by Himself to maintain.

Moses' intercessory prayer succeeded, although he apparently felt from subsequent action that he had only won a temporary reprieve. **Jehovah repented of the evil which he said he would do unto his people.** Connell has well interpreted this statement.

> An anthropomorphic expression adapting the infinite ways of God to the finite minds of men. God does not repent as men do, as though He had erred or was too weak-minded to carry out His purposes. When God 'repents' He changes, not His eternal purposes, but the course of events which He had previously stated, because the prayers or altered demeanour of His people alter the conditions under which He had originally made the statement.[198]

[198] Connell, *op. cit.*, p. 129.

b. Human Judgment and Intercession (32:15-35)

15 And Moses turned, and went down from the mount, with the two tables of the testimony in his hand; tables that were written on both their sides; on the one side and on the other were they written. 16 And the tables were the work of God, and the writing was the writing of God, graven upon the tables. 17 And when Joshua heard the noise of the people as they shouted, he said unto Moses, There is a noise of war in the camp. 18 And he said, It is not the voice of them that shout for mastery, neither is it the voice of them that cry for being overcome; but the noise of them that sing do I hear. 19 And it came to pass, as soon as he came nigh unto the camp, that he saw the calf and the dancing: and Moses' anger waxed hot, and he cast the tables out of his hands, and brake them beneath the mount. 20 And he took the calf which they had made, and burnt it with fire, and ground it to powder, and strewed it upon the water, and made the children of Israel drink of it.

21 And Moses said unto Aaron, What did this people unto thee, that thou hast brought a great sin upon them? 22 And Aaron said, Let not the anger of my lord wax hot: thou knowest the people, that they are *set* on evil. 23 For they said unto me, Make us gods, which shall go before us; for as for this Moses, the man that brought us up out of the land of Egypt, we know not what is become of him. 24 And I said unto them, Whosoever hath any gold, let them break it off: so they gave it me; and I cast it into the fire, and there came out this calf.

25 And when Moses saw that the people were broken loose (for Aaron had let them loose for a derision among their enemies), 26 then Moses stood in the gate of the camp, and said, Whoso is on Jehovah's side, *let him come* unto me. And all the sons of Levi gathered themselves together unto him. 27 And he said unto them, Thus saith Jehovah, the God of Israel, Put ye every man his sword upon his thigh, and go to and fro from gate to gate throughout the camp, and slay every man his brother, and every man his companion, and every man his neighbor. 28 And the sons of Levi did according to the word of Moses: and there fell of the people that day about three thousand men. 29 And Moses said, Consecrate yourselves to-day to Jehovah, yea, every man against his son, and against

his brother; that he may bestow upon you a blessing this day.

30 And it came to pass on the morrow, that Moses said unto the people, Ye have sinned a great sin: and now I will go up unto Jehovah; peradventure I shall make atonement for your sin. 31 And Moses returned unto Jehovah, and said, Oh, this people have sinned a great sin, and have made them gods of gold. 32 Yet now, if thou wilt forgive their sin —; and if not, blot me, I pray thee, out of thy book which thou hast written. 33 And Jehovah said unto Moses, Whosoever hath sinned against me, him will I blot out of my book. 34 And now go, lead the people unto *the place* of which I have spoken unto thee: behold, mine angel shall go before thee; nevertheless in the day when I visit, I will visit their sin upon them. 35 And Jehovah smote the people, because they made the calf, which Aaron made.

Moses started down the mountain, carrying the two tables of stone, written on both sides with the hand of God. When he reached the place where Joshua still waited, Joshua was alarmed. He was hearing cries from the camp and feared that they had been attacked. But Moses pointed out that it was neither a cry of victory nor of terror. Then they apparently rounded a bend in the trail and could see the camp below them. There was the idol with an abandoned multitude dancing about it. Moses had sought to turn Jehovah's anger, but the sight was too much for him. He threw the tables of the testimony to the ground, breaking the sacred stones into fragments. Israel had already broken the covenant in fact, and such sacred objects as these had no place in a camp so full of sin. Then Moses rushed down to the camp, and with none of the timidity which had hindered his acceptance of Jehovah's call at the burning bush, threw down the idol, burned it, pulverized it, and strewed it upon the brook which ran out of Sinai (Deut. 9:21) so that they were forced to drink the dust of their sin. Under sufficient heat, the wooden core of the idol would have easily been consumed, leaving only the shell of gold to be beaten into powder. No doubt Moses called others to his assistance in the actual execution of this destruction.

Then he turned on Aaron, asking what the people could possibly have done to him that he led them into such a sin. Aaron's excuse was as pathetically weak as was Adam's in Eden: the people pressured him, and when he put the gold into the fire the calf came out of it all by itself! Moses later revealed that the Lord almost destroyed Aaron at this time, but he was saved by Moses' intercession (Deut. 9:20).

Moses' return, his anger, and even the destruction of the image, had not completely stopped the wild orgy of the people. They were **broken loose** or were completely uninhibited. So Moses called out what in Hebrew is only three words: Who for Jehovah? To me! The ones who moved quickly to help him were his tribal relatives, the Levites. Some of them too had been involved in the national sin and apparently still were (v. 29). But many of them had refrained from it from the beginning, or at least since Moses' return. He commanded them to take their swords and march through the camp, slaying those who apparently were still leading the wild celebration, even if in so doing they had to kill brothers, companions, and neighbors. The Levites obeyed, slaying 3,000 revelers. By such radical action the tumult ended. The Levites' obedience had consecrated them or "filled their hands" unto Jehovah, and shortly afterward they were given a semi-priestly position as helpers to the house of Aaron (Num. 3:5ff.).

The next day Moses told the people that they had **sinned a great sin,** but that he would go back up the mountain to see if he could make **atonement** for their sin. The Israelitish sacrificial system was not yet in operation, and despite his previous background and recent instruction concerning the new system of worship, Moses does not seem to have thought that any animal sacrifice would suffice for a sin so basic and so flagrant. In his intercessory prayer which followed on the mountain side, Moses asked the Lord to forgive His people, but if not to blot him out too. The book Moses referred to was probably not "the book of life" mentioned in Revelation 20:12, and it is doubtful if he had a clear concept of life after death, or of himself being accursed there. Rather this is probably a metaphorical concept, thinking of living men as those whom the Lord had "written" in His book as being still alive (see also Ps. 69:28; Isa. 4:3; Mal. 3:16). It seems as if Moses thought perhaps a human sacrifice, that of himself, might atone. But this was not enough. Only Christ could provide perfect atonement, and that higher revelation must await a later day. The Lord told him that only those who had sinned would be blotted out or die. Moses was to return to lead Israel to the promised land. The nation would survive and the covenant with the patriarchs would be fulfilled. Jehovah's **angel** would lead the way. But the guilty would not escape. The Lord would **visit their sin upon them,** and accordingly He **smote the people,** apparently with a pestilence. Moses' second intercession had secured the survival of the nation, but not of all the individuals involved.

c. Divine Judgment and Intercession (33:1-23)

1 And Jehovah spake unto Moses, Depart, go up hence, thou and the people that thou hast brought up out of the land of Egypt, unto the land of which I sware unto Abraham, to Isaac, and to Jacob, saying, Unto thy seed will I give it: 2 and I will send an angel before thee; and I will drive out the Canaanite, the Amorite, and the Hittite, and the Perizzite, the Hivite, and the Jebusite: 3 unto a land flowing with milk and honey: for I will not go up in the midst of thee; for thou art a stiffnecked people; lest I consume thee in the way. 4 And when the people heard these evil tidings, they mourned: and no man did put on him his ornaments. 5 And Jehovah said unto Moses, Say unto the children of Israel, Ye are a stiffnecked people; if I go up into the midst of thee for one moment, I shall consume thee: therefore now put off thy ornaments from thee, that I may know what to do unto thee. 6 And the children of Israel stripped themselves of their ornaments from mount Horeb onward.

7 Now Moses used to take the tent and to pitch it without the camp, afar off from the camp; and he called it, The tent of meeting. And it came to pass, that every one that sought Jehovah went out unto the tent of meeting, which was without the camp. 8 And it came to pass, when Moses went out unto the Tent, that all the people rose up, and stood, every man at his tent door, and looked after Moses, until he was gone into the

Tent. 9 And it came to pass, when Moses entered into the Tent, the pillar of cloud descended, and stood at the door of the Tent: and *Jehovah* spake with Moses. 10 And all the people saw the pillar of cloud stand at the door of the Tent: and all the people rose up and worshipped, every man at his tent door. 11 And Jehovah spake unto Moses face to face, as a man speaketh unto his friend. And he turned again into the camp: but his minister Joshua, the son of Nun, a young man, departed not out of the Tent.

12 And Moses said unto Jehovah, See, thou sayest unto me, Bring up this people: and thou hast not let me know whom thou wilt send with me. Yet thou hast said, I know thee by name, and thou hast also found favor in my sight. 13 Now therefore, I pray thee, if I have found favor in thy sight, show me now thy ways, that I may know thee, to the end that I may find favor in thy sight: and consider that this nation is thy people. 14 And he said, My presence shall go *with thee,* and I will give thee rest. 15 And he said unto him, If thy presence go not *with me,* carry us not up hence. 16 For wherein now shall it be known that I have found favor in thy sight, I and thy people? Is it not in that thou goest with us, so that we are separated, I and thy people, from all the people that are upon the face of the earth? 17 And Jehovah said unto Moses, I will do this thing also that thou hast spoken; for thou hast found favor in my sight, and I know thee by name. 18 And he said, Show me, I pray thee, thy glory. 19 And he said, I will make all my goodness pass before thee, and will proclaim the name of Jehovah before thee; and I will be gracious to whom I will be gracious, and will show mercy on whom I will show mercy. 20 And he said, Thou canst not see my face; for man shall not see me and live. 21 And Jehovah said, Behold, there is a place by me, and thou shalt stand upon the rock: 22 and it shall come to pass, while my glory passeth by, that I will put thee in a cleft of the rock, and will cover thee with my hand until I have passed by: 23 and I will take away my hand, and thou shalt see my back; but my face shall not be seen.

The Lord now proceeded to explain to Moses the plain implications of His remark in 32:34, "my angel shall go before thee." He says that Moses is to depart with Israel for Canaan, in order that He may fulfill His promise to the patriarchs. An angel will precede them to drive out the present inhabitants of the land, but Jehovah Himself will not go up in their midst, for His holiness would destroy them because of their stubbornness. In the promises of the covenant, the Lord had also said that He would send an angel before them. But that angel was so closely identified with Him, having His name in him (23:21), that He must have been the preincarnate Christ (see comments on 23:20-33). The angel now mentioned was of a different order altogether. Sin had led to the withdrawal of the divine presence.

When Moses relayed this news to Israel, the entire nation **mourned**. In obedience to Jehovah's instructions to Moses, they stripped themselves of their **ornaments** and apparently never put them back on **from mount Horeb onward**. Some of their ornaments had been used in the composition of the idol. The remaining ones were a painful reminder of that apostasy. They were later to be used in the construction of the tabernacle (35:22). The people had full reason to mourn the withdrawal of the divine presence. Prior to this time it had been Moses' custom to pitch a tent, called **The tent of meeting** at some distance from the camp. Moses went regularly to the tent to commune with Jehovah, and the people often watched him enter the tent, and also watched the cloudy pillar descend upon the tent as Moses conversed with the Lord. They would bow in worship at their own tent doors. And when they needed counsel, it was to this tent that they came that Moses might interpret God's laws for them. Here the Lord spoke to Moses directly **as a man speaketh unto his friend** — no crutches like dreams or visions or mere impressions. Moses went to the tent and returned, but Joshua seems to have been there constantly as Moses' attendant and assistant. Now this intimate fellowship was to be brought to an end. Critical scholars have claimed that the primitive tent of meeting mentioned here is a conflicting tradition about a cruder place of worship than the portable temple just described by Jehovah to Moses. But this is simply a pre-tabernacle stage, a tent Moses set aside more or less of his own volition, in the months between the Exodus and the construction of the tabernacle, in which to seek the divine will. Although it may be mentioned at the time of Jethro's visit (18:7), it is doubtful whether even the sacrifice offered by Jethro had any direct connection with the tent (see comments on 18:1-27).

But now Moses again takes up the office of the intercessor. He points out that the Lord has still given him the same heavy responsibility, but left him in complete confusion about his angelic helper. The Lord had spoken approvingly of Moses, and if He meant it, Moses asked for a fuller understanding of His ways so that he might find favor in His sight. He reminded the Lord again that **this nation is thy people**. Moses was not willing to settle for a lower level of fellowship, for a mere fulfillment of the covenant with the patriarchs. He was wanting a renewal of the covenant so recently established and so tragically broken. Now came the answer he had been hoping for. The Lord declared that His presence would also go, and He would give Moses **rest** — the rest and security of His companionship. Moses was quick to catch at the least hint of consent on Jehovah's part, and he said that if Jehovah was not also to go, that he would prefer that Israel not budge from the spot. There was no other way that Jehovah's approval of Moses (and Moses is quick to add of **thy people**) would be evident to the world at large except through His presence which separated them from all other peoples. Again the Lord assured Moses that He would grant his request.

Then Moses pressed a further request. He wanted to see the glory of God. He had spoken to the Lord directly as a friend. He had tarried in His presence forty days and nights. He had been closer to Him than any man had ever been. And yet Moses felt shut out from the fullness of the divine glory. The Lord granted this request too, insofar as Moses could bear it. He would cause His goodness to pass before Moses, proclaiming the divine name, revealing His grace and mercy as before He had revealed His justice. But Moses could not see His face and live. Instead, he would stand on a rock, and when Jehovah passed by, He would put Moses in a cleft of the rock, covering him with His hand. When He had passed, Moses could see

His back, but not His face. As Driver puts it, Moses would see "only the after-glow, which He leaves behind Him, but which may still suggest faintly what the full brilliancy of His presence must be."[199] What Moses really experienced is beyond the knowledge of folk less privileged. Perhaps Paul would have partially understood (II Cor. 12:1ff.). But the experience had to be put into anthropomorphic terms to make it in any sense intelligible.

2. The Revelation of God to Moses (34:1-9)

1 And Jehovah said unto Moses, Hew thee two tables of stone like unto the first: and I will write upon the tables the words that were on the first tables, which thou brakest. 2 And be ready by the morning, and come up in the morning unto mount Sinai, and present thyself there to me on the top of the mount. 3 And no man shall come up with thee; neither let any man be seen throughout all the mount; neither let the flocks nor herds feed before that mount. 4 And he hewed two tables of stone like unto the first; and Moses rose up early in the morning, and went up unto mount Sinai, as Jehovah had commanded him, and took in his hand two tables of stone. 5 And Jehovah descended in the cloud, and stood with him there, and proclaimed the name of Jehovah. 6 And Jehovah passed by before him, and proclaimed, Jehovah, Jehovah, a God merciful and gracious, slow to anger, and abundant in lovingkindness and truth; 7 keeping lovingkindness for thousands, forgiving iniquity and transgression and sin; and that will by no means clear *the guilty*, visiting the iniquity of the fathers upon the children, and upon the children's children, upon the third and upon the fourth generation. 8 And Moses made haste, and bowed his head toward the earth, and worshipped. 9 And he said, If now I have found favor in thy sight, O Lord, let the Lord, I pray thee, go in the midst of us; for it is a stiffnecked people; and pardon our iniquity and our sin, and take us for thine inheritance.

The Lord now gave instructions to Moses as to how he was to prepare for the renewal of the covenant and for the special revelation of the divine glory. He was to hew out two tables of stone

and bring them into the mount for the Lord to use in rewriting the Ten Commandments. This one scar of the broken covenant would remain. The other tables had been made by the Lord as well as inscribed by Him (32:16); the second set was to be manmade, although the Lord would still write upon them. He was to be ready by the following morning, and was to ascend Sinai alone, not permitting even the flocks and herds to graze upon its lower slopes.

Obediently Moses presented himself before Jehovah in the mount the next morning, carrying the two tablets. And the Lord **descended in the cloud,** and **stood with him,** proclaiming **the name of Jehovah.** And He passed by before Moses as He had promised, proclaiming His divine character in much the same terms as those contained in the Second Commandment (20:5-6), but with an added introduction which stressed appropriately that He was **merciful and gracious, slow to anger,** and **abundant in lovingkindness and truth.** Once actually this near the divine glory, Moses was himself quick to bow his head and worship. But he took advantage of the opportunity to present once again his intercession, asking that if he had indeed found favor in the Lord's sight that the Lord would go in the midst of His people. He admitted that they were a **stiffnecked people,** but he asked that the Lord would forgive them and take them for His **inheritance.**

3. The Restatement of the Covenant (34:10-26)

a. The Restatement of the Promises (34:10-11)

10 And he said, Behold, I make a covenant: before all thy people I will do marvels, such as have not been wrought in all the earth, nor in any nation; and all the people among which thou art shall see the work of Jehovah; for it is a terrible thing that I do with thee. 11 Observe thou that which I command thee this day: behold, I drive out before thee the Amorite, and the Canaanite, and the Hittite, and the Perizzite, and the Hivite, and the Jebusite.

The Lord now made His forgiveness concrete with a restatement and renewal of the covenant. Most of what He says is quite similar to the miscellaneous rules and the conditions and advantages of the covenant recorded in chapter 23. All of what He says is found either in the Ten Commandments or the balance of the Book of the Covenant. So it is a restatement of the broken covenant, summing up those points which especially need emphasis after Israel's fall into idolatry.

First there is a restatement of the promises of the covenant, remarking first of all that He **will do marvels** before Israel such as had never before been wrought on earth. These marvels were identified as the driving out of the Canaanite nations before them (cf. 23:20-33, especially vv. 22b-23, 27-31).

b. **The Restatement of the Conditions (34:12-26)**

12 Take heed to thyself, lest thou make a covenant with the inhabitants of the land whither thou goest, lest it be for a snare in the midst of thee: 13 but ye shall break down their altars, and dash in pieces their pillars, and ye shall cut down their Asherim 14 (for thou shalt worship no other god: for Jehovah, whose name is Jealous, is a jealous God); 15 lest thou make a covenant with the inhabitants of the land, and they play the harlot after their gods, and sacrifice unto their gods, and one call thee and thou eat of his sacrifice; 16 and thou take of their daughters unto thy sons, and their daughters play the harlot after their gods, and make thy sons play the harlot after their gods. 17 Thou shalt make thee no molten gods.

18 The feast of unleavened bread shalt thou keep. Seven days shalt thou eat unleavened bread, as I commanded thee, at the time appointed in the month Abib; for in the month Abib thou camest out from Egypt. 19 All that openeth the womb is mine; and all thy cattle that is male, the firstlings of cow and sheep. 20 And the firstling of an ass thou shalt redeem with a lamb: and if thou wilt not redeem it, then thou shalt break its neck. All the first-born of thy sons thou shalt redeem. And none shall appear before me empty.

21 Six days thou shalt work, but on the seventh day thou shalt rest: in plowing time and in harvest thou shalt rest. 22 And thou shalt observe the feast of weeks, *even* of the first-fruits of wheat harvest, and the feast of ingathering at the year's end. 23 Three times in the year shall all thy males appear before the Lord Jehovah, the God of Israel. 24 For I will cast out nations before thee, and enlarge thy borders: neither shall any man desire thy land, when thou goest up to appear before Jehovah thy God three times in the year.

25 Thou shalt not offer the blood of my sacrifice with leavened bread; neither shall the sacrifice of the feast of the passover be left unto the morning. 26 The first of the first-fruits of thy ground thou shalt bring unto the house of Jehovah thy God. Thou shalt not boil a kid in its mother's milk.

The references in verses 27-28 have been misread by some critical scholars, and they have claimed to find in verses 12-26 another set of ten commandments, the so-called "ritual decalogue,"[200] supposedly older than the set found in Exodus 20 and contradictory to the account there. But such an interpretation misses the whole point of this section. It is extracted from the Book of the Covenant and restated, not to the cancellation of the rest of the original covenant, but to the stressing of those elements of it which especially needed emphasis in the light of what Israel had so recently done. Ten commandments can only be drawn from it by a forced and arbitrary classification. Rawlinson points out that it naturally divides into twelve, which we may list as follows:[201]

(1) No treaty is to be made with the Canaanite nations, v. 12 (cf. 23:32-33 — the closing conditions of the covenant are thus the opening ones in the restatement).

(2) The Canaanite altars, sacred pillars, and Asherim (mentioned here for the first time) are to be utterly destroyed, v. 13 (cf. 23:24). Verses 14-16 explain the dangers inherent in the things prohibited in these two commandments, verse 14 virtually reproducing the First Commandment and part of the Second (20:3, 5), and verses 15-16 explaining how friendship with the heathen Canaanites could easily lead to idolatry.

(3) No molten images were to be made, v. 17 (cf. 20:23).

200 Rylaarsdam, *op. cit.*, I, 1076ff.   201 Rawlinson, *The Pulpit Commentary: Exodus*, II, 369.

(4) The Feast of Unleavened Bread is to be kept, v. 18. (This is almost an exact reproduction of 23:15.)

(5) The first-born are to be sacrificed or redeemed, vv. 19-20 (cf. 22:29b-30).

(6) The Sabbath is to be observed, with new emphasis on its observation even in the busiest seasons of the year — **plowing** and **harvest, v. 21** (cf. the Fourth Commandment, 20:8-11, and 23:12).

(7) The Feast of Pentecost or Weeks is to be observed, v. 22a (cf. 23:16a).

(8) The Feast of Tabernacles or Ingathering is to be observed, v. 22b (cf. 23:16b).

(9) At the times of the three great feasts all the males are to appear before the Lord, v. 23 (cf. 23:14, 17). Verse 24 is a striking assurance that if they were obedient in this respect, the Lord would protect their lands while they were gone from home.

(10) No leaven was to be used in sacrifice, nor any of the Passover sacrifice left until the next morning, v. 25 (cf. 23:18).

(11) The first-fruits of all produce were to be offered at the house of the Lord, v. 26a (cf. 23:19a).

(12) No kid was to be boiled in its mother's milk, v. 26b (cf. 23:19b).

These twelve commandments break up into three groups: 1-3 deal generally with idolatry, the sin into which Israel had just fallen; 4-11 deal with those religious holy days and feasts sanctioned by Jehovah, and some of the offerings connected with them — Israel need not look to paganism for religious celebrations if they observed the ones Jehovah had planned; and 12 deals with a now poorly understood pagan ritual which may have been involved in the wild orgies before the golden calf. The Lord renewed the covenant by stressing those points Israel had been most prone to forget.

4. The Rewriting of the Covenant (34:27-28)

27 And Jehovah said unto Moses, Write thou these words: for after the tenor of these words I have made a covenant with thee and with Israel. 28 And he was

there with Jehovah forty days and forty nights; he did neither eat bread, nor drink water. And he wrote upon the tables the words of the covenant, the ten commandments.

Two writings are spoken of in these verses: the recording of the restatement of the covenant done by Moses at Jehovah's command, and the rewriting by Jehovah upon the new tablets of stone of **the words of the covenant** which were still basic, **the ten commandments,** or as the Hebrew literally reads, "the ten words." These were the Ten Commandments of 20:2-17.

Moses tarried again in the presence of Jehovah forty days and nights, in a state of complete fast. Later he related that part of the time was spent in intercession (Deut. 9:18-20, 25-29).

5. The Result of Moses' Experience (34:29-35)

29 And it came to pass, when Moses came down from mount Sinai with the two tables of the testimony in Moses' hand, when he came down from the mount, that Moses knew not that the skin of his face shone by reason of his speaking with him. 30 And when Aaron and all the children of Israel saw Moses, behold, the skin of his face shone; and they were afraid to come nigh him. 31 And Moses called unto them; and Aaron and all the rulers of the congregation returned unto him: and Moses spake to them. 32 And afterward all the children of Israel came nigh: and he gave them in commandment all that Jehovah had spoken with him in mount Sinai. 33 And when Moses had done speaking with them, he put a veil on his face. 34 But when Moses went in before Jehovah to speak with him, he took the veil off, until he came out; and he came out, and spake unto the children of Israel that which he was commanded. 35 And the children of Israel saw the face of Moses, that the skin of Moses' face shone; and Moses put the veil upon his face again, until he went in to speak with him.

When Moses came down from Sinai with the second set of stone tablets, he was unaware that **the skin of his face shone,** or as the Hebrew literally reads, "sent out rays" or "horns." This had come about as he tarried in the presence of God, striking evidence that he had indeed had a closer contact with the glory of God than ever before. Aaron and the people apparently fled from him because of this strange glow. But Aaron and the elders came back when Moses called them, and afterward the entire nation assembled to hear Moses' report on the renewal of the covenant. By the time Moses finished his report, he was aware of what had happened to him. He accordingly covered his face with a veil which he took off only when going back before Jehovah. The glow of the divine glory "was a badge of his high office as the ambassador of God. No testimonial needed to be produced. He bore his credentials on his very face."[202] But the world was not yet ready for even this faint, temporary reflection of the divine glory. The full revelation of the divine glory must await the day of Christ (II Cor. 3:12-18).

E. TRAINING THROUGH SERVICE (35:1—40:38)

1. The Centrality of the Sabbath (35:1-3)

1 And Moses assembled all the congregation of the children of Israel, and said unto them, These are the words which Jehovah hath commanded, that ye should do them. 2 Six days shall work be done; but on the seventh day there shall be to you a holy day, a sabbath of solemn rest to Jehovah: whosoever doeth any work therein shall be put to death. 3 Ye shall kindle no fire throughout your habitations upon the sabbath day.

Now that the breach of the covenant had been repaired, the thread of the account as interrupted at the end of chapter 31 is resumed. The work of constructing the tabernacle which had been assigned Moses in the mount was now to be undertaken. He began it with the special words of admonition about the Sabbath with which Jehovah had concluded His instructions (31:12-17). Only 31:15 is actually quoted. And a new statement is added, prohibiting the kindling of fires upon the Sabbath. The preparation of food was permitted according to 12:16. Thus it is possible, as some scholars have suggested, that just as this special admonition was a warning not

to construct the house of worship on the Sabbath Day, just so this is a warning that the metalworkers are not to kindle their fires on that day.[203]

2. The Call to Offering and Service (35:4—36:7)

4 And Moses spake unto all the congregation of the children of Israel, saying, This is the thing which Jehovah commanded, saying, 5 Take ye from among you an offering unto Jehovah; whosoever is of a willing heart, let him bring it, Jehovah's offering: gold, and silver, and brass, 6 and blue, and purple, and scarlet, and fine linen, and goats' hair, 7 and rams' skins dyed red, and sealskins, and acacia wood, 8 and oil for the light, and spices for the anointing oil, and for the sweet incense, 9 and onyx stones, and stones to be set, for the ephod, and for the breastplate.

10 And let every wise-hearted man among you come, and make all that Jehovah hath commanded: 11 the tabernacle, its tent, and its covering, its clasps, and its boards, its bars, its pillars, and its sockets; 12 the ark, and the staves thereof, the mercy-seat, and the veil of the screen; 13 the table, and its staves, and all its vessels, and the showbread; 14 the candlestick also for the light, and its vessels, and its lamps, and the oil for the light; 15 and the altar of incense, and its staves, and the anointing oil, and the sweet incense, and the screen for the door, at the door of the tabernacle; 16 the altar of burnt-offering, with its grating of brass, its staves, and all its vessels, the laver and its base; 17 the hangings of the court, the pillars thereof, and their sockets, and the screen for the gate of the court; 18 the pins of the tabernacle, and the pins of the court, and their cords; 19 the finely wrought garments, for ministering in the holy place, the holy garments for Aaron the priest, and the garments of his sons, to minister in the priest's office.

20 And all the congregation of the children of Israel departed from the presence of Moses. 21 And they came, every one whose heart stirred him up, and every one whom his spirit made willing, *and* brought Jehovah's offering, for the work of the tent of meeting, and for all the service thereof, and for the holy garments. 22 And they came, both men and women, as many as were willing-hearted, *and* brought brooches, and ear-

[202] Robert Jamieson, A. R. Fausset, and David Brown, *Commentary Critical and Explanatory on the Whole Bible*, pp. 70-71.   [203] Rylaarsdam, *op. cit.*, I, 1082.

rings, and signet-rings, and armlets, all jewels of gold; even every man that offered an offering of gold unto Jehovah. 23 And every man, with whom was found blue, and purple, and scarlet, and fine linen, and goats' *hair,* and rams' skins dyed red, and sealskins, brought them. 24 Every one that did offer an offering of silver and brass brought Jehovah's offering; and every man, with whom was found acacia wood for any work of the service, brought it. 25 And all the women that were wise-hearted did spin with their hands, and brought that which they had spun, the blue, and the purple, the scarlet, and the fine linen. 26 And all the women whose heart stirred them up in wisdom spun the goats' *hair.* 27 And the rulers brought the onyx stones, and the stones to be set, for the ephod, and for the breastplate; 28 and the spice, and the oil; for the light, and for the anointing oil, and for the sweet incense. 29 The children of Israel brought a freewill-offering unto Jehovah; every man and woman, whose heart made them willing to bring for all the work, which Jehovah had commanded to be made by Moses.

30 And Moses said unto the children of Israel, See, Jehovah hath called by name Bezalel the son of Uri, the son of Hur, of the tribe of Judah; 31 and he hath filled him with the Spirit of God, in wisdom, in understanding, and in knowledge, and in all manner of workmanship; 32 and to devise skilful works, to work in gold, and in silver, and in brass, 33 and in cutting of stones for setting, and in carving of wood, to work in all manner of skilful workmanship. 34 And he hath put in his heart that he may teach, both he, and Oholiab, the son of Ahisamach, of the tribe of Dan. 35 Them hath he filled with wisdom of heart, to work all manner of workmanship, of the engraver, and of the skilful workman, and of the embroiderer, in blue, and in purple, in scarlet, and in fine linen, and of the weaver, even of them that do any workmanship, and of them that devise skilful works. 1 And Bezalel and Oholiab shall work, and every wise-hearted man, in whom Jehovah hath put wisdom and understanding to know how to work all the work for the service of the sanctuary, according to all that Jehovah hath commanded.

2 And Moses called Bezalel and Oholiab, and every wise-hearted man, in whose heart Jehovah had put wisdom, even every one whose heart stirred him up to come unto the work to do it: 3 and they received of Moses all the offering which the children of Israel had brought for the work of the service of the sanctuary, wherewith to make it. And they brought yet unto him freewill-offerings every morning. 4 And all the wise men, that wrought all the work of the sanctuary, came every man from his work which they wrought; 5 and they spake unto Moses, saying, The people bring much more than enough for the service of the work which Jehovah commanded to make. 6 And Moses gave commandment, and they caused it to be proclaimed throughout the camp, saying, Let neither man nor woman make any more work for the offering of the sanctuary. So the people were restrained from bringing. 7 For the stuff they had was sufficient for all the work to make it, and too much.

The second step was the announcement of the freewill-offering and of the materials which would be needed (35:4-9; cf. 25:2-7). The third step was an invitation by Moses to the skilled workers among the people to volunteer for service, and to aid them in knowing whose services would be needed, he listed the objects which were to be made (35:10-19). Then in 35:20-29, the people brought the offering, the people bringing the personal ornaments which they had stripped off themselves in 33:6, each person who had some of the materials contributing them, the women spinning additional material that they might give it, and the rulers offering precious stones and other valuable items. Then in 35:30—36:1, Moses announced the divine appointment and equipment of Bezalel and Oholiab to supervise the project and opened the door again for others to volunteer to assist them (cf. 31:2-6). In 36:2-7, Moses called these two men to a central place, and selected others from among the volunteers, and turned over to them the rapidly accumulating materials. Shortly afterward they came to ask that the offering be stopped, for more had been received than was needed. A chastened Israel had indeed given a model offering!

3. The Construction of the Tabernacle (36:8-38)

8 And all the wise-hearted men among them that wrought the work made the tabernacle with ten curtains; of fine twined linen, and blue, and purple, and

scarlet, with cherubim, the work of the skilful workman, *Bezalel* made them. 9 The length of each curtain was eight and twenty cubits, and the breadth of each curtain four cubits: all the curtains had one measure. 10 And he coupled five curtains one to another: and *the other* five curtains he coupled one to another. 11 And he made loops of blue upon the edge of the one curtain from the selvedge in the coupling: likewise he made in the edge of the curtain that was outmost in the second coupling. 12 Fifty loops made he in the one curtain, and fifty loops made he in the edge of the curtain that was in the second coupling: the loops were opposite one to another. 13 And he made fifty clasps of gold, and coupled the curtains one to another with the clasps: so the tabernacle was one. 14 And he made curtains of goats' *hair* for a tent over the tabernacle: eleven curtains he made them. 15 The length of each curtain was thirty cubits, and four cubits the breadth of each curtain: the eleven curtains had one measure. 16 And he coupled five curtains by themselves, and six curtains by themselves. 17 And he made fifty loops on the edge of the curtain that was outmost in the coupling, and fifty loops made he upon the edge of the curtain which was *outmost in* the second coupling. 18 And he made fifty clasps of brass to couple the tent together, that it might be one. 19 And he made a covering for the tent of rams' skins dyed red, and a covering of sealskins above. 20 And he made the boards for the tabernacle, of acacia wood, standing up. 21 Ten cubits was the length of a board, and a cubit and a half the breadth of each board. 22 Each board had two tenons, joined one to another: thus did he make for all the boards of the tabernacle. 23 And he made the boards for the tabernacle: twenty boards for the south side southward; 24 and he made forty sockets of silver under the twenty boards; two sockets under one board for its two tenons, and two sockets under another board for its two tenons. 25 And for the second side of the tabernacle, on the north side, he made twenty boards, 26 and their forty sockets of silver; two sockets under one board, and two sockets under another board. 27 And for the hinder part of the tabernacle westward he made six boards. 28 And two boards made he for the corners of the tabernacle in the hinder part. 29 And they were double beneath; and in like manner they were entire unto the top thereof unto one ring: thus he did to both of them

in the two corners. 30 And there were eight boards, and their sockets of silver, sixteen sockets; under every board two sockets.

31 And he made bars of acacia wood; five for the boards of the one side of the tabernacle, 32 and five bars for the boards of the other side of the tabernacle, and five bars for the boards of the tabernacle for the hinder part westward. 33 And he made the middle bar to pass through in the midst of the boards from the one end to the other. 34 And he overlaid the boards with gold, and made their rings of gold for places for the bars, and overlaid the bars with gold.

35 And he made the veil of blue, and purple, and scarlet, and fine twined linen: with cherubim, the work of the skilful workman, made he it. 36 And he made thereunto four pillars of acacia, and overlaid them with gold: their hooks were of gold; and he cast for them four sockets of silver. 37 And he made a screen for the door of the Tent, of blue, and purple, and scarlet, and fine twined linen, the work of the embroiderer; 38 and the five pillars of it with their hooks: and he overlaid their capitals and their fillets with gold; and their five sockets were of brass.

Jehovah's instructions to Moses had begun with the ark and moved out to the courtyard. But Bezalel and his helpers began with the tabernacle itself, first the inner curtains or "dwelling," then the tent and the skin-coverings, then the framework, finally the veil and the screen. These verses are nearly a verbatim reproduction of chapter 26 (see the comments there for the details and symbolism).

4. The Contents of the Tabernacle (37:1-29)

1 And Bezalel made the ark of acacia wood: two cubits and a half was the length of it, and a cubit and a half the breadth of it, and a cubit and a half the height of it. 2 And he overlaid it with pure gold within and without, and made a crown of gold to it round about. 3 And he cast for it four rings of gold, in the four feet thereof; even two rings on the one side of it, and two rings on the other side of it. 4 And he made staves of acacia wood, and overlaid them with gold. 5 And he put the staves into the rings on the sides of the ark, to bear the ark. 6 And he made a mercy-seat of pure gold: two cubits and a half *was* the length thereof, and a cubit and a half

the breadth thereof. 7 And he made two cherubim of gold; of beaten work made he them, at the two ends of the mercy-seat; 8 one cherub at the one end, and one cherub at the other end: of one piece with the mercy-seat made he the cherubim at the two ends thereof. 9 And the cherubim spread out their wings on high, covering the mercy-seat with their wings, with their faces one to another; toward the mercy-seat were the faces of the cherubim.

10 And he made the table of acacia wood: two cubits *was* the length thereof, and a cubit the breadth thereof, and a cubit and a half the height thereof. 11 And he overlaid it with pure gold, and made thereto a crown round about. 12 And he made unto it a border of a handbreadth round about, and made a golden crown to the border thereof round about. 13 And he cast for it four rings of gold, and put the rings in the four corners that were on the feet thereof. 14 Close by the border were the rings, the places for the staves to bear the table. 15 And he made the staves of acacia wood, and overlaid them with gold, to bear the table. 16 And he made the vessels which were upon the table, the dishes thereof, and the spoons thereof, and the bowls thereof, and the flagons thereof, wherewith to pour out, of pure gold.

17 And he made the candlestick of pure gold: of beaten work made he the candlestick, even its base, and its shaft; its cups, its knops, and its flowers, were of one piece with it. 18 And there were six branches going out of the sides thereof; three branches of the candlestick out of the one side thereof, and three branches of the candlestick out of the other side thereof: 19 three cups made like almond-blossoms in one branch, a knop and a flower; and three cups made like almond-blossoms in the other branch, a knop and a flower: so for the six branches going out of the candlestick. 20 And in the candlestick were four cups made like almond-blossoms, the knops thereof, and the flowers thereof; 21 and a knop under two branches of one piece with it, and a knop under two branches of one piece with it, and a knop under two branches of one piece with it, for the six branches going out of it. 22 Their knops and their branches were of one piece with it: the whole of it was one beaten work of pure gold. 23 And he made the lamps thereof, seven, and the snuffers thereof, and the snuff-dishes thereof, of pure gold. 24 Of a talent of pure gold made he it, and all the vessels thereof.

25 And he made an altar of incense of acacia wood: a cubit was the length thereof, and a cubit the breadth thereof, foursquare; and two cubits was the height thereof; the horns thereof were of one piece with it. 26 And he overlaid it with pure gold, the top thereof, and the sides thereof round about, and the horns of it: and he made unto it a crown of gold round about. 27 And he made for it two golden rings under the crown thereof, upon the two ribs thereof, upon the two sides of it, for places for staves wherewith to bear it. 28 And he made the staves of acacia wood, and overlaid them with gold. 29 And he made the holy anointing oil, and the pure incense of sweet spices, after the art of the perfumer.

After the house of worship itself had been constructed, Bezalel and his helpers moved on to its contents. The order given in Jehovah's instructions, beginning with the ark and ending with the candlestick, was also followed in the actual construction. Verses 1-24 are an almost exact reproduction of 25:10-40. Verses 25-28 add the altar of incense which was mentioned much later in the instructions (30:1-6), and verse 29 briefly mentions the anointing oil and incense described at length in the final instructions (30:22-38). (For the fashion and meaning of the various items, see comments on the passages cited.)

5. The Court of the Tabernacle (38:1-20)

1 And he made the altar of burnt-offering of acacia wood: five cubits was the length thereof, and five cubits the breadth thereof, foursquare; and three cubits the height thereof. 2 And he made the horns thereof upon the four corners of it; the horns thereof were of one piece with it: and he overlaid it with brass. 3 And he made all the vessels of the altar, the pots, and the shovels, and the basins, the flesh-hooks, and the firepans; all the vessels thereof made he of brass. 4 And he made for the altar a grating of network of brass, under the ledge round it beneath, reaching half-way up. 5 And he cast four rings for the four ends of the grating of brass, to be places for the staves. 6 And he made the staves of acacia wood, and overlaid them with brass. 7 And he put the staves into

the rings on the sides of the altar, wherewith to bear it; he made it hollow with planks.

8 And he made the laver of brass, and the base thereof of brass, of the mirrors of the ministering women that ministered at the door of the tent of meeting.

9 And he made the court: for the south side southward the hangings of the court were of fine twined linen, a hundred cubits; 10 their pillars were twenty, and their sockets twenty, of brass; the hooks of the pillars and their fillets were of silver. 11 And for the north side a hundred cubits, their pillars twenty, and their sockets twenty, of brass; the hooks of the pillars, and their fillets, of silver. 12 And for the west side were hangings of fifty cubits, their pillars ten, and their sockets ten; the hooks of the pillars, and their fillets, of silver. 13 And for the east side eastward fifty cubits. 14 The hangings for the one side *of the gate* were fifteen cubits; their pillars three, and their sockets three; 15 and so for the other side: on this hand and on that hand by the gate of the court were hangings of fifteen cubits; their pillars three, and their sockets three. 16 All the hangings of the court round about were of fine twined linen. 17 And the sockets for the pillars, and their fillets, of silver; and the overlaying of their capitals, of silver; and all the pillars of the court were filleted with silver. 18 And the screen for the gate of the court was the work of the embroiderer, of blue, and purple, and scarlet, and fine twined linen: and twenty cubits was the length, and the height in the breadth was five cubits, answerable to the hangings of the court. 19 And their pillars were four, and their sockets four, of brass; their hooks of silver, and the overlaying of their capitals, and their fillets, of silver. 20 And all the pins of the tabernacle, and of the court round about, were of brass.

After the house and its interior furnishings were completed, Bezalel and his helpers proceeded to the courtyard, just as the instructions had indicated. Here they made the altar of burnt-offering and the hangings of the court, verses 1-7, 9-20 essentially repeating the contents of 27:1-19. The one alteration is the insertion between these items of the bronze laver, described previously in 30: 18. Verse 8 adds the information that it was made of the bronze mirrors of the women who helped with the work in the tabernacle courtyard. (For details about the fashion and significance of the various items, see comments on the passages cited.)

6. The Cost of the Tabernacle (38:21-31)

21 This is the sum of *the things for* the tabernacle, even the tabernacle of the testimony, as they were counted, according to the commandment of Moses, for the service of the Levites, by the hand of Ithamar, the son of Aaron the priest. 22 And Bezalel the son of Uri, the son of Hur, of the tribe of Judah, made all that Jehovah commanded Moses. 23 And with him was Oholiab, the son of Ahisamach, of the tribe of Dan, an engraver, and a skilful workman, and an embroiderer in blue, and in purple, and in scarlet, and in fine linen.

24 All the gold that was used for the work in all the work of the sanctuary, even the gold of the offering, was twenty and nine talents, and seven hundred and thirty shekels, after the shekel of the sanctuary. 25 And the silver of them that were numbered of the congregation was a hundred talents, and a thousand seven hundred and threescore fifteen shekels, after the shekel of the sanctuary: 26 a beka a head, *that is,* half a shekel, after the shekel of the sanctuary, for every one that passed over to them that were numbered, from twenty years old and upward, for six hundred thousand and three thousand and five hundred and fifty men. 27 And the hundred talents of silver were for casting the sockets of the sanctuary, and the sockets of the veil; a hundred sockets for the hundred talents, a talent for a socket. 28 And of the thousand seven hundred seventy and five *shekels* he made hooks for the pillars, and overlaid their capitals, and made fillets for them. 29 And the brass of the offering was seventy talents, and two thousand and four hundred shekels. 30 And therewith he made the sockets to the door of the tent of meeting, and the brazen altar, and the brazen grating for it, and all the vessels of the altar, 31 and the sockets of the court round about, and the sockets of the gate of the court, and all the pins of the tabernacle, and all the pins of the court round about.

With the completion of the house of worship and its furnishings, there is an accounting of the laborers and the cost. In addition to the two supervising laborers, there is mention made now of Ithamar, one of the sons of Aaron, who took inventory of all the items before they were turned over to the Levites for their care and maintenance. This would indicate that the census taken in Numbers 1–4 with its appointment of the Levites to the charge of the sanctuary took place at about this time. Such is apparently assumed in the book of Numbers (see Num. 7:1–8:26 but cf. Exod. 40:17 and Num. 1:7). And it would explain the institution of the poll-tax or census-tax in conjunction with the instructions for the building of the tabernacle (Exod. 30:11-16).

The accounting of the metals used in building the sanctuary and its precincts is largely a total of all the various amounts mentioned in the instructions. It is an imposing list indeed. Some critical scholars have questioned the possibility of a group of nomads having such immense wealth at their disposal. Modern value of the materials would probably run to two or three million dollars. But these were no ordinary nomads. They were a people blessed by Jehovah. And they had just recently marched out of Egypt, bearing much of that great nation's wealth (12:35-36).

7. The Clothing of the Priests (39:1-31)

1 And of the blue, and purple, and scarlet, they made finely wrought garments, for ministering in the holy place, and made the holy garments for Aaron; as Jehovah commanded Moses.

2 And he made the ephod of gold, blue, and purple, and scarlet, and fine twined linen. 3 And they did beat the gold into thin plates, and cut it into wires, to work it in the blue, and in the purple, and in the scarlet, and in the fine linen, the work of the skilful workman. 4 They made shoulder-pieces for it, joined together; at the two ends was it joined together. 5 And the skilfully woven band, that was upon it, wherewith to gird it on, was of the same piece *and* like the work thereof; of gold, of blue, and purple, and scarlet, and fine twined linen; as Jehovah commanded Moses.

6 And they wrought the onyx stones, inclosed in settings of gold, graven with the engravings of a signet, according to the names of the children of Israel. 7 And he put them on the shoulder-pieces of the ephod, to be stones of memorial for the children of Israel; as Jehovah commanded Moses.

8 And he made the breastplate, the work of the skilful workman, like the work of the ephod; of gold, of blue, and purple, and scarlet, and fine twined linen. 9 It was foursquare; they made the breastplate double: a span was the length thereof, and a span the breadth thereof, being double. 10 And they set in it four rows of stones. A row of sardius, topaz, and carbuncle was the first row; 11 and the second row, an emerald, a sapphire, and a diamond; 12 and the third row, a jacinth, an agate, and an amethyst; 13 and the fourth row, a beryl, an onyx, and a jasper: they were inclosed in inclosings of gold in their settings. 14 And the stones were according to the names of the children of Israel, twelve, according to their names; like the engravings of a signet, every one according to his name, for the twelve tribes. 15 And they made upon the breastplate chains like cords, of wreathen work of pure gold. 16 And they made two settings of gold, and two gold rings, and put the two rings on the two ends of the breastplate. 17 And they put the two wreathen chains of gold in the two rings at the ends of the breastplate. 18 And the *other* two ends of the two wreathen chains they put on the two settings, and put them on the shoulder-pieces of the ephod, in the forepart thereof. 19 And they made two rings of gold, and put them upon the two ends of the breastplate, upon the edge thereof, which was toward the side of the ephod inward. 20 And they made two rings of gold, and put them on the two shoulder-pieces of the ephod underneath, in the forepart thereof, close by the coupling thereof, above the skilfully woven band of the ephod. 21 And they did bind the breastplate by the rings thereof unto the rings of the ephod with a lace of blue, that it might be upon the skilfully woven band of the ephod, and that the breastplate might not be loosed from the ephod; as Jehovah commanded Moses.

22 And he made the robe of the ephod of woven work, all of blue; 23 and the hole of the robe in the midst thereof, as the hole of a coat of mail, with a binding round about the hole of it, that it should not be rent. 24 And they made upon the skirts of the robe pomegranates of blue, and purple, and scarlet, *and* twined *linen,* 25 And they made bells of pure gold, and put the bells between the pomegranates upon the skirts of the robe round about, between the pomegranates; 26 a bell and a pomegranate, a bell and a pomegranate, upon the skirts of the robe round about, to minister in; as Jehovah commanded Moses.

27 And they made the coats of fine li-

nen of woven work for Aaron, and for his sons, 28 and the mitre of fine linen, and the goodly head-tires of fine linen, and the linen breeches of fine twined linen, 29 and the girdle of fine twined linen, and blue, and purple, and scarlet, the work of the embroiderer; as Jehovah commanded Moses.

30 And they made the plate of the holy crown of pure gold, and wrote upon it a writing, like the engravings of a signet, HOLY TO JEHOVAH. 31 And they tied unto it a lace of blue, to fasten it upon the mitre above; as Jehovah commanded Moses.

With the completion of the sanctuary and its precincts, Bezalel and his helpers proceeded to the garments of the priests. Oholiab was probably the one in charge of this part of the work (38:23). This section is a fairly exact reproduction of the instructions given in 28:6-43. (For details as to the fashion and meaning of the various items, see comments on the passage cited.)

8. The Completion of the Tabernacle (39:32-43)

32 Thus was finished all the work of the tabernacle of the tent of meeting: and the children of Israel did according to all that Jehovah commanded Moses; so did they. 33 And they brought the tabernacle unto Moses, the Tent, and all its furniture, its clasps, its boards, its bars, and its pillars, and its sockets; 34 and the covering of rams' skins dyed red, and the covering of sealskins, and the veil of the screen; 35 the ark of the testimony, and the staves thereof, and the mercy-seat; 36 the table, all the vessels thereof, and the showbread; 37 the pure candlestick, the lamps thereof, even the lamps to be set in order, and all the vessels thereof, and the oil for the light; 38 and the golden altar, and the anointing oil, and the sweet incense, and the screen for the door of the Tent; 39 the brazen altar, and its grating of brass, its staves, and all its vessels, the laver and its base; 40 the hangings of the court, its pillars, and its sockets, and the screen for the gate of the court, the cords thereof, and the pins thereof, and all the instruments of the service of the tabernacle, for the tent of meeting; 41 the finely wrought garments for ministering in the holy place, and the holy garments for Aaron the priest, and the garments of his sons, to minister in the priest's office. 42 According to all that Jehovah commanded Moses, so

the children of Israel did all the work. 43 And Moses saw all the work, and, behold, they had done it; as Jehovah had commanded, even so had they done it: and Moses blessed them.

Now everything was completed. And Bezalel and Oholiab and their assistants presented the finished items to Moses. When Moses examined them, he observed that all things had been done according to the divine instructions given him in the mount. And he **blessed** those who had labored so lovingly and so faithfully.

9. The Consecration of the Tabernacle (40:1-38)

a. Divine Instruction (40:1-15)

1 And Jehovah spake unto Moses, saying, 2 On the first day of the first month shalt thou rear up the tabernacle of the tent of meeting. 3 And thou shalt put therein the ark of the testimony, and thou shalt screen the ark with the veil. 4 And thou shalt bring in the table, and set in order the things that are upon it; and thou shalt bring in the candlestick, and light the lamps thereof. 5 And thou shalt set the golden altar for incense before the ark of the testimony, and put the screen of the door to the tabernacle. 6 And thou shalt set the altar of burnt-offering before the door of the tabernacle of the tent of meeting. 7 And thou shalt set the laver between the tent of meeting and the altar, and shalt put water therein. 8 And thou shalt set up the court round about, and hang up the screen of the gate of the court. 9 And thou shalt take the anointing oil, and anoint the tabernacle, and all that is therein, and shalt hallow it, and all the furniture thereof: and it shall be holy. 10 And thou shalt anoint the altar of burnt-offering, and all its vessels, and sanctify the altar: and the altar shall be most holy. 11 And thou shalt anoint the laver and its base, and sanctify it. 12 And thou shalt bring Aaron and his sons unto the door of the tent of meeting, and shalt wash them with water. 13 And thou shalt put upon Aaron the holy garments; and thou shalt anoint him, and sanctify him, that he may minister unto me in the priest's office. 14 And thou shalt bring his sons, and put coats upon them; 15 and thou shalt anoint them, as thou didst anoint their father, that they may minister unto me in the priest's office: and their anointing shall be to them for an everlasting priesthood throughout their generations.

New instructions were now in order. The Lord told Moses that the tabernacle was to be erected on **the first day of the first month,** just two weeks short of one year after they left Egypt, and just two weeks before they would celebrate the first anniversary of the Passover. They had now been at Sinai for nine months (cf. 19:1 and comments there), nearly three of which are accounted for in Moses' two forty-day periods on the mountain in Jehovah's presence. No doubt the actual building of the tabernacle required a great deal of time.

The Lord instructed Moses as to the order in which things were to be erected or put into place, and the relative positions of the various items. Beginning in verse 9, He gave instructions concerning the anointing with the holy anointing oil of the tabernacle and its interior furnishings, of the items in the courtyard, and of the priests. The instructions concerning the anointing of the building and its contents and precincts had been given in 30:26-29, and of the priests in 29:1-35. (For further details and symbolism, see comments under the passages cited.)

b. Human Action (40:16-33)

16 Thus did Moses: according to all that Jehovah commanded him, so did he.

17 And it came to pass in the first month in the second year, on the first day of the month, that the tabernacle was reared up. 18 And Moses reared up the tabernacle, and laid its sockets, and set up the boards thereof, and put in the bars thereof, and reared up its pillars. 19 And he spread the tent over the tabernacle, and put the covering of the tent above upon it; as Jehovah commanded Moses. 20 And he took and put the testimony into the ark, and set the staves on the ark, and put the mercy-seat above upon the ark: 21 and he brought the ark into the tabernacle, and set up the veil of the screen, and screened the ark of the testimony; as Jehovah commanded Moses. 22 And he put the table in the tent of meeting, upon the side of the tabernacle northward, without the veil. 23 And he set the bread in order upon it before Jehovah; as Jehovah commanded Moses. 24 And he put the candlestick in the tent of meet-

ing, over against the table, on the side of the tabernacle southward. 25 And he lighted the lamps before Jehovah; as Jehovah commanded Moses. 26 And he put the golden altar in the tent of meeting before the veil: 27 and he burnt thereon incense of sweet spices; as Jehovah commanded Moses. 28 And he put the screen of the door to the tabernacle. 29 And he set the altar of burnt-offering at the door of the tabernacle of the tent of meeting, and offered upon it the burnt-offering and the meal-offering; as Jehovah commanded Moses. 30 And he set the laver between the tent of meeting and the altar, and put water therein, wherewith to wash. 31 And Moses and Aaron and his sons washed their hands and their feet thereat; 32 when they went into the tent of meeting, and when they came near unto the altar, they washed; as Jehovah commanded Moses. 33 And he reared up the court round about the tabernacle and the altar, and set up the screen of the gate of the court. So Moses finished the work.

Now the instructions the Lord has just given as well as all that had been started or implied earlier is carried out to the finest detail. The building is erected, and reference is even made to the burning of incense upon the golden altar and to the washing of the hands and feet of Moses and Aaron and Aaron's sons in the laver. No mention had been made of Moses' continuing to serve as a priest, but he apparently did so at least until the formal ordination of Aaron.

c. Divine Sanction (40:34-38)

34 Then the cloud covered the tent of meeting, and the glory of Jehovah filled the tabernacle. 35 And Moses was not able to enter into the tent of meeting, because the cloud abode thereon, and the glory of Jehovah filled the tabernacle. 36 And when the cloud was taken up from over the tabernacle, the children of Israel went onward, throughout all their journeys: 37 but if the cloud was not taken up, then they journeyed not till the day that it was taken up. 38 For the cloud of Jehovah was upon the tabernacle by day, and there was fire therein by night, in the sight of all the house of Israel, throughout all their journeys.

When the structure had been completed, the cloud of Jehovah's glorious presence settled down, covering it and filling it until even Moses could not enter. Thus His approval was expressed. And while the cloud apparently lifted over the tabernacle after awhile so the prescribed worship could take place, the divine presence was among the people to stay. When the cloud lifted from the tabernacle, it was time to march. But as long as the cloud tarried, it was time to stay.

Bibliography

I. COMMENTARIES

Allis, Oswald T. *God Spake by Moses.* Nutley, N. J.: The Presbyterian and Reformed Publishing Company, 1958.

Baxter, J. Sidlow. *Explore the Book.* Vol. I. Grand Rapids: Zondervan, 1960.

Chadwick, G. A. *The Book of Exodus,* "The Expositor's Bible." Ed. W. Robertson Nicoll. New York: Hodder and Stoughton, n. d.

Clarke, Adam. *The Holy Bible with a Commentary and Critical Notes.* Vol. I. New York-Nashville: Abingdon-Cokesbury, rep., n.d.

Connell, J. Clement. "Exodus," *The New Bible Commentary.* Ed. Francis Davidson. Grand Rapids: Eerdmans, 1963.

Driver, S. R. *The Book of Exodus,* "The Cambridge Bible for Schools and Colleges." Ed. A. F. Kirkpatrick. Cambridge, 1911.

Goldman, Solomon. *From Slavery to Freedom,* Vol. III of "The Book of Human Destiny." New York: Abelard-Schuman, 1958.

Jamieson, Robert, A. R. Fausset, and David Brown. *Commentary Critical and Explanatory on the Whole Bible.* 1 vol. Grand Rapids: Zondervan, rep., n.d.

Johnson, Philip C. "Exodus," *The Wycliffe Bible Commentary.* Eds. Charles F. Pfeiffer and Everett F. Harrison. Chicago: Moody, 1963.

Keil, C. F., and F. Delitzsch. *Biblical Commentary on the Old Testament: the Pentateuch.* 3 vols. Grand Rapids: Eerdmans, rep., n.d.

McNeile, A. H. *The Book of Exodus,* "Westminster Commentaries." Ed. Walter Lock. London: Methuen, 1908.

Noth, Martin. *Exodus, a Commentary,* "The Old Testament Library." Eds. G. Ernest Wright, *et al.* Trans. J. S. Bowden. London: SCM, 1952.

Park, J. Edgar. "The Book of Exodus" (Exposition), *The Interpreter's Bible.* Ed. George Arthur Buttrick. Vol. I. New York-Nashville: Abingdon, 1952.

Rawlinson, George. "Exodus," *Commentary on the Whole Bible.* Ed. Charles John Ellicott. Vol. I. Grand Rapids: Zondervan, rep., n.d.

————. *The Pulpit Commentary: Exodus.* Eds. H. D. M. Spence and Joseph S. Exell. 2 vols., bound with *Genesis* as Vol. I of the reprint. Grand Rapids: Eerdmans, rep. 1958.

Rylaarsdam, J. Coert. "The Book of Exodus" (Introduction and Exegesis), *The Interpreter's Bible.* Ed. George Arthur Buttrick. Vol. I. New York-Nashville: Abingdon, 1952.

II. OTHER REFERENCE WORKS

Albright, William Foxwell. "Recent Discoveries in Bible Lands," in Robert Young, *Analytical Concordance to the Bible.* New York: Funk and Wagnalls, 1936.

————. "The Rediscovery of the Biblical World," in *The Westminster Historical Atlas to the Bible.* Eds. George Ernest Wright and Floyd Vivian Filson. Philadelphia: Westminster, 1946.

Blaikie, William G., rev. by Charles D. Matthews. *A Manual of Bible History.* New York: Ronald Press, 1940.

Blauw, Johannes. *The Missionary Nature of the Church.* New York: McGraw-Hill, 1962.

Brown, Francis, S. R. Driver, and Charles A. Briggs, eds. *A Hebrew and English Lexicon of the Old Testament.* Oxford: Clarendon, rep., 1959.

Buber, Martin. *Moses,* "The East and West Library." London: Phaidon, 1946.

Chappell, Clovis G. *Ten Rules for Living.* New York-Nashville: Abingdon-Cokesbury, 1938.

Coffman, James Burton. *The Ten Commandments, Yesterday and Today.* Westwood, N. J.: Revell, 1961.

Finegan, Jack. *Let My People Go, a Journey Through Exodus.* New York and Evanston: Harper and Row, 1963.

Free, Joseph P. *Archaeology and Bible History.* Rev. ed. Wheaton, Ill.: Scripture Press, 1962.

Girdlestone, Robert Baker. *Synonyms of the Old Testament.* Grand Rapids: Eerdmans, rep. 1948.

Gregory, James F. "The Holiness of God," in *Entire Sanctification: Studies in Christian Holiness,* "Aldersgate Doctrinal Studies." Eds. Paul L. Kindschi, Lee Haines, *et al.* Marion, Ind.: The Wesley Press, 1964.

Hastings, James, ed. *A Dictionary of the Bible.* 5 vols. New York: Scribner, 1898.

Hurlbut, Jesse Lyman. *A Bible Atlas.* New York: Rand McNally, 1943.

Jackson, Samuel Macauley, ed. *The New Schaff-Herzog Encyclopedia of Religious Knowledge.* Grand Rapids: Baker, rep. 1951.

Josephus, Flavius. *Complete Works.* Trans. William Whiston. Grand Rapids: Kregel, 1964.

Loetscher, Lefferts A., ed. *Twentieth Century Encyclopedia of Religious Knowledge.* 2 vols. Grand Rapids: Baker, 1955.

Mickelsen, A. Berkeley. "Romans," *The Wycliffe Bible Commentary.* Eds. Charles F. Pfeiffer and Everett F. Harrison. Chicago: Moody, 1963.

Pfeiffer, Charles F. *Egypt and the Exodus.* Grand Rapids: Baker, 1964.

Pfeiffer, Robert H. *Introduction to the Old Testament.* New York: Harper, 1948.

Purkiser, W. T., ed. *Exploring the Old Testament.* Kansas City, Mo.: Beacon Hill, 1964.

Sandmel, Samuel. *The Hebrew Scriptures: an Introduction to Their Literature and Religious Ideas.* New York: Alfred A. Knopf, 1963.

Smith, William. *Smith's Bible Dictionary.* Rev. ed. Philadelphia: A. J. Holman, n.d.

Thayer, Joseph Henry. *A Greek-English Lexicon of the New Testament.* Corrected edition. New York: American Book Company, 1889.

Thomas, D. Winton, ed. *Documents from Old Testament Times,* "Harper Torchbooks — Cloister Library." New York: Harper, 1961.

Trueblood, Elton. *Foundations for Reconstruction.* Rev. ed. New York: Harper, 1961.

Unger, Merrill F. *Archaeology and the Old Testament.* Grand Rapids: Zondervan, 1954.

————, ed. *Unger's Bible Dictionary.* Chicago: Moody, 1957.

von Rad, Gerhard. *Old Testament Theology.* Vol. I, "The Theology of Israel's Historical Traditions." Trans. D. M. G. Stalker. New York: Harper, 1962.

Wiley, H. Orton. *Christian Theology.* 3 vols. Kansas City, Mo.: Beacon Hill, 1940.

Wright, George Ernest, and Floyd Vivian Filson, eds. *The Westminster Historical Atlas to the Bible.* Philadelphia: Westminster, 1946.

Young, Edward J. *An Introduction to the Old Testament.* Rev. ed. Grand Rapids: Eerdmans, 1960.

Young, Robert. *Analytical Concordance to the Bible.* New York: Funk and Wagnalls, rep. 1936.

III. BIBLE VERSIONS

American Standard Version of *The Holy Bible.* New York: Thomas Nelson, 1901.

King James Version of *The Holy Bible.* 1611 (1st ed.) .

Meek, Theophile J. "Exodus," in *The Bible, an American Translation,* Old Testament ed. by J. M. Powis Smith, New Testament trans. by Edgar J. Goodspeed. Chicago: University of Chicago Press, 1939.

Moffatt, James. *A New Translation of the Holy Bible Containing the Old and New Testaments.* New York and London: Harper, 1954.

The Revised Standard Version of the Holy Bible. New York: Thomas Nelson, 1952.

Verkuyl, Gerrit, ed. The Holy Bible: *The Berkeley Version in Modern English.* Grand Rapids: Zondervan, 1959.

The Book of Leviticus
by Armor D. Peisker

Editor's Preface to Leviticus

The author of the commentary on the book of Leviticus for Volume I of the *Wesleyan Bible Commentary* is the Reverend Armor D. Peisker, General Editor of the Pilgrim Holiness Church. This office involves editing of the *Pilgrim Holiness Advocate*, the official organ of his denomination, and of the church's Sunday school literature.

Mr. Peisker was graduated from Colorado College with the A.B. degree *(cum laude)*, and he received the M.A. degree from Butler University, where he did his graduate studies and thesis in the field of Old Testament.

Mr. Peisker is an ordained minister in the Pilgrim Holiness Church. Positions which he has held in the service of his denomination include the presidency of Colorado Springs Bible Training School and, for about fifteen years, offices in the Foreign Missions Department. Prior to his present editorial position he was editor of his denomination's Sunday school literature, to which he personally contributed adult curriculum material. For a period of five years he wrote a weekly newspaper column entitled "Gospel Guideposts" for the *Frankfort* (Indiana) *Morning Times*. He has been a frequent contributor to religious periodicals. While serving in the Department of Foreign Missions of his church Mr. Peisker paid visits to Mexico and the West Indies.

For many Bible readers the book of Leviticus has been a dry and uninteresting Old Testament book, consisting of detailed codes of ceremonial and civil regulations that seemed to belong to a bygone day and people, but which bore no relevance to the Christian religion or modern society. In his commentary on Leviticus Mr. Peisker brings to the reader new and fresh insights into the deeper spiritual meanings of these ancient Hebraic codes. These bring to light the essence of the same divinely revealed truth, though expressed in a different form, as that which is made explicit in Christ and the Christianity of the New Testament.

Perhaps no greater commentary on Leviticus exists than the New Testament Epistle to the Hebrews. There the implicit divine truth of Leviticus is made challengingly explicit. Out of his rich background of scholarship and writing, and in a style that is lucid and stimulating, Mr. Peisker gives us a commentary on Leviticus that reveals anew, as St. Augustine conceived it, that in the Old Testament the New is *concealed,* and in the New Testament the Old is *revealed.* Perhaps of no part of the Old Testament is this insight truer than of Leviticus.

It is a pleasure to commend this exposition of Leviticus to the readers of the *Wesleyan Bible Commentary.*

CHAS. W. CARTER
General Editor
Wesleyan Bible Commentary

Outline

Introduction

How can one acceptably approach God and have fellowship with Him? This is the age-old query. Job, of ancient times, asked, "How can a man be just with God?" (Job 9:2). And we still ponder it. Jesus' disciples besought Him, "Teach us to pray." We still desire this. The third book of the Pentateuch gives answers we all seek.

We should not then turn aside from studying it because the title sounds difficult, nor because we may not at first see any relevancy between its strict ecclesiastical laws and the freedom of present-day Christian worship. The detailed Levitical laws, indeed, do not have the significance for us they did for Old Testament worshipers, but it is nevertheless true that without some comprehension of the truths of Leviticus we cannot understand the real character of God as the Holy One, nor the life and work of Christ. Nor can we without it understand the importance of the sacrificial, devoted, and holy life which the New Testament sets up as the Christian norm.

The supposedly dry, meaningless pages of Leviticus will actually glow with spiritual light if we read them aright. For through them shines the fact that God was always near His people, seeking to make them aware of the opportunity of worship. We need, as we read, to realize that as the Hebrew church carried out its ritualistic worship in penitence and faith, and with thanksgiving, our own God actually met with them. In a very real sense Jesus, the Savior, was present. And we need to realize that the Levitical commands which the Israelites obeyed literally foreshadowed Christ's completed work of atonement and His present position as our High Priest. The Levitical rites are to us pictures or emblems of our salvation and Christian walk. The New Testament book of Hebrews is a helpful guide to the understanding of these things.

By these emblems God would teach us the deep truths of His redemptive purposes and of His grace. He uses the earthly symbols in Leviticus as visual aids to bring within the range of our capacity views of the Savior's spiritual work which we could not otherwise comprehend. The great Day of Atonement, for example, illumines for us the significance of Calvary. The explanation of that day is:

> The life of the flesh is in the blood; and I have given it to you upon the altar to make atonement for your souls: for it is the blood that maketh atonement by reason of the life (Lev. 17:11).

Leviticus is definitely related to the preceding books of Genesis and Exodus. In Genesis we read of the creation of man in God's high and holy image, of his fall into sin, of God's purpose to bring the race back to Himself through a chosen people, Israel. In Exodus we read of God's continued working with His people, especially in His bringing them out of Egyptian bondage, giving the law, and the erection of His sanctuary in their midst. In Leviticus we read how the delivered or saved people were to have constant access to Jehovah, and how they were enabled to live holily in His presence.

Even after their miraculous Exodus from Egypt, God's chosen people were inclined to forsake His true worship. For example, at the very time He was meeting intimately with Moses in their behalf on Sinai, the people at the foot of the mount engaged in a wild, idolatrous orgy (Exod. 32:1-6). Only the mercy of God, manifested in answer to Moses' intercession, spared them from utter destruction (Exod. 32:7-14).

Between the events of that dreadful day and those with which Leviticus opens (during the latter part of the year at Sinai), a central house of worship, the tabernacle, had been provided. There God gave visible evidence of His presence among His people. The priests, the descendants of Levi, had been appointed to stand before God for the people. But those priests needed a guidebook to direct them in their ministrations of worship and in their efforts to restore the people to divine favor, should they fail or fall away from Jehovah. Aware of this need, God summoned Moses to come into His presence that He might communicate to him the necessary information. Leviticus is the resulting guidebook. It develops and enlarges upon the ceremonial laws of Exodus and becomes the basic directive for Judaism's worship and religious practice.

To approach God and to maintain fellowship with Him, the Israelites, redeemed out of Egyptian bondage, must be holy. They must separate themselves from sin and unto God. Holiness is, then, the principal theme of Leviticus. The subject is first mentioned specifically in chapter 11, verse 45. The key verse of the entire book is the succinct divine admonition, "Ye shall be holy; for I Jehovah your God am holy" (19:2).

By divinely ordained rituals, the priests were consecrated, set apart, and made holy that they might be worthy mediators between God and the people. Each individual Israelite was also required to follow carefully specified rules in worship and conduct that he might be holy before his God. The nation as a whole was likewise expected to remain separate, to stand out as a holy nation apart from all the surrounding peoples. National sacrifices and feasts were to be regularly observed in the fear of the Lord.

It is true that the holiness taught in Leviticus is ritualistic, but from those rituals basic truths stand out which apply to us now if we who are redeemed out of the bondage of sin would enjoy a spiritual experience of holiness of heart and life. The rituals by which the people were made holy involved the blood of sacrifice, and the consecration of the worshiper to God through identifying himself with his choice offering, and cleansing. These are the essential elements in our sanctification.

Christ on Calvary is our sacrifice.

> If the blood of goats and bulls, and the ashes of a heifer sprinkling them that have been defiled, sanctify unto the cleanness of the flesh: how much more shall the blood of Christ, who through the eternal Spirit offered himself without blemish unto God, cleanse your conscience from dead works to serve the living God? (Heb. 9:13, 14).

If we would benefit from the blood of Christ, we must give ourselves over unto God, as Paul said:

> I beseech you therefore, brethren, by the mercies of God, to present your bodies a living sacrifice, holy, acceptable to God, which is your spiritual service. And be not fashioned according to this world: but be ye transformed by the renewing of your mind, that ye may prove what is the good and acceptable and perfect will of God (Rom. 12:1, 2).

A primary factor in our sanctification is that our natures are cleansed so that from the heart we do the will of God. "God, who knoweth the heart, bare them witness, giving them the holy Spirit, even as he did unto us . . . cleansing their hearts by faith" (Acts 15:8, 9).

> This is the covenant that I will make with the house of Israel after those days, saith Jehovah: I will put my law in their inward parts, and in their heart will I write it; and I will be their God, and they shall be my people (Jer. 31:33; cf. Heb. 8:8-12; 10:16, 17).

(For additional introductory information see General Introduction to the Pentateuch at the front of this volume.)

Commentary on Leviticus

I. HOW TO APPROACH GOD (LEV. 1:1—16:34)

Leviticus is not the title assigned to the third book of the Pentateuch in the Hebrew Bible. That name came into our English versions from the Greek Septuagint of about the third century B.C. The Hebrew title is a single word, the the first word of the Hebrew text. Translated into English it is, "and He called."

"And He called." This is an especially significant title for a book which teaches us how to approach God and how to keep in fellowship with Him. For sinful men do not of themselves seek after the Lord; rather they go from Him. They tend to hide from His presence (Gen. 3:8). Always it has been God's loving call for men which has initiated any approach to Him (Gen. 3:9; 4:9; II Sam. 12:1, 7; Acts 9:3, 4; Ps. 119:155; Isa. 65:24; John 3:16, 17). No man has ever been at liberty to set up his own terms of approach to God.

A. LAWS DEALING WITH SACRIFICES (1:1—7:38)

Sacrifice — a sacrifice acceptable to God — is the basis of all true worship. Man is in himself guilty and unclean. He needs a sacrifice to free him from guilt and to cleanse away his defilement (Heb. 9:22).

To show that sin is actually sinful, that holiness is necessary before the Lord, and to indicate how the people could be free from condemnation, God established a system of sacrifices and offerings.

The institution of sacrifices to God was not new. Sacrifices date back to the first family. Noah sacrificed. But here in the book of Leviticus the institution is systematized. It is here arranged so as to meet the various phases of man's need, and to point toward the ultimate complete provision for that need in the promised Redeemer (Matt. 26:26-29; Heb. 10:1-10).

The first seven chapters of Leviticus are, in a certain sense, a manual of sacrifice, for here are the regulations for carrying through the five main types of offerings.

1. The Whole Burnt-Offering (1:1-17; 6:8-13)

This was an individual expression of devotion, of thanksgiving, of worship. It was not like the sprinkled blood spoken of in Exodus whereby the people were to be redeemed from Egypt. This is an offering to meet the needs of a redeemed people in their approach to their Savior.

The offering might consist of a bull, a sheep, a goat, a pigeon, or a turtle dove, depending upon the ability of the worshiper to provide. The Hebrew word rendered "burnt-offering" means "that which ascends," and is descriptive of the fact that the offering was to be wholly consumed on the altar. All of the sacrifice ascended to God in a flame and smoke. By it the worshiper sought nothing from God for himself; rather, in the symbol of his wholly consumed offering, he gave himself completely to the Lord. It speaks to us of Christ's sacrifice for us, and it calls us to a total commitment of ourselves to Him (cf. Rom. 12:1-2).

a. Of the Herd (1:1-9)

1 And Jehovah called unto Moses, and spake unto him out of the tent of meeting, saying, 2 Speak unto the children of Israel, and say unto them, When any man of you offereth an oblation unto Jehovah, ye shall offer your oblation of the cattle, *even* of the herd and of the flock.

3 If his oblation be a burnt-offering of the herd, he shall offer it a male without blemish: he shall offer it at the door of the tent of meeting, that he may be accepted before Jehovah. 4 And he shall lay his hand upon the head of the burnt-offering; and it shall be accepted for him to make atonement for him.

299

5 And he shall kill the bullock before Jehovah: and Aaron's sons, the priests, shall present the blood, and sprinkle the blood round about upon the altar that is at the door of the tent of meeting. 6 And he shall flay the burnt-offering, and cut it into its pieces. 7 And the sons of Aaron the priest shall put fire upon the altar, and lay wood in order upon the fire; 8 and Aaron's sons, the priests, shall lay the pieces, the head, and the fat, in order upon the wood that is on the fire which is upon the altar: 9 but its inwards and its legs shall he wash with water. And the priest shall burn the whole on the altar, for a burnt-offering, an offering made by fire, of a sweet savor unto Jehovah.

This time (vv. 1, 2) Moses was summoned not to the fiery mount of judgment, but to the **tent of meeting** or tabernacle — to the sanctuary of sacrifice and worship, indicative of God's mercy. At Sinai only Moses dared to draw near to God. But now Jehovah makes a way for every Israelite to worship in the divine presence. He began the instruction regarding that approach by pointing out what a man should do who might want to **offer an oblation** or make a gift, as the Hebrew word *corban* indicates (cf. Mark 7:11). The root meaning of this term is "to bring near," and it suggests God's purpose here for His people. The term is used throughout Leviticus for various kinds of offerings by which man approached God, and through which God, in turn, drew near to men (cf. Jas. 4:8).

The animal brought for the burnt-offering (vv. 3, 4) was to be a perfect specimen. It was offered **at the door of the tent of meeting,** that is, at the brazen altar in the court of the tabernacle (Exod. 40:6). In contrast to such offerings as are prescribed in 4:2, 3 and 5:15, this was to be brought voluntarily (cf. KJV). The offerer was to **lay his hand upon the head** of his offering, thereby identifying himself with the sacrifice. He thus actually became one with his offering in consecration to God (cf. Rom. 12:1). By his oneness with the offering, the offerer became acceptable before the Lord, the offering making atonement for him. To atone literally suggests "to cover over." So it was that the offerer's sins were covered from the eyes of the holy God who can never look with favor upon sin

(Hab. 1:13; cf. Ps. 51:1, 9; 103:12; Isa. 43:25; 44:22; Mic. 7:19; Heb. 10:1-4).

The burnt-offering being a type of Christ, the application of this to us today sets forth the fact that it is as we identify ourselves with Christ, give ourselves wholly to Him, become one with Him, that we may find acceptance with God (I John 4:17; 5:20; I Cor. 6:17; Eph. 1:6; 5:30; Col. 2:10).

Whether the offerer himself, or an officer of the tabernacle, actually killed the animal is not clear in the Hebrew text (vv. 5, 6), but it is certain that taking the blood and applying it to the altar was a priestly function. Putting this blood, the seat of the animal's life, against the sacred altar symbolized the giving of the offerer's life to God and acknowledged God's active participation in the atonement ceremony; and, pointing forward to Jesus' offering of Himself, it was efficacious in forgiveness and in reconciling the offerer to God (I Pet. 1:2).

The animal was skinned (the skin becoming the property of the functioning priest), and cut **into its pieces,** i.e., according to its joints (Exod. 12:46; Num. 9:12; John 19:36).

Verses 7-9 describe the further activity of the priest in sacrificing the burnt-offering. For a more complete picture of the situation, however, chapter 6:8-13 should be read along with these verses. This fire-offering was a pleasing fragrance to the Lord. The application of a human characteristic to God here is simply a figurative and graphic way of saying that the Lord took pleasure in the voluntary burnt-offerings of His people — offerings by which they demonstrated their aspiration after Him, their purpose to do His will, and their self-surrender to Him (see Eph. 5:2; Phil. 4:18; I Pet. 2:5).

b. Of the Flock (1:10-13)

10 And if his oblation be of the flock, of the sheep, or of the goats, for a burnt-offering; he shall offer it a male without blemish. 11 And he shall kill it on the side of the altar northward before Jehovah: and Aaron's sons, the priests, shall sprinkle its blood upon the altar round about. 12 And he shall cut it into its pieces, with its head and its fat; and the priest shall lay them in order on

the wood that is on the fire which is upon the altar: 13 but the inwards and the legs shall he wash with water. And the priest shall offer the whole, and burn it upon the altar: it is a burnt-offering, an offering made by fire, of a sweet savor unto Jehovah.

The ritual here for offering a sheep or a goat was the same as in the offering of a bull. It is mentioned in this connection that the animal was to be killed on the north side of the altar. This, however, applied to all sacrifices except the peace-offering.

c. Of Birds (1:14-17)

14 And if his oblation to Jehovah be a burnt-offering of birds, then he shall offer his oblation of turtle-doves, or of young pigeons. 15 And the priest shall bring it unto the altar, and wring off its head, and burn it on the altar; and the blood thereof shall be drained out on the side of the altar; 16 and he shall take away its crop with the filth thereof, and cast it beside the altar on the east part, in the place of the ashes: 17 and he shall rend it by the wings thereof, *but* shall not divide it asunder. And the priest shall burn it upon the altar, upon the wood that is upon the fire: it is a burnt-offering, an offering made by fire, of a sweet savor unto Jehovah.

As in some other instances, where the offerer was too poor to offer either a bull, a ram, or a goat, he could offer a pigeon or a turtle dove (Lev. 5:7-10). In making such an offering, the pattern was simpler, but in general quite the same as that followed in the other instances. The poor man worshiping with an offering of only a little bird, which he may have caught in a bush, was as acceptable to God as the rich man who brought the largest and most perfect specimen out of his vast herd (cf. II Cor. 8:12).

2. The Meal-Offering (2:1-16; 6:14-23)

This voluntary offering of thanksgiving, usually made in connection with the animal sacrifices (Lev. 7:11-14; 8:26; 9:4; Num. 15:1-16), consisted in the main of grain or grain products. **Meal** or "cereal" offering, titles used in the ASV and the RSV respectively, are therefore more definitive than the "meat" offering of the KJV. To understand the significance of the latter title one must interpret it in the broad sense of a "food" offering (see Berkeley Version).

In contrast to the burnt-offering in which there was always the giving of a life to God, the **meal-offering** was made from wheat. This grain required man's diligent cultivation. Then, before it could be offered it had to be harvested and further processed by man. As the burnt-offering represented the offerer giving his life — himself — to God, the **meal-offering** represented the worshiper giving to God of his food, the fruits of his labors. By this act the offerer acknowledged that his material benefits came through the aid and goodness of God.

The duty signified in this Old Testament ritual is still our obligation. We must give over to God for His purposes not only our persons, but all of our works and their results. All secular labor and its profits, as well as all religious service and its accomplishments, are to be laid at the feet of Christ (I Cor. 10:31). For, after all, our capacities are gifts of God, entrusted to us for stewardship. Our attainments, accumulations, and accomplishments increase our responsibilities and must be consecrated to the Lord. They are but resources for ever-widening usefulness in building God's kingdom.

The **meal-offering** might be offered in several forms: as **fine flour** (v. 1), i.e., white flour; as cooked into bread or wafers (vv. 4, 5, 7); or as grain crushed and parched (v. 14).

a. Of Uncooked Fine Flour (2:1-3)

1 And when any one offereth an oblation of a meal-offering unto Jehovah, his oblation shall be of fine flour; and he shall pour oil upon it, and put frankincense thereon: 2 and he shall bring it to Aaron's sons the priests; and he shall take thereout his handful of the fine flour thereof, and of the oil thereof, with all the frankincense thereof. And the priest shall burn *it as* the memorial thereof upon the altar, an offering made by fire, of a sweet savor unto Jehovah: 3 and that which is left of the meal-offering shall be Aaron's and his sons': it is a thing most holy of the offerings of Jehovah made by fire.

When the offering was uncooked in the form of flour, olive oil was mixed with the flour (7:10), or poured over the meal. Olive oil was not only a principal food product of the people, as was the flour, but it represented the gracious presence of the Holy Spirit in illumination and sanctification.

Placed upon the offering was some frankincense, a fragrant gum resin easily ground into powder which emitted a balsamlike odor when burning. Added here to the meal thank-offering it was symbolic of the worshiper's sincere prayer and joyful praise as he sought to be remembered favorably before the Lord.

Salt was also an ingredient in all of the meal-offerings (v. 13), representative of God's perpetual covenant of salvation and fellowship with His people (Num. 18:19) — the covenant upon which the whole sacrificial system rested.

Having prepared his offering from not less than three quarts of flour (Num. 28: 12), the officer brought it to the priest at the tabernacle (v. 2). From this the priest took out one handful to burn upon the altar, making sure that he included in this portion all of the frankincense.

The Hebrew term for **memorial** (v. 2) implies more than a calling of God's attention to an absent offerer whom He might have forgotten. It was, indeed, as the worshiper's immediate presence before the Lord.

The unburned portion was considered most holy (v. 3), for, consecrated to God, it was to serve as food for the priest without whose aid the offering could not be made. By eating of this, the priest — who foreshadowed Christ, our Priest — identified himself with the worshiper in his approach to God (cf. 6:14-18).

b. Of Bread (2:4-16)

4 And when thou offerest an oblation of a meal-offering baken in the oven, it shall be unleavened cakes of fine flour mingled with oil, or unleavened wafers anointed with oil. 5 And if thy oblation be a meal-offering of the baking-pan, it shall be of fine flour unleavened, mingled with oil. 6 Thou shalt part it in pieces, and pour oil thereon: it is a meal-offering. 7 And if thy oblation be a meal-offering of the frying-pan, it shall be made of fine flour with oil. 8 And thou shalt bring the meal-offering that is made of these things unto Jehovah: and it shall be presented unto the priest, and he shall bring it unto the altar.

9 And the priest shall take up from the meal-offering the memorial thereof, and shall burn it upon the altar, an offering made by fire, of a sweet savor unto Jehovah. 10 And that which is left of the meal-offering shall be Aaron's and his sons': it is a thing most holy of the offerings of Jehovah made by fire.

11 No meal-offering, which ye shall offer unto Jehovah, shall be made with leaven; for ye shall burn no leaven, nor any honey, as an offering made by fire unto Jehovah. 12 As an oblation of first-*fruits* ye shall offer them unto Jehovah: but they shall not come up for a sweet savor on the altar. 13 And every oblation of thy meal-offering shalt thou season with salt; neither shalt thou suffer the salt of the covenant of thy God to be lacking from thy meal-offering: with all thine oblations thou shalt offer salt.

14 And if thou offer a meal-offering of first-fruits unto Jehovah, thou shalt offer for the meal-offering of thy first-fruits grain in the ear parched with fire, bruised grain of the fresh ear. 15 And thou shalt put oil upon it, and lay frankincense thereon: it is a meal-offering. 16 And the priest shall burn the memorial of it, part of the bruised grain thereof, and part of the oil thereof, with all the frankincense thereof: it is an offering made by fire unto Jehovah.

The offering could be made in the form of bread or wafers prepared in several ways: in an **oven;** in a **baking-pan,** i.e., a flat plate or griddle; in a **frying-pan** or roaster (cf. Berkeley Version); or fresh **grain** could be crushed and parched. But regardless of how the offering was prepared, neither **leaven** nor **honey** (a term which included boiled down fruit juices) was permitted (vv. 11, 12), because these were commonly associated with fermentation and suggested corruption.

The method used for preparing the offering might be determined by the means available to the worshiper, but one form of offering was as acceptable to the Lord as another. This suggests to us that regardless of our capacities — great or small — or the form of our possessions and labors, God will through the work of Christ accept our consecration of them. He will use us in His work so long as we are free from leaven, or all that is corrupt in our lives; so long as we possess the oil of the Holy Spirit, illuminating and sanctifying us; so long as our service is fragrant with the frankincense of joy and adoration; and so long as we rely by faith upon the salt of God's everlasting covenant with us through His Son.

3. The Peace-Offering (3:1-17; cf. 7:11-38)

1 And if his oblation be a sacrifice of peace-offerings; if he offer of the herd, whether male or female, he shall offer it without blemish before Jehovah. 2 And he shall lay his hand upon the head of his oblation, and kill it at the door of the tent of meeting: and Aaron's sons the priests shall sprinkle the blood upon the altar round about. 3 And he shall offer of the sacrifice of peace-offerings an offering made by fire unto Jehovah; the fat that covereth the inwards, and all the fat that is upon the inwards, 4 and the two kidneys, and the fat that is on them, which is by the loins, and the caul upon the liver, with the kidneys, shall he take away. 5 And Aaron's sons shall burn it on the altar upon the burnt-offering, which is upon the wood that is on the fire: it is an offering made by fire, of a sweet savor unto Jehovah.

6 And if his oblation for a sacrifice of peace-offerings unto Jehovah be of the flock; male or female, he shall offer it without blemish. 7 If he offer a lamb for his oblation, then shall he offer it before Jehovah; 8 and he shall lay his hand upon the head of his oblation, and kill it before the tent of meeting: and Aaron's sons shall sprinkle the blood thereof upon the altar round about. 9 And he shall offer of the sacrifice of peace-offerings an offering made by fire unto Jehovah; the fat thereof, the fat tail entire, he shall take away hard by the backbone; and the fat that covereth the inwards, and all the fat that is upon the inwards, 10 and the two kidneys, and the fat that is upon them, which is by the loins, and the caul upon the liver, with the kidneys, shall he take away. 11 And the priest shall burn it upon the altar: it is the food of the offering made by fire unto Jehovah.

12 And if his oblation be a goat, then he shall offer it before Jehovah: 13 and he shall lay his hand upon the head of it, and kill it before the tent of meeting; and the sons of Aaron shall sprinkle the blood thereof upon the altar round about. 14 And he shall offer thereof his oblation, *even* an offering made by fire unto Jehovah; the fat that covereth the inwards, and all the fat that is upon the inwards, 15 and the two kidneys, and the fat that is upon them, which is by the loins, and the caul upon the liver, with

the kidneys, shall he take away. 16 And the priest shall burn them upon the altar: it is the food of the offering made by fire, for a sweet savor; all the fat is Jehovah's. 17 It shall be a perpetual statute throughout your generations in all your dwellings, that ye shall eat neither fat nor blood.

The separation between the secular and the sacred, so common in our society, would have been foreign to Israel. Religion was involved in all of the Israelites' affairs. Particularly were the important events in Jewish life related to God through prayer and thanksgiving.

Activities connected with the peace-offering highlight this involvement of religion, especially in the social life of the people. Under the New Testament covenant, religion certainly should cover no less of life than it did under the old. So we Christians can find instruction and encouragement here.

The peace-offering, the most common type of sacrifice, provided a delightful combination of worship and social fellowship. Family and friends could join the offerer in a covenant meal after the offering had been made at the altar in the tabernacle court. The meal based upon portions of the consecrated offering was symbolic of the peace and fellowship existing between God and His people.

Such a voluntary offering might be made in recognition of unmerited and unexpected blessings. It was then known as a thank- or praise-offering. A peace-offering might also be made in fulfillment of a vow. Then it was designated as a votive-offering. Or a peace-offering might be made simply as an expression of love for God. This type was called a freewill-offering (7:11-34).

The Israelites, joyfully eating together of the consecrated sacrificial animal, whose blood had been shed and sprinkled in atonement for sin, provide a striking symbol of the way in which Christians now may, in happy fellowship, spiritually partake of Christ who, by giving Himself, became our salvation and our peace. He declared: "The bread which I will give is my flesh, for the life of the world . . . . My flesh is meat indeed . . . . He that eateth me, he also shall live because of me" (John 6:51, 55, 57; see also Eph. 2:14-16; Acts 13:47; Heb. 5:9; 9:28).

Leviticus 7:11-38 gives instructions for disposal of various parts of the sacrificial animals. Directions for the sacred meal to follow the offering are given in 7:11-34 and 19:5-8.

Since it was a voluntary offering, the worshiper was free to choose an animal — male or female — of the cattle, sheep, or goats. The offering must, however, be **without blemish** (3:1). In the case of the freewill-offering, it would seem (22:21-25) that a bull or lamb with a slight imperfection ("a part too long or too short," 22:23, RSV) might have been accepted if it were the best the offerer had. Adam Clarke, however, makes this observation:

> It was the opinion of the Jews, and it appears to be correct, that none of these imperfect animals were ever offered on the altar; but the person who made the freewill offering of such things as he had, sold the animal and gave its price for the support of the sanctuary.[1]

In this connection it is interesting to note that the Septuagint translates Leviticus 22:25 thus: "And a calf or a sheep with the ears cut off, or that has lost its tail, thou shalt slay them for thyself; but they shall not be accepted for the vow."

As in the case of the burnt-offering, the worshiper here identified himself with his offering (v. 2), and the blood of the victim was sprinkled upon the altar. (For the significance of this see comments on 1:1-3.)

Whereas in the burnt-offering the whole animal was offered on the altar, in this instance only the fat was removed from the offering and burned before the Lord (vv. 3, 4). This portion was considered among the Jews to be the most valuable part of the animal. Special instructions were given for removing and offering the tail of a sheep (v. 9). The type of sheep raised by the Israelites was similar to some still raised in the Near East. They had tails weighing as much as ten to fifteen pounds, composed of a particularly choice substance in character between fat and marrow. It was ordinarily mixed with other portions of meat as a luxury or used instead of butter.

A meal-offering was also to accompany the peace-offering (7:11-14; see notes on chapter 2).

The breast of the animal and the right shoulder, considered the best of the meat, were consecrated as food for the priests (7:28-34). The rest of the victim was then returned to the worshiper for the festive meal. It had to be consumed within two days. Should any meat of the offered victim remain to the third day, it was to be burned with fire lest it spoil (7:15-18; 19:5-8).

The peace-offering which served as an expiation, and also as food for priest and worshiper, represented Christ, who was the sacrificial victim for our salvation, and is also the source of our spiritual sustenance. "Take, eat; this is my body," He said (Matt. 26:26). By daily feeding on Him we may live and grow unto life eternal.

We must keep in mind, however, that only those who were ceremonially clean could partake worthily of the peace-offering (7:19-21). This suggests the solemn fact that we can partake worthily of Christ only as we keep ourselves morally clean, "unspotted from the world" (Jas. 1:27); "hating even the garment spotted by the flesh" (Jude 23). It is Peter who admonishes us, "Like as he who called you is holy, be ye yourselves also holy in all manner of living; because it is written, 'Ye shall be holy; for I am holy' " (I Pet. 1:15).

4. The Sin-Offering (4:1-5, 13-14; 6:24-30)

It is dangerous to wink at sin. It is a serious offense to make light of any disobedience towards God. It is a grave error deliberately to go against the known will of God with some such excuse: "Oh well, God will forgive me for anything anytime."

Even the Old Testament Hebrews learned by their rituals that they could not sin with impunity. They knew that they could not deliberately transgress God's laws and then come and easily counteract the sin merely by making a sacrifice. They learned also that ignorance was no excuse for sin.

The sin-offering brought the people face to face with the gravity of all disobedience toward God. For no provision was made for high-handed sinning (Num. 15:30). The sin-offering had no connec-

---

[1] Adam Clarke, *The Holy Bible Containing the Old and New Testaments*, I, 584.

tion with presumptuous, defiant rebellion against God. This offering was efficacious for those in Israel who might have offended the holiness of God unknowingly as, for example, having become involved inadvertently in ceremonial uncleanness (4:2, 13, 22, 27; 5:2, 3).

Similarly, we today need the atoning blood of Christ to cover our mistakes and whatever shortcomings may flow from our faulty human nature. For regardless of how pure our motives may be, we shall always in this life be subject to what John Wesley spoke of as involuntary transgressions of the divine law (see Ps. 19:12). When such inadvertent mistakes and faults become known to us, however, we need to acknowledge and correct them. For there is the awful possibility that those unintentional transgressions may become deliberate sins which will bring us into judgment (Heb. 2:3; 10:26, 31; II Pet. 2:20, 21).

The sin-offering availed when a man may have erred through infirmity or weakness, as in failing to testify as a witness regarding a known crime when witnesses were publicly summoned (5:1). Such a failure might result in a miscarriage of justice. This suggests that the people of God are always to be responsible citizens (see Matt. 22:21; Rom. 13:6, 7; I Pet. 2:13-17).

Another example of the kind of sins for which the sin-offering was acceptable is when one had inadvertently made a rash vow (5:4). This teaches us that all who serve God should be sober and watchful so as to avoid involvement in unwise, hasty actions and promises (see I Thess. 5:6; I Pet. 4:7).

For such sins the offerer was to sacrifice the sin-offering when he became aware of the fact that he had sinned. Even though these were sins committed in ignorance and without deliberation, repentance was to accompany the offering, for sacrifice had no magical means of atonement (5:5).

So it is that forgiveness always involves both repentance and reliance upon atonement. We can trust in the merits of Christ, our sin-offering, only after we have acknowledged and forsaken our evil (see Luke 24:47; Acts 17:30; Tit. 2:11, 12). But having repented, we must trust in Christ's atonement, for repentance alone will not bring us into divine favor (II Cor. 5:21).

The three sacrifices outlined in the earlier chapters of Leviticus — the burnt-offering, the meal-offering, and the peace-offering — had been known and offered long before God's instructions on Sinai, but the sin-offering was instituted at the mount. And while the other offerings were made in dedication and praise, the sin-offering was sacrificed in repentance for sins which had not only broken man's fellowship with God, but which had actually injured the offender's own personality. The primary meaning of the Hebrew root translated here as sin and sin-offering is "to miss," to "fall short of," and implies that the person who has missed God's way, who has fallen short of His purposes, not only displeased God, but actually injured his own true self, and so long as he remains without atonement his character is defective. This would suggest to us that in a very real sense we cannot break God's laws. Disobeying them breaks or injures only ourselves.

It was a blessed fact that a sin-offering was provided to restore Israelites of all classes: the priest, the congregation as a whole, the ruler, and the common man. The significance of this offering has its fulfillment in the person and work of Jesus Christ, who is the one eternally effectual sin-offering for all men. He who is both High Priest and Victim offered Himself for us, so that we have "boldness to enter into the holy place by the blood of Jesus" (Heb. 10:19).

a. For Priest (4:1-12)

1 And Jehovah spake unto Moses, saying, 2 Speak unto the children of Israel, saying, If any one shall sin unwittingly, in any of the things which Jehovah hath commanded not to be done, and shall do any one of them: 3 if the anointed priest shall sin so as to bring guilt on the people, then let him offer for his sin, which he hath sinned, a young bullock without blemish unto Jehovah for a sin-offering. 4 And he shall bring the bullock unto the door of the tent of meeting before Jehovah; and he shall lay his hand upon the head of the bullock, and kill the bullock before Jehovah. 5 And the anointed priest shall take of the blood of the bullock, and bring it to the tent of meeting:

6 and the priest shall dip his finger in the blood, and sprinkle of the blood seven times before Jehovah, before the veil of the sanctuary. 7 And the priest shall put of the blood upon the horns of the altar of sweet incense before Jehovah, which is in the tent of meeting; and all the blood of the bullock shall he pour out at the base of the altar of burnt-offering, which is at the door of the tent of meeting. 8 And all the fat of the bullock of the sin-offering he shall take off from it; the fat that covereth the inwards, and all the fat that is upon the inwards, 9 and the two kidneys, and the fat that is upon them, which is by the loins, and the caul upon the liver, with the kidneys, shall he take away, 10 as it is taken off from the ox of the sacrifice of peace-offerings: and the priest shall burn them upon the altar of burnt-offering. 11 And the skin of the bullock, and all its flesh, with its head, and with its legs, and its inwards, and its dung, 12 even the whole bullock shall he carry forth without the camp unto a clean place, where the ashes are poured out, and burn it on wood with fire: where the ashes are poured out shall it be burnt.

The **anointed priest** has reference to the high priest (3:12; see also Heb. 5:1-4). His sin was particularly grave, for while he was indeed one of the Israelites, he was also the representative of the entire nation before the Lord. His sin, therefore, brought guilt upon the whole congregation (v. 3). Accordingly, he was required to bring the most valuable gift of all offerings, a bull, and must identify himself with it (v. 4; see also comments on 1:3, 4).

Those who serve the Lord and the church as ministers in any capacity should have a particular carefulness to see that their lives are kept acceptable before God. For God looks upon a man's guilt in the light of his knowledge of the truth, and of his rank and station. The influence and example of a minister reaches far, so any sin or shortcoming in his life is particularly reprehensible.

Since the high priest ministered before God in the Holy Place of the tabernacle, he by his sin defiled that Holy Place, and he must sprinkle the atoning blood of the sin-offering before the veil of the Holy Place (see Exod. 26:31-33). He was to do this **seven times** (v. 6), for among the Jews the number seven suggested com-

pleteness. And since he ministered before the golden altar (Exod. 3:1-10) in offering incense as the prayers of the people before the Lord, he had by his sin defiled that holy altar and must apply some of the blood upon the horns of that golden altar (v. 7).

The fat of the sacrificial victim was to be burned on the brazen altar in the tabernacle court, as in the case of the peace-offering (3:3, 4), but the flesh of the animal with which the sinful priest had identified himself and which had been offered for his atonement could not be partaken of by the priests. It had to be wholly burned outside of the camp, out of the Lord's sight (v. 12; 6:24-30; see also Heb. 13:10-13).

b. For Congregation (4:13-21)

13 And if the whole congregation of Israel err, and the thing be hid from the eyes of the assembly, and they have done any of the things which Jehovah hath commanded not to be done, and are guilty; 14 when the sin wherein they have sinned is known, then the assembly shall offer a young bullock for a sin-offering, and bring it before the tent of meeting. 15 And the elders of the congregation shall lay their hands upon the head of the bullock before Jehovah; and the bullock shall be killed before Jehovah. 16 And the anointed priest shall bring of the blood of the bullock to the tent of meeting: 17 and the priest shall dip his finger in the blood, and sprinkle it seven times before Jehovah, before the veil. 18 And he shall put of the blood upon the horns of the altar which is before Jehovah, that is in the tent of meeting; and all the blood shall he pour out at the base of the altar of burnt-offering, which is at the door of the tent of meeting. 19 And all the fat thereof shall he take off from it, and burn it upon the altar. 20 Thus shall he do with the bullock; as he did with the bullock of the sin-offering, so shall he do with this; and the priest shall make atonement for them, and they shall be forgiven. 21 And he shall carry forth the bullock without the camp, and burn it as he burned the first bullock: it is the sin-offering for the assembly.

The ritual here is the same as for the priest, because Israel was looked upon as "a kingdom of priests" (Exod. 19:6). As representatives of all Israel, the elders of the nation were to lay their hands upon the head of the sacrificial victim, thus identifying the whole congregation with the sacrifice.

God has always held groups and nations responsible for their conduct, and He continues to do so now. This is true in spite of the present-day trend to neutralize religious influence in government. God is still the ruler of the affairs of all nations, and they are under obligation to recognize His authority and His righteous demands. The plain language of the Second Psalm is still God's word to men.

c. For Ruler (4:22-26)

22 When a ruler sinneth, and doeth unwittingly any one of all the things which Jehovah his God hath commanded not to be done, and is guilty; 23 if his sin, wherein he hath sinned, be made known to him, he shall bring for his oblation a goat, a male without blemish. 24 And he shall lay his hand upon the head of the goat, and kill it in the place where they kill the burnt-offering before Jehovah: it is a sin-offering. 25 And the priest shall take of the blood of the sin-offering with his finger, and put it upon the horns of the altar of burnt-offering; and the blood thereof shall he pour out at the base of the altar of burnt-offering. 26 And all the fat thereof shall he burn upon the altar, as the fat of the sacrifice of peace-offerings; and the priest shall make atonement for him as concerning his sin, and he shall be forgiven.

When a ruler in Israel was seeking forgiveness, a male goat rather than a bull was offered. The blood in this case was not sprinkled before the veil nor placed upon the incense altar, for the ruler did not minister before the Lord in the Holy Place. But the blood was applied to the horns of the brazen altar in the court, and the meat was eaten by the priests (6:24-30).

It is God who sets up rulers in the land, and they are responsible to Him. In a world where democratic processes are more and more in vogue, men in high places are largely influenced by party pressures and the desire for votes from their constituencies. But worthy rulers must consider of greater importance the righteous demands of God, and in the fear of God, cast their weight on the side of right. God does not waive His authority out of deference to political expediency.

d. For Common Man (4:27—5:13)

(1) Sins of Ignorance (4:27-35)

27 And if any one of the common people sin unwittingly, in doing any of the things which Jehovah hath commanded not to be done, and be guilty; 28 if his sin, which he hath sinned, be made known to him, then he shall bring for his oblation a goat, a female without blemish, for his sin which he hath sinned. 29 And he shall lay his hand upon the head of the sin-offering, and kill the sin-offering in the place of burnt-offering. 30 And the priest shall take of the blood thereof with his finger, and put it upon the horns of the altar of burnt-offering; and all the blood thereof shall he pour out at the base of the altar. 31 And all the fat thereof shall he take away, as the fat is taken away from off the sacrifice of peace-offerings; and the priest shall burn it upon the altar for a sweet savor unto Jehovah; and the priest shall make atonement for him, and he shall be forgiven.

32 And if he bring a lamb as his oblation for a sin-offering, he shall bring it a female without blemish. 33 And he shall lay his hand upon the head of the sin-offering, and kill it for a sin-offering in the place where they kill the burnt-offering. 34 And the priest shall take of the blood of the sin-offering with his finger, and put it upon the horns of the altar of burnt-offering; and all the blood thereof shall he pour out at the base of the altar. 35 And all the fat thereof shall he take away, as the fat of the lamb is taken away from the sacrifice of peace-offerings; and the priest shall burn them on the altar, upon the offerings of Jehovah made by fire; and the priest shall make atonement for him as touching his sin that he hath sinned, and he shall be forgiven.

In this case a female goat or an ewe lamb could serve as a sacrifice and was offered in the same manner as that for the ruler.

If, however, the offender was too poor for either the goat or the lamb, he might bring two turtle doves or two pigeons (5:7-10). Because of the impossibility of separating the fat of the small bird from the rest of the flesh, as in the case of the larger animals, and burning it on the altar, all of the flesh of one of the birds was burned on the altar, while that of the second bird was given to the priest for his portion. For the extremely poor who could not provide even two birds, three quarts of white flour could be offered, as in the case of the meal-offering (chap. 2). It was different from the meal-offering, however, in that no oil or frankincense was to be added in the sin-offering. The handful of flour offered as a **memorial** (2:2) was burned before the Lord on the same altar as the animal sin-offerings (5:11-13).

God is gracious, and by accepting this simple sacrifice, the most wretched in Israel could find forgiveness and salvation.

(2) Sin of Neglect (5:1-13)

1 And if any one sin, in that he heareth the voice of adjuration, he being a witness, whether he hath seen or known, if he do not utter it, then he shall bear his iniquity. 2 Or if any one touch any unclean thing, whether it be the carcass of an unclean beast, or the carcass of unclean cattle, or the carcass of unclean creeping things, and it be hidden from him, and he be unclean, then he shall be guilty. 3 Or if he touch the uncleanness of man, whatsoever his uncleanness be wherewith he is unclean, and it be hid from him; when he knoweth of it, then he shall be guilty. 4 Or if any one swear rashly with his lips to do evil, or to do good, whatsoever it be that a man shall utter rashly with an oath, and it be hid from him; when he knoweth of it, then he shall be guilty in one of these *things*. 5 And it shall be, when he shall be guilty in one of these *things*, that he shall confess that wherein he hath sinned: 6 and he shall bring his trespass-offering unto Jehovah for his sin which he hath sinned, a female from the flock, a lamb or a goat, for a sin-offering; and the priest shall make atonement for him as concerning his sin.

7 And if his means suffice not for a lamb, then he shall bring his trespass-offering for that wherein he hath sinned, two turtle-doves, or two young pigeons, unto Jehovah; one for a sin-offering, and the other for a burnt-offering. 8 And he shall bring them unto the priest, who shall offer that which is for the sin-offering first, and wring off its head from its neck, but shall not divide it

asunder: 9 and he shall sprinkle of the blood of the sin-offering upon the side of the altar; and the rest of the blood shall be drained out at the base of the altar: it is a sin-offering. 10 And he shall offer the second for a burnt-offering, according to the ordinance; and the priest shall make atonement for him as concerning his sin which he hath sinned, and he shall be forgiven.

11 But if his means suffice not for two turtle-doves, or two young pigeons, then he shall bring his oblation for that wherein he hath sinned, the tenth part of an ephah of fine flour for a sin-offering: he shall put no oil upon it, neither shall he put any frankincense thereon; for it is a sin-offering. 12 And he shall bring it to the priest, and the priest shall take his handful of it as the memorial thereof, and burn it on the altar, upon the offerings of Jehovah made by fire: it is a sin-offering. 13 And the priest shall make atonement for him as touching his sin that he hath sinned in any of these things, and he shall be forgiven: and *the remnant* shall be the priest's, as the meal-offering.

From reading verses 6 and 7 in the King James Version it might appear that this section has reference to the trespass-offering rather than to the sin-offering. However, the American Standard margin indicates that the Hebrew term for "trespass offering" in verse 6 can be rendered "for his guilt," and so the phrase can read: "He shall bring for his guilt unto Jehovah. . . ." The Septuagint also is helpful here. It reads: "He shall bring for his transgressions against the Lord, for the sin which he hath sinned. . . ."

It seems certain for this reason that the verses here refer to the sin-offering of the previous chapter. This is further indicated by the fact that the victim for the trespass-offering, referred to in later verses of this chapter, was always a ram (for comments on these verses, see discussion on chapter 4).

5. The Trespass-Offering (5:14—6:7; 7:1-10).

The Hebrew word translated "trespass" in this passage means an invasion of the rights of others, especially in respect to property or service. Such encroachment, whether done knowingly or ignorantly, is wrong. To correct the wrong requires restitution and compensation to the person injured. So while in the eyes of the ritual law of Israel all trespasses were sins, all sins were not trespasses.

God, therefore, specified a different sacrifice to provide expiation when an Israelite defrauded or injured another person in respect to material things than He did when the man had committed an offence which did not infringe directly upon the rights of others. This sacrifice was known as the trespass or guilt (RSV) offering. Offering of the sacrifice was always accompanied by the worshiper making, so far as possible, full reparations to the person wronged. This involved making restitution and paying an additional twenty percent compensation (5:16; 6:5). If the reparations could not be made to the one offended or a near relative, the amount involved was to be paid to the priest (Num. 5:5-10). Such a costly offering would tend to make the people conscious of the price of sin.

The fact that the ram had to be offered, as well as reparations made, indicates that sin against one's fellow men is also sin against God (Matt. 5:23, 24; 19:19b; 22:37-40; I Thess. 4:6; Jas. 4:11). To settle the matter acceptably, then, requires His forgiveness as surely as it requires the favor of the party offended.

The sacrifice here was slain by the priest, as in the case of the sin-offering (7:1-8), and was accompanied with a meal-offering (7:8-10). In the case of the trespass-offering, however, the blood of the victim was not applied to the horns of the altar of burnt-offerings, as in the case of the sacrifice of the sin-offering (4:1-26), but was sprinkled **round about the altar** (7:2), probably to emphasize the satisfaction for a trespass.

Since it is hardly conceivable that all of the people could be guilty of the type of transgression considered here, the trespass-offering always had reference to the guilt of an individual, never to that of the entire congregation of Israel, as was sometimes the case with the sin-offering.

Regardless of the rank or means of the offerer, the animal required for the offering was always a **ram of the flock** (5:15, 18; 6:6). This suggests that God does not respect persons when it comes to making full satisfaction for a trespass. A man who may have defrauded his neighbor —

whether in large or small matters — remains, regardless of his condition, debtor before God until full restitution is made. Debt is debt by whomsoever it is owed.

Unlike victims in other sacrifices, the ram for the trespass-offering was to be appraised, and its value must in no case fall below two full-weight shekels of the sanctuary (5:15, 18; 6:6). It is significant that the sanctuary shekel is specified here, for that was of standard weight, whereas the shekel of the people was often of light weight. This would remind Israel, and us, that we are not to measure our conduct towards others by the judgment of men, but by God's standard of absolute righteousness (see II Cor. 10:12-18).

The law regarding the trespass-offering was divided into two sections: trespasses in things which by law or an act of consecration were considered as belonging to the Lord, and trespasses in things pertaining to men.

a. In Respect to God (5:14-19)

14 And Jehovah spake unto Moses, saying, 15 If any one commit a trespass, and sin unwittingly, in the holy things of Jehovah; then he shall bring his trespass-offering unto Jehovah, a ram without blemish out of the flock, according to thy estimation in silver by shekels, after the shekel of the sanctuary, for a trespass-offering: 16 and he shall make restitution for that which he hath done amiss in the holy thing, and shall add the fifth part thereto, and give it unto the priest; and the priest shall make atonement for him with the ram of the trespass-offering, and he shall be forgiven. 17 And if any one sin, and do any of the things which Jehovah hath commanded not to be done; though he knew it not, yet is he guilty, and shall bear his iniquity. 18 And he shall bring a ram without blemish out of the flock, according to thy estimation, for a trespass-offering, unto the priest; and the priest shall make atonement for him concerning the thing wherein he erred unwittingly and knew it not, and he shall be forgiven. 19 It is a trespass-offering: he is certainly guilty before Jehovah.

The holy things of Jehovah (v. 15) refer to such matters as a man's inadvertent eating of the flesh of the firstling of his cattle, or the flesh of a sin-offering, or perhaps using his tithe for himself.

Verses 14-16 apply to instances where the Israelite could determine the value involved in his trespass. Verses 17-19 deal with situations where the man was aware of a trespass, but was unable to determine the precise measure of his offence.

This shows that God claimed from His own people certain rights to their material possessions. Jehovah sternly reminded Israel of this in such passages as Malachi 3:8, 9. And the New Testament would teach us that God still desires that we use our material possessions liberally for the advancement of His work (Matt. 19:21, 22; 25:34-39; Luke 6:38; Acts 20:35; I Cor. 16:2; II Cor. 8:1-14; 9:6, 7; Eph. 4:28; I Tim. 6:17-19; I John 3:17) .

b. In Respect to Man (6:1—7:38)

1 And Jehovah spake unto Moses, saying, 2 If any one sin, and commit a trespass against Jehovah, and deal falsely with his neighbor in a matter of deposit, or of bargain, or of robbery, or have oppressed his neighbor, 3 or have found that which was lost, and deal falsely therein, and swear to a lie; in any of all these things that a man doeth, sinning therein; 4 then it shall be, if he hath sinned, and is guilty, that he shall restore that which he took by robbery, or the thing which he hath gotten by oppression, or the deposit which was committed to him, or the lost thing which he found, 5 or anything about which he hath sworn falsely; he shall even restore it in full, and shall add the fifth part more thereto: unto him to whom it appertaineth shall he give it, in the day of his being found guilty. 6 And he shall bring his trespass-offering unto Jehovah, a ram without blemish out of the flock, according to thy estimation, for a trespass-offering, unto the priest: 7 and the priest shall make atonement for him before Jehovah; and he shall be forgiven concerning whatsoever he doeth so as to be guilty thereby.

8 And Jehovah spake unto Moses, saying, 9 Command Aaron and his sons, saying, This is the law of the burnt-offering: the burnt-offering shall be on the hearth upon the altar all night unto the morning; and the fire of the altar shall be kept burning thereon. 10 And the priest shall put on his linen garment, and his linen breeches shall he put upon his flesh; and he shall take up the ashes whereto the fire hath consumed the burnt-offering on the altar, and he shall

put them beside the altar. 11 And he shall put off his garments, and put on other garments, and carry forth the ashes without the camp unto a clean place. 12 And the fire upon the altar shall be kept burning thereon, it shall not go out; and the priest shall burn wood on it every morning: and he shall lay the burnt-offering in order upon it, and shall burn thereon the fat of the peace-offerings. 13 Fire shall be kept burning upon the altar continually; it shall not go out.

14 And this is the law of the meal-offering: the sons of Aaron shall offer it before Jehovah, before the altar. 15 And he shall take up therefrom his handful, of the fine flour of the meal-offering, and of the oil thereof, and all the frankincense which is upon the meal-offering, and shall burn it upon the altar for a sweet savor, as the memorial thereof, unto Jehovah. 16 And that which is left thereof shall Aaron and his sons eat: it shall be eaten without leaven in a holy place; in the court of the tent of meeting they shall eat it. 17 It shall not be baken with leaven. I have given it as their portion of my offerings made by fire; it is most holy, as the sin-offering, and as the trespass-offering. 18 Every male among the children of Aaron shall eat of it, as *his* portion for ever throughout your generations, from the offerings of Jehovah made by fire: whosoever toucheth them shall be holy.

19 And Jehovah spake unto Moses, saying, 20 This is the oblation of Aaron and of his sons, which they shall offer unto Jehovah in the day when he is anointed: the tenth part of an ephah of fine flour for a meal-offering perpetually, half of it in the morning, and half thereof in the evening. 21 On a baking-pan it shall be made with oil; when it is soaked, thou shalt bring it in: in baken pieces shalt thou offer the meal-offering for a sweet savor unto Jehovah. 22 And the anointed priest that shall be in his stead from among his sons shall offer it: by a statute for ever it shall be wholly burnt unto Jehovah. 23 And every meal-offering of the priest shall be wholly burnt: it shall not be eaten.

24 And Jehovah spake unto Moses, saying, 25 Speak unto Aaron and to his sons, saying, This is the law of the sin-offering: in the place where the burnt-offering is killed shall the sin-offering be killed before Jehovah: it is most holy. 26 The priest that offereth it for sin shall eat it: in a holy place shall it be eaten, in the court of the tent of meeting. 27 Whatsoever shall touch the flesh

thereof shall be holy; and when there is sprinkled of the blood thereof upon any garment, thou shalt wash that whereon it was sprinkled in a holy place. 28 But the earthen vessel wherein it is boiled shall be broken; and if it be boiled in a brazen vessel, it shall be scoured, and rinsed in water. 29 Every male among the priests shall eat thereof: it is most holy. 30 And no sin-offering, whereof any of the blood is brought into the tent of meeting to make atonement in the holy place, shall be eaten: it shall be burnt with fire.

1 And this is the law of the trespass-offering: it is most holy. 2 In the place where they kill the burnt-offering shall they kill the trespass-offering; and the blood thereof shall he sprinkle upon the altar round about. 3 And he shall offer of it all the fat thereof: the fat tail, and the fat that covereth the inwards, 4 and the two kidneys, and the fat that is on them, which is by the loins, and the caul upon the liver, with the kidneys, shall he take away; 5 and the priest shall burn them upon the altar for an offering made by fire unto Jehovah: it is a trespass-offering. 6 Every male among the priests shall eat thereof: it shall be eaten in a holy place: it is most holy. 7 As is the sin-offering, so is the trespass-offering; there is one law for them: the priest that maketh atonement therewith, he shall have it. 8 And the priest that offereth any man's burnt-offering, even the priest shall have to himself the skin of the burnt-offering which he hath offered. 9 And every meal-offering that is baken in the oven, and all that is dressed in the frying-pan, and on the baking-pan, shall be the priest's that offereth it. 10 And every meal offering, mingled with oil, or dry, shall all the sons of Aaron have, one as well as another.

11 And this is the law of the sacrifice of peace-offerings, which one shall offer unto Jehovah. 12 If he offer it for a thanksgiving, then he shall offer with the sacrifice of thanksgiving unleavened cakes mingled with oil, and unleavened wafers anointed with oil, and cakes mingled with oil, of fine flour soaked. 13 With cakes of leavened bread he shall offer his oblation with the sacrifice of his peace-offerings for thanksgiving. 14 And of it he shall offer one out of each oblation for a heave-offering unto Jehovah; it shall be the priest's that sprinkleth the blood of the peace-offerings.

15 And the flesh of the sacrifice of his peace-offerings for thanksgiving shall be eaten on the day of his oblation; he shall not leave any of it until the morning. 16 But if the sacrifice of his oblation be a vow, or a freewill-offering, it shall be eaten on the day that he offereth his sacrifice; and on the morrow that which remaineth of it shall be eaten: 17 but that which remaineth of the flesh of the sacrifice on the third day shall be burnt with fire. 18 And if any of the flesh of the sacrifice of his peace-offerings be eaten on the third day, it shall not be accepted, neither shall it be imputed unto him that offereth it: it shall be an abomination, and the soul that eateth of it shall bear his iniquity.

19 And the flesh that toucheth any unclean thing shall not be eaten; it shall be burnt with fire. And as for the flesh, every one that is clean shall eat thereof: 20 but the soul that eateth of the flesh of the sacrifice of the peace-offerings, that pertain unto Jehovah, having his uncleanness upon him, that soul shall be cut off from his people. 21 And when any one shall touch any unclean thing, the uncleanness of man, or an unclean beast, or any unclean abomination, and eat of the flesh of the sacrifice of peace-offerings, which pertain unto Jehovah, that soul shall be cut off from his people.

22 And Jehovah spake unto Moses, saying, 23 Speak unto the children of Israel, saying, Ye shall eat no fat, of ox, or sheep, or goat. 24 And the fat of that which dieth of itself, and the fat of that which is torn of beasts, may be used for any other service; but ye shall in no wise eat of it. 25 For whosoever eateth the fat of the beast, of which men offer an offering made by fire unto Jehovah, even the soul that eateth it shall be cut off from his people. 26 And ye shall eat no manner of blood, whether it be of bird or of beast, in any of your dwellings. 27 Whosoever it be that eateth any blood, that soul shall be cut off from his people.

28 And Jehovah spake unto Moses, saying, 29 Speak unto the children of Israel, saying, He that offereth the sacrifice of his peace-offerings unto Jehovah shall bring his oblation unto Jehovah out of the sacrifice of his peace-offerings: 30 his own hands shall bring the offerings of Jehovah made by fire; the fat with the breast shall he bring, that the breast may be waved for a wave-offering before Jehovah. 31 And the priest shall burn the fat upon the altar; but the breast shall be Aaron's and his sons'. 32 And the right thigh shall ye give unto the priest for a heave-offering out of the sacrifices of your peace-offerings. 33 He among the sons of Aaron that offereth the blood of

the peace-offerings, and the fat, shall have the right thigh for a portion. 34 For the wave-breast and the heave-thigh have I taken out of the sacrifices of their peace-offerings, and have given them unto Aaron the priest and unto his sons as *their* portion for ever from the children of Israel.

35 This is the anointing-portion of Aaron, and the anointing-portion of his sons, out of the offerings of Jehovah made by fire, in the day when he presented them to minister unto Jehovah in the priest's office; 36 which Jehovah commanded to be given them of the children of Israel, in the day that he anointed them. It is *their* portion for ever throughout their generations.

37 This is the law of the burnt-offering, of the meal-offering, and of the sin-offering, and of the trespass-offering, and of the consecration, and of the sacrifice of peace-offerings; 38 which Jehovah commanded Moses in mount Sinai, in the day that he commanded the children of Israel to offer their oblations unto Jehovah, in the wilderness of Sinai.

To indicate the type of offences meant, reference is made to several typical examples implying intentional embezzlement, plunder, and fraud. **In a matter of deposit, or of bargain** (v. 2), literally implies "something delivered him to keep, or in fellowship" (see LXX and KJV). The RSV also suggests the same rendering of the phrase: "In a matter of deposit or security." This applies to a man who sold or used for himself something which another had entrusted to him for safekeeping. **Robbery** (v. 2) may involve violent seizure or fraudulent maneuvering. **Oppressed his neighbor** suggests taking advantage of another's circumstance to extort from him anything or any service to which one has no right. **Found that which is lost** (v. 3) applies to a man who upon finding something of value denies it to the rightful owner (compare this section with Exod. 22:7-15 and Num. 5:5-10).

The fact that the offender should **be forgiven** only after restitution and the making of proper sacrifice would teach Israel the same need for repentance (which involves undoing what has been done amiss) and for bringing forth "fruit worthy of repentance" (Matt. 3:8), as John the Baptist later proclaimed.

The trespass-offering presents a clear picture of the work of Christ, who as our trespass-offering made full reparations before God for us whose debt of sin was beyond any power of ours to repay fully (Rom. 10:4; see Isa. 53:5). Isaiah 53:10 would also indicate this, for the word there translated "offering for sin" means also **trespass-offering** in the Leviticus passage under consideration (see margin 53:10, ASV). The fact that sins are referred to as "debts" in Matthew 6:12 is also suggestive in this respect.

For comments on verses 8-13 see section 1, the whole burnt-offering (1:1-17). For comments on verses 14-23 see section 2, the meal-offering (2:1-16). For comments on verses 24-30 refer to section 4, the sin-offering (4:1—5:13).

For comments on verses 1-10 see section 5, the trespass-offering (5:14—6:7). For comments on verses 11-38 see section 3, the peace-offering (3:1-17).

B. A PRIESTHOOD ESTABLISHED (8:1—10:20)

Up until this time the patriarchal order had prevailed — an order in which the father served as the family priest. He, as head of his family, was the mediator between his dependents and God. He was responsible to lead his household in the worship and service of Jehovah. Job is a notable example of this (Job 1:5). Except for the reference to Melchizedek as priest in Genesis 14:18, no official priest is previously mentioned. Now, however, as Israel became a nation, the Lord gave instructions for the setting apart of a certain tribe to serve as priests for the entire nation. Of that tribe He selected a family to administer the rites at the tabernacle, and of that family he indicated a particular man to serve as the great or high priest.

The more we understand of this the more significant becomes the fact that in the New Testament Church Christ is the High Priest (Heb. 2:17, 18; 7-9; 10:11-14); and all believers, through Him, are priests with direct access to God for themselves and for others (Rom. 15:16; Heb. 4:14-16; 10:15-22; I Pet. 2:4-10; Rev. 1:4-6). The Christian ministry is made up of those within the universal priesthood of the whole Christian Church who give themselves at the call of the

Spirit to serve in special capacities of spiritual work and leadership.

Throughout Israel's history the priestly function was different and distinct from the prophetical. The prophet represented God to the people; the priest represented the prayers and sacrifices of the people to the Lord (Exod. 28:1-43; Lev. 16:1-34). The Hebrew terms themselves indicate these differences. The word translated "prophet" means literally "one who speaks by inspiration," whereas the term for "priest" is literally "a mediator." The prophet was a preacher, speaking Jehovah's message to the people; the priest's task involved petition and worship, the discerning of the will of God (Num. 27: 21; Deut. 33:8), and the teaching of the law of the Lord.

1. The Priests Set Apart (8:1-36)

In the earlier chapters we have seen that God was very specific in His demands regarding the ritual and form of worship. Now we note that He was also greatly concerned about the people who were to carry out those rituals. They were to be consecrated, set apart from others for God's singular service. They were to be sanctified. Isaiah later declared the truth of what we see being carried out here when he said that those who would bear the vessels of the Lord must be clean (Isa. 52:11).

While we recognize in these rituals a shadow of better things to come (Heb. 10:1), they were not merely symbols of those better things. They were acts of real worship and consecration. As the participants engaged in the ceremonies with penitence, prayer, and sincere devotion they actually received forgiveness, the favor of God, and His grace for the work to which they were called.

Nevertheless, what was provided for the priest of Israel in the way of outward consecration from the secular and profane was a striking forecast and symbol of the greater provision made for all New Testament believers in Christ, namely, their sanctification and inward cleansing from the power and defilement of sin in human nature. And just as surely as God insisted upon the priests being consecrated and cleansed before they could engage in their priestly offices, so we who would do effective work for Christ

must separate ourselves from sin to God, and through obedient faith receive through the Holy Spirit the cleansing made available for us in the blood of Christ. In fact, the Greek New Testament word for priest stresses this, for it implies "the holy one"; "the consecrated one." The priests in Israel were anointed with literal blood and oil symbolizing the atoning Sacrifice, Jesus Christ, and the Spirit — who were to come later. In the New Testament Church the symbols are not required, for the reality has come.

a. Who, What, and Where (8:1-4)

1 And Jehovah spake unto Moses, saying, 2 Take Aaron and his sons with him, and the garments, and the anointing oil, and the bullock of the sin-offering, and the two rams, and the basket of unleavened bread; 3 and assemble thou all the congregation at the door of the tent of meeting. 4 And Moses did as Jehovah commanded him; and the congregation was assembled at the door of the tent of meeting.

God chose the tribe of Levi — of which Moses was a member — to serve as priests in Israel, claiming them for Himself in lieu of the first-born of all the tribes whose lives were spared in the Exodus (Num. 8:14-19). Within the larger circle of Levites, there was, however, a distinction made between Aaron and his sons and the rest of the Levites. Only the family of Aaron was to minister before the Lord in the sanctuary, while others were to help in various capacities as priestly assistants (Num. 3:1-13). Aaron was himself to function as the high priest, and succeeding high priests were to be selected from the house of Aaron. So it was that at the ordination ceremony only **Aaron and his sons** (v. 2) were set apart.

The garments for the priests, and the other items needed for the ordination ceremonies spoken of in the detailed plans for this ceremony recorded in Exodus 28 and 29 (comments on which see) were all taken to the tabernacle as Aaron and his sons "went up" with Moses for the sacred occasion.

b. How (8:5-36)

5 And Moses said unto the congregation, This is the thing which Jehovah hath commanded to be done.

6 And Moses brought Aaron and his sons, and washed them with water. 7 And he put upon him the coat, and girded him with the girdle, and clothed him with the robe, and put the ephod upon him, and he girded him with the skilfully woven band of the ephod, and bound it unto him therewith. 8 And he placed the breastplate upon him: and in the breastplate he put the Urim and the Thummim. 9 And he set the mitre upon his head; and upon the mitre, in front, did he set the golden plate, the holy crown; as Jehovah commanded Moses.

10 And Moses took the anointing oil, and anointed the tabernacle and all that was therein, and sanctified them. 11 And he sprinkled thereof upon the altar seven times, and anointed the altar and all its vessels, and the laver and its base, to sanctify them. 12 And he poured of the anointing oil upon Aaron's head, and anointed him, to sanctify him. 13 And Moses brought Aaron's sons, and clothed them with coats, and girded them with girdles, and bound head-tires upon them; as Jehovah commanded Moses.

14 And he brought the bullock of the sin-offering: and Aaron and his sons laid their hands upon the head of the bullock of the sin-offering. 15 And he slew it; and Moses took the blood, and put it upon the horns of the altar round about with his finger, and purified the altar, and poured out the blood at the base of the altar, and sanctified it, to make atonement for it. 16 And he took all the fat that was upon the inwards, and the caul of the liver, and the two kidneys, and their fat; and Moses burned it upon the altar. 17 But the bullock, and its skin, and its flesh, and its dung, he burnt with fire without the camp; as Jehovah commanded Moses.

18 And he presented the ram of the burnt-offering: and Aaron and his sons laid their hands upon the head of the ram. 19 And he killed it; and Moses sprinkled the blood upon the altar round about. 20 And he cut the ram into its pieces; and Moses burnt the head, and the pieces, and the fat. 21 And he washed the inwards and the legs with water; and Moses burnt the whole ram upon the altar: it was a burnt-offering for a sweet savor: it was an offering made by fire unto Jehovah; as Jehovah commanded Moses.

22 And he presented the other ram, the ram of consecration: and Aaron and his sons laid their hands upon the head of the ram. 23 And he slew it; and Moses took of the blood thereof, and put it upon the tip of Aaron's right ear, and upon the thumb of his right hand, and upon the great toe of his right foot. 24 And he brought Aaron's sons; and Moses put of the blood upon the tip of their right ear, and upon the thumb of their right hand, and upon the great toe of their right foot: and Moses sprinkled the blood upon the altar round about. 25 And he took the fat, and the fat tail, and all the fat that was upon the inwards, and the caul of the liver, and the two kidneys, and their fat, and the right thigh: 26 and out of the basket of unleavened bread, that was before Jehovah, he took one unleavened cake, and one cake of oiled bread, and one wafer, and placed them on the fat, and upon the right thigh: 27 and he put the whole upon the hands of Aaron, and upon the hands of his sons, and waved them for a wave-offering before Jehovah. 28 And Moses took them from off their hands, and burnt them on the altar upon the burnt-offering: they were a consecration for a sweet savor: it was an offering made by fire unto Jehovah. 29 And Moses took the breast, and waved it for a wave-offering before Jehovah: it was Moses' portion of the ram of consecration; as Jehovah commanded Moses.

30 And Moses took of the anointing oil, and of the blood which was upon the altar, and sprinkled it upon Aaron, upon his garments, and upon his sons, and upon his sons' garments with him, and sanctified Aaron, his garments, and his sons, and his sons' garments with him.

31 And Moses said unto Aaron and to his sons, Boil the flesh at the door of the tent of meeting: and there eat it and the bread that is in the basket of consecration, as I commanded, saying, Aaron and his sons shall eat it. 32 And that which remaineth of the flesh and of the bread shall ye burn with fire. 33 And ye shall not go out from the door of the tent of meeting seven days, until the days of your consecration be fulfilled: for he shall consecrate you seven days. 34 As hath been done this day, so Jehovah hath commanded to do, to make atonement for you. 35 And at the door of the tent of meeting shall ye abide day and night seven days, and keep the charge of Jehovah, that ye die not: for so I am commanded. 36 And Aaron and his sons did all the things which Jehovah commanded by Moses.

How the ordination ceremony was to be conducted so as to impress both priests and people with God's holiness had been outlined in the Exodus passage just cited, and here Moses carries through according to those divine instructions.

The consecration activities involved four particular requirements which were highly significant — highly significant not only to the Aaronic priesthood, but also in their symbolism for us who are to serve as a "holy priesthood" (I Pet. 2:5) in our own generation. There was washing, symbolic of the moral cleansing of heart and life (Tit. 3:5). There was the investiture, the putting on of special clothing, typical of justification and the putting on of the garments of righteousness (Rev. 19:8). There was anointing, suggestive of sanctification which brings the anointing of the Holy Spirit (Acts 10: 38; John 3:34; I John 2:20). There was sacrifice, indicative of acceptance with the Lord (Heb. 10:19-31).

The ceremony included also the making of four of the offerings discussed under chapters 1—4:12 (which comments see). They were offered here, however, not in the order presented previously, but in the order of experience. The sin-offering, which speaks of forgiveness and reconciliation, was followed by the burnt-offering, indicative of consecration. There was the meal-offering (usually made in connection with the animal sacrifices) which speaks of service. The climax of the occasion was the peace-offering which provides communion with God and fellowship with the brethren. The peace-offering in this instance is referred to as the offering of **consecration** (v. 22) or, as the Hebrew term implies, an offering "to fill the hands," that is, an offering by which the participants were invested with an office with a special task to do. Its administration in this case differed from the ordinary peace-offering in that the priest's portion was assigned to Moses, since he acted as priest on behalf of Aaron and his sons; and in that since Aaron and his sons were to remain seven days at the tabernacle, repeating the offering each day, they were to eat the meat of the peace-offering on the day offered, rather than having to wait until the day following (7:15-18).

In this particular ritual, different from the ordinary peace-offering, the whole body was symbolically consecrated by the anointing of the priest's ear, thumb, and toe with blood (indicative of atonement),

and with oil (suggestive of the anointing of the Holy Spirit). This highlights how the ear is to be quickened to hear the Word of God, the hand quickened to do His work, and the feet quickened to walk in the way of His commandments. It suggests also how true religion affects the whole of life. The cleansing blood and the anointing oil do make a difference in what we listen to, what we do, and where we go. Cleansed from sin and anointed by the Holy Spirit, all of our active powers and every aspect of our living reflect the holy and righteous benefits of Christ's salvation.

Continuing the ordination ceremony for seven days (seven being the number of perfection and completeness), indicated to the priest that his consecration must be a complete one; his body, soul, time, and talents were to be wholly devoted to God and to the service of His people.

2. The Priests Begin Their Ministry (9:1-24)

The immediate demands made upon the newly consecrated priests call attention to the fact that they were not ordained to remain idle. They were not given so much as a day's relief from duty that they might go home to receive the congratulations and commendations of their friends and loved ones for the honors that had come to them. Their hands were at once filled with the work of their pressing ministry (see comments on 8:22).

This is currently relevant. To be set aside as a minister of the Lord is an honor which brings rich spiritual benefits. Whoever aspires to be an overseer in the church, the Apostle Paul told Timothy, seeks for a noble task (I Tim. 3:1). But to be so consecrated and ordained brings immediate and urgent responsibility. The man worthy of the minister's honor and benefits must be prepared and ready to assume the incumbent burdens. His call brings him almost unlimited opportunity, but it also involves a lifetime of hard, often heart-breaking work, and it carries with it a solemn charge to redeem the time, to gather the over-ripened harvest while it is still day.

a. The Priests Receive Instructions (9:1-7)

1 And it came to pass on the eighth day, that Moses called Aaron and his sons, and the elders of Israel; 2 and he said unto Aaron, Take thee a calf of the herd for a sin-offering, and a ram for a burnt-offering, without blemish, and offer them before Jehovah. 3 And unto the children of Israel thou shalt speak, saying, Take ye a he-goat for a sin-offering; and a calf and a lamb, both a year old, without blemish, for a burnt-offering; 4 and an ox and a ram for peace-offerings, to sacrifice before Jehovah; and a meal-offering mingled with oil: for to-day Jehovah appeareth unto you. 5 And they brought that which Moses commanded before the tent of meeting: and all the congregation drew near and stood before Jehovah. 6 And Moses said, This is the thing which Jehovah commanded that ye should do: and the glory of Jehovah shall appear unto you. 7 And Moses said unto Aaron, Draw near unto the altar, and offer thy sin-offering, and thy burnt-offering, and make atonement for thyself, and for the people; and offer the oblation of the people, and make atonement for them; as Jehovah commanded.

Up to this time Moses had served as priest, but now at the end of the seven-day ordination ceremony of Aaron and his sons (8:33) a new order began. Aaron and his sons were to begin their duty of offering the sacrifices before the Lord. In particular, they were to prepare immediately for an assembly of the whole congregation of Israel that God might visibly manifest Himself to them and thus show His approval and ratify what had just been done in setting up an official priesthood. The **elders of Israel** (v. 1), or heads of the various tribes, were also called up, told of the proposed gathering, and probably were instructed regarding their responsibilities in the preparations.

Things must be readied for sacrifices for the priests and the people. (For the method of administering these and their significance see notes on chapters 1-7.)

b. The Priests Offer Sacrifices for Themselves (9:8-14)

8 So Aaron drew near unto the altar, and slew the calf of the sin-offering, which was for himself. 9 And the sons of Aaron

presented the blood unto him; and he dipped his finger in the blood, and put it upon the horns of the altar, and poured out the blood at the base of the altar: 10 but the fat, and the kidneys, and the caul from the liver of the sin-offering, he burnt upon the altar; as Jehovah commanded Moses. 11 And the flesh and the skin he burnt with fire without the camp.

12 And he slew the burnt-offering; and Aaron's sons delivered unto him the blood, and he sprinkled it upon the altar round about. 13 And they delivered the burnt-offering unto him, piece by piece, and the head: and he burnt them upon the altar. 14 And he washed the inwards and the legs, and burnt them upon the burnt-offerings on the altar.

Although Aaron and his sons had been made priests, they were still only men, and before they could sacrifice acceptably for the people they must offer a sin-offering and a burnt-offering in their own behalf. It is good, however, to know that our High Priest, Jesus Christ, was sinless and did not need to offer for Himself. We are told: "Such a high priest became us, holy, guileless, undefiled, separated from sinners, and made higher than the heavens; who needeth not daily, like those high priests, to offer up sacrifices, first for his own sins, and then for the sins of the people: for this he did once for all, when he offered up himself" (Heb. 7:26, 27).

In the order of the sacrifices here offered by the priests for themselves, there is a parable for us who today would minister for the Lord in any capacity at all. First there was the offering for sin, then there was the offering of consecration. In our lives too the sin problem must first be cared for, and then there must be consecration of ourselves to the will and work of God. Before we can effectively witness to God's saving grace, we must ourselves have been forgiven and have committed ourselves utterly to the Lord. The husbandman must be a partaker of the fruits he seeks to impart to others (I Tim. 2:6).

c. The Priests Offer Sacrifices for the People (9:15-21)

15 And he presented the people's oblation, and took the goat of the sin-offering which was for the people, and slew it,

and offered it for sin, as the first. 16 And he presented the burnt-offering, and offered it according to the ordinance. 17 And he presented the meal-offering, and filled his hand therefrom, and burnt it upon the altar, besides the burnt-offering of the morning.

18 He slew also the ox and the ram, the sacrifice of peace-offerings, which was for the people: and Aaron's sons delivered unto him the blood, which he sprinkled upon the altar round about, 19 and the fat of the ox and of the ram, the fat tail, and that which covereth *the inwards*, and the kidneys, and the caul of the liver: 20 and they put the fat upon the breasts, and he burnt the fat upon the altar: 21 and the breasts and the right thigh Aaron waved for a wave-offering before Jehovah; as Moses commanded.

The order of the sacrifices for the congregation here is no accident. The people needed first of all the benefits of the sin-offering. They needed also the benefits of the burnt-offering and the meal-offering. That is, they needed forgiveness. They needed to surrender themselves and the fruits of their hands to the Lord. Only then could they acceptably offer the peace-offering and participate in its sacrificial feast.

There is a significant analogy here also of the usual order of development in Christian experience. Awakened by the Holy Spirit to our spiritual need, we are usually first of all concerned about forgiveness of sin and acceptance with the Lord. Hence faith first apprehends Christ as the sin-offering, as the One who "bare our sins in his body" (I Pet. 2:24). We are also led to see Christ as the One who in lowly consecration to the Father's will accomplished His purpose. And so we are called to a total commitment of ourselves to the Lord, and through His grace are enabled to live righteously in His sight. But in this condition we do not walk far until we find that an evil nature abides within us which has unforeseen strength to overcome and lead us into sin again. This prepares us, still in accord with the order of the grace set forth in the sacrifices, to lay hold upon Christ by faith, to feed upon Him as our peace-offering. He thus becomes our sanctification, and we become partakers of His full salvation.

d. The Priests' Sacrifices Bring God's Blessing (9:22-24)

22 And Aaron lifted up his hands toward the people, and blessed them; and he came down from offering the sin-offering, and the burnt-offering, and the peace-offerings. 23 And Moses and Aaron went into the tent of meeting, and came out, and blessed the people: and the glory of Jehovah appeared unto all the people. 24 And there came forth fire from before Jehovah, and consumed upon the altar the burnt-offering and the fat: and when all the people saw it, they shouted, and fell on their faces.

Having confidently carried out the commands of the Lord, Aaron lifted his hands in benediction toward the people, probably following the formula of Numbers 6:25, 26; and came down the steps which led from the great altar where he had been making sacrifice. He and Moses then went into the immediate presence of God in the tabernacle where Aaron was probably inducted into the offices required there and came out to bless the people.

To show His pleasure with the faith and obedience of His servants, the Lord manifested His splendor, probably by means of the Shekinah, or by the fiery cloud of divine presence over the tabernacle, and by sending fire which quickly consumed the smoldering sacrifice.

Obedience and faith never fail to bring the blessing of God. The preacher or layman whose soul is not occasionally thrilled with the reality of God's presence and glory is most likely failing somewhere in obedience and trust. "For it is the God who said, 'Let light shine out of darkness,' who hath shone in our hearts to give the light of the knowledge of the glory of God in the face of Christ" (II Cor. 4:6, RSV). And God's manifest blessing brings the same response from His devout believers today that it did among the congregation of Israel who shouted and bowed low before Him: a response of joyful praise and holy reverence.

3. Sacrilege Brings Judgment (10:1-20)

God's manifest glory, as related in the previous chapters, was evidence of His pleasure in the acceptable worship of His people. But in this chapter the fire of blessing becomes the fire of judgment.

It is a startling reminder that to have witnessed and shared in a manifestation of God's presence does not give one immunity from judgment in case of wrongdoing. Rather, the more we know of God's grace and power, the more strictly we shall be held to account for every failure to honor and exalt the Lord. Indeed, any careless, irresponsible attitude or action is entirely out of place in a Christian. Repentance and a turning to God begets a carefulness which must be continual (cf. Eph. 5:15-17). It is a carefulness such as is referred to by the Apostle Paul in writing to the Corinthians following their correction of unbecoming conduct among them. "Behold what earnestness this very thing, this godly sorrow, has produced in you, what vindication of yourselves, what indignation, what fear, what longing, what zeal, what avenging of wrong! In everything you demonstrated yourselves to be innocent in the matter" (II Cor. 7:11, NASB).

a. Two Priests Worship Arbitrarily (10:1-7)

1 And Nadab and Abihu, the sons of Aaron, took each of them his censer, and put fire therein, and laid incense thereon, and offered strange fire before Jehovah, which he had not commanded them. 2 And there came forth fire from before Jehovah, and devoured them, and they died before Jehovah. 3 Then Moses said unto Aaron, This is it that Jehovah spake, saying, I will be sanctified in them that come nigh me, and before all the people I will be glorified. And Aaron held his peace. 4 And Moses called Mishael and Elzaphan, the sons of Uzziel the uncle of Aaron, and said unto them, Draw near, carry your brethren from before the sanctuary out of the camp. 5 So they drew near, and carried them in their coats out of the camp, as Moses had said. 6 And Moses said unto Aaron, and unto Eleazar and unto Ithamar, his sons, Let not the hair of your heads go loose, neither rend your clothes; that ye die not, and that he be not wroth with all the congregation: but let your brethren, the whole house of Israel, bewail the burning which Jehovah hath kindled. 7 And ye shall not go out from the door of the tent of meeting, lest ye die; for the anointing oil of Jehovah is upon you. And they did according to the word of Moses.

Nadab and Abihu, the eldest sons of Aaron, acting impulsively, gravely sinned. Some implications of their failure are obscure, but it is clear that on their own initiative they presumed to worship in a way God had not commanded them (v. 1).

From Leviticus 16:12 it appears that fire for the censers had to be taken from the altar's sacred flame (see Num. 16:46). Perhaps they failed in this. Leviticus 16:1, 2 suggests that they may have pressed their way beyond the sacred veil of the tabernacle into the immediate presence of the Shekinah where only the high priest was to enter.

Furthermore, there were no instructions to burn incense on this particular occasion (chaps. 8, 9). Then, when they did choose to do this, they did so with no regard to the divine order for such worship (Exod. 30). The time for burning incense before the golden altar had not arrived, for this was to be done morning and evening. Also, incense was to be burned only by the high priest or by the common priests one at a time according to assignment (Exod. 30:9; Luke 1:9). But Nadab and Abihu, over-stimulated perhaps by the manifestations just experienced, overcome, maybe, with pride and ambition, or perhaps through rivalry or jealousy, presumed to take precedence over their father and rushed in together to offer incense simultaneously. The **strange** or "unholy" (RSV) **fire** may then well refer to offering of incense arbitrarily in defiance of God's laws.

Priests were considered near to the Lord in that they had access to the Holy Place, and they were to lift God up and glorify Him before the people (v. 3). Because Nadab and Abihu failed so grossly in this and set a public example of human will-worship, they were destroyed (v. 2). The Lord is indeed a consuming fire (Heb. 12:29). Our attitude toward Him determines whether that fire will hallow or destroy us.

The priests were not the first men, nor were they the last, who deemed one kind of fire as good as another, who attempted to lay down their own conditions for honoring the Lord. The second man on earth tried this. Cain well knew what a proper sacrifice involved (Gen. 4:6, 7), but he persisted in his own desired religious pattern. And to this day many men are prone to be religious, would even appear Christian, but all the while follow their own fancies and inclinations. They hope that somehow God will condescend to be pleased with their manner of life and worship. They would have Him serve them. But they neither humble themselves to please Him, nor seek to serve Him as He has indicated in His Word they should. It remains true, nevertheless, that God's worship and work must be done according to His will.

Moses called in cousins of Aaron and himself (Exod. 6:22) to carry out the slain priests (v. 4). So it was that the dead men, still dressed in their white priestly tunics or **coats,** in which they had just been consecrated for holy service, were carried outside the camp for burial (v. 5). The people throughout the congregation mourned the tragedy. And we may be sure that Aaron was deeply shaken. But because he and his remaining sons were engaged in their priestly duties, they were forbidden to show any of the common signs of mourning such as letting their hair hang loose (that is, according to the Septuagint, going bareheaded) or rending their clothes.

b. God Gives Further Instructions to Aaron (10:8-11)

8 And Jehovah spake unto Aaron, saying, 9 Drink no wine nor strong drink, thou, nor thy sons with thee, when ye go into the tent of meeting, that ye die not: it shall be a statute for ever throughout your generations: 10 and that ye may make a distinction between the holy and the common, and between the unclean and the clean; 11 and that ye may teach the children of Israel all the statutes which Jehovah hath spoken unto them by Moses.

The fact that God at this particular time forbade the use of intoxicants by the ministering priests in the tabernacle may indicate that Nadab and Abihu had been drunk. It is possible, and apparently probable, that they had been careless and irresponsible because they were addled from their drinking. This has a very personal application for all of us as Christians, for we are very really a body of priests unto the Lord. We are not only obligated to refrain from be-

fuddling intoxicants, but from all other pursuits which blunt our spiritual perception, dim our vision to behold the needs of lost men, or otherwise adversely affect our service.

c. Other Priests Affected (10:12-20)

12 And Moses spake unto Aaron, and unto Eleazar and unto Ithamar, his sons that were left, Take the meal-offering that remaineth of the offerings of Jehovah made by fire, and eat it without leaven beside the altar; for it is most holy; 13 and ye shall eat it in a holy place, because it is thy portion, and thy sons' portion, of the offerings of Jehovah made by fire: for so I am commanded. 14 And the wave-breast and the heave-thigh shall ye eat in a clean place, thou, and thy sons, and thy daughters with thee: for they are given as thy portion, and thy sons' portion, out of the sacrifices of the peace-offerings of the children of Israel. 15 The heave-thigh and the wave-breast shall they bring with the offerings made by fire of the fat, to wave it for a wave-offering before Jehovah: and it shall be thine, and thy sons' with thee, as a portion for ever; as Jehovah hath commanded.

16 And Moses diligently sought the goat of the sin-offering, and, behold, it was burnt: and he was angry with Eleazar and with Ithamar, the sons of Aaron that were left, saying, 17 Wherefore have ye not eaten the sin-offering in the place of the sanctuary, seeing it is most holy, and he hath given it you to bear the iniquity of the congregation, to make atonement for them before Jehovah? 18 Behold, the blood of it was not brought into the sanctuary within: ye should certainly have eaten it in the sanctuary, as I commanded. 19 And Aaron spake unto Moses, Behold, this day have they offered their sin-offering and their burnt-offering before Jehovah; and there have befallen me such things as these: and if I had eaten the sin-offering to-day, would it have been well-pleasing in the sight of Jehovah? 20 And when Moses heard *that,* it was well-pleasing in his sight.

It would appear that the tragic judgment had fallen before the priests had eaten their portions of the meal-offering and the peace-offering (9:12-20; 2:1-16; 6:14-23; 3:1-17; 7:11-38; Exod. 29:27). So affected were they by the circumstances that they hardly knew what to do; but they were instructed to go ahead with their duties (vv. 12-15). Overcome by the situations, the priests had also failed to properly eat their portion of the sin-offering and had burned their part of the goat given for the people's sin (9:15, 16), as they customarily did with their own sin-offering (vv. 16, 17; see also 4:27-33; 5:1-13). Nor had the sacrificial blood from the sin-offering been properly taken into the sanctuary. When Aaron was reproved for this, his reply indicated that he and his sons were so deeply grieved by the loss of their loved ones that they simply could not eat and, furthermore, they feared that they may have been considered involved in and contaminated by the sins of Nadab and Abihu and so did not consider themselves worthy to mediate the sins of the people. Moses recognized the sincerity and reasonableness of the plea. So it was that judgment was mingled with mercy.

C. DISTINGUISHING CLEAN AND UNCLEAN (11:1—15:33)

These chapters continue with the subject, "How to Approach God." (See Outline in front of Introduction.) Previous sections have dealt with matters pertaining to the sanctuary. This one, however, has to do with matters concerning Israel's daily living. Any effectual approach to God, this would say to us, involves more than our attitudes and activities at a place of public worship.

It suggests that if we would come into the divine presence our whole manner of living must receive attention. True worship on the Lord's Day will be preceded by six days of faithfulness toward God. It is difficult, for example, to sing with conviction at church, "I'm a Child of the King," if all week we have lived like a prodigal or an orphan.

1. Distinguishing Clean and Unclean Animals (11:1-47)

The terms "clean" and "unclean" as used here do not mean that the animals so described were either dirty or not dirty. The meaning is that for the Israelites they were proper or improper for food, or that contact with their dead bodies made an Israelite ceremonially unfit for worship and for association with other people. This is not the first mention of distinguishing between these two classes of animals, for Noah was appar-

ently aware of some such division (Gen. 7:2).

a. Clean and Unclean Animals as They Relate to Diet (11:1-23)

1 And Jehovah spake unto Moses and to Aaron, saying unto them, 2 Speak unto the children of Israel, saying, These are the living things which ye may eat among all the beasts that are on the earth. 3 Whatsoever parteth the hoof, and is clovenfooted, *and* cheweth the cud, among the beasts, that may ye eat. 4 Nevertheless these shall ye not eat of them that chew the cud, or of them that part the hoof: the camel, because he cheweth the cud but parteth not the hoof, he is unclean unto you. 5 And the coney, because he cheweth the cud but parteth not the hoof, he is unclean unto you. 6 And the hare, because she cheweth the cud but parteth not the hoof, she is unclean unto you. 7 And the swine, because he parteth the hoof, and is clovenfooted, but cheweth not the cud, he is unclean unto you. 8 Of their flesh ye shall not eat, and their carcasses ye shall not touch; they are unclean unto you.

9 These may ye eat of all that are in the waters: whatsoever hath fins and scales in the waters, in the seas, and in the rivers, that may ye eat. 10 And all that have not fins and scales in the seas, and in the rivers, of all that move in the waters, and of all the living creatures that are in the waters, they are an abomination unto you, 11 and they shall be an abomination unto you; ye shall not eat of their flesh, and their carcasses ye shall have in abomination. 12 Whatsoever hath no fins nor scales in the waters, that is an abomination unto you.

13 And these ye shall have in abomination among the birds; they shall not be eaten, they are an abomination: the eagle, and the gier-eagle, and the ospray, 14 and the kite, and the falcon after its kind, 15 every raven after its kind, 16 and the ostrich, and the night-hawk, and the sea-mew, and the hawk after its kind, 17 and the little owl, and the cormorant, and the great owl, 18 and the horned owl, and the pelican, and the vulture, 19 and the stork, the heron after its kind, and the hoopoe, and the bat.

20 All winged creeping things that go upon all fours are an abomination unto you. 21 Yet these may ye eat of all winged creeping things that go upon all fours, which have legs above their feet, wherewith to leap upon the earth; 22 even these of them ye may eat: the locust after its kind, and the bald locust after

its kind, and the cricket after its kind. 23 But all winged creeping things, which have four feet, are an abomination unto you.

The distinguishing marks of those animals considered proper for food were selected in a simple, practical manner which the common people could easily recognize. They fell into four classes: quadrupeds (vv. 2-8); water animals (vv. 9-12); birds (vv. 13-19); and insects (vv. 20-23).

Those accepted for food among the first group had two distinguishing marks. They must be ruminants and they must have completely divided hoofs. To illustrate, four specific animals are cited which are unclean because they do not meet both of these requirements: the camel, the coney or rock badger, the hare, and the hog. The fact that two of these, coney and hare, are not actually ruminants (i.e., do not chew the cud), although their jaws are in almost constant motion and so give that appearance, suggests that the classification of the animals is empirical, though not strictly scientific (see also Deut. 14:4).

Sea foods were limited to those fish which have both fins and scales.

Only unclean birds — most of them birds of prey and feeders upon carrion — are listed. The identification of some of these is very uncertain now, as a comparison of different translations of this section will indicate.

Among the insects, the Israelites were permitted to eat four classes of locusts distinguished by their long hind legs especially adapted for jumping.

b. Clean and Unclean Animals as They Relate to Physical Contact (11:24-43)

24 And by these ye shall become unclean: whosoever toucheth the carcass of them shall be unclean until the even; 25 and whosoever beareth *aught* of the carcass of them shall wash his clothes, and be unclean until the even. 26 Every beast which parteth the hoof, and is not clovenfooted, nor cheweth the cud, is unclean unto you: every one that toucheth them shall be unclean. 27 And whatsoever goeth upon its paws, among all beasts that go on all fours, they are unclean unto you: whoso toucheth their

carcass shall be unclean until the even. 28 And he that beareth the carcass of them shall wash his clothes, and be unclean until the even: they are unclean unto you.

29 And these are they which are unclean unto you among the creeping things that creep upon the earth: the weasel, and the mouse, and the great lizard after its kind, 30 and the gecko, and the land-crocodile, and the lizard, and the sand-lizard, and the chameleon. 31 These are they which are unclean to you among all that creep: whosoever doth touch them, when they are dead, shall be unclean until the even. 32 And upon whatsoever any of them, when they are dead, doth fall, it shall be unclean; whether it be any vessel of wood, or raiment, or skin, or sack, whatsoever vessel it be, wherewith any work is done, it must be put into water, and it shall be unclean until the even; then shall it be clean. 33 And every earthen vessel, whereinto any of them falleth, whatsoever is in it shall be unclean, and it ye shall break. 34 All food *therein* which may be eaten, that on which water cometh, shall be unclean; and all drink that may be drunk in every *such* vessel shall be unclean. 35 And everything whereupon *any part* of their carcass falleth shall be unclean; whether oven, or range for pots, it shall be broken in pieces: they are unclean, and shall be unclean unto you. 36 Nevertheless a fountain or a pit wherein is a gathering of water shall be clean: but that which toucheth their carcass shall be unclean. 37 And if *aught* of their carcass fall upon any sowing seed which is to be sown, it is clean. 38 But if water be put upon the seed, and *aught* of their carcass fall thereon, it is unclean unto you.

39 And if any beast, of which ye may eat, die; he that toucheth the carcass thereof shall be unclean until the even. 40 And he that eateth of the carcass of it shall wash his clothes, and be unclean until the even: he also that beareth the carcass of it shall wash his clothes, and be unclean until the even.

41 And every creeping thing that creepeth upon the earth is an abomination; it shall not be eaten. 42 Whatsoever goeth upon the belly, and whatsoever goeth upon all fours, or whatsoever hath many feet, even all creeping things that creep upon the earth, them ye shall not eat; for they are an abomination. 43 Ye shall not make yourselves abominable with any creeping thing that creepeth, neither shall ye make yourselves unclean with them, that ye should be defiled thereby.

Animals improper for food might be touched or handled without uncleanness so long as they were alive, but contact with the dead body of such an animal was considered unclean. To be unclean from such contact was, however, not considered morally wrong, unless there had been deliberate contempt for the law, for somebody must touch dead animals to remove them, etc. It did not, therefore, interrupt spiritual communion with God in prayer, but this physical contact did bring a temporary ceremonial unfitness for worship at the tabernacle and for mingling with one's neighbors (vv. 24-28).

Objects of clothing and cooking vessels were also considered unclean if the carcass of an unclean creature had contacted them. They must be ceremonially cleansed in water and not used until evening. In case the contaminated vessel or piece of equipment was of earthenware, it was to be broken and no longer used in preparing food (vv. 39-43).

c. Reasons for Distinguishing Clean from Unclean (11:44-47)

44 For I am Jehovah your God: sanctify yourselves therefore, and be ye holy; for I am holy: neither shall ye defile yourselves with any manner of creeping thing that moveth upon the earth. 45 For I am Jehovah that brought you up out of the land of Egypt, to be your God: ye shall therefore be holy, for I am holy.

46 This is the law of the beast, and of the bird, and of every living creature that moveth in the waters, and of every creature that creepeth upon the earth; 47 to make a distinction between the unclean and the clean, and between the living thing that may be eaten and the living thing that may not be eaten.

Wholesomeness as food was doubtless involved in the selection of clean animals. Sanitation was probably a consideration in regulations regarding handling of dead animals, etc. And there was the factor of separating Israel as a people; for to observe many of these rules would make it impossible for the Israelites to mingle freely and intimately with surrounding nations. Whether Israel understood these aspects or not, the fact that God made these requirements and insisted upon their observance was an almost constant reminder to the people that they were under divine authority.

Furthermore, by these regulations in temporal matters God was teaching Israel important truths regarding Himself and their relationship to Him. These rules were enacted because of the covenant which prevailed between Jehovah and His people by which Israel was set apart as particular servants of God (Exod. 19:26). As God's people (Exod. 22:31) the Israelites were to avoid all impurity in order that the holy God might tabernacle among them (v. 45; 15:31; 18:1-5; 20:22-26; 26:11, 12). In this teaching process ceremonial cleanness spoke of holiness (Ezek. 30:24; Lev. 15:31; Ezek. 22:26; Isa. 35:8; 52:1; Rev. 21:27); and ceremonial uncleanness spoke of sin which only God could remove (Lev. 16:16, 30; 5:3, 4; Job 14:4; Ps. 51:10-12; II Chron. 30:19; Isa. 4:4; Ezek. 36:25, 29; Zech. 3:4).

These matters are also an object lesson for us today. It is true that the Hebrew ceremonial laws distinguishing clean and unclean have been done away in Christ (Col. 2:16, 20-23); and to insist on applying them to ourselves brings no end of trouble and confusion. Nevertheless, the principle remains that true religion is concerned not only with those things which have a conspicuously spiritual nature — faith, doctrine, and worship — but with the whole of life. The Apostle Paul expressed this when he wrote: "whether therefore ye eat, or drink, or whatever ye do, do all to the glory of God" (I Cor. 10:31).

The dietary laws in Israel indicate God's concern for the bodies of His people, and would remind us that we cannot with impunity carelessly disregard or neglect physical laws. Our bodies are, after all, not our own. They are the temples of the Holy Spirit (I Cor. 6:19). They would also call our attention to the fact that while we are to carry on normal lives and mingle with our fellow men, we are to be separate from them in our attitudes and actions toward evil and toward temporal materialistic evaluations of this world (II Cor. 6:14-18; Matt. 6: 33).

These laws, aimed at teaching the Hebrew nation elements of purity and holiness, suggest to us that if we would approach God and would hope to worship Him in the beauty of holiness, we must be spiritually clean — we must be saved from sin and from the corruption of this world, holy within and righteous without (John 15:3; 13:10; I John 1:7; Eph. 5:25, 26; Heb. 10:2, 21, 22).

2. Distinguishing Clean and Unclean Persons, Garments and Dwellings (12:1—13:59)

a. Purification of a Woman after Childbirth (12:1-8)

1 And Jehovah spake unto Moses, saying, 2 Speak unto the children of Israel, saying, If a woman conceive seed, and bear a man-child, then she shall be unclean seven days; as in the days of the impurity of her sickness shall she be unclean. 3 And in the eighth day the flesh of his foreskin shall be circumcised. 4 And she shall continue in the blood of *her* purifying three and thirty days; she shall touch no hallowed thing, nor come into the sanctuary, until the days of her purifying be fulfilled. 5 But if she bear a maid-child, then she shall be unclean two weeks, as in her impurity; and she shall continue in the blood of *her* purifying threescore and six days.

6 And when the days of her purifying are fulfilled, for a son, or for a daughter, she shall bring a lamb a year old for a burnt-offering, and a young pigeon, or a turtle-dove, for a sin-offering, unto the door of the tent of meeting, unto the priest: 7 and he shall offer it before Jehovah, and make atonement for her; and she shall be cleansed from the fountain of her blood. This is the law for her that beareth, whether a male or a female. 8 And if her means suffice not for a lamb, then she shall take two turtle-doves, or two young pigeons; the one for a burnt-offering, and the other for a sin-offering: and the priest shall make atonement for her, and she shall be clean.

"Children are a heritage of Jehovah," the psalmist declared; and so it was that the birth of a child in Israel was a joyous event (Ps. 127, 128). The uncleanness attached in this chapter to childbirth and the necessary purification ritual to be entered into by the mother do not, then, imply that marriage and proper sexual relations therein are sinful. We should note, however, that the laws in Israel banned all sensuality and sexual

activity in connection with God's worship (Exod. 19:15; 20:26; Lev. 15:16-18). This was in marked contrast to the licentious religious practices associated with the fertility cults of the surrounding peoples.

The rites connected with childbirth do, nevertheless, indicate that the birth of a child was considered to be a solemn as well as a happy event. The regulations attached to the purification of a woman following childbirth served to impress upon the parents their moral and spiritual responsibility toward their newborn child, for he was by nature born with a corrupt nature, bent to evil, and in need of their parental teaching and guidance, and of God's salvation made available in His merciful provisions of atonement.

The regulations here indicate that after the birth of a son, the mother was to stay in seclusion a week, as was ordinarily the case "at the time of her menstruation" (v. 2, RSV; see 15:19-24). The baby boy was then to be circumcised. The mother was to remain at home for about another month (33 days). After that she was to go to the tabernacle with a burnt-offering and a sin-offering (see also 15:25-30). A beautiful and instructive commentary on the regulation here is found in connection with Mary of Nazareth and her Son born in Bethlehem (Luke 2:21-24).

No reason is given for requiring a longer period of seclusion for the mother in case she gave birth to a daughter.

Circumcision was to the Israelite more than a physical rite. Through this the son was formally brought into the household of God, made a partaker of the covenant benefits between Jehovah and His people (Rom. 2:28, 29). From Leviticus 26:41, it would appear that it was also looked upon as a symbol of the "circumcision of the heart" which is mentioned with greater significance in the New Testament (Col. 2:10, 11; Phil. 3:3; Rom. 4:11). John Wesley saw in this a symbol of heart cleansing in entire sanctification.

As is the case in connection with clean and unclean animals, so the demands of this chapter do not carry over to our times, but they should make it clear to us that God has deep concern in every aspect of marriage and of home life. None of us can, therefore, disregard the considerable teaching of His Word relative to the sacredness and the solemn obligations involved in these relationships.

b. Distinguishing Leprous Persons (13:1-46)

1 And Jehovah spake unto Moses and unto Aaron, saying, 2 When a man shall have in the skin of his flesh a rising, or a scab, or a bright spot, and it become in the skin of his flesh the plague of leprosy, then he shall be brought unto Aaron the priest, or unto one of his sons the priests: 3 and the priest shall look on the plague in the skin of the flesh: and if the hair in the plague be turned white, and the appearance of the plague be deeper than the skin of his flesh, it is the plague of leprosy; and the priest shall look on him, and pronounce him unclean. 4 And if the bright spot be white in the skin of his flesh, and the appearance thereof be not deeper than the skin, and the hair thereof be not turned white, then the priest shall shut up *him that hath* the plague seven days: 5 and the priest shall look on him the seventh day: and, behold, if in his eyes the plague be at a stay, and the plague be not spread in the skin, then the priest shall shut him up seven days more: 6 and the priest shall look on him again the seventh day; and, behold, if the plague be dim, and the plague be not spread in the skin, then the priest shall pronounce him clean: it is a scab: and he shall wash his clothes, and be clean. 7 But if the scab spread abroad in the skin, after that he hath showed himself to the priest for his cleansing, he shall show himself to the priest again: 8 and the priest shall look; and, behold, if the scab be spread in the skin, then the priest shall pronounce him unclean: it is leprosy.

9 When the plague of leprosy is in a man, then he shall be brought unto the priest; 10 and the priest shall look; and, behold, if there be a white rising in the skin, and it have turned the hair white, and there be quick raw flesh in the rising, 11 it is an old leprosy in the skin of his flesh, and the priest shall pronounce him unclean: he shall not shut him up; for he is unclean. 12 And if the leprosy break out abroad in the skin, and the leprosy cover all the skin of *him that hath* the plague from his head even to his feet, as far as appeareth to the priest; 13 then the priest shall look; and, behold, if the leprosy have covered all his flesh, he shall pronounce *him* clean *that hath* the plague: it is all turned white: he is clean.

14 But whensoever raw flesh appeareth in him, he shall be unclean. 15 And the priest shall look on the raw flesh, and pronounce him unclean: the raw flesh is unclean: it is leprosy. 16 Or if the raw flesh turn again, and be changed unto white, then he shall come unto the priest; 17 and the priest shall look on him; and, behold, if the plague be turned into white, then the priest shall pronounce *him* clean *that hath* the plague: he is clean.

18 And when the flesh hath in the skin thereof a boil, and it is healed, 19 and in the place of the boil there is a white rising, or a bright spot, reddish-white, then it shall be showed to the priest; 20 and the priest shall look; and, behold, if the appearance thereof be lower than the skin, and the hair thereof be turned white, then the priest shall pronounce him unclean: it is the plague of leprosy, it hath broken out in the boil. 21 But if the priest look on it, and, behold, there be no white hairs therein, and it be not lower than the skin, but be dim; then the priest shall shut him up seven days: 22 and if it spread abroad in the skin, then the priest shall pronounce him unclean: it is a plague. 23 But if the bright spot stay in its place, and be not spread, it is the scar of the boil; and the priest shall pronounce him clean.

24 Or when the flesh hath in the skin thereof a burning by fire, and the quick *flesh* of the burning become a bright spot, reddish-white, or white; 25 then the priest shall look upon it; and, behold, if the hair in the bright spot be turned white, and the appearance thereof be deeper than the skin; it is leprosy, it hath broken out in the burning: and the priest shall pronounce him unclean: it is the plague of leprosy. 26 But if the priest look on it, and, behold, there be no white hair in the bright spot, and it be no lower than the skin, but be dim; then the priest shall shut him up seven days: 27 and the priest shall look upon him the seventh day: if it spread abroad in the skin, then the priest shall pronounce him unclean: it is the plague of leprosy. 28 And if the bright spot stay in its place, and be not spread in the skin, but be dim; it is the rising of the burning, and the priest shall pronounce him clean: for it is the scar of the burning.

29 And when a man or woman hath a plague upon the head or upon the beard, 30 then the priest shall look on the plague; and, behold, if the appearance thereof be deeper than the skin, and there be in it yellow thin hair, then the priest shall pronounce him unclean: it

is a scall, it is leprosy of the head or of the beard. 31 And if the priest look on the plague of the scall, and, behold, the appearance thereof be not deeper than the skin, and there be no black hair in it, then the priest shall shut up *him that hath* the plague of the scall seven days: 32 and in the seventh day the priest shall look on the plague; and, behold, if the scall be not spread, and there be in it no yellow hair, and the appearance of the scall be not deeper than the skin, 33 then he shall be shaven, but the scall shall he not shave; and the priest shall shut up *him that hath* the scall seven days more: 34 and in the seventh day the priest shall look on the scall; and, behold, if the scall be not spread in the skin, and the appearance thereof be not deeper than the skin; then the priest shall pronounce him clean: and he shall wash his clothes, and be clean. 35 But if the scall spread abroad in the skin after his cleansing, 36 then the priest shall look on him; and, behold, if the scall be spread in the skin, the priest shall not seek for the yellow hair; he is unclean. 37 But if in his eyes the scall be at a stay, and black hair be grown up therein; the scall is healed, he is clean: and the priest shall pronounce him clean.

38 And when a man or a woman hath in the skin of the flesh bright spots, even white bright spots; 39 then the priest shall look; and, behold, if the bright spots in the skin of their flesh be of a dull white, it is a tetter, it hath broken out in the skin; he is clean.

40 And if a man's hair be fallen off his head, he is bald; *yet* is he clean. 41 And if his hair be fallen off from the front part of his head, he is forehead bald; *yet* is he clean. 42 But if there be in the bald head, or the bald forehead, a reddish-white plague; it is leprosy breaking out in his bald head, or his bald forehead. 43 Then the priest shall look upon him; and, behold, if the rising of the plague be reddish-white in his bald head, or in his bald forehead, as the appearance of leprosy in the skin of the flesh; 44 he is a leprous man, he is unclean: the priest shall surely pronounce him unclean; his plague is in his head.

45 And the leper in whom the plague is, his clothes shall be rent, and the hair of his head shall go loose, and he shall cover his upper lip, and shall cry, Unclean, unclean. 46 All the days wherein the plague is in him he shall be unclean; he is unclean: he shall dwell alone; without the camp shall his dwelling be.

The word translated **leprosy** here is a general term which includes various skin disorders whose prominent feature was "whiteness" such as we now see in leucoderma and psoriasis. No mention is made of symptoms connected with what we know now as anesthetic leprosy which affects the nerve trunks, particularly at the extremities which become increasingly numb and ultimately lose vitality. Care in detecting these chronic skin diseases, which might be transmitted to others, was important, so they could be discovered in the early stages and isolated, thereby preventing their spread.

Should suspicious skin eruptions appear — a swollen place or an eruption (RSV) or a bright spot — the affected person was to present himself to the priest for examination (vv. 1-8). If the priest was not sure of the diagnosis, the patient might be isolated outside the camp so that the priest might make further observations.

If a person had an open sore in a white swelling where the hair was also white, he was to present himself to the priest for diagnosis. The priest was to declare a person with all of these symptoms leprous and unclean. Further observation was considered pointless (vv. 9-17). Should, however, the skin of the patient appear white with no open sores, the priest would consider it a noncontagious case, and the patient could return to his tent.

A boil which had healed might be the source of leprosy. Should a white or reddish-white spot appear in a sunken place where a boil had been, and if the hair of the area turned white, the priest diagnosed this as leprosy (vv. 18-23). If some of these symptoms were, however, not present, the patient was held and isolated for further observation.

A burned place on the skin might become leprous (vv. 24-28), and should the symptoms appear here as in the case of a boil, it would be considered leprous.

If an itching disease attacked the skin of the head or beard, causing the hair to turn yellow, and if a scab or scale appeared lower than the normal skin surface, the patient was unclean (vv. 29-37). It is thought that this may have been what we now know as ringworm.

Several symptoms are listed (vv. 38-

44) which do not necessarily indicate a patient should be declared unclean.

If a person was found to be really leprous he was to go into isolation outside the camp of Israel (vv. 45, 46). He must appear as a mourner (10:6), mourning actually his own sure death. As one of the signs of mourning he was to cover **his upper lip.** That is, he was to pull his beard up over his head to hide his face in shame and embarrassment (cf. Ezek. 24:17, 22; Mic. 3:7).

Leprosy with its small, obscure beginnings; its rapid spread; its contagion; its unspeakable loathsomeness; and its ultimate outcome in death provides a realistic picture of sin's tragic work in the lives of men.

c. Distinguishing Leprous Garments (13:47-59)

47 The garment also that the plague of leprosy is in, whether it be a woollen garment, or a linen garment; 48 whether it be in warp, or woof; of linen, or of woollen; whether in a skin, or in anything made of skin; 49 if the plague be greenish or reddish in the garment, or in the skin, or in the warp, or in the woof, or in anything of skin; it is the plague of leprosy, and shall be showed unto the priest. 50 And the priest shall look upon the plague, and shut up *that which hath* the plague seven days: 51 and he shall look on the plague on the seventh day: if the plague be spread in the garment, either in the warp, or in the woof, or in the skin, whatever service skin is used for; the plague is a fretting leprosy; it is unclean. 52 And he shall burn the garment, whether the warp or the woof, in woollen or in linen, or anything of skin, wherein the plague is: for it is a fretting leprosy; it shall be burnt in the fire.

53 And if the priest shall look, and, behold, the plague be not spread in the garment, either in the warp, or in the woof, or in anything of skin; 54 then the priest shall command that they wash the thing wherein the plague is, and he shall shut it up seven days more: 55 and the priest shall look, after that the plague is washed; and, behold, if the plague have not changed its color, and the plague be not spread, it is unclean; thou shalt burn it in the fire: it is a fret, whether the bareness be within or without. 56 And if the priest look, and, behold, the plague be dim after the washing thereof, then he shall rend it out of the garment, or out of the skin, or out of

the warp, or out of the woof: 57 and if it appear still in the garment, either in the warp, or in the woof, or in anything of skin, it is breaking out: thou shalt burn that wherein the plague is with fire. 58 And the garment, either the warp, or the woof, or whatsoever thing of skin it be, which thou shalt wash, if the plague be departed from them, then it shall be washed the second time, and shall be clean.

59 This is the law of the plague of leprosy in a garment of woollen or linen, either in the warp, or the woof, or anything of skin, to pronounce it clean, or to pronounce it unclean.

The garment also that the plague of leprosy is in refers to the garment affected by mold or mildew; **whether warp, or woof** implies that the rule which follows applies to both woven and knitted materials. **Whether in a skin,** i.e., in leather, **or anything made of skin** (vv. 47, 48). When an Israelite found greenish or reddish patches of mold or mildew in any of his garments he was to bring the affected piece to the priest who, after examining it, was to isolate it for a week. If at the end of the week the mold or mildew had spread it was considered to be a **fretting leprosy.** "To fret" actually means "to gnaw" or to make holes in. It described not simply a superficial affection, but one which was penetrating and persistent. Such a rotting or corroding condition was considered malignant. The garment so affected was considered unclean and must be destroyed by burning it in fire (vv. 49-52).

If, however, the mildew or mold had not spread during the week, the garment was to be washed and isolated for another seven days. If the washing did not change the appearance of the affected portion, the garment was considered unclean and must be burned (vv. 53-55). Should the washing, on the other hand, make the spot less noticeable, the affected portion was to be torn out, but the garment was not to be destroyed (v. 56). The destruction of all such garments might have worked a real hardship upon the poor in Israel (cf. Deut. 24:10-13). If, however, the affection **appeared still** or again (RSV), i.e., reappeared later in the garment from which the patch had been torn, the garment must be destroyed without further examination (v. 57). Those garments where the patch of mildew or mold disappeared in the test wash were to be washed again and then were considered ceremonially clean, suitable for continued use (vv. 58, 59).

This concern for garments in Israel reminds us that in both Testaments garments are frequently used as a symbol of one's manner of life (Isa. 61:10; 64:6; Zech. 3:4; Jude 23; Rev. 3:4, 18; 7:14; 16:15). The care taken by the Israelites to avoid ceremonial uncleanness by wearing questionable garments teaches us as Christians the importance of being clothed with the garments of righteousness: of having a manner of life that is thoroughly upright in the sight of God and men (Eph. 2:2, 3; 4: 20-24; Phil. 1:27; 3:20; Col. 3:7-10; I Tim. 4:12; Tit. 3:3-5; Heb. 13:5-7; Jas. 1:27; I Pet. 1:15-18; 2:12; 3:1-16; II Pet. 3:11).

It was the priest, not the next door neighbor, nor even the nearest relative, who was to determine whether or not the garment was unclean. And it was the priest who prescribed the process for cleansing that which he had declared unclean. Similarly, as we walk through life we are to keep ourselves unspotted, not through following mere human judgment. Not by comparing ourselves with others. To do this will bring us into confusion (II Cor. 10:12). We must determine our course of living before God and among men by going to our Priest, Jesus Christ, who speaks to us through His Word, the Bible, and through the Holy Spirit, whom He has sent to lead us into all truth (John 16:13, 14).

The burning of the infected garment suggests judgment upon evil, and reminds us that there can be no trifling with sin. If, in the light of God's Word and under the dealings of the Holy Spirit, we find anything in our lives which is out of harmony with the spirit and teaching of Jesus Christ, there is to be no temporizing, no compromising of the issue. There is but one thing to do: give up that attitude, that habit. For in every facet of life we are to be conformed to His image (Rom. 8:29, 30).

d. Cleansing and Restoration of the Leper (14:1-32)

1 And Jehovah spake unto Moses, saying, 2 This shall be the law of the leper in the day of his cleansing: he shall be brought unto the priest: 3 and the priest shall go forth out of the camp; and the priest shall look; and, behold, if the plague of leprosy be healed in the leper, 4 then shall the priest command to take for him that is to be cleansed two living clean birds, and cedar-wood, and scarlet, and hyssop: 5 and the priest shall command to kill one of the birds in an earthen vessel over running water. 6 As for the living bird, he shall take it, and the cedar-wood, and the scarlet, and the hyssop, and shall dip them and the living bird in the blood of the bird that was killed over the running water: 7 and he shall sprinkle upon him that is to be cleansed from the leprosy seven times, and shall pronounce him clean, and shall let go the living bird into the open field. 8 And he that is to be cleansed shall wash his clothes, and shave off all his hair, and bathe himself in water; and he shall be clean: and after that he shall come into the camp, but shall dwell outside his tent seven days. 9 And it shall be on the seventh day, that he shall shave all his hair off his head and his beard and his eyebrows, even all his hair he shall shave off: and he shall wash his clothes, and he shall bathe his flesh in water, and he shall be clean.

10 And on the eighth day he shall take two he-lambs without blemish, and one ewe-lamb a year old without blemish, and three tenth parts *of an ephah* of fine flour for a meal-offering, mingled with oil, and one log of oil. 11 And the priest that cleanseth him shall set the man that is to be cleansed, and those things, before Jehovah, at the door of the tent of meeting. 12 And the priest shall take one of the he-lambs, and offer him for a trespass-offering, and the log of oil, and wave them for a wave-offering before Jehovah: 13 and he shall kill the he-lamb in the place where they kill the sin-offering and the burnt-offering, in the place of the sanctuary: for as the sin-offering is the priest's, so is the trespass-offering: it is most holy. 14 And the priest shall take of the blood of the trespass-offering, and the priest shall put it upon the tip of the right ear of him that is to be cleansed, and upon the thumb of his right hand, and upon the great toe of his right foot. 15 And the priest shall take of the log of oil, and pour it into the palm of his own left hand; 16 and the priest shall dip his right finger in the oil that is in his left hand, and shall sprinkle of the oil with his finger seven times before Jehovah. 17 And of the rest of the oil that is in his hand shall the priest put upon the

tip of the right ear of him that is to be cleansed, and upon the thumb of his right hand, and upon the great toe of his right foot, upon the blood of the trespass-offering: 18 and the rest of the oil that is in the priest's hand he shall put upon the head of him that is to be cleansed: and the priest shall make atonement for him before Jehovah. 19 And the priest shall offer the sin-offering, and make atonement for him that is to be cleansed because of his uncleanness: and afterward he shall kill the burnt-offering; 20 and the priest shall offer the burnt-offering and the meal-offering upon the altar: and the priest shall make atonement for him, and he shall be clean.

21 And if he be poor, and cannot get so much, then he shall take one he-lamb for a trespass-offering to be waved, to make atonement for him, and one tenth part *of an ephah* of fine flour mingled with oil for a meal-offering, and a log of oil; 22 and two turtle-doves, or two young pigeons, such as he is able to get; and the one shall be a sin-offering, and the other a burnt-offering. 23 And on the eighth day he shall bring them for his cleansing unto the priest, unto the door of the tent of meeting, before Jehovah: 24 and the priest shall take the lamb of the trespass-offering, and the log of oil, and the priest shall wave them for a wave-offering before Jehovah. 25 And he shall kill the lamb of the trespass-offering; and the priest shall take of the blood of the trespass-offering, and put it upon the tip of the right ear of him that is to be cleansed, and upon the thumb of his right hand, and upon the great toe of his right foot. 26 And the priest shall pour of the oil into the palm of his own left hand; 27 and the priest shall sprinkle with his right finger some of the oil that is in his left hand seven times before Jehovah: 28 and the priest shall put of the oil that is in his hand upon the tip of the right ear of him that is to be cleansed, and upon the thumb of his right hand, and upon the great toe of his right foot, upon the place of the blood of the trespass-offering: 29 and the rest of the oil that is in the priest's hand he shall put upon the head of him that is to be cleansed, to make atonement for him before Jehovah. 30 And he shall offer one of the turtle-doves, or of the young pigeons, such as he is able to get, 31 even such as he is able to get, the one for a sin-offering, and the other for a burnt-offering, with the meal-offering:

and the priest shall make atonement for him that is to be cleansed before Jehovah. 32 This is the law of him in whom is the plague of leprosy, who is not able to get *that which pertaineth* to his cleansing.

Whenever a leper felt himself cured, he could not just come back into camp and take his place there again. A priest was to go outside the camp where the leper was isolated to determine if indeed the disease were cured (vv. 1-3). If the leper was found to be well again, the priest was to lead him in a ritual to provide for his ceremonial cleansing and his restoration to society and the sanctuary.

Leprosy being a type of sin and the priest a foreshadowing of Christ, and the leper needing the priest's mediation for his restoration has very inspiring suggestions for us.

> The whole work of reinstating the outcast in his lost privileges begins in this act of the priest going forth to the place of the leper's banishment. The coming forth of Christ Jesus to us, to where we were in our banishment, that was the initial incident in our restoration to God. No one but the priest could come nigh a leper without contracting defilement; no one but the sacred person of our divine Priest could approach us "in our sins" and also bring the unclean life back to purity and privilege.[2]

The objects to be secured for the first part of the ritual were: **two living clean** (11:13-19) **birds, some cedar-wood** (perhaps juniper) and some spun (LXX) **scarlet** or scarlet string (Berkeley), some branches of a leafy plant called **hyssop** (Exod. 12:22), and an earthen vessel containing running or living water, i.e., pure water from a flowing stream or spring. The scarlet string was probably used to tie the birds to the bundles of cedar-wood and hyssop. The priest was to kill one of the birds over the vessel so that the blood would go into the water (v. 5). The remaining objects were each to be dipped in the blood of the slain bird which had mingled with the fresh, pure water; and the leper was sprinkled seven times — seven indicating completeness — with the blood and water mixture. Thereupon the priest declared the person clean and released the living bird.

---

2 W. H. Jellis, "Leviticus," *Preacher's Commentary*, p. 182.

In the bird flying away, the leper could joyfully visualize his own uncleanness being borne away (vv. 6, 7), and we can see that as the slain bird sacrificed speaks to us of our Savior who was offered up for trespasses, so the living bird speaks to us of our resurrected Lord, raised for our justification (Rom. 4:25).

Isolated outside the camp there could be no sacrifice before the altar, but the whole ceremony stressed purification and symbolized the restoration to life of one who had been considered as dead to his people and to the service of God in the tabernacle. Hyssop (Exod. 12:22; Ps. 51:7) was on different occasions used as indicative of cleansing. Cedar and scarlet also had a prominent place in suggesting purification (Num. 19). Furthermore, the type of wood here implied [cedar or juniper] was almost incorruptible and symbolized the impartation of new life free from corruption. Scarlet also spoke of life and health.

After the priest had accomplished his work, the leper washed his clothes, shaved off all of his hair, and bathed. In this way the outward marks of his past isolated life were removed, as well as all probability of contagion of others when he would come into camp. He was now permitted to return to the society of his brethren in Israel.

The fact that the suppliant participated first in the cleansing ritual administered by the priest before cleansing himself reminds us that we are not able by any righteous efforts of our own to save and free ourselves from the leprosy of sin. But having been saved by the blood of Christ, we are definitely responsible to cleanse our outward lives of all evil ways and defilement. We are to see to it that our conduct is worthy of Him who has delivered us, worthy of His Church which we are to represent among men, and such as will have no tendency to contaminate or lead astray other members of Christ's Church.

The leper was not yet, however, permitted to return to the worship at the tabernacle nor to the intimacies of the family circle. For while he was delivered from the power of death, he was not yet clean from ceremonial defilement of the dead.

There is yet persisting such a connection of his old self with his old leprous self as precludes him from yet entering the more immediate presence of God. The reality of this analogy will appear to any one who compares the rites which now follow (vss. 10-20) with those appointed for the Nazarite, when defiled by the dead (Num. 4:9-12).[3]

For another week he must remain outside his tent home and from the place of the sanctuary. This may have been a precautionary measure to provide additional time for any reappearance of the skin eruption. It might also have served as a spiritual discipline to remind the man, now restored to his people, how reverently and cautiously, after his defilement, he must venture into the presence of God and the full responsibilities of life.

On the seventh day after his cleansing outside the camp, the leper was again to wash his clothes, shave and bathe. Then on the eighth day he was to begin his new life of complete restoration and freedom by taking to the priest before the Lord at the tabernacle **two he-lambs without blemish, and one ewe-lamb without blemish, and three tenth parts of an ephah of fine flour** [an ephah was a measure equal to three-eighths to two-thirds of a bushel] and **one log** of olive oil [a log was a measure equal to a little more than half a pint].

The priest would meet him there **at the door of the tent of meeting**, i.e., before the brazen altar in the court of the tabernacle (vv. 9-11; cf. 1:3). One of the he-lambs was offered there as a trespass-offering (5:14—6:7; 7:1-10). **Wave-offering** applies to the portions of the sacrifice to become the possession of the priest and denotes a special ceremony consisting of holding the right shoulder of the victim [it would appear here that the whole animal with the oil was waved] horizontally and moving it forward toward the altar and backward away from the altar, signifying that the portion was the Lord's but was given back to the priest by Him (v. 12).

The two other animals were offered: the ewe-lamb as a sin-offering (4:1—5:13; 6:24-30), and the other as a burnt-offering (1:1-17; 6:8-13). Each of these sacri-

3 S. H. Kellogg, "Leviticus," *An Exposition of the Bible*, I, 325.

fices, as was the custom, was accompanied with a meal-offering (2:1-16; 6:14-23), there being three portions of the white flour provided (v. 10) from the beginning. The leper was anointed with the blood of the trespass-offering and then with the oil (vv. 13-20). If the leper were poor, he might substitute two pigeons or two doves for lambs for the sin-offering and burnt-offering (vv. 21-32; cf. 4:27-35; 5:7-10). By these offerings the cured leper was restored to full rights and privileges of a living member of the people of the living God.

The special prominence given to the trespass-offering in this ceremony may be accounted for in that the trespass-offering represented reparation and satisfaction for loss of service. The leper who had been excluded from the camp had not been able to fulfill his obligations to God and his fellow men in service and worship. This sacrifice made amends for this lack.

The similarity of the ceremony here described with that of the consecration of the priest (Lev. 8) suggests that the leper, who had been barred from association with his fellow Israelites and from the opportunities of worship at the synagogue, is now restored or consecrated and cleansed so that he may again participate in the service of his covenant God and enjoy again the fellowship with God's happy people.

> Although the leper is constantly described as "unclean" and not as a sinner, despite the fact that the "stroke" of leprosy may, as in the case of Miriam, be the punishment for grievous sin, it seems proper to see in the fact that leprosy is dealt with so elaborately, an indication that this particularly loathsome and intractable disease is to be regarded as a type of that indwelling sin in which all the afflictions and ills of mankind have their cause and origin. If death is the curse pronounced by God upon sin and contact with death is defiling, then disease which undermines health and is a stepping-stone to death carries with it a certain defilement whether it be infectous in the medical sense or not.[4]

In restoring the leper to his place among God's people, the priest first applied the blood of the lamb, and then on top of the blood applied the anointing oil. This suggests to us that in providing

for our deliverance from the leprosy of sin, Christ's blood is applied to our hearts in forgiveness and regeneration, and subsequently the Holy Spirit, symbolized by the oil, comes in His cleansing, empowering work, sanctifying us wholly. Jesus called attention to the fact that the world could not receive the infilling of the Spirit. He comes to cleanse and fill only those who have entered into covenant with God through the blood of Christ (John 14:15-17; cf. Acts 2:38).

e. Distinguishing Clean and Unclean Dwellings (14:33-57)

33 And Jehovah spake unto Moses and unto Aaron, saying, 34 When ye are come into the land of Canaan, which I give to you for a possession, and I put the plague of leprosy in a house of the land of your possession; 35 then he that owneth the house shall come and tell the priest, saying, There seemeth to me to be as it were a plague in the house. 36 And the priest shall command that they empty the house, before the priest goeth in to see the plague, that all that is in the house be not made unclean: and afterward the priest shall go in to see the house: 37 and he shall look on the plague; and, behold, if the plague be in the walls of the house with hollow streaks, greenish or reddish, and the appearance thereof be lower than the wall; 38 then the priest shall go out of the house to the door of the house, and shut up the house seven days. 39 And the priest shall come again the seventh day, and shall look; and, behold, if the plague be spread in the walls of the house; 40 then the priest shall command that they take out the stones in which the plague is, and cast them into an unclean place without the city: 41 and he shall cause the house to be scraped within round about, and they shall pour out the mortar, that they scrape off, without the city into an unclean place: 42 and they shall take other stones, and put them in the place of those stones; and he shall take other mortar, and shall plaster the house.

43 And if the plague come again, and break out in the house, after that he hath taken out the stones, and after he hath scraped the house, and after it is plastered; 44 then the priest shall come in and look; and, behold, if the plague be spread in the house, it is a fretting leprosy in the house: it is unclean. 45 And he shall break down the house, the stones of it, and the timber thereof, and all the

---

[4] O. T. Allis, "Leviticus," *The New Bible Commentary*, p. 147.

mortar of the house; and he shall carry them forth out of the city into an unclean place. 46 Moreover he that goeth into the house all the while that it is shut up shall be unclean until the even. 47 And he that lieth in the house shall wash his clothes; and he that eateth in the house shall wash his clothes.

48 And if the priest shall come in, and look, and, behold, the plague hath not spread in the house, after the house was plastered; then the priest shall pronounce the house clean, because the plague is healed. 49 And he shall take to cleanse the house two birds, and cedar-wood, and scarlet, and hyssop: 50 and he shall kill one of the birds in an earthen vessel over running water: 51 and he shall take the cedar-wood, and the hyssop, and the scarlet, and the living bird, and dip them in the blood of the slain bird, and in the running water, and sprinkle the house seven times: 52 and he shall cleanse the house with the blood of the bird, and with the running water, and with the living bird, and with the cedar-wood, and with the hyssop, and with the scarlet: 53 but he shall let go the living bird out of the city into the open field: so shall he make atonement for the house; and it shall be clean.

54 This is the law for all manner of plague of leprosy, and for a scall, 55 and for the leprosy of a garment, and for a house, 56 and for a rising, and for a scab, and for a bright spot; 57 to teach when it is unclean, and when it is clean: this is the law of leprosy.

Israel was at this time living in tents, but they were here given instructions to guide them in the future when they should arrive in Palestine and live in stone houses. **The plague of leprosy in a house** probably refers to some kind of mold or rot. The fact that the Lord speaks of putting this into the house does not necessarily imply that every house where such a condition was found had been cursed of God because of some sin of the builder or of the occupants; for the Bible frequently passes over secondary causes and agencies.

The method of determining whether or not a house was unclean followed the same principles as those for distinguishing clean and unclean garments (13:47-59). The ritual prescribed for cleansing the house is the same as the initial ceremony followed in cleansing the healed leper (vv. 1-7).

This religious consideration of a situation which would appear to us today to be purely secular, illustrates, as do the social aspects of the peace-offering (3:1-17; 7:11-38), that religion affected all phases of Israel's life. And it would teach us that holiness can often be expressed through material things. Our religion should influence the appearance of our homes. They should be free from all that defiles or corrodes the moral and spiritual lives of our families. They should not only be free from all that has the appearance of evil, but they should be maintained in a manner positively conducive to godly living and in a manner which speaks of our faith to all who enter.

f. Cleansing from Sexual Discharges (15:1-33)

1 And Jehovah spake unto Moses and to Aaron, saying, 2 Speak unto the children of Israel, and say unto them, When any man hath an issue out of his flesh, because of his issue he is unclean. 3 And this shall be his uncleanness in his issue: whether his flesh run with his issue, or his flesh be stopped from his issue, it is his uncleanness. 4 Every bed whereon he that hath the issue lieth shall be unclean; and everything whereon he sitteth shall be unclean. 5 And whosoever toucheth his bed shall wash his clothes, and bathe himself in water, and be unclean until the even. 6 And he that sitteth on anything whereon he that hath the issue sat shall wash his clothes, and bathe himself in water, and be unclean until the even. 7 And he that toucheth the flesh of him that hath the issue shall wash his clothes, and bathe himself in water, and be unclean until the even. 8 And if he that hath the issue spit upon him that is clean, then he shall wash his clothes, and bathe himself in water, and be unclean until the even. 9 And what saddle soever he that hath the issue rideth upon shall be unclean. 10 And whosoever toucheth anything that was under him shall be unclean until the even: and he that beareth those things shall wash his clothes, and bathe himself in water, and be unclean until the even. 11 And whomsoever he that hath the issue toucheth, without having rinsed his hands in water, he shall wash his clothes, and bathe himself in water, and be unclean until the even. 12 And the earthen vessel, which he that hath the issue toucheth, shall be broken;

and every vessel of wood shall be rinsed in water.

13 And when he that hath an issue is cleansed of his issue, then he shall number to himself seven days for his cleansing, and wash his clothes; and he shall bathe his flesh in running water, and shall be clean. 14 And on the eighth day he shall take to him two turtle-doves, or two young pigeons, and come before Jehovah unto the door of the tent of meeting, and give them unto the priest: 15 and the priest shall offer them, the one for a sin-offering, and the other for a burnt-offering, and the priest shall make atonement for him before Jehovah for his issue.

16 And if any man's seed of copulation go out from him, then he shall bathe all his flesh in water, and be unclean until the even. 17 And every garment, and every skin, whereon is the seed of copulation, shall be washed with water, and be unclean until the even. 18 The woman also with whom a man shall lie with seed of copulation, they shall both bathe themselves in water, and be unclean until the even.

19 And if a woman have an issue, *and* her issue in her flesh be blood, she shall be in her impurity seven days: and whosoever toucheth her shall be unclean until the even. 20 And everything that she lieth upon in her impurity shall be unclean: everything also that she sitteth upon shall be unclean. 21 And whosoever toucheth her bed shall wash his clothes, and bathe himself in water, and be unclean until the even. 22 And whosoever toucheth anything that she sitteth upon shall wash his clothes, and bathe himself in water, and be unclean until the even. 23 And if it be on the bed, or on anything whereon she sitteth, when he toucheth it, he shall be unclean until the even. 24 And if any man lie with her, and her impurity be upon him, he shall be unclean seven days; and every bed whereon he lieth shall be unclean.

25 And if a woman have an issue of her blood many days not in the time of her impurity, or if she have an issue beyond the time of her impurity; all the days of the issue of her uncleanness she shall be as in the days of her impurity: she is unclean. 26 Every bed whereon she lieth all the days of her issue shall be unto her as the bed of her impurity: and everything whereon she sitteth shall be unclean, as the uncleanness of her impurity. 27 And whosoever toucheth those things shall be unclean, and shall wash his clothes, and bathe himself in water, and be unclean until the even. 28 But if she be cleansed of her issue, then she shall

number to herself seven days, and after that she shall be clean. 29 And on the eighth day she shall take unto her two turtle-doves, or two young pigeons, and bring them unto the priest, to the door of the tent of meeting. 30 And the priest shall offer the one for a sin-offering, and the other for a burnt-offering; and the priest shall make atonement for her before Jehovah for the issue of her uncleanness.

31 Thus shall ye separate the children of Israel from their uncleanness, that they die not in their uncleanness, when they defile my tabernacle that is in the midst of them.

32 This is the law of him that hath an issue, and of him whose seed of copulation goeth from him, so that he is unclean thereby; 33 and of her that is sick with her impurity, and of him that hath an issue, of the man, and of the woman, and of him that lieth with her that is unclean.

This chapter deals with the cleansing from ceremonial uncleanness connected with sexual emissions, both abnormal and normal, of both men and women. It is helpful to consider this chapter along with chapter 12 which deals with the ceremonial uncleanness attached to childbirth.

First is discussed the ritual involved in cleansing a man from ceremonal uncleanness resulting from an abnormal **issue of his flesh,** "running of the reins," KJV margin; "discharge," ASV; "running discharge," Amplified Old Testament (hereafter AOT).

This issue apparently refers to a mild form of gonorrhea (v. 3, LXX); however, the more virulent form of the disease known today did not appear until the fifteenth century A.D. The man thus afflicted was considered ceremonially unclean (v. 2), and while not isolated outside the camp, he was, like all others who were unclean, not permitted — under penalty of death — to attend the religious gatherings at the tabernacle and was not to make physical contact with other people. In fact, whatever he touched, whether persons or things, became ceremonially contaminated (vv. 4-12).

This uncleanness which made life so difficult for himself and others prevailed as long as the disease persisted. If, however, he should become cured from the affliction, he could be ceremonially cleansed and restored to a normal life by ceremonial bathing in water from a spring or running stream, by washing his clothes, and offering two turtle doves or two pigeons for a sin-offering (4:1—5:13; 6:24-30) and a burnt-offering (vv. 13-15; 1:1-17; 6:8-13; Ezek. 36:25).

The second type of uncleanness dealt with in this chapter concerned any man who should have **seed of copulation go out from him** (i.e., have a normal emission of semen other than in the sex act). Such a man would be ceremonially **unclean until the even.** Then in order to be acceptable to take his place again in society he was to bathe privately and wash the items which he had contacted during his uncleanness. No public offerings were required.

A third form of uncleanness considered here had to do with a woman during her normal menstrual discharge. She was considered unclean for seven days. Her cleansing was obtained at the end of that period by bathing and by the washing of those items contacted during her uncleanness. No public offerings were required.

A fourth form of uncleanness concerned a woman suffering a discharge other than that of the menstrual period (cf. Matt. 9:20-22). She was considered unclean for the length of the time such a discharge persisted (cf. Ezek. 36:17). To become ceremonially clean again after she was cured, she must provide two pigeons or turtle doves to the priest for a sin-offering (4:1—5:13; 6:24-30) and a burnt-offering (1:1-17; 6:8-13).

In the strict rules outlined in this chapter there were evident hygienic and health benefits for individuals and for the nation as a whole. They banned self-destroying indulgences, established habits of cleanliness, and arrested contamination of loathsome disease.

But there was more to these rules than this. While normal sex life in Israelite homes was encouraged, the rules of this chapter put wholesome restraints upon all people and set forth God's demand for purity. God knew human weakness, and to help His people to live the pure life He made transgression troublesome, shameful, and expensive.

Furthermore, these rules set Israel apart

from the pagan people about them. For their neighbors not only lived quite without sexual restraints, but many of their religious rites actually involved licentious practices which encouraged immorality of the basest order.

The uncleanness of this chapter, a type of sinfulness, would teach us that sinfulness is contagious, that evil persons tend to contaminate anything or anybody they touch.

The uncleanness spoken of in this chapter was a secret thing which might be known only to the person affected. This suggests that men may be sinful without others knowing of it. "There may be a very correct exterior life, and yet a cherishing of pride, and lust, and unbelief, and a secret painting of the walls with imagery, as much unfitting us for society and the pure and good as any open and outbroken wickedness."[5] Cleansing is needed for these secret sins as surely as for open sins.

It would also show us that disciplined sex activity in marriage is proper and good, but that unrestrained sex can be disastrous. Nathaniel Micklem comments thus:

> There have been those who have sought to live as if the sexual had no place in their lives. This leads to disaster. Not less disastrous is a purely materialistic or purely physical notion of sex. Man is neither an angel nor a beast, but a person, compact of body and soul in indissoluble union while life lasts . . . . A guiding principle for Christians is that the sexual nature of man must be frankly recognized by him and accepted, and must also be kept in due place by reverence for his spiritual nature."[6]

There is much in the New Testament which speaks to the proper Christian attitude toward sex. We read: "Let marriage be held in honor among all, and let the bed be undefiled: for fornicators and adulterers God will judge" (Heb. 13:4). "This is the will of God, even your sanctification, that ye abstain from fornication" (I Thess. 4:3). The word translated here as "fornication" refers to all forms of sex expression contrary to God's law. To abide by this instruction immediately separates us from a vast num-

5 J. A. Seiss, "Leviticus," *Biblical Illustrator*, p. 192.
6 Nathaniel Micklem, *The Interpreter's Bible*, II, 75.

ber about us. For we live in a day of frightful moral laxity.

As Christians we are to live transformed lives by the power of Christ through His Holy Spirit. We are not given any excuse for falling into sexual sin. The Apostle Paul writes of this forcibly in his Epistle to the Thessalonians. He says:

> God's plan is to make you holy, and that entails first of all a clean cut with sexual immorality. Every one of you should learn to control his body, keeping it pure and treating it with respect, and never regarding it as an instrument for self-gratification, as do pagans with no knowledge of God. You cannot break this rule without in some way cheating your fellow men. And you must remember that God will punish all who do offend in this matter, and we have warned you how we have seen this work out in our experience of life. The calling of God is not to impurity but to the most thorough purity, and anyone who makes light of the matter is not making light of man's ruling but of God's command. It is not for nothing that the Spirit God gives us is called the Holy Spirit (I Thess. 4:3-8, Phillips).

The gospel not only teaches us that God demands purity in deed, but that He also demands purity of thought and desire (Matt. 5:27-32).

The ceremonially contaminating emanations from the human body which made attendance impossible at the tabernacle where God met His people, remind us of the distressing vileness which flows out of the unregenerated heart which keeps us away from God. The Apostle Paul spoke of this when he wrote, "I know that in me, that is, in my flesh, dwelleth no good thing" (Rom. 7:18; cf. Matt. 12:34, 35; Gal. 5:19-21). Such inherent spiritual uncleanness naturally drives us away from the holy God and involves us in acts of disobedience to His law. Such uncleanness makes it impossible for us to approach God and to live in His favor. For God sees not only our sins of action but also the defilement of our inner being. But He has in His love come to our side. He has in Christ provided for the forgiveness of our transgressions and our regeneration (I Cor. 15:3; John 1:12, 13). He has also provided in Christ for the cleansing away of the inherent sin principle (Acts 15:9; John 17:14-19).

So it is that in Christ we may not only be saved from our sins, but we may be sanctified, cleansed from our sin (cf. I John 1:7).

D. CEREMONY FOR THE ANNUAL DAY OF ATONEMENT (16:1-34)

The Lord instructed Moses regarding the Day of Atonement, which was to become an annual occasion when reparations were to be made and forgiveness granted for all the sins of all Israelites — from the high priest to the most obscure child (vv. 16, 21, 30, 33; Heb. 10:1, 2; I John 1:7-9). It was to be the climactic event in Jewish expiatory ceremonials. In the events of this day all of the lesser acts of atonement culminated. While the holiness of God and the sinfulness of sin are set forth, special stress is laid here upon the completeness of the pardon offered to the sinner and to his restoration to divine favor. This was to be a day in which Israel was to give its most solemn expression of repentance, faith, and worship (cf. 23:26-32; 25:9; Num. 29:7-11; Ezek. 45:18-20).

This, the most important of all the holy ordinances with which the book of Leviticus deals, has been referred to as the "Good Friday of the Old Testament." And this chapter of Leviticus may be said to be to the complete system of Mosaic types what Isaiah 53 is to all of that prophet's Messianic proclamations. This chapter, in giving us the instructions regarding the Day of Atonement, does, indeed, set forth most clearly Christ's atoning work. This passage also supplied the New Testament writer of the epistle to the Hebrew Christians with his most striking and most significant typology.

This was a day in which Israelites, characteristically arrogant and self-willed (cf. Deut. 8:2, 3, 16), were to humble themselves before the Lord (vv. 29, 31; 23:27, 32; Num. 29:7). As an outward indication of their inward sorrow and penitence, the people were to spend the day in fasting. It came, in fact, to be referred to as "the fast" (cf. Acts 27:9). In this respect the Day of Atonement contrasts with the annual feasts, especially the Feast of Tabernacles (23:40; cf. Deut. 12:7, 12), which were occasions of rejoicing and festivity.

1. The Preparation of the High Priest (16:1-10)

1 And Jehovah spake unto Moses, after the death of the two sons of Aaron, when they drew near before Jehovah, and died; 2 and Jehovah said unto Moses, Speak unto Aaron thy brother, that he come not at all times into the holy place within the veil, before the mercy-seat which is upon the ark; that he die not: for I will appear in the cloud upon the mercy-seat. 3 Herewith shall Aaron come into the holy place: with a young bullock for a sin-offering, and a ram for a burnt-offering. 4 He shall put on the holy linen coat, and he shall have the linen breeches upon his flesh, and shall be girded with the linen girdle, and with the linen mitre shall he be attired: they are the holy garments; and he shall bathe his flesh in water, and put them on. 5 And he shall take of the congregation of the children of Israel two he-goats for a sin-offering, and one ram for a burnt-offering.

6 And Aaron shall present the bullock of the sin-offering, which is for himself, and make atonement for himself, and for his house. 7 And he shall take the two goats, and set them before Jehovah at the door of the tent of meeting. 8 And Aaron shall cast lots upon the two goats; one lot for Jehovah, and the other lot for Azazel. 9 And Aaron shall present the goat upon which the lot fell for Jehovah, and offer him for a sin-offering. 10 But the goat, on which the lot fell for Azazel, shall be set alive before Jehovah, to make atonement for him, to send him away for Azazel into the wilderness.

Following instructions regarding distinguishing the clean from the unclean (chaps. 11-15), the Leviticus account resumes from 10:2 where the **death of the two sons of Aaron** is related (v. 1). These sons, Nadab and Abihu, were priests who had met tragic deaths as a divine punishment for sacrilege in attempting to make offerings not in accord with the divine instructions. Their sudden fiery judgment was still fresh in the minds of the remaining priests. The Lord, therefore, took occasion of this to begin His solemn rules for observing the Day of Atonement by calling Moses' attention to the fact that Aaron, the high priest, Moses' brother, was not to frequent the especially sacred precincts of the **holy place within the veil**, i.e., the Holy of Holies of the

tabernacle (Exod. 26:31-35), where was located the **mercy-seat** (Exod. 25:17-21), upon which appeared a **cloud** (Exod. 40: 34-38) indicative of God's immediate presence (v. 2; cf. Heb. 9:7-15; 25-28). Under penalty of death, he was to enter there only once each year (vv. 29, 34; cf. Heb. 9:7), and then only in a most holy act of atonement to be carried out in the manner specified in the following verses. While some of the priests ministered daily before the veil at the golden altar, none could go beyond the veil.

The Day of Atonement was to be observed annually on the tenth day of the seventh month, Tishri (our September or October). The observance was to begin at sundown of the ninth day and continue until sundown of the tenth day. To prepare himself for his functions, the high priest was, however, according to Jewish writers, to present himself at the tabernacle and remain there quite alone for the entire preceding week. During this time he was to abstain from all that would render him ceremonially unclean or disturb his devotions.

On the evening of the ninth day he ate lightly, and throughout the night maintained a vigil. On the morning of the tenth day he bathed and dressed himself, not in the usual ornate garments of the high priest, but in the holy white linen attire of a humble penitent (v. 4; cf. Exod. 28).

In preparation for the sacrifices to follow, he was to have at hand a bullock and a ram, respectively, for a sin-offering (4:1—5:13; 6:24-30) and burnt-offering (1:1-17; 6:8-13) for himself and his priest sons. As sacrifices for the people he was also to have at hand two identical he-goats for a sin-offering and a ram for a burnt-offering (vv. 5, 6, 24).

The goats of the people having been brought into the court **at the door of the tent of meeting**, at the north of the brazen altar, the high priest was to cast lots to determine which goat would be sacrificed **for Jehovah** and which one would be for **Azazel** (for "removal," margin; the "dismissed one," Berkeley; a "scapegoat," LXX: vv. 8-10).

While the ceremonies which followed these preparations overlapped in many points, it seems that there were to be three distinct rites: the sacrifice for the priests, the sacrifice for the people, and the ceremony involving the scapegoat.

2. The Sacrifice for the Priests (16:11-14)

11 And Aaron shall present the bullock of the sin-offering, which is for himself, and shall make atonement for himself, and for his house, and shall kill the bullock of the sin-offering which is for himself. 12 And he shall take a censer full of coals of fire from off the altar before Jehovah, and his hands full of sweet incense beaten small, and bring it within the veil: 13 and he shall put the incense upon the fire before Jehovah, that the cloud of the incense may cover the mercy-seat that is upon the testimony, that he die not: 14 and he shall take of the blood of the bullock, and sprinkle it with his finger upon the mercy-seat on the east; and before the mercy-seat shall he sprinkle of the blood with his finger seven times.

Since the priests themselves were sinners, before the high priest could sacrifice for the people he must offer a sacrifice for his own sins. The sacrifice for the high priest and his house of priests was to be a young bull (v. 11), the same as a priest's private offering (4:3-11). Before slaying this animal in the court area (cf. Ezek. 40:35-43), the high priest was to place his hands upon the animal's head, while confessing his sins and those of his sons.

Following the slaughter of the bull, the high priest was to enter the Holy of Holies for the first of several times during the day. He was to carry into the Holy of Holies a censer which he had filled with burning coals from the brazen altar. The censer he was to carry in his right hand, and a container of incense in his left hand (v. 12). Placing the censer on the floor, he was to empty the incense on the burning coals. This would cause a cloud of fragrant smoke to cover the mercy-seat (v. 13). The purpose of the rising smoke, Moses was told, was that Aaron, the priest, ministering in the immediate presence of God might die not (v. 2). This might well remind the high priest of Exodus 33:20, which states that no man can look upon God and live. The rising of the smoke would, as it were, protect the high priest from beholding God, whose very presence was considered to be on the mercy-seat.

This high respect and wholesome fear of God's holiness is very different from the concept of some who think of God as a kind, companionable person who can be approached at any time, in any way, in the most familiar fashion. It is true that the New Testament speaks of God as our Father. But He is always a *holy* Father. Even the New Testament refers to Him as "a consuming fire" (Heb. 12:29). And we are solemnly reminded that "it is a fearful thing to fall into the hands of the living God" (Heb. 10:31).

Although the New Testament does not countenance that familiarity with God which sooner or later breeds disrespect or even contempt, it does indicate better, more intimate things for us than those enjoyed by the Old Testament believers. We are taught that the veil which separated God from the people was rent by Christ (Matt. 27:51), so that through Him we may now have direct, personal access to the Father (Rom. 5:2; Eph. 2:18; 3:12; Heb. 10:19). What none but the high priest could do, all of us may do now in Christ. What the high priest could do but once each year, we may now in Christ do at all times.

The rent veil not only gives us access to God in prayer now, but it opens the door of heaven to us for an everlasting abode in His presence. As Melville reminds us,

> We may not only draw nigh to God now in prayer, but we shall draw nigh to him hereafter in person. We shall rise from the dust; we shall tread the firmament, we shall enter by the gates of pearl, and we shall walk the streets of gold. Blessed be God for this rent veil! Like a window opened in the sky, there have come forth through it the shinings of eternity, the promises of immortality, rich and lively visions of the inheritance of the saints in light. [7]

There is, indeed, an inspiring suggestion of what the gospel teaches about Christ as we read verse 2 from the LXX, along with such passages as Romans 3:25; I John 2:2; and 4:10 where Christ is referred to as our "propitiation." In the LXX "mercy seat" becomes "propitiatory." The passage reads: "I will ap-

[7] Henry Melville, *Butler's Bible Work*, II, 418.

pear in a cloud on the propitiatory." Christ is our Mercy Seat, our Propitiatory. In Him we come into the very presence of God, and through Him we shall live in the very presence of God forever.

Having placed the censer on the floor at the foot of the ark, the high priest then was to go out of the Holy of Holies (backward, according to the Talmud, so as not to turn his back toward Jehovah) and return to the court. There he was to secure the basin of blood from the bull slain for his sins, and those of the priests, and withdraw again into the Holy of Holies. On this second entrance into the presence of God, with his finger he was to sprinkle blood seven times in front of, or on the east side of the mercy-seat, signifying the covering of his own sins and those of all the priests (v. 14).

3. The Sacrifice for the People (16:15-19)

15 Then shall he kill the goat of the sin-offering that is for the people, and bring his blood within the veil, and do with his blood as he did with the blood of the bullock, and sprinkle it upon the mercy-seat, and before the mercy-seat: 16 and he shall make atonement for the holy place, because of the uncleanness of the children of Israel, and because of their transgressions, even all their sins: and so shall he do for the tent of meeting, that dwelleth with them in the midst of their uncleannesses. 17 And there shall be no man in the tent of meeting when he goeth in to make atonement in the holy place, until he come out, and have made atonement for himself, and for his household, and for all the assembly of Israel. 18 And he shall go out unto the altar that is before Jehovah, and make atonement for it, and shall take of the blood of the bullock, and of the blood of the goat, and put it upon the horns of the altar round about. 19 And he shall sprinkle of the blood upon it with his finger seven times, and cleanse it, and hallow it from the uncleanness of the children of Israel.

Following his sprinkling of the blood before the mercy-seat for himself and the other priests, the high priest, leaving the vessel of blood in the Holy of Holies, was to come back into the court to perform the rites of atonement for the people. The sacrifice in this case was to be the goat on which the lot had fallen for Jehovah (v. 8). The blood of this animal slain for the sins of the people was to be put into a vessel, and with it the high priest again was to enter the Holy of Holies and sprinkle some of the blood before the mercy-seat as he did with the blood of the bull (v. 15).

Then he was to combine the blood of both animals and sprinkle seven times the horns of the golden altar of incense, which was a symbol of the prayers of all Israel. This altar stood in the Holy Place before the veil which separated the Holy Place from the Most Holy (vv. 18, 19; cf. Exod. 30:10). Some scholars feel that the altar referred to here is the altar of burnt-offering in the court (see AOT, v. 18).

This rite was to make atonement for the altar and tabernacle which had been ceremonially defiled by the sins of the people. It would assure the people of forgiveness, of the effectiveness of the regularly prescribed worship in the now cleansed tabernacle. It was also to assure the presence of the holy God in the midst of a sinful people (cf. Heb. 2:17; 9:22-24). The remainder of the blood was to be taken back to the court and poured out at the base of the brazen altar.

Although on other occasions the high priest was assisted by his sons, on the Day of Atonement he was required to minister alone (v. 17). This reminds us that Jesus, our High Priest, trod the winepress alone for us (Isa. 63:3).

4. The Scapegoat (16:20-22)

20 And when he hath made an end of atoning for the holy place, and the tent of meeting, and the altar, he shall present the live goat: 21 and Aaron shall lay both his hands upon the head of the live goat, and confess over him all the iniquities of the children of Israel, and all their transgressions, even all their sins; and he shall put them upon the head of the goat, and shall send him away by the hand of a man that is in readiness into the wilderness: 22 and the goat shall bear upon him all their iniquities unto a solitary land: and he shall let go the goat in the wilderness.

The high priest was now to go to the scapegoat, the animal whose lot designated him for Azazel (cf. v. 8). Placing his hands upon the animal, he was to confess the sins of the people, and then turn the animal over to a man that is in

readiness (a man previously appointed) to lead the goat away outside the camp **and let go the goat into the wilderness.** This symbolized the carrying away of the people's sins (cf. Ps. 103:12; Isa. 38:17; 53: 11; Mic. 7:9). As the goat slain for the people's sacrifice illustrates the covering of sin by the blood of Christ for sin's expiation, so the sending away of this animal illustrates the carrying away of sin by Christ's death and resurrection (cf. John 1:29; Rom. 4:25; Heb. 9:1—10:18; I Pet. 2:24).

Some authorities call attention to the fact that the word *Azazel* not only means what is suggested in the comments on verses 8-10, but also an evil spirit, and thus represents Satan. So in this way it is pointed out that the scapegoat being sent away into the wilderness symbolizes an announcement to Satan that the sacrifice of the other animal has destroyed his power over sinners.

5. Completing the Offerings (16:23-28)

23 And Aaron shall come into the tent of meeting, and shall put off the linen garments, which he put on when he went into the holy place, and shall leave them there: 24 and he shall bathe his flesh in water in a holy place, and put on his garments, and come forth, and offer his burnt-offering and the burnt-offering of the people, and make atonement for himself and for the people. 25 And the fat of the sin-offering shall he burn upon the altar. 26 And he that letteth go the goat for Azazel shall wash his clothes, and bathe his flesh in water, and afterward he shall come into the camp. 27 And the bullock of the sin-offering, and the goat of the sin-offering, whose blood was brought in to make atonement in the holy place, shall be carried forth without the camp; and they shall burn in the fire their skins, and their flesh, and their dung. 28 And he that burneth them shall wash his clothes, and bathe his flesh in water, and afterward he shall come into the camp.

The high priest, bathed and adorned in the magnificent robes of his high office (Exod. 28:20), now stands at the brazen altar in the court where he is to offer the burnt-offering for himself and his sons and the sacrifice for the people (v. 42). The atonement completed, the entire congregation of Israel dedicates itself to God, and is accepted.

What remained of the sacrificial animals was to be taken outside the camp by a man previously appointed. There those remains were to be burned (cf. Heb. 13:11-13). Both the man who had thus disposed of the remains of the sacrifices, and the one who had led out the scapegoat, were to be considered unclean, and before returning to the camp they were to bathe and wash their garments.

The high priest then was to give his blessing to all of the nation, representatives of which would gather outside the tabernacle court.

6. Instruction for Perpetuating the Day of Atonement (16:29-34)

29 And it shall be a statute for ever unto you: in the seventh month, on the tenth day of the month, ye shall afflict your souls, and shall do no manner of work, the home-born, or the stranger that sojourneth among you: 30 for on this day shall atonement be made for you, to cleanse you; from all your sins shall ye be clean before Jehovah. 31 It is a sabbath of solemn rest unto you, and ye shall afflict your souls; it is a statute for ever. 32 And the priest, who shall be anointed and who shall be consecrated to be priest in his father's stead, shall make the atonement, and shall put on the linen garments, even the holy garments: 33 and he shall make atonement for the holy sanctuary; and he shall make atonement for the tent of meeting and for the altar; and he shall make atonement for the priests and for all the people of the assembly. 34 And this shall be an everlasting statute unto you, to make atonement for the children of Israel because of all their sins once in the year. And he did as Jehovah commanded Moses.

The Day of Atonement, a holy sabbath of solemn rest, was to be free from work and secular interest, and was to be observed annually (Isa. 58:13; see also the opening comments at the beginning of this chapter).

Present-day Jews observe the Day of Atonement each fall, referring to the occasion as *Yom* (day) *Kippur* (covering or atonement).

There is much in this chapter to remind us of the New Testament gospel with its emphasis upon the remission of sins and the presence of God made available in Christ, who is both our Sacrifice and our High Priest, who laid aside His celestial garments to become one with us (Heb. 2:17).

The Epistle to the Hebrews in particular, both by resemblance and by contrast, draws helpful lessons in this regard. Hebrews 9:26 suggests to us that the sacrifice at the brazen altar speaks to us of the death of Christ. Hebrews 9:24 uses the priest's entering into the Holy of Holies as a type of Christ's intercession for us. Hebrews 9:28 reminds us that the return of the priest to the congregation speaks to us of Christ's second coming.

Hebrews makes much of the atoning work of Christ as our High Priest (Heb. 4:14). The high priest had to enter the Holy of Holies every year to offer sacrifices of bulls and goats for himself as well as the people. Jesus Christ, however, entered into the heavenly sanctuary offering His own blood once for all. His offering was not for Himself, for He was without sin; but it was for the sins of others. And by His blood He assures us of eternal redemption (Heb. 9, 10).

Conspicuous in this chapter is also the place of repentance and faith by which men prepare themselves for the benefits of the atonement. Writing of the importance of the Israelites personally "afflicting their souls," or repenting on the Day of Atonement, S. H. Kellogg says:

> This most distinctly taught, that howsoever complete atonement may be, and howsoever, in making that atonement through a sacrificial victim, the sinner himself has no part, yet apart from his personal repentance for his sins, that atonement shall profit him nothing; nay, it was declared (23:29) that if any man should fail on this point, God would cut him off from his people. The law abides as regards the greater sacrifice of Christ; except we repent, we shall even because of that sacrifice, only the more terribly perish; because not even this supreme exhibition of the holy love and justice of God has moved us to renounce sin[8] (compare I John 1:9 and Romans 5:8-11).

II. HOW TO KEEP IN FELLOWSHIP WITH GOD (Lev. 17:1—27:34)

The holy God calls: that is the message of Leviticus (see Introduction). That God who calls also provides atonement whereby sinful men may approach Him, may actually come into His very presence (chaps. 1-16). He also provides a way whereby His redeemed people may be holy and have a continuing walk of fellowship with Him. It is to this holy life of continuing fellowship that we now give attention.

These chapters may well be referred to as "The Holiness Code" because there is frequent reference to need for sanctification or holiness in the lives of those people who would walk with the holy God. The sanctification or holiness of which these chapters speak is ritualistic and involves largely a separation of the people from those things considered to be ceremonially unclean. But those rituals provide for us earthly symbols or pictures from which we may gather spiritual, heavenly truth that we may understand better what holy living includes. An illustration of this is seen when the Apostle Peter, exhorting Christian believers to be holy in all manner of life, quotes from this section (I Pet. 1:14-16).

A. LAWS GOVERNING ISRAEL'S LIFE AS A HOLY PEOPLE (17:1—26:46)

1. The Law of Holy Living (17:1—20:27)

Israel, redeemed by the Lord, is called unto holiness, a holiness evidenced in a total separation from the ways of the heathen about them (18:3). The regulations of these four chapters are intended to enforce that separation by specific commands and prohibitions.

a. Separation in Preparation and Use of Food (17:1-16)

(1) Meats Acceptable as Sacrifices (17:1-9)

1 And Jehovah spake unto Moses, saying, 2 Speak unto Aaron, and unto his sons, and unto all the children of Israel, and say unto them: This is the thing which Jehovah hath commanded, saying, 3 What man soever there be of the house of Israel, that killeth an ox, or lamb, or goat, in the camp, or that killeth it without the camp, 4 and hath not brought it unto the door of the tent of meeting, to offer it as an oblation unto Jehovah before the tabernacle of Jehovah: blood shall be imputed unto that man; he hath

---

8 Kellogg, op. cit., p. 303.

shed blood; and that man shall be cut off from among his people: 5 to the end that the children of Israel may bring their sacrifices which they sacrifice in the open field, even that they may bring them unto Jehovah, unto the door of the tent of meeting, unto the priest, and sacrifice them for sacrifices of peace-offerings unto Jehovah. 6 And the priest shall sprinkle the blood upon the altar of Jehovah at the door of the tent of meeting, and burn the fat for a sweet savor unto Jehovah. 7 And they shall no more sacrifice their sacrifices unto the he-goats, after which they play the harlot. This shall be a statute for ever unto them throughout their generations.

8 And thou shalt say unto them, Whatsoever man there be of the house of Israel, or of the strangers that sojourn among them, that offereth a burnt-offering or sacrifice, 9 and bringeth it not unto the door of the tent of meeting, to sacrifice it unto Jehovah; that man shall be cut off from his people.

The Israelites were permitted to eat various types of animals referred to as "clean" (chap. 11). But not all of these clean animals were acceptable for sacrifice in the worship of the Lord. The regulations here have to do with those animals slaughtered for food which were also acceptable as sacrifices for worship at the tabernacle as prescribed in chapters 1 through 7.

The slaying of any such animal, **ox, or lamb, or goat,** was to be done at **the door of the tent of meeting** (vv. 3, 4), and was to be treated as a peace-offering (3:1-17; 7:11-38). This would emphasize the fact that the animals slain for food were to be prepared and eaten with thanksgiving and praise.

Speaking of this regulation Kellogg explains:

The terms of this law suppose a camp life; indeed, the camp is explicitly named (vs. 3). That which was enjoined was quite practicable under the conditions of life in the wilderness, when, at the best, flesh was scarce and the people dwelt compactly together; but would have been utterly inapplicable and impracticable at a later date, after they were settled throughout the land of Canaan, then to have slaughtered all beasts used for food at the central sanctuary would have been impossible. Hence we find that, as we should expect, the modified law of

Deuteronomy (12:15, 16, 20-24) assuming the previous existence of this earlier law, explicitly rescinds it.[9]

A principal reason for this regulation was that the children of Israel no more sacrifice their sacrifices unto the he-goats (goat-like gods or demons, or field spirits, AOT), after which they play the harlot (v. 7; cf. 19:4; 26:1, 30). This regulation was to stop the practice of all pagan rites common in Egypt and still practiced by some of the Israelites in connection with the preparation of their daily food (cf. Exod. 34:15f.; Lev. 20:5f.).

This regulation opened the way to stress the fact that no sacrifice of any kind was to be offered at any other place than at the central sanctuary, either by the Israelites themselves or by **strangers,** Gentiles who might be living among them. No idolatry or anything which might be associated with it was to be permitted in the camp of God's holy people (vv. 8, 9). They were married to the Lord, as it were. They were to be faithful, therefore, and worship only Him.

This ceremonial regulation regarding the preparation and use of meat teaches us that our daily supply of food should, so to speak, be brought before the Lord: we are to recognize that it has come from Him, and that it is, therefore, to be used only as it might glorify Him. This attitude of mind and heart will, indeed, help to set us apart from the self-sufficient, ungrateful, God-ignoring men of the world. Jesus sought to instill this spirit in His disciples when He taught them to pray: "Give us this day our daily bread."

This would also remind us that all worship directed other than to our Lord is not true worship (cf. John 14:6; Acts 4:12).

(2) Meats Not Acceptable as Sacrifices (17:10-16)

10 And whatsoever man there be of the house of Israel, or of the strangers that sojourn among them, that eateth any manner of blood, I will set my face against that soul that eateth blood, and will cut him off from among his people. 11 For the life of the flesh is in the blood; and I have given it to you upon the altar to make atonement for your souls:

for it is the blood that maketh atonement by reason of the life. 12 Therefore I said unto the children of Israel, No soul of you shall eat blood, neither shall any stranger that sojourneth among you eat blood. 13 And whatsoever man there be of the children of Israel, or of the strangers that sojourn among them, who taketh in hunting any beast or bird that may be eaten; he shall pour out the blood thereof, and cover it with dust.

14 For as to the life of all flesh, the blood thereof is *all one* with the life thereof: therefore I said unto the children of Israel, Ye shall eat the blood of no manner of flesh; for the life of all flesh is the blood thereof: whosoever eateth it shall be cut off. 15 And every soul that eateth that which dieth of itself, or that which is torn of beasts, whether he be homeborn or a sojourner, he shall wash his clothes, and bathe himself in water, and be unclean until the even: then shall he be clean. 16 But if he wash them not, nor bathe his flesh, then he shall bear his iniquity.

In preparing clean animals or birds taken in hunting for food (v. 13), careful attention was to be given to the handling of the blood. Whereas the blood of animals used for sacrifice or slain before the tabernacle was poured out at the foot of the brazen altar and drained away by a conduit, the blood of animals killed in the hunt was to be poured out on the ground and covered respectfully with dust (v. 14; cf. Deut. 12:16). The eating of animals which had not been bled in accord with these regulations was forbidden; and if anyone did eat such meat accidentally, not knowing how the meat had been prepared, he was, upon learning of his error, to wash his clothes and bathe. He was considered unfit to associate with his fellows or to worship at the tabernacle until sundown. Under no circumstances were Israelites to eat blood.

The reason for forbidding the eating of blood was, the Lord declared, because **the life of the flesh is in the blood; and I have given it to you upon the altar to make atonement for your souls** (v. 11; cf. Gen. 9:4). So it would appear that this regulation was intended to impress the people with a respect for life, all life. It was also to keep ever before them the sacredness of the blood as being the

means of atonement and salvation. They must always be reminded that without the shedding of blood there is no remission of sin (cf. Acts 15:20, 29; 21:25).

There may have been sanitary and hygienic reasons also for this regulation; for it is true that the blood of the animals might well have been infected with germs and parasites of many kinds injurious to the health of the people.

This regard for the blood also teaches us a regard for life. It should impress us with the fact that everything connected with God and His revelation to us through Christ, who shed His blood for us, must never be treated lightly. It must always be regarded with the utmost respect and reverence.

b. Unlawful Marriages and Sex Relations (18:1-30)

The Lord continued His emphasis upon the need for holiness in Israel. He said the people were not to conform their manner of life to that of the people among whom they lived, but were to be guided by His laws. His statutes were to set the standard for their conduct. To follow them assured fullness of life (cf. Deut. 30:15-20). He then specified certain demands regarding their sexual behavior. As B. W. Anderson points out: "The basis for these laws is not irrational taboo but the covenant relationship which sets Israel apart for the service of God (Exod. 19:3-6). As a holy and consecrated people (Exod. 22:31), Israelites must avoid all impurity in order that the holy God may tabernacle in their midst (15:31)."[10]

(1) Unlawful Marriages (18:1-19)

1 And Jehovah spake unto Moses, saying, 2 Speak unto the children of Israel, and say unto them, I am Jehovah your God. 3 After the doings of the land of Egypt, wherein ye dwelt, shall ye not do: and after the doings of the land of Canaan, whither I bring you, shall ye not do; neither shall ye walk in their statutes. 4 Mine ordinances shall ye do, and my statutes shall ye keep, to walk therein: I am Jehovah your God. 5 Ye shall therefore keep my statutes, and mine ordinances; which if a man do, he shall live in them: I am Jehovah. 6 None of you shall approach to any that are near of kin to him, to uncover

10 B. W. Anderson, *The Oxford Annotated Bible*, p. 135.

their nakedness: I am Jehovah. 7 The nakedness of thy father, even the nakedness of thy mother, shalt thou not uncover: she is thy mother; thou shalt not uncover her nakedness. 8 The nakedness of thy father's wife shalt thou not uncover; it is thy father's nakedness. 9 The nakedness of thy sister, the daughter of thy father, or the daughter of thy mother, whether born at home, or born abroad, even their nakedness thou shalt not uncover. 10 The nakedness of thy son's daughter, or of thy daughter's daughter, even their nakedness thou shalt not uncover: for theirs is thine own nakedness. 11 The nakedness of thy father's wife's daughter, begotten of thy father, she is thy sister, thou shalt not uncover her nakedness. 12 Thou shalt not uncover the nakedness of thy father's sister: she is thy father's near kinswoman. 13 Thou shalt not uncover the nakedness of thy mother's sister: for she is thy mother's near kinswoman. 14 Thou shalt not uncover the nakedness of thy father's brother, thou shalt not approach to his wife: she is thine aunt. 15 Thou shalt not uncover the nakedness of thy daughter-in-law: she is thy son's wife; thou shalt not uncover her nakedness. 16 Thou shalt not uncover the nakedness of thy brother's wife: it is thy brother's nakedness. 17 Thou shalt not uncover the nakedness of a woman and her daughter; thou shalt not take her son's daughter, or her daughter's daughter, to uncover her nakedness; they are near kinswomen: it is wickedness. 18 And thou shalt not take a wife to her sister, to be a rival *to her*, to uncover her nakedness, besides the other in her life-time.

19 And thou shalt not approach unto a woman to uncover her nakedness, as long as she is impure by her uncleanness.

The phrase **uncover the nakedness of** which recurs frequently here refers, at least sometimes (from the implications of v. 18), to actual marriage (see vv. 7, 19, 20). The use of such an expression seems to stress the fact that such unions as are condemned here cannot be true marriages, but result more from fleshly passion than from natural and holy affections (cf. v. 14). The reason given for these prohibitions, however, is that the parties involved are near of kin. This may imply that the marriage of near kinsfolk is unnatural and improper. But it also may take into consideration the well-

established fact that marriages between near relatives are likely to be barren or to produce unhealthy children.

The significance of verse 18 is clearer in the Berkeley rendering: "While your wife is still living do not take her sister for a rival to expose her nakedness."

Verse 19 refers most likely to the consummating of marriage (cf. 2:18 and 15:24).

Modern marriage laws are very largely based upon the principles stated in this passage.

(2) Heinous Sins to Avoid (18:20-23)

20 And thou shalt not lie carnally with thy neighbor's wife, to defile thyself with her. 21 And thou shalt not give any of thy seed to make them pass through *the fire* to Molech; neither shalt thou profane the name of thy God: I am Jehovah. 22 Thou shalt not lie with mankind, as with womankind: it is abomination. 23 And thou shalt not lie with any beast to defile thyself therewith; neither shall any woman stand before a beast, to lie down thereto: it is confusion.

The implications of verse 21 are more evident through reading the RSV: "You shall not give any of your children to devote them by fire to Molech, and so profane the name of your God: I am the Lord." Molech was an Ammonite deity (I Kings 11:7) to whom infants were sacrificed. While often the infants were first slain and then burned as an offering to the heathen deity (cf. 20:2-5; II Kings 17:31; Jer. 7:31; 19:5; Ezek. 16:20f.), there is evidence that live infants were on occasions put into the idol's arms to perish in flames burning within the idol. Such an abomination was particularly abhorrent to Jehovah (cf. v. 22 with I Cor. 6:9, 10).

The horribly degrading sins described in these verses are known to have been commonly practiced in Egypt from which Israel had just come, as well as in other cultured nations of that day. They were in many instances actually a part of the religious rites connected with heathen deities in Egypt and Canaan. The men and women who so prostituted themselves for the gods were called sacred or holy. To refrain from all of these base sins would, then, make Israel stand out prominently as a witness to the true holiness of Jehovah.

(3) Summary and General Warning (18:24-30)

24 Defile not ye yourselves in any of these things: for in all these the nations are defiled which I cast out from before you; 25 and the land is defiled: therefore I do visit the iniquity thereof upon it, and the land vomiteth out her inhabitants. 26 Ye therefore shall keep my statutes and mine ordinances, and shall not do any of these abominations; neither the home-born, nor the stranger that sojourneth among you 27 (for all these abominations have the men of the land done, that were before you, and the land is defiled); 28 that the land vomit not you out also, when ye defile it, as it vomited out the nation that was before you. 29 For whosoever shall do any of these abominations, even the souls that do them shall be cut off from among their people. 30 Therefore shall ye keep my charge, that ye practise not any of these abominable customs, which were practised before you, and that ye defile not yourselves therein: I am Jehovah your God.

Pointing out that it was for this kind of living that judgment would fall upon the nations in Palestine for which Israel was destined, Jehovah also warned Israel that to practice such sins would bring similar judgment.

All of God's instructions concerning marriage, together with His prohibitions and warnings against improper sexual relationships, remind us that sexual immorality is not simply a personal matter. It is that to be sure; but by promiscuity whole **nations are defiled** (v. 24). There is much history to prove that such immorality undermines a civilization and leads only to national destruction.

c. Miscellaneous Moral Requirements (19:1-37)

The precepts and prohibitions of this chapter do not set forth a complete enumeration of all moral or ceremonial duties; they are rather illustrations of how the Israelites were to apply to their daily lives the injunction: **Ye shall be holy, for I Jehovah your God am holy** (v. 2). This command is the key verse of the entire book of Leviticus (see Introduc-

tion). It is the keynote which resounds throughout all of the law (cf. Matt. 5:48; I Pet. 1:15). The chapter falls into three principal parts.

(1) Honor Parents, Reverence God (19:1-8)

1 And Jehovah spake unto Moses, saying, 2 Speak unto all the congregation of the children of Israel, and say unto them, Ye shall be holy; for I Jehovah your God am holy. 3 Ye shall fear every man his mother, and his father; and ye shall keep my sabbaths: I am Jehovah your God. 4 Turn ye not unto idols, nor make to yourselves molten gods: I am Jehovah your God.

5 And when ye offer a sacrifice of peace-offerings unto Jehovah, ye shall offer it that ye may be accepted. 6 It shall be eaten the same day ye offer it, and on the morrow: and if aught remain until the third day, it shall be burnt with fire. 7 And if it be eaten at all on the third day, it is an abomination; it shall not be accepted: 8 but every one that eateth it shall bear his iniquity, because he hath profaned the holy thing of Jehovah: and that soul shall be cut off from his people.

Fear ("give due respect," AOT) . . . **mother, . . . father . . . keep my sabbaths. . . . Turn ye not unto idols** (vv. 3, 4). These are portions of the decalogue (Exod. 20:12, 8-11, 3-6) and point up fundamental, inseparable requirements in all social and religious life. Without respect for parents there can be no enduring social order, and without such respect there is likely to be little regard for or understanding of God, our heavenly Father. There can be no satisfactory worship of God without observing His holy days and without giving the Lord our wholehearted devotion. Furthermore, without proper observance of the Lord's days and without undivided devotion in the home it is impossible to teach our children properly in the ways of God.

By living respectably, by precept, and by wise discipline, parents are responsible to command respect. This is essential, for it is in the home that children learn best to respect authority, to be considerate of others, and to obey law. Furthermore, worthy parents, by example and by precept, provide their children with a noble concept of what our heavenly

Father is like, so that the children will desire to be His.

Special stress may be given here to the observance of the Lord's holy days and to seeking first His kingdom, because these demands have always come into sharp conflict with man's love of gain and his eager pursuit for material security. In all ages these requirements have provided a test of one's consecration and real spiritual depth.

The passage regarding eating the peace-offering (vv. 5-8) would further impress upon Israel the need for proper reverence for God. The peace-offering was one of the most delightful rites in Israel's program of worship. It was offered to express love and appreciation for God, for such things as His unmerited favor and for His answers to prayer. The occasion of the offering was a sacred but happy time of fellowship with God and with one's friends. Stressing the importance of not holding meat from the offering over to the third day would teach the folly of false economy which seeks to save at the expense of obedience to the holy God. These verses become significant as they are considered along with the more complete instructions regarding this rite (3:1-7; 7:11-38).

(2) Requirements, Man to Man (19:9-18)

9 And when ye reap the harvest of your land, thou shalt not wholly reap the corners of thy field, neither shalt thou gather the gleaning of thy harvest. 10 And thou shalt not glean thy vineyard, neither shalt thou gather the fallen fruit of thy vineyard; thou shalt leave them for the poor and for the sojourner: I am Jehovah your God.

11 Ye shall not steal; neither shall ye deal falsely, nor lie one to another. 12 And ye shall not swear by my name falsely, and profane the name of thy God: I am Jehovah.

13 Thou shalt not oppress thy neighbor, nor rob him: the wages of a hired servant shall not abide with thee all night until the morning. 14 Thou shalt not curse the deaf, nor put a stumbling-block before the blind; but thou shalt fear thy God: I am Jehovah.

15 Ye shall do no unrighteousness in judgment: thou shalt not respect the person of the poor, nor honor the person of the mighty: but in righteousness shalt thou judge thy neighbor. 16 Thou shalt not go up and down as a talebearer among thy people: neither shalt thou stand against the blood of thy neighbor: I am Jehovah.

17 Thou shalt not hate thy brother in thy heart: thou shalt surely rebuke thy neighbor, and not bear sin because of him. 18 Thou shalt not take vengeance, nor bear any grudge against the children of thy people; but thou shalt love thy neighbor as thyself: I am Jehovah.

This passage consists of five groups of laws designed to regulate human relations in Israel. It follows rather closely the second table of the decalogue (Exod. 20:12-17).

The first set of precepts (vv. 9, 10), looking forward to the day when Israel would be settled in Palestine, speaks of considerations to be given to the poor in Israel, both to the Hebrews and to the Gentiles who, not able to own land in Israel, might be in special need. Land-owners were not to harvest their grain fields to the very corners, nor to pick up from the ground what might have fallen. They were not to strip the grape vines, nor to pick up the grapes which might have fallen to the ground. They were purposely to leave grain and fruit for the poor to gather for themselves (cf. 25:23). These precepts would tend to curb undue selfishness and to test the landowner's consideration of God's laws.

While our current social order differs from that of Israel, God is still concerned about the poor and expects us personally to find ways of helping them. And it is still true that we are all only stewards of whatever may have come into our possession (cf. Matt. 25:34-46; Acts 2:44, 45; Gal. 2:10; Jas. 1:27).

The second set of precepts (vv. 11, 12) condemns especially stealing and defrauding, which frequently come to involve lying and false swearing, or perjury, in an effort to keep what has been secured dishonestly.

Stealing, Martin Luther said, is to get another man's property wrongfully into our possession. In that light, to steal and to defraud or cheat become quite synonymous. And the ways to steal or cheat in our complex society are almost endless. T. C. Meyers lists the following:

Padding an expense account on a smaller scale, cheating the government on income tax even in small amounts, buying on credit without the possibility or intention of paying, keeping the change when a clerk makes a mistake, pushing the scales upward when the butcher weighs the meat, cheating on examinations, running red lights in traffic, telling little falsehoods for status' sake in social dealings, passing along gossip about another person that might rob him of his good name, gambling. . . . When we see need and do nothing about it. . . . The man who will not work but expects the government to keep him up when he is able to work is a thief. . . . To fail to give a good day's work in return for a day's pay is stealing. We can steal by doing nothing. To withhold evidence that would free an innocent man from punishment is stealing. To hear someone disparage another person, assassinate another's character, and keep silent, this is robbery of the worst sort.[11]

While the first set of rules had particular application to the man of means, these apply to all men, rich or poor. A poor man has no more right to steal from the rich than does the rich man have a right to take advantage of the poor or to withhold from another man what is his due.

A third set of rules (vv. 13, 14) condemns oppression and violence. Because the laborer's reserves were generally limited, it was required that employers pay their employees each day in order that their families might not be in want. While this is not the custom now, it is still wrong to hold back wages unduly. The New Testament is emphatic here too (Jas. 5:4).

The fourth set of laws (vv. 15, 16) demands absolute justice in court trials. Whether a man is rich or poor is to have no place in determining his guilt or innocence. To **stand against the blood of thy neighbor** condemns the offering of slanderous or false witness whereby one seeks to get his fellow man put to death (cf. Exod. 23:7). And the Talmud's interpretation is helpful: "Thou shalt not stand silent by, when thy neighbor's life is in danger in the court of judgment and thy testimony might save him."

The final set of precepts (vv. 17, 18) goes behind all of the acts involved in the preceding laws, and deals with the state of heart which prompts those acts.

In the light of this passage we are to rebuke sin, even when the wrong does not harm us. Yet we are not to seek to avenge wrong, even though we are injured by it. We are not to be envious and begrudge our fellow man any good he may have, even though he be an evildoer and we feel him to be undeserving. Whether he be friend or foe, good or evil, we are to love him as ourselves (cf. Exod. 23:4, 5; Mark 12:31).

Neighbor here seems to have reference to the fellow Israelite, one of the **children of thy people**. The term is, however, broadened in verse 34 to include the non-Israelite sojourner (cf. Lev. 25:35-55; Deut. 10:18, 19; Luke 10:29-33).

(3) All Aspects of Life Included (19:19-37)

19 Ye shall keep my statutes. Thou shalt not let thy cattle gender with a diverse kind: thou shalt not sow thy field with two kinds of seed: neither shall there come upon thee a garment of two kinds of stuff mingled together. 20 And whosoever lieth carnally with a woman, that is a bondmaid, betrothed to a husband, and not at all redeemed, nor freedom given her; they shall be punished; they shall not be put to death, because she was not free. 21 And he shall bring his trespass-offering unto Jehovah, unto the door of the tent of meeting, even a ram for a trespass-offering. 22 And the priest shall make atonement for him with the ram of the trespass-offering before Jehovah for his sin which he hath sinned: and the sin which he hath sinned shall be forgiven him.

23 And when ye shall come into the land, and shall have planted all manner of trees for food, then ye shall count the fruit thereof as their uncircumcision: three years shall they be as uncircumcised unto you; it shall not be eaten. 24 But in the fourth year all the fruit thereof shall be holy, for giving praise unto Jehovah. 25 And in the fifth year shall ye eat of the fruit thereof, that it may yield unto you the increase thereof: I am Jehovah your God.

26 Ye shall not eat anything with the blood: neither shall ye use enchantments, nor practise augury. 27 Ye shall not round the corners of your heads, neither shalt thou mar the corners of thy beard. 28 Ye shall not make any cuttings in your flesh for the dead, nor print any marks upon you: I am Jehovah.

11 T. C. Meyers, *Thunder on the Mountain*, pp. 124, 126.

29 Profane not thy daughter, to make her a harlot; lest the land fall to whoredom, and the land become full of wickedness. 30 Ye shall keep my sabbaths, and reverence my sanctuary: I am Jehovah.

31 Turn ye not unto them that have familiar spirits, nor unto the wizards; seek them not out, to be defiled by them: I am Jehovah your God.

32 Thou shalt rise up before the hoary head, and honor the face of the old man, and thou shalt fear thy God: I am Jehovah.

33 And if a stranger sojourn with thee in your land, ye shall not. do him wrong. 34 The stranger that sojourneth with you shall be unto you as the home-born among you, and thou shalt love him as thyself; for ye were sojourners in the land of Egypt: I am Jehovah your God.

35 Ye shall do no unrighteousness in judgment, in measures of length, of weight, or of quantity. 36 Just balances, just weights, a just ephah, and a just hin, shall ye have: I am Jehovah your God, who brought you out of the land of Egypt. 37 And ye shall observe all my statutes, and all mine ordinances, and do them: I am Jehovah.

This section begins and ends with an exhortation to obedience and, as O. T. Allis points out, "it almost seems as if an element of contrast had been intentionally introduced to emphasize the fact that every department and phase of life is covered by the ordinances of God."[12]

Cattle (v. 19), a broader term than herd or flock, includes both clean and unclean animals. It is not possible to understand now just why Jehovah forbade the Israelites to develop hybrid animals and plants. But it may well be that He desired thereby to cultivate in the minds of the Israelites a reverence for the divinely established order in nature (cf. Deut. 22:9-11). This stipulation would have prohibited the breeding of mules; so it is quite likely that those mentioned in David's time (I Kings 10:25) were imported.

A trespass with a slave concubine (vv. 20-22; cf. Exod. 21:7-11) received legal clemency rather than death, as in the case of a free woman (Deut. 22:23, 24), because the woman involved was not free and was considered to be the property of another.

The reason for a law which countenanced both slavery and concubinage can probably be accounted for in Jesus' statement regarding the reason for divorce, "because of the hardness of men's hearts" (Matt. 18:9). Nevertheless, the principle introduced in this law which recognized the slave girl as a person with rights which were being taken advantage of rather than as simply a chattel, in due time required the total abolition of slavery.

The restriction against using the fruit from a young tree until the fifth year (vv. 23-25) probably is based upon the general requirement that the first-fruits are to be consecrated to the Lord. The yield of the first years was considered of such inferior quality as to be unworthy of the Lord. By the fourth year, however, the fruit was thought to be good enough to be consecrated to the Lord. For the first three years then, the tree was looked upon as was an **uncircumcised** child, one not yet consecrated.

We may well learn from this that God and His interests are to have priority over ourselves and our interests.

The next several restrictions condemned heathen practices unworthy of God's holy people (vv. 26-29). The significance of verse 26 becomes clearer in the Berkeley translation: "Make use of neither fortune telling or witchcraft practice."

Pagan men often cut their hair and beards in certain ways to honor their idols and to show which of the deities they worshiped. For an Israelite to adopt a fashion associated with idolatry would misrepresent him as a worshiper of the true and living God (v. 27).

Pagans often cut their flesh in hopeless mourning (v. 28; cf. Deut. 14:1; Amos 8:10; Isa. 22:12; Jer. 16:6; Mic. 1:16). Perhaps something of the implication of God's prohibition here is found in I Thessalonians 4:13 where the Christian is told to "sorrow not, even as the rest, who have no hope."

To give one's daughters to become harlot priestesses at the temple whose fees went to the upkeep of the religion was also a common pagan practice, but an abomination to the Lord.

The Israelites were to shun spiritualist mediums and the **wizards** or "knowing

12 Allis, op. cit., p. 153.

ones" who are said to enter into them (v. 31; cf. I Sam. 28:3; II Kings 21:6; 23:24).

The ephah was equal to three eighths to two thirds of a bushel. The hin was a liquid measure containing about one gallon (v. 36).

d. Penalties for Transgression (20:1-21)

1 And Jehovah spake unto Moses, saying, 2 Moreover, thou shalt say to the children of Israel, Whosoever he be of the children of Israel, or of the strangers that sojourn in Israel, that giveth of his seed unto Molech; he shall surely be put to death: the people of the land shall stone him with stones. 3 I also will set my face against that man, and will cut him off from among his people; because he hath given of his seed unto Molech, to defile my sanctuary, and to profane my holy name. 4 And if the people of the land do at all hide their eyes from that man, when he giveth of his seed unto Molech, and put him not to death; 5 then I will set my face against that man, and against his family, and will cut him off, and all that play the harlot after him, to play the harlot with Molech, from among their people.

6 And the soul that turneth unto them that have familiar spirits, and unto the wizards, to play the harlot after them, I will even set my face against that soul, and will cut him off from among his people. 7 Sanctify yourselves therefore, and be ye holy; for I am Jehovah your God. 8 And ye shall keep my statutes, and do them: I am Jehovah who sanctifieth you. 9 For every one that curseth his father or his mother shall surely be put to death: he hath cursed his father or his mother; his blood shall be upon him. 10 And the man that committeth adultery with another man's wife, even he that committeth adultery with his neighbor's wife, the adulterer and the adulteress shall surely be put to death. 11 And the man that lieth with his father's wife hath uncovered his father's nakedness: both of them shall surely be put to death; their blood shall be upon them. 12 And if a man lie with his daughter-in-law, both of them shall surely be put to death: they have wrought confusion; their blood shall be upon them. 13 And if a man lie with mankind, as with womankind, both of them have committed abomination: they shall surely be put to death; their blood shall be upon them. 14 And if a man take a wife and her mother, it is wickedness: they shall be burnt with fire, both he and they; that there be no wickedness among you. 15 And if a man lie with a beast, he shall surely be put to death: and ye shall slay the beast. 16 And if a woman approach unto any beast, and lie down thereto, thou shalt kill the woman, and the beast: they shall surely be put to death; their blood shall be upon them.

17 And if a man shall take his sister, his father's daughter, or his mother's daughter, and see her nakedness, and she see his nakedness; it is a shameful thing; and they shall be cut off in the sight of the children of their people: he hath uncovered his sister's nakedness; he shall bear his iniquity. 18 And if a man shall lie with a woman having her sickness, and shall uncover her nakedness; he hath made naked her fountain, and she hath uncovered the fountain of her blood: and both of them shall be cut off from among their people. 19 And thou shalt not uncover the nakedness of thy mother's sister, nor of thy father's sister; for he hath made naked his near kin: they shall bear their iniquity. 20 And if a man shall lie with his uncle's wife, he hath uncovered his uncle's nakedness: they shall bear their sin; they shall die childless. 21 And if a man shall take his brother's wife, it is impurity: he hath uncovered his brother's nakedness; they shall be childless.

To insure obedience to rightful authority, it never has been enough simply to appeal to men's consciences. It has always been necessary to declare and execute penalties for disobedience. It is not surprising, then, to find this passage which lists penalties for numerous transgressions already condemned in earlier sections of the book of Leviticus. This list makes no pretense of being Israel's complete penal code. But it deals simply with a selection of crimes commented upon particularly in the two preceding chapters.

In this list the following offences were punishable by death: the worship of Molech (vv. 1-5); witchcraft (vv. 6, 27); disrespect for parents (v. 9; cf. Exod. 21:15); and numerous sex vices (vv. 10-16). For some other offences capital punishment was not decreed (vv. 17-21).

Moses' time was very different from ours, and we may not now understand just why some cases were handled with such severity. It is neither possible nor desirable that this code be applied literally in our situation. But there are principles regarding administering justice and in dealing with offenders which we should note and heed.

A prime object of these penalties was to satisfy justice and to instill in Israel a respect for authority (Num. 35:33). This must be an abiding purpose in all statutes and enforcement agencies. In our day, however, capital punishment is being generally abrogated; and in our desire to help rehabilitate individual lawbreakers we often tend to bend the law to meet what we think are immediate needs of the individual caught in its meshes. So it is we often undermine the authority of law and leave it quite ineffective.

Another reason for the strict enforcement of heavy penalties was to rid society of those debased criminal elements which tended to corrupt the whole nation. This speaks to our problem of widespread and deeply entrenched criminal elements, a problem we seem unable to solve and in many instances even unwilling to face honestly.

Another principle seen here is that unfaithfulness toward God and sins against the family are considered among the gravest of transgressions, meriting most severe punishment. In our day, to fight for freedom, to disbelieve in God and to practice atheism are considered smart and right. Disrespect for parents and disregard for marriage vows are a common way of life. Abnormal sexual practices so strongly condemned in this Leviticus code are becoming accepted in "respectable" circles.

All of this would teach us that we are obligated to keep teeth in our laws by careful, strict enforcement; we are obligated to administer justice so as to deepen a general regard for law; in every teaching ministry of the church we must impress our people with the fact that government, law, and order are of God (Rom. 13:1-7; I Tim. 2:2-4); that justice must rule among us (Ezek. 45:9); that evildoers must be punished and their corrupting influence upon others stopped; that wisdom begins with faith and fear of God (Ps. 111:10); that marriage and family life are not merely convenient civil arrangements, but are divinely established institutions (Mark 10:4-9).

The laws and penalties of the "Holiness Code," of which this chapter is the conclusion, makes it clear that the end of government and of life is not to obtain man's material needs, but rather uprightness. And we may be sure that God will in due course enforce His will in this regard. In spite of widespread unbelief and disobedience to God's laws, He still rules the world. He will not abdicate His place of righteous authority in order to submit His laws to the sanction of popular vote.

e. Conclusions Regarding Holy Living (20:22-27)

22 Ye shall therefore keep all my statutes, and all mine ordinances, and do them; that the land, whither I bring you to dwell therein, vomit you not out. 23 And ye shall not walk in the customs of the nation, which I cast out before you: for they did all these things, and therefore I abhorred them. 24 But I have said unto you, Ye shall inherit their land, and I will give it unto you to possess it, a land flowing with milk and honey: I am Jehovah your God, who hath separated you from the peoples. 25 Ye shall therefore make a distinction between the clean beast and the unclean, and between the unclean fowl and the clean: and ye shall not make your souls abominable by beast, or by bird, or by anything wherewith the ground teemeth, which I have separated from you as unclean. 26 And ye shall be holy unto me: for I, Jehovah, am holy, and have set you apart from the peoples, that ye should be mine.

27 A man also or a woman that hath a familiar spirit, or that is a wizard, shall surely be put to death: they shall stone them with stones; their blood shall be upon them.

This is a summary of promises and admonitions which the Lord had previously spoken to Israel (cf. especially such passages as 11; 18:28ff., and Exod. 3:8, 17). It seems clear that a principal aim of the dietary laws and other ceremonial demands placed upon Israel was to promote a definite separation between that nation and the Canaanites whose land they were to possess.

If the Israelites were to be the people of the holy God, they must keep themselves wholly separated unto Him (cf. II Cor. 6:14-18; Jer. 31:1, 9). Verse 27 emphasizes this along with verse 6 and 19:26.

2. Holiness of the Priests (21:1—22:33)

Israel was a kingdom of priests consecrated unto Jehovah for His service (Exod. 19:5, 6). As such, the people served in a threefold capacity: the congregation, the ordinary priests, and the high priest. This was in accord with the threefold division of the tabernacle: the court, the Holy Place, and the Holy of Holies.

Chapters 17 through 20 contain laws which set the congregation apart from surrounding nations. God gives precepts which set the priests apart from the rest of the congregation for their most holy ministry before the Lord at the sanctuary. These involve holiness in personal relationships, in physical well-being, in freedom from ceremonial defilement, and in sacrifices.

a. Holiness in Personal Relationships (21:1-15)

1 And Jehovah said unto Moses, Speak unto the priests, the sons of Aaron, and say unto them, There shall none defile himself for the dead among his people; 2 except for his kin, that is near unto him, for his mother, and for his father, and for his son, and for his daughter, and for his brother, 3 and for his sister a virgin, that is near unto him, that hath had no husband; for her may he defile himself. 4 He shall not defile himself, *being* a chief man among his people, to profane himself. 5 They shall not make baldness upon their head, neither shall they shave off the corner of their beard, nor make any cuttings in their flesh. 6 They shall be holy unto their God, and not profane the name of their God; for the offerings of Jehovah made by fire, the bread of their God, they do offer: therefore they shall be holy. 7 They shall not take a woman that is a harlot, or profane; neither shall they take a woman put away from her husband: for he is holy unto his God. 8 Thou shalt sanctify him therefore; for he offereth the bread of thy God: he shall be holy unto thee; for I Jehovah, who sanctify you, am holy. 9 And the daughter of any priest, if she profane herself by playing the harlot, she profaneth her father: she shall be burnt with fire.

10 And he that is the high priest among his brethren, upon whose head the anointing oil is poured, and that is consecrated to put on the garments, shall not let the hair of his head go loose, nor rend his clothes; 11 neither shall he go in to any dead body, nor defile himself for his father, or for his mother; 12 neither shall he go out of the sanctuary, nor profane the sanctuary of his God; for the crown of the anointing oil of his God is upon him: I am Jehovah. 13 And he shall take a wife in her virginity. 14 A widow, or one divorced, or a profane woman, a harlot, these shall he not take: but a virgin of his own people shall he take to wife. 15 And he shall not profane his seed among his people: for I am Jehovah who sanctifieth him.

If all of the congregation was to be holy, separated, and devoted to Jehovah, how much more true was this of the priests, for it was they who were required to stand between the people and Jehovah and it was they who were to be as God to the people (see comments on 10:2, 3).

The ceremonial laws regarding separation which applied to Israel have been done away in Christ. But, Kellogg reminds us that

> as contrasted with the world without, it is not enough that Christians should be equally correct and moral in life with the best men of the world; though too many seem to be living under that impression. They must be more than this; they must be holy. God will wink at things in others which He will not deal lightly with in them. And so, again within the church, those who occupy various positions of dignity as teachers and rulers of God's flock are just in that degree laid under the more stringent obligations to holiness of life and walk[13] (cf. I Pet. 2:1-5).

Death had come into the world because of sin, and the priests were to avoid contact with corpses, except in the case of their own next of kin (vv. 1-3; cf. Ezek. 44:25). While the priest's wife is not mentioned, she would naturally be considered as an exception along with the next of kin; for under the law she was considered to be nearer to her husband than even his parents.

Furthermore, as priests they were not to show outward signs of mourning in case of death, as did their pagan neighbors by shaving their heads, disfiguring their beards, and cutting their flesh (v. 5). The reason given for these rules is

[13] Kellogg, *op. cit.*, p. 345.

that the priest was **chief among his people** (v. 4), and his principal function was to minister before God by offering "sacrifices of the Lord as the gifts of their God" (v. 6, LXX).

These regulations were not given to depreciate earthly relationships, but to magnify the priestly office as transcending even the most sacred of earthly ties and to point out that even in life's extremities, God is the priests' portion and their comfort.

These facts cannot but remind us of the New Testament message to all of us who have a place in the priesthood of Christian believers: "He that loveth father or mother more than me is not worthy of me; and he that loveth son or daughter more than me is not worthy of me" (Matt. 10:37). "Those that have wives may be as though they had none; and those that weep, as though they wept not" (I Cor. 7:29, 30). "Sorrow not, even as the rest, who have no hope. For if we believe that Jesus died and rose again, even so them also that are asleep in Jesus will God bring with him" (I Thess. 4:13, 14).

The priest was also to be holy in his marriage and home relationships. His wife and children were to be persons worthy of a place beside a man set aside for God's holy service (vv. 7-9).

Because the high priest had been anointed in consecration to wear the special garments of the particularly sacred and unique office, the demands upon him were even more rigid than those of the ordinary priests. He was not to participate at all in mourning for the dead. He was not even permitted to go to the place where his father and mother might lie in death. **Neither shall he go out of the sanctuary** (v. 12) does not imply that he stayed always at the tabernacle, but rather that he must not leave his work at God's house to honor the dead.

The high priest's choice of a wife was more limited than that of the other priests. He must marry a virgin Israelite (cf. I Tim. 3:2-7; Tit. 1:7-9). This rule was to safeguard his future family. An unworthy marriage might greatly lessen the chances that his children would be worthy of taking their places as successors in his holy office (vv. 10-15).

b. Holiness in Physical Perfection (21:16-24)

16 And Jehovah spake unto Moses, saying, 17 Speak unto Aaron, saying, Whosoever he be of thy seed throughout their generations that hath a blemish, let him not approach to offer the bread of his God. 18 For whatsoever man he be that hath a blemish, he shall not approach: a blind man, or a lame, or he that hath a flat nose, or anything superfluous, 19 or a man that is broken-footed, or broken-handed, 20 or crook-backed, or a dwarf, or that hath a blemish in his eye, or is scurvy, or scabbed, or hath his stones broken; 21 no man of the seed of Aaron the priest, that hath a blemish, shall come nigh to offer the offerings of Jehovah made by fire: he hath a blemish; he shall not come nigh to offer the bread of his God. 22 He shall eat the bread of his God, both of the most holy, and of the holy: 23 only he shall not go in unto the veil, nor come nigh unto the altar, because he hath a blemish; that he profane not my sanctuaries: for I am Jehovah who sanctifieth them. 24 So Moses spake unto Aaron, and to his sons, and unto all the children of Israel.

Just as the animals offered in sacrifice were to be perfect specimens (22:17-25), so the priests who offered those sacrifices were to be without physical defect (vv. 16-21). While a physically defective member of the priestly family was debarred from holy service at the sanctuary, such an unfortunate person was not prohibited from sharing in the food and supplies which were allowed for the sustaining of the priests and their families (v. 22).

c. Holiness in Freedom from Defilement (22:1-16)

1 And Jehovah spake unto Moses, saying, 2 Speak unto Aaron and to his sons, that they separate themselves from the holy things of the children of Israel, which they hallow unto me, and that they profane not my holy name: I am Jehovah. 3 Say unto them, Whosoever he be of all your seed throughout your generations, that approacheth unto the holy things, which the children of Israel hallow unto Jehovah, having his uncleanness upon him, that soul shall be cut off from before me: I am Jehovah. 4 What man soever of the seed of Aaron is a leper, or hath an issue; he shall not eat

of the holy things, until he be clean.
And whoso toucheth anything that is
unclean by the dead, or a man whose
seed goeth from him; 5 or whosoever
toucheth any creeping thing, whereby he
may be made unclean, or a man of whom
he may take uncleanness, whatsoever uncleanness he hath; 6 the soul that toucheth any such shall be unclean until the
even, and shall not eat of the holy
things, unless he bathe his flesh in water.
7 And when the sun is down, he shall be
clean; and afterward he shall eat of the
holy things, because it is his bread. 8
That which dieth of itself, or is torn of
beasts, he shall not eat, to defile himself
therewith: I am Jehovah. 9 They shall
therefore keep my charge, lest they bear
sin for it, and die therein, if they profane it: I am Jehovah who sanctifieth
them.

10 There shall no stranger eat of the
holy thing: a sojourner of the priest's, or
a hired servant, shall not eat of the holy
thing. 11 But if a priest buy any soul,
the purchase of his money, he shall eat
of it; and such as are born in his house,
they shall eat of his bread. 12 And if a
priest's daughter be married unto a
stranger, she shall not eat of the heave-
offering of the holy things. 13 But if a
priest's daughter be a widow, or divorced,
and have no child, and be returned unto
her father's house, as in her youth, she
shall eat of her father's bread: but there
shall no stranger eat thereof. 14 And if
a man eat of the holy thing unwittingly,
then he shall put the fifth part thereof
unto it, and shall give unto the priest
the holy thing. 15 And they shall not
profane the holy things of the children
of Israel, which they offer unto Jehovah,
16 and so cause them to bear the iniquity
that bringeth guilt, when they eat their
holy things: for I am Jehovah who sanctifieth them.

For reasons set forth in chapters 11-15,
the priests were subject to ceremonial defilement just as were the other Israelites.
When for any cause priests were so defiled, they were not to partake of the
portion of the dedicated sacrifices or **holy
things** which was allotted to the priests
(see the regulations concerning leprosy,
13:1-46; on having an issue, 15:3; one
whose seed went from him, 15:16-18;
Heb. 5:2; 7:28; and creeping things, 11:
24-28) . **Stranger** (v. 10) refers to a layman
outside the priest's immediate household.
The priest's purchase of a **soul** really
means a "slave" (RSV, v. 11).

d. Holiness in Sacrificing (22:17-33)

17 And Jehovah spake unto Moses, saying, 18 Speak unto Aaron, and to his
sons, and unto all the children of Israel,
and say unto them, Whosoever he be of
the house of Israel, or of the sojourners
in Israel, that offereth his oblation, whether it be any of their vows, or any of their
freewill-offerings, which they offer unto
Jehovah for a burnt-offering; 19 that ye
may be accepted, *ye shall offer* a male
without blemish, of the bullocks, of the
sheep, or of the goats. 20 But whatsoever
hath a blemish, that shall ye not offer: for
it shall not be acceptable for you. 21 And
whosoever offereth a sacrifice of peace-
offerings unto Jehovah to accomplish a
vow, or for a freewill-offering, of the
herd or of the flock, it shall be perfect
to be accepted; there shall be no blemish
therein. 22 Blind, or broken, or maimed,
or having a wen, or scurvy, or scabbed, ye
shall not offer these unto Jehovah, nor
make an offering by fire of them upon
the altar unto Jehovah. 23 Either a bullock or a lamb that hath anything superfluous or lacking in his parts, that
mayest thou offer for a freewill-offering;
but for a vow it shall not be accepted.
24 That which hath its stones bruised, or
crushed, or broken, or cut, ye shall not
offer unto Jehovah; neither shall ye do
thus in your land. 25 Neither from the
hand of a foreigner shall ye offer the
bread of your God of any of these; because their corruption is in them, there
is a blemish in them: they shall not be
accepted for you.

26 And Jehovah spake unto Moses,
saying, 27 When a bullock, or a sheep,
or a goat, is brought forth, then it shall
be seven days under the dam; and from
the eighth day and thenceforth it shall
be accepted for the oblation of an offering made by fire unto Jehovah. 28 And
whether it be cow or ewe, ye shall not
kill it and its young both in one day.
29 And when ye sacrifice a sacrifice of
thanksgiving unto Jehovah, ye shall sacrifice it that ye may be accepted. 30 On
the same day it shall be eaten; ye shall
leave none of it until the morning: I am
Jehovah. 31 Therefore shall ye keep
my commandments, and do them: I am
Jehovah. 32 And ye shall not profane
my holy name; but I will be hallowed
among the children of Israel: I am Jehovah who halloweth you, 33 who brought
you out of the land of Egypt, to be your
God: I am Jehovah.

This is a summary regarding the acceptable sacrifices. Details regarding these

are set forth in the first seven chapters of Leviticus: **burnt-offering** (v. 18; cf. 1:1-17; 6:8-13), **peace-offerings** (v. 21) and **sacrifice of thanksgiving** (v. 29; cf. 3:1-17; 7:11-38). **Seven days under the dam** means that it "shall remain seven days with its mother" (v. 27, RSV). The sacrifice must be at least eight days old.

3. Holiness of the Nation (23:1—24:23)

Seven special convocations were to become an established part of Israel's life. They were all holy days, occasions which would draw the people aside from regular secular activities to worship; and in some instances to commemorate notable events in the nation's history. Uniquely Israelite, these holy days further set the Hebrews apart as different from the surrounding pagan nations. And by observing these days, the people witnessed to their faith in Jehovah who created their nation and continually sustained it.

a. The Holy Convocations (23:1-44)

Two Hebrew words, *moed* and *hag*, are used when referring to these gatherings. The former implies an "appointed meeting or season," the emphasis being upon the time. The latter term means "festival." Coming from a root meaning "to dance," it emphasizes gladness and festivity. While in the KJV both words are translated "feast," in the ASV the first is translated **set feast** with a marginal note "appointed season"; and the second is there rendered simply **feast**. All of these holy days are called convocations because on them the people were to come together for united, public participation. In each instance the people were summoned to the meetings by the blowing of silver trumpets (Num. 10:1-10).

(1) The Sabbath (23:1-3)

1 And Jehovah spake unto Moses, saying, 2 Speak unto the children of Israel, and say unto them, The set feasts of Jehovah, which ye shall proclaim to be holy convocations, even these are my set feasts. 3 Six days shall work be done: but on the seventh day is a sabbath of solemn rest, a holy convocation; ye shall do no manner of work: it is a sabbath unto Jehovah in all your dwellings.

Six days shall work be done, but on the seventh day is a sabbath of solemn rest (v. 3). Wherever the Sabbath is commanded, it is referred to, not as day number seven nor as the seventh day of the week, but as the seventh day following six days of labor (Exod. 20:9, 10; Deut. 5:13, 14). In this connection Purkiser comments: "It may be sufficient to point out that the spiritual observance of one day a week literally fulfils the requirements of the seventh commandment, and to read 'Saturday' into the commandment is to interpolate something which is not there."[14]

Special emphasis is made regarding this day being free from toil. During other sacred religious gatherings usual household tasks were permitted, but not on the Sabbath. On this day no manner of work was to be done. This would prevent excuses for failing to gather for the public worship and would remind us Christians that the Lord's Day is a "holy convocation" in which public worship is not optional, but a duty (cf. Heb. 10:25).

Two reasons are given in the Bible for the observance of the Sabbath as a day for rest and worship. In the first place, it is said to be a looking back, a memorial of God's rest after the creation (Exod. 20:11).

In the second place, it is suggested that it is to be a looking forward to a promised redemption. God's sabbatic rest had been interrupted by sin. His good work was marred (Gen. 3:17, 18; Rom. 8:20). In such a state God could no longer rest. He became involved then, as it were, in the work of a new creation designed ultimately to restore both man and nature to their sabbatic perfection. This was to be achieved through a promised Redeemer.

So it is that rest and redemption are predominant themes throughout the activities in the series of Israel's appointed holy days. Some stress one phase and some another. Both ideas stand out in the Sabbath observance. This seems to be suggested in Exodus 31:13: "Verily ye shall keep my sabbaths: for it is a sign between me and you throughout your generations; that ye may know that I am Jehovah who sanctifieth you." And on another occasion Jehovah told Israel that

---

[14] W. T. Purkiser, "Leviticus," *Aldersgate Biblical Series*, p. 52.

they were to observe the Sabbath to commemorate the Exodus (Deut. 5:15) by which event He undertook to bring them out of bondage into His rest. The Exodus was, indeed, a pledge of that greater rest which God has promised through the redemptive acts of Jesus Christ. The New Testament writer to Hebrew Christians writes of this effectively in the fourth chapter of his epistle.

(2) The Passover and Feast of Unleavened Bread (23:4-8)

4 These are the set feasts of Jehovah, even holy convocations, which ye shall proclaim in their appointed season. 5 In the first month, on the fourteenth day of the month at even, is Jehovah's passover. 6 And on the fifteenth day of the same month is the feast of unleavened bread unto Jehovah: seven days ye shall eat unleavened bread. 7 In the first day ye shall have a holy convocation: ye shall do no servile work. 8 But ye shall offer an offering made by fire unto Jehovah seven days: in the seventh day is a holy convocation; ye shall do no servile work.

The Sabbath differed from the other holy days referred to in this chapter in that it was a weekly observance while the others were annual affairs.

First among the annual feasts was the Passover (v. 5), which was held on the evening before the full moon of the month Nisan (March-April). Contemporary Jews still observe this holy day each spring during the Christian Eastertide. No description of its observance is given here, but details are prescribed in Exodus 12.

The Passover was not a convocation, but was observed strictly as a family feast in the homes of the people. Neither aliens, sojourners, nor hired servants could participate (Exod. 12:43-49). In case of a small family, neighbors might be invited to share the paschal meal. It was held in sacred commemoration of the Hebrews' exemption from the stroke of the death angel in Egypt. As an evidence of their faith and obedience toward Jehovah, the Hebrew slaves killed a lamb and applied its blood to the lintels and doorposts of their houses and ate the meat to sustain them on their flight to freedom.

In like manner, the later Jews slew a Passover lamb and partook of its meat.

Like the Sabbath, however, the Passover was not only historical. It was also typical. It looked forward as well as backward. The rite was a foreshadowing of the great facts and consequences of Christ's sacrifice. This is suggested first of all by the fact that the Hebrew word for Passover is a derivative of a term meaning "to propitiate." And we remember that in writing of Jesus, John said: "He is the propitiation for our sins; and not for ours only, but also for the whole world. . . ." "Herein is love, not that we loved God, but that he loved us, and sent his Son to be the propitiation for our sins" (I John 2:2; 4:10).

Further illustration of this is seen in the fact that Christ was crucified at the Passover season. It may be that He suffered on the day before the sacrifice of the Passover lamb, since the Hebrew day ended at six p.m. But under the new covenant Good Friday takes the place of the Passover. In this regard the Apostle Paul declares: "Our passover also hath been sacrificed, even Christ" (I Cor. 5:7). And the command not to break a bone of the paschal lamb (Exod. 12:46) is applied to Christ (John 19:36).

So it is that the Passover prefigured a deliverance far greater than that from Egyptian slavery. It speaks of deliverance from Satan and dread of the wrath to come. For even as applying the blood of the Passover victim saved the early Hebrews from the death angel, so the Spirit's application of the blood of Christ to the hearts of those who believe saves from the tyranny and the wages of sin, even death (cf. Rom. 6:23; I Cor. 6:11; Eph. 1:7; Heb. 9:14; I Pet. 1:19; I John 1:7; Rev. 1:5).

Furthermore, as the blood at the door was the only means of safety from an inevitable judgment, so the blood of Christ is the only means whereby we may escape an inevitable and eternal judgment (Acts 4:12).

Then, just as it was not enough to slay the paschal lamb, so it is not enough that Christ should have died. Only in applying the blood to the door was the firstborn safe. So we can be assured of safety only as through faith we have the efficacy of the Savior's blood applied to our hearts (cf. Heb. 10:19-25).

The Passover also speaks to us of the significance of our Christian Lord's Supper. By our observance we show the Lord's death. As the devout Israelite observed the Passover with the slain lamb, he did it with expectancy of entering into the promised land; so we too eat, expecting Him, even our Savior, to come again to bring us to our heavenly home (I Cor. 11:26).

The observance of the Passover was followed immediately the next day by the beginning of the Feast of Unleavened Bread (vv. 6-8). The two occasions are treated here, as in other passages, as two phases of one celebration (cf. Exod. 12:14-20).

The Feast of Unleavened Bread got its name from the fact that for its duration of seven days no leaven was permitted in the houses of the people. They ate their food unleavened, as did their forefathers fleeing from Egypt.

Whereas the Passover rite had special significance in relation to the slaying of the first-born, the Feast of Unleavened Bread emphasized the Exodus itself.

The first day and the last day of the feast were to be holy convocations in which **no servile work** was to be done (v. 7). The implication was that while the people were not to engage in their field work nor that of their craft or profession, different from the Sabbath, they were free to cook their meals and do such essential tasks.

On the intervening days the people carried on their activities quite as usual with the exception that they used unleavened bread, and at the tabernacle made special sacrifices in addition to the regular daily offerings.

Leaven was here a symbol of corruption, though not always so used in the Scriptures (cf. Matt. 13:33). The pains to which the people went to clean their houses of all leaven, and to refrain from eating any during the festival, represented their determined separation from the corruption of the world and sin unto God and His holiness.

It was in the light of this symbolism that the Apostle Paul could appeal so earnestly and graphically to the Corinthian Christians to live pure, holy lives.

"Purge out the old leaven," he said to them, "that ye may be a new lump, even as ye are unleavened" (cf. Heb. 5:1-8).

(3) The Offering of First-Fruits (23:9-14)

9 And Jehovah spake unto Moses, saying, 10 Speak unto the children of Israel, and say unto them, When ye are come into the land which I give unto you, and shall reap the harvest thereof, then ye shall bring the sheaf of the first-fruits of your harvest unto the priest: 11 and he shall wave the sheaf before Jehovah, to be accepted for you: on the morrow after the sabbath the priest shall wave it. 12 And in the day when ye wave the sheaf, ye shall offer a he-lamb without blemish a year old for a burnt-offering unto Jehovah. 13 And the meal-offering thereof shall be two tenth parts *of an ephah* of fine flour mingled with oil, an offering made by fire unto Jehovah for a sweet savor; and the drink-offering thereof shall be of wine, the fourth part of a hin. 14 And ye shall eat neither bread, nor parched grain, nor fresh ears, until this selfsame day, until ye have brought the oblation of your God: it is a statute for ever throughout your generations in all your dwellings.

The instructions for this offering were given in anticipation of Israel's settlement in Palestine (v. 10). There are three other occasions in the book of Leviticus where the same procedure is followed (14:34; 19:23; 25:2).

When the people had become established in their own land, they were to observe an offering of first-fruits on the day following the final Sabbath of the Feast of Unleavened Board (cf. Deut. 26:5-10). This would come normally at the beginning of barley harvest in what is now our month of April.

This observance involved the bringing of a sheaf of the grain to the priest, who would present it before the Lord and sacrifice a burnt-offering with its meal- and drink-offerings (cf. 1:1-17; 6:8-13; 2:1-16; 6:14-23; Exod. 29:38-42).

The single sheaf of grain offered by the priest represented the complete harvest as belonging to God. So the people were not permitted to eat any of their grain in any form until they had recognized God's ownership with this offering of thanksgiving and consecration (v. 14). In their festival of unleavened bread they had symbolized the fact that they themselves belonged to the Lord; now in this rite they show further that all they possess also belongs to Him.

This would remind us that we are not free to spend our own energies, abilities or income first upon ourselves and then, if there is a surplus, share with the Lord. Our first-fruits belong to God. Kingdom interests have priority (Luke 12:31). All we are and have belongs to God. We are but stewards (Ps. 24:1; Rom. 6:13; 12:1, 2).

The Apostle Paul seems to have this law in mind when he applies its symbolism to the Gentile Christians (Rom. 8:23); to the ancestors of the Jews (Rom. 11:16); to individual Christians (Rom. 16:5); and to Christ (I Cor. 15:20, 23). Other similar New Testament references are also significant (see Jas. 1:18; Rev. 14:4).

(4) The Feast of Weeks or Pentecost (23:15-22)

15 And ye shall count unto you from the morrow after the sabbath, from the day that ye brought the sheaf of the wave-offering; seven sabbaths shall there be complete: 16 even unto the morrow after the seventh sabbath shall ye number fifty days; and ye shall offer a new meal-offering unto Jehovah. 17 Ye shall bring out of your habitations two wave-loaves of two tenth parts *of an ephah*: they shall be of fine flour, they shall be baken with leaven, for first-fruits unto Jehovah. 18 And ye shall present with the bread seven lambs without blemish a year old, and one young bullock, and two rams: they shall be a burnt-offering unto Jehovah, with their meal-offering, and their drink-offerings, even an offering made by fire, of a sweet savor unto Jehovah. 19 And ye shall offer one he-goat for a sin-offering, and two he-lambs a year old for a sacrifice of peace-offerings. 20 And the priest shall wave them with the bread of the first-fruits for a wave-offering before Jehovah, with the two lambs: they shall be holy to Jehovah for the priest. 21 And ye shall make proclamation on the selfsame day; there shall be a holy convocation unto you; ye

shall do no servile work: it is a statute forever in all your dwellings throughout your generations.

Some seven weeks, fifty days to be exact, after the offering of the first-fruits the Feast of Weeks was to be held as a holy convocation free from servile work. The name by which the feast later became known, Pentecost, comes from the Greek word meaning fifty.

The first-fruits offering was to mark the very beginning of the harvest. Since the first grain to ripen would be barley, a barley sheaf was to be offered. The Feast of Weeks was to mark the close of the grain harvest. The last of the grains to be reaped was the wheat. The grain in this case was offered in the form of a special **new** (i.e., of new grain) **meal-offering** (v. 16; cf. 2:1-16; 6:14-23). The meal-offering was in the form of bread. This was an unusual meal-offering in that the bread was leavened. It was, in fact, to be just like that which they ate daily in their homes. Since it contained leaven, here symbolizing corruption, none of it could be burned at God's altar. It was to be offered as a wave-offering (v. 20; cf. 14:12).

The **ephah** was equivalent to three-eighths to two-thirds of a bushel. This special wave-offering was to be accompanied by **burnt-offerings** (1:1-17; 6:8-13), with their regular **meal-offering** (2:1-16; 6:14-23) and **drink-offerings** (Exod. 29:40f.; Num. 28:7), as well as with **peace-offerings** (3:1-17; 7:11-38).

Since this was to be a harvest festival, it was not out of place to remind the people at the time of the requirement about permitting the poor to glean their fields (v. 22; cf. 19:9). For at this season they should be particularly aware of being stewards of God's abundance. The harvest was, after all, of God's doing. Kellogg says:

This festival, as one of the sabbatic series, celebrated the rest after the labors of the grain harvest, a symbol of the great sabbatism to follow that harvest which is the "end of the age," Matthew 19:39. As a consecration, it dedicated unto God the daily food of the nation for the coming year. As passover reminded them that God was the Creator of Israel, so herein, receiving their daily bread from Him, they were reminded that He was also the Sustainer of Israel; while the full accompaniment of burnt-offerings and peace-offerings expressed their full consecration and happy state of friendship with Jehovah, secured through the expiation of the sin-offering.[15]

This feast is particularly significant to Christians, for it was during one of its observances that the early Church was baptized with the Holy Spirit. It occurred with the coming of the Holy Spirit to 120 faithful disciples of Jesus who, in obedience to His instructions, were waiting in an upper room in Jerusalem (Acts 2).

In this way the Feast of Pentecost prefigured the ministry of the Holy Spirit in His sanctifying influences, cleansing and empowering the hearts and lives of those who open themselves to Him. In this light the harvest festival of Israel speaks to us of the fruit, the harvest of the Spirit in the lives of those in whom He dwells: "love, joy, peace, longsuffering, kindness, goodness, faithfulness, meekness, self-control" (Gal. 5:22).

By this feast, especially marked by the offering of bread like that which they daily ate, we are reminded of Him who came to be one among us, providing us with daily bread from heaven for our spiritual sustenance (John 6:35).

(5) The Feast of Trumpets (23:23-25)

22 And when ye reap the harvest of your land, thou shalt not wholly reap the corners of thy field, neither shalt thou gather the gleaning of thy harvest: thou shalt leave them for the poor, and for the sojourner: I am Jehovah your God. 23 And Jehovah spake unto Moses, saying, 24 Speak unto the children of Israel, saying, In the seventh month, on the first day of the month, shall be a solemn rest unto you, a memorial of blowing of trumpets, a holy convocation. 25 Ye shall do no servile work; and ye shall offer an offering made by fire unto Jehovah.

The number seven had particular significance in Israel. It was the sacred number of perfection. It is not surprising then that the seventh month, Tishri (our September-October), in the Hebrew calendar was marked by three special occasions: the Feast of Trumpets, the Day of Atonement, and the Feast of Tabernacles.

The first day of this month was the Hebrews' New Year's Day — the beginning of their civil year. Even to the present time, Jews celebrate this occasion each fall with a holiday known as "rosh hashshanah," the beginning of the year.

Originally the day was to be observed as a holy convocation in which regular work and business were to be put aside.

The day was to be announced by the joyous blasts of many trumpets throughout the land. Actually, the Hebrew text does not contain the word *trumpet*, but rather a word which indicates either shouting or blowing a blast. It may well be that both the shouting of the people and the blowing of the trumpets were involved. According to Jewish tradition, the blasts were blown not upon the silver trumpet of Numbers 10:2-10, commonly used by the priests at the sanctuary, but rather upon the ram's horn used on other especially solemn occasions (cf. Josh. 6). Everyone in Israel anywhere throughout the land was urged this day to blow his ram's horn. It was a day of special gladness.

While the whole congregation was not required to gather at the sanctuary on this day, the priests did offer additional sacrifices at the altar besides the daily sacrifices.

The blowing of the trumpets may have been considered as God reminding the people of their duty to Him and of the need for preparing themselves for the particularly significant holy days which the month ahead held for them. It may also have been that the Hebrews thought of it as a reminder of God's steadfast love toward them and their fathers; a glad proclamation of their call to and unique position in the divine favor.

Indeed, the trumpet is frequently used in Scripture as an image of the voice or Word of God. So it is that the proclaiming of God's faithfulness on the Feast of Trumpets might well be considered a type of the New Testament account of the proclamation of the gospel through Christ and His Church. This very image is so used if, as many think, Isaiah 27:13 refers to the conversion of the nations to faith in Christ. The prophet there declares, "It shall come to pass in that day, that a great trumpet shall be blown." And how true it is that the sounding forth of the gospel proclaimed a glorious new beginning!

(6) The Day of Atonement (23:26-32)

26 And Jehovah spake unto Moses, saying, 27 Howbeit on the tenth day of this seventh month is the day of atonement: it shall be a holy convocation unto you, and ye shall afflict your souls; and ye shall offer an offering made by fire unto Jehovah. 28 And ye shall do no manner of work in that same day; for it is a day of atonement, to make atonement for you before Jehovah your God. 29 For whatsoever soul it be that shall not be afflicted in that same day; he shall be cut off from his people. 30 And whatsoever soul it be that doeth any manner of work in that same day, that soul will I destroy from among his people. 31 Ye shall do no manner of work: it is a statute for ever throughout your generations in all your dwellings. 32 It shall be unto you a sabbath of solemn rest, and ye shall afflict your souls: in the ninth day of the month at even, from even unto even, shall ye keep your sabbath.

Nine days after the Hebrew New Year's celebration was to come the most solemn day of all — the Day of Atonement. It was to be a day of fasting, a day of humbling before God for all Israel. It was a day of special sacrifices; the only day of the whole year when even the high priest approached into the immediate presence of Jehovah in the Most Holy Place of the tabernacle. It was on this day that the expiatory sacrifices, offered in sincere repentance and with faith, gave assurance that all sin was removed and that Israel could rest in Jehovah's loving favor. It was a day foreshadowing the complete salvation God provides through Christ Jesus.

The detailed instructions regarding the observance of this high day are given in chapter 16 where there are rather full comments.

(7) The Feast of Tabernacles (23:33-44)

33 And Jehovah spake unto Moses, saying, 34 Speak unto the children of Israel, saying, On the fifteenth day of this seventh month is the feast of tabernacles for seven days unto Jehovah. 35 On the first day shall be a holy convocation: ye shall do no servile work. 36 Seven days ye shall offer an offering made by fire unto Jehovah: on the eighth day shall be a holy convocation unto you; and ye shall offer an offering made by fire unto Jehovah: it is a solemn assembly; ye shall do no servile work.

37 These are the set feasts of Jehovah, which ye shall proclaim to be holy convocations, to offer an offering made by fire unto Jehovah, a burnt-offering, and a meal-offering, a sacrifice, and drink-offerings, each on its own day; 38 besides the sabbaths of Jehovah, and besides your gifts, and besides all your vows, and besides all your freewill-offerings, which ye give unto Jehovah.

39 Howbeit on the fifteenth day of the seventh month, when ye have gathered in the fruits of the land, ye shall keep the feast of Jehovah seven days: on the first day shall be a solemn rest, and on the eighth day shall be a solemn rest. 40 And ye shall take you on the first day the fruit of goodly trees, branches of palm-trees, and boughs of thick trees, and willows of the brook; and ye shall rejoice before Jehovah your God seven days. 41 And ye shall keep it a feast unto Jehovah seven days in the year: it is a statute for ever throughout your generations; ye shall keep it in the seventh month. 42 Ye shall dwell in booths seven days; all that are home-born in Israel shall dwell in booths; 43 that your generations may know that I made the children of Israel to dwell ·in booths, when I brought them out of the land of Egypt: Ĩ am Jehovah your God. 44 And Moses declared unto the children of Israel the set feasts of Jehovah.

Two weeks after the Day of Atonement the Israelites were to begin a week-long celebration known as **the feast of tabernacles** or booths (v. 34), so called because for the duration of the festivities the people were to live in temporary booths made of **branches of palm trees, and boughs of thick trees, and willows of the brook** (v. 40). This was done to commemorate the temporary dwellings of Israel during the long wilderness wanderings. It was also to remind the present generation of God's care and guidance of their forefathers through those difficult years when they had no fields, no crops, and no permanent abiding place. And it was to impress upon them what every generation needs to be reminded of: "that man doth not live by bread only, but by everything that proceedeth out of the mouth of Jehovah doth man live" (Deut. 8:3).

Furthermore, coming at the close of the harvest of fruit trees and vineyards (v. 39), it was to be a special time of thanksgiving and rejoicing before the Lord (v. 40; cf. Deut. 16:13-15). It was their annual thanksgiving festival. Attesting to the sincere gratitude of the people toward the Lord, they gave special attention and consideration to the Levites who had no portion in the land, and to the fatherless, the widow, and even to the Gentile sojourner among them.

The first and eighth days were to be holy days of convocation free from ordinary work and business (vv. 35, 36). All week long there was also to be much activity at the sanctuary with the offering of a great many special sacrifices. For example, this week involved the largest number of burnt-offerings of any of the feasts, consisting of a total of seventy bulls. Details of all this are given in Numbers 29:12-38.

This joyous thanksgiving feast calls to mind that many of Israel's holy days were marked by gladness, and evidences the fact that the Israelites' walk with Jehovah brought them much happiness. Theirs was a religion of joy. Even their Sabbaths, which may appear austere to us, were not days of stern repression and forbidding gloom. They were rather days of rest and rejoicing pointing forward to the eternal joy of the consummated kingdom, the Sabbath rest which remains for the people of God (Heb. 4:9).

What was true of the religion of the Old Testament is much more true of that proclaimed in the New. In all times and among all peoples those who trust in Jehovah and order their lives by His precepts find the joy of the Lord to be their strength (Neh. 8:10).

b. The Holy Light and Bread (24:1-9)

Israel was to be a holy nation separated unto the holy God. To help maintain this sacred relationship all of the people were continually to observe numerous holy convocations unique to the history and life of the nation. Among these was the Sabbath, a weekly day of rest and worship. Other stipulated holy days and festivals were to be observed annually.

But holy living involves more than weekly and annual convocations. It must be a daily, hourly affair. So it was that between Sabbaths, the priests were to make daily sacrifices and keep up a constant routine of service at the sanctuary. Two phases of the priests' daily functions are brought to attention here: keeping the light burning in the golden lampstand in the Holy Place of the tabernacle, and supplying the showbread continually displayed on a table in the same room.

Why these matters should be discussed just here is not clear. But it does not seem strange to place the descriptions of these priestly functions immediately following instructions for the annual thanksgiving feast celebrating the harvest of fruit and grain. This placement might well point up the fact that the priests were dependent upon the people sharing their harvests, if the work of God was to continue.

So it ever is. If holiness is to characterize any nation, holiness must characterize generally the individuals who make up that nation. No one group, not even a consecrated, devoted body of priests or ministers, can make a nation holy. In the situation before us we see ways whereby a holy people and a holy priesthood were to cooperate in the worship of God and in maintaining a nation worthy of His name.

(1) The Oil for the Lamp (24:1-4)

1 And Jehovah spake unto Moses, saying, 2 Command the children of Israel, that they bring unto thee pure olive oil beaten for the light, to cause a lamp to burn continually. 3 Without the veil of the testimony, in the tent of meeting, shall Aaron keep it in order from evening to morning before Jehovah continually: it shall be a statute for ever throughout your generations. 4 He shall keep in order the lamps upon the pure candlestick before Jehovah continually.

The lamp referred to here is the golden lampstand described in Exodus 25:31-40 which was to stand in the south side of the Holy Place separated from the Most Holy Place by the **veil of the testimony** (v. 3). It was made of a single shaft with three branches on either side. At the top of the central shaft and of each branch was an oil container shaped like an almond blossom. A light was to keep burning continually in each of the seven containers **from evening to morning** (v. 3). It was the task of Aaron (v. 4) and his sons (Exod. 27:21) to **keep it in order.** But it was for the people to supply by freewill-offerings the olive oil which was to provide the fuel for the lights. The oil was to be only of the best quality, obtained by merely beating or bruising the olives in a mortar or mill without application of heat (v. 2).

Zechariah (4:1-14) used a similar lampstand to symbolize the nation of Israel, God's congregation, as the giver of light to all the world. The light burning in the Holy Place of the sanctuary in the center of Israel's camp might well be a similar symbol. And since oil, the source of the light, is generally typical of the Holy Spirit, the same emphasis appears here as in Zechariah. The light burns effectively "not by might, nor by power, but by my Spirit, saith Jehovah of hosts" (Zech. 4:6).

This all may in turn well foreshadow the Christian Church and its salvation influence throughout the earth. The Lord Himself declared of His people: "Ye are the light of the world . . . . let your light shine before men; that they may see your good works, and glorify your Father who is in heaven" (Matt. 5:14, 16). This truth is set forth again by the Revelator who saw in his vision the collective Church through the ages represented by seven lampstands among which Christ walked robed in high-priestly vesture (Rev. 1).

That the light might keep burning brightly, the priests were to work diligently with the lamps each day, trimming and cleaning. This suggests that only that True Light which shines to all men (John 1:9) is eternally luminous and lustrous. All of us as lesser lights are responsible to keep our lights burning (Luke 12:35). This is especially illustrated in the experience of the foolishly neglectful virgins who found their lights going out (Matt. 25:8).

How great is the Christian's personal responsibility here! Darkness may brood over the world outside, but the light in the sanctuary must continually shine.

Outside, the gloom of error and darkness of delusion may spread, but within Christ's Church "the light of the knowledge of the glory of God" must shine on. Outside, men may love darkness and dwell therein because their deeds are evil. But within Christ's Church men must love light. Their deeds must be deeds of truth so that by them the light manifests the work of God to the world (John 3:19-21).

(2) The Bread of the Sanctuary (24:5-9)

5 And thou shalt take fine flour, and bake twelve cakes thereof: two tenth parts *of an ephah* shall be in one cake. 6 And thou shalt set them in two rows, six on a row, upon the pure table before Jehovah. 7 And thou shalt put pure frankincense upon each row, that it may be to the bread for a memorial, even an offering made by fire unto Jehovah. 8 Every sabbath day he shall set it in order before Jehovah continually; it is on the behalf of the children of Israel, an everlasting covenant. 9 And it shall be for Aaron and his sons; and they shall eat it in a holy place: for it is most holy unto him of the offerings of Jehovah made by fire by a perpetual statute.

Standing on the north side of the Holy Place, opposite the golden lampstand, was a golden table described in Exodus 25:23-30. Upon this table there was to be a constant supply of bread — twelve loaves, one for each tribe in Israel. This bread, baked by the Levites from flour furnished by the people, was called showbread, literally, "bread of the face" or "bread of the presence" because it was placed before the face of the Lord, that is, in His presence.

The loaves were to be arranged in two rows, or perhaps two piles of six loaves each (v. 6 and margin). On or beside (v. 7, AOT) each row or pile of loaves there was to be a bowl or spoon of frankincense which was to be burned before the Lord each Sabbath (probably on the golden altar of incense) when the new supply of bread was placed on the table. It was placed on the table in such a way that the table would never be empty as a continual memorial to the everlasting covenant between Jehovah and His people (v. 8).

Like the meal-offering made in the

outer court (2:1-16; 6:14-23) the loaves on the table in the Holy Place were to symbolize the consecration unto the Lord of the results of the labor of the hands. The twelve loaves on the table, representing the whole nation, implied that the Lord desires the consecration of the nation as well as of individuals — the nation with all of the potential of its collective organization.

The table upon which the bread was laid, made of acacia wood overlaid with gold, is commonly recognized as a symbol of Christ. This being so, we are reminded that only as we or our gifts are laid upon Christ can they be accepted before the Lord.

c. Punishment for Blasphemy (24:10-23)

10 And the son of an Israelitish woman, whose father was an Egyptian, went out among the children of Israel; and the son of the Israelitish woman and a man of Israel strove together in the camp: 11 and the son of the Israelitish woman blasphemed the Name, and cursed; and they brought him unto Moses. And his mother's name was Shelomith, the daughter of Dibri, of the tribe of Dan. 12 And they put him in ward, that it might be declared unto them at the mouth of Jehovah.

13 And Jehovah spake unto Moses, saying, 14 Bring forth him that hath cursed without the camp; and let all that heard him lay their hands upon his head, and let all the congregation stone him. 15 And thou shalt speak unto the children of Israel, saying, Whosoever curseth his God shall bear his sin. 16 And he that blasphemeth the name of Jehovah, he shall surely be put to death; all the congregation shall certainly stone him: as well the sojourner, as the home-born, when he blasphemeth the name of Jehovah, shall be put to death. 17 And he that smiteth any man mortally shall surely be put to death. 18 And he that smiteth a beast mortally shall make it good, life for life. 19 And if a man cause a blemish in his neighbor; as he hath done, so shall it be done to him: 20 breach for breach, eye for eye, tooth for tooth; as he hath caused a blemish in a man, so shall it be rendered unto him. 21 And he that killeth a beast shall make it good: and he that killeth a man shall be put to death. 22 Ye shall have one manner of law, as well for the sojourner, as for the home-born: for I am Jehovah

your God. 23 And Moses spake to the children of Israel; and they brought forth him that had cursed out of the camp, and stoned him with stones. And the children of Israel did as Jehovah commanded Moses.

In a holy nation blasphemy cannot be tolerated. When, therefore, the son of an Israelite woman profaned God's name, the judges knew that something must be done. But what? This is the first mention of such a sin. The judges had probably not met such a situation before.

There were two problems. What was to be the penalty for blasphemy? Should the same penalty apply to all in Israel, the man of mixed blood as well as the pure-bred Israelite? The offender was put in confinement until the authorities could obtain divine direction.

The Lord made it clear (probably by Urim and Thummim) that blasphemy was a heinous sin, and demanded the death penalty. Furthermore, the penalty must be applied to all who might offend, whether they were home-born or Gentile sojourners.

Verses 17-22 deal with a series of violent crimes already discussed in Exodus 21:12, 23-36. They may be inserted here in order to highlight by association the seriousness of blasphemy, and they may be mentioned also to indicate that the penalty of each of those sins was to be the same for all people in Israel, as was the penalty for profanity. No exceptions were to be allowed.

To us death seems an unduly stern penalty for the crime. It is, however, impossible for us to judge Israel's civil laws objectively from our vantage point. But irreverence and disrespect for God, which blasphemous profanity displays, is a grievous sin any time, anywhere, because reverence for God lies at the very foundation of even common morality. Furthermore, profanity is a particularly corrupting evil. It influences others quickly and tragically. Death may have been as much a penalty to rid the community of this vile spot of infection as to prescribe a penalty fitting the offence. For as Nathaniel Micklem comments: "Disaster must descend upon the land where the Name is cursed, the lordship of the living God repudiated, no matter whether the offender is a native Israelite or a resident alien."[16]

4. Directions Concerning the Land (25:1—26:46)

The earlier chapters of Leviticus set forth numerous graphic ways in which God sought to impress Israel with the fact that they themselves and all the products of their hands and fields were peculiarly the Lord's and that they were to show forth His holiness among the nations.

Now the laws regarding the land stress the fact that the very fields upon which they are utterly dependent for sustenance belong to Jehovah. Ownership of any plot of ground was not vested in a man, but in God. This fact is parallel to the customs of most primitive peoples to the present where land is held in trusteeship by the clan and is inalienable.

Not only would these laws emphasize the fact that "the earth is the Lord's," but they would also be strong deterrents to individual covetousness in Israel; and throughout the land they would tend greatly to curb economic exploitation.

a. The Sabbatical Year (25:1-7)

1 And Jehovah spake unto Moses in mount Sinai, saying, 2 Speak unto the children of Israel, and say unto them, When ye come into the land which I give you, then shall the land keep a sabbath unto Jehovah. 3 Six years thou shalt sow thy field, and six years thou shalt prune thy vineyard, and gather in the fruits thereof; 4 but in the seventh year shall be a sabbath of solemn rest for the land, a sabbath unto Jehovah: thou shalt neither sow thy field, nor prune thy vineyard. 5 That which groweth of itself of thy harvest thou shalt not reap, and the grapes of thy undressed vine thou shalt not gather: it shall be a year of solemn rest for the land. 6 And the sabbath of the land shall be for food for you; for thee, and for thy servant and for thy maid, and for thy hired servant and for thy stranger, who sojourn with thee. 7 And for thy cattle, and for the beasts that are in thy land, shall all the increase thereof be for food.

The law of the sabbatical year stipulated that the land possessed by the He-brews was to lie fallow for one year in every seven years. Not only were no grains to be sown, but during this time olive groves and vineyards were to remain unattended.

During this year whatever the land produced of itself was not to be harvested and stored as usual by the owner or tenant, but was to be left for public consumption. The poor, the slave, and the stranger could partake of it freely.

The charity motive was, indeed, one reason for this practice (Exod. 23:10, 11). Another indication of the spirit of charity which was to predominate during the sabbatical year was the fact that those people who had borrowed money were not obligated during this year to make payment on their debts (Deut. 15:1-11). The plan was also to provide **rest for the land** (v. 5). An even more important purpose was to point up the fact that the land really belonged to Jehovah, who would give it back to His people for stewardship (v. 2).

The sabbatical year was to begin at the end of Israel's seventh ecclesiastical month (see notes on 23:23-25). It is not stated, however, when the people, after their arrival in Palestine, were to begin their calculation for the seventh year for this observance. But it would seem likely that they would not do so until they quite generally possessed the land and the tribes were settled in their portions (Josh. 5:12).

There were apparently no special religious gatherings required, but Deuteronomy 31:10 suggests that it was to be a year spent in the teaching and training of Israel in the laws of Jehovah. Furthermore, to carry out the demands of this law and thus to prove the promises of God would impress Israel with the reality of Jehovah's presence and providence and train them in habits of trust and confidence (vv. 20-22). Not only so, but obedience to this law would make Israel conspicuous among the other peoples of Palestine. It would, therefore, provide a remarkable opportunity for witnessing to their faith as they sought to answer questions bound to arise among outsiders with whom they would come in contact.

---

[16] Micklem, *op. cit.*, p. 119.

b. The Year of Jubilee (25:8-55)

Every fiftieth year at the close of the Day of Atonement ram's horn trumpets resounded throughout the land proclaiming the year of jubilee — so called from the Hebrew word *yobhel,* meaning "ram," whose horn was used in the proclamation. The sabbatical rules for resting the land (vv. 1-7) were in force during this extraordinary year; but there were additional regulations which provided even greater liberties and more freedom.

(1) Rules for Its Observation (25:8-22)

8 And thou shalt number seven sabbaths of years unto thee, seven times seven years; and there shall be unto thee the days of seven sabbaths of years, even forty and nine years. 9 Then shalt thou send abroad the loud trumpet on the tenth day of the seventh month; in the day of atonement shall ye send abroad the trumpet throughout all your land. 10 And ye shall hallow the fiftieth year, and proclaim liberty throughout the land unto all the inhabitants thereof: it shall be a jubilee unto you; and ye shall return every man unto his possession, and ye shall return every man unto his family. 11 A jubilee shall that fiftieth year be unto you: ye shall not sow, neither reap that which groweth of itself in it, nor gather *the grapes* in it of the undressed vines. 12 For it is a jubilee; it shall be holy unto you: ye shall eat the increase thereof out of the field. 13 In this year of jubilee ye shall return every man unto his possession. 14 And if thou sell aught unto thy neighbor, or buy of thy neighbor's hand, ye shall not wrong one another. 15 According to the number of years after the jubilee thou shalt buy of thy neighbor, *and* according unto the number of years of the crops he shall sell unto thee. 16 According to the multitude of the years thou shalt increase the price thereof, and according to the fewness of the years thou shalt diminish the price of it; for the number of the crops doth he sell unto thee. 17 And ye shall not wrong one another; but thou shalt fear thy God: for I am Jehovah your God. 18 Wherefore ye shall do my statutes, and keep mine ordinances and do them; and ye shall dwell in the land in safety. 19 And the land shall yield its fruit, and ye shall eat your fill, and dwell therein in safety. 20 And if ye shall say, What shall we eat the seventh year? behold, we shall not sow, nor gather in our increase; 21 then I will command my blessing upon you in the sixth year, and it shall bring forth fruit for the three years. 22 And ye shall sow the eighth year, and eat of the fruits, the old store; until the ninth year, until its fruits come in, ye shall eat the old store.

On the year of jubilee all land reverted back to the original family free of encumbrances (vv. 10, 13). So it was that no one was to be able to buy land in Israel in perpetuity (v. 23). It was really a matter of leasing. The amount of rent to be paid was reckoned upon the approximate value of crops in the remaining years before jubilee (vv. 14-16). This regulation naturally made for the careful preservation of genealogies. And because of the law no one family could grow exorbitantly rich by permanently adding property to property; nor could any family be doomed to perpetual poverty, for whatever possessions might have been lost were restored every fifty years.

To keep the sabbatical laws regarding the land brought special blessings from God. He declared that in the sixth year previous to the observance of the sabbatical year there would be a "bumper crop" so that they could lay up in store. If there were not then enough supplies obtainable from the untilled land, there would still be plenty of food for all (vv. 18-22; cf. II Kings 19:29; Isa. 37:30). Even when the year of jubilee followed a sabbatical year, there would be food enough in the sixth-year crop for two following years (v. 21).

On the year of jubilee slaves were freed (vv. 10, 39-43), and debtors were absolved (Deut. 15:2, 3).

The prophet Isaiah (61:1-3) alluded to the proclamation of the jubilee year when he spoke those remarkable words which Jesus read in the Nazareth synagogue and declared were fulfilled in Himself (Luke 4:16-20). And how true it is that Christ through His work of redemption has freed us from the bondage of sin and slavery to Satan and has restored us into the glorious liberty of the children of God. And whomsoever the Son makes free is free indeed (John 8:36; Rom. 6:18, 22; 8:2).

(2) The Law of Redemption (25: 23-34)

23 And the land shall not be sold in perpetuity; for the land is mine: for ye are strangers and sojourners with me. 24 And in all the land of your possession ye shall grant a redemption for the land. 25 If thy brother be waxed poor, and sell some of his possession, then shall his kinsman that is next unto him come, and shall redeem that which his brother hath sold. 26 And if a man have no one to redeem it, and he be waxed rich and find sufficient to redeem it; 27 then let him reckon the years of the sale thereof, and restore the overplus unto the man to whom he sold it; and he shall return unto his possession. 28 But if he be not able to get it back for himself, then that which he hath sold shall remain in the hand of him that hath bought it until the year of jubilee: and in the jubilee it shall go out, and he shall return unto his possession.

29 And if a man sell a dwelling-house in a walled city, then he may redeem it within a whole year after it is sold; for a full year shall he have the right of redemption. 30 And if it be not redeemed within the space of a full year, then the house that is in the walled city shall be made sure in perpetuity to him that bought it, throughout his generations: it shall not go out in the jubilee. 31 But the houses of the villages which have no wall round about them shall be reckoned with the fields of the country: they may be redeemed, and they shall go out in the jubilee. 32 Nevertheless the cities of the Levites, the houses of the cities of their possession, may the Levites redeem at any time. 33 And if one of the Levites redeem, then the house that was sold, and the city of his possession, shall go out in the jubilee; for the houses of the cities of the Levites are their possession among the children of Israel. 34 But the field of the suburbs of their cities may not be sold; for it is their perpetual possession.

The concept upon which this law was based is explained in verse 23. The idea was that Israelites were to be **strangers and sojourners** on land which did not rightly belong to them, but which the Lord was giving them as an inheritance. The land was then a stewardship from Jehovah, not private property to be bought and sold for any personal profit. The law opposed the swallowing up of ancestral holdings (I Kings 21:3; Isa.

5:8). No land was to be sold forever from the family who obtained it at the original division and allotment of Canaan.

Even before the year of jubilee land could be redeemed. If, for example, a landholder would come into financial straits and need to sell his property, he might do so. But if then, a near kinsman (literally, "redeemer") would have sufficient funds to buy back the property lost, he might do so at any time, so that the land would revert to the original family (cf. Ruth 4).

This illustrates what Christ has done in a spiritual sense for us. He became *man*, a near kinsman, a redeemer, and redeemed the inheritance which we forfeited through sin (Eph. 1:3-14).

If the man who sold his property should later become financially able, he might buy back the land by restoring to the buyer money in proportion to the years yet remaining until the jubilee year (vv. 24-27).

There was to be exception made in the case of city houses not belonging to Levites. In this case, if the house sold was not redeemed within a year it would become the buyer's in perpetuity (vv. 29, 30). This was to be permitted because city houses were not considered necessary means of support as were the fields. This also gave opportunity for proselytes to own property; and city property was suitable for those engaged in a trade or a craft.

If, however, a Levite's house were to be sold, it could be redeemed at any time, even after a year had elapsed. And if not redeemed (v. 33, margin) it would return to him at the jubilee year. For the property given the Levites for service at the sanctuary was to remain permanently in their possession (vv. 32, 33; cf. Num. 35:1-8).

(3) Treatment of the Poor (25:35-55)

35 And if thy brother be waxed poor, and his hand fail with thee; then thou shalt uphold him: *as* a stranger and a sojourner shall he live with thee. 36 Take thou no interest of him or increase, but fear thy God; that thy brother may live with thee. 37 Thou shalt not give him thy money upon interest, nor give him thy victuals for increase. 38 I am Jehovah your God, who brought you forth

out of the land of Egypt, to give you the land of Canaan, *and* to be your God.

39 And if thy brother be waxed poor with thee, and sell himself unto thee; thou shalt not make him to serve as a bondservant. 40 As a hired servant, and as a sojourner, he shall be with thee; he shall serve with thee unto the year of jubilee: 41 then shall he go out from thee, he and his children with him, and shall return unto his own family, and unto the possession of his fathers shall he return. 42 For they are my servants, whom I brought forth out of the land of Egypt: they shall not be sold as bondmen. 43 Thou shalt not rule over him with rigor, but shalt fear thy God. 44 And as for thy bondmen, and thy bondmaids, whom thou shalt have; of the nations that are round about you, of them shall ye buy bondmen and bondmaids. 45 Moreover of the children of the strangers that sojourn among you, of them shall ye buy, and of their families that are with you, which they have begotten in your land: and they shall be your possession. 46 And ye shall make them an inheritance for your children after you, to hold for a possession; of them shall ye take your bondmen for ever: but over your brethren the children of Israel ye shall not rule, one over another, with rigor.

47 And if a stranger or sojourner with thee be waxed rich, and thy brother be waxed poor beside him, and sell himself unto the stranger *or* sojourner with thee, or to the stock of the stranger's family; 48 after that he is sold he may be redeemed: one of his brethren may redeem him; 49 or his uncle, or his uncle's son, may redeem him, or any that is nigh of kin unto him of his family may redeem him: or if he be waxed rich, he may redeem himself. 50 And he shall reckon with him that bought him from the year that he sold himself to him unto the year of jubilee: and the price of his sale shall be according unto the number of years; according to the time of a hired servant shall he be with him. 51 If there be yet many years, according unto them he shall give back the price of his redemption out of the money that he was bought for. 52 And if there remain but few years unto the year of jubilee, then he shall reckon with him; according unto his years shall he give back the price of his redemption. 53 As a servant hired year by year shall he be with him: he shall not rule with rigor over him in thy sight. 54 And if he be not redeemed by these *means*, then he shall go out in the year of jubilee, he, and his children with

him. 55 For unto me the children of Israel are servants; they are my servants whom I brought forth out of the land of Egypt: I am Jehovah your God.

If a fellow Israelite were to become in need, he was to be maintained. If he borrowed money, no interest was to be charged him. If he needed to buy food, the food was to be sold to him without profit (vv. 35-38; Exod. 22:25).

No Israelite was to be permitted to buy one of his brethren as a slave. A poor man was, however, to be able to sell himself as a hired servant for six years, or until the year of jubilee, if the jubilee year should come first (vv. 39-43; cf. Exod. 21:1-6; Deut. 15:12-18).

It was to be permissible, however, for the Israelites to have slaves from among non-Israelites (vv. 44-66). Should an Israelite become poor and sell himself to serve a non-Israelite resident of the land as a hired servant until the year of jubilee, in the interim he might be redeemed by a near kinsman; or if he became able, he might also redeem himself by repaying the employer money in proportion to the time remaining until jubilee year (vv. 47-55).

c. Prosperity for Obedience (26:1-13)

1 Ye shall make you no idols, neither shall ye rear you up a graven image, or a pillar, neither shall ye place any figured stone in your land, to bow down unto it: for I am Jehovah your God. 2 Ye shall keep my sabbaths, and reverence my sanctuary: I am Jehovah.

3 If ye walk in my statutes, and keep my commandments, and do them; 4 then I will give your rains in their season, and the land shall yield its increase, and the trees of the field shall yield their fruit. 5 And your threshing shall reach unto the vintage, and the vintage shall reach unto the sowing time; and ye shall eat your bread to the full, and dwell in your land safely. 6 And I will give peace in the land, and ye shall lie down, and none shall make you afraid: and I will cause evil beasts to cease out of the land, neither shall the sword go through your land. 7 And ye shall chase your enemies, and they shall fall before you by the sword. 8 And five of you shall chase a hundred, and a hundred of you shall chase ten thousand; and your enemies shall fall before you by the sword. 9 And I will have respect unto you, and make you fruitful, and multiply you, and

will establish my covenant with you. 10
And ye shall eat old store long kept, and
ye shall bring forth the old because of
the new. 11 And I will set my tabernacle among you: and my soul shall not
abhor you. 12 And I will walk among
you, and will be your God, and ye shall
be my people. 13 I am Jehovah your
God, who brought you forth out of the
land of Egypt, that ye shall not be their
bondmen; and I have broken the bars
of your yoke, and made you go upright.

The importance of keeping the laws of
Jehovah are summed up in Deuteronomy
30:15. And here God points out that
the choice is up to the people. If they
chose obedience, there would be blessing (cf. Exod. 19:5, 6). But if they
chose disobedience, there would be judgment. This was to be true not only for
Israel, but for all men in all times (cf.
John 3:16-21).

Before speaking of the blessing which
comes from obedience to His law, Jehovah gives a final warning and exhortation. There must be no idolatry, but
complete loyalty to the true God. There
must be diligent keeping of the Sabbaths.
There must be a reverence for the place
of worship where God in a very special
way manifested Himself among them.
These three demands may well be considered as a summary of the fundamental
commandments of the law.

An obedient people would be blessed
by a supply of physical needs, peace,
power in the face of all enemies (v. 8),
and the presence of God who would have
fellowship with His people (v. 12).

The meaning of verse 1 seems clearer
as expressed in the LXX: "Ye shall not
make to yourselves gods made with hands,
or graven; neither shall ye rear up a
pillar for yourselves, neither shall ye set
up a stone for an object in your land to
worship it."

Establish my covenant with you (v. 9).
This is a confirmation of Jehovah's promises to Abraham (Gen. 12:2; 13:16; 15:5;
17:5, 6; 18:18; 22:17, 18).

The significance of verse 10 is that
crops would be in such abundance that
the people would be able to lay up in
store large amounts to last a long time.
They would, in fact, have to clear out
stored supplies in order to make room
for the new crops.

I will set my tabernacle among you
. . . . I will walk among you. These
words have been gloriously fulfilled to
us through Christ, of whom John wrote:
"The Word [Christ] became flesh [human,
incarnate] and tabernacled — fixed His
tent flesh, lived awhile — among us; and
we saw His glory" (John 1:14, ANT).
Bars of your yoke. This reference to the
wooden pieces which extended down from
the yoke on each side of the oxen's
head and were fastened with thongs reminds Israel of her bondage in Egypt
from which Jehovah had given deliverance. **Make you go upright.** In Egypt the
Israelites' backs had been bent when as
slaves they toiled for their cruel masters.
Like oxen in the yoke they had pulled
and carried heavy loads. Now they were
free men. They could lift their heads
and walk upright as God intends all men
to do (v. 13).

d. Poverty for Disobedience (26:14-45)

14 But if ye will not hearken unto me,
and will not do all these commandments;
15 and if ye shall reject my statutes, and
if your soul abhor mine ordinances, so
that ye will not do all my commandments,
but break my covenant; 16 I also will do
this unto you: I will appoint terror over
you, even consumption and fever, that
shall consume the eyes, and make the
soul to pine away; and ye shall sow your
seed in vain, for your enemies shall eat
it. 17 And I will set my face against you,
and ye shall be smitten before your enemies: they that hate you shall rule over
you; and ye shall flee when none pursueth you. 18 And if ye will not yet for
these things hearken unto me, then I will
chastise you seven times more for your
sins. 19 And I will break the pride of
your power: and I will make your heaven
as iron, and your earth as brass; 20 and
your strength shall be spent in vain; for
your land shall not yield its increase,
neither shall the trees of the land yield
their fruit.

21 And if ye walk contrary unto me, and
will not hearken unto me, I will bring
seven times more plagues upon you
according to your sins. 22 And I will
send the beast of the field among you,
which shall rob you of your children,
and destroy your cattle, and make you
few in number; and your ways shall become desolate.

23 And if by these things ye will not
be reformed unto me, but will walk con-

trary unto me; 24 then will I also walk contrary unto you; and I will smite you, even I, seven times for your sins. 25 And I will bring a sword upon you, that shall execute the vengeance of the covenant; and ye shall be gathered together within your cities: and I will send the pestilence among you; and ye shall be delivered into the hand of the enemy. 26 When I break your staff of bread, ten women shall bake your bread in one oven, and they shall deliver your bread again by weight: and ye shall eat, and not be satisfied.

27 And if ye will not for all this hearken unto me, but walk contrary unto me; 28 then I will walk contrary unto you in wrath; and I also will chastise you seven times for your sins. 29 And ye shall eat the flesh of your sons, and the flesh of your daughters shall ye eat. 30 And I will destroy your high places, and cut down your sun-images, and cast your dead bodies upon the bodies of your idols: and my soul shall abhor you. 31 And I will make your cities a waste, and will bring your sanctuaries unto desolation, and I will not smell the savor of your sweet odors. 32 And I will bring the land into desolation; and your enemies that dwell therein shall be astonished at it. 33 And you will I scatter among the nations, and I will draw out the sword after you: and your land shall be a desolation, and your cities shall be a waste.

34 Then shall the land enjoy its sabbaths, as long as it lieth desolate, and ye are in your enemies' land; even then shall the land rest, and enjoy its sabbaths. 35 As long as it lieth desolate it shall have rest, even the rest which it had not in your sabbaths, when ye dwelt upon it. 36 And as for them that are left of you, I will send a faintness into their heart in the lands of their enemies: and the sound of a driven leaf shall chase them; and they shall flee, as one fleeth from the sword; and they shall fall when none pursueth. 37 And they shall stumble one upon another, as it were before the sword, when none pursueth: and ye shall have no power to stand before your enemies. 38 And ye shall perish among the nations, and the land of your enemies shall eat you up. 39 And they that are left of you shall pine away in their iniquity in your enemies' lands; and also in the iniquity of their fathers shall they pine away with them.

40 And they shall confess their iniquity, and the iniquity of their fathers, in their trespass which they trespassed against me, and also that, because they walked contrary unto me, 41 I also walked contrary unto them, and brought them into the land of their enemies: if then their uncircumcised heart be humbled, and they then accept of the punishment of their iniquity; 42 then will I remember my covenant with Jacob; and also my covenant with Isaac, and also my covenant with Abraham will I remember; and I will remember the land. 43 The land also shall be left by them, and shall enjoy its sabbaths, while it lieth desolate without them: and they shall accept of the punishment of their iniquity; because, even because they rejected mine ordinances, and their soul abhorred my statutes. 44 And yet for all that, when they are in the land of their enemies, I will not reject them, neither will I abhor them, to destroy them utterly, and to break my covenant with them; for I am Jehovah their God; 45 but I will for their sakes remember the covenant of their ancestors, whom I brought forth out of the land of Egypt in the sight of the nations, that I might be their God: I am Jehovah.

46 These are the statutes and ordinances and laws, which Jehovah made between him and the children of Israel in mount Sinai by Moses.

The chastisements that were to come for disobedience are related in more detail than the blessings that would come from obedience. Even where love and promises of reward fail, fear of judgment does serve in many cases to turn men from evil.

Four principal judgments were threatened: pestilence (vv. 16, 25); famine (v. 19); wild beasts (v. 22); war and the accompanying desolations (vv. 25-39). These are in glaring contrast to the rewards of obedience (cf. vv. 7, 8; see also Jeremiah 15:3f; Ezek. 14:12-21).

Seven times is to be understood as sevenfold (vv. 18, 21, 24, 28). The climax of poverty and desolation would come with the Israelites being carried away captive. The land would then have the rest which had been denied it by Israel's failing to observe the sabbatical and jubilee years (v. 34; cf. II Chron. 36:21; Jer. 25:8-11; 27:6-8; 29:10). Such judgments would result in repentance, forgiveness, and restoration to Palestine (vv. 40-45; Deut. 30:1-5). **Uncircumcised heart** refers to the person whose spirit is unresponsive to the will of Jehovah (v. 41; cf. Jer. 4:4).

B. RELIGIOUS VOWS AND TITHES (27:1-34)

Love and gratitude to God often prompted men to make a special gift to the Lord above what they conceived to be their duty. This chapter gives instructions concerning the giving of such gifts. It is in marked contrast to preceding chapters, for what has gone before concerned duties and obligations upon all Israelites. This speaks of vows which are made in response to a noble religious impulse, but are obligatory on no one (cf. Deut. 23:22).

A man might consecrate or devote to the Lord persons (vv. 1-8), beasts (vv. 9-13), houses and lands (vv. 14-25). There were, however, certain items which could not be thus given to the Lord, for by law they were already His: the firstlings among the beasts (vv. 26, 27), things which God had banned (vv. 28, 29), and the tithes (vv. 30-33).

Should a man wish to reclaim for his own use something previously dedicated to the Lord, he might in some cases do so by paying to the Lord money according to the schedule set up under each type of offering.

1. Vowing of Persons (27:1-8)

1 And Jehovah spake unto Moses, saying, 2 Speak unto the children of Israel, and say unto them, When a man shall accomplish a vow, the persons shall be for Jehovah by thy estimation. 3 And thy estimation shall be of the male from twenty years old even unto sixty years old, even thy estimation shall be fifty shekels of silver, after the shekel of the sanctuary. 4 And if it be a female, then thy estimation shall be thirty shekels. 5 And if it be from five years old even unto twenty years old, then thy estimation shall be of the male twenty shekels, and for the female ten shekels. 6 And if it be from a month old even unto five years old, then thy estimation shall be of the male five shekels of silver, and for the female thy estimation shall be three shekels of silver. 7 And if it be from sixty years old and upward; if it be a male, then thy estimation shall be fifteen shekels, and for the female ten shekels. 8 But if he be poorer than thy estimation, then he shall be set before the priest, and the priest shall value him; according to the ability of him that vowed shall the priest value him.

The idea of verse 2 is that whenever a person would make a special vow or promise regarding himself or another over whom he had authority, the person devoted should be reckoned as in fact belonging to Jehovah.

However, it was not possible at that time to have place in direct service at the tabernacle for all who would so devote themselves. The Levites were appointed to care for such service. But these sincere people could fulfill their holy desire by substituting money for their services. A regular scale of values was set, based upon sex and age, the highest price being set for men at their peak of capacity for labor.

Should a person want to give himself to the Lord, and lacked even the low amount of money stipulated, he could do so by coming to the priest and expressing his desire. The priest would, thereupon, set a price commensurate with his ability to pay.

What the actual assigned values would be in our money is quite impossible for us to say, for we have no sure information about the value of a shekel before the Greek period. At that time it was worth approximately sixty-four cents, though its purchasing power would be considerably more. The Berkeley Version, by translating shekels as dollars, probably helps us to obtain the significance of the passage.

2. Vowing of Animals (27:9-13)

9 And if it be a beast, whereof men offer an oblation unto Jehovah, all that any man giveth of such unto Jehovah shall be holy. 10 He shall not alter it, nor change it, a good for a bad, or a bad for a good: and if he shall at all change beast for beast, then both it and that for which it is changed shall be holy. 11 And if it be any unclean beast, of which they do not offer an oblation unto Jehovah, then he shall set the beast before the priest; 12 and the priest shall value it, whether it be good or bad: as thou the priest valuest it, so shall it be. 13 But if he will indeed redeem it, then he shall add the fifth part thereof unto thy estimation.

A man might desire to consecrate some of his domestic animals to Jehovah. He might do this, but he must hold to his promise and not later change an inferior animal for the one originally promised.

If the animal given was suitable for sacrifice at the tabernacle altar, the animal itself must be given over for sanctuary service. If, however, the animal was not suitable for sacrifice, the priest was to set a price upon it, and it would be sold. The proceeds from the sale were to go toward the upkeep of the sanctuary. If, however, the offerer decided that he wanted the latter type of animal back for his own use, he could receive it back by paying a fifth more than the appraised selling price.

3. Vowing of Houses and Lands (27:14-25)

14 And when a man shall sanctify his house to be holy unto Jehovah, then the priest shall estimate it, whether it be good or bad: as the priest shall estimate it, so shall it stand. 15 And if he that sanctifieth it will redeem his house, then he shall add the fifth part of the money of thy estimation unto it, and it shall be his.
16 And if a man shall sanctify unto Jehovah part of the field of his possession, then thy estimation shall be according to the sowing thereof: the sowing of a homer of barley *shall be valued* at fifty shekels of silver. 17 If he sanctify his field from the year of jubilee, according to thy estimation it shall stand. 18 But if he sanctify his field after the jubilee, then the priest shall reckon unto him the money according to the years that remain unto the year of jubilee; and an abatement shall be made from thy estimation. 19 And if he that sanctified the field will indeed redeem it, then he shall add the fifth part of the money of thy estimation unto it, and it shall be assured to him. 20 And if he will not redeem the field, or if he have sold the field to another man, it shall not be redeemed any more: 21 but the field, when it goeth out in the jubilee, shall be holy unto Jehovah, as a field devoted: the possession thereof shall be the priest's. 22 And if he sanctify unto Jehovah a field which he hath bought, which is not of the field of his possession; 23 then the priest shall reckon unto him the worth of thy estimation unto the year of jubilee: and he shall give thine estimation in that day, as a holy thing unto Jehovah. 24 In the year of jubilee the field shall return unto him of whom it was bought, even to him to whom the possession of the land belongeth. 25 And

all thy estimations shall be according to the shekel of the sanctuary: twenty gerahs shall be the shekel.

Should a man want to give his house to the Lord, he might do so. In such a case, the priest was to estimate its value and the house could be sold. It seems, however, that should the man want to remain living there, he might do so by considering the house as the property of the Lord and by paying an established rental fee. Should he decide he wanted to get the house back, he could do so by paying into the sanctuary treasury an amount a fifth more than the estimated selling price.

In case a man wanted to give to the Lord a field which was his by inheritance, he might do so (vv. 16-21). The priest was then to determine the value of the field on the basis of fifty shekels, for as much land as would be sown with a homer of barley. The capacity of a homer, like the value of a shekel, is uncertain. Various authorities give capacities varying from three-and-eight-tenths bushels to about twelve bushels.

The evaluation of the land would vary according to the length of time to the jubilee year. The owner might continue to use the land, but he would have to pay the established price into the sanctuary treasury. It appears he could do this in annual installments, or as otherwise it might be agreed upon. Should he finally desire to remove from the land the obligation of the vow, he might do so by adding a fifth of the original price and paying this into the treasury. Without such a redemption, it would be freed of the vow's obligation in the year of jubilee.

If, however, the man should sell the land he had dedicated to the Lord and had not redeemed, it would not come back to him in the jubilee, but would become the property of the Levites. This probably was a penalty applied for selling what was really not his to sell, for it had been given by him to the Lord.

If a man wanted to dedicate a piece of land which he had not inherited but had bought for a price, he might do so (vv. 22-24) in the same manner as the person who dedicated inherited land. But the appraised value must be paid in full immediately and could not be made in installments. In the year of jubilee, the land would then revert to the original owner.

Trying to apply the Old Testament rules about vows has sometimes led to great error, even sin. In fact, New Testament Christian living seems to have no place for binding oneself to a vow to give to God what one is not duty bound to do. For through the obligation of grateful love to the Lord for His redeeming love for us, there is no part of our being or of our possessions which does not from the beginning of our walk with Him belong to Him. The Apostle Paul set forth this essential Christian devotement of all to God. He declared: "The love of Christ constraineth us;· because we thus judge, that one died for all, therefore all died; and he died for all, that they that live should no longer live unto themselves, but unto him who for our sakes died and rose again" (II Cor. 5:14, 15).

4. Exclusions from the Vow (27:26-34)

26 Only the firstling among beasts, which is made a firstling to Jehovah, no man shall sanctify it; whether it be ox or sheep, it is Jehovah's. 27 And if it be of an unclean beast, then he shall ransom it according to thine estimation, and shall add unto it the fifth part thereof: or if it be not redeemed, then it shall be sold according to thy estimation.
28 Notwithstanding, no devoted thing, that a man shall devote unto Jehovah of all that he hath, whether of man or beast, or of the field of his possession, shall be sold or redeemed: every devoted thing is most holy unto Jehovah. 29 No one devoted, that shall be devoted from among men, shall be ransomed; he shall surely be put to death.
30 And all the tithe of the land, whether of the seed of the land, or of the fruit of the tree, is Jehovah's: it is holy unto Jehovah. 31 And if a man will redeem aught of his tithe, he shall add unto it the fifth part thereof. 32 And all the tithe of the herd or the flock, whatsoever passeth under the rod, the tenth shall be holy unto Jehovah. 33 He shall not search whether it be good or bad, neither shall he change it: and if he change it at all, then both it and that for which it is changed shall be holy; it shall not be redeemed.
34 These are the commandments, which Jehovah commanded Moses for the children of Israel in mount Sinai.

There were three classes of property which might not be dedicated to the Lord. The firstlings among the clean animals could not be dedicated, for they were by law already the property of the Lord (vv. 26, 27; cf. Exod. 13:2; Deut. 15:19-23). Any person or property which was under the ban of the Lord, such as, for example, the booty in Jericho (Josh. 6:19), was not to be used at all, nor even dedicated to the Lord (vv. 23, 29). Achan, who kept such booty (Josh. 7:1, 13), was in turn put under ban and fell under the sentence of capital punishment. Neither he himself nor anyone else could buy off the Lord for Achan and secure his release.

The tithe, or the tenth of the increase of the crops, as well as the increase of the herds and flocks, was already the Lord's and so could not be dedicated (vv. 30-33). Should a man, however, prefer to pay his tithe in money rather than in kind, he was permitted to do so by paying a fifth more than the actually appraised value of the tithe. This did not apply, however, to clean animals suitable for sacrifice at the altar.

Whatsoever passeth under the rod (v. 32), refers to the counting of the animals to determine the tithe. Sheep, for example, were counted one by one as they passed under the shepherd's rod as they entered the fold.

The Old Testament law of the tithe would teach us Christians that the giving of our money is not to be a matter of caprice and impulse. There needs to be regular, systematic, and proportionate giving to the work of the Lord. We are to lay aside regularly as God prospers us (I Cor. 16:2). But the New Testament suggests to us that the tithe is but an average minimum. We are taught now that we are to abound in the grace of giving. The reason for this generosity the Apostle Paul gives: "For ye know the grace of our Lord Jesus Christ, that, though he was rich, yet for your sakes he became poor, that ye through his poverty might become rich" (II Cor. 8:9). There is much in the book of Leviticus which does not directly apply to us in the

Christian Church. But there is an important, even essential, lesson for us in the laws and rituals of the book. S. H. Kellogg expresses it so well in these words:

For the individual and for the nation, holiness consisting in full consecration of body and soul to the Lord, and separation from all that defileth, is the divine ideal, to the attainment of which Jew and Gentile alike are called. And the only way of this attainment is through the atoning Sacrifice, and the mediation of the High Priest appointed of God; and the only evidence of its attainment is a joyful obedience, hearty and unreserved, to all the commandments of God. For us all it stands written: "Ye shall be holy; for I, Jehovah, your God, am holy."[17]

[17] Kellogg, *op. cit.*, p. 379.

Bibliography

Allis, O. T. "Leviticus," *The New Bible Commentary*. Ed. F. Davidson. Grand Rapids: Eerdmans, 1954.

Anderson, B. W. *The Oxford Annotated Bible*. New York: Oxford, 1962.

Angus, Joseph. *The Bible Handbook*. New York: Revell, 1952.

Bonar, Andrew A. *Leviticus*. Grand Rapids: Zondervan, 1959.

Butler, J. G. *Bible Work*. Vol. II. New York: Funk and Wagnalls, 1889.

Buttrick, G. A. (ed.). *The Interpreter's Dictionary of the Bible*. Vols. III and IV. New York: Abingdon, 1962.

Carmichael, P. H. *Understanding the Books of the Old Testament*. Richmond: John Knox, 1963.

Clarke, Adam. "Leviticus," *Commentary and Critical Notes*. Vol. I. New York: T. Mason and G. Lane, 1837.

Exell, Joseph S. "Leviticus," *The Biblical Illustrator*. New York: Revell, n.d.

Fallows, S. (ed.). *Bible Encyclopedia*. Vols. II and III. Chicago: Howard Severance, 1911.

Griffith Thomas, W. H. *Through the Pentateuch Chapter by Chapter*. Grand Rapids: Eerdmans, rep. 1957.

Habershon. *The Study of the Types*. Grand Rapids: Kregel, 1957.

Henry, Matthew. "Leviticus," *Commentary on the Whole Bible*. Vol. I. New York: Revell, n.d.

Jacobson, H. *Bible Knowledge*. Vol. I. Chicago: Scripture Press, 1957.

Jacobus, M. W., Lane, E. C., Zenos, A. C. (eds.). *Bible Dictionary*. New York: Funk and Wagnalls, 1936.

Jamieson, Robert, Fausset, A. D., Brown, David (eds.). "Leviticus," *A Commentary on the Old and New Testaments*. Vol. I. Grand Rapids: Eerdmans, 1948.

Jellis, W. H. "Leviticus," *Preacher's Commentary*. New York: Funk and Wagnalls, 1892.

Jukes, Andrew. *The Law of the Offerings*. New York: Revell, n.d.

Kellogg, S. H. "Leviticus," *An Exposition of the Bible*. Vol. I. Hartford: S. S. Scranton, 1903.

Lampe, G. W. H. and Woollcombe, K. J. *Essays on Typology*. Napierville, Ill.: Allenson, 1957.

Mackintosh, C. H. *Notes on the Book of Leviticus*. New York: Revell, n.d.

Mead, W. R., Stoddart, J. D. (eds.). *Dictionary of Texts*. Vol. I. New York: Doran, n.d.

Melville, Henry. *Butler's Bible Work*. New York: Funk and Wagnalls, 1890.

Meyers, T. C. *Thunder on the Mountain*. New York: Abingdon, 1965.

Micklem, Nathaniel. "Leviticus," *The Interpreter's Bible*. Vol. II. New York: Abingdon, 1953.

Morgan, G. Campbell. *Exposition of the Whole Bible*. Westwood, N. J.: Revell, 1959.

Purkiser, W. T. "Leviticus," *Aldersgate Biblical Series*. Winona Lake: Light and Life Press, 1961.

————. *Exploring the Old Testament*. Kansas City: Beacon Hill, 1961.

Schultz, S. J. *The Old Testament Speaks*. New York: Harper, 1960.

Seiss, J. A. "Leviticus," *Biblical Illustrator*. New York: Revell, n.d.

The Book of Numbers

by Howard A. Hanke

Editor's Preface to Numbers and Deuteronomy

Dr. Howard A. Hanke, Professor of Bible at Asbury College, Wilmore, Kentucky, is the author of the expositions on Numbers and Deuteronomy in Volume I of the *Wesleyan Bible Commentary*. Dr. Hanke received his B.A. degree from Asbury College, his B.D. degree from Perkins School of Theology, and his Th.D. from Iliff School of Theology. His major field is Old Testament Religion and Literature, and the subject of his doctoral dissertation was "The Origin and Development of the Baal Religion." He is an ordained minister in the Rocky Mountain Conference of the Methodist Church, and he did pastoral service in Denver, Colorado, until the time of his call to his present professorship at Asbury College in 1950.

Dr. Hanke holds membership in the Evangelical Theological Society, the National Education Association and the National Association of Professors of Hebrew. He is the Educational Director and Seminar Instructor in Bible Lands Seminars, an accredited study-travel organization through which Asbury Theological Seminary and Asbury College give academic credit. He has also served on the summer faculty of New York University.

Dr. Hanke's published works include *The Keystone of Christian Doctrine* (Eerdmans, 1952), *The Tabernacle in the Wilderness* (Eerdmans, 1953), *Christ and the Church in the Old Testament* (Zondervan, 1957, a Pathway Book Club selection), *From Eden to Eternity* (Eerdmans, 1960, cited by E.T.S. as one of the top twenty-five evangelical books published in 1960); *The Validity of the Virgin Birth* (Zondervan, 1963, cited by E. T. S. as one of the top twenty-five evangelical books published in 1963 and used as a major selection by the Pinebrook Book Club and the Christian Family Book Club).

Dr. Hanke is also contributor to *The Wycliff Bible Commentary, The Wycliff Bible Encyclopedia* and *The Berkeley Bible,* of which he is a member of the translation staff. He has been a contributor to such journals as *The Christian Advocate, United Evangelical Action* and *The Herald.*

Dr. Hanke has traveled widely in the Bible Lands, Europe, the world mission fields and the Iron Curtain countries, where he has had many consultations with leading scholars. He has visited almost all of the major archaeological sites in Egypt, Greece, Iran, Iraq, Israel, Italy, Jordan, Lebanon, and Turkey, as well as many of the islands of the Mediterranean Sea. He has retraced the steps of Moses from Egypt to Palestine many times, and he has made a special survey of the entire geographical area in which the events recorded in Numbers and Deuteronomy actually took place.

Dr. Hanke is listed in *Who's Who in American Methodism* (1952 and 1955); *Who's Who in American Education* (1964-65); *Who's Who in the South and Southwest* (1964-65); *Directory of American Scholars* (Vol. IV, 1964), and *Contemporary Authors* (1964).

The author's many years of varied and enriching experiences in graduate study, pastoral work, college teaching, writing and extensive travels and research in the Bible Lands eminently qualify him to write the expositions on these important Old Testament books for Volume I of the *Wesleyan Bible Commentary*. It is the General Editor's pleasure to commend Dr. Hanke's commentaries on Numbers and Deuteronomy to the readers of the *Wesleyan Bible Commentary*.

CHAS. W. CARTER
General Editor
The Wesleyan Bible Commentary

Outline

377

Introduction

The book of Numbers is the fourth in the Pentateuch, and describes the numbering of the people while camping at Mt. Sinai. The English name is derived from the Latin Vulgate *Numeri* ("Numbers"), but actually the numbering of the tribes appears only in chapters 1, 2, 3 and 26.

In most Hebrew Bibles the title is *Bemidbar* ("in the wilderness"), and this is perhaps a more relevant title than "Numbers," since most of the content describes the wanderings of the people in the wilderness.

The book is divided into three main parts.

Part I (1:1—10:10). Israel is now camped on the plain at the base of Mt. Sinai. The tabernacle has been built, the law has been given and the priesthood has been established. The religious rites and rituals have been clearly outlined under the leadership of Aaron, the high priest, and his sons.

Each tribe is identified by the name of one of the twelve sons of Jacob (the two sons of Joseph, Ephraim and Manasseh, are known as half-tribes). Each tribe has its assigned place in respect to the tabernacle, and the tribe of Levi is commissioned to assume responsibility for service, maintenance and moving of the tabernacle. The Levites number 22,273 at this time (chaps. 1-3).

Each person in the tribe of Levi is to serve the cause from age thirty to fifty, after which he is exempt from further service (chap. 4).

Strict rules of sanitation are to be observed. Unclean persons are to be removed outside the camp (chap. 5). Rules for the Nazarite vow are defined (chap. 6). A detailed account of the tabernacle offering by the princes or chiefs of the twelve tribes is given (chap. 7). The Levites are consecrated to their respective services (chap. 8). Rules for the Passover are given, and the date is set for the fourteenth of the first month

of the second year after departure from Egypt (chap. 9). Moses is commanded to make two silver trumpets to be used in announcing the forward march of the Israelites. Details for dismantling the tabernacle are given (chap. 10).

Part II (10:11—22:40). This tells of Israel's journey from Mt. Sinai to the plains of Moab. The judgment of a plague is pronounced upon many for their murmurings (chap. 11). The marriage of Moses to a Cushite wife results in sedition by Aaron and his sister Miriam, who is afflicted with leprosy (chap. 12). Twelve men, one from each tribe, are sent to Canaan for forty days to spy out the land. Only Joshua and Caleb urge the people to go on in to possess the land (chap. 13).

The pessimism produced by the ten other spies results in murmurings and plans to go back to Egypt. God pronounces judgment upon all who are twenty years old and over for their rebellious attitude. The abortive attack upon the Amalekites results in defeat (chap. 14). Directions for conducting worship in the new land are given (chap. 15). The judgment of God comes upon Korah, Dathan, Abiram and their associates for insurrection against Moses. They suffer death by being swallowed by the earth (chap. 16).

The proof that God had called Aaron and his sons to the priesthood is established by the budding of Aaron's rod (chap. 17). The priests and Levites are to be supported by the offerings and the tithe (chap. 18). Purification ordinances in connection with a red heifer are given (chap. 19). Miriam dies and Moses is informed he will not lead the people into the promised land because of his disobedience. The king of Edom refuses to give passage to the Israelites. Aaron is defrocked at Mt. Hor and dies soon thereafter. Eleazar, his son, becomes his successor (chap. 20). Arad, one of the Canaanitish kings, attacks

Israel and is defeated. The people murmur for lack of bread and water. God punishes them for their lack of faith by sending fiery serpents into their midst. They are offered healing by looking up at the brazen serpent which God commanded Moses to elevate on a pole. Sihon, king of the Amorites, and Og, king of Bashan, are defeated (chap. 21).

When Israel arrives in Moab, King Balak sends for the prophet Balaam to pronounce curses upon them (chap. 22).

Part III (23:1—36:13). This finds the Israelites on the plains of Moab. Balak offers sacrifices to his gods, but Balaam prophesies good concerning Israel (chap. 23). Balaam continues to favor Israel, whereupon Balak dismisses him (chap. 24). The evil effects of Balaam's doubleminded ministry are expressed in Israel's adultery with the women of Moab and Midian (chap. 25). A second census is taken, with a total count of 601,730. Only Joshua and Caleb are among those of the first census (chap. 26).

A reform movement makes daughters eligible to inherit property. Moses is permitted to view the promised land from Mt. Abarim, but is forbidden to enter. Joshua is appointed his successor (chap. 27).

Laws related to burnt-offerings, the Sabbath, the Passover, the first-fruits, etc., are repeated (chap. 28). Further instruction is given with respect to the feast days (chap. 29). Miscellaneous vows and ordinances concerning vows are given (chap. 30).

The Israelites gain a great victory over the people of Midian and slay their five kings and Balaam the prophet (chap. 31). The children of Reuben, Gad and the half-tribe of Manasseh request and receive permission to settle on the east side of the Jordan, with the stipulation that they first help their brethren possess the rest of the land (chap. 32).

The journey of the Israelites from Egypt to Canaan is reviewed (chap. 33). The borders of the land are defined and a formula is worked out for dividing the land (chap. 34). The Levites are assigned forty-eight cities of which six are to be cities of refuge (chap. 35). The laws of inheritance are given. Daughters to whom paternal inheritance descends are not to marry outside their own tribes (chaps. 36-37).

The period covered by this book is between thirty-eight and thirty-nine years.

(For date, authorship and additional introductory information see General Introduction to the Pentateuch at the front of this volume.)

Commentary on Numbers

I. GOD'S COMMAND TO NUMBER THE PEOPLE (Num. 1:1—4:49)

A. THE FORMULA FOR NUMBERING THE PEOPLE (1:1-4)

1 And Jehovah spake unto Moses in the wilderness of Sinai, in the tent of meeting, on the first day of the second month, in the second year after they were come out of the land of Egypt, saying, 2 Take ye the sum of all the congregation of the children of Israel, by their families, by their fathers' houses, according to the number of the names, every male, by their polls; 3 from twenty years old and upward, all that are able to go forth to war in Israel, thou and Aaron shall number them by their hosts. 4 And with you there shall be a man of every tribe; every one head of his fathers' house.

The setting for this numbering is the plain at the base of Mt. Sinai where the tribes had been camping for about ten months (Exod. 19:1). The declaration that **Jehovah spake unto Moses in the wilderness** is one of the eighty or more instances in this book where Moses is referred to as the receiver of divine communication. This internal evidence gives strong support to the assumption that Moses was, in sum and substance, the author of this book. Certainly no other person was more eminently qualified to make such an authoritative record.

God had led His covenant people out of the slave camps in Egypt for the purpose of giving them full national status and a recognized identity as an independent people out of which one day the Messiah would come. During this encampment at Sinai three essential institutions for communion with and worship of God were established. One, the tent of meeting or the tabernacle where the proper sacrificial offerings were made and where the priests carried on the redemptive ritual; two, the priesthood, of which Aaron was the great high priest; and three, the tablets of stone or the Ten Commandments.

The time had now come for them to organize as a great army so that they could continue their journey toward Canaan with confidence and assurance. Many enemy tribes and nations stood between them and the promised land, which could be possessed only with a strong, well-organized army under the direction and power of God. This was necessary so,

1. That they might see he [God] had not forgotten his promise to Abraham, but was multiplying his posterity. 2 That they might observe due order in their march toward the promised land. 3. That the tribes and families might be properly distinguished; that all litigations concerning property, inheritance, etc., might, in all future times, be prevented. 4 That the promise concerning the Messiah might be known to have its due accomplishment, when in the fulness of time God should send him from the seed of Abraham through the house of David. And, 5. That they might know their strength for war; for although they should ever consider God as the protector and defense, yet it was necessary that they should be assured of their own fitness, naturally speaking, to cope with any ordinary difficulty.[1]

The task usually assigned to a military draft board was given to Moses and Aaron. Every male twenty years of age and capable of meeting the physical requirements for military service was to be counted and inducted into the army. Each tribal regiment was to be identified with its respective tribal head. It is to be noted that in the numbering, only qualified males were counted; no women, children, strangers, or Levites were included.

[1] Adam Clarke, *The Holy Bible Containing the Old and New Testaments . . . With a Commentary and Critical Notes*, I, 609.

B. THE TRIBAL HEADS (1:5-19)

5. And these are the names of the men that shall stand with you. Of Reuben: Elizur the son of Shedeur. 6 Of Simeon: Shelumiel the son of Zurishaddai. 7 Of Judah: Nahshon the son of Amminadab. 8 Of Issachar: Nethanel the son of Zuar. 9 Of Zebulun: Eliab the son of Helon. 10 Of the children of Joseph: Of Ephraim: Elishama the son of Ammihud. Of Manasseh: Gamaliel the son of Pedahzur. 11 Of Benjamin: Abidan the son of Gideoni. 12 Of Dan: Ahiezer the son of Ammishaddai. 13 Of Asher: Pagiel the son of Ochran. 14 Of Gad: Eliasaph the son of Deuel. 15 Of Naphtali: Ahira the son of Enan. 16 These are they that were called of the congregation, the princes of the tribes of their fathers; they were the heads of the thousands of Israel. 17 And Moses and Aaron took these men that are mentioned by name: 18 and they assembled all the congregation together on the first day of the second month; and they declared their pedigrees after their families, by their fathers' houses, according to the number of the names, from twenty years old and upward, by their polls. 19 As Jehovah commanded Moses, so he numbered them in the wilderness of Sinai.

One exegete reminds us that

. . . almost every one of these names in the Hebrew embodies some reference to God. . . These Hebrew names were carefully chosen, and gave the bearers of them something high to live up to in their relation to God . . . Elizur means "My God is a rock," Shedeur, "Shaddi is light," Shelumiel, "My friend is God," Zurishaddae, "Shaddae is a rock," Nahshon (an ancestor of David and of Jesus Christ), "Serpent," Amminadab, "the divine kinsman is beautiful," Nethanel, "God gave," Zuar, "Little One," Eliab, "God is father," etc.[2]

Efforts have been made to show that this list of names is not historically valid but no real evidence has been produced to support this contention. Archaeological evidence strongly supports the authenticity of the biblical record. One of the greatest Old Testament scholars, Nelson Glueck, says, "It may be stated categorically that no archaeological discovery has ever controverted a Biblical reference."[3]

C. THE NUMBERING (1:20-46)

20 And the children of Reuben, Israel's first-born, their generations, by their families, by their fathers' houses, according to the number of the names, by their polls, every male from twenty years old and upward, all that were able to go forth to war; 21 those that were numbered of them, of the tribe of Reuben, were forty and six thousand and five hundred.

22 Of the children of Simeon, their generations, by their families, by their fathers' houses, those that were numbered thereof according to the number of the names, by their polls, every male from twenty years old and upward, all that were able to go forth to war; 23 those that were numbered of them, of the tribe of Simeon, were fifty and nine thousand and three hundred.

24 Of the children of Gad, their generations, by their families, by their fathers' houses, according to the number of the names, from twenty years old and upward, all that were able to go forth to war; 25 those that were numbered of them, of the tribe of Gad, were forty and five thousand six hundred and fifty.

26 Of the children of Judah, their generations, by their families, by their fathers' houses, according to the number of the names, from twenty years old and upward, all that were able to go forth to war; 27 those that were numbered of them, of the tribe of Judah, were threescore and fourteen thousand and six hundred.

28 Of the children of Issachar, their generations, by their families, by their fathers' houses, according to the number of the names, from twenty years old and upward, all that were able to go forth to war; 29 those that were numbered of them, of the tribe of Issachar, were fifty and four thousand and four hundred.

30 Of the children of Zebulun, their generations, by their families, by their fathers' houses, according to the number of the names, from twenty years old and upward, all that were able to go forth to war; 31 those that were numbered of them, of the tribe of Zebulun, were fifty and seven thousand and four hundred.

32 Of the children of Joseph, *namely*, of the children of Ephraim, their generations, by their families, by their fathers' houses, according to the number of the names, from twenty years old and upward, all that were able to go forth to war; 33 those that were numbered of

[2] John Marsh, "Numbers," *The Interpreter's Bible*, II, 144.
[3] Nelson Glueck, *Rivers in the Desert*, p. 31.

them, of the tribe of Manasseh, were forty thousand and five hundred.

34 Of the children of Manasseh, their generations, by their families, by their fathers' houses, according to the number of the names, from twenty years old and upward, all that were able to go forth to war; 35 those that were numbered of them, of the tribe of Manasseh, were thirty and two thousand and two hundred.

36 Of the children of Benjamin, their generations, by their families, by their fathers' houses, according to the number of the names, from twenty years old and upward, all that were able to go forth to war; 37 those that were numbered of them, of the tribe of Benjamin, were thirty and five thousand and four hundred.

38 Of the children of Dan, their generations, by their families, by their fathers' houses, according to the number of the names, from twenty years old and upward, all that were able to go forth to war; 39 those that were numbered of them, of the tribe of Dan, were threescore and two thousand and seven hundred.

40 Of the children of Asher, their generations, by their families, by their fathers' houses, according to the number of the names, from twenty years old and upward, all that were able to go forth to war; 41 those that were numbered of them, of the tribe of Asher, were forty and one thousand and five hundred.

42 Of the children of Naphtali, their generations, by their families, by their fathers' houses, according to the number of the names, from twenty years old and upward, all that were able to go forth to war; 43 those that were numbered of them, of the tribe of Naphtali, were fifty and three thousand and four hundred.

44 These are they that were numbered, whom Moses and Aaron numbered, and the princes of Israel, being twelve men: they were each one for his fathers' house. 45 So all they that were numbered of the children of Israel by their fathers' houses, from twenty years old and upward, all that were able to go forth to war in Israel; 46 even all they that were numbered were six hundred thousand and three thousand and five hundred and fifty.

Despite the hardship which the Hebrews suffered in Egypt, God's people had greatly increased in number from the seventy souls that went to Egypt (Gen. 46:27). God's promise and plan cannot fail (Gen. 16:5).

Some liberal scholars are prone to question the accuracy of this number, not on the basis of the Bible text, but on the basis of rationalization and a refusal to recognize providential care and divine intervention. One scholar in this tradition says, "The total number 603,550 is unhistorical. If this number were correct the total population would have been over 2,000,000. No land, fertile or otherwise could support such a group."[4]

D. THE LEVITES (1:47-54)

47 But the Levites after the tribe of their fathers were not numbered among them. 48 For Jehovah spake unto Moses, saying, 49 Only the tribe of Levi thou shalt not number, neither shalt thou take the sum of them among the children of Israel; 50 but appoint thou the Levites over the tabernacle of the testimony, and over all the furniture thereof, and over all that belongeth to it: they shall bear the tabernacle, and all the furniture thereof; and they shall minister unto it, and shall encamp round about the tabernacle. 51 And when the tabernacle setteth forward, the Levites shall take it down; and when the tabernacle is to be pitched, the Levites shall set it up: and the stranger that cometh nigh shall be put to death. 52 And the children of Israel shall pitch their tents, every man by his own camp, and every man by his own standard, according to their hosts. 53 But the Levites shall encamp round about the tabernacle of the testimony, that there be no wrath upon the congregation of the children of Israel: and the Levites shall keep the charge of the tabernacle of the testimony. 54 Thus did the children of Israel; according to all that Jehovah commanded Moses, so did they.

The Levites were excluded from the military census because they had the responsibility of transporting the tabernacle and conducting religious services. Their place of encampment was adjacent to the tabernacle where they could readily attend to any demands.

The architectural wonders of man grace the nations of the earth. None is greater than that which God revealed to Moses in the desert at Mt. Sinai. God instructed Moses on Mt. Sinai to build "according to all that I show thee after the pattern of the tabernacle, and the pattern of the instruments thereof, even so shall ye make it" (Heb. 8:5). Over fifty times it is said of Moses, "as the Lord commanded Moses, so did he." A careful study of the tabernacle makes obvious that God chooses to accomplish the greatest number of ends by the fewest and simplest means possible. Every detail had spiritual as well as functional implications.

The plan and specifications revealed to Moses were comprehensive and complete. The kind of wood, the colors, the skins, the rings, the stones, the embroidery, the lamps and the candlestick and even the priest's robes — all were to convey truth, not only for Moses and his people but for those that were afar off. It is significant that God gave only two chapters in the Bible to the creation of the world and the fall of man, while he set apart no less than fifty chapters for the subject of the tabernacle. Every detail in the tabernacle declares the Lord Jesus Christ, who became flesh and tabernacled among us.

The outside of the tabernacle was commonplace and unattractive. It was made out of drab badgers' skins. But when we come inside we find ourselves surrounded by shining gold; looking up to the curtained roof, we see the wings of the cherubim woven in blue and purple and scarlet and fine twined linen . . . so it is with Christ Himself. The natural man, beholding Him, sees no beauty that he should desire Him, but to those who know the Lord Jesus Christ, His beauty satisfies their souls.[5]

E. CAMP ORGANIZATION (2:1-34)

1 And Jehovah spake unto Moses and unto Aaron, saying, 2 The children of Israel shall encamp every man by his own standard, with the ensigns of their fathers' houses: over against the tent of meeting shall they encamp round about. 3 And those that encamp on the east side toward the sunrising shall be they of the standard of the camp of Judah, according to their hosts: and the prince of the children of Judah shall be Nahshon the son of Amminadab. 4 And his host, and those that were numbered of them, were threescore and fourteen thousand and six hundred. 5 And those that encamp next unto him shall be the tribe

of Issachar: and the prince of the children of Issachar shall be Nethanel the son of Zuar. 6 And his host, and those that were numbered thereof, were fifty and four thousand and four hundred. 7 And the tribe of Zebulun: and the prince of the children of Zebulun shall be Eliab the son of Helon. 8 And his host, and those that were numbered thereof, were fifty and seven thousand and four hundred. 9 All that were numbered of the camp of Judah were a hundred thousand and fourscore thousand and six thousand and four hundred, according to their hosts. They shall set forth first.

10 On the south side shall be the standard of the camp of Reuben according to their hosts: and the prince of the children of Reuben shall be Elizur the son of Shedeur. 11 And his host, and those that were numbered thereof, were forty and six thousand and five hundred. 12 And those that encamp next unto him shall be the tribe of Simeon: and the prince of the children of Simeon shall be Shelumiel the son of Zurishaddai. 13 And his host, and those that were numbered of them, were fifty and nine thousand and three hundred. 14 And the tribe of Gad: and the prince of the children of Gad shall be Eliasaph the son of Reuel. 15 And his host, and those that were numbered of them, were forty and five thousand and six hundred and fifty. 16 All that were numbered of the camp of Reuben were a hundred thousand and fifty and one thousand and four hundred and fifty, according to their hosts. And they shall set forth second.

17 Then the tent of meeting shall set forward, with the camp of the Levites in the midst of the camps: as they encamp, so shall they set forward, every man in his place, by their standards.

18 On the west side shall be the standard of the camp of Ephraim according to their hosts: and the prince of the children of Ephraim shall be Elishama the son of Ammihud. 19 And his host, and those that were numbered of them, were forty thousand and five hundred. 20 And next unto him shall be the tribe of Manasseh: and the prince of the children of Manasseh shall be Gamaliel the son of Pedahzur. 21 And his host, and those that were numbered of them, were thirty and two thousand and two hundred. 22 And the tribe of Benjamin: and the prince of the children of Benjamin shall be Abidan the son of Gideoni. 23 And his host, and those that were num-

---

[5] Howard A. Hanke, *The Tabernacle in the Wilderness*, p. 12.

bered of them, were thirty and five thousand and four hundred. 24 All that were numbered of the camp of Ephraim were a hundred thousand and eight thousand and a hundred, according to their hosts. And they shall set forth third.

25 On the north side shall be the standard of the camp of Dan according to their hosts: and the prince of the children of Dan shall be Ahiezer the son of Ammishaddai. 26 And his host, and those that were numbered of them, were threescore and two thousand and seven hundred. 27 And those that encamp next unto him shall be the tribe of Asher: and the prince of the children of Asher shall be Pagiel the son of Ochran. 28 And his hosts, and those that were numbered of them, were forty and one thousand and five hundred. 29 And the tribe of Naphtali: and the prince of the children of Naphtali shall be Ahira the son of Enan. 30 And his host, and those that were numbered of them, were fifty and three thousand and four hundred. 31 All that were numbered of the camp of Dan were a hundred thousand and fifty and seven thousand and six hundred. They shall set forth hindmost by their standards.

32 These are they that were numbered of the children of Israel by their fathers' houses: all that were numbered of the camps according to their hosts were six hundred thousand and three thousand and five hundred and fifty. 33 But the Levites were not numbered among the children of Israel; as Jehovah commanded Moses. 34 Thus did the children of Israel; according to all that Jehovah commanded Moses, so they encamped by their standards, and so they set forward, every one by their families, according to their fathers' houses.

It is evident that strict military precision prevailed and that each tribe marched behind its own regimental identification. It is supposed that the standard is what we would call a flag. It is to be acknowledged that the entire Exodus story, apart from God's miraculous supervision and intervention, would be fantastic and impossible. Certainly the terrain over which they traveled was bleak and barren and, with the exception of an occasional oasis, the land could not support even a fraction of the number which this great army contained. Critics with naturalistic leanings are skeptical of the entire Exodus story and some go

so far as to deny that there was an Exodus under the leadership of Moses. The popular, critical view held by many liberal scholars is that the Pentateuch was not written by Moses but by men centuries later. A typical scholar in this tradition says,

> When it is remembered that the writers of these chapters were remote in both time and place from the events they record . . . it will be recognized that the writers act, so to speak, "by faith and not by sight." The picture here painted of those ancient times are ideas, clear enough in the minds of the writers, but hardly to be interpreted as historical records in the modern sense of the term.[6]

The born-again Christian with faith in the Bible as God's infallible Word need not be distressed at this point. It is a fact that such critical theories are based upon speculation and not upon biblical fact or content. The Bible-believing Christian takes faith in the fact that over eighty references refer to Mosaic authorship in this book alone. One scholar says, "One must ask whether pious frauds inserted the words 'The Lord spake unto Moses' to give their literary work a ring of authority."[7]

The order of the camp and the tribal arrangement is suggestive of the perfection characterizing all that God does. There were four standards or banners — one for each of the four sides of the tabernacle (vv. 3, 10, 18, 25). The priests and Levites camped nearest the tabernacle to protect it against ceremonial uncleanness.

Prophetic implications are to be found in the position of the camp of Judah. Its location to the east is not accidental but intentional (v. 3). From very early times in Hebrew history a great leader was looked for. Very early biblical records give us sketches about the Holy One that was to come. Through his prophetic telescope Moses is inspired to tell us that the Messiah would come out of the tribe of Judah (Gen. 49:10). The location of the camp of Judah conveys the idea that as the sun arising in the east ushers in the dawn of a new day, so the tribe of Judah located eastward would

6 Lindsay B. Longacre, "Numbers," *Abingdon Bible Commentary*, p. 299.
7 Elmer Smick, "Numbers," *The Wycliff Bible Commentary*, p. 112.

usher in the "Sun of Righteousness" with healing for all nations.[8]

This symbolism is carried over in our Christian hymnody to denote the gate of heaven in the words, "I will meet you in the morning, just inside the eastern gate over there."

While the tabernacle was being moved, one-half of the tribes marched before it and the other half brought up the rear. The priests and Levites were in the middle directing the movement.

Thus did the children of Israel: according to all that Jehovah commanded Moses (v. 34). It should be noted that a happy state of affairs existed in the camp of Israel when the people were obedient. On the other hand, no measure has been devised by which to assuage the misery and heartache which attached itself to the Israelites when they were disobedient. It is eternally true that disobedience in any area of life brings trouble and despair.

F. AARON AND HIS SONS (3:1-4)

1 Now these are the generations of Aaron and Moses in the day that Jehovah spake with Moses in mount Sinai. 2 And these are the names of the sons of Aaron: Nadab the first-born, and Abihu, Eleazar, and Ithamar. 3 These are the names of the sons of Aaron, the priests that were anointed, whom he consecrated to minister in the priest's office. 4 And Nadab and Abihu died before Jehovah, when they offered strange fire before Jehovah, in the wilderness of Sinai, and they had no children; and Eleazar and Ithamar ministered in the priest's office in the presence of Aaron their father.

Since these facts have been previously stated it is apparent that the names are repeated here as a reaffirmation of the true Levitical leadership.

Nadab and Abihu died before Jehovah when they offered strange fire (v. 4). We are not sure as to what this strange fire was, but we do recall that the functions in and around the tabernacle had to be exercised with the greatest degree of propriety. It is to be noted that the court of the tabernacle had one entrance — the gate facing east — and that those who tried to gain admittance by crawling

under or climbing over the eight-foot linen fence suffered immediate death. The linen fence served as the line of demarcation between the world of sin on the outside and the redemptive court on the inside. Entrance could be made into the redemptive court only by way of the gate (Exod. 27:9-21). Efforts to gain admittance over the fence resulted in sure and certain death. Touching the fence was fatal. The eastern gate was the one and only way into the court of God's favor (Exod. 27:9-19; 38:9-20). Jesus said on one occasion, "He that entereth not by the door into the sheepfold, but climbeth up some other way is a thief and a robber" (John 10:1). Climbing over the fence is representative of man's efforts to gain salvation through humanistic efforts. Many have been the plans whereby Christ and His cross are avoided, but none have met the measurement of God's standard. The fence around the tabernacle with its one gate is suggestive of Christ as the only door to salvation. Jesus said, "I am the door, by me, if any man enter in he shall be saved" (John 10:9). In another place He said, "No man cometh unto the Father but by me" (John 14:6).[9]

In reference to this **strange fire,** one scholar says:

In view of Lev. 16:12 (cf. Nu. 16:46; Rev. 8:5) we may suppose that the sin lay in the use of common fire taken from the altar. But this phrase *strange fire* is wide enough to cover any breach of the laws regarding the preparation and use of incense (see Ex. 30:1-10; 34-38). Lev. 16:1-2 might also lead us to infer that Nadab and Abihu presumptuously penetrated into the Holy of Holies.[10]

Further attention should be called to God's expectations when animal offerings were presented. No human agency was to provide the fire; instead,

He sent his own fire as the emblem of his presence and the means of consummating the sacrifice. Here we find Aaron's sons neglecting the Divine ordinance, and offering incense with strange fire, that is common fire, fire not of celestial origin; and therefore the fire of God consumed them. So the very fire which, if properly applied, would have sanctified and consumed their gift, became now the very instrument of their destruction.[11]

---

[8] Hanke, *op. cit.,* p. 13.   [9] *Ibid.,* p. 14.

[10] J. R. Dummelow (ed.), *A Commentary on the Holy Bible,* p. 91.   [11] Clarke, *op. cit.,* I, 537.

G. THE LEVITICAL TRIBE (3:5-13)

5 And Jehovah spake unto Moses, saying, 6 Bring the tribe of Levi near, and set them before Aaron the priest, that they may minister unto him. 7 And they shall keep his charge, and the charge of the whole congregation before the tent of meeting, to do the service of the tabernacle. 8 And they shall keep all the furniture of the tent of meeting, and the charge of the children of Israel, to do the service of the tabernacle. 9 And thou shalt give the Levites unto Aaron and to his sons: they are wholly given unto him on the behalf of the children of Israel. 10 And thou shalt appoint Aaron and his sons, and they shall keep their priesthood: and the stranger that cometh nigh shall be put to death. 11 And Jehovah spake unto Moses, saying, 12 And I, behold, I have taken the Levites from among the children of Israel instead of all the first-born that openeth the womb among the children of Israel; and the Levites shall be mine: 13 for all the first-born are mine; on the day that I smote all the first-born in the land of Egypt I hallowed unto me all the first-born in Israel, both man and beast; mine they shall be: I am Jehovah.

A general statement of order is here given regarding the priests and Levites. It appears that the first-born sons in Egypt who escaped the death angel were the first ones to serve in the tabernacle, and that they are now supplanted by the Levites (v. 10).

The Levites had the full responsibility of putting up, maintaining and taking down the tabernacle and of carrying it and its utensils when the Israelites were on the move. They were subservient to the priests (v. 10) and performed the most common tasks of caring for the tabernacle. The priests, on the other hand, attended to all the matters in connection with the sacrifices, including the showbread, the libations, the incense and the sprinkling of the blood. They were the special servants of God.

H. THE LEVITICAL FAMILIES (3:14-21).

14 And Jehovah spake unto Moses in the wilderness of Sinai, saying, 15 Number the children of Levi by their fathers' houses, by their families: every male from a month old and upward

shalt thou number them. 16 And Moses numbered them according to the word of Jehovah, as he was commanded. 17 And these were the sons of Levi by their names: Gershon, and Kohath, and Merari. 18 And these are the names of the sons of Gershon by their families: Libni and Shimei. 19 And the sons of Kohath by their families: Amram, and Izhar, Hebron, and Uzziel. 20 And the sons of Merari by their families: Mahli and Mushi. These are the families of the Levites according to their fathers' houses.

21 Of Gershon was the family of the Libnites, and the family of the Shimeites: these are the families of the Gershonites.

It should be noted that the Levites were not numbered at the first census, but that they are now to undergo a private count, and that the census is to start with all the males who are a month old, instead of twenty years old and upward as was the case with the other tribes.

The numbering of the tribes was done by Moses and Aaron. The numbering of the Levites was to be executed by Moses alone. In this connection Adam Clarke comments:

> For as the money with which the first-born of Israel, who exceeded the number of Levites, were redeemed, was to be paid to Aaron and his sons (3:48), it was decent that he, whose advantage it was that the number of the first-born of Israel should exceed, should not be authorized to take that number himself.[12]

I. THE DUTIES OF THE SONS OF LEVI (3:22-39).

22 Those that were numbered of them, according to the number of all the males, from a month old and upward, even those that were numbered of them were seven thousand and five hundred. 23 The families of the Gershonites shall encamp behind the tabernacle westward. 24 And the prince of the fathers' house of the Gershonites shall be Eliasaph the son of Lael. 25 And the charge of the sons of Gershon in the tent of meeting shall be the tabernacle, and the Tent, the covering thereof, and the screen for the door of the tent of meeting, 26 and the hangings of the court, and the screen for the door of the court, which is by the tabernacle, and by the altar round about, and the cords of it for all the service thereof.

12 Ibid., I, 625.

27 And of Kohath was the family of the Amramites, and the family of the Isharites, and the family of the Hebronites, and the family of the Uzzielites: these are the families of the Kohathites. 28 According to the number of all the males, from a month old and upward, there were eight thousand and six hundred, keeping the charge of the sanctuary. 29 The families of the sons of Kohath shall encamp on the side of the tabernacle southward. 30 And the prince of the fathers' house of the families of the Kohathites shall be Elizaphan the son of Uzziel. 31 And their charge shall be the ark, and the table, and the candlestick, and the altars, and the vessels of the sanctuary wherewith they minister, and the screen, and all the service thereof. 32 And Eleazar the son of Aaron the priest shall be prince of the princes of the Levites, *and have* the oversight of them that keep the charge of the sanctuary.

33 Of Merari was the family of the Mahlites, and the family of the Mushites: these are the families of Merari. 34 And those that were numbered of them, according to the number of all the males, from a month old and upward, were six thousand and two hundred. 35 And the prince of the fathers' house of the families of Merari was Zuriel the son of Abihail: they shall encamp on the side of the tabernacle northward. 36 And the appointed charge of the sons of Merari shall be the boards of the tabernacle, and the bars thereof, and the pillars thereof, and the sockets thereof, and all the instruments thereof, and all the service thereof, 37 and the pillars of the court round about, and their sockets, and their pins, and their cords.

38 And those that encamp before the tabernacle eastward, before the tent of meeting toward the sunrising, shall be Moses, and Aaron and his sons, keeping the charge of the sanctuary for the charge of the children of Israel; and the stranger that cometh nigh shall be put to death. 39 All that were numbered of the Levites, whom Moses and Aaron numbered at the commandment of Jehovah, by their families, all the males from a month old and upward, were twenty and two thousand.

We note that there were 7,500 Gershonites, 8,600 Kohathites (v. 28), and 6,200 Merarites (v. 34), or a grand total of 22,300. However, in verse 39 we read that there was a total of **twenty and two thousand.** There is obviously a discrepancy of 300. This is due, perhaps, to the Hebrew numbering system. The Hebrew consonant "caph" (500) and the "resh" (200) are written so nearly alike that a slight deviation of the downward stroke could make the difference. The symbol for 200 is similar in shape to the symbol for 500. This scribal mistake was obviously made at a very early date because the same mistake is carried over into the Septuagint.

J. THE FIRST-BORN REDEEMED (3:40-51)

40 And Jehovah said unto Moses, Number all the first-born males of the children of Israel from a month old and upward, and take the number of their names. 41 And thou shalt take the Levites for me (I am Jehovah) instead of all the first-born among the children of Israel; and the cattle of the Levites instead of all the firstlings among the cattle of the children of Israel. 42 And Moses numbered, as Jehovah commanded him, all the first-born among the children of Israel. 43 And all the first-born males according to the number of names, from a month old and upward, of those that were numbered of them, were twenty and two thousand two hundred and three score and thirteen.

44 And Jehovah spake unto Moses, saying, 45 Take the Levites instead of all the first-born among the children of Israel, and the cattle of the Levites instead of their cattle; and the Levites shall be mine: I am Jehovah. 46 And for the redemption of the two hundred and threescore and thirteen of the first-born of the children of Israel, that are over and above *the number of* the Levites, 47 thou shalt take five shekels apiece by the poll; after the shekel of the sanctuary shalt thou take them (the shekel is twenty gerahs): 48 and thou shalt give the money, wherewith the odd number of them is redeemed, unto Aaron and to his sons. 49 And Moses took the redemption-money from them that were over and above them that were redeemed by the Levites; 50 from the first-born of the children of Israel took he the money, a thousand three hundred and threescore and five *shekels,* after the shekel of the sanctuary: 51 and Moses gave the redemption-money unto Aaron and to his sons, according to the word of Jehovah, as Jehovah commanded Moses.

In this passage we find that there were 273 more of the first-born than there were Levites. The redemption price was five shekels each (vv. 46-48). This creates the problem of collecting the total redemption price of 1365 shekels from 22,273 persons.

Clark quotes the speculation of Rabbi Solomon Jarachi: "Moses took 22,000 slips of parchment, and wrote on each a son of Levi, and 273 others, on which he wrote five shekels; then he mixed them in a basket, and each man took out one; those who drew the slips on which five shekels were written paid the money; the others went free."[13] He surmises that the difference was probably paid out of the general fund.

K. THE DUTIES OF THE KOHATHITES (4:1-15)

1 And Jehovah spake unto Moses and unto Aaron, saying, 2 Take the sum of the sons of Kohath from among the sons of Levi, by their families, by their fathers' houses, 3 from thirty years old and upward even until fifty years old, all that enter upon the service, to do the work in the tent of meeting. 4 This is the service of the sons of Kohath in the tent of meeting, *about* the most holy things: 5 when the camp setteth forward, Aaron shall go in, and his sons, and they shall take down the veil of the screen, and cover the ark of the testimony with it, 6 and shall put thereon a covering of sealskin, and shall spread over it a cloth all of blue, and shall put in the staves thereof. 7 And upon the table of showbread they shall spread a cloth of blue, and put thereon the dishes, and the spoons, and the bowls and the cups wherewith to pour out; and the continual bread shall be thereon: 8 and they shall spread upon them a cloth of scarlet, and cover the same with a covering of sealskin, and shall put in the staves thereof. 9 And they shall take a cloth of blue, and cover the candlestick of the light, and its lamps, and its snuffers, and its snuffdishes, and all the oil vessels thereof, wherewith they minister unto it: 10 and they shall put it and all the vessels thereof within a covering of sealskin, and shall put it upon the frame. 11 And upon the golden altar they shall spread a cloth of blue, and cover it with a covering of sealskin, and shall put in the staves thereof: 12 and they shall take all the vessels of ministry, wherewith they minister in the sanctuary, and put them in a cloth of blue, and cover them with a covering of sealskin, and shall put them on the frame. 13 And they

shall take away the ashes from the altar, and spread a purple cloth thereon: 14 And they shall put upon it all the vessels thereof, wherewith they minister about it, the firepans, the flesh-hooks, and the shovels, and the basins, all the vessels of the altar; and they shall spread upon it a covering of sealskin, and put in the staves thereof. 15 And when Aaron and his sons have made an end of covering the sanctuary, and all the furniture of the sanctuary, as the camp is to set forward; after that, the sons of Kohath shall come to bear it: but they shall not touch the sanctuary, lest they die. These things are the burden of the sons of Kohath in the tent of meeting.

Take the sum of the sons of Kohath (v. 2). It appears that Kohath was the second son of Levi, but his family is mentioned first, perhaps because this was the family of Moses and Aaron (3:19; cf. Exod. 6:18-20).

From thirty years old and upward (v. 3a). It is to be noted that the age for beginning Levitical service is stated to be twenty in II Chronicles 31:17 and in Ezra 3:8; in 8:24 it is twenty-five. Thus we have the ages of twenty, twenty-five, and thirty. Some critical scholars would insist that there is a contradiction, but this is not necessarily true. It can be pointed out that the matter of age decreased with the advance of time. The age was set at thirty during the period in the wilderness when service was extremely severe and required the service of both mental and physical maturity. It appears that the Levites went into an apprenticeship service at twenty-five and began their public service at thirty. It may be assumed that the "sons of the prophets" also underwent an apprenticeship period before they became full-time prophets.[14]

In David's time, when the tabernacle was established at Shiloh and the rigors of nomadic desert life no longer existed, the beginning age for Levitical service was reduced to twenty. It should also be noted that the educational process had been greatly accelerated by this time, thus making a younger age more feasible. Perhaps an apprenticeship is also involved.

Public service of twenty to thirty years was considered to be a legitimate and

[13] *Ibid.,* I, 627.   [14] *Ibid.*

reasonable norm. It is still the accepted formula for retirement in the military and other areas of endeavor. This was indeed a merciful and benevolent ordinance, which would ease the burden of those with years of faithful service and open the ranks for incoming young men.

When the signal was given by God for the Israelites to begin their march, it was the responsibility of Aaron and his sons to go first into the tabernacle to remove and pack the most sacred objects. The ark was to be draped with the veil and over this was to be placed a protective "badger skin" (v. 6 — KJV). The table of showbread was to be covered with a blue cloth and on this the sacrificial vessels of the tabernacle were to be placed (v. 7).

After the preliminary work had been done by Aaron and his sons, the sons of Kohath were to come and carry the equipment. Thus the Kohathites could carry the covered equipment without suffering the consequences of death by directly touching the holy things (vv. 15, 20).

L. THE DUTIES OF ELEAZAR, SON OF AARON (4:16-20)

16 And the charge of Eleazar the son of Aaron the priest shall be the oil for the light, and the sweet incense, and the continual meal-offering, and the anointing oil, the charge of all the tabernacle, and of all that therein is, the sanctuary, and the furniture thereof.

17 And Jehovah spake unto Moses and unto Aaron, saying, 18 Cut ye not off the tribe of the families of the Kohathites from among the Levites; 19 but thus do unto them, that they may live, and not die, when they approach unto the most holy things: Aaron and his sons shall go in, and appoint them every one to his service and to his burden; 20 but they shall not go in to see the sanctuary even for a moment, lest they die.

It seems apparent that Eleazar was to be general superintendent over all the tabernacle service and over the most sacred objects. No intrusion into the sanctuary was to be tolerated while the holy things were uncovered. Only when they were properly shielded from view could the Kohathites enter to perform their duties (vv. 16-20).

M. THE DUTIES OF THE GERSHONITES (4:21-28).

21 And Jehovah spake unto Moses, saying, 22 Take the sum of the sons of Gershon also, by their fathers' houses, by their families; 23 from thirty years old and upward until fifty years old shalt thou number them; all that enter in to wait upon the service, to do the work in the tent of meeting. 24 This is the service of the families of the Gershonites, in serving and in bearing burdens: 25 they shall bear the curtains of the tabernacle, and the tent of meeting, its covering, and the covering of sealskin that is above upon it, and the screen for the door of the tent of meeting, 26 and the hangings of the court, and the screen for the door of the gate of the court, which is by the tabernacle and by the altar round about, and their cords, and all the instruments of their service, and whatsoever shall be done with them: therein shall they serve. 27 At the commandment of Aaron and his sons shall be all the service of the sons of the Gershonites, in all their burden, and in all their service; and ye shall appoint unto them in charge all their burden. 28 This is the service of the families of the sons of the Gershonites in the tent of meeting: and their charge shall be under the hand of Ithamar the son of Aaron the priest.

The Gershonites from thirty to fifty years old were to carry the hangings or curtains of the tabernacle and the court which surrounded it. Aaron's son Ithamar was to be the chief supervisor (v. 28).

N. THE DUTIES OF THE MERARITES (4:29-49)

29 As for the sons of Merari, thou shalt number them by their families, by their fathers' houses; 30 from thirty years old and upward even unto fifty years old shalt thou number them, every one that entereth upon the service, to do the work of the tent of meeting. 31 And this is the charge of their burden, according to all their service in the tent of meeting: the boards of the tabernacle, and the bars thereof, and the pillars thereof, and the sockets thereof, 32 and the pillars of the court round about, and their sockets, and their pins, and their cords, with all their instruments, and with all their service: and by name ye shall appoint the instruments of the charge of their burden. 33 This is the service of the families of the sons of Merari, according to all

their service, in the tent of meeting, under the hand of Ithamar the son of Aaron the priest.

34 And Moses and Aaron and the princes of the congregation numbered the sons of the Kohathites by their families, and by their fathers' houses, 35 from thirty years old and upward even unto fifty years old, every one that entered upon the service, for work in the tent of meeting: 36 and those that were numbered of them by their families were two thousand seven hundred and fifty. 37 These are they that were numbered of the families of the Kohathites, all that did serve in the tent of meeting, whom Moses and Aaron numbered according to the commandment of Jehovah by Moses.

38 And those that were numbered of the sons of Gershon, their families, and by their fathers' houses, 39 from thirty years old and upward even unto fifty years old, every one that entered upon the service, for work in the tent of meeting, 40 even those that were numbered of them, by their families, by their fathers' houses, were two thousand and six hundred and thirty. 41 These are they that were numbered of the families of the sons of Gershon, all that did serve in the tent of meeting, whom Moses and Aaron numbered according to the commandment of Jehovah.

42 And those that were numbered of the families of the sons of Merari, by their families, by their fathers' houses, 43 from thirty years old and upward even unto fifty years old, every one that entered upon the service, for work in the tent of meeting, 44 even those that were numbered of them by their families, were three thousand and two hundred. 45 These are they that were numbered of the families of the sons of Merari, whom Moses and Aaron numbered according to the commandment of Jehovah by Moses.

46 All those that were numbered of the Levites, whom Moses and Aaron and the princes of Israel numbered, by their families, and by their fathers' houses, 47 from thirty years old and upward even unto fifty years old, every one that entered in to do the work of service, and the work of bearing burdens in the tent of meeting, 48 even those that were numbered of them, were eight thousand and five hundred and fourscore. 49 According to the commandment of Jehovah they were numbered by Moses, every one according to his service, and according to his burden: thus were they numbered of him, as Jehovah commanded Moses.

The Merarites from thirty to fifty years old (v. 30) were to carry the framework of the tabernacle, including the boards, the bars, the pillars and the sockets, the pins and the ropes. Aaron's son Ithamar was also the supervisor of the Merarites (v. 39).

II. MISCELLANEOUS LAWS (Num. 5:1-31)

A. CEREMONIAL CLEANLINESS OF THE CAMP (5:1-4)

1 And Jehovah spake unto Moses, saying, 2 Command the children of Israel, that they put out of the camp every leper, and everyone that hath an issue, and whosoever is unclean by the dead: 3 both male and female shall ye put out, without the camp shall ye put them; that they defile not their camp, in the midst whereof I dwell. 4 And the children of Israel did so, and put them out without the camp; as Jehovah spake unto Moses, so did the children of Israel.

It can be assumed that those who had serious infirmities and infectious diseases were assigned a special isolation area outside the main camp of the Israelites. The camp, God's dwelling-place among His people, had to be kept clean. Today we assign the sick and the diseased to hospitals and sanatoriums for obvious reasons. Lepers were always excluded from the cities. Those with festering sores and bodily discharge were excluded, as were those who handled the dead. In an assemblage of this size it was essential that no undue risks be taken for fear of starting an epidemic.

It is evident that a spiritual implication is here involved. Since the camp was the habitation of God, it had to be kept spiritually pure, and physical cleanliness was a symbol of this purity. John Wesley is credited with saying that "cleanliness is next to godliness," and this may be part of the implication here. The ceremonially unclean were not to fraternize in the camp until they submitted themselves to a cleansing process.

B. RESTITUTION FOR GUILT (5:5-10)

5 And Jehovah spake unto Moses, saying, 6 Speak unto the children of Israel, When a man or woman shall commit any sin that men commit, so as to trespass

against Jehovah, and that soul shall be guilty; 7 then he shall confess his sin which he hath done: and he shall make restitution for his guilt in full, and add unto it the fifth part thereof, and give it unto him in respect of whom he hath been guilty. 8 But if the man have no kinsman to whom restitution may be made for the guilt, the restitution for guilt which is made unto Jehovah shall be the priest's; besides the ram of the atonement, whereby atonement shall be made for him. 9 And every heave-offering of all the holy things of the children of Israel, which they present unto the priest, shall be his. 10 And every man's hallowed things shall be his: whatsoever any man giveth the priest, it shall be his.

The sin to which reference is here made was an offense against a fellow man, and in every instance full restitution was to be made. This idea is also expressed by Zacchaeus in Luke 19:8.

In addition to making restitution, it was required of the offender to add one-fifth the value of the thing compensated for. This might be a measure of interest to compensate the wronged person for the lost earning power. It is central in the redemptive economy of God that restitution must be made before full forgiveness can be reached. Clarke comments thus:

> When a man has done wrong to his neighbour, though, on his repentance, and faith in our Lord Jesus, God forgives him his sin, yet he requires him to make restitution to the person injured, if it lie in the compass of his power. If he do not, God will take care to exact it in the course of his providence. Such respect has he for the dictates of infinite justice that nothing of this kind shall pass unnoticed. Several instances of this have already occurred in this history, and we shall see several more. No man should expect mercy at the hand of God who, having wronged his neighbour, refuses, when he has it in his power to make restitution.[15]

Frequently the offender was deprived of making restitution directly to the offended because of death or some other reason, and in this case the offender could make things right in his own heart by paying the restitution to the priest, or God's representative. In ad-

dition, the offender was required to offer a ram for his expiation (v. 6).

C. THE TEST OF MARITAL INFIDELITY (5:11-31)

11 And Jehovah spake unto Moses, saying, 12 Speak unto the children of Israel, and say unto them, If any man's wife go aside, and commit a trespass against him, 13 and a man lie with her carnally, and it be hid from the eyes of her husband, and be kept close, and she be defiled, and there be no witness against her, and she be not taken in the act; 14 and the spirit of jealousy come upon him, and he be jealous of his wife, and she be defiled: or if the spirit of jealousy come upon him, and he be jealous of his wife, and she be not defiled: 15 then shall the man bring his wife unto the priest, and shall bring her oblation for her, the tenth part of an ephah of barley meal; he shall pour no oil upon it, nor put frankincense thereon; for it is a meal-offering of jealousy, a meal-offering of memorial, bringing iniquity to remembrance.

16 And the priest shall bring her near, and set her before Jehovah: 17 and the priest shall take holy water in an earthen vessel; and of the dust that is on the floor of the tabernacle the priest shall take, and put it into the water. 18 And the priest shall set the woman before Jehovah, and let the hair of the woman's head go loose, and put the meal-offering of memorial in her hands, which is the meal-offering of jealousy: and the priest shall have in his hand the water of bitterness that causeth the curse. 19 And the priest shall cause her to swear, and shall say unto the woman, If no man have lain with thee, and if thou have not gone aside to uncleanness, being under thy husband, be thou free from this water of bitterness that causeth the curse. 20 But if thou have gone aside, being under thy husband, and if thou be defiled, and some man have lain with thee besides thy husband: 21 then the priest shall cause the woman to swear with the oath of cursing, and the priest shall say unto the woman, Jehovah make thee a curse and an oath among thy people, when Jehovah doth make thy thigh to fall away, and thy body to swell; 22 and this water that causeth the curse shall go into thy bowels, and make thy body to swell, and thy thigh to fall away. And the woman shall say, Amen, Amen.

23 And the priest shall write these curses in a book, and he shall blot them

[15] *Ibid.*, I, 242.

out into the water of bitterness: 24 and he shall make the woman drink the water of bitterness that causeth the curse; and the water that causeth the curse shall enter into her *and become* bitter. 25 And the priest shall take the meal-offering of jealousy out of the woman's hand, and shall wave the meal-offering before Jehovah, and bring it unto the altar: 26 and the priest shall take a handful of the meal-offering, as the memorial thereof, and burn it upon the altar, and afterward shall make the woman drink the water. 27 And when he hath made her drink the water, then it shall come to pass, if she be defiled, and have committed a trespass against her husband, that the water that causeth the curse shall enter into her *and become* bitter, and her body shall swell, and her thigh shall fall away: and the woman shall be a curse among her people. 28 And if the woman be not defiled, but be clean; then she shall be free, and shall conceive seed.

29 This is the law of jealousy, when a wife, being under her husband, goeth aside, and is defiled; 30 or when the spirit of jealousy cometh upon a man, and he is jealous of his wife; then shall he set the woman before Jehovah, and the priest shall execute upon her all this law. 31 And the man shall be free from iniquity, and that woman shall bear her iniquity.

This section deals with the question of whether a man's wife has been unfaithful to her marriage vow. A formula is here presented to determine guilt or innocence. In order to understand the severity of this trial by ordeal one must appreciate the seriousness of the offense. Adultery, both physical and spiritual, is one of the most serious of all sins. Certainly this trial by ordeal was reason to avoid the appearance of such an offense. It made mandatory the greatest discretion.

The biblical view of marital infidelity is clearly expressed in the commandment: "Thou shalt not commit adultery" (Exod. 20:14). The punishment of the adulterer can be understood only when the seriousness of the offense is fully realized.

It is evident that the high standard of the Levitical law helped greatly to maintain a high degree of marital purity in Israel (see Lev. 20:10).

Her body shall swell and her thigh shall fall away (v. 27). The most scholar-

ly treatment of this text still leaves much to be desired. One scholar says:

It is obvious that the swelling of the body may refer to pregnancy. The I.C.C. suggests that the falling thigh means premature birth (p. 48) . . . We would translate this phrase as follows, "Her body shall swell and she shall give birth (or give an untimely birth), and that woman shall become a curse in the midst of her people" . . . there is no evidence that this law was practiced at any time except during the period of Moses' leadership.[16]

D. THE NAZARITE VOW (6:1-21)

1 And Jehovah spake unto Moses, saying, 2 Speak unto the children of Israel, and say unto them, When either man or woman shall make a special vow, the vow of a Nazirite, to separate himself unto Jehovah, 3 he shall separate himself from wine and strong drink; he shall drink no vinegar of wine, or vinegar of strong drink, neither shall he drink any juice of grapes, nor eat fresh grapes or dried. 4 All the days of his separation shall he eat nothing that is made of the grape-vine, from the kernels even to the husk.

5 All the days of his vow of separation there shall no razor come upon his head: until the days be fulfilled, in which he separateth himself unto Jehovah, he shall be holy; he shall let the locks of the hair of his head grow long.

6 All the days that he separateth himself unto Jehovah he shall not come near to a dead body. 7 He shall not make himself unclean for his father, or for his mother, for his brother, or for his sister, when they die; because his separation unto God is upon his head. 8 All the days of his separation he is holy unto Jehovah.

9 And if any man die very suddenly beside him, and he defile the head of his separation; then he shall shave his head in the day of his cleansing, on the seventh day shall he shave it. 10 And on the eighth day he shall bring two turtle-doves, or two young pigeons, to the priest, to the door of the tent of meeting: 11 and the priest shall offer one for a sin-offering, and the other for a burnt-offering, and make atonement for him, for that he sinned by reason of the dead, and shall hallow his head that same day. 12 And he shall separate unto Jehovah the days of his separation, and shall bring a he-lamb a year old for a tres-

pass-offering: but the former days shall be void, because his separation was defiled.

13 And this is the law of the Nazirite, when the days of his separation are fulfilled: he shall be brought unto the door of the tent of meeting: 14 and he shall offer his oblation unto Jehovah, one he-lamb a year old without blemish for a burnt-offering, and one ewe-lamb a year old without blemish for a sin-offering, and one ram without blemish for peace-offerings, 15 and a basket of unleavened bread, cakes of fine flour mingled with oil, and unleavened wafers anointed with oil, and their meal-offering, and their drink-offerings. 16 And the priest shall present them before Jehovah, and shall offer his sin-offering, and his burnt-offering: 17 and he shall offer the ram for a sacrifice of peace-offerings unto Jehovah, with the basket of unleavened bread: the priest shall offer also the meal-offering thereof, and the drink-offering thereof. 18 And the Nazirite shall shave the head of his separation at the door of the tent of meeting, and shall take the hair of the head of his separation, and put it on the fire which is under the sacrifice of peace-offerings. 19 And the priest shall take the boiled shoulder of the ram, and one unleavened cake out of the basket, and one unleavened wafer, and shall put them upon the hands of the Nazirite, after he hath shaven *the head of* his separation; 20 and the priest shall wave them for a wave-offering before Jehovah; this is holy for the priest, together with the wave-breast and heave-thigh: and after that the Nazirite may drink wine.

21 This is the law of the Nazirite who voweth, *and of* his oblation unto Jehovah for his separation, besides that which he is able to get: according to his vow which he voweth, so he must do after the law of his separation.

The vow of a Nazarite was associated with a devout dedication for a special service, either limited or for life. The Nazarite committed himself to strict and stringent disciplines, including total abstinence from alcoholic beverages (v. 3). He was not to shave himself (v. 5), nor was he to touch the dead (vv. 6-7).

During the period of the vow the person was expected to let his hair grow and at the end of the separation period he offered his shorn hair to the Lord as a sacrifice by burning it.

It is to be noted that the case of Samson (Judg. 13-16) was different in that he did not assume the vow himself, but the obligation was placed upon him before birth by the command that he was to be a Nazarite all his life (Judg. 13:5, 7, 13-14).

E. THE PRIESTLY BENEDICTION (6:22-27)

22 And Jehovah spake unto Moses, saying, 23 Speak unto Aaron and unto his sons, saying, On this wise ye shall bless the children of Israel: ye shall say unto them,

24 Jehovah bless thee, and keep thee:
25 Jehovah make his face to shine upon thee, and be gracious unto thee:
26 Jehovah lift up his countenance upon thee, and give thee peace.
27 So shall they put my name upon the children of Israel; and I will bless them.

The grammar of this passage has been objected to by some critical scholars as has the inclusion of this benediction in this context. One critic says:

There could be no better illustration of the promiscuous character of this document than the occurrence of this beautiful benediction in the midst of the mechanical details of the vows and offerings.[17]

It would appear, however, that this priestly benediction is most proper and congenial to this context. It was the duty of the priests to make the blessing of the Lord upon the people (see Deut. 10:8; 21:5; and Lev. 9:22-23).

This priestly benediction contains three double clauses of increasing length and intensity and in both the name of the Lord is used (vv. 24-26). This is somewhat similar to the culminating hallelujah chorus of Psalm 150. An affinity is seen here to the threefold Christian benediction (II Cor. 13:14; see also Ps. 4:6; 29:11; 31:16; 67; 80:3, 7, 19). The words **make his face to shine upon thee** (v. 25) are a common Hebrew expression to denote happiness (see Prov. 16:15). The opposite is true when the face is darkened (Joel 2:6). The Hebrew word for peace (*shalom*, v. 26) is the most often used word in Israel today, and means, among other things, health, good will, peace of mind, friendship, etc.

Clarke paraphrases the benediction thus:

1. May God speak good unto thee, by giving thee his excellent promises! . . . May he preserve thee in the possession of all the good thou hast, and from all the evil with which thou art threatened. 2. May the Holy Trinity illuminate thy heart, giving thee the true knowledge of thyself and of thy Maker; and may he show thee his graciousness in pardoning thy sins, and supporting thy soul! 3. May God give thee communion with the Father, Son, and the Spirit, with a constant sense of his approbation; and grant thee prosperity in thy soul, and in all thy secular affairs.[18]

F. THE OFFERINGS OF THE TRIBAL HEADS (7:1-89)

1 And it came to pass on the day that Moses had made an end of setting up the tabernacle, and had anointed it and sanctified it, and all the furniture thereof, and the altar and all the vessels thereof, and had anointed them and sanctified them; 2 that the princes of Israel, the heads of their fathers' houses, offered. These were the princes of the tribes, these are they that were over them that were numbered: 3 and they brought their oblation before Jehovah, six covered wagons, and twelve oxen; a wagon for every two of the princes, and for each one an ox: and they presented them before the tabernacle. 4 And Jehovah spake unto Moses, saying, 5 Take it of them, that they may be *used* in doing the service of the tent of meeting; and thou shalt give them unto the Levites, to every man according to his service. 6 And Moses took the wagons and the oxen, and gave them unto the Levites. 7 Two wagons and four oxen he gave unto the sons of Gershon, according to their service: 8 and four wagons and eight oxen he gave unto the sons of Merari, according unto their service, under the hand of Ithamar the son of Aaron the priest. 9 But unto the sons of Kohath he gave none, because the service of the sanctuary belonged unto them; they bare it upon their shoulders. 10 And the princes offered for the dedication of the altar in the day that it was anointed, even the princes offered their oblation before the altar. 11 And Jehovah said unto Moses, They shall offer their oblation, each prince on his day, for the dedication of the altar.

12 And he that offered his oblation the first day was Nahshon the son of Amminadab, of the tribe of Judah: 13 and his oblation was one silver platter, the weight whereof was a hundred and thirty *shekels*, one silver bowl of seventy shekels, after the shekel of the sanctuary; both of them full of fine flour mingled with oil for a meal-offering; 14 one golden spoon of ten *shekels*, full of incense; 15 one young bullock, one ram, one he-lamb a year old, for a burnt-offering; 16 one male of the goats for a sin-offering; 17 and for the sacrifice of peace-offerings, two oxen, five rams, five he-goats, five he-lambs a year old: this was the oblation of Nahshon the son of Amminadab.

18 On the second day Nethanel the son of Zuar, prince of Issachar, did offer: 19 he offered for his oblation one silver platter, the weight whereof was a hundred and thirty *shekels*, one silver bowl of seventy shekels, after the shekel of the sanctuary; both of them full of fine flour mingled with oil for a meal-offering; 20 one golden spoon of ten *shekels*, full of incense; 21 one young bullock, one ram, one he-lamb a year old, for a burnt-offering; 22 one male of the goats for a sin-offering; 23 and for the sacrifice of peace-offerings, two oxen, five rams, five he-goats, five he-lambs a year old: this was the oblation of Nahshon the son of Zuar.

24 On the third day Eliab the son of Helon, prince of the children of Zebulun: 25 his oblation was one silver platter, the weight whereof was a hundred and thirty *shekels*, one silver bowl of seventy shekels, after the shekel of the sanctuary; both of them full of fine flour mingled with oil for a meal-offering; 26 one golden spoon of ten *shekels*, full of incense; 27 one young bullock, one ram, one he-lamb a year old, for a burnt-offering; 28 one male of the goats for a sin-offering; 29 and for the sacrifice of peace-offerings, two oxen, five rams, five he-goats, five he-lambs a year old: this was the oblation of Eliab the son of Helon.

30 On the fourth day Elizur the son of Shedeur, prince of the children of Reuben: 31 his oblation was one silver platter, the weight whereof was a hundred and thirty *shekels*, one silver bowl of seventy shekels, after the shekel of the sanctuary; both of them full of fine flour mingled with oil for a meal-offering; 32 one golden spoon of ten *shekels*, full of incense; 33 one young bullock, one ram, one he-lamb a year old, for a burnt-offering; 34 one male of the goats for a

sin-offering; 35 and for the sacrifice of peace-offerings, two oxen, five rams, five he-goats, five he-lambs a year old: this was the oblation of Elizur the son of Shedeur.

36 On the fifth day Shelumiel the son of Zurishaddai, prince of the children of Simeon: 37 his oblation was one silver platter, the weight whereof was a hundred and thirty *shekels,* one silver bowl of seventy shekels, after the shekel of the sanctuary; both of them full of fine flour mingled with oil for a meal-offering; 38 one golden spoon of ten *shekels,* full of incense; 39 one young bullock, one ram, one he-lamb a year old, for a burnt-offering; 40 one male of the goats for a sin-offering; 41 and for the sacrifice of peace-offerings, two oxen, five rams, five he-goats, five he-lambs a year old: this was the oblation of Shelumiel the son of Zurishaddai.

42 On the sixth day Eliasaph the son of Deuel, prince of the children of Gad: 43 his oblation was one silver platter, the weight whereof was a hundred and thirty *shekels,* one silver bowl of seventy shekels, after the shekel of the sanctuary; both of them full of fine flour mingled with oil for a meal-offering; 44 one golden spoon of ten *shekels,* full of incense; 45 one young bullock, one ram, one he-lamb a year old, for a burnt-offering; 46 one male of the goats for a sin-offering; 47 and for the sacrifice of peace-offerings, two oxen, five rams, five he-goats, five he-lambs a year old: this was the oblation of Eliasaph the son of Deuel.

48 On the seventh day Elishama the son of Ammihud, prince of the children of Ephraim: 49 his oblation was one silver platter, the weight whereof was a hundred and thirty *shekels,* one silver bowl of seventy shekels, after the shekel of the sanctuary; both of them full of fine flour mingled with oil for a meal-offering; 50 one golden spoon of ten *shekels,* full of incense; 51 one young bullock, one ram, one he-lamb a year old, for a burnt-offering; 52 one male of the goats for a sin-offering; 53 and for the sacrifice of peace-offerings, two oxen, five rams, five he-goats, five he-lambs a year old: this was the oblation of Elishama the son of Ammihud.

54 On the eighth day Gamaliel the son of Pedahzur, prince of the children of Manasseh: 55 his oblation was one silver platter, the weight whereof was a hundred and thirty *shekels,* one silver bowl of seventy shekels, after the shekel of the sanctuary; both of them full of fine flour mingled with oil for a meal-offering; 56 one golden spoon of ten *shekels,*

full of incense; 57 one young bullock, one ram, one he-lamb a year old, for a burnt-offering; 58 one male of the goats for a sin-offering; 59 and for the sacrifice of peace-offerings, two oxen, five rams, five he-goats, five he-lambs a year old: this was the oblation of Gamaliel the son of Pedahzur.

60 On the ninth day Abidan the son of Gideoni, prince of the children of Benjamin: 61 his oblation was one silver platter, the weight whereof was a hundred and thirty *shekels,* one silver bowl of seventy shekels, after the shekel of the sanctuary; both of them full of fine flour mingled with oil for a meal-offering; 62 one golden spoon of ten *shekels,* full of incense; 63 one young bullock, one ram, one he-lamb a year old, for a burnt-offering; 64 one male of the goats for a sin-offering; 65 and for the sacrifice of peace-offerings, two oxen, five rams, five he-goats, five he-lambs a year old: this was the oblation of Abidan the son of Gideoni.

66 On the tenth day Ahiezer the son of Ammishaddai, prince of the children of Dan: 67 his oblation was one silver platter, the weight whereof was a hundred and thirty *shekels,* one silver bowl of seventy shekels, after the shekel of the sanctuary; both of them full of fine flour mingled with oil for a meal-offering; 68 one golden spoon of ten *shekels,* full of incense; 69 one young bullock, one ram, one he-lamb a year old, for a burnt-offering; 70 one male of the goats for a sin-offering; 71 and for the sacrifice of peace-offerings, two oxen, five rams, five he-goats, five he-lambs a year old: this was the oblation of Ahiezer the son of Ammishaddai.

72 On the eleventh day Pagiel the son of Ochran, prince of the children of Asher: 73 his oblation was one silver platter, the weight whereof was a hundred and thirty *shekels,* one silver bowl of seventy shekels, after the shekel of the sanctuary; both of them full of fine flour mingled with oil for a meal-offering; 74 one golden spoon of ten *shekels,* full of incense; 75 one young bullock, one ram, one he-lamb a year old, for a burnt-offering; 76 one male of the goats for a sin-offering; 77 and for the sacrifice of peace-offerings, two oxen, five rams, five he-goats, five he-lambs a year old: this was the oblation of Pagiel the son of Ochran.

78 On the twelfth day Ahira the son of Enan, prince of the children of Naphtali: 79 his oblation was one silver platter, the weight whereof was a hundred and thirty *shekels,* one silver bowl of

seventy shekels, after the shekel of the sanctuary; both of them full of fine flour mingled with oil for a meal-offering; 80 one golden spoon of ten *shekels*, full of incense; 81 one young bullock, one ram, one he-lamb a year old, for a burnt-offering; 82 one male of the goats for a sin-offering; 83 and for the sacrifice of peace-offerings, two oxen, five rams, five he-goats, five he-lambs a year old: this was the oblation of Ahira the son of Enan.

84 This was the dedication of the altar, in the day when it was anointed, by the princes of Israel: twelve silver platters, twelve silver bowls, twelve golden spoons; 85 each silver platter *weighing* a hundred and thirty *shekels*, and each bowl seventy; all the silver of the vessels two thousand and four hundred *shekels*, after the shekel of the sanctuary; 86 the twelve golden spoons, full of incense, *weighing* ten *shekels* apiece, after the shekel of the sanctuary; all the gold of the spoons a hundred and twenty *shekels*; 87 all the oxen for the burnt-offering twelve bullocks, the rams twelve, the he-lambs a year old twelve, and their meal-offering; and the males of the goats for a sin-offering twelve; 88 and all the oxen for the sacrifice of peace-offerings twenty and four bullocks, the rams sixty, the he-goats sixty, the he-lambs a year old sixty. This was the dedication of the altar, after that it was anointed.

89 And when Moses went into the tent of meeting to speak with him, then he heard the Voice speaking unto him from above the mercy-seat that was upon the ark of the testimony, from between the two cherubim: and he spake unto him.

It appears that six covered or "tilted" wagons drawn by two oxen each were designated as vehicles in which the heavier parts of the tabernacle and its equipment were to be transported. The sons of Gershon were given only two wagons because they carried only the curtains, coverings and hangings (v. 25). Additional wagons were assigned to the sons of Merari because they were responsible for transporting the heavy tabernacle equipment — the boards, pillars and sockets of the tabernacle (vv. 31, 32). The sons of Kohath had the responsibility of carrying the most sacred tabernacle equipment — the ark, table, candlestick, altar, etc. These objects were to be carried on their shoulders, and so to

receive the most careful personal attention. All possibility of desecration and/or damage, such as would be incurred by runaway draft animals, was to be avoided. Every tribal head was to make a special offering on his respective day.

Nahshon . . . of Judah was the one to make the first offerings as enumerated in verses 13-17. The Israelites made identical offerings in kind and quantity in the order of their march (chap. 2), as enumerated in verses 12, 18, 24, 30, 36, 42, 48, 54, 60, 66, 72, and 78. It should be pointed out that each tribe was equally indebted to God, and that each gave testimonial recognition of this sense of obligation.

The sacrificial vessels and the sacrificial animals were to be clean. This is suggestive of the holy purity that was expected of those who officiated before the Lord. The entire sacrificial ritual was designed to express faith in and dedication to Jehovah God. The people were always to give their best to the Lord.[19]

The symbolical import was the Lamb that was slain "from the foundation of the world" (Rev. 13:8) for the "remission of sins, and sanctification through faith, and in the work of the Holy Ghost, in the communion and feeling whereof they rejoiced before God."[20]

Moses . . . heard the Voice (v. 89). Moses saw no visible manifestation (theophany), but the voice he heard was that of the Almighty. There are many instances, however, when some visible manifestation of deity appeared in Old Testament times. On numerous occasions the "angel" making his appearance in the Old Testament was actually Christ (Jehovah). "The angel of the Lord" came in human form to Abraham, Hagar, and Lot, to Moses and Joshua, to the Israelites at Bochim, to Gideon and Manoah. While any angel sent to execute the commands of God might be called the angel of the Lord (II Sam. 24:16; I Kings 19:5, 7), yet mention is made of an angel under circumstances that justify one in thinking always of the same angel, who is distinguished from Jehovah, and yet identified with Him (Gen. 16:10, 13; 22:11, 12, 15, 16; Exod. 3:2, 4; Josh. 5:13-15; 6:2; Zech. 1:10-13), who revealed the

---

[19] *Ibid.*, I, 641.   [20] *Ibid.*

face of God (Gen. 32:30), in whom was Jehovah's name (Exod. 23:21), and whose presence was equivalent to Jehovah's presence (Exod. 32:34; 33:14; Isa. 63:9). The angel of the Lord thus appears as a manifestation of Jehovah Himself, one with Jehovah and yet different from Him.[21]

G. THE GOLDEN CANDLESTICK (8:1-4)

1 And Jehovah spake unto Moses, saying, 2 Speak unto Aaron, and say unto him, When thou lightest the lamps, the seven lamps shall give light in front of the candlestick. 3 And Aaron did so; he lighted the lamps thereof *so as to give light* in front of the candlestick, as Jehovah commanded Moses. 4 And this was the work of the candlestick, beaten work of gold; unto the base thereof, *and* unto the flowers thereof, it was beaten work: according unto the pattern which Jehovah had showed Moses, so he made the candlestick.

This is another instance among many where the Lord speaks directly to Moses, thus confirming Mosaic authorship. Moses is commanded to assign the responsibility of lighting the golden candlestick to Aaron.

Light is a very important provision in creation, and it is to be noted that light was the first created object in the natural world. Physical light dispels darkness and spiritual light dispels spiritual darkness. Light is essential to existence. It is that which clothes everything with beauty and color. It is that which gives glory to the rainbow and the ruby. It is that which makes the diamond anything but a bit of charcoal. It is that which makes the human face so full of loveliness; and it is that which gives us everything that is beautiful in our human relationships and in all the wonder of the natural world.

Many of the figures used in the Bible in relation to God are figures of light. The pillar of fire and the burning bush remind us of the words of Jesus Christ when He said, "I am the light of the world" (John 8:12). The golden candlestick was the first object that met the gaze of the priest. God wants the pure light of His divine illumination to shine

forth in His Church, so that His light may find expression in and through us.

We must point out at least one more important fact — the candlestick had to be filled with oil each day. The officiating priest had to trim the wick and keep it clean and pure. This tells us that we, too, must be attended to each day by way of prayer, the study of God's Word, and service. We must keep the light burning at all times.[22]

Josephus tells us that these seven lights represented the sun, moon and the five planets (*Antiquities*, III, 6, 7). The twenty-fifth chapter of Exodus should be read in this connection.

H. THE SANCTIFICATION OF THE LEVITES (8:5-22)

5 And Jehovah spake unto Moses, saying, 6 Take the Levites from among the children of Israel, and cleanse them. 7 And thus shalt thou do unto them, to cleanse them: sprinkle the water of expiation upon them, and let them cause a razor to pass over all their flesh, and let them wash their clothes, and cleanse themselves. 8 Then let them take a young bullock, and its meal-offering, fine flour mingled with oil; and another young bullock shalt thou take for a sin-offering. 9 And thou shalt present the Levites before the tent of meeting: and thou shalt assemble the whole congregation of the children of Israel: 10 and thou shalt present the Levites before Jehovah. And the children of Israel shall lay their hands upon the Levites: 11 and Aaron shall offer the Levites before Jehovah for a wave-offering, on the behalf of the children of Israel, that it may be theirs to do the service of Jehovah. 12 And the Levites shall lay their hands upon the heads of the bullocks: and offer thou the one for a sin-offering, and the other for a burnt-offering, unto Jehovah, to make atonement for the Levites. 13 And thou shalt set the Levites before Aaron, and before his sons, and offer them for a wave-offering unto Jehovah.

14 Thus shalt thou separate the Levites from among the children of Israel; and the Levites shall be mine. 15 And after that shall the Levites go in to do the service of the tent of meeting: and thou shalt cleanse them, and offer them for a wave-offering. 16 For they are wholly given unto me from among the children of Israel; instead of all that openeth

[21] Howard A. Hanke, *Christ and the Church in the Old Testament*, p. 40.
[22] Hanke, *op. cit.*, pp. 18, 19.

the womb, even the first-born of all the children of Israel, have I taken them unto me. 17 For all the first-born among the children of Israel are mine, both man and beast: on the day that I smote all the first-born in the land of Egypt I sanctified them for myself. 18 And I have taken the Levites instead of all the first-born among the children of Israel. 19 And I have given the Levites as a gift to Aaron and to his sons from among the children of Israel, to do the service of the children of Israel in the tent of meeting, and to make atonement for the children of Israel; that there be no plague among the children of Israel, when the children of Israel come nigh unto the sanctuary. 20 Thus did Moses, and Aaron, and all the congregation of the children of Israel, unto the Levites: according unto all that Jehovah commanded Moses touching the Levites, so did the children of Israel unto them. 21 And the Levites purified themselves from sin, and they washed their clothes: and Aaron offered them for a wave-offering before Jehovah; and Aaron made atonement for them to cleanse them. 22 And after that went the Levites in to do their service in the tent of meeting before Aaron, and before his sons: as Jehovah had commanded Moses concerning the Levites, so did they unto them.

It is evident that human vessels — the Lord's servants — must be cleansed from their sins before they can officiate in the presence of God. Before a priest could render service in the tabernacle, he had to undergo thorough ceremonial cleansing.

Just inside the gate was the brazen altar where the sin question had to be settled before anyone could go into the redemptive court (Exod. 27:1-8). The brass out of which the altar was made is suggestive of judgment for sin. In the wilderness Moses lifted up the brazen serpent which provided healing for the bodies of those who had been afflicted (Num. 21:9 and John 3:14-18). The brazen serpent typified Christ upon the cross, made sin for us who knew no sin: "that we might be made the righteousness of God in Him" (II Cor. 5:21).

The brazen altar stood directly in the entrance, and no one could gain admittance to the court without first accounting for sin by offering a perfect

sacrifice without spot or blemish. Does this not suggest the rigid requirement for salvation today — that of repenting for sin and confessing Christ before we can come to a saving experience?

The Hebrews presented a choice animal as a sin-offering, whereas we present ourselves and plead the atoning merits of the Lamb who was slain for us. It is of interest to note that this pattern of sacrifice dates back to the days of the flood when Noah stepped out of the ark and offered sacrifices to God (Gen. 8:18-20). This practice was continued by the Jewish church until the Lamb of God was offered on the altar for our sins.[23]

But not only was it necessary to atone for the sins of commission; it was also necessary for the priests to be sanctified. This sanctification of the spirit is expressed in the brazen laver at which each priest was required to officiate after he made an offering for sin and before he went into the tabernacle to perform service in the name of the Lord.

The children of Israel shall put their hands upon the Levites (v. 10). The laying on of hands was a ritual of identification and transference. In this way the people identified themselves officially with the priesthood and the plan of salvation the Lord had revealed to Moses and the priests. By so doing they expressed their own need for saving and sanctifying power and at the same time expressed their faith and confidence in the priestly leadership. Perhaps this was a Levitical way of expressing a "vote of confidence."

Smick says, "By this art the truth was conveyed pictorially that these Levites were substitutes for the first-born in the service of the sanctuary. The early church continued such well known practices as the laying on of hands (Acts 6:6; I Tim. 4:14)."[24]

The Levites had a personal need with regard to being cleansed from sin. Only after they had satisfied the ceremonial requirement of the sin-offering could they officiate in the tabernacle. Service in the name of the Lord required complete dedication, for the Lord Himself said, "I sanctified them for myself" (v.

---

[23] *Ibid.*, pp. 15, 16.   [24] *Op. cit.*, p. 123.

17). Both the priests and the people were to be a peculiar people, holy unto the Lord (Lev. 19:2; I Chron. 16:29). This is the standard for the people of God in all ages as affirmed by the New Testament writers (Luke 1:74; Heb. 12:14; I Pet. 1:16; II Pet. 3:11; etc.).

I. THE LEVITICAL AGE CLASSIFICATION (8:23-26)

23 And Jehovah spake unto Moses, saying, 24 This is that which belongeth unto the Levites: from twenty and five years old and upward they shall go in to wait upon the service in the work of the tent of meeting: 25 and from the age of fifty years they shall cease waiting upon the work, and shall serve no more, 26 but shall minister with their brethren in the tent of meeting, to keep the charge, and shall do no service. Thus shalt thou do unto the Levites touching their charges.

Verse 24 seems to be in disagreement with 4:35, but for a likely explanation see comments on 4:3a.

J. THE SECOND PASSOVER (9:1-14)

1 And Jehovah spake unto Moses in the wilderness of Sinai, in the first month of the second year after they were come out of the land of Egypt, saying, 2 Moreover let the children of Israel keep the passover in its appointed season. 3 In the fourteenth day of this month, at even, ye shall keep it in its appointed season: according to all the statutes of it, and according to all the ordinances thereof, shall ye keep it. 4 And Moses spake unto the children of Israel, that they should keep the passover. 5 And they kept the passover in the first *month*, on the fourteenth day of the month, at even, in the wilderness of Sinai: according to all that Jehovah commanded Moses, so did the children of Israel. 6 And there were certain men, who were unclean by reason of the dead body of a man, so that they could not keep the passover on that day: and they came before Moses and before Aaron on that day: 7 and those men said unto him, We are unclean by reason of the dead body of a man: wherefore are we kept back, that we may not offer the oblation of Jehovah in its appointed season among the children of Israel? 8 And Moses said unto them, Stay ye, that I may hear what Jehovah will command concerning you.

9 And Jehovah spake unto Moses, saying, 10 Speak unto the children of Israel, saying, If any man of you or of your generations shall be unclean by reason of a dead body, or be on a journey afar off, yet he shall keep the passover unto Jehovah. 11 In the second month on the fourteenth day at even they shall keep it; they shall eat it with unleavened bread and bitter herbs: 12 they shall leave none of it unto the morning, nor break a bone thereof: according to all the statute of the passover they shall keep it. 13 But the man that is clean, and is not on a journey, and forbeareth to keep the passover, that soul shall be cut off from his people; because he offered not the oblation of Jehovah in its appointed season, that man shall bear his sin. 14 And if a stranger shall sojourn among you, and will keep the passover unto Jehovah; according to the statute of the passover, and according to the ordinance thereof, so shall he do: ye shall have one statute, both for the sojourner, and for him that is born in the land.

The Passover was to be an eternal memorial unto the Lord, and was to be observed by all Israel. For one reason or another, some of the Israelites were otherwise occupied at the regular Passover. A special Passover service was conducted for those who had become ceremonially unclean while attending to the burial of the dead (v. 7), and for those who were on a journey (v. 10) and could not be present at the regular time.

Verse 12 follows the exact pattern of the first Passover in Egypt (Exod. 12:46). Later when Christ, the Passover Lamb, was offered on the cross this same pattern is expressed "that the scripture should be fulfilled, a bone of him shall not be broken" (John 19:36).

The Israelitish Passover was in the highest sense a sacrament. The ceremony of its observance was divinely prescribed, and the solemn obligation and acknowledgment were continuously renewed. In renewing this obligation of fidelity to God, the Israelite ate the paschal lamb and unleavened bread in solemn token of the deliverance past, and in religious anticipation of the infinitely greater thing which this signified.[25]

The importance of the memorial is reflected in the serious consequences for those who did not observe the Passover, but who were readily available (v. 13).

[25] Howard A. Hanke, *From Eden to Eternity*, pp. 71-72.

It is always necessary for sin to be borne by someone — either the Redeemer, symbolically expressed in the paschal lamb, or the sinner himself. Those who refused to observe the Passover, who did not avail themselves of the provision for transferring their sins to the sin-bearer, were cut off from the people. In this ritualistic picture one may discern the idea of free moral choice. It has always been "whosoever will may come."

Even the stranger coming into camp could appropriate the redemptive work of the Savior, which was prefigured and symbolized in the passover lamb. Such converts were required to submit to circumcision (Exod. 12:48, 49).

K. THE GUIDING PILLAR OF FIRE (9:15-23)

15 And on the day that the tabernacle was reared up the cloud covered the tabernacle, even the tent of the testimony: and at even it was upon the tabernacle as it were the appearance of fire, until morning. 16 So it was alway: the cloud covered it, and the appearance of fire by night. 17 And whenever the cloud was taken up from over the Tent, then after that the children of Israel journeyed: and in the place where the cloud abode, there the children of Israel encamped. 18 At the commandment of Jehovah the children of Israel journeyed, and at the commandment of Jehovah they encamped: as long as the cloud abode upon the tabernacle they remained encamped. 19 And when the cloud tarried upon the tabernacle many days, then the children of Israel kept the charge of Jehovah, and journeyed not. 20 And sometimes the cloud was a few days upon the tabernacle; then according to the commandment of Jehovah they remained encamped, and according to the commandment of Jehovah they journeyed. 21 And sometimes the cloud was from evening until morning; and when the cloud was taken up in the morning, they journeyed: or if it continued by day and by night, when the cloud was taken up, they journeyed. 22 Whether it were two days, or a month, or a year, that the cloud tarried upon the tabernacle, abiding thereon, the children of Israel remained encamped, and journeyed not; but when it was taken up, they journeyed. 23 At the commandment of Jehovah they encamped, and at the commandment of Jehovah they jour-

neyed: they kept the charge of Jehovah, at the commandment of Jehovah by Moses.

The pillar of cloud directed the movement of the people. The cloud hung over the Holy of Holies by day, and by night it took on the form of a pillar of fire. **Whenever the cloud was taken up from over the Tent, then after that the children of Israel journeyed; and in the place where the cloud abode, there the children of Israel encamped** (v. 17). It is said that the length of time the Israelites camped in one place varied from **two days** to **a year** (v. 22).

Travel in the desert was hard and exhausting. Most of the terrain was desert sand and rock with only an occasional oasis. Nevertheless the Lord provided rest periods commensurate with their need (v. 23).

The pillar of cloud speaks to us of the presence of God through His Holy Spirit. During the day the pillar took the shape of a mushrooming cloud so that they might be guided as well as be protected from the hot desert sun. At night the pillar turned into a column of fire so that the people might have visible evidence of God's presence. It is interesting to note that the pillar was a light for the Hebrews but utter darkness for the Egyptians. So it is with Christians and sinners. The believer receives light and revelation from God, but to the sinner this mystical intelligence is foolishness (I Cor. 2:11-14).

It is to be noted that when the Hebrews began to move out of Egypt, Pharaoh and his army gave pursuit. So it is with a seeker when he takes steps to leave spiritual Egypt. Satan always makes it difficult for the repentant soul to make his escape. He always makes a last desperate attempt to keep the captive from crossing the "red sea" (see 13:21-22).[26]

Spiritual significance is seen in the pillar of cloud by Paul: "All our fathers were under the cloud, and all passed through the sea; and did all eat the same spiritual meat: and did all drink the same spiritual drink; for they drank of that spiritual rock that followed them,

---

[26] Hanke, *The Tabernacle in the Wilderness*, pp. 35, 36.

and that Rock was Christ" (I Cor. 10:1, KJV).

Grace Saxe sees in the wilderness experience a parallel to the journey of the Church through the wilderness of the world. She points out that

. . . as God conducted the Israelites from Egypt through the barren wilderness, protecting them from danger, supplying their needs, teaching them, training them, and eventually bringing them into the rich land of Canaan, their permanent home, so Christ is, at this time, gathering together a people for His name, taking them through a hostile world, protecting, providing, teaching, training and preparing them for their eternal home.[27]

L. THE SIGNAL TO MARCH (10:1-10)

1 And Jehovah spake unto Moses, saying, 2 Make thee two trumpets of silver; of beaten work shalt thou make them: and thou shalt use them for the calling of the congregation, and for the journeying of the camps. 3 And when they shall blow them, all the congregation shall gather themselves unto thee at the door of the tent of meeting. 4 And if they blow but one, then the princes, the heads of the thousands of Israel, shall gather themselves unto thee. 5 And when ye blow an alarm, the camps that lie on the east side shall take their journey. 6 And when ye blow an alarm the second time, the camps that lie on the south side shall take their journey: they shall blow an alarm for their journeys. 7 But when the assembly is to be gathered together, ye shall blow, but ye shall not sound an alarm. 8 And the sons of Aaron, the priests, shall blow the trumpets; and they shall be to you for a statute for ever throughout your generations. 9 And when ye go to war in your land against the adversary that oppresseth you, then ye shall sound an alarm with the trumpets; and ye shall be remembered before Jehovah your God, and ye shall be saved from your enemies. 10 Also in the day of your gladness, and in your set feasts, and in the beginnings of your months, ye shall blow the trumpets over your burnt-offerings, and over the sacrifices of your peace-offerings; and they shall be to you for a memorial before your God: I am Jehovah your God.

It has been pointed out that the total number of Israelites was between two and three million. The silver trumpets were to be the means through which Moses would communicate with his people. The high granite mountain cliffs on each side of the valley of encampment provided a sounding board for the reverberation of trumpet blasts. Two trumpet blasts were the signal for all the people to assemble themselves in the proximity of the tabernacle door (v. 3). One trumpet blast was the signal for the princes to assemble (v. 4). It is probable that there were variations of sound somewhat like the various calls given by an army bugler. A single alarm was the signal for the eastward division to march (v. 5), and a second alarm started movement by the divisions to the south of the tabernacle. It would seem that there would be a third and fourth alarm for the other divisions. Apparently there is a defect in the Masoretic text because the Septuagint contains these additional words: "And ye shall sound a third alarm, and the camps pitched westward shall move forward; and ye shall sound a fourth alarm, and they that encamp toward the north shall move forward: they shall sound an alarm at their departure" (v. 6b, LXX).

When the danger of war threatened, the people were to be called together for deliberation. Smick says:

For an account of the use of the trumpets in a time of distress, see II Chr. 13:12-15. In battle the people "cried unto the Lord and the priests sounded with the trumpets." Indeed, the trumpets as an "ordinance forever" symbolized dependence on God. Similarly prayer, as a more articulate expression of that dependence, reminds God to bless his people.[28]

The trumpets were to be used upon every occasion — in time of gladness, during solemn days and religious festivals (v. 10).

III. THE MARCH FROM SINAI TO KADESH-BARNEA (Num. 10:11-12:16)

A. THE ENCAMPMENT AT PARAN (10:11-36)

11 And it came to pass in the second year, in the second month, on the twentieth day of the month, that the cloud was taken up from over the taber-

---

[27] Grace Saxe, *Studies in Hebrews*, p. 1.   [28] *Op. cit.*, p. 125.

nacle of the testimony. 12 And the children of Israel set forward according to their journeys out of the wilderness of Sinai; and the cloud abode in the wilderness of Paran. 13 And they first took their journey according to the commandment of Jehovah by Moses. 14 And in the first *place* the standard of the camp of the children of Judah set forward according to their hosts: and over his host was Nahshon the son of Amminadab. 15 And over the host of the tribe of the children of Issachar was Nethanel the son of Zuar. 16 And over the host of the tribe of the children of Zebulun was Eliab the son of Helon.

17 And the tabernacle was taken down; and the sons of Gershon and the sons of Merari, who bare the tabernacle, set forward. 18 And the standard of the camp of Reuben set forward according to their hosts: and over his host was Elizur the son of Shedeur. 19 And over the host of the tribe of the children of Simeon was Shelumiel the son of Zurishaddai. 20 And over the host of the tribe of the children of Gad was Eliasaph the son of Deuel.

21 And the Kohathites set forward, bearing the sanctuary: and *the others* did set up the tabernacle against their coming. 22 And the standard of the camp of the children of Ephraim set forward according to their hosts: and over his host was Elishama the son of Ammihud. 23 And over the host of the tribe of the children of Manasseh was Gamaliel the son of Pedahzur. 24 And over the host of the tribe of the children of Benjamin was Abidan the son of Gideoni.

25 And the standard of the camp of the children of Dan, which was the rearward of all the camps, set forward according to their hosts: and over his host was Ahiezer the son of Ammishaddai. 26 And over the host of the tribe of the children of Asher was Pagiel the son of Ochran. 27 And over the host of the tribe of the children of Naphtali was Ahira the son of Enan. 28 Thus were the journeyings of the children of Israel according to their hosts; and they set forward.

29 And Moses said unto Hobab, the son of Reuel the Midianite, Moses' father-in-law, We are journeying unto the place of which Jehovah said, I will give it you: come thou with us, and we will do thee good; for Jehovah hath spoken good concerning Israel. 30 And he said unto him, I will not go; but I will depart to mine own land, and to my kindred. 31 And he said, Leave us not, I pray thee; forasmuch as thou knowest how we are to encamp in the wilderness, and thou

shalt be to us instead of eyes. 3 And it shall be, if thou go with us, yea, it shall be, that what good soever Jehovah shall do unto us, the same will we do unto thee.

33 And they set forward from the mount of Jehovah three days' journey; and the ark of the covenant of Jehovah went before them three days' journey, to seek out a resting-place for them. 34 And the cloud of Jehovah was over them by day, when they set forward from the camp.

35 And it came to pass, when the ark set forward, that Moses said, Rise up, O Jehovah, and let thine enemies be scattered; and let them that hate thee flee before thee. 36 And when it rested, he said, Return, O Jehovah, unto the ten thousands of the thousands of Israel.

The Israelites have been camping in the shadow of Mt. Sinai for almost one year. The time has now come for them to move on toward the promised land. Later when Moses reviewed the history of the wilderness march in the land of Moab, he supplied the words which are missing from the text in Numbers: "Ye have dwelt long enough in this mountain: turn you and take your journey and go . . ." (Deut. 1:6-7).

The marching order of the tribes is listed as follows, with Judah at the head and Naphtali bringing up the rear: Judah, Issachar, Zebulun, Gershonites and Merarites carrying the tabernacle, Reuben, Simeon, Gad, the Kohathites with the sanctuary, Ephraim, Manasseh, Benjamin, Dan, Asher and Naphtali (vv. 14-27).

Moses said unto Hobab (v. 29). Hobab was the brother-in-law of Moses. New and strange land lay on toward Canaan, and Moses needed a strong frontiersman, a Davy Crockett or Daniel Boone type, to lead the way through the wilderness, which, it can be assumed, Hobab knew very well. Apparently the marching Israelites did not meet up with Hobab until they had been on the march for several days.

Come thou with us (v. 29). Moses extends a personal invitation for Hobab to join the Israelites, but Hobab replies, I **will not go; but I will depart to mine own land and mine own kindred** (v. 30)

Leave us not (v. 31). Moses makes an impassioned plea to Hobab to **be to us instead of eyes** (v. 31). It is difficult to ascertain from the text whether Hobab responded to this final plea. From such scriptures as Judges 1:16; 4:11; and I Samuel 15:6 it would appear that Hobab changed his mind and went with Israel. The above scriptures show that his posterity was resident later on in Canaan.

One might question the need for Hobab's guide service when they had the pillar of cloud to guide them. Clarke gives a likely explanation:

> The cloud directed their general journeys, but not their particular excursions. Parties took several journeys while the grand army lay still. They therefore needed such a person as Hobab, who was well acquainted with the desert, to direct these particular excursions (see chap. 8, 20, 31, 32, etc.); to point them out watering places, and places where they might meet with fuel, etc., etc. What man cannot do under the direction of God's providence, do for himself, God will do in the way of special mercy. He could have directed them to the fountains and to the places of fuel, but Hobab can do this, therefore let Hobab be employed; and let Hobab know for his encouragement that, while he is serving others in the way of God's providence, he is securing his own best interests. On these grounds Hobab should be invited, and for this reason Hobab should go. Man cannot do God's work; and God will not do the work which he has qualified and commanded man to perform. Thus then the Lord is ever seen, even while he is helping man by man.[29]

B. THE JUDGMENT OF THE LORD AT TABERAH (11:1-9)

1 And the people were as murmurers, *speaking* evil in the ears of Jehovah: and when Jehovah heard it, his anger was kindled; and the fire of Jehovah burnt among them, and devoured in the uttermost part of the camp. 2 And the people cried unto Moses; and Moses prayed unto Jehovah, and the fire abated. 3 And the name of that place was called Taberah, because the fire of Jehovah burnt among them.

4 And the mixed multitude that was among them lusted exceedingly: and the children of Israel also wept again, and said, Who shall give us flesh to eat? 5 We remember the fish, which we did eat in Egypt for nought; the cucumbers, and the melons, and the leeks, and the onions, and the garlic: 6 but now our soul is dried away; there is nothing at all save this manna to look upon. 7 And the manna was like coriander seed, and the appearance thereof as the appearance of bdellium. 8 The people went about, and gathered it, and ground it in mills, or beat it in mortars, and boiled it in pots, and made cakes of it: and the taste of it was as the taste of fresh oil. 9 And when the dew fell upon the camp in the night, the manna fell upon it.

The Berkeley Version gives a better rendering of the statement of verse 1a: "Now the people complained of misfortune in the Lord's hearing." It is true that the people had enjoyed providential oversight and that all of their needs had been met, but at the same time their human nature had to be considered. There are times when faith is weak, as is attested by the apostles when they said, "Lord, increase our faith" (Luke 17:5).

The physical terrain in which the Israelites were traveling was a bleak and barren desert wasteland. Granite mountains without vegetation leered at them from every hand. One visit to this desert wilderness engenders a bit of human understanding of their complaint.

The seriousness of the situation is revealed in the judgment God brought upon them. It is quite possible that the complaining was actually a symptom of deep-seated sin in the lives of the people. Doubt usually follows acts of sin, and sin follows doubt.

We are told (v. 1c) that the fire of the Lord consumed the ones on the outer edge of the camp, and this is typical. When people commit sin they withdraw at some distance from the altar. It did not take long, however, for the people to cry out in repentance and for mercy. When Moses prayed, the judgment of the Lord was stayed. The place of the burning was Taberah, which means "burning."

Not all of the people who left Egypt were "spiritual Israelites." Some were of physical descent, but not all were of spiritual descent, as indicated by Paul: "They which are of faith, the same are the children of Abraham" (Gal. 3:7; see also John 8:37-41). The **mixed multitude** represents those in every age who pretend to be followers of the Lord, but are not.

The conflict between the forces of good and evil in the world is evident on every hand. Every means and method is used by Satan and his angels to frustrate and destroy God's redemptive program (see Job 1:7ff.; Luke 4:6; Acts 26:18, II Cor. 4:3, 4; Eph. 6:12; II Thess. 2:9; etc.). Satan's most effective efforts have been made through imitation, half-truths, and counterfeit. Satan has counterfeits for all the good things of God. There is in the world today a counterfeit church made up of people (inside the visible church and out) who are motivated by Satan. The "church in the wilderness" (Acts 7:38) had to contend with this counterfeit group known as the **mixed multitude** (v. 4; Exod. 12:38), the "congregation of evildoers" (Ps. 26:5), the "assembly of the wicked," etc. In the book of Revelation this "church" is referred to as the "synagogue of Satan" (Rev. 2:9; 3:9; see also Acts 6:9).[30]

The Apis-bull cult was a very popular religion in Egypt, and it is evident that some who left Egypt were addicted to this worship. This is evidenced when Moses ascended the mount and the people made the golden calf. It is said that they made a "molten calf," and it appears that the **mixed multitude** had a mold on hand with which to mold the calf (Exod. 31:2-6). It is also likely that the mold was brought from Egypt and was readily available at this time. The moral and spiritual character of this multitude is evident. Clarke says:

> This mongrel people, who had comparatively little of the knowledge of God, feeling their difficulty and fatigues of the journey, were the first to complain; and then we find the children of Israel joined them in their complainings, and made a common cause with these semi-infidels.[31]

The manna was as coriander seed (v. 7). Theologians have engaged in a great deal of speculation as to what the manna was. Liberal scholars endeavor to provide a purely naturalistic explanation. Representative of this school of thought is this statement: "The manna as described in this connection had much in common with a sugary sap that in June and July exudes from a kind of Tamarisk growing in the Sinaitic peninsula. It is possible that this natural product may form the basis of the account."[32] Others suggest that the manna referred to was "leichen," which has been used by the Arabs in time of great need for bread. To the devout student of the Bible there is no problem here. It was obviously a supernatural substance given in a miraculous way. Clarke's statement is probably most satisfactory for evangelical Christians:

> The sacred historian has given us the most circumstantial proofs that it was a supernatural and miraculous supply; that nothing of the kind had ever been seen before, and probably nothing like it has ever afterwards appeared. That it was a type of our blessed Redeemer, and of the salvation which he has provided for man, there can be no doubt, for in this way it is applied by Christ; and from it we may gather this general conclusion, that salvation is of the Lord. The Israelites must have perished in the wilderness, had not God fed them with bread from heaven; and every human soul must have perished, had not Jesus Christ come down from heaven, and given himself for the life of the world.[33]

C. THE DISCOURAGEMENT OF MOSES (11:10-15)

10 And Moses heard the people weeping throughout their families, every man at the door of his tent: and the anger of Jehovah was kindled greatly; and Moses was displeased. 11 And Moses said unto Jehovah, Wherefore hast thou dealt ill with thy servant? and wherefore have I not found favor in thy sight, that thou layest the burden of all this people upon me? 12 Have I conceived all this people? have I brought them forth, that thou shouldest say unto me, Carry them in thy bosom, as a nursing-father carrieth the sucking child, unto the land which thou swarest unto their fathers? 13 Whence should I have flesh to give unto all this people? for they weep unto me, saying, Give us flesh, that we may eat. 14 I am not able to bear all this people alone, because it is too heavy for me. 15 And if thou deal thus with me, kill me, I pray thee, out of hand, if I have

30 Hanke, *Christ and the Church in the Old Testament*, p. 131.   31 *Op. cit.*, I, 653.
32 Longacre, *op. cit.*, p. 302.   33 *Op. cit.*, I, 387.

found favor in thy sight; and let me not see my wretchedness.

The times must have been very difficult for Moses. He no doubt was doing all that he could do to make the people comfortable under the circumstances, and yet the people wept. He must have felt as does a mother with a limited food supply for her baby.

But despite the justification which the people may have had for their attitude, the Lord was not pleased with them. For a short period Moses' own faith was greatly tested. Human nature does become dominant at times. Even Jesus our Lord must have felt this when he said, "My God, my God, why hast thou forsaken me?" (Matt. 27:46).

The distress and wretchedness is graphically described in verse 11 and the verses following. Moses pleads with the Lord that his life may be taken so he will be spared his grief and wretchedness (v. 15). The human burden is evidently too great for Moses to bear.

D. THE SEVENTY ELDERS (11:16-25)

16 And Jehovah said unto Moses, Gather unto me seventy men of the elders of Israel, whom thou knowest to be the elders of the people, and officers over them; and bring them unto the tent of meeting, that they may stand there with thee. 17 And I will come down and talk with thee there: and I will take of the Spirit which is upon thee, and will put it upon them; and they shall bear the burden of the people with thee, that thou bear it not thyself alone. 18 And say thou unto the people, Sanctify yourselves against to-morrow, and ye shall eat flesh; for ye have wept in the ears of Jehovah, saying, Who shall give us flesh to eat? for it was well with us in Egypt: therefore Jehovah will give you flesh, and ye shall eat. 19 Ye shall not eat one day, nor two days, nor five days, neither ten days, nor twenty days, 20 but a whole month, until it come out at your nostrils, and it be loathsome unto you; because that ye have rejected Jehovah who is among you, and have wept before him, saying, Why came we forth out of Egypt? 21 And Moses said, The people, among whom I am, are six hundred thousand footmen; and thou hast said, I will give them flesh, that they may eat a whole month. 22 Shall flocks and herds be slain for them, to suffice them? or shall all the fish of the sea be gathered together for them, to suffice them? 23 And Jehovah said unto Moses, Is Jehovah's hand waxed short? now shalt thou see whether my word shall come to pass unto thee or not.

24 And Moses went out, and told the people the words of Jehovah: and he gathered seventy men of the elders of the people, and set them round about the Tent. 25 And Jehovah came down in the cloud, and spake unto him, and took of the Spirit that was upon him, and put it upon the seventy elders: and it came to pass, that, when the Spirit rested upon them, they prophesied, but they did so no more.

It is evident that a contributing factor to the discouragement which Moses experienced was linked to physical exhaustion. Moses did what many executives do today — he tried to do everything himself.

The Lord now instructs Moses to appoint a cabinet — elders and officers — to help him in his gigantic administrative task. This is an extension of the organizational setup Jethro suggested to Moses when judicial problems developed (Exod. 18:13ff.). This is probably the origin of the Sanhedrin — the council of seventy.

The statement in verse 17 involves the entire matter of the degree to which people in the Old Testament received the Spirit of God or the Holy Spirit. It appears that the bestowal of God's Spirit upon people in the Old Testament was reserved primarily for special occasions and specially appointed persons — usually prophets, priests and kings. Such instances can be found in connection with Balaam (Num. 24:2), Othniel (Judg. 3:10), Gideon (Judg. 6:34), Samson (Judg. 14:6), Saul (I Sam. 10:10), David (I Sam. 16:13), etc.

A universal bestowal of God's Spirit was prophesied by one of the prophets (Joel 2:28), and the outpouring of the Holy Spirit on the Day of Pentecost is identified by Peter as the fulfillment of this prophecy (Acts 2:16ff.). It is an attested fact throughout Scripture that the residence of the Holy Spirit is essential for administering the work of the Lord. In this post-apostolic period all believers are holy priests of God (I Pet. 2:5; Rev. 1:6; 20:6). This relationship is known as "the priesthood of believers."

Ministers of God can bear the burden of divine administration only with the impowering presence of the divine Spirit. The power of God comes only with the bestowal of the Holy Spirit (Luke 24:49; Acts 1:8; Mic. 3:8).

The anointing of God's Spirit is closely related to sanctification. It is the Wesleyan view that when a believer makes a complete consecration as suggested by Paul (Rom 12:1), God in turn baptizes the believer with the Holy Spirit (Matt. 3:11), and the result is sanctification of the believer — the removal of the carnal nature. The word *sanctify* has a twofold meaning: first, the act of the believer in setting himself aside in complete dedication; and, second, the response of God in His bestowal of the Holy Spirit's baptism or anointing. It is obvious that God cannot do His part until the believer presents himself as a sacrifice without spot or blemish upon the altar.

The reference in verse 18 is a direction to the people to sanctify themselves, that is, to set themselves apart for anointing. It is always a foregone conclusion that when the believer sanctifies himself, God will respond with His sanctifying grace. Clarke says: "The gracious God never called a man to perform a work without furnishing him with adequate strength; and to refuse to do it on the pretense of inability is a little short of rebellion against God."[34]

The Wesleyan position is best expressed in the Article of Religion on "Sanctification":

Sanctification is the renewal of our fallen nature by the Holy Ghost, received through faith in Jesus Christ, whose blood atonement cleanseth from all sin; whereby we are washed from its pollution, saved from its power, and are enabled, through grace, to love God with all our hearts and to walk in his holy commandments blameless.[35]

For some reason the ideal diet for the people in the desert was manna. Even though flesh, for some reason, was not good for them at this time, God finally promised to give them a diet of meat for a whole month. This extended meat diet, however, was to have a most unpleasant after-effect (v. 20).

Shall flocks and herds be slain? (v. 22). Once again the faith of Moses is greatly tested. He observes that there are six hundred thousand footmen (soldiers), and he cannot comprehend how all this multitude can be fed with flesh short of killing all "the flocks and the herds" and bringing in all the fish from the sea.

Is the Lord's hand waxed short? (v. 23). We could paraphrase thus: Hast thou forgotten the miracles which I have already performed? Or thinkest thou that my power is decreased? The power that is unlimited can never be diminished.[36]

When the Spirit rested upon them they prophesied (v. 25a). This can be understood to mean that the elders performed civil and sacred functions, including exhorting the people to peaceful submission and dedication to God. This is an emergency situation resulting from the fearful judgment that came upon the "mixed multitude." This was a time for the renewal of faith and confidence in God's providential care and leadership. It is not known whether the seventy elders prophesied only on this one occasion and never again, or whether they made only one statement on each issue in the same sense that it is said, "Shakespeare never repeats." In view of the growing complexity of the task it would seem that the true meaning would be the latter. The Berkeley Version renders the text thus: "After the Spirit had come upon them, they prophesied once, but not again." The Septuagint says, "They prophesied and ceased."

E. THE PROPHECY OF ELDAD AND MEDAD (11:26-30)

26 But there remained two men in the camp, the name of the one was Eldad, and the name of the other Medad: and the Spirit rested upon them; and they were of them that were written, but had not gone out unto the Tent; and they prophesied in the camp. 27 And there ran a young man, and told Moses, and said, Eldad and Medad do prophesy in the camp. 28 And Joshua the son of Nun, the minister of Moses, one of his chosen men, answered and said, My lord Moses, forbid them. 29 And Moses said unto him, Art thou jealous for my sake?

[34] *Op. cit.*, I, 654.   [35] *Discipline of the Methodist Church*, paragraph 86.   [36] Clarke, *op. cit.*, I, 655.

would that all Jehovah's people were prophets, that Jehovah would put his Spirit upon them! 30 And Moses gat him into the camp, he and the elders of Israel.

It is possible that Eldad and Medad were two of the seventy elders, but were hindered for some reason from presenting themselves at the tabernacle at the appointed time. Joshua was over-anxious about these two men who prophesied after the other elders ended their services. Joshua wanted Moses to forbid them from prophesying, but Moses took the same position that our Lord took in a similar situation where John became disturbed because some other evangelists were using different techniques from his own for casting out demons. Jesus said to him, "Forbid them not, for he that is not against us is for us" (Luke 9:49-50; see also Luke 9:51-56). Instead of being alarmed, Moses expressed the wish that many of the people would be thus endowed and so motivated.

The fact that Joshua's anxiety (v. 29) was unjustified is indicated in Moses' reply. Moses expresses the motive that should characterize every spokesman for the Lord. He is not desirous of maintaining his position by unworthy means. He is willing and, in fact, anxious, that others, duly appointed by God, should also exercise the prophetic gift.

F. THE QUAILS AND THE PLAGUE (11:31-35)

31 And there went forth a wind from Jehovah, and brought quails from the sea, and let them fall by the camp, about a day's journey on this side, and a day's journey on the other side, round about the camp, and about two cubits above the face of the earth. 32 And the people rose up all that day, and all the night, and all the next day, and gathered the quails: he that gathered least gathered ten homers: and they spread them all abroad for themselves round about the camp. 33 While the flesh was yet between their teeth, ere it was chewed, the anger of Jehovah was kindled against the people, and Jehovah smote the people with a very great plague. 34 And the name of that place was called Kibroth-hattaavah, because there they buried the people that lusted. 35 From Kibroth-hattaavah the people journeyed unto Hazeroth; and they abode at Hazeroth.

It is to be observed that frequently the miraculous nature of an event is related to time, place and circumstance. The Lord uses natural means in bringing about miraculous ends. Remember, the Lord "caused the sea to go back by a strong east wind all that night" when Moses and the Israelites were being pursued by Pharaoh and his army (Exod. 14:21). After the quails flew across the sea, they fell exhausted in the wilderness. Even today, natives mount huge nets between high poles in this area so that the in-coming quails hit these snares, and fall stunned to the ground. At certain seasons in the year quails are most plentiful and very cheap in the markets in this area. The miracle is to be seen in the extremely strong wind, which caused the quails to come within the bounds of the camp rather than along the seashore. Frequently trans-Atlantic planes make the crossing in several hours less than the regular schedule because of a strong "tail wind," and this principle could easily apply here. We note that this was apparently a special wind sent by the Lord to accomplish a certain objective.

And let them fall by the camp . . . about two cubits above the face of the earth (v. 31b). An imaginary difficulty has been created here by some exegetes who suppose that the quails literally covered the entire earth or that they fell two cubits deep (about three feet) within the area of the camp. The Hebrew text does not support this view. The truth of the matter is that the quails flew in great numbers within two feet above the ground and that the people could easily reach out and catch or club them. The Septuagint renders this passage thus, "as it were two cubits from the earth." The Vulgate reads, "and they flew in the air, two cubits high above the ground."

The people rose up all that day, and all the night (v. 32). It is clear that the people were required to exercise initiative by standing up to gather the quails, perhaps in sacks and baskets. They were still on the wing and would soon be out of their reach if they did not capture them; the exhausted quails would recuperate quickly.

We do not know exactly what the plague was which smote the people, but it is possible that the quails were diseased. It is a known fact that rabbits carry a certain type of disease which causes fever, and if the blood comes in contact with a cut or wound it frequently results in death. Perhaps the foreknowledge of this condition is why the Lord wanted them to stay on their diet of manna. Apparently many of the people died during this plague. The Hebrew word **Kibroth-hattaavah** (v. 34) literally means: "The graves of greed."

G. THE INSURRECTION OF MIRIAM AND AARON (12:1-16)

1 And Miriam and Aaron spake against Moses because of the Cushite woman whom he had married; for he had married a Cushite woman. 2 And they said, Hath Jehovah indeed spoken only with Moses? hath he not spoken also with us? And Jehovah heard it. 3 Now the man Moses was very meek, above all the men that were upon the face of the earth. 4 And Jehovah spake suddenly unto Moses, and unto Aaron, and unto Miriam, Come out ye three unto the tent of meeting. And they three came out. 5 And Jehovah came down in a pillar of cloud, and stood at the door of the Tent, and called Aaron and Miriam; and they both came forth. 6 And he said, Hear now my words: if there be a prophet among you, I Jehovah will make myself known unto him in a vision, I will speak with him in a dream. 7 My servant Moses is not so; he is faithful in all my house: 8 with him will I speak mouth to mouth, even manifestly, and not in dark speeches; and the form of Jehovah shall he behold: wherefore then were ye not afraid to speak against my servant, against Moses? 9 And the anger of Jehovah was kindled against them; and he departed. 10 And the cloud removed from over the Tent; and, behold, Miriam was leprous, as *white as* snow: and Aaron looked upon Miriam, and, behold, she was leprous. 11 And Aaron said unto Moses, Oh, my lord, lay not, I pray thee, sin upon us, for that we have done foolishly, and for that we have sinned. 12 Let her not, I pray, be as one dead, of whom the flesh is half consumed when he cometh out of his mother's womb. 13 And Moses cried unto Jehovah, saying, Heal her, O God, I beseech thee. 14 And Jehovah said unto Moses, If her father had but spit in her face, should she not be ashamed seven days? let her be shut up without the camp seven days, and after that she shall be brought in again. 15 And Miriam was shut up without the camp seven days: and the people journeyed not till Miriam was brought in again.

16 And afterward the people journeyed from Hazeroth, and encamped in the wilderness of Paran.

Miriam and Aaron complained about Moses' marriage to an Ethiopian (or Cushite) woman, but their true motive for this criticism is found in their jealousy of the power and influence of Moses. It is not clear whether the Cushite woman was Moses' first wife or his second wife after the death of his first wife Zipporah. This is a general statement without any indication as to when or where. Perhaps this had been smoldering in their minds for a long time and now becomes the subtle excuse for attacking Moses. One scholar explains it thus:

> Views of this person have been of two general classes: (1) She is to be identified with Zipporah (Exod. 2:21 and elsewhere), Moses' Midianitish wife, who is here called "the Cushite," either in scorn of her dark complexion (cf. Jer. 13:23) and foreign origin . . . or as a consequence of an erroneous notion of the late age when this apocryphal addition, "because of the Cushite," etc., was inserted in the narrative (so Wellhausen). And (2) She is a woman whom Moses took to wife after the death of Zipporah, really a Cushite (Ethiopian) by race.[37]

It is to be noted that Aaron was the high priest in Israel, but apparently he was not granted the gift of prophecy. "Using Moses' marriage to the Ethiopian woman as a pretext to start a whispering campaign against their brother, Miriam and Aaron challenge Moses' sole right to speak for God."[38]

Moses was very meek (v. 3). It appears that the Hebrew word *anav* here translated **meek** is not rightly understood in this context. It is the judgment of some that this word is used in the Old Testament context to mean "depressed" or "affected." It is obvious that such an attack from his own brother and sister would have a depressing effect upon him.[39]

[37] J. Oscar Boyd, "Cushite," *International Standard Bible Encyclopedia*, III, 769.
[38] Smick, *op. cit.*, p. 129.   [39] Clarke, *op. cit.*, I, 657.

Jehovah spake suddenly unto Moses, and unto Aaron and unto Miriam (v. 4). The Lord's response toward this rebellious attitude is here brought into quick focus. The Lord is displeased and is determined to settle the matter at once. The subjects in question are instructed to assemble at the tabernacle where differences were customarily settled.

The Lord came down in the pillar of cloud to mediate the difference (for comment on God speaking to man, see notes on 7:89). One writer calls attention to the two main terms in which deity is referred to in the Old Testament. It is his contention that the name Jehovah (from *Yhwh*) is the intimate personal covenant name by which God (*Elohim*), the trinitarian God, communicates with His people. Under this interpretation, Jehovah in the Old Testament is finally revealed in the New Testament as Jesus Christ.[40]

Verse 6 is most difficult, but not impossible. The question is raised as to whether there is a prophet in Israel other than Moses. This is a Semitic figure of speech and a way of saying that there is not another prophet. Longacre paraphrases this passage thus:

> *Listen to me!*
> *If there be a prophet of Jehovah*
> *among you,*
> *In a vision do I make myself known*
> *to him,*
> *In a dream do I speak to him.*
> *Not so is my servant Moses:*
> *In all my affairs he is fully trusted,*
> *By word of mouth do I speak with*
> *him.*
> *Straightforwardly and not in mystic*
> *enigmas.*
> *Jehovah's very form doth he behold.*
> *Why then do you not fear to speak*
> *Against my servant, against Moses.*[41]

It is evident that Aaron wants to be equal with Moses but does not have the courage to declare his desires directly to Jehovah; he turns to Moses instead. Moses comes out of this episode the unique leader of Israel.

The anger of Jehovah was kindled (v. 9). The Lord settles the question as to who is the primary leader. Moses is justified by the words of the Lord while

the error of the rebellious Aaron and Miriam is indicated through the judgment that came upon Miriam. We do not know why Aaron was not afflicted, but it is quite likely that Miriam was the instigator of the mutiny. Clarke says that if he had "been smitten . . . the priesthood itself would have fallen in contempt." For the sake of the office, ministers are sometimes spared exposure. It is a fair assumption, however, that in the end an accounting will come to all men, irrespective of their station in life.

If her father had but spit in her face (v. 14). Spitting in a person's face was a sign of shame and contempt imposed on wrongdoers, but even they could be absolved of their disgrace by some kind of ceremonial cleansing. In like manner, Miriam's offense was shameful, but she too could be restored to communal acceptance, by being expelled from camp for seven days. This would no doubt give her ample time to think about her sin and to repent. Then, too, by that time the people would be in a state of forgetfulness and Miriam could once again take her rightful place in Israel. It has been said that "time heals all wounds."

And Miriam was shut out (v. 15). Miriam served her sentence for seven days and was then restored to camp. The journey to the wilderness of Paran was delayed until Miriam returned.

IV. THE ENCAMPMENT AT KADESH-BARNEA (Num. 13:1— 14:45)

A. THE SPIES SENT INTO CANAAN (13:1-25)

1 And Jehovah spake unto Moses, saying, 2 Send thou men, that they may spy out the land of Canaan, which I give unto the children of Israel: of every tribe of their fathers shall ye send a man, every one a prince among them. 3 And Moses sent them from the wilderness of Paran according to the commandment of Jehovah: all of them men who were heads of the children of Israel. 4 And these were their names: Of the tribe of Reuben, Shammua the son of Zaccur. 5 Of the tribe of Simeon, Shaphat the son of Hori. 6 Of the tribe of Judah, Caleb the son of Jephunneh. 7 Of the tribe of Issachar, Igal the son

---

[40] Hanke, *Christ and the Church in the Old Testament*, pp. 36ff.   [41] *Op. cit.*, p. 303.

of Joseph. 8 Of the tribe of Ephraim, Hoshea the son of Nun. 9 Of the tribe of Benjamin, Palti the son of Raphu. 10 Of the tribe of Zebulun, Gaddiel the son of Sodi. 11 Of the tribe of Joseph, *namely*, of the tribe of Manasseh, Gaddi the son of Susi. 12 Of the tribe of Dan, Ammiel the son of Gemalli. 13 Of the tribe of Asher, Sethur the son of Michael. 14 Of the tribe of Naphtali, Nahbi the son of Vophsi. 15 Of the tribe of Gad, Geuel the son of Machi. 16 These are the names of the men that Moses sent to spy out the land. And Moses called Hoshea the son of Nun Joshua.

17 And Moses sent them to spy out the land of Canaan, and said unto them, Get you up this way by the South, and go up into the hill-country: 18 and see the land, what it is; and the people that dwell therein, whether they are strong or weak, whether they are few or many; 19 and what the land is that they dwell in, whether it is good or bad; and what cities they are that they dwell in, whether in camps, or in strongholds; 20 and what the land is, whether it is fat or lean, whether there is wood therein, or not. And be ye of good courage, and bring of the fruit of the land. Now the time was the time of the first-ripe grapes.

21 So they went up, and spied out the land from wilderness of Zin unto Rehob, to the entrance of Hamath. 22 And they went up by the South, and came unto Hebron; and Ahiman, Sheshai, and Talmai, the children of Anak, were there. (Now Hebron was built seven years before Zoan in Egypt.) 23 And they came unto the valley of Eshcol, and cut down from thence a branch with one cluster of grapes, and they bare it upon a staff between two; *they brought* also of the pomegranates, and of the figs. 24 That place was called the valley of Eshcol, because of the cluster which the children of Israel cut down from thence. 25 And they returned from spying out the land at the end of forty days.

Send thou men, that they may spy out the land (v. 2). From the reference in Deuteronomy 1:19-24, it appears that the Lord agreed to let them send out spies only after the people made a demand for such a procedure. It is not said whether this was the Lord's first choice for them, but it is apparent that He did not oppose such an intelligent approach. After the people made such a request the Lord commanded Moses to set up the me-

chanics for sending out the spies. This passage might be thus paraphrased: "The people have demanded that spies be sent out, so I will authorize Moses to work out a plan by which every tribe will be represented in the venture."

All of them were heads of the children of Israel (v. 3). In the party of spies Shammua represented Reuben (v. 4); Shaphat, Simeon (v. 5); Caleb, Judah (v. 5); Igal, Issachar (v. 7); Hoshea, Ephraim (v. 8); Palti, Benjamin (v. 9); Gaddiel, Zebulun (v. 10); Gaddi, Joseph through Manasseh (v. 11); Ammiel, Dan (v. 12); Sethur, Asher (v. 13); Nahbi, Naphtali (v. 14); and Geuel, Gad (v. 15).

Moses changed Hoshea's name to Joshua, meaning or signifying "saved" or a "savior" or "salvation." Clarke suggests that this change of name came when he had victory over Amalek (see Exod. 17: 13-14).[42]

We are told that:

Moses added the covenant name of God (*Yhwh*) to the name Oshea ("deliverance"). This name for God is translated JEHOVAH in the ASV and in a few places in the AV, but the latter usually renders it *LORD*. According to Exod. 3:14-15, the name designates God as the great "I AM", eternal and personal in his being. It also reminded Israel that he was the covenant-maker, who gave the promises to the fathers — Abraham, Isaac, and Jacob.[43]

The spies were to survey the land (v. 18) and to evaluate the people's capabilities with regard to making war. Special consideration was to be given as to how fruitful and productive the land was. They were to observe what kind of houses the people lived in, because this would determine the question of whether the people were permanent residents and well-entrenched, or whether they lived as nomadic tent dwellers. All of these considerations are important when an army moves into a territory. The spies were to bring back some of the fruit of the land so that Moses and the people could see, firsthand, what kind of land they would finally take over. It is stated that this was the time of the **first-ripe grapes.**

The spies made a wide sweep through the southern part of Canaan and finally

[42] *Op. cit.*, I, 660.   [43] Smick, *op. cit.*, p. 130.

arrived at Hebron, the old home town of Abraham. Apparently this area had now come under the control of the gigantic descendants of Anak. In the Eshcol country they found an abundance of fruit, including grapes, pomegranates and figs (v. 23). When this writer visited this same area a few years ago, the grape vines were loaded with such large bunches of grapes that to keep them from falling to the ground the owners propped up the vines with large tree limbs. It was, and still is, a land "flowing with milk and honey." As evidence of their findings they brought back samples of the land's productivity. One specimen was a large cluster of grapes which they suspended on poles carried by two men. After they searched the land for forty days, they returned to camp.

B. THE REPORT OF THE SPIES (13:26-33)

26 And they went and came to Moses, and to Aaron, and to all the congregation of the children of Israel, unto the wilderness of Paran, to Kadesh; and brought back word unto them, and unto all the congregation, and showed them the fruit of the land. 27 And they told him, and said, We came unto the land whither thou sentest us; and surely it floweth with milk and honey; and this is the fruit of it. 28 Howbeit the people that dwell in the land are strong, and the cities are fortified, *and* very great: and moreover we saw the children of Anak there. 29 Amalek dwelleth in the land of the South: and the Hittite, and the Jebusite, and the Amorite, dwell in the hill-country; and the Canaanite dwelleth by the sea, and along by the side of the Jordan.
30 And Caleb stilled the people before Moses, and said, Let us go up at once, and possess it; for we are well able to overcome it. 31 But the men that went up with him said, We are not able to go up against the people; for they are stronger than we. 32 And they brought up an evil report of the land which they had spied out unto the children of Israel, saying, The land, through which we have gone to spy it out, is a land that eateth up the inhabitants thereof; and all the people that we saw in it are men of great stature. 33 And there we saw the Nephilim, the sons of Anak, who come of the Nephilim: and we were in our own sight as grasshoppers, and so we were in their sight.

Upon their return the spies immediately reported to central intelligence so their findings could be evaluated. The people were called in to see the produce which the spies brought back to camp. There was both a majority and a minority report. Both agreed that the land was desirable to have and that it was indeed a land flowing with milk and honey. The majority, however, emphasized the fact that the people were strong and that their cities were indeed walled, and, in their opinion, would be most difficult to overcome. The children of Anak apparently terrified this group. In case the Anakites were not enough to frighten the people, they called attention also to the Amalekites who lived in the south, the Hittites and the Jebusites who lived in the mountains and the Canaanites who lived near the sea and near the Jordan River (v. 29).

Caleb and Joshua made the minority report. Caleb immediately addressed the people and assured them that they were able and should go at once to possess the land. The majority group, however, insisted that it was impossible for Israel to capture the land. With the "eyes of doubt" they could only see the greatness of the enemy. They were overcome with every kind of defeatism.

A land that eateth up the inhabitants (v. 32a). This reference indicates that the inhabitants were warlike and that there was continual strife in the land. In other words, the land was so rich and fruitful that there was perpetual strife and struggle for control. The majority felt that a land which so many struggled and fought for would be difficult to keep.

It is evident that the children of Anak were men of great stature (v. 33b), much larger than were the Israelites. It is quite probable that the "giant" Goliath and his family were of their race. The majority group saw themselves as grasshoppers in comparison.

There are in our midst today those who are spiritually related to the ten spies. They acknowledge that the experience of salvation is good and to be desired, but they continually sound a pessimistic note to the effect that we cannot totally conquer sin. They insist that we must "sin in word and deed" every day. Clarke writes:

"Sin," say they, "cannot be destroyed in this life — it will always dwell in you — the Anakim cannot be conquered — we are but as grasshoppers against the Anakim," etc., etc. Here and there a Joshua and a Caleb, trusting alone in the power of God, armed with faith in the infinite efficacy of that blood which cleanses from all unrighteousness, boldly stand forth and say: "Their defence is departed from them, and the Lord is with us; let us go up at once and possess the land, for we are well able to overcome." We can do all things through Christ strengthening us: he will purify us unto himself, and give us that rest from sin here which his death has procured and his word has promised.[44]

C. THE EFFECT OF THE SPIES' REPORT (14:1-45)

1 And all the congregation lifted up their voice, and cried; and the people wept that night. 2 And all the children of Israel murmured against Moses and against Aaron: and the whole congregation said unto them, Would that we had died in the land of Egypt! or would that we had died in this wilderness! 3 And wherefore doth Jehovah bring us unto this land, to fall by the sword? Our wives and our little ones will be a prey: were it not better for us to return into Egypt? 4 And they said one to another, Let us make a captain, and let us return into Egypt. 5 Then Moses and Aaron fell on their faces before all the assembly of the congregation of the children of Israel. 6 And Joshua the son of Nun and Caleb the son of Jephunneh, who were of them that spied out the land, rent their clothes: 7 and they spake unto all the congregation of the children of Israel, saying, The land, which we passed through to spy it out, is an exceeding good land. 8 If Jehovah delight in us, then he will bring us into this land, and give it unto us; a land which floweth with milk and honey. 9 Only rebel not against Jehovah, neither fear ye the people of the land; for they are bread for us: their defence is removed from over them, and Jehovah is with us: fear them not. 10 But all the congregation bade stone them with stones. And the glory of Jehovah appeared in the tent

of meeting unto all the children of Israel.

11 And Jehovah said unto Moses, How long will this people despise me? and how long will they not believe in me, for all the signs which I have wrought among them? 12 I will smite them with the pestilence, and disinherit them, and will make of thee a nation greater and mightier than they.

13 And Moses said unto Jehovah, Then the Egyptians will hear it; for thou broughtest up this people in thy might from among them; 14 and they will tell it to the inhabitants of this land. They have heard that thou Jehovah art in the midst of this people; for thou Jehovah art seen face to face, and thy cloud standeth over them, and thou goest before them, in a pillar of cloud by day, and in a pillar of fire by night. 15 Now if thou shalt kill this people as one man, then the nations which have heard the fame of thee will speak, saying, 16 Because Jehovah was not able to bring this people into the land which he sware unto them, therefore he hath slain them in the wilderness. 17 And now, I pray thee, let the power of the Lord be great, according as thou hast spoken, saying, 18 Jehovah is slow to anger, and abundant in lovingkindness, forgiving iniquity and transgression; and that will by no means clear *the guilty,* visiting the iniquity of the fathers upon the children, upon the third and upon the fourth generation. 19 Pardon, I pray thee, the iniquity of this people according unto the greatness of thy lovingkindness, and according as thou hast forgiven this people, from Egypt even until now.

20 And Jehovah said, I have pardoned according to thy word: 21 but in very deed, as I live, and as all the earth shall be filled with the glory of Jehovah; 22 because all those men that have seen my glory, and my signs, which I wrought in Egypt and in the wilderness, yet have tempted me these ten times, and have not hearkened to my voice; 23 surely they shall not see the land which I sware unto their fathers, neither shall any of them that despised me see it: 24 but my servant Caleb, because he had another spirit with him, and hath followed me fully, him will I bring into the land whereinto he went; and his seed shall possess it. 25 Now the Amalekite and the Canaanite dwell in the valley: to-morrow turn ye, and get you into

---

[44] Clarke, *op. cit.,* I, 662.

the wilderness by the way to the Red Sea.

26 And Jehovah spake unto Moses and unto Aaron, saying, 27 How long *shall I bear* with this evil congregation, that murmur against me? I have heard the murmurings of the children of Israel, which they murmur against me. 28 Say unto them, As I live, saith Jehovah, surely as ye have spoken in mine ears, so will I do to you: 29 your dead bodies shall fall in this wilderness; and all that were numbered of you, according to your whole number, from twenty years old and upward, that have murmured against me, 30 surely ye shall not come into the land, concerning which I sware that I would make you dwell therein, save Caleb the son of Jephunneh, and Joshua the son of Nun. 31 But your little ones, that ye said should be a prey, them will I bring in, and they shall know the land which ye have rejected. 32 But as for you, your dead bodies shall fall in this wilderness. 33 And your children shall be wanderers in the wilderness forty years, and shall bear your whoredoms, until your dead bodies be consumed in the wilderness. 34 After the number of the days in which ye spied out the land, even forty days, for every day a year, shall ye bear your iniquities, even forty years, and ye shall know my alienation. 35 I, Jehovah, have spoken, surely this will I do unto all this evil congregation, that are gathered together against me: in this wilderness they shall be consumed, and there they shall die.

36 And the men, whom Moses sent to spy out the land, who returned, and made all the congregation to murmur against him, by bringing up an evil report against the land, 37 even those men that did bring up an evil report of the land, died by the plague before Jehovah. 38 But Joshua the son of Nun, and Caleb the son of Jephunneh, remained alive of those men that went to spy out the land.

39 And Moses told these words unto all the children of Israel: and the people mourned greatly. 40 And they rose up early in the morning, and gat them up to the top of the mountain, saying, Lo, we are here, and will go up unto the place which Jehovah hath promised: for we have sinned. 41 And Moses said, Wherefore now do ye transgress the commandment of Jehovah, seeing it shall not prosper? 42 Go not up, for Jehovah is not among you; that ye be not smitten down before your enemies. 43 For there the Amalekite and the Canaanite are before you, and ye shall fall by the sword: because ye are turned back from following Jehovah, therefore Jehovah will not be with you. 44 But they presumed to go up to the top of the mountain: nevertheless the ark of the covenant of Jehovah, and Moses, departed not out of the camp. 45 Then the Amalekite came down, and the Canaanite who dwelt in that mountain, and smote them and beat them down, even unto Hormah.

As they heard the report, the people gave evidence to a degraded state of mind. Instead of expressing faith and hope, they gave themselves to pessimism and defeat, and felt sorry for themselves. They found fault with Moses and Aaron and lamented the fact that they did not die in Egypt, or at best, in the wilderness (v. 2). They even accused the Lord of deliberately bringing them to this place to **fall by the sword** (v. 3).

The people accepted the defeatist attitude expressed by the ten spies and decided to renounce the authority of Moses. They talked in terms of giving up their journey to Canaan and returning to Egypt with its "flesh-pots of sin." They are now reaping the consequences of lingering too long in the wilderness. God's plan had been for them to go on and possess the land of Canaan, but they now find themselves discouraged and strangers to the grace of God.

The seriousness of the situation is evidenced by the impassioned plea of Moses and Aaron before the Lord. Joshua and Caleb also joined in this emergency prayer meeting. The act of tearing their clothing (v. 6) was an expression of humility and utter desperation and a cry for help from the Lord.

Joshua and Caleb made an impassioned plea to the people to exercise common sense and to consider the providential care the Lord had exercised over them. They reiterated that the land of Canaan was **an exceeding good land** and that the people could expect the same faithful care the Lord had shown them since they left Egypt. They were assured that the Lord would bring them safely into the land **which floweth with milk and honey** (v. 8).

There were some conditions, however: they were to desist from their rebellion and they were not to fear **the people of the land.**

They are bread for us (v. 9b). This is, no doubt, a colloquial expression, and means that the difficulty which the people appear to present will be overcome as easily as people eat bread. Their strong, walled cities and fortifications will be overcome through the power of Almighty God, even as was evidenced later at Jericho.

In utter disregard and contempt for the preaching of the leaders, the people rejected their earnest pleas and asked that they be stoned. This indicates the depth of the people's apostasy. They have now reached the point of no return in their evil imaginations. God's punishment cannot be longer delayed.

The Lord manifested Himself in the tabernacle to deal with this critical situation. The evil determination to stone the Lord's faithful spokesman was stayed by the Lord's intervention. He had something to say to rebellious Israel. Verse 11 shows that even the Lord's patience can be limited. One writer says:

> This question gives us a revealing insight into the nature of God. It is not only man who cries, "How long, O Lord?" but God who also cries, "How long, O Man?" God's patience with man should keep man patient still with his brother man, and patient too, toward God. But man should remember that there may be limits even to the patience of God.[45]

The Lord pronounces His indignation (v. 12a), and along with it the judgment that is to befall the rebellious people. From verse 12b it appears that the Lord will bring an end to adult Israel and will build a new nation out of Joshua and Caleb and those under twenty years of age. The new nation is to exemplify the spirit of Moses, Aaron, Joshua and Caleb.

Moses engages in a bit of arguing with the Lord (v. 18). He points out that the Egyptians will get news of such severe judgment as is proposed and they in turn will communicate this information to the Canaanites. So far the inhabitants of the land had been informed (perhaps by the Egyptians) that the Lord was a God who appeared **face to face** and that He led His people on their way by means of a pillar of cloud and fire (v. 14). The dialogue between Moses and the Lord continues.

Moses points out that if all the people were destroyed the news would get out that the all-powerful God of Israel was defeated because He could not bring the people into the land He had promised them (v. 16).

Jehovah is slow to anger, and abundant in lovingkindness (v. 18a). This is a repetition of Exodus 34:6-7. Moses observes that the power of the Lord is great, but this greatness is characterized by mercy and forgiveness.

By no means clearing the guilty (v. 18b). But it must be remembered that sin results in punishment. If the sinner refuses to repent he must suffer the consequences. Sinners may be justified at the cross through repentance and confession or be judged and punished in the divine court of justice. Sin is of such a nature that its evil effects may be transmitted to the third and fourth generation. It is a fact even today that certain diseases, biological weaknesses and social pathologies express themselves in the offspring.

Moses makes an impassioned plea for the Lord to pardon the people (v. 19). The Lord promises pardon, but it must be remembered that pardon cannot become effective unless the sinner repents of and confesses his sins.

It is evident that the adult population over twenty years of age refused to repent. In their own self-will they had gone down the road of apostasy to a point of no return. It is evident that there is a distinction between backsliding and apostasy. It is quite probable that apostasy and the unpardonable sin are intimately related. This idea is suggested in such passages as Isaiah 63:10, Matthew 12:31, Acts 5:3, and Romans 1:24 (see also Rom. 1:18-32; Heb. 6:4). The subsequent punishment was death in the wilderness (v. 23).

Caleb was a bold and courageous spirit who had a willingness to follow the directions of the Lord. His spirit was so fused with the Spirit of the Lord that he had risen above human inquietudes and earthly fears. God's witness to Caleb was that he **hath followed me fully** (v. 24b). One exegete says:

> "Follow fully" derives from a root meaning "to fill," and is used to express the consecration of the priest ("fill his hand,"

3:3). It also means "to overflow" or "to do anything in abundance without holding back," whether for evil or for good (Job 16:10). Caleb abandoned himself completely to God, who in turn "abundanced" Caleb by "filling his hand," to do the divine will. A perfect example of consecration.[46]

It was John Wesley's position that when a person had experienced justification (salvation, new birth, conversion) it was God's will that he go on to Christian perfection, namely, to entire sanctification. This is what the disciples experienced on the Day of Pentecost. This is a necessary experience before a person can minister in the name of the Lord with power and consistent sustaining grace. This Spirit-baptism comes to believers when the conditions laid down in Romans 12:1-2 are met. Men endued with the power of God are men filled with the Holy Spirit (see Acts 1:8).

This experience of entire sanctification is frequently compared to the land of Canaan into which the Israelites were commanded to go. Canaan was their ultimate goal. It was the land that God had promised to the Hebrew children. It was a land flowing with milk and honey, where the grapes of Eshcol grew so big that they hung to the ground. This land was their reward for going all the way — not just part of the way.

God also offers us the "milk and honey" experience if we consecrate ourselves completely to Him for service. We too can live in the land where pomegranates and grapes abound. Paul gives us the formula: "I beseech you therefore, brethren, by the mercies of God, that ye present your bodies a living sacrifice, holy and acceptable unto God, which is your reasonable service" (Rom. 12:1).

It is the will of God that all believers should be filled with the Holy Spirit, and this can come about only by obeying the divine injunction: "wait for the promise of the Father."

When the members of the infant Church in Jerusalem met the condition "they were all filled with the Holy Spirit." This blessed Canaan experience is a believer's privilege, a believer's birthright and a believer's obligation. God has provided it, and He expects every believer to appropriate it.

A complete surrender to God with the resultant infilling of the Holy Spirit will save Christians, both young and old, from wasting many precious years in the wilderness. It was God's desire for the Hebrews to go immediately to possess the land, but because of their unbelief, they doomed themselves to aimless wanderings in the snake-infested desert. What folly! Why should any believer spend torturous years in the wilderness when the murmuring brooks of Canaan and the grapes of Eshcol beckon him on.

God intends that every believer should be radiant, happy and victorious. Pentecost changed the early believers from a state of uncertainty to one of victory and joy. What God did for the early Christians He wills to do for all believers.[47]

The judgment of the Lord is about to be administered (v. 29). All Israelites from twenty years old and upward are to die in the desert. They have forfeited their right to live because of their repeated and insistent rebellion against the Lord and their refusal to live a decent moral life. The courts today recognize the fact that certain crimes, if committed, can bring forfeiture of personal freedom, or even of life itself.

Caleb and Joshua were the only adults who were permitted to enter the land of Canaan, along with the younger generation. In Wesleyan theology, as in most Christian theology, there is the doctrine of the "age of accountability." It is assumed that a child is innocent in the sight of God until he attains the age at which he knows right from wrong. The child must at that time make a choice either to accept Jesus Christ as Lord and Savior or, consequently, suffer the state of the unjustified. It appears that this idea is suggested in the younger generation of Israel that is to go on into the promised land.

Israel is to suffer privation and desert misery for forty years (v. 33). The length of this punishment is intimately associated with the basis for Israel's punishment, namely, the refusal to accept the favorable minority report which was made after forty days of spying out the land. In order that they might never

---

[46] Smick, op. cit., p. 132.   [47] Hanke, The Tabernacle in the Wilderness, p. 36.

forget the reason for their punishment, the sentence was based upon the formula — one year for each day, or **forty days, for every day a year** (v. 34). The figure forty was to become a figurative symbol of the "forty days of folly."

The Lord's judgment struck immediately upon the ten unfaithful spies. They were struck dead where they stood. Paul warns the Corinthians against the judgment that came upon the Israelites. Apparently there was a condition in Corinth that was closely akin to this wilderness experience (see I Cor. 10:1-12).

The writer of the Epistle to the Hebrews warns his readers that there is danger of divine judgment, and he cites the forty years' judgment in the wilderness (see Heb. 3:16-19).

Only Joshua and Caleb of the adult population escaped the desert judgment. They did so because they obeyed and followed the command of the Lord. We are told that these things were for an example to us (I Cor. 10:6). This is a warning to preachers of God's Word. The plan of salvation must be honestly and fearlessly presented at all times.

They rose up early . . . and gat them up to the top of the mountain (v. 40). The Lord had commanded that they return to the wilderness, but instead they reiterated their rebellious attitude by attacking their enemies. It should be pointed out that an attack was to be preceded by a command from the Lord. The Israelites expressed their indifference to God's command by doing the very opposite of what they were commanded to do. Clarke comments on this passage thus:

> They found themselves on the very borders of the land, and they heard God say they should not enter it, but should be consumed by a forty years' wandering in the wilderness; notwithstanding, they are determined to render vain this purpose of God, probably supposing that the temporary sorrow they felt for their late rebellion would be accepted as a sufficient atonement for their crimes. They accordingly went up, and were cut down by their enemies; and why? God went not with them. How vain is the counsel of man against the wisdom of God! Nature, poor, fallen human nature, is ever running into extremes. This

miserable people, a short time ago, thought that though they had Omnipotence with them they could not conquer and possess the land! Now they imagine that though God himself go not with them, yet they shall be sufficient to drive out the inhabitants, and take possession of their country! Man is ever supposing he can either do all things or do nothing; he is therefore sometimes presumptuous, and at other times in despair. Who but an apostle, or one under the influence of the same Spirit, can say, I can do all things through Christ who strengtheneth me?[48]

There is an obvious difference between presumption and divinely inspired faith. They took this action on their own initiative and self-sufficiency. Against the will of God they attacked the enemy, and thus they suffered serious military defeat.

V. THE YEARS OF WANDERING IN THE WILDERNESS (Num. 15:1—20:29)

A. THE CEREMONIAL FORMULA (15:1-31)

1 And Jehovah spake unto Moses, saying, 2 Speak unto the children of Israel, and say unto them, When ye are come into the land of your habitations, which I give unto you, 3 and will make an offering by fire unto Jehovah, a burnt-offering, or a sacrifice, to accomplish a vow, or as a freewill-offering, or in your set feasts, to make a sweet savor unto Jehovah, of the herd, or of the flock; 4 then shall he that offereth his oblation offer unto Jehovah a meal offering of a tenth part *of an ephah* of fine flour mingled with the fourth part of a hin of oil: 5 and wine for the drink-offering, the fourth part of a hin shalt thou prepare with the burnt-offering, or for the sacrifice, for each lamb. 6 Or for a ram, thou shalt prepare for a meal-offering two tenth parts *of an ephah* of fine flour mingled with the third part of a hin of oil: 7 and for the drink-offering thou shalt offer the third part of a hin of wine, of a sweet savor unto Jehovah. 8 And when thou preparest a bullock for a burnt-offering, or for a sacrifice, to accomplish a vow, or for peace-offerings unto Jehovah; 9 then shall he offer with the bullock a meal-offering of three tenth parts *of an ephah* of fine flour mingled with half a hin of

oil: 10 and thou shalt offer for the drink-offering half a hin of wine, for an offering made by fire, of a sweet savor unto Jehovah.

11 Thus shall it be done for each bullock, or for each ram, or for each of the he-lambs, or of the kids. 12 According to the number that ye shall prepare, so shall ye do to every one according to their number. 13 All that are home-born shall do these things after this manner, in offering an offering made by fire, of a sweet savor unto Jehovah. 14 And if a stranger sojourn with you, or whosoever may be among you throughout your generations, and will offer an offering made by fire, of a sweet savor unto Jehovah; as ye do, so he shall do. 15 For the assembly, there shall be one statute for you, and for the stranger that sojourneth *with you,* a statute for ever throughout your generations: as ye are, so shall the sojourner be before Jehovah. 16 One law and one ordinance shall be for you, and for the stranger that sojourneth with you.

17 And Jehovah spake unto Moses, saying, 18 Speak unto the children of Israel, and say unto them, When ye come into the land whither I bring you, 19 then it shall be, that, when ye eat of the bread of the land, ye shall offer up a heave-offering unto Jehovah. 20 Of the first of your dough ye shall offer up a cake for a heave-offering: as the heave-offering of the threshing-floor, so shall ye heave it. 21 Of the first of your dough ye shall give unto Jehovah a heave-offering throughout your generations.

22 And when ye shall err, and not observe all these commandments, which Jehovah hath spoken unto Moses, 23 even all that Jehovah hath commanded you by Moses, from the day that Jehovah gave commandment, and onward throughout your generations; 24 then it shall be, if it be done unwittingly, without the knowledge of the congregation, that all the congregation shall offer one young bullock for a burnt-offering, for a sweet savor unto Jehovah, with the meal-offering thereof, and the drink-offering thereof, according to the ordinance, and one he-goat for a sin-offering. 25 And the priest shall make atonement for all the congregation of the children of Israel, and they shall be forgiven; for it was an error, and they have brought their oblation, an offering made by fire unto Jehovah, and their sin-offering before Jehovah, for their error: 26 and all the congregation of the children of Israel shall be forgiven, and the stranger that sojourneth among them; for in respect of all the people it was done unwittingly.

27 And if one person sin unwittingly, then he shall offer a she-goat a year old for a sin-offering. 28 And the priest shall make atonement for the soul that erreth, when he sinneth unwittingly, before Jehovah, to make atonement for him; and he shall be forgiven. 29 Ye shall have one law for him that doeth aught unwittingly, for him that is home-born among the children of Israel, and for the stranger that sojourneth among them. 30 But the soul that doeth aught with a high hand, whether he be home-born or a sojourner, the same blasphemeth Jehovah; and that soul shall be cut off from among his people. 31 Because he hath despised the word of Jehovah, and hath broken his commandment, that soul shall utterly be cut off; his iniquity shall be upon him.

It appears that the Lord is now giving the Israelites a special preparatory course in the Levitical ritual for the time when they shall enter the land. It is apparent that certain phases of the offerings here specified were not intended for the wilderness but rather for the promised land. Bringing an offering to the Lord (v. 3) signifies

an offering or gift by which a person has access unto God: and this receives light from the universal custom that prevails in the east, no man being permitted to approach the presence of a superior without a present or gift; the offering thus brought was called *korban,* which properly means the introduction offering or offering of access.[49]

The instruction given here is a repetition of that which has been given before (see Lev. 1—7). One writer says:

There is little in these rules that is not already contained in the laws given at Sinai for the priests. The purpose of this section is an indirect one. It focuses attention on the certainty that God will bring His people into the Promised Land (cf. verses 2 and 18). Just when they have failed so miserably, and a whole generation has been doomed to die in the wilderness, specific stress is laid on God's plan for His people in Canaan, and indirect means of giving them assurance that His promises will be carried out in due time.[50]

[49] *Ibid.,* I, 508.   [50] A. A. MacRae, "Numbers," *The New Bible Commentary,* p. 181.

The amount of meal and flour was determined by the size of the sacrifice. A lamb (v. 5), a ram (v. 6), and a bullock (v. 8), each required their respective proportions. Verse 13 would suggest that the instructions are directed to the young generation under twenty years of age. The Septuagint renders this passage thus: "Every native of the country shall do thus."

Strangers or neighboring worshipers of other gods were always welcome to convert to the religion of Jehovah God. The basic condition for salvation was the same for all men, and so it is today. It has always been, "Jesus Christ the same yesterday, today and forever" (Heb. 13: 8). This idea is clearly stated in the words, as ye do, so shall he do (v. 14b). This is further emphasized in the next verse, there shall be one statute for you, and for the stranger that sojourneth with you . . . as ye are, so shall the sojourner be before Jehovah (v. 15). Verse 18 indicates that the instructions in these passages have a future connotation. The dough offering is related to a thanksgiving to the Lord for His bounty and goodness. The word *dough* comes from the Hebrew word *arisa* and means coarse grain. One exegete suggests that

> the fact that this heave offering of coarse grain is called *teruma,* "a contribution," indicates that it was for priestly consumption, while the fine flour of Lev. 23:13 was to be a fire offering, a pleasing savor unto the Lord.[51]

An infraction which fell in the category of verse 24a was to be dealt with in a spirit of understanding. The Wesleyan interpretation of real sin would be limited to an evil act or violation of God's law, done willfully and on purpose. By definition, "Sin is a willful transgression against a known law of God." I John 3:4 is so understood under this definition of sin.

It is obvious that the same evil act might be committed under circumstances which would absolve the person of guilt. Because of the infirmity of the flesh it is possible to become involved in acts which are not intentional. A limited or impaired sense of sight, hearing, smell or other sensory perception might be the underlying cause for an act which would be evil, but would not be considered sin. In a court at law the principle of motive is always an important consideration. Even though an act is not done because of an evil motive, there must be some kind of public acknowledgment of the infraction (v. 24b). An apology or plea for pardon is an acceptable expression for a social infraction done unintentionally. Even such an act in ignorance required an offering or public expression unto the Lord. There was a single standard for both the born Israelite and the Israelite by adoption.

The person who acted with evil intention or a high hand was to be expelled from camp fellowship. This applied to both the "born" Israelite and the stranger, or "adopted Israelite." The seriousness of the offense is expressed in these words, that soul shall utterly be cut off; his iniquity shall be upon him (v. 31). It is probable that the incidents in Hebrews 4:4-8 and 10:26-31 are closely akin to this situation.

B. JUDGMENT OF SABBATH DESE-CRATION (15:32-36)

32 And while the children of Israel were in the wilderness, they found a man gathering sticks upon the sabbath day. 33 And they that found him gathering sticks brought him unto Moses and Aaron, and unto all the congregation. 34 And they put him in ward, because it had not been declared what should be done to him. 35 And Jehovah said unto Moses, The man shall surely be put to death: all the congregation shall stone him with stones without the camp. 36 And all the congregation brought him without the camp, and stoned him to death with stones; as Jehovah commanded Moses.

It appears that the man in question in verse 32 committed the sin referred to in verse 30. The KJV translates this passage thus: "The soul that doeth ought presumptuously." Obviously the man despised and repudiated the commandment of God, and his punishment was commensurate with his deed. Rebellion against law and order always results in serious trouble. The man was gathering sticks on the Sabbath (v. 33), but the

51 Smick, *op. cit.,* p. 133.

crux of the matter is not so much what he was doing as the fact that he had denied God's authority. It is the rebellious spirit of which the act is a symptom.

The Sabbath violator was placed in confinement until he could be tried by a legally constituted tribunal or court. The Lord commands that the man is to be put to death (v. 35). The congregation is appointed as the executioner: they are to stone him. The punishment was harsh but the infraction challenged the very authority of God.

C. THE BORDER OF THEIR GARMENTS (15:37-41)

37 And Jehovah spake unto Moses, saying, 38 Speak unto the children of Israel, and bid them that they make them fringes in the borders of their garments throughout their generations, and that they put upon the fringe of each border a cord of blue: 39 and it shall be unto you for a fringe, that ye may look upon it, and remember all the commandments of Jehovah, and do them; and that ye follow not after your own heart and your own eyes, after which ye use to play the harlot; 40 that ye may remember and do all my commandments, and be holy unto your God. 41 I am Jehovah your God, who brought you out of the land of Egypt, to be your God: I am Jehovah your God.

Symbols have always been means whereby spiritual values have been conveyed. The cross and the crown are familiar Christian symbols to symbolize suffering and victory. The **fringes in the borders of their garments** were to be emblematic or symbolic of God's commandments. These fringes were visible reminders that they were subject to the commandments. The people were to look upon these fringes and be reminded that they were to be a holy people and subject to the commandments of the Lord.

D. THE REBELLION OF KORAH (16:1-35)

1 Now Korah, the son of Izhar, the son of Kohath, the son of Levi, with Dathan and Abiram, the sons of Eliab, and On, the son of Peleth, sons of Reuben, took *men*: 2 and they rose up before Moses, with certain of the children of Israel, two hundred and fifty princes of the congregation, called to the assembly, men of renown; 3 and they assembled themselves together against Moses and against Aaron, and said unto them, Ye take too much upon you, seeing all the congregation are holy, every one of them, and Jehovah is among them: wherefore then lift ye up yourselves above the assembly of Jehovah?

4 And when Moses heard it, he fell upon his face: 5 and he spake unto Korah and unto all his company, saying, In the morning Jehovah will show who are his, and who is holy, and will cause him to come near unto him: even him whom he shall choose will he cause to come near unto him. 6 This do: take you censers, Korah, and all his company; 7 and put fire in them, and put incense upon them before Jehovah tomorrow: and it shall be that the man whom Jehovah doth choose, he *shall be* holy: ye take too much upon you, ye sons of Levi. 8 And Moses said unto Korah, Hear now, ye sons of Levi: 9 *seemeth it but* a small thing unto you, that the God of Israel hath separated you from the congregation of Israel, to bring you near to himself, to do the service of the tabernacle of Jehovah, and to stand before the congregation to minister unto them; 10 and that he hath brought thee near, and all thy brethren the sons of Levi with thee? and seek ye the priesthood also? 11 Therefore thou and all thy company are gathered together against Jehovah: and Aaron, what is he that ye murmur against him?

12 And Moses sent to call Dathan and Abiram, the sons of Eliab; and they said, We will not come up: 13 is it a small thing that thou hast brought us up out of a land flowing with milk and honey, to kill us in the wilderness, but thou must needs make thyself also a prince over us? 14 Moreover thou hast not brought us into a land flowing with milk and honey, nor given us inheritance of fields and vineyards: wilt thou put out the eyes of these men? we will not come up.

15 And Moses was very wroth, and said unto Jehovah, Respect not thou their offering: I have not taken one ass from them, neither have I hurt one of them. 16 And Moses said unto Korah, Be thou and all thy company before Jehovah, thou, and they, and Aaron, to-morrow: 17 and take ye every man his censer, and put incense upon them, and bring ye before Jehovah every man his censer, two hundred and fifty censers; thou also, and Aaron, each his censer. 18 And they took every man his censer, and put fire in them, and laid incense thereon, and

stood at the door of the tent of meeting with Moses and Aaron. 19 And Korah assembled all the congregation against them unto the door of the tent of meeting: and the glory of Jehovah appeared unto all the congregation.

20 And Jehovah spake unto Moses and unto Aaron, saying, 21 Separate yourselves from among this congregation, that I may consume them in a moment. 22 And they fell upon their faces, and said, O God, the God of the spirits of all flesh, shall one man sin, and wilt thou be wroth with all the congregation? 23 And Jehovah spake unto Moses, saying, 24 Speak unto the congregation, saying, Get you up from about the tabernacle of Korah, Dathan, and Abiram. 25 And Moses rose up and went unto Dathan and Abiram; and the elders of Israel followed him. 26 And he spake unto the congregation, saying, Depart, I pray you, from the tents of these wicked men, and touch nothing of theirs, lest ye be consumed in all their sins. 27 So they gat them up from the tabernacle of Korah, Dathan, and Abiram, on every side: and Dathan and Abiram came out, and stood at the door of their tents, and their wives, and their sons, and their little ones. 28 And Moses said, Hereby ye shall know that Jehovah hath sent me to do all these works; for *I have* not *done them* of mine own mind. 29 If these men die the common death of all men, or if they be visited after the visitation of all men; then Jehovah hath not sent me. 30 But if Jehovah make a new thing, and the ground open its mouth, and swallow them up, with all that appertain unto them, and they go down alive into Sheol; then ye shall understand that these men have despised Jehovah.

31 And it came to pass, as he made an end of speaking all these words, that the ground clave asunder that was under them; 32 and the earth opened its mouth, and swallowed them up, and their households, and all the men that appertained unto Korah, and all their goods. 33 So they, and all that appertained to them, went down alive into Sheol: and the earth closed upon them, and they perished from among the assembly. 34 And all Israel that were round about them fled at the cry of them; for they said, Lest the earth swallow us up. 35 And fire came forth from Jehovah, and devoured the two hundred and fifty men that offered the incense.

The apostate nature of some tribal leaders is further expressed in the rebellion of Korah. The Lord had expressed His displeasure over the rebellious attitude of the people only a short time before, but irrespective of this warning Korah was determined to push the issue further. It should be pointed out that Korah was the chief instigator in this plot, and this is verified by the fact that the word **men** is not in the original Hebrew text. The Septuagint reads thus, "and Core the son of Isaar the son of Caath the son of Levi . . . spake." The word "spake" appears here instead of **took men.** It is evident in other parts of Scripture where reference is made to this event that it is attributed to Korah (26:9 and Jude 11).

Ye take too much upon you (v. 3). This paraphrased might read: "You are taking more authority than has been granted you." This is, of course, a false premise in the light of the context. Moses certainly was their legitimate leader, and this had been demonstrated before. It is apparent that Korah, Dathan and Abiram are overcome with jealousy. They accuse Moses of setting himself up as an arrogant, self-appointed leader.

The Lord will be the judge in this matter, which is to be directed by a determinative ritual. Of this text Marsh says:

> Moses' reply . . . is to invite Korah and his fellows to a sort of trial by ordeal. They shall bring on the morrow fire pans with incense, and Yahweh himself will choose who is to be holy and so come near to burn . . . The whole arrangement of the Israelite camp was governed by the fact that the holier a man was, the nearer he could come to Yahweh's trysting tent.[52]

Moses calls Korah's attention to the fact that he has underestimated his offense and has overestimated his rights and privileges (vv. 8-9). Not only had Korah sought the priestly function but he also induced some fellow Levites to seek the same (v. 10). After rebuking Korah, Moses sends for Dathan and Abiram, but they refuse to make their appearance; rather, they inject a further irrelevance into the matter at hand. They criticize Moses for not providing productive fields and vineyards in the desert (v. 13). Smick makes this comment:

52 *Op. cit.,* II, 221.

Dathan and Abiram refused to come out of the tabernacle to face Moses but sent bitter complaint (vv. 12-14). Korah, on the other hand, and his 250 "princes" (not all but many being Levites; vv. 7, 8; 27:3) appeared with censers in hand, to prove that they were holy and could perform this priestly duty. Suddenly the glory of the Lord appeared at the door of the Tabernacle; and the Lord upheld Moses' authority by opening the earth to swallow the three leaders of the rebellion, with their houses and possessions (v. 32). A further judgment of fire devoured the company of censer-bearers.[53]

Respect not their offering (v. 15). Acceptable sacrifices must be accompanied by a pure motive. Clarke says, "God never has blessed, and never can bless, any scheme of salvation which is not of his own appointment."[54]

The time has now come when a clear distinction is to be made between the true leaders and the "would-be" counterfeit leaders (v. 21). Moses and the congregation are to withdraw themselves from the site of divine judgment and execution. Definite action must be taken at once in order to avoid the disaster that is to come upon the guilty rebels. God is about to give a public demonstration regarding the question of leadership. Moses advises the people that if their leaders live to die a normal death they can then be assured that he was not their leader (v. 29). But if the Lord invokes a peculiar kind of death upon the leaders, the congregation is to understand that the Lord has expressed His displeasure toward the rebels and has thereby vindicated His claim to leadership (v. 30). Immediately after this statement the surface of the earth cracked open under the feet of the rebels and they all fell into the horrible pit created by the supernatural earthquake.

After the earthquake swallowed Korah, Dathan and Abiram, fire from heaven fell upon the two hundred and fifty men that offered incense.

E. THE VINDICATION OF AARON'S PRIESTHOOD (16:36—17:13)

36 And Jehovah spake unto Moses, saying, 37 Speak unto Eleazar the son of Aaron the priest, that he take up the censers out of the burning, and scatter thou the fire yonder; for they are holy, 38 even the censers of these sinners against their own lives; and let them be made beaten plates for a covering of the altar: for they offered them before Jehovah; therefore they are holy; and they shall be a sign unto the children of Israel. 39 And Eleazar the priest took the brazen censers, which they that were burnt had offered; and they beat them out for a covering of the altar, 40 to be a memorial unto the children of Israel, to the end that no stranger, that is not of the seed of Aaron, come near to burn incense before Jehovah; that he be not as Korah, and as his company: as Jehovah spake unto him by Moses.

41 But on the morrow all the congregation of the children of Israel murmured against Moses and against Aaron, saying, Ye have killed the people of Jehovah. 42 And it came to pass, when the congregation was assembled against Moses and against Aaron, that they looked toward the tent of meeting: and, behold, the cloud covered it, and the glory of Jehovah appeared. 43 And Moses and Aaron came to the front of the tent of meeting. 44 And Jehovah spake unto Moses, saying, 45 Get you up from among this congregation, that I may consume them in a moment. And they fell upon their faces. 46 And Moses said unto Aaron, Take thy censer, and put fire therein from off the altar, and lay incense thereon, and carry it quickly unto the congregation, and make atonement for them: for there is wrath gone out from Jehovah; the plague is begun. 47 And Aaron took as Moses spake, and ran into the midst of the assembly; and, behold, the plague was begun among the people: and he put on the incense, and made atonement for the people. 48 And he stood between the dead and the living; and the plague was stayed. 49 Now they that died by the plague were fourteen thousand and seven hundred, besides them that died about the matter of Korah. 50 And Aaron returned unto Moses unto the door of the tent of meeting: and the plague was stayed.

1 And Jehovah spake unto Moses, saying, 2 Speak unto the children of Israel, and take of them rods, one for each fathers' house, of all their princes according to their fathers' houses, twelve rods: write thou every man's name upon his rod. 3 And thou shalt write Aaron's name upon the rod of Levi; for there shall be one rod for each head of their fathers' houses. 4 And thou shalt lay

---

[53] Op. cit., p. 134.   [54] Op. cit., I, 671.

them up in the tent of meeting before the testimony, where I meet with you. 5 And it shall come to pass, that the rod of the man whom I shall choose shall bud: and I will make to cease from me the murmurings of the children of Israel, which they murmur against you. 6 And Moses spake unto the children of Israel; and all their princes gave him rods, for each prince one, according to their fathers' houses, even twelve rods: and the rod of Aaron was among their rods. 7 And Moses laid up the rods before Jehovah in the tent of the testimony.

8 And it came to pass on the morrow, that Moses went into the tent of the testimony; and, behold, the rod of Aaron for the house of Levi was budded, and put forth buds, and produced blossoms, and bare ripe almonds. 9 And Moses brought out all the rods from before Jehovah unto all the children of Israel: and they looked, and took every man his rod. 10 And Jehovah said unto Moses, Put back the rod of Aaron before the testimony, to be kept for a token against the children of rebellion; that thou mayest make an end of their murmurings against me, that they die not. 11 Thus did Moses: as Jehovah commanded him, so did he.

12 And the children of Israel spake unto Moses, saying, Behold, we perish, we are undone, we are all undone. 13 Every one that cometh near, that cometh near unto the tabernacle of Jehovah, dieth: shall we perish all of us?

The Lord commanded Moses to have Eleazar the son of Aaron make a covering for the altar out of the bronze censers, which had belonged to the two hundred and fifty who had been destroyed by fire (v. 38).

The covering on the altar was to be a reminder to the congregation that the Lord has a plan and a design in worship and that only those qualified to affiliate dare assume this responsibility (see comments on 3:4). It seems incredible that the people should continue their complaining after they had witnessed the fearful judgment which the Lord had imposed. The Lord commanded Moses to separate himself from the murmuring people so that punishment could be imposed upon them (v. 45). Moses made a last-minute effort to intercede for the people, but the plague had begun to exact its toll. Apparently the plague be-

gan on one side of the camp but was stopped before it got out of control. We do not know what the plague was, but apparently it spread rapidly, and 14,700 people died from it before Aaron could stay the epidemic (v. 49).[55]

Take them rods, one for each fathers' house (v. 2). By now the people were so confused about authority and legal leadership that a further step was necessary to quiet their minds, and to settle forever the dispute as to the resident tribe for the priesthood. The Lord uses an illustrated object lesson through which He conveys the truth of the matter. Each tribal head is to bring his staff or sceptre, the officially recognized sign of a political sovereign. Each staff bore the name of its tribal chief, i.e., the names of the sons of Jacob. Each tribal head is commanded to lay his staff on the ground, **before the testimony,** presumably inside the enclosed court in front of the tabernacle proper in which the ark of the covenant was contained.

It is decreed by the Lord that the deciding factor of priesthood shall be the rod which **shall bud.** The owner of the rod which becomes alive and blossoms out with buds shall be the true priestly head. The demonstration in this situation is so obviously miraculous that no one could doubt as to which tribe was the divinely appointed priestly tribe. Aaron's staff budded, blossomed and bore almonds **on the morrow** or during the night. Clarke makes this observation:

Every thing in this miracle is so far beyond the power of nature, that no doubt could remain on the minds of the people, or the envious chiefs, of the Divine appointment of Aaron, and of the especial interference of God in this case. To see a piece of wood long cut off from the parent stock, without bark or moisture remaining, laid up in a dry place for a single night, with others in the same circumstances — to see such a piece of wood resume and evince the perfection of vegetative life, budding, blossoming, and bringing forth ripe fruit at the same time, must be such a demonstration of the peculiar interference of God, as to silence every doubt and satisfy every scruple. It is worthy of remark that a sceptre, or staff of office, resuming its vegetative life, was considered an absolute impossibility among the ancients; and as they were accustomed to swear by their sceptres, this circumstance was added to establish and confirm the oath.[56]

The ark of the covenant housed in the Holy of Holies or the inner sanctum of the tabernacle was to contain the testimony, i.e., the items which attested God's providential and miraculous oversight (Exod. 25:16). These items of testimony were the tablets of the law, a pot of manna and Aaron's rod which budded. Two golden cherubim, one at each end, were to be attached to the cover of the ark or mercy-seat (Exod. 25:19). The room in which the ark was located was a perfect cube. Above the ark hovered the Shekinah glory. Once each year on the Day of Atonement, the high priest carried the names of the people on his breast and shoulders and made peace with God for their sins. The Holy of Holies was the secret place of the Most High where all repentant sinners could enter in the representation of the high priest. View of the inside was obstructed by the veil. Now the veil has been rent in twain and all believers are priests in the faith and may go personally to the mercy-seat. When the sinner meets the condition at the foot of the cross, the veil for him becomes "rent in twain" and it is then that he can rejoice over the invitation: "Having therefore, brethren, boldness to enter the holiest by the blood of Jesus, by a new and living way, which he has consecrated for us, through the veil, that is to say his flesh; and having an high priest over the house of God; let us draw nigh with a true heart in full assurance of faith, having our hearts sprinkled from an evil conscience, and our bodies washed with pure water" (Heb. 10:19-22).

The apostate condition in which the people find themselves is expressed in their inability to comprehend spiritual truth. They are given over to one hysterical extremity after another. The unrepentant sinner does not see the truth, but rather he endeavors to rationalize his self-righteousness. Frequently a sinner is so unaware of spiritual relevance that he desecrates the holy with his very presence. Only an animal without spot or blemish was to be offered on the altar.

No person has a right to handle holy things without first having his defilement cleansed with the blood of the Lamb. "Present your bodies a living sacrifice, holy and acceptable unto God," is and always has been the basis on which a person can come into the presence of the Lord God.[57]

F. THE DUTIES OF AARON AND HIS SONS (18:1-32)

1 And Jehovah said unto Aaron, Thou and thy sons and thy fathers' house with thee shall bear the iniquity of the sanctuary; and thou and thy sons with thee shall bear the iniquity of your priesthood. 2 And thy brethren also, the tribe of Levi, the tribe of thy father, bring thou near with thee, that they may be joined unto thee, and minister unto thee: but thou and thy sons with thee shall be before the tent of the testimony. 3 And they shall keep thy charge, and the charge of all the Tent: only they shall not come nigh unto the vessels of the sanctuary and unto the altar, that they die not, neither they, nor ye. 4 And they shall be joined unto thee, and keep the charge of the tent of meeting, for all the service of the Tent: and a stranger shall not come nigh unto you. 5 And ye shall keep the charge of the sanctuary, and the charge of the altar; that there be wrath no more upon the children of Israel. 6 And I, behold, I have taken your brethren the Levites from among the children of Israel: to you they are a gift, given unto Jehovah, to do the service of the tent of meeting. 7 And thou and thy sons with thee shall keep your priesthood for everything of the altar, and for that within the veil; and ye shall serve: I give you the priesthood as a service of gift: and the stranger that cometh nigh shall be put to death.

8 And Jehovah spake unto Aaron, And I, behold, I have given thee the charge of my heave-offerings, even all the hallowed things of the children of Israel; unto thee have I given them by reason of the anointing, and to thy sons, as a portion for ever. 9 This shall be thine of the most holy things, *reserved* from the fire: every oblation of theirs, even every meal-offering of theirs, and every sin-offering of theirs, and every trespass-offering of theirs, which they shall render unto me, shall be most holy for thee and for thy sons. 10 As the most holy things shalt thou eat thereof; every male shall eat thereof: it shall be holy

unto thee. 11 And this is thine: the heave-offering of their gift, even all the wave-offerings of the children of Israel; I have given them unto thee, and to thy sons and to thy daughters with thee, as a portion for ever; every one that is clean in thy house shall eat thereof. 12 All the best of the oil, and all the best of the vintage, and of the grain, the first-fruits of them which they give unto Jehovah, to thee have I given them. 13 The first-ripe fruits of all that is in their land, which they bring unto Jehovah, shall be thine; every one that is clean in thy house shall eat thereof. 14 Everything devoted in Israel shall be thine. 15 Everything that openeth the womb, of all flesh which they offer unto Jehovah, both of man and beast shall be thine: nevertheless the first-born of man shalt thou surely redeem, and the firstling of unclean beasts shalt thou redeem. 16 And those that are to be redeemed of them from a month old shalt thou redeem, according to thine estimation, for the money of five shekels, after the shekel of the sanctuary (the same is twenty gerahs). 17 But the firstling of a cow, or the firstling of a sheep, or the firstling of a goat, thou shalt not redeem; they are holy: thou shalt sprinkle their blood upon the altar, and shalt burn their fat for an offering made by fire, for a sweet savor unto Jehovah. 18 And the flesh of them shall be thine, as the wave-breast and as the right thigh, it shall be thine. 19 All the heave-offerings of the holy things, which the children of Israel offer unto Jehovah, have I given thee, and thy sons and thy daughters with thee, as a portion for ever: it is a covenant of salt for ever before Jehovah unto thee and to thy seed with thee. 20 And Jehovah said unto Aaron, Thou shalt have no inheritance in their land, neither shalt thou have any portion among them: I am thy portion and thine inheritance among the children of Israel.

21 And unto the children of Levi, behold, I have given all the tithe in Israel for an inheritance, in return for their service which they serve, even the service of the tent of meeting. 22 And henceforth the children of Israel shall not come nigh the tent of meeting, lest they bear sin, and die. 23 But the Levites shall do the service of the tent of meeting, and they shall bear their iniquity: it shall be a statute for ever throughout your generations; and among the children of Israel they shall have no inheritance. 24 For the tithe of the children of Israel, which they offer as a heave-offering unto Jehovah, I have given to the Levites for an inheritance: therefore I have said unto them, Among the children of Israel they shall have no inheritance.

25 And Jehovah spake unto Moses, saying, 26 Moreover thou shalt speak unto the Levites, and say unto them, When ye take of the children of Israel the tithe which I have given you from them for your inheritance, then ye shall offer up a heave-offering of it for Jehovah, a tithe of the tithe. 27 And your heave-offering shall be reckoned unto you, as though it were the grain of the threshing-floor, and as the fulness of the winepress. 28 Thus ye also shall offer a heave-offering unto Jehovah of all your tithes, which ye receive of the children of Israel; and thereof ye shall give Jehovah's heave-offering to Aaron the priest. 29 Out of all your gifts ye shall offer every heave-offering of Jehovah, of all the best thereof, even the hallowed part thereof out of it. 30 Therefore thou shalt say unto them, When ye heave the best thereof from it, then it shall be reckoned unto the Levites as the increase of the threshing-floor, and as the increase of the winepress. 31 And ye shall eat it in every place, ye and your households: for it is your reward in return for your service in the tent of meeting. 32 And ye shall bear no sin by reason of it, when ye have heaved from it the best thereof; and ye shall not profane the holy things of the children of Israel, that ye die not.

The Lord had confirmed the Levitical priesthood by miraculous interference, but this divine privilege carried with it tremendous responsibility. They were answerable for the legal and religious pollutions that might ensue.

A careful distinction of service is set forth in verse 2. Only the priests were to officiate in the tabernacle. Their brethren, also Levites, were to discharge the incidental services in connection with the tabernacle worship services, but were not to touch nor come near the **vessels of the sanctuary** (v. 3). Strangers could submit to the Levitical ritual and become members of the tabernacle congregation, but the privilege of coming into contact with the sacrificial vessels was forbidden. A violation of this ordinance carried the penalty of death (v. 7).

When Jehovah spoke unto Aaron (v. 8), He once again emphasized and delineated the exclusive duties of Aaron and his sons. They were to be in charge of the **heave-offerings** (v. 8), the **meal-offerings**, the **sin-offering** and the **trespass-offering** (v. 9). These sacrificial offerings were to be **holy**, or without blemish, and were to be **reserved from the fire** for food on the table of the priests. Parts of the offerings of grain and meat were intended for the priestly diet.

A clean, sanctified life was always required for participating in any of the ritualistic services. God has always demanded that man give his best, his choicest possession, in his expression of devotion. It has always been, "My best for God." It was understood that the Levites, without earthly inheritance, were to be supported by the tithes and offerings of the people. By providing for God's chosen servants the people were rendering service and devotion unto the Lord. Jesus described the nature of this transaction when He said, "In as much as ye have done it unto one of the least of these my brethren, ye have done it unto me" (Matt. 25:40). The people were to bring the best of everything — the best oil, the best wine and the best wheat.

All of life was to have a definite relationship to the Lord. The first-fruits and the first-born were considered to be the choicest specimens of the fields and the herds. The redemption of the first-born has always been looked upon by the Jews with dignity and reverence. To the Christian this rite has some connotations associated with the christening of a child. Clarke gives the following description of this rite:

> Redemption of the first-born is one of the rites which is still practiced among the Jews. According to Leo of Modena, it is performed in the following manner: When the child is thirty days old, the father sends for one of the descendants of Aaron: several persons being assembled on the occasion, the father brings a cup containing several pieces of gold and silver coin. The priest then takes the child into his arms and addressing himself to the mother, says: "Is this thy son?" Mother: "Yes." Priest: "Hast thou never had another child, male or female, a miscarriage or untimely birth?" Mother: "No." Priest: "This being the case, this child as first-born belongs to me." Then, turning to the father, he says: "If it be thy desire to have this child, thou must redeem it." Father: "I present thee with this gold and silver for this purpose." Priest: "Thou dost wish, therefore, to redeem the child?" Father: "I do wish so to do." The priest then, turning himself to the assembly, says: "Very well; this child as first-born, is mine, as it is written in Bemidbar (Num. 18:16). Thou shalt redeem the first-born of a month old for five shekels, but I shall content myself with this in exchange." He then takes two gold crowns or thereabouts, and returns the child to his parents.[58]

The heave-offerings were to be used for the support of the Levites, and this provision was identified as **a covenant of salt** because **salt** was a substance which purified, preserved, and sustained. As salt is a preserving agent for food, so the Levites were to take on the preserving quality of salt in their religious and social relationship to Israel. Jesus must have had this in mind when He said, "Salt is good: but if even the salt have lost its savor, wherewith shall it be seasoned? It is fit neither for the land nor for the dunghill: men cast it out" (Luke 14:33-34). Salt gives zest and flavor to our physical food, and the spiritual salt — the gospel — gives meaning and purpose to life. Paul exhorts the Colossians thus: "Let your speech be always with grace, seasoned with salt, that ye may know how ye ought to answer each one" (Col. 4:6).

The priestly tribe was to be supported by a portion of the tithes and offerings and was to be denied a regular physical inheritance in Canaan. They were to assume that the Lord Himself would always be their satisfying portion. The Levites were to receive a tenth of all the productivity of the land. Clarke points out that they had forty-eight cities and that the total land area of these cities was 53,000 acres, and this compared with the total acreage of 11,264,000 was a very small percentage. It may be pointed out, however, that what the Levites received was considerable. Their remuneration was small, but they enjoyed independence and a comfortable living. This is the ideal pattern for a Christian minister — that he be able to give his entire time and attention to caring for the congregation; that the congregation in turn supply his needs in a modest way, short of excess.[59]

As the people had an obligation to bring their tithe to the Levites, so the Levites had an obligation to bring the tithe of the tithes to the priests for their support. "My best for God" (v. 29) was the consistent criteria for all. Even the Levites were to follow this standard (v. 30).

The high standard of living above sin is always the prevailing norm for the Lord's people. A departure from this standard results in death.

G. THE ORDINANCE OF THE RED HEIFER (19:1-22)

1 And Jehovah spake unto Moses and unto Aaron, saying, 2 This is the statute of the law which Jehovah hath commanded, saying, Speak unto the children of Israel, that they bring thee a red heifer without spot, wherein is no blemish, *and* upon which never came yoke. 3 And ye shall give her unto Eleazar the priest, and he shall bring her forth without the camp, and one shall slay her before his face: 4 and Eleazar the priest shall take of her blood with his finger, and sprinkle of her blood toward the front of the tent of meeting seven times. 5 And one shall burn the heifer in his sight; her skin, and her flesh, and her blood, with her dung, shall he burn: 6 and the priest shall take cedarwood, and hyssop, and scarlet, and cast it into the midst of the burning of the heifer. 7 Then the priest shall wash his clothes, and he shall bathe his flesh in water, and afterward he shall come into the camp, and the priest shall be unclean until the even. 8 And he that burneth her shall wash his clothes in water, and bathe his flesh in water, and shall be unclean until the even. 9 And a man that is clean shall gather up the ashes of the heifer, and lay them up without the camp in a clean place; and it shall be kept for the congregation of the children of Israel for a water for impurity: it is a sin-offering. 10 And he that gathereth the ashes of the heifer shall wash his clothes, and be unclean until the even: and it shall be unto the children of Israel, and unto the stranger that sojourneth among them, for a statute for ever.

11 He that toucheth the dead body of any man shall be unclean seven days: 12 the same shall purify himself there-with on the third day, and on the seventh day he shall be clean: but if he purify not himself the third day, then the seventh day he shall not be clean. 13 Whosoever toucheth a dead person, the body of a man that hath died, and purifieth not himself, defileth the tabernacle of Jehovah; and that soul shall be cut off from Israel: because the water for impurity was not sprinkled upon him, he shall be unclean; his uncleanness is yet upon him.

14 This is the law when a man dieth in a tent: every one that cometh into the tent, and every one that is in the tent, shall be unclean seven days. 15 And every open vessel, which hath no covering bound upon it, is unclean. 16 And whosoever in the open field toucheth one that is slain with a sword, or a dead body, or a bone of a man, or a grave, shall be unclean seven days. 17 And for the unclean they shall take of the ashes of the burning of the sin-offering; and running water shall be put thereto in a vessel: 18 and a clean person shall take hyssop, and dip it in the water, and sprinkle it upon the tent, and upon all the vessels, and upon the persons that were there, and upon him that touched the bone, or the slain, or the dead, or the grave: 19 and the clean person shall sprinkle upon the unclean on the third day, and on the seventh day: and on the seventh day he shall purify him; and he shall wash his clothes, and bathe himself in water, and shall be clean at even.

20 But the man that shall be unclean, and shall not purify himself, that soul shall be cut off from the midst of the assembly, because he hath defiled the sanctuary of Jehovah: the water for impurity hath not been sprinkled upon him; he is unclean. 21 And it shall be a perpetual statute unto them: and he that sprinkleth the water for impurity shall wash his clothes; and he that toucheth the water for impurity shall be unclean until even. 22 And whatsoever the unclean person toucheth shall be unclean; and the soul that toucheth it shall be unclean until even.

Speak . . . that they bring thee a red heifer without spot (v. 2). It has been pointed out that this is the only case in which the color of the victim is specified.[60] The red heifer rite is one in which the entire congregation had an interest. This is an instance when a single, specific animal was offered in

[59] *Ibid.*, I, 677.
[60] Robert Jamieson, "Numbers," *A Commentary on the Old and New Testament,* p. 241.

behalf of the entire nation of Israel. Each person had some part in making provision for this **red heifer** without spot or blemish. A heifer is here designated in opposition to the Apis-bull cult in Egypt. Of this rite one commentator says:

> We have here the divine appointment concerning the solemn burning of a red heifer to ashes, and the preserving of the ashes, that of them might be made, not a beautifying, but a purifying water, for that was the utmost the law reached to; it offered not to adorn as the gospel does, but to cleanse only. This burning of the heifer . . . was typical of the death and sufferings of Christ, by which he intended not only to satisfy God's justice, but to purify and pacify our consciences, that we may have peace with God, and also peace in our own bosoms.[61]

The sacrifice was taken outside the camp according to the requirements of the law (Lev. 24:14). This speaks to us of our Lord Jesus Christ who "suffered without the gate" (Heb. 13:12) that He might sanctify us through His own blood. After the animal was slain outside the camp Eleazar was commanded to dip his finger in the blood and sprinkle it directly before the tabernacle. The ritual involving the sprinkling of the blood was central in all sacrifices of atonement. This particular rite was not conducted at the altar but rather toward the sanctuary. This act of worship was suggestive of the satisfaction made to God by the death of Jesus Christ, the Lamb slain "from the foundation of the world" (Rev. 13:8).[62]

The ashes of the heifer were to be carefully gathered up by a clean person and preserved without the camp in a clean place to be used as the occasion demanded. The ashes were to be mixed with water and used in connection with the cleansing ritual (v. 15). Any person who had contact with something dead — even the ashes of a sacrificial animal — was considered to be unclean for **seven days** (v. 11). The cleansing process involved the sprinkling of the water of separation upon the unclean person (v. 13). The ashes of the heifer were always available when need arose. The ceremonial uncleanness here in question included exposure to dead bodies, open

vessels, the bone of a dead man or a grave (vv. 14-16).

Ashes mixed with water make one of the best scouring agents known and are frequently used by those who camp out. This may be symbolic of the ceremonial cleansing which was to be effected by the administration of this mixture. Matthew Henry gives the following illuminating information:

> These ashes are said to be laid up here as a "purification for sin," because, though they were intended only to purify from ceremonial uncleanness, yet they were a type of that purification for sin which our Lord Jesus made by his death . . . Now observe, (1) That the water of purification was made so by the ashes of a heifer, whose blood was sprinkled before the sanctuary; so that which cleanses our conscience, is the abiding virtue of the death of Christ: it is his blood that "cleanses from all sin" (I Jn. 1:7). (2) That the ashes were sufficient for all the people; there needed not to be a fresh heifer slain for every person or family that had occasion to be purified, but this one was enough for all, even for strangers that "sojourned among them;" (vs. 10). And even so, there is virtue enough in the blood of Christ for all that repent and believe the gospel, for every Israelite; and not for their sins only, but for the "sins of the whole world," (I Jn. 2:2). (3) That these ashes were capable of being preserved without waste to many ages. No bodily substance is so incorruptible as ashes are, which made them a very fit emblem of the everlasting efficacy of the sacrifice of Christ. He is able to save, and, in order to do that, able to cleanse to the uttermost, both persons and times. (4) These ashes were laid up as a stock or treasure, for the constant purifications of Israel from their pollutions; so the blood of Christ is laid up for us in the word and sacraments, as an inexhaustible fountain of merit, to which by faith we may have recourse daily, for the purging of our conscience; see Zech. 13:1.[63]

H. THE DEATH OF MIRIAM (20:1)

1 And the children of Israel, even the whole congregation, came into the wilderness of Zin in the first month: and the people abode in Kadesh; and Miriam died there, and was buried there.

---

[61] Matthew Henry, *A Commentary on the Holy Bible*, p. 382.   [62] *Ibid.*   [63] *Ibid.*

The Israelites have now come to the last phase of their journey. They have been on the way for about thirty-eight years (Deut. 1:22, 23; 2:4). On the assumption that Miriam was about ten years old at the birth of her brother Moses, she was about one hundred and thirty years old at death. Clarke says that she appears to have died about four months before her brother Aaron (33:38) and eleven before her brother Moses; so that these three, the most eminent of the Israelites, died in the space of one year.

I. THE TERRIBLE THIRST AT MERIBAH (20:2-6)

2 And there was no water for the congregation: and they assembled themselves together against Moses and against Aaron. 3 And the people strove with Moses, and spake, saying, Would that we had died when our brethren died before Jehovah! 4 And why have ye brought the assembly of Jehovah into this wilderness, that we should die there, we and our beasts? 5 And wherefore have ye made us to come up out of Egypt, to bring us in unto this evil place? it is no place of seed, or of figs, or of vines, or of pomegranates; neither is there any water to drink. 6 And Moses and Aaron went from the presence of the assembly unto the door of the tent of meeting, and fell upon their faces: and the glory of Jehovah appeared unto them.

The Israelites have now moved away from a semi-oasis area and into parched, waterless desert country. All of the water supply has been exhausted, and the people face with terror the prospects of having their bones bleach in the burning desert sand and sun. Only he who has traversed this terrain can possibly know how fearful this section of the country is, if one is dependent upon one's own resources. The nearness of the desert dangers greatly accelerated the doubt of the people, and consequently they complained to Moses. Their plight was so desperate that they lamented the fact that they did not perish earlier with their brethren (v. 3). They even expressed regret that Moses had led the people out of Egypt (v. 5).

In desperation Moses and Aaron turned to the Lord for direction. At the door of the tabernacle the **glory of Jehovah** appeared unto them. We note that in the KJV the "glory" and the "person" of the Lord are the same.

J. WATER FROM THE ROCK (20:7-13)

7 And Jehovah spake unto Moses, saying, 8 Take the rod, and assemble the congregation, thou, and Aaron thy brother, and speak ye unto the rock before their eyes, that it give forth its water; and thou shalt bring forth to them water out of the rock; so thou shalt give the congregation and their cattle drink. 9 And Moses took the rod from before Jehovah, as he commanded him.

10 And Moses and Aaron gathered the assembly together before the rock, and he said unto them, Hear now, ye rebels; shall we bring you forth water out of this rock? 11 And Moses lifted up his hand, and smote the rock with his rod twice: and water came forth abundantly, and the congregation drank, and their cattle. 12 And Jehovah said unto Moses and Aaron, Because ye believed not in me, to sanctify me in the eyes of the children of Israel, therefore ye shall not bring this assembly into the land which I have given them. 13 These are the waters of Meribah; because the children of Israel strove with Jehovah, and he was sanctified in them.

The Lord acknowledged the desperate situation of the people and commanded Moses to take his rod or sceptre in hand and to speak unto the rock. Moses had the Lord's assurance that an abundant supply of water would flow out of the rock. The pilgrim making the journey from Suez to St. Catherine's Monastery has his attention called to a large rock about the size of a small room. According to tradition, this is the rock which supplied the Israelites with water. It is probable that this rock has more traditional or figurative significance than historical reality, but one is able to see a large rock in the general area where this miracle took place.

Hear now, ye rebels (v. 10). The manner in which they address the people would suggest that both Moses and Aaron have almost reached a nervous breaking point.

In his anxiety Moses apparently misunderstood God's command or ignored it. The Lord had commanded him to speak to the rock, but instead he smote it twice with his rod. Despite Moses' disobedience, the Lord made the water to flow and the congregation along with their beasts were satisfied. There is a great difficulty at this point as to why Moses forfeited his right to enter the promised land. Clarke gives some very plausible explanations:

> What was the offence for which Moses was excluded from the promised land? It appears to have consisted in some or all of the following particulars: 1. God had commanded him (ver. 8) to take the rod in his hand, and go and SPEAK to the rock, and it should give forth water. It seems Moses did not think speaking would be sufficient, therefore he smote the rock without any command so to do. 2. He did this twice, which certainly in this case indicated a great perturbation of spirit, and want of attention to the presence of God. 3. He permitted his spirit to be carried away by a sense of the people's disobedience, and thus, being provoked, he was led to speak unadvisedly with his lips: Hear now ye rebels (ver. 10). 4. He did not acknowledge God in the miracle which was about to be wrought, but took the honour to himself and Aaron: "Must *we* fetch you water out of this rock?" Thus it plainly appears that they did not properly believe in God, and did not honour him in the sight of the people; for in their presence they seem to express doubt whether the thing could be done. As Aaron appears to have been consenting in the above particulars, therefore he is also excluded from the promised land.[64]

K. THE ENMITY OF EDOM (20:14-22)

14 And Moses sent messengers from Kadesh unto the king of Edom, Thus saith thy brother Israel, Thou knowest all the travail that hath befallen us: 15 how our fathers went down into Egypt, and we dwelt in Egypt a long time; and the Egyptians dealt ill with us, and our fathers: 16 and when we cried unto Jehovah, he heard our voice, and sent an angel, and brought us forth out of Egypt: and, behold, we are in Kadesh, a city in the uttermost of thy border. 17 Let us pass, I pray thee, through thy land: we will not pass through field or through vineyard, neither will we drink of the water of the wells; we will go along the king's highway; we will not turn aside to the right hand nor to the left, until we have passed thy border.

18 And Edom said unto them, Thou shalt not pass through me, lest I come out with the sword against thee. 19 And the children of Israel said unto him, We will go up by the highway; and if we drink of thy water, I and my cattle, then will I give the price thereof: let me only, without *doing* anything *else*, pass through on my feet. 20 And he said, Thou shalt not pass through. And Edom came out against him with much people, and with a strong hand. 21 Thus Edom refused to give Israel passage through his border: wherefore Israel turned away from him.

22 And they journeyed from Kadesh: and the children of Israel, even the whole congregation, came unto mount Hor.

Moses appeals to the king of Edom for safe passage through his kingdom (v. 14). He refers to himself as **thy brother Israel**. The Edomites were the "cousins" of Israel through their relationship to Esau, the brother of Jacob. Esau was the progenitor of the Edomites and Jacob of the Israelites. The messengers of Moses are instructed to bring the king of Edom up to date on Israel's stay in Egypt (v. 15) and how the Lord had delivered them (v. 16).

The king of Edom is given assurance that the Israelites will pass through his land without causing the damage that is usually done by an invading or passing army. They promise not to bother the vineyards and not to drink of the water in the wells without paying (v. 19). They also promise to stay on the highway, which appears to be one of the public roadways through his land.

Thou shalt not pass through (v. 20). The enmity which had no doubt been smoldering in the hearts of the Edomites is here expressed. The king refuses to grant them permission for free and safe passage. It appears, however, that only this clan of Edomites expressed this hostility, for later a more friendly attitude is expressed by some Edomites (see Deut. 2:29). When the Edomites refused to grant permission for their passage, they continued on their way through more difficult terrain and made their way to Mt. Hor (v. 22).

L. THE DEATH OF AARON (20:23-29)

23 And Jehovah spake unto Moses and Aaron in mount Hor, by the border of

the land of Edom, saying, 24 Aaron shall be gathered unto his people; for he shall not enter into the land which I have given unto the children of Israel, because ye rebelled against my word at the waters of Meribah. 25 Take Aaron and Eleazar his son, and bring them up unto mount Hor; 26 and strip Aaron of his garments, and put them upon Eleazar his son: and Aaron shall be gathered *unto his people,* and shall die there. 27 And Moses did as Jehovah commanded: and they went up into mount Hor in the sight of all the congregation. 28 And Moses stripped Aaron of his garments, and put them upon Eleazar his son; and Aaron died there on the top of the mount: and Moses and Eleazar came down from the mount. 29 And when all the congregation saw that Aaron was dead, they wept for Aaron thirty days, even all the house of Israel.

The time has now come for Aaron to end his earthly pilgrimage. Aaron and Eleazar are commanded to go to the top of Mt. Hor. There Aaron is to be stripped of his priestly robes and Eleazar is to be officially ordained as the successor to Aaron, the high priest (v. 26) .

The modern visitor to Petra has his attention called to Mt. Hor, the mountain on which tradition says Aaron was buried. A stone mausoleum has been placed there.

Neither Moses, Miriam nor Aaron was permitted to bring the Israelites into the promised land. All three had shown some expression of disobedience. The actual entry into Canaan was reserved for Joshua, who was a type of our Lord Jesus Christ, and for Caleb. Only Christ can lead believers into the experience of sanctified rest.[65]

VI. THE MARCH TO MOAB (Num. 21:1-35)

A. VICTORY OVER KING ARAD (21: 1-4)

1 And the Canaanite, the king of Arad, who dwelt in the South, heard tell that Israel came by the way of Atharim; and he fought against Israel, and took some of them captive. 2 And Israel vowed a vow unto Jehovah, and said, If thou wilt indeed deliver this people into my hand, then I will utterly destroy their cities. 3 And Jehovah hearkened to the voice of Israel, and delivered up the Canaanites;

and they utterly destroyed them and their cities: and the name of the place was called Hormah. 4 And they journeyed from mount Hor by the way to the Red Sea, to compass the land of Edom: and the soul of the people was much discouraged because of the way.

Israel is on the march again and has now traveled to a point on the eastern fringe of Edom under the control of King Arad the Canaanite. News had come to him of Israel's conquests.

Came by the way of Atharim (v. 1b). The KJV renders the passage thus: "came by the way of the spies." It has been speculated that this was an area visited by the twelve spies, but this is not probable because the location is far removed from the route which the spies took. It is more likely that Atharim is the name of a place — a town or a community.

Arad was no more friendly to Israel than was the king of Edom. He declared war on them and took some prisoners.

Israel made a covenant with the Lord that they would destroy the cities of Canaan if they were given military victory. Subsequently the Canaanites were defeated and destroyed. A difficulty appears here, however, because the Canaanites were not completely destroyed at this time.

Some scholars believe that verse 3 was added afterward by Joshua or Ezra, after the total destruction was actually accomplished. It can be pointed out that the **Arad** mentioned here is mentioned among those destroyed by Joshua at a later date (see Josh. 12:14). The Israelites were dedicated to the destruction of the enemy, but frequently it was not done at the moment, but rather at a later time.[66]

The Israelites had taken a circular route around the southern end of Edom and now find themselves in a desolate desert area on the eastern border of Edom in what is now the Maan community. The modern visitor to Maan finds the place infested with flies and other insects and unbearable heat, especially in the summer months. There is little or no natural vegetation in this area. Only the burning desert sun and sand are there to welcome the stranger.

[65] *Ibid.,* I, 682.   [66] *Ibid.,* I, 683.

B. THE SERPENT OF BRASS (21:5-22)

5 And the people spake against God, and against Moses, Wherefore have ye brought us up out of Egypt to die in the wilderness? for there is no bread, and there is no water; and our soul loatheth this light bread. 6 And Jehovah sent fiery serpents among the people, and they bit the people; and much people of Israel died. 7 And the people came to Moses, and said, We have sinned, because we have spoken against Jehovah, and against thee; pray unto Jehovah, that he take away the serpents from us. And Moses prayed for the people. 8 And Jehovah said unto Moses, Make thee a fiery serpent, and set it upon a standard: and it shall come to pass, that every one that is bitten, when he seeth it, shall live. 9 And Moses made a serpent of brass, and set it upon the standard: and it came to pass, that if a serpent had bitten any man, when he looked unto the serpent of brass, he lived.

10 And the children of Israel journeyed, and encamped in Oboth. 11 And they journeyed from Oboth, and encamped at Iye-abarim, in the wilderness which is before Moab, toward the sunrising. 12 From thence they journeyed, and encamped in the valley of Zered. 13 From thence they journeyed, and encamped on the other side of the Arnon, which is in the wilderness, that cometh out of the border of the Amorites: for the Arnon is the border of Moab, between Moab and the Amorites. 14 Wherefore it is said in the book of the Wars of Jehovah,

Vaheb in Suphah,
And the valleys of the Arnon,
15 And the slope of the valleys
That inclineth toward the dwelling of Ar.
And leaneth upon the border of Moab.
16 And from thence *they journeyed* to Beer: that is the well whereof Jehovah said unto Moses, Gather the people together, and I will give them water.
17 Then sang Israel this song:
Spring up, O well; sing ye unto it:
18 The well, which the princes digged,
Which the nobles of the people delved,
With the sceptre, *and* with their staves.
And from the wilderness *they journeyed* to Mattanah; 19 and from Mattanah to Nahaliel; and from Nahaliel to Bamoth; 20 and from Bamoth to the valley that is in the field of Moab, to the top of Pisgah, which looketh down upon the desert.
21 And Israel sent messengers unto Sihon king of the Amorites, saying, 22

Let me pass through thy land: we will not turn aside into field, or into vineyard; we will not drink of the water of the wells: we will go by the king's highway, until we have passed thy border.

Once again the natural environment discourages the people and causes them to complain about their hardships. Once again they lament the fact that they have been taken out of Egypt to **die in the wilderness**. There is no bread or water, and they are sick and tired of manna, or **light bread**. Another translation for **light bread** is "vile bread." This term comes from the Hebrew word *hakkelokel*, meaning "insubstantial or light."

The Israelites are now in real trouble (v. 6). Not only do they find themselves in naturally unfriendly surroundings but their camp becomes infested with snakes. It would be difficult to imagine what life would be like if our homes should suddenly become infested with poisonous snakes. Many of the people were bitten and died. Obviously the serpents had been in the wilderness all the time, but now the Lord releases His restraint and turns them loose. The people show some evidence of repentance (v. 7). They beg Moses to ask the Lord that the serpents be taken away.

Make thee a fiery serpent (v. 8). Moses is to fashion a serpent out of brass and place it on a pole in the camp of Israel. It is quite likely that the pole had a cross piece near the top so that the serpent could be made to stay on the pole and not slide down. The brazen serpent would have a shiny appearance and would be easily discernible in the camp. The KJV renders verse 8d thus: "when he looketh upon it, shall live." The cure for their infection was obviously supernatural. Those who had not died from the sting or the bite of the serpents could be healed by looking in faith upon the object which symbolized their Sin-bearer. Henry says: "The Jews themselves say that it was not the sight of the brazen serpent that cured them, but in looking up to it, they looked up to God as the Lord that healed them."[67]

The redemptive significance of this event is brought out in our Savior's reference. Said He, "As Moses lifted up the serpent in the wilderness, even so must

---

[67] *Op. cit.*, I, 388.

the Son of man be lifted up; that whosoever believeth in him should not perish but have eternal life" (John 3:14-15, KJV). We are told that our Lord was made sin for us — our sins were actually placed upon Him, and in this sense He became our Sin-bearer. Clarke says:

> From our Lord's words we may learn, 1. That as the serpent was lifted up on the pole or ensign, so Jesus Christ was lifted up on the cross. 2. That as the Israelites were to look at the brazen serpent, so sinners must look to Christ for salvation. 3. That as God provided no other remedy than this *looking,* for the wounded Israelites, so he has provided no other way of salvation than faith in the blood of his Son. 4. That as he who looked at the brazen serpent was cured and did live, so he that believeth on the Lord Jesus Christ shall not perish, but have eternal life. 5. That as neither the serpent, nor looking at it, but the invisible power of God healed the people, so neither the cross of Christ, nor his merely being crucified, but the pardon he has bought by his blood, communicated by the powerful energy of his Spirit, saves the souls of men.[68]

The Israelites moved ahead at a rather rapid pace. They rested at Oboth, at Iye-abarim (v. 11), and in the valley of Zered (v. 12). After a little longer sojourn near the Arnon River, which is the border **between Moab and the Amorites** (v. 13), they continued on their way to Beer, the place of the well (v. 16). Here Israel had a song fest (v. 17), and continued on to Pisgah, with several stops in between (v. 20).

Israel sent messengers unto Sihon (v. 21). Once again Israel faces a formidable enemy in the king of the Amorites.

Let me pass through (v. 22). They assure Sihon that they will not molest the fields or vineyards but will go right through on the "King's highway," which apparently was a public thoroughfare.

C. THE DEFEAT OF SIHON (21:23-35)

23 And Sihon would not suffer Israel to pass through his border: but Sihon gathered all his people together, and went out against Israel into the wilderness, and came to Jahaz; and he fought against Israel. 24 And Israel smote him with the edge of the sword, and possessed

his land from the Arnon unto the Jabbok, even unto the children of Ammon; for the border of the children of Ammon was strong. 25 And Israel took all these cities: and Israel dwelt in all the cities of the Amorites, in Heshbon, and in all the towns thereof. 26 For Heshbon was the city of Sihon the king of the Amorites, who had fought against the former king of Moab, and taken all his land out of his hand, even unto the Arnon. 27 Wherefore they that speak in proverbs say,

Come ye to Heshbon;
Let the city of Sihon be built and established:
28 For a fire is gone out of Heshbon,
A flame from the city of Sihon:
It hath devoured Ar of Moab,
The lords of the high places of the Arnon.
29 Woe to thee, Moab!
Thou art undone, O people of Chemosh:
He hath given his sons as fugitives,
And his daughters into captivity,
Unto Sihon king of the Amorites.
30 We have shot at them; Heshbon is perished even unto Dibon,
And we have laid waste even unto Nophah,
Which *reacheth* unto Medeba.

31 Thus Israel dwelt in the land of the Amorites. 32 And Moses sent to spy out Jazer; and they took the towns thereof, and drove out the Amorites that were there.

33 And they turned and went up by the way of Bashan: and Og the king of Bashan went out against them, he and all his people, to battle at Edrei. 34 And Jehovah said unto Moses, Fear him not: for I have delivered him into thy hand, and all his people, and his land; and thou shalt do to him as thou didst unto Sihon king of the Amorites, who dwelt at Heshbon. 35 So they smote him, and his sons and all his people, until there was none left him remaining: and they possessed his land.

Sihon marshalled his forces and attacked Israel, but his attack was unsuccessful. Israel, in turn, attacked and conquered the Amorites and passed through their land from the Arnon to the Jabbok River (v. 24), right to the border of Ammon. It appears that Israel stayed in this area for several months, or even longer (vv. 25-32). Finally they again

[68] *Op. cit.,* I, 685.

started their journey and were confronted with Og the king of Bashan.

Jehovah said unto Moses (v. 34). The Lord assures Moses that he will have victory over Og in the same way that he conquered Sihon.

So they smote him (v. 35). It appears that Moses' conquest was complete and that all semblance of King Og's government was destroyed.

VII. ARRIVAL IN MOAB (Num. 22:1—25:18)

A. THE KING OF MOAB (22:1-4)

1 And the children of Israel journeyed, and encamped in the plains of Moab beyond the Jordan at Jericho.

2 And Balak the son of Zippor saw all that Israel had done to the Amorites. 3 And Moab was sore afraid of the people, because they were many: and Moab was distressed because of the children of Israel. 4 And Moab said unto the elders of Midian, Now will this multitude lick up all that is round about us as the ox licketh up the grass of the field. And Balak the son of Zippor was king of Moab at that time.

After occupying Bashan for a short period they marched on into Moab on the east bank of the Jordan with Jericho just to the west of them and beyond the river. Zippor, king of the Moabites (v. 4), had received reports of Israel's military success against the Amorites and the Bashanites and was fearful that he might suffer a similar fate.

B. THE CALL OF BALAAM (22:5-35)

5 And he sent messengers unto Balaam the son of Beor, to Pethor, which is by the River, to the land of the children of his people, to call him, saying, Behold, there is a people come out from Egypt: behold, they cover the face of the earth, and they abide over against me. 6 Come now therefore, I pray thee, curse me this people; for they are too mighty for me: peradventure I shall prevail, that we may smite them, and that I may drive them out of the land; for I know that he whom thou blessest is blessed, and he whom thou cursest is cursed.

7 And the elders of Moab and the elders of Midian departed with the rewards of divination in their hand; and they came unto Balaam, and spake unto him the words of Balak. 8 And he said unto them, Lodge here this night, and I will bring you word again, as Jehovah shall speak unto me: and the princes of Moab abode with Balaam. 9 And God came unto Balaam, and said, What men are these with thee? 10 And Balaam said unto God, Balak the son of Zippor, king of Moab, hath sent unto me, *saying,* 11 Behold, the people that is come out of Egypt, it covereth the face of the earth: now, come curse me them; peradventure I shall be able to fight against them, and shall drive them out. 12 And God said unto Balaam, Thou shalt not go with them; thou shalt not curse the people; for they are blessed. 13 And Balaam rose up in the morning, and said unto the princes of Balak, Get you into your land; for Jehovah refuseth to give me leave to go with you. 14 And the princes of Moab rose up, and they went unto Balak, and said, Balaam refuseth to come with us.

15 And Balak sent yet again princes, more, and more honorable than they. 16 And they came to Balaam, and said to him, Thus saith Balak the son of Zippor, Let nothing, I pray thee, hinder thee from coming unto me: 17 for I will promote thee unto very great honor, and whatsoever thou sayest unto me I will do: come therefore, I pray thee, curse me this people. 18 And Balaam answered and said unto the servants of Balak, If Balak would give me his house full of silver and gold, I cannot go beyond the word of Jehovah my God, to do less or more. 19 Now therefore, I pray you, tarry ye also here this night, that I may know what Jehovah will speak unto me more. 20 And God came unto Balaam at night, and said unto him, If the men are come to call thee, rise up, go with them; but only the word which I speak unto thee, that shalt thou do.

21 And Balaam rose up in the morning, and saddled his ass, and went with the princes of Moab. 22 And God's anger was kindled because he went; and the angel of Jehovah placed himself in the way for an adversary against him. Now he was riding upon his ass, and his two servants were with him. 23 And the ass saw the angel of Jehovah standing in the way, with his sword drawn in his hand; and the ass turned aside out of the way, and went into the field: and Balaam smote the ass, to turn her into the way. 24 Then the angel of Jehovah stood in a narrow path between the vineyards, a wall being on this side, and a wall on that side. 25 And the ass saw the angel of Jehovah, and she thrust herself unto the wall, and crushed Ba-

laam's foot against the wall: and he smote her again. 26 And the angel of Jehovah went further, and stood in a narrow place, where was no way to turn either to the right hand or to the left. 27 And the ass saw the angel of Jehovah, and she lay down under Balaam: and Balaam's anger was kindled, and he smote the ass with his staff. 28 And Jehovah opened the mouth of the ass, and she said unto Balaam, What have I done unto thee, that thou hast smitten me these three times? 29 And Balaam said unto the ass, Because thou hast mocked me: I would there were a sword in my hand, for now I had killed thee. 30 And the ass said unto Balaam, Am not I thine ass, upon which thou hast ridden all thy life long unto this day? was I ever wont to do so unto thee? And he said, Nay.

31 Then Jehovah opened the eyes of Balaam, and he saw the angel of Jehovah standing in the way, with his sword drawn in his hand; and he bowed his head, and fell on his face. 32 And the angel of Jehovah said unto him, Wherefore hast thou smitten thine ass these three times? behold, I am come forth for an adversary, because thy way is perverse before me: 33 and the ass saw me, and turned aside before me these three times: unless she had turned aside from me, surely now I had even slain thee, and saved her alive. 34 And Balaam said unto the angel of Jehovah, I have sinned; for I knew not that thou stoodest in the way against me: now therefore, if it displease thee, I will get me back again. 35 And the angel of Jehovah said unto Balaam, Go with the men; but only the word that I shall speak unto thee, that thou shalt speak. So Balaam went with the princes of Balak.

The king of Moab decided to engage the service of Balaam, a black magic artist, to cast a curse upon the Israelites. Balaam lived in Pethor, which appears to have been located near the Euphrates River in Mesopotamia. He was evidently at one time a true prophet of Jehovah (see Num. 21:27), but he had taken unto himself some strange powers of sorcery and divination. It appears that both prophets and sorcerers had the power to cast an evil spell upon people, and in fact to impose a curse upon them (see Gen. 9:25; Ps. 6:20; Josh. 6:26; Jer. 17:5, 6).[69]

It was customary to offer a special prophet some kind of material gift as an expression of confidence. It is obvious that Balaam was very covetous and hard to please. Peter gives us this insight into the character of Balaam: They "have forsaken the right way and are gone astray following the way of Balaam the son of Bosor, who loved the wages of unrighteousness" (II Pet. 2:15).

Henry gives this evaluation of Balaam:

Balaam had been a great prophet, who, for the accomplishment of his predictions, and the answers of his prayers, both for good and evil, had been looked upon justly as a man of great interest with God; but that growing proud and covetous, God departed from him, and then, to support his sinking credit, he betook himself to diabolical arts. He is called a prophet (II Pet. 2:16), because he had been one, or, perhaps, he had raised his reputation from the first by his magical charms, as Simon Magres, who bewitched the people so far that he was called "The great power of God" (Acts 8:10).[70]

As Jehovah shall speak to me (v. 8). This is a very difficult passage, but it is apparent that Balaam at least goes through the motions of a true prophet. He apparently has some kind of discourse with God.

Thou shalt not go with them; thou shalt not curse the people (v. 12). We have a difficult Hebrew sentence construction here. It should read, "Thou shalt not go with the people to curse them." Balaam was at liberty to go along, but he had strict orders to refrain from hurting the people with his "black magic." When activity came to a standstill Balak's princes invited Balaam to go home with them, but Balaam refused to go. The princes of Balak went back to their king and advised him that Balaam refused to come along (v. 14).

Balak made another effort to get Balaam to cooperate by sending still higher officials (v. 15), probably the secretary of state and his staff. This new delegation extended a special invitation for Balaam to visit Balak at his palace (v. 16). Balak promised to bestow great honor to Balaam if he would only perform his "black magic." Balaam then revealed his true nature by demanding a much higher price for his services than had been offered.

[69] Ibid., I, 690.   [70] Op. cit., I, 391.

Balaam was fearful of the Lord and purposely set the price so high that even King Balak would not pay it. Balaam knew from past experience that he could not frustrate the purpose of God. He was strongly tempted with glory and riches, but his fear of God prevented him from going beyond a certain point in opposition to Jehovah.[71]

Balaam kept Balak's princes in a state of uncertainty by saying he wanted to consult with God during the night (v. 19). The will of God had been revealed to Balaam earlier (v. 12). God did not want him to go with the princes (v. 22). MacRae says:

> The Lord's will was already known to him. He should have immediately repeated his previous refusal, since there was no new fact which could possibly warrant a reopening of the question. However, instead of following the known will of God, Balaam declared that he would again seek to learn God's will in the matter (vs. 19, 20) — This was in itself an act of disloyalty to God. Once God's will is clear, it is not honoring Him to seek further light: What He now deserves is immediate and unquestioning obedience.
>
> Balaam's new request for knowledge of God's will was due only to his greed for the rich gifts that the men had brought . . . Instead of repeating what Balaam already knew, God apparently granted Balaam's desire. In this case, Balaam did carry out his intention, but only the supernatural power of God enabled him to do so. Since he said only what God desired, the expected profits did not materialize. He would have been better off if he had stayed at home.[72]

The revelations of God are usually seen only by those who are interested. Verse 23 is an example of the opposition the Lord gave Balaam in his journey toward Moab. Henry makes this comment:

> The holy angels are adversaries to sin, and perhaps are employed more than we are aware of in preventing it, particularly in opposing those that have any ill design against God's church and people, for whom Michael our prince stands up, Dan. 12:1, 10, 21. What a comfort this is to all that wish well to the Israel of God, that he never suffers wicked men to form any attempt against them without

sending his holy angels forth to break this attempt, and secure his little ones.[73]

The angel of Jehovah . . . stood in a narrow place (v. 26). Here is further evidence of God's opposition to Balaam's journey to see Balak. In the next few verses the ass becomes the victim of sin's circumstance. When the ass saw that the passage was blocked by the angel she lay down, whereupon Balaam whipped the beast (v. 27).

Jehovah opened the mouth of the ass (v. 28). Balaam shows no surprise at the unusual ability on the part of the beast to speak. Smick queries:

> Did the ass give forth audible sound, or was this merely an experience in the mind of Balaam? The truth is probably to be found on both sides. While the appearance of the angel and the voice of the ass were not hallucinations, it seems that they were seen and heard by Balaam only and not by the others who were present — as was the case several times in the New Testament (Acts 9:7; 2:9; Jn. 12:28, 29). On the road to Damascus there were physical phenomena which only Paul understood; so Balaam because of a combination of mental and spiritual distractions, could not see the angel until God opened his eyes. Nor could others have understood the ass unless God had given them this ability.[74]

By now Balaam's anger is so aroused that he would kill the ass if he had a sword in his possession (v. 29). The ass pleads with Balaam and tries to bring him to his senses. Finally Balaam is given the power to see the angel of Jehovah standing in the way with his sword drawn. Apparently Balaam becomes terrified and falls on his face. The angel rebukes Balaam for the harsh treatment he has imposed upon the ass (v. 32). The angel informs Balaam that he owes his life to the ass. The angel says, **unless she had turned aside from me, surely now I had even slain thee, and saved her life** (v. 33).

I have sinned (v. 34). Balaam is now confronted with irrefutable evidence of his wicked way, and confesses his sin. Balaam expresses a willingness to turn back, but the angel commands him to go with the men. However, he is warned to speak only the words which the Lord wants spoken (vv. 34, 35).

71 Clarke, op. cit., I, 691.   72 Op. cit., p. 188.   73 Op. cit., I, 393.   74 Op. cit., p. 142.

C. BALAAM'S ARRIVAL IN MOAB (22:36-41)

36 And when Balak heard that Balaam was come, he went out to meet him unto the City of Moab, which is on the border of the Arnon, which is in the utmost part of the border. 37 And Balak said unto Balaam, Did I not earnestly send unto thee to call thee? wherefore camest thou not unto me? am I not able indeed to promote thee to honor? 38 And Balaam said unto Balak, Lo, I am come unto thee: have I now any power at all to speak anything? the word that God putteth in my mouth, that shall I speak. 39 And Balaam went with Balak, and they came unto Kiriath-huzoth. 40 And Balak sacrificed oxen and sheep, and sent to Balaam, and to the princes that were with him.

41 And it came to pass in the morning, that Balak took Balaam, and brought him up into the high places of Baal; and he saw from thence the utmost part of the people.

Advance messengers informed King Balak that Balaam was coming, so a royal welcome was arranged for Balaam at the edge of the city of Moab. When the two men met, Balak rebuked Balaam for not coming the first time (v. 37).

The word that God putteth into my mouth (v. 38). Balaam is faced with the problem of trying to obey the Lord and also to please the king, but decides in favor of the Lord.

Balak sacrificed oxen and sheep (v. 39). Apparently Balak made a special offering to the Baal gods with hopes of accomplishing the end for which he had Balaam come. Balak assumes that it will be easier for Balaam to pronounce his curse upon Israel by standing at some distance, so he is taken to a great high place from which he can view the people and pronounce the curse. This would make the curse more impersonal. This is the principle so relevant to many social and moral evils today, e.g., it is not too difficult for the bombardier to drop his bombs upon helpless women and children if it is done from a great height.

D. BALAAM'S FIRST SACRIFICE (23:1-12)

1 And Balaam said unto Balak, Build me here seven altars, and prepare me here seven bullocks and seven rams. 2 And Balak did as Balaam had spoken; and Balak and Balaam offered on every altar a bullock and a ram. 3 And Balaam said unto Balak, Stand by thy burnt-offering, and I will go: peradventure Jehovah will come to meet me; and whosoever he showeth me I will tell thee. And he went to a bare height. 4 And God met Balaam: and he said unto him, I have prepared the seven altars, and I have offered up a bullock and a ram on every altar. 5 And Jehovah put a word in Balaam's mouth, and said, Return unto Balak, and thus thou shalt speak. 6 And he returned unto him, and, lo, he was standing by his burnt-offering, he, and all the princes of Moab. 7 And he took up his parable, and said,

> From Aram hath Balak brought me,
> The king of Moab from the mountains of the East:
> Come, curse me Jacob,
> And come, defy Israel.
>
> 8 How shall I curse, whom God hath not cursed?
> And how shall I defy, whom Jehovah hath not defied?
>
> 9 For from the top of the rocks I see him,
> And from the hills I behold him:
> Lo, it is a people that dwelleth alone,
> And shall not be reckoned among the nations.
>
> 10 Who can count the dust of Jacob,
> Or number the fourth part of Israel?
> Let me die the death of the righteous,
> And let my last end be like his!

11 And Balak said unto Balaam, What hast thou done unto me? I took thee to curse mine enemies, and, behold, thou hast blessed them altogether. 12 And he answered and said, Must I not take heed to speak that which Jehovah putteth in my mouth?

Building seven altars was not characteristic of Jehovah-worship; one altar was enough. It is evident that heathen influence comes into focus here. Balaam wants to put on a big show to convince Balak that he is trying to do what is expected of him. In his heart, however, he is determined to stay within the bounds the Lord has laid out for him.

Standing in proximity of the offering identified the worshiper with the sacrifice (v. 3). Of this passage Clarke says:

> We have already seen that blessing and cursing in this way were considered as religious rites, and therefore must be always preceded by sacrifice. See this exemplified in the case of Isaac, before he blessed Jacob and Esau, Gen. 27. The venison

that was brought to Isaac, of which he did eat, was properly the preparatory sacrifice.[75]

And he took up his parable, and said (v. 7). It has been observed by some scholars that this poetry reflects the age of Moses in its subject matter, form, technical language and the proper names. One exegete says:

> Balaam calls each poem a *mashal,* translated "parable" in 23:7, 18; 24:3, 15. *Mashal* cannot be limited to either parable or proverb; rather, it is so broad that it applies to all "Wisdom" literature. Hebrew poetry has as its main feature parallelism of thoughts, lines, and stanzas, in appositional, oppositional, or progressive form. The Balaam oracles display all this, and in addition they have an archaic and often Aramaic flavor, which points to the antiquity and origin (from Aram) of the character who speaks.[76]

Verses 7 to 10 are in the form of a poem and convey the idea that Balaam has a desire to share in the providential blessings of Israel, e.g., many seed (v. 10) and God's special favor (v. 8).

Balak said unto Balaam, What hast thou done unto me? (v. 11). It is beginning to dawn upon Balak that he has been betrayed (v. 11). When Balak questions Balaam about his work, Balaam clearly admits that he has been saying only that which Jehovah has permitted him to say.

E. BALAAM'S SECOND SACRIFICE (23:13-26)

13 And Balak said unto him, Come, I pray thee, with me unto another place, from whence thou mayest see them; thou shalt see but the utmost part of them, and shalt not see them all: and curse me them from thence. 14 And he took him into the field of Zophim, to the top of Pisgah, and built seven altars, and offered up a bullock and a ram on every altar. 15 And he said unto Balak, Stand here by thy burnt-offering, while I meet *Jehovah* yonder. 16 And Jehovah met Balaam, and put a word in his mouth, and said, Return unto Balak, and thus shalt thou speak. 17 And he came to him, and, lo, he was standing by his burnt-offering, and the princes of Moab with him. And Balak said unto

him, What hath Jehovah spoken? 18 And he took up his parable, and said, Rise up, Balak, and hear; Hearken unto me, thou son of Zippor: 19 God is not a man, that he should lie, Neither the son of man, that he should repent: Hath he said, and will he not do it? Or hath he spoken, and will he not make it good? 20 Behold, I have received *commandment* to bless: And he hath blessed, and I cannot reverse it. 21 He hath not beheld iniquity in Jacob; Neither hath he seen perverseness in Israel: Jehovah his God is with him, And the shout of a king is among them. 22 God bringeth them forth out of Egypt; He hath as it were the strength of the wild-ox. 23 Surely there is no enchantment with Jacob; Neither is there any divination with Israel: Now shall it be said of Jacob and of Israel, What hath God wrought! 24 Behold, the people riseth up as a lioness, And as a lion doth he lift himself up: He shall not lie down until he eat of the prey, And drink the blood of the slain. 25 And Balak said unto Balaam, Neither curse them at all, nor bless them at all. 26 But Balaam answered and said unto Balak, Told not I thee, saying, All that Jehovah speaketh, that I must do?

Balak makes another attempt to get Balaam to curse Israel, trying once again to have the job done at a distance — from atop a high place. This time, however, Balak takes him to a place where he can see only a part of the people, thinking that he would be more willing to pronounce the curse upon a segment than the whole (v. 14). Clarke says:

> Balak thought that the sight of such an immense camp had intimidated Balaam, and this he might gather from what he said in the tenth verse: "Who can count the dust of Jacob, etc." He thought therefore that he might get Balaam to curse them in detached parties, till the whole camp should be devoted to destruction by successive execrations.[77]

[75] *Op. cit.,* I, 694.　　[76] Smick, *op. cit.,* p. 142.　　[77] *Op. cit.,* I, 695.

Once again Balaam tries to confuse the issue (v. 15). He permits Balak to build seven altars to Baal and then switches over to having a conference with Jehovah. Jehovah reiterates His word to Balaam (v. 16), and when Balak asks Balaam what Jehovah has said (v. 17) the issue is further confused by Balaam's speaking in a poetical parable rather than giving a direct answer. It is Jehovah who holds dominant control over Balaam. One scholar observes:

> Balaam here sees the Lord as the One who forces him to bless Israel because He must bring to pass His promised word. The Lord is the source of His people's strength; so no incantation can be effective against them. Balaam concludes by likening Israel to a stalking lion, that catches and devours its prey.[78]

Balak is now quite upset over Balaam's vacillating, delaying tactics (v. 25). It becomes evident that Balaam is trying to play both ends toward the middle— to please both Balak and Jehovah. Balak is now fearful that Balaam may show his total and complete sympathy for Israel. Balak takes the position that Balaam should not bless Israel if he will not curse them. Balaam points out to Balak that he must obey Jehovah (v. 26).

F. BALAAM'S THIRD SACRIFICE (23: 27—24:14)

27 And Balak said unto Balaam, Come now, I will take thee unto another place; peradventure it will please God that thou mayest curse me them from thence. 28 And Balak took Balaam unto the top of Peor, that looketh down upon the desert. 29 And Balaam said unto Balak, Build me here seven altars, and prepare me here seven bullocks and seven rams. 30 And Balak did as Balaam had said, and offered up a bullock and a ram on every altar. 1 And when Balaam saw that it pleased Jehovah to bless Israel, he went not, as at the other times, to meet with enchantments, but he set his face toward the wilderness. 2 And Balaam lifted up his eyes, and he saw Israel dwelling according to their tribes; and the Spirit of God came upon him. 3 And he took up his parable, and said,
Balaam the son of Beor saith,
And the man whose eye was closed saith;

4 He saith, who heareth the words of God,
Who seeth the vision of the Almighty,
Falling down, and having his eyes open:
5 How goodly are thy tents, O Jacob,
Thy tabernacles, O Israel!
6 As valleys are they spread forth,
As gardens by the river-side,
As lign-aloes which Jehovah hath planted,
As cedar-trees beside the waters.
7 Water shall flow from his buckets,
And his seed shall be in many waters,
And his king shall be higher than Agag,
And his kingdom shall be exalted.
8 God bringeth him forth out of Egypt;
He hath as it were the strength of the wild-ox:
He shall eat up the nations his adversaries,
And shall break their bones in pieces,
And smite *them* through with his arrows.
9 He couched, he lay down as a lion,
And as a lioness; who shall rouse him up?
Blessed be every one that blesseth thee,
And cursed be every one that curseth thee.

10 And Balak's anger was kindled against Balaam, and he smote his hands together; and Balak said unto Balaam, I called thee to curse mine enemies, and, behold, thou hast altogether blessed them these three times. 11 Therefore now flee thou to thy place: I thought to promote thee unto great honor; but, lo, Jehovah hath kept thee back from honor. 12 And Balaam said unto Balak, Spake I not also to thy messengers that thou sentest unto me, saying, 13 If Balak would give me his house full of silver and gold, I cannot go beyond the word of Jehovah, to do either good or bad of mine own mind; what Jehovah speaketh, that will I speak? 14 And now, behold, I go unto my people: come, *and* I will advertise thee what this people shall do to thy people in the latter days.

In order to break this chain of thought, Balak induces Balaam to visit another high place (Mt. Peor), thinking that Jehovah might change his mind and permit Balaam to curse Israel. Once again seven altars are built and the sacrifices offered. It appears that Balaam is now convinced that the Lord wants Israel blessed, and he

---

[78] Smick, *op. cit.*, p. 143.

makes no further efforts at ascertaining whether the Lord has changed his mind. Once again Balaam avoids any direct confrontation with Balak by reciting a poetical parable describing the favor Israel enjoys with the Lord. Israel is compared to a garden by the river-side, and is strong and mighty as a lioness (vv. 3-9). It appears from Balaam's prophetic statements concerning Israel's victory over her enemies, that he had insights obtained directly from Jehovah. A hidden force apparently drove Balaam to saying and doing things he did not want to do.[79]

Balak has become thoroughly disgusted with Balaam (v. 10) and plainly says to him that he has blessed Israel three times instead of doing what he had been ordered to do — curse Israel. Balak tells Balaam to remove himself out of his country and go home (v. 11). Balaam tells Balak that he would not go against the word of the Lord for a "house full of silver and gold."

G. BALAAM'S PROPHECY AT PEOR (24:15-25)

15 And he took up his parable, and said,
Balaam the son of Beor saith,
And the man whose eye was closed saith;
16 He saith, who heareth the words of God,
And knoweth the knowledge of the Most High,
Who seeth the vision of the Almighty,
Falling down, and having his eyes open:
17 I see him, but not now;
I behold him, but not nigh:
There shall come forth a star out of Jacob,
And a sceptre shall rise out of Israel,
And shall smite through the corners of Moab,
And break down all the sons of tumult.
18 And Edom shall be a possession,
Seir also shall be a possession, *who were* his enemies;
While Israel doeth valiantly.
19 And out of Jacob shall one have dominion,
And shall destroy the remnant from the city.
20 And he looked on Amalek, and took up his parable, and said,

Amalek was the first of the nations;
But his latter end shall come to destruction.
21 And he looked on the Kenite, and took up his parable, and said,
Strong is thy dwelling-place,
And thy nest is set in the rock.
22 Nevertheless Kain shall be wasted,
Until Asshur shall carry thee away captive.
23 And he took up his parable, and said,
Alas, who shall live when God doeth this?
24 But ships *shall come* from the coast of Kittim,
And they shall afflict Asshur, and shall afflict Eber;
And he also shall come to destruction.
25 And Balaam rose up, and went and returned to his place; and Balak also went his way.

And he took up his parable (v. 15). For the fourth time Balaam shrouds the issue in a poetical parable in which he predicts the downfall of Moab, Edom, Amalek, and Asshur. It is evident that Balaam strikes a Messianic note in this parable (v. 17). The Balaam-Balak episode has now ended and the prophet goes back home. Clarke says:

1. It appears . . . that Balaam knew and worshipped the true God.
2. That he had been a true prophet . . .
3. That he did practice some illicit branches of knowledge.
4. That though he was a believer in the true God, yet he was covetous, "he loved the wages of unrighteousness."
5. That it does not appear that . . . he wished to curse Israel when he found they were the servants of the true God.
6. That it is possible he did not know this at first. Balak had told him that there was a numerous people come out of Egypt . . . marauders, wandering hordes, freebooters.
7. That as soon as he found it displeased God he cheerfully offered to return and did not advance till he had not only the permission, but the authority of God to proceed.
8. That when he came in view of the Israelites' camp he did not attempt to make use of any means of sorcery.[80]

The fact remains, however, that Israel did suffer through the influence of Balaam. It is evident that the greatest harm which Balaam brought upon Israel was in persuading them to marry among the

[79] Cf. Clarke, *op. cit.*, I, 698.   [80] *Ibid.*, I, 700.

Moabites. By so doing, they established blood ties with the unbelievers and in turn were enticed to sacrifice to the Moabite gods. It was the Moabite women and not Balaam that actually influenced the Israelites to go astray.[81]

H. ISRAEL COMMITS ADULTERY IN MOAB (25:1-18)

1 And Israel abode in Shittim; and the people began to play the harlot with the daughters of Moab: 2 for they called the people unto the sacrifices of their gods; and the people did eat, and bowed down to their gods. 3 And Israel joined himself unto Baal-peor: and the anger of Jehovah was kindled against Israel. 4 And Jehovah said unto Moses, Take all the chiefs of the people, and hang them up unto Jehovah before the sun, that the fierce anger of Jehovah may turn away from Israel. 5 And Moses said unto the judges of Israel, Slay ye every one his men that have joined themselves unto Baal-peor.

6 And, behold, one of the children of Israel came and brought unto his brethren a Midianitish woman in the sight of Moses, and in the sight of all the congregation of the children of Israel, while they were weeping at the door of the tent of meeting. 7 And when Phinehas, the son of Eleazar, the son of Aaron the priest, saw it, he rose up from the midst of the congregation, and took a spear in his hand; 8 and he went after the man of Israel into the pavilion, and thrust both of them through, the man of Israel, and the woman through her body. So the plague was stayed from the children of Israel. 9 And those that died by the plague were twenty and four thousand.

10 And Jehovah spake unto Moses, saying, 11 Phinehas, the son of Eleazar, the son of Aaron the priest, hath turned my wrath away from the children of Israel, in that he was jealous with my jealousy among them, so that I consumed not the children of Israel in my jealousy. 12 Wherefore say, Behold, I give unto him my covenant of peace: 13 and it shall be unto him, and to his seed after him, the covenant of an everlasting priesthood; because he was jealous for his God, and made atonement for the children of Israel.

14 Now the name of the man of Israel that was slain, who was slain with the Midianitish woman, was Zimri, the son of Salu, a prince of a fathers' house among the Simeonites. 15 And the name of the Midianitish woman that was slain was Cozbi, the daughter of Zur; he was head of the people of a fathers' house in Midian.

16 And Jehovah spake unto Moses, saying, 17 Vex the Midianites, and smite them; 18 for they vex you with their wiles, wherewith they have beguiled you in the matter of Peor, and in the matter of Cozbi, the daughter of the prince of Midian, their sister, who was slain on the day of the plague in the matter of Peor.

Not only did the people of Israel commit adultery with the daughters of Moab; they also committed spiritual adultery by bowing down and worshiping the Baal gods (v. 2). The anger of the Lord was provoked against the leaders of Israel for leading the people into idolatry and adultery. Moses was commanded to execute those leaders who were responsible for this terrible development. They were to be executed by hanging **before the sun.** It can be assumed that this meant executing them in the most conspicuous place, in the daytime.[82]

The apostate audacity which some of the people expressed is seen in the situation where an Israelite brought an unclean heathen woman into the precincts of the place of worship. It has been suggested that the woman was a common prostitute (Vulgate), but it is more likely that this was a matrimonial union. Such a marriage was in direct opposition to the law of God. The seriousness of this offense is seen in the fact that the rest of the congregation was in a state of humiliation and prayer in front of the tabernacle. This might be compared to a bunch of rowdies disturbing a church service.

When the high priest saw this shameful demonstration, he took a spear and executed both the man and the woman on the spot (vv. 7-8). Clarke suggests that this act could be justified only by the "pressing exigencies of the case."

Apparently the execution of this man and woman brought the matter to a conclusion. Twenty-four thousand people died because of the plague the Lord had imposed upon the people for their shameful conduct (v. 9). The Lord looked upon the execution of the couple as a vindication of His judgment. Phinehas had acted on behalf of the Lord, and therefore received His sanction and blessing (vv. 11-12).

The name of the man (v. 14). For the first time the names of the man and the woman who committed the horrible sacrilege are given. Zimri from the tribe of Simeon was the man, and Cozbi the Midianite was the woman here in question.

Vex the Midianites (v. 17). Moses is ordered to take full vengeance upon the Midianites because of the evil which they had caused. The full import of this attack is given in 31:1-20.

VIII. ISRAEL'S SECOND NUMBERING (Num. 26:1-65)

A. DIRECTIONS FOR THE CENSUS (26:1-4)

1 And it came to pass after the plague, that Jehovah spake unto Moses and unto Eleazar the son of Aaron the priest, saying, 2 Take the sum of all the congregation of the children of Israel, from twenty years old and upward, by their fathers' houses, all that are able to go forth to war in Israel. 3 And Moses and Eleazar the priest spake with them in the plains of Moab by the Jordan at Jericho, saying, 4 *Take the sum of the people,* from twenty years old and upward; as Jehovah commanded Moses and the children of Israel, that came forth out of the land of Egypt.

The time has now come for final preparation before entering the promised land. The census is to be brought up to date so that there may be an equitable distribution of the land. Those twenty years old and upward are to be numbered and made available for service in the army. Moses and Eleazar are now in charge since Aaron died at Mt. Hor.

B. TAKING THE CENSUS (26:5-51)

5 Reuben, the first-born of Israel; the sons of Reuben: *of* Hanoch the family of the Hanochites; of Pallu, the family of the Palluites; 6 of Hezron, the family of the Hezronites; of Carmi, the family of the Carmites. 7 These are the families of the Reubenites; and they that were numbered of them were forty and three thousand and seven hundred and thirty. 8 And the sons of Pallu: Eliab. 9 And the sons of Eliab: Nemuel, and Dathan,

and Abiram. These are that Dathan and Abiram, who were called of the congregation, who strove against Moses and against Aaron in the company of Korah, when they strove against Jehovah, 10 and the earth opened its mouth, and swallowed them up together with Korah, when that company died; what time the fire devoured two hundred and fifty men, and they became a sign. 11 Notwithstanding, the sons of Korah died not.

12 The sons of Simeon after their families: of Nemuel, the family of the Nemuelites; of Jamin, the family of the Jaminites; of Jachin, the family of the Jachinites; 13 of Zerah, the family of the Zerahites; of Shaul, the family of the Shaulites. 14 These are the families of the Simeonites, twenty and two thousand and two hundred.

15 The sons of Gad after their families: of Zephon, the family of the Zephonites; of Haggi, the family of the Haggites; of Shuni, the family of the Shunites: 16 of Ozni, the family of the Oznites; of Eri, the family of the Erites; 17 of Arod, the family of the Arodites; of Areli, the family of the Arelites. 18 These are the families of the sons of Gad according to those that were numbered of them, forty thousand and five hundred.

19 The sons of Judah: Er and Onan; and Er and Onan died in the land of Canaan. 20 And the sons of Judah after their families were: of Shelah, the family of the Shelanites; of Perez, the family of the Perezites; of Zerah, the family of the Zerahites. 21 And the sons of Perez were: of Hezron, the family of the Hezronites; of Hamul, the family of the Hamulites. 22 These are the families of Judah according to those that were numbered of them, threescore and sixteen thousand and five hundred.

23 The sons of Issachar after their families: *of* Tola, the family of the Tolaites; of Puvah, the family of the Punites; 24 of Jashub, the family of the Jashubites; of Shimron, the family of the Shimronites. 25 These are the families of Issachar according to those that were numbered of them, threescore and four thousand and three hundred.

26 The sons of Zebulun after their families: of Sered, the family of the Seredites; of Elon, the family of the Elonites; of Jahleel, the family of the Jahleelites. 27 These are the families of the Zebulunites according to those that were numbered of them, threescore thousand and five hundred.

28 The sons of Joseph after their families: Manasseh and Ephraim. 29 The sons of Manasseh: of Machir, the family

of the Machirites; and Machir begat Gilead: of Gilead, the family of the Gileadites. 30 These are the sons of Gilead: *of* Iezer, the family of the Iezerites; of Helek, the family of the Helekites; 31 and *of* Asriel, the family of the Asrielites; and *of* Shechem, the family of the Shechemites; 32 and *of* Shemida, the family of the Shemidaites; and *of* Hepher, the family of the Hepherites. 33 And Zelophehad the son of Hepher had no sons, but daughters: and the names of the daughters of Zelophehad were Mahlah, and Noah, Hoglah, Milcah, and Tirzah. 34 These are the families of Manasseh; and they that were numbered of them were fifty and two thousand and seven hundred.

35 These are the sons of Ephraim after their families: of Shuthelah, the family of the Shuthelahites; of Becher, the family of the Becherites; of Tahan, the family of the Tahanites. 36 And these are the sons of Shuthelah: of Eran, the family of the Eranites. 37 These are the families of the sons of Ephraim according to those that were numbered of them, thirty and two thousand and five hundred. These are the sons of Joseph after their families.

38 The sons of Benjamin after their families: of Bela, the family of the Belaites; of Ashbel, the family of the Ashbelites; of Ahiram, the family of the Ahiramites; 39 of Shupham, the family of the Shuphamites; of Hupham, the family of the Huphamites. 40 And the sons of Bela were Ard and Naaman: *of Ard*, the family of the Ardites; of Naaman, the family of the Naamites. 41 These are the sons of Benjamin after their families; and they that were numbered of them were forty and five thousand and six hundred.

42 These are the sons of Dan after their families: of Shuham, the family of the Shuhamites. These are the families of Dan after their families. 43 All the families of the Shuhamites, according to those that were numbered of them, were threescore and four thousand and four hundred.

44 The sons of Asher after their families: of Imnah, the family of the Imnites; of Ishvi, the family of the Ishvites; of Beriah, the family of the Beriites. 45 Of the sons of Beriah: of Heber, the family of the Heberites; of Malchiel, the family of the Malchielites. 46 And the name of the daughter of Asher was Serah. 47 These are the families of the sons of Asher according to those that were numbered

of them, fifty and three thousand and four hundred.

48 The sons of Naphtali after their families: of Jahzeel, the family of the Jahzeelites; of Guni, the family of the Gunites; 49 of Jezer, the family of the Jezerites; of Shillem, the family of the Shillemites. 50 These are the families of Naphtali according to their families; and they that were numbered of them were forty and five thousand and four hundred.

51 These are they that were numbered of the children of Israel, six hundred thousand and a thousand seven hundred and thirty.

Reference to detail in this section will be reserved for the biblical text. It is to be noted that the sins of the nation have exacted their toll on the population (vv. 7-51). Instead of showing a sizeable increase, the final count shows a decrease as compared with the previous census. For sake of comparison, we list the present as well as the previous census:

	Now	Before	
Reuben	43,730	46,500	2,770 decrease
Simeon	22,200	59,300	37,100 decrease
Gad	40,500	45,650	5,150 decrease
Judah	76,500	74,600	1,900 increase
Issachar	64,300	54,400	9,900 increase
Zebulun	60,500	57,400	3,100 increase
Manasseh	52,700	32,200	20,500 increase
Ephraim	32,500	40,500	8,000 decrease
Benjamin	45,600	35,400	10,200 increase
Dan	64,400	62,700	1,700 increase
Asher	53,400	41,500	11,900 increase
Naphtali	45,400	53,400	8,000 decrease
Total	601,730	603,550	1,820 decrease in 38 years

Decrease in all, 61,020 Increase in all, 59,200[83]

C. DISTRIBUTION OF THE LAND (26:52-56)

52 And Jehovah spake unto Moses, saying, 53 Unto these the land shall be divided for an inheritance according to the number of names. 54 To the more thou shalt give the more inheritance, and to the fewer thou shalt give the less inheritance: to every one according to those that were numbered of him shall his inheritance be given. 55 Notwithstanding, the land shall be divided by

83 *Ibid.*, I, 706.

lot: according to the names of the tribes of their fathers they shall inherit. 56 According to the lot shall their inheritance be divided between the more and the fewer.

The size of the inheritance was to be determined by the number in each tribe. The tribes with the greatest numbers were to get the largest inheritance. The division was to be made by the drawing of lots. The lots or portions were so disposed or arranged that the larger tribes did not draw a small inheritance. Dummelow says,

> The casting of lots is of the nature of an appeal to God, and was resorted to in order to detect a culprit (Josh. 7:14, I Sam. 14:42), to select an office-bearer (I Chr. 24:4, 5, Acts 1:26), or to make a division of property as here (also Mat. 27:35). In the case before us, lots were cast to determine the locality of each tribe's inheritance, but its size was regulated by the number of the names; the relative fertility of each locality being also no doubt taken into consideration. The twelve lots, which would be tablets of wood or stone, each inscribed with the name of a tribe, were probably put in an urn; and, as the name of each portion of land was called out, the high priest or representative of a tribe (34:16-29) drew a lot, and the tribe whose name was drawn inherited that territory. The precise boundaries would be adjusted afterwards, according to the population shown by the census.[84]

D. A CENSUS OF THE LEVITES (26:57-65)

57 And these are they that were numbered of the Levites after their families: of Gershon, the family of the Gershonites; of Kohath, the family of the Kohathites; of Merari, the family of the Merarites. 58 These are the families of Levi: the family of the Libnites, the family of the Hebronites, the family of the Mahlites, the family of the Mushites, the family of the Korahites. And Kohath begat Amram. 59 And the name of Amram's wife was Jochebed, the daughter of Levi, who was born to Levi in Egypt: and she bare unto Amram Aaron and Moses, and Miriam their sister. 60 And unto Aaron were born Nadab and Abihu, Eleazar and Ithamar. 61 And Nadab and Abihu died, when they offered strange fire before Jehovah. 62 And they that

were numbered of them were twenty and three thousand, every male from a month old and upward: for they were not numbered among the children of Israel, because there was no inheritance given them among the children of Israel.

63 These are they that were numbered by Moses and Eleazar the priest, who numbered the children of Israel in the plains of Moab by the Jordan at Jericho. 64 But among these there was not a man of them that were numbered by Moses and Aaron the priest, who numbered the children of Israel in the wilderness of Sinai. 65 For Jehovah had said to them, They shall surely die in the wilderness. And there was not left a man of them, save Caleb the son of Jephunneh, and Joshua the son of Nun.

The priestly tribe has now increased from 22,000 to 23,000, a net gain of one thousand.

Only Joshua and Caleb remain from the first numbering. The sentence of death for those over twenty at the first numbering has now been carried out.

IX. THE LAW OF INHERITANCE (Num. 27:1-11)

1 Then drew near the daughters of Zelophehad, the son of Hepher, the son of Gilead, the son of Machir, the son of Manasseh, of the families of Manasseh the son of Joseph; and these are the names of his daughters: Mahlah, Noah, and Hoglah, and Milcah, and Tirzah. 2 And they stood before Moses, and before Eleazar the priest, and before the princes and all the congregation, at the door of the tent of meeting, saying, 3 Our father died in the wilderness, and he was not among the company of them that gathered themselves together against Jehovah in the company of Korah: but he died in his own sin; and he had no sons. 4 Why should the name of our father be taken away from among his family, because he had no son? Give unto us a possession among the brethren of our father. 5 And Moses brought their cause before Jehovah.

6 And Jehovah spake unto Moses, saying, 7 The daughters of Zelophehad speak right: thou shalt surely give them a possession of an inheritance among their father's brethren; and thou shalt cause the inheritance of their father to pass unto them. 8 And thou shalt

speak unto the children of Israel, saying, If a man die, and have no son, then ye shall cause his inheritance to pass unto his daughter. 9 And if he have no daughter, then ye shall give his inheritance unto his brethren. 10 And if he have no brethren, then ye shall give his inheritance unto his father's brethren. 11 And if his father have no brethren, then ye shall give his inheritance unto his kinsman that is next to him of his family, and he shall possess it: and it shall be unto the children of Israel a statute *and* ordinance, as Jehovah commanded Moses.

A legal problem of inheritance has developed. The Manassite Zelophehad had five daughters and no sons. According to the existing law only sons could inherit property. One exegete has analyzed the situation thus:

These daughters pointed out that if they, as daughters, could not inherit land, then their father's inheritance would be lost. God confirmed to Moses the well-known provision by which daughters might inherit land (Josh. 17:3-6). But the next in line of inheritance were to be paternal brothers of the deceased, then paternal uncles, and then the nearest kinsman. However, the daughters were to be free to marry, and their children would continue their father's genealogy and inherit his land. Thus was Jair in the line of Manasseh in 32:41 and Deut. 3:14. Similar to this was the law of levirate marriage, by which a widow without children married the nearest kin of her husband, that his name and inheritance might not be cut off. Both of these laws were based on the principle that the land which the Lord gave to a family should never be sold or allowed to pass out of that family (Lev. 25:23).[85]

The Lord confirms the claims of the daughters. **If a man die** (v. 8). The Lord gives the order in which the succession shall be. If a man has no sons, his inheritance shall go to his daughter, and if he has no daughter, then it shall go to his brothers (v. 7). If he has no brothers, the inheritance shall go to his father's brothers, or his uncles (v. 10). If he has no uncles, then the inheritance is to go to the next of kin (v. 11).

X. MOSES PREPARES FOR DEATH (Num. 27:12-23)

A. MOSES' DEATH (27:12-14)

12 And Jehovah said unto Moses, Get thee up into this mountain of Abarim, and behold the land which I have given unto the children of Israel. 13 And when thou hast seen it, thou also shalt be gathered unto thy people, as Aaron thy brother was gathered; 14 because ye rebelled against my word in the wilderness of Zin, in the strife of the congregation, to sanctify me at the waters before their eyes. (These are the waters of Meribah of Kadesh in the wilderness of Zin.)

The time has now come for Moses to go to his final reward. He is commanded to ascend a certain mountain which is identified as Mt. Nebo (Deut. 32:49), the highest peak in the **Abarim** range.

B. JOSHUA APPOINTED MOSES' SUCCESSOR (27:15-23)

15 And Moses spake unto Jehovah, saying, 16 Let Jehovah, the God of the spirits of all flesh, appoint a man over the congregation, 17 who may go out before them, and who may come in before them, and who may lead them out, and who may bring them in; that the congregation of Jehovah be not as sheep which have no shepherd. 18 And Jehovah said unto Moses, Take thee Joshua the son of Nun, a man in whom is the Spirit, and lay thy hand upon him; 19 and set him before Eleazar the priest, and before all the congregation; and give him a charge in their sight. 20 And thou shalt put of thine honor upon him, that all the congregation of the children of Israel may obey. 21 And he shall stand before Eleazar the priest, who shall inquire for him by the judgment of the Urim before Jehovah: at his word shall they go out, and at his word they shall come in, both he, and all the children of Israel with him, even all the congregation. 22 And Moses did as Jehovah commanded him; and he took Joshua, and set him before Eleazar the priest, and before all the congregation: 23 and he laid his hands upon him, and gave him a charge, as Jehovah spake by Moses.

Moses is very much concerned that a capable leader should be his successor. The Lord commands Moses to appoint

85 Smick, *op. cit.*, p. 146.

Joshua, a man of spiritual grace, to take charge. It is fitting and proper that any religious leader should be filled with the Spirit of God. Clarke says, "How miserably qualified is that man for the work of God who is not guided and influenced by the Holy Ghost."[86]

Eleazar, the high priest, is to perform the inaugural ceremony in the presence of the people (v. 19). Moses is to express his approval and affirm God's choice in the matter (v. 20). It is to be noted that Eleazar is to be the direct contact with the Lord and that he in turn is to convey divine intelligence to Joshua.

XI. PUBLIC OFFERINGS (Num. 28:1— 29:40)

A. THE OFFERINGS COMMANDED (28:1-2)

1 And Jehovah spake unto Moses, saying, 2 Command the children of Israel, and say unto them, My oblation, my food for my offerings made by fire, of a sweet savor unto me, shall ye observe to offer unto me in their due season.

In this and the following chapter the ritual program is given in outline, as it was also given in Leviticus 23. There is this difference, however: the implications at this point have special reference to activity after Israel possesses the promised land. Why the precepts are repeated so many times we do not know, but it is evident that the people had daily, weekly, monthly and yearly interruptions, because of their unsettled state in the wilderness, and needed to be reminded just before they were to enter the land of plenty. It is also to be noted that a new generation, ignorant of many past events, had now taken the leadership.[87]

The reference here to food for God (v. 2) is to be interpreted ceremonially. Smick makes this comment:

God's food here referred to was not that which the priests received as their due, but rather the food that went up in smoke at the fire offerings. The thought is that God eats and drinks with his worshipers, which, far from being a primitive notion, is carried over into the N.T. in the parallel ordinance of the Lord's table, the Communion.[88]

B. THE DAILY OFFERINGS DEFINED (28:3-8)

3 And thou shalt say unto them, This is the offering made by fire which ye shall offer unto Jehovah: he-lambs a year old without blemish, two day by day, for a continual burnt-offering. 4 The one lamb shalt thou offer in the morning, and the other lamb shalt thou offer at even; 5 and the tenth part of an ephah of fine flour for a meal-offering, mingled with the fourth part of a hin of beaten oil. 6 It is a continual burnt-offering, which was ordained in mount Sinai for a sweet savor, an offering made by fire unto Jehovah. 7 And the drink-offering thereof shall be the fourth part of a hin for the one lamb: in the holy place shalt thou pour out a drink-offering of strong drink unto Jehovah. 8 And the other lamb shalt thou offer at even: as the meal-offering of the morning, and as the drink-offering thereof, thou shalt offer it, an offering made by fire, of a sweet savor unto Jehovah.

Each day two he-lambs without blemish were to be offered — one in the morning and the other in the evening. This offering was an expression of the people's faith and devotion to the Lord, and it also helped to make them constantly aware of their utter dependence upon Him.

The fine flour (v. 5) was very expensive in labor and time. Many hours were required to make this fine flour, and it too represented "My best for the Lord," as did the "lambs without blemish." The constant and eternal covenant relationship and demand is indicated in the continuity and the systematic nature of the burnt-offering (v. 6).

C. THE SABBATH OFFERING (28:9-10)

9 And on the sabbath day two he-lambs a year old without blemish, and two tenth parts of an ephah of fine flour for a meal-offering, mingled with oil, and the drink-offering thereof: 10 this is the burnt-offering of every sabbath, besides the continual burnt-offering, and the drink-offering thereof.

On the Sabbath Day two additional he-lambs were to be offered to make them peculiarly aware of the Sabbath and its demands.

---

[86] Op. cit., I, 709.   [87] Ibid., I, 710.   [88] Op. cit., pp. 147, 148.

D. THE MONTHLY OFFERINGS (28: 11-15)

11 And in the beginnings of your months ye shall offer a burnt-offering unto Jehovah: two young bullocks, and one ram, seven he-lambs a year old without blemish; 12 and three tenth parts *of an ephah* of fine flour for a meal-offering, mingled with oil, for each bullock; and two tenth parts of fine flour for a meal-offering, mingled with oil, for the one ram; 13 and a tenth part of fine flour mingled with oil for a meal-offering unto every lamb; for a burnt-offering of a sweet savor, an offering made by fire unto Jehovah. 14 And their drink-offerings shall be half a hin of wine for a bullock, and the third part of a hin for the ram, and the fourth part of a hin for a lamb: this is the burnt-offering of every month throughout the months of the year. 15 And one he-goat for a sin-offering unto Jehovah; it shall be offered besides the continual burnt-offering, and the drink-offering thereof.

A special offering at the first of each month was to be made to the Lord. The offering was to consist of two young bullocks, one ram, seven lambs a year old and a kid or he-goat.

E. THE YEARLY OFFERINGS (28:16—29:40)

16 And in the first month, on the fourteenth day of the month, is Jehovah's passover. 17 And on the fifteenth day of this month shall be a feast: seven days shall unleavened bread be eaten. 18 In the first day shall be a holy convocation: ye shall do no servile work; 19 but ye shall offer an offering made by fire, a burnt-offering unto Jehovah: two young bullocks, and one ram, and seven he-lambs a year old; they shall be unto you without blemish; 20 and their meal-offering, fine flour mingled with oil: three tenth parts shall ye offer for a bullock, and two tenth parts for the ram; 21 a tenth part shalt thou offer for every lamb of the seven lambs; 22 and one he-goat for a sin-offering, to make atonement for you. 23 Ye shall offer these besides the burnt-offering of the morning, which is for a continual burnt-offering. 24 After this manner ye shall offer daily, for seven days, the food of the offering made by fire, of a sweet savor unto Jehovah: it shall be offered besides the continual burnt-offering, and the drink-offering thereof.

25 And on the seventh day ye shall have a holy convocation; ye shall do no servile work.

26 Also in the day of the first-fruits, when ye offer a new meal-offering unto Jehovah in your *feast of* weeks, ye shall have a holy convocation; ye shall do no servile work; 27 but ye shall offer a burnt-offering for a sweet savor unto Jehovah: two young bullocks, one ram, seven he-lambs a year old; 28 and their meal-offering, fine flour mingled with oil, three tenth parts for each bullock, two tenth parts for the one ram, 29 a tenth part for every lamb of the seven lambs; 30 one he-goat, to make atonement for you. 31 Besides the continual burnt-offering, and the meal-offering thereof, ye shall offer them (they shall be unto you without blemish), and their drink-offerings.

1 And in the seventh month, on the first day of the month, ye shall have a holy convocation; ye shall do no servile work: it is a day of blowing of trumpets unto you. 2 And ye shall offer a burnt-offering for a sweet savor unto Jehovah: one young bullock, one ram, seven he-lambs a year old without blemish; 3 and their meal-offering, fine flour mingled with oil, three tenth parts for the bullock, two tenth parts for the ram; 4 and one tenth part for every lamb of the seven lambs; 5 and one he-goat for a sin-offering, to make atonement for you; 6 besides the burnt-offering of the new moon, and the meal-offering thereof, and the continual burnt-offering and the meal-offering thereof, and their drink-offerings, according unto their ordinance, for a sweet savor, an offering made by fire unto Jehovah.

7 And on the tenth day of this seventh month ye shall have a holy convocation; and ye shall afflict your souls: ye shall do no manner of work; 8 but ye shall offer a burnt-offering unto Jehovah for a sweet savor: one young bullock, one ram, seven he-lambs a year old; they shall be unto you without blemish; 9 and their meal-offering, fine flour mingled with oil, three tenth parts for the bullock, two tenth parts for the one ram, 10 a tenth part for every lamb of the seven lambs: 11 one he-goat for a sin-offering; besides the sin-offering of atonement, and the continual burnt-offering, and the meal-offering thereof, and their drink-offerings.

12 And on the fifteenth day of the seventh month ye shall have a holy convocation; ye shall do no servile work, and ye shall keep a feast unto Jehovah seven days: 13 and ye shall offer a burnt-

offering, an offering made by fire, of a sweet savor unto Jehovah; thirteen young bullocks, two rams, fourteen he-lambs a year old; they shall be without blemish; 14 and their meal-offering, fine flour mingled with oil, three tenth parts for every bullock of the thirteen bullocks, two tenth parts for each ram of the two rams, 15 and a tenth part for every lamb of the fourteen lambs; 16 and one he-goat for a sin-offering; besides the continual burnt-offering, the meal-offering thereof, and the drink-offering thereof.

17 And on the second day *ye shall offer* twelve young bullocks, two rams, fourteen he-lambs a year old without blemish; 18 and their meal-offering and their drink-offerings for the bullocks, for the rams, and for the lambs, according to their number, after the ordinance; 19 and one he-goat for a sin-offering; besides the continual burnt-offering, and the meal-offering thereof, and their drink-offerings.

20 And on the third day eleven bullocks, two rams, fourteen he-lambs a year old without blemish; 21 and their meal-offering and their drink-offerings for the bullocks, for the rams, and for the lambs, according to their number, after the ordinance; 22 and one he-goat for a sin-offering; besides the continual burnt-offering, and the meal-offering thereof, and the drink-offering thereof.

23 And on the fourth day ten bullocks, two rams, fourteen he-lambs a year old without blemish; 24 their meal-offering and their drink-offerings for the bullocks, for the rams, and for the lambs, according to their number, after the ordinance; 25 and one he-goat for a sin-offering; besides the continual burnt-offering, the meal-offering thereof, and the drink-offering thereof.

26 And on the fifth day nine bullocks, two rams, fourteen he-lambs a year old without blemish; 27 and their meal-offering and their drink-offerings for the bullocks, for the rams, and for the lambs, according to their number, after the ordinance; 28 and one he-goat for a sin-offering; besides the continual burnt-offering, and the meal-offering thereof, and the drink-offering thereof.

29 And on the sixth day eight bullocks, two rams, fourteen he-lambs a year old without blemish; 30 and their meal-offering and their drink-offerings for the bullocks, for the rams, and for the lambs, according to their number, after the ordinance; 31 and one he-goat for a sin-offering; besides the continual burnt-

offering, the meal-offering thereof, and the drink-offerings thereof.

32 And on the seventh day seven bullocks, two rams, fourteen he-lambs a year old without blemish; 33 and their meal-offering and their drink-offerings for the bullocks, for the rams, and for the lambs, according to their number, after the ordinance; 34 and one he-goat for a sin-offering; besides the continual burnt-offering, the meal-offering thereof, and the drink-offering thereof.

35 On the eighth day ye shall have a solemn assembly: ye shall do no servile work; 36 but ye shall offer a burnt-offering, an offering made by fire, of a sweet savor unto Jehovah: one bullock, one ram, seven he-lambs a year old without blemish; 37 their meal-offering and their drink-offerings for the bullock, for the ram, and for the lambs, shall be according to their number, after the ordinance: 38 and one he-goat for a sin-offering; besides the continual burnt-offering, and the meal-offering thereof, and the drink-offering thereof.

39 These ye shall offer unto Jehovah in your set feasts, besides your vows, and your freewill-offerings, for your burnt-offerings, and for your meal-offerings, and for your drink-offerings, and for your peace-offerings. 40 And Moses told the children of Israel according to all that Jehovah commanded Moses.

1. Feast of Unleavened Bread (28:16-25)

No offering was appointed for the Passover because the offerings were to be made by the priests. The Passover lamb was directly related to family participation. The Feast of Unleavened Bread was to be eaten from the first through the seventh day. They were to do no **servile** work (v. 18) during this period.

2. Feast of Weeks (28:26-31)

The day of the first-fruits (v. 26) was also called the Day of First-Fruits and the Feast of Pentecost.

3. Feast of Trumpets (29:1-6)

In the seventh month on the first day (v. 1) was the beginning of Israel's civil year and an occasion for festive activity. This **holy convocation** was ushered in by the blast of trumpets, work was stopped and a burnt-offering was made unto the Lord.

4. Day of Atonement (29:7-11)

The tenth day of this seventh month (v. 7) was the Day of Atonement, and it was one of the most important feast days in Israel's calendar. It is still celebrated by the Jews, however on a greatly modified scale. On this day the high priest sacrificed a bullock for himself and his fellow priests. Next he placed the censer with live coals inside the Holy of Holies so that the smoke might cover the mercy-seat. He then sprinkled blood from the bullock upon the mercy-seat and the floor.

After the high priest made an atonement for himself and his house (Lev. 16:6) two goats were presented "before the Lord at the door of the tabernacle of the congregation. And Aaron cast lots upon the goats; one lot for the Lord, and the other lot for the scapegoat. . . . And Aaron shall lay both his hands upon the head of the live goat, and confess over him all the iniquities of the children of Israel, and all their transgressions in all their sins, putting them upon the head of the goat, and shall send him away by the hand of a fit man into the wilderness" (Lev. 16:8-9, 21-22).

The blood of the goat killed for a sin-offering was taken within the veil and sprinkled upon and before the mercy-seat "because of the uncleanness of the children of Israel and because of their transgressions in all their sins" (Lev. 16:16).

The time the high priest spent behind the veil was always an occasion of anxiety and suspense. As long as the high priest moved about behind the veil the golden bells on his garment gave forth a tinkling sound and the people knew that all was well. Silence in the inner sanctum indicated that the priest had completed his ministration before the Lord and that he was standing before the mercy-seat waiting for Jehovah to indicate His pleasure by a quivering motion of the Shekinah glory. There was to be "a golden bell and a pomegranate, upon the hem of the robe round about. And it shall be upon Aaron to minister: and his sound shall be heard when he goeth into the holy place before the Lord, and when he cometh out, that he die not" (Exod. 28:35).

Tradition has it that a scarlet cord was tied around the high priest's leg so that he could be dragged out if he suffered death inside. It meant certain death for the high priest if he went into the presence of Jehovah without being ceremonially clean and fit to officiate for the people. Only holy, set-aside people could come into the presence of the Lord God (Exod. 19:22; II Sam. 6:7-8).

There was a season of rejoicing among the worshipers when the short period of silence was broken by the tinkling bells. The sounding of the bells meant that all was well and that the sin problem had been settled for another year.

The Jews of today go through the motions of this great feast day but deny the significance that made the Day of Atonement relevant when it was instituted. Clarke says:

> The great day of atonement, and the sacrifices, rites, and ceremonies prescribed for it, were commanded to be solemnized by the Jews through the whole of their dispensation, and as long as God should acknowledge them for his people: yet in the present day scarcely a shadow of these things remains; there is no longer a scape-goat, nor a goat for sacrifice, provided by them in any place. They are sinners, and they are without an atonement. How strange it is that they do not see that the essence of their religion is gone, and that consequently God has thrown them entirely out of covenant with himself! The true expiation, the Christ crucified, they refuse to receive, and are consequently without temple, altar, scape-goat, atonement, or any means of salvation! The state of the Gentile world is bad, but that of the Jews is doubly deplorable. Their total excision excepted, wrath is come upon them to the uttermost. What a proof is this of the truth of the predictions in their own law, and of those in the Gospel of Christ! Who, with the Jews and the Bible before his eyes, can doubt the truth of that Bible as a Divine revelation? Had this people been extinct, we might have doubted whether there were ever a people on the earth that acknowledged such a law, or observed such ordinances; but the people, their law, and their prophets are still in being, and all proclaim what God has wrought, and that he has now ceased to work among them, because they have refused to receive and profit by the great atonement; and yet he preserves them alive, and in a state of complete separation from all the people of the earth

in all places of their dispersion! How powerfully does the preservation of the Jews as a distinct people bear testimony at once to the truth of their own law which they acknowledge, and the Gospel of Christ which they reject![89]

5. Feast of Tabernacles (29:12-40)

This feast began on the fifteenth day of the month and lasted for eight days. It was unusually expressive and joyful, as was the Feast of Thanksgiving (Lev. 23:33-43). Smick says:

This feast was the climax of the religious year. The attention paid to the offering of bullocks each day indicates the importance of the feast. Seventy bullocks in all were offered, beginning with thirteen on the first day, twelve on the second, and so on, down to seven on the seventh day. Then followed an eighth day sabbath of offerings. All this was in addition to the regular daily offerings. As in the case of the monthly blowing of trumpets (10:10), it is assumed here that such details as dwelling in booths are well known (Lev. 23:40-44). Animal sacrifices were multiplied at this season because it was a "feast" (*hag*) not a "fast." Except for the Passover and the Day of Atonement, when there was afflicting of souls, the people were in festival mood on their special days. Though some sin offerings were always prescribed, most of these offerings were consecration and thanksgiving offerings.[90]

XII. THE LAW CONCERNING VOWS (Num. 30:1-16)

A. A MAN'S VOW (30:1-2)

1 And Moses spake unto the heads of the tribes of the children of Israel, saying, This is the thing which Jehovah hath commanded. 2 When a man voweth a vow unto Jehovah, or sweareth an oath to bind his soul with a bond, he shall not break his word; he shall do according to all that proceedeth out of his mouth.

A vow or promise in the sight of God is a serious and solemn thing. We are not to make vain or idle vows or promises.

B. A WOMAN'S VOW (30:3-16)

3 Also when a woman voweth a vow unto Jehovah, and bindeth herself by a bond, being in her father's house, in her youth, 4 and her father heareth her vow, and her bond wherewith she hath bound her soul, and her father holdeth his peace at her; then all her vows shall stand, and every bond wherewith she hath bound her soul shall stand. 5 But if her father disallow her in the day that he heareth, none of her vows, or of her bonds wherewith she hath bound her soul, shall stand: and Jehovah will forgive her, because her father disallowed her.

6 And if she be *married* to a husband, while her vows are upon her, or the rash utterance of her lips, wherewith she hath bound her soul, 7 and her husband hear it, and hold his peace at her in the day that he heareth it; then her vows shall stand, and her bonds wherewith she hath bound her soul shall stand. 8 But if her husband disallow her in the day that he heareth it, then he shall make void her vow which is upon her, and the rash utterance of her lips, wherewith she hath bound her soul: and Jehovah will forgive her.

9 But the vow of a widow, or of her that is divorced, *even* everything wherewith she hath bound her soul, shall stand against her. 10 And if she vowed in her husband's house, or bound her soul by a bond with an oath, 11 and her husband heard it, and held his peace at her, and disallowed her not; then all her vows shall stand, and every bond wherewith she bound her soul shall stand. 12 But if her husband made them null and void in the day that he heard them, then whatsoever proceeded out of her lips concerning her vows, or concerning the bond of her soul, shall not stand: her husband hath made them void; and Jehovah will forgive her.

13 Every vow, and every binding oath to afflict the soul, her husband may establish it, or her husband may make it void. 14 But if her husband altogether hold his peace at her from day to day, then he establisheth all her vows, or all her bonds, which are upon her: he hath established them, because he held his peace at her in the day that he heard them. 15 But if he shall make them null and void after that he hath heard them, then he shall bear her iniquity. 16 These are the statutes, which Jehovah commanded Moses, between a man and his wife, between a father and his daughter, being in her youth, in her father's house.

There is no double standard with the Lord. A vow is a vow regardless of the

[89] *Op. cit.*, I, 565, 566.   [90] *Op. cit.*, p. 148.

sex of the person. Every culture must have a way of making human intentions binding. A vow or promise may take the form of both a sworn statement or a signed document. A well-known exegete says:

> An important aspect of family life is brought out in this chapter. The Bible never considers a woman as a mere chattel. Her individuality is stressed and respected. A mature woman who lives alone is answerable only to God (vs. 9). A woman who is a member of a family is subject to a definite but limited oversight by the head of that family.
>
> The chapter begins by asserting that a man who makes a vow is bound by it, and cannot revoke it. A young woman who is living in her father's house, or a married woman, can make a vow, and must fulfil it unless her father or husband (as the case may be) cancels it. This he can do, if he chooses, on the day when he first hears of it, but not later on. If he interferes at a later time, he is as guilty before the Lord as if he had broken a vow which he had made himself (vs. 15).[91]

XIII. JUDGMENT UPON THE MIDIANITES (Num. 31:1-54)

A. ISRAEL TAKES VENGEANCE (31:1-20)

1 And Jehovah spake unto Moses, saying, 2 Avenge the children of Israel of the Midianites: afterward shalt thou be gathered unto thy people. 3 And Moses spake unto the people, saying, Arm ye men from among you for the war, that they may go against Midian, to execute Jehovah's vengeance on Midian. 4 Of every tribe a thousand, throughout all the tribes of Israel, shall ye send to the war. 5 So there were delivered, out of the thousands of Israel, a thousand of every tribe, twelve thousand armed for war. 6 And Moses sent them, a thousand of every tribe, to the war, them and Phinehas the son of Eleazar the priest, to the war, with the vessels of the sanctuary and the trumpets for the alarm in his hand. 7 And they warred against Midian, as Jehovah commanded Moses; and they slew every male. 8 And they slew the kings of Midian with the rest of their slain: Evi, and Rekem, and Zur, and Hur, and Reba, the five kings of Midian: Balaam also the son of Beor they slew with the sword. 9 And the children of Israel took captive the women of Midian and their little ones; and all their cattle, and all their flocks, and all their goods, they took for a prey. 10 And all their cities in the places wherein they dwelt, and all their encampments, they burnt with fire. 11 And they took all the spoil, and all the prey, both of man and of beast. 12 And they brought the captives, and the prey, and the spoil, unto Moses, and unto Eleazar the priest, and unto the congregation of the children of Israel, unto the camp at the plains of Moab, which are by the Jordan at Jericho.

13 And Moses, and Eleazar the priest, and all the princes of the congregation, went forth to meet them without the camp. 14 And Moses was wroth with the officers of the host, the captains of thousands and the captains of hundreds, who came from the service of the war. 15 And Moses said unto them, Have ye saved all the women alive? 16 Behold, these caused the children of Israel, through the counsel of Balaam, to commit trespass against Jehovah in the matter of Peor, and so the plague was among the congregation of Jehovah. 17 Now therefore kill every male among the little ones, and kill every woman that hath known man by lying with him. 18 But all the women-children, that have not known man by lying with him, keep alive for yourselves. 19 And encamp ye without the camp seven days: whosoever hath killed any person, and whosoever hath touched any slain, purify yourselves on the third day and on the seventh day, ye and your captives. 20 And as to every garment, and all that is made of skin, and all work of goats' *hair*, and all things made of wood, ye shall purify yourselves.

The seriousness of sin in the sight of God is here expressed. The Lord commanded that the Midianites were to be destroyed because their life of degradation and sin had reached the point where it endangered other people. "The wages of sin is death" (Rom. 6:23). This was not a personal quarrel between two peoples—it was a matter with which God was vitally concerned. The Midianites were idolaters and this was offensive to Jehovah; it required His attention. Personal attitudes and desires of revenge were irrelevant at this point. The seriousness of the situation is evident — their souls and bodies were jeopardized by this evil influence.[92]

91 MacRae, *op. cit.*, p. 192.   92 Clarke, *op. cit.*, I, 715, 716.

Each tribe made a contribution to the war effort. **Phinehas, the son of Eleazar the priest** (v. 6), was sent with the expedition. The leadership of God in this was symbolized by the presence of holy objects. The ark and its contents were to lead the way. It is probable that Phinehas was sent because his father Eleazar was advanced in years and could not endure the rigors of army maneuvers. It is not stated, but Joshua was probably in command of the military operation.

The unusual nature of this war is revealed in the fact that peaceful surrender was not offered to the Midianites. They had sinned so extensively against Jehovah that judgment was their due. The "cup of their iniquity" was full, and they had to be destroyed to keep their degradation from infecting Israel.[93]

The fearful judgment of death and destruction at the hands of the Israelites is beyond description. The people had committed what John calls "the sin unto death." Smick points out that the commandment in this instance is "no justification for any of the holy wars of the Christian era for the simple reason that in this era there has been no Moses to learn through revelation just when and where the sovereign God wills to avenge himself."[94]

It is to be noted that Balaam now receives his just reward. He induced the Israelites to commit sensuous sins and to eat food offered to idols. Balaam's disgrace is referred to by the New Testament writers (Jude 11; Rev. 2:14).

The judgment imposed upon the men, and apparently their wives, is harsh indeed, and apart from the ultimate consequences of sin there is no explanation. However, it must be remembered that God is the author and supporter of life and that He has absolute wisdom and administers unquestionable justice. It must be assumed that the harsh physical judgment did not preclude mercy for their souls, and certainly the children were taken safely into heaven.[95] The fearful nature of this event is seen in the minute ritualistic cleansing to which all participants were to submit themselves (vv. 19-20).

B. THE DIVISION OF THE SPOILS (31:21-54)

21 And Eleazar the priest said unto the men of war that went to the battle, This is the statute of the law which Jehovah hath commanded Moses: 22 howbeit the gold, and the silver, the brass, the iron, the tin, and the lead, 23 everything that may abide the fire, ye shall make to go through the fire, and it shall be clean; nevertheless it shall be purified with the water for impurity: and all that abideth not the fire ye shall make go through the water. 24 And ye shall wash your clothes on the seventh day, and ye shall be clean; and afterward ye shall come into the camp.

25 And Jehovah spake unto Moses, saying, 26 Take the sum of the prey that was taken, both of man and of beast, thou, and Eleazar the priest, and the heads of the fathers' *houses* of the congregation; 27 and divide the prey into two parts: between the men skilled in war, that went out to battle, and all the congregation. 28 And levy a tribute unto Jehovah of the men of war that went out to battle: one soul of five hundred, *both* of the persons, and of the oxen, and of the asses, and of the flocks: 29 take it of their half, and give it unto Eleazar the priest, for Jehovah's heave-offering. 30 And of the children of Israel's half, thou shalt take one drawn out of every fifty, of the persons, of the oxen, of the asses, and of the flocks, *even* of all the cattle, and give them unto the Levites, that keep the charge of the tabernacle of Jehovah. 31 And Moses and Eleazar the priest did as Jehovah commanded Moses.

32 Now the prey, over and above the booty which the men of war took, was six hundred thousand and seventy thousand and five thousand sheep, 33 and threescore and twelve thousand oxen, 34 and threescore and one thousand asses, 35 and thirty and two thousand persons in all, of the women that had not known man by lying with him. 36 And the half, which was the portion of them that went out to war, was in number three hundred thousand and thirty thousand and seven thousand and five hundred sheep: 37 and Jehovah's tribute of the sheep was six hundred and threescore and fifteen. 38 And the oxen were thirty and six thousand; of which Jehovah's tribute was threescore and twelve. 39 And the asses were thirty thousand and five hundred; of which Jehovah's tribute was threescore and one. 40 And the persons were sixteen

---

[93] *Ibid.,* I, 716.   [94] *Op. cit.,* p. 150.   [95] Clarke, *op. cit.,* I, 716.

thousand; of whom Jehovah's tribute was thirty and two persons. 41 And Moses gave the tribute, which was Jehovah's heave-offering, unto Eleazar the priest, as Jehovah commanded Moses.

42 And of the children of Israel's half, which Moses divided off from the men that warred 43 (now the congregation's half was three hundred thousand and thirty thousand, seven thousand and five hundred sheep, 44 and thirty and six thousand oxen, 45 and thirty thousand and five hundred asses, 46 and sixteen thousand persons), 47 even of the children of Israel's half, Moses took one drawn out of every fifty, both of man and of beast, and gave them unto the Levites, that kept the charge of the tabernacle of Jehovah; as Jehovah commanded Moses.

48 And the officers that were over the thousands of the host, the captains of thousands, and the captains of hundreds, came near unto Moses; 49 and they said unto Moses, Thy servants have taken the sum of the men of war that are under our charge, and there lacketh not one man of us. 50 And we have brought Jehovah's oblation, what every man hath gotten, of jewels of gold, ankle-chains, and bracelets, signet-rings, ear-rings, and armlets, to make atonement for our souls before Jehovah. 51 And Moses and Eleazar the priest took the gold of them, even all wrought jewels. 52 And all the gold of the heave-offering that they offered up to Jehovah, of the captains of thousands, and of the captains of hundreds, was sixteen thousand seven hundred and fifty shekels. 53 (For the men of war had taken booty, every man for himself.) 54 And Moses and Eleazar the priest took the gold of the captains of thousands and of hundreds, and brought it into the tent of meeting, for a memorial for the children of Israel before Jehovah.

The men of war were to turn over one five-hundredth part of the spoil to the Levites, either for sacrifice or for personal use. The congregation was to turn over one-fiftieth part of their share of spoil to the Levites. The war spoil was quite large. The Israelites took 32,000 females prisoner, 61,000 asses, 72,000 oxen, and 675,000 sheep. It is apparent that a great deal of spoil was taken from the Midianites which was not registered in the general accounting. Of this spoil the soldiers gave a considerable portion as an offering unto the Lord (v. 52).

XIV. REUBEN, GAD AND HALF OF MANASSEH SETTLE EAST OF THE JORDAN (Num. 32:1-42)

A. THE REQUEST OF REUBEN AND GAD (32:1-27)

1 Now the children of Reuben and the children of Gad had a very great multitude of cattle: and when they saw the land of Jazer, and the land of Gilead, that, behold, the place was a place for cattle; 2 the children of Gad and the children of Reuben came and spake unto Moses, and to Eleazar the priest, and unto the princes of the congregation, saying, 3 Ataroth, and Dibon, and Jazer, and Nimrah, and Heshbon, and Elealeh, and Sebam, and Nebo, and Beon, 4 the land which Jehovah smote before the congregation of Israel, is a land for cattle; and thy servants have cattle. 5 And they said, If we have found favor in thy sight, let this land be given unto thy servants for a possession; bring us not over the Jordan.

6 And Moses said unto the children of Gad and the children of Reuben, Shall your brethren go to the war, and shall ye sit here? 7 And wherefore discourage ye the heart of the children of Israel from going over into the land which Jehovah hath given them? 8 Thus did your fathers, when I sent them from Kadesh-barnea to see the land. 9 For when they went up unto the valley of Eshcol, and saw the land, they discouraged the heart of the children of Israel, that they should not go into the land which Jehovah had given them. 10 And Jehovah's anger was kindled in that day, and he sware, saying, 11 Surely none of the men that came up out of Egypt, from twenty years old and upward, shall see 'the land which I sware unto Abraham, unto Isaac, and unto Jacob; because they have not wholly followed me: 12 save Caleb the son of Jephunneh the Kenizzite, and Joshua the son of Nun; because they have wholly followed Jehovah. 13 And Jehovah's anger was kindled against Israel, and he made them wander to and fro in the wilderness forty years, until all the generation, that had done evil in the sight of Jehovah, was consumed. 14 And, behold, ye are risen up in your fathers' stead, an increase of sinful men, to augment yet the fierce anger of Jehovah toward Israel. 15 For if ye turn away from after him, he will yet again leave them in the wilderness; and ye will destroy all this people.

16 And they came near unto him, and

said, We will build sheepfolds here for our cattle, and cities for our little ones: 17 but we ourselves will be ready armed to go before the children of Israel, until we have brought them unto their place: and our little ones shall dwell in the fortified cities because of the inhabitants of the land. 18 We will not return unto our houses, until the children of Israel have inherited every man his inheritance. 19 For we will not inherit with them on the other side of the Jordan, and forward; because our inheritance is fallen to us on this side of the Jordan eastward.

20 And Moses said unto them, If ye will do this thing, if ye will arm yourselves to go before Jehovah to the war, 21 and every armed man of you will pass over the Jordan before Jehovah, until he hath driven out his enemies from before him, 22 and the land is subdued before Jehovah; then afterward ye shall return, and be guiltless towards Jehovah, and towards Israel; and this land shall be unto you for a possession before Jehovah. 23 But if ye will not do so, behold, ye have sinned against Jehovah; and be sure your sin will find you out. 24 Build you cities for your little ones, and folds for your sheep; and do that which hath proceeded out of your mouth. 25 And the children of Gad and the children of Reuben spake unto Moses, saying, Thy servants will do as my lord commandeth. 26 Our little ones, our wives, our flocks, and all our cattle, shall be there in the cities of Gilead; 27 but thy servants will pass over, every man that is armed for war, before Jehovah to battle, as my lord saith.

Reuben and Gad had many cattle and were weary from the hardships of driving the herd. When they saw that the lands of Gilead and Jazer were suitable for grazing cattle they requested permission of Moses to settle down on the east side of the Jordan River (vv. 2-5). Moses raised the question as to why they should be granted this special privilege when much fighting still remained before the rest of the brethren could settle down in the land beyond the river. Furthermore, Moses pointed out that this would have an adverse psychological effect upon the brethren and would invite jealousy on their part. Moses suggests that this would have the same effect upon the morale of the people as the evil report of the spies did thirty-seven years earlier.

Reuben and Gad propose that they build enclosures for their cattle and temporary shelter or cities for their children (v. 16). It has been suggested that they repaired the cities of the Amorites which they had taken. It appears that the wives stayed with the children and the cattle while the men crossed over Jordan to help subdue the inhabitants of Canaan (v. 26). Gad and Manasseh agree that they will not make claim to land on the other side (western) of the Jordan and that after they help secure the inheritance of the other tribes they will return to their own (vv. 18, 19). Moses agrees to let Gad and Manasseh carry out their proposal, but points out that if they do not abide by their agreement they will be sinning against Jehovah (v. 23).

B. THE REQUEST IS OFFICIALLY RECOGNIZED (32:28-42)

28 So Moses gave charge concerning them to Eleazar the priest, and to Joshua the son of Nun, and to the heads of the fathers' *houses* of the tribes of the children of Israel. 29 And Moses said unto them, If the children of Gad and the children of Reuben will pass with you over the Jordan, every man that is armed to battle, before Jehovah, and the land shall be subdued before you; then ye shall give them the land of Gilead for a possession: 30 but if they will not pass over with you armed, they shall have possessions among you in the land of Canaan. 31 And the children of Gad and the children of Reuben answered, saying, As Jehovah hath said unto thy servants, so will we do. 32 We will pass over armed before Jehovah into the land of Canaan, and the possession of our inheritance *shall remain* with us beyond the Jordan.

33 And Moses gave unto them, even to the children of Gad, and to the children of Reuben, and unto the half-tribe of Manasseh the son of Joseph, the kingdom of Sihon king of the Amorites, and the kingdom of Og king of Bashan, the land, according to the cities thereof with *their* borders, even the cities of the land round about. 34 And the children of Gad built Dibon, and Ataroth, and Aroer, 35 and Atroth-shophan, and Jazer, and Jogbehah, 36 and Beth-nimrah, and Beth-haran: fortified cities, and folds for sheep. 37 And the children of Reuben built Heshbon, and Elealeh, and Kiriathaim, 38 and Nebo, and Baal-meon, (their names being changed,) and Sib-

mah: and they gave other names unto the cities which they builded. 39 And the children of Machir the son of Manasseh went to Gilead, and took it, and dispossessed the Amorites that were therein. 40 And Moses gave Gilead unto Machir the son of Manasseh; and he dwelt therein. 41 And Jair the son of Manasseh went and took the towns thereof, and called them Havvoth-jair. 42 And Nobah went and took Kenath, and the villages thereof, and called it Nobah, after his own name.

The matter now becomes official, and the substance of the agreement is transmitted to Eleazar the priest and to Joshua and to the heads of the tribes of Israel who will have the responsibility to see that the agreement is carried out. As soon as Reuben and Gad fulfill their agreement they will be at liberty to return to Gilead (v. 29). Reuben and Gad reaffirm the agreement. The half-tribe of Manasseh is also included in the land allotment on the east side of the Jordan River.

XV. A SUMMARY OF ISRAEL'S JOURNEY (Num. 33:1-49)

1 These are the journeys of the children of Israel, when they went forth out of the land of Egypt by their hosts under the hand of Moses and Aaron. 2 And Moses wrote their goings out according to their journeys by the commandment of Jehovah: and these are their journeys according to their goings out. 3 And they journeyed from Rameses in the first month, on the fifteenth day of the first month; on the morrow after the passover the children of Israel went out with a high hand in the sight of all the Egyptians, 4 while the Egyptians were burying all their first-born, whom Jehovah had smitten among them: upon their gods also Jehovah executed judgments.

5 And the children of Israel journeyed from Rameses, and encamped in Succoth. 6 And they journeyed from Succoth, and encamped in Etham, which is in the edge of the wilderness. 7 And they journeyed from Etham, and turned back unto Pi-hahiroth, which is before Baal-zephon: and they encamped before Migdol. 8 And they journeyed from before Hahiroth, and passed through the midst of the sea into the wilderness: and they went three days' journey in the wilderness of Etham, and encamped in Marah. 9 And they journeyed from Marah, and

came unto Elim: and in Elim were twelve springs of water, and threescore and ten palm-trees; and they encamped there. 10 And they journeyed from Elim, and encamped by the Red Sea. 11 And they journeyed from the Red Sea, and encamped in the wilderness of Sin. 12 And they journeyed from the wilderness of Sin, and encamped in Dophkah. 13 And they journeyed from Dophkah, and encamped in Alush. 14 And they journeyed from Alush, and encamped in Rephidim, where was no water for the people to drink. 15 And they journeyed from Rephidim, and encamped in the wilderness of Sinai. 16 And they journeyed from the wilderness of Sinai, and encamped in Kibroth-hattaavah. 17 And they journeyed from Kibroth-hattaavah, and encamped in Hazeroth. 18 And they journeyed from Hazeroth, and encamped in Rithmah. 19 And they journeyed from Rithmah, and encamped in Rimmon-perez. 20 And they journeyed from Rimmon-perez, and encamped in Libnah. 21 And they journeyed from Libnah, and encamped in Rissah. 22 And they journeyed from Rissah, and encamped in Kehelathah. 23 And they journeyed from Kehelathah, and encamped in mount Shepher. 24 And they journeyed from mount Shepher, and encamped in Haradah. 25 And they journeyed from Haradah, and encamped in Makheloth. 26 And they journeyed from Makheloth, and encamped in Tahath. 27 And they journeyed from Tahath, and encamped in Terah. 28 And they journeyed from Terah, and encamped in Mithkah. 29 And they journeyed from Mithkah, and encamped in Hashmonah. 30 And they journeyed from Hashmonah, and encamped in Moseroth. 31 And they journeyed from Moseroth, and encamped in Bene-jaakan. 32 And they journeyed from Bene-jaakan, and encamped in Hor-haggidgad. 33 And they journeyed from Hor-haggidgad, and encamped in Jotbathah. 34 And they journeyed from Jotbathah, and encamped in Abronah. 35 And they journeyed from Abronah, and encamped in Ezion-geber. 36 And they journeyed from Ezion-geber, and encamped in the wilderness of Zin (the same is Kadesh). 37 And they journeyed from Kadesh, and encamped in mount Hor, in the edge of the land of Edom.

38 And Aaron the priest went up into mount Hor at the commandment of Jehovah, and died there, in the fortieth year after the children of Israel were come out of the land of Egypt, in the fifth month, on the first day of the month. 39 And Aaron was a hundred

and twenty and three years old when he died in mount Hor.

40 And the Canaanite, the king of Arad, who dwelt in the South in the land of Canaan, heard of the coming of the children of Israel.

41 And they journeyed from mount Hor, and encamped in Zalmonah. 42 And they journeyed from Zalmonah, and encamped in Punon. 43 And they journeyed from Punon, and encamped in Oboth. 44 And they journeyed from Oboth, and encamped in Iye-abarim, in the border of Moab. 45 And they journeyed from Iyim, and encamped in Dibon-gad. 46 And they journeyed from Dibon-gad, and encamped in Almon-diblathaim. 47 And they journeyed from Almon-diblathaim, and encamped in the mountains of Abarim, before Nebo. 48 And they journeyed from the mountains of Abarim, and encamped in the plains of Moab by the Jordan at Jericho. 49 And they encamped by the Jordan, from Beth-jeshimoth even unto Abel-shittim in the plains of Moab.

Time is taken now for making a written historical transcript of Israel's journey from Egypt to their present location. Many spiritual implications and applications may be drawn from this wilderness journey. A study of the places, persons and things shows definite spiritual meaning.

1. *Egypt.* The land of Egypt was the land of Ham, which means "black." The descriptive phrase, "black as sin" is well known and applies very well to Egypt since the name is a synonym for sin (Rev. 11:8-9). It was the land of bondage for the Hebrews, and as such their plight was almost hopeless. Their own resources were not sufficient to deal with the problem at hand. They were dependent upon help from the outside such as God gave to them through His servant Moses. Egypt is a type of the world of sin, and sinners struggling therein find the going hard.

2. *Pharaoh.* This Egyptian king ruled Egypt with an iron hand. A picture of satanic designs is presented in Exodus 1:7-22. Truly, here is a picture of Satan himself, who as "the prince of the world" holds his slaves in the bondage of sin. "Israel sighed by reason of the bondage and they cried and their cry came up unto God by reason of the bondage" (Exod. 2:23). Is this not a picture of

sinners, who, when they cry out to God in true repentance, get a sympathetic response from God?

3. *The Children of Israel.* The Hebrew children typify the people who become dissatisfied with the wages of sin and honestly long for a better life. When people are ready to turn from sin to righteousness there is always a great leader who is ready to take them from Egypt to Canaan. "Whosoever will may come." Even one sinner is important enough for the Guide of Heaven to lead an exodus to the promised land. Our Lord not only delivers us out of Egypt but He goes with us every step of the way.

4. *Moses.* Moses is a type of Christ who leads the people out of the land of sin. He was given to the people at just the right time, even as Christ came forth when the "fulness of the time was come." Moses is compared to Christ, the Great Deliverer (Deut. 18:15; Acts 2:23). He was "called the son of Pharaoh's daughter," but chose rather to "suffer afflictions with the people of God than to enjoy the pleasures of sin for a season" (Heb. 11:24-25). Moses was rich in every sense of the word. As the son of Pharaoh's daughter he was in line for the throne. He had all the social and economic advantages of Egypt at his command, but he chose rather to suffer poverty and privation with his people. Jesus, too, was rich, yet for our sakes He became poor that we through His poverty might become rich (II Cor. 8:9; Phil. 2:5-8).

Moses was rejected by his people. When Moses received his call to service he said, "behold, they will not believe me, nor hearken unto my voice: for they will say, The Lord hath not appeared unto thee" (Exod. 4:1). Jesus also "came unto his own, and his own received him not" (John 1:11).

God sent credentials with Moses so that the people might know that he was sent of God. The miracles that Moses performed were akin to the miracles of Christ. The miracles of Christ, as those of Moses, were intended to give credence to His divine commission.

From the Hebrews' desire to sacrifice unto God we learn that we cannot build our altar of worship in the "land of sin."

Pharaoh wanted them to offer their sacrifices within his borders. Moses was divinely compelled to go "three days' journey" from the land.

It is also necessary for true believers to get out of "Egypt." "Friendship with the world is enmity with God" (I John 2:15-17). It is impossible to serve the God of heaven and the god of this evil world at the same time. We must serve either one or the other (Matt. 6:24).

5. *Pharaoh's Imitations.* Pharaoh called his magicians together, and they duplicated many of the miracles. Satan also has a counterfeit religion, and its borders run so close to the genuine that many are deceived. Satan is religious, and as long as he can keep the people satisfied with a humanistic, rationalistic brand of religion he is happy. Imitating the real thing is much more effective than outright infidelity. Religion with some semblance of reality is always dangerous because there is enough truth in it to make it attractive. God wants fully committed Christians. Compromise is not in the true believer's rulebook. Without compromise Moses stated the case plainly and to the point: "There shall not an hoof be left behind" (Exod. 10:26). God demands complete separation from the world, sin and the will of Satan.

6. *The Passover* (Exod. 12:1ff.). In the Passover we see the redemptive work of Christ. The lamb was to be without spot or blemish, and its blood was to be sprinkled upon the doorpost and the lintel so that the death angel could see it. The applied blood was the key to life: without the blood, death was sure and certain. Paul tells us that "Christ, our passover, is sacrificed for us" (I Cor. 5:7). The importance of Christ's blood is symbolized in the blood of the Passover lamb. Jehovah informed the people that "the blood shall be to you for a token upon the houses where ye are: and when I see the blood I will pass over you" (Exod. 12:13). Many people in Egypt were good, moral, law-abiding citizens, but this was not enough. Only the blood availed.

With the assurance of safety the Hebrews were able to feast upon their lamb with peace of mind. They enjoyed communion and fellowship such as only the redeemed can have. The feast is not for unbelievers, but for those who have been redeemed by the blood of the Lamb.

7. *The Red Sea* (Exod. 14:9ff.). The children of Israel had now been delivered by the blood. At the Red Sea they were delivered from Egypt by the power of God. The Red Sea opened a path for the Hebrews, but when they had crossed, the angry waves closed in on Pharaoh and his men. The Red Sea means death — a separation from the forces of sin. The Red Sea experience might be called a type of water baptism marking the end of service to Satan and the beginning of service to God.

8. *The Redemption Song* (Exod. 15:1-21). When the Hebrews saw that Pharaoh and his army had been drowned in the sea they sang a song of victory. Is this not the thing that happens when we cross the red sea of salvation? Do we not find within us a compelling urge to sing the glad songs of Zion as an expression of praise and thanksgiving to God for saving us from our enemy, the devil? When we look at Calvary and see that our own sins are gone, we too enter into an understanding of the hymns that have been sung by the saints of other days. The song of Moses is a type of the Christian hymn.

9. *The Wilderness* (Exod. 17:1ff.). After the people had been redeemed for a few weeks the trials and hardships began to press in upon them. In the light of these physical hardships many began to think about the flesh pots and the garlic of Egypt. The natural outlook for survival was very dark. Wilderness testings came to them from every hand. This experience symbolizes the sad experiences many believers go through who do not hasten on to complete consecration. Neglecting prayer, Bible study and service is one of the wilderness dangers that believers must avoid. Every believer should become established by making his complete dedication to God. This is our reasonable service (Rom. 12:1-2). Clarke notes that the book of Numbers is the first recorded travel diary:

> We may consider the whole book of Numbers as a diary, and indeed the first book of travels ever published. Dr. Shaw, Dr. Pococke, and several others, have endeavored to mark out the route of the

Israelites, through this great, dreary, and trackless desert, and have ascertained many of the stages here described. Indeed there are sufficient evidences of this important journey still remaining, for the descriptions of many are so particular that the places are readily ascertained by them; but this is not the case with all. Israel was the Church of God in the wilderness, and its unsettled, wandering state under Moses may point out the unsettled state of religion under the law. Their being brought, after the death of Moses, into the promised rest by Joshua, may point out the establishment, fixedness, and certainty of that salvation provided by Jesus Christ, of whom Joshua, in name and conduct, was a remarkable type.[96]

XVI. LAWS REGARDING THE PROMISED LAND (Num. 33:50— 36:13)

A. CANAANITES TO BE DRIVEN OUT (33:50-56)

50 And Jehovah spake unto Moses in the plains of Moab by the Jordan at Jericho, saying, 51 Speak unto the children of Israel, and say unto them, When ye pass over the Jordan into the land of Canaan, 52 then ye shall drive out all the inhabitants of the land from before you, and destroy all their figured *stones*, and destroy all their molten images, and demolish all their high places: 53 and ye shall take possession of the land, and dwell therein; for unto you have I given the land to possess it. 54 And ye shall inherit the land by lot according to your families; to the more ye shall give the more inheritance, and to the fewer thou shalt give the less inheritance: wheresoever the lot falleth to any man, that shall be his; according to the tribes of your fathers shall ye inherit. 55 But if ye will not drive out the inhabitants of the land from before you, then shall those that ye let remain of them be as pricks in your eyes, and as thorns in your sides, and they shall vex you in the land wherein ye dwell. 56 And it shall come to pass, that, as I thought to do unto them, so will I do unto you.

The Lord commanded the Israelites to do a thorough job of driving the Canaanites from the land. It is quite likely that they had gained possession of the land by force at an earlier age, and they

were to suffer the same treatment they imposed upon former inhabitants.

The depraved nature of the Canaanites made it necessary that they be removed from the land for fear of infecting God's people with their lewd and sensuous worship of the reproductive forces of nature. Included in this cultic worship was temple prostitution and immorality of the most depraved kind. Clarke makes this comment:

> It has been usual among pious men to consider these Canaanites remaining in the land, as emblems of indwelling sin; and it must be granted that what those remaining Canaanites were to the people of Israel, who were disobedient to God, such is indwelling sin to all those who will not have the blood of the covenant to cleanse them from all unrighteousness. For a time, while conscience is tender, such persons feel themselves straitened in all their goings, hindered in all their religious services, and distressed beyond measure because of the law — the authority and power of sin, which they find warring in their members: by and by the eye of their mind becomes obscured by the constant piercings of sin, till at last, fatally persuaded that sin must dwell in them as long as they live, they accommodate their minds to their situation, their consciences cease to be tender, and they content themselves with expecting redemption where and when it has never been promised, i.e. beyond the grave![97]

The Canaanite system of worship was idolatry of the basest kind. Many kinds of sensuous and sexual symbols, pictures and objects characterized their ritual. Representations of the male sex organs (called poles) were prominently displayed at the "High Places" where worship was carried on. The sex act became a kind of sympathetic overture to the gods of nature, who in turn were expected to make the land fertile and the animals productive. All of these ritualistic objects were to be completely destroyed, and the inhabitants were to be driven out. The Lord warns the people that they will suffer serious consequences if they do not follow explicit orders. If the Canaanites are allowed to remain they will be as **pricks** in their eyes and **thorns** in their sides. These metaphors and figures of speech convey the warning that if they

[96] *Ibid.*, I, 721.   [97] *Ibid.*, I, 725.

permit these depraved idolaters to remain in the land they will be plagued and harassed on every side.

B. INSTRUCTIONS FOR ENTERING CANAAN (34:1-29)

1 And Jehovah spake unto Moses, saying, 2 Command the children of Israel, and say unto them, When ye come into the land of Canaan (this is the land that shall fall unto you for an inheritance, even the land of Canaan according to the borders thereof), 3 then your south quarter shall be from the wilderness of Zin along by the side of Edom, and your south border shall be from the end of the Salt Sea eastward; 4 and your border shall turn about southward of the ascent of Akrabbim, and pass along to Zin; and the goings out thereof shall be southward of Kadesh-barnea; and it shall go forth to Hazar-addar, and pass along to Azmon; 5 and the border shall turn about from Azmon unto the brook of Egypt, and the goings out thereof shall be at the sea.

6 And for the western border, ye shall have the great sea and the border *thereof*: this shall be your west border.

7 And this shall be your north border: from the great sea ye shall mark out for you mount Hor; 8 from mount Hor ye shall mark out unto the entrance of Hamath; and the goings out of the border shall be at Zedad; 9 and the border shall go forth to Ziphron, and the goings out thereof shall be at Hazar-enan: this shall be your north border.

10 And ye shall mark out your east border from Hazar-enan to Shepham; 11 and the border shall go down from Shepham to Riblah, on the east side of Ain; and the border shall go down, and shall reach unto the side of the sea of Chinnereth eastward; 12 and the border shall go down to the Jordan, and the goings out thereof shall be at the Salt Sea. This shall be your land according to the borders thereof round about.

13 And Moses commanded the children of Israel, saying, This is the land which ye shall inherit by lot, which Jehovah hath commanded to give unto the nine tribes, and to the half-tribe: 14 for the tribe of the children of Reuben according to their fathers' houses, and the tribe of the children of Gad according to their fathers' houses, have received, and the half-tribe of Manasseh have received, their inheritance: 15 the two tribes and the half-tribe have received their inheritance beyond the Jordan at Jericho eastward, toward the sun-rising.

16 And Jehovah spake unto Moses, saying, 17 These are the names of the men that shall divide the land unto you for inheritance: Eleazar the priest, and Joshua the son of Nun. 18 And ye shall take one prince of every tribe, to divide the land for inheritance. 19 And these are the names of the men: Of the tribe of Judah, Caleb the son of Jephunneh. 20 And of the tribe of the children of Simeon, Shemuel the son of Ammihud. 21 Of the tribe of Benjamin, Elidad the son of Chislon. 22 And of the tribe of the children of Dan a prince, Bukki the son of Jogli. 23 Of the children of Joseph: of the tribe of the children of Manasseh a prince, Hanniel the son of Ephod. 24 And of the tribe of the children of Ephraim a prince, Kemuel the son of Shiphtan. 25 And of the tribe of the children of Zebulun a prince, Elizaphan the son of Parnach. 26 And of the tribe of the children of Issachar a prince, Paltiel the son of Azzan. 27 And of the tribe of the children of Asher a prince, Ahihud the son of Shelomi. 28 And of the tribe of the children of Naphtali a prince, Pedahel the son of Ammihud. 29 These are they whom Jehovah commanded to divide the inheritance unto the children of Israel in the land of Canaan.

Special instructions are now given in matters of borders and boundary lines. The southern border is to be the inhabitable lands on the southern extremity of the Dead Sea. It is not likely that the borders extended into the barren desert areas which surrounded the Dead Sea on the south and east. One scholar explains the situation thus:

> The southern border: this started from the southern extremity of the Dead Sea, here called the Salt Sea (vs. 3), and proceeded in a S. W. direction to the Ascent of Akrabbim, i.e. "of scorpions" (vs. 4), a row of cliffs about 8 miles distant; thence it passed by way of Kadesh-Barnea to the River of Egypt, where it reached the Mediterranean Sea (vs. 5). The "River of Egypt" is not the Nile but a brook, now identified with the Wady el-Arish, flowing into the sea about 20 miles south of Gaza. It is frequently mentioned as the S. W. border of Canaan (see I Kings 8:65, II Kings 24:7, II Chr. 7:8, Isa. 25:12). This southern boundary was also the boundary

of Judah and Simeon (see Josh. 15:1-4, 19:9) .98

The western border (v. 6). The great sea here referred to is the Mediterranean Sea. The preface great is used to distinguish the Mediterranean Sea from lesser bodies of water such as the Dead Sea or the Sea of Galilee.

Your north border (v. 7). The Mt. Hor here referred to is not the mountain in Edom, but is probably some peak in the Lebanon range.

The side of the sea of Chinnereth eastward (v. 11) is the Sea of Tiberias, but better known as Lake Galilee. Part of the eastern border was to be along the Jordan River southward to the Dead Sea. This river is well known in both the Old and New Testaments. The Lord wrought many miracles — the flow of the river was stopped temporarily; both Elijah and Elisha separated its waters; Naaman, the Syrian, came here to take his "seven dips" (II Kings 5:1-14) , and it was here where John the Baptist baptized Jesus our Lord, and where the voice of God was heard concerning Him (Matt. 3:16, 17; Mark 1:5-11) .99

The promised land was cradled in natural protective barriers. The Mediterranean Sea flanked it on the west, the mountains protected it to the north, a belt of desert country in the east made it difficult for enemies to approach and the desert mountains and sand in the south provided a kind of buffer between Israel and the enemies to the south.

The land of Canaan is described by Jehovah as a good land — a land flowing with streams, where there was an abundance of wheat, barley, grapes, figs, pomegranates, olive oil and honey. There was also an abundance of iron and copper for their agricultural and industrial development (Deut. 8:7-9) .100

It is acknowledged that Reuben, Gad and the half-tribe of Manasseh were permitted to settle on the east side of the Jordan (v. 15) . Eleazar and Joshua were to divide the land among tribal heads (v. 17) . In the remaining verses the prince of each tribe is named.

C. CITIES OF REFUGE (35:1-34)

1 And Jehovah spake unto Moses in the plains of Moab by the Jordan at Jericho, saying, 2 Command the children of Israel, that they give unto the Levites of the inheritance of their possession cities to dwell in; and suburbs for the cities round about them shall ye give unto the Levites. 3 And the cities shall they have to dwell in; and their suburbs shall be for their cattle, and for their substance, and for all their beasts. 4 And the suburbs of the cities, which ye shall give unto the Levites, shall be from the wall of the city and outward a thousand cubits round about. 5 And ye shall measure without the city for the east side two thousand cubits, and for the south side two thousand cubits, and for the west side two thousand cubits, and for the north side two thousand cubits, the city being in the midst. This shall be to them the suburbs of the cities. 6 And the cities which ye shall give unto the Levites, they shall be the six cities of refuge, which ye shall give for the manslayer to flee unto: and besides them ye shall give forty and two cities. 7 All the cities which ye shall give to the Levites shall be forty and eight cities; them *shall ye give* with their suburbs. 8 And concerning the cities which ye shall give of the possession of the children of Israel, from the many ye shall take many; and from the few ye shall take few: every one according to his inheritance which he inheriteth shall give of his cities unto the Levites.

9 And Jehovah spake unto Moses, saying, 10 Speak unto the children of Israel, and say unto them, When ye pass over the Jordan into the land of Canaan, 11 then ye shall appoint you cities to be cities of refuge for you, that the manslayer that killeth any person unwittingly may flee thither. 12 And the cities shall be unto you for refuge from the avenger, that the manslayer die not, until he stand before the congregation for judgment. 13 And the cities which ye shall give shall be for you six cities of refuge. 14 Ye shall give three cities beyond the Jordan, and three cities shall ye give in the land of Canaan; they shall be cities of refuge. 15 For the children of Israel, and for the stranger and for the sojourner among them, shall these six cities be for refuge; that every one that killeth any person unwittingly may flee thither.

16 But if he smote him with an instrument of iron, so that he died, he is a murderer: the murderer shall surely be put to death. 17 And if he smote him with a stone in the hand,

98 Dummelow, op. cit., p. 120.   99 Clarke, op. cit., I, 727.   100 Ibid.

whereby a man may die, and he died, he is a murderer: the murderer shall surely be put to death. 18 Or if he smote him with a weapon of wood in the hand, whereby a man may die, and he died, he is a murderer: the murderer shall surely be put to death. 19 The avenger of blood shall himself put the murderer to death: when he meeteth him, he shall put him to death. 20 And if he thrust him of hatred, or hurled at him, lying in wait, so that he died, 21 or in enmity smote him with his hand, so that he died; he that smote him shall surely be put to death; he is a murderer: the avenger of blood shall put the murderer to death, when he meeteth him.

22 But if he thrust him suddenly without enmity, or hurled upon him anything without lying in wait, 23 or with any stone, whereby a man may die, seeing him not, and cast it upon him, so that he died, and he was not his enemy, neither sought his harm; 24 then the congregation shall judge between the smiter and the avenger of blood according to these ordinances; 25 and the congregation shall deliver the manslayer out of the hand of the avenger of blood, and the congregation shall restore him to his city of refuge, whither he was fled: and he shall dwell therein until the death of the high priest, who was anointed with the holy oil. 26 But if the manslayer shall at any time go beyond the border of his city of refuge, whither he fleeth, 27 and the avenger of blood find him without the border of his city of refuge, and the avenger of blood slay the manslayer; he shall not be guilty of blood, 28 because he should have remained in his city of refuge until the death of the high priest: but after the death of the high priest the manslayer shall return into the land of his possession.

29 And these things shall be for a statute *and* ordinance unto you throughout your generations in all your dwellings. 30 Whoso killeth any person, the murderer shall be slain at the mouth of witnesses: but one witness shall not testify against any person that he die. 31 Moreover ye shall take no ransom for the life of a murderer, that is guilty of death; but he shall surely be put to death. 32 And ye shall take no ransom for him that is fled to his city of refuge, that he may come again to dwell in the land, until the death of the priest. 33 So ye shall not pollute the land wherein ye are: for blood, it polluteth the land; and no expiation can be made for the land for the blood that is shed therein, but by the blood of him that shed it. 34 And thou shalt not defile the land which ye inhabit, in the midst of which I dwell: for I, Jehovah, dwell in the midst of the children of Israel.

The tribe of Levi was set aside to administer the religious affairs. They were not to engage in secular activities or pursuits but were to give their entire time to serve in a priestly capacity. One commentator says:

The tribe of Levi received no part of the land of Canaan as their inheritance (18:20-24, 26:62). By way of compensation they received the tithes for their support (18:21). It is here further provided that 48 cities with their suburbs be allotted to them out of the inheritance of the other tribes, for the maintenance of themselves and their herds. The carrying out of this injunction is recorded in Josh. 21, where it is also noted that the priests (the sons of Aaron) received 13 of these cities (vs. 4). The people as well as the priests and Levites, benefited by this arrangement, for the latter being dispersed throughout the land were able to instruct the people in the law and worship of God. On the duty of the priests and Levites to teach the people, see (Lev. 10:11; Deut. 17:8, 9; 33:10; II Chr. 19:8-10) .[101]

The measurements enumerated in verse 5 are most difficult to understand. It is probable that the area of the city was not considered in this formula. The city was conceived as a mathematical point, and all measurement to or from the city was reckoned from the absolute center or the "zero mile stone." The bounds of the city extended for 2,000 cubits in each of the four directions, thus giving a band of 2,000 cubits width on each side of the city.

It was the custom in Moses' day for the kinsmen of a murdered person to pursue and slay the murderer, a practice known in anthropology as "blood vengeance." Frequently innocent men died in a manner similar to mob action today. The cities of refuge were to be sanctuaries to which the accused person could go

101 Dummelow, *op. cit.*, p. 120.

until he could have a fair trial (see v. 12). If the death was accidental the person would be absolved of guilt and set free (vv. 11, 22-25), but if it was willful murder, the guilty person was to be put to death (vv. 16-21). Three of these cities were located on the east side of the Jordan and three on the west (see v. 14).

The Levites were to have supervision and control of the six cities of refuge, and in addition they were to have forty-two other cities, for a total of forty-eight. The purchase price of these cities was to be subsidized by the people. The amount each contributed was determined by the size of his inheritance (v. 8).

The congregation was to be the judge and jury to determine if death was accidental or by willful murder. The man who was thus declared innocent was to live in the city of refuge until the death of the high priest. It was declared that if the **manslayer** departed from the city of refuge before the death of the high priest, he would be considered **guilty of blood,** and would do so at the peril of his own life. After the death of the high priest he could **return to the land of his possession** (vv. 24-28). The seriousness of taking life is reflected in the supreme penalty which was imposed upon the murderer (vv. 30-34). One writer observes:

> Murder is such a serious crime that it cannot be atoned for by the payment of a money fine; nor can the man who has unintentionally killed another, purchase his release from the city of refuge before the death of the high priest. St. Peter reminds Christians that they were not redeemed with silver or gold but with the precious blood of Christ (I Pet. 1:18, 19).[102]

D. LEGISLATION REGARDING INHERITANCE (36:1-13)

1 And the heads of the fathers' *houses* of the family of the children of Gilead, the son of Machir, the son of Manasseh, of the families of the sons of Joseph, came near, and spake before Moses, and before the princes, the heads of the fathers' *houses* of the children of Israel: 2 and they said, Jehovah commanded my lord to give the land for inheritance by lot to the children of Israel: and my lord was commanded by Jehovah to give the inheritance of Zelophehad our brother unto his daughters. 3 And if they be married to any of the sons of the *other* tribes of the children of Israel, then will their inheritance be taken away from the inheritance of our fathers, and will be added to the inheritance of the tribe whereunto they shall belong: so will it be taken away from the lot of our inheritance. 4 And when the jubilee of the children of Israel shall be, then will their inheritance be added unto the inheritance of the tribe whereunto they shall belong: so will their inheritance be taken away from the inheritance of the tribe of our fathers.

5 And Moses commanded the children of Israel according to the word of Jehovah, saying, The tribe of the sons of Joseph speaketh right. 6 This is the thing which Jehovah doth command concerning the daughters of Zelophehad, saying, Let them be married to whom they think best; only into the family of the tribe of their father shall they be married. 7 So shall no inheritance of the children of Israel remove from tribe to tribe; for the children of Israel shall cleave every one to the inheritance of the tribe of his fathers. 8 And every daughter, that possesseth an inheritance in any tribe of the children of Israel, shall be wife unto one of the family of the tribe of her father, that the children of Israel may possess every man the inheritance of his fathers. 9 So shall no inheritance remove from one tribe to another tribe; for the tribes of the children of Israel shall cleave every one to his own inheritance.

10 Even as Jehovah commanded Moses, so did the daughters of Zelophehad: 11 for Mahlah, Tirzah, and Hoglah, and Milcah, and Noah, the daughters of Zelophehad, were married unto their father's brothers' sons. 12 They were married into the families of the sons of Manasseh the son of Joseph; and their inheritance remained in the tribe of the family of their father.

13 These are the commandments and the ordinances which Jehovah commanded by Moses unto the children of Israel in the plains of Moab by the Jordan at Jericho.

The problem of inheritance became more complex as the tribes grew in number, and the daughters began to marry outside their own tribe. One writer gives this interpretation:

102 *Ibid.,* p. 121.

Elders from the tribe of Manasseh complained that the legislation given concerning the daughters of Zelophehad (chap. 27) could result in the loss of Zelophehad's portion of their inheritance should his daughters marry outside their tribe. Moses under divine authority, agreed with this and required that the daughters of Zelophehad marry within their own tribe, Manasseh. The property was inalienable and could not be removed even from tribe to tribe (vs. 7). The principle of inalienable property Israel held in common with Near Eastern peoples long before she merged as a nation. The real estate contracts of a fifteenth century north Mesopotamian town, Nuzu, center around this principle. It continued to control the thinking of faithful Israelites even in the days of Ahab and Naboth (I Kings 21:3). Thus these women had to marry their paternal cousins (Num. 36:11), who could have been second or third cousins.[103]

[103] Smick, *op. cit.*, p. 154.

Bibliography

Anderson, C. A. "The Book of Numbers." *Old Testament Commentary*. Eds. H. C. Alleman and E. E. Flack. Philadelphia: Muhlenberg, 1948.

Boyd, J. Oscar. "Cushite." *International Standard Bible Encyclopedia*. Grand Rapids: Eerdmans, 1952 reprint.

Butzer, Albert G. "Numbers." *The Interpreter's Bible*. Vol. II. New York: Abingdon-Cokesbury, 1953.

Clarke, Adam. *The Holy Bible Containing the Old and New Testaments With a Commentary and Critical Notes*, Vols. I & II. New York: Abingdon-Cokesbury, n.d.

Discipline of the Methodist Church. Paragraph 86. New York: Abingdon-Cokesbury.

Dummelow, J. R. (ed.). *A Commentary on the Holy Bible*. New York: Macmillan, 1943.

Glueck, Nelson. *Rivers in the Desert*. New York: Farrar, Straus and Cudahy, 1959.

Gray, C. B. "Numbers." *International Critical Commentary*. 2nd edition. Edinburgh: T. and T. Clark, 1912.

Hanke, Howard A. *Christ and the Church in the Old Testament*. Grand Rapids: Zondervan, 1957.

————. *From Eden to Eternity*. Grand Rapids: Eerdmans, 1960.

————. *The Tabernacle in the Wilderness*. Grand Rapids: Eerdmans, 1952.

Henry, Matthew. *A Commentary on the Holy Bible*. New York: Funk and Wagnalls.

Jamieson, Robert. "Numbers." *A Commentary on the Old and New Testament*. Eds. R. Jamieson, A. R. Fausset, and D. Brown. New York: Revell, n.d.

Keil, C. F., and Delitzsch, F. *The Pentateuch*. Vol. III. Grand Rapids: Eerdmans, 1956 reprint.

Lange, J. P. "Numbers." *A Commentary on the Holy Scriptures*. Ed. J. P. Lange. Grand Rapids: Zondervan, 1956 reprint.

Longacre, Lindsey B. "Numbers." *The Abingdon Bible Commentary*. Eds. F. C. Eiselen *et al*. Nashville: Abingdon, 1929.

MacRae, A. A. "Numbers." *The New Bible Commentary*. Eds. F. Davidson *et al*. Grand Rapids: Eerdmans, 1953.

Marsh, John. "Numbers." *The Interpreter's Bible*. Ed. G. A. Buttrick. Vol. 2. New York: Abingdon-Cokesbury, 1953.

Saxe, Grace. *Studies in Hebrews*. Chicago: Moody, 1958.

Smick, Elmer. "Numbers." *The Wycliff Bible Commentary*. Eds. C. F. Pfeiffer and E. F. Harrison, Chicago: Moody, 1962.

The Book of Deuteronomy

by Howard A. Hanke

Outline

Introduction

The title "Deuteronomy," as it appears in our English Bible, is an anglicized form of the Greek compound word *Deuteronomion,* which means "second law" (*deuteros*=second; *nomos*=law). This Greek term is an interpretative paraphrase of the Hebrew title *Aleh Hadebarim,* which means "These are the words." In some of the Hebrew commentaries the rabbis call this book *Misneh Torah,* which means "the repetition of the law." Others call it *Sepher Tukhhuth,* which means "the book of reproofs."

This book is rightly referred to as "the second law" because it contains the Levitical laws and ordinances in a more concise and systematic form than previously given. (For date and authorship see General Introduction.)

HISTORICAL BACKGROUND

The book of Deuteronomy contains a record of Israel's activity in the wilderness over a five-week period, beginning on the first day of the eleventh month of the fortieth year after the Israelites left Egypt, and ending one lunar month later. The historical record extends seven days after the death of Moses at the age of 120.

A new generation had now grown up. Of the people who left Egypt, only Moses, Joshua and Caleb were still alive. The rebellious older generation had died in the wilderness. Most of the new adult generation was too young to remember anything of significance about the events of forty years in the wilderness. For their benefit Moses restates and records these events. Moses is very explicit in pointing out the importance of fearing, loving and obeying Jehovah. Moses repeats and explains the Ten Commandments, the ordinances, and the Levitical laws, and adds some which he had not delivered before.

The whole law is restated and reaffirmed in a most solemn manner, with an assurance that great blessings are in store for Israel when they obey, and fearful punishment when they disobey their God. The covenant between Jehovah and Abraham, Isaac and Jacob is revealed and restated to be equally binding upon this generation.

Prophetic statements concerning future events are clearly stated. Each tribe is prophetically blessed. Before his death Moses is permitted to view the promised land from the peak of Mt. Pisgah, the highest point in the Nebo or Abarim range. After viewing the land Moses died and was privately buried by God. At the end of the last chapter Joshua is introduced as Moses' successor. A thumbnail sketch of each chapter is given below:

1. Moses reviews the events which took place between Mt. Horeb and Kadesh.
2. Israel's journey from Kadesh to the Amorite country, where King Sihon was defeated, is narrated.
3. The conflict with Og, king of Bashan, and the division of the land formerly belonging to Kings Og and Sihon among the tribes of Reuben, Gad and Manasseh are described.
4. Moses exhorts the people to obey the laws of Jehovah and reminds them of the serious consequences awaiting them for disobedience. Bezer, Ramoth and Golan, on the east side of Jordan, are designated as cities of refuge.
5. Moses repeats the Ten Commandments and explains to the people what the law at Sinai meant to their fathers.
6. The people are exhorted to love Jehovah with all their hearts and are promised an abundance of good things.
7. Jehovah commands the people to destroy the Canaanites completely.
8. Moses reviews the many mercies which the people enjoyed in the wilderness and urges the new gen-

eration not to forfeit Jehovah's blessings through indifference and disobedience.

9. The people are informed that they will soon cross over the Jordan River, not because of their goodness but because of Jehovah's mercy.

10. Moses tells the people about the tragic events in connection with the second tablets of the law and reviews the events in their journey from Beeroth to Jotbathah. The Levites are chosen and the rite of circumcision is spiritualized by applying it to the heart.

11. Moses projects the mighty blessings Jehovah will bestow upon His people if they obey. The formulas of blessing at Mt. Gerizim and of cursing at Mt. Ebal are given.

12. The Israelites are commanded to destroy all vestiges of Canaanite idolatry and to make suitable animal sacrifices and offerings for their sins.

13. The people are warned against false prophets and idolatry.

14. A warning is given against practicing the heathen custom of cutting themselves at funerals. The law of clean and unclean animals is discussed and the people's duty of supporting the Levites is reiterated.

15. The people are to observe a whole year of rest every seventh year.

16. The feasts of Passover, Pentecost and Tabernacles are discussed. Judges and officers are appointed for judicial oversight.

17. The penalty for idolatry is defined; superior judges are to try the most difficult cases; and the duties of a king are projected.

18. Divination or fortune-telling is condemned; a great prophet is foretold; and ways of distinguishing false prophets are enumerated.

19. Regulations governing cities of refuge are given.

20. The philosophy of war is discussed; special regulations for military service are presented, and military disposition of the conquered Canaanites is explained.

21. Proper procedure for determining guilt when the murderer is missing is given; marriage with captives and the rights of the first-born are discussed.

22. Social regulations pertaining to lost property are given; suitable apparel for men and women is delineated; rules and regulations involving virginity and adultery are given.

23. Restrictions to be imposed upon eunuchs, bastards, harlots, Moabites and Ammonites are enumerated.

24. Laws concerning marriage, newlyweds, pledges and wages are listed.

25. Penal limitations are defined; laws regarding the remarriage of widows are stated.

26. The ceremonies relative to offering first-fruits and tithes are described; complete consecration to Jehovah is a declared obligation.

27. The words of the law are to be written on stone monuments and erected on Mt. Ebal; certain tribes standing on Mt. Gerizim are to bless the people for obedience, and other tribes on Mt. Ebal are to curse the people for disobedience.

28. The blessings for faithfulness and curses for disobedience are enumerated.

29. The covenant of Jehovah is interpreted to be binding on the present generation, as it was to their fathers.

30. Jehovah promises pardon for the penitent and punishment for the unrepentant sinner.

31. At the age of 120 Moses delivers a copy of the law to the priests, who are to read it to the congregation every seven years.

32. Moses gives a prophetical-historical song, and then is commanded to view the promised land from the peak of Mt. Nebo.

33. The twelve tribes receive their respective blessings.

34. Moses views the promised land from the top of Mt. Nebo, and then dies and is buried privately by Jehovah. At this point Joshua takes command. (For date, authorship and additional introductory information see General Introduction to the Pentateuch at the front of this volume.)

Commentary on Deuteronomy

I. MOSES REVIEWS THE LORD'S COVENANT (Deut. 1:1—4:43)

A. INTRODUCTION (1:1-8)

1 These are the words which Moses spake unto all Israel beyond the Jordan in the wilderness, in the Arabah over against Suph, between Paran, and Tophel, and Laban, and Hazeroth, and Di-za-hab. 2 It is eleven days' *journey* from Horeb by the way of mount Seir unto Kadesh-barnea. 3 And it came to pass in the fortieth year, in the eleventh month, on the first day of the month, that Moses spake unto the children of Israel, according unto all that Jehovah had given him in commandment unto them; 4 after he had smitten Sihon the king of the Amorites, who dwelt in Heshbon, and Og the king of Bashan, who dwelt in Ashtaroth, at Edrei. 5 Beyond the Jordan, in the land of Moab, began Moses to declare this law, saying, 6 Jehovah our God spake unto us in Horeb, saying, Ye have dwelt long enough in this mountain: 7 turn you, and take your journey, and go to the hill-country of the Amorites, and unto all *the places* nigh thereunto, in the Arabah, in the hill-country, and in the lowland, and in the South, and by the sea-shore, the land of the Canaanites, and Lebanon, as far as the great river, the river Euphrates. 8 Behold, I have set the land before you: go in and possess the land which Jehovah sware unto your fathers, to Abraham, to Isaac, and to Jacob, to give unto them and to their seed after them.

The life of Moses has been long and eventful. He has led the people out of Egypt to the plains of Moab, or the area adjacent thereto, where the Israelites are to make preparation for entering and possessing the land of Canaan. Shortly before his death, in the vicinity of Mt. Nebo, Moses calls the tribes to a general assembly at which he reviews the journey from Egypt to Moab. This is done, prob-

ably, for the benefit of the members of the young generation from twenty years old and upward who have now attained adulthood, and are to become the leaders in Israel. Many references are made to Moses as the spokesman. One writer says:

> The name of Moses occurs ninety-nine times in the New Testament and every reference throws light on this book. This is the first of several notices that the words were originally spoken; afterwards they came to be written. The ten commandments provide a parallel. Moses spoke to *all Israel*. This is one of the characteristic phrases of Deuteronomy. Called to lead the people at the time when they are being welded into a nation, Moses envisages the nation as a whole.[1]

The exact place where this discourse took place is not easy to identify. The KJV makes reference to an area "over against the Red *Sea*," but it is to be noted that *Sea* is italicized and does not appear in the Hebrew text. The ASV is the more accurate rendering and reads, **in the Arabah.** The Arabah is the trough-shaped valley extending from the Dead Sea to the Gulf of Akaba.

It took only eleven days for the Israelites to journey from Horeb to Kadesh-barnea. Even though they were only a few miles from the promised land, they were not permitted to enter it until the rebellious adult generation was dead. For the next thirty-eight and a half years they wandered around in the wilderness within view of Canaan. It was in the fortieth year after they left Egypt that Moses spoke his farewell message to the people (v. 3). This was a sad year for the Israelites. In the first month Miriam died (Num. 20), during the fifth month Aaron died (Num. 33:38), and at the end of the year Moses died.[2]

They had been camping near Mt.

[1] Quoted by G. T. Manley, "Deuteronomy," *The New Bible Commentary*, p. 197.
[2] Adam Clarke, *The Holy Bible Containing the Old and New Testaments . . . With a Commentary and Critical Notes*, I, 737.

Sinai for about one year. This is where they received the law, the priesthood and the tabernacle. With these three institutions they were in a position to carry on formal religious services. The time had now come for them to move forward toward their land of promise (v. 7).

The area which was assigned to the Israelites was very large. Apparently the Mediterranean Sea and the Euphrates River were to be theirs to occupy. Clarke says:

> Thus Moses fixes the bounds of the land, to which on all quarters the territories of the Israelites might be extended, should the land of Canaan, properly so called, be found insufficient for them. Their South border might extend to the mount of the Amorites; their West to the borders of the Mediterranean Sea; their North to Lebanon; and their East border to the river Euphrates: and to this extent Solomon reigned; (see I Kings 4:21). So that in his time, at least, the promise to Abraham was literally fulfilled.[3]

B. THE APPOINTMENT OF JUDGES (1:9-18; see also Exod. 18:13-27)

9 And I spake unto you at that time, saying, I am not able to bear you myself alone: 10 Jehovah your God hath multiplied you, and, behold, ye are this day as the stars of heaven for multitude. 11 Jehovah, the God of your fathers, make you a thousand times as many as ye are, and bless you, as he hath promised you! 12 How can I myself alone bear your cumbrance, and your burden, and your strife? 13 Take you wise men, and understanding, and known, according to your tribes, and I will make them heads over you. 14 And ye answered me, and said, The thing which thou hast spoken is good for us to do. 15 So I took the heads of your tribes, wise men, and known, and made them heads over you, captains of thousands, and captains of hundreds, and captains of fifties, and captains of tens, and officers, according to your tribes. 16 And I charged your judges at that time, saying, Hear the causes between your brethren, and judge righteously between a man and his brother, and the sojourner that is with him. 17 Ye shall not respect persons in judgment; ye shall hear the small and the great alike; ye shall not be afraid of the face of man; for the judgment is God's: and the cause that is too hard for you ye shall bring unto me, and I

will hear it. 18 And I commanded you at that time all the things which ye should do.

God had promised Abraham that his people would become a nation compared to the multitudes of the stars in the heavens (see Gen. 15:5). This promise was made at the time when Abraham did not have a male heir. Through divine intervention his wife Sarah conceived and bore Isaac. Jacob was born to Isaac and became the father of twelve sons (Gen. 29 and 30). This was the beginning of the twelve tribes of Israel, whose numbers can now be compared to **the stars of heaven for multitude** (v. 10). This greatly multiplied number is the basis for encouragement and faith in the promises of God. Kline says:

> The very circumstance that gave rise to the need for these judicial assistants to Moses, namely, the multiplication of Abraham's seed, was itself evidence of the Lord's faithfulness in fulfilling his promises (Gen. 12:2; 15:5) and thus afforded encouragement to Israel to advance in faith to take possession of Canaan. God's faithful mediator, reflecting the goodness of the Lord, prayed for the full realization of all the promises of the Abrahamic Covenant (vs. 11).[4]

The judicial responsibility for such a large number of people was more than Moses could discharge. He was commanded to appoint judicial assistants from among the most learned wise men (v. 13). From the statement **according to your tribes** it appears that each of these men was to be selected to serve the tribe of which he was a member.

The organization was similar to that which is operational in military organizations today. There were to be chief captains over a thousand men, and then this larger group was to be subdivided into groups of one hundred, which a lower-rank captain would command. These groups of one hundred were to be further subdivided into groups of ten, over which there was to be a lesser captain. In this arrangement it was possible to communicate with the entire nation by calling together the chief captains; justice could be administered at each level. If no satisfactory solution was found

---

[3] Ibid., I, 738.   [4] Meredith G. Kline, "Deuteronomy," The Wycliff Bible Commentary, p. 157.

at a lower level an appeal could be made to the next higher judicial category right on up to Moses himself — the supreme captain (see v. 17). Clarke says:

> What a curious and well-regulated economy was that of the Israelites! See its order and arrangement: 1 God, the King and Supreme Judge; 2 Moses, God's prime minister; 3 The priests, consulting him by *Urim* and *Thummim*; 4 The chiefs or princes of the twelve tribes; 5 Chiliarchs, or captains over thousands; 6 Centurions, or captains over hundreds; 7 Tribunes, or captains over fifty men; 8 Decurions, or captains over ten men; and 9 Officers, persons who might be employed by the different chiefs in executing particular commands. All these held their authority from God, and yet were subject and accountable to each other.[5]

This judicial system was to be absolutely just and fair to all, irrespective of their economic status (v. 17). It was clearly understood that in their administration the judges were acting in behalf of and in the place of God Himself. All of the judgments were to be in keeping with the concept that God was a holy and righteous judge and showed partiality to no man. This idea is expressed also in Deuteronomy 16:18 and John 7:24.

C. THE SPIES SENT FROM KADESH-BARNEA (1:19-33; see also Num. 13:1-33)

19 And we journeyed from Horeb, and went through all that great and terrible wilderness which ye saw, by the way to the hill-country of the Amorites, as Jehovah our God commanded us; and we came to Kadesh-barnea. 20 And I said unto you, Ye are come unto the hill-country of the Amorites, which Jehovah our God giveth unto us. 21 Behold, Jehovah thy God hath set the land before thee: go up, take possession, as Jehovah, the God of thy fathers, hath spoken unto thee; fear not, neither be dismayed. 22 And ye came near unto me every one of you, and said, Let us send men before us, that they may search the land for us, and bring us word again of the way by which we must go up, and the cities unto which we shall come. 23 And the thing pleased me well; and I took twelve men of you, one man for every tribe: 24 and they turned and went

up into the hill-country, and came unto the valley of Eshcol, and spied it out. 25 And they took of the fruit of the land in their hands, and brought it down unto us, and brought us word again, and said, It is a good land which Jehovah our God giveth unto us.

26 Yet ye would not go up, but rebelled against the commandment of Jehovah your God: 27 and ye murmured in your tents, and said, Because Jehovah hated us, he hath brought us forth out of the land of Egypt, to deliver us into the hand of the Amorites, to destroy us. 28 Whither are we going up? our brethren have made our heart to melt, saying, The people are greater and taller than we; the cities are great and fortified up to heaven; and moreover we have seen the sons of the Anakim there. 29 Then I said unto you, Dread not, neither be afraid of them. 30 Jehovah your God who goeth before you, he will fight for you, according to all that he did for you in Egypt before your eyes, 31 and in the wilderness, where thou hast seen how that Jehovah thy God bare thee, as a man doth bear his son, in all the way that ye went, until ye came unto this place. 32 Yet in this thing ye did not believe Jehovah your God, 33 who went before you in the way, to seek you out a place to pitch your tents in, in fire by night, to show you by what way ye should go, and in the cloud by day.

The people are commanded to enter the land of Canaan and possess it (v. 21). They are assured by the Lord that they have nothing to fear as long as they are obedient. Jehovah had commanded Moses to send spies into the land of Canaan to assess the land (v. 22; see also Num. 1:1ff.). Perhaps the purpose of this command was to encourage the people and stimulate their faith by giving them an opportunity to see the fruits of the land. It may also have been intended to give the leaders an opportunity to formulate their military strategy. The delegation of spies was to have representation from each of the tribes except the tribe of Levi (v. 23). Since the tribe of Joseph became two tribes (Gen. 48:8-22), and the priestly tribe of Levi was not numbered among the tribes (Num. 1:47f.), there were twelve spies (see Num. 13:4ff.). The spies brought back large quantities of the delicious fruit with the statement: "Surely it floweth with milk

---

[5] *Op. cit.*, I, 739.

and honey: and this is the fruit of it"
(Num. 13:27). The spies were all agreed
that the promised land was a good land
and to be desired. They even acknowledged, **It is a good land which Jehovah
our God giveth unto us** (v. 25).

Even though the land was fruitful,
there was an element of doubt as to
whether they were strong enough, militarily, to take the land. The ten evil
spies were afraid of the Anakim and their
strong, fortified cities (see Num. 13:28-
29). The tribes were induced to adopt
this defeatist interpretation of the situation. They **rebelled against the commandment of Jehovah.**

After the hardships of the desert began
to become more pronounced the people
began to blame Jehovah for all of their
troubles. They accused the Lord of
bringing them out of Egypt for the purpose of delivering them into the hands
of the Amorites. They indulged in self-
pity and accused the Lord of hating them.
The people were assured that the Lord
would fight their battles for them, even
as the Lord had undertaken for them in
their escape from Egypt and in their
survival in the wilderness thus far (vv.
30-31). Even though the Lord had given
them providential oversight and had
taken care of their needs the people refused to march on into the promised
land.

D. JUDGMENT PRONOUNCED UP-
ON ISRAEL (1:34-40; see also Num.
14:20-35)

34 And Jehovah heard the voice of
your words, and was wroth, and sware,
saying, 35 Surely there shall not one of
these men of this evil generation see the
good land, which I sware to give unto
your fathers, 36 save Caleb the son of
Jephunneh; he shall see it; and to him
will I give the land that he hath trodden upon, and to his children, because
he hath wholly followed Jehovah. 37 Also
Jehovah was angry with me for your
sakes, saying, Thou also shalt not go in
thither: 38 Joshua the son of Nun,
who standeth before thee, he shall go in
thither; encourage thou him; for he shall
cause Israel to inherit it. 39 Moreover
your little ones, and your children, that
this day have no knowledge of good or
evil, they shall go in thither, and unto

them will I give it, and they shall possess
it. 40 But as for you, turn you, and take
your journey into the wilderness by the
way to the Red Sea.

When the people refused to do as
Jehovah had commanded they were left
to take care of themselves. The Lord
withdrew His providential oversight and
pronounced a forty-year judgment of
hardship and wilderness wanderings. It
was decreed that not one of the adult
generation except Joshua and Caleb was
to see the promised land. The Lord said,
"Your dead bodies shall fall in this
wilderness . . . from twenty years old
and upward" (see Num. 14:29-33). Only
Joshua and Caleb, the two faithful spies
who said, "Let us go up at once and
possess it; for we are well able to overcome it," were actually to enter the land
of Canaan. Manley says:

Moses' thoughts now turn to the two men
of his contemporaries who were faithful,
Caleb and Joshua. The story of Caleb is
full of inspiration to all who are prepared wholly to follow the Lord. He is
mentioned first as being probably the
elder and the chief spokesman. *The
Lord was angry with me for your sakes.*
God's judgments are impartial, and
when Moses rebelled he too had incurred God's anger. The exact nature
of his sin is not made clear, but both
in transgression and in punishment he
was identified with the older generation.
As Moses begins to think of Caleb's entry
the bitterness of his own exclusion forces
itself forward, mitigated by the thought
of the transference of his charge to
Joshua, his trusted minister.[6]

E. ISRAEL'S DEFEAT AT HORMAH
(1:41-46)

41 Then ye answered and said unto me,
We have sinned against Jehovah, we
will go up and fight, according to all
that Jehovah our God commanded us.
And ye girded on every man his weapons
of war, and were forward to go up into
the hill-country. 42 And Jehovah said
unto me, Say unto them, Go not up,
neither fight; for I am not among you;
lest ye be smitten before your enemies.
43 So I spake unto you, and ye hearkened
not; but ye rebelled against the commandment of Jehovah, and were presumptuous, and went up into the hill-
country. 44 And the Amorites, that

6 *Op. cit.,* p. 199.

dwelt in that hill-country, came out against you, and chased you, as bees do, and beat you down in Seir, even unto Hormah. 45 And ye returned and wept before Jehovah; but Jehovah hearkened not to your voice, nor gave ear unto you. 46 So ye abode in Kadesh many days, according unto the days that ye abode *there.*

It is possible to persist in rebellion against God so long that punishment cannot be averted. The Israelites had "pushed their luck" too far and had reached the "point of no return" as far as punishment was concerned. In a superficial way the people admitted that they had sinned against the Lord, but true repentance was not evident. There was no indication of true godly sorrow such as results in salvation. We are told that "the sorrow of the world worketh death" (II Cor. 7:10). Their true heart condition is reflected in their determined effort to fight the enemy even though Jehovah had said, **Go not up, neither fight; for I am not among you; lest ye be smitten before your enemies** (v. 42). In their presumptuous self-sufficiency the people made a frontal attack against the Amorites, only to suffer humiliating defeat. Henry makes the following observation:

> God reminded them of their foolish and fruitless attempt to get this sentence reversed when it was too late. They tried to get Him to reverse his sentence by their reformation in one particular; whereas they had refused to go up against the Canaanites, now they would go up in all haste, and they girded on their weapons of war for that purpose. Thus, when the door is shut, and the day of grace over, there will be found those that stand without and knock. But this, which looked like a reformation, proved but a farther rebellion; God, by Moses, prohibited the attempt. "Yet they went presumptuously up to the hill." Acting now in contempt of the threatening, as before in contempt of the promise, as if they were governed by a spirit of contradiction; and it sped accordingly. They were chased and destroyed, and by this defeat which they suffered, when they had provoked God to leave them, they were taught what success they might have had if they had kept themselves in His love.

They also tried to get Him to reverse his sentence by their prayers and tears. "They returned and wept before the Lord." While they were fretting and quarreling, it is said "they wept that night;" those were tears of rebellion *against* God. . . . Note, tears of discontent must be wept over again; the sorrow of the world worketh death, and is to be repented of; it is not so with godly sorrow, *that* will end in joy. But their weeping was all to no purpose. "The Lord would not hearken to your voice, because ye would not hearken to his;" the decree was gone forth, and like Esau, they found no place of repentance, though they sought it carefully with tears.[7]

F. A REVIEW OF THE WILDERNESS EXPERIENCE (2:1-25)

1 Then we turned, and took our journey into the wilderness by the way to the Red Sea, as Jehovah spake unto me; and we compassed mount Seir many days. 2 And Jehovah spake unto me, saying, 3 Ye have encompassed this mountain long enough: turn you northward. 4 And command thou the people, saying, Ye are to pass through the border of your brethren the children of Esau, that dwell in Seir, and they will be afraid of you. Take ye good heed unto yourselves therefore; 5 contend not with them; for I will not give you of their land, no, not so much as for the sole of the foot to tread on; because I have given mount Seir unto Esau for a possession. 6 Ye shall purchase food of them for money, that ye may eat; and ye shall also buy water of them for money, that ye may drink. 7 For Jehovah thy God hath blessed thee in all the work of thy hand; he hath known thy walking through this great wilderness: these forty years Jehovah thy God hath been with thee; thou hast lacked nothing. 8 So we passed by from our brethren the children of Esau, that dwell in Seir, from the way of the Arabah from Elath and from Ezion-geber.

And we turned and passed by the way of the wilderness of Moab. 9 And Jehovah said unto me, Vex not Moab, neither contend with them in battle; for I will not give thee of his land for a possession; because I have given Ar unto the children of Lot for a possession. 10 (The Emim dwelt therein aforetime, a people great, and many, and tall, as the Anakim: 11 these also are accounted Rephaim, as the Anakim; but the Moab-

---

[7] Matthew Henry, *A Commentary on the Holy Bible,* II, 427.

ites call them Emim. 12 The Horites also dwelt in Seir aforetime, but the children of Esau succeeded them; and they destroyed them from before them, and dwelt in their stead; as Israel did unto the land of his possession, which Jehovah gave unto them.) 13 Now rise up, and get over the brook Zered. And we went over the brook Zered. 14 And the days in which we came from Kadesh-barnea, until we were come over the brook Zered, were thirty and eight years; until all the generation of the men of war were consumed from the midst of the camp, as Jehovah sware unto them. 15 Moreover the hand of Jehovah was against them, to destroy them from the midst of the camp, until they were consumed.

16 So it came to pass, when all the men of war were consumed and dead from among the people, 17 that Jehovah spake unto me, saying, 18 Thou art this day to pass over Ar, the border of Moab: 19 and when thou comest nigh over against the children of Ammon, vex them not, nor contend with them; for I will not give thee of the land of the children of Ammon for a possession; because I have given it unto the children of Lot for a possession. 20 (That also is accounted a land of Rephaim: Rephaim dwelt therein aforetime; but the Ammonites call them Zamzummim, 21 a people great, and many, and tall, as the Anakim; but Jehovah destroyed them before them; and they succeeded them, and dwelt in their stead; 22 as he did for the children of Esau, that dwell in Seir, when he destroyed the Horites from before them; and they succeeded them, and dwelt in their stead even unto this day. 23 And the Avvim, that dwelt in villages as far as Gaza, the Caphtorim, that came forth out of Caphtor, destroyed them, and dwelt in their stead.) 24 Rise ye up, take your journey, and pass over the valley of the Arnon: behold, I have given into thy hand Sihon the Amorite, king of Heshbon, and his land; begin to possess it, and contend with him in battle. 25 This day will I begin to put the dread of thee and the fear of thee upon the peoples that are under the whole heaven, who shall hear the report of thee, and shall tremble, and be in anguish because of thee.

It is evident that the period referred to in verse 1 relates itself to the forty-year period of wilderness wanderings. The people defied God and made a pre-

sumptuous attack upon Canaan with the hope that they could escape God's judgment. This unwarranted military indulgence resulted in complete disaster and ended in the wilderness graves.[8]

The mandate issued earlier to advance into Canaan is now repeated (v. 3). The exact route is difficult to identify because many of the places named are not now known, but the general route prescribed took them north of Edom and then on a southern detour down the Arabah back to the Gulf of Akabah and into the vicinity of Mt. Seir.

The enmity between the two brothers Esau and Jacob transmits itself into succeeding generations. At this time Esau blocks Israel's entry into Seir (Num. 20: 20). Later, Esau's descendants, the Edomites, aid and abet the Babylonians in their attack upon Jerusalem (see Obadiah).

Take ye good heed . . . contend not with them (vv. 4, 5). The Israelites are warned not to attack Esau or to renew old grievances. Kline says:

> The struggle for the birthright was long since settled; Canaan was Jacob's. Nevertheless, Esau had his possession, too, in Mount Seir (cf. Gen. 36), and Israel was forbidden to contend for it. (See Deut. 23:7, 8 for the relatively privileged position of the Edomites in Israel's assembly.) When the policy dictated by the Lord was followed, the Edomites refused passage through their land, thus compelling Israel to make a circuit about their borders. The Numbers passage (Num. 20:14ff.) does not say that the Edomites refused to sell provisions to the Israelites once it was clear that Israel was content to go around Edom. Moreover, Deut. 2:6 and 29 do not clearly state that Edom did sell provisions to Israel. For even 2:29a possibly refers only to the last clause in verse 28 (cf. 2:29b with 23:3, 4). Hence there is no contradiction between Numbers and Deuteronomy on this matter.[9]

Old wounds must be left to heal, and Israel is to do this by keeping her distance. The Israelites were commanded to treat the Edomites with respect and not to meddle in their affairs. They were to forgive and forget, even though the Edomites treated them unkindly. They were permitted to have some contact with

---

8 Kline, *op. cit.*, p. 158.   9 *Ibid.*, p. 158.

the Edomites, but only on a purely business basis. It is quite likely that Israel's limited association with the Edomites was similar to that which any passing stranger might have. The Israelites were to trade with them as neighbors and in a business manner. They were to pay for the meat and water which they used. They were to conduct themselves respectfully, even in relationship to their enemies.[10]

The Israelites faithfully obeyed the commandment of Jehovah to avoid unnecessary intercourse with the Edomites. To the north was Moab, where the descendants of Lot and Abraham lived. Here again the Israelites were commanded not to fight the Moabites. The Lord had given them providential oversight and had supplied all of their needs. Clarke says:

> God had given them much property, and therefore they had no need of plunder; they had gold and silver to buy the provender they needed, and therefore God would not permit them to take any thing by violence. Lot possessed this country after the destruction of Sodom and Gomorrah. Its inhabitants were generally esteemed as giants; probably they were a hardy, fierce, and terrible people, who lived, like the wandering Arabs, on the plunder of others. This was sufficient to gain them the appellation of giants, or men of prodigious stature.[11]

The Zered River or brook empties into the southern end of the Dead Sea and forms the southern boundary of Moab. With what faith and courage the people have left they are commanded to cross the rugged gorge cut by the mountain torrents of the Zered during the rainy seasons when cloudbursts are not uncommon. During the thirty-eight years spent in their wanderings between Kadesh-barnea and the brook Zered the adult generation died. A new generation is now ready to take over (vv. 14-17). The day of march has come (v. 18): Israel is now ready to possess the land which they could have taken nearly forty years before. They are now approaching Ammon located east and north of Moab (Deut. 2:18, 19; cf. 8b; Num. 21:11ff.).

Once again the Lord commands the people not to make trouble with a nation of people — this time the Ammonites (v. 19). Twice already they have been commanded to pass peaceably by nations in their pathway, i.e., Edom and Moab. It should be noted that Canaan was their destination, and that they were always to keep this fact uppermost in their mind. They could easily become so involved in the entanglements en route that they might forfeit their destination. This should also be a warning to Christians to avoid entanglements in the "wilderness of the world" through which they are passing. Henry says:

> The caution was given them, not to meddle with the Moabites or Ammonites, whom they must not disseize, nor so much as disturb in their possessions. Though the Moabites aimed to ruin Israel, Num. 22:6, yet Israel must not aim to ruin them. If others design us a mischief, that will not justify us in designing them a mischief. But why must not the Moabites and Ammonites be meddled with? 1. Because they were the children of Lot, (vs. 19) righteous Lot, who kept his integrity in Sodom. Note, children often fare the better in this world for the piety of their ancestors; the seed of the upright, though they degenerate, yet are blessed with temporal good things. 2. Because the land they were possessed of was what God had given them, and he did not design it for Israel. Even wicked men have a right to their worldly possessions, and must not be wronged. The tares are allowed their place in the field, and must not be rooted out until the harvest. God gives and preserves outward blessings to wicked men, to show that these are not the best things, but he has better in store for his own children.[12]

Rise ye up . . . pass over the valley of Arnon (v. 24). The valley of Arnon marked the southern boundary of the Amorites. Sihon, king of the Amorites, ruled from the Arnon to the Jabbok River, and to cross the Jordan River it was necessary to bring Israel within the borders of Sihon's kingdom. A spot near the Jordan River was their so-called launching site. Kline points out:

> The Amorites were protected by no such inviolability as the Edomites, Moabites, and Ammonites. The fact that an offer

[10] Henry, *op. cit.*, II, 427.   [11] *Op. cit.*, I, 742.   [12] *Op. cit.*, II, 428.

of peace was made to Sihon (2:26) indicates that his land in Trans-Jordania (which had earlier belonged to the Moabites and Ammonites; cf. Josh. 13:25; 21:26; Jud. 11:13) was not a part of Israel's promised land proper (cf. Deut. 20:10).

It was indeed the time when the Amorites should have ripened for judgment, which had been set as the hour for Israel's conquest of Canaan (cf. Gen. 15:16). With the spread of these Amorites across the Jordan, there was a corresponding extension of the territory that would fall into Israel's possession by conquest. Therefore a new divine order met Israel at the Arnon: "Begin to take possession and contend."[13]

G. ISRAEL CONQUERS SIHON
(2:26-37; see also Num. 21:21-30)

26 And I sent messengers out of the wilderness of Kedemoth unto Sihon king of Heshbon with words of peace, saying, 27 Let me pass through thy land: I will go along by the highway, I will turn neither unto the right hand nor to the left. 28 Thou shalt sell me food for money, that I may eat; and give me water for money, that I may drink: only let me pass through on my feet; 29 as the children of Esau that dwell in Seir, and the Moabites that dwell in Ar, did unto me; until I shall pass over the Jordan into the land which Jehovah our God giveth us. 30 But Sihon king of Heshbon would not let us pass by him; for Jehovah thy God hardened his spirit, and made his heart obstinate, that he might deliver him into thy hand, as at this day. 31 And Jehovah said unto me, Behold, I have begun to deliver up Sihon and his land before thee: begin to possess, that thou mayest inherit his land. 32 Then Sihon came out against us, he and all his people, unto battle at Jahaz. 33 And Jehovah our God delivered him up before us; and we smote him, and his sons, and all his people. 34 And we took all his cities at that time, and utterly destroyed every inhabited city, with the women and the little ones; we left none remaining: 35 only the cattle we took for a prey unto ourselves, with the spoil of the cities which we had taken. 36 From Aroer, which is on the edge of the valley of the Arnon, and from the city that is in the valley, even unto Gilead, there was not a city too high for us; Jehovah our God delivered up all before us: 37 only to the land

of the children of Ammon thou camest not near; all the side of the river Jabbok, and the cities of the hill-country, and wheresoever Jehovah our God forbade us.

The Israelites approached Sihon in a most conciliatory spirit. All they asked of King Sihon was the privilege of passing over the public highway. They assured him that they would stay on the road and that they would pay with money for all the food and water they should need during the period of their passage. Moses proffered peace to Sihon with the opportunity of trade with his people. By doing so, Moses did not disobey God, and in the end it left Sihon inexcusable for what happened.

Jehovah thy God hardened his spirit, and made his heart obstinate (v. 30). This is a difficult passage, and must be considered carefully in its total context. In Exodus 7:13 a similar passage is found. There it is stated that the Lord hardened Pharaoh's heart. First, it must be recognized that Sihon as well as Pharaoh was by choice outside the grace of God. Both were sinners by choice. Within this context God elects to use men as they are in carrying out His divine mission and plan. To put it bluntly: God uses both saints and sinners in His over-all plan to bring about redemptive ends. Clarke makes the following comment with regard to Pharaoh, and it can be assumed that the same principle applies to Sihon:

> The case of Pharaoh has given rise to many fierce controversies, and to several strange and conflicting opinions. Would men but look at the whole account without the medium of their respective creeds, they would find little difficulty to apprehend the truth. When the subject in question is a person who has hardened his own heart by frequently resisting the grace and spirit of God, it is but just and right that God should withhold those graces which he has repeatedly offered, and which the sinner has despised and rejected.[14]

The destruction of Sihon's kingdom was ruthless and complete. The sinful state of this nation had come to full fruition. Jehovah is given full credit for their victory (v. 36). Henry makes this

---

[13] Op cit., p. 159.   [14] Op. cit., I, 312.

observation with regard to Israel's conduct:

They put all the Amorites to the sword, men, women, and children (vs. 33, 34). This they did as the executioners of God's wrath; now the measure of the Amorites' iniquity was full (Gen. 25:16), and the longer it was in the filling, the sorer was the reckoning at last. This was one of the devoted nations; they died not as Israel's enemies, but as sacrifices to divine justice, in the offering of which sacrifices Israel was employed, as a kingdom of priests. . . . They took possession of all they had: their cities (vs. 34), their goods (vs. 35), and their land (vs. 36). The wealth of the sinner is laid up for the just. What a new world did Israel now come into! Most of them were born, and had lived all their days, in a vast howling wilderness, where they knew not what either fields or cities were, had no houses to dwell in, and neither sowed nor reaped: and now of a sudden to become masters of a country so well built, so well husbanded, this made amends for their long waiting, and yet it was but the earnest of a great deal more. Much more joyful will the change be which holy souls will experience, when they remove out of the wilderness of this world, to the better country, that is, the heavenly; to the city that has foundations.[15]

H. ISRAEL CONQUERS OG OF BASHAN (3:1-11; see also Num. 21: 31-35)

1 Then we turned, and went up the way to Bashan: and Og the king of Bashan came out against us, he and all his people, unto battle at Edrei. 2 And Jehovah said unto me, Fear him not; for I have delivered him, and all his people, and his land, into thy hand; and thou shalt do unto him as thou didst unto Sihon king of the Amorites, who dwelt at Heshbon. 3 So Jehovah our God delivered into our hand Og also, the king of Bashan, and all his people: and we smote him until none was left to him remaining. 4 And we took all his cities at that time; there was not a city which we took not from them; threescore cities, all the region of Argob, the kingdom of Og in Bashan. 5 All these were cities fortified with high walls, gates, and bars; besides the unwalled towns a great many. 6 And we utterly destroyed them, as we did unto Sihon king of

Heshbon, utterly destroying every inhabited city, with the women and the little ones. 7 But all the cattle, and the spoil of the cities, we took for a prey unto ourselves. 8 And we took the land at that time out of the hand of the two kings of the Amorites that were beyond the Jordan, from the valley of the Arnon unto mount Hermon 9 (which Hermon the Sidonians call Sirion, and the Amorites call it Senir); 10 all the cities of the plain, and all Gilead, and all Bashan, unto Salecah and Edrei, cities of the kingdom of Og in Bashan. 11 (For only Og king of Bashan remained of the remnant of the Rephaim; behold, his bedstead was a bedstead of iron; is it not in Rabbah of the children of Ammon? nine cubits was the length thereof, and four cubits the breadth of it, after the cubit of a man.)

Og, the king of Bashan, and his people had forfeited their right to continued existence because of the degree of sin into which they had evolved. They were to receive the same ruthless punishment that was imposed upon Sihon, king of the Amorites (v. 2). The natural strength of the Hebrews was inadequate to conquer Og. All the cities of Bashan were walled, fortified cities. Under the direction and with the power of the Lord the Hebrews were able to destroy completely this powerful military nation (see notes on 2:34).

Og was a formidable prince. He was the last survivor of a race of giants, and as such had great strength. His bedstead was preserved by the Ammonites, and it gives us suggestions of how great his strength was. His weight may be estimated by the materials of his bedstead: it was of iron, as if a bedstead of wood would not have been sufficient to support him. The size of the bed gives some indication of the size of the man: it was nine cubits long, and four cubits broad. If a cubit be assumed to be half a yard, the bed was four and a half yards long, and two yards broad. If he be allowed two extra cubits for free movement he may still have been three and a half yards high, double the stature of an ordinary man, and well-proportioned.

Even with all the strength of Og, the Israelites smote him (v. 3). We see that when God pleads His people's cause, He

15 *Op. cit.*, II, 429.

can deal with giants as with grasshoppers. No man's might can protect him against the Almighty. The army of Og was very powerful, for he had the command of sixty fortified cities, besides unwalled towns (v. 5). Yet all this was nothing before God's people of Israel when they came with a commission to destroy him.[16]

The Hebrews took full possession of the conquered land. They now had in their control all the fruitful country east of Jordan between the River Arnon and Mount Hermon (v. 8). Moses was to be deprived of entering the promised land, but was encouraged to see, in the victory of Israel, the promises of God fulfilled in its behalf.

I. REUBEN, GAD AND MANASSEH SETTLE EAST OF THE JORDAN (3:12-22; see also Num. 32:1-42)

12 And this land we took in possession at that time: from Aroer, which is by the valley of the Arnon, and half the hill-country of Gilead, and the cities thereof, gave I unto the Reubenites and to the Gadites: 13 and the rest of Gilead, and all Bashan, the kingdom of Og, gave I unto the half-tribe of Manasseh; all the region of Argob, even all Bashan. (The same is called the land of Rephaim. 14 Jair the son of Manasseh took all the region of Argob, unto the border of the Geshurites and the Maacathites, and called them, even Bashan, after his own name, Havvoth-jair, unto this day.) 15 And I gave Gilead unto Machir. 16 And unto the Reubenites and unto the Gadites I gave from Gilead even unto the valley of the Arnon, the middle of the valley, and the border *thereof*, even unto the river Jabbok, which is the border of the children of Ammon; 17 the Arabah also, and the Jordan and the border *thereof*, from Chinnereth even unto the sea of the Arabah, the Salt Sea, under the slopes of Pisgah eastward.

18 And I commanded you at that time, saying, Jehovah your God hath given you this land to possess it: ye shall pass over armed before your brethren the children of Israel, all the men of valor. 19 But your wives, and your little ones, and your cattle (I know that ye have much cattle), shall abide in your cities which I have given you, 20 until Jehovah give rest unto your brethren, as unto you, and they also possess the land which Jehovah your God giveth them beyond the Jordan: then shall ye return every man unto his pos-

session, which I have given you. 21 And I commanded Joshua at that time, saying, Thine eyes have seen all that Jehovah your God hath done unto these two kingdoms whither thou goest over. 22 Ye shall not fear them; for Jehovah your God, he it is that fighteth for you.

After the conquest of the area east of the Jordan a division was made of the land among those who requested to settle there. Joseph's allotment was divided between Ephraim and Manasseh. Manasseh received one-half of his inheritance on the east side of the Jordan and the other on the west. One-half of the hill country of Gilead went to the Reubenites and to the Gadites. The rest of Gilead and all of Bashan were given to Manasseh (v. 13). It was strictly understood that the two-and-one-half tribes who settled on the east side of the Jordan River were to cross over and help the rest of the tribes possess their inheritance before they were to settle down in their land (see notes on Num. 32:1-27). Henry says:

Moses repeats the condition of the grant which they had already agreed to (vs. 18-20): that they should send a strong detachment over Jordan to lead the van in the conquest of Canaan, who should not return to their families, at least not to settle (though for a time they might retire thither into winter-quarters at the end of a campaign) till they had seen their brethren in as full possession of their respective allotments, as themselves were now in of theirs. They must hereby be taught not to look at their own things only, but at the things of others (Phil. 2:4). When we are at rest, we should desire to see our brethren at rest too, and should be ready to do what we can towards it; for we are not born for ourselves, but are members one of another.[17]

The wives and the children of the two-and-one-half tribes were to stay in the shelter of the cities on the east side of the Jordan River, while the men went over to help their brethren possess their allotted territory (v. 19).

J. MOSES IS FORBIDDEN TO ENTER CANAAN (3:23-29)

23 And I besought Jehovah at that time, saying, 24 O Lord Jehovah, thou

---

[16] *Ibid.*, II, 429.   [17] *Op. cit.*, II, 430.

hast begun to show thy servant thy greatness, and thy strong hand: for what god is there in heaven or in earth, that can do according to thy works, and according to thy mighty acts? 25 Let me go over, I pray thee, and see the good land that is beyond the Jordan, that goodly mountain, and Lebanon. 26 But Jehovah was wroth with me for your sakes, and hearkened not unto me; and Jehovah said unto me, Let it suffice thee; speak no more unto me of this matter. 27 Get thee up unto the top of Pisgah, and lift up thine eyes westward, and northward, and southward, and eastward, and behold with thine eyes: for thou shalt not go over this Jordan. 28 But charge Joshua, and encourage him, and strengthen him; for he shall go over before this people, and he shall cause them to inherit the land which thou shalt see. 29 So we abode in the valley over against Bethpeor.

Moses gives testimony to the greatness of the Lord and pleads that he may have the privilege of at least entering the land of Canaan, but this privilege is denied him (v. 26). The prayer of Moses recorded in these two verses is very touching. Moses had suffered much in body and mind in bringing the people to the borders of Canaan, and yet he was not permitted to enter the promised land. However, God did permit him to view the land from afar.[18]

Even though Moses was denied the privilege of crossing over to Canaan, the Lord arranged for him to view the promised land from the top of Mt. Pisgah, a high point in the Nebo (Abarim) range. A view at this point is very advantageous and satisfying. From this place it is possible to see the fertile Jericho area as well as the beautiful hill country around Jerusalem and Hebron. This view assured Moses that the land was indeed good and to be desired. Joshua was commissioned to lead the people into the land of promise (v. 28).

K. MOSES COMMANDS OBEDIENCE
(4:1-8)

1 And now, O Israel, hearken unto the statutes and unto the ordinances, which I teach you, to do them; that ye may live, and go in and possess the land which Jehovah, the God of your fathers, giveth you. 2 Ye shall not add unto the word

which I command you, neither shall ye diminish from it, that ye may keep the commandments of Jehovah your God which I command you. 3 Your eyes have seen what Jehovah did because of Baal-peor; for all the men that followed Baal-peor, Jehovah thy God hath destroyed them from the midst of thee. 4 But ye that did cleave unto Jehovah your God are alive every one of you this day. 5 Behold, I have taught you statutes and ordinances, even as Jehovah my God commanded me, that ye should do so in the midst of the land whither ye go in to possess it. 6 Keep therefore and do them; for this is your wisdom and your understanding in the sight of the peoples, that shall hear all these statutes, and say, Surely this great nation is a wise and understanding people. 7 For what great nation is there, that hath a god so nigh unto them, as Jehovah our God is whensoever we call upon him? 8 And what great nation is there, that hath statutes and ordinances so righteous as all this law, which I set before you this day?

The rights and privileges of Canaan demanded absolute obedience. The Israelites were to keep the ordinances and statutes which had been spelled out during their journey. Moses emphasized the importance of faithful dedication to God. By "hearken, O Israel" is meant not only to listen but to listen attentively when the Book of the Law was read so that they might translate the written word into everyday life.[19]

God's laws are immutable and must not be amended or abridged. The Israelites were to refrain from adding to the law because God's law was perfectly conceived and revealed and any addition would be an adulteration. On the other hand, they were not to leave some part of the law unobserved. They were not to omit the good which the law required. Scott says:

> Moses commands obedience to the statutes and judgments. This will insure life, entrance into and possession of the land. The laws are not to be tampered with in the interests of human weakness. The experience at Baalpeor (i.e., the place sacred to the local god of Peor) was a warning. Those who turned to heathenism are dead; those who resolutely clung to Jehovah are alive. If Israel will only be obedient, then his wisdom will be proved and his religion and morality will

---

[18] Clarke, op. cit., I, 745.   [19] Henry, op. cit., II, 432.

excite the admiration of surrounding nations.[20]

All of the religious systems of the world at this time were wicked, obscene and demoralizing. Nature cults involving sex in their ritual were prevalent on every hand. The moral and religious state of this heathen culture are well described by Paul (see Rom. 1:18-32).

Even the nations of the world recognized that Israel had something unique and to be desired. The nations of the earth have borrowed from Israel's legal, moral and civil codes. If the Mosaic element were to be removed from the laws of civilized nations, little of value would remain.[21]

L. WARNINGS AGAINST IDOLATRY (4:9-40)

9 Only take heed to thyself, and keep thy soul diligently, lest thou forget the things which thine eyes saw, and lest they depart from thy heart all the days of thy life; but make them known unto thy children and thy children's children; 10 the day that thou stoodest before Jehovah thy God in Horeb, when Jehovah said unto me, Assemble me the people, and I will make them hear my words, that they may learn to fear me all the days that they live upon the earth, and that they may teach their children. 11 And ye came near and stood under the mountain; and the mountain burned with fire unto the heart of heaven, with darkness, cloud, and thick darkness. 12 And Jehovah spake unto you out of the midst of the fire: ye heard the voice of words, but ye saw no form; only *ye heard* a voice. 13 And he declared unto you his covenant, which he commanded you to perform, even the ten commandments; and he wrote them upon two tables of stone. 14 And Jehovah commanded me at that time to teach you statutes and ordinances, that ye might do them in the land whither ye go over to possess it.

15 Take ye therefore good heed unto yourselves; for ye saw no manner of form on the day that Jehovah spake unto you in Horeb out of the midst of the fire; 16 lest ye corrupt yourselves, and make you a graven image in the form of any figure, the likeness of male or female, 17 the likeness of any beast that is on the earth, the likeness of any winged bird that flieth in the heavens, 18 the likeness of anything that creepeth on the ground, the likeness of any fish that is in the water under the earth; 19 and lest thou lift up thine eyes unto heaven, and when thou seest the sun and the moon and the stars, even all the host of heaven, thou be drawn away and worship them, and serve them, which Jehovah thy God hath allotted unto all the peoples under the whole heaven. 20 But Jehovah hath taken you, and brought you forth out of the iron furnace, out of Egypt, to be unto him a people of inheritance, as at this day. 21 Furthermore Jehovah was angry with me for your sakes, and sware that I should not go over the Jordan, and that I should not go in unto that good land, which Jehovah thy God giveth thee for an inheritance: 22 but I must die in this land, I must not go over the Jordan; but ye shall go over, and possess that good land. 23 Take heed unto yourselves, lest ye forget the covenant of Jehovah your God, which he made with you, and make you a graven image in the form of anything which Jehovah thy God hath forbidden thee. 24 For Jehovah thy God is a devouring fire, a jealous God.

25 When thou shalt beget children, and children's children, and ye shall have been long in the land, and shall corrupt yourselves, and make a graven image in the form of anything, and shall do that which is evil in the sight of Jehovah thy God, to provoke him to anger; 26 I call heaven and earth to witness against you this day, that ye shall soon utterly perish from off the land whereunto ye go over the Jordan to possess it; ye shall not prolong your days upon it, but shall utterly be destroyed. 27 And Jehovah will scatter you among the peoples, and ye shall be left few in number among the nations, whither Jehovah shall lead you away. 28 And there ye shall serve gods, the work of men's hands, wood and stone, which neither see, nor hear, nor eat, nor smell. 29 But from thence ye shall seek Jehovah thy God, and thou shalt find him, when thou searchest after him with all thy heart and with all thy soul. 30 When thou art in tribulation, and all these things are come upon thee, in the latter days thou shalt return to Jehovah thy God, and hearken unto his voice: 31 for Jehovah thy God is a merciful God; he will not fail thee, neither destroy thee, nor forget the covenant of thy fathers which he sware unto them.

32 For ask now of the days that are past, which were before thee, since the

---

[20] D. Russell Scott, "Deuteronomy," *Abingdon Bible Commentary*, p. 324. [21] Clarke, *op. cit.*, I, 747.

day that God created man upon the earth, and from the one end of heaven unto the other, whether there hath been *any such thing* as this great thing is, or hath been heard like it? 33 Did ever a people hear the voice of God speaking out of the midst of the fire, as thou hast heard, and live? 34 Or hath God assayed to go and take him a nation from the midst of *another* nation, by trials, by signs, and by wonders, and by war, and by a mighty hand, and by an outstretched arm, and by great terrors, according to all that Jehovah your God did for you in Egypt before your eyes? 35 Unto thee it was showed, that thou mightest know that Jehovah he is God; there is none else besides him. 36 Out of heaven he made thee to hear his voice, that he might instruct thee: and upon earth he made thee to see his great fire; and thou heardest his words out of the midst of the fire. 37 And because he loved thy fathers, therefore he chose their seed after them, and brought thee out with his presence, with his great power, out of Egypt; 38 to drive out nations from before thee greater and mightier than thou, to bring thee in, to give thee their land for an inheritance, as at this day. 39 Know therefore this day, and lay it to thy heart, that Jehovah he is God in heaven above and upon the earth beneath: there is none else. 40 And thou shalt keep his statutes, and his commandments, which I command thee this day, that it may go well with thee, and with thy children after thee, and that thou mayest prolong thy days in the land, which Jehovah thy God giveth thee, for ever.

The children of God were to be constantly mindful of their ultimate and eternal interests. Soul as well as body was to be carefully considered in their over-all activities. The Levitical ritual was to be a constant reminder to them that they were "chosen people" to accomplish a "holy mission" for the Lord. Much depended upon them, because in the possession of the Israelite nation were the reception, preservation and recording of the "holy oracles." They were God's human channel through which the Messiah was to be revealed. Spiritual diligence is always demanded in the interest of spiritual integrity. Clarke says:

It is not sufficient to lay up divine things in the memory, they must be laid up in

the heart. "Thy word have I hidden in my heart," says David, "that I might not sin against thee." The life of God in the soul of man can alone preserve the soul to life everlasting; and this grace must be retained all the days of our life. When Adam fell, his condition was not meliorated by the reflection that he had been once in paradise; nor does it avail Satan now that he was once an angel of light. Those who let the grace of God depart from their hearts, lose that grace; and those who lose the grace, fall from the grace; and as some have fallen and risen no more, so may others; therefore take heed to thyself. Were it impossible for men finally to fall from the grace of God, exhortations of this kind had never been given, because they would have been unnecessary, and God never does an unnecessary thing.[22]

The older generation is now dead and those of twenty years old and upward have now become the leaders. Since they are too young to know or remember much about the wilderness experience, Moses reviews for them the providential care God has exercised over them. Not only are they to be informed, but they are to teach their children in the ways of the Lord. It is obvious that the rebellious, sinful generation that died in the wilderness had so apostatized that they were not able, nor did they have a mind to teach this generation now being addressed by Moses. (The spiritual significance of the wilderness journey is given in comments under Num. 33:1-41.)

The appearances of deity to man in the Old Testament are shrouded in mystery (v. 15). The angel (*Malak*) of God or of Jehovah is a frequent mode of God's manifestation of Himself in human form, for special purposes. In many passages it is assumed that God and His angel are the same being, and the names are used synonymously (Gen. 16:7ff.; 22:15, 16; Exod. 3:2-4; Judg. 2:4, 5). The angel's identification with the Messiah and the Logos (Word-Christ) is obvious and evident — the latter terms being more definite in their expression of God's revelation to man. Here Christ carries on the office of Redeemer in behalf of God's over-all redemptive program during the Old Testament period.

Professor Sauer is in agreement. He

[22] *Op. cit.*, I, 747.

points out that the "spiritual significance of the covenant with Abraham is also the reason, in the history of redemption, that the angel of the Lord comes forward." As the church fathers had already recognized, this is no less a person than the Son of God Himself, the Word (John 1:1; Rev. 19:13; Prov. 8:22, 23), who appeared later in Christ (John 1:14). Therefore He plainly calls Himself "God" (Exod. 3:2, 6), and is so named (Exod. 3:2). Nothing is more fitting than that just here the Son of God Himself should appear, indicating at one and the same time His oneness with God and also a certain self-distinction from God. To the father of the "seed" (Gal. 3:6) appears the "Seed" Himself as the "messenger," the "angel of the Lord" (Gen. 22:11, 15), and from now on through the whole Old Testament there runs an organic unfolding of this veiled self-revelation of the Son; from the "angel of the Lord" (Gen. 16:7), to the "angel of his presence" (Isa. 63:9; Exod. 33:14; 23:20-21), on to the "messenger of the covenant" (Mal. 3:1), to Jehovah Himself, who will come suddenly to His temple (Mal. 3:1).[23]

The Israelites were constantly warned to avoid animal and human images of all kinds, such as characterized the heathen religions of the world (v. 16). Clarke says:

> However God chose to appear or manifest himself, he took care never to assume any describable form. He would have no image worship, because he is a spirit, and they who worship him must worship him in Spirit and in truth. These outward things tend to draw the mind out of itself, and diffuse it on sensible, if not sensual, objects; and thus spiritual worship is prevented, and the Holy Ghost grieved. Persons acting in this way can never know much of the religion of the heart.[24]

Brought you forth out of the iron furnace (v. 20). It is apparent that the Israelites were compelled to do the most difficult work in Egypt, that having to do with building of all kinds, including digging, smelting and associated tasks in a foundry.

Jehovah was angry with me (v. 21).

Moses explains to the people that the promise to Israel will be realized by Israel as a nation, but that he, as their leader, will not be permitted to enter the promised land (see comments on Num. 20:12). Moses warns the people that they are to keep the covenant of Jehovah and to refrain from making any graven images.

Even though Moses did not get to enter the land of Canaan, he was permitted to see the land from afar and made to realize that all his efforts were not in vain. He was given the assurance that the covenant between Israel and Jehovah was still in effect. One ancient divine once said, "There is more joy in the penitential mournings of a believer than in all the mirth of a wicked man."[25]

Pisgah was the ridge from which the most inspiring views of the promised land could be obtained. The following poetical observation is significant:

> The springs, or pourings forth of Pisgah, fertilizing the land, may suggest a discourse on the joys and various advantages that flow from heavenly prospects. How much the present life is benefited and beautified by thoughts and purposes that flow from views of the heavenly life. Every true Pisgah in our life, i.e., every point of exalted meditation, should be a fountain-head of holy thought and action.[26]

Jehovah thy God is a devouring fire (v. 24). The people are reminded that even though the Lord loves them and gives them providential oversight, they will be punished for disobedience. God can express His designs of love only when His people are obedient. The law of obedience applies to all areas of human conduct and experience. God is a jealous God, and He tolerates no competition. He is a consuming fire and brings judgment upon all who permit their affections to be misdirected.[27]

Jehovah will scatter you (v. 27). One of the penalties which was to be imposed upon Israel for disobedience was that they would lose their homes and national identity for longer or shorter periods of time, depending on how long it took them to repent and make their peace with the Lord. The book of Judges gives

---

[23] Howard A. Hanke, *Christ and the Church in the Old Testament*, p. 40.   [24] *Op. cit.*, I, 748.
[25] James Cooper Gray and George M. Adams, *Gray and Adams Bible Commentary*, p. 475.
[26] *Ibid.*, p. 475.   [27] Henry, *op. cit.*, II, 433.

an example of how this judgment actually worked.

Jehovah thy God is a merciful God (v. 31). The God of heaven is strict in His demands, though merciful, and "not wishing that any should perish, but that all should come to repentance" (II Pet. 3:9).

M. CITIES OF REFUGE EAST OF THE JORDAN (4:41-43)

41 Then Moses set apart three cities beyond the Jordan toward the sunrising; 42 that the manslayer might flee thither, that slayeth his neighbor unawares, and hated him not in time past; and that fleeing unto one of these cities he might live: 43 *namely*, Bezer in the wilderness, in the plain country, for the Reubenites; and Ramoth in Gilead, for the Gadites; and Golan in Bashan, for the Manassites.

These cities were to be places of refuge where a **manslayer** could get protection of the law until he could be fairly tried by his superiors. This gave the man protection who accidentally killed someone but who might otherwise be lynched by the kinsmen of the slain man.

If a man neglected to flee to the city of refuge he did so at his own peril. If the avenger of blood overtook him on the way his blood was upon his own head because he did not avail himself of the security which God had provided.

If it was ascertained that the manslayer in question was innocent of intentional murder or that the death was accidental, he was free to go his way, and it was decreed that the avenger of blood could not molest him. He was, however, required to stay away from his own house and patrimony until the death of the high priest. As long as he stayed in the protective area of the city or suburbs, he was safe from harm, but if he ventured forth, he removed himself from the protective custody of the law.[28]

N. MOSES REVIEWS THE LAW (4:44-49)

44 And this is the law which Moses set before the children of Israel: 45 these are the testimonies, and the statutes, and the ordinances, which Moses spake unto the children of Israel, when they came forth out of Egypt, 46 beyond the Jordan, in the valley over against Beth-peor, in the land of Sihon king of the Amorites, who dwelt at Heshbon, whom Moses and the children of Israel smote, when they came forth out of Egypt. 47 And they took his land in possession, and the land of Og king of Bashan, the two kings of the Amorites, who were beyond the Jordan toward the sunrising; 48 from Aroer, which is on the edge of the valley of the Arnon, even unto mount Sion (the same is Hermon), 49 and all the Arabah beyond the Jordan eastward, even unto the sea of the Arabah, under the slopes of Pisgah.

This section is a summary of the conquests on the east side of the Jordan River. Manley points out:

The place and time of the second discourse are carefully defined. It was given in full view of Beth-Peor, which adds piquancy to its warnings, and of Pisgah (vs. 49), which sheds light on its promises. Sion (vs. 48) as a name for Hermon is found only here. The word "testimony" denotes a solemn assertion or witness. God's testimonies are the declaration of His character, will and purpose, as contained in Holy Scripture. In Exod. 25:21, 22, the ten commandments are called the "testimony," and in II Kings 11:12 we are told that Jehoiada delivered "the testimony" to Jehoash, which may have been the whole or part of this book of Deuteronomy. "This is the law" probably refers to chapters 5-26, which are presented as one discourse.[29]

II. SPECIFICATIONS OF THE COVENANT LIFE (Deut. 5:1 — 26:19)

A. THE TEN COMMANDMENTS (5:1-21; see also Exod. 20:1-7)

1 And Moses called unto all Israel, and said unto them, Hear, O Israel, the statutes and the ordinances which I speak in your ears this day, that ye may learn them, and observe to do them. 2 Jehovah our God made a covenant with us in Horeb. 3 Jehovah made not this covenant with our fathers, but with us, even us, who are all of us here alive this day. 4 Jehovah spake with you face to face in the mount out of the midst of the fire 5 (I stood between Jehovah and you at that time, to show you the word of Jehovah: for ye were afraid because of the fire, and went not up into the mount), saying,

---

[28] *Ibid.*, I, 421.   [29] *Op. cit.*, p. 203.

6 I am Jehovah thy God, who brought thee out of the land of Egypt, out of the house of bondage.

7 Thou shalt have no other gods before me.

8 Thou shalt not make unto thee a graven image, *nor* any likeness *of anything* that is in heaven above, or that is in the earth beneath, or that is in the water under the earth: 9 thou shalt not bow down thyself unto them, nor serve them; for I, Jehovah, thy God, am a jealous God, visiting the iniquity of the fathers upon the children, and upon the third and upon the fourth generation of them that hate me; 10 and showing lovingkindness unto thousands of them that love me and keep my commandments.

11 Thou shalt not take the name of Jehovah thy God in vain: for Jehovah will not hold him guiltless that taketh his name in vain.

12 Observe the sabbath day, to keep it holy, as Jehovah thy God commanded thee. 13 Six days shalt thou labor, and do all thy work; 14 but the seventh day is a sabbath unto Jehovah thy God: *in it* thou shalt not do any work, thou, nor thy son, nor thy daughter, nor thy manservant, nor thy maid-servant, nor thine ox, nor thine ass, nor any of thy cattle, nor thy stranger that is within thy gates; that thy man-servant and thy maid-servant may rest as well as thou. 15 And thou shalt remember that thou wast a servant in the land of Egypt, and Jehovah thy God brought thee out thence by a mighty hand and by an outstretched arm: therefore Jehovah thy God commanded thee to keep the sabbath day.

16 Honor thy father and thy mother, as Jehovah thy God commanded thee; that thy days may be long, and that it may go well with thee, in the land which Jehovah thy God giveth thee.

17 Thou shalt not kill.

18 Neither shalt thou commit adultery.

19 Neither shalt thou steal.

20 Neither shalt thou bear false witness against thy neighbor.

21 Neither shalt thou covet thy neighbor's wife; neither shalt thou desire thy neighbor's house, his field, or his manservant, or his maid-servant, his ox, or his ass, or anything that is thy neighbor's.

The time has now come for a general conference at which all Israel is expected to be present. The most vital and intimate tenets of their faith are now about to be reviewed for the benefit of the younger generation of Israel,

which has now taken charge and needs to be impressed with the essentials of the covenant between Jehovah and Israel. Israel is to learn thoroughly the ordinances and to observe them. The covenant which was made at Horeb is actually the same covenant which Jehovah had made with Abraham. This is a continuing covenant frequently restated and interpreted, and is just as valid with this new generation as with the generation now dead. The spiritual impact of this covenant is still in effect today. Kline makes the following comment:

> When suzerainty treaties were renewed, the stipulations, which constituted the long and crucial central section of the covenant, were repeated but with modifications, especially such as were necessary to meet the changing situation. So Moses rehearsed and reformulated the requirements promulgated in the Sinaitic Covenant. Furthermore, just as treaty stipulations customarily began with the fundamental and general demand for the vassal's absolute allegiance to the suzerain, and then proceeded to various specific requirements, so Moses now confronted Israel with the primary demand for consecration to the Lord (vv. 5-11) and then with the ancillary stipulations of covenant life (vv. 12-26).[30]

The Ten Commandments which Moses is about to review (see notes on Exod. 20) are the most perfect legal codes of behavior which have ever come to man. Many of the laws of the nations of the world contain the sum and substance of these laws. These laws are so designed that when humanity conforms to them, society moves along with the greatest degree of peace and harmony. When these laws are broken the greatest discord and confusion result. These ancient codes of law might be called expressions of love by God toward humanity, for in keeping them, man enjoys the greatest probability of physical, mental and moral well-being. It is truly said, "For this is the love of God, that we keep his commandments: and his commandments are not grievous" (I John 5:3).

When theologians are impelled to write upon the Ten Commandments they feel as one must feel if commanded to drain the oceans dry by using a dipper. All

---

[30] *Op. cit.,* p. 162.

comments that can be made about the commandments are only feeble mutterings when placed by the side of the Decalogue itself.

Theologians have recognized a twofold division in the Ten Commandments. The first division includes the first, second, third, and fourth commandments and deals with man's relationship to God. Our entire system of theology rests in this first section and conveys to man the reverence and service he is to render his Creator. The second division contains the last six commandments and teaches man his moral and ethical obligations toward his fellow men. These are the rules and regulations which make possible a happy and orderly society. When these priciples are ignored society tends to disintegrate.

The Ten Commandments are repeated here expressly for the purpose of impressing the new generation with the fact that they were relevant and applicable to their time and circumstance. There is always danger that old truths may be considered out of date and irrelevant to the contemporary scene.

The version of the commandments in Deuteronomy is slightly different from that in Exodus, as the Lord's Prayer in Matthew, chapter four, is different from the version in Luke, chapter eleven. Let us now consider each commandment in the order given:

THE FIRST COMMANDMENT

Thou shalt have no other gods before me (v. 7). Jehovah is the God of the universe and a jealous God (v. 9). His love tolerates no divided loyalty. Israel is to be a "holy nation," separated from the heathen practice of worshiping many gods. By many providential acts and miracles God had communicated to the Israelites the fact that He was their God and that besides Him there was no other deity. Of this commandment Clarke says:

> This commandment prohibits every species of mental idolatry, and all inordinate attachment to earthly and sensible things. As God is the fountain of happiness, and no intelligent creature can be happy but through him, whoever seeks happiness in the creature is necessarily an idolater; as he puts the creature

in the place of the Creator, expecting that from the gratification of his passions, in the use or abuse of earthly things, which is to be found in God alone. The very first commandment of the whole series is divinely calculated to prevent man's misery and promote his happiness, by taking him off from all false dependence and leading him to God himself, the fountain of all good.[31]

THE SECOND COMMANDMENT

Thou shalt not make unto thee a graven image (v. 8). Israel was to have no representations of deity in the likeness of man or animal. One of the violations Israel feared most was blasphemy, and this is expressed in their unwillingness to vocalize the name of God (see comments on verse 11). The prohibition of carved or graven images cut at the very taproot of all heathen religions and known idolatry. Imagery of every kind in the entire universe came under this commandment. They were to have no **likeness of anything that is in heaven above, or that is in the earth beneath, or that is in the water under the earth.** It can be pointed out that modern Israel uses representations of trees, flowers and other plants on its coins and stamps instead of the likeness of a person.

Visiting the iniquity of the fathers (v. 9). It must be assumed that if the children walk in the same evil way as did their parents, they too will be punished. It must always be remembered that Jehovah is a just and righteous God and that no person can suffer damnation without an opportunity to accept saving grace. It can be assumed that as the covenant was made with the nation of Israel and had corporate relevance, so also is the matter of the judgment of God upon the children of Israel in succeeding generations.

Showing lovingkindness (v. 10). The love of God is clearly expressed at this point. Obedience is the key to a wonderful providential oversight. The rewards of walking in God's will are many and may be compared to the pleasure one may enjoy in travel, as long as one stays on the right road. Deviations and detours from the main highway of life — God's will — are fraught with difficulties

31 Op. cit., I, 402.

and suffering. The "Highway of Holiness" is the way of happiness and offers the greatest degree of well-being.

THE THIRD COMMANDMENT

Thou shalt not take the name of Jehovah thy God in vain (v. 11). This is one of the commandments that is violated in many ways. Any profane or idle utterance of the name of God or swearing falsely in the name of God is using the sacred name in vain. The Jews of Old Testament times were so fearful of using the name of God in vain, that, in order to avoid the possibility of such an offense, they changed the pronunciation of Jehovah's name. It is the opinion of many that the two divine names, *God* (Elohim) and *Lord* (Yhwh), are designations of the trinitarian Godhead and the second person (Christ) respectively, although this is held in question by certain other scholars.

If the name *Yhwh* (Jehovah) has been confusing to the modern critics, it was more so to the apostate religious leaders of the Old Testament Church. One Bible scholar says, "For 2000 years before our Lord came to earth the Jewish priests argued about how to pronounce the name *Yhwh*. As a result of this constant quarrel over the name, they split up into many sects. Caiaphas, the high priest said, 'It is the want of being able to pronounce *Yhwh* (Jesus to us) in its full sense, that has caused so much dissension among the Jews.' "[32]

The name of Jehovah can be used in only two ways — in vain or in reverence. It is obvious that no person can accept Him or correctly give utterance to His name until He truly becomes his personal Lord and Savior. Paul brought this out forcibly when he preached to the men of Israel about the prophecies, saying, "They that dwell at Jerusalem, and their rulers, because they knew him not, nor yet the voices of the prophets which are read every sabbath day, they have fulfilled them in condemning him. And though they found no cause of death in him, yet desired they Pilate that he should be slain" (Acts 13:27, 28). Since they could not truthfully call His name, they reacted and sought to kill Him. The name of Jesus is relevant only as a term in worship or as a caption to a curse. A person either takes the name of the Lord in adoration or he takes it in vain. Between these two extremes there is no significant use of the name. Christ Jesus is either Lord of all, or He is not Lord at all.

According to II Timothy 2:19, to name the name of Christ Jesus is to belong to Him; the naming of His name on the part of the Gentiles signified their acceptance as God's people (Acts 15:17); to "hold fast his name" was to be true to Him as made known (Rev. 2:13; 3:8); to be "gathered together in his name," and to "do all things in his name," were acknowledgments of Him (Matt. 18:20; Col. 3:17). To know His name is to love and worship Him. To know but ignore His name is to crucify Him, as was done by those who did not know Him. With respect to using the name of Jehovah in vain, one commentator observes:

> Consider what the profane use of this name suggests. 1. An irreverent heart; no deep regard for the honor of God; 2. A lying heart: a heart conscious of its own habitual rectitude would not invoke the name of the Most High in confirmation of its utterances.

> Consider why this use of the Holy Name was forbidden. 1. To induce a profound respect for the name and nature of God; 2. To secure the habit of simple and truthful speech.[33]

THE FOURTH COMMANDMENT

Observe the sabbath day, to keep it holy (v. 12). This is one of the commandments which is ignored to a large extent in the secular culture that characterizes our day. More and more pressure of all kinds is being applied to outlaw "blue laws" and other Lord's Day ordinances. The day of rest — now known as Sunday by non-Jewish people — has been looked upon with a great deal of respect. A day for rest and public worship has been the very foundation of the way of life of Jew and Gentile alike.

It is assumed that the importance of the Lord's Day is the fact of one rest day in seven, rather than the day itself. Man

[32] Theodore Fitch, *Authority and Power Through Jesus' Name*, p. 32.
[33] Gray and Adams, *op. cit.*, p. 477.

is so constituted that his physical and mental interests are best served when he observes the weekly rest day. The Sabbath Day was especially created for the over-all well-being of man. One scholar says:

> The rabbis seemed to think that the Sabbath was an end in itself, an institution to which the pious Israelite must subject all his personal interests; in other words, that man was made for the Sabbath: man might suffer hardship, but the institution must be preserved inviolate. Jesus, on the contrary, taught that the Sabbath was made for man's benefit. If there should arise a conflict between man's needs and the letter of the Law, man's higher interests and needs must take precedence over the law of the Sabbath.[34]

After the rupture between the Messiah-believing and the Messiah-rejecting Jews, the Christian Church began to observe the first day of the week. Sampey says:

> The early Christians kept the 7th day as a Sabbath, much after the fashion of other Jews. Gradually the 1st day of the week came to be recognized as the day on which the followers of Jesus would meet for worship. The resurrection of Our Lord on that day made it for Christians the most joyous day of all the week. . . . The early Christians brought over into their mode of observing the Lord's Day the best elements of the Jewish Sabbath, without its onerous restrictions.[35]

We read and hear a great deal about resting on the Sabbath or Lord's Day, but it is seldom that anything is said about the second part of this commandment. It would seem that it is equally offensive to idle away the six work days in the week. There is a tendency in the present day to do as little as one can for as much as one can receive. Idle time is becoming a great problem, and this is seen in the adult and juvenile delinquency of the present era. Leisure time without some compensating responsibility and activity tends to destroy moral and ethical obligations and attitudes.

THE FIFTH COMMANDMENT

Honor thy father and thy mother (v. 16). The cradle is the place where re-

spect for law and authority begins. Honor and respect for parental authority is the foundation on which respect for the authority of God and the civil laws rests. When honor and respect for parents is disregarded there is little likelihood that the principle of respect will find expression in other areas of life.

A peculiar respect is due to parents which no one else can claim. During the early formative years parents stand in the place of God to their children, and therefore disrespect toward parents is disrespect toward God.

There is a twofold emphasis in this commandment. Children are not only to be obedient and kindly affectioned toward their parents, but they are also to refrain from any hurtful activity or attitude. Parents are to have the first place of honor and respect. This concept is diametrically opposed to the atheistic, Communistic philosophy that the state is the highest good and that the state must receive primary consideration, even if it means spying on or betraying one's parents. This philosophy depreciates the judgment of parents and appreciates that of the children who are not yet mature enough to make judgments in many areas of life. Some unknown sage has said, "God has given parents brains to use for their children until the children can grow some of their own."

Generally speaking, children who respect and obey their parents have the greatest probability of success and well-being. Wisdom and knowledge of good, when passed on from parent to child, can be the determining factor in a child's ultimate state in life. Teaching children the fear and knowledge of God is one basic treasure which no one else can convey because of the peculiar, intimate nearness of parents to children. Manley says:

> This fifth commandment deals with the most sacred of human relationships, that of parenthood. The name of Father applies first of all to God, and when He allows men to share it He ennobles them accordingly. Men choose their own friends, but parents are the gift of God, His instruments in bringing them to birth, a ministry which has no parallel. For this reason parents must be honoured. The promise of length of days in the

[34] John Richard Sampey, "Sabbath," *International Standard Bible Encyclopedia*, IV, 2631.   [35] *Ibid.*

land, which is equally God's gift, is an incentive to obedience. Honour to parents is limited by the honour due to God who is supreme. By studying the life of Christ we can see how both allegiances can be perfectly combined (Matt. 10:37; 19:29; Luke 2:49, 51) .[36]

THE SIXTH COMMANDMENT

Thou shalt not kill (v. 17) . This commandment forbids murder, but does not, in the judgment of most people, apply to the death penalty imposed by law for a major crime. It is stated in the Scriptures: "Whoso sheddeth man's blood, by man shall his blood be shed" (Gen. 9:6). The idea that certain circumstances warrant the death penalty is brought out in such Scriptures as Exodus 21:29; 22:20; 35:2; Leviticus 20:10; Deuteronomy 13:9; 17:12; and 21:21.

Jesus emphasized the fact that murder not only includes the act of wantonly taking someone's life, but even the intent of the heart (see Matt. 5:21ff.) . In a certain sense, taking a man's life could be anything that degrades him and deprives him of the full and rich life God wants him to enjoy.

THE SEVENTH COMMANDMENT

Neither shalt thou commit adultery (v. 18) . Adultery, or infidelity by married people, has been looked upon by civilized society as one of the most destructive acts against society and the individual. The command not to commit adultery is a fence intended to shield us from many forms of social, psychological and personal harm.

Sexual intercourse carries with it great responsibility, and is to be engaged in only by those who commit themselves to each other in holy matrimony. The sex act is the seal and symbol of a divine union, blessed of God and sacred. Outside of the true love which finds its final expression in marriage, the sex act becomes, in the end, repulsive and vulgar, and usually ends in disgust. The rise of sexual immorality in this age is a symptom of the cancerous moral and spiritual decay now eating itself into the very soul of society.

The act of adultery is stealing rights and privileges from one person and giving them to someone else. Adultery is an act of cruelty against the person to whom fidelity was pledged at the marriage altar. Illicit sex acts can result in such social pathologies as venereal disease, unwanted children left as a burden upon society, disintegration of personality, suicide and crime.

The consent of the mind to adultery and the act itself are expressly forbidden in the Scriptures. Jesus said, "Whosoever looketh upon a woman to lust after her hath committed adultery with her already in his heart" (Matt. 5:28, KJV) .

Generally speaking, adultery refers to sexual intercourse among married people outside their own marriage bed, and fornication refers to all sorts of pre- and extramarital sex relations. But both are equally forbidden in the Scriptures (see Matt. 5:28, 32; Acts 15:29; I Cor. 5:1; 6:18; 7:2; and Eph. 5:3) . Stress is placed upon this seventh commandment because in the beginning God instituted marriage and used it to signify His love to His people, and the union between Christ and His Church. This mystical union between Christ and His Church is fittingly compared to the sacred relationship in an ideal marriage. The essential aspect of fidelity is obvious. On the other hand, it can be pointed out that adultery is used figuratively to designate spiritual unfaithfulness toward God. When the Israelites turned to other gods, it was said that they were committing spiritual adultery or whoredoms (see Judg. 2:17; 8:27; I Chron. 5:25; Ps. 106:39; Ezek. 6:9; 20:30; 23:35; Hos. 4:12; 5:4; 9:1) .

THE EIGHTH COMMANDMENT

Neither shalt thou steal (v. 19) . This commandment has to do with our own wealth as well as that of our neighbor. Stealing has many applications, both personal and social. We can steal from ourselves and our family by sinful spending and by miserliness. The misuse of things which have value can result in stealing. A father can steal from his family by squandering or gambling away his money. Depriving a person of his good name and character is theft. Shrewd business relations related to employment,

---

[36] *Op. cit.*, p. 205.

rents, wages, debts, etc. can become theft. There is almost no end to the ways in which a person can steal, when the spirit of honesty and integrity are absent. The Christian standard must never be compromised; both goods and the gospel are sacred trusts from God.

THE NINTH COMMANDMENT

Neither shalt thou bear false witness against thy neighbor (v. 20). This commandment is closely related to the eighth commandment in that a person can suffer loss of valuable considerations by the falsifying of the truth. A false witness in court can impose loss of property and even loss of a good name upon an innocent person. One does not even have to be in court to bear false witness. Repeating of a harmful tale or rumor can do an equal amount of damage to a person's life. Manley says:

> Though the ninth commandment is negative in form, it may be given a positive content. It sets the false in contrast to the true; by forbidding the one, it enforces the other. Our witness, our testimony, must be true. The Christian, like his Master, must bear witness to the truth, and how can he do this except by bearing witness to Him who is the truth?[37]

THE TENTH COMMANDMENT

Neither shalt thou covet (v. 21). This, the last commandment, is very closely related to many of the other commandments. Another's possession is coveted by a person before he steals it — whether that possession be his neighbor's wife or some material thing. Desiring the house or wife or estate of another shows that one is discontented with his own lot in life. If one is truly in love with Christ, he is confident that He is leading in every circumstance of his life. When we know that He is leading, life takes on excitement and true meaning. We want nothing more. Then we can say with Paul, "I have learned, in whatsoever state I am, therewith to be content" (Phil. 4:11). This commandment forbids coveting anything that belongs to one's neighbor; a close walk with Christ only will enable one to obey it.

B. THE PEOPLE REQUEST A MEDIATOR (5:22-33)

22 These words Jehovah spake unto all your assembly in the mount out of the midst of the fire, of the cloud, and of the thick darkness, with a great voice: and he added no more. And he wrote them upon two tables of stone, and gave them unto me. 23 And it came to pass, when ye heard the voice out of the midst of the darkness, while the mountain was burning with fire, that ye came near unto me, even all the heads of your tribes, and your elders; 24 and ye said, Behold, Jehovah our God hath showed us his glory and his greatness, and we have heard his voice out of the midst of the fire: we have seen this day that God doth speak with man, and he liveth. 25 Now therefore why should we die? for this great fire will consume us: if we hear the voice of Jehovah our God any more, then we shall die. 26 For who is there of all flesh, that hath heard the voice of the living God speaking out of the midst of the fire, as we have, and lived? 27 Go thou near, and hear all that Jehovah our God shall say: and speak thou unto us all that Jehovah our God shall speak unto thee; and we will hear it, and do it.

28 And Jehovah heard the voice of your words, when ye spake unto me; and Jehovah said unto me, I have heard the voice of the words of this people, which they have spoken unto thee: they have well said all that they have spoken. 29 Oh that there were such a heart in them, that they would fear me, and keep all my commandments always, that it might be well with them, and with their children for ever! 30 Go say to them, Return ye to your tents. 31 But as for thee, stand thou here by me, and I will speak unto thee all the commandment, and the statutes, and the ordinances, which thou shalt teach them, that they may do them in the land which I give them to possess it. 32 Ye shall observe to do therefore as Jehovah your God hath commanded you: ye shall not turn aside to the right hand or to the left. 33 Ye shall walk in all the way which Jehovah your God hath commanded you, that ye may live, and that it may be well with you, and that ye may prolong your days in the land which ye shall possess.

The circumstances of giving the law on Mt. Sinai are repeated here. It ap-

[37] *Ibid.*

pears that the voice of Jehovah was sufficiently loud that all of the assembly below could hear (v. 23). After giving the law orally, Jehovah wrote it on tablets of stone.

When the people heard the voice of Jehovah and saw the fire on top of Mt. Sinai, they were terror-stricken. The experience of hearing God Himself speak was so awful that they feared for their very lives (v. 25). On previous occasions the Lord had appeared, or made Himself manifest, to select individuals (Gen. 16: 7ff.; 22:15-16; Exod. 3:2-4), but now a peculiar manifestation of His power is given in the holy fire and His voice on Mt. Sinai (v. 26). Since the camp of Israel was located in a deep valley between two mountains, the reverberations of Jehovah's voice must have been awe-inspiring and fearful. His voice would echo and re-echo all along the valley.

God's appearance to man has always been a terrible experience, from the time God sought Adam in the garden to the time that man was sought out in the incarnation of Jesus Christ. The people requested that henceforth Jehovah would speak to Moses and not to them directly (v. 27). It is probable that many in Israel were guilty of sin, and when a man sins a pronouncement of the law is always disturbing and painful. The people felt that they could more easily receive God's law through a secondary channel — that being Moses. This is suggestive of the mediatorial nature of revelation. It is evident that many of the people were not sincere. The people had fear of God because of their guilty consciences, and not because of a desire to do God's commandments.

After the people were ordered to go back to their tents (v. 30), Moses was commanded to linger on top of the Mount so that Jehovah could teach him **the commandment, and the statutes, and the ordinances,** which he was in turn to teach the people. In addition to the Ten Commandments as such, Jehovah gave Moses the technical details and the practical applications of the laws (v. 31). Jehovah once again emphasized the importance of absolute obedience (vv. 32-33).

C. THE GREAT COMMANDMENT (6:1-9; see also Matt. 22:36-40)

1 Now this is the commandment, the statutes, and the ordinances, which Jehovah your God commanded to teach you, that ye might do them in the land whither ye go over to possess it; 2 that thou mightest fear Jehovah thy God, to keep all his statutes and his commandments, which I command thee, thou, and thy son, and thy son's son, all the days of thy life; and that thy days may be prolonged. 3 Hear therefore, O Israel, and observe to do it; that it may be well with thee, and that ye may increase mightily, as Jehovah, the God of thy fathers, hath promised unto thee, in a land flowing with milk and honey.

4 Hear, O Israel: Jehovah our God is one Jehovah: 5 and thou shalt love Jehovah thy God with all thy heart, and with all thy soul, and with all thy might. 6 And these words, which I command thee this day, shall be upon thy heart; 7 and thou shalt teach them diligently unto thy children, and shalt talk of them when thou sittest in thy house, and when thou walkest by the way, and when thou liest down, and when thou risest up. 8 And thou shalt bind them for a sign upon thy hand, and they shall be for frontlets between thine eyes. 9 And thou shalt write them upon the door-posts of thy house, and upon thy gates.

The people are reminded that they are to put the laws of Jehovah into daily practice. The Israelites are to be a peculiar people — a holy nation — distinguished from the nations of the world by a peculiar dedication to Jehovah, the great Lawgiver.

The laws of Jehovah are to be taught to the children so that they may enjoy long years of prosperity and happiness (v. 2). The fact that Jehovah is the one and only God is again reiterated (v. 4).

Thou shalt love Jehovah thy God (v. 5). In the previous chapter we studied each of the Ten Commandments and their man-to-God and man-to-man relationships. These commandments were written on tablets of stone, but if these laws are to be relevant to man's need they must be engraved upon the tablets of the heart. In this great commandment of love all the commandments are consolidated and gathered together. Here the largely negative commandments become positive. It is to be observed that this supreme love to God would preclude breaking any of the written commandments. A supreme love for God, such as is commanded here, is the sum and substance of all Christian experience.

When the Pharisees asked what the "great commandment" was, Jesus reminded them of what Moses said about the supreme love of man toward God. In addition to quoting Deuteronomy 6:5 Jesus also quoted Leviticus 19:18, which reads, "Thou shalt love thy neighbor as thyself." Of these two statements — love of God and man — Jesus said, "On these two commandments the whole law hangeth, and the prophets" (Matt. 22:40). "The love of God is presented in both the Old and New Testaments as the ruling disposition of the heart from which obedience springs, thus permitting no change in devotion."[38] Thus it is seen that the basic nature of religion has always demanded complete and supreme devotion to God.

It should be acknowledged that this commandment of perfect love creates a difficult theological problem. The mere command to love does not instill love nor does it motivate an attitude of love. This has been resolved by Wesleyan theologians through the doctrine of "entire sanctification" — a measure of grace subsequent to conversion whereby the heart is cleansed from the carnal nature and filled with perfect love. The term "perfect love" is sometimes used synonymously with the term "entire sanctification." (For a definition of sanctification as given in the Discipline of the Methodist Church see comments on Num. 11:18.)

What is implied in loving God with all the heart, soul, mind, and strength? (1) To love God with all one's heart implies being ready to give up, do or suffer anything in order to please and glorify Him; having neither love nor hatred, hope nor fear, inclination nor aversion, desire nor delight, but as they relate to God, and are regulated by Him. (2) To love God with all one's soul implies being ready to give up life for His sake — to endure all sorts of torments, and to be deprived of all kinds of comforts, rather than dishonor God. (3) To love God with all one's strength implies exerting all the powers of one's body and soul in the service of God. (4) To love God with all one's mind implies applying oneself only to know God, and His holy will.[39]

The agreement of the doctrinal teachings in the Old and New Testaments is clearly revealed in all their parts. It is obvious that revelation, whether in the Old Testament or the New, is substantially the same and manifests itself through common agencies and means; the basic redemptive tenets are essentially the same, irrespective of their time or place in history, because God transcends time. Man's inspiration is an experience resulting from divine revelation, and the product is reflected in the redemptive narrative originating with the Adamic era (Acts 2:22ff.; 3:17, 18, 21ff.). The redemptive principle is first expressed in the blood sacrifice offered by Abel, and in subsequent generations. The written word becomes divine intelligence to man as the Holy Spirit bears witness in his heart. Through revelation man lays hold of divine truth which cannot be reached by reason alone, and cannot be reduced to some rational system of man without the direct aid of the Spirit of God. "The Scriptures contain a body of truth which God seeks to communicate to man. This body of truth is known as the deposit of faith. . . . The Bible reveals its message to those who seek to know the truth in order that they may follow it."[40] It is the "faith which was once delivered to the saints" (Jude 3).

When redemptive revelation was given, both by word and in written form during the period preceding the incarnation, the Savior, Jesus Christ, was an active participant with the Father and the Holy Spirit. God through Christ is the redemptive Agent in the Old Testament dispensation; whereas Christ became the redemptive Agent, Coordinator and Witness during the New Testament period. The Savior came not to establish some new doctrine, but to confirm and fulfill the redemptive plan provisionally given and foretold in the Old Testament. The New Testament is a historical statement of the prophetic pronouncements in the

---

[38] Howard A. Hanke, *From Eden to Eternity*, p. 129.
[39] Adam Clarke, *The New Testament of Our Lord and Saviour Jesus Christ*, I, 215.
[40] Holmes Rolston, "Revelation," *Twentieth Century Encyclopedia of Religious Knowledge*, II, 971.

Old Testament that were fulfilled in the New (Luke 24:44; see also Acts 3:18, 21).

James clearly states that by revelation the prophets spoke in the name of Christ (Jas. 5:10). Luke says that the law and the prophets served the redemptive purpose until the coming of John the Baptist. In speaking of Christ Philip said: "We have found him, of whom Moses in the law and the prophets did write" (John 1:45). Evidently Christ in the Old Testament is identical with Christ in the New. Peter clearly states that "all the prophets witness" to Christ and that through His name all believers "receive remission of sins" (Acts 10:43). Paul, in his message to Agrippa, bases salvation on belief in the Messiah to whom the prophets testified (Acts 26:27). Christ affirmed that the "golden rule" was the very foundation of the law and the prophets (Matt. 7:12). Christ is the eternal theme in the Scriptures, and it is He whom God promised "afore by the prophets" (Rom. 1:2). The righteousness of God in Christ was manifested in and witnessed to by the law and the prophets (Rom. 3:21). The Spirit of Christ, which was in the prophets, testified of the sufferings of Christ and the glory that should follow (I Pet. 1:10, 11).[41]

Thou shalt teach them diligently (v. 7). If our society is to be a continuing and expanding Christian community it is necessary for parents to teach the Bible to their children, both by precept and example. It was the diligent teaching of the Scriptures that made the Hebrew people a fit channel through which the Messiah could be revealed.

Much of the teaching in the days of Moses was by word of mouth. Biblical concepts and precepts were repeated over and over so that the teachings became a part of their memory. Writing, as such, was limited to the scrolls in the possession of the prophets and religious leaders. The parents attended the reading of the biblical passages, memorized them and then taught them to their children. They were to teach their children in the ways of the Lord while they were sitting in their homes, and while they were walking, as well as when they went to bed and immediately upon arising. In addition, they were to tie Scripture passages to their hands and upon their foreheads (v. 9). This practice was adopted from the Jews by the Mohammedans and reduced to a form of legalistic idolatry.

D. PUNISHMENT FOR DISOBEDIENCE (6:10-25)

10 And it shall be, when Jehovah thy God shall bring thee into the land which he sware unto thy fathers, to Abraham, to Isaac, and to Jacob, to give thee, great and goodly cities, which thou buildedst not, 11 and houses full of all good things, which thou filledst not, and cisterns hewn out, which thou hewedst not, vineyards and olive-trees, which thou plantedst not, and thou shalt eat and be full; 12 then beware lest thou forget Jehovah, who brought thee forth out of the land of Egypt, out of the house of bondage. 13 Thou shalt fear Jehovah thy God; and him shalt thou serve, and shalt swear by his name. 14 Ye shall not go after other gods, of the gods of the peoples that are round about you; 15 for Jehovah thy God in the midst of thee is a jealous God; lest the anger of Jehovah thy God be kindled against thee, and he destroy thee from off the face of the earth.

16 Ye shall not tempt Jehovah your God, as ye tempted him in Massah. 17 Ye shall diligently keep the commandments of Jehovah your God, and his testimonies, and his statutes, which he hath commanded thee. 18 And thou shalt do that which is right and good in the sight of Jehovah; that it may be well with thee, and that thou mayest go in and possess the good land which Jehovah sware unto thy fathers, 19 to thrust out all thine enemies from before thee, as Jehovah hath spoken.

20 When thy son asketh thee in time to come, saying, What mean the testimonies, and the statutes, and the ordinances, which Jehovah our God hath commanded you? 21 then thou shalt say unto thy son, We were Pharaoh's bondmen in Egypt: and Jehovah brought us out of Egypt with a mighty hand; 22 and Jehovah showed signs and wonders, great and sore, upon Egypt, upon Pharaoh, and upon all his house, before our eyes; 23 and he brought us out from thence, that he might bring us in, to give us the land which he sware unto our fathers. 24 And Jehovah commanded us to do all these statutes, to fear Jehovah our God, for our good always, that he might preserve us alive, as at this day. 25 And it shall be righteousness unto us, if

---

[41] Howard A. Hanke, *Christ and the Church in the Old Testament*, p. 57.

we observe to do all this commandment before Jehovah our God, as he hath commanded us.

Jehovah promises the Israelites **goodly cities** and **houses full of all good things** and **cisterns hewn out** and **vineyards and olive-trees** (vv. 10, 11). But in the midst of this wealth there is danger of forgetting the source of all blessings; there is danger of apostasy (v. 12).

They are warned against the gods of the Canaanites (v. 14), and are reminded that Jehovah is a jealous God who will impose severe punishment for spiritual infidelity (v. 15). They are cautioned against making again the mistake made at Massah, where they raised the question: "Is Jehovah among us or not?" (Exod. 17:7).

As a safeguard against backsliding they are to think constantly upon the words of the Lord, as well as keep the commandments and testimonies of God (v. 17). Israel's spiritual life is to be such an integral part of its cultural pattern that it will be normal and natural for the sons of the younger generation to ask questions and learn the sacred history of Israel's development and deliverance (vv. 20-25).

E. ISRAEL WARNED AGAINST IDOLATRY (7:1-5)

1 When Jehovah thy God shall bring thee into the land whither thou goest to possess it, and shall cast out many nations before thee, the Hittite, and the Girgashite, and the Amorite, and the Canaanite, and the Perizzite, and the Hivite, and the Jebusite, seven nations greater and mightier than thou; 2 and when Jehovah thy God shall deliver them up before thee, and thou shalt smite them; then thou shalt utterly destroy them: thou shalt make no covenant with them, nor show mercy unto them; 3 neither shalt thou make marriages with them; thy daughter thou shalt not give unto his son, nor his daughter shalt thou take unto thy son. 4 For he will turn away thy son from following me, that they may serve other gods: so will the anger of Jehovah be kindled against you, and he will destroy thee quickly. 5 But thus shall ye deal with them: ye shall break down their altars, and dash in pieces their pillars, and hew down their Asher-

im, and burn their graven images with fire.

The promises of Jehovah are explicit. On the assumption that Israel will obey and practice the commandments, it will take over the land occupied by the idolatrous heathen nations. It should be pointed out that these heathen nations had forcefully taken the land from others and that the land did not actually belong to them. These heathen people had become so degenerate and corrupt that they had forfeited the right to live (v. 2). This is still recognized by law in the case of murderers, rapists, and kidnappers. It must be remembered that the holy and righteous Jehovah God was and is no respecter of persons (see Deut. 10:17; Eph. 6:9; Col. 3:25).

Israel can expect the favor and providential protection of the Lord only if it is faithful and does not adopt the abominable customs and habits of the Canaanites. To avoid this possibility, the sons and daughters of Israel are not to marry the sons and daughters of the Canaanites (v. 3-5). As a further precaution, Israel is commanded to destroy completely the altars, idols, and places of worship where the degrading sex-perverted orgies were practiced. One writer gives this graphic description of the Canaanite religion:

> Baal was their principal god; Ashtoreth, Baal's wife, their principal goddess. She was the personification of the reproductive principle in nature. Ishtar was her Babylonian name; Astarte her Greek and Roman name. Baalim, the plural of Baal, were images of Baal. Ashtaroth, the plural of Ashtoreth. Ashera was a sacred pole, cone of stone, or a tree trunk, representing the goddess. Temples of Baal and Ashtoreth were usually together. Priestesses were temple prostitutes. Sodomites were male temple prostitutes. The worship of Baal, Ashtoreth, and other Canaanite gods consisted in the most extravagant orgies; their temples were centers of vice.[42]

F. ISRAEL TO BE A HOLY PEOPLE (7:6-11)

6 For thou art a holy people unto Jehovah thy God: Jehovah thy God hath chosen thee to be a people for his own possession, above all peoples that are

---

[42] Henry H. Halley, *Bible Handbook*, p. 160.

upon the face of the earth. 7 Jehovah did not set his love upon you, nor choose you, because ye were more in number than any people; for ye were the fewest of all peoples: 8 but because Jehovah loveth you, and because he would keep the oath which he sware unto your fathers, hath Jehovah brought you out with a mighty hand, and redeemed you out of the house of bondage, from the hand of Pharaoh king of Egypt. 9 Know therefore that Jehovah thy God, he is God, the faithful God, who keepeth covenant and lovingkindness with them that love him and keep his commandments to a thousand generations, 10 and repayeth them that hate him to their face, to destroy them: he will not be slack to him that hateth him, he will repay him to his face. 11 Thou shalt therefore keep the commandment, and the statutes, and the ordinances, which I command thee this day, to do them.

The people of God are to be, and indeed will be, a peculiar people because they have deity residing within. This residence of God within makes them creatures not only of this world but also of the spiritual realm. The peculiar characteristic of holiness is to be a personal reality in the life of the individual, as suggested by the Hebrew word for peculiar, *segullah*. This was a quality which was not and could not be inherited.

The statement about being holy is repeated in Deuteronomy 14:2. This idea of personal holiness and God's indwelling is more clearly elucidated in the New Testament. The idea of personal holiness is reaffirmed by Peter in these words: "Because it is written, Be ye holy, for I am holy" (I Pet. 1:16), and Peter is here quoting from Exodus 11:45. It is obvious that there is no double standard in man's relationship to God. This was an essential requirement in the Old Testament, as it is in the New Testament. Holiness of life is everywhere enjoined (see Lev. 19:2; I Chron. 16:29; Luke 1:74, 75; II Cor. 7:1; Eph. 4:24; Heb. 12:14; II Pet. 3:11). The idea that our body is a residence or temple of the Holy Spirit is further delineated in such passages as I Corinthians 3:16, Ephesians 2:20-22 and I Peter 2:5.

It must be remembered that Israel was not chosen arbitrarily as a favorite nation by Jehovah, but was chosen rather for a special purpose and mission, namely, (1) to receive and preserve the Holy Oracles, and (2) to provide the human line through which the Messiah was to come. The special benefits which Israel was to enjoy for obedience were in effect those to be enjoyed by all people who obey God. Heathen people could become believers and receive the blessings promised to all who obey His commands in spirit.

In a spiritual sense, a heathen could become a Hebrew (saved person), just as today a sinner may become a Christian. To become a spiritual Hebrew or a spiritual child of Abraham was to become a believer. This relationship came by faith and not by physical descent from Abraham (see John 8:33-59 and Heb. 11).

All of the promises God made for the benefit of Israel were contingent upon Israel's walk in the path of holiness prescribed in the laws given to Moses. Jehovah promised these special benefits to the people in **a thousand generations** (v. 9), or to all generations in the future who walk in the way of holiness.

G. BLESSINGS FOR OBEDIENCE (7:12-26)

12 And it shall come to pass, because ye hearken to these ordinances, and keep and do them, that Jehovah thy God will keep with thee the covenant and the lovingkindness which he sware unto thy fathers: 13 and he will love thee, and bless thee, and multiply thee; he will also bless the fruit of thy body and the fruit of thy ground, thy grain and thy new wine and thine oil, the increase of thy cattle and the young of thy flock, in the land which he sware unto thy fathers to give thee. 14 Thou shalt be blessed above all peoples: there shall not be male or female barren among you, or among your cattle. 15 And Jehovah will take away from thee all sickness; and none of the evil diseases of Egypt, which thou knowest, will he put upon thee, but will lay them upon all them that hate thee. 16 And thou shalt consume all the peoples that Jehovah thy God shall deliver unto thee; thine eyes shall not pity them: neither shalt thou serve their gods; for that will be a snare unto thee.

17 If thou shalt say in thy heart, These nations are more than I; how can I dispossess them? 18 thou shalt not be afraid of them: thou shalt well remember what Jehovah thy God did unto Pharaoh, and unto all Egypt; 19 the great trials

which thine eyes saw, and the signs, and the wonders, and the mighty hand, and the outstretched arm, whereby Jehovah thy God brought thee out: so shall Jehovah thy God do unto all the peoples of whom thou art afraid. 20 Moreover Jehovah thy God will send the hornet among them, until they that are left, and hide themselves, perish from before thee. 21 Thou shalt not be affrighted at them; for Jehovah thy God is in the midst of thee, a great God and a terrible. 22 And Jehovah thy God will cast out those nations before thee by little and little: thou mayest not consume them at once, lest the beasts of the field increase upon thee. 23 But Jehovah thy God will deliver them up before thee, and will discomfit them with a great discomfiture, until they be destroyed. 24 And he will deliver their kings into thy hand, and thou shalt make their name to perish from under heaven: there shall no man be able to stand before thee, until thou have destroyed them. 25 The graven images of their gods shall ye burn with fire: thou shalt not covet the silver or the gold that is on them, nor take it unto thee, lest thou be snared therein; for it is an abomination to Jehovah thy God. 26 And thou shalt not bring an abomination into thy house, and become a devoted thing like unto it: thou shalt utterly detest it, and thou shalt utterly abhor it; for it is a devoted thing.

The covenant which Jehovah made with the fathers is a continuing agreement and is applicable to every generation. The rewards for walking in the path Jehovah has outlined are many. God will love them, bless them and multiply them (v. 12). He will bless the fruit of their body and the fruit of the ground, as well as the flocks and herds (v. 13). Furthermore, the walk of grace and holiness will give them freedom from sickness and the evil diseases of Egypt (v. 15). They will be victorious in war (v. 16); but all these blessings are contingent upon their fidelity to Jehovah. They are warned against the temptation to dignify and glamorize the heathen nations and are reminded of what Jehovah did to Pharaoh (v. 18). Jehovah will marshal all His power against their enemies, even to the extent of sending hornets to discomfit the enemy (v. 20). In return for this protective leadership Israel is to destroy the enemy and its images (vv. 25-26).

H. CANAAN, A LAND OF PLENTY (8:1-10)

1 All the commandment which I command thee this day shall ye observe to do, that ye may live, and multiply, and go in and possess the land which Jehovah sware unto your fathers. 2 And thou shalt remember all the way which Jehovah thy God hath led thee these forty years in the wilderness, that he might humble thee, to prove thee, to know what was in thy heart, whether thou wouldest keep his commandments, or not. 3 And he humbled thee, and suffered thee to hunger, and fed thee with manna, which thou knewest not, neither did thy fathers know; that he might make thee know that man doth not live by bread only, but by everything that proceedeth out of the mouth of Jehovah doth man live. 4 Thy raiment waxed not old upon thee, neither did thy foot swell, these forty years. 5 And thou shalt consider in thy heart, that, as a man chasteneth his son, so Jehovah thy God chasteneth thee. 6 And thou shalt keep the commandments of Jehovah thy God, to walk in his ways, and to fear him. 7 For Jehovah thy God bringeth thee into a good land, a land of brooks of water, of fountains and springs, flowing forth in valleys and hills; 8 a land of wheat and barley, and vines and fig-trees and pomegranates; a land of olive-trees and honey; 9 a land wherein thou shalt eat bread without scarceness, thou shalt not lack anything in it; a land whose stones are iron, and out of whose hills thou mayest dig copper. 10 And thou shalt eat and be full, and thou shalt bless Jehovah thy God for the good land which he hath given thee.

Israel's obedience and dedication is to be total and absolute, and on the basis of this complete commitment it is to enjoy bounteous provisions in the land of Canaan. Henry makes the following observation:

Now that the Israelites were come of age, and were entering upon their inheritance, they must be reminded of the discipline they had been under during their minority, and the method God had taken to train them up for himself. The wilderness was the school in which they had been for forty years boarded and taught, under tutors and governors; and this was a time to bring it all to remembrance. It is very good for us to remember all the ways both of God's providence and grace, by which he has led us hitherto through this wilderness, that we may be prevailed with cheerfully to serve him and trust in him. Here let us set up our Ebenezer.[43]

The mind of man is fickle and very forgetful, especially with regard to benefits and blessings bestowed by someone else, including the blessings of God. The Israelites are reminded that man has a body as well as a spirit and that both parts must be fed. Jehovah says to them: **Man doth not live by bread only, but by everything that proceedeth out of the mouth of Jehovah doth man live** (v. 3). Later Jesus quoted this passage on the Mount of Temptation (Matt. 4:4), indicating that the body and spirit have the same need in every age.

As a man chasteneth his son (v. 5). Chastening is an expression of love, whether administered by parents or by God. The psalmist says, "Blessed is the man whom thou chasteneth, O Lord" (Ps. 94:12; see also Prov. 3:11; Jer. 10:24; John 15:2). In the Apocalypse it is stated, "As many as I love, I rebuke and chasten: be zealous therefore, and repent" (Rev. 3:19). It is evident that the chastening of the Lord is intended as a means of grace.

Jehovah thy God bringeth thee into a good land (v. 7). The fruitful state of Canaan is again mentioned. All of the wonderful things which were missing in the desert are to be enjoyed in the land of their inheritance: brooks of water, fountains and springs, wheat and barley, vines and fig trees and pomegranates, olive trees and honey, bread without scarceness, stones of iron and copper. These are some of the bounteous provisions in the promised land.

I. THE DANGER OF FORGETTING GOD (8:11-20)

11 Beware lest thou forget Jehovah thy God, in not keeping his commandments, and his ordinances, and his statutes, which I command thee this day: 12 lest, when thou hast eaten and art full, and hast built goodly houses, and dwelt therein; 13 and when thy herds and thy flocks multiply, and thy silver and thy gold is multiplied, and all that thou hast is multiplied; 14 then thy heart be lifted up, and thou forget Jehovah thy God, who brought thee forth out of the land of Egypt, out of the house of bondage; 15

who led thee through the great and terrible wilderness, *wherein were* fiery serpents and scorpions, and thirsty ground where was no water; who brought thee forth water out of the rock of flint; 16 who fed thee in the wilderness with manna, which thy fathers knew not; that he might humble thee, and that he might prove thee, to do thee good at thy latter end: 17 and *lest* thou say in thy heart, My power and the might of my hand hath gotten me this wealth. 18 But thou shalt remember Jehovah thy God, for it is he that giveth thee power to get wealth; that he may establish his covenant which he sware unto thy fathers, as at this day. 19 And it shall be, if thou shalt forget Jehovah thy God, and walk after other gods, and serve them, and worship them, I testify against you this day that ye shall surely perish. 20 As the nations that Jehovah maketh to perish before you, so shall ye perish; because ye would not hearken unto the voice of Jehovah your God.

This section is a reiteration of the many dangers and temptations which Israel will face in the land of plenty (see notes on Deut. 4:9).

J. THE CANAANITES TO BE DESTROYED (9:1-5)

1 Hear, O Israel: thou art to pass over the Jordan this day, to go in to dispossess nations greater and mightier than thyself, cities great and fortified up to heaven, 2 a people great and tall, the sons of the Anakim, whom thou knowest, and of whom thou hast heard say, Who can stand before the sons of Anak? 3 Know therefore this day, that Jehovah thy God is he who goeth over before thee as a devouring fire; he will destroy them, and he will bring them down before thee: so shalt thou drive them out, and make them to perish quickly, as Jehovah hath spoken unto thee. 4 Speak not thou in thy heart, after that Jehovah thy God hath thrust them out from before thee, saying, For my righteousness Jehovah hath brought me in to possess this land; whereas for the wickedness of these nations Jehovah doth drive them out from before thee. 5 Not for thy righteousness, or for the uprightness of thy heart, dost thou go in to possess their land; but for the wickedness of these nations Jehovah thy God doth drive them out from before thee, and that he may establish the

word which Jehovah sware unto thy fathers, to Abraham, to Isaac, and to Jacob.

The day of march has come, but with the command to move forward is the reminder that the cities in Canaan are **great and fortified up to heaven** and its people **great and tall.** These great people are the sons of Anak (see Gen. 6:4; Num. 13:33; Deut. 2:11; 3:11; Josh. 17:15; II Sam. 21:16-20).

The Israelites are also reminded that they are not sufficiently strong to conquer the land, and that Jehovah will go before them as a **devouring fire** (vv. 2-3). Jehovah cautions the people against indulging in self-admiration and arrogant egotism (v. 4). Their victory will be realized because of the mercy and love of Jehovah and not because of their own self-righteousness. Coupled with this is the extreme wickedness of the Canaanites upon which Jehovah will bring judgment through His obedient people. Jehovah will make this an occasion for memorializing His covenant with Abraham, Isaac and Jacob (v. 5). Clarke makes this timely observation:

> It was not by any sovereign act of God that these Canaanites were cast out, but for their wickedness; they had transgressed the law of their Creator; they had resisted his Spirit, and could no longer be tolerated. The Israelites were to possess their land, not because they deserved it, but first, because they were less wicked than the others; and secondly, because God thus chose to begin the great work of his salvation among men.[44]

K. ISRAEL'S REBELLION AT HOREB (9:6-29)

6 Know therefore, that Jehovah thy God giveth thee not this good land to possess it for thy righteousness; for thou art a stiffnecked people. 7 Remember, forget thou not, how thou provokedst Jehovah thy God to wrath in the wilderness: from the day that thou wentest forth out of the land of Egypt, until ye came unto this place, ye have been rebellious against Jehovah. 8 Also in Horeb ye provoked Jehovah to wrath, and Jehovah was angry with you to destroy you. 9 When I was gone up into the mount to receive the tables of stone, even the tables of the covenant which

Jehovah made with you, then I abode in the mount forty days and forty nights; I did neither eat bread nor drink water. 10 And Jehovah delivered unto me the two tables of stone written with the finger of God; and on them *was written* according to all the words, which Jehovah spake with you in the mount out of the midst of the fire in the day of assembly. 11 And it came to pass at the end of forty days and forty nights, that Jehovah gave me the two tables of stone, even the tables of the covenant. 12 And Jehovah said unto me, Arise, get thee down quickly from hence; for thy people that thou hast brought forth out of Egypt have corrupted themselves; they are quickly turned aside out of the way which I commanded them; they have made them a molten image. 13 Furthermore Jehovah spake unto me, saying, I have seen this people, and, behold, it is a stiffnecked people: 14 let me alone, that I may destroy them, and blot out their name from under heaven; and I will make of thee a nation mightier and greater than they. 15 So I turned and came down from the mount, and the mount was burning with fire: and the two tables of the covenant were in my two hands. 16 And I looked, and, behold, ye had sinned against Jehovah your God; ye had made you a molten calf: ye had turned aside quickly out of the way which Jehovah had commanded you. 17 And I took hold of the two tables, and cast them out of my two hands, and brake them before your eyes. 18 And I fell down before Jehovah, as at the first, forty days and forty nights; I did neither eat bread nor drink water; because of all your sin which ye sinned, in doing that which was evil in the sight of Jehovah, to provoke him to anger. 19 For I was afraid of the anger and hot displeasure, wherewith Jehovah was wroth against you to destroy you. But Jehovah hearkened unto me that time also. 20 And Jehovah was very angry with Aaron to destroy him: and I prayed for Aaron also at the same time. 21 And I took your sin, the calf which ye had made, and burnt it with fire, and stamped it, grinding it very small, until it was as fine as dust: and I cast the dust thereof into the brook that descended out of the mount.

22 And at Taberah, and at Massah, and at Kibroth-hattaavah, ye provoked Jehovah to wrath. 23 And when Jehovah sent you from Kadesh-barnea, saying, Go up and possess the land which I have given you; then ye rebelled against the

commandment of Jehovah your God, and
ye believed him not, nor hearkened to
his voice. 24 Ye have been rebellious
against Jehovah from the day that I
knew you.

25 So I fell down before Jehovah the
forty days and forty nights that I fell
down, because Jehovah had said he would
destroy you. 26 And I prayed unto Jehovah, and said, O Lord Jehovah, destroy
not thy people and thine inheritance,
that thou hast redeemed through thy
greatness, that thou hast brought forth out
of Egypt with a mighty hand. 27 Remember thy servants, Abraham, Isaac, and
Jacob; look not unto the stubbornness
of this people, nor to their wickedness,
nor to their sin, 28 lest the land whence
thou broughtest us out say, Because Jehovah was not able to bring them into the
land which he promised unto them, and
because he hated them, he hath brought
them out to slay them in the wilderness.
29 Yet they are thy people and thine
inheritance, which thou broughtest out
by thy great power and by thine outstretched arm.

The Lord constantly reminded the
Israelites that the favor they enjoyed was
not due to their own righteousness, for
they had traditionally shown a **stiffnecked** or rebellious attitude. They were
reminded that their disobedience and self-
will invoked the wrath of Jehovah upon
them in the wilderness (see Num. 14:22).
This rebellious attitude had been consistent and continuous from the time they
left Egypt (v. 7). Moses reminded the
people of the shameful idolatry practiced
while he was receiving the tablets of the
law on Mt. Sinai. The seriousness of the
occasion is reflected in the fact that Moses
fasted for forty days and forty nights (vv.
9-11).

Before the Israelites even fought the
battle against the Canaanites, Moses
warned them that when they obtained
the victory they would have a tendency
to feel proud and self-righteous about
it. But he warns them here against committing this sin. They had repeatedly
shown themselves to be a fractious, cove-
nant-breaking people. They had been
spared and preserved in covenant relationship with God only through the
Lord's merciful renewal of the broken
covenant in response to the pleas of
Moses interceding for them.

A most grievous case of Israel's faithlessness took place at the very time
the covenant was being solemnized at
Horeb. Israel had just sworn allegiance
to God and vowed obedience to His
commandments (Exod. 24). Indeed, it
was while the Lord was in the very process
of inscribing the treaty on the duplicate
stone documents that Israel broke the
covenant by engaging in idolatry. In
that hour the wrath of God blazed and
Israel was at the brink of destruction.[45]

It is to be noted that the tablets of the
law came only after agonizing prayer and
travail. Great things in life do not came
easy nor without some mortification of
the flesh. While Moses was experiencing
a great measure of grace upon the mount,
the people of Israel debased themselves
by worshiping a representation of Egypt's
calf, or the Apis bull-god (see Exod. 32:
12). When Moses saw what the people
were doing he was so emotionally overcome that he broke the tablets of stone
by throwing them down upon the rocky
mountain slope (v. 17).

It was with the greatest degree of discipline and self-perseverance that Moses
maintained his own faith. He fasted
and prayed forty days (possibly twice, see
v. 25) that God's anger would be turned
away from the people.

L. THE SECOND TABLES OF STONE (10:1-11)

1 At that time Jehovah said unto me,
Hew thee two tables of stone like unto
the first, and come up unto me into the
mount, and make thee an ark of wood.
2 And I will write on the tables the
words that were on the first tables which
thou brakest, and thou shalt put them in
the ark. 3 So I made an ark of acacia
wood, and hewed two tables of stone
like unto the first, and went up into the
mount, having the two tables in my
hand. 4 And he wrote on the tables, according to the first writing, the ten commandments, which Jehovah spake unto
you in the mount out of the midst of the
fire in the day of the assembly: and
Jehovah gave them unto me. 5 And I
turned and came down from the mount,
and put the tables in the ark which I
had made; and there they are as Jehovah commanded me. 6 (And the children of Israel journeyed from Beeroth
Bene-jaakan to Moserah. There Aaron

[45] See Kline, *op. cit.*, p. 167.

died, and there he was buried; and Eleazar his son ministered in the priest's office in his stead. 7 From thence they journeyed unto Gudgodah; and from Gudgodah to Jotbathah, a land of brooks of water. 8 At that time Jehovah set apart the tribe of Levi, to bear the ark of the covenant of Jehovah, to stand before Jehovah to minister unto him, and to bless in his name, unto this day. 9 Wherefore Levi hath no portion nor inheritance with his brethren; Jehovah is his inheritance, according as Jehovah thy God spake unto him.) 10 And I stayed in the mount, as at the first time, forty days and forty nights: and Jehovah hearkened unto me that time also; Jehovah would not destroy thee. 11 And Jehovah said unto me, Arise, take thy journey before the people; and they shall go in and possess the land, which I sware unto their fathers to give unto them.

The first two tables were provided by Jehovah Himself (Exod. 32:16, 19), whereas Moses is now commanded to provide tables wrought by his own hands. Jehovah promises to write the same words on them that were on the first (v. 2). The tablets, when completed, are to be placed in the ark of the covenant. A description of this ark is found in Exodus 25:10ff. The material quoted in verses 6 and 7 is probably a fragment from an old itinerary and is very incomplete. (For a complete text of the events here described, see Num. 33:31-39.) [46]

The priesthood is to reside in the tribe of Levi; this tribe was sanctified for the purpose of administering the rites and ritual before Jehovah God. The tribe of Levi is to have no land allotment such as is to be given to the other tribes, but is to be supported by the tithes and offerings from the other tribes (see comments on Num. 18:20-29; v. 10, see comments on Deut. 9:11).

M. REQUIREMENTS FOR A HOLY LIFE (10:12-22).

12 And now, Israel, what doth Jehovah thy God require of thee, but to fear Jehovah thy God, to walk in all his ways, and to love him, and to serve Jehovah thy God with all thy heart and with all thy soul, 13 to keep the commandments of Jehovah, and his statutes, which I command thee this day for thy

good? 14 Behold, unto Jehovah thy God belongeth heaven and the heaven of heavens, the earth, with all that is therein. 15 Only Jehovah had a delight in thy fathers to love them, and he chose their seed after them, even you above all peoples, as at this day. 16 Circumcise therefore the foreskin of your heart, and be no more stiffnecked. 17 For Jehovah your God, he is God of gods, and Lord of lords, the great God, the mighty, and the terrible, who regardeth not persons, nor taketh reward. 18 He doth execute justice for the fatherless and widow, and loveth the sojourner, in giving him food and raiment. 19 Love ye therefore the sojourner; for ye were sojourners in the land of Egypt. 20 Thou shalt fear Jehovah thy God; him shalt thou serve; and to him shalt thou cleave, and by his name shalt thou swear. 21 He is thy praise, and he is thy God, that hath done for thee these great and terrible things, which thine eyes have seen. 22 Thy fathers went down into Egypt with threescore and ten persons; and now Jehovah thy God hath made thee as the stars of heaven for multitude.

What doth Jehovah thy God require of thee? (v. 12). The answer is given immediately. Jehovah requires that the Israelites should fear Him and walk in all His ways and love Him and **serve Jehovah thy God with all thy heart and with all thy soul** (v. 12); they are to keep the commandments and the statutes of Jehovah (v. 13). The supreme love of Jehovah is given as the keystone to keeping all of the commandments (see comments on Deut. 6:5). The sovereignty and majesty of God is clearly elucidated (v. 14). A historical background of Jehovah's providential care of Israel is here given this young generation (v. 15).

Physical circumcision was the initiatory rite into covenant relationship between Jehovah and Abraham (Gen. 17:1-10). But this was only the outer expression of an inner spiritual circumcision.

For the Old Testament Church the rite of circumcision was the symbol of faith, by which believers were distinguished from the heathen people; the rite effected admission to the fellowship of the covenant people, securing for the individual his share in the promises and saving benefits provided by God from the

[46] See G. Ernest Wright, "Deuteronomy," *The Interpreter's Bible*, II, 397, and Clarke, *op. cit.*, I, 722f., 768.

foundation of the world (Rev. 13:8). It is evident that ethical demands are made on one that is spiritually circumcised, i.e., "born again and inwardly purified." It binds him to obedience to God, whose covenant sign he bears in his body, and to a blameless walk before Him (Gen. 17:1). Thus it is the symbol of the renewal and purification of the heart. The spiritual significance is brought out in the use of the phrase "uncircumcision of heart" to note a want of receptivity to the things of God (Lev. 26:41; Jer. 9:25; Ezek. 44:7); while on the other hand the purification of the heart by which it becomes receptive to the things of God, and capable of executing God's will, is called circumcision of the heart (v. 16; 30:6).

From this evidence, it will be seen that the physical operation (circumcision) is a sign of a spiritual operation wrought on the heart by the Holy Spirit. "Circumcision of heart" means spiritual renewal and purification. The words "circumcision" and "baptism" are terms dealing with a rite or ceremony subsequent to conversion. In the Old and New Testaments an exercise of faith in God's redemptive provision preceded the rite — circumcision or baptism, as the case may be. It can be noted that Abraham was "spiritually circumcised" before he submitted to the physical operation of circumcision (Rom. 4:11). Neither circumcision nor baptism was relevant or significant apart from the supernatural operation — conversion of the heart — through the Holy Spirit (I Cor. 7:19).

Paul says, "Jesus Christ was a minister of the circumcision for the truth of God, to confirm the promises made unto the fathers" (Rom. 15:8). By the time of John the Baptist, water-baptism had become the general mode of initiating a believer into the Christian faith. By the time Paul became a believer in Christ Jesus, circumcision was practiced by the Church only on occasion, to avoid offending the Jews (Acts 16:3). Gradually baptism with water superseded circumcision.

Reference to sprinkling of water and cleansing from filthiness is common in the Old Testament (Num. 8:7; Ezek. 36:25). It is certain that John the Baptist found in such passages the ground for his practice of baptizing the Jewish believers who sought "to flee from the wrath to come" (John 1:25-28; see also Matt. 3:7). In the baptism of John a connecting link between the Old and New Testament Church is clearly seen. It has always been necessary for sinful man to accept the promised regeneration, so lovingly offered by Jehovah. The renewing and cleansing so often referred to is in reality the circumcision of the heart (Deut. 30:6) in contradistinction to the flesh, the token of the Abrahamic covenant.[47]

Jehovah is the great and mighty God with personal interest in all of His creation. He is no respecter of persons (see comments on Deut. 1:17). He executes justice for the orphans and widows and shows benevolent interest to strangers (v. 18). Israel is to show lovingkindness to the underprivileged, even as Jehovah has shown kindness to His people (vv. 19-22).[48]

N. GOD'S GREATNESS (11:1-7)

1 Therefore thou shalt love Jehovah thy God, and keep his charge, and his statutes, and his ordinances, and his commandments, alway. 2 And know ye this day: for I *speak* not with your children that have not known, and that have not seen the chastisement of Jehovah your God, his greatness, his mighty hand, and his outstretched arm, 3 and his signs, and his works, which he did in the midst of Egypt unto Pharaoh the king of Egypt, and unto all his land; 4 and what he did unto the army of Egypt, unto their horses, and to their chariots; how he made the water of the Red Sea to overflow them as they pursued after you, and how Jehovah hath destroyed them unto this day; 5 and what he did unto you in the wilderness, until ye came unto this place; 6 and what he did unto Dathan and Abiram, the sons of Eliab, the son of Reuben; how the earth opened its mouth, and swallowed them up, and their households, and their tents, and every living thing that followed them, in the midst of all Israel: 7 but your eyes have seen all the great work of Jehovah which he did.

Without supreme love for God there can be no obedience and no happiness of

[47] Hanke, *Christ and the Church in the Old Testament*, pp. 102-03.
[48] R. V. G. Tasker, *The Old Testament in the New Testament*, pp. 147-48.

the soul. Jehovah demands absolute and complete commitment, and by a miracle of grace resulting in love all the law is fulfilled (see comments on Deut. 6:5).

O. THE BLESSINGS AND DANGERS IN CANAAN (11:8-32)

8 Therefore shall ye keep all the commandment which I command thee this day, that ye may be strong, and go in and possess the land, whither ye go over to possess it; 9 and that ye may prolong your days in the land, which Jehovah sware unto your fathers to give unto them and to their seed, a land flowing with milk and honey. 10 For the land, whither thou goest in to possess it, is not as the land of Egypt, from whence ye came out, where thou sowedst thy seed, and wateredst it with thy foot, as a garden of herbs; 11 but the land, whither ye go over to possess it, is a land of hills and valleys, *and* drinketh water of the rain of heaven, 12 a land which Jehovah thy God careth for: the eyes of Jehovah thy God are always upon it, from the beginning of the year even unto the end of the year.

13 And it shall come to pass, if ye shall hearken diligently unto my commandments which I command you this day to love Jehovah your God, and to serve him with all your heart and with all your soul, 14 that I will give the rain of your land in its season, the former rain and the latter rain, that thou mayest gather in thy grain, and thy new wine, and thine oil. 15 And I will give grass in thy fields for thy cattle, and thou shalt eat and be full. 16 Take heed to yourselves, lest your heart be deceived, and ye turn aside, and serve other gods, and worship them; 17 and the anger of Jehovah be kindled against you, and he shut up the heavens, so that there shall be no rain, and the land shall not yield its fruit; and ye perish quickly from off the good land which Jehovah giveth you.

18 Therefore shall ye lay up these my words in your heart and in your soul; and ye shall bind them for a sign upon your hand, and they shall be for frontlets between your eyes. 19 And ye shall teach them your children, talking of them, when thou sittest in thy house, and when thou walkest by the way, and when thou liest down, and when thou risest up. 20 And thou shalt write them upon the doorposts of thy house, and upon thy gates; 21 that your days may be multiplied, and the days of your children, in the land which Jehovah sware unto your fathers to give them, as the days of the heavens above the earth. 22 For if ye shall diligently keep all this commandment which I command you, to do it, to love Jehovah your God, to walk in all his ways, and to cleave unto him; 23 then will Jehovah drive out all these nations from before you, and ye shall dispossess nations greater and mightier than yourselves. 24 Every place whereon the sole of your foot shall tread shall be yours: from the wilderness, and Lebanon, from the river, the river Euphrates, even unto the hinder sea shall be your border. 25 There shall no man be able to stand before you: Jehovah your God shall lay the fear of you and the dread of you upon all the land that ye shall tread upon, as he hath spoken unto you.

26 Behold, I set before you this day a blessing and a curse: 27 the blessing, if ye shall hearken unto the commandments of Jehovah your God, which I command you this day; 28 and the curse, if ye shall not hearken unto the commandments of Jehovah your God, but turn aside out of the way which I command you this day, to go after other gods, which ye have not known. 29 And it shall come to pass, when Jehovah thy God shall bring thee into the land whither thou goest to possess it, that thou shalt set the blessing upon mount Gerizim, and the curse upon mount Ebal. 30 Are they not beyond the Jordan, behind the way of the going down of the sun, in the land of the Canaanites that dwell in the Arabah, over against Gilgal, beside the oaks of Moreh? 31 For ye are to pass over the Jordan to go in to possess the land which Jehovah your God giveth you, and ye shall possess it, and dwell therein. 32 And ye shall observe to do all the statutes and the ordinances which I set before you this day.

In the sight of God the laws are regarded as one, and the breaking of any commandment brings with it the judgment of all the commandments (see Jas. 2:10). A clean moral life, such as is expected by God of His people, will give the Israelites the mental and physical strength necessary for subduing the Canaanites and possessing the promised land. In addition, a moral life will add extra years of life to the Israelites (v. 9).

The Israelites had very unhappy memories of working in the fields of Egypt. Since it seldom rains in Egypt, moisture for raising crops had to be supplied by the flooding Nile. Controlling these floods for effective crop production required building canals, terraces, dams and ditches. Water had to be collected in ponds and channeled into the fields when needed. At some seasons in the year it was necessary to elevate the water from the ponds and canals by means of crude animal- and human-powered water wheels and cylindrical pumps.

The extensive expenditure of physical energy in the blazing heat of Egypt made life for the field worker, and especially the slave, very difficult. In addition to working in the fields, the Israelites were compelled to make bricks and other building materials in off-season periods when no work was needed in the fields.

The Lord encourages the weary Israelites by telling them that the promised land is a place where they sow their seed and where the rains come down from heaven to water the land. In this new land they will not have to suffer the harsh privations and hardships of Egypt, nor will they suffer from the intense heat. The Lord will send the **former rain** at planting time and the **latter rain** for maturing their crops (v. 14). Even the pasture land will give natural grazing for their cattle (v. 15).

The Israelites were constantly warned against the temptation to forget their God in times when they were enjoying prosperity (see notes on Deut. 4:9). God's people are to subject themselves to the strictest religious discipline including the memorization of the commandments and ordinances of the Lord. Turning to the gods of Canaan will result in judgment; rain will cease and the fields will not yield their fruit and they will perish (v. 17).

In order to be constantly reminded of Jehovah's demands upon them they were not only to memorize the law, but they were to bind portions of the law on their hands and foreheads. Clarke gives an interesting explanation of this custom.

> The Jews wrote the following four portions of the law upon slips of parchment or vellum: "Sanctify unto me the first-born," Exod. 13:2-10. "And it shall be, when the Lord shall bring thee into the land," Exod. 13:11-16. "Hear, O Israel, the Lord our God is one Lord," Deut. 6:4-9. "And it shall come to pass, if ye shall hearken diligently," Deut.

11:13-21. These four portions, making in all 30 verses, written as mentioned above, and covered with leather, they tied to the forehead and to the hand or arm.

> In the process of time the spirit of this law was lost in the letter, and when the word was not in their mouth, nor the law in their heart, they had their phylacteries on their heads and on their hands. And the Pharisees, who in our Lord's time affected extraordinary piety, made their phylacteries very broad, that they might have many sentences written upon them, or the ordinary portions in very large and observable letters.[49]

Ye shall teach them your children (v. 19). The Jews are known for their close-knit family life. Through the ages they have maintained a great degree of racial integrity. Teaching the children the laws of Jehovah has always been an integral part of Jewish home life. In addition, certain parts of the law were to be written upon the doorposts of the homes and on the gates (v. 20). It is still a custom among orthodox Jews to fasten a small object or container called a *mazuza*, upon the doorpost of their homes. The *mazuza* contains a copy of Deuteronomy 4:4-9. It is required by law in Israel today to affix a *mazuza* inside the front doorpost of every building. A *mazuza* can be seen on the doorpost of every room in every hotel in Israel. It must be pointed out, however, that these external signs can and do become legalistic trappings without spiritual significance.

The borders of Israel were to extend from Lebanon in the north to the wilderness in the south, and from the Euphrates River in the east to the Mediterranean Sea in the west. The Israelites were to view their land in the spirit of reverent fear because of the blessing which would come upon Israel for obedience and, conversely, the curse for disobedience (vv. 25-28).

Mt. Gerizim is a peak 2849 feet above sea level. With Mt. Ebal (2077 feet above sea level) it forms the valley in which ancient Canaanitish Shechem was located. From the slopes of Gerizim Joshua later pronounced the blessing which would come when Israel obeyed the law (see Josh. 8:33-35). On the slopes of Ebal Joshua later erected an altar, and from it he pronounced the curses that would follow disobedience of the law. At the present time a colony of Samaritans lives on the hillside of Mt. Gerizim, holding in possession a very ancient copy of the Pentateuch.

P. GOD TO BE WORSHIPED IN A CENTRAL PLACE (12:1-28)

1 These are the statutes and the ordinances which ye shall observe to do in the land which Jehovah, the God of thy fathers, hath given thee to possess it, all the days that ye live upon the earth. 2 Ye shall surely destroy all the places wherein the nations that ye shall dispossess served their gods, upon the high mountains, and upon the hills, and under every green tree: 3 and ye shall break down their altars, and dash in pieces their pillars, and burn their Asherim with fire; and ye shall hew down the graven images of their gods; and ye shall destroy their name out of that place. 4 Ye shall not do so unto Jehovah your God. 5 But unto the place which Jehovah your God shall choose out of all your tribes, to put his name there, even unto his habitation shall ye seek, and thither thou shalt come; 6 and thither ye shall bring your burnt-offerings, and your sacrifices, and your tithes, and the heave-offering of your hand, and your vows, and your freewill-offerings, and the firstlings of your herd and of your flock: 7 and there ye shall eat before Jehovah your God, and ye shall rejoice in all that ye put your hand unto, ye and your households, wherein Jehovah thy God hath blessed thee. 8 Ye shall not do after all the things that we do here this day, every man whatsoever is right in his own eyes; 9 for ye are not as yet come to the rest and to the inheritance, which Jehovah thy God giveth thee. 10 But when ye go over the Jordan, and dwell in the land which Jehovah your God causeth you to inherit, and he giveth you rest from all your enemies round about, so that ye dwell in safety; 11 then it shall come to pass that to the place which Jehovah your God shall choose, to cause his name to dwell there, thither shall ye bring all that I command you: your burnt-offerings, and your sacrifices, your tithes, and the heave-offering of your hand, and all your choice vows which ye vow unto Jehovah. 12 And ye shall rejoice before Jehovah your God, ye, and your sons, and your daughters, and your men-servants, and your maid-servants, and the Levite that is within your gates, forasmuch as he hath no portion nor inheritance with you. 13 Take heed to thyself that thou offer not thy burnt-offerings in every place that thou seest; 14 but in the place which Jehovah shall choose in one of thy tribes, there thou shalt offer thy burnt-offerings, and there thou shalt do all that I command thee.

15 Notwithstanding, thou mayest kill and eat flesh within all thy gates, after all the desire of thy soul, according to the blessing of Jehovah thy God which he hath given thee: the unclean and the clean may eat thereof, as of the gazelle, and as of the hart. 16 Only ye shall not eat the blood; thou shalt pour it out upon the earth as water. 17 Thou mayest not eat within thy gates the tithe of thy grain, or of the new wine, or of thine oil, or the firstlings of thy herd or of thy flock, nor any of thy vows which thou vowest, nor thy freewill-offerings, nor the heave-offering of thy hand; 18 but thou shalt eat them before Jehovah thy God in the place which Jehovah thy God shall choose, thou, and thy son, and thy daughter, and thy man-servant, and thy maid-servant, and the Levite that is within thy gates: and thou shalt rejoice before Jehovah thy God in all that thou puttest thy hand unto. 19 Take heed to thyself that thou forsake not the Levite as long as thou livest in thy land.

20 When Jehovah thy God shall enlarge thy border, as he hath promised thee, and thou shalt say, I will eat flesh, because thy soul desireth to eat flesh; thou mayest eat flesh, after all the desire of thy soul. 21 If the place which Jehovah thy God shall choose, to put his name there, be too far from thee, then thou shalt kill of thy herd and of thy flock, which Jehovah hath given thee, as I have commanded thee; and thou mayest eat within thy gates, after all the desire of thy soul. 22 Even as the gazelle and as the hart is eaten, so thou shalt eat thereof: the unclean and the clean may eat thereof alike. 23 Only be sure that thou eat not the blood: for the blood is the life; and thou shalt not eat the life with the flesh. 24 Thou shalt not eat it; thou shalt pour it out upon the earth as water. 25 Thou shalt not eat it; that it may go well with thee, and with thy children after thee, when thou shalt do that which is right in the eyes of Jehovah. 26 Only thy holy things which thou hast, and thy vows, thou shalt take, and go unto the place which Jehovah shall choose; 27 and thou shalt offer thy burnt-offerings, the flesh and the blood, upon the altar of Jehovah thy God; and the blood of thy sacrifices shall be poured out upon the altar of Jehovah thy God;

and thou shalt eat the flesh. 28 Observe and hear all these words which I command thee, that it may go well with thee, and with thy children after thee for ever, when thou doest that which is good and right in the eyes of Jehovah thy God.

The imperative nature of Jehovah's laws is here clearly stated. There could be no compromise: every detail of the law had to be obeyed if Israel was to retain God's favor. These laws were immutable and eternal and were equally binding upon the present as well as all future generations. Israel was to express its faith by obedience. Its social, spiritual and moral well-being was clearly related to these ordinances. Obedience to the laws of Jehovah was the key to the "good life," and in the continual practice of them Israel was to be distinguished from the degenerate heathen nations, upon whom the judgment of God was about to be imposed.

The Canaanite society had become so morally corrupt that every semblance of its culture was to be destroyed. Its idols, statues, temples, altars and high places of worship were to be completely obliterated lest they should become a snare and a temptation to Israel (see comments on Num. 33:52).

Jehovah had given the Israelites a carefully worked out ritual which was designed to help them keep their minds upon the reason for their existence. Each sacrifice and offering expressed some peculiar aspect or facet of salvation (see comments on Num. 28:1ff.). The blood sacrifice was symbolic of the blood of the Lamb slain "from the foundation of the world" (Rev. 13:8). One day the great Redeemer would come as a personification of that which they enacted in their ritualistic expression of faith. Obviously the references to sacrifices and offerings in this book are restatements of that which had been given before. Kline says:

As normative religious practice was concerned, there was nothing essentially new about this law even in Moses' day. In patriarchal times, when a succession of altars was built in the course of the patriarch's journeyings, there was apparently but one central family altar at any given time. Similarly, in the Sinaitic

legislation (Ex. 20:24), Israel's place of sacrifice is identified with the central place where God recorded his name (i.e., revealed his glorious nature); by special supernatural theophany, the place of God's visible symbolic dwelling in the midst of her people.[50]

There is one difference in the Deuteronomic expectation: Israel's place of worship is to change from the portable tabernacle to a permanently built temple. Israel is to enjoy a degree of rest after crossing the Jordan River (vv. 10, 11).

Ye shall rejoice (v. 12). The religion of Jehovah was characterized by a degree of joy and jubilation. The book of Psalms — the Hebrew hymnal — is pregnant with such expressions as joy, praise, thanksgiving and gladness. Only the Hebrew-Christian religion has jubilation as its central keynote.[51]

The entire Levitical ritual was filled with spiritual significance and prophetic implications of good things to come. Every minute detail was clearly elucidated by Jehovah, even to the extent of the places where Israel was to present its burnt-offerings. There was always danger that the sensuous nature religion might tempt the Israelites to mix some of the heathen ritual with their own. Clarke says:

To prevent idolatry and bring about a perfect uniformity in the Divine worship, which at that time was essentially necessary; because every rite and ceremony had a determinate meaning, and pointed out the good things which were to come, therefore one place must be established where these rites and ceremonies should be carefully and punctually observed. Had it not been so, every man would have formed his worship according to his own mind, and the whole beauty and importance of the grand representative system would have been destroyed, and the Messiah and the glories of his kingdom could not have been seen through the medium of the Jewish ritual.[52]

Verse 16 is a reaffirmation of the law forbidding the eating of blood (see Lev. 17:12). This prohibition had been passed down from generation to generation. The penalty for eating blood was very severe: the guilty were to be excommunicated

[50] Op. cit., p. 171.   [51] Hanke, From Eden to Eternity, pp. 173ff.   [52] Op. cit., I, 773.

from fellowship with Israel. Eating blood was so strongly forbidden because blood literally contained a living principle which unites and feeds all the living parts of the body. Even a more serious consideration is found in the fact that this life-giving fluid (blood) makes atonement for the soul. God ordained that the blood should be poured out within the framework of a most reverent and respectful ceremony. Henry remarks:

> God appointed the sprinkling or pouring out of the blood of the sacrifice upon the altar, to signify that the life of the sacrifice was given to God instead of the sinner's life, and as a ransom or counterprice for it; therefore 'without shedding of blood there was no remission' (Heb. 9:22). For this reason they must eat no blood, and . . . it was then a very good reason; for God would by this means preserve the honour of that way of atonement which he had instituted, and kept up in the minds of the people a reverent regard to it. The blood of the covenant being then a sensible object, no blood must be either eaten, or trodden under foot as a common thing.[53]

Jehovah designated a certain place where the "community of faith" could meet together in His presence to eat in a common fellowship. Eating together helps men and women to get better acquainted and to share with each other their faith. Eating in a framework of Christian fellowship can be done to the glory of God.

The attitude of the people toward the ministerial members was to be one of respect and reverence. The Levites had no inheritance or private income and were obliged to render service in the worship service in behalf of the people. If the offerings were withheld the Levites would perish. The Christian Church also recognizes the importance of a full-time ministry. Every pastor, ideally speaking, should give all his time and service in ministering salvation and spiritual growth to the souls of men, and this can be done only when the congregation is faithful with its tithes and offerings. The church is greatly impoverished when the pastor must divide his energies between his pastoral charge and some outside economic interest.

Q. THE DANGER OF IDOLATRY (12:29—14:2)

29 When Jehovah thy God shall cut off the nations from before thee, whither thou goest in to dispossess them, and thou dispossessest them, and dwellest in their land; 30 take heed to thyself that thou be not ensnared to follow them, after that they are destroyed from before thee; and that thou inquire not after their gods, saying, How do these nations serve their gods? even so will I do likewise. 31 Thou shalt not do so unto Jehovah thy God: for every abomination to Jehovah, which he hateth, have they done unto their gods; for even their sons and their daughters do they burn in the fire to their gods. 32 What thing soever I command you, that shall ye observe to do: thou shalt not add thereto, nor diminish from it.

1 If there arise in the midst of thee a prophet, or a dreamer of dreams, and he give thee a sign or a wonder, 2 and the sign or the wonder come to pass, whereof he spake unto thee, saying, Let us go after other gods, which thou hast not known, and let us serve them; 3 thou shalt not hearken unto the words of that prophet, or unto that dreamer of dreams: for Jehovah your God proveth you, to know whether ye love Jehovah your God with all your heart and with all your soul. 4 Ye shall walk after Jehovah your God, and fear him, and keep his commandments, and obey his voice, and ye shall serve him, and cleave unto him. 5 And that prophet, or that dreamer of dreams, shall be put to death, because he hath spoken rebellion against Jehovah your God, who brought you out of the land of Egypt, and redeemed thee out of the house of bondage, to draw thee aside out of the way which Jehovah thy God commanded thee to walk in. So shalt thou put away the evil from the midst of thee.

6 If thy brother, the son of thy mother, or thy son, or thy daughter, or the wife of thy bosom, or thy friend, that is as thine own soul, entice thee secretly, saying, Let us go and serve other gods, which thou hast not known, thou, nor thy fathers; 7 of the gods of the peoples that are round about you, nigh unto thee, or far off from thee, from the one end of the earth even unto the other end of the earth; 8 thou shalt not consent unto him, nor hearken unto him; neither shall thine eye pity him, neither shalt thou spare, neither shalt thou conceal him:

---

[53] Op. cit., I, 300.

9 but thou shalt surely kill him; thy hand shall be first upon him to put him to death, and afterwards the hand of all the people. 10 And thou shalt stone him to death with stones, because he hath sought to draw thee away from Jehovah thy God, who brought thee out of the land of Egypt, out of the house of bondage. 11 And all Israel shall hear, and fear, and shall do no more any such wickedness as this is in the midst of thee.

12 If thou shalt hear tell concerning one of thy cities, which Jehovah thy God giveth thee to dwell there, saying, 13 Certain base fellows are gone out from the midst of thee, and have drawn away the inhabitants of their city, saying, Let us go and serve other gods, which ye have not known; 14 then shalt thou inquire, and make search, and ask diligently; and, behold, if it be truth, and the thing certain, that such abomination is wrought in the midst of thee, 15 thou shalt surely smite the inhabitants of that city with the edge of the sword, destroying it utterly, and all that is therein and the cattle thereof, with the edge of the sword. 16 And thou shalt gather all the spoil of it into the midst of the street thereof, and shalt burn with fire the city, and all the spoil thereof every whit, unto Jehovah thy God: and it shall be a heap for ever; it shall not be built again. 17 And there shall cleave nought of the devoted thing to thy hand; that Jehovah may turn from the fierceness of his anger, and show thee mercy, and have compassion upon thee, and multiply thee, as he hath sworn unto thy fathers; 18 when thou shalt hearken to the voice of Jehovah thy God, to keep all his commandments which I command thee this day, to do that which is right in the eyes of Jehovah thy God.

1 Ye are the children of Jehovah your God: ye shall not cut yourselves, nor make any baldness between your eyes for the dead. 2 For thou art a holy people unto Jehovah thy God, and Jehovah hath chosen thee to be a people for his own possession, above all peoples that are upon the face of the earth.

The Canaanite nations had sinned beyond the point of no return. The judgment of God could no longer be stayed, and as a result they were to be destroyed and the Israelites were to possess the land which they had forfeited through their persistent moral degradation. At the same time, the Israelites were warned of a similar judgment if they adopted the religious practices of the heathen nations. Upon arrival in Canaan God's people would observe that their enemies had indeed prospered, and they too might be tempted to **inquire after their gods** (v. 30). Jehovah informed "the people of the covenant" that the Canaanites had committed **every abomination** imaginable, and for this they were being destroyed. Let Israel be warned lest a terrible judgment come upon it. The Israelites were to rely solely upon the leadership of Jehovah; they were to observe all the law, and were not to **add thereto nor diminish from it** (v. 32).

Jehovah warns His people of a secondary danger — that of false prophets arising in their midst. The danger of prophetic "wolves in sheep's clothing" has always been a very serious danger, and is one against which Jesus warned His disciples (see Matt. 7:15). Kline says:

> Intimation of the prophetic institution to be established in Israel had already been given. God's self-disclosure to the prophets would be through the media of vision and dream (Num. 12:5; cf. Deut. 18:15ff.). Even if one with impressive credentials to the effect that he was a channel of revelation (1b, 2a) should incite Israel to render allegiance and tribute to other gods (ab; cf. 3b, 5b), his counsel must be despised (3a; cf. Gal. 1:8, 9).[54]

Israel is advised that she can best resist the overtures of temptation by close association with Jehovah and by keeping His commandments (v. 4). The seriousness of persuading believers to forsake Jehovah is seen in the supreme penalty imposed upon it. The prophet guilty of this offense was to be put to death for his crime against Jehovah and also to prevent him from doing further harm. Removing the guilt could be accomplished only by removing the guilty. Only through the supreme penalty could the infection be kept from spreading.[55]

The supreme penalty was to be imposed upon a prophet as well as a relative or close friend without consideration for the person's social status (vv. 6-7). The means of execution was to be stoning, and the person approached by the false prophet was to take the initiative in

[54] Op. cit., p. 172.   [55] Henry, op. cit., II, 455.

bringing the guilty one to judgment (vv. 8-11).

The burden of reporting the offender rested upon each individual. Just to hear about some activity along this line was sufficient reason for a person to initiate an investigation (vv. 12-14). In some situations whole cities were to be destroyed and the spoils were to be burned (vv. 15-18).

The children of Israel were commanded to refrain from adopting the cultural and religious practices of the Canaanites. Among the most offensive was the practice of cutting and mutilating their bodies during a religious exercise, as was done by the Baal priests in the contest with Elijah on Mt. Carmel (see I Kings 18:28; see also Lev. 19:28; 21:5; I Cor. 6:15; and I Tim. 5:23; cf. Deut. 7:6-11 with comments).

R. CLEAN AND UNCLEAN FOODS (14:3-21)

3 Thou shalt not eat any abominable thing. 4 These are the beasts which ye may eat: the ox, the sheep, and the goat, 5 the hart, and the gazelle, and the roebuck, and the wild goat, and the pygarg, and the antelope, and the chamois. 6 And every beast that parteth the hoof, and hath the hoof cloven in two, *and* cheweth the cud, among the beasts, that may ye eat. 7 Nevertheless these ye shall not eat of them that chew the cud, or of them that have the hoof cloven: The camel, and the hare, and the coney, because they chew the cud but part not the hoof, they are unclean unto you. 8 And the swine, because he parteth the hoof but cheweth not the cud, he is unclean unto you: of their flesh ye shall not eat, and their carcasses ye shall not touch.

9 These ye may eat of all that are in the waters: whatsoever hath fins and scales may ye eat; 10 and whatsoever hath not fins and scales ye shall not eat; it is unclean unto you.

11 Of all clean birds ye may eat. 12 But these are they of which ye shall not eat: the eagle, and the gier-eagle, and the ospray, 13 and the glede, and the falcon, and the kite after its kind, 14 and every raven after its kind, 15 and the ostrich, and the night-hawk, and the sea-mew, and the hawk after its kind, 16 the little owl, and the great owl, and the horned owl, 17 and the pelican, and the vulture, and the cormorant, 18 and the stork, and the heron after its kind, and the hoopoe,

and the bat. 19 And all winged creeping things are unclean unto you: they shall not be eaten. 20 Of all clean birds ye may eat.

21 Ye shall not eat of anything that dieth of itself: thou mayest give it unto the sojourner that is within thy gates, that he may eat it; or thou mayest sell it unto a foreigner: for thou art a holy people unto Jehovah thy God. Thou shalt not boil a kid in its mother's milk.

The problem of keeping Israel separated from the idolatrous world involved positive affirmations as well as negative taboos. Some of the things which the people were forbidden to eat were things which the heathen used in their religious orgies. In addition, there were dietary restrictions in the interest of health and sanitation. Trichinosis is a dreaded intestinal disease caused by the trichinae (worms) found in pork not thoroughly cooked. This disease is almost incurable, even in our modern age of miracle drugs and medical procedures. Many people are allergic to pork products and suffer painful symptoms of various sorts, including headaches. Science is still in the process of discovering some of the functional aspects of the dietary restrictions imposed upon the Israelites. The clean and unclean animals are enumerated in verses 4-20.

Boiling a kid in his mother's milk was an ancient Canaanite practice in connection with their religious ritual. The Jews still interpret this passage to mean that they were not to eat meat and milk dishes at the same meal. In modern Israel, kosher restaurants and hotels (most are kosher by law) do not serve milk in any form when meat is being served. This restriction applies even to cream in coffee. In order to insure that no dish on which meat has been served comes into contact with milk foods, two separate sets of dishes are used — usually of different colors.

S. THE LAW OF THE TITHE (14:22-29)

22 Thou shalt surely tithe all the increase of thy seed, that which cometh forth from the field year by year. 23 And thou shalt eat before Jehovah thy God, in the place which he shall choose, to cause his name to dwell there, the tithe of thy grain, of thy new wine, and

of thine oil, and the firstlings of thy
herd and of thy flock; that thou mayest
learn to fear Jehovah thy God always.
24 And if the way be too long for thee,
so that thou art not able to carry it,
because the place is too far from thee,
which Jehovah thy God shall choose, to
set his name there, when Jehovah thy
God shall bless thee; 25 then shalt thou
turn it into money, and bind up the
money in thy hand, and shalt go unto
the place which Jehovah thy God shall
choose: 26 and thou shalt bestow the
money for whatsoever thy soul desireth,
for oxen, or for sheep, or for wine, or
for strong drink, or for whatsoever thy
soul asketh of thee; and thou shalt eat
there before Jehovah thy God, and thou
shalt rejoice, thou and thy household.
27 And the Levite that is within thy
gates, thou shalt not forsake him; for he
hath no portion nor inheritance with
thee.
28 At the end of every three years thou
shalt bring forth all the tithe of thine increase in the same year, and shalt lay it
up within thy gates: 29 and the Levite,
because he hath no portion nor inheritance with thee, and the sojourner, and
the fatherless, and the widow, that are
within thy gates, shall come, and shall
eat and be satisfied; that Jehovah thy
God may bless thee in all the work of thy
hand which thou doest.

The first tithe was to be given to the
Levites, but the second tithe was to be
eaten before the Lord by the Israelites
during the first and second year. During
the third year this tithe was to be given
to the Levites and to the poor (see Deut.
14:28-29). In the fourth and fifth years
it was again eaten by the owners. In the
sixth year it was given to the poor, and
then came the seventh or sabbatical year
when all people had things in common.[56]

T. THE SABBATICAL YEAR (15:1-6).

1 At the end of every seven years thou
shalt make a release. 2 And this is the
manner of the release: every creditor
shall release that which he hath lent
unto his neighbor; he shall not exact
it of his neighbor and his brother; because Jehovah's release hath been proclaimed. 3 Of a foreigner thou mayest
exact it: but whatsoever of thine is with
thy brother thy hand shall release.
4 Howbeit there shall be no poor with
thee (for Jehovah will surely bless thee

in the land which Jehovah thy God
giveth thee for an inheritance to possess
it), 5 if only thou diligently hearken
unto the voice of Jehovah thy God, to
observe to do all this commandment
which I command thee this day. 6 For
Jehovah thy God will bless thee, as he
promised thee: and thou shalt lend unto
many nations, but thou shalt not borrow;
and thou shalt rule over many nations,
but they shall not rule over thee.

The children of Israel were commanded to observe a special sabbath year
every seventh year. This was a special
year when the people ceased from their
labor and the fields were to "rest and be
still," i.e., the land was to lie fallow after
being worked for six years (see Exod.
23:10ff.). The poor people and the animals were to glean what they could in
the resting fields while the others lived
on what they had saved during the six
working years. This ordinance applied
also to the release of Hebrew slaves
(Exod. 21:1-6). Even debts were to
be cancelled in the seventh year. Loans
were to be renewed for the foreigner, but
the obligation of a kinsman or neighbor
was to be cancelled. This practice has become obsolete among the Jews since the
development of long-term credit.

U. LENDING TO THE POOR (15:7-11)

7 If there be with thee a poor man,
one of thy brethren, within any of thy
gates in thy land which Jehovah thy God
giveth thee, thou shalt not harden thy
heart, nor shut thy hand from thy poor
brother; 8 but thou shalt surely open thy
hand unto him, and shalt surely lend
him sufficient for his need in that which
he wanteth. 9 Beware that there be not
a base thought in thy heart, saying, The
seventh year, the year of release, is at
hand; and thine eye be evil against thy
poor brother, and thou give him nought;
and he cry unto Jehovah against thee,
and it be sin unto thee. 10 Thou shalt
surely give him, and thy heart shall not
be grieved when thou givest unto him;
because that for this thing Jehovah thy
God will bless thee in all thy work, and
in all that thou puttest thy hand unto.
11 For the poor will never cease out of
the land: therefore I command thee,
saying, Thou shalt surely open thy
hand unto thy brother, to thy needy, and
to thy poor, in thy land.

---

[56] Clarke, op. cit., I, 778.

The Israelites were to consider the fact that the land they possessed was a gift from Jehovah. They were to look with compassion upon the needy and make available to them loans under reasonable terms and conditions (v. 8). They were to give from a generous heart and not hesitate to lend because of the soon-approaching sabbatical year when all debts were to be cancelled (v. 9). The Israelites were assured of God's blessing if they would lend and give with a heart of benevolence (v. 10). There would always be the poor whose needs had to be satisfied by those who had an excess of goods (v. 11).

V. TREATMENT OF SERVANTS (15: 12-18)

12 If thy brother, a Hebrew man, or a Hebrew woman, be sold unto thee, and serve thee six years; then in the seventh year thou shalt let him go free from thee. 13 And when thou lettest him go free from thee, thou shalt not let him go empty: 14 thou shalt furnish him liberally out of thy flock, and out of thy thresh-ing-floor, and out of thy winepress; as Jehovah thy God hath blessed thee thou shalt give unto him. 15 And thou shalt remember that thou wast a bondman in the land of Egypt, and Jehovah thy God redeemed thee: therefore I command thee this thing to-day. 16 And it shall be, if he say unto thee, I will not go out from thee; because he loveth thee and thy house, because he is well with thee; 17 then thou shalt take an awl, and thrust it through his ear unto the door, and he shall be thy servant for ever. And also unto thy maid-servant thou shalt do likewise. 18 It shall not seem hard unto thee, when thou lettest him go free from thee; for to the double of the hire of a hireling hath he served thee six years: and Jehovah thy God will bless thee in all that thou doest.

There were several ways by which a Hebrew might become a slave. In extreme poverty a person might elect to sell himself as a slave so that his debt could be paid. In desperation a father might sell his children to someone so that the family economy could be resolved. A thief who could not repay what he had stolen could sell himself so that restitution might be made. However, at the end of the six years all slaves were to be set free. When the slave was liberated the former owner was to provide a reasonable amount of substance so that the freed man could get started on his own (vv. 13-14). The Israelites were constantly to remember that they themselves were once slaves in Egypt and that Jehovah had redeemed them (vv. 15-16). The liberator was assured that Jehovah's blessings would rest upon him.

W. THE OFFERING OF FIRSTLINGS (15:19-23)

19 All the firstling males that are born of thy herd and of thy flock thou shalt sanctify unto Jehovah thy God: thou shalt do no work with the firstling of thy herd, nor shear the firstling of thy flock. 20 Thou shalt eat it before Jehovah thy God year by year in the place which Jehovah shall choose, thou and thy household. 21 And if it have any blemish, *as if it be* lame or blind, any ill blemish whatsoever, thou shalt not sacrifice it unto Jehovah thy God. 22 Thou shalt eat it within thy gates: the unclean and the clean *shall eat it* alike, as the gazelle, and as the hart. 23 Only thou shalt not eat the blood thereof; thou shalt pour it out upon the ground as water.

The rule of sacrifice was "My best for the Lord." The first-fruits from the land and the firstlings of the herd usually bring a premium price on the market. Israel was to sanctify the firstlings and to eat them ceremonially before the Lord at the time and place designated by Jehovah (v. 20). This ritual was also to commemorate the sparing of Israel's first-born in Egypt (Exod. 13:2ff.). Only the animals which were without spot or blemish were to be sacrificed to the Lord (v. 21). The people were again warned not to eat the blood (v. 23; see also comments on Deut. 12:16).

X. THE THREE ANNUAL FEASTS (16:1-17)

1 Observe the month of Abib, and keep the passover unto Jehovah thy God; for in the month of Abib Jehovah thy God brought thee forth out of Egypt by night. 2 And thou shalt sacrifice the passover unto Jehovah thy God, of the flock and the herd, in the place which Jehovah shall choose, to cause his name to dwell there. 3 Thou shalt eat no leavened bread with it; seven days shalt

thou eat unleavened bread therewith, even the bread of affliction; for thou camest forth out of the land of Egypt in haste: that thou mayest remember the day when thou camest forth out of the land of Egypt all the days of thy life. 4 And there shall be no leaven seen with thee in all thy borders seven days; neither shall any of the flesh, which thou sacrificest the first day at even, remain all night until the morning. 5 Thou mayest not sacrifice the passover within any of thy gates, which Jehovah thy God giveth thee; 6 but at the place which Jehovah thy God shall choose, to cause his name to dwell in, there thou shalt sacrifice the passover at even, at the going down of the sun, at the season that thou camest forth out of Egypt. 7 And thou shalt roast and eat it in the place which Jehovah thy God shall choose: and thou shalt turn in the morning, and go unto thy tents. 8 Six days thou shalt eat unleavened bread; and on the seventh day shall be a solemn assembly to Jehovah thy God; thou shalt do no work *therein*.

9 Seven weeks shalt thou number unto thee: from the time thou beginnest to put the sickle to the standing grain shalt thou begin to number seven weeks. 10 And thou shalt keep the feast of weeks unto Jehovah thy God with a tribute of a freewill-offering of thy hand, which thou shalt give, according as Jehovah thy God blesseth thee: 11 and thou shalt rejoice before Jehovah thy God, thou, and thy son, and thy daughter, and thy man-servant, and thy maid-servant, and the Levite that is within thy gates, and the sojourner, and the fatherless, and the widow, that are in the midst of thee, in the place which Jehovah thy God shall choose, to cause his name to dwell there. 12 And thou shalt remember that thou wast a bondman in Egypt: and thou shalt observe and do these statutes.

13 Thou shalt keep the feast of tabernacles seven days, after that thou hast gathered in from thy threshing-floor and from thy winepress: 14 and thou shalt rejoice in thy feast, thou, and thy son, and thy daughter, and thy man-servant, and thy maid-servant, and the Levite, and the sojourner, and the fatherless, and the widow, that are within thy gates. 15 Seven days shalt thou keep a feast unto Jehovah thy God in the place which Jehovah shall choose; because Jehovah thy God will bless thee in all thine increase, and in all the work of thy hands, and thou shalt be altogether joyful. 16 Three

times in a year shall all thy males appear before Jehovah thy God in the place which he shall choose: in the feast of unleavened bread, and in the feast of weeks, and in the feast of tabernacles; and they shall not appear before Jehovah empty: 17 every man shall give as he is able, according to the blessing of Jehovah thy God which he hath given thee.

The Mosaic law instituted three historic feasts at which every adult male in good health was required to be present. These three feasts were: (1) the Passover (Lev. 23:5-8), (2) the Feast of Weeks (Exod. 23:16; 34:22; Num. 28:26; and Acts 2:1), and (3) the Feast of Tabernacles (Lev. 23:34-44).

The Passover was a sacred and solemn feast for Israel in which the passing of the death angel in Egypt was brought to remembrance. Only one week in the month of Abib was to be given to the festive program, but the three preceding meals were to be a period of solemn preparation in anticipation of this glorious event. During the feast week they were to eat no leavened bread (here a symbol of evil) as a reminder of the fearful conditions in Egypt out of which Jehovah had delivered them (v. 3). The Passover sacrifice was not just another sacrifice, but it was the sacrifice which could be offered only at the place and time Jehovah appointed (vv. 4-6). During the first six days of the Passover feast the Israelites were to eat only unleavened bread, and the seventh day was to culminate in a solemn assembly to Jehovah when all work ceased (v. 8).

The Feast of Weeks or Pentecost came on the fiftieth day after the Passover, and originally had an agricultural significance. Rabbinical calculation makes it the day of the giving of the law on Mt. Sinai.[57] Old Testament believers celebrated the Day of Pentecost in remembrance of the giving of the law on Mt. Sinai; New Testament believers celebrate it in remembrance of the baptism with the Holy Spirit in the Upper Room. Many Christians see a significant analogy in the giving of the law at Mt. Sinai fifty days after the Passover and the baptism of the Holy Spirit upon the disciples in the Upper Room fifty days after the resurrection of Jesus Christ[58] (see comments on

[57] Ella Davis Isaacs, "Feasts and Fasts," *The International Standard Bible Encyclopedia*, II, 1103.
[58] Madeline S. Miller and J. Lane Miller, "Pentecost," *Harper's Bible Dictionary*, pp. 536, 537.

Acts 2ff. in the *Wesleyan Bible Commentary*, Vol. IV).

The Feast of Tabernacles was also called the Feast of Booths or of Ingathering, and it came five days after the Day of Atonement and lasted from seven to eight days (Lev. 23:34-36). This festival came at the harvest time of grapes, olives and other fruits, and marked the beginning of the new civil year (Deut. 16:13-17). It was an occasion when families moved into tents in the fields and celebrated thanksgiving — a time of great rejoicing and fellowship among the Israelites (vv. 14-15). It was also a time when people made offerings to the Lord according to the blessings they had received from Jehovah (vv. 16-17). The modern camp meeting, especially when people live in tents, forms an obvious analogy.

III. JUDICIAL JUSTICE (Deut. 16:18—21:23)

A. APPOINTMENT OF JUDGES (16:18-20)

18 Judges and officers shalt thou make thee in all thy gates, which Jehovah thy God giveth thee, according to thy tribes; and they shall judge the people with righteous judgment. 19 Thou shalt not wrest justice: thou shalt not respect persons; neither shalt thou take a bribe; for a bribe doth blind the eyes of the wise, and pervert the words of the righteous. 20 That which is altogether just shalt thou follow, that thou mayest live, and inherit the land which Jehovah thy God giveth thee.

The nation of Israel was so large that it became necessary to divide it into small segments with a judge or officer in charge of each group. The judges were commanded to administer justice to all the people and were not to have "respect of persons" because of wealth or other social considerations. Justice and fair treatment were to be rendered regardless of state or place in society (v. 19). The judges were warned against the danger of taking gifts or bribes.

B. WARNING AGAINST IMAGES (16:21-22)

21 Thou shalt not plant thee an Asherah of any kind of tree beside the altar of Jehovah thy God, which thou shalt make thee. 22 Neither shalt thou set thee up a pillar; which Jehovah thy God hateth.

The Israelites were warned against planting groves of trees near the altar of the Lord because the native Canaanites worshiped their images and idols in groves of trees. There was danger that Israel might become careless and adopt some of the heathen ritual in its worship of Jehovah (v. 22).

C. BLEMISHED SACRIFICES FORBIDDEN (17:1)

1 Thou shalt not sacrifice unto Jehovah thy God an ox, or a sheep, wherein is a blemish, *or* anything evil; for that is an abomination unto Jehovah thy God.

The perfect sacrificial animal symbolized the devotion and affection the worshiper had for the Lord. The offering coming from a heart motivated by love is the finest. As children of God, our best for the Lord is always the proper measurement of that which we offer. God is a holy God who tolerates no divided devotion or loyalty. Nothing must excel that which we offer to Him. The Christian standard of offering is prophetically projected in the animal sacrifices. Paul states the Christian standard thus: "I beseech you therefore, brethren, by the mercies of God, that you present your bodies a living sacrifice, holy, acceptable to God" (Rom. 12:1; for additional material on this subject see comments on Deut. 15:19-23).

D. THE PUNISHMENT OF IDOLATERS (17:2-7)

2 If there be found in the midst of thee, within any of thy gates which Jehovah thy God giveth thee, man or woman, that doeth that which is evil in the sight of Jehovah thy God, in transgressing his covenant, 3 and hath gone and served other gods, and worshipped them, or the sun, or the moon, or any of the host of heaven, which I have not commanded, 4 and it be told thee, and thou hast heard of it; then shalt thou inquire diligently; and, behold, if it be true, and the thing certain, that such abomination is wrought in Israel, 5 then shalt thou bring forth that man or that woman, who hath done this evil thing, unto thy gates, even the

man or the woman; and thou shalt stone them to death with stones. 6 At the mouth of two witnesses, or three witnesses, shall he that is to die be put to death; at the mouth of one witness he shall not be put to death. 7 The hand of the witnesses shall be first upon him to put him to death, and afterward the hand of all the people. So thou shalt put away the evil from the midst of thee.

The seriousness with which the Lord looked upon spiritual infidelity is expressed in the supreme punishment which was to be imposed upon those who deviated from true Jehovah-worship. The individual had the responsibility of being alert to any infractions within the camp and was commanded to report those who worshiped other gods. However, a warning was given against making reports on the basis of rumor or heresy. Each person was obligated to **inquire diligently** or to investigate thoroughly the report to ascertain if it was true and beyond question (v. 4). After the report of evil was verified the investigator had the further responsibility of bringing the guilty one to the **gates** where the congregation was to stone him (v. 5). It was necessary to have from two to three witnesses before the death penalty could be carried out. The law specified that the witnesses were to cast the first stone.

E. THE LAW OF APPEAL (17:8-13)

8 If there arise a matter too hard for thee in judgment, between blood and blood, between plea and plea, and between stroke and stroke, being matters of controversy within thy gates; then shalt thou arise, and get thee up unto the place which Jehovah thy God shall choose; 9 and thou shalt come unto the priests the Levites, and unto the judge that shall be in those days: and thou shalt inquire; and they shall show thee the sentence of judgment. 10 And thou shalt do according to the tenor of the sentence which they shall show thee from that place which Jehovah shall choose; and thou shalt observe to do according to all that they shall teach thee: 11 according to the tenor of the law which they shall teach thee, and according to the judgment which they shall tell thee, thou shalt do; thou shalt not turn aside from the sentence which they shall show thee, to the right hand, nor to the left. 12 And the

man that doeth presumptuously, in not hearkening unto the priest that standeth to minister there before Jehovah thy God, or unto the judge, even that man shall die: and thou shalt put away the evil from Israel. 13 And all the people shall hear, and fear, and do no more presumptuously.

It was conceivable that the local judges or magistrates might not be sufficiently trained in matters of the law to decide some cases involving legal technicalities. The priests and Levites were specially trained in legal matters and were considered to be the best qualified to pass on these difficult cases (vv. 9-11).[59]

Those who refused to abide by the decision of this high tribunal were considered to be in rebellion against law and authority and lost all further rights of protection under the law. A person guilty of rebellion was to be put to death.

F. LAWS CONCERNING A KING (17: 14-20)

14 When thou art come unto the land which Jehovah thy God giveth thee, and shalt possess it, and shalt dwell therein, and shalt say, I will set a king over me, like all the nations that are round about me; 15 thou shalt surely set him king over thee, whom Jehovah thy God shall choose: one from among thy brethren shalt thou set king over thee; thou mayest not put a foreigner over thee, who is not thy brother. 16 Only he shall not multiply horses to himself, nor cause the people to return to Egypt, to the end that he may multiply horses; forasmuch as Jehovah hath said unto you, Ye shall henceforth return no more that way. 17 Neither shall he multiply wives to himself, that his heart turn not away: neither shall he greatly multiply to himself silver and gold.

18 And it shall be, when he sitteth upon the throne of his kingdom, that he shall write him a copy of this law in a book, out of *that which is* before the priests the Levites: 19 and it shall be with him, and he shall read therein all the days of his life; that he may learn to fear Jehovah his God, to keep all the words of this law and these statutes, to do them; 20 that his heart be not lifted up above his brethren, and that he turn not aside from the commandment, to the right hand, or to the left: to the end that he may prolong his days in his kingdom,

he and his children, in the midst of Israel.

A prophetic projection is expressed in verse 14 of a time when the Israelites will be settled in the land of Canaan and will demand a king patterned after the kings in the nations around them (see I Sam. 8:5ff.). The king the people will choose will be **one from among thy brethren** and not a foreigner (v. 15). Clarke says,

> It was on the ground of this command that the Jews proposed that insidious question to our Lord, "Is it lawful to give tribute to Caesar, or no?" Matt. 22:17; for they were then under the authority of a foreign power. Had Christ said Yes, then they would have condemned him by this law; had he said NO, then they would have accused him to Caesar.[60]

The idea of a king was anathema to Jehovah because the king, to some of the surrounding peoples, was a god. To the Israelites only Jehovah was to be King (cf. Exod. 15:18; 19:5-6; Deut. 33:5; Judg. 8:23). Horses were widely used by some of the heathen nations in conducting aggressive wars. The Israelites were warned against putting their trust in "horses and chariots" instead of God. The psalmist makes this timely reference, "Some trust in chariots and some in horses: but we will remember the name of the Lord our God" (Ps. 20:7). Later King Solomon disregarded this warning and began his decline and destruction (see I Kings 4:26; 10:26-29).

Marriage is always presented in the Bible as a sacred relationship between a man and a woman. One wife and one husband is the divine standard. Even though many men in the Scriptures had more than one wife, this was never the divine norm for man. This idea of monogamous marriage is expressed in these words, "Therefore shall a man leave his father and his mother, and shall cleave unto his wife, and they shall be one flesh" (Gen. 2:4).

Solomon sinned against this divine command and brought ruin upon himself. He adopted the heathen custom of bigamous marriages, and, in the interest of political and economic expediency, married many of the heathen women. The violation of this legal norm brought ruin and destruction, not only upon himself but also upon his nation (I Kings 11:1-11).

The future king of Israel was to be well versed in the laws of Jehovah. He was to have a personal copy of the Scriptures so that he might **read therein all the days of his life.** Through the reading of the divine law the king was to learn reverent fear for Jehovah and to understand fully the nature of his divine office (v. 19). The king was always to exercise a great degree of humility and to walk circumspectly before the Lord (v. 20).

G. SUPPORT OF THE LEVITES (18: 1-8)

1 The priests the Levites, *even* all the tribe of Levi, shall have no portion nor inheritance with Israel: they shall eat the offerings of Jehovah made by fire, and his inheritance. 2 And they shall have no inheritance among their brethren: Jehovah is their inheritance, as he hath spoken unto them. 3 And this shall be the priests' due from the people, from them that offer a sacrifice, whether it be ox or sheep, that they shall give unto the priest the shoulder, and the two cheeks, and the maw. 4 The first-fruits of thy grain, of thy new wine, and of thine oil, and the first of the fleece of thy sheep, shalt thou give him. 5 For Jehovah thy God hath chosen him out of all thy tribes, to stand to minister in the name of Jehovah, him and his sons for ever.

6 And if a Levite come from any of thy gates out of all Israel, where he sojourneth, and come with all the desire of his soul unto the place which Jehovah shall choose; 7 then he shall minister in the name of Jehovah his God, as all his brethren the Levites do, who stand there before Jehovah. 8 They shall have like portions to eat, besides that which cometh of the sale of his patrimony.

In the wisdom of God there was to be a priestly tribe whose sole responsibility was the spiritual needs of Israel. The Levites were to have no outside secular interests or responsibilities but to give themselves entirely to administering spiritual matters. The other tribes were obligated to support the Levites with their tithes and offerings (see comments

---

[60] *Ibid.*, I, 783.

on Num. 18:20ff.). Henry makes this comment:

> Care is taken that the priests entangle not themselves with the affairs of this life, nor enrich themselves with the wealth of this world; they have better things to mind. They "shall have no part nor inheritance with Israel," that is, no share either in the spoils taken in war, or in the land that was to be divided by lot, v. 1. Their warfare and husbandry are both spiritual, and enough to fill their hands both with work and profit, and to content them. "The Lord is their inheritance" v. 2. Note thôse that have God for their inheritance, according to the new covenant, should not be greedy of great things in the world; neither gripe what they have, nor grasp at more, but look upon all present things with the indifference which becomes those that believe God to be all-sufficient . . . the people must provide for them. They must have their "due from the people," v. 3. Their maintenance must not depend upon the generosity of the people, but they must be by law entitled to it. He that is taught in the word, ought in justice to communicate to him that teaches him; and he that has the benefit of solemn religious assemblies, to contribute to the comfortable support of those that preside in such assemblies.[61]

H. WARNING AGAINST HEATHEN PRACTICES (18:9-14)

9 When thou art come into the land which Jehovah thy God giveth thee, thou shalt not learn to do after the abominations of those nations. 10 There shall not be found with thee any one that maketh his son or his daughter to pass through the fire, one that useth divination, one that practiseth augury, or an enchanter, or a sorcerer, 11 or a charmer, or a consulter with a familiar spirit, or a wizard, or a necromancer. 12 For whosoever doeth these things is an abomination unto Jehovah: and because of these abominations Jehovah thy God doth drive them out from before thee. 13 Thou shalt be perfect with Jehovah thy God. 14 For these nations, that thou shalt dispossess, hearken unto them that practise augury, and unto diviners; but as for thee, Jehovah thy God hath not suffered thee so to do.

The Israelites were warned against adopting the sensuous practices of the Canaanites after they had taken possession of their inheritance. The occult superstitions, sorcery, divination and spiritualism of the heathen peoples were to be avoided.[62]

The infectious nature of the idolatrous customs in Canaan is indicated in the frequent warnings Jehovah gives His people. It was the custom among the heathen inhabitants of Canaan to consecrate their children to the god Moloch by making them pass through the fire, and frequently to have them completely consumed (see Lev. 18:21). Divination and the various arts of fortune-telling — witchcraft, charms, incantations — were customarily used by these heathen worshipers. These divinational arts are presented in the Scriptures as an evil to be avoided (see Deut. 18:11; I Sam. 28:11; Isa. 2:6; 8:19; Mal. 3:5; Acts 8:11; Rev. 18:23). Verse 12 says, **whosoever doeth these things is an abomination unto Jehovah,** and it was because of these wicked practices that the Canaanites had forfeited their right to life and land. By these practices they expressed their apostate condition (v. 12). It should be pointed out that Jehovah's priest Melchizedek had made available to the Canaanites the redemptive message.

Thou shalt be perfect (v. 13). There was no compromise in the dedication which was required by Jehovah. The doctrine of Christian perfection is a cardinal tenet in the faith of many denominations. For a further development of this doctrine see comments on Numbers 11:18ff.

I. A PROPHET LIKE MOSES PROMISED (18:15-22)

15 Jehovah thy God will raise up unto thee a prophet from the midst of thee, of thy brethren, like unto me; unto him ye shall hearken; 16 according to all that thou desiredst of Jehovah thy God in Horeb in the day of the assembly, saying, Let me not hear again the voice of Jehovah my God, neither let me see this great fire any more, that I die not. 17 And Jehovah said unto me, They have well said that which they have spoken. 18 I will raise them up a prophet from among their brethren, like unto thee; and I will put my words in his mouth, and he shall speak unto them all that I

61 Op. cit., II, 465.   62 Kline, op. cit., p. 181.

shall command him. 19 And it shall come to pass, that whosoever will not hearken unto my words which he shall speak in my name, I will require it of him.

20 But the prophet, that shall speak a word presumptuously in my name, which I have not commanded him to speak, or that shall speak in the name of other gods, that same prophet shall die. 21 And if thou say in thy heart, How shall we know the word which Jehovah hath not spoken? 22 when a prophet speaketh in the name of Jehovah, if the thing follow not, nor come to pass, that is the thing which Jehovah hath not spoken: the prophet hath spoken it presumptuously, thou shalt not be afraid of him.

God will raise up unto thee a prophet (v. 15). It is commonly agreed by scholars that this reference has prophetic significance, not only for the immediate future in the succession of prophets but also with regard to the coming of Christ the Messiah. This is the clearest promise of the Messianic prophecies and is so recognized in Acts 3:22 and 7:37. This prophecy was the focal point when the Christian believers said, "This is of a truth, the Prophet that should come into the world" (John 6:14; see also John 1:45). This prophetic statement is of such import and significance that the fulfillment of it would result in a momentous climax of grace. Henry says:

> God had made it clear that there should come a Prophet, great above all the prophets, by whom God would make known himself and his will to the children of men more fully and clearly than ever he had done before. He is 'the light of the world,' as prophecy was of the Jewish church, John 8:12. He is the Word by whom God speaks to us, John 1:1; Heb. 1:2. . . . In his birth he should be one of the nation, should live among them, and be sent to them . . . he should be like unto Moses, only as much above him, as the other prophets came short of him.[63]

The prophetic office carried with it grave responsibility. To speak lightly or falsely was an offense calling for the death penalty. In some instances a test of time was necessary to determine if a prophet spoke the truth (v. 22).

J. CITIES OF REFUGE (19:1-14; see also Num. 35:9-28)

1 When Jehovah thy God shall cut off the nations, whose land Jehovah thy God giveth thee, and thou succeedest them, and dwellest in their cities, and in their houses; 2 thou shalt set apart three cities for thee in the midst of thy land, which Jehovah thy God giveth thee to possess it. 3 Thou shalt prepare thee the way, and divide the borders of thy land, which Jehovah thy God causeth thee to inherit, into three parts, that every manslayer may flee thither.

4 And this is the case of the manslayer, that shall flee thither and live: whoso killeth his neighbor unawares, and hated him not in time past; 5 as when a man goeth into the forest with his neighbor to hew wood, and his hand fetcheth a stroke with the axe to cut down the tree, and the head slippeth from the helve, and lighteth upon his neighbor, so that he dieth; he shall flee unto one of these cities and live: 6 lest the avenger of blood pursue the manslayer, while his heart is hot, and overtake him, because the way is long, and smite him mortally; whereas he was not worthy of death, inasmuch as he hated him not in time past. 7 Wherefore I command thee, saying, Thou shalt set apart three cities for thee. 8 And if Jehovah thy God enlarge thy border, as he hath sworn unto thy fathers, and give thee all the land which he promised to give unto thy fathers; 9 if thou shalt keep all this commandment to do it, which I command thee this day, to love Jehovah thy God, and to walk ever in his ways; then shalt thou add three cities more for thee, besides these three: 10 that innocent blood be not shed in the midst of thy land, which Jehovah thy God giveth thee for an inheritance, and so blood be upon thee.

11 But if any man hate his neighbor, and lie in wait for him, and rise up against him, and smite him mortally so that he dieth, and he flee into one of these cities; 12 then the elders of his city shall send and fetch him thence, and deliver him into the hand of the avenger of blood, that he may die. 13 Thine eye shall not pity him, but thou shalt put away the innocent blood from Israel, that it may go well with thee.

14 Thou shalt not remove thy neighbor's landmark, which they of old time have set, in thine inheritance which thou

---

[63] *Op. cit.*, II, 466, 467. Some of the other major Messianic prophecies are here listed: Gen. 3:15; 17:19; 18:18; Ps. 16:10; 22:16, 18; 27:12; 34:20; 41:9; 68:18; 69:21; 109:7, 8; 110:4; Isa. 7:14; 9:7; 11:2; 50:6; 53:3ff.; Jer. 31:15; Dan. 9:25; Hos. 11:1; Zech. 9:9; 11:12, 13; 12:10.

shall inherit, in the land that Jehovah thy God giveth thee to possess it.

According to the law given to the sons of Noah, a man who killed a man was to be killed by a fellow man (Gen. 4:6). We now have a more precise definition of this law in the recognition of motive. The cities of refuge were instituted to provide protection for a man who accidentally and unintentionally killed someone. The killer was permitted to flee to the city of refuge and stay there under the protection of the law until his motive could be determined. According to Jewish tradition the roads to these cities were broad and kept in a good state of repair so that a man so involved had no difficulty in getting to one before a mob could lynch him (v. 3). Three cities of refuge had already been established on the east side of the Jordan; now three additional cities are designated on the west side (Deut. 4:41). The land was to be divided into three sections so that a city of refuge would be centrally located in each area. Henry gives the following spiritual analysis:

> Christ is not a refuge at a distance which we must ascend, or go down to the deep for, but the word is nigh us, and Christ is the word, Rom. 10:8. The gospel brings salvation to our door, and there it knocks for admission. And, to make the flight of the delinquent the more easy, the way must be prepared, that led to the city of refuge. Probably, they had causeways or streetways leading to those cities, and the Jews say, that the magistrates of Israel, upon one certain day in the year, sent out messengers to see that those roads were in good repair, and they were to remove stumbling-blocks, mend bridges that were broken, and, where two ways met, they were to set up a Mercurial post, with finger to point the way, on which was engraved in great letters, Miklat, Miklat; Refuge, Refuge.[64]

(See also comments on Num. 35:6 and Deut. 4:41-43.)

The necessity of keeping all the law was frequently reiterated (see also Jas. 2:10). Jehovah demanded complete commitment — not just identification. In a prophetic light, three additional cities were to be added on condition that the Israelites obeyed the law as set forth. Kline says:

Moses looked beyond the near future and the section of the three western cities to a more remote future, when Israelite expansion — in accordance with the divine purpose (1:7; 11:24; 12:20) — would necessitate nine instead of six cities of refuge. There is no historical notice of compliance with this command.[65]

The cities of refuge were not intended to be preserves where a murderer might escape punishment, but they were instituted for the protection of the innocent man. Motive and circumstance were deciding factors as to whether a man was a murderer or a victim of circumstance. If convicted, the murderer was to be forcibly removed and delivered to the avenger of blood (vv. 11-13).

Before fences came into use a man's property line was marked out by a pile of stones at its corners. Thus it was possible to steal some land by moving the pile of stones. A man's property represented his means of life, and moving the markers was considered a serious offense. It is the design and will of God that man should be absolutely honest in his relationship to his fellow man. Every man should know what belongs to him and what belongs to his neighbor. Boundary lines were surveyed and staked, and the legality of the stone markers was declared by Jehovah. This concept of ownership is a moral law and is binding upon us as well as the ancients. This is an application of the commandment, "Thou shalt not steal" (Exod. 20:15).

K. THE LAW CONCERNING WITNESSES (19:15-21)

15 One witness shall not rise up against a man for any iniquity, or for any sin, in any sin that he sinneth: at the mouth of two witnesses, or at the mouth of three witnesses, shall a matter be established. 16 If an unrighteous witness rise up against any man to testify against him of wrongdoing, 17 then both the men, between whom the controversy is, shall stand before Jehovah, before the priests and the judges that shall be in those days; 18 and the judges shall make diligent inquisition: and, behold, if the witness be a false witness, and have testified falsely against his brother; 19 then shall ye do unto him, as he had thought to do unto his brother: so shalt thou put away the

64 Op. cit., II, 468.   65 Op. cit., p. 82.

evil from the midst of thee. 20 And those that remain shall hear, and fear, and shall henceforth commit no more any such evil in the midst of thee. 21 And thine eyes shall not pity; life *shall go* for life, eye for eye, tooth for tooth, hand for hand, foot for foot.

Legal action in court was of such serious consequence that no verdict could be finalized with only one witness. Conviction required at least two witnesses whose testimonies were in agreement. Two or more witnesses were required so that no person could be punished because of a personal grudge or some selfish ambition. Perjury was and still is a very serious offense (see II Cor. 13:1).

In the event that there was only one witness the case was referred to the priests and judges, who were to make a thorough investigation of both the accuser and the accused (vv. 12-18). If it was ascertained that the accuser brought false accusation, he was in turn to receive the punishment that would have fallen upon the accused if he had been guilty (v. 19). The disposition of such a case was to be an example and a warning to each individual Israelite. No pity was to be shown the guilty offender, whether he was the accuser or the accused. The law was exact and explicit — **life shall go for life, eye for eye, tooth for tooth** . . . (vv. 20-21).

L. WARFARE AND EXEMPTIONS FROM SERVICE (20:1-20)

1 When thou goest forth to battle against thine enemies, and seest horses, and chariots, *and* a people more than thou, thou shalt not be afraid of them; for Jehovah thy God is with thee, who brought thee up out of the land of Egypt. 2 And it shall be, when ye draw nigh unto the battle, that the priest shall approach and speak unto the people, 3 and shall say unto them, Hear, O Israel, ye draw nigh this day unto battle against your enemies: let not your heart faint; fear not, nor tremble, neither be ye affrighted at them; 4 for Jehovah your God is he that goeth with you, to fight for you against your enemies, to save you. 5 And the officers shall speak unto the people, saying, What man is there that hath built a new house, and hath not dedicated it? let him go and return to his house, lest he die in the battle, and another man dedicate it. 6 And what man is there that hath planted a vineyard, and hath not used the fruit thereof? let him go and return unto his house, lest he die in the battle, and another man use the fruit thereof. 7 And what man is there that hath betrothed a wife, and hath not taken her? let him go and return unto his house, lest he die in the battle, and another man take her. 8 And the officers shall speak further unto the people, and they shall say, What man is there that is fearful and fainthearted? let him go and return unto his house, lest his brethren's heart melt as his heart. 9 And it shall be, when the officers have made an end of speaking unto the people, that they shall appoint captains of hosts at the head of the people.

10 When thou drawest nigh unto a city to fight against it, then proclaim peace unto it. 11 And it shall be, if it make thee answer of peace, and open unto thee, then it shall be, that all the people that are found therein shall become tributary unto thee, and shall serve thee. 12 And if it will make no peace with thee, but will make war against thee, then thou shalt besiege it: 13 and when Jehovah thy God delivereth it into thy hand, thou shalt smite every male thereof with the edge of the sword: 14 but the women, and the little ones, and the cattle, and all that is in the city, even all the spoil thereof, shalt thou take for a prey unto thyself; and thou shalt eat the spoil of thine enemies, which Jehovah thy God hath given thee. 15 Thus shalt thou do unto all the cities which are very far off from thee, which are not of the cities of these nations. 16 But of the cities of these peoples, that Jehovah thy God giveth thee for an inheritance, thou shalt save alive nothing that breatheth: 17 but thou shalt utterly destroy them: the Hittite, and the Amorite, the Canaanite, and the Perizzite, the Hivite, and the Jebusite; as Jehovah thy God hath commanded thee; 18 that they teach you not to do after all their abominations, which they have done unto their gods; so would ye sin against Jehovah your God.

19 When thou shalt besiege a city a long time, in making war against it to take it, thou shalt not destroy the trees thereof by wielding an axe against them; for thou mayest eat of them, and thou shalt not cut them down; for is the tree of the field man, that it should be besieged of thee? 20 Only the trees of which thou knowest that they are not trees for food, thou shalt destroy and cut them down; and thou shalt build bulwarks against the city that maketh war with thee, until it fall.

The Lord conditioned the people for the battles which were ahead in the land of Canaan. The physical power in the hands of the enemy — horses and chariots — was to be a secondary consideration. Over against the powerful Canaanites was Almighty God, who would deliver them and lead them to victory. They were reminded that the God who led them out of Egypt and sustained them in the wilderness was still their God.

The people were to have their attention focused upon God, their spiritual strength. What is more fitting than a worship service in the face of danger! Jehovah was their strength and would fight the battle for the people when they were in tune with Him (vv. 2-4).

It was the custom among the Israelites to dedicate their house to Jehovah with prayer, praise and thanksgiving. It was believed that this secured God's presence and blessing. It is the practice of some Christian churches to this day to consecrate to the Lord the church building, an organ, or a home.

Only those with courageous hearts and a complete dedication to the cause could effectively serve in the army. If a man had divided loyalty it was better that he return to his home than enter into battle because his presence would be a hindrance to the other men. Perhaps this is what Jesus had in mind when he made reference to the plowman (see comments on Luke 9:62 in the *Wesleyan Bible Commentary*, Vol. IV). If a man owned a house that had not been dedicated he would do well to settle his private business first. Later he could go into battle with the feeling that all business matters had been settled (v. 5). If a man had not harvested his vineyard he should go home and attend to this matter (v. 6). If a man was engaged to a girl he would best serve the cause by completing the marriage (v. 7).

The armies of Israel were not to attack a Canaanite city until the inhabitants had received fair notice to surrender without resistance. Even in dealing with its enemies Israel was required to observe justice and honor. Upon surrender the enemy people were to become the slaves of the Israelites (v. 11). If the city refused to surrender, Israel was commanded to make an all-out attack, killing all the males (v. 13), while women and children were to be taken captive. The spoil of the city was to become the property of the Israelites (v. 14). This harsh treatment should be evaluated in the light of the utter moral degeneration of the Canaanites (for additional comment on this subject see Num. 31:2 and Deut. 7:1-5).

The trees of the field provided life-sustaining food for humanity. Olives, figs, dates, nuts and other fruits were staples in the oriental diet. It took many years of growth before some trees produced. For this reason it was a serious crime to mutilate or destroy a tree. It was permissible, however, to cut down trees which were not fruit-bearing. These could be used for tools, buildings and instruments of war, as well as for fortifications (v. 20).

M. EXPIATION FOR UNTRACED MURDER (21:1-9).

1 If one be found slain in the land which Jehovah thy God giveth thee to possess it, lying in the field, and it be not known who hath smitten him; 2 then thy elders and thy judges shall come forth, and they shall measure unto the cities which are round about him that is slain: 3 and it shall be, that the city which is nearest unto the slain man, even the elders of that city shall take a heifer of the herd, which hath not been wrought with, and which hath not drawn in the yoke; 4 and the elders of that city shall bring down the heifer unto a valley with running water, which is neither plowed nor sown, and shall break the heifer's neck there in the valley. 5 And the priests the sons of Levi shall come near; for them Jehovah thy God hath chosen to minister unto him, and to bless in the name of Jehovah; and according to their word shall every controversy and every stroke be. 6 And all the elders of that city, who are nearest unto the slain man, shall wash their hands over the heifer whose neck was broken in the valley; 7 and they shall answer and say, Our hands have not shed this blood, neither have our eyes seen it. 8 Forgive, O Jehovah, thy people Israel, whom thou hast redeemed, and suffer not innocent blood *to remain* in the midst of thy people Israel. And the blood shall be forgiven them. 9 So shalt thou put away the innocent blood from the midst of thee, when thou shalt do that which is right in the eyes of Jehovah.

The opening verses in this chapter describe judicial procedure where the guilty murderer could not be traced. Henry says:

> Care had been taken by some preceding laws for the vigorous and effectual prosecution of a wilful murderer, ch. 19.11 . . . the putting of whom to death was the putting away of the guilt of blood from the land; but if that could not be done, the murderer not being discovered, they must not think that the land was in no danger of contracting any pollution because it was not through any neglect of theirs that the murderer was unpunished; no, a great solemnity is here provided for the putting away of the guilty, as an expression of their dread and detestation of that sin.[66]

The elders residing in the city which was closest to the slain man were to break the neck of an unworked heifer in an uncultivated valley with running water (v. 6). After this part of the ritual they were to wash their hands over the heifer and testify that they had not shed the blood of the murdered man, and ask Jehovah not to allow innocent blood to remain in their midst. Thus they were absolved from all possible ceremonial or moral pollution (vv. 7-9). This idea was expressed, both personally and collectively, when Pilate washed his hands at the trial of Jesus (Matt. 27:24).

N. MISCELLANEOUS LAWS (21:10-22)

10 When thou goest forth to battle against thine enemies, and Jehovah thy God delivereth them into thy hands, and thou carriest them away captive, 11 and seest among the captives a beautiful woman, and thou hast a desire unto her, and wouldest take her to thee to wife; 12 then thou shalt bring her home to thy house; and she shall shave her head, and pare her nails; 13 and she shall put the raiment of her captivity from off her, and shall remain in thy house, and bewail her father and her mother a full month: and after that thou shalt go in unto her, and be her husband, and she shall be thy wife. 14 And it shall be, if thou have no delight in her, then thou shalt let her go whither she will; but thou shalt not sell her at all for money, thou shalt not deal with her as a slave, because thou hast humbled her.

15 If a man have two wives, the one beloved, and the other hated, and they have borne him children, both the beloved and the hated; and if the first-born son be hers that was hated; 16 then it shall be, in the day that he causeth his sons to inherit that which he hath, that he may not make the son of the beloved the first-born before the son of the hated, who is the first-born: 17 but he shall acknowledge the first-born, the son of the hated, by giving him a double portion of all that he hath; for he is the beginning of his strength; the right of the first-born is his.

18 If a man have a stubborn and rebellious son, that will not obey the voice of his father, or the voice of his mother, and, though they chasten him, will not hearken unto them; 19 then shall his father and his mother lay hold on him, and bring him out unto the elders of his city, and unto the gate of his place; 20 and they shall say unto the elders of his city, This our son is stubborn and rebellious, he will not obey our voice; he is a glutton, and a drunkard. 21 And all the men of his city shall stone him to death with stones: so shalt thou put away the evil from the midst of thee; and all Israel shall hear, and fear.

22 And if a man have committed a sin worthy of death, and he be put to death, and thou hang him on a tree; 23 his body shall not remain all night upon the tree, but thou shalt surely bury him the same day; for he that is hanged is accursed of God; that thou defile not thy land which Jehovah thy God giveth thee for an inheritance.

According to ancient heathen custom all things captured in a war were legitimate spoils. Women were forcibly taken and subjected to the carnal desire of men, but the law of Jehovah required that human dignity be applied to all women — free or captive. If an Israelite was attracted to a beautiful captive girl he could take her as his wife only after certain conditions were met. The ritual to which she was to submit included shaving her head and manicuring her fingernails. She was to live in the man's house for one month during which time she was to show evidence of repentance and to renounce the life practiced by her father and mother (vv. 12-13). Kline comments:

The case of a captive woman (vv. 10, 11; cf. 20:14; contrast 7:3) is used as a case in point for establishing the rights of the wife, perhaps because the principle would obviously apply a fortiori in the case of an Israelite wife. On the purificatory acts of verses 12b, 13a, which signified removal from captive-slave status, compare Lev. 14:8; Num. 8:7. On the month's mourning, see Num. 20:29 and Deut. 34:8. This period would provide for the achieving of inward composure for beginning a new life, as well as for an appropriate expression of filial piety.[67]

If the marriage failed to work out satisfactorily the man was to set the woman free — she was not to be sold as a slave. A man's authority did not include the power to enslave his wife or to sell her as a slave. The dissolution of marriage was to be exercised according to the law of divorce (see Deut. 24:1-4).

The word **hated** (v. 15) should more correctly read "loved less." A man might love both wives but one would be more endearing than the other, as in the case of Jacob's love for Leah and Rachel (see Gen. 29:16ff.). We note that polygamy did exist under the Mosaic administration, but it was never approved by Jehovah (see Matt. 19:8). The Mosaic law required of the parents that they give their children their rights without partiality or favor (vv. 16-17).

The seriousness of a rebellious attitude is reflected in the penalty that was to be imposed upon a rebellious son. Rebellion, of any kind, against authority — secular or divine — was not to be tolerated. If the son became rebellious against parental authority he was to be taken to the elders or proper authorities for punishment, and the punishment for rebellion was death by stoning (vv. 19-21).

The law stipulated that a person who was executed by hanging was to be taken down the same day. The sun was not to set on the dead body while still hanging. It was deemed that the law had been satisfied and public justice had been exercised when a criminal was pronounced dead. No good cause could be served by extended exposure of the dead body beyond the day of execution. Death by hanging carried with it a peculiar public disgrace; it expressed the curse

that God placed upon criminality (v. 23).

IV. THE SANCTITY OF DIVINE ORDER (Deut. 22:1—25:19)

A. ASSISTING FALLEN BEASTS (22:1-4)

1 Thou shalt not see thy brother's ox or his sheep go astray, and hide thyself from them: thou shalt surely bring them again unto thy brother. 2 And if thy brother be not nigh unto thee, or if thou know him not, then thou shalt bring it home to thy house, and it shall be with thee until thy brother seek after it, and thou shalt restore it to him. 3 And so shalt thou do with his ass; and so shalt thou do with his garment; and so shalt thou do with every lost thing of thy brother's, which he hath lost, and thou hast found: thou mayest not hide thyself. 4 Thou shalt not see thy brother's ass or his ox fallen down by the way, and hide thyself from them: thou shalt surely help him to lift them up again.

The command to show mercy to a fallen beast is an extension of the command, "Thou shalt love thy neighbor as thyself" (Lev. 19:18). The Golden Rule expresses the spirit and attitude which one human being should possess in his relationship to his fellow man and his possessions. There is both a humane and an economic aspect in helping a neighbor to recover one of his lost beasts of burden or some other property. To see a brother's animal in distress was sufficient reason for a man to lend a helping hand.

B. WARNING AGAINST INTERCHANGE OF GARMENTS (22:5)

5 A woman shall not wear that which pertaineth unto a man, neither shall a man put on a woman's garment; for whosoever doeth these things is an abomination unto Jehovah thy God.

The Lord created man and woman with different physiological features and each was to function in his or her respective area of life. It is a fundamental principle of life that society is best served when women exercise their God-endowed functions, and likewise when men per-

[67] Op. cit., p. 184.

form the tasks allotted to them. Nothing is more confusing than when women pose as men and when men pose as women. Kline observes:

> It is the fundamental principle which underlies the opening requirement of this section that the distinction between man and woman should not be blurred by one's appropriating the characteristic articles of the other (Deut. 22:5). God created them male and female, with distinctive natures and functions; specifically, in the divinely established order of authority, man is the head of the woman as together they reign over the earth. The Lord created the various "kinds" in the vegetable and animal kingdom (Gen. 1:11ff.). Israel was so to treat these "kinds" that they would be preserved in their distinctive natures (Deut. 22:6, 7, 9-11; cf. Lev. 19:19).[68]

C. MISCELLANEOUS LAWS (22:6-12)

6 If a bird's nest chance to be before thee in the way, in any tree or on the ground, with young ones or eggs, and the dam sitting upon the young, or upon the eggs, thou shalt not take the dam with the young: 7 thou shalt surely let the dam go, but the young thou mayest take unto thyself; that it may be well with thee, and that thou mayest prolong thy days.

8 When thou buildest a new house, then thou shalt make a battlement for thy roof, that thou bring not blood upon thy house, if any man fall from thence.

9 Thou shalt not sow thy vineyard with two kinds of seed, lest the whole fruit be forfeited, the seed which thou hast sown, and the increase of the vineyard. 10 Thou shalt not plow with an ox and an ass together. 11 Thou shalt not wear a mingled stuff, wool and linen together.

12 Thou shalt make thee fringes upon the four borders of thy vesture, wherewith thou coverest thyself.

The spirit of mercy expressed here is also to apply in matters so small as birds in a nest which has been dislodged from a tree limb. The finder of a bird's nest on the ground was to take the small birds into protective custody so that they would not be endangered by predatory beasts. The dam or female parent was to be liberated in order that she might help to perpetuate her kind. It is quite likely that a person who expresses cruelty to helpless animals will also express cruelty to his fellow creatures.

A builder was to provide proper scaffolding for his workers to prevent them from suffering hurtful falls (v. 8). This is recognized practice today in the buildings trade.

This writer has been privileged to observe agricultural methods in the Near East. Frequently a farmer, too poor to own two draft animals of the same kind, hitches his camel with a cow or his ox with an ass. When two animals of different size and strength are hitched to a plow there is confusion. The short-legged animal is overworked because it must take two or three steps for a single step by the larger animal. Clarke says:

> Two beasts of a different species cannot associate comfortably together, and on this ground never pull pleasantly either in cart or plough; and every farmer knows that it is of considerable consequence to the comfort of the cattle to put them together that have an affection for each other. This may be very frequently remarked in certain cattle, which, on this account, are termed true yoke-fellows. After all, it is very probable that the general design was to prevent improper alliances in civil and religious life. And to this St. Paul seems evidently to refer, II Cor. 6:14; BE YE NOT UNEQUALLY YOKED TOGETHER WITH UNBELIEVERS; which is simply to be understood as prohibiting all intercourse between Christians and idolaters in social, matrimonial and religious life.[69]

Thou shalt not wear mingled stuff (v. 11). Wool and linen have different qualities with regard to shrinkage when washed. This unequal balance tends to draw the garment out of shape and to form a rough, irregular texture.

D. LAWS CONCERNING CHASTITY (22:13-30)

13 If any man take a wife, and go in unto her, and hate her, 14 and lay shameful things to her charge, and bring up an evil name upon her, and say, I took this woman, and when I came nigh to her, I found not in her the tokens of virginity; 15 then shall the father of the damsel, and her mother, take and bring forth the tokens of the damsel's virginity unto the elders of the city in the gate;

[68] Ibid., p. 185.   [69] Op. cit., I, 795.

16 and the damsel's father shall say unto the elders, I gave my daughter unto this man to wife, and he hateth her; 17 and, lo, he hath laid shameful things *to her charge*, saying, I found not in thy daughter the tokens of virginity; and yet these are the tokens of my daughter's virginity. And they shall spread the garment before the elders of the city. 18 And the elders of that city shall take the man and chastise him; 19 and they shall fine him a hundred *shekels* of silver, and give them unto the father of the damsel, because he hath brought up an evil name upon a virgin of Israel: and she shall be his wife; he may not put her away all his days. 20 But if this thing be true, that the tokens of virginity were not found in the damsel; 21 then they shall bring out the damsel to the door of her father's house, and the men of her city shall stone her to death with stones, because she hath wrought folly in Israel, to play the harlot in her father's house: so shalt thou put away the evil from the midst of thee.

22 If a man be found lying with a woman married to a husband, then they shall both of them die, the man that lay with the woman, and the woman: so shalt thou put away the evil from Israel.

23 If there be a damsel that is a virgin betrothed unto a husband, and a man find her in the city, and lie with her; 24 then ye shall bring them both out unto the gate of that city, and ye shall stone them to death with stones; the damsel, because she cried not, being in the city; and the man, because he hath humbled his neighbor's wife: so thou shalt put away the evil from the midst of thee.

25 But if the man find the damsel that is betrothed in the field, and the man force her, and lie with her; then the man only that lay with her shall die: 26 but unto the damsel thou shalt do nothing; there is in the damsel no sin worthy of death: for as when a man riseth against his neighbor, and slayeth him, even so is this matter; 27 for he found her in the field, the betrothed damsel cried, and there was none to save her.

28 If a man find a damsel that is a virgin, that is not betrothed, and lay hold on her, and lie with her, and they be found; 29 then the man that lay with her shall give unto the damsel's father fifty *shekels* of silver, and she shall be his wife, because he hath humbled her; he may not put her away all his days.

30 A man shall not take his father's wife, and shall not uncover his father's skirt.

The laws of Jehovah were very exact and explicit with regard to marriage and a bride's virginity. If a husband of a new bride brought false accusations against his wife the elders were to punish him severely and force him to pay compensation to the bride's father (vv. 18-19). In addition, he was obligated to keep his wife without possibility of divorce (v. 19b). On the other hand, if the bride was guilty of unchastity she was to be stoned. The laws of Jehovah regarding illicit sexual relationship were very strict, and anyone who took lightly the matter of sex outside wedlock was in serious trouble. The judicial responsibility of Israel's leaders was very exact (Deut. 5:18; 19:12; 21:2-6, 19, 20; 20:7-9; Lev. 18:20, 29; 20:10). The only permissible practice of sexual intercourse was between a man and his wife (vv. 23-30).

E. CERTAIN CLASSES TO BE EXCLUDED FROM RELIGIOUS COMMUNION (23:1-8)

1 He that is wounded in the stones, or hath his privy member cut off, shall not enter into the assembly of Jehovah.

2 A bastard shall not enter into the assembly of Jehovah; even to the tenth generation shall none of his enter into the assembly of Jehovah.

3 An Ammonite or a Moabite shall not enter into the assembly of Jehovah; even to the tenth generation shall none belonging to them enter into the assembly of Jehovah for ever: 4 because they met you not with bread and with water in the way, when ye came forth out of Egypt, and because they hired against thee Balaam the son of Beor from Pethor of Mesopotamia, to curse thee. 5 Nevertheless Jehovah thy God would not hearken unto Balaam; but Jehovah thy God turned the curse into a blessing unto thee, because Jehovah thy God loved thee. 6 Thou shalt not seek their peace nor their prosperity all thy days for ever.

7 Thou shalt not abhor an Edomite; for he is thy brother: thou shalt not abhor an Egyptian; because thou wast a sojourner in his land. 8 The children of the third generation that are born unto them shall enter into the assembly of Jehovah.

The only animal sacrifice that was acceptable to the Lord was one without "spot or blemish." This ideal was transmitted to those who entered or exercised service in the precincts of the tabernacle. An afflicted person was not to partake of these special privileges.[70]

F. LAWS OF CLEANLINESS (23:9-14)

9 When thou goest forth in camp against thine enemies, then thou shalt keep thee from every evil thing. 10 If there be among you any man, that is not clean by reason of that which chanceth him by night, then shall he go abroad out of the camp, he shall not come within the camp: 11 but it shall be, when evening cometh on, he shall bathe himself in water; and when the sun is down, he shall come within the camp. 12 Thou shalt have a place also without the camp, whither thou shalt go forth abroad: 13 and thou shalt have a paddle among thy weapons; and it shall be, when thou sittest down abroad, thou shalt dig therewith, and shalt turn back and cover that which cometh from thee: 14 for Jehovah thy God walketh in the midst of camp, to deliver thee, and to give up thine enemies before thee; therefore shall thy camp be holy, that he may not see an unclean thing in thee, and turn away from thee.

As the Israelites increased in number, social and sanitary problems increased. They were to be clean and free from moral and ceremonial pollution as well as natural pollution. The camp of the Lord was to be clean and have nothing offensive in it. Henry aptly remarks:

It is strange that the divine law, or at least the solemn order and direction of Moses, should extend to a thing of this nature; but the design of it was to teach them, (1) Modesty and a good decorum; nature itself teaches them thus to distinguish themselves from beasts that know no shame. (2) Cleanliness, and (though not niceness, yet) neatness, even in their camp. Impurity is offensive to the senses God has endued us with, prejudicial to the health, a wrong to the comfort of human life and an evidence of a careless slothful temper of mind. (3) Purity from the pollution of sin; if there must be this care taken to preserve the body clean and sweet, much more should we be solicitous to keep the mind so. (4) A reverence of the divine majesty. This is the reason here given; for the Lord thy God walketh by his ark, the special token of his presence in the midst of thy camp; with

respect to that external symbol this external purity is required, which (though not insisted on in the letter when that reason ceases, yet) teaches us to preserve inward purity of soul, in consideration of the eye of God, which is always upon us. By this expression of respect to the presence of God among them, they were taught both to fortify themselves against sin, and to encourage themselves against their enemies with the consideration of that presence. (5) A regard one to another. The filthiness of one is noisome to many; this law of cleanliness therefore teaches us not to do that which will be justly offensive to our brethren, and grieve them. It is a law against nuisances.[71]

G. THE LAWS OF HUMAN RELATIONS (23:15—25:16)

15 Thou shalt not deliver unto his master a servant that is escaped from his master unto thee: 16 he shall dwell with thee, in the midst of thee, in the place which he shall choose within one of thy gates, where it pleaseth him best: thou shalt not oppress him.

17 There shall be no prostitute of the daughters of Israel, neither shall there be a sodomite of the sons of Israel. 18 Thou shalt not bring the hire of a harlot, or the wages of a dog, into the house of Jehovah thy God for any vow: for even both these are an abomination unto Jehovah thy God.

19 Thou shalt not lend upon interest to thy brother; interest of money, interest of victuals, interest of anything that is lent upon interest. 20 Unto a foreigner thou mayest lend upon interest; but unto thy brother thou shalt not lend upon interest, that Jehovah thy God may bless thee in all that thou puttest thy hand unto, in the land whither thou goest in to possess it.

21 When thou shalt vow a vow unto Jehovah thy God, thou shalt not be slack to pay it: for Jehovah thy God will surely require it of thee; and it would be sin in thee. 22 But if thou shalt forbear to vow, it shall be no sin in thee. 23 That which is gone out of thy lips thou shalt observe and do; according as thou hast vowed unto Jehovah thy God, a freewill-offering, which thou hast promised with thy mouth.

24 When thou comest into thy neighbor's vineyard, then thou mayest eat of grapes thy fill at thine own pleasure; but thou shalt not put any in thy vessel. 25

[70] For comments on Balaam (vv. 4-5) see Numbers 22:5ff.   [71] Op. cit., II, 478.

When thou comest into thy neighbor's standing grain, then thou mayest pluck the ears with thy hand; but thou shalt not move a sickle unto thy neighbor's standing grain.

1 When a man taketh a wife, and marrieth her, then it shall be, if she find no favor in his eyes, because he hath found some unseemly thing in her, that he shall write her a bill of divorcement, and give it in her hand, and send her out of his house. 2 And when she is departed out of his house, she may go and be another man's *wife*. 3 And if the latter husband hate her, and write her a bill of divorcement, and give it in her hand, and send her out of his house; or if the latter husband die, who took her to be his wife; 4 her former husband, who sent her away, may not take her again to be his wife, after that she is defiled; for that is abomination before Jehovah: and thou shalt not cause the land to sin, which Jehovah thy God giveth thee for an inheritance.

5 When a man taketh a new wife, he shall not go out in the host, neither shall he be charged with any business: he shall be free at home one year, and shall cheer his wife whom he hath taken.

6 No man shall take the mill or the upper millstone to pledge; for he taketh *a man's* life to pledge.

7 If a man be found stealing any of his brethren of the children of Israel, and he deal with him as a slave, or sell him; then that thief shall die: so shalt thou put away the evil from the midst of thee.

8 Take heed in the plague of leprosy, that thou observe diligently, and do according to all that the priests the Levites shall teach you: as I commanded them, so ye shall observe to do. 9 Remember what Jehovah thy God did unto Miriam by the way as ye came forth out of Egypt.

10 When thou dost lend thy neighbor any manner of loan, thou shalt not go into his house to fetch his pledge. 11 Thou shalt stand without, and the man to whom thou dost lend shall bring forth the pledge without unto thee. 12 And if he be a poor man, thou shalt not sleep with his pledge; 13 thou shalt surely restore to him the pledge when the sun goes down, that he may sleep in his garment, and bless thee: and it shall be righteousness unto thee before Jehovah thy God.

14 Thou shalt not oppress a hired servant that is poor and needy, whether he be of thy brethren, or of thy sojourners that are in thy land within thy gates: 15 in his day thou shalt give him his hire, neither shall the sun go down upon it (for he is poor, and setteth his heart upon it); lest he cry against thee unto Jehovah, and it be sin unto thee.

16 The fathers shall not be put to death for the children, neither shall the children be put to death for the fathers: every man shall be put to death for his own sin.

17 Thou shalt not wrest the justice *due* to the sojourner, *or* to the fatherless, nor take the widow's raiment to pledge; 18 but thou shalt remember that thou wast a bondman in Egypt, and Jehovah thy God redeemed thee thence: therefore I command thee to do this thing.

19 When thou reapest thy harvest in thy field, and hast forgot a sheaf in the field, thou shalt not go again to fetch it: it shall be for the sojourner, for the fatherless, and for the widow; that Jehovah thy God may bless thee in all the work of thy hands. 20 When thou beatest thine olive-tree, thou shalt not go over the boughs again: it shall be for the sojourner, for the fatherless, and for the widow. 21 When thou gatherest *the grapes* of thy vineyard, thou shalt not glean it after thee: it shall be for the sojourner, for the fatherless, and for the widow. 22 And thou shalt remember that thou wast a bondman in the land of Egypt: therefore I command thee to do this thing.

1 If there be a controversy between men, and they come unto judgment, and *the judges* judge them; then they shall justify the righteous, and condemn the wicked. 2 And it shall be, if the wicked man be worthy to be beaten, that the judge shall cause him to lie down, and to be beaten before his face, according to his wickedness, by number. 3 Forty stripes he may give him, he shall not exceed; lest, if he should exceed, and beat him above these with many stripes, then thy brother should seem vile unto thee.

4 Thou shalt not muzzle the ox when he treadeth out *the grain*.

5 If brethren dwell together, and one of them die, and have no son, the wife of the dead shall not be married without unto a stranger: her husband's brother shall go in unto her, and take her to him to wife, and perform the duty of a husband's brother unto her. 6 And it shall be, that the first-born that she beareth shall succeed in the name of his brother that is dead, that his name be not blotted out of Israel. 7 And if the man like not to take his brother's wife, then his brother's wife shall go up to the gate unto the elders, and say, My husband's

brother refuseth to raise up unto his brother a name in Israel; he will not perform the duty of a husband's brother unto me. 8 Then the elders of his city shall call him, and speak unto him: and if he stand, and say, I like not to take her; 9 then shall his brother's wife come unto him in the presence of the elders, and loose his shoe from off his foot, and spit in his face; and she shall answer and say, So shall it be done unto the man that doth not build up his brother's house. 10 And his name shall be called in Israel, The house of him that hath his shoe loosed.

11 When men strive together one with another, and the wife of the one draweth near to deliver her husband out of the hand of him that smiteth him, and putteth forth her hand, and taketh him by the secrets; 12 then thou shalt cut off her hand, thine eye shall have no pity.

13 Thou shalt not have in thy bag diverse weights, a great and a small. 14 Thou shalt not have in thy house diverse measures, a great and a small. 15 A perfect and just weight shalt thou have; a perfect and just measure shalt thou have: that thy days may be long in the land which Jehovah thy God giveth thee. 16 For all that do such things, *even* all that do unrighteously, are an abomination unto Jehovah thy God.

Utmost compassion was to be shown the slave who escaped from his heathen master in order to join himself to God's people. The slave was to receive the privilege of asylum and an opportunity to become a worshiper of Jehovah.

All forms of prostitution and sexual perversion were offensive to Jehovah's moral law. Gains from this profession were not to be given as an offering. The land of Israel was to provide no shelter for that which was unclean. The Israelites were the "chosen" of God and were to conduct themselves as His children.

The Israelites were forbidden to lend with usury to fellow Israelites (v. 19). Their landholding represented no investment on their part because it had been given them by the Lord. They were to have all things in common and to share with each other the bounty of the land. It was permissible to borrow and lend on the basis of having the principal returned without interest. On the other hand, they were permitted to charge interest on a loan to a foreigner who lived by trade.

Making a vow was optional. However, when a person made a vow he was expected to keep it. Jehovah encouraged His people to give free expression of religious love in their everyday life. They were to give out of a heart of love rather than from the legal compunction of a vow. God did not encourage a sense of carelessness or indifference in those who made a vow (see Lev. 27; Num. 30:2ff.).

If a man passed through a neighbor's vineyard or grain field he was permitted to eat what he could to satisfy his hunger, but he was not permitted to carry anything away for future need. The law of compassion stipulated that there was a social obligation to feed a poor hungry man, but this provision was not to be abused. Taking away some grain or fruit in a vessel was considered theft (see Matt. 12:1ff.; Mark 2:23; Luke 6:1).

It is apparent that a Jew could put away his wife if he found some uncleanness in her (v. 1). It was not sufficient that he should have a dislike for her or that he become interested in some other woman; he had to show that there was some unpleasant characteristic in her which made his marriage incompatible. It is evident that something less serious than adultery could be the ground for a man's dissolving his marriage. On the other hand, adultery was an offense for which the death penalty was exacted (see Deut. 22:13ff.; Lev. 20:10).

It was necessary to give the woman something in writing which was verified by witnesses. This legal document absolved her of any serious misconduct and made it possible for her to marry someone else as though her husband were actually dead. If her second husband died or divorced her she might marry a third time, but not her first husband (v. 4). Divorce was an abnormal thing and was permitted by Moses only because of the hardness of a man's heart. This toleration was abrogated by our Lord (see Matt. 19:9; Mark 10:6-9; cf. Gen. 2:23-24).

In the interest of establishing a new marriage a man was given an extended leave of absence from his work or business and excused from all military obligations. This tended to preserve and confirm the love between newly married couples. If the husband was forced to absent himself from his wife there was danger that their love might cool and possibly be alienated by someone else. This rule suggests the importance the Hebrews placed upon the sanctity of the home and marriage.[72] This is probably the origin of the customary honeymoon.

The family mill was a very important object in the economy of a family, for it was in the mill that flour was ground for daily use. It was expressly forbidden for a man to jeopardize family well-being by giving a loan or pledge on his millstone because there was danger that he might not be able to pay the loan, and thus forfeit the means for preparing the family food. No legal device could be attached to the little mill which ground the corn and protected the wife's livelihood.

The crime of kidnapping was very serious, and punishable by death. This is similar to the kidnapping laws in many states of America.

A person to whom a loan was made was not to have his pawn or pledge forcibly taken. The debtor was to be given ample time to surrender voluntarily "his collateral." A poor man who pawned his sleeping garments was to have them returned to him by bedtime for the Lord's sake (vv. 11-13). A poor man lived from "hand to mouth." At the end of the day he was to be paid his wages so that he could buy food for his family (v. 15).

Each individual Israelite was responsible for his own acts and was to receive commensurate punishment. A father could not assume the death penalty for his child, nor was a child to assume it for his father. All social classes in Israel were to receive absolute justice and to enjoy all legal rights (see comments on Deut. 1:17; 10:17).

Sustenance was to be provided for the poor, the orphans and the widows by leaving some grain in the field at harvest time (v. 19). Grain which had been overlooked or spilled was to remain in the field so that the needy would be able to glean enough to meet their need. The corners of the field were not to be harvested, nor was every grape in the vineyard, or every olive on a tree to be gathered (see Lev. 19:9-10). When Naomi and Ruth returned from Moab to Bethlehem they sustained themselves by gleaning in the field of Boaz (see Ruth 2:1ff.). This is the biblical background for much of our social service today.

In case of a disagreement, the two contestants were to be brought before the judges. If the guilty party was to receive a public whipping it was to be done in the presence of the judges, in order to limit the beating to forty stripes (vv. 2-3). Paul is said to have received one stripe short of this limit (II Cor. 11:24), to allow a safe margin in counting. Forty stripes was legal and permissible punishment, but more than this was considered to be cruel and illegal. The individual dignity of the creature made in God's own image is here expressed.

The work animal was entitled to eat from the field while it labored. A man is entitled to his just reward as suggested in I Timothy 5:8 (see also I Cor. 9:9).

In order to keep a family alive, the dead man's brother was to marry the widow. However, if the man found no favor in the widow he was to appear before the elders of the city, at which time a ceremony was performed. The widow was to loose his shoe and spit in his face as a reproach for his refusal to build up his brother's house (vv. 5-9). The ceremony is described in detail in Ruth 4:1ff. (see also Matt. 22:24; Mark 12:19; and Luke 20:28).

Fair ground-rules were to be observed when two men fought. If the wife of the smitten husband joined in the fight, she was not to injure or mutilate the sexual organs of the one who was beating her husband. If she did, her hand was to be cut off. Individual dignity was to be respected because each man bore the mark of God's covenant through circumcision. Kline says:

> That this forbidden act of mutilating the reproductive organ includes contempt for the covenant sign and not just indecency is suggested by the apparent similarity in the nature of the punishment and the sign, both involving a mutilation of the body. Weight is added to this interpretation by the fact that apart from this, only the *lex talionis* (see Deut. 19:21) calls for such penal mutilation.[73]

The principle of the Golden Rule was to be applied in all business transactions.

---

[72] Gray and Adams, *op. cit.*, p. 519.   [73] *Op. cit.*, p. 189.

No one was to have two different weights or measurements. A **perfect and just weight** was to be the norm (see also Lev. 19:35, 36). Any standard contrary to this was an abomination to Jehovah (vv. 14-15).

H. AMALEK TO BE BLOTTED OUT (25:17-19)

17 Remember what Amalek did unto thee by the way as ye came forth out of Egypt; 18 how he met thee by the way, and smote the hindmost of thee, all that were feeble behind thee, when thou wast faint and weary; and he feared not God. 19 Therefore it shall be, when Jehovah thy God hath given thee rest from all thine enemies round about, in the land which Jehovah thy God giveth thee for an inheritance to possess it, that thou shalt blot out the remembrance of Amalek from under heaven; thou shalt not forget.

The remembrance of how Amalek had attacked them in their journey from Egypt, having no regard for the feeble, faint and weary among them, was to be preserved, not for personal revenge, but as a reminder that Jehovah had the final word. It did develop that Amalek was finally blotted out of existence, while Israel, who suffered temporarily at his hands, was about to enter the precincts of her glory.

I. THE FIRST-FRUITS AND THE TITHE (26:1-19)

1 And it shall be, when thou art come in unto the land which Jehovah thy God giveth thee for an inheritance, and possessest it, and dwellest therein, 2 that thou shalt take of the first of all the fruit of the ground, which thou shalt bring in from thy land that Jehovah thy God giveth thee; and thou shalt put it in a basket, and shalt go unto the place which Jehovah thy God shall choose, to cause his name to dwell there. 3 And thou shalt come unto the priest that shall be in those days, and say unto him, I profess this day unto Jehovah thy God, that I am come unto the land which Jehovah sware unto our fathers to give us. 4 And the priest shall take the basket out of thy hand, and set it down before the altar of Jehovah thy God. 5 And thou shalt answer and say before Jehovah thy God, A Syrian ready to perish was my father; and he went down into Egypt, and

sojourned there, few in number; and he became there a nation, great, mighty, and populous. 6 And the Egyptians dealt ill with us, and afflicted us, and laid upon us hard bondage: 7 and we cried unto Jehovah, the God of our fathers, and Jehovah heard our voice, and saw our affliction, and our toil, and our oppression; 8 and Jehovah brought us forth out of Egypt with a mighty hand, and with an outstretched arm, and with great terribleness, and with signs, and with wonders; 9 and he hath brought us into this place, and hath given us this land, a land flowing with milk and honey. 10 And now, behold, I have brought the first of the fruit of the ground, which thou, O Jehovah, hast given me. And thou shalt set it down before Jehovah thy God, and worship before Jehovah thy God: 11 and thou shalt rejoice in all the good which Jehovah thy God hath given unto thee, and unto thy house, thou, and the Levite, and the sojourner that is in the midst of thee. 12 When thou hast made an end of tithing all the tithe of thine increase in the third year, which is the year of tithing, then thou shalt give it unto the Levite, to the sojourner, to the fatherless, and to the widow, that they may eat within thy gates, and be filled. 13 And thou shalt say before Jehovah thy God, I have put away the hallowed things out of my house, and also have given them unto the Levite, and unto the sojourner, to the fatherless, and to the widow, according to all thy commandment which thou hast commanded me: I have not transgressed any of thy commandments, neither have I forgotten them: 14 I have not eaten thereof in my mourning, neither have I put away thereof, being unclean, nor given thereof for the dead: I have hearkened to the voice of Jehovah my God; I have done according to all that thou hast commanded me. 15 Look down from thy holy habitation, from heaven, and bless thy people Israel, and the ground which thou hast given us, as thou swarest unto our fathers, a land flowing with milk and honey.

16 This day Jehovah thy God commandeth thee to do these statutes and ordinances: thou shalt therefore keep and do them with all thy heart, and with all thy soul. 17 Thou hast avouched Jehovah this day to be thy God, and that thou wouldest walk in his ways, and keep his statutes, and his commandments, and his ordinances, and hearken unto his voice: 18 and Jehovah hath avouched thee this day to be a people

for his own possession, as he hath promised thee, and that thou shouldest keep all his commandments; 19 and to make thee high above all nations that he hath made, in praise, and in name, and in honor; and that thou mayest be a holy people unto Jehovah thy God, as he hath spoken.

The Israelites were to observe a special thanksgiving to Jehovah at the time of the first-fruits, or the day after the Passover (Lev. 23:10). Every man was to bring for himself a basket of first-fruits on the Feast of Pentecost, which was the end of the harvest. This ritual was intended to keep the Israelites in constant remembrance that the Lord had delivered them through many difficult situations. In the course of the ritual the worshiper was to give a verbal testimony as well as to recite a portion of history attesting the providential oversight Jehovah had given Israel (vv. 5-11).

A Syrian ready to perish (v. 5b). The marginal note in the ASV text translates **Syrian** to read **Aramaean.** Clarke gives the following interpretation:

> It is pretty evident, from the text, that by a Syrian we are to understand Jacob, so called from his long residence in Syria with his father-in-law Laban. And his "being ready to perish" may signify the hard usage and severe labour he had had in Laban's service, by which his life might have often been in imminent danger.[74]

In the third year from the sabbatical year the Levites were to **tithe their tithe,** or give a special offering amounting to ten percent of the tithe, to **the Levites, to the sojourner, to the fatherless, and to the widow.** This giving was to be followed by a testimonial of compliance to Jehovah (vv. 13-15).

The worship of the Israelites was to be reactivated by love for the Lord. This is the thing that Jesus tried to re-establish among the Jews when He commented on the commandments (see Matt. 22:26-40). Absolute obedience of the law, motivated by their love for Jehovah, would be the condition by which Israel would become a great and mighty nation. She was to be a holy people unto the Lord (see comments on Deut. 7:6ff.).

Op. cit., I, 804.

V. INSCRIPTION OF THE LAW, BLESSINGS AND CURSINGS (Deut. 27:1—28:68)

A. INSCRIPTION OF THE LAW (27:1-8)

1 And Moses and the elders of Israel commanded the people, saying, Keep all the commandment which I command you this day. 2 And it shall be on the day when ye shall pass over the Jordan unto the land which Jehovah thy God giveth thee, that thou shalt set thee up great stones, and plaster them with plaster: 3 and thou shalt write upon them all the words of this law, when thou art passed over; that thou mayest go in unto the land which Jehovah thy God giveth thee, a land flowing with milk and honey, as Jehovah, the God of thy fathers, hath promised thee. 4 And it shall be, when ye are passed over the Jordan, that ye shall set up these stones, which I command you this day, in mount Ebal, and thou shalt plaster them with plaster. 5 And there shalt thou build an altar unto Jehovah thy God, an altar of stones: thou shalt lift up no iron *tool* upon them. 6 Thou shalt build the altar of Jehovah thy God of unhewn stones; and thou shalt offer burnt-offerings thereon unto Jehovah thy God: 7 and thou shalt sacrifice peace-offerings, and shalt eat there; and thou shalt rejoice before Jehovah thy God. 8 And thou shalt write upon the stones all the words of this law very plainly.

Heretofore the Israelites possessed very few written documents. Most of the laws and ordinances were committed to memory and passed from father to son. The people were now entering their permanent home and were to erect monuments on which the laws of Jehovah were to be recorded. These were to be perpetual reminders that they were the "chosen people," with a peculiar mission and purpose. It should be pointed out that the two main responsibilities assigned to these chosen people were: (1) to receive and preserve the laws and ordinances of Jehovah, which later became the Holy Scriptures; (2) to be the human channel through which God would send the Messiah.

In addition to the monuments, they were to build a permanent altar out of unfinished stones on which to make their sacrificial offerings. Jehovah spoke to the people through the words on the monuments, and on the altar of sacrifice the people spoke to God. Thus there was a system of communion between the people and Jehovah.

B. OBEDIENCE COMMANDED (27:9-10)

9 And Moses and all the priests the Levites spake unto all Israel, saying, Keep silence, and hearken, O Israel: This day thou art become the people of Jehovah thy God. 10 Thou shalt therefore obey the voice of Jehovah thy God, and do his commandments and his statutes, which I command thee this day.

Obedience and absolute loyalty to Jehovah are emphasized many times. The frequency with which the command to obedience is reiterated indicates the essential importance of a complete commitment.

C. THE CURSES AT MT. EBAL (27: 11-26)

11 And Moses charged the people the same day, saying, 12 These shall stand upon mount Gerizim to bless the people, when ye are passed over the Jordan: Simeon, and Levi, and Judah, and Issachar, and Joseph, and Benjamin. 13 And these shall stand upon mount Ebal for the curse: Reuben, Gad, and Asher, and Zebulun, Dan, and Naphtali. 14 And the Levites shall answer, and say unto all the men of Israel with a loud voice.

15 Cursed be the man that maketh a graven or molten image, an abomination unto Jehovah, the work of the hands of the craftsman, and setteth it up in secret. And all the people shall answer and say, Amen.

16 Cursed be he that setteth light by his father or his mother. And all the people shall say, Amen.

17 Cursed be he that removeth his neighbor's landmark. And all the people shall say, Amen.

18 Cursed be he that maketh the blind to wander out of the way. And all the people shall say, Amen.

19 Cursed be he that wresteth the justice *due* to the sojourner, fatherless, and widow. And all the people shall say, Amen.

20 Cursed be he that lieth with his father's wife, because he hath uncovered his father's skirt. And all the people shall say, Amen.

21 Cursed be he that lieth with any manner of beast. And all the people shall say, Amen.

22 Cursed be he that lieth with his sister, the daughter of his father, or the daughter of his mother. And all the people shall say, Amen.

23 Cursed be he that lieth with his mother-in-law. And all the people shall say, Amen.

24 Cursed be he that smiteth his neighbor in secret. And all the people shall say, Amen.

25 Cursed be he that taketh a bribe to slay an innocent person. And all the people shall say, Amen.

26 Cursed be he that confirmeth not the words of this law to do them. And all the people shall say, Amen.

It is generally understood that the tribes of Reuben, Gad, Asher, Zebulun, Dan, and Nephtali were to stand on the slopes of Mt. Ebal facing the opposite slope of Mt. Gerizim, to pronounce the curses of Jehovah when the people transgressed. In contrast, the six tribes, Simeon, Levi, Judah, Issachar, Joseph, and Benjamin, all descended from Jacob's wives Leah and Rachel, were to stand on the slopes of Mt. Gerizim and pronounce Jehovah's blessings upon the people when they obeyed the laws of Jehovah (v. 11). Kline comments thus:

> Whether the two sets of tribes were to fulfill their respective roles unto curse and blessing simply by having either curse or blessing formulae directed toward them, or by themselves reciting or at least assenting to one or the other is not stated. In chapter 28 there appear matching sets of six blessings (vv. 3-6) and six curses (vv. 16-19); it seems difficult to dissociate these from the present two sets of six tribes.
>
> The ark of the covenant and the Levitical priests were to be stationed between Ebal and Gerizim (Deut. 27:14). They must lead Israel in the oath of ratification, consisting of a series of twelve self-maledictions (Deut. 27:15-26). The repeated "Cursed be" identifies the covenant-breaker's fate with that of the serpent (cf. Gen. 3:14). The "Amen" response was the customary formula of assent.[75]

---

[75] *Op. cit.*, p. 192.

D. THE BLESSINGS AT MT. GERIZIM (28:1-14)

1 And it shall come to pass, if thou shalt hearken diligently unto the voice of Jehovah thy God, to observe to do all his commandments which I command thee this day, that Jehovah thy God will set thee on high above all the nations of the earth: 2 and all these blessings shall come upon thee, and overtake thee, if thou shalt hearken unto the voice of Jehovah thy God. 3 Blessed shalt thou be in the city, and blessed shalt thou be in the field. 4 Blessed shall be the fruit of thy body, and the fruit of thy ground, and the fruit of thy beasts, the increase of thy cattle, and the young of thy flock. 5 Blessed shall be thy basket and thy kneading-trough. 6 Blessed shalt thou be when thou comest in, and blessed shalt thou be when thou goest out.

7 Jehovah will cause thine enemies that rise up against thee to be smitten before thee: they shall come out against thee one way, and shall flee before thee seven ways. 8 Jehovah will command the blessing upon thee in thy barns, and in all that thou puttest thy hand unto; and he will bless thee in the land which Jehovah thy God giveth thee. 9 Jehovah will establish thee for a holy people unto himself, as he hath sworn unto thee; if thou shalt keep the commandments of Jehovah thy God, and walk in his ways. 10 And all the peoples of the earth shall see that thou art called by the name of Jehovah; and they shall be afraid of thee. 11 And Jehovah will make thee plenteous for good, in the fruit of thy body, and in the fruit of thy cattle, and in the fruit of thy ground, in the land which Jehovah sware unto thy fathers to give thee. 12 Jehovah will open unto thee his good treasure the heavens, to give the rain of thy land in its season, and to bless all the work of thy hand: and thou shalt lend unto many nations, and thou shalt not borrow. 13 And Jehovah will make thee the head, and not the tail; and thou shalt be above only, and thou shalt not be beneath; if thou shalt hearken unto the commandments of Jehovah thy God, which I command thee this day, to observe and to do *them*, 14 and shalt not turn aside from any of the words which I command you this day, to the right hand, or to the left, to go after other gods to serve them.

The bounteous blessings which the Israelites were to enjoy in their new land were contingent upon absolute and full obedience to the stipulations set down by Jehovah. They were not "chosen people" as such, but chosen to be a "show window" for the holiness and righteousness of God. They had the great responsibility of demonstrating to the heathen world the nature of God.

Jehovah was a holy God and they as His children were to be a holy people (see Lev. 11:44-45; I Pet. 1:13-16). It cannot be too strongly emphasized that the people of God were to be sanctified in all manner of conversation and conduct. They were to be a peculiar and a strange people as compared with the heathen society, with its evil practices, into which they were now being thrust. They were to be set on high so that they could let their light shine in a crooked and perverse society (v. 1; see comments on Num. 11:18ff.).

The blessings which they were to enjoy would transcend all bounds. This blessed or happy state would be theirs to enjoy in all relationships of life (vv. 3-6). They were to have protection against their heathen enemies (v. 7), and their barns were to be full (v. 8) if they kept the commandments of Jehovah (v. 9). Their example was to be a testimony to the peoples of the earth (v. 10). On this condition they would enjoy a population increase, and their cattle would multiply (v. 11). The nations of the world would pay them homage. But all this was dependent on whether they observed and obeyed the commands of Jehovah (vv. 12-14).

E. THE CONSEQUENCES FOR DISOBEDIENCE (28:15-68)

15 But it shall come to pass, if thou wilt not hearken unto the voice of Jehovah thy God, to observe to do all his commandments and his statutes which I command thee this day, that all these curses shall come upon thee, and overtake thee. 16 Cursed shalt thou be in the city, and cursed shalt thou be in the field. 17 Cursed shall be thy basket and thy kneading-trough. 18 Cursed shall be the fruit of thy body, and the fruit of thy ground, the increase of thy cattle, and the young of thy flock. 19 Cursed shalt thou be when thou comest in, and cursed shalt thou be when thou goest out.

20 Jehovah will send upon thee cursing, discomfiture, and rebuke, in all that thou puttest thy hand unto to do, until thou

be destroyed, and until thou perish quickly; because of the evil of thy doings, whereby thou hast forsaken me. 21 Jehovah will make the pestilence cleave unto thee, until he have consumed thee from off the land, whither thou goest in to possess it. 22 Jehovah will smite thee with consumption, and with fever, and with inflammation, and with fiery heat, and with the sword, and with blasting, and with mildew; and they shall pursue thee until thou perish. 23 And thy heaven that is over thy head shall be brass, and the earth that is under thee shall be iron. 24 Jehovah will make the rain of thy land powder and dust: from heaven shall it come down upon thee, until thou be destroyed.

25 Jehovah will cause thee to be smitten before thine enemies; thou shalt go out one way against them, and shalt flee seven ways before them: and thou shalt be tossed to and fro among all the kingdoms of the earth. 26 And thy dead body shall be food unto all birds of the heavens, and unto the beasts of the earth; and there shall be none to frighten them away. 27 Jehovah will smite thee with the boil of Egypt, and with the emerods, and with the scurvy, and with the itch, whereof thou canst not be healed. 28 Jehovah will smite thee with madness, and with blindness, and with astonishment of heart; 29 and thou shalt grope at noonday, as the blind gropeth in darkness, and thou shalt not prosper in thy ways; and thou shalt be only oppressed and robbed alway, and there shall be none to save thee. 30 Thou shalt betroth a wife, and another man shall lie with her: thou shalt build a house, and thou shalt not dwell therein: and thou shalt plant a vineyard, and shalt not use the fruit thereof. 31. Thine ox shall be slain before thine eyes, and thou shalt not eat thereof: thine ass shall be violently taken away from before thy face: thy sheep shall be given unto thine enemies, and thou shalt have none to save thee. 32 Thy sons and thy daughters shall be given unto another people; and thine eyes shall look, and fail with longing for them all the day: and there shall be nought in the power of thy hand. 33 The fruit of thy ground, and all thy labors, shall a nation which thou knowest not eat up; and thou shalt be only oppressed and crushed alway; 34 so that thou shalt be mad for the sight of thine eyes which thou shalt see. 35 Jehovah will smite thee in the knees, and in the legs, with a sore boil, whereof thou canst not be healed, from

the sole of thy foot unto the crown of thy head.

36 Jehovah will bring thee, and thy king whom thou shalt set over thee, unto a nation that thou hast not known, thou nor thy fathers; and there shalt thou serve other gods, wood and stone. 37 And thou shalt become an astonishment, a proverb, and a byword, among all the peoples whither Jehovah shall lead thee away. 38 Thou shalt carry much seed out into the field, and shalt gather little in; for the locust shall consume it. 39 Thou shalt plant vineyards and dress them, but thou shalt neither drink of the wine, nor gather *the grapes;* for the worm shall eat them. 40 Thou shalt have olive-trees throughout all thy borders, but thou shalt not anoint thyself with the oil; for thine olive shall cast *its fruit.* 41 Thou shalt beget sons and daughters, but they shall not be thine; for they shall go into captivity. 42 All thy trees and the fruit of thy ground shall the locust possess. 43 The sojourner that is in the midst of thee shall mount up above thee higher and higher; and thou shalt come down lower and lower. 44 He shall lend to thee, and thou shalt not lend to him: he shall be the head, and thou shalt be the tail. 45 And all these curses shall come upon thee, and shall pursue thee, and overtake thee, till thou be destroyed; because thou hearkenedst not unto the voice of Jehovah thy God, to keep his commandments and his statutes which he commanded thee: 46 and they shall be upon thee for a sign and for a wonder, and upon thy seed for ever.

47 Because thou servedst not Jehovah thy God with joyfulness, and with gladness of heart, by reason of the abundance of all things; 48 therefore shalt thou serve thine enemies that Jehovah shall send against thee, in hunger, and in thirst, and in nakedness, and in want of all things: and he shall put a yoke of iron upon thy neck, until he have destroyed thee. 49 Jehovah will bring a nation against thee from far, from the end of the earth, as the eagle flieth; a nation whose tongue thou shalt not understand; 50 a nation of fierce countenance, that shall not regard the person of the old, nor show favor to the young, 51 and shall eat the fruit of thy cattle, and the fruit of thy ground, until thou be destroyed; that also shall not leave thee grain, new wine, or oil, the increase of thy cattle, or the young of thy flock, until they have caused thee to perish. 52 And they shall besiege thee in all thy gates, until thy high and fortified walls come down, wherein thou trustedst, throughout all thy land; and

they shall besiege thee in all thy gates throughout all thy land, which Jehovah thy God hath given thee. 53 And thou shalt eat the fruit of thine own body, the flesh of thy sons and of thy daughters, whom Jehovah thy God hath given thee, in the siege and in the distress wherewith thine enemies shall distress thee. 54 The man that is tender among you, and very delicate, his eye shall be evil toward his brother, and toward the wife of his bosom, and toward the remnant of his children whom he hath remaining; 55 so that he will not give to any of them of the flesh of his children whom he shall eat, because he hath nothing left him, in the siege and in the distress wherewith thine enemy shall distress thee in all thy gates. 56 The tender and delicate woman among you, who would not adventure to set the sole of her foot upon the ground for delicateness and tenderness, her eye shall be evil toward the husband of her bosom, and toward her son, and toward her daughter, 57 and toward her young one that cometh out from between her feet, and toward her children whom she shall bear; for she shall eat them for want of all things secretly, in the siege and in the distress wherewith thine enemy shall distress thee in thy gates.

58 If thou wilt not observe to do all the words of this law that are written in this book, that thou mayest fear this glorious and fearful name, JEHOVAH THY GOD; 59 then Jehovah will make thy plagues wonderful, and the plagues of thy seed, even great plagues, and of long continuance, and sore sicknesses, and of long continuance. 60 And he will bring upon thee again all the diseases of Egypt, which thou wast afraid of; and they shall cleave unto thee. 61 Also every sickness, and every plague, which is not written in the book of this law, them will Jehovah bring upon thee, until thou be destroyed. 62 And ye shall be left few in number, whereas ye were as the stars of heaven for multitude; because thou didst not hearken unto the voice of Jehovah thy God. 63 And it shall come to pass, that, as Jehovah rejoiced over you to do you good, and to multiply you, so Jehovah will rejoice over you to cause you to perish, and to destroy you; and ye shall be plucked from off the land whither thou goest in to possess it. 64 And Jehovah will scatter thee among all peoples, from the one end of the earth even unto the other end of the earth; and there thou shalt serve other gods, which thou hast not known, thou nor thy fathers, even wood and stone. 65 And among these nations shalt thou find no ease, and

there shall be no rest for the sole of thy foot: but Jehovah will give thee there a trembling heart, and failing of eyes, and pining of soul; 66 and thy life shall hang in doubt before thee; and thou shalt fear night and day, and shalt have no assurance of thy life. 67 In the morning thou shalt say, Would it were even! and at even thou shalt say, Would it were morning! for the fear of thy heart which thou shalt fear, and for the sight of thine eyes which thou shalt see. 68 And Jehovah will bring thee into Egypt again with ships, by the way whereof I said unto thee, Thou shalt see it no more again: and there ye shall sell yourselves unto your enemies for bondmen and for bondwomen, and no man shall buy you.

The punishment for disobedience was to be severe. The curse of God would rest upon them in every area and aspect of life. The fearful curses which were to come upon Israel for disobedience are enumerated in all of their horrible detail in verses 16-68.

VI. RENEWAL OF GOD'S COVENANT (Deut. 29:1-29)

A. MOSES CALLS THE PEOPLE TO RENEWAL (29:1-9)

1 These are the words of the covenant which Jehovah commanded Moses to make with the children of Israel in the land of Moab, besides the covenant which he made with them in Horeb.

2 And Moses called unto all Israel, and said unto them, Ye have seen all that Jehovah did before your eyes in the land of Egypt unto Pharaoh, and unto all his servants, and unto all his land; 3 the great trials which thine eyes saw, the signs, and those great wonders: 4 but Jehovah hath not given you a heart to know, and eyes to see, and ears to hear, unto this day. 5 And I have led you forty years in the wilderness: your clothes are not waxed old upon you, and thy shoe is not waxed old upon thy foot. 6 Ye have not eaten bread, neither have ye drunk wine or strong drink; that ye may know that I am Jehovah your God. 7 And when ye came unto this place, Sihon the king of Heshbon, and Og the king of Bashan, came out against us unto battle, and we smote them: 8 and we took their land, and gave it for an inheritance unto the Reubenites, and to the Gadites, and to the half-tribe of the Manassites. 9 Keep therefore the words of this cove-

nant, and do them, that ye may prosper in all that ye do.

It is apparent that verse 1 should be the last verse in the previous chapter since the matter in verse 2 is entirely different. It appears as the sixty-ninth verse in the most correct copies of the Hebrew Bible. Scholars are not agreed as to whether this verse is a summary statement or whether it is the heading to a new address.

The covenant which was made here was a renewal of that given at Horeb, which renewed the covenant with Abraham, which in turn renewed the covenant with Adam. Each generation had the benefit of a formal renewal of previous covenants. The Scofield Bible designates this as the Palestine covenant.

Moses is now nearing the end of his earthly pilgrimage (v. 2). A new generation has grown up which is ready to possess the land promised to Israel. The Israelites are reminded of the providential care Jehovah has given His people during the trials and tribulations in Egypt and in the desert. They are reminded that while they wandered forty years in the wilderness neither their clothes nor shoes wore out (vv. 3-9).

B. THE COVENANT ETERNALLY BINDING (29:10-21)

10 Ye stand this day all of you before Jehovah your God, your heads, your tribes, your elders, and your officers, even all the men of Israel, 11 your little ones, your wives, and thy sojourner that is in the midst of thy camps, from the hewer of thy wood unto the drawer of thy water; 12 that thou mayest enter into the covenant of Jehovah thy God, and into his oath, which Jehovah thy God maketh with thee this day; 13 that he may establish thee this day unto himself for a people, and that he may be unto thee a God, as he spake unto thee, and as he sware unto thy fathers, to Abraham, to Isaac, and to Jacob. 14 Neither with you only do I make this covenant and this oath, 15 but with him that standeth here with us this day before Jehovah our God, and also with him that is not here with us this day 16 (for ye know how we dwelt in the land of Egypt, and how we came through the midst of the nations through which ye passed; 17 and ye have seen their abominations, and their idols, wood and stone,

silver and gold, which were among them) ; 18 lest there should be among you man, or woman, or family, or tribe, whose heart turneth away this day from Jehovah our God, to go to serve the gods of those nations; lest there should be among you a root that beareth gall and wormwood; 19 and it come to pass, when he heareth the words of this curse, that he bless himself in his heart, saying, I shall have peace, though I walk in the stubbornness of my heart, to destroy the moist with the dry. 20 Jehovah will not pardon him, but then the anger of Jehovah and his jealousy will smoke against that man, and all the curse that is written in this book shall lie upon him, and Jehovah will blot out his name from under heaven. 21 And Jehovah will set him apart unto evil out of all the tribes of Israel, according to all the curses of the covenant that is written in this book of the law.

The covenant which had been in effect over the ages is about to be restated for the new generation (v. 10). The covenant between Jehovah and Israel was vitally relevant and important to every soul in Israel; therefore every individual was called upon to present himself at this grand assembly. Every person, from the priests down to the hewers of wood and the drawers of water, was to be a vital part of this holy company (vv. 11-12).

That he may establish thee (v. 13). In addition to initial possession of the land the people were to become firmly established in it. Their identification with Jehovah was to be deeply rooted in a complete dedication. This eternal covenant had a backward look to Abraham as well as a forward look to those yet unborn (vv. 14-16).

Ye have seen their abominations (v. 17). The people are reminded of the abominable idol worship which they had seen in their journey from Egypt, and they are told that they will encounter it in the new land.

C. JUDGMENT FOR APOSTASY (29:22-29)

22 And the generation to come, your children that shall rise up after you, and the foreigner that shall come from a far land, shall say, when they see the plagues of that land, and the sicknesses wherewith Jehovah hath made it sick; 23 and that the whole land thereof is brimstone, and

salt, *and* a burning, *that* it is not sown, nor beareth, nor any grass groweth therein, like the overthrow of Sodom and Gomorrah, Admah and Zeboiim, which Jehovah overthrew in his anger, and in his wrath: 24 even all the nations shall say, Wherefore hath Jehovah done thus unto this land? what meaneth the heat of this great anger? 25 Then men shall say, Because they forsook the covenant of Jehovah, the God of their fathers, which he made with them when he brought them forth out of the land of Egypt, 26 and went and served other gods, and worshipped them, gods that they knew not, and that he had not given unto them: 27 therefore the anger of Jehovah was kindled against this land, to bring upon it all the curse that is written in this book; 28 and Jehovah rooted them out of their land in anger, and in wrath, and in great indignation, and cast them into another land, as at this day. 29 The secret things belong unto Jehovah our God; but the things that are revealed belong unto us and to our children for ever, that we may do all the words of this law.

Moses here projects a description of that which will prevail in Israel when the people turn their face from Jehovah in apostasy. This description is prophetic, in part, of Israel's captivity to the Assyrians in 722 B. C. and the Babylonian captivity of Judah in 606 B. C. The foreigner coming into the land will make reference to the sickness of the land — both physically and spiritually. The surrounding nations are made to ask the question: **Wherefore hath Jehovah done this unto this land?** In dramatic dialogue they will give this answer, **Because they forsook the covenant of Jehovah, the God of their fathers** (vv. 23-29).

D. CONDITIONS FOR
RESTORATION (30:1-14)

1 And it shall come to pass, when all these things are come upon thee, the blessing and the curse, which I have set before thee, and thou shalt call them to mind among all the nations, whither Jehovah thy God hath driven thee, 2 and shalt return unto Jehovah thy God, and shalt obey his voice according to all that I command thee this day, thou and thy children, with all thy heart, and with all thy soul; 3 that then Jehovah thy God will turn thy captivity, and have compassion upon thee, and will return and gather thee from all the peoples, whither

Jehovah thy God hath scattered thee. 4 If *any of* thine outcasts be in the uttermost parts of heaven, from thence will Jehovah thy God gather thee, and from thence will he fetch thee: 5 and Jehovah thy God will bring thee into the land which thy fathers possessed, and thou shalt possess it; and he will do thee good, and multiply thee above thy fathers. 6 And Jehovah thy God will circumcise thy heart, and the heart of thy seed, to love Jehovah thy God with all thy heart, and with all thy soul, that thou mayest live. 7 And Jehovah thy God will put all these curses upon thine enemies, and on them that hate thee, that persecuted thee. 8 And thou shalt return and obey the voice of Jehovah, and do all his commandments which I command thee this day. 9 And Jehovah thy God will make thee plenteous in all the work of thy hand, in the fruit of thy body, and in the fruit of thy cattle, and in the fruit of thy ground, for good: for Jehovah will again rejoice over thee for good, as he rejoiced over thy fathers; 10 if thou shalt obey the voice of Jehovah thy God, to keep his commandments and his statutes which are written in this book of the law; if thou turn unto Jehovah thy God with all thy heart, and with all thy soul.

11 For this commandment which I command thee this day, it is not too hard for thee, neither is it far off. 12 It is not in heaven, that thou shouldest say, Who shall go up for us to heaven, and bring it unto us, and make us to hear it, that we may do it? 13 Neither is it beyond the sea, that thou shouldest say, Who shall go over the sea for us, and bring it unto us, and make us to hear it, that we may do it? 14 But the word is very nigh unto thee, in thy mouth, and in thy heart, that thou mayest do it.

This prophetic and dramatic dialogue extends to the point where the people repent and are restored. It is especially prophetic of the period of the judges and also of the time when the people are restored after the Babylonian captivity. If the people would truly repent Jehovah would show compassion (v. 3), and permit them to be restored to the land which their fathers possessed (vv. 4-5).

Thy God will circumcise thy heart (v. 6; see comments on Deut. 10:16).

After receiving their punishment and repenting of their sins God's people will once again enjoy the grace and favor of Jehovah (v. 9). They will be fruitful and multiply in all areas of life. The commands of God are always reasonable and possible to obey (v. 11). The relationship with Jehovah is to be a present-tense, here-and-now fellowship. The people are to obey in the present and Jehovah will reward in the present. This relationship is not a far-distant, heavenly reality, nor is it to be had in far-distant lands, but it is to be theirs in their hearts now, in the very land in which they are to dwell (vv. 12-14).

E. THE CHOICE BETWEEN LIFE AND DEATH (30:15-20)

15 See, I have set before thee this day life and good, and death and evil; 16 in that I command thee this day to love Jehovah thy God, to walk in his ways, and to keep his commandments and his statutes and his ordinances, that thou mayest live and multiply, and that Jehovah thy God may bless thee in the land whither thou goest in to possess it. 17 But if thy heart turn away, and thou wilt not hear, but shalt be drawn away, and worship other gods, and serve them; 18 I denounce unto you this day, that ye shall surely perish; ye shall not prolong your days in the land, whither thou passest over the Jordan to go in to possess it. 19 I call heaven and earth to witness against you this day, that I have set before thee life and death, the blessing and the curse: therefore choose life, that thou mayest live, thou and thy seed; 20 to love Jehovah thy God, to obey his voice, and to cleave unto him; for he is thy life, and the length of thy days; that thou mayest dwell in the land which Jehovah sware unto thy fathers, to Abraham, to Isaac, and to Jacob, to give them.

Jehovah makes a projection of the good and the evil (v. 15). Only Israel can make the choice between the two (vv. 16-19). These were set before the children of Israel, according to Clarke, for the following reasons:

1 That they might comprehend their import. 2 That they might feel their importance. 3 That they might choose life and the path of believing, loving obedience that led to it. 4 That they and their posterity, thus choosing life and refusing evil, might be the favorites of God in time and eternity.

Were there no such thing as free will in man, who could reconcile these sayings either with sincerity or common sense?

God has made the human will free, and there is no power or influence either in heaven, earth, or hell, except the power of God, that can deprive it of its free volitions; of its power to will and nill, to choose and refuse, to act or not act or force it to sin against God. Hence man is accountable for his actions, because they are his; were he necessitated by fate, or sovereign constraint, they could not be his. Hence he is rewardable, hence he is punishable. God, in his creation, willed that the human creature should be free, and he formed his soul accordingly; and the Law and Gospel, the promise and precept, and the doctrine of eternal life, are all constructed on this ground; that is, they all necessarily suppose the freedom of the human will: nor could it be will if it were not free, because the principle of freedom or liberty is necessarily implied in the idea of volition.[76]

The motivation toward God must always be love. This love is evidenced by keeping the commandments (see John 14:15, 23).

F. JOSHUA COMMISSIONED TO SUCCEED MOSES (31:1-23)

1 And Moses went and spake these words unto all Israel. 2 And he said unto them, I am a hundred and twenty years old this day; I can no more go out and come in: and Jehovah hath said unto me, Thou shalt not go over this Jordan. 3 Jehovah thy God, he will go over before thee; he will destroy these nations from before thee, and thou shalt dispossess them: *and* Joshua, he shall go over before thee, as Jehovah hath spoken. 4 And Jehovah will do unto them as he did to Sihon and to Og, the kings of the Amorites, and unto their land; whom he destroyed. 5 And Jehovah will deliver them up before you, and ye shall do unto them according unto all the commandment which I have commanded you. 6 Be strong and of good courage, fear not, nor be affrighted at them: for Jehovah thy God, he it is that doth go with thee; he will not fail thee, nor forsake thee. 7 And Moses called unto Joshua, and said unto him in the sight of all Israel, Be strong and of good courage: for thou shalt go with this people into the land which Jehovah hath sworn unto their fathers to give them; and thou shalt cause them to inherit it. 8 And Jehovah, he it is that doth go before thee; he will be with thee, he will not fail thee, neither

[76] *Op. cit.*, I, 819-20.

forsake thee: fear not, neither be dismayed.

9 And Moses wrote this law, and delivered it unto the priests the sons of Levi, that bare the ark of the covenant of Jehovah, and unto all the elders of Israel. 10 And Moses commanded them, saying, At the end of *every* seven years, in the set time of the year of release, in the feast of tabernacles, 11 when all Israel is come to appear before Jehovah thy God in the place which he shall choose, thou shalt read this law before all Israel in their hearing. 12 Assemble the people, the men and the women and the little ones, and thy sojourner that is within thy gates, that they may hear, and that they may learn, and fear Jehovah your God, and observe to do all the words of this law; 13 and that their children, who have not known, may hear, and learn to fear Jehovah your God, as long as ye live in the land whither ye go over the Jordan to possess it.

14 And Jehovah said unto Moses, Behold, thy days approach that thou must die: call Joshua, and present yourselves in the tent of meeting, that I may give him a charge. And Moses and Joshua went, and presented themselves in the tent of meeting. 15 And Jehovah appeared in the Tent in a pillar of cloud: and the pillar of cloud stood over the door of the Tent. 16 And Jehovah said unto Moses, Behold, thou shalt sleep with thy fathers; and this people will rise up, and play the harlot after the strange gods of the land, whither they go to be among them, and will forsake me, and break my covenant which I have made with them. 17 Then my anger shall be kindled against them in that day, and I will forsake them, and I will hide my face from them, and they shall be devoured, and many evils and troubles shall come upon them; so that they will say in that day, Are not these evils come upon us because our God is not among us? 18 And I will surely hide my face in that day for all the evil which they shall have wrought, in that they are turned unto other gods. 19 Now therefore write ye this song for you, and teach thou it the children of Israel: put it in their mouths, that this song may be a witness for me against the children of Israel. 20 For when I shall have brought them into the land which I sware unto their fathers, flowing with milk and honey, and they shall have eaten and filled themselves, and waxed fat; then will they turn unto other gods, and serve them, and despise me, and break my covenant. 21 And it shall come to pass, when many evils and troubles are come

upon them, that this song shall testify before them as a witness; for it shall not be forgotten out of the mouths of their seed: for I know their imagination which they frame this day, before I have brought them into the land which I sware. 22 So Moses wrote this song the same day, and taught it the children of Israel. 23 And he gave Joshua the son of Nun a charge, and said, Be strong and of good courage; for thou shalt bring the children of Israel into the land which I sware unto them: and I will be with thee.

Moses is now one hundred and twenty years old, and the time for his heavenly reward is near. Moses assures the people that they will cross the Jordan under the able leadership of Joshua, and that Jehovah will lead the way to remove all obstacles in their way, if they remain obedient (vv. 4-5). Moses entreats Joshua to be strong and of good courage because Jehovah has covenanted with His people to lead them into the land (v. 8).

Moses committed the contents of the book of Deuteronomy to writing. Since this book contained Jehovah's contractual agreement, copies were made. One copy was placed in the hands of the Levites and priests and the other copy was placed beside the ark (v. 23) as a testimonial and a ready reference in case the working copy was damaged, mutilated or destroyed. This book was to be read before the entire congregation of Israel at the end of every sabbatical year. Thus the older generation would be reminded and the new generation informed with regard to Jehovah's covenant relationship to Israel (vv. 10-13).

The time for Moses' departure had come (v. 14). The transference of leadership was to be made in the tabernacle. Jehovah's presence was attested by the pillar of cloud that stood over the door (v. 15). The Old Testament concept of immortality is clearly stressed in the words: **thou shalt sleep with thy fathers** (v. 16; see also Job 19:25-27; Ps. 16:10; Eccl. 12:7; Dan. 12:2).

Through the foreknowledge of God, Israel's intermittent backsliding is here projected (vv. 17-18; see comments on Deut. 29:22ff.).

The word of Jehovah committed to the mind and memory in the form of song would serve as a strengthening and stabilizing force when they entered the promised land and began to enjoy a settled life. The edifying effect of songs with religious content cannot be overestimated (vv. 20-23). Conversely, the evil effect of sensuous, lust-stimulating songs, as is sometimes seen today, can greatly influence and encourage immorality. Most commercial and many ideological products, both harmful and good, are sold in our contemporary society with the aid of a musical jingle.

Music can be a vehicle for the glory of God or it can be the means of moral degradation. Songs and choruses about the things of God should be taught our children on every occasion. Children should be taught early in life to "make a joyful noise unto the Lord."

G. THE LAW TO BE PLACED IN THE ARK (31:24-29)

24 And it came to pass, when Moses had made an end of writing the words of this law in a book, until they were finished, 25 that Moses commanded the Levites, that bare the ark of the covenant of Jehovah, saying, 26 Take this book of the law, and put it by the side of the ark of the covenant of Jehovah your God, that it may be there for a witness against thee. 27 For I know thy rebellion, and thy stiff neck: behold, while I am yet alive with you this day, ye have been rebellious against Jehovah; and how much more after my death? 28 Assemble unto me all the elders of your tribes, and your officers, that I may speak these words in their ears, and call heaven and earth to witness against them. 29 For I know that after my death ye will utterly corrupt yourselves, and turn aside from the way which I have commanded you; and evil will befall you in the latter days; because ye will do that which is evil in the sight of Jehovah, to provoke him to anger through the work of your hands.

The two tables of the law were to be placed inside the ark and a complete copy of the Levitical laws was to be deposited in a box beside the ark. It is probable that in the days of Josiah the working copy had been lost or destroyed and that this second copy from the box was produced (II Chron. 34:14ff.; see comments on Deut. 31:9).

Moses expresses concern over Israel's future (v. 27) because he has seen the people rebel and defy Jehovah on nu-

merous occasions. The foreknowledge of God is revealed to Moses. The song of Moses is to be recited in the interest of the Israelites and in view of their foreseen rebellion (vv. 28-29; see comments on Deut. 29:22ff.).

VII. ISRAEL'S SONGS OF PRAISE (Deut. 31:30—33:29)

A. MOSES' SONG OF DELIVERANCE (31:30—32:52)

30 And Moses spake in the ears of all the assembly of Israel the words of this song, until they were finished.

1 Give ear, ye heavens, and I will speak;
And let the earth hear the words of my mouth.
2 My doctrine shall drop as the rain;
My speech shall distil as the dew,
As the small rain upon the tender grass,
And as the showers upon the herb.
3 For I will proclaim the name of Jehovah:
Ascribe ye greatness unto our God.
4 The Rock, his work is perfect;
For all his ways are justice:
A God of faithfulness and without iniquity,
Just and right is he.
5 They have dealt corruptly with him, *they are* not his children, *it is* their blemish;
They are a perverse and crooked generation.
6 Do ye thus requite Jehovah,
O foolish people and unwise?
Is not he thy father that hath bought thee?
He hath made thee, and established thee.
7 Remember the days of old,
Consider the years of many generations:
Ask thy father, and he will show thee;
Thine elders, and they will tell thee.
8 When the Most High gave to the nations their inheritance,
When he separated the children of men,
He set the bounds of the peoples
According to the number of the children of Israel.
9 For Jehovah's portion is his people;
Jacob is the lot of his inheritance.
10 He found him in a desert land,
And in the waste howling wilderness;
He compassed him about, he cared for him,

He kept him as the apple of his eye.
11 As an eagle that stirreth up her nest,
That fluttereth over her young,
He spread abroad his wings, he took
them,
He bare them on his pinions.
12 Jehovah alone did lead him,
And there was no foreign god with
him.
And he did eat the increase of the
field;
And he made him to suck honey out
of the rock,
And oil out of the flinty rock;
14 Butter of the herd, and milk of the
flock,
With fat of lambs,
And rams of the breed of Bashan, and
goats,
With the finest of the wheat;
And of the blood of the grape thou
drankest wine.
15 But Jeshurun waxed fat, and kicked:
Thou art waxed fat, thou art grown
thick, thou art become sleek;
Then he forsook God who made him,
And lightly esteemed the Rock of his
salvation.
16 They moved him to jealousy with
strange *gods;*
With abominations provoked they him
to anger.
17 They sacrificed unto demons, *which
were* no God,
To gods that they knew not,
To new *gods* that came up of late,
Which your fathers dreaded not.
18 Of the Rock that begat thee thou art
unmindful,
And hast forgotten God that gave thee
birth.
19 And Jehovah saw *it,* and abhorred
them,
Because of the provocation of his sons
and his daughters.
20 And he said, I will hide my face from
them,
I will see what their end shall be:
For they are a very perverse generation,
Children in whom is no faithfulness.
21 They have moved me to jealousy with
that which is not God;
They have provoked me to anger
with their vanities:
And I will move them to jealousy
with those that are not a people;
I will provoke them to anger with a
foolish nation.
22 For a fire is kindled in mine anger,
And burneth unto the lowest Sheol,
And devoureth the earth with its
increase,

And setteth on fire the foundations
of the mountains.
23 I will heap evils upon them;
I will spend mine arrows upon them:
24 *They shall be* wasted with hunger,
and devoured with burning heat
And bitter destruction;
And the teeth of beasts will I send
upon them,
With the poison of crawling things
of the dust.
25 Without shall the sword bereave,
And in the chambers terror;
It shall destroy both young man and
virgin,
The suckling with the man of gray
hairs.
26 I said, I would scatter them afar,
I would make the remembrance of
them to cease from among men;
27 Were it not that I feared the provocation of the enemy,
Lest their adversaries should judge
amiss,
Lest they should say, Our hand is
exalted,
And Jehovah hath not done all this.
28 For they are a nation void of counsel,
And there is no understanding in
them.
29 Oh that they were wise, that they
understood this,
That they would consider their latter
end!
30 How should one chase a thousand,
And two put ten thousand to flight,
Except their Rock had sold them,
And Jehovah had delivered them up?
31 For their rock is not as our Rock,
Even our enemies themselves being
judges.
32 For their vine is of the vine of Sodom,
And of the fields of Gomorrah:
Their grapes are grapes of gall,
Their clusters are bitter:
33 Their wine is the poison of serpents,
And the cruel venom of asps.
34 Is not this laid up in store with me,
Sealed up among my treasures?
35 Vengeance is mine, and recompense,
At the time when their foot shall slide:
For the day of their calamity is at
hand,
And the things that are to come upon
them shall make haste.
36 For Jehovah will judge his people,
And repent himself for his servants;
When he seeth that *their* power is
gone,
And there is none *remaining,* shut
up or left at large.
37 And he will say, Where are their
gods,
The rock in which they took refuge;

38 Which did eat the fat of their sacrifices,
And drank the wine of their drink-offering?
Let them rise up and help you,
Let them be your protection.
39 See now that I, even I, am he,
And there is no god with me:
I kill, and I make alive;
I wound, and I heal:
And there is none that can deliver out of my hand.
40 For I lift up my hand to heaven,
And say, As I live for ever,
41 If I whet my glittering sword,
And my hand take hold on judgment;
I will render vengeance to mine adversaries,
And will recompense them that hate me.
42 I will make mine arrows drunk with blood,
And my sword shall devour flesh;
With the blood of the slain and the captives,
From the head of the leaders of the enemy.
43 Rejoice, O ye nations, *with* his people:
For he will avenge the blood of his servants,
And will render vengeance to his adversaries,
And will make expiation for his land, for his people.
44 And Moses came and spake all the words of this song in the ears of the people, he, and Hoshea the son of Nun. 45 And Moses made an end of speaking all these words to all Israel; 46 and he said unto them, Set your heart unto all the words which I testify unto you this day, which ye shall command your children to observe to do, *even* all the words of this law. 47 For it is no vain thing for you; because it is your life, and through this thing ye shall prolong your days in the land, whither ye go over the Jordan to possess it.
48 And Jehovah spake unto Moses that selfsame day, saying, 49 Get thee up into this mountain of Abarim, unto mount Nebo, which is in the land of Moab, that is over against Jericho; and behold the land of Canaan, which I give unto the children of Israel for a possession; 50 and die in the mount whither thou goest up, and be gathered unto thy people, as Aaron thy brother died in mount Hor, and was gathered unto his people: 51 because ye trespassed against me in the midst of the children of Israel at the waters of Meribah of Kadesh, in the wil-

derness of Zin; because ye sanctified me not in the midst of the children of Israel. 52 For thou shalt see the land before thee; but thou shalt not go thither into the land which I give the children of Israel.

This song has been the subject of much comment by commentators. The best literary critics are agreed that it is an example of excellent poetical composition. Some of the objectives of this poem are: (1) to emphasize and magnify the glory and majesty of God; (2) to show the interest true believers have in God as their friend; (3) to show the dangers in departing from God; (4) to remind them of their providential heritage; (5) to leave a written record of warning to posterity with regard to apostasy; (6) to show that even people under great providential oversight can turn away from the living God to worship idols and indulge in heathen immorality; (7) to show the patience and long-suffering which God possesses in behalf of His people; and (8) to show that ultimately the grace and goodness of God will triumph in the lives of those who are faithful to the end. Clarke says:

> All this is done with such strength and elegance of diction, with such appropriate, energetic, and impressive figures and metaphors, and in such a powerful torrent of that soul-penetrating, pure poetic spirit that comes glowing from the bosom of God, that the reader is alternately elated or depressed, filled with compunction or confidence, with despair or hope, according to the quick transitions of the inimitable writer to the different topics which form the subject of this incomparable and wondrously varied ode. May that Spirit by which it was dictated give it its fullest, most durable, and most effectual impression upon the mind of every reader![77]

The first three verses of chapter 32 are an invocation or summons to the people to give their attention and to be witnesses of the covenant between themselves and Jehovah.

It is to be noted that the word **Rock** (v. 4) is capitalized and denotes deity and obviously has reference to Jehovah, the God of the Israelites. This term is used six times in this chapter and about eighteen times in other parts of the Old

[77] *Ibid.*, I, 832.

Testament. Attention should be called to the fact that the word **Rock** is capitalized only when reference is made to Jehovah (see vv. 31, 37; also I Sam. 2:2; II Sam. 22:2-3; Ps. 18:2, 31; 31:3).

The two principal names for deity in the Old Testament are Elohim and the consonantal form Yhwh. *Elohim* is translated "God" in most versions. *Yhwh* is translated "Lord" in the King James Version, "Jehovah" in the American Revised Version, and "Yahweh" in some of the modern translations. There is some evidence to suggest that "Jehovah" in the Old Testament signifies the second person of the Trinity.[78]

With reference to the "rock" in Jesus' conversation with Peter (Matt. 16:18), it is evident that that "rock" is the "Rock" referred to many times in the Old Testament, and that "Rock" is actually Christ, as is suggested in Paul's address to the Corinthians. There it is clearly stated that "they drank of that spiritual Rock that followed them; and that Rock was Christ" (I Cor. 10:4). Thus it is established that the names "Rock" and "Christ" are used interchangeably without regard to time or period.[79]

Verses 7 to 14 contain an inspirational ballad in which Israel's historic perspective is reviewed. All the verses deal with some aspect of Jehovah's providential care of His people. The many blessings enjoyed by the people of God are enumerated. Kline says:

> The Lord, coming to seek and to save that which was lost, found homeless Israel helpless in the desert. He cherished his people as jealously as does a man that which is most precious to him, or as an eagle cherishes its young (vs. 11). The figure might be interpreted of the deliverance from Egypt as well as of the guidance of Canaan. In the Lord's strength Israel advanced in majestic triumph through Trans-Jordan (cf. 2:31ff.) and over mountainous Canaan to feast on all the choicest offerings of field and flock (vv. 13b, 14).[80]

The word **Jeshurun** (v. 15) is a Hebrew word meaning "the upright," and is a designation used for Israel. It is used prophetically as a reproach for the apos-

tasy in which Israel had indulged in the past and would again indulge in the future. Clarke suggests that this prophecy was spoken as a warning in that the evil might not take place. He notes that if the evil was absolutely unavoidable, no blame could attach itself to Israel. A marked example is seen in I Samuel 23:11ff. where a prediction appears in almost absolute form, and yet the evil was prevented because the person received the prediction as a warning.[81]

Lightly esteemed the Rock of his salvation (v. 15b). Israel is here pictured as thinking too highly of herself and thereby lightly esteeming the God of her salvation (for comments on "Rock" see Deut. 32:4ff.). It is a matter bordering on self-deification.

They sacrificed unto demons (v. 17). The depth of their degradation is indicated in the object of their affection. Instead of offering sacrifices to Jehovah, they offered them to demons.

I will hide my face from them (v. 20). Jehovah's covenant with His people was contingent upon absolute fidelity. Israel has now dedicated herself to rival image-gods, and Jehovah has pronounced the curse of extinction. The fire of Jehovah's jealousy will burn them in the lowest Sheol (vv. 21-22). They are to suffer with burning heat and the ravages of wild beasts (vv. 23-25). They are to be scattered in faraway places (vv. 26-27).

Jehovah is willing to temper His judgment and stay His vengeance upon Israel because of the encouragement and consolation which complete destruction would give her enemies — even the enemies of Jehovah. God's compassion dictates that a remnant should be spared. God has pronounced Israel to be a foolish nation, but wishes she were wise. If Israel could only anticipate her glorious future.

Consider their latter end (v. 29b). This will be the time when they will be host to the Messiah. If they could think on this, they would be more temperate. It is always important to think in terms of ultimate ends rather than in terms of temporary expediencies. The latter end of life and the future state of the soul

---

[78] Wacker, W. L., "Name," *International Standard Bible Encyclopedia*, IV, 2112; see also Hanke, *Christ and the Church in the Old Testament*, pp. 15ff., 36ff.

[79] Hanke, *From Eden to Eternity*, pp. 17, 75, 109, 110. [80] *Op. cit.*, pp. 199, 200.

[81] Clarke, *op. cit.*, I, 827, 828.

are always more important than the satisfaction of fleshly appetites, lest one sell his birthright for a mess of pottage (Gen. 25:29ff.). If Israel had not forsaken Jehovah, one enemy could not have chased a thousand Israelites, nor could two put ten thousand to flight (v. 30).

The nature of Israel's enemies is like Sodom and Gomorrah, and their vine is bitter and poisonous, producing nothing but mischief and misery to all who come in contact with them (v. 32). The day of calamity is not far distant (vv. 33-35). **Jehovah will judge his people** (v. 36). Jehovah has absolute power over Israel and a right to punish her, but in the day of her calamity He will show mercy. Jehovah will chide Israel and mockingly ask, **Where are their gods, the rock in which they took refuge?** (vv. 37f.). Jehovah now pushes the heathen gods aside and declares Himself to be the true and living God who has power to kill and to make alive (vv. 40-43).

Moses probably addressed the people from the tabernacle after Jehovah had given him the preceding prophetic song. He again reminded his people that they could please Jehovah only when they served Him in a true dedication of love. They were to teach their children all the words of the law, for in obedience to the law they would find preservation of life and length of days (v. 47). **Jehovah spake unto Moses** (v. 48). Jehovah commanded Moses to journey to the top of Mt. Nebo where he was to view the promised land. After viewing the land of Canaan Moses would die and be gathered unto his people.

B. MOSES' SONG OF BLESSING ON THE TRIBES OF ISRAEL (33:1-29)

1 And this is the blessing, wherewith Moses the man of God blessed the children of Israel before his death. 2 And he said,
Jehovah came from Sinai,
And rose from Seir unto them;
He shined forth from mount Paran,
And he came from the ten thousands of holy ones:
At his right hand was a fiery law for them.
3 Yea, he loveth the people;
All his saints are in thy hand:
And they sat down at thy feet;
Every one shall receive of thy words.
4 Moses commanded us a law,

An inheritance for the assembly of Jacob.
5 And he was king in Jeshurun,
When the heads of the people were gathered,
All the tribes of Israel together.
6 Let Reuben live, and not die;
Nor let his men be few.
7 And this is *the blessing* of Judah: and he said,
Hear, Jehovah, the voice of Judah,
And bring him in unto his people.
With his hands he contended for himself;
And thou shalt be a help against his adversaries.
8 And of Levi he said,
Thy Thummim and thy Urim are with thy godly one,
Whom thou didst prove at Massah,
With whom thou didst strive at the waters of Meribah;
9 Who said of his father, and of his mother, I have not seen him;
Neither did he acknowledge his brethren,
Nor knew he his own children.
For they have observed thy word,
And keep thy covenant.
10 They shall teach Jacob thine ordinances,
And Israel thy law:
They shall put incense before thee,
And whole burnt-offering upon thine altar.
11 Bless, Jehovah, his substance,
And accept the work of his hands:
Smite through the loins of them that rise up against him,
And of them that hate him, that they rise not again.
12 Of Benjamin he said,
The beloved of Jehovah shall dwell in safety by him;
He covereth him all the day long,
And he dwelleth between his shoulders.
13 And of Joseph he said,
Blessed of Jehovah be his land,
For the precious things of heaven, for the dew,
And for the deep that coucheth beneath,
14 And for the precious things of the fruits of the sun,
And for the precious things of the growth of the moons,
15 And for the chief things of the ancient mountains,
And for the precious things of the everlasting hills,
16 And for the precious things of the earth and the fulness thereof,

And the good will of him that dwelt
in the bush.
Let *the blessing* come upon the head
of Joseph,
And upon the crown of the head of
him that was separate from his
brethren.

17 The firstling of his herd, majesty is
his;
And his horns are the horns of the
wild-ox:
With them he shall push the peoples
all of them, *even* the ends of the
earth:
And they are the ten thousands of
Ephraim,
And they are the thousands of Manasseh.

18 And of Zebulun he said,
Rejoice, Zebulun, in thy going out;
And, Issachar, in thy tents.

19 They shall call the peoples unto the
mountain;
There shall they offer sacrifices of
righteousness:
For they shall suck the abundance of
the seas,
And the hidden treasures of the sand.

20 And of Gad he said,
Blessed be he that enlargeth Gad:
He dwelleth as a lioness,
And teareth the arm, yea, the crown
of the head.

21 And he provided the first part for himself,
For there was the lawgiver's portion
reserved;
And he came *with* the heads of the
people;
He executed the righteousness of Jehovah,
And his ordinances with Israel.

22 And of Dan he said,
Dan is a lion's whelp,
That leapeth forth from Bashan.

23 And of Naphtali he said,
O Naphtali, satisfied with favor,
And full with the blessing of Jehovah,
Possess thou the west and the south.

24 And of Asher he said,
Blessed be Asher with children;
Let him be acceptable unto his breth-
ren,
And let him dip his foot in oil.

25 Thy bars shall be iron and brass;
And as thy days, so shall thy strength
be.

26 There is none like unto God, O
Jeshurun,
Who rideth upon the heavens for thy
help,
And in his excellency on the skies.

27 The eternal God is *thy* dwelling-place,

And underneath are the everlasting
arms.
And he thrust out the enemy from
before thee,
And said, Destroy.

28 And Israel dwelleth in safety,
The fountain of Jacob alone,
In a land of grain and new wine;
Yea, his heavens drop down dew.

29 Happy art thou, O Israel:
Who is like unto thee, a people saved
by Jehovah,
The shield of thy help,
And the sword of thy excellency!
And thine enemies shall submit them-
selves unto thee;
And thou shalt tread upon their high
places.

The general purpose of this blessing is
to inform the new generation of the
foundation on which this and all other
invocations are expressed. Jehovah had
manifested His majestic glory in Mt.
Sinai (Exod. 31:18), at Seir (Num. 24:
18; Deut. 2:12), at Paran (Num. 14:10),
and at Meribah-Kadesh (Num. 20:1ff.).
In each place Jehovah manifested His
glory in a fiery appearance.

All considerations of judgment and
punishment for disobedience were to
be interpreted within the context of
Jehovah's love for His people. This love
was always manifest, whether Israel enjoyed blessings or experienced judgment.
Punishment was given only as a chastisement to direct the attention of the people
back to God, as a divine corrective and
not vindication. Jehovah had consecrated
Israel unto Himself and had ordained
that she should be a holy people — a
holy nation, peculiar and different from
the degenerate society around them. The
Israelites were to be bright and shining
lights in a dark and sin-drenched world.
To dramatize His majestic holiness, Jehovah displayed His glory on several
occasions (vv. 4-5).

Reuben had committed a sin with his
father's concubine (Gen. 49:3, 4), and
had participated in the rebellion with
Korah (Num. 16:1ff.), but Jehovah decrees that a remnant of his descendants
shall live. Great is the mercy of God
when His people humble themselves and
repent. The Lord is "not willing that any
should perish, but that all should come
to repentance" (II Pet. 3:9).

Symbolic significance is seen in the

stones assigned to each of the twelve sons of Jacob. The emerald was assigned to Reuben because the emerald is sea green in color. The man who was as unstable as water found his name in a stone the color of which suggested the ever-rolling, restless sea.

Judah was the vessel chosen by Jehovah through which the Messiah would be manifested. Judah was assigned the sardius (ruby) stone because "he washed his garments in wine, and his clothes in the blood of grapes" (Gen. 49:11). One further analogy might be drawn here in that the Savior who shed His blood on the cross came from the tribe of Judah. Obviously, no stone other than the blood-red ruby could better or more forcibly convey the idea of atonement. Kline says:

> The blessing for royal Judah (Leah's fourth son) is, in effect, the prayer that Jacob's prophetic blessing on him might be fulfilled (cf. Gen. 49:9-12), that Judah might be enabled to accomplish the kingly task of conquering the adversaries and thence return to his people to receive their obedience.[82]

The tribe of Levi was chosen to serve the priestly functions. Aaron was chosen as the high priest and was called the holy or godly one. The high priest wore a breastplate over his heart on which were imbedded twelve stones — one for each tribe. The Urim and Thummim were placed underneath the breastplate near his heart. These objects were used to determine the will of God in certain matters. The Israelites were reminded of the sad events at Meribah in which both Moses and Aaron were involved (see Exod. 17).

Who said of his father (v. 9). Exegetes are not agreed on the identity of the person. Some think reference is made to all tribes, some see here a reference to the Messiah, and others think that the tribe of Levi is involved. It is probable that Aaron and the tribe of Levi are here referred to. Clarke says:

> The law had strictly enjoined that if the father, mother, brother, or child of the high priest should die, he must not mourn for them, but act as if they were not his kindred; (see Lev. 21:11, 12). Neither must Aaron mourn for his sons

Nadab and Abihu, though not only their death, but the circumstances of it, were the most affliction that could possibly affect a parent's heart. Besides, the high priest was forbidden on pain of death, to go out from the door of the tabernacle, (Lev. 10:2-7) for God would have them more to regard their function and duty in his service, than any natural affection whatever.

> And herein Christ was figured, who, when he was told that his mother and brethren stood without and wished to speak with him, said: "Who is my mother, and who are my brethren? whosoever shall do the will of my father who is in heaven, the same is my brother and sister and mother."[83]

The Levites were to be the religious teachers in Israel. All aspects of Jehovah-worship were to be acted out in the ceremonies and sacrifices. Each ritualistic act was to foreshadow some aspect of Jehovah's redemptive plan in Christ the Lamb of God. For this faithful service the tribe of Levi was to receive the blessings of God. Even though the priestly tribe had no earthly inheritance, its needs were to be met by the tithes and offerings of the people. The Levites would be blessed in proportion to the prosperity of the people, and their economic well-being was contingent upon a holy, godly, obedient life (v. 11).

The reference to the beloved of Jehovah (v. 12) is an allusion to the special affection Jacob had for Benjamin (Gen. 49:27f.). Moses relates the peculiar fertility which characterized the portion of the land which was assigned to the descendants of Joseph (v. 13). Mention is made of the dews which come upon this dry soil, and the abundant supplies of underground water. Clearly set forth is the abundance of the fertile soil which Ephraim and Manasseh, the sons of Jacob, will enjoy (vv. 14-17).

Zebulun's inheritance was located on the coast where conditions were most favorable for traffic and commerce upon the seas (see Gen. 49:13).

As Zebulun would prosper in shipping, so Issachar would prosper in his fertile agricultural domain. Clarke says: "By their traffic with the Gentiles (for so I think ammim should be understood here) they shall be the instruments in God's hands of converting many to the true faith; so that instead of sacrificing to idols they should offer sacrifices of righteousness."[84]

The tribe of Gad settled on the east side of the Jordan, but crossed over with his brothers to help subdue the land for them. After the west side was secured he went back to his earlier possession. Gad's portion was extensive and his ability to protect his property was as the strength of a lioness. When the Israelites had conquered the kingdoms of Sihon and Og, request was made to Moses by the tribe of Gad to settle on the east side of the Jordan River. This request was approved on the condition that his men cross over and help their brothers conquer and possess their portions. Gad was the first one to select a homestead.

Bashan, the land allotted to Dan, was a kind of jungle wilderness infested with lions. Moses probably intended to point out that the people of Dan were strong and able to live a kind of predatory life in this kind of environment.

Naphtali, satisfied with favor (v. 23). Some understand this passage to describe the neighborly goodwill which the tribe of Naphtali would enjoy (see Gen. 49: 21). Others interpret **favor** to mean that they would enjoy "special favor with Jehovah." The land which this tribe possessed was fertile and very productive.[85]

Moses prays for and prophesies four things for Asher: (1) that he will be blessed with children, (2) that his children will be good neighbors, (3) that his land will produce abundantly, and (4) that his strength shall be great (v. 25).

There is none like unto the God of Jeshurun (v. 26). This is an expression of particular affection. The God of Israel is exalted (see comments on Deut. 32: 15ff.). Jehovah is the great and mighty living God, unlike any of the heathen gods with which Israel has come in contact. Arms are symbols of power (v. 27b). Jehovah's arms cradle Israel — the Old Testament Church. His providential care is always directed toward His people when they trust and obey.

The mystical Church is to survive all adversities and abide forever. It is obvious that when Christ said to Peter, "the gates of hell shall not prevail against it (the Church)," He used the eternal tense. This statement rightly interpreted means that the gates of hell never have prevailed against it, the gates of hell are not now prevailing against it, and the gates of hell never will prevail against it (Matt. 16:18). The citadels of sin and Satan can never withstand the offensive attacks of God's spiritual army. Christ is the triumphant head over the Church now as He was the triumphant head over the Church under the name of Jehovah in the Old Testament. The redemptive message of the Old Testament is the redemptive message of the New Testament.[86]

Israel dwelleth in safety (v. 28). The day is not too far distant when Israel will cease from her desert wanderings and settle down in a land flowing with milk and honey. It is a land of much grain and wine; the heavens water the plains with dew during the dry season. The people of Israel will be happy because they are a saved people — a redeemed people. They shall be victorious against their enemies (v. 29).

VIII. THE DEATH OF MOSES (Deut. 34:1-12)

A. THE PLACE OF MOSES' DEATH (34:1-8)

1 And Moses went up from the plains of Moab unto mount Nebo, to the top of Pisgah, that is over against Jericho. And Jehovah showed him all the land of Gilead, unto Dan, 2 and all Naphtali, and the land of Ephraim and Manasseh, and all the land of Judah, unto the hinder sea, 3 and the South, and the Plain of the valley of Jericho the city of palm-trees, unto Zoar. 4 And Jehovah said unto him, This is the land which I sware unto Abraham, unto Isaac, and unto Jacob, saying, I will give it unto thy seed: I have caused thee to see it with thine eyes, but thou shalt not go over thither. 5 So Moses the servant of Jehovah died there in the land of Moab, according to the word of Jehovah. 6 And he buried him in the valley in the land of Moab over against Beth-

[84] *Op. cit.*, I, 837.   [85] Henry, *op. cit.*, II, 513.
[86] Hanke, *Christ and the Church in the Old Testament*, p. 25.

peor: but no man knoweth of his sepulchre unto this day. 7 And Moses was a hundred and twenty years old when he died: his eye was not dim, nor his natural force abated. 8 And the children of Israel wept for Moses in the plains of Moab thirty days: so the days of weeping in the mourning for Moses were ended.

It can be assumed that Moses concluded his writing ministry with his prophetic blessing upon the twelve tribes of Israel (33:29). Since this chapter deals with the death and burial of Moses, someone else must have written it. Some scholars think that Ezra was the author of this chapter, while others credit it to Joshua. It is quite possible that the thirty-fourth chapter of Deuteronomy was formerly the first chapter of the book of Joshua. The mechanical possibility of this is most reasonable in that the early manuscripts did not have chapter or verse divisions, nor did the text contain points and pauses. Sometimes several books were sewed together in continuous order on a roll, and when the scrolls were organized into books it was quite possible that the beginning of one book might be transferred to the end of another.

A great deal of mystery enshrouds the burial of Moses. Jude suggests that there was a struggle for the body of Moses between Michael the archangel and the devil (Jude 9). The secret of Moses' tomb has never been discovered and probably never will be. It is quite likely that Jehovah buried Moses in a secret place so that the people would not deify their departed leader, as the Buddhists, Confucianists and certain other religionists do theirs. There was danger that they might commit idolatry by paying divine homage to a man. In retrospect, Moses had the qualities that could well have challenged the idolatrous tendencies which the people had expressed on several occasions. It appears that Moses was physically well preserved when he died, having good eyesight and being still virile and strong.

The children of Israel wept (v. 8). It

is understandable why the death of Moses would be a very sad occasion for Israel. Moses had been a true and faithful servant of Jehovah and a lover of his people, and at his death all of these sterling qualities were greatly magnified in the thinking of the people. They had every reason to weep and mourn for their dead hero.

B. JOSHUA TAKES COMMAND (34:9-12)

9 And Joshua the son of Nun was full of the spirit of wisdom; for Moses had laid his hands upon him: and the children of Israel hearkened unto him, and did as Jehovah commanded Moses. 10 And there hath not arisen a prophet since in Israel like unto Moses, whom Jehovah knew face to face, 11 in all the signs and the wonders, which Jehovah sent him to do in the land of Egypt, to Pharaoh, and to all his servants, and to all his land, 12 and in all the mighty hand, and in all the great terror, which Moses wrought in the sight of all Israel.

Joshua had come up through the ranks. He had demonstrated on every occasion his trustworthiness and reliability. He had been one of the two faithful spies and had assisted Moses numerous times. Now the well-earned responsibility of leading his people to possess the land is placed upon his shoulders. Joshua was a man of great strength of moral character, as well as being versed in the wisdom of his day. Moses confirmed Jehovah's choice by laying his hands upon Joshua, and the children of Israel enthusiastically responded by pledging their allegiance to him.

There hath not arisen a prophet (v. 10). It is quite obvious that Moses was Israel's greatest prophet. Words are inadequate to express the magnitude of his greatness. He had given up his option to the throne of Egypt to lead a group of unorganized slaves to the promised land. The writer of Hebrews gives a most fitting tribute to this great man Moses (see Heb. 11:24-29).

Bibliography

Clarke, Adam. *The Holy Bible Containing the Old and New Testament . . . With a Commentary and Critical Notes.* Vol. I. New York: Abingdon-Cokesbury, n.d.

Fitch, Theodore. *Authority and Power Through Jesus' Name.* Council Bluffs: Theodore Fitch Publisher, 1955.

Gray, James Cooper and George M. Adams. *Gray and Adams Bible Commentary.* Grand Rapids: Zondervan, n.d.

Halley, Henry H. *Bible Handbook.* Grand Rapids: Zondervan, 1962.

Hanke, Howard A. *Christ and the Church in the Old Testament.* Grand Rapids: Zondervan, 1957.

————. *From Eden to Eternity.* Grand Rapids: Eerdmans, 1960.

————. *The Tabernacle in the Wilderness.* Grand Rapids: Eerdmans, 1963.

Henry, Matthew. *A Commentary on the Holy Bible.* Vol. II. New York: Funk and Wagnalls, n.d.

Isaacs, Ella Davis. "Feasts and Fasts." *The International Standard Bible Encyclopedia.* Vol. II. Grand Rapids: Eerdmans, 1939.

Kline, Meredith G. "Deuteronomy." *The Wycliff Bible Commentary.* Chicago: Moody, 1962.

Manley, G. T. "Deuteronomy." *The New Bible Commentary.* Grand Rapids: Eerdmans, 1953.

Miller, Madeline S. and J. Lane Miller. "Pentecost." *Harper's Bible Dictionary.* New York: Harper and Row, 1955.

Rolston, Holmes. "Revelation." *Twentieth Century Encyclopedia of Religious Knowledge.* Vol. II. Grand Rapids: Baker, 1955.

Sampey, John Richard. "Sabbath." *International Standard Bible Encyclopedia.* Vol. IV. Grand Rapids: Eerdmans, 1939.

Scott, D. Russell. "Deuteronomy." *Abingdon Bible Commentary.* New York: Abingdon-Cokesbury, 1929.

Tasker, R. V. G. *The Old Testament in the New Testament.* Grand Rapids: Eerdmans, 1954.

Wacker, W. L. "Names." *International Standard Bible Encyclopedia.* Vol. IV. Grand Rapids: Eerdmans, 1939.

Wright, G. Ernest. "Deuteronomy." *The Interpreter's Bible.* Vol. II. Nashville: Abingdon-Cokesbury, 1953.

Volume One

Part II

JOSHUA – ESTHER

CHARLES R. WILSON

Head of Religion Department
Taylor University

Contents

General Introduction to the Historical Books

by

Charles R. Wilson

Through a series of extraordinary historical events, a new community called Israel came into being. The religion of this community differed decisively from that of other ancient peoples. Of the various explanations for this difference, the most adequate one is to be found by analysis of the peculiar intimate connection which existed between the religion and the history of this distinctive people.

Although much has been said about the comparison of the literature of Israel with that of other ancient civilizations of the Near East, it remains that the most obvious difference is the unrelenting concern which the Israelites had for their history. This is the cardinal point made by G. Ernest Wright in his influential monograph, *God Who Acts*.[1]

This undeviating concern for their historical traditions is remarkably evident in the literature of the Israelites, especially the Old Testament. In the course of the formation of the Old Testament, there have appeared two general patterns for the arrangement of the books. The one arrangement is found in the Hebrew Bibles and the other first appeared in the Greek Septuagint, which is dated sometime during the third or second century B.C.

The Hebrew Bibles have the books arranged in three divisions: *Torah* ("the Law"), *Nevi'im* ("the Prophets") and *Ketuvim* ("the Writings"). In the Septuagint the books of the Old Testament were arranged in four divisions instead of three. There were the Pentateuch, the Historical Books, the Poetical and Wisdom Books and the Prophetic Books. This Septuagint arrangement is used in the Bibles of the English-speaking people.

The Historical Books give the history of God's relationship with Israel. The material which is incorporated into these books stresses God's gracious acts of lovingkindness toward Israel. Israel, in turn, was charged with the responsibility of obedience to the law. When Israel failed to obey, God dealt in acts of judgment. Israel was called of God to be His chosen people in fulfilling His redemptive purpose for all people.

Much more than merely factual material is found in the Historical Books. They are essentially meaningful interpretations of the facts of Israel's history. They do more than preserve Israel's past; they provide revelations of the God of Israel through the historical situations.

There are two dominant strands of historical writing in the Historical Books. The first is the prophetic strand, which interprets Israel's history largely by means of what may be called the Deuteronomic principle. The second is the priestly strand, which views that history largely from what may be called the chronicler's point of view. Some acquaintance with these two strands is indispensable in the study of the Historical Books. In order to grasp as adequately as possible the significance of these interpretations of Israel's history, the following discussion concerning them is necessary.

The book of Deuteronomy provides the basis for the Deuteronomic principle. That this book has exercised immense influence upon the Historical Books has often been acknowledged. In Deuteronomy, great stress is placed upon Israel's responsibility in the covenant-relation which that people sustained with Jehovah, the God of Israel. Above everything else, Israel was charged with complete, unquestioning, undivided loyalty to God.

[1] G. E. Wright, *God Who Acts* (London: SCM, 1952), p. 39.

This was the supreme condition upon which Israel was given the promised land of Canaan. A serious earnestness pervades the entire book. There is constant emphasis that what God has given He can take again. The promised land was God's gracious gift to Israel as an inheritance, but it was a conditional gift. If Israel remained loyally obedient to the law, God would faithfully preserve the inheritance for His people; but if the Israelites became disloyal and disobedient, God would disinherit them and take the land from them.

While in the Septuagint arrangement of the Historical Books there is no subdivision, the arrangement found in the Hebrew Bible does have subdivisions. The second division, *Nevi'im* ("the Prophets"), has two subdivisions, the "Former Prophets," which include Joshua, Judges, I and II Samuel and I and II Kings, and the "Latter Prophets." The four books classified as the former prophets in the Hebrew Bible recount Israel's history from the entrance into the promised land under Joshua to the exile from the land by Nebuchadnezzar of Babylon, a period approximating seven hundred years.

Joshua records the remarkable conquest and explains its realization in terms of Israel's loyalty. Judges reveals the unstable period of settlement in the land. By means of a cyclical pattern, the history of the period is portrayed as one of disloyalty followed by judgment, which in turn was followed by repentance and gracious deliverance. The cyclical pattern of the history of the judges has been drawn up on the basis of the Deuteronomic principle. The history of the period has received that meaningful interpretation at the hands of the prophetic tradition.

The account of Israel's history found in Samuel and Kings is a narration of developments during the monarchy. On the whole, the prophetic movement gave an unfavorable account of the monarchy. Kings is concluded with Israel in Babylonian exile. The serious view of the law and the covenant which is found in Deuteronomy is the criterion by which the former prophets judged the period of the monarchy.

The second strand of historical writing found in the Historical Books is the priestly, which views Israel's history from the chronicler's perspective. In this viewpoint, great stress is placed upon the temple cultus and those elements which contribute to it. This emphasis is dominant in I and II Chronicles, Ezra and Nehemiah. These books form a historical unit in describing Israel's history from the reign of King David, in the eleventh century B.C., to the period of reform under Ezra and Nehemiah, in the fifth century B.C., a period of approximately six hundred years.

The priestly strand of historical narration is also described as the chronicler's interpretation, since the book of Chronicles is recognized as the product of the priestly tradition. The chronicler's account of Israel's history places the accent upon loyalty to the temple and its cultus. The chronicler's insistence is that the temple is the place where all Israel is to worship Jehovah, for it is divinely appointed.

Many factors were related to this holy sanctuary and contributed to it. There were the laws which provided for the priests and Levites as well as the entire sacrificial system. There was the Davidic dynasty which provided and maintained the temple and its services. There was the ark of the covenant which was kept in the temple. The very land on which the temple was erected was holy unto the Lord. From the chronicler's point of view, Israel's history was written and interpreted in the light of loyalty to the temple and its religious services. Because of this viewpoint, the chronicler extols the Davidic list of kings as well as the city of Jerusalem. At the same time, he practically ignores the Northern Kingdom and its destiny, except as it impinges on the kingdom of Judah.

The Historical Books were written, not merely to preserve the past, but to instruct, by drawing upon the realities of history. The writers might be compared to preachers and teachers. Whether of the prophetic or priestly tradition and emphasis, these men documented their profound conviction that Israel owed loyalty to God, the Lord of history. The Historical Books, like sermons, were written to persuade Israel that repentance for past sins and renewal of faithfulness to the Lord Jehovah were obligatory.

The biblical writers unequivocally affirmed that God had revealed Himself through Israel's past and was continuing to do so. His revelation was purposeful for the salvation of all people. He chose Israel and laid upon this select people of extraordinary origins a missionary responsibility of world-wide dimensions. Israel was to be a light for all nations. Failure to follow the Lord Jehovah in this great calling resulted in the divine use of other nations as instruments of chastisement upon Israel.

Even though Israel had not fulfilled her mission, despite divine correction, God sent His Son to fulfill His redemptive purpose, and He made the Church the heir of Israel's missionary obligation. Since the Church has been commissioned to proclaim the good news of God's redemptive activity, the history of ancient Israel is meaningful and important to the Church of our century as well as to the Church throughout its history. The living God is still active in the ongoing of history to bestow blessings as well as judgments.

Powerful and persuasive sermonic materials abound in the Historical Books. Although there is the temptation to select isolated texts and make applications which disregard the context, diligent attention to the meaningful history given in the Historical Books will open up new and marvelous vistas of divine truth as it has been given in the history of Israel.

The Book of Joshua
by Charles R. Wilson

Editor's Preface to the Old Testament
Historical Books

The author of the commentaries on the Historical Books of the Old Testament (Joshua through Esther) for the *Wesleyan Bible Commentary* is Professor Charles R. Wilson, Ph.D. Dr. Wilson was born in Iowa and reared in the state of Kansas. He is the eldest son of the late Dr. Oliver G. Wilson, widely and favorably known as a minister and educator in the Wesleyan Methodist Church and editor of the *Wesleyan Methodist,* the official organ of his denomination.

Dr. Wilson attended Miltonvale College, and he holds the A.B. degree from Northwestern State College at Alva, Oklahoma, the B.D. from Asbury Theological Seminary, the M.A. in philosophy from Syracuse University, and the Ph. D. in theology from Vanderbilt University. He also did graduate study at Capital University.

He holds membership in the Society of Biblical Literature and Exegesis and the American Association of University Professors, and is listed in the Directory of American Scholars. He is co-editor with Martin W. Cox of the editorial writings of Dr. Oliver G. Wilson, *Boundless Horizons* (Zondervan, 1960), and he has contributed numerous articles to religious periodicals and scholarly journals.

Dr. Wilson was ordained to the ministry of the Wesleyan Methodist Church of America by the Kansas Conference in 1939. He served churches of his denomination for three years in Kansas, three years in Oklahoma and two years in Ohio. For two years he served a Presbyterian church in Tennessee, and a Methodist church in New York for one year. For two years he was assistant pastor of the Houghton College Church.

Professor Wilson began his teaching career at Miltonvale College in 1948 where he served for eight years, the last three years as the Chairman of the Department of Theology. For six years from 1959 through 1965 he was Professor of Bible and Theology at Houghton College. Dr. Wilson is presently Head of the Department of Religion and Professor of Philosophy and Religion at Taylor University.

From a background of many years of enrichment through graduate study, Christian ministry and teaching of the Old Testament in the college classroom, Dr. Wilson has written the commentaries on the Historical Books of the Old Testament for the *Wesleyan Bible Commentary*. His understanding of the historical background, structure, purpose and message of these books, expressed in a delightful narrative style of writing, makes his commentary both pleasant and profitable reading. It is with pleasure that these expositions are commended to the readers of the *Wesleyan Bible Commentary*.

CHAS. W. CARTER
General Editor
Wesleyan Bible Commentary

Outline

9

Introduction

Joshua is the first book in the group of writings in the Old Testament termed the "Former Prophets."[1] Joshua, Judges, Samuel and Kings constitute this group. These writings trace the history of Israel from the entrance into Canaan in the thirteenth century B.C., to the exile from Canaan in the sixth century B.C.[2] Written from the historical perspective of the prophets of Israel, these books not only provide factual reality concerning Israel's history, but they also reveal profound conceptions of that history and stimulating challenges in the light of the historical events.

I. LITERARY COMPOSITION

Discussions regarding the composition of Joshua may be roughly classified into three categories. In the first category are those discussions classified under the widely-held critical approach. Proponents of these discussions seek to solve the problem of the composition of Joshua in terms of the proposed Pentateuch documents, J, E, D, P. These discussions are so prevalent that one well-known contemporary scholar affirms: "This approach . . . is adopted by almost all introductions and commentaries."[3] However, it must be recognized that some scholars of equal note do not find this view satisfactory.

A second approach, which is one of long standing, includes those discussions which consider Joshua, or a contemporary, as the author. The following statement is representative of this approach: "The title of this book is derived from the pious and valiant leader whose achievements it relates, and who is com-

monly supposed to have been its author."[4] This second approach has emphasized that the book of Joshua was written during the times in which the events it records were occurring. This seems to be naïve principally because there are references in the book which apply to the time of the monarchy, such as the Jebusites inhabiting Jerusalem (15:63) and Canaanites serving the people of the tribe of Ephraim (16:10).

A third approach, which appears to mediate between the first and second, considers the authorship to be attributable to a "Deuteronomist." J. P. U. Lilley gives an excellent statement of this mediating position. He says, "The Deuteronomist may be considered the author, inasmuch as one cannot extract the 'deuteronomic passages' from the narrative and leave complete or intelligible 'source documents.' "[5] While there are indications of contemporary sources, there are some statements in the book of Joshua which are appropriately related to the time of the monarchy (e.g., Josh. 15:63; 16:10). For the "Deuteronomist," as Lilley points out, the primary principle of interpreting the events comprising Israel's conquest of the land of Canaan was that obedience to the law of God was necessary for success. This key principle is explicit in the charge which Jehovah gave to Joshua: "Be strong and of good courage; for thou shalt cause this people to inherit the land which I sware unto their fathers to give them. Only be strong and very courageous, to observe to do according to all the law, . . . that thou mayest have good success whithersoever thou goest" (Josh. 1:6, 7).

[1] See General Introduction to the Historical Books.
[2] Cf. K. A. Kitchen and T. C. Mitchell, "Chronology of the Old Testament," *The New Bible Dictionary*, ed. J. D. Douglas, pp. 212-23.
[3] John Bright, "Joshua: Introduction and Exegesis," *The Interpreter's Bible*, eds. G. A. Buttrick et al., II, 541.
[4] R. Jamieson, A. R. Fausset, D. Brown, *A Commentary, Critical and Explanatory on the Whole Bible*, p. 7.
[5] J. P. U. Lilley, "Joshua, Book of," NBD, p. 662. See also the General Introduction to the Historical Books.

II. HISTORICAL SIGNIFICANCE

There are two reasons for the historical significance of the book of Joshua. The first is that the narratives in the book are grounded in history. Their historical occurrence can be validated. They are not fanciful imaginings and legendary tales, but are recognized as trustworthy historical accounts which refer to events in the life of ancient Israel.

The dominant note being sounded in contemporary critical scholarship is well stated as follows: "When we come to the narratives of the conquest, the external evidence at our disposal is considerable and important. In the light of it, the historicity of such a conquest ought no longer to be denied."[6]

There are two main theories of the historical dating of the conquest. Each claims biblical and archaeological support. The first theory dates the conquest in the fifteenth century B.C. The biblical evidence is derived from I Kings 6:1, in which it is recorded that the Exodus from Egypt occurred 480 years before Solomon began construction of the temple. This construction began in 967 B.C., making the date of the Exodus to be 1447 B.C. and the date of the conquest 40 years later, 1407 B.C. For the strength of the first position see discussion in Exodus in this volume.

The second theory begins with Exodus 1:11, in which it is stated that the Israelites while in Egyptian bondage built treasure cities, Pithon and Raamses. These cities were built during the reign of Rameses II, 1290-1224 B.C., the Pharaoh of Egypt at the time of Israel's oppression. The conquest is dated about 1240 B.C. This second theory appears to be the stronger of the two in the light of available evidence.[7]

The second reason for the historical significance of the book of Joshua is that it relates how God revealed Himself through His mighty acts in history. The book of Joshua stands first in the list of books known in the Hebrew text as the Former Prophets and in the English text as the Historical Books. Since the English text shows the influence of the Greek Septuagint in the matter of arrangement of the books, greater accuracy in understanding the significance of Joshua is obtained if the writing is considered in the light of its being a reflection of the viewpoint of the prophets.

The Former Prophets is a designation of authorship. It refers to writings composed by prophets and seers. Their historiography was unique in that their historical writing was not only to preserve the records of the past but also, and much more important, to bear witness to the wondrous deeds of God and to reveal profound insight and understanding of God's dealings with Israel.

The unanimity in modern biblical studies concerning the centrality of history in the Bible is quite enlightening and impressive. History is understood to be the arena where events occur that have profound significance. "According to the unanimous view of the biblical writers, the meaning of the events resides in a meeting of men with God."[8] This is why F. F. Bruce affirms:

> The divine revelation which the Old Testament records was conveyed in two principal ways — by mighty works and prophetic words. . . . This interplay of mighty work and prophetic word explains why history and prophecy are so intermingled throughout its pages.[9]

The ancient Hebrews were preoccupied with the study of history because of the connection they observed between history and their religion. They portrayed their "religion to a considerable degree by telling its history . . . by the narration and exposition of historical events in general."[10] They discovered that the events which were significant and the values which were important were found not by studying man in nature but in contemplating man, and the ways of God with man, in history.

The book of Joshua is history, but it is history written with a religious concern. It is the kind of historical writing that not only records the happenings but also explains those happenings religiously.

[6] John Bright, A History of Israel, p. 117.
[7] See the article by K. A. Kitchen and T. C. Mitchell, "Chronology of the Old Testament," NBD, pp. 215, 216. Also cf. discussion by Lee Haines in "Exodus," WBC.
[8] C. H. Dodd, The Bible Today, p. 99.   [9] F. F. Bruce, "Bible," NBD, p. 149.
[10] Herbert Butterfield, Christianity and History, p. 3.

The book is an account of God's hand at work in the whole story of the conquest and division of the land of Canaan.

III. MORAL AND SPIRITUAL VALUES

Joshua, as a part of the Former Prophets, is history written for a religious reason. It shows the dealings of God with His people.

Moreover, the narratives in Joshua consistently reflect profound respect for the law. Now the law influenced immeasurably the prophetic conception of history. Obedience to the law and loyalty to God who gave it were demanded by the "Deuteronomist." There was utter abhorrence for the perennial tendency to disobey the law and lapse into idolatry.

The book of Joshua re-enforces this outlook by giving an account of the conquest and division of Canaan. The story of Israel's history as told in Joshua is a demonstration wrought out in the arena of history that Israel gained the promised land because God fought for His obedient chosen people. Historical evidence supports the view that God is faithful to obedient Israel. While this is not the whole story of Israel, it is the lesson which the "Deuteronomist" has drawn from the historical happenings of the conquest.

Another significant value which the book of Joshua affords is derived from a study of the principle of *cherem* employed in the warfare of the conquest. According to this principle, people as well as places in Canaan were "utterly destroyed," "put to the ban," "devoted." This principle has shocked many who read the book of Joshua. It is an offense to their finer sensibilities. However, more is involved than simply offending sensitive emotions. There is an extremely difficult moral problem involved. Did God really command Israel utterly to destroy the inhabitants of Canaan? If so, was this inconsistent with the law given by God which commands "Thou shalt not kill"?

Serious attempts to deal with this problem have followed two general lines of thought. The traditional orthodox thinking has been along the line of moral retribution. This approach presupposes

that if there is to be a moral order functioning in the world there must be admitted the dread possibility of judgment upon those who deviate from that order. It follows from this that the principle of *cherem* is defined as an expression of moral retribution upon immoral individuals.

A corollary of the idea of retribution is the idea of prophylaxis, which involves the taking of such necessary measures as will insulate the uninfected from infection with the impurity of the immoral.

The traditional view has moved in the direction of preserving moral law and order, embodying as it does the characteristic of impersonalness, even at the expense of moral human beings who possess personality.

The preservation of moral order at the expense of the moral individual subjects the realm of the personal to the realm of the impersonal. Yet this is not in keeping with God's covenant with Israel. That covenant was a relationship established between a personal God and His people. Thus, the covenant idea enhances the personal realm and carries with it opportunities and responsibilities which transcend the realm of the impersonal. While there is the impersonal moral order, a moral personality is not inferior to it. Thus, Rahab and those with her in her house in Jericho, and even the Gibeonites who entered into a covenant with Israel, although under the sentence of death, by faith escaped destruction.

Modern critical thinking has been along the line of the primitive nature of Israel's religious conceptions. This approach presupposes that God's revelation to Israel was limited by the inability of Israel to grasp a higher and loftier idea of God. As a result, Israel understood God to be a warring deity who commanded the complete destruction of His enemies.

The modern critical view has tended to downgrade the religion of ancient Israel by holding that its primitive character obstructed an adequate revelation of deity. Yet the great prophets of Israel were not so inclined. The concern of the prophetic message was that Israel return to her former relation with God and the covenant responsibilities which the law of God required. The failure of Israel to heed the prophetic call brought disastrous consequences.

In seeking a more constructive understanding of the principle of *cherem*, N. H. Snaith has well explained its meaning by contrasting it with its opposite, *qodesh*, which is translated "holiness":

> One god's *qodesh* was another god's *cherem*. The devotees of one god therefore destroyed all they could capture of the other god's property . . . .[11]

This was common practice among all Semitic peoples. It was based upon the belief that the gods possessed everything as well as everyone within the area of their domain. This meant that the land of Canaan as well as all the inhabitants of the land were considered the property of the gods of Canaan. Because the land and its people were *qodesh* to the nature gods of the Canaanites, they were *cherem* to Jehovah, the Lord of history, who had entered into covenant with a people, giving them the promise of a land wherein God would make them a blessing to all peoples (Gen. 12:1-3; 15:18; Exod. 6: 2-8; 19:5, 6; Josh. 6:17-21).

It is highly significant that application of *cherem* yielded the right of way to the exercise of faith. Joshua records the outstanding example of the Canaanite, Rahab of Jericho, who by faith embraced the covenant relation with Jehovah and became *qodesh* rather than *cherem* (Josh. 6:17; Heb. 11:31; Jas. 2:24-26). The personal God who entered into covenant with Abraham and who fulfilled His promise to Israel is faithful to those who covenant with him, regardless of whether they are Israelite or Canaanite, Jew or Gentile.

A third value of the book of Joshua lies in the story of the occupation of the promised land. This story reveals the profoundly significant fulfillment of a promise, for the land of Canaan, so strategically located in the geographical center of the ancient world, was to become the arena in which God's redemptive activity in behalf of His people would become a blessing to all peoples.

Canaan was not an isolated hinter-land, hidden from the nations of the earth. Rather, it was a frontier-land which opened toward all nations. The central geographical position of Canaan carried with it a central mission for Israel, Jehovah's covenant people: "In thee shall all the families of the earth be blessed" (Gen. 12:3).

Often the point of Canaan as a "land of promise" has been missed completely. It was not according to God's redemptive work that Israel was to look upon Canaan as a possession because it was promised. Rather, Israel was to look upon Canaan as a commission giving God the occasion to fulfill His promise of redemption to all peoples.[12]

[11] Norman H. Snaith, *The Distinctive Ideas of the Old Testament*, p. 40.
[12] Cf. J. McKee Adams, *Biblical Backgrounds*, pp. 69ff.; Johannes Blauw, *The Missionary Nature of the Church*, pp. 17ff.; H. H. Rowley, *The Biblical Doctrine of Election*, pp. 65-67.

Commentary on Joshua

I. THE WORD OF THE LORD TO JOSHUA AND JOSHUA'S RESPONSE (Josh. 1:1-18)

The keynote of the book of Joshua is the faithfulness of God to fulfill His promises to Israel. When He called Moses to lead this people out of Egypt, He promised them a land for their inheritance (cf. Exod. 3:8, 17; 6:8). Later, when he called Joshua to be Moses' successor, He reaffirmed that promise (vv. 1-2).

A. THE WORD OF THE LORD TO JOSHUA (1:1-9)

While the manner in which the Lord communicated to Joshua may appear to be described ambiguously, the purpose is unmistakably clear, namely, to commission Joshua to the task of leading Israel into the promised land, as well as to command him to obey the law of the Lord.

1. Commissioning to a Task (1:1-5)

1 Now it came to pass after the death of Moses the servant of Jehovah, that Jehovah spake unto Joshua the son of Nun, Moses' minister, saying, 2 Moses my servant is dead; now therefore arise, go over this Jordan, thou, and all this people, unto the land which I do give to them, even to the children of Israel. 3 Every place that the sole of your foot shall tread upon, to you have I given it, as I spake unto Moses. 4 From the wilderness, and this Lebanon, even unto the great river, the river Euphrates, all the land of the Hittites, and unto the great sea toward the going down of the sun, shall be your border. 5 There shall not any man be able to stand before thee all the days of thy life: as I was with Moses, so I will be with thee; I will not fail thee, nor forsake thee.

The manner in which the Lord communicated to Joshua is referred to as "speaking." When it is written, **Jehovah spake unto Joshua** (v. 1), the difficulty is to understand how God spoke. Did God use a voice and speak a language to Joshua? If not, then has anthropomorphic language been employed to indicate that God crossed the boundary between the divine and the human in order to communicate to Joshua? People who maintain a biblical faith in God have known what it is to hear the Lord speaking, even though they realize that no voice, as we use the term, was heard. Doubtless, we have said: "The Lord said to me . . . ." As a result, we have easily communicated to others what the Lord said, but we never find it easy to describe precisely how the Lord said it.

Again and again, the biblical writers express no doubt as to the fact that God has spoken; however, they seem to struggle with a certain ambiguity as they indicate the manner in which God has spoken. An over-all view of the Bible indicates that biblical personalities were able to recognize through such aspects of their being as intuition or conscience that the Lord was speaking. Such personalities were more sensitively attuned to the voice of God than is modern man. While the means by which God spoke to Joshua remain enigmatic, the purpose is remarkably clear, **Jehovah spoke unto Joshua . . . arise, go . . . unto the land which I do give to them, even to the children of Israel** (v. 2).

The word of the Lord to Joshua was, in the first place, a commission to lead the people of Israel into the promised land (v. 2). The ideal boundaries of this land included all the land bounded by the wilderness of Zin on the south, the Euphrates River on the north, the Mediterranean Sea on the west and the land of Gilead on the east (v. 4; cf. Gen. 15:18; Exod. 23:31; Deut. 34:1-2). The land of Gilead was already occupied by Reuben, Gad and half of Manasseh (Num. 32).

As I was with Moses, so I will be with thee (v. 5). These divine words were particularly meaningful to Joshua. He was born in slavery, but since the days of the Exodus he had been an eyewitness to the mighty works of the living God wrought through Moses. He had seen the waters of the Red Sea part as Moses stretched his rod over them. He had seen water gush out of the rock at Rephidim as Moses struck it. He had seen the hostile Amalekites repulsed when Moses held up his hands before the Lord. He had seen Sihon and Og utterly defeated when Moses led Israel against them. In the light of all that God had accomplished through Moses, the divine promise to Joshua was powerfully assuring.

Joshua possessed admirable qualifications for succeeding Moses as Israel's leader. From the human standpoint he would appear as the outstanding candidate. For one thing, he was of one of the leading tribes (Josh. 19:49, 50; I Chron. 7:27). Ephraim, being of the house of Joseph, had vied with Judah for tribal supremacy. To be of the tribe of Ephraim was indicative of an excellent tribal background for leadership.

Furthermore, Joshua had shown himself to be capable of outstanding generalship. In the battle against the Amalekites he achieved a decisive victory (Exod. 17:13).

Also, he had shown undaunted faith in the Lord when he voted with the minority to invade Canaan from Kadesh-barnea (Num. 14:6-9).

Joshua had been in close association with Moses from the time of the Exodus to the arrival at the border of the promised land (Exod. 17:9; 24:13; 33:11; Deut. 31:14).

Admirable as were these qualifications, they were insufficient to qualify Joshua as Moses' successor. What was absolutely essential was the divine presence. Just as Moses' remarkable leadership rested on the reality of that presence so did Joshua's. **There shall not any man be able to stand before thee all the days of thy life** (v. 5). "It was at the call of God that all his potentialities were called forth, and that call brought to the leadership of Israel a man assured of his divine commission."[1]

I will not fail thee, nor forsake thee (v. 5). With Joshua's commission fortified by the promise of the divine presence, there was the encouragement to be courageous. This task involved the Lord. Wherever Joshua must go in order to fulfill his divine commission, the presence of the Lord would go with him.

The task of possessing Canaan is not to be viewed as a desperate foray of fanatical savages motivated by aggression and banditry. This was not a campaign carried on to strengthen a nation or an ideology at the expense of conquered peoples. Rather, this was the Lord marching on in the course of history in order that He might establish His people in the land which He had given them and thus that they might be a blessing to all people.

For some time it has been the pattern of critical historians to discredit the actual occurrence of an invasion of Canaan by Israel under Joshua's leadership. According to this view, if Joshua were a historical personality he was an insignificant tribal hero of Ephraim whose fame increased as Ephraim, his own tribe, gained prominence. In time the legendary story of Joshua heralded him as a hero of Israel.[2]

However, mounting evidence makes such an interpretation of the historicity of Joshua inadequate. Archaeological findings abundantly attest that a great onslaught upon Canaan took place in the thirteenth century. This onslaught destroyed such places as Debir and Lachish in the southern part. Hazor, in the north, was destroyed in the same century.[3] The biblical account of the conquest bears the marks of genuine historical events.

On the basis of archaeological evidence John Bright concludes: "When we come to the narratives of the conquest, the external evidence at our disposal is considerable and important. In the light of it, the historicity of such a conquest ought no longer to be denied."[4]

[1] H. J. Blair, "Joshua," *New Bible Commentary*, p. 223.
[2] Robert H. Pfeiffer, *Introduction to the Old Testament*, pp. 296-301.
[3] Y. Yadin, "Excavations at Hazor," *The Biblical Archaeologist*, XIX (February, 1956), pp. 2-11.
[4] John Bright, *A History of Israel*, p. 117.

2. Commanding Obedience (1:6-9)

6 Be strong and of good courage; for thou shalt cause this people to inherit the land which I sware unto their fathers to give them. 7 Only be strong and very courageous, to observe to do according to all the law, which Moses my servant commanded thee: turn not from it to the right hand or to the left, that thou mayest have good success whithersoever thou goest. 8 This book of the law shall not depart out of thy mouth, but thou shalt meditate thereon day and night, that thou mayest observe to do according to all that is written therein: for then thou shalt make thy way prosperous, and then thou shalt have good success. 9 Have not I commanded thee? Be strong and of good courage; be not affrighted, neither be thou dismayed: for Jehovah thy God is with thee whithersoever thou goest.

Joshua's commission was re-enforced with a specific condition for success: **This book of the law shall not depart out of thy mouth, but thou shalt meditate thereon day and night, that thou mayest observe to do according to all that is written therein: for then thou shalt make thy way prosperous, and then thou shalt have good success.** The condition upon which success was promised was obedience to the commandment of the Lord. Such obedience was to be rewarded with victory and success. **Only be strong and very courageous, to observe to do according to all the law** (v. 7).

The commandment of obedience was a necessary corollary to the commissioning for a task. If the Lord assigned the task, then the Lord was free to assign the means by which the end was to be accomplished. This was the case with Joshua. The command was obedience to the already known will of God. The law had already been given, and Joshua was asked to obey that which he already knew. Strength and courage were necessary for the coming forward movement, but they were also necessary for obedience to the law of God.

The rewards promised for obedience were important and very encouraging. Prosperity and success were to come to the obedient. God had given the command and He likewise gave the promise of reward. In each case, the word of the Lord held the initiative and challenged Joshua to respond in obedient faith.

B. THE RESPONSE OF JOSHUA (1:10-18)

Joshua's response to the Lord was not so much in word as in deed. He began making preparations for crossing Jordan and persuaded the Trans-Jordan tribes to assist the invasion.

1. Preparing to Cross Jordan (1:10, 11)

10 Then Joshua commanded the officers of the people, saying, 11 Pass through the midst of the camp, and command the people, saying, Prepare you victuals; for within three days ye are to pass over this Jordan, to go in to possess the land, which Jehovah your God giveth you to possess it.

Joshua's obedient response to the **word** of the Lord was implicit in his charge to the officers of the people (v. 10). These men had constituted a familiar part of Israel's organization since the time of the departure from Sinai (Deut. 1:15). Here on the east side of the Jordan their responsibility was to execute Joshua's directive and mobilize Israel for this important advance. All Israel was informed that the time to possess the inheritance promised to the patriarchs had come. The Lord God of Israel **giveth you to possess** it (v. 11). Israel was to cross over Jordan within three days and receive the inheritance which the Lord would give (v. 11). Of course, there were battles to be fought, but the Lord gives victory. Divine giving was to come as there was obedience to the divine command. This is frustrating to those who hope that divine giving will relieve them of conscious, obedient effort. Doubt as to God's faithfulness to give may arise when there is lack of obedience. The fault then is not divine failure to give but human failure to obey the divine word.

2. Persuading the Trans-Jordan Tribes (1:12-18)

12 And to the Reubenites, and to the Gadites, and to the half-tribe of Manasseh, spake Joshua, saying, 13 Remember the word which Moses commanded you, saying, Jehovah your God giveth you rest, and will give you this land. 14 Your wives, your little ones, and your cattle, shall abide in the land which Moses gave you beyond the Jordan; but ye shall

pass over before your brethren armed, all the mighty men of valor, and shall help them; 15 until Jehovah have given your brethren rest, as *he hath given you*, and they also have possessed the land which Jehovah your God giveth them: then ye shall return unto the land of your possession, and possess it, which Moses the servant of Jehovah gave you beyond the Jordan toward the sunrising. 16 And they answered Joshua, saying, All that thou hast commanded us we will do, and whithersoever thou sendest us we will go. 17 According as we hearkened unto Moses in all things, so will we hearken unto thee: only Jehovah thy God be with thee, as he was with Moses. 18 Whosoever he be that shall rebel against thy commandment, and shall not hearken unto thy words in all that thou commandest him, he shall be put to death: only be strong and of good courage.

From the time of the conquest of the Trans-Jordan nations, including the Moabites and the Amorites, some of the Israelites were content to accept these conquered areas as their inheritance. The tribes involved were Reuben, Gad and half of Manasseh (Num. 32). Accordingly, both Moses and Joshua reminded these tribes that they were responsible to assist the other tribes when the time came for them to possess their inheritance (cf. Num. 32; Josh. 1). Moses had said that the tribes desiring Trans-Jordan inheritances would be as rebellious to the Lord, if they did not aid their fellow tribes, as were the Israelites at Kadesh-barnea who feared to go forward and possess the land.

Joshua's call for assistance and his reminder of that former occasion at Kadesh-barnea caused the two-and-one-half tribes to respond in complete obedience. **All that thou commandest us we will do, and withersoever thou sendest us we will go** (v. 16).

II. SPIES IN JERICHO (Josh. 2:1-24)

A. THE MISSION OF THE SPIES TO JERICHO (2:1-7)

The spies were to find the best possible routes by which Israel might execute the invasion and determine as far as possible the resources of the inhabitants. They endeavored to remain as anony-

mous as possible, but the king of Jericho heard of their presence and tried in vain to capture them.

1. The Task Involved (2:1a)

1a And Joshua the son of Nun sent out of Shittim two men as spies secretly, saying, Go, view the land, and Jericho.

The usual route for the invasion of Palestine from Egypt was from the south or southwest. Nearly forty years earlier Israel had made an unsuccessful attempt from the south (Num. 14). However, Palestine was well prepared to resist attack from that direction.

The eastern frontier had been regarded by the Canaanites as impregnable because of the Dead Sea and the deep Jordan valley with its rapid and unfordable stream. Consequently, there was considerably less expectancy of an invasion from the east.

However, under Moses' leadership, Israel had arrived on the east side of the Jordan and had conquered the nations of that area. The inhabitants of Canaan became alarmed. All Jericho became fearful.

When Joshua became Moses' successor he was divinely commissioned to cross over the Jordan River and possess the land. This meant that Jericho must be captured, for it was necessary to move past Jericho in order to gain access to the passes that led up from the floor of the Jordan valley, one thousand and more feet above sea level, where such places as Ai and Bethel were located. This first move, like all initial efforts, was important, for, if successful, it would give a decided advantage.

The spies were ordered by Joshua to spy out the land and also Jericho. To this twofold task the spies gave themselves at great personal risk.

2. The Actions of the Spies (2:1b)

1b And they went, and came into the house of a harlot whose name was Rahab, and lay there.

The spies followed a careful plan to avoid suspicion and detection. They followed one of the harlots of Jericho to her house. Although many attempts have been made to represent Rahab as an innkeeper, there remain doubts. The location of the house on the city wall was advantageous for escape. All this was an earnest and precautionary attempt to hide their true mission. The perils were great and death the end if they were discovered. Yet with courageous faith they readily risked their lives for the success of the venture. They are exemplary of so many anonymous and unsung heroes who yet await full recognition for their efforts.

3. The Reactions of the King of Jericho (2:2-7)

2 And it was told the king of Jericho, saying, Behold, there came men in hither to-night of the children of Israel to search out the land. 3 And the king of Jericho sent unto Rahab, saying, Bring forth the men that are come to thee, that are entered into thy house; for they are come to search out the land. 4 And the woman took the two men, and hid them; and she said, Yea, the men came unto me, but I knew not whence they were: 5 and it came to pass about the time of the shutting of the gate, when it was dark, that the men went out; whither the men went I know not: pursue after them quickly; for ye will overtake them. 6 But she had brought them up to the roof, and hid them with the stalks of flax, which she had laid in order upon the roof. 7 And the men pursued after them the way to the Jordan unto the fords: and as soon as they that pursued after them were gone out, they shut the gate.

The efforts of the spies to remain undetected were in vain. Even that very night the king of Jericho was informed of spies in the city. He knew of their being at Rahab's house.

The king's demand that Rahab bring forth the spies was answered by her denial of the knowledge of their whereabouts. The king respected the privacy of the woman and did not require that his messenger be admitted. It was a custom of the ancients to observe the privacy of women.

The reply of Rahab involved falsehood and traitorous conduct toward her king and city. How can this be explained when she is cited as an example of faith (Heb. 11:31)? A possible explanation may be given by realizing that she was fully convinced that it was futile to fight against the God of Israel. Even if the spies were put to death, it would make no difference in the ultimate result. Jericho was doomed. To reveal the spies would not save a single life, but would only anger the Israelites. At the same time, to conceal the spies would harm no one. Rahab's choice appeared to be: reveal the spies and sacrifice all hope of life; conceal the spies and have hope that somehow she and her family would be spared.

B. THE CONVERSATION OF THE SPIES WITH RAHAB (2:8-21)

Rahab's conversation with the spies while betraying fear also bespoke faith. Her urgent plea for mercy was rewarded by the spies' covenant to spare her and those with her.

1. The Plea of Rahab for Mercy (2:8-14)

8 And before they were laid down, she came up unto them upon the roof; 9 and she said unto the men, I know that Jehovah hath given you the land, and that the fear of you is fallen upon us, and that all the inhabitants of the land melt away before you. 10 For we have heard how Jehovah dried up the water of the Red Sea before you, when ye came out of Egypt; and what ye did unto the two kings of the Amorites, that were beyond the Jordan, unto Sihon and to Og, whom ye utterly destroyed. 11 And as soon as we had heard it, our hearts did melt, neither did there remain any more spirit in any man, because of you: for Jehovah your God, he is God in heaven above, and on earth beneath. 12 Now therefore, I pray you, swear unto me by Jehovah, since I have dealt kindly with you, that ye also will deal kindly with my father's house, and give me a true token; 13 and that ye will save alive my father, and my mother, and my brethren, and my sisters, and all that they have, and will deliver our lives from death. 14 And the men said unto her, Our life for yours, if ye utter not this our business; and it shall be, when Jehovah giveth us the land, that we will deal kindly and truly with thee.

Jehovah your God, he is God in heaven above, and on earth beneath (v. 11). Here is Rahab's remarkable confession of faith. Here is the reason for her actions in behalf of the spies. Her only hope of escape from being utterly destroyed lay in kindness to them. It was futile to try to withstand the God of Israel. Kindness towards His people was her only hope. This was the crucible out of which her desperate faith emerged. She had faith that God would show kindness: **I pray you . . . since I have dealt kindly with you, that ye also will deal kindly with my father's house** (v. 12). Into her dark and tragic life had come hope that the God of Israel was a God of kindness and compassion to the alien and foreigner.

2. The Covenant with Rahab (2:15-21)

15 Then she let them down by a cord through the window; for her house was upon the side of the wall, and she dwelt upon the wall. 16 And she said unto them, Get you to the mountain, lest the pursuers light upon you; and hide yourselves there three days, until the pursuers be returned: and afterward may ye go your way. 17 And the men said unto her, We will be guiltless of this thine oath which thou hast made us to swear. 18 Behold, when we come into the land, thou shalt bind this line of scarlet thread in the window which thou didst let us down by: and thou shalt gather unto thee into the house thy father, and thy mother, and thy brethren, and all thy father's household. 19 And it shall be, that whosoever shall go out of the doors of thy house into the street, his blood shall be upon his head, and we shall be guiltless: and whosoever shall be with thee in the house, his blood shall be on our head, if any hand be upon him. 20 But if thou utter this our business, then we shall be guiltless of thine oath which thou hast made us to swear. 21 And she said, According unto your words, so be it. And she sent them away, and they departed: and she bound the scarlet line in the window.

The spies covenanted with Rahab to deal kindly with her and her family. In return, Rahab was to fulfill three requirements: (1) The scarlet thread given to her by the spies was to be hung from the window. (2) All of the household of Rahab's father were to be in Rahab's house. (3) Rahab was to conceal the identity of the spies and their mission.

Rahab agreed to these requirements and the spies departed. They were let down over the wall by a cord from Rahab's house. Rahab showed her faith in the promise of the spies as **she bound the scarlet line in the window** (v. 21).

C. THE RETURN OF THE SPIES TO JOSHUA (2:22-24)

Heeding Rahab's suggestions, the spies returned to Joshua and reported all that had happened.

1. The Spies Follow Rahab's Directions (2:22)

22 And they went, and came unto the mountain, and abode there three days, until the pursuers were returned: and the pursuers sought them throughout all the way, but found them not.

Following the advice given by Rahab the spies were able to make their escape and to return undetected to the camp of Israel. Pursuers from Jericho hunted for them in vain.

2. The Spies Report to Joshua (2:23, 24)

23 Then the two men returned, and descended from the mountain, and passed over, and came to Joshua the son of Nun; and they told him all that had befallen them. 24 And they said unto Joshua, Truly Jehovah hath delivered into our hands all the land; and moreover all the inhabitants of the land do melt away before us.

The spies reported to Joshua all that had happened. The events had convinced them that the inhabitants of the land were in panic and fear. This indicated to them that the promise of the Lord was being fulfilled (cf. 1:5, 6).

III. CROSSING THE JORDAN (Josh. 3:1—4:24)

A. THE CROSSING ORDERED (3:1-13)

Divinely given instructions were relayed to all Israel by Joshua. Meanwhile, the Lord promised to do marvels in behalf of Israel as they crossed over to their promised land.

1. The Directions Given by Joshua (3:1-6, 9-13)

1 And Joshua rose up early in the morning; and they removed from Shittim, and came to the Jordan, he and all the children of Israel; and they lodged there before they passed over. 2 And it came to pass after three days, that the officers

went through the midst of the camp; 3 and they commanded the people, saying, When ye see the ark of the covenant of Jehovah your God, and the priests the Levites bearing it, then ye shall remove from your place, and go after it. 4 Yet there shall be a space between you and it, about two thousand cubits by measure: come not near unto it, that ye may know the way by which ye must go; for ye have not passed this way heretofore. 5 And Joshua said unto the people, Sanctify yourselves; for to-morrow Jehovah will do wonders among you. 6 And Joshua spake unto the priests, saying, Take up the ark of the covenant, and pass over before the people. And they took up the ark of the covenant, and went before the people.

9 And Joshua said unto the children of Israel, Come hither, and hear the words of Jehovah your God. 10 And Joshua said, Hereby ye shall know that the living God is among you, and that he will without fail drive out from before you the Canaanite, and the Hittite, and the Hivite, and the Perizzite, and the Girgashite, and the Amorite, and the Jebusite. 11 Behold, the ark of the covenant of the Lord of all the earth passeth over before you into the Jordan. 12 Now therefore take you twelve men out of the tribes of Israel, for every tribe a man. 13 And it shall come to pass, when the soles of the feet of the priests that bear the ark of Jehovah, the Lord of all the earth, shall rest in the waters of the Jordan, that the waters of the Jordan shall be cut off, even the waters that come down from above; and they shall stand in one heap.

The washings and abstentions required to sanctify the people were preparations for being in the presence of the holy God engaged in wondrous workings. **The living God is among you, he will without fail drive out from before you the Canaanite** (v. 10).

The priests, appointed guardians of the ark of the covenant, were instructed to move the ark from its place in the tabernacle in preparation for the crossing. The ark was the symbol of the presence of the Lord. The priests were responsible to see that the divine symbol was in its place.

2. The Promise Made by the Lord (3:7, 8)

7 And Jehovah said unto Joshua, This day will I begin to magnify thee in the sight of all Israel, that they may know that, as I was with Moses, so I will be with thee. 8 And thou shalt command the priests that bear the ark of the covenant, saying, When ye are come to the brink of the waters of the Jordan, ye shall stand still in the Jordan.

This divine pledge to Joshua reaffirmed the earlier promise (1:5) with the additional statement that God's mighty working was to be for all Israel to see. **This day will I begin to magnify thee in the sight of all Israel** (v. 7).

B. THE CROSSING ACCOMPLISHED (3:14-17)

The phenomenal miracle of Israel's crossing the Jordan was accomplished by the Lord while Israel obeyed His instructions.

1. The Ark of the Covenant Positioned (3:14, 15)

14 And it came to pass, when the people removed from their tents, to pass over the Jordan, the priests that bare the ark of the covenant being before the people; 15 and when they that bare the ark were come unto the Jordan, and the feet of the priests that bare the ark were dipped in the brink of the water (for the Jordan overfloweth all its banks all the time of harvest),

As the priests bore the ark of the covenant forward to the Jordan River, overflowing because hot weather was melting the snow of the Lebanon mountains, all Israel moved forward expectantly. It was the ark of the covenant which was to make a way for Israel, for it indicated the presence of Jehovah was leading His people.

2. The Waters of Jericho Blocked (3:16, 17)

16 that the waters which came down from above stood, and rose up in one heap, a great way off, at Adam, the city that is beside Zarethan; and those that went down toward the sea of the Arabah, even the Salt Sea, were wholly cut off: and the people passed over right against Jericho. 17 And the priests that bare the ark of the covenant of Jehovah stood firm on dry ground in the midst of the Jordan; and all Israel passed over on dry ground, until all the nation were passed clean over the Jordan.

While Israel acknowledged that God had provided passage across Jordan, apparently there was knowledge of a cave-in of the river banks some distance up the river (v. 16). It was the harvest season. This arrived in the Jordan valley during April when spring rains and melting snow from the Lebanon mountains were causing the river to crest at flood stage.[5]

Normal fording of the river was impossible. However, as the priests bearing the ark of the covenant stepped into the swirling waters of the raging torrent the river began to recede until it was possible for the Israelites to walk across. The river was checked at a spot called Adam, identified as Tell ed-Damiyeh, near the junction of the Jabbok and the Jordan fifteen to twenty miles from Jericho (v. 16).[6] Garstang cites an earthquake shock in 1927 which completely blocked the Jordan for over twenty-one hours.[7] It is possible that sections of the high clay banks of the river collapsed into the river at Adam coincident with Israel's crossing. Whatever may have been the "natural" cause for the damming of the river, the "religious" explanation acknowledges divine intervention.

C. THE CROSSING MEMORIALIZED (4:1-24)

Israel brought stones from the river bottom for the purpose of erecting a memorial to the miraculous power of the Lord.

1. By Stones from the River Bottom (4:1-18)

1 And it came to pass, when all the nation were clean passed over the Jordan, that Jehovah spake unto Joshua, saying, 2 Take you twelve men out of the people, out of every tribe a man, 3 and command ye them, saying, Take you hence out of the midst of the Jordan, out of the place where the priests' feet stood firm, twelve stones, and carry them over with you, and lay them down in the lodging-place, where ye shall lodge this night. 4 Then Joshua called the twelve men, whom he had prepared of the children of Israel, out of every tribe a man: 5 and Joshua said unto them, Pass over before the ark of Jehovah your God into the midst of the Jordan, and take you

up every man of you a stone upon his shoulder, according unto the number of the tribes of the children of Israel; 6 that this may be a sign among you, that, when your children ask in time to come, saying, What mean ye by these stones? 7 then ye shall say unto them, Because the waters of the Jordan were cut off before the ark of the covenant of Jehovah; when it passed over the Jordan, the waters of the Jordan were cut off: and these stones shall be for a memorial unto the children of Israel for ever.

8 And the children of Israel did so as Joshua commanded, and took up twelve stones out of the midst of the Jordan, as Jehovah spake unto Joshua, according to the number of the tribes of the children of Israel; and they carried them over with them unto the place where they lodged, and laid them down there. 9 And Joshua set up twelve stones in the midst of the Jordan, in the place where the feet of the priests that bare the ark of the covenant stood: and they are there unto this day. 10 For the priests that bare the ark stood in the midst of the Jordan, until everything was finished that Jehovah commanded Joshua to speak unto the people, according to all that Moses commanded Joshua: and the people hasted and passed over. 11 And it came to pass, when all the people were clean passed over, that the ark of Jehovah passed over, and the priests, in the presence of the people. 12 And the children of Reuben, and the children of Gad, and the half-tribe of Manasseh, passed over armed before the children of Israel, as Moses spake unto them: 13 about forty thousand ready armed for war passed over before Jehovah unto battle, to the plains of Jericho. 14 On that day Jehovah magnified Joshua in the sight of all Israel; and they feared him, as they feared Moses, all the days of his life.

15 And Jehovah spake unto Joshua, saying, 16 Command the priests that bear the ark of the testimony, that they come up out of the Jordan. 17 Joshua therefore commanded the priests, saying, Come ye up out of the Jordan. 18 And it came to pass, when the priests that bare the ark of the covenant of Jehovah were come up out of the midst of the Jordan, and the soles of the priests' feet were lifted up unto the dry ground, that the waters of the Jordan returned unto their place, and went over all its banks, as aforetime.

---

[5] Cf. John Bright, "Joshua," *The Interpreter's Bible*, p. 567.   [6] *Ibid.*, p. 568.
[7] Cf. John Garstang, *Foundations of Bible History: Joshua, Judges*, pp. 136-37.

The stones taken from the bed of the Jordan River signalized a remarkable phenomenon. At the season of the year when the Jordan was at flood-tide, a large host of men, women, and children had only to obey the divine word and walk forward into the river. The water fell away before the presence of the ark of the covenant.

2. At Gilgal Where Israel Encamped (4:19-24)

19 And the people came up out of the Jordan on the tenth day of the first month, and encamped in Gilgal, on the east border of Jericho. 20 And those twelve stones, which they took out of the Jordan, did Joshua set up in Gilgal. 21 And he spake unto the children of Israel, saying, When your children shall ask their fathers in time to come, saying, What mean these stones? 22 then ye shall let your children know, saying, Israel came over this Jordan on dry land. 23 For Jehovah your God dried up the waters of the Jordan from before you, until ye were passed over, as Jehovah your God did to the Red Sea, which he dried up from before us, until we were passed over; 24 that all the peoples of the earth may know the hand of Jehovah, that it is mighty; that ye may fear Jehovah your God for ever.

Gilgal marked the first encampment for Israel in the promised land proper. Here the stones were erected to serve as a perennial symbol of the method by which Israel entered Canaan. Children were to be instructed concerning the significance of the memorial. They were to be told the incredible but true story of how the stones were gathered from the bottom of the river. Not only they but all people were to know **the hand of Jehovah, that it is mighty** (v. 24).

IV. EVENTS AT GILGAL (Josh. 5:1-15)

A. THE EVENTS IMPLEMENTING ISRAEL'S OBEDIENCE TO GOD'S LAW (5:1-12)

At Gilgal Israel was required to express her obedience to the law by restoring the observance of circumcision and the Passover.

1. Circumcision Accomplished (5:1-9)

1 And it came to pass, when all the kings of the Amorites, that were beyond the Jordan westward, and all the kings of the Canaanites, that were by the sea, heard how that Jehovah had dried up the waters of the Jordan from before the children of Israel, until we were passed over, that their heart melted, neither was there spirit in them any more, because of the children of Israel.

2 At that time Jehovah said unto Joshua, Make thee knives of flint, and circumcise again the children of Israel the second time. 3 And Joshua made him knives of flint, and circumcised the children of Israel at the hill of the foreskins. 4 And this is the cause why Joshua did circumcise: all the people that came forth out of Egypt, that were males, even all the men of war, died in the wilderness by the way, after they came forth out of Egypt. 5 For all the people that came out were circumcised; but all the people that were born in the wilderness by the way as they came forth out of Egypt, they had not circumcised. 6 For the children of Israel walked forty years in the wilderness, till all the nation, even the men of war that came forth out of Egypt, were consumed, because they hearkened not unto the voice of Jehovah: unto whom Jehovah sware that he would not let them see the land which Jehovah sware unto their fathers that he would give us, a land flowing with milk and honey. 7 And their children, whom he raised up in their stead, them did Joshua circumcise: for they were uncircumcised, because they had not circumcised them by the way. 8 And it came to pass, when they had done circumcising all the nation, that they abode in their places in the camp, till they were whole. 9 And Jehovah said unto Joshua, This day have I rolled away the reproach of Egypt from off you. Wherefore the name of that place was called Gilgal, unto this day.

Circumcision was a rite of initiation into the covenant community of Israel. It had been neglected since the disaster at Kadesh-barnea because the covenant people had been under divine chastisement for forty years. Upon the completion of circumcision under Joshua's leadership, the word of the Lord came to Joshua, **This day have I rolled away the reproach of Egypt from off you** (v. 9).

Circumcision is identified in the Old Testament with the covenant which the Lord made with Abraham (Gen. 17:10-14). "Circumcision signifies the gracious movement of God to men, and only derivatively . . . the consecration of man to God. This truth underlies Jos. 5:2ff."[8]

The restoration of this rite signified not merely an outward act of commitment to the covenant but more profoundly a spiritual acknowledgment of obedience in the covenant relation (Gen. 17:10).

To speak of the circumcising of the heart is to indicate obedience to the covenant-making God (cf. Deut. 30:6 with Rom. 2:29). It is possible to profess obedience through a display of outward evidences, but true obedience known to God is not guilty of hypocrisy. While we look on the outward appearance, God looks upon the heart. As Israel heard the divine announcement of the removal of the reproach of bondage because the covenant sign of circumcision had been restored, so we may hear similar good news from the Lord as we respond in obedience.

2. The Passover Observed (5:10-12)

10 And the children of Israel encamped in Gilgal; and they kept the passover on the fourteenth day of the month at even in the plains of Jericho. 11 And they did eat of the produce of the land on the morrow after the passover, unleavened cakes and parched grain, in the selfsame day. 12 And the manna ceased on the morrow, after they had eaten of the produce of the land; neither had the children of Israel manna any more; but they did eat of the fruit of the land of Canaan that year.

There is no evidence that the Israelites had observed the Passover since the days when they were at Mount Sinai (Num. 9:4). Now, as part of their reconsecration, the people of God observed this important meal that commemorated the Exodus.

The observance of the Passover memorialized to all the Israelites that their exit from bondage to become a special people of God was by means of power surpassing their own. God in His graciousness and faithfulness had brought them out of Egypt.

Christians are continually reminded of Jesus Christ as our Passover. As we partake of the Lord's Supper, we acknowledge that it memorializes our deliverance from sin through the power of one who is victor over sin and death.

B. AN EVENT AFFIRMING GOD'S PRESENCE (5:13-15)

As Joshua prepared to enter upon the conquest there came to him the prince of the Lord, before whom Joshua bowed in loyalty.

1. The Appearance of the Prince of the Lord (5:13, 14)

13 And it came to pass, when Joshua was by Jericho, that he lifted up his eyes and looked, and, behold, there stood a man over against him with his sword drawn in his hand: and Joshua went unto him, and said unto him, Art thou for us, or for our adversaries? 14 And he said, Nay; but *as* prince of the host of Jehovah am I now come. And Joshua fell on his face to the earth, and did worship, and said unto him, What saith my lord unto his servant?

The heavenly visitor is not identified as the Lord, but the distinction between the angel of the Lord and the Lord Himself is not sharply drawn in the Old Testament. This prince attests the presence of the Lord and generates the expectation of divine activity in the coming conquest. His words affirm that the army of Israel is only part of the army supporting Joshua. The hosts of the Lord are poised for the event.

In the course of history it is necessary to admit that national preparedness and arms races do not ultimately decide the outcome of strategic crises. Again and again, history reveals that crises were not resolved simply on the basis of material power. The biblical writers continually affirm that there is a divine dimension in the course of events. To ignore this is to neglect to reckon with all the factors that are involved in the historical processes. In our day, as then, nations are not only implicated with other nations but also with the Lord of history.

2. Joshua's Position as Servant to the Prince (5:15)

15 And the prince of Jehovah's hosts said unto Joshua, Put off thy shoe from off thy foot; for the place whereon thou standest is holy. And Joshua did so.

When Joshua heard the stranger identify himself as the prince of the host of

---

[8] J. A. Motyer, "Circumcision," NBD, p. 223.

Jehovah, he recognized the presence of the Lord and replied, "What saith my Lord unto his servant?" (v. 14). When the prince informed Joshua of the sanctity of the occasion Joshua removed his shoes to symbolize his reverence for and submission to the Lord.

V. CENTRAL CAMPAIGN (Josh. 6:1–8:35)

A. VICTORY AT JERICHO (6:1-27)

The initial effort in the conquest was the taking of Jericho. Israel's obedience made possible the miraculous victory. Only Rahab and those with her were spared.

1. Divine Instructions to Joshua (6:1-7)

1 Now Jericho was straitly shut up because of the children of Israel: none went out, and none came in. 2 And Jehovah said unto Joshua, See, I have given into thy hand Jericho, and the king thereof, and the mighty men of valor. 3 And ye shall compass the city, all the men of war, going about the city once. Thus shalt thou do six days. 4 And seven priests shall bear seven trumpets of rams' horns before the ark: and the seventh day ye shall compass the city seven times, and the priests shall blow the trumpets. 5 And it shall be, that, when they make a long blast with the ram's horn, and when ye hear the sound of the trumpet, all the people shall shout with a great shout; and the wall of the city shall fall down flat, and the people shall go up every man straight before him. 6 And Joshua the son of Nun called the priests, and said unto them, Take up the ark of the covenant, and let seven priests bear seven trumpets of rams' horns before the ark of Jehovah. 7 And they said unto the people, Pass on, and compass the city, and let the armed men pass on before the ark of Jehovah.

Explicit instructions were given concerning the procession around Jericho. Seven priests with trumpets were to be followed by the ark. These were in the middle of the procession, for Joshua placed the armed warriors in the vanguard and the rearguard. A great shout from the army was to climax the seventh time around the city on the seventh day. The divine promise was that this would

be the signal that would bring about the collapse of the walls. Then each one of the Israelites was to advance upon the city. This meant a forward charge directly into the dust and rubble of debris where defenceless dead were lying. Extraordinary loyalty on the part of each individual was demanded. However, the Lord had spoken to Joshua, **See, I have given into thy hand Jericho** (v. 2).

2. Israel's Obedience to the Lord (6:8-19)

8 And it was so, that, when Joshua had spoken unto the people, the seven priests bearing the seven trumpets of rams' horns before Jehovah passed on, and blew the trumpets: and the ark of the covenant of Jehovah followed them. 9 And the armed men went before the priests that blew the trumpets, and the rearward went after the ark, *the priests* blowing the trumpets as they went. 10 And Joshua commanded the people, saying, Ye shall not shout, nor let your voice be heard, neither shall any word proceed out of your mouth, until the day I bid you shout; then shall ye shout. 11 So he caused the ark of Jehovah to compass the city, going about it once: and they came into the camp, and lodged in the camp.

12 And Joshua rose early in the morning, and the priests took up the ark of Jehovah. 13 And the seven priests bearing the seven trumpets of rams' horns before the ark of Jehovah went on continually, and blew the trumpets: and the armed men went before them; and the rearward came after the ark of Jehovah, *the priests* blowing the trumpets as they went. 14 And the second day they compassed the city once, and returned into the camp: so they did six days.

15 And it came to pass on the seventh day, that they rose early at the dawning of the day, and compassed the city after the same manner seven times: only on that day they compassed the city seven times. 16 And it came to pass at the seventh time, when the priests blew the trumpets, Joshua said unto the people, Shout; for Jehovah hath given you the city. 17 And the city shall be devoted, even it and all that is therein, to Jehovah: only Rahab the harlot shall live, she and all that are with her in the house, because she hid the messengers that we sent. 18 But as for you, only keep yourselves from the devoted thing, lest when ye have devoted it, ye take of the devoted thing; so would ye make the camp

of Israel accursed, and trouble it. 19 But all the silver, and gold, and vessels of brass and iron, are holy unto Jehovah: they shall come into the treasury of Jehovah.

This was indeed an incredible kind of assault on a walled city so strongly fortified: fighting men in battle array, but no battle. The only activity involved was the thirteen circuits of the city and the occasional trumpet blasts. However, the warriors demonstrated their loyalty and military discipline as well as religious obedience. They maintained their places in the procession in which the ark of the covenant was carried.

Upon the signal from Joshua there sounded a long, piercing blast on the trumpets and a triumphant, thunderous shout from the army of Israel. The walls of Jericho collapsed amid mighty rumblings and billowing clouds of dust.

The signal from Joshua included an important announcement that deserves a special comment. When Joshua said, **Shout; for Jehovah hath given you the city,** he added, **And the city shall be devoted . . . to Jehovah. . . . But as for you, only keep yourselves from the devoted thing** (vv. 16-18). To be **devoted** denoted an irrevocable removal from any common usage and a total commitment unto the Lord. This removal from common usage meant either irrevocable condemnation to destruction or irrevocable consecration to deity. In the case of Jericho as in the case of places on the east side of the Jordan (Deut. 2:34), persons and objects consecrated to false gods were corrupt as well as corrupting. They were fit for nothing but destruction or *cherem* lest those who spared them be corrupted. To devote or ban persons or things from common use was not the right of any individual but was in the nature of an official condemnation pronounced by God through His servants (Lev. 27:28, 29).

This ban was because of the divinely instituted conviction that whatever corrupted the religion of the people of Israel and led to compromising relationships with idolatrous peoples was to be committed to the divine act of destruction. Compromise on the part of Israel with foreign gods violated the law of

covenant Israel and was a dangerous peril. As a surgeon removes at any cost the complete diseased cancerous growth that endangers the life of the patient, so complete separation from the idolatry of Canaan was necessary if the Israelites were to survive as the people of God. They had no right to those things that would imperil their distinctive, worshipful obedience to the Lord of all the earth (3:13).[9]

> The religion of Yahweh had to be preserved and kept pure at all costs if the nation was to survive. Consequently no treatment was too drastic in order to safeguard it. There is a powerful lesson here. . . . Anything that hinders the onward march of God, and . . . his purpose, must be eliminated.[10]

The words of Jesus re-enforce this standpoint: "Whoso shall cause one of these little ones that believe on me to stumble . . . a great millstone should be hanged about his neck. . . . If thy hand or thy foot causeth thee to stumble, cut it off . . ." (Matt. 18:6, 8).

3. Jericho Destroyed but Rahab Spared (6:20—7:1)

20 So the people shouted, and *the priests* blew the trumpets: and it came to pass, when the people heard the sound of the trumpet, that the people shouted with a great shout, and the wall fell down flat, so that the people went up into the city, every man straight before him, and they took the city. 21 And they utterly destroyed all that was in the city, both man and woman, both young and old, and ox, and sheep, and ass, with the edge of the sword. 22 And Joshua said unto the two men that had spied out the land, Go into the harlot's house, and bring out thence the woman, and all that she hath, as ye sware unto her. 23 And the young men the spies went in, and brought out Rahab, and her father, and her mother, and her brethren, and all that she had; all her kindred also they brought out; and they set them without the camp of Israel. 24 And they burnt the city with fire, and all that was therein; only the silver, and the gold, and the vessels of brass and of iron, they put into the treasury of the house of Jehovah. 25 But Rahab the harlot, and her father's household, and all that she had, did Joshua

---

[9] See Introduction.   [10] J. R. Sizoo, "Joshua," IB, p. 581.

save alive; and she dwelt in the midst of Israel unto this day, because she hid the messengers, whom Joshua sent to spy out Jericho. 26 And Joshua charged them with an oath at that time, saying, Cursed be the man before Jehovah, that riseth up and buildeth this city Jericho: with the loss of the first-born shall he lay the foundation thereof, and with the loss of his youngest son shall he set up the gates of it. 27 So Jehovah was with Joshua; and his fame was in all the land. 1 But the children of Israel committed a trespass in the devoted thing; for Achan, the son of Carmi, the son of Zabdi, the son of Zerah, of the tribe of Judah, took of the devoted thing: and the anger of Jehovah was kindled against the children of Israel.

At the sound of the trumpets and the shout of the warriors, the walls of Jericho fell. Without hesitation the warriors proved loyal and bold. Straight ahead they went into the dust and smoke and rubble, **and they took the city** (v. 20). To be sure, the divine power had crushed the walls, but it was with heroic faith that the army of Israel surged forward on the dangerous mission of conquest.

In obedience to God, rather than in enslavement to powerful, ugly dispositions which warfare inflames, the armed men of Israel **utterly destroyed** ("devoted," margin) **all that was in the city** (v. 21).

The only exceptions were Rahab and her father's household. Joshua honored the pledge which the spies of Israel had made with Rahab. Apparently, Rahab's house, identified by the scarlet cord, was undamaged in the holocaust at Jericho. Rahab and her relatives seeking refuge in her house on the wall were safe and were taken from the house to the vicinity of the camp of Israel.

Surely one of the keys in explaining this exception was the faith of Rahab. This is indicated by New Testament references to her (Heb. 11:31; Jas. 2:25). Her own testimony to the spies expressed her faith: "I know that the Lord hath given you the land" (Josh. 2:9). She believed so sincerely and so completely in the God of Israel that she risked being caught as a traitor to her own city rather than surrender the spies of Israel to her king's messengers.

B. ATTACK AGAINST AI (7:2—8:29)

When Joshua set out to capture Ai he was full of confidence inspired by the conquest of Jericho, but he was greatly pained and shocked by defeat at Ai.

1. Unsuccessful First Assault (7:2-9)

2 And Joshua sent men from Jericho to Ai, which is beside Beth-aven, on the east side of Beth-el, and spake unto them, saying, Go up and spy out the land. And the men went up and spied out Ai. 3 And they returned to Joshua, and said unto him, Let not all the people go up; but let about two or three thousand men go up and smite Ai; make not all the people to toil thither; for they are but few. 4 So there went up thither of the people about three thousand men; and they fled before the men of Ai. 5 And the men of Ai smote of them about thirty and six men; and they chased them *from* before the gate even unto Shebarim, and smote them at the descent: and the hearts of the people melted, and became as water.

6 And Joshua rent his clothes, and fell to the earth upon his face before the ark of Jehovah until the evening, he and the elders of Israel; and they put dust upon their heads. 7 And Joshua said, Alas, O Lord Jehovah, wherefore hast thou at all brought this people over the Jordan, to deliver us into the hand of the Amorites, to cause us to perish? would that we had been content and dwelt beyond the Jordan! 8 Oh, Lord, what shall I say, after that Israel hath turned their backs before their enemies! 9 For the Canaanites and all the inhabitants of the land will hear of it, and will compass us round, and cut off our name from the earth: and what wilt thou do for thy great name?

The conquest of Jericho had been a pledge of future success. However, the gracious, powerful presence of the Lord leading on to victory was conditioned upon the continuing obedience of each Israelite.

Joshua's advance against Ai was up the steep incline from the Jordan valley to the western plateau. Soldiers from Ai attacked, and Israel fell back demoralized and defeated.

The defeat created panic among the Israelites, and Joshua's anguished cry revealed his own wavering faith: **Oh, Lord, what shall I say, after that Israel hath turned their backs before their ene-**

mies! . . . and what wilt thou do for thy great name? (vv. 8, 9).

2. Achan Discovered (7:10-26)

10 And Jehovah said unto Joshua, Get thee up; wherefore art thou thus fallen upon thy face? 11 Israel hath sinned; yea, they have even transgressed my covenant which I commanded them: yea, they have even taken of the devoted thing, and have also stolen, and dissembled also; and they have even put it among their own stuff. 12 Therefore the children of Israel cannot stand before their enemies; they turn their backs before their enemies, because they are become accursed: I will not be with you any more, except ye destroy the devoted thing from among you. 13 Up, sanctify the people, and say, Sanctify yourselves against to-morrow: for thus saith Jehovah, the God of Israel, There is a devoted thing in the midst of thee, O Israel; thou canst not stand before thine enemies, until ye take away the devoted thing from among you. 14 In the morning therefore ye shall be brought near by your tribes: and it shall be, that the tribe which Jehovah taketh shall come near by families; and the family which Jehovah shall take shall come near by households; and the households which Jehovah shall take shall come near man by man. 15 And it shall be, that he that is taken with the devoted thing shall be burnt with fire, he and all that he hath; because he hath transgressed the covenant of Jehovah, and because he hath wrought folly in Israel.

16 So Joshua rose up early in the morning, and brought Israel near by their tribes; and the tribe of Judah was taken: 17 and he brought near the family of Judah; and he took the family of the Zerahites: and he brought near the family of the Zerahites man by man; and Zabdi was taken: 18 and he brought near his household man by man; and Achan, the son of Carmi, the son of Zabdi, the son of Zerah, of the tribe of Judah, was taken. 19 And Joshua said unto Achan, My son, give, I pray thee, glory to Jehovah, the God of Israel, and make confession unto him; and tell me now what thou hast done; hide it not from me. 20 And Achan answered Joshua, and said, Of a truth I have sinned against Jehovah, the God of Israel, and thus and thus have I done: 21 when I saw among the spoil a goodly Babylonish mantle, and two hundred shekels of silver, and a wedge of gold of fifty shekels weight, then I coveted them, and took them; and,

behold, they are hid in the earth in the midst of my tent, and the silver under it. 22 So Joshua sent messengers, and they ran unto the tent; and, behold, it was hid in his tent, and the silver under it. 23 And they took them from the midst of the tent, and brought them unto Joshua, and unto all the children of Israel; and they laid them down before Jehovah. 24 And Joshua, and all Israel with him, took Achan the son of Zerah, and the silver, and the mantle, and the wedge of gold, and his sons, and his daughters, and his oxen, and his asses, and his sheep, and his tent, and all that he had: and they brought them up unto the valley of Achor. 25 And Joshua said, Why hast thou troubled us? Jehovah shall trouble thee this day. And all Israel stoned him with stones; and they burned them with fire, and stoned them with stones. 26 And they raised over him a great heap of stones, unto this day; and Jehovah turned from the fierceness of his anger. Wherefore the name of that place was called, The valley of Achor, unto this day.

Achan had violated the command of the Lord to devote everything in Jericho to the Lord (v. 11). Nothing was to be for common use.

Joshua was instructed by the Lord of the violation and was told to cast lots to discover the guilty party. The lot pointed to Achan, of the tribe of Judah.

Achan's confession revealed the reason for his violation of the ban: **I coveted them, and took them** (v. 21). Achan, in a passion of covetousness, had allowed covetousness rather than obedience to control him. He came first and God second. This selfish priority had expelled the first pair from Eden, and it brought frightening judgment upon Achan. He, by taking of the thing that was banned, brought himself under the ban. He died by the stones hurled by his fellow Israelites. He who **troubled** Israel was left in the **valley of Achor,** which means "troubling" (vv. 25, 26).

3. Successful Second Assault (8:1-29)

1 And Jehovah said unto Joshua, Fear not, neither be thou dismayed: take all the people of war with thee, and arise, go up to Ai; see, I have given into thy hand the king of Ai, and his people, and his city, and his land; 2 and thou shalt do to Ai and her king as thou didst unto Jericho and her king: only the spoil thereof,

and the cattle thereof, shall ye take for a prey unto yourselves: set thee an ambush for the city behind it.

3 So Joshua arose, and all the people of war, to go up to Ai: and Joshua chose out thirty thousand men, the mighty men of valor, and sent them forth by night. 4 And he commanded them, saying, Behold, ye shall lie in ambush against the city, behind the city; go not very far from the city, but be ye all ready: 5 and I, and all the people that are with me, will approach unto the city. And it shall come to pass, when they come out against us, as at the first, that we will flee before them; 6 and they will come out after us, till we have drawn them away from the city; for they will say, They flee before us, as at the first: so we will flee before them; 7 and ye shall rise up from the ambush, and take possession of the city: for Jehovah your God will deliver it into your hand. 8 And it shall be, when ye have seized upon the city, that ye shall set the city on fire; according to the word of Jehovah shall ye do: see, I have commanded you. 9 And Joshua sent them forth; and they went to the ambushment, and abode between Beth-el and Ai, on the west side of Ai: but Joshua lodged that night among the people.

10 And Joshua arose up early in the morning, and mustered the people, and went up, he and the elders of Israel, before the people to Ai. 11 And all the people, *even* the *men of* war that were with him, went up, and drew nigh, and came before the city, and encamped on the north side of Ai: now there was a valley between him and Ai. 12 And he took about five thousand men, and set them in ambush between Beth-el and Ai, on the west side of the city. 13 So they set the people, even all the host that was on the north of the city, and their liers-in-wait that were on the west of the city; and Joshua went that night into the midst of the valley. 14 And it came to pass, when the king of Ai saw it, that they hasted and rose up early, and the men of the city went out against Israel to battle, he and all his people, at the time appointed, before the Arabah; but he knew not that there was an ambush against him behind the city. 15 And Joshua and all Israel made as if they were beaten before them, and fled by the way of the wilderness. 16 And all the people that were in the city were called together to pursue after them: and they pursued after Joshua, and were drawn away from the city. 17 And there was not a man left in Ai or Beth-el, that went

not out after Israel: and they left the city open, and pursued after Israel.

18 And Jehovah said unto Joshua, Stretch out the javelin that is in thy hand. And Joshua stretched out the javelin that was in his hand toward the city. 19 And the ambush arose quickly out of their place, and they ran as soon as he had stretched out his hand, and entered into the city, and took it; and they hasted and set the city on fire. 20 And when the men of Ai looked behind them, they saw, and, behold, the smoke of the city ascended up to heaven, and they had no power to flee this way or that way: and the people that fled to the wilderness turned back upon the pursuers. 21 And when Joshua and all Israel saw that the ambush had taken the city, and that the smoke of the city ascended, then they turned again, and slew the men of Ai. 22 And the others came forth out of the city against them; so they were in the midst of Israel, some on this side, and some on that side: and they smote them, so that they let none of them remain or escape. 23 And the king of Ai they took alive, and brought him to Joshua.

24 And it came to pass, when Israel had made an end of slaying all the inhabitants of Ai in the field, in the wilderness wherein they pursued them, and they were all fallen by the edge of the sword, until they were consumed, that all Israel returned unto Ai, and smote it with the edge of the sword. 25 And all that fell that day, both of men and women, were twelve thousand, even all the men of Ai. 26 For Joshua drew not back his hand, wherewith he stretched out the javelin, until he had utterly destroyed all the inhabitants of Ai. 27 Only the cattle and the spoil of that city Israel took for a prey unto themselves, according unto the word of Jehovah which he commanded Joshua. 28 So Joshua burnt Ai, and made it a heap for ever, even a desolation, unto this day. 29 And the king of Ai he hanged on a tree until the eventide: and at the going down of the sun Joshua commanded, and they took his body down from the tree, and cast it at the entrance of the gate of the city, and raised thereon a great heap of stones, unto this day.

Joshua's battle plan for the second assault upon Ai was carefully laid. While the main force created a diversion the special striking force lying in ambush was to attack. Coordination of the movements of the two bodies of soldiers was extremely important.

Joshua's second attempt on Ai was undertaken not only after severe judgment upon the transgressor, Achan, but also after marshalling all the fighting men and planning a complex battle maneuver involving diversion tactics and ambush. The plan was successful, for the king of Ai pursued the Israelites and left his city defenceless before the striking force that had been in ambush. As a result, the city was destroyed by fire and left desolate.

C. COVENANT RENEWAL AT MOUNT EBAL (8:30-35)

With important military advances into central Canaan achieved, Joshua called for a renewal of the covenant at Shechem.

1. Sacrifices Offered (8:30, 31)

30 Then Joshua built an altar unto Jehovah, the God of Israel, in mount Ebal, 31 as Moses the servant of Jehovah commanded the children of Israel, as it is written in the book of the law of Moses, an altar of unhewn stones, upon which no man had lifted up any iron: and they offered thereon burnt-offerings unto Jehovah, and sacrificed peace-offerings.

The instructions given in Deuteronomy 11:29, 30 were carried out. An altar was erected upon which sacrifices were offered to God for what He had done. The deep wedge which Joshua had driven into the heart of Canaan by taking Jericho and Ai was climaxed with religious observances. The altar was a visible testimony to the faith by which Israel had triumphed over the Canaanites.

2. The Law Read (8:32-35)

32 And he wrote there upon the stones a copy of the law of Moses, which he wrote, in the presence of the children of Israel. 33 And all Israel, and their elders and officers, and their judges, stood on this side of the ark and on that side before the priests the Levites, that bare the ark of the covenant of Jehovah, as well the sojourner as the homeborn; half of them in front of mount Gerizim, and half of them in front of mount Ebal; as Moses the servant of Jehovah had commanded at the first, that they should bless the people of Israel. 34 And afterward he read all the words of the law, the blessing and the curse, according to all that is written in the book of the law. 35 There was not a word of all that Moses commanded, which Joshua read not before all the assembly of Israel, and the women, and the little ones, and the sojourners that were among them.

Joshua read a copy of the law of Moses in the presence of all the people on Mount Ebal and Mount Gerizim. It is profoundly significant that the people of Israel pledged themselves to keep God's law. As soon as they had gained a solid foothold in the new land, rather than forget former vows and neglect reverent obedience, they renewed their covenant to keep the law of God.

VI. SOUTHERN CAMPAIGN (Josh. 9:1—10:43)

A. STRATEGY OF THE GIBEONITES (9:1-27)

As consternation increased throughout the land, the Gibeonites resorted to a ruse for purposes of self-preservation.

1. Deceitfulness Toward Israel (9:1-15)

1 And it came to pass, when all the kings that were beyond the Jordan, in the hill-country, and in the lowland, and on all the shore of the great sea in front of Lebanon, the Hittite, and the Amorite, the Canaanite, the Perizzite, the Hivite, and the Jebusite, heard thereof; 2 that they gathered themselves together, to fight with Joshua and with Israel, with one accord.
3 But when the inhabitants of Gibeon heard what Joshua had done unto Jericho and to Ai, 4 they also did work wilily, and went and made as if they had been ambassadors, and took old sacks upon their asses, and wine-skins, old and rent and bound up, 5 and old and patched shoes upon their feet, and old garments upon them; and all the bread of their provision was dry and was become mouldy. 6 And they went to Joshua unto the camp at Gilgal, and said unto him, and to the men of Israel, We are come from a far country: now therefore make ye a covenant with us. 7 And the men of Israel said unto the Hivites, Peradventure ye dwell among us; and how shall we make a covenant with you? 8 And they said unto Joshua, We are thy servants. And Joshua said unto them, Who are ye? and from whence come ye? 9 And they said unto him, From a very far country thy servants are come be-

cause of the name of Jehovah thy God: for we have heard the fame of him, and all that he did in Egypt, 10 and all that he did to the two kings of the Amorites, that were beyond the Jordan, to Sihon king of Heshbon, and to Og king of Bashan, who was at Ashtaroth. 11 And our elders and all the inhabitants of our country spake to us, saying, Take provision in your hand for the journey, and go to meet them, and say unto them, We are your servants: and now make ye a covenant with us. 12 This our bread we took hot for our provision out of our houses on the day we came forth to go unto you; but now, behold, it is dry, and is become mouldy: 13 and these wine-skins, which we filled, were new; and, behold, they are rent: and these our garments and our shoes are become old by reason of the very long journey. 14 And the men took of their provision, and asked not counsel at the mouth of Jehovah. 15 And Joshua made peace with them, and made a covenant with them, to let them live: and the princes of the congregation sware unto them.

The success of Israel against Jericho and Ai created contrasting reactions among the inhabitants of the land. On the one hand, there were attempts at organized resistance. Kings gathered their armies together to fight Israel (vv. 1, 2) On the other hand, there was deceitful defection to the Israelites by the Gibeonite cities (vv. 3-5).

The Gibeonites, also called Hivites, sent representatives to Israel to **make a covenant** (v. 6). Their motivation was self-interest. Their reaction to the news of the fate of Jericho and Ai was self-preservation. Their realistic outlook is embodied in the old colloquialism, "If you can't lick 'em, join 'em!"

Their attempt to join Israel was fraudulent. They appeared at the camp of Israel as weary travelers who had come a great distance. Their clothes were ragged and dirty. Their food was spoiled. Their own words were, **We are come from a far country** (v. 6).

Now Israel had been specifically instructed regarding covenants. There were to be no covenants, or leagues, with the inhabitants of Canaan (Exod. 23:32; 34:12; Deut. 7:2). Moreover, the elders of Israel pondered the possibility that these strangers might be neighbors, **Peradventure ye dwell among us** (v. 7).

Nevertheless, Joshua and the elders of Israel proceeded to enter upon an important agreement, namely, a covenant with the Gibeonites. It is strange that this covenant was made apparently without seeking divine counsel (v. 14). It was an important decision to make, and the circumstances were shrouded in mystery. It was time to seek the Lord for guidance, but Israel seemed unaware of trickery and peril. The elders of Israel were lax and careless. They were blind to the fact that they were the victims of an elaborate fraud.

It is a fact in human existence that any advance which individuals as well as communities achieve encounters resistance. Those who are advancing to their promised land encounter not only brutal frontal resistance but also evasive, delaying maneuvers that capitalize on laxity, flatter pride, and mock our stupid self-confidence. Israel shortly discovered her failure to inquire of the Lord and her folly in making a covenant with the Gibeonites.

2. Disciplined by Israel (9:16-27)

16 And it came to pass at the end of three days after they had made a covenant with them, that they heard that they were their neighbors, and that they dwelt among them. 17 And the children of Israel journeyed, and came unto their cities on the third day. Now their cities were Gibeon, and Chephirah, and Beeroth, and Kiriath-jearim. 18 And the children of Israel smote them not, because the princes of the congregation had sworn unto them by Jehovah, the God of Israel. And all the congregation murmured against the princes. 19 But all the princes said unto all the congregation, We have sworn unto them by Jehovah, the God of Israel: now therefore we may not touch them. 20 This we will do to them, and let them live; lest wrath be upon us, because of the oath which we sware unto them. 21 And the princes said unto them, Let them live: so they became hewers of wood and drawers of water unto all the congregation, as the princes had spoken unto them.

22 And Joshua called for them, and he spake unto them, saying, Wherefore have ye beguiled us, saying, We are very far from you; when ye dwell among us? 23 Now therefore ye are cursed, and there shall never fail to be of you bondmen, both hewers of wood and drawers of water for the house of my God. 24 And

they answered Joshua, and said, Because it was certainly told thy servants, how that Jehovah thy God commanded his servant Moses to give you all the land, and to destroy all the inhabitants of the land from before you; therefore we were sore afraid for our lives because of you, and have done this thing. 25 And now, behold, we are in thy hand: as it seemeth good and right unto thee to do unto us, do. 26 And so did he unto them, and delivered them out of the hand of the children of Israel, that they slew them not. 27 And Joshua made them that day hewers of wood and drawers of water for the congregation, and for the altar of Jehovah, unto this day, in the place which he should choose.

Israel discovered she had been tricked when, three days later, she came to the cities of the Gibeonites. Plainly, Israel was under obligation to devote even the Gibeonites to destruction, but at the same time the princes of Israel had voluntarily entered into a covenant with the Gibeonites. What course of action was Israel to follow when faced with this dilemma?

The elders insisted that it was imperative to keep the covenant, even at the risk of violating the principle of *cherem,* which required devoting the Gibeonites to destruction. However, the covenant terms were qualified to the extent that the Gibeonites were reduced to the status of slaves. **Ye are cursed,** said Joshua, possibly intending to suggest a qualified *cherem* (v. 23).

Without resistance, the Gibeonites accepted their new status in the covenant relation. **We are in thy hand: as it seemeth good and right unto thee to do unto us, do** (v. 25). Joshua sentenced them to be **hewers of wood and drawers of water** (v. 23).

The capitulation of the Gibeonites provided Joshua with an important military advantage. A direct thrust southward by the warriors of Israel was now possible without danger of being cut off from the base of operations at Gilgal.

While it must be acknowledged that Israel's covenant with the Hivites of Gibeon transgressed the law of the Lord, the mercy of the Lord was extended toward this people. Just as earlier when the individual person, Rahab, together with those with her, had by faith escaped the destruction which befell the inhabitants of Jericho, so later when the people of Gibeon, although engaged in deceit, submitted to the covenant terms, they expressed a faith which God countenanced. As evidence of this, we recall that it was for the Gibeonites as well as for Israel that the Lord wrought the miracle of the battle of Beth-horon (10:7-15). Just as Rahab had contributed to the overthrow of Jericho by aiding the spies, so the Hivites contributed to the conquest of southern Canaan by defecting to Israel.

In the light of such historical events there is revealed the redeeming grace of the Lord amid circumstances that might seem to thwart it. We are so accustomed to the viewpoint that we must be worthy to receive God's free grace that we limit the revelation of grace to those occasions when we consider that we are worthy. Rahab and the Hivites had little to commend them to the care and love of God, yet they received it in boundless measure through faith.

B. CONQUEST OF THE SOUTHERN COALITION (10:1-43)

Because of Gibeon's defection to Israel she was attacked by a southern coalition of kings. Israel responded to Gibeon's danger and routed the attackers.

1. Gibeon Attacked by the Southern Coalition (10:1-5)

1 Now it came to pass, when Adoni-zedek king of Jerusalem heard how Joshua had taken Ai, and had utterly destroyed it (as he had done to Jericho and her king, so he had done to Ai and her king), and how the inhabitants of Gibeon had made peace with Israel, and were among them; 2 that they feared greatly, because Gibeon was a great city, as one of the royal cities, and because it was greater than Ai, and all the men thereof were mighty. 3 Wherefore Adoni-zedek king of Jerusalem sent unto Hoham king of Hebron, and unto Piram king of Jarmuth, and unto Japhia king of Lachish, and unto Debir king of Eglon, saying, 4 Come up unto me, and help me, and let us smite Gibeon; for it hath made peace with Joshua and with the children of Israel. 5 Therefore the five kings of the Amorites, the king of Jerusalem, the king of Hebron, the king of Jarmuth, the king of Lachish, the king of Eglon, gathered themselves together,

and went up, they and all their hosts, and encamped against Gibeon, and made war against it.

Gibeon's defection to Israel created two reactions among the kings of southern Canaan. In the first place, there was a decided increase of fear. Gibeon, with its formidable defences and mighty men, no longer provided protection against Israel. In the second place, there was determined action. The king of Jerusalem, Adoni-zedek, formed a coalition against the Gibeonites to punish them for their treachery.

2. Israel Allied with Gibeon (10:6-27)

6 And the men of Gibeon sent unto Joshua to the camp to Gilgal, saying, Slack not thy hand from thy servants; come up to us quickly, and save us, and help us: for all the kings of the Amorites that dwell in the hill-country are gathered together against us. 7 So Joshua went up from Gilgal, he, and all the people of war with him, and all the mighty men of valor. 8 And Jehovah said unto Joshua, Fear them not: for I have delivered them into thy hands; there shall not a man of them stand before thee. 9 Joshua therefore came upon them suddenly; for he went up from Gilgal all the night. 10 And Jehovah discomfited them before Israel, and he slew them with a great slaughter at Gibeon, and chased them by the way of the ascent of Beth-horon, and smote them to Azekah, and unto Makkedah. 11 And it came to pass, as they fled from before Israel, while they were at the descent of Beth-horon, that Jehovah cast down great stones from heaven upon them unto Azekah, and they died: they were more who died with the hailstones than they whom the children of Israel slew with the sword. 12 Then spake Joshua to Jehovah in the day when Jehovah delivered up the Amorites before the children of Israel; and he said in the sight of Israel,

Sun, stand thou still upon Gibeon;
And thou, Moon, in the valley of
Aijalon.
13   And the sun stood still, and the
moon stayed,
Until the nation had avenged themselves of their enemies.
Is not this written in the book of Jashar? And the sun stayed in the midst of heaven, and hasted not to go down about a whole day. 14 And there was no day like that before it or after it, that

Jehovah hearkened unto the voice of a man: for Jehovah fought for Israel. 15 And Joshua returned, and all Israel with him, unto the camp to Gilgal. 16 And these five kings fled, and hid themselves in the cave at Makkedah. 17 And it was told Joshua, saying, The five kings are found, hidden in the cave at Makkedah. 18 And Joshua said, Roll great stones unto the mouth of the cave, and set men by it to keep them: 19 but stay not ye; pursue after your enemies, and smite the hindmost of them; suffer them not to enter into their cities: for Jehovah your God hath delivered them into your hand. 20 And it came to pass, when Joshua and the children of Israel had made an end of slaying them with a very great slaughter, till they were consumed, and the remnant which remained of them had entered into the fortified cities, 21 that all the people returned to the camp to Joshua at Makkedah in peace: none moved his tongue against any of the children of Israel. 22 Then said Joshua, Open the mouth of the cave, and bring forth those five kings unto me out of the cave. 23 And they did so, and brought forth the five kings unto him out of the cave, the king of Jerusalem, the king of Hebron, the king of Jarmuth, the king of Lachish, the king of Eglon. 24 And it came to pass, when they brought forth those kings unto Joshua, that Joshua called for all the men of Israel, and said unto the chiefs of the men of war that went with him, Come near, put your feet upon the necks of these kings. And they came near, and put their feet upon the necks of them. 25 And Joshua said unto them, Fear not, nor be dismayed; be strong and of good courage: for thus shall Jehovah do to all your enemies against whom ye fight. 26 And afterward Joshua smote them, and put them to death, and hanged them on five trees; and they were hanging upon the trees until the evening. 27 And it came to pass at the time of the going down of the sun, that Joshua commanded, and they took them down off the trees, and cast them into the cave wherein they had hidden themselves, and laid great stones on the mouth of the cave, unto this very day.

The Gibeonites were unprepared to war against the armies of the five southern kings of Jerusalem, Hebron, Jarmuth, Lachish and Eglon. Their appeal to Joshua was answered by Joshua's all night march from Gilgal (v. 9). The distance was about twenty miles from the base camp in the Jordan valley. The strenuous march was up a steep mountain pass from an elevation of about a thousand feet below sea level to more than twenty-five hundred feet above sea level on the western plateau.

It was probably early morning when Joshua and his men launched their surprise attack on the armies besieging Gibeon. **Jehovah discomfited** the besiegers by the aggressive rush of the Israelites (vv. 9, 10). It was through the speed of Joshua's men as they rushed forward that the Lord worked to create panic among the enemy. Moreover, **he slew them and chased them,** and **Jehovah cast down great stones from heaven** (vv. 10, 11). Here was the living Lord leading His warriors in the battle. Joshua and his men were engaged in conflict on the Lord's side. Their faithfulness enabled their Lord to overwhelm the adversary.

The poem from the book of Jashar, a collection of songs praising the heroes of Israel, voices Joshua's prayer calling the sun and the moon to his aid.

What Joshua needed more than anything else, from the human standpoint and according to the context, was opportunity for a surprise attack. There are various explanations as to what actually happened. It may be that Joshua prayed for and received a prolonging of the darkness before the dawning light of the new day. His prayer was answered by the heavy cloud cover of the hailstorm which effectively aided Joshua's surprise attack and which later loosed a barrage of hailstones upon the fleeing enemy.[11]

The victory at Gibeon and Beth-horon initiated the full thrust of the southern campaign. The five southern kings were trapped in a cave at Makkedah and slain.

3. Areas Occupied (10:28-43)

28 And Joshua took Makkedah on that day, and smote it with the edge of the sword, and the king thereof: he utterly destroyed them and all the souls that were therein; he left none remaining; and he did to the king of Makkedah as he had done unto the king of Jericho. 29 And Joshua passed from Makkedah, and all Israel with him, unto Libnah, and fought against Libnah: 30 and Je-

hovah delivered it also, and the king thereof, into the hand of Israel; and he smote it with the edge of the sword, and all the souls that were therein; he left none remaining in it; and he did unto the king thereof as he had done unto the king of Jericho. 31 And Joshua passed from Libnah, and all Israel with him, unto Lachish, and encamped against it, and fought against it: 32 and Jehovah delivered Lachish into the hand of Israel; and he took it on the second day, and smote it with the edge of the sword, and all the souls that were therein, according to all that he had done to Libnah.

33 Then Horam king of Gezer came up to help Lachish; and Joshua smote him and his people, until he had left him none remaining.

34 And Joshua passed from Lachish, and all Israel with him, unto Eglon; and they encamped against it, and fought against it; 35 and they took it on that day, and smote it with the edge of the sword; and all the souls that were therein he utterly destroyed that day, according to all that he had done to Eglon.

36 And Joshua went up from Eglon, and all Israel with him, unto Hebron; and they fought against it: 37 and they took it, and smote it with the edge of the sword, and the king thereof, and all the cities thereof, and all the souls that were therein; he left none remaining, according to all that he had done to Eglon; but he utterly destroyed it, and all the souls that were therein.

38 And Joshua returned, and all Israel with him, to Debir, and fought against it: 39 and he took it, and the king thereof, and all the cities thereof; and they smote them with the edge of the sword, and utterly destroyed all the souls that were therein; he left none remaining: as he had done to Hebron, so he did to Debir, and to the king thereof; as he had done also to Libnah, and to the king thereof.

40 So Joshua smote all the land, the hill-country, and the South, and the lowland, and the slopes, and all their kings: he left none remaining, but he utterly destroyed all that breathed, as Jehovah, the God of Israel, commanded. 41 And Joshua smote them from Kadesh-barnea even unto Gaza, and all the country of Goshen, even unto Gibeon. 42 And all these kings and their land did Joshua take at one time, because Jehovah, the God of Israel, fought for Israel. 43 And Joshua returned, and all Israel with him, unto the camp to Gilgal.

---

11 Blair, *op. cit.*, p. 231.

This report of Joshua's southern conquest lists first the cities of the low-lying hills of the Shephelah. These cities were in strategic locations guarding the approaches to the southern highlands. In each case the town with its people was laid under *cherem*.

Joshua turned from the foothills to the highlands. First he took Hebron, about ninety miles south of Jerusalem. The *cherem* is likewise applied to the cities of the highlands. Archaeological investigation has confirmed the overthrow of some of the southern cities by violence and fire.[12]

VII. NORTHERN CAMPAIGN
(Josh. 11:1-15)

A. JABIN'S FORMATION OF THE NORTHERN COALITION (11:1-5)

1 And it came to pass, when Jabin king of Hazor heard thereof, that he sent to Jobab king of Madon, and to the king of Shimron, and to the king of Achshaph, 2 and to the kings that were on the north, in the hill-country, and in the Arabah south of Chinneroth, and in the lowland, and in the heights of Dor on the west, 3 to the Canaanite on the east and on the west, and the Amorite, and the Hittite, and the Perizzite, and the Jebusite in the hill-country, and the Hivite under Hermon in the land of Mizpah. 4 And they went out, they and all their hosts with them, much people, even as the sand that is upon the seashore in multitude, with horses and chariots very many. 5 And all these kings met together; and they came and encamped together at the waters of Merom, to fight with Israel.

In Canaan's northland Jabin, king of Hazor, rallied numerous kings to join in the fight to halt the victorious Israelites, just as in Canaan's southland Adoni-zedek, king of Jerusalem, had persuaded kings to unite forces against the threatening advance of Joshua and his men.

On the wide plains near the waters of Merom, Jabin marshalled a vast army of men and chariots. While most maps identify Merom with Lake Huleh, the most likely location of this stream is ten miles west of the Jordan River where large springs form a stream flowing southward by the village of Meiron into the Sea of Galilee.[13] Jabin's army was **even as the sand that is upon the sea-shore in multitude, with horses and chariots very many** (v. 4).

News of the capture of Jericho and the rout of the combined armies of the southern coalition doubtless compelled the northern kings to realize the extreme crisis which they faced. Under the mounting pressure of this crisis the kings readied an unusually large defending army with weapons and fortified this powerful army with horses and chariots.

B. JOSHUA'S VICTORY OVER THE NORTHERN COALITION (11:6-15)

6 And Jehovah said unto Joshua, Be not afraid because of them; for to-morrow at this time will I deliver them up all slain before Israel: thou shalt hock their horses, and burn their chariots with fire. 7 So Joshua came, and all the people of war with him, against them by the waters of Merom suddenly, and fell upon them. 8 And Jehovah delivered them into the hand of Israel, and they smote them, and chased them unto great Sidon, and unto Misrephoth-maim, and unto the valley of Mizpeh eastward; and they smote them, until they left them none remaining. 9 And Joshua did unto them as Jehovah bade him: he hocked their horses, and burnt their chariots with fire.

10 And Joshua turned back at that time, and took Hazor, and smote the king thereof with the sword:· for Hazor beforetime was the head of all those kingdoms. 11 And they smote all the souls that were therein with the edge of the sword, utterly destroying them; there was none left that breathed: and he burnt Hazor with fire. 12 And all the cities of those kings, and all the kings of them, did Joshua take, and he smote them with the edge of the sword, and utterly destroyed them; as Moses the servant of Jehovah commanded. 13 But as for the cities that stood on their mounds, Israel burned none of them, save Hazor only; that did Joshua burn. 14 And all the spoil of these cities, and the cattle, the children of Israel took for a prey unto themselves; but every man they smote with the edge of the sword, until they had destroyed them, neither left they

[12] W. F. Albright, *Archaeology of Palestine and the Bible*, p. 108.
[13] J. P. U. Lilley, "Merom (Waters of)," NBD, p. 810. Cf. *The Westminster Historical Atlas*, eds. G. E. Wright and F. V. Filson.

any that breathed. 15 As Jehovah commanded Moses his servant, so did Moses command Joshua: and so did Joshua; he left nothing undone of all that Jehovah commanded Moses.

Apparently Jabin was not intending to launch a military offensive against Joshua, who was engaged in fighting in the hill country, since the horses and chariots were useful only on the plains. However, he endeavored to be prepared to battle against Joshua in the most advantageous way possible. Moreover, he had a fast and powerful striking force against the foot soldiers of Israel. He had chariots that moved with amazing swiftness. The charioteers carried long lances that struck down foot soldiers who had comparatively short weapons such as swords.

However, Joshua used the same tactics of surprise that he had used at Gibeon. He came **suddenly, and fell upon them** (v. 7). **And Jehovah delivered them into the hand of Israel** (v. 8).

The battle filled the Canaanites with panic. Israel witnessed the futility of trusting in horses and chariots. Trust in the Lord and obedience to His will were factors that made Israel's conquest irresistible.

The *cherem* was again put into effect, but there were limitations. Except for Hazor, the cities were not destroyed. The inhabitants of the cities were destroyed, but the livestock and other possessions were taken by Israel.

The keynote of obedience is sounded in the recounting of Joshua's successes in the north. **As Jehovah commanded . . . so did Joshua; he left nothing undone . . .** (v. 15). As far as the biblical account is concerned, the remarkable conquest under Joshua's leadership is to be explained as the result of faith and obedience. These two essentials are intertwined throughout the life of Joshua. They identify the kind of leadership which enabled Israel to enter the promised land.

The period of the conquest was not a Christian era, but it offers illumination to the Christian who is committed to a life of obedient faith and faithful obedience. For one thing, a Christian is involved in a covenant relationship with God, and such a relationship has the essential characteristic of faithfulness. Just as Joshua was charged to give faithful obedience to the law, so also a Christian is commissioned to give faithful obedience to Jesus Christ, the "mediator of a better covenant" (Heb. 8:6). For, just as the Lord was faithful to Joshua, so He is faithful to Christians through His covenant made in Jesus Christ.

Furthermore, a Christian is called upon to enter his "land of promise." This is a call not so much to enter upon a possession as to enter upon a commission. A Christian is called not so much to acquire an inheritance as to share the gospel of Jesus Christ. The call to enter the "land of promise" is a call to interpret the spirit of the conquest in terms of spiritual compassion rather than in terms of carnal aggression.

VIII. CONCLUSION OF THE CONQUEST (Josh. 11:16—12:24)

A. TERRITORIES CONQUERED (11:16-23)

16 So Joshua took all that land, the hill-country, and all the South, and all the land of Goshen, and the lowland, and the Arabah, and the hill-country of Israel, and the lowland of the same; 17 from mount Halak, that goeth up to Seir, even unto Baal-gad in the valley of Lebanon under mount Hermon; and all their kings he took, and smote them, and put them to death. 18 Joshua made war a long .time with all those kings. 19 There was not a city that made peace with the children of Israel, save the Hivites the inhabitants of Gibeon: they took all in battle. 20 For it was of Jehovah to harden their hearts, to come against Israel in battle, that he might utterly destroy them, that they might have no favor, but that he might destroy them, as Jehovah commanded Moses.

21 And Joshua came at that time, and cut off the Anakim from the hill-country, from Hebron, from Debir, from Anab, and from all the hill-country of Judah, and from all the hill-country of Israel: Joshua utterly destroyed them with their cities. 22 There was none of the Anakim left in the land of the children of Israel: only in Gaza, in Gath, and in Ashdod, did some remain. 23 So Joshua took the whole land, according to all that Jehovah spake unto Moses; and Joshua gave it for an inheritance unto Israel according to their divisions by their tribes. And the land had rest from war.

The two decisive battles of the conquest were fought at Beth-horon and

Merom. In both Joshua had utilized to a remarkable degree the element of surprise. In both the Lord had smitten and chased the resisting armies (cf. 10:9 with 11:8). This resulted in shattering any further efforts toward large coalitions of organized resistance. Many pockets of resistance remained, and continued efforts were put forth by Israel to make possible settlement in the land.

According to the summary of the territories conquered, the whole of Canaan was included, from Mount Halak, south of Beersheba, north to Baal-gad, in the vicinity of Mount Hermon.

Throughout the land not a city or people made peace with Israel except the inhabitants of Gibeon (v. 19). The Canaanites did not want to make peace; rather, they came against Israel in battle (v. 20). It was of Jehovah to harden their hearts (v. 20).

It is very difficult to perceive the biblical viewpoint regarding the hardening of the heart. Perhaps centuries of well-meaning theological debate have confused the issue.

The hardening of the heart in the context of the Old Testament viewpoint does not refer to resisting personal salvation when confronted by one engaged in evangelism. The inhabitants of Canaan were not being evangelized, as we use the term. Rather, they were confronted by the Lord of history in the ongoing of historical events. Their creaturely resistance inevitably involved them with the Lord of creation, and out of that involvement there developed a divine activity which acted against them. The essential problem involved from the Arminian viewpoint is that of human freedom.

B. KINGS CONQUERED (12:1-24)

After the narration of kings conquered by Moses on the east side of the Jordan, the account tells of kings conquered by Joshua on the west side of the Jordan.

1. By Moses East of Jordan (12:1-6)

1 Now these are the kings of the land, whom the children of Israel smote, and possessed their land beyond the Jordan toward the sunrising, from the valley of the Arnon unto mount Hermon, and all the Arabah eastward: 2 Sihon king of the Amorites, who dwelt in Heshbon, and ruled from Aroer, which is on the edge of the valley of the Arnon, and *the city that is in* the middle of the valley and half Gilead, even unto the river Jabbok, the border of the children of Ammon; 3 and the Arabah unto the sea of Chinneroth, eastward, and unto the sea of the Arabah, even the Salt Sea, eastward, the way to Beth-jeshimoth; and on the south, under the slopes of Pisgah: 4 and the border of Og king of Bashan, of the remnant of the Rephaim, who dwelt at Ashtaroth and at Edrei, 5 and ruled in mount Hermon, and in Salecah, and in all Bashan, unto the border of the Geshurites and the Maacathites, and half Gilead, the border of Sihon king of Heshbon. 6 Moses the servant of Jehovah and the children of Israel smote them: and Moses the servant of Jehovah gave it for a possession unto the Reubenites, and the Gadites, and the half-tribe of Manasseh.

This chapter summarizes the conquest of Canaan. First, there is given the list of kings who were conquered by Israel under Moses' leadership on the east side of the Jordan River.

The Trans-Jordan territory was allotted to Reuben, Gad and half of Manasseh. Numbers 32 recounts the request of these tribes for this inheritance and Moses' acknowledgment.

2. By Joshua West of Jordan (12:7-24)

7 And these are the kings of the land whom Joshua and the children of Israel smote beyond the Jordan westward, from Baal-gad in the valley of Lebanon even unto mount Halak, that goeth up to Seir (and Joshua gave it unto the tribes of Israel for a possession according to their divisions; 8 in the hill-country, and in the lowland, and in the Arabah, and in the slopes, and in the wilderness, and in the South; the Hittite, the Amorite, and the Canaanite, the Perizzite, the Hivite, and the Jebusite): 9 the king of Jericho, one; the king of Ai, which is beside Beth-el, one; 10 the king of Jerusalem, one; the king of Hebron, one; 11 the king of Jarmuth, one; the king of Lachish, one; 12 the king of Eglon, one; the king of Gezer, one; 13 the king of Debir, one; the king of Geder, one; 14 the king of Hormah, one; the king of Arad, one; 15 the king of Libnah, one; the king of Adullam, one; 16 the king of Makkedah, one; the king of Beth-el, one; 17 the king of Tappuah, one; the king of Hepher, one; 18 the king of Aphek, one;

the king of Lassharon, one; 19 the king of Madon, one; the king of Hazor, one; 20 the king of Shimron-meron, one; the king of Achshaph, one; 21 the king of Taanach, one; the king of Megiddo, one; 22 the king of Kedesh, one; the king of Jokneam in Carmel, one; 23 the king of Dor in the height of Dor, one; the king of Goiim in Gilgal, one; 24 the king of Tirzah, one: all the kings thirty and one.

Under Joshua's leadership, Israel had moved into the land west of Jordan and won some outstanding battles. Generally speaking, the kings of the land had merely local authority, usually extending over a city and its outlying districts. However, in the face of threatening invasion, the kings tended to band together. Since they were not closely united there were only two major coalitions, one defeated at Beth-horon and the other at Hazor.

IX. CONFIRMATION OF THE TRANS-JORDAN INHERITANCE (Josh. 13:1-33)

A. THE COMMAND OF THE LORD (13:1-7)

1 Now Joshua was old and well stricken in years; and Jehovah said unto him, Thou art old and well stricken in years, and there remaineth yet very much land to be possessed. 2 This is the land that yet remaineth: all the regions of the Philistines, and all the Geshurites; 3 from the Shihor, which is before Egypt, even unto the border of Ekron northward, which is reckoned to the Canaanites; the five lords of the Philistines; the Gazites, and the Ashdodites, the Ashkelonites, the Gittites, and the Ekronites; also the Avvim, 4 on the south; all the land of the Canaanites, and Mearah that belongeth to the Sidonians, unto Aphek, to the border of the Amorites; 5 and the land of the Gebalites, and all Lebanon, toward the sunrising, from Baal-gad under mount Hermon unto the entrance of Hamath; 6 all the inhabitants of the hill-country from Lebanon unto Misrephoth-maim, even all the Sidonians; them will I drive out from before the children of Israel: only allot thou it unto Israel for an inheritance, as I have commanded thee. 7 Now therefore divide this land for an inheritance unto the nine tribes, and the half-tribe of Manasseh.

Here begins the second part of the book of Joshua: the history of the division of the land among the tribes. The chapter begins with a reference to the Lord giving instruction to the aging Joshua. Divine guidance was as necessary in the establishing of an inheritance as in the conquering of it in the first place.

God is as important during the postwar period as during days of war. As the battle is not necessarily to the strong so the peace is not necessarily to the wise, if God is relegated out of the discussions. This is as true for the troubled twentieth-century international scene as it was for ancient Israel. Amid the changing times this truth remains unchanged.

Even though **there remaineth yet very much land to be possessed** (v. 1), Joshua was to divide the entire area since ultimate possession was assured: **Them will I drive out from before the children of Israel** (v. 6). The chief sections where strong resistance remained were on the southwest coast where the Philistines were located, and in the northern section of the country, including the Sidonians.

B. JOSHUA'S CONFIRMATION OF THE TRANS-JORDAN INHERITANCE (13:8-14)

8 With him the Reubenites and the Gadites received their inheritance, which Moses gave them, beyond the Jordan eastward, even as Moses the servant of Jehovah gave them: 9 from Aroer, that is on the edge of the valley of the Arnon, and the city that is in the middle of the valley, and all the plain of Medeba unto Dibon; 10 and all the cities of Sihon king of the Amorites, who reigned in Heshbon, unto the border of the children of Ammon; 11 and Gilead, and the border of the Geshurites and Maacathites, and all mount Hermon, and all Bashan unto Salecah; 12 all the kingdom of Og in Bashan, who reigned in Ashtaroth and in Edrei (the same was left of the remnant of the Rephaim); for these did Moses smite, and drove them out. 13 Nevertheless the children of Israel drove not out the Geshurites, nor the Maacathites: but Geshur and Maacath dwell in the midst of Israel unto this day. 14 Only unto the tribe of Levi he gave no inheritance; the offerings of Jehovah, the God of Israel, made by fire are his inheritance, as he spake unto him.

Joshua confirmed the inheritance which Moses had given to Reuben, Gad and half of Manasseh on the east side of the Jordan (v. 8). This confirmation indicated Joshua's integrity. He was faithful to the promises made by Moses.

How often changing situations are allowed to alter agreements made in good faith. Much had transpired since the days of Moses, but Joshua did not forget or qualify Moses' promise to the two-and-one-half tribes. More such persons of integrity are needed in all walks of life.

C. REUBEN'S INHERITANCE (13:15-23)

15 And Moses gave unto the tribe of the children of Reuben according to their families. 16 And their border was from Aroer, that is on the edge of the valley of the Arnon, and the city that is in the middle of the valley, and all the plain by Medeba; 17 Heshbon, and all its cities that are in the plain; Dibon, and Bamoth-baal, and Beth-baal-meon, 18 and Jahaz, and Kedemoth, and Mephaath, 19 and Kiriathaim, and Sibmah, and Zereth-shahar in the mount of the valley, 20 and Beth-peor, and the slopes of Pisgah, and Beth-jeshimoth, 21 and all the cities of the plain, and all the kingdom of Sihon king of the Amorites, who reigned in Heshbon, whom Moses smote with the chiefs of Midian, Evi, and Rekem, and Zur, and Hur, and Reba, the princes of Sihon, that dwelt in the land. 22 Balaam also the son of Beor, the soothsayer, did the children of Israel slay with the sword among the rest of their slain. 23 And the border of the children of Reuben was the Jordan, and the border thereof. This was the inheritance of the children of Reuben according to their families, the cities and the villages thereof.

While Moses had already allotted the Trans-Jordan land to Reuben, Gad and the half-tribe of Manasseh, it became Joshua's responsibility to fix the specific boundaries. Reuben was placed in the south, Gad in the center and Manasseh in the north.

The tribe of Reuben was of Jacob's first-born son and was the first to have its inheritance accurately defined. The land assigned to this tribe was bounded on the west by the Dead Sea, on the south by the Arnon River, on the east by the Ammonites. This area, while the

smallest of the three inheritances, embraced the kingdom of Sihon. To the south were the Moabites and to the east were the Ammonites, both of which were not to be troubled by Israel, according to divine command (cf. Deut. 2:9, 19).

D. GAD'S INHERITANCE (13:24-28)

24 And Moses gave unto the tribe of Gad, unto the children of Gad, according to their families. 25 And their border was Jazer, and all the cities of Gilead, and half the land of the children of Ammon, unto Aroer that is before Rabbah; 26 and from Heshbon unto Ramath-mizpeh, and Betonim; and from Mahanaim unto the border of Debir; 27 and in the valley, Beth-haram, and Beth-nimrah, and Succoth, and Zaphon, the rest of the kingdom of Sihon king of Heshbon, the Jordan and the border thereof, unto the uttermost part of the sea of Chinnereth beyond the Jordan eastward. 28 This is the inheritance of the children of Gad according to their families, the cities and the villages thereof.

The territory of Gad was bounded on the west by the Jordan River, on the south by the tribe of Reuben, on the east by Ammon, on the north by Manasseh. The half of the land of the children of Ammon occupied by Gad was seized from Sihon, who had taken it from the Ammonites (v. 25).

E. HALF OF MANASSEH'S INHERITANCE (13:29-33)

29 And Moses gave inheritance unto the half-tribe of Manasseh: and it was for the half-tribe of the children of Manasseh according to their families. 30 And their border was from Mahanaim, all Bashan, all the kingdom of Og king of Bashan, and all the towns of Jair, which are in Bashan, threescore cities: 31 and half Gilead, and Ashtaroth, and Edrei, the cities of the kingdom of Og in Bashan, were for the children of Machir the son of Manasseh, even for the half of the children of Machir according to their families.

32 These are the inheritances which Moses distributed in the plains of Moab, beyond the Jordan at Jericho, eastward. 33 But unto the tribe of Levi Moses gave no inheritance: Jehovah, the God of Israel, is their inheritance, as he spake unto them.

The largest portion of the Trans-Jordan territory was occupied by the half-tribe of Manasseh. This area included half of Gilead and all of Bashan. It was bounded on the west by the Sea of Galilee and the Jordan valley and on the south by Gad. Its eastern and northern frontiers were exposed to constant threat of attack by nomads. Brave men of Manasseh defended this frontier with courage. Life was not easy for them and their families, for their inheritance often was in peril.

X. INHERITANCE OF JUDAH AND JOSEPH (Josh. 14:1—17:18)

A. JUDAH'S INHERITANCE (14:1—15:63)

The history of the division of the land now relates the boundaries of the two leading houses of Israel, that of Judah and Joseph, with Joseph being divided into two tribes, Ephraim and Manasseh.

1. Caleb's Request (14:1-15)

1 And these are the inheritances which the children of Israel took in the land of Canaan, which Eleazar the priest, and Joshua the son of Nun, and the heads of the fathers' *houses* of the tribes of the children of Israel, distributed unto them, 2 by the lot of their inheritance, as Jehovah commanded by Moses, for the nine tribes, and for the half-tribe. 3 For Moses had given the inheritance of the two tribes and the half-tribe beyond the Jordan: but unto the Levites he gave no inheritance among them. 4 For the children of Joseph were two tribes, Manasseh and Ephraim: and they gave no portion unto the Levites in the land, save cities to dwell in, with the suburbs thereof for their cattle and for their substance. 5 As Jehovah commanded Moses, so the children of Israel did; and they divided the land.
6 Then the children of Judah drew nigh unto Joshua in Gilgal: and Caleb the son of Jephunneh the Kenizzite said unto him, Thou knowest the thing that Jehovah spake unto Moses the man of God concerning me and concerning thee in Kadesh-barnea. 7 Forty years old was I when Moses the servant of Jehovah sent me from Kadesh-barnea to spy out the land; and I brought him word again as it was in my heart. 8 Nevertheless my brethren that went up with me made the heart of the people melt; but I wholly

followed Jehovah my God. 9 And Moses sware on that day, saying, Surely the land whereon thy foot hath trodden shall be an inheritance to thee and to thy children for ever, because thou hast wholly followed Jehovah my God. 10 And now, behold, Jehovah hath kept me alive, as he spake, these forty and five years, from the time that Jehovah spake this word unto Moses, while Israel walked in the wilderness: and now, lo, I am this day fourscore and five years old. 11 As yet I am as strong this day as I was in the day that Moses sent me: as my strength was then, even so is my strength now, for war, and to go out and to come in. 12 Now therefore give me this hill-country, whereof Jehovah spake in that day; for thou heardest in that day how the Anakim were there, and cities great and fortified: it may be that Jehovah will be with me, and I shall drive them out, as Jehovah spake.
13 And Joshua blessed him; and he gave Hebron unto Caleb the son of Jephunneh for an inheritance. 14 Therefore Hebron became the inheritance of Caleb the son of Jephunneh the Kenizzite unto this day; because that he wholly followed Jehovah, the God of Israel. 15 Now the name of Hebron beforetime was Kiriath-arba; *which Arba was* the greatest man among the Anakim. And the land had rest from war.

The opening verses of chapter 14 are introductory and are followed by the account of Caleb's request. Apparently before the allotment began Caleb came to Joshua with a reminder that at Kadesh-barnea he had been one of the twelve spies. His complete confidence in God had caused Moses to promise, **Surely the land whereon thy foot hath trodden shall be an inheritance to thee** (v. 9; cf. Num. 14:24).

Of the twelve spies sent out from Kadesh-barnea only Caleb and Joshua returned with a confident report. When God sentenced Israel to death in the wilderness, only Caleb and Joshua were exempted and promised an inheritance in Canaan. Caleb's request to Joshua implied that he not only was promised an inheritance but also was given the opportunity to choose it. All others, except Joshua, were assigned their inheritance by lot. Joshua's request is recorded in Joshua 19:50.

With confidence and courage undiminished by the war of conquest, Caleb referred to God's faithfulness in preserving him until the present. **Jehovah hath kept me alive, as he spake** (v. 10).

He then requested, **Now therefore give me this hill-country, whereof Jehovah spake in that day** (v. 12). Caleb refused the opportunity to choose an inheritance where he could retire quietly in his older years. He chose, rather, an inheritance occupied by the frighteningly powerful Anakim. His courage and faith never shone more brightly.

Now when the time had come to enter upon the promised inheritance, Caleb's example of faith and courage should have been a powerful inspiration to all the tribes. Had all Israel followed his example the account recorded in Judges would have been greatly altered. What actually happened was that just as at Kadesh so at the opportunity to possess the inheritance, Israel, generally speaking, refused to rise up to the divine command.

Joshua blessed Caleb and granted his request. Caleb received Hebron **because that he wholly followed Jehovah, the God of Israel** (v. 14).

Caleb is an excellent example of a committed person. He trusted in the God of Israel without reservation. His life is a powerful persuasion to follow the Lord regardless of the circumstances.

2. Judah's Boundaries (15:1-63)

1 And the lot for the tribe of the children of Judah according to their families was unto the border of Edom, even to the wilderness of Zin southward, at the uttermost part of the south. 2 And their south border was from the uttermost part of the Salt Sea, from the bay that looketh southward; 3 and it went out southward of the ascent of Akrabbim, and passed along to Zin, and went up by the south of Kadesh-barnea, and passed along by Hezron, and went up to Addar, and turned about to Karka; 4 and it passed along to Azmon, and went out at the brook of Egypt; and the goings out of the border were at the sea: this shall be your south border. 5 And the east border was the Salt Sea, even unto the end of the Jordan. And the border of the north quarter was from the bay of the sea at the end of the Jordan; 6 and the border went up to Beth-hoglah, and passed along by the north of Beth-arabah; and the border went up to the stone of Bohan the son of Reuben; 7 and the border went

up to Debir from the valley of Achor, and so northward, looking toward Gilgal, that is over against the ascent of Adummim, which is on the south side of the river; and the border passed along to the waters of En-shemesh, and the goings out thereof were at En-rogel; 8 and the border went up by the valley of the son of Hinnom unto the side of the Jebusite southward (the same is Jerusalem); and the border went up to the top of the mountain that lieth before the valley of Hinnom westward, which is at the uttermost part of the vale of Rephaim northward; 9 and the border extended from the top of the mountain unto the fountain of the waters of Nephtoah, and went out to the cities of mount Ephron; and the border extended to Baalah (the same is Kiriath-jearim); 10 and the border turned about from Baalah westward unto mount Seir, and passed along unto the side of mount Jearim on the north (the same is Chesalon), and went down to Beth-shemesh, and passed along by Timnah; 11 and the border went out unto the side of Ekron northward; and the border extended to Shikkeron, and passed along to mount Baalah, and went out at Jabneel; and the goings out of the border were at the sea. 12 And the west border was to the great sea, and the border *thereof*. This is the border of the children of Judah round about according to their families.

13 And unto Caleb the son of Jephunneh he gave a portion among the children of Judah, according to the commandment of Jehovah to Joshua, even Kiriatharba, *which Arba was* the father of Anak (the same is Hebron). 14 And Caleb drove out thence the three sons of Anak: Sheshai, and Ahiman, and Talmai, the children of Anak. 15 And he went up thence against the inhabitants of Debir: now the name of Debir beforetime was Kiriath-sepher. 16 And Caleb said, He that smiteth Kiriath-sepher, and taketh it, to him will I give Achsah my daughter to wife. 17 And Othniel the son of Kenaz, the brother of Caleb, took it: and he gave him Achsah his daughter to wife. 18 And it came to pass, when she came *unto him*, that she moved him to ask of her father a field: and she alighted from off her ass; and Caleb said unto her, What wouldest thou? 19 And she said, Give me a blessing; for that thou hast set me in the land of the South, give me also springs of water. And he gave her the upper springs and the nether springs.

20 This is the inheritance of the tribe of the children of Judah according to their families.

21 And the uttermost cities of the tribe of the children of Judah toward the border of Edom in the South were Kabzeel, and Eder, and Jagur, 22 and Kinah, and Dimonah, and Adadah, 23 and Kedesh, and Hazor, and Ithnan, 24 Ziph, and Telem, and Bealoth, 25 and Hazor-hadattah, and Kerioth-hezron (the same is Hazor), 26 Amam, and Shema, and Moladah, 27 and Hazar-gaddah, and Heshmon, and Beth-pelet, 28 and Hazar-shual, and Beer-sheba, and Biziothiah, 29 Baalah, and Iim, and Ezem, 30 and Eltolad, and Chesil, and Hormah, 31 and Ziklag, and Madmannah, and Sansannah, 32 and Lebaoth, and Shilhim, and Ain, and Rimmon: all the cities are twenty and nine, with their villages.

33 In the lowland, Eshtaol, and Zorah, and Ashnah, and Zanoah, and En-gannim, Tappuah, and Enam, 35 Jarmuth, and Adullam, Socoh, and Azekah, 36 and Shaaraim, and Adithaim, and Gederah, and Gederothaim; fourteen cities with their villages.

37 Zenan, and Hadashah, and Migdal-gad, 38 and Dilean, and Mizpeh, and Joktheel, 39 Lachish, and Bozkath, and Eglon, 40 and Cabbon, and Lahmam, and Chitlish, 41 and Gederoth, Beth-dagon, and Naamah, and Makkedah; sixteen cities with their villages.

42 Libnah, and Ether, and Ashan, 43 and Iphtah, and Ashnah, and Nezib, 44 and Keilah, and Achzib, and Mareshah; nine cities with their villages.

45 Ekron, with its towns and its villages; 46 from Ekron even unto the sea, all that were by the side of Ashdod, with their villages.

47 Ashdod, its towns and its villages; Gaza, its towns and its villages; unto the brook of Egypt, and the great sea, and the border thereof.

48 And in the hill-country, Shamir, and Jattir, and Socoh, 49 and Dannah, and Kiriath-sannah (the same is Debir), 50 and Anab, and Eshtemoh, and Anim, 51 and Goshen, and Holon, and Giloh; eleven cities with their villages.

52 Arab, and Dumah, and Eshan, 53 and Janim, and Beth-tappuah, and Aphekah, 54 and Humtah, and Kiriath-arba (the same is Hebron), and Zior; nine cities with their villages.

55 Maon, Carmel, and Ziph, and Jutah, 56 and Jezreel, and Jokdeam, and Zanoah, 57 Kain, Gibeah, and Timnah; ten cities with their villages.

58 Halhul, Beth-zur, and Gedor, 59 and Maarath, and Beth-anoth, and Eltekon; six cities with their villages.

60 Kiriath-baal (the same is Kiriath-jearim), and Rabbah; two cities with their villages.

61 In the wilderness, Beth-arabah, Middin, and Secacah, 62 and Nibshan, and the City of Salt, and Engedi; six cities with their villages.

63 And as for the Jebusites, the inhabitants of Jerusalem, the children of Judah could not drive them out: but the Jebusites dwell with the children of Judah at Jerusalem unto this day.

The southern boundary ran from the southern tip of the Dead Sea southwest to a point near Kadesh-barnea, northwest along the river of Egypt to the Mediterranean. The northern boundary began at the mouth of the Jordan River and followed an irregular line due west to the coast. The boundary passed along the Hinnon Valley, which was on the southern border of Jerusalem. The Dead Sea was the eastern boundary, while the Mediterranean was the western boundary.

Into this territory Caleb came to possess his inheritance. He took Hebron and promised his daughter, Achsah, to whomever took Debir. Othniel took the city and married the daughter. She then asked a "present" (v. 19, margin) of her father. She said, **Thou hast set me in the land of the South, give me also springs of water** (v. 19).

Water was scarce in the south country, the plateau known as the Negeb. To be located where one did not have access to water made living little more than existing. Caleb's daughter saw that something more important than land was needed. Water was also needed.

The story seems to provide an analogy of life. Life needs more than a location; it must have nourishment from spiritual refreshment. Individuals, families and churches find that there is more to life than a location where one can build. There must be opportunities for spiritual and moral refreshing.

The tribe of Judah had many cities in its inheritance. The city of Jerusalem lay alongside of the northern boundary of Judah as it passed along the Hinnon Valley. Apparently, Judah made a serious attempt to drive out the Jebusites, but it was unsuccessful.

B. JOSEPH'S INHERITANCE
(16:1—17:18)

Ephraim and half of Manasseh were given inheritance on the west side of the

Jordan. However, a measure of dissatisfaction was expressed by these tribes.

1. Ephraim's Share (16:1-10)

1 And the lot came out for the children of Joseph from the Jordan at Jericho, at the waters of Jericho on the east, even the wilderness, going up from Jericho through the hill-country to Beth-el; 2 and it went out from Beth-el to Luz, and passed along unto the border of the Archites to Ataroth; 3 and it went down westward to the border of the Japhletites, unto the border of Beth-horon the nether, even unto Gezer; and the goings out thereof were at the sea. 4 And the children of Joseph, Manasseh and Ephraim, took their inheritance.

5 And the border of the children of Ephraim according to their families was *thus*: the border of their inheritance eastward was Ataroth-addar, unto Beth-horon the upper; 6 and the border went out westward at Michmethath on the north; and the border turned about eastward, unto Taanath-shiloh, and passed along it on the east of Janoah; 7 and it went down from Janoah to Ataroth, and to Naarah, and reached unto Jericho, and went out at the Jordan. 8 From Tappuah the border went along westward to the brook of Kanah; and the goings out thereof were at the sea. This is the inheritance of the tribe of the children of Ephraim according to their families; 9 together with the cities which were set apart for the children of Ephraim in the midst of the inheritance of the children of Manasseh, all the cities with their villages. 10 And they drove not out the Canaanites that dwelt in Gezer: but the Canaanites dwell in the midst of Ephraim unto this day, and are become servants to do taskwork.

The house of Joseph formed two tribes, Ephraim and Manasseh. A single lot was cast for these two tribes so they might be located side by side.

After an over-all designation of the location of the house of Joseph, the territory of Ephraim is outlined. The southern border extended westward from Bethel to Gezer and on toward the sea. The northern border was an irregular one generally in line with Michmethath and the brook Kanah. Apparently, the territory was not large enough for the tribe of Ephraim since cities were set apart for . . . Ephraim in the midst of the inheritance . . . of Manasseh (v. 9).

Ephraim did not drive out the Canaanites completely. Instead, they made them servants. This is not in keeping with the principle of *cherem* which had been divinely imposed upon the inhabitants of the land.

2. Half of Manasseh's Share (17:1-13)

1 And *this* was the lot for the tribe of Manasseh; for he was the first-born of Joseph. As for Machir the first-born of Manasseh, the father of Gilead, because he was a man of war, therefore he had Gilead and Bashan. 2 So *the lot* was for the rest of the children of Manasseh according to their families: for the children of Abiezer, and for the children of Helek, and for the children of Asriel, and for the children of Shechem, and for the children of Hepher, and for the children of Shemida: these were the male children of Manasseh the son of Joseph according to their families. 3 But Zelophehad, the son of Hepher, the son of Gilead, the son of Machir, the son of Manasseh, had no sons, but daughters: and these are the names of his daughters: Mahlah, and Noah, Hoglah, Milcah, and Tirzah. 4 And they came near before Eleazar the priest, and before Joshua the son of Nun, and before the princes, saying, Jehovah commanded Moses to give us an inheritance among our brethren: therefore according to the commandment of Jehovah he gave them an inheritance among the brethren of their father. 5 And there fell ten parts to Manasseh, besides the land of Gilead and Bashan, which is beyond the Jordan; 6 because the daughters of Manasseh had an inheritance among his sons. And the land of Gilead belonged unto the rest of the sons of Manasseh.

7 And the border of Manasseh was from Asher to Michmethath, which is before Shechem; and the border went along to the right hand, unto the inhabitants of En-tappuah. 8 The land of Tappuah belonged to Manasseh; but Tappuah on the border of Manasseh belonged to the children of Ephraim. 9 And the border went down unto the brook of Kanah, southward of the brook: these cities belonged to Ephraim among the cities of Manasseh: and the border of Manasseh was on the north side of the brook, and the goings out thereof were at the sea: 10 southward it was Ephraim's, and northward it was Manasseh's, and the sea was his border; and they reached to Asher on the north, and to Issachar on the east. 11 And Manasseh had in Issachar and in Asher Beth-shean and its towns, and Ibleam and its

towns, and the inhabitants of Dor and its towns, and the inhabitants of En-dor and its towns, and the inhabitants of Taanach and its towns, and the inhabitants of Megiddo and its towns, even the three heights. 12 Yet the children of Manasseh could not drive out *the inhabitants of those cities; but the Canaanites would dwell in that land.* 13 And it came to pass, when the children of Israel were waxed strong, that they put the Canaanites to taskwork, and did not utterly drive them out.

The southern border of Manasseh touched along the northern border of Ephraim. The northern border was fringed by the powerful Canaanite fortresses of Beth-shean, Ibleam, Taanach and Megiddo, which guarded the fertile plain of Esdraelon.

These fortress cities proved too much for Manasseh and remained free for some time to come from domination by Israel.

3. Dissatisfaction Regarding the Inheritance (17:14-18)

14 And the children of Joseph spake unto Joshua, saying, Why hast thou given me but one lot and one part for an inheritance, seeing I am a great people, forasmuch as hitherto Jehovah hath blessed me? 15 And Joshua said unto them, If thou be a great people, get thee up to the forest, and cut down for thyself there in the land of the Perizzites and of the Rephaim; since the hill-country of Ephraim is too narrow for thee. 16 And the children of Joseph said, The hill-country is not enough for us: and all the Canaanites that dwell in the land of the valley have chariots of iron, both they who are in Beth-shean and its towns, and they who are in the valley of Jezreel. 17 And Joshua spake unto the house of Joseph, even to Ephraim and to Manasseh, saying, Thou art a great people, and hast great power; thou shalt not have one lot only: 18 but the hill-country shall be thine; for though it is a forest, thou shalt cut it down, and the goings out thereof shall be thine; for thou shalt drive out the Canaanites, though they have chariots of iron, and though they are strong.

The house of Joseph complained to Joshua regarding the one lot it received. **I am a great people** (v. 14) refers to numbers rather than to power. The people were crowded in their inheritance.

Joshua's answer was that there would be sufficient room if the forests were cleared and the Canaanites were driven out of the valleys. Accomplishment of these objectives would require hard work and fearless fighting, but Joshua was confident that the tasks could be accomplished. He challenged the house of Joseph to vigorous action.

The strategic fortress cities guarding the plain of Esdraelon were given as an inheritance to Manasseh. Joshua's challenge seems to have caused no response, for Manasseh never occupied those cities. Not until the monarchy were these strongholds captured.

XI. INHERITANCE FOR THE SEVEN REMAINING TRIBES (Josh. 18:1— 19:51)

A. JOSHUA'S INSTRUCTIONS (18:1-10)

1 And the whole congregation of the children of Israel assembled themselves together at Shiloh, and set up the tent of meeting there: and the land was subdued before them. 2 And there remained among the children of Israel seven tribes, which had not yet divided their inheritance. 3 And Joshua said unto the children of Israel, How long are ye slack to go in to possess the land, which Jehovah, the God of your fathers, hath given you? 4 Appoint for you three men of each tribe: and I will send them, and they shall arise, and walk through the land, and describe it according to their inheritance; and they shall come unto me. 5 And they shall divide it into seven portions: Judah shall abide in his border on the south, and the house of Joseph shall abide in their border on the north. 6 And ye shall describe the land into seven portions, and bring *the description* hither to me; and I will cast lots for you here before Jehovah our God. 7 For the Levites have no portion among you; for the priesthood of Jehovah is their inheritance: and Gad and Reuben and the half-tribe of Manasseh have received their inheritance beyond the Jordan eastward, which Moses the servant of Jehovah gave them.

8 And the men arose, and went: and Joshua charged them that went to describe the land, saying, Go and walk through the land, and describe it, and come again to me; and I will cast lots for you before Jehovah in Shiloh. 9 And the

men went and passed through the land, and described it by cities into seven portions in a book; and they came to Joshua unto the camp at Shiloh. 10 And Joshua cast lots for them in Shiloh before Jehovah: and there Joshua divided the land unto the children of Israel according to their divisions.

Joshua's instructions regarding inheritances for the remaining tribes were given at Shiloh. After Judah and Joseph had received their inheritances and had departed from Gilgal to their new land, Joshua ordered that the permanent camp be moved from Gilgal to Shiloh.

The movement of the camp included the movement of the tabernacle. Shiloh was especially suitable as a location for the tabernacle because of its central location among the tribes. It remained at Shiloh for many years. The Philistine attack on Shiloh during the days of Samuel marked the end of the residence of the tabernacle there.

With the houses of Judah and Joseph occupied in possessing their inheritance, Joshua observed the apathy of the seven remaining tribes: **How long are ye slack to go in to possess the land** (v. 3). These tribes were still without inheritances, and Joshua was concerned about their indifference.

Joshua arranged for three men from each of the seven tribes to take a survey of the land which yet remained. This area was divided into seven portions and lots were cast.

B. BENJAMIN'S INHERITANCE (18:11-28)

11 And the lot of the tribe of the children of Benjamin came up according to their families: and the border of their lot went out between the children of Judah and the children of Joseph. 12 And their border on the north quarter was from the Jordan; and the border went up to the side of Jericho on the north, and went up through the hill-country westward; and the goings out thereof were at the wilderness of Beth-aven. 13 And the border passed along from thence to Luz, to the side of Luz (the same is Beth-el), southward; and the border went down to Ataroth-addar, by the mountain that lieth on the south of Beth-horon the nether. 14 And the border extended *thence*, and turned about on the west quarter southward, from the mountain

that lieth before Beth-horon southward; and the goings out thereof were at Kiriath-baal (the same is Kiriath-jearim), a city of the children of Judah: this was the west quarter. 15 And the south quarter was from the uttermost part of Kiriath-jearim; and the border went out westward, and went out to the fountain of the waters of Nephtoah; 16 and the border went down to the uttermost part of the mountain that lieth before the valley of the son of Hinnom, which is in the vale of Rephaim northward; and it went down to the valley of Hinnom, to the side of the Jebusite southward, and went down to En-rogel; 17 and it extended northward, and went out at En-shemesh, and went out to Geliloth, which is over against the ascent of Adummim; and it went down to the stone of Bohan the son of Reuben; 18 and it passed along to the side over against the Arabah northward, and went down unto the Arabah; 19 and the border passed along to the side of Beth-hoglah northward; and the goings out of the border were at the north bay of the Salt Sea, at the south end of the Jordan: this was the south border. 29 And the Jordan was the border of it on the east quarter. This was the inheritance of the children of Benjamin, by the borders thereof round about, according to their families.

21 Now the cities of the tribe of the children of Benjamin according to their families were Jericho, and Beth-hoglah, and Emek-keziz, 22 and Beth-arabah, and Zemaraim, and Beth-el, 23 and Avvim, and Parah, and Ophrah, 24 and Chephar-ammoni, and Ophni, and Geba; twelve cities with their villages: 25 Gibeon, and Ramah, and Beeroth, 26 and Mizpeh, and Chephirah, and Mozah, 27 and Rekem, and Irpeel, and Taralah, 28 and Zelah, Eleph, and the Jebusite (the same is Jerusalem), Gibeath, *and* Kiriath; fourteen cities with their villages. This is the inheritance of the children of Benjamin according to their families.

Benjamin was allotted an inheritance between that of Judah and Ephraim. This position served as a buffer between the two great, competing houses of Israel, Judah on the south and Joseph on the north.

C. SIMEON'S INHERITANCE (19:1-9)

1 And the second lot came out for Simeon, even for the tribe of the children of Simeon according to their families: and their inheritance was in the midst of the inheritance of the children

of Judah. 2 And they had for their inheritance Beer-sheba, or Sheba, and Moladah, 3 and Hazar-shual, and Balah, and Ezem, 4 and Eltolad, and Bethul, and Hormah, 5 and Ziklag, and Beth-marcaboth, and Hazar-susah, 6 and Beth-lebaoth, and Sharuhen; thirteen cities with their villages: 7 Ain, Rimmon, and Ether, and Ashan; four cities with their villages: 8 and all the villages that were round about these cities to Baalath-beer, Ramah of the South. This is the inheritance of the tribe of the children of Simeon according to their families. 9 Out of the part of the children of Judah was the inheritance of the children of Simeon; for the portion of the children of Judah was too much for them: therefore the children of Simeon had inheritance in the midst of their inheritance.

It had become evident that Judah had too large an inheritance. **The portion of the children of Judah was too much for them** (v. 9). Therefore, when Simeon's lot was determined, the inheritance was in the southern part of Judah's portion. Simeon was a small, weak tribe, and, before many years had passed, it lost its identity and was absorbed into the tribe of Judah.

D. ZEBULUN'S INHERITANCE (19:10-16)

10 And the third lot came up for the children of Zebulun according to their families. And the border of their inheritance was unto Sarid; 11 and their border went up westward, even to Maralah, and reached to Dabbesheth; and it reached to the brook that is before Jokneam; 12 and it turned from Sarid eastward toward the sunrising unto the border of Chisloth-tabor; and it went out to Daberath, and went up to Japhia; 13 and from thence it passed along eastward to Gath-hepher, to Eth-kazin; and it went out at Rimmon which stretcheth unto Neah; 14 and the border turned about it on the north to Hannathon; and the goings out thereof were at the valley of Iphtah-el; 15 and Kattath, and Nahalal, and Shimron, and Idalah, and Bethlehem: twelve cities with their villages. 16 This is the inheritance of the children of Zebulun according to their families, these cities with their villages.

To Zebulun was given a part of the fertile inland plain of Esdraelon. Along this plain extended the important trade route of many centuries. It was known as the "Way to the Sea." However, the tribe of Zebulun was of minor importance in the history of Israel. With all the potential for abundance located in the bounds of Zebulun's inheritance, the tribe appeared to be satisfied with a mediocre existence and little or no influence.

E. ISSACHAR'S INHERITANCE (19:17-23)

17 The fourth lot came out for Issachar, even for the children of Issachar according to their families. 18 And their border was unto Jezreel, and Chesulloth, and Shunem, 19 and Hapharaim, and Shion, and Anaharath, 20 and Rabbith, and Kishion, and Ebez, 21 and Remeth, and En-gannim, and En-haddah, and Beth-pazzez, 22 and the border reached to Tabor, and Shahazumah, and Bethshemesh; and the goings out of their border were at the Jordan: sixteen cities with their villages. 23 This is the inheritance of the tribe of the children of Issachar according to their families, the cities with their villages.

Issachar's territory was between the fertile land of Zebulun and the inheritance of Manasseh. It included the plain of Jezreel and part of the plain of Esdraelon. The tribe was apparently one of the larger tribes, numerically, with excellent opportunities for prosperity. Yet it remained relatively uninfluential.

F. ASHER'S INHERITANCE (19:24-31)

24 And the fifth lot came out for the tribe of the children of Asher according to their families. 25 And their border was Helkath, and Hali, and Beten, and Achshaph, 26 and Allammelech, and Amad, and Mishal; and it reached to Carmel westward, and to Shihor-libnath; 27 and it turned toward the sunrising to Beth-dagon, and reached to Zebulun, and to the valley of Iphtah-el northward to Beth-emek and Neiel; and it went out to Cabul on the left hand, 28 and Ebron, and Rehob, and Hammon, and Kanah, even unto great Sidon; 29 and the border turned to Ramah, and to the fortified city of Tyre; and the border turned to Hosah; and the goings out thereof were at the sea by the region of Achzib; 30 Ummah also, and Aphek, and Rehob: twenty and two cities with their villages. 31 This is the inheritance of the tribe of the children of Asher according to their families, these cities with their villages.

The tribe of Asher obtained the important maritime plain and mountain territory north of Zebulun. The area had excellent soil and climate. Mineral resources, especially iron, were in the mountains. However, this tribe continued in relative obscurity along with her sister tribes of the productive northern part of Canaan.

G. NAPHTALI'S INHERITANCE (19:32-39)

32 The sixth lot came out for the children of Naphtali, even for the children of Naphtali according to their families. 33 And their border was from Heleph, from the oak in Zaanannim, and Adaminekeb, and Jabneel, unto Lakkum; and the goings out thereof were at the Jordan; 34 and the border turned westward to Aznoth-tabor, and went out from thence to Hukkok; and it reached to Zebulun on the south, and reached to Asher on the west, and to Judah at the Jordan toward the sunrising. 35 And the fortified cities were Ziddim, Zer, and Hammath, Rakkath, and Chinnereth, 36 and Adamah, and Ramah, and Hazor, 37 and Kedesh, and Edrei, and En-hazor, 38 and Iron, and Migdal-el, Horem, and Beth-anath, and Beth-shemesh; nineteen cities with their villages. 39 This is the inheritance of the tribe of the children of Naphtali according to their families, the cities with their villages.

Naphtali was bounded on the west by the tribe of Asher and on the east by the Jordan River. Included in this geographical territory were fertile lands and rich forests. A considerable portion of the territory consisted of the mountains of Galilee.

H. DAN'S INHERITANCE (19:40-48)

40 The seventh lot came out for the tribe of the children of Dan according to their families. 41 And the border of their inheritance was Zorah, and Eshtaol, and Irshemesh, 42 and Shaalabbin, and Aijalon, and Ithlah, 43 and Elon, and Timnah, and Ekron, 44 and Eltekeh, and Gibbethon, and Baalath, 45 and Jehud, and Bene-berak, and Gath-rimmon, 46 and Me-jarkon, and Rakkon, with the border over against Joppa. 47 And the border of the children of Dan went out beyond them; for the children of Dan went up and fought against Leshem, and took it, and smote it with the edge of the sword, and possessed it, and dwelt therein, and

called Leshem, Dan, after the name of Dan their father. 48 This is the inheritance of the tribe of the children of Dan according to their families, these cities with their villages.

Dan's settlement was bounded on the south by Judah's territory, on the east and north by Benjamin and Ephraim, on the west by the seacoast. Rich and fertile land was included in this small area. The tribe of Dan engaged in a bitter struggle to dislodge their enemies from the fertile areas. Being unsuccessful, the Danites migrated to the source of the Jordan at the foot of Mt. Hermon (Judg. I8). Here on the northern fringe of their allotted inheritance Dan faced the constant threat of invasion from the north.

I. JOSHUA'S INHERITANCE (19:49-51)

49 So they made an end of distributing the land for inheritance by the borders thereof; and the children of Israel gave an inheritance to Joshua the son of Nun in the midst of them: 50 according to the commandment of Jehovah they gave him the city which he asked, even Timnath-serah in the hill-country of Ephraim; and he built the city, and dwelt therein.

51 These are the inheritances, which Eleazar the priest, and Joshua the son of Nun, and the heads of the fathers' *houses* of the tribes of the children of Israel, distributed for inheritance by lot in Shiloh before Jehovah, at the door of the tent of meeting. So they made an end of dividing the land.

After all of the tribes had received their inheritance, Joshua was given his inheritance in the tribe of Ephraim. Joshua's personal interests were taken care of only after the needs of all others had been provided. His desire to see that Caleb and each of the tribes were given inheritances shows a selfless leader, concerned not so much about himself as those for whom he was responsible. This is an essential characteristic of leaders.

XII. CITIES FOR SPECIAL SERVICE (Josh. 20:1—21:45)

A. CITIES OF REFUGE (20:1-9)

1 And Jehovah spake unto Joshua, saying, 2 Speak to the children of Israel, say-

ing, Assign you the cities of refuge, whereof I spake unto you by Moses, 3 that the manslayer that killeth any person unwittingly *and* unawares may flee thither: and they shall be unto you for a refuge from the avenger of blood. 4 And he shall flee unto one of those cities, and shall stand at the entrance of the gate of the city, and declare his cause in the ears of the elders of that city; and they shall take him into the city unto them, and give him a place, that he may dwell among them. 5 And if the avenger of blood pursue after him, then they shall not deliver up the manslayer into his hand; because he smote his neighbor unawares, and hated him not beforetime. 6 And he shall dwell in that city, until he stand before the congregation for judgment, until the death of the high priest that shall be in those days: then shall the manslayer return, and come unto his own city, and unto his own house, unto the city from whence he fled.

7 And they set apart Kedesh in Galilee in the hill-country of Naphtali, and Shechem in the hill-country of Ephraim, and Kiriath-arba (the same is Hebron) in the hill-country of Judah. 8 And beyond the Jordan at Jericho eastward, they assigned Bezer in the wilderness in the plain out of the tribe of Reuben, and Ramoth in Gilead out of the tribe of Gad, and Golan in Bashan out of the tribe of Manasseh. 9 These were the appointed cities for all the children of Israel, and for the stranger that sojourneth among them, that whosoever killeth any person unwittingly might flee thither, and not die by the hand of the avenger of blood, until he stood before the congregation.

The custom of blood revenge, sometimes termed the "blood-feud" or the "law of blood," is of long standing. Biblical origins are found in Genesis. The word of the Lord to Noah was, "Whoso sheddeth man's blood, by man shall his blood be shed" (Gen. 9:6). While this law has been viewed as an attempt to regulate a custom deeply rooted in society, it is preferable to view it as a profound vindication of the sacredness of human life.

Cities of refuge were determined in order that the unintentional murderer could have respite from the custom of blood revenge. These cities offered no refuge for intentional murderers. However, if an unintentional murderer fled

to a city of refuge he was under its protection until judged by the congregation as to his intent. If the judgment rendered was that his crime was unintentional, the slayer was to remain in the city until the death of the high priest. He was then free to leave the city without the threat of being slain.

"It may be said that the institution of the cities of refuge served mainly to prevent excesses which might develop from the execution of what is usually called 'blood-feud'."[14]

Little is known concerning this practice of asylum for the unintentional murderer. References to it are in I Kings 1 and 2. Possibly, as the central authority of the monarchy was established in Canaan, the need for the right of refuge for the unintentional murderer was no longer necessary.

The cities of refuge were all Levite cities. This suggests the part which ministers and Christian workers should have in society. Just as the Levites assisted in obtaining a place in the community of citizens, so ministers are able to assist in the rehabilitation of those who have need (cf. vv. 4, 5).

B. CITIES FOR LEVITES (21:1-45)

1 Then came near the heads of fathers' *houses* of the Levites unto Eleazar the priest, and unto Joshua the son of Nun, and unto the heads of fathers' *houses* of the tribes of the children of Israel; 2 and they spake unto them at Shiloh in the land of Canaan, saying, Jehovah commanded by Moses to give us cities to dwell in, with the suburbs thereof for our cattle. 3 And the children of Israel gave unto the Levites out of their inheritance, according to the commandment of Jehovah, these cities with their suburbs.

4 And the lot came out for the families of the Kohathites: and the children of Aaron the priest, who were of the Levites, had by lot out of the tribe of Judah, and out of the tribe of the Simeonites, and out of the tribe of Benjamin, thirteen cities.

5 And the rest of the children of Kohath had by lot out of the families of the tribe of Ephraim, and out of the tribe of Dan, and out of the half-tribe of Manasseh, ten cities.

6 And the children of Gershon had by lot out of the families of the tribe of Issachar, and out of the tribe of Asher,

[14] N. H. Ridderbos, "Cities of Refuge," NBD, p. 234.

and out of the tribe of Naphtali, and out of the half-tribe of Manasseh in Bashan, thirteen cities.

7 The children of Merari according to their families had out of the tribe of Reuben, and out of the tribe of Gad, and out of the tribe of Zebulun, twelve cities.

8 And the children of Israel gave by lot unto the Levites these cities with their suburbs, as Jehovah commanded by Moses. And they gave out of the tribe of the children of Judah, and out of the tribe of the children of Simeon, these cities which are *here* mentioned by name: 10 and they were for the children of Aaron, of the families of the Kohathites, who were of the children of Levi; for theirs was the first lot. 11 And they gave them Kiriath-arba, *which Arba was* the father of Anak (the same is Hebron), in the hill-country of Judah, with the suburbs thereof round about it. 12 But the fields of the city, and the villages thereof, gave they to Caleb the son of Jephunneh for his possession.

13 And unto the children of Aaron the priest they gave Hebron with its suburbs, the city of refuge for the manslayer, and Libnah with its suburbs, 14 and Jattir with its suburbs, and Eshtemoa with its suburbs, 15 and Holon with its suburbs, and Debir with its suburbs, 16 and Ain with its suburbs, and Juttah with its suburbs, *and* Beth-shemesh with its suburbs; nine cities out of those two tribes. 17 And out of the tribe of Benjamin, Gibeon with its suburbs, Geba with its suburbs, 18 Anathoth with its suburbs, and Almon with its suburbs; four cities. 19 All the cities of the children of Aaron, the priests, were thirteen cities with their suburbs.

20 And the families of the children of Kohath, the Levites, even the rest of the children of Kohath, they had the cities of their lot out of the tribe of Ephraim. 21 And they gave them Shechem with its suburbs in the hill-country of Ephraim, the city of refuge for the manslayer, and Gezer with its suburbs, 22 and Kibzaim with its suburbs, and Beth-horon with its suburbs; four cities. 23 And out of the tribe of Dan, Elteke with its suburbs, Gibbethon with its suburbs, 24 Aijalon with its suburbs, Gath-rimmon with its suburbs; four cities. 25 And out of the half-tribe of Manasseh, Taanach with its suburbs, and Gath-rimmon with its suburbs; two cities. 26 All the cities of the families of the rest of the children of Kohath were ten with their suburbs.

27 And unto the children of Gershon, of the families of the Levites, out of the half-tribe of Manasseh *they* gave Golan in Bashan with its suburbs, the city of refuge for the manslayer, and Be-eshterah with its suburbs; two cities. 28 And out of the tribe of Issachar, Kishion with its suburbs, Daberath with its suburbs, 29 Jarmuth with its suburbs, Engannim with its suburbs; four cities. 30 And out of the tribe of Asher, Mishal with its suburbs, Abdon with its suburbs, 31 Helkath with its suburbs, and Rehob with its suburbs; four cities. 32 And out of the tribe of Naphtali, Kedesh in Galilee with its suburbs, the city of refuge for the manslayer, and Hammoth-dor with its suburbs, and Kartan with its suburbs; three cities. 33 All the cities of the Gershonites according to their families were thirteen cities with their suburbs.

34 And unto the families of the children of Merari, the rest of the Levites, out of the tribe of Zebulun, Jokneam with its suburbs, and Kartah with its suburbs, 35 Dimnah with its suburbs, Nahalal with its suburbs; four cities. 36 And out of the tribe of Reuben, Bezer with its suburbs, and Jahaz with its suburbs, 37 Kedemoth with its suburbs, and Mephaath with its suburbs; four cities. 38 And out of the tribe of Gad, Ramoth in Gilead with its suburbs, the city of refuge for the manslayer, and Mahanaim with its suburbs, 39 Heshbon with its suburbs, Jazer with its suburbs; four cities in all. 40 All *these were* the cities of the children of Merari according to their families, even the rest of the families of the Levites; and their lot was twelve cities.

41 All the cities of the Levites in the midst of the possession of the children of Israel were forty and eight cities with their suburbs. 42 These cities were every one with their suburbs round about them: thus it was with all these cities.

43 So Jehovah gave unto Israel all the land which he sware to give unto their fathers; and they possessed it, and dwelt therein. 44 And Jehovah gave them rest round about, according to all that he sware unto their fathers: and there stood not a man of all their enemies before them; Jehovah delivered all their enemies into their hand. 45 There failed not aught of any good thing which Jehovah had spoken unto the house of Israel; all came to pass.

Although the tribe of Levi was given no inheritance, specified cities were set aside for the Levites. A total of forty-eight cities scattered throughout the tribes were designated as Levitical cities. "The Levitical cities do not seem to have been the exclusive possession of the tribe, but rather the Levites had certain privileges within them. . . . Their pasture land could not be sold at all, but remained their perpetual possession (Lev. XXV. 32-34)."[15]

The Levites first came into prominence at Mt. Sinai upon the occasion of Israel's worship of the golden calf. After Aaron, of the tribe of Levi, had led Israel into apostasy and idolatry, the sons of Levi displayed faithfulness to God by punishing many of the unfaithful. "This display of fidelity to God may partially account for the signal responsibilities given the tribe in the pentateuchal legislation."[16]

The Levites may well have been distributed throughout Israel to be perpetual witnesses for God among the people. They performed religious duties, expounded the law and preserved the history of Israel in chronicles and writings. They kept the religion of Israel related to everyday life, for they dwelt among the people.

The concluding verses of Joshua 21 form the conclusion to the account of the division of the land. In a sweeping generality, the assertion is made that God had fulfilled His promise of a promised land.

While not all the inhabitants were destroyed, nor all the land conquered, yet Israel had entered upon the promised possession. God was faithful. **There failed not aught of any good thing which Jehovah had spoken unto the house of Israel; all came to pass** (v. 45).

XIII. RETURN OF THE TRANS-JORDAN TRIBES ·(Josh. 22:1-34)

A. COMMENDATION BY JOSHUA (22:1-9)

1 Then Joshua called the Reubenites, and the Gadites, and the half-tribe of Manasseh, 2 and said unto them, Ye have kept all that Moses the servant of Jehovah commanded you, and have hearkened unto my voice in all that I commanded you: 3 ye have not left your brethren these many days unto this day, but have kept the charge of the commandment of Jehovah your God. 4 And now Jehovah your God hath given rest unto your brethren, as he spake unto them: therefore now turn ye, and get

you unto your tents, unto the land of your possession, which Moses the servant of Jehovah gave you beyond the Jordan. 5 Only take diligent heed to do the commandment and the law which Moses the servant of Jehovah commanded you, to love Jehovah your God, and to walk in all his ways, and keep his commandments, and to cleave unto him, and to serve him with all your heart and with all your soul. 6 So Joshua blessed them, and sent them away; and they went unto their tents.

7 Now to the one half-tribe of Manaseh Moses had given *inheritance* in Bashan; but unto the other half gave Joshua among their brethren beyond the Jordan westward. Moreover when Joshua sent them away unto their tents, he blessed them, 8 and spake unto them, saying, Return with much wealth unto your tents, and with very much cattle, with silver, and with gold, and with brass, and with iron, and with very much raiment: divide the spoil of your enemies with your brethren. 9 And the children of Reuben and the children of Gad and the half-tribe of Manasseh returned, and departed from the children of Israel out of Shiloh, which is in the land of Canaan, to go unto the land of Gilead, to the land of their possession, whereof they were possessed, according to the commandment of Jehovah by Moses.

Earlier, while still on the east side of the Jordan, three tribes, Reuben, Gad and half of Manasseh, had requested that the Trans-Jordan area which Israel had conquered be allotted to them. Moses agreed on the stipulation that these three tribes fight with the others in the conquest of the land on the west side. The three tribes pledged to enter the fight until "the children of Israel have inherited every man his inheritance" (Num. 32:18). These tribes continued faithful throughout the conquest under Joshua.

Finally, with every Israelite provided an inheritance, Joshua prepared to provide honorable discharges for the men of the three Trans-Jordan tribes.

The keynote of Joshua's commendation of these tribes is their obedience. He specifically referred to the fact that they **have kept all that Moses . . . commanded . . . and . . . all that I commanded** (v. 2). He was acutely aware that their obedience had been sacrificial.

---

[15] D. A. Hubbard, "Priests and Levites," NBD, p. 1029.   [16] *Ibid.*, p. 1028.

It had cost them separation from loved ones and struggle against hostile enemies. Notwithstanding the sacrifice, they were faithfully obedient: **Ye have not left your brethren these many days** (v. 3). This obedience expressed itself in *patriotism* to the community of Israel and in *piety* to God.

The returning tribes were urged to continue their loving obedience to the Lord. **Take diligent heed to do the commandment . . . to love Jehovah . . . to serve him with all your heart . . . (v. 5).**

B. CRISIS AMONG THE TRIBES (22:10-34)

On their way to their homes the three tribes built an altar beside the Jordan River. This was rumored among the tribes as idolatry and almost provoked war. Conflict was averted and the altar was recognized as a memorial.

1. Building an Altar (22:10)

10 And when they came unto the region about the Jordan, that is in the land of Canaan, the children of Reuben and the children of Gad and the half-tribe of Manasseh built there an altar by the Jordan, a great altar to look upon.

The two-and-one-half tribes were journeying home. As they came to the Jordan they proceeded to erect an altar of remembrance out of stones. Apparently these tribes realized that their inheritance was separated more than desirable from the tribes on the west side of the Jordan. The depth of the central *Arabah,* or gorge, through which the Jordan flows and which reaches great depths at the Dead Sea, is one of the deepest depressions of exposed land surface in the world. There is no question but that it was an important factor affecting the proximity of the tribes of Israel. Those on the east side of the Jordan were considered to be separated from the other tribes by reason of the Jordanian gorge.

"The problem of the two and one-half tribes was how to keep alive and strong the ties of comradeship. . . . So they built the high altar of remembrance near the bank of the river Jordan. It was to

stand as an eternal monument to their oneness."[17]

2. Misunderstanding About the Altar (22:11-20)

11 And the children of Israel heard say, Behold, the children of Reuben and the children of Gad and the half-tribe of Manasseh have built an altar in the fore-front of the land of Canaan, in the region about the Jordan, on the side that pertaineth to the children of Israel. 12 And when the children of Israel heard of it, the whole congregation of the children of Israel gathered themselves together at Shiloh, to go up against them to war.

13 And the children of Israel sent unto the children of Reuben, and to the children of Gad, and to the half-tribe of Manasseh, into the land of Gilead, Phinehas the son of Eleazar the priest, 14 and with him ten princes, one prince of a fathers' house for each of the tribes of Israel; and they were every one of them head of their fathers' houses among the thousands of Israel. 15 And they came unto the children of Reuben, and to the children of Gad, and to the half-tribe of Manasseh, unto the land of Gilead, and they spake with them, saying, 16 Thus saith the whole congregation of Jehovah, What trespass is this that ye have committed against the God of Israel, to turn away this day from following Jehovah, in that ye have builded you an altar, to rebel this day against Jehovah? 17 Is the iniquity of Peor too little for us, from which we have not cleansed ourselves unto this day, although there came a plague upon the congregation of Jehovah, 18 that ye must turn away this day from following Jehovah? and it will be, seeing ye rebel to-day against Jehovah, that to-morrow he will be wroth with the whole congregation of Israel. 19 Howbeit, if the land of your possession be unclean, then pass ye over unto the land of the possession of Jehovah, wherein Jehovah's tabernacle dwelleth, and take possession among us: but rebel not against Jehovah, nor rebel against us, in building you an altar besides the altar of Jehovah our God. 20 Did not Achan the son of Zerah commit a trespass in the devoted thing, and wrath fell upon all the congregation of Israel? and that man perished not alone in his iniquity.

The threat of civil war suddenly mushroomed in Israel. The discovery of this great altar beside Jordan caused an

---

[17] Sizoo, *op. cit.,* pp. 657-58.

assembly of the elders of the western tribes at Shiloh to consider going to war against the eastern tribes (v. 12).

The reason for the crisis was misunderstanding. Without any attempt to learn the reasons which prompted the erection of the altar the western tribes were deciding upon war.

The problems of misunderstanding and unreasonableness are still with the human race. "The problem of all time is how to put the round table of common negotiation in place of the arbitrament of the sword."[18]

This particular problem was over a religious issue. One of the ironic facts of history is that religious issues, instead of uniting brothers, have often divided them. Religion has caused many wars. "It has built barricades instead of bridges, walls instead of windows."[19]

3. Vindicating the Presence of the Altar (22:21-29)

21 Then the children of Reuben and the children of Gad and the half-tribe of Manasseh answered, and spake unto the heads of the thousands of Israel, 22 The Mighty One, God, Jehovah, the Mighty One, God, Jehovah, he knoweth; and Israel he shall know: if it be in rebellion, or if in trespass against Jehovah (save thou us not this day), 23 that we have built us an altar to turn away from following Jehovah; or if to offer thereon burnt-offering or meal-offering, or if to offer sacrifices of peace-offerings thereon, let Jehovah himself require it; 24 and if we have not *rather* out of carefulness done this, *and* of purpose, saying, In time to come your children might speak unto our children, saying, What have ye to do with Jehovah, the God of Israel? 25 for Jehovah hath made the Jordan a border between us and you, ye children of Reuben and children of Gad; ye have no portion in Jehovah: so might your children make our children cease from fearing Jehovah. 26 Therefore we said, Let us now prepare to build us an altar, not for burnt-offering, nor for sacrifice: 27 but it shall be a witness between us and you, and between our generations after us, that we may do the service of Jehovah before him with our burnt-offerings, and with our sacrifices, and with our peace-offerings; that your children may not say to our children in time to come, Ye have no portion in Jehovah. 28

Therefore said we, It shall be, when they so say to us or to our generations in time to come, that we shall say, Behold the pattern of the altar of Jehovah, which our fathers made, not for burnt-offering, nor for sacrifice; but it is a witness between us and you. 29 Far be it from us that we should rebel against Jehovah, and turn away this day from following Jehovah, to build an altar for burnt-offering, for meal-offering, or for sacrifice, besides the altar of Jehovah our God that is before his tabernacle.

A commission from the congregation of Israel went to the Trans-Jordan tribes to obtain an explanation. The demand for an explanation came from people who were fearful of judgment from the Lord. This implication is clear from the reference which is made to **Achan the son of Zerah** (v. 20). They feared that all Israel would stand condemned.

The Trans-Jordan spokesmen were deeply affected by the accusation of apostasy and rebellion. Their shock is evident in the broken and abrupt language of their reply. There is evidence of a deeply wounded love. The two-and-one-half tribes had been engaged in erecting a monument testifying to their unitedness with all Israel, but it had only provoked talk of war.

However, in their explanation for the altar, the tribes asserted that it was erected as a symbol of tribal unity. It was to **be a witness between us and you, and between our generations after us, that we may do the service of Jehovah . . .** (v. 27). It was a sign to all that the Trans-Jordan tribes had a share in the inheritance of a promised land.

4. Accepting the Altar (22:30-34)

30 And when Phinehas the priest, and the princes of the congregation, even the heads of the thousands of Israel that were with him, heard the words that the children of Gad and the children of Manasseh spake, it pleased them well. 31 And Phinehas the son of Eleazar the priest said unto the children of Reuben, and to the children of Gad, and to the children of Manasseh, This day we know that Jehovah is in the midst of us, because ye have not committed this trespass against Jehovah: now have ye delivered the children of Israel out of the hand of Jehovah. 32 And Phinehas the son of Eleazar the

---

[18] *Ibid.,* p. 658.   [19] *Ibid.,* p. 659.

priest, and the princes, returned from the children of Reuben, and from the children of Gad, out of the land of Gilead, unto the land of Canaan, to the children of Israel, and brought them word again. 33 And the thing pleased the children of Israel; and the children of Israel blessed God, and spake no more of going up against them to war, to destroy the land wherein the children of Reuben and the children of Gad dwelt. 34 And the children of Gad called the altar *Ed*: For, *said they*, it is a witness between us that Jehovah is God.

The congregation of Israel was kind in offering to make room for the two-and-one-half tribes on the west side of the Jordan if necessary (see 22:19). This was evidence of their deep concern for the Trans-Jordan tribes, and it is commendable.

Furthermore, when the congregation heard the explanation for the altar they readily and cheerfully accepted it. This, too, is commendable. Reconciliation was effected and the altar stood as a perpetual witness.

"The name of the altar is lacking in the M. T. and in most of the versions. The reading **Ed** (witness) is a surmise based on the Syriac and the contest."[20]

XIV. JOSHUA'S FAREWELL ADDRESS (Josh. 23:1-16)

A. PROMISE OF FULL POSSESSION OF CANAAN (23:1-10)

"This chapter balances the introduction in 1:1-9 admirably, gathering together many of the themes enunciated there and throughout the book, and drawing from them lessons for the guidance of Israel in the future."[21]

1. Inspiration out of the Past (23:1-3)

1 And it came to pass after many days, when Jehovah had given rest unto Israel from all their enemies round about, and Joshua was old and well stricken in years; 2 that Joshua called for all Israel, for their elders and for their heads, and for their judges and for their officers, and said unto them, I am old and well stricken in years: 3 and ye have seen all that Jehovah your God hath done unto all these nations because of you; for

Jehovah your God, he it is that hath fought for you.

Joshua called to remembrance the past events: **Ye have seen all that Jehovah your God hath done . . . he it is that hath fought for you** (v. 3). Recollection of the conquest called to mind the many occasions of divine help. Each occasion provided added inspiration as it was related to the others.

There was the battle of Jericho when the walls were flattened. There was the battle of Beth-horon when hail stones pummeled a great army. There was Hazor when the chariots of iron proved utterly helpless against Israel. In all this, God was engaged in historic acts of revelation to inspire His people.

2. Confirmation as to the Future (23:4-10)

4 Behold, I have allotted unto you these nations that remain, to be an inheritance for your tribes, from the Jordan, with all the nations that I have cut off, even unto the great sea toward the going down of the sun. 5 And Jehovah your God, he will thrust them out from before you, and drive them from out of your sight; and ye shall possess their land, as Jehovah your God spake unto you. 6 Therefore be ye very courageous to keep and to do all that is written in the book of the law of Moses, that ye turn not aside therefrom to the right hand or to the left; 7 that ye come not among these nations, these that remain among you; neither make mention of the name of their gods, nor cause to swear *by them*, neither serve them, nor bow down yourselves unto them; 8 but cleave unto Jehovah your God, as ye have done unto this day. 9 For Jehovah hath driven out from before you great nations and strong: but as for you, no man hath stood before you unto this day. 10 One man of you shall chase a thousand; for Jehovah your God, he it is that fighteth for you, as he spake unto you.

Jehovah your God, he will thrust them out from before you . . . and ye shall possess their land . . . (v. 5). The task of complete conquest remained unfinished. Each tribe had its own inheritance to secure from entrenched inhabitants. Nevertheless, as God had fought for

Israel in the past, He would continue to do so in the future.

However, the insistence upon obedience is enforced: **Therefore be ye very courageous to keep and to do all that is written in the book of the law of Moses** (v. 6). Furthermore, there was to be no compromise with the inhabitants, . . . **come not among these nations, these that remain among you** (v. 7).

"Verse 10 should be translated not as future but as a generalization of their experience — 'One of you could put a thousand to flight because it is the Lord your God who has fought for you.' "[22]

B. PERIL OF FATAL PUNISHMENT (23:11-16)

11 Take good heed therefore unto yourselves, that ye love Jehovah your God. 12 Else if ye do at all go back, and cleave unto the remnant of these nations, even these that remain among you, and make marriages with them, and go in unto them, and they to you; 13 know for a certainty that Jehovah your God will no more drive these nations from out of your sight; but they shall be a snare and a trap unto you, and a scourge in your sides, and thorns in your eyes, until ye perish from off this good land which Jehovah your God hath given you. 14 And, behold, this day I am going the way of all the earth: and ye know in all your hearts and in all your souls, that not one thing hath failed of all the good things which Jehovah your God spake concerning you; all are come to pass unto you, not one thing hath failed thereof. 15 And it shall come to pass, that as all the good things are come upon you of which Jehovah your God spake unto you, so will Jehovah bring upon you all the evil things, until he have destroyed you from off this good land which Jehovah your God hath given unto you. 16 When ye transgress the covenant of Jehovah your God, which he commanded you, and go and serve other gods, and bow down yourselves to them; then will the anger of Jehovah be kindled against you, and ye shall perish quickly from off the good land which he hath given unto you.

Joshua plainly warned that disobedience was to be punished severely. Disobedience would bring about a loss of God's help. As a consequence, Israel would **perish quickly from off the good land** (v. 16)

If Israel joined with the other nations and ceased to love the Lord, then those nations would become **a snare . . . and a scourge . . . and thorns . . . to** Israel (v. 13).

"Here we have the core and substance of the theology of the Deuteronomic writers — unswerving obedience to the law of God or complete destruction and extinction."[23]

Joshua uttered a sublime statement of faith in God's providence when he declared, **Behold, this day I am going the way of all the earth: . . . not one thing hath failed of all the good things which Jehovah your God spake concerning you** (v. 14). Out of his wide and varied experience of God in war as well as peace, Joshua affirmed that the divine presence was the greatest and most trustworthy influence in his life.

XV. COVENANT AT SHECHEM (Josh. 24:1-33)

A. JOSHUA'S REVIEW OF ISRAEL'S HISTORY (24:1-15)

1 And Joshua gathered all the tribes of Israel to Shechem, and called for the elders of Israel, and for their heads, and for their judges, and for their officers; and they presented themselves before God. 2 And Joshua said unto all the people, Thus saith Jehovah, the God of Israel, Your fathers dwelt of old time beyond the River, even Terah, the father of Abraham, and the father of Nahor: and they served other gods. 3 And I took your father Abraham from beyond the River, and led him throughout all the land of Canaan, and multiplied his seed, and gave him Isaac. 4 And I gave unto Isaac Jacob and Esau: and I gave unto Esau mount Seir, to possess it; and Jacob and his children went down into Egypt. 5 And I sent Moses and Aaron, and I plagued Egypt, according to that which I did in the midst thereof: and afterward I brought you out. 6 And I brought your fathers out of Egypt: and ye came unto the sea; and the Egyptians pursued after your fathers with chariots and with horsemen unto the Red Sea. 7 And when they cried out unto Jehovah, he put darkness between you and the Egyptians, and

[22] Blair, *op. cit.*, p. 235.   [23] Sizoo, *op. cit.*, p. 666.

brought the sea upon them, and covered them: and your eyes saw what I did in Egypt: and ye dwelt in the wilderness many days. 8 And I brought you into the land of the Amorites, that dwelt beyond the Jordan: and they fought with you; and I gave them into your hand, and ye possessed their land; and I destroyed them from before you. 9 Then Balak the son of Zippor, king of Moab, arose and fought against Israel: and he sent and called Balaam the son of Beor to curse you; 10 but I would not hearken unto Balaam; therefore he blessed you still: so I delivered you out of his hand. 11 And ye went over the Jordan, and came unto Jericho: and the men of Jericho fought against you, the Amorite, and the Perizzite, and the Canaanite, and the Hittite, and the Girgashite, the Hivite, and the Jebusite; and I delivered them into your hand. 12 And I sent the hornet before you, which drove them out from before you, even the two kings of the Amorites; not with thy sword, nor with thy bow. 13 And I gave you a land whereon thou hadst not labored, and cities which ye built not, and ye dwell therein; of vineyards and oliveyards which ye planted not do ye eat.

14 Now therefore fear Jehovah, and serve him in sincerity and in truth; and put away the gods which your fathers served beyond the River, and in Egypt; and serve ye Jehovah. 15 And if it seem evil unto you to serve Jehovah, choose you this day whom ye will serve; whether the gods which your fathers served that were beyond the River, or the gods of the Amorites, in whose land ye dwell: but as for me and my house, we will serve Jehovah.

This chapter is one of the most important in the entire Old Testament. Here is given the account of an important assembly of Israel at Shechem, strategically located between Mount Gerizim and Mount Ebal. In the presence of the assembled Israelites Joshua related outstanding events in their history. He began with the patriarchal period (vv. 1-4) and moved on to the events of the Exodus (vv. 5-7) and the conquest (vv. 8-13).

On the basis of this review of events, Joshua called Israel to decision. **Choose you this day whom ye will serve** (v. 15). Either serve the tribal deities of the neighboring nations or **fear Jehovah, and serve him in sincerity and in truth** (v.

14). **As for me and my house, we will serve Jehovah** (v. 15).

B. ISRAEL'S RESPONSE TO THE REVIEW OF GOD'S MIGHTY ACTS (24:16-24)

16 And the people answered and said, Far be it from us that we should forsake Jehovah, to serve other gods; 17 for Jehovah our God, he it is that brought us and our fathers up out of the land of Egypt, from the house of bondage, and that did those great signs in our sight, and preserved us in all the way wherein we went, and among all the peoples through the midst of whom we passed; 18 and Jehovah drove out from before us all the peoples, even the Amorites that dwelt in the land: therefore we also serve Jehovah; for he is our God. 19 And Joshua said unto the people, Ye cannot serve Jehovah; for he is a holy God; he is a jealous God; he will not forgive your transgression nor your sins. 20 If ye forsake Jehovah, and serve foreign gods, then he will turn and do you evil, and consume you, after that he hath done you good. 21 And the people said unto Joshua, Nay; but we will serve Jehovah. 22 And Joshua said unto the people, Ye are witnesses against yourselves that ye have chosen you Jehovah, to serve him. And they said, We are witnesses. 23 Now therefore put away, *said he*, the foreign gods which are among you, and incline your heart unto Jehovah, the God of Israel. 24 And the people said unto Joshua, Jehovah our God will we serve, and unto his voice will we hearken.

The people of Israel responded in faith: **We also will serve Jehovah; for he is our God** (v. 18). Here is sincere acknowledgment that no other explanation sufficed to account for Israel's past history and present standing than the mighty acts of the living God. Here was a people, on the basis of personal and collective experience of God, declaring their intention to serve Him and none other.

Joshua's reply repudiated the merely enthusiastic and exuberant decision. The claim of the holy God demands more than decision of the *lips*. There must be decision of the *life*. More than convenient loyalty is required. There must be consecrated, steadfast obedience. The people affirmed their genuine determination to serve the Lord (v. 21).

C. ISRAEL'S COVENANT WITH THE LORD RENEWED (24:25-28)

25 So Joshua made a covenant with the people that day, and set them a statute and an ordinance in Shechem. 26 And Joshua wrote these words in the book of the law of God; and he took a great stone, and set it up there under the oak that was by the sanctuary of Jehovah. 27 And Joshua said unto all the people, Behold, this stone shall be a witness against us; for it hath heard all the words of Jehovah which he spake unto us: it shall be therefore a witness against you, lest ye deny your God. 28 So Joshua sent the people away, every man unto his inheritance.

On the basis of Israel's decision to serve the Lord and no other god, Joshua bound them to their decision in the most significant manner possible, namely, renewing the covenant that was made originally at Sinai. The covenant renewal bound Israel to her great decision, **We will serve Jehovah** (v. 21).

With the renewing of the covenant a great stone was set up under an oak tree at Shechem as a witness to Israel's declaration and covenant to serve God.

D. EPILOGUE (24:29-33)

29 And it came to pass after these things, that Joshua the son of Nun, the servant of Jehovah, died, being a hundred and ten years old. 30 And they buried him in the border of his inheritance in Timnath-serah, which is in the hill-country of Ephraim, on the north of the mountain of Gaash. 31 And Israel served Jehovah all the days of Joshua, and all the days of the elders that outlived Joshua, and had known all the work of Jehovah, that he had wrought for Israel.

32 And the bones of Joseph, which the children of Israel brought up out of Egypt, buried they in Shechem, in the parcel of ground which Jacob bought of the sons of Hamor the father of Shechem for a hundred pieces of money: and they became the inheritance of the children of Joseph. 33 And Eleazar the son of Aaron died; and they buried him in the hill of Phinehas his son, which was given him in the hill-country of Ephraim.

The book of Joshua concludes with the account of three burials, that of Joshua, Joseph and Eleazar.

Bibliography

I. EXEGETICAL AND HISTORICAL VALUE

Adams, J. McKee. *Biblical Backgrounds.* Nashville: Broadman, 1934.

Albright, W. F. *Archaeology and the Religion of Israel.* 3rd ed. Baltimore: John Hopkins, 1953.

————. *Archaeology of Palestine and the Bible.* Harmondsworth: Penguin Books, 1949.

Blair, H. J. "Joshua." *The New Bible Commentary.* Eds. F. Davidson, A. M. Stibbs, E. F. Kevan. Grand Rapids: Eerdmans, 1953.

Blauw, Johannes. *The Missionary Nature of the Church.* New York: McGraw-Hill, 1962.

Bright, John. *A History of Israel.* Philadelphia: Westminster, 1959.

————. "Joshua: Introduction and Exegesis." *The Interpreter's Bible.* Eds. G. A. Buttrick *et al.* Vol. II. New York and Nashville: Abingdon, 1953.

Butterfield, Herbert. *Christianity and History.* New York: Scribner, 1950.

Dodd, C. H. *The Bible Today.* New York: Macmillan, 1947.

Douglas, J. D. *The New Bible Dictionary.* Grand Rapids: Eerdmans, 1962.

Garstang, John. *Foundations of Bible History: Joshua, Judges.* London: Constable, 1931.

Maclear, G. F. "Joshua." *The Cambridge Bible for Schools and Colleges.* Ed. J. J. S. Perowne. Cambridge, 1889.

Pfeiffer, Robert H. *Introduction to the Old Testament.* New York: Harper, 1948.

Rowley, H. H. *The Biblical Doctrine of Election.* London: Lutterworth, 1950.

————. *From Joseph to Joshua.* London: Oxford, 1950.

Snaith, Norman H. *The Distinctive Ideas of the Old Testament,* Philadelphia: Westminster, 1946.

Wright, G. E., and F. V. Filson (eds.). *The Westminster Historical Atlas.* Revised. Philadelphia: Westminster, 1956.

II. EXPOSITORY AND PRACTICAL VALUE

Clarke, Adam. *Clarke's Commentary: Joshua to Esther.* Reprint. New York and Nashville: Abingdon, n.d.

Hastings, J. and E. (eds.). *The Speaker's Bible.* Reprint. Grand Rapids: Baker, n.d.

Maclaren, Alexander. *Expositions of Holy Scripture: Deuteronomy through II Samuel.* New York: Doran, n.d.

Marchant, F. G. "Joshua." *Preacher's Homiletical Commentary.* New York: Funk and Wagnalls, 1892.

Redpath, Alan. *Victorious Christian Living: Studies in the Book of Joshua.* Intro. by Paul S. Rees. New York: Revell, 1955.

Sizoo, J. R. "Joshua: Exposition." *The Interpreter's Bible.* Eds. G. A. Buttrick *et al.* Vol. II. New York and Nashville: Abingdon, 1953.

Spence, H. D. M., and J. S. Exell (eds.). *The Pulpit Commentary.* New York: Funk and Wagnalls, n.d.

Stevenson, Dwight E. *Preaching on the Books of the Old Testament.* New York: Harper, 1961.

The Book of Judges

by Charles R. Wilson

Outline

Introduction

Judges is the second book in the group of writings in the Old Testament termed the "Former Prophets."[1] Joshua, Judges, Samuel and Kings constitute this group. While Joshua recounts a series of lightning thrusts by the Israelites under Joshua, resulting in the conquest of Canaan, Judges portrays a series of astonishing deliverances in behalf of the Israelites during the prolonged period of settlement in Canaan.

I. TITLE

The title of the book is derived from the name given to a series of persons who were raised up in a remarkable manner to "judge" Israel. The historical occasion of Israel's settlement in the promised land was one of turbulence and struggle. When the Israelites turned to the Lord in prayer and repentance He "raised up judges, who saved them" (Judg. 2:16). The Hebrew word *shophet,* translated "judge," is close in meaning to "king."[2] This reveals that the judges in Israel had more than legal arbitration responsibilities. The term *saviour* (3:9) involved the broader meanings of leader and deliverer as well as arbiter.

The manner in which the judges were raised up to deliver Israel was that they were possessed by the Spirit of God and received spiritual power for the task. This spiritual power, or divine *charisma,* gave authority to those possessed by it, and they in turn inspired the warriors of the tribes in overthrowing those nations subjecting them to oppression.

II. COMPOSITION

There are evidences that parts of Judges are older than the book as we have it. For example, the song of Deb-orah (5:1-31) originated in the period contemporary with the event it celebrates. "The Jebusites in Jerusalem" (1:21) indicates a date earlier than David's capture of Jerusalem. "The Canaanites in Gezer" (1:29) refers to the Gezer prior to Solomon's acquisition.

Most of the book, while composed of much ancient material, has been arranged to bring out a distinctive viewpoint of Israel's history. That viewpoint is treated in Judges 2:11—3:6. The main part, which tells of repeated declensions, oppressions and deliverances, is set in a recurring frame of reference (cf. Judg. 2:18, 19). The latter part includes two narratives which have not been incorporated into the distinctive framework. They are the occasions of image-worship in Dan and the rape at Gibeah recorded in chapters 17 to 21. These serve to illustrate the turbulent conditions during the period of settlement.

The distinctive viewpoint which the book in its present form sets forth is that the God of Israel led His people by a constant discipline in order that they might come to a clearer and more complete understanding of Himself and His requirements.

F. F. Bruce has considered the date for the origin of the well-defined view of history which appears throughout the main part of Judges. His judgment is:

> The author's 'philosophy of history' may suggest a date after Josiah's reformation (621 B.C.), which was based on the recovery of the Deuteronomic law-code.[3]

Judges, though a composite of such ancient material, was formed into the systematic writing as we have it fairly late in the history of Israel. The determinative factor in this conclusion is that the systematized character of Judges results from a

---

[1] See General Introduction to the Historical Books.
[2] B. W. Anderson, *Understanding the Old Testament,* p. 105.
[3] F. F. Bruce, "Judges," *The New Bible Commentary,* ed. by F. Davidson, A. M. Stibbs and E. F. Kevan, p. 237.

view of history that became well defined as a result of the insight of the prophets.

III. HISTORY OF THE PERIOD

The dates for the period of the judges may be set between 1250 and 1050 B.C.[4] This includes the history of Israel from the death of Joshua to the rise of the monarchy under Saul.

Joshua's death may be dated in 1417 B.C., as seen from comparing the following references: Exod. 17:8f.; 16:35; Josh. 24:29; I Kings 6:1. This would make the period of the judges roughly to have been 367 years. An alternative view is a later dating of Joshua's death.

Under the leadership of Joshua, Israel was able to enter Canaan. During the period of the judges Israel struggled with the problem of becoming established in the promised land.

The endeavor of the Israelites to enter into the land of Canaan and to establish themselves upon their inheritance was contemporary with a significant migration of peoples throughout the Middle East. Canaan was the focal point for migrating peoples, some coming by land, others coming by sea. Those who came by land were the Habiru, semi-nomadic peoples found in various parts of western Asia from the eighteenth to the thirteenth century B. C. During the fourteenth century they attacked the cities of Canaan. Correspondence recorded on the Tell el-Amarna tablets relates urgent calls to the Egyptian Pharaoh, Akhnaton, from provincial rulers of the cities of Canaan for help against the Habiru. "The word 'Habiru' may be identical with 'Hebrews,' . . . though these Habiru are probably not to be identified with the Israelites led by Joshua."[5]

Those people who came by sea were Aegeans. These first attempted to land in Egypt during the thirteenth century B. C., but were repulsed by the Egyptian Pharaoh, Merenptah. Unable to gain territory in Egypt, these sea raiders settled on the coast of Canaan and quickly exercised considerable control over a sizable territory. They came to be known as Philistines. From their name was derived the name Palestine, another name for the land of Canaan.

The efforts of the Israelites to settle in Canaan were marked by struggle. According to John Bright, available archaeological evidence "shows that the twelfth and eleventh centuries were as disturbed as any in the history of Palestine."[6] The book of Judges describes the period as turbulent and marked by critical periods of idolatry and consequent oppression. Intermittently there were comparatively peaceful times.

In attempting an analysis of this troublesome era of Israel's history we shall, first, observe the cultural transition in which Israel was involved and, second, explore the resulting religious tension. It is beyond the scope of this introduction to engage in any exhaustive analysis; rather, only a brief survey for practical purposes is given.

Israel's cultural transition was the change-over from a semi-nomadic, pastoral way of life to a cultural pattern largely devoted to agricultural and urban development. In some respects this occurred quite rapidly. "Israel in general, with surprising speed, became a nation of small farmers."[7] Not only were the Israelites able to shift from a pastoral to an agrarian pattern of living, but they were also able to make excellent progress in urban development. At first, Israelite towns were incredibly crude. "By the eleventh century, however, as Israelites learned the techniques of farming and building, a decided improvement may be noted."[8]

The culture of the Canaanites was immeasurably advanced over that of the incoming Israelites, who had been reduced to slavery for many years. It was inevitable that the Israelites would borrow from Canaanite culture to improve their own lot in Canaan. Furthermore, since the religion of the Canaanites was seemingly inextricably bound up with the agrarian life of the people, it seemed to the Israelites that the Canaanite religion was a necessary part of the Canaanite culture.

Canaanite religion consisted of the worship of Baal and Ashtaroth (cf. Judg. 2:13) .

[4] *Ibid.*, p. 237. Cf. "Chronology of the O. T.," *New Bible Dictionary.*   [5] *Ibid.*, p. 236.
[6] John Bright, *A History of Israel*, p. 117.   [7] *Ibid.*, p. 155.   [8] *Loc. cit.*

The title 'Baal' means 'lord' or 'owner,' and designates the male deity who owns the land and controls its fertility.[9]

The fertility of the land was viewed from the religious standpoint, its productivity dependent upon the sexual relations between Baal and his consort.

Moreover, the Canaanites believed that they could cooperate with these divine fertility powers and thereby insure the welfare and productivity of the land. Therefore, sacred prostitution was a prominent feature in Baal-worship. The man identifying himself with Baal and the woman identifying herself with Ashtaroth could induce divine relations for the sake of productivity.

This Canaanite conception of Baal identified deity with *nature*. This was far removed from the Israelite conception of Jehovah as the *Lord of history*. Yet the Israelites were continually tempted to blur the distinction. Here was the glory of the prophetic insight. The prophets saw with incisive clarity that Israel must keep herself from the worship of Baal, for it was idolatry and sin in the presence of Jehovah. To engage in Baal-worship was to incur the displeasure and discipline of the Lord.

The history of the period, as written from the standpoint of the prophets, is one in which religious tension dominates Israel's struggle.

IV. MORAL AND SPIRITUAL VALUES

The history of the period of the judges was the story of God's activity regarding His people and the other nations. The fundamental factor in the developments and events for this era was Jehovah. This was clearly observed by the writers of the Former Prophets.

The book of Judges is based upon a way of viewing history that emerged as a clearly definable outlook in the time of the prophets. F. F. Bruce states the view as follows:

> The cause of prosperity is found in obedience to the will of God . . . ; adversity is the sure sequel to departure from this strait path.[10]

The structure of the book of Judges clearly reflects this viewpoint.

The stories about Israel and the judges treat historical reality in an interpretative and meaningful way. From Othniel to Samson, the efforts of the various heroic judges are described according to the well-defined viewpoint that prosperity follows obedience to God while oppression comes as judgment for disobedience. Through the ongoing of Israel's history God disciplined His people to obey Him.

The timeless relevance of the book of Judges lies in its positive affirmation that the factor of discipline is an important element in the historical process. History is purposive and meaningful to those who believe that God is active in the events of life for the purpose of disciplining His people for His service. This powerfully dynamic conception of the God who is involved in history is relevant for all time.

[9] Anderson, *op. cit.*, p. 97.
[10] Bruce, *op. cit.*, p. 237.

Commentary on Judges

I. TRIBAL CONQUEST
(Judg. 1:1–2:5)

Joshua was dead. With his leadership ended, the first phase of the conquest was complete. The next phase was the occupation of the tribal inheritances. Since pockets of resistance remained in the various tribal allotments, these had to be conquered if the tribes were to possess their inheritance with a sense of security.

A. JUDAH (1:1-21)

1 And it came to pass after the death of Joshua, that the children of Israel asked of Jehovah, saying, Who shall go up for us first against the Canaanites, to fight against them? 2 And Jehovah said, Judah shall go up: behold, I have delivered the land into his hand. 3 And Judah said unto Simeon his brother, Come up with me into my lot, that we may fight against the Canaanites; and I likewise will go with thee into thy lot. So Simeon went with him. 4 And Judah went up; and Jehovah delivered the Canaanites and the Perizzites into their hand: and they smote of them in Bezek ten thousand men. 5 And they found Adoni-bezek in Bezek; and they fought against him, and they smote the Canaanites and the Perizzites. 6 But Adoni-bezek fled; and they pursued after him, and caught him, and cut off his thumbs and his great toes. 7 And Adoni-bezek said, Threescore and ten kings, having their thumbs and their great toes cut off, gathered *their food* under my table: as I have done, so God hath requited me. And they brought him to Jerusalem, and he died there.

8 And the children of Judah fought against Jerusalem, and took it, and smote it with the edge of the sword, and set the city on fire. 9 And afterward the children of Judah went down to fight against the Canaanites that dwelt in the hill-country, and in the South, and in the lowland. 10 And Judah went against the Canaanites that dwelt in Hebron (now the name of Hebron beforetime was Kiriath-arba); and they smote Sheshai, and Ahiman, and Talmai.

11 And from thence he went against the inhabitants of Debir. (Now the name of Debir beforetime was Kiriath-sepher.) 12 And Caleb said, He that smiteth Kiriath-sepher, and taketh it, to him will I give Achsah my daughter to wife. 13 And Othniel the son of Kenaz, Caleb's younger brother, took it: and he gave him Achsah his daughter to wife. 14 And it came to pass, when she came *unto him,* that she moved him to ask of her father a field: and she alighted from off her ass; and Caleb said unto her, What wouldest thou? 15 And she said unto him, Give me a blessing; for that thou hast set me in the land of the South, give me also springs of water. And Caleb gave her the upper springs and the nether springs.

16 And the children of the Kenite, Moses' brother-in-law, went up out of the city of palm-trees with the children of Judah into the wilderness of Judah, which is in the south of Arad; and they went and dwelt with the people. 17 And Judah went with Simeon his brother, and they smote the Canaanites that inhabited Zephath, and utterly destroyed it. And the name of the city was called Hormah. 18 Also Judah took Gaza with the border thereof, and Ashkelon with the border thereof, and Ekron with the border thereof. 19 And Jehovah was with Judah; and he drove out *the inhabitants of* the hill-country; for he could not drive out the inhabitants of the valley, because they had chariots of iron. 20 And they gave Hebron unto Caleb, as Moses had spoken: and he drove out thence the three sons of Anak. 21 And the children of Benjamin did not drive out the Jebusites that inhabited Jerusalem; but the Jebusites dwell with the children of Benjamin in Jerusalem unto this day.

The word of the Lord commissioned the tribe of Judah to lead in this new phase of occupation. Earlier, Judah had been the first tribe to obtain an inheritance located on the west side of the Jordan River (Josh. 15). These two important "firsts" for Judah underscore the importance of the distinctive blessing which Jacob pronounced upon his son Judah (Gen. 49). This fourth son of Jacob, also the fourth son of Jacob's first wife, Leah, occupied a leading part in Israel's history through his descendants. The biblical account clearly indicates that this was not by chance. Divine providence was actively engaged in the role of the tribe of Judah.

The book of Judges opens with a query on the part of the tribes of Israel, **Who shall go up for us first against the Canaanites, to fight against them?** (v. 1). The divinely given answer is, **Judah shall go up** (v. 2). From the biblical point of view the explanation for Judah's leading role in the occupation was her obedient response to the word of the Lord. Just as the man Joshua responded to the divine word to him, so later the people of the tribe of Judah unitedly responded to God's word to them.

Judah asked the tribe of Simeon to join in this initial tribal effort of occupation since Simeon's inheritance was to be carved out of Judah's (cf. Josh. 15:26-32; 19:1-9; Judg. 1:3; I Chron. 4:28-33). **And Jehovah delivered the Canaanites and the Perizzites into their hand** (v. 4). The occupation account begins on the high note of invincibility, with Judah and Simeon conquering through the power of the Lord.

The apparent atrocity dealt Adonibezek is best understood in the light of the *lex talionis* (law of retaliation). His admission of guilt, **as I have done, so God hath requited me** (v. 7), carried with it the admission of retribution for his own cruelty. This ancient warring king recognized that judgment had fallen upon him because of the evils he had committed. Wars do have the element of judgment in them. Not only was this the case among ancient peoples, but it is true for modern nations as well. There is always the tendency to oversimplify such a complex fact of reality as war; nevertheless, the Bible portrays the element of judgment in many of the wars it records.

The account of the capture of Jerusalem must be studied in the light of related Scriptures (cf. Josh. 15:63; Judg. 1:8, 21; II Sam. 5:6ff.). Myers says:

There is no valid reason, however, why there should not have been two destructions of Jerusalem, as was the case of Debir, Eglon, Beth-shemesh, Bethel and elsewhere.[1]

The story of the occupation of Debir given in Judges 1:11-15 is almost word for word a parallel of Joshua 15:15-19. The uniquely important element of this story is the gift which Caleb gave to his daughter, Achsah, the wife of Othniel, who had received her as a reward for the capture of Debir. This necessitated Caleb's daughter dwelling with her husband in **the land of the South** (v. 15), the arid territory of the Negeb.

Need for water was constant. Achsah requested that Caleb give her **springs of water** (v. 15). This required giving adjoining land which had springs. Caleb granted her request.

As with Caleb's daughter, there are people who have been given dry and arid areas of life. Their life is difficult because of a serious lack of necessary resources. They greatly need **the upper and the nether springs** (v. 15). Unless needed refreshment and vital resources are made available, life may become intolerable. As Caleb granted his daughter's request, so God is ready to grant our request for adequate resources for living.

The children of the Kenite, Moses' brother-in-law, went up . . . and dwelt with the people. And Judah . . . smote the Canaanites . . . (vv. 16, 17). The accepted meaning is not **brother-in-law** but "father-in-law."[2]

While the Kenites, a nomad people who associated with the tribes of Israel and who accompanied Judah and Simeon on their occupation, were content to settle among the inhabitants of the land, Judah and Simeon were not so inclined. The difference lies in the fact that **Jehovah was with Judah; and he drove out the inhabitants of the hill-country** (v. 19).

What was involved was the risk inherent in the intermingling of peoples of different religions. To the extent that Judah mingled with the Canaanites, to that extent she risked the adulteration of her Jehovah-worship. If she were able to retain her religious faith and still amalgamate with the Canaanites there

[1] J. M. Myers, "Introduction and Exegesis of Judges," *The Interpreter's Bible*, II, 541.
[2] F. F. Bruce, "Judges," *New Bible Dictionary*, p. 679.

would be no problem. However, the history of religion in general and of Israel's religion in particular indicates that it is an open question whether it is possible to reach the place where this is not a problem. Separation removes the possibility of influence because a barrier is erected. Intermingling imperils the possibility of retaining distinctiveness. Too much may be lost in the process. The tribe of Benjamin faced this problem, for it could not drive out the Jebusites from Jerusalem. **The Jebusites dwell with the children of Benjamin in Jerusalem unto this day** (v. 21).

B. JOSEPH (1:22-29)

22 And the house of Joseph, they also went up against Beth-el; and Jehovah was with them. 23 And the house of Joseph sent to spy out Beth-el. (Now the name of the city beforetime was Luz.) 24 And the watchers saw a man come forth out of the city, and they said unto him, Show us, we pray thee, the entrance into the city, and we will deal kindly with thee. 25 And he showed them the entrance into the city; and they smote the city with the edge of the sword; but they let the man go and all his family. 26 And the man went into the land of the Hittites, and built a city, and called the name thereof Luz, which is the name thereof unto his day.

27 And Manasseh did not drive out *the inhabitants of* Beth-shean and its towns, nor *of* Taanach and its towns, nor the inhabitants of Dor and its towns, nor the inhabitants of Ibleam and its towns, nor the inhabitants of Megiddo and its towns; but the Canaanites would dwell in that land. 28 And it came to pass, when Israel was waxed strong, that they put the Canaanites to taskwork, and did not utterly drive them out.

29 And Ephraim drove not out the Canaanites that dwelt in Gezer; but the Canaanites dwelt in Gezer among them.

While the tribe of Judah exercised leadership among the tribes by reason of its favored position, the house of Joseph was a perennial challenger. Just as when Joshua allocated the promised land by lot, giving Judah the first lot and Joseph the second lot, so later, when Judah left to claim her inheritance, Joseph followed. **Manasseh did not drive out . . . Beth-shean . . . Taanach . . . Dor . . . Ibleam . . . Megiddo** (v. 27). Manasseh was the

elder son of Joseph and founded the tribe bearing his name. This tribe found a strong chain of Canaanite fortresses along its northern boundary. These fortresses were a serious threat to any attempt at uniting Israel, for they separated the Joseph tribes of Ephraim and Manasseh from the northern tribes. Some were not conquered until the time of David, two hundred years later.

Ephraim drove not out . . . Gezer (v. 29). Gezer was on the southwestern corner of the inheritance of Ephraim and some eighteen miles west of Jerusalem. Jerusalem was conquered by David, but Gezer remained unconquered until the time of Solomon.

C. ZEBULUN, ASHER, NAPHTALI, DAN (1:30-36)

30 Zebulun drove not out the inhabitants of Kitron, nor the inhabitants of Nahalol; but the Canaanites dwelt among them, and became subject to taskwork.

31 Asher drove not out the inhabitants of Acco, nor the inhabitants of Sidon, nor of Ahlab, nor of Achzib, nor of Helbah, nor of Aphik, nor of Rehob; 32 but the Asherites dwelt among the Canaanites, the inhabitants of the land; for they did not drive them out.

33 Naphtali drove not out the inhabitants of Beth-shemesh, nor the inhabitants of Beth-anath; but he dwelt among the Canaanites, the inhabitants of the land: nevertheless the inhabitants of Beth-shemesh and of Beth-anath became subject to taskwork.

34 And the Amorites forced the children of Dan into the hill-country; for they would not suffer them to come down to the valley; 35 but the Amorites would dwell in mount Heres, in Aijalon, and in Shaalbim: yet the hand of the house of Joseph prevailed, so that they became subject to taskwork. 36 And the border of the Amorites was from the ascent of Akrabbim, from the rock, and upward.

These tribes, with the exception of Dan, were initially located in the northern part of the land. The tribe of Dan in part soon migrated north because of the pressure exerted by the Amorites. So before the period of the judges came to an end all the tribes were, in part at least, in the northern sector.

Significantly, these tribes were unsuccessful in their occupation efforts. Instead, a strained co-existence resulted, with the Canaanites occasionally regimented into forced-labor companies. To the extent that the influence of the Canaanites affected Israel's religion her woes increased. This perilous development gave rise to a singular event to which attention must now be devoted.

D. "FROM GILGAL TO BOCHIM" (2:1-5)

1 And the angel of Jehovah came up from Gilgal to Bochim. And he said, I made you to go up out of Egypt, and have brought you unto the land which I sware unto your fathers; and I said, I will never break my covenant with you: 2 and ye shall make no covenant with the inhabitants of this land; ye shall break down their altars. But ye have not hearkened unto my voice: why have ye done this? 3 Wherefore I also said, I will not drive them out from before you; but they shall be as thorns in your sides, and their gods shall be a snare unto you. 4 And it came to pass, when the angel of Jehovah spake these words unto all the children of Israel, that the people lifted up their voice, and wept. 5 And they called the name of that place Bochim: and they sacrificed there unto Jehovah.

As Israel continued to adjust to the existing situation of her many Canaanite neighbors, a new appearance of **the angel of Jehovah** occurred (v. 1). Earlier, as the conquest was about to begin under Joshua, "the prince of the host of Jehovah" appeared at Gilgal (Josh. 5:14).

Now a new period has begun, one marked by compromise rather than by conquest. The angel of Jehovah came up from Gilgal to Bochim, not to announce a new conquest but to declare that the heathen power of the Canaanites would remain near the tribes of Israel as judgment upon their disobedience. What had happened since entrance into Canaan was aptly summed up in the phrase, **from Gilgal to Bochim** (v. 1).

Gilgal, which means "rolling," was so named because it signified that God had "rolled away the reproach of Egypt" (Josh. 5:9). Israel was no longer a slave nation; she was a free nation entering upon her promised land. The Lord of history was with her.

Bochim, which means "weeping," signified that the people realized that the judgment of the Lord was upon their failures. As an emancipated nation Israel was destined to occupy the land of Canaan. Instead, the tribes of Israel had accommodated themselves to the inhabitants of the land. This resulted in divine displeasure.

All Israel entered upon an occasion of repentance and sacrifice to the Lord. True worship to the God of Israel lasted for a brief time but gave way to alternating periods of apostasy.

II. INTRODUCTION TO THE JUDGES (Judg. 2:6—3:6)

The introduction to the accounts of the judges includes the last years of Joshua and the explication of the structure of the narratives of the judges.

A. JOSHUA'S FINAL DAYS (2:6-10)

6 Now when Joshua had sent the people away, the children of Israel went every man unto his inheritance to possess the land. 7 And the people served Jehovah all the days of Joshua, and all the days of the elders that outlived Joshua, who had seen all the great work of Jehovah that he had wrought for Israel. 8 And Joshua the son of Nun, the servant of Jehovah, died, being a hundred and ten years old. 9 And they buried him in the border of his inheritance in Timnath-heres, in the hill-country of Ephraim, on the north of the mountain of Gaash. 10 And also all that generation were gathered unto their fathers: and there arose another generation after them, that knew not Jehovah, nor yet the work which he had wrought for Israel.

This passage specifically relates the period of the judges to the time of Joshua so that a continuity is established. Joshua's dismissal of the people (v. 6) refers to their assembly at Shechem where the covenant relation with the Lord had been renewed (cf. Josh. 24).

From this time of covenant renewal until the death of Joshua **the people served Jehovah** (v. 7). The explicit reason for this faithful service was that these Israelites **who had seen all the great work of Jehovah . . . for Israel** were constantly reminded by Joshua concerning that which they had witnessed (v. 7).

However, with the death of Joshua a new era commenced with the rise of the second generation which had not witnessed the work . . . wrought for Israel (v. 10).

Ministers are particularly aware of this gap between generations. Illustrations may have a powerful impact upon those who have shared in the experiences illustrated, while others who have no such firsthand acquaintance are unimpressed. Just as this second generation of Israelites was unimpressed by witness to the great works of God, so many remain indifferent to the good news of the gospel. There is lacking a vital firsthand awareness of God and His redemption. Consequently, preaching falls on idle ears, not only because the hearers lack a vital sense of the divine, but also because the preacher may lack a consciousness of God as well.

B. ISRAEL'S DEFECTION (2:11-15)

11 And the children of Israel did that which was evil in the sight of Jehovah, and served the Baalim; 12 and they forsook Jehovah, the God of their fathers, who brought them out of the land of Egypt, and followed other gods, of the gods of the peoples that were round about them, and bowed themselves down unto them: and they provoked Jehovah to anger. 13 And they forsook Jehovah, and served Baal and the Ashtaroth. 14 And the anger of Jehovah was kindled against Israel, and he delivered them into the hands of spoilers that despoiled them; and he sold them into the hands of their enemies round about, so that they could not any longer stand before their enemies. 15 Whithersoever they went out, the hand of Jehovah was against them for evil, as Jehovah had spoken, and as Jehovah had sworn unto them: and they were sore distressed.

To understand the temptation of Israel to forsake Jehovah her God and to serve Baal and the Ashtaroth, some knowledge of the religion of Baal is needed. Baal-worship was the dominant religion of the Canaanites at this time. *Baal,* meaning "lord," was the name given to the male deity who owned the land and governed its fertility. The personal name of the female consort of Baal was Ashtaroth.

The Canaanites viewed the marvelous productivity of nature from a religious standpoint. The grape vineyards and the grain fields were owned by Baal and their productivity depended upon the sexual relations between him and the female deity, Ashtaroth.

The people endeavored to induce this intercourse between Baal and Ashtaroth by temple rituals that imitated the relations between the two deities. Thus, the magic power of the temple ritual of the Canaanites stimulated Baal in his fertility actions with his consort. The Canaanites performed their erotic rituals in an attempt to stimulate the rhythms of the agricultural realm.

The Ras Shamra tablets, first discovered in 1929 on the coast of northern Syria, give firsthand information about the Canaanite religious practices and rituals. Baal-worship was ingrained into the agricultural practices of the people. Anderson says:

> To have ignored the Baal rites in those days would have seemed as impractical as for a modern farmer to ignore science in the cultivation of the land.[3]

The Canaanite religion, on the one hand, maintained that the divine powers were disclosed in the realm of nature through sex and the mystery of fertility. There was a recurring cycle in this religion grounded in nature. As the Canaanite looked upon nature he saw evidence of this recurring cyclical pattern.

The religion of Israel, on the other hand, held that the power of the divine was disclosed in the realm of history. It was in this realm that the non-recurring events such as the Exodus and the Sinaitic covenant revealed the Jehovah who had chosen to enter into covenant relation with Israel. Jehovah was not stimulated by the magic of ritual; He called Israel to trust and obey. The Canaanite religion forced Israel to face a vital question: Was the meaning and purpose for Israel's existence realized in her relation to the divine powers within nature, or in her relation to the God of history?

Israel's defection from Jehovah to Baal is evidence that she sought to find the meaning and purpose for her existence in her relation to the powers within nature. Yet the God of history would not allow her to pursue her quest along this line. **The anger of Jehovah was kindled against Israel . . . and he sold them into the hands of their enemies . . .** (v. 14).

3 Bernhard W. Anderson, *Understanding the Old Testament,* p. 100.

C. JEHOVAH'S DELIVERANCE (2:16-19).

16 And Jehovah raised up judges, who saved them out of the hand of those that despoiled them. 17 And yet they hearkened not unto their judges; for they played the harlot after other gods, and bowed themselves down unto them: they turned aside quickly out of the way wherein their fathers walked, obeying the commandments of Jehovah; *but* they did not so. 18 And when Jehovah raised them up judges, then Jehovah was with the judge, and saved them out of the hand of their enemies all the days of the judge: for it repented Jehovah because of their groaning by reason of them that oppressed them and vexed them. 19 But it came to pass, when the judge was dead, that they turned back, and dealt more corruptly than their fathers, in following other gods to serve them, and to bow down unto them; they ceased not from their doings, nor from their stubborn way.

In order to understand Judges 2:6—3:6 as an introduction to the accounts of the judges, it is necessary to realize that the author is here giving a definite view of history. As Payne says,

> The author of Judges was . . . not simply recording events, but then interpreting the facts on the basis of an explicit philosophy of history.[4]

This Deuteronomic view of history followed a specific pattern: when Israel sinned and disobeyed, the Lord punished with oppression; when Israel repented, the Lord sent His Spirit upon judges who delivered the people from oppression.

This view of history does not allow for a straightforward chronicling of the events during the period of the judges. The main interest centered not upon a chronicle of events but upon the lesson which the events of this period revealed. In this connection, Moore writes:

> This general introduction contains an interpretation and judgment of the history of the whole period. . . . The lesson of the history is . . . the chief thing.[5]

This lesson is illustrated by means of the cyclical pattern used for giving the stories of the judges. Because Israel had sinned she was oppressed. Because of great distress by reason of her oppression Israel cried to the Lord in repentance and He raised up deliverers. These were special persons whom the Spirit of the Lord anointed and endowed with special abilities.

The history of Israel is evidence of the truth of this view. On the basis of the reliability of the historical data, this Deuteronomic view of history is relevant to the contemporary scene. The preacher has authority to declare that sin is under judgment and that a people who sins against God will be punished. On the other hand, the oppressed nation that repents may receive mercy.

D. ISRAEL'S DISCIPLINE (2:20—3:6)

20 And the anger of Jehovah was kindled against Israel; and he said, Because this nation have transgressed my covenant which I commanded their fathers, and have not hearkened unto my voice; 21 I also will not henceforth drive out any from before them of the nations that Joshua left when he died; 22 that by them I may prove Israel, whether they will keep the way of Jehovah to walk therein, as their fathers did keep it, or not. 23 So Jehovah left those nations, without driving them out hastily; neither delivered he them into the hand of Joshua.

1 Now these are the nations which Jehovah left, to prove Israel by them, even as many *of Israel* as had not known all the wars of Canaan; 2 only that the generations of the children of Israel might know, to teach them war, at the least such as beforetime knew nothing thereof: 3 *namely*, the five lords of the Philistines, and all the Canaanites, and the Sidonians, and the Hivites that dwelt in mount Lebanon, from mount Baal-hermon unto the entrance of Hamath. 4 And they were *left*, to prove Israel by them, to know whether they would hearken unto the commandments of Jehovah, which he commanded their fathers by Moses. 5 And the children of Israel dwelt among the Canaanites, the Hittites, and the Amorites, and the Perizzites, and the Hivites, and the Jebusites: 6 and they took their daughters to be their wives, and gave their own daughters to their sons and served their gods.

---

[4] J. B. Payne, "Judges," NBD, p. 679.
[5] G. F. Moore, "A Critical and Exegetical Commentary on Judges," *International Critical Commentary*, 2nd ed., pp. 62, 63.

Israel's persistent defection caused the anger of Jehovah to be kindled (v. 20). The divine word declared, Because this nation have transgressed my covenant . . . I also will not henceforth drive out any from before them of the nations . . . that by them I may prove Israel (vv. 20-22).

Israel's failure to conquer the promised land completely was interpreted to be a means through which God was to test the faithfulness of His people. From simply the historical point of view Israel had failed. Yet biblical history is the interpretation of developments as well as the recording of them. Why had Israel failed? Transgression was the obvious explanation, but it was not the complete explanation. The Deuteronomic explanation includes another dimension in the answer: Israel had transgressed, but God was acting redemptively in this very situation of transgression. This actual activity of God for good, precisely in the crux of Israel's evil activity, helps in understanding God's concern for history.

The God of Israel did not force the trial upon Israel through absolute, sovereign power. Rather, this evil situation was the occasion for God to test His people. The process appears to have the semblance of cruelty, but that is because we forget that God is using an evil development in Israel's history to accomplish merciful redemption. The astonishing and incomprehensible fact is that God's redemptive activity was wrought out in the very circumstances that caused Israel to transgress. The very presence and pressure of the Canaanites with their culture and religion, while being a temptation to Israel to capitulate, served also as a means of proving and purifying Israel.

This appears to be a mark of the gracious providence of God which is observable throughout the cosmos. Nations as well as individuals develop in this manner. To be sure, this has the appearance of a calculated risk. There is no inherent guarantee that the development of a nation or of an individual life will be accomplished.

Yet just as wise parents realize that the sheltered child who never faces temptation and opposition is not developing as he should, so God knows the necessity of developing His children. As many in later life acknowledge their debt to the test, the opposition, the affliction, so the author, looking back, saw the providence of God in Israel's history during the turbulent times of the judges. So Jehovah left those nations, without driving them out hastily (v. 23).

III. OTHNIEL, EHUD, SHAMGAR (Judg. 3:7-31)

A. ISRAEL'S DEFECTION AND DIVINE DELIVERANCE BY OTHNIEL (3:7-11)

7 And the children of Israel did that which was evil in the sight of Jehovah, and forgat Jehovah their God, and served the Baalim and the Asheroth. 8 Therefore the anger of Jehovah was kindled against Israel, and he sold them into the hand of Cushan-rishathaim king of Mesopotamia: and the children of Israel served Cushan-rishathaim eight years. 9 And when the children of Israel cried unto Jehovah, Jehovah raised up a saviour to the children of Israel, who saved them, even Othniel the son of Kenaz, Caleb's younger brother. 10 And the Spirit of Jehovah came upon him, and he judged Israel; and he went out to war, and Jehovah delivered Cushan-rishathaim king of Mesopotamia into his hand: and his hand prevailed against Cushan-rishathaim. 11 And the land had rest forty years. And Othniel the son of Kenaz died.

The first historical incident of the period of the judges is the invasion by the king of Mesopotamia because Israel served the Baalim and the Asheroth (v. 7).

According to Garstang,

The oppression evidently affected chiefly, if not entirely, the southernmost tribes, and did not call for a general effort to drive out the invaders.[6]

It is really impossible to determine the territorial extent of the oppression because the record is fragmentary. It is strange that a king from Mesopotamia should have been repulsed by a deliverer from the southern part of Judah. Othniel had received his inheritance in the Negeb in southern Judah.

To what extent, geographically, the

---

[6] John Garstang, *Foundations of Bible History, Joshua and Judges*, p. 264.

land was oppressed is not known. What is known is that the people of the oppressed territory **cried unto the Lord** (v. 9). The nature deities, Baal and Ashtaroth, were helpless when the historical reality of war and servitude confronted the Israelites. Historical reality compelled Israel in humiliation to acknowledge that not Baal but Jehovah was the Lord of history.

Jehovah raised up a saviour . . . even Othniel (v. 9). Doubtless this younger brother of Caleb had firsthand knowledge of Caleb's heroic service to God and to Israel. Now the Lord called the younger brother to deliver Israel.

The Spirit of Jehovah came upon him (v. 10). With the Spirit of God upon him, Othniel went forth from Judah **and he judged Israel; and he went out to war** (v. 10). Othniel's Spirit-directed field generalship overpowered the occupation forces of the king of Mesopotamia and hurled them back from the borders of the tribes. Here was clear-cut victory, comparable to the victories of Joshua and of Othniel's older brother, Caleb. However, its objective was limited, for Othniel was not fighting to complete the conquest of the land. His mission was to remove the oppressive judgment of God upon disobedient Israel. It remained to be seen whether Israel would prove true to Jehovah when the disciplinary chastisement was removed.

B. ISRAEL'S DEFECTION AND DIVINE DELIVERANCE BY EHUD (3:12-30)

12 And the children of Israel again did that which was evil in the sight of Jehovah: and Jehovah strengthened Eglon the king of Moab against Israel, because they had done that which was evil in the sight of Jehovah. 13 And he gathered unto him the children of Ammon and Amalek; and he went and smote Israel, and they possessed the city of palm-trees. 14 And the children of Israel served Eglon the king of Moab eighteen years. 15 But when the children of Israel cried unto Jehovah, Jehovah raised them up a saviour, Ehud the son of Gera, the Benjamite, a man left-handed. And the children of Israel sent tribute by him unto Eglon the king of Moab. 16 And Ehud made him a sword which had two edges, a cubit in length; and he girded it under his raiment upon his right

thigh. 17 And he offered the tribute unto Eglon king of Moab: now Eglon was a very fat man. 18 And when he had made an end of offering the tribute, he sent away the people that bare the tribute. 19 But he himself turned back from the quarries that were by Gilgal, and said, I have a secret errand unto thee, O king. And he said, Keep silence. And all that stood by him went out from him. 20 And Ehud came unto him; and he was sitting by himself alone in the cool upper room. And Ehud said, I have a message from God unto thee. And he arose out of his seat. 21 And Ehud put forth his left hand, and took the sword from his right thigh, and thrust it into his body: 22 and the haft also went in after the blade; and the fat closed upon the blade, for he drew not the sword out of his body; and it came out behind. 23 Then Ehud went forth into the porch, and shut the doors of the upper room upon him, and locked them.

24 Now when he was gone out, his servants came; and they saw, and, behold, the doors of the upper room were locked; and they said, Surely he is covering his feet in the upper chamber. 25 And they tarried till they were ashamed; and, behold, he opened not the doors of the upper room: therefore they took the key, and opened *them;* and, behold, their lord was fallen down dead on the earth.

26 And Ehud escaped while they tarried, and passed beyond the quarries, and escaped unto Seirah. 27 And it came to pass, when he was come, that he blew a trumpet in the hill-country of Ephraim; and the children of Israel went down with him from the hill-country, and he before them. 28 And he said unto them, Follow after me; for Jehovah hath delivered your enemies the Moabites into your hand. And they went down after him, and took the fords of the Jordan against the Moabites, and suffered not a man to pass over. 29 And they smote of Moab at that time about ten thousand men, every lusty man, and every man of valor; and there escaped not a man. 30 So Moab was subdued that day under the hand of Israel. And the land had rest fourscore years.

The historical narrative reveals that Israel could not resist temptation, and **again did that which was evil . . .** (v. 12). As a result, invaders from the east crossed the Jordan and captured Jericho. Moabites, Ammonites and Amalekites formed an impressive threat to the well-being of the southern and central tribes.

For eighteen years this confederation of foreign might dominated the central territory.

Finally, Israel turned from nature worship and again called upon the Lord of history. **Jehovah raised them up a saviour, Ehud . . . the Benjamite** (v. 15).

Ehud's tribal territory had been affected by the Moabite invasion. Throughout the years of occupation the Moabites had demanded tribute money from the central tribes. On this particular occasion, Ehud was selected by his people to head the delegation taking the regular tribute to Eglon, king of Moab. He carefully plotted to strike a blow for the freedom of his people.

After the delegation had paid the tribute, Ehud requested and was granted a private audience with the king. Doubtless Ehud's left-handedness was an important element of surprise, a kind of secret weapon in its own right. King Eglon would not expect the manipulation of a dagger with the left hand.

The element of surprise is always an important factor at critical moments. This applies to individuals as well as to nations. It applies to the forces working for God and His people as well as the forces working for evil and oppression.

Followers of the Lord need to consider their own capabilities and aptitudes. They may possess just the faculty that will result, under God, in some outstanding achievement. "Little is much if God is in it."

C. DIVINE DELIVERANCE BY SHAMGAR (3:31)

31 And after him was Shamgar the son of Anath, who smote of the Philistines six hundred men with an ox-goad: and he also saved Israel.

After Ehud's notable victory over the Moabites, who had come from the east side of the Jordan, there came from the southwest a force of Philistines into Judah. They were challenged by one man armed with an ox-goad — a long-handled, pointed stick. This lone challenger smote six hundred Philistines of the invading force. F. F. Bruce allows that this man, Shamgar, the son of Anath, may have been a Canaanite whose exploit afforded

the neighboring Israelites some relief.[7] Regardless of his nationality, Shamgar also saved Israel (v. 31).

IV. DEBORAH AND BARAK (Judg. 4:1–5:31)

The Canaanite oppression under Jabin and divine deliverance by the prophetess Deborah and the warrior Barak is given in two accounts, one in prose (chap. 4) and one in poetry (chap. 5).

A. THE PROSE STORY (4:1-24)

The prose account tells of a woman, Deborah, who amid an increasingly serious crisis challenged a warrior, Barak, to lead the army of Israel against an ever-growing tyranny of the Canaanites and to an astonishing and overwhelming victory.

1. The Oppression by the Canaanites (4:1-3)

1 And the children of Israel again did that which was evil in the sight of Jehovah, when Ehud was dead. 2 And Jehovah sold them into the hand of Jabin king of Canaan, that reigned in Hazor; the captain of whose host was Sisera, who dwelt in Harosheth of the Gentiles. 3 And the children of Israel cried unto Jehovah: for he had nine hundred chariots of iron; and twenty years he mightily oppressed the children of Israel.

Previous accounts in Judges of oppressions of the Israelites indicate that the southern and central parts of Canaan were affected. Now, oppression occurred in the northern part. Tribes such as Issachar, Zebulun and Naphtali were directly affected the most. In a larger sense, the national unity of Israel was involved.

Garstang gives an excellent account of the historical occasion for this oppression. His view is that Sisera had gained territory in the plain of Acco at Harosheth and had made an alliance with Jabin of Hazor in the form of mercenary service. Sisera embarked upon a period of unrestrained tyranny which threatened the very existence of several northern tribes and imperiled all the tribes. Garstang says:

This state of affairs plunged Israel in jeopardy. . . . It was at this crisis, the

---

[7] Bruce, *op. cit.*, p. 1170.

gravest which had menaced the growing nation, that Deborah the prophetess arose and gathered the tribes together, 'a mother in Israel.'[8]

The author of Judges asserts that Israel's disobedience was the cause of the oppression. As the people recognized this and **cried unto Jehovah** (v. 3) there came promise of divine help. Here is a crystal-clear example of the Deuteronomic understanding of the history of Israel. As long as Israel wholly followed the Lord there was progress towards complete occupation of the land and possession of the inheritance. However, when Israel sinned she was in jeopardy, and was subjected to the peril of tyranny.

2. The Command of the Lord (4:4-11)

4 Now Deborah, a prophetess, the wife of Lappidoth, she judged Israel at that time. 5 And she dwelt under the palm-tree of Deborah between Ramah and Beth-el in the hill-country of Ephraim: and the children of Israel came up to her for judgment. 6 And she sent and called Barak the son of Abinoam out of Kedesh-naphtali, and said unto him, Hath not Jehovah, the God of Israel, commanded, *saying*, Go and draw unto mount Tabor, and take with thee ten thousand men of the children of Naphtali and of the children of Zebulun? 7 And I will draw unto thee, to the river Kishon, Sisera, the captain of Jabin's army, with his chariots and his multitude; and I will deliver him into thy hand. 8 And Barak said unto her, If thou wilt go with me, then I will go; but if thou wilt not go with me, I will not go. 9 And she said, I will surely go with thee: notwithstanding, the journey that thou takest shall not be for thine honor; for Jehovah will sell Sisera into the hand of a woman. And Deborah arose, and went with Barak to Kedesh. 10 And Barak called Zebulun and Naphtali together to Kedesh; and there went up ten thousand men at his feet: and Deborah went up with him. 11 Now Heber the Kenite had separated himself from the Kenites, even from the children of Hobab the brother-in-law of Moses, and had pitched his tent as far as the oak in Zaanannim, which is by Kedesh.

During a part of the twenty years that Sisera had engaged in expanding his tyrannical regime over the northern part of Canaan, Deborah was active in central Canaan as a charismatic leader. Her spirit of prophecy and her wisdom in settling disputes had caused her name and work to be known to many. The Spirit of the Lord was upon her.

To this woman, who saw the oppressive condition of the tribes and who knew of their repentance, came the command of the Lord: **Go . . . and I will draw . . . Sisera . . . and . . . deliver him into your hand** (vv. 6, 7). The crisis was serious and deliverance was imperative. Deborah sent for Barak, who lived in the territory which was affected the most by Sisera's activities and who may have been Sisera's prisoner for a time.[9]

The summons for Barak came from the Lord through the prophetess. She told Barak to assemble ten thousand fighting men at Mount Tabor, which is located about fifteen miles east of Harosheth and on the northern side of the plain of Esdraelon. For Sisera to engage in combat with Barak, it was necessary for him to move his chariots across the plain to the place of battle. As long as Barak kept his men in the hill country it was impossible for Sisera's chariots to do battle effectively.

In all of this obedience to the command of the Lord there appears in striking contrast the forthright courage of Deborah and the faltering hesitancy of Barak. In reply to her summons, **Go and draw unto mount Tabor** (v. 6), Barak answered, **If thou wilt go with me, then I will go; but if thou wilt not go with me, I will not go** (v. 8). Unhesitatingly, Deborah replied, **I will surely go with thee**, and courageously she **arose, and went with Barak** (v. 9). The confident and decisive courage of Deborah was a powerful force upon Barak and his men. This is always so. A person who is powerfully moved by convictions in a moment of crisis has great influence upon the uncertain and hesitating person. When those convictions are in harmony with the will of God, this forthrightness is a great force in stirring others to accept their God-given responsibilities.

8 Garstang, *op. cit.*, p. 294.
9 G. A. Cooke, "Barak," *Dictionary of the Bible*, ed. by J. Hastings, I, 246.

Because of Barak's hesitancy another element was injected into the scene. Deborah foretold that a woman rather than Barak would destroy Sisera. This woman was Jael, a Kenite who had come with her husband from southern Canaan to Kedesh in the plain of Esdraelon. Her loyalty to the Israelites rather than to the Canaanites is a stirring parallel to the faith and loyalty of Rahab the Canaanite at Jericho, when Joshua led Israel to triumph (Josh. 2).

3. The Battle of Kishon (4:12-16)

12 And they told Sisera that Barak the son of Abinoam was gone up to mount Tabor. 13 And Sisera gathered together all his chariots, even nine hundred chariots of iron, and all the people that were with him, from Harosheth of the Gentiles, unto the river Kishon. 14 And Deborah said unto Barak, Up; for this is the day in which Jehovah hath delivered Sisera into thy hand; is not Jehovah gone out before thee? So Barak went down from mount Tabor, and ten thousand men after him. 15 And Jehovah discomfited Sisera, and all his chariots, and all his host, with the edge of the sword before Barak; and Sisera alighted from his chariot, and fled away on his feet. 16 But Barak pursued after the chariots, and after the host, unto Harosheth of the Gentiles: and all the host of Sisera fell by the edge of the sword; there was not a man left.

Barak made no attempt to hide his movements as he assembled his men at Mount Tabor. Sisera was told of the movements of the Israelites. He **gathered together all his chariots, even nine hundred chariots of iron, and all the people that were with him** (v. 13). This was a most formidable force arrayed against Barak. Israel had nothing equivalent to Sisera's chariots of iron. Furthermore, Israel was not prepared for war. Men were not trained; weapons were totally inadequate.

However, it was not Sisera that took the offensive. As he was maneuvering his army into position against Barak, it was the prophetess that saw the moment of opportunity. Just as maneuvers reached the critical stage, rain began to fall and turned to such a downpour that the battlefield became a quagmire and the little Kishon became a raging torrent. Deborah commanded, **Up; for this is the day in which Jehovah hath delivered Sisera into thy hand; is not Jehovah gone out before thee?** (v. 14). Upon receiving this message from the prophetess, Barak rallied his men and went forth to battle against Sisera. On that day the Lord of history defeated Sisera through the combination of men and nature. The victory removed the oppression upon the northern tribes, improved the progress toward increased union of the tribes of Israel, and caused Israel to know that the Lord rewards faithful obedience.

4. The Death of Sisera (4:17-24)

17 Howbeit Sisera fled away on his feet to the tent of Jael the wife of Heber the Kenite; for there was peace between Jabin the king of Hazor and the house of Heber the Kenite. 18 And Jael went out to meet Sisera, and said unto him, Turn in, my lord, turn in to me; fear not. And he turned in unto her into the tent, and she covered him with a rug. 19 And he said unto her, Give me, I pray thee, a little water to drink; for I am thirsty. And she opened a bottle of milk, and gave him drink, and covered him. 20 And he said unto her, Stand in the door of the tent, and it shall be, when any man doth come and inquire of thee, and say, Is there any man here? that thou shalt say, No. 21 Then Jael Heber's wife took a tent-pin, and took a hammer in her hand, and went softly unto him, and smote the pin into his temples, and it pierced through into the ground; for he was in a deep sleep; so he swooned and died. 22 And, behold, as Barak pursued Sisera, Jael came out to meet him, and said unto him, Come, and I will show thee the man whom thou seekest. And he came unto her; and, behold, Sisera lay dead, and the tent-pin was in his temples.

23 So God subdued on that day Jabin the king of Canaan before the children of Israel. 24 And the hand of the children of Israel prevailed more and more against Jabin the king of Canaan, until they had destroyed Jabin king of Canaan.

Sisera, realizing catastrophe had fallen upon him, left his chariot and fled from the battlefield on foot. He had not gone far until he came to the tent of Jael, the wife of Heber the Kenite. Sisera apparently saw no cause for distrusting these Kenites who had migrated to the north and were on peaceful terms with Jabin, king of Hazor. Jael welcomed him and gave him food and a place to sleep.

While Sisera slept Jael killed him. When Barak came by she went out to him and told him she would show him the man he was seeking. When Barak saw that the man was Sisera, he doubtless remembered the prophecy of Deborah. The Israelites proclaimed this Kenite woman a national heroine.

B. THE POETIC SONG (5:1-31)

Bruce states:
The song of Deborah has been preserved from the 12th century B.C. with its language practically unmodernized. . . . It was evidently composed on the morrow of the victory which it celebrates.[10]

It is "the almost unanimous judgment of scholars" that its origin was "contemporary with the events it describes. . . . Hence as a source for the history of the period it is unsurpassed."[11]

The song is arbitrarily divided into six strophes of comparable length in the ASV. This artificiality of the balanced structuring of the song is downgraded by some, but it does not appear to be a serious concern in the over-all picture portrayed by the song. This balance of six fairly equal strophes by competent scholars, though not above criticism, raises no serious problem for our study.

1. Praise (5:1-5)

1 Then sang Deborah and Barak the son of Abinoam' on that day, saying,
2 For that the leaders took the lead in Israel,
For that the people offered themselves willingly,
Bless ye Jehovah.
3 Hear, O ye kings; give ear, O ye princes;
I, *even* I, will sing unto Jehovah;
I will sing praise to Jehovah, the God of Israel.
4 Jehovah, when thou wentest forth out of Seir,
When thou marchedst out of the field of Edom,
The earth trembled, the heavens also dropped,
Yea, the clouds dropped water.
5 The mountains quaked at the presence of Jehovah,
Even yon Sinai at the presence of Jehovah, the God of Israel.

The song of Deborah begins with praise because of the victory which the Lord accomplished for Israel. Essentially, this song was dedicated to the Lord because of His active presence with His people and His ordering of the elements of nature against the enemies of His people. There is evident in this song an almost overwhelming sense of divine participation in the total scene, beginning with God's summons to Deborah and Barak and culminating in the victorious battle against Sisera. From first to last it had been the Lord.

The spontaneity of praise is reflected in the contemporaneous origin of this song. Immediately Israel, led by Deborah, burst forth into jubilant praise.

This note of spontaneous, jubilant praise for God's presence is part of the heritage of the Judeo-Christian tradition. Again and again, people within this tradition have given praise to God because they have had vital occasion to do so. The living Lord still is actively present, and awareness of His great deliverances still occasions praise.

2. Oppression (5:6-11)

6 In the days of Shamgar the son of Anath,
In the days of Jael, the highways were unoccupied,
And the travellers walked through byways.
7 The rulers ceased in Israel, they ceased,
Until that I Deborah arose,
That I arose a mother in Israel.
8 They chose new gods;
Then was war in the gates:
Was there a shield or spear seen Among forty thousand in Israel?
9 My heart is toward the governors of Israel,
That offered themselves willingly among the people:
Bless ye Jehovah.
10 Tell *of it*, ye that ride on white asses,
Ye that sit on rich carpets,
And ye that walk by the way.
11 Far from the noise of archers, in the places of drawing water,
There shall they rehearse the righteous acts of Jehovah,
Even the righteous acts of his rule in Israel.
Then the people of Jehovah went down to the gates.

---

[10] Bruce, *op. cit.*, p. 303.   [11] Myers, *op. cit.*, II, 717, 718.

The song relates the developments in chronological sequence. The oppression had become critical. The locale included the plain of Esdraelon and the valley of Jezreel. The tribe of Issachar which had inherited this area was especially imperiled and helpless to ward off the might of Sisera. However, control of this area was not only oppressive to the local tribe, but **the highways were unoccupied** (v. 6). Normally busy travel routes connecting Mesopotamia and Egypt passed through this territory. These main arteries of travel and commerce were now unused, thus jeopardizing international commerce. Also, the unity of the tribal league of Israel was impossible. The northern tribes such as Asher, Naphtali, Zebulun and Dan were isolated from the central and southern tribes. The whole scene is depicted graphically by the reference to travel having shifted from the highways to the by-ways. Here travelers could move with less likelihood of detection by the ruling power.

The international scene offered little prospect for relief from this oppression. Egypt, as well as Mesopotamia, was in no position to interfere with Sisera's ambitions for an expanding empire. Those two nations were occupied with their own internal concerns.

The tribes of Israel were unprepared and ill-organized. There was insufficient equipment to put enough armed Israelites on the battlefield to offer serious resistance to Sisera.

3. Roll Call (5:12-18)

12 Awake, awake, Deborah;
    Awake, awake, utter a song:
    Arise, Barak, and lead away thy captives, thou son of Abinoam.
13 Then came down a remnant of the nobles *and* the people;
    Jehovah came down for me against the mighty.
14 Out of Ephraim *came down* they whose root is in Amalek;
    After thee, Benjamin, among thy peoples;
    Out of Machir came down governors,
    And out of Zebulun they that handle the marshal's staff.
15 And the princes of Issachar were with Deborah;
    As was Issachar, so was Barak;

Into the valley they rushed forth at his feet.
    By the watercourses of Reuben
    There were great resolves of heart.
16 Why sattest thou among the sheepfolds,
    To hear the pipings for the flocks?
    At the watercourses of Reuben
    There were great searchings of heart.
17 Gilead abode beyond the Jordan:
    And Dan, why did he remain in ships?
    Asher sat still at the haven of the sea,
    And abode by his creeks.
18 Zebulun was a people that jeoparded their lives unto the death,
    And Naphtali, upon the high places of the field.

First called to awake to the occasion were Deborah and Barak. They resolved to free their people from the Canaanites. Accordingly, the tribes of Israel were summoned. Those that responded indicate the locale threatened by Sisera's tyranny. Ephraim, Benjamin, Machir (Manasseh), Zebulun and Naphtali rallied to aid Issachar. Especially the two tribes which were closest to the distress caused by Sisera were cited for heroism. **Zebulun was a people that jeoparded their lives unto the death, and Naphtali, upon the high places of the field** (v. 18).

Four tribes were given severe rebukes for their unresponsiveness to the call to arms. They were Reuben, Gilead (Gad), Dan and Asher, all located on the periphery of the troubled area. While Reuben had **great resolves of heart** and **great searchings of heart**, there was no decisive action (vv. 15, 16). This was the essence of the rebuke. More than pious sentiment and compassionate thoughts were needed. Overt assistance was called for, but the danger seemed too far away. However, the composer of the song of Deborah looked upon Sisera as a threat to all of Israel.[12]

4. Battle (5:19-23)

19 The kings came forth and fought;
    Then fought the kings of Canaan,
    In Taanach by the waters of Megiddo:
    They took no gain of money.
20 From heaven fought the stars,
    From their courses they fought against Sisera.
21 The river Kishon swept them away,
    That ancient river, the river Kishon.
    O my soul, march on with strength.

22 Then did the horsehoofs stamp
   By reason of the prancings, the
   prancings of their strong ones.
23 Curse ye Meroz, said the angel of
   Jehovah,
   Curse ye bitterly the inhabitants
   thereof,
   Because they came not to the help of
   Jehovah,
   To the help of Jehovah against the
   mighty.

For the first time after the settlement in Canaan the majority of the tribes acted unitedly.[13] It is possible to place Deborah about midway in the period of the judges. Much of the credit for bringing about this united effort must be attributed to the Spirit-anointed genius and courage of this woman-prophetess.

Sisera's mobile army, moving swiftly by means of the iron chariots, attacked the united armies of the tribes of Israel at the Kishon River. However, a great rainstorm deluged the battle area, and the flooding Kishon swept the proud charioteers and their steeds away. This outstanding victory can be accounted for only by what God did through the implementation of natural forces. The song of Deborah clearly expresses the faith of ancient Israel in the God of heaven and earth. More than natural phenomena are here involved. The historical character of God's activity is inherent in Israel's faith.

The reference to Meroz in verse 23 is highly uncertain. A likely explanation is that it refers to a village in Issachar near the battle scene which refused to join the Israelites, possibly for fear of reprisals from Sisera. If this is true it illustrates the displeasure of God upon those who through lack of faith regard their own safety and well-being more highly than the ongoing of the Kingdom of God.

5. Jael (5:24-27)

24 Blessed above women shall Jael be,
   The wife of Heber the Kenite;
   Blessed shall she be above women in
   the tent.
25 He asked water, *and* she gave him
   milk;
   She brought him butter in a lordly
   dish.
26 She put her hand to the tent-pin,

And her right hand to the workmen's
   hammer;
   And with the hammer she smote
   Sisera, she smote through his head;
   Yea, she pierced and struck through
   his temples.
27 At her feet he bowed, he fell, he lay;
   At her feet he bowed, he fell:
   Where he bowed, there he fell down
   dead.

Certain of the tribes of Israel and Meroz were singled out with justifiable criticism. They were blamed for inaction in a time of crisis that demanded resolute bravery. Their failure to act indicated their lack of faith.

On the other hand, other tribes, together with Jael, a Kenite, were cited for courageous action. The tent of Heber, the Kenite, was not far from the battle scene. After the heavy rain and the flooded river had caused Sisera's army to panic, Sisera was running for his very life. In his flight he came to Heber's tent.

Jael, the wife of Heber, while manifesting atrocious ethics, expressed a faith and loyalty that won for her the acclaim of the song of Deborah. The paradox seems difficult to resolve. Jael may have been accountable for wrong conduct, but the whole point of the song of Deborah is that a crisis demanded action against an aggressor. The God of Israel expected His people to meet the crisis with courageous faith. Even a foreign woman expressed her allegiance. For this she was justly praised. The action of Jael, though not without its moral difficulties from the contemporary point of view, stands in vivid contrast to the indecisiveness of tribes who were on the periphery. This woman in the very midst of the critically oppressed region made a memorable contribution to the victory over Sisera.

6. The Mother of Sisera (5:28-31)

28 Through the window she looked forth,
   and cried,
   The mother of Sisera *cried* through
   the lattice,
   Why is his chariot so long in coming?
   Why tarry the wheels of his chariots?
29 Her wise ladies answered her,
   Yea, she returned answer to herself,
30 Have they not found, have they not
   divided the spoil?

---

[13] Cooke, "Deborah," *Dictionary of the Bible*, I, 578.

A damsel, two damsels to every man;
To Sisera a spoil of dyed garments,
A spoil of dyed garments embroidered,
Of dyed garments embroidered on
    both sides, on the necks of the spoil?
31 So let all thine enemies perish, O
    Jehovah:
But let them that love him be as the
    sun when he goeth forth in his
    might.
And the land had rest forty years.

The closing scene in the song of Deborah is that of the mother of Sisera anxiously awaiting the return of her son who will never return. She and her court attendants desperately hope against hope. The scene remains unfinished, and we are left to imagine the impact that the news of her son's death had upon this waiting mother.

The song of Deborah closes with the prayer that all of the enemies of the Lord may perish and that the friends of the Lord may bring blessing upon the land (v. 31).

V. GIDEON (Judg. 6:1—8:32)

The story of Gideon is one of the longer stories in the book of Judges. However, the same basic cyclical pattern of defection, punishment and deliverance which occurs again and again in the accounts of other judges occurs in the account of Gideon also. The Israelites disobeyed the Lord; the Lord delivered them into the hand of the Midianites for seven years; and the Spirit of the Lord came upon Gideon for the purpose of delivering his people. By far the greatest attention is given to the deliverance accomplished by the Lord through Gideon.

A. MIDIANITE RAIDS (6:1-10)

1 And the children of Israel did that which was evil in the sight of Jehovah: and Jehovah delivered them into the hand of Midian seven years. 2 And the hand of Midian prevailed against Israel; and because of Midian the children of Israel made them the dens which are in the mountains, and the caves, and the strongholds. 3 And so it was, when Israel had sown, that the Midianites came up, and the Amalekites, and the children of the east; they came up against them; 4 and they encamped against them, and destroyed the increase of the earth, till thou come unto Gaza, and left no sustenance in Israel, neither sheep, nor ox,

nor ass. 5 For they came up with their cattle and their tents; they came in as locusts for multitude; both they and their camels were without number: and they came into the land to destroy it. 6 And Israel was brought very low because of Midian; and the children of Israel cried unto Jehovah.

7 And it came to pass, when the children of Israel cried unto Jehovah because of Midian, 8 that Jehovah sent a prophet unto the children of Israel: and he said unto them, Thus saith Jehovah, the God of Israel, I brought you up from Egypt, and brought you forth out of the house of bondage; 9 and I delivered you out of the hand of the Egyptians, and out of the hand of all that oppressed you, and drove them out from before you, and gave you their land; 10 and I said unto you, I am Jehovah your God; ye shall not fear the gods of the Amorites, in whose land ye dwell. But ye have not hearkened unto my voice.

The children of Israel did that which was evil in the sight of Jehovah (v. 1). As a consequence, they were plagued by nomads from desert areas of the Arabian peninsula. Marauding bands of Midianite and Amalekite nomads, riding camels, crossed the Jordan valley and entered the plain of Esdraelon. They made their raids at the harvest season and plundered the crops of Israelites.

This happened annually for a period of seven years. The Israelites were again in desperate circumstances. Although they had diligently prepared the soil and planted the seed, they were thwarted in their attempts to reap a harvest. The fierce Midianites on their swift camels terrorized the land during the harvest season. Their forays surprised and overwhelmed the Israelites.

Having suffered years of this humiliating and impoverishing treatment, the Israelites began to pray to the Lord. The divine response to their prayers came first in the presence of an anonymous prophet. His message to Israel was that, although the gracious God of Israel had declared He was their God, they had not acknowledged His Lordship.

It is true that the Midianites had their own evil, selfish motives for plundering Israel: they were not consciously intent upon doing the service of Jehovah. However, the point to keep clearly in mind is that the Lord of history was using developments of historical character to accomplish His redemptive purposes for Israel. These were the means He was using to cause Israel to repent and return to Him. This profound concept of history undergirds the stories of the judges whom God anointed with His Spirit.

B. CALL OF GIDEON (6:11-32)

Gideon was of the tribe of West Manasseh (v. 15). His family lived at Ophrah. Harvest season had come and Gideon was helping gather in the grain. Normally, the grain was threshed on the ground in the open. However, the times were not normal because of the raids of the Midianites.

Gideon was harvesting grain in a **winepress** (v. 11), a large vat for crushing grapes. He kept noise to a minimum as he beat the straw. Hidden in the vat Gideon beat out the grain in small quantities. Though fearful of the Midianites, the need for food compelled him, as well as other Israelites, to harvest in unusual ways.

1. First Phase of the Call: Appearance of the Divine Messenger (6:11-24)

11 And the angel of Jehovah came, and sat under the oak which was in Ophrah, that pertained unto Joash the Abiezrite: and his son Gideon was beating out wheat in the winepress, to hide it from the Midianites. 12 And the angel of Jehovah appeared unto him, and said unto him, Jehovah. is with thee, thou mighty man of valor. 13 And Gideon said unto him, Oh, my lord, if Jehovah is with us, why then is all this befallen us? and where are all his wondrous works which our fathers told us of, saying, Did not Jehovah bring us up from Egypt? but now Jehovah hath cast us off, and delivered us into the hand of Midian. 14 And Jehovah looked upon him, and said, Go in this thy might, and save Israel from the hand of Midian: have not I sent thee? 15 And he said unto him, Oh, Lord, wherewith shall I save Israel? behold, my family is the poorest in Manasseh, and I am the least in my father's house. 16 And Jehovah said unto him, Surely I will be with thee, and thou shalt smite the Midianites as one man. 17 And he said unto him, If now I have found favor in thy sight, then show me a sign that it is thou that talkest with me. 18 Depart not hence, I pray thee, until I come unto thee, and bring forth my present, and lay it before thee. And he said, I will tarry until thou come again.

19 And Gideon went in, and made ready a kid, and unleavened cakes of an ephah of meal: the flesh he put in a basket, and he put the broth in a pot, and brought it out unto him under the oak, and presented it. 20 And the angel of God said unto him, Take the flesh and the unleavened cakes, and lay them upon this rock, and pour out the broth. And he did so. 21 Then the angel of Jehovah put forth the end of the staff that was in his hand, and touched the flesh and the unleavened cakes; and there went up fire out of the rock, and consumed the flesh and the unleavened cakes; and the angel of Jehovah departed out of his sight. 22 And Gideon saw that he was the angel of Jehovah; and Gideon said, Alas, O Lord Jehovah! forasmuch as I have seen the angel of Jehovah face to face. 23 And Jehovah said unto him, Peace be unto thee; fear not: thou shalt not die. 24 Then Gideon built an altar there unto Jehovah, and called it Jehovah-shalom: unto this day it is yet in Ophrah of the Abiezrites.

Gideon may have hidden well enough to escape detection by the Midianites, but God found him. In an unusual word of greeting, **the angel of Jehovah appeared unto him, and said unto him, Jehovah is with thee, thou mighty man of valor** (v. 12). At that particular time and place Gideon did not appear to be exemplary for his courage. He was hiding from the Midianites. If some passing band of Midianites were to discover him, they would rob him of what little he had, and he was helpless to resist them. Yet the angel called him a **mighty man of valor.**

Unaware of the identity of the messenger, Gideon replied, **If Jehovah is with us, why then is all this befallen us?** (v. 13). There is pathos in Gideon's question. He identified himself with his people. In his great concern over the conditions in Israel he replied, in effect, "Why say that Jehovah is with me when He has forsaken my people, the Israel of the Lord?"

The voice of command came to Gideon, **Go . . . save Israel . . .** (v. 14). He recoiled at the command, for he considered himself as the least of Israel and of his father's house. However, this mark of humility was a key to his outstanding deliverance of Israel. It is always a characteristic which God is pleased to use in His service. Some people, aware of their supposed humility, become proud. However, humility is not conscious of itself.

Unaware of the majesty of the person with whom he was speaking, Gideon expressed a desire to bring his visitor an offering. This included meat, cakes and broth. The visitor asked that this be placed upon a particular rock, from which fire came and consumed the food. At this the visitor vanished and Gideon realized with terror that he had looked upon the angel of Jehovah. He feared that the result would be death, but the word of the Lord to him was, **Peace be unto thee; fear not** (v. 23).

Gideon built an altar . . . and called it Jehovah-shalom (v. 24). An important and decisive change had come to Gideon. Prior to this he had been threshing grain in a wine press. He was filled with discouragement and despair; he was anxious and fearful. Now that he had met the Lord he had received the gracious, comforting words of peace and assurance.

Gideon's altar was a sign of an important change in his life. He had transferred his loyalties from Baal to the God who had given peace, something that Baal could not give. Further, Gideon's altar signified the reality of the peace which had come to him. Even amid the trying and frustrating circumstances occasioned by the marauding Midianites Gideon had received the peace of God.

2. Second Phase of the Call: Break Down the Altar to Baal (6:25-32)

25 And it came to pass the same night, that Jehovah said unto him, Take thy father's bullock, even the second bullock seven years old, and throw down the altar of Baal that thy father hath, and cut down the Asherah that is by it; 26 and build an altar unto Jehovah thy God upon the top of this stronghold, in the orderly manner, and take the second bullock, and offer a burnt-offering with the wood of the Asherah which thou shalt cut down. 27 Then Gideon took ten men of his servants, and did as Jehovah had spoken unto him: and it came to pass, because he feared his father's household and the men of the city, so that he could not do it by day, that he did it by night.

28 And when the men of the city arose early in the morning, behold, the altar of Baal was broken down, and the Asherah was cut down that was by it, and the second bullock was offered upon the altar that was built. 29 And they said one to another, Who hath done this thing? And when they inquired and asked, they said, Gideon the son of Joash hath done this thing. 30 Then the men of the city said unto Joash, Bring out thy son, that he may die, because he hath broken down the altar of Baal, and because he hath cut down the Asherah that was by it. 31 And Joash said unto all that stood against him, Will ye contend for Baal? or will ye save him? he that will contend for him, let him be put to death whilst it is yet morning: if he be a god, let him contend for himself, because one hath broken down his altar. 32 Therefore on that day he called him Jerubbaal, saying, Let Baal contend against him, because he hath broken down his altar.

The second phase of Gideon's call was to break down the altar of Baal which belonged to his father. Until this time, Gideon apparently saw no conflict between Baal-worship and Jehovah-worship. Yet this command signified that idolatry must be removed from within Israel before the outward enemies of Israel could be repelled. There must be a religious crusade against Baal before Israel would be ready to wage war against Midian. This is continually relevant. Doing the will of the God of peace means beginning at home to adjust to God's purposes before one is ready for service beyond.

Apparently aware of the uproar the pulling down of the altar of Baal would cause, Gideon performed this deed at night with the aid of servants. The next day there was considerable commotion about it. When it was discovered that Gideon was responsible the men of the city demanded his death. It may seem incredible that Gideon's townspeople were ready to kill him for this, but the incident shows all too clearly how entrenched the Baalism of the Canaanites had become in Israel. Israel, whom God intended to possess the land of Canaan, was now possessed by the god of the Canaanites.

Here is the grave peril in which the would-be followers of God so often stand.

Joash was ordered to surrender his son to death at the hands of the people. However, he refused, declaring that Baal must fight for himself. Anyone who would fight for Baal must face the possibility of death. Here was Gideon's first encouragement from human sources. His own father, apparently very influential in the town, had taken his stand on the side of Jehovah and Gideon. It had been a tense situation, with Gideon in real danger. The tide turned, however, and they called Gideon Jerubbaal, meaning that Gideon had defied Baal and gotten away with it. Baal himself must take any countermeasures that were to be taken.

The result was a new awareness of an awakening hope. The Lord was about to visit His people in mercy. The leader was the least member of the poorest family of the tribe of Manasseh — yet this man had received the peace of Jehovah and had defied Baal.

C. FLEECE TEST (6:33-40)

33 Then all the Midianites and the Amalekites and the children of the east assembled themselves together; and they passed over, and encamped in the valley of Jezreel. 34 But the Spirit of Jehovah came upon Gideon; and he blew a trumpet; and Abiezer was gathered together after him. 35 And he sent messengers throughout all Manasseh; and they also were gathered together after him: and he sent messengers unto Asher, and unto Zebulun, and unto Naphtali; and they came up to meet them.

36 And Gideon said unto God, If thou wilt save Israel by my hand, as thou hast spoken, 37 behold, I will put a fleece of wool on the threshing-floor; if there be dew on the fleece only, and it be dry upon all the ground, then shall I know that thou wilt save Israel by my hand, as thou hast spoken. 38 And it was so; for he rose up early on the morrow, and pressed the fleece together, and wrung the dew out of the fleece, a bowlful of water. 39 And Gideon said unto God, Let not thine anger be kindled against me, and I will speak but this once: let me make trial, I pray thee, but this once with the fleece; let it now be dry only upon the fleece, and upon all the ground let there be dew. 40 And God did so that night: for it was dry upon the fleece only, and there was dew on all the ground.

As in previous years the beginning of a new harvest season signaled the renewal of plunderings by the Midianites. They encamped in the valley of Jezreel, a most fruitful area. They seized the harvest and killed Israelites. Probably at this time the brothers of Gideon were killed at Tabor (8:18, 19).

Upon previous forays by the Midianites Gideon had looked on in helpless anger and frustration. Upon this occasion, the **Spirit of Jehovah came upon Gideon** (v. 34). The circumstances were the same; the man was the same. The great difference was in the coming of the Spirit of God upon the man. The marginal note gives the literal meaning of **came upon** as "clothed itself with." This expression denotes complete possession. Gideon became a God-possessed man. Deeper than possessing is being possessed.

As a result of this coming of the Spirit of God, Gideon sounded a trumpet call to arms. The first response came from the members of his own clan. They knew what had happened in Ophrah, and they were ready to follow Gideon, the one who had defied Baal and who now was preparing to battle against the Midianites. Here were those who knew Gideon best ready to join with him. The movement grew, with Manasseh, Asher, Zebulun and Naphtali responding to Gideon's summons.

Gideon found himself facing a climactic situation. The invading Midianites still stalked the land and Gideon had to decide whether to go on with his efforts or to withdraw. He could still turn back, but if he chose to continue his effort to drive out the Midianites there would be no turning back, for he would be forced to fight the Midianites. He would set in motion forces that by their very momentum would precipitate conflict.

In that supreme moment of decision Gideon made a test: **If thou wilt save Israel by my hand, as thou hast spoken, behold, I will put a fleece of wool on the threshing-floor** (vv. 36, 37). This was not a reflection of doubt but, rather, of dependency. Gideon had been reared amid Baal-worship. His knowledge of the ways of God was based upon past history.

"Where are all his wondrous works which our fathers told us . . ." (v. 13)? Present circumstances were very critical and Gideon knew it, but he had no firsthand knowledge of the power of God. So he asked for a sign and it was granted. Twice by the fleece test the Lord indicated that He would deliver Israel by means of Gideon.

D. DIVINE GUIDANCE TO GIDEON (7:1-14)

1 Then Jerubbaal, who is Gideon, and all the people that were with him, rose up early, and encamped beside the spring of Harod: and the camp of Midian was on the north side of them, by the hill of Moreh, in the valley.

2 And Jehovah said unto Gideon, The people that are with thee are too many for me to give the Midianites into their hand, lest Israel vaunt themselves against me, saying, Mine own hand hath saved me. 3 Now therefore proclaim in the ears of the people, saying, Whosoever is fearful and trembling, let him return and depart from mount Gilead. And there returned of the people twenty and two thousand; and there remained ten thousand.

4 And Jehovah said unto Gideon, The people are yet too many; bring them down unto the water, and I will try them for thee there: and it shall be, that of whom I say unto thee, This shall go with thee, the same shall go with thee; and of whomsoever I say unto thee, This shall not go with thee, the same shall not go. 5 So he brought down the people unto the water: and Jehovah said unto Gideon, Every one that lappeth of the water with his tongue, as a dog lappeth, him shalt thou set by himself; likewise every one that boweth down upon his knees to drink. 6 And the number of them that lapped, putting their hand to their mouth, was three hundred men: but all the rest of the people bowed down upon their knees to drink water. 7 And Jehovah said unto Gideon, By the three hundred men that lapped will I save you, and deliver the Midianites into thy hand; and let all the people go every man unto his place. 8 So the people took victuals in their hand, and their trumpets; and he sent all the men of Israel every man unto his tent, but retained the three hundred men: and the camp of Midian was beneath him in the valley.

9 And it came to pass the same night, that Jehovah said unto him, Arise, get thee down into the camp; for I have delivered it into thy hand. 10 But if thou fear to go down, go thou with Purah thy servant down to the camp: 11 and thou shalt hear what they say; and afterward shall thy hands be strengthened to go down into the camp. Then went he down with Purah his servant unto the outermost part of the armed men that were in the camp. 12 And the Midianites and the Amalekites and all the children of the east lay along in the valley like locusts for multitude; and their camels were without number, as the sand which is upon the seashore for multitude. 13 And when Gideon was come, behold, there was a man telling a dream unto his fellow; and he said, Behold, I dreamed a dream; and, lo, a cake of barley bread tumbled into the camp of Midian, and came unto the tent, and smote it so that it fell, and turned it upside down, so that the tent lay flat. 14 And his fellow answered and said, This is nothing else save the sword of Gideon the son of Joash, a man of Israel: into his hand God hath delivered Midian, and all the host.

As the climactic day of battle with the Midianites approached, two important instructions were given to Gideon by the Lord. One required the reduction of Gideon's army; the other required Gideon to spy out the Midianite camp under cover of darkness.

The first directive concerning the size of Gideon's army was aimed at the preservation of the Lord's glory. A total of thirty-two thousand men had answered Gideon's call to battle. This obviously was not as large a number as that of the Midianites, who were said to be **like locusts for multitude; and their camels were without number, as the sand which is upon the seashore for multitude** (v. 12). Yet it was sufficiently large that it might cause the Israelites to pride themselves on the victory (v. 2).

As many as were fearful were permitted to leave. Almost seventy per cent fell in this group, leaving ten thousand. Yet this was still too many. Further reduction was accomplished by the simple "lap test." Ninety-seven per cent of the ten thousand failed this test. This left three hundred, less than one per cent of the original thirty-two thousand. With this number of warriors Gideon dared to challenge one hundred thirty-five thousand (8:10).

That night Gideon was given his second directive. He was to spy out the Midianite camp. While performing this dangerous mission, Gideon overheard a Midianite relating a dream concerning a barley cake tumbling into the camp. The barley cake was a common food for the poor in the days of oppressed Israel. As interpreted by the companion of the Midianite it signified the coming of Gideon and the defeat of Midian (v. 14). To Gideon, this was a victory omen.

E. DEFEAT OF MIDIAN (7:15—8:21)

15 And it was so, when Gideon heard the telling of the dream, and the interpretation thereof, that he worshipped; and he returned into the camp of Israel, and said, Arise; for Jehovah hath delivered into your hand the host of Midian. 16 And he divided the three hundred men into three companies, and he put into the hands of all of them trumpets, and empty pitchers, with torches within the pitchers. 17 And he said unto them, Look on me, and do likewise: and, behold, when I come to the outermost part of the camp, it shall be that, as I do, so shall ye do. 18 When I blow the trumpet, I and all that are with me, then blow ye the trumpets also on every side of all the camp, and say, For Jehovah and for Gideon.

19 So Gideon, and the hundred men that were with him, came unto the outermost part of the camp in the beginning of the middle watch, when they had but newly set the watch: and they blew the trumpets, and brake in pieces the pitchers that were in their hands. 20 And the three companies blew the trumpets, and brake the pitchers, and held the torches in their left hands, and the trumpets in their right hands wherewith to blow; and they cried, The sword of Jehovah and of Gideon. 21 And they stood every man in his place round about the camp; and all the host ran; and they shouted, and put *them* to flight. 22 And they blew the three hundred trumpets, and Jehovah set every man's sword against his fellow, and against all the host; and the host fled as far as Beth-shittah toward Zererah, as far as the border of Abel-meholah, by Tabbath. 23 And the men of Israel were gathered together out of Naphtali, and out of Asher, and out of all Manasseh, and pursued after Midian.

24 And Gideon sent messengers throughout all the hill-country of Ephraim, saying, Come down against Midian, and take before them the waters, as far as Beth-barah, even the Jordan. So all the men of Ephraim were gathered together, and took the waters as far as Beth-barah, even the Jordan. 25 And they took the two princes of Midian, Oreb and Zeeb; and they slew Oreb at the rock of Oreb, and Zeeb they slew at the winepress of Zeeb, and pursued Midian: and they brought the heads of Oreb and Zeeb to Gideon beyond the Jordan.

1 And the men of Ephraim said unto him, Why hast thou served us thus, that thou callest us not, when thou wentest to fight with Midian? And they did chide with him sharply. 2 And he said unto them, What have I now done in comparison with you? Is not the gleaning of the grapes of Ephraim better than the vintage of Abiezer? 3 God hath delivered into your hand the princes of Midian, Oreb and Zeeb: and what was I able to do in comparison with you? Then their anger was abated toward him, when he had said that.

4 And Gideon came to the Jordan, *and* passed over, he, and the three hundred men that were with him, faint, yet pursuing. 5 And he said unto the men of Succoth, Give, I pray you, loaves of bread unto the people that follow me; for they are faint, and I am pursuing after Zebah and Zalmunna, the kings of Midian. 6 And the princes of Succoth said, Are the hands of Zebah and Zalmunna now in thy hand, that we should give bread unto thine army? 7 And Gideon said, Therefore when Jehovah hath delivered Zebah and Zalmunna into my hand, then I will tear your flesh with the thorns of the wilderness and with briers. 8 And he went up thence to Penuel, and spake unto them in like manner; and the men of Penuel answered him as the men of Succoth had answered. 9 And he spake also unto the men of Penuel, saying, When I come again in peace, I will break down this tower.

10 Now Zebah and Zalmunna were in Karkor, and their hosts with them, about fifteen thousand men, all that were left of all the host of the children of the east; for there fell a hundred and twenty thousand men that drew sword. 11 And Gideon went up by the way of them that dwelt in tents on the east of Nobah and Jogbehah, and smote the host; for the host was secure. 12 And Zebah and Zalmunna fled; and he pursued after them; and he took the two kings of

Midian, Zebah and Zalmunna, and discomfited all the host.

13 And Gideon the son of Joash returned from the battle from the ascent of Heres. 14 And he caught a young man of the men of Succoth, and inquired of him: and he described for him the princes of Succoth, and the elders thereof, seventy and seven men. 15 And he came unto the men of Succoth, and said, Behold Zebah and Zalmunna, concerning whom ye did taunt me, saying, Are the hands of Zebah and Zalmunna now in thy hand, that we should give bread unto thy men that are weary? 16 And he took the elders of the city, and thorns of the wilderness and briers, and with them he taught the men of Succoth. 17 And he brake down the tower of Penuel, and slew the men of the city. 18 Then said he unto Zebah and Zalmunna, What manner of men were they whom ye slew at Tabor? And they answered, As thou art, so were they; each one resembled the children of a king. 19 And he said, They were my brethren, the sons of my mother: as Jehovah liveth, if ye had saved them alive, I would not slay you. 20 And he said unto Jether his firstborn, Up, and slay them. But the youth drew not his sword; for he feared, because he was yet a youth. 21 Then Zebah and Zalmunna said, Rise thou, and fall upon us; for as the man is, so is his strength. And Gideon arose, and slew Zebah and Zalmunna, and took the crescents that were on their camels' necks.

Gideon realized that the Midianites were afraid. His battle strategy was to capitalize on this fear. Under cover of darkness his three hundred men surrounded the camp. Upon signal, they blew trumpets and held aloft lighted torches. They also lifted their voices and shouted, **The sword of Jehovah and of Gideon** (v. 20). The Midianites were terrorized, as indicated by the fact that they began fighting each other (v. 22). It seems evident that the Midianites had some fear of retaliation for their years of plundering in Israel. Being responsible also for the death of some of Gideon's brothers, they must have been aware of the possibility of reprisals (cf. 8:18, 19). The Lord enabled Gideon to utilize their fears to the advantage of Israel.

The Midianites fled eastward toward the Jordan with Gideon's warriors following. Others who had volunteered but had been excluded from the select three hundred now joined in the pursuit (v. 23). The men of Ephraim were also alerted and moved to block passage across the fords of the Jordan. This obstructed the retreat of the Midianites.

The Ephraimites captured the Midianite chiefs, Oreb and Zeeb (v. 25). This fact was recalled by Gideon when he faced the Ephraimites after the battle. They were angry because they had not been summoned before the battle. Their displeasure was probably because they were not given a chance to share in the spoils of war rather than because they were not called upon to fight. Gideon reminded the Ephraimites that they had done greater than he, for they had captured the Midianite chiefs. **God hath delivered into your hand the princes of Midian . . . and what was I able to do in comparison with you?** (v. 3). Thus were the men of Ephraim mollified.

Gideon's handling of this affair gives insight into his character. Faced by a jealous and angry company of fellow Israelites, Gideon might have precipitated a civil war had he answered them in anger. However, his handling of this affair is a model in human relations. Instead of criticism, he expressed congratulations for their achievement. Furthermore, he considered their achievement greater than his. It is little wonder that their anger was appeased. How much useless and corrupting strife might be avoided if individuals would assume Gideon's role of peacemaker, being willing to recognize the worth of what others have accomplished and minimizing what they themselves have done.

Gideon and his three hundred men, **faint, yet pursuing** (v. 4), passed over the Jordan after the fleeing Midianites. This persistent pursuit by Gideon was a complete surprise to the Midianites, who when they reached **Karkor** failed to set a watch and were thrown into a panic by the appearance of Gideon and his men (vv. 10, 11).

The pursuing Israelites lacked adequate provisions and became weak and faint. Gideon expected assistance from the Israelites on the east side of the Jordan, specifically the Gadites. However, he was disappointed when the princes of both Succoth and Penuel refused to give aid. Their refusal may have been motivated by fear of retaliation from the Midianites. Their fear caused them to reveal a dismal apathy toward national loyalty. They were desperately striving to maintain an existence which was in constant peril because of the roving bands of desert nomads. Gideon's efforts appeared to them to be hopeless and futile.

Gideon's demeanor toward the Gadites was wholly different from that toward the angry Ephraimites. He was so incensed at the Gadites that he threatened to teach them a lesson upon his return from the chase. The Gadites may have thought there was no need to worry about Gideon's threat, but they learned differently. He returned from capturing the kings of Midian and severely chastised them.

What can be said about Gideon's conduct on the east side of the Jordan? There must have been some reason for his persistent pursuit of the Midianites and his fierce anger with the Gadites. Apparently, Gideon was seeking to revenge the death of his own brothers (vv. 18, 19), and perhaps of others. He was powerfully moved to follow after the Midianites, even when others considered it futile. When this strong motivation to gain revenge for the death of his fellow men was frustrated by the taunts of the Gadites, he became exceedingly angry at them also, for they seemed to him to be assisting the marauding Midianites. Here is Gideon the hero, much obsessed by the spirit of retaliation. It is an open question as to how fully possessed by the Spirit of God Gideon was as he expressed this spirit of revenge. There may be a marked difference between what God wills and what even a man of God may do in moments of his weakened humanity.

F. GIDEON'S EPHOD (8:22-32)

22 Then the men of Israel said unto Gideon, Rule thou over us, both thou, and thy son, and thy son's son also; for thou hast saved us out of the hand of Midian. 23 And Gideon said unto them, I will not rule over you, neither shall my son rule over you: Jehovah shall rule over you. 24 And Gideon said unto them, I would make a request of you, that ye would give me every man the ear-rings of his spoil. (For they had golden ear-

rings, because they were Ishmaelites.) 25 And they answered, We will willingly give them. And they spread a garment, and did cast therein every man the ear-rings of his spoil. 26 And the weight of the golden ear-rings that he requested was a thousand and seven hundred *shekels* of gold; besides the crescents, and the pendants, and the purple raiment that was on the kings of Midian, and besides the chains that were about their camels' necks. 27 And Gideon made an ephod thereof, and put it in his city, even in Ophrah: and all Israel played the harlot after it there; and it became a snare unto Gideon, and to his house. 28 So Midian was subdued before the children of Israel, and they lifted up their heads no more. And the land had rest forty years in the days of Gideon.

29 And Jerubbaal the son of Joash went and dwelt in his own house. 30 And Gideon had threescore and ten sons of his body begotten; for he had many wives. 31 And his concubine that was in Shechem, she also bare him a son, and he called his name Abimelech. 32 And Gideon the son of Joash died in a good old age, and was buried in the sepulchre of Joash his father, in Ophrah of the Abiezrites.

Gideon's successful routing of the Midianites drew the tribes of Israel together. He was elevated to a place of strength and leadership and was offered the position of king. Here was a great test of Gideon's loyalty to God. To accept the kingship would violate the theocracy, and this violation he refused to commit. His reply to their offer was an uncompromising, **Jehovah shall rule over you** (v. 23).

Gideon countered the request of the men of Israel with a request of his own. He asked that every man give him the **ear-rings** of his spoil (v. 24). Those who had joined in gathering up the spoils of the victory over the Midianites willingly surrendered them, and Gideon made an ephod from them and set it up in Ophrah, his home town in Manasseh. The reference to the ephod here, as in Judges 17:5 and 18:14-20, appears to be somewhat enigmatic. Just what the ephod was, scholars are not certain. Possibly after all Gideon took undue credit to himself for the victories won by making himself a token of his leadership that robbed God of the glory and turned the people to idolatry.

Ophrah had been a memorable place to Gideon. Here the angel of Jehovah appeared to him while he furtively harvested grain in a wine press. Here he defied Baal by destroying the altar of Baal. Here he erected an altar to Jehovah and worshiped. It is of interest, then, that in Ophrah Gideon put the ephod, which was probably intended to memorialize what God had accomplished through Gideon.

Whatever may have been the reason for making the ephod and placing it in Ophrah, the object became a source of temptation and caused Israel to sin: **All Israel played the harlot after it** (v. 27). Even well-intended memorials to divine blessings and victories may become, unwittingly, objects of idolatry that corrupt the worship of God and preclude spiritual progress.

Thus Gideon, who had overthrown Baal-worship, unwittingly prepared the way back to idolatry. Apparently Gideon intended that the ephod in Ophrah should glorify God, but gradually it led away from God. An originally good intention on the part of Gideon became actualized into an evil deed by Israel. This has happened to many well-intentioned persons.

VI. ABIMELECH, TOLA, JAIR
(Judg. 8:33—10:5)

The story of Abimelech is a lengthy sequel to the Gideon story. It is followed by the accounts of two minor judges. One, named Tola, judged Israel in Ephraim. The other, named Jair, judged Israel in Gilead.

A. ABIMELECH (8:33—9:57)

Following the death of Gideon, his native tribe Manasseh soon forgot Jehovah and the house of Gideon. Abimelech, the son of Gideon, aspired to become king, a position which Gideon had rejected. The story of his brief rule and its end illustrates the ageless truth of the precept: As you sow so shall you reap.

1. Declension in Manasseh (8:33-35)

33 And it came to pass, as soon as Gideon was dead, that the children of Israel turned again, and played the harlot after the Baalim, and made Baalberith their god. 34 And the children of Israel remembered not Jehovah their God, who had delivered them out of the hand of all their enemies on every side; 35 neither showed they kindness to the house of Jerubbaal, *who is* Gideon, according to all the goodness which he had showed unto Israel.

The deliverance from the Midianites did not impress the Israelites for long, according to the sacred historian. Neither God nor Gideon was remembered with gratitude. **Israel remembered not Jehovah . . . neither showed they kindness to the house of Jerubbaal, who is Gideon . . .** (vv. 34, 35). This was the cyclical pattern beginning again. However, the Lord did not chasten the people in the usual fashion. Thus, the story of Abimelech shows some variation.

2. Abimelech, King of Shechem (9:1-6)

1 And Abimelech the son of Jerubbaal went to Shechem unto his mother's brethren, and spake with them, and with all the family of the house of his mother's father, saying, 2 Speak, I pray you, in the ears of all the men of Shechem, Whether is better for you, that all the sons of Jerubbaal, who are threescore and ten persons, rule over you, or that one rule over you? remember also that I am your bone and your flesh. 3 And his mother's brethren spake of him in the ears of all the men of Shechem all these words: and their hearts inclined to follow Abimelech; for they said, He is our brother. 4 And they gave him threescore and ten *pieces* of silver out of the house of Baal-berith, wherewith Abimelech hired vain and light fellows, who followed him. 5 And he went unto his father's house at Ophrah, and slew his brethren the sons of Jerubbaal, being threescore and ten persons, upon one stone: but Jotham the youngest son of Jerubbaal was left; for he hid himself. 6 And all the men of Shechem assembled themselves together, and all the house of Millo, and went and made Abimelech king, by the oak of the pillar that was in Shechem.

Abimelech was the son of Gideon by his concubine who lived in Shechem, one of the oldest cities in Canaan (8:31). Shechem, located in the half of Manasseh west of the Jordan, was not far from Gideon's home, Ophrah. Here the story of Abimelech centers. Because of the developments depicted in the account,

Jacob Myers considers it to be one of the most instructive in Judges.[14] It bears out the concept given in earlier parts of Judges that the Canaanites continued to live in the land and that there was intermingling with the Israelites. The Shechemites exemplified this intermingling. Abimelech's mother being a Shechemite, he claimed Shechemite citizenship. It may well be she was a Canaanite, making Abimelech half-Israelite and half-Canaanite.

If Abimelech were part Canaanite, this ancestry would in part explain his aspiration for kingship, since the idea of a king was definitely a Canaanite idea at this time. It is significant that this is one of the earliest instances that show the desire of the people for a king. Undue centralization of governmental powers has never been characteristic of the revealed divine will or the ideals of true democracy based upon divine principles.

Abimelech had certain factors in his favor when he made known his aspirations to be king. For one thing, he was known as the son of the deliverer, Gideon. For another, he was closely related to the Shechemites, who favored the idea of a king.

His first step was to appeal to his relatives in Shechem. They responded favorably to him because he championed the cause of a king and because he was their relative. They even took of the wealth of the temple of Baal-berith in Shechem and provided Abimelech with financial help. He used this assistance to hire men to go with him to Ophrah to do away with all rival contenders among the Israelite sons of Gideon. After this, there being no rival except young Jotham who escaped the purge, the men of Shechem made Abimelech king. His kingdom did not become large. It included an area less than the size of West Manasseh.

3. Jotham's Fable (9:7-21)

7 And when they told it to Jotham, he went and stood on the top of mount Gerizim, and lifted up his voice, and cried, and said unto them, Hearken unto me, ye men of Shechem, that God may hearken unto you. 8 The trees went forth on a time to anoint a king over them; and they said unto the olive-tree,

Reign thou over us. 9 But the olive-tree said unto them, Should I leave my fatness, wherewith by me they honor God and man, and go to wave to and fro over the trees? 10 And the trees said to the fig-tree, Come thou, and reign over us. 11 But the fig-tree said unto them, Should I leave my sweetness, and my good fruit, and go to wave to and fro over the trees? 12 And the trees said unto the vine, Come thou, and reign over us. 13 And the vine said unto them, Should I leave my new wine, which cheereth God and man, and go to wave to and fro over the trees? 14 Then said all the trees unto the bramble, Come thou, and reign over us. 15 And the bramble said unto the trees, If in truth ye anoint me king over you, then come and take refuge in my shade; and if not, let fire come out of the bramble, and devour the cedars of Lebanon. 16 Now therefore, if ye have dealt truly and uprightly, in that ye have made Abimelech king, and if ye have dealt well with Jerubbaal and his house, and have done unto him according to the deserving of his hands 17 (for my father fought for you, and adventured his life, and delivered you out of the hand of Midian: 18 and ye are risen up against my father's house this day, and have slain his sons, threescore and ten persons, upon one stone, and have made Abimelech, the son of his maid-servant, king over the men of Shechem, because he is your brother); 19 if ye then have dealt truly and uprightly with Jerubbaal and with his house this day, then rejoice ye in Abimelech, and let him also rejoice in you: 20 but if not, let fire come out from Abimelech, and devour the men of Shechem, and the house of Millo; and let fire come out from the men of Shechem, and from the house of Millo, and devour Abimelech. 21 And Jotham ran away, and fled, and went to Beer, and dwelt there, for fear of Abimelech his brother.

Young Jotham climbed to one of the overhanging heights of Mount Gerizim which towered above Shechem and uttered a fable which was heard by the Shechemites who were assembled for the coronation of the king.

According to Jotham's fable, the trees offered the kingship of their realm first to the olive tree, then to the fig tree, afterwards to the vine and, because these refused the offer, finally to the bramble, the least qualified.

---

[14] Myers, *op. cit.*, II, 751.

The obvious point of the fable is contempt for kingship. This low opinion of the idea of a king may well reflect an early date of writing. Furthermore, the application of the bramble to Abimelech reflects contempt for Abimelech. In addition to likening Abimelech to the bramble, Jotham deliberately refers to Abimelech as the son of a slave concubine. He ascribed to the Shechemite woman "a status inferior to her real one."[15]

According to Jotham's fable, the bramble provided the crown with considerable pride and boasting, promising the protection it could not really give. The bramble's boast gives the lesson of the fable, namely, it is absurd for other trees to seek refuge in the shade of the bramble when it is powerless to provide that refuge.[16] Likewise, Jotham's estimate of Abimelech was a low one. He considered him unworthy of the kingly office.

Jotham did not omit making the application of his fable as definite as possible, but he did so in a way not expected. The main point of the application is that the Shechemites had not **dealt well with Jerubbaal** . . . (v. 16). Jotham declared that they slew Gideon's legitimate sons and gave the kingship to an undeserving one. Therefore, Jotham's curse is, **let fire come out from Abimelech, and devour the men of Shechem . . . and let fire come out from the men of Shechem . . . and devour Abimelech** (v. 20). The course of events saw this come to pass. Abimelech set fire to the men of Shechem, while he in turn was crushed by a heavy millstone. The effect of Jotham's words was to stir up such strong feelings against him that he fled in fear of reprisal (v. 21). The individual who dares to go against the opinions and wishes of the masses will still find that he must bear their misunderstanding and hatred.

4. Revolt Against Abimelech (9:22-57)

22 And Abimelech was prince over Israel three years. 23 And God sent an evil spirit between Abimelech and the men of Shechem; and the men of Shechem dealt treacherously with Abimelech: 24 that the violence done to the threescore and ten sons of Jerubbaal might come, and that their blood might be laid upon Abimelech their brother, who slew them, and upon the men of Shechem, who strengthened his hands to slay his brethren. 25 And the men of Shechem set liers-in-wait for him on the tops of the mountains, and they robbed all that came along that way by them: and it was told Abimelech.

26 And Gaal the son of Ebed came with his brethren, and went over to Shechem; and the men of Shechem put their trust in him. 27 And they went out into the field, and gathered their vineyards, and trod *the grapes,* and held festival, and went into the house of their god, and did eat and drink, and cursed Abimelech. 28 And Gaal the son of Ebed said, Who is Abimelech, and who is Shechem, that we should serve him? is not he the son of Jerubbaal? and Zebul his officer? serve ye the men of Hamor the father of Shechem: but why should we serve him? 29 And would that this people were under my hand! then would I remove Abimelech. And he said to Abimelech, Increase thine army, and come out.

30 And when Zebul the ruler of the city heard the words of Gaal the son of Ebed, his anger was kindled. 31 And he sent messengers unto Abimelech craftily, saying, Behold, Gaal the son of Ebed and his brethren are come to Shechem; and, behold, they constrain the city *to take part* against thee. 32 Now therefore, up by night, thou and the people that are with thee, and lie in wait in the field: 33 and it shall be, that in the morning, as soon as the sun is up, thou shalt rise early, and rush upon the city; and, behold, when he and the people that are with him come out against thee, then mayest thou do to them as thou shalt find occasion.

34 And Abimelech rose up, and all the people that were with him, by night, and they laid wait against Shechem in four companies. 35 And Gaal the son of Ebed went out, and stood in the entrance of the gate of the city: and Abimelech rose up, and the people that were with him, from the ambushment. 36 And when Gaal saw the people, he said to Zebul, Behold, there come people down from the tops of the mountains. And Zebul said unto him, Thou seest the shadow of the mountains as if they were men. 37 And Gaal spake again and said, See, there come people down by the middle of the land, and one company cometh by the way of the oak of Meonenim. 38 Then said Zebul unto him, Where is now thy mouth, that thou saidst, Who is Abimelech, that we should serve him? is not this the people that thou hast despised?

[15] Bruce, *op. cit.,* p. 248.   [16] Myers, *op. cit.,* II, 754.

go out now, I pray, and fight with them. 39 And Gaal went out before the men of Shechem, and fought with Abimelech. 40 And Abimelech chased him, and he fled before him, and there fell many wounded, even unto the entrance of the gate.

41 And Abimelech dwelt at Arumah: and Zebul drove out Gaal and his brethren, that they should not dwell in Shechem. 42 And it came to pass on the morrow, that the people went out into the field; and they told Abimelech. 43 And he took the people, and divided them into three companies, and laid wait in the field; and he looked, and, behold, the people came forth out of the city; and he rose up against them, and smote them. 44 And Abimelech, and the companies that were with him, rushed forward, and stood in the entrance of the gate of the city: and the two companies rushed upon all that were in the field, and smote them. 45 And Abimelech fought against the city all that day; and he took the city, and slew the people that were therein: and he beat down the city, and sowed it with salt.

46 And when all the men of the tower of Shechem heard thereof, they entered into the stronghold of the house of Elberith. 47 And it was told Abimelech that all the men of the tower of Shechem were gathered together. 48 And Abimelech gat him up to mount Zalmon, he and all the people that were with him; and Abimelech took an axe in his hand, and cut down a bough from the trees, and took it up, and laid it on his shoulder: and he said unto the people that were with him, What ye have seen me do, make haste, and do as I have done. 49 And all the people likewise cut down every man his bough, and followed Abimelech, and put them to the stronghold, and set the stronghold on fire upon them; so that all the men of the tower of Shechem died also, about a thousand men and women.

50 Then went Abimelech to Thebez, and encamped against Thebez, and took it. 51 But there was a strong tower within the city, and thither fled all the men and women, and all they of the city, and shut themselves in, and gat them up to the roof of the tower. 52 And Abimelech came unto the tower, and fought against it, and drew near unto the door of the tower to burn it with fire. 53 And a certain woman cast an upper millstone upon Abimelech's head, and brake his skull. 54 Then he called hastily unto the young man his armor-bearer, and said unto him, Draw thy sword, and kill me, that men say not of me, A woman slew him. And his young man thrust him through, and he died. 55 And when the men of Israel saw that Abimelech was dead, they departed every man unto his place. 56 Thus God requited the wickedness of Abimelech, which he did unto his father, in slaying his seventy brethren; 57 and all the wickedness of the men of Shechem did God requite upon their heads: and upon them came the curse of Jotham the son of Jerubbaal.

Abimelech's rule was for a period of three years. Divine judgment upon him and the Shechemites was initiated by the presence of **an evil spirit between Abimelech and the men of Shechem** (v. 23). It is difficult to understand that **God sent an evil spirit.** Essentially, it involved a lack of mutual confidence. The Shechemites were acting disloyally; so Abimelech was seeking revenge. The significant reason given was that the death of the sons of Gideon might be recompensed (v. 24). Abimelech had dealt cruelly with them. Inevitably, he must reap the harvest of the cruelty he had sown. This is the outstanding lesson of the story of Abimelech, and it re-enforces the historian's analysis of Israel's history during the period of the judges. The cyclical pattern emphasizes the idea of judgment and retribution.

The Shechemite revolt appears to have a measure of ambiguity surrounding it. It took the form of robbing merchant caravans passing through Manasseh. If Abimelech had promised safe passage, the Shechemite ambushments of these caravans proved his promised protection was worthless. In this manner, their treachery destroyed his attempt to establish the prestige of his kingship. Moreover, this deprived Abimelech of revenue from merchants passing through his realm.

A new development in the story was the appearance in Shechem of Gaal, a leader of a roving band that attempted to take advantage of the strained relations between Abimelech and the Shechemites.[17] Apparently Abimelech was dwelling in nearby Arumah while a subordinate named Zebul governed Shechem. Gaal won the friendship of the Shechemites and then delivered a tirade against Abimelech. His main point was that Abime-

---

[17] J. P. U. Lilley, *New Bible Dictionary*, p. 445.

lech was at least half-Israelite. **Is he not the son of Jerubbaal?** (v. 28). Gaal called upon the Shechemites, **Serve ye the men of Hamor the father of Shechem** (v. 28). Hamor was the Canaanite ruler of Shechem in the time of Jacob (cf. Gen. 33: 19). Gaal's reference to Hamor the Canaanite implies that many of the Shechemites looked to their Canaanite heritage.

Zebul reported these developments to Abimelech, who came in force and routed Gaal. Meanwhile, Abimelech dealt the Shechemites a devastating blow. First, he destroyed the city (v. 45). Next, he burned the tower of Shechem where the people had sought refuge (v. 49). Then Abimelech went to nearby Thebez, which had participated in the revolt, and prepared to set fire to the tower of Thebez (v. 52). At the proper moment, a woman on the tower dropped a millstone, which crushed the head of Abimelech. He died by the sword-thrust of his armorbearer to save him from death by a woman.

The story of Abimelech closes with the clearly stated moral: **God required the wickedness of Abimelech . . . and all the wickedness of the men of Shechem did God requite upon their heads** (vv. 56, 57). It is noteworthy that the very element that helped Abimelech to power under questionable circumstances was the element that revolted against him and brought his downfall. Furthermore, it should be emphasized that the story of Abimelech is the story of reaping what one sows.

B. TOLA AND JAIR (10:1-5)

1 And after Abimelech there arose to save Israel Tola the son of Puah, the son of Dodo, a man of Issachar; and he dwelt in Shamir in the hill-country of Ephraim. 2 And he judged Israel twenty and three years, and died, and was buried in Shamir. 3 And after him arose Jair, the Gileadite; and he judged Israel twenty and two years. 4 And he had thirty sons that rode on thirty ass colts, and they had thirty cities, which are called Havvothjair unto this day, which are in the land of Gilead. 5 And Jair died, and was buried in Kamon.

It is of interest to note how Tola is introduced. **After Abimelech there arose**

to save Israel Tola . . . (v. 1). After the selfish effort of Abimelech, which lasted three years, there arose a deliverer out of Issachar named Tola who for twenty-three years served well as an arbitrator in Ephraim.

After Tola there arose a deliverer named Jair, on the east side of the Jordan in Gilead. Jair was a man of wealth. His thirty sons had thirty cities in Gilead. For twenty-two years this wealthy and influential Israelite served as arbitrator in Gilead by means of the Spirit of the Lord that rested upon him.

VII. JEPHTHAH, IBZAN, ELON, ABDON (Judg. 10:6–12:15)

From Jair to Samuel there appeared widespread defection in Israel and, consequently, there was widespread oppression. Israel followed after the gods of the bordering nations, Syria, Ammon, Moab, Philistia and Phoenicia (v. 6).

Because of Israel's idolatry during this period there occurred a sweeping oppression covering most of the land. From the west came the Philistines, and from the east came the Ammonites (v. 7). The Philistinian aggression lasted forty years, and the developments under that oppression are given in connection with Samson and Samuel. The Ammonite domination lasted about half as long and was effectually overthrown by Jephthah.

A. JEPHTHAH (10:6–12:7)

The historian's account of the story of Jephthah is given in the usual cyclical manner of declension, discipline and deliverance.

1. Ammonite Oppression (10:6-18)

6 And the children of Israel again did that which was evil in the sight of Jehovah, and served the Baalim, and the Ashtaroth, and the gods of Syria, and the gods of Sidon, and the gods of Moab, and the gods of the children of Ammon, and the gods of the Philistines; and they forsook Jehovah, and served him not. 7 And the anger of Jehovah was kindled against Israel, and he sold them into the hand of the Philistines, and into the hand of the children of Ammon. 8 And they vexed and oppressed the children of Israel that year: eighteen years *oppressed they* all the children of

Israel that were beyond the Jordan in the land of the Amorites, which is in Gilead. 9 And the children of Ammon passed over the Jordan to fight also against Judah, and against Benjamin; so that Israel was sore distressed.

10 And the children of Israel cried unto Jehovah, saying, We have sinned against thee, even because we have forsaken our God, and have served the Baalim. 11 And Jehovah said unto the children of Israel, *Did* not *I save you* from the Egyptians, and from the Amorites, from the children of Ammon, and from the Philistines? 12 The Sidonians also, and the Amalekites, and the Maonites, did oppress you; and ye cried unto me, and I saved you out of their hand. 13 Yet ye have forsaken me, and served other gods: wherefore I will save you no more. 14 Go and cry unto the gods which ye have chosen; let them save you in the time of your distress. 15 And the children of Israel said unto Jehovah, We have sinned: do thou unto us whatsoever seemeth good unto thee; only deliver us, we pray thee, this day. 16 And they put away the foreign gods from among them, and served Jehovah; and his soul was grieved for the misery of Israel.

17 Then the children of Ammon were gathered together, and encamped in Gilead. And the children of Israel assembled themselves together, and encamped in Mizpah. 18 And the people, the princes of Gilead, said one to another, What man is he that will begin to fight against the children of Ammon? he shall be head over all the inhabitants of Gilead.

Both the cause of the oppression, idolatry, and the oppression itself appear to have been widespread. The penetration of idolatry was from all directions and into the great majority of the tribes. The combination of Philistia and Ammon made a strong threat to the security of Israel. The Philistines dominated the land west of the Jordan while the Ammonites not only controlled Gilead but also threatened several tribes on the west side of the Jordan (vv. 8, 9).

The crisis was serious and caused Israel to acknowledge her sin and cry unto the Lord. The reply from the Lord was unexpected, **Go and cry unto the gods which ye have chosen; let them save you in the time of your distress** (v. 14). How often man erects his humanly conceived gods, but in the time of trouble he often realizes their inadequacy to deliver him. So the Israelites were aware of the failure

of the gods which they had chosen. Instead of praying to these gods, **Israel put away the foreign gods . . . and served Jehovah** (v. 16).

Because of the great suffering of Israel and because of the resolute forsaking of foreign gods, the Lord **was grieved for the misery of Israel** (v. 16). Moreover, the Israelites in Gilead began a search for a leader who would deliver them from the Ammonites. Their hope was not only in what God would do but also in what they must do. Their prayers were accompanied by resolute turning from their idolatry and definite searching for a man to lead them in battle. They accepted responsibility for positive action.

2. Jephthah's Deliverance (11:1-40)

1 Now Jephthah the Gileadite was a mighty man of valor, and he was the son of a harlot: and Gilead begat Jephthah. 2 And Gilead's wife bare him sons; and when his wife's sons grew up, they drove out Jephthah, and said unto him, Thou shalt not inherit in our father's house; for thou art the son of another woman. 3 Then Jephthah fled from his brethren, and dwelt in the land of Tob: and there were gathered vain fellows to Jephthah, and they went out with him.

4 And it came to pass after a while, that the children of Ammon made war against Israel. 5 And it was so, that, when the children of Ammon made war against Israel, the elders of Gilead went to fetch Jephthah out of the land of Tob; 6 and they said unto Jephthah, Come and be our chief, that we may fight with the children of Ammon. 7 And Jephthah said unto the elders of Gilead, Did not ye hate me, and drive me out of my father's house? and why are ye come unto me now when ye are in distress? 8 And the elders of Gilead said unto Jephthah, Therefore are we turned again to thee now, that thou mayest go with us, and fight with the children of Ammon; and thou shalt be our head over all the inhabitants of Gilead. 9 And Jephthah said unto the elders of Gilead, If ye bring me home again to fight with the children of Ammon, and Jehovah deliver them before me, shall I be your head? 10 And the elders of Gilead said unto Jephthah, Jehovah shall be witness between us; surely according to thy word so will we do. 11 Then Jephthah went with the elders of Gilead, and the people made him head and chief over

them: and Jephthah spake all his words before Jehovah in Mizpah.

12 And Jephthah sent messengers unto the king of the children of Ammon, saying, What hast thou to do with me, that thou art come unto me to fight against my land? 13 And the king of the children of Ammon answered unto the messengers of Jephthah, Because Israel took away my land, when he came up out of Egypt, from the Arnon even unto the Jabbok, and unto the Jordan; now therefore restore those *lands* again peaceably. 14 And Jephthah sent messengers again unto the king of the children of Ammon; 15 and he said unto him, Thus saith Jephthah: Israel took not away the land of Moab, nor the land of the children of Ammon; 16 but when they came up from Egypt, and Israel went through the wilderness unto the Red Sea, and came to Kadesh; 17 then Israel sent messengers unto the king of Edom, saying, Let me, I pray thee, pass through thy land; but the king of Edom hearkened not. And in like manner he sent unto the king of Moab; but he would not: and Israel abode in Kadesh. 18 Then they went through the wilderness, and went around the land of Edom, and the land of Moab, and came by the east side of the land of Moab, and they encamped on the other side of the Arnon; but they came not within the border of Moab, for the Arnon was the border of Moab. 19 And Israel sent messengers unto Sihon king of the Amorites, the king of Heshbon; and Israel said unto him, Let us pass, we pray thee, through thy land unto my place. 20 But Sihon trusted not Israel to pass through his border; but Sihon gathered all his people together, and encamped in Jahaz, and fought against Israel. 21 And Jehovah, the God of Israel, delivered Sihon and all his people into the hand of Israel, and they smote them: so Israel possessed all the land of the Amorites, the inhabitants of that country. 22 And they possessed all the border of the Amorites, from the Arnon even unto the Jabbok, and from the wilderness even unto the Jordan. 23 So now Jehovah, the God of Israel, hath dispossessed the Amorites from before his people Israel, and shouldest thou possess them? 24 Wilt not thou possess that which Chemosh thy god giveth thee to possess? So whomsoever Jehovah our God hath dispossessed from before us, them will we possess. 25 And now art thou anything better than Balak the son of Zippor, king of Moab? did he ever strive against Israel, or did he ever fight against them? 26 While Israel dwelt in Heshbon and its towns, and in

Aroer and its towns, and in all the cities that are along by the side of the Arnon, three hundred years; wherefore did ye not recover them within that time? 27 I therefore have not sinned against thee, but thou doest me wrong to war against me: Jehovah, the Judge, be judge this day between the children of Israel and the children of Ammon. 28 Howbeit the king of the children of Ammon hearkened not unto the words of Jephthah which he sent him.

29 Then the Spirit of Jehovah came upon Jephthah, and he passed over Gilead and Manasseh, and passed over Mizpeh of Gilead, and from Mizpeh of Gilead he passed over unto the children of Ammon. 30 And Jephthah vowed a vow unto Jehovah, and said, If thou wilt indeed deliver the children of Ammon into my hand, 31 then it shall be, that whatsoever cometh forth from the doors of my house to meet me, when I return in peace from the children of Ammon, it shall be Jehovah's, and I will offer it up for a burnt-offering. 32 So Jephthah passed over unto the children of Ammon to fight against them; and Jehovah delivered them into his hand. 33 And he smote them from Aroer until thou come to Minnith, even twenty cities, and unto Abel-cheramim, with a very great slaughter. So the children of Ammon were subdued before the children of Israel.

34 And Jephthah came to Mizpah unto his house; and, behold, his daughter came out to meet him with timbrels and with dances: and she was his only child; besides her he had neither son nor daughter. 35 And it came to pass, when he saw her, that he rent his clothes, and said, Alas, my daughter! thou hast brought me very low, and thou art one of them that trouble me; for I have opened my mouth unto Jehovah, and I cannot go back. 36 And she said unto him, My father, thou hast opened thy mouth unto Jehovah; do unto me according to that which hath proceeded out of thy mouth, forasmuch as Jehovah hath taken vengeance for thee on thine enemies, even on the children of Ammon. 37 And she said unto her father, Let this thing be done for me: let me alone two months, that I may depart and go down upon the mountains, and bewail my virginity, I and my companions. 38 And he said, Go. And he sent her away for two months: and she departed, she and her companions, and bewailed her virginity upon the mountains. 39 And it came to pass at the end of two months, that she returned unto her father, who did with her according to his vow which he had

vowed: and she knew not man. And it was a custom in Israel, 40 that the daughters of Israel went yearly to celebrate the daughter of Jephthah the Gileadite four days in a year.

The Israelites in Gilead were in great need of leadership in order to resist Ammon effectively. In this crisis they turned to a man whom they formerly considered undesirable. Jephthah, like Abimelech, was half-Canaanite and was rejected by his father's family (v. 2). Doubtless embittered, he left home for the land of Tob, probably north of Ammon and east of that part of Manasseh located east of the Jordan River. In this area he lived the life of an outlaw but established a reputation for unquestioned courage. In his free-swinging style of living he supported himself and his men by raiding Syrian and Ammonite villages. At the same time his surroundings were influencing his life and thought. Away from his father's family he lived amid a mixture of religious beliefs. Whatever religion Jephthah had must have been under foreign influence.

The Israelites needed a man of heroic courage, and none had greater reputation for daring bravery than this exiled chief who was leader of a band of **vain fellows** (v. 3). Crises often bring about strange changes. Jephthah, at one time undesirable, was now the desired leader against Ammon, for he **was a mighty man of valor** (v. 1). He was surprised to learn that he was wanted; until now he had been shunned (v. 7). It was doubtless humiliating to the princes of Israel in Gilead to seek Jephthah, whom earlier they had banished. Driven by the crisis, they asked him to be their leader. This happens again and again. Crises reveal leaders.

Jephthah consented to lead Israel against Ammon on the condition that he would be made chief (v. 9). To this the princes agreed (v. 10). The agreement was concluded by calling Jehovah as witness (vv. 10, 11).

Jephthah entered upon a lengthy defense against the claim of the king of Ammon that the land belonged to the Ammonites (vv. 12-28). Essentially, the core of his defense was that Israel owed its possession of the land to Jehovah

(v. 23). The argument was that since the God of Israel had given the land to Israel He was stronger than the gods of Ammon and Moab (v. 24). Moreover, since Ammon had made no claim to the land for three hundred years there was no valid reason for doing so now (vv. 26, 27). Jephthah refused to acknowledge any wrongdoing on Israel's part; rather, Ammon was charged with wrongdoing in provoking the battle. Jehovah was called upon to be the judge between Israel and Ammon (v. 27).

This defense established Jephthah in a righteous cause, and it is not without significance that immediately following this defense Jephthah received spiritual re-enforcement. **Then the Spirit of Jehovah came upon Jephthah** . . . (v. 29).

Empowered by the Spirit of the Lord, Jephthah summoned the fighting men of Israel who lived in Gilead. He confronted the great host of Ammon which had oppressed the Israelites for years and was flushed with a sense of power.

Jephthah had already argued with the king of Ammon that the God of Israel was responsible for Israel's possessing the land. He moved forward to the battle knowing that he was taking his life in his hands but expecting that the Lord would prove His superiority over the gods of Ammon (v. 29; cf. 12:3). In the light of this, Jephthah vowed to make a burnt-offering to the Lord (vv. 30, 31). "The language of the vow suggests that he had a human sacrifice in mind."[18]

Assuring himself that he had made a vow commensurate with his expectations of what Jehovah would do, Jephthah led Israel against Ammon. He accomplished a complete victory and turned homeward.

He was overwhelmed with grief when he returned to find that his daughter, his only child, was the first living thing that came forth to meet him (vv. 34, 35; cf. v. 30). Bruce writes:

> Although human sacrifice was strictly forbidden to Israelites, we need not be surprised at a man of Jephthah's half-Canaanite antecedents following Canaanite usage in this matter.[19]

Human sacrifices were connected with the worship of Phoenicia, Syria and Ammon. No doubt the vow-making by Jephthah

[18] Myers, *op. cit.*, II, 679.   [19] Bruce, *op. cit.*, p. 250.

was associated with his heathen surroundings in the land of Tob.

The homecoming of the victorious Jephthah is made more vivid in the light of the fact that he dearly loved his only daughter. He had been unwanted by his own family. What he had been deprived of in the way of love and understanding he had given to his child. Now, the thought of having to take her life to fulfill his vow stabbed him deeply. Jephthah faced a greater conflict than he had faced with the Ammonites. It was a conflict of interests: should he keep his daughter or keep his vow? His courageous resolve was, **I have opened my mouth unto Jehovah, and I cannot go back** (v. 35). His daughter responded in willing submission and courage. She truly was of the same heroic character as her father. There is pathos in the realization that this son of a harlot who suffered great humiliation and loneliness because of the treatment he was given by his own people would have developed such strong affection for his only child and yet, to keep his pledge, would offer her very life. No son would continue the fame of her father; no child would think of her as mother. The daughter requested, **Let me alone . . . that I may . . . bewail my virginity . . .** (v. 37).

Her father granted her request and, afterwards, fulfilled his vow. The statement that Jephthah **did with her according to his vow** may be understood as implying her actual sacrifice,[20] though some scholars think that it was a "sacrifice" of the girl to a celibate life, rather than a "human sacrifice" in death.

3. Ephraimite Jealousy (12:1-7)

1 And the men of Ephraim were gathered together, and passed northward; and they said unto Jephthah, Wherefore passedst thou over to fight against the children of Ammon, and didst not call us to go with thee? we will burn thy house upon thee with fire. 2 And Jephthah said unto them, I and my people were at great strife with the children of Ammon; and when I called you, ye saved me not out of their hand. 3 And when I saw that ye saved me not, I put my life in my hand, and passed over against the children of Ammon, and

Jehovah delivered them into my hand: wherefore then are ye come up unto me this day, to fight against me? 4 Then Jephthah gathered together all the men of Gilead, and fought with Ephraim; and the men of Gilead smote Ephraim, because they said, Ye are fugitives of Ephraim, ye Gileadites, in the midst of Ephraim, *and* in the midst of Manasseh. 5 And the Gileadites took the fords of the Jordan against the Ephraimites. And it was so, that, when *any of* the fugitives of Ephraim said, Let me go over, the men of Gilead said unto him, Art thou an Ephraimite? If he said, Nay; 6 then said they unto him, Say now Shibboleth; and he said Sibboleth; for he could not frame to pronounce it right: then they laid hold on him, and slew him at the fords of the Jordan. And there fell at that time of Ephraim forty and two thousand.

7 And Jephthah judged Israel six years. Then died Jephthah the Gileadite, and was buried in *one of* the cities of Gilead.

Jephthah, his house silent and his heart sorrowing because of the loss of his only child, was reproached and threatened by the jealous tribe of Ephraim: **We will burn thy house upon thee with fire** (v. 1). This exile from home, who had been able to salvage from the cruelties of life a home and family, later lost his only child and now was threatened with the loss of his home.

When he inquired why Ephraim wanted to fight he was taunted with the sneer, **Ye are fugitives of Ephraim, ye Gileadites** (v. 4). These insulting words shouted at Jephthah were not unchallenged. He had known the life of a fugitive, but he had proven himself a mighty man of courage. He entered into civil war with the Ephraimites, who had crossed Jordan in force.

The tribe of Ephraim had a history of this sort of highhandedness in claiming superiority. At the time of the allotment of Canaan, this tribe wanted more land because it was a great people (Josh. 17: 14). When Gideon defeated Midian, Ephraim was resentful because it had not been called to help (Judg. 8:1). Jephthah also stirred Ephraimite resentment (v. 1). Pride of position tends to resentment and jealousy whenever recognition is not forthcoming.

The battle between Ephraim and Gil-

---

[20] *Loc. cit.*

ead was won by Jephthah. Retreating Ephraimites found the fords of the Jordan River controlled by Gileadites. Those who attempted to cross the river were given the accent test to tell whether they were Ephraimites or not. The test word was "Shibboleth," but an Ephraimite pronounced it "Sibboleth." Every Ephraimite discovered by this method was put to death. Incidentally, the word *Shibboleth* means "ear of corn."[21]

The storm that swirled about the Shibboleth of Jephthah's time has never completely ended, for the word has become a favorite watchword for groups which emphasize their so-called distinctives. It is a separatist word and is used as a clarion call to distinguish friend from foe.

Verbal differences sometimes engender controversy and civil war. They may develop into violent quarrels which involve the sacrifice of the finest people and the destruction of outstanding reputations.

The Ephraimites' pride of pre-eminence as shown in their attitude toward the Gadites who lived in Gilead and the Gadites' spirit of retaliation as shown in their readiness to fight the Ephraimites when accused of desertion were signs of a sick relationship, potentially dangerous.

Ephraim's self-centered attitude of indispensability and God's angry spirit of revenge aroused by Ephraim's name-calling were circumstances which caused the Gadites to enforce rigid intolerance by means of the Shibboleth. As in the case of Ephraim and Gad, so in our contemporary relationships, the Shibboleths are not so important as their causes. Why do people construct and enforce their Shibboleths? This question more often than not requires an answer that stands as an indictment against, rather than as a justification for, our Shibboleths.

B. IBZAN, ELON, ABDON (12:8-15)

8 And after him Ibzan of Bethlehem judged Israel. 9 And he had thirty sons; and thirty daughters he sent abroad, and thirty daughters he brought in from abroad for his sons. And he judged Israel seven years. 10 And Ibzan died, and was buried at Beth-lehem.

11 And after him Elon the Zebulunite judged Israel; and he judged Israel ten years. 12 And Elon the Zebulunite died, and was buried in Aijalon in the land of Zebulun.

13 And after him Abdon the son of Hillel the Pirathonite judged Israel. 14 And he had forty sons and thirty sons' sons, that rode on threescore and ten ass colts: and he judged Israel eight years. 15 And Abdon the son of Hillel the Pirathonite died, and was buried in Pirathon in the land of Ephraim, in the hill-country of the Amalekites.

These three minor judges who were active following Jephthah's career were located on the west side of the Jordan River. Ibzan was apparently a man of wealth and influence, as demonstrated by the number of his sons and daughters. Bethlehem may have been the town located in Zebulun. His seven years of judging may have had their share of crises but nothing is recorded about them. If the Philistines were in the land there may have been troublesome times (cf. Judg. 10:6, 7).

Elon was of the tribe of Zebulun and judged Israel ten years. Abdon was of the tribe of Ephraim. References to his family and cattle indicate that he, like Ibzan, was a judge of considerable wealth and influence. His judgeship lasted eight years.

VIII. SAMSON (Judg. 13:1—16:31)

The historian, having given the account of the Ammonite oppression on the east side of the Jordan River, and Jephthah's deliverance, turns to the account of the Philistine oppression on the west side of the river, and Samson's resistance (13:1; cf. 10:6, 7). "Jehovah delivered them into the hand of the Philistines forty years" (13:1). "These forty years lasted at least until the second battle of Ebenezer (I Sam. 7: 10ff.) . . . ."[22] The account of Samson spans a period of at least twenty years (15:20). Apparently Samson and Samuel were contemporaries, with Samson being the older. Samson was not born until the Philistine oppression was afflicting the land, and he was to have a significant role as judge. "He shall begin to save Israel out of the hand of the Philistines" (13:5). This would place him in the same period as Samuel. Furthermore, the lives of both men were involved in the

---

[21] *Ibid.*, p 251.   [22] *Loc. cit.*

crisis resulting from the Philistine oppression.

Samson was of the tribe of Dan and the village of Zorah, located in the Shephelah about fourteen miles west of Jerusalem. His life story from birth to death is recounted in the book of Judges, covered in more detail than any of the other judges.

A. CIRCUMSTANCES OF SAMSON'S BIRTH (13:1-25)

1 And the children of Israel again did that which was evil in the sight of Jehovah; and Jehovah delivered them into the hand of the Philistines forty years. 2 And there was a certain man of Zorah, of the family of the Danites, whose name was Manoah; and his wife was barren, and bare not. 3 And the angel of Jehovah appeared unto the woman, and said unto her, Behold now, thou art barren, and bearest not; but thou shalt conceive, and bear a son. 4 Now therefore beware, I pray thee, and drink no wine nor strong drink, and eat not any unclean thing: 5 for, lo, thou shalt conceive, and bear a son; and no razor shall come upon his head; for the child shall be a Nazirite unto God from the womb: and he shall begin to save Israel out of the hand of the Philistines. 6 Then the woman came and told her husband, saying, A man of God came unto me, and his countenance was like the countenance of the angel of God, very terrible; and I asked him not whence he was, neither told he me his name: 7 but he said unto me, Behold, thou shalt conceive, and bear a son; and now drink no wine nor strong drink, and eat not any unclean thing; for the child shall be a Nazirite unto God from the womb to the day of his death.

8 Then Manoah entreated Jehovah, and said, Oh, Lord, I pray thee, let the man of God whom thou didst send come again unto us, and teach us what we shall do unto the child that shall be born. 9 And God hearkened to the voice of Manoah; and the angel of God came again unto the woman as she sat in the field: but Manoah her husband was not with her. 10 And the woman made haste, and ran, and told her husband, and said unto him, Behold, the man hath appeared unto me, that came unto me the *other* day. 11 And Manoah arose, and went after his wife, and came to the man, and said unto him, Art thou the man that spakest unto the woman? And he

said, I am. 12 And Manoah said, Now let thy words come to pass: what shall be the ordering of the child, and *how* shall we do unto him? 13 And the angel of Jehovah said unto Manoah, Of all that I said unto the woman let her beware. 14 She may not eat of anything that cometh of the vine, neither let her drink wine or strong drink, nor eat any unclean thing; all that I commanded her let her observe.

15 And Manoah said unto the angel of Jehovah, I pray thee, let us detain thee, that we may make ready a kid for thee. 16 And the angel of Jehovah said unto Manoah, Though thou detain me, I will not eat of thy bread; and if thou wilt make ready a burnt-offering, thou must offer it unto Jehovah. For Manoah knew not that he was the angel of Jehovah. 17 And Manoah said unto the angel of Jehovah, What is thy name, that, when thy words come to pass, we may do thee honor? 18 And the angel of Jehovah said unto him, Wherefore askest thou after my name, seeing it is wonderful? 19 So Manoah took the kid with the meal-offering, and offered it upon the rock unto Jehovah: and *the angel* did wondrously; and Manoah and his wife looked on. 20 For it came to pass, when the flame went up toward heaven from off the altar, that the angel of Jehovah ascended in the flame of the altar: and Manoah and his wife looked on; and they fell on their faces to the ground.

21 But the angel of Jehovah did no more appear to Manoah or to his wife. Then Manoah knew that he was the angel of Jehovah. 22 And Manoah said unto his wife, We shall surely die, because we have seen God. 23 But his wife said unto him, If Jehovah were pleased to kill us, he would not have received a burnt-offering and a meal-offering at our hand, neither would he have showed us all these things, nor would at this time have told such things as these. 24 And the woman bare a son, and called his name Samson: and the child grew, and Jehovah blessed him. 25 And the Spirit of Jehovah began to move him in Mahaneh-dan, between Zorah and Eshtaol.

The story of Samson opens with a visit from **the angel of the Lord** to the wife of Manoah of the tribe of Dan. This man and wife had no children, but the angel announced that the woman was to bear a child and **the child shall be a Nazirite unto God** . . . (v. 5). The word **Nazirite** refers to "one who is set apart, dedicated to the Lord."[23]

---

[23] Myers, *op. cit.*, II, 777.

One of the instructive aspects related to the birth narrative of Samson has to do with the responsibility of his parents. Since the child was to be a Nazirite, the angel of the Lord instructed the wife of Manoah to rear him in the Nazirite manner (v. 4). A dedicated son needs dedicated parents both as a heritage and as an example. A parent owes this to his child.

Furthermore, after hearing his wife's account of the visitation by the angel of the Lord, Manoah prayed, **Let the man of God . . . teach us what we shall do unto the child that shall be born** (v. 8).

In spite of the fact that Samson did not measure up to the ideal of a dedicated person, a decisive factor throughout his life was that he was a child of promise who was reared amid righteous influences by devout parents. Samson's ancestral heritage stands in contrast to that of Jephthah of Gad.

Manoah, unaware that the person who announced the birth of Samson was the angel of the Lord, offered to prepare a meal for the visitor. Not until the messenger mysteriously ascended in the flame of a burnt-offering he invited Manoah to make did the realization come to Manoah, **We have seen God** (v. 22).

Fear gripped Manoah as he told his wife, **We shall surely die, because we have seen God** (v. 22). However, his wife had the clearer perception of the meaning of what was happening. She remonstrated with her husband, **If Jehovah were pleased to kill us, he would not . . . at this time have told us such things as these** (v. 22). There are people who, like Manoah, fear that God has put them away from Him. They also need the encouragement of Manoah's wife. They need to see before them the God-given task. It dispels the illusion that God has abandoned them. If there is a call to service, there is the corollary of the divine presence.

And the woman bare a son, and called his name Samson (v. 24). The angel of Jehovah had promised Manoah and his wife that their son would **begin to save Israel** (v. 5). As Samson grew, **Jehovah blessed him. And the Spirit of Jehovah began to move him . . .** (vv. 24, 25). The promise and fulfillment specifically related to delivering Israel from the Philistines. When the Spirit of the Lord came upon Samson and began to move him, he was impelled to take action against the Philistines. The following episode in the life of Samson was essentially an effort on his part to provoke the hostility of the Philistines.

B. THE WOMAN OF TIMNAH (14:1—15:8)

1 And Samson went down to Timnah, and saw a woman in Timnah of the daughters of the Philistines. 2 And he came up, and told his father and his mother, and said, I have seen a woman in Timnah of the daughters of the Philistines: now therefore get her for me to wife. 3 Then his father and his mother said unto him, Is there never a woman among the daughters of thy brethren, or among all my people, that thou goest to take a wife of the uncircumcised Philistines? And Samson said unto his father, Get her for me; for she pleaseth me well. 4 But his father and his mother knew not that it was of Jehovah; for he sought an occasion against the Philistines. Now at that time the Philistines had rule over Israel.

5 Then went Samson down, and his father and his mother, to Timnah, and came to the vineyards of Timnah: and, behold, a young lion roared against him. 6 And the Spirit of Jehovah came mightily upon him, and he rent him as he would have rent a kid; and he had nothing in his hand: but he told not his father or his mother what he had done. 7 And he went down, and talked with the woman; and she pleased Samson well. 8 And after a while he returned to take her; and he turned aside to see the carcass of the lion: and, behold, there was a swarm of bees in the body of the lion, and honey. 9 And he took it into his hands, and went on, eating as he went; and he came to his father and mother, and gave unto them, and they did eat: but he told them not that he had taken the honey out of the body of the lion.

10 And his father went down unto the woman: and Samson made there a feast; for so used the young men to do. 11 And it came to pass, when they saw him, that they brought thirty companions to be with him. 12 And Samson said unto them, Let me now put forth a riddle unto you: if ye can declare it unto me within the seven days of the feast, and find it out, then I will give you thirty linen garments and thirty changes of raiment; 13 but if ye cannot declare it unto me, then shall ye give me thirty

linen garments and thirty changes of raiment. And they said unto him, Put forth thy riddle, that we may hear it. 14 And he said unto them,

Out of the eater came forth food,
And out of the strong came forth sweetness.

And they could not in three days declare the riddle.

15 And it came to pass on the seventh day, that they said unto Samson's wife, Entice thy husband, that he may declare unto us the riddle, lest we burn thee and thy father's house with fire: have ye called us to impoverish us? is it not so? 16 And Samson's wife wept before him, and said, Thou dost but hate me, and lovest me not: thou hast put forth a riddle unto the children of my people, and hast not told it me. And he said unto her, Behold, I have not told it my father nor my mother, and shall I tell thee? 17 And she wept before him the seven days, while their feast lasted: and it came to pass on the seventh day, that he told her, because she pressed him sore; and she told the riddle to the children of her people. 18 And the men of the city said unto him on the seventh day before the sun went down, What is sweeter than honey? and what is stronger than a lion? And he said unto them,

If ye had not plowed with my heifer,
Ye had not found out my riddle.

19 And the Spirit of Jehovah came mightily upon him, and he went down to Ashkelon, and smote thirty men of them, and took their spoil, and gave the changes of raiment unto them that declared the riddle. And his anger was kindled, and he went up to his father's house. 20 But Samson's wife was given to his companion, whom he had used as his friend.

1 But it came to pass after a while, in the time of wheat harvest, that Samson visited his wife with a kid; and he said, I will go in to my wife into the chamber. But her father would not suffer him to go in. 2 And her father said, I verily thought that thou hadst utterly hated her; therefore I gave her to thy companion: is not her younger sister fairer than she? take her, I pray thee, instead of her. 3 And Samson said unto them, This time shall I be blameless in regard of the Philistines, when I do them a mischief. 4 And Samson went and caught three hundred foxes, and took firebrands, and turned tail to tail, and put a firebrand in the midst between every two tails. 5 And when he had set the brands

on fire, he let them go into the standing grain of the Philistines, and burnt up both the shocks and the standing grain, and also the olive-yards. 6 Then the Philistines said, Who hath done this? And they said, Samson, the son-in-law of the Timnite, because he hath taken his wife, and given her to his companion. And the Philistines came up, and burnt her and her father with fire. 7 And Samson said unto them, If ye do after this manner, surely I will be avenged of you, and after that I will cease. 8 And he smote them hip and thigh with a great slaughter: and he went down and dwelt in the cleft of the rock of Etam.

It is significant that the story of Samson opens with the statement, "And the children of Israel again did that which was evil in the sight of Jehovah; and Jehovah delivered them into the hand of the Philistines forty years" (13:1). We hear no cry of distress from Israel because of this oppression. Rather, co-existence was the popular theme. "Biblical sources and archaeological remains are at one in exhibiting a period of intermingling between Israelites and Philistines. . . .[24] These two peoples lived side by side without much difficulty. Even though Samson's father disapproved of Samson's desire to marry the woman of Timnah (v. 3), he did not prevent the marriage. "The Samson episodes reflect an unsettled situation when as yet there was no open warfare between the two peoples."[25]

In the light of these backgrounds, it is necessary to realize that Israel apparently was apathetic toward Samson. Even though the Spirit of Jehovah was upon him for the purpose of delivering Israel from the Philistines, co-existence rather than deliverance was the popular desire.

While there were serious irregularities in the behavior of Samson the Nazirite, it appears that he was a man ahead of his time and, consequently, unwelcomed. He moved to deliver Israel, but Israel was unimpressed. Not until the serious crises connected with the first battle at Ebenezer did Israel shake off her apathy and seek deliverance (cf. I Sam. 4).

All of this is for the purpose of offering some illumination on the strange circumstances surrounding Samson's first romance and marriage. When the Spirit of Jehovah was beginning to stir Samson to move against the Philistines, he saw a Philistine woman in Timnah who would serve his purpose. This strange complex is revealed by the historian in the following manner. **Samson said unto his father, Get her for me; for she pleaseth me well. But his father and mother knew not that it was of Jehovah; for he sought an occasion against the Philistines** (v. 3, 4).

Against the wish of his parents, Samson persisted in his desire to marry the woman of Timnah. Yet this persistence involved more than the love of a man for a woman; it was also an occasion for provoking the Philistines to open hostility. Such a development, supposedly, would rally Israel behind the Spirit-clothed deliverer. However, there was no such response on the part of Israel.

Leaders continually face this difficulty. Some who might have made a great contribution to humanity never have the opportunity because they appear to have been out of step with their contemporaries and the times in which they lived. Others, less capable of contributing to the welfare of humanity, appear at the opportune time and place and accomplish phenomenal good. Samson was never able to rally an army and arouse the people.

The marriage of Samson reveals a strained relation in the household of Manoah. It was customary for parents to arrange the marriage of their children, but it appears that Samson's parents did not arrange his. They sought to fulfill the divine directives in rearing this child of promise, their only child. His persistence in a marriage of which they did not approve was extremely difficult for them, and more so since they could not perceive any activity of the Lord in it.

Samson's marriage was not in any sense ordinary. Not only did he arrange it himself and select Philistines as attendants, but the bride remained at her parents' home and was visited by Samson.

Samson's slaying of a young lion on the way to the wedding provided him with a riddle for the guests at the marriage festivities. A prize was promised if the riddle were solved during that seven-day period.

Through threats made to Samson's bride, the men found out the answer, but they waited to give it until the sun was going down on the seventh day (v. 18). This would seem to be a plot on the part of these Philistines to humiliate and nettle Samson just before he entered the privacy of the wedding night.

Samson, who had sought to provoke the Philistines, found himself so angry that he never fully consummated the wedding (v. 19). Rather, after he had made proper payment for the wager he had made, he went home to his parents. His angry departure demanded forthright action on the part of the bride's parents to save her from great humiliation. **But Samson's wife was given to his companion, whom he had used as his friend** (v. 20). Apparently, she was given to the best man.

Later, Samson returned to Timnah and sought the woman he had deserted in anger. Her father refused Samson admittance. **I verily thought thou hadst utterly hated her** (v. 2). She had revealed the secret of the riddle and her father thought Samson hated her for this. However, the father implied that he had done wrong, for he offered him a younger sister: **Is not her younger sister fairer than she? Take her, I pray thee, instead of her** (v. 2).

However, Samson considered that he had a just cause for retaliation. **This time shall I be blameless in regard to the Philistines, when I do them a mischief** (v. 3). The mischief consisted of tying flaming torches to foxes, which dashed in panic through the grainfields of the Philistines. The destructive inferno incensed the Philistines, who sought out Samson's wife **and burnt her and her father with fire** (v. 6). Earlier she had been threatened by the Philistines seeking the answer to Samson's riddle — **Lest we burn thee and thy father's house with fire** (v. 15).

This retaliatory deed against Samson's wife aroused Samson, and **he smote them hip and thigh with a great slaughter** (v. 8). By now the Philistines were so thoroughly aroused that Samson went into hiding **in the cleft of the rock of Etam** (v. 8).

The incident of Samson and the woman at Timnah has served to point up at least two developments. First, the Israelites were largely content to co-exist with the Philistines, even though the element of oppression was involved. Second, Samson did not succeed in rallying Israel to resist the Philistines. The next episode emphasizes this failure.

C. SAMSON'S VICTORY AT LEHI (15:9-20)

9 Then the Philistines went up, and encamped in Judah, and spread themselves in Lehi. 10 And the men of Judah said, Why are ye come up against us? And they said, To bind Samson are we come up, to do to him as he hath done to us. 11 Then three thousand men of Judah went down to the cleft of the rock of Etam, and said to Samson, Knowest thou not that the Philistines are rulers over us? what then is this that thou hast done unto us? And he said unto them, As they did unto me, so have I done unto them. 12 And they said unto him, We are come down to bind thee, that we may deliver thee into the hand of the Philistines. And Samson said unto them, Swear unto me, that ye will not fall upon me yourselves. 13 And they spake unto him, saying, No; but we will bind thee fast, and deliver thee into their hand: but surely we will not kill thee. And they bound him with two new ropes, and brought him up from the rock.

14 When he came unto Lehi, the Philistines shouted as they met him: and the Spirit of Jehovah came mightily upon him, and the ropes that were upon his arms became as flax that was burnt with fire, and his bands dropped from off his hands. 15 And he found a fresh jawbone of an ass, and put forth his hand, and took it, and smote a thousand men therewith. 16 And Samson said,

With the jawbone of an ass, heaps upon heaps,

With the jawbone of an ass have I smitten a thousand men.

17 And it came to pass, when he had made an end of speaking, that he cast away the jawbone out of his hand; and that place was called Ramath-lehi. 18 And he was sore athirst, and called on Jehovah, and said, Thou hast given this great deliverance by the hand of thy servant; and now shall I die for thirst, and fall into the hand of the uncircumcised. 19 But God clave the hollow place that is in Lehi, and there came water thereout; and when he had drunk, his spirit came again, and he revived: wherefore the name thereof was called En-hakkore, which is in Lehi, unto this day.

20 And he judged Israel in the days of the Philistines twenty years.

The Philistines came in considerable force to take Samson prisoner. The tribe of Judah was distressed by their appearance, and upon learning why they had come, offered to give them aid in taking Samson. Three thousand men of Judah found Samson and remonstrated with him: Knowest thou not that the Philistines are rulers over us? (v. 11). Their obvious apathy resented Samson's disturbance of the status quo. They delivered Samson bound with ropes to the Philistines who were at Lehi, but the Spirit of Jehovah came mightily upon him and with a jawbone he waged a victorious one-man battle with his would-be captors.

The sequel to the battle showed the strong man, Samson, in a moment of weakness. Because of thirst, he feared he would die and fall into the hands of the conquered in his moment of triumph. This would have been utter humiliation.

D. SAMSON IN GAZA (16:1-3)

1 And Samson went to Gaza, and saw there a harlot, and went in unto her. 2 *And it was told* the Gazites, saying, Samson is come hither. And they compassed him in, and laid wait for him all night in the gate of the city, and were quiet all the night, saying, *Let be* till morning light, then we will kill him. 3 And Samson lay till midnight, and arose at midnight, and laid hold of the doors of the gate of the city, and the two posts, and plucked them up, bar and all, and put them upon his shoulders, and carried them up to the top of the mountain that is before Hebron.

Samson's efforts to deliver Israel from the Philistines reached their highest point of heroism when he defeated the Philistines at Lehi. His love for a daughter of a Philistine dwelling in Timnah had furnished the occasion for a series of happenings which culminated in the battle at that place. Samson had shown himself superior to the Philistines, but Israel had not rallied to his leadership.

Beginning with the account of his lust for a Philistine harlot in Gaza, the story of Samson moves rapidly to his tragic, though heroic, death. Only in his hour of death does the strong man rise above his sensualism and degradation.

There is no reason given for Samson's journey to Gaza, which was about thirty-eight miles southwest of Zorah and about the same distance from Hebron. However, in Gaza he spent the night with a harlot. The Philistines, hearing of Samson's presence, surrounded the city all night. They plotted to kill him the next day.

Samson arose at midnight in order to leave the city. Finding the city gates locked he escaped the Philistines by lifting the barred gates on his shoulders and carrying them to Hebron (v. 3). "This was the worst humiliation he could have inflicted on his enemies, because city gates symbolized national strength."[26]

E. SAMSON AND DELILAH (16:4-22)

4 And it came to pass afterward, that he loved a woman in the valley of Sorek, whose name was Delilah. 5 And the lords of the Philistines came up unto her, and said unto her, Entice him, and see wherein his great strength lieth, and by what means we may prevail against him, that we may bind him to afflict him: and we will give thee every one of us eleven hundred *pieces* of silver. 6 And Delilah said to Samson, Tell me, I pray thee, wherein thy great strength lieth, and wherewith thou mightest be bound to afflict thee. 7 And Samson said unto her, If they bind me with seven green withes that were never dried, then shall I become weak, and be as another man. 8 Then the lords of the Philistines brought up to her seven green withes which had not been dried, and she bound him with them. 9 Now she had liers-in-wait abiding in the inner chamber. And she said unto him, The Philistines are upon thee, Samson. And he brake the withes, as a string of tow is broken when it toucheth the fire. So his strength was not known.

10 And Delilah said unto Samson, Behold, thou hast mocked me, and told me lies: now tell me, I pray thee, wherewith thou mightest be bound. 11 And he said unto her, If they only bind me with new ropes wherewith no work hath been done, then shall I become weak, and be as another man. 12 So Delilah took new ropes, and bound him therewith, and said unto him, The Philistines are upon thee, Samson. And the liers-in-wait

were abiding in the inner chamber. And he brake them from off his arms like a thread.

13 And Delilah said unto Samson, Hitherto thou hast mocked me, and told me lies: tell me wherewith thou mightest be bound. And he said unto her, If thou weavest the seven locks of my head with the web. 14 And she fastened it with the pin, and said unto him, The Philistines are upon thee, Samson. And he awaked out of his sleep, and plucked away the pin of the beam, and the web.

15 And she said unto him, How canst thou say, I love thee, when thy heart is not with me? thou hast mocked me these three times, and hast not told me wherein thy great strength lieth. 16 And it came to pass, when she pressed him daily with her words, and urged him, that his soul was vexed unto death. 17 And he told her all his heart, and said unto her, There hath not come a razor upon my head; for I have been a Nazirite unto God from my mother's womb: if I be shaven, then my strength will go from me, and I shall become weak, and be like any other man.

18 And when Delilah saw that he had told her all his heart, she sent and called for the lords of the Philistines, saying, Come up this once, for he hath told me all his heart. Then the lords of the Philistines came up unto her, and brought the money in their hand. 19 And she made him sleep upon her knees; and she called for a man, and shaved off the seven locks of his head; and she began to afflict him, and his strength went from him. 20 And she said, The Philistines are upon thee, Samson. And he awoke out of his sleep, and said, I will go out as at other times, and shake myself free. But he knew not that Jehovah was departed from him. 21 And the Philistines laid hold on him, and put out his eyes; and they brought him down to Gaza, and bound him with fetters of brass; and he did grind in the prison-house. 22 Howbeit the hair of his head began to grow again after he was shaven.

This episode was a humiliating one for Samson and took place just a short distance from Zorah. Samson loved a woman in the valley of Sorek named Delilah. Her name is Semitic in origin, but she probably was a Philistine. When the Philistines knew of the romance, they offered a fabulous bribe to Delilah if she could discover the secret of Samson's phenomenal strength. Myers comments:

> Since the value of a silver shekel was somewhere between sixty and sixty-five cents, the price for Samson's betrayal was for that time enormous. . . .[27]

To Delilah the lure of the bribe was stronger than her love for Samson, and she urged him to tell her the secret of his strength.

The entire incident of Delilah's effort to discover Samson's secret seems to be in the form of a playful game. In reality it was a very dangerous sport indeed, for Samson's very freedom and eyesight were involved. Samson foolishly courted disaster thinking that Delilah was playing with him.

Delilah failed in her first two attempts, first with **withes** (bowstrings), second with **new ropes**. She pursued relentlessly, for a great prize was at stake. On the third attempt she pleaded so intently that he could withstand her no longer: **And it came to pass, when she pressed him daily with her words, and urged him, that his soul was vexed unto death. And he told her . . . if I be shaven, then my strength will go from me . . . (vv. 16, 17).**

In the meantime, she contacted the Philistines: **Come up this once, for he hath told me all his heart (v. 18).** Apparently they had given up, but she persuaded them to return to their hiding place in the next room. Samson came to visit and was lulled to sleep. As Delilah cut his hair, **she began to afflict him, and his strength went from him (v. 19).**

When Delilah awakened Samson with the words, **The Philistines are upon thee, Samson,** he prepared to arise as before, but his strength was gone. **He knew not that Jehovah was departed from him (v. 20).** For the first time in twenty years Samson was taken captive by the Philistines. They secured him with fetters of brass and blinded him. He spent his time grinding meal in the prison at Gaza.

As time passed, Samson's hair grew long again and apparently his strength began to return. This prepares for the final episode.

F. SAMSON'S LAST DAYS (16:23-31)

23 And the lords of the Philistines gathered them together to offer a great sacrifice unto Dagon their god, and to rejoice; for they said, Our god hath delivered Samson our enemy into our hand. 24 And when the people saw him, they praised their god; for they said, Our god hath delivered into our hand our enemy, and the destroyer of our country, who hath slain many of us. 25 And it came to pass, when their hearts were merry, that they said, Call for Samson, that he may make us sport. And they called for Samson out of the prison-house; and he made sport before them. And they set him between the pillars: 26 and Samson said unto the lad that held him by the hand, Suffer me that I may feel the pillars whereupon the house resteth, that I may lean upon them. 27 Now the house was full of men and women; and all the lords of the Philistines were there; and there were upon the roof about three thousand men and women, that beheld while Samson made sport.

28 And Samson called unto Jehovah, and said, O Lord Jehovah, remember me, I pray thee, and strengthen me, I pray thee, only this once, O God, that I may be at once avenged of the Philistines for my two eyes. 29 And Samson took hold of the two middle pillars upon which the house rested, and leaned upon them, the one with his right hand, and the other with his left. 30 And Samson said, Let me die with the Philistines. And he bowed himself with all his might; and the house fell upon the lords, and upon all the people that were therein. So the dead that he slew at his death were more than they that he slew in his life. 31 Then his brethren and all the house of his father came down, and took him, and brought him up, and buried him between Zorah and Eshtaol in the burying-place of Manoah his father. And he judged Israel twenty years.

The Philistines finally had their troublemaker where he would cause no more trouble. However, as Samson pondered his lot during the days he spent grinding in Gaza, he doubtless thought much about the loss of his sight. His final request had to do with recompense for this loss (cf. v. 28).

As the Philistines gathered to offer thanks unto their god, Dagon, at the temple in Gaza, they decided to have

[27] *Ibid.*, II, 792.

Samson brought before them to **make sport** (v. 25). Possibly they meant for him to perform some of his feats of strength.

Because his captors had blinded him he was lead about by one to whom he made a request, **Suffer me that I may feel the pillars whereupon the house resteth, that I may lean upon them** (v. 26).

With a prayer, **O Lord Jehovah . . . strengthen me . . . that I may be avenged . . . for my two eyes,** and with a mighty surge of strength, **he bowed himself with all his might** (vv. 28, 30). The temple of Dagon fell with disastrous results. Samson regained his strength only to expend it in a vengeful holocaust of destruction and death.

It was a catastrophic end for a life begun with the promise, "He shall begin to save Israel out of the hand of the Philistines" (13:5). Through Samson the Lord "sought an occasion against the Philistines" (14:4). His final words, however, were, **Let me die with the Philistines** (v. 30). One comes away from the story of Samson with a feeling of pathos. This life which began with such great promise, in its final moments pulled down everything within reach, leaving a great heap of rubble. Such tragic mishandling of life and its responsibilities happens all too frequently. Not only is this mishandling a tragedy in itself, but it tends to strike out against everything and everyone within reach.

There is another viewpoint from which to reflect upon Samson's end, namely, how the destructive feat of Samson affected the religious outlook of the Philistines. Samson had caused the Philistines much trouble during his lifetime and at his death he destroyed the temple of Dagon.

In this he had vindicated the honor of Jehovah, God of Israel, against Dagon, the god of Philistia. This religious reversal made a great impression upon the Philistines. They were not only in deep mourning over the death of so many fellow-countrymen and the destruction of their temple, but also in dread fear of Jehovah of Israel. Singularly enough, a mishandled life became an instrument by which the God of history acted in the arena of history.

IX. APPENDICES (Judg. 17:1—21:25)

With the story of Samson the history of Israel as recounted in the book of Judges comes to a close. Attached to this history of Israel are two appendices. The first gives the account of image-worship in the tribe of Dan, while the second gives the account of a rape at Gibeah in Benjamin. These accounts are not concerned with the cyclical developments of disobedience, discipline and deliverance which occur in the stories of the judges. Rather, these accounts give insight into the internal state of affairs during the period of the judges. They are invaluable as sources for a study of what it was like to live in the land of Israel in those days.

A. IMAGE-WORSHIP IN DAN (17:1— 18:31)

This is the story of the seizure of the images of Micah, an Ephraimite, by the Danites, and the removal of those images to Laish, where the Danites relocated and instituted an idolatrous shrine.

1. Micah's Image-Worship (17:1-13)

1 And there was a man of the hill-country of Ephraim, whose name was Micah. 2 And he said unto his mother, The eleven hundred *pieces* of silver that were taken from thee, about which thou didst utter a curse, and didst also speak it in mine ears, behold, the silver is with me; I took it. And his mother said, Blessed be my son of Jehovah. 3 And he restored the eleven hundred *pieces* of silver to his mother; and his mother said, I verily dedicate the silver unto Jehovah from my hand for my son, to make a graven image and a molten image: now therefore I will restore it unto thee. 4 And when he restored the money unto his mother, his mother took two hundred *pieces* of silver, and gave them to the founder, who made thereof a graven image and a molten image: and it was in the house of Micah. 5 And the man Micah had a house of gods, and he made an ephod, and teraphim, and consecrated one of his sons, who became his priest. 6 In those days there was no king in Israel: every man did that which was right in his own eyes.

7 And there was a young man out of Beth-lehem-judah, of the family of Judah, who was a Levite; and he sojourned there. 8 And the man departed out of the city, out of Beth-lehem-judah, to sojourn where he could find *a place;* and he came to

the hill-country of Ephraim to the house of Micah, as he journeyed. 9 And Micah said unto him, Whence comest thou? And he said unto him, I am a Levite of Beth-lehem-judah, and I go to sojourn where I may find *a place*. 10 And Micah said unto him, Dwell with me, and be unto me a father and a priest, and I will give thee ten *pieces* of silver by the year, and a suit of apparel, and thy victuals. So the Levite went in. 11 And the Levite was content to dwell with the man; and the young man was unto him as one of his sons. 12 And Micah consecrated the Levite, and the young man became his priest, and was in the house of Micah. 13 Then said Micah, Now know I that Jehovah will do me good, seeing I have a Levite to my priest.

Micah, an Ephraimite, had stolen money from his mother. He had a change of mind, however, when he learned it was money which had been given to the Lord, and he returned it. Part of the money was dedicated by Micah's mother to be made into an image and put in Micah's house. Whether there was more than one image is uncertain.

Moreover, Micah was visited by a wandering Levite, and he proceeded to offer him the position of priest in his house. This Levite, Jonathan, was Moses' grandson (v. 30). His presence was reassuring to the idolatrous Micah, who thought this would please the Lord. **Now know I that Jehovah will do me good, seeing I have a Levite to my priest** (v. 13). There are many persons who, like Micah, rationalize to the extent of expecting God's blessing upon their idolatry and sin because they observe some form of obedience to the divine law.

2. The Migration of Dan (18:1-31)

1 In those days there was no king in Israel: and in those days the tribe of the Danites sought them an inheritance to dwell in; for unto that day *their* inheritance had not fallen unto them among the tribes of Israel. 2 And the children of Dan sent of their family five men from their whole number, men of valor, from Zorah, and from Eshtaol, to spy out the land, and to search it; and they said unto them, Go, search the land. And they came to the hill-country of Ephraim, unto the house of Micah, and lodged there. 3 When they were by the house of Micah, they knew the voice of the young man the Levite; and they turned

aside thither, and said unto him, Who brought thee hither? and what doest thou in this place? and what hast thou here? 4 And he said unto them, Thus and thus hath Micah dealt with me, and he hath hired me, and I am become his priest. 5 And they said unto him, Ask counsel, we pray thee, of God, that we may know whether our way which we go shall be prosperous. 6 And the priest said unto them, Go in peace: before Jehovah is your way wherein ye go.

7 Then the five men departed, and came to Laish, and saw the people that were therein, how they dwelt in security, after the manner of the Sidonians, quiet and secure; for there was none in the land, possessing authority, that might put *them* to shame in anything, and they were far from the Sidonians, and had no dealings with any man. 8 And they came unto their brethren to Zorah and Eshtaol: and their brethren said unto them, What *say* ye? 9 And they said, Arise, and let us go against them; for we have seen the land, and, behold, it is very good: and are ye still? be not slothful to go and to enter in to possess the land. 10 When ye go, ye shall come unto a people secure, and the land is large; for God hath given it into your hand, a place where there is no want of anything that is in the earth.

11 And there set forth from thence of the family of the Danites, out of Zorah and out of Eshtaol, six hundred men girt with weapons of war. 12 And they went up, and encamped in Kiriath-jearim, in Judah: wherefore they called that place Mahaneh-dan unto this day; behold, it is behind Kiriath-jearim. 13 And they passed thence unto the hill-country of Ephraim, and came unto the house of Micah.

14 Then answered the five men that went to spy out the country of Laish, and said unto their brethren, Do ye know that there is in these houses an ephod, and teraphim, and a graven image, and a molten image? now therefore consider what ye have to do. 15 And they turned aside thither, and came to the house of the young man the Levite, even unto the house of Micah, and asked him of his welfare. 16 And the six hundred men girt with their weapons of war, who were of the children of Dan, stood by the entrance of the gate. 17 And the five men that went to spy out the land went up, and came in thither, and took the graven image, and the ephod, and the teraphim, and the molten image: and the priest stood by the entrance of the gate with the six hundred men girt with weapons of war. 18 And when these went into

Micah's house, and fetched the graven image, the ephod, and the teraphim, and the molten image, the priest said unto them, What do ye? 19 And they said unto him, Hold thy peace, lay thy hand upon thy mouth, and go with us, and be to us a father and a priest: is it better for thee to be priest unto the house of one man, or to be priest unto a tribe and a family in Israel? 20 And the priest's heart was glad, and he took the ephod, and the teraphim, and the graven image, and went in the midst of the people.

21 So they turned and departed, and put the little ones and the cattle and the goods before them. 22 When they were a good way from the house of Micah, the men that were in the houses near to Micah's house were gathered together, and overtook the children of Dan. 23 And they cried unto the children of Dan. And they turned their faces and said unto Micah, What aileth thee, that thou comest with such a company? 24 And he said, Ye have taken away my gods which I made, and the priest, and are gone away, and what have I more? and how then say ye unto me, What aileth thee? 25 And the children of Dan said unto him, Let not thy voice be heard among us, lest angry fellows fall upon you, and thou lose thy life, with the lives of thy household. 26 And the children of Dan went their way: and when Micah saw that they were too strong for him, he turned and went back into his house.

27 And they took that which Micah had made, and the priest whom he had, and came unto Laish, unto a people quiet and secure, and smote them with the edge of the sword; and they burnt the city with fire. 28 And there was no deliverer, because it was far from Sidon, and they had no dealings with any man; and it was in the valley that lieth by Beth-rehob. And they built the city, and dwelt therein. 29 And they called the name of the city Dan, after the name of Dan their father, who was born unto Israel: howbeit the name of the city was Laish at the first. 30 And the children of Dan set up for themselves the graven image; and Jonathan, the son of Gershom, the son of Moses, he and his sons were priests to the tribe of the Danites until the day of the captivity of the land. 31 So they set them up Micah's graven image which he made, all the time that the house of God was in Shiloh.

Because of the increasing pressure from the native inhabitants in the inheritance of Dan, the people of this tribe recognized the impossibility of redeeming their inheritance and sought another location. It was a period of uncertainty for the tribe of Dan. **In those days the tribe of the Danites sought them an inheritance to dwell in** (v. 1).

Therefore, the Danites sent five men to find a place where they could relocate. They happened upon Micah's residence and inquired of Micah's Levite concerning their venture. He replied, **Go in peace: before Jehovah is your way wherein ye go** (v. 6). Reassured, they went on northward to Laish. They viewed the territory in which Laish was located and were delighted with it as **a place where there is no want of anything** . . . (v. 10).

They returned to their people and reported. While not all of the Danites responded, some six hundred men with their families prepared to relocate. Their journey was by way of Micah's house in Ephraim.

When they arrived at Micah's house they used the threat of force plus persuasion to obtain his image and his priest. They then continued on to Laish and captured the unsuspecting city, devastating it with fire.

A new city was erected on the site and called Dan. Here the stolen image was enshrined and the grandson of Moses, Jonathan, together with his successors, continued their priestly function **until the day of the captivity of the land** (v. 30). This is a probable reference to the conquest of Galilee by Tiglath-pileser III of Assyria in 732 B.C.[28]

For Dan to have a continuing priesthood descended from Moses enhanced its prestige enormously. The antiquity of the cult of Dan may have been equal to that of Shiloh, where the tabernacle was erected and the Aaronic priesthood ministered until about the time of the first battle of Ebenezer (I Sam. 4). **So they set them up Micah's graven image which he made, all the time that the house of God was in Shiloh** (v. 31).

B. RAPE AT GIBEAH (19:1—21:25)

The book of Judges has as its final narrative a horrendous outrage that stood

28 Cf. Bruce, op. cit., p. 255.

out as an epitome of wickedness for centuries to come. The eighth-century prophet Hosea made reference to it: "They have deeply corrupted themselves, as in the days of Gibeah" (Hos. 9:9).

1. The Levite and His Concubine (19: 1-30)

1 And it came to pass in those days, when there was no king in Israel, that there was a certain Levite sojourning on the farther side of the hill-country of Ephraim, who took to him a concubine out of Beth-lehem-judah. 2 And his concubine played the harlot against him, and went away from him unto her father's house to Beth-lehem-judah, and was there the space of four months. 3 And her husband arose, and went after her, to speak kindly unto her, to bring her again, having his servant with him, and a couple of asses: and she brought him into her father's house; and when the father of the damsel saw him, he rejoiced to meet him. 4 And his father-in-law, the damsel's father, retained him; and he abode with him three days: so they did eat and drink, and lodged there. 5 And it came to pass on the fourth day, that they arose early in the morning, and he rose up to depart: and the damsel's father said unto his son-in-law, Strengthen thy heart with a morsel of bread, and afterward ye shall go your way. 6 So they sat down, and did eat and drink, both of them together: and the damsel's father said unto the man, Be pleased, I pray thee, to tarry all night, and let thy heart be merry. 7 And the man rose up to depart; but his father-in-law urged him, and he lodged there again. 8 And he arose early in the morning on the fifth day to depart; and the damsel's father said, Strengthen thy heart, I pray thee, and tarry ye until the day declineth; and they did eat, both of them. 9 And when the man rose up to depart, he, and his concubine, and his servant, his father-in-law, the damsel's father, said unto him, Behold, now the day draweth toward evening, I pray you tarry all night: behold, the day groweth to an end, lodge here, that thy heart may be merry; and tomorrow get you early on your way, that thou mayest go home. 10 But the man would not tarry that night, but he rose up and departed, and came over against Jebus (the same is Jerusalem) : and there were with him a couple of asses saddled; his concubine also was with him. 11 When they were by Jebus, the day was far spent; and the servant said unto his master, Come, I pray thee, and let us turn aside into this city of the Jebusites, and lodge in it. 12 And his master said unto him, We will not turn aside into the city of a foreigner, that is not of the children of Israel; but we will pass over to Gibeah. 13 And he said unto his servant, Come and let us draw near to one of these places; and we will lodge in Gibeah, or in Ramah. 14 So they passed on and went their way; and the sun went down upon them near to Gibeah, which belongeth to Benjamin. 15 And they turned aside thither, to go in to lodge in Gibeah: and he went in, and sat him down in the street of the city; for there was no man that took them into his house to lodge.

16 And, behold, there came an old man from his work out of the field at even: now the man was of the hill-country of Ephraim, and he sojourned in Gibeah; but the men of the place were Benjamites. 17 And he lifted up his eyes, and saw the wayfaring man in the street of the city; and the old man said, Whither goest thou? and whence comest thou? 18 And he said unto him, We are passing from Beth-lehem-judah unto the farther side of the hill-country of Ephraim; from thence am I, and I went to Beth-lehem-judah: and I am *now* going to the house of Jehovah; and there is no man that taketh me into his house. 19 Yet there is both straw and provender for our asses; and there is bread and wine also for me, and for thy handmaid, and for the young man that is with thy servants: there is no want of anything. 20 And the old man said, Peace be unto thee; howsoever let all thy wants lie upon me; only lodge not in the street. 21 So he brought him into his house, and gave the asses fodder; and they washed their feet, and did eat and drink.

22 As they were making their hearts merry, behold, the men of the city, certain base fellows, beset the house round about, beating at the door; and they spake to the master of the house, the old man, saying, Bring forth the man that came into thy house, that we may know him. 23 And the man, the master of the house, went out unto them, and said unto them, Nay, my brethren, I pray you, do not so wickedly; seeing that this man is come into my house, do not this folly. 24 Behold, here is my daughter a virgin, and his concubine; them I will bring out now, and humble ye them, and do with them what seemeth good unto you: but unto this man do not any such folly. 25 But the men would not hearken to him: so the man laid hold on his concu-

bine, and brought her forth unto them; and they knew her, and abused her all the night until the morning: and when the day began to spring, they let her go. 26 Then came the woman in the dawning of the day, and fell down at the door of the man's house where her lord was, till it was light.

27 And her lord rose up in the morning, and opened the doors of the house, and went out to go his way; and, behold, the woman his concubine was fallen down at the door of the house, with her hands upon the threshold. 28 And he said unto her, Up, and let us be going; but none answered: then he took her up upon the ass; and the man rose up, and gat him unto his place. 29 And when he was come into his house, he took a knife, and laid hold on his concubine, and divided her, limb by limb, into twelve pieces, and sent her throughout all the borders of Israel. 30 And it was so, that all that saw it said, There was no such deed done nor seen from the day that the children of Israel came up out of the land of Egypt unto this day: consider it, take counsel, and speak.

Since Gibeah in Benjamin lay between Ephraim to the north and Judah to the south, it is necessary to remember that the Levite of Ephraim passed through Benjamin on his way to win back his unfaithful concubine who had gone to Judah. He accomplished a happy reunion and spent several days of celebration in Judah.

On his return to Ephraim, the Levite and his concubine lodged overnight in Gibeah. The one man in the place that offered hospitality to the strangers was not a Benjaminite. He was a fellow-Ephraimite who was sojourning in Gibeah (v. 16). The Benjaminites of the city made no effort to be hospitable, for the Levite said, **There is no man that taketh me into his house** (v. 18). The sojourning Ephraimite replied, **Let all thy wants lie upon me** (v. 20).

While the guests were enjoying this hospitality, certain rascals of the city demanded to have access to them for base sexuality. When the situation appeared to be out of control the Levite thrust out his concubine for their indulgence. After a night of being subjected to repeated raping she died.

The next day the Levite continued homeward. He carried the body of his concubine to his home, divided it into twelve pieces and sent a piece to each tribe.

2. War Against Benjamin (20:1-48)

1 Then all the children of Israel went out, and the congregation was assembled as one man, from Dan even to Beer-sheba, with the land of Gilead, unto Jehovah at Mizpah. 2 And the chiefs of all the people, even of all the tribes of Israel, presented themselves in the assembly of the people of God, four hundred thousand footmen that drew sword. 3 (Now the children of Israel were gone up to Mizpah.) And the children of Israel said, Tell us, how was this wickedness brought to pass? 4 And the Levite, the husband of the woman that was murdered, answered and said, I came into Gibeah that belongeth to Benjamin, I and my concubine, to lodge. 5 And the men of Gibeah rose against me, and beset the house round about me by night; me they thought to have slain, and my concubine they forced, and she is dead. 6 And I took my concubine, and cut her in pieces, and sent her throughout all the country of the inheritance of Israel; for they have committed lewdness and folly in Israel. 7 Behold, ye children of Israel, all of you, give here your advice and counsel.

8 And all the people arose as one man, saying, We will not any of us go to his tent, neither will we any of us turn unto his house. 9 But now this is the thing which we will do to Gibeah: we will go up against it by lot; 10 and we will take ten men of a hundred throughout all the tribes of Israel, and a hundred of a thousand, and a thousand out of ten thousand, to fetch victuals for the people, that they may do, when they come to Gibeah of Benjamin, according to all the folly that they have wrought in Israel. 11 So all the men of Israel were gathered against the city, knit together as one man.

12 And the tribes of Israel sent men through all the tribe of Benjamin, saying, What wickedness is this that is come to pass among you? 13 Now therefore deliver up the men, the base fellows, that are in Gibeah, that we may put them to death, and put away evil from Israel. But Benjamin would not hearken to the voice of their brethren the children of Israel. 14 And the children of Benjamin gathered themselves together out of the cities unto Gibeah, to go out to battle against the children of Israel. 15 And the children of Benjamin were numbered on that day out of the cities

twenty and six thousand men that drew sword, besides the inhabitants of Gibeah, who were numbered seven hundred chosen men. 16 Among all this people there were seven hundred chosen men left-handed; every one could sling stones at a hairbreadth, and not miss.

17 And the men of Israel, besides Benjamin, were numbered four hundred thousand men that drew sword: all these were men of war. 18 And the children of Israel arose, and went up to Beth-el, and asked counsel of God; and they said, Who shall go up for us first to battle against the children of Benjamin? And Jehovah said, Judah *shall go up* first.

19 And the children of Israel rose up in the morning, and encamped against Gibeah. 20 And the men of Israel went out to battle against Benjamin; and the men of Israel set the battle in array against them at Gibeah. 21 And the children of Benjamin came forth out of Gibeah, and destroyed down to the ground of the Israelites on that day twenty and two thousand men. 22 And the people, the men of Israel, encouraged themselves, and set the battle again in array in the place where they set themselves in array the first day. 23 And the children of Israel went up and wept before Jehovah until even; and they asked of Jehovah, saying, Shall I again draw nigh to battle against the children of Benjamin my brother? And Jehovah said, Go up against him.

24 And the children of Israel came near against the children of Benjamin the second day. 25 And Benjamin went forth against them out of Gibeah the second day, and destroyed down to the ground of the children of Israel again eighteen thousand men; all these drew the sword. 26 Then all the children of Israel, and all the people, went up, and came unto Beth-el, and wept, and sat there before Jehovah, and fasted that day until even; and they offered burnt-offerings and peace-offerings before Jehovah. 27 And the children of Israel asked of Jehovah (for the ark of the covenant of God was there in those days, 28 and Phinehas, the son of Eleazar, the son of Aaron, stood before it in those days), saying, Shall I yet again go out to battle against the children of Benjamin my brother, or shall I cease? And Jehovah said, Go up; for to-morrow I will deliver him into thy hand.

29 And Israel set liers-in-wait against Gibeah round about. 30 And the children of Israel went up against the children of Benjamin on the third day, and set themselves in array against Gibeah,

as at other times. 31 And the children of Benjamin went out against the people, and were drawn away from the city; and they began to smite and kill of the people, as at other times, in the highways, of which one goeth up to Beth-el, and the other to Gibeah, in the field, about thirty men of Israel. 32 And the children of Benjamin said, They are smitten down before us, as at the first. But the children of Israel said, Let us flee, and draw them away from the city unto the highways. 33 And all the men of Israel rose up out of their place, and set themselves in array at Baal-tamar: and the liers-in-wait of Israel brake forth out of their place, even out of Maareh-geba. 34 And there came over against Gibeah ten thousand chosen men out of all Israel, and the battle was sore; but they knew not that evil was close upon them. 35 And Jehovah smote Benjamin before Israel; and the children of Israel destroyed of Benjamin that day twenty and five thousand and a hundred men: all these drew the sword.

36 So the children of Benjamin saw that they were smitten; for the men of Israel gave place to Benjamin, because they trusted unto the liers-in-wait whom they had set against Gibeah. 37 And the liers-in-wait hasted, and rushed upon Gibeah; and the liers-in-wait drew themselves along, and smote all the city with the edge of the sword. 38 Now the appointed sign between the men of Israel and the liers-in-wait was, that they should make a great cloud of smoke rise up out of the city. 39 And the men of Israel turned in the battle, and Benjamin began to smite and kill of the men of Israel about thirty persons; for they said, Surely they are smitten down before us, as in the first battle. 40 But when the cloud began to arise up out of the city in a pillar of smoke, the Benjamites looked behind them; and, behold, the whole of the city went up *in smoke* to heaven. 41 And the men of Israel turned, and the men of Benjamin were dismayed: for they saw that evil was come upon them. 42 Therefore they turned their backs before the men of Israel unto the way of the wilderness; but the battle followed hard after them; and they that came out of the cities destroyed them in the midst thereof. 43 They inclosed the Benjamites round about, *and* chased them, *and* trod them down at *their* resting-place, as far as over against Gibeah toward the sunrising. 44 And there fell of Benjamin eighteen thousand men; all these *were* men of valor. 45 And they turned and fled toward the wilderness

unto the rock of Rimmon: and they gleaned of them in the highways five thousand men, and followed hard after them unto Gidom, and smote of them two thousand men. 46 So that all who fell that day of Benjamin were twenty and five thousand men that drew the sword; all these *were* men of valor. 47 But six hundred men turned and fled toward the wilderness unto the rock of Rimmon, and abode in the rock of Rimmon four months. 48 And the men of Israel turned again upon the children of Benjamin, and smote them with the edge of the sword, both the entire city, and the cattle, and all that they found: moreover all the cities which they found they set on fire.

The Levite's drastic call for justice had a powerful effect upon the tribes. The revolting crime at Gibeah united Israel in a singular way. The tribes were as one in opposition to so ruthless a deed, that is, all save the tribe of Benjamin and the Gadites of Jabesh-gilead.

The tribes of Israel assembled a congregation at Mizpah, located about three miles west of Gibeah, and decided that the deed against the Levite must be avenged. There was remarkable unity in the proposed course of action. **So all the men of Israel were gathered against the city, knit together as one man** (v. 11).

The tribe of Benjamin was ordered to surrender the culprits, but Benjamin refused. War was the only alternative. Divine guidance was sought and Judah was ordered to launch the attack (v. 18). The first two attacks upon Gibeah and the Benjaminites were repulsed, but the third attack routed the defenders and Gibeah was completely destroyed by fire. Apparently other parts of Benjamin were ravaged by the invading Israelites. **All the cities which they found they set on fire** (v. 48). The conquest of Benjamin was utter and complete. The tribe was almost annihilated in this ruthless battle.

3. Attempts to Restore Benjamin (21: 1-25)

1 Now the men of Israel had sworn in Mizpah, saying, There shall not any of us give his daughter unto Benjamin to wife. 2 And the people came to Beth-el, and sat there till even before God, and lifted up their voices, and wept sore. 3 And they said, O Jehovah, the God of Israel, why is this come to pass in Israel, that there should be to-day one tribe lacking in Israel? 4 And it came to pass on the morrow, that the people rose early, and built there an altar, and offered burnt-offerings and peace-offerings. 5 And the children of Israel said, Who is there among all the tribes of Israel that came not up in the assembly unto Jehovah? For they had made a great oath concerning him that came not up unto Jehovah to Mizpah, saying, He shall surely be put to death. 6 And the children of Israel repented them for Benjamin their brother, and said, There is one tribe cut off from Israel this day. 7 How shall we do for wives for them that remain, seeing we have sworn by Jehovah that we will not give them of our daughters to wives?

8 And they said, What one is there of the tribes of Israel that came not up unto Jehovah to Mizpah? And, behold, there came none to the camp from Jabesh-gilead to the assembly. 9 For when the people were numbered, behold, there were none of the inhabitants of Jabesh-gilead there. 10 And the congregation sent thither twelve thousand men of the valiantest, and commanded them, saying, Go and smite the inhabitants of Jabesh-gilead with the edge of the sword, with the women and the little ones. 11 And this is the thing that ye shall do: ye shall utterly destroy every male, and every woman that hath lain by man. 12 And they found among the inhabitants of Jabesh-gilead four hundred young virgins, that had not known man by lying with him; and they brought them unto the camp to Shiloh, which is in the land of Canaan.

13 And the whole congregation sent and spake to the children of Benjamin that were in the rock of Rimmon, and proclaimed peace unto them. 14 And Benjamin returned at that time; and they gave them the women whom they had saved alive of the women of Jabesh-gilead: and yet so they sufficed them not. 15 And the people repented them for Benjamin, because that Jehovah had made a breach in the tribes of Israel.

16 Then the elders of the congregation said, How shall we do for wives for them that remain, seeing the women are destroyed out of Benjamin? 17 And they said, There must be an inheritance for them that are escaped of Benjamin, that a tribe be not blotted out from Israel. 18 Howbeit we may not give them wives of our daughters; for the children of Israel had sworn, saying, Cursed be he that giveth a wife to Benjamin. 19 And they said, Behold, there is a feast

of Jehovah from year to year in Shiloh, which is on the north of Beth-el, on the east side of the highway that goeth up from Beth-el to Shechem, and on the south of Lebonah. 20 And they commanded the children of Benjamin, saying, Go and lie in wait in the vineyards; 21 and see, and, behold, if the daughters of Shiloh come out to dance in the dances, then come ye out of the vineyards, and catch you every man his wife of the daughters of Shiloh, and go to the land of Benjamin. 22 And it shall be, when their fathers or their brethren come to complain unto us, that we will say unto them, Grant them graciously unto us; because we took not for each man *of them* his wife in battle, neither did ye give them unto them; else would ye now be guilty. 23 And the children of Benjamin did so, and took them wives, according to their number, of them that danced, whom they carried off: and they went and returned unto their inheritance, and built the cities, and dwelt in them. 24 And the children of Israel departed thence at that time, every man to his tribe and to his family, and they went out from thence every man to his inheritance.

25 In those days there was no king in Israel: every man did that which was right in his own eyes.

In the aftermath of the carnage of Benjamin, Israel came together at Bethel in great mourning over Benjamin. **O Jehovah . . . why is this come to pass in Israel, that there should be to-day one tribe lacking in Israel?** (v. 3). **And the children of Israel repented them for Benjamin . . .** (v. 6).

As they pondered how Benjamin might be restored, it was remembered that they had vowed at Mizpah concerning any who failed to take part in the avenging of the Levite, **He shall surely be put to death** (v. 5).

They discovered that no one from Jabesh-gilead in the tribe of Gad had been present; so Jabesh-gilead was put to the sword and its virgins were brought as wives for the few remaining Benjaminites (v. 14). As the number of these virgins was insufficient, it was decided that the Benjaminites still lacking wives were to go to Shiloh in Ephraim and seize a daughter of the people of that city. In this manner the retention of the tribe of Benjamin was accomplished.

So the Israelites endeavored to heal the deep wound caused by their civil war. Meanwhile, the decimated tribe of Benjamin began life where it had left off by returning to the land of its inheritance and building cities.

These two accounts of life in the land of Israel during the period of the judges re-enforce the historian's point of view that the situation in the land prior to the monarchy was not as satisfactory and orderly as in the time of the kings. A recurring refrain is, **In those days there was no king in Israel** (17:6; 18:1; 19:1; 21:25). The corollary to this is, **Every man did that which was right in his own eyes** (17:6; 21:25). The point is that the historian sees Israel's lot improved by the coming of the monarchy.

Bibliography

I. EXEGETICAL AND HISTORICAL VALUE

Albright, W. F. *Archaeology and the Religion of Israel*. 3rd ed. Baltimore: John Hopkins, 1953.

Anderson, Bernhard W. *Understanding the Old Testament*. Englewood Cliffs, N. J.: Prentice-Hall, 1957.

Bright, John. *A History of Israel*. Philadelphia: Westminster, 1959.

Bruce, F. F. "Judges." *New Bible Commentary*. Eds. F. Davidson *et al.* Grand Rapids: Eerdmans, 1953.

Cooke, G. A. "Barak." *Dictionary of the Bible*. Ed. J. Hastings. Vol. I. New York: Scribner, 1902.

Garstang, John. *Foundations of Bible History: Joshua, Judges*. London: Constable, 1931.

Moore, G. F. "A Critical and Exegetical Commentary on Judges." *International Critical Commentary*. Edinburgh: T. & T. Clark, 1908.

Myers, Jacob M. "Judges: Introduction and Exegesis." *The Interpreter's Bible*. Eds. G. A. Buttrick *et al.* Vol. II. New York and Nashville: Abingdon, 1953.

Schultz, Samuel J. *The Old Testament Speaks*. New York: Harper and Row, 1960.

Wright, G. E., and F. V. Filson (eds.). *The Westminster Historical Atlas*. Revised. Philadelphia: Westminster, 1956.

II. EXPOSITORY AND PRACTICAL VALUE

Elliott, Phillips P. "Judges: Exposition." *The Interpreter's Bible*. Eds. G. A. Buttrick *et al.* Vol. II, New York and Nashville: Abingdon, 1953.

Lange, John P. *Commentary on the Holy Scripture: Joshua, Judges, Ruth*. Trans. and ed. Philip Schaff. Reprint. Grand Rapids: Zondervan, n.d.

Maclaren, Alexander. *Expositions of Holy Scripture: Deuteronomy through II Samuel*. New York: Doran, n.d.

Morgan, G. Campbell. *Living Messages of the Books of the Bible: Genesis to Malachi*. Revell, 1912.

Nicoll, W. Robertson. *The Expositor's Bible*. Vol. II. Grand Rapids: Eerdmans, 1940.

Rust, Eric C. "Judges, Ruth, I and II Samuel." *The Layman's Bible Commentary*. Eds. B. H. Kelly *et al.* Vol. VI. Richmond, Va.: John Knox, 1959.

Stevenson, Dwight E. *Preaching on the Books of the Old Testament*. New York: Harper, 1961.

Tombs, Lawrence E. "Nation Making." *Bible Guides*. Eds. William Barclay and F. F. Bruce. No. 4. New York and Nashville: Abingdon, n.d.

The Book of Ruth

by Charles R. Wilson

Outline

Introduction

Ruth, a Moabitess, was so full of loving-kindness that Israel could not let her be forgotten. Although an alien, she was a leading personality in one of the most beautiful Old Testament stories of filial faithfulness. Her story is told in the book of Ruth.

I. PLACE IN THE CANON

The book of Ruth appears in the third division of the Hebrew Bible, the *Ketuvim* or Writings, the other two divisions being the *Torah* or Law and the *Nevi'im* or Prophets. This threefold division appears to have become established by 200 B.C. " 'The Wisdom of Jesus ben Sirach' written in about 200 B.C. includes, in chapters XLIV-XLIX, references to all the books of the Law and of the Prophets, and to part of the Writings."[1] The third division, the Writings, was formed later than the others.

The translators of the Septuagint, who began their work in the third century B.C., disregarded the divisions of the Prophets and the Writings. For one thing, they placed Ruth after Judges because the subject matter refers to the times of the judges (Ruth 1:1). Whether or not the book of Ruth was originally placed in juxtaposition with Judges is impossible to determine. As a result, the issue as to whether the Hebrew Bible or the Septuagint has the book in the proper place is incapable of being resolved. It may be assumed, however, that the arrangement in the Hebrew Bible is correct.

II. COMPOSITION

The story of Ruth is a marvel of descriptive writing. There has been considerable comment as to whether this story is the product of earlier or later composition. "In any case, the structure of the book reveals the consummate art of the ancient Hebrew narrators."[2] Elements in such a structure include balance, as Orpah over against Ruth; economy of language, as the description of life in Bethlehem; inclusion of details, as Ruth saving a portion of her meal for Naomi; the prolonging of suspense, as the occasion of the nearer kinsman's answer regarding the inheritance.

There is a remarkable charm about the story. The relationships which existed between a woman and her daughters-in-law, between Boaz and his field workers, between the leading men at the gate and those who sought settlements, indicate a pattern for social relationships. Amid the turbulent period of the judges it presents a quiet pastoral scene in which people were faithful to God and loving toward their fellow men. Even a foreigner was identified with the life of Israel and was able to make a contribution to its well-being. Though an alien, Ruth is portrayed as kind, loyal and self-giving. The climax of the story is reached when Ruth, who appeared to have no future, was married to Boaz and entered the genealogy of the great king of Israel, David.

III. HISTORICAL SIGNIFICANCE

No single explanation fully sets forth the significance of this book. There are, however, some that give valuable aid toward this end. One is that it supplies a genealogy for David, the greatest of the Hebrew kings. Another is that it emphasizes integration and pleads for the inclusion of aliens in the community of Israel. With such an emphasis the book of Ruth makes explicit what is implicit in the Genesis genealogies, namely, that in the great plan and purpose of God all peoples are included and man-made racial barriers are disregarded. Still another ex-

---

[1] G. T. Manley, *The New Bible Handbook*, p. 30.
[2] Louise P. Smith, "Ruth: Introduction and Exegesis," *The Interpreter's Bible*, p. 830.

planation is that it is a protest against exclusivism and separatism. This seems to require dating the book during the time of Ezra and Nehemiah, a time of strict prohibition of mixed marriages. It is also a plea for humanitarian care for the childless widow so that the next of kin would assume responsibility. Finally, it is the narration of an intense and lasting friendship between an Israelite and a Moabite, the one a mother and the other a daughter-in-law. The story traces the course of events in Naomi's life from initial comfort through losses to final comfort, with Ruth providing love and devotion surpassing that of seven sons (4:5). Ruth's plea, "Entreat me not to leave thee, . . . for whither thou goest, I will go" (1:16), is an expression of that indissolvable friendship.

Generally speaking, the dating of the origin of the book has in a large measure determined its significance, with an earlier dating associated with providing David a genealogy, and a later dating associated with a plea for racial tolerance. If the problem of dating is relegated to a position of minor importance, the timeless significance of the true value of friendship of individuals of whatever race who have a common religious faith assumes major importance.

Commentary on Ruth

I. ELIMELECH'S MIGRATION TO MOAB (Ruth 1:1-5)

1 And it came to pass in the days when the judges judged, that there was a famine in the land. And a certain man of Bethlehem-judah went to sojourn in the country of Moab, he, and his wife, and his two sons. 2 And the name of the man was Elimelech, and the name of his wife Naomi, and the name of his two sons Mahlon and Chilion, Ephrathites of Bethlehem-judah. And they came into the country of Moab, and continued there. 3 And Elimelech, Naomi's husband, died; and she was left, and her two sons. 4 And they took them wives of the women of Moab; the name of the one was Orpah, and the name of the other Ruth: and they dwelt there about ten years. 5 And Mahlon and Chilion died both of them; and the woman was left of her two children and of her husband.

The beautiful story of Ruth has its setting **in the days when the judges judged** (v. 1). It all began as a result of a serious famine in Judah. A critical scarcity made life in Judah intolerable for an Israelite named Elimelech. To escape the threat of starvation, he and his wife, Naomi, together with their sons, Mahlon and Chilion, left their inheritance in Bethlehem and journeyed to Moab.

It was a desperate move for Elimelech. It meant leaving familiar faces and surroundings. It involved the risk of travel during the uneasy period of the judges. It required considerable adjustments to a new culture and a foreign way of life.

Geographically, the distance from Bethlehem to Moab was not great for those days. A journey of about fifty miles was involved. The heart of Moab was the plateau which lay east of the Dead Sea between the Arnon and the Zered wadis, which drain into the Dead Sea.

Culturally and religiously, however, the distance was immense. Unlike the confederation of the tribes of Israel, the kingdom of Moab was highly organized. There were excellent buildings and strong fortifications. There was considerable agricultural and pastoral activity. The religion of the Moabites was devoted to Chemosh and worship of Chemosh included human sacrifice.

Elimelech and his family attempted to make a new start in this foreign land. They left a famine-stricken country only to encounter further reverses. First, there was the death of Elimelech (v. 3). Second, there was the loss of the two sons who, having married Moabite women, lived ten years and died (v. 5). Third, the bereaved wives were left childless.

While some have attempted to show that these reverses came as a result of migration to an alien land and marriage to foreign wives, there is no proof that such was the case.

II. NAOMI AND HER DAUGHTERS-IN-LAW (Ruth 1:6-22)

Receiving news that the famine in Judah was at an end, Naomi decided to return to her homeland. Her daughters-in-law, Orpah and Ruth, also decided to go with her.

A. NAOMI'S PERSUASION (1:6-14)

6 Then she arose with her daughters-in-law, that she might return from the country of Moab: for she had heard in the country of Moab how that Jehovah had visited his people in giving them bread. 7 And she went forth out of the place where she was, and her two daughters-in-law with her; and they went on the way to return unto the land of Judah. 8 And Naomi said unto her two daughters-in-law, Go, return each of you to her mother's house: Jehovah deal kindly with you, as ye have dealt with the dead, and with me. 9 Jehovah grant you that ye may find rest, each of you in the house of her husband. Then she kissed them, and they lifted up their voice, and wept. 10 And they said unto her,

Nay, but we will return with thee unto thy people. 11 And Naomi said, Turn again, my daughters: why will ye go with me? have I yet sons in my womb, that they may be your husbands? 12 Turn again, my daughters, go your way; for I am too old to have a husband. If I should even have hope, if I should even have a husband tonight, and should also bear sons; 13 would ye therefore tarry till they were grown? would ye therefore stay from having husbands? nay, my daughters; for it grieveth me much for your sakes, for the hand of Jehovah is gone forth against me. 14 And they lifted up their voice, and wept again: and Orpah kissed her mother-in-law; but Ruth clave unto her.

Naomi endeavored to persuade her daughters-in-law to remain in Moab. **Go, return each of you to her mother's house** (v. 8). Naomi's reference is to the women's quarters. **Jehovah deal kindly with you** (v. 8). The Hebrew term *chesed* is variously translated "lovingkindness," "goodness," "loyalty." Naomi was desirous that God would grant *chesed* to her daughters-in-law even though they were outside Israel and aliens to the covenant. **Jehovah grant you that ye may find rest, each of you in the house of her husband** (v. 9). The pronoun **her** here refers to their respective mothers, hence the meaning is that they should return to their parental homes. Naomi reveals the utter helplessness of widows without children as she urges Orpah and Ruth to go back where they would find security and kindness in the family home.

Notwithstanding her plea, Naomi faced daughters-in-law who were resolute in their determination to go with her. **Nay, but we will return with thee unto thy people** (v. 10). Orpah and Ruth had proved themselves kindly in their dealings, not only with their husbands who were no longer living, but now also with their mother-in-law who was in the depth of a living death of loneliness and self-incrimination. Naomi revealed her deep guilt feeling when she said, **For it grieveth me much for your sakes, for the hand of Jehovah is gone forth against me** (v. 13 margin: "It is far more bitter for me than for you"). Yet Orpah and Ruth were willing to risk their future in an alien land in order to help Naomi.

B. RUTH'S PERSISTENCE (1:15-22)

15 And she said, Behold, thy sister-in-law is gone back unto her people, and unto her god: return thou after thy sister-in-law. 16 And Ruth said, Entreat me not to leave thee, and to return from following after thee; for whither thou goest, I will go; and where thou lodgest, I will lodge; thy people shall be my people, and thy God my God; 17 where thou diest, will I die, and there will I be buried: Jehovah do so to me, and more also, if aught but death part thee and me. 18 And when she saw that she was stedfastly minded to go with her, she left off speaking unto her.

19 So they two went until they came to Beth-lehem. And it came to pass, when they were come to Beth-lehem, that all the city was moved about them, and *the women* said, Is this Naomi? 20 And she said unto them, Call me not Naomi, call me Mara; for the Almighty hath dealt very bitterly with me. 21 I went out full, and Jehovah hath brought me home again empty; why call ye me Naomi, seeing Jehovah hath testified against me, and the Almighty hath afflicted me? 22 So Naomi returned, and Ruth the Moabitess, her daughter-in-law, with her, who returned out of the country of Moab: and they came to Beth-lehem in the beginning of barley harvest.

Because of Naomi's persuasion, Orpah relented and, bidding farewell, returned to her people. Naomi attempted to use Orpah's decision to influence Ruth, **Behold, thy sister-in-law is gone back unto her people, and unto her god** (v. 15). However, Ruth was unwilling to follow her sister-in-law and return to the security of her people and the worship of the god of Moab. She was as firmly committed to kind and devoted treatment to her mother-in-law as she had been to her husband (cf. Naomi's remarks in v. 8).

Naomi had been greatly shaken in her faith by the recent harsh experiences to which she had been subjected. She reacted bitterly as she saw her life under divine judgment. Without hesitation and without reservation Ruth entered into Naomi's trying ordeal and gave selfless devotion to her.

Notwithstanding what Naomi had said concerning the judgment of the Lord toward her, Ruth resolutely declared, **Entreat me not to leave thee . . . whither thou goest, I will go . . . thy people shall be my people, and thy God my God . . .**

Jehovah do so to me, and more also, if aught but death part thee and me (vv. 16, 17). Her words constitute an exquisite expression of resolution. Although Naomi had offered nothing but uncertainty and frustration, Ruth was not looking at the circumstances as she declared her decision to go with Naomi.

More than natural affection motivated Ruth. Not only was she resolute in her purpose of giving selfless devotion to a grief-stricken and bitter mother-in-law, but also she was determined to join Naomi's people in worshiping the true God. She was ready to renounce her ancestral worship, for she had come to a knowledge of the God who had had raised up a distinctive people. Presumably, Elimelech and his family had brought her that knowledge.

Rather than return to her former life, Ruth preferred to risk everything and go with Naomi. Determination to help others and to serve the only true and living God always requires resolute faith and decision.

The two of them arrived in Bethlehem to the surprise of the inhabitants. **Is this Naomi?** (v. 19). This was an expression of amazement at seeing Naomi returning in such a mournful condition. Naomi's reply indicates that her afflictions had left their mark upon her spirit. **Call me not Naomi, call me Mara; for the Almighty hath dealt very bitterly with me** (v. 20). The contrast between the former name, Naomi, meaning "pleasant," and the latter name, Mara, meaning "bitter," is quite significant in the light of the fact that she blamed God for her troubles. On more than one occasion she had complained because of what to her was harsh treatment by the Lord (cf. vv. 13, 20-21; 2:20). Nevertheless, Ruth stayed by her side in gracious devotion and also maintained an abiding faith in God in spite of her circumstances. Although Ruth was a foreigner, her devotion to Naomi and her faith in God made a memorable impression upon the inhabitants of Bethlehem.

III. RUTH IN THE FIELD OF BOAZ (Ruth 2:1-23)

It was necessary to find some means of livelihood. Voluntarily, Ruth, though an alien, offered to glean in the harvest field in order to provide for Naomi and herself.

A. RUTH'S REMARKABLE OPPORTUNITY (2:1-7)

1 And Naomi had a kinsman of her husband's, a mighty man of wealth, of the family of Elimelech; and his name was Boaz. 2 And Ruth the Moabitess said unto Naomi, Let me now go to the field, and glean among the ears of grain after him in whose sight I shall find favor. And she said unto her, Go, my daughter. 3 And she went, and came and gleaned in the field after the reapers: and her hap was to light on the portion of the field belonging unto Boaz, who was of the family of Elimelech. 4 And, behold, Boaz came from Beth-lehem, and said unto the reapers, Jehovah be with you. And they answered him, Jehovah bless thee. 5 Then said Boaz unto his servant that was set over the reapers, Whose damsel is this? 6 And the servant that was set over the reapers answered and said, It is the Moabitish damsel that came back with Naomi out of the country of Moab: 7 and she said, Let me glean, I pray you, and gather after the reapers among the sheaves. So she came, and hath continued even from the morning until now, save that she tarried a little in the house.

Ruth willingly went forth to seek for work. Being a stranger, she hardly knew where to begin her search. **And her hap was to light on the portion of the field belonging unto Boaz, who was of the family of Elimelech** (v. 3). The overseer granted her permission to glean. What appears for the moment to be chance (hap) frequently proves to be the hand of God; and so it was with Ruth, as subsequent events revealed.

B. BOAZ'S READY BENEVOLENCE (2:8-16)

8 Then said Boaz unto Ruth, Hearest thou not, my daughter? Go not to glean in another field, neither pass from hence, but abide here fast by my maidens. 9 Let thine eyes be on the field that they do reap, and go thou after them: have I not charged the young men that they shall not touch thee? and when thou art athirst, go unto the vessels, and drink of that which the young men have drawn. 10 Then she fell on her face, and bowed herself to the ground, and said unto him, Why have I found favor in thy sight, that thou shouldest take knowledge of me, seeing I am a foreigner? 11 And Boaz answered and said unto her, It hath fully been showed me, all that thou hast done unto thy mother-in-

law since the death of thy husband; and how thou hast left thy father and thy mother, and the land of thy nativity, and art come to a people that thou knewest not heretofore. 12 Jehovah recompense thy work, and a full reward be given thee of Jehovah, the God of Israel, under whose wings thou art come to take refuge. 13 Then she said, Let me find favor in thy sight, my lord; for that thou hast comforted me, and for that thou hast spoken kindly unto thy handmaid, though I be not as one of thy handmaids.

14 And at meal-time Boaz said unto her, Come hither, and eat of the bread, and dip thy morsel in the vinegar. And she sat beside the reapers; and they reached her parched grain, and she did eat, and was sufficed, and left thereof. 15 And when she was risen up to glean, Boaz commanded his young men, saying, Let her glean even among the sheaves, and reproach her not. 16 And also pull out some for her from the bundles, and leave it, and let her glean, and rebuke her not.

When Boaz discovered the stranger among the gleaners, he was informed that she was the Moabite woman who had returned with Naomi. Upon hearing this, he went to Ruth and urged her to continue to work in his field. In addition, he allowed her to drink from the fresh water reserved for the reapers and at mealtime invited her to a special place at their table. His ready benevolence so deeply affected Ruth that she bowed reverently before him (v. 10). Then she spoke, **Why have I found favor in thy sight . . . seeing I am a foreigner?** (v. 10).

Boaz explained that he had heard of Ruth's kindness to her mother in law and of her severing home ties in order to come to dwell among unknown people (v. 11). **Jehovah recompense thy work, and a full reward be given thee of Jehovah, the God of Israel, under whose wings thou art come to take refuge** (v. 12). Even more than showing kindness to her mother-in-law and identifying herself with the people of Israel, Ruth had come to find refuge in Jehovah. As a true representative of Israel's high calling to be a blessing to all people, Boaz bestowed a blessing on Ruth who was a stranger to the covenant which Jehovah had with Israel. To a profound degree, Boaz was fulfilling the true calling which every Israelite as well as the community of Israel was obligated to ful-

fill (cf. "a kingdom of priests," Exod. 19:6).

C. NAOMI'S REVERENT GRATITUDE (2:17-23)

17 So she gleaned in the field until even; and she beat out that which she had gleaned, and it was about an ephah of barley. 18 And she took it up, and went into the city; and her mother-in-law saw what she had gleaned: and she brought forth and gave to her that which she had left after she was sufficed. 19 And her mother-in-law said unto her, Where hast thou gleaned to-day? and where hast thou wrought? blessed be he that did take knowledge of thee. And she showed her mother-in-law with whom she had wrought, and said, The man's name with whom I wrought to-day is Boaz. 20 And Naomi said unto her daughter-in-law, Blessed be he of Jehovah, who hath not left off his kindness to the living and to the dead. And Naomi said unto her, The man is nigh of kin unto us, one of our near kinsmen. 21 And Ruth the Moabitess said, Yea, he said unto me, Thou shalt keep fast by my young men, until they have ended all my harvest. 22 And Naomi said unto Ruth her daughter-in-law, It is good, my daughter, that thou go out with his maidens, and that they meet thee not in any other field. 23 So she kept fast by the maidens of Boaz, to glean unto the end of barley harvest and of wheat harvest; and she dwelt with her mother-in-law.

When Ruth returned to Naomi at the evening-time, she told of her day's work. **The man's name with whom I wrought today is Boaz** (v. 19). Upon hearing this, Naomi declared reverently, **Blessed be he of Jehovah, who hath not left off his kindness to the living and to the dead** (v. 20). Naomi saw that Boaz was their divinely chosen benefactor. God was still gracious to them, even though they had sustained the loss of their husbands. Furthermore, since Boaz was a near kin to Naomi he had the right to redeem Elimelech's inheritance (v. 20). Such a fortunate turn of events was of the greatest encouragement to Naomi.

IV. RUTH AT BOAZ'S THRESHING-FLOOR (Ruth 3:1-18)

As a result of the circumstances which had developed because of Boaz's interest in Ruth, Naomi proposed a plan to provide future security for Ruth through marriage.

A. THE MOTIVE (3:1-5)

1 And Naomi her mother-in-law said unto her, My daughter, shall I not seek rest for thee, that it may be well with thee? 2 And now is not Boaz our kinsman, with whose maidens thou wast? Behold, he winnoweth barley to-night in the threshing-floor. 3 Wash thyself therefore, and anoint thee, and put thy raiment upon thee, and get thee down to the threshing-floor; but make not thyself known unto the man, until he shall have done eating and drinking. 4 And it shall be, when he lieth down, that thou shalt mark the place where he shall lie, and thou shalt go in, and uncover his feet, and lay thee down; and he will tell thee what thou shalt do. 5 And she said unto her, All that thou sayest I will do.

Naomi asked Ruth, **My daughter, shall I not seek rest for thee, that it may be well with thee?** (v. 1). The idea of "rest" implied marriage. It was the responsibility of the parents, ordinarily, to arrange for a marriage. Although Naomi was entitled to seek a near kinsman to redeem Elimelech's inheritance, she realized that Boaz's favored treatment of Ruth might well indicate that here was a kinsman who would not only redeem Elimelech's inheritance but, because of his interest in Ruth, would desire her in marriage. Not only would the inheritance be redeemed but Ruth would be given security and the expectation of posterity.

B. THE METHOD (3:6-9)

6 And she went down unto the threshing-floor, and did according to all that her mother-in-law bade her. 7 And when Boaz had eaten and drunk, and his heart was merry, he went to lie down at the end of the heap of grain: and she came softly, and uncovered his feet, and laid her down. 8 And it came to pass at midnight, that the man was afraid, and turned himself; and, behold, a woman lay at his feet. 9 And he said, Who art thou? And she answered, I am Ruth thy handmaid: spread therefore thy skirt over thy handmaid; for thou art a near kinsman.

At night Ruth went to the threshing-floor where Boaz had been winnowing grain. Rather than leave his harvest un-

protected he simply slept at the threshing-floor.

Following Naomi's advice, Ruth lay down at Boaz's feet and waited. During the night he awakened, and was startled to find someone near him. Ruth revealed her identity and requested Boaz's protection because he was a near kinsman. Implied in her request was the hope that Boaz would marry her. It was a bold venture on her part, but Naomi had encouraged her to do this in the hope that Boaz's admiration for Ruth and his responsibility as kinsman would cause him to give Ruth the security of marriage.

C. THE MAN (3:10-18)

10 And he said, Blessed be thou of Jehovah, my daughter: thou hast showed more kindness in the latter end than at the beginning, inasmuch as thou followedst not young men, whether poor or rich. 11 And now, my daughter, fear not; I will do to thee all that thou sayest; for all the city of my people doth know that thou art a worthy woman. 12 And now it is true that I am a near kinsman; howbeit there is a kinsman nearer than I. 13 Tarry this night, and it shall be in the morning, that if he will perform unto thee the part of a kinsman, well; let him do the kinsman's part: but if he will not do the part of a kinsman to thee, then will I do the part of a kinsman to thee, as Jehovah liveth: lie down until the morning.

14 And she lay at his feet until the morning: and she rose up before one could discern another. For he said, Let it not be known that the woman came to the threshing-floor. 15 And he said, Bring the mantle that is upon thee, and hold it: and she held it; and he measured six *measures* of barley, and laid it on her: and he went into the city. 16 And when she came to her mother-in-law, she said, Who art thou, my daughter? And she told her all that the man had done to her. 17 And she said, These six *measures* of barley gave he me; for he said, Go not empty unto thy mother-in-law. 18 Then said she, Sit still, my daughter, until thou know how the matter will fall; for the man will not rest, until he have finished the thing this day.

Although modern Occidentals may be surprised at Ruth's advances, Boaz is reported by the ancient oriental writer as pleased with her approach to him. He said, **Thou hast showed more kindness in the latter end than at the beginning, inas-**

much as thou followedst not young men (v. 10). The "kindness" of which Boaz spoke was that which Ruth had already shown to Elimelech and Naomi as well as to her own deceased husband (v. 8). It was the manner in which Naomi had spoken of Boaz and his beneficence (v. 20). Boaz saw Ruth's advances as an expression of her "kindness" in being willing to become the wife of an aging man rather than a handsome younger man. This impressed him greatly. He expressed no concern over their racial and cultural differences. Perhaps the suggestion may be found in this remarkable incident that true human understanding and love are, after all, the only adequate solutions to the man-made racial problems. He saw in her person the embodiment of "kindness" and his own deep "kindness" responded.

Boaz assured Ruth, **I will do to thee all that thou sayest** (v. 11). His "kindness" was more than sentimentality and compassion. It was a decisive concern for Ruth's well-being. It involved volition and decision, motivated not so much by feelings as by providential influence. Boaz was "kind" not only because of human love and affection but also because of divine love and concern. His actions exemplified godliness toward an alien whose faith in Jehovah had found its expression in "kindness."

Because of a nearer kinsman, Boaz, in his integrity, told Ruth that the law of the kinsman must be respected. However, Boaz promised, **If he will not do the part of a kinsman to thee, then I will . . . as Jehovah liveth** (v. 13).

V. BOAZ AND ELIMELECH'S INHERITANCE (Ruth 4:1-17)

In keeping with his promise to Ruth, the very next morning Boaz went to the gate of the city to settle the matter of Elimelech's inheritance. Calling to the nearer kinsman, Boaz proceeded to discuss the matter.

A. THE PROBLEM OF THE NEARER KINSMAN (4:1-6)

1 Now Boaz went up to the gate, and sat him down there: and, behold, the near kinsman of whom Boaz spake came by; unto whom he said, Ho, such a one! turn aside, sit down here. And he turned aside, and sat down. 2 And he took ten men of the elders of the city, and said, Sit ye down here. And they sat down. 3 And he said unto the near kinsman, Naomi, that is come again out of the country of Moab, selleth the parcel of land, which was our brother Elimelech's: 4 and I thought to disclose it unto thee, saying, Buy it before them that sit here, and before the elders of my people. If thou wilt redeem it, redeem it: but if thou wilt not redeem it, then tell me, that I may know; for there is none to redeem it besides thee; and I am after thee. And he said, I will redeem it. 5 Then said Boaz, What day thou buyest the field of the hand of Naomi, thou must buy it also of Ruth the Moabitess, the wife of the dead, to raise up the name of the dead upon his inheritance. 6 And the near kinsman said, I cannot redeem it for myself, lest I mar mine own inheritance: take thou my right of redemption on thee; for I cannot redeem it.

Boaz pointed out to the nearer kinsman that Naomi's plight had necessitated her selling the inheritance of Elimelech (v. 3). The law provided that the nearest kinsman was obligated to redeem, that is, buy back the inheritance from the one who had controlling possession, in order that it might be retained as the family inheritance (cf. Lev. 25:25; Deut. 25:5-10). When he heard of the need for redeeming the inheritance, the nearer kinsman replied, **I will redeem it** (v. 4).

Upon hearing this, Boaz said, **What day thou buyest the field of the hand of Naomi, thou must buy it also of Ruth the Moabitess . . . to raise up the name of the dead upon his inheritance** (v. 5). This explanation caused the kinsman to realize that redeeming Elimelech's inheritance would affect the value of his own inheritance. He said, **I cannot redeem it for myself, lest I mar my own inheritance** (v. 6).

B. THE PURCHASE OF BOAZ (4:7-12)

7 Now this was the custom in former time in Israel concerning redeeming and concerning exchanging, to confirm all things: a man drew off his shoe, and gave it to his neighbor; and this was the manner of attestation in Israel. 8 So the near kinsman said unto Boaz, Buy it for thyself. And he drew off his shoe. 9 And Boaz said unto the elders, and unto all the people, Ye are witnesses this day, that I have bought all that was Elimelech's, and all

that was Chilion's and Mahlon's, of the hand of Naomi. 10 Moreover Ruth the Moabitess, the wife of Mahlon, have I purchased to be my wife, to raise up the name of the dead upon his inheritance, that the name of the dead be not cut off from among his brethren, and from the gate of his place: ye are witnesses this day. 11 And all the people that were in the gate, and the elders, said, We are witnesses. Jehovah make the woman that is come into thy house like Rachel and like Leah, which two did build the house of Israel: and do thou worthily in Ephrathah, and be famous in Beth-lehem: 12 and let thy house be like the house of Perez, whom Tamar bare unto Judah, of the seed which Jehovah shall give thee of this young woman.

When the nearer kinsman gave the sign of removing his shoe, confirming his decision regarding the inheritance, Boaz said, **Ye are witnesses this day that I have bought all . . . of the hand of Naomi. Moreover Ruth the Moabitess have I purchased to be my wife, to raise up the name of the dead upon his inheritance** (vv. 9, 10).

Boaz "bought" Naomi's inheritance and "purchased" Ruth as his wife. The same Hebrew word used in the two instances means "to obtain." Boaz declared himself responsible for the inheritance and for a wife.

In the former time (v. 7) is an indication that the incident of Boaz redeeming the inheritance occurred during some period when Deuteronomy 25:5-10 was no longer observed. However, it vividly and appropriately illustrates the responsibilities of the near kinsman. By fulfilling the levirate law, Boaz had preserved the inheritance of Elimelech and pledged the continuation of the family of Mahlon, the son of Elimelech and the deceased husband of Ruth.

In a much larger sense, the Christian view holds that the example of Boaz's fulfilling the levirate law is an expression of the rich symbolism of Christ as the nearer kinsman, who came not to destroy but to fulfill the law (cf. Matt. 5:7). In fulfilling the law, Jesus Christ made possible our sharing in the fullness of eternal life.

There followed a blessing by the elders, including a wish that he be rewarded for his kindness by a family of twelve sons.

This is implicit in the reference to Rachel and Leah who provided Jacob with twelve sons (v. 11). The blessing also includes the wish that just as Perez continued the line of Judah, even though he was a twin, so also might the son of Boaz continue the line of Boaz.

C. THE PRAISE GIVEN TO RUTH (4:13-17)

13 So Boaz took Ruth, and she became his wife; and he went in unto her, and Jehovah gave her conception, and she bare a son. 14 And the women said unto Naomi, Blessed be Jehovah, who hath not left thee this day without a near kinsman; and let his name be famous in Israel. 15 And he shall be unto thee a restorer of life, and a nourisher of thine old age; for thy daughter-in-law, who loveth thee, who is better to thee than seven sons, hath borne him. 16 And Naomi took the child, and laid it in her bosom, and became nurse unto it. 17 And the women her neighbors gave it a name, saying, There is a son born to Naomi; and they called his name Obed: he is the father of Jesse, the father of David.

Boaz and Ruth were married, and after a time a son was born. Then the women uttered a most befitting eulogy to Ruth. They said to Naomi, **Blessed be Jehovah, who hath not left thee this day without a near kinsman . . . for thy daughter-in-law, who loveth thee, who is better to thee than seven sons, hath borne him** (vv. 14, 15).

Although an alien, Ruth had expressed such devoted love to Naomi that she won the affection of all who knew of her kindness. The story implies that the women of Bethlehem would have been delighted if they could have been the recipients of the lovingkindness which this alien had shown to Naomi. The kindly quality of Ruth's love won for her a permanent welcome in Bethlehem and a secure marriage in the home of Boaz.

VI. THE GENEALOGY (Ruth 4:18-22)

18 Now these are the generations of Perez: Perez begat Hezron, 19 and Hezron begat Ram, and Ram begat Amminadab, 20 and Amminadab begat Nahshon, and Nahshon begat Salmon, 21 and Salmon begat Boaz, and Boaz begat Obed, 22 and Obed begat Jesse, and Jesse begat David.

The genealogy begins with the son of Judah, who began the line of descent that continued through Boaz and Obed and climaxed with David. It was intended to give in abbreviated manner the line from Judah to David. This line, which would finally culminate in Christ, had foreign blood since Ruth was from Moab. Thus Ruth the Moabitess not only became an honored woman in Israel but an ancestress of the great Redeemer Jesus Christ.

Bibliography

I. Exegetical and Historical Value

Graham, W. C. "Ruth." *The Abingdon Bible Commentary*. New York-Nashville: Abingdon-Cokesbury, 1929.

Gray, M. "Ruth, Book of." *The New Bible Dictionary*. Ed. J. D. Douglas. Grand Rapids: Eerdmans, 1962.

Keil, C. F. and F. Delitzsch. *Biblical Commentary on the Old Testament*. Reprint. Grand Rapids: Eerdmans, 1956.

Macdonald, A. "Ruth." *New Bible Commentary*. Eds. F. Davidson *et al.* Grand Rapids: Eerdmans, 1953.

Manley, G. T. *New Bible Handbook*. Chicago: Inter-Varsity, 1947.

Smith, L. P. "Ruth: Introduction and Exegesis." *The Interpreter's Bible*. Eds. G. A. Buttrick *et al.* Vol. II. New York-Nashville: Abingdon, 1953.

Wright, G. E. and F. V. Filson (eds.). *The Westminster Historical Atlas*. Philadelphia: Westminster, 1945.

II. Expository and Practical Value

Clarke, Adam. *Commentary*. Vol. II. London: Ward, n. d.

Cleland, J. T. "Ruth: Exposition." *The Interpreter's Bible*. Eds. G. A. Buttrick *et al.* Vol. II. New York-Nashville: Abingdon, 1953.

Lange, J. P. *Commentary on the Holy Scripture*. Reprint. Vol. IV. Grand Rapids: Zondervan, n. d.

Nicoll, W. Robertson (ed.). *The Expositor's Bible*. Vol. II. Reprint. Grand Rapids: Eerdmans, 1940.

Spence, H. D. M. and J. S. Exell (eds.). *The Pulpit Commentary*. Vol. VIII. New York and London: Funk and Wagnalls, n. d.

The First Book of Samuel

by Charles R. Wilson

Outline

Introduction

The books of Samuel cover one of the most important periods in Israel's history. This period of approximately one hundred years began with the birth of Samuel and ended with the last days of David's reign. During this time Israel passed from a loose tribal confederation to a strong monarchy acknowledged as a ranking power by surrounding nations. This astounding transformation accounts for the significance of this comparatively brief period.[1]

I. TITLE

I and II Samuel originally formed a single book called "Samuel" in the Hebrew Scriptures. I and II Kings were also combined to form the book called "Kings."

The translators of the Greek Septuagint regarded these books as a complete history of the kingdom of Israel, so they united them under one title, "Books of the Kingdom." Furthermore, they divided "Samuel" and "Kings," making a total of four divisions under the one title. The four divisions were called "First Book of the Kingdom," "Second Book of the Kingdom," etc. Jerome's Latin Vulgate, while changing the title to "Book of the Kings," retained the four divisions.

Since 1516, when Daniel Blomberg effected a compromise in the edition of the Bible which he published, English Bibles have restored the original titles of "Samuel" and "Kings" and have retained the four divisions as arranged by the Septuagint. The King James Version has even retained the Latin Vulgate's titles for the divisions as subtitles; for example, "The First Book of Samuel" has the subtitle, "The First Book of the Kings," etc.

II. COMPILATION

The books of Samuel were compiled from sources by one who was well informed about this important period in Israel's history. There were records preserved by Samuel, Nathan and Gad (I Sam. 10:25; I Chron. 29:29). There were royal records such as David ordered to be kept (I Chron. 27:24). There were compilations of poetic literature such as the book of Jasher (II Sam. 1:18). "The evidence clearly indicates that the books are a compilation."[2]

There is a decided emphasis on the recognition that much of the source material for I and II Samuel is contemporaneous with the events given. Sources are extraordinarily full and are of great historical value. According to John Bright, information about this period is adequate and accurate so that we are "better informed about this period than any comparable one in Israel's history."[3]

The books of Samuel are acknowledged as outstanding examples of historical writing. "It is no exaggeration to say that these books form the earliest and finest examples known to man of developed historical writing."[4]

Not only are these books outstanding from a historical standpoint, but also in their setting forth of the "Deuteronomic" principle. This principle is basic to the books and is explicitly given by an unknown prophet of the Lord: "Them that honor me I will honor, and they that despise me shall be lightly esteemed" (I Sam. 2:30).

III. HISTORICAL SIGNIFICANCE

The books of Samuel were written not merely to narrate historical events of preceding times but also to teach the moral and religious lessons which the

---

[1] Cf. John Bright, A History of Israel, p. 163.
[2] A. M. Renwick, "I and II Samuel," New Bible Commentary, ed. by F. Davidson, A. M. Stibbs, E. F. Kevan, p. 262.
[3] Bright, op. cit., p. 163.   [4] The Westminster Study Edition of the Holy Bible, p. 369.

divine discipline had wrought out in the arena of historic activity.

The authenticity and completeness of the history of Israel recorded in the books of Samuel give great emphasis to the significance of history in the Bible. It was through the outworking of the historical processes that God revealed His acts. The compiler of Samuel was aware of that and perceived that what had happened in the course of Israel's history was vital to his contemporaries for their instruction and admonition concerning God's activity in their time.

The Apostle Paul was astutely aware of the significance of this divine discipline in the historic process and the lessons accorded thereby when he wrote to the Corinthians: "Now these things happened unto them by way of example; and they are written for our admonition" (I Cor. 10:11).

Not only was Paul aware of the importance of the historical, but he was also sensitive to the lessons of moral and spiritual significance which are gained by perceiving the discipline of God. To the task of making explicit some of the larger moral and spiritual lessons of the books of Samuel, we now turn.

IV. MORAL AND SPIRITUAL VALUE

Viewing the books of Samuel as an integral part of the history of the kingdom of Israel, we need to make explicit the specific values which inhere in these writings as they relate to us and to nations of our time.

It is helpful to keep in the foreground the fact that the books of Samuel record the history of an important transitional period in Israel's history. From a loose tribal confederation Israel passed into a powerful and prosperous monarchy. No longer were the people thinking of their land as "a land of promise," for it was now their possession.

Early in this important period of change, the Israelites asked for a king (I Sam. 8:4, 19, 20). This request triggered a series of historical events that brought about far-reaching changes for Israel.

Israel's request, as far as can be determined, was the result of a serious emergency due to the increasingly powerful Philistines, a well-organized, well-armed military people, who threatened to dominate Canaan. Furthermore, Israel's request was made with reluctance, since it involved a step toward a new authoritarian order which was foreign to Israel. Although Israel hoped that Saul would accomplish the formation of a nation, he did not bring to pass the new order. It was with David that a new and different Israel emerged. In a series of incredibly brilliant wars, David smashed the Philistine threat, captured numerous Canaanite towns, including Jerusalem, and conquered an empire stretching from the Gulf of Aqabah on the south to Syria far to the north. Israel was transformed from a struggling tribal league to a militant empire dominating the surrounding nations.

The incredible achievement accomplished by David made a memorable impression, for he had secured the promised inheritance. He had made Israel a kingdom and he had subdued the surrounding nations.

In the background, however, lurked an insidious and perilous temptation, namely, the identifying of the kingdom created by David with Israel's destiny as a people of promise, and the equating of citizenship in the newly created state with the divine purpose for Israel that she should be "a kingdom of priests, and a holy nation" (Exod. 19:6).

Israel's request for a king was a threat to her true destiny. Yet Israel's cultural dilemma seemed to demand a king. The Philistines were an ominous and dangerous peril to the very existence of Israel. "Unlike previous foes, the Philistines did not pose a limited threat..., they threatened Israel in her totality and with her life."[5] Self-preservation motivated Israel to be like other nations. Yet, Israel's destiny was not linked with being like the nations but with being a blessing to the nations. She was called to fill a priestly role as a people presenting God to the nations.[6] Israel was to demonstrate the active presence of God in the ongoing of history.

It cannot be ignored, that if God would reveal His presence to the nations of the world through Israel, then Israel must undergo the experience of becoming a

---

[5] Bright, op. cit., p. 164.   [6] Cf. J. Blauw, The Missionary Nature of the Church, p. 26.

nation, just as surely as God must undergo the experience of the incarnation. Yet if Israel yielded to the temptation to identify a human kingdom with the divine kingdom she would be yielding to idolatry.

This is always a treacherous temptation, for it leads to a false faith. It generates faith in the visible authority of earthly power rather than faith in the kingly authority of the Lord of heaven and earth. This tendency to trust in that which is like the nations of the earth is continually in evidence, and it induces, subtly, the subservience of religion to the state. When the state is conceived as the creator of security, power and prosperity then religion is remolded, almost imperceptibly, to serve the state.

A vivid illustration of this in the Christian era occurred in the fourth century A.D. with the conversion of the Roman Emperor, Constantine. This ushered in an uncomfortably close alliance between Christianity and the state. With the state providing protection and prosperity for the church, it seemed most appropriate for the church to reciprocate by acknowledging and approving the state. This was clearly expressed by Eusebius, the outstanding church historian of the fourth century A.D.[7]

The history of Israel was very closely interwoven with the prophets. More specifically, the political history of Israel was always closely associated with prophecy.[8] The beginnings of this close association are clearly discernible in Samuel's relationships with Saul and the people of Israel. With the transition from a tribal people to a state there was the development of the prophetic order under Samuel's leadership (I Sam. 10:5, 6; 19:18-24).

The spirit of prophecy as exercised by Samuel and those who succeeded him was a continuing challenge and corrective to the monarchy. The prophet of the Lord more than any other individual was enabled to interpret the course of events and to declare the will of God in the historical situation.

The prophet did not speak in his own right. Rather, he declared what God had spoken to him. A remarkable illustration of the faithfulness of the true prophet is

to be found in Samuel. His call to be a prophet was the occasion for a jolting message concerning the destruction of the house of Eli (I Sam. 3:10-18). Saul's disobedience regarding the Amalekites was the cause for Samuel's shattering message concerning the divine rejection of Saul (I Sam. 15:16-31).

Although the prophet was truly God's spokesman in the political history of Israel, he was subject to the temptation of loyalty to the king. In such servitude, he declared pleasing prophecies to the king. Samuel and those of the true prophetic tradition shunned this temptation with vigor. They gave complete obedience to the Spirit of God which possessed them.

The Spirit-filled individual cannot professionalize his God-given gift without invoking divine displeasure. The spirit of prophecy is subject to God alone. Discernment and interpretation of the ongoing of history cannot be made the tool of human institutions and still retain divinely given clarity concerning the will of God. Samuel is a remarkable illustration of the faithfulness of the true prophet who challenged the king to do the will of God.

A third value of the books of Samuel is the description of the person and character of David. Especially II Samuel 9-20 provides a series of excellent episodes in the life of David which are extraordinarily revealing.

The picture given of David has a darker as well as a brighter side. On the darker side, David is depicted as a military warrior engaged in deeds of cruelty common to his times (II Sam. 8:2). He engaged in deceit (I Sam. 27:8-12). He committed adultery and murder (II Sam. 11:2-17). As a father he lacked the proper balance between justice and mercy in dealing with his family problems (cf. II Sam. 14:28-33 and 15:1-6). The troubles of David's later life and the judgment upon his house may be traced to David's great sin. Though it was pardoned, its consequences were felt throughout the whole of his later years.

On the brighter side, David was a charming individual, inspiring love and devotion on the part of those with whom he was associated (I Chron. 12:1-22). He is set forth as an example of true repentance. The Fifty-first Psalm is a profound

---

[7] Cf. C. N. Cochrane, *Christianity and Classical Culture*, pp. 183-86.
[8] B. Anderson, *Understanding the Old Testament*, p. 187.

revelation of the inner spirit of the penitent David. As an encouragement to repentance, David's penitence reveals the assurance of forgiveness for every truly penitent individual.

In two respects David became an ideal for later times. First, he was remembered as just and patriotic. Second, he was remembered as Israel's kingly ideal. As Israel's history moved forward and the glory of the Davidic era faded, there developed a Messianic consciousness. Israel associated the Messianic hope with a renewed and reconstructed kingdom to be accomplished by a "son of David" (II Sam. 7:12-16).

The study of the life and character of David as portrayed in the books of Samuel is productive in that it shows a typical human being beset by the creatureliness of his existence as well as blessed by the providence of God. On the one hand, he was challenged by the prophet Nathan for his wickedness: "Thou art the man" (II Sam. 12:7). On the other hand, he was declared to be "a man after his [God's] own heart" (I Sam. 13:14).

Commentary on First Samuel

I. CONSECRATED AND CALLED (I Sam. 1:1—4:1a)

Samuel appeared on the stage of Israel's history as a result of the prayer of Hannah, the childless wife of Elkanah. While still a child he was dedicated to the Lord and reared in the sanctuary at Shiloh. While ministering to the chief priest, Eli, Samuel was active in the service of the tabernacle. He was summoned to be a prophet through a vision of the Lord in the night.

A. A SON IS BORN (1:1-28)

Elkanah, who was of the tribe of Ephraim, faithfully journeyed to the sanctuary in Shiloh each year to worship the Lord. However, Elkanah had a serious problem in his family that came to have a great influence upon his religious life.

1. The Plight of Hannah (1:1-8)

1 Now there was a certain man of Ramathaim-zophim, of the hill-country of Ephraim, and his name was Elkanah, the son of Jeroham, the son of Elihu, the son of Tohu, the son of Zuph, an Ephraimite: 2 and he had two wives; the name of the one was Hannah, and the name of the other Peninnah: and Peninnah had children, but Hannah had no children. 3 And this man went up out of his city from year to year to worship and to sacrifice unto Jehovah of hosts in Shiloh. And the two sons of Eli, Hophni and Phinehas, priests unto Jehovah, were there. 4 And when the day came that Elkanah sacrificed, he gave to Peninnah his wife, and to all her sons and her daughters, portions: 5 but unto Hannah he gave a double portion; for he loved Hannah, but Jehovah had shut up her womb. 6 And her rival provoked her sore, to make her fret, because Jehovah had shut up her womb. 7 And *as* he did so year by year, when she went up to the house of Jehovah, so she provoked her; therefore she wept, and did not eat. 8 And Elkanah her husband said unto her, Han-

nah, why weepest thou? and why eatest thou not? and why is thy heart grieved? am not I better to thee than ten sons?

Elkanah had two wives. This was the reason for a very unwholesome family relationship, especially since one of the wives, Hannah, was without children. Not only was the other wife, Peninnah, inclined to jealousy, but Hannah herself was bitter. Elkanah was involved by reason of his expressions of favoritism. Apparently he married Hannah because he loved her, while he had married Peninnah in order to have children.

Hannah's childlessness was attributed to the direct action of the Lord. Barrenness was looked upon as a sign of divine displeasure (cf. Deut. 7:13, 14). Peninnah doubtless accused Hannah concerning her misfortune, saying that it was punishment for sin.

This has happened again and again. Not only have jealous individuals wielded this dagger of untruth to the hurt of many an innocent victim but also well-meaning people thrust this idea upon sensitive souls and leave a wounded conscience that never heals.

Hannah was not being punished for sin. She was childless, it is true, but she was not being punished. Elkanah loved her; moreover, the Lord loved her. Peninnah despised and harassed her. She even brought the Lord in on her side: **And her rival provoked her sore, to make her fret, because Jehovah had shut up her womb** (v. 6). Peninnah was no authority on the reason for Hannah's childlessness. She was using it as a religious weapon against one who was dearer to Elkanah than she was.

How imperative it is when confronted by life's inexplicable situations that we avoid explanations and solutions which not only impinge upon the inviolate integrity of the Almighty but also inflict irreparable harm upon those who are His creatures, at the same time giving us a false sense of superiority.

2. The Promise of Samuel (1:9-20)

9 So Hannah rose up after they had eaten in Shiloh, and after they had drunk. Now Eli the priest was sitting upon his seat by the door-post of the temple of Jehovah. 10 And she was in bitterness of soul, and prayed unto Jehovah, and wept sore. 11 And she vowed a vow, and said, O Jehovah of hosts, if thou wilt indeed look on the affliction of thy handmaid, and remember me, and not forget thy handmaid, but wilt give unto thy handmaid a man-child, then I will give him unto Jehovah all the days of his life, and there shall no razor come upon his head. 12 And it came to pass, as she continued praying before Jehovah, that Eli marked her mouth. 13 Now Hannah, she spake in her heart; only her lips moved, but her voice was not heard: therefore Eli thought she had been drunken. 14 And Eli said unto her, How long wilt thou be drunken? put away thy wine from thee. 15 And Hannah answered and said, No, my lord, I am a woman of a sorrowful spirit: I have drunk neither wine nor strong drink, but I poured out my soul before Jehovah. 16 Count not thy handmaid for a wicked woman; for out of the abundance of my complaint and my provocation have I spoken hitherto. 17 Then Eli answered and said, Go in peace; and the God of Israel grant thy petition that thou hast asked of him. 18 And she said, Let thy handmaid find favor in thy sight. So the woman went her way, and did eat; and her countenance was no more *sad*.

19 And they rose up in the morning early, and worshipped before Jehovah, and returned, and came to their house to Ramah. And Elkanah knew Hannah his wife; and Jehovah remembered her; 20 and it came to pass, when the time was come about, that Hannah conceived, and bare a son; and she called his name Samuel, *saying*, Because I have asked him of Jehovah.

At the time of the yearly sacrifice, Elkanah and his family journeyed to Shiloh to worship the Lord. Upon this particular occasion Hannah was in deep distress because of Peninnah: **And she was in bitterness of soul, and prayed unto Jehovah, and wept sore** (v. 10).

Hannah was nearly defeated by her lot. She was not a model in her reactions to one of life's great disappointments. Her prayer was not so much that she might develop right reactions and dispositions as that she might have a child and so retaliate against Peninnah: **O Jehovah of hosts, if thou . . . wilt give unto thy handmaid a man-child, then will I give him unto Jehovah . . .** (v. 11). She explained, **For out of the abundance of my complaint and my provocation have I spoken hitherto** (v. 16).

Amid these distressing and difficult circumstances, Jehovah of hosts wrought a great thing in Israel by the birth of Samuel. The totality of this great thing was not apparent immediately, for this infant was not yet ready to go forth to save Israel and to declare the word of the Lord. Yet in due time Samuel was to be strategically important in the history of Israel.

While it is readily granted that the family life of Elkanah was unattractive, it is necessary to recognize the fact that the Lord of hosts entered into this dismal set of human relations and began a saving work in Israel. The Lord remembered Hannah. However, Hannah was remembered not simply in order to appease her retaliatory spirit toward Peninnah but that she might render service to God and her people. Because of the divine activity in the episode, the birth of Samuel was not merely the placating of a bitter, childless woman but the providing of a priest, a judge, a prophet for Israel.

3. The Presentation to the Lord (1: 21-28)

21 And the man Elkanah, and all his house, went up to offer unto Jehovah the yearly sacrifice, and his vow. 22 But Hannah went not up; for she said unto her husband, *I will not go up* until the child be weaned; and then I will bring him, that he may appear before Jehovah, and there abide for ever. 23 And Elkanah her husband said unto her, Do what seemeth thee good; tarry until thou have weaned him; only Jehovah establish his word. So the woman tarried and gave her son suck, until she weaned him. 24 And when she had weaned him, she took him up with her, with three bullocks, and one ephah of meal, and a bottle of wine, and brought him unto the house of Jehovah in Shiloh: and the child was young. 25 And they slew the bullock, and brought the child to Eli. 26 And she said, Oh, my lord, as thy soul liveth, my lord, I am the woman that stood by thee here, praying

unto Jehovah. 27 For this child I prayed; and Jehovah hath given me my petition which I asked of him: 28 therefore also I have granted him to Jehovah; as long as he liveth he is granted to Jehovah. And he worshipped Jehovah there.

Hannah was loyal to the momentous vow which she had made to the Lord. To have a son had meant much to her as a wife, but to be faithful to the Lord meant much more. So, in response to divine thoughtfulness in giving her a son, she presented Samuel to Eli who kept the sanctuary at Shiloh. It was a presentation which was complete and irrevocable. **I have granted him to Jehovah; as long as he liveth he is granted to Jehovah** (v. 28).

Here is dedicated integrity. She kept her pledge. It is this about Hannah and her child that is so pregnant with feeling. Notwithstanding her mother-love and the delights of pleasing her beloved Elkanah with a first-born man-child, Hannah faithfully performed her vow.

In the final analysis a key indication of character is faithfulness to one's promises. This is seldom acknowledged by those who make promises easily and carelessly. Yet this is the key virtue of Hannah. She kept her word and gave her son to be God's oracle to Israel.

B. THE SONG OF HANNAH (2:1-10)

1. Ascription of Praise to the Lord (2:1-2)

1 And Hannah prayed, and said:
My heart exulteth in Jehovah;
My horn is exalted in Jehovah;
My mouth is enlarged over mine enemies;
Because I rejoice in thy salvation.
2 There is none holy as Jehovah;
For there is none besides thee,
Neither is there any rock like our God.

The song of Hannah begins with praise to the Lord for what He has wrought. **Mine horn is exalted** is a metaphor drawn from wild life (v. 1). It depicts a victorious animal carrying its head high. **My mouth is enlarged** refers to gaping, an ancient gesture of contempt (v. 1).

The song declared, **There is none holy as Jehovah** (v. 2). Furthermore, Jehovah is the supreme **rock** on whom one can rest

secure (v. 2). Hannah was blessed not only with the answer to her prayer but with an awareness of the presence of God.

2. Acknowledgment of the Lord's Sovereignty (2:3-8)

3 Talk no more so exceeding proudly;
Let not arrogancy come out of your mouth;
For Jehovah is a God of knowledge,
And by him actions are weighed.
4 The bows of the mighty men are broken;
And they that stumbled are girded with strength.
5 They that were full have hired out themselves for bread;
And they that were hungry have ceased *to hunger*:
Yea, the barren hath borne seven;
And she that hath many children languisheth.
6 Jehovah killeth, and maketh alive:
He bringeth down to Sheol, and bringeth up.
7 Jehovah maketh poor, and maketh rich:
He bringeth low, he also lifteth up.
8 He raiseth up the poor out of the dust,
He lifteth up the needy from the dunghill,
To make them sit with princes,
And inherit the throne of glory:
For the pillars of the earth are Jehovah's,
And he hath set the world upon them.

The song of Hannah moves on to an awareness of divine sovereignty. **For Jehovah is a God of knowledge, and by him actions are weighed** (v. 3). With this figure of the scales weighing actions there is introduced the sovereignty of God.

The verses which follow show the changes in the fortunes of people. These changes, however, are not because of the caprice of an arbitrary sovereign but are seen as rewards or punishments. The mighty are humbled; the stumbling are strengthened. The full have become hirelings; the hungry have become full. The barren is happy; the mother with many children sorrows.

This sovereignty is not capricious, but responsible. God as Creator and Preserver of the universe fulfills His moral obligation: **For the pillars of the earth are Jehovah's, and he hath set the world upon them** (v. 8).

3. Announcement of the Messiah of the Lord (2:9-10)

9 He will keep the feet of his holy ones;
But the wicked shall be put to silence
in darkness;
For by strength shall no man prevail.
10 They that strive with Jehovah shall be
broken to pieces;
Against them will he thunder in heaven:
Jehovah will judge the ends of the earth;
And he will give strength unto his king,
And exalt the horn of his anointed.

In the last two verses of the song of Hannah there is a shift from the present to the Messianic future. Particularly, the reference to the coming of the Messiah is evident in the words, **And he will give strength unto his king, and exalt the horn of his anointed** (v. 10). "These terms are best taken as referring to the Messianic king, the same who is the theme of the second Psalm."[1]

C. THE MISCONDUCT OF ELI'S HOUSEHOLD (2:11-26)

11 And Elkanah went to Ramah to his house. And the child did minister unto Jehovah before Eli the priest.
12 Now the sons of Eli were base men; they knew not Jehovah. 13 And the custom of the priests with the people was, that, when any man offered sacrifice, the priest's servant came, while the flesh was boiling, with a flesh-hook of three teeth in his hand; 14 and he struck it into the pan, or kettle, or caldron, or pot; all that the flesh-hook brought up the priest took therewith. So they did in Shiloh unto all the Israelites that came thither. 15 Yea, before they burnt the fat, the priest's servant came, and said to the man that sacrificed, Give flesh to roast for the priest; for he will not have boiled flesh of thee, but raw. 16 And if the man said unto him, They will surely burn the fat first, and then take as much as thy soul desireth; then he would say, Nay, but thou shalt give it me now: and if not, I will take it by force. 17 And the sin of the young men was very great before Jehovah; for the men despised the offering of Jehovah.
18 But Samuel ministered before Jehovah, being a child, girded with a linen ephod. 19 Moreover his mother made him a little robe, and brought it to him from year to year, when she came up with her husband to offer the yearly sacrifice. 20 And Eli blessed Elkanah and his wife, and said, Jehovah give thee seed of this woman for the petition which was asked of Jehovah. And they went unto their own home. 21 And Jehovah visited Hannah, and she conceived, and bare three sons and two daughters. And the child Samuel grew before Jehovah.

22 Now Eli was very old; and he heard all that his sons did unto all Israel, and how that they lay with the women that did service at the door of the tent of meeting. 23 And he said unto them, Why do ye such things? for I hear of your evil dealings from all this people. 24 Nay, my sons; for it is no good report that I hear: ye make Jehovah's people to transgress. 25 If one man sin against another, God shall judge him; but if a man sin against Jehovah, who shall entreat for him? Notwithstanding, they hearkened not unto the voice of their father, because Jehovah was minded to slay them. 26 And the child Samuel grew on, and increased in favor both with Jehovah, and also with men.

The sons of Eli, Hophni and Phinehas, were living in open disregard of the Lord. **Now the sons of Eli were base men; they knew not Jehovah** (v. 12). "'Did not acknowledge the Lord' more nearly reproduces the thought of the original."[2] These men were committing at least two major sins. Worshipers were being robbed of that part of the sacrifice which they themselves were to consume in their sacrificial meal at the sanctuary. Also, the Lord was insulted in that the priests took that part of the sacrifice which they desired before the Lord had received His part.

Although the aging Eli was aware of the evil behavior of his sons, he was unable to change their ways. There is a tendency to pass more severe condemnation upon Eli here than is warranted, namely, that his rebuke was weak and feeble. Let it be remembered, however, that Eli was a **very old** and feeble man. Not long after this, when he died of injuries sustained in a fall, he was "ninety and eight years old; and his eyes were set, so that he could not see" (4:15). If the fact that Eli was a **very old** man is given proper recognition, one must also realize that his sons were mature adults and would not be so readily guided by the advice of their aged father.

There was a firm warning in Eli's words, **If a man sin against Jehovah, who shall entreat for him?** (v. 25). Eli spoke

[1] A. R. S. Kennedy, "Samuel," *The Century Bible*, p. 45.   [2] *Ibid.*, p. 45.

truly to his sons, yet they would not listen. **Notwithstanding they hearkened not unto the voice of their father, because Jehovah was minded to slay them** (v. 25). It is indefensible to claim that it would have been futile for the sons of Eli to listen to their father because the Lord had determined to destroy them anyway.

Rather, this judgment upon them is best understood in the light of the Deuteronomic conception of history. Sin brings judgment, but repentance brings deliverance. There is a "hardening of the heart," but it is accomplished not by a sovereign act of God but by the deliberate act of man in his resistance to God's known will and mercy.

D. THE MESSAGE BY A MAN OF GOD (2:27-36)

27 And there came a man of God unto Eli, and said unto him, Thus saith Jehovah, Did I reveal myself unto the house of thy father, when they were in Egypt *in bondage* to Pharaoh's house? 28 and did I choose him out of all the tribes of Israel to be my priest, to go up unto mine altar, to burn incense, to wear an ephod before me? and did I give unto the house of thy father all the offerings of the children of Israel made by fire? 29 Wherefore kick ye at my sacrifice and at mine offering, which I have commanded in *my* habitation, and honorest thy sons above me, to make yourselves fat with the chiefest of all the offerings of Israel my people? 30 Therefore Jehovah, the God of Israel, saith, I said indeed that thy house, and the house of thy father, should walk before me for ever: but now Jehovah saith, Be it far from me; for them that honor me I will honor, and they that despise me shall be lightly esteemed. 31 Behold, the days come, that I will cut off thine arm, and the arm of thy father's house, that there shall not be an old man in thy house. 32 And thou shalt behold the affliction of *my* habitation, in all the wealth which *God* shall give Israel; and there shall not be an old man in thy house for ever. 33 And the man of thine, *whom* I shall not cut off from mine altar, *shall be* to consume thine eyes, and to grieve thy heart; and all the increase of thy house shall die in the flower of their age. 34 And this shall be the sign unto thee, that shall come upon thy two sons, on Hophni and Phinehas: in one day they shall die both of them. 35 And I will raise me up a faithful priest, that shall do according to that which is in my heart and in my mind: and I will build him a sure

house; and he shall walk before mine anointed for ever. 36 And it shall come to pass, that every one that is left in thy house shall come and bow down to him for a piece of silver and a loaf of bread, and shall say, Put me, I pray thee, into one of the priests' offices, that I may eat a morsel of bread.

A man of God appeared in Shiloh to bring the message of the Lord to Eli. It was a message of doom. This prophet made an incisive observation about Eli that, to a large degree, makes it possible for us to see the error of Eli's ways: **Wherefore kick ye at my sacrifice . . . , and honorest thy sons above me?** (v. 29). This question which the Lord asked Eli through the man of God reveals the besetting sin of Eli. He yielded to the temptation to favor his children at the expense of the loyalty he owed unto the Lord.

This was no late tendency appearing in his old age. It had been a tendency of such long standing that in old age Eli was helpless to correct the habits of life that had become fixed. He must reap what he had sown. It must have been heartbreaking for him to hear the pronouncement, **and all the increase of thy house shall die in the flower of their age** (v. 33).

Through the man of God the Lord made the promise, **I will raise me up a faithful priest, that shall do according to that which is in my heart and in my mind** (v. 35).

E. THE SUMMONS TO SAMUEL (3:1—4:1a)

1. The Call of God (3:1-14)

1 And the child Samuel ministered unto Jehovah before Eli. And the word of Jehovah was precious in those days; there was no frequent vision. 2 And it came to pass at that time, when Eli was laid down in his place (now his eyes had begun to wax dim, so that he could not see), 3 and the lamp of God was not yet gone out, and Samuel was laid down *to sleep*, in the temple of Jehovah, where the ark of God was; 4 that Jehovah called Samuel: and he said, Here am I. 5 And he ran unto Eli, and said, Here am I; for thou calledst me. And he said, I called not; lie down again. And he went and lay down. 6 And Jehovah called yet again, Samuel. And Samuel arose and went to Eli, and said,

Here am I; for thou calledst me. And he answered, I called not, my son; lie down again. 7 Now Samuel did not yet know Jehovah, neither was the word of Jehovah yet revealed unto him. 8 And Jehovah called Samuel again the third time. And he arose and went to Eli, and said, Here am I; for thou calledst me. And Eli perceived that Jehovah had called the child. 9 Therefore Eli said unto Samuel, Go, lie down: and it shall be, if he call thee, that thou shalt say, Speak, Jehovah; for thy servant heareth. So Samuel went and lay down in his place.

10 And Jehovah came, and stood, and called as at other times, Samuel, Samuel. Then Samuel said, Speak; for thy servant heareth. 11 And Jehovah said to Samuel, Behold, I will do a thing in Israel, at which both the ears of every one that heareth it shall tingle. 12 In that day I will perform against Eli all that I have spoken concerning his house, from the beginning even unto the end. 13 For I have told him that I will judge his house for ever, for the iniquity which he knew, because his sons did bring a curse upon themselves, and he restrained them not. 14 And therefore I have sworn unto the house of Eli, that the iniquity of Eli's house shall not be expiated with sacrifice nor offering for ever.

Samuel had reached an important period of his life. He is described as a **child,** but that is no definitive indication of his age. The original word may refer to one of any age between an infant and an adult of forty years (cf. I Sam. 4:21; II Chron. 13:7). Josephus refers to Samuel as twelve years of age (*Antiquities* V. 10. 4).

The word of Jehovah was precious in those days; there was no frequent vision (v. 1). The word of the Lord and the vision which Samuel witnessed, as recorded in this chapter, were so infrequent during this period in Israel that Samuel was immediately recognized as a prophet.

This phenomenal revelation occurred during the night. Samuel was awakened by someone calling his name. Supposing that the aging Eli, who was going blind, had called, Samuel went to him (vv. 2, 5). Eli had not called. After the third interruption, **Eli perceived that Jehovah had called the child** (v. 8).

Although active in the service of the sanctuary and helpful to Eli, Samuel was totally uninformed regarding the recep-

tion of a revelation from the Lord. It was necessary for the old priest to counsel him. Eli's sons were unresponsive to their father's spiritual understanding and advice. Samuel, however, listened and obeyed.

When the call of God came again, Samuel responded, **Speak; for thy servant heareth** (v. 10). As a result of Samuel's readiness to heed the voice of the Lord, he became aware also of the presence of the Lord. **And Jehovah came, and stood, and called as at other times, Samuel, Samuel** (v. 10).

The Lord revealed to Samuel that impending punishment was about to come to Eli's household. **Behold, I will do a thing in Israel** is better rendered according to the literal translation, "I am doing a thing in Israel" (v. 11).[3] The punishment was at hand.

Furthermore, the Lord revealed why the punishment was coming upon Eli: **For I have told him that I will judge his house forever, for the iniquity which he knew, because his sons did bring a curse upon themselves, and he restrained them not** (v. 13). Eli had not been the responsible priest and father he should have been.

2. The Communication to Eli (3:15—4:1a)

15 And Samuel lay until the morning, and opened the doors of the house of Jehovah. And Samuel feared to show Eli the vision. 16 Then Eli called Samuel, and said, Samuel, my son. And he said, Here am I. 17 And he said, What is the thing that *Jehovah* hath spoken unto thee? I pray thee, hide it not from me: God do so to thee, and more also, if thou hide anything from me of all the things that he spake unto thee. 18 And Samuel told him every whit, and hid nothing from him. And he said, It is Jehovah: let him do what seemeth him good.

19 And Samuel grew, and Jehovah was with him, and did let none of his words fall to the ground. 20 And all Israel from Dan even to Beer-sheba knew that Samuel was established to be a prophet of Jehovah. 21 And Jehovah appeared again in Shiloh; for Jehovah revealed himself to Samuel in Shiloh by the word of Jehovah. 1 And the word of Samuel came to all Israel.

Samuel slept no more that night. The first revelation and the accompanying message had greatly impressed him. Samuel

---

[3] Renwick, *op. cit.,* p. 265.

was fearful about telling Eli, but Eli called him to learn what the Lord had said to him.

In response to the question, Samuel told him everything: **He hid nothing from him** (v. 18). Eli accepted the message with what seemed to be a resigned attitude: **It is Jehovah: let him do what seemeth him good** (v. 18).

From this time onward Samuel became the recognized leader of the religious life of the people (v. 20). From Dan to Beersheba Israelites came to Samuel at Shiloh. Moreover, the word of the Lord through Samuel was spread throughout Israel. This marked an important difference from the times when there were rare occurrences of the word of the Lord (cf. 3:1). Samuel's willing response to the Lord had released Israel from the dearth of divine revelation (vv. 19-21). Now it was possible to hear the word of God.

II. "THE GLORY IS DEPARTED" (I Sam. 4:1b—7:2)

The book of Samuel shifts from the person of Samuel to events surrounding the ark of the Lord. A real crisis developed in Israel in connection with the ark. Its capture by the Philistines and later return marked an epochal time in the history of Israel.

A. ISRAEL SUBDUED BY THE PHILISTINES (4:1b-11)

Now Israel went out against the Philistines to battle, and encamped beside Ebenezer: and the Philistines encamped in Aphek. 2 And the Philistines put themselves in array against Israel: and when they joined battle, Israel was smitten before the Philistines; and they slew of the army in the field about four thousand men. 3 And when the people were come into the camp, the elders of Israel said, Wherefore hath Jehovah smitten us to-day before the Philistines? Let us fetch the ark of the covenant of Jehovah out of Shiloh unto us, that it may come among us, and save us out of the hand of our enemies. 4 So the people sent to Shiloh; and they brought from thence the ark of the covenant of Jehovah of hosts, who sitteth *above* the cherubim: and the two sons of Eli, Hophni and Phinehas, were there with the ark of the covenant of God.
5 And when the ark of the covenant of Jehovah came into the camp, all Israel shouted with a great shout, so that the earth rang again. 6 And when the Philistines heard the noise of the shout, they said, What meaneth the noise of this great shout in the camp of the Hebrews? And they understood that the ark of Jehovah was come into the camp. 7 And the Philistines were afraid, for they said, God is come into the camp. And they said, Woe unto us! for there hath not been such a thing heretofore. 8 Woe unto us! who shall deliver us out of the hand of these mighty gods? these are the gods that smote the Egyptians with all manner of plagues in the wilderness. 9 Be strong, and quit yourselves like men, O ye Philistines, that ye be not servants unto the Hebrews, as they have been to you: quit yourselves like men, and fight. 10 And the Philistines fought, and Israel was smitten, and they fled every man to his tent: and there was a very great slaughter; for there fell of Israel thirty thousand footmen. 11 And the ark of God was taken; and the two sons of Eli, Hophni and Phinehas, were slain.

The Philistines first began oppressing the Israelites even before the birth of Samson who judged Israel twenty years (Judg. 15:20). "The judgeship of Eli and Samson must have been partly contemporaneous . . . ."[4] During the year that Eli was ninety-eight years old the Philistines engaged in one of their numerous battles with the Israelites (cf. vv. 2, 15). Israel was defeated.

Upon returning to the camp the elders of Israel inquired, **Wherefore hath Jehovah smitten us today before the Philistines?** This question was of importance because it was an acknowledgment that Israel's defeat was not by reason of Jehovah's weakness but His strength. He was not weaker than Dagon, the god of the Philistines. Israel's defeat was in some inexplicable way an act of God. He was the Lord of Israel, but He was also able to accommodate Philistinian aggression for His purpose.

Israel decided to bring the ark from Shiloh to the camp and regroup for another battle against the Philistines. This greatly encouraged the fighting men in the camp, for the ark was equated with the presence of the Lord. On the other hand, when the Philistines heard of the ark in the camp of Israel they were greatly dismayed.

---

4 *Ibid.*

Accompanying the ark were the sons of Eli, Hophni and Phinehas. Again the battle lines formed, with the Philistines fighting in order that they would not be taken as slaves (v. 9). Events happened quickly. Israel was defeated, Hophni and Phinehas were killed and the ark of God was captured.

B. ELI SHOCKED BY THE NEWS (4:12-22)

12 And there ran a man of Benjamin out of the army, and came to Shiloh the same day, with his clothes rent, and with earth upon his head. 13 And when he came, lo, Eli was sitting upon his seat by the way-side watching; for his heart trembled for the ark of God. And when the man came into the city, and told it, all the city cried out. 14 And when Eli heard the noise of the crying, he said, What meaneth the noise of this tumult? And the man hasted, and came and told Eli. 15 Now Eli was ninety and eight years old; and his eyes were set, so that he could not see. 16 And the man said unto Eli, I am he that came out of the army, and I fled to-day out of the army. And he said, How went the matter, my son? 17 And he that brought the tidings answered and said, Israel is fled before the Philistines, and there hath been also a great slaughter among the people, and thy two sons also, Hophni and Phinehas, are dead, and the ark of God is taken. 18 And it came to pass, when he made mention of the ark of God, that *Eli* fell from off his seat backward by the side of the gate; and his neck brake, and he died: for he was an old man, and heavy. And he had judged Israel forty years.

19 And his daughter-in-law, Phinehas' wife, was with child, near to be delivered: and when she heard the tidings that the ark of God was taken, and that her father-in-law and her husband were dead, she bowed herself and brought forth; for her pains came upon her. 20 And about the time of her death the women that stood by her said unto her, Fear not; for thou hast brought forth a son. But she answered not, neither did she regard it. 21 And she named the child Ichabod, saying, The glory is departed from Israel; because the ark of God was taken, and because of her father-in-law and her husband. 22 And she said, The glory is departed from Israel; for the ark of God is taken.

One of the men of Israel ran from the scene of battle to Shiloh to report the disastrous developments. He told of the defeat of Israel and the great loss of life which the army had sustained. He reported the death of Eli's sons and the capture of the ark by the Philistines.

When Eli heard that the ark of God was captured, it was more than the old priest could bear. He fell and broke his neck. He died as a result.

Eli's daughter-in-law, the wife of Phinehas, was nearing the time of childbirth. The tragic news brought her to labor and just as she gave birth to a son she died from the shock and overstrain. The child was given a haunting name. He was called **Ichabod** (v. 21). The word is primarily a reference to the loss of the ark. **The glory is departed from Israel** (v. 21).

The defeat was overwhelming. Shiloh was completely destroyed and the priests slain. Apparently, the Philistines not only captured the ark but also destroyed the sanctuary at Shiloh (cf. Ps. 78:60-64; Jer. 7:12; 26:9). This was a major disaster for Israel. Shiloh was never again a center for Israel's religion. Doubtless Samuel escaped with some of the sacred vessels and endeavored to reorganize the life of the people. The day that the glory departed from Israel was dark indeed. It is always a dark day in the life of any man or people when the light of God is extinguished from that life (cf. John 13:30).

C. DAGON SMITTEN BY THE LORD (5:1-12)

1 Now the Philistines had taken the ark of God, and they brought it from Ebenezer unto Ashdod. 2 And the Philistines took the ark of God, and brought it into the house of Dagon, and set it by Dagon. 3 And when they of Ashdod arose early on the morrow, behold, Dagon was fallen upon his face to the ground before the ark of Jehovah. And they took Dagon, and set him in his place again. 4 And when they arose early on the morrow morning, behold, Dagon was fallen upon his face to the ground before the ark of Jehovah; and the head of Dagon and both the palms of his hands *lay* cut off upon the threshold; only *the stump of* Dagon was left to him. 5 Therefore neither the priests of Dagon, nor any that come into Dagon's house, tread on the threshold of Dagon in Ashdod, unto this day.

6 But the hand of Jehovah was heavy upon them of Ashdod, and he destroyed them, and smote them with tumors, even Ashdod and the borders thereof. 7 And when the men of Ashdod saw that it was so, they said, The ark of the God of Is-

rael shall not abide with us; for his hand is sore upon us, and upon Dagon our god. 8 They sent therefore and gathered all the lords of the Philistines unto them, and said, What shall we do with the ark of the God of Israel? And they answered, Let the ark of the God of Israel be carried about unto Gath. And they carried the ark of the God of Israel *thither*. 9 And it was so, that, after they had carried it about, the hand of Jehovah was against the city with a very great discomfiture: and he smote the men of the city, both small and great; and tumors brake out upon them. 10 So they sent the ark of God to Ekron. And it came to pass, as the ark of God came to Ekron, that the Ekronites cried out, saying, They have brought about the ark of the God of Israel to us, to slay us and our people. 11 They sent therefore and gathered together all the lords of the Philistines, and they said, Send away the ark of the God of Israel, and let it go again to its own place, that it slay us not, and our people. For there was a deadly discomfiture throughout all the city; the hand of God was very heavy there. 12 And the men that died not were smitten with the tumors; and the cry of the city went up to heaven.

The victorious Philistines took the ark of God to Ashdod and placed it in the temple of Dagon, the Philistine deity. Not only was Dagon thrown down and broken, but also the Philistines of Ashdod were plagued with **tumors** (v. 6).

As a result, the Philistines concluded that the God of Israel was stronger than their own god. The men of Ashdod said, **The ark of the God of Israel shall not abide with us; for his hand is sore upon us, and upon Dagon our god** (v. 7).

Here is a distinctive contrast between the attitude of the plagued Philistines and of the defeated Israelites. Israel concluded that the Lord had left Israel at the mercy of her Philistinian adversary, while the Philistines of Ashdod thought their plague was because Dagon was unable to withstand the stronger deity of Israel. "For the sons of this world are for their own generation wiser than the sons of the light" (Luke 16:8).

D. THE ARK SENT BACK TO ISRAEL (6:1–7:2)

1 And the ark of Jehovah was in the country of the Philistines seven months. 2 And the Philistines called for the priests and the diviners, saying, What shall we do with the ark of Jehovah? show us where-with we shall send it to its place. 3 And they said, If ye send away the ark of the God of Israel, send it not empty; but by all means return him a trespass-offering: then ye shall be healed, and it shall be known to you why his hand is not removed from you. 4 Then said they, What shall be the trespass-offering which we shall return to him? And they said, Five golden tumors, and five golden mice, *according to* the number of the lords of the Philistines; for one plague was on you all, and on your lords. 5 Wherefore ye shall make images of your tumors, and images of your mice that mar the land; and ye shall give glory unto the God of Israel: peradventure he will lighten his hand from off you, and from off your gods, and from off your land. 6 Wherefore then do ye harden your hearts, as the Egyptians and Pharaoh hardened their hearts? When he had wrought wonderfully among them, did they not let the people go, and they departed? 7 Now therefore take and prepare you a new cart, and two milch kine, on which there hath come no yoke; and tie the kine to the cart, and bring their calves home from them; 8 and take the ark of Jehovah and lay it upon the cart; and put the jewels of gold, which ye return him for a trespass-offering, in a coffer by the side thereof; and send it away, that it may go. 9 And see; if it goeth up by the way of its own border to Beth-shemesh, then he hath done us this great evil: but if not, then we shall know that it is not his hand that smote us; it was a chance that happened to us.

10 And the men did so, and took two milch kine, and tied them to the cart, and shut up their calves at home; 11 and they put the ark of Jehovah upon the cart, and the coffer with the mice of gold and the images of their tumors. 12 And the kine took the straight way by the way to Beth-shemesh; they went along the highway, lowing as they went, and turned not aside to the right hand or to the left; and the lords of the Philistines went after them unto the border of Beth-shemesh. 13 And they of Beth-shemesh were reaping their wheat harvest in the valley; and they lifted up their eyes, and saw the ark, and rejoiced to see it. 14 And the cart came into the field of Joshua the Beth-shemite, and stood there, where there was a great stone: and they clave the wood of the cart, and offered up the kine for a burnt-offering unto Jehovah. 15 And the Levites took down the ark of Jehovah, and the coffer that was with it, wherein the jewels of gold were, and put them on the great stone: and the men of Beth-shemesh offered burnt-offerings and sacrificed sacrifices the same

day unto Jehovah. 16 And when the five lords of the Philistines had seen it, they returned to Ekron the same day.

17 And these are the golden tumors which the Philistines returned for a trespass-offering unto Jehovah: for Ashdod one, for Gaza one, for Ashkelon one, for Gath one, for Ekron one; 18 and the golden mice, according to the number of all the cities of the Philistines belonging to the five lords, both of fortified cities and of country villages, even unto the great stone, whereon they set down the ark of Jehovah, *which stone remaineth* unto this day in the field of Joshua the Beth-shemite.

19 And he smote of the men of Beth-shemesh, because they had looked into the ark of Jehovah, he smote of the people seventy men, *and* fifty thousand men; and the people mourned, because Jehovah had smitten the people with a great slaughter. 20 And the men of Beth-shemesh said, Who is able to stand before Jehovah, this holy God? and to whom shall he go up from us? 21 And they sent messengers to the inhabitants of Kiriath-jearim, saying, The Philistines have brought back the ark of Jehovah; come ye down, and fetch it up to you.

1 And the men of Kiriath-jearim came, and fetched up the ark of Jehovah, and brought it into the house of Abinadab in the hill, and sanctified Eleazar his son to keep the ark of Jehovah. 2 And it came to pass, from the day that the ark abode in Kiriath-jearim, that the time was long; for it was twenty years: and all the house of Israel lamented after Jehovah.

The Philistines realized the urgent necessity of getting rid of the ark of Jehovah. The immediate question was, **What shall we do with the ark of Jehovah?** (v. 2). They decided to send the ark away and accompany it with a trespass offering of five golden tumors and mice (vv. 3, 4).

A cart was prepared to carry the ark. Two young, untrained cows were selected to pull the cart. All of this was part of a master plan to determine whether or not the God of Israel, who was equated with the ark, was really the One who had struck at the Philistines with the dreadful plague.

Their test was to determine where the ark would be carried by the young cows when they were sent away: **And see; if it goeth up by the way of its own border to Beth-shemesh, then he hath done us this great evil: but if not, then we shall know**

that it is not his hand that smote us; it was a chance that happened to us (v. 9).

Their problem was to determine whether it was God or accident that visited them with affliction. This is a problem that constantly emerges in the ongoing stream of events. How can it be treated?

The Philistines provide one method. They sought to remove the last vestige of doubt about their particular circumstance. The fallacy of this method is one of oversimplification. In an effort to determine whether God or accident was the solution, they allowed an element of chance to figure in the method. Although in this case the Philistines arrived at the right answer, their method remains faulty. The Christian approach to affliction must not be in terms of trying to find the source of affliction but in accepting affliction as a discipline of life. There must be an attempt to understand the reverses of life in the light of God's providential care.

The young cows took the cart bearing the ark straight to Beth-shemesh in Israel (v. 12). When the Israelites saw the ark they rejoiced and offered a burnt-offering unto Jehovah.

However, their joy quickly turned to terror because the Israelites at Beth-shemesh who looked into the ark were smitten to death. Messengers were sent to the men of Kiriath-jearim, some nine miles northeast of Beth-shemesh, to come and get the ark. This was done and the ark remained there for twenty years.

The times were difficult. Philistine power menaced Israel. Shiloh was occupied; the ark was left at Kiriath-jearim; idolatry flourished; Samuel was greatly limited in his efforts. **All the house of Israel lamented after Jehovah** (v. 2).

III. VICTORY AT MIZPAH (I Sam. 7:3-17)

Following the series of disheartening circumstances involving the ark of Jehovah, Samuel became the hope of Israel and the leader of reform.

A. SAMUEL SUMMONS TO MIZPAH (7:3-6)

3 And Samuel spake unto all the house of Israel, saying, If ye do return unto Jehovah with all your heart, then put away the foreign gods and the Ashtaroth from among you, and direct your hearts unto Jehovah,

and serve him only; and he will deliver you out of the hand of the Philistines. 4 Then the children of Israel did put away the Baalim and the Ashtaroth, and served Jehovah only.

5 And Samuel said, Gather all Israel to Mizpah, and I will pray for you unto Jehovah. 6 And they gathered together to Mizpah, and drew water, and poured it out before Jehovah, and fasted on that day, and said there, We have sinned against Jehovah. And Samuel judged the children of Israel in Mizpah.

Samuel called upon all Israel to return unto the Lord. Idolatry flourished, and the hearts of the Israelites were seeking after other gods. The setting is similar to that which is described in the book of Judges. Verses 3 and 4 have all the marks of the framework of Judges (cf. Judg. 10:10-16). The scene definitely shows Samuel in the role of judge, or savior.

The promise of Samuel was, If ye do return unto Jehovah . . . he will deliver you out of the hand of the Philistines (v. 3). The response of Israel was one of obedience. Then the children of Israel did put away the Baalim and the Ashtaroth, and served Jehovah only (v. 4).

Samuel called for an assembly of Israel at Mizpah, a place about five miles northwest of Jerusalem. It was a significant day for Israel because it was an occasion of national humiliation and repentance. The Philistines were suspicious of this national assembly and prepared to put down any attempt to revolt. Samuel offered a lamb as a whole burnt-offering and prayed.

B. JEHOVAH SUBDUES THE PHILISTINES (7:7-11)

7 And when the Philistines heard that the children of Israel were gathered together to Mizpah, the lords of the Philistines went up against Israel. And when the children of Israel heard it, they were afraid of the Philistines. 8 And the children of Israel said to Samuel, Cease not to cry unto Jehovah our God for us, that he will save us out of the hand of the Philistines. 9 And Samuel took a sucking lamb, and offered it for a whole burnt-offering unto Jehovah: and Samuel cried unto Jehovah for Israel; and Jehovah answered him. 10 And as Samuel was offering up the burnt-offering, the Philistines drew near to battle against Israel; but Jehovah thundered with a great thunder on that day upon the Philistines, and discomfited them; and they were smitten down before Israel. 11 And the men of Israel went out of Mizpah, and pursued the Philistines, and smote them, until they came under Beth-car.

As the Philistines drew near to battle, Jehovah answered the prayer of Samuel: **Jehovah thundered with a great thunder** (v. 10). The Philistines were seized with panic and disastrously smitten. Divine intervention in answer to prayer assures victory.

C. EBENEZER, STONE OF HELP (7:12-14)

12 Then Samuel took a stone, and set it between Mizpah and Shen, and called the name of it Eben-ezer, saying, Hitherto hath Jehovah helped us. 13 So the Philistines were subdued, and they came no more within the border of Israel: and the hand of Jehovah was against the Philistines all the days of Samuel. 14 And the cities which the Philistines had taken from Israel were restored to Israel, from Ekron even unto Gath; and the border thereof did Israel deliver out of the hand of the Philistines. And there was peace between Israel and the Amorites.

On the same battlefield where Israel lost the ark some twenty years before, Samuel set up a stone commemorating this remarkable victory over the Philistines. He named it **Eben-ezer, saying, Hitherto hath Jehovah helped us** (v. 12). There are certain definite landmarks of victory in the life of every person and nation that has experienced the divine intervention in times of distress.

D. SAMUEL, SAVIOR IN ISRAEL (7:15-17)

15 And Samuel judged Israel all the days of his life. 16 And he went from year to year in circuit to Bethel, and Gilgal, and Mizpah; and he judged Israel in all those places. 17 And his return was to Ramah, for there was his house; and there he judged Israel: and he built there an altar unto Jehovah.

So complete and decisive was this victory at Mizpah that the Philistines were unable to battle the Israelites successfully during the time of Samuel's judgeship. It is granted that the Philistines continued to menace Israel, and, during the reign of Saul, they seriously jeopardized his kingdom. However, Mizpah was a momentous victory and Samuel, Israel's judge, or savior, recognized it by the memorial called Ebenezer. Such memorials are always an encouragement to faith in periods of severe attack.

IV. "MAKE US A KING" (I Sam. 8: 1-22)

Samuel judged Israel with uprightness. As a fearless prophet he declared the will of the Lord, and as a faithful priest he worshiped the Lord before the altar. However, his decision to include his sons in judging Israel was unsatisfactory because of their misconduct (v. 3). In this he appears to have been influenced, however unconsciously, by the example of Eli. Thus we are reminded of the powerful, though perhaps ever so subtle, influence of personal example.

A. THE PEOPLE'S REQUEST (8:1-9)

1 And it came to pass, when Samuel was old, that he made his sons judges over Israel. 2 Now the name of his first-born was Joel; and the name of his second, Abijah: they were judges in Beer-sheba. 3 And his sons walked not in his ways, but turned aside after lucre, and took bribes, and perverted justice. 4 Then all the elders of Israel gathered themselves together, and came to Samuel unto Ramah; 5 and they said unto him, Behold, thou art old, and thy sons walk not in thy ways: now make us a king to judge us like all the nations. 6 But the thing displeased Samuel, when they said, Give us a king to judge us. And Samuel prayed unto Jehovah. 7 And Jehovah said unto Samuel, Hearken unto the voice of the people in all that they say unto thee; for they have not rejected thee, but they have rejected me, that I should not be king over them. 8 According to all the works which they have done since the day that I brought them up out of Egypt even unto this day, in that they have forsaken me, and served other gods, so do they also unto thee. 9 Now therefore hearken unto their voice: howbeit thou shalt protest solemnly unto them, and shalt show them the manner of the king that shall reign over them.

From the narrative it seems that the precipitating development which may have caused the elders of the various tribes to gather together to make request of Samuel was the misconduct of his sons. This development may have been the proverbial "last straw," but there were more important developments that were of greater influence and implication than this.

For one thing, Israel had developed a new sense of solidarity and unity under Samuel's leadership. This was something new in the disruptive period of the judges. Generally, the tribes of Israel had remained loosely organized and largely independent of one another, except in their common religious loyalty.

Even this common religious bond was severely tested by the tendency to idolatry. Yet oppressions occurred and served to drive them to repentance, whereupon God would raise up a saving judge.

The new spirit in Israel had its beginning with the victory at Mizpah. Ebenezer was the sign of a new outlook and solidarity. Increasingly, there was a desire for national unity. In several of the tribes it was no longer the glory and prosperity of Judah or Ephraim, but the glory of Israel that was sought. In all of this Samuel himself was a key factor.

Another decisive development was a corollary with the first. It was a desire to organize in such a way as to preserve best this national solidarity. It seemed obvious to the elders of Israel that the best-known method of political organization for this purpose was a king to rule over the people. This was the practice all about Israel. If it sufficed for other peoples it would suffice for Israel, was their logical conclusion.

So the elders of Israel requested of Samuel, **Make us a king to judge us like all the nations** (v. 5). This was no affront to Samuel, as is sometimes indicated. Rather, these elders, having a sense of well-being under Samuel's judgeship, did not usurp Samuel's authority but, rather, trusted in Samuel to help further the new spirit in Israel.

The really disturbing element in the request of the elders of Israel for a king was revealed by the Lord to Samuel: **for they have not rejected thee, but they have rejected me, that I should not be king over them** (v. 7).

It is true that God was King over Israel during the period of history from Moses through Samuel. The rule of God is commonly known as the period of theocracy. During this time charismatic leaders were raised up by God to serve Israel. These included judges, prophets and priests.

God could have remained King during the period known as the monarchy. However, the elders of Israel saw their crisis from the wrong viewpoint. They saw their situation as demanding political security comparable to what they saw among the surrounding nations. They should have seen their situation as demanding religious loyalty to the Lord of hosts.

"Israel has been called in her election by Yahweh to be preacher and example, prophet and priest for the nations."[5] Israel had not been called to establish an ideal politic. However, in the decision to have a king was implicit the establishment of a rival to Israel's supreme calling. Instead of one history essentially religious, Israel chose to inaugurate a rival history essentially political.

In the course of the history of the monarchy, the kings were continually challenged by the prophets who sought to preserve Israel's religious history. "Israel was called to religious leadership of the world, and the verdict of history is . . . her entry into world politics . . . [was] a fundamental mistake."[6]

B. SAMUEL'S PROTEST (8:10-23)

10 And Samuel told all the words of Jehovah unto the people that asked of him a king. 11 And he said, This will be the manner of the king that shall reign over you: he will take your sons, and appoint them unto him, for his chariots, and to be his horsemen; and they shall run before his chariots; 12 and he will appoint them unto him for captains of thousands, and captains of fifties; and *he will set some* to plow his ground, and to reap his harvest, and to make his instruments of war, and the instruments of his chariots. 13 And he will take your daughters to be perfumers, and to be cooks, and to be bakers. 14 And he will take your fields, and your vineyards, and your oliveyards, even the best of them, and give them to his servants. 15 And he will take the tenth of your seed, and of your vineyards, and give to his officers, and to his servants. 16 And he will take your men-servants, and your maid-servants, and your goodliest young men, and your asses, and put them to his work. 17 He will take the tenth of your flocks: and ye shall be his servants. 18 And ye shall cry out in that day because of

your king whom ye shall have chosen you; and Jehovah will not answer you in that day.

19 But the people refused to hearken unto the voice of Samuel; and they said, Nay; but we will have a king over us, 20 that we also may be like all the nations, and that our king may judge us, and go out before us, and fight our battles. 21 And Samuel heard all the words of the people, and he rehearsed them in the ears of Jehovah. 22 And Jehovah said to Samuel, Hearken unto their voice, and make them a king. And Samuel said unto the men of Israel, Go ye every man unto his city.

Samuel prayed unto the Lord (v. 6). The Lord answered Samuel and revealed, among other things, that Samuel was to protest the request of the leaders and disclose to them the basic kingly rights which belonged to a monarch (v. 9).

The king had the right to require military service and forced labor (vv. 11-13). He was entitled to appropriate the land of his subjects (v. 14). He was to levy taxes and to assemble a retinue of servants for the royal court (vv. 15, 16). All of the Israelites were to be his subjects (v. 17).

This remarkable protest emerging from the prophetic tradition expressed clearly the implications of a monarchy and the peril it posed to a people who served Jehovah as King.

But **the people refused to hearken unto the voice of Samuel** (v. 19). This was a momentous decision, the consequences of which are written large in the history of Israel. In the light of it, the word of the Lord came to Samuel, **Hearken unto their voice, and make them a king** (v. 22).

V. SAUL MADE KING (I Sam. 9:1— 11:15)

Saul was the first-born son of a Benjamite named Kish, who lived at Gibeah, four miles north of Jerusalem. Kish was **a mighty man of wealth** (margin, v. 1). Saul was in the prime of life. The phrase, **a young man and a goodly**, does not refer to Saul's youth but to his maturity of life. "The original denotes a man 'in the prime of manhood.' "[7]

[5] Blauw, *op. cit.*, p. 28.
[6] G. B. Caird, "Introduction and Exegesis of I and II Samuel," *The Interpreter's Bible*, eds. G. A. Buttrick *et al.*, II, 919, 920.   [7] Kennedy, *op. cit.*, p. 77.

A. SAUL'S SEARCH (9:1-14)

1 Now there was a man of Benjamin, whose name was Kish, the son of Abiel, the son of Zeror, the son of Becorath, the son of Aphiah, the son of a Benjamite, a mighty man of valor. 2 And he had a son, whose name was Saul, a young man and a goodly: and there was not among the children of Israel a goodlier person than he: from his shoulders and upward he was higher than any of the people. 3 And the asses of Kish, Saul's father, were lost. And Kish said to Saul his son, Take now one of the servants with thee, and arise, go seek the asses. 4 And he passed through the hill-country of Ephraim, and passed through the land of Shalishah, but they found them not: then they passed through the land of Shaalim, and there they were not: and he passed through the land of the Benjamites, but they found them not.

5 When they were come to the land of Zuph, Saul said to his servant that was with him, Come, and let us return, lest my father leave off caring for the asses, and be anxious for us. 6 And he said unto him, Behold now, there is in this city a man of God, and he is a man that is held in honor; all that he saith cometh surely to pass: now let us go thither; peradventure he can tell us concerning our journey whereon we go. 7 Then said Saul to his servant, But, behold, if we go, what shall we bring the man? for the bread is spent in our vessels, and there is not a present to bring to the man of God: what have we? 8 And the servant answered Saul again, and said, Behold, I have in my hand the fourth part of a shekel of silver: that will I give to the man of God, to tell us our way. 9 (Beforetime in Israel, when a man went to inquire of God, thus he said, Come, and let us go to the seer; for he that is now called a Prophet was beforetime called a Seer.) 10 Then said Saul to his servant, Well said; come, let us go. So they went unto the city where the man of God was.

11 As they went up the ascent to the city, they found young maidens going out to draw water, and said unto them, Is the seer here? 12 And they answered them, and said, He is; behold, *he is* before thee: make haste now, for he is come to-day into the city; for the people have a sacrifice to-day in the high place. 13 As soon as ye are come into the city, ye shall straightway find him, before he goeth up to the high place to eat; for the people will not eat until he come, because he doth bless the sacrifice; *and* afterwards they eat that are bidden. Now therefore get you up; for at this time ye shall find him. 14 And they went up to the city; *and* as they came within the city, behold, Samuel came out toward them, to go up to the high place.

The first meeting of Saul and Samuel might seem to involve an element of chance. It came about through the search for straying animals which belonged to Saul's father. However, it was not chance but providence that explains this important meeting of two men, one to be anointed king of Israel by the other before they parted.

Saul and his servant had searched diligently for the lost asses and were about to return home lest his father become anxious about their safety (v. 5). They knew they were in the **land of Zuph,** and the servant recalled that there lived **a man of God** in the city who was **held in honor** (vv. 5, 6). The place was Samuel's home town.

B. SAUL SERVED THE PRIME PORTION (9:15-27)

15 Now Jehovah had revealed unto Samuel a day before Saul came, saying, 16 To-morrow about this time I will send thee a man out of the land of Benjamin, and thou shalt anoint him to be prince over my people Israel; and he shall save my people out of the hand of the Philistines: for I have looked upon my people, because their cry is come unto me. 17 And when Samuel saw Saul, Jehovah said unto him, Behold, the man of whom I spake to thee! this same shall have authority over my people. 18 Then Saul drew near to Samuel in the gate, and said, Tell me, I pray thee, where the seer's house is. 19 And Samuel answered Saul, and said, I am the seer; go up before me unto the high place, for ye shall eat with me to-day: and in the morning I will let thee go, and will tell thee all that is in thy heart. 20 And as for thine asses that were lost three days ago, set not thy mind on them; for they are found. And for whom is all that is desirable in Israel? Is it not for thee, and for all thy father's house? 21 And Saul answered and said, Am not I a Benjamite, of the smallest of the tribes of Israel? and my family the least of all the families of the tribe of Benjamin? wherefore then speakest thou to me after this manner?

22 And Samuel took Saul and his servant, and brought them into the guest-chamber, and made them sit in the chiefest place among them that were bidden, who were about thirty persons. 23 And Samuel said unto the cook, Bring the portion which I gave thee, of which I said unto

thee, Set it by thee. 24 And the cook took up the thigh, and that which was upon it, and set it before Saul. And *Samuel* said, Behold, that which hath been reserved! set it before thee and eat; because unto the appointed time hath it been kept for thee, for I said, I have invited the people. So Saul did eat with Samuel that day.

25 And when they were come down from the high place into the city, he communed with Saul upon the housetop. 26 And they arose early: and it came to pass about the spring of the day, that Samuel called to Saul on the housetop, saying, Up, that I may send thee away. And Saul arose, and they went out both of them, he and Samuel, abroad. 27 As they were going down at the end of the city, Samuel said to Saul, Bid the servant pass on before us (and he passed on), but stand thou still first, that I may cause thee to hear the word of God.

Samuel was aware that he was to meet the man whom God had chosen to be king. **Jehovah had uncovered the ear of Samuel** (margin, v. 15). The divine message came audibly rather than visibly. **To-morrow about this time I will send thee a man . . . and thou shalt anoint him** (v. 16).

When Saul and his servant came to Ramah to inquire of the man of God concerning the lost asses, the first person they met was Samuel, and they inquired of him where the **seer** lived (v. 18).

Samuel disclosed his identity: **I am the seer** (v. 19). What Samuel had to say in the next few utterances caused Saul great amazement.

For one thing, Samuel said that he would tell Saul what was on his, not Samuel's mind: **I . . . will tell thee all that is in thy heart** (v. 19). In the light of what we know about Saul we can well understand these words as indicating "that Saul had brooded in secret over the tyranny of the Philistines."[8] He may have had some formative plans for resisting this tyranny. For another thing, when Samuel referred to the honor and advantages in Israel that were to be given Saul, Saul replied in words of great self-abasement (vv. 20, 21). He could not understand why great honor should come to him when he was from the little tribe of Benjamin.

Samuel took Saul into a room used for sacrificial feasts and gave him the place of honor among the thirty guests. Saul was served the priests' portion of the sacrifice; this belonged to Samuel but was reserved for Saul on this occasion.

C. SAUL SHOWN SIGNS (10:1-16)

1 Then Samuel took the vial of oil, and poured it upon his head, and kissed him, and said, Is it not that Jehovah hath anointed thee to be prince over his inheritance? 2 When thou art departed from me to-day, then thou shalt find two men by Rachel's sepulchre, in the border of Benjamin at Zelzah; and they will say unto thee, The asses which thou wentest to seek are found; and, lo, thy father hath left off caring for the asses, and is anxious for you, saying, What shall I do for my son? 3 Then shalt thou go on forward from thence, and thou shalt come to the oak of Tabor; and there shall meet thee there three men going up to God to Beth-el, one carrying three kids, and another carrying three loaves of bread, and another carrying a bottle of wine: 4 and they will salute thee, and give thee two loaves of bread, which thou shalt receive of their hand. 5 After that thou shalt come to the hill of God, where is the garrison of the Philistines: and it shall come to pass, when thou art come thither to the city, that thou shalt meet a band of prophets coming down from the high place with a psaltery, and a timbrel, and a pipe, and a harp, before them; and they will be prophesying: 6 and the Spirit of Jehovah will come mightily upon thee, and thou shalt prophesy with them, and shalt be turned into another man. 7 And let it be, when these signs are come unto thee, that thou do as occasion shall serve thee; for God is with thee. 8 And thou shalt go down before me to Gilgal; and, behold, I will come down unto thee, to offer burnt-offerings, and to sacrifice sacrifices of peace-offerings: seven days shalt thou tarry, till I come unto thee, and show thee what thou shalt do.

9 And it was so, that, when he had turned his back to go from Samuel, God gave him another heart: and all those signs came to pass that day. 10 And when they came thither to the hill, behold, a band of prophets met him; and the Spirit of God came mightily upon him, and he prophesied among them. 11 And it came to pass, when all that knew him beforetime saw that, behold, he prophesied with the prophets, then the people said one to another, What is this that is come unto the son of Kish? Is Saul also among the prophets? 12 And one of the same place

8 *Ibid.*, p. 81.

answered and said, And who is their father? Therefore it became a proverb, Is Saul also among the prophets? 13 And when he had made an end of prophesying, he came to the high place.

14 And Saul's uncle said unto him and to his servant, Whither went ye? And he said, To seek the asses; and when we saw that they were not found, we came to Samuel. 15 And Saul's uncle said, Tell me, I pray thee, what Samuel said unto you. 16 And Saul said unto his uncle, He told us plainly that the asses were found. But concerning the matter of the kingdom, whereof Samuel spake, he told him not.

The day following Samuel's feast honoring Saul, Samuel privately anointed Saul on the outskirts of Ramah, just as Saul was departing for his home in Gibeah. Then Samuel gave Saul three signs verifying the fact of his kingly authority: two men by Rachel's sepulchre (v. 2); three men by the oak of Tabor (v. 3); a band of prophets near Gibeah (v. 5).

Saul was told that when he saw these signs fulfilled he was to take the first opportunity to exercise his kingly role; God was with him (v. 7). This opportunity came within a few weeks when the men of Jabesh-gilead appealed for help against the Ammonites.

D. SAUL SELECTED AT MIZPAH (10:17-27)

17 And Samuel called the people together unto Jehovah to Mizpah; 18 and he said unto the children of Israel, Thus saith Jehovah, the God of Israel, I brought up Israel out of Egypt, and I delivered you out of the hand of the Egyptians, and out of the hand of all the kingdoms that oppressed you: 19 but ye have this day rejected your God, who himself saveth you out of all your calamities and your distresses; and ye have said unto him, Nay, but set a king over us. Now therefore present yourselves before Jehovah by your tribes, and by your thousands. 20 So Samuel brought all the tribes of Israel near, and the tribe of Benjamin was taken. 21 And he brought the tribe of Benjamin near by their families; and the family of the Matrites was taken; and Saul the son of Kish was taken: but when they sought him, he could not be found. 22 Therefore they asked of Jehovah further, Is there yet a man to come hither? And Jehovah answered, Behold, he hath hid himself among the baggage. 23 And they ran and fetched him thence; and when he stood among the people, he was higher than any of the people from his shoulders and upward. 24 And Samuel said to all the people, See ye him whom Jehovah hath chosen, that there is none like him among all the people? And all the people shouted, and said, Long live the king.

25 Then Samuel told the people the manner of the kingdom, and wrote it in a book, and laid it up before Jehovah. And Samuel sent all the people away, every man to his house. 26 And Saul also went to his house to Gibeah; and there went with him the host, whose hearts God had touched. 27 But certain worthless fellows said, How shall this man save us? And they despised him, and brought him no present. But he held his peace.

Samuel called upon the people of Israel to assemble at Mizpah. He recalled the gracious deliverances which the Lord had wrought for Israel and acknowledged that the people were insisting upon a king.

Since Israel was satisfied with nothing less, Samuel prepared to select a king by sacred lot. The lot fell upon Saul, and Samuel declared, **See ye whom Jehovah hath chosen . . . . And all the people shouted, and said, Long live the king** (v. 24).

Having selected their king, the people returned to their homes. As Saul returned to Gibeah, he was accompanied by a group of brave and loyal men **whose hearts God had touched** (v. 26). Not only was the God of Israel granting Israel a king, but also He was stirring up a hard core of loyal men who would help Saul as he asserted his claims and rights as a monarch. God's callings are always accompanied by His ability to execute the task.

Doubtless, there were men motivated by purely human motives to help Saul get his kingly rule under way. Since the people had chosen to have a king they were humanly disposed to help the king. With the Lord of Israel, however, it was different. Although He had not desired that Israel should have a king, He willingly encouraged loyalty to the king. God cooperates with infirm human beings and overrules their mistakes as best He can for the good of His total cause, where there is not open rebellion against the principles of right.

E. SAUL SANCTIONED AS KING (11: 1-15)

1 Then Nahash the Ammonite came up, and encamped against Jabesh-gilead: and all the men of Jabesh said unto Nahash, Make a covenant with us, and we will serve thee. 2 And Nahash the Ammonite said unto them, On this condition will I make it with you, that all your right eyes be put out; and I will lay it for a reproach upon all Israel. 3 And the elders of Jabesh said unto him, Give us seven days' respite, that we may send messengers unto all the borders of Israel; and then, if there be none to save us, we will come out to thee. 4 Then came the messengers to Gibeah of Saul, and spake these words in the ears of the people: and all the people lifted up their voice, and wept. 5 And, behold, Saul came following the oxen out of the field; and Saul said, What aileth the people that they weep? And they told him the words of the men of Jabesh. 6 And the Spirit of God came mightily upon Saul when he heard those words, and his anger was kindled greatly. 7 And he took a yoke of oxen, and cut them in pieces, and sent them throughout all the borders of Israel by the hand of messengers, saying, Whosoever cometh not forth after Saul and after Samuel, so shall it be done unto his oxen. And the dread of Jehovah fell on the people, and they came out as one man. 8 And he numbered them in Bezek; and the children of Israel were three hundred thousand, and the men of Judah thirty thousand. 9 And they said unto the messengers that came, Thus shall ye say unto the men of Jabesh-gilead, To-morrow, by the time the sun is hot, ye shall have deliverance. And the messengers came and told the men of Jabesh; and they were glad. 10 Therefore the men of Jabesh said, To-morrow we will come out unto you, and ye shall do with us all that seemeth good unto you. 11 And it was so on the morrow, that Saul put the people in three companies; and they came into the midst of the camp in the morning watch, and smote the Ammonites until the heat of the day: and it came to pass, that they that remained were scattered, so that not two of them were left together.

12 And the people said unto Samuel, Who is he that said, Shall Saul reign over us? bring the men, that we may put them to death. 13 And Saul said, There shall not a man be put to death this day; for to-day Jehovah hath wrought deliverance in Israel.

14 Then said Samuel to the people, Come, and let us go to Gilgal, and renew the kingdom there. 15 And all the people went to Gilgal; and there they made Saul king before Jehovah in Gilgal; and there they offered sacrifices of peace-offerings before Jehovah; and there Saul and all the men of Israel rejoiced greatly.

The threat of the Ammonites to enslave the people of Jabesh-gilead provided Saul with the opportunity to show his kingly power. Samuel had encouraged Saul to do this (v. 7).

Jabesh-gilead was located in the tribe of Gad on the east side of the Jordan. Messengers hurried throughout Israel seeking aid against the threat of the Ammonites. Arriving in Gibeah of the tribe of Benjamin they told the people of their peril.

When Saul heard the story he was mightily moved upon by the Spirit of God and called upon Israel to follow him. A great response from the tribes gave Saul a strong army, which he deployed against the Ammonites and won a smashing victory (v. 11). As a result, the people were jubilant over their king. In the very nature of humanity there seems to be a demand for an occasion in which a leader may demonstrate his worth before he is given the full confidence of those he would lead or govern.

Samuel's address was not, strictly speaking, a farewell speech. Rather than withdrawing to private life, Samuel continued in the vigorous role of prophet until his death a few years before that of Saul.

As Saul assumed the role of political leader, Samuel took the opportunity of reviewing his own leadership in Israel. He then entered upon an important interpretation of history. It was an occasion marked by divine approval in the form of a great rainstorm.

VI. SAMUEL'S ADDRESS (I Sam. 12:1-25)

A. PERSUASIVE VINDICATION OF HIMSELF (12:1-5)

1 And Samuel said unto all Israel, Behold, I have hearkened unto your voice in all that ye said unto me, and have made a king over you. 2 And now, behold, the king walketh before you; and I am old and grayheaded; and, behold, my sons are with you: and I have walked before you from my youth unto this day. 3 Here I am: witness against me before Jehovah, and before his anointed: whose ox have I taken? or whose ass have I taken? or whom

have I defrauded? whom have I oppressed? or of whose hand have I taken a ransom to blind mine eyes therewith? and I will restore it you. 4 And they said, Thou hast not defrauded us, nor oppressed us, neither hast thou taken aught of any man's hand. 5 And he said unto them, Jehovah is witness against you, and his anointed is witness this day, that ye have not found aught in my hand. And they said, He is witness.

Samuel's vindication was concerned with his conduct as a judge. The examples which he mentioned relate to judicial honesty and integrity. His long period of service as a judge was blameless.

He challenged the people to expose any injustice he might have committed. **Whose ox have I taken? . . . whom have I defrauded? . . . of whose hand have I taken a bribe to blind my eyes therewith? and I will restore it you** (v. 3).

The people responded that he had been upright and just. Samuel accepted their response and called upon both God and the king to witness their testimony (v. 5). Thus he closed his career having the honor and respect of his people and the favor of God. How different from that of Samson or Eli. His was a life well lived and a service well rendered. What a blessed ending for any leader.

B. PROFOUND VIEW OF HISTORY (12:6-15)

6 And Samuel said unto the people, It is Jehovah that appointed Moses and Aaron, and that brought your fathers up out of the land of Egypt. 7 Now therefore stand still, that I may plead with you before Jehovah concerning all the righteous acts of Jehovah, which he did to you and to your fathers. 8 When Jacob was come into Egypt, and your fathers cried unto Jehovah, then Jehovah sent Moses and Aaron, who brought forth your fathers out of Egypt, and made them to dwell in this place. 9 But they forgat Jehovah their God; and he sold them into the hand of Sisera, captain of the host of Hazor, and into the hand of the Philistines, and into the hand of the king of Moab; and they fought against them. 10 And they cried unto Jehovah, and said, We have sinned, because we have forsaken Jehovah, and have served the Baalim and the Ashtaroth: but now deliver us out of the hand of our enemies, and we will serve thee. 11 And Jehovah sent Jerubbaal, and Bedan, and Jephthah, and Samuel, and delivered you

out of the hand of your enemies on every side; and ye dwelt in safety. 12 And when ye saw that Nahash the king of the children of Ammon came against you, ye said unto me, Nay, but a king shall reign over us; when Jehovah your God was your king. 13 Now therefore behold the king whom ye have chosen, and whom ye have asked for: and, behold, Jehovah hath set a king over you. 14 If ye will fear Jehovah, and serve him, and hearken unto his voice, and not rebel against the commandment of Jehovah, and both ye and also the king that reigneth over you be followers of Jehovah your God, *well:* 15 but if ye will not hearken unto the voice of Jehovah, but rebel against the commandment of Jehovah, then will the hand of Jehovah be against you, as it was against your fathers.

The view of history given here is the same as that which provides the structure of the book of Judges (cf. Judg. 2:11-19). It appears frequently in the Old Testament. It may be summarized as follows: when the people of Israel are loyal to Jehovah, they prosper and flourish; when they forsake Jehovah for other gods, they are punished and humbled.

As Samuel spoke of the history of Israel, he drew upon instances in Israel's history which substantiated his view. **Now therefore stand still, that I may plead with you before Jehovah concerning all the righteous acts of Jehovah, which he did to you and to your fathers** (v. 7).

Samuel cited the oppressions of the Egyptians, Canaanites, Philistines and Moabites. He mentioned the deliverances of Gideon, Barak and Samuel himself.

However, Samuel warned Israel regarding the venture into the political arena. A king had been selected to rule over Israel even though Jehovah was King. The view of history which Samuel had already mentioned was still the decisive factor in Israel's life. King or no king, if the people of Israel forsook God, then He would punish them (vv. 13-15).

While Israel wanted to be like other nations politically, Samuel warned that Israel was expected to be faithful to Jehovah. In this way, all nations would behold her distinctive religious loyalty.

C. PROVIDENTIAL VERIFICATION OF SAMUEL'S MESSAGE (12:16-25)

16 Now therefore stand still and see this great thing, which Jehovah will do before

your eyes. 17 Is it not wheat harvest to-day? I will call unto Jehovah, that he may send thunder and rain; and ye shall know and see that your wickedness is great, which ye have done in the sight of Jehovah, in asking you a king. 18 So Samuel called unto Jehovah; and Jehovah sent thunder and rain that day: and all the people greatly feared Jehovah and Samuel.

19 And all the people said unto Samuel, Pray for thy servants unto Jehovah thy God, that we die not; for we have added unto all our sins *this* evil, to ask us a king. 20 And Samuel said unto the people, Fear not: ye have indeed done all this evil; yet turn not aside from following Jehovah, but serve Jehovah with all your heart: 21 and turn ye not aside; for *then would ye go* after vain things which cannot profit nor deliver, for they are vain. 22 For Jehovah will not forsake his people for his great name's sake, because it hath pleased Jehovah to make you a people unto himself. 23 Moreover as for me, far be it from me that I should sin against Jehovah in ceasing to pray for you: but I will instruct you in the good and the right way. 24 Only fear Jehovah, and serve him in truth with all your heart; for consider how great things he hath done for you. 25 But if ye shall still do wickedly, ye shall be consumed, both ye and your king.

It was the time of the wheat harvest. Rain during harvest was as unlikely as snow during the summer. Yet Samuel called upon the Lord to send rain as a sign confirming his words, **and Jehovah sent thunder and rain that day** (v. 18).

This caused the people to be afraid, and they said to Samuel, **Pray for thy servants unto Jehovah thy God, that we die not** (v. 19). Samuel reassured the people, **Fear not . . . yet turn not aside from following Jehovah, but serve Jehovah with all your heart: and turn ye not aside** (vv. 20, 21).

He reminded them that it had pleased the Lord to make them a **people unto himself** (v. 22). They were told to fear Jehovah and serve him in truth. If they did wickedly, Samuel declared, **Ye shall be consumed, both ye and your king** (v. 25).

VII. SAUL AND HIS TASK (I Sam. 13: 1—14:52)

When the Lord revealed to Samuel that He would send him a man of the tribe of Benjamin to be anointed as king

over Israel, He said: ". . . and he shall save my people out of the hand of the Philistines" (I Sam. 9:16). Saul entered upon this lifework by preparing for a major war with the Philistines. His son Jonathan proved himself to be a very important lieutenant and a courageous leader.

A. THE PHILISTINE THREAT AND SAUL'S FOOLISH SACRIFICE (13: 1-23)

1 Saul was [*forty*] years old when he began to reign; and when he had reigned two years over Israel, 2 Saul chose him three thousand men of Israel, whereof two thousand were with Saul in Michmash and in the mount of Beth-el, and a thousand were with Jonathan in Gibeah of Benjamin: and the rest of the people he sent every man to his tent. 3 And Jonathan smote the garrison of the Philistines that was in Geba; and the Philistines heard of it. And Saul blew the trumpet throughout all the land, saying, Let the Hebrews hear. 4 And all Israel heard say that Saul had smitten the garrison of the Philistines, and also that Israel was had in abomination with the Philistines. And the people were gathered together after Saul to Gilgal.

5 And the Philistines assembled themselves together to fight with Israel, thirty thousand chariots, and six thousand horsemen, and people as the sand which is on the sea-shore in multitude: and they came up, and encamped in Michmash, eastward of Beth-aven. 6 When the men of Israel saw that they were in a strait (for the people were distressed), then the people did hide themselves in caves, and in thickets, and in rocks, and in coverts, and in pits. 7 Now some of the Hebrews had gone over the Jordan to the land of Gad and Gilead; but as for Saul, he was yet in Gilgal, and all the people followed him trembling.

8 And he tarried seven days, according to the set time that Samuel *had appointed*: but Samuel came not to Gilgal; and the people were scattered from him. 9 And Saul said, Bring hither the burnt-offering to me, and the peace-offerings. And he offered the burnt-offering. 10 And it came to pass that, as soon as he had made an end of offering the burnt-offering, behold, Samuel came; and Saul went out to meet him, that he might salute him. 11 And Samuel said, What hast thou done? And Saul said, Because I saw that the people were scattered from me, and that thou camest not within the days appointed, and that the Philistines assembled themselves together at Michmash; 12 therefore said I, Now will the Philistines come down upon

me to Gilgal, and I have not entreated the favor of Jehovah: I forced myself therefore, and offered the burnt-offering. 13 And Samuel said to Saul, Thou hast done foolishly; thou hast not kept the commandment of Jehovah thy God, which he commanded thee: for now would Jehovah have established thy kingdom upon Israel for ever. 14 But now thy kingdom shall not continue: Jehovah hath sought him a man after his own heart, and Jehovah hath appointed him to be prince over his people, because thou hast not kept that which Jehovah commanded thee. 15 And Samuel arose, and gat him up from Gilgal unto Gibeah of Benjamin.

And Saul numbered the people that were present with him, about six hundred men. 16 And Saul, and Jonathan his son, and the people that were present with them, abode in Geba of Benjamin: but the Philistines encamped in Michmash. 17 And the spoilers came out of the camp of the Philistines in three companies: one company turned unto the way that leadeth to Ophrah, unto the land of Shual; 18 and another company turned the way to Beth-horon; and another company turned the way of the border that looketh down upon the valley of Zeboim toward the wilderness. 19 Now there was no smith found throughout all the land of Israel; for the Philistines said, Lest the Hebrews make them swords or spears: 20 but all the Israelites went down to the Philistines, to sharpen every man his share, and his coulter, and his axe, and his mattock; 21 yet they had a file for the mattocks, and for the coulters, and for the forks, and for the axes, and to set the goads. 22 So it came to pass in the day of battle, that there was neither sword nor spear found in the hand of any of the people that were with Saul and Jonathan: but with Saul and with Jonathan his son was there found. 23 And the garrison of the Philistines went out unto the pass of Michmash.

The first significant effort of the new king of Israel was to build up a standing army ready for combat. This was absolutely necessary if he were to battle successfully the strong and deeply entrenched Philistines. **Saul chose him three thousand men of Israel** (v. 2). His army was not a motley band of volunteers but a well-trained army of handpicked soldiers. They were the prime examples of excellent military prowess.

Jonathan had a thousand men with him and made the initial engagement with the Philistines at Geba. This alerted the Philistines as to what was taking place, so

they immediately prepared to put down any uprising in Israel (v. 5). Their large numbers and powerful weapons terrorized many in Israel.

Even Saul was unable to conduct himself with the poise and calmness which the crisis demanded. Samuel had instructed Saul in Ramah, on the day he had secretly anointed him to be king of Israel, to go to Gilgal and wait for Samuel to come and offer burnt-offerings and show Saul what to do (10:8).

However, the king did not wait for the priest-prophet, but assumed the role of priest and offered his own burnt-offering. When Samuel arrived, his judgment was, **Thou hast done foolishly; thou hast not kept the commandment of Jehovah thy God, which he commanded thee** (v. 13).

Saul proceeded with his military preparedness, but his army was inadequately equipped. This was because the Philistines had foresight enough to outlaw any Israelite working with metal. All tools and weapons had to be procured from the Philistines (vv. 19, 20). Therefore, one of Saul's great problems was arming his soldiers for battle (v. 22).

B. JONATHAN'S VICTORY AND SAUL'S RASH VOW (14:1-52)

1 Now it fell upon a day, that Jonathan the son of Saul said unto the young man that bare his armor, Come, and let us go over to the Philistines' garrison, that is on yonder side. But he told not his father. 2 And Saul abode in the uttermost part of Gibeah under the pomegranate-tree which is in Migron: and the people that were with him were about six hundred men; 3 and Ahijah, the son of Ahitub, Ichabod's brother, the son of Phinehas, the son of Eli, the priest of Jehovah in Shiloh, wearing an ephod. And the people knew not that Jonathan was gone. 4 And between the passes, by which Jonathan sought to go over unto the Philistines' garrison, there was a rocky crag on the one side, and a rocky crag on the other side: and the name of the one was Bozez, and the name of the other Seneh. 5 The one crag rose up on the north in front of Michmash, and the other on the south in front of Geba.

6 And Jonathan said to the young man that bare his armor, Come, and let us go over unto the garrison of these uncircumcised: it may be that Jehovah will work for us; for there is no restraint to Jehovah to save by many or by few. 7 And his

armorbearer said unto him, Do all that is in thy heart: turn thee, behold, I am with thee according to thy heart. 8 Then said Jonathan, Behold, we will pass over unto the men, and we will disclose ourselves unto them. 9 If they say thus unto us, Tarry until we come to you; then we will stand still in our place, and will not go up unto them. 10 But if they say thus, Come up unto us; then we will go up; for Jehovah hath delivered them into our hand: and this shall be the sign unto us. 11 And both of them disclosed themselves unto the garrison of the Philistines: and the Philistines said, Behold, the Hebrews come forth out of the holes where they had hid themselves. 12 And the men of the garrison answered Jonathan and his armorbearer, and said, Come up to us, and we will show you a thing. And Jonathan said unto his armorbearer, Come up after me; for Jehovah hath delivered them into the hand of Israel. 13 And Jonathan climbed up upon his hands and upon his feet, and his armorbearer after him: and they fell before Jonathan; and his armorbearer slew them after him. 14 And that first slaughter, which Jonathan and his armorbearer made, was about twenty men, within as it were half a furrow's length in an acre of land. 15 And there was a trembling in the camp, in the field, and among all the people; the garrison, and the spoilers, they also trembled; and the earth quaked: so there was an exceeding great trembling.

16 And the watchmen of Saul in Gibeah of Benjamin looked; and, behold, the multitude melted away, and they went *hither* and thither. 17 Then said Saul unto the people that were with him, Number now, and see who is gone from us. And when they had numbered, behold, Jonathan and his armorbearer were not there. 18 And Saul said unto Ahijah, Bring hither the ark of God. For the ark of God was *there* at that time with the children of Israel. 19 And it came to pass, while Saul talked unto the priest, that the tumult that was in the camp of the Philistines went on and increased: and Saul said unto the priest, Withdraw thy hand. 20 And Saul and all the people that were with him were gathered together, and came to the battle: and, behold, every man's sword was against his fellow, *and there was* a very great discomfiture. 21 Now the Hebrews that were with the Philistines as beforetime, and that went up with them into the camp, *from the country* round about, even they also *turned* to be with the Israelites that were with Saul and Jonathan. 22 Likewise all the men of Israel that had hid themselves in the hill-country of Ephraim, when they heard that the Philistines fled,

even they also followed hard after them in the battle. 23 So Jehovah saved Israel that day: and the battle passed over by Beth-aven.

24 And the men of Israel were distressed that day; for Saul had adjured the people, saying, Cursed be the man that eateth any food until it be evening, and I be avenged on mine enemies. So none of the people tasted food. 25 And all the people came into the forest; and there was honey upon the ground. 26 And when the people were come unto the forest, behold, the honey dropped: but no man put his hand to his mouth; for the people feared the oath. 27 But Jonathan heard not when his father charged the people with the oath: wherefore he put forth the end of the rod that was in his hand, and dipped it in the honeycomb, and put his hand to his mouth; and his eyes were enlightened. 28 Then answered one of the people, and said, Thy father straitly charged the people with an oath, saying, Cursed be the man that eateth food this day. And the people were faint. 29 Then said Jonathan, My father hath troubled the land: see, I pray you, how mine eyes have been enlightened, because I tasted a little of this honey. 30 How much more, if haply the people had eaten freely to-day of the spoil of their enemies which they found? for now hath there been no great slaughter among the Philistines.

31 And they smote of the Philistines that day from Michmash to Aijalon. And the people were very faint; 32 and the people flew upon the spoil, and took sheep, and oxen, and calves, and slew them on the ground; and the people did eat them with the blood. 33 Then they told Saul, saying, Behold, the people sin against Jehovah, in that they eat with the blood. And he said, Ye have dealt treacherously: roll a great stone unto me this day. 34 And Saul said, Disperse yourselves among the people, and say unto them, Bring me hither every man his ox, and every man his sheep, and slay them here, and eat; and sin not against Jehovah in eating with the blood. And all the people brought every man his ox with him that night, and slew them there. 35 And Saul built an altar unto Jehovah: the same was the first altar that he built unto Jehovah.

36 And Saul said, Let us go down after the Philistines by night, and take spoil among them until the morning light, and let us not leave a man of them. And they said, Do whatsoever seemeth good unto thee. Then said the priest, Let us draw near hither unto God. 37 And Saul asked counsel of God, Shall I go down after the Philistines? wilt thou deliver them into the

hand of Israel? But he answered him not that day. 38 And Saul said, Draw nigh hither, all ye chiefs of the people; and know and see wherein this sin hath been this day. 39 For, as Jehovah liveth, who saveth Israel, though it be in Jonathan my son, he shall surely die. But there was not a man among all the people that answered him. 40 Then said he unto all Israel, Be ye on one side, and I and Jonathan my son will be on the other side. And the people said unto Saul, Do what seemeth good unto thee. 41 Therefore Saul said unto Jehovah, the God of Israel, Show the right. And Jonathan and Saul were taken *by lot*; but the people escaped. 42 And Saul said, Cast *lots* between me and Jonathan my son. And Jonathan was taken.

43 Then Saul said to Jonathan, Tell me what thou hast done. And Jonathan told him, and said, I did certainly taste a little honey with the end of the rod that was in my hand; and, lo, I must die. 44 And Saul said, God do so and more also; for thou shalt surely die, Jonathan. 45 And the people said unto Saul, Shall Jonathan die, who hath wrought this great salvation in Israel? Far from it: as Jehovah liveth, there shall not one hair of his head fall to the ground; for he hath wrought with God this day. So the people rescued Jonathan, that he died not. 46 Then Saul went up from following the Philistines; and the Philistines went to their own place.

47 Now when Saul had taken the kingdom over Israel, he fought against all his enemies on every side, against Moab, and against the children of Ammon, and against Edom, and against the kings of Zobah, and against the Philistines: and whithersoever he turned himself, he put *them* to the worse. 48 And he did valiantly, and smote the Amalekites, and delivered Israel out of the hands of them that despoiled them.

49 Now the sons of Saul were Jonathan, and Ishvi, and Malchishua; and the names of his two daughters were these: the name of the first-born Merab, and the name of the younger Michal: 50 and the name of Saul's wife was Ahinoam the daughter of Ahimaaz. And the name of the captain of his host was Abner the son of Ner, Saul's uncle. 51 And Kish was the father of Saul; and Ner the father of Abner was the son of Abiel.

52 And there was sore war against the Philistines all the days of Saul: and when Saul saw any mighty man, or any valiant man, he took him unto him.

As Jonathan had initiated the war with the Philistines by the first skirmish at Geba, so he moved first again as the tempo of the war increased. Jonathan must be recognized as a first-rate soldier who was always ready to wage war offensively.

Many Israelites were in hiding and Saul's army was trembling while encamped at Gilgal (cf. 13:6, 7). Jonathan and his armor-bearer, whether fearful or not the record does not say, proceeded on a bold venture. **Come, and let us go over to the Philistines' garrison** (v. 1). Just the two of them went forth to the garrison. They may well have had fears even as the rest, but they were not so obsessed with anxieties that they were impotent and helpless. Indeed, they were under the extreme pressure of the crisis like all the rest, but they were able to think and act heroically. This is to their glory. A certain amount of legitimate fear prevents excessive self-confidence and fosters reliance upon God for help in dangerous emergencies.

Fundamental to their heroism was their faith in Jehovah, so well expressed by Jonathan. **It may be that Jehovah will work for us; for there is no restraint to Jehovah to save by many or by few** (v. 6). Jonathan's armor-bearer was of the same mind, for he said, **I am with thee according to thy heart** (v. 7).

Their courageous faith was their great weapon. As they engaged the Philistines of the garrison there came divine re-enforcement in the form of an earthquake. **There was a trembling in the camp . . . so there was a trembling of God** (margin, v. 15).

Saul was informed of the strange happenings among the Philistines, so he summoned the priest to determine whether or not he should send his army against the Philistines. Before the priest could receive a divine message from the ephod he carried, Saul ordered his men to attack. The Philistines were routed. **So Jehovah saved Israel that day** (v. 23).

Saul was so excited, apparently, at the remarkable victory that he ordered his men to continue the battle without taking any food. He laid a curse upon any that would eat until he had been avenged of his enemies, the Philistines (v. 24). Here is Saul in an all-out effort to accomplish the task to which he was commissioned.

However, Jonathan and his armor-bearer were not present when the curse was announced. Therefore, when Jonathan found honey and ate it (v. 27) he did so in ignorance of the consequences.

Possibly Jonathan would have been undetected if Saul had not been anxious to pursue the Philistines throughout the night. The priest insisted that Saul should seek divine counsel (v. 36). When the priest attempted to obtain an answer from the ephod, there was no answer. Saul was alarmed because to him this was an indication of the presence of sin (v. 38).

The ephod was consulted and Jonathan was exposed. Saul prepared for the execution of Jonathan because he had violated the curse by eating honey. However, the men who were fighting under Saul were so incensed by this royal edict that they resisted and provided a ransom for Jonathan (v. 45). The penalty for breaking Saul's rash vow was never executed, and well that it was not for the sake of Israel, as such would have deprived them of their efficient military leader and probably wrought havoc for them.

In the crisis for which Saul was raised up, namely, delivering Israel from the Philistines, he had not shown superior qualities of leadership. He was excitable and impetuous. He failed to respect instructions given to him, and he forced rash restrictions upon others. His son Jonathan appeared to be a man of more stable character and firmer faith.

VIII. "TO OBEY IS BETTER" (I Sam. 15:1-35)

The Amalekites were among the oldest enemies of the Israelites. Both traced their lineage back to Isaac and Abraham, the Amalekites by way of Esau and the Israelites by way of Jacob, who became known by the name Israel as a result of events at Peniel. There had existed long-standing hatred which had its first appearance in Esau's hatred of Jacob.

The Amalekites had wantonly attacked the Israelites during their journey from Egypt and after their entrance into the promised land (cf. Exod. 17:8-16; Num. 14:45; Judg. 3:13; 7:12). It may be, according to I Samuel 15:33, that Samuel knew of recent atrocities committed by the Amalekites. Against this unrelenting foe of Israel there had been pronounced the *cherem* (Deut. 25:17-19).[9]

Samuel, the religious leader of Israel, came to Saul, the securely established political leader, with a reminder that he, Samuel, had performed the will of God in anointing Saul to be king. The reminder was accompanied by a divine command, **Now go and smite Amalek, and utterly destroy all that they have . . .** (v. 3).

A. SAUL'S DISOBEDIENCE (15:1-9)

1 And Samuel said unto Saul, Jehovah sent me to anoint thee to be king over his people, over Israel: now therefore hearken thou unto the voice of the words of Jehovah. 2 Thus saith Jehovah of hosts, I have marked that which Amalek did to Israel, how he set himself against him in the way, when he came up out of Egypt. 3 Now go and smite Amalek, and utterly destroy all that they have, and spare them not; but slay both man and woman, infant and suckling, ox and sheep, camel and ass.

4 And Saul summoned the people, and numbered them in Telaim, two hundred thousand footmen, and ten thousand men of Judah. 5 And Saul came to the city of Amalek, and laid wait in the valley. 6 And Saul said unto the Kenites, Go, depart, get you down from among the Amalekites, lest I destroy you with them; for ye showed kindness to all the children of Israel, when they came up out of Egypt. So the Kenites departed from among the Amalekites. 7 And Saul smote the Amalekites, from Havilah as thou goest to Shur, that is before Egypt. 8 And he took Agag the king of the Amalekites alive, and utterly destroyed all the people with the edge of the sword. 9 But Saul and the people spared Agag, and the best of the sheep, and of the oxen, and of the fatlings, and the lambs, and all that was good, and would not utterly destroy them: but everything that was vile and refuse, that they destroyed utterly.

Saul made preparations to execute the *cherem*. Gathering a large force, he moved into the Negeb and struck a devastating blow. The Amalekites were completely overpowered.

The spoil of battle was enormous. Apparently, the Israelites were unable to resist the temptation to save much of the best which fell into their hands. However, it is not easy for us to understand how they could so flagrantly disregard the *cherem*. All Jewish history, from the time of Achan forward, stood as witness against them. Moreover, Saul's recent determina-

---

[9] Cf. the discussion on the *cherem* in Joshua, pp. 563f.

tion to kill his own son who had un-wittingly violated his rash vow, stood as an indictment against Saul's sparing Agag (cf. 14:44 with 15:9). It is quite impossible for a person of rash disposition to be consistent in character or conduct.

Here is a glaring example of unjustified self-assurance. Saul did what he wanted to do. He may have been more or less innocent of the charge of malicious insolence and self-will or he may have been motivated by a radical stubbornness. Perhaps he is best understood as moving from that spirit of humility and timidity that caused him to hide among the stuff when he had been selected king at Mizpah to that point where his life became possessed by violent neurosis and spiritual solitariness.

Saul might well have occupied himself with a spiritual inventory. He could have profited by taking a comprehensive look at himself as king. He needed to see himself in perspective. The direction he was going was sufficient to give him warning signals.

Life offers us the opportunity of sizing up the course we are pursuing. As Saul needed to check himself regarding the progress of his relations with the Lord, so do we. The higher our office or position, the more difficult it becomes for us to accept instruction or warning from others. It should be remembered that no man is wholly sufficient unto himself.

B. GOD'S DISMISSAL (15:10-35)

10 Then came the word of Jehovah unto Samuel, saying, 11 It repenteth me that I have set up Saul to be king; for he is turned back from following me, and hath not performed my commandments. And Samuel was wroth; and he cried unto Jehovah all night. 12 And Samuel rose early to meet Saul in the morning; and it was told Samuel, saying, Saul came to Carmel, and, behold, he set him up a monument, and turned, and passed on, and went down to Gilgal. 13 And Samuel came to Saul; and Saul said unto him, Blessed be thou of Jehovah: I have performed the commandment of Jehovah. 14 And Samuel said, What meaneth then this bleating of the sheep in mine ears, and the lowing of the oxen which I hear? 15 And Saul said, They have brought them from the Amalekites: for the people spared the best of the sheep and of the oxen, to sacrifice unto Jehovah thy God; and the rest we have utterly destroyed. 16 Then Samuel said unto Saul, Stay, and I will tell thee what Jehovah hath said to me this night. And he said unto him, Say on.

17 And Samuel said, Though thou wast little in thine own sight, wast thou not made the head of the tribes of Israel? And Jehovah anointed thee king over Israel; 18 and Jehovah sent thee on a journey, and said, Go, and utterly destroy the sinners the Amalekites, and fight against them until they be consumed. 19 Wherefore then didst thou not obey the voice of Jehovah, but didst fly upon the spoil, and didst that which was evil in the sight of Jehovah? 20 And Saul said unto Samuel, Yea, I have obeyed the voice of Jehovah, and have gone the way which Jehovah sent me, and have brought Agag the king of Amalek, and have utterly destroyed the Amalekites. 21 But the people took of the spoil, sheep and oxen, the chief of the devoted things, to sacrifice unto Jehovah thy God in Gilgal. 22 And Samuel said, Hath Jehovah as great delight in burnt-offerings and sacrifices, as in obeying the voice of Jehovah? Behold, to obey is better than sacrifice, and to hearken than the fat of rams. 23 For rebellion is as the sin of witchcraft, and stubbornness is as idolatry and teraphim. Because thou hast rejected the word of Jehovah, he hath also rejected thee from being king.

24 And Saul said unto Samuel, I have sinned; for I have transgressed the commandment of Jehovah, and thy words, because I feared the people, and obeyed their voice. 25 Now therefore, I pray thee, pardon my sin, and turn again with me, that I may worship Jehovah. 26 And Samuel said unto Saul, I will not return with thee; for thou hast rejected the word of Jehovah, and Jehovah hath rejected thee from being king over Israel. 27 And as Samuel turned about to go away, Saul laid hold upon the skirt of his robe, and it rent. 28 And Samuel said unto him, Jehovah hath rent the kingdom of Israel from thee this day, and hath given it to a neighbor of thine, that is better than thou. 29 And also the Strength of Israel will not lie nor repent; for he is not a man, that he should repent. 30 Then he said, I have sinned: yet honor me now, I pray thee, before the elders of my people, and before Israel, and turn again with me, that I may worship Jehovah thy God. 31 So Samuel turned again after Saul; and Saul worshipped Jehovah.

32 Then said Samuel, Bring ye hither to me Agag the king of the Amalekites. And Agag came unto him cheerfully. And Agag said, Surely the bitterness of death is past. 33 And Samuel said, As thy sword hath made women childless, so shall thy mother

be childless among women. And Samuel hewed Agag in pieces before Jehovah in Gilgal.

34 Then Samuel went to Ramah; and Saul went up to his house to Gibeah of Saul. 35 And Samuel came no more to see Saul until the day of his death; for Samuel mourned for Saul: and Jehovah repented that he had made Saul king over Israel.

The scene shifts to Ramah where Samuel received a divine message, **It repenteth me that I have set up Saul to be king; for he is turned back from following me . . .** (v. 11). Divine repentance is best understood in terms of God's re-arrangement of the stewardship or dispensation which relates to Israel. This does not interpret deity in terms of divine caprice, but it does interpret deity in terms of human fickleness and instability. Where man fails in fulfilling his stewardship, God "repents" by finding a replacement (cf. Acts 1:15-26).

Under divine approval, Saul was dismissed as king. This caused intense feelings for Samuel when he heard the divine communication: **And Samuel was wroth; and he cried unto the Lord all night** (v. 11).

Samuel left Ramah for Gilgal where he confronted Saul with his violation of *cherem.* Saul replied that the Amalekites were destroyed and the spoil of battle which was brought back to Gilgal was devoted as a sacrifice to the Lord (v. 21).

Upon-hearing this, Samuel replied, **Behold, to obey is better than sacrifice, and to hearken than the fat of rams** (v. 22). God desired obedience to the command He had given in preference to a sacrifice. Saul's evasion of the divine command was declared to be as wicked as witchcraft and idolatry (v. 23).

Saul was given the word of the Lord regarding his dismissal, **Jehovah hath rent the kingdom of Israel from thee this day** (v. 28). Then Samuel turned to the task of completing the *cherem.* Agag was dealt with as required.

Samuel came no more to see Saul . . . Samuel mourned for Saul: and Jehovah repented that he had made Saul king over Israel (v. 35).

IX. DAVID CHOSEN (I Sam. 16:1—18:9)

Samuel was deeply grieved by the divine rejection of Saul, and his mind apparently lingered upon the momentous implications. However, he was abruptly confronted by the word of the Lord and commissioned to go to the house of Jesse in Bethlehem which belonged to Judah.

A. DAVID ANOINTED BY SAMUEL (16:1-13)

1 And Jehovah said unto Samuel, How long wilt thou mourn for Saul, seeing I have rejected him from being king over Israel? fill thy horn with oil, and go: I will send thee to Jesse the Beth-lehemite; for I have provided me a king among his sons. 2 And Samuel said, How can I go? if Saul hear it, he will kill me. And Jehovah said, Take a heifer with thee, and say, I am come to sacrifice to Jehovah. 3 And call Jesse to the sacrifice, and I will show thee what thou shalt do: and thou shalt anoint unto me him whom I name unto thee. 4 And Samuel did that which Jehovah spake, and came to Beth-lehem. And the elders of the city came to meet him trembling, and said, Comest thou peaceably? 5 And he said, Peaceably; I am come to sacrifice unto Jehovah: sanctify yourselves, and come with me to the sacrifice. And he sanctified Jesse and his sons, and called them to the sacrifice.

6 And it came to pass, when they were come, that he looked on Eliab, and said, Surely Jehovah's anointed is before him. 7 But Jehovah said unto Samuel, Look not on his countenance, or on the height of his stature; because I have rejected him: for *Jehovah seeth* not as man seeth; for man looketh on the outward appearance, but Jehovah looketh on the heart. 8 Then Jesse called Abinadab, and made him pass before Samuel. And he said, Neither hath Jehovah chosen this. 9 Then Jesse made Shammah to pass by. And he said, Neither hath Jehovah chosen this. 10 And Jesse made seven of his sons to pass before Samuel. And Samuel said unto Jesse, Jehovah hath not chosen these. 11 And Samuel said unto Jesse, Are here all thy children? And he said, There remaineth yet the youngest, and, behold, he is keeping the sheep. And Samuel said unto Jesse, Send and fetch him; for we will not sit down till he come hither. 12 And he sent, and brought him in. Now he was ruddy, and withal of a beautiful countenance, and goodly to look upon. And Jehovah said, Arise, anoint him; for this is he. 13 Then Samuel took the horn of oil, and anointed him in the midst of his brethren: and the Spirit of Jehovah came mightily upon David from that day forward. So Samuel rose up, and went to Ramah.

The word of Jehovah to Samuel was arresting, **I will send thee to Jesse . . . I have provided me a king among his sons** (v. 1). However, Samuel not only grieved over Saul; he actually feared him. Saul was impetuous. He could spare Agag, but he could all but execute the death sentence on his own son. He had been told the bad news that he was rejected as king. His reactions were unpredictable. Samuel feared that Saul would kill him if it were known that Samuel had anointed his successor. From what we know of Saul, particularly in his relations to David, it may well be that Samuel's fears were well founded, although, generally, Samuel was fearless regardless of the peril.

Samuel was to take a heifer and say, **I am come to sacrifice to Jehovah** (v. 3). This was customary; meanwhile, he was to anoint the son of Jesse who would be designated by the Lord.

Arriving at the house of Jesse, Samuel made plans for the sacrifice and the accompanying sacrificial meal. When it was ready and Jesse's sons were assembled, Samuel anointed David. **And the Spirit of Jehovah came mightily upon David . . .** (v. 13).

B. DAVID PRESENTED TO SAUL (16: 14-23)

14 Now the Spirit of Jehovah departed from Saul, and an evil spirit from Jehovah troubled him. 15 And Saul's servants said unto him, Behold now, an evil spirit from God troubleth thee. 16 Let our lord now command thy servants, that are before thee, to seek out a man who is a skilful player on the harp: and it shall come to pass, when the evil spirit from God is upon thee, that he shall play with his hand, and thou shalt be well. 17 And Saul said unto his servants, Provide me now a man that can play well, and bring him to me. 18 Then answered one of the young men, and said, Behold, I have seen a son of Jesse the Beth-lehemite, that is skilful in playing, and a mighty man of valor, and a man of war, and prudent in speech, and a comely person; and Jehovah is with him. 19 Wherefore Saul sent messengers unto Jesse, and said, Send me David thy son, who is with the sheep. 20 And Jesse took an ass *laden* with bread, and a bottle of wine, and a kid, and sent them by David his son unto Saul. 21 And David came to Saul, and stood before him: and he loved him greatly; and he became his armorbearer. 22 And Saul sent to Jesse, saying, Let David, I pray thee, stand before me; for he hath found favor in my sight. 23 And it came to pass, when the *evil* spirit from God was upon Saul, that David took the harp, and played with his hand: so Saul was refreshed, and was well, and the evil spirit departed from him.

While **the Spirit of Jehovah came mightily upon David . . . the Spirit of Jehovah departed from Saul** (vv. 13, 14). While David developed in those virtues nurtured by the Spirit, Saul deteriorated to a state bordering on insanity.

> All antiquity was at one in ascribing . . . mind-sickness . . . to evil spirits . . . since Yahweh was supreme in the realm of spirits, the evil spirit could only come from Him and by His permission.[10]

Saul's greatest problem, doubtless, involved an evil conscience and an awareness of the absence of God. Without God man usually attempts to be his own God.

The influence of music upon morbidity was and still is widely recognized. Saul's servants informed him of the young David and of his musical ability. David was brought before Saul. As David played his harp, Saul was refreshed and he **loved him greatly** (v. 21).

C. DAVID ENLISTED AGAINST GOLIATH (17:1-58)

1 Now the Philistines gathered together their armies to battle; and they were gathered together at Socoh, which belongeth to Judah, and encamped between Socoh and Azekah, in Ephes-dammim. 2 And Saul and the men of Israel were gathered together, and encamped in the vale of Elah, and set the battle in array against the Philistines. 3 And the Philistines stood on the mountain on the one side, and Israel stood on the mountain on the other side: and there was a valley between them. 4 And there went out a champion out of the camp of the Philistines, named Goliath, of Gath, whose height was six cubits and a span. 5 And he had a helmet of brass upon his head, and he was clad with a coat of mail; and the weight of the coat was five thousand shekels of brass. 6 And he had greaves of brass upon his legs, and a javelin of brass between his shoulders. 7 And the staff of his spear was like a weaver's beam; and his spear's head *weighed* six hundred shekels

10 Kennedy, *op. cit.*, p. 119.

of iron: and his shield-bearer went before him. 8 And he stood and cried unto the armies of Israel, and said unto them, Why are ye come out to set your battle in array? am not I a Philistine, and ye servants to Saul? choose you a man for you, and let him come down to me. 9 If he be able to fight with me, and kill me, then will we be your servants; but if I prevail against him, and kill him, then shall ye be our servants, and serve us. 10 And the Philistine said, I defy the armies of Israel this day; give me a man, that we may fight together. 11 And when Saul and all Israel heard these words of the Philistine, they were dismayed, and greatly afraid.

12 Now David was the son of that Ephrathite of Beth-lehem-judah, whose name was Jesse; and he had eight sons: and the man was an old man in the days of Saul, stricken *in years* among men. 13 And the three eldest sons of Jesse had gone after Saul to the battle: and the names of his three sons that went to the battle were Eliab the first-born, and next unto him Abinadab, and the third Shammah. 14 And David was the youngest; and the three eldest followed Saul. 15 Now David went to and fro from Saul to feed his father's sheep at Beth-lehem. 16 And the Philistine drew near morning and evening, and presented himself forty days.

17 And Jesse said unto David his son, Take now for thy brethren an ephah of this parched grain, and these ten loaves, and carry *them* quickly to the camp to thy brethren; 18 and bring these ten cheeses unto the captain of their thousand, and look how thy brethren fare, and take their pledge. 19 Now Saul, and they, and all the men of Israel, were in the vale of Elah, fighting with the Philistines. 20 And David rose up early in the morning, and left the sheep with a keeper, and took, and went, as Jesse had commanded him; and he came to the place of the wagons, as the host which was going forth to the fight shouted for the battle. 21 And Israel and the Philistines put the battle in array, army against army. 22 And David left his baggage in the hand of the keeper of the baggage, and ran to the army, and came and saluted his brethren. 23 And as he talked with them, behold, there came up the champion, the Philistine of Gath, Goliath by name, out of the ranks of the Philistines, and spake according to the same words: and David heard them. 24 And all the men of Israel, when they saw the man, fled from him, and were sore afraid. 25 And the men of Israel said, Have ye seen this man that is come up? surely to defy Israel is he come up: and it shall be, that the man who killeth him,

the king will enrich him with great riches, and will give him his daughter, and make his father's house free in Israel. 26 And David spake to the men that stood by him, saying, What shall be done to the man that killeth this Philistine, and taketh away the reproach from Israel? for who is this uncircumcised Philistine, that he should defy the armies of the living God? 27 And the people answered him after this manner, saying, So shall it be done to the man that killeth him.

28 And Eliab his eldest brother heard when he spake unto the men; and Eliab's anger was kindled against David, and he said, Why art thou come down? and with whom hast thou left those few sheep in the wilderness? I know thy pride, and the naughtiness of thy heart; for thou art come down that thou mightest see the battle. 29 And David said, What have I now done? Is there not a cause? 30 And he turned away from him toward another, and spake after the same manner: and the people answered him again after the former manner.

31 And when the words were heard which David spake, they rehearsed them before Saul; and he sent for him. 32 And David said to Saul, Let no man's heart fail because of him; thy servant will go and fight with this Philistine. 33 And Saul said to David, Thou art not able to go against this Philistine to fight with him; for thou art but a youth, and he a man of war from his youth. 34 And David said unto Saul, Thy servant was keeping his father's sheep; and when there came a lion, or a bear, and took a lamb out of the flock, 35 I went out after him, and smote him, and delivered it out of his mouth; and when he arose against me, I caught him by his beard, and smote him, and slew him. 36 Thy servant smote both the lion and the bear: and this uncircumcised Philistine shall be as one of them, seeing he hath defied the armies of the living God. 37 And David said, Jehovah that delivered me out of the paw of the lion, and out of the paw of the bear, he will deliver me out of the hand of this Philistine. And Saul said unto David, Go, and Jehovah shall be with thee. 38 And Saul clad David with his apparel, and he put a helmet of brass upon his head, and he clad him with a coat of mail. 39 And David girded his sword upon his apparel, and he assayed to go; for he had not proved it. And David said unto Saul, I cannot go with these; for I have not proved them. And David put them off him. 40 And he took his staff in his hand, and chose him five smooth stones out of the brook, and put them in the shepherd's bag which

he had, even in his wallet; and his sling was in his hand: and he drew near to the Philistine.

41 And the Philistine came on and drew near unto David; and the man that bare the shield went before him. 42 And when the Philistine looked about, and saw David, he disdained him; for he was but a youth, and ruddy, and withal of a fair countenance. 43 And the Philistine said unto David, Am I a dog, that thou comest to me with staves? And the Philistine cursed David by his gods. 44 And the Philistine said to David, Come to me, and I will give thy flesh unto the birds of the heavens, and to the beasts of the field. 45 Then said David to the Philistine, Thou comest to me with a sword, and with a spear, and with a javelin: but I come to thee in the name of Jehovah of hosts, the God of the armies of Israel, whom thou hast defied. 46 This day will Jehovah deliver thee into my hand; and I will smite thee, and take thy head from off thee; and I will give the dead bodies of the host of the Philistines this day unto the birds of the heavens, and to the wild beasts of the earth; that all the earth may know that there is a God in Israel, 47 and that all this assembly may know that Jehovah saveth not with sword and spear: for the battle is Jehovah's, and he will give you into our hand. 48 And it came to pass, when the Philistine arose, and came and drew nigh to meet David, that David hastened, and ran toward the army to meet the Philistine. 49 And David put his hand in his bag, and took hence a stone, and slang it, and smote the Philistine in his forehead; and the stone sank into his forehead, and he fell upon his face to the earth.

50 So David prevailed over the Philistine with a sling and with a stone, and smote the Philistine, and slew him; but there was no sword in the hand of David. 51 Then David ran, and stood over the Philistine, and took his sword, and drew it out of the sheath thereof, and slew him, and cut off his head therewith. And when the Philistines saw that their champion was dead, they fled. 52 And the men of Israel and of Judah arose, and shouted, and pursued the Philistines, until thou comest to Gai, and to the gates of Ekron. And the wounded of the Philistines fell down by the way to Shaaraim, even unto Gath, and unto Ekron. 53 And the children of Israel returned from chasing after the Philistines, and they plundered their camp. 54 And David took the head of the Philistine, and brought it to Jerusalem; but he put his armor in his tent.

55 And when Saul saw David go forth against the Philistine, he said unto Abner, the captain of the host, Abner, whose son is this youth? And Abner said, As thy soul liveth, O King, I cannot tell. 56 And the king said, Inquire thou whose son the stripling is. 57 And as David returned from the slaughter of the Philistine, Abner took him, and brought him before Saul with the head of the Philistine in his hand. 58 And Saul said to him, Whose son art thou, thou young man? And David answered, I am the son of thy servant Jesse the Beth-lehemite.

Throughout the reign of Saul a state of war existed between the Philistines and the Israelites. Israel was unable to enjoy a sense of national security because of the constant threat of invasion from Philistia.

Upon one of these penetrations into Israel, the Philistine warriors pushed as far as the well-known valley of Elah about sixteen miles southwest of Jerusalem before encountering the army of Israel.

While the two armies faced one another across the valley, the Philistine, Goliath, dared any Israelite to engage him in a single encounter. His reported size of between nine and ten feet and his powerful soldierly physique were awesome to behold. His very presence and arrogant boast created panic among the soldiers of Israel: **And all the men of Israel, when they saw the man, fled from him, and were sore afraid** (v. 24).

Now David went to and fro from Saul to feed his father's sheep at Beth-lehem (v. 15). His father took occasion to send David to the battlefront to inquire about his brothers. When David arrived, he heard Goliath make his challenge. It disturbed him and he said, **Who is this uncircumcised Philistine, that he should defy the armies of the living God?** (v. 26).

David's outburst angered his brother Eliab, who apparently thought the only proper place for this young brother was at home doing his father's bidding. However, David was so outspoken about the haughtiness of Goliath that even Saul was impressed. Furthermore, David expressed such contagious confidence in God that he changed the whole morale of Saul's camp. **Jehovah . . . will deliver me out of the hand of this Philistine** (v. 37).

As David went forth to accept the challenge of Goliath, he expressed the basis of his faith as he said, **Thou comest to me with a sword . . . but I come to thee in the name of Jehovah of hosts** (v.

45). With unerring aim, David struck the giant with a stone hurled from his sling. When the Philistines saw that their mighty champion was dead, they made a fast retreat. It was a resounding victory because of David's confidence and courage, elements of faith which are always essential, but especially in times of peril.

D. DAVID LOVED BY JONATHAN (18:1-9)

1 And it came to pass, when he had made an end of speaking unto Saul, that the soul of Jonathan was knit with the soul of David, and Jonathan loved him as his own soul. 2 And Saul took him that day, and would let him go no more home to his father's house. 3 Then Jonathan and David made a covenant, because he loved him as his own soul. 4 And Jonathan stripped himself of the robe that was upon him, and gave it to David, and his apparel, even to his sword, and to his bow, and to his girdle. 5 And David went out whithersoever Saul sent him, *and* behaved himself wisely: and Saul set him over the men of war, and it was good in the sight of all the people, and also in the sight of Saul's servants.

6 And it came to pass as they came, when David returned from the slaughter of the Philistine, that the women came out of all the cities of Israel, singing and dancing, to meet king Saul, with timbrels, with joy, and with instruments of music. 7 And the women sang one to another as they played, and said,

Saul hath slain his thousands,
And David his ten thousands.

8 And Saul was very wroth, and this saying displeased him; and he said, They have ascribed unto David ten thousands, and to me they have ascribed but thousands; and what can he have more but the kingdom? 9 And Saul eyed David from that day and forward.

The whole episode of David fighting Goliath in the name of Jehovah was of great interest to Jonathan. Earlier, Jonathan and his armor-bearer had courageously fought a whole garrison of Philistines because they were convinced that Jehovah would deliver the Philistines into their hands (14:6, 12, 15). David, likewise, challenged Goliath, "the battle is Jehovah's, and he will give you into our hand" (17:47).

The result seemed to be that Jonathan was mightily impressed with David. Jona-

than loved him as his own soul (v. 1). The motive for Jonathan's love appeared to be that he saw in David a true, courageous warrior who like himself had trusted God against overwhelming odds and had lived to tell about it. No other two in Israel, as far as the account goes, had ventured so far in exposing themselves to real danger, yet with the firm conviction that God was with them to give victory.

Doubtless this is not the full explanation for Jonathan's love, but it is quite true that people of like characters and ideals are often, though not always, drawn together. Nor is it possible to explain why David loved Jonathan as he did. There was an affectionate covenant between them, apparently initiated by Jonathan (v. 3).

X. SAUL'S ESTRANGEMENT FROM DAVID (I Sam. 18:10—19:17)

From the time of David's victory over Goliath, the relationship between Saul and David deteriorated. The reason seems to be the people's enthusiasm for David. As Saul returned from the battle against the Philistines, the welcoming throng was jubilant. While Saul was honored by the singing, greater honor went to David. This greatly displeased Saul, and he became intensely jealous. It was the great English scientist and divine, Henry Drummond, who said, "Envy is a feeling of ill-will to those who are in the same line as ourselves" (*The Greatest Thing in the World*, p. 17). It issues from a sense of insecurity and fear.

This was not the only occasion that the people affected Saul's outlook. When he was selected king at Mizpah he hid from the people among the stuff (10:22). When he was informed by Samuel that God had rejected him as king, Saul pleaded with Samuel not to desert him in the presence of the elders of Israel (v. 30). Once again, in the scene before us, Saul showed keen sensitivity to popular reaction.

Emotionally as well as socially insecure, Saul soon betrayed himself. Jealousy began its insidious poisoning of his total personality. Frightened about his own status, he regarded David with fear and reacted with envy and jealousy.

A. SAUL INCENSED BY JEALOUSY (18:10-30)

10 And it came to pass on the morrow, that an evil spirit from God came mightily upon Saul, and he prophesied in the midst of the house: and David played with his hand, as he did day by day. And Saul had his spear in his hand; 11 and Saul cast the spear; for he said, I will smite David even to the wall. And David avoided out of his presence twice. 12 And Saul was afraid of David, because Jehovah was with him, and was departed from Saul. 13 Therefore Saul removed him from him, and made him his captain over a thousand; and he went out and came in before the people. 14 And David behaved himself wisely in all his ways; and Jehovah was with him. 15 And when Saul saw that he behaved himself very wisely, he stood in awe of him. 16 But all Israel and Judah loved David; for he went out and came in before them.

17 And Saul said to David, Behold, my elder daughter Merab, her will I give thee to wife: only be thou valiant for me, and fight Jehovah's battles. For Saul said, Let not my hand be upon him, but let the hand of the Philistines be upon him. 18 And David said unto Saul, Who am I, and what is my life, or my father's family in Israel, that I should be son-in-law to the king? 19 But it came to pass at the time when Merab, Saul's daughter, should have been given to David, that she was given unto Adriel the Meholathite to wife. 20 And Michal, Saul's daughter, loved David: and they told Saul, and the thing pleased him. 21 And Saul said, I will give him her, that she may be a snare to him, and that the hand of the Philistines may be against him. Wherefore Saul said to David, Thou shalt this day be my son-in-law a second time.

22 And Saul commanded his servants, saying, Commune with David secretly, and say, Behold, the king hath delight in thee, and all his servants love thee: now therefore be the king's son-in-law. 23 And Saul's servants spake those words in the ears of David. And David said, Seemeth it to you a light thing to be the king's son-in-law, seeing that I am a poor man, and lightly esteemed? 24 And the servants of Saul told him, saying, On this manner spake David. 25 And Saul said, Thus shall ye say to David, The king desireth not any dowry, but a hundred foreskins of the Philistines, to be avenged of the king's enemies. Now Saul thought to make David fall by the hand of the Philistines. 26 And when his servants told David these words, it pleased David well to be the king's son-

in-law. And the days were not expired; 27 and David arose and went, he and his men, and slew of the Philistines two hundred men; and David brought their foreskins, and they gave them in full number to the king, that he might be the king's son-in-law. And Saul gave him Michal his daughter to wife. 28 And Saul saw and knew that Jehovah was with David; and Michal, Saul's daughter, loved him. 29 And Saul was yet the more afraid of David; and Saul was David's enemy continually.

30 Then the princes of the Philistines went forth: and it came to pass, as often as they went forth, that David behaved himself more wisely than all the servants of Saul; so that his name was much set by.

While the popular acclaim accorded David provided the occasion for Saul's jealousy, it did not necessarily follow that he must be jealous. Within his own person there was a reaction to this popular acclaim for David that was dark and sinister and evil. Saul's jealousy emerged from the labyrinth of his own personality, and it involved not only insecurity and fear but also sin and culpability.

Saul's conduct toward David was affected by the poison of jealousy. For one thing, he removed David from the court and placed him over a fighting contingent (v. 13). For another, he promised David his daughter, Merab, but reneged on the promise (v. 19). Furthermore, he consorted with his servants in a plot to have David killed by promising his daughter, Michal, to David (vv. 25, 26).

Jealousy is a deadly foe to human relations. What Saul was doing is all too typical of the actions of the jealous. Jealousy seeks to attack and destroy. It becomes a murderous passion with the intent to kill, that the object of fear may be removed. In so doing, it manifests its own weakness and insecurity.

B. SAUL INTENT UPON MURDER (19:1-17)

1 And Saul spake to Jonathan his son, and to all his servants, that they should slay David. But Jonathan, Saul's son, delighted much in David. 2 And Jonathan told David, saying, Saul my father seeketh to slay thee: now therefore, I pray thee, take heed to thyself in the morning, and abide in a secret place, and hide thyself: 3 and I will go out and stand beside my father in the field where thou art, and I

will commune with my father of thee; and if I see aught, I will tell thee. 4 And Jonathan spake good of David unto Saul his father, and said unto him, Let not the king sin against his servant, against David; because he hath not sinned against thee, and because his works have been to thee-ward very good: 5 for he put his life in his hand, and smote the Philistine, and Jehovah wrought a great victory for all Israel: thou sawest it, and didst rejoice; wherefore then wilt thou sin against innocent blood, to slay David without a cause? 6 And Saul hearkened unto the voice of Jonathan: and Saul sware, As Jehovah liveth, he shall not be put to death. 7 And Jonathan called David, and Jonathan showed him all those things. And Jonathan brought David to Saul, and he was in his presence, as beforetime.

8 And there was war again: and David went out, and fought with the Philistines, and slew them with a great slaughter; and they fled before him. 9 And an evil spirit from Jehovah was upon Saul, as he sat in his house with his spear in his hand; and David was playing with his hand. 10 And Saul sought to smite David even to the wall with the spear; but he slipped away out of Saul's presence, and he smote the spear into the wall: and David fled, and escaped that night. 11 And Saul sent messengers unto David's house, to watch him, and to slay him in the morning: and Michal, David's wife, told him, saying, If thou save not thy life to-night, to-morrow thou wilt be slain. 12 So Michal let David down through the window: and he went, and fled, and escaped. 13 And Michal took the teraphim, and laid it in the bed, and put a pillow of goats' *hair* at the head thereof, and covered it with the clothes. 14 And when Saul sent messengers to take David, she said, He is sick. 15 And Saul sent the messengers to see David, saying, Bring him up to me in the bed, that I may slay him. 16 And when the messengers came in, behold, the teraphim was in the bed, with the pillow of goats' *hair* at the head thereof. 17 And Saul said unto Michal, Why hast thou deceived me thus, and let mine enemy go, so that he is escaped? And Michal answered Saul, He said unto me, Let me go; why should I kill thee?

And Saul spake to Jonathan his son, and to all his servants, that they should slay David (v. 1). Saul was so completely mastered by jealous hatred that he talked openly of his intention to kill David. He sought the help of Jonathan as well as others.

However, Jonathan attempted to dissuade his father. He made an impressive intercession in David's behalf (vv. 4, 5). He concluded by asking Saul, **Wherefore then wilt thou sin against innocent blood, to slay David without a cause?** Saul's attitude toward David was wholly unjustified, and for a time Jonathan had helped him to see this. Saul affirmed that David would not die (v. 6).

David's next successes against the Philistines recreated the occasion of popular acclaim, and Saul's murderous intent became so deadly that David was warned by Michal, his wife, to flee. David escaped through a window and fled to Samuel in Ramah (vv. 11, 12).

XI. DAVID A FUGITIVE (I Sam. 19:18—26:25)

The events in Israel related by these chapters vividly depict a demented and despotic Saul utterly incapacitated for his royal responsibilities. Nevertheless, in spite of his frenzied hunt for David, he still wielded impressive authority over a sufficient number who willingly remained loyal to him.

A. DAVID'S FLIGHT FROM SAUL (19:18—22:23)

This account shows David, son-in-law of the king and commander in the army, treated by Saul as a hunted criminal.

1. To Samuel (19:18-24)

18 Now David fled, and escaped, and came to Samuel to Ramah, and told him all that Saul had done to him. And he and Samuel went and dwelt in Naioth. 19 And it was told Saul, saying, Behold, David is at Naioth in Ramah. 20 And Saul sent messengers to take David: and when they saw the company of the prophets prophesying, and Samuel standing as head over them, the Spirit of God came upon the messengers of Saul, and they also prophesied. 21 And when it was told Saul, he sent other messengers, and they also prophesied. And Saul sent messengers again the third time, and they also prophesied. 22 Then went he also to Ramah, and came to the great well that is in Secu: and he asked and said, Where are Samuel and David? And one said, Behold, they are at Naioth in Ramah. 23 And he went thither to Naioth in Ramah: and the Spirit of God came upon him also, and he went on, and prophesied,

until he came to Naioth in Ramah. 24 And he also stripped off his clothes, and he also prophesied before Samuel, and lay down naked all that day and all that night. Wherefore they say, Is Saul also among the prophets?

David fled from Saul's court in Gibeah to Samuel in Ramah. **Naioth** was apparently a group of buildings at Ramah in which Samuel conducted a school for prophets.[11]

When Samuel was informed of David's presence in Ramah, he sent messengers on three occasions to seize David. Each time they prophesied. Saul then came himself but was seized in a spirit of ecstasy and prophesied also. While it may be difficult to define precisely the nature of this prophetic experience it is safe to assume that it involved only the fringes of Saul's emotional life, for it left him with the same hatred and inner turmoil with which he struggled before it occurred.

2. To Jonathan (20:1-42)

1 And David fled from Naioth in Ramah, and came and said before Jonathan, What have I done? what is mine iniquity? and what is my sin before thy father, that he seeketh my life? 2 And he said unto him, Far from it; thou shalt not die: behold, my father doeth nothing either great or small, but that he discloseth it unto me; and why should my father hide this thing from me? it is not so. 3 And David sware moreover, and said, Thy father knoweth well that I have found favor in thine eyes; and he saith, Let not Jonathan know this, lest he be grieved: but truly as Jehovah liveth, and as thy soul liveth, there is but a step between me and death. 4 Then said Jonathan unto David, Whatsoever thy soul desireth, I will even do it for thee. 5 And David said unto Jonathan, Behold, to-morrow is the new moon, and I should not fail to sit with the king at meat: but let me go, that I may hide myself in the field unto the third day at even. 6 If thy father miss me at all, then say, David earnestly asked leave of me that he might run to Beth-lehem his city; for it is the yearly sacrifice there for all the family. 7 If he say thus, It is well; thy servant shall have peace: but if he be wroth, then know that evil is determined by him. 8 Therefore deal kindly with thy servant; for thou hast brought thy servant into a covenant of Jehovah with thee: but if there be in me iniquity, slay

me thyself; for why shouldest thou bring me to thy father? 9 And Jonathan said, Far be it from thee; for if I should at all know that evil were determined by my father to come upon thee, then would not I tell it thee? 10 Then said David to Jonathan, Who shall tell me if perchance thy father answer thee roughly? 11 And Jonathan said unto David, Come, and let us go out into the field. And they went out both of them into the field.

12 And Jonathan said unto David, Jehovah, the God of Israel, *be witness*: when I have sounded my father about this time to-morrow, *or* the third day, behold, if there be good toward David, shall I not then send unto thee, and disclose it unto thee? 13 Jehovah do so to Jonathan, and more also, should it please my father to do thee evil, if I disclose it not unto thee, and send thee away, that thou mayest go in peace: and Jehovah be with thee, as he hath been with my father. 14 And thou shalt not only while yet I live show me the loving-kindness of Jehovah, that I die not; 15 but also thou shalt not cut off thy kindness from my house for ever; no, not when Jehovah hath cut off the enemies of David every one from the face of the earth. 16 So Jonathan made a covenant with the house of David, *saying*, And Jehovah will require it at the hand of David's enemies.

17 And Jonathan caused David to swear again, for the love that he had to him; for he loved him as he loved his own soul. 18 Then Jonathan said unto him, To-morrow is the new moon: and thou wilt be missed, because thy seat will be empty. 19 And when thou hast stayed three days, thou shalt go down quickly, and come to the place where thou didst hide thyself when the business was in hand, and shalt remain by the stone Ezel. 20 And I will shoot three arrows on the side thereof, as though I shot at a mark. 21 And, behold, I will send the lad, *saying*, Go, find the arrows. If I say unto the lad, Behold, the arrows are on this side of thee; take them, and come; for there is peace to thee and no hurt, as Jehovah liveth. 22 But if I say thus unto the boy, Behold, the arrows are beyond thee; go thy way; for Jehovah hath sent thee away. 23 And as touching the matter which thou and I have spoken of, behold, Jehovah is between thee and me for ever.

24 So David hid himself in the field: and when the new moon was come, the king sat him down to eat food. 25 And the king sat upon his seat, as at other times, even upon the seat by the wall; and Jonathan stood up, and Abner sat by Saul's side: but David's place was empty. 26 Nevertheless

[11] *Ibid.*, p. 138.

Saul spake not anything that day: for he thought, Something hath befallen him, he is not clean; surely he is not clean. 27 And it came to pass on the morrow after the new moon, *which was* the second *day,* that David's place was empty: and Saul said unto Jonathan his son, Wherefore cometh not the son of Jesse to meat, neither yesterday, nor to-day? 28 And Jonathan answered Saul, David earnestly asked leave of me to go to Beth-lehem: 29 and he said, Let me go, I pray thee; for our family hath a sacrifice in the city; and my brother, he hath commanded me *to be there*: and now, if I have found favor in thine eyes, let me get away, I pray thee, and see my brethren. Therefore he is not come unto the king's table.

30 Then Saul's anger was kindled against Jonathan, and he said unto him, Thou son of a perverse rebellious woman, do not I know that thou hast chosen the son of Jesse to thine own shame, and unto the shame of thy mother's nakedness? 31 For as long as the son of Jesse liveth upon the ground, thou shalt not be established, nor thy kingdom. Wherefore now send and fetch him unto me, for he shall surely die. 32 And Jonathan answered Saul his father, and said unto him, Wherefore should he be put to death? what hath he done? 33 And Saul cast his spear at him to smite him; whereby Jonathan knew that it was determined of his father to put David to death. 34 So Jonathan arose from the table in fierce anger, and did eat no food the second day of the month; for he was grieved for David, because his father had done him shame.

35 And it came to pass in the morning, that Jonathan went out into the field at the time appointed with David, and a little lad with him. 36 And he said unto his lad, Run, find now the arrows which I shoot. And as the lad ran, he shot an arrow beyond him. 37 And when the lad was come to the place of the arrow which Jonathan had shot, Jonathan cried after the lad, and said, Is not the arrow beyond thee? 38 And Jonathan cried after the lad, Make speed, haste, stay not. And Jonathan's lad gathered up the arrows, and came to his master. 39 But the lad knew not anything: only Jonathan and David knew the matter. 40 And Jonathan gave his weapons unto his lad, and said unto him, Go, carry them to the city. 41 And as soon as the lad was gone, David arose out of *a place* toward the South, and fell on his face to the ground, and bowed himself three times: and they kissed one another, and wept one with another, until David exceeded. 42 And Jonathan said to David, Go in peace, forasmuch as we have sworn both of us in the name of Jehovah, saying, Jehovah shall be between me and thee, and between my seed and thy seed, for ever. And he arose and departed: and Jonathan went into the city.

Developments at Naioth in Ramah gave David time to flee to Gibeah and consult with his trusted friend Jonathan. It was incredible news to Jonathan that Saul was once again seeking to kill David (v. 2). David replied in words that impressed Jonathan greatly concerning the seriousness of the situation, **there is but a step between me and death** (v. 3).

Jonathan immediately pledged himself to do all he could for David. **Whatsoever thy soul desireth, I will even do it for thee** (v. 4). David urged that they put forth a test. It involved the royal feast which Saul held for the leaders of his kingdom every new moon (v. 5). David would absent himself, and if Saul were angered because of David's absence this would reveal that Saul had murderous intent. Jonathan was to note Saul's reactions and report to David at a pre-arranged time and place (vv. 18-22).

At the royal feast Saul became so enraged not only at David's absence but also at Jonathan's explanation that he caused Jonathan to rise in anger and leave the table (vv. 30-34). David was informed by Jonathan that Saul had expressed great rage. This meant that David must remain clear of Saul. One wrong step would mean death (cf. v. 3).

3. To Ahimelech (21:1—22:5)

1 Then came David to Nob to Ahimelech the priest: and Ahimelech came to meet David trembling, and said unto him, Why art thou alone, and no man with thee? 2 And David said unto Ahimelech the priest, The king hath commanded me a business, and hath said unto me, Let no man know anything of the business whereabout I send thee, and what I have commanded thee: and I have appointed the young men to such and such a place. 3 Now therefore what is under thy hand? give me five loaves of bread in my hand, or whatsoever is present. 4 And the priest answered David, and said, There is no common bread under my hand, but there is holy bread; if only the young men have kept themselves from women. 5 And David answered the priest, and said unto him, Of a truth women have been kept from us about these three days; when I came out, the vessels of the young men were holy, though it was but a com-

mon journey; how much more then to-day shall their vessels be holy? 6 So the priest gave him holy *bread*; for there was no bread there but the showbread, that was taken from before Jehovah, to put hot bread in the day when it was taken away.

7 Now a certain man of the servants of Saul was there that day, detained before Jehovah; and his name was Doeg the Edomite, the chiefest of the herdsmen that belonged to Saul. 8 And David said unto Ahimelech, And is there not here under thy hand spear or sword? for I have neither brought my sword nor my weapons with me, because the king's business required haste. 9 And the priest said, The sword of Goliath the Philistine, whom thou slewest in the vale of Elah, behold, it is here wrapped in a cloth behind the ephod: if thou wilt take that, take it; for there is no other save that here. And David said, There is none like that; give it me.

10 And David arose, and fled that day for fear of Saul, and went to Achish the king of Gath. 11 And the servants of Achish said unto him, Is not this David the king of the land? did they not sing one to another of him in dances, saying,

Saul hath slain his thousands,
And David his ten thousands?

12 And David laid up these words in his heart, and was sore afraid of Achish the king of Gath. 13 And he changed his behavior before them, and feigned himself mad in their hands, and scrabbled on the doors of the gate, and let his spittle fall down upon his beard. 14 Then said Achish unto his servants, Lo, ye see the man is mad; wherefore then have ye brought him to me? 15 Do I lack madmen, that ye have brought this fellow to play the madman in my presence? shall this fellow come into my house?

1 David therefore departed thence, and escaped to the cave of Adullam: and when his brethren and all his father's house heard it, they went down thither to him. 2 And every one that was in distress, and every one that was in debt, and every one that was discontented, gathered themselves unto him; and he became captain over them: and there were with him about four hundred men.

3 And David went thence to Mizpeh of Moab: and he said unto the king of Moab, Let my father and my mother, I pray thee, come forth, *and be* with you, till I know what God will do for me. 4 And he brought them before the king of Moab: and they dwelt with him all the while that David was in the stronghold. 5 And the prophet Gad said unto David, Abide not in the stronghold; depart, and get thee into

the land of Judah. Then David departed, and came into the forest of Hereth.

The precise location of Nob is unknown. It must have been within a few miles of Gibeah.[12] Ahimelech was priest. In I Samuel 14:3, he was referred to as belonging to the line of Eli. David came to Ahimelech but declined to expose his peril. Rather, he led Ahimelech to believe that he was on an urgent mission for King Saul (v. 2). Ahimelech, unaware of the tragic relationship existing between Saul and David, received David, fed him and those with him and gave him a sword, Goliath's sword. David departed and became known as a rebel leader. **And everyone that was in distress and . . . in debt and . . . discontented, gathered themselves unto him; and he became captain over them** (v. 2).

4. The Sequel (22:6-23)

6 And Saul heard that David was discovered, and the men that were with him: now Saul was sitting in Gibeah, under the tamarisk-tree in Ramah, with his spear in his hand, and all his servants were standing about him. 7 And Saul said unto his servants that stood about him, Hear now, ye Benjamites; will the son of Jesse give every one of you fields and vineyards, will he make you all captains of thousands and captains of hundreds, 8 that all of you have conspired against me, and there is none that discloseth to me when my son maketh a league with the son of Jesse, and there is none of you that is sorry for me, or discloseth unto me that my son hath stirred up my servant against me, to lie in wait, as at this day? 9 Then answered Doeg the Edomite, who stood by the servants of Saul, and said, I saw the son of Jesse coming to Nob, to Ahimelech the son of Ahitub. 10 And he inquired of Jehovah for him, and gave him victuals, and gave him the sword of Goliath the Philistine.

11 Then the king sent to call Ahimelech the priest, the son of Ahitub, and all his father's house, the priests that were in Nob: and they came all of them to the king. 12 And Saul said, Hear now, thou son of Ahitub. And he answered, Here I am, my lord. 13 And Saul said unto him, Why have ye conspired against me, thou and the son of Jesse, in that thou hast given him bread, and a sword, and hast inquired of God for him, that he should rise against me, to lie in wait, as at this day? 14 Then Ahimelech answered the

king, and said, And who among all thy servants is so faithful as David, who is the king's son-in-law, and is taken into thy council, and is honorable in thy house? Have I to-day begun to inquire of God for him? be it far from me: let not the king impute anything unto his servant, nor to all the house of my father; for thy servant knoweth nothing of all this, less or more. 16 And the king said, Thou shalt surely die, Ahimelech, thou, and all thy father's house. 17 And the king said unto the guard that stood about him, Turn, and slay the priests of Jehovah; because their hand also is with David, and because they knew that he fled, and did not disclose it to me. But the servants of the king would not put forth their hand to fall upon the priests of Jehovah. 18 And the king said to Doeg, Turn thou, and fall upon the priests. And Doeg the Edomite turned, and he fell upon the priests, and he slew on that day fourscore and five persons that did wear a linen ephod. 19 And Nob, the city of the priests, smote he with the edge of the sword, both men and women, children and sucklings, and oxen and asses and sheep, with the edge of the sword.

20 And one of the sons of Ahimelech, the son of Ahitub, named Abiathar, escaped, and fled after David. 21 And Abiathar told David that Saul had slain Jehovah's priests. 22 And David said unto Abiathar, I knew on that day, when Doeg the Edomite was there, that he would surely tell Saul: I have occasioned *the death* of all the persons of thy father's house. 23 Abide thou with me, fear not; for he that seeketh my life seeketh thy life: for with me thou shalt be in safeguard.

Saul was ready to use any means to get rid of David. He called an assembly of his servants at Gibeah and railed on them for their conspiracy of silence (vv. 7, 8).

One of his servants was present who had seen David with Ahimelech. Doeg, an Edomite, who was trusted by Saul with important responsibilities and who catered to Saul's whims and fancies, revealed to Saul what had transpired between Ahimelech and David at Nob. This implicated the priests and implied they were a party to a conspiracy against Saul.

Upon hearing this, Saul summoned Ahimelech and the other priests and angrily eyed them as traitors. **Thou shalt surely die, Ahimelech, thou, and all thy father's house** (v. 16). The king's atrocious conduct had engendered passive resistance among his guards, and they

refused to execute his command that the priests be executed. Only Doeg performed the terrible deed (v. 18). One son of Ahimelech named Abiathar escaped and joined David (vv. 20-23). David summed up the incident by saying to Abiathar, **I knew on that day, when Doeg the Edomite was there, that he would surely tell Saul** (v. 22).

B. DAVID'S FIGHT FOR KEILAH AND THE SEQUEL (23:1—24:22)

The Philistines continued their encroachment upon the land of Israel. They attacked Keilah, located in the Shephelah overlooking the valley of Elah, and sought to reduce the city to submission by starvation.

1. David's Fight (23:1-6)

1 And they told David, saying, Behold, the Philistines are fighting against Keilah, and are robbing the threshing-floors. 2 Therefore David inquired of Jehovah, saying, Shall I go and smite these Philistines? And Jehovah said unto David, Go, and smite the Philistines, and save Keilah. 3 And David's men said unto him, Behold, we are afraid here in Judah: how much more then if we go to Keilah against the armies of the Philistines? 4 Then David inquired of Jehovah yet again. And Jehovah answered him, and said, Arise, go down to Keilah; for I will deliver the Philistines into thy hand. 5 And David and his men went to Keilah, and fought with the Philistines, and brought away their cattle, and slew them with a great slaughter. So David saved the inhabitants of Keilah. 6 And it came to pass, when Abiathar the son of Ahimelech fled to David to Keilah, that he came down with an ephod in his hand.

David heard of the robbery taking place at Keilah, and inquired of the Lord as to what assistance he might give his own people against the Philistines. He was able to inquire of the Lord through an ephod which Abiathar had brought with him from Nob (cf. 22:20; 23:6). This oracle provided an affirmative answer to David's questions. David went to Keilah, overpowered the Philistines and saved the city.

2. The Sequel (23:7—24:22)

7 And it was told Saul that David was come to Keilah. And Saul said, God hath delivered him into my hand; for he is shut

in, by entering into a town that hath gates and bars. 8 And Saul summoned all the people to war, to go down to Keilah, to besiege David and his men. 9 And David knew that Saul was devising mischief against him; and he said to Abiathar the priest, Bring hither the ephod. 10 Then said David, O Jehovah, the God of Israel, thy servant hath surely heard that Saul seeketh to come to Keilah, to destroy the city for my sake. 11 Will the men of Keilah deliver me up into his hand? will Saul come down, as thy servant hath heard? O Jehovah, the God of Israel, I beseech thee, tell thy servant. And Jehovah said, He will come down. 12 Then said David, Will the men of Keilah deliver up me and my men into the hand of Saul? And Jehovah said, They will deliver thee up. 13 Then David and his men, who were about six hundred, arose and departed out of Keilah, and went whithersoever they could go. And it was told Saul that David was escaped from Keilah; and he forbare to go forth. 14 And David abode in the wilderness in the strongholds, and remained in the hill-country in the wilderness of Ziph. And Saul sought him every day, but God delivered him not into his hand.

15 And David saw that Saul was come out to seek his life: and David was in the wilderness of Ziph in the wood. 16 And Jonathan, Saul's son, arose, and went to David into the wood, and strengthened his hand in God. 17 And he said unto him, Fear not; for the hand of Saul my father shall not find thee; and thou shalt be king over Israel, and I shall be next unto thee; and that also Saul my father knoweth. 18 And they two made a covenant before Jehovah: and David abode in the wood, and Jonathan went to his house.

19 Then came up the Ziphites to Saul to Gibeah, saying, Doth not David hide himself with us in the strongholds in the wood, in the hill of Hachilah, which is on the south of the desert? 20 Now therefore, O king, come down, according to all the desire of thy soul to come down; and our part shall be to deliver him up into the king's hand. 21 And Saul said, Blessed be ye of Jehovah; for ye have had compassion on me. 22 Go, I pray you, make yet more sure, and know and see his place where his haunt is, and who hath seen him there; for it is told me that he dealeth very subtly. 23 See therefore, and take knowledge of all the lurking-places where he hideth himself, and come ye again to me of a certainty, and I will go with you: and it shall come to pass, if he be in the land, that I will search him out among all the thousands of Judah.

24 And they arose, and went to Ziph before Saul: but David and his men were in the wilderness of Maon, in the Arabah on the south of the desert. 25 And Saul and his men went to seek him. And they told David: wherefore he came down to the rock, and abode in the wilderness of Maon. And when Saul heard *that*, he pursued after David in the wilderness of Maon. 26 And Saul went on this side of the mountain, and David and his men on that side of the mountain: and David made haste to get away for fear of Saul; for Saul and his men compassed David and his men round about to take them. 27 But there came a messenger unto Saul, saying, Haste thee, and come; for the Philistines have made a raid upon the land. 28 So Saul returned from pursuing after David, and went against the Philistines: therefore they called that place Selahammahlekoth. 29 And David went up from thence, and dwelt in the strongholds of En-gedi.

1 And it came to pass, when Saul was returned from following the Philistines, that it was told him, saying, Behold, David is in the wilderness of En-gedi. 2 Then Saul took three thousand chosen men out of all Israel, and went to seek David and his men upon the rocks of the wild goats. 3 And he came to the sheep-cotes by the way, where was a cave; and Saul went in to cover his feet. Now David and his men were abiding in the innermost parts of the cave. 4 And the men of David said unto him, Behold, the day of which Jehovah said unto thee, Behold, I will deliver thine enemy into thy hand, and thou shalt do to him as it shall seem good unto thee. Then David arose, and cut off the skirt of Saul's robe privily. 5 And it came to pass afterward, that David's heart smote him, because he had cut off Saul's skirt. 6 And he said unto his men, Jehovah forbid that I should do this thing unto my lord, Jehovah's anointed, to put forth my hand against him, seeing he is Jehovah's anointed. 7 So David checked his men with these words, and suffered them not to rise against Saul. And Saul rose up out of the cave, and went on his way.

8 David also arose afterward, and went out of the cave, and cried after Saul, saying, My lord the king. And when Saul looked behind him, David bowed with his face to the earth, and did obeisance. 9 And David said to Saul, Wherefore hearkenest thou to men's words, saying, Behold, David seeketh thy hurt? 10 Behold, this day thine eyes have seen how that Jehovah had delivered thee to-day into my hand in the cave: and some bade me kill thee; but *mine eye* spared thee; and I said, I will not put forth my hand against my lord; for he is Jehovah's anointed. 11 Moreover, my father, see,

yea, see the skirt of thy robe in my hand; for in that I cut off the skirt of thy robe, and killed thee not, know thou and see that there is neither evil nor transgression in my hand, and I have not sinned against thee, though thou huntest after my life to take it. 12 Jehovah judge between me and thee, and Jehovah avenge me of thee; but my hand shall not be upon thee. 13 As saith the proverb of the ancients, Out of the wicked cometh forth wickedness; but my hand shall not be upon thee. 14 After whom is the king of Israel come out? after whom dost thou pursue? after a dead dog, after a flea. 15 Jehovah therefore be judge, and give sentence between me and thee, and see, and plead my cause, and deliver me out of thy hand.

16 And it came to pass, when David had made an end of speaking these words unto Saul, that Saul said, Is this thy voice, my son David? And Saul lifted up his voice, and wept. 17 And he said to David, Thou art more righteous than I; for thou hast rendered unto me good, whereas I have rendered unto thee evil. 18 And thou hast declared this day how that thou hast dealt well with me, forasmuch as when Jehovah had delivered me up into thy hand, thou killedst me not. 19 For if a man find his enemy, will he let him go well away? wherefore Jehovah reward thee good for that which thou hast done unto me this day. 20 And now, behold, I know that thou shalt surely be king, and that the kingdom of Israel shall be established in thy hand. 21 Swear now therefore unto me by Jehovah, that thou wilt not cut off my seed after me, and that thou wilt not destroy my name out of my father's house. 22 And David sware unto Saul. And Saul went home; but David and his men gat them up unto the stronghold.

Saul, upon hearing that David was at Keilah, deluded himself that God was with him against David. And Saul said, God hath delivered him into my hand (v. 7). This was impossible. Saul himself had been responsible for driving Abiathar the priest to David and it was through him that David was directed to go to Keilah.

David said to Abiathar, Bring hither the ephod (v. 9). Then in most earnest language David spread his peril before the Lord and asked for guidance. The Lord answered explicitly and clearly by means of the ephod (vv. 11, 12). Doubtless to David's surprise, the Lord revealed that the men of Keilah whom David had liberated from the Philistines would sur-

render David to Saul (v. 12). By means of the guidance thus received, David evaded Saul and came into the wilderness of Ziph located about four miles southeast of Hebron (v. 15). From there he went south into the wilderness of Maon. Saul and his men, aided by the Ziphites, were about to catch David and his men when news came of a Philistine invasion (v. 27). It was necessary to engage the Philistines immediately, so Saul was unable to close in on David. Thus a perilous situation for David was relieved by the raid of the Philistines.

When Saul returned to Gibeah from pursuing the band of raiding Philistines he was informed that David was in the wilderness of En-gedi situated along the western shore of the Dead Sea. This was wild and rocky country. Apparently, the Ziphites, malicious foes of David and loyal to Saul, had tracked David to this desolate area.

Soon Saul was in the area with some of his select soldiers. He was relentless in his determination to destroy David. Unwittingly, Saul and his men entered the very cave in which David was hiding. David's men saw the incident as providential: Behold, the day of which Jehovah said unto thee, Behold, I will deliver thine enemy into thy hand (v. 4). To them it seemed that God had put Saul within David's power. However, though David held in his hand the sword of Goliath and though his men were eager to destroy Saul, he restrained the impulse to attack.

The basic factor in his magnanimity toward Saul was the religious motive: Jehovah forbid that I should do this thing unto my lord, Jehovah's anointed . . . (v. 6). David still saw Saul as his superior and respected him because he was the anointed of the Lord. Doubtless David was greatly troubled over Saul's personal grudge against him, but when sorely tempted to retaliate with the same intent as Saul had toward him, he could not and, at the same time, remain true to his conscience. While Saul seemed to have no conscience toward David, David had a clear conscience as to his attitudes and actions toward Saul. The difference lay in the religious character of the two men. Saul was deluding himself concerning the help of the Lord, while David was defending his restraint on the grounds of his religious integrity (cf. 23:7 with 23: 10-12).

Where the religious motive for conduct is warped or absent, almost any behavior can be rationalized as being acceptable. Where that motive is soundly based on right relationship with God, there is realized a capacity to do the right thing, even when pressed to do the expedient thing.

When Saul left the cave and had departed a little distance, David came to the entrance and called to Saul. In his words to Saul, he revealed that he could not understand why Saul wanted to kill him. When he showed Saul how easily he might have killed him in the cave, the king appeared impressed. He even admitted to David, **Thou art more righteous than I; for thou hast rendered unto me good, whereas I have rendered unto thee evil** (v. 17). Also, Saul withdrew his men from pursuing David and returned to Gibeah.

C. DAVID FOUND IN MAON, AND THE SEQUEL (25:1-44)

1 And Samuel died; and all Israel gathered themselves together, and lamented him, and buried him in his house at Ramah. And David arose, and went down to the wilderness of Paran.

2 And there was a man in Maon, whose possessions were in Carmel; and the man was very great, and he had three thousand sheep, and a thousand goats: and he was shearing his sheep in Carmel. 3 Now the name of the man was Nabal; and the name of his wife Abigail; and the woman was of good understanding, and of a beautiful countenance: but the man was churlish and evil in his doings; and he was of the house of Caleb. 4 And David heard in the wilderness that Nabal was shearing his sheep. 5 And David sent ten young men, and David said unto the young men, Get you up to Carmel, and go to Nabal, and greet him in my name: 6 and thus shall ye say to him that liveth in *prosperity*, Peace be unto thee, and peace be to thy house, and peace be unto all that thou hast. 7 And now I have heard that thou hast shearers: thy shepherds have now been with us, and we did them no hurt, neither was there aught missing unto them, all the while they were in Carmel. 8 Ask thy young men, and they will tell thee: wherefore let the young men find favor in thine eyes; for we come in a good day: give, I pray thee, whatsoever

cometh to thy hand, unto thy servants, and to thy son David.

9 And when David's young men came, they spake to Nabal according to all those words in the name of David, and ceased. 10 And Nabal answered David's servants, and said, Who is David? and who is the son of Jesse? there are many servants now-a-days that break away every man from his master. 11 Shall I then take my bread, and my water, and my flesh that I have killed for my shearers, and give it unto men of whom I know not whence they are? 12 So David's young men turned on their way, and went back, and came and told him according to all these words. 13 And David said unto his men, Gird ye on every man his sword. And they girded on every man his sword; and David also girded on his sword: and there went up after David about four hundred men; and two hundred abode by the baggage.

14 But one of the young men told Abigail, Nabal's wife, saying, Behold, David sent messengers out of the wilderness to salute our master; and he railed at them. 15 But the men were very good unto us, and we were not hurt, neither missed we anything as long as we went with them, when we were in the fields: 16 they were a wall unto us both by night and by day, all the while we were with them keeping the sheep. 17 Now therefore know and consider what thou wilt do; for evil is determined against our master, and against all his house: for he is such a worthless fellow, that one cannot speak to him.

18 Then Abigail made haste, and took two hundred loaves, and two bottles of wine, and five sheep ready dressed, and five measures of parched grain, and a hundred clusters of raisins, and two hundred cakes of figs, and laid them on asses. 19 And she said unto her young men, Go on before me; behold, I come after you. But she told not her husband Nabal. 20 And it was so, as she rode on her ass, and came down by the covert of the mountain, that, behold, David and his men came down toward her; and she met them. 21 Now David had said, Surely in vain have I kept all that this fellow hath in the wilderness, so that nothing was missed of all that pertained unto him: and he hath returned me evil for good. 22 God do so unto the enemies of David, and more also, if I leave of all that pertain to him by the morning light so much as one man-child.

23 And when Abigail saw David, she hasted, and alighted from her ass, and fell before David on her face, and bowed herself to the ground. 24 And she fell at his feet, and said, Upon me, my lord, upon me be the iniquity; and let thy handmaid,

I pray thee, speak in thine ears, and hear thou the words of thy handmaid. 25 Let not my lord, I pray thee, regard this worthless fellow, even Nabal; for as his name is, so is he; Nabal is his name, and folly is with him: but I thy handmaid saw not the young men of my lord, whom thou didst send. 26 Now therefore, my lord, as Jehovah liveth, and as thy soul liveth, seeing Jehovah hath withholden thee from bloodguiltiness, and from avenging thyself with thine own hand, now therefore let thine enemies, and them that seek evil to my lord, be as Nabal. 27 And now this present which thy servant hath brought unto my lord, let it be given unto the young men that follow my lord. 28 Forgive, I pray thee, the trespass of thy handmaid: for Jehovah will certainly make my lord a sure house, because my lord fighteth the battles of Jehovah; and evil shall not be found in thee all thy days. 29 And though man be risen up to pursue thee, and to seek thy soul, yet the soul of my lord shall be bound in the bundle of life with Jehovah thy God; and the souls of thine enemies, them shall he sling out, as from the hollow of a sling. 30 And it shall come to pass, when Jehovah shall have done to my lord according to all the good that he hath spoken concerning thee, and shall have appointed thee prince over Israel, 31 that this shall be no grief unto thee, nor offence of heart unto my lord, either that thou hast shed blood without cause, or that my lord hath avenged himself. And when Jehovah shall have dealt well with my lord, then remember thy handmaid.

32 And David said to Abigail, Blessed be Jehovah, the God of Israel, who sent thee this day to meet me: 33 and blessed be thy discretion, and blessed be thou, that hast kept me this day from bloodguiltiness, and from avenging myself with mine own hand. 34 For in very deed, as Jehovah, the God of Israel, liveth, who hath withholden me from hurting thee, except thou hadst hasted and come to meet me, surely there had not been left unto Nabal by the morning light so much as one man-child. 35 So David received of her hand that which she had brought him: and he said unto her, Go up in peace to thy house; see, I have hearkened to thy voice, and have accepted thy person.

36 And Abigail came to Nabal; and, behold, he held a feast in his house, like the feast of a king; and Nabal's heart was merry within him, for he was very drunken: wherefore she told him nothing, less or more, until the morning light. 37 And it came to pass in the morning, when the wine was gone out of Nabal, that his wife told him these things, and his heart died within him, and he became as a stone. 38 And it came to pass about ten days after, that Jehovah smote Nabal, so that he died.

39 And when David heard that Nabal was dead, he said, Blessed be Jehovah, that hath pleaded the cause of my reproach from the hand of Nabal, and hath kept back his servant from evil: and the evil-doing of Nabal hath Jehovah returned upon his own head. And David sent and spake concerning Abigail, to take her to him to wife. 40 And when the servants of David were come to Abigail to Carmel, they spake unto her, saying, David hath sent us unto thee, to take thee to him to wife. 41 And she arose, and bowed herself with her face to the earth, and said, Behold, thy handmaid is a servant to wash the feet of the servants of my lord. 42 And Abigail hasted, and arose, and rode upon an ass, with five damsels of hers that followed her; and she went after the messengers of David, and became his wife.

43 David also took Ahinoam of Jezreel; and they became both of them his wives. 44 Now Saul had given Michal his daughter, David's wife, to Palti the son of Laish, who was of Gallim.

The Septuagint reads "Maon" instead of **Paran**, which is in keeping with the context (cf. vv. 1, 2). Carmel was located near Hebron and is not to be confused with the mount near the plain of Esdraelon.

David requested of Nabal, who lived in that area, that he and his men might receive adequate recompense for the protection they were able to afford him against marauding bands.

Nabal insulted David's messengers and so angered David that he came against Nabal with drawn sword and intent to destroy Nabal and all he had (vv. 21, 22).

Abigail, the wife of Nabal, was told by one of the servants of David's protection and Nabal's refusal (vv. 14-17). Quickly she acted to provide the proper recompense. Admitting that her husband had acted as a "fool," for that was the meaning of Nabal, she gave David a present. Because he was kept from murder by Abigail's action, David gave praise to God, who had sent her to meet him (vv. 32-35). Furthermore, when Nabal died shortly, because of apparent excesses and a stroke, David sent some of his men to bring Abigail to be his wife (vv. 39-42).

D. DAVID FOLLOWED TO ZIPH (26: 1-25)

1 And the Ziphites came unto Saul to Gibeah, saying, Doth not David hide himself in the hill of Hachilah, which is before the desert? 2 Then Saul arose, and went down to the wilderness of Ziph, having three thousand chosen men of Israel with him, to seek David in the wilderness of Ziph. 3 And Saul encamped in the hill of Hachilah, which is before the desert, by the way. But David abode in the wilderness, and he saw that Saul came after him into the wilderness. 4 David therefore sent out spies, and understood that Saul was come of a certainty. 5 And David arose, and came to the place where Saul had encamped; and David beheld the place where Saul lay, and Abner the son of Ner, the captain of his host: and Saul lay within the place of the wagons, and the people were encamped round about him.

6 Then answered David and said to Ahimelech the Hittite, and to Abishai the son of Zeruiah, brother to Joab, saying, Who will go down with me to Saul to the camp? And Abishai said, I will go down with thee. 7 So David and Abishai came to the people by night: and, behold, Saul lay sleeping within the place of the wagons, with his spear stuck in the ground at his head; and Abner and the people lay round about him. 8 Then said Abishai to David, God hath delivered up thine enemy into thy hand this day: now therefore let me smite him, I pray thee, with the spear to the earth at one stroke, and I will not smite him the second time. 9 And David said to Abishai, Destroy him not; for who can put forth his hand against Jehovah's anointed, and be guiltless? 10 And David said, As Jehovah liveth, Jehovah will smite him; or his day shall come to die; or he shall go down into battle, and perish. 11 Jehovah forbid that I should put forth my hand against Jehovah's anointed: but now take, I pray thee, the spear that is at his head, and the cruse of water, and let us go. 12 So David took the spear and the cruse of water from Saul's head; and they gat them away: and no man saw it, nor knew it, neither did any awake; for they were all asleep, because a deep sleep from Jehovah was fallen upon them.

13 Then David went over to the other side, and stood on the top of the mountain afar off; a great space being between them; 14 and David cried to the people, and to Abner the son of Ner, saying, Answerest thou not, Abner? Then Abner answered and said, Who art thou that criest to the king? 15 And David said to Abner, Art not thou a *valiant* man? and who is like to thee in Israel? wherefore then hast thou not kept watch over thy lord the king? for there came one of the people in to destroy the king thy lord. 16 This thing is not good that thou hast done. As Jehovah liveth, ye are worthy to die, because ye have not kept watch over your lord, Jehovah's anointed. And now see where the king's spear is, and the cruse of water that was at his head.

17 And Saul knew David's voice, and said, Is this thy voice, my son David? And David said, It is my voice, my lord, O king. 18 And he said, Wherefore doth my lord pursue after his servant? for what have I done? or what evil is in my hand? 19 Now therefore, I pray thee, let my lord the king hear the words of his servant. If it be Jehovah that hath stirred thee up against me, let him accept an offering: but if it be the children of men, cursed be they before Jehovah; for they have driven me out this day that I should not cleave unto the inheritance of Jehovah, saying, Go, serve other gods. 20 Now therefore, let not my blood fall to the earth away from the presence of Jehovah: for the king of Israel is come out to seek a flea, as when one doth hunt a partridge in the mountains.

21 Then said Saul, I have sinned: return, my son David; for I will no more do thee harm, because my life was precious in thine eyes this day: behold, I have played the fool, and have erred exceedingly. 22 And David answered and said, Behold the spear, O king! let then one of the young men come over and fetch it. 23 And Jehovah will render to every man his righteousness and his faithfulness; forasmuch as Jehovah delivered thee into my hand to-day, and I would not put forth my hand against Jehovah's anointed. 24 And, behold, as thy life was much set by this day in mine eyes, so let my life be much set by in the eyes of Jehovah, and let him deliver me out of all tribulation. 25 Then Saul said to David, Blessed be thou, my son David: thou shalt both do mightily, and shalt surely prevail. So David went his way, and Saul returned to his place.

The Ziphites informed Saul of David's presence in the wilderness of Ziph. Saul came with specially selected soldiers to destroy David. However, David's spies kept him informed of Saul's movements.

At night David and Abishai managed a daring sortie into the camp of Saul. Because a deep sleep from Jehovah was fallen upon them (v. 12), David and his companion were able to remove Saul's spear and water vessel.

When they were at a safe distance, David awakened Saul's sleeping encampment. Saul recognized the voice of David and answered him (v. 17). He became contrite and repentant when he discovered that David had been near enough to him to take his life.

Then David put Saul in a real dilemma with significant implications. If the Lord had antagonized Saul against David, then David was willing to make an offering and be reconciled to the Lord. However, if men had been responsible, then let thêm be under the curse of the Lord for banishing David from the land in which the Lord was worshiped (v. 19).

Either horn of the dilemma forced Saul to recognize his own wrongdoing. He was keeping David from his right to serve the Lord. David's contention was correct, and Saul stood condemned for sinning against God and David.

This encounter between Saul and David seems to have ended in ambiguity. Saul's effort at reconciliation did not create a mutual climate of trust and friendship. Rather, after this encounter David turned in despair to take refuge among the Philistines (cf. 27:1). Here, in the life and conduct of Saul, is a marked example of the triumph of perverted desires and purposes over the dictates of sound, clear logic and natural human obligations. Such a course can only lead to self-destruction.

XII. THE FALL OF SAUL (I Sam. 27:1—31:13)

David's plight had become desperate. Having been pursued from wilderness to wilderness in the territory of Judah, his native tribe, he came to the despairing conclusion that he must leave his homeland. **I shall now perish one day by the hand of Saul: there is nothing better for me than that I should escape into the land of the Philistines** (v. 1). Such a temporary emotional reaction on David's part serves well to reveal his basic humanity which he shares with all honest and sincere followers of God. It may be regarded as a virtue rather than a vice since it reveals his recognition of human limitations and forced him to greater dependence upon God (cf. Jas. 5:17).

A. DAVID AT ZIKLAG (27:1-12)

1 And David said in his heart, I shall now perish one day by the hand of Saul: there is nothing better for me than that I

should escape into the land of the Philistines; and Saul will despair of me, to seek me any more in all the borders of Israel: so shall I escape out of his hand. 2 And David arose, and passed over, he and the six hundred men that were with him, unto Achish the son of Maoch, king of Gath. 3 And David dwelt with Achish at Gath, he and his men, every man with his household, even David with his two wives, Ahinoam the Jezreelitess, and Abigail the Carmelitess, Nabal's wife. 4 And it was told Saul that David was fled to Gath: and he sought no more again for him.

5 And David said unto Achish, If now I have found favor in thine eyes, let them give me a place in one of the cities in the country, that I may dwell there: for why should thy servant dwell in the royal city with thee? 6 Then Achish gave him Ziklag that day: wherefore Ziklag pertaineth unto the kings of Judah unto this day. 7 And the number of the days that David dwelt in the country of the Philistines was a full year and four months.

8 And David and his men went up, and made a raid upon the Geshurites, and the Girzites, and the Amalekites; for those *nations* were the inhabitants of the land, who were of old, as thou goest to Shur, even unto the land of Egypt. 9 And David smote the land, and saved neither man nor woman alive, and took away the sheep, and the oxen, and the asses, and the camels, and the apparel; and he returned, and came to Achish. 10 And Achish said, Against whom have ye made a raid to-day? And David said, Against the South of Judah, and against the South of the Jerahmeelites, and against the South of the Kenites. 11 And David saved neither man nor woman alive, to bring them to Gath, saying, Lest they should tell of us, saying, So did David, and so hath been his manner all the while he hath dwelt in the country of the Philistines. 12 And Achish believed David, saying, He hath made his people Israel utterly to abhor him; therefore he shall be my servant for ever.

Contrary to what might have been expected as a result of Saul's encounter with David at Ziph, David found himself driven to seek what he had desperately wanted to avoid, namely, the protection of Saul's mortal enemies, the Philistines. This was done only as a last and desperate venture.

David went to Achish, king of Gath, and requested permission to dwell in one of the remote villages controlled by the political center of Gath. Achish granted him permission to dwell in Ziklag. **And it**

was told Saul that David was fled to Gath;
and he sought no more again for him
(v. 4). David remained in the land of the
Philistines for a little more than a year
(v. 7).

During this period of exile in Philistia,
David led his men in numerous raids.
Apparently, David had made arrangements with Achish for making these raids.
It may be inferred that Achish was to receive a share of the booty taken in each
raid (cf. vv. 9 and 11).

David appears in a very unsatisfactory
light during this time, for these raids involved the destruction of whole settlements and practicing bold deceit toward
Achish who had granted him protection.
His prime purpose appeared to be to
use these means to persuade Achish of
his loyalty to him. At least he succeeded
in this rather low objective, for Achish
believed him and let it be known that
David could always remain. **Therefore he
shall be my servant for ever** (v. 12).
David's conduct here must be understood
in the light of the undeveloped ethic
of his times, not to be judged by the
standards of New Testament Christian
ethics (cf. Acts 17:30).

B. SAUL AT ENDOR (28:1-25)

1 And it came to pass in those days, that
the Philistines gathered their hosts together
for warfare, to fight with Israel. And
Achish said unto David, Know thou assuredly, that thou shalt go out with me in
the host, thou and thy men. 2 And David
said to Achish, Therefore thou shalt know
what thy servant will do. And Achish said
to David, Therefore will I make thee
keeper of my head for ever.

3 Now Samuel was dead, and all Israel
had lamented him, and buried him in
Ramah, even in his own city. And Saul
had put away those that had familiar
spirits, and the wizards, out of the land. 4
And the Philistines gathered themselves
together, and came and encamped in
Shunem: and Saul gathered all Israel together, and they encamped in Gilboa. 5
And when Saul saw the host of the Philistines, he was afraid, and his heart
trembled greatly. 6 And when Saul inquired of Jehovah, Jehovah answered him
not, neither by dreams, nor by Urim, nor
by prophets. 7 Then said Saul unto his
servants, Seek me a woman that hath a
familiar spirit, that I may go to her, and
inquire of her. And his servants said to

him, Behold, there is a woman that hath
a familiar spirit at En-dor.

8 And Saul disguised himself, and put
on other raiment, and went, he and two
men with him, and they came to the
woman by night: and he said, Divine unto
me, I pray thee, by the familiar spirit, and
bring me up whomsoever I shall name
unto thee. 9 And the woman said unto
him, Behold, thou knowest what Saul hath
done, how he hath cut off those that have
familiar spirits, and the wizards, out of the
land: wherefore then layest thou a snare
for my life, to cause me to die? 10 And
Saul sware to her by Jehovah, saying, As
Jehovah liveth, there shall no punishment
happen to thee for this thing. 11 Then
said the woman, Whom shall I bring up
unto thee? And he said, Bring me up
Samuel. 12 And when the woman saw
Samuel, she cried with a loud voice; and
the woman spake to Saul, saying, Why
hast thou deceived me? for thou art Saul.
13 And the king said unto her, Be not
afraid: for what seest thou? And the
woman said unto Saul, I see a god coming
up out of the earth. 14 And he said unto
her, What form is he of? And she said, An
old man cometh up; and he is covered
with a robe. And Saul perceived that it was
Samuel, and he bowed with his face to the
ground, and did obeisance.

15 And Samuel said to Saul, Why hast
thou disquieted me, to bring me up? And
Saul answered, I am sore distressed; for
the Philistines make war against me, and
God is departed from me, and answereth
me no more, neither by prophets, nor by
dreams: therefore I have called thee, that
thou mayest make known unto me what I
shall do. 16 And Samuel said, Wherefore
then dost thou ask of me, seeing Jehovah
is departed from thee, and is become thine
adversary? 17 And Jehovah hath done unto
thee, as he spake by me: and Jehovah hath
rent the kingdom out of thy hand, and
given it to thy neighbor, even to David. 18
Because thou obeyedst not the voice of
Jehovah, and didst not execute his fierce
wrath upon Amalek, therefore hath Jehovah done this thing unto thee this day.
19 Moreover Jehovah will deliver Israel also
with thee into the hand of the Philistines;
and to-morrow shalt thou and thy sons be
with me: Jehovah will deliver the host of
Israel also into the hand of the Philistines.

20 Then Saul fell straightway his full
length upon the earth, and was sore afraid,
because of the words of Samuel: and there
was no strength in him; for he had eaten
no bread all the day, nor all the night. 21
And the woman came unto Saul, and saw
that he was sore troubled, and said unto
him, Behold, thy handmaid hath hearkened

unto thy voice, and I have put my life in my hand, and have hearkened unto thy words which thou spakest unto me. 22 Now therefore, I pray thee, hearken thou also unto the voice of thy handmaid, and let me set a morsel of bread before thee; and eat, that thou mayest have strength, when thou goest on thy way. 23 But he refused, and said, I will not eat. But his servants, together with the woman, constrained him; and he hearkened unto their voice. So he arose from the earth, and sat upon the bed. 24 And the woman had a fatted calf in the house; and she hasted, and killed it; and she took flour, and kneaded it, and did bake unleavened bread thereof: 25 and she brought it before Saul, and before his servants; and they did eat. Then they rose up, and went away that night.

The Philistines prepared for a major onslaught against Saul. Achish was joining with other lords of the Philistines for a decisive victory.

When Saul saw the build-up of the Philistine forces he became fearful (v. 5). He needed help as greatly as he had ever needed it, but in his hour of extremity he knew it was futile to inquire of the Lord. **Jehovah answered him not, neither by dreams, nor by Urim, nor by prophets** (v. 6). It had become unmistakably clear to Saul that the Lord would not answer him.

In despair rather than defiance, Saul turned to an alternative source of help. He said to his servants, **Seek me a woman that hath a familiar spirit, that I may go to her, and inquire of her** (v. 7). It is impossible to determine Saul's motivation, but if any significance is allowed for his mental deterioration since the day of Samuel's severe rebuke to him regarding his disposition of the Amalekites, Saul was in mental anguish as well as in spiritual alienation. Not only was a breakdown near, but also God was absent.

As a consequence of this combination of factors, rather than as deliberate defiance, Saul turned to what God had forbidden, namely, a person with a familiar spirit (cf. Lev. 19:31; 20:27). Disguised, Saul and two men went at night to a woman at Endor. Apparently unrecognized, he requested of her, **Divine unto me . . . by the familiar spirit, and bring me up whomsoever I shall name unto thee** (v. 8).

Because of Saul's earlier decree outlawing necromancy, the woman feared entrapment (cf. v. 3). Her fears having been allayed, she asked, **Whom shall I bring up unto thee?** (v. 11). The reply was, **Bring me up Samuel** (v. 11). As the woman intensified her powers, the situation became charged with psychic activity. Suddenly, the woman was terrified as she realized Saul's identity and all that was involved in his request.

Careful examination of this incident at Endor has given rise to two widely held explanations obtained by two different methods. There is the explanation which asserts that Saul was in the presence of Samuel. This conclusion is reached by recognition of the objective elements in the incident. The second explanation asserts that Samuel was not actually present. This conclusion is reached by stressing the subjective elements.

It is possible to explain the incident by recognizing that both objective and subjective elements were involved, by admitting both historical and psychological elements. Historically speaking, everyone was acquainted with Samuel's declarations regarding the Lord's displeasure with Saul. It was common knowledge that Samuel and Saul had not seen each other for years. With this historical knowledge as background, the woman of Endor saw the whole situation when she heard the request for Samuel.

Psychologically speaking, the woman perceived intuitively, rather than visually, that there was a being arising. When she made this known to Saul he impulsively decided that it was Samuel.

As a result of this hasty judgment, Saul began conversation, not by verbalizing with an objective reality but rather musing in the presence of a psychological phenomenon. All that had occurred in former days now had become very real to Saul in an experience that was indeed traumatic for him.

The whole episode was devastating to Saul. Upon the realization that he was coming to the end of his life in defeat and disgrace, he was so overwhelmed that he fainted. With this sense of impending disaster, Saul faced the coming battle with the Philistines.

C. THE PHILISTINES AT APHEK (29:1—30:31)

1 Now the Philistines gathered together all their hosts to Aphek: and the Israelites encamped by the fountain which is in Jezreel. 2 And the lords of the Philistines passed on by hundreds, and by thousands; and David and his men passed on in the rearward with Achish. 3 Then said the princes of the Philistines, What *do* these Hebrews *here?* And Achish said unto the princes of the Philistines, Is not this David, the servant of Saul the king of Israel, who hath been with me these days, or *rather* these years, and I have found no fault in him since he fell away *unto me* unto this day? 4 But the princes of the Philistines were wroth with him; and the princes of the Philistines said unto him, Make the man return, that he may go back to his place where thou hast appointed him, and let him not go down with us to battle, lest in the battle he become an adversary to us: for wherewith should this *fellow* reconcile himself unto his lord? should it not be with the heads of these men? 5 Is not this David, of whom they sang one to another in dances, saying,

Saul hath slain his thousands,
And David his ten thousands?

6 Then Achish called David, and said unto him, As Jehovah liveth, thou hast been upright, and thy going out and thy coming in with me in the host is good in my sight; for I have not found evil in thee since the day of thy coming unto me unto this day: nevertheless the lords favor thee not. 7 Wherefore now return, and go in peace, that thou displease not the lords of the Philistines. 8 And David said unto Achish, But what have I done? and what hast thou found in thy servant so long as I have been before thee unto this day, that I may not go and fight against the enemies of my lord the king? 9 And Achish answered and said to David, I know that thou art good in my sight, as an angel of God: notwithstanding the princes of the Philistines have said, He shall not go up with us to the battle. 10 Wherefore now rise up early in the morning with the servants of thy lord that are come with thee; and as soon as ye are up early in the morning, and have light, depart. 11 So David rose up early, he and his men, to depart in the morning, to return into the land of the Philistines. And the Philistines went up to Jezreel.

1 And it came to pass, when David and his men were come to Ziklag on the third day, that the Amalekites had made a raid upon the South, and upon Ziklag, and had smitten Ziklag, and burned it with fire, 2 and had taken captive the women *and all*

that were therein, both small and great: they slew not any, but carried them off, and went their way. 3 And when David and his men came to the city, behold, it was burned with fire; and their wives, and their sons, and their daughters, were taken captive. 4 Then David and the people that were with him lifted up their voice and wept, until they had no more power to weep. 5 And David's two wives were taken captive, Ahinoam the Jezreelitess, and Abigail the wife of Nabal the Carmelite. 6 And David was greatly distressed; for the people spake of stoning him, because the soul of all the people was grieved, every man for his sons and for his daughters: but David strengthened himself in Jehovah his God.

7 And David said to Abiathar the priest, the son of Ahimelech, I pray thee bring me hither the ephod. And Abiathar brought thither the ephod to David. 8 And David inquired of Jehovah, saying, If I pursue after this troop, shall I overtake them? And he answered him, Pursue; for thou shalt surely overtake *them,* and shalt without fail recover *all.* 9 So David went, he and the six hundred men that were with him, and came to the brook Besor, where those that were left behind stayed. 10 But David pursued, he and four hundred men; for two hundred stayed behind, who were so faint that they could not go over the brook Besor.

11 And they found an Egyptian in the field, and brought him to David, and gave him bread, and he did eat; and they gave him water to drink; 12 and they gave him a piece of a cake of figs, and two clusters of raisins: and when he had eaten, his spirit came again to him; for he had eaten no bread, nor drunk any water, three days and three nights. 13 And David said unto him, To whom belongest thou? and whence art thou? And he said, I am a young man of Egypt, servant to an Amalekite; and my master left me, because three days ago I fell sick. 14 We made a raid upon the South of the Cherethites, and upon that which belongeth to Judah, and upon the South of Caleb; and we burned Ziklag with fire. 15 And David said to him, Wilt thou bring me down to this troop? And he said, Swear unto me by God, that thou wilt neither kill me, nor deliver me up into the hands of my master, and I will bring thee down to this troop.

16 And when he had brought him down, behold, they were spread abroad over all the ground, eating and drinking, and dancing, because of all the great spoil that they had taken out of the land of the Philistines, and out of the land of Judah. 17 And David smote them from the twilight

even unto the evening of the next day: and there escaped not a man of them, save four hundred young men, who rode upon camels and fled. 18 And David recovered all that the Amalekites had taken; and David rescued his two wives. 19 And there was nothing lacking to them, neither small nor great, neither sons nor daughters, neither spoil, nor anything that they had taken to them: David brought back all. 20 And David took all the flocks and the herds, *which* they drove before those *other* cattle, and said, This is David's spoil.

21 And David came to the two hundred men, who were so faint that they could not follow David, whom also they had made to abide at the brook Besor; and they went forth to meet David, and to meet the people that were with him: and when David came near to the people, he saluted them. 22 Then answered all the wicked men and base fellows, of those that went with David, and said, Because they went not with us, we will not give them aught of the spoil that we have recovered, save to every man his wife and his children, that he may lead them away, and depart. 23 Then said David, Ye shall not do so, my brethren, with that which Jehovah hath given unto us, who hath preserved us, and delivered the troop that came against us into our hand. 24 And who will hearken unto you in this matter? for as his share is that goeth down to the battle, so shall his share be that tarrieth by the baggage: they shall share alike. 25 And it was so from that day forward, that he made it a statute and an ordinance for Israel unto this day.

26 And when David came to Ziklag, he sent of the spoil unto the elders of Judah, even to his friends, saying, Behold, a present for you of the spoil of the enemies of Jehovah: 27 to them that were in Beth-el, and to them that were in Ramoth of the South, and to them that were in Jattir, 28 and to them that were in Aroer, and to them that were in Siphmoth, and to them that were in Eshtemoa, 29 and to them that were in Racal, and to them that were in the cities of the Jerahmeelites, and to them that were in the cities of the Kenites, 30 and to them that were in Hormah, and to them that were in Borashan, and to them that were in Athach, 31 and to them that were in Hebron, and to all the places where David himself and his men were wont to haunt.

While the army of Israel mobilized its strength at the foot of Mount Gilboa, the Philistines gathered at Aphek, probably on the plain of Sharon, an advantageous place for an attack on central Palestine.

David and his men were with the Philistines because of the order given by Achish (cf. 28:1). However, other lords of the Philistines refused to trust David and ordered his return to Ziklag (v. 4). Achish complied and made David return while the Philistines went on to engage the Israelites at Mount Gilboa (v. 11).

When David and his men reached Ziklag they were angered and grieved to find that the city, along with other cities, had been subjected to a dreadful raid by the Amalekites. David, however, trusted in God and called for Abiathar to bring the ephod in order to determine whether or not to pursue the Amalekites. He received an affirmative answer and pursued the raiders. He found a dying servant of the band whom he nourished sufficiently until he could tell about himself and his masters. He gave David information that enabled him to overtake and overpower the raiding band (vv. 16-20).

David recovered all he had lost and much more. Moreover, he required that fair distribution be made. **As his share is that goeth down to the battle, so shall his share be that tarrieth by the baggage: they shall share alike** (v. 24).

Also, David used the occasion as an opportunity to show himself friendly and hospitable to the elders of various cities in Judah (vv. 26-31). This was an expression of his gratitude to those who had befriended him (cf. v. 30). Also, it was excellent diplomacy, for it indicated David's loyalty to his own tribe of Judah.

D. THE BATTLE AT MOUNT GILBOA (31:1-13; cf. I Chron. 10:1-14)

1 Now the Philistines fought against Israel: and the men of Israel fled from before the Philistines, and fell down slain in mount Gilboa. 2 And the Philistines followed hard upon Saul and upon his sons; and the Philistines slew Jonathan, and Abinadab, and Malchishua, the sons of Saul. 3 And the battle went sore against Saul, and the archers overtook him; and he was greatly distressed by reason of the archers. 4 Then said Saul to his armorbearer, Draw thy sword, and thrust me through therewith, lest these uncircumcised come and thrust me through, and abuse me. But his armorbearer would not; for he was sore afraid. Therefore Saul took his sword, and fell upon it. 5 And when his armorbearer saw that Saul was dead, he likewise fell upon his sword, and died

with him. 6 So Saul died, and his three sons, and his armorbearer, and all his men, that same day together.

7 And when the men of Israel that were on the other side of the valley, and they that were beyond the Jordan, saw that the men of Israel fled, and that Saul and his sons were dead, they forsook the cities, and fled; and the Philistines came and dwelt in them. 8 And it came to pass on the morrow, when the Philistines came to strip the slain, that they found Saul and his three sons fallen in mount Gilboa. 9 And they cut off his head, and stripped off his armor, and sent into the land of the Philistines round about, to carry the tidings unto the house of their idols, and to the people. 10 And they put his armor in the house of the Ashtaroth; and they fastened his body to the wall of Beth-shan. 11 And when the inhabitants of Jabesh-gilead heard concerning him that which the Philistines had done to Saul, 12 all the valiant men arose, and went all night, and took the body of Saul and the bodies of his sons from the wall of Beth-shan; and they came to Jabesh, and burnt them there. 13 And they took their bones, and buried them under the tamarisk-tree in Jabesh, and fasted seven days.

The Philistines and the Israelites joined battle at Mount Gilboa. The outcome was not long in doubt: **And the battle went sore against Saul** (v. 3). Saul's three sons, including Jonathan, were slain. The enemy archers discovered Saul and apparently wounded him (v. 3). Rather than suffer Philistinian atrocities, Saul chose to die. He told his armor-bearer to complete the deed which the archers had begun. When the young man refused, Saul laboriously placed his sword in position and fell on it (v. 4).

"The paradoxical thing about suicide is that men turn to it when they can think of nothing but themselves."[13] When nothing exists for the man but himself, there is no reason for him to exist.

The final act of vengeance upon Saul by the Philistines was to hang his decapitated body on the city wall of Beth-shan and place his armor in the temple of Ashtaroth. Israelites from east of the Jordan crossed over and took Saul's body to Jabesh-gilead to bury it. So the career of the first king of Israel came to its tragic end.

[13] J. C. Shroeder, "I Samuel, Exposition," *The Interpreter's Bible*, II, 1040.

The Second Book of Samuel

by Charles R. Wilson

Outline

Commentary on Second Samuel

I. DAVID'S DIRGE (II Sam. 1:1-27)

The chapter begins with an explanation of Saul's death and moves on to a remarkable poem composed by David in lamentation over the death of Saul.

A. ITS CAUSE (1:1-16)

1 And it came to pass after the death of Saul, when David was returned from the slaughter of the Amalekites, and David had abode two days in Ziklag; 2 it came to pass on the third day, that, behold, a man came out of the camp from Saul, with his clothes rent, and earth upon his head: and so it was, when he came to David, that he fell to the earth, and did obeisance. 3 And David said unto him, From whence comest thou? And he said unto him, Out of the camp of Israel am I escaped. 4 And David said unto him, How went the matter? I pray thee, tell me. And he answered, The people are fled from the battle, and many of the people also are fallen and dead; and Saul and Jonathan his son are dead also. 5 And David said unto the young man that told him, How knowest thou that Saul and Jonathan his son are dead? 6 And the young man that told him said, As I happened by chance upon mount Gilboa, behold, Saul was leaning upon his spear; and, lo, the chariots and the horsemen followed hard after him. 7 And when he looked behind him, he saw me, and called unto me. And I answered, Here am I. 8 And he said unto me, Who art thou? And I answered him, I am an Amalekite. 9 And he said unto me, Stand, I pray thee, beside me, and slay me; for anguish hath taken hold of me, because my life is yet whole in me. 10 So I stood beside him, and slew him, because I was sure that he could not live after that he was fallen: and I took the crown that was upon his head, and the bracelet that was on his arm, and have brought them hither unto my lord. 11 Then David took hold on his clothes, and rent them; and likewise all the men that were with him: 12 and they mourned, and wept, and fasted until even, for Saul, and for Jonathan his son, and for the people of Jehovah, and for the house of Israel; because they were fallen by the sword. 13 And David said unto the young man that told him, Whence art thou? And he answered, I am the son of a sojourner, an Amalekite. 14 And David said unto him, How wast thou not afraid to put forth thy hand to destroy Jehovah's anointed? 15 And David called one of the young men, and said, Go near, and fall upon him. And he smote him, so that he died. 16 And David said unto him, Thy blood be upon thy head; for thy mouth hath testified against thee, saying, I have slain Jehovah's anointed.

David was in Ziklag, having returned from his pursuit of the Amalekites, who had plundered his city along with others (cf. I Sam. 30). A stranger appeared in the city and reported the death of Saul (v. 4).

The account of Saul's death as given by this stranger, who was an Amalekite, was apparently a fanciful tale of his own invention. It is impossible to reconcile it with the account of Saul's death recorded in I Samuel 31.

While the Amalekite's story of the death of Saul was false, it is entirely possible that his reference to being associated with Saul's encampment was true. When asked from where he had come, he replied, **Out of the camp of Israel am I escaped** (v. 3).

He may have had some association with Saul's army as a camp worker. "The word *ger* (stranger) means a foreigner admitted to a modified civil status in Israel. . . ."[14]

The Amalekite hurried from Mount Gilboa to David in Ziklag to tell David the outcome of the battle. He must have been well acquainted with the situation

---

[14] Renwick, *op. cit.*, p. 279.

in Israel, particularly the relationship existing between Saul and David. He knew where to find David, living in exile in the land of the Philistines. He knew that David was the great challenger to the throne of Israel. His eagerness to reach David with his story of Saul's death was prompted by a covetous desire to gain recognition from David.

The Amalekite's report was not received as he probably expected. Instead of starting a jubilant celebration, the report plunged David's company into mourning (vv. 11, 12). Although David now had access to the throne, the national crisis was far more important to him than personal gain. The plight of the nation of Israel was indeed perilous because of the defeat by the uncircumcised Philistines. Saul, the Lord's anointed, and Jonathan, David's dearest friend, were dead. The army of Israel was helpless to halt the Philistines and the nation was once more exposed to the danger of being completely conquered.

It must be noted that David was not only greatly concerned over this new crisis in Israel but also devoutly reverent toward **Jehovah's anointed** (v. 14). This was David's attitude continually (cf. I Sam. 24:6; 26:9, 11, 16), and it is an attitude that should characterize all soberminded leaders. Because the Amalekite violated what to David was significantly sacred, David ordered that he be executed.

B. ITS CONTENT (1:17-27)

And David lamented with this lamentation over Saul and over Jonathan his son (v. 17). The original Hebrew term, *quinah,* is the technical term for a lamentation or dirge for the dead.[15]

This early Hebrew poem in commemoration of the deaths of Saul and Jonathan divides into two parts. The first refers to their deaths as bringing a supreme tragedy to the nation (vv. 19-22). The second refers to their personal virtues (vv. 23-27).

1. National Trouble (1:17-22)

17 And David lamented with this lamentation over Saul and over Jonathan his son 18 (and he bade them teach the

children of Judah *the song of* the bow: behold, it is written in the book of Jashar) :
19 Thy glory, O Israel, is slain upon thy high places!
How are the mighty fallen!
20 Tell it not in Gath,
Publish it not in the streets of Ashkelon;
Lest the daughters of the Philistines rejoice,
Lest the daughters of the uncircumcised triumph.
21 Ye mountains of Gilboa,
Let there be no dew nor rain upon you, neither fields of offerings:
For there the shield of the mighty was vilely cast away,
The shield of Saul, not anointed with oil.
22 From the blood of the slain, from the fat of the mighty,
The bow of Jonathan turned not back,
And the sword of Saul returned not empty.

How are the mighty fallen! (v. 19). This moving refrain is oft repeated (cf. 1:25, 27). David was keenly aware of Israel's time of trouble. Not only had Israel's leaders been vanquished, but the nation's humiliation had been published among the Philistines. In Gath and Ashkelon the news had triggered victory celebrations.

David's mournful dirge includes a curse upon the scene of the disaster. **Ye mountains of Gilboa, let there be no dew nor rain upon you** (v. 21).

2. Personal Tribute (1:23-27)

23 Saul and Jonathan were lovely and pleasant in their lives,
And in their death they were not divided:
They were swifter than eagles,
They were stronger than lions.
24 Ye daughters of Israel, weep over Saul,
Who clothed you in scarlet delicately,
Who put ornaments of gold upon your apparel.
25 How are the mighty fallen in the midst of the battle!
Jonathan is slain upon thy high places.
26 I am distressed for thee, my brother Jonathan:
Very pleasant hast thou been unto me:

---

[15] Kennedy, *op. cit.,* p. 194.

Thy love to me was wonderful,
Passing the love of women.
27 How are the mighty fallen,
And the weapons of war perished!

David here pays tribute to the brave deeds of Saul and Jonathan. They **were lovely and pleasant in their lives** (v. 23). While there was much about Saul's personality that was unattractive, there was a reciprocal loyalty and love between father and son. David, who was unable to generate loyalty in his own sons comparable to that of Jonathan for Saul, saw this sterling quality in Saul's relationship with his son. **And in their death they were not divided** (v. 23).

David reached the climax of his dirge in his passionate expression of sorrow over the fate of Jonathan his friend. Jonathan's love had been wonderful to David, who had lived in constant bewilderment regarding Saul's murderous hate toward him. Jonathan's death left a great emptiness in his life, for Jonathan had shared with David a friendship that far surpassed the ordinary.

II. RIVALRY FOR THE KINGDOM (II Sam. 2:1—4:12)

The throne of Israel was unoccupied, and the nation had no plans for a successor to Saul. There was no reason for David to remain in exile longer. As was his custom, however, David sought to know the will of God concerning what he should do.

A. DAVID IN HEBRON (2:1-7)

1 And it came to pass after this, that David inquired of Jehovah, saying, Shall I go up into any of the cities of Judah? And Jehovah said unto him, Go up. And David said, Whither shall I go up? And he said, Unto Hebron. 2 So David went up thither, and his two wives also, Ahinoam the Jezreelitess, and Abigail the wife of Nabal the Carmelite. 3 And his men that were with him did David bring up, every man with his household: and they dwelt in the cities of Hebron. 4 And the men of Judah came, and there they anointed David king over the house of Judah.

And they told David, saying, The men of Jabesh-gilead were they that buried Saul. 5 And David sent messengers unto the men of Jabesh-gilead, and said unto them, Blessed be ye of Jehovah, that ye have showed this kindness unto your lord, even unto Saul, and have buried him. 6 And now Jehovah show loving-kindness and truth unto you: and I also will requite you this kindness, because ye have done this thing. 7 Now therefore let your hands be strong, and be ye valiant; for Saul your lord is dead, and also the house of Judah have anointed me king over them.

By means of a series of questions, David was able to know that God willed his moving from Ziklag to Hebron in Judah. David's own tribe was first to approve him as successor to Saul. **And the men of Judah came, and there they anointed David king over the house of Judah** (v. 4).

David had maintained friendly relations with his native tribe while he was in exile. He had made presents to the cities of Judah from the spoil of his raids (cf. I Sam. 30:26-31). Furthermore, in seeking the will of God, David had no sound reason for going elsewhere than to Judah. Since he was returning from exile, it was to be expected that he would return to his own tribe. Hebron was easy to defend and had not been a target of the Philistines.

Basically, David exercised faith in the will of God, but that faith was implemented by sound practical sense. There seems to be a strange tendency to equate the will of God with the illogical and irrational, but David did not so understand divine guidance. Again and again David inquired concerning God's will, and he followed it in keeping with practical wisdom. It is ordinarily possible for one to follow the will of God if it can be interpreted in terms of the sane, consistent, orderly ongoings of life. Otherwise, a sincere believer seeking the will of God finds his course of action constantly frustrated, for he is not certain what is the will of God.

David was told that Saul had been buried by men from Jabesh-gilead (v. 4b). These people had not forgotten what Saul had done for them in the early part of his reign (cf. I Sam. 11). Thus he sent a message of commendation to them for their kindness to Saul. Further, he offered a gentle hint that since Saul was dead and Judah had made David king, the men of Jabesh-gilead might transfer their loyalty from Saul to himself.

B. ISH-BOSHETH IN MAHANAIM (2:8-11)

8 Now Abner the son of Ner, captain of Saul's host, had taken Ish-bosheth the son of Saul, and brought him over to Mahanaim; 9 and he made him king over Gilead, and over the Ashurites, and over Jezreel, and over Ephraim, and over Benjamin, and over all Israel. 10 Ish-bosheth, Saul's son, was forty years old when he began to reign over Israel, and he reigned two years. But the house of Judah followed David. 11 And the time that David was king in Hebron over the house of Judah was seven years and six months.

Rivalry for the throne of Israel developed when Abner, commander of Saul's army and a cousin of the fallen king, proclaimed Ish-bosheth, a son of Saul, as Saul's successor. Mahanaim, the chief city in Gilead, was selected as the capital (v. 8). The Gileadites had proved themselves loyal to Saul since his defeat of the Ammonites in their behalf (I Sam. 11). Abner's actions indicate an able and astute general who put his king in as favorable a position as possible.

C. CIVIL WAR (2:12—3:5)

12 And Abner the son of Ner, and the servants of Ish-bosheth the son of Saul, went out from Mahanaim to Gibeon. 13 And Joab the son of Zeruiah, and the servants of David, went out, and met them by the pool of Gibeon; and they sat down, the one on the one side of the pool, and the other on the other side of the pool. 14 And Abner said to Joab, Let the young men, I pray thee, arise and play before us. And Joab said, Let them arise. 15 Then they arose and went over by number: twelve for Benjamin, and for Ish-bosheth the son of Saul, and twelve of the servants of David. 16 And they caught every one his fellow by the head, and *thrust* his sword in his fellow's side; so they fell down together: wherefore that place was called Helkath-hazzurim, which is in Gibeon. 17 And the battle was very sore that day; and Abner was beaten, and the men of Israel, before the servants of David.

18 And the three sons of Zeruiah were there, Joab, and Abishai, and Asahel: and Asahel was as light of foot as a wild roe.

19 And Asahel pursued after Abner; and in going he turned not to the right hand nor to the left from following Abner. 20 Then Abner looked behind him, and said, Is it thou, Asahel? And he answered, It is I. 21 And Abner said to him, Turn thee aside to thy right hand or to thy left, and lay thee hold on one of the young men, and take thee his armor. But Asahel would not turn aside from following him. 22 And Abner said again to Asahel, Turn thee aside from following me: wherefore should I smite thee to the ground? how then should I hold up my face to Joab thy brother? 23 Howbeit he refused to turn aside: wherefore Abner with the hinder end of the spear smote him in the body, so that the spear came out behind him; and he fell down there, and died in the same place: and it came to pass, that as many as came to the place where Asahel fell down and died stood still.

24 But Joab and Abishai pursued after Abner: and the sun went down when they were come to the hill of Ammah, that lieth before Giah by the way of the wilderness of Gibeon. 25 And the children of Benjamin gathered themselves together after Abner, and became one band, and stood on the top of a hill. 26 Then Abner called to Joab, and said, Shall the sword devour for ever? knowest thou not that it will be bitterness in the latter end? how long shall it be then, ere thou bid the people return from following their brethren? 27 And Joab said, As God liveth, if thou hadst not spoken, surely then in the morning the people had gone away, nor followed every one his brother. 28 So Joab blew the trumpet; and all the people stood still, and pursued after Israel no more, neither fought they any more. 29 And Abner and his men went all that night through the Arabah; and they passed over the Jordan, and went through all Bithron, and came to Mahanaim.

30 And Joab returned from following Abner: and when he had gathered all the people together, there lacked of David's servants nineteen men and Asahel. 31 But the servants of David had smitten of Benjamin, and of Abner's men, *so that* three hundred and threescore men died. 32 And they took up Asahel, and buried him in the sepulchre of his father, which was in Beth-lehem. And Joab and his men went all night, and the day brake upon them at Hebron.

1 Now there was long war between the house of Saul and the house of David: and David waxed stronger and stronger,

but the house of Saul waxed weaker and weaker.

2 And unto David were sons born in Hebron: and his first-born was Amnon, of Ahinoam the Jezreelitess; 3 and his second, Chileab, of Abigail the wife of Nabal the Carmelite; and the third, Absalom the son of Maacah the daughter of Talmai king of Geshur; 4 and the fourth, Adonijah the son of Haggith; and the fifth, Shephatiah the son of Abital; 5 and the sixth, Ithream, of Eglah, David's wife. These were born to David in Hebron.

"These verses describe the age-old sordid chain of circumstances which lead to war."[16] The first link is increasing tension between two nations. There occurs the precipitating incident that provokes the outbreak of hostilities. Then follows the all-out war, the uncertain outcome, the truce and finally the unstable peace.

The reason for the appearance of Abner and his men at Gibeon is unknown. Gibeon was about six miles northwest of Jerusalem. David's general, Joab, came from Hebron, about twenty miles south of Jerusalem, with his men, to meet force with force.

Abner laid down a challenge, **Let the young men . . . play before us** (v. 14). It may not be possible to ascertain Abner's motive for this, but in the light of the chain reaction which prompts wars, it is possible to say that Abner deliberately provoked an incident that carried the live possibility of war. The sword-play was calculated to evoke increased tension and stir up the will to fight. The incident exploded into a full-blown battle. **And the battle was very sore that day; and Abner was beaten** (v. 17).

The young brother of Joab, Asahel, an inexperienced but passionate fighter, pursued the skillful and experienced Abner. He was no match for Abner and died from a spear wound inflicted upon him (v. 23). Moreover, his impetuosity stirred up a bitter feud between Joab and Abner which had far-reaching results for the kingdom as well as for David (cf. II Sam. 3; I Kings 2). While youth can on occasion contribute phenomenally to an enterprise, e.g., young David's victory over Goliath, it is possible for an impetuous, inexperienced youth to compli-

cate matters seriously or even tragically, as is seen in Asahel's rash action.

D. ABNER'S REVOLT (3:6-39)

6 And it came to pass, while there was war between the house of Saul and the house of David, that Abner made himself strong in the house of Saul. 7 Now Saul had a concubine, whose name was Rizpah, the daughter of Aiah: and *Ish-bosheth* said to Abner, Wherefore hast thou gone in unto my father's concubine? 8 Then was Abner very wroth for the words of Ish-bosheth, and said, Am I a dog's head that belongeth to Judah? This day do I show kindness unto the house of Saul thy father, to his brethren, and to his friends, and have not delivered thee into the hand of David; and yet thou chargest me this day with a fault concerning this woman. 9 God do so to Abner, and more also, if, as Jehovah hath sworn to David, I do not even so to him; 10 to transfer the kingdom from the house of Saul, and to set up the throne of David over Israel and over Judah, from Dan even to Beer-sheba. 11 And he could not answer Abner another word, because he feared him.

12 And Abner sent messengers to David on his behalf, saying, Whose is the land? saying *also*, Make thy league with me, and, behold, my hand shall be with thee, to bring about all Israel unto thee. 13 And he said, Well; I will make a league with thee; but one thing I require of thee: that is, thou shall not see my face, except thou first bring Michal, Saul's daughter, when thou comest to see my face. 14 And David sent messengers to Ish-bosheth, Saul's son, saying, Deliver me my wife Michal, whom I betrothed to me for a hundred foreskins of the Philistines. 15 And Ish-bosheth sent, and took her from her husband, even from Paltiel the son of Laish. 16 And her husband went with her, weeping as he went, and followed her to Bahurim. Then said Abner unto him, Go, return: and he returned.

17 And Abner had communication with the elders of Israel, saying, In times past ye sought for David to be king over you: 18 now then do it; for Jehovah hath spoken of David, saying, By the hand of my servant David I will save my people Israel out of the hand of the Philistines, and out of the hand of all their enemies. 19 And Abner also spake in the ears of Benjamin: and Abner went also to speak in the ears of David in Hebron all that seemed good to Israel, and to the whole

---

[16] G. Little, "Exposition of II Samuel," *The Interpreter's Bible*, II, 1051.

house of Benjamin. 20 So Abner came to David to Hebron, and twenty men with him. And David made Abner and the men that were with him a feast. 21 And Abner said unto David, I will arise and go, and will gather all Israel unto my lord the king, that they may make a covenant with thee, and that thou mayest reign over all that thy soul desireth. And David sent Abner away; and he went in peace.

22 And, behold, the servants of David and Joab came from a foray, and brought in a great spoil with them: but Abner was not with David in Hebron; for he had sent him away, and he was gone in peace. 23 When Joab and all the host that was with him were come, they told Joab, saying, Abner the son of Ner came to the king, and he hath sent him away, and he is gone in peace. 24 Then Joab came to the king, and said, What hast thou done? behold, Abner came unto thee; why is it that thou hast sent him away, and he is quite gone? 25 Thou knowest Abner the son of Ner, that he came to deceive thee, and to know thy going out and thy coming in, and to know all that thou doest. 26 And when Joab was come out from David, he sent messengers after Abner, and they brought him back from the well of Sirah: but David knew it not.

27 And when Abner was returned to Hebron, Joab took him aside into the midst of the gate to speak with him quietly, and smote him there in the body, so that he died, for the blood of Asahel his brother. 28 And afterward, when David heard it, he said, I and my kingdom are guiltless before Jehovah for ever of the blood of Abner the son of Ner: 29 let it fall upon the head of Joab, and upon all his father's house; and let there not fail from the house of Joab one that hath an issue, or that is a leper, or that leaneth on a staff, or that falleth by the sword, or that lacketh bread. 30 So Joab and Abishai his brother slew Abner, because he had killed their brother Asahel at Gibeon in the battle.

31 And David said to Joab, and to all the people that were with him, Rend your clothes, and gird you with sackcloth, and mourn before Abner. And king David followed the bier. 32 And they buried Abner in Hebron: and the king lifted up his voice, and wept at the grave of Abner; and all the people wept. 33 And the king lamented for Abner, and said,

Should Abner die as a fool dieth?

34 Thy hands were not bound, nor thy feet put into fetters:
As a man falleth before the children of iniquity, so didst thou fall.

And all the people wept again over him. 35 And all the people came to cause David to eat bread while it was yet day; but David sware, saying, God do so to me, and more also, if I taste bread, or aught else, till the sun be down. 36 And all the people took notice of it, and it pleased them; as whatsoever the king did pleased all the people. 37 So all the people and all Israel understood that day that it was not of the king to slay Abner the son of Ner. 38 And the king said unto his servants, Know ye not that there is a prince and a great man fallen this day in Israel? 39 And I am this day weak, though anointed king; and these men the sons of Zeruiah are too hard for me: Jehovah reward the evil-doer according to his wickedness.

The war between David and Ish-bosheth continued. While the house of Saul weakened during this period, the house of David grew stronger (cf. 3:1). **Abner made himself strong in the house of Saul** (v. 6). The authority and adequacy of Ish-bosheth's rule weakened, while Abner personally continued to benefit himself.

Finally, Abner was so bold in his arrogance that he violated the rights of the king and consorted with one of the royal concubines, Rizpah (v. 7). Ish-bosheth's objection was based on the inviolate rights of the king, but Abner deliberately misunderstood, claiming that his taking Rizpah momentarily was merely a trifling incident.

This incident provided Abner an excuse for transferring his loyalty from the house of Saul to the house of David (vv. 8-11). He sent messengers to David for the purpose of establishing friendly relations.

David welcomed the messengers and promised to make a league with Abner if Michal, whom Saul had betrothed to him, were restored to him. Saul had changed his plans and given her to Paltiel (cf. I Sam. 25:44). Abner forced her separation, and she was sent to David (vv. 15, 16).

Paltiel was innocently victimized by reason of political intrigue. David demanded Michal because this restored his relationship to the house of Saul and would place him in a very strong position as successor to Saul. Abner forcibly executed Michal's return to David in order that he might be in a strong political position in the league between the house of David and the house of Saul. He was Saul's cousin and may have aspired to become David's lieutenant. This would have provided a really explosive situation because Joab would have challenged Abner's bid for position in the new league.

However, Abner was unable to complete his league with David because of bold treachery on the part of Joab (v. 27). When David heard of the assassination of Abner he took strong measures to show the people of Israel that he regretted this deed and that he was not a party to it. His imprecation upon Joab and his lamentation for Abner reflect this (vv. 28, 29, 33, 34). **So all the people and all Israel understood that day that it was not of the king to slay Abner** (v. 37). David gave a generous tribute to Abner. **Know ye not that there is a prince and a great man fallen this day in Israel?** (v. 38). He also acknowledged a weakness in his control of Joab. **And I am this day weak, though anointed king; and these men of Zeruiah are too hard for me** (v. 39; cf. 2:18).

E. ISH-BOSHETH'S ASSASSINATION (4:1-12)

1 And when *Ish-bosheth*, Saul's son, heard that Abner was dead in Hebron, his hands became feeble, and all the Israelites were troubled. 2 And *Ish-bosheth*, Saul's son, had two men that were captains of bands: the name of the one was Baanah, and the name of the other Rechab, the sons of Rimmon the Beerothite, of the children of Benjamin (for Beeroth also is reckoned to Benjamin: 3 and the Beerothites fled to Gittaim, and have been sojourners there until this day).

4 Now Jonathan, Saul's son, had a son that was lame of his feet. He was five years old when the tidings came of Saul and Jonathan out of Jezreel; and his nurse took him up, and fled: and it came to pass, as she made haste to flee, that he fell, and became lame. And his name was Mephibosheth.

5 And the sons of Rimmon the Beerothite, Rechab and Baanah, went, and came about the heat of the day to the house of Ish-bosheth, as he took his rest at noon. 6 And they came thither into the midst of the house, as though they would have fetched wheat; and they smote him in the body: and Rechab and Baanah his brother escaped. 7 Now when they came into the house, as he lay on his bed in his bedchamber, they smote him, and slew him, and beheaded him, and took his head, and went by the way of the Arabah all night. 8 And they brought the head of Ish-bosheth unto David to Hebron, and said to the king, Behold, the head of Ish-bosheth, the son of Saul, thine enemy, who sought thy life; and Jehovah hath avenged my lord the king this day of Saul, and of his seed. 9 And David answered Rechab and Baanah his brother, the sons of Rimmon the Beerothite, and said unto them, As Jehovah liveth, who hath redeemed my soul out of all adversity, 10 when one told me, saying, Behold, Saul is dead, thinking to have brought good tidings, I took hold of him, and slew him in Ziklag, which was the reward I gave him for his tidings. 11 How much more, when wicked men have slain a righteous person in his own house upon his bed, shall I not now require his blood of your hand, and take you away from the earth? 12 And David commanded his young men, and they slew them, and cut off their hands and their feet, and hanged them up beside the pool in Hebron. But they took the head of Ish-bosheth, and buried it in the grave of Abner in Hebron.

Upon hearing of the death of Abner, Ish-bosheth and his supporters were fearful for their cause. This situation worsened when two of his captains plotted to kill Ish-bosheth. Being successful in their effort they came to tell David. In their story to David they affirmed, **Jehovah hath avenged my lord the king this day of Saul, and of his seed** (v. 8). They claimed that the deed committed against Ish-bosheth was an act of God. David powerfully rejected their claim which implied that everything that happens must be because God wills it. His own experience had included much adversity which was not because of God but because of jealous Saul (cf. v. 9). Moreover, when the Amalekite had come to David and reported what he claimed to have done to Saul, David utterly rejected him. Here again David was pronounced in his outlook on historical occurrences. He refused to believe that what had happened to Ish-bosheth was predetermined by God.

III. JERUSALEM, THE CITY OF DAVID (II Sam. 5:1-25)

The vicious circumstances which surrounded the deaths of Abner and Ish-bosheth ended the period of rivalry between the house of David and the house of Saul. The Philistines remained a constant threat to the welfare and security of Israel. Under these circumstances, representatives of the various tribes of Israel agreed upon David as their king.

A. DAVID, KING OF ALL ISRAEL (5:1-5; cf. I Chron. 11:1-3; 12:23-40)

1 Then came all the tribes of Israel to David unto Hebron, and spake, saying, Behold, we are thy bone and thy flesh. 2 In times past, when Saul was king over us, it was thou that leddest out and broughtest in Israel: and Jehovah said to thee, Thou shalt be shepherd of my people Israel, and thou shalt be prince over Israel. 3 So all the elders of Israel came to the king to Hebron; and king David made a covenant with them in Hebron before Jehovah: and they anointed David king over Israel. 4 David was thirty years old when he began to reign, and he reigned forty years. 5 In Hebron he reigned over Judah seven years and six months; and in Jerusalem he reigned thirty and three years over all Israel and Judah.

Representative elders from all the tribes came to David at Hebron. They were still convinced that the course they desired to pursue was that of a monarchy. Samuel's prophetic declarations earlier and Saul's disappointing reign of approximately forty years were not sufficient to deter them.

Lacking the leadership of a prophet, such as Samuel at the time of Saul's selection as king, the elders conferred with David. **Behold, we are thy bone and thy flesh** (v. 1). They acknowledged that the Lord was with him in order that he should be **prince over Israel** (v. 2).

David made a covenant with them . . . and they anointed David king over Israel (v. 3). The covenant relation which was established must have provided for

an equality among the tribes, Judah having no greater claim than the other tribes.

At last David had arrived at the kingship of Israel. Since a youth he had been selected as king. However, before the kingship was attained he had absorbed hard trials and violent reverses. Rather than attempting to force events to bring him to this high position, David had the capacity and insight to make the events steppingstones rather than stones of stumbling. He raised anxious questions concerning some situations, but he never lost his spiritual insight and the ability to capitalize on what life had thrust upon him.

David's life and thought during those years between the anointing by Samuel at Bethlehem and the anointing by the elders of Israel at Hebron provide a magnificent example of life at its finest. What happens to an individual is not so important as his reactions. The acts of history do not overrule the actions or reactions of a man; rather, they are the occasions that reveal the real man.

B. DAVID, CONQUEROR OF JERUSALEM (5:6-16; cf. I Chron. 11:4-9)

6 And the king and his men went to Jerusalem against the Jebusites, the inhabitants of the land, who spake unto David, saying, Except thou take away the blind and the lame, thou shalt not come in hither; thinking, David cannot come in hither. 7 Nevertheless David took the stronghold of Zion; the same is the city of David. 8 And David said on that day, Whosoever smiteth the Jebusites, let him get up to the watercourse, and *smite* the lame and the blind, that are hated of David's soul. Wherefore they say, There are the blind and the lame; he cannot come into the house. 9 And David dwelt in the stronghold, and called it the city of David. And David built round about from Millo and inward. 10 And David waxed greater and greater; for Jehovah, the God of hosts, was with him.

11 And Hiram king of Tyre sent messengers to David, and cedar-trees, and carpenters, and masons; and they built David a house. 12 And David perceived that Jehovah had established him king over Israel, and that he had exalted his kingdom for his people Israel's sake.

13 And David took him more concubines and wives out of Jerusalem, after he was come from Hebron; and there were yet sons and daughters born to David. 14 And these are the names of those that were born unto him in Jerusalem: Shammua, and Shobab, and Nathan, and Solomon, 15 and Ibhar, and Elishua, and Nepheg, and Japhia, 16 and Elishama, and Eliada, and Eliphelet.

Jerusalem was the ancient capital of the Jebusites, who had withstood all attempts of the Israelites to occupy their city. Even in the time of David, approximately three centuries since the days of Joshua and Jerusalem, Jerusalem still defied occupation by Israel.

When David became king of all Israel he was faced with the problem of securing a capital that would serve the nation. Hebron had served well as the capital city for Judah, but it was not ideally located for a national capital.

David decided to seize Jerusalem. It was a neutral city as far as Israel's history was concerned. It was also a border city between Judah to the south and Benjamin to the north. The recent rivalry for the throne had occurred between David of Judah and Ish-bosheth of Benjamin. For David to seek a city on the border of Judah and Benjamin was a strong move for unity and harmony. Likewise, it appealed to all the tribes to the north. "The narrative represents the capture of Jerusalem as the first act of David's reign."[17]

When David and his army approached the city they were taunted by the Jebusites, **Except thou take away the blind and the lame, thou shalt not come in hither** (v. 6). Nevertheless, through a remarkable feat of heroism, David captured the city. His strategy was to enter the city by **the watercourse** (v. 8). Archaeology gives evidence of a water tunnel from the Gihon spring.[18]

Jerusalem was renamed **the city of David** (v. 9). Since David's personal army had captured it, Jerusalem became his personal possession. This was a significant conquest before all Israel. Doubtless it greatly enhanced David's authority and prestige.

C. DAVID, VICTOR OVER PHILISTIA (5:17-25; cf. I Chron. 14:8-17)

17 And when the Philistines heard that they had anointed David king over Israel, all the Philistines went up to seek David; and David heard of it, and went down to the stronghold. 18 Now the Philistines had come and spread themselves in the valley of Rephaim. 19 And David inquired of Jehovah, saying, Shall I go up against the Philistines? wilt thou deliver them into my hand? And Jehovah said unto David, Go up; for I will certainly deliver the Philistines into thy hand. 20 And David came to Baal-perazim, and David smote them there; and he said, Jehovah hath broken mine enemies before me, like the breach of waters. Therefore he called the name of that place Baal-perazim. 21 And they left their images there; and David and his men took them away.

22 And the Philistines came up yet again, and spread themselves in the valley of Rephaim. 23 And when David inquired of Jehovah, he said, Thou shalt not go up: make a circuit behind them, and come upon them over against the mulberry-trees. 24 And it shall be, when thou hearest the sound of marching in the tops of the mulberry-trees, that then thou shalt bestir thyself; for then is Jehovah gone out before thee to smite the host of the Philistines. 25 And David did so, as Jehovah commanded him, and smote the Philistines from Geba until thou come to Gezer.

When the Philistines heard that Israel was reunited and that David was king, they proceeded to take action lest David strengthen Israel sufficiently to break the power of Philistia over Israel. David heard that their army was near Jerusalem and he **inquired of Jehovah, saying, Shall I go up against the Philistines?** (v. 19). The answer of the Lord was, **Go up; for I will certainly deliver the Philistines into thy hand** (v. 19).

Again the Philistines returned to engage in battle with David. When David inquired of the Lord for guidance he was instructed to come up from the rear and wait near some mulberry trees (v. 23). When there came **the sound of marching in the tops of the mulberry-trees** David

[17] Caird, op. cit., II, 1069.
[18] S. R. Driver, Notes on the Hebrew Text and the Topography of the Books of Samuel, 2nd ed., p. 260.

was to attack (v. 24). The result was a stunning defeat for the Philistines.

Over and over again in the ongoing of God's work there has been the sound, or evidence, of God already having gone forth. In the moment of faith, as the sound of marching was heard, there have been those valiant ones who were alert and sensitive to the signs and wrought great exploits. When God has gone forth and there is the sound of marching, no one has any more important obligation than to bestir himself.

IV. THE ARK OF GOD MOVED TO JERUSALEM (II Sam. 6:1-23)

The ark of God had remained neglected for many years. Since that tragic day when Israel lost the ark in the battle against the Philistines, it had been housed in a temporary shelter at Kiriath-jearim under the care of Eleazar (cf. I Sam. 7:1, 2). David, however, aimed to make Jerusalem not only the political but also the religious center of the nation.

A. DAVID'S ACTIVITY (6:1-15; cf. I Chron. 13:1-14; 15:1—16:43)

1 And David again gathered together all the chosen men of Israel, thirty thousand. 2 And David arose, and went with all the people that were with him, from Baale-Judah, to bring up from thence the ark of God, which is called by the Name, even the name of Jehovah of hosts that sitteth *above* the cherubim. 3 And they set the ark of God upon a new cart, and brought it out of the house of Abinadab that was in the hill: and Uzzah and Ahio, the sons of Abinadab, drove the new cart. 4 And they brought it out of the house of Abinadab, which was in the hill, with the ark of God: and Ahio went before the ark. 5 And David and all the house of Israel played before Jehovah with all manner of *instruments made of* firwood, and with harps, and with psalteries, and with timbrels, and with castanets, and with cymbals.

6 And when they came to the threshing-floor of Nacon, Uzzah put forth *his hand* to the ark of God, and took hold of it; for the oxen stumbled. 7 And the anger of Jehovah was kindled against Uzzah; and God smote him there for his error; and there he died by the ark of God. 8 And David was displeased, because Jehovah had broken forth upon Uzzah; and he called that place Perezuzzah, unto this day. 9 And David was afraid of Jehovah that day; and he said, How shall the ark of Jehovah come unto me? 10 So David would not remove the ark of Jehovah unto him into the city of David; but David carried it aside into the house of Obed-edom the Gittite. 11 And the ark of Jehovah remained in the house of Obed-edom the Gittite three months: and Jehovah blessed Obed-edom, and all his house.

12 And it was told king David, saying, Jehovah hath blessed the house of Obed-edom and all that pertaineth unto him, because of the ark of God. And David went and brought up the ark of God from the house of Obed-edom into the city of David with joy. 13 And it was so, that, when they that bare the ark of Jehovah had gone six paces, he sacrificed an ox and a fatling. 14 And David danced before Jehovah with all his might; and David was girded with a linen ephod. 15 So David and all the house of Israel brought up the ark of Jehovah with shouting, and with the sound of the trumpet.

And David arose . . . to bring up the ark of God, which is called by . . . the name of Jehovah of hosts that sitteth above the cherubim (v. 2). As the ark was placed upon a new cart for removal to Jerusalem, David and the people with him joined in a procession. There was music and ritual for the occasion.

In the course of the procession, Uzzah, son of Abinadab, who had provided shelter for the ark at his home at Kiriath-jearim, touched the ark on one occasion when the oxen were difficult to control (v. 6). As a result, he died because of **the anger of Jehovah** (v. 7).

In reading the account of Uzzah's death, some are inclined to judge the incident upon the basis of their subjective reactions. They express surprise that such an irrevocable judgment as death should befall one who had committed a seemingly innocent deed based upon the honorable motive of trying to avoid an accident. It is preferable to judge the incident in the light of David's reactions rather than our own. **David was displeased. . . . And David was afraid of Jehovah that day** (vv. 8, 9). The apparent reactions were mingled. David was provoked because his great undertaking of bringing the ark to Jerusalem was interrupted. He was fearful because he did not know how to complete his effort. How shall the ark of Jehovah come unto me? (v. 9).

Whether it is acceptable to us or not, David's reactions seem little concerned about Uzzah, but greatly interested in getting on with the activity at hand. Uzzah's death was incidental to the more important matter of completing an effort which involved the interest of all Israel and which identified the newly created monarchy as preserver of Israel's religious institutions. In this David was far wiser than Saul, who neglected the ark and drove the priests fom him.

Since the house of Obed-edom prospered, it appears that the anger of the Lord had passed. A renewed effort was launched. And it was so, that when they that bare the ark of Jehovah had gone six paces, he sacrificed an ox and a fatling (v. 13). The distance of six paces indicated a test as to whether the Lord was willing for the procession to continue. Amid considerable acclaim and shouting, the ark was carried up to Jerusalem (v. 15).

B. MICHAL OFFENDED (6:16-23; cf. I Chron. 15:29)

16 And it was so, as the ark of Jehovah came into the city of David, that Michal the daughter of Saul looked out at the window, and saw king David leaping and dancing before Jehovah; and she despised him in her heart. 17 And they brought in the ark of Jehovah, and set it in its place, in the midst of the tent that David had pitched for it; and David offered burnt-offerings and peace-offerings before Jehovah. 18 And when David had made an end of offering the burnt-offering and the peace-offerings, he blessed the people in the name of Jehovah of hosts. 19 And he dealt among all the people, even among the whole multitude of Israel, both to men and women, to every one a cake of bread, and a portion of flesh, and a cake of raisins. So all the people departed every one to his house.

20 Then David returned to bless his household. And Michal the daughter of Saul came out to meet David, and said, How glorious was the king of Israel to-day, who uncovered himself to-day in the eyes of the handmaids of his servants, as one of the vain fellows shamelessly uncovereth himself! 21 And David said unto Michal, It was before Jehovah, who chose me above thy father, and above all his house, to appoint me prince over the people of Jehovah, over Israel: therefore will I play before Jehovah. 22 And I will be yet more vile than this, and will be base in mine own sight: but of the handmaids of whom thou hast spoken, of them shall I be had in honor. 23 And Michal the daughter of Saul had no child unto the day of her death.

The daughter whom Saul had given to David as his wife seems to have had the same inclinations as her father toward the ark and its honor. She was offended because David danced naked before the ark. To her, David had behaved himself as a perverted exhibitionist in the presence of innocent girls. David's reply was that his nakedness was before Jehovah and his conduct before the maidens was such as to enhance his person in their eyes (v. 22). To our sensitiveness, David's reply seems inappropriate.

V. THE DESTINY OF DAVID'S DYNASTY (II Sam. 7:1-29)

This chapter is largely concerned with a message from the Lord to David as given through the prophet Nathan. David's response to the prophecy was a prayer of humble thanksgiving.

A. THE PROPHECY OF NATHAN (7:1-17; cf. I Chron. 17:1-15)

1 And it came to pass, when the king dwelt in his house, and Jehovah had given him rest from all his enemies round about, 2 that the king said unto Nathan the prophet, See now, I dwell in a house of cedar, but the ark of God dwelleth within curtains. 3 And Nathan said to the king, Go, do all that is in thy heart; for Jehovah is with thee. 4 And it came to pass the same night, that the word of Jehovah came unto Nathan, saying, 5 Go and tell my servant David, Thus saith Jehovah, Shalt thou build me a house for me to dwell in? 6 for I have not dwelt in a house since the day that I brought up the children of Israel out of Egypt, even to this day, but have walked in a tent and in a tabernacle. 7 In all places wherein I have walked with all the children of Israel, spake I a word with any of the tribes of Israel, whom I commanded to be shepherd of my people Israel, saying, Why have ye not built me a house of cedar? 8 Now therefore thus shalt thou

say unto my servant David, Thus saith Jehovah of hosts, I took thee from the sheepcote, from following the sheep, that thou shouldest be prince over my people, over Israel; 9 and I have been with thee whithersoever thou wentest, and have cut off all thine enemies from before thee; and I will make thee a great name, like unto the name of the great ones that are in the earth. 10 And I will appoint a place for my people Israel, and will plant them, that they may dwell in their own place, and be moved no more; neither shall the children of wickedness afflict them any more, as at the first, 11 and *as* from the day that I commanded judges to be over my people Israel; and I will cause thee to rest from all thine enemies. Moreover Jehovah telleth thee that Jehovah will make thee a house. 12 When thy days are fulfilled, and thou shalt sleep with thy fathers, I will set up thy seed after thee, that shall proceed out of thy bowels, and I will establish his kingdom. 13 He shall build a house for my name, and I will establish the throne of his kingdom for ever. 14 I will be his father, and he shall be my son: if he commit iniquity, I will chasten him with the rod of men, and with the stripes of the children of men; 15 but my lovingkindness shall not depart from him, as I took it from Saul, whom I put away before thee. 16 And thy house and thy kingdom shall be made sure for ever before thee: thy throne shall be established for ever. 17 According to all these words, and according to all this vision, so did Nathan speak unto David.

When first mentioned in the history of Israel Nathan was already David's most important spiritual counsellor. Although nothing is recorded concerning the activities of Nathan prior to this incident, in all probability he had risen to his present position by reason of his outstanding service as a prophet.

David confided to Nathan that it appeared necessary to build a house for the ark of God. Jerusalem had become the political as well as the religious center of Israel. David himself dwelt in a regal residence of cedar, but the ark of God had no such royal building.

Nathan gave to David an important message concerning the building of this house. The essential point of the message was: it was not David who was to build a

house, that is, a temple for the ark of God, but Jehovah who was to build a house, that is, a dynasty for David (cf. II Sam. 7:5, 11).[19]

Nathan reminded David of what the God of Israel had done for His people as well as for David. Furthermore, God purposed to continue His work. **I will appoint a place for my people Israel . . . that they may dwell in their own place. . . . Moreover Jehovah telleth thee that Jehovah will make thee a house** (vv. 10, 11).

David was moved to build a temple when he observed the great contrast between his own sturdy house of cedar and the inadequate housing for the ark of God. It seemed important to him that the ark should have much better housing. May there not be a lesson here for those who live in luxurious modern homes while they worship in dilapidated and antiquated churches? Should the house of the worshiper be better than that of the One worshiped?

However, the prophet of the Lord declared that it was not David who would build a house for Jehovah, but it was Jehovah who would build a house for David. Here is a perennially relevant truth, that God deigns to dwell in temples consisting of human lives fulfilling divine purposes, rather than lavish temples made with human hands.

Here is the distinctive contrast between the worship of the Lord of history who chose Israel as His people and David as their king and the worship of the gods of nature so revered by the Canaanites. This is not to imply that the Lord of all is divorced from nature, for He is Creator of nature. Yet, it is to affirm that the redemptive purpose of God is oriented not so much in nature as in history. Consequently, God has purposed to dwell in Israel, a people called to covenant relation with Him. He also purposed to establish the dynasty of David forever.

The expectation of David's everlasting kingdom contributed extensively to the Messianic hope. Even after the downfall of David's kingdom many Jews centered their hopes on the coming of David's greater Son. New Testament writers were convinced that Jesus Christ was the

---

[19] Kennedy, *op. cit.*, p. 223.

fulfillment of the Messianic hope (cf. Luke 1:31-33; Acts 2:29-31; 12:22, 23; Heb. 1:5).

B. THE PRAYER OF DAVID (7:18-29; cf. I Chron. 17:16-27)

18 Then David the king went in, and sat before Jehovah; and he said, Who am I, O Lord Jehovah, and what is my house, that thou hast brought me thus far? 19 And this was yet a small thing in thine eyes, O Lord Jehovah; but thou hast spoken also of thy servant's house for a great while to come; and this *too* after the manner of men, O Lord Jehovah! 20 And what can David say more unto thee? for thou knowest thy servant, O Lord Jehovah. 21 For thy word's sake, and according to thine own heart, hast thou wrought all this greatness, to make thy servant know it. 22 Wherefore thou art great, O Jehovah God: for there is none like thee, neither is there any God besides thee, according to all that we have heard with our ears. 23 And what one nation in the earth is like thy people, even like Israel, whom God went to redeem unto himself for a people, and to make him a name, and to do great things for you, and terrible things for thy land, before thy people, whom thou redeemedst to thee out of Egypt, *from* the nations and their gods? 24 And thou didst establish to thyself thy people Israel to be a people unto thee for ever; and thou, Jehovah, becamest their God. 25 And now, O Jehovah God, the word that thou hast spoken concerning thy servant, and concerning his house, confirm thou it for ever, and do as thou hast spoken. 26 And let thy name be magnified for ever, saying, Jehovah of hosts is God over Israel; and the house of thy servant David shall be established before thee. 27 For thou, O Jehovah of hosts, the God of Israel, hast revealed to thy servant, saying, I will build thee a house: therefore hath thy servant found in his heart to pray this prayer unto thee. 28 And now, O Lord Jehovah, thou art God, and thy words are truth, and thou hast promised this good thing unto thy servant: 29 now therefore let it please thee to bless the house of thy servant, that it may continue for ever before thee; for thou, O Lord Jehovah, hast spoken it: and with thy blessing let the house of thy servant be blessed for ever.

David's prayer expressed a sense of wonder and awe. He was astonished that God should establish his dynasty on the throne of Israel. **Who am I, O Lord Jehovah, and what is my house, that thou hast brought me thus far?** (v. 18).

Out of his sense of awe David expressed great respect for the ways of God. **For thy word's sake, and according to thine own heart, hast thou wrought all this greatness, to make thy servant know it** (v. 21).

David was acutely aware of the activity of the Almighty. As he reflected upon Israel's history and upon his own powerful position, he acknowledged that the Lord had accomplished these remarkable achievements. **Wherefore thou art great, O Jehovah God: for there is none like thee** (v. 22).

Fully aware of the activity of deity, not only in Israel's history but also in his own personal life, David petitioned the Lord to fulfill His promise regarding the establishment of the dynasty of David (v. 25).

From a sense of overwhelming awe at the presence of the word of the Lord, David was moved to a profound faith in that word. What Jehovah had declared, David believed would be fulfilled. **And now, O Lord Jehovah . . . thy words are truth, . . . let it please thee to bless the house of thy servant, that it may continue for ever before thee; for thou, O Lord Jehovah, hast spoken it** (vv. 28, 29).

While David gave full acknowledgment to the sovereignty of God's word, he was also aware of his own responsibility concerning the fulfillment of the divine promise. It is impossible to impose a determinism upon David in the light of his prayer offered in a spirit of mingled surprise and trust. He willingly and gratefully responded to the divine word in order that he might share in the promise.

VI. RÉSUMÉ OF DAVID'S REIGN (II Sam. 8:1-18)

The sacred historian gives an extremely concise résumé of David's military and political accomplishments. In the light of the divine promise given in the preceding chapter, the achievements of David are given with a definite reserve and brevity that highlights the divine activity in behalf of the dynasty of David.

A. MILITARY (8:1-14; cf. I Chron. 18: 1-13)

1 And after this it came to pass, that David smote the Philistines, and subdued them: and David took the bridle of the mother city out of the hand of the Philistines.

2 And he smote Moab, and measured them with the line, making them to lie down on the ground; and he measured two lines to put to death, and one full line to keep alive. And the Moabites became servants to David, and brought tribute.

3 David smote also Hadadezer the son of Rehob, king of Zobah, as he went to recover his dominion at the River. 4 And David took from him a thousand and seven hundred horsemen, and twenty thousand footmen: and David hocked all the chariot horses, but reserved of them for a hundred chariots. 5 And when the Syrians of Damascus came to succor Hadadezer king of Zobah, David smote of the Syrians two and twenty thousand men. 6 Then David put garrisons in Syria of Damascus; and the Syrians became servants to David, and brought tribute. And Jehovah gave victory to David whithersoever he went. 7 And David took the shields of gold that were on the servants of Hadadezer, and brought them to Jerusalem. 8 And from Betah and from Berothai, cities of Hadadezer, king David took exceeding much brass.

9 And when Toi king of Hamath heard that David had smitten all the host of Hadadezer, 10 then Toi sent Joram his son unto king David, to salute him, and to bless him, because he had fought against Hadadezer and smitten him: for Hadadezer had wars with Toi. And *Joram* brought with him vessels of silver, and vessels of gold, and vessels of brass: 11 these also did king David dedicate unto Jehovah, with the silver and gold that he dedicated of all the nations which he subdued; 12 of Syria, and of Moab, and of the children of Ammon, and of the Philistines, and of Amalek, and of the spoil of Hadadezer, son of Rehob, king of Zobah.

13 And David gat him a name when he returned from smiting the Syrians in the Valley of Salt, even eighteen thousand men. 14 And he put garrisons in Edom; throughout all Edom put he garrisons, and all the Edomites became servants to David. And Jehovah gave victory to David whithersoever he went.

Although this account of David's wars is only in summary form, it reveals remarkable military successes against other nations. It may well be that before David launched any significant foreign war he embarked upon the conquest of unconquered territories within his kingdom. For this reason David's initial military efforts were against the Philistines (v. 1).

Since the Philistines controlled large portions of Canaan, David's conquest caused many of the territories aligned with the Philistines to transfer their allegiance to him. The conquest of the Philistines, therefore, not only removed the constant threat posed by this warring nation, but it also consolidated and unified the kingdom under David to a degree far surpassing that achieved by Saul.

For unknown reasons, David's campaign against Moab was accompanied by terrible punishment. Two-thirds of the prisoners were put to death (v. 2). This was a sharp turn in the relationships between David and the Moabites which had existed when he was a fugitive from Saul (I Sam. 22:3, 4). David's conquest of Moab was sufficient to keep that country subject to Israel for the next century and a half.

David's battle against Hadadezer, king of Zobah, evidently was but an incident in what was really a great war against the Ammonites and their allies. The circumstances of this war are described in II Samuel 10:6-19, but the battle with Hadadezer is mentioned in this section (vv. 3-5).

Other nations were conquered. A summary listing of all of the nations includes Philistia, Moab, Syria, Ammon, Zobah, Amalek and Edom (vv. 12-14). With dramatic suddenness these achievements skyrocketed Israel into being the foremost nation in that part of the world.

This brought about a sweeping change from the former tribal league that had made David king. A complex empire had come into being, with the tribes of Israel comprising the lesser part of it. The center of this new power was not to be found in the tribes of Israel but in David himself.

The capital city, Jerusalem, was David's personal possession as a result of its conquest by David's personal army. The subjugated nations were subject to David and administered by him. There developed a phenomenal centralization of power in all of these developments. David's remarkable expansion of the kingdom was possible because the Lord gave victory to David whithersoever he went (v. 14).

B. POLITICAL (8:15-18; cf. I Chron. 18: 14-17)

15 And David reigned over all Israel; and David executed justice and righteousness unto all his people. 16 And Joab the son of Zeruiah was over the host; and Jehoshaphat the son of Ahilud was recorder; 17 and Zadok the son of Ahitub, and Ahimelech the son of Abiathar, were priests; and Seraiah was scribe; 18 and Benaiah the son of Jehoiada *was over* the Cherethites and the Pelethites; and David's sons were chief ministers.

David's new empire required administration. Except for two lists of administrative officers not much is known about his organizational set-up (cf. II Sam. 8:15-18; 20:23-26). "Lacking native precedent, David patterned his bureaucracy, at least in part, on Egyptian models."[20] Regardless of whether or not we know the structure of David's administration, we are told that David executed justice and righteousness unto all his people (v. 15).

VII. DAVID'S KINDNESS (II Sam. 9:1-13)

David had reached the zenith of his power and proceeded to arrange an incredible kindness.

A. REASON FOR THE KINDNESS (9: 1-8)

1 And David said, Is there yet any that is left of the house of Saul, that I may show him kindness for Jonathan's sake? 2 And there was of the house of Saul a servant whose name was Ziba, and they called him unto David; and the king said unto him, Art thou Ziba? And he said, Thy servant is he. 3 And the king said, Is there not yet any of the house of Saul, that I may show the kindness of God unto him? And Ziba said unto the king, Jonathan hath yet a son, who is lame of his feet. 4 And the king said unto him, Where is he? And Ziba said unto the king, Behold, he is in the house of Machir the son of Ammiel, in Lo-debar. 5 Then king David sent, and fetched him

out of the house of Machir the son of Ammiel, from Lo-debar. 6 And Mephibosheth, the son of Jonathan, the son of Saul, came unto David, and fell on his face, and did obeisance. And David said, Mephibosheth. And he answered, Behold, thy servant! 7 And David said unto him, Fear not; for I will surely show thee kindness for Jonathan thy father's sake, and will restore thee all the land of Saul thy father; and thou shalt eat bread at my table continually. 8 And he did obeisance, and said, What is thy servant, that thou shouldest look upon such a dead dog as I am?

It was customary among the nations in and around Palestine for the dynasty in power to destroy all members of the previous dynasty.[21] If David were inclined to follow the accepted custom, the dynasty of Saul was in peril. Yet the powerful monarch had not desired to follow custom. Instead, he desired to show kindness to the previous dynasty. Is there yet any that is left of the house of Saul, that I may show him kindness for Jonathan's sake? (v. 1).

The reason given for this desire to show kindness was twofold: because of Jonathan and because of the kindness of God (v. 3). Not only was David aware of his obligation to Jonathan, recorded in I Samuel 20:14-16, but also he was eager to share the love and mercy of God with any of the former dynasty.

David's kindness far transcended the accepted custom among kings. It was patterned according to the lovingkindness of the Lord which had been shown toward David.

Realization of that love transforms customary relationships. Just as the love of God worked marvelously to change the relation between the dynasty of David and that of Saul, so also it works the same in any relationship where people seek to share it.

B. RECITAL OF THE KINDNESS (9: 9-13)

9 Then the king called to Ziba, Saul's servant, and said unto him, All that pertained to Saul and to all his house have I given unto thy master's son. 10 And thou shalt till the land for him, thou, and thy sons, and thy servants; and thou shalt

[20] Bright, *op. cit.*, p. 184.   [21] Caird, *op. cit.*, p. 1093.

bring in *the fruits,* that thy master's son may have bread to eat: but Mephibosheth thy master's son shall eat bread alway at my table. Now Ziba had fifteen sons and twenty servants. 11 Then said Ziba unto the king, According to all that my lord the king commandeth his servant, so shall thy servant do. As for Mephibosheth, *said the king,* he shall eat at my table, as one of the king's sons. 12 And Mephibosheth had a young son, whose name was Mica. And all that dwelt in the house of Ziba were servants unto Mephibosheth. 13 So Mephibosheth dwelt in Jerusalem; for he did eat continually at the king's table. And he was lame in both his feet.

When told of lame Mephibosheth, David had him brought into his presence and arranged for "the kindness of God" to be implemented in specific ways. One of Saul's faithful servants, Ziba, was given the task of caring for Mephibosheth (v. 9).

As custodian of the inheritance of Saul, Ziba was commissioned, along with his family, to cultivate the land. Income from this source would enable Mephibosheth to afford his own home in Jerusalem. Furthermore, David extended to Mephibosheth the signal honor of eating at the royal table (v. 11). This was outstanding protection, for anyone who ate at the king's table was in comfortable security. David's own experience with Saul enabled him to understand how much this would mean to Mephibosheth. Experience always makes possible a truer understanding of the other person.

VIII. WAR AGAINST AMMON (II Sam. 10:1—12:31)

The war against Ammon was one of David's great wars. It began because of an ignominious insult on the part of Ammon and it set the stage for David's disgraceful affair with Bathsheba.

A. INSULT TO DAVID (10:1-5; cf. I Chron. 19:1-5)

1 And it came to pass after this, that the king of the children of Ammon died, and Hanun his son reigned in his stead. 2 And David said, I will show kindness unto Hanun the son of Nahash, as his father showed kindness unto me. So David sent by his servants to comfort him

concerning his father. And David's servants came into the land of the children of Ammon. 3 But the princes of the children of Ammon said unto Hanun their lord, Thinkest thou that David doth honor thy father, in that he hath sent comforters unto thee? hath not David sent his servants unto thee to search the city, and to spy it out, and to overthrow it? 4 So Hanun took David's servants, and shaved off the one half of their beards, and cut off their garments in the middle, even to their buttocks, and sent them away. 5 When they told it unto David, he sent to meet them; for the men were greatly ashamed. And the king said, Tarry at Jericho until your beards be grown, and then return.

A strong, friendly relationship had existed between David and Nahash, king of Ammon. The use of the important word, **kindness,** indicates they were bound together by some significant agreement or treaty (v. 2).

Upon hearing of the death of the king of Ammon, David sent emissaries with condolences to the new king, Hanun, son of Nahash. The emissaries were taken for spies and treated shamefully. The Ammonites were treacherous and cruel themselves. It was a simple matter to project their own character upon David. They were aware of his remarkable exploits in building the kingdom of Israel, and they were concerned about preserving their own nation against any wily trick on the part of David.

Their misunderstanding of David's motive for sending men to Ammon prompted the Ammonites to seize the Israelites. This mishandling of inviolate representatives of the strong royal dynasty of Israel so angered David that he prepared for war against Ammon.

What may be a wonderful relationship between people can evaporate when good motives are misinterpreted. Suspicious people often err in this. While caution is always in order, suspicion which emerges out of an evil heart is never in order, for it invariably leads to ruptured friendships.

B. FIRST CAMPAIGN (10:6-19; cf. I Chron. 19:6-19)

6 And when the children of Ammon saw that they were become odious to David, the children of Ammon sent and

hired the Syrians of Beth-rehob, and the Syrians of Zobah, twenty thousand footmen, and the king of Maacah with a thousand men, and the men of Tob twelve thousand men. 7 And when David heard of it, he sent Joab, and all the host of the mighty men. 8 And the children of Ammon came out, and put the battle in array at the entrance of the gate: and the Syrians of Zobah and of Rehob, and the men of Tob and Maacah, were by themselves in the field.

9 Now when Joab saw that the battle was set against him before and behind, he chose of all the choice men of Israel, and put them in array against the Syrians: 10 and the rest of the people he committed into the hand of Abishai his brother; and he put them in array against the children of Ammon. 11 And he said, If the Syrians be too strong for me, then thou shalt help me; but if the children of Ammon be too strong for thee, then I will come and help thee. 12 Be of good courage, and let us play the man for our people, and for the cities of our God: and Jehovah do that which seemeth him good. 13 So Joab and the people that were with him drew nigh unto the battle against the Syrians: and they fled before him. 14 And when the children of Ammon saw that the Syrians were fled, they likewise fled before Abishai, and entered into the city. Then Joab returned from the children of Ammon, and came to Jerusalem.

15 And when the Syrians saw that they were put to the worse before Israel, they gathered themselves together. 16 And Hadarezer sent, and brought out the Syrians that were beyond the River: and they came to Helam, with Shobach the captain of the host of Hadarezer at their head. 17 And it was told David; and he gathered all Israel together, and passed over the Jordan, and came to Helam. And the Syrians set themselves in array against David, and fought with him. 18 And the Syrians fled before Israel; and David slew of the Syrians *the men of* seven hundred chariots, and forty thousand horsemen, and smote Shobach the captain of their host, so that he died there. 19 And when all the kings that were servants to Hadarezer saw that they were put to the worse before Israel, they made peace with Israel, and served them. So the Syrians feared to help the children of Ammon any more.

When the Ammonites realized that their mistreatment of David's representatives had precipitated a state of war between Israel and Ammon, they sought aid from the Syrians located to the north of them. Meanwhile, David sent his army under Joab's command against the Ammonite capital, Rabbah.

The Syrians came upon the Israelites near Rabbah (v. 14). Joab deployed part of his army under the command of Abishai, his brother, against the Ammonites who came out of Rabbah, while he took the rest of the army to attack the Syrians in the field.

There was an implicit resignation to the will of the Lord in Joab's words to Abishai as the two commanders prepared for battle. **Be of good courage, and let us play the man for our people, and for the cities of our God: and Jehovah do that which seemeth him good** (v. 12).

Joab and his men attacked the Syrians first and they retreated. The Ammonites then retired to the safety of their city walls. The Syrians were sent re-enforcements, but David moved to intercept the fresh troops. The ensuing battle resulted in an important victory for David while the Syrian commander met his death (v. 18). As a result, the Syrians withdrew their help from Ammon. **So the Syrians feared to help the children of Ammon any more** (v. 19).

The second campaign included a prolonged siege of Rabbah, the capital of Ammon, and its ultimate occupation. Meanwhile in Jerusalem there occurred the affair between David and Bathsheba.

C. SECOND CAMPAIGN (11:1–12:31)

1. Siege of Rabbah (11:1; cf. I Chron. 20:1)

1 And it came to pass, at the return of the year, at the time when kings go out *to battle,* that David sent Joab, and his servants with him, and all Israel; and they destroyed the children of Ammon, and besieged Rabbah. But David tarried at Jerusalem.

The following spring siege operations were resumed at Rabbah. This marked the opening of the second campaign against Ammon. David sent Joab to Rabbah, located about twenty miles east of the Jordan, while he remained at Jerusalem. It is misleading to insist that David remained in Jerusalem to enjoy idleness and as a consequence was tempted to desire Bathsheba. This misses the point and ignores the larger perspective of David's career. The only reason we are told that David remained at Jerusalem is that it is essential to the incident which follows.

2. David's Sin (11:2-27)

2 And it came to pass at eventide, that David arose from off his bed, and walked upon the roof of the king's house: and from the roof he saw a woman bathing; and the woman was very beautiful to look upon. 3 And David sent and inquired after the woman. And one said, Is not this Bath-sheba, the daughter of Eliam, the wife of Uriah the Hittite? 4 And David sent messengers, and took her; and she came in unto him, and he lay with her (for she was purified from her uncleanness) ; and she returned unto her house. 5 And the woman conceived; and she sent and told David, and said, I am with child.

6 And David sent to Joab, *saying*, Send me Uriah the Hittite. And Joab sent Uriah to David. 7 And when Uriah was come unto him, David asked of him how Joab did, and how the people fared, and how the war prospered. 8 And David said to Uriah, Go down to thy house, and wash thy feet. And Uriah departed out of the king's house, and there followed him a mess *of food* from the king. 9 But Uriah slept at the door of the king's house with all the servants of his lord, and went not down to his house. 10 And when they had told David, saying, Uriah went not down unto his house, David said unto Uriah, Art thou not come from a journey? wherefore didst thou not go down unto thy house? 11 And Uriah said unto David, The ark, and Israel, and Judah, abide in booths; and my lord Joab, and the servants of my lord, are encamped in the open field; shall I then go into my house, to eat and to drink, and to lie with my wife? as thou livest, and as thy soul liveth, I will not do this thing. 12 And David said to Uriah, Tarry here to-day also, and to-morrow I will let thee depart. So Uriah abode in Jerusalem that day, and the morrow. 13 And when David had called him, he did eat and drink before him; and he made him drunk: and at even he went out to lie on his bed with the servants of his lord, but went not down to his house.

14 And it came to pass in the morning, that David wrote a letter to Joab, and sent it by the hand of Uriah. 15 And he wrote in the letter, saying, Set ye Uriah in the forefront of the hottest battle, and retire ye from him, that he may be smitten, and die. 16 And it came to pass, when Joab kept watch upon the city, that he assigned Uriah unto the place where he knew that valiant men were. 17 And the men of the city went out, and fought with Joab: and there fell some of the people, even of the servants of David; and Uriah the Hittite died also. 18 Then Joab sent and told David all the things concerning the war; 19 and he charged the messenger, saying, When thou hast made an end of telling all the things concerning the war unto the king, 20 it shall be that, if the king's wrath arise, and he say unto thee, Wherefore went ye so nigh unto the city to fight? knew ye not that they would shoot from the wall? 21 Who smote Abimelech the son of Jerubbesheth? did not a woman cast an upper millstone upon him from the wall, so that he died at Thebez? why went ye so nigh the wall? then shalt thou say, Thy servant Uriah the Hittite is dead also.

22 So the messenger went, and came and showed David all that Joab had sent him for. 23 And the messenger said unto David, The men prevailed against us, and came out unto us into the field, and we were upon them even unto the entrance of the gate. 24 And the shooters shot at thy servants from off the wall; and some of the king's servants are dead, and thy servant Uriah the Hittite is dead also. 25 Then David said unto the messenger, Thus shalt thou say unto Joab, Let not this thing displease thee, for the sword devoureth one as well as another; make thy battle more strong against the city, and overthrow it: and encourage thou him.

26 And when the wife of Uriah heard that Uriah her husband was dead, she made lamentation for her husband. 27 And when the mourning was past, David sent and took her home to his house, and she became his wife, and bare him a son. But the thing that David had done displeased Jehovah.

David had reached unprecedented heights in his drive to build and enlarge the kingdom. His unbroken series of conquests had carried him to the place of absolute and unquestioned power. What could be denied one whose successes had been so outstanding? What could be unlawful for so favored a ruler? The moment of greatest self-security may become one's moment of greatest insecurity.

It must have been in this frame of

mind and disposition that **David arose from off his bed, and walked upon the roof of the king's house** (v. 2). For as he looked from the roof-top **he saw a woman bathing** (v. 2). He desired this beautiful woman and, summoning her to the palace, he committed the sin of adultery with her. This was a violation of the seventh commandment and was a crime punishable by death (cf. Exod. 20:14; Lev. 20:10).

The woman was Bathsheba, the daughter of Eliam and the wife of Uriah. Both men were among the select of David's mighty men (23:34, 39). Eliam was the son of Ahithophel, a famous royal counsellor who later espoused the rebellion of Absalom, possibly as retaliation for the disgrace David had brought upon his family in the affair with his granddaughter, Bathsheba (cf. 15:12).

When Bathsheba sent a message to David telling him, **I am with child,** David sent for Uriah at Rabbah (vv. 5, 6). When this one who was numbered among David's most heroic and trusted warriors appeared before the king, David inquired about the siege at the capital city of Ammon. After this he arranged for Uriah to go home.

Uriah would not go because of his sense of responsibility and because of his loyalty to his fellow warriors. While the ark of God was at the scene of the siege and while his fellows slept in the open fields Uriah considered it an unworthy gesture to spend his time at ease in the comfort of his home (v. 11).

It seems incredible that David made another and still more disreputable attempt to break down Uriah's heroic self-control. Even though intoxicated Uriah still retained his sense of honor (v. 13).

Failing in this, David sent Uriah back to the siege of Rabbah. He also sent a message with Uriah to Joab, which in reality was Uriah's death sentence (v. 15). Joab executed David's order by placing Uriah in a company that was ordered to charge the city. He died from wounds received in that fatal charge (v. 17).

Joab reported to David that Uriah was dead. David sent a message of encouragement to Joab and urged that the seige continue (v. 25). Meanwhile, Bathsheba lamented the death of Uriah for the customary period. When the time for mourning was ended, David took Bathsheba **to be his wife.** It appeared to David that this unseemly affair was solved even though underhanded methods had been employed. **But the thing that David had done displeased Jehovah** (v. 27).

3. David Reprimanded (12:1-25)

1 And Jehovah sent Nathan unto David. And he came unto him, and said unto him, There were two men in one city; the one rich, and the other poor. 2 The rich man had exceeding many flocks and herds; 3 but the poor man had nothing, save one little ewe lamb, which he had bought and nourished up: and it grew up together with him, and with his children; it did eat of his own morsel, and drank of his own cup, and lay in his bosom, and was unto him as a daughter. 4 And there came a traveller unto the rich man, and he spared to take of his own flock and of his own herd, to dress for the wayfaring man that was come unto him, but took the poor man's lamb, and dressed it for the man that was come to him. 5 And David's anger was greatly kindled against the man; and he said to Nathan, As Jehovah liveth, the man that hath done this is worthy to die: 6 and he shall restore the lamb fourfold, because he did this thing, and because he had no pity.

7 And Nathan said to David, Thou art the man. Thus saith Jehovah, the God of Israel, I anointed thee king over Israel, and I delivered thee out of the hand of Saul; 8 and I gave thee thy master's house, and thy master's wives into thy bosom, and gave thee the house of Israel and of Judah; and if that had been too little, I would have added unto thee such and such things. 9 Wherefore hast thou despised the word of Jehovah, to do that which is evil in his sight? thou hast smitten Uriah the Hittite with the sword, and hast taken his wife to be thy wife, and hast slain him with the sword of the children of Ammon. 10 Now therefore the sword shall never depart from thy house, because thou hast despised me, and hast taken the wife of Uriah the Hittite to be thy wife. 11 Thus saith Jehovah, Behold, I will raise up evil against thee out of thine own house; and I will take thy wives before thine eyes, and give them unto thy neighbor, and he shall lie with thy wives in the sight of this sun. 12 For thou didst it secretly: but I will do this thing before all Israel,

and before the sun. 13 And David said unto Nathan, I have sinned against Jehovah. And Nathan said unto David, Jehovah also hath put away thy sin; thou shalt not die. 14 Howbeit, because by this deed thou hast given great occasion to the enemies of Jehovah to blaspheme, the child also that is born unto thee shall surely die. 15 And Nathan departed unto his house.

And Jehovah struck the child that Uriah's wife bare unto David, and it was very sick. 16 David therefore besought God for the child; and David fasted, and went in, and lay all night upon the earth. 17 And the elders of his house arose, *and stood* beside him, to raise him up from the earth: but he would not, neither did he eat bread with them. 18 And it came to pass on the seventh day, that the child died. And the servants of David feared to tell him that the child was dead; for they said, Behold, while the child was yet alive, we spake unto him, and he hearkened not unto our voice: how will he then vex himself, if we tell him that the child is dead! 19 But when David saw that his servants were whispering together, David perceived that the child was dead; and David said unto his servants, Is the child dead? And they said, He is dead. 20 Then David arose from the earth, and washed, and anointed himself, and changed his apparel; and he came into the house of Jehovah, and worshipped: then he came to his own house; and when he required, they set bread before him, and he did eat. 21 Then said his servants unto him, What thing is this that thou hast done? thou didst fast and weep for the child, while it was alive; but when the child was dead, thou didst rise and eat bread. 22 And he said, While the child was yet alive, I fasted and wept: for I said, Who knoweth whether Jehovah will not be gracious to me, that the child may live? 23 But now he is dead, wherefore should I fast? can I bring him back again? I shall go to him, but he will not return to me.

24 And David comforted Bath-sheba his wife, and went in unto her, and lay with her: and she bare a son, and he called his name Solomon. And Jehovah loved him; 25 and he sent by the hand of Nathan the prophet; and he called his name Jedidiah, for Jehovah's sake.

The Lord, displeased at what David had done, commissioned his prophet to speak to the king. Nathan's message to the king began with a story of high-handed oppression of a poor man by a wealthy neighbor. In this parable Nathan dealt with only one sin, namely, the theft of the poor man's one little ewe lamb (v. 4). The point of the parable is specifically given in the words of Nathan to David: **Wherefore hast thou despised the word of Jehovah, to do that which is evil in his sight? thou hast smitten Uriah the Hittite with the sword, and hast taken his wife** ... (v. 9).

David listened to the parable and, before Nathan made the application, burst out in anger against the wealthy neighbor. **As Jehovah liveth, the man** ... **is worthy to die: and he shall restore the lamb fourfold, because he did this thing, and because he had no pity** (v. 5).

Nathan jolted David with the blunt rejoinder, **Thou art the man** (v. 7). He reminded David that the God of Israel had given him much — deliverance from Saul, the customary obtaining of his predecessor's wives, the kingdom of Israel. David had become exceedingly rich and powerful, and he could have had more (v. 8).

Instead, David resorted to ruthless oppression in order to gain what he desired. He had no pity. For this sin he was given a stinging rebuke. Nathan told him that **the sword shall never depart from thy house,** indicating the family feuds which would develop (v. 10). Also, Nathan anticipated Absalom's rebellion when he said, **Thus saith Jehovah, Behold, I will raise up evil against thee out of thine own house** (v. 11). Moreover, Nathan said, **The child also that is born unto thee shall surely die** (v. 14).

According to Nathan, divine punishment for David's sin included (1) feuds within his family, (2) insubordination within his own household, (3) death of the illegitimate, new-born child. Such was the punishment which came upon David's house, and it was written large in the course of Israel's history.

David did not suffer punishment upon his own person, except indirectly. However, the psychological impact of the reverses which came upon his family undoubtedly made a profound impression upon him. Furthermore, Nathan's blistering reprimand, instead of enraging David, occasioned profound penitence on his part. Evidence of this is the well-known Fifty-first Psalm which carries the ascription, "A Psalm of David; when Nathan the prophet came unto him, after he had gone in to Bath-sheba."

David's repentance caused Nathan to speak words which imply that had David not repented he may well have paid for his sin with his life. When David said, **I have sinned against Jehovah**, Nathan absolved him of his sin: **Jehovah also hath put away thy sin**, and added, **thou shalt not die** (v. 13).

While David did not die for his sin, because of his repentance, his evil deed caused a chain of events that brought tragedy, humiliation and disgrace. The responsibility for these results rested upon David. At the same time, the biblical viewpoint asserts that the activity of God was intertwined in the ongoing of that history in which the consequences of David's sin were coming to pass.

It is an oversimplification to assert, on the one hand, that David's punishment was caused entirely by what he had done, and, on the other hand, that David's punishment was wholly the activity of divine sovereignty. Rather, there was an interaction between David's disobedience to God's will and God's displeasure because of the disobedience. The subtlety of this interaction has been a major source of misunderstanding regarding the relationship between the dignity of man and the sovereignty of God.

The reprimand by Nathan was in part shortly fulfilled when David's child sickened and died. In time, David and Bathsheba had another son to whom the name Solomon was given. David was assured of restored relations with God when Nathan came and christened the child Jedidiah, meaning "Beloved of Jehovah" (v. 25, margin). It was a sign of God's favor not only upon David and his married relationship with Bathsheba but also upon the son born of that relationship.

4. Capture of Rabbah (12:26-31; cf. I Chron. 20:1-3)

26 Now Joab fought against Rabbah of the children of Ammon, and took the royal city. 27 And Joab sent messengers to David, and said, I have fought against Rabbah; yea, I have taken the city of waters. 28 Now therefore gather the rest of the people together, and encamp against the city, and take it; lest I take the city, and it be called after my name. 29 And David gathered all the people together, and went to Rabbah, and fought against it, and took it. 30 And he took the crown of their king from off his head; and the weight thereof was a talent of gold, and *in it were* precious stones; and it was set on David's head. And he brought forth the spoil of the city, exceeding much. 31 And he brought forth the people that were therein, and put them under saws, and under harrows of iron, and under axes of iron, and made them pass through the brickkiln: and thus did he unto all the cities of the children of Ammon. And David and all the people returned unto Jerusalem.

This continues the narrative of David's great war with Ammon, which was discontinued after II Samuel 11:1. Joab and his army had carried on the siege of Rabbah and the Ammonite defense was beginning to weaken. He reported to David, **I have taken the city of waters** (v. 27). Apparently, he had effectively deprived the city of its water supply, making a prolonged defense against the siege impossible.

Knowing this, Joab sent messengers to tell David to come and direct the victorious charge against beleaguered Rabbah, or else Joab would take it and name it after him (v. 28). David came and directed the battle against the city. The outcome was a decisive victory for David (vv. 29, 30).

The Ammonites were subjugated to David's rule. Whether they were savagely tortured or merely subjected to hard labor is an old controversy. The text indicates torture while the marginal rendering favors hard labor. Kennedy renders the verse as follows: "and he set them to saws and iron picks and iron axes and made them labour at the brick moulds."[22]

The war with Ammon was a significant one for David. In one respect, it was the battleground for one of David's great military successes. David's empire expanded rapidly to the north and east as a result. In another respect, the war was the background for David's great moral failure. Sexual desire erupted and demolished the character of a great man with high principles of justice and honor. Mil-

22 Kennedy, *op. cit.*, p. 250.

itary prowess never compensates for loss of moral rectitude.

IX. AMNON AND ABSALOM (II Sam. 13:1—14:33)

From this point to the end of II Samuel 20, the narration of the history of David's reign focuses upon trouble within the royal household. Behind all the causes that enter into the making of this history was the great weakness of David in governing his own household.

This troublesome problem in David's family life was placed immediately after the story of David's adultery with Bathsheba as a testimony against the violation of the most sacred bond of family life. Adultery carries with it consequences which no man can prohibit, notwithstanding the many who in these times claim that such a sin carries no consequence.

A. AMNON'S RAPE OF TAMAR (13:1-19)

1 And it came to pass after this, that Absalom the son of David had a fair sister, whose name was Tamar; and Amnon the son of David loved her. 2 And Amnon was so vexed that he fell sick because of his sister Tamar; for she was a virgin; and it seemed hard to Amnon to do anything unto her. 3 But Amnon had a friend, whose name was Jonadab, the son of Shimeah, David's brother: and Jonadab was a very subtle man. 4 And he said unto him, Why, O son of the king, art thou thus lean from day to day? wilt thou not tell me? And Amnon said unto him, I love Tamar, my brother Absalom's sister. 5 And Jonadab said unto him, Lay thee down on thy bed, and feign thyself sick: and when thy father cometh to see thee, say unto him, Let my sister Tamar come, I pray thee, and give me bread to eat, and dress the food in my sight, that I may see it, and eat it from her hand. 6 So Amnon lay down, and feigned himself sick: and when the king was come to see him, Amnon said unto the king, Let my sister Tamar come, I pray thee, and make me a couple of cakes in my sight, that I may eat from her hand.

7 Then David sent home to Tamar, saying, Go now to thy brother Amnon's house, and dress him food. 8 So Tamar went to her brother Amnon's house; and he was laid down. And she took dough, and kneaded it, and made cakes in his sight, and did bake the cakes. 9 And she took the pan, and poured them out before him; but he refused to eat. And Amnon said, Have out all men from me. And they went out every man from him. 10 And Amnon said unto Tamar, Bring the food into the chamber, that I may eat from thy hand. And Tamar took the cakes which she had made, and brought them into the chamber to Amnon her brother. 11 And when she had brought them near unto him to eat, he took hold of her, and said unto her, Come, lie with me, my sister. 12 And she answered him, Nay, my brother, do not force me; for no such thing ought to be done in Israel: do not thou this folly. 13 And I, whither shall I carry my shame? and as for thee, thou wilt be as one of the fools in Israel. Now therefore, I pray thee, speak unto the king; for he will not withhold me from thee. 14 Howbeit he would not hearken unto her voice; but being stronger than she, he forced her, and lay with her.

15 Then Amnon hated her with exceeding great hatred; for the hatred wherewith he hated her was greater than the love wherewith he had loved her. And Amnon said unto her, Arise, be gone. 16 And she said unto him, Not so, because this great wrong in putting me forth is *worse* than the other that thou didst unto me. But he would not hearken unto her. 17 Then he called his servant that ministered unto him, and said, Put now this woman out from me, and bolt the door after her. 18 And she had a garment of divers colors upon her; for with such robes were the king's daughters that were virgins apparelled. Then his servant brought her out, and bolted the door after her. 19 And Tamar put ashes on her head, and rent her garment of divers colors that was on her; and she laid her hand on her head, and went her way, crying aloud as she went.

Although Amnon was the first of David's sons to bring reproach upon the royal house, Absalom, who is the central figure in the tragic events of the following chapters, is mentioned first. **Absalom the son of David had a fair sister, whose name was Tamar** (v. 1). Absalom and Tamar were full brother and sister, children of Maacah, daughter of the king of Geshur, a small Aramean nation never driven out of the inheritance of East Manasseh.

Amnon was David's first-born, the son of Ahinoam of Jezreel, located in the inheritance of Issachar, and a half-brother to Absalom and Tamar. Strong sexual passions toward Tamar debilitated Amnon because of the frustration he encountered. **It seemed hard to Amnon to do anything unto her** (v. 2). The fact that she was kept in seclusion in David's harem accounted for this.

Through the shrewdness of Jonadab, a scheme was devised by which Tamar was sent by the king to Amnon's quarters, where he could vent his passions (v. 5). Jonadab was smart enough in scheming to help Amnon get what he wanted, but he gave him no advice on how to avoid the consequences of his passionate act. There are many who play the part of a Jonadab. They may never be declared guilty, but they surely are accomplices in the crime.

The scheme was executed flawlessly, and Amnon gained the object of his desire. However, the sin was not pleasant to Amnon and he despised Tamar (v. 15). She left his presence and lamented, rending her garment and putting ashes upon her head (v. 19).

B. ABSALOM'S REVENGE AGAINST AMNON (13:20-39)

20 And Absalom her brother said unto her, Hath Amnon thy brother been with thee? but now hold thy peace, my sister: he is thy brother; take not this thing to heart. So Tamar remained desolate in her brother Absalom's house. 21 But when king David heard of all these things, he was very wroth. 22 And Absalom spake unto Amnon neither good nor bad; for Absalom hated Amnon, because he had forced his sister Tamar.

23 And it came to pass after two full years, that Absalom had sheep-shearers in Baal-hazor, which is beside Ephraim: and Absalom invited all the king's sons. 24 And Absalom came to the king, and said, Behold now, thy servant hath sheep-shearers; let the king, I pray thee, and his servants go with thy servant. 25 And the king said to Absalom, Nay, my son, let us not all go, lest we be burdensome unto thee. And he pressed him: howbeit he would not go, but blessed him. 26 Then said Absalom, If not, I pray thee, let my brother Amnon go with us. And the king said unto him, Why should he go with thee? 27 But Absalom pressed him, and he let Amnon and all the king's sons go with him. 28 And Absalom commanded his servants, saying, Mark ye now, when Amnon's heart is merry with wine; and when I say unto you, Smite Amnon, then kill him; fear not; have not I commanded you? be courageous, and be valiant. 29 And the servants of Absalom did unto Amnon as Absalom had commanded. Then all the king's sons arose, and every man gat him up upon his mule, and fled.

30 And it came to pass, while they were in the way, that the tidings came to David, saying, Absalom hath slain all the king's sons, and there is not one of them left. 31 Then the king arose, and rent his garments, and lay on the earth; and all his servants stood by with their clothes rent. 32 And Jonadab, the son of Shimeah, David's brother, answered and said, Let not my lord suppose that they have slain all the young men the king's sons; for Amnon only is dead: for by the appointment of Absalom this hath been determined from the day that he forced his sister Tamar. 33 Now therefore let not my lord the king take the thing to his heart, to think that all the king's sons are dead: for Amnon only is dead. 34 But Absalom fled. And the young man that kept the watch lifted up his eyes, and looked, and, behold, there came much people by the way of the hill-side behind him. 35 And Jonadab said unto the king, Behold, the king's sons are come: as thy servant said, so it is. 36 And it came to pass, as soon as he had made an end of speaking, that, behold, the king's sons came, and lifted up their voice, and wept: and the king also and all his servants wept very sore.

37 But Absalom fled, and went to Talmai the son of Ammihur, king of Geshur, And *David* mourned for his son every day. 38 So Absalom fled, and went to Geshur, and was there three years. 39 And *the soul of* king David longed to go forth unto Absalom: for he was comforted concerning Amnon, seeing he was dead.

When David heard of Amnon's crime, **he was very wroth** (v. 21). However, because David did nothing about punishing Amnon, Absalom bitterly watched for an opportunity for revenge. Jonadab, who was a keen observer of people and who had seen something wrong with Amnon, also kept his eye upon Absalom. He later told David that he had watched the countenance of Absalom since the wrong done to Tamar, and it bore a warning scowl continually (v. 32).

After two years, in connection with the annual sheep-shearing festivities, Absalom arranged to kill Amnon (vv. 28, 29). When the deed was committed Absalom fled to his mother's native land, Geshur (v. 37). He remained there three years. Meanwhile, David longed to see Absalom (vv. 38, 39).

C. DAVID'S RECONCILIATION WITH ABSALOM (14:1-33)

Joab was the important person who made possible Absalom's return to Jerusalem from Geshur. He accomplished this in two stages.

1. Partial Reconciliation (14:1-27)

1 Now Joab the son of Zeruiah perceived that the king's heart was toward Absalom. 2 And Joab sent to Tekoa, and fetched thence a wise woman, and said unto her, I pray thee, feign thyself to be a mourner, and put on mourning apparel, I pray thee, and anoint not thyself with oil, but be as a woman that hath a long time mourned for the dead: 3 and go in to the king, and speak on this manner unto him. So Joab put the words in her mouth.

4 And when the woman of Tekoa spake to the king, she fell on her face to the ground, and did obeisance, and said, Help, O king. 5 And the king said unto her, What aileth thee? And she answered, Of a truth I am a widow, and my husband is dead. 6 And thy handmaid had two sons, and they two strove together in the field, and there was none to part them, but the one smote the other, and killed him. 7 And, behold, the whole family is risen against thy handmaid, and they say, Deliver him that smote his brother, that we may kill him for the life of his brother whom he slew, and so destroy the heir also. Thus will they quench my coal which is left, and will leave to my husband neither name nor remainder upon the face of the earth.

8 And the king said unto the woman, Go to thy house, and I will give charge concerning thee. 9 And the woman of Tekoa said unto the king, My lord, O king, the iniquity be on me, and on my father's house; and the king and his throne be guiltless. 10 And the king said, Whosoever saith aught unto thee, bring him to me, and he shall not touch thee any more. 11 Then said she, I pray thee, let the king remember Jehovah thy God, that the avenger of blood destroy not any more, lest they destroy my son. And he said, As Jehovah liveth, there shall not one hair of thy son fall to the earth.

12 Then the woman said, Let thy handmaid, I pray thee, speak a word unto my lord the king. And he said, Say on. 13 And the woman said, Wherefore then hast thou devised such a thing against the people of God? for in speaking this word the king is as one that is guilty, in that the king doth not fetch home again his banished one. 14 For we must needs die, and are as water spilt on the ground, which cannot be gathered up again; neither doth God take away life, but deviseth means, that he that is banished be not an outcast from him. 15 Now therefore seeing that I am come to speak this word unto my lord the king, it is because the people have made me afraid: and thy handmaid said, I will now speak unto the king; it may be that the king will perform the request of his servant. 16 For the king will hear, to deliver his servant out of the hand of the man that would destroy me and my son together out of the inheritance of God. 17 Then thy handmaid said, Let, I pray thee, the word of my lord the king be comfortable; for as an angel of God, so is my lord the king to discern good and bad: and Jehovah thy God be with thee.

18 Then the king answered and said unto the woman, Hide not from me, I pray thee, aught that I shall ask thee. And the woman said, Let my lord the king now speak. 19 And the king said, Is the hand of Joab with thee in all this? And the woman answered and said, As thy soul liveth, my lord the king, none can turn to the right hand or to the left from aught that my lord the king hath spoken; for thy servant Joab, he bade me, and he put all these words in the mouth of thy handmaid; 20 to change the face of the matter hath thy servant Joab done this thing: and my lord is wise, according to the wisdom of an angel of God, to know all things that are in the earth.

21 And the king said unto Joab, Behold now, I have done this thing: go therefore, bring the young man Absalom back. 22 And Joab fell to the ground on his face, and did obeisance, and blessed the king; and Joab said, To-day thy servant knoweth that I have found favor in thy sight, my lord, O king, in that the king hath performed the request of his servant. 23 So Joab arose and went to Geshur, and brought Absalom to Jerusalem. 24 And the king said, Let him turn to his own house, but let him not

see my face. So Absalom turned to his own house, and saw not the king's face.

25 Now in all Israel there was none to be so much praised as Absalom for his beauty: from the sole of his foot even to the crown of his head there was no blemish in him. 26 And when he cut the hair of his head (now it was at every year's end that he cut it; because it was heavy on him, therefore he cut it); he weighed the hair of his head at two hundred shekels, after the king's weight. 27 And unto Absalom there were born three sons, and one daughter, whose name was Tamar: she was a woman of a fair countenance.

The first stage of reuniting David and Absalom was only partial. It consisted of Joab's gaining permission from David to bring Absalom to Jerusalem, but for two years Absalom remained in partial disfavor.

Joab's interest in bringing Absalom back to Jerusalem was motivated by David's attitude. **Now Joab . . . perceived that the king's heart was toward Absalom** (v. 1). Realizing this, Joab secured the assistance of a woman from nearby Tekoa to plead a hypothetical case in which she sought David's help (vv. 6, 7).

David granted her plea, but she continued by applying her parable to David's relationship with Absalom (vv. 13, 14). Whereupon, David inquired if Joab had instigated this plot, and he permitted him to bring Absalom back to Jerusalem. There was one important restriction made by the king: **Let him turn to his own house, but let him not see my face** (v. 24).

Reconciliation was not complete. It appears that David was unnecessarily severe with Absalom at this time. With Amnon it had been different, for David unwisely did nothing (cf. 13:21; 14:24). This vacillating treatment indicated a serious defect in David's character.

Had David been fully reconciled to Absalom upon the latter's return to Jerusalem, he might have escaped the humiliation of Absalom's later rebellion. Instead, David compelled his son to brood longer in a relationship of estrangement, for David refused to see him for two years, even though Absalom was at Jerusalem.

2. Complete Reconciliation (14:28-33)

28 And Absalom dwelt two full years in Jerusalem; and he saw not the king's face. 29 Then Absalom sent for Joab, to send him to the king; but he would not come to him: and he sent again a second time, but he would not come. 30 Therefore he said unto his servants, See, Joab's field is near mine, and he hath barley there; go and set it on fire. And Absalom's servants set the field on fire. 31 Then Joab arose, and came to Absalom unto his house, and said unto him, Wherefore have thy servants set my field on fire? 32 And Absalom answered Joab, Behold, I sent unto thee, saying, Come hither, that I may send thee to the king, to say, Wherefore am I come from Geshur? it were better for me to be there still. Now therefore let me see the king's face; and if there be iniquity in me, let him kill me. 33 So Joab came to the king, and told him; and when he had called for Absalom, he came to the king, and bowed himself on his face to the ground before the king: and the king kissed Absalom.

After two years, Absalom was still in disfavor with the king. Joab was not interested in helping the reconciliation further until Absalom ordered his servants to set Joab's field afire. This brought Joab to Absalom and ultimately prodded him to persuade David to arrange for Absalom to come to the royal house. When David saw Absalom he gave him the kiss of reconciliation (v. 33).

X. ABSALOM'S REBELLION (II Sam. 15:1—19:43)

The most serious crisis which developed within the royal household of David was Absalom's attempt to usurp the kingdom. However, Absalom was killed in the attempt and the rebellion was crushed.

A. ABSALOM'S CONSPIRACY (15:1-12)

1 And it came to pass after this, that Absalom prepared him a chariot and horses, and fifty men to run before him. 2 And Absalom rose up early, and stood beside the way of the gate: and it was so, that, when any man had a suit which should come to the king for judgment, then Absalom called unto him, and said, Of what city art thou? And he said, Thy servant is of one of the tribes of Israel. 3

And Absalom said unto him, See, thy matters are good and right; but there is no man deputed of the king to hear thee. 4 Absalom said moreover, Oh that I were made judge in the land, that every man who hath any suit or cause might come unto me, and I would do him justice! 5 And it was so, that, when any man came nigh to do him obeisance, he put forth his hand, and took hold of him, and kissed him. 6 And on this manner did Absalom to all Israel that came to the king for judgment: so Absalom stole the hearts of the men of Israel.

7 And it came to pass at the end of forty years, that Absalom said unto the king, I pray thee, let me go and pay my vow, which I have vowed unto Jehovah, in Hebron. 8 For thy servant vowed a vow while I abode at Geshur in Syria, saying, If Jehovah shall indeed bring me again to Jerusalem, then I will serve Jehovah. 9 And the king said unto him, Go in peace. So he arose, and went to Hebron. 10 But Absalom sent spies throughout all the tribes of Israel, saying, As soon as ye hear the sound of the trumpet, then ye shall say, Absalom is king in Hebron. 11 And with Absalom went two hundred men out of Jerusalem, that were invited, and went in their simplicity; and they knew not anything. 12 And Absalom sent for Ahithophel the Gilonite, David's counsellor, from his city, even from Giloh, while he was offering the sacrifices. And the conspiracy was strong; for the people increased continually with Absalom.

The narrative recorded in II Samue' 13-20 is a chain of closely related events, the origin of which was David's sin against Uriah. Absalom's conspiracy was the overt action of an embittered, arrogant son against his father whom he despised. David had crushed resistance and revolt wherever it appeared throughout his realm and frontiers. Apparently, he little suspected revolt within his own household So often is this the case, but a man is really no stronger than his weakest point. David's weakness appeared in his relationships with his own sons. He administered the affairs of his kingdom with remarkable authority, but he erred regrettably in administering his own family.

Absalom's methods of gaining popularity and preparing the way for seizing the throne were very effective, although unscrupulous. He downgraded the present regime (v. 3). He made great promise of providing for the injustices and grievances if he were in power (v. 4). He showed a fawning interest in people because of what they could make possible for him (v. 5). So Absalom stole the hearts of the men of Israel (v. 6). This does not mean that he won their affection and loyalty. Rather, he deceived them just as Jacob deceived Laban (cf. Gen. 31:20, 26).

Within four years Absalom was prepared for his attempt to gain the kingdom. His steps in precipitating the uprising were full of treachery. He began by using a religious cloak as a cover (v. 7). He resorted to spies to spread the news of the impending overthrow (v. 10). He cultivated the support of the highly influential counsellor in David's court, Ahithophel, grandfather of Bathsheba, generally understood to have been embittered toward David because of the scandalous deed involving his granddaughter (v. 12).

B. DAVID'S RETREAT (15:13—16:14)

13 And there came a messenger to David, saying, The hearts of the men of Israel are after Absalom. 14 And David said unto all his servants that were with him at Jerusalem, Arise, and let us flee; for else none of us shall escape from Absalom: make speed to depart, lest he overtake us quickly, and bring down evil upon us, and smite the city with the edge of the sword. 15 And the king's servants said unto the king, Behold, thy servants are ready to do whatsoever my lord the king shall choose. 16 And the king went forth, and all his household after him. And the king left ten women, that were concubines, to keep the house. 17 And the king went forth, and all the people after him; and they tarried in Bethmerhak. 18 And all his servants passed on beside him; and all the Cherethites, and all the Pelethites, and all the Gittites, six hundred men that came after him from Gath, passed on before the king.

19 Then said the king to Ittai the Gittite, Wherefore goest thou also with us? return, and abide with the king: for thou art a foreigner, and also an exile; return to thine own place. 20 Whereas thou camest but yesterday, should I this day make thee go up and down with us, seeing I go whither I may? return thou, and take back thy brethren; mercy and truth be with thee. 21 And Ittai answered

the king, and said, As Jehovah liveth, and as my lord the king liveth, surely in what place my lord the king shall be, whether for death or for life, even there also will thy servant be. 22 And David said to Ittai, Go and pass over. And Ittai the Gittite passed over, and all his men, and all the little ones that were with him. 23 And all the country wept with a loud voice, and all the people passed over: the king also himself passed over the brook Kidron, and all the people passed over, toward the way of the wilderness.

24 And, lo, Zadok also *came*, and all the Levites with him, bearing the ark of the covenant of God; and they set down the ark of God; and Abiathar went up, until all the people had done passing out of the city. 25 And the king said unto Zadok, Carry back the ark of God into the city: if I shall find favor in the eyes of Jehovah, he will bring me again, and show me both it, and his habitation: 26 but if he say thus, I have no delight in thee; behold, here am I, let him do to me as seemeth good unto him. 27 The king said also unto Zadok the priest, Art thou *not* a seer? return into the city in peace, and your two sons with you, Ahimaaz thy son, and Jonathan the son of Abiathar. 28 See, I will tarry at the fords of the wilderness, until there come word from you to certify me. 29 Zadok therefore and Abiathar carried the ark of God again to Jerusalem: and they abode there.

30 And David went up by the ascent of the *mount of* Olives, and wept as he went up; and he had his head covered, and went barefoot: and all the people that were with him covered every man his head, and they went up, weeping as they went up. 31 And one told David, saying, Ahithophel is among the conspirators with Absalom. And David said, O Jehovah, I pray thee, turn the counsel of Ahithophel into foolishness. 32 And it came to pass, that, when David was come to the top *of the ascent*, where God was worshipped, behold, Hushai the Archite came to meet him with his coat rent, and earth upon his head. 33 And David said unto him, If thou passest on with me, then thou wilt be a burden unto me: 34 but if thou return to the city, and say unto Absalom, I will be thy servant, O king; as I have been thy father's servant in time past, so will I now be thy servant; then wilt thou defeat for me the counsel of Ahithophel. 35 And hast thou not there with thee Zadok and Abiathar the priests? therefore it shall be, that what thing soever thou shalt hear out of the king's house, thou shalt tell it to Zadok and Abiathar the priests. 36 Behold, they have there with them their two sons, Ahimaaz, Zadok's son, and Jonathan, Abiathar's son; and by them ye shall send unto me everything that ye shall hear. 37 So Hushai, David's friend, came into the city; and Absalom came into Jerusalem.

1 And when David was a little past the top *of the ascent*, behold, Ziba the servant of Mephibosheth met him, with a couple of asses saddled, and upon them two hundred loaves of bread, and a hundred clusters of raisins, and a hundred of summer fruits, and a bottle of wine. 2 And the king said unto Ziba, what meanest thou by these? And Ziba said, The asses are for the king's household to ride on; and the bread and summer fruit for the young men to eat; and the wine, that such as are faint in the wilderness may drink. 3 And the king said, And where is thy master's son? And Ziba said unto the king, Behold, he abideth at Jerusalem; for he said, To-day will the house of Israel restore me the kingdom of my father. 4 Then said the king to Ziba, Behold, thine is all that pertaineth unto Mephibosheth. And Ziba said, I do obeisance; let me find favor in thy sight, my lord, O king.

5 And when king David came to Bahurim, behold, there came out thence a man of the family of the house of Saul, whose name was Shimei, the son of Gera; he came out, and cursed still as he came. 6 And he cast stones at David, and at all the servants of king David: and all the people and all the mighty men were on his right hand and on his left. 7 And thus said Shimei when he cursed, Begone, begone, thou man of blood, and base fellow: 8 Jehovah hath returned upon thee all the blood of the house of Saul, in whose stead thou hast reigned; and Jehovah hath delivered the kingdom into the hand of Absalom thy son; and, behold, thou art *taken* in thine own mischief, because thou art a man of blood.

9 Then said Abishai the son of Zeruiah unto the king, Why should this dead dog curse my lord the king? let me go over, I pray thee, and take off his head. 10 And the king said, What have I to do with you, ye sons of Zeruiah? Because he curseth, and because Jehovah hath said unto him, Curse David; who then shall say, Wherefore hast thou done so? 11 And David said to Abishai, and to all his servants, Behold, my son, who came forth from my bowels, seeketh my life: how much more *may* this Benjamite now *do it?* let him alone, and let him curse; for

Jehovah hath bidden him. 12 It may be that Jehovah will look on the wrong done unto me, and that Jehovah will requite me good for *his* cursing of me this day. 13 So David and his men went by the way; and Shimei went along on the hillside over against him, and cursed as he went, and threw stones at him, and cast dust. 14 And the king, and all the people that were with him, came weary; and he refreshed himself there.

According to the narrative, David was taken by complete surprise when messengers informed him of Absalom's conspiracy in Hebron. **Arise, and let us flee; for else none of us shall escape from Absalom** (v. 14).

Apparently, David ordered the exodus from the strongly fortified capital because he feared treachery from within the city and even within his royal court. At last he had become fully aware of this serious peril. Perhaps earlier he might have dealt with his treacherous son, Absalom, before such widespread support of his mutiny had developed. It was now too late for that. Rather, David retreated from Jerusalem across the Jordan River to Mahanaim. The whole incident reveals the weakness of David's uneasy conscience. His own treachery against Uriah came back to haunt him in the feared treachery of Absalom.

David's retreat in the face of the conspiracy of Absalom is recorded in the most detailed manner of any incident in the recorded history of the Hebrews.[23] It is not our purpose to explore it extensively, but it is poignant and powerful because of the detailed references to emotions and loyalties which motivate human nature.

There was Ittai, only recently a member of the court, but his expression of loyalty ranks with that of Ruth (cf. v. 21 with Ruth 1:16, 17). There was Zadok the priest, who was urged by David to return to Jerusalem to watch developments (v. 25). A priest caring for the ark of God could remain in Jerusalem as a spy for David without arousing suspicion. Zadok loyally followed David's order. There was Hushai, who showed his devotion to David by being willing to return to Jerusalem to counteract the counsel and influence of Ahithophel to Absalom (vv. 33, 34).

Two individuals are revealed in the narrative of the retreat as hoping to gain for themselves by the turn of events. Ziba was hopeful that if David were able to quell the revolt, he would bestow gratuitous favors upon Ziba (vv. 3, 4). Shimei hoped that David would be banished, making it possible for the overthrow of Saul to be avenged (v. 8). Shimei was of the tribe of Benjamin, from which Saul had come. David's spirit of humility in the face of Shimei's bitter denunciation is commendable and is a perennial example to those subjected to criticism (vv. 11, 12).

C. ABSALOM'S OCCUPANCY (16:15— 17:29)

15 And Absalom, and all the people, the men of Israel, came to Jerusalem, and Ahithophel with him. 16 And it came to pass, when Hushai the Archite, David's friend, was come unto Absalom, that Hushai said unto Absalom, *Long* live the king, *Long* live the king. 17 And Absalom said to Hushai, Is this thy kindness to thy friend? why wentest thou not with thy friend? 18 And Hushai said unto Absalom, Nay; but whom Jehovah, and this people, and all the men of Israel have chosen, his will I be, and with him will I abide. 19 And again, whom should I serve? *should I* not *serve* in the presence of his son? as I have served in thy father's presence, so will I be in thy presence.

20 Then said Absalom to Ahithophel, Give your counsel what we shall do. 21 And Ahithophel said unto Absalom, Go in unto thy father's concubines, that he hath left to keep the house; and all Israel will hear that thou art abhorred of thy father: then will the hands of all that are with thee be strong. 22 So they spread Absalom a tent upon the top of the house; and Absalom went in unto his father's concubines in the sight of all Israel. 23 And the counsel of Ahithophel, which he gave in those days, was as if a man inquired at the oracle of God: so was all the counsel of Ahithophel both with David and with Absalom.

1 Moreover Ahithophel said unto Absalom, Let me now choose out twelve thousand men, and I will arise and pursue after David this night: 2 and I will come upon him while he is weary and weak-handed, and will make him afraid;

23 *Ibid.*, p. 264.

and all the people that are with him shall flee; and I will smite the king only; 3 and I will bring back all the people unto thee: the man whom thou seekest is as if all returned: so all the people shall be in peace. 4 And the saying pleased Absalom well, and all the elders of Israel.

5 Then said Absalom, Call now Hushai the Archite also, and let us hear likewise what he saith. 6 And when Hushai was come to Absalom, Absalom spake unto him, saying, Ahithophel hath spoken after this manner: shall we do *after* his saying? if not, speak thou. 7 And Hushai said unto Absalom, The counsel that Ahithophel hath given this time is not good. 8 Hushai said moreover, Thou knowest thy father and his men, that they are mighty men, and they are chafed in their minds, as a bear robbed of her whelps in the field; and thy father is a man of war, and will not lodge with the people. 9 Behold, he is hid now in some pit, or in some *other* place: and it will come to pass, when some of them are fallen at the first, that whosoever heareth it will say, There is a slaughter among the people that follow Absalom. 10 And even he that is valiant, whose heart is as the heart of a lion, will utterly melt; for all Israel knoweth that thy father is a mighty man, and they that are with him are valiant men. 11 But I counsel that all Israel be gathered together unto thee, from Dan even to Beer-sheba, as the sand that is by the sea for multitude; and that thou go to battle in thine own person. 12 So shall we come upon him in some place where he shall be found, and we will light upon him as the dew falleth on the ground; and of him and of all the men that are with him we will not leave so much as one. 13 Moreover, if he be gotten into a city, then shall all Israel bring ropes to that city, and we will draw it into the river, until there be not one small stone found there. 14 And Absalom and all the men of Israel said, The counsel of Hushai the Archite is better than the counsel of Ahithophel. For Jehovah had ordained to defeat the good counsel of Ahithophel, to the intent that Jehovah might bring evil upon Absalom.

15 Then said Hushai unto Zadok and to Abiathar the priests, Thus and thus did Ahithophel counsel Absalom and the elders of Israel; and thus and thus have I counselled. 16 Now therefore send quickly, and tell David, saying, Lodge not this night at the fords of the wilderness, but by all means pass over; lest the king be swallowed up, and all the people that are

with him. 17 Now Jonathan and Ahimaaz were staying by En-rogel; and a maidservant used to go and tell them; and they went and told king David: for they might not be seen to come into the city. 18 But a lad saw them, and told Absalom: and they went both of them away quickly, and came to the house of a man in Bahurim, who had a well in his court; and they went down thither. 19 And the woman took and spread the covering over the well's mouth, and strewed bruised grain thereon; and nothing was known. 20 And Absalom's servants came to the woman to the house; and they said, Where are Ahimaaz and Jonathan? And the woman said unto them, They are gone over the brook of water. And when they had sought and could not find them, they returned to Jerusalem.

21 And it came to pass, after they were departed, that they came up out of the well, and went and told king David; and they said unto David, Arise ye, and pass quickly over the water; for thus hath Ahithophel counselled against you. 22 Then David arose, and all the people that were with him, and they passed over the Jordan: by the morning light there lacked not one of them that was not gone over the Jordan. 23 And when Ahithophel saw that his counsel was not followed, he saddled his ass, and arose, and gat him home, unto his city, and set his house in order, and hanged himself; and he died, and was buried in the sepulchre of his father.

24 Then David came to Mahanaim. And Absalom passed over the Jordan, he and all the men of Israel with him. 25 And Absalom set Amasa over the host instead of Joab. Now Amasa was the son of a man, whose name was Ithra the Israelite, that went in to Abigal the daughter of Nahash, sister to Zeruiah, Joab's mother. 26 And Israel and Absalom encamped in the land of Gilead.

27 And it came to pass, when David was come to Mahanaim, that Shobi the son of Nahash of Rabbah of the children of Ammon, and Machir the son of Ammiel of Lo-debar, and Barzillai the Gileadite of Rogelim, 28 brought beds, and basins, and earthen vessels, and wheat, and barley, and meal, and parched *grain,* and beans, and lentils, and parched *pulse,* 29 and honey, and butter, and sheep, and cheese of the herd, for David, and for the people that were with him, to eat: for they said, The people are hungry, and weary, and thirsty, in the wilderness.

And Absalom, and all the people, the men of Israel, came to Jerusalem, and Ahithophel with him (v. 15). Among those who welcomed Absalom into the city was Hushai, who won the confidence of the proud Absalom with profuse flattery (vv. 18, 19).

Since the harem of an oriental monarch was the legacy of his successor, one of the first steps which Ahithophel advised Absalom to take was to possess David's harem (v. 21).

Ahithophel's counsel was highly regarded. It was **as if a man inquired at the oracle of God** (v. 23). One of the strange phenomena of human nature is the confidence that is often placed in the embittered, prejudiced person. Ahithophel had been an astute counsellor to David. The best explanation of his switch to Absalom is David's affair with Bathsheba. His counsel regarding possession of David's harem revealed his complete severance from David.

A lengthy account of the rivalry that occurred between Ahithophel and Hushai in counselling Absalom is climaxed with Absalom's conclusion that the counsel of Hushai is better than that of Ahithophel essentially because of Hushai's flattery (vv. 1-14). The historian's explanation of this is: **For Jehovah had ordained to defeat the good counsel of Ahithophel, to the intent that Jehovah might bring evil upon Absalom** (v. 14).

D. ABSALOM'S DEFEAT (18:1-33)

1 And David numbered the people that were with him, and set captains of thousands and captains of hundreds over them. 2 And David sent forth the people, a third part under the hand of Joab, and a third part under the hand of Abishai the son of Zeruiah, Joab's brother, and a third part under the hand of Ittai the Gittite. And the king said unto the people, I will surely go forth with you myself also. 3 But the people said, Thou shalt not go forth: for if we flee away, they will not care for us; neither if half of us die, will they care for us: but thou art worth ten thousand of us; therefore now it is better that thou be ready to succor us out of the city. 4 And the king said unto them, What seemeth you best I will do. And the king stood by the gateside, and all the people went out by hundreds and by thousands. 5 And the

king commanded Joab and Abishai and Ittai, saying, Deal gently for my sake with the young man, even with Absalom. And all the people heard when the king gave all the captains charge concerning Absalom.

6 So the people went out into the field against Israel: and the battle was in the forest of Ephraim. 7 And the people of Israel were smitten there before the servants of David, and there was a great slaughter there that day of twenty thousand men. 8 For the battle was there spread over the face of all the country; and the forest devoured more people that day than the sword devoured.

9 And Absalom chanced to meet the servants of David. And Absalom was riding upon his mule, and the mule went under the thick boughs of a great oak, and his head caught hold of the oak, and he was taken up between heaven and earth; and the mule that was under him went on. 10 And a certain man saw it, and told Joab, and said, Behold, I saw Absalom hanging in an oak. 11 And Joab said unto the man that told him, And, behold, thou sawest it, and why didst thou not smite him there to the ground? and I would have given thee ten *pieces of* silver, and a girdle. 12 And the man said unto Joab, Though I should receive a thousand *pieces of* silver in my hand, yet would I not put forth my hand against the king's son: for in our hearing the king charged thee and Abishai and Ittai, saying, Beware that none touch the young man Absalom. 13 Otherwise if I had dealt falsely against his life (and there is no matter hid from the king), then thou thyself wouldest have set thyself against *me*. 14 Then said Joab, I may not tarry thus with thee. And he took three darts in his hand, and thrust them through the heart of Absalom, while he was yet alive in the midst of the oak. 15 And ten young men that bare Joab's armor compassed about and smote Absalom, and slew him.

16 And Joab blew the trumpet, and the people returned from pursuing after Israel; for Joab held back the people. 17 And they took Absalom, and cast him into the great pit in the forest, and raised over him a very great heap of stones: and all Israel fled every one to his tent. 18 Now Absalom in his lifetime had taken and reared up for himself the pillar, which is in the king's dale; for he said, I have no son to keep my name in remembrance: and he called the pillar after his own name; and it is called Absalom's monument, unto this day.

19 Then said Ahimaaz the son of Zadok, Let me now run, and bear the king tidings, how that Jehovah hath avenged him of his enemies. 20 And Joab said unto him, Thou shalt not be the bearer of tidings this day, but thou shalt bear tidings another day; but this day thou shalt bear no tidings, because the king's son is dead. 21 Then said Joab to the Cushite, Go, tell the king what thou hast seen. And the Cushite bowed himself unto Joab, and ran. 22 Then said Ahimaaz the son of Zadok yet again to Joab, But come what may, let me, I pray thee, also run after the Cushite. And Joab said, Wherefore wilt thou run, my son, seeing that thou wilt have no reward for the tidings? 23 But come what may, said he, I will run. And he said unto him, Run. Then Ahimaaz ran by the way of the Plain, and outran the Cushite.

24 Now David was sitting between the two gates: and the watchman went up to the roof of the gate unto the wall, and lifted up his eyes, and looked, and, behold, a man running alone. 25 And the watchman cried, and told the king. And the king said, If he be alone, there is tidings in his mouth. And he came apace, and drew near. 26 And the watchman saw another man running; and the watchman called unto the porter, and said, Behold, another man running alone. And the king said, He also bringeth tidings. 27 And the watchman said, I think the running of the foremost is like the running of Ahimaaz the son of Zadok. And the king said, He is a good man, and cometh with good tidings.

28 And Ahimaaz called, and said unto the king, All is well. And he bowed himself before the king with his face to the earth, and said, Blessed be Jehovah thy God, who hath delivered up the men that lifted up their hand against my lord the king. 29 And the king said, Is it well with the young man Absalom? And Ahimaaz answered, When Joab sent the king's servant, even me thy servant, I saw a great tumult, but I knew not what it was. 30 And the king said, Turn aside, and stand here. And he turned aside, and stood still.

31 And, behold, the Cushite came; and the Cushite said, Tidings for my lord the king; for Jehovah hath avenged thee this day of all them that rose up against thee. 32 And the king said unto the Cushite, Is it well with the young man Absalom? And the Cushite answered, The enemies of my lord the king, and all that rise up against thee to do thee hurt, be as that young man is. 33 And the king was much

moved, and went up to the chamber over the gate, and wept: and as he went, thus he said, O my son Absalom, my son, my son Absalom! would I had died for thee, O Absalom, my son, my son!

David had located temporary headquarters at Mahanaim on the east side of the Jordan. Absalom, having assembled his army, pursued David with the intent of killing him and reigning as his successor. The battle between the two forces occurred in the forest of Ephraim east of the Jordan River (v. 6). It was an overwhelming defeat for Absalom (v. 8). Absalom himself was slain by Joab (v. 14). This was contrary to David's orders.

It is pathetic to observe that David had concern only for his son on that day of battle. The crisis involved his own future as well as the welfare of his loyal troops, yet David was preoccupied with an obsession for Absalom (vv. 5, 12, 29, 32). Yet Absalom had nothing but bitter animosity to return (cf. 17:4). When the news reached David that Absalom was dead, David mourned, **O my son Absalom, my son, my son Absalom! would I had died for thee, O Absalom, my son, my son!** (v. 33). David's anguish arose not only out of the tragedy of Absalom's death but more basically out of his own failure with his son.

E. DAVID'S RETURN (19:1-43)

1 And it was told Joab, Behold, the king weepeth and mourneth for Absalom. 2 And the victory that day was turned into mourning unto all the people; for the people heard say that day, The king grieveth for his son. 3 And the people gat them by stealth that day into the city, as people that are ashamed steal away when they flee in battle. 4 And the king covered his face, and the king cried with a loud voice, O my son Absalom, O Absalom, my son, my son! 5 And Joab came into the house to the king, and said, Thou hast shamed this day the faces of all thy servants, who this day have saved thy life, and the lives of thy sons and of thy daughters, and the lives of thy wives, and the lives of thy concubines; 6 in that thou lovest them that hate thee, and hatest them that love thee. For thou hast declared this day, that princes and servants are nought unto thee: for this day I perceive, that if Absalom had lived, and all we had died this day, then it had

pleased thee well. 7 Now therefore arise, go forth, and speak comfortably unto thy servants; for I swear by Jehovah, if thou go not forth, there will not tarry a man with thee this night: and that will be worse unto thee than all the evil that hath befallen thee from thy youth until now. 8 Then the king arose, and sat in the gate. And they told unto all the people, saying, Behold, the king is sitting in the gate: and all the people came before the king.

Now Israel had fled every man to his tent. 9 And all the people were at strife throughout all the tribes of Israel, saying, The king delivered us out of the hand of our enemies, and he saved us out of the hand of the Philistines; and now he is fled out of the land from Absalom. 10 And Absalom, whom we anointed over us, is dead in battle. Now therefore why speak ye not a word of bringing the king back?

11 And king David sent to Zadok and to Abiathar the priests, saying, Speak unto the elders of Judah, saying, Why are ye the last to bring the king back to his house? seeing the speech of all Israel is come to the king, *to bring him* to his house. 12 Ye are my brethren, ye are my bone and my flesh: wherefore then are ye the last to bring back the king? 13 And say ye to Amasa, Art thou not my bone and my flesh? God do so to me, and more also, if thou be not captain of the host before me continually in the room of Joab. 14 And he bowed the heart of all the men of Judah, even as *the heart of* one man; so that they sent unto the king, *saying,* Return thou, and all thy servants. 15 So the king returned, and came to the Jordan. And Judah came to Gilgal, to go to meet the king, to bring the king over the Jordan.

16 And Shimei the son of Gera, the Benjamite, who was of Bahurim, hasted and came down with the men of Judah to meet king David. 17 And there were a thousand men of Benjamin with him, and Ziba the servant of the house of Saul, and his fifteen sons and his twenty servants with him; and they went through the Jordan in the presence of the king. 18 And there went over a ferry-boat to bring over the king's household, and to do what he thought good. And Shimei the son of Gera fell down before the king, when he was come over the Jordan. 19 And he said unto the king, Let not my lord impute iniquity unto me, neither do thou remember that which thy servant did perversely the day that my lord the king went out of

Jerusalem, that the king should take it to his heart. 20 For thy servant doth know that I have sinned: therefore, behold, I am come this day the first of all the house of Joseph to go down to meet my lord the king.

21 But Abishai the son of Zeruiah answered and said, Shall not Shimei be put to death for this, because he cursed Jehovah's anointed! 22 And David said, What have I to do with you, ye sons of Zeruiah, that ye should this day be adversaries unto me? shall there any man be put to death this day in Israel? for do not I know that I am this day king over Israel? 23 And the king said unto Shimei, Thou shalt not die. And the king sware unto him.

24 And Mephibosheth the son of Saul came down to meet the king; and he had neither dressed his feet, nor trimmed his beard, nor washed his clothes, from the day the king departed until the day he came home in peace. 25 And it came to pass, when he was come to Jerusalem to meet the king, that the king said unto him, Wherefore wentest not thou with me, Mephibosheth? 26 And he answered, My lord, O king, my servant deceived me: for thy servant said, I will saddle me an ass, that I may ride thereon, and go with the king; because thy servant is lame. 27 And he hath slandered thy servant unto my lord the king; but my lord the king is as an angel of God: do therefore what is good in thine eyes. 28 For all my father's house were but dead men before my lord the king; yet didst thou set thy servant among them that did eat at thine own table. What right therefore have I yet that I should cry any more unto the king? 29 And the king said unto him, Why speakest thou any more of thy matters? I say, Thou and Ziba divide the land. 30 And Mephibosheth said unto the king, Yea, let him take all, forasmuch as my lord the king is come in peace unto his own house.

31 And Barzillai the Gileadite came down from Rogelim; and he went over the Jordan with the king, to conduct him over the Jordan. 32 Now Barzillai was a very aged man, even fourscore years old: and he had provided the king with sustenance while he lay at Mahanaim; for he was a very great man. 33 And the king said unto Barzillai, Come thou over with me, and I will sustain thee with me in Jerusalem. 34 And Barzillai said unto the king, How many are the days of the years of my life, that I should go up with the king unto Jerusalem? 35 I am this day fourscore years old: can I discern between

good and bad? can thy servant taste what I eat or what I drink? can I hear any more the voice of singing men and singing women? wherefore then should thy servant be yet a burden unto my lord the king? 36 Thy servant would but just go over the Jordan with the king: and why should the king recompense it me with such a reward? 37 Let thy servant, I pray thee, turn back again, that I may die in mine own city, by the grave of my father and my mother. But behold, thy servant Chimham; let him go over with my lord the king; and do to him what shall seem good unto thee. 38 And the king answered, Chimham shall go over with me, and I will do to him that which shall seem good unto thee: and whatsoever thou shalt require of me, that will I do for thee. 39 And all the people went over the Jordan, and the king went over: and the king kissed Barzillai, and blessed him; and he returned unto his own place.

40 So the king went over to Gilgal, and Chimham went over with him: and all the people of Judah brought the king over, and also half the people of Israel. 41 And, behold, all the men of Israel came to the king, and said unto the king, Why have our brethren the men of Judah stolen thee away, and brought the king, and his household, over the Jordan, and all David's men with him? 42 And all the men of Judah answered the men of Israel, Because the king is near of kin to us: wherefore then are ye angry for this matter? have we eaten at all at the king's cost? or hath he given us any gift? 43 And the men of Israel answered the men of Judah, and said, We have ten parts in the king, and we have also more *right* in David than ye: why then did ye despise us, that our advice should not be first had in bringing back our king? And the words of the men of Judah were fiercer than the words of the men of Israel.

David's personal grief was undermining the welfare of the kingdom. Joab was keenly aware of the situation (v. 7). He aroused David sufficiently that David went forth to assume his kingly role: **Then the king arose, and sat in the gate** (v. 8).

David returned to Jerusalem escorted by the men of Judah whom he had privately urged to instigate such a move (vv. 11-15). He made Amasa, his nephew, the new army commander in place of Joab (v. 13).

The northern tribes complained that they had the better right to bring David back to Jerusalem since there were more of them. This incensed the men of Judah and an angry argument followed (vv. 42, 43). These divisive, tribal jealousies had been submerged during the strong personal rule of David, but they had not been eliminated. It is an enlightening commentary on the weakening of David's rule that the tribes were again quarreling among themselves.

XI. SHEBA'S REBELLION (II Sam. 20: 1-26)

1 And there happened to be there a base fellow, whose name was Sheba, the son of Bichri, a Benjamite: and he blew the trumpet, and said, We have no portion in David, neither have we inheritance in the son of Jesse: every man to his tents, O Israel. 2 So all the men of Israel went up from following David, and followed Sheba the son of Bichri; but the men of Judah clave unto their king, from the Jordan even to Jerusalem.

3 And David came to his house at Jerusalem; and the king took the ten women his concubines, whom he had left to keep the house, and put them in ward, and provided them with sustenance, but went not in unto them. So they were shut up unto the day of their death, living in widowhood.

4 Then said the king to Amasa, Call me the men of Judah together within three days, and be thou here present. 5 So Amasa went to call *the men of* Judah together; but he tarried longer than the set time which he had appointed him. 6 And David said to Abishai, Now will Sheba the son of Bichri do us more harm than did Absalom: take thou thy lord's servants, and pursue after him, lest he get him fortified cities, and escape out of our sight. 7 And there went out after him Joab's men, and the Cherethites and the Pelethites, and all the mighty men; and they went out of Jerusalem, to pursue after Sheba the son of Bichri. 8 When they were at the great stone which is in Gibeon, Amasa came to meet them. And Joab was girded with his apparel of war that he had put on, and thereon was a girdle with a sword fastened upon his loins in the sheath thereof; and as he went forth it fell out. And Joab said to Amasa, Is it well with thee, my brother? And Joab took Amasa by the beard with his right hand to kiss him. 10 But Amasa

took no heed to the sword that was in
Joab's hand: so he smote him therewith
in the body, and shed out his bowels to
the ground, and struck him not again;
and he died.

And Joab and Abishai his brother pursued after Sheba the son of Bichri. 11
And there stood by him one of Joab's
young men, and said, He that favoreth
Joab, and he that is for David, let him
follow Joab. 12 And Amasa lay wallowing
in his blood in the midst of the highway.
And when the man saw that all the
people stood still, he carried Amasa out
of the highway into the field, and cast a
garment over him, when he saw that
every one that came by him stood still. 13
When he was removed out of the highway, all the people went on after Joab, to
pursue after Sheba the son of Bichri.

14 And he went through all the tribes
of Israel unto Abel, and to Beth-maacah,
and all the Berites: and they were
gathered together, and went also after
him. 15 And they came and besieged him
in Abel of Beth-maacah, and they cast up
a mound against the city, and it stood
against the rampart; and all the people
that were with Joab battered the wall, to
throw it down. 16 Then cried a wise
woman out of the city, Hear, hear; say, I
pray you, unto Joab, Come near hither,
that I may speak with thee. 17 And he
came near unto her; and the woman said,
Art thou Joab? And he answered, I am.
Then she said unto him, Hear the words
of thy handmaid. And he answered, I do
hear. 18 Then she spake, saying, They were
wont to speak in old time, saying, They
shall surely ask *counsel* at Abel: and so
they ended *the matter.* 19 I am of them
that are peaceable and faithful in Israel:
thou seekest to destroy a city and a
mother in Israel: why wilt thou swallow
up the inheritance of Jehovah? 20 And
Joab answered and said, Far be it, far be
it from me, that I should swallow up or
destroy. 21 The matter is not so: but a
man of the hill-country of Ephraim, Sheba the son of Bichri by name, hath lifted
up his hand against the king, even against
David; deliver him only, and I will
depart from the city. And the woman
said unto Joab, Behold, his head shall be
thrown to thee over the wall. 22 Then
the woman went unto all the people in
her wisdom. And they cut off the head of
Sheba the son of Bichri, and threw it
out to Joab. And he blew the trumpet,
and they were dispersed from the city,
every man to his tent. And Joab returned
to Jerusalem unto the king.

23 Now Joab was over all the host of
Israel; and Benaiah the son of Jehoiada
was over the Cherethites and over the
Pelethites; 24 and Adoram was over the
men subject to taskwork; and Jehoshaphat
the son of Ahilud was the recorder; 25
and Sheva was scribe; and Zadok
and Abiathar were priests; 26 and also
Ira the Jairite was chief minister unto
David.

Sheba was of the tribe of Benjamin
and, when the northern tribes quarreled
with Judah over bringing David to
Jerusalem, he called for a general revolt
against David's rule (v. 1).

David, meanwhile, gave orders to his
new commander, Amasa, to assemble the
warriors of Judah, but Amasa delayed (v.
5). Therefore, David gave orders to
Abishai, for he was aware that Joab,
brother of Abishai, would join to aid
him. Once the men were assembled and
pursuit of Sheba was begun, Amasa appeared. As Joab met him, he treacherously drove a sword into Amasa, fatally
wounding him (v. 10).

Automatically, Joab assumed command,
as the narrative reports: **And Joab and
Abishai his brother pursued after Sheba**
(v. 10). The pursuit took them to Abel of
Beth-maacah, located in the northern-
most region of Israel in the tribe of
Naphtali (v. 15). Although Sheba's rebellion was already broken, Joab knew what
impressive salutary effect the tireless
search and quick dispatch of the rebel
would have upon other would-be rebels.

The citizens of Abel had no enthusiasm for Sheba's cause, and they assassinated him. When Joab was given the
head of Sheba, he ordered the expedition
to cease its attack upon the city (v. 22).

Joab, although a ruthless man of war,
refrained from the murder of the innocent villagers of Abel. He thus avoided
an incident that would have made the
harmony of the tribes more difficult.
Coupled with Joab's remarkable military
prowess was a keen sense of judgment.
His intense loyalty to David was no less
remarkable.

XII. APPENDIX (II Sam. 21:1—24:25)

"Chapters XXI-XXIV are made up of
six appendices placed at the end of the
second book of Samuel so as not to inter-

rupt David's history."[24] The contents of these chapters are of varied character. The six sections contain narrative as well as poetry.

A. FAMINE (21:1-14)

1 And there was a famine in the days of David three years, year after year; and David sought the face of Jehovah. And Jehovah said, It is for Saul, and for his bloody house, because he put to death the Gibeonites. 2 And the king called the Gibeonites, and said unto them (now the Gibeonites were not of the children of Israel, but of the remnant of the Amorites; and the children of Israel had sworn unto them: and Saul sought to slay them in his zeal for the children of Israel and Judah) ; 3 and David said unto the Gibeonites, What shall I do for you? and wherewith shall I make atonement, that ye may bless the inheritance of Jehovah? 4 And the Gibeonites said unto him, It is no matter of silver or gold between us and Saul, or his house; neither is it for us to put any man to death in Israel. And he said, What ye shall say, that will I do for you. 5 And they said unto the king, The man that consumed us, and that devised against us, *that* we should be destroyed from remaining in any of the borders of Israel, 6 let seven men of his sons be delivered unto us, and we will hang them up unto Jehovah in Gibeah of Saul, the chosen of Jehovah. And the king said, I will give them.

7 But the king spared Mephibosheth, the son of Jonathan the son of Saul, because of Jehovah's oath that was between them, between David and Jonathan the son of Saul. 8 But the king took the two sons of Rizpah the daughter of Aiah, whom she bare unto Saul, Armoni and Mephibosheth; and the five sons of Michal the daughter of Saul, whom she bare to Adriel the son of Barzillai the Meholathite: 9 and he delivered them into the hands of the Gibeonites, and they hanged them in the mountain before Jehovah, and they fell *all* seven together. And they were put to death in the days of harvest, in the first days, at the beginning of barley harvest.

10 And Rizpah the daughter of Aiah took sackcloth, and spread it for her upon the rock, from the beginning of harvest until water was poured upon them from heaven; and she suffered neither the birds of the heavens to rest on them by day, nor the beasts of the field by night. 11 And it was told David what Rizpah the daughter of Aiah, the concubine of Saul, had done.

12 And David went and took the bones of Saul and the bones of Jonathan his son from the men of Jabesh-gilead, who had stolen them from the street of Bethshan, where the Philistines had hanged them, in the day that the Philistines slew Saul in Gilboa: 13 and he brought up from thence the bones of Saul and the bones of Jonathan his son: and they gathered the bones of them that were hanged. 14 And they buried the bones of Saul and Jonathan his son in the country of Benjamin in Zela, in the sepulchre of Kish his father: and they performed all that the king commanded. And after that God was entreated for the land.

A three years' famine apparently near the beginning of David's reign plagued the land. The word of the Lord revealed to David that the famine was due to Saul's violation of the covenant which had been made centuries before between Joshua and the Gibeonites.

David inquired of the Gibeonites as to what atonement could be made to rectify the wrong done by Saul (v. 3). The Gibeonites asked that seven of Saul's sons be given as an atonement (v. 6). They were left hanging for several months, until the start of the fall rains (v. 10).

The mother of two of the sons, Rizpah, was grieved and continued a devoted and harrowing vigil over all of the bodies during the time they hung exposed. The faithfulness of her long vigil moved David to have the bones of these seven sons given a decent burial with Saul and Jonathan (vv. 13, 14). **After that God was intreated for the land** (v. 14). With the coming of the rains, there was the realization that atonement was adequate.

B. WAR (21:15-22; cf. I Chron. 20:4-8)

15 And the Philistines had war again with Israel; and David went down, and his servants with him, and fought against the Philistines. And David waxed faint; 16 and Ishbi-benob, who was of the sons of the giant, the weight of whose spear was three hundred *shekels* of brass in weight, he being girded with a new *sword*, thought to have slain David. 17 But Abishai the son of Zeruiah succored him, and smote the Philistine, and killed

24 Renwick, *op. cit.*, p. 290; cf. Kennedy, *op. cit.*, p. 296.

him. Then the men of David sware unto him, saying, Thou shalt go no more out with us to battle, that thou quench not the lamp of Israel.

18 And it came to pass after this, that there was again war with the Philistines at Gob: then Sibbecai the Hushathite slew Saph, who was of the sons of the giant. 19 And there was again war with the Philistines at Gob; and Elhanan the son of Jaare-oregim the Beth-lehemite slew Goliath the Gittite, the staff of whose spear was like a weaver's beam. 20 And there was again war at Gath, where was a man of great stature, that had on every hand six fingers, and on every foot six toes, four and twenty in number; and he also was born to the giant. 21 And when he defied Israel, Jonathan the son of Shimei, David's brother, slew him. 22 These four were born to the giant in Gath; and they fell by the hand of David, and by the hand of his servants.

This is a brief account of David's early battles with the Philistines about the time of the capture of Jerusalem. In one of the battles David had a narrow escape in which he was almost killed (v. 16). Thereafter, his men demanded that he refrain from going into battle. He was to them the only hope for Israel (v. 17).

C. PSALM (22:1-51)

1 And David spake unto Jehovah the words of this song in the day that Jehovah delivered him out of the hand of all his enemies, and out of the hand of Saul: 2 and he said,

Jehovah is my rock, and my fortress, and my deliverer, even mine;
3 God, my rock, in him will I take refuge;
My shield, and the horn of my salvation, my high tower, and my refuge;
My saviour, thou savest me from violence.
4 I will call upon Jehovah, who is worthy to be praised:
So shall I be saved from mine enemies.
5 For the waves of death compassed me;
The floods of ungodliness made me afraid:
6 The cords of Sheol were round about me:
The snares of death came upon me.
7 In my distress I called upon Jehovah;
Yea, I called unto my God:
And he heard my voice out of his temple,
And my cry *came* into his ears.

8 Then the earth shook and trembled,
The foundations of heaven quaked
And were shaken, because he was wroth.
9 There went up a smoke out of his nostrils,
And fire out of his mouth devoured:
Coals were kindled by it.
10 He bowed the heavens also, and came down;
And thick darkness was under his feet.
11 And he rode upon a cherub, and did fly;
Yea, he was seen upon the wings of the wind.
12 And he made darkness pavilions round about him,
Gathering of waters, thick clouds of the skies.
13 At the brightness before him
Coals of fire were kindled.
14 Jehovah thundered from heaven,
And the Most High uttered his voice.
15 And he sent out arrows, and scattered them;
Lightning, and discomfited them.
16 Then the channels of the sea appeared,
The foundations of the world were laid bare,
By the rebuke of Jehovah,
At the blast of the breath of his nostrils.
17 He sent from on high, he took me;
He drew me out of many waters;
18 He delivered me from my strong enemy,
From them that hated me; for they were too mighty for me.
19 They came upon me in the day of my calamity;
But Jehovah was my stay.
20 He brought me forth also into a large place;
He delivered me, because he delighted in me.
21 Jehovah rewarded me according to my righteousness;
According to the cleanness of my hands hath he recompensed me.
22 For I have kept the ways of Jehovah,
And have not wickedly departed from my God.
23 For all his ordinances were before me;
And as for his statutes, I did not depart from them.
24 I was also perfect toward him;
And I kept myself from mine iniquity.
25 Therefore hath Jehovah recompensed me according to my righteousness,
According to my cleanness in his eyesight.

26 With the merciful thou wilt show thyself merciful;
With the perfect man thou wilt show
thyself perfect;

27 With the pure thou wilt show thyself pure;
And with the perverse thou wilt show
thyself froward.

28 And the afflicted people thou wilt save;
But thine eyes are upon the haughty,
that thou mayest bring them down.

29 For thou art my lamp, O Jehovah;
And Jehovah will lighten my darkness.

30 For by thee I run upon a troop;
By my God do I leap over a wall.

31 As for God, his way is perfect:
The word of Jehovah is tried;
He is a shield unto all them that take
refuge in him.

32 For who is God, save Jehovah?
And who is a rock, save our God?

33 God is my strong fortress;
And he guideth the perfect in his way.

34 He maketh his feet like hinds' feet,
And setteth me upon my high places.

35 He teacheth my hands to war,
So that mine arms do bend a bow of
brass.

36 Thou hast also given me the shield
of thy salvation;
And thy gentleness hath made me
great.

37 Thou hast enlarged my steps under
me;
And my feet have not slipped.

38 I have pursued mine enemies, and
destroyed them;
Neither did I turn again till they were
consumed.

39 And I have consumed them, and smitten them through, so that they cannot arise:
Yea, they are fallen under my feet.

40 For thou hast girded me with strength
unto the battle;
Thou hast subdued under me those
that rose up against me.

41 Thou hast also made mine enemies
turn their backs unto me,
That I might cut off them that hate
me.

42 They looked, but there was none to
save;
Even unto Jehovah, but he answered
them not.

43 Then did I beat them small as the
dust of the earth,
I did crush them as the mire of
the streets, and did spread them
abroad.

44 Thou also hast delivered me from
the strivings of my people;

Thou hast kept me to be the head of
the nations:
A people whom I have not known shall
serve me.

45 The foreigners shall submit themselves
unto me:
As soon as they hear of me, they shall
obey me.

46 The foreigners shall fade away,
And shall come trembling out of their
close places.

47 Jehovah liveth; and blessed be my
rock;
And exalted be God, the rock of my
salvation,

48 Even the God that executeth vengeance
for me,
And that bringeth down peoples under
me,

49 And that bringeth me forth from
mine enemies:
Yea, thou liftest me up above them
that rise up against me;
Thou deliverest me from the violent
man.

50 Therefore I will give thanks unto thee,
O Jehovah, among the nations,
And will sing praises unto thy name.

51 Great deliverance giveth he to his
king,
And showeth lovingkindness to his
anointed,
To David and to his seed, for evermore.

This psalm is almost identical with
Psalm 18. It is a thanksgiving hymn for
deliverance from Saul and for victories
over enemies. It may refer to the conquests of II Samuel 8 which secured the
throne of David and the kingdom of
Israel. For an exposition of this psalm see
"The Psalms" in the *Wesleyan Bible
Commentary*, Vol. II.

D. FAREWELL (23:1-7)

1 Now these are the last words of David.
David the son of Jesse saith,
And the man who was raised on high
saith,
The anointed of the God of Jacob,
And the sweet psalmist of Israel:

2 The Spirit of Jehovah spake by me,
And his word was upon my tongue.

3 The God of Israel said,
The Rock of Israel spake to me:
One that ruleth over men righteously,
That ruleth in the fear of God,

4 *He shall be* as the light of the morning, when the sun riseth,
A morning without clouds,

When the tender grass *springeth* out of
  the earth,
Through clear shining after rain.
5 Verily my house is not so with God;
  Yet he hath made with me an ever-
    lasting covenant,
  Ordered in all things, and sure:
  For it is all my salvation, and all *my*
    desire,
  Although he maketh it not to grow.
6 But the ungodly shall be all of them
    as thorns to be thrust away,
  Because they cannot be taken with the
    hand;
7 But the man that toucheth them
  Must be armed with iron and the
    staff of a spear:
  And they shall be utterly burned with
    fire in *their* place.

This poetical section presents the farewell words of David. It reveals a number of aspects of David's life. First, he
was a composer of psalms (v. 1). Second,
he spoke as a prophet of the Lord (v. 2).
Third, he was the embodiment of justice
(v. 3). Fourth, his dynasty was permanently established by **an everlasting
covenant** (v. 5).

Hebrew poets were accustomed to compose last words which served to highlight
the characteristics of the person to whom
they referred. In the case of David, his
farewell words significantly point to his
poetry, prophecy, justice and everlasting
dynasty. These were the durable aspects
of his life.

E. MIGHTY MEN (23:8-39; cf. I Chron. 11:10-47)

8 These are the names of the mighty
men whom David had: Josheb-basshebeth
a Tahchemonite, chief of the captains;
the same was Adino the Eznite, against
eight hundred slain at one time.
9 And after him was Eleazar the son of
Dodai the son of an Ahohite, one of the
three mighty men with David, when they
defied the Philistines that were there
gathered together to battle, and the men
of Israel were gone away. 10 He arose,
and smote the Philistines until his hand
was weary, and his hand clave unto the
sword; and Jehovah wrought a great victory that day; and the people returned
after him only to take spoil.
11 And after him was Shammah the
son of Agee a Hararite. And the Philistines were gathered together into a
troop, where was a plot of ground full
of lentils; and the people fled from the
Philistines. 12 But he stood in the midst
of the plot, and defended it, and slew the
Philistines; and Jehovah wrought a great
victory.
13 And three of the thirty chief men
went down, and came to David in the
harvest time unto the cave of Adullam;
and the troop of the Philistines was encamped in the valley of Rephaim. 14 And
David was then in the stronghold; and
the garrison of the Philistines was then in
Beth-lehem. 15 And David longed, and
said, Oh that one would give me water to
drink of the well of Beth-lehem, which is
by the gate! 16 And the three mighty
men brake through the host of the Philistines, and drew water out of the well of
Beth-lehem, that was by the gate, and
took it, and brought it to David: but he
would not drink thereof, but poured it
out unto Jehovah. 17 And he said, Be it
far from me, O Jehovah, that I should do
this: *shall I drink* the blood of the men
that went in jeopardy of their lives?
therefore he would not drink it. These
things did the three mighty men.
18 And Abishai, the brother of Joab,
the son of Zeruiah, was chief of the
three. And he lifted up his spear against
three hundred and slew them, and had a
name among the three. 19 Was he not
most honorable of the three? therefore he
was made their captain: howbeit he attained not unto the *first* three.
20 And Benaiah the son of Jehoiada,
the son of a valiant man of Kabzeel, who
had done mighty deeds, he slew the two
sons of Ariel of Moab: he went down also
and slew a lion in the midst of a pit in
time of snow. 21 And he slew an Egyptian,
a goodly man: and the Egyptian had
a spear in his hand; but he went down to
him with a staff, and plucked the spear
out of the Egyptian's hand, and slew him
with his own spear. 22 These things did
Benaiah the son of Jehoiada, and had a
name among the three mighty men. 23
He was more honorable than the thirty,
but he attained not to the *first* three.
And David set him over his guard.
24 Asahel the brother of Joab was one
of the thirty; Elhanan the son of Dodo of
Beth-lehem, 25 Shammah the Harodite,
Elika the Harodite, 26 Helez the Paltite,
Ira the son of Ikkesh the Tekoite, 27
Abiezer the Anathothite, Mebunnai the
Hushathite, 28 Zalmon the Ahohite, Maharai the Netophathite, 29 Heleb the son
of Baanah the Netophathite, Ittai the son
of Ribai of Gibeah of the children of
Benjamin, 30 Benaiah a Pirathonite, Hid-
dai of the brooks of Gaash, 31 Abialbon
the Arbathite, Azmaveth the Barhumite,

32 Eliahba the Shaalbonite, the sons of Jashen, Jonathan, 33 Shammah the Hararite, Ahiam the son of Sharar the Ararite, 34 Eliphelet the son of Ahasbai, the son of the Maacathite, Eliam the son of Ahithophel the Gilonite, 35 Hezro the Carmelite, Paarai the Arbite, 36 Igal the son of Nathan of Zobah, Bani the Gadite, 37 Zelek the Ammonite, Naharai the Beerothite, armorbearers to Joab the son of Zeruiah, 38 Ira the Ithrite, Gareb the Ithrite, 39 Uriah the Hittite: thirty and seven in all.

This list of David's mighty men was drawn up while David was still reigning in Hebron. As vacancies occurred new men were inducted. The original list refers to those who helped David in his rise to power.

There were two orders, the order of "The Three," apparently gained by outstanding heroism, and the order of "The Thirty," composed of those who went beyond the line of duty. Joab is conspicuously absent. He may have been in a class by himself. Asahel, brother of Joab, was chief of "The Thirty" (v. 18).[25] However, since Asahel was slain by Abner, Saul's commander, this list refers to the original number of mighty men (cf. 2:18ff.). Doubtless, changes occurred as war decimated the list.

To achieve a place in the order of "The Three" required some outstanding military achievement. It is not known what these men did to achieve the honor, but examples of their bravery as members of the order are given.

The Philistines enter the picture to a great extent as they provided the occasions for heroism. The incident of three of "The Thirty" obtaining David a drink of water from the well at Bethlehem when the Philistines were encamped there is a well-known example of devotion as well as bravery. These men readily risked their lives to provide David his wish (vv. 15, 16).

F. CENSUS (24:1-25; cf. I Chron. 21:1-30)

1 And again the anger of Jehovah was kindled against Israel, and he moved David against them, saying, Go, number Israel and Judah. 2 And the king said to Joab the captain of the host, who was

with him, Go now to and fro through all the tribes of Israel, from Dan even to Beer-sheba, and number ye the people, that I may know the sum of the people. 3 And Joab said unto the king, Now Jehovah thy God add unto the people, how many soever they may be, a hundredfold; and may the eyes of my lord the king see it: but why doth my lord the king delight in this thing? 4 Notwithstanding, the king's word prevailed against Joab, and against the captains of the host. And Joab and the captains of the host went out from the presence of the king, to number the people of Israel. 5 And they passed over the Jordan, and encamped in Aroer, on the right side of the city that is in the middle of the valley of Gad, and unto Jazer: 6 then they came to Gilead, and to the land of Tahtim-hodshi; and they came to Dan-jaan, and round about to Sidon, 7 and came to the stronghold of Tyre, and to all the cities of the Hivites, and of the Canaanites; and they went out to the south of Judah, at Beer-sheba. 8 So when they had gone to and fro through all the land, they came to Jerusalem at the end of nine months and twenty days. 9 And Joab gave up the sum of the numbering of the people unto the king: and there were in Israel eight hundred thousand valiant men that drew the sword; and the men of Judah were five hundred thousand men.

10 And David's heart smote him after that he had numbered the people. And David said unto Jehovah, I have sinned greatly in that which I have done: but now, O Jehovah, put away, I beseech thee, the iniquity of thy servant; for I have done very foolishly. 11 And when David rose up in the morning, the word of Jehovah came unto the prophet Gad, David's seer, saying, 12 Go and speak unto David, Thus saith Jehovah, I offer thee three things: choose thee one of them, that I may do it unto thee. 13 So Gad came to David, and told him, and said unto him, Shall seven years of famine come unto thee in thy land? or wilt thou flee three months before thy foes while they pursue thee? or shall there be three days' pestilence in thy land? now advise thee, and consider what answer I shall return to him that sent me. 14 And David said unto Gad, I am in a great strait: let us fall now into the hand of Jehovah; for his mercies are great; and let me not fall into the hand of man.

15 So Jehovah sent a pestilence upon

---

[25] There is close similarity in the Hebrew words for "three" and "thirty." Abishai was not one of "The Three," but he was chief of "The Thirty."

Israel from the morning even to the time appointed; and there died of the people from Dan even to Beer-sheba seventy thousand men. 16 And when the angel stretched out his hand toward Jerusalem to destroy it, Jehovah repented him of the evil, and said to the angel that destroyed the people, It is enough; now stay thy hand. And the angel of Jehovah was by the threshing-floor of Araunah the Jebusite. 17 And David spake unto Jehovah when he saw the angel that smote the people, and said, Lo, I have sinned, and I have done perversely; but these sheep, what have they done? let thy hand, I pray thee, be against me, and against my father's house.

18 And Gad came that day to David, and said unto him, Go up, rear an altar unto Jehovah in the threshing-floor of Araunah the Jebusite. 19 And David went up according to the saying of Gad, as Jehovah commanded. 20 And Araunah looked forth, and saw the king and his servants coming on toward him: and Araunah went out, and bowed himself before the king with his face to the ground. 21 And Araunah said, Wherefore is my lord the king come to his servant? And David said, To buy the threshing-floor of thee, to build an altar unto Jehovah, that the plague may be stayed from the people. 22 And Araunah said unto David, Let my lord the king take and offer up what seemeth good unto him: behold, the oxen for the burnt-offering, and the threshing instruments and the yokes of the oxen for the wood: 23 all this, O king, doth Araunah give unto the king. And Araunah said unto the king, Jehovah thy God accept thee. 24 And the king said unto Araunah, Nay; but I will verily buy it of thee at a price; neither will I offer burnt-offerings unto Jehovah my God which cost me nothing. So David bought the threshing-floor and the oxen for fifty shekels of silver. 25 And David built there an altar unto Jehovah, and offered burnt-offerings and peace-offerings. So Jehovah was entreated for the land, and the plague was stayed from Israel.

Famine came upon Israel because of Saul's violation of the covenant relation in massacring the Gibeonites (21:1). Pestilence afflicted Israel because of David's sin in taking a census. It is much more difficult to ascertain the sinfulness of taking a census.

It appears that the census was primarily a military measure (v. 9). It is possible that the sin consisted in the aspiration of achieving the chief place among the nations. David, on this premise, sinned in the census-taking in that he sought to prepare Israel for political leadership among the nations. However, Israel was called not to be great among the nations but to witness to the redeeming activity of God, Israel being the leading recipient of this activity and, therefore, largely responsible for sharing it with the nations of the earth. Following this line of reasoning, it would appear that David aspired to· make Israel politically dominant, whereas God desired to make Israel religiously missionary in outlook.

Upon the completion of the census David was aware of his sin (v. 10). He confessed his wrong even before the arrival of the prophet (v. 11). Placing himself and his kingdom at the mercy of the Lord, David prayed, **Let us fall now into the hand of Jehovah** (v. 14). Pestilence afflicted the land in the form of a death-dealing plague. The manpower that David had hoped to rely upon in his military might was reduced drastically.

A theophany appeared unto David as he was by the threshing-floor of Araunah the Jebusite located on Mount Moriah in Jerusalem. The prophet told David to build an altar there. David arranged with Araunah to buy the threshing-floor, saying: **I will verily buy it of thee at a price; neither will I offer burnt-offerings unto Jehovah my God which cost me nothing** (v. 24). This outstanding statement of David gives the essential idea underlying all true sacrifice, namely, there is cost involved. David was determined to offer true sacrifice unto the Lord. The Lord's response was seen in causing the plague to cease (v. 25).

Bibliography

I. EXEGETICAL AND HISTORICAL VALUE

Anderson, B. *Understanding the Old Testament.* Englewood Cliffs, N. J.: Prentice-Hall, 1957.

Blauw, J. *The Missionary Nature of the Church.* New York: McGraw-Hill, 1962.

Bright, John. *A History of Israel.* Philadelphia: Westminster, 1951.

Caird, George B. "First and Second Samuel: Introduction and Exegesis." *The Interpreter's Bible.* Eds. G. A. Buttrick *et al.* Vol. II. New York and Nashville: Abingdon, 1953.

Cochrane, C. N. *Christianity and Classical Culture.* New York: Oxford, 1961.

Driver, S. R. *Notes on the Hebrew Text and the Topography of the Books of Samuel,* 2nd ed. Oxford, 1913.

Kennedy, A. R. S. "The Book of Samuel." *The New Century Bible.* London: Caxton, n.d.

Kirkpatrick, A. F. "First Samuel." *The Cambridge Bible for Schools and Colleges.* Ed. J. J. S. Perowne. Cambridge, 1890.

————. "Second Samuel." *The Cambridge Bible for Schools and Colleges.* Ed. J. J. S. Perowne. Cambridge, 1884.

Renwick, A. M. "I and II Samuel." *New Bible Commentary.* Eds. F. Davidson *et al.* Grand Rapids: Eerdmans, 1953.

Wright, G. E. and F. V. Filson (eds.). *The Westminster Historical Atlas.* Philadelphia: Westminster, 1945.

II. EXPOSITORY AND PRACTICAL VALUE

Lange, J. P. *Commentary on the Holy Scripture.* Reprint. Vol. V. Grand Rapids: Zondervan, n.d.

Little, G. "II Samuel: Exposition." *The Interpreter's Bible.* Eds. G. A. Buttrick *et al.* Vol. II. New York and Nashville: Abingdon, 1953.

Maclaren, A. *Expositions of Holy Scripture.* Vol. II. New York: Doran, n.d.

Nicoll, W. Robertson (ed.). *The Expositor's Bible.* Vol. II. Reprint. Grand Rapids: Eerdmans, 1940.

Spence, H. D. M. and J. S. Exell (eds.). *Pulpit Commentary.* Vol. 9. New York and London: Funk and Wagnalls.

Stevenson, Dwight E. *Preaching on the Books of the Old Testament.* New York: Harper, 1961.

The First Book of Kings

by Charles R. Wilson

Outline

Introduction

The two books of Kings originally formed a single work, the fourth and last book of that section of the Hebrew Bible called the "Former Prophets." This work begins where Samuel ends, namely, the last days of David's reign. It includes Solomon's reign, the revolt of the northern tribes, and the parallel histories of the Northern and Southern Kingdoms until the fall of the former in 721 B. C. and of the latter in 586 B. C. It concludes with an account of Jehoiachin's release from Babylonian imprisonment after being held a prisoner for thirty-seven years. The time span covered by Kings is over four hundred years.

I. COMPOSITION

It is generally accepted that Kings was written about the close of the seventh century B. C., soon after the death of King Josiah. C. F. Burney was of the opinion that the main writing of Kings was done before the destruction of the Southern Kingdom, while those parts which require exilic dating are later additions and interpolations.[1]

The compiler remains anonymous, but he does identify some of his major sources and acknowledges dependence upon others. For the account of the reign of Solomon, given in I Kings 1-11, his source was "the book of the acts of Solomon" (I Kings 11:41). For the account of the Northern Kingdom there are seventeen references to "the book of the chronicles of the kings of Israel" (I Kings 14:19, etc.). For the account of the Southern Kingdom there are fifteen references to "the book of the chronicles of the kings of Judah" (I Kings 14:29, etc.). There were the annals of the royal courts as well as the histories written by the prophets which provided additional sources. "The cycles of stories about Elijah and Elisha may have been preserved independently."[2]

The narrative in Kings was meant as a continuation of the narrative in Samuel. In giving the account of the reign of Solomon, the compiler continually refers to divine revelation given to David at the time of his intense interest in building a temple unto the Lord at Jerusalem (II Sam. 7:1-17).[3]

Of major interest to the compiler of Kings is the divine declaration to David regarding his son: "If he commit iniquity, I will chasten him with the rod of men, and with the stripes of the children of men" (II Sam. 7:14). This is shown in David's final words to his successor, Solomon: "Keep the charge of Jehovah thy God, to walk in his ways, to keep his statutes and his commandments ... according to that which is written in the law of Moses ... that Jehovah may establish his word which he spake concerning me, saying, If thy children ... walk before me in truth with all their heart ... there shall not fail thee ... a man on the throne of Israel" (I Kings 2:3, 4).

Highly significant in this is the place held by the law. Just as Deuteronomic influence impregnated the first three books of the Former Prophets, namely, Joshua, Judges and Samuel, so that influence is to be found in the fourth and last book, Kings. If the descendants of David maintained wholehearted allegiance to God, there would not fail to be an heir on the throne. If they forsook God, the Davidic line would be broken, the temple destroyed and Jerusalem left desolate.

By the skillful use of his main sources, which give the histories of Solomon and both the Northern and Southern Kingdoms, the compiler of Kings gives a sober and realistic account of the history of the

---

[1] C. F. Burney, "Kings, I and II," *A Dictionary of the Bible*, edited by J. Hastings, II, 862.
[2] J. C. J. Waite, "Kings, Books of," *New Bible Dictionary*, edited by J. D. Douglas, p. 699.
[3] Cf. II Sam. 7:12-14; I Kings 2:1-4; 6:11-13; 8:17-20; 9:3-9; 11:30-39.

monarchy based upon Deuteronomic principles (Deut. 27—29). Writing his account in the even-glow of the kingdom of Judah, the compiler, while maintaining strong allegiance to the Davidic dynasty, the temple and Jerusalem, shows with blazing clarity that the tragedy which came upon the kingdom was a supreme example of divine retribution. The story of Israel from David's death to the thirty-seventh year of Jehoiachin's captivity is an actual working out, in the ongoing of history, of the reality of divine judgment upon a covenant people who had become unfaithful and compromising in their worship of Jehovah.

II. HISTORY FROM THE THEOLOGICAL PERSPECTIVE

"The religious standpoint of the writer of Kings is that of the Book of Deuteronomy."[4] The Deuteronomic standpoint laid primary emphasis upon wholeheartedness faithfulness to Jehovah as Israel's only God. This emphasis was based upon the fact that Jehovah had chosen Israel from among the nations so that through Israel all nations might be blessed. Yet Israel was unfaithful. Not only did the kings of the monarchy willfully violate the covenant which God made with David (II Sam. 7:8-16) but also the covenant which God made with Israel at Shechem (Deut. 29:1-22). The Shechem covenant provided the Deuteronomic criteria by which the history of the monarchy was written.

Kings is history written purposefully. The compiler's aim was not primarily descriptive, according to which recorded history simply informs concerning the past. Rather, the compiler's aim was primarily didactic, according to which recorded history gives instruction, guidance and admonition. He sought to instruct his generation and succeeding generations concerning covenant unfaithfulness and its tragic end. He graphically admonished by means of historical reality the tragic harvest of religious irresponsibility and infidelity written large in the history of a nation. Gray says: "We look in vain in Kings for any consciousness of

the positive destiny of Israel among the peoples of the earth...."[5] Rather, Israel was intent on serving other gods and following after the nations. When Kings was written, the nation was reaching the end of the way. Again Gray states: "This was a time for mourning and humiliation for Israel, and the opportunity to bring home to her that sin brought divine retribution."[6] Kings reveals powerful pathos as it instructs and admonishes the remnant of Israel to repent and return to the covenant-keeping God and His world-wide commission for her. It has been well said:

> The remarkable note is that when all was lost, someone found the history of that tragic period worth recording as a lesson of God's discipline of His people.[7]

III. MORAL AND SPIRITUAL VALUE

Kings provides far more religious instruction than a superficial reading would indicate. It is the final book in a four-volumed set known as the Former Prophets. These books record Israel's history from the time of the entrance into the promised land under Joshua during the thirteenth century B. C. until the exile into Babylon during the seventh century B. C., a span of time covering approximately six centuries.

A. THE IMPORTANCE OF HISTORY

Like Joshua, Judges and Samuel, Kings is historical. It was written not merely to preserve the past but to persuade that generation which was contemporary with the time of writing, as well as succeeding generations. It was like an illustrated sermon instructing the people to repentance and renewed allegiance to Jehovah.

History was important because it was meaningful and purposeful. The history of Israel's monarchy from David's death to Jehoiachin's release was a meaningful period, from the Kings standpoint, because a faithless and recalcitrant covenant people was under divine chastening and discipline through the instrumentality of alien peoples. This was seen clearly by the

---

4 Burney, op. cit., p. 857.   5 J. Gray, I and II Kings, p. 42.   6 Ibid., p. 43.
7 J. A. Montgomery and H. S. Gehman, "A Critical and Exegetical Commentary on the Books of Kings," International Critical Commentary, pp. 44, 45.

prophets as they preached repentance and faithfulness.

History continues to be important and meaningful to those who recognize the contributions of the prophetic standpoint. What is happening in our time may have momentous significance if we explore the developments with the forthright integrity and humble faith of the prophets. God reveals as He wills, and His saving activity continues in history.

B. DISCIPLINE ACCORDING TO THE DEUTERONOMIC PRINCIPLE

The influence of Deuteronomy upon the Former Prophets is generally recognized. According to this book, Israel was given the opportunity of life and good and blessing if she remained faithful to her covenant with Jehovah (Deut. 30:15-20). On the other hand, she would receive death and evil and cursing if she desecrated the covenant. That opportunity had not become obsolete because God was the living God who was active in history vindicating His covenant faithfulness. What had happened during the monarchy was historical evidence to the Deuteronomists that God was disciplining His covenant-desecrating people.

The living God exercises unalterable faithfulness to the covenant, be it the old or the new. When the covenant relationship which He has made is marred, He acts in disciplining judgment through the ongoing process of historical events. If the covenant people of Jehovah do not keep faith, God in His faithfulness deals with the unfaithfulness of His people through the discipline of the stern realities of history.

C. JEHOVAH ALONE IS GOD

Outstanding among the values of Kings is the unequivocal affirmation that Jehovah alone is God. He is not one God among many. He is altogether other than the nature deities. He is the covenant God who acts in history to accomplish His purpose.

The recurring theme of the prophets was that there was no God but Jehovah. Yet the perennial sin of Israel was that of treating Jehovah as one among many. Her relations with other nations together with the political and cultural interchanges were at the root of the tendency to acknowledge other gods. The cultures of the surrounding nations were so impregnated with their nature religions that in adopting the culture of a people the Israelites tended to adulterate their Jehovah-worship.

Commentary on First Kings

I. THE STRUGGLE OVER SUCCESSION (I Kings 1:1—2:46)

The monarchy of Israel had no provision for determining the succession to the throne. Saul and David were selected by God and the people (cf. I Sam. 10:17-24 and II Sam. 5:1-3). However, the son of Saul, Ish-bosheth, was made king by the authority of Abner, captain of Saul's army (II Sam. 2:8-9). Furthermore, there were the possibilities of the tradition of primogeniture, by which the first-born son was considered the heir, and the personal choice of the ruling monarch, David.

A. RIVALS FOR THE THRONE (1:1-53)

Adonijah apparently was a qualified heir to the throne since he was the oldest surviving son of David. However, Solomon's claim to the throne was by reason of David's promise (1:13, 17).

1. David's Incapacity (1:1-4)

1 Now king David was old and stricken in years; and they covered him with clothes, but he gat no heat. 2 Wherefore his servants said unto him, Let there be sought for my lord the king a young virgin: and let her stand before the king, and cherish him; and let her lie in thy bosom, that my lord the king may get heat. 3 So they sought for a fair damsel throughout all the borders of Israel, and found Abishag the Shunammite, and brought her to the king. 4 And the damsel was very fair; and she cherished the king, and ministered to him; but the king knew her not.

These verses may involve more than David's loss of physical vigor. It may indicate that his loss of sexual vigor imperiled his capacity to reproduce, a capacity which was a necessary requirement of the neighboring Canaanite kings.

Although David did not indulge in the Canaanite fertility cult, his sexual impotence was of real concern to the royal court. The fact that Abishag was procured to excite him sexually shows the extent to which the royal court of David was influenced by the Canaanite cult of fertility. It was an indication that Israel was becoming "like all the nations" (I Sam. 8:20).

2. Adonijah's Claim (1:5-10)

5 Then Adonijah the son of Haggith exalted himself, saying, I will be king: and he prepared him chariots and horsemen, and fifty men to run before him. 6 And his father had not displeased him at any time in saying, Why hast thou done so? and he was also a very goodly man; and he was born after Absalom. 7 And he conferred with Joab the son of Zeruiah, and with Abiathar the priest: and they following Adonijah helped him. 8 But Zadok the priest, and Benaiah the son of Jehoiada, and Nathan the prophet, and Shimei, and Rei, and the mighty men that belong to David, were not with Adonijah. 9 And Adonijah slew sheep and oxen and fatlings by the stone of Zoheleth, which is beside En-rogel; and he called all his brethren, the king's sons, and all the men of Judah, the king's servants: 10 but Nathan the prophet, and Benaiah, and the mighty men, and Solomon his brother, he called not.

Adonijah . . . exalted himself, saying, I will be king (v. 5). Since David showed signs that he was no longer able to fulfill the requirements of king, a likely candidate to succeed him was his oldest living son, Adonijah. He had been permitted by David to enhance his status with **chariots and horsemen** (vv. 5, 6). He was **a very goodly man**, a phrase referring to his handsome appearance (v. 6). He had the support of Joab, David's long-time trusted general, and Abiathar, the priest, who escaped Saul's massacre of the priests at

Nob and joined David while he was a fugitive from Saul (I Sam. 22:20). His brothers, **the king's sons,** except Solomon, and **the men of Judah** were supporting his move to become king (v. 9).

Adonijah invited his supporters to a feast at En-rogel, a spring located near the confluence of the Kidron and Hinnon valleys on the outskirts of Jerusalem. This signaled the beginning of Adonijah's uprising.

It is significant that Adonijah did not invite the opposition, including Nathan the prophet, Benaiah and the mighty men, and Solomon. This exclusion indicates

> that Adonijah was not prepared for "peaceful coexistence", to which, by ancient Semitic convention, he would have been committed by such a meal.[1]

Obviously, Adonijah thought that his forces were strong enough to destroy the opposition. Later he realized his enormous error.

3. Solomon's Counter-Claim (1:11-40)

11 Then Nathan spake unto Bath-sheba the mother of Solomon, saying, Hast thou not heard that Adonijah the son of Haggith doth reign, and David our lord knoweth it not? 12 Now therefore come, let me, I pray thee, give thee counsel, that thou mayest save thine own life, and the life of thy son Solomon. 13 Go and get thee in unto king David, and say unto him, Didst not thou, my lord, O king, swear unto thy handmaid, saying, Assuredly Solomon thy son shall reign after me, and he shall sit upon my throne? why then doth Adonijah reign? 14 Behold, while thou yet talkest there with the king, I also will come in after thee, and confirm thy words.

15 And Bath-sheba went in unto the king into the chamber: and the king was very old; and Abishag the Shunammite was ministering unto the king. 16 And Bath-sheba bowed, and did obeisance unto the king. And the king said, What wouldest thou? 17 And she said unto him, My lord, thou swarest by Jehovah thy God unto thy handmaid, *saying,* Assuredly Solomon thy son shall reign after me, and he shall sit upon my throne. 18 And now, behold, Adonijah reigneth; and thou, my lord the king, knowest it not: 19 and he hath slain oxen and fatlings and sheep in abundance, and hath called

all the sons of the king, and Abiathar the priest, and Joab the captain of the host; but Solomon thy servant hath he not called. 20 And thou, my lord the king, the eyes of all Israel are upon thee, that thou shouldest tell them who shall sit on the throne of my lord the king after him. 21 Otherwise it will come to pass, when my lord the king shall sleep with his fathers, that I and my son Solomon shall be counted offenders.

22 And, lo, while she yet talked with the king, Nathan the prophet came in. 23 And they told the king, saying, Behold, Nathan the prophet. And when he was come in before the king, he bowed himself before the king with his face to the ground. 24 And Nathan said, My lord, O king, hast thou said, Adonijah shall reign after me, and he shall sit upon my throne? 25 For he is gone down this day, and hath slain oxen and fatlings and sheep in abundance, and hath called all the king's sons, and the captains of the host, and Abiathar the priest; and, behold, they are eating and drinking before him, and say, *Long* live king Adonijah. 26 But me, even me thy servant, and Zadok the priest, and Benaiah the son of Jehoiada, and thy servant Solomon, hath he not called. 27 Is this thing done by my lord the king, and thou hast not showed unto thy servants who should sit on the throne of my lord the king after him?

28 Then king David answered and said, Call to me Bath-sheba. And she came into the king's presence, and stood before the king. 29 And the king sware, and said, As Jehovah liveth, who hath redeemed my soul out of all adversity, 30 verily as I sware unto thee by Jehovah, the God of Israel, saying, Assuredly Solomon thy son shall reign after me, and he shall sit upon my throne in my stead; verily so will I do this day. 31 Then Bath-sheba bowed with her face to the earth, and did obeisance to the king, and said, Let my lord king David live for ever.

32 And king David said, Call to me Zadok the priest, and Nathan the prophet, and Benaiah the son of Jehoiada. And they came before the king. 33 And the king said unto them, Take with you the servants of your lord, and cause Solomon my son to ride upon mine own mule, and bring him down to Gihon: 34 and let Zadok the priest and Nathan the prophet anoint him there king over Israel; and blow ye the trumpet, and say, *Long* live king Solomon. 35 Then ye shall come up

---

[1] John Gray, *I and II Kings,* p. 83.

after him, and he shall come and sit upon my throne; for he shall be king in my stead; and I have appointed him to be prince over Israel and over Judah. 36 And Benaiah the son of Jehoiada answered the king, and said, Amen: Jehovah, the God of my lord the king, say so *too*. 37 As Jehovah hath been with my lord the king, even so be he with Solomon, and make his throne greater than the throne of my lord king David.

38 So Zadok the priest, and Nathan the prophet, and Benaiah the son of Jehoiada, and the Cherethites and the Pelethites, went down, and caused Solomon to ride upon king David's mule, and brought him to Gihon. 39 And Zadok the priest took the horn of oil out of the Tent, and anointed Solomon. And they blew the trumpet; and all the people said, *Long* live king Solomon. 40 And all the people came up after him, and the people piped with pipes, and rejoiced with great joy, so that the earth rent with the sound of them.

Nathan the prophet initiated countermoves to block Adonijah's effort to gain the throne. He spoke to Bathsheba, the mother of Solomon, ... let me ... **give thee counsel, that thou mayest save thine own life, and the life of thy son Solomon** (v. 12). This reveals his awareness of the cleavage within the house of David which had Adonijah and Solomon on opposite sides. He was astutely aware of the implications of Adonijah's exclusion of Solomon as well as himself from the uprising meal at En-rogel (cf. vv. 1, 10). His counsel to Bathsheba indicates that he considered her life and the life of her son in mortal peril.

Nathan's approach to Bathsheba adroitly injected the reminder that Adonijah was the son of a rival wife, Haggith (v. 11). He also reminded Bathsheba of a promise which David had made to her, **Assuredly Solomon thy son shall reign after me** (v. 13).

Bathsheba acted according to Nathan's counsel. She went to the king, and he acknowledged his promise (v. 30). Accordingly, while Adonijah conducted his feast at En-rogel, David had Solomon anointed at **Gihon,** the famous Virgin's Spring in the Kidron Valley (v. 38). Solomon's role in the struggle for succession appears to be more passive than that of Adonijah.

4. Failure of Adonijah's Plan (1:41-53)

41 And Adonijah and all the guests that were with him heard it as they had made an end of eating. And when Joab heard the sound of the trumpet, he said, Wherefore is this noise of the city being in an uproar? 42 While he yet spake, behold, Jonathan the son of Abiathar the priest came: and Adonijah said, Come in; for thou art a worthy man, and bringest good tidings. 43 And Jonathan answered and said to Adonijah, Verily our lord king David hath made Solomon king: 44 and the king hath sent with him Zadok the priest, and Nathan the prophet, and Benaiah the son of Jehoiada, and the Cherethites and the Pelethites; and they have caused him to ride upon the king's mule; 45 and Zadok the priest and Nathan the prophet have anointed him king in Gihon; and they are come up from thence rejoicing, so that the city rang again. This is the noise that ye have heard. 46 And also Solomon sitteth on the throne of the kingdom. 47 And moreover the king's servants came to bless our lord king David, saying, Thy God make the name of Solomon better than thy name, and make his throne greater than thy throne: and the king bowed himself upon the bed. 48 And also thus said the king, Blessed be Jehovah, the God of Israel, who hath given one to sit on my throne this day, mine eyes even seeing it.

49 And all the guests of Adonijah were afraid, and rose up, and went every man his way. 50 And Adonijah feared because of Solomon; and he arose, and went, and caught hold on the horns of the altar. 51 And it was told Solomon, saying, Behold, Adonijah feareth king Solomon; for, lo, he hath laid hold on the horns of the altar, saying, Let king Solomon swear unto me first that he will not slay his servant with the sword. 52 And Solomon said, If he shall show himself a worthy man, there shall not a hair of him fall to the earth; but if wickedness be found in him, he shall die. 53 So king Solomon sent, and they brought him down from the altar. And he came and did obeisance to king Solomon; and Solomon said unto him, Go to thy house.

During the feasting at En-rogel, Adonijah's company heard the tumult of the people as Solomon was anointed king. In panic, the supporters of Adonijah dispersed, while Adonijah himself hurried to the great altar for refuge. "Though the right of sanctuary is not expressly mentioned in the law, it is implied by Exodus 21:14."[2]

Adonijah's plea was, **Let king Solomon swear unto me first that he will not slay his servant with the sword** (v. 51). He expected severe treatment from Solomon, presumably the same kind of treatment he would have given Solomon had the situation been reversed.

Solomon promised, **If he shall show himself a worthy man, there shall not a hair of him fall to the earth** (v. 52). Because Adonijah came before the king and acknowledged Solomon's sovereignty, his life was spared.

Although Adonijah's cause was lost, his precipitation of the crisis over David's successor brought out the solution to the problem. David himself selected his successor. Israel's first and second kings were designated by God and selected by the people. Israel's third king was the choice of the ruling monarch, King David.

B. DAVID'S COUNSEL TO SOLOMON (2:1-12)

David, having come to the end of his life, now gives final counsel to Solomon. The unusual factor involved is that the counsel, given in two distinct sections, hardly appears unified in outlook and spirit. In the first section the outlook and temper is one of encouraging faithful obedience to God, while in the second section there is the call for realistic and practical action in order to protect the accession of Solomon to the throne.

1. Obey the Lord (2:1-4)

1 Now the days of David drew nigh that he should die; and he charged Solomon his son, saying, 2 I am going the way of all the earth: be thou strong therefore, and show thyself a man; 3 and keep the charge of Jehovah thy God, to walk in his ways, to keep his statutes, *and* his commandments, and his ordinances, and his testimonies, according to that which is written in the law of Moses, that thou mayest prosper in all that thou doest, and whithersoever thou turnest thyself; 4 that Jehovah may establish his word which he spake concerning me, saying, If thy children take heed to their way, to walk before me in truth with all their heart and with all their soul, there shall

not fail thee (said he) a man on the throne of Israel.

This section is Deuteronomic in character, in the sense that Solomon is promised prosperity in all his reign if he would zealously obey the Deuteronomic law. On the other hand, disobedience would bring the chastening of the Lord.

2. Judge the Political Opponents (2:5-12)

5 Moreover thou knowest also what Joab the son of Zeruiah did unto me, even what he did to the two captains of the hosts of Israel, unto Abner the son of Ner, and unto Amasa the son of Jether, whom he slew, and shed the blood of war in peace, and put the blood of war upon his girdle that was about his loins, and in his shoes that were on his feet. 6 Do therefore according to thy wisdom, and let not his hoar head go down to Sheol in peace. 7 But show kindness unto the sons of Barzillai the Gileadite, and let them be of those that eat at thy table; for so they came to me when I fled from Absalom thy brother. 8 And, behold, there is with thee Shimei the son of Gera, the Benjamite, of Bahurim, who cursed me with a grievous curse in the day when I went to Mahanaim; but he came down to meet me at the Jordan, and I sware to him by Jehovah, saying, I will not put thee to death with the sword. 9 Now therefore hold him not guiltless, for thou art a wise man; and thou wilt know what thou oughtest to do unto him, and thou shalt bring his hoar head down to Sheol with blood.

10 And David slept with his fathers, and was buried in the city of David. 11 And the days that David reigned over Israel were forty years: seven years reigned he in Hebron, and thirty and three years reigned he in Jerusalem. 12 And Solomon sat upon the throne of David his father; and his kingdom was established greatly.

In this section of David's final counsel to Solomon, the stress is on young Solomon's realistic handling of some situations which have come to him as a legacy from the reign of his father. David specifically mentions two problems, namely, Joab (vv. 5-6) and Shimei (vv. 8-9). In order to maintain a strong Davidic dynasty, these two men must be eliminated. David

---

[2] H. L. Ellison, "I and II Kings," *New Bible Commentary*, ed. by F. Davidson *et al.*, p. 303.

also mentions one pledge of good-will which Solomon should maintain, namely, the royal pledge to the house of the aged Barzillai (v. 7).

C. SOLOMON'S PURGE (2:13-46)

13 Then Adonijah the son of Haggith came to Bath-sheba the mother of Solomon. And she said, Comest thou peaceably? And he said, Peaceably. 14 He said moreover, I have somewhat to say unto thee. And she said, Say on. 15 And he said, Thou knowest that the kingdom was mine, and that all Israel set their faces on me, that I should reign: howbeit the kingdom is turned about, and is become my brother's; for it was his from Jehovah. 16 And now I ask one petition of thee; deny me not. And she said unto him, Say on. 17 And he said, Speak, I pray thee, unto Solomon the king (for he will not say thee nay), that he give me Abishag the Shunammite to wife. 18 And Bath-sheba said, Well; I will speak for thee unto the king.

19 Bath-sheba therefore went unto king Solomon, to speak unto him for Adonijah. And the king rose up to meet her, and bowed himself unto her, and sat down on his throne, and caused a throne to be set for the king's mother; and she sat on his right hand. 20 Then she said, I ask one small petition of thee; deny me not. And the king said unto her, Ask on, my mother; for I will not deny thee. 21 And she said, Let Abishag the Shunammite be given to Adonijah thy brother to wife. 22 And king Solomon answered and said unto his mother, And why dost thou ask Abishag the Shunammite for Adonijah? ask for him the kingdom also; for he is mine elder brother; even for him, and for Abiathar the priest, and for Joab the son of Zeruiah. 23 Then king Solomon sware by Jehovah, saying, God do so to me, and more also, if Adonijah hath not spoken this word against his own life. 24 Now therefore as Jehovah liveth, who hath established me, and set me on the throne of David my father, and who hath made me a house, as he promised, surely Adonijah shall be put to death this day. 25 And king Solomon sent by Benaiah the son of Jehoiada; and he fell upon him, so that he died.

26 And unto Abiathar the priest said the king, Get thee to Anathoth, unto thine own fields; for thou art worthy of death: but I will not at this time put thee to death, because thou barest the ark of the Lord Jehovah before David my father, and because thou wast afflicted in all wherein my father was afflicted. 27 So Solomon thrust out Abiathar from being priest unto Jehovah, that he might fulfil the word of Jehovah, which he spake concerning the house of Eli in Shiloh.

28 And the tidings came to Joab; for Joab had turned after Adonijah, though he turned not after Absalom. And Joab fled unto the Tent of Jehovah, and caught hold on the horns of the altar. 29 And it was told king Solomon, Joab is fled unto the Tent of Jehovah, and, behold, he is by the altar. Then Solomon sent Benaiah the son of Jehoiada, saying, Go, fall upon him. 30 And Benaiah came to the Tent of Jehovah, and said unto him, Thus saith the king, Come forth. And he said, Nay; but I will die here. And Benaiah brought the king word again, saying, Thus said Joab, and thus he answered me. 31 And the king said unto him, Do as he hath said, and fall upon him, and bury him; that thou mayest take away the blood, which Joab shed without cause, from me and from my father's house. 32 And Jehovah will return his blood upon his own head, because he fell upon two men more righteous and better than he, and slew them with the sword, and my father David knew it not, *to wit,* Abner the son of Ner, captain of the host of Israel, and Amasa the son of Jether, captain of the host of Judah. 33 So shall their blood return upon the head of Joab, and upon the head of his seed for ever: but unto David, and unto his seed, and unto his house, and unto his throne, shall there be peace for ever from Jehovah. 34 Then Benaiah the son of Jehoiada went up, and fell upon him, and slew him; and he was buried in his own house in the wilderness. 35 And the king put Benaiah the son of Jehoiada in his room over the host; and Zadok the priest did the king put in the room of Abiathar.

36 And the king sent and called for Shimei, and said unto him, Build thee a house in Jerusalem, and dwell there, and go not forth thence any whither. 37 For on the day thou goest out, and passest over the brook Kidron, know thou for certain that thou shalt surely die: thy blood shall be upon thine own head. 38 And Shimei said unto the king, The saying is good: as my lord the king hath said, so will thy servant do. And Shimei dwelt in Jerusalem many days.

39 And it came to pass at the end of three years, that two of the servants of Shimei ran away unto Achish, son of Maacah, king of Gath. And they told

Shimei, saying, Behold, thy servants are in Gath. 40 And Shimei arose, and saddled his ass, and went to Gath to Achish, to seek his servants; and Shimei went, and brought his servants from Gath. 41 And it was told Solomon that Shimei had gone from Jerusalem to Gath, and was come again. 42 And the king sent and called for Shimei, and said unto him, Did I not adjure thee by Jehovah, and protest unto thee, saying, Know for certain, that on the day thou goest out, and walkest abroad any whither, thou shalt surely die? and thou saidst unto me, The saying that I have heard is good. 43 Why then hast thou not kept the oath of Jehovah, and the commandment that I have charged thee with? 44 The king said moreover to Shimei, thou knowest all the wickedness which thy heart is privy to, that thou didst to David my father: therefore Jehovah shall return thy wickedness upon thine own head. 45 But king Solomon shall be blessed, and the throne of David shall be established before Jehovah for ever. 46 So the king commanded Benaiah the son of Jehoiada; and he went out, and fell upon him, so that he died. And the kingdom was established in the hand of Solomon.

Solomon proceeds in a determined and effective manner to eliminate existing threats to the continued prosperity and success of the dynasty of David.

One such threat appears when Adonijah requests Abishag (vv. 13-25). Solomon interprets the request as a renewed attempt on the part of Adonijah to gain the throne (v. 22). There was an ancient Semitic custom that the man who inherited the women of a deceased king became his successor (cf. II Sam. 16:20-23).

Solomon next turns his attention to the allies of Adonijah, namely, Abiathar and Joab. Abiathar was a priest and not subject to the royal decree of death. However, Solomon banishes him from the royal court and religious sanctuary (v. 26).

Joab, hearing of Solomon's purge, seeks refuge at the altar. This is to no avail, for he is slain (v. 34). If the altar had provided sanctuary for Joab, this would have set an important precedent. Needless to say, the precedent would have proved impractical.

There is the problem of Shimei still remaining. Solomon decrees that Shimei remain in Jerusalem under what may be described as surveillance. Any departure

from Jerusalem will be a violation of this decree. The penalty for violation is death (v. 37). Because Shimei violates this decree, he is put to death (v. 46).

Solomon effectively executed the counsel of his father David. By such firm and realistic measures as he executed during the purge at the beginning of his reign, Solomon secured the kingdom (v. 46).

II. THE WISDOM AND ADMINISTRATION OF SOLOMON
(I Kings 3:1—4:34)

Solomon inherited a strong kingdom from his father. He had great aspirations to enhance the prestige of his rule and implemented those aspirations by morally reprehensible as well as morally responsible activities.

A. WISDOM (3:1-28)

While Solomon was pursuing his political aims, he met the God of Israel in an encounter at Gibeon. Out of that encounter came a humbled Solomon who had received a new heart.

1. Prayer for Wisdom (3:1-15)

1 And Solomon made affinity with Pharaoh king of Egypt, and took Pharaoh's daughter, and brought her into the city of David, until he had made an end of building his own house, and the house of Jehovah, and the wall of Jerusalem round about. 2 Only the people sacrificed in the high places, because there was no house built for the name of Jehovah until those days. 3 And Solomon loved Jehovah, walking in the statutes of David his father: only he sacrificed and burnt incense in the high places.

4 And the king went to Gibeon to sacrifice there; for that was the great high place: a thousand burnt-offerings did Solomon offer upon that altar. 5 In Gibeon Jehovah appeared to Solomon in a dream by night; and God said, Ask what I shall give thee. 6 And Solomon said, Thou hast showed unto thy servant David my father great lovingkindness, according as he walked before thee in truth, and in righteousness, and in uprightness of heart with thee; and thou hast kept for him this great lovingkindness, that thou hast given him a son to sit on his throne, as it is this day. 7 And now, O Jehovah my God, thou hast made thy servant king instead of David my

father: and I am but a little child; I know not how to go out or come in. 8 And thy servant is in the midst of thy people which thou hast chosen, a great people, that cannot be numbered nor counted for multitude. 9 Give thy servant therefore an understanding heart to judge thy people, that I may discern between good and evil; for who is able to judge this thy great people?

10 And the speech pleased the Lord, that Solomon had asked this thing. 11 And God said unto him, Because thou hast asked this thing, and hast not asked for thyself long life, neither hast asked riches for thyself, nor hast asked the life of thine enemies, but hast asked for thyself understanding to discern justice; 12 behold, I have done according to thy word: lo, I have given thee a wise and an understanding heart; so that there hath been none like thee before thee, neither after thee shall any arise like unto thee. 13 And I have also given thee that which thou hast not asked, both riches and honor, so that there shall not be any among the kings like unto thee, all thy days. 14 And if thou wilt walk in my ways, to keep my statutes and my commandments, as thy father David did walk, then I will lengthen thy days. 15 And Solomon awoke; and, behold, it was a dream: and he came to Jerusalem, and stood before the ark of the covenant of Jehovah, and offered up burnt-offerings, and offered peace-offerings, and made a feast to all his servants.

After Solomon had secured his reign by removing all rivals, as related in I Kings 2, he sought to improve his political career by using not only marriage but also religion for political expediency. **Solomon made affinity with Pharaoh king of Egypt, and took Pharaoh's daughter** (v. 1). The alliance with Egypt strengthened Solomon's rule. He also **sacrificed and burnt incense in the high places** (v. 3). Solomon's political aspirations apparently motivated his reprehensible religious activities. He seemed possessed with one concern above all others: to be successful in his rule over the kingdom. To succeed in this he used marriage, as was commonly done by ancient monarchs, to serve his international diplomacy. He also bowed before religious shrines in order to obtain any possible help from that source.

Notwithstanding these efforts of Solomon to secure his political future, the incident which occurred to him at Gibeon was of an altogether different ordering. This was not one of Solomon's political daydreams. This was a compelling dream given by God.

In a dream, Solomon was confronted by the Lord Jehovah. He expressed a basic honesty in this meeting as he admitted his inward concern about governing the strong state of Israel. He acknowledged a sense of unpreparedness and inadequacy. Behind his facade of international diplomacy and religious practice, Solomon in the presence of God acknowledged his own weakness. **I am but a little child; I know not how to go out or come in** (v. 7).

Solomon could forego engaging in marriage and in religion for political purposes, but he could not forego the help of God in his reign. At Gibeon, Solomon met the Lord, and he was humbled. It is true that he did not always maintain the humility which he showed at Gibeon, but the experience of the divine that came to him corrected his spiritual focus at least momentarily. His ambitious efforts to secure his political future seemed impotent in the presence of the Lord of Israel. **God said, Ask what I shall give thee** (v. 5). Solomon answered in humility, **Give thy servant therefore an understanding heart to judge this people** (v. 9).

Solomon's previously aggressive political activities appear in decided contrast to his humble request for an understanding heart. In the presence of the self-revealing God of Israel Solomon faced the problem deep within himself. He lacked inner resources for directing the affairs of state. Above all else he sensed the need for understanding in order to judge rightly. To meet this need, he looked to God and found the answer to his anxiety. **I have given thee a wise and an understanding heart** (v. 12). Solomon's prayer was answered. The divine help needed to purge the dross of political egoism was granted to him. Rather than to promote his own security, Solomon was divinely enabled to enter fully into the cases of his people which needed a verdict of justice and, with profound insight, to render just judgments.

2. Practice of Wisdom (3:16-28)

16 Then there came two women that were harlots, unto the king, and stood before him. 17 And the one woman said, Oh, my lord, I and this woman dwell in one house; and I was delivered of a child with her in the house. 18 And it came to pass the third day after I was delivered, that this woman was delivered also; and we were together; there was no stranger with us in the house, save we two in the house. 19 And this woman's child died in the night, because she lay upon it. 20 And she arose at midnight, and took my son from beside me, while thy handmaid slept, and laid it in her bosom, and laid her dead child in my bosom. 21 And when I rose in the morning to give my child suck, behold, it was dead; but when I had looked at it in the morning, behold, it was not my son, whom I did bear. 22 And the other woman said, Nay; but the living is my son, and the dead is thy son. And this said, No; but the dead is thy son, and the living is my son. Thus they spake before the king.

23 Then said the king, The one saith, This is my son that liveth, and thy son is the dead: and the other saith, Nay; but thy son is the dead, and my son is the living. 24 And the king said, Fetch me a sword. And they brought a sword before the king. 25 And the king said, Divide the living child in two, and give half to the one, and half to the other. 26 Then spake the woman whose the living child was unto the king, for her heart yearned over her son, and she said, Oh, my lord, give her the living child, and in no wise slay it. But the other said, It shall be neither mine nor thine; divide it. 27 Then the king answered and said, Give her the living child, and in no wise slay it: she is the mother thereof. 28 And all Israel heard of the judgment which the king had judged; and they feared the king: for they saw that the wisdom of God was in him, to do justice.

Why was the crass incident of two harlots quarreling over a child selected from any number of incidents to express the wisdom of Solomon? There is no answer, but it can be said that this dramatic story, though linked with sordidness, is also linked with Solomon's understanding heart by the connecting link of love. Solomon employed the test of love to determine the true mother of the child. Through love he found the truth. Having found the true mother, he administered justice by giving her the child. Solomon progressed through three stages: (1) he began with an understanding heart, (2) he employed the test of love, (3) he rendered justice. **And all Israel heard of the judgment ... for they saw that the wisdom of God was in him, to do justice** (v. 28).

The practice of wisdom is perennially relevant. As Solomon rendered justice by means of an understanding and empathetic attitude, so is justice to be granted to those seeking it. No arbitrary ruling in itself is sufficient. Decisions must be based upon that kind of understanding Samuel had in mind in another context when he said, "Man looketh on the outward appearance, but Jehovah looketh on the heart" (I Sam. 16:7).

B. ADMINISTRATION (4:1-34)

Solomon's reign was, for those times, a model of organizational efficiency. His remarkable administration over the large empire was possible because of capable personnel.

1. The Personnel in his Administration (4:1-19)

1 And king Solomon was king over all Israel. 2 And these were the princes whom he had: Azariah the son of Zadok, the priest; 3 Elihoreph and Ahijah, the sons of Shisha, scribes; Jehoshaphat the son of Ahilud, the recorder; 4 and Benaiah the son of Jehoiada was over the host; and Zadok and Abiathar were priests; 5 and Azariah the son of Nathan was over the officers; and Zabud the son of Nathan was chief minister, and the king's friend; 6 and Ahishar was over the household; and Adoniram the son of Abda was over the men subject to taskwork.

7 And Solomon had twelve officers over all Israel, who provided victuals for the king and his household: each man had to make provision for a month in the year. 8 And these are their names: Ben-hur, in the hill-country of Ephraim; 9 Bendeker, in Makaz, and in Shaalbim, and Beth-shemesh, and Elon-beth-hanan; 10 Ben-hesed, in Arubboth (to him pertained Socoh, and all the land of Hepher); 11 Ben-abinadab, in all the height of Dor (he had Taphath the daughter of Solomon to wife); 12 Baana the son of Ahilud, in Taanach and Megiddo, and all Beth-shean which is beside Zarethan, beneath Jezreel, from Beth-shean to

Abel-meholah, as far as beyond Jokmeam; 13 Ben-geber, in Ramoth-gilead (to him *pertained* the towns of Jair the son of Manasseh, which are in Gilead; *even* to him *pertained* the region of Argob, which is in Bashan, threescore great cities with walls and brazen bars) ; 14 Ahinadab the son of Iddo, in Mahanaim; 15 Ahimaaz, in Naphtali (he also took Basemath the daughter of Solomon to wife) ; 16 Baana the son of Hushai, in Asher and Bealoth; 17 Jehoshaphat the son of Paruah, in Issachar; 18 Shimei the son of Ela, in Benjamin; 19 Geber the son of Uri, in the land of Gilead, the country of Sihon king of the Amorites and of Og king of Bashan; and *he was* the only officer that was in the land.

There were two categories of personnel in Solomon's administration. There were the **princes** (v. 2) who were the highest officials in his court. Also, there were the twelve officers (v. 7) who were district governors, each assigned to a particular geographical part of the kingdom. It is quite significant that the list of districts and their governors omits Judah. Apparently, Judah was exempt from providing supplies for the court and military, a chief obligation laid upon the districts (cf. vv. 22-23, 27-28) .

This preference shown to Solomon's own tribe was extremely unwise. Since the posterity of the line of Joseph through Ephraim and Manasseh continually competed with Judah for leadership among the tribes, Solomon's unwise districting of the kingdom definitely contributed to the disruption of the monarchy at his death. He may have had an "understanding heart" for the harlot who was the true mother, but he did not have such a heart for the old tribal loyalties lying deep in the bosom of many Israelites.

This problem continually thwarts enterprising institutions. A leader who tends toward favoritism generates a reaction or backlash. He may escape the consequences, but the institution or group does not.

2. The Prosperity of his Administration (4:20-34)

20 Judah and Israel were many as the sand which is by the sea in multitude, eating and drinking and making merry. 21 And Solomon ruled over all the kingdoms from the River unto the land of the Philistines, and unto the border of Egypt: they brought tribute, and served Solomon all the days of his life. 22 And Solomon's provision for one day was thirty measures of fine flour, and threescore measures of meal, 23 ten fat oxen, and twenty oxen out of the pastures, and a hundred sheep, besides harts, and gazelles, and roebucks, and fatted fowl. 24 For he had dominion over all *the region* on this side the River, from Tiphsah even to Gaza, over all the kings on this side the River: and he had peace on all sides round about him. 25 And Judah and Israel dwelt safely, every man under his vine and under his fig-tree, from Dan even to Beer-sheba, all the days of Solomon. 26 And Solomon had forty thousand stalls of horses for his chariots, and twelve thousand horsemen. 27 And those officers provided victuals for king Solomon, and for all that came unto king Solomon's table, every man in his month; they let nothing be lacking. 28 Barley also and straw for the horses and swift steeds brought they unto the place where *the officers* were, every man according to his charge.

29 And God gave Solomon wisdom and understanding exceeding much, and largeness of heart, even as the sand that is on the sea-shore. 30 And Solomon's wisdom excelled the wisdom of all the children of the east, and all the wisdom of Egypt. 31 For he was wiser than all men; than Ethan the Ezrahite, and Heman, and Calcol, and Darda, the sons of Mahol: and his fame was in all the nations round about. 32 And he spake three thousand proverbs; and his songs were a thousand and five. 33 And he spake of trees, from the cedar that is in Lebanon even unto the hyssop that springeth out of the wall: he spake also of beasts, and of birds, and of creeping things, and of fishes. 34 And there came of all peoples to hear the wisdom of Solomon, from all kings of the earth, who had heard of his wisdom.

This is a picture of the splendor of Solomon, his power, wealth and wisdom. His regal magnificence is described according to the promises which God made to him at Gibeon (I Kings 3:11-14) . It is proof of God's favor.

While it is true that material prosperity may be the reward of righteousness, it is not necessary to assume that it is the result of righteousness only. In fact, material prosperity can and does result in godless unrighteousness.

III. SOLOMON'S EARLIER ENTER-
PRISES (I Kings 5:1—9:25)

Solomon's reign was marked by an important building program, the most impressive building being the temple.

A. HELP FROM HIRAM (5:1-18; cf. II Chron. 2:1-16)

1 And Hiram king of Tyre sent his servants unto Solomon; for he had heard that they had anointed him king in the room of his father: for Hiram was ever a lover of David. 2 And Solomon sent to Hiram, saying, 3 Thou knowest how that David my father could not build a house for the name of Jehovah his God for the wars which were about him on every side, until Jehovah put them under the soles of his feet. 4 But now Jehovah my God hath given me rest on every side; there is neither adversary, nor evil occurrence. 5 And, behold, I purpose to build a house for the name of Jehovah my God, as Jehovah spake unto David my father, saying, Thy son, whom I will set upon thy throne in thy room, he shall build the house for my name. 6 Now therefore command thou that they cut me cedar-trees out of Lebanon; and my servants shall be with thy servants; and I will give thee hire for thy servants according to all that thou shalt say: for thou knowest that there is not among us any that knoweth how to cut timber like unto the Sidonians.

7 And it came to pass, when Hiram heard the words of Solomon, that he rejoiced greatly, and said, Blessed be Jehovah this day, who hath given unto David a wise son over this great people. 8 And Hiram sent to Solomon, saying, I have heard *the message* which thou hast sent unto me: I will do all thy desire concerning timber of cedar, and concerning timber of fir. 9 My servants shall bring them down from Lebanon unto the sea; and I will make them into rafts to go by sea unto the place that thou shalt appoint me, and will cause them to be broken up there, and thou shalt receive them; and thou shalt accomplish my desire, in giving food for my household. 10 So Hiram gave Solomon timber of cedar and timber of fir according to all his desire. 11 And Solomon gave Hiram twenty thousand measures of wheat for food to his household, and twenty measures of pure oil: thus gave Solomon to Hiram year by year. 12 And Jehovah gave

Solomon wisdom, as he promised him; and there was peace between Hiram and Solomon; and they two made a league together.

13 And king Solomon raised a levy out of all Israel; and the levy was thirty thousand men. 14 And he sent them to Lebanon, ten thousand a month by courses; a month they were in Lebanon, and two months at home: and Adoniram was over the men subject to taskwork. 15 And Solomon had threescore and ten thousand that bare burdens, and fourscore thousand that were hewers in the mountains; 16 besides Solomon's chief officers that were over the work, three thousand and three hundred, who bare rule over the people that wrought in the work. 17 And the king commanded, and they hewed out great stones, costly stones, to lay the foundation of the house with wrought stone. 18 And Solomon's builders and Hiram's builders and the Gebalites did fashion them, and prepared the timber and the stones to build the house.

Hiram, king of Tyre, a friend of David, sent emissaries to Solomon, who, in turn, communicated to Hiram an important message. **I purpose to build a house for the name of Jehovah my God** (v. 5).

"In the time of Solomon, Tyre was a rising power and was soon to dominate . . . the whole of southern Phoenicia."[3] The friendly relations between this rising power and the impressive nation of Israel provided for mutual assistance. Hiram needed access to the vital trade routes through Israel as well as trade with Israel. Solomon needed Phoenician materials and artisans. Solomon frankly acknowledged his need for the skilled Phoenician workmen: **There is not among us any that knoweth how to cut timber like unto the Sidonians** (v. 6).

This passage relating the help which Hiram was willing to provide Solomon concludes with a statement that reveals the faithfulness of the Lord Jehovah to Solomon and at the same time depicts an intimate relationship developing between Solomon and Hiram. **And Jehovah gave Solomon wisdom, as he promised him; and there was peace between Hiram and Solomon; and they two made a league together** (v. 12).

The first part of this verse shows Jehovah faithful to what He had promised

3 Gray, *op. cit.*, p. 144.

Solomon at Gibeon (I Kings 2:12). The second strikes a jarring note when viewed in relation to the first. The relationship between Hiram and Solomon was one of peace (v. 12). Since there was no threat of war, the essential meaning of peace is *rapprochement,* a cozy relationship. It was this sense of intimate relationship that prompted these rulers to make a league, literally, to "cut a covenant" (v. 12). This involved the offering of religious sacrifices to the gods of the participants. "This was a solemn religious action involving Solomon in a recognition of Hiram's gods."[4] In the type of alliance which Solomon made with Hiram, the God of Israel was placed on the same level as the gods of Hiram. This being the case, Solomon's covenant involved religious compromise for the sake of political support in building the temple. This was, to say the least, an incongruous situation. Notwithstanding Jehovah's faithfulness, Solomon was not reciprocating with the same fidelity. His construction programs and international involvements, even though motivated by religious concerns, were encroaching on his first responsibility, namely, loyal obedience to his God.

B. SOLOMON'S TEMPLE (6:1-38; cf. II Chron. 3:1-14)

1 And it came to pass in the four hundred and eightieth year after the children of Israel were come out of the land of Egypt, in the fourth year of Solomon's reign over Israel, in the month Ziv, which is the second month, that he began to build the house of Jehovah. 2 And the house which king Solomon built for Jehovah, the length thereof was threescore cubits, and the breadth thereof twenty *cubits,* and the height thereof thirty cubits. 3 And the porch before the temple of the house, twenty cubits was the length thereof according to the breadth of the house; *and* ten cubits was the breadth thereof before the house. 4 And for the house he made windows of fixed lattice-work. 5 And against the wall of the house he built stories round about, against the walls of the house round about, both of the temple and of the oracle; and he made side-chambers round about. 6 The nethermost story was five cubits broad, and the middle was six

cubits broad, and the third was seven cubits broad; for on the outside he made offsets *in the wall* of the house round about, that *the beams* should not have hold in the walls of the house. 7 And the house, when it was in building, was built of stone made ready at the quarry; and there was neither hammer nor axe nor any tool of iron heard in the house, while it was in building. 8 The door for the middle side-chambers was in the right side of the house: and they went up by winding stairs into the middle *story,* and out of the middle into the third. 9 So he built the house, and finished it; and he covered the house with beams and planks of cedar. 10 And he built the stories against all the house, each five cubits high: and they rested on the house with timber of cedar.

11 And the word of Jehovah came to Solomon, saying, 12 Concerning this house which thou art building, if thou wilt walk in my statutes, and execute mine ordinances, and keep all my commandments to walk in them; then will I establish my word with thee, which I spake unto David thy father. 13 And I will dwell among the children of Israel, and will not forsake my people Israel.

14 So Solomon built the house, and finished it. 15 And he built the walls of the house within with boards of cedar: from the floor of the house unto the walls of the ceiling, he covered them on the inside with wood; and he covered the floor of the house with boards of fir. 16 And he built twenty cubits on the hinder part of the house with boards of cedar from the floor unto the walls *of the ceiling:* he built *them* for it within, for an oracle, even for the most holy place. 17 And the house, that is, the temple before the oracle, was forty cubits *long.* 18 And there was cedar on the house within, carved with knops and open flowers: all was cedar; there was no stone seen. 19 And he prepared an oracle in the midst of the house within, to set there the ark of the covenant of Jehovah. 20 And within the oracle was *a space of* twenty cubits in length, and twenty cubits in breadth, and twenty cubits in the height thereof; and he overlaid it with pure gold: and he covered the altar with cedar. 21 So Solomon overlaid the house within with pure gold: and he drew chains of gold across before the oracle; and he overlaid it with gold. 22 And the whole house he overlaid with gold, until all the house was finished: also the whole

---

[4] Ellison, *op. cit.,* p. 306.

altar that belonged to the oracle he overlaid with gold.

23 And in the oracle he made two cherubim of olive-wood, each ten cubits high. 24 And five cubits was the one wing of the cherub, and five cubits the other wing of the cherub: from the uttermost part of the one wing unto the uttermost part of the other were ten cubits. 25 And the other cherub was ten cubits: both the cherubim were of one measure and one form. 26 The height of the one cherub was ten cubits, and so was it of the other cherub. 27 And he set the cherubim within the inner house; and the wings of the cherubim were stretched forth, so that the wing of the one touched the one wall, and the wing of the other cherub touched the other wall; and their wings touched one another in the midst of the house. 28 And he overlaid the cherubim with gold.

29 And he carved all the walls of the house round about with carved figures of cherubim and palm-trees and open flowers, within and without. 30 And the floor of the house he overlaid with gold, within and without. 31 And for the entrance of the oracle he made doors of olive-wood: the lintel *and* door-posts were a fifth part *of the wall.* 32 So *he made* two doors of olive-wood; and he carved upon them carvings of cherubim and palm-trees and open flowers, and overlaid them with gold; and he spread the gold upon the cherubim, and upon the palm-trees. 33 So also made he for the entrance of the temple door-posts of olive-wood, out of a fourth part *of the wall;* 34 and two doors of firwood: the two leaves of the one door were folding, and the two leaves of the other door were folding. 35 And he carved *thereon* cherubim and palm-trees and open flowers; and he overlaid them with gold fitted upon the graven work. 36 And he built the inner court with three courses of hewn stone, and a course of cedar beams.

37 In the fourth year was the foundation of the house of Jehovah laid, in the month Ziv. 38 And in the eleventh year, in the month Bul, which is the eighth month, was the house finished throughout all the parts thereof, and according to all the fashion of it. So was he seven years in building it.

Of all the projects in Solomon's ambitious building program, the building of the temple was the most important. A proportionately extended account is given of its erection, design and furnishings.

Construction of the temple began during the fourth year of Solomon's reign. **And it came to pass in the four hundred and eightieth year after the children of Israel were come out of the land of Egypt, in the fourth year of Solomon's reign . . . that he began to build the house of Jehovah (v. 1).** Although this verse holds the cardinal clue to dating the Exodus in the fifteenth century B.C., the evidence of recent archaeology together with evidence gleaned from the study of tribal genealogies results in a thirteenth century B.C. dating.[5]

The size of the temple was sixty by twenty cubits (about ninety feet by thirty feet). This was twice the floor space of the tabernacle. Its height was thirty cubits (about forty-five feet). It was a great architectural achievement for the tenth century B. C.

The structural features of the temple also included a **porch** for the front entrance and **side-chambers** for use by the priests (vv. 3, 5).

The interior features of the temple included the large room referred to as the **house** (v. 15) and **the most holy place** referred to as the **oracle** (v. 16). The interior was covered with cedar and overlaid with gold.

Perhaps the most surprising feature was the placing of two cherubim in the Holy of Holies. If nothing but the ark of the covenant were placed in the Holy of Holies of the tabernacle, according to the directive given to Moses at Mount Sinai, why did Solomon have cherubim as well as the ark of the covenant in the Holy of Holies of the temple? The answer seems to lie in the function which they served. Either they served primarily as a symbolic protection for the ark of the covenant or as a symbolic support for the throne of the Lord.[6] In view of the fact that Phoenician craftsmen actively engaged in the work as well as contributed ideas and suggestions, it is probable that the cherubim indicate Phoenician influence. The Phoenicians are known to have used winged figures to support the throne of a king.[7]

[5] Cf. John Garstang, *Foundations of Bible History: Joshua, Judges;* H. H. Rowley, *From Joseph to Joshua.*
[6] Gray, *op. cit.,* p. 162.   [7] *Ibid.*

This development coupled with the covenant between Solomon and Hiram, together with the religious implications involved, put a severe strain on Solomon's unequivocal loyalty to the Jehovah of Israel. Foreign political influences were inextricably bound up with religion.

C. SOLOMON'S PALACE (7:1-12)

1 And Solomon was building his own house thirteen years, and he finished all his house. 2 For he built the house of the forest of Lebanon; the length thereof was a hundred cubits, and the breadth thereof fifty cubits, and the height thereof thirty cubits, upon four rows of cedar pillars, with cedar beams upon the pillars. 3 And it was covered with cedar above over the forty and five beams, that were upon the pillars; fifteen in a row. 4 And there were beams in three rows, and window was over against window in three ranks. 5 And all the doors and posts were made square with beams: and window was over against window in three ranks. 6 And he made the porch of pillars; the length thereof was fifty cubits, and the breadth thereof thirty cubits; and a porch before them; and pillars and a threshold before them. 7 And he made the porch of the throne where he was to judge, even the porch of judgment: and it was covered with cedar from floor to floor. 8 And his house where he was to dwell, the other court within the porch, was of the like work. He made also a house for Pharaoh's daughter (whom Solomon had taken to wife), like unto this porch.

9 All these were of costly stones, even of hewn stone, according to measure, sawed with saws, within and without, even from the foundation unto the coping, and so on the outside unto the great court. 10 And the foundation was of costly stones, even great stones, stones of ten cubits, and stones of eight cubits. 11 And above were costly stones, even hewn stone, according to measure, and cedar-wood. 12 And the great court round about had three courses of hewn stone, and a course of cedar beams; like as the inner court of the house of Jehovah, and the porch of the house.

Solomon's building project on Mount Moriah consisted of a large complex of buildings, the most noteworthy being the temple. An approximate plan of this whole complex together with the courts of the buildings has been attempted by T. W. Davies.[8]

While seven years were required to complete the building of the temple, a single magnificent edifice, only thirteen years were needed to complete a palace complex consisting of public as well as private quarters. Included in the public buildings were **the house of the forest of Lebanon** (v. 2), generally understood to have been a large public hall; **the porch of pillars** (v. 6), perhaps a portico leading into the next-mentioned enclosure; and **the porch of judgment** (v. 7), likely a hall for rendering justice. Included in the private buildings of the palace complex were Solomon's house **where he was to dwell** (v. 8), meaning the royal residence, and **a house for Pharaoh's daughter** (v. 8), more likely a reference to the harem rather than a private house.

Looking at Solomon's building project realistically, it seems unlikely that he is deserving of the extensive criticism leveled at him for requiring thirteen years to build the palace complex when seven years were required for the temple. Rather than to inject a moral question into the picture, it is preferable to consider the matter in an amoral context, as builders do when they compare the time required for one job as against the time required for another.

D. TEMPLE FURNISHINGS (7:13-51; cf. II Chron. 3:15—4:22)

13 And king Solomon sent and fetched Hiram out of Tyre. 14 He was the son of a widow of the tribe of Naphtali, and his father was a man of Tyre, a worker in brass; and he was filled with wisdom and understanding and skill, to work all works in brass. And he came to king Solomon, and wrought all his work. 15 For he fashioned the two pillars of brass, eighteen cubits high apiece: and a line of twelve cubits compassed either of them about. 16 And he made two capitals of molten brass, to set upon the tops of the pillars: the height of the one capital was five cubits, and the height of the other capital was five cubits. 17 There were nets of checker-work, and wreaths of chain-work, for the capitals which were

8 T. W. Davies, "Temple," *Hastings Dictionary of the Bible*, IV, 695ff.; cf. W. Shaw Caldecott and James Orr, "Temple," *International Standard Bible Encyclopedia*, ed. by James Orr, V, 2930ff.

upon the top of the pillars; seven for the one capital, and seven for the other capital. 18 So he made the pillars; and there were two rows round about upon the one network, to cover the capitals that were upon the top of the pillars: and so did he for the other capital. 19 And the capitals that were upon the top of the pillars in the porch were of lily-work, four cubits. 20 And there were capitals above also upon the two pillars, close by the belly which was beside the network: and the pomegranates were two hundred, in rows round about upon the other capital. 21 And he set up the pillars at the porch of the temple: and he set up the right pillar, and called the name thereof Jachin; and he set up the left pillar, and called the name thereof Boaz. 22 And upon the top of the pillars was lily-work: so was the work of the pillars finished.

23 And he made the molten sea of ten cubits from brim to brim, round in compass, and the height thereof was five cubits; and a line of thirty cubits compassed it round about. 24 And under the brim of it round about there were knops which did compass it, for ten cubits, compassing the sea round about: the knops were in two rows, cast when it was cast. 25 It stood upon twelve oxen, three looking toward the north, and three looking toward the west, and three looking toward the south, and three looking toward the east; and the sea was set upon them above, and all their hinder parts were inward. 26 And it was a handbreadth thick; and the brim thereof was wrought like the brim of a cup, like the flower of a lily: it held two thousand baths.

27 And he made the ten bases of brass; four cubits was the length of one base, and four cubits the breadth thereof, and three cubits the height of it. 28 And the work of the bases was on this manner: they had panels; and there were panels between the ledges; 29 and on the panels that were between the ledges were lions, oxen, and cherubim; and upon the ledges there was a pedestal above; and beneath the lions and oxen were wreaths of hanging work. 30 And every base had four brazen wheels, and axles of brass; and the four feet thereof had undersetters: beneath the laver were the undersetters molten, with wreaths at the side of each. 31 And the mouth of it within the capital and above was a cubit: and the mouth thereof was round after the work of a pedestal, a cubit and a half; and also upon the mouth of it were gravings, and their panels were foursquare, not round.

32 And the four wheels were underneath the panels; and the axletrees of the wheels were in the base: and the height of a wheel was a cubit and half a cubit. 33 And the work of the wheels was like the work of a chariot wheel: their axletrees, and their felloes, and their spokes, and their naves, were all molten. 34 And there were four undersetters at the four corners of each base: the undersetters thereof were of the base itself. 35 And in the top of the base was there a round compass half a cubit high; and on the top of the base the stays thereof and the panels thereof were of the same. 36 And on the plates of the stays thereof, and on the panels thereof, he graved cherubim, lions, and palm-trees, according to the space of each, with wreaths round about. 37 After this manner he made the ten bases: all of them had one casting, one measure, and one form.

38 And he made ten lavers of brass: one laver contained forty baths; and every laver was four cubits; and upon every one of the ten bases one laver. 39 And he set the bases, five on the right side of the house, and five on the left side of the house: and he set the sea on the right side of the house eastward, toward the south.

40 And Hiram made the lavers, and the shovels, and the basins. So Hiram made an end of doing all the work that he wrought for king Solomon in the house of Jehovah: 41 the two pillars, and the two bowls of the capitals that were on the top of the pillars; and the two networks to cover the two bowls of the capitals that were on the top of the pillars; 42 and the four hundred pomegranates for the two networks; two rows of pomegranates for each network, to cover the two bowls of the capitals that were upon the pillars; 43 and the ten bases, and the ten lavers on the bases; 44 and the one sea, and the twelve oxen under the sea; 45 and the pots, and the shovels, and the basins: even all these vessels, which Hiram made for king Solomon, in the house of Jehovah, were of burnished brass. 46 In the plain of the Jordan did the king cast them, in the clay ground between Succoth and Zarethan. 47 And Solomon left all the vessels *unweighed*, because they were exceeding many: the weight of the brass could not be found out.

48 And Solomon made all the vessels that were in the house of Jehovah: the golden altar, and the table whereupon the showbread was, of gold; 49 and the

candlesticks, five on the right side, and five on the left, before the oracle, of pure gold; and the flowers, and the lamps, and the tongs, of gold; 50 and the cups, and the snuffers, and the basins, and the spoons, and the firepans, of pure gold; and the hinges, both for the doors of the inner house, the most holy place, and for the doors of the house, to wit, of the temple, of gold.

51 Thus all the work that king Solomon wrought in the house of Jehovah was finished. And Solomon brought in the things which David his father had dedicated, even the silver, and the gold, and the vessels, and put them in the treasuries of the house of Jehovah.

Solomon secured a skilled bronze-worker named Hiram, whose mother was an Israelite but whose father was a man of Tyre (v. 14). Excellent craftsmen were not to be found in Israel.

Hiram constructed two free-standing bronze pillars eighteen cubits high (27 feet), each with a capital (bowl, cf. v. 41) of five cubits (7½ feet) placed on top. These were placed on the porch of the temple and were called Jachin ("He shall establish") and Boaz ("In it is strength"), but no explanation of their function is given (v. 21). "The names . . . may reflect the relationship of God and king."[9] Jachin may refer to God in His mighty acts while Boaz may refer to the king's dependence upon God's activity.

The bronze sea constructed by Hiram probably symbolized the sea (v. 23). Gray thinks that "the containing the waters may have symbolized the triumph of Cosmos over Chaos, the ordering powers of Providence in Nature."[10] The bronze work of Hiram also included the lavers, and the shovels, and the basins (v. 40).

In addition to the bronze furnishings constructed by Hiram, Solomon had numerous objects of gold fashioned for the temple (vv. 48-50).

E. DEDICATORY PROCESSIONAL (8:1-11; cf. II Chron. 5:2-14)

1 Then Solomon assembled the elders of Israel, and all the heads of the tribes, the princes of the fathers' houses of the children of Israel, unto king Solomon in Jerusalem, to bring up the ark of the covenant of Jehovah out of the city of David, which is Zion. 2 And all the men of Israel assembled themselves unto king Solomon at the feast, in the month Ethanim, which is the seventh month. 3 And all the elders of Israel came, and the priests took up the ark. 4 And they brought up the ark of Jehovah, and the tent of meeting, and all the holy vessels that were in the Tent; even these did the priests and the Levites bring up. 5 And king Solomon and all the congregation of Israel, that were assembled unto him, were with him before the ark, sacrificing sheep and oxen, that could not be counted nor numbered for multitude. 6 And the priests brought in the ark of the covenant of Jehovah unto its place, into the oracle of the house, to the most holy place, even under the wings of the cherubim. 7 For the cherubim spread forth their wings over the place of the ark, and the cherubim covered the ark and the staves thereof above. 8 And the staves were so long that the ends of the staves were seen from the holy place before the oracle; but they were not seen without: and there they are unto this day. 9 There was nothing in the ark save the two tables of stone which Moses put there at Horeb, when Jehovah made a covenant with the children of Israel, when they came out of the land of Egypt. 10 And it came to pass, when the priests were come out of the holy place, that the cloud filled the house of Jehovah, 11 so that the priests could not stand to minister by reason of the cloud; for the glory of Jehovah filled the house of Jehovah.

Upon the occasion of the dedication of the temple Solomon arranged for the ark of the covenant to be brought from the tent located in the city to the Most Holy Place in the temple (vv. 1, 4, 6). It was a memorable procession, for it climaxed Solomon's efforts to provide a residence for Jehovah and the ark of the covenant.

When the priests were come out of the holy place . . . the glory of Jehovah filled the house of Jehovah (vv. 10, 11). The presence of the Lord was manifest in the dense cloud. Solomon and the people knew that Jehovah had made the temple His habitation.

F. SOLOMON'S ADDRESS (8:12-21; cf. II Chron. 6:1-11)

12 Then spake Solomon, Jehovah hath said that he would dwell in the thick darkness. 13 I have surely built thee a

---

[9] Gray, op. cit., p. 175.   [10] Ibid., p. 177.

house of habitation, a place for thee to dwell in for ever. 14 And the king turned his face about, and blessed all the assembly of Israel: and all the assembly of Israel stood. 15 And he said, Blessed be Jehovah, the God of Israel, who spake with his mouth unto David my father, and hath with his hand fulfilled it, saying, 16 Since the day that I brought forth my people Israel out of Egypt, I chose no city out of all the tribes of Israel to build a house, that my name might be there; but I chose David to be over my people Israel. 17 Now it was in the heart of David my father to build a house for the name of Jehovah, the God of Israel. 18 But Jehovah said unto David my father, Whereas it was in thy heart to build a house for my name, thou didst well that it was in thy heart: 19 nevertheless thou shalt not build the house; but thy son that shall come forth out of thy loins, he shall build the house for my name. 20 And Jehovah hath established his word that he spake; for I am risen up in the room of David my father, and sit on the throne of Israel, as Jehovah promised, and have built the house for the name of Jehovah, the God of Israel. 21 And there have I set a place for the ark, wherein is the covenant of Jehovah, which he made with our fathers, when he brought them out of the land of Egypt.

Solomon's address to the assembly of Israel was an historical recapitulation of the developments involved in the project of building the temple from the time David expressed interest in building it. Solomon looked upon the temple as the fulfillment of God's covenant with David (v. 20). In a more sweeping view, he looked upon the completion of this building which housed the ark of the covenant as ending the probationary period begun with the Exodus and reaching this position of permanence (cf. 4:16, 21)

G. SOLOMON'S PRAYER AND BENE- DICTION (8:22-61; cf. II Chron. 6: 12-42)

22 And Solomon stood before the altar of Jehovah in the presence of all the assembly of Israel, and spread forth his hands toward heaven; 23 and he said, O Jehovah, the God of Israel, there is no God like thee, in heaven above, or on earth beneath; who keepest covenant and lovingkindness with thy servants, that walk before thee with all their heart; 24 who hast kept with thy servant David my father that which thou didst promise him: yea, thou spakest with thy mouth, and hast fulfilled it with thy hand, as it is this day. 25 Now therefore, O Jehovah, the God of Israel, keep with thy servant David my father that which thou hast promised him, saying, There shall not fail thee a man in my sight to sit on the throne of Israel, if only thy children take heed to their way, to walk before me as thou hast walked before me. 26 Now therefore, O God of Israel, let thy word, I pray thee, be verified, which thou spakest unto thy servant David my father.

27 But will God in very deed dwell on the earth? behold, heaven and the heaven of heavens cannot contain thee; how much less this house that I have builded! 28 Yet have thou respect unto the prayer of thy servant, and to his supplication, O Jehovah my God, to hearken unto the cry and to the prayer which thy servant prayeth before thee this day; 29 that thine eyes may be open toward this house night and day, even toward the place whereof thou hast said, My name shall be there; to hearken unto the prayer which thy servant shall pray toward this place. 30 And hearken thou to the supplication of thy servant, and of thy people Israel, when they shall pray toward this place: yea, hear thou in heaven thy dwelling-place; and when thou hearest, forgive.

31 If a man sin against his neighbor, and an oath be laid upon him to cause him to swear, and he come and swear before thine altar in this house; 32 then hear thou in heaven, and do, and judge thy servants, condemning the wicked, to bring his way upon his own head, and justifying the righteous, to give him according to his righteousness.

33 When thy people Israel are smitten down before the enemy, because they have sinned against thee; if they turn again to thee, and confess thy name, and pray and make supplication unto thee in this house: 34 then hear thou in heaven, and forgive the sin of thy people Israel, and bring them again unto the land which thou gavest unto their fathers.

35 When heaven is shut up, and there is no rain, because they have sinned against thee; if they pray toward this place, and confess thy name, and turn from their sin, when thou dost afflict them: 36 then hear thou in heaven, and forgive the sin of thy servants, and of thy people Israel, when thou teachest them the good way wherein they should walk; and send rain upon thy land, which thou

hast given to thy people for an inheritance.

37 If there be in the land famine, if there be pestilence, if there be blasting or mildew, locust or caterpillar; if their enemy besiege them in the land of their cities; whatsoever plague, whatsoever sickness there be; 38 what prayer and supplication soever be made by any man, or by all thy people Israel, who shall know ever man the plague of his own heart, and spread forth his hands toward this house: 39 then hear thou in heaven thy dwelling-place, and forgive, and do, and render unto every man according to all his ways, whose heart thou knowest; (for thou, even thou only, knowest the hearts of all the children of men;) 40 that they may fear thee all the days that they live in the land which thou gavest unto our fathers.

41 Moreover concerning the foreigner, that is not of thy people Israel, when he shall come out of a far country for thy name's sake 42 (for they shall hear of thy great name, and of thy mighty hand, and of thine outstretched arm); when he shall come and pray toward this house; 43 hear thou in heaven thy dwelling-place, and do according to all that the foreigner calleth to thee for; that all the peoples of the earth may know thy name, to fear thee, as doth thy people Israel, and that they may know that this house which I have built is called by thy name.

44 If thy people go out to battle against their enemy, by whatsoever way thou shalt send them, and they pray unto Jehovah toward the city which thou hast chosen, and toward the house which I have built for thy name; 45 then hear thou in heaven their prayer and their supplication, and maintain their cause.

46 If they sin against thee (for there is no man that sinneth not), and thou be angry with them, and deliver them to the enemy, so that they carry them away captive unto the land of the enemy, far off or near; 47 yet if they shall bethink themselves in the land whither they are carried captive, and turn again, and make supplication unto thee in the land of them that carried them captive, saying, We have sinned, and have done perversely, we have dealt wickedly; 48 if they return unto thee with all their heart and with all their soul in the land of their enemies, who carried them captive, and pray unto thee toward their land, which thou gavest unto their fathers, the city which thou hast chosen, and the house which I have built for thy name: 49 then

hear thou their prayer and their supplication in heaven thy dwelling-place, and maintain their cause; 50 and forgive thy people who have sinned against thee, and all their transgressions wherein they have transgressed against thee; and give them compassion before those who carried them captive, that they may have compassion on them 51 (for they are thy people, and thine inheritance, which thou broughtest forth out of Egypt, from the midst of the furnace of iron); 52 that thine eyes may be open unto the supplication of thy servant, and unto the supplication of thy people Israel, to hearken unto them whensoever they cry unto thee. 53 For thou didst separate them from among all the peoples of the earth, to be thine inheritance, as thou spakest by Moses thy servant, when thou broughtest our fathers out of Egypt, O Lord Jehovah.

54 And it was so, that, when Solomon had made an end of praying all this prayer and supplication unto Jehovah, he arose from before the altar of Jehovah, from kneeling on his knees with his hands spread forth toward heaven. 55 And he stood, and blessed all the assembly of Israel with a loud voice, saying, 56 Blessed be Jehovah, that hath given rest unto his people Israel, according to all that he promised: there hath not failed one word of all his good promise, which he promised by Moses his servant. 57 Jehovah our God be with us, as he was with our fathers: let him not leave us, nor forsake us; 58 that he may incline our hearts unto him, to walk in all his ways, and to keep his commandments, and his statutes, and his ordinances, which he commanded our fathers. 59 And let these my words, wherewith I have made supplication before Jehovah, be nigh unto Jehovah our God day and night, that he maintain the cause of his servant, and the cause of his people Israel, as every day shall require; 60 that all the peoples of the earth may know that Jehovah, he is God; there is none else. 61 Let your heart therefore be perfect with Jehovah our God, to walk in his statutes, and to keep his commandments, as at this day.

First, Solomon prayed with thanksgiving for the covenant-faithfulness of God toward David and his heir (vv. 22-24). Second, he prayed for the establishment of the Davidic dynasty, conditional upon the Deuteronomic way of life, namely, obedience (vv. 25, 26). Third, he prayed that the temple might be a place of prayer where Israel could find forgiveness (vv. 27-30). Fourth, he listed seven specific examples of need when prayer might be made unto the Lord, and prayed that God would hear the prayer of the petitioner (vv. 31-53).

Solomon's dedicatory prayer doubtless was prepared beforehand, careful thought being given to it. The prayer begins with thanksgiving to God for His faithfulness toward David. Next, the emphasis falls upon the faithful obedience of Israel. Then follows supplication for the temple, that it might fulfill the purpose for which it was built, namely, that here people may pray and God may forgive. The numerous specific examples which constitute the remainder of the prayer are essentially an emphasis on the central purpose of the temple. It was to be a house of prayer and forgiveness.

Having completed this memorable prayer, Solomon arose and pronounced an eloquent benediction (vv. 54-61). Its stress was upon the covenant relationship: **Jehovah our God be with us** (v. 57); **Let your heart be perfect with Jehovah our God . . . to keep his commandments** (v. 61). The distinctive emphasis in the covenantal relation between God and Israel was that God would be Israel's God if Israel would be obedient. Solomon's benediction reveals an awareness of this.

H. DEDICATORY SACRIFICES (8:62-66; cf. II Chron. 7:4-10)

62 And the king, and all Israel with him, offered sacrifice before Jehovah. 63 And Solomon offered for the sacrifice of peace-offerings, which he offered unto Jehovah, two and twenty thousand oxen, and a hundred and twenty thousand sheep. So the king and all the children of Israel dedicated the house of Jehovah. 64 The same day did the king hallow the middle of the court that was before the house of Jehovah; for there he offered the burnt-offering, and the meal-offering, and the fat of the peace-offerings, because the brazen altar that was before Jehovah was too little to receive the burnt-offering, and the meal-offering, and the fat of the peace-offerings. 65 So Solomon held the feast at that time, and all Israel with him, a great assembly, from the entrance of Hamath unto the brook of Egypt, before Jehovah our God, seven days and seven days, even fourteen days. 66 On the eighth day he sent the people away; and they blessed the king, and went unto their tents joyful and glad of heart for all the goodness that Jehovah had showed unto David his servant, and to Israel his people.

The dedication of the temple was completed with the offering of **the sacrifice of peace-offerings** (v. 63). According to the law, when there was the sacrifice of a peace-offering, the greater part of the sacrifice was to be eaten for food (Lev. 7:15). A peace-offering was a sacrifice for the purpose of having a meal together, the blood, fat and entrails being burned upon the altar and the flesh being eaten by the worshipers.[11]

I. JEHOVAH'S COVENANT WITH SOLOMON (9:1-9; cf. II Chron. 7:11-22)

1 And it came to pass, when Solomon had finished the building of the house of Jehovah, and the king's house, and all Solomon's desire which he was pleased to do, 2 that Jehovah appeared to Solomon the second time, as he had appeared unto him at Gibeon. 3 And Jehovah said unto him, I have heard thy prayer and thy supplication, that thou hast made before me: I have hallowed this house, which thou hast built, to put my name there for ever; and mine eyes and my heart shall be there perpetually. 4 And as for thee, if thou wilt walk before me, as David thy father walked, in integrity of heart, and in uprightness, to do according to all that I have commanded thee, and wilt keep my statutes and mine ordinances; 5 then I will establish the throne of thy kingdom over Israel for ever, according as I promised to David thy father, saying, There shall not fail thee a man upon the throne of Israel. 6 But if ye shall turn away from following me, ye or your children, and not keep my commandments and my statutes which I have set before you, but shall go and serve other gods, and worship them; 7 then will I cut off Israel out of the land which I have given them; and this house, which I have hallowed for my name, will I cast out of my sight; and Israel shall be a proverb and a byword among all peoples. 8 And though this house is so high, yet shall every one that passeth by it be

11 *Ibid.*, p. 216.

astonished, and shall hiss; and they shall say, Why hath Jehovah done thus unto this land, and to this house? 9 and they shall answer, Because they forsook Jehovah their God, who brought forth their fathers out of the land of Egypt, and laid hold on other gods, and worshipped them, and served them: therefore hath Jehovah brought all this evil upon them.

Just as the Lord had appeared to Solomon at Gibeon and granted his request for "an understanding heart" (I Kings 3:12), so now He granted Solomon's request for the temple: **I have heard thy prayer . . . I have hallowed this house which thou hast built, to put my name there for ever** (v. 3).

Solomon was assured that God had accepted this building as His dwelling-place. However, God's blessing would be upon the throne of David and upon the temple of Solomon only if He were faithfully obeyed. If God were rejected, He declared, **Then will I cut off Israel out of the land . . . and this house . . . will I cast out of my sight** (v. 7).

In the light of this covenant between the Lord and Solomon at the dedication of the temple, it is helpful to give in broad strokes the general picture of the history of the temple.

Solomon's temple lasted only four centuries, and, for the major part of the time, they were centuries of dishonor and disgrace for the temple. Shortly after Solomon's death, Shishak of Egypt plundered it. At least six times during its existence it was despoiled and robbed. Its sanctity was polluted: Ahaz provided the temple with a Syrian altar while Manasseh placed an idol in it.

Although the temple was destroyed by the Babylonians, it was not really destroyed until it had been degraded by the Israelites themselves. Solomon gave great emphasis to the centralizing and externalizing of Jehovah-worship. All Israel looked toward the temple at Jerusalem for the habitation of the Lord. The sacrificial system functioned in this central location. This was Solomon's supreme religious contribution. Yet the Lord warned Solomon that if Israel were disobedient, the temple would become a solemn monument of divine judgment (vv. 8, 9).

J. SOLOMON'S OTHER ENTERPRISES (9:10-28; cf. II Chron. 8:1-17)

10 And it came to pass at the end of twenty years, wherein Solomon had built the two houses, the house of Jehovah and the king's house 11 (now Hiram the king of Tyre had furnished Solomon with cedar-trees and fir-trees, and with gold, according to all his desire), that then king Solomon gave Hiram twenty cities in the land of Galilee. 12 And Hiram came out from Tyre to see the cities which Solomon had given him; and they pleased him not. 13 And he said, What cities are these which thou hast given me, my brother? And he called them the land of Cabul unto this day. 14 And Hiram sent to the king sixscore talents of gold.

15 And this is the reason of the levy which king Solomon raised, to build the house of Jehovah, and his own house, and Millo, and the wall of Jerusalem, and Hazor, and Megiddo, and Gezer. 16 Pharaoh king of Egypt had gone up, and taken Gezer, and burnt it with fire, and slain the Canaanites that dwelt in the city, and given it for a portion unto his daughter, Solomon's wife. 17 And Solomon built Gezer, and Beth-horon the nether, 18 and Baalath, and Tamar in the wilderness, in the land, 19 and all the store-cities that Solomon had, and the cities for his chariots, and the cities for his horsemen, and that which Solomon desired to build for his pleasure in Jerusalem, and in Lebanon, and in all the land of his dominion. 20 As for all the people that were left of the Amorites, the Hittites, the Perizzites, the Hivites, and the Jebusites, who were not of the children of Israel; 21 their children that were left after them in the land, whom the children of Israel were not able utterly to destroy, of them did Solomon raise a levy of bondservants unto this day. 22 But of the children of Israel did Solomon make no bondservants; but they were the men of war, and his servants, and his princes, and his captains, and rulers of his chariots and of his horsemen.

23 These were the chief officers that were over Solomon's work, five hundred and fifty, who bare rule over the people that wrought in the work.

24 But Pharaoh's daughter came up out of the city of David unto her house which *Solomon* had built for her: then did he build Millo.

25 And three times in a year did Solomon offer burnt-offerings and peace-offerings upon the altar which he built unto Jehovah, burning incense therewith,

upon the altar that was before Jehovah. So he finished the house.

26 And king Solomon made a navy of ships in Ezion-geber, which is beside Eloth, on the shore of the Red Sea, in the land of Edom. 27 And Hiram sent in the navy his servants, shipmen that had knowledge of the sea, with the servants of Solomon. 28 And they came to Ophir, and fetched from thence gold, four hundred and twenty talents, and brought it to king Solomon.

This section contains miscellaneous accounts of Solomon's enterprises. One effort was to obtain more gold (v. 14). The obvious explanation for this effort was that Solomon's way of living required it.

Another enterprise was the exploitation of forced labor to work on the extensive building projects (v. 15). Such labor was used in building the temple and the royal palace and was continued on other projects, notably the **store-cities** (v. 19).

Moreover, a third enterprise was the construction of ships at Ezion-geber and using them to import gold from Ophir (vv. 26, 28). "In view of the biblical tradition that Ophir was in Arabia, ... it is safest to regard Ophir as South Arabia."[12]

These efforts on the part of Solomon were for the purpose of enhancing the splendor of his reign, but only at considerable risk. Such enterprises do not encourage the development of an understanding heart and wise administration. They encourage exploitation and ruthlessness. Ultimately Solomon's son, Rehoboam, would pay a high price for some of Solomon's enterprises which were controversial and reprehensible.

IV. SOLOMON'S FORTUNE AND FAILURE (I Kings 10:1—11:43)

Solomon's political fortune is vividly illustrated by the visit of the queen of Sheba (chap. 10); his religious failure is poignantly revealed in the religious influence of his foreign wives (chap. 11).

A. POLITICAL FORTUNE (10:1-29)

The divine promise given to Solomon at Gibeon was fulfilled, and the wisdom of God in him was a wonder to many. Foreign dignitaries desired to visit him and brought lavish gifts which added to his wealth and affluence.

1. The Visit of the Queen of Sheba (10:1-13; cf. II Chron. 9:1-12)

1 And when the queen of Sheba heard of the fame of Solomon concerning the name of Jehovah, she came to prove him with hard questions. 2 And she came to Jerusalem with a very great train, with camels that bare spices, and very much gold, and precious stones; and when she was come to Solomon, she communed with him of all that was in her heart. 3 And Solomon told her all her questions: there was not anything hid from the king which he told her not. 4 And when the queen of Sheba had seen all the wisdom of Solomon, and the house that he had built, 5 and the food of his table, and the sitting of his servants, and the attendance of his ministers, and their apparel, and his cupbearers, and his ascent by which he went up unto the house of Jehovah; there was no more spirit in her. 6 And she said to the king, It was a true report that I heard in mine own land of thine acts, and of thy wisdom. 7 Howbeit I believed not the words, until I came, and mine eyes had seen it: and, behold, the half was not told me; thy wisdom and prosperity exceed the fame which I heard. 8 Happy are thy men, happy are these thy servants, that stand continually before thee, *and* that hear thy wisdom. 9 Blessed be Jehovah thy God, who delighted in thee, to set thee on the throne of Israel: because Jehovah loved Israel for ever, therefore made he thee king, to do justice and righteousness. 10 And she gave the king a hundred and twenty talents of gold, and of spices very great store, and precious stones: there came no more such abundance of spices as these which the queen of Sheba gave to king Solomon.

11 And the navy also of Hiram, that brought gold from Ophir, brought in from Ophir great plenty of almug-trees and precious stones. 12 And the king made of the almug-trees pillars for the house of Jehovah, and for the king's house, harps also and psalteries for the singers: there came no such almug-trees, nor were seen, unto this day.

13 And king Solomon gave to the queen of Sheba all her desire, whatsoever she asked, besides that which Solomon

---

[12] *Ibid.*, p. 238.

gave her of his royal bounty. So she turned, and went to her own land, she and her servants.

While an important reason for the visit of the queen of Sheba may have been to make a trade agreement with Solomon, the emphasis in the Kings narrative is on the interest she had in observing firsthand his wisdom and royal splendor. This was a supreme moment for Solomon to engage in the high calling God had given Israel, His chosen people. Of the line of Abraham, Solomon was one of those through whom God promised to bless all nations (cf. Gen. 12:3).

In his solemn prayer offered at the dedication of the temple, Solomon had prayed concerning the foreigner: "When he shall come and pray ... hear thou ... that all the peoples of the earth may know thy name ... as doth thy people Israel" (8:42, 43). His petition was that by means of the temple the foreigner might know the Lord. The visit of the queen of Sheba provided an opportunity for this.

When the queen saw the magnificence of the temple and listened to Solomon's wisdom she was enthralled with the wonder of it all: **Behold, the half was not told me** (v. 7). However, she was not persuaded by it all to worship the Lord of Israel. Solomon's emphasis on Israel's institutional religion greatly impressed the queen of Sheba with what the Lord had done for Israel, but it did not impel her to become converted. She returned to the religion of Sheba.

Great churches, throngs of worshipers, expansive programs may impress others that God is with us and that He is a great God, but this does not of itself impel those impressed to become inquirers. They think of God as our God, not as their God. It is imperative that we be more concerned to invite others to the Lord of all than to impress them with God's benefits to us. The poignant note in the story of the visit of the queen of Sheba is that she returned to her homeland to worship at the shrines of her gods, notwithstanding the impression Solomon's temple made upon her regarding the God of Israel and all His benefits.

2. The Wealth and Affluence of Solomon (10:14-29; cf. II Chron. 9:13-28)

14 Now the weight of gold that came to Solomon in one year was six hundred threescore and six talents of gold, 15 besides *that which* the traders *brought*, and the traffic of the merchants, and of all the kings of the mingled people, and of the governors of the country. 16 And king Solomon made two hundred bucklers of beaten gold; six hundred *shekels* of gold went to one buckler. 17 And *he made* three hundred shields of beaten gold; three pounds of gold went to one shield: and the king put them in the house of the forest of Lebanon. 18 Moreover the king made a great throne of ivory, and overlaid it with the finest gold. 19 There were six steps to the throne, and the top of the throne was round behind; and there were stays on either side by the place of the seat, and two lions standing beside the stays. 20 And twelve lions stood there on the one side and on the other upon the six steps: there was not the like made in any kingdom. 21 And all king Solomon's drinking vessels were of gold, and all the vessels of the house of the forest of Lebanon were of pure gold: none were of silver; it was nothing accounted of in the days of Solomon. 22 For the king had at sea a navy of Tarshish with the navy of Hiram: once every three years came the navy of Tarshish, bringing gold, and silver, ivory, and apes, and peacocks.

23 So king Solomon exceeded all the kings of the earth in riches and in wisdom. 24 And all the earth sought the presence of Solomon, to hear his wisdom, which God had put in his heart. 25 And they brought every man his tribute, vessels of silver, and vessels of gold, and raiment, and armor, and spices, horses, and mules, a rate year by year.

26 And Solomon gathered together chariots and horsemen: and he had a thousand and four hundred chariots, and twelve thousand horsemen, that he bestowed in the chariot cities, and with the king at Jerusalem. 27 And the king made silver to be in Jerusalem as stones, and cedars made he to be as the sycamore-trees that are in the lowland, for abundance. 28 And the horses which Solomon had were brought out of Egypt; and the king's merchants received them in droves, each drove at a price. 29 And a chariot came up and went out of Egypt for six hundred *shekels* of silver, and a horse for a hundred and fifty; and so for all the kings of the Hittites, and for the kings of

Syria, did they bring them out by their means.

This account of the glory of Solomon, composed of unconnected details taken from the royal archives, resulted from the impression made upon the queen of Sheba. The writer was delighted with Solomon's splendor as he recorded specific items that contributed to the good fortune of the king. There was the fabulous inflow of gold (vv. 14, 15), the majestic throne of ivory (v. 18) and the expansive horse market (v. 29). Solomon had reached the zenith of his reign and the peak of his power and influence.

B. RELIGIOUS FAILURE (11:1-43)

Notwithstanding all the political fortune Solomon gained because of the divine blessing which had been promised upon his reign, he proceeded on a course that ended in religious failure.

Since his marriages were, for the most part, motivated by political considerations, namely, establishing closer political as well as cultural ties with surrounding nations, it inevitably followed that there must be tolerance and broadmindedness regarding the native religions of the wives of Solomon's harem. Otherwise, instead of political profit, Solomon would face the hostility of the nations because he deprived their native daughters of the religion of their homeland. Thus Solomon was willing to allow his wives to continue in their religion.

1. The Influence of Foreign Religions (11:1-8)

1 Now king Solomon loved many foreign women, together with the daughter of Pharaoh, women of the Moabites, Ammonites, Edomites, Sidonians, and Hittites; 2 of the nations concerning which Jehovah said unto the children of Israel, Ye shall not go among them, neither shall they come among you; for surely they will turn away your heart after their gods: Solomon clave unto these in love. 3 And he had seven hundred wives, princesses, and three hundred concubines; and his wives turned away his heart. 4 For it came to pass, when Solomon was old, that his wives turned away his heart after other gods; and his heart was not perfect with Jehovah his God, as was the

heart of David his father. 5 For Solomon went after Ashtoreth the goddess of the Sidonians, and after Milcom the abomination of the Ammonites. 6 And Solomon did that which was evil in the sight of Jehovah, and went not fully after Jehovah, as did David his father. 7 Then did Solomon build a high place for Chemosh the abomination of Moab, in the mount that is before Jerusalem, and for Molech the abomination of the children of Ammon. 8 And so did he for all his foreign wives, who burnt incense and sacrificed unto their gods.

Solomon's reign was impregnated with political aspirations that continually imperiled the integrity of Israel's Jehovah-worship. He was intent upon reigning well. A major source of help to him was international diplomacy and trade. The times were peaceful and he could easily enhance his political power through foreign marriages. Therefore many such marriages were arranged. These many foreign wives were not evidence of mere sensuality on Solomon's part. "Solomon's marriages . . . had a political significance."[13]

Foreign influences made important inroads into the life and religion of Israel during Solomon's reign. The temple, to a great extent modified by foreign craftsmen and skilled workmen, symbolized these influences. Jerusalem, the capital, received a great influx of foreign ambassadors and merchantmen who brought new ideas and customs along with their wealth. Solomon delighted in all of this. His tolerant hospitality, incited by political aspirations and commercial expansion, led him to religious syncretism and compromise. **Then did Solomon build a high place for Chemosh the abomination of Moab, in the mount that is before Jerusalem, and for Molech the abomination of the children of Ammon** (v. 7).

2. The Judgment of Jehovah (11:9-43)

Notwithstanding Solomon's intent to secure political glory at the expense of true Jehovah-worship, the God of Israel acted to disturb the cordial relations with surrounding nations, as well as to generate revolt within the kingdom of Israel.

---

[13] *Ibid.*, p. 254.

a. Declaration of the Break-up of the Kingdom (11:9-13)

9 And Jehovah was angry with Solomon, because his heart was turned away from Jehovah, the God of Israel, who had appeared unto him twice, 10 and had commanded him concerning this thing, that he should not go after other gods: but he kept not that which Jehovah commanded. 11 Wherefore Jehovah said unto Solomon, Forasmuch as this is done of thee, and thou hast not kept my covenant and my statutes, which I have commanded thee, I will surely rend the kingdom from thee, and will give it to thy servant. 12 Notwithstanding in thy days I will not do it, for David thy father's sake: but I will rend it out of the hand of thy son. 13 Howbeit I will not rend away all the kingdom; but I will give one tribe to thy son, for David my servant's sake, and for Jerusalem's sake which I have chosen.

And Jehovah was angry with Solomon (v. 9). Solomon's course of action had been satisfactory to himself because he had gained fame and fortune. Yet his course occasioned divine judgment because of disobedience: **he kept not that which Jehovah commanded** (v. 10).

Solomon was reminded of the two theophanies to him and their affirmation of the Davidic covenant (cf. 11:9; 3:5-15; 9:1-9). Those theophanies had conveyed to Solomon conditional blessings, but because of his disobedience the house of David had forfeited the kingdom. **I will not rend away all the kingdom; but I will give one tribe to thy son, for David my servant's sake, and for Jerusalem's sake which I have chosen** (v. 13).

b. Revolution Within the Kingdom (11:14-43)

14 And Jehovah raised up an adversary unto Solomon, Hadad the Edomite: he was of the king's seed in Edom. 15 For it came to pass, when David was in Edom, and Joab the captain of the host was gone up to bury the slain, and had smitten every male in Edom 16 (for Joab and all Israel remained there six months, until he had cut off every male in Edom); 17 that Hadad fled, he and certain Edomites of his father's servants with him, to go into Egypt, Hadad being yet a little child. 18 And they arose out of Midian, and came to Paran; and they took men with them out of Paran, and they came to Egypt, unto Pharaoh king of Egypt, who gave him a house, and appointed him victuals, and gave him land. 19 And Hadad found great favor in the sight of Pharaoh, so that he gave him to wife the sister of his own wife, the sister of Tahpenes the queen. 20 And the sister of Tahpenes bare him Genubath his son, whom Tahpenes weaned in Pharaoh's house; and Genubath was in Pharaoh's house among the sons of Pharaoh. 21 And when Hadad heard in Egypt that David slept with his fathers, and that Joab the captain of the host was dead, Hadad said to Pharaoh, Let me depart, that I may go to mine own country. 22 Then Pharaoh said unto him, But what hast thou lacked with me, that, behold, thou seekest to go to thine own country? And he answered, Nothing: howbeit only let me depart.

23 And God raised up *another* adversary unto him, Rezon the son of Eliada, who had fled from his lord Hadadezer king of Zobah. 24 And he gathered men unto him, and became captain over a troop, when David slew them *of Zobah*: and they went to Damascus, and dwelt therein, and reigned in Damascus. 25 And he was an adversary to Israel all the days of Solomon, besides the mischief that Hadad *did*: and he abhorred Israel, and reigned over Syria.

26 And Jeroboam the son of Nebat, an Ephraïmite of Zeredah, a servant of Solomon, whose mother's name was Zeruah, a widow, he also lifted up his hand against the king. 27 And this was the reason why he lifted up his hand against the king: Solomon built Millo, and repaired the breach of the city of David his father. 28 And the man Jeroboam was a mighty man of valor; and Solomon saw the young man that he was industrious, and he gave him charge over all the labor of the house of Joseph. 29 And it came to pass at that time, when Jeroboam went out of Jerusalem, that the prophet Ahijah the Shilonite found him in the way; now *Ahijah* had clad himself with a new garment; and they two were alone in the field. 30 And Ahijah laid hold of the new garment that was on him, and rent it in twelve pieces. 31 And he said to Jeroboam, Take thee ten pieces; for thus saith Jehovah, the God of Israel, Behold, I will rend the kingdom out of the hand of Solomon, and will give ten tribes to thee 32 (but he shall have one tribe, for my servant David's sake and for Jerusalem's sake, the city which I have chosen out of all the tribes of Israel); 33 because that they have forsaken me, and have worshipped Ashtoreth the goddess of the Sidonians, Chemosh the god of

Moab, and Milcom the god of the children of Ammon; and they have not walked in my ways, to do that which is right in mine eyes, and *to keep* my statutes and mine ordinances, as did David his father. 34 Howbeit I will not take the whole kingdom out of his hand; but I will make him prince all the days of his life, for David my servant's sake whom I chose, who kept my commandments and my statutes; 35 but I will take the kingdom out of his son's hand, and will give it unto thee, even ten tribes. 36 And unto his son will I give one tribe, that David my servant may have a lamp alway before me in Jerusalem, the city which I have chosen me to put my name there. 37 And I will take thee, and thou shalt reign according to all that thy soul desireth, and shalt be king over Israel. 38 And it shall be, if thou wilt hearken unto all that I command thee, and wilt walk in my ways, and do that which is right in mine eyes, to keep my statutes and my commandments, as David my servant did; that I will be with thee, and will build thee a sure house, as I built for David, and will give Israel unto thee. 39 And I will for this afflict the seed of David, but not for ever. 40 Solomon sought therefore to kill Jeroboam; but Jeroboam arose, and fled into Egypt, unto Shishak king of Egypt, and was in Egypt until the death of Solomon.

41 Now the rest of the acts of Solomon, and all that he did, and his wisdom, are they not written in the book of the acts of Solomon? 42 And the time that Solomon reigned in Jerusalem over all Israel was forty years. 43 And Solomon slept with his fathers, and was buried in the city of David his father: and Rehoboam his son reigned in his stead.

This account of the revolutionary foment in Solomon's empire is in three parts: Hadad's revolt in Edom (vv. 14-22), Rezon's revolt in Syria (vv. 23-25), and Jeroboam of the house of Joseph and his abortive revolt (vv. 26-40).

Two of the leaders, Hadad and Jeroboam, although initiating separate revolts for different reasons, secured the protection and favor of Solomon's ally, Egypt. Such developments were severe reverses to Solomon's political relationships, for he had a treaty with Egypt and had married Pharaoh's daughter (I Kings 3:1).

Although Solomon had become a religious eclectic for political expediency, Jehovah refused to become a God among the gods. **Jehovah raised up an adversary unto Solomon** (v. 14; cf. v. 23). "Adversary" comes from the Hebrew word for Satan. With reference to Solomon's adversary, the Hebrew word is a common noun, but in time the word came to be a proper noun referring to the motivator of evil impulses.[14]

In our human finitude it is impossible to trace through the complex maze of historical situations the activity of providence and to see that activity with clarity. However, divine revelation leaves no doubt that providence does invade the affairs of nations.

In each of the three revolutionary efforts under consideration there smoldered a resentment of long standing. In Hadad's case, there had been a massacre of Edomites during David's reign (vv. 15-17). Rezon escaped when David slew the Syrians fighting for Hadadezer, king of Zobah, and became the leader of a company of bandits (vv. 23-24). Shortly after David's death, Rezon captured Damascus for his stronghold and withstood pressure from Solomon. In time, this stronghold became the center of a strong rival to Israel, namely, Syria.

Jeroboam's revolt occurred at Jerusalem. He was an Ephraimite of the line of Joseph (v. 26). Long-standing rivalry existed between the lines of Judah and Joseph. During the era of the monarchy, during which time David established Jerusalem and Solomon centralized worship at the temple, the house of Joseph must have resented the dominance of the house of Judah. When Solomon oppressed Ephraim along with other tribes by drafting Israelites for forced labor on construction work at Jerusalem, Jeroboam attempted a revolt (vv. 26-28). The failure of this revolt resulted in his flight to Egypt, but he waited for another chance. That time came after the death of Solomon.

These three uprisings during Solomon's reign were the result of Solomon's enemies' attempt to retaliate. In some remarkable manner, however, these upris-

---

[14] *Ibid.*, pp. 263-64.

ings were called upon to fulfill a purpose that transcended retaliation. They fulfilled a dual purpose: human retaliation motivated by hate, and divine justice motivated by love.

V. THE GREAT REVOLT (I Kings 12:1-24)

Solomon's oppressive policies had undermined his efforts to achieve political fame and security. Immediately following his death, pent-up resentment exploded and shattered the solidarity of the kingdom which Solomon had sought to establish.

A. REQUEST TO REHOBOAM (12:1-5; cf. II Chron. 10:1-5)

1 And Rehoboam went to Shechem: for all Israel were come to Shechem to make him king. 2 And it came to pass, when Jeroboam the son of Nebat heard of it (for he was yet in Egypt, whither he had fled from the presence of king Solomon, and Jeroboam dwelt in Egypt, 3 and they sent and called him), that Jeroboam and all the assembly of Israel came, and spake unto Rehoboam, saying, 4 Thy father made our yoke grievous: now therefore make thou the grievous service of thy father, and his heavy yoke which he put upon us, lighter, and we will serve thee. 5 And he said unto them, Depart yet for three days, then come again to me. And the people departed.

When Rehoboam was made king of Israel he was confronted with a request. The leaders of Israel said, **Thy father made our yoke grevious: now therefore make ... his heavy yoke ... lighter, and we will serve thee** (v. 4).

Instead of compliments for Solomon's regal splendor there were complaints for his rigorous oppression. However, the request was not motivated by a sincere desire to return unto the Lord, but by a secular desire for a more congenial materialistic economy. If Rehoboam granted the request, Israel promised to serve the king faithfully. Yet this was not Israel's primary problem. The God of Israel had been insulted and treated as one god among many. Not material benefits from the king but merciful forgiveness from Jehovah was Israel's need in this crisis.

B. REPLY FROM REHOBOAM (12:6-15; cf. II Chron. 10:6-15)

6 And king Rehoboam took counsel with the old men, that had stood before Solomon his father while he yet lived, saying, What counsel give ye me to return answer to this people? 7 And they spake unto him, saying, If thou wilt be a servant unto this people this day, and wilt serve them, and answer them, and speak good words to them, then they will be thy servants for ever. 8 But he forsook the counsel of the old men which they had given him, and took counsel with the young men that were grown up with him, that stood before him. 9 And he said unto them, What counsel give ye, that we may return answer to this people, who have spoken to me, saying, Make the yoke that thy father did put upon us lighter? 10 And the young men that were grown up with him spake unto him, saying, Thus shalt thou say unto this people that spake unto thee, saying, Thy father made our yoke heavy, but make thou it lighter unto us; thus shalt thou speak unto them, My little finger is thicker than my father's loins. 11 And now whereas my father did lade you with a heavy yoke, I will add to your yoke: my father chastised you with whips, but I will chastise you with scorpions.

12 So Jeroboam and all the people came to Rehoboam the third day, as the king bade, saying, Come to me again the third day. 13 And the king answered the people roughly, and forsook the counsel of the old men which they had given him, 14 and spake to them after the counsel of the young men, saying, My father made your yoke heavy, but I will add to your yoke: my father chastised you with whips, but I will chastise you with scorpions. 15 So the king hearkened not unto the people; for it was a thing brought about of Jehovah, that he might establish his word, which Jehovah spake by Ahijah the Shilonite to Jeroboam the son of Nebat.

My father made your yoke heavy, but I will add to your yoke (v. 14). With these words, the arrogant Rehoboam rejected any easing of the oppression instituted by Solomon. He might have been able to avert the secession had he been in a more conciliatory mood. His contemptuous treatment of the request cost him dearly.

C. REBELLION OF ISRAEL (12:16-20; cf. II Chron. 10:16-19)

16 And when all Israel saw that the king hearkened not unto them, the people answered the king, saying, What portion have we in David? neither have we inheritance in the son of Jesse: to your tents, O Israel: now see to thine own house, David. So Israel departed unto their tents. 17 But as for the children of Israel that dwelt in the cities of Judah, Rehoboam reigned over them. 18 Then king Rehoboam sent Adoram, who was over the men subject to taskwork; and all Israel stoned him to death with stones. And king Rehoboam made speed to get him up to his chariot, to flee to Jerusalem. 19 So Israel rebelled against the house of David unto this day. 20 And it came to pass, when all Israel heard that Jeroboam was returned, that they sent and called him unto the congregation, and made him king over all Israel: there was none that followed the house of David, but the tribe of Judah only.

Upon receiving such impudent treatment from Rehoboam, all the tribes of Israel, except Judah and Benjamin, exclaimed, **What portion have we in David? . . . to your tents, O Israel: now see to thine own house, David** (v. 16). Whereupon, the northern tribes rebelled against Rehoboam and made Jeroboam their king (vv. 19, 20).

Meanwhile, Rehoboam followed up his declaration of increasing the burdens of the people by sending Adoram to enforce allegiance. Adoram was the most hated man in the kingdom because he was overseer of the slave labor. He was stoned.

D. REPRISAL ATTEMPTED (12:21-24; cf. II Chron. 11:1-4)

21 And when Rehoboam was come to Jerusalem, he assembled all the house of Judah, and the tribe of Benjamin, a hundred and fourscore thousand chosen men, that were warriors, to fight against the house of Israel, to bring the kingdom again to Rehoboam the son of Solomon. 22 But the word of God came unto Shemaiah the man of God, saying, 23 Speak unto Rehoboam the son of Solomon, king of Judah, and unto all the house of Judah and Benjamin, and to the rest of the people, saying, 24 Thus saith Jehovah, Ye shall not go up, nor fight against your brethren the children of Israel: return every man to his house; for this thing is of me. So they hearkened unto the word of Jehovah, and returned and went their way, according to the word of Jehovah.

Rehoboam proceeded to organize military might against the seceding tribes. His plan was to crush the revolt. However, a prophet of the Lord warned Rehoboam that he should not pursue Israel (v. 24).

The hard facts of the political scene compelled Rehoboam to revise his plans. He was compelled to realize that the leader of the northern tribes, Jeroboam, had a zealous following, while his own authority was in doubt. Furthermore, Egypt, a rising power, had shown kindness to Jeroboam when he was in exile. Within five years Egypt did invade Judah (I Kings 14:25). Rehoboam must have realized early the threat which Egypt posed to Judah. Rather than engage in war against the northern tribes immediately he sought to build adequate fortifications against invasion.

VI. THE NORTHERN KINGDOM DURING THE TENTH CENTURY B. C. (I Kings 12:25—14:20; 15:25-32)

The catastrophe of the schism of the kingdom occurred during the latter part of the tenth century B.C. (ca. 930). With the selection of Jeroboam, the son of Nebat, the ten northern states inaugurated a new kingdom called Israel. This kingdom continued until overthrown by Assyria in the eighth century B. C. (ca. 720).

A. THE RELIGIOUS EXPEDIENCY OF JEROBOAM (12:25-33)

25 Then Jeroboam built Shechem in the hill-country of Ephraim, and dwelt therein; and he went out from thence, and built Penuel. 26 And Jeroboam said in his heart, Now will the kingdom return to the house of David: 27 if this people go up to offer sacrifices in the house of Jehovah at Jerusalem, then will the heart of this people turn again unto their lord, even unto Rehoboam king of Judah; and they will kill me, and return to Rehoboam king of Judah. 28 Whereupon the king took counsel, and made two calves of gold; and he said unto them, It is too much for you to go up to Jerusalem: behold thy gods, O Israel,

which brought thee up out of the land of Egypt. 29 And he set the one in Beth-el, and the other put he in Dan. 30 And this thing became a sin; for the people went *to worship* before the one, even unto Dan. 31 And he made houses of high places, and made priests from among all the people, that were not of the sons of Levi. 32 And Jeroboam ordained a feast in the eighth month, on the fifteenth day of the month, like unto the feast that is in Judah, and he went up unto the altar; so did he in Beth-el, sacrificing unto the calves that he had made: and he placed in Beth-el the priests of the high places that he had made. 33 And he went up unto the altar which he had made in Beth-el on the fifteenth day in the eighth month, even in the month which he had devised of his own heart: and he ordained a feast for the children of Israel, and went up unto the altar, to burn incense.

Although Jeroboam had some outstanding political advantages over his rival Rehoboam, who ruled in Jerusalem, he was greatly concerned over the religious disadvantages he confronted. Politically, he controlled vastly greater territory and population. Also, he had contacts with the revived Egyptian nation, which, though formerly friendly to Solomon, became a serious threat to the kingdom of Judah.

Religiously, however, Jeroboam realized that he confronted an enormous disadvantage which outweighed his political advantages. **Now will the kingdom return unto the house of David: if this people go up to offer sacrifices in the house of Jehovah at Jerusalem, then will the heart of this people turn again unto their lord, even unto Rehoboam king of Judah** (v. 27).

A major element in the temple worship was the observance of Jehovah's covenant with David and his dynasty. Jeroboam saw the peril of having the subjects of his kingdom participating in temple worship which looked upon all rule except Davidic as illegitimate. "The problem of theological legitimacy, which all ancient kingships required, was particularly acute in his case."[15] Jeroboam had the task of creating a nation where none had existed, and he needed a state religion, that is, official cultic endorsement: **Whereupon the king took counsel, and made two calves of gold** (v. 28). "The infamous calves were probably not representations of deity but pedestals on which the invisible Yahweh was supposed to stand."[16]

The religion of Jehovah from its inception has never been a means to an end. If the history of Israel's religion shows anything, it shows that the worship of Jehovah is for the purpose of "the glory of God." To adulterate that purpose is to invite compromise and expediency.

B. THE RIGHTEOUS EFFORTS OF THE PROPHETS (13:1—14:20; 15:25-32)

Jeroboam's religious innovations were rejected by the Lord. A prophet from Judah and Ahijah from Ephraim declared the judgment of the Lord not only upon Jeroboam's religious policies but also upon his reign.

1. The Man of God from Judah (13:1-32)

An unnamed prophet of the Lord came from the kingdom ruled by Rehoboam to denounce the religious institutions of Jeroboam's kingdom.

a. Obedience to the Word of Jehovah (13:1-10)

1 And, behold, there came a man of God out of Judah by the word of Jehovah unto Beth-el: and Jeroboam was standing by the altar to burn incense. 2 And he cried against the altar by the word of Jehovah, and said, O altar, altar, thus saith Jehovah: Behold, a son shall be born unto the house of David, Josiah by name; and upon thee shall he sacrifice the priests of the high places that burn incense upon thee, and men's bones shall they burn upon thee. 3 And he gave a sign the same day, saying, This is the sign which Jehovah hath spoken: Behold, the altar shall be rent, and the ashes that are upon it shall be poured out. 4 And it came to pass, when the king heard the saying of the man of God, which he cried against the altar in Beth-el, that Jeroboam put forth his hand from the altar, saying, Lay hold on him. And his hand, which he put forth against him, dried

15 John Bright, *A History of Israel*, p. 217.
16 D. A. Hubbard, "Jeroboam," *The New Bible Dictionary*, ed. by J. D. Douglas, p. 614; cf. W. F. Albright, *From the Stone Age to Christianity*, 2nd ed., pp. 299-301.

up, so that he could not draw it back again to him. 5 The altar also was rent, and the ashes poured out from the altar, according to the sign which the man of God had given by the word of Jehovah. 6 And the king answered and said unto the man of God, Entreat now the favor of Jehovah thy God, and pray for me, that my hand may be restored me again. And the man of God entreated Jehovah, and the king's hand was restored him again, and became as it was before. 7 And the king said unto the man of God, Come home with me, and refresh thyself, and I will give thee a reward. 8 And the man of God said unto the king, If thou wilt give me half thy house, I will not go in with thee, neither will I eat bread nor drink water in this place; 9 for so was it charged me by the word of Jehovah, saying, Thou shalt eat no bread, nor drink water, neither return by the way that thou camest. 10 So he went another way, and returned not by the way that he came to Beth-el.

There came a man of God out of Judah by the word of Jehovah unto Beth-el (v. 1). This man of God was not merely bringing "the word of Jehovah." He was being brought by it. "The word of Jehovah" in relation to the prophet had a certain dynamic and compulsion. The man of God was obediently responsive to it. Not only did he come to Bethel but he also delivered his message **by the word of Jehovah** (v. 2).

The fulfillment of this prophecy is in II Kings 23:15, 16, and the details of its fulfillment were inserted when the prediction came to pass. "The compiler of the Book of Kings gathered his material from various sources, and did his work after Josiah was dead."[17]

Following the incident at the altar, Jeroboam invited the prophet to come and refresh himself, but the invitation was refused. The prophet declared that he had been so instructed **by the word of Jehovah** (v. 9). Up to this point in the narrative the prophet from Judah fully obeyed the commission given "by the word of Jehovah."

b. Disobedience to the Word of Jehovah (13:11-22)

11 Now there dwelt an old prophet in Beth-el; and one of his sons came and told him all the works that the man of God had done that day in Beth-el: the words which he had spoken unto the king, them also they told unto their father. 12 And their father said unto them, What way went he? Now his sons had seen what way the man of God went, that came from Judah. 13 And he said unto his sons, Saddle me the ass. So they saddled him the ass; and he rode thereon. 14 And he went after the man of God, and found him sitting under an oak; and he said unto him, Art thou the man of God that camest from Judah? And he said, I am. 15 Then he said unto him, Come home with me, and eat bread. 16 And he said, I may not return with thee, nor go in with thee; neither will I eat bread nor drink water with thee in this place: 17 for it was said to me by the word of Jehovah, Thou shalt eat no bread nor drink water there, nor turn again to go by the way that thou camest. 18 And he said unto him, I also am a prophet as thou art; and an angel spake unto me by the word of Jehovah, saying, Bring him back with thee into thy house, that he may eat bread and drink water. *But* he lied unto him. 19 So he went back with him, and did eat bread in his house, and drank water.

20 And it came to pass, as they sat at the table, that the word of Jehovah came unto the prophet that brought him back; 21 and he cried unto the man of God that came from Judah, saying, Thus saith Jehovah, Forasmuch as thou hast been disobedient unto the mouth of Jehovah, and hast not kept the commandment which Jehovah thy God commanded thee, 22 but camest back, and hast eaten bread and drunk water in the place of which he said to thee, Eat no bread, and drink no water; thy body shall not come unto the sepulchre of thy fathers.

The word of God was the only sure guide for the man of God from Judah. When confronted by an old prophet of Bethel the man of God acknowledged that he was under orders given **by the word of Jehovah** (v. 17). However, he accepted the invitation of the old prophet when he subtly claimed, **An angel spake unto me by the word of Jehovah** (v. 18). An intermediary, an angel, was used by the old prophet to avoid a direct lie in the name of God. The man of God violated the ban of eating with residents of a kingdom which was under divine disfavor. He became disobedient by allowing a false substitute to take the place of the direct revelation given by the mouth of Jehovah (v. 21).

c. The Sequel (13:23-32)

23 And it came to pass, after he had eaten bread, and after he had drunk, that he saddled for him the ass, *to wit,* for the prophet whom he had brought back. 24 And when he was gone, a lion met him by the way, and slew him: and his body was cast in the way, and the ass stood by it; the lion also stood by the body. 25 And, behold, men passed by, and saw the body cast in the way, and the lion standing by the body; and they came and told it in the city where the old prophet dwelt. 26 And when the prophet that brought him back from the way heard thereof, he said, It is the man of God, who was disobedient unto the mouth of Jehovah: therefore Jehovah hath delivered him unto the lion, which hath torn him, and slain him, according to the word of Jehovah, which he spake unto him. 27 And he spake to his sons, saying, Saddle me the ass. And they saddled it. 28 And he went and found his body cast in the way, and the ass and the lion standing by the body: the lion had not eaten the body, nor torn the ass. 29 And the prophet took up the body of the man of God, and laid it upon the ass, and brought it back; and he came to the city of the old prophet, to mourn, and to bury him. 30 And he laid his body in his own grave; and they mourned over him, *saying,* Alas, my brother! 31 And it came to pass, after he had buried him, that he spake to his sons, saying, When I am dead, then bury me in the sepulchre wherein the man of God is buried; lay my bones beside his bones. 32 For the saying which he cried by the word of Jehovah against the altar in Beth-el, and against all the houses of the high places which are in the cities of Samaria, shall surely come to pass.

Because the man of God was disobedient to the word of Jehovah, which he had publicly declared and publicly disobeyed, he came under judgment and died (v. 24). When the news was carried to the old prophet in Bethel he provided a place of burial for the man of God and mourned his death. The entire account of this man of God reflects the solemn responsibility of one who is commissioned "by the word of Jehovah." When confronted by "thus saith the Lord," there is no alternative but obedience. To disobey brings judgment, not always immediate, but ultimately inevitable.

2. The Prophet Ahijah of Shiloh (13:33—14:20; 15:25-32)

Ahijah the Shilonite was of the house of Joseph and the tribe of Ephraim (14:2). The sickness of Abijah, son of Jeroboam, provided the occasion for the prophet Ahijah to deliver an important prophecy regarding the house of Jeroboam.

a. The Occasion (13:33—14:5)

33 After this thing Jeroboam returned not from his evil way, but made again from among all the people priests of the high places: whosoever would, he consecrated him, that there might be priests of the high places. 34 And this thing became sin unto the house of Jeroboam, even to cut it off, and to destroy it from off the face of the earth.

1 At that time Abijah the son of Jeroboam fell sick. 2 And Jeroboam said to his wife, Arise, I pray thee, and disguise thyself, that thou be not known to be the wife of Jeroboam; and get thee to Shiloh: behold, there is Ahijah the prophet, who spake concerning me that I should be king over this people. 3 And take with thee ten loaves, and cakes, and a cruse of honey, and go to him: he will tell thee what shall become of the child. 4 And Jeroboam's wife did so, and arose, and went to Shiloh, and came to the house of Ahijah. Now Ahijah could not see; for his eyes were set by reason of his age. 5 And Jehovah said unto Ahijah, Behold, the wife of Jeroboam cometh to inquire of thee concerning her son; for he is sick: thus and thus shalt thou say unto her; for it will be, when she cometh in, that she will feign herself to be another woman.

After this thing Jeroboam returned not from his evil way. . . . At that time Abijah the son of Jeroboam fell sick (v. 33; v. 1). These were the circumstances which prepared the way for the prophecy of Ahijah. The wife of Jeroboam went in disguise to Shiloh to inquire concerning the sick child (v. 4). It is obvious that Ahijah had refused to endorse Jeroboam's religious practices and was no longer in touch with the king.

b. The Prophecy (14:6-16)

6 And it was so, when Ahijah heard the sound of her feet, as she came in at the door, that he said, Come in, thou wife of Jeroboam; why feignest thou thyself to be another? for I am sent to thee with heavy tidings. 7 Go, tell Jeroboam, thus saith Jehovah, the God of Israel: Forasmuch as I exalted thee from among the people, and made thee prince over my people Israel, 8 and rent the kingdom away from the house of David, and gave it thee; and yet thou hast not been as my servant David, who kept my commandments, and who followed me with all his heart, to do that only which was right in mine eyes, 9 but hast done evil above all that were before thee, and hast gone and made thee other gods, and molten images, to provoke me to anger, and hast cast me behind thy back: 10 therefore, behold, I will bring evil upon the house of Jeroboam, and will cut off from Jeroboam every man-child, him that is shut up and him that is left at large in Israel, and will utterly sweep away the house of Jeroboam, as a man sweepeth away dung, till it be all gone. 11 Him that dieth of Jeroboam in the city shall the dogs eat; and him that dieth in the field shall the birds of the heavens eat: for Jehovah hath spoken it. 12 Arise thou therefore, get thee to thy house: *and* when thy feet enter into the city, the child shall die. 13 And all Israel shall mourn for him, and bury him; for he only of Jeroboam shall come to the grave, because in him there is found some good thing toward Jehovah, the God of Israel, in the house of Jeroboam. 14 Moreover Jehovah will raise him up a king over Israel, who shall cut off the house of Jeroboam that day: but what? even now. 15 For Jehovah will smite Israel, as a reed is shaken in the water; and he will root up Israel out of this good land which he gave to their fathers, and will scatter them beyond the River, because they have made their Asherim, provoking Jehovah to anger. 16 And he will give Israel up because of the sins of Jeroboam, which he hath sinned, and wherewith he hath made Israel to sin.

Ahijah the prophet made the occasion of the queen's visit the occasion for delivering the message of judgment. Even though Jeroboam was elevated by the God of Israel to be king, he had acknowledged other gods (v. 9). This was intolerable, and for this the dynasty of Jeroboam was to be rejected (v. 10). **Jehovah**

will raise him up a king over Israel, who shall cut off the house of Jeroboam that day (v. 14). Furthermore, Ahijah declared that the king's son would die (v. 12).

c. The Fulfillment (14:17-20; 15:25-32)

17 And Jeroboam's wife arose, and departed, and came to Tirzah: *and* as she came to the threshold of the house, the child died. 18 And all Israel buried him, and mourned for him, according to the word of Jehovah, which he spake by his servant Ahijah the prophet.

19 And the rest of the acts of Jeroboam, how he warred, and how he reigned, behold, they are written in the book of the chronicles of the kings of Israel. 20 And the days which Jeroboam reigned were two and twenty years: and he slept with his fathers, and Nadab his son reigned in his stead.

25 And Nadab the son of Jeroboam began to reign over Israel in the second year of Asa king of Judah; and he reigned over Israel two years. 26 And he did that which was evil in the sight of Jehovah, and walked in the way of his father, and in his sin wherewith he made Israel to sin. 27 And Baasha the son of Ahijah, of the house of Issachar, conspired against him; and Baasha smote him at Gibbethon, which belonged to the Philistines; for Nadab and all Israel were laying siege to Gibbethon. 28 Even in the third year of Asa king of Judah did Baasha slay him, and reigned in his stead. 29 And it came to pass that, as soon as he was king, he smote all the house of Jeroboam: he left not to Jeroboam any that breathed, until he had destroyed him; according unto the saying of Jehovah, which he spake by his servant Ahijah the Shilonite; 30 for the sins of Jeroboam which he sinned, and wherewith he made Israel to sin, because of his provocation wherewith he provoked Jehovah, the God of Israel, to anger.

31 Now the rest of the acts of Nadab, and all that he did, are they not written in the book of the chronicles of the kings of Israel? 32 And there was war between Asa and Baasha king of Israel all their days.

Jeroboam continued to reign until his death and was succeeded by his son, Nadab, before Ahijah's prophecy was fulfilled. Nadab was engaged in a siege of Gibbethon, seeking to take it from the Philistines when he was murdered by a usurper, Baasha of Issachar. To protect himself, Baasha slew all the house of Jeroboam to remove any avenger who might seek his life.

VII. THE SOUTHERN KINGDOM DURING THE TENTH CENTURY B.C. (I Kings 14:21—15:24)

Even though the northern tribes of Israel revolted about 930 B.C., the kings of the line of David continued to rule in Jerusalem. From the time of the revolt until the close of the tenth century, three Davidic kings had ascended the throne: Rehoboam, who ruled until about 915 B.C.; Abijam (Abijah in Chronicles), who ruled until 912 B.C.; and Asa, who ruled from 912 B.C. until 875 B.C. The first twenty years of the Southern Kingdom were marked by retrogression. This was followed by a period of reformation under Asa.

A. RETROGRESSION UNDER REHOBOAM AND ABIJAM (14:21—15:8; cf. II Chron. 12:1—13:22)

21 And Rehoboam the son of Solomon reigned in Judah. Rehoboam was forty and one years old when he began to reign, and he reigned seventeen years in Jerusalem, the city which Jehovah had chosen out of all the tribes of Israel, to put his name there: and his mother's name was Naamah the Ammonitess. 22 And Judah did that which was evil in the sight of Jehovah, and they provoked him to jealousy with their sins which they committed, above all that their fathers had done. 23 For they also built them high places, and pillars, and Asherim, on every high hill, and under every green tree; 24 and there were also sodomites in the land: they did according to all the abominations of the nations which Jehovah drove out before the children of Israel.

25 And it came to pass in the fifth year of king Rehoboam, that Shishak king of Egypt came up against Jerusalem; 26 and he took away the treasures of the house of Jehovah, and the treasures of the king's house; he even took away all: and he took away all the shields of gold which Solomon had made. 27 And king Rehoboam made in their stead shields of brass, and committed them to the hands of the captains of the guard, who kept the door of the king's house. 28 And it

was so, that, as oft as the king went into the house of Jehovah, the guard bare them, and brought them back into the guard-chamber.

29 Now the rest of the acts of Rehoboam, and all that he did, are they not written in the book of the chronicles of the kings of Judah? 30 And there was war between Rehoboam and Jeroboam continually. 31 And Rehoboam slept with his fathers, and was buried with his fathers in the city of David: and his mother's name was Naamah the Ammonitess. And Abijam his son reigned in his stead.

1 Now in the eighteenth year of king Jeroboam the son of Nebat began Abijam to reign over Judah. 2 Three years reigned he in Jerusalem: and his mother's name was Maacah the daughter of Abishalom. 3 And he walked in all the sins of his father, which he had done before him; and his heart was not perfect with Jehovah his God, as the heart of David his father. 4 Nevertheless for David's sake did Jehovah his God give him a lamp in Jerusalem, to set up his son after him, and to establish Jerusalem; 5 because David did that which was right in the eyes of Jehovah, and turned not aside from anything that he commanded him all the days of his life, save only in the matter of Uriah the Hittite. 6 Now there was war between Rehoboam and Jeroboam all the days of his life.

7 And the rest of the acts of Abijam, and all that he did, are they not written in the book of the chronicles of the kings of Judah? And there was war between Abijam and Jeroboam. 8 And Abijam slept with his fathers; and they buried him in the city of David: and Asa his son reigned in his stead.

The retrogression which occurred under Rehoboam and Abijam was an increasing syncretism of Jehovah-worship with Baal-worship. Jehovah was considered a god among the gods. Temple worship continued, but altars were erected and groves were planted for Baal-worship (vv. 22, 23).

Accordingly, the Southern Kingdom proceeded upon a course that was marred by religious apostasy. This apostasy was not the only lamentable development, for during the fifth year of Rehoboam's reign, Shishak of Egypt invaded Jerusalem. He demanded an enormous amount of tribute, including treasures from the temple.

The account of Shishak's invasion as recorded in Kings puts the stress upon the losses which the temple of Solomon sustained. Since the temple worship was devoted to Jehovah, the temple losses were very important to the prophetic tradition.

However, Shishak's account of this invasion, as it is inscribed on one of the pylons of the temple at Karnak (ancient Thebes), reveals extensive penetration into both Judah and Israel.[18] A comparison of the account in Kings and the account at Karnak reveals the prophetic concern over the temple losses. Such losses were additional causes for concern in addition to the decline of unadulterated Jehovah-worship.

Rehoboam was able to restore his political realm, which had suffered under Shishak's invasion, but he made no attempt at religious reform. Rather, the deterioration of true Jehovah-worship continued throughout the seventeen years of Rehoboam's rule and the three years of Abijam's rule.

B. REFORMATION UNDER ASA
(15:9-24; cf. II Chron. 14:1—15:18)

9 And in the twentieth year of Jeroboam king of Israel began Asa to reign over Judah. 10 And forty and one years reigned he in Jerusalem: and his mother's name was Maacah the daughter of Abishalom. 11 And Asa did that which was right in the eyes of Jehovah, as did David his father. 12 And he put away the sodomites out of the land, and removed all the idols that his fathers had made. 13 And also Maacah his mother he removed from being queen, because she had made an abominable image for an Asherah; and Asa cut down her image, and burnt it at the brook Kidron. 14 But the high places were not taken away: nevertheless the heart of Asa was perfect with Jehovah all his days. 15 And he brought into the house of Jehovah the things that his father had dedicated, and the things that himself had dedicated, silver, and gold, and vessels.

16 And there was war between Asa and Baasha king of Israel all their days. 17 And Baasha king of Israel went up against Judah, and built Ramah, that he might not suffer any one to go out or come in to Asa king of Judah. 18 Then Asa took all the silver and the gold that

were left in the treasures of the house of Jehovah, and the treasures of the king's house, and delivered them into the hand of his servants; and king Asa sent them to Ben-hadad, the son of Tabrimmon, the son of Hezion, king of Syria, that dwelt at Damascus, saying, 19 *There is* a league between me and thee, between my father and thy father: behold, I have sent unto thee a present of silver and gold; go, break thy league with Baasha king of Israel, that he may depart from me. 20 And Ben-hadad hearkened unto king Asa, and sent the captains of his armies against the cities of Israel, and smote Ijon, and Dan, and Abel-beth-maacah, and all Chinneroth, with all the land of Naphtali. 21 And it came to pass, when Baasha heard thereof, that he left off building Ramah, and dwelt in Tirzah. 22 Then king Asa made a proclamation unto all Judah; none was exempted: and they carried away the stones of Ramah, and the timber thereof, wherewith Baasha had builded; and king Asa built therewith Geba of Benjamin, and Mizpah.

23 Now the rest of all the acts of Asa, and all his might, and all that he did, and the cities which he built, are they not written in the book of the chronicles of the kings of Judah? But in the time of his old age he was diseased in his feet. 24 And Asa slept with his fathers, and was buried with his fathers in the city of David his father; and Jehoshaphat his son reigned in his stead.

Asa began his reign in the tenth century (ca. 910 B.C.) and continued well into the ninth (ca. 875 B. C.). His reformation was marked by acts which pleased the Lord: **And Asa did that which was right in the eyes of Jehovah** (v. 11). This included a clear and decisive break with idolatry and a return to pure Jehovah-worship. He did not take away the high places; **nevertheless the heart of Asa was perfect with Jehovah all his days** (v. 14). Because of his unequivocal stand Asa was declared to be perfect in his relationship with Jehovah, this perfection being of a simplified order, namely, worshiping God only.

Asa's grandmother, Maacah, the queen-mother, was a zealous devotee to an image she had made. She was not his mother as indicated in verse 13 (cf. 15:2 where Maacah is mother of Abijam).

18 Gray, *op. cit.,* pp. 312-13.

Maacah **had made an abominable image for an Asherah** (v. 13). "This may mean as an image of the goddess."[19] This goddess was Baal's consort.

. To maintain his resolute rejection of idolatry, Asa had to sever personal relationships with Maacah, his grandmother. He removed her from her official position as queen-mother and destroyed her image with fire. Apparently either Maacah preferred her idol to her royal position and the Jehovah-worship of Asa, or she was an object of judgment, because she was unwilling to part with her image. In either case, the focus is on Asa's determined reform, which was not to be hindered by the strong ties of human relationship. God's will and pleasure were the important concern for Asa. All else was secondary, including his grandmother's image.

During the reign of Asa there were outbreaks of fighting between the hostile kingdoms of Judah and Israel. The Kings account refers to one occasion, the strengthening and fortifying of Ramah by Baasha, the northern king, usurper of the Northern Kingdom by the overthrow of Nadab, Jeroboam's son. Ramah was on the border of the two kingdoms.

Asa's military strategy to counterbalance this threat to the Southern Kingdom was to enter into an alliance with Syria. This required Baasha to fortify the frontier of the Northern Kingdom facing Syria. As a result of Asa's shrewd military and diplomatic strategy, Baasha withdrew his threat and evacuated Ramah.

VIII. THE NORTHERN KINGDOM DURING THE FIRST HALF OF THE NINTH CENTURY B.C.
(I Kings 15:33—22:40)

A. PART ONE (15:33—16:28)

As the Northern Kingdom entered the ninth century the new dynasty of Baasha from the tribe of Issachar had usurped the throne. For about a quarter of a century the kingdom was under this regime. Late in the second decade of the ninth century (ca. 822 B. C.) a captain over the chariots named Zimri staged an uprising which put him on the throne for a brief period of days (vv. 10, 15). How-

ever, he failed to obtain the support of the army commander, Omri, who destroyed him and claimed the throne. Omri launched one of the two major dynasties of the Northern Kingdom, the other being that of Jehu in the eighth century B. C.

1. The Rise and Fall of the Dynasty of Baasha (15:33—16:14)

33 In the third year of Asa king of Judah began Baasha the son of Ahijah to reign over all Israel in Tirzah, *and reigned* twenty and four years. 34 And he did that which was evil in the sight of Jehovah, and walked in the way of Jeroboam, and in his sin wherewith he made Israel to sin. 1 And the word of Jehovah came to Jehu the son of Hanani against Baasha, saying, 2 Forasmuch as I exalted thee out of the dust, and made thee prince over my people Israel, and thou hast walked in the way of Jeroboam, and hast made my people Israel to sin, to provoke me to anger with their sins; 3 behold, I will utterly sweep away Baasha and his house; and I will make thy house like the house of Jeroboam the son of Nebat. 4 Him that dieth of Baasha in the city shall the dogs eat; and him that dieth of his in the field shall the birds of the heavens eat.

5 Now the rest of the acts of Baasha, and what he did, and his might, are they not written in the book of the chronicles of the kings of Israel? 6 And Baasha slept with his fathers, and was buried in Tirzah; and Elah his son reigned in his stead. 7 And moreover by the prophet Jehu the son of Hanani came the word of Jehovah against Baasha, and against his house, both because of all the evil that he did in the sight of Jehovah, to provoke him to anger with the work of his hands, in being like the house of Jeroboam, and because he smote him.

8 In the twenty and sixth year of Asa king of Judah began Elah the son of Baasha to reign over Israel in Tirzah, *and reigned* two years. 9 And his servant Zimri, captain of half his chariots, conspired against him. Now he was in Tirzah, drinking himself drunk in the house of Arza, who was over the household in Tirzah: 10 and Zimri went in and smote him, and killed him, in the twenty and seventh year of Asa king of Judah, and reigned in his stead. 11 And it came to pass, when he began to reign, as soon as he sat on his throne, that he smote all

---

[19] Norman H. Snaith, "The First and Second Book of Kings: Introduction and Exegesis," *The Interpreter's Bible*, III, 134.

the house of Baasha: he left him not a single man-child, neither of his kinsfolks, nor of his friends. 12 Thus did Zimri destroy all the house of Baasha, according to the word of Jehovah, which he spake against Baasha by Jehu the prophet, 13 for all the sins of Baasha, and the sins of Elah his son, which they sinned, and wherewith they made Israel to sin, to provoke Jehovah, the God of Israel, to anger with their vanities. 14 Now the rest of the acts of Elah, and all that he did, are they not written in the book of the chronicles of the kings of Israel?

With the usurpation of the throne by Baasha, a new tribe challenged the leadership which the tribe of Ephraim had produced in the dynasty of Jeroboam, the son of Nebat. Baasha was of the tribe of Issachar (v. 27). Little contribution by way of leadership ever came from this tribe. On this rare occasion, the tribal heritage contributed little to enable Baasha to rise to the heights. He failed to fulfill the expectations of the prophet Ahijah, who had declared, "Jehovah will raise him up a king over Israel, who shall cut off the house of Jeroboam that day" (I Kings 14:14). Baasha's rise to power had the quality of brutal usurpation about it, yet at the same time Jehovah used Baasha in judgment upon Jeroboam. A certain tension and ambiguity is inherent in any explanation of God's use of Baasha because of the problem of relating good and evil. Baasha's evil assassination of Nadab, the son of Jeroboam, was in a very real sense divine judgment upon Jeroboam. The penetration of the good purpose of God into the evil intention of man defies reason, but it is the prophet's explanation for the downfall of the dynasty of Jeroboam.

Since Baasha persisted in the ways of Jeroboam, he likewise faced the message of divine judgment, this time given through the prophet Jehu, the son of Hanani. **And the word of the Lord came ... against Baasha, saying ... I will utterly sweep away Baasha and his house; and I will make thy house like the house of Jeroboam the son of Nebat** (vv. 1-3).

Although Baasha ruled a total of twenty-four years, the judgment of the Lord did not come until the second year after his death, during the reign of his son, Elah. Zimri usurped the throne and fulfilled not only his selfish lust for power

but also the divine purpose with regard to Baasha (vv. 12, 13).

2. The Reign of Zimri (16:15-20)

15 In the twenty and seventh year of Asa king of Judah did Zimri reign seven days in Tirzah. Now the people were encamped against Gibbethon, which belonged to the Philistines. 16 And the people that were encamped heard say, Zimri hath conspired, and hath also smitten the king: wherefore all Israel made Omri, the captain of the host, king over Israel that day in the camp. 17 And Omri went up from Gibbethon, and all Israel with him, and they besieged Tirzah. 18 And it came to pass, when Zimri saw that the city was taken, that he went into the castle of the king's house, and burnt the king's house over him with fire, and died, 19 for his sins which he sinned in doing that which was evil in the sight of Jehovah, in walking in the way of Jeroboam, and in his sin which he did, to make Israel to sin. 20 Now the rest of the acts of Zimri, and his treason that he wrought, are they not written in the book of the chronicles of the kings of Israel?

Zimri gained the throne of the Northern Kingdom by assassinating Elah, the king, who was feasting and drinking in Tirzah, the capital (vv. 9, 10). The conspiracy was successful in destroying the house of Baasha, and Zimri began his rule in Tirzah.

His reign, however, was brief (v. 15). Resistance to his claim to the throne came from the army. The commander of the army, Omri, laid siege to Tirzah, and when Zimri saw that his cause was lost, he took his own life through an act of arson (v. 18). The verdict on his reign is summarized as **the treason that he wrought** (v. 20).

3. The Rise of the Dynasty of Omri (16:21-28)

21 Then were the people of Israel divided into two parts: half of the people followed Tibni the son of Ginath, to make him king; and half followed Omri. 22 But the people that followed Omri prevailed against the people that followed Tibni the son of Ginath: so Tibni died, and Omri reigned. 23 In the thirty and first year of Asa king of Judah began Omri to reign over Israel, *and reigned* twelve years: six years reigned he in Tirzah. 24 **And he bought the hill Samaria of She-**

mer for two talents of silver; and he built on the hill, and called the name of the city which he built, after the name of Shemer, the owner of the hill, Samaria. 25 And Omri did that which was evil in the sight of Jehovah, and dealt wickedly above all that were before him. 26 For he walked in all the way of Jeroboam the son of Nebat, and in his sins wherewith he made Israel to sin, to provoke Jehovah, the God of Israel, to anger with their vanities. 27 Now the rest of the acts of Omri which he did, and his might that he showed, are they not written in the book of the chronicles of the kings of Israel? 28 So Omri slept with his fathers, and was buried in Samaria; and Ahab his son reigned in his stead.

Although Omri had succeeded in removing Zimri, he was confronted with a rival named Tibni, who was seeking the throne. The civil struggle which occurred resulted in Tibni's death, leaving Omri in firm control of the kingdom.

Omri was an important ruler in the Northern Kingdom for twelve years during the early part of the ninth century (ca. 882-871 B. C.). While the scriptural account is meager, archaeological evidence obtained from the Moabite stone and from the court records of the Assyrian monarch, Shalmaneser II, shows Omri a ruler of considerable importance. He showed noteworthy ability by recovering the unity of the kingdom that had been split by loyalties to Zimri, Tibni and himself. He left his impress upon Moab, a neighboring state, and Assyria, the great international power with its capital at Nineveh. He purchased a site as a personal possession, and built a city-state within a state to bequeath to his descendants, so founding a dynasty.[20] This capital was named Samaria and was located on a hill rising about three hundred feet above the surrounding plain. It became a strong fortress capital.

Notwithstanding Omri's importance, he was sweepingly condemned for ruling wickedly during his reign of twelve years. **Omri did that which was evil in the sight of Jehovah, and dealt wickedly above all that were before him** (v. 25).

From the standpoint of secular history, Omri left a profound impression upon his contemporaries, as archaeology indis-

putably attests. He left his mark on the world. This is the criterion of success for many, but the writer of Kings is not among them. From his standpoint, Omri is not significant and is dismissed with a few verses. Omri was unimpressed by religious concerns, except to continue the religion of the kingdom as instituted by Jeroboam, the son of Nebat. He had a wrong sense of values in that he treated religion as a perfunctory part of the state.

B. PART TWO (16:29—22:40)

The reign of Omri greatly improved the Northern Kingdom. He drastically reduced, if not halted altogether, the long civil strife between the Northern and Southern Kingdoms which had been waged intermittently by Jeroboam and Baasha. This period of hostilities, extending over a period of about a half-century, had been costly to both kingdoms. Omri's rule resulted in peace and prosperity.

Yet Omri's rule was judged by the prophets as a wicked one. Furthermore, he headed a dynasty which continued for almost a half-century and which met the resistance of the prophets of Jehovah. From the standpoint of the Kings account, prophets such as Elijah, Micaiah and Elisha were the truly important defenders of Israel's faith, while the kings of the Omri dynasty were wicked destroyers of that faith.

1. King Ahab of the Dynasty of Omri (16:29-34)

29 And in the thirty and eighth year of Asa king of Judah began Ahab the son of Omri to reign over Israel: and Ahab the son of Omri reigned over Israel in Samaria twenty and two years. 30 And Ahab the son of Omri did that which was evil in the sight of Jehovah above all that were before him. 31 And it came to pass, as if it had been a light thing for him to walk in the sins of Jeroboam the son of Nebat, that he took to wife Jezebel the daughter of Ethbaal king of the Sidonians, and went and served Baal, and worshipped him. 32 And he reared up an altar for Baal in the house of Baal, which he had built in Samaria. 33 And Ahab made the Asherah; and Ahab did yet more to provoke

[20] Gray, *op. cit.*, p. 331.

Jehovah, the God of Israel, to anger than all the kings of Israel that were before him. 34 In his days did Hiel the Bethelite build Jericho: he laid the foundation thereof with the loss of Abiram his first-born, and set up the gates thereof with the loss of his youngest son Segub, according to the word of Jehovah, which he spake by Joshua the son of Nun.

Omri was succeeded by his son, Ahab, whose outstanding reign continued for twenty-two years (v. 29). Ahab was a successful ruler and an astute statesman. He achieved fame as a builder of cities, and devoted his energies to peace and prosperity. As a result, he formed close ties with the Phoenicians and married Jezebel of Sidon to strengthen those ties. He was highly successful in some of his battles against Syria. He continued a strong and friendly alliance with the Southern Kingdom. Yet all of this is insignificant in the account as given in Kings.

What is really significant about Ahab, from the prophets' viewpoint, is his resounding collision with the prophetic order. What was of highest interest for the compiler of Kings was Elijah's confrontation with Ahab and Jezebel, together with the willfully wicked response of the latter.

The confrontation came about because Ahab had married the daughter of the Sidonian king and joined her in the worship of Baal. **And it came to pass, as if it had been a light thing for him to walk in the sins of Jeroboam ... that he took to wife Jezebel . . . and went and served Baal, and worshipped him. . . . Ahab did yet more to provoke Jehovah ... than all the kings of Israel that were before him** (vv. 31-33).

2. The Prophet Elijah and the Great Famine in Ahab's Reign (17:1—19:21)

The Elijah story opens abruptly during the notable and plentiful reign of Ahab with a declaration which directly challenged Ahab and Jezebel and their Baal-worship. **As Jehovah . . . liveth . . . there shall not be dew nor rain these years** (v. 1). Baal-worship was essentially a fertility cult, and the activities of Baal with his consort provided for the fertility of

nature. Baal was the lord of sky and weather. It was in this sphere of Baal's strength that the living God made His challenge when He, through Elijah, declared that natural processes were to be disturbed. Elijah's declaration appears to have had little impact upon the affluent and prosperous kingdom.

a. Hiding by Cherith (17:1-7)

1 And Elijah the Tishbite, who was of the sojourners of Gilead, said unto Ahab, As Jehovah, the God of Israel, liveth, before whom I stand, there shall not be dew nor rain these years, but according to my word. 2 And the word of Jehovah came unto him, saying, 3 Get thee hence, and turn thee eastward, and hide thyself by the brook Cherith, that is before the Jordan. 4 And it shall be, that thou shalt drink of the brook; and I have commanded the ravens to feed thee there. 5 So he went and did according unto the word of Jehovah; for he went and dwelt by the brook Cherith, that is before the Jordan. 6 And the ravens brought him bread and flesh in the morning, and bread and flesh in the evening; and he drank of the brook. 7 And it came to pass after a while, that the brook dried up, because there was no rain in the land.

The Elijah narrative does not follow the national scene and portray the increasing difficulties occasioned by the prolonged drought. Instead, it follows the activities of Elijah during this period. Leaving Samaria, Elijah found seclusion by the brook Cherith while the power of the living God stopped the normal process of rainfall. Meanwhile, as the period of drought lengthened, there can be no doubt that the worshipers of Baal increased their activities greatly in an attempt to encourage Baal to send rain. However, as the weeks, months and even years passed, Baal gave no relief to the drought-stricken area. Elijah remained in seclusion while *the word of God* revealed its superiority to *the work of Baal*.

He went and dwelt by the brook Cherith, that is before the Jordan (v. 5).[21] While the location of Cherith is unknown, it was not outside the sphere of providence. According to the narrative, the marvel of a solitary prophet in the care of the living God was more noteworthy than the methods adopted by the

---

[21] Cf. *Revised Standard Version*: "that is east of the Jordan."

Omri dynasty to meet the national emergency brought about by the drought.

b. Waiting at Zarephath (17:8-24)

8 And the word of Jehovah came unto him, saying, 9 Arise, get thee to Zarephath, which belongeth to Sidon, and dwell there: behold, I have commanded a widow there to sustain thee. 10 So he arose and went to Zarephath; and when he came to the gate of the city, behold, a widow was there gathering sticks: and he called to her, and said, Fetch me, I pray thee, a little water in a vessel, that I may drink. 11 And as she was going to fetch it, he called to her, and said, Bring me, I pray thee, a morsel of bread in thy hand. 12 And she said, As Jehovah thy God liveth, I have not a cake, but a handful of meal in the jar, and a little oil in the cruse: and, behold, I am gathering two sticks, that I may go in and dress it for me and my son, that we may eat it, and die. 13 And Elijah said unto her, Fear not; go and do as thou hast said; but make me thereof a little cake first, and bring it forth unto me, and afterward make for thee and for thy son. 14 For thus saith Jehovah, the God of Israel, The jar of meal shall not waste, neither shall the cruse of oil fail, until the day that Jehovah sendeth rain upon the earth. 15 And she went and did according to the saying of Elijah: and she, and he, and her house, did eat *many* days. 16 The jar of meal wasted not, neither did the cruse of oil fail, according to the word of Jehovah, which he spake by Elijah.

17 And it came to pass after these things, that the son of the woman, the mistress of the house, fell sick; and his sickness was so sore, that there was no breath left in him. 18 And she said unto Elijah, What have I to do with thee, O thou man of God? thou art come unto me to bring my sin to remembrance, and to slay my son! 19 And he said unto her, Give me thy son. And he took him out of her bosom, and carried him up into the chamber, where he abode, and laid him upon his own bed. 20 And he cried unto Jehovah, and said, O Jehovah my God, hast thou also brought evil upon the widow with whom I sojourn, by slaying her son? 21 And he stretched himself upon the child three times, and cried unto Jehovah, and said, O Jehovah my God, I pray thee, let this child's soul come into him again. 22 And Jehovah hearkened unto the voice of Elijah; and the soul of the child came into him

again, and he revived. 23 And Elijah took the child, and brought him down out of the chamber into the house, and delivered him unto his mother; and Elijah said, See, thy son liveth. 24 And the woman said to Elijah, Now I know that thou art a man of God, and that the word of Jehovah in thy mouth is truth.

After the brook Cherith dried up, Elijah was directed by the word of the Lord to go to Zarephath. This village was in Sidon and was governed by King Ethbaal, father of Jezebel. The drought covering the kingdom of Ahab extended to the kingdom of Ethbaal, showing that the living God controlled the sky and weather of Sidon as well as Samaria.

When Elijah arrived at Zarephath, he found a widow in desperate plight because of the drought. She and her son were starving. She doubtless worshiped Baal, but Baal had not eased her critical need.

There were many families and widows in that foreign land who were in need, but one particular widow received Elijah (v. 15). Because of this woman's great faith the entire incident of Elijah at Zarephath was recounted by Jesus when He was illustrating the fact that no prophet is accepted in his own country. Regarding this, Jesus said, "There were many widows in Israel in the days of Elijah ... when there came a great famine over all the land; and unto none of them was Elijah sent, but only to Zarephath, in the land of Sidon, unto a woman that was a widow" (Luke 4:26). From Jesus' point of view, this incident which happened to a family outside of Israel that worshiped Baal, occurred because there was faith in God and His prophet Elijah.

Elijah learned an important lesson here, namely, that the mission of God was wider than he thought. Elijah was a devoted and zealous prophet for Jehovah of Israel. He passionately opposed Baal of Sidon. Yet he was sent to a village under the authority of Sidon and found a willing and obedient disciple in the widow of Zarephath.

This was a necessary part of Elijah's experience. He needed to see the largeness of God and His purpose. At Zarephath, Elijah was given opportunity to realize God's larger concerns. John

Wesley was aware of the greatness of the heart of God and declared, "The world is my parish."

Elijah at Zarephath is a lesson for the missionary who goes to a foreign field, not simply a land of darkness and heathenism, but more appropriately a land where souls are waiting to give faith and loyalty to God. Elijah went to a foreign land to discover that God was already there. Any missionary may, and in fact to be effective must, go in the confidence of the faithfulness of God to all men.

c. Contesting at Carmel (18:1-46)

1 And it came to pass after many days, that the word of Jehovah came to Elijah, in the third year, saying, Go, show thyself unto Ahab; and I will send rain upon the earth. 2 And Elijah went to show himself unto Ahab. And the famine was sore in Samaria. 3 And Ahab called Obadiah, who was over the household. (Now Obadiah feared Jehovah greatly: 4 for it was so, when Jezebel cut off the prophets of Jehovah, that Obadiah took a hundred prophets, and hid them by fifty in a cave, and fed them with bread and water.) 5 And Ahab said unto Obadiah, Go through the land, unto all the fountains of water, and unto all the brooks: peradventure we may find grass and save the horses and mules alive, that we lose not all the beasts. 6 So they divided the land between them to pass throughout it: Ahab went one way by himself, and Obadiah went another way by himself.

7 And as Obadiah was in the way, behold, Elijah met him: and he knew him, and fell on his face, and said, Is it thou, my lord Elijah? 8 And he answered him, It is I: go, tell thy lord, Behold, Elijah *is here.* 9 And he said, Wherein have I sinned, that thou wouldest deliver thy servant into the hand of Ahab, to slay me? 10 As Jehovah thy God liveth, there is no nation or kingdom, whither my lord hath not sent to seek thee: and when they said, He is not here, he took an oath of the kingdom and nation, that they found thee not. 11 And now thou sayest, Go, tell thy lord, Behold, Elijah *is here.* 12 And it will come to pass, as soon as I am gone from thee, that the Spirit of Jehovah will carry thee whither I know not; and so when I come and tell Ahab, and he cannot find thee, he will slay me: but I thy servant fear Jehovah from my youth. 13 Was it not told my lord what I did when Jezebel slew the prophets of Jehovah, how I hid a hundred men of Jehovah's prophets by fifty in a cave, and fed them with bread and water? 14 And now thou sayest, Go, tell thy lord, Behold, Elijah *is here;* and he will slay me. 15 And Elijah said, As Jehovah of hosts liveth, before whom I stand, I will surely show myself unto him today.

16 So Obadiah went to meet Ahab, and told him; and Ahab went to meet Elijah. 17 And it came to pass, when Ahab saw Elijah, that Ahab said unto him, Is it thou, thou troubler of Israel? 18 And he answered, I have not troubled Israel; but thou, and thy father's house, in that ye have forsaken the commandments of Jehovah, and thou hast followed the Baalim. 19 Now therefore send, and gather to me all Israel unto mount Carmel, and the prophets of Baal four hundred and fifty, and the prophets of the Asherah four hundred, that eat at Jezebel's table.

20 So Ahab sent unto all the children of Israel, and gathered the prophets together unto mount Carmel. 21 And Elijah came near unto all the people, and said, How long go ye limping between the two sides? If Jehovah be God, follow him; but if Baal, then follow him. And the people answered him not a word. 22 Then said Elijah unto the people, I, even I only, am left a prophet of Jehovah; but Baal's prophets are four hundred and fifty men. 23 Let them therefore give us two bullocks; and let them choose one bullock for themselves, and cut it in pieces, and lay it on the wood, and put no fire under; and I will dress the other bullock, and lay it on the wood, and put no fire under. 24 And call ye on the name of your god, and I will call on the name of Jehovah: and the God that answereth by fire, let him be God. And all the people answered and said, It is well spoken.

25 And Elijah said unto the prophets of Baal, Choose you one bullock for yourselves, and dress it first; for ye are many; and call on the name of your god, but put no fire under. 26 And they took the bullock which was given them, and they dressed it, and called on the name of Baal from morning even until noon, saying, O Baal, hear us. But there was no voice, nor any that answered. And they leaped about the altar which was made. 27 And it came to pass at noon, that Elijah mocked them, and said, Cry aloud; for he is a god: either he is musing, or he is gone aside, or he is on a journey, or peradventure he sleepeth and must be awaked. 28 And they cried aloud, and cut themselves after their manner with knives

and lances, till the blood gushed out upon them. 29 And it was so, when midday was past, that they prophesied until the time of the offering of the *evening* oblation; but there was neither voice, nor any to answer, nor any that regarded.

30 And Elijah said unto all the people, Come near unto me; and all the people came near unto him. And he repaired the altar of Jehovah that was thrown down. 31 And Elijah took twelve stones, according to the number of the tribes of the sons of Jacob, unto whom the word of Jehovah came, saying, Israel shall be thy name. 32 And with the stones he built an altar in the name of Jehovah; and he made a trench about the altar, as great as would contain two measures of seed. 33 And he put the wood in order, and cut the bullock in pieces, and laid it on the wood. And he said, Fill four jars with water, and pour it on the burnt-offering, and on the wood. 34 And he said, Do it the second time; and they did it the second time. And he said, Do it the third time; and they did it the third time. 35 And the water ran round about the altar; and he filled the trench also with water. 36 And it came to pass at the time of the offering of the *evening* oblation, that Elijah the prophet came near, and said, O Jehovah, the God of Abraham, of Isaac, and of Israel, let it be known this day that thou art God in Israel, and that I am thy servant, and that I have done all these things at thy word. 37 Hear me, O Jehovah, hear me, that this people may know that thou, Jehovah, art God, and *that* thou hast turned their heart back again. 38 Then the fire of Jehovah fell, and consumed the burnt-offering, and the wood, and the stones, and the dust, and licked up the water that was in the trench. 39 And when all the people saw it, they fell on their faces: and they said, Jehovah, he is God; Jehovah, he is God. 40 And Elijah said unto them, Take the prophets of Baal; let not one of them escape. And they took them; and Elijah brought them down to the brook Kishon, and slew them there.

41 And Elijah said unto Ahab, Get thee up, eat and drink; for there is the sound of abundance of rain. 42 So Ahab went up to eat and to drink. And Elijah went up to the top of Carmel; and he bowed himself down upon the earth, and put his face between his knees. 43 And he said to his servant, Go up now, look toward the sea. And he went up, and looked, and said, There is nothing. And he said, Go again seven times. 44 And it came to pass at the seventh time, that he said, Behold, there ariseth a cloud out of the sea, as small as a man's hand. And he said, Go up, say unto Ahab, Make ready *thy chariot,* and get thee down, that the rain stop thee not. 45 And it came to pass in a little while, that the heavens grew black with clouds and wind, and there was a great rain. And Ahab rode, and went to Jezreel: 46 and the hand of Jehovah was on Elijah; and he girded up his loins, and ran before Ahab to the entrance of Jezreel.

Elijah's first major task had been the annunciation of the drought (I Kings 17). His second major task was the announcement of a contest on Mount Carmel (I Kings 18). The reason for the contest must have been to find out how to end the drought. Whoever was responsible for it could bring it to an end. Was Baal or was Jehovah responsible?

Elijah was told that Jehovah was about to send rain. This is the main point at issue, and it involves the whole chapter, as is clearly stated in the opening verse. **And it came to pass, after many days, that the word of Jehovah came to Elijah, in the third year, saying, Go, show thyself unto Ahab; and I will send rain upon the earth** (v. 1). The contest on Mount Carmel was between Jehovah, the God of Israel, and Baal, the nature god of sky and weather. The god who sent rain would prove himself to be God in Israel. Elijah's challenge was, **The God that answereth by fire, let him be God** (v. 24). The fundamental issue was rainfall, and this is not to be obscured by the falling of fire to consume the sacrifice. God declared to Elijah that He was sending rain.

Sustained by this divine promise, Elijah prepared to meet Ahab. As Elijah returned to Israel from Zarephath in Phoenicia, he chanced to meet the governor of Ahab's household, Obadiah. This man was in a most unusual position. He had the high honor and responsibility of managing the royal house of King Ahab and Queen Jezebel, a house devoted to Baal-worship. Yet Obadiah was a faithful worshiper of Jehovah. He had shown heroism of faith by helping prophets of Jehovah who were persecuted by the royal family (v. 4). This good man honored the Lord in spite of an evil and compromising environment.

When Ahab was informed by Obadiah as to the whereabouts of Elijah, he came to the place immediately and confronted Elijah with a denunciatory question: **Is it thou, thou troubler of Israel?** (v. 17). Ahab looked upon Elijah as a man who stirred up needless trouble in Israel. As far as Ahab was concerned, the mattter of accommodating Jehovah-worship to Baal-worship was not a crime, but a necessary expedient for the welfare of the state.

Surprisingly, Ahab did not consider himself an apostate. "Though Ahab never officially ceased to be a Jehovah worshiper . . . he seems to have given his wife a fairly free hand to propagate her faith."[22] He retained a band of prophets of Jehovah at his court (I Kings 22:6, 11, 12). The names of his children which are known, Ahaziah, Jehoram and Athaliah, were all compounded with Jehovah (Yahweh). He gave evidence that Jehovah-worship was tolerated in his kingdom. Therefore, he did not conceive of himself as responsible for Israel's troubles.

Elijah saw Israel's troubles as caused by Ahab's tolerance. **I have not troubled Israel; but thou, and thy father's house, in that ye have forsaken the commandments of Jehovah, and thou hast followed Baalim** (v. 18). Ahab tried to mix the two religions, but Elijah called for a decision of undivided loyalty. A contest of the two deities was arranged. The place was on Mount Carmel (v. 19).

Representatives from various parts of Ahab's kingdom were summoned by the king to the promontory of Mount Carmel overlooking the Mediterranean Sea. In the presence of King Ahab, the prophets of Baal and the people of the kingdom, Elijah issued an ultimatum. **How long go ye limping between the two sides? If Jehovah be God, follow him; but if Baal, then follow him** (v. 21).

The intolerance of Elijah collided with the tolerance of Ahab. For Elijah the importance of undivided loyalty in religion transcended all other considerations, including national well-being. The issue raised by Elijah is a perennial one. Religion is not for purposes of expediency and accommodation. It is not a means to an end. Religion must reckon with the ultimate, and all else, even the state,

must remain subservient to the religious ultimate. Where religious loyalties become divided, the crucial decision must be made as to the *ultimate* religious loyalty. This is basic in the monotheism of Judaism and Christianity.

For Ahab, religious accommodation was the best policy; for Elijah, undivided religious loyalty was the only policy. In the light of a three-year drought, the contest on Mount Carmel was to give empirical evidence to all Israel that the god which answered by fire demanded undivided allegiance. **The God that answereth by fire, let him be God** (v. 24). The people gave their assent (v. 24).

The prophets of Baal were given first opportunity. Having prepared the sacrifice, they spent the day in prayers and frenzied activity, but from Baal **there was neither voice, nor any answer, nor any that regarded** (v. 29).

At the time of the evening sacrifice, Elijah prepared the old altar of Jehovah that had been in disrepair for some time (v. 30). Having put the sacrifice in place, he ordered water poured on it as part of the ritual related to the bringing of rain. Elijah had made the issue of rain the central issue in the contest.

Elijah's prayer petitioned God to act, **that this people may know that thou, Jehovah, art God** (v. 37). The prayer was brief, but its central petition is clear: let Jehovah show Himself to be God. Jehovah answered by sending fire. The people responded, **Jehovah, he is God** (v. 39). Elijah urged Ahab to complete the ritual of the sacrifice with great haste because rain was on the way (v. 41). Before Ahab could finish the sacrificial meal and drive to Jezreel, the heavens were heavy with clouds, **and there was a great rain** (v. 45).

It was a dramatic and climactic moment, the result of a long, severe drought, and a compelling revelation to the dynasty of Omri, particularly Ahab, and to the people of the Northern Kingdom that Jehovah is God. Jehovah was greater than Baal and He tolerated no compromise or division of loyalties. Israel had responded in faith, acknowledging only Jehovah to be God. The great fam-

[22] Ellison, *op. cit.*, p. 315.

ine and its termination were under Jehovah's control, rather than Baal's.

d. Fleeing to Horeb (19:1-21)

1 And Ahab told Jezebel all that Elijah had done, and withal how he had slain all the prophets with the sword. 2 Then Jezebel sent a messenger unto Elijah, saying, So let the gods do to me, and more also, if I make not thy life as the life of one of them by to-morrow about this time. 3 And when he saw that, he arose, and went for his life, and came to Beersheba, which belongeth to Judah, and left his servant there. 4 But he himself went a day's journey into the wilderness, and came and sat down under a juniper-tree: and he requested for himself that he might die, and said, It is enough; now, O Jehovah, take away my life; for I am not better than my fathers. 5 And he lay down and slept under a juniper-tree; and, behold, an angel touched him, and said unto him, Arise and eat. 6 And he looked, and, behold, there was at his head a cake baken on the coals, and a cruse of water. And he did eat and drink, and laid him down again. 7 And the angel of Jehovah came again the second time, and touched him, and said, Arise and eat, because the journey is too great for thee. 8 And he arose, and did eat and drink, and went in the strength of that food forty days and forty nights unto Horeb the mount of God.

9 And he came thither unto a cave, and lodged there; and, behold, the word of Jehovah came to him, and he said unto him, What doest thou here, Elijah? 10 And he said, I have been very jealous for Jehovah, the God of hosts; for the children of Israel have forsaken thy covenant, thrown down thine altars, and slain thy prophets with the sword: and I, even I only, am left; and they seek my life, to take it away. 11 And he said, Go forth, and stand upon the mount before Jehovah. And, behold, Jehovah passed by, and a great and strong wind rent the mountains, and brake in pieces the rocks before Jehovah; but Jehovah was not in the wind: and after the wind an earthquake; but Jehovah was not in the earthquake: 12 and after the earthquake a fire; but Jehovah was not in the fire: and after the fire a still small voice. 13 And it was so, when Elijah heard it, that he wrapped his face in his mantle, and went out, and stood in the entrance of the cave. And, behold, there came a voice unto him, and said, What doest thou here, Elijah? 14 And he said, I have been

very jealous for Jehovah, the God of hosts; for the children of Israel have forsaken thy covenant, thrown down thine altars, and slain thy prophets with the sword; and I, even I only, am left; and they seek my life, to take it away.

15 And Jehovah said unto him, Go, return on thy way to the wilderness of Damascus: and when thou comest, thou shalt anoint Hazael to be king over Syria; 16 and Jehu the son of Nimshi shalt thou anoint to be king over Israel: and Elisha the son of Shaphat of Abel-meholah shalt thou anoint to be prophet in thy room. 17 And it shall come to pass, that him that escapeth from the sword of Hazael shall Jehu slay; and him that escapeth from the sword of Jehu shall Elisha slay. 18 Yet will I leave *me* seven thousand in Israel, all the knees which have not bowed unto Baal, and every mouth which hath not kissed him.

19 So he departed thence, and found Elisha the son of Shaphat, who was plowing, with twelve yoke *of oxen* before him, and he with the twelfth: and Elijah passed over unto him, and cast his mantle upon him. 20 And he left the oxen, and ran after Elijah, and said, Let me, I pray thee, kiss my father and my mother, and then I will follow thee. And he said unto him, Go back again; for what have I done to thee? 21 And he returned from following him, and took the yoke of oxen, and slew them, and boiled their flesh with the instruments of the oxen, and gave unto the people, and they did eat. Then he arose, and went after Elijah, and ministered unto him.

While Elijah was at last able to bring Israel to a decision after a period of prolonged drought and a remarkable contest on Mount Carmel, he was unable to influence Jezebel. She was as zealous in her loyalty to Baal as Elijah in his loyalty to Jehovah. However, she had the secular power of the state at her command. Ultimately, God accomplished the overthrow of her authority and the downfall of the dynasty, but during the time of Elijah the worshippers of Jehovah passed through a trying ordeal. The ordering of divine justice in history does not always occur even when it seems appropriate. The problem of immediate justice remains an enigma in our universe to those who rely upon human rationality rather than faith in a righteous and just God.

Jezebel considered that her threatening

message to Elijah (v. 2) was founded on legitimate grievances. He had ordered the execution of the prophets of Baal at Mount Carmel, and she was seeking to avenge their death. The Baal crisis in the Northern Kingdom had reached a desperate and deadly stage. Prophets of Baal as well as prophets of Jehovah were forced to face the reality of martyrdom.

Elijah fled southward, passing through the Southern Kingdom where King Jehoshaphat ruled in Jerusalem. This God-fearing king had embarked upon a perilous political expedient, a friendly alliance with Elijah's foe, King Ahab. Passing through Beersheba, Elijah continued in the direction of Mount Horeb, more commonly called Mount Sinai. Coming to a lonely juniper tree, Elijah admitted utter defeat: **It is enough, now, O Jehovah, take away my life** (v. 4).

The despair that was stabbing Elijah's heroic faith was overwhelming because of an unanswered question: Was Jehovah really God when Jezebel's power remained intact? Amid his doubts and fears, Elijah longed to die. Yet Jehovah mercifully supplied nourishment in order that Elijah might proceed on the long journey that would lead him to a remarkable new understanding of the ways of God.

When Elijah arrived at Mount Horeb (Sinai), he was asked by the Lord, **What doest thou here, Elijah?** (v. 9). His explanation was that an apostate Israel was seeking to take his life (v. 10). Whereupon there came a great wind, followed by an earthquake, and finally by a fire. Afterwards there was **a sound of gentle stillness** (v. 12, margin). "There is nothing to indicate to us whether the sound was articulate or not ... but ... the prophet ... knew ... to present himself before Jehovah."[23] **And it was so, when Elijah heard it, that he wrapped his face in his mantle, and went out, and stood in the entrance of the cave** (v. 13). "The revelation was not one for the eye, but for the spirit, of the prophet."[24] The Lord came to Elijah, not in the wind, the earthquake, or the fire, but in the stilling of them. Elijah did not wrap his mantle about him in worship because of the dramatic natural phenomena, but because of the presence of the Lord in the gentle silence.

Out of that memorable silence came a voice questioning, **What doest thou here, Elijah?** (v. 13). The question was a direct challenge to Elijah's melancholy loneliness. He was, in reality, a fugitive from the places where history was being made.

The Hebrew concern for history is one of the outstanding contributions of this people. Elijah, standing tall in the line of Hebrew prophets concerned with the history of Israel, found Mount Horeb and the awesome silence an occasion for recommissioning. He was sent back to the land where history was being made.

The relevance of Elijah's flight to Mount Horeb and the meaningful experience of the "sound of gentle stillness," together with the call to return to the mainstream of human living, is profound. Every century has more than its share of Jehovah-worshipers who flee from the responsibilities of grappling with the realities of history. They retire to the cloisters and to the retreats where they continue in the faith, isolated from and insulated against the actual realities of life and the ongoing of history. The call of God, as well as the challenge of history, is to move out into the current of life and fulfill God-given responsibilities in spite of the threat of martyrdom.

Elijah's journey to Mount Horeb reveals the profound regard he had for the Mosaic tradition in Israel. In a sense, Elijah represented the whole prophetic movement. The prophets were concerned that Israel return to the Mosaic covenant. Their spirit of reform was not with an eye to the future but with an eye to the past. Yet this did not mean that they were anachronistic and dwelling upon an unrecoverable past. Elijah and all the other prophets were keenly aware of the relevance of their efforts. They saw the deeper and abiding implications of the covenant and of God's ways in history.[25]

3. War Between Ahab of Israel and Ben-hadad of Syria (20:1-43)

1 And Ben-hadad the king of Syria gathered all his host together; and there were thirty and two kings with him, and

---

[23] Lumby, *op. cit.*, p. 202.   [24] *Ibid.*
[25] Cf. B. Anderson, *Understanding the Old Testament*, pp. 211-12.

horses and chariots: and he went up and besieged Samaria, and fought against it. 2 And he sent messengers to Ahab king of Israel, into the city, and said unto him, Thus saith Ben-hadad, 3 Thy silver and thy gold is mine; thy wives also and thy children, even the goodliest, are mine. 4 And the king of Israel answered and said, It is according to thy saying, my lord, O king; I am thine, and all that I have. 5 And the messengers came again, and said, Thus speaketh Ben-hadad, saying, I sent indeed unto thee, saying, Thou shalt deliver me thy silver, and thy gold, and thy wives, and thy children; 6 but I will send my servants unto thee to-morrow about this time, and they shall search thy house, and the houses of thy servants; and it shall be, that whatsoever is pleasant in thine eyes, they shall put it in their hand, and take it away.

7 Then the king of Israel called all the elders of the land, and said, Mark, I pray you, and see how this man seeketh mischief: for he sent unto me for my wives, and for my children, and for my silver, and for my gold; and I denied him not. 8 And all the elders and all the people said unto him, Hearken thou not, neither consent. 9 Wherefore he said unto the messengers of Ben-hadad, Tell my lord the king, All that thou didst send for to thy servant at the first I will do; but this thing I may not do. And the messengers departed, and brought him word again. 10 And Ben-hadad sent unto him, and said, The gods do so unto me, and more also, if the dust of Samaria shall suffice for handfuls for all the people that follow me. 11 And the king of Israel answered and said, Tell him, Let not him that girdeth on *his armor* boast himself as he that putteth it off. 12 And it came to pass, when *Ben-hadad* heard this message, as he was drinking, he and the kings, in the pavilions, that he said unto his servants, Set *yourselves in array.* And they set *themselves in array* against the city.

13 And, behold, a prophet came near unto Ahab king of Israel, and said, Thus saith Jehovah, Hast thou seen all this great multitude? behold, I will deliver it into thy hand this day; and thou shalt know that I am Jehovah. 14 And Ahab said, By whom? And he said, Thus saith Jehovah, By the young men of the princes of the provinces. Then he said, Who shall begin the battle? And he answered, Thou. 15 Then he mustered the young men of the princes of the provinces, and they were two hundred and thirty-two: and after them he mustered all the peo-

ple, even all the children of Israel, being seven thousand.

16 And they went out at noon. But Ben-hadad was drinking himself drunk in the pavilions, he and the kings, the thirty and two kings that helped him. 17 And the young men of the princes of the provinces went out first; and Ben-hadad sent out, and they told him, saying, There are men come out from Samaria. 18 And he said, Whether they are come out for peace, take them alive; or whether they are come out for war, take them alive. 19 So these went out of the city, the young men of the princes of the provinces, and the army which followed them. 20 And they slew every one his man; and the Syrians fled, and Israel pursued them: and Ben-hadad the king of Syria escaped on a horse with horsemen. 21 And the king of Israel went out, and smote the horses and chariots, and slew the Syrians with a great slaughter.

22 And the prophet came near to the king of Israel, and said unto him, Go, strengthen thyself, and mark, and see what thou doest; for at the return of the year the king of Syria will come up against thee. 23 And the servants of the king of Syria said unto him, Their god is a god of the hills; therefore they were stronger than we: but let us fight against them in the plain, and surely we shall be stronger than they. 24 And do this thing: take the kings away, every man out of his place, and put captains in their room; 25 and number thee an army, like the army that thou hast lost, horse for horse, and chariot for chariot; and we will fight against them in the plain, and surely we shall be stronger than they. And he hearkened unto their voice, and did so.

26 And it came to pass at the return of the year, that Ben-hadad mustered the Syrians, and went up to Aphek, to fight against Israel. 27 And the children of Israel were mustered, and were victualled, and went against them: and the children of Israel encamped before them like two little flocks of kids; but the Syrians filled the country. 28 And a man of God came near and spake unto the king of Israel and said, Thus saith Jehovah, Because the Syrians have said, Jehovah is a god of the hills, but he is not a god of the valleys; therefore will I deliver all this great multitude into thy hand, and ye shall know that I am Jehovah. 29 And they encamped one over against the other seven days. And so it was, that in the seventh day the battle was joined; and the children of Israel slew of the Syrians a hundred thousand footmen in

one day. 30 But the rest fled to Aphek, into the city; and the wall fell upon twenty and seven thousand men that were left. And Ben-hadad fled, and came into the city, into an inner chamber.

31 And his servants said unto him, Behold now, we have heard that the kings of the house of Israel are merciful kings: let us, we pray thee, put sackcloth on our loins, and ropes upon our heads, and go out to the king of Israel: peradventure he will save thy life. 32 So they girded sackcloth on their loins, and *put* ropes on their heads, and came to the king of Israel, and said, Thy servant Ben-hadad saith, I pray thee, let me live. And he said, Is he yet alive? he is my brother. 33 Now the men observed diligently, and hasted to catch whether it were his mind; and they said, Thy brother Ben-hadad. Then he said, Go ye, bring him. Then Ben-hadad came forth to him; and he caused him to come up into the chariot. 34 And *Ben-hadad* said unto him, The cities which my father took from thy father I will restore; and thou shalt make streets for thee in Damascus, as my father made in Samaria. And I, *said Ahab*, will let thee go with this covenant. So he made a covenant with him, and let him go.

35 And a certain man of the sons of the prophets said unto his fellow by the word of Jehovah, Smite me, I pray thee. And the man refused to smite him. 36 Then said he unto him, Because thou hast not obeyed the voice of Jehovah, behold, as soon as thou art departed from me, a lion shall slay thee. And as soon as he was departed from him, a lion found him, and slew him. 37 Then he found another man, and said, Smite me, I pray thee. And the man smote him, smiting and wounding him. 38 So the prophet departed, and waited for the king by the way, and disguised himself with his headband over his eyes. 39 And as the king passed by, he cried unto the king; and he said, Thy servant went out into the midst of the battle; and, behold, a man turned aside, and brought a man unto me, and said, Keep this man: if by any means he be missing, then shall thy life be for his life, or else thou shalt pay a talent of silver. 40 And as thy servant was busy here and there, he was gone. And the king of Israel said unto him, So shall thy judgment be; thyself hast decided it. 41 And he hasted, and took the headband away from his eyes; and the king of Israel discerned him that he was of the prophets. 42 And he said unto him, Thus saith Jehovah, Because thou hast let go out of thy hand the man whom I had devoted to destruction, therefore thy life shall go for his life, and thy people for his people. 43 And the king of Israel went to his house heavy and displeased, and came to Samaria.

The narrative of Elijah is interrupted by an account of hostilities between Ahab and Ben-hadad. Ahab is the central figure, and he appears in quite a different light. Prophets are shown supporting him (vv. 13f., 22f., 28). One prophet is reported to have rebuked him for the remarkable leniency with which he treated Ben-hadad, who was captured as a war prisoner (vv. 35-43).

Ben-hadad of Syria provoked the hostilities largely because of his attempt to coerce Ahab into an alliance against Assyria. For a time Ahab was compelled to acknowledge Ben-hadad as overlord (vv. 2-4). As Ben-hadad was pressing his demands by armed force and invasion, a prophet counselled Ahab as to an offensive maneuver that brought a decisive military victory to Ahab (v. 21). A second battle, a year later, resulted in the capture and release of Ben-hadad (v. 34). This unusual leniency on the part of Ahab had important political implications of international importance. It enabled him to enter an alliance of smaller nations, including Syria, against the awesome power of Assyria. Moreover, Syria was able to provide strong protection for the Northern Kingdom against Assyria under Shalmaneser III.

Within three years the alliance between Ahab and Ben-hadad was put to a real test at the battle of Qarqar, 853 B. C., on the Orontes River near Hamath against Assyria. Although the battle of Qarqar is not mentioned in the Kings account, Ahab's important participation in it is attested to in Assyrian annals, and a grave crisis for the Northern Kingdom was averted. Had Shalmaneser III won the battle of Qarqar the history of Northern Kingdom of the ninth century might have been different.

The developments recorded in this chapter provide a glimpse of the international political arena in which Ahab moved. In the light of his involvements, he was in a position to see the peril which confronted his realm. In all of this there is no indication that he sought

Jehovah. His rule and his international affinities reveal no commitment other than to self and security. For a time, his policy was effective. Yet, it may be remembered that the God of Israel had spoken at Mount Horeb commissioning Elijah to anoint Jehu (I Kings 19:16). This foretold the downfall of the dynasty of Omri. While only approximation in chronology is possible, the time lapse between Elijah's commission of Jehu at Mount Horeb and the downfall of the dynasty of Omri was about a score of years. At best, Ahab's efforts were temporary.

4. Naboth's Vineyard (21:1-29)

1 And it came to pass after these things, that Naboth the Jezreelite had a vineyard, which was in Jezreel, hard by the palace of Ahab king of Samaria. 2 And Ahab spake unto Naboth, saying, Give me thy vineyard, that I may have it for a garden of herbs, because it is near unto my house; and I will give thee for it a better vineyard than it: or, if it seem good to thee, I will give thee the worth of it in money. 3 And Naboth said to Ahab, Jehovah forbid it me, that I should give the inheritance of my fathers unto thee. 4 And Ahab came into his house heavy and displeased because of the word which Naboth the Jezreelite had spoken to him; for he had said, I will not give thee the inheritance of my fathers. And he laid him down upon his bed, and turned away his face, and would eat no bread.

5 But Jezebel his wife came to him, and said unto him, Why is thy spirit so sad, that thou eatest no bread? 6 And he said unto her, Because I spake unto Naboth the Jezreelite, and said unto him, Give me thy vineyard for money; or else, if it please thee, I will give thee *another* vineyard for it: and he answered, I will not give thee my vineyard. 7 And Jezebel his wife said unto him, Dost thou now govern the kingdom of Israel? arise, and eat bread, and let thy heart be merry: I will give thee the vineyard of Naboth the Jezreelite. 8 So she wrote letters in Ahab's name, and sealed them with his seal, and sent the letters unto the elders and to the nobles that were in his city, *and* that dwelt with Naboth. 9 And she wrote in the letters, saying, Proclaim a fast, and set Naboth on high among the people: 10 and set two men, base fellows, before him, and let them bear witness against him, saying, Thou didst curse God and

the king. And then carry him out, and stone him to death.

11 And the men of his city, even the elders and the nobles who dwelt in his city, did as Jezebel had sent unto them, according as it was written in the letters which she had sent unto them. 12 They proclaimed a fast, and set Naboth on high among the people. 13 And the two men, the base fellows, came in and sat before him: and the base fellows bare witness against him, even against Naboth, in the presence of the people, saying, Naboth did curse God and the king. Then they carried him forth out of the city, and stoned him to death with stones. 14 Then they sent to Jezebel, saying, Naboth is stoned, and is dead. 15 And it came to pass, when Jezebel heard that Naboth was stoned, and was dead, that Jezebel said to Ahab, Arise, take possession of the vineyard of Naboth the Jezreelite, which he refused to give thee for money; for Naboth is not alive, but dead. 16 And it came to pass, when Ahab heard that Naboth was dead, that Ahab rose up to go down to the vineyard of Naboth the Jezreelite, to take possession of it.

17 And the word of Jehovah came to Elijah the Tishbite, saying, 18 Arise, go down to meet Ahab king of Israel, who dwelleth in Samaria: behold, he is in the vineyard of Naboth, whither he is gone down to take possession of it. 19 And thou shalt speak unto him, saying, Thus saith Jehovah, Hast thou killed, and also taken possession? And thou shalt speak unto him, saying, Thus saith Jehovah, In the place where dogs licked the blood of Naboth shall dogs lick thy blood, even thine. 20 And Ahab said to Elijah, Hast thou found me, O mine enemy? And he answered, I have found thee, because thou hast sold thyself to do that which is evil in the sight of Jehovah. 21 Behold, I will bring evil upon thee, and will utterly sweep thee away and will cut off from Ahab every man-child, and him that is shut up and him that is left at large in Israel: 22 and I will make thy house like the house of Jeroboam the son of Nebat, and like the house of Baasha the son of Ahijah for the provocation wherewith thou hast provoked me to anger, and hast made Israel to sin. 23 And of Jezebel also spake Jehovah, saying, The dogs shall eat Jezebel by the rampart of Jezreel. 24 Him that dieth of Ahab in the city the dogs shall eat; and him that dieth in the field shall the birds of the heavens eat. 25 (But there was none like unto Ahab, who did sell himself to do that which was

evil in the sight of Jehovah, whom Jezebel his wife stirred up. 26 And he did very abominably in following idols, according to all that the Amorites did, whom Jehovah cast out before the children of Israel.)

27 And it came to pass, when Ahab heard those words, that he rent his clothes, and put sackcloth upon his flesh, and fasted, and lay in sackcloth, and went softly. 28 And the word of Jehovah came to Elijah the Tishbite, saying, 29 Seest thou how Ahab humbleth himself before me? because he humbleth himself before me, I will not bring the evil in his days; but in his son's day will I bring the evil upon his house.

Attention to the narrative of Elijah is resumed in this chapter. Although Ahab's petty greed, his partnership with Jezebel, and his claim of Naboth's vineyard constitute an episode of unrelieved blackness, Elijah's bold rebuke constitutes an essential concern for social justice.

The episode occurred over a piece of land which belonged to Naboth's vineyard at Jezreel, where the summer palace of the Omri dynasty was located. Since this piece of land adjoined the royal property, Ahab desired it to satisfy a whim. **Give me thy vineyard, that I may have it for a garden of herbs, because it is near unto my house** (v. 2).

Naboth refused. **Jehovah forbid it me, that I should give the inheritance of my fathers unto thee** (v. 3). Ahab was generous in his offer of other land or money, but Naboth's refusal was based on an altogether different principle, a religious one. The land belonged to the family estate by reason of inheritance. Jehovah, the God of Israel, had provided that inheritance. Naboth considered himself the responsible steward of this divine inheritance. It was not his prerogative to dispose of the property. Although Ahab recognized this basic hereditary principle in Israel, Jezebel did not. Her religion of Baal placed no such limitations as hereditary rights on the exercise of royal powers. Baalism was accommodated to what later became known as "the divine right of kings."

Jezebel resorted to treachery, under the pretense of legality. As a result, the people of Jezreel stoned Naboth and his sons

(v. 13; cf. II Kings 9:26). When Ahab was informed by Jezebel that Naboth was dead, he went to take possession of the disputed vineyard (v. 16). While Ahab was in the vineyard, planning what he would do with this newly acquired property, there occurred another dramatic confrontation of Ahab and Elijah. A thunderous judgment against this outrageous crime was delivered by the fearless prophet (vv. 21-24). As a consequence, Ahab repented in sackcloth and ashes (v. 27).

While the contest on Mount Carmel was a vivid expression of the conflict between Jehovah-worship and Baal-worship in the field of religious loyalties, the vineyard of Naboth was an excellent example of that conflict in the field of social relationships.[26] Elijah was representative of the great prophetic tradition in championing the social righteousness of the Mosaic tradition. Baalism tended toward favoring the aristocracy and its resulting social inequalities. Such a religion tolerated the social injustices which "first-class citizens" forced upon the "second-class citizens." Jehovah-worship stood unalterably opposed to such social inequality.

5. Ahab's Death (22:1-40)

Ahab's rule continued in the Northern Kingdom for twenty-two years (I Kings 16:29). The events of this chapter occasioned his death during the middle of the ninth century B. C. He was trying to force Ben-hadad of Syria to keep a promise to cede Ramoth-gilead to Israel (cf. I Kings 20:34). In the ensuing battle, Ahab was mortally wounded.

a. Counsel of War (22:1-12; cf. II Chron. 18:1-11)

1 And they continued three years without war between Syria and Israel. 2 And it came to pass in the third year, that Jehoshaphat the king of Judah came down to the king of Israel. 3 And the king of Israel said unto his servants, Know ye that Ramoth-gilead is ours, and we are still, and take it not out of the hand of the king of Syria? 4 And he said unto Jehoshaphat, Wilt thou go with me to battle to Ramoth-gilead? And Jehoshaphat said to the king of Israel, I am as

26 *Ibid.*, p. 213.

thou art, my people as thy people, my horses as thy horses.

5 And Jehoshaphat said unto the king of Israel, Inquire first, I pray thee, for the word of Jehovah. 6 Then the king of Israel gathered the prophets together, about four hundred men, and said unto them, Shall I go against Ramoth-gilead to battle, or shall I forbear? And they said, Go up; for the Lord will deliver it into the hand of the king. 7 But Jehoshaphat said, Is there not here a prophet of Jehovah besides, that we may inquire of him? 8 And the king of Israel said unto Jehoshaphat, There is yet one man by whom we may inquire of Jehovah, Micaiah the son of Imlah: but I hate him; for he doth not prophesy good concerning me, but evil. And Jehoshaphat said, Let not the king say so. 9 Then the king of Israel called an officer, and said, Fetch quickly Micaiah the son of Imlah. 10 Now the king of Israel and Jehoshaphat the king of Judah were sitting each on his throne, arrayed in their robes, in an open place at the entrance of the gate of Samaria; and all the prophets were prophesying before them. 11 And Zedekiah the son of Chenaanah made him horns of iron, and said, Thus saith Jehovah, With these shalt thou push the Syrians, until they be consumed. 12 And all the prophets prophesied so, saying, Go up to Ramoth-gilead, and prosper; for Jehovah will deliver it into the hand of the king.

Upon the occasion of a royal visit by Jehoshaphat, king of the Southern Kingdom, Ahab declared, Know ye that Ramoth-gilead is ours, and we are still, and take it not out of the hand of the king of Syria? (v. 3). Ramoth-gilead was a key fortress dominating the approach to the heart of the Northern Kingdom from the direction of Syria. Possession of it by the Northern Kingdom was essential in the event of war between the two countries. Ben-hadad had promised it to Ahab as part settlement of a war fought some three years earlier (20:34). The promise had not been fulfilled.

Ahab asked Jehoshaphat for military assistance to take Ramoth-gilead by force. Jehoshaphat declared his willingness to assist Ahab, although he requested, Inquire first, I pray thee, for the word of Jehovah (v. 5). Ahab complied. Then the king of Israel gathered the prophets to-

gether, about four hundred men, and said unto them, Shall I go against Ramoth-gilead to battle, or shall I forbear? And they said, Go up; for the Lord will deliver it into the hand of the king (v. 6). According to these "yes-men," the will of Jehovah and the counsel of war by Ahab coincided completely.

The God-fearing Jehoshaphat was not satisfied. Upon inquiry, he was told of another prophet: There is yet one man by whom we may inquire of Jehovah, Micaiah the son of Imlah: but I hate him; for he doth not prophesy good concerning me, but evil (v. 8). Jehoshaphat remonstrated, Let not the king say so (v. 8). Why Ahab omitted reference to Elijah is unknown.

These two kings depict two contrasting attitudes representative of the kings of Israel. Ahab considered the prophets of Israel as agents of the kings, willing to give them the counsel and word they desired. Jehoshaphat regarded the prophets as agents of divine revelation. Furthermore, the four hundred prophets led by Zedekiah conform admirably to Ahab's conception of the prophets. However, Micaiah followed the course of divinely ordained prophets. "This passage significantly anticipates the difference and, indeed, antipathy between the great figures of prophecy such as Amos . . . and those termed by them 'false prophets'."[27]

b. Prophecy of Micaiah (22:13-28; cf. II Chron. 18:12-27)

13 And the messenger that went to call Micaiah spake unto him, saying, Behold now, the words of the prophets *declare* good unto the king with one mouth: let thy word, I pray thee, be like the word of one of them, and speak thou good. 14 And Micaiah said, As Jehovah liveth, what Jehovah saith unto me, that will I speak. 15 And when he was come to the king, the king said unto him, Micaiah, shall we go to Ramoth-gilead to battle, or shall we forbear? And he answered him, Go up and prosper; and Jehovah will deliver it into the hand of the king. 16 And the king said unto him, How many times shall I adjure thee that thou speak unto me nothing but the truth in the name of Jehovah? 17 And he said, I saw all Israel scattered upon the mountains, as sheep that have no shepherd: and

27 Gray, op. cit., p. 399.

Jehovah said, These have no master; let them return every man to his house in peace. 18 And the king of Israel said to Jehoshaphat, Did I not tell thee that he would not prophesy good concerning me, but evil? 19 And *Micaiah* said, Therefore hear thou the word of Jehovah: I saw Jehovah sitting on his throne, and all the host of heaven standing by him on his right hand and on his left. 20 And Jehovah said, Who shall entice Ahab, that he may go up and fall at Ramoth-gilead? And one said on this manner; and another said on that manner. 21 And there came forth a spirit, and stood before Jehovah, and said, I will entice him. 22 And Jehovah said unto him, Wherewith? And he said, I will go forth, and will be a lying spirit in the mouth of all his prophets. And he said, Thou shalt entice him, and shalt prevail also: go forth, and do so. 23 Now therefore, behold, Jehovah hath put a lying spirit in the mouth of all these thy prophets; and Jehovah hath spoken evil concerning thee.

24 Then Zedekiah the son of Chenaanah came near, and smote Micaiah on the cheek, and said, Which way went the Spirit of Jehovah from me to speak unto thee? 25 And Micaiah said, Behold, thou shalt see on that day, when thou shalt go into an inner chamber to hide thyself. 26 And the king of Israel said, Take Micaiah, and carry him back unto Amon the governor of the city, and to Joash the king's son; 27 and say, Thus saith the king, Put this fellow in the prison, and feed him with bread of affliction and with water of affliction until I come in peace. 28 And Micaiah said, If thou return at all in peace, Jehovah hath not spoken by me. And he said, Hear, ye peoples, all of you.

Micaiah's prophecy revealed that the four hundred prophets were deceived in order that Ahab might be lured to his death. **Now therefore, behold, Jehovah hath put a lying spirit in the mouth of all these thy prophets** (v. 23). Micaiah believed that this was the means by which God in judgment would bring destruction upon Ahab.

It is beside the point to focus attention on the notion that God deliberately deceived Ahab. This casts suspicion on divine integrity. Too limited a view of God and His ways in history might encourage such attention on God's deceitfulness. However, in the light of Ahab's use of the prophets to his advantage and of his

antipathy to true prophets such as Elijah and Micaiah, it is to be expected that he had apostatized. In some inexplicable manner, God was actively working through Ahab's "yes-men" to accomplish divine judgment. In a very profound sense, God accomplished righteous judgment through the prophets who surrendered to the political pressures of the king. This is to put the emphasis upon God's activity in human history, rather than upon God's accountability for deceit.

Ahab's reward to Micaiah was imprisonment (v. 27). This was the treatment Zedekiah gave Jeremiah a century and a half later (Jer. 37:38). Micaiah was ready to let his message stand the test of historical actuality: **If thou return at all in peace, Jehovah hath not spoken by me** (v. 28).

c. Judgment on Ahab (22:29-40; cf. II Chron. 18:28-34)

29 So the king of Israel and Jehoshaphat the king of Judah went up to Ramoth-gilead. 30 And the king of Israel said unto Jehoshaphat, I will disguise myself, and go into the battle; but put thou on thy robes. And the king of Israel disguised himself, and went into the battle. 31 Now the king of Syria had commanded the thirty and two captains of his chariots, saying, Fight neither with small nor great, save only with the king of Israel. 32 And it came to pass, when the captains of the chariots saw Jehoshaphat, that they said, Surely it is the king of Israel; and they turned aside to fight against him: and Jehoshaphat cried out. 33 And it came to pass, when the captains of the chariots saw that it was not the king of Israel, that they turned back from pursuing him. 34 And a certain man drew his bow at a venture, and smote the king of Israel between the joints of the armor: wherefore he said unto the driver of his chariot, Turn thy hand, and carry me out of the host; for I am sore wounded. 35 And the battle increased that day: and the king was stayed up in his chariot against the Syrians, and died at even; and the blood ran out of the wound into the bottom of the chariot. 36 And there went a cry throughout the host about the going down of the sun, saying, Every man to his city, and every man to his country. 37 So the king died, and was brought to Samaria; and they buried the king in Samaria. 38 And they washed the chariot

by the pool of Samaria; and the dogs licked up his blood (now the harlots washed themselves *there*) ; according unto the word of Jehovah which he spake. 39 Now the rest of the acts of Ahab, and all that he did, and the ivory house which he built, and all the cities that he built, are they not written in the book of the chronicles of the kings of Israel? 40 So Ahab slept with his fathers; and Ahaziah his son reigned in his stead.

Ahab and Jehoshaphat took their forces to seize Ramoth-gilead. Ben-hadad prepared to offer stout resistance, notwithstanding his promise (cf. 20:34). Ahab disguised himself as a common soldier. This was not to increase Jehoshaphat's prowess but was apparently to thwart Micaiah's prophecy.

During the battle a Syrian shot an arrow at one of the enemy, little realizing that it was Ahab. The phrase, **at a venture** (v. 34), means innocently, not aware of the great importance of the shot. The Syrian knew he was shooting one of the enemy, but he did not know who it was.

How often people find themselves, just as this anonymous Syrian archer, involved in some circumstance far beyond their understanding. Yet, though such circumstances seem happenstance, the divine purpose is accomplished through them, as in the case of God's judgment upon Ahab.

This is not to affirm a divine determinism of history that makes Ahab irresponsible for himself and his deeds. Rather, it shows that in the complex ongoing of historical reality, God is not a helpless deity amid the intricate complexities, but He is the active Lord of history.

C. A PARENTHESIS: JEHOSHA-PHAT'S POLICIES (22:41-50; cf. II Chron. 17, 19, 20)

41 And Jehoshaphat the son of Asa began to reign over Judah in the fourth year of Ahab king of Israel. 42 Jehoshaphat was thirty and five years old when he began to reign; and he reigned twenty and five years in Jerusalem. And his mother's name was Azubah the daughter of Shilhi. 43 And he walked in all the way of Asa his father; he turned not aside from it, doing that which was right in the eyes of Jehovah: howbeit the high places were not taken away; the people still sacrificed and burnt incense in the high places. 44 And Jehoshaphat made peace with the king of Israel.

45 Now the rest of the acts of Jehoshaphat, and his might that he showed, and how he warred, are they not written in the book of the chronicles of the kings of Judah? 46 And the remnant of the sodomites, that remained in the days of his father Asa, he put away out of the land. 47 And there was no king in Edom: a deputy was king. 48 Jehoshaphat made ships of Tarshish to go to Ophir for gold: but they went not; for the ships were broken at Ezion-geber. 49 Then said Ahaziah the son of Ahab unto Jehoshaphat, Let my servants go with thy servants in the ships. But Jehoshaphat would not. 50 And Jehoshaphat slept with his fathers, and was buried with his fathers in the city of David his father; and Jehoram his son reigned in his stead.

Before continuing the history of the Northern Kingdom during the ninth century B. C., the Kings account includes a brief section on Jehoshaphat, king of the Southern Kingdom, who was contemporary with Ahab, Ahaziah and Jehoram. Jehoshaphat's religious policy is shown in marked contrast to that of Ahab. He **walked in all the way of Asa his father; doing that which was right in the eyes of Jehovah** (v. 43). However, his political policy was in remarkable unity with Ahab's: **Jehoshaphat made peace with the king of Israel** (v. 44). This was a most unusual development. In some unique manner, Jehoshaphat managed a religious policy for his kingdom that faithfully maintained the worship of Jehovah and at the same time manipulated a political policy that embraced the Omri dynasty. After his reign, Jehoshaphat's political policy endangered the worship of Jehovah in the Southern Kingdom.

D. THE ACCESSION OF AHAZIAH (22:51-53)

51 Ahaziah the son of Ahab began to reign over Israel in Samaria in the seventeenth year of Jehoshaphat king of Judah, and he reigned two years over Israel. 52 And he did that which was evil in the sight of Jehovah, and walked in the way of his father, and in the way of his mother, and in the way of Jeroboam the son of Nebat, wherein he made Israel to sin. 53 And he served Baal, and worshipped him, and provoked to anger

Jehovah, the God of Israel, according to all that his father had done.

Ahaziah was reared in a royal house of religious compromise. His father, Ahab, had prophets which essayed to prophesy in the name of Jehovah but in reality aimed to please the king. His mother, Jezebel, was a devout worshiper of Baal and had zealously propagated her religion in Israel. Her influence was as great during the reign of Ahaziah as it had been during the reign of Ahab. Ahaziah must not be considered as a victim of circumstances, unfortunate to have parents of the religious outlook of Ahab and Jezebel. Ultimately, his own personal choices involved him in the religious outlook of his parents. **And he did that which was evil in the sight of Jehovah, and walked in the way of his father, and in the way of his mother, and in the way of Jeroboam the son of Nebat** (v. 52).

The Second Book of Kings

by Charles R. Wilson

Outline

293

Commentary on Second Kings

I. THE NORTHERN KINGDOM DURING THE MIDDLE OF THE NINTH CENTURY B.C. (II Kings 1:1–10:31)

A. PART ONE (1:1–3:27)

1. King Ahaziah of the Omri Dynasty (1:1-18)

1 And Moab rebelled against Israel after the death of Ahab. 2 And Ahaziah fell down through the lattice in his upper chamber that was in Samaria, and was sick: and he sent unto them, Go, inquire of Baal-zebub, the god of Ekron, whether I shall recover of this sickness. 3 But the angel of Jehovah said to Elijah the Tishbite, Arise, go up to meet the messengers of the king of Samaria, and say unto them, Is it because there is no God in Israel, that ye go to inquire of Baal-zebub, the god of Ekron? 4 Now therefore thus saith Jehovah, Thou shalt not come down from the bed whither thou art gone up, but shalt surely die. And Elijah departed.

5 And the messengers returned unto him, and he said unto them, Why is it that ye are returned? 6 And they said unto him, There came up a man to meet us, and said unto us, Go, turn again unto the king that sent you, and say unto him, Thus saith Jehovah, Is it because there is no God in Israel, that thou sendest to inquire of Baal-zebub, the god of Ekron? therefore thou shalt not come down from the bed whither thou art gone up, but shalt surely die. 7 And he said unto them, What manner of man was he that came up to meet you, and told you these words? 8 And they answered him, He was a hairy man, and girt with a girdle of leather about his loins. And he said, It is Elijah the Tishbite.

9 Then the king sent unto him a captain of fifty with his fifty. And he went up to him: and, behold, he was sitting on the top of the hill. And he spake unto him, O man of God, the king hath said, Come down. 10 And Elijah answered and said to the captain of fifty, If I be a man of God, let fire come down from heaven,

and consume thee and thy fifty. And there came down fire from heaven, and consumed him and his fifty. 11 And again he sent unto him another captain of fifty with his fifty. And he answered and said unto him, O man of God, thus hath the king said, Come down quickly. 12 And Elijah answered and said unto them, If I be a man of God, let fire come down from heaven, and consume thee and thy fifty. And the fire of God came down from heaven, and consumed him and his fifty. 13 And again he sent the captain of a third fifty with his fifty. And the third captain of fifty went up, and came and fell on his knees before Elijah, and besought him, and said unto him, O man of God, I pray thee, let my life, and the life of these fifty thy servants, be precious in thy sight. 14 Behold, there came fire down from heaven, and consumed the two former captains of fifty with their fifties; but now let my life be precious in thy sight. 15 And the angel of Jehovah said unto Elijah, Go down with him: be not afraid of him. And he arose, and went down with him unto the king. 16 And he said unto him, Thus saith Jehovah, Forasmuch as thou hast sent messengers to inquire of Baal-zebub, the god of Ekron, is it because there is no God in Israel to inquire of his word? therefore thou shalt not come down from the bed whither thou art gone up, but shalt surely die.

17 So he died according to the word of Jehovah which Elijah had spoken. And Jehoram began to reign in his stead in the second year of Jehoram the son of Jehoshaphat king of Judah; because he had no son. 18 Now the rest of the acts of Ahaziah which he did, are they not written in the book of the chronicles of the kings of Israel?

Ahaziah's brief reign of two years was filled with misfortune. There were two important events to which reference is made in this passage. The first of these, the Moabite rebellion, is only mentioned (v. 1). However, the important archaeological discovery, the Moabite Stone, gives a more complete picture. The Moabite king had inscribed upon it the account of his successful revolt from Israel. He gloried in Chemosh, the god of Moab, which made possible victory over Israel and her gods.

The second event, Ahaziah's fatal fall, together with Elijah's intervention, is given in greater detail (vv. 2-18). The Kings account explains that in the midst of his personal calamity Ahaziah turned to yet another deity: **Go, inquire of Baal-zebub, the god of Ekron, whether I shall recover of this sickness** (v. 2). Ekron was the most northern of the Philistine cities.

Because Ahaziah did this, Jehovah sent Elijah with a message: **Is it because there is no God in Israel, that ye go to inquire of Baal-zebub, the god of Ekron?** (v. 3). Because Ahaziah had sought the help of Baal-zebub, Elijah declared that he would die. The implication is not that Ahaziah would have been healed had he sought the help of Jehovah. Rather, Elijah's assertion was that the natural misfortune of a fatal injury was the occasion of divine judgment on Ahaziah because of his idolatry. It is humanly impossible to tell whether such misfortunes are instruments of divine judgment upon individuals. There is a temptation to rashness by asserting either a "yes" or "no" explanation, when, in reality, the real answer is known only to God and to whomsoever He wills to reveal it. **But the angel of Jehovah said to Elijah the Tishbite, Arise, go . . . and say . . .** (v. 3) Even in this instance, all that the divine word really asserted was that it was useless for Ahaziah to expect to recover. **So he died according to the word of Jehovah which Elijah had spoken** (v. 17).

Elijah's confrontation with Ahaziah shows the unequivocal stand which Elijah maintained against the idolatry and arrogance of the Omri dynasty. Ahaziah was compelled to face death with no deity ready to help him. He retaliated by sending a captain and his armed men to seize and punish Elijah. The first two captains addressed Elijah in mockery and scorn, **O man of God, the king hath said, Come down** (vv. 9, 11). With disdain and irreverence, these armed companies

treated God and his prophet outrageously and provoked judgment upon themselves.[28] Their disrespect and scorn was comparable to that of Ahaziah.

2. Elisha Succeeds Elijah (2:1-25)

1 And it came to pass, when Jehovah would take up Elijah by a whirlwind into heaven, that Elijah went with Elisha from Gilgal. 2 And Elijah said unto Elisha, Tarry here, I pray thee; for Jehovah hath sent me as far as Beth-el. And Elisha said, As Jehovah liveth, and as thy soul liveth, I will not leave thee. So they went down to Beth-el. 3 And the sons of the prophets that were at Beth-el came forth to Elisha, and said unto him, Knowest thou that Jehovah will take away thy master from thy head to-day? And he said, Yea, I know it; hold ye your peace. 4 And Elijah said unto him, Elisha, tarry here, I pray thee; for Jehovah hath sent me to Jericho. And he said, As Jehovah liveth, and as thy soul liveth, I will not leave thee. So they came to Jericho. 5 And the sons of the prophets that were at Jericho came near to Elisha, and said unto him, Knowest thou that Jehovah will take away thy master from thy head to-day? And he answered, Yea, I know it; hold ye your peace. 6 And Elijah said unto him, Tarry here, I pray thee; for Jehovah hath sent me to the Jordan. And he said, As Jehovah liveth, and as thy soul liveth, I will not leave thee. And they two went on. 7 And fifty men of the sons of the prophets went, and stood over against them afar off: and they two stood by the Jordan. 8 And Elijah took his mantle, and wrapped it together, and smote the waters, and they were divided hither and thither, so that they two went over on dry ground. 9 And it came to pass, when they were gone over, that Elijah said unto Elisha, Ask what I shall do for thee, before I am taken from thee. And Elisha said, I pray thee, let a double portion of thy spirit be upon me. 10 And he said, Thou hast asked a hard thing: *nevertheless,* if thou see me when I am taken from thee, it shall be so unto thee; but if not, it shall not be so. 11 And it came to pass, as they still went on, and talked, that, behold, *there appeared* a chariot of fire, and horses of fire, which parted them both asunder; and Elijah went up by a whirlwind into heaven. 12 And Elisha saw it, and he cried, My father, my father, the

---

[28] Lumby, *op. cit.,* p. 5.

chariots of Israel and the horsemen thereof!

And he saw him no more: and he took hold of his own clothes, and rent them in two pieces. 13 He took up also the mantle of Elijah that fell from him, and went back, and stood by the bank of the Jordan. 14 And he took the mantle of Elijah that fell from him, and smote the waters, and said, Where is Jehovah, the God of Elijah? and when he also had smitten the waters, they were divided hither and thither; and Elisha went over.

15 And when the sons of the prophets that were at Jericho over against him saw him, they said, The spirit of Elijah doth rest on Elisha. And they came to meet him, and bowed themselves to the ground before him. 16 And they said unto him, Behold now, there are with thy servants fifty strong men; let them go, we pray thee, and seek thy master, lest the Spirit of Jehovah hath taken him up, and cast him upon some mountain, or into some valley. And he said, Ye shall not send. 17 And when they urged him till he was ashamed, he said, Send. They sent therefore fifty men; and they sought three days, but found him not. 18 And they came back to him, while he tarried at Jericho; and he said unto them, Did I not say unto you, Go not?

19 And the men of the city said unto Elisha, Behold, we pray thee, the situation of this city is pleasant, as my lord seeth: but the water is bad, and the land miscarrieth. 20 And he said, Bring me a new cruse, and put salt therein. And they brought it to him. 21 And he went forth unto the spring of the waters, and cast salt therein, and said, Thus saith Jehovah, I have healed these waters; there shall not be from thence any more death or miscarrying. 22 So the waters were healed unto this day, according to the word of Elisha which he spake.

23 And he went up from thence unto Beth-el; and as he was going up by the way, there came forth young lads out of the city, and mocked him, and said unto him, Go up, thou baldhead; go up, thou baldhead. 24 And he looked behind him and saw them, and cursed them in the name of Jehovah. And there came forth two she-bears out of the wood, and tare forty and two lads of them. 25 And he went from thence to mount Carmel, and from thence he returned to Samaria.

Elijah had been subjected to the threat of death. He had carried on a life or death struggle in the name of Jehovah against Baal-worship. Prophets of Jehovah as well as prophets of Baal had gone to their death as a result. Kings had come under divine judgment. Both Ahab and Ahaziah had died, as the word of the Lord through Elijah had declared.

The day finally came when Elijah must reckon with the future. However, instead of being given a burial, he was taken upward by a whirlwind (v. 11).

Not only Elijah but also Elisha and the bands of prophets in Bethel and Jericho were conscious of the momentous occasion (cf. vv. 1-3, 5, 7, 9). There is no reason given for Elijah's request that Elisha return from accompanying him. However, that request highlights Elisha's determination to go with Elijah (v. 2). Elisha had become a devoted and loyal friend of Elijah. Other conspicuous examples of such friendship are: Ruth to Naomi, Jonathan to David, Timothy to Paul.

It cannot be without significance that Elijah visited Gilgal, Bethel and Jericho (vv. 1, 2, 4). At each of these places there resided a colony of prophets (cf. vv. 3, 5; II Kings 4:38). Elijah's visit to each colony may have been to inspire their loyalty to Jehovah.

The visitation to the colonies of prophets completed, Elijah and Elisha crossed the Jordan River by means of the miraculous parting of the water. Then Elijah said to Elisha, **Ask what I shall do for thee, before I am taken from thee** (v. 9). At last the event of which both were aware was explicitly mentioned. Elijah was to be taken. However, before that occurrence, he offered to help Elisha in whatever way Elisha needed.

Such an occasion as Elisha's can be most revealing. His master was about to depart and was offering whatever help Elisha might choose. What would his request be? Out of his inmost desire he requested: **I pray thee, let a double portion of thy spirit be upon me** (v. 9). This entreaty revealed Elisha's earnest desire to succeed Elijah in his prophetic responsibility. Here was no glamorous or appealing choice during the Omri dynasty. Nevertheless, it revealed the heroic stuff of Elisha.

There is a most illuminating lesson of the power of influence drawn from a comparison of King Ahaziah and Elisha the prophet. The king was under the strong influence of idolatry by reason of the royal family, but Elisha was faithful to Jehovah by reason of the influence of Elijah. This graphically illustrates the general picture of the kings and the prophets of the Northern Kingdom. The political leaders resorted to religious expediency and compromise, while the prophets denounced that policy and preached that Jehovah alone is God. Judgment was visited upon the kings, but belated honor was accorded the prophets by later generations.

Upon Elijah's departure Elisha was granted the seal of his prophetic commissioning as successor to Elijah. He saw the true, though neglected, power of God which was available for Israel: **My father, my father, the chariots of Israel and the horsemen thereof!** (v. 12). The vision of the chariots was the pledge that Elisha's request was granted (cf. v. 9).

Upon returning to the Jordan, Elisha must have made the dividing of the river a test as to the fulfillment of his request. Prophets who beheld it, hurried to bow in Elisha's presence (v. 15). As he came to Jericho he gave aid to the city by miraculously purifying the spring providing water for the city. On his way from Jericho to Bethel he uttered a curse upon a group of disrespectful boys.

3. King Jehoram, the Last of the Omri Dynasty (3:1-27)

1 Now Jehoram the son of Ahab began to reign over Israel in Samaria in the eighteenth year of Jehoshaphat king of Judah, and reigned twelve years. 2 And he did that which was evil in the sight of Jehovah, but not like his father, and like his mother; for he put away the pillar of Baal that his father had made. 3 Nevertheless he cleaved unto the sins of Jeroboam the son of Nebat, wherewith he made Israel to sin; he departed not therefrom.

4 Now Mesha king of Moab was a sheep-master; and he rendered unto the king of Israel the wool of a hundred thousand lambs, and of a hundred thousand rams. 5 But it came to pass, when Ahab was dead, that the king of Moab rebelled against the king of Israel. 6 And king Jehoram went out of Samaria at that time, and mustered all Israel. 7 And he went and sent to Jehoshaphat the king of Judah, saying, The king of Moab hath rebelled against me: wilt thou go with me against Moab to battle? And he said, I

will go up: I am as thou art, my people as thy people, my horses as thy horses. 8 And he said, Which way shall we go up? And he answered, The way of the wilderness of Edom. 9 So the king of Israel went, and the king of Judah, and the king of Edom; and they made a circuit of seven days' journey: and there was no water for the host, nor for the beasts that followed them. 10 And the king of Israel said, Alas! for Jehovah hath called these three kings together to deliver them into the hand of Moab. 11 But Jehoshaphat said, Is there not here a prophet of Jehovah, that we may inquire of Jehovah by him? And one of the king of Israel's servants answered and said, Elisha the son of Shaphat is here, who poured water on the hands of Elijah. 12 And Jehoshaphat said, The word of Jehovah is with him. So the king of Israel and Jehoshaphat and the king of Edom went down to him.

13 And Elisha said unto the king of Israel, What have I to do with thee? get thee to the prophets of thy father, and to the prophets of thy mother. And the king of Israel said unto him, Nay; for Jehovah hath called these three kings together to deliver them into the hand of Moab. 14 And Elisha said, As Jehovah of hosts liveth, before whom I stand, surely, were it not that I regard the presence of Jehoshaphat the king of Judah, I would not look toward thee, nor see thee. 15 But now bring me a minstrel. And it came to pass, when the minstrel played, that the hand of Jehovah came upon him. 6 And he said, Thus saith Jehovah, Make this valley full of trenches. 17 For thus saith Jehovah, Ye shall not see wind, neither shall ye see rain; yet that valley shall be filled with water, and ye shall drink, both ye and your cattle and your beasts. 18 And this is but a light thing in the sight of Jehovah: he will also deliver the Moabites into your hand. 19 And ye shall smite every fortified city, and every choice city, and shall fell every good tree, and stop all fountains of water, and mar every good piece of land with stones. 20 And it came to pass in the morning, about the time of offering the oblation, that, behold, there came water by the way of Edom, and the country was filled with water.

21 Now when all the Moabites heard that the kings were come up to fight against them, they gathered themselves together, all that were able to put on armor, and upward, and stood on the border. 22 And they rose up early in the morning, and the sun shone upon the

water, and the Moabites saw the water over against them as red as blood: 23 and they said, This is blood; the kings are surely destroyed, and they have smitten each man his fellow: now therefore, Moab, to the spoil. 24 And when they came to the camp of Israel, the Israelites rose up and smote the Moabites, so that they fled before them; and they went forward into the land smiting the Moabites. 25 And they beat down the cities; and on every good piece of land they cast every man his stone, and filled it; and they stopped all the fountains of water, and felled all the good trees, until in Kir-haraseth *only* they left the stones thereof; howbeit the slingers went about it, and smote it. 26 And when the king of Moab saw that the battle was too sore for him, he took with him seven hundred men that drew sword, to break through unto the king of Edom; but they could not. 27 Then he took his eldest son that should have reigned in his stead, and offered him for a burnt-offering upon the wall. And there was great wrath against Israel: and they departed from him, and returned to their own land.

Moab had revolted from Israel about the time of or shortly after Ahab's death. Ahaziah's injury cut short his reign before any action could be taken. Jehoram, his brother, became king and prepared to restore sovereignty over Moab. The coalition which he formed to march against Moab included the Southern Kingdom and Edom, along with the Northern Kingdom. This was a most unlikely coalition, inasmuch as Israel and Judah had engaged in much civil war and Edom was a natural ally of Moab. Jehoram proceeded toward Moab by the circuitous route of Edom and found himself depleted of an adequate water supply (v. 9).

Jehoshaphat, king of Judah, inquired if a prophet of the Lord were present. Elisha was found. It is significant that no matter how successful Jehoram had been in organizing his coalition against Moab, the venture would have failed if water could not be found. Elisha was ready to help only because of Jehoshaphat, the God-fearing king of Judah (v. 14). He ordered the valley to be made full of trenches (v. 16).

Meanwhile, rain was falling on the distant hills of Edom while the Moabite army was mobilizing at its frontier on the other side of the dry valley. The next morning, Jehoram's men saw what they so desperately needed, **There came water by way of Edom** (v. 20). Meanwhile, the Moabites saw the same sight, but they interpreted it altogether differently. **This is blood; the kings are surely destroyed** (margin: **have surely fought together**), **and they have smitten each man his fellow** (v. 23). Since the Moabites realized that Jehoram's army was a heterogeneous coalition of rival nations, they hastily concluded that internal warfare had decimated the invading force.

When the Moabites descended into the valley they were attacked by Jehoram's forces and overwhelmed. The Israelites pressed their advantage and conquered all but the last fortified city of Moab, Kir-haraseth. In utter desperation, the king of Moab sacrificed his son to Chemosh (v. 27). **And there was great wrath against Israel: and they departed from him** (v. 27). A possible explanation is that the kings of Judah and Edom became angry at the king of Israel for having caused such a desperate deed as that of Mesha's offering his son.[29] The result was the break-up of the coalition. In the Moabite Stone, Mesha attributes this to the anger of Chemosh.

B. PART TWO (4:1—8:29)

This section is largely concerned with a special narrative describing the activity of Elisha. The stories portray the remarkable power and prestige which attended his work. They are in two general groups. The first group includes Elisha's private activity among individuals, families and communities. The second group includes his public activity in national and international history, particularly with reference to the history of Israel and Syria.

1. Elisha Narratives (4:1—8:15)

Since these narratives focus upon Elisha, and since he is mentioned in connection with the reigns of Jehoram (ca. 849-842 B. C.) and Jehoash (ca. 801-786 B. C.), approximately a half-century may be covered by these stories. However, little attention is given to chronology and

29 Lumby, *op. cit.*, p. 32.

to the names of the Israelite kings. Because of the limitations, it is impossible to determine the time in which the events took place. Though some of the events took place in the middle of the ninth century B.C., others doubtless occurred in the latter part of the century.

a. The Widow's Oil (4:1-7)

1 Now there cried a certain woman of the wives of the sons of the prophets unto Elisha, saying, Thy servant my husband is dead; and thou knowest that thy servant did fear Jehovah: and the creditor is come to take unto him my two children to be bondmen. 2 And Elisha said unto her, What shall I do for thee? tell me; what hast thou in the house? And she said, Thy handmaid hath not anything in the house, save a pot of oil. 3 Then he said, Go, borrow thee vessels abroad of all thy neighbors, even empty vessels; borrow not a few. 4 And thou shalt go in, and shut the door upon thee and upon thy sons, and pour out into all those vessels; and thou shalt set aside that which is full. 5 So she went from him, and shut the door upon her and upon her sons; they brought *the vessels* to her, and she poured out. 6 And it came to pass, when the vessels were full, that she said unto her son, Bring me yet a vessel. And he said unto her, There is not a vessel more. And the oil stayed. 7 Then she came and told the man of God. And he said, Go, sell the oil, and pay thy debt, and live thou and thy sons of the rest.

Like several of Elisha's miracles, the miraculous supply of oil was to help those associated with the schools of the prophets. In this instance, a widow of a deceased prophet was unable to pay a debt. Her appeal to Elisha was answered by his appeal to her faith. **Go, borrow thee vessels abroad of all thy neighbors, even empty vessels; borrow not a few** (v. 3). "The quantity of oil was limited only by her faith in collecting empty vessels."[30] As she poured out the oil, she filled vessel after vessel. Finally, when she had filled them all, she called to her son for another vessel. He answered, **There is not a vessel more** (v. 6).

The widow's faith was more complex than simply passive acceptance of the prophet's word. It involved the activity of finding **not a few** empty vessels to contain an increased amount of that which she already had, the anointing oil. The amount of oil which she received was in direct proportion to the amount she was prepared to receive. It was according to her faith. Her extremity was God's opportunity.

b. The Shunammite's Son (4:8-37)

8 And it fell on a day, that Elisha passed to Shunem, where was a great woman; and she constrained him to eat bread. And so it was that as oft as he passed by, he turned in thither to eat bread. 9 And she said unto her husband, Behold now, I perceive that this is a holy man of God, that passeth by us continually. 10 Let us make, I pray thee, a little chamber on the wall; and let us set for him there a bed, and a table, and a seat, and a candlestick: and it shall be, when he cometh to us, that he shall turn in thither. 11 And it fell on a day, that he came thither, and he turned into the chamber and lay there. 12 And he said to Gehazi his servant, Call this Shunammite. And when he had called her, she stood before him. 13 And he said unto him, Say now unto her, Behold, thou hast been careful for us with all this care; what is to be done for thee? wouldest thou be spoken for to the king, or to the captain of the host? And she answered, I dwell among mine own people. 14 And he said, What then is to be done for her? And Gehazi answered, Verily she hath no son, and her husband is old. 15 And he said, Call her. And when he had called her, she stood in the door. 16 And he said, At this season, when the time cometh round, thou shalt embrace a son. And she said, Nay, my lord, thou man of God, do not lie unto thy handmaid.

17 And the woman conceived, and bare a son at that season, when the time came round, as Elisha had said unto her. 18 And when the child was grown, it fell on a day, that he went out to his father to the reapers. 19 And he said unto his father, My head, my head. And he said to his servant, Carry him to his mother. 20 And when he had taken him, and brought him to his mother, he sat on her knees till noon, and then died. 21 And she went up and laid him on the bed of the man of God, and shut *the door* upon him, and went out. 22 And she called unto her husband, and said, Send me, I pray thee, one of the servants, and one of the asses, that I may run to the man of God, and come again. 23 And he said,

---

[30] Snaith, *op. cit.*, p. 203.

Wherefore wilt thou go to him to-day? it is neither new moon nor sabbath. And she said, It shall be well. 24 Then she saddled an ass, and said to her servant, Drive, and go forward; slacken me not the riding, except I bid thee. 25 So she went, and came unto the man of God to mount Carmel.

And it came to pass, when the man of God saw her afar off, that he said to Gehazi his servant, Behold, yonder is the Shunammite: 26 run, I pray thee, now to meet her, and say unto her, Is it well with thee? is it well with thy husband? is it well with the child? And she answered, It is well. 27 And when she came to the man of God to the hill, she caught hold of his feet. And Gehazi came near to thrust her away; but the man of God said, Let her alone: for her soul is vexed within her; and Jehovah hath hid it from me, and hath not told me. 28 Then she said, Did I desire a son of my lord? did I not say, Do not deceive me? 29 Then he said to Gehazi, Gird up thy loins, and take my staff in thy hand, and go thy way: if thou meet any man, salute him not; and if any salute thee, answer him not again: and lay my staff upon the face of the child. 30 And the mother of the child said, As Jehovah liveth, and as thy soul liveth, I will not leave thee. And he arose, and followed her. 31 And Gehazi passed on before them, and laid the staff upon the face of the child; but there was neither voice, nor hearing. Wherefore he returned to meet him, and told him, saying, The child is not awaked.

32 And when Elisha was come into the house, behold, the child was dead, and laid upon his bed. 33 He went in therefore, and shut the door upon them twain, and prayed unto Jehovah. 34 And he went up, and lay upon the child, and put his mouth upon his mouth, and his eyes upon his eyes, and his hands upon his hands: and he stretched himself upon him; and the flesh of the child waxed warm. 35 Then he returned, and walked in the house once to and fro; and went up, and stretched himself upon him: and the child sneezed seven times, and the child opened his eyes. 36 And he called Gehazi, and said, Call this Shunammite. So he called her. And when she was come in unto him, he said, Take up thy son. 37 Then she went in, and fell at his feet, and bowed herself to the ground; and she took up her son, and went out.

This is a remarkable story in that the son was miraculously given to a childless couple and was miraculously restored to life when apparently dead. The man, woman and child remain anonymous, for the focus of the story is upon Elisha as the miracle-working prophet of the Lord.

Shunem was located a few miles north of Jezreel, the summer residence of the Omri dynasty. Elisha passed through Shunem when traveling either from Samaria or Jezreel to Mount Carmel. When his journeys became known to a rich and influential woman of Shunem, she persuaded her husband to provide a special room for Elisha's convenience (vv. 9-10).

To show his gratitude Elisha asked if he should make mention of her to the king. She replied that there was no need. Further inquiry disclosed a great and secret longing. Although prosperous, she was childless, an immense disappointment to the ancient orientals. Elisha's gratitude prompted him to promise her a son (v. 16). A son was born as promised.

The narrative passes over a number of years and resumes with the grown son working in the harvest. He sickened and died, apparently from sunstroke. The Shunammite's delight became despair, and she appealed to the prophet. **Did I desire a son of my lord? did I not say, Do not deceive me?** (v. 28). The words sounded reproachful and made it clear to Elisha that she felt it would have been better for her if she had never had a child than to undergo the sorrow of losing him. In great sympathy and with miraculous power Elisha came and revived the son (vv. 33-35). The entire story reveals great kindness and sympathetic understanding on the part of the prophet.

c. Death in the Pot (4:38-41)

38 And Elisha came again to Gilgal. And there was a dearth in the land; and the sons of the prophets were sitting before him; and he said unto his servant, Set on the great pot, and boil pottage for the son of the prophets. 39 And one went out into the field to gather herbs, and found a wild vine, and gathered thereof wild gourds his lap full, and came and shred them into the pot of pottage; for they knew them not. 40 So they poured out for the men to eat. And it came to pass, as they were eating of the pottage, that they cried out, and said, O man of God, there is death in the pot. And they could not eat thereof. 41 But he said, Then bring meal. And he cast it into the

pot; and he said, Pour out for the people, that they may eat. And there was no harm in the pot.

Gilgal was a center of prophetic activity and probably was visited occasionally by Elisha. **The sons of the prophets were sitting before him** (v. 38). This was a period of instruction. Elisha was teaching this colony out of the wealth of his own prophetic understanding.

While so occupied, Elisha directed that the usual meager meal be prepared. Since it was a time of famine, the usual vegetation was unavailable. However, a wild vine with gourds was found. This was put in the great pot, but it was found to be poisonous. Elijah miraculously remedied the pottage by the use of meal.

There is a symbolic meaning that is appropriate. Just as Elisha was able to make the bitter, poisonous pottage palatable, so he was able to give instruction to the prophets whereby their ministry might be nourishing rather than harmful.

d. Twenty Loaves (4:42-44)

42 And there came a man from Baal-shalishah, and brought the man of God bread of the first-fruits, twenty loaves of barley, and fresh ears of grain in his sack. And he said, Give unto the people, that they may eat. 43 And his servant said, What, should I set this before a hundred men? But he said, Give the people, that they may eat; for thus saith Jehovah, They shall eat, and shall leave thereof. 44 So he set it before them, and they did eat, and left thereof, according to the word of Jehovah.

There lived at Baal-shalishah, a place not far from Gilgal, a man who gave food to the colony of prophets (v. 42). Elisha prepared to distribute the food among the one hundred prophets in the colony. Gehazi considered the food supply far too limited. Yet the story shows Elisha's unwavering trust in the Lord. **Give the people, that they may eat; for thus saith Jehovah, They shall eat, and shall leave thereof** (v. 43).

e. Naaman the Leper (5:1-27)

1 Now Naaman, captain of the host of the king of Syria, was a great man with his master, and honorable, because by him Jehovah had given victory unto Syria: he was also a mighty man of valor, *but he was* a leper. 2 And the Syrians had gone out in bands, and had brought away captive out of the land of Israel a little maiden; and she waited on Naaman's wife. 3 And she said unto her mistress, Would that my lord were with the prophet that is in Samaria! then would he recover him of his leprosy. 4 And one went in, and told his lord, saying, Thus and thus said the maiden that is of the land of Israel. 5 And the king of Syria said, Go now, and I will send a letter unto the king of Israel. And he departed, and took with him ten talents of silver, and six thousand *pieces* of gold, and ten changes of raiment. 6 And he brought the letter to the king of Israel, saying, And now when this letter is come unto thee, behold, I have sent Naaman my servant to thee, that thou mayest recover him of his leprosy. 7 And it came to pass, when the king of Israel had read the letter, that he rent his clothes, and said, Am I God, to kill and to make alive, that this man doth send unto me to recover a man of his leprosy? but consider, I pray you, and see how he seeketh a quarrel against me.

8 And it was so, when Elisha the man of God heard that the king of Israel had rent his clothes, that he sent to the king, saying, Wherefore hast thou rent thy clothes? let him come now to me, and he shall know that there is a prophet in Israel. 9 So Naaman came with his horses and with his chariots, and stood at the door of the house of Elisha. 10 And Elisha sent a messenger unto him, saying, Go and wash in the Jordan seven times, and thy flesh shall come again to thee, and thou shalt be clean. 11 But Naaman was wroth, and went away, and said, Behold, I thought, He will surely come out to me, and stand, and call on the name of Jehovah his God, and wave his hand over the place, and recover the leper. 12 Are not Abanah and Pharpar, the rivers of Damascus, better than all the waters of Israel? may I not wash in them, and be clean? So he turned and went away in a rage. 13 And his servants came near, and spake unto him, and said, My father, if the prophet had bid thee do some great thing, wouldest thou not have done it? how much rather then, when he saith to thee, Wash, and be clean? 14 Then went he down, and dipped *himself* seven times in the Jordan, according to the saying of the man of God; and his flesh came again like unto the flesh of a little child, and he was clean.

15 And he returned to the man of

God, he and all his company, and came, and stood before him; and he said, Behold now, I know that there is no God in all the earth, but in Israel: now therefore, I pray thee, take a present of thy servant. 16 But he said, As Jehovah liveth, before whom I stand, I will receive none. And he urged him to take it; but he refused. 17 And Naaman said, If not, yet, I pray thee, let there be given to thy servant two mules' burden of earth; for thy servant will henceforth offer neither burnt-offering nor sacrifice unto other gods, but unto Jehovah. 18 In this thing Jehovah pardon thy servant: when my master goeth into the house of Rimmon to worship there, and he leaneth on my hand, and I bow myself in the house of Rimmon, when I bow myself in the house of Rimmon, Jehovah pardon thy servant in this thing. 19 And he said unto him, Go in peace. So he departed from him a little way.

20 But Gehazi, the servant of Elisha the man of God, said, Behold, my master hath spared this Naaman the Syrian, in not receiving at his hands that which he brought: as Jehovah liveth, I will run after him, and take somewhat of him. 21 So Gehazi followed after Naaman. And when Naaman saw one running after him, he alighted from the chariot to meet him, and said, Is all well? 22 And he said, All is well. My master hath sent me, saying, Behold, even now there are come to me from the hill-country of Ephraim two young men of the sons of the prophets; give them, I pray thee, a talent of silver, and two changes of raiment. 23 And Naaman said, Be pleased to take two talents. And he urged him, and bound two talents of silver in two bags, with two changes of raiment, and laid them upon two of his servants; and they bare them before him. 24 And when he came to the hill, he took them from their hand, and bestowed them in the house; and he let the men go, and they departed. 25 But he went in, and stood before his master. And Elisha said unto him, Whence comest thou, Gehazi? And he said, Thy servant went no whither. 26 And he said unto him, Went not my heart *with thee,* when the man turned from his chariot to meet thee? Is it a time to receive money, and to receive garments, and oliveyards and vineyards, and sheep and oxen, and menservants and maid-servants? 27 The leprosy therefore of Naaman shall cleave unto thee, and unto thy seed for ever. And he went out from his presence a leper *as white* as snow.

This narrative of Elisha's healing the leprosy of Naaman shows the prophet active in international affairs. The two countries, Israel and Syria, were brought into direct contact, not in war as was so often the case, but in peace.

The victory achieved through Elisha could have been a lesson to Israel as to the power of God to turn the enemies of Israel to a belief in and worship of the true God, if Israel were to repent and turn from idolatry.

The story of Naaman occurred during a period of uneasy peace because the Syrians had earlier made forays into Israel (v. 2). The little Israelite girl who was taken captive during one of these sporadic attacks was made to serve the wife of Naaman. She was another Israelite who knew of the true God, despite the false religions existing in the Northern Kingdom. It must have been an occasion of great sorrow when she was carried away into Syria. Yet she provided the setting for the confrontation of the two nations.

Upon hearing through her about the possibility of a cure for Naaman, the Syrian king sent him to Samaria, capital of the Northern Kingdom. When Elisha heard of the coming of Naaman he sent a message to the king asking that Naaman be sent to him, **and he shall know that there is a prophet in Israel** (v. 8).

When Naaman appeared at the house of Elisha in Samaria, the prophet directed him to go to the Jordan River and wash seven times (v. 10). Elisha prescribed a river in Israel as part of the proof that there was a prophet in Israel. Naaman, however, despised the Jordan and contemplated the beautiful rivers of his own land (v. 12). The point of the curing of Naaman was to demonstrate to Syria as well as to Israel that Elisha was a true prophet of the Jehovah of Israel. Immeasurable credit is due to the anonymous Israelite maiden and the servants of Naaman for their invaluable assistance in informing Naaman of healing for his leprosy and persuading him to obey the command of Elisha. **Then he went down, and dipped . . . and he was clean** (v. 14).

In gratitude, Naaman returned to Elisha with extravagant gifts. Elisha, typical of the prophets, lived frugally. All of this wealth would have cared for his needs for a long time. However, he refused everything. Gehazi, Elisha's servant, had willingly endured the privations of one associated with the prophets until this time. Temptation engulfed him, and he followed after Naaman and requested some of the treasure. Upon returning to Elisha, Gehazi was punished by becoming leprous.

The whole story has a rhythmic pattern expressed antithetically. Naaman is pictured as proud when sick but humble when healed. Naaman the heathen is a leper at the beginning, but Gehazi the servant of the prophet is a leper at the end.

f. The Axhead (6:1-7)

1 And the sons of the prophets said unto Elisha, Behold now, the place where we dwell before thee is too strait for us. 2 Let us go, we pray thee, unto the Jordan, and take thence every man a beam, and let us make us a place there, where we may dwell. And he answered, Go ye. 3 And one said, Be pleased, I pray thee, to go with thy servants. And he answered, I will go. 4 So he went with them. And when they came to the Jordan, they cut down wood. 5 But as one was felling a beam, the axehead fell into the water; and he cried, and said, Alas, my master! for it was borrowed. 6 And the man of God said, Where fell it? And he showed him the place. And he cut down a stick, and cast it in thither, and made the iron to swim. 7 And he said, Take it up to thee. So he put out his hand, and took it.

During Elisha's ministry, the prophets in the Northern Kingdom continued their colonies. One such colony became larger than its facilities could accommodate. Seeking out Elisha, the prophets proposed to enlarge their quarters. Elisha went with them to the wooded area alongside the Jordan. One of the men lost his ax, but Elisha miraculously recovered it. **And he . . . made the iron to swim** (v. 6).

g. Sightless Syrians (6:8-23)

8 Now the king of Syria was warring against Israel; and he took counsel with his servants, saying, In such and such a place shall be my camp. 9 And the man of God sent unto the king of Israel, saying, Beware that thou pass not such a place; for thither the Syrians are coming down. 10 And the king of Israel sent to the place which the man of God told him and warned him of; and he saved himself there, not once nor twice. 11 And the heart of the king of Syria was sore troubled for this thing; and he called his servants, and said unto them, Will ye not show me which of us is for the king of Israel? 12 And one of his servants said, Nay, my lord, O king; but Elisha, the prophet that is in Israel, telleth the king of Israel the words that thou speakest in thy bedchamber. 13 And he said, Go and see where he is, that I may send and fetch him. And it was told him, saying, Behold, he is in Dothan.

14 Therefore sent he thither horses, and chariots, and a great host: and they came by night, and compassed the city about. 15 And when the servant of the man of God was risen early, and gone forth, behold, a host with horses and chariots was round about the city. And his servant said unto him, Alas, my master! how shall we do? 16 And he answered, Fear not; for they that are with us are more than they that are with them. 17 And Elisha prayed, and said, Jehovah, I pray thee, open his eyes, that he may see. And Jehovah opened the eyes of the young man; and he saw: and, behold, the mountain was full of horses and chariots of fire round about Elisha. 18 And when they came down to him, Elisha prayed unto Jehovah, and said, Smite this people, I pray thee, with blindness. And he smote them with blindness according to the word of Elisha. 19 And Elisha said unto them, This is not the way, neither is this the city: follow me, and I will bring you to the man whom ye seek. And he led them to Samaria.

20 And it came to pass, when they were come into Samaria, that Elisha said, Jehovah, open the eyes of these men, that they may see. And Jehovah opened their eyes, and they saw; and, behold, they were in the midst of Samaria. 21 And the king of Israel said unto Elisha, when he saw them, My father, shall I smite them? shall I smite them? 22 And he answered, Thou shalt not smite them: wouldest thou smite those whom thou hast taken captive with thy sword and with thy bow? set bread and water before them, that they may eat and drink, and go to their master. 23 And he prepared great provision for them; and when they had eaten and drunk, he sent them away, and they went to their master. And the bands of Syria came no more into the land of Israel.

Relationships between the Northern Kingdom and Syria had deteriorated to a state of war. The Syrian king sought to capture the king of Israel. The names of these kings were unnecessary for the narrative because the important personality was Elisha, the man of God in Israel.

When the Syrian king was informed that Elisha was telling the king of Israel the location of the Syrian bands, he led his united forces at night to Dothan where Elisha was (vv. 13-14). The next morning when Elisha faced the problems of the day, he offered two prayers. One was for his servant, unnamed but no longer Gehazi (cf. II Kings 8:4-6): **Jehovah, I pray thee, open his eyes, that he may see** (v. 17). The young man saw **the mountain ... full of horses and chariots of fire round about Elisha** (v. 7). The second prayer was regarding the Syrians: **Smite this people, I pray thee, with blindness** (v. 18).

Escorting the blind Syrian warriors to Samaria, Elisha directed the king of Israel to feed them and release them, an unprecedented act of kindness. **And the bands of Syria came no more into the land of Israel** (v. 23). What could not have been accomplished by revenge was accomplished by kindness.

h. Siege of Samaria (6:24—7:20)

24 And it came to pass after this, that Ben-hadad king of Syria gathered all his host, and went up, and besieged Samaria. 25 And there was a great famine in Samaria: and, behold, they besieged it, until an ass's head was sold for fourscore *pieces* of silver, and the fourth part of a kab of dove's dung for five *pieces* of silver. 26 And as the king of Israel was passing by upon the wall, there cried a woman unto him, saying, Help, my lord, O king. 27 And he said, If Jehovah do not help thee, whence shall I help thee? out of the threshing-floor, or out of the wine-press? 28 And the king said unto her, What aileth thee? And she answered, This woman said unto me, Give thy son, that we may eat him to-day, and we will eat my son to-morrow. 29 So we boiled my son, and did eat him: and I said unto her on the next day, Give thy son, that we may eat him; and she hath hid her son. 30 And it came to pass, when the king heard the words of the woman, that he rent his clothes (now he was passing by upon the wall); and the people

looked, and, behold, he had sackcloth within upon his flesh. 31 Then he said, God do so to me, and more also, if the head of Elisha the son of Shaphat shall stand on him this day.

32 But Elisha was sitting in his house, and the elders were sitting with him; and *the king* sent a man from before him: but ere the messenger came to him, he said to the elders, See ye how this son of a murderer hath sent to take away my head? look, when the messenger cometh, shut the door, and hold the door fast against him: is not the sound of his master's feet behind him? 33 And while he was yet talking with them, behold, the messenger came down unto him: and he said, Behold, this evil is of Jehovah; why should I wait for Jehovah any longer? 1 And Elisha said, Hear ye the word of Jehovah: thus saith Jehovah, To-morrow about this time shall a measure of fine flour be *sold* for a shekel, and two measures of barley for a shekel, in the gate of Samaria. 2 Then the captain on whose hand the king leaned answered the man of God, and said, Behold, if Jehovah should make windows in heaven, might this thing be? And he said, Behold, thou shalt see it with thine eyes, but shalt not eat thereof.

3 Now there were four leprous men at the entrance of the gate: and they said one to another, Why sit we here until we die? 4 If we say, We will enter into the city, then the famine is in the city, and we shall die there; and if we sit still here, we die also. Now therefore come, and let us fall unto the host of the Syrians: if they save us alive, we shall live; and if they kill us, we shall but die. 5 And they rose up in the twilight, to go unto the camp of the Syrians; and when they were come to the outermost part of the camp of the Syrians, behold, there was no man there. 6 For the Lord had made the host of the Syrians to hear a noise of chariots, and a noise of horses, even the noise of a great host: and they said one to another, Lo, the king of Israel hath hired against us the kings of the Hittites, and the kings of the Egyptians, to come upon us. 7 Wherefore they arose and fled in the twilight, and left their tents, and their horses, and their asses, even the camp as it was, and fled for their life. 8 And when these lepers came to the outermost part of the camp, they went into one tent, and did eat and drink, and carried thence silver, and gold, and raiment, and went and hid it; and they came back, and entered into

another tent, and carried thence also, and went and hid it.

9 Then they said one to another, We do not well; this day is a day of good tidings, and we hold our peace: if we tarry till the morning light, punishment will overtake us; now therefore come, let us go and tell the king's household. 10 So they came and called unto the porter of the city; and they told them, saying, We came to the camp of the Syrians, and, behold, there was no man there, neither voice of man, but the horses tied, and the asses tied, and the tents as they were. 11 And he called the porters; and they told it to the king's household within. 12 And the king arose in the night, and said unto his servants, I will now show you what the Syrians have done to us. They know that we are hungry; therefore are they gone out of the camp to hide themselves in the field, saying, When they come out of the city, we shall take them alive, and get into the city. 13 And one of his servants answered and said, Let some take, I pray thee, five of the horses that remain, which are left in the city (behold, they are as all the multitude of Israel that are left in it; behold, they are as all the multitude of Israel that are consumed) ; and let us send and see. 14 They took therefore two chariots with horses; and the king sent after the host of the Syrians, saying, Go and see. 15 And they went after them unto the Jordan: and, lo, all the way was full of garments and vessels, which the Syrians had cast away in their haste. And the messengers returned, and told the king.

16 And the people went out, and plundered the camp of the Syrians. So a measure of fine flour was *sold* for a shekel, and two measures of barley for a shekel, according to the word of Jehovah. 17 And the king appointed the captain on whose hand he leaned to have the charge of the gate: and the people trod upon him in the gate, and he died as the man of God had said, who spake when the king came down to him. 18 And it came to pass, as the man of God had spoken to the king, saying, Two measures of barley for a shekel, and a measure of fine flour for a shekel, shall be to-morrow about this time in the gate of Samaria; 19 and that captain answered the man of God, and said, Now, behold, if Jehovah should make windows in heaven, might such a thing be? and he said, Behold, thou shalt see it with thine eyes, but shalt not eat thereof: 20 it came to pass even so unto

him; for the people trod upon him in the gate, and he died.

Elisha continues to be the most important figure as the Elisha narratives move on. "The king of Israel is probably Jehoahaz son of Jehu, the Syrian king is probably Ben-hadad son of . . . Hazael."[31] However, there is considerable uncertainty as to the historical setting. It is possible to understand it as a belated sequel to the preceding incident. In that incident, kind-hearted Elisha had directed the king of Israel to return the captive Syrians (cf. 6:23). When some time had elapsed, Syria returned in force and laid siege to Samaria. The king of Israel reproachfully threatened, **God do so to me, and more also, if the head of Elisha the son of Shaphat shall stand on him this day** (v. 31).

As far as the king of Israel was concerned, Elisha was responsible for the calamity of Samaria's siege. A messenger was sent from the king to put Elisha to death (v. 32).

Meanwhile in his house Elisha revealed to those with him that the king was sending a messenger to kill him and also that the king had had a sudden change of heart and was coming close behind the messenger to stop him. The word of the Lord to Elisha was that help was on the way for the beleaguered city. **To-morrow about this time shall a measure of fine flour be sold for a shekel** (v. 1). It sounded fantastic to declare that the very next day the starving city would have a bountiful food supply.

However, that night the Syrians were thrown into panic by extraordinary noises (v. 6). They retreated in great haste, for they feared that Israel had hired outside help. Four anonymous lepers who were dying of starvation made the remarkable discovery and brought the good news to Samaria (vv. 9-10).

i. The Shunammite's Land (8:1-6)

1 Now Elisha had spoken unto the woman, whose son he had restored to life, saying, Arise, and go thou and thy household, and sojourn wheresoever thou canst sojourn: for Jehovah hath called for a famine; and it shall also come upon the land seven years. 2 And the woman arose, and did according to the word of the

---

[31] Snaith, *op. cit.*, p. 219.

man of God; and she went with her household, and sojourned in the land of the Philistines seven years. 3 And it came to pass at the seven years' end, that the woman returned out of the land of the Philistines: and she went forth to cry unto the king for her house and for her land. 4 Now the king was talking with Gehazi the servant of the man of God, saying, Tell me, I pray thee, all the great things that Elisha hath done. 5 And it came to pass, as he was telling the king how he had restored to life him that was dead, that, behold, the woman, whose son he had restored to life, cried to the king for her house and for her land. And Gehazi said, My lord, O king, this is the woman, and this is her son, whom Elisha restored to life. 6 And when the king asked the woman, she told him. So the king appointed unto her a certain officer, saying, Restore all that was hers, and all the fruits of the field since the day that she left the land, even until now.

Elisha had advised the woman of Shunem that because of a coming famine she should leave her homeland for a time. She accepted his counsel and went to Philistia. Her land passed to the control of the king. Upon her return, she appealed to the king for her land just at the time of Gehazi's audience with the king. Gehazi was telling the king of Elisha's great work. When the Shunammite woman appeared before the king, Gehazi said, My lord, O king, this is the woman, and this is her son, whom Elisha restored to life (v. 5). The king was so impressed that he restored her land. This story emphasizes the great influence which Elisha exerted, even upon the king.

j. Hazael and Elisha (8:7-15)

7 And Elisha came to Damascus; and Ben-hadad the king of Syria was sick; and it was told him, saying, The man of God is come hither. 8 And the king said unto Hazael, Take a present in thy hand, and go, meet the man of God, and inquire of Jehovah by him, saying, Shall I recover of this sickness? 9 So Hazael went to meet him, and took a present with him, even of every good thing of Damascus, forty camels' burden, and came and stood before him, and said, Thy son Ben-hadad king of Syria hath sent me to thee, saying, Shall I recover of this sickness? 10 And Elisha said unto him, Go, say unto him, Thou shalt surely recover; howbeit Jehovah hath showed me that he shall

surely die. 11 And he settled his countenance stedfastly *upon him*, until he was ashamed: and the man of God wept. 12 And Hazael said, Why weepeth my lord? And he answered, Because I know the evil that thou wilt do unto the children of Israel: their strongholds wilt thou set on fire, and their young men wilt thou slay with the sword, and wilt dash in pieces their little ones, and rip up their women with child. 13 And Hazael said, But what is thy servant, who is but a dog, that he should do this great thing? And Elisha answered, Jehovah hath showed me that thou shalt be king over Syria. 14 Then he departed from Elisha, and came to his master; who said to him, What said Elisha to thee? And he answered, He told me that thou wouldest surely recover. 15 And it came to pass on the morrow, that he took the coverlet, and dipped it in water, and spread it on his face, so that he died: and Hazael reigned in his stead.

Just as the preceding narrative showed the high regard in which Elisha was held by the king of the Northern Kingdom, so this narrative shows the high regard in which Elisha was held by the king of Syria. Hearing that Elisha was in the vicinity of Damascus, Ben-hadad, who was very ill, sent a high-ranking official, Hazael, with a very costly gift, to inquire if he would recover (vv. 8-9).

Just as surely as Elisha rejected Naaman's lavish gift so doubtless he rejected Ben-hadad's on the principle that his revelations were not for sale or subject to bribes. Nevertheless, Elisha said that the king would recover.

In confrontation with Hazael, Elisha became aware of a revelation other than the king's recovery. He perceived that he was looking at one who would usurp the throne of Syria and also be an instrument of divine judgment against Israel (vv. 12-13). The account shows that Hazael did obtain the throne (v. 15).

2. Jehoram and Ahaziah of the Southern Kingdom (8:16-29; cf. II Chron. 21:1—22:6)

16 And in the fifth year of Joram the son of Ahab king of Israel, Jehoshaphat being then king of Judah, Jehoram the son of Jehoshaphat king of Judah began to reign. 17 Thirty and two years old was he when he began to reign; and he reigned eight years in Jerusalem. 18 And

he walked in the way of the kings of Israel, as did the house of Ahab: for he had the daughter of Ahab to wife; and he did that which was evil in the sight of Jehovah. 19 Howbeit Jehovah would not destroy Judah, for David his servant's sake, as he promised him to give unto him a lamp for his children alway.

20 In his days Edom revolted from under the hand of Judah, and made a king over themselves. 21 Then Joram passed over to Zair, and all his chariots with him: and he rose up by night, and smote the Edomites that compassed him about, and the captains of the chariots; and the people fled to their tents. 22 So Edom revolted from under the hand of Judah unto this day. Then did Libnah revolt at the same time. 23 And the rest of the acts of Joram, and all that he did, are they not written in the book of the chronicles of the kings of Judah? 24 And Joram slept with his fathers, and was buried with his fathers in the city of David; and Ahaziah his son reigned in his stead.

25 In the twelfth year of Joram the son of Ahab king of Israel did Ahaziah the son of Jehoram king of Judah begin to reign. 26 Two and twenty years old was Ahaziah when he began to reign; and he reigned one year in Jerusalem. And his mother's name was Athaliah the daughter of Omri king of Israel. 27 And he walked in the way of the house of Ahab, and did that which was evil in the sight of Jehovah, as did the house of Ahab; for he was the son-in-law of the house of Ahab. 28 And he went with Joram the son of Ahab to war against Hazael king of Syria at Ramoth-gilead: and the Syrians wounded Joram. 29 And king Joram returned to be healed in Jezreel of the wounds which the Syrians had given him at Ramah, when he fought against Hazael king of Syria. And Ahaziah the son of Jehoram king of Judah went down to see Joram the son of Ahab in Jezreel, because he was sick.

Although the Kings account has had primary concern for developments in the Northern Kingdom during the remarkable period of Elijah and Elisha, the outstanding ninth-century prophets, the contemporary developments in the Southern Kingdom have been included.

Jehoram of the Davidic dynasty ruled in Jerusalem for eight years (ca. 849-842; v. 17). This was contemporary with Jehoram, the last of the Omri dynasty in Samaria. Many of the Elisha incidents occurred during this time. No comparable prophet was active in the Southern Kingdom.

Nevertheless, it would appear that such a prophet was needed, for Jehoram of Jerusalem had married the sister of Jehoram of Samaria. She was the daughter of Ahab and Jezebel (v. 18). **Howbeit Jehovah would not destroy Judah, for David his servant's sake, as he promised him to give unto him a lamp for his children alway** (v. 19). It grew very dark in Judah during the days of Jehoram, but a light was kept burning. This was because of divine providence. Providence remains an abiding reality and cannot be eliminated from the ongoing of history.

Succeeding Jehoram on the throne in Jerusalem was Ahaziah, grandson of Ahab and Jezebel (v. 26). His reign was very brief, only one year, because of his involvement with the dynasty of Omri (vv. 28-29).

C. PART THREE (9:1—10:31)

This part of the history of the Northern Kingdom during the middle of the ninth century B. C. included the dethroning of the powerful Omri dynasty, which had lasted almost four decades, and the overthrowing of Baal-worship, the religious trademark of the Omri rulers.

1. Omri Dynasty Dethroned by Jehu (9:1—10:17)

The man who was able to oust the Omri dynasty was Jehu, a powerful army general.

a. Jehu Anointed (9:1-13)

1 And Elisha the prophet called one of the sons of the prophets, and said unto him, Gird up thy loins, and take this vial of oil in thy hand, and go to Ramoth-gilead. 2 And when thou comest thither, look out there Jehu the son of Jehoshaphat the son of Nimshi, and go in, and make him arise up from among his brethren, and carry him to an inner chamber. 3 Then take the vial of oil, and pour it on his head, and say, Thus saith Jehovah, I have anointed thee king over Israel. Then open the door, and flee, and tarry not. 4 So the young man, even the young man the prophet, went to Ramoth-gilead. 5 And when he came, behold, the captains of the host were sitting; and he said, I have an errand to thee, O captain. And Jehu said, Unto

which of us all? And he said, To thee, O captain. 6 And he arose, and went into the house; and he poured the oil on his head, and said unto him, Thus saith Jehovah, the God of Israel, I have anointed thee king over the people of Jehovah, even over Israel. 7 And thou shalt smite the house of Ahab thy master, that I may avenge the blood of my servants the prophets, and the blood of all the servants of Jehovah, at the hand of Jezebel. 8 For the whole house of Ahab shall perish; and I will cut off from Ahab every man-child, and him that is shut up and him that is left at large in Israel. 9 And I will make the house of Ahab like the house of Jeroboam the son of Nebat, and like the house of Baasha the son of Ahijah. 10 And the dogs shall eat Jezebel in the portion of Jezreel, and there shall be none to bury her. And he opened the door, and fled.

11 Then Jehu came forth to the servants of his lord: and one said unto him, Is all well? wherefore came this mad fellow to thee? And he said unto them, Ye know the man and what his talk was. 12 And they said, It is false; tell us now. And he said, Thus and thus spake he to me, saying, Thus saith Jehovah, I have anointed thee king over Israel. 13 Then they hasted, and took every man his garment, and put it under him on the top of the stairs, and blew the trumpet, saying, Jehu is king.

Elijah and Elisha had been the faithful messengers of Jehovah to Israel for approximately three decades, yet the kingdom persisted in apostasy. Moreover, the political situation was deteriorating. The point had been reached where revolt was a real threat to the kingdom.

At this critical period, Elisha perceived the course of action to follow. Knowing through his prophetic calling the political restlessness, he sent one of his disciples to Ramoth-gilead where the army was engaged in trying to take this frontier city from Syria. It had been a bone of contention between the two nations for decades. The disciple was instructed to anoint Jehu, one of the captains and apparently the dynamic spirit of the war chieftains (v. 5).

When the disciple had completed his mission, Jehu confided to his fellow captains that the man had said, **Thus saith Jehovah, I have anointed thee king over Israel** (v. 12). They rallied to his support and exclaimed, **Jehu is king** (v. 13).

b. Jehoram Assassinated (9:14-29)

14 So Jehu the son of Jehoshaphat the son of Nimshi conspired against Joram. (Now Joram was keeping Ramoth-gilead, he and all Israel, because of Hazael king of Syria; 15 but king Joram was returned to be healed in Jezreel of the wounds which the Syrians had given him, when he fought with Hazael king of Syria.) And Jehu said, If this be your mind, then let none escape and go forth out of the city, to go to tell it in Jezreel. 16 So Jehu rode in a chariot, and went to Jezreel; for Joram lay there. And Ahaziah king of Judah was come down to see Joram.

17 Now the watchman was standing on the tower in Jezreel, and he spied the company of Jehu as he came, and said, I see a company. And Joram said, Take a horseman, and send to meet them, and let him say, Is it peace? 18 So there went one on horseback to meet him, and said, Thus saith the king, Is it peace? And Jehu said, What hast thou to do with peace? turn thee behind me. And the watchman told, saying, The messenger came to them, but he cometh not back. 19 Then he sent out a second on horseback, who came to them, and said, Thus saith the king, Is it peace? And Jehu answered, What hast thou to do with peace? turn thee behind me. 20 And the watchman told, saying, He came even unto them, and cometh not back: and the driving is like the driving of Jehu the son of Nimshi; for he driveth furiously.

21 And Joram said, Make ready. And they made ready his chariot. And Joram king of Israel and Ahaziah king of Judah went out, each in his chariot, and they went out to meet Jehu, and found him in the portion of Naboth the Jezreelite. 22 And it came to pass, when Joram saw Jehu, that he said, Is it peace, Jehu? And he answered, What peace, so long as the whoredoms of thy mother Jezebel and her witchcrafts are so many? 23 And Joram turned his hands, and fled, and said to Ahaziah, There is treachery, O Ahaziah. 24 And Jehu drew his bow with his full strength, and smote Joram between his arms; and the arrow went out at his heart, and he sunk down in his chariot. 25 Then said *Jehu* to Bidkar his captain, Take up, and cast him in the portion of the field of Naboth the Jezreelite; for remember how that, when I and thou rode together after Ahab his father, Jehovah laid this burden upon him: 26 Surely I have seen yesterday the blood of Naboth, and the blood of his sons, saith Jehovah; and I will requite

thee in this plat, saith Jehovah. Now therefore take and cast him into the plat *of ground*, according to the word of Jehovah.

27 But when Ahaziah the king of Judah saw this, he fled by the way of the garden-house. And Jehu followed after him, and said, Smite him also in the chariot: *and they smote him* at the ascent of Gûr, which is by Ibleam. And he fled to Megiddo, and died there. 28 And his servants carried him in a chariot to Jerusalem, and buried him in his sepulchre with his fathers in the city of David.

29 And in the eleventh year of Joram the son of Ahab began Ahaziah to reign over Judah.

Having gained the support of the military captains, Jehu plotted to attack King Jehoram, who was convalescing in Jezreel from battle wounds received at Ramoth-gilead. Jehu was an aggressive leader and led his men with great speed. He led a contingent at his usual breakneck pace to Jezreel, where he killed Jehoram and pursued Ahaziah, king of Judah, and finally killed him (vv. 24, 27).

c. Jezebel Assaulted (9:30-37)

30 And when Jehu was come to Jezreel, Jezebel heard of it; and she painted her eyes, and attired her head, and looked out at the window. 31 And as Jehu entered in at the gate, she said, Is it peace, thou Zimri, thy master's murderer? 32 And he lifted up his face to the window, and said, Who is on my side? who? And there looked out to him two or three eunuchs. 33 And he said, Throw her down. So they threw her down; and some of her blood was sprinkled on the wall, and on the horses: and he trod her under foot. 34 And when he was come in, he did eat and drink; and he said, See now to this cursed woman, and bury her; for she is a king's daughter. 35 And they went to bury her; but they found no more of her than the skull, and the feet, and the palms of her hands. 36 Wherefore they came back, and told him. And he said, This is the word of Jehovah, which he spake by his servant Elijah the Tishbite, saying, In the portion of Jezreel shall the dogs eat the flesh of Jezebel; 37 and the body of Jezebel shall be as dung upon the face of the field in the portion of Jezreel, so that they shall not say, This is Jezebel.

Jezebel heard that the king, her son, had been killed. However, she met Jehu with defiance as indicated in her greeting: **Is it peace, thou Zimri, thy master's murderer?** (v. 31). Her reference to Zimri was well chosen to indicate her attitude. Zimri destroyed the dynasty of Baasha and ruled only seven days before Omri usurped the throne (cf. I Kings 16:9-15). Jezebel's last recorded words, leveled at one who was about to destroy her, indicate a proud, arrogant spirit, unbowed even in the face of death. She died as she had lived. As far as she was concerned, the God of Israel counted for little.

d. Jezreel Atrocity (10:1-17)

1 Now Ahab had seventy sons in Samaria. And Jehu wrote letters, and sent to Samaria, unto the rulers of Jezreel, even the elders, and unto them that brought up *the sons of* Ahab, saying, 2 And now as soon as this letter cometh to you, seeing your master's sons are with you, and there are with you chariots and horses, a fortified city also, and armor; 3 look ye out the best and meetest of your master's sons, and set him on his father's throne, and fight for your master's house. 4 But they were exceedingly afraid, and said, Behold, the two kings stood not before him: how then shall we stand? 5 And he that was over the household, and he that was over the city, the elders also, and they that brought up *the children,* sent to Jehu, saying, We are thy servants, and will do all that thou shalt bid us; we will not make any man king: do thou that which is good in thine eyes. 6 Then he wrote a letter the second time to them, saying, If ye be on my side, and if ye will hearken unto my voice, take ye the heads of the men your master's sons, and come to me to Jezreel by to-morrow this time. Now the king's sons, being seventy persons, were with the great men of the city, who brought them up. 7 And it came to pass, when the letter came to them, that they took the king's sons, and slew them, even seventy persons, and put their heads in baskets, and sent them unto him to Jezreel. 8 And there came a messenger, and told him, saying, They have brought the heads of the king's sons. And he said, Lay ye them in two heaps at the entrance of the gate until the morning. 9 And it came to pass in the morning, that he went out, and stood, and said to all the people, Ye are righteous: behold, I conspired against my master, and slew him; but who smote all

these? 10 Know now that there shall fall unto the earth nothing of the word of Jehovah, which Jehovah spake concerning the house of Ahab: for Jehovah hath done that which he spake by his servant Elijah. 11 So Jehu smote all that remained of the house of Ahab in Jezreel, and all his great men, and his familiar friends, and his priests, until he left him none remaining.

12 And he arose and departed, and went to Samaria. And as he was at the shearing-house of the shepherds in the way, 13 Jehu met with the brethren of Ahaziah king of Judah, and said, Who are ye? And they answered, We are the brethren of Ahaziah: and we go down to salute the children of the king and the children of the queen. 14 And he said, Take them alive. And they took them alive, and slew them at the pit of the shearing-house, even two and forty men; neither left he any of them.

15 And when he was departed thence, he lighted on Jehonadab the son of Rechab coming to meet him; and he saluted him, and said to him, Is thy heart right, as my heart is with thy heart? And Jehonadab answered, It is. If it be, give me thy hand. And he gave him his hand; and he took him up to him into the chariot. 16 And he said, Come with me, and see my zeal for Jehovah. So they made him ride in his chariot. 17 And when he came to Samaria, he smote all that remained unto Ahab in Samaria, till he had destroyed him, according to the word of Jehovah, which he spake to Elijah.

Jehu acted swiftly to destroy all the descendants of Ahab. There were seventy of them in Samaria, and they were entrusted to the supervision of the **great men of the city, who brought them up** (v. 6). Jehu challenged those who were in charge of these sons to resist if they dared (v. 3). He notified them, **If ye be on my side . . . take ye the heads of the men, your master's sons, and come to me to Jezreel by to-morrow this time** (v. 6).

When the men of the city complied, Jehu stood before the people of Jezreel and appealed to them, **Ye are righteous** (v. 9). "It is significant here that Jehu is appealing to the people of Yahweh."[32] He sought to be exonerated of any major blame for the assassination of the king in the light of the decapitation of Ahab's sons. **Who smote all these?** (v. 9). He further exonerated himself by an appeal to the prophecy of Elijah, **Jehovah hath done that which he spake by his servant Elijah** (v. 10).

How was it possible for Jehu to claim that God could use him, when he executed such a merciless and bloody purge? It is true that the judgment of the Lord was being accomplished, but it is not true that Jehu was anointed with the spirit of a prophet when he made his claim. Furthermore, since God is profoundly active in history, it is difficult to ascertain the divine activity at every juncture in the movement of history. At this particular crisis in the Northern Kingdom one dynasty was disappearing and another was emerging. The process involved elements of good and elements of evil. To us, in retrospect, it seems entirely brutal and evil; to those of biblical understanding it was impregnated with divine activity.

From the standpoint of the prophets, the dynasty of Omri had violated Jehovah-worship and become enmeshed in foreign alliances. From the standpoint of the army, Jehoram's military setbacks cost him the confidence of his captains. From the standpoint of the people, the aristocracy of Samaria had lived affluently at the expense of the masses. A revolution was in the offing. While these causes contributed to the explosion, and while Jehu was the human leader on whom the responsibility fell for taking the helm and directing affairs, the Kings account is unequivocal in its insistence that the Lord of history was the dominant factor. In our contemporary cultural revolution we have an analogous situation. The civil rights movement is a powerful revolution. As it progresses, certain factions of the movement use violence, yet this does not condemn the whole program as evil. In fact, there is powerful biblical persuasion for seeing the total movement as an occasion for God to reveal His purposes.

2. Baal-Worship Overthrown by Jehu (10:8-36)

18 And Jehu gathered all the people together, and said unto them, Ahab served Baal a little; but Jehu will serve him much. 19 Now therefore call unto

32 Gray, *op. cit.*, p. 501.

me all the prophets of Baal, all his worshippers, and all his priests; let none be wanting: for I have a great sacrifice *to do* to Baal; whosoever shall be wanting, he shall not live. But Jehu did it in subtlety, to the intent that he might destroy the worshippers of Baal. 20 And Jehu said, Sanctify a solemn assembly for Baal. And they proclaimed it. 21 And Jehu sent through all Israel: and all the worshippers of Baal came, so that there was not a man left that came not. And they came into the house of Baal; and the house of Baal was filled from one end to another. 22 And he said unto him that was over the vestry, Bring forth vestments for all the worshippers of Baal. And he brought them forth vestments. 23 And Jehu went, and Jehonadab the son of Rechab, into the house of Baal; and he said unto the worshippers of Baal, Search, and look that there be here with you none of the servants of Jehovah, but the worshippers of Baal only. 24 And they went in to offer sacrifices and burnt-offerings. Now Jehu had appointed him fourscore men without, and said, If any of the men whom I bring into your hands escape, *he that letteth him go,* his life shall be for the life of him.

25 And it came to pass, as soon as he had made an end of offering the burnt-offering, that Jehu said to the guard and to the captains, Go in, and slay them; let none come forth. And they smote them with the edge of the sword; and the guard and the captains cast them out, and went to the city of the house of Baal. 26 And they brought forth the pillars that were in the house of Baal, and burned them. 27 And they brake down the pillar of Baal, and brake down the house of Baal, and made it a draught-house, unto this day. 28 Thus Jehu destroyed Baal out of Israel.

29 Howbeit from the sins of Jeroboam the son of Nebat, wherewith he made Israel to sin, Jehu departed not from after them, *to wit,* the golden calves that were in Beth-el, and that were in Dan. 30 And Jehovah said unto Jehu, Because thou hast done well in executing that which is right in mine eyes, *and* hast done unto the house of Ahab according to all that was in my heart, thy sons of the fourth generation shall sit on the throne of Israel. 31 But Jehu took no heed to walk in the law of Jehovah, the God of Israel, with all his heart: he departed not from the sins of Jeroboam, wherewith he made Israel to sin.

32 In those days Jehovah began to cut off from Israel: and Hazael smote them in all the borders of Israel; 33 from the Jordan eastward, all the land of Gilead, the Gadites, and the Reubenites, and the Manassites, from Aroer, which is by the valley of the Arnon, even Gilead and Bashan. 34 Now the rest of the acts of Jehu, and all that he did, and all his might, are they not written in the book of the chronicles of the kings of Israel? 35 And Jehu slept with his fathers; and they buried him in Samaria. And Jehoahaz his son reigned in his stead. 36 And the time that Jehu reigned over Israel in Samaria was twenty and eight years.

Having completed the extinction of the royal line of Omri with atrocious savagery, Jehu declared, **Ahab served Baal a little; but Jehu will serve him much** (v. 18). This was a deception; its purpose was to lure Baal-worshipers into their temple, from which he allowed none to escape (v. 25). The temple of Baal was completely demolished.

Jehu's blood-bath was an event of horror in the Northern Kingdom. It did save the country from becoming thoroughly identified with Baalism, but the price paid was exorbitant. The nation was paralyzed internally as well as alienated from Judah because of Jehu's murder of Ahaziah, king at Jerusalem, and from Phoenicia, because of the death of Jezebel and all the Baal-worshipers. A century later there was still the realization that Jehu had been needlessly savage. "Yet a little while, and I will avenge the blood of Jezebel upon the house of Jehu" (Hos. 1:4).

II. SYNCHRONIZED HISTORY OF THE NORTHERN AND SOUTHERN KINGDOMS DURING THE LATTER PART OF THE NINTH CENTURY AND DURING THE EIGHTH CENTURY UNTIL THE FALL OF THE NORTHERN KINGDOM (II Kings 11:1—17:41)

The histories of the two kingdoms for the next sixty years (ca. 842-783 B. C.) are synchronized in the Kings account. First, there is the account of the Southern Kingdom to the close of the ninth century B. C. The usurpation by Athaliah and the reign of Joash are included. Second, there is the account of the Northern Kingdom to the close of the ninth century B. C., and into the early part of the eighth century B. C. This period covers the reigns of Jehu, Jehoahaz and Jehoash. It also includes the last days of Elisha and the confrontation which occurred between Jehoash of Israel and Amaziah of Judah.

The full sweep of Jehu's revolt in the Northern Kingdom carried into the Southern Kingdom. When news of Ahaziah's death reached Athaliah she embarked upon a purge in Jerusalem.

A. ATHALIAH (11:1-3; cf. II Chron. 22:10-12)

1 Now when Athaliah the mother of Ahaziah saw that her son was dead, she arose and destroyed all the seed royal. 2 But Jehosheba, the daughter of king Joram, sister of Ahaziah, took Joash the son of Ahaziah, and stole him away from among the king's sons that were slain, even him and his nurse, *and put them* in the bed-chamber; and they hid him from Athaliah, so that he was not slain; 3 and he was with her hid in the house of Jehovah six years. And Athaliah reigned over the land.

Upon the death of Ahaziah, the queen-mother, Athaliah, daughter of Ahab and Jezebel, acted swiftly to control the royal situation in Jerusalem. She ordered the extinction of all of the line of David and seized the authority of the monarchy. For six years she ruled (v. 3).

However, her attempt to destroy the royal family completely was foiled by the wife of Jehoiada the high priest, Jehosheba (v. 2). "She was no doubt the half-sister of Ahaziah, the daughter of Joram by another mother than Athaliah."[33]

B. JOASH (11:4—12:21)

For six years Jehoiada and Jehosheba kept Joash hidden from Athaliah, the ruling monarch in Jerusalem. Meanwhile, there was extensive plotting to restore the Davidic line by making Joash king.

1. Accession of Joash (11:4-20; cf. II Chron. 23:1-21)

4 And in the seventh year Jehoiada sent and fetched the captains over hundreds of the Carites and of the guard,

and brought them to him into the house of Jehovah; and he made a covenant with them, and took an oath of them in the house of Jehovah, and showed them the king's son. 5 And he commanded them, saying, This is the thing that ye shall do: a third part of you, that come in on the sabbath, shall be keepers of the watch of the king's house; 6 and a third part shall be at the gate Sur; and a third part at the gate behind the guard: so shall ye keep the watch of the house, and be a barrier. 7 And the two companies of you, even all that go forth on the sabbath, shall keep the watch of the house of Jehovah about the king. 8 And ye shall compass the king round about, every man with his weapons in his hand; and he that cometh within the ranks, let him be slain: and be ye with the king when he goeth out, and when he cometh in.

9 And the captains over hundreds did according to all that Jehoiada the priest commanded; and they took every man his men, those that were to come in on the sabbath, with those that were to go out on the sabbath, and came to Jehoiada the priest. 10 And the priest delivered to the captains over hundreds the spears and shields that had been king David's, which were in the house of Jehovah. 11 And the guard stood, every man with his weapons in his hand, from the right side of the house to the left side of the house, along by the altar and the house, by the king round about. 12 Then he brought out the king's son, and put the crown upon him, and *gave him* the testimony; and they made him king, and anointed him; and they clapped their hands, and said, *Long* live the king.

13 And when Athaliah heard the noise of the guard *and of* the people, she came to the people into the house of Jehovah: 14 and she looked, and, behold, the king stood by the pillar, as the manner was, and the captains and the trumpets by the king; and all the people of the land rejoiced, and blew trumpets. Then Athaliah rent her clothes, and cried, Treason! treason! 15 And Jehoiada the priest commanded the captains of hundreds that were set over the host, and said unto them, Have her forth between the ranks; and him that followeth her slay with the sword. For the priest said, Let her not be slain in the house of Jehovah. 16 So they made way for her; and she went by the way of the horses' entry to the king's house: and there was she slain.

17 And Jehoiada made a covenant be-

tween Jehovah and the king and the people, that they should be Jehovah's people; between the king also and the people. 18 And all the people of the land went to the house of Baal, and brake it down; his altars and his images brake they in pieces thoroughly, and slew Mattan the priest of Baal before the altars. And the priest appointed officers over the house of Jehovah. 19 And he took the captains over hundreds, and the Carites, and the guard, and all the people of the land; and they brought down the king from the house of Jehovah, and came by the way of the gate of the guard unto the king's house. And he sat on the throne of the kings. 20 So all the people of the land rejoiced, and the city was quiet. And Athaliah they had slain with the sword at the king's house.

Joash was but one year old when he was rescued from the infamous plot of Athaliah. By the time he was seven the insurrection against Athaliah was in readiness. It included the priesthood, the military and the people (cf. vv. 4, 11, 14). Jehoiada's plan to make Joash king was executed without Athaliah's knowledge until it was too late (cf. vv. 12-14). Devoid of sovereign authority, Athaliah was slain (v. 16). Given the opportunity to declare allegiance to Jehovah, **Jehoiada made a covenant between Jehovah and the king and the people, that they should be Jehovah's people** (v. 17).

2. Allegiance of Joash (11:21—12:16; cf. II Chron. 24:1-14)

21 Jehoash was seven years old when he began to reign. 1 In the seventh year of Jehu began Jehoash to reign; and he reigned forty years in Jerusalem: and his mother's name was Zibiah of Beer-sheba. 2 And Jehoash did that which was right in the eyes of Jehovah all his days wherein Jehoiada the priest instructed him. 3 Howbeit the high places were not taken away; the people still sacrificed and burnt incense in the high places.
4 And Jehoash said to the priests, All the money of the hallowed things that is brought into the house of Jehovah, in current money, the money of the persons for whom each man is rated, and all the money that it cometh into any man's heart to bring into the house of Jehovah, 5 let the priests take it to them, every man from his acquaintance; and they shall repair the breaches of the house, wheresoever any breach shall be found. 6

But it was so, that in the three and twentieth year of king Jehoash the priests had not repaired the breaches of the house. 7 Then king Jehoash called for Jehoiada the priest, and for the *other* priests, and said unto them, Why repair ye not the breaches of the house? now therefore take no *more* money from your acquaintance, but deliver it for the breaches of the house. 8 And the priests consented that they should take no *more* money from the people, neither repair the breaches of the house.
9 But Jehoiada the priest took a chest, and bored a hole in the lid of it, and set it beside the altar, on the right side as one cometh into the house of Jehovah: and the priests that kept the threshold put therein all the money that was brought into the house of Jehovah. 10 And it was so, when they saw that there was much money in the chest, that the king's scribe and the high priest came up, and they put up in bags and counted the money that was found in the house of Jehovah. 11 And they gave the money that was weighed out into the hands of them that did the work, that had the oversight of the house of Jehovah: and they paid it out to the carpenters and the builders, that wrought upon the house of Jehovah, 12 and to the masons and the hewers of stone, and for buying timber and hewn stone to repair the breaches of the house of Jehovah, and for all that was laid out for the house to repair it. 13 But there were not made for the house of Jehovah cups of silver, snuffers, basins, trumpets, any vessels of gold, or vessels of silver, of the money that was brought into the house of Jehovah; 14 for they gave that to them that did the work, and repaired therewith the house of Jehovah. 15 Moreover they reckoned not with the men, into whose hand they delivered the money to give to them that did the work; for they dealt faithfully. 16 The money for the trespass-offerings, and the money for the sin-offerings, was not brought into the house of Jehovah: it was the priests'.

Joash ruled until the close of the ninth century B. C., a period of four decades. He began to rule at the age of seven. During the lifetime of Jehoiada, Joash received direct priestly influence. **And Jehoash did that which was right in the eyes of Jehovah all his days wherein Jehoiada the priest instructed him** (v. 2).

As a result of this priestly influence, Joash's allegiance to Jehovah was expressed largely through his repair and purification of the temple. As long as Joash had the influence of Jehoiada he was faithful to God and zealous for the upkeep of the temple. He was the originator of the "Joash chest" plan (v. 9).

3. Assassination of Joash (12:17-21; cf. II Chron. 24:23-27)

17 Then Hazael king of Syria went up, and fought against Gath, and took it; and Hazael set his face to go up to Jerusalem. 18 And Jehoash king of Judah took all the hallowed things that Jehoshaphat and Jehoram and Ahaziah, his fathers, kings of Judah, had dedicated, and his own hallowed things, and all the gold that was found in the treasures of the house of Jehovah, and of the king's house, and sent it to Hazael king of Syria: and he went away from Jerusalem. 19 Now the rest of the acts of Joash, and all that he did, are they not written in the book of the chronicles of the kings of Judah? 20 And his servants arose, and made a conspiracy, and smote Joash at the house of Millo, *on the way* that goeth down to Silla. 21 For Jozacar the son of Shimeath, and Jehozabad the son of Shomer, his servants, smote him, and he died; and they buried him with his fathers in the city of David: and Amaziah his son reigned in his stead.

During the reign of Joash a series of developments so undermined his rule that he became bitterly disliked. These included the death of his devout advisor, Jehoiada, and certain military reverses. So hated was he by his servants that they conspired to assassinate him (v. 21).

After Jehu's rule of almost three decades, his son Jehoahaz came to the throne in Samaria. His rule of seventeen years ended at the close of the ninth century B. C. It was a period of helplessness for Israel. Jehoahaz was hardly more than a vassal to Hazael, king of Syria. Under Jehoash, the son of Jehoahaz, a remarkable recovery was begun.

C. JEHOAHAZ (13:1-9)

1 In the three and twentieth year of Joash the son of Ahaziah, king of Judah, Jehoahaz the son of Jehu began to reign over Israel in Samaria, *and reigned* seventeen years. 2 And he did that which was evil in the sight of Jehovah, and followed the sins of Jeroboam the son of Nebat, wherewith he made Israel to sin; he departed not therefrom. 3 And the anger of Jehovah was kindled against Israel, and he delivered them into the hand of Hazael king of Syria, and into the hand of Ben-hadad the son of Hazael, continually. 4 And Jehoahaz besought Jehovah, and Jehovah hearkened unto him; for he saw the oppression of Israel, how that the king of Syria oppressed them. 5 (And Jehovah gave Israel a saviour, so that they went out from under the hand of the Syrians; and the children of Israel dwelt in their tents as beforetime. 6 Nevertheless they departed not from the sins of the house of Jeroboam, wherewith he made Israel to sin, but walked therein: and there remained the Asherah also in Samaria.) 7 For he left not to Jehoahaz of the people save fifty horsemen, and ten chariots, and ten thousand footmen; for the king of Syria destroyed them, and made them like the dust in threshing. 8 Now the rest of the acts of Jehoahaz, and all that he did, and his might, are they not written in the book of the chronicles of the kings of Israel? 9 And Jehoahaz slept with his fathers; and they buried him in Samaria: and Joash his son reigned in his stead.

During the reign of Jehoahaz the outlook for the Northern Kingdom was very bleak. Hazael's oppression reduced Jehoahaz to a status of dependency upon Syria. The explanation given in the Kings account is a religious one. **And the anger of Jehovah was kindled against Israel, and he delivered them into the hand of Hazael king of Syria . . . continually** (v. 3).

Intercession followed oppression. **Jehoahaz besought Jehovah, and Jehovah hearkened unto him; for he saw the oppression of Israel** (v. 4). Although this prayer was heard, Jehoahaz did not live to see the deliverance of Israel from her oppression. His grandson, Jeroboam, the son of Jehoash, became the "saviour" whom Jehovah gave to Israel (v. 5).[34]

It is important to realize that Jehoahaz held the key not only to the divinely instituted oppression but also to the divinely granted salvation. He was not a victim of circumstances nor was he elect unto salvation, leaving him irresponsible in both instances. His oppression was because of his wilful transgression. His salvation was because of penitent inter-

---

cession. He offers helpful insight into man's relation to God.

D. JEHOASH (13:10-25)

10 In the thirty and seventh year of Joash king of Judah began Jehoash the son of Jehoahaz to reign over Israel in Samaria, *and reigned* sixteen years. 11 And he did that which was evil in the sight of Jehovah; he departed not from all the sins of Jeroboam the son of Nebat, wherewith he made Israel to sin; but he walked therein. 12 Now the rest of the acts of Joash, and all that he did, and his might wherewith he fought against Amaziah king of Judah, are they not written in the book of the chronicles of the kings of Israel? 13 And Joash slept with his fathers; and Jeroboam sat upon his throne: and Joash was buried in Samaria with the kings of Israel.

14 Now Elisha was fallen sick of his sickness whereof he died: and Joash the king of Israel came down unto him, and wept over him, and said, My father, my father, the chariots of Israel and the horsemen thereof! 15 And Elisha said unto him, Take bow and arrows; and he took unto him bow and arrows. 16 And he said to the king of Israel, Put thy hand upon the bow; and he put his hand *upon it.* And Elisha laid his hands upon the king's hands. 17 And he said, Open the window eastward; and he opened it. Then Elisha said, Shoot; and he shot. And he said, Jehovah's arrow of victory, even the arrow of victory over Syria; for thou shalt smite the Syrians in Aphek, till thou have consumed them. 18 And he said, Take the arrows; and he took them. And he said unto the king of Israel, Smite upon the ground; and he smote thrice, and stayed. 19 And the man of God was wroth with him, and said, Thou shouldest have smitten five or six times: then hadst thou smitten Syria till thou hadst consumed it; whereas now thou shalt smite Syria but thrice.

20 And Elisha died, and they buried him. Now the bands of the Moabites invaded the land at the coming in of the year. 21 And it came to pass, as they were burying a man, that, behold, they spied a band; and they cast the man into the sepulchre of Elisha: and as soon as the man touched the bones of Elisha, he revived, and stood up on his feet.

22 And Hazael king of Syria oppressed Israel all the days of Jehoahaz. 23 But Jehovah was gracious unto them, and had compassion on them, and had respect unto them, because of his covenant with Abraham, Isaac, and Jacob, and would not destroy them, neither cast he them from his presence as yet. 24 And Hazael king of Syria died; and Ben-hadad his son reigned in his stead. 25 And Jehoash the son of Jehoahaz took again out of the hand of Ben-hadad the son of Hazael the cities which he had taken out of the hand of Jehoahaz his father by war. Three times did Joash smite him, and recovered the cities of Israel.

Jehoash ruled during the first fifteen years of the eighth century B. C. The outlook for the Northern Kingdom brightened greatly. "Israel's resurgence began with Jehoash ... who came to the throne just after the Assyrians had crippled Damascus."[35] Jehoash recovered the cities which his father had lost (v. 25). Apparently, the Syrians were completely ejected from the kingdom.

Of importance during the reign of Jehoash is the account of the last days of Elisha. He had not appeared in Israel's history since the coronation of Jehu at least fifty years prior to the events recorded in this passage. As news spread that he was sick, Jehoash the king came to him and wept over his approaching demise (v. 14). This was indicative of the high esteem in which Elisha was held.

Elisha offered Jehoash a formula for victory over Syria through the symbolism of the arrows (v. 17). Jehoash was reluctant to do more than shoot three arrows. Elisha remonstrated with him that he had stopped so soon (v. 19).

E. HOSTILE CONFRONTATION OF THE REIGNS OF AMAZIAH AND JEHOASH (14:1-22; cf. II Chron. 25:1-28)

1 In the second year of Joash son of Joahaz king of Israel began Amaziah the son of Joash king of Judah to reign. 2 He was twenty and five years old when he began to reign; and he reigned twenty and nine years in Jerusalem: and his mother's name was Jehoaddin of Jerusalem. 3 And he did that which was right in the eyes of Jehovah, yet not like David his father: he did according to all that Joash his father had done. 4 Howbeit the high places were not taken away: the people still sacrificed and burnt

35 Bright, *op. cit.*, p. 238.

incense in the high places. 5 And it came to pass, as soon as the kingdom was established in his hand, that he slew his servants who had slain the king his father: 6 but the children of the murderers he put not to death; according to that which is written in the book of the law of Moses, as Jehovah commanded, saying, The fathers shall not be put to death for the children, nor the children be put to death for the fathers; but every man shall die for his own sin. 7 He slew of Edom in the Valley of Salt ten thousand, and took Sela by war, and called the name of it Joktheel, unto this day.

8 Then Amaziah sent messengers to Jehoash, the son of Jehoahaz son of Jehu, king of Israel, saying, Come, let us look one another in the face. 9 And Jehoash the king of Israel sent to Amaziah king of Judah, saying, The thistle that was in Lebanon sent to the cedar that was in Lebanon, saying, Give thy daughter to my son to wife: and there passed by a wild beast that was in Lebanon, and trod down the thistle. 10 Thou hast indeed smitten Edom, and thy heart hath lifted thee up: glory thereof, and abide at home; for why shouldest thou meddle in *thy* hurt, that thou shouldest fall, even thou, and Judah with thee?

11 But Amaziah would not hear. So Jehoash king of Israel went up; and he and Amaziah king of Judah looked one another in the face at Beth-shemesh, which belongeth to Judah. 12 And Judah was put to the worse before Israel; and they fled every man to his tent. 13 And Jehoash king of Israel took Amaziah king of Judah, the son of Jehoash the son of Ahaziah, at Beth-shemesh, and came to Jerusalem, and brake down the wall of Jerusalem from the gate of Ephraim unto the corner gate, four hundred cubits. 14 And he took all the gold and silver, and all the vessels that were found in the house of Jehovah, and in the treasures of the king's house, the hostages also, and returned to Samaria.

15 Now the rest of the acts of Jehoash which he did, and his might, and how he fought with Amaziah king of Judah, are they not written in the book of the chronicles of the kings of Israel? 16 And Jehoash slept with his fathers, and was buried in Samaria with the kings of Israel; and Jeroboam his son reigned in his stead.

17 And Amaziah the son of Joash king of Judah lived after the death of Jehoash son of Jehoahaz king of Israel fifteen years. 18 Now the rest of the acts of Amaziah, are they not written in the book of the chronicles of the kings of Judah? 19 And they made a conspiracy against him in Jerusalem; and he fled to Lachish: but they sent after him to Lachish, and slew him there. 20 And they brought him upon horses; and he was buried at Jerusalem with his fathers in the city of David. 21 And all the people of Judah took Azariah, who was sixteen years old, and made him king in the room of his father Amaziah. 22 He built Elath, and restored it to Judah, after that the king slept with his fathers.

Jehoash and Amaziah were contemporary. While Jehoash was beginning the task of restoring the prosperity of the Northern Kingdom, Amaziah was also displaying qualities of capable rule. Flushed with victory over Edom, Amaziah persisted in provoking Jehoash (vv. 10-11).

Jehoash's parable of the thistle, cedar and wild beast has become a well-known story illustrating meddling in affairs not one's own (v. 9). Amaziah was overly confident and could not be deterred. In the battle which ensued he was severely beaten. He discovered what happens to little thistles that think they are big cedars.

The resurgence of the two kingdoms reached its apex under the long and capable rule of Jeroboam, the son of Jehoash, and Azariah (Uzziah), of the dynasty of David. Jeroboam ruled over forty years, while Azariah ruled over fifty years (cf. 14:23; 15:2).

F. JEROBOAM OF THE JEHU DYNASTY (14:23-29)

23 In the fifteenth year of Amaziah the son of Joash king of Judah Jeroboam the son of Joash king of Israel began to reign in Samaria, *and reigned* forty and one years. 24 And he did that which was evil in the sight of Jehovah: he departed not from all the sins of Jeroboam the son of Nebat, wherewith he made Israel to sin. 25 He restored the border of Israel from the entrance of Hamath unto the sea of the Arabah, according to the word of Jehovah, the God of Israel, which he spake by his servant Jonah the son of Amittai, the prophet, who was of Gath-hepher. 26 For Jehovah saw the affliction of Israel, that it was very bitter; for there was none shut up nor left at large, neither was there any helper for Israel. 27 And Jehovah said not that he would blot

out the name of Israel from under heaven; but he saved them by the hand of Jeroboam the son of Joash.

28 Now the rest of the acts of Jeroboam, and all that he did, and his might, how he warred, and how he recovered Damascus, and Hamath, *which had belonged* to Judah, for Israel, are they not written in the book of the chronicles of the kings of Israel? 29 And Jeroboam slept with his fathers, even with the kings of Israel; and Zechariah his son reigned in his stead.

"Jeroboam II was by far the most successful of all the kings of Israel."[36] The solid accomplishments of his father provided a foundation on which he was able to raise the Northern Kingdom to a level of material prosperity unheard of in the annals of her history.

He expanded the boundaries of the kingdom and his sovereignty some two hundred miles north of Samaria. A period of peace, productivity and prosperity made life luxurious and plentiful.

However, for a true picture of the religion and morals of the kingdom under Jeroboam, the son of Jehoash, one must turn to the writings of Amos and Hosea. Because a nation is affluent, it does not follow that it is righteous. The glowing picture of a healthy kingdom with a bright future gives only one side of the story. The other side as depicted by the prophets is a grim portrayal of a nation mortally ill and in an advanced stage of decadence religiously, socially and morally. "The eighth century in Israel reached its mid-point on a note of hideous dissonance."[37]

G. AZARIAH (UZZIAH) OF THE DAVIDIC DYNASTY (15:1-7; cf. II Chron. 26:3-23)

1 In the twenty and seventh year of Jeroboam king of Israel began Azariah son of Amaziah king of Judah to reign. 2 Sixteen years old was he when he began to reign; and he reigned two and fifty years in Jerusalem: and his mother's name was Jecoliah of Jerusalem. 3 And he did that which was right in the eyes of Jehovah, according to all that his father Amaziah had done. 4 Howbeit the high places were not taken away: the people still sacrificed and burnt incense in the high places. 5 And Jehovah smote the

king, so that he was a leper unto the day of his death, and dwelt in a separate house. And Jotham the king's son was over the household, judging the people of the land. 6 Now the rest of the acts of Azariah, and all that he did, are they not written in the book of the chronicles of the kings of Judah? 7 And Azariah slept with his fathers; and they buried him with his fathers in the city of David: and Jotham his son reigned in his stead.

The Kings account of Jeroboam of Israel and Azariah of Judah is remarkably brief. The Chronicles account is much more in keeping with the significance of their respective reigns. It is obvious that the Kings account is preoccupied with the shaping up of the religious situation in the Northern Kingdom. After this brief glimpse at the fifty-two-year rule of Azariah, the Kings compiler is chiefly concerned in this chapter over the political decline and religious decay of the Northern Kingdom. Within twenty years after Azariah's reign came to a close, the Northern Kingdom fell to the Assyrian conqueror.

H. TWO DECADES OF DECLINE IN THE NORTHERN KINGDOM (15: 8-31)

8 In the thirty and eighth year of Azariah king of Judah did Zechariah the son of Jeroboam reign over Israel in Samaria six months. 9 And he did that which was evil in the sight of Jehovah, as his fathers had done: he departed not from the sins of Jeroboam the son of Nebat, wherewith he made Israel to sin. 10 And Shallum the son of Jabesh conspired against him, and smote him before the people, and slew him, and reigned in his stead. 11 Now the rest of the acts of Zechariah, behold, they are written in the book of the chronicles of the kings of Israel. 12 This was the word of Jehovah which he spake unto Jehu, saying, Thy sons to the fourth generation shall sit upon the throne of Israel. And so it came to pass.

13 Shallum the son of Jabesh began to reign in the nine and thirtieth year of Uzziah king of Judah; and he reigned the space of a month in Samaria. 14 And Menahem the son of Gadi went up from Tirzah, and came to Samaria, and smote Shallum the son of Jabesh in Samaria, and slew him, and reigned in his stead.

[36] Snaith, *op. cit.*, p. 264.   [37] Bright, *op. cit.*, p. 248.

15 Now the rest of the acts of Shallum, and his conspiracy which he made, behold, they are written in the book of the chronicles of the kings of Israel. 16 Then Menahem smote Tiphsah, and all that were therein, and the borders thereof, from Tirzah: because they opened not to him, therefore he smote it; and all the women therein that were with child he ripped up.

17 In the nine and thirtieth year of Azariah king of Judah began Menahem the son of Gadi to reign over Israel, *and reigned* ten years in Samaria. 18 And he did that which was evil in the sight of Jehovah: he departed not all his days from the sins of Jeroboam the son of Nebat, wherewith he made Israel to sin. 19 There came against the land Pul the king of Assyria; and Menahem gave Pul a thousand talents of silver, that his hand might be with him to confirm the kingdom in his hand. 20 And Menahem exacted the money of Israel, even of all the mighty men of wealth, of each man fifty shekels of silver, to give to the king of Assyria. So the king of Assyria turned back, and stayed not there in the land. 21 Now the rest of the acts of Menahem, and all that he did, are they not written in the book of the chronicles of the kings of Israel? 22 And Menahem slept with his fathers; and Pekahiah his son reigned in his stead.

23 In the fiftieth year of Azariah king of Judah Pekahiah the son of Menahem began to reign over Israel in Samaria, *and reigned* two years. 24 And he did that which was evil in the sight of Jehovah: he departed not from the sins of Jeroboam the son of Nebat, wherewith he made Israel to sin. 25 And Pekah the son of Remaliah, his captain, conspired against him, and smote him in Samaria, in the castle of the king's house, with Argob and Arieh; and with him were fifty men of the Gileadites: and he slew him, and reigned in his stead. 26 Now the rest of the acts of Pekahiah, and all that he did, behold, they are written in the book of the chronicles of the kings of Israel.

27 In the two and fiftieth year of Azariah king of Judah Pekah the son of Remaliah began to reign over Israel in Samaria, *and reigned* twenty years. 28 And he did that which was evil in the sight of Jehovah: he departed not from the sins of Jeroboam the son of Nebat, wherewith he made Israel to sin. 29 In the days of Pekah king of Israel came Tiglath-pileser king of Assyria, and took Ijon, and Abel-beth-maacah, and Janoah, and Kedesh, and Hazor, and Gilead, and Galilee, all the land of Naphtali; and he carried them captive to Assyria. 30 And Hoshea the son of Elah made a conspiracy against Pekah the son of Remaliah, and smote him, and slew him, and reigned in his stead, in the twentieth year of Jotham the son of Uzziah. 31 Now the rest of the acts of Pekah, and all that he did, behold, they are written in the book of the chronicles of the kings of Israel.

Jeroboam, son of Jehoash, ended his rule about the midpoint of the eighth century B. C. During the next two decades the Northern Kingdom deteriorated swiftly because of anarchy and chaos. Just as Israel was called upon to face the greatest foreign threat of her entire history, the revived and powerful Assyria, she found herself in the clutches of conspiracy and disintegration. Six kings ascended the throne at Samaria. Four of them met death by political violence. Internal dissension was sinking the ship of state.

Jeroboam was succeeded by Zechariah, his son, the fifth king of the Jehu dynasty. Zechariah reigned only six months (v. 8). This ended the Jehu dynasty which had ruled the Northern Kingdom for almost a century, from the middle of the ninth to the middle of the eighth century B. C.

The leader of the conspiracy against Zechariah was Shallum, but his rule lasted only one month (v. 13): His assassin, Menahem, was on the throne when the powerful Assyrian army threatened. Menahem quickly submitted and paid tribute (v. 20).

The son of Menahem, Pekahiah, ruled but two years when a conspiracy led by Pekah brought about his death (v. 25). During Pekah's rule, Assyria occupied much of the territory of the Northern Kingdom (v. 29). Meanwhile, internal revolt flared. Hoshea conspired against Pekah and murdered him (v. 30).

I. JOTHAM AND AHAZ OF THE DAVIDIC DYNASTY (15:32—16:20)

The synchronization of the histories of the two kingdoms is continued with the brief account of two southern kings.

1. Jotham (15:32-38; cf. II Chron. 27:1-9)

32 In the second year of Pekah the son of Remaliah king of Israel began Jotham the son of Uzziah king of Judah to reign. 33 Five and twenty years old was he when he began to reign; and he reigned sixteen years in Jerusalem: and his mother's name was Jerusha the daughter of Zadok. 34 And he did that which was right in the eyes of Jehovah; he did according to all that his father Uzziah had done. 35 Howbeit the high places were not taken away: the people still sacrificed and burned incense in the high places. He built the upper gate of the house of Jehovah. 36 Now the rest of the acts of Jotham, and all that he did, are they not written in the book of the chronicles of the kings of Judah? 37 In those days Jehovah began to send against Judah Rezin the king of Syria, and Pekah the son of Remaliah. 38 And Jotham slept with his fathers, and was buried with his fathers in the city of David his father: and Ahaz his son reigned in his stead.

Jotham was a Jehovah-worshiper. **He did that which was right in the eyes of Jehovah** (v. 34). He also endeavored to follow in the steps of Uzziah, his influential father. During his reign, his kingdom had repercussions from the international crisis. Assyria's pressure on Syria and the Northern Kingdom caused these two countries to seek the assistance of the Southern Kingdom (v. 37).

2. Ahaz (16:1-20; cf. II Chron. 28:1-27)

1 In the seventeenth year of Pekah the son of Remaliah Ahaz the son of Jotham king of Judah began to reign. 2 Twenty years old was Ahaz when he began to reign; and he reigned sixteen years in Jerusalem: and he did not that which was right in the eyes of Jehovah his God, like David his father. 3 But he walked in the way of the kings of Israel, yea, and made his son to pass through the fire, according to the abominations of the nations, whom Jehovah cast out from before the children of Israel. 4 And he sacrificed and burnt incense in the high places, and on the hills, and under every green tree.

5 Then Rezin king of Syria and Pekah son of Remaliah king of Israel came up to Jerusalem to war: and they besieged Ahaz, but could not overcome him. 6 At that time Rezin king of Syria recovered Elath to Syria, and drove the Jews from Elath; and the Syrians came to Elath, and dwelt there, unto this day.

7 So Ahaz sent messengers to Tiglath-pileser king of Assyria, saying, I am thy servant and thy son: come up, and save me out of the hand of the king of Syria, and out of the hand of the king of Israel, who rise up against me. 8 And Ahaz took the silver and gold that was found in the house of Jehovah, and in the treasures of the king's house, and sent it for a present to the king of Assyria. 9 And the king of Assyria hearkened unto him; and the king of Assyria went up against Damascus, and took it, and carried *the people of* it captive to Kir, and slew Rezin.

10 And king Ahaz went to Damascus to meet Tiglath-pileser king of Assyria, and saw the altar that was at Damascus; and king Ahaz sent to Urijah the priest the fashion of the altar, and the pattern of it, according to all the workmanship thereof. 11 And Urijah the priest built an altar: according to all that king Ahaz had sent from Damascus, so did Urijah the priest make it against the coming of king Ahaz from Damascus. 12 And when the king was come from Damascus, the king saw the altar: and the king drew near unto the altar, and offered thereon. 13 And he burnt his burnt-offering and his meal-offering, and poured his drink-offering, and sprinkled the blood of his peace-offerings, upon the altar. 14 And the brazen altar, which was before Jehovah, he brought from the forefront of the house, from between his altar and the house of Jehovah, and put it on the north side of his altar. 15 And king Ahaz commanded Urijah the priest, saying, Upon the great altar burn the morning burnt-offering, and the evening meal-offering, and the king's burnt-offering, and his meal-offering, with the burnt-offering of all the people of the land, and their meal-offering, and their drink-offerings; and sprinkle upon it all the blood of the burnt-offering, and all the blood of the sacrifice: but the brazen altar shall be for me to inquire by. 16 Thus did Urijah the priest, according to all that king Ahaz commanded.

17 And king Ahaz cut off the panels of the bases, and removed the laver from off them, and took down the sea from off the brazen oxen that were under it, and put it upon a pavement of stone. 18 And the covered way for the sabbath that they had built in the house, and the king's entry without, turned he unto the house

of Jehovah, because of the king of Assyria. 19 Now the rest of the acts of Ahaz which he did, are they not written in the book of the chronicles of the kings of Judah? 20 And Ahaz slept with his fathers, and was buried with his fathers in the city of David: and Hezekiah his son reigned in his stead.

While the Northern Kingdom was in its agony of final disintegration, the Southern Kingdom was approaching a crisis. Surrounded by hostile nations, Edom, Philistia, the Northern Kingdom and Syria, Ahaz resolved upon a political expedient which the prophet Isaiah resisted (cf. Isa. 7-8). Ahaz resolved to appeal to Assyria. His appeal and bribe to Assyria brought a response. **The king of Assyria went up against Damascus, and took it** (v. 9). What Assyria did to Israel is described in II Kings 17. Ahaz relied upon power politics, but such expediency for the sake of self-interest was disastrous.

Ahaz made a visit to Damascus to give full submission to Tiglath-pileser of Assyria (v. 10). While there he was greatly impressed with an Assyrian altar, so much so that he had one like it erected at Jerusalem. As a result of his submission to Assyria, Ahaz made some religious innovations in the worship at Jerusalem. "Ahaz was doing honour to the gods of Assyria."[38] Among the nations of antiquity nothing was purely secular. When international agreements were made, there was implicit in them the agreement of the gods of the nations involved. When the agreements were between unequal parties, the gods of the junior partner submitted to the gods of the senior partner. This happened to the Southern Kingdom when Ahaz capitulated to Assyria and copied the Assyrian altar. Isaiah vigorously opposed regarding Jehovah as a junior deity in His relationship to the Assyrian deities.

J. THE FALL OF THE NORTHERN KINGDOM (17:1-41)

The Kings compiler returns to the history of the Northern Kingdom. The finale is about to be given.

[38] Ellison, *op. cit.*, p. 326.

1. Hoshea Conquered by Assyria (17:1-6)

1 In the twelfth year of Ahaz king of Judah began Hoshea the son of Elah to reign in Samaria over Israel, *and reigned* nine years. 2 And he did that which was evil in the sight of Jehovah, yet not as the kings of Israel that were before him. 3 Against him came up Shalmaneser king of Assyria; and Hoshea became his servant, and brought him tribute. 4 And the king of Assyria found conspiracy in Hoshea; for he had sent messengers to So king of Egypt, and offered no tribute to the king of Assyria, as he had done year by year: therefore the king of Assyria shut him up, and bound him in prison. 5 Then the king of Assyria came up throughout all the land, and went up to Samaria, and besieged it three years. 6 In the ninth year of Hoshea the king of Assyria took Samaria, and carried Israel away unto Assyria, and placed them in Halah, and on the Habor, the river of Gozan, and in the cities of the Medes.

Because Hoshea violated his relationship to Assyria as a tribute-paying vassal to that nation, he was besieged. For three years, Samaria withstood before surrendering (v. 5). The inhabitants were deported and their identity lost.

2. In Retrospect (17:7-23)

7 And it was so, because the children of Israel had sinned against Jehovah their God, who brought them up out of the land of Egypt from under the hand of Pharaoh king of Egypt, and had feared other gods, 8 and walked in the statutes of the nations, whom Jehovah cast out from before the children of Israel, and of the kings of Israel, which they made. 9 And the children of Israel did secretly things that were not right against Jehovah their God: and they built them high places in all their cities, from the tower of the watchmen to the fortified city; 10 and they set them up pillars and Asherim upon every high hill, and under every green tree; 11 and there they burnt incense in all the high places, as did the nations whom Jehovah carried away before them; and they wrought wicked things to provoke Jehovah to anger; 12 and they served idols, whereof Jehovah had said unto them, Ye shall not do this thing. 13 Yet Jehovah testified unto Israel, and unto Judah, by every prophet, and every seer, saying, Turn ye from your evil ways, and

keep my commandments and my statutes, according to all the law which I commanded your fathers, and which I sent to you by my servants the prophets. 14 Notwithstanding, they would not hear, but hardened their neck, like to the neck of their fathers, who believed not in Jehovah their God. 15 And they rejected his statutes, and his covenant that he made with their fathers, and his testimonies which he testified unto them; and they followed vanity, and became vain, and *went* after the nations that were round about them, concerning whom Jehovah had charged them that they should not do like them. 16 And they forsook all the commandments of Jehovah their God, and made them molten images, even two calves, and made an Asherah, and worshipped all the host of heaven, and served Baal. 17 And they caused their sons and their daughters to pass through the fire, and used divination and enchantments, and sold themselves to do that which was evil in the sight of Jehovah, to provoke him to anger. 18 Therefore Jehovah was very angry with Israel, and removed them out of his sight: there was none left but the tribe of Judah only.

19 Also Judah kept not the commandments of Jehovah their God, but walked in the statutes of Israel which they made. 20 And Jehovah rejected all the seed of Israel, and afflicted them, and delivered them into the hand of spoilers, until he had cast them out of his sight. 21 For he rent Israel from the house of David; and they made Jeroboam the son of Nebat king: and Jeroboam drove Israel from following Jehovah, and made them sin a great sin. 22 And the children of Israel walked in all the sins of Jeroboam which he did; they departed not from them; 23 until Jehovah removed Israel out of his sight, as he spake by all his servants the prophets. So Israel was carried away out of their own land to Assyria unto this day.

With the fall of Samaria, the last stronghold of the Northern Kingdom was captured by Assyria. This occurred in the latter part of the eighth century (ca. 721 B. C.). This event was cause for the compiler to pause and reflect upon the course which Israel had taken.

He forthrightly declared that Israel's destruction was because of sin. **And it was so, because the children of Israel had sinned against Jehovah their God** (v. 7). Israel's sinful acts are considered in the

special context of God's saving acts. Before the sins of Israel are enumerated, the salvation of God is set forth. That salvation included, first of all, deliverance from bondage by **Jehovah their God, who brought them out of the land of Egypt** (v. 8).

Second, it included an inheritance which God gave to Israel when he subdued the kings of Canaan (v. 8).

Third, it included the sending of prophets who warned the people to turn from their evil ways (v. 13).

Israel's sinful acts were violations of God's saving acts. The people **had sinned against Jehovah their God . . . and had feared other gods** (v. 7). Israel's sin involved acknowledgment and worship of other gods, sometimes in addition to and sometimes in preference to the God of their deliverance.

Second, Israel's sin included violations of God's covenant demands. **And they rejected his statutes, and his covenant that he made with their fathers** (v. 15). Israel's delivering God had made demands of His people and had given explicit expression to those demands through the law. Although the Israelites had promised to keep the commandments, they failed to do so.

Third, Israel's sin included the calf-worship instituted by Jeroboam, the son of Nebat, on the occasion of the great revolt of the ten northern tribes in the tenth century B. C. **And they forsook all the commandments of Jehovah their God, and made them molten images, even two calves, . . . and served Baal** (v. 16). Israel's calf-worship severed her from faithful worship at the temple in Jerusalem and patriotic allegiance to the throne of David. The Kings account emphasizes that the catastrophe which befell the Northern Kingdom occurred because of her, as Norman Snaith puts it, "breaking away from loyalty to the throne of David and worshipping . . . at a temple other than that of Jerusalem."[39]

Israel's threefold sin was rebellion against God's saving acts in history: (1) the Exodus, (2) the prophets, (3) the kingdom under David. Israel violated the covenant, resisted the prophets, and rejected the rule of David. **Therefore**

---

[39] Snaith, *op. cit.*, p. 280.

Jehovah was very angry with Israel, and removed them out of his sight: and there was none left but the tribe of Judah only (v. 18).

3. The Assyrian Resettlement (17:24-41)

24 And the king of Assyria brought men from Babylon, and from Cuthah, and from Avva, and from Hamath and Sepharvaim, and placed them in the cities of Samaria instead of the children of Israel; and they possessed Samaria, and dwelt in the cities thereof. 25 And so it was, at the beginning of their dwelling there, that they feared not Jehovah: therefore Jehovah sent lions among them, which killed some of them. 26 Wherefore they spake to the king of Assyria, saying, The nations which thou hast carried away, and placed in the cities of Samaria, know not the law of the god of the land: therefore he hath sent lions among them, and, behold, they slay them, because they know not the law of the god of the land.

27 Then the king of Assyria command-ed, saying, Carry thither one of the priests whom ye brought from thence; and let them go and dwell there, and let him teach them the law of the god of the land. 28 So one of the priests whom they had carried away from Samaria came and dwelt in Beth-el, and taught them how they should fear Jehovah. 29 Howbeit every nation made gods of their own, and put them in the houses of the high places which the Samaritans had made, every nation in their cities wherein they dwelt. 30 And the men of Babylon made Suc-coth-benoth, and the men of Cuth made Nergal, and the men of Hamath made Ashima, 31 and the Avvites made Nibhaz and Tartak; and the Sepharvites burnt their children in the fire to Adrammelech and Anammelech, the gods of Sephar-vaim. 32 So they feared Jehovah, and made unto them from among themselves priests of the high places, who sacrificed for them in the houses of the high pla-ces. 33 They feared Jehovah, and served their own gods, after the manner of the nations from among whom they had been carried away.

34 Unto this day they do after the former manner: they fear not Jehovah, neither do they after their statutes, or after their ordinances, or after the law or after the commandment which Jehovah commanded the children of Jacob, whom he named Israel; 35 with whom Jehovah

had made a covenant, and charged them, saying, Ye shall not fear other gods, nor bow yourselves to them, nor serve them, nor sacrifice to them: 36 but Jehovah, who brought you up out of the land of Egypt with great power and with an outstretched arm, him shall ye fear, and unto him shall ye bow yourselves, and to him shall ye sacrifice: 37 and the statutes and the ordinances, and the law and the commandment, which he wrote for you, ye shall observe to do for evermore; and ye shall not fear other gods: 38 and the covenant that I have made with you ye shall not forget; neither shall ye fear other gods: 39 but Jehovah your God shall ye fear; and he will deliver you out of the hand of all your enemies. 40 How-beit they did not hearken, but they did after their former manner. 41 So these nations feared Jehovah, and served their graven images; their children likewise, and their children's children, as did their fathers, so do they unto this day.

After deporting the important citizens of the Northern Kingdom, the Assyrian policy called for importing people from the eastern part of the empire to aug-ment the less important Israelites who were as so many cattle to the Assyrian king.

Religious anarchy followed. The peo-ple were attacked by wild beasts because of their religious deviations (v. 25). Not-withstanding the efforts of a priest of Israel who was returned to instruct the people how to worship Jehovah, wholesale religious tolerance and syncre-tism developed. **They feared Jehovah, and served their own gods** (v. 33).

Unto this day they do after the former manner: they fear not Jehovah (v. 34). "The worship of Jehovah, merely be-cause they regard Him as the local deity of the land, is no worship at all."[40] These people may have thought they were worshiping Jehovah, even though they included Him with other deities. This idea appears in verses 32, 33 and 41. However, the compiler of Kings knew that worship of Jehovah required the abandonment of all worship to any other god, for there is no God but Jehovah (vv. 34-35). This was the unequivocal stand of the prophets and must be basic to any renewal of biblical religion.

40 Lumby, op. cit., p. 178.

III. THE SOUTHERN KINGDOM DURING THE REIGN OF HEZEKIAH IN THE LATTER PART OF THE EIGHTH CENTURY (II Kings 18:1—20:21)

Through the reign of Ahaz, the Southern Kingdom was allied with Assyria and remained submissive. While the Northern Kingdom was under Assyrian attack, the Southern Kingdom maintained strict neutrality. Hezekiah, the son of Ahaz, reversed this policy and struggled to free the kingdom from Assyria's domination. It was a hazardous policy and turned out to be only a "stop-gap" effort, which was ended by Hezekiah's son, Manasseh.

A. HEZEKIAH'S REFORMATION IN THE SOUTHERN KINGDOM (18: 1-12; cf. II Chron. 29:1—31:21)

1 Now it came to pass in the third year of Hoshea son of Elah king of Israel, that Hezekiah the son of Ahaz king of Judah began to reign. 2 Twenty and five years old was he when he began to reign; and he reigned twenty and nine years in Jerusalem: and his mother's name was Abi the daughter of Zechariah. 3 And he did that which was right in the eyes of Jehovah, according to all that David his father had done. 4 He removed the high places, and brake the pillars, and cut down the Asherah: and he brake in pieces the brazen serpent that Moses had made; for unto those days the children of Israel did burn incense to it; and he called it Nehushtan. 5 He trusted in Jehovah, the God of Israel; so that after him was none like him among all the kings of Judah, nor *among them* that were before him. 6 For he clave to Jehovah; he departed not from following him, but kept his commandments, which Jehovah commanded Moses. 7 And Jehovah was with him; whithersoever he went forth he prospered: and he rebelled against the king of Assyria, and served him not. 8 He smote the Philistines unto Gaza and the borders thereof, from the tower of the watchmen to the fortified city.

9 And it came to pass in the fourth year of king Hezekiah, which was the seventh year of Hoshea son of Elah king of Israel, that Shalmaneser king of Assyria came up against Samaria, and besieged it. 10 And at the end of three years they took it: in the sixth year of Hezekiah, which was the ninth year of Hoshea king of Israel, Samaria was taken. 11 And the king of Assyria carried Israel away unto Assyria, and put them in Halah, and on the Habor, the river of Gozan, and in the cities of the Medes, 12 because they obeyed not the voice of Jehovah their God, but transgressed his covenant, even all that Moses the servant of Jehovah commanded, and would not hear it, nor do it.

Hezekiah began his reign under grim conditions. Politically, Assyria was poised to conquer the entire territory between its boundary and the boundary of Egypt. Religiously, the Northern Kingdom had turned from Jehovah to other gods. The Southern Kingdom under Ahaz had followed the same course (II Kings 16:3).

Hezekiah sought to reform religion. Instead of frantically pursuing a foreign policy of expediency and "power politics," he pursued a positive religious policy. **He removed the high places, and brake the pillars, and cut down the Asherah.... He trusted in Jehovah, the God of Israel** (vv. 4-5).

The primacy which Hezekiah gave to religious reforms was well pleasing to the Lord. **And Jehovah was with him; whithersoever he went forth he prospered** (v. 7). This description is optimistic, but it needs to be read in the light of the sober danger confronting the kingdom. Hezekiah was not able to drive Assyria out of entrenched positions, but he was able to defend Jerusalem and parts of his kingdom.

B. HEZEKIAH'S RESISTANCE TO ASSYRIA (18:13—19:37; cf. II Chron. 32: 1-23)

13 Now in the fourteenth year of king Hezekiah did Sennacherib king of Assyria come up against all the fortified cities of Judah, and took them. 14 And Hezekiah king of Judah sent to the king of Assyria to Lachish, saying, I have offended; return from me: that which thou puttest on me will I bear. And the king of Assyria appointed unto Hezekiah king of Judah three hundred talents of silver and thirty talents of gold. 15 And Hezekiah gave *him* all the silver that was found in the house of Jehovah, and in the treasures of the king's house. 16 At that time did Hezekiah cut off *the gold from* the doors of the temple of Jehovah, and *from* the pillars which Hezekiah king of Judah had overlaid, and gave it to the king of Assy-

ria. 17 And the king of Assyria sent Tartan and Rab-saris and Rabshakeh from Lachish to king Hezekiah with a great army unto Jerusalem. And they went up and came to Jerusalem. And when they were come up, they came and stood by the conduit of the upper pool, which is in the highway of the fuller's field. 18 And when they had called to the king, there came out to them Eliakim the son of Hilkiah, who was over the household, and Shebnah the scribe, and Joah the son of Asaph the recorder.

19 And Rabshakeh said unto them, Say ye now to Hezekiah, Thus saith the great king, the king of Assyria, What confidence is this wherein thou trustest? 20 Thou sayest (but they are but vain words), *There is* counsel and strength for the war. Now on whom dost thou trust, that thou hast rebelled against me? 21 Now, behold, thou trustest upon the staff of this bruised reed, even upon Egypt; whereon if a man lean, it will go into his hand, and pierce it: so is Pharaoh king of Egypt unto all that trust on him. 22 But if ye say unto me, We trust in Jehovah our God; is not that he, whose high places and whose altars Hezekiah hath taken away, and hath said to Judah and to Jerusalem, Ye shall worship before this altar in Jerusalem? 23 Now therefore, I pray thee, give pledges to my master the king of Assyria, and I will give thee two thousand horses, if thou be able on thy part to set riders upon them. 24 How then canst thou turn away the face of one captain of the least of my master's servants, and put thy trust on Egypt for chariots and for horsemen? 25 Am I now come up without Jehovah against this place to destroy it? Jehovah said unto me, Go up against this land, and destroy it.

26 Then said Eliakim the son of Hilkiah, and Shebnah, and Joah, unto Rabshakeh, Speak, I pray thee, to thy servants in the Syrian language; for we understand it: and speak not with us in the Jews' language, in the ears of the people that are on the wall. 27 But Rabshakeh said unto them, Hath my master sent me to thy master, and to thee, to speak these words? *hath he* not *sent me* to the men that sit on the wall, to eat their own dung, and to drink their own water with you? 28 Then Rabshakeh stood, and cried with a loud voice in the Jews' language, and spake, saying, Hear ye the word of the great king, the king of Assyria. 29 Thus saith the king, Let not Hezekiah deceive you; for he will not be able to deliver you out of his hand: 30

neither let Hezekiah make you trust in Jehovah, saying, Jehovah will surely deliver us, and this city shall not be given into the hand of the king of Assyria. 31 Hearken not to Hezekiah: for thus saith the king of Assyria, Make your peace with me, and come out to me; and eat ye every one of his vine, and every one of his fig-tree, and drink ye every one the waters of his own cistern; 32 until I come and take you away to a land like your own land, a land of grain and new wine, a land of bread and vineyards, a land of olive-trees and of honey, that ye may live, and not die: and hearken not unto Hezekiah, when he persuadeth you, saying, Jehovah will deliver us. 33 Hath any of the gods of the nations ever delivered his land out of the hand of the king of Assyria? 34 Where are the gods of Hamath, and of Arpad? where are the gods of Sepharvaim, of Hena, and Ivvah? have they delivered Samaria out of my hand? 35 Who are they among all the gods of the countries, that have delivered their country out of my hand, that Jehovah should deliver Jerusalem out of my hand?

36 But the people held their peace, and answered him not a word; for the king's commandment was, saying, Answer him not. 37 Then came Eliakim the son of Hilkiah, who was over the household, and Shebna the scribe, and Joah the son of Asaph the recorder, to Hezekiah with their clothes rent, and told him the words of Rabshakeh.

1 And it came to pass, when king Hezekiah heard it, that he rent his clothes, and covered himself with sackcloth, and went into the house of Jehovah. 2 And he sent Eliakim, who was over the household, and Shebna the scribe, and the elders of the priests, covered with sackcloth, unto Isaiah the prophet the son of Amoz. 3 And they said unto him, Thus saith Hezekiah, This day is a day of trouble, and of rebuke, and of contumely; for the children are come to the birth, and there is not strength to bring forth. 4 It may be Jehovah thy God will hear all the words of Rabshakeh, whom the king of Assyria his master hath sent to defy the living God, and will rebuke the words which Jehovah thy God hath heard: wherefore lift up thy prayer for the remnant that is left. 5 So the servants of king Hezekiah came to Isaiah. 6 And Isaiah said unto them, Thus shall ye say to your master, Thus saith Jehovah, Be not afraid of the words that thou hast heard, wherewith the servants of the king of Assyria have blasphemed me. 7 Behold, I will put a spirit in him, and he

shall hear tidings, and shall return to his own land; and I will cause him to fall by the sword in his own land.

8 So Rabshakeh returned, and found the king of Assyria warring against Libnah; for he had heard that he was departed from Lachish. 9 And when he heard say of Tirhakah king of Ethiopia, Behold, he is come out to fight against thee, he sent messengers again unto Hezekiah, saying, 10 Thus shall ye speak to Hezekiah king of Judah, saying, Let not thy God in whom thou trustest deceive thee, saying, Jerusalem shall not be given into the hand of the king of Assyria. 11 Behold, thou hast heard what the kings of Assyria have done to all lands, by destroying them utterly: and shalt thou be delivered? 12 Have the gods of the nations delivered them, which my fathers have destroyed, Gozan, and Haran, and Rezeph, and the children of Eden that were in Telassar? 13 Where is the king of Hamath, and the king of Arpad, and the king of the city of Sepharvaim, of Hena, and Ivvah?

14 And Hezekiah received the letter from the hand of the messengers, and read it; and Hezekiah went up unto the house of Jehovah, and spread it before Jehovah. 15 And Hezekiah prayed before Jehovah, and said, O Jehovah, the God of Israel, that sittest *above* the cherubim, thou art the God, even thou alone, of all the kingdoms of the earth; thou hast made heaven and earth. 16 Incline thine ear, O Jehovah, and hear; open thine eyes, O Jehovah, and see; and hear the words of Sennacherib, wherewith he hath sent him to defy the living God. 17 Of a truth, Jehovah, the kings of Assyria have laid waste the nations and their lands, 18 and have cast their gods into the fire; for they were no gods, but the work of men's hands, wood and stone; therefore they have destroyed them. 19 Now therefore, O Jehovah our God, save thou us, I beseech thee, out of his hand, that all the kingdoms of the earth may know that thou Jehovah art God alone.

20 Then Isaiah the son of Amoz sent to Hezekiah, saying, Thus saith Jehovah, the God of Israel, Whereas thou hast prayed to me against Sennacherib king of Assyria, I have heard *thee*. 21 This is the word that Jehovah hath spoken concerning him: The virgin daughter of Zion hath despised thee and laughed thee to scorn; the daughter of Jerusalem hath shaken her head at thee. 22 Whom hast thou defied and blasphemed? and against whom hast thou exalted thy voice and lifted up thine eyes on high? *even* against

the Holy One of Israel. 23 By thy messengers thou hast defied the Lord, and hast said, With the multitude of my chariots am I come up to the height of the mountains, to the innermost parts of Lebanon; and I will cut down the tall cedars thereof, and the choice fir-trees thereof; and I will enter into his farthest lodging-place, the forest of his fruitful field. 24 I have digged and drunk strange waters, and with the sole of my feet will I dry up all the rivers of Egypt.

25 Hast thou not heard how I have done it long ago, and formed it of ancient times? now have I brought it to pass, that it should be thine to lay waste fortified cities into ruinous heaps. 26 Therefore their inhabitants were of small power, they were dismayed and confounded; they were as the grass of the field, and as the green herb, as the grass on the housetops, and as grain blasted before it is grown up. 27 But I know thy sitting down, and thy going out, and thy coming in, and thy raging against me. 28 Because of thy raging against me, and because thine arrogancy is come up into mine ears, therefore will I put my hook in thy nose, and my bridle in thy lips, and I will turn thee back by the way by which thou camest.

29 And this shall be the sign unto thee: ye shall eat this year that which groweth of itself, and in the second year that which springeth of the same; and in the third year sow ye, and reap, and plant vineyards, and eat the fruit thereof. 30 And the remnant that is escaped of the house of Judah shall again take root downward, and bear fruit upward. 31 For out of Jerusalem shall go forth a remnant, and out of mount Zion they that shall escape: the zeal of Jehovah shall perform this. 32 Therefore thus saith Jehovah concerning the king of Assyria, He shall not come unto this city, nor shoot an arrow there, neither shall he come before it with shield, nor cast up a mound against it. 33 By the way that he came, by the same shall he return, and he shall not come unto this city, saith Jehovah. 34 For I will defend this city to save it, for mine own sake, and for my servant David's sake.

35 And it came to pass that night, that the angel of Jehovah went forth, and smote in the camp of the Assyrians a hundred fourscore and five thousand: and when men arose early in the morning, behold, these were all dead bodies. 36 So Sennacherib king of Assyria departed, and went and returned, and dwelt at Nineveh. 37 And it came to pass, as he

was worshipping in the house of Nisroch his god, that Adrammelech and Sharezer smote him with the sword: and they escaped into the land of Ararat. And Esar-haddon his son reigned in his stead.

Now in the fourteenth year of king Hezekiah did Sennacherib king of Assyria come up against all the fortified cities of Judah, and took them (v. 13). This campaign occurred in 701 B.C.[41] It moved southward along the coast, conquering Phoenicia and Philistia. The fortified cities of Judah were captured and Jerusalem was besieged.

Fully aware of the desperate peril of the city, Hezekiah sent to Sennacherib who was engaged at Lachish on the boundary between Judah and Philistia, and asked for peace (v. 14). Sennacherib's terms were so high that Hezekiah was compelled to give all of the wealth of the temple and the royal treasury (v. 16).

Unappeased and forced to reckon with Egyptian forces coming to Hezekiah's aid, Sennacherib demanded the surrender of Jerusalem (vv. 17, 21, 31). Hezekiah refused to surrender even though Sennacherib's messenger, Rabshakeh, boasted, Who are they among all the gods of the countries, that have delivered their country out of my hand, that Jehovah should deliver Jerusalem out of my hand? (v. 35).

Sennacherib had delivered his final ultimatum. Hezekiah knew that the crisis had reached the critical stage. He sent to the prophet Isaiah, This is a day of trouble, and of rebuke, and of contumely; for children are come to birth, and there is not strength to bring forth (v. 3). In the time of this grave crisis Judah did not have the needed resources.

Isaiah's reply reminded Hezekiah of the blasphemy of the Assyrians (v. 6). He then declared what God was about to do. I will put a spirit in him, and he shall hear tidings, and shall return to his own land (v. 7). "Panic in its various degrees was thought by the Hebrews to be the consequence of the spirit of God."[42] Isaiah declared that the invading supernatural influence would change Sennacherib's plans.

The crisis deepened by reason of a letter which Sennacherib sent to Heze-

kiah (vv. 9-13). In that time of trouble Hezekiah, instead of relying upon an alliance with Egypt, went up unto the house of Jehovah. . . . And Hezekiah prayed before Jehovah (vv. 14-15). Turning from the temptation to become entangled in foreign alliances, Hezekiah prayed. It was the most important activity in which he could engage. He had pursued other possibilities, such as help from Egypt, but he realized their futility. All of the nations, including Syria, Israel, Tyre, which had tried to ally themselves against Assyria had been conquered.

Rather than panic, Hezekiah prayed. The prayer consisted of three parts: (1) invocation (v. 15), (2) confession (vv. 16-18), and (3) supplication (v. 19). The invocation was addressed to the true God. The confession was a description of the need which Sennacherib had occasioned and the defiance which he had for the living God. The supplication was that God would save Jerusalem, not for Jerusalem's sake, but for the Lord's sake. O Jehovah our God, save thou us . . . that all the kingdoms of the earth may know that thou Jehovah art God alone (v. 19).

Isaiah sent a remarkable message to Hezekiah (vv. 20-34). It included both a sign of singular scorn for Sennacherib (vv. 20-28) and a sign of sovereign salvation for Jerusalem (vv. 29-34). The zeal of Jehovah shall perform this (v. 31). This was an extremely valuable emphasis set forth by Isaiah, for it stressed God's concern and activity in salvation. "The deliverance . . . of the people will not be due to any automatic working out of history, or to any natural or economic causes."[43] Rather, the deliverance will be accomplished by the living God. This is a perennial hope for all people.

That night the angel of Jehovah went forth, and smote in the camp of the Assyrians a hundred fourscore and five thousand (v. 35). Troubled Sennacherib was compelled to return to Nineveh, and Jerusalem was free, at least for a time.

C. HEZEKIAH'S RECOVERY FROM ILLNESS (20:1-11; cf. II Chron. 32:24)

1 In those days was Hezekiah sick unto death. And Isaiah the prophet the son of

---

[41] Bright, op. cit., p. 268.   [42] Gray, op. cit., p. 622.   [43] Snaith, op. cit., p. 303.

Amoz came to him, and said unto him, Thus saith Jehovah, Set thy house in order; for thou shalt die, and not live. 2 Then he turned his face to the wall, and prayed unto Jehovah, saying, 3 Remember now, O Jehovah, I beseech thee, how I have walked before thee in truth and with a perfect heart, and have done that which is good in thy sight. And Hezekiah wept sore. 4 And it came to pass, before Isaiah was gone out into the middle part of the city, that the word of Jehovah came to him, saying, 5 Turn back, and say to Hezekiah the prince of my people, Thus saith Jehovah, the God of David thy father, I have heard thy prayer, I have seen thy tears: behold, I will heal thee; on the third day thou shalt go up unto the house of Jehovah. 6 And I will add unto thy days fifteen years; and I will deliver thee and this city out of the hand of the king of Assyria; and I will defend this city for mine own sake, and for my servant David's sake. 7 And Isaiah said, Take a cake of figs. And they took and laid it on the boil, and he recovered.

8 And Hezekiah said unto Isaiah, What shall be the sign that Jehovah will heal me, and that I shall go up unto the house of Jehovah the third day? 9 And Isaiah said, This shall be the sign unto thee from Jehovah, that Jehovah will do the thing that he hath spoken: shall the shadow go forward ten steps, or go back ten steps? 10 And Hezekiah answered, It is a light thing for the shadow to decline ten steps: nay, but let the shadow return backward ten steps. 11 And Isaiah the prophet cried unto Jehovah; and he brought the shadow ten steps backward, by which it had gone down on the dial of Ahaz.

For some unrevealed reason, Hezekiah became **sick unto death** (v. 1). Isaiah informed him of the seriousness of his case and advised him to arrange his affairs. Doubtless this included designating his successor to the throne as well as providing for his family.

Hezekiah apparently looked upon his demise at this particular juncture in his life as divine punishment, for it was coming upon him while he was in the midst of his life and work. He shared the belief of his times that the wicked are punished by early death while the righteous are rewarded by long life.[44]

44 *Ibid.*, p. 305.

The illness was made a matter of prayer, and Hezekiah was healed. Moreover, he was given a sign; Jehovah **brought the shadow ten steps backward, by which it had gone down on the dial of Ahaz** (v. 11). It is impossible to explain this sign, but its symbolism is significant. Hezekiah's life was to be lengthened just as surely as the shadow climbed backward.

Hezekiah's illness holds an important lesson. Isaiah's announcement of Hezekiah's untimely death and its subsequent annulment were determined, not so much by a determinism beyond all control of Hezekiah, but rather by his relationship with God. From the standpoint of Hezekiah, it was his prayer that made possible the divine healing. Human responsibility and divine activity were involved.

D. HEZEKIAH'S RECEPTION OF THE BABYLONIANS (20:12-21; cf. II Chron. 32:31)

12 At that time Berodach-baladan the son of Baladan, king of Babylon, sent letters and a present unto Hezekiah; for he had heard that Hezekiah had been sick. 13 And Hezekiah hearkened unto them, and showed them all the house of his precious things, the silver, and the gold, and the spices, and the precious oil, and the house of his armor, and all that was found in his treasures: there was nothing in his house, nor in all his dominion, that Hezekiah showed them not. 14 Then came Isaiah the prophet unto king Hezekiah, and said unto him, What said these men? and from whence came they unto thee? And Hezekiah said, They are come from a far country, even from Babylon. 15 And he said, What have they seen in thy house? And Hezekiah answered, All that is in my house have they seen: there is nothing among my treasures that I have not showed them.

16 And Isaiah said unto Hezekiah, Hear the word of Jehovah. 17 Behold, the days come, that all that is in thy house, and that which thy fathers have laid up in store unto this day, shall be carried to Babylon: nothing shall be left, saith Jehovah. 18 And of thy sons that shall issue from thee, whom thou shalt beget, shall they take away; and they shall be eunuchs in the palace of the king of Babylon. 19 Then said Hezekiah unto Isaiah, Good is the word of Jehovah

which thou hast spoken. He said moreover, Is it not so, if peace and truth shall be in my days? 20 Now the rest of the acts of Hezekiah, and all his might, and how he made the pool, and the conduit, and brought water into the city, are they not written in the book of the chronicles of the kings of Judah? 21 And Hezekiah slept with his fathers; and Manasseh his son reigned in his stead.

This is a disquieting incident, for it shows Hezekiah lapsing into an attitude of pride. The Babylonians had come to Hezekiah for two reasons. The first was largely a pretext in order that the second might be accomplished without the Assyrians being aware of it. The pretext was Hezekiah's illness. The real reason was to form an alliance against Assyria.

Hezekiah was flattered by the suggestion of an alliance with Babylon. Self-confidently, he showed them his resources and treasures. However, Isaiah was disturbed and asked, **What have they seen in thy house?** (v. 15). He did not approve of Hezekiah's proud display to the Babylonians, for he saw that he was merely exchanging one enemy for another. He declared that Babylon would ultimately crush Jerusalem (v. 17).

Isaiah's question to Hezekiah is a haunting one. Hezekiah's great defense was not in weapons and treasures but in Jehovah. Yet, Hezekiah was delighted that the Babylonians were interested in what his kingdom could provide in an alliance. Isaiah saw the king's grievous error and rebuked him. Hezekiah was humbled, but the opportunity was gone. Babylon continued on its pagan course and returned to crush Jerusalem in about a century. Opportunities to give a faithful witness to the living God cannot be recalled. History cannot reverse itself, but it does produce a tragic harvest from neglected opportunities.

IV. THE SOUTHERN KINGDOM DURING THE FIRST HALF OF THE SEVENTH CENTURY (II Kings 21:1-26)

The reign of Manasseh was longer than that of any other of the Davidic kings. Assyria was at the peak of its power and influence at the time and brought the Southern Kingdom under its influence.

A. MANASSEH (21:1-18; cf. II Chron. 33:1-20)

1 Manasseh was twelve years old when he began to reign; and he reigned five and fifty years in Jerusalem: and his mother's name was Hephzibah. 2 And he did that which was evil in the sight of Jehovah, after the abominations of the nations whom Jehovah cast out before the children of Israel. 3 For he built again the high places which Hezekiah his father had destroyed; and he reared up altars for Baal, and made an Asherah, as did Ahab king of Israel, and worshipped all the host of heaven, and served them. 4 And he built altars in the house of Jehovah, whereof Jehovah said, In Jerusalem will I put my name. 5 And he built altars for all the host of heaven in the two courts of the house of Jehovah. 6 And he made his son to pass through the fire, and practised augury, and used enchantments, and dealt with them that had familiar spirits, and with wizards: he wrought much evil in the sight of Jehovah, to provoke him to anger. 7 And he set the graven image of Asherah, that he had made, in the house of which Jehovah said to David and to Solomon his son, In this house, and in Jerusalem, which I have chosen out of all the tribes of Israel, will I put my name for ever; 8 neither will I cause the feet of Israel to wander any more out of the land which I gave their fathers, if only they will observe to do according to all that I have commanded them, and according to all the law that my servant Moses commanded them. 9 But they hearkened not: and Manasseh seduced them to do that which is evil more than did the nations whom Jehovah destroyed before the children of Israel.

10 And Jehovah spake by his servants the prophets, saying, 11 Because Manasseh king of Judah hath done these abominations, and hath done wickedly above all that the Amorites did, that were before him, and hath made Judah also to sin with his idols; 12 therefore thus saith Jehovah, the God of Israel, Behold, I bring such evil upon Jerusalem and Judah, that whosoever heareth of it, both his ears shall tingle. 13 And I will stretch over Jerusalem the line of Samaria, and the plummet of the house of Ahab; and I will wipe Jerusalem as a man wipeth a dish, wiping it and turning it upside down. 14 And I will cast off the remnant of mine inheritance, and deliver them into the hand of their enemies; and they shall become a prey and a spoil to all their enemies; 15 because they have done

that which is evil in my sight, and have provoked me to anger, since the day their fathers came forth out of Egypt, even unto this day.

16 Moreover Manasseh shed innocent blood very much, till he had filled Jerusalem from one end to another; besides his sin wherewith he made Judah to sin, in doing that which was evil in the sight of Jehovah. 17 Now the rest of the acts of Manasseh, and all that he did, and his sin that he sinned, are they not written in the book of the chronicles of the kings of Judah? 18 And Manasseh slept with his fathers, and was buried in the garden of his own house, in the garden of Uzza: and Amon his son reigned in his stead.

The reign of Manasseh extended fifty-five years and has been described as "Judah's Dark Age."[45] For approximately half a century he promoted Baalism. **He reared up altars for Baal . . . as did Ahab king of Israel** (v. 3). He followed the astral cult of Assyria in that he **worshipped all the host of heaven, and served them** (v. 3). Doubtless he was under Assyrian pressure to do this. "As a vassal, Manasseh of course had to pay homage to his overlord's gods."[46] He even built altars to these astral deities in the temple of Jehovah (v. 5). Manasseh desired to appease Assyria, but he accomplished this only at terrible cost. Israel's distinctive worship of Jehovah, the only God, was in danger of being lost.

Prophets raised their voices in opposition to this apostasy. **And Jehovah spake by his servants the prophets** (v. 10). Yet there was a dearth of prophets, for not one single prophet can be identified by name as prophesying during the half-century reign of Manasseh. Doubtless Manasseh was merciless in his attempt to silence the word of Jehovah. **Moreover Manasseh shed innocent blood very much** (v. 16). He was denounced as the worst king of the Davidic line for whose sin, Jehovah declared, **I will wipe Jerusalem as a man wipeth a dish** (v. 13). Manasseh's reign was one of peace and his death came without violence, but judgment awaited the kingdom in another fifty years.

B. AMON (21:19-26; cf. II Chron. 33:21-25)

19 Amon was twenty and two years old when he began to reign; and he reigned two years in Jerusalem: and his mother's name was Meshullemeth the daughter of Haruz of Jotbah. 20 And he did that which was evil in the sight of Jehovah, as did Manasseh his father. 21 And he walked in all the way that his father walked in, and served the idols that his father served, and worshipped them: 22 and he forsook Jehovah, the God of his fathers, and walked not in the way of Jehovah. 23 And the servants of Amon conspired against him, and put the king to death in his own house. 24 But the people of the land slew all them that had conspired against king Amon; and the people of the land made Josiah his son king in his stead. 25 Now the rest of the acts of Amon which he did, are they not written in the book of the chronicles of the kings of Judah? 26 And he was buried in his sepulchre in the garden of Uzza: and Josiah his son reigned in his stead.

Amon ruled as his father Manasseh had done. After two years his courtiers conspired against him and killed him. The reason may have been political, since Egypt was gaining in power and posed as a possible threat to Assyrian occupancy of Palestine.

The people avenged Amon's death by putting the conspirators to death and making his son, Josiah, king (v. 24).

V. JOSIAH'S REIGN AND REFORMATION DURING THE SECOND HALF OF THE SEVENTH CENTURY (II Kings 22:1—23:30)

Josiah ruled thirty-one years in Jerusalem (640-609 B.C.). He was only eight years of age at the beginning of his reign (v. 1). This was because of the abbreviated reign of Amon, his father. On the international scene, Assyria was weakening as a world power. "Assyria, plagued by unrest at home, had quite lost effective control of the west and was no longer in a position to interfere."[47] The Southern Kingdom under King Josiah found itself free of foreign domination.

[45] Anderson, op. cit., p. 293.   [46] Bright, op. cit., p. 290.   [47] Ibid., p. 295.

A. JOSIAH'S TIMELY REFORM (22: 1—23:27)

Josiah's reform was outstanding in the history of the Southern Kingdom. "In the mind of the Bible writers it so far overshadowed all of Josiah's other royal acts that they tell us virtually nothing else about him."[48] The reform is described in three stages that may be likened to the stages of a tree: the root, the shoot, the fruit.

1. The Root of the Reform—Repair of the Temple (22:1-7; cf. II Chron. 34: 1-14)

1 Josiah was eight years old when he began to reign; and he reigned thirty and one years in Jerusalem: and his mother's name was Jedidah the daughter of Adaiah of Bozkath. 2 And he did that which was right in the eyes of Jehovah, and walked in all the way of David his father, and turned not aside to the right hand or to the left.

3 And it came to pass in the eighteenth year of king Josiah, that the king sent Shaphan, the son of Azaliah the son of Meshullam, the scribe, to the house of Jehovah, saying, 4 Go up to Hilkiah the high priest, that he may sum the money which is brought into the house of Jehovah, which the keepers of the threshold have gathered of the people: 5 and let them deliver it into the hand of the workmen that have the oversight of the house of Jehovah; and let them give it to the workmen that are in the house of Jehovah, to repair the breaches of the house, 6 unto the carpenters, and to the builders, and to the masons, and for buying timber and hewn stone to repair the house. 7 Howbeit there was no reckoning made with them of the money that was delivered into their hand; for they dealt faithfully.

The reform began in Josiah's eighteenth year, during the tenth year of his reign, when he proceeded to repair the temple. "The event on which all else in Josiah's reformation seems to hinge is the restoration of the temple."[49] In the course of repairs came the discovery of a copy of the Book of the Law. **Hilkiah the high priest said unto Shaphan the scribe, I have found the book of the law in the house of Jehovah** (v. 8).

It comes as a shock to learn that the law of God was lost in the house of God. When that happens, the situation has reached an extreme point of decadence. Both the temple and the law had been neglected and desecrated for the more than half-century rule of Manasseh and Amon.

2. The Shoot of the Reform— Reading the Book of the Law (22:8-20; cf. II Chron. 34:15-28)

8 And Hilkiah the high priest said unto Shaphan the scribe, I have found the book of the law in the house of Jehovah. And Hilkiah delivered the book to Shaphan, and he read it. 9 And Shaphan the scribe came to the king, and brought the king word again, and said, Thy servants have emptied out the money that was found in the house, and have delivered it into the hand of the workmen that have the oversight of the house of Jehovah. 10 And Shaphan the scribe told the king, saying, Hilkiah the priest hath delivered me a book. And Shaphan read it before the king. 11 And it came to pass, when the king had heard the words of the book of the law, that he rent his clothes. 12 And the king commanded Hilkiah the priest, and Ahikam the son of Shaphan, and Achbor the son of Micaiah, and Shaphan the scribe, and Isaiah the king's servant, saying, 13 Go ye, inquire of Jehovah for me, and for the people, and for all Judah, concerning the words of this book that is found; for great is the wrath of Jehovah that is kindled against us, because our fathers have not hearkened unto the words of this book, to do according unto all that which is written concerning us.

14 So Hilkiah the priest, and Ahikam, and Achbor, and Shaphan, and Isaiah, went unto Huldah the prophetess, the wife of Shallum the son of Tikvah, the son of Harhas, keeper of the wardrobe (now she dwelt in Jerusalem in the second quarter) ; and they communed with her. 15 And she said unto them, Thus saith Jehovah, the God of Israel: Tell ye the man that sent you unto me, 16 Thus saith Jehovah, Behold, I will bring evil upon this place, and upon the inhabitants thereof, even all the words of the book which the king of Judah hath read. 17 Because they have forsaken me, and have burned incense unto other gods, that they might provoke me to anger with all the work of their hands, therefore my wrath shall be kindled against

---

[48] *Ibid.*, pp. 295-96.   [49] Lumby, *op. cit.*, p. 225.

this place, and it shall not be quenched. 18 But unto the king of Judah, who sent you to inquire of Jehovah, thus shall ye say to him, Thus saith Jehovah, the God of Israel: As touching the words which thou hast heard, 19 because thy heart was tender, and thou didst humble thyself before Jehovah, when thou heardest what I spake against this place, and against the inhabitants thereof, that they should become a desolation and a curse, and hast rent thy clothes, and wept before me; I also have heard thee, saith Jehovah. 20 Therefore, behold, I will gather thee to thy fathers, and thou shalt be gathered to thy grave in peace, neither shall thine eyes see all the evil which I will bring upon this place. And they brought the king word again.

When the Book of the Law was read before the king, the activity which it generated was awesome. First, the king was penitent. The reading of the law revealed the ignorance of the king, for the law revealed how far the nation had departed from Jehovah and how perilous was its standing before Jehovah (vv. 11, 13).

Second, the prophetess Huldah prophesied that the desecration of the law carried its own judgment. **Because they have forsaken me ... therefore my wrath shall be kindled against this place, and it shall not be quenched** (v. 17). However, because Josiah was repentant, the prophetess promised that the judgment of the Lord would not come during his reign (v. 20).

3. **The Fruit of the Reform — Response to the Law (23:1-27; cf. II Chron. 34:29–35:19)**

1 And the king sent, and they gathered unto him all the elders of Judah and of Jerusalem. 2 And the king went up to the house of Jehovah, and all the men of Judah and all the inhabitants of Jerusalem with him, and the priests, and the prophets, and all the people, both small and great: and he read in their ears all the words of the book of the covenant which was found in the house of Jehovah. 3 And the king stood by the pillar, and made a covenant before Jehovah, to walk after Jehovah, and to keep his commandments, and his testimonies, and his statutes, with all *his* heart, and all *his* soul, to confirm the words of this covenant that were written in this book: and all the people stood to the covenant.

4 And the king commanded Hilkiah the high priest, and the priests of the second order, and the keepers of the threshold, to bring forth out of the temple of Jehovah all the vessels that were made for Baal, and for the Asherah, and for all the host of heaven; and he burned them without Jerusalem in the fields of the Kidron, and carried the ashes of them unto Beth-el. 5 And he put down the idolatrous priests, whom the kings of Judah had ordained to burn incense in the high places in the cities of Judah, and in the places round about Jerusalem; them also that burned incense unto Baal, to the sun, and to the moon, and to the planets, and to all the host of heaven. 6 And he brought out the Asherah from the house of Jehovah, without Jerusalem, unto the brook Kidron, and burned it at the brook Kidron, and beat it to dust, and cast the dust thereof upon the graves of the common people. 7 And he brake down the houses of the sodomites, that were in the house of Jehovah, where the women wove hangings for the Asherah. 8 And he brought all the priests out of the cities of Judah, and defiled the high places where the priests had burned incense, from Geba to Beer-sheba; and he brake down the high places of the gates that were at the entrance of the gate of Joshua the governor of the city, which were on a man's left hand at the gate of the city. 9 Nevertheless the priests of the high places came not up to the altar of Jehovah in Jerusalem, but they did eat unleavened bread among their brethren. 10 And he defiled Topheth, which is in the valley of the children of Hinnom, that no man might make his son or his daughter to pass through the fire to Molech. 11 And he took away the horses that the kings of Judah had given to the sun, at the entrance of the house of Jehovah, by the chamber of Nathan-melech the chamberlain, which was in the precincts; and he burned the chariots of the sun with fire. 12 And the altars that were on the roof of the upper chamber of Ahaz, which the kings of Judah had made, and the altars which Manasseh had made in the two courts of the house of Jehovah, did the king break down, and beat *them* down from thence, and cast the dust of them into the brook Kidron. 13 And the high places that were before Jerusalem, which were on the right hand of the mount of corruption, which Solomon the king of Israel had builded for Ashtoreth the abomination of the Sidonians, and for Chemosh the abomination of Moab, and for Milcom the abomination

of the children of Ammon, did the king defile. 14 And he brake in pieces the pillars, and cut down the Asherim, and filled their places with the bones of men.

15 Moreover the altar that was at Bethel, and the high place which Jeroboam the son of Nebat, who made Israel to sin, had made, even the altar and the high place he brake down; and he burned the high place and beat it to dust, and burned the Asherah. 16 And as Josiah turned himself, he spied the sepulchres that were there in the mount; and he sent, and took the bones out of the sepulchres, and burned them upon the altar, and defiled it, according to the word of Jehovah which the man of God proclaimed, who proclaimed these things. 17 Then he said, What monument is that which I see? And the men of the city told him, It is the sepulchre of the man of God, who came from Judah, and proclaimed these things that thou hast done against the altar of Bethel. 18 And he said, Let him be; let no man move his bones. So they let his bones alone, with the bones of the prophet that came out of Samaria. 19 And all the houses also of the high places that were in the cities of Samaria, which the kings of Israel had made to provoke *Jehovah* to anger, Josiah took away, and did to them according to all the acts that he had done in Beth-el. 20 And he slew all the priests of the high places that were there, upon the altars, and burned men's bones upon them; and he returned to Jerusalem.

21 And the king commanded all the people, saying, Keep the passover unto Jehovah your God, as it is written in this book of the covenant. 22 Surely there was not kept such a passover from the days of the judges that judged Israel, nor in all the days of the kings of Israel, nor of the kings of Judah; 23 but in the eighteenth year of king Josiah was this passover kept to Jehovah in Jerusalem.

24 Moreover them that had familiar spirits, and the wizards, and the teraphim, and the idols, and all the abominations that were seen in the land of Judah and in Jerusalem, did Josiah put away, that he might confirm the words of the law which were written in the book that Hilkiah the priest found in the house of Jehovah. 25 And like unto him was there no king before him, that turned to Jehovah with all his heart, and with all his soul, and with all his might, according to all the law of Moses; neither after him arose there any like him.

26 Notwithstanding, Jehovah turned not from the fierceness of his great wrath, wherewith his anger was kindled against Judah, because of all the provocations wherewith Manasseh had provoked him. 27 And Jehovah said, I will remove Judah also out of my sight, as I have removed Israel, and I will cast off this city which I have chosen, even Jerusalem, and the house of which I said, My name shall be there.

First of all, Josiah and the elders of the kingdom renewed the covenant of the law. **And the king ... made a covenant before Jehovah ... to keep his commandments ... and all the people stood to the covenant** (v. 3).

Second, Josiah performed the responsibilities which the covenant relationship demanded. Idolatry was removed and the shrines destroyed. "In general, he began in the temple, continued in Jerusalem, passed over to the Mount of Olives, and thence throughout the country."[50]

Third, the observance of the Passover was renewed according to the requirements of the Book of the Covenant (v. 21). It had been long neglected, but Josiah gave it national significance.

B. JOSIAH'S UNTIMELY DEATH (23: 28-30; cf. II Chron. 35:20-24)

28 Now the rest of the acts of Josiah, and all that he did, are they not written in the book of the chronicles of the kings of Judah? 29 In his days Pharaoh-necoh king of Egypt went up against the king of Assyria to the river Euphrates: and king Josiah went against him; and *Pharaoh-necoh* slew him at Megiddo, when he had seen him. 30 And his servants carried him in a chariot dead from Megiddo, and brought him to Jerusalem, and buried him in his own sepulchre. And the people of the land took Jehoahaz the son of Josiah, and anointed him, and made him king in his father's stead.

As long as Josiah ruled, the reform movement was maintained. However, a certain measure of doubt hangs over the effectiveness of it, largely because of the silence of the very important prophet, Jeremiah, who was contemporary with Josiah. Apparently, the reform lacked in-

---

[50] Snaith, *op. cit.*, p. 320.

ner depth despite its outer breadth. Its stress on form and ceremony may have resulted in superficiality.

Notwithstanding the kingdom reform, developments of international moment were swiftly reaching a climax. The Assyrian capital, Nineveh, was captured by the Babylonians and the Medes in 612 B. C. As a result, Babylon looked toward possession of Syria and Palestine, formerly dominated by Assyria. Egypt, however, hurried to support the remnants of Assyrian resistance.

Whether Josiah was tempted, as Hezekiah was a century earlier, to become an ally of Babylon is not known, but he certainly did not want an Egypto-Assyrian victory over Babylon. That would put him at the mercy of Egypt. He endeavored to block the Egyptians at Megiddo and was killed in battle in 609 B. C. His suicidal action was not significant in the international crisis, for the Egyptian monarch, Neco II, moved on to the Euphrates River. For the next few years, Egypt dominated all of Palestine and Syria. Meanwhile Jehoahaz, the son of Josiah, ruled in Jerusalem amid an impending crisis in which Egypt and Babylon were involved in the fortunes of Judah.

VI. THE LAST YEARS OF THE SOUTHERN KINGDOM (II Kings 23:31—25:30)

With Josiah's passing, the fortunes of the Southern Kingdom deteriorated rapidly. Egyptian control was seriously threatened by Babylon, and religious decline set in at Jerusalem.

A. EGYPTIAN DOMINATION (23:31-37; cf. II Chron. 36:1-4)

31 Jehoahaz was twenty and three years old when he began to reign; and he reigned three months in Jerusalem: and his mother's name was Hamutal the daughter of Jeremiah of Libnah. 32 And he did that which was evil in the sight of Jehovah, according to all that his fathers had done. 33 And Pharaoh-necoh put him in bonds at Riblah in the land of Hamath, that he might not reign in Jerusalem; and put the land to the tribute of a hundred talents of silver, and a talent of gold. 34 And Pharaoh-necoh made Eliakim the son of Josiah king in the room of Josiah his father, and changed his name to Jehoiakim: but he took Jehoahaz away; and he came to Egypt, and died there. 35 And Jehoiakim gave the silver and the gold to Pharaoh; but he taxed the land to give the money according to the commandment of Pharaoh: he exacted the silver and the gold of the people of the land, of every one according to his taxation, to give it unto Pharaoh-necoh.

36 Jehoiakim was twenty and five years old when he began to reign; and he reigned eleven years in Jerusalem: and his mother's name was Zebidah the daughter of Pedaiah of Rumah. 37 And he did that which was evil in the sight of Jehovah, according to all that his fathers had done.

For a few years, that is, between 609 and 605 B. C., Egypt's control extended over Palestine and Syria. Although Josiah was succeeded by his son Jehoahaz, the Egyptian monarch dethroned him within three months, presumably because he endeavored to continue Josiah's policies of political nationalism.

His brother, Eliakim, whose name Neco changed to Jehoiakim, was placed on the throne, and he ruled eleven years (vv. 34, 36). Jehoiakim remained a vassal of Neco. His rule was vigorously opposed by the prophet Jeremiah.

B. BABYLONIAN INVASION (24:1—25:21)

In 605 B. C. Egyptian control of Palestine and Syria ended with a decisive defeat at Carchemish on the Euphrates River. The power of Babylon moved southward, and Egyptian forces retreated to the homeland.

1. First Stage (24:1-7; cf. II Chron. 37:5-8)

1 In his days Nebuchadnezzar king of Babylon came up, and Jehoiakim became his servant three years: then he turned and rebelled against him. 2 And Jehovah sent against him bands of the Chaldeans, and bands of the Syrians, and bands of the Moabites, and bands of the children of Ammon, and sent them against Judah to destroy it, according to the word of Jehovah, which he spake by his servants the prophets. 3 Surely at the commandment of Jehovah came this upon Judah, to remove them out of his sight, for the

sins of Manasseh, according to all that he did, 4 and also for the innocent blood that he shed; for he filled Jerusalem with innocent blood: and Jehovah would not pardon. 5 Now the rest of the acts of Jehoiakim, and all that he did, are they not written in the book of the chronicles of the kings of Judah? 6 So Jehoiakim slept with his fathers; and Jehoiachin his son reigned in his stead. 7 And the king of Egypt came not again any more out of his land; for the king of Babylon had taken, from the brook of Egypt unto the river Euphrates, all that pertained to the king of Egypt.

Jehoiakim was compelled to admit the sovereignty of Nebuchadnezzar. He remained subject for three years and then rebelled (v. 1). It proved to be a fatal error, for Nebuchadnezzar ordered Judah to be destroyed (v. 2). The Kings account inserts the dimension of judgment at this point. **Surely at the commandment of Jehovah came this upon Judah; to remove them out of his sight, for the sins of Manasseh** (v. 3).

2. Second Stage (24:8-17; cf. II Chron. 36:9, 10)

8 Jehoiachin was eighteen years old when he began to reign; and he reigned in Jerusalem three months: and his mother's name was Nehushta the daughter of El-nathan of Jerusalem. 9 And he did that which was evil in the sight of Jehovah, according to all that his father had done. 10 At that time the servants of Nebuchadnezzar king of Babylon came up to Jerusalem, and the city was besieged. 11 And Nebuchadnezzar king of Babylon came unto the city, while his servants were besieging it; 12 and Jehoiachin the king of Judah went out to the king of Babylon, he, and his mother, and his servants, and his princes, and his officers: and the king of Babylon took him in the eighth year of his reign. 13 And he carried out thence all the treasures of the house of Jehovah, and the treasures of the king's house, and cut in pieces all the vessels of gold, which Solomon king of Israel had made in the temple of Jehovah, as Jehovah had said. 14 And he carried away all Jerusalem, and all the princes, and all the mighty men of valor, even ten thousand captives, and all the craftsmen and the smiths; none remained, save the poorest sort of the people of the land. 15 And he carried away Jehoiachin to Babylon; and the king's mother, and the king's wives, and his officers, and the chief men of the land, carried he into captivity from Jerusalem to Babylon. 16 And all the men of might, even seven thousand, and the craftsmen and the smiths a thousand, all of them strong and apt for war, even them the king of Babylon brought captive to Babylon. 17 And the king of Babylon made Mattaniah, *Jehoiachin's* father's brother, king in his stead, and changed his name to Zedekiah.

In 598 B. C. Nebuchadnezzar marched the Babylonian army toward Judah. Jehoiakim died before Nebuchadnezzar arrived, presumably assassinated. His son, Jehoiachin, became ruler in Judah, but ruled only three months and surrendered to Nebuchadnezzar (v. 8). Jehoiachin, his mother, important officials and leading citizens, together with many of the treasures of Judah, were carried to Babylon (vv. 13-15). Zedekiah was placed on the throne (v. 17).

3. Third Stage (24:18—25:21; cf. II Chron. 36:11-21)

18 Zedekiah was twenty and one years old when he began to reign; and he reigned eleven years in Jerusalem: and his mother's name was Hamutal the daughter of Jeremiah of Libnah. 19 And he did that which was evil in the sight of Jehovah, according to all that Jehoiakim had done. 20 For through the anger of Jehovah did it come to pass in Jerusalem and Judah, until he had cast them out from his presence.

And Zedekiah rebelled against the king of Babylon. 1 And it came to pass in the ninth year of his reign, in the tenth month, in the tenth day of the month, that Nebuchadnezzar king of Babylon came, he and all his army, against Jerusalem, and encamped against it; and they built forts against it round about. 2 So the city was besieged unto the eleventh year of king Zedekiah. 3 On the ninth day of the *fourth* month the famine was sore in the city, so that there was no bread for the people of the land. 4 Then a breach was made in the city, and all the men of war *fled* by night by the way of the gate between the two walls, which was by the king's garden (now the Chaldeans were against the city round about) ; and *the king* went by the way of the Arabah. 5 But the army of the Chaldeans pursued after the king, and overtook him in the plains of Jericho; and all his army was scattered from him. 6 Then they took the king, and carried him up unto the king of Babylon to Riblah; and they gave judgment upon him. 7 And they slew the sons of Zedekiah before his eyes, and put out the eyes of Zedekiah, and bound him in fetters, and carried him to Babylon.

8 Now in the fifth month, on the seventh day of the month, which was the nineteenth year of king Nebuchadnezzar, king of Babylon, came Nebuzaradan the captain of the guard, a servant of the king of Babylon, unto Jerusalem. 9 And he burnt the house of Jehovah, and the king's house; and all the houses of Jerusalem, even every great house, burnt he with fire. 10 And all the army of the Chaldeans, that were *with* the captain of the guard, brake down the walls of Jerusalem round about. 11 And the residue of the people that were left in the city, and those that fell away, that fell to the king of Babylon, and the residue of the multitude, did Nebuzaradan the captain of the guard carry away captive. 12 But the captain of the guard left of the poorest of the land to be vinedressers and husbandmen.

13 And the pillars of brass that were in the house of Jehovah, and the bases and the brazen sea that were in the house of Jehovah, did the Chaldeans break in pieces, and carried the brass of them to Babylon. 14 And the pots, and the shovels, and the snuffers, and the spoons, and all the vessels of brass wherewith they ministered, took they away. 15 And the firepans, and the basins, that which was of gold, in gold, and that which was of silver, in silver, the captain of the guard took away. 16 The two pillars, the one sea, and the bases, which Solomon had made for the house of Jehovah, the brass of all these vessels was without weight. 17 The height of the one pillar was eighteen cubits, and a capital of brass was upon it; and the height of the capital was three cubits, with network and pomegranates upon the capital round about, all of brass: and like unto these had the second pillar with network.

18 And the captain of the guard took Seraiah the chief priest, and Zephaniah the second priest, and the three keepers of the threshold: 19 and out of the city he took an officer that was set over the men of war; and five men of them that saw the king's face, who were found in the city;

and the scribe, the captain of the host, who mustered the people of the land; and threescore men of the people of the land that were found in the city. 20 And Nebuzaradan the captain of the guard took them, and brought them to the king of Babylon to Riblah. 21 And the king of Babylon smote them, and put them to death at Riblah in the land of Hamath. So Judah was carried away captive out of his land.

Jehoiakim's rule and abortive revolt against Nebuchadnezzar had brought a major crisis to Judah within a quarter of a century after the impressive resurgence under Josiah, Judah's great reformer. Certain chief cities such as Lachish had been severely damaged. The economy had declined sharply and the population reduced greatly.

Zedekiah profited very little, if any, from the bitter experiences of Jehoiakim. Although he ruled eleven years, a number of those years were devoted to conniving plots to gain independence. Jeremiah consistently repudiated Zedekiah's revolutionary ambitions.

Finally, rebellion broke out, and Zedekiah declared independence from Babylon. Babylonian reaction was immediate and catastrophic. A systematic conquest of city after city was begun in 588 B.C. (v. 1). Finally, Jerusalem lay under siege. In 587 B. C. the Babylonians breached the walls and captured the city (v. 4). Zedekiah was captured, blinded and taken to Babylon (vv. 6-7). A month later Jerusalem was burned and its walls wrecked (vv. 9-10). Certain important officers and citizens were executed (vv. 18-21). **So Judah was carried away captive out of his land** (v. 21).

C. GEDALIAH ASSASSINATED (25:22-26)

22 And as for the people that were left in the land of Judah, whom Nebuchadnezzar king of Babylon had left, even over them he made Gedaliah the son of Ahikam, the son of Shaphan, governor. 23 Now when all the captains of the forces, they and their men, heard that the king of Babylon had made Gedaliah governor, they came to Gedaliah to Mizpah, even

Ishmael the son of Nethaniah, and Johanan the son of Kareah, and Seraiah the son of Tanhumeth the Netophathite, and Jaazaniah the son of the Maacathite, they and their men. 24 And Gedaliah sware to them and to their men, and said unto them, Fear not because of the servants of the Chaldeans: dwell in the land, and serve the king of Babylon, and it shall be well with you. 25 But it came to pass in the seventh month, that Ishmael the son of Nethaniah, the son of Elishama of the seed royal, came, and ten men with him, and smote Gedaliah, so that he died, and the Jews and the Chaldeans that were with him at Mizpah. 26 And all the people, both small and great, and the captains of the forces, arose, and came to Egypt; for they were afraid of the Chaldeans.

After the destruction of Jerusalem, the land was made a province of Babylon and Gedaliah was made governor. His seat of government was apparently at Mizpah (v. 23). However, the effort was a failure, for within a year he was assassinated (v. 25).

D. JEHOIACHIN GRANTED CLEMENCY (25:27-30)

27 And it came to pass in the seven and thirtieth year of the captivity of Jehoiachin king of Judah, in the twelfth month, on the seven and twentieth day of the month, that Evilmerodach king of Babylon, in the year that he began to reign, did lift up the head of Jehoiachin king of Judah out of prison; 28 and he spake kindly to him, and set his throne above the throne of the kings that were with him in Babylon, 29 and changed his prison garments. And *Jehoiachin* did eat bread before him continually all the days of his life: 30 and for his allowance, there was a continual allowance given him of the king, every day a portion, all the days of his life.

The Kings account closes on the optimistic note of clemency for Jehoiachin. After thirty-seven years of captivity, he was released from prison and restored to favor (vv. 27-28). Evil-merodach had succeeded Nebuchadnezzar as ruler of Babylon, and this deed marked a distinct policy change in Babylon.

Bibliography

I. Exegetical and Historical Value

Albright, W. F. *From the Stone Age to Christianity*. Garden City, N. Y.: Doubleday, 1957.

Anderson, B. *Understanding the Old Testament*. Englewood Cliffs, N. J.: Prentice-Hall, 1957.

Bahr, The Rev. Dr. *The Book of Kings*. "Commentary on the Holy Scriptures." Ed. John Peter Lange. Reprint. Grand Rapids: Zondervan, n.d.

Bright, John. *A History of Israel*. Philadelphia: Westminster, 1951.

Burney, C. F. "Kings, I and II." *A Dictionary of the Bible*. Ed. J. Hastings. Vol. II. New York: Scribner, 1902.

Clarke, Adam. *Commentary and Critical Notes*. Vol. II. New York and Nashville: Abingdon, n.d.

Crockett, W. D. *A Harmony of the Books of Samuel, Kings and Chronicles*. Grand Rapids: Baker, rep., 1951.

Davies, T. W. "Temple." *Hastings Dictionary of the Bible*. Vol. IV. New York: Scribner: 1902.

Ellison, H. L. "I and II Kings." *The New Bible Commentary*. Eds. F. Davidson *et al.* Grand Rapids: Eerdmans, 1953.

Gordon, Cyrus H. *Introduction to Old Testament Times*. Ventnor, 1953.

Gray, John. *I and II Kings*. Philadelphia: Westminster, 1963.

Kaufmann, Yehezhel. *The Religion of Israel From Its Beginning to the Babylonian Exile*. Trans. and abr. by M. Greenberg. Chicago: University of Chicago, 1960.

Lumby, J. R. "The First Book of Kings." *The Cambridge Bible for Schools and Colleges*. Ed. J. J. S. Perowne. Cambridge: University Press, 1896.

————. "The Second Book of Kings." *The Cambridge Bible for Schools and Colleges*. Ed. J. J. S. Perowne. Cambridge: University Press, 1889.

Montgomery, J. A. and H. S. Gehman. "The Book of Kings." *International Critical Commentary*. Edinburgh: T. and T. Clark, 1951.

Pritchard, J. B. *The Ancient Near East: An Anthology of Texts and Pictures*. Princeton: University Press, 1958.

Schultz, Samuel. *The Old Testament Speaks*. New York: Harper, 1960.

Simpson, D. C. "First and Second Kings." *The Abingdon Bible Commentary*. Eds. F. C. Eiselen, E. Lewis, D. G. Downey. New York and Nashville: Abingdon-Cokesbury, 1929.

Skinner, John. "Kings." *The New Century Bible*. New York: Oxford, 1904.

Smith, G. A. *The Historical Geography of the Holy Land*. London: Hodder and Stoughton, 1935.

Snaith, Norman H. "The First and Second Books of Kings: Introduction and Exegesis." *The Interpreter's Bible*. Eds. G. A. Buttrick *et al.* Vol. III. New York and Nashville: Abingdon, 1954.

Thiele, Edwin. *The Mysterious Numbers of the Hebrew Kings*. Chicago: University of Chicago, 1951.

Waite, J. C. J. "Books of Kings." *The New Bible Dictionary*. Eds. J. D. Douglas *et al.* Grand Rapids: Eerdmans, 1962.

Wright, G. E. and F. V. Filson (eds.). *The Westminster Historical Atlas*. Philadelphia: Westminster, 1945.

II. Expository and Practical Value

Calkins, Raymond. "Exposition of II Kings." *The Interpreter's Bible*. Eds. G. A. Buttrick *et al.* Vol. III. New York and Nashville: Abingdon, 1954.

Edersheim, Alfred. *History of Israel and Judah From the Birth of Solomon to the Reign of Ahab*. New York: Revell, 1880.

————. *History of Israel and Judah From the Reign of Ahab to the Decline of the Two Kingdoms*. New York: Revell, 1885.

————. *History of Israel and Judah From the Decline of the Two Kingdoms to the Assyrian and Babylonian Captivity*. New York: Revell, 1887.

Farrar, F. W. "The First Book of Kings." *The Expositor's Bible*. Ed. W. Robertson Nicoll. Vol. II. Reprint. Grand Rapids: Eerdmans, 1940.

———. "The Second Book of Kings." *The Expositor's Bible.* Ed. W. Robertson Nicoll. Vol. II. Reprint. Grand Rapids: Eerdmans, 1940.

Sockman, Ralph W. "Exposition of I Kings." *The Interpreter's Bible.* Eds. G. A. Buttrick *et al.* Vol. III. New York and Nashville: Abingdon, 1954.

Thompson, J. A. "I and II Kings." *The Biblical Expositor.* Ed. Carl F. H. Henry. Vol. I. Philadelphia: Holman, 1960.

The First Book of Chronicles

by Charles R. Wilson

Outline

Introduction

Besides the historical writings of the "prophets," namely, Joshua, Judges, Samuel and Kings, there appear other historical writings in the Old Testament, namely, Ruth, Esther, Ezra, Nehemiah and Chronicles. In the Hebrew Bible the historical writings of the prophets appear under the second group of Old Testament books, "the Prophets," while the other historical writings appear under the third group, "the Writings." In the third century B.C. the Greek Septuagint revised the threefold grouping of Old Testament books of "Law," "Prophets," and "Writings" and, among other changes, grouped all the historical books together. Ruth was placed between Judges and Samuel because it contained a story related to the period of the judges. Chronicles, Ezra, Nehemiah and Esther were placed after Kings. English Bibles follow the order of the Septuagint rather than the Hebrew Bible in the arrangement of these historical books.

I. TITLE

In the earliest Hebrew manuscripts, Chronicles was considered one book entitled "Events of the Times." In the Greek Septuagint, the book was placed after Kings and divided into two parts called "Supplements," inasmuch as they were considered supplementary to the Kings. In the Latin Vulgate of the fourth century A.D., the title was changed to *Chronicorum,* from which has been derived the English title, "Chronicles."

The evidence appears conclusive that an original unity of Chronicles, Ezra and Nehemiah existed. "There is general agreement that all three (four) books were originally one work."[1]

An important corollary of this general agreement is that the majority of scholars assign the date of these writings between the last half of the fourth and the first half of the third century B.C.

However, if credence be given the idea that this work was written as soon as possible after the success of the separation policy instituted under Ezra and Nehemiah, just as Kings was written in the afterglow of the success and prosperity of Josiah, then it is preferable to consider a date very soon after the date for the separation policy, namely, the latter third of the fifth century B.C.[2]

II. PURPOSE

Chronicles is post-exilic in origin and, consequently, reflects the post-exilic period. Far-reaching crises had occurred in the community of Israel since the reign of David during the tenth century B.C., some six hundred to seven hundred years earlier. There was the catastrophic division of the kingdom in the latter part of the tenth century B.C., with the Northern Kingdom disintegrating in slightly over two hundred years, 721 B.C. There was the disastrous collapse of the Southern Kingdom in the sixth century B. C. The period of exile in Babylon during the sixth century B.C. was followed by the momentous return of a remnant and the building of a second temple. Hope mounted high as the sixth century came to a close.

After a period of lesser significance, other Jews returned from the exile in Babylon to Jerusalem. There were few barriers between the Jews of the returning exiles and the inhabitants of the surrounding countries. As a result, a definite amalgamating process developed. During

---

[1] N. H. Snaith, "The Historical Books," *The Old Testament and Modern Study,* ed. H. H. Rowley, p. 107. Reasons favoring the common authorship of Chronicles, Ezra, and Nehemiah are considered at length by E. L. Curtis and A. A. Madsen, "The Books of Chronicles," *The International Critical Commentary,* pp. 3-5.

[2] *Ibid.,* p. 108.

the latter part of the fifth century B.C. there came from Babylon two important personalities who instituted reform and separatism. This movement continued under their leadership into the fourth century B.C.

In the aftermath of the results achieved during these post-exilic reforms, the chronicler wrote for the post-exilic Jewish community which considered Jerusalem and its temple the center of Jewry. The community centered everything in the temple worship and the written law. While it was no longer possible to consider Jerusalem as the center and capital of an independent kingdom, it was possible to establish it as the center of a religious community. It was this post-exilic religious community and its Levitical order that was the primary concern of the chronicler.

He had at least two objectives in writing the pre-exilic history of this community. The first objective was to show that God had carried forward His great purpose for Israel through the Southern Kingdom and the Davidic dynasty. The northern territory, during the time of the chronicler, was inhabited by Samaritans, a people of mixed traditions who considered themselves true descendants of pre-exilic Israel. The chronicler's viewpoint was that the Southern Kingdom was the true pre-exilic Israel, and Jerusalem was the holy city of God and His people. Attention centered upon the Davidic kings as well as the temple and its Levitical institutions.

The second objective was to reveal that God blessed those who worshiped Him according to the requirements of the law but chastened those who defected in their worship. True Jehovah-worship had been instituted in Jerusalem, and the law had ordained the Levitical establishment. As the chronicler wrote the pre-exilic history of Israel, he held up to his contemporaries the history of the past in order that it might be a mirror in which they might behold the gracious results which follow obedience and the dire consequences which follow disobedience. From the Levitical point of view, obedience rested fundamentally on observances of the Levitical order of worship and the moral requirements of the law.

III. HISTORICAL CHARACTER

Chronicles is written from a practical point of view. Israel's history is narrated in such a way as to teach specific lessons. By itself, Chronicles gives an unbalanced view of Israel's history. For example, it is weighted in favor of the Davidic kingdom, while the Northern Kingdom is largely ignored. It is also weighted in favor of the Levitical ceremonial worship at the temple, as compared with the prophetic demand for moral righteousness before the Lord of heaven and earth.

Nevertheless, it is clear that the chronicler took it for granted that his readers had a knowledge of the content of Samuel and Kings. He was not intent upon writing the history of Israel from the same viewpoint as the writers of those histories, which depicted impartially the good as well as the bad. The prophetic tradition resolutely showed the unvarnished truth regarding Israel's history. The chronicler had more hortatory aims, for he intently endeavored to show the Jewish community of his day how it could prosper under the blessing of Jehovah. He drew from the pre-exilic history of Israel those features which made possible the accomplishment of his aims.

There are problems concerned with the historical accuracy of the Chronicles account. There are apparent discrepancies between Chronicles and Samuel and Kings unresolved at present. There are problems regarding statistics recorded in the Chronicles. Notwithstanding these difficulties, there is an authentication of the historical character of Chronicles. The book is not to be written off as a fanciful interpretation of Israel's history. Rather, it is to be considered as a deeply religious view of God's activity in history, an activity that includes elements of both grace and judgment.

IV. MORAL AND SPIRITUAL VALUE

Chronicles is a remarkable book when studied from the standpoint of the chronicler. There are two values to be gained in following this pattern of study. The first is the apprehension of a clearly delineated religious view of history. The second is the appreciation for an institutionally oriented manner of worship which is acceptable to God.

A. A RELIGIOUS VIEW OF HISTORY

While Chronicles contains the account of Israel from the time of David until the collapse of the kingdom, the account is rightly understood only if it has conveyed the fundamental belief held by the chronicler that God is active in the ongoing history of His people. Again and again, when there was triumph or tragedy in Israel's history, the chronicler went behind the scenes in search for the religious causes involved. On occasions of triumph, he found the underlying cause was invariably religious obedience; on occasions of tragedy, the cause was disobedience. For the chronicler, God was the ultimate explanation for the triumph as well as for the tragedy.

This religious view of history, in which there is astute awareness that God is active in history, may be vigorously challenged in this modern era. The trend toward a naturalistic view of history is a very strong rival. Such a view affirms that all causes are natural causes, and all other explanations are superstitions.

The chronicler's religious view attests to belief in the realm of the supernatural. The transcendent God has injected into history a moral and spiritual dimension which cannot be ignored with impunity.

This supernaturalistic view of history may not provide the total solution to the problem of prosperity and perversity, but it affords the most important ingredients in any solution. The chronicler's insistence that we learn to order our lives before God on the basis of the lessons from the past is of great concern to everyone.

B. AN ACCEPTABLE MANNER OF WORSHIP

The worship of Jehovah at the temple in Jerusalem was, for the chronicler, the only acceptable worship of God. This had been made clear in the history of Israel. Consequently, worship of God was to be through prescribed forms and in a prescribed manner. Essentially nothing was left to spontaneity and enthusiasm. The law gave minute prescriptions regarding the acceptable manner of worship.

There is perennial value in this, although free churches largely ignore this fact. Such omission has effects which have not been wholesome by any means. It is imperative that worshipers of the most high God give the chronicler a serious hearing in order that they may be "doers of the word."

Christian ministers and their congregations need a liturgical concern. Chronicles is a biblical source for giving impetus to such a concern. Our worship cannot be left to be developed according to our fancy. Rather, it must conform to divine requirements. Judgment which is not even recognized as judgment has visited many congregations and many worshipers because of unacceptable worship.

One of the enduring values of Chronicles is the religious emphasis given to the institutional forms of religion. Religious life depends upon forms, ceremonies and institutions. Any emphasis upon the individual and his religion must not be at the expense of the religious institution and its significance for acceptable worship.

Commentary on First Chronicles

I. GENEALOGIES WITH MAJOR INTEREST IN THE DAVIDIC AND THE LEVITICAL LINES (I Chron. 1:1–9:44)

The first nine chapters of the Chronicles account occupy themselves with genealogical information. This genealogical interest is based upon a profound and sacred regard for the political institution of the Davidic dynasty and the religious institution of the Levitical priesthood.

A. GENEALOGIES FROM GENESIS (1:1–2:2)

The chronicler assumed that his readers had a familiarity with the genealogies in Genesis.

1. From Adam to Abraham (1:1-27)

1 Adam, Seth, Enosh, 2 Kenan, Mahalalel, Jared, 3 Enoch, Methuselah, Lamech, 4 Noah, Shem, Ham, and Japheth.
5 The sons of Japheth: Gomer, and Magog, and Madai, and Javan, and Tubal, and Meshech, and Tiras. 6 And the sons of Gomer: Ashkenaz, and Diphath, and Togarmah. 7 And the sons of Javan: Elishah, and Tarshish, Kittim, and Rodanim.
8 The sons of Ham: Cush, and Mizraim, Put, and Canaan. 9 And the sons of Cush: Seba, and Havilah, and Sabta, and Raama, and Sabteca. And the sons of Raamah: Sheba, and Dedan. 10 And Cush begat Nimrod; he began to be a mighty one in the earth. 11 And Mizraim begat Ludim, and Anamim, and Lehabim, and Naphtuhim, 12 and Pathrusim, and Casluhim (from whence came the Philistines), and Caphtorim. 13 And Canaan begat Sidon his first-born, and Heth, 14 and the Jebusite, and the Amorite, and the Girgashite, 15 and the Hivite, and the Arkite, and the Sinite, 16 and the Arvadite, and the Zemarite, and the Hamathite.
17 The sons of Shem: Elam, and Asshur, and Arpachshad, and Lud, and Aram, and Uz, and Hul, and Gether, and Meshech. 18 And Arpachshad begat Shelah, and Shelah begat Eber. 19 And unto Eber were born two sons: the name of the one was Peleg; for in his days the earth was divided; and his brother's name was Joktan. 20 And Joktan begat Almodad, and Sheleph, and Hazarmaveth, and Jerah, 21 and Hadoram, and Uzal, and Diklah, 22 and Ebal, and Abimael, and Sheba, 23 and Ophir, and Havilah, and Jobab. All these were the sons of Joktan.
24 Shem, Arpachshad, Shelah, 25 Eber, Peleg, Reu, 26 Serug, Nahor, Terah, 27 Abram (the same is Abraham).

The genealogies begin with Adam, created in the image of God and the source of all races. The chronicler, though avowedly concentrating upon the Davidic line and the Levitical families, by beginning with Adam, reveals an awareness of the Creator-God and the common bond of all races. Because of this beginning, all the tables which follow imply that the chronicler believed an invaluable service could be rendered to God and humanity through the faithful preservation of the two revered institutions of Judah, the Davidic kingship and the Levitical priesthood. This profound regard for institutions as they minister through faithful service is valid. When, however, institutions demand undeviating loyalty at the expense of loyalty to God and concern for individuals their true purpose has been lost. Even the chronicler had to reckon with the tempting point of view which prefers the impersonal institution to the individual person. The tension of institutionalism versus individualism is a perennial tension and seems to be a part of the human predicament.

The genealogy from Adam to Abraham traces the line of Adam through Seth to Noah and his son Shem. Although there are digressions, these serve to complement the essential line of descent.

2. From Abraham to Judah (1:28—2:2)

28 The sons of Abraham: Isaac, and Ishmael. 29 These are their generations: the first-born of Ishmael, Nebaioth; then Kedar, and Adbeel, and Mibsam, 30 Mishma, and Dumah, Massa, Hadad, and Tema, 31 Jetur, Naphish, and Kedemah. These are the sons of Ishmael.

32 And the sons of Keturah, Abraham's concubine: she bare Zimran, and Jokshan, and Medan, and Midian, and Ishbak, and Shuah. And the sons of Jokshan: Sheba, and Dedan. 33 And the sons of Midian: Ephah, and Epher, and Hanoch, and Abida, and Eldaah. All these were the sons of Keturah.

34 And Abraham begat Isaac. The sons of Isaac: Esau, and Israel.

35 The sons of Esau: Eliphaz, Reuel, and Jeush, and Jalam, and Korah. 36 The sons of Eliphaz: Teman, and Omar, Zephi, and Gatam, Kenaz, and Timna, and Amalek. 37 The sons of Reuel: Nahath, Zerah, Shammah, and Mizzah.

38 And the sons of Seir: Lotan, and Shobal, and Zibeon, and Anah, and Dishon, and Ezer, and Dishan. 39 And the sons of Lotan: Hori, and Homam; and Timna was Lotan's sister. 40 The sons of Shobal: Alian, and Manahath, and Ebal, Shephi, and Onam. And the sons of Zibeon: Aiah, and Anah. 41 The sons Anah: Dishon. And the sons of Dishon: Hamran, and Eshban, and Ithran, and Cheran. 42 The sons of Ezer: Bilhan, and Zaavan, Jaakan. The sons of Dishan: Uz, and Aran.

43 Now these are the kings that reigned in the land of Edom, before there reigned any king over the children of Israel: Bela the son of Beor; and the name of his city was Dinhabah. 44 And Bela died, and Jobab the son of Zerah of Bozrah reigned in his stead. 45 And Jobab died, and Husham of the land of the Temanites reigned in his stead. 46 And Husham died, and Hadad the son of Bedad, who smote Midian in the field of Moab, reigned in his stead; and the name of his city was Avith. 47 And Hadad died, and Samlah of Masrekah reigned in his stead. 48 And Samlah died, and Shaul of Rehoboth by the River reigned in his stead. 49 And Shaul died, and Baal-hanan the son of Achbor reigned in his stead. 50 And Baal-hanan died, and Hadad reigned in his stead; and the name of his city was Pai: and his wife's name was Mehetabel,

the daughter of Matred, the daughter of Me-zahab. 51 And Hadad died.

And the chiefs of Edom were: chief Timna, chief Aliah, chief Jetheth, 52 chief Oholibamah, chief Elah, chief Pinon, 53 chief Kenaz, chief Teman, chief Mibzar, 54 chief Magdiel, chief Iram. These are the chiefs of Edom.

1 These are the sons of Israel: Reuben, Simeon, Levi, and Judah, Issachar, and Zebulun, 2 Dan, Joseph, and Benjamin, Naphtali, Gad, and Asher.

The line of descent from Abraham to Judah includes Isaac and Israel. However, there are digressions which include the descendants of Abraham by way of Ishmael and Keturah, and the descendants of Isaac by way of Esau.

B. GENEALOGY OF JUDAH AND SIMEON (2:3—4:43)

The tribe of Simeon lost its identity during the period of the judges. Judah more or less absorbed the tribal distinctives of Simeon until Simeon tended to cease to have a distinctive existence. Nevertheless, the chronicler faithfully preserved the genealogy of this tribe and, as a result, actually preserved its identity.

1. From Judah to David (2:3-17)

3 The sons of Judah: Er, and Onan, and Shelah; which three were born unto him of Shua's daughter the Canaanitess. And Er, Judah's first-born, was wicked in the sight of Jehovah; and he slew him. 4 And Tamar his daughter-in-law bare him Perez and Zerah. All the sons of Judah were five.

5 The sons of Perez: Hezron, and Hamul. 6 And the sons of Zerah: Zimri, and Ethan, and Heman, and Calcol, and Dara; five of them in all. 7 And the sons of Carmi: Achar, the troubler of Israel, who committed a trespass in the devoted thing. 8 And the sons of Ethan: Azariah.

9 The sons also of Hezron, that were born unto him: Jerahmeel, and Ram, and Chelubai. 10 And Ram begat Amminadab, and Amminadab begat Nahshon, prince of the children of Judah; 11 and Nahshon begat Salma, and Salma begat Boaz, 12 and Boaz begat Obed, and Obed begat Jesse; 13 and Jesse begat his first-born Eliab, and Abinadab the second, and Shimea the third, 14 Nethanel the fourth, Raddai the fifth, 15 Ozem the

sixth, David the seventh; 16 and their sisters were Zeruiah and Abigail. And the sons of Zeruiah: Abishai, and Joab, and Asahel, three. 17 And Abigail bare Amasa; and the father of Amasa was Jether the Ishmaelite.

The genealogy from Judah to David descends by way of Perez, the son of Judah, Boaz, Naomi's near kinsman who married Ruth the Moabitess, Obed, the first-born of Boaz and Ruth, and his son Jesse, who as well as being the grandson of Boaz and Ruth was also the father of David, Israel's most illustrious king.

The eldest son of Perez was Hezron (v. 5). The list of Hezron's descendants begins with verse 9. Of special importance in that list is the name **Chelubai** (v. 9). "Chelubai is a variant spelling of Caleb."[1] The name *Caleb* is used of the same man in verse 18. The interpretation of the identity of this man to a large extent affects the interpretation of the nationality of a large portion of the tribe of Judah.

One interpretation is that this man is Caleb the Kenezite (cf. Num. 13:6; Josh. 14:6; I Chron. 4:15).[2] Another is the assumption that this Caleb lived prior to Caleb the Kenezite, one of the twelve spies.[3] The first interpretation makes a considerable part of the tribe of Judah non-Israelite. The second assumes the existence of a Caleb in Judah heretofore unidentified. It is impossible to offer an unquestioned interpretation of this problem.

2. Descendants of Caleb and Jerahmeel (2:18-55)

18 And Caleb the son of Hezron begat *children* of Azubah *his* wife, and of Jerioth; and these were her sons: Jesher, and Shobab, and Ardon. 19 And Azubah died, and Caleb took unto him Ephrath, who bare him Hur. 20 And Hur begat Uri, and Uri begat Bezalel.

21 And afterward Hezron went in to the daughter of Machir the father of Gilead, whom he took *to wife* when he was threescore years old; and she bare him Segub. 22 And Segub begat Jair, who had three and twenty cities in the land of Gilead. 23 And Geshur and Aram took the towns of Jair from them, with Ken-

ath, and the villages thereof, even threescore cities. All these were the sons of Machir the father of Gilead. 24 And after that Hezron was dead in Caleb-ephrathah, then Abijah Hezron's wife bare him Ashhur the father of Tekoa.

25 And the sons of Jerahmeel the first-born of Hezron were Ram the first-born, and Bunah, and Oren, and Ozem, Ahijah. 26 And Jerahmeel had another wife, whose name was Atarah; she was the mother of Onam. 27 And the sons of Ram the first-born of Jerahmeel were Maaz, and Jamin, and Eker. 28 And the sons of Onam were Shammai, and Jada. And the sons of Shammai: Nadab, and Abishur. 29 And the name of the wife of Abishur was Abihail; and she bare him Ahban, and Molid. 30 And the sons of Nadab: Seled, and Appaim; but Seled died without children. 31 And the sons of Appaim: Ishi. And the sons of Ishi: Sheshan. And the sons of Sheshan: Ahlai. 32 And the sons of Jada the brother of Shammai: Jether, and Jonathan; and Jether died without children. 33 And the sons of Jonathan: Peleth, and Zaza. These were the sons of Jerahmeel. 34 Now Sheshan had no sons, but daughters. And Sheshan had a servant, an Egyptian, whose name was Jarha. 35 And Sheshan gave his daughter to Jarha his servant to wife; and she bare him Attai. 36 And Attai begat Nathan, and Nathan begat Zabad, 37 and Zabad begat Ephlal, and Ephlal begat Obed, 38 and Obed begat Jehu, and Jehu begat Azariah, 39 and Azariah begat Helez, and Helez begat Eleasah, 40 and Eleasah begat Sismai, and Sismai begat Shallum, 41 and Shallum begat Jekamiah, and Jekamiah begat Elishama.

42 And the sons of Caleb the brother of Jerahmeel were Mesha his first-born, who was the father of Ziph; and the sons of Mareshah the father of Hebron. 43 And the sons of Hebron: Korah, and Tappuah, and Rekem, and Shema. 44 And Shema begat Raham, the father of Jorkeam; and Rekem begat Shammai. 45 And the son of Shammai was Maon; and Maon was the father of Beth-zur. 46 And Ephah, Caleb's concubine, bare Haran, and Moza, and Gazez; and Haran begat Gazez. 47 And the sons of Jahdai: Regem, and Jothan, and Geshan, and Pelet, and Ephah, and Shaaph. 48 Maacah, Caleb's concubine, bare Sheber and Tirhanah. 49 She bare also Shaaph the father of Madmannah, Sheva the father

---

[1] W. A. L. Elmslie, "First and Second Chronicles: Introduction and Exegesis," *The Interpreter's Bible*, III, 353.
[2] *Ibid.*   [3] H. L. Ellison, "I and II Chronicles," *New Bible Commentary*, p. 342.

of Machbena, and the father of Gibea; and the daughter of Caleb was Achsah.

50 These were the sons of Caleb, the son of Hur, the first-born of Ephrathah: Shobal the father of Kiriath-jearim, 51 Salma the father of Beth-lehem, Hareph the father of Beth-gader. 52 And Shobal the father of Kiriath-jearim had sons: Haroeh, half of the Menuhoth. 53 And the families of Kiriath-jearim: the Ithrites, and the Puthites, and the Shumathites, and the Mishraites; of them came the Zorathites and the Eshtaolites. 54 The sons of Salma: Beth-lehem, and the Netophathites, Atroth-beth-joab, and half of the Manahathites, the Zorites. 55 And the families of scribes that dwelt at Jabez: the Tirathites, the Shimeathites, the Sucathites. These are the Kenites that came of Hammath, the father of the house of Rechab.

Caleb and Jerahmeel were sons of Hezron, who in turn was the grandson of Judah (cf. 2:3, 4 and 5). Their genealogies provide an expanded genealogy of Judah.

3. Descendants of David (3:1-24)

1 Now these were the sons of David, that were born unto him in Hebron: the first-born, Amnon, of Ahinoam the Jezreelitess; the second, Daniel, of Abigail the Carmelitess; 2 the third, Absalom the son of Maacah the daughter of Talmai king of Geshur; the fourth, Adonijah the son of Haggith; 3 the fifth, Shephatiah of Abital; the sixth, Ithream by Eglah his wife: 4 six were born unto him in Hebron; and there he reigned seven years and six months. And in Jerusalem he reigned thirty and three years; 5 and these were born unto him in Jerusalem: Shimea, and Shobab, and Nathan, and Solomon, four, of Bathshua the daughter of Ammiel; 6 and Ibhar, and Elishama, and Eliphelet, 7 and Nogah, and Nepheg, and Japhia, 8 and Elishama, and Eliada, and Eliphelet, nine. 9 All these were the sons of David, besides the sons of the concubines; and Tamar was their sister.

10 And Solomon's son was Rehoboam, Abijah his son, Asa his son, Jehoshaphat his son, 11 Joram his son, Ahaziah his son, Joash his son, 12 Amaziah his son, Azariah his son, Jotham his son, 13 Ahaz his son, Hezekiah his son, Manasseh his son, 14 Amon his son, Josiah his son. 15 And the sons of Josiah: the first-born Johanan, the second Jehoiakim, the third Zedekiah, the fourth Shallum. 16 And the sons of Jehoiakim: Jeconiah his son,

Zedekiah his son. 17 And the sons of Jeconiah, the captive: Shealtiel his son, 18 and Malchiram, and Pedaiah, and Shenazzar, Jekamiah, Hoshama, and Nedabiah. 19 And the sons of Pedaiah: Zerubbabel, and Shimei. And the sons of Zerubbabel: Meshullam, and Hananiah; and Shelomith was their sister; 20 and Hashubah, and Ohel, and Berechiah, and Hasadiah, Jushabhesed, five. 21 And the sons of Hananiah: Pelatiah, and Jeshaiah; the sons of Rephaiah, the sons of Arnan, the sons of Obadiah, the sons of Shecaniah. 22 And the sons of Shecaniah: Shemaiah. And the sons of Shemaiah: Hattush, and Igal, and Bariah, and Neariah, and Shaphat, six. 23 And the sons of Neariah: Elioenai, and Hizkiah, and Azrikam, three. 24 And the sons of Elioenai: Hodaviah, and Eliashib, and Pelaiah, and Akkub, and Johanan, and Delaiah, and Anani, seven.

There are three stages in the genealogical list of David's descendants: (1) the sons of David (vv. 1-9), (2) the royal descendants of David from Solomon to Zedekiah (vv. 10-16), and (3) the descendants of David from the fall of the kingdom (vv. 17-24). The first stage has reference to David's royal family, the second stage gives the succession of the royal dynasty, and the third stage lists descendants of David from the time of the captivity.

Zerubbabel was made the first governor of Jerusalem by the Persians during the return of the remnant from exile. He is mentioned in verse 19. This descendant of David governing the remnant in Jerusalem gave some hope of a restoration of the kingly line of David.

4. Another Genealogy of Judah (4:1-23)

1 The sons of Judah: Perez, Hezron, and Carmi, and Hur, and Shobal. 2 And Reaiah the son of Shobal begat Jahath; and Jahath begat Ahumai and Lahad. These are the families of the Zorathites. 3 And these were the sons of the father of Etam: Jezreel, and Ishma, and Idbash; and the name of their sister was Hazzelelponi; 4 and Penuel the father of Gedor, and Ezer the father of Hushah. These are the sons of Hur, the first-born of Ephrathah, the father of Beth-lehem. 5 And Ashhur the father of Tekoa had two wives, Helah and Naarah. 6 And Naarah bare him Ahuzzam, and Hepher, and Temeni, and Haahashtari. These were the sons of Naarah. 7 And the sons of

Helah were Zereth, Izhar, and Ethnan. 8 And Hakkoz begat Anub, and Zobebah, and the families of Aharhel the son of Harum. 9 And Jabez was more honorable than his brethren: and his mother called his name Jabez, saying, Because I bare him with sorrow. 10 And Jabez called on the God of Israel, saying, Oh that thou wouldest bless me indeed, and enlarge my border, and that thy hand might be with me, and that thou wouldest keep me from evil, that it be not to my sorrow! And God granted him that which he requested. 11 And Chelub the brother of Shuhah begat Mehir, who was the father of Eshton. 12 And Eshton begat Beth-rapha, and Paseah, and Tehinnah the father of Ir-nahash. These are the men of Recah. 13 And the sons of Kenaz: Othniel, and Seraiah. And the sons of Othniel: Hathath. 14 And Meonothai begat Ophrah: and Seraiah begat Joab the father of Ge-harashim; for they were craftsmen. 15 And the sons of Caleb the son of Jephunneh: Iru, Elah, and Naam; and the sons of Elah; and Kenaz. 16 And the sons of Jehallelel: Ziph, and Ziphah, Tiria, and Asarel. 17 And the sons of Ezrah: Jether, and Mered, and Epher, and Jalon; and she bare Miriam, and Shammai, and Ishbah the father of Eshtemoa. 18 And his wife the Jewess bare Jered the father of Gedor, and Heber the father of Soco, and Jekuthiel the father of Zanoah. And these are the sons of Bithiah the daughter of Pharaoh, whom Mered took. 19 And the sons of the wife of Hodiah, the sister of Naham, were the father of Keilah the Garmite, and Eshtemoa the Maacathite. 20 And the sons of Shimon: Amnon, and Rinnah, Ben-hanan, and Tilon. And the sons of Ishi: Zoheth, and Ben-zoheth. 21 The sons of Shelah the son of Judah: Er the father of Lecah, and Laadah the father of Mareshah, and the families of the house of them that wrought fine linen, of the house of Ashbea; 22 and Jokim, and the men of Cozeba, and Joash, and Saraph, who had dominion in Moab, and Jashubi-lehem. And the records are ancient. 23 These were the potters, and the inhabitants of Netaim and Gederah: there they dwelt with the king for his work.

This collection is fragmentary when compared with the genealogy of Judah given in I Chronicles 2. Of the names given here, two should be noted. Carmi should be Caleb (v. 1; cf. 2:9, 19, 50). The second is Jabez (vv. 1, 10). Jabez

means "giving sorrow." For some reason his mother had given him this depressing name. In his prayer Jabez asked **that it be not to my sorrow** (v. 10). In his problem over the meaning of his name, Jabez offers a fitting example. He made it a matter of prayer. **And God granted that which he requested** (v. 10).

5. Descendants of Simeon (4:24-43)

24 The sons of Simeon: Nemuel, and Jamin, Jarib, Zerah, Shaul; 25 Shallum his son, Mibsam his son, Mishma his son. 26 And the sons of Mishma: Hammuel his son, Zaccur his son, Shimei his son. 27 And Shimei had sixteen sons and six daughters; but his brethren had not many children, neither did all their family multiply like to the children of Judah. 28 And they dwelt at Beer-sheba, and Moladah, and Hazar-shual, 29 and at Bilhah, and at Ezem, and at Tolad, 30 and at Bethuel, and at Hormah, and at Ziklag, 31 and at Beth-marcaboth, and Hazar-susim, and at Beth-biri, and at Shaaraim. These were their cities unto the reign of David. 32 And their villages were Etam, and Ain, Rimmon, and Tochen, and Ashan, five cities; 33 and all their villages that were round about the same cities, unto Baal. These were their habitations, and they have their genealogy. 34 And Meshobab, and Jamlech, and Joshah the son of Amaziah, 35 and Joel, and Jehu the son of Joshibiah, the son of Seraiah, the son of Asiel, 36 and Elioenai, and Jaakobah, and Jeshohaiah, and Asaiah, and Adiel, and Jesimiel, and Benaiah, 37 and Ziza the son of Shiphi, the son of Allon, the son of Jedaiah, the son of Shimri, the son of Shemaiah—38 these mentioned by name were princes in their families: and their fathers' houses increased greatly. 39 And they went to the entrance of Gedor, even unto the east side of the valley, to seek pasture for their flocks. 40 And they found fat pasture and good, and the land was wide, and quiet, and peaceable; for they that dwelt there aforetime were of Ham. 41 And these written by name came in the days of Hezekiah king of Judah, and smote their tents, and the Meunim that were found there, and destroyed them utterly unto this day, and dwelt in their stead; because there was pasture there for their flocks. 42 And some of them, even of the sons of Simeon, five hundred men, went to mount Seir, having for their captains Pelatiah, and Neariah, and Rephaiah, and Uzziel, the sons of Ishi. 43

And they smote the remnant of the Amalekites that escaped, and have dwelt there unto this day.

According to the chronicler, the tribe of Simeon preserved its identity in genealogical lists. From the standpoint of Israel's other historians, Simeon appears to have become absorbed into Judah so as to lose its identity in Israel's history.

C. GENEALOGIES OF THE TRANS-JORDAN TRIBES (5:1-26)

1 And the sons of Reuben the first-born of Israel (for he was the first-born; but, forasmuch as he defiled his father's couch, his birthright was given unto the sons of Joseph the son of Israel; and the genealogy is not to be reckoned after the birthright. 2 For Judah prevailed above his brethren, and of him came the prince; but the birthright was Joseph's), 3 the sons of Reuben the first-born of Israel: Hanoch, and Pallu, Hezron, and Carmi. 4 The sons of Joel: Shemaiah his son, Gog his son, Shimei his son, 5 Micah his son, Reaiah his son, Baal his son, 6 Beerah his son, whom Tilgath-pilneser king of Assyria carried away captive: he was prince of the Reubenites. 7 And his brethren by their families, when the genealogy of their generations was reckoned: the chief, Jeiel, and Zechariah, 8 and Bela the son of Azaz, the son of Shema, the son of Joel, who dwelt in Aroer, even unto Nebo and Baal-meon: 9 and eastward he dwelt even unto the entrance of the wilderness from the river Euphrates, because their cattle were multiplied in the land of Gilead. 10 And in the days of Saul, they made war with the Hagrites, who fell by their hand; and they dwelt in their tents throughout all the *land* east of Gilead.

11 And the sons of Gad dwelt over against them, in the land of Bashan unto Salecah: 12 Joel the chief, and Shapham the second, and Janai, and Shaphat in Bashan. 13 And their brethren of their fathers' houses: Michael, and Meshullam, and Sheba, and Jorai, and Jacan, and Zia, and Eber, seven. 14 These were the sons of Abihail, the son of Huri, the son of Jaroah, the son of Gilead, the son of Michael, the son of Jeshishai, the son of Jahdo, the son of Buz; 15 Ahi the son of Abdiel, the son of Guni, chief of their fathers' houses. 16 And they dwelt in Gilead in Bashan, and in its towns, and in all the suburbs of Sharon, as far as their borders. 17 All these were reckoned by genealogies in the days of Jotham king of Judah, and in the days of Jeroboam king of Israel.

18 The sons of Reuben, and the Gadites, and the half-tribe of Manasseh, of valiant men, men able to bear buckler and sword, and to shoot with bow, and skilful in war, were forty and four thousand seven hundred and threescore, that were able to go forth to war. 19 And they made war with the Hagrites, with Jetur, and Naphish, and Nodab. 20 And they were helped against them, and the Hagrites were delivered into their hand, and all that were with them; for they cried to God in the battle, and he was entreated of them, because they put their trust in him. 21 And they took away their cattle; of their camels fifty thousand, and of sheep two hundred and fifty thousand, and of asses two thousand, and of men a hundred thousand. 22 For there fell many slain, because the war was of God. And they dwelt in their stead until the captivity.

23 And the children of the half-tribe of Manasseh dwelt in the land: they increased from Bashan unto Baal-hermon and Senir and mount Hermon. 24 And these were the heads of their fathers' houses: even Epher, and Ishi, and Eliel, and Azriel, and Jeremiah, and Hodaviah, and Jahdiel, mighty men of valor, famous men, heads of their fathers' houses.

25 And they trespassed against the God of their fathers, and played the harlot after the gods of the peoples of the land, whom God destroyed before them. 26 And the God of Israel stirred up the spirit of Pul king of Assyria, and the spirit of Tilgath-pilneser king of Assyria, and he carried them away, even the Reubenites, and the Gadites, and the half-tribe of Manasseh, and brought them unto Halah, and Habor, and Hara, and to the river of Gozan, unto this day.

This chapter traces the descendants of the tribes of Israel which settled on the east side of the Jordan River. There are two instructive incidents involving all three tribes.

The first incident was the war against the Hagrites during the period of conquest. The Israelites received the help of the Lord **because they put their trust in him** (v. 20). It was an impressive conquest by the Trans-Jordan tribes, and they continued to occupy the land **until the captivity** (v. 22).

The second incident involved the conquest of these tribes by Assyria during the destruction of the Northern Kingdom. The reason was, **they trespassed against the God of their fathers** (v. 25). The chronicler implies that these tribes went so far away from God that they passed the point of no return, something which the tribe of Judah did not do.

D. GENEALOGIES OF LEVI (6:1-81)

This long chapter of eighty-one verses is wholly devoted to the priestly tribe. Here is a vivid illustration of the chronicler's conception of who is important in his review of Israel's history. Only to the kingly tribe of Judah has he devoted more space.

1. Aaron's High Priestly Line (6:1-15)

1 The sons of Levi: Gershon, Kohath, and Merari. 2 And the sons of Kohath: Amram, Izhar, and Hebron, and Uzziel. 3 And the children of Amram: Aaron, and Moses, and Miriam. And the sons of Aaron: Nadab, and Abihu, Eleazar, and Ithamar. 4 Eleazar begat Phinehas, Phinehas begat Abishua, 5 and Abishua begat Bukki, and Bukki begat Uzzi, 6 and Uzzi begat Zerahiah, and Zerahiah begat Meraioth, 7 Meraioth begat Amariah, and Amariah begat Ahitub, 8 and Ahitub begat Zadok, and Zadok begat Ahimaaz, 9 and Ahimaaz begat Azariah, and Azariah begat Johanan, 10 and Johanan begat Azariah (he it is that executed the priest's office in the house that Solomon built in Jerusalem), 11 and Azariah begat Amariah, and Amariah begat Ahitub, 12 and Ahitub begat Zadok, and Zadok begat Shallum, 13 and Shallum begat Hilkiah, and Hilkiah begat Azariah, 14 and Azariah begat Seraiah, and Seraiah begat Jehozadak; 15 and Jehozadak went *into captivity*, when Jehovah carried away Judah and Jerusalem by the hand of Nebuchadnezzar.

This list is obviously incomplete. It begins with Aaron and continues to Jehozadak at the time of the destruction of the temple in Jerusalem in the sixth century B.C. However, there is no reference to the priests at Shiloh, including the house of Eli, nor is there the inclusion of Jehoiada (cf. II Chron. 22:11), Urijah (II Kings 16:11) and Azariah (II Chron. 26:20).

2. Other Levitical Genealogies (6:16-53)

16 The sons of Levi: Gershom, Kohath, and Merari. 17 And these are the names of the sons of Gershom: Libni and Shimei. 18 And the sons of Kohath were Amram, and Izhar, and Hebron, and Uzziel. 19 The sons of Merari: Mahli and Mushi. And these are the families of the Levites according to their fathers' *houses*. 20 Of Gershom: Libni his son, Jahath his son, Zimmah his son, 21 Joah his son, Iddo his son, Zerah his son, Jeatherai his son. 22 The sons of Kohath: Amminadab his son, Korah his son, Assir his son, 23 Elkanah his son, and Ebiasaph his son, and Assir his son, 24 Tahath his son, Uriel his son, Uzziah his son, and Shaul his son. 25 And the sons of Elkanah: Amasai, and Ahimoth. 26 As for Elkanah, the sons of Elkanah: Zophai his son, and Nahath his son, 27 Eliab his son, Jeroham his son, Elkanah his son. 28 And the sons of Samuel: the first-born, *Joel*, and the second Abijah. 29 The sons of Merari: Mahli, Libni his son, Shimei his son, Uzzah his son, 30 Shimea his son, Haggiah his son, Asaiah his son.

31 And these are they whom David set over the service of song in the house of Jehovah, after that the ark had rest. 32 And they ministered with song before the tabernacle of the tent of meeting, until Solomon had built the house of Jehovah in Jerusalem: and they waited on their office according to their order. 33 And these are they that waited, and their sons. Of the sons of the Kohathites: Heman the singer, the son of Joel, the son of Samuel, 34 the son of Elkanah, the son of Jeroham, the son of Eliel, the son of Toah, 35 the son of Zuph, the son of Elkanah, the son of Mahath, the son of Amasai, 36 the son of Elkanah, the son of Joel, the son of Azariah, the son of Zephaniah, 37 the son of Tahath, the son of Assir, the son of Ebiasaph, the son of Korah, 38 the son of Izhar, the son of Kohath, the son of Levi, the son of Israel. 39 And his brother Asaph, who stood on his right hand, even Asaph the son of Berechiah, the son of Shimea, 40 the son of Michael, the son of Baaseiah, the son of Malchijah, 41 the son of Ethni, the son of Zerah, the son of Adaiah, 42 the son of Ethan, the son of Zimmah, the son of Shimei, 43 the son of Jahath, the son of Gershom, the son of Levi. 44 And on the left hand their brethren the sons of Merari: Ethan the son of Kishi, the son of Abdi, the son of Malluch, 45 the son of Hashabiah, the son of Amaziah, the son of Hilkiah, 46 the son of Amzi, the son of Bani, the son of

Shemer, 47 the son of Mahli, the son of Mushi, the son of Merari, the son of Levi. 48 And their brethren the Levites were appointed for all the service of the tabernacle of the house of God.

49 But Aaron and his sons offered upon the altar of burnt-offering, and upon the altar of incense, for all the work of the most holy place, and to make atonement for Israel, according to all that Moses the servant of God had commanded. 50 And these are the sons of Aaron: Eleazar his son, Phinehas his son, Abishua his son, 51 Bukki his son, Uzzi his son, Zerahiah his son, 52 Meraioth his son, Amariah his son, Ahitub his son, 53 Zadok his son, Ahimaaz his son.

The sons of Levi: Gershom, Kohath, and Merari (v. 16). The sons of Levi were responsible for the worship of the Israelites. Their authority derived from their descent from any one of these three great Levitical families.

Among the lists of Levites were those who provided the musical portion of worship, and their descendants. They were appointed by David (v. 31).

3. Levitical Cities (6:54-81)

54 Now these are their dwelling-places according to their encampments in their borders: to the sons of Aaron, of the families of the Kohathites (for theirs was the *first* lot), 55 to them they gave Hebron in the land of Judah, and the suburbs thereof round about it; 56 but the fields of the city, and the villages thereof, they gave to Caleb the son of Jephunneh. 57 And to the sons of Aaron they gave the cities of refuge, Hebron; Libnah also with its suburbs, and Jattir, and Eshtemoa with its suburbs, 58 and Hilen with its suburbs, Debir with its suburbs, 59 and Ashan with its suburbs, and Beth-shemesh with its suburbs; 60 and out of the tribe of Benjamin, Geba with its suburbs, and Allemeth with its suburbs, and Anathoth with its suburbs. All their cities throughout their families were thirteen cities.

61 And unto the rest of the sons of Kohath *were given* by lot, out of the family of the tribe, out of the half-tribe, the half of Manasseh, ten cities. 62 And to the sons of Gershom, according to their families, out of the tribe of Issachar, and out of the tribe of Asher, and out of the tribe of Naphtali, and out of the tribe of Manasseh in Bashan, thirteen cities. 63 Unto the sons of Merari *were given* by lot, according to their families,

out of the tribe of Reuben, and out of the tribe of Gad, and out of the tribe of Zebulun, twelve cities. 64 And the children of Israel gave to the Levites the cities with their suburbs. 65 And they gave by lot out of the tribe of the children of Judah, and out of the tribe of the children of Simeon, and out of the tribe of the children of Benjamin, these cities which are mentioned by name.

66 And some of the families of the sons of Kohath had cities of their borders out of the tribe of Ephraim. 67 And they gave unto them the cities of refuge, Shechem in the hill-country of Ephraim with its suburbs; Gezer also with its suburbs, 68 and Jokmeam with its suburbs, and Beth-horon with its suburbs, 69 and Aijalon with its suburbs, and Gath-rimmon with its suburbs; 70 and out of the half-tribe of Manasseh, Aner with its suburbs, and Bileam with its suburbs, for the rest of the family of the sons of Kohath.

71 Unto the sons of Gershom *were given*, out of the family of the half-tribe of Manasseh, Golan in Bashan with its suburbs, and Ashtaroth with its suburbs; 72 and out of the tribe of Issachar, Kedesh with its suburbs, Daberath with its suburbs, 73 and Ramoth with its suburbs, and Anem with its suburbs; 74 and out of the tribe of Asher, Mashal with its suburbs, and Abdon with its suburbs, 75 and Hukok with its suburbs, and Rehob with its suburbs; 76 and out of the tribe of Naphtali, Kedesh in Galilee with its suburbs, and Hammon with its suburbs, and Kiriathaim with its suburbs.

77 Unto the rest of *the Levites*, the sons of Merari, *were given*, out of the tribe of Zebulun, Rimmono with its suburbs, Tabor with its suburbs; 78 and beyond the Jordan at Jericho, on the east side of the Jordan, *were given them*, out of the tribe of Reuben, Bezer in the wilderness with its suburbs, and Jahzah with its suburbs, 79 and Kedemoth with its suburbs, and Mephaath with its suburbs; 80 and out of the tribe of Gad, Ramoth in Gilead with its suburbs, and Mahanaim with its suburbs, 81 and Heshbon with its suburbs, and Jazer with its suburbs.

These verses refer to cities mentioned in Joshua (cf. Josh. 29:9-25, 33, 40). The Levitical cities were distributed throughout the tribal inheritance to insure the distribution of the Levites among the various tribes.

E. GENEALOGIES OF THE NORTHERN TRIBES (7:1-40)

The lists in this chapter include those of the northern tribes. Since the tribe of Judah was the primary concern of the chronicler, those tribes involved in its history are given fuller treatment than the other tribes.

1. Issachar, Benjamin, (Zebulun), (Dan), Naphtali, Manasseh (7:1-19)

1 And of the sons of Issachar: Tola, and Puah, Jashub, and Shimron, four. 2 And the sons of Tola: Uzzi, and Rephaiah, and Jeriel, and Jahmai, and Ibsam, and Shemuel, heads of their fathers' houses, to wit, of Tola; mighty men of valor in their generations: their number in the days of David was two and twenty thousand and six hundred. 3 And the sons of Uzzi: Izrahiah. And the sons of Izrahiah: Michael, and Obadiah, and Joel, Isshiah, five; all of them chief men. 4 And with them, by their generations, after their fathers' houses, were bands of the host for war, six and thirty thousand; for they had many wives and sons. 5 And their brethren among all the families of Issachar, mighty men of valor, reckoned in all by genealogy, were fourscore and seven thousand.

6 The sons of Benjamin: Bela, and Becher, and Jediael, three. 7 And the sons of Bela: Ezbon, and Uzzi, and Uzziel, and Jerimoth, and Iri, five; heads of fathers' houses, mighty men of valor; and they were reckoned by genealogy twenty and two thousand and thirty and four. 8 And the sons of Becher: Zemirah, and Joash, and Eliezer, and Elioenai, and Omri, and Jeremoth, and Abijah, and Anathoth, and Alemeth. All these were the sons of Becher. 9 And they were reckoned by genealogy, after their generations, heads of their fathers' houses, mighty men of valor, twenty thousand and two hundred. 10 And the sons of Jediael: Bilhan. And the sons of Bilhan: Jeush, and Benjamin, and Ehud, and Chenaanah, and Zethan, and Tarshish, and Ahishahar. 11 All these were sons of Jediael, according to the heads of their fathers' houses, mighty men of valor, seventeen thousand and two hundred, that were able to go forth in the host for war. 12 Shuppim also, and Huppim, the sons of Ir, Hushim, the sons of Aher.

13 The sons of Naphtali: Jahziel, and Guni, and Jezer, and Shallum, the sons of Bilhah.

14 The sons of Manasseh: Asriel, whom his concubine the Aramitess bare; she bare Machir the father of Gilead. 15 And Machir took a wife of Huppim and Shuppim, whose sister's name was Maacah; and the name of the second was Zelophehad: and Zelophehad had daughters. 16 And Maacah the wife of Machir bare a son, and she called his name Peresh; and the name of his brother was Sheresh; and his sons were Ulam and Rakem. 17 And the sons of Ulam: Bedan. These were the sons of Gilead the son of Machir, the son of Manasseh. 18 And his sister Hammolecheth bare Ishhod, and Abiezer, and Mahlah. 19 And the sons of Shemida were Ahian, and Shechem, and Likhi, and Aniam.

In giving the genealogy of Issachar the number of the military men is given. These men are described as **mighty men of valor in their generations** (v. 2). The military support which Issachar provided David during his wars must have been significant.

Since the authentic genealogy of Benjamin is in 8:1-40, it is very widely held that the genealogy given in 7:6-11 is not for Benjamin but for Zebulun.[4] Of this tribe there was a considerable number **that were able to go forth in the host for war** (v. 11).

The genealogy of Dan is generally considered to be given in verse 12. This is by way of the same factors which entered into the identification of Zebulun.

2. Ephraim and Asher (7:20-40)

20 And the sons of Ephraim: Shuthelah, and Bered his son, and Tahath his son, and Eleadah his son, and Tahath his son, 21 and Zabad his son, and Shuthelah his son, and Ezer, and Elead, whom the men of Gath that were born in the land slew, because they came down to take away their cattle. 22 And Ephraim their father mourned many days, and his brethren came to comfort him. 23 And he went in to his wife, and she conceived, and bare a son, and he called his name Beriah, because it went evil with his house. 24 And his daughter was Sheerah, who built Beth-horon the nether and the upper, and Uzzensheerah. 25 And Rephah was his son, and Resheph, and Telah his son, and Tahan his son. 26 Ladan his son, Ammihud his son, El-

4 Ibid., p. 344; cf. Elmslie, op. cit., p. 372.

ishama his son, 27 Nun his son, Joshua his son.

28 And their possessions and habitations were Beth-el and the towns thereof, and eastward Naaran, and westward Gezer, with the towns thereof; Shechem also and the towns thereof, unto Azzah and the towns thereof; 29 and by the borders of the children of Manasseh, Beth-shean and its towns, Taanach and its towns, Megiddo and its towns, Dor and its towns. In these dwelt the children of Joseph the son of Israel.

30 The sons of Asher: Imnah, and Ishvah, and Ishvi, and Beriah, and Serah their sister. 31 And the sons of Beriah: Heber, and Malchiel, who was the father of Birzaith. 32 And Heber begat Japhlet, and Shomer, and Hotham, and Shua their sister. 33 And the sons of Japhlet: Pasach, and Bimhal, and Ashvath. These are the children of Japhlet. 34 And the sons of Shemer: Ahi, and Rohgah, Jehubbah, and Aram. 35 And the sons of Helem his brother: Zophah, and Imna, and Shelesh, and Amal. 36 The sons of Zophah: Suah, and Harnepher, and Shual, and Beri, and Imrah, 37 Bezer, and Hod, and Shamma, and Shilshah, and Ithran, and Beera. 38 And the sons of Jether: Jephunneh, and Pispa, and Ara. 39 And the sons of Ulla: Arah, and Hanniel, and Rizia. 40 All these were the children of the princes. And the number of them reckoned by genealogy for service in war was twenty and six thousand men.

In the genealogy of Ephraim, the most complete ancestral list of Joshua is given (vv. 25-27). Otherwise, there is an ominous brevity in listing the descendants of Ephraim as though the chronicler were deliberately downgrading the Joseph tribes because of their leading role in the great secession from the Davidic kingdom and the Aaronic priesthood.

F. BENJAMIN'S GENEALOGY ELABORATED (8:1-40)

1 And Benjamin begat Bela his first-born, Ashbel the second, and Aharah the third, 2 Nohah the fourth, and Rapha the fifth. 3 And Bela had sons: Addar, and Gera, and Abihud, 4 and Abishua, and Naaman, and Ahoah, 5 and Gera, and Shephuphan, and Huram. 6 And these are the sons of Ehud: these are the heads of fathers' houses of the inhabitants of Geba, and they carried them captive to Manahath: 7 and Naaman, and Ahijah, and Gera, he carried them cap-

tive; and he begat Uzza and Ahihud. 8 And Shaharaim begat children in the field of Moab, after he had sent them away; Hushim and Baara were his wives. 9 And he begat of Hodesh his wife, Jobab, and Zibia, and Mesha, and Malcam, 10 and Jeuz, and Shachia, and Mirmah. These were his sons, heads of fathers' houses. 11 And of Hushim he begat Abitub and Elpaal. 12 And the sons of Elpaal: Eber, and Misham, and Shemed, who built Ono and Lod, with the towns thereof; 13 and Beriah, and Shema, who were heads of fathers' houses of the inhabitants of Aijalon, who put to flight the inhabitants of Gath; 14 and Ahio, Shashak, and Jeremoth, 15 and Zebadiah, and Arad, and Eder, 16 and Michael, and Ishpah, and Joha, the sons of Beriah, 17 and Zebadiah, and Meshullam, and Hizki, and Heber, 18 and Ishmerai, and Izliah, and Jobab, the sons of Elpaal, 19 and Jakim, and Zichri, and Zabdi, 20 and Elienai, and Zillethai, and Eliel, 21 and Adaiah, and Beraiah, and Shimrath, the sons of Shimei, 22 and Ishpan, and Eber, and Eliel, 23 and Abdon, and Zichri, and Hanan, 24 and Hananiah, and Elam, and Anthothijah, 25 and Iphdeiah, and Penuel, the sons of Shashak, 26 and Shamsherai, and Shehariah, and Athaliah, 27 and Jaareshiah, and Elijah, and Zichri, the sons of Jeroham. 28 These were heads of fathers' houses throughout their generations, chief men: these dwelt in Jerusalem.

29 And in Gibeon there dwelt the father of Gibeon, Jeiel, whose wife's name was Maacah; 30 and his first-born son Abdon, and Zur, and Kish, and Baal, and Nadab, 31 and Gedor, and Ahio, and Zecher. 32 And Mikloth begat Shimeah. And they also dwelt with their brethren in Jerusalem, over against their brethren. 33 And Ner begat Kish; and Kish begat Saul; and Saul begat Jonathan, and Malchi-shua, and Abinadab, and Eshbaal. 34 And the son of Jonathan was Merib-baal; and Merib-baal begat Micah. 35 And the sons of Micah: Pithon, and Melech, and Tarea, and Ahaz. 36 And Ahaz begat Jehoaddah; and Jehoaddah begat Alemeth, and Azmaveth, and Zimri; and Zimri begat Moza. 37 And Moza begat Binea; Raphah was his son, Eleasah his son, Azel his son. 38 And Azel had six sons, whose names are these: Azrikam, Bocheru, and Ishmael, and Sheariah, and Obadiah, and Hanan. All these were the sons of Azel. 39 And the sons of Eshek his brother: Ulam his first-born, Jeush the second, and Eliphelet the third. 40 And the sons of Ulam were mighty men of valor, arch-

ers, and had many sons, and sons' sons, a hundred and fifty. All these were of the sons of Benjamin.

Although this chapter contains very little more than a list of names, it is intended to stand as a tribute to the loyalty of this tribe to the Davidic dynasty. When the northern tribes revolted, Benjamin remained with Judah.

This genealogy includes the house of Saul (vv. 29-40). Although Saul was David's bitter enemy, the tribe of Benjamin, from which he came, remained loyal to David and his line.

G. THE RETURNING REMNANT (9: 1-34)

1 So all Israel were reckoned by genealogies; and, behold, they are written in the book of the kings of Israel. And Judah was carried away captive to Babylon for their transgression. 2 Now the first inhabitants that dwelt in their possessions in their cities were Israel, the priests, the Levites, and the Nethinim. 3 And in Jerusalem dwelt of the children of Judah, and of the children of Benjamin, and of the children of Ephraim and Manasseh: 4 Uthai the son of Ammihud, the son of Omri, the son of Imri, the son of Bani, of the children of Perez the son of Judah. 5 And of the Shilonites: Asaiah the first-born, and his sons. 6 And of the sons of Zerah: Jeuel, and their brethren, six hundred and ninety. 7 And of the sons of Benjamin: Sallu the son of Meshullam, the son of Hodaviah, the son of Hassenuah, 8 and Ibneiah the son of Jeroham, and Elah the son of Uzzi, the son of Michri, and Meshullam the son of Shephatiah, the son of Reuel, the son of Ibnijah; 9 and their brethren, according to their generations, nine hundred and fifty and six. All these men were heads of fathers' *houses* by their fathers' houses.

10 And of the priests: Jedaiah, and Jehoiarib, Jachin, 11 and Azariah the son of Hilkiah, the son of Meshullam, the son of Zadok, the son of Meraioth, the son of Ahitub, the ruler of the house of God; 12 and Adaiah the son of Jeroham, the son of Pashhur, the son of Malchijah, and Maasai the son of Adiel, the son of Jahzerah, the son of Meshullam, the son of Meshillemith, the son of Immer; 13 and their brethren, heads of their fathers' houses, a thousand and seven hundred and threescore; very able men for the work of the service of the house of God.

14 And of the Levites: Shemaiah the son of Hasshub, the son of Azrikam, the son of Hashabiah, of the sons of Merari; 15 and Bakbakkar, Heresh, and Galal, and Mattaniah the son of Mica, the son of Zichri, the son of Asaph, 16 and Obadiah the son of Shemaiah, the son of Galal, the son of Jeduthun, and Berechiah the son of Asa, the son of Elkanah, that dwelt in the villages of the Netophathites.

17 And the porters: Shallum, and Akkub, and Talmon, and Ahiman, and their brethren (Shallum was the chief), 18 who hitherto *waited* in the king's gate eastward: they were the porters for the camp of the children of Levi. 19 And Shallum the son of Kore, the son of Ebiasaph, the son of Korah, and his brethren, of his father's house, the Korahites, were over the work of the service, keepers of the thresholds of the tent: and their fathers had been over the camp of Jehovah, keepers of the entry. 20 And Phinehas the son of Eleazar was ruler over them in time past, *and* Jehovah was with him. 21 Zechariah the son of Meshelemiah was porter of the door of the tent of meeting. 22 All these that were chosen to be porters in the thresholds were two hundred and twelve. These were reckoned by genealogy in their villages, whom David and Samuel the seer did ordain in their office of trust. 23 So they and their children had the oversight of the gates of the house of Jehovah, even the house of the tent, by wards. 24 On the four sides were the porters, toward the east, west, north, and south. 25 And their brethren, in their villages, were to come in every seven days from time to time to be with them: 26 for the four chief porters, who were Levites, were in an office of trust, and were over the chambers and over the treasuries in the house of God. 27 And they lodged round about the house of God, because the charge *thereof* was upon them; and to them pertained the opening thereof morning by morning.

28 And certain of them had charge of the vessels of service; for by count were these brought in and by count were these taken out. 29 Some of them also were appointed over the furniture, and over all the vessels of the sanctuary, and over the fine flour, and the wine, and the oil, and the frankincense, and the spices. 30 And some of the sons of the priests prepared the confection of the spices. 31 And Mattithiah, one of the Levites, who was the first-born of Shallum the Korahite, had the office of trust over the things that were baked in pans. 32 And some of their brethren, of the sons of the Kohathites,

were over the showbread, to prepare it every sabbath.

33 And these are the singers, heads of fathers' *houses* of the Levites, *who dwelt* in the chambers *and were* free *from other service;* for they were employed in their work day and night. 34 These were heads of fathers' *houses* of the Levites, throughout their generations, chief men: these dwelt at Jerusalem.

The chronicler makes no attempt to relate the list of names in this chapter with the genealogies in the preceding chapters. The latter provide the genealogical framework of the history of Israel, while the lists in this chapter stress the post-exilic community of Jews as the legitimate genealogical sequel to that history.

The post-exilic Jewish community was primarily a religious one centering upon the priests. Around this company of priests were the Levites, including both porters and singers. The priests were responsible for the religious well-being of the community, and the chronicler describes them as **very able men for the work of the service of the house of God** (v. 13). They were courageous in maintaining the righteousness and purity which the service of God required. Although the period was one of trial and discouragement, the priests served the religious needs of the community with valor. This is the perennial calling of those who are set apart for the service of the house of God.

H. SAUL'S ANCESTRY AND POSTERITY (9:35-44)

35 And in Gibeon there dwelt the father of Gibeon, Jeiel, whose wife's name was Maachah; 36 and his first-born son Abdon, and Zur, and Kish, and Baal, and Ner, and Nadab, 37 and Gedor, and Ahio, and Zechariah, and Mikloth. 38 And Mikloth begat Shimeam. And they also dwelt with their brethren in Jerusalem, over against their brethren. 39 And Ner begat Kish; and Kish begat Saul; and Saul begat Jonathan, and Malchishua, and Abinadab, and Eshbaal. 40 And the son of Jonathan was Merib-baal; and Merib-baal begat Micah. 41 And the sons of Micah: Pithon, and Melech, and Tahrea, *and Ahaz.* 42 And Ahaz begat Jarah; and Jarah begat Alemeth, and Azmaveth, and Zimri; and Zimri begat Moza; 43 and Moza begat Binea; and Rephaiah his son, Eleasah his son, Azel

his son. 44 And Azel had six sons, whose names are these: Azrikam, Bocheru, and Ishmael, and Sheariah, and Obadiah, and Hanan: these were the sons of Azel.

This list of Saul's ancestors as well as his descendants is given as the immediate prelude to the chronicler's history of David and his dynasty (cf. 8:29-40).

II. THE REIGN OF DAVID (I Chron. 10:1—29:30)

The shorter genealogical division of Chronicles includes I Chronicles 1-9. The longer historical division includes I Chronicles 10—II Chronicles 36. This historical division depicts the history of Israel from the reign of King David to the return of the remnant from exile. Chronologically, this is from the tenth century B.C. to the sixth century B. C.

A. THE DEATH OF SAUL (10:1-14; cf. I Sam. 31:1-13)

1 Now the Philistines fought against Israel: and the men of Israel fled from before the Philistines, and fell down slain in mount Gilboa. 2 And the Philistines followed hard after Saul and after his sons; and the Philistines slew Jonathan, and Abinadab, and Malchishua, the sons of Saul. 3 And the battle went sore against Saul, and the archers overtook him; and he was distressed by reason of the archers. 4 Then said Saul unto his armorbearer, Draw thy sword, and thrust me through therewith, lest these uncircumcised come and abuse me. But his armorbearer would not; for he was sore afraid. Therefore Saul took his sword, and fell upon it. 5 And when his armorbearer saw that Saul was dead, he likewise fell upon his sword, and died. 6 So Saul died, and his three sons; and all his house died together.

7 And when all the men of Israel that were in the valley saw that they fled, and that Saul and his sons were dead, they forsook their cities, and fled; and the Philistines came and dwelt in them. 8 And it came to pass on the morrow, when the Philistines came to strip the slain, that they found Saul and his sons fallen in mount Gilboa. 9 And they stripped him, and took his head, and his armor, and sent into the land of the Philistines round about, to carry the tidings unto their idols, and to the people. 10 And they put his armor in the house of their gods, and fastened his

head in the house of Dagon. 11 And when all Jabesh-gilead heard all that the Philistines had done to Saul, 12 all the valiant men arose, and took away the body of Saul, and the bodies of his sons, and brought them to Jabesh, and buried their bones under the oak in Jabesh, and fasted seven days.

13 So Saul died for his trespass which he committed against Jehovah, because of the word of Jehovah, which he kept not; and also for that he asked counsel of one that had a familiar spirit, to inquire *thereby*, 14 and inquired not of Jehovah: therefore he slew him, and turned the kingdom unto David the son of Jesse.

This is the sole historical reference which is made to Saul's life and activity. A careful appraisal of it gives something of the chronicler's interpretation of history. Saul could not be ignored because he had been the anointed of God to be king over Israel. However, he had been rejected and his line denied the throne. Because of God's rejection of Saul, the chronicler includes only the account of his death. This sole incident from the career of Saul is offered as proof that he was rejected, and, therefore, is not to be included among the royalty of Israel. So Saul died for his trespass which he committed against Jehovah ... therefore he slew him, and turned the kingdom unto David the son of Jesse (vv. 13, 14).

B. DAVID, KING OVER ISRAEL (11: 1-3)

1 Then all Israel gathered themselves to David unto Hebron, saying, Behold, we are thy bone and thy flesh. 2 In times past, even when Saul was king, it was thou that leddest out and broughtest in Israel: and Jehovah thy God said unto thee, Thou shalt be shepherd of my people Israel, and thou shalt be prince over my people Israel. 3 So all the elders of Israel came to the king to Hebron; and David made a covenant with them in Hebron before Jehovah; and they anointed David king over Israel, according to the word of Jehovah by Samuel.

The transition from the reign of Saul to the reign of David is recounted with unusual brevity. There is nothing concerning the reign of Ish-bosheth, the son of Saul, and the period of warfare between the house of David and the house of Saul.

C. JERUSALEM, THE CITY OF DAVID (11:4-9)

4 And David and all Israel went to Jerusalem (the same is Jebus) ; and the Jebusites, the inhabitants of the land, were there. 5 And the inhabitants of Jebus said to David, Thou shalt not come in hither. Nevertheless David took the stronghold of Zion; the same is the city of David. 6 And David said, Whosoever smiteth the Jebusites first shall be chief and captain. And Joab the son of Zeruiah went up first, and was made chief. 7 And David dwelt in the stronghold; therefore they called it the city of David. 8 And he built the city round about, from Millo even round about; and Joab repaired the rest of the city. 9 And David waxed greater and greater; for Jehovah of hosts was with him.

The impression is that an immediate sequel to David's coronation was the occupation of Jerusalem. This was a great achievement, and the city was known as the city of David (v. 7).

D. DAVID'S MILITARY ADHERENTS (11:10—12:40)

In these sections there are names, deeds and statistics of men who were loyal to David. The compilations are not meant to say that these all joined David before he became king. Rather, it is to say that the list of David's heroes is placed conveniently at the beginning of his reign.

1. The Mighty Men (11:10-47)

10 Now these are the chief of the mighty men whom David had, who showed themselves strong with him in his kingdom, together with all Israel, to make him king, according to the word of Jehovah concerning Israel. 11 And this is the number of the mighty men whom David had: Jashobeam, the son of a Hachmonite, the chief of the thirty; he lifted up his spear against three hundred and slew them at one time. 12 And after him was Eleazar the son of Dodo, the Ahohite, who was one of the three mighty men. 13 He was with David at Pas-dammim, and there the Philistines were gathered together to battle, where was a plot of ground full of barley; and the people fled from before the Philistines. 14 And they stood in the midst of the plot, and defended it, and slew the

Philistines; and Jehovah saved them by a great victory.

15 And three of the thirty chief men went down to the rock to David, into the cave of Adullam; and the host of the Philistines were encamped in the valley of Rephaim. 16 And David was then in the stronghold, and the garrison of the Philistines was then in Beth-lehem. 17 And David longed, and said, Oh that one would give me water to drink of the well of Beth-lehem, which is by the gate! 18 And the three brake through the host of the Philistines, and drew water out of the well of Beth-lehem, that was by the gate, and took it, and brought it to David: but David would not drink thereof, but poured it out unto Jehovah, 19 and said, My God forbid it me, that I should do this: shall I drink the blood of these men that have put their lives in jeopardy? for with *the jeopardy of* their lives they brought it. Therefore he would not drink it. These things did the three mighty men.

20 And Abishai, the brother of Joab, he was chief of the three; for he lifted up his spear against three hundred and slew them, and had a name among the three. 21 Of the three, he was more honorable than the two, and was made their captain: howbeit he attained not to the *first* three.

22 Benaiah the son of Jehoiada, the son of a valiant man of Kabzeel, who had done mighty deeds, he slew the two *sons of* Ariel of Moab: he went down also and slew a lion in the midst of a pit in time of snow. 23 And he slew an Egyptian, a man of great stature, five cubits high; and in the Egyptian's hand was a spear like a weaver's beam; and he went down to him with a staff, and plucked the spear out of the Egyptian's hand, and slew him with his own spear. 24 These things did Benaiah the son of Jehoiada, and had a name among the three mighty men. 25 Behold, he was more honorable than the thirty, but he attained not to the *first* three: and David set him over his guard.

26 Also the mighty men of the armies: Asahel the brother of Joab, Elhanan the son of Dodo of Beth-lehem, 27 Shammoth the Harorite, Helez the Pelonite, 28 Ira the son of Ikkesh the Tekoite, Abiezer the Anathothite, 29 Sibbecai the Hushathite, Ilai the Ahohite, 30 Maharai the Netophathite, Heled the son of Baanah the Netophathite, 31 Ithai the son of Ribai of Gibeah of the children of Benjamin, Benaiah the Pirathonite, 32 Hurai of the brooks of Gaash, Abiel the

Arbathite, 33 Azmaveth the Baharumite, Eliahba the Shaalbonite, 34 the sons of Hashem the Gizonite, Jonathan the son of Shagee the Hararite, 35 Ahiam the son of Sacar the Hararite, Eliphal the son of Ur, 36 Hepher the Mecherathite, Ahijah the Pelonite, 37 Hezro the Carmelite, Naarai the son of Ezbai, 38 Joel brother of Nathan, Mibhar the son of Hagri, 39 Zelek the Ammonite, Naharai the Berothite, the armorbearer of Joab the son of Zeruiah, 40 Ira the Ithrite, Gareb the Ithrite, 41 Uriah the Hittite, Zabad the son of Ahlai, 42 Adina the son of Shiza the Reubenite, a chief of the Reubenites, and thirty with him, 43 Hanan the son of Maacah, and Joshaphat the Mithnite, 44 Uzzia the Ashterathite, Shama and Jeiel the sons of Hotham the Aroerite, 45 Jediael the son of Shimri, and Joha his brother, the Tizite, 46 Eliel the Mahavite, and Jeribai, and Joshaviah, the sons of Elnaam, and Ithmah the Moabite, 47 Eliel, and Obed, and Jaasiel the Mezobaite.

On this passage see the notes on the parallel passage in II Samuel 23:8-39.

2. Friends in Exile (12:1-22)

1 Now these are they that came to David to Ziklag, while he yet kept himself close because of Saul the son of Kish; and they were among the mighty men, his helpers in war. 2 They were armed with bows, and could use both the right hand and the left in slinging stones and in shooting arrows from the bow: they were of Saul's brethren of Benjamin. 3 The chief was Ahiezer; then Joash, the sons of Shemaah the Gibeathite, and Jeziel, and Pelet, the sons of Azmaveth, and Beracah, and Jehu the Anathothite, 4 and Ishmaiah the Gibeonite, a mighty man among the thirty, and over the thirty, and Jeremiah, and Jahaziel, and Johanan, and Jozabad the Gederathite, 5 Eluzai, and Jerimoth, and Bealiah, and Shemariah, and Shephatiah the Haruphite, 6 Elkanah, and Isshiah, and Azarel, and Joezer, and Jashobeam, the Korahites, 7 and Joelah, and Zebadiah, the sons of Jeroham of Gedor.

8 And of the Gadites there separated themselves unto David to the stronghold in the wilderness, mighty men of valor, men trained for war, that could handle shield and spear; whose faces were like the faces of lions, and they were as swift as the roes upon the mountains: 9 Ezer the chief, Obadiah the second, Eliab the third, 10 Mishmannah the fourth, Jere-

miah the fifth, 11 Attai the sixth, Eliel the seventh, 12 Johanan the eighth, Elzabad the ninth, 13 Jeremiah the tenth, Machbannai the eleventh. 14 These of the sons of Gad were captains of the host: he that was least was equal to a hundred, and the greatest to a thousand. 15 These are they that went over the Jordan in the first month, when it had overflowed all its banks; and they put to flight all them of the valleys, both toward the east and toward the west.

16 And there came of the children of Benjamin and Judah to the stronghold unto David. 17 And David went out to meet them, and answered and said unto them, If ye be come peaceably unto me to help me, my heart shall be knit unto you; but if *ye be come* to betray me to mine adversaries, seeing there is no wrong in my hands, the God of our fathers look thereon, and rebuke it. 18 Then the Spirit came upon Amasai, who was chief of the thirty, *and he said,* Thine are we, David, and on thy side, thou son of Jesse: peace, peace be unto thee, and peace be to thy helpers; for thy God helpeth thee. Then David received them, and made them captains of the band.

19 Of Manasseh also there fell away some to David, when he came with the Philistines against Saul to battle: but they helped them not; for the lords of the Philistines upon advisement sent him away, saying, He will fall away to his master Saul to the jeopardy of our heads. 20 As he went to Ziklag, there fell to him of Manasseh, Adnah, and Jozabad, and Jediael, and Michael, and Jozabad, and Elihu, and Zillethai, captains of thousands that were of Manasseh. 21 And they helped David against the band of rovers: for they were all mighty men of valor, and were captains in the host. 22 For from day to day men came to David to help him, until there was a great host, like the host of God.

This passage is peculiar to the chronicler. It emphasizes the fact that in the days of David's exile fighting men of great skill and valor came to him. These courageous warriors are described vividly: **they could use both the right hand and the left** (v. 2); **men trained for war, that could handle shield and spear** (v. 8); **they were all mighty men of valor** (v. 21).

3. Warriors in Hebron (12:23-40)

23 And these are the numbers of the heads of them that were armed for war, who came to David to Hebron, to turn the kingdom of Saul to him, according to the word of Jehovah. 24 The children of Judah that bare shield and spear were six thousand and eight hundred, armed for war. 25 Of the children of Simeon, mighty men of valor for the war, seven thousand and one hundred. 26 Of the children of Levi four thousand and six hundred. 27 And Jehoiada was the leader of *the house of* Aaron; and with him were three thousand and seven hundred, 28 and Zadok, a young man mighty of valor, and of his father's house twenty and two captains. 29 And of the children of Benjamin, the brethren of Saul, three thousand: for hitherto the greatest part of them had kept their allegiance to the house of Saul. 30 And of the children of Ephraim twenty thousand and eight hundred, mighty men of valor, famous men in their fathers' houses. 31 And of the half-tribe of Manasseh eighteen thousand, who were mentioned by name, to come and make David king. 32 And of the children of Issachar, men that had understanding of the times, to know what Israel ought to do, the heads of them were two hundred; and all their brethren were at their commandment. 33 Of Zebulun, such as were able to go out in the host, that could set the battle in array, with all manner of instruments of war, fifty thousand, and that could order *the battle array, and were* not of double heart. 34 And of Naphtali a thousand captains, and with them with shield and spear thirty and seven thousand. 35 And of the Danites that could set the battle in array, twenty and eight thousand and six hundred. 36 And of Asher, such as were able to go out in the host, that could set the battle in array, forty thousand. 37 And on the other side of the Jordan, of the Reubenites, and the Gadites, and of the half-tribe of Manasseh, with all manner of instruments of war for the battle, a hundred and twenty thousand.

38 All these, being men of war, that could order the battle array, came with a perfect heart to Hebron, to make David king over all Israel: and all the rest also of Israel were of one heart to make David king. 39 And they were there with David three days, eating and drinking; for their brethren had made preparation for them. 40 Moreover they that were nigh unto them, *even* as far as Issachar and Zebulun and Naphtali, brought bread on asses, and on camels, and on mules, and on oxen, victuals of meal, cakes of figs, and clusters of raisins, and wine, and oil, and oxen, and sheep in abundance: for there was joy in Israel.

This is another passage peculiar to Chronicles. David was settled in Hebron after the death of Saul. There came to him considerable re-enforcements **to turn the kingdom of Saul to him, according to the word of Jehovah** (v. 23).

The force of what is here being said is that David had the support of a great many from all of the tribes. That he became king was not only the will of God but also the will of a great host of patriotic followers.

E. DAVID AND THE ARK (13:1—16:43)

After capturing Jerusalem and establishing it as "the city of David" and the capital of the nation, David was primarily concerned to restore the ark of the covenant to its rightful place in the religious life of the nation. The Chronicles account gives much space to the ark of the covenant.

1. The Ark Brought from Kiriath-jearim (13:1-14; cf. II Sam. 6)

1 And David consulted with the captains of thousands and of hundreds, even with every leader. 2 And David said unto all the assembly of Israel, If it seem good unto you, and if it be of Jehovah our God, let us send abroad every where unto our brethren that are left in all the land of Israel, with whom the priests and Levites are in their cities that have suburbs, that they may gather themselves unto us; 3 and let us bring again the ark of our God to us: for we sought not unto it in the days of Saul. 4 And all the assembly said that they would do so; for the thing was right in the eyes of all the people. 5 So David assembled all Israel together, from the Shihor *the brook* of Egypt even unto the entrance of Hamath, to bring the ark of God from Kiriath-jearim. 6 And David went up, and all Israel, to Baalah, *that is,* to Kiriath-jearim, which belonged to Judah, to bring up from thence the ark of God Jehovah that sitteth *above* the cherubim, that is called by the Name. 7 And they carried the ark of God upon a new cart, *and brought it* out of the house of Abinadab: and Uzza and Ahio drove the cart. 8 And David and all Israel played before God with all their might, even with songs, and with harps, and with psalteries, and with timbrels, and with cymbals, and with trumpets. 9 And when they came unto the thresh-ing-floor of Chidon, Uzza put forth his hand to hold the ark; for the oxen stumbled. 10 And the anger of Jehovah was kindled against Uzza, and he smote him, because he put forth his hand to the ark; and there he died before God. 11 And David was displeased, because Jehovah had broken forth upon Uzza: and he called that place Perez-uzza, unto this day. 12 And David was afraid of God that day, saying, How shall I bring the ark of God home to me? 13 So David removed not the ark unto him into the city of David, but carried it aside into the house of Obed-edom the Gittite. 14 And the ark of God remained with the family of Obed-edom in his house three months: and Jehovah blessed the house of Obed-edom, and all that he had.

David purposed to obtain the ark and place it in the capital of his kingdom. Moreover, he sought the cooperation of all Israel, and this was willingly granted. "The chronicler is obviously making more of the occasion than the writer of Samuel."[5] This is true because of his intent of writing a religious history of Israel in which the ark of the covenant has a central place.

There is revealed an intriguing sequence of moods which came to David in the course of moving the ark from Kiriath-jearim. First is the solemn mood of the formal procession (v. 6). Second is the jubilant mood accompanying the transportation of the ark (v. 8). Third is the mood of disquietude because of the tragic fate of Uzza (v. 11). Fourth is the mood of fear (v. 12). This series of moods points to a concern of the chronicler to which he gave much attention, namely, reverence in religious order and worship. True and acceptable reverence is coupled with correctness in order and worship. David needed more than mood; he needed form which was acceptable to God. Worship to God cannot be determined by disposition alone, according to the chronicler. He considered correct form essential. This is a valid emphasis often slighted in non-liturgical services of worship.

2. Insertion: David's Defeat of the Philistines (14:1-17; cf. II Sam. 5:11-25)

1 And Hiram king of Tyre sent messengers to David, and cedar-trees, and masons, and carpenters, to build him a

house. 2 And David perceived that Jehovah had established him king over Israel; for his kingdom was exalted on high, for his people Israel's sake.

3 And David took more wives at Jerusalem; and David begat more sons and daughters. And these are the names of the children whom he had in Jerusalem: Shammua, and Shobab, Nathan, and Solomon, 5 and Ibhar, and Elishua, and Elpelet, 6 and Nogah, and Nepheg, and Japhia, 7 and Elishama, and Beeliada, and Eliphelet.

8 And when the Philistines heard that David was anointed king over all Israel, all the Philistines went up to seek David: and David heard of it, and went out against them. 9 Now the Philistines had come and made a raid in the valley of Rephaim. 10 And David inquired of God, saying, Shall I go up against the Philistines? and wilt thou deliver them into my hand? And Jehovah said unto him, Go up; for I will deliver them into thy hand. 11 So they came up to Baal-perazim, and David smote them there; and David said, God hath broken mine enemies by my hand, like the breach of waters. Therefore they called the name of that place Baal-perazim. 12 And they left their gods there; and David gave commandment, and they were burned with fire.

13 And the Philistines yet again made a raid in the valley. 14 And David inquired again of God; and God said unto him, Thou shalt not go up after them: turn away from them, and come upon them over against the mulberry-trees. 15 And it shall be, when thou hearest the sound of marching in the tops of the mulberry-trees, that then thou shalt go out to battle; for God is gone out before thee to smite the host of the Philistines. 16 And David did as God commanded him: and they smote the host of the Philistines from Gibeon even to Gezer. 17 And the fame of David went out into all lands; and Jehovah brought the fear of him upon all nations.

This chapter interrupts the account of bringing the ark of the covenant to Jerusalem. After references to David's palace and family, the chronicler proceeds to describe David's important victories over the Philistines. **And when the Philistines heard that David was anointed king over all Israel, all the Philistines went up to seek David** (v. 8). Because David faithfully inquired of the Lord, he was able to gain two impressive victories

over the Philistines. **And the fame of David went out into all lands** (v. 17).

3. The Ark Brought to Jerusalem (15: 1–16:6; cf. II Sam. 6:12-19)

1 And *David* made him houses in the city of David; and he prepared a place for the ark of God, and pitched for it a tent. 2 Then David said, None ought to carry the ark of God but the Levites: for them hath Jehovah chosen to carry the ark of God, and to minister unto him for ever. 3 And David assembled all Israel at Jerusalem, to bring up the ark of Jehovah unto its place, which he had prepared for it. 4 And David gathered together the sons of Aaron, and the Levites: 5 of the sons of Kohath, Uriel the chief, and his brethren a hundred and twenty; 6 of the sons of Merari, Asaiah the chief, and his brethren two hundred and twenty; 7 of the sons of Gershom, Joel the chief, and his brethren a hundred and thirty; 8 of the sons of Elizaphan, Shemaiah the chief, and his brethren two hundred; 9 of the sons of Hebron, Eliel the chief, and his brethren fourscore; 10 of the sons of Uzziel, Amminadab the chief, and his brethren a hundred and twelve. 11 And David called for Zadok and Abiathar the priests, and for the Levites, for Uriel, Asaiah, and Joel, Shemaiah, and Eliel, and Amminadab, 12 and said unto them, Ye are the heads of the fathers' *houses* of the Levites: sanctify yourselves, both ye and your brethren, that ye may bring up the ark of Jehovah, the God of Israel, unto *the place* that I have prepared for it. 13 For because ye *bare it* not at the first, Jehovah our God made a breach upon us, for that we sought him not according to the ordinance. 14 So the priests and the Levites sanctified themselves to bring up the ark of Jehovah, the God of Israel. 15 And the children of the Levites bare the ark of God upon their shoulders with the staves thereon, as Moses commanded according to the word of Jehovah.

16 And David spake to the chief of the Levites to appoint their brethren the singers, with instruments of music, psalteries and harps and cymbals, sounding aloud and lifting up the voice with joy. 17 So the Levites appointed Heman the son of Joel; and of his brethren, Asaph the son of Berechiah; and of the sons of Merari their brethren, Ethan the son of Kushaiah; 18 and with them their brethren of the second degree, Zechariah, Ben, and Jaaziel, and Shemiramoth, and Jehiel, and Unni, Eliab, and Benaiah, and

Maaseiah, and Mattithiah. and Eliphelehu, and Mikneiah, and Obed-edom, and Jeiel, the doorkeepers. 19 So the singers, Heman, Asaph, and Ethan, *were appointed*, with cymbals of brass to sound aloud; 20 and Zechariah, and Aziel, and Shemiramoth, and Jehiel, and Unni, and Eliab, and Maaseiah, and Benaiah, with psalteries set to Alamoth; 21 and Mattithiah, and Eliphelehu, and Mikneiah, and Obed-edom, and Jeiel, and Azaziah, with harps set to the Sheminith, to lead. 22 And Chenaniah, chief of the Levites, was over the song: he instructed about the song, because he was skilful. 23 And Berechiah and Elkanah were doorkeepers for the ark. 24 And Shebaniah, and Joshaphat, and Nethanel, and Amasai, and Zechariah, and Benaiah, and Eliezer, the priests, did blow the trumpets before the ark of God; and Obed-edom and Jehiah were doorkeepers for the ark.

25 So David, and the elders of Israel, and the captains over thousands, went to bring up the ark of the covenant of Jehovah out of the house of Obed-edom with joy. 26 And it came to pass, when God helped the Levites that bare the ark of the covenant of Jehovah, that they sacrificed seven bullocks and seven rams. 27 And David was clothed with a robe of fine* linen, and all the Levites that bare the ark, and the singers, and Chenaniah the master of the song *with* the singers: and David had upon him an ephod of linen. 28 Thus all Israel brought up the ark of the covenant of Jehovah with shouting, and with sound of the cornet, and with trumpets, and with cymbals, sounding aloud with psalteries and harps.

29 And it came to pass, as the ark of the covenant of Jehovah came to the city of David, that Michal the daughter of Saul looked out at the window, and saw king David dancing and playing; and she despised him in her heart.

1 And they brought in the ark of God, and set it in the midst of the tent that David had pitched for it: and they offered burnt-offerings and peace-offerings before God. 2 And when David had made an end of offering the burnt-offering and the peace-offerings, he blessed the people in the name of Jehovah. 3 And he dealt to every one of Israel, both man and woman, to every one a loaf of bread, and a portion *of flesh*, and a cake of raisins.

4 And he appointed certain of the Levites to minister before the ark of Jehovah, and to celebrate and to thank and praise Jehovah, the God of Israel: 5 Asaph the chief, and second to him Zechariah, Jeiel, and Shemiramoth, and Jehiel, and Mattithiah, and Eliab, and Benaiah, and Obed-edom, and Jeiel, with psalteries and with harps; and Asaph with cymbals, sounding aloud; 6 and Benaiah and Jahaziel the priests with trumpets continually, before the ark of the covenant of God.

David renewed his efforts to have the ark of the covenant brought to Jerusalem. He learned from his first attempt that the transportation of the ark should be by the Levites. **None ought to carry the ark of God but the Levites: for them hath God chosen to carry the ark of God, and to minister unto him for ever** (v. 2; cf. vv. 11-13).

After careful instructions and preparations, the ceremonial procession bore the ark to Jerusalem. Accompanying the Levitical bearers were the appointed musicians and singers, together with David (vv. 27, 28). By reason of the correctness of procedure in handling the ark, the procession moved without incident into Jerusalem. It occasioned great enthusiasm, and David joined in the dancing and playing (v. 29). It appeared to Michal the queen that David was acting beneath his kingly dignity (v. 29). Yet David had learned a valuable lesson in worship to God, and he was joyous over the results. It is ever an occasion of joy to realize that correctness and appropriateness in worship is blessed of God.

4. A Psalm of Praise (16:7-36)

7 Then on that day did David first ordain to give thanks unto Jehovah, by the hand of Asaph and his brethren.
8 O give thanks unto Jehovah, call upon his name;
   Make known his doings among the peoples.
9 Sing unto him, sing praises unto him;
   Talk ye of all his marvellous works.
10 Glory ye in his holy name;
   Let the heart of them rejoice that seek Jehovah.
11 Seek ye Jehovah and his strength;
   Seek his face evermore.
12 Remember his marvellous works that he hath done,
   His wonders, and the judgments of his mouth,
13 O ye seed of Israel his servant,
   Ye children of Jacob, his chosen ones.
14 He is Jehovah our God;
   His judgments are in all the earth.

15 Remember his covenant for ever,
  The word which he commanded to a thousand generations,
16 *The covenant* which he made with Abraham,
  And his oath unto Isaac,
17 And confirmed the same unto Jacob for a statute,
  To Israel for an everlasting covenant,
18 Saying, Unto thee will I give the land of Canaan,
  The lot of your inheritance;
19 When ye were but a few men in number,
  Yea, very few, and sojourners in it;
20 And they went about from nation to nation,
  And from one kingdom to another people.
21 He suffered no man to do them wrong;
  Yea, he reproved kings for their sakes,
22 *Saying*, Touch not mine anointed ones,
  And do my prophets no harm.
23 Sing unto Jehovah, all the earth;
  Show forth his salvation from day to day.
24 Declare his glory among the nations,
  His marvellous works among all the peoples.
25 For great is Jehovah, and greatly to be praised:
  He also is to be feared above all gods.
26 For all the gods of the peoples are idols:
  But Jehovah made the heavens.
27 Honor and majesty are before him:
  Strength and gladness are in his place.
28 Ascribe unto Jehovah, ye kindreds of the peoples,
  Ascribe unto Jehovah glory and strength;
29 Ascribe unto Jehovah the glory due unto his name:
  Bring an offering, and come before him;
  Worship Jehovah in holy array.
30 Tremble before him, all the earth:
  The world also is established that it cannot be moved.
31 Let the heavens be glad, and let the earth rejoice;
  And let them say among the nations, Jehovah reigneth.
32 Let the sea roar, and the fulness thereof;
  Let the field exult, and all that is therein;
33 Then shall the trees of the wood sing for joy before Jehovah;
  For he cometh to judge the earth.
34 O give thanks unto Jehovah; for he is good;

For his lovingkindness *endureth* for ever.
35 And say ye, Save us, O God of our salvation,
  And gather us together and deliver us from the nations,
  To give thanks unto thy holy name,
  And to triumph in thy praise.
36 Blessed be Jehovah, the God of Israel,
  From everlasting even to everlasting.
And all the people said, Amen, and praised Jehovah.

This psalm is a composite of parts of three canonical psalms: the first movement (vv. 8-22) is from Psalm 105:1-15; the second movement (vv. 23-33) is from Psalm 96:1b-13a; and the third movement (vv. 34-36) is from Psalm 106:1, 47-48. The compilation was by one thoroughly acquainted with the psalms and contained most appropriate selections. It was an opportune occasion for David to render a psalm, and the selection was in keeping with the occasion. "None of the three Psalms used is Davidic and all are later, possibly even post exilic."[6] Evidently no existing psalm was suitable, so a composite was formed. For further commentary the relevant passages in the Psalms should be studied.

5. Religious Service (16:37-43)

37 So he left there, before the ark of the covenant of Jehovah, Asaph and his brethren, to minister before the ark continually, as every day's work required; 38 and Obed-edom with their brethren, threescore and eight; Obed-edom also the son of Jeduthun and Hosah to be doorkeepers; 39 and Zadok the priest, and his brethren the priests, before the tabernacle of Jehovah in the high place that was at Gibeon, 40 to offer burnt-offerings unto Jehovah upon the altar of burnt-offering continually morning and evening, even according to all that is written in the law of Jehovah, which he commanded unto Israel; 41 and with them Heman and Jeduthun, and the rest that were chosen, who were mentioned by name, to give thanks to Jehovah, because his lovingkindness *endureth* for ever; 42 and with them Heman and Jeduthun *with* trumpets and cymbals for those that should sound aloud, and *with* instruments for the songs of God; and the sons of Jeduthun to be at the gate. 43

[6] *Ibid.*, p. 348.

And all the people departed every man to his house: and David returned to bless his house.

With the ark properly and safely brought to Jerusalem, David proceeded to arrange for adequate ministration of religious worship. Assignments were made for the daily schedule (v. 37). Zadok and the priests were responsible for continual sacrifices (vv. 39, 40). The musicians were to provide testimonials of praise (vv. 41, 42). With the return of the ark to the center of Israel's religious and cultural life, David had accomplished a revitalization of religious devotion along liturgical and ceremonial lines. Great emphasis was given to the responsibilities of the priests and Levites and their helpers. This kind of reviving may not be understood by churches which give little or no attention to form and liturgy, but it is clearly understood by the liturgical and confessional churches. Without doubt, John Wesley with his liturgical concern appreciatively studied it.

F. DAVID'S TEMPLE PLANS (17:1-27)

The fact that the ark was sheltered by a tent while the king lived in a palace, caused David to aspire to build a temple for the ark.

1. The Message of the Prophet (17:1-15; cf. II Sam. 7:1-17)

1 And it came to pass, when David dwelt in his house, that David said to Nathan the prophet, Lo, I dwell in a house of cedar, but the ark of the covenant of Jehovah *dwelleth* under curtains. 2 And Nathan said unto David, Do all that is in thy heart; for God is with thee. 3 And it came to pass the same night, that the word of God came to Nathan, saying, 4 Go and tell David my servant, Thus saith Jehovah, Thou shalt not build me a house to dwell in; 5 for I have not dwelt in a house since the day that I brought up Israel, unto this day, but have gone from tent to tent, and from *one* tabernacle *to another*. 6 In all places wherein I have walked with all Israel, spake I a word with any of the judges of Israel, whom I commanded to be shepherd of my people, saying, Why have ye not built me a house of cedar? 7 Now therefore thus shalt thou say unto my servant David, Thus saith Jehovah of hosts, I took thee from the sheepcote, from following the sheep, that thou shouldest be prince over my people Israel: 8 and I have been with thee whithersoever thou hast gone, and have cut off all thine enemies from before thee; and I will make thee a name, like unto the name of the great ones that are in the earth. 9 And I will appoint a place for my people Israel, and will plant them, that they may dwell in their own place, and be moved no more; neither shall the children of wickedness waste them any more, as at the first, 10 and *as* from the day that I commanded judges to be over my people Israel; and I will subdue all thine enemies. Moreover I tell thee that Jehovah will build thee a house. 11 And it shall come to pass, when thy days are fulfilled that thou must go to be with thy fathers, that I will set up thy seed after thee, who shall be of thy sons; and I will establish his kingdom. 12 He shall build me a house, and I will establish his throne for ever. 13 I will be his father, and he shall be my son: and I will not take my lovingkindness away from him, as I took it from him that was before thee; 14 but I will settle him in my house and in my kingdom for ever; and his throne shall be established for ever. 15 According to all these words, and according to all this vision, so did Nathan speak unto David.

When David expressed his aspiration concerning building the temple, Nathan the prophet seemed agreeable, until he received a message from the Lord. That message denied David the opportunity of fulfilling his desire. Nathan's readiness to deliver the message to David was a great test of the prophet's fidelity to the Lord. David had supreme political power, and for Nathan to deny the powerful monarch an opportunity to fulfill his aspirations was perilous. Although Nathan was fully aware of what David wanted to do, he had a clear understanding of the divine message. True to the tradition of the prophets, Nathan courageously challenged the political sovereign. The prophets have left us a challenging tradition. Political authority still needs to hear the message of the Lord through prophets.

2. The Prayer of the King (17:16-27; cf. II Sam. 7:18-29)

16 Then David the king went in, and sat before Jehovah; and he said, Who am

I, O Jehovah God, and what is my house, that thou hast brought me thus far? 17 And this was a small thing in thine eyes, O God; but thou hast spoken of thy servant's house for a great while to come, and hast regarded me according to the estate of a man of high degree, O Jehovah God. 18 What can David *say* yet more unto thee concerning the honor which is done to thy servant? for thou knowest thy servant. 19 O Jehovah, for thy servant's sake, and according to thine own heart, hast thou wrought all this greatness, to make known all *these* great things. 20 O Jehovah, there is none like thee, neither is there any God besides thee, according to all that we have heard with our ears. 21 And what one nation in the earth is like thy people Israel, whom God went to redeem unto himself for a people, to make thee a name by great and terrible things, in driving out nations from before thy people, whom thou redeemedst out of Egypt? 22 For thy people Israel didst thou make thine own people for ever; and thou, Jehovah, becamest their God. 23 And now, O Jehovah, let the word that thou hast spoken concerning thy servant, and concerning his house, be established for ever, and do as thou hast spoken. 24 And let thy name be established and magnified for ever, saying, Jehovah of hosts is the God of Israel, even a God to Israel: and the house of David thy servant is established before thee. 25 For thou, O my God, hast revealed to thy servant that thou wilt build him a house: therefore hath thy servant found *in his heart* to pray before thee. 26 And now, O Jehovah, thou art God, and hast promised this good thing unto thy servant: 27 and now it hath pleased thee to bless the house of thy servant, that it may continue for ever before thee: for thou, O Jehovah, hast blessed, and it is blessed for ever.

David's response in prayer was one of abounding gratitude for the amazing activity of divine grace. He willingly relented his aspiration to build the temple, for he acknowledged that his relationship with God was dependent, not so much upon what he desired to do for God, as upon what God was doing for him. In any relationship which man has with God, it is vitally necessary to realize that what is done is to be done according to the will of God.

G. DAVID'S WARS (18:1—20:8)

David's wars are recounted in Chronicles in such a way as to show that David utilized his wars for the purpose of obtaining a large store of wealth and treasures in preparation for a temple of the Lord (cf. II Sam. 7:1ff. with I Chron. 18:1ff.).

1. David's Victories (18:1-13; cf. II Sam. 8:1-14)

1 And after this it came to pass, that David smote the Philistines, and subdued them, and took Gath and its towns out of the hand of the Philistines. 2 And he smote Moab; and the Moabites became servants to David, and brought tribute.

3 And David smote Hadarezer king of Zobah unto Hamath, as he went to establish his dominion by the river Euphrates. 4 And David took from him a thousand chariots, and seven thousand horsemen, and twenty thousand footmen; and David hocked all the chariot horses, but reserved of them for a hundred chariots. 5 And when the Syrians of Damascus came to succor Hadarezer king of Zobah, David smote of the Syrians two and twenty thousand men. 6 Then David put *garrisons* in Syria of Damascus; and the Syrians became servants to David, and brought tribute. And Jehovah gave victory to David whithersoever he went. 7 And David took the shields of gold that were on the servants of Hadarezer, and brought them to Jerusalem. 8 And from Tibhath and from Cun, cities of Hadarezer, David took very much brass, wherewith Solomon made the brazen sea, and the pillars, and the vessels of brass.

9 And when Tou king of Hamath heard that David had smitten all the host of Hadarezer king of Zobah, 10 he sent Hadoram his son to king David, to salute him, and to bless him, because he had fought against Hadarezer and smitten him (for Hadarezer had wars with Tou); and *he had with him* all manner of vessels of gold and silver and brass. 11 These also did king David dedicate unto Jehovah, with the silver and the gold that he carried away from all the nations; from Edom, and from Moab, and from the children of Ammon, and from the Philistines, and from Amalek.

12 Moreover Abishai the son of Zeruiah smote of the Edomites in the Valley of Salt eighteen thousand. 13 And he put garrisons in Edom; and all the Edomites became servants to David. And Jehovah gave victory to David whithersoever he went.

With slight variations the Chronicles account is almost the same as the Samuel account (cf. II Sam. 8:1-14). There are references by the chronicler to David's wars as occasions for David to take spoils of war from other countries in order to have materials ready for building a temple. **And from ... cities of Hadarezer, David took very much brass, wherewith Solomon made the brazen sea, and the pillars, and the vessels of brass** (v. 8; cf. vv. 7, 10, 11). Neither David nor the chronicler seems to convey awareness of the moral problem involved in dedicating the confiscated wealth of other nations to a temple for Jehovah God. In the light of the righteousness of God, it is necessary to cultivate a conscience regarding such matters. David's wars were approved by the chronicler since they made possible adequate materials for the temple. However, the noble end did not justify the ignoble means. The chronicler sees David's victories as given by God (I Chron. 18:13). Is it not possible that the principle is the same as that which directed Joshua to slay the Canaanites (cf. Gen. 15:16; II Kings 21:11)?

2. Parenthesis: David's Officers (18:14-17; cf. II Sam. 8:15-18)

14 And David reigned over all Israel; and he executed justice and righteousness unto all his people. 15 And Joab the son of Zeruiah was over the host, and Jehoshaphat the son of Ahilud was recorder; 16 and Zadok the son of Ahitub, and Abimelech the son of Abiathar, were priests; and Shavsha was scribe; 17 and Benaiah the son of Jehoiada was over the Cherethites and the Pelethites; and the sons of David were chief about the king.

This passage is similar to the parallel passage in Samuel.

3. The Ammonite Campaign (19:1—20:3; cf. II Sam. 10:1—11:1; 12:26-31)

1 And it came to pass after this, that Nahash the king of the children of Ammon died, and his son reigned in his stead. 2 And David said, I will show kindness unto Hanun the son of Nahash, because his father showed kindness to me. So David sent messengers to comfort him concerning his father. And David's servants came into the land of the children of Ammon to Hanun, to comfort him. 3 But the princes of the children of Ammon said to Hanun, Thinkest thou that David doth honor thy father, in that he hath sent comforters unto thee? are not his servants come unto thee to search, and to overthrow, and to spy out the land? 4 So Hanun took David's servants, and shaved them, and cut off their garments in the middle, even to their buttocks, and sent them away. 5 Then there went certain persons, and told David how the men were served. And he sent to meet them; for the men were greatly ashamed. And the king said, Tarry at Jericho until your beards be grown, and then return.

6 And when the children of Ammon saw that they had made themselves odious to David, Hanun and the children of Ammon sent a thousand talents of silver to hire them chariots and horsemen out of Mesopotamia, and out of Aram-maacah, and out of Zobah. 7 So they hired them thirty and two thousand chariots, and the king of Maacah and his people, who came and encamped before Medeba. And the children of Ammon gathered themselves together from their cities, and came to battle. 8 And when David heard of it, he sent Joab, and all the host of the mighty men. 9 And the children of Ammon came out, and put the battle in array at the gate of the city: and the kings that were come were by themselves in the field.

10 Now when Joab saw that the battle was set against him before and behind, he chose of all the choice men of Israel, and put them in array against the Syrians. 11 And the rest of the people he committed into the hand of Abishai his brother; and they put themselves in array against the children of Ammon. 12 And he said, If the Syrians be too strong for me, then thou shalt help me; but if the children of Ammon be too strong for thee, then I will help thee. 13 Be of good courage, and let us play the man for our people, and for the cities of our God: and Jehovah do that which seemeth him good. 14 So Joab and the people that were with him drew nigh before the Syrians unto the battle; and they fled before him. 15 And when the children of Ammon saw that the Syrians were fled, they likewise fled before Abishai his brother, and entered into the city. Then Joab came to Jerusalem.

16 And when the Syrians saw that they were put to the worse before Israel, they sent messengers, and drew forth the Syrians that were beyond the River, with Shophach the captain of the host of Had-

arezer at their head. 17 And it was told David; and he gathered all Israel together, and passed over the Jordan, and came upon them, and set the battle in array against them. So when David had put the battle in array against the Syrians, they fought with him. 18 And the Syrians fled before Israel; and David slew of the Syrians *the men of* seven thousand chariots, and forty thousand footmen, and killed Shophach the captain of the host. 19 And when the servants of Hadarezer saw that they were put to the worse before Israel, they made peace with David, and served him: neither would the Syrians help the children of Ammon any more.

1 And it came to pass, at the time of the return of the year, at the time when kings go out *to battle,* that Joab led forth the army, and wasted the country of the children of Ammon, and came and besieged Rabbah. But David tarried at Jerusalem. And Joab smote Rabbah, and overthrew it. 2 And David took the crown of their king from off his head, and found it to weigh a talent of gold, and there were precious stones in it; and it was set upon David's head: and he brought forth the spoil of the city, exceeding much. 3 And he brought forth the people that were therein, and cut *them* with saws, and with harrows of iron, and with axes. And thus did David unto all the cities of the children of Ammon. And David and all the people returned to Jerusalem.

The only significant variation in the Chronicles account from the Samuel account is the omission of David's affair with Bathsheba, including the death of Uriah. Since the Chronicles account exalted the political institution of the Davidic dynasty and the religious institution of worship in Jerusalem, this unseemly incident in the life of David is omitted.

4. The Philistine Conflict (20:4-8; cf. II Sam. 21:18-22)

4 And it came to pass after this, that there arose war at Gezer with the Philistines: then Sibbecai the Hushathite slew Sippai, of the sons of the giant; and they were subdued. 5 And there was again war with the Philistines; and Elhanan the son of Jair slew Lahmi the brother of Goliath the Gittite, the staff of whose spear was like a weaver's beam. 6 And there was again war at Gath, where was a man of great stature, whose fingers and toes were four and twenty, six *on each hand,* and

six *on each foot;* and he also was born unto the giant. 7 And when he defied Israel, Jonathan the son of Shimea David's brother slew him. 8 These were born unto the giant in Gath; and they fell by the hand of David, and by the hand of his servants.

Since there is no important variation from the Samuel account, see the notes on the parallel passage in II Samuel.

H. DAVID'S CENSUS AND ITS SEQUEL (21:1—22:19)

The chronicler has not recorded this presumptuous sin as a story without purpose but as an account contributing to the explanation for the site of the temple and how that location was obtained.

1. The Census and the Pestilence (21:1-17; cf. II Sam. 24:1-17)

1 And Satan stood up against Israel, and moved David to number Israel. 2 And David said to Joab and to the princes of the people, Go, number Israel from Beer-sheba even to Dan; and bring me word, that I may know the sum of them. 3 And Joab said, Jehovah make his people a hundred times as many as they are: but, my lord the king, are they not all my lord's servants? why doth my lord require this thing? why will he be a cause of guilt unto Israel? 4 Nevertheless the king's word prevailed against Joab. Wherefore Joab departed, and went throughout all Israel, and came to Jerusalem. 5 And Joab gave up the sum of the numbering of the people unto David. And all they of Israel were a thousand thousand and a hundred thousand men that drew sword: and Judah was four hundred threescore and ten thousand men that drew sword. 6 But Levi and Benjamin counted he not among them; for the king's word was abominable to Joab. 7 And God was displeased with this thing; therefore he smote Israel. 8 And David said unto God, I have sinned greatly, in that I have done this thing: but now put away, I beseech thee, the iniquity of thy servant; for I have done very foolishly.

9 And Jehovah spake unto Gad, David's seer, saying, 10 Go and speak unto David, saying, Thus saith Jehovah, I offer thee three things: choose thee one of them, that I may do it unto thee. 11 So Gad came to David, and said unto him, Thus saith Jehovah, Take which thou wilt: 12 either three years of famine; or

three months to be consumed before thy foes, while the sword of thine enemies overtaketh thee; or else three days the sword of Jehovah, even pestilence in the land, and the angel of Jehovah destroying throughout all the borders of Israel. Now therefore consider what answer I shall return to him that sent me. 13 And David said unto Gad, I am in a great strait: let me fall, I pray, into the hand of Jehovah; for very great are his mercies: and let me not fall into the hand of man. 14 So Jehovah sent a pestilence upon Israel; and there fell of Israel seventy thousand men. 15 And God sent an angel unto Jerusalem to destroy it: and as he was about to destroy, Jehovah beheld, and he repented him of the evil, and said to the destroying angel, It is enough; now stay thy hand. And the angel of Jehovah was standing by the threshing-floor of Ornan the Jebusite. 16 And David lifted up his eyes, and saw the angel of Jehovah standing between earth and heaven, having a drawn sword in his hand stretched out over Jerusalem. Then David and the elders, clothed in sackcloth, fell upon their faces. 17 And David said unto God, Is it not I that commanded the people to be numbered? Even I it is that have sinned and done very wickedly; but these sheep, what have they done? let thy hand, I pray thee, O Jehovah my God, be against me, and against my father's house; but not against thy people, that they should be plagued.

While the Samuel account explains the act of David taking the census as originating with God, the Chronicles account gives a refinement of that explanation. Fully aware that Satan is an agent of God, the chronicler sets forth the moral test to which David succumbed. While there is no doubt that Satan is the enemy of God, there is reason to believe that just as wicked men can serve God in His purposes so can Satan. The Chronicles account helps us to see our moral accountability. Moral testing is part of life, and we are to live with this realization before us. Note the account in II Samuel.

2. The Sacrifice and the Temple Site (21:18—22:1; cf. II Sam. 24:18-25)

18 Then the angel of Jehovah commanded Gad to say to David, that David should go up, and rear an altar unto Jehovah in the threshing-floor of Ornan the Jebusite. 19 And David went up at the saying of Gad, which he spake in the name of Jehovah. 20 And Ornan turned back, and saw the angel; and his four sons that were with him hid themselves. Now Ornan was threshing wheat. 21 And as David came to Ornan, Ornan looked and saw David, and went out of the threshing-floor, and bowed himself to David with his face to the ground. 22 Then David said to Ornan, Give me the place of this threshing-floor, that I may build thereon an altar unto Jehovah: for the full price shalt thou give it me, that the plague may be stayed from the people. 23 And Ornan said unto David, Take it to thee, and let my lord the king do that which is good in his eyes: lo, I give *thee* the oxen for burnt-offerings, and the threshing instruments for wood, and the wheat for the meal-offering; I give it all. 24 And king David said to Ornan, Nay; but I will verily buy it for the full price: for I will not take that which is thine for Jehovah, nor offer a burnt-offering without cost. 25 So David gave to Ornan for the place six hundred shekels of gold by weight. 26 And David built there an altar unto Jehovah, and offered burnt-offerings and peace-offerings, and called upon Jehovah; and he answered him from heaven by fire upon the altar of burnt-offering. 27 And Jehovah commanded the angel; and he put up his sword again into the sheath thereof.

28 At that time, when David saw that Jehovah had answered him in the threshing-floor of Ornan the Jebusite, then he sacrificed there. 29 For the tabernacle of Jehovah which Moses made in the wilderness, and the altar of burnt-offering, were at that time in the high place at Gibeon. 30 But David could not go before it to inquire of God; for he was afraid because of the sword of the angel of Jehovah. 1 Then David said, This is the house of Jehovah God, and this is the altar of burnt-offering for Israel.

David's confession of sin regarding the census resulted in the divine word instructing him through the mouth of the prophet to go to the threshing-floor of Ornan the Jebusite and erect an altar unto Jehovah (v. 18). Upon his arrival at the location, David discovered Ornan hiding because of his fear of a heavenly visitor, the angel of Jehovah, who had interrupted his threshing.

David related to Ornan the purpose of his coming. Upon hearing this, Ornan willingly agreed to give David possession of the place. David arranged to purchase the site and then had an altar for sacrifice erected (vv. 26-27). By reason of the sacrifice, **Jehovah commanded the angel; and he put up his sword** (v. 27).

The terrible pestilence was removed from the people, and David realized that God had received the sacrifice offered on Ornan's threshing-floor. As a result, he determined that this place of sacrifice was to be the site of the temple. **This is the house of Jehovah God, and this is the altar of burnt-offering for Israel** (v. 1). "The purpose of these verses is to show how, as a consequence of the census and plague, the threshing-place became the consecrated site of the temple."[7] What began as a presumptuous sin of census-taking had as its sequel a memorable sign of divine blessing. When David repented and offered sacrifice to God, there came fire from heaven and consumed the sacrifice (v. 26). There also came the divine confirmation that Ornan's threshing-floor was to be the site for the temple (v. 1).

While the entire incident regarding the census-taking and the sacrifice indicates the weakness of man, the more important truth is the revelation of the grace of God. In a manner that eludes analysis, God made provision for a place of worship. Mount Moriah became a most sacred spot, for here Solomon built the temple unto the Lord.

3. David's Temple Preparations (22:2-5)

2 And David commanded to gather together the sojourners that were in the land of Israel; and he set masons to hew wrought stones to build the house of God. 3 And David prepared iron in abundance for the nails for the doors of the gates, and for the couplings; and brass in abundance without weight; 4 and cedar-trees without number: for the Sidonians and they of Tyre brought cedar-trees in abundance to David. 5 And David said, Solomon my son is young and tender, and the house that is to be builded for Jehovah must be exceeding magnificent, of fame and of glory throughout all countries: I will therefore make preparation for it. So David prepared abundantly before his death.

Although David did not build the temple, he engaged in extensive preparations for it (v. 5). The materials which he amassed included stone, brass and cedar lumber.

4. David's Charge Concerning the Temple (22:6-19)

6 Then he called for Solomon his son, and charged him to build a house for Jehovah, the God of Israel. 7 And David said to Solomon his son, As for me, it was in my heart to build a house unto the name of Jehovah my God. 8 But the word of Jehovah came to me, saying, Thou hast shed blood abundantly, and hast made great wars: thou shalt not build a house unto my name, because thou hast shed much blood upon the earth in my sight. 9 Behold, a son shall be born to thee, who shall be a man of rest; and I will give him rest from all his enemies round about; for his name shall be Solomon, and I will give peace and quietness unto Israel in his days. 10 He shall build a house for my name; and he shall be my son, and I will be his father; and I will establish the throne of his kingdom over Israel for ever. 11 Now, my son, Jehovah be with thee; and prosper thou, and build the house of Jehovah thy God, as he hath spoken concerning thee. 12 Only Jehovah give thee discretion and understanding, and give thee charge concerning Israel; that so thou mayest keep the law of Jehovah thy God. 13 Then shalt thou prosper, if thou observe to do the statutes and the ordinances which Jehovah charged Moses with concerning Israel: be strong, and of good courage; fear not, neither be dismayed. 14 Now, behold, in my affliction I have prepared for the house of Jehovah a hundred thousand talents of gold, and a thousand thousand talents of silver, and of brass and iron without weight; for it is in abundance: timber also and stone have I prepared; and thou mayest add thereto. 15 Moreover there are workmen with thee in abundance, hewers and workers of stone and timber, and all men that are skilful in every manner of work: 16 of the gold, the silver, and the brass, and the iron, there is no number. Arise and be doing, and Jehovah be with thee.

17 David also commanded all the princes of Israel to help Solomon his son, *saying*, 18 Is not Jehovah your God with you? and hath he not given you rest on every side? for he hath delivered the inhabitants of the land into my hand; and the land is subdued before Jehovah, and before his people. 19 Now set your

[7] Edward L. Curtis and Albert A. Madsen, "The Books of Chronicles, A Critical and Exegetical Commentary," *International Critical Commentary*, p. 254.

heart and your soul to seek after Jehovah your God; arise therefore, and build ye the sanctuary of Jehovah God, to bring the ark of the covenant of Jehovah, and the holy vessels of God, into the house that is to be built to the name of Jehovah.

This charge which David made to Solomon was given shortly before David's death. It included a legacy given by the king. In some measure, this legacy may be regarded as parallel to that given in I Kings 2:2-9.

Of prime importance in David's words was the matter of the construction of the temple. This was the task which Solomon was to give priority (v. 6). Of similar importance was David's insistence on faithful observance of the law (v. 12). In order that Solomon would keep the law, David prayed, **Only Jehovah give thee discretion and understanding ... so thou mayest keep the law of Jehovah** (v. 12).

As a final charge, David urged Solomon, **Arise and be doing, and Jehovah be with thee** (v. 16). According to the Chronicles account, the great aspiration of David was the erection of the temple. Even in old age, the vision had not dimmed. He had labored diligently and prayed fervently that his son would be able to execute the task.

Moreover, David challenged the princes to give aid to Solomon. These civic leaders had given undeviating loyalty to David (v. 18). They were called upon to give Solomon every assistance necessary in order to accomplish the task of erecting the temple (v. 19).

I. DAVID'S ORGANIZATION OF THE RELIGIOUS OFFICERS (23:1—26:32)

According to Chronicles, David gave careful attention to the organization of the Levites according to their duties, in order that there would be efficient performance of the temple ministries. This emphasized David's prime concern for the temple and its functions.

The chronicler's emphasis on David's concern for the temple is a striking lesson for all laymen. Regarding the temple and its purpose, David was ineligible to contribute in a priestly or Levitical manner. Notwithstanding his kingly power, he was a layman in so far as the religious institutions were concerned. Yet he was dynamic and influential. Any layman can be an interested and participating builder of such divinely ordained institutions as the church and its auxiliaries. Note the remarkable influence of David.

1. Division of the Levites (23:1-32)

1 Now David was old and full of days; and he made Solomon his son king over Israel. 2 And he gathered together all the princes of Israel, with the priests and the Levites. 3 And the Levites were numbered from thirty years old and upward: and their number by their polls, man by man, was thirty and eight thousand. 4 Of these, twenty and four thousand were to oversee the work of the house of Jehovah; and six thousand were officers and judges; 5 and four thousand were doorkeepers; and four thousand praised Jehovah with the instruments which I made, *said David*, to praise therewith. 6 And David divided them into courses according to the sons of Levi: Gershon, Kohath, and Merari.

7 Of the Gershonites: Ladan and Shimei. 8 The sons of Ladan: Jehiel the chief, and Zetham, and Joel, three. 9 The sons of Shimei: Shelomoth, and Haziel, and Haran, three. These were the heads of the fathers' *houses* of Ladan. 10 And the sons of Shimei: Jahath, Zina, and Jeush, and Beriah. These four were the sons of Shimei. 11 And Jahath was the chief, and Zizah the second: but Jeush and Beriah had not many sons; therefore they became a fathers' house in one reckoning.

12 The sons of Kohath: Amram, Izhar, Hebron, and Uzziel, four. 13 The sons of Amram: Aaron and Moses; and Aaron was separated, that he should sanctify the most holy things, he and his sons, for ever, to burn incense before Jehovah, to minister unto him, and to bless in his name, for ever. 14 But as for Moses the man of God, his sons were named among the tribe of Levi. 15 The sons of Moses: Gershom and Eliezer. 16 The sons of Gershom: Shebuel the chief. 17 And the sons of Eliezer were: Rehabiah the chief; and Eliezer had no other sons; but the sons of Rehabiah were very many. 18 The sons of Izhar: Shelomith the chief. 19 The sons of Hebron: Jeriah the chief, Amariah the second, Jahaziel the third, and Jekameam the fourth. 20 The sons of Uzziel: Micah the chief, and Isshiah the second.

21 The sons of Merari: Mahli and Mushi. The sons of Mahli: Eleazar and

Kish. 22 And Eleazar died, and had no sons, but daughters only: and their brethren the sons of Kish took them *to wife*. 23 The sons of Mushi: Mahli, and Eder, and Jeremoth, three.

24 These were the sons of Levi after their fathers' houses, even the heads of the fathers' *houses* of those of them that were counted, in the number of names by their polls, who did the work for the service of the house of Jehovah, from twenty years old and upward. 25 For David said, Jehovah, the God of Israel, hath given rest unto his people; and he dwelleth in Jerusalem for ever: 26 and also the Levites shall no more have need to carry the tabernacle and all the vessels of it for the service thereof. 27 For by the last words of David the sons of Levi were numbered, from twenty years old and upward. 28 For their office was to wait on the sons of Aaron for the service of the house of Jehovah, in the courts, and in the chambers, and in the purifying of all holy things, even the work of the service of the house of God; 29 for the showbread also, and for the fine flour for a meal-offering, whether of unleavened wafers, or of that which is baked in the pan, or of that which is soaked, and for all manner of measure and size; 30 and to stand every morning to thank and praise Jehovah, and likewise at even; 31 and to offer all burnt-offerings unto Jehovah, on the sabbaths, on the new moons, and on the set feasts, in number according to the ordinance concerning them, continually before Jehovah; 32 and that they should keep the charge of the tent of meeting, and the charge of the holy place, and the charge of the sons of Aaron their brethren, for the service of the house of Jehovah.

The account of the transfer of the kingdom from David to Solomon is introduced by showing primary concern for the adequate classification of the Levites. This evidence further documents the viewpoint of Chronicles that David was greatly desirous of consolidating Israel's Jehovah-worship under the Levitical order.

David arranged for the Levitical divisions according to age (vv. 6-23). A section of the next chapter is similar to this passage (cf. 24:20-31). Not only did David arrange the Levites into groups or divisions, but also he altered the age requirement for Levites who were admitted for

the first time to perform the temple services. The age limit was lowered from thirty to twenty years of age (vv. 24-27; cf. 23:3). "The importance of this section is that it shows ... the law could be changed by lawful authority. . . ."[8] As lawful authority David ordered a change in the Levitical age without deliberating as to whether this was acceptable to Mosaic tradition.

2. Division of Aaron's Sons (24:1-19)

1 And the courses of the sons of Aaron *were these*. The sons of Aaron: Nadab and Abihu, Eleazar and Ithamar. 2 But Nadab and Abihu died before their father, and had no children: therefore Eleazar and Ithamar executed the priest's office. 3 And David with Zadok of the sons of Eleazar, and Ahimelech of the sons of Ithamar, divided them according to their ordering in their service. 4 And there were more chief men found of the sons of Eleazar than of the sons of Ithamar; and *thus* were they divided: of the sons of Eleazar there were sixteen, heads of fathers' houses; and of the sons of Ithamar, according to their fathers' houses, eight. 5 Thus were they divided by lot, one sort with another; for there were princes of the sanctuary, and princes of God, both of the sons of Eleazar, and of the sons of Ithamar. 6 And Shemaiah the son of Nethanel the scribe, who was of the Levites, wrote them in the presence of the king, and the princes, and Zadok the priest, and Ahimelech the son of Abiathar, and the heads of the fathers' *houses* of the priests and of the Levites; one fathers' house being taken for Eleazar, and one taken for Ithamar.

7 Now the first lot came forth to Jehoiarib, the second to Jedaiah, 8 the third to Harim, the fourth to Seorim, 9 the fifth to Malchijah, the sixth to Mijamin, 10 the seventh to Hakkoz, the eighth to Abijah, 11 the ninth to Jeshua, the tenth to Shecaniah, 12 the eleventh to Eliashib, the twelfth to Jakim, 13 the thirteenth to Huppah, the fourteenth to Jeshebeab, 14 the fifteenth to Bilgah, the sixteenth to Immer, 15 the seventeenth to Hezir, the eighteenth to Happizzez, 16 the nineteenth to Pethahiah, the twentieth to Jehezkel, 17 the one and twentieth to Jachin, the two and twentieth to Gamul, 18 the three and twentieth to Delaiah, the four and twentieth to Maaziah. 19 This was the ordering of them in their service, to come into the house of Jeho-

8 Ellison, *op. cit.*, p. 351.

vah according to the ordinance *given* unto them by Aaron their father, as Jehovah, the God of Israel, had commanded him.

The Chronicles account faithfully portrays David actively organizing the temple personnel, even though the edifice would not be built during his lifetime.

3. Division of the Other Sons of Levi (24:20-31)

20 And of the rest of the sons of Levi: of the sons of Amram, Shubael; of the sons of Shubael, Jehdeiah. 21 Of Rehabiah: of the sons of Rehabiah, Isshiah the chief. 22 Of the Izharites, Shelomoth; of the sons of Shelomoth, Jahath. 23 And the sons of *Hebron*: Jeriah *the chief*, Amariah the second, Jahaziel the third, Jekameam the fourth. 24 The sons of Uzziel, Micah; of the sons of Micah, Shamir. 25 The brother of Micah, Isshiah; of the sons of Isshiah, Zechariah. 26 The sons of Merari: Mahli and Mushi; the sons of Jaaziah: Beno. 27 The sons of Merari: of Jaaziah, Beno, and Shoham, and Zaccur, and Ibri. 28 Of Mahli: Eleazar, who had no sons. 29 Of Kish; the sons of Kish: Jerahmeel. 30 And the sons of Mushi: Mahli, and Eder, and Jerimoth. These were the sons of the Levites after their fathers' houses. 31 These likewise cast lots even as their brethren the sons of Aaron in the presence of David the king, and Zadok, and Ahimelech, and the heads of the fathers' *houses* of the priests and of the Levites; the fathers' *houses* of the chief even as those of his younger brother.

See the similar passage in I Chronicles 23:6-23 and notes.

4. Division of Select Singers (25:1-31)

1 Moreover David and the captains of the host set apart for the service certain of the sons of Asaph, and of Heman, and of Jeduthun, who should prophesy with harps, with psalteries, and with cymbals: and the number of them that did the work according to their service was: 2 of the sons of Asaph: Zaccur, and Joseph, and Nethaniah, and Asharelah, the sons of Asaph, under the hand of Asaph, who prophesied after the order of the king. 3 Of Jeduthun; the sons of Jeduthun: Gedaliah, and Zeri, and Jeshaiah, Hashabiah, and Mattithiah, six, under the hands of their father Jeduthun with the harp, who prophesied in giving thanks and praising Jehovah. 4 Of Heman; the sons of Heman: Bukkiah, Mattaniah, Uzziel, Shebuel, and Jerimoth, Hananiah, Hanani, Eliathah, Giddalti, and Romamti-ezer, Joshbekashah, Mallothi, Hothir, Mahazioth. 5 All these were the sons of Heman the king's seer in the words of God, to lift up the horn. And God gave to Heman fourteen sons and three daughters. 6 All these were under the hands of their father for song in the house of Jehovah, with cymbals, psalteries, and harps, for the service of the house of God; Asaph, Jeduthun, and Heman being under the order of the king. 7 And the number of them, with their brethren that were instructed in singing unto Jehovah, even all that were skilful, was two hundred fourscore and eight. 8 And they cast lots for their offices, all alike, as well the small as the great, the teacher as the scholar.

9 Now the first lot came forth for Asaph to Joseph: the second to Gedaliah; he and his brethren and sons were twelve: 10 the third to Zaccur, his sons and his brethren, twelve: 11 the fourth to Izri, his sons and his brethren, twelve: 12 the fifth to Nethaniah, his sons and his brethren, twelve: 13 the sixth to Bukkiah, his sons and his brethren, twelve: 14 the seventh to Jesharelah, his sons and his brethren, twelve: 15 the eighth to Jeshaiah, his sons and his brethren, twelve: 16 the ninth to Mattaniah, his sons and his brethren, twelve: 17 the tenth to Shimei, his sons and his brethren, twelve: 18 the eleventh to Azarel, his sons and his brethren, twelve: 19 the twelfth to Hashabiah, his sons and his brethren, twelve: 20 for the thirteenth, Shubael, his sons and his brethren, twelve: 21 for the fourteenth, Mattithiah, his sons and his brethren, twelve: 22 for the fifteenth to Jeremoth, his sons and his brethren, twelve: 23 for the sixteenth to Hananiah, his sons and his brethren, twelve: 24 for the seventeenth to Joshbekashah, his sons and his brethren, twelve: 25 for the eighteenth to Hanani, his sons and his brethren, twelve: 26 for the nineteenth to Mallothi, his sons and his brethren, twelve: 27 for the twentieth to Eliathah, his sons and his brethren, twelve: 28 for the one and twentieth to Hothir, his sons and his brethren, twelve: 29 for the two and twentieth to Giddalti, his sons and his brethren, twelve: 30 for the three and twentieth to Mahazioth, his sons and his brethren, twelve: 31 for the four and twentieth to Romamti-ezer, his sons and his brethren, twelve.

It seems quite clear that David arranged for professional prophets to be part of the temple personnel. Since there were select musicians, **who should prophesy with harp, with psalteries, and with cymbals** (v. 1), it appears that they were given the responsibility to prophesy to the accompaniment of music. It is well known that many prophetic utterances were in poetic form. Here the prophetic ministry was incorporated into the institutional worship of the temple.

5. Division of the Doorkeepers (26:1-19)

1 For the courses of the doorkeepers: of the Korahites, Meshelemiah the son of Kore, of the sons of Asaph. 2 And Meshelemiah had sons: Zechariah the firstborn, Jediael the second, Zebadiah the third, Jathniel the fourth, 3 Elam the fifth, Jehohanan the sixth, Eliehoenai the seventh. 4 And Obed-edom had sons: Shemaiah the first-born, Jehozabad the second, Joah the third, and Sacar the fourth, and Nethanel the fifth, 5 Ammiel the sixth, Issachar the seventh, Peullethai the eighth; for God blessed him. 6 Also unto Shemaiah his son were sons born, that ruled over the house of their father; for they were mighty men of valor. 7 The sons of Shemaiah: Othni, and Rephael, and Obed, Elzabad, whose brethren were valiant men, Elihu, and Semachiah. 8 All these were of the sons of Obed-edom: they and their sons and their brethren, able men in strength for the service; threescore and two of Obed-edom. 9 And Meshelemiah had sons and brethren, valiant men, eighteen. 10 Also Hosah, of the children of Merari, had sons: Shimri the chief (for though he was not the firstborn, yet his father made him chief) , 11 Hilkiah the second, Tebaliah the third, Zechariah the fourth: all the sons and brethren of Hosah were thirteen. 12 Of these were the courses of the doorkeepers, even of the chief men, having offices like their brethren, to minister in the house of Jehovah. 13 And they cast lots, as well the small as the great, according to their fathers' houses, for every gate. 14 And the lot eastward fell to Shelemiah. Then for Zechariah his son, a discreet counsellor, they cast lots; and his lot came out northward. 15 To Obed-edom southward; and to his sons the store-house. 16 To Shuppim and Hosah westward, by the gate of Shallecheth, at the causeway that goeth up, watch against watch. 17 Eastward were six Levites, northward four a day, southward four a day, and for the store-house two and two. 18 For Parbar westward, four at the causeway, and two at Parbar. 19

These were the courses of the doorkeepers; of the sons of the Korahites, and of the sons of Merari.

Nothing was omitted in David's meticulous arrangements for the temple and its functions. Along with Levites, priests and prophets, there were the porters who were responsible for the temple supplies. The king deemed their tasks an integral part of the temple complex and so made their office a part of the institution of the temple.

6. Division of Various Levitical Officers (26:20-32)

20 And of the Levites, Ahijah was over the treasures of the house of God, and over the treasures of the dedicated things. 21 The sons of Ladan, the sons of the Gershonites belonging to Ladan, the heads of the fathers' *houses* belonging to Ladan the Gershonite: Jehieli. 22 The sons of Jehieli: Zetham, and Joel his brother, over the treasures of the house of Jehovah. 23 Of the Amramites, of the Izharites, of the Hebronites, of the Uzzielites: 24 and Shebuel the son of Gershon, the son of Moses, was ruler over the treasures. 25 And his brethren: of Eliezer *came* Rehabiah his son, and Jeshaiah his son, and Joram his son, and Zichri his son, and Shelomoth his son. 26 This Shelomoth and his brethren were over all the treasures of the dedicated things, which David the king, and the heads of the fathers' *houses,* the captains over thousands and hundreds, and the captains of the host, had dedicated. 27 Out of the spoil won in battles did they dedicate to repair the house of Jehovah. 28 And all that Samuel the seer, and Saul the son of Kish, and Abner the son of Ner, and Joab the son of Zeruiah, had dedicated, whosoever had dedicated anything, it was under the hand of Shelomoth, and of his brethren.

29 Of the Izharites, Chenaniah and his sons were for the outward business over Israel, for officers and judges. 30 Of the Hebronites, Hashabiah and his brethren, men of valor, a thousand and seven hundred, had the oversight of Israel beyond the Jordan westward, for all the business of Jehovah, and for the service of the king. 31 Of the Hebronites was Jerijah the chief, even of the Hebronites, according to their generations by fathers' *houses.* In the fortieth year of the reign of David they were sought for, and there were found among them mighty men of valor at Jazer of Gilead. 32 And his brethren, men of valor, were two thou-

sand and seven hundred, heads of fathers' *houses*, whom king David made overseers over the Reubenites, and the Gadites, and the half-tribe of the Manassites, for every matter pertaining to God, and for the affairs of the king.

This passage includes various categories not already included. The organization of the temple personnel was nothing less than phenomenal. Doubtless, many who tend to criticize church organization are unaware of the highly complex organization of the temple and its services.

J. DAVID'S ORGANIZATION OF CIVIL OFFICERS (27:1-34)

Not only did David concentrate on the religious organization of the temple but he also skillfully planned the political organization of the kingdom. Three classifications of civil officials are discernible.

1. Army Captains (27:1-15)

1 Now the children of Israel after their number, *to wit*, the heads of fathers' *houses* and the captains of thousands and of hundreds, and their officers that served the king, in any matter of the courses which came in and went out month by month throughout all the months of the year—of every course were twenty and four thousand. 2 Over the first course for the first month was Jashobeam the son of Zabdiel: and in his course were twenty and four thousand. 3 *He was* of the children of Perez, the chief of all the captains of the host for the first month. 4 And over the course of the second month was Dodai the Ahohite, and his course; and Mikloth the ruler: and in his course were twenty and four thousand. 5 The third captain of the host for the third month was Benaiah, the son of Jehoiada the priest, chief: and in his course were twenty and four thousand. 6 This is that Benaiah, who was the mighty man of the thirty, and over the thirty: and *of* his course was Ammizabad his son. 7 The fourth *captain* for the fourth month was Asahel the brother of Joab, and Zebadiah his son after him: and in his course were twenty and four thousand. 8 The fifth captain for the fifth month was Shamhuth the Izrahite: and in his course were twenty and four thousand. 9 The sixth *captain* for the sixth month was Ira the son of Ikkesh the Tekoite: and in his course were twenty and four thousand. 10 The seventh *captain* for the seventh month was Helez the Pelonite, of the children of Ephraim: and in his course were twenty and four thousand. 11 The eighth *captain* for the eighth month was Sibbecai the Hushathite, of the Zerahites: and in his course were twenty and four thousand. 12 The ninth *captain* for the ninth month was Abiezer the Anathothite, of the Benjamites: and in his course were twenty and four thousand. 13 The tenth *captain* for the tenth month was Maharai the Netophathite, of the Zerahites: and in his course were twenty and four thousand. 14 The eleventh *captain* for the eleventh month was Benaiah the Pirathonite, of the children of Ephraim: and in his course were twenty and four thousand. 15 The twelfth *captain* for the twelfth month was Heldai the Netophathite, of Othniel: and in his course were twenty and four thousand.

These army captains had as their responsibility the safety of the king. As the royal bodyguard these captains rotated in their service. Over a period of a year they all had taken their time of service.

2. Tribal Princes (27:16-24)

16 Furthermore over the tribes of Israel: of the Reubenites was Eliezer the son of Zichri the ruler: of the Simeonites, Shephatiah the son of Maacah: 17 of Levi, Hashabiah the son of Kemuel: of Aaron, Zadok: 18 of Judah, Elihu, one of the brethren of David: of Issachar, Omri the son of Michael: 19 of Zebulun, Ishmaiah the son of Obadiah: of Naphtali, Jeremoth the son of Azriel: 20 of the children of Ephraim, Hoshea the son of Azaziah: of the half-tribe of Manasseh, Joel the son of Pedaiah: 21 of the half-tribe of Manasseh in Gilead, Iddo the son of Zechariah: of Benjamin, Jaasiel the son of Abner: 22 of Dan, Azarel the son of Jeroham. These were the captains of the tribes of Israel. 23 But David took not the number of them from twenty years old and under, because Jehovah had said he would increase Israel like to the stars of heaven. 24 Joab the son of Zeruiah began to number, but finished not; and there came wrath for this upon Israel; neither was the number put into the account in the chronicles of king David.

Although David's strong centralized monarchy did much to reduce tribal authority, he did recognize the tribal structure of Israel's organization. Official recognition was by way of the appointment of tribal princes. There was a total of thirteen princes. Two tribes are omitted from the list of those having tribal princes, namely, Gad and Asher. No explanation is provided.

3. Royal Officers (27:25-34)

25 And over the king's treasures was Azmaveth the son of Adiel: and over the treasures in the fields, in the cities, and in the villages, and in the castles, was Jonathan the son of Uzziah: 26 and over them that did the work of the field for tillage of the ground was Ezri the son of Chelub: 27 and over the vineyards was Shimei the Ramathite: and over the increase of the vineyards for the winecellars was Zabdi the Shiphmite: 28 and over the olive-trees and the sycamore-trees that were in the lowland was Baal-hanan the Gederite: and over the cellars of oil was Joash: 29 and over the herds that fed in Sharon was Shitrai the Sharonite: and over the herds that were in the valleys was Shaphat the son of Adlai: 30 and over the camels was Obil the Ishmaelite: and over the asses was Jehdeiah the Meronothite: and over the flocks was Jaziz the Hagrite. 31 All these were the rulers of the substance which was king David's.

32 Also Jonathan, David's uncle, was a counsellor, a man of understanding, and a scribe: and Jehiel the son of Hachmoni was with the king's sons: 33 and Ahithophel was the king's counsellor: and Hushai the Archite was the king's friend: 34 and after Ahithophel was Jehoiada the son of Benaiah, and Abiathar: and the captain of the king's host was Joab.

The royal officers included stewards over the royal treasures as well as managers of the vineyards, camels, flocks and the like. **All these were the rulers of the substance which was king David's** (v. 31).

In addition to the stewards there were counsellors. As the name implies, these were advisors to the king.

K. DAVID'S DISCOURSE ON THE TEMPLE (28:1—29:30)

In this concluding section on David, the chronicler places the farewell speech of the king. The major theme is the temple.

1. Solomon Endorsed (28:1-10)

1 And David assembled all the princes of Israel, the princes of the tribes, and the captains of the companies that served the king by course, and the captains of thousands, and the captains of hundreds, and the rulers over all the substance and possessions of the king and of his sons, with the officers, and the mighty men, even all the mighty men of valor, unto Jerusalem. 2 Then David the king stood up upon his feet, and said, Hear me, my brethren, and my people: as for me, it was in my heart to build a house of rest for the ark of the covenant of Jehovah, and for the footstool of our God; and I had made ready for the building. 3 But God said unto me, Thou shalt not build a house for my name, because thou art a man of war, and hast shed blood. 4 Howbeit Jehovah, the God of Israel, chose me out of all the house of my father to be king over Israel for ever: for he hath chosen Judah to be prince; and in the house of Judah, the house of my father; and among the sons of my father he took pleasure in me to make me king over all Israel; 5 and of all my sons (for Jehovah hath given me many sons), he hath chosen Solomon my son to sit upon the throne of the kingdom of Jehovah over Israel. 6 And he said unto me, Solomon thy son, he shall build my house and my courts; for I have chosen him to be my son, and I will be his father. 7 And I will establish his kingdom for ever, if he be constant to do my commandments and mine ordinances, as at this day. 8 Now therefore, in the sight of all Israel, the assembly of Jehovah, and in the audience of our God, observe and seek out all the commandments of Jehovah your God; that ye may possess this good land, and leave it for an inheritance to your children after you for ever.

9 And thou, Solomon my son, know thou the God of thy father, and serve him with a perfect heart and with a willing mind; for Jehovah searcheth all hearts, and understandeth all the imaginations of the thoughts. If thou seek him, he will be found of thee; but if thou forsake him, he will cast thee off for ever. 10 Take heed now; for Jehovah hath chosen thee to build a house for the sanctuary: be strong, and do it.

David began his farewell speech with a reference to his chief concern, namely, the building of the temple. After acknowledging that he was not given the opportunity of building it, he declared that Solomon, the chosen of the Lord, would build it (vv. 5-6).

2. Plans for the Temple (28:11-19)

11 Then David gave to Solomon his son the pattern of the porch *of the temple,* and of the houses thereof, and of the treasuries thereof, and of the upper rooms thereof, and of the inner chambers thereof, and of the place of the mercy-seat; 12 and the pattern of all that he had by the Spirit, for the courts of the house of Jehovah, and for all the chambers round about, for the treasuries of the house of God, and for the treasuries of the dedicated things; 13 also for the courses of the priests and the Levites, and for all the work of the service of the house of Jehovah, and for all the vessels of service in the house of Jehovah; 14 of gold by weight for the *vessels of* gold, for all vessels of every kind of service; *of silver* for all the vessels of silver by weight, for all vessels of every kind of service; 15 by weight also for the candle-sticks of gold, and for the lamps thereof, of gold, by weight for every candlestick and for the lamps thereof; and for the candlesticks of silver, *silver* by weight for *every* candlestick and for the lamps thereof, according to the use of every candle-stick; 16 and the gold by weight for the tables of showbread, for every table; and silver for the tables of silver; 17 and the flesh-hooks, and the basins, and the cups, of pure gold; and for the golden bowls by weight for every bowl; and for the silver bowls by weight for every bowl; 18 and for the altar of incense refined gold by weight; and gold for the pattern of the chariot, *even* the cherubim, that spread out *their wings,* and covered the ark of the covenant of Jehovah. 19 All this, *said David,* have I been made to understand in writing from the hand of Jehovah, even all the works of this pattern.

Then David gave to Solomon his son the pattern . . . (v. 11). This pattern included David's plans for the various parts of the temple complex. According to the chronicler's account, David received the pattern for the temple by direct revelation from God. Just as the plan for the tabernacle was authoritatively given by God to Moses, so was the plan for the temple given to David.

3. Encouragement to Solomon (28:20-21)

20 And David said to Solomon his son, Be strong and of good courage, and do it: fear not, nor be dismayed; for Jehovah God, even my God, is with thee; he will

not fail thee, nor forsake thee, until all the work for the service of the house of Jehovah be finished. 21 And, behold, there are the courses of the priests and the Levites, for all the service of the house of God: and there shall be with thee in all manner of work every willing man that hath skill, for any manner of service: also the captains and all the people will be wholly at thy commandment.

This passage resumes the thought of I Chronicles 28:10. David found the source of encouragement in divine help. He said to Solomon, **Be strong . . . for Jehovah . . . is with thee; he will not fail thee . . . until all the work for . . . the house of Jehovah be finished** (v. 20). Abiding faith in such a source of encouragement as God Himself has never been misplaced. God is faithful.

4. Appeal for Generous Gifts (29:1-9)

1 And David the king said unto all the assembly, Solomon my son, whom alone God hath chosen, is yet young and tender, and the work is great; for the palace is not for man, but for Jehovah God. 2 Now I have prepared with all my might for the house of my God the gold for the *things of* gold, and the silver for the *things of* silver, and the brass for the *things of* brass, the iron for the *things of* iron, and wood for the *things of* wood; onyx stones, and *stones* to be set, stones for inlaid work, and of divers colors, and all manner of precious stones, and marble stones in abundance. 3 Moreover also, because I have set my affection on the house of my God, seeing that I have a treasure of mine own of gold and silver, I give it unto the house of my God, over and above all that I have prepared for the holy house, 4 even three thousand talents of gold, of the gold of Ophir, and seven thousand talents of refined silver, wherewith to overlay the walls of the houses; 5 of gold for the *things of* gold, and of silver for the *things of* silver, and for all manner of work *to be made* by the hands of artificers. Who then offereth willingly to consecrate himself this day unto Jehovah?

6 Then the princes of the fathers' *houses,* and the princes of the tribes of Israel, and the captains of thousands and of hundreds, with the rulers over the king's work, offered willingly; 7 and they gave for the service of the house of God of gold five thousand talents and ten thousand darics, and of silver ten thousand talents, and of brass eighteen thou-

sand talents, and of iron a hundred thousand talents. 8 And they with whom *precious* stones were found gave them to the treasure of the house of Jehovah, under the hand of Jehiel the Gershonite. 9 Then the people rejoiced, for that they offered willingly, because with a perfect heart they offered willingly to Jehovah: and David the king also rejoiced with great joy.

David's appeal to the people for generous gifts was most effective because of the example he set for them. He announced that he was giving a huge gift from his own private fortune (vv. 3-5). In the light of this generosity he urged all to give (v. 5). The people responded willingly and liberally (v. 6). This was an eloquent and moving moment for David. His life nearly ended, he was greatly uplifted by the realization that the temple would be built. The people were showing their complete loyalty to the total effort. Many have experienced similar elation as a long-planned project became a reality. Others have become disillusioned and broken in spirit because their ideals were never realized. In any case, what is more important is that our ideals and purposes conform to the glory and honor of God. Certainly David here set a worthy example for all servants of God who approach the end of life with an accumulation of material possessions. When such possessions are given or willed to the Church of Christ there is a transfer of credit from the temporal to the eternal bank, rather than the dissipation of such resources through the disposal of estates (Matt. 6:19, 20).

5. Prayer of Thanksgiving (29:10-19)

10 Wherefore David blessed Jehovah before all the assembly; and David said, Blessed be thou, O Jehovah, the God of Israel our father, for ever and ever. 11 Thine, O Jehovah, is the greatness, and the power, and the glory, and the victory, and the majesty: for all that is in the heavens and in the earth *is thine;* thine is the kingdom, O Jehovah, and thou art exalted as head above all. 12 Both riches and honor come of thee, and thou rulest over all; and in thy hand is power and might; and in thy hand it is to make great, and to give strength unto all. 13 Now therefore, our God, we thank thee, and praise thy glorious name. 14 But who am I, and what is my people, that we

should be able to offer so willingly after this sort? for all things come of thee, and of thine own have we given thee. 15 For we are strangers before thee, and sojourners, as all our fathers were: our days on the earth are as a shadow, and there is no abiding. 16 O Jehovah our God, all this store that we have prepared to build thee a house for thy holy name cometh of thy hand, and is all thine own. 17 I know also, my God, that thou triest the heart, and hast pleasure in uprightness. As for me, in the uprightness of my heart I have willingly offered all these things: and now have I seen with joy thy people that are present here, offer willingly unto thee. 18 O Jehovah, the God of Abraham, of Isaac, and of Israel, our fathers, keep this for ever in the imagination of the thoughts of the heart of thy people, and prepare their heart unto thee; 19 and give unto Solomon my son a perfect heart, to keep thy commandments, thy testimonies, and thy statutes, and to do all these things, and to build the palace, for which I have made provision.

At this high moment, David offered a prayer of thanksgiving. It included acknowledgment of divine majesty and is one of the finest expressions of human gratitude. It is a model thanksgiving prayer.

6. A Day of Gladness (29:20-25)

20 And David said to all the assembly, Now bless Jehovah your God. And all the assembly blessed Jehovah, the God of their fathers, and bowed down their heads, and worshipped Jehovah, and the king. 21 And they sacrificed sacrifices unto Jehovah, and offered burnt-offerings unto Jehovah, on the morrow after that day, even a thousand bullocks, a thousand rams, and a thousand lambs, with their drink-offerings, and sacrifices in abundance for all Israel, 22 and did eat and drink before Jehovah on that day with great gladness.

And they made Solomon the son of David king the second time, and anointed him unto Jehovah to be prince, and Zadok to be priest. 23 Then Solomon sat on the throne of Jehovah as king instead of David his father, and prospered; and all Israel obeyed him. 24 And all the princes, and the mighty men, and all the sons likewise of king David, submitted themselves unto Solomon the king. 25 And Jehovah magnified Solomon exceedingly in the sight of all Israel, and bestowed upon him such royal majesty as had not been on any king before him in Israel.

The day of David's final farewell was a memorable one. After his discourse and prayer, there were many sacrifices and great rejoicing. **And they sacrificed sacrifices unto Jehovah . . . and did eat and drink before Jehovah on that day with great gladness** (vv. 21-22) .

7. Summary (29:26-30)

26 Now David the son of Jesse reigned over all Israel. 27 And the time that he reigned over Israel was forty years; seven years reigned he in Hebron, and thirty and three *years* reigned he in Jerusalem.

28 And he died in a good old age, full of days, riches, and honor: and Solomon his son reigned in his stead. 29 Now the acts of David the king, first and last, behold, they are written in the history of Samuel the seer, and in the history of Nathan the prophet, and in the history of Gad the seer, 30 with all his reign and his might, and the times that went over him, and over Israel, and over all the kingdoms of the countries.

And he died in a good old age, full of days, riches, and honor (v. 28) . With these words, the chronicler concludes his glowing account of David, who more than any other individual made the temple possible.

The Second Book of Chronicles

by Charles R. Wilson

Outline

Commentary on Second Chronicles

I. THE REIGN OF SOLOMON (II Chron. 1:1—9:31)

The chronicler's account of Solomon establishing himself as the successor to David is given without mention of the ruthless measures taken against his opponents (compare II Chron. 1 with I Kings 1 and 2).

A. SOLOMON'S WISDOM AND WEALTH (1:1-17; cf. I Kings 3:4-15; 10:26-29)

1 And Solomon the son of David was strengthened in his kingdom, and Jehovah his God was with him, and magnified him exceedingly. 2 And Solomon spake unto all Israel, to the captains of thousands and of hundreds, and to the judges, and to every prince in all Israel, the heads of the fathers' *houses.* 3 So Solomon, and all the assembly with him, went to the high place that was at Gibeon; for there was the tent of meeting of God, which Moses the servant of Jehovah had made in the wilderness. 4 But the ark of God had David brought up from Kiriath-jearim to the *place* that David had prepared for it; for he had pitched a tent for it at Jerusalem. 5 Moreover the brazen altar, that Bezalel the son of Uri, the son of Hur, had made, was there before the tabernacle of Jehovah: and Solomon and the assembly sought unto it. 6 And Solomon went up thither to the brazen altar before Jehovah, which was at the tent of the meeting, and offered a thousand burnt-offerings upon it.

7 In that night did God appear unto Solomon, and said unto him, Ask what I shall give thee. 8 And Solomon said unto God, Thou hast showed great lovingkindness unto David my father, and hast made me king in his stead. 9 Now, O Jehovah God, let thy promise unto David my father be established; for thou hast made me king over a people like the dust of the earth in multitude. 10 Give me now wisdom and knowledge, that I may go out and come in before this people; for who can judge this thy people, that is so great? 11 And God said to Solomon, Because this was in thy heart, and thou hast not asked riches, wealth, or honor, nor the life of them that hate thee, neither yet hast asked long life; but hast asked wisdom and knowledge for thyself, that thou mayest judge my people, over whom I have made thee king: 12 wisdom and knowledge is granted unto thee; and I will give thee riches, and wealth, and honor, such as none of the kings have had that have been before thee; neither shall there any after thee have the like. 13 So Solomon came from the high place that was at Gibeon, from before the tent of meeting, unto Jerusalem; and he reigned over Israel.

14 And Solomon gathered chariots and horsemen: and he had a thousand and four hundred chariots, and twelve thousand horsemen, that he placed in the chariot cities, and with the king at Jerusalem. 15 And the king made silver and gold to be in Jerusalem as stones, and cedars made he to be as the sycamore-trees that are in the lowland, for abundance. 16 And the horses which Solomon had were brought out of Egypt; the king's merchants received them in droves, each drove at a price. 17 And they fetched up and brought out of Egypt a chariot for six hundred *shekels* of silver, and a horse for a hundred and fifty: and so for all the kings of the Hittites, and the kings of Syria, did they bring them out by their means.

Solomon began his reign by engaging in a sacred act of worship at Gibeon, **for there was the tent of meeting of God** (v. 3). Even though the ark of the covenant was not there, the God of the covenant met with Solomon and communed with him at Gibeon (see notes on the parallel passage in I Kings).

B. SOLOMON'S PURPOSE TO BUILD A TEMPLE (2:1-18; cf. I Kings 5:1-12)

1 Now Solomon purposed to build a house for the name of Jehovah, and a

house for his kingdom. 2 And Solomon counted out threescore and ten thousand men to bear burdens, and fourscore thousand men that were hewers in the mountains, and three thousand and six hundred to oversee them. 3 And Solomon sent to Huram the king of Tyre, saying, As thou didst deal with David my father, and didst send him cedars to build him a house to dwell therein, *even so deal with me.* 4 Behold, I am about to build a house for the name of Jehovah my God, to dedicate it to him, and to burn before him incense of sweet spices, and for the continual showbread, and for the burnt-offerings morning and evening, on the sabbaths, and on the new moons, and on the set feasts of Jehovah our God. This is *an ordinance* for ever to Israel. 5 And the house which I build is great; for great is our God above all gods. 6 But who is able to build him a house, seeing heaven and the heaven of heavens cannot contain him? who am I then, that I should build him a house, save only to burn incense before him? 7 Now therefore send me a man skilful to work in gold, and in silver, and in brass, and in iron, and in purple, and crimson, and blue, and that knoweth how to grave *all manner of* gravings, *to be* with the skilful men that are with me in Judah and in Jerusalem, whom David my father did provide. 8 Send me also cedar-trees, fir-trees, and algum-trees, out of Lebanon; for I know that thy servants know how to cut timber in Lebanon. And, behold, my servants shall be with thy servants, 9 even to prepare me timber in abundance; for the house which I am about to build shall be great and wonderful. 10 And, behold, I will give to thy servants, the hewers that cut timber, twenty thousand measures of beaten wheat, and twenty thousand measures of barley, and twenty thousand baths of wine, and twenty thousand baths of oil. 11 Then Huram the king of Tyre answered in writing, which he sent to Solomon, Because Jehovah loveth his people, he hath made thee king over them. 12 Huram said moreover, Blessed be Jehovah, the God of Israel, that made heaven and earth, who hath given to David the king a wise son, endued with discretion and understanding, that should build a house for Jehovah, and a house for his kingdom. 13 And now I have sent a skilful man, endued with understanding, of Huram my father's, 14 the son of a woman of the daughters of Dan; and his father was a man of Tyre, skilful to work

in gold, and in silver, in brass, in iron, in stone, and in timber, in purple, in blue, and in fine linen, and in crimson, also to grave any manner of graving, and to devise any device; that there may be *a place* appointed unto him with thy skilful men, and with the skilful men of my lord David thy father. 15 Now therefore the wheat and the barley, the oil and the wine, which my lord hath spoken of, let him send unto his servants: 16 and we will cut wood out of Lebanon, as much as thou shalt need; and we will bring it to thee in floats by sea to Joppa; and thou shalt carry it up to Jerusalem.

17 And Solomon numbered all the sojourners that were in the land of Israel, after the numbering wherewith David his father had numbered them; and they were found a hundred and fifty thousand and three thousand and six hundred. 18 And he set threescore and ten thousand of them to bear burdens, and fourscore thousand that were hewers in the mountains, and three thousand and six hundred overseers to set the people at work.

Now Solomon purposed to build a house for the name of Jehovah (v. 1). In giving the account of the correspondence with Huram, the king of Tyre, relative to building the temple, the Chronicles account is considerably expanded compared to the account in Kings. In Chronicles, the form used for the king of Tyre is Huram, while in Samuel and Kings it is Hiram.

Solomon's purpose to build the temple was one thing; however, the means for accomplishing that purpose were quite another thing. "Archaeology has fully borne out Israel's backwardness in the arts at this time."[9] Although Solomon indicated that he had some skilled labor, what he had was inadequate for the great enterprise. Whereupon he sent to Tyre for a skilled craftsman (v. 7).

Although Solomon had a magnificent purpose for building the temple, he was keenly aware of the greatness and transcendence of God. **And the house which I build is great; for great is our God above all gods. But who is able to build him a house, seeing heaven and the heaven of heavens cannot contain him?** (vv. 5-6). Solomon's stated purpose was not so

9 *Ibid.,* p. 354.

much the erection of a temple in which the transcendent God might dwell as a central place where all Israel might gather to worship Him. God is greater than any building.

Erection of a magnificent building for the worship of God can be the means of assisting the cultivation of a high sense of God. When there is the right purpose of heart, a massive, majestic cathedral built to worship God can be an amazing and awe-inspiring testimony of faith in the transcendent Lord.

Where such cathedrals are not possible, less imposing buildings should express the worshipers' sincere spirit of reverence and worship. In the construction of churches, one of the prime purposes is the erection of a structure which testifies to all who behold it that the worshipers have an exalted conception of the Lord Jehovah. Solomon has given us an admirable example.

C. THE TEMPLE AND ITS FURNISHINGS (3:1—5:1)

The Chronicles account of the temple includes its location, its interior and its furnishings.

1. The Location (3:1-4; cf. I Kings 6:2-10)

1 Then Solomon began to build the house of Jehovah at Jerusalem on mount Moriah, where *Jehovah* appeared unto David his father, which he made ready in the place that David had appointed, in the threshing-floor of Ornan the Jebusite. 2 And he began to build in the *second day* of the second month, in the fourth year of his reign. 3 Now these are the foundations which Solomon laid for the building of the house of God. The length by cubits after the first measure was threescore cubits, and the breadth twenty cubits. 4 And the porch that was before *the house*, the length of it, according to the breadth of the house, was twenty cubits, and the height a hundred and twenty; and he overlaid it within with pure gold.

Then Solomon began to build the house of Jehovah at Jerusalem on mount Moriah (v. 1). It was on this site that David had witnessed earlier divine judgment tempered with divine mercy (cf. I Chron. 21:28—22:1). He had left instructions for the location of the temple; therefore, Solomon's action was the execution of his father's instructions.

It was not until the second month of the fourth year of his reign that Solomon commenced construction. If his reign commenced in 971/70 B.C., then construction of the temple began in 967/66 B.C. The dimensions of the foundations were large for buildings of that time, but they do not seem so large when compared with the dimensions of modern buildings. The foundation measured about ninety by thirty feet (v. 3).

2. The Interior (3:5-14; cf. I Kings 6:14-35)

5 And the greater house he ceiled with fir-wood, which he overlaid with fine gold, and wrought thereon palm-trees and chains. 6 And he garnished the house with precious stones for beauty: and the gold was gold of Parvaim. 7 He overlaid also the house, the beams, the thresholds, and the walls thereof, and the doors thereof, with gold; and graved cherubim on the walls.

8 And he made the most holy house: the length thereof, according to the breadth of the house, was twenty cubits, and the breadth thereof twenty cubits; and he overlaid it with fine gold, amounting to six hundred talents. 9 And the weight of the nails was fifty shekels of gold. And he overlaid the upper chambers with gold.

10 And in the most holy house he made two cherubim of image work; and they overlaid them with gold. 11 And the wings of the cherubim were twenty cubits long: the wing of the one *cherub* was five cubits, reaching to the wall of the house; and the other wing was *likewise* five cubits, reaching to the wing of the other cherub. 12 And the wing of the other cherub was five cubits, reaching to the wall of the house; and the other wing was five cubits *also*, joining to the wing of the other cherub. 13 The wings of these cherubim spread themselves forth twenty cubits: and they stood on their feet, and their faces were toward the house. 14 And he made the veil of blue, and purple, and crimson, and fine linen, and wrought cherubim thereon.

See notes on the parallel passage in Kings.

3. The Bronze Pillars (3:15-17; cf. I Kings 7:15-22)

15 Also he made before the house two pillars of thirty and five cubits high, and the capital that was on the top of each of them was five cubits. 16 And he made chains in the oracle, and put *them* on the tops of the pillars; and he made a hundred pomegranates, and put them on the chains. 17 And he set up the pillars before the temple, one on the right hand, and the other on the left; and called the name of that on the right hand Jachin, and the name of that on the left Boaz.

See notes on the parallel passage in Kings.

4. The Furnishings (4:1—5:1; cf. I Kings 7:23-51)

1 Moreover he made an altar of brass, twenty cubits the length thereof, and twenty cubits the breadth thereof, and ten cubits the height thereof. 2 Also he made the molten sea of ten cubits from brim to brim, round in compass; and the height thereof was five cubits; and a line of thirty cubits compassed it round about. 3 And under it was the likeness of oxen, which did compass it round about, for ten cubits, compassing the sea round about. The oxen were in two rows, cast when it was cast. 4 It stood upon twelve oxen, three looking toward the north, and three looking toward the west, and three looking toward the south, and three looking toward the east: and the sea was set upon them above, and all their hinder parts were inward. 5 And it was a handbreadth thick; and the brim thereof was wrought like the brim of a cup, like the flower of a lily: it received and held three thousand baths. 6 He made also ten lavers, and put five on the right hand, and five on the left, to wash in them; such things as belonged to the burnt-offering they washed in them; but the sea was for the priests to wash in. 7 And he made the ten candlesticks of gold according to the ordinance concerning them; and he set them in the temple, five on the right hand, and five on the left. 8 He made also ten tables, and placed them in the temple, five on the right side, and five on the left. And he made a hundred basins of gold. 9 Furthermore he made the court of the priests, and the great court, and doors for the court, and overlaid the doors of them with brass. 10 And he set the sea on the right side *of the house* eastward, toward the south. 11 And

Huram made the pots, and the shovels, and the basins.

So Huram made an end of doing the work that he wrought for king Solomon in the house of God: 12 the two pillars, and the bowls, and the two capitals which were on the top of the pillars, and the two networks to cover the two bowls of the capitals that were on the top of the pillars, 13 and the four hundred pomegranates for the two networks; two rows of pomegranates for each network, to cover the two bowls of the capitals that were upon the pillars. 14 He made also the bases, and the lavers made he upon the bases; 15 one sea, and the twelve oxen under it. 16 The pots also, and the shovels, and the flesh-hooks, and all the vessels thereof, did Huram his father make for king Solomon, for the house of Jehovah, of bright brass. 17 In the plain of the Jordan did the king cast them, in the clay ground between Succoth and Zeredah. 18 Thus Solomon made all these vessels in great abundance: for the weight of the brass could not be found out.

19 And Solomon made all the vessels that were in the house of God, the golden altar also, and the tables whereon was the showbread; 20 and the candlesticks with their lamps, to burn according to the ordinance before the oracle, of pure gold; 21 and the flowers, and the lamps, and the tongs, of gold, and that perfect gold; 22 and the snuffers, and the basins, and the spoons, and the firepans, of pure gold. And as for the entry of the house, the inner doors thereof for the most holy place, and the doors of the house, *to wit*, of the temple, were of gold.

1 Thus all the work that Solomon wrought for the house of Jehovah was finished. And Solomon brought in the things that David his father had dedicated, even the silver, and the gold, and all the vessels, and put them in the treasuries of the house of God.

See notes on the parallel passage in Kings.

D. THE DEDICATION OF THE TEMPLE (5:2—7:22)

Except for a few additions mainly concerned with liturgy, this section is nearly parallel with I Kings 8:1-66.

1. The Ark Moved to the Temple (5:2-14; cf. I Kings 8:1-11)

2 Then Solomon assembled the elders of Israel, and all the heads of the tribes,

the princes of the fathers' *houses* of the children of Israel, unto Jerusalem, to bring up the ark of the covenant of Jehovah out of the city of David, which is Zion. 3 And all the men of Israel assembled themselves unto the king at the feast, which was *in* the seventh month. 4 And all the elders of Israel came: and the Levites took up the ark; 5 and they brought up the ark, and the tent of meeting, and all the holy vessels that were in the Tent; these did the priests the Levites bring up. 6 And king Solomon and all the congregation of Israel, that were assembled unto him, were before the ark, sacrificing sheep and oxen, that could not be counted nor numbered for multitude. 7 And the priests brought in the ark of the covenant of Jehovah unto its place, into the oracle of the house, to the most holy place, even under the wings of the cherubim. 8 For the cherubim spread forth their wings over the place of the ark, and the cherubim covered the ark and the staves thereof above. 9 And the staves were so long that the ends of the staves were seen from the ark before the oracle; but they were not seen without: and there it is unto this day. 10 There was nothing in the ark save the two tables which Moses put *there* at Horeb, when Jehovah made a covenant with the children of Israel, when they came out of Egypt.

11 And it came to pass, when the priests were come out of the holy place (for all the priests that were present had sanctified themselves, and did not keep their courses; 12 also the Levites who were the singers, all of them, even Asaph, Heman, Jeduthun, and their sons and their brethren, arrayed in fine linen, with cymbals and psalteries and harps, stood at the east end of the altar, and with them a hundred and twenty priests sounding with trumpets) ; 13 it came to pass, when the trumpeters and singers were as one, to make one sound to be heard in praising and thanking Jehovah; and when they lifted up their voice with the trumpets and cymbals and instruments of music, and praised Jehovah, *saying*, For he is good; for his lovingkindness *endureth* for ever; that then the house was filled with a cloud, even the house of Jehovah, 14 so that the priests could not stand to minister by reason of the cloud: for the glory of Jehovah filled the house of God.

See notes on the parallel passage in I Kings.

2. The Address of Solomon (6:1-11; cf. I Kings 8:12-21)

1 Then spake Solomon, Jehovah hath said that he would dwell in the thick darkness. 2 But I have built thee a house of habitation, and a place for thee to dwell in for ever. 3 And the king turned his face, and blessed all the assembly of Israel: and all the assembly of Israel stood.

4 And he said, Blessed be Jehovah, the God of Israel, who spake with his mouth unto David my father, and hath with his hands fulfilled it, saying, 5 Since the day that I brought forth my people out of the land of Egypt, I chose no city out of all the tribes of Israel to build a house in, that my name might be there; neither chose I any man to be prince over my people Israel: 6 but I have chosen Jerusalem, that my name might be there, and have chosen David to be over my people Israel. 7 Now it was in the heart of David my father to build a house for the name of Jehovah, the God of Israel. 8 But Jehovah said unto David my father, Whereas it was in thy heart to build a house for my name, thou didst well that it was in thy heart: 9 nevertheless thou shalt not build the house; but thy son that shall come forth out of thy loins, he shall build the house for my name. 10 And Jehovah hath performed his word that he spake; for I am risen up in the room of David my father, and sit on the throne of Israel, as Jehovah promised, and have built the house for the name of Jehovah, the God of Israel. 11 And there have I set the ark, wherein is the covenant of Jehovah, which he made with the children of Israel.

See notes on the parallel passage in I Kings.

3. The Prayer of Dedication (6:12-42; cf. I Kings 8:22-53)

12 And he stood before the altar of Jehovah in the presence of all the assembly of Israel, and spread forth his hands 13 (for Solomon had made a brazen scaffold, five cubits long, and five cubits broad, and three cubits high, and had set it in the midst of the court; and upon it he stood, and kneeled down upon his knees before all the assembly of Israel, and spread forth his hands toward heaven) ; 14 and he said, O Jehovah, the God of Israel, there is no God like thee, in heaven, or on earth; who keepest covenant and lovingkindness with thy servants, that walk before thee with all their

heart; 15 who hast kept with thy servant David my father that which thou didst promise him: yea, thou spakest with thy mouth, and hast fulfilled it with thy hand, as it is this day. 16 Now therefore, O Jehovah, the God of Israel, keep with thy servant David my father that which thou hast promised him, saying, There shall not fail thee a man in my sight to sit on the throne of Israel, if only thy children take heed to their way, to walk in my law as thou hast walked before me. 17 Now therefore, O Jehovah, the God of Israel, let thy word be verified, which thou spakest unto thy servant David.

18 But will God in very deed dwell with men on the earth? behold, heaven and the heaven of heavens cannot contain thee; how much less this house which I have builded! 19 Yet have thou respect unto the prayer of thy servant, and to his supplication, O Jehovah my God, to hearken unto the cry and to the prayer which thy servant prayeth before thee; 20 that thine eyes may be open toward this house day and night, even toward the place whereof thou hast said that thou wouldest put thy name there; to hearken unto the prayer which thy servant shall pray toward this place. 21 And hearken thou to the supplications of thy servant, and of thy people Israel, when they shall pray toward this place: yea, hear thou from thy dwelling-place, even from heaven; and when thou hearest, forgive.

22 If a man sin against his neighbor, and an oath be laid upon him to cause him to swear, and he come *and* swear before thine altar in this house; 23 then hear thou from heaven, and do, and judge thy servants, requiting the wicked, to bring his way upon his own head; and justifying the righteous, to give him according to his righteousness.

24 And if thy people Israel be smitten down before the enemy, because they have sinned against thee, and shall turn again and confess thy name, and pray and make supplication before thee in this house; 25 then hear thou from heaven, and forgive the sin of thy people Israel, and bring them again unto the land which thou gavest to them and to their fathers.

26 When the heavens are shut up, and there is no rain, because they have sinned against thee; if they pray toward this place, and confess thy name, and turn from their sin, when thou dost afflict them: 27 then hear thou in heaven, and forgive the sin of thy servants, and of thy people Israel, when thou teachest them

the good way wherein they should walk; and send rain upon thy land, which thou hast given to thy people for an inheritance.

28 If there be in the land famine, if there be pestilence, if there be blasting or mildew, locust or caterpillar; if their enemies besiege them in the land of their cities; whatsoever plague or whatsoever sickness there be; 29 what prayer and supplication soever be made by any man, or by all thy people Israel, who shall know every man his own plague and his own sorrow, and shall spread forth his hands toward this house: 30 then hear thou from heaven thy dwelling-place, and forgive, and render unto every man according to all his ways, whose heart thou knowest (for thou, even thou only, knowest the hearts of the children of men); 31 that they may fear thee, to walk in thy ways, so long as they live in the land which thou gavest unto our fathers.

32 Moreover concerning the foreigner, that is not of thy people Israel, when he shall come from a far country for thy great name's sake, and thy mighty hand, and thine outstretched arm; when they shall come and pray toward this house: 33 then hear thou from heaven, even from thy dwelling-place, and do according to all that the foreigner calleth to thee for; that all the peoples of the earth may know thy name, and fear thee, as doth thy people Israel, and that they may know that this house which I have built is called by thy name.

34 If thy people go out to battle against their enemies, by whatsoever way thou shalt send them, and they pray unto thee toward this city which thou hast chosen, and the house which I have built for thy name; 35 then hear thou from heaven their prayer and their supplication, and maintain their cause.

36 If they sin against thee (for there is no man that sinneth not), and thou be angry with them, and deliver them to the enemy, so that they carry them away captive unto a land far off or near; 37 yet if they shall bethink themselves in the land whither they are carried captive, and turn again, and make supplication unto thee in the land of their captivity, saying, We have sinned, we have done perversely, and have dealt wickedly; 38 if they return unto thee with all their heart and with all their soul in the land of their captivity, whither they have carried them captive, and pray toward their land, which thou gavest unto their fathers, and the city which thou hast cho-

sen, and toward the house which I have built for thy name; 39 then hear thou from heaven, even from thy dwelling-place, their prayer and their supplications, and maintain their cause, and forgive thy people who have sinned against thee.

40 Now, O my God, let, I beseech thee, thine eyes be open, and let thine ears be attent, unto the prayer that is made in this place. 41 Now therefore arise, O Jehovah God, into thy resting-place, thou, and the ark of thy strength: let thy priests, O Jehovah God, be clothed with salvation, and let thy saints rejoice in goodness. 42 O Jehovah God, turn not away the face of thine anointed: remember *thy* lovingkindnesses to David thy servant.

See notes on the parallel passage in I Kings.

4. The Glory of Jehovah (7:1-3)

1 Now when Solomon had made an end of praying, the fire came down from heaven, and consumed the burnt-offering and the sacrifices; and the glory of Jehovah filled the house. 2 And the priests could not enter into the house of Jehovah, because the glory of Jehovah filled Jehovah's house. 3 And all the children of Israel looked on, when the fire came down, and the glory of Jehovah was upon the house; and they bowed themselves with their faces to the ground upon the pavement, and worshipped, and gave thanks unto Jehovah, *saying*, For he is good; for his lovingkindness *endureth* for ever.

This passage does not appear in I Kings. However, it reveals in a most impressive way the divine favor upon Solomon's efforts to build the temple. The fire of the Lord consumed the sacrifices, while the glory of the Lord filled the temple (v. 1). When the people beheld the divine outpouring of fire and glory, they bowed in worship, saying, **For he is good; for his lovingkindness endureth for ever** (v. 3).

Here is manifested the spirit of true worship. Notwithstanding the magnificent structure which was the work of their hands, the people of Israel witnessed a remarkable divine manifestation which called forth a response of gratitude for the goodness of the Lord. Such worship is possible anywhere. It does not necessarily depend upon buildings and furnishings.

Rather, it is born out of God's revelation and our response.

5. The Feast of Dedication (7:4-10; cf. I Kings 8:62-66)

4 Then the king and all the people offered sacrifice before Jehovah. 5 And king Solomon offered a sacrifice of twenty and two thousand oxen, and a hundred and twenty thousand sheep. So the king and all the people dedicated the house of God. 6 And the priests stood, according to their offices; the Levites also with instruments of music of Jehovah, which David the king had made to give thanks unto Jehovah (for his lovingkindness *endureth* for ever), when David praised by their ministry: and the priests sounded trumpets before them; and all Israel stood. 7 Moreover Solomon hallowed the middle of the court that was before the house of Jehovah; for there he offered the burnt-offerings, and the fat of the peace-offerings, because the brazen altar which Solomon had made was not able to receive the burnt-offering, and the meal-offering, and the fat.

8 So Solomon held the feast at that time seven days, and all Israel with him, a very great assembly, from the entrance of Hamath unto the brook of Egypt. 9 And on the eighth day they held a solemn assembly: for they kept the dedication of the altar seven days, and the feast seven days. 10 And on the three and twentieth day of the seventh month he sent the people away unto their tents, joyful and glad of heart for the goodness that Jehovah had showed unto David, and to Solomon, and to Israel his people.

See notes on the parallel passage in I Kings.

6. The Revelation to Solomon (7:11-22)

11 Thus Solomon finished the house of Jehovah, and the king's house: and all that came into Solomon's heart to make in the house of Jehovah, and in his own house, he prosperously effected. 12 And Jehovah appeared to Solomon by night, and said unto him, I have heard thy prayer, and have chosen this place to myself for a house of sacrifice. 13 If I shut up the heavens so that there is no rain, or if I command the locust to devour the land, or if I send pestilence among my people; 14 if my people, who are called by my name, shall humble themselves, and pray, and seek my face, and turn from their wicked ways; then

will I hear from heaven, and will forgive their sin, and will heal their land. 15 Now mine eyes shall be open, and mine ears attent, unto the prayer that is made in this place. 16 For now have I chosen and hallowed this house, that my name may be there for ever; and mine eyes and my heart shall be there perpetually. 17 And as for thee, if thou wilt walk before me as David thy father walked, and do according to all that I have commanded thee, and wilt keep my statutes and mine ordinances; 18 then I will establish the throne of thy kingdom, according as I covenanted with David thy father, saying, There shall not fail thee a man to be ruler in Israel.

19 But if ye turn away, and forsake my statutes and my commandments which I have set before you, and shall go and serve other gods, and worship them; 20 then will I pluck them up by the roots out of my land which I have given them; and this house, which I have hallowed for my name, will I cast out of my sight, and I will make it a proverb and a byword among all peoples. 21 And this house, which is so high, every one that passeth by it shall be astonished, and shall say, Why hath Jehovah done thus unto this land, and to this house? 22 And they shall answer, Because they forsook Jehovah, the God of their fathers, who brought them forth out of the land of Egypt, and laid hold on other gods, and worshipped them, and served them: therefore hath he brought all this evil upon them.

E. SURVEY OF SOLOMON'S RULE (8:1—9:31)

Except for the chronicler's omission of I Kings 9:11-16 and his addition of II Chronicles 8:13-16, this passage is nearly parallel with I Kings 9:10—10:29 plus I Kings 11:41-43.

1. Building Enterprises (8:1-11; cf. I Kings 9:10-24)

1 And it came to pass at the end of twenty years, wherein Solomon had built the house of Jehovah, and his own house, 2 that the cities which Huram had given to Solomon, Solomon built them, and caused the children of Israel to dwell there.

3 And Solomon went to Hamath-zobah, and prevailed against it. 4 And he built Tadmor in the wilderness, and all the store-cities, which he built in Hamath. 5 Also he built Beth-horon the upper,

and Beth-horon the nether, fortified cities, with walls, gates, and bars; 6 and Baalath, and all the store-cities that Solomon had, and all the cities for his chariots, and the cities for his horsemen, and all that Solomon desired to build for his pleasure in Jerusalem, and in Lebanon, and in all the land of his dominion.

7 As for all the people that were left of the Hittites, and the Amorites, and the Perizzites, and the Hivites, and the Jebusites, that were not of Israel; 8 of their children that were left after them in the land, whom the children of Israel consumed not, of them did Solomon raise a levy *of bondservants* unto this day. 9 But of the children of Israel did Solomon make no servants for his work; but they were men of war, and chief of his captains, and rulers of his chariots and of his horsemen. 10 And these were the chief officers of king Solomon, even two hundred and fifty, that bare rule over the people.

11 And Solomon brought up the daughter of Pharaoh out of the city of David unto the house that he had built for her; for he said, My wife shall not dwell in the house of David king of Israel, because the places are holy, whereunto the ark of Jehovah hath come.

See notes on the parallel passage in 1 Kings.

2. Worship of Jehovah (8:12-16; cf. I Kings 9:25)

12 Then Solomon offered burnt-offerings unto Jehovah on the altar of Jehovah, which he had built before the porch, 13 even as the duty of every day required, offering according to the commandment of Moses, on the sabbaths, and on the new moons, and on the set feasts, three times in the year, *even* in the feast of unleavened bread, and in the feast of weeks, and in the feast of tabernacles. 14 And he appointed, according to the ordinance of David his father, the courses of the priests to their service, and the Levites to their offices, to praise, and to minister before the priests, as the duty of every day required; the doorkeepers also by their courses at every gate: for so had David the man of God commanded. 15 And they departed not from the commandment of the king unto the priests and Levites concerning any matter, or concerning the treasures.

16 Now all the work of Solomon was prepared unto the day of the foundation of the house of Jehovah, and until it was

finished. *So* the house of Jehovah was completed.

See notes on the parallel passage in I Kings.

3. Trade (8:17-18; cf. I Kings 9:26-28)

17 Then went Solomon to Ezion-geber, and to Eloth, on the seashore in the land of Edom. 18 And Huram sent him by the hands of his servants ships, and servants that had knowledge of the sea; and they came with the servants of Solomon to Ophir, and fetched from thence four hundred and fifty talents of gold, and brought them to king Solomon.

See notes on the parallel passage in I Kings.

4. The Queen of Sheba (9:1-12; cf. I Kings 10:1-10)

1 And when the queen of Sheba heard of the fame of Solomon, she came to prove Solomon with hard questions at Jerusalem, with a very great train, and camels that bare spices, and gold in abundance, and precious stones: and when she was come to Solomon, she communed with him of all that was in her heart. 2 And Solomon told her all her questions; and there was not anything hid from Solomon which he told her not. 3 And when the queen of Sheba had seen the wisdom of Solomon, and the house that he had built, 4 and the food of his table, and the sitting of his servants, and the attendance of his ministers, and their apparel, his cupbearers also, and their apparel, and his ascent by which he went up unto the house of Jehovah; there was no more spirit in her. 5 And she said to the king, It was a true report that I heard in mine own land of thine acts, and of thy wisdom. 6 Howbeit I believed not their words, until I came, and mine eyes had seen it; and, behold, the half of the greatness of thy wisdom was not told me: thou exceedest the fame that I heard. 7 Happy are thy men, and happy are these thy servants, that stand continually before thee, and hear thy wisdom. 8 Blessed be Jehovah thy God, who delighted in thee, to set thee on his throne, to be king for Jehovah thy God: because thy God loved Israel, to establish them for ever, therefore made he thee king over them, to do justice and righteousness.

9 And she gave the king a hundred and twenty talents of gold, and spices in great abundance, and precious stones: neither was there any such spice as the queen of Sheba gave to king Solomon. 10 And the servants also of Huram, and the servants of Solomon, that brought gold from Ophir, brought algum-trees and precious stones. 11 And the king made of the algum-trees terraces for the house of Jehovah, and for the king's house, and harps and psalteries for the singers: and there were none such seen before in the land of Judah. 12 And king Solomon gave to the queen of Sheba all her desire, whatsoever she asked, besides that which she had brought unto the king. So she turned, and went to her own land, she and her servants.

See notes on the parallel passage in I Kings.

5. Summary of Wealth and Power (9: 13-28; cf. I Kings 10:11-29)

13 Now the weight of gold that came to Solomon in one year was six hundred and threescore and six talents of gold, 14 besides that which the traders and merchants brought: and all the kings of Arabia and the governors of the country brought gold and silver to Solomon. 15 And king Solomon made two hundred bucklers of beaten gold; six hundred *shekels* of beaten gold went to one buckler. 16 And *he made* three hundred shields of beaten gold; three hundred *shekels* of gold went to one shield: and the king put them in the house of the forest of Lebanon. 17 Moreover the king made a great throne of ivory, and overlaid it with pure gold. 18 And there were six steps to the throne, with a footstool of gold, which were fastened to the throne, and stays on either side by the place of the seat, and two lions standing beside the stays. 19 And twelve lions stood there on the one side and on the other upon the six steps: there was not the like made in any kingdom. 20 And all king Solomon's drinking vessels were of gold, and all the vessels of the house of the forest of Lebanon were of pure gold: silver was nothing accounted of in the days of Solomon. 21 For the king had ships that went to Tarshish with the servants of Huram; once every three years came the ships of Tarshish, bringing gold, and silver, ivory, and apes, and peacocks.

22 So king Solomon exceeded all the kings of the earth in riches and wisdom. 23 And all the kings of the earth sought the presence of Solomon, to hear his wisdom, which God had put in his heart. 24 And they brought every man his tribute, vessels of silver, and vessels of gold, and raiment, armor, and spices, horses, and

mules, a rate year by year. 25 And Solomon had four thousand stalls for horses and chariots, and twelve thousand horsemen, that he bestowed in the chariot cities, and with the king at Jerusalem. 26 And he ruled over all the kings from the River even unto the land of the Philistines, and to the border of Egypt. 27 And the king made silver to be in Jerusalem as stones, and cedars made he to be as the sycamore-trees that are in the lowland, for abundance. 28 And they brought horses for Solomon out of Egypt, and out of all lands.

See notes on the parallel passage in I Kings.

6. Conclusion of Solomon's Reign (9: 29-31; cf. I Kings 11:41-43)

29 Now the rest of the acts of Solomon, first and last, are they not written in the history of Nathan the prophet, and in the prophecy of Ahijah the Shilonite, and in the visions of Iddo the seer concerning Jeroboam the son of Nebat? 30 And Solomon reigned in Jerusalem over all Israel forty years. 31 And Solomon slept with his fathers, and he was buried in the city of David his father: and Rehoboam his son reigned in his stead.

See notes on the parallel passage in I Kings.

II. THE KINGDOM OF JUDAH (II Chron. 10:1—36:23)

Of major interest to the chronicler in his history of the kingdom are the Davidic dynasty and temple worship as administered according to the Levitical order.

A. REIGN OF DAVIDIC KINGS DURING THE LATTER PART OF THE TENTH CENTURY B.C. (10: 1—13:22)

Solomon's successor to the throne of David was his son, Rehoboam. He, in turn, was followed by Abijah.

1. Rehoboam (10:1—12:16)

The reign of Rehoboam was inaugurated about 930 B.C.[10]

a. Rebellion (10:1-19; cf. I Kings 12: 1-20)

1 And Rehoboam went to Shechem; for all Israel were come to Shechem to make him king. 2 And it came to pass, when Jeroboam the son of Nebat heard of it (for he was in Egypt, whither he had fled from the presence of king Solomon), that Jeroboam returned out of Egypt. 3 And they sent and called him; and Jeroboam and all Israel came, and they spake to Rehoboam, saying, 4 Thy father made our yoke grievous: now therefore make thou the grievous service of thy father, and his heavy yoke which he put upon us, lighter, and we will serve thee. 5 And he said unto them, Come again unto me after three days. And the people departed.

6 And king Rehoboam took counsel with the old men, that had stood before Solomon his father while he yet lived, saying, What counsel give ye me to return answer to this people? 7 And they spake unto him, saying, If thou be kind to this people, and please them, and speak good words to them, then they will be thy servants for ever. 8 But he forsook the counsel of the old men which they had given him, and took counsel with the young men that were grown up with him, that stood before him. 9 And he said unto them, What counsel give ye, that we may return answer to this people, who have spoken to me, saying, Make the yoke that thy father did put upon us lighter? 10 And the young men that were grown up with him spake unto him, saying, Thus shalt thou say unto the people that spake unto thee, saying, Thy father made our yoke heavy, but make thou it lighter unto us; thus shalt thou say unto them, My little finger is thicker than my father's loins. 11 And now whereas my father did lade you with a heavy yoke, I will add to your yoke: my father chastised you with whips, but I *will chastise you* with scorpions.

12 So Jeroboam and all the people came to Rehoboam the third day, as the king bade, saying, Come to me again the third day. 13 And the king answered them roughly; and king Rehoboam forsook the counsel of the old men, 14 and spake to them after the counsel of the young men, saying, My father made your yoke heavy, but I will add thereto: my father chastised you with whips, but I *will chastise you* with scorpions. 15 So the king hearkened not unto the people; for it was brought about of God, that Jehovah might establish his word, which he spake by Ahijah the Shilonite to Jeroboam the son of Nebat.

16 And when all Israel saw that the

---

[10] E. Thiele, *The Mysterious Numbers of the Hebrew Kings.*

king hearkened not unto them, the people answered the king, saying, What portion have we in David? neither have we inheritance in the son of Jesse: every man to your tents, O Israel: now see to thine own house, David. So all Israel departed unto their tents. 17 But as for the children of Israel that dwelt in the cities of Judah, Rehoboam reigned over them. 18 Then king Rehoboam sent Hadoram, who was over the men subject to taskwork; and the children of Israel stoned him to death with stones. And king Rehoboam made speed to get him up to his chariot, to flee to Jerusalem. 19 So Israel rebelled against the house of David unto this day.

From the chronicler's viewpoint, the rebellion of the northern tribes against the dynasty of David and the worship at the temple was apostasy.[11] While frank to acknowledge that Rehoboam provoked the rebellion, the chronicler omits consideration of any defects in the Davidic regime. There is an indirect acknowledgment of wrongs inflicted by Solomon in the words of the people, **Thy father made our yoke grievous** (v. 4). However, this did not justify revolt.

b. Rehoboam over Judah and Benjamin (11:1-23)

1 And when Rehoboam was come to Jerusalem, he assembled the house of Judah and Benjamin, a hundred and fourscore thousand chosen men, that were warriors, to fight against Israel, to bring the kingdom again to Rehoboam. 2 But the word of Jehovah came to Shemaiah the man of God, saying, 3 Speak unto Rehoboam the son of Solomon, king of Judah, and to all Israel in Judah and Benjamin, saying, 4 Thus saith Jehovah, Ye shall not go up, nor fight against your brethren: return every man to his house; for this thing is of me. So they hearkened unto the words of Jehovah, and returned from going against Jeroboam.

5 And Rehoboam dwelt in Jerusalem, and built cities for defence in Judah. 6 He built Beth-lehem, and Etam, and Tekoa, 7 and Beth-zur, and Soco, and Adullam, 8 and Gath, and Mareshah, and Ziph, 9 and Adoraim, and Lachish, and Azekah, 10 and Zorah, and Aijalon, and Hebron, which are in Judah and in Benjamin, fortified cities. 11 And he fortified the strongholds, and put captains in them, and stores of victuals, and oil and

wine. 12 And in every city *he put* shields and spears, and made them exceeding strong. And Judah and Benjamin belonged to him.

13 And the priests and the Levites that were in all Israel resorted to him out of all their border. 14 For the Levites left their suburbs and their possession, and came to Judah and Jerusalem: for Jeroboam and his sons cast them off, that they should not execute the priest's office unto Jehovah; 15 and he appointed him priests for the high places, and for the he-goats, and for the calves which he had made. 16 And after them, out of all the tribes of Israel, such as set their hearts to seek Jehovah, the God of Israel, came to Jerusalem to sacrifice unto Jehovah, the God of their fathers. 17 So they strengthened the kingdom of Judah, and made Rehoboam the son of Solomon strong, three years; for they walked three years in the way of David and Solomon.

18 And Rehoboam took him a wife, Mahalath the daughter of Jerimoth the son of David, *and of* Abihail the daughter of Eliab the son of Jesse; 19 and she bare him sons: Jeush, and Shemariah, and Zaham. 20 And after her he took Maacah the daughter of Absalom; and she bare him Abijah, and Attai, and Ziza, and Shelomith. 21 And Rehoboam loved Maacah the daughter of Absalom above all his wives and his concubines (for he took eighteen wives and threescore concubines, and begat twenty and eight sons and threescore daughters). 22 And Rehoboam appointed Abijah the son of Maacah to be chief, *even* the prince among his brethren; for *he was minded* to make him king. 23 And he dealt wisely, and dispersed of all his sons throughout all the lands of Judah and Benjamin, unto every fortified city: and he gave them victuals in abundance. And he sought *for them* many wives.

There is reluctance on the part of the Chronicles account to acknowledge more than necessary the extent of the rebellion. For example, in quoting the word of the Lord to Shemaiah, **Speak unto Rehoboam ... and to all Israel in Judah and Benjamin** (v. 3), there is given the suggestion that many members of the northern tribes remained loyal to the kingdom, even when it necessitated migration to loyal territory. There is the mention of the migration of the Levites,

11 Ellison, *op. cit.*, p. 356.

who lived among the northern tribes, to Jerusalem (v. 13).

Alert to possible invasion by the northern tribes, which had the greater military power and resources, Rehoboam was forced to erect extensive defenses (vv. 5-12). This was the lamentable state of affairs to which the kingdom was brought as a result of the arrogance of power. Rehoboam's abuse of the power within his control so wounded the nation of Israel that recovery was never effected. Arrogance continually plagues human relations. It has no place in fulfilling the redemptive mission which God has given to His people.

c. Egyptian Invasion of Judah (12: 1-16; cf. I Kings 14:25-31)

1 And it came to pass, when the kingdom of Rehoboam was established, and he was strong, that he forsook the law of Jehovah, and all Israel with him. 2 And it came to pass in the fifth year of king Rehoboam, that Shishak king of Egypt came up against Jerusalem, because they had trespassed against Jehovah, 3 with twelve hundred chariots, and threescore thousand horsemen. And the people were without number that came with him out of Egypt: the Lubim, the Sukkiim, and the Ethiopians. 4 And he took the fortified cities which pertained to Judah, and came unto Jerusalem. 5 Now Shemaiah the prophet came to Rehoboam, and to the princes of Judah, that were gathered together to Jerusalem because of Shishak, and said unto them, Thus saith Jehovah, Ye have forsaken me, therefore have I also left you in the hand of Shishak. 6 Then the princes of Israel and the king humbled themselves; and they said, Jehovah is righteous. 7 And when Jehovah saw that they humbled themselves, the word of Jehovah came to Shemaiah, saying, They have humbled themselves: I will not destroy them; but I will grant them some deliverance, and my wrath shall not be poured out upon Jerusalem by the hand of Shishak. 8 Nevertheless they shall be his servants, that they may know my service, and the service of the kingdoms of the countries. 9 So Shishak king of Egypt came up against Jerusalem, and took away the treasures of the house of Jehovah, and the treasures of the king's house; he took all away: he took away also the shields of gold which Solomon had made. 10 And king Rehoboam made in their stead shields of brass, and committed them to the hands of the captains of the guard, that kept the door of the king's house. 11 And it was so, that, as oft as the king entered into the house of Jehovah, the guard came and bare them, and brought them back into the guard-chamber. 12 And when he humbled himself, the wrath of Jehovah turned from him, so as not to destroy him altogether: and moreover in Judah there were good things *found*.

13 So king Rehoboam strengthened himself in Jerusalem, and reigned: for Rehoboam was forty and one years old when he began to reign, and he reigned seventeen years in Jerusalem, the city which Jehovah had chosen out of all the tribes of Israel, to put his name there: and his mother's name was Naamah the Ammonitess. 14 And he did that which was evil, because he set not his heart to seek Jehovah.

15 Now the acts of Rehoboam, first and last, are they not written in the histories of Shemaiah the prophet and of Iddo the seer, after the manner of genealogies? And there were wars between Rehoboam and Jeroboam continually. 16 And Rehoboam slept with his fathers, and was buried in the city of David: and Abijah his son reigned in his stead.

The invasion of Shishak of Egypt was regarded by the chronicler as the result of the sin committed by Rehoboam; **he forsook the law of Jehovah** (v. 1). **Thus saith the Lord, ye have forsaken me, therefore have I left you in the hand of Shishak** (v. 5). The strong rebuke delivered by Shemaiah the prophet caused Rehoboam to repent. The chronicler makes a point of the fact that although the invasion brought about the loss of treasures in the kingdom (v. 9), it could have been much worse, even the destruction of the kingdom itself (v. 7).

2. Abijah (13:1-22; cf. I Kings 15:1-8)

1 In the eighteenth year of king Jeroboam began Abijah to reign over Judah. 2 Three years reigned he in Jerusalem: and his mother's name was Micaiah the daughter of Uriel of Gibeah. And there was war between Abijah and Jeroboam. 3 And Abijah joined battle with an army of valiant men of war, even four hundred thousand chosen men: and Jeroboam set the battle in array against him with eight hundred thousand chosen men, who were mighty men of valor. 4 And Abijah stood up upon mount Zemaraim, which is in

the hill-country of Ephraim, and said, Hear me, O Jeroboam and all Israel: 5 Ought ye not to know that Jehovah, the God of Israel, gave the kingdom over Israel to David for ever, even to him and to his sons by a covenant of salt? 6 Yet Jeroboam the son of Nebat, the servant of Solomon the son of David, rose up, and rebelled against his lord. 7 And there were gathered unto him worthless men, base fellows, that strengthened themselves against Rehoboam the son of Solomon, when Rehoboam was young and tender-hearted, and could not withstand them. 8 And now ye think to withstand the kingdom of Jehovah in the hand of the sons of David; and ye are a great multitude, and there are with you the golden calves which Jeroboam made you for gods. 9 Have ye not driven out the priests of Jehovah, the sons of Aaron, and the Levites, and made you priests after the manner of the peoples of *other* lands? so that whosoever cometh to consecrate himself with a young bullock and seven rams, the same may be a priest of *them that are* no gods. 10 But as for us, Jehovah is our God, and we have not forsaken him; and *we have* priests ministering unto Jehovah, the sons of Aaron, and the Levites in their work: 11 and they burn unto Jehovah every morning and every evening burnt-offerings and sweet incense: the showbread also *set they* in order upon the pure table; and the candlestick of gold with the lamps thereof, to burn every evening: for we keep the charge of Jehovah our God; but ye have forsaken him. 12 And, behold, God is with us at our head, and his priests with the trumpets of alarm to sound an alarm against you. O children of Israel, fight ye not against Jehovah, the God of your fathers; for ye shall not prosper.

13 But Jeroboam caused an ambushment to come about behind them: so they were before Judah, and the ambushment was behind them. 14 And when Judah looked back, behold, the battle was before and behind them; and they cried unto Jehovah, and the priests sounded with the trumpets. 15 Then the men of Judah gave a shout: and as the men of Judah shouted, it came to pass, that God smote Jeroboam and all Israel before Abijah and Judah. 16 And the children of Israel fled before Judah; and God delivered them into their hand. 17 And Abijah and his people slew them with a great slaughter: so there fell down slain of Israel five hundred thousand chosen men. 18 Thus the children of Israel were brought under at that time, and the

children of Judah prevailed, because they relied upon Jehovah, the God of their fathers. 19 And Abijah pursued after Jeroboam, and took the cities from him, Beth-el with the towns thereof, and Jeshanah with the towns thereof, and Ephron with the towns thereof. 20 Neither did Jeroboam recover strength again in the days of Abijah: and Jehovah smote him, and he died. 21 But Abijah waxed mighty, and took unto himself fourteen wives, and begat twenty and two sons, and sixteen daughters. 22 And the rest of the acts of Abijah, and his ways, and his sayings, are written in the commentary of the prophet Iddo.

There is no parallel in I Kings for the battle at Zemaraim (v. 4). Rather, the Kings account gives a general description of Abijah's reign. However, the Chronicles account includes this battle since it portrays Abijah in a holy crusade. The king claimed that the rebellion of the northern tribes was instigated by hardened characters who had imposed upon the youthful Rehoboam (v. 7). Therefore Abijah declared that the time had come for a holy war. God was on the side of Judah; it was folly to fight against Him (v. 12). In the battle, Abijah was victorious (v. 18). However, the victory was hardly more than the recapture of a few border towns, and even these were not retained long.

The chronicler's account of Abijah's activity is set in the larger context of the apostasy of the northern tribes. They were wrong in persisting in their separation from the rule of the house of David. Therefore, Abijah, Rehoboam's successor, was the divine instrument of chastisement upon these rebellious ones.

B. REFORMS OF ASA AND JEHOSHAPHAT FROM THE CLOSE OF THE TENTH CENTURY TO THE MIDDLE OF THE NINTH CENTURY B.C. (14:1—20:37)

This was a period of approximately sixty-five years. Asa ruled about forty-one years and his successor, Jehoshaphat, about twenty-five years. Both kings registered considerable progress in the types of reform important from the viewpoint of the chronicler, who had a great interest in the Levitical form of temple worship.

1. Asa (14:1—16:14; cf. I Kings 15:9-24)

The Chronicles account is considerably expanded in comparison with the Kings account.

a. Reform (14:1-8)

1 So Abijah slept with his fathers, and they buried him in the city of David; and Asa his son reigned in his stead. In his days the land was quiet ten years. 2 And Asa did that which was good and right in the eyes of Jehovah his God: 3 for he took away the foreign altars, and the high places, and brake down the pillars, and hewed down the Asherim, 4 and commanded Judah to seek Jehovah, the God of their fathers, and to do the law and the commandment. 5 Also he took away out of all the cities of Judah the high places and the sun-images: and the kingdom was quiet before him. 6 And he built fortified cities in Judah; for the land was quiet, and he had no war in those years, because Jehovah had given him rest. 7 For he said unto Judah, Let us build these cities, and make about them walls, and towers, gates, and bars; the land is yet before us, because we have sought Jehovah our God; we have sought him, and he hath given us rest on every side. So they built and prospered. 8 And Asa had an army that bare bucklers and spears, out of Judah three hundred thousand; and out of Benjamin, that bare shields and drew bows, two hundred and fourscore thousand: all these were mighty men of valor.

Asa was well pleasing to the Lord. Not only did he remove idolatrous worship but he also commanded obedience to the law of Jehovah (vv. 2-5). This intensive reform was rewarded with a welcomed period of peace. **We have sought him, and he hath given us rest on every side** (v. 7).

b. Victory (14:9-15)

9 And there came out against them Zerah the Ethiopian with an army of a thousand thousand, and three hundred chariots; and he came unto Mareshah. 10 Then Asa went out to meet him, and they set the battle in array in the valley of Zephathah at Mareshah. 11 And Asa cried unto Jehovah his God, and said, Jehovah, there is none besides thee to help, between the mighty and him that hath no strength: help us, O Jehovah our God; for we rely on thee, and in thy name are we come against this multitude.

O Jehovah, thou art our God; let not man prevail against thee. 12 So Jehovah smote the Ethiopians before Asa, and before Judah; and the Ethiopians fled. 13 And Asa and the people that were with him pursued them unto Gerar: and there fell of the Ethiopians so many that they could not recover themselves; for they were destroyed before Jehovah, and before his host; and they carried away very much booty. 14 And they smote all the cities round about Gerar; for the fear of Jehovah came upon them: and they despoiled all the cities; for there was much spoil in them. 15 They smote also the tents of cattle, and carried away sheep in abundance, and camels, and returned to Jerusalem.

After his diligent religious reform honoring the Lord, Asa faced a critical situation. Invasion by Zerah threatened his kingdom. In earnest, believing prayer, he said, **Jehovah, there is none besides thee to help, between the mighty and him that hath no strength** (v. 11). Admitting utter weakness in himself, Asa affirmed great faith in the might of the Lord. He was not disillusioned, for through the power of the Lord he realized a remarkable deliverance (v. 12). Again and again, the strength of the Lord has been revealed in behalf of those who confess to weakness and cast themselves upon Him in utter dependence.

c. Faithfulness (15:1-19)

1 And the Spirit of God came upon Azariah the son of Oded: 2 and he went out to meet Asa, and said unto him, Hear ye me, Asa, and all Judah and Benjamin: Jehovah is with you, while ye are with him; and if ye seek him, he will be found of you; but if ye forsake him, he will forsake you. 3 Now for a long season Israel was without the true God, and without a teaching priest, and without law: 4 but when in their distress they turned unto Jehovah, the God of Israel, and sought him, he was found of them. 5 And in those times there was no peace to him that went out, nor to him that came in; but great vexations were upon all the inhabitants of the lands. 6 And they were broken in pieces, nation against nation, and city against city; for God did vex them with all adversity. 7 But be ye strong, and let not your hands be slack; for your work shall be rewarded.

8 And when Asa heard these words, and the prophecy of Oded the prophet,

he took courage, and put away the abominations out of all the land of Judah and Benjamin, and out of the cities which he had taken from the hill-country of Ephraim; and he renewed the altar of Jehovah, that was before the porch of Jehovah. 9 And he gathered all Judah and Benjamin, and them that sojourned with them out of Ephraim and Manasseh, and out of Simeon: for they fell to him out of Israel in abundance, when they saw that Jehovah his God was with him. 10 So they gathered themselves together at Jerusalem in the third month, in the fifteenth year of the reign of Asa. 11 And they sacrificed unto Jehovah in that day, of the spoil which they had brought, seven hundred oxen and seven thousand sheep. 12 And they entered into the covenant to seek Jehovah, the God of their fathers, with all their heart and with all their soul; 13 and that whosoever would not seek Jehovah, the God of Israel, should be put to death, whether small or great, whether man or woman. 14 And they sware unto Jehovah with a loud voice, and with shouting, and with trumpets, and with cornets. 15 And all Judah rejoiced at the oath; for they had sworn with all their heart, and sought him with their whole desire; and he was found of them: and Jehovah gave them rest round about.

16 And also Maacah, the mother of Asa the king, he removed from being queen, because she had made an abominable image for an Asherah and Asa cut down her image, and made dust of it, and burnt it at the brook Kidron. 17 But the high places were not taken away out of Israel: nevertheless the heart of Asa was perfect all his days. 18 And he brought into the house of God the things that his father had dedicated, and that he himself had dedicated, silver, and gold, and vessels. 19 And there was no more war unto the five and thirtieth year of the reign of Asa.

There is no other reference to the prophet Azariah than the account given of him in Chronicles. He prophesied in the days of Asa, and the burden of his prophecy was in harmony with the viewpoint of the chronicler. **Jehovah is with you, while you are with him** (v. 2). Azariah's message to Asa was that Asa's faithfulness in reform found favor with God, for God would be with him.

This inspired Asa with courage to take further measures of reform (v. 8). He called upon Judah and those from the

northern tribes who had migrated to the territory of Judah to come before the Lord and offer sacrifices (vv. 9-12). Because Asa carried out numerous reforms, the chronicler observed that many of the inhabitants of the northern tribes migrated to Asa's kingdom, **for they fell to him out of Israel in abundance, when they saw that Jehovah his God was with him** (v. 9).

With the offering of sacrifices, Asa and all the people renewed the covenant with the Lord. **And all Judah rejoiced at the oath** (v. 15). The people who migrated from the northern tribes participated in all this. The inhabitants of Judah were excellent examples in their glad reception of those who came out of the northern tribes to join their faithful worship. Christians do well to emulate this exemplary conduct toward those who may have departed from the company of the faithful for a time, but who later return.

d. Weakness in Faith (16:1-14; cf. I Kings 15:16-22)

1 In the six and thirtieth year of the reign of Asa, Baasha king of Israel went up against Judah, and built Ramah, that he might not suffer any one to go out or come in to Asa king of Judah. 2 Then Asa brought out silver and gold out of the treasures of the house of Jehovah and of the king's house, and sent to Ben-hadad king of Syria, that dwelt at Damascus, saying, 3 *There is* a league between me and thee, as *there was* between my father and thy father: behold, I have sent thee silver and gold; go, break thy league with Baasha king of Israel, that he may depart from me. 4 And Ben-hadad hearkened unto king Asa, and sent the captains of his armies against the cities of Israel; and they smote Ijon, and Dan, and Abel-maim, and all the store-cities of Naphtali. 5 And it came to pass, when Baasha heard thereof, that he left off building Ramah, and let his work cease. 6 Then Asa the king took all Judah; and they carried away the stones of Ramah, and the timber thereof, wherewith Baasha had builded; and he built therewith Geba and Mizpah.

7 And at that time Hanani the seer came to Asa king of Judah, and said unto him, Because thou hast relied on the king of Syria, and hast not relied on Jehovah thy God, therefore is the host of the king of Syria escaped out of thy hand. 8 Were

not the Ethiopians and the Lubim a huge host, with chariots and horsemen exceeding many? yet, because thou didst rely on Jehovah, he delivered them into thy hand. 9 For the eyes of Jehovah run to and fro throughout the whole earth, to show himself strong in the behalf of them whose heart is perfect toward him. Herein thou hast done foolishly; for from henceforth thou shalt have wars. 10 Then Asa was wroth with the seer, and put him in the prison-house; for he was in a rage with him because of this thing. And Asa oppressed some of the people at the same time.

11 And, behold, the acts of Asa, first and last, lo, they are written in the book of the kings of Judah and Israel. 12 And in the thirty and ninth year of his reign Asa was diseased in his feet; his disease was exceeding great: yet in his disease he sought not to Jehovah, but to the physicians. 13 And Asa slept with his fathers, and died in the one and fortieth year of his reign. 14 And they buried him in his own sepulchres, which he had hewn out for himself in the city of David, and laid him in the bed which was filled with sweet odors and divers kinds *of spices* prepared by the perfumers' art: and they made a very great burning for him.

During his reign Asa was threatened by the king of the northern tribes, Baasha. As far as the chronicler was concerned, Asa committed a great sin when he gave the treasure from the temple to the king of Syria, Ben-hadad, and by this means persuaded him to break his treaty with Baasha and declare war on the Northern Kingdom (vv. 2-4).

Hanani, encountered only in this incident and mentioned only by the chronicler, declared that if Asa had relied upon Jehovah as he did when threatened by Zerah, he could have overpowered not only Baasha but even the combined strength of Baasha and Ben-hadad (vv. 7-8). **For the eyes of Jehovah run to and fro throughout the whole earth, to show himself strong in behalf of them whose heart is perfect toward him** (v. 9). This was the climactic declaration in Hanani's rebuke. Buying friendship with the temple treasure, Asa had entered into foreign alliances instead of relying by faith upon the Lord.

Asa added to his iniquity by imprisoning the prophet who rebuked him and oppressing those who sympathized with

the prophet (v. 10). In addition, when Asa became afflicted with diseased feet he called for the physicians and neglected to call upon the Lord (v. 12). Anything symptomatic of a deteriorating and weakening faith is significantly serious. It is absolutely essential to watch for warning signals. As faith deteriorates, there is the subtle changing of directions from going the way God wills to going the way self wills.

2. Jehoshaphat (17:1—20:37)

As with the chronicler's account of Asa, so the account of Jehoshaphat is considerably expanded in comparison with the Kings account (cf. 17:1—20:37 with I Kings 22:1-35, 41-43, 48-49).

a. Reign (17:1-19)

1 And Jehoshaphat his son reigned in his stead, and strengthened himself against Israel. 2 And he placed forces in all the fortified cities of Judah, and set garrisons in the land of Judah, and in the cities of Ephraim, which Asa his father had taken. 3 And Jehovah was with Jehoshaphat, because he walked in the first ways of his father David, and sought not unto the Baalim, 4 but sought to the God of his father, and walked in his commandments, and not after the doings of Israel. 5 Therefore Jehovah established the kingdom in his hand; and all Judah brought to Jehoshaphat tribute; and he had riches and honor in abundance. 6 And his heart was lifted up in the ways of Jehovah: and furthermore he took away the high places and the Asherim out of Judah.

7 Also in the third year of his reign he sent his princes, even Ben-hail, and Obadiah, and Zechariah, and Nethanel, and Micaiah, to teach in the cities of Judah; 8 and with them the Levites, even Shemaiah, and Nethaniah, and Zebadiah, and Asahel, and Shemiramoth, and Jehonathan, and Adonijah, and Tobijah, and Tobadonijah, the Levites; and with them Elishama and Jehoram, the priests. 9 And they taught in Judah, having the book of the law of Jehovah with them; and they went about throughout all the cities of Judah, and taught among the people.

10 And the fear of Jehovah fell upon all the kingdoms of the lands that were round about Judah, so that they made no war against Jehoshaphat. 11 And some of the Philistines brought Jehoshaphat presents, and silver for tribute; the Arabians also brought him flocks, seven thousand and seven hundred rams, and seven thou-

sand and seven hundred he-goats. 12 And Jehoshaphat waxed great exceedingly; and he built in Judah castles and cities of store. 13 And he had many works in the cities of Judah; and men of war, mighty men of valor, in Jerusalem. 14 And this was the numbering of them according to their fathers' houses: Of Judah, the captains of thousands: Adnah the captain, and with him mighty men of valor three hundred thousand; 15 and next to him Jehohanan the captain, and with him two hundred and fourscore thousand; 16 and next to him Amasiah the son of Zichri, who willingly offered himself unto Jehovah; and with him two hundred thousand mighty men of valor. 17 And of Benjamin: Eliada a mighty man of valor, and with him two hundred thousand armed with bow and shield; 18 and next to him Jehozabad, and with him a hundred and fourscore thousand ready prepared for war. 19 These were they that waited on the king, besides those whom the king put in the fortified cities throughout all Judah.

Jehoshaphat's reign was characterized by two major enterprises: building extensive fortifications against attack (v. 2), and following after Jehovah (v. 4). As a result of Jehoshaphat's obedience to the Lord, his kingdom became strong (v. 5). The strength of Judah was re-enforced by the efforts of the king to provide instruction in the law. Princes and Levites gave instruction in the law throughout the cities of the land. **And they taught in Judah, having the book of the law of Jehovah with them** (v. 9).

The history of Judaism not only is a remarkable history in itself but includes an outstanding system of religious education. A Jew was required to observe religious education as a lifelong activity, not merely a childhood diversion during odd moments. The history of Christianity does not usually reveal that same high quality of religious instruction. It is vitally necessary for Christians to give themselves to Christian instruction and learning in order to know their religious heritage and to live their Christian faith meaningfully.

b. Alliance (18:1—19:3; cf. I Kings 22:1-38)

1 Now Jehoshaphat had riches and honor in abundance; and he joined affinity with Ahab. 2 And after certain years he went down to Ahab to Samaria. And Ahab killed sheep and oxen for him in abundance, and for the people that were with him, and moved him to go up *with him* to Ramoth-gilead. 3 And Ahab king of Israel said unto Jehoshaphat king of Judah, Wilt thou go with me to Ramoth-gilead? And he answered him, I am as thou art, and my people as thy people; and *we will be* with thee in the war.

4 And Jehoshaphat said unto the king of Israel, Inquire first, I pray thee, for the word of Jehovah. 5 Then the king of Israel gathered the prophets together, four hundred men, and said unto them, Shall we go to Ramoth-gilead to battle, or shall I forbear? And they said, Go up; for God will deliver it into the hand of the king. 6 But Jehoshaphat said, Is there not here a prophet of Jehovah besides, that we may inquire of him? 7 And the king of Israel said unto Jehoshaphat, There is yet one man by whom we may inquire of Jehovah: but I hate him; for he never prophesieth good concerning me, but always evil: the same is Micaiah the son of Imla. And Jehoshaphat said, Let not the king say so. 8 Then the king of Israel called an officer, and said, Fetch quickly Micaiah the son of Imla. 9 Now the king of Israel and Jehoshaphat the king of Judah sat each on his throne, arrayed in their robes, and they were sitting in an open place at the entrance of the gate of Samaria; and all the prophets were prophesying before them. 10 And Zedekiah the son of Chenaanah made him horns of iron and said, Thus saith Jehovah, With these shalt thou push the Syrians, until they be consumed. 11 And all the prophets prophesied so, saying, Go up to Ramoth-gilead, and prosper; for Jehovah will deliver it into the hand of the king.

12 And the messenger that went to call Micaiah spake to him, saying, Behold, the words of the prophets *declare* good to the king with one mouth: let thy word therefore, I pray thee, be like one of theirs, and speak thou good. 13 And Micaiah said, As Jehovah liveth, what my God saith, that will I speak. 14 And when he was come to the king, the king said unto him, Micaiah, shall we go to Ramoth-gilead to battle, or shall I forbear? And he said, Go ye up, and prosper; and they shall be delivered into your hand. 15 And the king said to him, How many times shall I adjure thee that thou speak unto me nothing but the truth in the name of Jehovah? 16 And he said, I saw all Israel scattered upon the mountains, as sheep that have no shepherd: and Jehovah said, These have no master; let

them return every man to his house in peace. 17 And the king of Israel said to Jehoshaphat, Did I not tell thee that he would not prophesy good concerning me, but evil? 18 And *Micaiah* said, Therefore hear ye the word of Jehovah: I saw Jehovah sitting upon his throne, and all the host of heaven standing on his right hand and on his left. 19 And Jehovah said, Who shall entice Ahab king of Israel, that he may go up and fall at Ramoth-gilead? And one spake saying after this manner, and another saying after that manner. 20 And there came forth a spirit, and stood before Jehovah, and said, I will entice him. And Jehovah said unto him, Wherewith? 21 And he said, I will go forth, and will be a lying spirit in the mouth of all his prophets. And he said, Thou shalt entice him, and shalt prevail also: go forth, and do so. 22 Now therefore, behold, Jehovah hath put a lying spirit in the mouth of these thy prophets; and Jehovah hath spoken evil concerning thee.

23 Then Zedekiah the son of Chenaanah came near, and smote Micaiah upon the cheek, and said, Which way went the Spirit of Jehovah from me to speak unto thee? 24 And Micaiah said, Behold, thou shalt see on that day, when thou shalt go into an inner chamber to hide thyself. 25 And the king of Israel said, Take ye Micaiah, and carry him back unto Amon the governor of the city, and to Joash the king's son; 26 and say, Thus saith the king, Put this fellow in the prison, and feed him with bread of affliction and with water of affliction, until I return in peace. 27 And Micaiah said, If thou return at all in peace, Jehovah hath not spoken by me. And he said, Hear, ye peoples, all of you.

28 So the king of Israel and Jehoshaphat the king of Judah went up to Ramoth-gilead. 29 And the king of Israel said unto Jehoshaphat, I will disguise myself, and go into the battle; but put thou on thy robes. So the king of Israel disguised himself; and they went into the battle. 30 Now the king of Syria had commanded the captains of his chariots, saying, Fight neither with small nor great, save only with the king of Israel. 31 And it came to pass, when the captains of the chariots saw Jehoshaphat, that they said, It is the king of Israel. Therefore they turned about to fight against him: but Jehoshaphat cried out, and Jehovah helped him; and God moved them *to depart* from him. 32 And it came to pass, when the captains of the chariots saw that it was not the king of Israel, that

they turned back from pursuing him. 33 And a certain man drew his bow at a venture, and smote the king of Israel between the joints of the armor: wherefore he said to the driver of the chariot, Turn thy hand, and carry me out of the host; for I am sore wounded. 34 And the battle increased that day: howbeit the king of Israel stayed himself up in his chariot against the Syrians until the even; and about the time of the going down of the sun he died.

1 And Jehoshaphat the king of Judah returned to his house in peace to Jerusalem. 2 And Jehu the son of Hanani the seer went out to meet him, and said to king Jehoshaphat, Shouldest thou help the wicked, and love them that hate Jehovah? for this thing wrath is upon thee from before Jehovah. 3 Nevertheless there are good things found in thee, in that thou hast put away the Asheroth out of the land, and hast set thy heart to seek God.

Now Jehoshaphat had riches and honor in abundance; and he joined affinity with Ahab (v. 1). The story of Jehoshaphat's alliance with Ahab as given in Chronicles is parallel with the Kings account, except that the chronicler has put Jehoshaphat in the center of the activity. The account begins with the implication that Jehoshaphat made a mistake. Although his kingdom was strong and prosperous, he formed an alliance with the Northern Kingdom. It was imperative for Ahab of the Northern Kingdom to find reinforcements to protect him from Syria, but Jehoshaphat needed no such assistance.

Nevertheless, the account indicates that the alliance was strengthened with the marriage of Athaliah, daughter of Ahab and Jezebel, to Jehoram, son of Jehoshaphat and heir to the throne in Jerusalem (cf. v. 1 and 21:6). The sequel to this marriage was disastrous. The way was opened for introducing Baalism into Judah (22:3ff.). As a result, the people of Judah were debased and eventually the Davidic dynasty was almost destroyed (22:10-12). In fact, Jehoshaphat's noteworthy reforms were obliterated.

The alliance stands as a grim reminder that there are incalculable risks taken in such involvements. Jehoshaphat was strong and may have calculated that the advantage was on his side. However, the account plainly reveals that while one can act as he chooses, he cannot determine the results of his actions. Jehu, the son of Hanani, brought the word of divine rebuke to the king: **Shouldest thou help the wicked, and love them that hate Jehovah? for this thing wrath is upon thee from before Jehovah** (v. 2). Nevertheless, in the main, Jehoshaphat continued to please God.

c. Justice (19:4-11)

4 And Jehoshaphat dwelt at Jerusalem: and he went out again among the people from Beer-sheba to the hill-country of Ephraim, and brought them back unto Jehovah, the God of their fathers. 5 And he set judges in the land throughout all the fortified cities of Judah, city by city, 6 and said to the judges, Consider what ye do: for ye judge not for man, but for Jehovah; and *he is* with you in the judgment. 7 Now therefore let the fear of Jehovah be upon you; take heed and do it: for there is no iniquity with Jehovah our God, nor respect of persons, nor taking of bribes.

8 Moreover in Jerusalem did Jehoshaphat set of the Levites and the priests, and of the heads of the fathers' *houses* of Israel, for the judgment of Jehovah, and for controversies. And they returned to Jerusalem. 9 And he charged them, saying, Thus shall ye do in the fear of Jehovah, faithfully, and with a perfect heart. 10 And whensoever any controversy shall come to you from your brethren that dwell in their cities, between blood and blood, between law and commandment, statutes and ordinances, ye shall warn them, that they be not guilty towards Jehovah, and so wrath come upon you and upon your brethren: this do, and ye shall not be guilty. 11 And, behold, Amariah the chief priest is over you in all matters of Jehovah; and Zebadiah the son of Ishmael, the ruler of the house of Judah, in all the king's matters: also the Levites shall be officers before you. Deal courageously, and Jehovah be with the good.

And Jehoshaphat . . . went out again among the people (v. 4). The work of reform was resumed with attention given to improving the administration of justice.

d. Victory Through Prayer (20:1-37)

1 And it came to pass after this, that the children of Moab, and the children of Ammon, and with them some of the Am-

monites, came against Jehoshaphat to battle. 2 Then there came some that told Jehoshaphat, saying, There cometh a great multitude against thee from beyond the sea from Syria; and, behold, they are in Hazazon-tamar (the same is En-gedi). 3 And Jehoshaphat feared, and set himself to seek unto Jehovah; and he proclaimed a fast throughout all Judah. 4 And Judah gathered themselves together, to seek *help* of Jehovah: even out of all the cities of Judah they came to seek Jehovah.

5 And Jehoshaphat stood in the assembly of Judah and Jerusalem, in the house of Jehovah, before the new court; 6 and he said, O Jehovah, the God of our fathers, art not thou God in heaven? and art not thou ruler over all the kingdoms of the nations? and in thy hand is power and might, so that none is able to withstand thee. 7 Didst not thou, O our God, drive out the inhabitants of this land before thy people Israel, and give it to the seed of Abraham thy friend for ever? 8 And they dwelt therein, and have built thee a sanctuary therein for thy name, saying, 9 If evil come upon us, the sword, judgment, or pestilence, or famine, we will stand before this house, and before thee (for thy name is in this house), and cry unto thee in our affliction, and thou wilt hear and save. 10 And now, behold, the children of Ammon and Moab and mount Seir, whom thou wouldest not let Israel invade, when they came out of the land of Egypt, but they turned aside from them, and destroyed them not; 11 behold, how they reward us, to come to cast us out of thy possession, which thou hast given us to inherit. 12 O our God, wilt thou not judge them? for we have no might against this great company that cometh against us; neither know we what to do: but our eyes are upon thee. 13 And all Judah stood before Jehovah, with their little ones, their wives, and their children.

14 Then upon Jahaziel the son of Zechariah, the son of Benaiah, the son of Jeiel, the son of Mattaniah, the Levite, of the sons of Asaph, came the Spirit of Jehovah in the midst of the assembly; 15 and he said, Hearken ye, all Judah, and ye inhabitants of Jerusalem, and thou king Jehoshaphat: Thus saith Jehovah unto you, Fear not ye, neither be dismayed by reason of this great multitude; for the battle is not yours, but God's. 16 To-morrow go ye down against them: behold, they come up by the ascent of Ziz; and ye shall find them at the end of the valley, before the wilderness of Jeru-

el. 17 Ye shall not need to fight in this *battle*: set yourselves, stand ye still, and see the salvation of Jehovah with you, O Judah and Jerusalem; fear not, nor be dismayed: to-morrow go out against them; for Jehovah is with you. 18 And Jehoshaphat bowed his head with his face to the ground; and all Judah and the inhabitants of Jerusalem fell down before Jehovah, worshipping Jehovah. 19 And the Levites, of the children of the Kohathites and of the children of the Korahites, stood up to praise Jehovah, the God of Israel, with an exceeding loud voice.

20 And they rose early in the morning, and went forth into the wilderness of Tekoa: and as they went forth, Jehoshaphat stood and said, Hear me, O Judah, and ye inhabitants of Jerusalem: believe in Jehovah your God, so shall ye be established; believe his prophets, so shall ye prosper. 21 And when he had taken counsel with the people, he appointed them that should sing unto Jehovah, and give praise in holy array, as they went out before the army, and say, Give thanks unto Jehovah; for his lovingkindness *endureth* for ever. 22 And when they began to sing and to praise, Jehovah set liers-in-wait against the children of Ammon, Moab, and mount Seir, that were come against Judah; and they were smitten. 23 For the children of Ammon and Moab stood up against the inhabitants of mount Seir, utterly to slay and destroy them: and when they had made an end of the inhabitants of Seir, every one helped to destroy another.

24 And when Judah came to the watch-tower of the wilderness, they looked upon the multitude; and, behold, they were dead bodies fallen to the earth, and there were none that escaped. 25 And when Jehoshaphat and his people came to take the spoil of them, they found among them in abundance both riches and dead bodies, and precious jewels, which they stripped off for themselves, more than they could carry away: and they were three days in taking the spoil, it was so much. 26 And on the fourth day they assembled themselves in the valley of Beracah; for there they blessed Jehovah: therefore the name of that place was called The valley of Beracah unto this day. 27 Then they returned, every man of Judah and Jerusalem, and Jehoshaphat in the forefront of them, to go again to Jerusalem with joy; for Jehovah had made them to rejoice over their enemies. 28 And they came to Jerusalem with psalteries and harps and trumpets unto the house of Jehovah. 29 And the fear of God was on all the kingdoms of the countries, when they heard that Jehovah fought against the enemies of Israel. 30 So the realm of Jehosphahat was quiet; for his God gave him rest round about.

31 And Jehoshaphat reigned over Judah: he was thirty and five years old when he began to reign; and he reigned twenty and five years in Jerusalem: and his mother's name was Azubah the daughter of Shilhi. 32 And he walked in the way of Asa his father, and turned not aside from it, doing that which was right in the eyes of Jehovah. 33 Howbeit the high places were not taken away; neither as yet had the people set their hearts unto the God of their fathers. 34 Now the rest of the acts of Jehoshaphat, first and last, behold, they are written in the history of Jehu the son of Hanani, which is inserted in the book of the kings of Israel.

35 And after this did Jehoshaphat king of Judah join himself with Ahaziah king of Israel; the same did very wickedly: 36 and he joined himself with him to make ships to go to Tarshish; and they made the ships in Ezion-geber. 37 Then Eliezer the son of Dodavahu of Mareshah prophesied against Jehoshaphat, saying, Because thou hast joined thyself with Ahaziah, Jehovah hath destroyed thy works. And the ships were broken, so that they were not able to go to Tarshish.

News came to Jehoshaphat of an impending invasion from Moab and Ammon. However, his first recorded thought was not of his powerful army but of the mighty Jehovah. He called upon the people to fast and to seek the help of the Lord (vv. 3-4). His memorable prayer recalled the divine help given in past days, recounted the national crisis of the present moment and expressed reliance upon the help of Jehovah for the future (vv. 5-13).

Jehovah answered by the living voice of a prophet named Jahaziel, a Levite belonging to the company of musicians. His "thus saith Jehovah" was: **The battle is not yours, but God's** (v. 15). On the strength of this word, Jehoshaphat greatly encouraged the people. **Hear me, O Judah ... believe in Jehovah your God, so shall ye be established; believe his prophets, so shall ye prosper** (v. 20). As the people gave praise unto the Lord, the invading army was destroyed. **Jehovah had made them to rejoice over their enemies** (v. 29).

C. REIGN OF DAVIDIC KINGS DURING THE MIDDLE OF THE NINTH CENTURY B.C. (21:1—23:21)

Following the reforming reigns of Asa and Jehoshaphat, there occurred a catastrophic decline in religious devotion lasting for almost fifteen years.

1. Jehoram (21:1-20; cf. II Kings 8:16-22)

1 And Jehoshaphat slept with his fathers, and was buried with his fathers in the city of David: and Jehoram his son reigned in his stead. 2 And he had brethren, the sons of Jehoshaphat: Azariah, and Jehiel, and Zechariah, and Azariah, and Michael, and Shephatiah; all these were the sons of Jehoshaphat king of Israel. 3 And their father gave them great gifts, of silver, and of gold, and of precious things, with fortified cities in Judah: but the kingdom gave he to Jehoram, because he was the first-born. 4 Now when Jehoram was risen up over the kingdom of his father, and had strengthened himself, he slew all his brethren with the sword, and divers also of the princes of Israel. 5 Jehoram was thirty and two years old when he began to reign; and he reigned eight years in Jerusalem. 6 And he walked in the way of the kings of Israel, as did the house of Ahab; for he had the daughter of Ahab to wife: and he did that which was evil in the sight of Jehovah. 7 Howbeit Jehovah would not destroy the house of David, because of the covenant that he had made with David, and as he promised to give a lamp to him and to his children alway.

8 In his days Edom revolted from under the hand of Judah, and made a king over themselves. 9 Then Jehoram passed over with his captains, and all his chariots with him: and he rose up by night, and smote the Edomites that compassed him about, and the captains of the chariots. 10 So Edom revolted from under the hand of Judah unto this day: then did Libnah revolt at the same time from under his hand, because he had forsaken Jehovah, the God of his fathers. 11 Moreover he made high places in the mountains of Judah, and made the inhabitants of Jerusalem to play the harlot, and led Judah astray. 12 And there

came a writing to him from Elijah the prophet, saying, Thus saith Jehovah, the God of David thy father, Because thou hast not walked in the ways of Jehoshaphat thy father, nor in the ways of Asa king of Judah, 13 but hast walked in the way of the kings of Israel, and hast made Judah and the inhabitants of Jerusalem to play the harlot, like as the house of Ahab did, and also hast slain thy brethren of thy father's house, who were better than thyself: 14 behold, Jehovah will smite with a great plague thy people, and thy children, and thy wives, and all thy substance; 15 and thou shalt have great sickness by disease of thy bowels, until thy bowels fall out by reason of the sickness, day by day.

16 And Jehovah stirred up against Jehoram the spirit of the Philistines, and of the Arabians that are beside the Ethiopians: 17 and they came up against Judah, and brake into it, and carried away all the substance that was found in the king's house, and his sons also, and his wives; so that there was never a son left him, save Jehoahaz, the youngest of his sons.

18 And after all this Jehovah smote him in his bowels with an incurable disease. 19 And it came to pass, in process of time, at the end of two years, that his bowels fell out by reason of his sickness, and he died of sore diseases. And his people made no burning for him, like the burning of his fathers. 20 Thirty and two years old was he when he began to reign, and he reigned in Jerusalem eight years: and he departed without being desired; and they buried him in the city of David, but not in the sepulchres of the kings.

With the passing of Jehoshaphat, the tragic sequel to his alliance with Ahab began to unfold. His son Jehoram was evil. **He walked in the ways of the kings of Israel, as did the house of Ahab** (v. 6). His rule was saturated with religious apostasy. When his eight-year rule was terminated, his people did not regret it: **he departed without being desired** (v. 20). That is a sad commentary on the departure of any man.

2. Ahaziah (22:1-9; cf. II Kings 8:25-29)

1 And the inhabitants of Jerusalem made Ahaziah his youngest son king in his stead; for the band of men that came with the Arabians to the camp had slain all the eldest. So Ahaziah the son of Jehoram king of Judah reigned. 2 Forty

and two years old was Ahaziah when he began to reign; and he reigned one year in Jerusalem: and his mother's name was Athaliah the daughter of Omri. 3 He also walked in the ways of the house of Ahab; for his mother was his counsellor to do wickedly. 4 And he did that which was evil in the sight of Jehovah, as did the house of Ahab; for they were his counsellors after the death of his father, to his destruction. 5 He walked also after their counsel, and went with Jehoram the son of Ahab king of Israel to war against Hazael king of Syria at Ramoth-gilead: and the Syrians wounded Joram. 6 And he returned to be healed in Jezreel of the wounds which they had given him at Ramah, when he fought against Hazael king of Syria. And Azariah the son of Jehoram king of Judah went down to see Jehoram the son of Ahab in Jezreel, because he was sick.

7 Now the destruction of Ahaziah was of God, in that he went unto Joram: for when he was come, he went out with Jehoram against Jehu the son of Nimshi, whom Jehovah had anointed to cut off the house of Ahab. 8 And it came to pass, when Jehu was executing judgment upon the house of Ahab, that he found the princes of Judah, and the sons of the brethren of Ahaziah, ministering to Ahaziah, and slew them. 9 And he sought Ahaziah, and they caught him (now he was hiding in Samaria), and they brought him to Jehu, and slew him; and they buried him, for they said, He is the son of Jehoshaphat, who sought Jehovah with all his heart. And the house of Ahaziah had no power to hold the kingdom.

Ahaziah, the youngest son of Jehoram, reigned for a year under the evil influence of his mother, Athaliah. **His mother was his counsellor to do wickedly** (v. 3). She was a devotee of Baal and antagonistic toward Jehovah. Her wickedness was a dominant influence in the royal household. The death of Ahaziah at the hand of Jehu was, from the chronicler's point of view, divine retribution for his wickedness (v. 7).

3. Athaliah's Usurpation and Overthrow (22:10—23:21; cf. II Kings 11:1-20)

10 Now when Athaliah the mother of Ahaziah saw that her son was dead, she arose and destroyed all the seed royal of the house of Judah. 11 But Jehosha-beath, the daughter of the king, took Joash the son of Ahaziah, and stole him away from among the king's sons that were slain, and put him and his nurse in the bedchamber. So Jehoshabeath, the daughter of king Jehoram, the wife of Jehoiada the priest (for she was the sister of Ahaziah), hid him from Athaliah, so that she slew him not. 12 And he was with them hid in the house of God six years: and Athaliah reigned over the land.

1 And in the seventh year Jehoiada strengthened himself, and took the captains of hundreds, Azariah the son of Jeroham, and Ishmael the son of Jehohanan, and Azariah the son of Obed, and Maaseiah the son of Adaiah, and Elishaphat the son of Zichri, into covenant with him. 2 And they went about in Judah, and gathered the Levites out of all the cities of Judah, and the heads of fathers' *houses* of Israel, and they came to Jerusalem. 3 And all the assembly made a covenant with the king in the house of God. And he said unto them, Behold, the king's son shall reign, as Jehovah hath spoken concerning the sons of David. 4 This is the thing that ye shall do: a third part of you, that come in on the sabbath, of the priests and of the Levites, shall be porters of the thresholds; 5 and a third part shall be at the king's house; and a third part at the gate of the foundation: and all the people shall be in the courts of the house of Jehovah. 6 But let none come into the house of Jehovah, save the priests, and they that minister of the Levites; they shall come in, for they are holy: but all the people shall keep the charge of Jehovah. 7 And the Levites shall compass the king round about, every man with his weapons in his hand; and whosoever cometh into the house, let him be slain: and be ye with the king when he cometh in, and when he goeth out.

8 So the Levites and all Judah did according to all that Jehoiada the priest commanded: and they took every man his men, those that were to come in on the sabbath, with those that were to go out on the sabbath; for Jehoiada the priest dismissed not the courses. 9 And Jehoiada the priest delivered to the captains of hundreds the spears, and bucklers, and shields, that had been king David's, which were in the house of God. 10 And he set all the people, every man with his weapon in his hand, from the right side of the house to the left side of the house, along by the altar and the house, by the king round about. 11 Then they brought

out the king's son, and put the crown upon him, and *gave him* the testimony, and made him king: and Jehoiada and his sons anointed him; and they said, *Long* live the king.

12 And when Athaliah heard the noise of the people running and praising the king, she came to the people into the house of Jehovah: 13 and she looked, and, behold, the king stood by his pillar at the entrance, and the captains and the trumpets by the king; and all the people of the land rejoiced, and blew trumpets; the singers also *played* on instruments of music, and led the singing of praise. Then Athaliah rent her clothes, and said, Treason! treason! 14 And Jehoiada the priest brought out the captains of hundreds that were set over the host, and said unto them, Have her forth between the ranks; and whoso followeth her, let him be slain with the sword: for the priest said, Slay her not in the house of Jehovah. 15 So they made way for her; and she went to the entrance of the horse gate to the king's house: and they slew her there.

16 And Jehoiada made a covenant between himself, and all the people, and the king, that they should be Jehovah's people. 17 And all the people went to the house of Baal, and brake it down, and brake his altars and his images in pieces, and slew Mattan the priest of Baal before the altars. 18 And Jehoiada appointed the officers of the house of Jehovah under the hand of the priests the Levites, whom David had distributed in the house of Jehovah, to offer the burnt-offerings of Jehovah, as it is written in the law of Moses, with rejoicing and with singing, according to the order of David. 19 And he set the porters at the gates of the house of Jehovah, that none that was unclean in anything should enter in. 20 And he took the captains of hundreds, and the nobles, and the governors of the people, and all the people of the land, and brought down the king from the house of Jehovah: and they came through the upper gate unto the king's house, and set the king upon the throne of the kingdom. 21 So all the people of the land rejoiced, and the city was quiet. And Athaliah they had slain with the sword.

The final stage of the sequel to Jehoshaphat's alliance with the northern king, Ahab, came when Athaliah seized the reins of authority about nine years after the death of Jehoshaphat. After attempting to annihilate all members of the royal household who could lay claim to the throne, she ruled tyrannically for six years (v. 12). She nearly obliterated the dynasty of David, but failed to seize Joash, who was taken into hiding.

The terrible consequences of Jehoshaphat's alliance had reached their ultimate fury, although he was not living to realize their terribleness. After six years, the high priest, Jehoiada, led a successful revolt and arranged for the coronation of the seven-year-old Joash. Athaliah charged that treason had been committed, but the only attention given to her was that she was slain by the sword (v. 15).

D. REFORMS OF JOASH DURING THE LATTER PART OF THE NINTH CENTURY B.C. (24:1-27; cf. II Kings 11:21—12:21)

Although the reign of Joash covered forty years, only two episodes have been retained by the chronicler: the repair of the temple and the invasion by Syria.

1. Repair of the Temple (24:1-14; cf. II Kings 11:21—12:16)

1 Joash was seven years old when he began to reign; and he reigned forty years in Jerusalem: and his mother's name was Zibiah, of Beer-sheba. 2 And Joash did that which was right in the eyes of Jehovah all the days of Jehoiada the priest. 3 And Jehoiada took for him two wives; and he begat sons and daughters.

4 And it came to pass after this, that Joash was minded to restore the house of Jehovah. 5 And he gathered together the priests and the Levites, and said to them, Go out unto the cities of Judah, and gather of all Israel money to repair the house of your God from year to year; and see that ye hasten the matter. Howbeit the Levites hastened it not. 6 And the king called for Jehoiada the chief, and said unto him, Why hast thou not required of the Levites to bring in out of Judah and out of Jerusalem the tax of Moses the servant of Jehovah, and of the assembly of Israel, for the tent of the testimony? 7 For the sons of Athaliah, that wicked woman, had broken up the house of God; and also all the dedicated things of the house of Jehovah did they bestow upon the Baalim.

8 So the king commanded, and they made a chest, and set it without at the gate of the house of Jehovah. 9 And they

made a proclamation through Judah and Jerusalem, to bring in for Jehovah the tax that Moses the servant of God laid upon Israel in the wilderness. 10 And all the princes and all the people rejoiced, and brought in, and cast into the chest, until they had made an end. 11 And it was so, that, at what time the chest was brought unto the king's officers by the hand of the Levites, and when they saw that there was much money, the king's scribe and the chief priest's officer came and emptied the chest, and took it, and carried it to its place again. Thus they did day by day, and gathered money in abundance. 12 And the king and Jehoiada gave it to such as did the work of the service of the house of Jehovah; and they hired masons and carpenters to restore the house of Jehovah, and also such as wrought iron and brass to repair the house of Jehovah. 13 So the workmen wrought, and the work of repairing went forward in their hands, and they set up the house of God in its state, and strengthened it. 14 And when they had made an end, they brought the rest of the money before the king and Jehoiada, whereof were made vessels for the house of Jehovah, even vessels wherewith to minister and to offer, and spoons, and vessels of gold and silver. And they offered burnt-offerings in the house of Jehovah continually all the days of Jehoiada.

The temple was in great need of repair because of Athaliah, the wife of Jehoram, and her sons (v. 7). The focal points of reform instituted during the reign of Joash were the repair and refurnishing of the temple. During his reign there was developed the idea of a "Joash chest," into which were placed the contributions of the people for the cost of repairing the temple. For the chronicler, this was a significant reform, inasmuch as it provided for the renovation of the temple and the restoration of Levitical worship.

2. Invasion by Syria (24:15-27; cf. II Kings 12:17-18)

15 But Jehoiada waxed old and was full of days, and he died; a hundred and thirty years old was he when he died. 16 And they buried him in the city of David among the kings, because he had done good in Israel, and toward God and his house. 17 Now after the death of Jehoiada came the princes of Judah, and made obeisance to the king. Then the king hearkened unto them. 18 And they forsook the house of Jehovah, the God of their fathers, and served the Asherim and the idols: and wrath came upon Judah and Jerusalem for this their guiltiness. 19 Yet he sent prophets to them, to bring them again unto Jehovah; and they testified against them: but they would not give ear.

20 And the Spirit of God came upon Zechariah the son of Jehoiada the priest; and he stood above the people, and said unto them, Thus saith God, Why transgress ye the commandments of Jehovah, so that ye cannot prosper? because ye have forsaken Jehovah, he hath also forsaken you. 21 And they conspired against him, and stoned him with stones at the commandment of the king in the court of the house of Jehovah. 22 Thus Joash the king remembered not the kindness which Jehoiada his father had done to him, but slew his son. And when he died, he said, Jehovah look upon it, and require it.

23 And it came to pass at the end of the year, that the army of the Syrians came up against him: and they came to Judah and Jerusalem, and destroyed all the princes of the people from among the people, and sent all the spoil of them unto the king of Damascus. 24 For the army of the Syrians came with a small company of men; and Jehovah delivered a very great host into their hand, because they had forsaken Jehovah, the God of their fathers. So they executed judgment upon Joash.

25 And when they were departed from him (for they left him very sick), his own servants conspired against him for the blood of the sons of Jehoiada the priest, and slew him on his bed, and he died; and they buried him in the city of David, but they buried him not in the sepulchres of the kings. 26 And these are they that conspired against him: Zabad the son of Shimeath the Ammonitess, and Jehozabad the son of Shimrith the Moabitess. 27 Now concerning his sons, and the greatness of the burdens laid upon him, and the rebuilding of the house of God, behold, they are written in the commentary of the book of the kings. And Amaziah his son reigned in his stead.

Joash was deeply indebted to Jehoiada the priest for establishing his reign and cultivating reform. Yet, this king committed a terrible crime. After the death of Jehoiada, Joash departed from the worship of Jehovah. He became so enraged at the prophet Zechariah, the son of Jehoiada, for rebuking this wickedness that he had him stoned to death. For this crime, Joash was made to pay a high price. Not only was his country invaded by Syria, but Joash was assassinated by his own servants (see vv. 24-25). One cannot escape the application of the truth that what one sows one also reaps.

E. REIGN OF DAVIDIC KINGS DURING THE EIGHTH CENTURY B. C. (25:1—28:27)

Before the chronicler reaches another period of reform in the history of Judah, he gives the reigns of four kings who ruled successively during the eighth century B.C. They were Amaziah, Uzziah, Jotham and Ahaz.

1. Amaziah (25:1-28; cf. II Kings 14: 1-20)

The account of Amaziah centers around two military efforts, one against Edom and the other against the Northern Kingdom. Although he initiated both efforts, Amaziah was successful only against Edom.

a. Against Edom (25:1-16; cf. II Kings 14:7)

1 Amaziah was twenty and five years old when he began to reign; and he reigned twenty and nine years in Jerusalem: and his mother's name was Jehoaddan, of Jerusalem. 2 And he did that which was right in the eyes of Jehovah, but not with a perfect heart. 3 Now it came to pass, when the kingdom was established unto him, that he slew his servants that had killed the king his father. 4 But he put not their children to death, but did according to that which is written in the law in the book of Moses, as Jehovah commanded, saying, The fathers shall not die for the children, neither shall the children die for the fathers; but every man shall die for his own sin.
5 Moreover Amaziah gathered Judah together, and ordered them according to their fathers' houses, under captains of thousands and captains of hundreds, even all Judah and Benjamin: and he numbered them from twenty years old and upward, and found them three hundred thousand chosen men, able to go forth to war, that could handle spear and shield.

6 He hired also a hundred thousand mighty men of valor out of Israel for a hundred talents of silver. 7 But there came a man of God to him, saying, O king, let not the army of Israel go with thee; for Jehovah is not with Israel, to wit, with all the children of Ephraim. 8 But if thou wilt go, do valiantly, be strong for the battle: God will cast thee down before the enemy; for God hath power to help, and to cast down. 9 And Amaziah said to the man of God, But what shall we do for the hundred talents which I have given to the army of Israel? And the man of God answered, Jehovah is able to give thee much more than this. 10 Then Amaziah separated them, to wit, the army that was come to him out of Ephraim, to go home again: wherefore their anger was greatly kindled against Judah, and they returned home in fierce anger. 11 And Amaziah took courage, and led forth his people, and went to the Valley of Salt, and smote of the children of Seir ten thousand. 12 And other ten thousand did the children of Judah carry away alive, and brought them unto the top of the rock, and cast them down from the top of the rock, so that they were all broken in pieces. 13 But the men of the army whom Amaziah sent back, that they should not go with him to battle, fell upon the cities of Judah, from Samaria even unto Beth-horon, and smote of them three thousand, and took much spoil.
14 Now it came to pass, after that Amaziah was come from the slaughter of the Edomites, that he brought the gods of the children of Seir, and set them up to be his gods, and bowed down himself before them, and burned incense unto them. 15 Wherefore the anger of Jehovah was kindled against Amaziah, and he sent unto him a prophet, who said unto him, Why hast thou sought after the gods of the people, which have not delivered their own people out of thy hand? 16 And it came to pass, as he talked with him, that the king said unto him, Have we made thee of the king's counsel? forbear; why shouldest thou be smitten? Then the prophet forbare, and said, I know that God hath determined to destroy thee, because thou hast done this, and hast not hearkened unto my counsel.

Amaziah's conquest of Edom is recounted in twelve verses in Chronicles, but is contained in only one verse in Kings. The reason for the expanded account in Chronicles is that it explains the outcome of the second military effort of

Amaziah, the effort against the Northern Kingdom which resulted in humiliating defeat for Amaziah.

When Amaziah defeated Edom, he returned to Jerusalem bringing the gods of the Edomites with him (v. 14). In typical oriental fashion, he began to worship these gods, for it was a prevalent belief among the ancient oriental rulers that conquerors gained added power through their conquests because the gods of the conquered nations thereafter served the conqueror. Although the kings of the chosen people of God were expressly forbidden to cultivate any relationship with foreign gods, Amaziah disobeyed. Because of his idolatry, the prophet of the Lord warned him, **I know that God hath determined to destroy thee, because thou hast done this** (v. 16).

b. Against Israel (25:17-28; cf. II Kings 14:8-16)

17 Then Amaziah king of Judah took advice, and sent to Joash, the son of Jehoahaz the son of Jehu, king of Israel, saying, Come, let us look one another in the face. 18 And Joash king of Israel sent to Amaziah king of Judah, saying, The thistle that was in Lebanon sent to the cedar that was in Lebanon, saying, Give thy daughter to my son to wife: and there passed by a wild beast that was in Lebanon, and trod down the thistle. 19 Thou sayest, Lo, thou hast smitten Edom; and thy heart lifteth thee up to boast: abide now at home; why shouldest thou meddle to *thy* hurt, that thou shouldest fall, even thou, and Judah with thee?

20 But Amaziah would not hear; for it was of God, that he might deliver them into the hand *of their enemies,* because they had sought after the gods of Edom. 21 So Joash king of Israel went up; and he and Amaziah king of Judah looked one another in the face at Beth-shemesh, which belongeth to Judah. 22 And Judah was put to the worse before Israel; and they fled every man to his tent. 23 And Joash king of Israel took Amaziah king of Judah, the son of Joash the son of Jehoahaz, at Beth-shemesh, and brought him to Jerusalem, and brake down the wall of Jerusalem from the gate of Ephraim unto the corner gate, four hundred cubits. 24 And *he took* all the gold and silver, and all the vessels that were found in the house of God with Obed-edom, and the treasures of the king's house, the hostages also, and returned to Samaria.

25 And Amaziah the son of Joash king of Judah lived after the death of Joash son of Jehoahaz king of Israel fifteen years. 26 Now the rest of the acts of Amaziah, first and last, behold, are they not written in the book of the kings of Judah and Israel? 27 Now from the time that Amaziah did turn away from following Jehovah they made a conspiracy against him in Jerusalem; and he fled to Lachish: but they sent after him to Lachish, and slew him there. 28 And they brought him upon horses, and buried him with his fathers in the city of Judah.

Then Amaziah king of Judah took advice, and sent to Joash ... saying, Come, let us look one another in the face (v. 17). This unique oriental expression was essentially a challenge. Amaziah dared Joash to a face-to-face encounter. It was an ultimatum with warlike overtones. Amaziah was over-confident. Flushed with victory over Edom, he was eager to expand his power to the north over the Northern Kingdom.

However, Amaziah had engaged in idolatry since his conquest of Edom, and God had warned him through His prophet. Nevertheless, the arrogant king proceeded with his plans for war, but encountered disaster on the field of battle. Unheeded warnings often result in disaster.

2. Uzziah (26:1-23; cf. II Kings 14:21-22; 15:1-7)

The reign of Uzziah was a long one (v. 3). The chronicler divides it into two periods: the first and longer period being highlighted by political success, and the second, shorter period highlighted by religious sacrilege.

a. Political Success (26:1-15)

1 And all the people of Judah took Uzziah, who was sixteen years old, and made him king in the room of his father Amaziah. 2 He built Eloth, and restored it to Judah, after that the king slept with his fathers. 3 Sixteen years old was Uzziah when he began to reign; and he reigned fifty and two years in Jerusalem: and his mother's name was Jechiliah, of Jerusalem. 4 And he did that which was right in the eyes of Jehovah, according to all that his father Amaziah had done. 5 And he set himself to seek God in the

days of Zechariah, who had understanding in the vision of God: and as long as he sought Jehovah, God made him to prosper.

6 And he went forth and warred against the Philistines, and brake down the wall of Gath, and the wall of Jabneh, and the wall of Ashdod; and he built cities in *the country of* Ashdod, and among the Philistines. 7 And God helped him against the Philistines, and against the Arabians that dwelt in Gur-baal, and the Meunim. 8 And the Ammonites gave tribute to Uzziah: and his name spread abroad even to the entrance of Egypt; for he waxed exceeding strong. 9 Moreover Uzziah built towers in Jerusalem at the corner gate, and at the valley gate, and at the turning *of the wall,* and fortified them. 10 And he built towers in the wilderness, and hewed out many cisterns, for he had much cattle; in the lowland also, and in the plain: *and he had* husbandmen and vinedressers in the mountains and in the fruitful fields; for he loved husbandry. 11 Moreover Uzziah had an army of fighting men, that went out to war by bands, according to the number of their reckoning made by Jeiel the scribe and Maaseiah the officer, under the hand of Hananiah, one of the king's captains. 12 The whole number of the heads of fathers' *houses,* even the mighty men of valor, was two thousand and six hundred. 13 And under their hand was an army, three hundred thousand and seven thousand and five hundred, that made war with mighty power, to help the king against the enemy. 14 And Uzziah prepared for them, even for all the host, shields, and spears, and helmets, and coats of mail, and bows, and stones for slinging. 15 And he made in Jerusalem engines, invented by skilful men, to be on the towers and upon the battlements, wherewith to shoot arrows and great stones. And his name spread far abroad; for he was marvellously helped, till he was strong.

Uzziah's reign was long and successful because **God made him to prosper** (v. 5). Faithfulness to God resulted in national prosperity and political success.

b. Religious Sacrilege (26:16-23)

16 But when he was strong, his heart was lifted up, so that he did corruptly, and he trespassed against Jehovah his God; for he went into the temple of Jehovah to burn incense upon the altar of incense. 17 And Azariah the priest went in after him, and with him fourscore priests of Jehovah, that were valiant men: 18 and they withstood Uzziah the king, and said unto him, It pertaineth not unto thee, Uzziah, to burn incense unto Jehovah, but to the priests the sons of Aaron, that are consecrated to burn incense: go out of the sanctuary; for thou hast trespassed; neither shall it be for thine honor from Jehovah God. 19 Then Uzziah was wroth; and he had a censer in his hand to burn incense; and while he was wroth with the priests, the leprosy brake forth in his forehead before the priests in the house of Jehovah, beside the altar of incense. 20 And Azariah the chief priest, and all the priests, looked upon him, and, behold, he was leprous in his forehead, and they thrust him out quickly from thence; yea, himself hasted also to go out, because Jehovah had smitten him. 21 And Uzziah the king was a leper unto the day of his death, and dwelt in a separate house, being a leper; for he was cut off from the house of Jehovah: and Jotham his son was over the king's house, judging the people of the land. 22 Now the rest of the acts of Uzziah, first and last, did Isaiah the prophet, the son of Amoz, write. 23 So Uzziah slept with his fathers; and they buried him with his fathers in the field of burial which belonged to the kings; for they said, He is a leper: and Jotham his son reigned in his stead.

Uzziah's political successes have been given extended treatment in the Chronicles account, but they have been omitted in the Kings account. The chronicler has given an extended account to make the contrast more vivid between Uzziah's success and his sacrilege. His success was because he sought the Lord; his sacrilege was because he trespassed against the law of the Lord. **But when he was strong, his heart was lifted up . . . and he trespassed against Jehovah his God** (v. 16).

One verse in Chronicles gives the account of Uzziah's act of pride (v. 16). However, the sequel to that one act is recounted in several verses. Uzziah was smitten with leprosy. When the priests saw the leprosy, they forced the king out of the temple lest he defile the sacred sanctuary. Discovering the leprosy, Uzziah knew that he was endangering the ceremonial purity of the temple and, **himself hasted also to go out** (v. 20).

Uzziah is an important illustration of the proverb, "Pride goeth before destruction, and a haughty spirit before a fall" (Prov. 16:18). No one is more surprised by such a fall than the proud one himself.

3. Jotham (27:1-9; cf. II Kings 15:32-38)

1 Jotham was twenty and five years old when he began to reign; and he reigned sixteen years in Jerusalem: and his mother's name was Jerushah the daughter of Zadok. 2 And he did that which was right in the eyes of Jehovah, according to all that his father Uzziah had done: howbeit he entered not into the temple of Jehovah. And the people did yet corruptly. 3 He built the upper gate of the house of Jehovah, and on the wall of Ophel he built much. 4 Moreover he built cities in the hill-country of Judah, and in the forests he built castles and towers. 5 He fought also with the king of the children of Ammon, and prevailed against them. And the children of Ammon gave him the same year a hundred talents of silver, and ten thousand measures of wheat, and ten thousand of barley. So much did the children of Ammon render unto him, in the second year also, and in the third. 6 So Jotham became mighty, because he ordered his ways before Jehovah his God. 7 Now the rest of the acts of Jotham, and all his wars, and his ways, behold, they are written in the book of the kings of Israel and Judah. 8 He was five and twenty years old when he began to reign, and reigned sixteen years in Jerusalem. 9 And Jotham slept with his fathers, and they buried him in the city of David: and Ahaz his son reigned in his stead.

Although Jotham has not been classified as one of the reforming kings, the chronicler does give the key which explains his reign. **So Jotham became mighty, because he ordered his ways before Jehovah his God** (v. 6). The decisive factor in the life of Jotham was the fact that he lived in obedience to God. Resolute ordering of one's life is essential in the exercise of obedience to God.

4. Ahaz (28:1-27; cf. II Kings 16:1-20)

1 Ahaz was twenty years old when he began to reign; and he reigned sixteen years in Jerusalem: and he did not that which was right in the eyes of Jehovah, like David his father; 2 but he walked in the ways of the kings of Israel, and made also molten images for the Baalim. 3

Moreover he burnt incense in the valley of the son of Hinnom, and burnt his children in the fire, according to the abominations of the nations whom Jehovah cast out before the children of Israel. 4 And he sacrificed and burnt incense in the high places, and on the hills, and under every green tree.

5 Wherefore Jehovah his God delivered him into the hand of the king of Syria; and they smote him, and carried away of his a great multitude of captives, and brought them to Damascus. And he was also delivered into the hand of the king of Israel, who smote him with a great slaughter. 6 For Pekah the son of Remaliah slew in Judah a hundred and twenty thousand in one day, all of them valiant men; because they had forsaken Jehovah, the God of their fathers. 7 And Zichri, a mighty man of Ephraim, slew Maaseiah the king's son, and Azrikam the ruler of the house, and Elkanah that was next to the king.

8 And the children of Israel carried away captive of their brethren two hundred thousand, women, sons, and daughters, and took also away much spoil from them, and brought the spoil to Samaria. 9 But a prophet of Jehovah was there, whose name was Oded: and he went out to meet the host that came to Samaria, and said unto them, Behold, because Jehovah, the God of your fathers, was wroth with Judah, he hath delivered them into your hand, and ye have slain them in a rage which hath reached up unto heaven. 10 And now ye purpose to keep under the children of Judah and Jerusalem for bondmen and bondwomen unto you: *but* are there not even with you trespasses of your own against Jehovah your God? 11 Now hear me therefore, and send back the captives, that ye have taken captive of your brethren; for the fierce wrath of Jehovah is upon you. 12 Then certain of the heads of the children of Ephraim, Azariah the son of Johanan, Berechiah the son of Meshillemoth, and Jehizkiah the son of Shallum, and Amasa the son of Hadlai, stood up against them that came from the war, 13 and said unto them, Ye shall not bring in the captives hither: for ye purpose that which will bring upon us a trespass against Jehovah, to add unto our sins and to our trespass; for our trespass is great, and there is fierce wrath against Israel. 14 So the armed men left the captives and the spoil before the princes and all the assembly. 15 And the men that have been mentioned by name rose up, and took the captives, and with the spoil clothed all

that were naked among them, and arrayed them, and shod them, and gave them to eat and to drink, and anointed them, and carried all the feeble of them upon asses, and brought them to Jericho, the city of palm-trees, unto their brethren: then they returned to Samaria. 16 At that time did king Ahaz send unto the kings of Assyria to help him. 17 For again the Edomites had come and smitten Judah, and carried away captives. 18 The Philistines also had invaded the cities of the lowland, and of the South of Judah, and had taken Beth-shemesh, and Aijalon, and Gederoth, and Soco with the towns thereof, and Timnah with the towns thereof, Gimzo also and the towns thereof: and they dwelt there. 19 For Jehovah brought Judah low because of Ahaz king of Israel; for he had dealt wantonly in Judah, and trespassed sore against Jehovah. 20 And Tilgath-pilneser king of Assyria came unto him, and distressed him, but strengthened him not. 21 For Ahaz took away a portion out of the house of Jehovah, and out of the house of the king and of the princes, and gave it unto the king of Assyria: but it helped him not.

22 And in the time of his distress did he trespass yet more against Jehovah, this same king Ahaz. 23 For he sacrificed unto the gods of Damascus, which smote him; and he said, Because the gods of the kings of Syria helped them, *therefore* will I sacrifice to them, that they may help me. But they were the ruin of him, and of all Israel. 24 And Ahaz gathered together the vessels of the house of God, and cut in pieces the vessels of the house of God, and shut up the doors of the house of Jehovah; and he made him altars in every corner of Jerusalem. 25 And in every city of Judah he made high places to burn incense unto other gods, and provoked to anger Jehovah, the God of his fathers. 26 Now the rest of his acts, and all his ways, first and last, behold, they are written in the book of the kings of Judah and Israel. 27 And Ahaz slept with his fathers, and they buried him in the city, even in Jerusalem; for they brought him not into the sepulchres of the kings of Israel: and Hezekiah his son reigned in his stead.

In Kings, Ahaz is depicted according to the Deuteronomic principle of explaining the history of Israel, namely, that disobedience results in the coming of divine judgment. In Chronicles, however, he is depicted according to the chronicler's method of analyzing the history of Israel, namely, that of attempting to get behind the historical occasions and give the religious explanation for the events. "Out of the historical materials, those facts which show how Ahaz, notwithstanding the heavy blows which Jahve inflicted upon him, always sinned more deeply against the Lord . . . are chosen. . . ."[12]

Although his predecessors on the throne of David had ruled with success and prosperity for about three-fourths of the eighth century, Ahaz wilfully apostatized from Jehovah. This apostasy resulted in some of the greatest military defeats and economic reverses that Judah ever had. Syria, Israel, Edom, Philistia, in separate engagements, brought humiliating defeats upon Judah. The chronicler's rationale is clear: **For Jehovah brought Judah low because of Ahaz king of Israel; for he had dealt wantonly in Judah, and trespassed sore against Jehovah** (v. 19).

Instead of returning to the Lord, Ahaz desecrated the temple by removing the sacred treasures in order that he might purchase the help of Assyria (v. 21). In his obstinacy, Ahaz refused to worship the almighty God. Instead, he worshiped the gods of his oppressors (v. 23). His stubborn determination towards apostasy provoked the anger of the Lord (v. 25). The divine judgment upon Ahaz's stubborn wilfulness is the chronicler's religious explanation for the disastrous reign of Ahaz. It is a warning to all.

F. REFORMS OF HEZEKIAH DURING THE LAST QUARTER OF THE EIGHTH CENTURY B.C. (29:1—32:33; cf. II Kings 18:1—20:21)

There were two highlights of the reign of Hezekiah, as that reign is recounted in both Kings and Chronicles. In Kings, the restoration of Jehovah-worship has been treated briefly, while the resistance movement against Sennacherib of Assyria has been given a much more expanded treatment. In Chronicles, this is reversed, with the restoration of Jehovah-worship receiving extensive treatment, while the resistance against Sennacherib is treated briefly.

12 C. F. Keil, "The Book of Chronicles," *Biblical Commentary on the Old Testament*, p. 433.

In the light of this reversal of emphasis, it is possible to observe the chronicler's real interest. He has sought to make clear the explanation for Hezekiah's incredible success in resisting Sennacherib. Because Hezekiah engaged in far-reaching reforms in which Jehovah-worship was restored according to the Levitical requirements, with the temple being pivotal in all of this, he was able to resist successfully the Assyrian invasion.

Whether or not our ecclesiastical tradition is rich in honorable and reverent ceremonies of worship, we are confronted with the chronicler's insistence that the recovery of true Jehovah-worship requires an emphasis upon the form of worship as well as the content.

1. Reform (29:1–31:21; cf. II Kings 18: 1-8)

The Chronicles account requires three chapters in describing the reform conducted by Hezekiah, while the Kings account requires only a few verses.

a. Cleansing the Temple (29:1-36)

1 Hezekiah began to reign when he was five and twenty years old; and he reigned nine and twenty years in Jerusalem: and his mother's name was Abijah, the daughter of Zechariah. 2 And he did that which was right in the eyes of Jehovah, according to all that David his father had done. 3 He in the first year of his reign, in the first month, opened the doors of the house of Jehovah, and repaired them. 4 And he brought in the priests and the Levites, and gathered them together into the broad place on the east, 5 and said unto them, Hear me, ye Levites; now sanctify yourselves, and sanctify the house of Jehovah, the God of your fathers, and carry forth the filthiness out of the holy place. 6 For our fathers have trespassed, and done that which was evil in the sight of Jehovah our God, and have forsaken him, and have turned away their faces from the habitation of Jehovah, and turned their backs. 7 Also they have shut up the doors of the porch, and put out the lamps, and have not burned incense nor offered burnt-offerings in the holy place unto the God of Israel. 8 Wherefore the wrath of Jehovah was upon Judah and Jerusalem, and he hath delivered them to be tossed to and fro, to be an astonishment, and a hissing, as ye see with your eyes. 9 For, lo, our fathers have fallen by the sword, and our sons and our daughters and our wives are in captivity for this. 10 Now it is in my heart to make a covenant with Jehovah, the God of Israel, that his fierce anger may turn away from us. 11 My sons, be not now negligent; for Jehovah hath chosen you to stand before him, to minister unto him, and that ye should be his ministers, and burn incense.

12 Then the Levites arose, Mahath, the son of Amasai, and Joel the son of Azariah, of the sons of the Kohathites; and of the sons of Merari, Kish the son of Abdi, and Azariah the son of Jehallelel; and of the Gershonites, Joah the son of Zimmah, and Eden the son of Joah; 13 and of the sons of Elizaphan, Shimri and Jeuel; and of the sons of Asaph, Zechariah and Mattaniah; 14 and of the sons of Heman, Jehuel and Shimei; and of the sons of Jeduthun, Shemaiah and Uzziel. 15 And they gathered their brethren, and sanctified themselves, and went in, according to the commandment of the king by the words of Jehovah, to cleanse the house of Jehovah. 16 And the priests went in unto the inner part of the house of Jehovah, to cleanse it, and brought out all the uncleanness that they found in the temple of Jehovah into the court of the house of Jehovah. And the Levites took it, to carry it out abroad to the brook Kidron. 17 Now they began on the first *day* of the first month to sanctify, and on the eighth day of the month came they to the porch of Jehovah; and they sanctified the house of Jehovah in eight days: and on the sixteenth day of the first month they made an end. 18 Then they went in to Hezekiah the king within *the palace,* and said, We have cleansed all the house of Jehovah, and the altar of burnt-offering, with all the vessels thereof, and the table of showbread, with all the vessels thereof. 19 Moreover all the vessels, which king Ahaz in his reign did cast away when he trespassed, have we prepared and sanctified; and, behold, they are before the altar of Jehovah.

20 Then Hezekiah the king arose early, and gathered the princes of the city, and went up to the house of Jehovah. 21 And they brought seven bullocks, and seven rams, and seven lambs, and seven he-goats, for a sin-offering for the kingdom and for the sanctuary and for Judah. And he commanded the priests the sons of Aaron to offer them on the altar of Jehovah. 22 So they killed the bullocks, and the priests received the blood, and sprinkled it on the altar: and they killed the rams, and sprinkled the blood upon the altar: they killed also the lambs, and

sprinkled the blood upon the altar. 23 And they brought near the he-goats for the sin-offering before the king and the assembly; and they laid their hands upon them: 24 and the priests killed them, and they made a sin-offering with their blood upon the altar, to make atonement for all Israel: for the king commanded *that* the burnt-offering and the sin-offering *should be made* for all Israel.

25 And he set the Levites in the house of Jehovah with cymbals, with psalteries, and with harps, according to the commandment of David, and of Gad the king's seer, and Nathan the prophet; for the commandment was of Jehovah by his prophets. 26 And the Levites stood with the instruments of David, and the priests with the trumpets. 27 And Hezekiah commanded to offer the burnt-offering upon the altar. And when the burnt-offering began, the song of Jehovah began also, and the trumpets, together with the instruments of David king of Israel. 28 And all the assembly worshipped, and the singers sang, and the trumpeters sounded; all this *continued* until the burnt-offering was finished.

29 And when they had made an end of offering, the king and all that were present with him bowed themselves and worshipped. 30 Moreover Hezekiah the king and the princes commanded the Levites to sing praises unto Jehovah with the words of David, and of Asaph the seer. And they sang praises with gladness, and they bowed their heads and worshipped.

31 Then Hezekiah answered and said, Now ye have consecrated yourselves unto Jehovah; come near and bring sacrifices and thank offerings into the house of Jehovah. And the assembly brought in sacrifices and thank-offerings; and as many as were of a willing heart *brought* burnt-offerings. 32 And the number of the burnt-offerings which the assembly brought was threescore and ten bullocks, a hundred rams, and two hundred lambs: all these were for a burnt-offering to Jehovah. 33 And the consecrated things were six hundred oxen and three thousand sheep. 34 But the priests were too few, so that they could not flay all the burnt-offerings: wherefore their brethren the Levites did help them, till the work was ended, and until the priests had sanctified themselves; for the Levites were more upright in heart to sanctify themselves than the priests. 35 And also the burnt-offerings were in abundance, with the fat of the peace-offerings, and with

the drink-offerings for every burnt-offering. So the service of the house of Jehovah was set in order. 36 And Hezekiah rejoiced, and all the people, because of that which God had prepared for the people: for the thing was done suddenly.

Although in the Chronicles account this cleansing is placed first in the reforms, it is not even mentioned in Kings. Not only is this cleansing placed first in Hezekiah's reforms, but also the Levitical institution is given the responsibility for carrying out the reform. In his speech, Hezekiah called upon the Levites to show their zeal and loyalty (vv. 5-11).

The Levites responded wholeheartedly (vv. 12-19). Upon completion of the cleansing and the offering of sacrifices, the worship of Jehovah was resumed in the temple. **So the service of the house of Jehovah was set in order** (v. 35). There was acknowledgment that God was in this (v. 36). God insists that worship be genuine and blesses those efforts which are put forth for more appropriate worship. Efforts to make the house of God a house of prayer are especially significant.

b. Celebrating the Passover (30:1-27)

This ceremony is not recorded in the Kings account. It was observed in Judah after the collapse of the Northern Kingdom in 722/21 B.C.

(1) Invitation (30:1-12)

1 And Hezekiah sent to all Israel and Judah, and wrote letters also to Ephraim and Manasseh, that they should come to the house of Jehovah at Jerusalem, to keep the passover unto Jehovah, the God of Israel. 2 For the king had taken counsel, and his princes, and all the assembly in Jerusalem, to keep the passover in the second month. 3 For they could not keep it at that time, because the priests had not sanctified themselves in sufficient number, neither had the people gathered themselves together to Jerusalem. 4 And the thing was right in the eyes of the king and of all the assembly. 5 So they established a decree to make proclamation throughout all Israel, from Beersheba even to Dan, that they should come to keep the passover unto Jehovah, the God of Israel, at Jerusalem: for they had not kept it in great numbers in such sort as it is written. 6 So the posts went with the letters from the king and his princes

throughout all Israel and Judah, and according to the commandment of the king, saying, Ye children of Israel, turn again unto Jehovah, the God of Abraham, Isaac, and Israel, that he may return to the remnant that are escaped of you out of the hand of the kings of Assyria. 7 And be not ye like your fathers, and like your brethren, who trespassed against Jehovah, the God of their fathers, so that he gave them up to desolation, as ye see. 8 Now be ye not stiffnecked, as your fathers were; but yield yourselves unto Jehovah, and enter into his sanctuary, which he hath sanctified for ever, and serve Jehovah your God, that his fierce anger may turn away from you. 9 For if ye turn again unto Jehovah, your brethren and your children shall find compassion before them that led them captive, and shall come again into this land: for Jehovah your God is gracious and merciful, and will not turn away his face from you, if ye return unto him.

10 So the posts passed from city to city through the country of Ephraim and Manasseh, even unto Zebulun: but they laughed them to scorn, and mocked them. 11 Nevertheless certain men of Asher and Manasseh and of Zebulun humbled themselves, and came to Jerusalem. 12 Also upon Judah came the hand of God to give them one heart, to do the commandment of the king and of the princes by the word of Jehovah.

Letters from Hezekiah were sent into all parts of his kingdom as well as into regions of the former Northern Kingdom. They contained a plea to the people of the northern tribes to return to the worship of Jehovah (vv. 6-8). The plea was strengthened by a reminder concerning the essential character of Jehovah: **for Jehovah your God is gracious and merciful, and will not turn away his face from you, if ye return unto him** (v. 9).

Hezekiah's messengers were given a mixed reception. While some were treated with mockery and scorn, others were hospitably received and their invitation accepted (vv. 10-11). Here is a vivid description of the relationship which God maintains with a wayward people. While His invitation is not irresistible, it is gracious.

The essential element in Israel's understanding of God, as He had revealed Himself through His relationship with His people, was grace. Although the Isra-

elites were a covenant people, they displayed faithlessness and disloyalty again and again. But even when the people of the northern tribes were no longer a part of a nation, they were not beyond the mercy and grace of the Lord. All of this is part of the significance of Hezekiah's invitation.

(2) Implementation (30:13-27)

13 And there assembled at Jerusalem much people to keep the feast of unleavened bread in the second month, a very great assembly. 14 And they arose and took away the altars that were in Jerusalem, and all the altars for incense took they away, and cast them into the brook Kidron. 15 Then they killed the passover on the fourteenth *day* of the second month: and the priests and the Levites were ashamed, and sanctified themselves, and brought burnt-offerings into the house of Jehovah. 16 And they stood in their place after their order, according to the law of Moses the man of God: the priests sprinkled the blood *which they received* of the hand of the Levites. 17 For there were many in the assembly that had not sanctified themselves: therefore the Levites had the charge of killing the passovers for every one that was not clean, to sanctify them unto Jehovah. 18 For a multitude of the people, even many of Ephraim and Manasseh, Issachar and Zebulun, had not cleansed themselves, yet did they eat the passover otherwise than it is written. For Hezekiah had prayed for them, saying, The good Jehovah pardon every one that setteth his heart to seek God, Jehovah, the God of his fathers, though *he be not cleansed* according to the purification of the sanctuary. 20 And Jehovah hearkened to Hezekiah, and healed the people. 21 And the children of Israel that were present at Jerusalem kept the feast of unleavened bread seven days with great gladness; and the Levites and the priests praised Jehovah day by day, *singing* with loud instruments unto Jehovah. 22 And Hezekiah spake comfortably unto all the Levites that had good understanding *in the service* of Jehovah. So they did eat throughout the feast for the seven days, offering sacrifices of peace-offerings, and making confession to Jehovah, the God of their fathers.

23 And the whole assembly took counsel to keep other seven days; and they kept *other* seven days with gladness. 24 For Hezekiah king of Judah did give to the assembly for offerings a thousand

bullocks and seven thousand sheep; and the princes gave to the assembly a thousand bullocks and ten thousand sheep: and a great number of priests sanctified themselves. 25 And all the assembly of Judah, with the priests and the Levites, and all the assembly that came out of Israel, and the sojourners that came out of the land of Israel, and that dwelt in Judah, rejoiced. 26 So there was great joy in Jerusalem; for since the time of Solomon the son of David king of Israel there was not the like in Jerusalem. 27 Then the priests the Levites arose and blessed the people: and their voice was heard, and their prayer came up to his holy habitation, even unto heaven.

Earlier the priests had cleansed the temple (II Chron. 29:16). Now the citizens cleanse the city of Jerusalem (v. 14). The reform included a civic as well as a religious movement, and laymen as well as clergy. Apparently the laymen were more zealous than the Levitical priests, for the priests were spurred to greater zeal (v. 15). Laymen may well lead in such reforms. Let the ministers bestir themselves, as did the Levites, and repent of the apathy that has come upon them.

The Passover lamb was slain and the event celebrated according to the law. Some from the northern tribes arrived too late to perform the ceremonial ablutions, which required several days for completion. Nevertheless Hezekiah prayed for them and the Levites gave them aid (vv. 17-20). The Lord is not so bound by His law that mercy is unavailing. Just as for those of the northern tribes who were too late for all the ceremonies of preparation, so for others, prayers were heard and the people forgiven (v. 20). This Passover observance was a memorable occasion. **Since the time of Solomon . . . there was not the like in Jerusalem** (v. 26).

c. Collecting the Offerings (31:1-21)

1 Now when all this was finished, all Israel that were present went out to the cities of Judah, and brake in pieces the pillars, and hewed down the Asherim, and brake down the high places and the altars out of all Judah and Benjamin, in Ephraim also and Manasseh, until they had destroyed them all. Then all the children of Israel returned, every man to his possession, into their own cities.

2 And Hezekiah appointed the courses of the priests and the Levites after their courses, every man according to his service, both the priests and the Levites, for burnt-offerings and for peace-offerings, to minister, and to give thanks, and to praise in the gates of the camp of Jehovah. 3 *He appointed* also the king's portion of his substance for the burnt-offerings, *to wit*, for the morning and evening burnt-offerings, and the burnt-offerings for the sabbaths, and for the new moons, and for the set feasts, as it is written in the law of Jehovah. 4 Moreover he commanded the people that dwelt in Jerusalem to give the portion of the priests and the Levites, that they might give themselves to the law of Jehovah. 5 And as soon as the commandment came abroad, the children of Israel gave in abundance the first-fruits of grain, new wine, and oil, and honey, and of all the increase of the field; and the tithe of all things brought they in abundantly. 6 And the children of Israel and Judah, that dwelt in the cities of Judah, they also brought in the tithe of oxen and sheep, and the tithe of dedicated things which were consecrated unto Jehovah their God, and laid them by heaps. 7 In the third month they began to lay the foundation of the heaps, and finished them in the seventh month. 8 And when Hezekiah and the princes came and saw the heaps, they blessed Jehovah, and his people Israel. 9 Then Hezekiah questioned the priests and the Levites concerning the heaps. 10 And Azariah the chief priest, of the house of Zadok, answered him and said, Since *the people* began to bring the oblations into the house of Jehovah, we have eaten and had enough, and have left plenty: for Jehovah hath blessed his people; and that which is left is this great store.

11 Then Hezekiah commanded to prepare chambers in the house of Jehovah; and they prepared them; 12 and they brought in the oblations and the tithes and the dedicated things faithfully. And over them Conaniah the Levite was ruler, and Shimei his brother was second; 13 and Jehiel, and Azaziah, and Nahath, and Asahel, and Jerimoth, and Jozabad, and Eliel, and Ismachiah, and Mahath, and Benaiah, were overseers under the hand of Conaniah and Shimei his brother, by the appointment of Hezekiah the king, and Azariah the ruler of the house of God. 14 And Kore the son of Imnah the Levite, the porter at the east *gate*, was over the freewill-offerings of God, to distribute the oblations of Jehovah, and the

most holy things. 15 And under him were Eden, and Miniamin, and Jeshua, and Shemaiah, Amariah, and Shecaniah, in the cities of the priests, in their office of trust, to give to their brethren by courses, as well to the great as to the small: 16 besides them that were reckoned by genealogy of males, from three years old and upward, even every one that entered into the house of Jehovah, as the duty of every day required, for their service in their offices according to their courses; 17 and them that were reckoned by genealogy of the priests by their fathers' houses, and the Levites from twenty years old and upward, in their offices by their courses; 18 and them that were reckoned by genealogy of all their little ones, their wives, and their sons, and their daughters, through all the congregation: for in their office of trust they sanctified themselves in holiness. 19 Also for the sons of Aaron the priests, that were in the fields of the suburbs of their cities, in every city, there were men that were mentioned by name, to give portions to all the males among the priests, and to all that were reckoned by genealogy among the Levites.

20 And thus did Hezekiah throughout all Judah; and he wrought that which was good and right and faithful before Jehovah his God. 21 And in every work that he began in the service of the house of God, and in the law, and in the commandments, to seek his God, he did it with all his heart, and prospered.

While this is not in the Kings account, it appears in the Chronicles account as evidence of the concern shown for the welfare of the priests and Levites. Hezekiah's reform included adequate provision and care for the servants of the Lord who ministered in the sanctuary.

The people gave so generously that Azariah the high priest declared: **Since the people began to bring the oblations into the house of Jehovah, we have eaten, and had enough, and have left plenty: for Jehovah hath blessed his people** (v. 10). Such a reform is continually needed. Many ministers have never received the benefits of such a blessing.

2. Resistance (32:1-33; cf. II Kings 18: 17—19:37)

1 After these things, and this faithfulness, Sennacherib king of Assyria came, and entered into Judah, and encamped against the fortified cities, and thought to win them for himself. 2 And when Hezekiah saw that Sennacherib was come, and that he was purposed to fight against Jerusalem, 3 he took counsel with his princes and his mighty men to stop the waters of the fountains which were without the city; and they helped him. 4 So there was gathered much people together, and they stopped all the fountains, and the brook that flowed through the midst of the land, saying, Why should the kings of Assyria come, and find much water? 5 And he took courage, and built up all the wall that was broken down, and raised *it* up to the towers, and the other wall without, and strengthened Millo *in* the city of David, and made weapons and shields in abundance. 6 And he set captains of war over the people, and gathered them together to him in the broad place at the gate of the city, and spake comfortably to them, saying, 7 Be strong and of good courage, be not afraid nor dismayed for the king of Assyria, nor for all the multitude that is with him; for there is a greater with us than with him: 8 with him is an arm of flesh; but with us is Jehovah our God to help us, and to fight our battles. And the people rested themselves upon the words of Hezekiah king of Judah.

9 After this did Sennacherib king of Assyria send his servants to Jerusalem (now he was before Lachish, and all his power with him), unto Hezekiah king of Judah, and unto all Judah that were at Jerusalem, saying, 10 Thus saith Sennacherib king of Assyria, Whereon do ye trust, that ye abide the siege in Jerusalem? 11 Doth not Hezekiah persuade you, to give you over to die by famine and by thirst, saying, Jehovah our God will deliver us out of the hand of the king of Assyria? 12 Hath not the same Hezekiah taken away his high places and his altars, and commanded Judah and Jerusalem, saying, Ye shall worship before one altar, and upon it shall ye burn incense? 13 Know ye not what I and my fathers have done unto all the peoples of the lands? Were the gods of the nations of the lands in any wise able to deliver their land out of my hand? 14 Who was there among all the gods of those nations which my fathers utterly destroyed, that could deliver his people out of my hand, that your God should be able to deliver you out of my hand? 15 Now therefore let not Hezekiah deceive you, nor persuade you after this manner, neither believe ye him; for no god of any nation or kingdom was able to deliver his people out of my hand, and out of the

hand of my fathers: how much less shall your God deliver you out of my hand?

16 And his servants spake yet more against Jehovah God, and against his servant Hezekiah. 17 He wrote also letters, to rail on Jehovah, the God of Israel, and to speak against him, saying, As the gods of the nations of the lands, which have not delivered their people out of my hand, so shall not the God of Hezekiah deliver his people out of my hand. 18 And they cried with a loud voice in the Jews' language unto the people of Jerusalem that were on the wall, to affright them, and to trouble them; that they might take the city. 19 And they spake of the God of Jerusalem, as of the gods of the peoples of the earth, which are the work of men's hands.

20 And Hezekiah the king, and Isaiah the prophet the son of Amoz, prayed because of this, and cried to heaven. 21 And Jehovah sent an angel, who cut off all the mighty men of valor, and the leaders and captains, in the camp of the king of Assyria. So he returned with shame of face to his own land. And when he was come into the house of his god, they that came forth from his own bowels slew him there with the sword. 22 Thus Jehovah saved Hezekiah and the inhabitants of Jerusalem from the hand of Sennacherib the king of Assyria, and from the hand of all *others,* and guided them on every side. 23 And many brought gifts unto Jehovah to Jerusalem, and precious things to Hezekiah king of Judah; so that he was exalted in the sight of all nations from thenceforth.

24 In those days Hezekiah was sick even unto death: and he prayed unto Jehovah; and he spake unto him, and gave him a sign. 25 But Hezekiah rendered not again according to the benefit done unto him; for his heart was lifted up: therefore there was wrath upon him, and upon Judah and Jerusalem. 26 Notwithstanding Hezekiah humbled himself for the pride of his heart, both he and the inhabitants of Jerusalem, so that the wrath of Jehovah came not upon them in the days of Hezekiah.

27 And Hezekiah had exceeding much riches and honor: and he provided him treasuries for silver, and for gold, and for precious stones, and for spices, and for shields, and for all manner of goodly vessels; 28 store-houses also for the increase of grain and new wine and oil; and stalls for all manner of beasts, and flocks in folds. 29 Moreover he provided him cities, and possessions of flocks and herds in abundance; for God had given him very much substance. 30 This same Hezekiah also stopped the upper spring of the waters of Gihon, and brought them straight down on the west side of the city of David. And Hezekiah prospered in all his works. 31 Howbeit in *the business of* the ambassadors of the princes of Babylon, who sent unto him to inquire of the wonder that was done in the land, God left him, to try him, that he might know all that was in his heart.

32 Now the rest of the acts of Hezekiah, and his good deeds, behold, they are written in the vision of Isaiah the prophet the son of Amoz, in the book of the kings of Judah and Israel. 33 And Hezekiah slept with his fathers, and they buried him in the ascent of the sepulchres of the sons of David: and all Judah and the inhabitants of Jerusalem did him honor at his death. And Manasseh his son reigned in his stead.

The chronicler's account of Sennacherib's campaign against Hezekiah is given solely as a proof of the power of God to deliver a faithful king.[13] In Hezekiah's great reform, the Levitical order of temple worship had been restored, and God had taken delight in the ceremony and liturgy of the services and sacrifices, not for their own sakes, but because they were evidence of genuine faith and worship. Through the measures of reform which he had taken, Hezekiah had become potentially impregnable, since he was able to rely upon the might of Jehovah.

It is important to observe the chronicler's viewpoint. He affirms that the reforms of Hezekiah explain his phenomenal resistance to Sennacherib. This is so unlike many who reform. They never think of reforming until they are overcome in a crisis; then they vow to live right and worship God. But because Hezekiah reformed before the day of crisis, he found strength in the time of crisis (vv. 1, 21). The result was that the fame of Hezekiah spread far (v. 23). Even ambassadors from Babylon came to confer with him (v. 31).

For the concluding events in Hezekiah's reign see the notes on the parallel passage in II Kings 20:1-21.

---

[13] W. R. Harvey-Jellie, "Chronicles," *The Century Bible,* p. 303; cf. Keil, *op. cit.,* p. 472.

G. REIGN OF DAVIDIC KINGS DURING THE FIRST HALF OF THE SEVENTH CENTURY B.C. (33:1-25)

1. Manasseh (33:1-20; cf. II Kings 21: 1-18)

1 Manasseh was twelve years old when he began to reign; and he reigned fifty and five years in Jerusalem. 2 And he did that which was evil in the sight of Jehovah, after the abominations of the nations whom Jehovah cast out before the children of Israel. 3 For he built again the high places which Hezekiah his father had broken down; and he reared up altars for the Baalim, and made Asheroth, and worshipped all the host of heaven, and served them. 4 And he built altars in the house of Jehovah, whereof Jehovah said, In Jerusalem shall my name be for ever. 5 And he built altars for all the host of heaven in the two courts of the house of Jehovah. 6 He also made his children to pass through the fire in the valley of the son of Hinnom; and he practised augury, and used enchantments, and practised sorcery, and dealt with them that had familiar spirits, and with wizards: he wrought much evil in the sight of Jehovah, to provoke him to anger. 7 And he set the graven image of the idol, which he had made, in the house of God, of which God said to David and to Solomon his son, In this house, and in Jerusalem, which I have chosen out of all the tribes of Israel, will I put my name for ever: 8 neither will I any more remove the foot of Israel from off the land which I have appointed for your fathers, if only they will observe to do all that I have commanded them, even all the law and the statutes and the ordinances given by Moses. 9 And Manasseh seduced Judah and the inhabitants of Jerusalem, so that they did evil more than did the nations whom Jehovah destroyed before the children of Israel. 10 And Jehovah spake to Manasseh, and to his people; but they gave no heed. 11 Wherefore Jehovah brought upon them the captains of the host of the king of Assyria, who took Manasseh in chains, and bound him with fetters, and carried him to Babylon. 12 And when he was in distress, he besought Jehovah his God, and humbled himself greatly before the God of his fathers. 13 And he prayed unto him; and he was entreated of him, and heard his supplication, and brought him again to Jerusalem into his kingdom. Then Manasseh knew that Jehovah he was God.

14 Now after this he built an outer wall to the city of David, on the west side of Gihon, in the valley, even to the entrance at the fish gate; and he compassed Ophel about with it, and raised it up to a very great height: and he put valiant captains in all the fortified cities of Judah. 15 And he took away the foreign gods, and the idol out of the house of Jehovah, and all the altars that he had built in the mount of the house of Jehovah, and in Jerusalem, and cast them out of the city. 16 And he built up the altar of Jehovah, and offered thereon sacrifices of peace-offerings and of thanksgiving, and commanded Judah to serve Jehovah, the God of Israel. 17 Nevertheless the people sacrificed still in the high places, but only unto Jehovah their God.

18 Now the rest of the acts of Manasseh, and his prayer unto his God, and the words of the seers that spake to him in the name of Jehovah, the God of Israel, behold, they are written among the acts of the kings of Israel. 19 His prayer also, and how God was entreated of him, and all his sin and his trespass, and the places wherein he built high places, and set up the Asherim and the graven images, before he humbled himself, behold, they are written in the history of Hozai. 20 So Manasseh slept with his fathers, and they buried him in his own house: and Amon his son reigned in his stead.

The Kings and Chronicles accounts of Manasseh's reign are closely parallel up to the point where Jehovah intervenes in righteous judgment. The Chronicles account describes Manasseh's being taken captive by the Babylonians. His prayer of repentance in captivity was heard and he was returned to Jerusalem. **Then Manasseh knew that Jehovah he was God** (v. 13).

The chronicler has endeavored to make clear the ways by which God dealt with Manasseh, one of the most wicked and idolatrous of the Davidic kings. He shows that Manasseh exercised an essential human characteristic when he chose to depart from the Lord, as well as when he chose to pray in humble repentance. More important, he also shows that God was ever present and relating Himself and His activity to Manasseh and his actions. When Manasseh sinned, God revealed Himself in judgment; when Manasseh repented, God revealed Himself in mercy. Sin brings judgment, while repentance brings mercy.

2. Amon (33:21-25; cf. II Kings 21:19-26)

21 Amon was twenty and two years old when he began to reign; and he reigned two years in Jerusalem. 22 And he did that which was evil in the sight of Jehovah, as did Manasseh his father; and Amon sacrificed unto all the graven images which Manasseh his father had made, and served them. 23 And he humbled not himself before Jehovah, as Manasseh his father had humbled himself; but this same Amon trespassed more and more. 24 And his servants conspired against him, and put him to death in his own house. 25 But the people of the land slew all them that had conspired against king Amon; and the people of the land made Josiah his son king in his stead.

See notes on the parallel passage in Kings.

H. REFORMS OF JOSIAH DURING THE SECOND HALF OF THE SEVENTH CENTURY B.C. (34:1–35:27; cf. II Kings 22:1–23:30)

1 Josiah was eight years old when he began to reign; and he reigned thirty and one years in Jerusalem. 2 And he did that which was right in the eyes of Jehovah, and walked in the ways of David his father, and turned not aside to the right hand or to the left. 3 For in the eighth year of his reign, while he was yet young, he began to seek after the God of David his father; and in the twelfth year he began to purge Judah and Jerusalem from the high places, and the Asherim, and the graven images, and the molten images. 4 And they brake down the altars of the Baalim in his presence; and the sun-images that were on high above them he hewed down; and the Asherim, and the graven images, and the molten images, he brake in pieces, and made dust of them, and strewed it upon the graves of them that had sacrificed unto them. 5 And he burnt the bones of the priests upon their altars, and purged Judah and Jerusalem. 6 And so did he in the cities of Manasseh and Ephraim and Simeon, even unto Naphtali, in their ruins round about. 7 And he brake down the altars, and beat the Asherim and the graven images into powder, and hewed down all the sun-images throughout all the land of Israel, and returned to Jerusalem.

8 Now in the eighteenth year of his reign, when he had purged the land and the house, he sent Shaphan the son of Azaliah, and Maaseiah the governor of the city, and Joah the son of Joahaz the recorder, to repair the house of Jehovah his God. 9 And they came to Hilkiah the high priest, and delivered the money that was brought into the house of God, which the Levites, the keepers of the threshold, had gathered of the hand of Manasseh and Ephraim, and of all the remnant of Israel, and of all Judah and Benjamin, and of the inhabitants of Jerusalem. 10 And they delivered it into the hand of the workmen that had the oversight of the house of Jehovah; and the workmen that wrought in the house of Jehovah gave it to mend and repair the house: 11 even to the carpenters and to the builders gave they it, to buy hewn stone, and timber for couplings, and to make beams for the houses which the kings of Judah had destroyed. 12 And the men did the work faithfully: and the overseers of them were Jahath and Obadiah, the Levites, of the sons of Merari; and Zechariah and Meshullam, of the sons of the Kohathites, to set it forward; and others of the Levites, all that were skilful with instruments of music. 13 Also they were over the bearers of burdens, and set forward all that did the work in every manner of service: and of the Levites there were scribes, and officers, and porters.

14 And when they brought out the money that was brought into the house of Jehovah, Hilkiah the priest found the book of the law of Jehovah given by Moses. 15 And Hilkiah answered and said to Shaphan the scribe, I have found the book of the law in the house of Jehovah. And Hilkiah delivered the book to Shaphan. 16 And Shaphan carried the book to the king, and moreover brought back word to the king, saying, All that was committed to thy servants, they are doing. 17 And they have emptied out the money that was found in the house of Jehovah, and have delivered it into the hand of the overseers, and into the hand of the workmen. 18 And Shaphan the scribe told the king, saying, Hilkiah the priest hath delivered me a book. And Shaphan read therein before the king. 19 And it came to pass, when the king had heard the words of the law, that he rent his clothes. 20 And the king commanded Hilkiah, and Ahikam the son of Shaphan, and Abdon the son of Micah, and Shaphan the scribe, and Asaiah the king's servant, saying, 21 Go ye, inquire of Jehovah for me, and for them that are left in

Israel and in Judah, concerning the words of the book that is found; for great is the wrath of Jehovah that is poured out upon us, because our fathers have not kept the word of Jehovah, to do according unto all that is written in this book.

22 So Hilkiah, and they whom the king *had commanded,* went to Huldah the prophetess, the wife of Shallum the son of Tokhath, the son of Hasrah, keeper of the wardrobe (now she dwelt in Jerusalem in the second quarter); and they spake to her to that effect. 23 And she said unto them, Thus saith Jehovah, the God of Israel: Tell ye the man that sent you unto me, 24 Thus saith Jehovah, Behold, I will bring evil upon this place, and upon the inhabitants thereof, even all the curses that are written in the book which they have read before the king of Judah. 25 Because they have forsaken me, and have burned incense unto other gods, that they might provoke me to anger with all the works of their hands; therefore is my wrath poured out upon this place, and it shall not be quenched. 26 But unto the king of Judah, who sent you to inquire of Jehovah, thus shall ye say to him, Thus saith Jehovah, the God of Israel: As touching the words which thou hast heard, 27 because thy heart was tender, and thou didst humble thyself before God, when thou heardest his words against this place, and against the inhabitants thereof, and hast humbled thyself before me, and hast rent thy clothes, and wept before me; I also have heard thee, saith Jehovah. 28 Behold, I will gather thee to thy fathers, and thou shalt be gathered to thy grave in peace, neither shall thine eyes see all the evil that I will bring upon this place, and upon the inhabitants thereof. And they brought back word to the king.

29 Then the king sent and gathered together all the elders of Judah and Jerusalem. 30 And the king went up to the house of Jehovah, and all the men of Judah and the inhabitants of Jerusalem, and the priests, and the Levites, and all the people, both great and small: and he read in their ears all the words of the book of the covenant that was found in the house of Jehovah. 31 And the king stood in his place, and made a covenant before Jehovah, to walk after Jehovah, and to keep his commandments, and his testimonies, and his statutes, with all his heart, and with all his soul, to perform the words of the covenant that were written in this book. 32 And he caused all that were found in Jerusalem and Benjamin to stand *to it.* And the inhabitants of Jerusalem did according to the covenant of God, the God of their fathers. 33 And Josiah took away all the abominations out of all the countries that pertained to the children of Israel, and made all that were found in Israel to serve, even to serve Jehovah their God. All his days they departed not from following Jehovah, the God of their fathers.

1 And Josiah kept a passover unto Jehovah in Jerusalem: and they killed the passover on the fourteenth *day* of the first month. 2 And he set the priests in their offices, and encouraged them to the service of the house of Jehovah. 3 And he said unto the Levites that taught all Israel, that were holy unto Jehovah, Put the holy ark in the house which Solomon the son of David king of Israel did build; there shall no more be a burden upon your shoulders. Now serve Jehovah your God, and his people Israel; 4 and prepare yourselves after your fathers' houses by your courses, according to the writing of David king of Israel, and according to the writing of Solomon his son. 5 And stand in the holy place according to the divisions of the fathers' houses of your brethren the children of the people, and *let there be for each* a portion of a fathers' house of the Levites. 6 And kill the passover, and sanctify yourselves, and prepare for your brethren, to do according to the word of Jehovah by Moses.

7 And Josiah gave to the children of the people, of the flock, lambs and kids, all of them for the passover-offerings, unto all that were present, to the number of thirty thousand, and three thousand bullocks: these were of the king's substance. 8 And his princes gave for a freewill-offering unto the people, to the priests, and to the Levites. Hilkiah and Zechariah and Jehiel, the rulers of the house of God, gave unto the priests for the passover-offerings two thousand and six hundred *small cattle,* and three hundred oxen. 9 Conaniah also, and Shemaiah and Nethanel, his brethren, and Hashabiah and Jeiel and Jozabad, the chiefs of the Levites, gave unto the Levites, for the passover-offerings five thousand *small cattle,* and five hundred oxen.

10 So the service was prepared, and the priests stood in their place, and the Levites by their courses, according to the king's commandment. 11 And they killed the passover, and the priests sprinkled *the blood which they received* of their

hand, and the Levites flayed them. 12 And they removed the burnt-offerings, that they might give them according to the division of the fathers' houses of the children of the people, to offer unto Jehovah, as it is written in the book of Moses. And so did they with the oxen. 13 And they roasted the passover with fire according to the ordinance: and the holy offerings boiled they in pots, and in caldrons, and in pans, and carried them quickly to all the children of the people. 14 And afterward they prepared for themselves, and for the priests, because the priests the sons of Aaron *were busied* in offering the burnt-offerings and the fat until night: therefore the Levites prepared for themselves, and for the priests the sons of Aaron. 15 And the singers the sons of Asaph were in their place, according to the commandment of David, and Asaph, and Heman, and Jeduthun the king's seer; and the porters were at every gate: they needed not to depart from their service; for their brethren the Levites prepared for them. 16 So all the service of Jehovah was prepared the same day, to keep the passover, and to offer burnt-offerings upon the altar of Jehovah, according to the commandment of king Josiah. 17 And the children of Israel that were present kept the passover at that time, and the feast of unleavened bread seven days. 18 And there was no passover like to that kept in Israel from the days of Samuel the prophet; neither did any of the kings of Israel keep such a passover as Josiah kept, and the priests, and the Levites, and all Judah and Israel that were present, and the inhabitants of Jerusalem. 19 In the eighteenth year of the reign of Josiah was this passover kept.

20 After all this, when Josiah had prepared the temple, Neco king of Egypt went up to fight against Carchemish by the Euphrates: and Josiah went out against him. 21 But he sent ambassadors to him, saying, What have I to do with thee, thou king of Judah? *I come* not against thee this day, but against the house wherewith I have war; and God hath commanded me to make haste: forbear thee from *meddling with* God, who is with me, that he destroy thee not. 22 Nevertheless Josiah would not turn his face from him, but disguised himself, that he might fight with him, and hearkened not unto the words of Neco from the mouth of God, and came to fight in the valley of Megiddo. 23 And the archers shot at king Josiah; and the king said to his servants, Have me away; for I am sore

wounded. 24 So his servants took him out of the chariot, and put him in the second chariot that he had, and brought him to Jerusalem; and he died, and was buried in the sepulchres of his fathers. And all Judah and Jerusalem mourned for Josiah. 25 And Jeremiah lamented for Josiah: and all the singing men and singing women spake of Josiah in their lamentations unto this day; and they made them an ordinance in Israel: and, behold, they are written in the lamentations. 26 Now the rest of the acts of Josiah, and his good deeds, according to that which is written in the law of Jehovah, 27 and his acts, first and last, behold, they are written in the book of the kings of Israel and Judah.

In the Kings account of Josiah's reform, the discovery of the Book of the Law was the event that initiated the great reform; in the Chronicles account, the discovery occurred during the course of the reform, which continued over a period of years. In keeping with this distinctive feature, the chronicler elaborately describes the great climax of the reform in the magnificent, unexcelled observance of the Passover.

Special effort is exercised by the chronicler to trace the progress of the reform. Ascending the throne at the age of eight years, Josiah began to seek the Lord at the age of sixteen (v. 3). Four years later, at the age of twenty, he began the actual reformation (v. 3). At twenty-six years of age, he commenced the repair of the temple, at which time the Book of the Law was discovered (v. 8). This discovery was followed by the renewal of the covenant and the observance of the Passover, all of these events occurring during the eighteenth year of his reign (v. 19).

For the chronicler, the observance of the Passover at the climax of the reform was of greatest significance. Here was one of the most illustrious kings of the Davidic dynasty proving the greatness of the Davidic line and showing a fond affection for the temple and the Levitical order of worship. This is the finale of the chronicler's account of the kingdom of David.

The formal occasion of the Passover was highly impregnated with the rich content of Israel's faith. Likewise, through our worship forms it is sometimes possible to worship God with a spiritual enrichment not found in inadequate worship forms. The chronicler seems to have had a heightened appreciation for form and ritual. When the symbolisms of formal worship are properly understood and used as means to a better understanding of God (not as ends in themselves) they may prove valuable to many worshipers today. However, God does not look with favor upon ritual *per se* (cf. Isa. 1:10-20; I Sam. 15:22). Jesus emphasized the importance of true spiritual worship over against empty and meaningless formalistic worship (John 4:21-24).

Josiah's death was extremely untimely. At the height of his reign, he was fatally wounded in battle (vv. 23-24). With his sudden and unexpected death, the hopes of the kingdom collapsed, and within a few years Babylon dominated the land.

I. REIGN OF DAVIDIC KINGS AT THE CLOSE OF THE SEVENTH AND THE BEGINNING OF THE SIXTH CENTURIES B.C. (36:1-21; cf. II Kings 23:31—25:21)

Within twenty-five years after the catastrophe of the sudden death of Josiah, the kingdom of David came to an end. The incorrigible religious perversity of the kings and people was the cause.

1. Jehoahaz (36:1-4; cf. II Kings 23:31-34)

1 Then the people of the land took Jehoahaz the son of Josiah, and made him king in his father's stead in Jerusalem. 2 Joahaz was twenty and three years old when he began to reign; and he reigned three months in Jerusalem. 3 And the king of Egypt deposed him at Jerusalem, and fined the land a hundred talents of silver and a talent of gold. 4 And the king of Egypt made Eliakim his brother king over Judah and Jerusalem, and changed his name to Jehoiakim. And Neco took Joahaz his brother, and carried him to Egypt.

See notes on the parallel passage in Kings.

2. Jehoiakim (36:5-8; cf. II Kings 23: 34—24:7)

5 Jehoiakim was twenty and five years old when he began to reign; and he reigned eleven years in Jerusalem: and he did that which was evil in the sight of Jehovah his God. 6 Against him came up Nebuchadnezzar king of Babylon, and bound him in fetters, to carry him to Babylon. 7 Nebuchadnezzar also carried of the vessels of the house of Jehovah to Babylon, and put them in his temple at Babylon. 8 Now the rest of the acts of Jehoiakim, and his abominations which he did, and that which was found in him, behold, they are written in the book of the kings of Israel and Judah: and Jehoiachin his son reigned in his stead.

See notes on the parallel passage in Kings.

3. Jehoiachin (36:9-10; cf. II Kings 24: 8-16)

9 Jehoiachin was eight years old when he began to reign; and he reigned three months and ten days in Jerusalem: and he did that which was evil in the sight of Jehovah. 10 And at the return of the year king Nebuchadnezzar sent, and ·brought him to Babylon, with the goodly vessels of the house of Jehovah, and made Zedekiah his brother king over Judah and Jerusalem.

See notes on the parallel passage in Kings.

4. Zedekiah (36:11-21; cf. II Kings 24: 17—25:21)

11 Zedekiah was twenty and one years old when he began to reign; and he reigned eleven years in Jerusalem: 12 and he did that which was evil in the sight of Jehovah his God; he humbled not himself before Jeremiah the prophet *speaking* from the mouth of Jehovah. 13 And he also rebelled against king Nebuchadnezzar, who had made him swear by God; but he stiffened his neck, and hardened his heart against turning unto Jehovah, the God of Israel. 14 Moreover all the chiefs of the priests, and the people, trespassed very greatly after all the abominations of the nations; and they polluted the house of Jehovah which he had hallowed in Jerusalem. 15 And Jehovah, the God of their fathers, sent to them by his messengers, rising up early and sending, because he had compassion on his people, and on his dwelling-place: 16 but they mocked the messengers of God, and despised his words, and scoffed at his prophets, until the wrath of Jehovah arose against his people, till there was no remedy.

17 Therefore he brought upon them the king of the Chaldeans, who slew their

young men with the sword in the house of their sanctuary, and had no compassion upon young man or virgin, old man or hoary-headed: he gave them all into his hand. 18 And all the vessels of the house of God, great and small, and the treasures of the house of Jehovah, and the treasures of the king, and of his princes, all these he brought to Babylon. 19 And they burnt the house of God, and brake down the wall of Jerusalem, and burnt all the palaces thereof with fire, and destroyed all the goodly vessels thereof. 20 And them that had escaped from the sword carried he away to Babylon; and they were servants to him and his sons until the reign of the kingdom of Persia: 21 to fulfil the word of Jehovah by the mouth of Jeremiah, until the land had enjoyed its sabbaths: *for* as long as it lay desolate it kept sabbath, to fulfil threescore and ten years.

See notes on the parallel passage in Kings.

J. EPILOGUE: THE RETURN (36:22-23)

22 Now in the first year of Cyrus king of Persia, that the word of Jehovah by the mouth of Jeremiah might be accomplished, Jehovah stirred up the spirit of Cyrus king of Persia, so that he made a proclamation throughout all his kingdom, and *put it* also in writing, saying, 23 Thus saith Cyrus king of Persia, All the kingdoms of the earth hath Jehovah, the God of heaven, given me; and he hath charged me to build him a house in Jerusalem, which is in Judah. Whosoever there is among you of all his people, Jehovah his God be with him, and let him go up.

The last chapter in Chronicles is not merely the delineation of tragedy. The chronicler had begun his account with genealogies going back to Adam; he concluded his account with the reign of Zedekiah, the last of the Davidic kings. Writing for Jews who had seen their temple built for the second time, he was astutely aware that they were granted a new beginning. Jehovah had stirred up the spirit of Cyrus, king of Persia, who decreed that he was commissioned to erect a house unto the Lord in Jerusalem (vv. 22-23).

While the Chronicles history of the kingdom was a warning against pride and perversity, it was also a consolation. God was so compassionate as to stir up the spirit of Cyrus to build a temple and give the Jews a new beginning. The temple of the restoration was a visible sign of God's mercy and love.

The Jews were given to understand that if they met the moral demands involved in the worship of the Lord in His holy temple, the divine glory would once again fill, not only the temple, but also the lives of all true worshipers. This is consolation to all men.

Bibliography

I. EXEGETICAL AND HISTORICAL VALUE

Beecher, W. J. "Chronicles." *The International Standard Bible Encyclopedia.* Ed. James Orr. Vol. I. Chicago: Howard-Severance, 1930.

Clarke, Adam. *Commentary and Critical Notes.* Vol. II. London: Ward, n.d.

Crockett, W. D. *A Harmony of the Books of Samuel, Kings, and Chronicles.* Reprint. Grand Rapids: Baker, 1951.

Curtis, E. L. and A. A. Madsen. "The Books of Chronicles." *The International Critical Commentary.* Edinburgh: T. and T. Clark, 1910.

Ellison, H. L. "I and II Chronicles." *The New Bible Commentary.* Eds. F. Davidson, A. M. Stibbs, E. F. Kevan. Grand Rapids: Eerdmans, 1953.

Elmslie, W. A. L. "First and Second Books of Chronicles: Introduction and Exegesis." *The Interpreter's Bible.* Vol. III. New York and Nashville: Abingdon, 1954.

Eiselen, F. C., E. Lewis, D. G. Downey (eds.). *The Abingdon Bible Commentary.* New York and Nashville: Abingdon-Cokesbury, 1929.

Harvey-Jellie, W. R. "Chronicles." *The Century Bible.* London: Caxton, n.d.

Keil, C. F. "The Book of the Chronicles." *Biblical Commentary on the Old Testament.* Reprint. Grand Rapids: Eerdmans, n.d.

Payne, J. B. "I and II Chronicles." *The Wycliffe Bible Commentary.* Eds. F. Pfeiffer and E. F. Harrison. Chicago: Moody Press, 1962.

Snaith, N. H. "The Historical Books." *The Old Testament and Modern Study.* Ed. H. H. Rowley. Oxford: Clarendon, 1951.

Zöckler, O. "The Books of Chronicles." *Commentary on the Holy Scripture.* Ed. J. P. Lange. Reprint. Grand Rapids: Zondervan, n.d.

II. EXPOSITORY AND PRACTICAL VALUE

Bennett, W. H. "The Books of Chronicles." *The Expositor's Bible.* Ed. W. R. Nicoll. Vol. II. Grand Rapids: Eerdmans, 1940.

Elmslie, W. A. L. "First and Second Books of Chronicles: Exposition." *The Interpreter's Bible.* Vol. III. New York and Nashville: Abingdon, 1954.

Stevenson, Dwight E. *Preaching on the Books of the Old Testament.* New York: Harper, 1961.

The Book of Ezra

by Charles R. Wilson

Outline

433

Introduction

Although Ezra and Nehemiah are two separate books in the English Bible, there is evidence that formerly they were one book. In the effort to establish a uniform Hebrew text of the Old Testament writings, the Masoretes of the sixth through the eighth centuries A.D. employed the special feature of placing notations at the end of a book.

There are no notations at the end of Ezra, but there are at the end of Nehemiah. These notations refer to both Ezra and Nehemiah. One specific notation states that Nehemiah 3:22 is the middle verse. This can mean only the middle of Ezra and Nehemiah when combined. Not until the sixteenth century A.D. was the practice of making Ezra and Nehemiah two books introduced.

I. COMPILATION

It is generally recognized that Ezra and Nehemiah have affinities with I and II Chronicles. The most satisfactory explanation for these resemblances is that these writings are the work of one compiler. "The opinion has become increasingly prevalent that . . . the compiler of Chronicles is the same as the compiler of Ezra and Nehemiah."[1]

The various sources used by the compiler included personal memoirs of Ezra and Nehemiah, incidents written about these two men, letters, decrees and genealogies. Two sections in Ezra are in Aramaic (4:7—6:18; 7:12-26). These consist almost entirely of royal decrees and letters.

These Aramaic sections have become the focal point in the current discussions regarding the dating of Ezra and Nehemiah.[2] If these sections represent the Aramaic of a later period, these writings must be dated accordingly, usually somewhere between 350 and 250 B.C. However, if these sections represent the Aramaic that was prevalent during that part of the period of the restoration included in the Old Testament narrative, these writings may reasonably be dated between 430 and 397 B.C.

Traditionally, the belief that Ezra preceded Nehemiah in returning to Jerusalem is associated with the belief that the book of Ezra preceded the book of Nehemiah. This appears valid on the basis of the following evidence. Ezra returned to Jerusalem in the seventh year of Artaxerxes (Ezra 7:7), while Nehemiah returned in the twentieth year (Neh. 2:1) and again in the thirty-second year of Artaxerxes (Neh. 13:6). This would place Nehemiah after Ezra, chronologically speaking. The arrangement of the books suggests the same relationship.

Since there is no identification of the Artaxerxes mentioned, there has been considerable inquiry as to which Artaxerxes was intended, since there were three Persian kings by that name: Artaxerxes I (465-424 B.C.), Artaxerxes II (404-358 B.C.) and Artaxerxes III (358-338 B.C.). Considering the identification of Artaxerxes as needing further study, it may be that the relation between Ezra and Nehemiah deserves consideration.

A related study is that of a comparison of Ezra and Nehemiah with I Esdras, one of the books of the Apocrypha. This book is a Greek version of that part of Chronicles, Ezra and Nehemiah from II Chronicles 35:1 to Ezra 10:44, with Nehemiah 8:1-12 at the end. Further attention to this study is impossible here, but it enters upon any detailed inquiry of the relation between Ezra and Nehemiah.

---

[1] H. E. Ryle, "Ezra and Nehemiah," *The Cambridge Bible for Schools and Colleges*, ed. J. J. S. Perowne, p. xxvi; cf. N. H. Snaith, "The Historical Books," *The Old Testament and Modern Study*, p. 107.
[2] N. H. Snaith, *ibid.*, p. 108.

II. HISTORICITY

As part of a larger literary activity, including I and II Chronicles, Ezra and Nehemiah, the latter two writings contain the account of the restoration of the Jewish community in Palestine and the establishment of the Levitical order as the orthodox worship of Jehovah in Jerusalem. The period of time covered in this historical account is somewhat less than a century and a half, depending upon the point of view (538-397 B.C.).

The restoration was a historic reality because of the favorable policy and economic assistance by Persian kings, notably Cyrus and Darius I in the sixth century B.C., and Artaxerxes I, Longimanus, in the fifth century B.C. The temple was completed under the leadership of Zerubbabel, the governor, and Jeshua, the high priest, during the sixth century B.C. The wall of Jerusalem was rebuilt and important reforms were achieved during the fifth century B.C. in order to preserve the racial and religious purity of the restored Jewish community. During this period Nehemiah, the governor, and Ezra, the priestly scribe, were the leaders.

III. HISTORICAL SIGNIFICANCE

Regardless of the point of view from which the books of Ezra and Nehemiah are approached, invaluable insight is gained concerning the compiler's appreciation for the heritage which the restored Jewish community at Jerusalem possessed, as well as his awareness of the destiny which that community was called upon to fulfill. The heritage was the covenant and its obligation, the law; the destiny was a separatist cultic orthodoxy.

The Jews who returned from exile looked upon themselves as the truly chosen people and upon their worship as the only orthodox one. The law was their authority. The leaders of this remnant found the company of the faithful in agreement with their efforts. Zerubbabel, Jeshua, Ezra and Nehemiah all had zealous support. However, the support was not unanimous, for there was compromise and apathy. Outright opposition flared. Nevertheless, in spite of the tensions, definite reforms were accomplished.

IV. MORAL AND SPIRITUAL VALUE

Among the significant contributions of Ezra and Nehemiah are a remarkable awareness of the intimate relationship between God and His people and a keen sensitivity to His providence. Both Ezra and Nehemiah were confident that God was in the whole endeavor (cf. Ezra 7:6, 9, 18, 27-28; Neh. 2:4, 8, 18, 20).

To a great degree the writings of Ezra and Nehemiah have been neglected because they appear so negative in character. Notwithstanding this factor, these men had a profound experience with God. Continually they affirmed that they were engaged in God's work. This confidence and courage never faltered.

There is the perennial need on the part of those engaged in the work of the Lord to have a conscious experience of His presence and guidance. This is possible amid the apathy and opposition of those around us.

A second value is the realization that Ezra's work was the practical implementation of the messages of the pre-exilic prophets. The great prophets such as Isaiah had warned against foreign religious influences and had declared judgment upon compromise. Ezra acknowledged this and sought by specific legalistic reforms to avoid all forms of adulteration. He feared divine judgment would follow compromise.

Although Judaism lost the benefits of cultural relations with other peoples, the identity of this religious community was maintained. Yet there was a rigid legalism that stifled the motivations which spring from deeper sources. John Wesley saw a wholesome corrective to religious legalism. While he emphasized the "methodical" aspect of Christianity, he emphasized even more its "spiritual" aspect, the Holy Spirit giving the true dynamic to holy living.

A third value is the example of the faithful stewardship of Nehemiah. This man constantly referred to the hope that his work for Jerusalem would be remembered by the Lord. Nehemiah was a eunuch without posterity. Given other circumstances his name and reputation might have extended no further than the royal palace in Persia. However, he saw his responsibility and accepted it. As a layman, he journeyed to Jerusalem and faced a virtually impossible task as well as vigorous opposition. With the help of the Lord, he revived a desolate Jewish community and sought to make it well-pleasing to God through reforms. He toiled diligently and sacrificed personal popularity in order to gain the divine commendation, "Well done." This deep desire was expressed in his prayer: "Remember me, O my God, for good" (Neh. 13:31).

Commentary on Ezra

I. A REMNANT RETURNS (Ezra 1:1–2:70)

The Jews dwelling in enforced exile in Babylon during the sixth century B.C. found to their good fortune that the conquest of Babylon by Cyrus of Persia in 539 B.C. held promise of a new day and a bright future for them.

A. THE ROYAL PROCLAMATION REGARDING THE TEMPLE (1:1-11; cf. I Esdras 2:1-12)

The coming of Cyrus upon the world scene heralded a new humanitarianism. Rulers of Assyria and Babylon had attacked the national identity of conquered countries by displacing whole populations. Cyrus, however, inaugurated his reign by granting displaced peoples the opportunity to return to their native lands.

1. The Reason (1:1-4)

1 Now in the first year of Cyrus king of Persia, that the word of Jehovah by the mouth of Jeremiah might be accomplished, Jehovah stirred up the spirit of Cyrus king of Persia, so that he made a proclamation throughout all his kingdom, and *put it* also in writing, saying, 2 Thus saith Cyrus king of Persia, All the kingdoms of the earth hath Jehovah, the God of heaven, given me; and he hath charged me to build him a house in Jerusalem, which is in Judah. 3 Whosoever there is among you of all his people, his God be with him, and let him go up to Jerusalem, which is in Judah, and build the house of Jehovah, the God of Israel (he is God), which is in Jerusalem. 4 And whosoever is left, in any place where he sojourneth, let the men of his place help him with silver, and with gold, and with goods, and with beasts, besides the freewill-offering for the house of God which is in Jerusalem.

In 538 B.C., during the first year of the reign of Cyrus over Babylon, he issued a royal proclamation that he was charged to build a house for Jehovah in Jerusalem (vv. 1-4). There are two other accounts of this proclamation in the book of Ezra (5:13-15 and 6:2-5). The accounts appear in one of the Aramaic sections and refer to the proclamation as an administrative order for the reconstruction of the temple in Jerusalem at royal expense. However, the account of the proclamation in the first chapter has a religious dimension. Cyrus is represented as a worshiper of Jehovah who authorizes the Jews to return to their homeland in order that they may restore the sanctuary in Jerusalem.

On the celebrated "Cyrus Cylinder," an archaeological discovery found at the site of ancient Babylon and dated 536 B.C., Cyrus has inscribed his conquests and generosities to the Babylonian god Marduk. He had it recorded that he returned all the idols to the captive peoples and granted these people permission to return to their homeland. Since the Jews had no idols, he allowed them to take the sacred vessels of their former temple with them.

2. The Response (1:5-11)

5 Then rose up the heads of fathers' *houses* of Judah and Benjamin, and the priests, and the Levites, even all whose spirit God had stirred to go up to build the house of Jehovah which is in Jerusalem. 6 And all they that were round about them strengthened their hands with vessels of silver, with gold, with goods, and with beasts, and with precious things, besides all that was willingly offered. 7 Also Cyrus the king brought forth the vessels of the house of Jehovah, which Nebuchadnezzar had brought forth out of Jerusalem, and had put in the house of his gods; 8 even those did Cyrus king of Persia bring forth by the hand of Mithredath the treasurer, and numbered them unto Sheshbazzar, the prince of Judah. 9 And this is the num-

ber of them: thirty platters of gold, a thousand platters of silver, nine and twenty knives, 10 thirty bowls of gold, silver bowls of a second sort four hundred and ten, and other vessels a thousand. 11 All the vessels of gold and of silver were five thousand and four hundred. All these did Sheshbazzar bring up, when they of the captivity were brought up from Babylon unto Jerusalem.

A company of Jews responded to the edict of Cyrus. They were stirred by God to return to Jerusalem in order to build the temple (v. 5). Just as Jehovah had stirred up the spirit of Cyrus, so He stirred up the spirit of those exiled Jews.

Sheshbazzar was commissioned by Cyrus to be the leader and to supervise the execution of the royal decree (v. 8). As soon as practical the journey to Jerusalem was begun. It is unlikely that a major exodus from Babylon occurred. Many Jews looked upon the nearly one-thousand-mile journey as very difficult and hazardous. Moreover, they were comfortably settled in Babylon, while the journey to Jerusalem to build a temple seemed so uncertain and costly. Only the more courageous and dedicated ones responded. This is repeatedly the case, for so often any attempt to do the will of God in advancing His cause involves the elements of venture and sacrifice.

B. THE REGISTER OF THE RETURNING JEWS (2:1-70; cf. Neh. 7:6-73; I Esdras 5:7-46)

1 Now these are the children of the province, that went up out of the captivity of those that had been carried away, whom Nebuchadnezzar the king of Babylon had carried away unto Babylon, and that returned unto Jerusalem and Judah, every one unto his city; 2 who came with Zerubbabel, Jeshua, Nehemiah, Seraiah, Reelaiah, Mordecai, Bilshan, Mispar, Bigvai, Rehum, Baanah.

The number of the men of the people of Israel: 3 The children of Parosh, two thousand a hundred seventy and two. 4 The children of Shephatiah, three hundred seventy and two. 5 The children of Arah, seven hundred seventy and five. 6 The children of Pahath-moab, of the children of Jeshua and Joab, two thousand eight hundred and twelve. 7 The children of Elam, a thousand two hundred fifty and four. 8 The children of Zattu, nine hundred forty and five. 9 The children of Zaccai, seven hundred and threescore. 10 The children of Bani, six hundred forty and two. 11 The children of Bebai, six hundred twenty and three. 12 The children of Azgad, a thousand two hundred twenty and two. 13 The children of Adonikam, six hundred sixty and six. 14 The children of Bigvai, two thousand fifty and six. 15 The children of Adin, four hundred fifty and four. 16 The children of Ater, of Hezekiah, ninety and eight. 17 The children of Bezai, three hundred twenty and three. 18 The children of Jorah, a hundred and twelve. 19 The children of Hashum, two hundred twenty and three. 20 The children of Gibbar, ninety and five. 21 The children of Beth-lehem, a hundred twenty and three. 22 The men of Netophah, fifty and six. 23 The men of Anathoth, a hundred twenty and eight. 24 The children of Azmaveth, forty and two. 25 The children of Kiriath-arim, Chephirah, and Beeroth, seven hundred and forty and three. 26 The children of Ramah and Geba, six hundred twenty and one. 27 The men of Michmas, a hundred twenty and two. 28 The men of Beth-el and Ai, two hundred twenty and three. 29 The children of Nebo, fifty and two. 30 The children of Magbish, a hundred fifty and six. 31 The children of the other Elam, a thousand two hundred fifty and four. 32 The children of Harim, three hundred and twenty. 33 The children of Lod, Hadid, and Ono, seven hundred twenty and five. 34 The children of Jericho, three hundred forty and five. 35 The children of Senaah, three thousand and six hundred and thirty.

36 The priests: the children of Jedaiah, of the house of Jeshua, nine hundred seventy and three. 37 The children of Immer, a thousand fifty and two. 38 The children of Pashhur, a thousand two hundred forty and seven. 39 The children of Harim, a thousand and seventeen.

40 The Levites: the children of Jeshua and Kadmiel, of the children of Hodaviah, seventy and four. 41 The singers: the children of Asaph, a hundred twenty and eight. 42 The children of the porters: the children of Shallum, the children of Ater, the children of Talmon, the children of Akkub, the children of Hatita, the children of Shobai, in all a hundred thirty and nine.

43 The Nethinim: the children of Ziha, the children of Hasupha, the children of Tabbaoth, 44 the children of Keros, the children of Siaha, the children

of Padon, 45 the children of Lebanah, the children of Hagabah, the children of Akkub, 46 the children of Hagab, the children of Shamlai, the children of Hanan, 47 the children of Giddel, the children of Gahar, the children of Reaiah, 48 the children of Rezin, the children of Nekoda, the children of Gazzam, 49 the children of Uzza, the children of Paseah, the children of Besai, 50 the children of Asnah, the children of Meunim, the children of Nephisim, 51 the children of Bakbuk, the children of Hakupha, the children of Harhur, 52 the children of Bazluth, the children of Mehida, the children of Harsha, 53 the children of Barkos, the children of Sisera, the children of Temah, 54 the children of Neziah, the children of Hatipha.

55 The children of Solomon's servants: the children of Sotai, the children of Hossophereth, the children of Peruda, 56 the children of Jaalah, the children of Darkon, the children of Giddel, 57 the children of Shephatiah, the children of Hattil, the children of Pochereth-hazzebaim, the children of Ami. 58 All the Nethinim, and the children of Solomon's servants, were three hundred ninety and two.

59 And these were they that went up from Tel-melah, Tel-harsha, Cherub, Addan, *and* Immer; but they could not show their fathers' houses, and their seed, whether they were of Israel: 60 the children of Delaiah, the children of Tobiah, the children of Nekoda, six hundred fifty and two. 61 And of the children of the priests: the children of Habaiah, the children of Hakkoz, the children of Barzillai, who took a wife of the daughters of Barzillai the Gileadite, and was called after their name. 62 These sought their register *among* those that were reckoned by genealogy, but they were not found: therefore were they deemed polluted and put from the priesthood. 63 And the governor said unto them, that they should not eat of the most holy things, till there stood up a priest with Urim and with Thummim.

64 The whole assembly together was forty and two thousand three hundred and threescore, 65 besides their menservants and their maid-servants, of whom there were seven thousand three hundred thirty and seven: and they had two hundred singing men and singing women. 66 Their horses were seven hundred thirty and six; their mules, two hundred forty and five; 67 their camels, four hundred thirty and five; *their* asses, six thousand seven hundred and twenty.

68 And some of the heads of fathers' *houses*, when they came to the house of Jehovah which is in Jerusalem, offered willingly for the house of God to set it up in its place: 69 they gave after their ability into the treasury of the work threescore and one thousand darics of gold, and five thousand pounds of silver, and one hundred priests' garments.

70 So the priests, and the Levites, and some of the people, and the singers, and the porters, and the Nethinim, dwelt in their cities, and all Israel in their cities.

This register is according to the following classifications: (1) by families (vv. 1-20), (2) by cities (vv. 21-35), by temple service (vv. 36-58), (4) by uncertified clans (vv. 59-63), (5) summary (vv. 64-70).

II. A TEMPLE UNTO THE LORD (Ezra 3:1—6:22)

No details are available concerning the journey. However, the returning Jews immediately began to carry out the royal decree.

A. BUILDING THE ALTAR OF SACRIFICE (3:1-7; cf. I Esdras 5:47-54)

1 And when the seventh month was come, and the children of Israel were in the cities, the people gathered themselves together as one man to Jerusalem. 2 Then stood up Jeshua the son of Jozadak, and his brethren the priests, and Zerubbabel the son of Shealtiel, and his brethren, and builded the altar of the God of Israel, to offer burnt-offerings thereon, as it is written in the law of Moses the man of God. 3 And they set the altar upon its base; for fear was upon them because of the peoples of the countries: and they offered burnt-offerings thereon unto Jehovah, even burnt-offerings morning and evening. 4 And they kept the feast of tabernacles, as it is written, and *offered* the daily burnt-offerings by number, according to the ordinance, as the duty of every day required; 5 and afterward the continual burnt-offering, and *the offerings* of the new moons, and of all the set feasts of Jehovah that were consecrated, and of every one that willingly offered a freewill-offering unto Jehovah. 6 From the first day of the seventh month began they to offer burnt-offerings unto Jehovah: but the foundation of the temple of Jehovah was not yet laid. 7 They gave money also

unto the masons, and to the carpenters; and food, and drink, and oil, unto them of Sidon, and to them of Tyre, to bring cedar-trees from Lebanon to the sea, unto Joppa, according to the grant that they had of Cyrus king of Persia.

One of the first recorded acts of the returning Jews was the erection of the altar of sacrifice; doubtless it was located on the site of the former altar. It was the first step in reinstating the Levitical order of sacrifice (v. 2). Likewise, it was putting God first in order that they might be delivered from their enemies: **fear was upon them because of the peoples of the countries** (v. 3). Their first concern was to restore the Levitical order of service and sacrifice. It was motivated, in part, by their seeking the help of the Lord against their adversaries. So today, individuals will revive their church-going habits or their private devotions when they face crises in which they realize their need of the help of the Lord.

B. BEGINNING THE TEMPLE (3:8-13; cf. I Esdras 5:55-65)

8 Now in the second year of their coming unto the house of God at Jerusalem, in the second month, began Zerubbabel the son of Shealtiel, and Jeshua the son of Jozadak, and the rest of their brethren the priests and the Levites, and all they that were come out of the captivity unto Jerusalem, and appointed the Levites, from twenty years old and upward, to have the oversight of the work of the house of Jehovah. 9 Then stood Jeshua with his sons and his brethren, Kadmiel and his sons, the sons of Judah, together, to have the oversight of the workmen in the house of God: the sons of Henadad, with their sons and their brethren the Levites. 10 And when the builders laid the foundation of the temple of Jehovah, they set the priests in their apparel with trumpets, and the Levites the sons of Asaph with cymbals, to praise Jehovah, after the order of David king of Israel. 11 And they sang one to another in praising and giving thanks unto Jehovah, *saying*, For he is good, for his lovingkindness *endureth* for ever toward Israel. And all the people shouted with a great shout, when they praised Jehovah, because the foundation of the house of Jehovah was laid. 12 But many of the priests and Levites and heads of fathers' *houses*, the old men that had seen the first house,

when the foundation of this house was laid before their eyes, wept with a loud voice; and many shouted aloud for joy: 13 so that the people could not discern the noise of the shout of joy from the noise of the weeping of the people; for the people shouted with a loud shout, and the noise was heard afar off.

With continued interest in the Levitical cultus, the account of the building of the temple makes clear that the Levites were made responsible for the task (v. 8). Two men were superintending the work: Zerubbabel, the son of Shealtiel, and Jeshua, the son of Jozadak (v. 8). Zerubbabel, who had succeeded Sheshbazzar, was the grandson of the Davidic king, Jehoiachin, who, in turn, was the grandson of the great and godly king Josiah. Jeshua, the high priest, was of the line of Zadok. Both men were of the finest Hebrew tradition—Zerubbabel of the line of David, and Jeshua (Joshua) of the line of Aaron.

The first stage in building the temple was the laying of the foundation (v. 9). There were mingled reactions to this. The tearful sighs of the older generation, which remembered the size and splendor of the former temple, were mingled with the joyful shouts of the younger generation, which had no fond memories of the former structure, but which had bright hopes for the future (v. 12). There is always a measure of stress in such situations. The older people cannot realize and appreciate the outlook of the younger, and vice versa.

C. BUILDING DELAYED BY OPPOSITION (4:1-24)

In addition to disappointment over the plans for the new temple, which did not compare in magnificence to the former temple, serious opposition came from the people of the land.

1. Earlier Opposition (4:1-5; cf. I Esdras 5:66-73)

1 Now when the adversaries of Judah and Benjamin heard that the children of the captivity were building a temple unto Jehovah, the God of Israel; 2 then they drew near to Zerubbabel, and to the heads of fathers' *houses*, and said unto them, Let us build with you; for we seek your God, as ye do; and we sacrifice unto

him since the days of Esar-haddon king of Assyria, who brought us up hither. 3 But Zerubbabel, and Jeshua, and the rest of the heads of fathers' *houses* of Israel, said unto them, Ye have nothing to do with us in building a house unto our God; but we ourselves together will build unto Jehovah, the God of Israel, as king Cyrus the king of Persia hath commanded us. 4 Then the people of the land weakened the hands of the people of Judah, and troubled them in building, 5 and hired counsellors against them, to frustrate their purpose, all the days of Cyrus king of Persia, even until the reign of Darius king of Persia.

The opposition was non-existent at first. In fact, the people of the land offered assistance: **Let us build with you; for we seek your God, as ye do** (v. 2). The people of the land were a mixture of races imported by Assyria during the eighth century B.C., some two centuries earlier. They had become known as Samaritans because they had come to accept rebuilt Samaria as their central city.

The Jews who returned from Babylonian exile were of the pure stock of Judah and Benjamin. Likewise, the priests and Levites were of the tribe of Levi. These people constituted a racially pure remnant, and they refused the offer of assistance from the Samaritans. **Ye have nothing to do with us in building a house unto our God** (v. 3).

Here was a singular exclusivism that was to persist and develop. From one point of view, it may be that the Jews were determined to restore their relationship with Jehovah, even at the risk of isolating themselves from other people, the very people to whom the Jews were divinely commissioned to be a blessing. It must be remembered that the events of the exile had been a series of hammer blows pounding into their understanding the fact that God had delivered His people into the hands of their enemies because of their rebelliousness and waywardness. The remnant was keenly mindful of that lesson. They were prepared to resist any temptation which might lead them into that same compromising position.

From another point of view, this tendency to exclusivism and particularism, this trend to think that God had

covenant relations for the racially pure Jews only, was not in harmony with the universal mission to which God had called His people. He had called them to be a blessing to all people. His grace and might were sufficient to enable them to resist being influenced by other nations in their religious faith.

It was not as necessary to retain a distinct identity, as important as that may have been, as it was for them to give themselves in service and sacrifice in order that God's purpose for every nation might be fulfilled.

2. Later Opposition (4:6-24; cf. I Esdras 2:16-30)

6 And in the reign of Ahasuerus, in the beginning of his reign, wrote they an accusation against the inhabitants of Judah and Jerusalem.

7 And in the days of Artaxerxes wrote Bishlam, Mithredath, Tabeel, and the rest of his companions, unto Artaxerxes king of Persia; and the writing of the letter was written in the Syrian *character,* and set forth in the Syrian *tongue.* 8 Rehum the chancellor and Shimshai the scribe wrote a letter against Jerusalem to Artaxerxes the king in this sort: 9 then *wrote* Rehum the chancellor, and Shimshai the scribe, and the rest of their companions, the Dinaites, and the Apharsathchites, the Tarpelites, the Apharsites, the Archevites, the Babylonians, the Shushanchites, the Dehaites, the Elamites, 10 and the rest of the nations whom the great and noble Osnappar brought over, and set in the city of Samaria, and in the rest *of the country* beyond the River, and so forth.

11 This is the copy of the letter that they sent unto Artaxerxes the king: Thy servants the men beyond the River, and so forth. 12 Be it known unto the king, that the Jews that came up from thee are come to us unto Jerusalem; they are building the rebellious and the bad city, and have finished the walls, and repaired the foundations. 13 Be it known now unto the king, that, if this city be builded, and the walls finished, they will not pay tribute, custom, or toll, and in the end it will be hurtful unto the kings. 14 Now because we eat the salt of the palace, and it is not meet for us to see the king's dishonor, therefore have we sent and certified the king; 15 that search may be made in the book of the records of thy fathers: so shalt thou find in the book of the records, and know that this city is a

rebellious city, and hurtful unto kings and provinces, and that they have moved sedition within the same of old time; for which cause was this city laid waste. 16 We certify the king that, if this city be builded, and the walls finished, by this means thou shalt have no portion beyond the River.

17 *Then* sent the king an answer unto Rehum the chancellor, and to Shimshai the scribe, and to the rest of their companions that dwell in Samaria, and in the rest *of the country* beyond the River: Peace, and so forth. 18 The letter which ye sent unto us hath been plainly read before me. 19 And I decreed, and search hath been made, and it is found that this city of old time hath made insurrection against kings, and that rebellion and sedition have been made therein. 20 There have been mighty kings also over Jerusalem, who have ruled over all *the country* beyond the River; and tribute, custom, and toll, was paid unto them. 21 Make ye now a decree to cause these men to cease, and that this city be not builded, until a decree shall be made by me. 22 And take heed that ye be not slack herein: why should damage grow to the hurt of the kings?

23 Then when the copy of king Artaxerxes' letter was read before Rehum, and Shimshai the scribe, and their companions, they went in haste to Jerusalem unto the Jews, and made them to cease by force and power. 24 Then ceased the work of the house of God which is at Jerusalem; and it ceased until the second year of the reign of Darius king of Persia.

Not only does the account at this point reveal such vigorous opposition that construction was delayed, but it also inserts accounts of later opposition in order to stress the fact that opposition of racially mixed people dwelling in the land was the major reason for the delay in the erection of the temple.

Two examples of later opposition are included. The first occurred in the form of a letter to Ahasuerus, or Xerxes (v. 6). This Persian king ruled during the fifth century (486-465 B.C.). The second occurred during the reign of Artaxerxes I, who succeeded Xerxes. Artaxerxes I (465-424 B.C.) received a complaint from the racially mixed people, who claimed that the Jews were preparing to defy the sovereign rule of the Persian king (v. 13). The complaint claimed

that the Jews were building a wall around Jerusalem. Artaxerxes I ordered construction to stop, and force was used to bring the work to a halt (v. 23).

D. BUILDING THE TEMPLE (5:1—6:22; cf. I Esdras 6:1—7:15)

1 Now the prophets, Haggai the prophet, and Zechariah the son of Iddo, prophesied unto the Jews that were in Judah and Jerusalem; in the name of the God of Israel *prophesied they* unto them. 2 Then rose up Zerubbabel the son of Shealtiel, and Jeshua the son of Jozadak, and began to build the house of God which is at Jerusalem; and with them were the prophets of God, helping them. 3 At the same time came to them Tattenai, the governor beyond the River, and Shethar-bozenai, and their companions, and said thus unto them, Who gave you a decree to build this house, and to finish this wall? 4 Then we told them after this manner, what the names of the men were that were making this building. 5 But the eye of their God was upon the elders of the Jews, and they did not make them cease, till the matter should come to Darius, and then answer should be returned by letter concerning it.

6 The copy of the letter that Tattenai, the governor beyond the River, and Shethar-bozenai, and his companions the Apharsachites, who were beyond the River, sent unto Darius the king; 7 they sent a letter unto him, wherein was written thus: Unto Darius the king, all peace. 8 Be it known unto the king, that we went into the province of Judah, to the house of the great God, which is builded with great stones, and timber is laid in the walls; and this work goeth on with diligence and prospereth in their hands. 9 Then asked we those elders, and said unto them thus, Who gave you a decree to build this house, and to finish this wall? 10 We asked them their names also, to certify thee, that we might write the names of the men that were at the head of them. 11 And thus they returned us answer, saying, We are the servants of the God of heaven and earth, and are building the house that was builded these many years ago, which a great king of Israel builded and finished. 12 But after that our fathers had provoked the God of heaven unto wrath, he gave them unto the hand of Nebuchadnezzar king of Babylon, the Chaldean, who destroyed this house, and carried the people away into Babylon. 13 But in the first year of Cyrus king of Babylon, Cyrus the king made a

decree to build this house of God. 14 And the gold and silver vessels also of the house of God, which Nebuchadnezzar took out of the temple that was in Jerusalem, and brought into the temple of Babylon, those did Cyrus the king take out of the temple of Babylon, and they were delivered unto one whose name was Sheshbazzar, whom he had made governor; 15 and he said unto him, Take these vessels, go, put them in the temple that is in Jerusalem, and let the house of God be builded in its place. 16 Then came the same Sheshbazzar, and laid the foundations of the house of God which is in Jerusalem: and since that time even until now hath it been in building, and yet it is not completed. 17 Now therefore, if it seem good to the king, let there be search made in the king's treasure-house, which is there at Babylon, whether it be so, that a decree was made of Cyrus the king to build this house of God at Jerusalem; and let the king send his pleasure to us concerning this matter.

1 Then Darius the king made a decree, and search was made in the house of the archives, where the treasures were laid up in Babylon. 2 And there was found at Achmetha, in the palace that is in the province of Media, a roll, and therein was thus written for a record: 3 In the first year of Cyrus the king, Cyrus the king made a decree: Concerning the house of God at Jerusalem, let the house be builded, the place where they offer sacrifices, and let the foundations thereof be strongly laid; the height thereof threescore cubits, and the breadth thereof threescore cubits; 4 with three courses of great stones, and a course of new timber: and let the expenses be given out of the king's house. 5 And also let the gold and silver vessels of the house of God, which Nebuchadnezzar took forth out of the temple which is at Jerusalem, and brought unto Babylon, be restored, and brought again unto the temple which is at Jerusalem, every one to its place; and thou shalt put them in the house of God.

6 Now therefore, Tattenai, governor beyond the River, Shethar-bozenai, and your companions the Apharsachites, who are beyond the River, be ye far from thence: 7 let the work of this house of God alone; let the governor of the Jews and the elders of the Jews build this house of God in its place. 8 Moreover I make a decree what ye shall do to these elders of the Jews for the building of this house of God: that of the king's goods, even of the tribute beyond the River,

expenses be given with all diligence unto these men, that they be not hindered. 9 And that which they have need of, both young bullocks, and rams, and lambs, for burnt-offerings to the God of heaven; *also* wheat, salt, wine, and oil, according to the word of the priests that are at Jerusalem, let it be given them day by day without fail; 10 that they may offer sacrifices of sweet savor unto the God of heaven, and pray for the life of the king, and of his sons. 11 Also I have made a decree, that whosoever shall alter this word, let a beam be pulled out from his house, and let him be lifted up and fastened thereon; and let his house be made a dunghill for this: 12 and the God that hath caused his name to dwell there overthrow all kings and peoples that shall put forth their hand to alter *the same*, to destroy this house of God which is at Jerusalem. I Darius have made a decree; let it be done with all diligence.

13 Then Tattenai, the governor beyond the River, Shethar-bozenai, and their companions, because that Darius the king had sent, did accordingly with all diligence. 14 And the elders of the Jews builded and prospered, through the prophesying of Haggai the prophet and Zechariah the son of Iddo. And they builded and finished it, according to the commandment of the God of Israel, and according to the decree of Cyrus, and Darius, and Artaxerxes king of Persia. 15 And this house was finished on the third day of the month Adar, which was in the sixth year of the reign of Darius the king.

16 And the children of Israel, the priests and the Levites, and the rest of the children of the captivity, kept the dedication of this house of God with joy. 17 And they offered at the dedication of this house of God a hundred bullocks, two hundred rams, four hundred lambs; and for a sin-offering for all Israel, twelve he-goats, according to the number of the tribes of Israel. 18 And they set the priests in their divisions, and the Levites in their courses, for the service of God, which is at Jerusalem; as it is written in the book of Moses.

19 And the children of the captivity kept the passover upon the fourteenth *day* of the first month. 20 For the priests and the Levites had purified themselves together; all of them were pure: and they killed the passover for all the children of the captivity, and for their brethren the priests, and for themselves. 21 And the children of Israel that were come again out of the captivity, and all such as had

separated themselves unto them from the filthiness of the nations of the land, to seek Jehovah, the God of Israel, did eat, 22 and kept the feast of unleavened bread seven days with joy: for Jehovah had made them joyful, and had turned the heart of the king of Assyria unto them, to strengthen their hands in the work of the house of God, the God of Israel.

Events of this part of the book of Ezra were contemporary with Haggai and Zechariah. During the second year of the reign of Darius I (520 B.C.) these prophets gave great impetus and inspiration to the resumption of the building of the temple (v. 2).

During this time the Persian governor in control of the territory of Syria and Palestine arrived to make an inspection of the activity. The governor, Tattenai by name, was unsatisfied with the explanation given by the Jews and sent to Darius I for counsel and instructions (vv. 6-17). The reply which the governor received from Darius was favorable to the Jews (6:1-12). Tattenai was instructed to give assistance wherever possible. He was to avoid any further interruption in the construction and building.

As a result of the dynamic influence of Haggai and Zechariah and the secular impetus of Darius I and Tattenai, the temple was completed within five years (515 B.C.). **And this house was finished on the third day of the month . . . in the sixth year of the reign of Darius the king** (v. 15). Upon completion of the temple the Passover was observed as part of the activity of dedication. Only those who were pure, that is, who had separated themselves from the ceremonially unclean people, were permitted to join in the Passover (vv. 20-21). The problem was not one between races, that is, between Jews and non-Jews, although that was involved. The problem was the worship of Jehovah according to the ceremonial requirements of the law. This cultic worship was threatened with pollution and adulteration by the participation of ceremonially unclean idolators.

The problem is a perennial one. How is cultic purity to be preserved without becoming so exclusive as to fail in fulfilling the divine call to be a blessing to all people? Christians who are aware of the delicate and sensitive problem of maintaining contact with non-Christians perpetually face this.

III. REFORM UNDER EZRA (Ezra 7:1— 10:44)

One of the most perplexing problems of the post-exilic period is the date of Ezra's arrival in Jerusalem. According to the textual evidence of Ezra 7:7, his arrival was in the seventh year of Artaxerxes. If this was Artaxerxes I, the date was 458 B.C. This, at least, provides a starting-point for Ezra's reform, according to the textual evidence immediately available.

A. GENEALOGY OF EZRA (7:1-10; cf. I Esdras 8:1-8)

1 Now after these things, in the reign of Artaxerxes king of Persia, Ezra the son of Seraiah, the son of Azariah, the son of Hilkiah, 2 the son of Shallum, the son of Zadok, the son of Ahitub, 3 the son of Amariah, the son of Azariah, the son of Meraioth, 4 the son of Zerahiah, the son of Uzzi, the son of Bukki, 5 the son of Abishua, the son of Phinehas, the son of Eleazar, the son of Aaron the chief priest— 6 this Ezra went up from Babylon. And he was a ready scribe in the law of Moses, which Jehovah, the God of Israel, had given; and the king granted him all his request, according to the hand of Jehovah his God upon him. 7 And there went up some of the children of Israel, and of the priests, and the Levites, and the singers, and the porters, and the Nethinim, unto Jerusalem, in the seventh year of Artaxerxes the king. 8 And he came to Jerusalem in the fifth month, which was in the seventh year of the king. 9 For upon the first *day* of the first month began he to go up from Babylon; and on the first *day* of the fifth month came he to Jerusalem, according to the good hand of his God upon him. 10 For Ezra had set his heart to seek the law of Jehovah, and to do it, and to teach in Israel statutes and ordinances.

The purpose of this genealogy is to show that Ezra was of the line of Aaron, the first high priest (v. 5). Being of the priestly line of Aaron greatly enhanced the genealogy of Ezra. Furthermore, he was a scribe (v. 6). During the time of Ezra, this designation was applied to those concerned with copying and interpreting the sacred law. "The name of Ezra is associated with the development of 'the scribe'. . . . He was the typical representative and. . . . founder of the later type of scribes."[1] Ezra greatly enhanced the position and authority of the scribes. A satisfactory, although concise, explanation is to be found in the following words: **For Ezra had set his heart to seek the law of Jehovah, and to do it, and to teach in Israel statutes and ordinances** (v. 10). He was the ideal Jewish scribe, dedicated to a threefold task: seeking to know the law, striving to obey it, and teaching it to others.

B. COMMISSION BY ARTAXERXES (7:11-28; cf. I Esdras 8:8-24)

11 Now this is the copy of the letter that the king Artaxerxes gave unto Ezra the priest, the scribe, even the scribe of the words of the commandments of Jehovah, and of his statutes to Israel: 12 Artaxerxes, king of kings, unto Ezra the priest, the scribe of the law of the God of heaven, perfect and so forth. 13 I make a decree, that all they of the people of Israel, and their priests and the Levites, in my realm, that are minded of their own free will to go to Jerusalem, go with thee. 14 Forasmuch as thou art sent of the king and his seven counsellors, to inquire concerning Judah and Jerusalem, according to the law of thy God which is in thy hand, 15 and to carry the silver and gold, which the king and his counsellors have freely offered unto the God of Israel, whose habitation is in Jerusalem, 16 and all the silver and gold that thou shalt find in all the province of Babylon, with the freewill-offering of the people, and of the priests, offering willingly for the house of their God which is in Jerusalem; 17 therefore thou shalt with all diligence buy with this money bullocks, rams, lambs, with their meal-offerings and their drink-offerings, and shalt offer them upon the altar of the house of your God which is in Jerusalem. 18 And whatsoever shall seem good to thee and to thy brethren to do with the rest of the silver and the gold, that do ye after the will of your God. 19 And the vessels that are given thee for the service of the house of thy God, deliver thou before the God of Jerusalem. 20 And whatsoever more shall be needful for the house of thy God, which thou shalt have

occasion to bestow, bestow it out of the king's treasure-house. 21 And I, even I Artaxerxes the king, do make a decree to all the treasurers that are beyond the River, that whatsoever Ezra the priest, the scribe of the law of the God of heaven, shall require of you, it be done with all diligence, 22 unto a hundred talents of silver, and to a hundred measures of wheat, and to a hundred baths of wine, and to a hundred baths of oil, and salt without prescribing how much. 23 Whatsoever is commanded by the God of heaven, let it be done exactly for the house of the God of heaven; for why should there be wrath against the realm of the king and his sons? 24 Also we certify you, that touching any of the priests and Levites, the singers, porters, Nethinim, or servants of this house of God, it shall not be lawful to impose tribute, custom, or toll, upon them. 25 And thou, Ezra, after the wisdom of thy God that is in thy hand, appoint magistrates and judges, who may judge all the people that are beyond the River, all such as know the laws of thy God; and teach ye him that knoweth them not. 26 And whosoever will not do the law of thy God, and the law of the king, let judgment be executed upon him with all diligence, whether it be unto death, or to banishment, or to confiscation of goods, or to imprisonment.

27 Blessed be Jehovah, the God of our fathers, who hath put such a thing as this in the king's heart, to beautify the house of Jehovah which is in Jerusalem; 28 and hath extended lovingkindness unto me before the king, and his counsellors, and before all the king's mighty princes. And I was strengthened according to the hand of Jehovah my God upon me, and I gathered together out of Israel chief men to go up with me.

Artaxerxes made a decree commissioning Ezra to return to Jerusalem in order to propagate the law of Jehovah. Permission was also given for a considerable company of Jews to make the journey with him (v. 13).

Ezra's commission included authority to teach and enforce the law. **Whosoever will not do the law of thy God, and the law of the king, let judgment be executed upon him with all diligence** (v. 26). Judgment included confiscation, imprisonment, banishment or death. Ezra was

---

[1] H. E. Ryle, "Ezra and Nehemiah," *The Cambridge Bible for Schools and Colleges,* ed. J. J. S. Perowne, p. 89.

given powerful authority to enforce his reforms and to require conformity to the Levitical law. All of this authority greatly aided him in the outward efforts of reform. While it enabled control of outward appearances, it was powerless to penetrate inwardly to the moods and dispositions of the people. This is the continual limitation of legalistic reforms, even though they do have a place.

C. CARAVAN TO JERUSALEM (8:1-36; cf. I Esdras 8:28-64)

1 Now these are the heads of their fathers' *houses,* and this is the genealogy of them that went up with me from Babylon, in the reign of Artaxerxes the king: 2 Of the sons of Phinehas, Gershom. Of the sons of Ithamar, Daniel. Of the sons of David, Hattush. 3 Of the sons of Shecaniah, of the sons of Parosh, Zechariah; and with him were reckoned by genealogy of the males a hundred and fifty. 4 Of the sons of Pahath-moab, Eliehoenai the son of Zerahiah; and with him two hundred males. 5 Of the sons of Shecaniah, the son of Jahaziel; and with him three hundred males. 6 And of the sons of Adin, Ebed the son of Jonathan; and with him fifty males. 7 And of the sons of Elam, Jeshaiah the son of Athaliah; and with him seventy males. 8 And of the sons of Shephatiah, Zebadiah the son of Michael; and with him fourscore males. 9 Of the sons of Joab, Obadiah the son of Jehiel; and with him two hundred and eighteen males. 10 And of the sons of Shelomith, the son of Josiphiah; and with him a hundred and threescore males. 11 And of the sons of Bebai, Zechariah the son of Bebai; and with him twenty and eight males. 12 And of the sons of Azgad, Johanan the son of Hakkatan; and with him a hundred and ten males. 13 And of the sons of Adonikam, *that were* the last; and these are their names: Eliphelet, Jeuel, and Shemaiah; and with them threescore males. 14 And of the sons of Bigvai, Uthai and Zabbud; and with them seventy males.

15 And I gathered them together to the river that runneth to Ahava; and there we encamped three days: and I viewed the people, and the priests, and found there none of the sons of Levi. 16 Then sent I for Eliezer, for Ariel, for Shemaiah, and for Elnathan, and for Jarib, and for Elnathan, and for Nathan, and for Zechariah, and for Meshullam, chief men; also for Joiarib, and for Elnathan, who were teachers. 17 And I sent them forth unto Iddo the chief at the place Casiphia; and I told them what they should say unto Iddo, *and* his brethren the Nethinim, at the place Casiphia, that they should bring unto us ministers for the house of our God. 18 And according to the good hand of our God upon us they brought us a man of discretion, of the sons of Mahli, the son of Levi, the son of Israel; and Sherebiah, with his sons and his brethren, eighteen; 19 and Hashabiah, and with him Jeshaiah of the sons of Merari, his brethren and their sons, twenty; 20 and of the Nethinim, whom David and the princes had given for the service of the Levites, two hundred and twenty Nethinim: all of them were mentioned by name.

21 Then I proclaimed a fast there, at the river Ahava, that we might humble ourselves before our God, to seek of him a straight way for us, and for our little ones, and for all our substance. 22 For I was ashamed to ask of the king a band of soldiers and horsemen to help us against the enemy in the way, because we had spoken unto the king, saying, The hand of our God is upon all them that seek him, for good; but his power and his wrath is against all them that forsake him. 23 So we fasted and besought our God for this: and he was entreated of us.

24 Then I set apart twelve of the chiefs of the priests, even Sherebiah, Hashabiah, and ten of their brethren with them, 25 and weighed unto them the silver and the gold, and the vessels, even the offering for the house of our God, which the king, and his counsellors, and his princes, and all Israel there present, had offered: 26 I weighed into their hand six hundred and fifty talents of silver, and silver vessels a hundred talents; of gold a hundred talents; 27 and twenty bowls of gold, of a thousand darics; and two vessels of fine bright brass, precious as gold. 28 And I said unto them, Ye are holy unto Jehovah, and the vessels are holy; and the silver and the gold are a freewill-offering unto Jehovah, the God of your fathers. 29 Watch ye, and keep them, until ye weigh them before the chiefs of the priests and the Levites, and the princes of the fathers' *houses* of Israel, at Jerusalem, in the chambers of the house of Jehovah. 30 So the priests and the Levites received the weight of the silver and the gold, and the vessels, to bring them to Jerusalem unto the house of our God.

31 Then we departed from the river Ahava on the twelfth *day* of the first month, to go unto Jerusalem: and the

hand of our God was upon us, and he delivered us from the hand of the enemy and the lier-in-wait by the way. 32 And we came to Jerusalem, and abode there three days. 33 And on the fourth day the silver and the gold and the vessels were weighed in the house of our God into the hand of Meremoth the son of Uriah the priest (and with him was Eleazar the son of Phinehas: and with them was Jozabad the son of Jeshua, and Noadiah the son of Binnui, the Levites) —34 the whole by number and by weight: and all the weight was written at that time.

35 The children of the captivity, that were come out of exile, offered burnt-offerings unto the God of Israel, twelve bullocks for all Israel, ninety and six rams, seventy and seven lambs, twelve he-goats for a sin-offering: all this was a burnt-offering unto Jehovah. 36 And they delivered the king's commissions unto the king's satraps, and to the governors beyond the River: and they furthered the people and the house of God.

Ezra gathered together those who were ready to journey with him to Jerusalem. Their purpose was to build a new community thoroughly indoctrinated in the law of God. The register of those who made the journey is given in verses 1-14.

One of the important ceremonies in preparation for the journey was Ezra's proclamation of a fast. Aware of the perils of the journey, he sought divine protection (vv. 21-22). In the course of the travel, the caravan may have encountered roving bands of robbers, but it successfully resisted any attacks (v. 31). Upon reaching Jerusalem, gifts were placed in the temple and a great burnt-offering was offered to the Lord (v. 35). It is always a mark of character to give thanks for protection and for kindness shown. These Jews gave thanks to God for reaching their destination safely.

D. REPORT OF THE PRINCES (9:1-4; cf. I Esdras 8:68-72)

1 Now when these things were done, the princes drew near unto me, saying, The people of Israel, and the priests and the Levites, have not separated themselves from the peoples of the lands, *doing* according to their abominations, even of the Canaanites, the Hittites, the Perizzites, the Jebusites, the Ammonites, the Moabites, the Egyptians, and the Amorites. 2 For they have taken of their daughters for themselves and for their sons, so that the holy seed have mingled themselves with the peoples of the lands: yea, the hand of the princes and rulers hath been chief in this trespass. 3 And when I heard this thing, I rent my garment and my robe, and plucked off the hair of my head and of my beard, and sat down confounded. 4 Then were assembled unto me every one that trembled at the words of the God of Israel, because of the trespass of them of the captivity; and I sat confounded until the evening oblation.

Before Ezra was ready to proceed with instruction in the law of God, he was informed of a situation which shocked him. Priests, Levites, public officials and leading citizens had mingled with the people of the land and married their women (v. 2).

E. REMORSE OF EZRA (9:5-15; cf. I Esdras 8:73-90)

5 And at the evening oblation I arose up from my humiliation, even with my garment and my robe rent; and I fell upon my knees, and spread out my hands unto Jehovah my God; 6 and I said, O my God, I am ashamed and blush to lift up my face to thee, my God; for our iniquities are increased over our head, and our guiltiness is grown up unto the heavens. 7 Since the days of our fathers we have been exceeding guilty unto this day; and for our iniquities have we, our kings, and our priests, been delivered into the hand of the kings of the lands, to the sword, to captivity, and to plunder, and to confusion of face, as it is this day. 8 And now for a little moment grace hath been showed from Jehovah our God, to leave us a remnant to escape, and to give us a nail in his holy place, that our God may lighten our eyes, and give us a little reviving in our bondage. 9 For we are bondmen; yet our God hath not forsaken us in our bondage, but hath extended lovingkindness unto us in the sight of the kings of Persia, to give us a reviving, to set up the house of our God, and to repair the ruins thereof, and to give us a wall in Judah and in Jerusalem. 10 And now, O our God, what shall we say after this? for we have forsaken thy commandments, 11 which thou hast commanded by thy servants the prophets, saying, The land, unto which ye go to possess it, is an unclean land through the uncleanness of

the peoples of the lands, through their abominations, which have filled it from one end to another with their filthiness: 12 now therefore give not your daughters unto their sons, neither take their daughters unto your sons, nor seek their peace or their prosperity for ever; that ye may be strong, and eat the good of the land, and leave it for an inheritance to your children for ever. 13 And after all that is come upon us for our evil deeds, and for our great guilt, seeing that thou our God hast punished us less than our iniquities deserve, and hast given us such a remnant, 14 shall we again break thy commandments, and join in affinity with the peoples that do these abominations? wouldest not thou be angry with us till thou hadst consumed us, so that there should be no remnant, nor any to escape? 15 O Jehovah, the God of Israel, thou art righteous; for we are left a remnant that is escaped, as it is this day: behold, we are before thee in our guiltiness; for none can stand before thee because of this.

Ezra's remorse was expressed in a prayer which included elements of confession and exhortation. He began with a confession of the wickedness of intermarriage in the sight of God (v. 6). He continued with an explanation for the exile and restoration (vv. 7-9). The exile was punishment for the sins of the people. Yet a remnant had been restored by the mercy of God. Ezra next referred to the law against intermarriage (vv. 10-12). His generation had sinned by violating this law. Finally, Ezra inquired as to whether or not God would annihilate the remnant (vv. 13-15). Here was earnest, intercessory prayer. Notwithstanding the peril which threatened the remnant, Ezra identified himself with the transgressors and prayed to God for forgiveness. This is truly a great example of intercession.

F. REFORM OF THE PEOPLE (10:1-17; cf. I Esdras 8:91—9:18)

1 Now while Ezra prayed and made confession, weeping and casting himself down before the house of God, there was gathered together unto him out of Israel a very great assembly of men and women and children; for the people wept very sore. 2 And Shecaniah the son of Jehiel, one of the sons of Elam, answered and said unto Ezra, We have trespassed against our God, and have married foreign women of the peoples of the land:

yet now there is hope for Israel concerning this thing. 3 Now therefore let us make a covenant with our God to put away all the wives, and such as are born of them, according to the counsel of my lord, and of those that tremble at the commandment of our God; and let it be done according to the law. 4 Arise; for the matter belongeth unto thee, and we are with thee: be of good courage, and do it.

5 Then arose Ezra, and made the chiefs of the priests, the Levites, and all Israel, to swear that they would do according to this word. So they sware. 6 Then Ezra rose up from before the house of God, and went into the chamber of Jehohanan the son of Eliashib: and when he came thither, he did eat no bread, nor drink water; for he mourned because of the trespass of them of the captivity. 7 And they made proclamation throughout Judah and Jerusalem unto all the children of the captivity, that they should gather themselves together unto Jerusalem; 8 and that whosoever came not within three days, according to the counsel of the princes and the elders, all his substance should be forfeited, and himself separated from the assembly of the captivity.

9 Then all the men of Judah and Benjamin gathered themselves together unto Jerusalem within the three days (it was the ninth month, on the twentieth day of the month); and all the people sat in the broad place before the house of God, trembling because of this matter, and for the great rain. 10 And Ezra the priest stood up, and said unto them, Ye have trespassed, and have married foreign women, to increase the guilt of Israel. 11 Now therefore make confession unto Jehovah, the God of your fathers, and do his pleasure; and separate yourselves from the peoples of the land, and from the foreign women. 12 Then all the assembly answered and said with a loud voice, As thou hast said concerning us, so must we do. 13 But the people are many, and it is a time of much rain, and we are not able to stand without: neither is this a work of one day or two; for we have greatly transgressed in this matter. 14 Let now our princes be appointed for all the assembly, and let all them that are in our cities that have married foreign women come at appointed times, and with them the elders of every city, and the judges thereof, until the fierce wrath of our God be turned from us, until this matter be despatched. 15 Only Jonathan the son of Asahel and Jahzeiah the son of Tikvah

stood up against this *matter*: and Meshullam and Shabbethai the Levite helped them.

16 And the children of the captivity did so. And Ezra the priest, *with* certain heads of fathers' *houses*, after their fathers' houses, and all of them by their names, were set apart; and they sat down in the first day of the tenth month to examine the matter. 17 And they made an end with all the men that had married foreign women by the first day of the first month.

The effect of Ezra's prayer on the people was very great. They feared that God would destroy them. One of the people, Shecaniah, suggested to Ezra that the way to escape the judgment of the Lord upon intermarriage was to have all the offenders separate themselves from their foreign wives and children (vv. 2, 3).

Ezra was called upon to lead the reform (v. 4). His first step was to secure an oath of allegiance from the priests, Levites and elders of the people (v. 5). Successive steps included a proclamation for all to assemble at the temple within three days (vv. 7-8). At the assembly Ezra called upon the people to make confession (vv. 10-11). He also called for the formal dissolution of the mixed marriages (v. 11).

The assembly approved a court of inquiry to deal with those involved in mixed marriages (v. 14). With Ezra as a member, this court proceeded to dissolve the mixed marriages. The work was completed in two months (vv. 16-17).

G. REGISTER OF THE MIXED MARRIAGES (10:18-44; cf. I Esdras 9:19-36)

18 And among the sons of the priests there were found that had married foreign women: *namely*, of the sons of Jeshua, the son of Jozadak, and his brethren, Maaseiah, and Eliezer, and Jarib, and Gedaliah. 19 And they gave their hand that they would put away their wives; and being guilty, *they offered* a ram of the flock for their guilt. 20 And of the sons of Immer: Hanani and Zebadiah. 21 And of the sons of Harim: Maaseiah, and Elijah, and Shemaiah, and Jehiel, and Uzziah. 22 And of the sons of Pashhur: Elioenai, Maaseiah, Ishmael, Nethanel, Jozabad, and Elasah.

23 And of the Levites: Jozabad, and Shimei, and Kelaiah (the same is Kelita), Pethahiah, Judah, and Eliezer.

24 And of the singers: Eliashib. And of the porters: Shallum, and Telem, and Uri.

25 And of Israel: Of the sons of Parosh: Ramiah, and Izziah, and Malchijah, and Mijamin, and Eleazar, and Malchijah, and Benaiah. 26 And of the sons of Elam: Mattaniah, Zechariah, and Jehiel, and Abdi, and Jeremoth, and Elijah. 27 And of the sons of Zattu: Elioenai, Eliashib, Mattaniah, and Jeremoth, and Zabad, and Aziza. 28 And of the sons of Bebai: Jehohanan, Hananiah, Zabbai, Athlai. 29 And of the sons of Bani: Meshullam, Malluch, and Adaiah, Jashub, and Sheal, Jeremoth. 30 And of the sons of Pahathmoab: Adna, and Chelal, Benaiah, Maaseiah, Mattaniah, Bezalel, and Binnui, and Manasseh. 31 And of the sons of Harim: Eliezer, Isshijah, Malchijah, Shemaiah, Shimeon, 32 Benjamin, Malluch, Shemariah. 33 Of the sons of Hashum: Mattenai, Mattattah, Zabad, Eliphelet, Jeremai, Manasseh, Shimei. 34 Of the sons of Bani: Maadai, Amran, and Uel, 35 Benaiah, Bedeiah, Cheluhi, 36 Vaniah, Meremoth, Eliashib, 37 Mattaniah, Mattenai, and Jaasu, 38 and Bani, and Binnui, Shimei, 39 and Shelemiah, and Nathan, and Adaiah, 40 Machnadebai, Shashai, Sharai, 41 Azarel, and Shelemiah, Shemariah, 42 Shallum, Amariah, Joseph. 43 Of the sons of Nebo: Jeiel, Mattithiah, Zabad, Zebina, Iddo, and Joel, Benaiah. 44 All these had taken foreign wives; and some of them had wives by whom they had children.

This list included members of the family of Jeshua, the high priest, as well as members of the priestly families (vv. 18, 20-22). Clergymen as well as laymen were involved.

Bibliography

I. Exegetical and Historical Value

Batten, Loring W. "The Books of Ezra and Nehemiah." *International Critical Commentary.* Eds. S. R. Driver, A. Plummer, C. A. Briggs. Edinburgh: T. & T. Clark, 1949.

Bowman, Raymond A. "The Book of Ezra and the Book of Nehemiah." *The Interpreter's Bible.* Eds. G. A. Buttrick *et al.* Vol. III. New York and Nashville: Abingdon, 1954.

Bright, John. *A History of Israel.* Philadelphia: Westminster, 1959.

Clarke, Adam. *Commentary and Critical Notes.* Vol. II. Reprint. New York and Nashville: Abingdon, n.d.

Complete Works of Flavius Josephus, The. Trans. William Whiston. Chicago: Thompson and Thomas, n.d.

Davies, T. W. "Ezra, Nehemiah and Esther," *The Century Bible.* London: Caxton, n.d.

Keil, C. F. and F. Delitzsch. "The Books of Ezra, Nehemiah, and Esther." *Biblical Commentary on the Old Testament.* Reprint. Grand Rapids: Eerdmans, n.d.

Pfeiffer, R. H. "Ezra and Nehemiah." *The Interpreter's Dictionary of the Bible.* Eds. G. A. Buttrick *et al.* Vol. II. New York and Nashville: Abingdon, 1962.

Pritchard, J. B. *The Ancient Near East: An Anthology of Texts and Pictures.* Princeton: University Press, 1958.

Rogers, Robert W. "Ezra and Nehemiah." *The Abingdon Bible Commentary.* Eds. F. C. Eiselen, E. Lewis, G. D. Downey. New York and Nashville: Abingdon-Cokesbury, 1929.

Rowley, H. H. *The Old Testament and Modern Study.* Oxford: Clarendon, 1952.

———. "The Chronological Order of Ezra and Nehemiah." *The Servant of the Lord and Other Essays on the Old Testament.* London: Lutterworth, 1952.

Ryle, H. E. "Ezra and Nehemiah." *The Cambridge Bible for Schools and Colleges.* Ed. J. J. S. Perowne. Cambridge: University Press, 1897.

Schultz, Samuel J. *The Old Testament Speaks.* New York: Harper, 1960.

Snaith, N. H. "The Historical Books." *The Old Testament and Modern Study.* Oxford: Clarendon, 1952.

Whitcomb, John C. "Ezra, Nehemiah and Esther." *The Wycliffe Bible Commentary.* Eds. C. F. Pfeiffer and E. F. Harrison. Chicago: Moody, 1962.

Wilson, R. Dick. "Ezra-Nehemiah." *The International Standard Bible Encyclopedia.* Ed. James Orr. Vol. II. Grand Rapids: Eerdmans, 1930.

Wright, S. Stafford. *The Date of Ezra's Coming to Jerusalem.* London: Tyndale, 1947.

———. "Ezra and Nehemiah." *The New Bible Commentary.* Eds. F. Davidson, A. M. Stibbs, E. F. Kevan. Grand Rapids: Eerdmans, 1953.

II. Expository and Practical Value

Adeney, Walter F. "The Books of Ezra, Nehemiah and Esther." *The Expositor's Bible.* Ed. W. Robertson Nicoll. Vol. II. Grand Rapids: Eerdmans, 1940.

Crosby, Howard. "Nehemiah." *Commentary.* Ed. J. P. Lange. Reprint. Grand Rapids: Zondervan, n.d.

Gilkey, Charles W. "The Book of Ezra and the Book of Nehemiah, Exposition." *The Interpreter's Bible.* Eds. G. A. Buttrick *et al.* Vol. III. New York and Nashville: Abingdon, 1954.

Rawlinson, G. "Ezra, Nehemiah, Esther." *The Pulpit Commentary.* Eds. H. D. M. Spence and J. S. Exell. Vol. XV. New York and London: Funk and Wagnalls, n.d.

Schultz, U. "Ezra." *Commentary.* Ed. J. P. Lange. Reprint. Grand Rapids: Zondervan, n.d.

Stevenson, Dwight E. *Preaching on the Books of the Old Testament.* New York: Harper, 1961.

The Book of Nehemiah

by Charles R. Wilson

Outline

Commentary on Nehemiah

I. NEHEMIAH, CUPBEARER TO THE KING (Neh. 1:1—2:8)

Unlike Ezra with his important priestly heritage and scribal training, Nehemiah was a layman who emerged from the crisis of the exile to make a memorable contribution to the welfare of his people.

A. CONCERN FOR JERUSALEM (1:1-11)

1 The words of Nehemiah the son of Hacaliah.

Now it came to pass in the month Chislev, in the twentieth year, as I was in Shushan the palace, 2 that Hanani, one of my brethren, came, he and certain men out of Judah; and I asked them concerning the Jews that had escaped, that were left of the captivity, and concerning Jerusalem. 3 And they said unto me, The remnant that are left of the captivity there in the province are in great affliction and reproach: the wall of Jerusalem also is broken down, and the gates thereof are burned with fire.

4 And it came to pass, when I heard these words, that I sat down and wept, and mourned certain days; and I fasted and prayed before the God of heaven, 5 and said, I beseech thee, O Jehovah, the God of heaven, the great and terrible God, that keepeth covenant and loving-kindness with them that love him and keep his commandments: 6 let thine ear now be attentive, and thine eyes open, that thou mayest hearken unto the prayer of thy servant, which I pray before thee at this time, day and night, for the children of Israel thy servants, while I confess the sins of the children of Israel, which we have sinned against thee. Yea, I and my father's house have sinned: 7 we have dealt very corruptly against thee, and have not kept the commandments, nor the statutes, nor the ordinances, which thou commandedst thy servant Moses. 8 Remember, I beseech thee, the word that thou commandedst thy servant Moses, saying, If ye trespass, I will scatter

you abroad among the peoples: 9 but if ye return unto me, and keep my commandments and do them, though your outcasts were in the uttermost part of the heavens, yet will I gather them from thence, and will bring them unto the place that I have chosen, to cause my name to dwell there. 10 Now these are thy servants and thy people, whom thou hast redeemed by thy great power, and by thy strong hand. 11 O Lord, I beseech thee, let now thine ear be attentive to the prayer of thy servant, and to the prayer of thy servants, who delight to fear thy name; and prosper, I pray thee, thy servant this day, and grant him mercy in the sight of this man.

The words of Nehemiah the son of Hacaliah (v. 1). With these words, Nehemiah began his personal account of the crisis in which he arose to important and responsible leadership. In a period when genealogies were very important, as evidenced by the lists in Chronicles, Ezra and Nehemiah, it is remarkably unusual to find Nehemiah's genealogy missing. Nothing more about his ancestry is known than that he was the son of Hacaliah (v. 1). It is impossible to determine from what tribe he came. Both Judah and Levi are possibilities, but there is no way, at present, to determine his genealogy. R. Dick Wilson (*International Standard Bible Encyclopedia*) intimates that Nehemiah and Zedekiah could be the "princes" mentioned in 9:38—which incidentally is verse 1 of chapter 10 in the Hebrew text. See also 2:3-5 and comments.

The process by which Nehemiah developed into a leader of his people began with the influence exerted upon him by a fellow Jew named Hanani (v. 2). He came to Nehemiah with a report of the great distress of the Jews in Jerusalem (v. 3). The incident occurred during the twentieth year of the reign of Artaxerxes I (v. 1; cf. 2:1), 445/44 B.C. It had been over ninety years since Cyrus had decreed that a temple be built in Jerusalem. Approximately seventy years had elapsed since the completion of that building.

During those years Persian culture reached its zenith, while the community of Jews in Palestine struggled to maintain a bare existence. There was decadence and disillusionment. Survival was precarious. Moreover, a catastrophe of sizable proportions had occurred a comparatively short time earlier (v. 3).

Nehemiah could have ignored the reports which he heard. He had a high and honorable position, cupbearer to the king (v. 11). Since he had no direct commission to assist in this distress, he might have excused himself. Yet he was deeply moved, and gave himself to fasting and prayer (v. 4). His concern for Jerusalem developed until it was more important than his concern for the king.

His prayer has points of resemblance with one by Ezra (Ezra 9:5-15), as well as with one by Daniel (Dan. 9:4-19). It was both a confession of sin and an appeal to the covenant promise. In the confession, Nehemiah identified himself with the wrongdoing (vv. 6-7). In the appeal, he trusted in the covenant promise, that God would gather His people to the chosen place if they would love Him and keep His commandments (vv. 5, 8-9).

B. COMMISSION BY ARTAXERXES (2:1-8)

Now I was cupbearer to the king. 1 And it came to pass in the month Nisan, in the twentieth year of Artaxerxes the king, when wine was before him, that I took up the wine, and gave it unto the king. Now I had not been *beforetime* sad in his presence. 2 And the king said unto me, Why is thy countenance sad, seeing thou art not sick? this is nothing else but sorrow of heart. Then I was very sore afraid. 3 And I said unto the king, Let the king live for ever: why should not my countenance be sad, when the city, the place of my fathers' sepulchres, lieth waste, and the gates thereof are consumed with fire? 4 Then the king said unto me, For what dost thou make request? So I prayed to the God of heaven. 5 And I said unto the king, If it please the king, and if thy servant have found favor in thy sight, that thou wouldest send me unto Judah, unto the city of my fathers' sepulchres, that I may build it. 6

And the king said unto me (the queen also sitting by him), For how long shall thy journey be? and when wilt thou return? So it pleased the king to send me; and I set him a time. 7 Moreover I said unto the king, If it please the king, let letters be given me to the governors beyond the River, that they may let me pass through till I come unto Judah; 8 and a letter unto Asaph the keeper of the king's forest, that he may give me timber to make beams for the gates of the castle which appertaineth to the house, and for the wall of the city, and for the house that I shall enter into. And the king granted me, according to the good hand of my God upon me.

Concern for Jerusalem continued to occupy Nehemiah's mind, and he considered what he should do. One day his great moment of opportunity arrived. When the king inquired as to the reason for his sadness, Nehemiah was fully prepared to state the matter tactfully and clearly. In his moment of opportunity he responded to the king prayerfully and decisively. **So I prayed to the God of heaven. And I said to the king** (vv. 4-5). In a real sense, God helps those who help themselves. Nehemiah had carefully prepared for this moment, and his prayer was that God would help him at this time. Many have realized this to be true in their lives.

If it please the king . . . send me unto Judah, unto the city of my fathers' sepulchres, that I may build it (v. 5). Nehemiah's request meant leaving the rich culture of Persia and going to a culturally sick and religiously weak land, his homeland, in order that he might devote himself to its survival. Yet his response to this challenge was eager and resolute. He was convinced that this was the call of God. **And the king granted me, according to the good hand of my God upon me** (v. 8).

II. NEHEMIAH BUILDS THE WALL OF JERUSALEM (Neh. 2:9—6:19)

Nehemiah made the journey to Jerusalem accompanied by a military escort. His arrival was not given a unanimous welcome, because there were those who desired control of Jerusalem but were deprived of their aspirations by the king's appointment of Nehemiah.

A. PROGRESS (2:9–3:32)

Nehemiah's account of the progress of rebuilding the wall of Jerusalem is in two parts: first, he gives a report of the preparations that were made; second, he lists the register of workers. He has not given a continuous report of the construction. Instead, there appear a series of vignettes giving glimpses of the work.

1. Preparation (2:9-20)

9 Then I came to the governors beyond the River, and gave them the king's letters. Now the king had sent with me captains of the army and horsemen. 10 And when Sanballat the Horonite, and Tobiah the servant, the Ammonite, heard of it, it grieved them exceedingly, for that there was come a man to seek the welfare of the children of Israel. 11 So I came to Jerusalem, and was there three days. 12 And I arose in the night, I and some few men with me; neither told I any man what my God put into my heart to do for Jerusalem; neither was there any beast with me, save the beast that I rode upon. 13 And I went out by night by the valley gate, even toward the jackal's well, and to the dung gate, and viewed the walls of Jerusalem, which were broken down, and the gates thereof were consumed with fire. 14 Then I went on to the fountain gate and to the king's pool: but there was no place for the beast that was under me to pass. 15 Then went I up in the night by the brook, and viewed the wall; and I turned back, and entered by the valley gate, and so returned. 16 And the rulers knew not whither I went, or what I did; neither had I as yet told it to the Jews, nor to the priests, nor to the nobles, nor to the rulers, nor to the rest that did the work. 17 Then said I unto them, Ye see the evil case that we are in, how Jerusalem lieth waste, and the gates thereof are burned with fire: come, and let us build up the wall of Jerusalem, that we be no more a reproach. 18 And I told them of the hand of my God which was good upon me, as also of the king's words that he had spoken unto me. And they said, Let us rise up and build. So they strengthened their hands for the good *work.* 19 But when Sanballat the Horonite, and Tobiah the servant, the Ammonite, and Geshem the Arabian, heard it, they laughed us to scorn, and despised us, and said, What is this thing that ye do? will ye rebel against the king? 20

Then answered I them, and said unto them, The God of heaven, he will prosper us; therefore we his servants will arise and build: but ye have no portion, nor right, nor memorial, in Jerusalem.

When Nehemiah arrived in Jerusalem with letters of authority, he made no grand proclamation of his plans (vv. 9, 12). Instead, his first activity was an inspection tour during the night without the knowledge of the inhabitants (vv. 12-15). His efforts to initiate the building program, which had become an insoluble problem before his arrival, indicate that Nehemiah exercised sound judgment. Careful study of his approach and methods can be invaluable to those engaged in building programs marred by the tensions of human differences.

After his inspection, Nehemiah wisely issued a call for cooperative action. This call reflected upon the reproach existing due to the state of affairs (v. 17). It also pointed out the existence of important resources, namely, the power of God and the decree of the Persian ruler (v. 18). The response of the people to Nehemiah's call was most gratifying: **Let us rise up and build** (v. 18).

2. Register (3:1-32)

1 Then Eliashib the high priest rose up with his brethren the priests, and they builded the sheep gate; they sanctified it, and set up the doors of it; even unto the tower of Hammeah they sanctified it, unto the tower of Hananel. 2 And next unto him builded the men of Jericho. And next to them builded Zaccur the son of Imri.

3 And the fish gate did the sons of Hassenaah build; they laid the beams thereof, and set up the doors thereof, the bolts thereof, and the bars thereof. 4 And next unto them repaired Meremoth the son of Uriah, the son of Hakkoz. And next unto them repaired Meshullam the son of Berechiah, the son of Meshezabel. And next unto them repaired Zadok the son of Baana. 5 And next unto them the Tekoites repaired; but their nobles put not their necks to the work of their lord.

6 And the old gate repaired Joiada the son of Paseah and Meshullam the son of Besodeiah; they laid the beams thereof, and set up the doors thereof, and the bolts thereof, and the bars thereof. 7 And next unto them repaired Melatiah the

Gibeonite, and Jadon the Meronothite, the men of Gibeon, and of Mizpah, *that appertained* to the throne of the governor beyond the River. 8 Next unto him repaired Uzziel the son of Harhaiah, goldsmiths. And next unto him repaired Hananiah one of the perfumers, and they fortified Jerusalem even unto the broad wall. 9 And next unto them repaired Rephaiah the son of Hur, the ruler of half the district of Jerusalem. 10 And next unto them repaired Jedaiah the son of Harumaph, over against his house. And next unto him repaired Hattush the son of Hashabneiah. 11 Malchijah the son of Harim, and Hashub the son of Pahath-moab, repaired another portion, and the tower of the furnaces. 12 And next unto him repaired Shallum the son of Hallohesh, the ruler of half the district of Jerusalem, he and his daughters.

13 The valley gate repaired Hanun, and the inhabitants of Zanoah; they built it, and set up the doors thereof, the bolts thereof, and the bars thereof, and a thousand cubits of the wall unto the dung gate.

14 And the dung gate repaired Malchijah the son of Rechab, the ruler of the district of Beth-haccherem; he built it, and set up the doors thereof, the bolts thereof, and the bars thereof.

15 And the fountain gate repaired Shallun the son of Colhozeh, the ruler of the district of Mizpah; he built it, and covered it, and set up the doors thereof, the bolts thereof, and the bars thereof, and the wall of the pool of Shelah by the king's garden, even unto the stairs that go down from the city of David. 16 After him repaired Nehemiah the son of Azbuk, the ruler of half the district of Beth-zur, unto the place over against the sepulchres of David, and unto the pool that was made, and unto the house of the mighty men. 17 After him repaired the Levites, Rehum the son of Bani. Next unto him repaired Hashabiah, the ruler of half the district of Keilah, for his district. 18 After him repaired their brethren, Bavvai the son of Henadad, the ruler of half the district of Keilah. 19 And next to him repaired Ezer the son of Jeshua, the ruler of Mizpah, another portion, over against the ascent to the armory at the turning *of the wall.* 20 After him Baruch the son of Zabbai earnestly repaired another portion, from the turning *of the wall* unto the door of the house of Eliashib the high priest. 21 After him repaired Meremoth the son of Uriah the son of Hakkoz another portion, from the door of the house of Eli-

ashib even to the end of the house of Eliashib. 22 And after him repaired the priests, the men of the Plain. 23 After them repaired Benjamin and Hasshub over against their house. After them repaired Azariah the son of Maaseiah the son of Ananiah beside his own house. 24 After him repaired Binnui the son of Henadad another portion, from the house of Azariah unto the turning *of the wall,* and unto the corner. 25 Palal the son of Uzai *repaired* over against the turning *of the wall,* and the tower that standeth out from the upper house of the king, which is by the court of the guard. After him Pedaiah the son of Parosh *repaired.* 26 (Now the Nethinim dwelt in Ophel, unto the place over against the water gate toward the east, and the tower that standeth out.) 27 After him the Tekoites repaired another portion, over against the great tower that standeth out, and unto the wall of Ophel.

28 Above the horse gate repaired the priests, every one over against his own house. 29 After them repaired Zadok the son of Immer over against his own house. And after him repaired Shemaiah the son of Shecaniah, the keeper of the east gate. 30 After him repaired Hananiah the son of Shelemiah, and Hanun the sixth son of Zalaph, another portion. After him repaired Meshullam the son of Berechiah over against his chamber. 31 After him repaired Malchijah one of the goldsmiths unto the house of the Nethinim, and of the merchants, over against the gate of Hammiphkad, and to the ascent of the corner. 32 And between the ascent of the corner and the sheep gate repaired the goldsmiths and the merchants.

This lengthy chapter records the various assignments of work upon the wall and the various groups which cooperated in the work. This is another one of those numerous lists which helped the post-exilic Jews to relate themselves not only to their rich heritage of the past but also to one another in their present community.

These lists were formal methods of identification with the true Jewish community. Those whose names did not appear in the listings were rejected by this exclusive religious group.

B. PROBLEMS (4:1—6:19)

The task of rebuilding the wall was enormous and every assistance was needed. However, the problems which arose added greatly to the task. These problems were of three types: external opposition, internal obstacles, and conspiracy against Nehemiah.

1. External Opposition (4:1-23)

1 But it came to pass that, when Sanballat heard that we were building the wall, he was wroth, and took great indignation, and mocked the Jews. 2 And he spake before his brethren and the army of Samaria, and said, What are these feeble Jews doing? will they fortify themselves? will they sacrifice? will they make an end in a day? will they revive the stones out of the heaps of rubbish, seeing they are burned? 3 Now Tobiah the Ammonite was by him, and he said, Even that which they are building, if a fox go up, he shall break down their stone wall. 4 Hear, O our God; for we are despised: and turn back their reproach upon their own head, and give them up for a spoil in a land of captivity; 5 and cover not their iniquity, and let not their sin be blotted out from before thee; for they have provoked *thee* to anger before the builders. 6 So we built the wall; and all the wall was joined together unto half *the height* thereof: for the people had a mind to work.

7 But it came to pass that, when Sanballat, and Tobiah, and the Arabians, and the Ammonites, and the Ashdodites, heard that the repairing of the walls of Jerusalem went forward, *and* that the breaches began to be stopped, then they were very wroth; 8 and they conspired all of them together to come and fight against Jerusalem, and to cause confusion therein. 9 But we made our prayer unto our God, and set a watch against them day and night, because of them. 10 And Judah said, The strength of the bearers of burdens is decayed, and there is much rubbish; so that we are not able to build the wall. 11 And our adversaries said, They shall not know, neither see, till we come into the midst of them, and slay them, and cause the work to cease. 12 And it came to pass that, when the Jews that dwelt by them came, they said unto us ten times from all places, Ye must return unto us. 13 Therefore set I in the lowest parts of the space behind the wall, in the open places, I set *there* the people after their families with their swords, their spears, and their bows. 14 And I looked, and rose up, and said unto the nobles, and to the rulers, and to the rest of the people, Be not ye afraid of them: remember the Lord, who is great and terrible, and fight for your brethren, your sons, and your daughters, your wives, and your houses.

15 And it came to pass, when our enemies heard that it was known unto us, and God had brought their counsel to nought, that we returned all of us to the wall, every one unto his work. 16 And it came to pass from that time forth, that half of my servants wrought in the work, and half of them held the spears, the shields, and the bows, and the coats of mail; and the rulers were behind all the house of Judah. 17 They that builded the wall and they that bare burdens laded themselves; every one with one of his hands wrought in the work, and with the other held his weapon; 18 and the builders, every one had his sword girded by his side, and so builded. And he that sounded the trumpet was by me. 19 And I said unto the nobles, and to the rulers and to the rest of the people, The work is great and large, and we are separated upon the wall, one far from another; 20 in what place soever ye hear the sound of the trumpet, resort ye thither unto us; our God will fight for us.

21 So we wrought in the work: and half of them held the spears from the rising of the morning till the stars appeared. 22 Likewise at the same time said I unto the people, Let every one with his servant lodge within Jerusalem, that in the night they may be a guard to us, and may labor in the day. 23 So neither I, nor my brethren, nor my servants, nor the men of the guard that followed me, none of us put off our clothes, every one *went with* his weapon *to* the water.

Although Nehemiah had full authority from the king to rebuild the wall, opposition arose from foes dwelling in Palestine. There was Sanballat, governor of Samaria according to the Elephantine papyri of this period. Although Sanballat was of Samaria, he considered himself a Jew and a worshiper of Jehovah. Later, a marriage by a member of his family with a member of the high priestly family of the Jews in Jerusalem strengthened his ties with Jerusalem (Neh. 13:28).

Allied with Sanballat was Tobiah, governor of Ammon. Tobiah was of Israelite origin and was a worshiper of Jehovah also. His family had come under Persian influence and had so favorably impressed the Persian rulers as to be given honors. Some members of the family line, including Tobiah, had served as governors of Ammon by appointment from the Persian kings. Both Tobiah and his son had married women of the nobles of Judah (Neh. 6:17-19).

Both Sanballat and Tobiah were accepted as Jews by the leading families of Jerusalem. Consequently, these men were angered by the fact that reforming Jews like Nehemiah considered them as heathen, having no right to the exclusive religious community in Judah.

Furthermore, these governors looked upon the building of the wall of Jerusalem as a political effort to establish Judah as a separate province with its own governor. Formation of this new province would necessitate new boundaries, with both Samaria and Ammon required to surrender some territory to Judah.

The opposition to Nehemiah involved various kinds of efforts to obstruct the building program. There was ridicule and mockery in the hope of destroying the morale of the builders (vv. 1-3). There was inciting of terroristic raids by bands of Ammonites and Arabs (vv. 7-12).

2. Internal Obstacles (5:1-19)

1 Then there arose a great cry of the people and of their wives against their brethren the Jews. 2 For there were that said, We, our sons and our daughters, are many: let us get grain, that we may eat and live. 3 Some also there were that said, We are mortgaging our fields, and our vineyards, and our houses: let us get grain, because of the dearth. 4 There were also that said, We have borrowed money for the king's tribute *upon* our fields and our vineyards. 5 Yet now our flesh is as the flesh of our brethren, our children as their children: and, lo, we bring into bondage our sons and our daughters to be servants, and some of our daughters are brought into bondage *already*: neither is it in our power to help it; for other men have our fields and our vineyards.

6 And I was very angry when I heard their cry and these words. 7 Then I consulted with myself, and contended with the nobles and the rulers, and said unto them, Ye exact usury, every one of his brother. And I held a great assembly against them. 8 And I said unto them, We after our ability have redeemed our brethren the Jews, that were sold unto the nations; and would ye even sell your brethren, and should they be sold unto us? Then held they their peace, and found never a word. 9 Also I said, The thing that ye do is not good: ought ye not to walk in the fear of our God, because of the reproach of the nations our enemies? 10 And I likewise, my brethren and my servants, do lend them money and grain. I pray you, let us leave off this usury. 11 Restore, I pray you, to them, even this day, their fields, their vineyards, their oliveyards, and their houses, also the hundredth part of the money, and of the grain, the new wine, and the oil, that ye exact of them. 12 Then said they, We will restore them, and will require nothing of them; so will we do, even as thou sayest. Then I called the priests, and took an oath of them, that they would do according to this promise. 13 Also I shook out my lap, and said, So God shake out every man from his house, and from his labor, that performeth not this promise; even thus be he shaken out, and emptied. And all the assembly said, Amen, and praised Jehovah. And the people did according to this promise.

14 Moreover from the time that I was appointed to be their governor in the land of Judah, from the twentieth year even unto the two and thirtieth year of Artaxerxes the king, *that is,* twelve years, I and my brethren have not eaten the bread of the governor. 15 But the former governors that were before me were chargeable unto the people, and took of them bread and wine, besides forty shekels of silver; yea, even their servants bare rule over the people: but so did not I, because of the fear of God. 16 Yea, also I continued in the work of this wall, neither bought we any land: and all my servants were gathered thither unto the work. 17 Moreover there were at my table, of the Jews and the rulers, a hundred and fifty men, besides those that came unto us from among the nations that were round about us. 18 Now that which was prepared for one day was one ox and six choice sheep; also fowls were prepared for me, and once in ten days store of all sorts of wine: yet for all this I demanded not the bread of the governor, because the bondage was heavy upon this people. 19 Remember unto me, O my God, for good, all that I have done for this people.

Nehemiah's problems included not only hostile enemies from the surrounding provinces but also difficulties within

Judah. For a number of years the Jews in Judah had been beset with economic problems, including famines, taxes and a variety of emergencies. Many had borrowed until their indebtedness had reduced them to the level of slaves. This deterioration of the economic situation finally reached such desperate proportions as to precipitate a crisis (vv. 1-5).

Nehemiah's methods of handling the crisis were direct and vigorous. He arranged for a face-to-face meeting with the Jews who controlled the wealth. Condemning them for trespassing against the law of usury and for trafficking in slave dealings (vv. 7-8), he appealed to them to cease from these evils. They consented to his appeal (v. 12). Nehemiah required them to take an oath and threatened any violators with expulsion (vv. 12-13).

Although his methods were rigorous, they alleviated the crisis. Yet they did not remedy the human problem of avarice. To threaten violators with expulsion is a deterrent to evil, but it is powerless to cleanse the evil heart of man.

3. Conspiracy Against Nehemiah (6:1-19)

1 Now it came to pass, when it was reported to Sanballat and Tobiah, and to Geshem the Arabian, and unto the rest of our enemies, that I had builded the wall, and that there was no breach left therein (though even unto that time I had not set up the doors in the gates), 2 that Sanballat and Geshem sent unto me saying, Come, let us meet together in *one of* the villages in the plain of Ono. But they thought to do me mischief. 3 And I sent messengers unto them, saying, I am doing a great work, so that I cannot come down: why should the work cease, whilst I leave it, and come down to you? 4 And they sent unto me four times after this sort; and I answered them after the same manner. 5 Then sent Sanballat his servant unto me in like manner the fifth time with an open letter in his hand, 6 wherein was written, It is reported among the nations, and Gashmu saith it, that thou and the Jews think to rebel; for which cause thou art building the wall: and thou wouldest be their king, according to these words. 7 And thou hast also appointed prophets to preach of thee at Jerusalem, saying, There is a king in Judah: and now shall it be reported to the king according to these words. Come now therefore, and let us take counsel together. 8 Then I sent unto him, saying, There are no such things done as thou sayest, but thou feignest them out of thine own heart. 9 For they all would have made us afraid, saying, Their hands shall be weakened from the work, that it be not done. But now, *O God,* strengthen thou my hands.

10 And I went unto the house of Shemaiah the son of Delaiah the son of Mehetabel, who was shut up; and he said, Let us meet together in the house of God, within the temple, and let us shut the doors of the temple: for they will come to slay thee; yea, in the night will they come to slay thee. 11 And I said, Should such a man as I flee? and who is there, that, being such as I, would go into the temple to save his life? I will not go in. 12 And I discerned, and, lo, God had not sent him; but he pronounced this prophecy against me: and Tobiah and Sanballat had hired him. 13 For this cause was he hired, that I should be afraid, and do so, and sin, and that they might have matter for an evil report, that they might reproach me. 14 Remember, O my God, Tobiah and Sanballat according to these their works, and also the prophetess Noadiah, and the rest of the prophets, that would have put me in fear.

15 So the wall was finished in the twenty and fifth *day* of *the month* Elul, in fifty and two days. 16 And it came to pass, when all our enemies heard *thereof,* that all the nations that were about us feared, and were much cast down in their own eyes; for they perceived that this work was wrought of our God. 17 Moreover in those days the nobles of Judah sent many letters unto Tobiah, and *the letters* of Tobiah came unto them. 18 For there were many in Judah sworn unto him, because he was the son-in-law of Shecaniah the son of Arah; and his son Jehohanan had taken the daughter of Meshullam the son of Berechiah to wife. 19 Also they spake of his good deeds before me, and reported my words to him. *And* Tobiah sent letters to put me in fear.

Nehemiah's alertness and the Jews' vigilance made possible the completion of the wall in spite of opposition. Nevertheless, Sanballat and Geshem launched a campaign of treachery against Nehemiah. They proposed that Nehemiah meet them in a neutral location in order to settle their differences (v. 2). It was an attempt to lure Nehemiah into a "trap."

His famous reply was: **I am doing a great work, so that I cannot come down** (v. 3).

Their plot having failed, Sanballat prepared an open letter charging Nehemiah with rebellion and demanding that there be a meeting to discuss this allegation (vv. 6-7). Nehemiah forthrightly denied the charge (v. 8).

Finally, two individuals were hired to prophesy that Nehemiah should seek the safety of the temple in order to avoid would-be assassins (vv. 10-11). Nehemiah discovered that it was part of a plot to accuse him of flagrant sacrilege for entering the temple.

Notwithstanding personal danger, Nehemiah continued to lead the rebuilding project. At last the wall was finished. Its completion was an overwhelming setback for his enemies. Furthermore, their ridicule changed to admiration and respect: **for they perceived that this work was wrought of our God** (v. 16). In spite of problems, Nehemiah persevered until the work was completed. It was an accomplishment due largely to God's blessing upon Nehemiah's qualities of leadership and character.

III. REGISTER OF THE RETURNING JEWS (Neh. 7:1-73a)

1 Now it came to pass, when the wall was built, and I had set up the doors, and the porters and the singers and the Levites were appointed, 2 that I gave my brother Hanani, and Hananiah the governor of the castle, charge over Jerusalem; for he was a faithful man, and feared God above many. 3 And I said unto them, Let not the gates of Jerusalem be opened until the sun be hot; and while they stand *on guard,* let them shut the doors, and bar ye them: and appoint watches of the inhabitants of Jerusalem, every one in his watch, and every one *to be* over against his house. 4 Now the city was wide and large; but the people were few therein, and the houses were not builded.

5 And my God put into my heart to gather together the nobles, and the rulers, and the people, that they might be reckoned by genealogy. And I found the book of the genealogy of them that came up at the first, and I found written therein: 6 These are the children of the province, that went up out of the captivity of those that had been carried away, whom Nebuchadnezzar the king of Babylon had carried away, and that returned unto Jerusalem and to Judah, every one unto his city; 7 who came with Zerubbabel, Jeshua, Nehemiah, Azariah, Raamiah, Nahamani, Mordecai, Bilshan, Mispereth, Bigvai, Nehum, Baanah.

The number of the men of the people of Israel: 8 The children of Parosh, two thousand a hundred and seventy and two. 9 The children of Shephatiah, three hundred seventy and two. 10 The children of Arah, six hundred fifty and two. 11 The children of Pahath-moab, of the children of Jeshua and Joab, two thousand and eight hundred *and* eighteen. 12 The children of Elam, a thousand two hundred fifty and four. 13 The children of Zattu, eight hundred forty and five. 14 The children of Zaccai, seven hundred and threescore. 15 The children of Binnui, six hundred forty and eight. 16 The children of Bebai, six hundred twenty and eight. 17 The children of Azgad, two thousand three hundred twenty and two. 18 The children of Adonikam, six hundred threescore and seven. 19 The children of Bigvai, two thousand threescore and seven. 20 The children of Adin, six hundred fifty and five. 21 The children of Ater, of Hezekiah, ninety and eight. 22 The children of Hashum, three hundred twenty and eight. 23 The children of Bezai, three hundred twenty and four. 24 The children of Hariph, a hundred and twelve. 25 The children of Gibeon, ninety and five. 26 The men of Bethlehem and Netophah, a hundred fourscore and eight. 27 The men of Anathoth, a hundred twenty and eight. 28 The men of Beth-azmaveth, forty and two. 29 The men of Kiriath-jearim, Chephirah, and Beeroth, seven hundred forty and three. 30 The men of Ramah and Geba, six hundred twenty and one. 31 The men of Michmas, a hundred and twenty and two. 32 The men of Beth-el and Ai, a hundred twenty and three. 33 The men of the other Nebo, fifty and two. 34 The children of the other Elam, a thousand two hundred fifty and four. 35 The children of Harim, three hundred and twenty. 36 The children of Jericho, three hundred forty and five. 37 The children of Lod, Hadid, and Ono, seven hundred twenty and one. 38 The children of Senaah, three thousand nine hundred and thirty.

39 The priests: The children of Jedaiah, of the house of Jeshua, nine hundred seventy and three. 40 The children of Immer, a thousand fifty and two. 41 The children of Pashhur, a thousand two

hundred forty and seven. 42 The children of Harim, a thousand *and* seventeen.

43 The Levites: the children of Jeshua, of Kadmiel, of the children of Hodevah, seventy and four. 44 The singers: the children of Asaph, a hundred forty and eight. 45 The porters: the children of Shallum, the children of Ater, the children of Talmon, the children of Akkub, the children of Hatita, the children of Shobai, a hundred thirty and eight.

46 The Nethinim: the children of Ziha, the children of Hasupha, the children of Tabbaoth, 47 the children of Keros, the children of Sia, the children of Padon, 48 the children of Lebana, the children of Hagaba, the children of Salmai, 49 the children of Hanan, the children of Giddel, the children of Gahar, 50 the children of Reaiah, the children of Rezin, the children of Nekoda, 51 the children of Gazzam, the children of Uzza, the children of Paseah, 52 the children of Besai, the children of Meunim, the children of Nephushesim, 53 the children of Bakbuk, the children of Hakupha, the children of Harhur, 54 the children of Bazlith, the children of Mehida, the children of Harsha, 55 the children of Barkos, the children of Sisera, the children of Temah, 56 the children of Neziah, the children of Hatipha.

57 The children of Solomon's servants: the children of Sotai, the children of Sophereth, the children of Perida, 58 the children of Jaala, the children of Darkon, the children of Giddel, 59 the children of Shephatiah, the children of Hattil, the children of Pochereth-hazzebaim, the children of Amon. 60 All the Nethinim, and the children of Solomon's servants, were three hundred ninety and two.

61 And these were they that went up from Tel-melah, Tel-harsha, Cherub, Addon, and Immer; but they could not show their fathers' houses, nor their seed, whether they were of Israel: 62 The children of Delaiah, the children of Tobiah, the children of Nekoda, six hundred forty and two. 63 And of the priests: the children of Hobaiah, the children of Hakkoz, the children of Barzillai, who took a wife of the daughters of Barzillai the Gileadite, and was called after their name. 64 These sought their register *among* those that were reckoned by genealogy, but it was not found: therefore were they deemed polluted and put from the priesthood. 65 And the governor said unto them, that they should not eat of the most holy things, till there stood up a priest with Urim and Thummim.

66 The whole assembly together was forty and two thousand three hundred and threescore, 67 besides their men-servants and their maid-servants, of whom there were seven thousand three hundred thirty and seven: and they had two hundred forty and five singing men and singing women. 68 Their horses were seven hundred thirty and six; their mules, two hundred forty and five; 69 *their* camels, four hundred thirty and five; *their* asses, six thousand seven hundred and twenty.

70 And some from among the heads of fathers' *houses* gave unto the work. The governor gave to the treasury a thousand darics of gold, fifty basins, five hundred and thirty priests' garments. 71 And some of the heads of fathers' *houses* gave into the treasury of the work twenty thousand darics of gold, and two thousand and two hundred pounds of silver. 72 And that which the rest of the people gave was twenty thousand darics of gold, and two thousand pounds of silver, and threescore and seven priests' garments.

73 So the priests, and the Levites, and the porters, and the singers, and some of the people, and the Nethinim, and all Israel, dwelt in their cities.

Nehemiah had led the great project of rebuilding the wall; however, few of the Jews were living within the walled city of Jerusalem. Building the wall was not enough; there must be an effort to get the people to move into the city. **Now the city was wide and large; and the people were few therein, and the houses were not builded** (v. 4).

Although the details are obscure as to Nehemiah's efforts, he launched a drive to get the people to move voluntarily. Others were selected by lot. Extended use was made of the list of those who had returned from Babylon. The list appears to have some slight variations from the one in Ezra 2.

IV. REFORM UNDER EZRA (Neh. 7: 73b—10:39)

This material forms part of the Ezra narrative, depicting events taking place after Nehemiah's first journey to Jerusalem in 445/44 B.C.

A. READING OF THE LAW (7:73b— 8:18)

And when the seventh month was come, the children of Israel were in their cities. 1 And all the people gathered themselves together as one man into the broad place that was before the water gate; and they spake unto Ezra the scribe to bring the book of the law of Moses, which Jehovah had commanded to Israel. 2 And Ezra the priest brought the law before the assembly, both men and women, and all that could hear with understanding, upon the first day of the seventh month. 3 And he read therein before the broad place that was before the water gate from early morning until midday, in the presence of the men and the women, and of those that could understand; and the ears of all the people were *attentive* unto the book of the law. 4 And Ezra the scribe stood upon a pulpit of wood, which they had made for the purpose; and beside him stood Mattithiah, and Shema, and Anaiah, and Uriah, and Hilkiah, and Maaseiah, on his right hand; and on his left hand, Pedaiah, and Mishael, and Malchijah, and Hashum, and Hashbaddanah, Zechariah, *and* Meshullam. 5 And Ezra opened the book in the sight of all the people (for he was above all the people) ; and when he opened it, all the people stood up. 6 And Ezra blessed Jehovah, the great God; and all the people answered, Amen, Amen, with the lifting up of their hands: and they bowed their heads, and worshipped Jehovah with their faces to the ground. 7 Also Jeshua, and Bani, and Sherebiah, Jamin, Akkub, Shabbethai, Hodiah, Maaseiah, Kelita, Azariah, Jozabad, Hanan, Pelaiah, and the Levites, caused the people to understand the law: and the people *stood* in their place. 8 And they read in the book, in the law of God, distinctly; and they gave the sense, so that they understood the reading.

9 And Nehemiah, who was the governor, and Ezra the priest the scribe, and the Levites that taught the people, said unto all the people, This day is holy unto Jehovah your God; mourn not, nor weep. For all the people wept, when they heard the words of the law. 10 Then he said unto them, Go your way, eat the fat, and drink the sweet, and send portions unto him for whom nothing is prepared; for this day is holy unto our Lord: neither be ye grieved; for the joy of Jehovah is your strength. 11 So the Levites stilled all the people, saying, Hold your peace, for the day is holy; neither be ye grieved. 12 And all the people went their way to eat, and to drink, and to send portions, and to make great mirth, because they had understood the words that were declared unto them.

13 And on the second day were gathered together the heads of fathers' *houses* of all the people, the priests, and the Levites, unto Ezra the scribe, even to give attention to the words of the law. 14 And they found written in the law, how that Jehovah had commanded by Moses, that the children of Israel should dwell in booths in the feast of the seventh month; 15 and that they should publish and proclaim in all their cities, and in Jerusalem, saying, Go forth unto the mount, and fetch olive branches, and branches of wild olive, and myrtle branches, and palm branches, and branches of thick trees, to make booths, as it is written. 16 So the people went forth, and brought them, and made themselves booths, every one upon the roof of his house, and in their courts, and in the courts of the house of God, and in the broad place of the water gate, and in the broad place of the gate of Ephraim. 17 And all the assembly of them that were come again out of the captivity made booths, and dwelt in the booths: for since the days of Jeshua the son of Nun unto that day had not the children of Israel done so. And there was very great gladness. 18 Also day by day, from the first day unto the last day, he read in the book of the law of God. And they kept the feast seven days; and on the eighth day was a solemn assembly, according unto the ordinance.

The last reference to Ezra was in relation to the court which was set up to dissolve the mixed marriages (Ezra 10). Meanwhile, an opportune time arrived for a major emphasis on the law. Any attempt to determine the chronological sequence would force certain issues which are beyond the scope of this endeavor.

Ezra came before the assembly of the people for the purpose of reading the law in their hearing (v. 3). As the people listened they were greatly impressed. **For all the people wept when they heard the words of the law** (v. 9). A certain sense of judgment and of guilt came upon them.

Ezra, however, was more concerned that the people should have a comprehensive awareness of God and their relation to Him than just a sense of guilt as they heard the law of God. He spoke to them, **Go your way . . . neither be ye grieved; for the joy of the Lord is your strength** (v. 10). They were encouraged to look upon the law as an occasion for gratitude and joy. To know God and His will as given in the law was the highest knowledge.

Yet, the very nature of the law is demanding. It yokes the conscience and the will with unyielding demands which human nature, being what it is apart from the Spirit of God, does not find joyful. Nevertheless, Ezra's affirmation was directed to a positive appreciation for the law and its disclosures. More than repentance for transgressions of the past is necessary. As the people look to the future, they must not forget God's law.

B. DEALING WITH SIN (9:1-38)

Ezra continued his reform through an effective teaching ministry conducted, in part, by means of public assemblies. One such convocation is referred to in Nehemiah 8, and another is referred to in this chapter.

1. Convocation (9:1-5)

1 Now in the twenty and fourth day of this month the children of Israel were assembled with fasting, and with sackcloth, and earth upon them. 2 And the seed of Israel separated themselves from all foreigners, and stood and confessed their sins, and the iniquities of their fathers. 3 And they stood up in their place, and read in the book of the law of Jehovah their God a fourth part of the day; and *another* fourth part they confessed, and worshipped Jehovah their God. 4 Then stood up upon the stairs of the Levites, Jeshua, and Bani, Kadmiel, Shebaniah, Bunni, Sherebiah, Bani, *and* Chenani, and cried with a loud voice unto Jehovah their God.

5 Then the Levites, Jeshua, and Kadmiel, Bani, Hashabneiah, Sherebiah, Hodiah, Shebaniah, *and* Pethahiah, said, Stand up and bless Jehovah your God from everlasting to everlasting; and blessed be thy glorious name, which is exalted above all blessing and praise.

The convocation consisted of reading from the law and making confession of sin (vv. 2-3). The purpose of this assembly was the signing of a declaration to abstain from mixed marriages (v. 38). This had been the cardinal sin against which Ezra stood unequivocally opposed. On the authority of the law, he rejected any compromise.

2. Confession (9:6-38)

6 Thou art Jehovah, even thou alone; thou hast made heaven, the heaven of heavens, with all their host, the earth and all things that are thereon, the seas and all that is in them, and thou preservest them all; and the host of heaven worshippeth thee. 7 Thou art Jehovah the God, who didst choose Abram, and broughtest him forth out of Ur of the Chaldees, and gavest him the name of Abraham, 8 and foundest his heart faithful before thee, and madest a covenant with him to give the land of the Canaanite, the Hittite, the Amorite, and the Perizzite, and the Jebusite, and the Girgashite, to give it unto his seed, and hast performed thy words; for thou art righteous.

9 And thou sawest the affliction of our fathers in Egypt, and heardest their cry by the Red Sea, 10 and showedst signs and wonders upon Pharaoh, and on all his servants, and on all the people of his land; for thou knewest that they dealt proudly against them, and didst get thee a name, as it is this day. 11 And thou didst divide the sea before them, so that they went through the midst of the sea on the dry land; and their pursuers thou didst cast into the depths, as a stone into the mighty waters. 12 Moreover in a pillar of cloud thou leddest them by day; and in a pillar of fire by night, to give them light in the way wherein they should go. 13 Thou camest down also upon mount Sinai, and spakest with them from heaven, and gavest them right ordinances and true laws, good statutes and commandments, 14 and madest known unto them thy holy sabbath, and commandedst them commandments, and statutes, and a law, by Moses thy servant, 15 and gavest them bread from heaven for their hunger, and broughtest forth water for them out of the rock for their thirst, and commandedst them that they should go in to possess the land which thou hadst sworn to give them.

16 But they and our fathers dealt proudly, and hardened their neck, and hearkened not to thy commandments, 17 and refused to obey, neither were mindful of thy wonders that thou didst among them, but hardened their neck, and in their rebellion appointed a captain to return to their bondage. But thou art a God ready to pardon, gracious and merciful, slow to anger, and abundant in lovingkindness, and forsookest them not. 18 Yea, when they had made them a molten calf, and said, This is thy God

that brought thee up out of Egypt, and had wrought great provocations; 19 yet thou in thy manifold mercies forsookest them not in the wilderness: the pillar of cloud departed not from over them by day, to lead them in the way; neither the pillar of fire by night, to show them light, and the way wherein they should go. 20 Thou gavest also thy good Spirit to instruct them, and withheldest not thy manna from their mouth, and gavest them water for their thirst. 21 Yea, forty years didst thou sustain them in the wilderness, *and* they lacked nothing; their clothes waxed not old, and their feet swelled not. 22 Moreover thou gavest them kingdoms and peoples, which thou didst allot after their portions: so they possessed the land of Sihon, even the land of the king of Heshbon, and the land of Og king of Bashan. 23 Their children also multipliedst thou as the stars of heaven, and broughtest them into the land concerning which thou didst say to their fathers, that they should go in to possess it. 24 So the children went in and possessed the land, and thou subduedst before them the inhabitants of the land, the Canaanites, and gavest them into their hands, with their kings, and the peoples of the land, that they might do with them as they would. 25 And they took fortified cities, and a fat land, and possessed houses full of all good things, cisterns hewn out, vineyards, and oliveyards, and fruit-trees in abundance: so they did eat, and were filled, and became fat, and delighted themselves in thy great goodness.

26 Nevertheless they were disobedient, and rebelled against thee, and cast thy law behind their back, and slew thy prophets that testified against them to turn them again unto thee, and they wrought great provocations. 27 Therefore thou deliveredst them into the hand of their adversaries, who distressed them: and in the time of their trouble, when they cried unto thee, thou heardest from heaven; and according to thy manifold mercies thou gavest them saviours who saved them out of the hand of their adversaries. 28 But after they had rest, they did evil again before thee; therefore leftest thou them in the hand of their enemies, so that they had the dominion over them: yet when they returned, and cried unto thee, thou heardest from heaven; and many times didst thou deliver them according to thy mercies, 29 and testifiedst against them, that thou mightest bring them again unto thy law. Yet they dealt proudly, and hearkened

not unto thy commandments, but sinned against thine ordinances (which if a man do, he shall live in them), and withdrew the shoulder, and hardened their neck, and would not hear. 30 Yet many years didst thou bear with them, and testifiedst against them by thy Spirit through thy prophets: yet would they not give ear: therefore gavest thou them into the hand of the peoples of the lands. 31 Nevertheless in thy manifold mercies thou didst not make a full end of them, nor forsake them; for thou art a gracious and merciful God.

32 Now therefore, our God, the great, the mighty, and the terrible God, who keepest covenant and lovingkindness, let not all the travail seem little before thee, that hath come upon us, on our kings, on our princes, and on our priests, and on our prophets, and on our fathers, and on all thy people, since the time of the kings of Assyria unto this day. 33 Howbeit thou art just in all that is come upon us; for thou hast dealt truly, but we have done wickedly; 34 neither have our kings, our princes, our priests, nor our fathers, kept thy law, nor hearkened unto thy commandments and thy testimonies wherewith thou didst testify against them. 35 For they have not served thee in their kingdom, and in thy great goodness that thou gavest them, and in the large and fat land which thou gavest before them, neither turned they from their wicked works. 36 Behold, we are servants this day, and as for the land that thou gavest unto our fathers to eat the fruit thereof and the good thereof, behold, we are servants in it.

37 And it yieldeth much increase unto the kings whom thou hast set over us because of our sins: also they have power over our bodies, and over our cattle, at their pleasure, and we are in great distress. 38 And yet for all this we make a sure covenant, and write it; and our princes, our Levites, *and* our priests, seal unto it.

Ezra used his occasions of public prayer as important opportunities to give instruction to his hearers. This is evident in his prayers recorded in Ezra 9 and Nehemiah 9. The theme of Ezra's prayer in this chapter is the lovingkindness of God to His covenant people who have been disobedient. This theme unfolds as Ezra makes a historical survey of God's relations with Israel. Seven outstanding periods are recounted in the history of Israel: the creation (v. 6), the patriarchs (vv.

7-8), the bondage in Egypt and wilderness wanderings (vv. 9-21), the occupation of Canaan (vv. 22-25), the monarchy (vv. 26-30a), the exile in Babylon (vv. 30b-35), and the return (v. 36).

Implicit in Ezra's prayer was the realization that no important disclosure of divine forgiveness had occurred since the exile (vv. 35-37). As a result, the prayer ended on a high note of faith. Since the people have confessed the sin of mixed marriages and have returned to the law, there is anticipated a notable manifestation of divine forgiveness which will usher in a new era of divine blessing and prosperity.

C. COVENANT OF OBEDIENCE (10: 1-39)

1 Now those that sealed were: Nehemiah the governor, the son of Hacaliah, and Zedekiah, 2 Seraiah, Azariah, Jeremiah, 3 Pashhur, Amariah, Malchijah, 4 Hattush, Shebaniah, Malluch, 5 Harim, Meremoth, Obadiah, 6 Daniel, Ginnethon, Baruch, 7 Meshullam, Abijah, Mijamin, 8 Maaziah, Bilgai, Shemaiah; these were the priests. 9 And the Levites: namely, Jeshua the son of Azaniah, Binnui of the sons of Henadad, Kadmeil; 10 and their brethren, Shebaniah, Hodiah, Kelita, Pelaiah, Hanan, 11 Mica, Rehob, Hashabiah, 12 Zaccur, Sherebiah, Shebaniah, 13 Hodiah, Bani, Beninu. 14 The chiefs of the people: Parosh, Pahath-moab, Elam, Zattu, Bani, 15 Bunni, Azgad, Bebai, 16 Adonijah, Bigvai, Adin, 17 Ater, Hezekiah, Azzur, 18 Hodiah, Hashum, Bezai, 19 Hariph, Anathoth, Nobai, 20 Magpiash, Meshullam, Hezir, 21 Meshezabel, Zadok, Jaddua, 22 Pelatiah, Hanan, Anaiah, 23 Hoshea, Hananiah, Hasshub, 24 Hallohesh, Pilha, Shobek, 25 Rehum, Hashabnah, Maaseiah, 26 and Ahiah, Hanan, Anan, 27 Malluch, Harim, Baanah.

28 And the rest of the people, the priests, the Levites, the porters, the singers, the Nethinim, and all they that had separated themselves from the peoples of the lands unto the law of God, their wives, their sons, and their daughters, every one that had knowledge and understanding; 29 they clave to their brethren, their nobles, and entered into a curse, and into an oath, to walk in God's law, which was given by Moses the servant of God, and to observe and do all the commandments of Jehovah our Lord, and his ordinances and his statutes; 30 and that we would not give our daughters unto the peoples of the land, nor take their daughters for our sons; 31 and if the peoples of the land bring wares or any grain on the sabbath day to sell, that we would not buy of them on the sabbath, or on a holy day; and that we would forego the seventh year, and the exaction of every debt.

32 Also we made ordinances for us, to charge ourselves yearly with the third part of a shekel for the service of the house of our God; 33 for the showbread, and for the continual meal-offering, and for the continual burnt-offering, for the sabbaths, for the new moons, for the set feasts, and for the holy things, and for the sin-offerings to make atonement for Israel, and for all the work of the house of our God. 34 And we cast lots, the priests, the Levites, and the people, for the wood-offering, to bring it into the house of our God, according to our fathers' houses, at times appointed, year by year, to burn upon the altar of Jehovah our God, as it is written in the law; 35 and to bring the first-fruits of our ground, and the first-fruits of all fruit of all manner of trees, year by year, unto the house of Jehovah; 36 also the first-born of our sons, and of our cattle, as it is written in the law, and the firstlings of our herds and of our flocks, to bring to the house of our God, unto the priests that minister in the house of our God; 37 and that we should bring the first-fruits of our dough, and our heave-offerings, and the fruit of all manner of trees, the new wine and the oil, unto the priests, to the chambers of the house of our God; and the tithes of our ground unto the Levites; for they, the Levites, take the tithes in all the cities of our tillage. 38 And the priest the son of Aaron shall be with the Levites, when the Levites take tithes: and the Levites shall bring up the tithe of the tithes unto the house of our God, to the chambers, into the treasure-house. 39 For the children of Israel and the children of Levi shall bring the heave-offering of the grain, of the new wine, and of the oil, unto the chambers, where are the vessels of the sanctuary, and the priests that minister, and the porters, and the singers: and we will not forsake the house of our God.

This was the culmination of Ezra's reform. Mixed marriages were renounced (vv. 28-30). Desecration of the Sabbath ceased (v. 31). The people pledged faithful support of the temple and its ritual

(vv. 31-39). **We will not forsake the house of our God** (v. 39).

V. REGISTER OF RETURNING JEWS (Neh. 11:1—12:26)

This passage includes four registers, their true nature being chiefly genealogical.

A. FAMILIES IN JERUSALEM (11:1-24)

1 And the princes of the people dwelt in Jerusalem: the rest of the people also cast lots, to bring one of ten to dwell in Jerusalem the holy city, and nine parts in the *other* cities. 2 And the people blessed all the men that willingly offered themselves to dwell in Jerusalem.

3 Now these are the chiefs of the province that dwelt in Jerusalem: but in the cities of Judah dwelt every one in his possession in their cities, *to wit*, Israel, the priests, and the Levites, and the Nethinim, and the children of Solomon's servants. 4 And in Jerusalem dwelt certain of the children of Judah, and of the children of Benjamin. Of the children of Judah: Athaiah the son of Uzziah, the son of Zechariah, the son of Amariah, the son of Shephatiah, the son of Mahalalel, of the children of Perez; 5 and Maaseiah the son of Baruch, the son of Colhozeh, the son of Hazaiah, the son of Adaiah, the son of Joiarib, the son of Zechariah, the son of the Shilonite. 6 All the sons of Perez that dwelt in Jerusalem were four hundred threescore and eight valiant men.

7 And these are the sons of Benjamin: Sallu the son of Meshullam, the son of Joed, the son of Pedaiah, the son of Kolaiah, the son of Maaseiah, the son of Ithiel, the son of Jeshaiah. 8 And after him Gabbai, Sallai, nine hundred twenty and eight. 9 And Joel the son of Zichri was their overseer; and Judah the son of Hassenuah was second over the city.

10 Of the priests: Jedaiah the son of Joiarib, Jachin, 11 Seraiah the son of Hilkiah, the son of Meshullam, the son of Zadok, the son of Meraioth, the son of Ahitub, the ruler of the house of God, 12 and their brethren that did the work of the house, eight hundred twenty and two; and Adaiah the son of Jeroham, the son of Pelaliah, the son of Amzi, the son of Zechariah, the son of Pashhur, the son of Malchijah, 13 and his brethren, chiefs of fathers' *houses*, two hundred forty and two; and Amashsai the son of Azarel, the son of Ahzai, the son of Meshillemoth, the son of Immer, 14 and their brethren, mighty men of valor, a hundred twenty and eight. And their overseer was Zabdiel, the son of Haggedolim.

15 And of the Levites: Shemaiah the son of Hasshub, the son of Azrikam, the son of Hashabiah, the son of Bunni; 16 and Shabbethai and Jozabad, of the chiefs of the Levites, who had the oversight of the outward business of the house of God; 17 and Mattaniah the son of Mica, the son of Zabdi, the son of Asaph, who was the chief to begin the thanksgiving in prayer, and Bakbukiah, the second among his brethren; and Abda the son of Shammua, the son of Galal, the son of Jeduthun. 18 All the Levites in the holy city were two hundred fourscore and four.

19 Moreover the porters, Akkub, Talmon, and their brethren, that kept watch at the gates, were a hundred seventy and two. 20 And the residue of Israel, of the priests, the Levites, were in all the cities of Judah, every one in his inheritance. 21 But the Nethinim dwelt in Ophel: and Ziha and Gishpa were over the Nethinim.

22 The overseer also of the Levites at Jerusalem was Uzzi the son of Bani, the son of Hashabiah, the son of Mattaniah, the son of Mica, of the sons of Asaph, the singers, over the business of the house of God. 23 For there was a commandment from the king concerning them, and a settled provision for the singers, as every day required. 24 And Pethahiah the son of Meshezabel, of the children of Zerah the son of Judah, was at the king's hand in all matters concerning the people.

B. FAMILIES IN VILLAGES SOUTH OF JERUSALEM (11:25-30)

25 And as for the villages, with their fields, some of the children of Judah dwelt in Kiriath-arba and the towns thereof, and in Dibon and the towns thereof, and in Jekabzeel and the villages thereof, 26 and in Jeshua, and in Moladah, and Beth-pelet, 27 and in Hazar-shual, and in Beer-sheba and the towns thereof, 28 and in Ziklag, and in Meconah and in the towns thereof, 29 and in En-rimmon, and in Zorah, and in Jarmuth, 30 Zanoah, Adullam, and their villages, Lachish and the fields thereof, Azekah and the towns thereof. So they encamped from Beer-sheba unto the valley of Hinnom.

C. FAMILIES IN VILLAGES NORTH OF JERUSALEM (11:31-36)

31 The children of Benjamin also *dwelt* from Geba *onward*, at Michmash and Aija, and at Beth-el and the towns thereof, 32 at Anathoth, Nob, Ananiah, 33 Hazor, Ramah, Gittaim, 34 Hadid, Zeboim, Neballat, 35 Lod, and Ono, the valley of craftsmen. 36 And of the Levites, certain courses in Judah *were joined* to Benjamin.

D. PRIESTS AND LEVITES (12:1-26)

1 Now these are the priests and the Levites that went up with Zerubbabel the son of Shealtiel, and Jeshua: Seraiah, Jeremiah, Ezra, 2 Amariah, Malluch, Hattush, 3 Shecaniah, Rehum, Meremoth, 4 Iddo, Ginnethoi, Abijah, 5 Mijamin, Maadiah, Bilgah, 6 Shemaiah, and Joiarib, Jedaiah, 7 Sallu, Amok, Hilkiah, Jedaiah. These were the chiefs of the priests and of their brethren in the days of Jeshua.

8 Moreover the Levites: Jeshua, Binnui, Kadmiel, Sherebiah, Judah, *and* Mattaniah, who was over the thanksgiving, he and his brethren. 9 Also Bakbukiah and Unno, their brethren, were over against them according to their offices. 10 And Jeshua begat Joiakim, and Joiakim begat Eliashib, and Eliashib begat Joiada, 11 and Joiada begat Jonathan, and Jonathan begat Jadua.

12 And in the days of Joiakim were priests, heads of fathers' *houses*: of Seraiah, Meraiah; of Jeremiah, Hananiah; 13 of Ezra, Meshullam; of Amariah, Jehohanan; 14 of Malluchi, Jonathan; of Shebaniah, Joseph; 15 of Harim, Adna; of Meraioth, Helkai; 16 of Iddo, Zechariah; of Ginnethon, Meshullam; 17 of Abijah, Zichri; of Miniamin, of Moadiah, Piltai; 18 of Bilgah, Shammua; of Shemaiah, Jehonathan; 19 and of Joiarib, Mattenai; of Jedaiah, Uzzi; 20 of Sallai, Kallai; of Amok, Eber; 21 of Hilkiah, Hashabiah; of Jedaiah, Nethanel.

22 As for the Levites, in the days of Eliashib, Joiada, and Johanan, and Jaddua, there were recorded the heads of fathers' *houses;* also the priests, in the reign of Darius the Persian. 23 The sons of Levi, heads of fathers' *houses,* were written in the book of the chronicles, even until the days of Johanan the son of Eliashib. 24 And the chiefs of the Levites: Hashabiah, Sherebiah, and Jeshua the son of Kadmiel, with their brethren over against them, to praise and give thanks, according to the commandment of David the man of God, watch next to watch. 25 Mattaniah, and Bakbukiah, Obadiah, Meshullam, Talmon, Akkub, were porters keeping the watch at the storehouses of the gates. 26 These were in the days of Joiakim the son of Jeshua, the son of Jozadak, and in the days of Nehemiah the governor, and of Ezra the priest the scribe.

VI. DEDICATION OF THE WALL (Neh. 12:27-43)

27 And at the dedication of the wall of Jerusalem they sought the Levites out of all their places, to bring them to Jerusalem, to keep the dedication with gladness, both with thanksgivings, and with singing, with cymbals, psalteries, and with harps. 28 And the sons of the singers gathered themselves together, both out of the plain round about Jerusalem, and from the villages of the Netophathites; 29 also from Beth-gilgal, and out of the fields of Geba and Azmaveth: for the singers had builded them villages round about Jerusalem. 30 And the priests and the Levites purified themselves; and they purified the people, and the gates, and the wall.

31 Then I brought up the princes of Judah upon the wall, and appointed two great companies that gave thanks and went in procession; *whereof one went* on the right hand upon the wall toward the dung gate: 32 and after them went Hoshaiah, and half of the princes of Judah, 33 and Azariah, Ezra, and Meshullam, 34 Judah, and Benjamin, and Shemaiah, and Jeremiah, 35 and certain of the priests' sons with trumpets: Zechariah the son of Jonathan, the son of Shemaiah, the son of Mattaniah, the son of Micaiah, the son of Zaccur, the son of Asaph; 36 and his brethren, Shemaiah, and Azarel, Milalai, Gilalai, Maai, Nethanel, and Judah, Hanani, with the mūsical instruments of David the man of God; and Ezra the scribe was before them. 37 And by the fountain gate, and straight before them, they went up by the stairs of the city of David, at the ascent of the wall, above the house of David, even unto the water gate eastward.

38 And the other company of them that gave thanks went to meet them, and I after them, with the half of the people, upon the wall, above the tower of the furnaces, even unto the broad wall, 39 and above the gate of Ephraim, and by the old gate, and by the fish gate, and the tower of Hananel, and the tower of Hammeah, even unto the sheep gate: and they

stood still in the gate of the guard. 40 So stood the two companies of them that gave thanks in the house of God, and I, and the half of the rulers with me; 41 and the priests, Eliakim, Maaseiah, Miniamin, Micaiah, Elioenai, Zechariah, and Hananiah, with trumpets; 42 and Maaseiah, and Shemaiah, and Eleazar, and Uzzi, and Jehohanan, and Malchijah, and Elam, and Ezer. And the singers sang loud with Jezrahiah their overseer. 43 And they offered great sacrifices that day, and rejoiced; for God had made them rejoice with great joy; and the women also and the children rejoiced: so that the joy of Jerusalem was heard even afar off.

On the day of dedication, the people assembled in two large companies upon the wall. Following separate routes, these two companies marched to the temple, where they participated in a combined service of thanksgiving and sacrifice. It was a time of joyousness: **so that the joy of Jerusalem was heard even afar off** (v. 43).

The dedication of the wall of Jerusalem was highly significant in depicting the diligent efforts to implement the separation of the Jews from the non-Jews. It gave a definite impetus to the particularistic tendencies of the returning Jews. The wall was an instrument of protection, and at the same time it was a symbol of separation. To the extent that it was such a symbol, the Jews were insulating themselves from other nations. However, from the inception of this special people, they were not called to be privileged recipients of divine blessing so much as they were to be special dispensers of divine grace to all people.

VII. REFORM UNDER NEHEMIAH (Neh. 12:44—13:31)

Nehemiah's concern for the welfare of the restored community of Jews in Palestine during the fifth century B.C. included not only the rebuilding of the wall of Jerusalem for the protection of the people but also the reforming of their religious and civic life.

A. REORGANIZATION OF THE TEMPLE TREASURY (12:44-47)

44 And on that day were men appointed over the chambers for the treasures, for the heave-offerings, for the first-fruits, and for the tithes, to gather into them, according to the fields of the cities, the portions appointed by the law for the priests and Levites: for Judah rejoiced for the priests and for the Levites that waited. 45 And they kept the charge of their God, and the charge of the purification, and *so did* the singers and the porters, according to the commandment of David, and of Solomon his son. 46 For in the days of David and Asaph of old there was a chief of the singers, and songs of praise and thanksgiving unto God. 47 And all Israel in the days of Zerubbabel, and in the days of Nehemiah, gave the portions of the singers and the porters, as every day required: and they set apart *that which was* for the Levites; and the Levites set apart *that which was* for the sons of Aaron.

This reform measure was aimed at giving adequate provision for the temple worship. Adequate arrangements were made to provide for the priests and Levites. Need for such reforms arose because of the mishandling of the portions allotted to the personnel which served at the temple.

Responsible leaders render a real service when they initiate reforms of this kind. Many churches are victimized by officials who intentionally or indifferently conduct the financial matters of a church in an unbusinesslike or unethical manner.

B. EXCLUSION OF FOREIGNERS (13:1-3)

1 On that day they read in the book of Moses in the audience of the people; and therein was found written, that an Ammonite and a Moabite should not enter into the assembly of God for ever, 2 because they met not the children of Israel with bread and with water, but hired Balaam against them, to curse them: howbeit our God turned the curse into a blessing. 3 And it came to pass, when they had heard the law, that they separated from Israel all the mixed multitude.

One of the important measures of Nehemiah's reform was the exclusion of foreigners from the community of Jews. Upon reading the law, it was found written therein that no Ammonite nor Moabite was to come into the assembly of Israel forever (v. 1; cf. Deut. 23:4-6). As a result of the knowledge of this law, the foreigners and strangers were separated from Israel.

C. EXPULSION OF TOBIAH (13:4-9)

4 Now before this, Eliashib the priest, who was appointed over the chambers of the house of our God, being allied unto Tobiah, 5 had prepared for him a great chamber, where aforetime they laid the meal-offerings, the frankincense, and the vessels, and the tithes of the grain, the new wine, and the oil, which were given by commandment to the Levites, and the singers, and the porters; and the heave-offerings for the priests. 6 But in all this *time* I was not at Jerusalem; for in the two and thirtieth year of Artaxerxes king of Babylon I went unto the king: and after certain days asked I leave of the king, 7 and I came to Jerusalem, and understood the evil that Eliashib had done for Tobiah, in preparing him a chamber in the courts of the house of God. 8 And it grieved me sore: therefore I cast forth all the household stuff of Tobiah out of the chamber. 9 Then I commanded, and they cleansed the chambers: and thither brought I again the vessels of the house of God, with the meal-offerings and the frankincense.

Tobiah was the co-antagonist with Sanballat against Nehemiah. As long as Nehemiah was in Jerusalem, he had resisted the efforts of Tobiah and Sanballat to collaborate with the Jews. However, after the wall was completed, Nehemiah made a journey to Persia. During his absence, Tobiah collaborated extensively with the citizens and priests at Jerusalem. Because of his royalty and because he was considered a worshiper of Jehovah, this collaborationist was welcomed into Jerusalem. The high priest, Eliashib, arranged accommodations for Tobiah in the temple precincts. These he occupied when he visited Jerusalem.

Upon Nehemiah's return to Jerusalem, he learned of these intolerable developments which had taken place during his absence. Greatly disturbed by these arrangements, Nehemiah rebuked Eliashib the high priest and ordered the temple purged in order that it might be used for its intended purpose, namely, worship of Jehovah (v. 9). Nehemiah met serious opposition because many of the Jews were collaborating with Tobiah (cf. Neh. 6:17-19).

The controversy over Tobiah was in regard to his vigorous opposition to Nehemiah's reform efforts. Exercising his civic authority, Nehemiah severed all relations with Tobiah and proceeded to strengthen his own political authority. While the religious issue was involved, the precipitating issue was civic order. Either Nehemiah was the authorized governor, or Tobiah could continue to create civic disorder.

A serious problem confronting all who occupy positions of authority is that of insubordination. The authority to rule requires the corollary of the discipline of obedience. Tobiah had refused to acknowledge Nehemiah's authority. As a result, Nehemiah exercised countermeasures and barred Tobiah from Jerusalem.

D. REFORM IN THE TITHE (13:10-14)

10 And I perceived that the portions of the Levites had not been given them; so that the Levites and the singers, that did the work, were fled every one to his field. 11 Then contended I with the rulers, and said, Why is the house of God forsaken? And I gathered them together, and set them in their place. 12 Then brought all Judah the tithe of the grain and the new wine and the oil unto the treasuries. 13 And I made treasurers over the treasuries, Shelemiah the priest, and Zadok the scribe, and of the Levites, Pedaiah: and next to them was Hanan the son of Zaccur, the son of Mattaniah; for they were counted faithful, and their business was to distribute unto their brethren. 14 Remember me, O my God, concerning this, and wipe not out my good deeds that I have done for the house of my God, and for the observances thereof.

The incident involving Tobiah was indirectly responsible for Nehemiah's discovery of a needed reform regarding the tithe. Having arranged for the purging of the temple, he set about reorganizing the temple treasury system in order to provide for the Levites.

E. SABBATH ENFORCEMENT (13:15-22)

15 In those days saw I in Judah some men treading winepresses on the sabbath, and bringing in sheaves, and lading asses *therewith;* as also wine, grapes, and figs,

and all manner of burdens, which they brought into Jerusalem on the sabbath day: and I testified *against them* in the day wherein they sold victuals. 16 There dwelt men of Tyre also therein, who brought in fish, and all manner of wares, and sold on the sabbath unto the children of Judah, and in Jerusalem. 17 Then I contended with the nobles of Judah, and said unto them, What evil thing is this that ye do, and profane the sabbath day? 18 Did not your fathers thus, and did not our God bring all this evil upon us, and upon this city? yet ye bring more wrath upon Israel by profaning the sabbath.

19 And it came to pass that, when the gates of Jerusalem began to be dark before the sabbath, I commanded that the doors should be shut, and commanded that they should not be opened till after the sabbath: and some of my servants set I over the gates, that there should no burden be brought in on the sabbath day. 20 So the merchants and sellers of all kind of wares lodged without Jerusalem once or twice. 21 Then I testified against them, and said unto them, Why lodge ye about the wall? if ye do so again, I will lay hands on you. From that time forth came they no more on the sabbath. 22 And I commanded the Levites that they should purify themselves, and that they should come and keep the gates, to sanctify the sabbath day. Remember unto me, O my God, this also, and spare me according to the greatness of thy lovingkindness.

Because there was evidence of the desecration of the law of the Sabbath, Nehemiah commanded that there must be obedience to the law. Moreover, he placed the Levites in the responsible position of enforcing the sanctity of the Sabbath.

F. PROHIBITION OF MIXED MARRIAGES (13:23-31)

23 In those days also saw I the Jews that had married women of Ashdod, of Ammon, *and* of Moab: 24 and their children spake half in the speech of Ashdod, and could not speak in the Jews' language, but according to the language of each people. 25 And I contended with them, and cursed them, and smote certain of them, and plucked off their hair, and made them swear by God, *saying*, Ye shall not give your daughters unto their sons, nor take their daughters for your sons, or for yourselves. 26 Did not Solomon king of Israel sin by these things? yet among many nations was there no king like him, and he was beloved of his God, and God made him king over all Israel: nevertheless even him did foreign women cause to sin. 27 Shall we then hearken unto you to do all this great evil, to trespass against our God in marrying foreign women?

28 And one of the sons of Joiada, the son of Eliashib the high priest, was son-in-law to Sanballat the Horonite: therefore I chased him from me. 29 Remember them, O my God, because they have defiled the priesthood, and the covenant of the priesthood, and of the Levites.

30 Thus cleansed I them from all foreigners, and appointed charges for the priests and for the Levites, every one in his work; 31 and for the wood-offering, at times appointed, and for the first-fruits. Remember me, O my God, for good.

Nehemiah's rebuilding project and reform measures were based on the conviction that if the Jewish community in Palestine were to survive, it had to maintain its exclusivistic policy. Nehemiah worked zealously for this policy when he built the wall, refused collaboration with Sanballat and Tobiah, demanded adequate provision for the priests and Levites and required the faithful observance of the law of the Sabbath.

There were influential Jews who refused to share this conviction with Nehemiah. Their opposition was not by open revolt but by subtle disregard for his policy. One of the issues was mixed marriages. The disregard which many Jews had shown caused Nehemiah to resort to public denunciations and violent actions in order to enforce his policy prohibiting mixed marriages (v. 25).

One of the most prominent and obstinate offenders was the grandson of Eliashib the high priest who was married to the daughter of Sanballat the Samaritan. Nehemiah banished him (v. 28).

This measure of forbidding mixed marriages proved to be the most difficult reform policy for Nehemiah to enforce, although he considered it of primary importance. The book of Nehemiah closes with signs of increasing tension between the two sides over this issue. There were the exclusivists who followed Nehemiah, and there were the inclusivists, such as Eliashib the high priest who officiated at the temple.

The issue tended to obliterate a greater issue, namely, that of missions and service. Nehemiah sought to retain the distinctive Jewish community by means of separation. His opponents did not see the importance of separation; they appreciated the opportunity for neighborliness with the people of the land. The greater issue confronting Nehemiah and the Jewish community was that of fulfilling the divine call to share the knowledge and lovingkindness of God with all people. This greater issue involved expendability. Every century, every country, even every Christian confronts the issue of survival versus expendability. The marvel of the Christian faith is that Christians follow One who was willing to be expendable. His sacrifice was approved by God in that He raised Him from the dead.

The Book of Esther

by Charles R. Wilson

Outline

Introduction

The book of Esther is the story of how a Jewish maiden became queen of Persia in the fifth century B.C., how Mordecai, her cousin, became grand vizier of the king, and how these two saved the Jews from an extermination plot by Haman, grand vizier of the king. The Jewish feast of Purim was established in commemoration of this deliverance from Haman's plot.

I. COMPOSITION

The book was written sometime after the death of Ahasuerus (v. 1). Since it is reasonable to identify Ahasuerus with Xerxes, the earliest dating for the book would be during the Persian period, sometime after 465 B.C. Generally speaking, there are two viewpoints regarding the time of composition. One viewpoint observes the book in terms of its authentic history and dates it comparatively near the events which it records. A second viewpoint observes the book in terms of its being a historical drama and dates it comparatively late, even as late as the Maccabean period (ca. 100 B.C.).

Approaching the story of Esther as authentic history is to date the book during the fifth century B.C. However, it is inexplicable that the story has not been confirmed by any Persian records, nor is it referred to by the New Testament writers.

II. HISTORICITY

As to the period of Jewish history between the completion of the temple in Jerusalem under the leadership of Zerubbabel and Jeshua in 515 B.C. and the middle of the next century, a period of about sixty years, the biblical record is almost completely silent. The story of Esther constitutes the main biblical source, and the events given in the book are dated in the third to the twelfth years of Ahasuerus (ca. 483-471 B.C.).

Contemporary critical studies of the book of Esther regard it as a historical novel.[1] The book does have some historical foundation.[2] Yet, it is an open question as to whether sufficient recognition has been given to the historical and archaeological confirmation of the amazingly accurate knowledge of Persian customs found in the book. There is reason to expect that the book of Esther will be recognized more and more for what its author claims it to be, namely, a recital of historical events.[3]

The purpose of the book of Esther is to provide the explanation for the observance of a festival for which no basis can be found in the law. The explanation is offered on the basis of a recital of Jewish history. For this reason, the authentic character of the history narrated in Esther is significant. Otherwise Purim cannot be considered based on a historical reality, but instead on historical drama. Such an explanation leaves much to be desired.

III. HISTORICAL SIGNIFICANCE

Since the book of Esther purports to explain the origin of Purim, it is necessary to offer some pertinent comments regarding Purim. This term is the Hebrew plural for *Pur*, a word meaning "lot." The word appears in connection with Haman's activities. "In the first month ... in the twelfth year of king Ahasuerus, they cast Pur, that is, the lot, before Haman ... to the twelfth month, which is the month Adar" (3:7).

---

[1] N. H. Snaith, "The Historical Books," *The Old Testament and Modern Study*, ed. by H. H. Rowley, p. 106.
[2] B. W. Anderson, "The Book of Esther: Introduction and Exegesis," *The Interpreter's Bible*, ed. by G. A. Buttrick *et al.*, III, 827.
[3] Samuel J. Schultz, *The Old Testament Speaks*, p. 261.

Haman had set the day of Jewish extermination by casting lots. The lot had designated the thirteenth day of Adar. However, the queen, Esther, and her kinsman, Mordecai, succeeded in neutralizing the appointed day of execution by securing from the king the right for Jewish retaliation on the same day. The result was a great massacre of the enemies of the Jews. Mordecai, as grand vizier, issued letters establishing Purim as a day of gladness.

IV. MORAL AND SPIRITUAL VALUES

Among the values which contribute to the significance of Esther and which give the story contemporary relevance is its explanation for anti-Semitism. According to the book, Haman's ugly attitude toward the Jews emerged out of an antipathy for a single obnoxious Jew, Mordecai by name (3:6). Mordecai's refusal to bow in the presence of Haman was related to another factor, namely, the separatism practiced by the Jews (3:8).

There is no doubt that anti-Semitism is a grim and scurrilous reality. Haman is representative of a line of hate-leaders who have persecuted and assaulted the Jews. The extermination of six million Jews during World War II is a shocking reminder of this criminal and inhuman disposition.

Anti-Semitism exists in the company of other inhuman antipathies such as apartheid, white supremacy, caste systems, racial discrimination and segregation The oppressions and cruelties to which human beings have been subjected because they were identified with a race, creed or color are unspeakably tragic.

The book of Esther describes in the most realistic manner the reaction of the Jews to this unjust oppression. This separatistic people was compelled to fight for survival. Esther and Mordecai did not pursue the course of separatism, regardless of consequences. Rather, they struggled valiantly and heroically to gain royal approval for the Jews. The edict granting the Jews the right to retaliate illustrates the determination and will of the Jews and their leaders to survive.

The problem which oppressed peoples face cannot be ignored. Oppression inevitably invites retaliation. Regardless of the race, creed or color of the oppressed people, the inhumanities heaped upon them create intolerable conditions. In the case of the Jews, Purim is an occasion of joy and gladness because the retaliatory actions were successful. The book of Esther does not come to grips with the ethical issues involved in retaliation. Christianity must grapple with the grim hatred which people, ruthlessly discriminated against, harbor against their oppressors in their desperate struggle to survive.

A second perennial value of the story of Esther is the courageous confrontation of the crisis by both Esther and Mordecai. On the part of Mordecai there was the clear-cut analysis of the crisis, when he sent the message to Esther, "Who knoweth whether thou art not come to the kingdom for such a time as this?" (4:14). On the part of Esther there was resolute decisiveness in meeting the crisis, "And if I perish, I perish" (4:16). Mordecai and Esther, against overwhelming odds, courageously pursued a course of action which resulted in a remarkable deliverance of the Jews. Haman's horrible plot to massacre the Jews was averted.

As a result, the story of Esther is especially favored by the Jews. Because of the outcome of the story, it has been passed from generation to generation with the same high regard which is associated with the story of Moses and the Exodus. The story of Esther is filled with tension packed events which have the capacity to shatter the courage of fearful participants, but these same events only serve to heighten the sense of purpose, as well as the resolute determination, of Esther and Mordecai.

A third value of the story is implicit in the unjust actions of Haman toward the Jews, as well as in the retaliatory action of the Jews, namely, the great need for repentance. Singularly absent in efforts to deal with anti-Semitic and other discriminatory movements is the element of repentance. Discriminatory movements, instead of fostering the spirit of humble repentance and human understanding, gender pride and intolerance. There is only one adequate remedy for such dispositions, and that is repentance.

There are great social evils of our times which need the prayers of the repentant heart. However, our repentance is often self-centered, as though sin is the act of an individual independent of others. Our repentance needs the larger dimensions of our sociological relationships in which we plead for the remission of the sins of our time which are committed wholesale, such as sins of whole races and classes against other races and classes of the human race.

Commentary on Esther

I. THE REIGN OF AHASUERUS (Esther 1:1—2:23)

Ahasuerus was the Persian ruler of the fifth century B.C. whom the Greeks referred to by the Greek name, Xerxes. The identity of Ahasuerus with Xerxes determines the dating of the events recorded in Esther during the first quarter of the fifth century B.C.

A. FESTIVE BANQUETING (1:1-12)

1 Now it came to pass in the days of Ahasuerus (this is Ahasuerus who reigned from India even unto Ethiopia, over a hundred and seven and twenty provinces), 2 that in those days, when the king Ahasuerus sat on the throne of his kingdom, which was in Shushan the palace, 3 in the third year of his reign, he made a feast unto all his princes and his servants; the power of Persia and Media, the nobles and princes of the provinces, being before him; 4 when he showed the riches of his glorious kingdom and the honor of his excellent majesty many days, even a hundred and fourscore days. 5 And when these days were fulfilled, the king made a feast unto all the people that were present in Shushan the palace, both great and small, seven days, in the court of the garden of the king's palace. 6 *There were hangings of* white *cloth, of* green, and *of* blue, fastened with cords of fine linen and purple to silver rings and pillars of marble: the couches were of gold and silver, upon a pavement of red, and white, and yellow, and black marble.
7 And they gave them drink in vessels of gold (the vessels being diverse one from another), and royal wine in abundance, according to the bounty of the king. 8 And the drinking was according to the law; none could compel: for so the king had appointed to all the officers of his house, that they should do according to every man's pleasure.
9 Also Vashti the queen made a feast for the women in the royal house which belonged to king Ahasuerus. 10 On the seventh day, when the heart of the king was merry with wine, he commanded Mehuman, Biztha, Harbona, Bigtha, and Abagtha, Zethar, and Carcas, the seven chamberlains that ministered in the presence of Ahasuerus the king, 11 to bring Vashti the queen before the king with the crown royal, to show the peoples and the princes her beauty; for she was fair to look on. 12 But the queen Vashti refused to come at the king's commandment by the chamberlains: therefore was the king very wroth, and his anger burned in him.

During the third year of his reign, Ahasuerus made a great feast (v. 3). According to the famous Greek historian, Herodotus, Ahasuerus called a great assembly at Shushan, the capital of Persia, in the year 483 B.C. to plan a military expedition against Greece. It is reasonable to consider the assembly referred to by Herodotus as the same event referred to in Esther as a great feast.

However, Herodotus saw the assembly as setting the stage for a war-crisis between Persia and Greece, while the biblical account narrates the feast as a necessary episode preparing the way for developments within Persia which were to have great significance for the Jews still in Babylon.

B. VASHTI DEPOSED (1:13-22)

13 Then the king said to the wise men, who knew the times (for so was the king's manner toward all that knew law and judgment; 14 and the next unto him were Carshena, Shethar, Admatha, Tarshish, Meres, Marsena, and Memucan, the seven princes of Persia and Media, who saw the king's face, and sat first in the kingdom), 15 What shall we do unto the queen Vashti according to law, because she hath not done the bidding of the king Ahasuerus by the chamberlains? 16 And Memucan answered before the king and the princes, Vashti the queen hath not done wrong to the king only, but also to all the princes, and to all the peoples

that are in all the provinces of the king Ahasuerus. 17 For this deed of the queen will come abroad unto all women, to make their husbands contemptible in their eyes, when it shall be reported, The king Ahasuerus commanded Vashti the queen to be brought in before him, but she came not. 18 And this day will the princesses of Persia and Media who have heard of the deed of the queen say *the like* unto all the king's princes. So *will there arise* much contempt and wrath. 19 If it please the king, let there go forth a royal commandment from him, and let it be written among the laws of the Persians and the Medes, that it be not altered, that Vashti come no more before king Ahasuerus; and let the king give her royal estate unto another that is better than she. 20 And when the king's decree which he shall make shall be published throughout all his kingdom (for it is great), all the wives will give to their husbands honor, both to great and small. 21 And the saying pleased the king and the princes; and the king did according to the word of Memucan: 22 for he sent letters into all the king's provinces, into every province according to the writing thereof, and to every people after their language, that every man should bear rule in his own house, and should speak according to the language of his people.

During the time of banqueting, the spirit of revelry mounted. In a supreme moment of ribald merriment, King Ahasuerus called for his queen, Vashti (vv. 10-11). He used the occasion of the feast to display the wealth and splendor of his kingdom (vv. 3-4). His command for Vashti to appear may have been the climax of his exhibition.

No explanation is given for the surprise refusal by Vashti (v. 12), but it appears likely that she resented being exhibited before the party. Her action, however, so angered the king that, though the occasion called for festivity, he initiated an order of business: **What shall we do unto the queen Vashti according to the law?** (v. 15).

The wise men counselled the king that because of her refusal Vashti should be banished from the king's presence (v. 19), lest their wives likewise act after her defiant example (v. 18). This counsel pleased the king, and he decreed that Vashti be deposed. Furthermore, the king sent letters throughout the empire ordering every man to rule his household (v. 22).

The subtle point involved was that the women were to submit to every rule and whim of their husbands, as Vashti was expected to submit to Ahasuerus. Such a relationship seriously jeopardizes the dignity of womanhood in any culture and in any century. A husband is not to rule his household after this manner.

C. ESTHER CHOSEN (2:1-18)

1 After these things, when the wrath of king Ahasuerus was pacified, he remembered Vashti, and what she had done, and what was decreed against her. 2 Then said the king's servants that ministered unto him, Let there be fair young virgins sought for the king: 3 and let the king appoint officers in all the provinces of his kingdom, that they may gather all the fair young virgins unto Shushan the palace, to the house of the women, unto the custody of Hegai the king's chamberlain, keeper of the women; and let their things for purification be given them; 4 and let the maiden that pleaseth the king be queen instead of Vashti. And the thing pleased the king; and he did so.

5 There was a certain Jew in Shushan the palace, whose name was Mordecai, the son of Jair, the son of Shimei, the son of Kish, a Benjamite, 6 who had been carried away from Jerusalem with the captives that had been carried away with Jeconiah king of Judah, whom Nebuchadnezzar the king of Babylon had carried away. 7 And he brought up Hadassah, that is, Esther, his uncle's daughter: for she had neither father nor mother, and the maiden was fair and beautiful; and when her father and mother were dead, Mordecai took her for his own daughter.

8 So it came to pass, when the king's commandment and his decree was heard, and when many maidens were gathered together unto Shushan the palace, to the custody of Hegai, that Esther was taken into the king's house, to the custody of Hegai, keeper of the women. 9 And the maiden pleased him, and she obtained kindness of him; and he speedily gave her her things for purification, with her portions, and the seven maidens who were meet to be given her out of the king's house: and he removed her and her maidens to the best place of the house of the women. 10 Esther had not made known her people nor her kindred; for Mordecai had charged her that she

should not make it known. 11 And Mordecai walked every day before the court of the women's house, to know how Esther did, and what would become of her. 12 Now when the turn of every maiden was come to go in to king Ahasuerus, after that it had been done to her according to the law for the women twelve months (for so were the days of their purifications accomplished, *to wit,* six months with oil of myrrh, and six months with sweet odors and with the things for the purifying of the women), 13 then in this wise came the maiden unto the king: Whatsoever she desired was given her to go with her out of the house of the women unto the king's house. 14 In the evening she went, and on the morrow she returned into the second house of the women, to the custody of Shaashgaz, the king's chamberlain, who kept the concubines: she came in unto the king no more, except the king delighted in her, and she were called by name. 15 Now when the turn of Esther, the daughter of Abihail the uncle of Mordecai, who had taken her for his daughter, was come to go in unto the king, she required nothing but what Hegai the king's chamberlain, the keeper of the women, appointed. And Esther obtained favor in the sight of all them that looked upon her.

16 So Esther was taken unto king Ahasuerus into his house royal in the tenth month, which is the month Tebeth, in the seventh year of his reign. 17 And the king loved Esther above all the women, and she obtained favor and kindness in his sight more than all the virgins; so that he set the royal crown upon her head, and made her queen instead of Vashti. 18 Then the king made a great feast unto all his princes and his servants, even Esther's feast; and he made a release to the provinces, and gave gifts, according to the bounty of the king.

The impetus for providing a successor to Vashti was the changing attitude of King Ahasuerus: **he remembered Vashti, and what she had done, and what was decreed against her** (v. 1). Whatever Ahasuerus may have been contemplating was lost in the flurry of royal activity to provide for assembling many beautiful candidates from whom the king would select one as queen, (vv. 2-4). This pleased the king.

Esther, with other candidates, was brought to the palace. Very wisely from her point of view, she heeded the counsel of Hegai, the royal keeper of the women: **Now when the turn of Esther ... was come to go in unto the king, she required nothing but what Hegai ... appointed** (v. 15).

Since the event of being presented to the king was extremely important to those entering the royal household, the young women attempted to be as attractive as possible. They hoped to impress the king and become his favorite. However, Esther's remarkable loveliness needed nothing to enhance it. **And the king loved Esther ... so that he set the royal crown upon her head, and made her queen instead of Vashti** (v. 17).

D. MORDECAI'S HEROISM (2:19-23)

19 And when the virgins were gathered together the second time, then Mordecai was sitting in the king's gate. 20 Esther had not yet made known her kindred nor her people; as Mordecai had charged her: for Esther did the commandment of Mordecai, like as when she was brought up with him. 21 In those days, while Mordecai was sitting in the king's gate, two of the king's chamberlains, Bigthan and Teresh, of those that kept the threshold, were wroth, and sought to lay hands on the king Ahasuerus. 22 And the thing became known to Mordecai, who showed it unto Esther the queen; and Esther told the king *thereof* in Mordecai's name. 23 And when inquisition was made of the matter, and it was found to be so, they were both hanged on a tree: and it was written in the book of the chronicles before the king.

This incident interrupts the main part of the narrative in order to relate an episode which vitally affects the main narrative in subsequent developments. A certain Jew named Mordecai had overheard a conspiracy against the king. Mordecai had been responsible for the upbringing of Esther (v. 7) as well as for some type of occupation at the palace (v. 5). When Mordecai sent a message to Esther, now reigning as queen, she informed the king. The conspirators were hanged, and the recording of the incident in the royal chronicles gave due recognition to Mordecai (v. 23; cf. 6:2).

II. THE PLOT OF HAMAN (Esther 3:1-15)

In the course of his reign, King Ahasuerus had occasion to promote one named Haman to the position of grand vizier, an office which ranked next in importance to the king. According to the decree of the king, all were compelled to bow to the grand vizier.

A. MORDECAI'S REFUSAL TO DO OBEISANCE TO HAMAN (3:1-6)

1 After these things did king Ahasuerus promote Haman the son of Hammedatha the Agagite, and advanced him, and set his seat above all the princes that were with him. 2 And all the king's servants, that were in the king's gate, bowed down, and did reverence to Haman; for the king had so commanded concerning him. But Mordecai bowed not down, nor did him reverence. 3 Then the king's servants, that were in the king's gate, said unto Mordecai, Why transgressest thou the king's commandment? 4 Now it came to pass, when they spake daily unto him, and he hearkened not unto them, that they told Haman, to see whether Mordecai's matters would stand: for he had told them that he was a Jew. 5 And when Haman saw that Mordecai bowed not down, nor did him reverence, then was Haman full of wrath. 6 But he thought scorn to lay hands on Mordecai alone; for they had made known to him the people of Mordecai: wherefore Haman sought to destroy all the Jews that were throughout the whole kingdom of Ahasuerus, even the people of Mordecai.

Mordecai's refusal to bow to Haman, the grand vizier, was explained in terms of his being a Jew (v. 4). This motive for refusal remains ambiguous. Nevertheless, Mordecai's refusal so stirred Haman's anger as to precipitate a most incredible plot. Haman's anger was no sudden, violent burst of passion, but a far more deadly form of anger that stalks its victim with deliberate intent to wreak terrible revenge. His plot was to exterminate Mordecai and the entire Jewish population (v. 6). He was willing to offer the king a fabulous bribe, ten thousand talents of silver (v. 9). His demented mind worked with remarkable efficiency, for, if the king agreed, Haman could pay the bribe by confiscating the possessions of those massacred.

The powerful passions of a human being can push his remarkable capacities to formulate incredible brutality. Yet, at the same time, the amazing mind of that creature can so manipulate the operation as to make it a profitable venture. Haman expected to make a fortune through confiscation. He is a clear example of the fallen condition of humanity, and the real pathos is that he gave no indication of regret for the immense wrong he had connived.

B. HAMAN'S REQUEST TO AHASUERUS (3:7-15)

7 In the first month, which is the month Nisan, in the twelfth year of king Ahasuerus, they cast Pur, that is, the lot, before Haman from day to day, and from month to month, to the twelfth month, which is the month Adar. 8 And Haman said unto king Ahasuerus, There is a certain people scattered abroad and dispersed among the peoples in all the provinces of thy kingdom; and their laws are diverse from those of every people; neither keep they the king's laws: therefore it is not for the king's profit to suffer them. 9 If it please the king, let it be written that they be destroyed: and I will pay ten thousand talents of silver into the hands of those that have the charge of the king's business, to bring it into the king's treasuries. 10 And the king took his ring from his hand, and gave it unto Haman the son of Hammedatha the Agagite, the Jews' enemy. 11 And the king said unto Haman, The silver is given to thee, the people also, to do with them as it seemeth good to thee. 12 Then were the king's scribes called in the first month, on the thirteenth day thereof; and there was written according to all that Haman commanded unto the king's satraps, and to the governors that were over every province, and to the princes of every people, to every province according to the writing thereof, and to every people after their language; in the name of king Ahasuerus was it written, and it was sealed with the king's ring. 13 And letters were sent by posts into all the king's provinces, to destroy, to slay, and to cause to perish, all Jews, both young and old, little children and women, in one day, even upon the thirteenth day of the twelfth month, which is the month Adar, and to take the spoil of them for a prey. 14 A copy of the writing, that the

decree should be given out in every province, was published unto all the peoples, that they should be ready against that day. 15 The posts went forth in haste by the king's commandment, and the decree was given out in Shushan the palace. And the king and Haman sat down to drink; but the city of Shushan was perplexed.

Haman's request that all the Jews be destroyed was based on his criticism of their separatistic manner of life: **There is a certain people ... and their laws are diverse ... neither keep they the king's law** (v. 8). Because of the tension created by the existence of a separatistically minded people in a totalitarian state, there is no tolerance possible. Unless the people devoted to separation can be made to give up their way of life in a totalitarian state, they face the wrath of those who control the state.

Haman's request was granted, and the royal decree was issued declaring the specific date on which the extermination was to occur: **destroy ... all Jews ... upon the thirteenth day of the twelfth month, which is the month Adar** (v. 13).

III. EVENTS LEADING TO THE DISCLOSURE OF THE PLOT BY ESTHER (Esther 4:1—8:2)

The die was cast. Haman had succeeded in obtaining an irrevocable decree from the Persian monarch, Ahasuerus. The execution of all the Jews had been ordered. The Jews reacted by commencing a prolonged period of mourning.

A. MORDECAI'S PERSUASION (4:1-17)

1 Now when Mordecai knew all that was done, Mordecai rent his clothes, and put on sackcloth with ashes, and went out into the midst of the city, and cried with a loud and a bitter cry; 2 and he came even before the king's gate: for none might enter within the king's gate clothed with sackcloth. 3 And in every province, whithersoever the king's commandment and his decree came, there was great mourning among the Jews, and fasting, and weeping, and wailing; and many lay in sackcloth and ashes.
4 And Esther's maidens and her chamberlains came and told it her; and the queen was exceedingly grieved: and she sent raiment to clothe Mordecai, and to take his sackcloth from off him; but he received it not. 5 Then called Esther for

Hathach, one of the king's chamberlains, whom he had appointed to attend upon her, and charged him to go to Mordecai, to know what this was, and why it was. 6 So Hathach went forth to Mordecai unto the broad place of the city, which was before the king's gate. 7 And Mordecai told him of all that had happened unto him, and the exact sum of the money that Haman had promised to pay to the king's treasuries for the Jews, to destroy them. 8 Also he gave him the copy of the writing of the decree that was given out in Shushan to destroy them, to show it unto Esther, and to declare it unto her, and to charge her that she should go in unto the king, to make supplication unto him, and to make request before him, for her people.
9 And Hathach came and told Esther the words of Mordecai. 10 Then Esther spake unto Hathach, and gave him a message unto Mordecai, *saying*: 11 All the king's servants, and the people of the king's provinces, do know, that whosoever, whether man or woman, shall come unto the king into the inner court, who is not called, there is one law for him, that he be put to death, except those to whom the king shall hold out the golden sceptre, that he may live: but I have not been called to come in unto the king these thirty days. 12 And they told to Mordecai Esther's words.
13 Then Mordecai bade them return answer unto Esther, Think not with thyself that thou shalt escape in the king's house, more than all the Jews. 14 For if thou altogether holdest thy peace at this time, then will relief and deliverance arise to the Jews from another place, but thou and thy father's house will perish: and who knoweth whether thou art not come to the kingdom for such a time as this? 15 Then Esther bade them return answer unto Mordecai, 16 Go, gather together all the Jews that are present in Shushan, and fast ye for me, and neither eat nor drink three days, night or day: I also and my maidens will fast in like manner; and so will I go in unto the king, which is not according to the law: and if I perish, I perish. 17 So Mordecai went his way, and did according to all that Esther had commanded him.

Mordecai entered upon the period of mourning and dressed himself in sackcloth. News came to Esther in the sheltered environs of the royal harem that Mordecai was attired in mourning garments (v. 4). Esther sent a messenger to Mordecai, and the messenger returned to tell her of the edict against the Jews. Furthermore, she prepared to go to the king to intercede for the Jews. With full awareness of the possible result of her act, she made her way to the king as she uttered those famous words: **if I perish, I perish** (v. 16). The most perilous moment was the instant he saw her. If Ahasuerus chose to reject her, Esther faced banishment and death. Such was the tremendous power and authority of the ancient monarch over his realm. However, when he saw her, Ahasuerus was pleased with her presence, and asked her to present her petition.

B. ESTHER'S BANQUET (5:1-8)

1 Now it came to pass on the third day, that Esther put on her royal apparel, and stood in the inner court of the king's house, over against the king's house: and the king sat upon his royal throne in the royal house, over against the entrance of the house. 2 And it was so, when the king saw Esther the queen standing in the court, that she obtained favor in his sight; and the king held out to Esther the golden sceptre that was in his hand. So Esther drew near, and touched the top of the sceptre. 3 Then said the king unto her, What wilt thou, queen Esther? and what is thy request? it shall be given thee even to the half of the kingdom. 4 And Esther said, If it seem good unto the king, let the king and Haman come this day unto the banquet that I have prepared for him.

5 Then the king said, Cause Haman to make haste, that it may be done as Esther hath said. So the king and Haman came to the banquet that Esther had prepared. 6 And the king said unto Esther at the banquet of wine, What is thy petition? and it shall be granted thee: and what is thy request? even to the half of the kingdom it shall be performed. 7 Then answered Esther, and said, My petition and my request is: 8 If I have found favor in the sight of the king, and if it please the king to grant my petition, and to perform my request, let the king and Haman come to the banquet that I shall prepare for them, and I will do to-morrow as the king hath said.

Esther's first step was to arrange for a banquet to which Ahasuerus and Haman were the invited guests. This secured her favor with the king. Because the crisis was great, she carefully sought to avoid any fatal misstep. Her astuteness in the situation is exemplary to all who face serious issues.

C. HAMAN'S RETALIATION AGAINST MORDECAI'S RESISTANCE (5:9-14)

9 Then went Haman forth that day joyful and glad of heart: but when Haman saw Mordecai in the king's gate, that he stood not up nor moved for him, he was filled with wrath against Mordecai. 10 Nevertheless Haman refrained himself, and went home; and he sent and fetched his friends and Zeresh his wife. 11 And Haman recounted unto them the glory of his riches, and the multitude of his children, and all the things wherein the king had promoted him, and how he had advanced him above the princes and servants of the king. 12 Haman said moreover, Yea, Esther the queen did let no man come in with the king unto the banquet that she had prepared but myself; and to-morrow also am I invited by her together with the king. 13 Yet all this availeth me nothing, so long as I see Mordecai the Jew sitting at the king's gate. 14 Then said Zeresh his wife and all his friends unto him, Let a gallows be made fifty cubits high, and in the morning speak thou unto the king that Mordecai may be hanged thereon: then go thou in merrily with the king unto the banquet. And the thing pleased Haman; and he caused the gallows to be made.

The main part of the narrative has been interrupted to relate the heightened tension between Haman and Mordecai. Because of the adamant attitude of Mordecai, Haman became so incensed, and so incensed his family and friends, that they suggested a gallows for Mordecai (v. 14). Following their advice and confident that Ahasuerus would concur, Haman had a gallows constructed. Spiteful anger is always perilous, since it can backlash with sudden fury.

D. AHASUERUS' RECOGNITION OF MORDECAI'S HEROISM (6:1-14)

1 On that night could not the king sleep; and he commanded to bring the book of records of the chronicles, and they were read before the king. 2 And it was found written, that Mordecai had told of **Bigthana** and **Teresh**, two of the

king's chamberlains, of those that kept the threshold, who had sought to lay hands on the king Ahasuerus. 3 And the king said, What honor and dignity hath been bestowed on Mordecai for this? Then said the king's servants that ministered unto him, There is nothing done for him. 4 And the king said, Who is in the court? Now Haman was come into the outward court of the king's house, to speak unto the king to hang Mordecai on the gallows that he had prepared for him. 5 And the king's servants said unto him, Behold, Haman standeth in the court. And the king said, Let him come in. 6 So Haman came in. And the king said unto him, What shall be done unto the man whom the king delighteth to honor? Now Haman said in his heart, To whom would the king delight to do honor more than to myself? 7 And Haman said unto the king, For the man whom the king delighteth to honor, 8 let royal apparel be brought which the king useth to wear, and the horse that the king rideth upon, and on the head of which a crown royal is set: 9 and let the apparel and the horse be delivered to the hand of one of the king's most noble princes, that they may array the man therewith whom the king delighteth to honor, and cause him to ride on horseback through the street of the city, and proclaim before him, Thus shall it be done to the man whom the king delighteth to honor.

10 Then the king said to Haman, Make haste, and take the apparel and the horse, as thou hast said, and do even so to Mordecai the Jew, that sitteth at the king's gate: let nothing fail of all that thou hast spoken. 11 Then took Haman the apparel and the horse, and arrayed Mordecai, and caused him to ride through the street of the city, and proclaimed before him, Thus shall it be done unto the man whom the king delighteth to honor. 12 And Mordecai came again to the king's gate. But Haman hasted to his house, mourning and having his head covered. 13 And Haman recounted unto Zeresh his wife and all his friends everything that had befallen him. Then said his wise men and Zeresh his wife unto him, If Mordecai, before whom thou hast begun to fall, be of the seed of the Jews, thou shalt not prevail against him, but shalt surely fall before him. 14 While they were yet talking with him, came the king's chamberlains, and hasted to bring Haman unto the banquet that Esther had prepared.

Before the main part of the story of Esther is resumed, there is the narration of an event during a sleepless night (v. 1). The king was listening to royal chronicles and heard of the earlier heroism of Mordecai (v. 2; cf. 2:21-23).

The next morning Haman waited for an audience with the king in order that he might request the hanging of Mordecai (v. 4). Not knowing that the king wished to honor Mordecai, he entered the king's presence. Before he was given opportunity to state his request, he was caused to listen to the king as he expressed a desire to bestow honor. Naturally, Haman thought that he was the one whom the king wished to elevate. Consequently, his astonishment was overwhelming when he learned that the king had Mordecai in mind (v. 10).

Upon returning to his wife and friends, Haman disclosed the incident. There was general agreement that the whole affair sounded a warning regarding the security of Haman's position. If Mordecai, before whom thou hast begun to fall, be of the seed of the Jews, thou shalt not prevail against him, but shall surely fall before him (v. 13).

E. ESTHER'S DISCLOSURE OF HAMAN'S PLOT (7:1–8:2)

1 So the king and Haman came to banquet with Esther the queen. 2 And the king said again unto Esther on the second day at the banquet of wine, What is thy petition, queen Esther? and it shall be granted thee: and what is thy request? even to the half of the kingdom it shall be performed. 3 Then Esther the queen answered and said, If I have found favor in thy sight, O king, and if it please the king, let my life be given me at my petition, and my people at my request: 4 for we are sold, I and my people, to be destroyed, to be slain, and to perish. But if we had been sold for bondmen and bondwomen, I had held my peace, although the adversary could not have compensated for the king's damage. 5 Then spake the king Ahasuerus and said unto Esther the queen, Who is he, and where is he, that durst presume in his heart to do so? 6 And Esther said, An adversary and an enemy, even this wicked Haman. Then Haman was afraid before the king and the queen. 7 And the king arose in his wrath from the banquet of wine *and went* into the palace garden:

and Haman stood up to make request for his life to Esther the queen; for he saw that there was evil determined against him by the king. 8 Then the king returned out of the palace garden into the place of the banquet of wine; and Haman was fallen upon the couch whereon Esther was. Then said the king, Will he even force the queen before me in the house? As the word went out of the king's mouth, they covered Haman's face. 9 Then said Harbonah, one of the chamberlains that were before the king, Behold also, the gallows fifty cubits high, which Haman hath made for Mordecai, who spake good for the king, standeth in the house of Haman. And the king said, Hang him thereon. 10 So they hanged Haman on the gallows that he had prepared for Mordecai. Then was the king's wrath pacified.

1 On that day did the king Ahasuerus give the house of Haman the Jews' enemy unto Esther the queen. And Mordecai came before the king; for Esther had told what he was unto her. 2 And the king took off his ring, which he had taken from Haman, and gave it unto Mordecai. And Esther set Mordecai over the house of Haman.

While Haman pondered the security of his future, the hour arrived for him to attend the second banquet with Ahasuerus and Esther (v. 1). In the course of the event, Esther disclosed to Ahasuerus, in the presence of Haman, the plot against the Jews and its significance (vv. 3-5).

Upon realizing that a sinister development had been in progress without his full knowledge of the facts and their implications, Ahasuerus became enraged (v. 7). Realizing that the anger of the king was implacable, Haman fell upon Esther's couch and besought from her a kind word in his behalf (v. 8). Misinterpreting Haman's nearness to the queen as an improper physical advance, the king's wrath was increased. Haman was ordered hanged on the gallows which he had prepared for Mordecai (vv. 8, 10).

Ahasuerus confiscated all of Haman's possessions and gave them to Esther (v. 1). Moreover, the king made Mordecai grand vizier in place of Haman, even though he was known to be a Jew (v. 2).

IV. THE DELIVERANCE OF THE JEWS (Esther 8:3—9:16)

Although Haman had been executed, the royal decree ordering the liquidation of the Jews on the thirteenth day of the twelfth month of Adar was still in effect.

A. ESTHER'S INTERCESSION (8:3-8)

3 And Esther spake yet again before the king, and fell down at his feet, and besought him with tears to put away the mischief of Haman the Agagite, and his device that he had devised against the Jews. 4 Then the king held out to Esther the golden sceptre. So Esther arose, and stood before the king. 5 And she said, If it please the king, and if I have found favor in his sight, and the thing seem right before the king, and I be pleasing in his eyes, let it be written to reverse the letters devised by Haman, the son of Hammedatha the Agagite, which he wrote to destroy the Jews that are in all the king's provinces: 6 for how can I endure to see the evil that shall come unto my people? or how can I endure to see the destruction of my kindred? 7 Then the king Ahasuerus said unto Esther the queen and to Mordecai the Jew, Behold, I have given Esther the house of Haman, and him they have hanged upon the gallows, because he laid his hand upon the Jews. 8 Write ye also to the Jews, as it pleaseth you, in the king's name, and seal it with the king's ring; for the writing which is written in the king's name, and sealed with the king's ring, may no man reverse.

Realizing the impending execution of the royal decree, Esther made intercession for her people by appealing for a reversal of the decree (v. 5). This was impossible to grant. However, the king did grant another decree which would, in effect, neutralize the former.

B. RETALIATION PERMITTED (8:9-17)

9 Then were the king's scribes called at that time, in the third month, which is the month Sivan, on the three and twentieth day thereof; and it was written according to all that Mordecai commanded unto the Jews, and to the satraps, and the governors and princes of the provinces which are from India unto Ethiopia, a hundred twenty and seven provinces, unto every province according to

the writing thereof, and unto every people after their language, and to the Jews according to their writing, and according to their language. 10 And he wrote in the name of king Ahasuerus, and sealed it with the king's ring, and sent letters by posts on horseback, riding on swift steeds that were used in the king's service, bred of the stud: 11 wherein the king granted the Jews that were in every city to gather themselves together, and to stand for their life, to destroy, to slay, and to cause to perish, all the power of the people and province that would assault them, *their* little ones and women, and to take the spoil of them for a prey, 12 upon one day in all the provinces of king Ahasuerus, *namely,* upon the thirteenth *day* of the twelfth month, which is the month Adar. 13 A copy of the writing, that the decree should be given out in every province, was published unto all the peoples, and that the Jews should be ready against that day to avenge themselves on their enemies. 14 So the posts that rode upon swift steeds that were used in the king's service went out, being hastened and pressed on by the king's commandment; and the decree was given out in Shushan the palace.

15 And Mordecai went forth from the presence of the king in royal apparel of blue and white, and with a great crown of gold, and with a robe of fine linen and purple: and the city of Shushan shouted and was glad. 16 The Jews had light and gladness, and joy and honor. 17 And in every province, and in every city, whithersoever the king's commandment and his decree came, the Jews had gladness and joy, a feast and a good day. And many from among the peoples of the land became Jews; for the fear of the Jews was fallen upon them.

As a result of the king's suggestion, Esther and Mordecai prepared a statement which was formed into a royal decree. It called for the Jews to rise in self-defense (vv. 11-12). This was a most unusual turn of events, yet it must not be overdrawn. Ahasuerus did not give his kingdom to the Jews to allow the massacre of his subjects. There were restrictions laid upon the Jews and these were carefully controlled by the king in order that he might keep this minority race under his rule.

C. THE JEWS DESTROY THEIR ENEMIES (9:1-16)

1 Now in the twelfth month, which is the month Adar, on the thirteenth day of the same, when the king's commandment and his decree drew near to be put in execution, on the day that the enemies of the Jews hoped to have rule over them (whereas it was turned to the contrary, that the Jews had rule over them that hated them), 2 the Jews gathered themselves together in their cities throughout all the provinces of the king Ahasuerus, to lay hand on such as sought their hurt: and no man could withstand them; for the fear of them was fallen upon all the peoples. 3 And all the princes of the provinces, and the satraps, and the governors, and they that did the king's business, helped the Jews; because the fear of Mordecai was fallen upon them. 4 For Mordecai was great in the king's house, and his fame went forth throughout all the provinces; for the man Mordecai waxed greater and greater. 5 And the Jews smote all their enemies with the stroke of the sword, and with slaughter and destruction, and did what they would unto them that hated them. 6 And in Shushan the palace the Jews slew and destroyed five hundred men. 7 And Parshandatha, and Dalphon, and Aspatha, 8 and Poratha, and Adalia, and Aridatha, 9 and Parmashta, and Arisai, and Aridai, and Vaizatha, 10 the ten sons of Haman the son of Hammedatha, the Jews' enemy, slew they; but on the spoil they laid not their hand.

11 On that day the number of those that were slain in Shushan the palace was brought before the king. 12 And the king said unto Esther the queen, The Jews have slain and destroyed five hundred men in Shushan the palace, and the ten sons of Haman; what then have they done in the rest of the king's provinces! Now what is thy petition? and it shall be granted thee: or what is thy request further? and it shall be done. 13 Then said Esther, If it please the king, let it be granted to the Jews that are in Shushan to do to-morrow also according unto this day's decree, and let Haman's ten sons be hanged upon the gallows. 14 And the king commanded it so to be done: and a decree was given out in Shushan; and they hanged Haman's ten sons. 15 And the Jews that were in Shushan gathered themselves together on the fourteenth day also of the month Adar, and slew three hundred men in Shushan; but on the spoil they laid not

their hand. 16 And the other Jews that were in the king's provinces gathered themselves together, and stood for their lives, and had rest from their enemies, and slew of them that hated them seventy and five thousand; but on the spoil they laid not their hand.

On the thirteenth day of the month Adar, the Jews held the upper hand and wreaked vengeance upon their enemies (v. 5). Included among those destroyed that day were the ten sons of Haman (v. 14).

V. THE PEAST OF PURIM (Esther 9:17 —10:3)

Up to this point in the book of Esther, the focal point has been the historical origin of the Jewish feast of Purim. The point of interest now is the action of Mordecai and Esther which legalized the feast as a Jewish festival, even though there was no requirement in the law.

A. MORDECAI'S LETTERS (9:17-32)

17 *This was done* on the thirteenth day of the month Adar; and on the fourteenth day of the same they rested, and made it a day of feasting and gladness. 18 But the Jews that were in Shushan assembled together on the thirteenth *day* thereof, and on the fourteenth thereof; and on the fifteenth *day* of the same they rested, and made it a day of feasting and gladness. 19 Therefore do the Jews of the villages, that dwell in the unwalled towns, make the fourteenth day of the month Adar *a day of* gladness and feasting, and a good day, and of sending portions one to another.
20 And Mordecai wrote these things, and sent letters unto all the Jews that were in all the provinces of the king Ahasuerus, both nigh and far, 21 to enjoin them that they should keep the fourteenth day of the month Adar, and the fifteenth day of the same, yearly, 22 as the days wherein the Jews had rest from their enemies, and the month which was turned unto them from sorrow to gladness, and from mourning into a good day; that they should make them days of feasting and gladness, and of sending portions one to another, and gifts to the poor. 23 And the Jews undertook to do as they had begun, and as Mordecai had written unto them; 24 because Haman the son of Hammedatha, the Agagite, the enemy of all the Jews, had plotted against

the Jews to destroy them, and had cast Pur, that is, the lot, to consume them, and to destroy them; 25 but when *the matter* came before the king, he commanded by letters that his wicked device, which he had devised against the Jews, should return upon his own head, and that he and his sons should be hanged on the gallows.
26 Wherefore they called these days Purim, after the name of Pur. Therefore because of all the words of this letter, and of that which they had seen concerning this matter, and that which had come unto them, 27 the Jews ordained, and took upon them, and upon their seed, and upon all such as joined themselves unto them, so that it should not fail, that they would keep these two days according to the writing thereof, and according to the appointed time thereof, every year; 28 and that these days should be remembered and kept throughout every generation, every family, every province, and every city; and that these days of Purim should not fail from among the Jews, nor the remembrance of them perish from their seed.
29 Then Esther the queen, the daughter of Abihail, and Mordecai the Jew, wrote with all authority to confirm this second letter of Purim. 30 And he sent letters unto all the Jews, to the hundred twenty and seven provinces of the kingdom of Ahasuerus, *with* words of peace and truth, 31 to confirm these days of Purim in their appointed times, according as Mordecai the Jew and Esther the queen had enjoined them, and as they had ordained for themselves and for their seed, in the matter of the fastings and their cry. 32 And the commandment of Esther confirmed these matters of Purim; and it was written in the book.

The thirteenth day of Adar was to have been a day of doom for the Jews; instead, it was turned into a day of retaliatory victory. Although it was a day of victory, it has continued to be observed as a day of fasting in commemoration of Esther's fasting (4:15-17). The fourteenth and fifteenth days of Adar are observed with feasting and giving of gifts in commemoration of the deliverance from Haman's efforts to destroy the Jews.

Wherefore they called these days Purim, after the name of Pur (v. 26). *Purim* is the Hebrew plural for *Pur*, which means "lot," from Haman's casting of lots (cf. 3:7). Mordecai sent letters establishing the festival of Purim to all Jews in Persia (cf. vv. 20, 30). This custom has continued unto this day.

B. MORDECAI'S GREATNESS (10:1-3)

1 And the king Ahasuerus laid a tribute upon the land, and upon the isles of the sea. 2 And all the acts of his power and of his might, and the full account of the greatness of Mordecai, whereunto the king advanced him, are they not written in the book of the chronicles of the kings of Media and Persia? 3 For Mordecai the Jew was next unto king Ahasuerus, and great among the Jews, and accepted of the multitude of his brethren, seeking the good of his people, and speaking peace to all his seed.

The story of the origin of Purim ended, as it began, with a description of the reign of Ahasuerus. However, the end is augmented by the presence of Mordecai as grand vizier and the significance of his policies (v. 3). Important among Mordecai's activities were those conducted for the welfare of the Jews.

Bibliography

I. Exegetical and Historical Value

Anderson, Bernhard W. "The Book of Esther: Introduction and Exegesis." *The Interpreter's Bible.* Eds. G. A. Buttrick *et al.* Vol. III. New York and Nashville: Abingdon, 1954.

Bravin, D. B. "The Book of Esther." *Old Testament Commentary.* Eds. H. C. Alleman and E. E. Flack. Philadelphia: Muhlenberg, 1951.

Bright, John. *A History of Israel.* Philadelphia: Westminster, 1959.

Cartledge, S. A. *A Conservative Introduction to the Old Testament.* Second edition. Athens, Ga.: University of Georgia Press, 1944.

Clarke, Adam. *Commentary and Critical Notes.* Vol. II. Reprint. New York and Nashville: Abingdon, n.d.

Complete Works of Flavius Josephus, The. Trans. William Whiston. Chicago: Thompson and Thomas, n.d.

Davies, T. W. "Ezra, Nehemiah and Esther." *The Century Bible.* London: Caxton, n.d.

Keil, C. F. and F. Delitzsch. "The Books of Ezra, Nehemiah and Esther." *Biblical Commentary on the Old Testament.* Reprint. Grand Rapids: Eerdmans, n.d.

MacDonald, A. "Esther." *The New Bible Commentary.* Eds. F. Davidson *et al.* Grand Rapids: Eerdmans, 1953.

Manley, G. T. *The New Bible Handbook.* Chicago: Inter-Varsity, 1963.

May, H. G. (ed.). *Oxford Bible Atlas.* New York: Oxford, 1962.

Pfeiffer, R. H. *Introduction to the Old Testament.* Revised. New York: Harper, 1948.

Pritchard, J. B. *The Ancient Near East: An Anthology of Texts and Pictures.* Princeton: University Press, 1958.

Rowley, H. H. *The Old Testament and Modern Study.* Oxford: Clarendon, 1952.

Schultz, Samuel J. *The Old Testament Speaks.* New York: Harper, 1960.

Snaith, N. H. "The Historical Books." *The Old Testament and Modern Study.* Oxford: Clarendon, 1952.

Whitcomb, John C. "Ezra, Nehemiah and Esther." *The Wycliff Bible Commentary.* Eds. C. F. Pfeiffer and E. F. Harrison. Chicago: Moody, 1962.

II. Expository and Practical Value

Adeney, Walter F. "The Books of Ezra, Nehemiah and Esther." *The Expositor's Bible.* Ed. W. Robertson Nicoll. Vol. II. Grand Rapids: Eerdmans, 1940.

Broomall, W. "Esther." *The Biblical Expositor.* Ed. C. F. H. Henry. Vol. I. Philadelphia: Holman, 1960.

Lichtenberger, Arthur C. "The Book of Esther: Exposition." *The Interpreter's Bible.* Eds. G. A. Buttrick *et al.* Vol. III. New York and Nashville: Abingdon, 1954.

Rawlinson, G. "Ezra, Nehemiah, Esther." *The Pulpit Commentary.* Eds. H. D. M. Spence and J. S. Exell. Vol. XV. New York and London: Funk and Wagnalls, n.d.

Stevenson, Dwight E. *Preaching on the Books of the Old Testament.* New York: Harper, 1961.